India

Sarina Singh

Lindsay Brown, Mark Elliott, Paul Harding, Abigail Hole
Patrick Horton, Kate James, Amy Karafin, Adam Karlin,
Anirban Das Mahapatra, Daniel McCrohan,
Amelia Thomas, Rafael Wlodarski

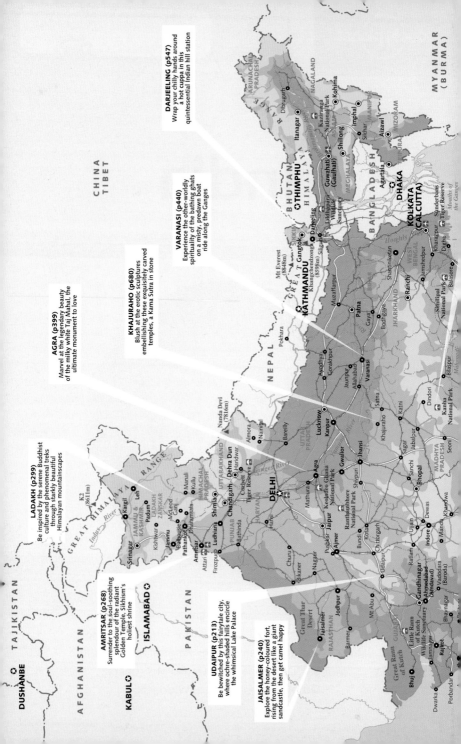

LADAKH (p299)
Be inspired by the serene Buddhist culture and phenomenal treks through starkly beautiful Himalayan mountainscapes

AMRITSAR (p268)
Surrender to the soul-soothing splendour of the radiant Golden Temple, Sikhism's holiest shrine

AGRA (p399)
Marvel at the legendary beauty of the milky white Taj Mahal, the ultimate monument to love

KHAJURAHO (p680)
Blush at the erotic sculptures embellishing these exquisitely carved temples, a Kama Sutra in stone

DARJEELING (p547)
Wrap your chilly hands around a hot cuppa in this quintessential Indian hill station

VARANASI (p440)
Experience the other-worldly spirituality of the bathing ghats on a misty, predawn boat ride along the Ganges

UDAIPUR (p213)
Be bewitched by this fairytale city, where ochre-shaded hills encircle the whimsical Lake Palace

JAISALMER (p240)
Explore the honey-coloured fort, rising from the desert like a giant sandcastle, then get camel happy

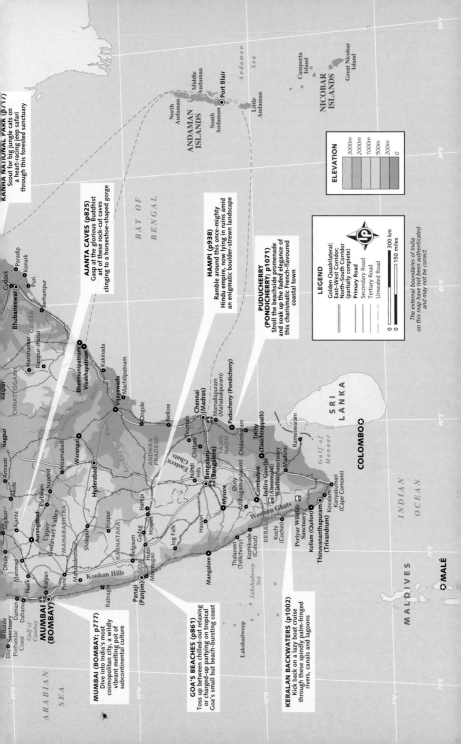

KANHA NATIONAL PARK (p710)
Scout for big jungle cats on a heart-racing jeep safari through this forested sanctuary

AJANTA CAVES (p825)
Gasp at the glorious Buddhist art of these rock-cut caves clinging to a horseshoe-shaped gorge

HAMPI (p938)
Ramble around this once-mighty Hindu empire, now lying in ruins amid an enigmatic boulder-strewn landscape

PUDUCHERRY (PONDICHERRY; p1071)
Stroll the beachside promenade and soak up the faded elegance of this charismatic French-flavoured coastal town

MUMBAI (BOMBAY; p777)
Dive into India's most cosmopolitan city, a wildly vibrant melting pot of subcontinental culture

GOA'S BEACHES (p861)
Toss up between chilled-out relaxing or charged-up partying on tropical Goa's small but beach-bursting coast

KERALAN BACKWATERS (p1002)
Kick back on a lazy boat cruise through these spindly palm-fringed rivers, canals and lagoons

ELEVATION

3000m
2000m
1000m
500m
200m
0

LEGEND

Golden Quadrilateral;
East-West Corridor;
North-South Corridor
(partially complete)
Primary Road
Secondary Road
Tertiary Road
Unsealed Road

0   300 km
0   150 miles

The external boundaries of India
on this map have not been authenticated
and may not be correct.

India Highlights

Home to one billion people and visited by countless travellers, India is many things. It is bustling and serene, heart-breaking and inspirational, state-of-the-art and timelessly traditional. It offers the traveller an unrivalled diversity of experiences, sights and sensations. We asked the Lonely Planet traveller community to suggest their favourites.

CHRIS MI

1 MONUMENT TO LOVE

The guide is right: the Taj Mahal (p404) is one sight that surpasses any hype. An elegant, beautiful monument to love that also betrays the megalomania of its owner; a perfect statement of humanity.

coeurdelion, Traveller

MUMBAI: MEGALOPOLIS

Mumbai (p777) is a truly cosmopolitan megalopolis that will leave you wondering long after you've left it. Everything you know about Indian society is multiplied here by a hundred and topped off with a tremendous energy. An absolute must-visit.

Robin Vermoesen, Traveller, Belgium

2

ORIEN HARVEY

THE KAMA SUTRA

Thousand-year-old erotic images adorn the well-preserved sandstone Hindu temples scattered throughout the Indian town of Khajuraho (p680). Many of the hundreds of orgy scenes defy the principles of gravity and anatomy while it seems horses were always, let's say, well loved.

Lisa Sinclair, Traveller, New Zealand

ANDERS BLOMQVIST

3

CHRIS ME

4 JAISALMER FORT

This 12th-century fort (p241) is a warren of narrow streets carved from sandstone, harbouring a palace, temples and hundreds of deceptively simple-looking *havelis* (traditional, ornately decorated residences). A quarter of the city's population lives here, surrounded by its 99 bastions.

anpl, Traveller

MARK DA

5 SEDUCTIVE HAMPI

The fascinating, far-flung ruins of Vijayanagar, near the village of Hampi (p938), once comprised a city of half a million. They're set in a strange and sublime boulder-strewn landscape that resonates with a magical and irresistibly seductive air.

anpl, Traveller

LAID-BACK LEH

Located high in the Indian region of Ladakh, Leh (p301) is a famous trading town from the southern Silk Road but the trading hasn't stopped. Tibetan masks, hats and Kashmiri boxes can be found cheaply, but look at the bead shops for lapis lazuli and amber bobbles.

dreno, Traveller

KAREN TRIST

ROW YOUR BOAT DOWN THE GANGES

Near the steps of Varanasi (p440), hire a boat and make your way to the middle of the river. Watch the pilgrims descend to the water, cupping their hands in prayer. Idle at the centre of Hinduism, and get caught in the eddy of India's heart.

Christopher Patch, Traveller, USA

PAUL BEINSSEN

 SENSATIONAL SIKKIM

This is one place which is sure to remain in my memory forever. Surrounded by the mighty snow-capped Himalaya, on an early morning one can see Khangchendzonga (p598), the second-largest peak in the Himalaya. The sun rays falling on the snowcapped mountains make it golden. A place where nature is at its best!

sharadab, Traveller

9 GO ON A CAMEL SAFARI

Take an overnight trip by camel into Rajasthan's Thar Desert (p246) to see gazelle, sleep on a sand dune, make chapati over an open fire, and meet desert-dwelling villagers who are capable of growing watermelons and wheat in sand.

cheryn, Traveller

A GOAN HOME

Nothing beats being invited to a Goan home (p858) to bask in the hospitality of the locals. They will buy the freshest fish and vegetables and create a meal that just goes together so well. It will leave you feeling totally *sossegado* (laid-back, contented).

Karishma Pais, Traveller, India

11

ANDERS BLOMQVIST

10

RICHARD I'ANSON

FATEHPUR SIKRI

Another of India's great lost cities, this one (p423) is within striking distance of the Taj Mahal. It's especially worth escaping the touts and exploring the backstreets of this magnificent fortified ghost town when it glows in the late afternoon sun.

anpl, Traveller

12

ANDERS BLOMQVIST

KOVALAM

Kovalam (p988) is Kerala's answer to Goa, and a good place to surf some very powerful waves in 'God's own country'. It's also exotic and peaceful, yet vibrant enough to keep you way longer than you've ever intended.

Robin Vermoesen, Traveller, Belgium

RICHARD I'AF

13 THE STREETS OF KOLKATA

Kolkata (Calcutta; p501): Children playing, men bathing, women washing; lives ebb and flow. Eating rice, selling bananas, sweeping dust; vivid colours glow. Taxis honking, autos beeping, cycle-wallahs running; harmony and chaos juxtapose.

Christopher Patch, Traveller, USA

ANTHONY PLUM

14 THE GOLDEN TEMPLE IN AMRITSAR

For Sikhs, a visit to the Golden Temple (p270) is the equivalent to a trip to Mecca for Muslims. Shimmering reflections of the temple, coupled with birdsong, create a scene of rare peace and beauty. For the full experience, stay in communal dorms with other pilgrims.

charliewalker, Traveller

A MINARET WITH A VIEW

From the top of Jama Masjid (p134) in Old Delhi, it seems possible to glimpse the whole of India – the entire nation just below your feet. Watch carefully the ordinary day unfold, and allow the humility to sink deep.

Christopher Patch, Traveller, USA

15

ANDERS BLOMQVIST

VIBRANT WEDDINGS

Among India's squalor is a pulsating society, rich in colour and energy. Nowhere is this more evident than at a wedding. Wedding receptions are where rituals and customs take a back seat to a feast of monumental proportions. Tease your palate with a vast array of divine offerings. Then torment your stomach by going back for more.

aboyabroad, Traveller

16

PAUL BEINSSEN

GARRY

17 MCLEOD GANJ

Sure, when you hear Dharamsala (p368) you may think Dalai Lama, but there is a thriving group of yogis hanging out in this diverse little town. Breathe the sweet clean air while standing on your head in the morning sun on a balcony overlooking the mountains.

horseanddog, Traveller

PATRICK H

18 GOING TO THE SHOPS IN KASHMIR

Feeling like an Arabian princess as you recline in a *shikara* (gondola-like boat). Sheltered by the sun under a colourful canopy, one leg skimming through the lotus leaves on Dal Lake (p287) as you go on your way to the market for a spot of shopping.

wavertree, Traveller

Contents

Destination India

Bamboozling. There's simply no other word that convincingly captures the enigma that is India. With its in-your-face diversity – from snow-dusted mountains to sun-washed beaches, tranquil temples to feisty festivals, lantern-lit villages to software-supremo cities – it's hardly surprising that this country has been dubbed the world's most multidimensional. Love it or loathe it – and most visitors see-saw between the two – India promises to jostle your entire being, and no matter where you go or what you do, it's a place you'll never forget.

FAST FACTS

Population: 1.027 billion (2001 census)

Unemployment rate: 7.2% (2008)

Average annual income: US$977

Population growth rate: 1.6%

Literacy rate: 65.38% (2001 census)

Families living in one-room homes: 42%

India's percentage of world population: 16.9%

Average cost of a big-city wedding: US$12,500

Life expectancy: 66 years (women) and 63 years (men)

Proportion of females to males: 933:1000 (2001 census)

Home to more than one billion people, the subcontinent bristles with an eclectic melange of ethnic groups, which translates into an intoxicating cultural cocktail for the traveller. For those seeking spiritual sustenance, India has oodles of sacrosanct sites and stirring philosophical epics, while history buffs will encounter gems from the past almost everywhere – from grand vestiges of the British Raj serenely peering over swarming spice bazaars to crumbling fortresses looming high above plunging ravines. Meanwhile, aficionados of the great outdoors can paddle in the shimmering waters of one of many balmy beaches, scout for big jungle cats on a blood-pumping wildlife safari, or simply inhale pine-scented air on a meditative forest walk. And then there's the food! From squidgy south Indian *idlis* (fermented rice cakes) to zesty north Indian curries, foodies can look forward to savouring a seductive smorgasbord of specialities.

Once you touch down on subcontinental soil, you'll quickly discover that cricket – India's sporting obsession – is one of the most spirited topics of conversation, along with the latest shenanigans in the razzle-dazzle world of Bollywood. However, it is politics – whether at the national, state or village level – that consistently dominates news headlines, with middle- and upper-class India also keenly keeping its finger on the pulse of international events. On the home front, economic matters feature high on the national political agenda. With one of the world's fastest-growing economies, India has certainly made giant strides over the past decade. However, despite averaging an annual growth rate of around 9% in recent years, vast sections of the country's billion-plus population have seen little benefit from the economic boom. Indeed, the government's ongoing challenge is to spread both the burden and bounty of India's fiscal prosperity. Not an easy task given that the gap between the haves and the have-nots is far from shrinking, and poverty (see p65) is set to spiral upwards if India's population rate continues to gallop beyond that of its economic growth.

For decades, overpopulation (see p66) has been at the core of many of the country's most pressing problems. Apart from the pressure that an expanding population is placing on India's already groaning infrastructure, analysts warn that it's just a matter of time before the mounting competition for resources ignites interminable communal conflict – not to mention bringing to cracking point an already overstretched health-care system. Analysts also predict that as the population continues to climb, so too will the number of children from low-income households who drop out of school in order to scrape together whatever they can to supplement meagre family earnings (see p63).

While India has unquestionably made laudable economic advancements, the government has been criticised for failing to sufficiently address its AIDS crisis (see p63) as well as a far more prolific and recent health epidemic – diabetes. Currently recording the world's highest number of diabetics, India registered close to 45 million cases in 2008, with health officials warning that this figure is likely to exceed 100 million in the next few years. Given its alarming growth rate, the government has pledged to beef up public risk awareness and prevention programmes.

When it comes to the environment, although there's legislation to protect ecosystems, activists cite government lethargy, paired with corruption down the ranks, for invariably exacerbating environmental degradation (see p102) and threatening endangered species (see p98). Climate change, deforestation, pollution and ever-expanding industrialisation are just some of the other issues the government is wrestling with.

The political challenges for India's government are no less daunting, especially in relation to ongoing communal friction, with the most incessant case being that between India and Pakistan over the disputed territory of Kashmir (see p53). Unresolved since the subcontinent's partition in 1947, the Kashmir impasse has been the catalyst for intensely rocky relations between the two countries ever since. While recent years have seen promising dialogue between Delhi and Islamabad, the November 2008 commando-style terrorist attacks in Mumbai swiftly saw hope turn to suspicion – see p57 for details.

On a more optimistic note, despite the dip in tourist arrivals immediately following the deadly 2008 Mumbai attacks, coupled with the global economic slump, government data indicates that India's foreign tourist arrivals in 2008 were pegged at 5.37 million – a 5.7% jump from the previous year. One of the most lucrative growth sectors is that of medical tourism (foreign travel to India for competitively priced medical treatment), which has projected earnings of a staggering US$2 billion by 2012. Furthermore, the World Travel & Tourism Council forecasts that India will secure the number-one position in regards to 10-year tourism growth potential.

So, what is it that's drawing more and more people to India? While the reasons vary intimately from person to person, for many it's the challenge of getting up close and personal with one of the planet's most intriguing countries…and quite possibly unravelling oneself along the way. But in all its chaotic glory, you'll soon discover that India is an eternal – and, if you tune into its unique rhythm, curiously melodic – work in progress. Indeed, for many visitors, this is precisely what makes her so deeply rewarding, so surprisingly addictive. Ultimately, it's all about taking a leap of faith and surrendering to the unknown: this is the India that nothing can ever prepare you for because its very essence – its elusive soul – lies cradled in its mystery.

Getting Started

Nothing can fully prepare you for India, but perhaps the one thing that best encapsulates this extraordinary country is its ability to inspire, frustrate, thrill and confound all at once.

Mind-bendingly multidimensional, India presents a wildly diverse spectrum of travel encounters. Some of these can be challenging, particularly for the first-time visitor: the poverty is confronting, Indian bureaucracy can be exasperating and the crush of humanity sometimes turns the simplest task into an energy-zapping battle. Even the most experienced travellers find their sanity frayed at some point, yet this is all part of the India experience. If you haven't visited this part of the planet before, set aside the first few days to simply acclimatise to the subcontinent's bamboozling symphony of sights, sounds, tastes and smells.

Get excited and knowledgable about your trip beforehand by reading up on India, especially its cultural framework. Doing so will augment your appreciation of the subcontinent's sights and traditions and also better equip you to hold more informed conversations with locals. Allow a few weeks of pretrip preparation to sort out immunisations and visas.

In terms of planning what to do once you arrive, the country's remarkable diversity can actually make it a veritable quagmire when nutting out itineraries. The key is to try not to squeeze in too much, as travelling often involves considerable distances and stamina. It's wise to factor in some flexibility, as things don't always run like clockwork in India – more than a few travellers have had their holidays marred by not being able to get their preferred train seats, or by being delayed by rescheduled transport services, for example. Flexibility will also allow spontaneity, whether it's simply spending an afternoon discussing samsara with a *pujari* (priest) whom you initially approached for directions after getting lost in a bazaar, or ditching travel plans with friends to join a short-staffed rural volunteer group you heard about while queuing for kebabs in Delhi. Regardless, your Indian sojourn is going to be a whole lot more enjoyable if you give yourself some time off purely to be.

WHEN TO GO

Climate plays a key factor in deciding when to visit India. You should keep in mind that climatic conditions in the far north are distinctly different to those of the extreme south.

See p1143 for more climate information.

Generally speaking, India's climate is defined by three seasons – the hot, the wet (monsoon) and the cool, each of which can vary in duration from north to south. The most pleasant time to visit most of the country is during the cooler period of November to around mid-February, although there are marked regional variations (see the Fast Facts boxes at the start of regional chapters for the best times to visit specific regions). If you're in India during the (hot) summer and (wet, humid) monsoon, cool relief can be found in the northern Himalayan region – consider pursuing 'The Great Himalayan Circuit' on p33.

Apart from the weather, the timing of certain festivals or special events may also influence when you wish to visit (see p26 and the Festivals In...boxes in regional chapters).

The Hot

The heat starts to build up in India from around February and by April it seriously warms up. It can get unbearably hot in May and June, with many

THE INDIA EXPERIENCE

There's a whole lot more to India than merely sightseeing:

- Activities that span from blood-pumping trekking to mind-soothing meditation (see p105)
- Courses – from getting sitar savvy to aligning your chakras (see p1142)
- Festivals that range from the wildly upbeat to the spiritually serene (see p26)
- Shopping, shopping and more shopping! (see p1154)
- Volunteering, whether it's teaching English at schools, lending a hand to clean up the countryside, or caring for injured animals (see p1165)

parts of the country experiencing temperatures of 40°C and above. Late in May the first signs of the monsoon are visible in some areas – high humidity, electrical storms, short rainstorms and dust storms that turn day into night. The hot season is the time to flee the baking plains and head for the cooler hills, and this is when hill stations are at their best (and busiest).

The Wet
When the monsoon finally arrives, it doesn't just suddenly appear. After some advance warning, the rain comes in steadily, generally starting around 1 June in the extreme south and sweeping north to cover the whole country (except Ladakh) by early July. The monsoon doesn't really cool things down; at first hot, dry and dusty weather is simply replaced by hot, humid and muddy conditions. It doesn't rain solidly all day, but it rains virtually every day; the water tends to come down in buckets for a while, followed by periods of sun, creating a fatiguing steam bath-like environment. The main monsoon comes from the southwest, but the southeast coast (and southern Kerala) is largely affected by the short and surprisingly heavy northeast monsoon, which brings rain from around October to early December.

The Cool
From around October the monsoon ends for most of the country and this is when India receives most tourists – however, by this time it's too cold to visit Ladakh (see p299). During October and November it's generally not too hot and not too cool (although October can still be uncomfortably warm and humid in some regions; see regional chapters). In the thick of winter (around mid-December to mid-January), Delhi and other northern cities can become astonishingly cold, especially at night. It certainly becomes bone-chillingly cold in the far north. In the far south, where it never gets truly cool, the temperatures become comfortably warm during this period.

COSTS & MONEY
On the financial front, India pleases all pockets. Accommodation ranges from simple backpacker lodgings to sumptuous top-end hotels, with some appealing midrange possibilities that won't bust the bank. A delicious array of eateries at all prices means you can fill your belly without emptying your moneybelt, and it's possible to zip around economically, as well thanks to the country's comprehensive public transport network.

As costs vary considerably nationwide, the best way of ascertaining how much money you'll require for your trip is to peruse the relevant regional chapters of this book. Be prepared to pay more in the larger cities such as Mumbai (Bombay) and Delhi, as well as at popular tourist destinations during peak season.

DON'T LEAVE HOME WITHOUT...

- Getting a visa (p1164) and travel insurance (p1149)
- Seeking advice about vaccinations (p1192) and taking adequate stock of prescription medication
- Nonrevealing clothes (women *and* men) – covering up will win you more respect and is essential when visiting sacred sites
- A well-concealed money belt (p1146)
- Sunscreen lotion and sunglasses
- A small torch (flashlight) for poorly lit streets and power cuts
- Good-quality earplugs to block out night din and for long bus/train trips
- Flip-flops (thongs) for shared or grotty bathrooms
- A shower cap and universal sink plug (uncommon except at top-end hotels)
- Tampons – sanitary pads are widely available but tampons are usually restricted to big (or touristy) cities
- Mosquito repellent (a mosquito net can also come in handy)
- A water bottle – if you use water-purification tablets or filters (see p1191) you'll help in the antiplastic crusade
- Sleeping-bag sheet – if you're unsure about hotel linen (especially at budget places) and for overnight train journeys
- Expecting the unexpected – India loves to toss up surprises

---

In relation to sightseeing, foreigners are often charged more than Indian citizens for entry into tourist sites (admission prices for foreigners are sometimes given in US dollars, payable in the rupee equivalent), and there may also be additional charges for still/video cameras.

When it comes to bedding down, hotel tariffs are usually higher in big cities (especially Mumbai) and tourist hot spots and may also be influenced by factors such as location, season and festivals. Given the vast differences nationwide, it's misleading for us to pinpoint a countrywide average accommodation price – see p1141 for more information, as well as the regional chapters 'Sleeping' sections. If you've got cash to splash, some of India's top-end hotels are among the world's finest, but be prepared to fork out at least US$200 per night at the better properties before even getting a whiff of room service. Surf the internet to investigate possible internet discounts.

So how does this all translate to a daily budget? Given the vast accommodation price differences across India, it's impossible to arrive at one neat figure. However, as an example, in Rajasthan you can expect to pay roughly between US$20 and US$25 per day if you stay in the cheapest hotels, travel on public buses, do limited sightseeing and eat basic meals. If you wish to stay at salubrious midrange hotels, dine at nicer restaurants, do a reasonable amount of sightseeing and largely travel by autorickshaw and taxi, you're looking at anywhere between US$40 and US$65 per day.

Eating out in India is sizzling-hot value, with budget restaurant meals for as little as Rs40 (even less at the more basic street eateries), and usually from around double that for a satiating midrange restaurant feed. At the more suave urban restaurants, main dishes generally hover between Rs150 and Rs350 to which you'll need to add the cost of side dishes, such as rice, and (usually) a tax of 10% to 12.5%.

HOW MUCH?

Toothpaste (100g): Rs28

Jute shoulder bag: from Rs50

One dozen bananas: Rs25

Small brass Ganesh: from Rs50

Sandalwood incense (15 sticks): from Rs20

TOP 10

INDIA

GREAT READS

With a riveting array of novels offering varied insights into India, there's no dearth of excellent bedtime-reading fodder – the below titles are just some of our favourites. For additional reading recommendations see p77, p24 and the boxed text, p782.

1 *The White Tiger* by Aravind Adiga
2 *The Inheritance of Loss* by Kiran Desai
3 *The God of Small Things* by Arundhati Roy
4 *Shantaram* by Gregory David Roberts
5 *Six Suspects* by Vikas Swarup
6 *Midnight's Children* by Salman Rushdie
7 *A Fine Balance* by Rohinton Mistry
8 *White Mughals* by William Dalrymple
9 *Sea of Poppies* by Amitav Ghosh
10 *A Suitable Boy* by Vikram Seth

MUST-SEE MOVIES

What better way to get all fired up about your trip than by holding your very own Indian movie marathon! The following is a small selection of acclaimed films that portray a diverse mix of Indian themes. Mainstream video stores outside India may not stock many (if any) Bollywood titles, but you shouldn't have any problem finding them at your local Indian video shop; if that fails, Indian grocery stores usually have at least one shelf bulging with rental DVDs.

To find out more about Indian cinema read p76.

1 *Earth, Water* and *Fire,* a trilogy directed by Deepa Mehta
2 *Slumdog Millionaire,* directed by Danny Boyle
3 *Being Cyrus,* directed by Homi Adajania
4 *Monsoon Wedding,* directed by Mira Nair; see also her other acclaimed films *The Namesake, Kama Sutra* and *Salaam Bombay!*
5 *Welcome to Sajjanpur,* directed by Shyam Benegal
6 *Lagaan,* written and directed by Ashutosh Gowariker
7 *Gandhi,* directed by Richard Attenborough; see also *Gandhi, My Father,* directed by Feroz Khan
8 *Mr & Mrs Iyer,* directed by Aparna Sen
9 *The Darjeeling Limited,* directed by Wes Anderson
10 *Black,* directed by Sanjay Leela Bhansali

FESTIVALS & EVENTS

India has a phenomenal variety of festivals – for further details see p26 and the 'Festivals In...' boxed texts in regional chapters. The following is just a drop in India's spectacular festival ocean.

1 Kumbh Mela (for dates see p837)
2 Festival of Dance (Feb/Mar); Madhya Pradesh (p671)
3 Rath Yatra (Jun/Jul); Orissa (p655) and Kolkata (Calcutta; p503)
4 Nehru Trophy Snake Boat Race (Aug); Kerala (p1001)
5 Ganesh Chaturthi (Aug/Sep); nationwide (p26), in Mumbai (p779) and Pune (p815)
6 Dussehra & Durga Puja (Sep/Oct); nationwide (p27) but especially in Mysore (p901), Kullu (p353) and Kolkata (p503)
7 Diwali (Oct/Nov); nationwide (p27)
8 Pushkar Camel Fair (Oct/Nov); Rajasthan (p199)
9 Sonepur Mela (Nov/Dec); Bihar (p574)
10 Festival of Carnatic Music & Dance (Dec/Jan); Tamil Nadu (p1043)

Regarding long-distance travel, there's a range of classes on trains and several bus types, resulting in considerable flexibility vis-à-vis comfort and price – regional chapters supply specific costs and also read p1178. Domestic air travel has become a lot more price competitive over recent years thanks to deregulation and good internet deals (see p1178). Within towns there's inexpensive public transport (see p1182), or perhaps you'd like to hire a car with driver, which is surprisingly good value if there are several of you to split the cost (see p1181).

TRAVEL LITERATURE

Bedazzled by wizardry since childhood, Tahir Shah travels through India to learn the art of illusion under the guidance of a mysterious master magician. *Sorcerer's Apprentice* chronicles his most extraordinary journey.

Edgy and engaging, *The Hungry Tide* by Amitav Ghosh explores the fortitude of the human spirit in the watery labyrinth of the Sunderbans, where crocodiles and man-eating tigers lurk.

Sacred Games, by Vikram Chandra, is a skilfully crafted and gripping thriller that takes the reader on an exhilarating journey through modern-day Mumbai's seedy underworld and beyond.

William Dalrymple's beautifully written travelogue, *City of Djinns,* traverses time to unpeel Delhi's intriguing layers, while *The Age of Kali* is a compilation of Dalrymple's insights gleaned from a decade of travelling the subcontinent.

Christopher Kremmer's *Inhaling the Mahatma* reveals the Australian author's multifarious encounters with India – that include a hijacking, riots, and falling in love – during and beyond his stint as a Delhi-based foreign correspondent in the early 1990s.

Hullabaloo in the Guava Orchard, by Kiran Desai, follows a bored post-office clerk and dreamer who retreats to the branches of a secluded guava tree in search of the contemplative life, only to be pursued by crowds of people seeking enlightenment.

William Sutcliffe's *Are You Experienced?* is the humorous tale of first-time backpacker Dave, who accompanies his best friend's girlfriend to India in an attempt to seduce her.

Gita Mehta's *Karma Cola* amusingly and cynically illustrates the cultural collision as India looks to the West for technology and modern methods, and the West descends upon India in search of wisdom and enlightenment.

An Area of Darkness, by VS Naipaul, published in 1964, describes the Nobel and Booker Prize–winning author's first visit to the subcontinent. Opinionated and unflinching, it's certainly a thought-provoking read as is his later travelogue, *India: A Million Mutinies Now,* published in 1990.

Chasing the Monsoon by Alexander Frater is an Englishman's story of his monsoon-chasing journey from Kovalam to Meghalaya, offering a captivating window into the monsoon's impact.

Anita Desai's *Journey to Ithaca* is the tale of two young Europeans, Matteo and Sophie, who go to India seeking enlightenment. While Matteo's ashram experience is spiritually affirming, Sophie's isn't quite so rosy.

Also see 'Great Reads' in the Top 10 box (p23).

> **'Chasing the Monsoon by Alexander Frater is an Englishman's story of his monsoon-chasing journey from Kovalam to Meghalaya'**

INTERNET RESOURCES

Events in India (www.eventsinindia.com) A handy site covering current happenings in major Indian cities.

Incredible India (www.incredibleindia.org) The official Indian government tourism site.

IndiaMike (www.indiamike.com) A popular forum which is a great place to tap into India's traveller grapevine.

Lonely Planet (www.lonelyplanet.com) Useful links, including the popular Thorn Tree Travel
Forum, where you can swap information with fellow travellers.

Maps of India (www.mapsofindia.com) Regional maps which includes thematic offerings such as
the locations of wildlife sanctuaries and hill stations.

World Newspapers (www.world-newspapers.com/india.html) Provides links to India's major
English-language national and regional publications, enabling you to stay tuned to what's happening where.

123india (www.123india.com) A portal with links to the arts, science, sport and more.

Events Calendar

Most festivals in India follow the Indian or Tibetan lunar calendars, tied to the moon's cycle, or the (changeable) Islamic calendar. Consequently, exact dates vary from year to year (consult tourist offices). Those listed here represent major national festivals, arranged according to the Indian lunar calendar; for details of regional festivals, see the regional chapters' Festivals in… boxed texts.

CHAITRA (MARCH/APRIL)

MAHAVIR JAYANTI
Jain festival that commemorates the birth of Mahavir, the founder of Jainism.

RAMANAVAMI
Hindus celebrate the birth of Rama with processions, music and feasting, and readings and enactments of scenes from the Ramayana.

EASTER
Christian holiday marking the Crucifixion and Resurrection of Jesus Christ.

VAISAKHA (APRIL/MAY)

BUDDHA JAYANTI
Celebrating Buddha's birth, enlightenment and attainment of nirvana (final release from the cycle of existence); this festival can fall in April, May or early June.

JYAISTHA (MAY/JUNE)

Only regional festivals fall in this period; see the regional chapters' Festivals in… boxed texts.

ASADHA (JUNE/JULY)

RATH YATRA (CAR FESTIVAL)
Effigies of Lord Jagannath (Vishnu as lord of the world) are hauled through cities on man-powered chariots, most famously in Puri (p646) in Orissa.

SRAVANA (JULY/AUGUST)

NAAG PANCHAMI
Hindu festival dedicated to Ananta, the serpent upon whose coils Vishnu rested between universes. Snakes are venerated as totems against monsoon flooding and other evils.

RAKSHA BANDHAN (NARIAL PURNIMA)
On the full moon, girls fix amulets known as *rakhis* to the wrists of brothers and close male friends to protect them in the coming year. Brothers reciprocate with gifts. Some people also worship the Vedic sea god Varuna.

RAMADAN (RAMAZAN)
Thirty days of dawn-to-dusk fasting mark the ninth month of the Islamic calendar. Celebrated around 12 August (2010), 1 August (2011) and 20 July (2012).

BHADRA (AUGUST/SEPTEMBER)

INDEPENDENCE DAY   15 Aug
This public holiday marks the anniversary of India's Independence (from Britain) in 1947. Celebrations are a countrywide expression of patriotism.

DRUKPA TESHI
A Buddhist festival celebrating the first teaching given by Siddhartha Gautama.

GANESH CHATURTHI
Hindus celebrate the birth of the elephant-headed god, Ganesh, with verve, particularly in Mumbai (see p841). Clay idols of Ganesh are paraded through the streets before being ceremonially immersed in rivers, tanks (reservoirs) or the sea.

JANMASTAMI
Hindus celebrate Krishna's birthday, particularly at his birthplace, Mathura (p425).

SHRAVAN PURNIMA
On this day of fasting, high-caste Hindus replace the sacred thread looped over their left shoulder.

PATETI
Parsis celebrate the Zoroastrian new year at this time, especially in Mumbai.

ASVINA (SEPTEMBER/OCTOBER)

NAVRATRI
This Hindu 'Festival of Nine Nights' leading up to Dussehra celebrates the goddess Durga in all her incarnations. Special folk dances are held, and the goddesses Lakshmi and Saraswati also receive

special praise. Festivities are particularly vibrant in Gujarat and Maharashtra.

DUSSEHRA
A Vaishnavite festival, celebrating the victory of the Hindu god Rama over the demon-king Ravana and the triumph of good over evil. Dussehra is big in Kullu (p353) and Mysore (p914), where effigies of Ravana and his cohorts are ritually burned.

DURGA PUJA
The conquest of good over evil, with the goddess Durga's victory over buffalo-headed demon Mahishasura. Celebrations occur around Dussehra, particularly in Kolkata (see p507), where thousands of images of the goddess are displayed then ritually immersed in rivers and water tanks.

GANDHI JAYANTI   2 Oct
This public holiday is a solemn celebration of Mohandas Gandhi's birth, with prayer meetings at his cremation site (Raj Ghat) in Delhi (see p134).

EID AL-FITR
Muslims celebrate the end of Ramadan with three days of festivities, starting 30 days after the start of the fast.

KARTIKA (OCTOBER/NOVEMBER)

DIWALI (DEEPAVALI)
On the 15th day of Kartika, Hindus joyfully celebrate the 'festival of lights' for five days, giving gifts, lighting fireworks, and burning butter and oil lamps to lead Lord Rama home from exile.

GOVARDHANA PUJA
A Vaishnavite Hindu festival commemorating the lifting of Govardhan Hill by Krishna; celebrated by Krishna devotees around India.

EID AL-ADHA
Muslims commemorate Ibrahim's readiness to sacrifice his son to God. It is around 16 November (2010), 6 November (2011) and 26 October (2012).

AGHAN (NOVEMBER/DECEMBER)

NANAK JAYANTI
The birthday of Guru Nanak, the founder of Sikhism, is celebrated with prayer readings and processions.

MUHARRAM
Shi'ia Muslims commemorate the martyrdom of the Prophet Mohammed's grandson Imam. Dates

are around 7 December (2010), 26 November (2011) and 15 November (2012).

PAUSA (DECEMBER/JANUARY)

CHRISTMAS DAY   25 Dec
Christians celebrate the birth of Jesus Christ.

MAGHA (JANUARY/FEBRUARY)

REPUBLIC DAY   26 Jan
This public holiday commemorates the founding of the Republic of India in 1950; the most spectacular celebrations are in Delhi, which holds a huge military parade along Rajpath and the Beating of the Retreat three days later.

PONGAL
A Tamil festival marking the end of the harvest season. Families in the south prepare pots of *pongal* (a mixture of rice, sugar, dhal and milk), symbolic of prosperity and abundance, then feed them to decorated and adorned cows.

VASANT PANCHAMI
Honouring Saraswati, the goddess of learning, Hindus dress in yellow and place books, musical instruments and other educational objects in front of idols of the goddess to receive her blessing.

LOSAR
Tibetan New Year – celebrated by Tantric Buddhists all over India, particularly in Himachal Pradesh, Sikkim, Ladakh and Zanskar. Dates can vary from region to region.

PHALGUNA (FEBRUARY/MARCH)

EID-MILAD-UN-NABI
Islamic festival celebrating the birth of the Prophet Mohammed. It falls around 26 February (2010), 15 February (2011) and 4 February (2012).

HOLI
One of North India's most ecstatic festivals; Hindus celebrate the beginning of spring by throwing coloured water and *gulal* (powder) at anyone within range. On the night before Holi, bonfires symbolise the demise of the evil demoness Holika.

SHIVARATRI
This day of Hindu fasting recalls the *tandava* (cosmic victory dance) of Lord Shiva. Temple processions are followed by the chanting of mantras and anointing of linga (phallic images of Shiva).

Itineraries
CLASSIC ROUTES

BEYOND THE GOLDEN TRIANGLE   10 Days
The Golden Triangle (Delhi–Agra–Jaipur–Delhi) is the all-time classic India quickie, but this trip goes that bit deeper.

Day one, take it slowly: visit tranquil **Humayun's Tomb** (p135), then later attend the sound-and-light show at the historic **Red Fort** (p134).

Next day, catch the train to **Agra** (p399) and gaze at the shimmering **Taj Mahal** (p404), before visiting the **Agra Fort** (p407). Spend day three surrounded by the ghosts of Mughals in the abandoned city of **Fatehpur Sikri** (p423).

On day four, return to Delhi and then fly direct to **Udaipur** (p213), to relax for a couple of days in Rajasthan's lake city, wander its bazaars and watch sunset from the **Monsoon Palace** (p217) before taking a train to visit the fascinating Dargah at **Ajmer** (p192). Then spend a day or two in the enchanting pilgrimage town of **Pushkar** (p195), before wending your way back to Delhi.

A twist on the classic 'Golden Triangle' (Delhi–Agra–Jaipur–Delhi) route. This geometric journey has a wider scope, going from Delhi to Agra, then flying into Rajasthan, to the gleaming white town of Udaipur, with a stop at pilgrimage centres Ajmer and Pushkar on the return.

A RAJASTHANI RAMBLE   **Two Weeks**

This much-loved circuit, which explores India's most colourful state, starts and ends in the bustling capital, Delhi.

Spend day one in Delhi, visiting the calm site of **Humayun's Tomb** (p135), before attending the sound-and-light show at the historic **Red Fort** (p134).

On day two, take the train to **Jaipur** (p168) to soak up the sights of the **Old City** (p169). Fill most of day three by exploring the fairy-tale fort at **Amber** (p182), then browse Jaipur's wonderful **emporiums** (p179).

On day four, take the bus to **Ajmer** (p192), where you can visit extraordinary Muslim shrine known as **Dargah** (p193), before taking a short bus ride to relax in the holy town of **Pushkar** (p195). Spend a few days here, chilling out and taking your time over the lakeside **temples** (p196) and then, on day seven, travel onward to the graceful lakeside whimsy of **Udaipur** (p213). Again, you can relax and sightsee here for a couple of days. Make time for an extravagant meal at the palace on the **lake** (p221).

Next, on day nine, take a taxi and visit **Kumbalgarh** (p224) and the temple at **Ranakpur** (p225) en route to the blue city, **Jodhpur** (p230). In Jodhpur you can admire the pastel-painted houses and magnificent **Mehrangarh Fort** (p231).

On day 11, take the bus or train through the desert to the ancient fortress of **Jaisalmer** (p240) to relive your *Arabian Nights* fantasies on a **camel safari** (see the boxed text, p246) in the dunes. Finally, on day 13, make your way back to Delhi, where you can visit the **Jama Masjid** (p134), dive into the surrounding **bazaars** (see the boxed text, p156), and finish off doing some last-minute **shopping** (p153).

This route starts in Delhi, then surveys Rajasthan's greatest hits: it takes in pink, blue, white and golden cities, and visits the region's mightiest forts and most exquisite temples. The circuit finishes on a high with a camel safari in the desert, before a day's exploration in Delhi.

A TASTE OF NORTH & SOUTH   Three Weeks

This north and south cocktail begins with a cultural feast, and ends with pure relaxation. Start by visiting the sights of **Delhi** (p129), then head to **Agra** (p399) and the **Taj Mahal** (p404), **Agra Fort** (p407) and **Fatehpur Sikri** (p423), as for the first itinerary. Next, if you have time, stop at **Keoladeo Ghana National Park** (p185), to see the rich birdlife, and then **Ranthambore National Park** (p201), to spot tigers, before heading to the Pink City of **Jaipur** (p168). Visit **Amber fort** (p182), browse the amazing **bazaars** (p179) of Jaipur and peek from behind the shutters at the **Hawa Mahal** (p169) before returning to Delhi to start the southern part of your trip.

Prepare to relax: fly south to **Kochi** (Cochin; p1013), where you can stay in evocative **Fort Cochin** (p1015), catch a **Kathakali performance** (p1023), and spend a couple of nights exploring this exotic spice port and eating in its delicious restaurants, before launching off into the backwaters of Kerala: head to **Alappuzha** (Alleppey; p999), and take a slow cruise in a houseboat, watching life on the water and kicking back. Next stop, the beach: try the less-visited sands around **Varkala** (p993), with its sea-cliffs and laid-back beaches. To experience Zenlike calm before taking your return flight from Kochi, do yoga and meditation at a local ashram and revel in **Ayurvedic treatments** (p994) such as synchronised massage.

For a smattering of the north, and a sprinkling of the south, this trip is ideal. Wallow in the cultural and artistic wealth of Delhi, Agra and Rajasthan before flying south for some serene relaxation, including boating in tranquil backwaters, yoga, massage and the beach.

ONCE AROUND NORTH INDIA   Two Months

Start this northern extravaganza in **Kolkata** (Calcutta; p501), finishing in **Delhi** (p119). Time your schedule so that the last leg through Ladakh falls between July and October, when the mountain passes are open (see p312).

Pass a few days enjoying the atmosphere and **food** (p522) in Kolkata, home to the **Victoria Memorial** (p508). Then head to **Bodhgaya** (p576), where Buddha attained enlightenment. Roll across the plains to the sacred city of **Varanasi** (p440), then to **Khajuraho** (p680), where temples drip with erotic carvings.

Head southwest through **Orchha** (p677) and **Jhansi** (p439) to **Sanchi** (p695), where Emperor Ashoka embraced Buddhism. In **Bhopal** (p689) pick up the train to **Jalgaon** (p828), a jumping-off point for the wonderful **Ajanta Caves** (p825).

Train it to **Mumbai** (Bombay; p777), then break north along the coast to **Ahmedabad** (Amdavad; p727). For a more peaceful slice of Gujarat, visit the mellow island of **Diu** (p749) and the tribal heartland of **Bhuj** (p770). Start your tour through Rajasthan in whimsical **Udaipur** (p213) and meander between here and **Jaipur** (p168), from where you can catch the train to Agra's **Taj Mahal** (p404).

Next, drop by **Delhi** (p119) to relish the **sights** (p129), **tastes** (p146) and **shopping** (p153) before dashing northeast to spot tigers in **Corbett Tiger Reserve** (p487) and practise yoga in **Rishikesh** (p475). Connect through **Dehra Dun** (p461) and **Chandigarh** (p256) to **Shimla** (p334), India's premier hill station.

Bus it to **Manali** (see the boxed text, p362) for some adrenalin-charged activities, then ride the mountain bus to Buddhist city, **Leh** (p301). If the political situation allows (see the boxed text, p283), head to **Srinagar** (p286) in Kashmir, then through **Jammu** (p282) to **McLeod Ganj** (p369).

Finish off the trip at **Amritsar** (p268) with its shimmering **Golden Temple** (p270) before one last train ride to Delhi. What a journey!

Kicking off in Kolkata and winding up in Delhi, this wide-ranging journey draws a snaking line through the highlights of Bihar, Uttar Pradesh, Madhya Pradesh, northern Maharashtra, Gujarat, Rajasthan, Uttarakhand, Himachal Pradesh, Ladakh, Kashmir and Punjab.

CIRCLING THE SOUTH
Two Months

Mumbai is the borderline between north and south, and the easiest starting point for exploring India's steamy southern tip. Time your trip to avoid the monsoon – the sunniest skies are from October to February.

Kick off in cosmopolitan **Mumbai** (p777) and make the most of the **shopping** (p804), **eating** (p798) and **drinking** (p801) before heading inland to **Ajanta** (p825) and **Ellora** (p822) to marvel at Maharashtra's finest cave art. Sashay southwest to **Goa** (p858) to laze on palm-fringed beaches before dosing up on history inland at wonderful **Hampi** (p938), with its temple ruins and giant boulders.

Next, rub shoulders with yuppies in the party bars of **Bengaluru** (Bangalore; p910) and smell the waft of incense in spicy **Mysore** (p914) with its extravagant **Maharaja's Palace** (p916). Feast on a banana-leaf **thali** (p919) before cruising south to Kerala, stopping at enigmatic **Kochi** (p1013) for a **Kathakali performance** (p1023). Cruise Kerala's languorous backwaters from **Alappuzha** (p999) before dipping your toes in the warm waters around **Varkala** (p993).

For a change of pace, go northwest to **Periyar Wildlife Sanctuary** (p1006) to spot elephants before visiting the Tamil temples in **Madurai** (p1094). Pop into **Trichy** (Tiruchirappalli; p1087) and **Thanjavur** (Tanjore; p1084) before slowing down the pace in French-flavoured **Puducherry** (Pondicherry; p1071). Dine on fine food in Tamil Nadu's busy capital, **Chennai** (Madras; p1052), before breaking north to admire the Mughal-era relics of **Hyderabad** (p959).

It's a long ride by train up the coast to **Bhubaneswar** (p645), the leaping-off point for **Puri** (p652), site of the famous **Rath Yatra chariot festival** (see the boxed text, p646). Drift north to the legendary Sun Temple at **Konark** (p657) before one last train ride northeast to **Kolkata** (p501).

A slice of the steamy south featuring beaches, cave temples, jungle reserves and some of South India's best and brightest cities. Allow at least two months to soak up the sights, sounds and sensations of the tropical south.

ROADS LESS TRAVELLED

SIKKIM & THE NORTHEAST STATES One Month

Surprisingly few people explore mountainous Sikkim and the tribal heartland of India's Northeast States. Permits are required, so plan your trip in advance, see p610 and p587. Also be aware of the security risks, see the boxed text, p611.

Obtain a Sikkim permit in **Siliguri** (p541), or **Darjeeling** (see the boxed text, p558), and sample India's most famous **teas** (p557). Then head to **Gangtok** (p588), the Sikkimese capital, and the surrounding **Buddhist monasteries** (p594).

Veer to **Namchi** (p596) for giant statues of Shiva and Padmasambhava, and to **Pelling** (p598), for **Pemayangtse Gompa** (p600) and Khangchendzonga views. Take the week-long trek from **Yuksom** (p602) to **Goecha La** (p603). Exit Sikkim via **Tashiding** (p605), returning to Siliguri for the journey east to Assam.

In **Guwahati** (p612), the Assamese capital, arrange tours and permits for Arunachal Pradesh, Nagaland, Mizoram, and Manipur. If you can't get a permit, try this loop: from Guwahati, head to **Manas** (p617) and **Kaziranga** (p618) National Parks to spot rare wildlife. Detour to sleepy **Shillong** (p637), and the waterfalls of **Cherrapunjee** (Sohra; p640). From **Agartala** (p633), capital of Tripura, head by air or land to **Bangladesh** (see the boxed text, p636).

With the right permits, head from Guwahati to Arunachal Pradesh for the stunning Buddhist monastery in the **Tawang Valley** (p626), or the tribal villages near **Ziro** (p623). A Nagaland permit opens up the capital **Kohima** (p627), and fascinating tribal villages around **Mon** (p629). Manipur permits are rarely granted, but there's a fair chance of eyeing Mizo culture in **Mizoram** (p631).

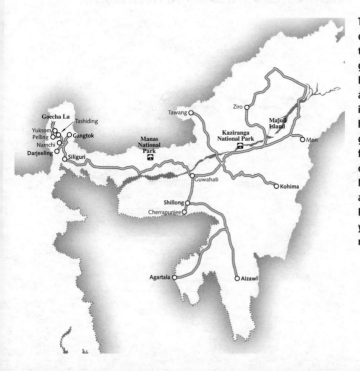

This is a journey off the beaten track through the gorgeous hills of Buddhist Sikkim and the rarely visited Northeast. You have the chance to get even further from the tourist circuit in tribal Nagaland, Mizoram and Arunachal Pradesh, providing you can obtain the required permits.

THE GREAT HIMALAYAN CIRCUIT   Four to Six Weeks

This rugged mountain odyssey can be started in Kashmir's **Srinagar** (p286), or in **Manali** (p357) in Himachal Pradesh, depending on the political situation – see the boxed text, p283. Note that the mountain passes are only open from July to October. Acute Mountain Sickness is also a hazard – see p1198.

Assuming things are safe, start off with a houseboat stay in **Srinagar** (p290) before embarking on the epic journey into the mountains. Start with the bone-shaking ride to **Kargil** (p295), the dusty gateway to remote **Zanskar** (p296). By bus or 4WD, head south through **Rangdum** (p296) to the monastery-strewn valley around **Padum** (p297), then return to Kargil for the coccyx-crunching ride on to **Ladakh** (p299). Break the journey east at **Lamayuru** (p322), **Alchi** (p321) and **Basgo** (p320), for awesome monastery paintings and sculptures.

On arrival in **Leh** (p301), take some time to unwind. Consider a **meditation course** (p307) and visit the local stupas, gompas and **palace** (p303). Join a tour over the world's highest road pass to the **Nubra Valley** (p323) and explore the Indus Valley by bus or rented motorcycle, visiting the monastery towns of **Stok** (p318), **Thiksey** (p326) and **Hemis** (p327).

Next, veer south over perilous mountain passes to **Keylong** (p391), the calm capital of Lahaul. Stroll to local **gompas** (p392), and travel by bus through parched deserts to **Kaza** (p393), the capital of Spiti. Obtain a permit for onward travel, then continue east to **Dhankar** (p395) and **Tabo** (p395) for more mesmerising Buddhist art.

With permit in hand, you can continue through knee-trembling mountain scenery to **Rekong Peo** (p345), capital of Kinnaur. Detour north to the pretty village of **Kalpa** (p346) to shake off the trail dust, then finish the journey with some creature comforts in **Shimla** (p334) – you've earned it!

A mountain odyssey, crossing over the world's highest motorable passes from Kashmir all the way to Kinnaur in Himachal Pradesh. Even when Kashmir is off limits, you can travel from Manali to Ladakh and finish the circuit from there.

THE TRIBAL CENTRE
Eight to 10 Weeks

Well off the radar of most travellers, the western plains are full of offbeat sights and fascinating glimpses of tribal India (see p109 for more information). However, security can be a concern in parts of Bihar – see p568.

Start in **Kolkata** (Calcutta; p501), Bengal's bustling cultural capital, before training it northeast to **Ranchi** (p582), gateway to **Betla (Palamau) National Park** (p583). Head back via Ranchi and **Gaya** (p575) to famous **Bodhgaya** (p576), the birthplace of Buddhism. Continue north via the Buddhist ruins at **Nalanda** (p581) to Bihar's capital, **Patna** (p568), to stock up on Mithila **tribal art** (p573).

Travel on to Madhya Pradesh through **Varanasi** (p440), detouring south past tiger- and leopard-inhabited **Bandhavgarh National Park** (p719) to **Jabalpur** (p713), for a boat cruise along the **Narmada River gorge** (p715). Take a side trip to **Kanha National Park** (p717) for another decent chance of spotting tigers.

Next, break east for **Bhopal** (p689), a surprising city that is rising above its tragic past. From here, you can detour to well-preserved Buddhist ruins at **Sanchi** (p695) and prehistoric painted caves at **Bhimbetka** (p695).

Next, trundle southeast to **Indore** (p704) for detours to the Mughal and Afghan ruins at **Mandu** (p709), the Hindu temples of **Ujjain** (p702) and the holy island of **Omkareshwar** (p707). From Indore, cut back across the state to **Jagdalpur** (p721) for visits to surrounding Bastar tribal areas.

More tribal visits are possible in nearby **Jeypore** (p663) in Orissa. For a change of scenery, head to the coast at **Gopalpur-on-Sea** (p660). Spot sea turtles at **Rushikulya** (p660) or take your binoculars to the bird-watching paradise of **Chilika Lake** (p659). Continue north through the capital, **Bhubaneswar** (p645), to the famous temples at **Puri** (p652) and **Konark** (p657). Finally, drift up the coast to Kolkata, with a detour to animal-packed **Similipal National Park** (p665).

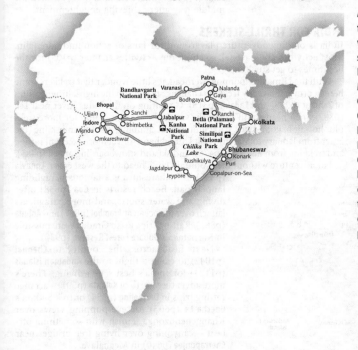

A looping circuit from Kolkata visiting the rarely seen sights of Bihar, Jharkhand, Madhya Pradesh, Chhattisgarh and Orissa – the tribal heartland of the Indian plains. Count on temples, historic ruins, encounters with tribal culture, and glorious national parks.

TAILORED TRIPS

THE BUDDHIST CIRCUIT

The Buddhist (or Lotus) Circuit is a pilgrims' trail in the footsteps of Buddha, connecting the sacred sites in Bihar and Uttar Pradesh where he walked and talked. A logical continuation of this circuit is Buddha's birthplace at Lumbini, an easy detour across the Nepal border from **Sunauli** (p456).

Begin in **Bodhgaya** (p576), the most sacred Buddhist site. **Mahabodhi Temple** (p576) is where Prince Siddhartha Gautama attained enlightenment and became Buddha, over 2500 years ago. Start your own path to enlightenment on a **meditation course** (p578) before heading to **Rajgir** (p580), where Buddha gave many sermons about the 'middle way'. Continue north until you reach the ruins of **Nalanda** (p581), marking the site of a vast and vanished Buddhist university.

At **Patna** (p568), see sculptures from Buddhist sites at **Patna Museum** (p570). You can detour here to **Vaishali** (p573), where Buddha preached his final sermon, and to **Kesariya** (p574), where he passed his begging bowl to his followers and began his final journey towards his birthplace at Lumbini. He died just short of the border at **Kushinagar** (p455). Heading here, you can visit **Sarnath** (p453), where Buddha first preached the middle way after achieving enlightenment.

INDIA FOR THRILL-SEEKERS

India is one big adventure playground for fans of action and adrenalin. Most activities are seasonal, so check the Activities chapter (p105) for the best times to get stuck in.

With the Himalaya looming overhead, it's little wonder that trekkers come here in droves. Start any trekking challenge in style on the high-altitude routes of **Zanskar** (p298) and **Ladakh** (p315). Go rafting on the Indus River near **Leh** (p307), then head south to **Manali** (see the boxed text, p362) for more treks plus hot-air balloon rides, paragliding, rock climbing, zorbing and skiing (the latter from January to March). Visit Uttarakhand for yet more excellent rafting and trekking from **Rishikesh** (p478), and ski and snowboarding at **Auli** (p485).

For adventure without the mountain chill, head to the west coast. **Lonavla**

(p836) in Maharashtra is a famous paragliding launch pad. Beach resorts in **Goa** (p858) offer diving and water sports, and more paragliders launch over the ocean at **Arambol** (p887) and **Anjuna** (p882). Rafting trips up to Grade IV are possible in Karnataka's **Dubare Forest Reserve** (p930).

Next, head across the country to **Chennai** (p1042) to catch a flight to the **Andaman Islands** (p1124) for India's best scuba-diving. There's more adventure north of **Kolkata** (p501) – arrange rafting trips in **Darjeeling** (p554) or trek Sikkim's **Goecha La** (p603) for eye-popping views over Khangchendzonga. Finish with something offbeat – canyoning over living tree bridges near **Cherrapunjee** (p640) in Meghalaya.

SAND, SEA & SACRED SITES

This route, from **Mumbai** (p777) to **Chennai** (p1042), blends some southern temples with the south's most beautiful beaches. To continue the beach theme, tag the sun-soaked **Andaman Islands** (p1120) to the end of this itinerary.

Start the search for sea and sand at Mumbai's **Chowpatty Beach** (p788) with a plate of the *bhelpuri* (crisp fried thin rounds of dough mixed with puffed rice, fried lentils, lemon juice, onion, herbs and chutney) while overlooking the Arabian Sea. Cruise to the stunning rock-cut temples on **Elephanta Island** (p809), then travel south to beach-blessed **Goa** (p858). Enjoy the best of the sand at **Arambol** (p887), **Vagator** (p885) and **Palolem** (p895), then continue along the coast to the sacred town of **Gokarna** (p935). Next, veer inland to the ruined Vijayanagar temples at **Hampi** (p938) and the Hoysala temples of **Belur** and **Halebid** (p924).

Connect through **Mangalore** (p930) and **Kochi** (p1013) to Kerala's seaside strip. Enjoy serious beach therapy in **Varkala** (p993) and **Kovalam** (p988), before jumping onto the train northeast to the awesome Sri Meenakshi Temple in **Madurai** (p1095). Continue north through the historic temple towns of **Trichy** (p1087), **Thanjavur** (p1084) and **Chidambaram** (p1079) and break the journey at the French-influenced seaside town of **Puducherry** (p1071).

Continuing north, detour inland to the captivating Arunachaleswar Temple in **Tiruvannamalai** (p1069), and follow the coast to **Mamallapuram** (Mahabalipuram; p1059), home to the famous rock-carved **Shore Temple** (p1060). Finally, finish your journey with a stroll along Chennai's **Marina Beach** (p1049).

History

India's story is one of the grand epics of world history. Throughout thousands of years of great civilisations, invasions, the birth of religions and countless cataclysms, India has time and again proved itself to be, in the words of its first prime minister, Jawaharlal Nehru, 'a bundle of contradictions held together by strong but invisible threads'. Indian history has always been a work in progress, a constant process of reinvention and accumulation that can ultimately prove elusive for those seeking to grasp its essential essence. And yet, from its myriad upheavals, a vibrant, diverse and thoroughly modern nation has emerged, as enduring as it is dynamic and increasingly geared to meet the multifarious challenges of the future.

INDUS VALLEY CIVILISATION

The Indus Valley, straddling the modern India–Pakistan border, is the cradle of civilisation on the Indian subcontinent. The first inhabitants of this region were nomadic tribes who cultivated land and kept domestic animals. Over thousands of years, an urban culture began to emerge from these tribes, particularly from 3500 BC. By 2500 BC large cities were well established, the focal points of what became known as the Harappan culture, which would flourish for more than 1000 years.

To learn more about the ancient Indus Valley civilisations, ramble around Harappa (www .harappa.com), which presents an illustrated yet scholarly overview.

The great cities of the Mature Harappan period were Moenjodaro and Harappa in present-day Pakistan, and Lothal (p737) near Ahmedabad. Lothal can be visited and from the precise, carefully laid-out street plan, some sense of this sophisticated 4500-year-old civilisation is still evident. Harappan cities often had a separate acropolis, suggesting a religious function, and the great tank at Moenjodaro may have been used for ritual bathing purposes. The major Harappan cities were also notable for their size – estimates put the population of Moenjodaro as high as at least 50,000.

By the middle of the 3rd millennium BC the Indus Valley culture was arguably the equal of other great civilisations emerging at the time. The Harappans traded with Mesopotamia, and developed a system of weights and measures and a highly developed art in the form of terracotta and bronze figurines. Recovered relics, including models of bullock carts and jewellery, offer the earliest evidence of a distinctive Indian culture. Indeed, many elements of Harappan culture would later become assimilated into Hinduism: clay figurines found at these sites suggest worship of a Mother goddess (later personified as Kali) and a male three-faced god sitting in the pose of a yogi (believed to be the historic Shiva) attended by four animals. Black stone pillars (associated with phallic worship of Shiva) and animal

TIMELINE

2600–1700 BC	1500 BC	1000 BC
The heyday of the Indus Valley civilisation. Spanning parts of Rajasthan, Gujarat and the Sindh province in present-day Pakistan, the settlement takes shape around metropolises such as Harappa and Moenjodaro.	The Indo-Aryan civilisation takes root in the fertile plains of the Indo-Gangetic basin. The settlers here speak an early form of Sanskrit, from which several Indian vernaculars, including Hindi, later evolve.	Indraprastha, Delhi's first incarnation, comes into being. Archaeological excavations at the site, where the Purana Qila now stands, continue even today, as more facts about this ancient capital keep emerging.

figures (the most prominent being the humped bull; later Shiva's mount, Nandi) have also been discovered.

EARLY INVASIONS & THE RISE OF RELIGIONS

The Harappan civilisation fell into decline from the beginning of the 2nd millennium BC. Some historians attribute the end of the empire to floods or decreased rainfall, which threatened the Harappans' agricultural base. The more enduring, if contentious, theory is that an Aryan invasion put paid to the Harappans, despite little archaeological proof or written reports in the ancient Indian texts to that effect. As a result, some nationalist historians argue that the Aryans (from a Sanskrit word meaning 'noble') were in fact the original inhabitants of India and that the invasion theory was actually invented by self-serving foreign conquerors. Others say that the arrival of Aryans was more of a gentle migration that gradually subsumed Harappan culture.

Those who defend the invasion theory believe that from around 1500 BC Aryan tribes from Afghanistan and Central Asia began to filter into northwest India. Despite their military superiority, their progress was gradual, with successive tribes fighting over territory and new arrivals pushing further east into the Ganges plain. Eventually these tribes controlled northern India as far as the Vindhya Hills. Many of the original inhabitants of northern India, the Dravidians, were pushed south.

The Hindu sacred scriptures, the Vedas (see p69), were written during this period of transition (1500–1200 BC) and the caste system became formalised.

As the Aryan tribes spread across the Ganges plain in the late 7th century BC, many were absorbed into 16 major kingdoms, which were, in turn, amalgamated into four large states. Out of these states arose the Nanda dynasty, which came to power in 364 BC, ruling over huge swathes of North India.

During this period, the Indian heartland narrowly avoided two invasions from the west which, if successful, could have significantly altered the path of Indian history. The first was by the Persian king Darius (521–486 BC), who annexed Punjab and Sindh (on either side of the modern India–Pakistan border). Alexander the Great advanced to India from Greece in 326 BC, but his troops refused to go beyond the Beas River in Himachal Pradesh. Alexander turned back without ever extending his power into India itself.

The period is also distinguished by the rise of two of India's most significant religions, Buddhism (p72) and Jainism (p72), which arose around 500 BC. Both questioned the Vedas and were critical of the caste system, although, unlike the Buddhists, the Jains never denied their Hindu heritage, and their faith never extended beyond India.

A History of India by Romila Thapar (Volume One) and Percival Spear (Volume Two) is one of the more thorough introductions to Indian history, from 1000 BC to Independent India.

563–483 BC	326 BC	321–185 BC
The life of Siddhartha Gautama (founder of Buddhism) who attained enlightenment beneath a Bodhi tree in Bodhgaya (Bihar) thereby transforming into the Buddha (Awakened One).	Alexander the Great invades India. He defeats King Porus in Punjab to enter the subcontinent, but a rebellion within his army keeps him from advancing beyond the Beas River in Himachal Pradesh.	India comes under the rule of the Maurya kings. Founded by Chandragupta Maurya, this Pan-Indian empire is ruled from Pataliputra (present-day Patna), and briefly adopts Buddhism during the reign of Emperor Ashoka.

MAP-DRAWING ARYAN-STYLE

While some historians dispute the origins of the Aryan presence in northern India, there's little argument that the subsequent Aryan kingdoms often adhered to one of history's more curious forms of territorial demarcation. Under the highly formalised ritual of *asvamedha* (horse sacrifice), a horse was allowed to roam freely, followed by a band of soldiers. If the horse's progress was impeded, the king would fight for the land in question. At the end of the prescribed period, the entire area over which the horse had wandered was taken to be the king's unchallenged territory. The horse was rewarded for its success or failure – which, it didn't matter – by being sacrificed. The system must have worked, because the ritual was still being performed centuries later by dynasties such as the Chalukyas of Badami (p946) to demonstrate the ruler's complete control over his kingdom.

THE MAURYAN EMPIRE & ITS AFTERMATH

If the Harappan culture was the cradle of Indian civilisation, Chandragupta Maurya was the founder of the first great Indian empire. He came to power in 321 BC, having seized the throne from the Nandas, and he soon expanded the empire to include the Indus Valley previously conquered by Alexander.

From its capital at Pataliputra (modern-day Patna), the Mauryan empire encompassed much of North India and reached as far south as modern-day Karnataka. The Mauryas were capable of securing control over such a vast realm through the use of an efficient bureaucracy, organised tiers of local government and a well-defined social order consisting of a rigid caste system.

The empire reached its peak under emperor Ashoka (see opposite). Such was Ashoka's power to lead and unite that after his death in 232 BC, no one could be found to hold the disparate elements of the Mauryan empire together. The empire rapidly disintegrated and collapsed altogether in 184 BC.

None of the empires that immediately followed could match the stability or enduring historical legacy of the Mauryans. The Sungas (184–70 BC), Kanvas (72–30 BC), Shakas (from 130 BC) and Kushanas (1st century BC until 1st century AD, and into the 3rd century in a diminished form) all had their turn, with the last briefly ruling over a massive area of North India and Central Asia.

Despite the multiplicity of ruling powers, this was a period of intense development. Trade with the Roman empire (overland, and by sea through the southern ports) became substantial during the 1st century AD; there was also overland trade with China.

Emperor Ashoka's ability to rule over his empire was assisted by a standing army consisting of roughly 9000 elephants, 30,000 cavalry and 600,000 infantry.

THE GOLDEN AGE OF THE GUPTAS

The empires that followed the Mauryans may have claimed large areas of Indian territory as their own, but many secured only nominal power over their realms. Throughout the subcontinent, small tribes and kingdoms effectively controlled territory and dominated local affairs.

AD 319–510	500–600	610
The golden era of the Gupta dynasty, the second of India's great empires after the Mauryas. This era is marked by a creative surge in literature and the arts.	The emergence of the Rajputs in Rajasthan. Hailing from three principal races supposedly of celestial origin, they form 36 separate clans which spread out to secure their own kingdoms across the region.	Prophet Mohammed establishes Islam. He soon invites the people of Mecca to adopt the new religion under the command of God, and his call is met with eager response.

AN ENLIGHTENED EMPEROR

Apart from the Mughals and then the British many centuries later, no other power controlled more Indian territory than the Mauryan empire. It's therefore fitting that it provided India with one of its most significant historical figures.

Emperor Ashoka's rule was characterised by a period of flourishing art and sculpture, while his reputation as a philosopher-king was enhanced by the rock-hewn edicts he used to both instruct his people and delineate the enormous span of his territory. Some of these moral teachings can still be seen, particularly the Ashokan edicts at Junagadh in Gujarat (p759).

Ashoka's reign also represented an undoubted historical high point for Buddhism. He embraced the religion in 262 BC, declaring it the state religion and cutting a radical swathe through the spiritual and social body of Hinduism. The extant highlights of Ashoka's Buddhist India are visible in Sarnath (p453) in Uttar Pradesh (on the spot where Buddha delivered his first sermon expounding the Noble Eightfold Path, or Middle Way to Enlightenment; see p72) and the stupas that the emperor built at Sanchi (p696) in Madhya Pradesh. Ashoka also sent missions abroad, and he is revered in Sri Lanka because he sent his son and daughter to carry Buddhism to the island.

The long shadow this emperor of the 3rd century BC still casts over India is evident from the fact that Ashoka's standard, which topped many pillars, is now the seal of modern-day India (four lions sitting back-to-back atop an abacus decorated with a frieze and the inscription 'truth alone triumphs') and its national emblem, chosen to reaffirm the ancient commitment to peace and goodwill.

In AD 319 Chandragupta I, the third king of one of these tribes, the little-known Guptas, came to prominence by a fortuitous marriage to the daughter of one of the most powerful tribes in the north, the Liccavis. The Gupta empire grew rapidly and under Chandragupta II (r 375–413) achieved its greatest extent. The Chinese pilgrim Fa-hsien, visiting India at the time, described a people 'rich and contented', ruled over by enlightened and just kings.

Poetry, literature and the arts flourished, with some of the finest work done at Ajanta (p825), Ellora (p822), Sanchi (p695) and Sarnath (p453). Towards the end of the Gupta period, Hinduism became the dominant religious force and its revival eclipsed Jainism and Buddhism; the latter in particular went into decline and, deprived of Ashoka's patronage, would never again be India's dominant religion.

The invasions of the Huns at the beginning of the 6th century signalled the end of this era, and in 510 the Gupta army was defeated by the Hun leader Toramana. Power in North India again devolved to a number of separate Hindu kingdoms.

> The concepts of zero and infinity are widely believed to have been devised by eminent Indian mathematicians during the reign of the Guptas.

THE HINDU SOUTH

Southern India has always laid claim to its own unique history. Insulated by distance from the political developments in the north, a separate set of

850	1026	1192
The Chola empire comes to power in South India, establishing itself as an especially formidable economic and military presence in Asia under the rule of Rajaraja Chola I and his son Rajendra Chola I.	Mahmud of Ghazni raids India for the last time, ransacking on this occasion the Hindu Somnath Temple in Gujarat, where he purportedly smashes the idol with his own hands.	Prithviraj Chauhan loses Delhi to Mohammed of Ghori. The defeat effectively ends Hindu supremacy in the region, exposing the subcontinent to subsequent Muslim invaders marching in from the northwest.

powerful kingdoms emerged, among them the Shatavahanas (who ruled over central India while the Kushanas held sway in the north), Kalingas and Vakatakas. But it was from the tribal territories on the fertile coastal plains that the greatest southern empires – the Cholas, Pandyas, Chalukyas, Cheras and Pallavas – came into their own.

The Chalukyas ruled mainly over the Deccan region of central India, although their power occasionally extended further north. With a capital at Badami in modern-day Karnataka, they ruled from 550 to 753 before falling to the Rashtrakutas. An eastern branch of the Chalukyas, with its capital at Kalyani in Karnataka, rose and ruled again from 972 to 1190.

In the far south, the Pallavas pioneered Dravidian architecture with its exuberant, almost baroque, style. The surviving architectural high points of Pallava rule are to be found in the Shore Temple (p1060) and Five Rathas (p1060) in Mamallapuram (Mahabalipuram), the temples of the erstwhile Pallava capital at Kanchipuram (p1065) and the Rock Fort Temple at Trichy (Tiruchirappalli; p1089).

The south's prosperity was based on long-established trading links with other civilisations, among them the Egyptians and Romans. In return for spices, pearls, ivory and silk, the Indians received Roman gold. Indian merchants also extended their influence to Southeast Asia. In 850 the Cholas rose to power and superseded the Pallavas. They soon set about turning the south's far-reaching trade influence into territorial conquest. Under the reign of Rajaraja Chola I (985–1014) they controlled almost the whole of South India, the Deccan plateau, Sri Lanka, parts of the Malay peninsula and the Sumatran-based Srivijaya kingdom.

Not all of their attention was focused overseas, however, and the Cholas left behind some of the finest examples of Dravidian architecture, most notably the sublime Brihadishwara Temple in Thanjavur (p1084) and Chidambaram's stunning Nataraja Temple (p1079). Both Thanjavur and Chidambaram served as Chola capitals.

India: A History by John Keay is an astute and readable account of subcontinental history spanning from the Harappan civilisation to Indian Independence.

Throughout, Hinduism remained the bedrock of South Indian culture.

THE MUSLIM NORTH

While South India guarded its resolutely Hindu character, North India was convulsed by Muslim armies invading from the northwest.

In the vanguard of Islamic expansion was Mahmud of Ghazni. Today, Ghazni is a nondescript little town between Kabul and Kandahar in Afghanistan. But in the early years of the 11th century, Mahmud turned it into one of the world's most glorious capital cities, which he largely funded by plundering his neighbours' territories. From 1001 to 1025 Mahmud conducted 17 raids into India, most infamously on the famous Shiva temple at Somnath (p755) in Gujarat. The Hindu force of 70,000 died trying to defend the temple, which eventually fell in early 1026. In the aftermath of

1206	1336	1398
Ghori is murdered during a prayer session while returning to Ghazni from a campaign in Lahore. In the absence of an heir, his kingdom is usurped by his generals. The Delhi Sultanate is born.	Foundation of the mighty Vijayanagar empire, named after its capital city, the ruins of which can be seen today in the vicinity of Hampi (in modern-day Karnataka).	Timur (Tamerlane) invades Delhi, on the pretext that the Sultans of Delhi are too tolerant with their Hindu subjects. He executes tens of thousands of Hindu captives before the battle for Delhi.

his victory, Mahmud, not particularly intent on acquiring new territory at this stage, transported a massive haul of gold and other booty back to his capital. These raids effectively shattered the balance of power in North India, allowing subsequent invaders to claim the territory for themselves.

Following Mahmud's death in 1033, Ghazni was seized by the Seljuqs and then fell to the Ghurs of western Afghanistan, who similarly had their eyes on the great Indian prize. The Ghur style of warfare was brutal – the Ghur general, Ala-ud-din, was known as 'Burner of the World'.

In 1191 Mohammed of Ghur advanced into India. Although defeated in a major battle against a confederacy of Hindu rulers, he returned the following year and routed his enemies. One of his generals, Qutb-ud-din, captured Delhi and was appointed governor; it was during his reign that the great Delhi landmark, the Qutb Minar complex (p163), was built. A separate Islamic empire was established in Bengal and within a short time almost the whole of North India was under Muslim control.

Following Mohammed's death in 1206, Qutb-ud-din became the first sultan of Delhi. His successor, Iltutmish, brought Bengal back under central control and defended the empire from an attempted Mongol invasion. Ala-ud-din Khilji came to power in 1296 and pushed the borders of the empire inexorably south, while simultaneously fending off further attacks by the Mongols.

'the Ghur general, Ala-ud-din, was known as Burner of the World'

NORTH MEETS SOUTH

Ala-ud-din died in 1320, and Mohammed Tughlaq ascended the throne in 1324. In 1328 Tughlaq took the southern strongholds of the Hoysala empire, which had centres at Belur, Halebid and Somnathpur. India was Tughlaq's for the taking.

However, while the empire of the pre-Mughal Muslims would achieve its greatest extent under Tughlaq's rule, his overreaching ambition also sowed the seeds of its disintegration. Unlike his forebears (including great rulers such as Ashoka), Tughlaq dreamed not only of extending his indirect influence over South India, but of controlling it directly as part of his empire.

After a series of successful campaigns Tughlaq decided to move the capital from Delhi to a more central location. The new capital was called Daulatabad and was near Aurangabad in Maharashtra. Not a man of half measures, Tughlaq sought to populate the new capital by forcefully marching the entire population of Delhi 1100km south, resulting in great loss of life. However, he soon realised that this left the north undefended and so the entire capital was moved north again. The superb hilltop fortress of Daulatabad (p821) stands as the last surviving monument to his megalomaniac vision.

The days of the Ghur empire were numbered. The last of the great sultans of Delhi, Firoz Shah, died in 1388 and the fate of the sultanate was sealed when Timur (Tamerlane) made a devastating raid from Samarkand (in

1469	1498	1510
Guru Nanak, the founder of the Sikh faith – which has millions of followers within and beyond India to the present day – is born in a village near Lahore (in modern-day Pakistan).	Vasco da Gama, a Portuguese voyager, discovers the sea route from Europe to India. He arrives in (present-day) Kerala and engages in trade with the local nobility.	Portuguese forces capture Goa under the command of Alfonso de Albuquerque, whose initial attempt was thwarted by the ruler, Sultan Adil Shah of Bijapur. However he succeeds a few months later following Shah's death.

Central Asia) into India in 1398. Timur's sacking of Delhi was truly merciless; some accounts say his soldiers slaughtered every Hindu inhabitant.

After Tughlaq's withdrawal from the south, several splinter kingdoms arose. The two most significant were the Islamic Bahmani sultanate, which emerged in 1345 with its capital at Gulbarga, and later Bidar (p952), and the Hindu Vijayanagar empire, founded in 1336 with its capital at Hampi (p938). The battles between the two were among the bloodiest communal violence in Indian history and ultimately resolved nothing in the two centuries before the Mughals ushered in a more enlightened age.

A History of South India from Prehistoric Times to the Fall of Vijayanagar by KA Nilakanta Sastri is arguably the most comprehensive (if heavy-going) history of this region.

THE MUGHALS

Even as Vijayanagar was experiencing its last days, the next great Indian empire was being founded. The Mughal empire was massive, and covered, at its height, almost the entire subcontinent. Its significance, however, lay not only in its size. Mughal emperors presided over a golden age of arts and literature and had a passion for building that resulted in some of the finest architecture in India. In particular, Shah Jahan's sublime Taj Mahal (p404) ranks as one of the wonders of the world.

The founder of the Mughal line, Babur (r 1526–30), was a descendant of both Genghis Khan and Timur (Tamerlane). In 1525, armed with this formidable lineage, he marched into Punjab from his capital at Kabul. With technological superiority brought by firearms, and consummate skill in simultaneously employing artillery and cavalry, Babur defeated the numerically superior armies of the sultan of Delhi at the Battle of Panipat in 1526.

Despite this initial success, Babur's son, Humayun (r 1530–56) was defeated by a powerful ruler of eastern India, Sher Shah, in 1539 and forced to withdraw to Iran. Following Sher Shah's death in 1545, Humayun returned to claim his kingdom, eventually conquering Delhi in 1555. He died the following year and was succeeded by his young son Akbar (r 1556–1605) who, during his 49-year reign, managed to extend and consolidate the empire until he ruled over a mammoth area.

True to his name, Akbar (which means 'great' in Arabic) was probably the greatest of the Mughals, for he not only had the military ability required of a ruler at that time, but was also a just and wise ruler and a man of culture. He saw, as previous Muslim rulers had not, that the number of Hindus in India was too great to subjugate. Although Akbar was no saint – reports of massacres of Hindus at Panipat and Chitrod tarnish his legacy – he remains known for integrating Hindus into his empire and skilfully using them as advisers, generals and administrators. Akbar also had a deep interest in religious matters, and spent many hours in discussion with religious experts of all persuasions, including Christians and Parsis.

Jehangir (r 1605–27) ascended to the throne following Akbar's death. Despite several challenges to the authority of Jehangir himself, the empire

1526	1540	1556
Babur becomes the first Mughal emperor after conquering Delhi. He stuns Rajasthan by routing its confederate force, gaining a technological edge on the battlefield thanks to the early introduction of matchlock muskets in his army.	The Sur dynasty briefly captures Delhi from the Mughals, after Sher Shah Suri's victory over Humayun in the Battle of Kanauj. The loss forces the Mughals to temporarily seek help from the Rajputs.	Hemu, a Hindu general in Adil Shah Suri's army, seizes Delhi after the accidental death of Humayun. He rules for barely a month before losing to Akbar in the Second Battle of Panipat.

THE STRUGGLE FOR THE SOUL OF INDIA

Founded as an alliance of Hindu kingdoms banding together to counter the threat from the Muslims, the Vijayanagar empire rapidly grew into one of India's wealthiest and greatest Hindu empires. Under the rule of Bukka I (c 1343–79), the majority of South India was brought under its control.

The Vijayanagans and the Bahmani sultanate, which was also based in South India, were evenly matched. The Vijayanagar armies occasionally got the upper hand, but generally the Bahmanis inflicted the worst defeats. The atrocities committed by both sides almost defy belief. In 1366 Bukka I responded to a perceived slight by capturing the Muslim stronghold of Mudkal and slaughtering every inhabitant bar one, who managed to escape and carry news of the attack to Mohammad Shah, the sultan. Mohammad swore that he would not rest until he had killed 100,000 Hindus. Instead, according to the Muslim historian Firishtah, 500,000 'infidels' were killed in the ensuing campaign.

Somehow, Vijayanagar survived. In 1482, following much intrigue and plotting in the royal court, the Bahmani sultanate disintegrated and five separate kingdoms, based on the major cities – Berar, Ahmednagar, Bijapur, Golconda and Ahmedabad – were formed. Of these, Bijapur (p949) and Ahmedabad (Amdavad; p727) still bear exceptional traces of this period of Islamic rule. With little realistic opposition from the north, the Hindu empire enjoyed a golden age of almost supreme power in the south. In 1520 the Hindu king Krishnadevaraya even took Bijapur.

Like Bahmani, however, Vijayanagar's fault lines were soon laid bare. A series of uprisings divided the kingdom fatally, just at a time when the Muslim sultanates were beginning to form a new alliance. In 1565 a Muslim coalition routed the Hindu armies at the Battle of Talikota. Hampi was destroyed. Although the last of the Vijayanagar line escaped and the dynasty limped on for several years, real power passed to local Muslim rulers or Hindu chiefs once loyal to the Vijayanagar kings. One of India's grisliest periods came to an end when the Bahmani kingdoms fell to the Mughals.

---

remained more or less intact. In periods of stability Jehangir took the opportunity to spend time in his beloved Kashmir, eventually dying en route there in 1627. He was succeeded by his son, Shah Jahan (r 1627–58), who secured his position as emperor by executing all male relatives who stood in his way. During his reign, some of the most vivid and permanent reminders of the Mughals' glory were constructed; in addition to the Taj Mahal, he also oversaw the construction of the mighty Red Fort (Lal Qila) in Delhi (p129) and converted the Agra Fort (p407) into a palace that would later become his prison.

The last of the great Mughals, Aurangzeb (r 1658–1707), imprisoned his father (Shah Jahan) and succeeded to the throne after a two-year struggle against his brothers. Aurangzeb devoted his resources to extending the empire's boundaries, and thus fell into much the same trap as that of Mohammed Tughlaq some 300 years earlier. He, too, tried moving his capital south (to

1600	1631	1674
Britain's Queen Elizabeth I grants the first trading charter to the East India Company on 31 December 1600, with the maiden voyage taking place in 1601 under the command of Sir James Lancaster.	Construction of the Taj Mahal begins in Agra after Shah Jahan, overcome with grief following the death of his wife Mumtaz Mahal, vows to build the most beautiful mausoleum in the world in her memory.	Shivaji establishes the Maratha kingdom, spanning western India and parts of the Deccan and North India. He assumes the supercilious title of Chhatrapati, which means 'Lord of the Universe'.

Aurangabad) and imposed heavy taxes to fund his military. A combination of decaying court life and dissatisfaction among the Hindu population at inflated taxes and religious intolerance weakened the Mughal grip.

The empire was also facing serious challenges from the Marathas in central India and, more significantly, the British in Bengal. With Aurangzeb's death in 1707, the empire's fortunes rapidly declined, and Delhi was sacked by Persia's Nadir Shah in 1739. Mughal 'emperors' continued to rule right up until the First War of Independence (aka Indian Uprising) in 1857, but they were emperors without an empire.

THE RAJPUTS & THE MARATHAS

Throughout the Mughal period, there remained strong Hindu powers, most notably the Rajputs. Centred in Rajasthan, the Rajputs were a proud warrior caste with a passionate belief in the dictates of chivalry, both in battle and in state affairs. The Rajputs opposed every foreign incursion into their territory, but were never united or adequately organised to deal with stronger forces on a long-term basis. When they weren't battling foreign oppression, they squandered their energies fighting each other. This eventually led to their territories becoming vassal states of the Mughal empire. Their prowess in battle, however, was acknowledged, and some of the best military men in the Mughal emperors' armies were Rajputs.

White Mughals by William Dalrymple tells the true story of an East India Company soldier who married an Indian Muslim princess, a tragic love story interwoven with harem politics, intrigue and espionage.

The Marathas were less picaresque but ultimately more effective. They first rose to prominence under their great leader Shivaji, who gathered popular support by championing the Hindu cause against the Muslim rulers. Between 1646 and 1680 Shivaji performed heroic acts in confronting the Mughals across most of central India. At one time, Shivaji was captured by the Mughals and taken to Agra but, naturally, he managed to escape and continue his adventures. Tales of his larger-than-life exploits are still popular with wandering storytellers. He is a particular hero in Maharashtra, where many of his wildest adventures took place. He's also revered for the fact that, as a lower-caste Shudra, he showed that great leaders don't have to be of the Kshatriya (soldier) caste.

Shivaji's son was captured, blinded and executed by Aurangzeb. His grandson wasn't made of the same sturdy stuff, so the Maratha empire continued under the Peshwas, hereditary government ministers who became the real rulers. They gradually took over more of the weakening Mughal empire's powers, first by supplying troops and then actually taking control of Mughal land.

The expansion of Maratha power came to an abrupt halt in 1761 at Panipat. In the town where Babur had won the battle that established the Mughal empire more than 200 years earlier, the Marathas were defeated by Ahmad Shah Durrani from Afghanistan. Maratha expansion to the west was halted, and although they consolidated their control over central India

1707	1739	1747
Death of Aurangzeb, the last of the Mughal greats. His demise triggers the gradual collapse of the Mughal empire, as anarchy and rebellion erupt across the country.	Nadir Shah plunders Delhi, and carries away with him the jewel-encrusted Peacock Throne as well as the Koh-i-noor, a magnificent diamond, which changes many hands to eventually become property of the British royalty.	Afghan ruler Ahmad Shah Durrani sweeps across northern India, capturing Lahore and Kashmir, sacking Delhi and dealing another blow to the rapidly contracting Mughal empire.

and the region known as Malwa, they were to fall to India's final imperial power, the British.

THE RISE OF EUROPEAN POWER

The British weren't the first European power to arrive in India, nor were they the last to leave – both of those 'honours' go to the Portuguese. In 1498 Vasco da Gama arrived on the coast of modern-day Kerala, having sailed around the Cape of Good Hope. Pioneering this route gave the Portuguese a century of monopolisation over Indian and far-Eastern trade with Europe. In 1510 they captured Goa, followed by Diu in 1531, two enclaves the Portuguese controlled until 1961. In its heyday, the trade flowing through 'Golden Goa' was said to rival that passing through Lisbon. In the long-term, however, the Portuguese didn't have the resources to maintain a worldwide empire and they were quickly eclipsed and isolated after the arrival of the British and French.

In 1600 Queen Elizabeth I granted a charter to a London trading company that gave it a monopoly on British trade with India. In 1613 representatives of the East India Company established their first trading post at Surat in Gujarat. Further British trading posts, which were administered and governed by representatives of the company, were established at Madras (Chennai) in 1640, Bengal in 1651 and Bombay (Mumbai) in 1668. Strange as it now seems, for nearly 250 years a commercial trading company and not the British government 'ruled' over British India.

By 1672 the French had established themselves at Pondicherry (Puducherry; p1071), an enclave they held even after the British departed and where unmistakable architectural traces of French elegance remain. The stage was set for more than a century of rivalry between the British and French for control of Indian trade. At one stage, under the guidance of a handful of talented and experienced commanders, the French appeared to hold the upper hand. In 1746 they took Madras (only to hand it back in 1749) and their success in placing their favoured candidate on the throne as Nizam of Hyderabad augured well for the future. But serious French aspirations effectively ended in 1750 when the directors of the French East India Company decided that their representatives were playing too much politics and doing too little trading. Key representatives were sacked and a settlement designed to end all ongoing political disputes was made with the British. Although the French company's profits may have risen in the short-term, the decision effectively removed France as a serious influence on the subcontinent.

BRITISH INDIA

By the early 19th century, India was effectively under British control, although there remained a patchwork of states, many nominally independent and governed by their own rulers, the maharajas (or similarly titled princes)

Plain Tales from the Raj by Charles Allen (ed.) is a fascinating series of interviews with people who played a role in British India on both sides of the table.

1757	1801	1857
Breaking out of its business mould, the East India Company registers its first military victory on Indian soil. Siraj-ud-Daulah, nawab of Bengal, is defeated by Robert Clive in the Battle of Plassey.	Ranjit Singh becomes maharaja (Great King) of the newly united Sikhs and forges a powerful new kingdom from his capital in Lahore (in present-day Pakistan).	The First War of Independence against the British takes place. In the absence of a national leader, the freedom fighters coerce the last Mughal king, Bahadur Shah Zafar, to proclaim himself emperor of India.

THE LAST MUGHAL *William Dalrymple*

Bahadur Shah Zafar, the last Mughal emperor of Delhi, was one of the most talented, tolerant and likeable of his remarkable dynasty. Born in 1775, when the British were still confined to the Indian shore, he saw his dynasty reduced to humiliating insignificance and the British transform themselves from simple traders into the most powerful military force in India.

Coming late to the throne, Zafar succeeded his father only in 1838, when it was already too late to reverse the inexorable political decline of the Mughals. Despite this he succeeded in creating around him a court culture of unparalleled brilliance, and partly through his patronage there took place in Delhi one of the greatest literary renaissances in Indian history.

Zafar was himself a mystic, poet and calligrapher of great charm and accomplishment, but his achievement was to nourish the talents of India's greatest love poet, Ghalib, and his rival Zauq. While the British progressively assumed more of the emperor's power, finally laying plans to remove the Mughals altogether from Shah Jahan's Red Fort, the court busied itself with the obsessive pursuit of the most cleverly turned love lyric, the most moving *ghazal*, the most perfect Urdu couplet. As military and economic realities of British power and territorial ambition closed in, the court was lost in a last idyll of pleasure gardens and poetic symposia.

All this was swept away on a May morning in 1857, when 300 mutinous sepoys rode into Delhi, massacred every British man, woman and child they could find, and declared Zafar their emperor. Zafar was powerless to resist being made the leader of an uprising he knew was doomed: an officerless army of peasant soldiers against the forces of the world's greatest military power. Within a month Delhi was surrounded by the British and the scene was set for one of the most pitiless sieges in Indian history.

The Siege of Delhi was the Raj's Stalingrad: a fight to the death between two powers, neither of whom could retreat. For the four hottest months of the Indian summer, the beautiful Mughal capital was bombarded by British artillery. There were unimaginable casualties, with both Indians and British starving, the city left without water, and the combatants on both sides driven to the limits of physical and mental endurance. Finally, on the 14 September 1857, the British attacked and took the city, sacking, massacring and looting as they went. Delhi was left an empty ruin.

India's Struggle for Independence by Bipan Chandra expertly chronicles the history of India from 1857 to 1947.

and nawabs. While these 'princely states' administered their own territories, a system of central government was developed. British bureaucratic models were replicated in the Indian government and civil service – a legacy that still exists. From 1784 onwards, the British government in London began to take a more direct role in supervising affairs in India, although the territory was still notionally administered by the East India Company until 1858.

Trade and profit continued to be the main focus of British rule in India, resulting in far-reaching changes. Iron and coal mining were developed and tea, coffee and cotton became key crops. A start was made on the vast rail network that's still in use today, irrigation projects were undertaken and the zamindar (landowner) system was encouraged. These absentee landlords eased the burden of administration and tax collection for the British, but contributed to the development of an impoverished and landless peasantry.

1858	1869	1885
British government assumes control over India – with power officially transferred from the East India Company to the Crown – beginning the period known as the British Raj, which lasts until India's independence in 1947.	The birth of Mohandas Karamchand Gandhi in Porbandar (Gujarat) – the man who would later become popularly known as Mahatma Gandhi and affectionately dubbed 'Father of the Nation'.	The Indian National Congress, India's first home-grown political organisation, is set up. It brings educated Indians together and plays a key role in India's enduring freedom struggle.

In the weeks that followed, the vengeful British oversaw the wholesale destruction of great areas of Mughal Delhi. The Red Fort was plundered and much of it – including the exquisite harem courts – was razed to the ground. Though the royal family had surrendered peacefully, all 10 of the emperor's surviving sons were shot in cold blood. The emperor himself was put on show trial in the ruins of his old palace, and sentenced to transportation. He left his beloved Delhi on a peasant's bullock cart. Separated from everyone and everything he loved, broken hearted, the last of the Great Mughals died in exile in Rangoon on Friday 7 November 1862, at the age of 87.

As Zafar himself wrote, just before his death:

Delhi was once a paradise,
Where Love held sway and reigned;
But its charm lies ravished now
And only ruins remain.

No tears were shed when shroudless they
Were laid in common graves;
No prayers were read for the noble dead,
Unmarked remain their graves

But things cannot remain, O Zafar,
Thus for who can tell?
Through God's great mercy and the Prophet
All may yet be well

William Dalrymple is the author of The Last Mughal

The British also imposed English as the local language of administration. For them, this was critical in a country with so many different languages, but it also kept the new rulers at arm's length from the Indian populace.

THE ROAD TO INDEPENDENCE

The desire among many Indians to be free from foreign rule remained. Opposition to the British began to increase at the turn of the 20th century, spearheaded by the Indian National Congress, the country's oldest political party, also known as the Congress Party and Congress (I).

It met for the first time in 1885 and soon began to push for participation in the government of India. A highly unpopular attempt by the British to partition Bengal in 1905 resulted in mass demonstrations and brought to light Hindu opposition to the division; the Muslim community formed its own

In 1909 the so-called Morley-Minto Reforms provided for limited Indian participation in government and introduced separate electorates for the country's different religious communities.

1911	1919	1940
British architect Edwin Lutyens begins work on New Delhi, the newest manifestation of Delhi, subsequently considered in architectural circles as one of the finest garden cities to have ever been built.	The massacre, on 13 April, of unarmed Indian protesters at Jallianwala Bagh in Amritsar (Punjab). Gandhi responds with his program of civil (nonviolent) disobedience against the British government.	The Muslim League adopts its Lahore Resolution, which champions greater Muslim autonomy in India. Subsequent campaigns throughout the 1940s for the creation of a separate Islamic nation are spearheaded by Mohammed Ali Jinnah.

BRITAIN'S SURGE TO POWER

The transformation of the British from traders to governors began almost by accident. Having been granted a licence to trade in Bengal by the Mughals, and following the establishment of a new trading post at Calcutta (Kolkata) in 1690, business began to expand rapidly. Under the apprehensive gaze of the nawab (local ruler), British trading activities became extensive and the 'factories' took on an increasingly permanent (and fortified) appearance.

Eventually the nawab decided that British power had grown far enough. In June 1756 he attacked Calcutta and, having taken the city, locked his British prisoners in a tiny cell. The space was so cramped and airless that many were dead by the following morning. The cell infamously became known as the 'Black Hole of Calcutta'.

Six months later, Robert Clive, an employee in the military service of the East India Company, led an expedition to retake Calcutta and entered into an agreement with one of the nawab's generals to overthrow the nawab himself. This he did in June 1757 at the Battle of Plassey (now called Palashi) and the general who had assisted him was placed on the throne. During the period that followed, with the British effectively in control of Bengal, the company's agents engaged in a period of unbridled profiteering. When a subsequent nawab finally took up arms to protect his own interests, he was defeated at the Battle of Baksar in 1764, a victory that confirmed the British as the paramount power in east India.

In 1771 Warren Hastings was made governor in Bengal. During his tenure the company greatly expanded its control. His astute statesmanship was aided by the fact that India at this time was experiencing a power vacuum created by the disintegration of the Mughal empire. The Marathas (p46), the only real Indian power to step into this gap, were divided among themselves. Hastings concluded a series of treaties with local rulers, including one with the main Maratha leader.

In the south, where Mughal influence had never been great, the picture was confused by the strong British–French rivalry, and one ruler was played off against another. This was never clearer than in the series of Mysore wars where Hyder Ali and his son, Tipu Sultan, waged a brave and determined campaign against the British. In the Fourth Mysore War (1789–99), Tipu Sultan was killed at Srirangapatnam and British power took another step forward. The long-running struggle with the Marathas was concluded in 1803, leaving only Punjab (held by the Sikhs) outside British control. Punjab finally fell in 1849 after the two Sikh Wars (1845–46 and 1848–49).

league and campaigned for protected rights in any future political settlement. As pressure rose, a split emerged in Hindu circles between moderates and radicals, the latter resorting to violence to publicise their aims.

With the outbreak of WWI, the political situation eased. India contributed hugely to the war (more than one million Indian volunteers were enlisted and sent overseas, suffering more than 100,000 casualties). The contribution was sanctioned by Congress leaders, largely on the expectation that it would be rewarded after the war was over. No such rewards transpired and disillusion was soon to follow. Disturbances were particularly persistent in Punjab and,

1942	1947	1947–48
Mahatma Gandhi launches the Quit India campaign, demanding that the British leave India without delay and allow the country to get on with the business of self-governance.	India gains independence on 15 August. Pakistan is formed a day earlier. Partition is followed by cross-border exodus, as tens of thousands of Hindus and Muslims brave communal riots to migrate to their respective nations.	First war between India and Pakistan takes place not long after the (procrastinating) maharaja of Kashmir signs the Instrument of Accession that cedes his state to India. Pakistan challenges the document's legality.

in April 1919, following riots in Amritsar, a British army contingent was sent to quell the unrest. Under direct orders of the officer in charge they ruthlessly fired into a crowd of unarmed protesters – see the boxed text on p272. News of the massacre spread rapidly throughout India, turning huge numbers of otherwise apolitical Indians into Congress supporters.

At this time, the Congress movement found a new leader in Mohandas Gandhi (see the box, p54). Not everyone involved in the struggle agreed with or followed Gandhi's policy of nonviolence, yet the Congress Party and Gandhi remained at the forefront of the push for independence.

As political power-sharing began to look more likely, and the mass movement led by Gandhi gained momentum, the Muslim reaction was to consider its own immediate future. The large Muslim minority had realised that an independent India would be dominated by Hindus and, despite Gandhi's fair-minded approach, others in the Congress Party may not be so willing to share power. By the 1930s Muslims were raising the possibility of a separate Islamic state.

A Princess Remembers by Gayatri Devi and Santha Rama Rau is the captivating memoir of the former maharani of Jaipur, the glamorous Gayatri Devi, born in 1919.

THE FIRST WAR OF INDEPENDENCE: THE INDIAN UPRISING

In 1857, half a century after having established firm control of India, the British suffered a serious setback. To this day, the causes of the Uprising (known at the time as the Indian Mutiny and subsequently labelled by nationalist historians as a War of Independence) are the subject of debate. The key factors included the influx of cheap goods, such as textiles, from Britain that destroyed many livelihoods; the dispossession of territories from many rulers; and taxes imposed on landowners.

The incident that's popularly held to have sparked the Uprising, however, took place at an army barracks in Meerut in Uttar Pradesh on 10 May 1857. A rumour leaked out that a new type of bullet was greased with what Hindus claimed was cow fat, while Muslims maintained that it came from pigs; pigs are considered unclean to Muslims, and cows are sacred to Hindus. Since loading a rifle involved biting the end off the waxed cartridge, these rumours provoked considerable unrest.

In Meerut, the situation was handled with a singular lack of judgment. The commanding officer lined up his soldiers and ordered them to bite off the ends of their issued bullets. Those who refused were immediately marched off to prison. The following morning, the soldiers of the garrison rebelled, shot their officers and marched to Delhi. Of the 74 Indian battalions of the Bengal army, seven (one of them Gurkhas) remained loyal, 20 were disarmed and the other 47 mutinied. The soldiers and peasants rallied around the ageing Mughal emperor in Delhi – see the box, p48. They held Delhi for some months and besieged the British Residency in Lucknow for five months before they were finally suppressed. The incident left festering scars on both sides.

Almost immediately the East India Company was wound up and direct control of the country was assumed by the British government, which announced its support for the existing rulers of the princely states, claiming they would not interfere in local matters as long as the states remained loyal to the British.

1948	1948–56	1952
Mahatma Gandhi is assassinated in New Delhi by Nathuram Godse on 30 January. Godse and his co-conspirator Narayan Apte are later tried, convicted and executed (by hanging).	Rajasthan takes shape, as the princely states form a beeline to sign the Instrument of Accession, giving up their territories which are incorporated into the newly formed Republic of India.	Elections are held in Rajasthan, and the state gets its first taste of democracy after centuries of monarchical rule. The Congress is the first party to be elected into office.

Political events were partially disrupted by WWII when large numbers of Congress supporters were jailed to prevent disruption to the war effort.

INDEPENDENCE & THE PARTITION OF INDIA

The Labour Party victory in the British elections in July 1945 dramatically altered the political landscape. For the first time, Indian independence was accepted as a legitimate goal. This new goodwill did not, however, translate into any new wisdom as to how to reconcile the divergent wishes of the two major Indian parties. Mohammed Ali Jinnah, the leader of the Muslim League, championed a separate Islamic state, while the Congress Party, led by Jawaharlal Nehru, campaigned for an independent greater India.

In early 1946 a British mission failed to bring the two sides together and the country slid closer towards civil war. A 'Direct Action Day', called by the Muslim League in August 1946, led to the slaughter of Hindus in Calcutta, which prompted reprisals against Muslims. In February 1947 the nervous British government made the momentous initial decision that Independence would come by June 1948 (however this date would later be brought forward). In the meantime, the viceroy, Lord Wavell, was replaced by Lord Louis Mountbatten.

The new viceroy encouraged the rival factions to agree upon a united India, but to no avail. A decision was made to divide the country, with Gandhi the only staunch opponent. Faced with increasing civil violence, Mountbatten made the precipitous decision to bring forward Independence to 15 August 1947.

The decision to divide the country into separate Hindu and Muslim territories was immensely tricky – indeed the question of where the dividing line should actually be drawn proved almost impossible. Some areas were clearly Hindu or Muslim, but others had evenly mixed populations, and there were isolated 'islands' of communities in areas predominantly settled by other religions. Moreover, the two overwhelmingly Muslim regions were on opposite sides of the country and, therefore, Pakistan would inevitably have an eastern and western half divided by a hostile India. The instability of this arrangement was self-evident, but it was to be 25 years before the predestined split finally came and East Pakistan became Bangladesh.

An independent British referee was given the odious task of drawing the borders, well aware that the effects would be catastrophic for countless people. The decisions were fraught with impossible dilemmas. Calcutta, with its Hindu majority, port facilities and jute mills, was divided from East Bengal, which had a Muslim majority, large-scale jute production, no mills and no port facilities. One million Bengalis became refugees in the mass movement across the new border.

The problem was far worse in Punjab, where intercommunity antagonisms were already running at fever pitch. Punjab, one of the most fertile and afflu-

Mahatma Gandhi reiterated that the leader of the Muslim League, Mohammed Ali Jinnah, should lead a united India, if that would prevent Partition.

In India's first post-Independence elections in 1951–52, the Congress Party won 364 of 489 seats but took just 45% of the popular vote.

1962	1964	1965
Border war (known as the Sino-Indian War) with China over the North-East Frontier Area and Ladakh. China successfully captures the disputed territory and ends the war with a unilateral ceasefire.	Prime Minister Jawaharlal Nehru dies of a heart attack. Independent India's first prime minister, he played a pivotal role in championing India's freedom from British rule.	Skirmishes in Kashmir and the disputed Rann of Kutch in Gujarat flare into the Second India–Pakistan War, which involved the biggest tank battles since WWII. The war ends with a UN-mandated ceasefire.

ent regions of the country, had large Muslim, Hindu and Sikh communities. The Sikhs had already campaigned unsuccessfully for their own state and now saw their homeland divided down the middle. The new border ran straight between Punjab's two major cities – Lahore and Amritsar. Prior to Independence, Lahore's population of 1.2 million included approximately 500,000 Hindus and 100,000 Sikhs. When the dust had finally settled, roughly 1000 Hindus and Sikhs remained.

It was clear that Punjab contained all the ingredients for an epic disaster, but the resulting bloodshed was far worse than anticipated. Huge population exchanges took place. Trains full of Muslims, fleeing westward, were held up and slaughtered by Hindu and Sikh mobs. Hindus and Sikhs fleeing to the east suffered the same fate at Muslim hands. The army that was sent to maintain order proved totally inadequate and, at times, all too ready to join the sectarian carnage. By the time the Punjab chaos had run its course, more than 10 million people had changed sides and at least 500,000 had been killed.

A golden oldie, *Gandhi*, directed by Richard Attenborough, is one of the few movies that adeptly captures the grand canvas that is India in tracing the country's rocky road to Independence.

THE KASHMIR CONFLICT

Kashmir is the most enduring symbol of the turbulent partition of India. In the lead up to Independence, the delicate task of drawing the India–Pakistan border was complicated by the fact that the 'princely states' in British India were nominally independent. As part of the settlement process, local rulers were asked which country they wished to belong to. Kashmir was a predominantly Muslim state with a Hindu maharaja, Hari Singh, who tried to delay his decision. A ragtag Pashtun (Pakistani) army crossed the border, intent on racing to Srinagar and annexing Kashmir for Pakistan. In the face of this advance, the maharaja panicked and requested armed assistance from India. The Indian army arrived only just in time to prevent the fall of Srinagar, and the maharaja signed the Instrument of Accession, tying Kashmir to India, in October 1947. The legality of the document was immediately disputed by Pakistan and the two nations went to war, just two months after Independence.

In 1948 the fledgling UN Security Council called for a referendum (which remains a central plank of Pakistani policy) to decide the status of Kashmir. A UN-brokered ceasefire in 1949 kept the two countries on either side of a demarcation line, called the Line of Control (LOC), with little else being resolved. Two-thirds of Kashmir fell on the Indian side of the LOC, which remains the frontier, but neither side accepts this as the official border. The Indian state of Jammu & Kashmir, as it has stood since that time, incorporates Ladakh (divided between Muslims and Buddhists), Jammu (with a Hindu majority) and the 130km-long, 55km-wide Kashmir Valley (with a Muslim majority and most of the state's inhabitants). On the Pakistani side, over three million Kashmiris live in Azad (Free) Kashmir.

1966	1971	1972
Indira Gandhi, daughter of Jawaharlal Nehru, becomes prime minister of India. She has been India's only female prime minister to this day.	East Pakistan champions independence from West Pakistan. India gets involved, sparking the Third India–Pakistan War. West Pakistan surrenders, losing sovereignty of East Pakistan, which becomes Bangladesh.	The Simla Agreement between India and Pakistan attempts to normalise relations. The Kashmiri ceasefire line is formalised as the 'Line of Control', and still remains the de-facto border between the two countries.

MAHATMA GANDHI

One of the great figures of the 20th century, Mohandas Karamchand Gandhi was born on 2 October 1869 in Porbandar, Gujarat. After studying in London (1888–91), he worked as a barrister in South Africa. Here, the young Gandhi became politicised, railing against the discrimination he encountered. He soon became the spokesman for the Indian community and championed equality for all.

Gandhi returned to India in 1915 with the doctrine of ahimsa (nonviolence) central to his political plans, and committed to a simple and disciplined lifestyle. He set up the Sabarmati Ashram in Ahmedabad, which was innovative for its admission of Untouchables.

Within a year, Gandhi had won his first victory, defending farmers in Bihar from exploitation. This was when it's said he first received the title 'Mahatma' (Great Soul) from an admirer. The passage of the discriminatory Rowlatt Acts (which allowed certain political cases to be tried without juries) in 1919 spurred him to further action and he organised a national protest. In the days that followed this hartal (strike), feelings ran high throughout the country. After the massacre of unarmed protesters in Amritsar (p272), a deeply shocked Gandhi immediately called off the movement.

By 1920 Gandhi was a key figure in the Indian National Congress, and he coordinated a national campaign of noncooperation or satyagraha (passive resistance) to British rule, with the effect of raising nationalist feeling while earning the lasting enmity of the British. In early 1930, Gandhi captured the imagination of the country, and the world, when he led a march of several thousand followers from Ahmedabad to Dandi on the coast of Gujarat. On arrival, Gandhi ceremoniously made salt by evaporating sea water, thus publicly defying the much-hated salt tax; not for the first time, he was imprisoned. Released in 1931 to represent the Indian National Congress at the second Round Table Conference in London, he won the hearts of many British people but failed to gain any real concessions from the government.

Disillusioned with politics, he resigned his parliamentary seat in 1934. He returned spectacularly to the fray in 1942 with the Quit India campaign, in which he urged the British to leave India immediately. His actions were deemed subversive and he and most of the Congress leadership were imprisoned.

In the frantic Independence bargaining that followed the end of WWII, Gandhi was largely excluded and watched helplessly as plans were made to partition the country – a dire tragedy in his eyes. Gandhi stood almost alone in urging tolerance and the preservation of a single India, and his work on behalf of members of all communities drew resentment from some Hindu hardliners. On his way to a prayer meeting in Delhi on 30 January 1948, he was assassinated by a Hindu zealot – there's a memorial at the spot where he was shot dead, known as Gandhi Smriti (p135).

Since the frontier was drawn, incursions across the LOC have occurred with dangerous regularity. Although India and Pakistan normalised – to some extent – relations in 1976, tensions remain incredibly high. Conflict within Kashmir itself began in earnest in 1989.

1975	1984	1991
In a questionable move, Prime Minister Indira Gandhi declares a state of emergency under Article 352 of the Indian Constitution, in response to growing civil unrest and political opposition.	Prime Minister Indira Gandhi is assassinated by two of her (Sikh) bodyguards after her highly controversial decision to have Indian troops storm Amritsar's Golden Temple, the Sikhs' holiest shrine.	Rajiv Gandhi is assassinated by a female suicide-bomber, who is a supporter of the Sri Lanka–based Liberation Tigers of Tamil Eelam (LTTE), while on the campaign trail in Tamil Nadu.

In the 1990s, skirmishes were an almost annual event. A militant fringe of Kashmiris turned to armed revolt against the Indian government, joined by waves of armed supporters from Afghanistan and Pakistan. Unfortunately, civilians proved as popular a target as soldiers. India accused Pakistan of assisting and directing the insurgents, while Pakistan countered that India was denying Kashmiris the right to self-determination. India–Pakistan relations reached their nadir in 1998 when the new Bharatiya Janata Party (BJP) government detonated five nuclear devices in the deserts of Rajasthan, after which Pakistan responded in kind. When Pakistan mounted an incursion across the LOC near Kargil, the spectre of nuclear conflict in one of the world's most volatile regions loomed.

Both parties stepped back from the brink amid a wave of international condemnation, although full-blown conflict remained a constant threat. The terrorist attack on the Indian parliament in December 2001 (the Indian government blamed Islamabad; Pakistan denied involvement) led to new sabre-rattling, while allegations persist of human-rights abuses by the Indian security forces in Kashmir.

By the time of the election of the Congress Party government of Prime Minister Manmohan Singh in 2004, relations were strained but reasonably cordial. Confidence-building measures – the re-opening of cross-border transport links, an Indian decision to withdraw a small number of troops, and Pakistan's softening of its rhetoric – had helped to calm the situation. However, the November 2008 terrorist attacks in Mumbai (see p57) have recently re-ignited tension between the south Asian neighbours.

For over six decades, both India and Pakistan have steadfastly viewed Kashmir as an inalienable part of their territory. The long-term viability of any substantive agreement will ultimately depend upon the extent to which the leaders of both nations can carry their countries along with them, for Kashmir has indeed become a cause célèbre and a matter of fervent national pride among both populations.

For further information, see p278.

INDEPENDENT INDIA

Jawaharlal Nehru tried to steer India towards a policy of nonalignment, balancing cordial relations with Britain and Commonwealth membership with moves towards the former USSR. The latter was due partly to conflicts with China, and US support for its arch-enemy Pakistan.

The 1960s and 1970s were tumultuous times for India. A border war with China in 1962, in what was then known as the North-East Frontier Area (NEFA; now the Northeast States) and Ladakh, resulted in the loss of Aksai Chin (Ladakh) and smaller NEFA areas. Wars with Pakistan in 1965 (over Kashmir) and 1971 (over Bangladesh) also contributed to a sense among many Indians of having enemies on all sides.

The Proudest Day – India's Long Road to Independence by Anthony Read and David Fisher is an engaging account of India's pre-Independence period.

The Dynasty: The Nehru-Gandhi Story by Jad Adams and Phillip Whitehead profiles post-Independent India's most famous political family, examining its successes and failures.

1992	**March 1998**	**May 1998**
Hindu–Muslim rivalry rears its ugly head once again as the Babri Masjid (mosque), claimed to be built on a Hindu shrine in Ayodhya (Uttar Pradesh), is demolished by Hindu zealots.	The Bharatiya Janata Party (BJP; Indian People's Party, founded in 1980), in alliance with several other parties, wins the national elections and Atal Behari Vajpayee is installed as India's Prime Minister.	India declares itself a nuclear power after conducting underground tests near the town of Pokaran in western Rajasthan. Pakistan follows suit, and the twin tests subject the subcontinental neighbours to global condemnation.

In the midst of it all, the hugely popular Nehru died in 1964 and his daughter Indira Gandhi (no relation to Mahatma Gandhi) was elected as prime minister in 1966.

Indira Gandhi, like Nehru before her, loomed large over the country she governed. Unlike Nehru, however, she was always a profoundly controversial figure whose historical legacy remains hotly disputed.

In 1975, facing serious opposition and unrest, she declared a state of emergency (which later became known as the Emergency). Freed of parliamentary constraints, Gandhi was able to boost the economy, control inflation remarkably well and decisively increase efficiency. On the negative side, political opponents often found themselves in prison, India's judicial system was turned into a puppet theatre and the press was fettered.

Gandhi's government was bundled out of office in the 1977 elections in favour of the Janata People's Party (JPP). The JPP founder, Jaya Prakash Narayan (JP), was an ageing Gandhian socialist who died soon after but is widely credited with having safeguarded Indian democracy. Once it was victorious, it soon became apparent that Janata lacked cohesive policies and a leader of Narayan's stature. Its leader, Morarji Desai, struggled to come to grips with the country's problems. With inflation soaring, unrest rising and the economy faltering, Janata fell apart in late 1979. The 1980 election brought Indira Gandhi back to power with a larger majority than ever before.

The Nehrus and the Gandhis is Tariq Ali's astute portrait-history of these families and the India over which they cast their long shadow.

CONTINUITY IN CONGRESS

Indira Gandhi grappled unsuccessfully with communal unrest in several regions, violent attacks on Dalits (the Scheduled Caste or Untouchables), numerous cases of police brutality and corruption, and the upheavals in the northeast and Punjab. In 1984, following an ill-considered decision to send in the Indian army to flush out armed Sikh separatists (demanding a separate Sikh state to be called Khalistan) from Amritsar's Golden Temple, Indira Gandhi was assassinated by her Sikh bodyguards. Her heavy-handed storming of the Sikhs' holiest temple was catastrophic and sparked bloody Hindu–Sikh riots that left more than 3000 people dead (mostly Sikhs who had been lynched). The quest for Khalistan has since been quashed.

In 1997 KR Narayanan became India's president, the first member of the lowest (Dalit; formerly known as Untouchable) Hindu caste to hold the position.

Indira Gandhi's son, Rajiv, a former pilot, became the next prime minister, with Congress winning in a landslide in 1984. However, after a brief golden reign, he was dragged down by corruption scandals and the inability to quell communal unrest, particularly in Punjab. In 1991 he, too, was assassinated in Tamil Nadu by a supporter of the Liberation Tigers of Tamil Eelam (LTTE; a Sri Lankan armed separatist group).

Narasimha Rao assumed the by-now-poisoned chalice that was leadership of the Congress Party and led it to victory at the polls in 1991. In 1992 the economy was given an enormous boost after the finance minister, Manmohan Singh, took the momentous step of partially floating the rupee

2001	May 2004	December 2004
On 26 January – India's Republic Day – Gujarat is rocked by a massive earthquake; more than 20,000 people are killed and around 167,000 others are injured.	Belonging to the Sikh faith, Manmohan Singh of the Congress Party becomes the first member of any religious minority community to hold India's highest elected office.	On 26 December a catastrophic tsunami batters coastal parts of eastern and southern India as well as the Andaman and Nicobar Islands, killing over 10,000 people and leaving hundreds of thousands homeless.

against a basket of 'hard' currencies. State subsidies were phased out and the once-moribund economy was also opened up, tentatively at first, to foreign investment, with multinationals drawn by an enormous pool of educated professionals and relatively low wages. The greatest exemplifier of this was India's emergence as a global software superpower (see p67).

A rapidly improving economy notwithstanding, the Rao government found itself mired in corruption scandals and failed to subdue rising communal tension, however it managed to stumble on until 1996. After losing the 1996 election, the Congress Party eventually regained power in 2004 under the leadership of another Gandhi – Sonia, the Italian-born wife of the late Rajiv Gandhi. The Bharatiya Janata Party's (BJP) planned national agitation campaign against the foreign origins of the Italian-born Congress leader was subverted by Sonia Gandhi's decision to step aside. The Congress Party's former finance minister, Manmohan Singh, was sworn in as prime minister.

RISING COMMUNAL TENSION

One of the most explosive cases of communal tension for India in the 1990s came on 6 December 1992, when Hindu zealots destroyed a mosque, the Babri Masjid, in Ayodhya (revered by Hindus as the birthplace of Rama) in Uttar Pradesh. Claiming the site as the former location of a Rama temple, the zealots patently used Ayodhya as an incendiary symbol for their call to 'return' India to its Hindu roots. The Hindu-revivalist BJP – which had become the main opposition party at the 1991 elections – did little to discourage the actions of those responsible for the mosque's destruction. Rioting flared across the north, leaving thousands dead; 257 people were killed and an estimated 1100 were wounded after a series of bomb blasts in Mumbai alone.

After the 1996 national elections, the BJP emerged as the largest party but only governed for two weeks as secular parties banded together to defeat its attempts to build a viable coalition. However, with the upsurge of Hindu nationalism and the disarray within the ranks of the Congress Party, momentum was with the BJP. It won the elections in 1998 and again in 1999, thereby becoming the first nonsecular party to hold national power in India.

The apparent moderacy and measured tones of Prime Minister Atal Behari Vajpayee were constantly offset by the more belligerent posture of other members of his government and many of the BJP's grassroots supporters. Although some attempts were certainly made at quieting the fears of India's minority communities, friction with Pakistan increased and communal tensions remained high.

In early 2002, 52 Hindu activists returning home from Ayodhya were burned to death in a train near Godhra in Gujarat. The deaths were initially blamed on a Muslim mob, an accusation fed by the regional BJP government in Gujarat. The subsequent riots left at least 2000 people dead and 12,000

In 2003 the Gujarat state assembly followed Madhya Pradesh, Orissa and Tamil Nadu in passing the Freedom of Religion Bill, designed to prevent religious conversions.

Political Resources – India (www.politicalre sources.net/India.htm) provides useful links to the major players and political parties in India.

2006	February 2007	July 2007
On 11 July seven bombs are detonated on suburban trains in Mumbai, India's commercial capital, leaving more than 200 people dead and over 700 others wounded.	On 18 February bomb blasts on a train travelling from Delhi to Lahore kill 68 passengers. The attack is believed to have been masterminded by Islamists intent on destabilising peace talks between India and Pakistan.	The country has its first woman, Pratibha Patil, sworn in as President of India. Patil was formerly the first female Governor of Rajasthan (2004 to 2007).

homeless, mainly Muslims. Government inquiries later cast considerable doubt on the cause of the fire, with an accident the most likely cause.

When Congress swept back to power in 2004, Prime Minister Manmohan Singh was openly enthusiastic about resuming productive peace talks with Pakistan over the disputed territory of Kashmir. However these talks came to an abrupt halt when communal tensions soared following the July 2006 train bombings in Mumbai that left more than 200 people dead. The Indian government pointed the finger at Pakistan, claiming that its intelligence had played a hand in the blasts – an accusation that Islamabad vehemently denied. Singh later recommended peace talks with Pakistan, but with suspicions running high on both sides of the border, the road to reconciliation was set to be a challenging one.

Adding further pressure to the peace process was the February 2007 terrorist bomb attack on a train travelling from Delhi to Lahore (Pakistan), which killed 68 commuters. The Indian and Pakistani governments vowed not to let the attack – suspected of being designed to specifically disrupt (improving) India–Pakistan relations – freeze bilateral peace talks. However, despite the Indian government's resolute stance, communal tension continued to fester, with 2008 proving to be one of the country's darkest years. In May 2008 a series of synchronised bomb blasts in Jaipur left over 60 people dead; in July of the same year bombings in Ahmedabad killed over 55; while September saw coordinated bomb explosions in Delhi kill at least 30 people. Investigations (ongoing) into all of these attacks have pointed the finger at hardline Islamist groups, with Delhi emphatically vowing to rein in terrorist activity. But for all its tough talk, the government was left speechless in late November 2008 when Mumbai, India's financial powerhouse, came under a spate of highly coordinated terror attacks – which included tourist landmarks like the iconic Taj Mahal Palace & Tower Hotel – that lasted three days and left over 173 people dead. At the time of writing, investigations were still being carried out, with links to Pakistan-based Islamic militant groups being actively pursued.

The Elephant, the Tiger & the Cellphone by Shashi Tharoor 'combines hard facts and statistics with personal opinion and observations' to explore historical elements that have shaped the intriguing puzzle that is 21st-century India.

October 2008	November 2008	2009
On October 22 India launches the Chandrayaan-1 spacecraft – the nation's first unmanned mission to the moon which will entail a two-year exploration of the lunar surface.	On November 26 a series of coordinated bombing and shooting attacks on landmark Mumbai sites (primarily in the city's south) lasts three days, killing over 173 people. One of the terrorists is caught alive.	The Congress-led alliance garners a decisive victory in India's general election. Manmohan Singh is reinstated as prime minister of the world's biggest democracy.

The Culture

THE NATIONAL PSYCHE

For travellers, one of the most enduring impressions of India is often the way everyday life is intertwined with the sacred: from the housewife who devoutly performs *puja* (prayers) at home each morning, to the shopkeeper who – regardless of how many eager-to-buy tourists may be in the store – rarely commences business until blessings have been sought from the gods.

Along with religion, family lies at the heart of Indian society. For the vast majority of Indians the idea of being unmarried and without children by one's mid-30s is unthinkable. Despite the rising number of nuclear families – primarily in larger cities such as Mumbai (Bombay), Bengaluru (Bangalore) and Delhi – the extended family remains a cornerstone in both urban and rural India, with males – usually the breadwinners – generally considered the head of the household.

With religion and family deemed so sacrosanct, don't be surprised or miffed if you are constantly grilled about these subjects yourself, especially beyond the larger cities, and receive curious (possibly disapproving) gawps if you don't 'fit the mould'. The first question travellers are invariably asked is their country of origin. This may be followed by questions on topics that might be considered somewhat inappropriate elsewhere, especially coming from a complete stranger. Apart from religion and marital status, frequently asked questions include age, qualifications, profession (possibly even income) and your impressions of India. This is simply innocuous probing, not intended to offend, and it's also perfectly acceptable for you to echo the same questions.

National pride has long existed on the subcontinent but has swelled in recent years as India attracts ever-increasing international kudos in the fields of information technology (IT), science, medicine, literature and film. Meanwhile, on the sporting arena there are rising stars on the tennis front, but it is cricket that reigns supreme with top players afforded superhero status. However, in 2008 the cricket pitch shared centre stage with the chessboard, when India's Viswanathan Anand defeated Russia's Vladimir Kramnik in the prestigious World Chess Championship, making Anand the first in chess history to nab the World Championship in three different categories: Knockout, Tournament and Match.

The country's robust economy – one of the world's fastest growing – is another source of prolific national pride. Also widely embraced as potent symbols of Indian honour and sovereignty are the advancements in nuclear and space technology – in 2008 India joined the elite global lunar club with its maiden unmanned mission to the moon.

In 21st-century India the juxtaposition of time-honoured and New Age flies in the face of some common stereotypes about the country. Sure you'll find tandoori chicken and men dressed in crumpled dhotis (long loincloths), but these days your tandoori chicken could well come atop a cheesy wood-fired pizza, and that dhoti-clad man you pass in the bazaar may be delivering instructions to his mergers and acquisitions office in London, on a mobile phone that makes yours look like a fossil.

LIFESTYLE
Traditional Culture
MARRIAGE, BIRTH & DEATH

Marriage is an exceptionally auspicious event for Indians and although 'love marriages' have spiralled upwards in recent times (mainly in urban hubs),

The Wonder That Was India by AL Basham offers incisive descriptions of Indian civilisations, major religions, origins of the caste system and social customs – a good thematic approach to weave the disparate strands together.

India has one of the planet's largest diasporas – over 26 million people – with Indian banks holding an estimated US$39 billion in Non-Resident Indian (NRI) accounts.

INDIA *Christopher Kremmer*

What is India? In a sprawling, teeming, extravagantly diverse land, what actually holds Indians together as a nation? The answer is culture, not the culture of Hindus or Muslims alone, nor simply the culture of the farmer or the cosmopolitan city dweller. Food matters, language too, but neither is the sole determinant of the Indian identity. It's a complex mixture of all of these elements.

Some like to define India by its contradictions and extremes. It's a land of tolerance, but also a place where bitter rivalries (especially in religious and political matters) occasionally explode, where the fantastic and mundane cohabitate cheek by jowl, like big rivers and parched plains, religious devotion and IT campuses. But contradictions alone can't explain the heart and soul of a place so distinctively different from China and the Middle East, let alone America, Europe and Australia. For me, India is its stories. The Sanskrit epics of the Ramayana and Mahabharata, the Bhagavad Gita, and the classical Urdu poetry of Ghalib. It's the stories of spiritual leaders like Gautama Buddha and Sri Ramakrishna, and of course Mahatma Gandhi, who achieved a unique synthesis of political and philosophical genius. India is the story of great empires, of Ashoka and the Chandraguptas, the Mughals and the Brits. But while empires have come and gone, the ordinary Indian farmer and trader, the soldier and the artist, the pandit and the *neta* (politician) have provided the human foundations upon which all these empires were built.

Yet India is more than the sum of all its parts. In my travels, it has been in those intimate moments, when seemingly nothing important is happening, that India's precious secrets are revealed. A glass of water offered by a village woman to slake the traveller's thirst on a baking hot day; a favourite paratha stall in a secret alleyway of Old Delhi; the sour-sweet smell of the first monsoon rains; the acrid odour of *bidis* (small, hand-rolled cigarettes); the dust-laden air that rushes through the missing windows of a ramshackle bus on a country road; even the eternal predations of enterprising, foreigner-fixated touts – these small encounters with a big country – a big-hearted country – are what stays with you long after memories of museums and temples have faded away.

Each of us has our own India. We treasure these memories, recalled with aching clarity, and hope that nothing changes. India is a work in progress, a painting on a shifting canvas, but there is also continuity amid the maelstrom. In Hindi, the word for 'hello' – *namaste* – also means 'goodbye'. The word for 'tomorrow' – *cul* – is the same as the word for 'yesterday'. And the word for 'journey' – *yatra* – also means 'pilgrimage'.

Christopher Kremmer is author of Inhaling the Mahatma.

most Hindu marriages are arranged. Discreet enquiries are made within the community. If a suitable match is not found, the help of professional matchmakers may be sought, or advertisements may be placed in newspapers and/or on the internet. The horoscopes are checked and, if propitious, there's a meeting between the two families. The legal marriage age in India is 18.

Dowry, although illegal, is still a key issue in many arranged marriages (primarily in the more conservative communities), with some families plunging into debt to raise the required cash and merchandise (from cars and computers to washing machines and televisions). Health workers claim that India's high rate of abortion of female foetuses (despite sex identification medical tests being banned in India, they still clandestinely occur in some clinics) is predominantly due to the financial burden of providing a daughter's dowry.

The Hindu wedding ceremony is officiated over by a priest and the marriage is formalised when the couple walk around a sacred fire seven times. Despite the existence of nuclear families, it's still the norm for a wife to live with her husband's family once married and assume the household duties outlined by her mother-in-law. Not surprisingly, the mother–daughter-in-law relationship can be a prickly one, as portrayed in the many Indian TV soap operas which largely revolve around this theme.

Divorce and remarriage is becoming more common (primarily in India's bigger cities), but divorce is still not granted by courts as a matter of routine and is generally frowned upon by society. Among the higher castes, widows are traditionally expected not to remarry and are admonished to wear white and live pious, celibate lives. Also see p74.

The birth of a child is another momentous occasion, with its own set of special ceremonies, which take place at various auspicious times during the early years of childhood. These include the casting of the child's first horoscope, name-giving, feeding the first solid food, and the first hair cutting.

Hindus cremate their dead, and funeral ceremonies are designed to purify and console both the living and the deceased. An important aspect of the proceedings is the *sharadda,* paying respect to one's ancestors by offering water and rice cakes. It's an observance that's repeated at each anniversary of the death. After the cremation the ashes are collected and, 13 days after the death (when blood relatives are deemed ritually pure), a member of the family usually scatters them in a holy river such as the Ganges, or in the ocean.

> Matchmaking has embraced the cyber age, with popular sites including www.shaadi.com, www.bharatmatrimony.com and, more recently, www.secondshaadi.com – for those trying a second time.

THE CASTE SYSTEM

Although the Indian constitution does not recognise the caste system, caste still wields considerable influence, especially in rural India, where the caste you are born into largely determines your social standing in the community. It can also influence one's vocational and marriage prospects. Castes are further divided into thousands of *jati,* groups of 'families' or social communities, which are sometimes but not always linked to occupation. Conservative Hindus will only marry someone of the same *jati.*

According to tradition, caste is the basic social structure of Hindu society. Living a righteous life and fulfilling your dharma (moral duty) raises your chances of being reborn into a higher caste and thus into better circumstances. Hindus are born into one of four varnas (castes): Brahmin (priests and scholars), Kshatriya (soldiers), Vaishya (merchants) and Shudra (labourers). The Brahmins were said to have emerged from the mouth of Lord Brahma at the moment of creation, Kshatriyas were said to have come from his arms, Vaishyas from his thighs and Shudras from his feet.

> Two insightful books about India's caste system are *Interrogating Caste* by Dipankar Gupta and *Translating Caste* edited by Tapan Basu.

Beneath the four main castes are the Dalits (formerly known as Untouchables), who hold menial jobs such as sweepers and latrine cleaners. The word 'pariah' is derived from the name of a Tamil Dalit group, the Paraiyars. Some Dalit leaders, such as the renowned Dr BR Ambedkar (1891–1956), sought to change their status by adopting another faith; in his case it was Buddhism. At the bottom of the social heap are the Denotified Tribes. They were known as the Criminal Tribes until 1952, when a reforming law officially recognised 198 tribes and castes. Many are nomadic or seminomadic tribes, forced by the wider community to eke out a living on society's fringes.

To improve the Dalits' position, the government reserves considerable numbers of public-sector jobs, parliamentary seats and university places for them. Today these quotas account for almost 25% of government jobs and university (student) positions. The situation varies regionally, as different political leaders chase caste vote-banks by promising to include them in reservations. The reservation system, while generally regarded in a favourable light, has also been criticised for unfairly blocking tertiary and employment opportunities for those who would have otherwise got positions on merit.

DOS & DON'TS

India has many time-honoured traditions and while you won't be expected to get everything 'right', common sense and courtesy will take you a long way. If in doubt about how you should behave (eg at a temple), watch what the locals do, or simply ask.

Dressing conservatively – women *and* men – wins a far warmer response from locals (women should also see p1170). Refrain from kissing and cuddling in public as this generally isn't condoned by society. Nudity in public is not on, and while bikinis may be acceptable on Goa's beaches, you should cover up (eg swim in knee-length shorts and a T-shirt) in less touristy places – use your judgement.

Religious Etiquette

Whenever visiting a sacred site, always dress and behave respectfully – don't wear shorts or sleeveless tops (this applies to men and women) and refrain from smoking. Loud and intrusive behaviour isn't appreciated, and neither are public displays of affection or kidding around.

Before entering a holy place, remove your shoes (tip the shoe-minder a few rupees when retrieving them) and check if photography is allowed. You're permitted to wear socks in most places of worship – often necessary during warmer months, when floors can be uncomfortably hot.

Religious etiquette advises against touching locals on the head, or directing the soles of your feet at a person, religious shrine or image of a deity. Religious protocol also advises against touching someone with your feet or touching a carving of a deity.

Head cover (for women and sometimes men) is required at some places of worship – especially *gurdwaras* (Sikh temples) and mosques – so carry a scarf just to be on the safe side. There are some sites that don't admit women and some that deny entry to nonadherents of their faith – enquire in advance. Women may be required to sit apart from men. Jain temples request the removal of leather items you may be wearing or carrying and may also request menstruating women not to enter.

Eating & Visiting Etiquette

If you're lucky enough to be invited to someone's home it's considered good manners to remove your shoes before entering the house, and to wash your hands before and after a meal. Wait to be served food or until you are invited to help yourself – if you're unsure about protocol, simply wait for your host to direct you.

It's customary to use your right hand for eating and other social acts such as shaking hands; the left hand is used for unsavoury actions such as toilet duties and removing dirty shoes. When drinking from a shared water container, hold it slightly above your mouth (thus avoiding contact between your lips and the mouth of the container).

Photography Etiquette

Exercise sensitivity when taking photos of people, especially women, who may find it offensive – obtain permission in advance.

Taking photos inside a shrine, at a funeral, at a religious ceremony or of people publicly bathing (including rivers) can also be offensive – ask first. Flash photography may be prohibited in certain areas of a shrine, or may not be permitted at all. Also see p1153 and p1145.

Other Tips for Travellers

To augment your chances of receiving the most accurate response when seeking directions from people on the street, refrain from posing questions in a leading manner. For instance, it's often best to ask, 'Which way to the museum?' rather than pointing and asking, 'Is this the way to the museum?' This is because you may well receive a fabricated answer (usually 'yes') if the person can't quite decipher your accent or simply didn't hear you properly. There is usually no malicious intent in this misinformation – people are just trying to be polite, as an unsympathetic 'no' can sound rather unfriendly.

It's also worth noting that the commonly used sideways wobble of the head doesn't necessarily mean 'no'. It can translate to: yes, maybe, or I have no idea.

DRESSING SUBCONTINENTAL STYLE

Widely worn by Indian women, the elegant sari comes in a single piece (between 5m and 9m long and 1m wide) and is ingeniously tucked and pleated into place without the need for pins or buttons. Worn with the sari is the choli (tight-fitting blouse) and a drawstring petticoat. The *palloo* is the part of the sari draped over the shoulder. Also commonly worn is the *salwar kameez*, a traditional dresslike tunic and trouser combination accompanied by a dupatta (long scarf). Saris and *salwar kameez* come in an appealing range of fabrics, designs and prices.

Traditional attire for men includes the dhoti, and in the south the lungi and the *mundu* are also commonly worn. The dhoti is a loose, long loincloth pulled up between the legs. The lungi is more like a sarong, with its end usually sewn up like a tube. The *mundu* is like a lungi but is always white.

There are regional and religious variations in costume – for example, you may see Muslim women wearing the all-enveloping burka.

PILGRIMAGE

Devout Hindus are expected to go on a *yatra* (pilgrimage) at least once a year. Pilgrimages are undertaken to implore the gods or goddesses to grant a wish, to take the ashes of a cremated relative to a holy river, or to gain spiritual merit. India has thousands of holy sites to which pilgrims travel; the elderly often make Varanasi (p440) their final one, as it's believed that dying in this sacred city releases a person from the cycle of rebirth.

Most festivals in India are rooted in religion and are thus a magnet for pilgrims. This is something that travellers should keep in mind, even at those festivals that may have a carnivalesque sheen (see boxed text, opposite).

Contemporary Issues

HIV & AIDS IN INDIA

In 2008 there were an estimated 2.4 million HIV-positive cases in India, according to UN and National AIDS Control Organisation (NACO) reports. However some analysts believe this is a conservative estimate, as many cases go unreported.

AVERT, the UK-based international HIV and AIDS charity, says that despite the widespread belief that HIV is confined to intravenous drug users and gay men, the bulk of infections in India are actually transmitted through heterosexual sex. It claims that a significant proportion of cases are women in monogamous relationships who have been infected by husbands who have had multiple sex partners, and that there has been an increasing trend of sexually active people aged between 15 and 44 becoming infected. AVERT asserts that HIV affects a diverse spectrum of the Indian community, but those who face a proportionately elevated risk include intravenous drug users, migrant workers, truck drivers and sex workers.

AIDS Sutra: Untold Stories from India reveals the human stories behind India's AIDS epidemic, with contributions from notable writers including Kiran Desai, Salman Rushdie and Vikram Seth.

In a country of more than one billion people, health officials warn that unless the government radically increases nationwide educational programs (especially promotion of condom use), the number of HIV-positive cases is set to dramatically spiral upwards. Campaigners purport that India's antigay laws (see p64) patently hamper treatment and education efforts.

CHILD LABOUR

Despite national legislation prohibiting child labour, human-rights groups believe India has *at least* 50 million (not the Indian government's estimation of 12.6 million) child labourers – the highest rate in the world. The International Labour Organisation (ILO) estimates that there are over 245 million children aged between five and 15 working as full-time labourers worldwide.

In India, poorly enforced laws, poverty and lack of a social-security system are cited as major causes of the problem. The harsh reality for many low-income families is that they simply can't afford to support their children, so they send them out to work in order to help make ends meet.

Recognising the need for tougher anti–child labour laws, in 2006 the Indian government ordered a ban against the employment of children aged below 14 as labourers in households and the hospitality trade, two areas known to have particularly high child labour numbers (reliable statistics unavailable). The ban is an addendum to existing legislation which already forbids the employment of children under the age of 14 in what it classifies as 'hazardous jobs' (eg glass factories, abattoirs). Employers who contravene the law face possible imprisonment, a hefty monetary fine, or both. The government has promised to appropriately rehabilitate displaced child labourers, but critics continue to be sceptical about its ability to effectively do so. They believe that many jobless children may well turn to begging and/or crime.

Human-rights organisations indicate that the vast majority of India's child labourers work in the agricultural industry, while others work on construction sites, or as rag pickers, household servants, carpet weavers (see p1156), brick makers and prostitutes. There are also believed to be some several hundred thousand children involved in the manufacture of *bidis* (small, hand-rolled cigarettes), who inhale large quantities of harmful tobacco dust and chemicals. Another hazardous industry employing children is that of fireworks manufacturing.

GAY & LESBIAN ISSUES

India has an estimated 2.5 million male homosexuals, according to NACO, however advocacy groups claim the figure is much higher and impossible to accurately ascertain given that homosexuality is illegal in India. Some reports suggest there are roughly 100 million gay, lesbian and transgender people in the country.

Section 377 of the national legislation forbids 'carnal intercourse against the order of nature' (that is, anal intercourse) and the penalties for transgression can theoretically be up to life imprisonment, plus a steep monetary fine. There's no law against lesbian sexual relations. Although this colonial-era law, which dates back to 1861, is rarely used to prosecute, it's allegedly used by authorities to harass, arrest and blackmail gay people.

In 2006 more than 100 high-profile personalities, including Nobel prize–winning economist, Amartya Sen, and literary stalwarts, Vikram Seth and Arundhati Roy, signed an open letter supporting a legal challenge that was lodged with the Delhi High Court. The case, which sought to overturn the country's antiquated antigay law, was unsuccessful. However, the ruling has since been challenged and high courts in a number of other Indian cities were also reviewing the antigay law at the time of writing. Activists are hopeful that sustained efforts will see Section 377 repealed in the near future.

While the more liberal sections of certain cities – such as Mumbai, Bengaluru, Delhi and Kolkata (Calcutta) – appear to be becoming more tolerant of homosexuality, gay life is still largely suppressed. As marriage is so important on the subcontinent, it's believed that most gay people stay in the closet or risk being disowned by their families and society. Nevertheless, freedom of expression is certainly growing. For instance, in 2008 there were Gay Pride marches for the first time ever in several Indian cities including Delhi, Kolkata and Bengaluru. And in 2003, Mumbai hosted the Larzish festival, India's pioneer queer film festival. This was quite a coup for the gay community, considering the hullabaloo raised by religious zealots over

Although roughly a third of India's population subsists on less than US$1 per day, the country has the world's fastest growing number of US$-millionaires; an estimated 125,000 in 2008.

HIJRAS

India's most visible nonheterosexual group is the *hijras*, a caste of transvestites and eunuchs who dress in women's clothing. Some are gay, some are hermaphrodites and some were unfortunate enough to be kidnapped and castrated. Since it has long been traditionally frowned upon to live openly as a gay man in India, *hijras* get around this by becoming, in effect, a third sex of sorts. They work mainly as uninvited entertainers at weddings and celebrations of the birth of male children, and possibly as prostitutes.

Read more about *hijras* in *The Invisibles* by Zia Jaffrey and *Ardhanarishvara the Androgyne* by Dr Alka Pande.

Deepa Mehta's film *Fire* (with lesbian themes), which was famously banned by the ultraconservative Shiv Sena party in 1998 (see also p76).

For details about gay support groups, publications and websites see p1148.

POVERTY

Raising the living standards of India's poor has been on the agenda for governments since Independence. However, recent World Bank estimates place around a third of the global poor in India. According to Indian government sources, there are around 220 million Indians living below the poverty line, 75% of them in rural areas. Many others live in horrendously overcrowded urban slums. Non-government groups cite poverty figures closer to 250 million. The worst affected states include Bihar, Orissa, Uttar Pradesh and Madhya Pradesh, which also have some of the nation's fastest growing population rates.

The major causes of poverty include illiteracy and a population growth level that is substantially exceeding India's economic growth rate. Although India's middle class is ballooning, there's still a marked disparity when it comes to the country's distribution of wealth. Around 25% (roughly 250 million) of India's population subsists on less than Rs20 per day, according to a 2007 report by the Government of India's National Commission for Enterprises in the Unorganized Sector (NCEUS).

In 2008 the average annual income per capita in India was US$977. India's minimum daily wage, which varies from state to state, was raised in 2007 from Rs66 per day to Rs80 per day, although this certainly isn't always the case in reality. Wages between industries vary, with state governments setting different minimums for different vocations, and there are occupations (such as household servants) which have no minimum wage structure at all. Women are often paid less, especially in areas such as construction and farming.

Prostitution and poverty are closely linked. A 2007 (Indian) Ministry of Women and Child Development report indicated that India is believed to have around 2.8 million (and growing) sex workers, with about 35% entering the trade before the age of 18. Some human-rights groups believe the number of prostitutes is far more – possibly as high as 15 million – with the majority in Mumbai.

Poverty accounts for India's ever-growing number of beggars, mainly located in the larger cities. For foreign visitors this is often the most confronting aspect of travelling in the subcontinent. Whether you give something is a matter of personal choice, though your money can often be put to better long-term use if given to a reputable charity. Or, you could work as a volunteer at a charitable organisation – for volunteering possibilities see p1165.

Chandni Bar, directed by Madhur Bhandarkar, offers a disturbingly realistic insight into the lives of women who, driven by poverty and often family pressure, work as dancers/prostitutes in the seedy bars of Mumbai (Bombay).

POPULATION

India has the world's second-largest population, estimated at 1.15 billion in 2008, and is tipped to exceed China as the planet's most populous nation by 2030. According to the Government of India's 'India: Urban Poverty Report 2009', 40% to 50% of India's total population is likely to be urban-based by 2030.

A population census is held every 10 years in India. The most recent was in 2001 and this revealed that India's population had risen by 21.34% in the previous decade. According to this census, Mumbai is India's most populated city, with an urban agglomeration population of 16.4 million; Kolkata ranks second with 13.2 million, with Delhi (12.8 million) and Chennai (Madras; 6.6 million) third and fourth. Despite India's many urban centres, the 2001 census revealed that the nation is still overwhelmingly rural, with an estimated 75% of the population living in the countryside.

For further official statistics, see the Census of India website, www.censusindia.net. For regional populations, see the Fast Facts boxes in regional chapters. Throughout this book, we've used the official 2001 census figures, which are now close to a decade old. The next census is scheduled for 2011.

Read more about India's tribal communities at www.tribal.nic.in, a site maintained by the Indian government's Ministry of Tribal Affairs.

RELIGION

From a mother performing *puja* for her child's forthcoming exams, to a mechanic who has renounced his material life and set off on the path to self-realisation, religion suffuses almost every aspect of life in India.

India's major religion, Hinduism, is practised by approximately 82% of the population. Along with Buddhism, Jainism and Zoroastrianism, it's one of the world's oldest extant religions, with roots extending beyond 1000 BC.

Islam is India's largest minority religion; around 12% of the population is Muslim. Islam is believed to have been introduced to northern India by invading armies (in the 16th and 17th centuries the Mughal empire controlled much of North India) and to the south by Arab traders.

Christians comprise about 2.3% of the population, with approximately 75% living in South India, while the Sikhs – estimated at around 1.9% of the population – are mostly found in the northern state of Punjab. Around 0.76% of the population is Buddhist, with Bodhgaya (Bihar) being a major pilgrimage destination. Jainism is followed by about 0.4% of the population, with the majority of Jains living in Gujarat and Mumbai. Parsis, adherents of Zoroastrianism, today number somewhere between 60,000 and 69,600 – a mere drop in the ocean of India's billion-plus population. Historically, Parsis settled in Gujarat and became farmers, however, during British rule they moved into commerce, forming a prosperous community in Mumbai (see boxed text, p789). Reports indicate that there are less than 5000 Jews left in India, most living in Mumbai and parts of South India.

Tribal religions have so merged with Hinduism and other mainstream religions that very few are now clearly identifiable. It's believed that some basic tenets of Hinduism may have originated in tribal culture.

For details about India's major religious festivals, see the Events Calendar (p26).

Unravelling the basic tenets of Hinduism are *Hinduism: An Introduction* by Shakunthala Jagannathan, *Essential Hinduism* by Steven Rosen, and *Hinduism: An Introduction* by Dharam Vir Singh.

Communal Conflict

Religion-based conflict has been a bloody part of India's history. The post-Independence partition of the country into Hindu India and Muslim Pakistan resulted in horrendous carnage and epic displacement (see p52).

Later bouts of major sectarian violence in India include the Hindu-Sikh riots of 1984, which led to the assassination of then prime minister Indira Gandhi (p56), and the politically fanned 1992 Ayodhya calamity (p57), which sparked ferocious Hindu-Muslim clashes.

A SOFTWARE SUPERPOWER

India's burgeoning information technology (IT) industry, born in the boom years of the 1990s and founded on India's highly skilled middle class and abundance of relatively inexpensive labour, has established the country as a major player in the world of technology.

Newspaper reports peg 2007's IT (including outsourcing) industry earnings at around US$55 billion, with projections for this to at least double by 2012. However, the 2008–09 global economic slow-down has put pressure on Indian IT firms, with job cuts, wage freezes and revised investment plans on the cards – only time will tell how the IT industry weathers the ongoing fiscal storm.

India's IT boom has transformed cities such as Hyderabad, nicknamed 'Cyberabad', and Bengaluru (Bangalore), known as 'India's Silicon Valley', into IT world leaders. Tamil Nadu, Karnataka and Andhra Pradesh now produce more than 50% of India's software exports, with emerging growth centres including Pune, Mumbai (Bombay), Delhi and Kolkata (Calcutta).

India has become an increasingly popular base for international call centres. Many of these centres put their staff through rigorous training courses to get them up to speed with the countries they'll be calling (mostly the UK, USA and Australia). These courses often include lessons on how to mimic foreign accents, and staff may also be given pseudo Western names as another means of bridging the cultural divide. Apart from the financial carrot, another incentive used by IT companies to lure well-qualified job seekers (from call-centre operators to software engineers) is the high standard of workplace comfort (see boxed text, p906).

Despite the IT boom playing a critical role in boosting the Indian economy, the industry does have its detractors, particularly those who claim that the country's IT growth is an entirely urban phenomenon, with little discernible impact upon the lives of the vast majority of Indians. The industry has also recently attracted negative press for various scandals, one of the most startling associated with Hyderabad-based IT giant, Satyam, which saw its chairman resign in early 2009 due to his involvement in serious accounting fraud. Despite the collective pros and cons, there is no doubt that IT will go down in history as one of India's great success stories.

The ongoing dispute between India and Pakistan over Kashmir is also perilously entwined in religious conflict. Since Partition, India and Pakistan have fought two wars over Kashmir and have had subsequent artillery exchanges, coming dangerously close to war in 1999. The festering dispute over this landlocked territory continues to fuel Hindu-Muslim animosity on both sides of the border – for more details see p53.

Hinduism

Hinduism has no founder or central authority and it isn't a proselytising religion. Essentially, Hindus believe in Brahman, who is eternal, uncreated and infinite; everything that exists emanates from Brahman and will ultimately return to it. The multitude of gods and goddesses are merely manifestations – knowable aspects of this formless phenomenon.

Hindus believe that earthly life is cyclical; you are born again and again (a process known as samsara), the quality of these rebirths being dependent upon your karma (conduct or action) in previous lives. Living a righteous life and fulfilling your dharma (moral code of behaviour; social duty) will enhance your chances of being born into a higher caste and better circumstances. Alternatively, if enough bad karma has accumulated, rebirth may take animal form. But it's only as a human that you can gain sufficient self-knowledge to escape the cycle of reincarnation and achieve moksha (liberation).

Did you know that blood-drinking Kali is another form of milk-giving Gauri? *Myth = Mithya: A Handbook of Hindu Mythology* by Devdutt Pattanaik sheds light on this and other intriguing Hindu folklores.

GODS & GODDESSES

All Hindu deities are regarded as a manifestation of Brahman, who is often described as having three main representations, the Trimurti: Brahma, Vishnu and Shiva.

ADIVASIS

India's Adivasis (tribal communities; Adivasi translates to 'original inhabitant' in Sanskrit) have origins that precede the Vedic Aryans and the Dravidians of the south. According to the 2001 census, India's Adivasis constitute 8.2% of the population (over 84 million people), with more than 400 different tribal groups. The literacy rate for Adivasis, as per the 2001 census, is just 29.6%; the national average is 65.4%.

Historically, contact between Adivasis and Hindu villagers on the plains rarely led to friction as there was little or no competition for resources and land. However, in recent decades an increasing number of Adivasis have been dispossessed of their ancestral land and turned into impoverished labourers. Although they still have political representation thanks to a parliamentary quota system, the dispossession and exploitation of Adivasis has reportedly sometimes been with the connivance of officialdom – an accusation the government denies. Whatever the arguments, unless more is done, the Adivasis' future is an uncertain one.

Read more about Adivasis in *Archaeology and History: Early Settlements in the Andaman Islands* by Zarine Cooper, *The Tribals of India* by Sunil Janah and *Tribes of India: The Struggle for Survival* by Christoph von Fürer-Haimendorf.

Brahman

The One; the ultimate reality. Brahman is formless, eternal and the source of all existence. Brahman is *nirguna* (without attributes), as opposed to all the other gods and goddesses, which are manifestations of Brahman and therefore *saguna* (with attributes).

Brahma

Only during the creation of the universe does Brahma play an active role. At other times he is in meditation. His consort is Saraswati, the goddess of learning, and his vehicle is a swan. He is sometimes shown sitting on a lotus that rises from Vishnu's navel, symbolising the interdependence of the gods. Brahma is generally depicted with four (crowned and bearded) heads, each turned towards a point of the compass.

Vishnu

The Hindu pantheon has around 330 million deities; those worshipped are a matter of personal choice or tradition.

The preserver or sustainer, Vishnu is associated with 'right action'. He protects and sustains all that is good in the world. He is usually depicted with four arms, holding a lotus, a conch shell (as it can be blown like a trumpet it symbolises the cosmic vibration from which all existence emanates), a discus and a mace. His consort is Lakshmi, the goddess of wealth, and his vehicle is Garuda, the man-bird creature. The Ganges is said to flow from his feet.

Shiva

Shiva is the destroyer, but without whom creation couldn't occur. Shiva's creative role is phallically symbolised by his representation as the frequently worshipped lingam. With 1008 names, Shiva takes many forms, including Nataraja, lord of the *tandava* (cosmic victory dance), who paces out the cosmos' creation and destruction.

Sometimes Shiva has snakes draped around his neck and is shown holding a trident (representative of the Trimurti) as a weapon while riding Nandi, his bull. Nandi symbolises power and potency, justice and moral order. Shiva's consort, Parvati, is capable of taking many forms.

Other Prominent Deities

Elephant-headed Ganesh is the god of good fortune, remover of obstacles, and patron of scribes (the broken tusk he holds was used to write sections of the

Mahabharata). His animal mount is a ratlike creature. How exactly Ganesh came to have an elephant's head is a story with several variations. One legend says that Ganesh was born to Parvati in the absence of his father (Shiva), so initially grew up not knowing him. One day, as Ganesh stood guard while his mother bathed, Shiva returned and asked to be let into Parvati's presence. Ganesh, who didn't recognise Shiva, refused. Enraged, Shiva lopped off Ganesh's head, only to later discover, much to his horror, that he had slaughtered his own son. He vowed to replace Ganesh's head with that of the first creature he came across, which happened to be an elephant.

Another prominent deity, Krishna is an incarnation of Vishnu sent to earth to fight for good and combat evil. His alliances with the *gopis* (milkmaids) and his love for Radha have inspired countless paintings and songs. Depicted with blue-hued skin, Krishna is often seen playing the flute.

Hanuman is the hero of the Ramayana and loyal ally of Rama; he embodies the concept of bhakti (devotion). Hanuman is the king of the monkeys, but is capable of taking on other forms.

Among the Shaivite (followers of the Shiva movement), Shakti – the goddess as mother and creator – is worshipped as a force in her own right. The concept of *shakti* is embodied in the ancient goddess Devi (divine mother), who is also manifested as Durga and, in a fiercer evil-destroying incarnation, Kali. Other widely worshipped goddesses include Lakshmi, the goddess of wealth, and Saraswati, the goddess of learning.

> Shiva is sometimes characterised as the lord of yoga, a Himalaya-dwelling ascetic with matted hair, an ash-smeared body and a third eye symbolising wisdom.

SACRED TEXTS

Hindu sacred texts fall into two categories: those believed to be the word of god (*shruti,* meaning 'heard') and those produced by people (smriti, meaning 'remembered'). The Vedas are regarded as *shruti* knowledge and are considered the authoritative basis for Hinduism. The oldest of the Vedic texts, the Rig-Veda, was compiled over 3000 years ago. Within its 1028 verses are prayers for prosperity and longevity as well as an explanation of the universe's origins. The Upanishads, the last parts of the Vedas, reflect on the mystery of death and emphasise the oneness of the universe. The oldest of the Vedic texts were written in Vedic Sanskrit (related to Old Persian). Later texts were composed in classical Sanskrit, but many have been translated into the vernacular.

The smriti texts comprise a collection of literature spanning centuries and include expositions on the proper performance of domestic ceremonies as well as the proper pursuit of government, economics and religious law. Among its well-known works are the Ramayana and Mahabharata, as well as the Puranas, which expand on the epics and promote the notion of the Trimurti. Unlike the Vedas, reading the Puranas is not restricted to initiated higher-caste males.

The Mahabharata

Thought to have been composed at some time around the 1st millennium BC, the Mahabharata focuses on the exploits of Krishna. By about 500 BC the

---

THE POWER OF OM

One of Hinduism's most venerated symbols is 'Om'. Pronounced 'aum', it's a highly propitious mantra (sacred word or syllable). The 'three' shape symbolises the creation, maintenance and destruction of the universe (and thus the holy Trimurti). The inverted *chandra* (crescent or half moon) represents the discursive mind and the *bindu* (dot) within it, Brahman.

Buddhists believe that, if repeated often enough with complete concentration, it will lead to a state of blissful emptiness.

THE SACRED SEVEN

The number seven has special significance in Hinduism. There are seven sacred Indian cities, each of which are major pilgrimage centres: Varanasi (p440), associated with Shiva; Haridwar (p469), where the Ganges enters the plains from the Himalaya; Ayodhya (p432), birthplace of Rama; Dwarka (p764), with the legendary capital of Krishna thought to be off the Gujarat coast; Mathura (p425), birthplace of Krishna; Kanchipuram (p1065), site of historic Shiva temples; and Ujjain (p702), venue every 12 years of the Kumbh Mela.

There are also seven sacred rivers: the Ganges (Ganga), Saraswati (thought to be underground), Yamuna, Indus, Narmada, Godavari and Cauvery.

Mahabharata had evolved into a far more complex creation with substantial additions, including the Bhagavad Gita (where Krishna proffers advice to Arjuna before a battle).

The story centres on conflict between the heroic gods (Pandavas) and the demons (Kauravas). Overseeing events is Krishna, who has taken on human form. Krishna acts as charioteer for the Pandava hero Arjuna, who eventually triumphs in a great battle with the Kauravas.

The Ramayana

Composed around the 3rd or 2nd century BC, the Ramayana is believed to be largely the work of one person, the poet Valmiki. Like the Mahabharata, it centres on conflict between the gods and demons.

The story goes that Dasharatha, the childless king of Ayodhya, called upon the gods to provide him with a son. His wife duly gave birth to a boy. But this child, named Rama, was in fact an incarnation of Vishnu, who had assumed human form to overthrow the demon king of Lanka, Ravana. The adult Rama, who won the hand of the princess Sita in a competition, was chosen by his father to inherit his kingdom. At the last minute Rama's stepmother intervened and demanded her son take Rama's place. Rama, Sita and Rama's brother, Lakshmana, were exiled and went off to the forests, where Rama and Lakshmana battled demons and dark forces. Ravana's sister attempted to seduce Rama. She was rejected and, in revenge, Ravana captured Sita and spirited her away to his palace in Lanka. Rama, assisted by an army of monkeys led by the loyal monkey god Hanuman, eventually found the palace, killed Ravana and rescued Sita. All returned victorious to Ayodhya, where Rama was crowned king.

SACRED ANIMALS & PLANTS

Animals, particularly snakes and cows, have long been worshipped in the subcontinent. For Hindus, the cow represents fertility and nurturing, while snakes (especially cobras) are associated with fertility and welfare. Naga stones (snake stones) serve the dual purpose of protecting humans from snakes and propitiating snake gods.

Plants can also have sacred associations, such as the banyan tree, which symbolises the Trimurti, while mango trees are symbolic of love – Shiva is believed to have married Parvati under one. Meanwhile, the lotus flower is believed to have emerged from the primeval waters and is connected to the mythical centre of the earth through its stem. Often found in the most polluted of waters, the lotus has the remarkable ability to blossom above murky depths. The centre of the lotus corresponds to the centre of the universe, the navel of the earth; all is held together by the stem and the eternal waters. This is how Hindus are reminded their own lives should be – like the fragile yet resolute lotus, an embodiment of beauty and strength. So revered is the lotus that today it's India's national flower.

Two recommended publications containing English translations of holy Hindu texts are *The Bhagavad Gita* by S Radhakrishnan and *The Valmiki Ramayana* by Romesh Dutt.

WORSHIP

Worship and ritual play a paramount role in Hinduism. In Hindu homes you'll often find a dedicated worship area, where members of the family pray to the deities of their choice. Beyond the home, Hindus worship at temples. *Puja* is a focal point of worship and ranges from silent prayer to elaborate ceremonies. Devotees leave the temple with a handful of *prasad* (temple-blessed food) which is humbly shared among friends and family. Other forms of worship include *aarti* (the auspicious lighting of lamps or candles) and the playing of soul-soothing bhajans (devotional songs).

A sadhu is someone who has surrendered all material possessions in pursuit of spirituality through meditation, the study of sacred texts, self-mortification and pilgrimage. Read more in *Sadhus: India's Mystic Holy Men* by Dolf Hartsuiker.

Islam

Islam was founded in Arabia by the Prophet Mohammed in the 7th century AD. The Arabic term *islam* means to surrender, and believers (Muslims) undertake to surrender to the will of Allah (God), which is revealed in the scriptures, the Quran. In this monotheistic religion, God's word is conveyed through prophets (messengers), of whom Mohammed is the most recent.

Following Mohammed's death, a succession dispute split the movement, and the legacy today is the Sunnis and the Shiites. Most Muslims in India are Sunnis. The Sunnis emphasise the 'well-trodden' path or the orthodox way. Shiites believe that only imams (exemplary leaders) can reveal the true meaning of the Quran.

All Muslims, however, share a belief in the Five Pillars of Islam: the shahada (declaration of faith: 'There is no God but Allah; Mohammed is his prophet'); prayer (ideally five times a day); the zakat (tax), in the form of a charitable donation; fasting (during Ramadan) for all except the sick, the very young, the elderly and those undertaking arduous journeys; and the haj (pilgrimage) to Mecca, which every Muslim aspires to do at least once.

To grasp the intricacies of Sikhism read *A History of the Sikhs* by Khushwant Singh, which comes in Volume One (1469–1839) and Volume Two (1839–2004).

Sikhism

Sikhism, founded in Punjab by Guru Nanak in the 15th century, began as a reaction against the caste system and Brahmin domination of ritual. Sikhs believe in one god and although they reject the worship of idols, some keep pictures of the 10 gurus as a point of focus. The Sikhs' holy book, the Guru Granth Sahib, contains the teachings of the 10 Sikh gurus, among others.

Like Hindus and Buddhists, Sikhs believe in rebirth and karma. In Sikhism, there's no ascetic or monastic tradition ending the cycles of rebirth.

Fundamental to Sikhs is the concept of Khalsa, or belief in a chosen race of soldier-saints who abide by strict codes of moral conduct (abstaining from alcohol, tobacco and drugs) and engage in a crusade for *dharmayudha*

GURU NANAK: SIKHISM'S FIRST GURU

Born in present-day Pakistan, Guru Nanak (1469–1539), the founder of Sikhism, was unimpressed with both Muslim and Hindu religious practices. Unlike many Indian holy men, he believed in family life and the value of hard work – he married, had two sons and worked as a farmer when not travelling around, preaching and singing self-composed *kirtan* (Sikh devotional songs) with his Muslim musician, Mardana. He performed miracles and emphasised meditation on God's name as the best way to enlightenment.

Nanak believed in equality centuries before it became fashionable and campaigned against the caste system. He was a practical guru – 'a person who makes an honest living and shares earnings with others recognises the way to God'. He appointed his most talented disciple to be his successor, not one of his sons.

His *kirtan* are still sung in *gurdwaras* (Sikh temples) and his picture hangs in millions of homes.

(righteousness). There are five *kakkars* (emblems) denoting the Khalsa brotherhood: *kesh* (the unshaven beard and uncut hair symbolising saintliness); *kangha* (comb to maintain the ritually uncut hair); *kaccha* (loose underwear symbolising modesty); *kirpan* (sabre or sword symbolising power and dignity); and *karra* (steel bangle symbolising fearlessness). Singh, literally 'Lion', is the name adopted by many Sikhs.

A belief in the equality of all beings lies at the heart of Sikhism. It's expressed in various practices, including *langar,* whereby people from all walks of life – regardless of caste and creed – sit side by side to share a complimentary meal prepared by volunteers in the communal kitchen of the *gurdwara* (Sikh temple).

Buddhism

Buddhism arose in the 6th century BC as a reaction against the strictures of Brahminical Hinduism. Buddha (Awakened One) is believed to have lived from about 563 BC to 483 BC. Formerly a prince (Siddhartha Gautama), the Buddha, at the age of 29, embarked on a quest for emancipation from the world of suffering. He achieved nirvana (the state of full awareness) at Bodhgaya (Bihar), aged 35. Critical of the caste system and the unthinking worship of gods, the Buddha urged his disciples to seek truth within their own experiences.

The Buddha taught that existence is based on Four Noble Truths – that life is rooted in suffering, that suffering is caused by craving, that one can find release from suffering by eliminating craving, and that the way to eliminate craving is by following the Noble Eightfold Path. This path consists of right understanding, right intention, right speech, right action, right livelihood, right effort, right awareness and right concentration. By successfully complying with these one can attain nirvana.

Buddhism had somewhat waned in parts of India by the turn of the 20th century. However, it saw a revival in the 1950s among intellectuals and Dalits who were disillusioned with the caste system. The number of followers has been further increased with the influx of Tibetan refugees. Both the current Dalai Lama and the 17th Karmapa reside in India (see p369 and p380).

> Set in Kerala against the backdrop of caste conflict and India's struggle for independence, *The House of Blue Mangoes* by David Davidar spans three generations of a Christian family.

Jainism

Jainism arose in the 6th century BC as a reaction against the caste restraints and rituals of Hinduism. It was founded by Mahavira, a contemporary of the Buddha.

Jains believe that liberation can be attained by achieving complete purity of the soul. Purity means shedding all *karman,* matter generated by one's actions that binds itself to the soul. By following various austerities (eg fasting and meditation) one can shed *karman* and purify the soul. Right conduct is essential, and fundamental to this is ahimsa (nonviolence) in thought and deed towards any living thing.

The religious disciplines of the laity are less severe than for monks, with some Jain monks going naked. The slightly less ascetic maintain a bare minimum of possessions including a broom, with which to sweep the path before them to avoid stepping on any living creature, and a piece of cloth that is tied over their mouth to prevent the accidental inhalation of insects.

Some notable Jain holy sites in India include Sravanabelagola (p924), Palitana (p748), Ranakpur (p225) and the Jain temples of Mt Abu (p226).

Christianity

There are various theories circulating about Christ's link to the subcontinent. Some, for instance, believe that Jesus spent his 'lost years' in India (see boxed text, p290), while others believe that Christianity arrived in South India with

ANATOMY OF A GOMPA

Parts of India, such as Sikkim and Ladakh, are known for their ornate, colourful gompas (Tibetan-style Buddhist monasteries). The focal point of a gompa is the *du-khang* (prayer hall), where monks assemble to chant passages from the sacred scriptures (morning prayers are a particularly atmospheric time to visit gompas). The walls may be covered in vivid murals or *thangkas* (cloth paintings) of *bodhisattvas* (enlightened beings) and *dharmapalas* (protector deities). By the entrance to the *du-khang* you'll usually find a mural depicting the Wheel of Life, a graphical representation of the core elements of Buddhist philosophy (see www.buddhanet.net/wheel1.htm for an interactive description of the Wheel of Life).

Most gompas hold *chaam* dances (ritual masked dances to celebrate the victory of good over evil) during major festivals. Dances to ward off evil feature masks of Mahakala, the Great Protector, usually dramatically adorned with a headdress of human skulls. The Durdag dance features skull masks depicting the Lords of the Cremation Grounds, while Shawa dancers wear masks of wild-eyed stags. These characters are often depicted with a third eye in the centre of their foreheads, signifying the need for inner reflection.

Another interesting activity at Buddhist monasteries is the production of butter sculptures, elaborate models made from coloured butter and dough. The sculptures are deliberately designed to decay, symbolising the impermanence of human existence. Many gompas also produce exquisite sand mandalas – geometric patterns made from sprinkled coloured sand, then destroyed to symbolise the futility of the physical plane.

St Thomas the Apostle in AD 52. However, many scholars say it's more likely Christianity arrived around the 4th century with a Syrian merchant, Thomas Cana, who set out for Kerala with around 400 families.

Catholicism established a strong presence in South India in the wake of Vasco da Gama's visit in 1498, and orders that have been active in the region include the Dominicans, Franciscans and Jesuits. Protestant missionaries are believed to have arrived from around the 18th century.

Zoroastrianism

Zoroastrianism, founded by Zoroaster (Zarathustra), had its inception in Persia in the 6th century BC and is based on the concept of dualism, whereby good and evil are locked in continuous battle. Zoroastrianism isn't quite monotheistic: good and evil entities coexist, although believers are enjoined to honour only the good. Humanity therefore has a choice. There's no conflict between body and soul: both are united in the good versus evil struggle. Humanity, although mortal, has components such as the soul, which are timeless; a pleasant afterlife depends on one's deeds, words and thoughts during earthly existence. But not every lapse is entered on the balance sheet and the errant soul is not called to account on the day of judgement for each and every misdemeanour.

Zoroastrianism was eclipsed in Persia by the rise of Islam in the 7th century and its followers, many of whom openly resisted this, suffered persecution. Over the following centuries, some immigrated to India, where they became known as Parsis. For more information, see p66 and p789.

WOMEN IN INDIA

Women in India are entitled to vote and own property. While the percentage of women in politics has risen over the past decade, they're still notably underrepresented in the national parliament, accounting for around 10% of parliamentary members.

Although the professions are still male dominated, women are steadily making inroads, especially in urban centres. Kerala was India's first state to break societal norms by recruiting female police officers in 1938. It was also the first state to establish an all-female police station (1973). For village women it's much more difficult to get ahead, but groups such as the Self-Employed Women's Association (SEWA) in Gujarat have shown what's possible. Here, socially disadvantaged women have been organised into unions, offering at least some lobbying power against discriminatory and exploitative work practices (see p736).

In low-income families, especially, girls can be regarded as a serious financial liability because at marriage a dowry must often be supplied. An Indian news report indicated that dowry-related deaths in 2006 stood at 7618 (around 12% higher than the previous year), with Uttar Pradesh and Bihar registering the most cases. However, this is likely to be a conservative figure given that many cases go unreported. For more about dowry see p59.

The Zoroastrian funerary ritual involves the 'Towers of Silence' where the corpse is laid out and exposed to vultures, which pick the bones clean.

For the urban middle-class woman, life is materially much more comfortable, but pressures still exist. Broadly speaking, she is far more likely to receive a tertiary education, but once married is still usually expected to 'fit in' with her in-laws and be a homemaker above all else. Like her village counterpart, if she fails to live up to expectations – even if it's just not being able to produce a grandson – the consequences can sometimes be dire, as demonstrated by the extreme practice of 'bride burning', wherein a wife is doused with flammable liquid and set alight. Reliable statistics are unavailable, but some women's groups claim that for every reported case, roughly 250 go unreported, and that less than 10% of the reported cases are pursued through the legal system.

According to the latest data from the Indian Home Ministry's National Crime Records Bureau (NCRB), in 2006 there was an eight-fold rise in the number of women raped since 1971 – the year rape cases were first compiled by the NCRB – jumping from seven to 53 reported cases per day (a 5.5% increase from 2005), with most incidents in Delhi. However, the figure is believed to be higher, as many rape cases go unreported.

Based on Rabindranath Tagore's novel, *Chokher Bali* (directed by Rituparno Ghosh) is a poignant film about a young widow living in early-20th-century Bengal who challenges the 'rules of widowhood' – something unthinkable in that era.

In October 2006, following women's civil rights campaigns, the Indian parliament passed a landmark bill (on top of existing legislation) which gives women who are suffering domestic violence increased protection and rights. Prior to this legislation, although women could lodge police complaints against abusive spouses, they weren't automatically entitled to a share of the marital property or to ongoing financial support. The new law purports that any form of physical, sexual (including marital rape), emotional and economic abuse entails not only domestic violence, but also human-rights violations. Perpetrators face imprisonment and fines. Under the new law, abused women are legally permitted to remain in the marital house. In addition, the law prohibits emotional and physical bullying in relation to dowry demands. Critics claim that many women, especially those outside India's larger cities, will still be reluctant to seek legal protection because of the social stigma involved.

Although the constitution allows for divorcees (and widows) to remarry, relatively few reportedly do so, simply because divorcees are traditionally considered outcasts from society, especially beyond big cities. Divorce rates in India are among the worlds' lowest, despite having risen from seven in 1000 in 1991, to 11 in 1000 in 2004. Although no reliable post-2004 statistics are available, divorce rates are reportedly growing by around 15% per annum, with most cases registered in urban India. One major Indian newspaper reported that there were around 9000 court-registered divorce cases in Delhi in 2007 – double the number some four years earlier.

Women travellers should also see p1170.

ARTS

Artistic beauty lies around almost every corner in India, whether it's the garishly painted trucks rattling down dusty rural roads or the exquisite, spidery body art of *mehndi* (henna). Indeed, a glowing highlight of subcontinental travel is its wealth of art treasures, from ancient temple architecture to a dynamic performing-arts scene.

Contemporary Indian artists have fused historical elements with edgy modern influences, creating art, dance and music that have won acclaim on both the domestic and international arenas.

Dance

Dance is an ancient Indian art form and is traditionally linked to mythology and classical literature. Dance can be divided into two main forms: classical and folk.

Classical dance is essentially based on well-defined traditional disciplines and includes:

- Bharata Natyam (also spelt *bharatanatyam*), which originated in Tamil Nadu, has been embraced throughout India.
- Kathakali, which has its roots in Kerala, is sometimes referred to as 'dance' but essentially is not – see p1022.
- Kathak, has Hindu and Islamic influences and was particularly popular with the Mughals. Kathak suffered a period of notoriety when it moved from the courts into houses where nautch (dancing) girls tantalised audiences with renditions of the Krishna and Radha love story. It was restored as a serious art form in the early 20th century.
- Manipuri, which has a delicate, lyrical flavour, hails from Manipur. It attracted a wider audience in the 1920s when the acclaimed Bengali writer Rabindranath Tagore invited one of its most revered exponents to teach at Shantiniketan (West Bengal).
- Kuchipudi is a 17th-century dance-drama that originated in the Andhra Pradesh village from which it takes its name. The story centres on the envious wife of Krishna.
- Odissi, claimed to be India's oldest classical dance form, was originally a temple art, and was later also performed at royal courts.

India's second major dance form, folk, is widespread and varied. It ranges from the high-spirited bhangra dance hailing from Punjab (see p265) to the theatrical dummy horse dances of Karnataka and Tamil Nadu, and the graceful fishers' dance of Orissa.

Pioneers of modern dance forms in India include Uday Shankar (older brother of sitar master Ravi), who once partnered Russian ballerina Anna Pavlova. Rabindranath Tagore was another innovator; in 1901 he set up a school at Shantiniketan (p538) that promoted the arts, including dance.

Music

Indian classical music traces its roots back to Vedic times, when religious poems chanted by priests were first collated in an anthology called the Rig-Veda. Over the millennia classical music has been shaped by many influences, and the legacy today is Carnatic (characteristic of South India) and Hindustani (the classical style of North India) music. With common origins, both share a number of features. Both use the raga (the melodic shape of the music) and tala (the rhythmic meter characterised by the number of beats); *tintal,* for example, has a tala of 16 beats. The audience follows the tala by clapping at the appropriate beat, which in *tintal* is at beats one, five and 13. There's no clap at the beat of nine; that's the *khali* (empty section), which

Sati: A Study of Widow Burning in India by Sakuntala Narasimhan looks at the startling history of *sati* (widow's suicide on her husband's funeral pyre; now banned) on the subcontinent.

Indian Classical Dance by Leela Venkataraman and Avinash Pasricha is a lavishly illustrated book covering various Indian dance forms, including Bharata Natyam, Odissi, Kuchipudi and Kathakali.

is indicated by a wave of the hand. Both the raga and the tala are used as a basis for composition and improvisation.

Both Carnatic and Hindustani music are performed by small ensembles, generally comprising three to six musicians, and both have many instruments in common. There's no fixed pitch, but there are differences between the two styles. Hindustani has been more heavily influenced by Persian musical conventions (a result of Mughal rule); Carnatic music, as it developed in South India, cleaves more closely to theory. The most striking difference, at least for those unfamiliar with India's classical forms, is Carnatic's greater use of voice.

One of the best-known Indian instruments is the sitar (large stringed instrument) with which the soloist plays the raga. Other stringed instruments include the sarod (which is plucked) and the sarangi (which is played with a bow). Also popular is the tabla (twin drums), which provides the tala. The drone, which runs on two basic notes, is provided by the oboelike *shehnai* or the stringed *tampura* (also spelt tamboura). The hand-pumped keyboard harmonium is used as a secondary melody instrument for vocal music.

Indian regional folk music is widespread and varied. Wandering musicians, magicians, snake charmers and storytellers often use song to entertain their audiences; the storyteller usually sings the tales from the great epics.

In North India you may come across qawwali (Islamic devotional singing), performed at mosques or at musical concerts. Qawwali concerts usually take the form of a *mehfil* (gathering) with a lead singer, a second singer, harmonium and tabla players, and a thunderous chorus of junior singers and clappers, all sitting cross-legged on the floor. The singer whips up the audience with lines of poetry, dramatic hand gestures and religious phrases as the two voices weave in and out, bouncing off each other to create an improvised, surging sound. On command the chorus dives in with a hypnotic and rhythmic refrain. Members of the audience often sway and shout out in ecstatic appreciation.

A completely different genre altogether, filmi music entails musical scores from Bollywood movies – modern (slower paced) love serenades feature among the predominantly hyperactive dance songs. To ascertain the latest filmi favourites, as well as in-vogue Indian pop singers, enquire at music stores.

Radio and TV have played a vital role in broadcasting different music styles – from soothing bhajans to booming Bollywood hits – to even the remotest corners of India.

Immerse yourself in India's vibrant performing-arts scene – especially classical dance and music – at Art India (www.artindia.net).

To tune into the melodious world of Hindustani classical music, including a glossary of musical terms, get a copy of *Nād: Understanding Raga Music* by Sandeep Bagchee.

Cinema

India's film industry was born in the late 19th century – the first major Indian-made motion picture, *Panorama of Calcutta*, was screened in 1899. India's first real feature film, *Raja Harishchandra*, was made during the silent era in 1913 and it's ultimately from this that Indian cinema traces its vibrant lineage.

Today, India's film industry is the biggest in the world – larger than Hollywood – and Mumbai, the Hindi-language film capital, is affectionately dubbed 'Bollywood'. India's other major film-producing cities include Chennai, Hyderabad and Bengaluru, with a number of other centres producing films in their own regional vernaculars. Big-budget films are often partly or entirely shot abroad, with some countries vigorously wooing Indian production companies because of the potential spin-off tourism revenue these films generate.

An average of 900 feature films are produced annually in India, with around 3.7 billion Bollywood movie tickets sold at the box office in 2006 alone. Apart from hundreds of millions of local Bollywood buffs, there are also millions of Non-Resident Indian (NRI) fans, who have played a significant role in catapulting Indian cinema onto the international arena.

Broadly speaking, there are two categories of Indian films. Most prominent is the mainstream movie – three hours and still running, these blockbusters are often tear-jerkers and are packed with dramatic twists interspersed with numerous song-and-dance performances. There are no explicit sex, or even kissing, scenes (although smooching is creeping into some Bollywood movies) in Indian films made for the local market; however, lack of nudity is often compensated for by heroines dressed in skimpy or body-hugging attire.

The second Indian film genre is art house, which adopts Indian 'reality' as its base. Generally speaking they are, or at least are supposed to be, socially and politically relevant. Usually made on infinitely smaller budgets than their commercial cousins, these films are the ones that win kudos at global film festivals and award ceremonies.

Set in Mumbai, *Slumdog Millionaire*, directed by British filmmaker Danny Boyle, is the latest international success story. Adapted from the novel *Q&A* by Indian diplomat/author Vikas Swarup, it scooped up eight Academy Awards in 2009, including Best Picture. However, amid the accolades, the film attracted criticism over its stereotypical depiction of India and allegedly exploitative use of child actors – accusations the filmmakers denied. In 1983, *Gandhi*, directed by Richard Attenborough, also seized eight Academy Awards, including Best Picture.

Indian-born Canadian filmmaker Deepa Mehta has also gained international acclaim for her trilogy, *Earth, Fire* and *Water.* Mehta faced various obstacles during and after filming, especially for *Fire,* with some nationalists burning down cinemas, claiming that the film's lesbian themes maligned Indian society and Hinduism.

For further film recommendations, see p23; for information about Bollywood and working as a film extra, see p788; and for more about Tamil films, see p1054.

Literature

India has a long tradition of Sanskrit literature, although works in the vernacular have contributed to a particularly rich legacy. In fact, it's claimed there are as many literary traditions as there are written languages.

Bengalis are traditionally credited with producing some of India's most celebrated literature, a movement often referred to as the Indian or Bengal Renaissance, which flourished from the 19th century with works by Bankim Chandra Chatterjee. But the man who to this day is mostly credited with first propelling India's cultural richness onto the world stage is Rabindranath Tagore, a Bengali who was awarded the Nobel Prize in Literature in 1913 for *Gitanjali* (see boxed text, p78).

India boasts an ever-growing list of internationally acclaimed authors. Some particularly prominent writers include Vikram Seth, best known for his award-winning epic novel *A Suitable Boy,* and Amitav Ghosh, who has won a number of accolades; his *Sea of Poppies* was shortlisted for the 2008 Man Booker Prize. Indeed, recent years have seen a number of Indian-born authors win the prestigious Man Booker Prize, the most recent being Aravind Adiga, who won in 2008 for his debut novel, *The White Tiger.* The prize went to Kiran Desai in 2006 for *The Inheritance of Loss;* Kiran Desai is the daughter of the award-winning Indian novelist Anita Desai, who has thrice been a Booker Prize nominee. In 1997, Arundhati Roy won the Booker Prize for her novel, *The God of Small Things,* while Salman Rushdie took this coveted award in 1981 for *Midnight's Children.*

Bedazzled by Bollywood? Get the low-down about celebrity happenings at Bollywood World (www .bollywoodworld.com), Bollywood Blitz (www .bollywoodblitz.com) and Bollywood Gossips (www .bollywoodgossips.net).

Encyclopedia of Indian Cinema by Ashish Rajadhyaksha and Paul Willemen chronicles India's fascinating cinematic history, spanning from 1897 to the 21st century.

Dip into details of English-language Indian literature – from historical to contemporary times – at Indian English Literature (www.indian englishliterature.com).

Trinidad-born Indian writer VS Naipaul has written widely about India and won many notable awards including the Booker Prize (1971) and the Nobel Prize in Literature (2001). UK-born Bengali writer Jhumpa Lahiri was awarded the 2000 Pulitzer Prize for Fiction for *Interpreter of Maladies*, a collection of short stories.

For further reading recommendations see p23 and for information about Tamil literature see p1050.

Architecture

Travellers will come across various forms of historic and contemporary temple architecture, India's most striking and revered form of construction. Although none of the wooden (occasionally brick) temples built in early times have survived the vagaries of the climate, by the advent of the Guptas (4th to 6th centuries AD) of North India, sacred structures of a new type were being constructed, and these set the standard for temples for several hundred years.

For Hindus, the square is a perfect shape, and complex rules govern the location, design and building of each temple, based on numerology, astrology, astronomy and religious principles. Essentially, a temple represents a map of the universe. At the centre is an unadorned space, the *garbhagriha* (inner sanctum), which is symbolic of the 'womb-cave' from which the universe is believed to have emerged. This provides a residence for the deity to which the temple is dedicated.

Hobnob with acclaimed local and international writers at Asia's biggest literary event, the Jaipur Literature Festival (www .jaipurliteraturefestival .org), held in late January in Jaipur (Rajasthan).

Above the shrine rises a superstructure known as a *vimana* in South India, and a *sikhara* in North India. The *sikhara* is curvilinear and topped with a grooved disk, on which sits a pot-shaped finial, while the *vimana* is stepped, with the grooved disk being replaced with a solid dome. Some temples have a *mandapa* (temple forechamber) connected to the sanctum by vestibules. These *mandapas* may also contain *vimanas* or *sikharas*.

A *gopuram* is a soaring pyramidal gateway tower of a Dravidian temple. The towering *gopurams* of various South Indian temple complexes (eg Madurai's Sri Meenakshi Temple, p1095) took ornamentation and monumentalism to new levels.

Commonly used for ritual bathing and religious ceremonies, as well as adding aesthetic appeal to places of worship, temple tanks have long been a focal point of temple activity. These often-vast, angular, engineered reservoirs of water, sometimes fed by rain, sometimes fed – via a complicated drainage system – by rivers, serve both sacred and secular purposes. The waters of

---

RABINDRANATH TAGORE

The brilliant and prolific poet, writer, artist and patriot Rabindranath Tagore has had an unparalleled impact on Bengali culture. Born to a prominent family in Kolkata (Calcutta) in 1861, he began writing as a young boy and never stopped, said to have been dictating his last poem only hours before his death in 1941.

Tagore is also largely credited with introducing India's historical and cultural richness to the Western world. He won the Nobel Prize in Literature in 1913 with his mystical collection of poems *Gitanjali* (Song Offerings), and in later years his lecture tours saw him carrying his message of human unity around Asia, America and Europe.

But for all his internationalism, Tagore's heart was firmly rooted in his homeland; a truth reflected in his many popular songs, sung by the masses, and in the lyrics of the national anthems of both India and Bangladesh. In 1915 Tagore was awarded a knighthood by the British, but he later surrendered it in protest of the 1919 Jallianwala Bagh Massacre in Amritsar (see p272).

For a taste of Tagore's work, get a copy of his *Selected Short Stories*.

some temple tanks are believed to have healing properties, while others are said to have the power to wash away sins. Devotees (as well as travellers) may be required to wash their feet in a temple tank before entering a place of worship.

From the outside, Jain temples can resemble Hindu ones, but inside they're often a riot of sculptural ornamentation, the very opposite of ascetic austerity. Meanwhile, *gurdwaras* (Sikh temples) can usually be identified by a *nishan sahib* (flagpole flying a triangular flag with the Sikh insignia). Amritsar's sublime Golden Temple (p270) is Sikhism's holiest shrine.

Stupas, which characterise Buddhist places of worship, essentially evolved from burial mounds. They served as repositories for relics of the Buddha and, later, other venerated souls. A relatively recent innovation is the addition of a *chaitya* (hall) leading up to the stupa itself. Bodhgaya (p576), where Siddhartha Gautama attained enlightenment and became the Buddha, has a collection of notable Buddhist monasteries and temples. The gompas (Buddhist monasteries; see p73) found in places such as Ladakh and Sikkim are characterised by distinctly Tibetan motifs.

India's Muslim invaders contributed their own architectural conventions, including arched cloisters and domes. The Mughals uniquely melded Persian, Indian and provincial styles. Examples include the tomb of Humayun in Delhi (p135), the fort at Agra (p407) and the city of Fatehpur Sikri (p423). Emperor Shah Jahan was responsible for some of India's most spectacular architectural creations, most notably the iconic Taj Mahal (p404).

One of the most striking differences between Hinduism and Islam is religious imagery. While Islamic art eschews any hint of idolatry or portrayal of God, it has evolved a rich heritage of calligraphic and decorative designs. In terms of mosque architecture, the basic design elements are similar worldwide. A large hall is dedicated to communal prayer and within the hall is a mihrab (niche) indicating the direction of Mecca. The faithful are called to prayer from minarets, placed at cardinal points.

Churches in India reflect the fashions and trends of typically European ecclesiastical architecture with many also incorporating Hindu decorative flourishes. The Portuguese, among others, made impressive attempts to replicate the great churches and cathedrals of their day.

> Architecture buffs will appreciate *Masterpieces of Traditional Indian Architecture* by Satish Grover and *The History of Architecture in India* by Christopher Tadgell, both of which include insights into temple architecture.

Painting

Around 1500 years ago artists covered the walls and ceilings of the Ajanta caves (p825) in western India with scenes from the Buddha's life. The figures are endowed with an unusual freedom and grace, and contrast with the next major style that emerged from this part of India in the 11th century.

India's Jain community created some particularly lavish temple art. However, after the Muslim conquest of Gujarat in 1299, the Jains turned their attention to illustrated manuscripts, which could be hidden away. These manuscripts are the only known form of Indian painting that survived the Islamic conquest of North India.

The Indo-Persian style – characterised by geometric design coupled with flowing form – developed from Islamic royal courts, although the depiction of the elongated eye is one convention that seems to have been retained from indigenous sources. The Persian influence blossomed when artisans fled to India following the 1507 Uzbek attack on Herat (in present-day Afghanistan), and with trade and gift-swapping between the Persian city of Shiraz, an established centre for miniature production, and Indian provincial sultans.

The 1526 victory by Babur at the Battle of Panipat ushered in the era of the Mughals in India. Although Babur and his son Humayun were both patrons of the arts, it's Humayun's son Akbar who is generally credited

> Discover more about India's diverse temple architecture (in addition to other temple-related information) at Temple Net (www.templenet. com).

THE FINE ART OF MEHNDI

Mehndi is the traditional art of painting a woman's hands (and sometimes feet) with intricate henna designs for auspicious ceremonies, such as marriage. If quality henna is used, the design, which is orange-brown, can last up to one month.

In touristy areas, *mehndi*-wallahs are adept at applying henna tattoo 'bands' on the arms, legs and lower back. If you're thinking about getting *mehndi* applied, allow at least a couple of hours for the design process and required drying time (during drying you can't use your hennaed hands). Once applied, henna usually fades faster the more you wash it and apply lotion.

It's always wise to request the artist to do a 'test' spot on your arm before proceeding, as nowadays some dyes contain chemicals that can cause allergies. If good-quality henna is used, you should not feel any pain during or after the procedure.

with developing the characteristic Mughal style. This painting style, often in colourful miniature form, largely depicts court life, architecture, battle and hunting scenes, as well as detailed portraits. Akbar recruited artists from far and wide, and artistic endeavour first centred on the production of illustrated manuscripts (topics varied from history to mythology), but later broadened into portraiture and the glorification of everyday events. European painting styles influenced some artists, and this influence occasionally reveals itself in experiments with motifs and perspective.

Akbar's son Jehangir also patronised painting, but he preferred portraiture, and his fascination with natural science resulted in a vibrant legacy of paintings of flowers and animals. Under Jehangir's son Shah Jahan, the Mughal style became less fluid, and although the bright colouring was eye-catching, the paintings lacked the vigour of before.

Various schools of miniature painting (small paintings crammed with detail) emerged in Rajasthan from around the 17th century. The subject matter ranged from royal processions to shikar (hunting expeditions), with many artists influenced by Mughal styles. The intense colours, still evident today in miniatures and frescoes in some Indian palaces, were often derived from crushed semiprecious stones, while the gold and silver colouring is in fact finely pounded pure gold and silver leaf.

By the 19th century, painting in North India was notably influenced by Western styles (especially English watercolours), giving rise to what has been dubbed the Company School, which had its centre in Delhi.

In 21st-century India, paintings by contemporary Indian artists have been selling at record numbers (and prices) around the world. One very successful online art auction house is the Mumbai-based **Saffronart** (www.saffronart.com). Online auctions promote feisty global bidding wars, largely accounting for the high success rate of Saffronart, which may also preview its paintings in Mumbai and New York prior to its major cyber auctions. Over recent years, international auction houses have been descending upon India, to either set up offices or secure gallery alliances, in order to grab a piece of the action of what they have identified as a major growth market.

Get arty with Indian Art *by Roy Craven,* Contemporary Indian Art: Other Realities *edited by Yashodhara Dalmia, and* Indian Miniature Painting *by Dr Daljeet and Professor PC Jain.*

Handicrafts

Over the centuries India's many ethnic groups have spawned a vivid artistic heritage that is both inventive and spiritually significant. Many crafts fulfil a practical need as much as an aesthetic one.

Crafts aren't confined to their region of origin – artists migrate and have sometimes been influenced by the ideas of other regions – which means you can come across, for example, a Kashmiri handicraft emporium anywhere in India.

There's a vast range of handicrafts produced in the subcontinent, with standouts including ceramics, jewellery, leatherwork, metalwork, stone carving, papier-mâché, woodwork and a sumptuous array of textiles. For more information about what's on offer, see p1154.

SPORT
Cricket

In India, it's all about cricket, cricket and cricket! Travellers who show even a slight interest in the game can expect to strike passionate conversations with people of all stripes, from taxi drivers to IT yuppies. Cutting across all echelons of society, cricket is more than just a national sporting obsession – it's a matter of enormous patriotism, especially evident whenever India plays against Pakistan. Matches between these South Asian neighbours – which have had rocky relations since Independence – attract especially high-spirited support, and the players of both sides are under colossal pressure to do their respective countries proud.

Today cricket – especially the recently rolled out Twenty20 format (see www.cricket20.com) – is big business in India, attracting lucrative sponsorship deals and celebrity status for its players, especially for high-profile personalities such as star batsman Sachin Tendulkar and ace-bowler Harbhajan Singh. The sport has not been without its murky side though, with Indian cricketers among those embroiled in match-fixing scandals over past years.

International matches are played at various Indian centres – for venues, dates and advance online ticket bookings (advisable) visit http://indiancricketleague.in/tickets.html. Many Indian newspapers also relay details of forthcoming matches.

India's first recorded cricket match was in 1721. It won its first test series in 1952 in Chennai against England.

Keep your finger on the cricketing pulse at **Cricinfo** (www.cricinfo.com) and **Cricbuzz** (www.cricbuzz.com).

Tennis

Although nowhere near as popular as cricket, tennis is steadily generating greater interest in India. Perhaps the biggest success story for India is the doubles team of Leander Paes and Mahesh Bhupathi, who won Wimbledon's prestigious title in 1999 – the first Indians ever to do so. More recently, Bhupathi and doubles partner Sania Mirza (also of India) won the Mixed Doubles title at the 2009 Australian Open, while Paes and his partner Cara Black (Zimbabwe) nabbed the 2008 US Open Mixed Doubles title.

At the 2005 Dubai Open, Indian wild card Sania Mirza first made international waves when she convincingly defeated 2004 US Open champion Svetlana Kuznetsova. Mirza, then ranked 97th, 90 spots behind Kuznetsova, became the first Indian woman to win a Women's Tennis Association Tour title. Mirza's 2009 Australian Open Mixed Doubles win secured her a place in history as India's first woman to win a Grand Slam event.

Traditional Indian Textiles, by John Gillow and Nicholas Barnard, explores India's beautiful regional textiles and includes sections on tie-dye, weaving, beadwork, brocades and even camel girths.

Cricket fans will be bowled over by *The Illustrated History of Indian Cricket* by Boria Majumdar and *The States of Indian Cricket* by Ramachandra Guha.

KOLAMS

Kolams, the striking and breathtakingly intricate rice-flour designs (also called *rangoli*) that adorn thresholds, especially in South India, are both auspicious and symbolic. *Kolams* are traditionally drawn at sunrise and are sometimes made of rice-flour paste, which may be eaten by little creatures – symbolising a reverence for even the smallest living things. Deities are deemed to be attracted to a beautiful *kolam*, which may also signal to sadhus (ascetics) that they will be offered food at a particular house. Some people believe that *kolams* protect against the evil eye.

The **All India Tennis Association** (AITA; www.aitatennis.com) has more information about the game in India.

Polo

Horse polo intermittently flourished in India (especially among Indian royalty) until Independence, after which patronage sharply declined due to lack of sufficient funds. Today there's a renewed interest in the game thanks to beefed-up sponsorship, although it still remains an elite sport and consequently fails to attract widespread public interest.

Travellers can catch a polo match, and hobnob with high society, during the cooler winter months at centres that include Delhi, Jaipur, Kolkata and Mumbai (check local newspapers for dates and venues). Polo is also occasionally played in Ladakh and Manipur.

The origins of polo are unclear. Believed to have roots in Persia and China some 2000 years back, in the subcontinent it's thought to have first been played in Baltistan (in present-day Pakistan). Polo publications claim that Emperor Akbar (who reigned in India from 1556 to 1605) first introduced rules to the game, but that polo, as it's played today, was largely influenced by a British cavalry regiment stationed in India during the 1870s. A set of international rules was implemented after WWI. The world's oldest surviving polo club, established in 1862, is in Kolkata – see **Calcutta Polo Club** (www.calcutt apolo.com).

Hockey

Keeping your finger on the pulse of Indian sporting news is just a click away on Sify Sports (www.sify.com/sports).

Despite being India's national sport, field hockey no longer enjoys the same following it once did, largely due to the unassailable popularity of cricket, which snatches most of India's sponsorship funding.

During its golden era, between 1928 and 1956, India won six consecutive Olympic gold medals in hockey; it later bagged two further Olympic gold medals, one in 1964 and the other in 1980.

There have been recent initiatives aimed at generating renewed interest in the game, with high-profile hockey clubs encouraging secondary school and tertiary students to join, resulting in some success. In early 2009, India's national men's/women's hockey world rankings were 11/14 respectively.

For those keen to tap into the hockey scene, two good places to begin are **Indian Hockey** (www.indianhockey.com) and **Indian Field Hockey** (www.bharatiya hockey.org).

Other Sports

The world's second most populous nation has copped derisive criticism for its dismal performances in recent Olympic Games, with critics pointing the finger at paltry sponsorship commitment, poor infrastructure/equipment and

---

KABADDI – KABADDI – KABADDI

A cross between 'touch' and a game of rugby without a ball, kabaddi is played around India but is particularly popular in the north Indian state of Punjab. While one of the players chants 'kabaddi' – and he can't stop or the other team of seven wins – the opposition has to get him to touch the centre line. The game frequently descends into a scrum, but one young player assured us there were rules: 'You're not supposed to punch him or put your hand over his mouth – that would be a foul.'

A less common, nine-a-side variation on this is *kho-kho*, in which a player chases his opponent around a line of eight sitting players.

lack of public interest – among other things. At the 2008 Olympics in Beijing, India won just three medals (all by men) – a gold medal for shooting (10m air rifle), a bronze for boxing and a bronze for wrestling. India only received one medal at the 2004 Athens Olympics – silver (for men's double-trap shooting). Meanwhile, at the 2000 Games in Sydney, a female weightlifter, Karnam Malleswari, was the only Indian to receive a medal (bronze), making her the first Indian woman to ever win an Olympic medal.

Football (soccer) has a reasonably strong following, especially in the country's east and south – for further details see **Indian Football** (www.indianfootball.com). In early 2009 India occupied the 148th spot in the FIFA world rankings.

Horse racing, held primarily in the cooler winter months, is especially popular in large cities including Mumbai, Mysore, Delhi, Kolkata, Hyderabad and Bengaluru; for more information, check out **India Race** (www.indiarace.com), **Equine India** (www.equineindia.com) and **Racing World** (www.racingworldindia.com).

Some lesser-known traditional sports that have survived over time include *kho-kho* and kabaddi (see boxed text, opposite), both of which are essentially elaborate games of tag.

For details about the 2010 Commonwealth Games in Delhi sprint straight to www. cwgdelhi2010.org.

MEDIA

According to the World Association of Newspapers (WAN) 2008 World Press Trends report, India is the second biggest market (after China) when it comes to newspaper circulation, with around 99 million copies sold daily. In 2007 there was an 11.2% jump in newspaper sales in India and a 35.5% rise in the five-year period.

On the whole, India's extensive print media – which entails tens of thousands of newspapers and magazines in a range of vernaculars – enjoys widespread freedom of expression. According to recent surveys, India's most highly read English-language newspapers are the **Times of India** (www.timesofindia .com), **The Hindu** (www.hinduonnet.com) and the **Hindustan Times** (www.hindustantimes. com). For other English-language dailies and news magazines, see p1139. Most publications have websites.

Indian TV was at one time dominated by the national (government-controlled) broadcaster **Doordarshan** (www.ddindia.gov.in); the introduction of satellite TV in the early 1990s revolutionised viewing habits by introducing hundreds of channels, from international news giants such as the BBC and CNN to a host of Indian regional channels broadcasting in local dialects.

Programs on the government-controlled **All India Radio** (AIR; www.allindiaradio. org), one of the world's biggest radio service providers, include news, interviews, music and sport. There are also mushrooming nationwide private FM channels that offer greater variety than the government broadcaster, including talkback on subjects, such as relationship issues, once considered taboo.

Consult local newspapers for TV and radio program details.

India's oldest English-language newspaper is the *Times of India* (title since 1861), first published biweekly in 1838 as *The Bombay Times and Journal of Commerce*.

For online links to national and regional Indian newspapers, see www.onlinenewspapers. com/india.htm.

Food & Drink

Through its food, you'll discover that India is a banquet expressed in colours, aromas, flavours, textures and personalities. Like so many aspects of India, its food, too, is an elusive thing to define because it's made up of so many regionally diverse dishes, all with their own preparation techniques and ingredients. It's the ancient vegetarian fare of the south, the meaty traditions of the Mughals, the glowing tandoor (clay oven) of Punjab and the Euro-Indian fusions of former colonies. It's the heavenly fragrance of spices, the juice of exotic fruits running down your chin and rich, fiery curries that will make your tastebuds stand to attention. Indeed it's the sheer diversity of what's on offer that makes eating your way through India so deliciously rewarding.

Because of the prices it can fetch, saffron can sometimes be adulterated, usually with safflower – this corrupted form is aptly dubbed as 'bastard saffron'.

STAPLES & SPECIALITIES
Spices

Christopher Columbus was actually looking for the black pepper of Kerala's Malabar Coast when he stumbled upon America. The region still grows the finest quality of the world's favourite spice, and it's integral to most savoury Indian dishes. Turmeric is the essence of most Indian curries, but coriander seeds are the most widely used spice and lend flavour and body to just about every savoury dish, while most Indian 'wet' dishes – commonly known as curries in the West – begin with the crackle of cumin seeds in hot oil. Tamarind is sometimes known as the 'Indian date' and is a popular souring agent in the south. The green cardamom of Kerala's Western Ghats is regarded as the world's best, and you'll find it in savouries, desserts and warming chai (tea). Saffron, the dried stigmas of crocus flowers grown in Kashmir, is so light it takes more than 1500 hand-plucked flowers to yield just one gram.

Symbolising purity and fertility, rice is used in Hindu wedding ceremonies and often as *puja* (holy offerings) in temples.

Just about every Indian dish is flavoured with a distinct combination of spices; there are as many masala (spice blend) recipes as there are villains in Bollywood movies.

Rice

Rice is a common staple, especially in South India. Long-grain white rice varieties are the most popular, served hot with just about any 'wet' cooked dish. Rice is often cooked up in a pilau (or pilaf; spiced rice dish) or biryani. From Assam's sticky rice in the far northeast to Kerala's red grains in the extreme south, you'll find countless regional varieties that locals will claim to be the best in India, though this honour is usually conceded to basmati, a fragrant long-grain variety which is widely exported around the world.

Spotlighting rice, *Finest Rice Recipes* by Sabina Sehgal Saikia shows just how versatile this humble grain is, with classy creations such as rice-crusted crab cakes.

Khichdi (or *khichri*), mostly cooked in North India, is a blend of lightly spiced rice and lentils. Rarely found on restaurant menus, it's mostly prepared in home kitchens to mollify upset tummies (we recommend it for Delhi Belly) – some restaurants may specially cook it if you give them adequate advance notice.

Bread

While rice is paramount in the south, wheat is the mainstay in the north. Roti, the generic term for Indian-style bread, is a name used interchangeably with chapati to describe the most common variety, the irresistible unleavened round bread made with whole-wheat flour and cooked on a *tawa* (hotplate). It may be smothered with ghee (clarified butter) or oil, but is eaten plain by the health conscious or those who can't afford ghee. In some places, rotis may be bigger and thicker than chapatis and possibly cooked in a *tandoor*.

Puri is deep-fried dough puffed up like a crispy balloon. *Kachori* is somewhat similar, but the dough has been pepped up with corn or dhal, which makes it considerably thicker. Flaky, unleavened *paratha* can be eaten as is or jazzed up with fillings such as paneer (soft, unfermented cheese). The thick, usually tear drop–shaped, naan is cooked in a tandoor and is especially divine when flavoured with garlic.

Dhal

While the staple of preference divides north and south, the whole of India is cheerfully united in its love for dhal (curried lentils or pulses). You may encounter up to 60 different pulses: the most common are *channa*, a slightly sweeter version of the yellow split pea; tiny yellow or green ovals called *moong* (mung beans); salmon-coloured *masoor* (red lentils); the ochre-coloured southern favourite, *tuvar* (yellow lentils; also known as *arhar*); *rajma* (kidney beans); *kabuli channa* (chickpeas); *urad* (black gram or lentils); and *lobhia* (black-eyed peas).

Meat

While India probably has more vegetarians than the rest of the world combined, it still has an extensive repertoire of carnivorous fare. Chicken, lamb and mutton (sometimes actually goat) are the mainstays; religious taboos make beef forbidden to Hindus and pork to Muslims.

In northern India you'll come across meat-dominated Mughlai cuisine, which includes rich curries, kebabs, koftas and biryanis. This spicy cuisine traces its history back to the (Islamic) Mughal empire that once reigned supreme in India.

Tandoori meat dishes are another North Indian favourite. The name is derived from the clay oven, or tandoor, in which the marinated meat is cooked.

Fish & Seafood

With around 7500km of coastline, it's no surprise that seafood is an important staple on the subcontinent, especially on the west coast, from Mumbai (Bombay) down to Kerala. Kerala is the biggest fishing state, while Goa boasts particularly succulent prawns and fiery fish curries, and the fishing communities of the Konkan Coast – sandwiched between these two states – are renowned for their seafood recipes. Few main meals in Orissa exclude fish, and in West Bengal, puddled with ponds and lakes, fish is king.

Fruit & Vegetables

Vegetables are usually served at every main meal across India, and *sabzi* (vegetables) is a word recognised in every Indian vernacular. They're generally cooked *sukhi* (dry) or *tari* (in a sauce) and within these two categories they can be fried, roasted, curried, stuffed, baked, mashed and combined (made into koftas) or dipped in batter to make a deep-fried pakora (fritter).

Potatoes are ubiquitous and popularly cooked with various masalas, with other vegetables, or mashed and fried for the street snack *aloo tikki* (mashed-potato patties). Onions are fried with other vegetables, ground into a paste for cooking with meats, and served raw as relishes. Heads of cauliflower are usually cooked dry on their own, with potatoes to make *aloo gobi* (potato-and-cauliflower curry), or with other vegetables such as carrots and beans. Fresh green peas turn up stir-fried with other vegetables in pilaus and biryanis and in one of North India's signature dishes, the magnificent *mattar paneer* (unfermented cheese and pea curry). *Baigan* (eggplant/aubergine) can be curried or sliced and deep-fried. Also popular is *saag* (a generic term for leafy

---

Containing handy tips, including how to best store spices, Monisha Bharadwaj's *The Indian Kitchen* is a slick cookbook with more than 200 traditional recipes.

Read more about Indian cuisine on p413.

Technically speaking, there's no such thing as an Indian 'curry' – the word, an anglicised derivative of the Tamil word *kari* (sauce), was used by the British as a term for any dish including spices.

greens), which can include mustard, spinach and fenugreek. Something a little more unusual is the bumpy-skinned *karela* (bitter gourd) which, like the delectable *bhindi* (okra), is commonly prepared dry with spices – both are a must try!

You'll find fruit fashioned into a *chatni* (chutney) or pickle, and also flavouring lassi (yoghurt-and-iced-water drink), *kulfi* (firm-textured ice cream) and other sweet treats. Citrus fruit such as oranges (which are often yellow-green in India), tangerines, pink and white grapefruits, kumquats and sweet limes are widely grown. Himachal Pradesh produces crunchy apples in autumn, while plump strawberries can be found in Kashmir during summer. Along the southern coast are refreshing tropical fruits such as pineapples and papayas. Mangoes abound during the summer months (especially April and May), with India boasting more than 500 varieties, the pick of the luscious bunch is the sweet Alphonso.

Pickles, Chutneys & Relishes

No Indian meal is really complete without one, and often all, of the above. A relish can be anything from a little pickled onion to a delicately crafted fusion of fruit, nuts and spices. One of the most popular meal accompaniments is raita (mildly spiced yoghurt, often containing shredded cucumber or diced pineapple; served chilled), which makes a tongue-cooling counter to spicy food. *Chatnis* can come in any number of varieties (sweet or savoury) and can be made from many different vegetables, fruits, herbs and spices. But you should proceed with caution before polishing off that pickled speck sitting on your thali; it will quite possibly be the hottest thing that you have ever tasted.

Dairy

Milk and milk products make a staggering contribution to Indian cuisine: *dahi* (curd/yoghurt) is commonly served with meals and is great for subduing heat; paneer is a godsend for the vegetarian majority; lassi is one in a host of nourishing sweet and savoury beverages; ghee is the traditional and pure cooking medium; and some of the finest *mithai* (Indian sweets) are made with milk.

Sweets

India has a wide and colourful jumble of, often sticky and squishy, *mithai* (sweets), most of them sinfully sugary. The main categories are *barfi* (a fudgelike milk-based sweet), soft *halwa* (made with vegetables, cereals, lentils, nuts or fruit), *ladoos* (sweet balls made of gram flour and semolina), and those made from *chhana* (unpressed paneer) such as *rasgullas* (cream-cheese balls flavoured with rose-water). There are also simpler – but equally scrumptious – offerings such as inimitable *jalebis* (orange-coloured coils of deep-fried batter dunked in sugar syrup; served hot) that you'll see all over the country.

Kheer (called *payasam* in the south) is one of the most popular after-meal desserts. It's a creamy rice pudding with a light, delicate flavour, enhanced with cardamom, saffron, pistachios, flaked almonds, chopped cashews or slivered dried fruit. Other favourites include *gulab jamuns*, deep-fried balls of dough soaked in rose-flavoured syrup, and *kulfi*, a firm-textured ice cream made with reduced milk and flavoured with any number of nuts (often pistachio), fruits and berries.

Each year, an estimated 14 tonnes of pure silver is converted into the edible foil that decorates many Indian sweets, especially during the Diwali festival.

The excellent *Complete Indian Cooking* by Mridula Baljekar, Rafi Fernandez, Shehzad Husain and Manisha Kanani contains '325 deliciously authentic recipes for the adventurous cook'. Recipes include chicken with green mango, masala mashed potatoes and Goan prawn curry.

The Anger of Aubergines: Stories of Women and Food by Bulbul Sharma is an amusing culinary analysis of social relationships interspersed with enticing recipes.

The Book of Indian Sweets by Satarupa Banerjee contains a tempting mix of regional sweet treats, from Bengali *rasgullas* to Goan *bebinca*.

THE MAGIC OF PAAN

Meals are often rounded off with *paan*, a fragrant mixture of betel nut (also called areca nut), lime paste, spices and condiments wrapped in an edible, silky *paan* leaf. Peddled by *paan*-wallahs, who are usually strategically positioned outside busy restaurants, *paan* is eaten as a digestive and mouth-freshener. The betel nut is mildly narcotic and some aficionados eat *paan* the same way heavy smokers consume cigarettes – over the years these people's teeth can become rotted red and black.

There are two basic types of *paan: mitha* (sweet) and *saadha* (with tobacco). A parcel of *mitha paan* is a splendid way to finish a satisfying meal. Pop the whole parcel in your mouth and chew slowly, allowing the juices to oooooooze.

DRINKS
Nonalcoholic Drinks

Chai (tea), the much-loved drink of the masses, is made with copious amounts of milk and sugar. A glass of steaming, frothy chai is the perfect antidote to the vicissitudes of life on the Indian road; the disembodied voice droning '*garam* chai, *garam* chai' (hot tea, hot tea) is likely to become one of the most familiar and welcome sounds of your trip. For those interested in taking a tea appreciation course see p543.

While chai is the choice of the nation, South Indians have long shared their loyalty with coffee. In recent years, though, the number of coffee-drinking North Indians has skyrocketed, with ever-multiplying branches of hip coffee chains, such as Barista and Café Coffee Day, widely found in what were once chai strongholds.

Masala soda is the quintessentially Indian soft drink that's available at many drinks stalls. It's a freshly opened bottle of fizzy soda, pepped up with lime, spices, salt and sugar. Also refreshing is *jal jeera*, made of lime juice, cumin, mint and rock salt. Sweet and savoury lassi, a yoghurt-based drink, is especially popular nationwide and is another wonderfully rejuvenating beverage.

Falooda is an interesting rose-flavoured drink made with milk, cream, nuts and strands of vermicelli, while *badam* milk (served hot or cold) is flavoured with almonds and saffron.

India has zillions of fresh-fruit juice vendors, however be wary of hygiene standards (see the box on p90). Some restaurants think nothing of adding salt or sugar to juice to intensify the flavours; ask the waiter to omit these if you don't want them.

For information about safely drinking water in India, see the boxed text, p1197.

Alcoholic Drinks

An estimated three-quarters of India's drinking population quaffs 'country liquor' such as the notorious arak (liquor distilled from coconut-palm sap, potatoes or rice) of the south. This is the poor-man's drink and millions are addicted to the stuff. Each year, many people are blinded or even killed by the methyl alcohol in illegal arak.

An interesting local drink is a clear spirit with a heady pungent flavour called *mahua*, distilled from the flower of the *mahua* tree. It's brewed in makeshift village stalls all over central India during March and April, when the trees bloom. *Mahua* is safe to drink as long as it comes from a trustworthy source. There have been cases of people being blinded after drinking *mahua* adulterated with methyl alcohol.

Legend says that Buddha, after falling asleep during meditation, decided to cut his eyelids off in an act of penance. The lids grew into the tea plant, which, when brewed, banished sleep.

Thin and crispy, pappadams (commonly referred to as pappad) are circle-shaped lentil- or chickpea-flour wafers served either before or with a meal.

The Chef's Special series has terrific (light-weight) cookbooks showcasing regional cuisines. Titles include *Bengali Kitchen, Goan Kitchen, Gujarati Kitchen, Kashmiri Kitchen, Punjabi Kitchen* and *South Indian Kitchen.*

Rice beer is brewed all over east and northeast India. In the Himalaya you'll find a grain alcohol called *raksi,* which is strong, has a mild charcoal flavour and tastes vaguely like scotch whisky.

Solan beer from Himachal Pradesh is made in one of the highest-altitude breweries in the world – 2440m.

Toddy, the sap from the palm tree, is drunk in coastal areas, especially Kerala, while feni is the primo Indian spirit, and the preserve of laid-back Goa. Coconut feni is light and rather unexceptional but the much more popular cashew feni – made from the fruit of the cashew tree – is worth a try.

About a quarter of India's drinks market comprises Indian Made Foreign Liquors (IMFLs), made with a base of rectified spirit. Recent years have seen a rise in the consumption of imported spirits, with a spiralling number of city watering holes and restaurants flaunting a dazzling array of domestic and foreign labels.

Beer is phenomenally popular everywhere, with the more upmarket bars and restaurants stocking local and foreign brands (Budweiser, Heineken, Corona and the like). Most of the domestic brands are straightforward Pilsners around the 5% alcohol mark; travellers champion Kingfisher.

Wine-drinking is on the rise, despite the domestic wine-producing industry still being relatively new. The favourable climate and soil conditions in certain areas – such as parts of Maharasthra and Karnataka – have spawned some commendable Indian wineries including Chateau Indage (www .indagevintners.com), Grover Vineyards (www.groverwines.com) and Sula Vineyards (www.sulawines.com). Domestic offerings include chardonnay, chenin blanc, sauvignon blanc, cabernet sauvignon, shiraz and zinfandel. Also see the 'Grapes of Worth' box on p816. Meanwhile, if you fancy sipping booze of the blue-blood ilk, traditional royal liqueurs of Rajasthan (once reserved for private consumption within royal families) are now sold at some city liquor shops, especially in Delhi and Jaipur. Ingredients range from aniseed, cardamom and saffron to rose, dates and mint. A popular choice is the 'Maharani Mahansar' (Rs1700 per bottle).

See p837 for details about India's major festivals.

CELEBRATIONS

Although most Hindu festivals have a religious core, many are also great occasions for spirited feasting. Sweets are considered the most luxurious of foods and almost every special occasion is celebrated with a mind-boggling range. *Karanjis,* crescent-shaped flour parcels stuffed with sweet *khoya* (milk solids) and nuts, are synonymous with Holi, the most rambunctious Hindu festival, and it wouldn't be the same without sticky *malpuas* (wheat pancakes dipped in syrup), *barfis* and *pedas* (multicoloured pieces of *khoya* and sugar). Pongal is the major harvest festival of the south and is most closely associated with the dish of the same name, made with the season's first rice, along with jaggery, nuts, raisins and spices. Diwali, the festival of lights, is the most widely celebrated national festival, and some regions have specific Diwali sweets; if you're in Mumbai dive into delicious *anarsa* (rice-flour cookies).

To delve into the wonderful world of Indian wine, clink – oops we mean click – on www .indianwine.com. Cheers!

Ramadan is the Islamic month of fasting, when Muslims abstain from eating, drinking or smoking between sunrise and sunset. Each day's fast is often broken with dates – considered auspicious – followed by fruit and fruit juices. On the final day of Ramadan, Eid al-Fitr, a lavish feast celebrates the end of the fast with nonvegetarian biryanis and a huge proliferation of special sweets.

WHERE TO EAT

India has oodles of restaurants, from ramshackle street eateries to swish five-star hotel offerings. Most midrange restaurants serve one of two basic genres: South Indian (which usually means the vegetarian food of Tamil Nadu and Karnataka) and North Indian (which comprises Punjabi/Mughlai fare). You'll also find the cuisines of neighbouring regions and states. Indians frequently migrate in search of work and these restaurants cater to the large communities seeking the familiar tastes of home.

Not to be confused with burger joints and pizzerias, restaurants in the south advertising 'fast food' are some of India's best. They serve the whole gamut of tiffin (snack) items and often have separate sweet counters. Many upmarket hotels have outstanding restaurants, usually with pan-Indian menus so you can explore various regional cuisines. Although they're not cheap, they're within splurging reach of most travellers. Some of India's more cosmopolitan cities, such as Mumbai, Delhi and Bengaluru (Bangalore), have an especially vibrant dining-out scene, with menus sporting everything from Indian and Mexican to Chinese and Mediterranean – peruse the Eating sections of those chapters for more details.

Dhabas (basic snack joints) are oases to millions of truck drivers, bus passengers and sundry travellers going anywhere by road. The original *dhabas* dot the North Indian landscape, but you'll find versions of them throughout the country. The rough-and-ready but hearty food served in these happy-go-lucky shacks has become a genre of its own known as '*dhaba* food'.

> For recipes online, try:
> www.recipesindian.com
> www.indiaexpress
> .com/cooking
> www.thokalath
> .com/cuisine
> www.indianfoodforever
> .com

Street Food

Whatever the time of day, food vendors are frying, boiling, roasting, peeling, simmering, mixing, juicing or baking some type of food and drink to lure peckish passers-by. Small operations usually have one special that they serve all day, while other vendors have different dishes for breakfast, lunch and dinner. The fare varies as you venture between neighbourhoods, towns and regions; it can be as simple as puffed rice or peanuts roasted in hot sand, as unexpected as a fried-egg sandwich, or as complex as the riot of different flavours known as *chaat* (savoury snack). For more about *chaat* read the box on p147.

Devilishly delicious deep-fried fare is the staple of the streets, and you'll find satiating samosas (deep-fried pastry triangles filled with spiced vegetables and less often meat), and *bhajia* (vegetable fritters) in varying degrees of spiciness. Much loved in Maharasthra is *vada pao,* a veg-burger of sorts, with a deep-fried potato patty in a bread bun served with hot chillies and tangy chutneys. Sublime kebabs doused in smooth curd and wrapped in warm Indian-style bread are most commonly found in neighbourhoods with a large Muslim community.

> Got the munchies? Grab *Street Foods of India* by Vimla and Deb Kumar Mukerji which has recipes of some of India's favourite snacks, from samosas and *bhelpuri* to *jalebis* and *kulfi.*

Platform Food

One of the thrills of travelling by rail is the culinary circus that greets you at almost every station. Roving vendors accost arriving trains, yelling and scampering up and down the carriages; fruit, *namkin* (savoury nibbles), omelettes and nuts are offered through the grills on the windows; and platform cooks try to lure you from the train with the sizzle of fresh samosas. Frequent rail travellers know which station is famous for which food item: Lonavla station in Maharashtra is known for *chikki* (nut and jaggery toffee), Agra for *peitha* (sweet crystallised pumpkin) and Dhaund near Delhi for biryani.

WHERE TO DRINK

Gujarat is India's only dry state but there are drinking laws in place all over the country, and each state may have regular dry days when the sale of alcohol from liquor shops is banned. To avoid paying high taxes, head for Goa, where booze isn't subject to the exorbitant levies of other states.

You'll find good watering holes in most big cities such as Mumbai, Bengaluru (Bangalore), Kolkata (Calcutta) and Delhi, which are usually at

---

STREET FOOD DOS & DON'TS

Tucking into street food is one of the joys of travelling in India – here are some tips to help avoid tummy troubles.

■ Give yourself a few days to adjust to the local cuisine, especially if you're not used to spicy food.

■ You know the rule about following a crowd – if the locals are avoiding a particular vendor, you should too. Also take notice of the profile of the customers – any place popular with families will probably be your safest bet.

■ Check how and where the vendor is cleaning the utensils, and how and where the food is covered. If the vendor is cooking in oil, have a peek to check it's clean. If the pots or surfaces are dirty, there are food scraps about or too many buzzing flies, don't be shy to make a hasty retreat.

■ Don't be put off when you order some deep-fried snack and the cook throws it back into the wok. It's common practice to partly cook the snacks first and then finish them off once they've been ordered. In fact, frying them hot again will kill any germs.

■ Unless a place is reputable (and busy), it's best to avoid eating meat from the street.

■ The hygiene standard at juice stalls is wildly variable, so exercise caution. Have the vendor press the juice in front of you and steer clear of anything stored in a jug or served in a glass (unless you're absolutely convinced of the washing standards).

■ Don't be tempted by glistening pre-sliced melon and other fruit, which keeps its luscious veneer with the regular dousing of (often dubious) water.

---

their liveliest on weekends. The more upmarket bars serve an impressive selection of domestic and imported drinks as well as draught beer. Many bars turn into music-thumping nightclubs anytime after 8pm although there are quiet lounge-bars to be found in some cities. In smaller towns the bar scene can be a seedy, male-dominated affair – not the kind of place thirsty female travellers should venture into alone. For details about a city's bars, see the Drinking sections of this book's regional chapters.

Stringent licensing laws discourage drinking in some restaurants but places that depend on the tourist rupee may covertly serve you beer in teapots and disguised glasses – but don't assume anything, at the risk of causing offence. Very few vegetarian restaurants serve alcohol.

VEGETARIANS & VEGANS

India produces some of the best vegetarian food you'll find anywhere on the planet. There's little understanding of veganism (the term 'pure vegetarian' means without eggs), and animal products such as milk, butter, ghee and curd are included in most Indian dishes. If you are vegan your first problem is likely to be getting the cook to completely understand your requirements.

For further information, surf the web – good places to begin include: **Indian Vegan** (www.indianvegan.com) and **Vegan World Network** (www.vegansworldnetwork.org).

HABITS & CUSTOMS

Three main meals a day is the norm in India. Breakfast is usually fairly light, maybe *idlis* (spongy, round, fermented rice cakes) and *sambar* (soupy lentil dish with cubed vegetables) in the south, and *parathas* in the north. The health-conscious (mostly the upper echelons of society) may restrict breakfast to fruit, cereal and/or toast. Lunch can be substantial (perhaps the local version of the thali) or light, especially for time-restricted office workers. Dinner is usually the main meal of the day. It's generally comprised of a few different

Celebrity chef Madhur Jaffrey has written best-selling cookbooks including *A Taste of India;* her fascinating memoir, *Climbing the Mango Trees,* includes 32 special family recipes.

preparations – several curried vegetable (maybe also meat) dishes and dhal, accompanied by rice and/or chapatis. Dishes are served all at once rather than as courses. Desserts are optional and most prevalent during festivals or other special occasions. Fruit often wraps up a meal. In many Indian homes dinner can be a late affair (post 9pm) depending on personal preference and possibly the season (eg late dinners during the warmer months). Restaurants usually spring to life after 9pm.

Food & Religion

For many in India, food is considered just as critical for fine-tuning the spirit as it is for sustaining the body. Broadly speaking, Hindus avoid foods that are thought to inhibit physical and spiritual development, although there are few hard-and-fast rules. The taboo on eating beef (the cow is holy to Hindus) is the most rigid restriction. Devout Hindus (and Jains) also avoid alcohol and foods such as garlic and onions, which are thought to heat the blood and arouse sexual desire. You may come across vegetarian restaurants that make it a point to advertise the absence of onion and garlic in their dishes for this reason. These items are also banned from most ashrams.

Some foods, such as dairy products, are considered innately pure and are eaten to cleanse the body, mind and spirit. Ayurveda, the ancient and complex science of life, health and longevity, also influences food customs (see the boxed text, p993).

Pork is taboo for Muslims and stimulants such as alcohol are avoided by the most devout. Halal is the term for all permitted foods, and haram for those prohibited. Fasting is considered an opportunity to earn the approval of Allah, to wipe the sin-slate clean and to understand the suffering of the poor.

Buddhists and Jains subscribe to the philosophy of ahimsa (nonviolence) and are mostly vegetarian. Jainism's central tenet is ultra-vegetarianism, and rigid restrictions are in place to avoid even potential injury to any living creature – Jains abstain from eating vegetables that grow underground because of the potential to harm insects during cultivation.

India's Sikh, Christian and Parsi communities have few or no restrictions on what they can eat.

> Food which is first offered to the gods at temples then shared among devotees is known as *prasad*.

> To explore the ayurvedic approach to food and life, get a copy of *Ayurveda: Life, Health & Longevity* by Robert E Svoboda.

COOKING COURSES

You might find yourself so inspired by Indian food that you want to take home a little Indian kitchen know-how – the listings below represent just a

---

EATING INDIAN-STYLE

Most people in India eat with their right hand. In the south, they use as much of the hand as is necessary, while elsewhere they use the tips of the fingers. The left hand is reserved for unsanitary actions such as removing grotty shoes. You can use your left hand for holding drinks and serving yourself from a communal bowl, but it shouldn't be used for bringing food to your mouth. Before and after a meal, it's good manners to wash your hands.

Once your meal is served, mix the food with your fingers. If you are having dhal and *sabzi* (vegetables), only mix the dhal into your rice and have the *sabzi* in small scoops with each mouthful. If you are having fish or meat curry, mix the gravy into your rice and take the flesh off the bones from the side of your plate. Scoop up lumps of the mix and, with your knuckles facing the dish, use your thumb to shovel the food into your mouth.

Indian children grow up with spicy food so there are rarely separate menus for them in restaurants. However there are plenty of dishes that don't have a spicy kick – roti, rice, (possibly) dhal, curd, soup, sandwiches etc – just ask if you're unsure. Small portions may be available at some restaurants.

sprinkling of the ever-increasing number of places offering cooking courses. Some are professionally run, others are very informal, and each is of varying duration. Most require at least a few days' advance notice.

Bhimsen's Cooking Class, **Lhamo's Kitchen**, **Nisha's Indian Cooking Course**, **Sangye's Kitchen** and **Tibetan Cooking School** (p374; McLeod Ganj, Himachal Pradesh)

Cook & Eat (p1017; Kochi, Kerala)

Holiday on the Menu (p867; Panaji, Goa)

Hotel Jamuna Resort (p192; Jhunjhunu, Rajasthan)

Hotel Krishna Niwas, **Noble Indian Cooking Classes**, **Shashi Cooking Classes** and **Spice Box** (p218; Udaipur, Rajasthan)

Kali Travel Home (p518; Kolkata, West Bengal)

Parul Puri (p139; Delhi)

Tannie Baig (p139; Delhi)

A growing number of homestays around Kerala offer cooking classes – two particularly promising places to ask around are Kumily (p1008) and Fort Cochin (p1019).

EAT YOUR WORDS
Useful Phrases

Do you accept credit cards?	*kyaa aap kredit kaard lete/letee haing?* (m/f)
What would you recommend?	*aap ke kyaal meng kyaa achchaa hogaa?*
I'm (a) vegetarian.	*maing... hoong shaakaahaaree*
I'd like the..., please.	*muje... chaahiye*
Please bring a/the...	*... laaiye*
bill	*bil*
fork	*kaangtaa*
glass	*glaas*
glass of wine	*sharaab kee kaa glaas*
knife	*chaakoo*
menu	*menyoo*
mineral water	*minral vaatar*
plate	*plet*
spoon	*chammach*
I don't eat...	*maing... naheeng kaataa/kaatee* (m/f)
Could you prepare a	*kyaa aap... ke binaa kaanaa taiyaar kar sakte/*
meal without...?	*saktee haing?* (m/f)
beef	*gaay ke gosht*
dairy products	*dood se banee cheezong*
fish	*machlee*
meat stock	*gosht ke staak*
pork	*suar ke gosht*
poultry	*murgee*
red meat (goat)	*bakree*
I'm allergic to...	*muje... kee elarjee hai*
nuts	*meve*
seafood	*machlee*
shellfish	*shelfish*

Food & Drink Glossary

achar	pickle
aloo	potato; also *alu*
aloo tikki	mashed-potato patty

appam	South Indian rice pancake
arak	liquor distilled from coconut milk, potatoes or rice
badam	almond
baigan	eggplant/aubergine; also known as *brinjal*
barfi	fudgelike sweet made from milk
bebinca	Goan 16-layer coconut cake whipped up with sugar, nutmeg, cardamom and egg yolks
besan	chickpea flour
betel	nut of the betel tree; chewed as a stimulant and digestive in *paan;* also called areca nut
bhajia	vegetable fritters
bhang lassi	blend of lassi and bhang (a derivative of marijuana)
bhelpuri	thin fried rounds of dough with rice, lentils, lemon juice, onion, herbs and chutney
bhindi	okra
biryani	fragrant spiced steamed rice with meat or vegetables
bonda	mashed-potato patty
chaat	savoury snack, may be seasoned with *chaat* masala
chach	buttermilk beverage
chai	tea
channa	spiced chickpeas
chapati	round unleavened Indian-style bread; also known as *roti*
chatni	chutney
chawal	rice
cheiku	small, sweet brown fruit
dahi	curd/yoghurt
dhal	curried lentil dish; a staple food of India
dhal makhani	black lentils and red kidney beans with cream and butter
dhansak	Parsi dish; meat, usually chicken, with curried lentils and rice
dosa	large South Indian savoury crepe
falooda	rose-flavoured drink made with milk, cream, nuts and vermicelli
faluda	long chickpea-flour noodles
farsan	savoury nibbles
feni	Goan liquor distilled from coconut milk or cashews
ghee	clarified butter
gobi	cauliflower
gram	legumes
gulab jamun	deep-fried balls of dough soaked in rose-flavoured syrup
halwa	soft sweet made with vegetables, cereals, lentils, nuts or fruit
idli	South Indian spongy, round, fermented rice cake
imli	tamarind
jaggery	hard, brown, sugarlike sweetener made from palm sap
jalebi	orange-coloured coils of deep-fried batter dunked in sugar syrup
karela	bitter gourd
keema	spiced minced meat
kheer	creamy rice pudding
khichdi	blend of lightly spiced rice and lentils; also *khichri*
kofta	minced vegetables or meat; often ball-shaped
korma	currylike braised dish
kulcha	soft leavened Indian-style bread
kulfi	flavoured (often with pistachio) firm-textured ice cream
ladoo	sweet ball made with gram flour and semolina; also *ladu*
lassi	yoghurt-and-iced-water drink
masala dosa	large South Indian savoury crepe *(dosa)* stuffed with spiced potatoes
mattar paneer	unfermented cheese and pea curry

methi	fenugreek
mishti doi	Bengali sweet; curd sweetened with jaggery
mithai	Indian sweets
molee	Keralan dish; fish pieces poached in coconut milk and spices
momo	Tibetan steamed or fried dumpling stuffed with vegetables or meat
mooli	white radish
naan	tandoor-cooked flat bread
namak	salt
namkin	savoury nibbles
pakora	bite-sized piece of vegetable dipped in chickpea-flour batter and deep-fried
palak paneer	unfermented cheese chunks in a puréed spinach gravy
paneer	soft, unfermented cheese made from milk curd
pani	water
pappadam	thin, crispy lentil or chickpea-flour circle-shaped wafer; commonly called *pappad*
paratha	Indian-style flaky bread (thicker than chapati) made with ghee and cooked on a hotplate; often stuffed with grated vegetables, paneer etc
phulka	a chapati that puffs up when briefly placed on an open flame
pilaf	see *pilau*
pilau	rice cooked in stock and flavoured with spices; also *pulau, pilao* or *pilaf*
pudina	mint
puri	flat savoury dough that puffs up when deep-fried; also *poori*
raita	mildly spiced yoghurt, often containing shredded cucumber or diced pineapple; served chilled
rasam	*dhal*-based broth flavoured with tamarind
rasgulla	cream-cheese balls flavoured with rose-water
rogan josh	rich, spicy lamb curry
saag	leafy greens
sabzi	vegetables
sambar	South Indian soupy lentil dish with cubed vegetables
samosa	deep-fried pastry triangles filled with spiced vegetables, sometimes meat
sonf	aniseed; used as a digestive and mouth-freshener, usually comes with the bill after a meal; also *saunf*
tandoor	clay oven
tawa	flat hotplate/iron griddle
thali	all-you-can-eat meal; stainless steel (sometimes silver) compartmentalised plate for meals
thukpa	hearty Tibetan noodle soup
tiffin	snack; also refers to meal container often made of stainless steel
tikka	spiced, often marinated, chunks of chicken, paneer etc
toddy	alcoholic drink, tapped from palm trees
tsampa	Tibetan staple of roast-barley flour
upma	*rava* (semolina) cooked with onions, spices, chilli peppers and coconut
uttapam	thick, savoury South Indian rice pancake with finely chopped onions, green chillies, coriander and coconut
vada	South Indian doughnut-shaped deep-fried lentil savoury
vindaloo	Goan dish; fiery curry in a marinade of vinegar and garlic

Environment

THE LAND

India is an incredibly diverse country with everything from steamy jungles and tropical rainforest, to arid deserts and the soaring peaks of the Himalaya. At 3,287,263 sq km, India is the second-largest Asian country after China, and it forms the vast bulk of the South Asian subcontinent – an ancient block of earth crust that slammed into Asia about 40 million years ago. India is composed of three major geographic features: Himalayan peaks and ridges along its northern borders, the vast alluvial floodplain of the Ganges and other rivers that run off south-facing slopes of the mountains and flow toward the Bay of Bengal, and the elevated Deccan Plateau that forms the core of India's triangular southern peninsula.

Read about wildlife, conservation and the environment in *Sanctuary Asia* (www.sanctuaryasia .com), a slick publication raising awareness about India's precious natural heritage.

The Himalaya

As the world's highest mountains – with the highest peak in India reaching 8598m tall – the Himalaya create an impregnable boundary that separates India from its neighbours in the north. This mighty 2500km-long wall of peaks and ridges formed when the Indian subcontinent broke away from Gondwanaland, a supercontinent in the Southern Hemisphere that included Africa, Antarctica, Australia and South America. All by itself, India drifted north and finally slammed slowly, but with immense force into the Eurasian continent about 40 million years ago. This collision buckled the soft sedimentary crust of Eurasia upward to form the Himalaya and many lesser wrinkles in the earth's crust that stretch across northern India from Afghanistan to Myanmar (Burma). Fossils of sea creatures from this time are found on 5000m-high Himalayan peaks, 800km from the nearest sea. This continental collision is an ongoing process and the Himalaya are still growing in height about 1cm per year and being pushed northward about 5cm a year.

When the Himalaya reached their great heights during the Pleistocene (less than 150,000 years ago), they began to block and alter weather systems, creating the monsoon climate that dominates India today, as well as forming a dry rain-shadow to the north.

Although it looks like a continuous range on a map, the Himalaya is actually a series of interlocking ridges, separated by countless valleys. Until the technology was created to run roads through the Himalaya, many of these valleys existed in complete isolation, preserving a diverse series of mountain cultures – with Muslims in Kashmir; Buddhists in Zanskar, Ladakh, Lahaul, Spiti, Sikkim and western Arunachal Pradesh; and Hindus in most of Himachal Pradesh and Uttarakhand (Uttaranchal).

Moving mountains make Northern India a volatile area for tectonic activity. Kashmir was rocked by a devastating earthquake in October 2005, killing 80,000 people.

The Indo-Gangetic Plains

Covering most of northern India, the vast alluvial plains of the sacred Ganges River drop just 200m between Delhi and the waterlogged wetlands of West Bengal, then joins forces with the Brahmaputra River from India's northeast before dumping into the sea in Bangladesh. These alluvial plains run in a west–east trough between the wall of the Himalaya to the north and the elevated tableland of the Deccan to the south, extending westward to include the most populous regions of Pakistan and eastward to include all of Bangladesh. Vast quantities of sediments from the neighbouring highlands accumulate on the plains to a depth of nearly 2km, creating fertile, well-watered agricultural land. This region is flat, homogenous and densely populated, but was once extensively forested and rich in wildlife.

The western portions of the Indo-Gangetic Plain merge into the Great Thar Desert in western Rajasthan, the site of a vanished prehistoric forest. Gujarat in the far west of India is separated from Sindh (Pakistan) by the Rann of Kutch – in the wet season, this brackish marshland floods to become a vast inland sea, but in the dry season (November to April) the waters recede, leaving isolated islands perched on an expansive plain.

The Deccan Plateau

South of the Indo-Gangetic (northern) plain, the land rises to the Deccan Plateau, marking the divide between the Mughal heartlands of North India and the Dravidian civilisations of the south. The Deccan is bound on either side by the Western and Eastern Ghats, which come together in their southern reaches to form the Nilgiri Hills in Tamil Nadu.

The 320,000-sq-km Deccan Plateau is the sole remaining visible portion of the much larger land mass that rafted north millions of years ago. The rest of this stable block of ancient earth crust is now rammed underneath the Himalayan uplift and buried under vast quantities of sediments on the Indo-Gangetic Plain. The plateau has been further covered by extensive lava flows and cut into numerous stepped shelves and narrow gorges by rushing rivers.

On the Deccan's western border, the Western Ghats drop sharply down to a narrow, coastal lowland to form a luxuriant slope of rainforest watered by monsoons out of the southwest. Rivers on the east slope of this range, such as the Godavari and the Krishna, drain eastwards across much of the plateau, crossing finally through a jumbled hilly region known as the Eastern Ghats to meet the Bay of Bengal.

The Islands

Offshore from India are a series of island groups, politically part of India but geographically linked to the landmasses of Southeast Asia and islands of the Indian Ocean. The Andaman and Nicobar Islands sit far out in the Bay of Bengal, while the coral atolls of Lakshadweep (300km west of Kerala) are a northerly extension of the Maldives islands, with a land area of just 32 sq km.

WILDLIFE

India has some of the richest biodiversity in the world, with 397 species of mammals, 1232 birds, 460 reptiles, 240 amphibians, and 2546 fish – among the highest counts for any country in the world. Understandably, wildlife-watching has become one of the country's prime tourist activities and there are dozens of national parks offering opportunities to spot rare and unusual wildlife. If you're keen on getting close to nature, see the boxed text, p100, detailing where and when to view wildlife.

Animals

The wildlife of India is fascinating and diverse, with many charismatic species both large and small. The country is a melting pot of animals from Europe, Asia, and ancient Gondwanaland that live in a wide range of habitats from lush mangrove swamps to icy alpine meadows.

India is best known for its signature species – elephants, tigers, monkeys, leopards, antelopes and rhinos – that roam the hills and plains of central and southern India. Most of these species are endangered by human competition for land and water, particularly in the overpopulated plains. Elephants and buffaloes are widely pressed into service as beasts of burden, but dwindling numbers of wild elephants, as well as one-horned Indian rhinos, and other

The popular guru Jaggi Vasudev has launched an ambitious project to plant 114 million new saplings in Tamil Nadu by 2016, increasing forest cover in the region by 10%. Visit http://projectgreen hands.org.

The Andaman and Nicobar Islands comprise 572 islands and are the peaks of a vast submerged mountain range extending almost 1000km between Myanmar (Burma) and Sumatra.

Visitors wanting an in-depth overview of India's habitats will want to read *Ecosystems of India*, edited by JRB Alfred.

wild animals struggle to survive in small protected patches of grassland and forest.

In east India, the Ganges and Yamuna Rivers merge and empty into the Bay of Bengal, creating the vast Sunderbans Delta – 80,000 sq km of mangrove swamps and watercourses that are home to tigers (estimated at 274 in 2004 and due to be recounted in 2009), crocodiles, fish, wild boars, sea turtles and snakes. Chitals (spotted deer) have evolved the ability to secrete salt from their glands to cope with this salt-laden environment.

India's national animal is the tiger, its national bird is the peacock and its national flower is the lotus. The national emblem of India is a column topped by three Asiatic lions.

The deserts of Rajasthan and Gujarat provide a home for desert-adapted species such as chinkaras (Indian gazelle), khurs (Asiatic wild asses), blackbucks (a large breed of antelope) and Indian wolves. The 1400-sq-km Sasan Gir Wildlife Sanctuary (p757) in Gujarat is the last refuge of the Asiatic lion, once found across India. Wilderness areas in the central plains provide a home to dholes (wild dogs), jackals, wolves, striped hyenas and numerous species of deer and antelope, including sambars, chitals, threatened mouse deer and muntjacs (barking deer).

India's primates range from the extremely rare hoolock gibbon and golden langur of the northeast, to species that are so common as to be a pest – most notably the stocky and aggressive rhesus macaque and the elegant grey langur. In the south, the role of loitering around temples and tourist sites is filled by the bonnet macaque. Threatened species clinging on in the rainforests of the south include lion-tailed macaques, glossy black Nilgiri langurs and slender loris, an adept insect-catcher with huge eyes for nocturnal hunting.

India has 460 species of reptiles, of which 50 are poisonous snakes. There are various species of cobra, including the legendary king cobra, the world's largest venomous snake, which grows up to 5m. For obvious reasons, snake charmers stick to smaller species! Nonvenomous snakes include the rat snake, the bright-green vine snake and the rock python. All live in the fear of the snake-killing mongoose, which has evolved ingenious techniques for hunting poisonous snakes, tricking the reptiles into striking repeatedly until they are exhausted, and then eating the head first to avoid being bitten.

The Wildlife Protection Society of India (www .wpsi-india.org) is a prominent wildlife-conservation organisation campaigning for animal welfare through education, lobbying and legal action against poachers.

In South India, the tropical forests of the Western Ghats contain one of the rarest bats on earth – the small Salim Ali's fruit bat – as well as flying lizards (technically gliders), sloth bears, leopards, jungle cats, hornbills, parrots and hundreds of other bird species – birders should check out the reserves listed on p105. Elephants and gaurs (Indian bison) also occur here, and the hills are the last remaining stronghold of the endangered Nilgiri tahr, or cloud goat.

The Himalaya harbours its own hardy range of creatures. Yaks and two-humped Bactrian camels are common domesticated animals, but extremely rare in the wild. Other herbivores include bharals (blue sheep), kiangs (Tibetan wild ass), Himalayan ibexes (a graceful mountain antelope), Himalayan tahrs (mountain goat) and rare Tibetan antelopes. Also found here are musk deer, hunted almost to extinction for the scent produced by the glands on their bellies. Recent attempts at captive breeding near Kedarnath (Uttarakhand) are providing some hope for this threatened species.

Predators of the Himalaya include black and brown bears, tigers, and the endangered snow leopard, an animal so elusive that many locals claim it can appear and disappear at will. Tiny populations cling on in Ladakh, Sikkim, Uttarakhand, Himachal Pradesh and Arunachal Pradesh. The rare red panda inhabits the bamboo thickets of the eastern Himalaya, particularly in Sikkim and Bhutan.

Cobras are believed to have power over the monsoon and are worshipped during the Naag Panchami festival each July/August; to the despair of animal-rights campaigners many snakes die from exhaustion and overfeeding.

Offshore, the Lakshadweep in the Indian Ocean and the Andaman and Nicobar Islands in the Bay of Bengal preserve classic coral atoll ecosystems. Bottlenose dolphins, coral reefs, sea turtles and tropical fish flourish beneath the water, while seabirds, reptiles, amphibians and butterflies thrive on land. The Andaman's small population of elephants has been known to swim up to 3km between islands. Another oddity found here is the coconut or robber crab, a 5kg tree-climbing monster that combs the beaches for broken coconuts.

ENDANGERED SPECIES

Serious bird-watchers will love the weighty *A Guide to the Birds of India* by Richard Grimmett, Carol Inskipp and Tim Inskipp; but for everyone else there's the slimmed-down *Pocket Guide to Birds of the Indian Subcontinent.*

Despite having amazing biodiversity, India faces a growing challenge from its exploding human population. At last count, India had 569 threatened species, comprising 247 species of plants, 89 species of mammals, 82 species of birds, 26 species of reptiles, 68 species of amphibians, 35 species of fish and 22 species of invertebrates.

Prior to 1972 India had only five national parks, so the Wildlife Protection Act was introduced that year to set aside parks and stem the abuse of wildlife. The act was followed by a string of similar pieces of legislation with bold ambitions but few teeth with which to enforce them. For example, the National Chambal Sanctuary set up to protect the last 200 gharial crocodiles in the wild is still the site of illegal sand-mining in plain view of a public highway, and local mafia gangs poach wildlife in the park at free will.

A rare success story has been Project Tiger, launched in 1973 to protect India's big mammals – see the boxed text, opposite. The main threats to wildlife continue to be habitat loss due to human encroachment, and poaching by criminals and even corrupt officials and businessmen at all levels of society. It is estimated that 846 tigers and 3140 leopards were poached between 1994 and 2008, while 320 elephants were poached from 2000 to 2008.

The bizarre gharial crocodile uses its extremely long, slender jaws like chopsticks to expertly snatch fish from the water.

All of India's wild cats, from leopards, to snow leopards, panthers and jungle cats, are facing extinction from habitat loss and poaching for the lucrative trade in skins and body parts for Chinese medicine. There are thought to be fewer than 3500 tigers, 1000 snow leopards and 300 Asiatic lions still alive in the wild. Spurious health benefits are linked to every part of the tiger, from the teeth to the penis, and a whole tiger carcass can fetch upwards of US$10,000. Government estimates suggest that India is losing 1% of its tigers every year to poachers.

Even highly protected rhinos are poached for the medicine trade – rhino horn is highly valued as an aphrodisiac and as a material for making handles for daggers in the Gulf. Elephants are regularly poached for ivory – we implore you not to support this trade by buying ivory souvenirs. Various species of deer are threatened by hunting for food and trophies, and the chiru, or Tibetan antelope, is nearly extinct because its hair is woven into wool for expensive shahtoosh shawls.

India's bear species are under threat and sloth bears are widely poached to be used as 'dancing bears' at tourist centres such as Agra and Jaipur – see the boxed text, p409. In the water, India's freshwater dolphins are in dire straits from pollution and human competition. The sea-turtle population on the Orissa coast also faces problems – see the boxed text, p661.

Plants

Though only 29 sq km in size, Keoladeo National Park is still the foremost birding site in India and has more than 400 species.

Once, India was almost entirely covered in forest; now India's total forest cover is estimated to be around 20%, although the Forest Survey of India has set an optimistic target of 33%. Despite widespread clearing of native habitats, the country boasts 49,219 plant species, of which around 5200 are endemic. Species on the southern peninsula show Malaysian ancestry, while desert plants in Rajasthan are more clearly allied with the Middle East, and conifer forests of the Himalaya derive from European and Siberian origins.

Outside of mountain forests found in the Himalaya, nearly all the lowland forests of India are subtypes of tropical forest, with native sal forests forming

---

HOORAY FOR PROJECT TIGER

When naturalist Jim Corbett first raised the alarm in the 1930s no one believed that tigers would ever be threatened. At the time it was believed there were 40,000 tigers in India, although no one had ever conducted a census. Then came Independence, which put guns into the hands of villagers who pushed into formerly off-limits hunting reserves to hunt for highly profitable tiger skins. By the time an official census was conducted in 1972, there were only 1800 tigers left and international outcry prompted Indira Gandhi to make the tiger the national symbol of India and set up **Project Tiger** (http://projecttiger.nic.in). The project has since established 27 tiger reserves that not only protect this top predator but all animals that live in the same habitats. After an initial round of successes, tiger numbers have recently plummeted to a new low of 1400 due to relentless poaching, so another $153 million and high-tech equipment have been devoted to the effort to stop this slide towards extinction.

---

the mainstay of the timber industry. Some of these tropical forests are true rainforest, staying green year-round, such as in the Western Ghats and in the northeast states, but most forests are deciduous and look surprisingly dusty and forlorn in the dry season. Fortunately, the leaf fall and dry vegetation makes wildlife viewing easier in otherwise dense woodlands.

High-value trees such as Indian rosewood, Malabar kino and teak have been virtually cleared from the Western Ghats, and sandalwood is endangered across India due to illegal logging for the incense and wood-carving industries. A bigger threat on forested lands is firewood harvesting, often carried out by landless peasants who squat on gazetted government land.

Several trees have significant religious value in India, including the silk-cotton tree, a big tree with spiny bark and large red flowers under which Pitamaha, the creator of the world, sat after his labours. Two well-known figs, the Banyan and Peepal, grow to immense size by dangling roots from their branches and fusing into massive multitrunked jungles of trunks and stems – one giant is nearly 200m across. It is said that Buddha achieved enlightenment while sitting under a peepul (also known as the bodhi tree).

The foothills and slopes of the Himalaya preserve classic montane species, including blue pine and deodar (Himalayan cedar) and deciduous forests of apple, chestnut, birch, plum and cinnamon. Above the snowline hardy plants such as anemones, edelweiss and gentians can be prolific, and one fabulous place to see them is at the Valley of the Flowers National Park.

India's hot deserts have their own unique species – the khejri tree and various strains of scrub acacia, adapted to the dry conditions. The hardy sea-buckthorn bush is the main fruiting shrub in the deserts of the Himalaya. All these indigenous species face a challenge from introduced species such as the eucalyptus, a water-hungry species introduced by the British to dry out malarial swamps.

NATIONAL PARKS & WILDLIFE SANCTUARIES

India has 97 national parks and 486 wildlife sanctuaries, which constitute about 5% of India's territory. An additional 70 parks have been authorised on paper but not yet implemented on the ground. There are also 14 biosphere reserves, overlapping many of the national parks and sanctuaries, providing safe migration channels for wildlife and allowing scientists to monitor biodiversity.

We strongly recommend visiting at least one national park or sanctuary on your travels – the experience of coming face-to-face with a wild elephant, rhino or tiger will stay with you for a lifetime, while your visit adds momentum to efforts to protect India's natural resources. Wildlife reserves tend to

Around 2000 plant species are described in Ayurveda (traditional Indian herbal medicine) and a further 91 plant species are used in *amchi* (Tibetan traditional medicine).

The Foundation for Revitalisation of Local Health Traditions has a search engine for medicinal plants at www.medicinalplants.in. Travellers with a serious interest should pick up CP Khare's *Encyclopedia Of Indian Medicinal Plants*.

MAJOR NATIONAL PARKS & WILDLIFE SANCTUARIES

Park/Sanctuary	Location	Features	Best time to visit	Page
Bandhavgarh National Park	Jabalpur, Madhya Pradesh	plains: tigers, leopards, deer, jackals, nilgais & boars	Nov-Apr	p719
Bhitarkanika Wildlife Sanctuary	northeast Orissa	estuarine mangrove forests: saltwater crocodiles, water monitors, pythons, wild boars & chitals	Dec-Feb	p667
Calimere (Kodikkarai) Wildlife & Bird Sanctuary	near Thanjavur, Tamil Nadu	coastal wetland: dolphins, sea turtles, crocodiles, flamingos, waterfowl, wading birds, mynas & barbets	Nov-Jan	p1083
Chandaka Wildlife Sanctuary	eastern Orissa	upland forest: muntjacs, mouse deer, leopards, hyenas & sloth bears	Oct-May	p652
Corbett Tiger Reserve	near Ramnagar, Uttarakhand	forest & river plains: tigers, leopards, dholes, elephants, crocodiles & 600 bird species	Mar-Jun	p487
Debrigarh Wildlife Sanctuary	near Sambalpur, Orissa	dry deciduous forest: tigers, leopards, deer, boars, sloth bears & bird life	Oct-May	p665
Dubare Forest Reserve	near Madikeri, Karnataka	interactive camp for retired working elephants	Sep-May	p930
Govind Wildlife Sanctuary & National Park	Saur-Sankri, Uttarakhand	mountain scenery: black & brown bears, snow leopards, deer & bird life	Apr-Jun & Sep-Nov	p483
Great Himalayan National Park	southeast of Kullu Valley, Himachal Pradesh	Himalayan mountains & community involvement: black & brown bears, bharal, leopards & snow leopards	Apr-Jun & Sep–mid-Nov	p349
Indira Gandhi (Annamalai) Wildlife Sanctuary	near Pollachi, Tamil Nadu	forested mountains: elephants, gaurs, tigers, jungle cats, bears, flying squirrels & civet cats	year-round, except in periods of drought	p1108
Jaldhapara Wildlife Sanctuary	northern West Bengal	forest & grasslands: rhinos, tigers, elephants & Bengal florican	mid-Oct–May	p544
Kanha National Park	Jabalpur, Madhya Pradesh	sal forest & open woodlands: barasinghas, tigers, leopards, dholes, gaurs & sambhars	Mar-Jun	p717
Kaziranga National Park	Assam, Northeast States	dense grassland & swamp: rhinos, buffaloes, barasinghas, elephants, tigers & birds of prey	Feb-Mar	p618
Keoladeo Ghana National Park	Bharatpur, Rajasthan	plains: eagles, cranes, flamingos, herons, storks & geese, pythons, jackals & deer	Oct–late Feb	p185
Little Rann Sanctuary	northwest Gujarat	desert region: flamingos, wild asses, wolves & caracals	Oct-Jun	p775
Mahatma Gandhi Marine National Park	Andaman & Nicobar Islands	mangrove forests & coral reefs	Nov-Apr	p1132
Manas National Park	near Guwahati, Assam	forest & grassland: rhinos, tigers, elephants, buffaloes & pygmy hogs	Nov-Apr	p617
Marine National Park	30km from Jamnagar, Gujarat	coral reefs & mangroves: finless porpoises, dugongs & sea turtles	Dec-Mar	p766
Nal Sarovar Bird Sanctuary	near Ahmedabad, Gujarat	vast lake & wetlands: indigenous & migratory birds, incl flamingos, pelicans & geese	Nov-Feb	p737

Park/Sanctuary	Location	Features	Best time to visit	Page
Nilgiri Biosphere Reserve (including Wayanad Wildlife Sanctuary & Bandipur, Nagarhole & Mudumalai National Parks)	Tamil Nadu, Karnataka & Kerala	forest: elephants, tigers, deer, gaurs, sambars, muntjacs, mouse deers, chitals & bonnet macaques	Mar-May (some areas year-round)	Mudumalai p1118, Bandipur p926, Nagarhole p926, Wayanad p1031
Panna National Park	near Khajuraho, Madhya Pradesh	dry deciduous forest: tigers, leopards, dholes, nilgais, chitals & sambars	Jan-May	p689
Pench Tiger Reserve	Madhya Pradesh	teak forest & grasslands: guars, hyenas, jungle cats & tigers	Feb-Apr	p716
Periyar Wildlife Sanctuary	Kumily, Kerala	wooded hills: lion-tailed macaques, elephants, gaurs, otters, dholes, pythons, kingfishers & fishing owls	Oct-Jun	p1006
Pin Valley National Park	Dhankar, Himachal Pradesh	pristine mountain scenery: snow leopards, ibexes, black bears & deer	Jul-Oct	p395
Rajaji National Park	near Haridwar, Uttarakhand	forested hills: elephants, tigers, leopards, deer & sloth bears	Mar-Jun	p474
Ranganathittu Bird Sanctuary	near Mysore, Karnataka	river & islands: storks, ibises, egrets, spoonbills & cormorants	Jun-Nov	p921
Ranthambore National Park	south of Jaipur, Rajasthan	dry forests around crocodile-filled lake: bird life incl painted storks, leopards, nilgais, crocodiles & tigers	Oct-Apr	p201
Sanjay Gandhi National Park	near Mumbai, Maharashtra	scenic city park: water birds, flying foxes & leopards	Aug-Apr	p809
Sariska Tiger Reserve	Sariska, Rajasthan	rocky wooded hills: tigers, peacocks, sambars, nilgais, boars & rhesus monkey	Nov-Mar	p188
Sasan Gir Wildlife Sanctuary	near Junagadh, Gujarat	desert oasis: Asiatic lions, leopards, crocodiles & nilgais	Dec-Apr	p757
Simlipal National Park	Balasore, Orissa	forest & waterfalls: tigers, leopards, elephants, crocodiles & bird life	Nov-Jun	p665
Sunderbans Tiger Reserve	southern West Bengal	mangrove forests: tigers, crocodiles & Gangetic dolphins	Oct-Mar	p534
Tadoba-Andhari Tiger Reserve	south of Nagpur, Maharashtra	deciduous forest, grasslands & wetlands: tigers, dholes, nilgais & gaurs	Feb-May	p831
Valley of Flowers National Park	near Joshimath, Uttarakhand	3500m above sea level: musk deer, Himalayan bears & butterflies & around 300 species of wildflower	mid-Jul–mid-Aug & mid-Sep–end Oct	p485
Vedantangal Bird Sanctuary	near, Chengalpattu Tamil Nadu	forest & lake: cormorants, egrets, herons, storks, ibises, spoonbills, grebes & pelicans	Nov-Jan	p1065
Velavadar National Park	near Bhavnagar, Gujarat	grasslands in delta region: blackbucks, nilgais & bird life	Dec-Mar	p748

A DAM TOO FAR?

The most controversial of India's many hydroelectric schemes is the Narmada Valley Development, a US$6-billion scheme to build 30 hydroelectric dams along the Narmada River in Madhya Pradesh, Rajasthan and Gujarat. Despite bringing benefits in terms of irrigation to thousands of villages and reducing desert encroachment into rural areas, the project will flood the tribal homelands of some 40,000 Adivasi (tribal) villagers, many of whom worship the waters as a deity. The government has promised to provide alternative accommodation, but thus far only 10% of the displaced peoples have found adequate farmland as compensation. The World Bank refused to fund the ongoing development, but Britain's Barclays Bank stepped in with loans and the Indian government has overruled every legal challenge to the development, despite some high-profile names joining the anti–Narmada Dam movement – including Booker Prize–winner Arundhati Roy. For the latest developments, see the **Friends of River Narmada website** (www.narmada.org).

---

be off the beaten track and infrastructure can be limited – book transport and accommodation in advance, and check opening times, permit requirements and entry fees before you visit. Many parks close to conduct a census of wildlife in the off-season, and monsoon rains can make wildlife-viewing tracks inaccessible.

Almost all parks offer jeep/van tours, but you can also search for wildlife on guided treks, boat trips and elephant safaris. For various safari possibilities, see p105.

Every argument has two sides: the pro–Narmada Dam lobby has launched its own campaign to publicise the virtues of the project – see www .supportnarmadadam.org and www.sardarsarov-ardam.org.

ENVIRONMENTAL ISSUES

With over a billion people, ever-expanding industrial and urban centres, and an expansive growth in chemical-intensive farming, India's environment is under tremendous threat. An estimated 65% of India's land is degraded in some way, and nearly all of that land is seriously degraded, with the government consistently falling short on most of its environmental protection goals due to lack of enforcement or willpower. Many problems experienced today are a direct result of the Green Revolution of the 1960s when a quantum leap in agricultural output was achieved using chemical fertilisers and pesticides, but at enormous cost to the environment, habitats, and wildlife populations.

Despite numerous new environmental laws since the 1984 Bhopal disaster (see the boxed text, p691), corruption continues to exacerbate environmental degradation – worst exemplified by the flagrant flouting of environmental rules by companies involved in hydroelectricity, mining, and uranium and oil exploration. Usually, the people most affected are low-caste rural farmers and Adivasis (tribal people) who have limited political representation and few resources to fight big businesses.

Between 11% and 27% of India's agricultural output is lost due to soil degradation from over-farming, rising soil salinity, loss of tree-cover and poor irrigation. The human cost is heart-rending, and lurking behind all these problems is a basic Malthusian truth: there are too many people for India to support at its current level of development.

While the Indian government could undoubtedly do more, some blame must also fall on Western farm subsidies that artificially reduce the cost of imported produce, undermining prices for Indian farmers. Western agribusiness also promote the use of nonpropagating, genetically modified (GM) seed stocks.

As anywhere, tourists tread a fine line between providing an incentive for change and making the problem worse. Many of the environmental problems in Goa (see the boxed text, p867) are a direct result of years of irresponsible development for tourism. Always consider your environmental impact while travelling in India, including while trekking (see p114) and diving (see p110).

Air Pollution

Industry and vehicle emissions is a serious concern, having increased four- to eight-fold over the past 20 years and catapulting India into the top ranks of countries with the most polluted air and highest levels of premature death due to air pollution. Indian diesel reportedly contains around 50 to 200 times more sulphur than European diesel and the ageing engines of Indian vehicles would fail most emissions tests in Europe or America. Delhi and Mumbai (Bombay) both tried to switch over their public transport to Compressed Natural Gas (CNG) but India's Supreme Court overturned those laws.

Unfortunately, national efforts to improve air-quality standards almost invariably fail due to lack of local enforcement. This problem occurs on the household level as well, with over half a million people a year dying from indoor air pollution – a result of continuing to burn with traditional wood or animal dung rather than switching to smokeless stoves or liquid gas offered by aid agencies.

> Air pollution in many Indian cities has been measured at more than double the maximum safe level recommended by the World Health Organization.

Climate Change

Changing climate patterns – linked to global carbon-emissions – have been creating dangerous extremes of weather in India. While India is a major polluter, in carbon emissions per capita it still ranks far behind America, Australia and Europe.

Increased monsoon rainfall has caused ever-worse flooding and destruction, including the devastating Gujarat and Maharashtra floods in 2005. In mountain deserts of Ladakh, increased rainfall is changing time-honoured farming patterns and threatening traditional mud-brick architecture. Conversely, other areas are experiencing reduced rainfall, causing drought and riots over access to water supplies. Islands in the Lakshadweep group as well as the low-lying plains of the Ganges delta are being inundated by rising sea levels.

Deforestation

Since Independence, some 53,000 sq km of India's forests have been cleared for logging and farming, or damaged by urban expansion, mining, industrialisation and river dams. The number of mangrove forests has halved since the early 1990s, reducing the nursery grounds for the fish that stock the Indian Ocean and Bay of Bengal.

> Noise pollution in major cities has been measured at over 90 decibels – more than one and a half times the recognised 'safe' limit. Bring earplugs!

India's first Five Year Plan in 1951 recognised the importance of forests for soil conservation, and various policies have been introduced to increase forest cover. Almost all have been flouted by officials, criminals and by ordinary people clearing forests for firewood and grazing in forest areas. Try to minimise the use of wood-burning stoves while you travel (this is less of an issue in areas with fast-growing pine species in the hills).

Officially, states are supposed to earmark an equivalent area for afforestation when an area is cleared, but enforcement is lax and land set aside may be unsuitable for forestry. On another front, invasive eucalyptus and other foreign plant species are swamping indigenous flora. Numerous charities are working with rural communities to encourage tree planting, and religious leaders like the Dalai Lama have joined the movement.

Water Resources

Arguably the biggest threat to public health in India is inadequate access to clean drinking water and proper sanitation. With the population set to double

Get the inside track on Indian environmental issues at Down to Earth (www.downtoearth.org .in), an online magazine that delves into stories overlooked by the mainstream media.

by 2050, agricultural, industrial and domestic water usage are all expected to spiral, despite government policies designed to control water use.

Rivers are also affected by run-off, industrial pollution and sewage contamination – the Sabarmati, Yamuna and Ganges are among the most polluted rivers on earth. At least 70% of the freshwater sources in India are now polluted in some way. In recent years, drought has devastated parts of the subcontinent (particularly Rajasthan and Gujarat) and has acted as a driving force for rural-to-urban migration.

Water distribution is another volatile issue. Since 1947 an estimated 35 million people in India have been displaced by major dams, mostly built for hydroelectricity projects to provide energy for this increasingly power-hungry nation. While hydroelectricity is one of the greener power sources, valleys across India are being sacrificed to create new power plants, and displaced people rarely receive adequate compensation – see the boxed texts, p102 and p346, for more on this issue.

Activities

India covers every terrain imaginable, from sun-baked deserts and moist rainforests to snow-dusted mountains and plunging ravines. With all this to play with, the opportunities for outdoor activities are endless. Choose from trekking, paragliding, mountaineering, jungle safaris, scuba-diving and elephant rides as well as yoga, meditation and much, much more. It would take a whole book to present all the options, but some of the most popular activities are covered in the following sections.

Choosing an Operator

Regardless of what you decide to do, you should exercise a little caution when choosing an operator. We receive regular reports of dodgy operators taking poorly equipped tourists into potentially dangerous situations. Remember that travel agents are only middlemen and the final decisions about safety and equipment come down to the people actually operating the trip. Check out all tour operators, trekking companies and activity providers carefully. Make sure that you know in advance what you're getting, then make sure you get what you paid for by having it put in writing.

Where possible, stick to companies that provide activities themselves, using their own guides and teaching staff. If you go through an agency, look for operators who are accredited by the Travel Agents Association of India (www.travelagentsofindia.com), the Indian Association of Tour Operators (www.iato.in) or the Adventure Tour Operators Association of India (www.atoai.org). Note that dodgy operators often change their names to sound like the trusted companies – consult official tourist offices for lists of government-approved operators and seek first-hand recommendations from fellow travellers.

Always check safety equipment before you set out and make sure you know what is included in the quoted price. If anything is substandard, let the operator know. If it refuses to make the necessary changes, go with another company. For any activity, make sure that you have adequate insurance – many travel-insurance policies have exclusions for risky activities, including such commonplace holiday activities as skiing, diving and trekking (see p1149).

The Wildlife Protection Society of India (www.wpsi-india.org/tiger) campaigns to save wildlife, especially tigers – see the website for tiger reserve locations, poaching statistics and more.

OUTDOOR ACTIVITIES

All sorts of activities are possible in the Indian outdoors, from trekking and mountaineering to wildlife safaris and white-water rafting, along with more laid-back pursuits such as elephant rides and boat tours.

MEETING THE WILDLIFE

India has some of the planet's most spectacular flora and fauna – from lumbering elephants and prowling tigers to desert orchids and trailing lianas. Here are some excellent ways to get up close and personal with Indian wildlife.

Bird-Watching

The subcontinent boasts some of the world's major bird-breeding and feeding grounds. Some places offer bird-spotting by boat (see regional chapters for comprehensive details). The following are prime bird-watching sites:

Andaman & Nicobar Islands Spot rare drongos and golden orioles on Havelock Island (p1133).

Goa Top spots to view all sorts of species are at Cotiago Wildlife Sanctuary (p896), and on the state's manifold river trips that can be arranged from almost every beach resort.

Gujarat Twitcher territory includes Khijadiya Bird Sanctuary (p766), the Little Rann Sanctuary (p775) and Nal Sarovar Bird Sanctuary (p737).

Haryana & Punjab There are several hundred species at Sultanpur Bird Sanctuary (p266).

Himachal Pradesh Catch glimpses of many species at the Great Himalayan National Park (p349).

Karnataka See storks, egrets, ibises and spoonbills at Karanji Lake Nature Park (p917), Ranganathittu Bird Sanctuary (p921), Bandipur National Park (p926) and Nagarhole National Park (p926).

Kerala View Indian bird species from May to July and migratory birds from October to February at Kumarakom Bird Sanctuary (p1005) and Thattekkad Bird Sanctuary (p1012).

Madhya Pradesh & Chhattisgarh Search for 250 species of birds at Pench Tiger Reserve (p716), Kanha National Park (p717), Bandhavgarh National Park (p719), Panna National Park (p689), Madhav National Park (p676), Satpura National Park (p699), Orchha Nature Reserve (p679) and Kanger Valley National Park (p724).

Mumbai Sanjay Gandhi National Park (p809) is home to almost 300 species of birds, and Sewri Creek (p791) is big with waders and pink flamingos.

Northeast States Try birding tours by raft at Potasali Eco-Camp (p618) near Tezpur in Assam.

Orissa Domestic species and migrating waterbirds are a feature at Similipal National Park (p665), Bhitarkanika Wildlife Sanctuary (p667) and Chilika Lake (p659).

> Birding in India and South Asia (www.birding.in) is a top cyber-spot to swoop into all things ornithological, right down to recommended bird-watching binoculars.

Rajasthan Birders can tick off numerous species at Keoladeo Ghana National Park (p185), Ranthambore National Park (p201) and Khichan (p239).

Sikkim Try the birding tours with Sikkim Tours & Travels (p591) in Gangtok and Khecheopalri Trekkers Hut Guest House (p601) at Khecheopalri Lake.

Tamil Nadu There's plenty to point binoculars at in Mudumalai National Park (p1118), Calimere Wildlife & Bird Sanctuary (p1083) and Vedantangal Bird Sanctuary (p1065).

West Bengal Bird-watching tours are offered by Kalimpong's Gurudongma Tours & Travels (p562).

Camel Treks

Camel safaris can be arranged in desert areas across India. Bum-numbing multiday safaris are especially popular in Rajasthan, typically starting from Jaisalmer (p246), Bikaner (p253), Khuri (p248) or Osiyan (p239) with camps set up each night beneath the stars. Short joy rides are also possible in those places, as well as in Pushkar (p196), Shekhawati (p189) and near Hunder (p325) in Ladakh's Nubra Valley, where Bactrian (two-humped) camels are descended from stock that used to ply the Himalayan trade routes until conflict with China sealed the routes to Tibet.

> Robyn Davidson's *Desert Places* is an account of the author's journey by camel with the Rabari (Rajasthani nomads) on their annual migration through the Thar Desert.

Elephant Rides & Safaris

A fun way to get close to wildlife is atop an elephant. Many of India's national parks have their own working elephants, which can be hired for safaris into areas that are inaccessible to jeeps and walkers. You might even find yourself just metres from a snarling Bengal tiger. As well as being a childhood dream for many travellers, elephant rides are much less disturbing to wildlife than noisy jeeps. To find out the best times to visit parks, see regional chapters and the boxed text, p100.

Bihar & Jharkhand Elephant safaris tour Jharkhand's Betla (Palamau) National Park (p583).

Goa Short elephant rides are possible at one of Ponda's spice plantations (p872).

Karnataka Elephant safaris go to India's largest elephant reserve at Bandipur National Park (p926) near Mysore. You can also interact with retired working elephants at Dubare Forest Reserve (p930) near Madikeri.

Kerala There are elephant rides at Periyar Wildlife Sanctuary (p1006) and at Kudanadu, 50km from Kochi (p1017).

Madhya Pradesh & Chhattisgarh Tiger-spotting elephant safaris go through Panna National Park (p689), Pench Tiger Reserve (p716), Kanha National Park (p717) and Bandhavgarh National Park (p719).

Northeast States One-horned rhinos can be spotted on elephant safaris at Kaziranga National Park (p618) and Pobitora National Park (p617), and other wildlife at Manas National Park (p617).

Tamil Nadu There's a slim chance you'll see a tiger, and good odds for spotting gaurs and spotted deer from an elephants back in Mudumalai National Park (p1118).

Uttarakhand Tigers may be seen on elephant rides in Corbett Tiger Reserve (p487) and Rajaji National Park (p474).

West Bengal Try the jumbo rides around Jaldhapara Wildlife Sanctuary (p544) to spot one-horned Indian rhinos.

Horse Rides

Horse riding is possible right around India, from gentle ambles in hill stations to more demanding trails through lowland forests. As well as these leisure rides, horses are used as transport on some *yatra* (pilgrimage) trekking routes. See the regional chapters for comprehensive details about all modes of horsing around.

Jeep Safaris

As well as elephant rides, there are numerous jeep safaris visiting national parks, tribal villages and remote temples and monasteries. You can normally arrange a custom itinerary, either with travel agents or directly with local jeep drivers – the regional chapters have details. Here are some popular options:

Mark Shand describes his journey across India by elephant in *Travels On My Elephant*, a compelling travelogue of a jumbo-sized adventure.

Bihar & Jharkhand Jeep tours to see wild beasties in Betla (Palamau) National Park (p583).

Gujarat Safaris to spot Asiatic lions in Sasan Gir Wildlife Sanctuary (p757) and wild ass and flamingos at Little Rann Sanctuary (p775).

Himachal Pradesh Trips go to monasteries, isolated villages and mountain viewpoints from Kaza (p393) in Lahaul and Spiti, as well as Manali (p359).

Jammu & Kashmir Jeeps tour to mountain passes and monasteries around Ladakh and Zanskar (see p314 and p307).

Karnataka Wildlife resorts offer safaris to Nagarhole National Park (p926), Bandipur National Park (p926) and other reserves.

Kerala Wildlife-spotting jeep tours drive through the forests of Wayanad Wildlife Sanctuary (p1031) as well as the areas surrounding Periyar Wildlife Sanctuary (p1006).

Madhya Pradesh & Chhattisgarh Tiger-spotting tours at Madhya Pradesh's three big tiger parks, Pench Tiger Reserve (p716), Kanha National Park (p717) and Bandhavgarh National Park (p719). Jeep safaris are also possible at Panna National Park (p689), Madhav National Park (p676), Satpura National Park (p699) and Kanger Valley National Park (p724).

Northeast States Jeeps travel to tribal villages in the Northeast States with Abor Country Travels from Itanagar (p623) and Himalayan Holidays from Bomdila (p625), or there are wildlife-spotting tours in Kaziranga National Park (p618) and Manas National Park (p617).

Orissa Animal-focused jeep safaris are offered in Similipal National Park (p665) and Badrama and Debrigarh Wildlife Sanctuaries (p665).

Rajasthan Spot wildlife by jeep in Ranthambore National Park (p201) and Sariska Tiger Reserve (p188) and the wildlife sanctuary at Kumbhalgarh (p224).

Sikkim Agencies in Gangtok (p591) arrange jeep tours to Buddhist villages and mountain valleys in north Sikkim.

Tamil Nadu Jeep tours are just one of several ways to scout for wildlife in Mudumalai National Park (p1118).

Uttarakhand Jeeps are used to spy tigers and deer in Rajaji National Park (p474) and Corbett Tiger Reserve (p487).

Wildlife-Watching by Boat

Viewing wildlife (beyond birds) by boat is possible at various places including the following:

Goa Dolphin-spotting boat trips set sail from almost every beach in Goa (p868).

Madhya Pradesh & Chhattisgarh There are crocodile-spotting trips at Raneh Falls (p689).

Northeast States Wildlife-spotting boat safaris at Manas National Park (p617).

Orissa Boat tours look for crocodiles, deer and birds at Bhitarkanika Wildlife Sanctuary (p667) and freshwater dolphins and birds at Chilika Lake (p659).

West Bengal Boat tours take you through the mangroves in the huge Sunderbans Tiger Reserve (p534).

OTHER ACTIVITIES

India is paradise for fans of the great outdoors. Trekking is possible throughout the country, from the steamy southern jungles to the wind-scoured valleys of the Himalaya. Among other adrenalin-charged activities, thrill-seekers can scuba dive, paraglide, raft, climb, kayak and zorb. See the following sections for some suggestions. Remember to take out adequate insurance cover for any 'adventure' activities before you travel.

Boat Tours

Boat tours operate all over India – the following cover a range of possibilities, from quick whizzes to multiday cruises. Also see Wildlife-Watching by Boat (p107).

Andaman & Nicobar Islands Boat and ferry trips go to outlying islands from Port Blair (p1131) and Mayabunder (p1136).

Goa River cruises are offered on the state's languid riverine stretches and from the capital, Panaji (p868). Fishing trips run from many beaches.

Gujarat Coral reef cruises go to Jamnagar's Marine National Park (p766).

Jammu & Kashmir In Srinagar, hire gondola-like *shikaras* for tours around serene Dal Lake (p287).

Karnataka Coracles unhurriedly drift up and down the meandering Tungabhadra River in Hampi (p938), while fishing boats offer sea rides in Gokarna (p935) and Malpe (p934).

Kerala Days of languorous drifting on the backwaters around Alleppey (p1002), or canoe tours from Kollam (Quilon; p998) and bamboo-raft tours in Periyar Wildlife Sanctuary (p1007). Houseboat trips are also available on the quieter backwaters around Kumarakom (p1005) and near Bekal in Northern Kerala (p1035).

Kolkata Cruises operate to watch the immersion of idols during the Durga Puja festival (p507).

Madhya Pradesh & Chhattisgarh Cruises go to the Marble Rocks near Jabalpur (p715) and along the holy Narmada River in Maheshwar (p708). There's jolly boating on Bhopal's Upper Lake (p692) and you can be rowed up to the water spray at Chitrakote Falls (p723). There's also pedal boating on the huge lake that borders Madhav National Park (p676) and at the holy ghats in Ujjain (p703).

Maharashtra Ride out to the mid-sea island fort of Murud (p831) on a sailboat.

Mumbai Boats cruise around Mumbai Harbour and to Elephanta Island (p794).

Northeast States Steamboat cruises along the Brahmaputra River in Assam with Jungle Travels India (p614).

Rajasthan Boat tours around Udaipur's Lake Pichola (p215).

Uttarakhand Rowboat tours on Nainital's Naini Lake (p490).

Uttar Pradesh Dawn tours of the ghats at Varanasi (p441 and p445), and sacred river cruises in Chitrakut (p438), Mathura (p426) and Allahabad (p434). Allahabad also has speed-boat trips, kayaking and waterskiing on the Yamuna River.

Canyoning

In Meghalaya, Cherrapunjee Holiday Resort (p641) offers unusual canyoning trips that use surreal 'living bridges' woven from living trees by local tribes. Canyoning is also possible from Manali (p363).

Caving

Millennia of torrential monsoon rains have hollowed out an amazing system of caves underneath the northeastern state of Meghalaya, including the 22km-long Krem Um Im-Liat Prah/Krem Labbit system, India's longest cave. Caving trips can be arranged through tour agents in Shillong (p637). However, this is serious caving and it's best to bring equipment from home.

Adivasis (tribal people) make up roughly 8% of the Indian population – more than 84 million people – and comprise some 450 different tribal groups.

Cultural Tours

Tours to tribal areas are permitted in several parts of India, providing a window into the traditional way of life of India's Adivasis (tribal people). Some tours can be quite exploitative but better tours employ tribal guides and try to minimise the effect of tourism on tribal people. Reputable tribal tours include the following:

Gujarat Stay with tribal Halepotra people in Gujarat's Shaam-e-Sarhad Rural Resort (p773) near Bhuj.

Jammu & Kashmir Travel agents in Leh (p307) can arrange tours and treks to tribal areas – also see the boxed text, p323.

Kerala Tours to Mannakudy tribal areas of Periyar Wildlife Sanctuary (p1007).

Madhya Pradesh & Chhattisgarh There are tribal tours with the Satpura Adventure Club in Pachmarhi (p701). The Government of India tourist office can organise homestays in Basari, a tribal village 27km east of Khajuraho (p686). For information on visiting remote tribal villages in Chhattisgarh, see p723, or go through the Chhattisgarh Tourism Board in Raipur (p720).

Northeast States You can arrange tours of tribal districts of the northeast states with travel agencies in Guwahati (p614), Dibrugarh (p622), Itanagar (p623), Kohima (p627), Aizawl (p632) and Bomdila (p625).

Orissa Tours to Orissa's tribal groups are available from Bhubaneswar or Puri – read the boxed text, p663.

Rajasthan There are tours of Bishnoi tribal villages from Jodhpur (p233).

Uttarakhand Visits to Gujjar buffalo herders in Rajaji National Park through Mohan's Adventure Tours (p471) in Haridwar.

Dive India (www.dive india.com), an Andaman Islands' dive company, has a comprehensive list of dive sites on its website.

Cycling & Motorcycling

Bicycle and motorcycle hire is widely available right across India, especially in areas that attract tourists – regional chapters have details of just some of the numerous rental places. For recommended motorcycle tours see p1185.

Diving, Snorkelling & Water Sports

The Andaman Islands are India's leading destination for scuba-diving, with world-class dive sites on well-preserved coral reefs, particularly around Havelock Island. Visibility is clearest from around December to March or April. Meanwhile, the Lakshadweep Islands offer more coral-atoll diving from mid-October to mid-May. Dive-certification courses and recreational dives are also possible in Goa.

Growing numbers of surfers are discovering the breaks off the island of Little Andaman (p1125), with the best waves generally between mid-March and mid-May.

Andaman & Nicobar Islands India's best diving is around Havelock Island (p1124).

Goa Numerous beach resorts offer diving courses, windsurfing and other holiday water sports (p861).

Kerala There is world-class diving between mid-October and mid-May on the little-visited Lakshadweep Islands (p1038).

Hang-Gliding & Paragliding

Goa, Himachal Pradesh and Maharashtra are the flying capitals of India. You can bring your own gear or arrange courses and tandem flights. Safety standards have been variable in the past – the government of Himachal Pradesh shut down all paragliding operators from 2004 to 2005 after a fatality – but things have since improved. Nevertheless, it's still worth contacting the state tourism departments for a safety update before leaping into the blue beyond. Himachal Tourism conducts the Himalayan Hang Gliding Rally in Billing (p383) every May.

RESPONSIBLE DIVING

To help preserve the ecology and beauty of reefs, observe the following guidelines when diving:

- Never use anchors on the reef and take care not to ground boats on coral.
- Avoid touching or disturbing living marine organisms – they can be damaged by even the gentlest contact. If you must hold on to the reef, only touch exposed rock or dead coral.
- Be conscious of your fins. Even without contact, the surge from fin strokes near the reef can damage delicate organisms. Kicking up clouds of sand can smother organisms.
- Practise and maintain proper buoyancy control. Major damage can be done by divers descending too fast and colliding with the reef.
- Don't collect or buy coral or shells.
- Ensure that you take home all your rubbish and any litter you may find. Plastics in particular are a serious threat to marine life.
- Do not feed fish.
- Choose a dive company with appropriate environmental policies and practices.

The best seasons for flying are October to June in Goa and Maharashtra, and March to June, and September to December in Himachal Pradesh.

Goa There are paragliding flights at Arambol (p887) and Anjuna (p882).

Himachal Pradesh Leisure paragliding is possible at Solang Nullah (p367) near Manali, and Billing (p383) near Dharamsala.

Kerala There are beginner paragliding classes or tandem flights in Munnar (p1010).

Madhya Pradesh & Chhattisgarh Go parasailing with Satpura Adventure Club in Pachmari (p701).

Maharashtra You can take courses and tandem paragliding flights at Lonavla (p836).

Kayaking & River Rafting

Across India, mighty rivers roar down from the hills and mountains, offering some fantastic opportunities for white-water rafting. Things aren't quite as organised as in nearby Nepal, but rivers in West Bengal, Sikkim, Himachal Pradesh, Uttarakhand and Ladakh provide the best rafting in North India, and Goa and Karnataka offer rafting trips down south. Rafting seasons for the different states are roughly as follows:

- Karnataka – October to January
- Himachal Pradesh – April to September or October
- Ladakh – July and August
- Maharashtra – July to September
- Uttarakhand – September to June
- West Bengal – September to November, March to June

Rafting is possible on at least 10 Indian rivers, from the jagged mountains of Ladakh to the steamy hinterland of Karnataka. See www .indiarafting.com for popular options.

The level of rapids varies from modest Grade II to raging Grade IV and most rafting operators offer multiday rafting safaris as well as short thrill rides. The five-day trip along the gorge of the Zanskar River in Ladakh is one of Asia's finest white-water runs. Catch these rivers while you can – India's rivers are being dammed for hydroelectric power at an alarming rate.

Himachal Pradesh White-water rafting trips on the Beas and Sutlej Rivers are organised through tour operators in Shimla (p334), Tattapani (p342), Kullu (p353) and Manali (p362).

Jammu & Kashmir Places in Leh (see p307) arrange kayaking and rafting in Ladakh.

Karnataka Kayaking and rafting trips can be organised with Bengaluru's Getoff ur ass (p907). White-water trips up to Grade IV are possible in Dubare Forest Reserve (p930).

Kerala Canoe trips on the backwaters of Kerala at Green Palms Homes (p1004) near Allepey. The tourist office in Kollam (p998) also arranges canoe tours of surrounding villages.

Madhya Pradesh & Chhattisgarh Rafting trips can be taken on the Betwa River in Orchha (p679), while kayaking is available on Upper Lake in Bhopal (p692).

Mumbai Rafting in Maharashtra is organised through Mumbai-based Outbound Adventure (p792), which offers rafting trips from around June to September.

Northeastern States Kayaking day trips on the mighty Brahmaputra with Purvi Discovery, Dibrugarh (Assam; p622).

Uttarakhand White-water rafting and kayaking trips on the Ganges and Alaknanda Rivers can be organised in Rishikesh (p478), Haridwar (p471) and Joshimath (p484).

Uttar Pradesh You can kayak on the holy Yamuna River in Allahabad (p436).

West Bengal Arrange rafting on the Rangeet and Teesta Rivers through agents in Darjeeling (p554) and Teesta Bazaar (p565).

Mark Shand's *River Dog* tells the diverting tale of a river journey along the Brahmaputra in Assam, in the company of a faithful hound.

Rock-Climbing & Mountaineering

For warm-weather climbers, there are some tremendous sandstone and granite climbing areas in Karnataka at Badami, Ramnagar, Savandurga, Anegundi and Hampi, India's premier bouldering region (p940). The Kullu Valley near Manali (p362) is another popular destination for sport climbers.

Climbing is on a mixture of bolts and traditional protection. Organised climbs can be arranged but serious climbers should bring gear from home – pack plenty of nuts, hexacentrics and cams, plus spare rolls of climbing tape for jamming cracks in sharp granite.

The main areas for proper mountaineering are Himachal Pradesh, Jammu and Kashmir, Uttarakhand and Sikkim.

Himachal Pradesh Mountaineering and rock-climbing trips can be organised in northern Himachal Pradesh from Manali (p362), Vashisht (p366) and McLeod Ganj (p374).

Jammu & Kashmir You can arrange mountaineering and trekking peak expeditions in Leh (p307) and Padum (p297). See also p317.

Sikkim Mountaineering and trekking expeditions can be organised in Khangchendzonga National Park in Gangtok (p591). See also the Goecha La Trek (p603).

Uttarakhand Arrange climbing and mountaineering expeditions in Uttarkashi (p482), Joshimath (p484), Nainital (p490), and Rishikesh (p478).

MOUNTAINEERING & CLIMBING COURSES

There are numerous private and government-run climbing organisations that offer mountaineering training courses, usually on set dates during the warmer summer months. Most include simple accommodation, meals and

---

MOUNTAINEERING IN INDIA

Mountaineers need permission from the **Indian Mountaineering Foundation** (IMF; www.indmount .org) in Delhi to climb most peaks over 6000m, and the expedition royalties are significant – foreigners are charged US$1200 to US$1650 per expedition, depending on the height of the peak. Many peaks lie in restricted areas near the China border and climbers must pay additional fees for inner-line and restricted-area permits, plus any national park fees that apply. Discounts are available for groups who make arrangements through approved travel agents within India – contact the IMF for more information on any aspect of mountaineering in India.

Fortunately, you don't have to be cashed-up to climb in India. There are numerous trekking peaks that can be climbed without permits or royalties, particularly in Ladakh, Zanskar, Lahaul, Spiti and Sikkim. The four-day ascent of Stok Kangri (6120m) – see p317 – is one of the most popular treks in India, providing a taste of high-altitude mountaineering (US$50 per person). However, you should be alert for the symptoms of Acute Mountain Sickness (see p1198) on any trek above 3000m. If you fancy some training before you embark on an expedition, there are several mountaineering courses that can start you down the path to becoming the next Reinhold Messner – see above for the list of course possibilities.

most of the equipment you need (bring your own warm-weather clothing). Reputable organisations include the following:

Himalayan Mountaineering Institute (www.exploredarjeeling.com/hmidarj.htm; Darjeeling) Climbing and mountaineering courses from March to December (p554).

Institute of Mountaineering & Allied Sports (www.dmas.gov.in; Manali) Mountaineering courses around Himachal Pradesh from May to October (p359).

Jawahar Institute of Mountaineering & Winter Sports (Kashmir; www.pahalgam .com/jimws.html) Summer mountaineering courses at all levels (p286).

Nainital Mountaineering Club (near Nainital) Outdoor rock-climbing courses close to Nainital (p490).

Nehru Institute of Mountaineering (www.nimindia.org; Uttarkashi) Winter mountaineering courses with a 6000m expedition (p482).

Tenzing Norgay Climbing Club (Darjeeling) Indoor and outdoor climbing courses (p554).

Skiing & Snowboarding

India's premier ski resort is at Gulmarg in Kashmir, but ongoing security concerns have pushed many skiers towards the smaller resorts in Uttarakhand and Himachal Pradesh. All skiing in India takes place on high-altitude meadows, with the best snows falling from around January to March. There are runs for skiers of all levels. Prices for equipment rental and ski passes are some of the world's lowest, but power cuts can stop the lifts for long periods.

Ladakh and Zanskar are popular trekking destinations – for details see p315 and p298.

Himachal Pradesh There's a small lift and ski lodges as well as a cable car under construction (scheduled for completion sometime in 2009) in Solang Nullah (p367). Lessons and ski hire are available and there's skiing for all levels. There are also expeditions to high-altitude powder on foot or by helicopter. Narkanda (p342) has less infrastructure than at Solang Nullah, but lessons are available and there's a portable ski-lift in season.

Jammu & Kashmir In Gulmarg (p294), chair and tow lifts plus a gondola cableway provide access to high-altitude powder. Lessons and rental are available and there are ski runs to suit all levels of experience.

Uttarakhand Auli (p485) has a gondola cableway, chairlift and rope-tow that can take you up 5km of beginner and intermediate slopes. Rental and lessons are available, and all levels of experience catered for.

Trekking

India presents some stunning trekking opportunities, particularly in the foothills of the Himalaya, with temples, Buddhist monasteries, remote lakes and mountain passes as popular destinations. Many trekking (and even road) passes are over 5000m in Ladakh. However, the trekking industry is not as well developed as in nearby Nepal. Trekking lodges are only found on a handful of routes and trekkers must carry everything they need, including food, tents, sleeping bags and emergency equipment. Drinking water isn't always available and trails are often poorly marked, with few people around to ask directions. Acute Mountain Sickness is also a risk on any routes over 3000m above sea level, including most routes in Ladakh, Zanskar and Lahaul and Spiti – see p1198 for more information.

Because of this, independent trekking can be risky. Most people opt for organised treks with local trekking agencies, though it is possible to hire your own porters, packhorses and guides through tourist offices. If you do make your own arrangements, work out an emergency plan for evacuation from the route. Tell someone at the trailhead where you are going and when you intend to be back, and never trek alone. On any organised trek, make sure you have all the equipment you need and ensure you know exactly what is included in the fee you pay. Proper travel insurance is essential – see p1149.

SAFETY GUIDELINES FOR TREKKING

Before embarking on a walking trip, consider the following points to ensure a safe and enjoyable experience:

- Pay any fees and possess any permits required by local authorities.
- Be sure you are healthy and feel comfortable walking for a sustained period.
- Obtain reliable information about physical and environmental conditions along your intended route (eg from park authorities).
- Be aware of local laws, regulations and etiquette about wildlife and the environment.
- Walk only in regions, and on trails, within your realm of experience.
- Be aware that weather conditions and terrain vary significantly from one region, or even from one trail, to another. Seasonal changes can significantly alter any trail. These differences influence the way walkers dress and the equipment they carry.
- Ask before you set out about the environmental characteristics that can affect your walk and how local, experienced walkers deal with these considerations.

The following areas offer some of India's best trekking:

Andaman & Nicobar Islands There are bird-watching jungle treks on Havelock Island (p1133).

Himachal Pradesh You can arrange treks to mountain passes, lakes and monasteries through agencies in Manali (p362), McLeod Ganj (p374), Bharmour (p389), Chamba (p388) and Kaza (p393). For popular routes see p331. Low-altitude treks are also possible in the Parvati Valley (p350) and the Great Himalayan National Park (p349) but see the boxed text, p350.

Jammu & Kashmir Organise treks in Ladakh and Zanskar through tour operators in Leh (p307) and Padum (p297). For popular routes, see p315 and p298. Treks are also possible at Gulmarg (p294), Pahalgam (p286) and Sonamarg (p294) in Jammu and Kashmir, but check the security situation first.

Karnataka Interesting treks around Karnataka with Bengaluru-based Getoff ur ass (p907) and agents and guest houses in Madikeri (p927).

Kerala There are guided wildlife-spotting treks in the Periyar Wildlife Sanctuary (p1006) and Wayanad Wildlife Sanctuary (p1031), and hill treks at Munnar (p1010 and p1012).

Madhya Pradesh & Chhattisgarh Arrange guided hill walks with Satpura Adventure Club in Pachmari (p701).

Rajasthan Mt Abu (p227) is the trekking hub of Rajasthan, with forest treks to spot wild bears. Hill treks can also be arranged in Nawalgarh (p191), Udaipur (p218) and Ranakpur (p225).

Sikkim Travel agencies in Gangtok (p591) and Yuksom (p602) arrange treks around Sikkim.

Tamil Nadu Guided treks in the buffer zone around Mudumalai National Park (p1118), and hill and jungle treks around Indira Gandhi (Annamalai) Wildlife Sanctuary (p1108), Ooty (Udhagamandalam; p1115) and Kodaikanal (p1105).

Uttarakhand You can organise treks to glaciers, mountain villages and Himalayan viewpoints, and pilgrimage treks to the Char Dham temples in Rishikesh (p478), Haridwar (p471), Uttarkashi (p482), Joshimath (p484) and Nainital (p490). See also p459.

West Bengal Various treks around Darjeeling (p559) including the dramatic Singalila Ridge.

Zorbing

Zorbing – rolling down mountain meadows in a giant plastic ball – is possible in Himachal Pradesh. Balls roll throughout the summer in Solang Nullah (p367) and Khajjiar (p386), near Dalhousie.

HOLISTIC & SPIRITUAL ACTIVITIES

Not all activities in India involve hauling yourself up mountains! Travellers with an interest in spirituality or alternative therapies will find an array of courses and treatments that strive to heal body, mind and spirit. Meditation,

RESPONSIBLE TREKKING

To help preserve the natural environment of India, consider the following tips when trekking.

Rubbish

- Carry out all your rubbish. Don't overlook easily forgotten items, such as silver paper, orange peel, cigarette butts and plastic wrappers. Empty packaging should be stored in a dedicated rubbish bag. Make an effort to carry out rubbish left by others.

- Never bury your rubbish: digging disturbs soil and ground cover and encourages erosion. Buried rubbish will likely be dug up by animals, who may be injured or poisoned by it. It may also take years to decompose.

- Minimise waste by taking minimal packaging and no more food than you'll need. Take reusable containers or stuff sacks.

- Sanitary napkins, tampons, condoms and toilet paper should be carried out despite the inconvenience. They burn and decompose poorly.

Human Waste Disposal

- Contamination of water sources by human faeces can lead to the transmission of all sorts of nasties. Where there is a toilet, please use it. Where there is none, bury your waste. Dig a small hole 15cm (6in) deep and at least 100m (320ft) from any watercourse. Cover the waste with soil and a rock. In snow, dig down to the soil.

- Ensure that these guidelines are applied to a portable toilet tent if one is being used by a large trekking party. Encourage all party members, including porters, to use the site.

Washing

- Don't use detergents or toothpaste in or near watercourses, even if they're biodegradable.

- For personal washing, use biodegradable soap and a water container (or even a lightweight, portable basin) at least 50m (160ft) away from the watercourse. Disperse the waste water widely to allow the soil to filter it fully.

- Wash cooking utensils 50m (160ft) from watercourses using a scourer, sand or snow instead of detergent.

Erosion

- Hillsides and mountain slopes, especially at high altitudes, are prone to erosion. Stick to existing tracks and avoid short cuts.

- If a well-used track passes through a mud patch, walk through the mud so as not to increase the size of the patch.

- Avoid removing the plant life that keeps topsoils in place.

ayurveda (Indian herbal medicine) and yoga, especially, are attracting an ever-increasing number of visitors to India.

ASHRAMS

India has dozens of ashrams – places of communal living established around the philosophies of a guru (spiritual guide/teacher). Codes of conduct vary, so make sure you're willing to abide by them before committing. See the boxed text, p116.

Andhra Pradesh Puttaparthi (Puttaparthi; p979) is the ashram of controversial but phenomenally popular guru Sri Sathya Sai Baba.

Kerala Matha Amrithanandamayi Mission (Alleppey; p1002) is famed for its female guru Amma –

Fires & Low-Impact Cooking

- Cutting wood causes deforestation – a major problem in India – so avoid open fires and stay in lodgings that don't use wood to cook or heat water where possible.
- Cook on a light-weight kerosene, alcohol or Shellite (white gas) stove and avoid those powered by disposable butane-gas canisters.
- If you're trekking with a guide and porters, supply stoves for the whole team. In alpine areas, ensure that all members are outfitted with enough clothing so that fires are not a necessity for warmth.
- Fires may be acceptable below the tree-line in areas that get very few visitors. If you light a fire, use an existing fireplace. Don't surround fires with rocks. Use only dead, fallen wood. Use minimal wood, just what you need for cooking. In huts, leave wood for the next person.
- Ensure that you fully extinguish a fire after use. Spread the embers and flood them with water.

Wildlife Conservation

- Do not engage in or encourage hunting – it is illegal in India.
- Don't buy items made from endangered species.
- Don't attempt to exterminate animals in huts. In wild places, they are likely to be protected native animals.
- Discourage the presence of wildlife by not leaving food scraps behind you. Place gear out of reach and tie packs to rafters or trees.
- Don't feed the wildlife as this can lead to animals becoming dependent on hand-outs, to unbalanced populations and to diseases.

Cultural Sensitivity

- Respect local cultural practices when interacting with communities, including attitudes to modesty.
- Observe official regulations in areas you visit. Many rules are there to protect the local way of life.
- Don't hand out pens, sweets or money to children; this promotes begging. If you wish to give, donate to local schools and community centres.
- Always seek permission from landowners if you intend to enter private property.
- Where possible, trek with a local guide. This way, money from tourism will directly benefit the people it affects.

'The Hugging Mother'. Sivananda Yoga Vedanta Dhanwantari Ashram (Trivandrum; p988) is a famous yoga centre, renowned for its hatha yoga courses. Sivagiri Mutt (Varkala; p994) is the most significant ashram devoted to Sree Narayana Guru.

Kolkata The universalist Ramakrishna Mission stressing the commonality of all religions has its headquarters at Belur Math (p518) with branches countrywide.

Maharashtra Sevagram houses the Brahmavidya Mandir Ashram (p830), established by Gandhi's disciple Vinoba Bhave, and the Sevagram Ashram (p830), founded by Gandhi himself. There's also Anandwan (see the boxed text; p830), the ashram founded by social activist Baba Amte near Nagpur, and Pune's Osho Meditation Resort (p846), which runs on the teachings of its founder, Osho.

Rajasthan The small Ashtang Yoga Ashram (Udaipur; p218) offers hatha yoga training. Brahma Kumaris Spiritual University (Mt Abu; p227) is the headquarters of the Brahma Kumaris organisation.

ASHRAMS & GURUS

Many people visit India specifically to spend time at an ashram – literally a 'place of striving' – for spiritual and personal enrichment. There are literally hundreds of gurus (the word means 'dispeller of darkness' or 'heavy with wisdom') offering their guidance on the path to perfection to millions of eager followers. However, a little caution is required. Some ashrams tread a fine line between spiritual community and personality cult, and there have been reports of questionable happenings at ashrams, often of a sexual nature. These allegations have touched some of the most popular spiritual communities, including the International Society for Krishna Consciousness and the International Sai Organisation of Sai Baba.

Choosing an ashram will depend on your spiritual leanings. All gurus have their own unique take on spiritual living, often with a focus on abstinence and meditation. All ashrams have a code of conduct, and visitors are usually required to adhere to strict rules, which may include a certain dress code, a daily regimen of yoga or meditation, and charitable work at social projects run by the ashram. The diet is almost always vegetarian and you may also be asked to abstain from eggs, tobacco, alcohol, garlic, onions, and 'black drinks' – ie anything containing caffeine, including tea and coke. Sex may be prohibited or positively encouraged – make sure you are comfortable with this before you stay.

Ashrams are generally run as charitable projects – though a number of gurus are reportedly multimillionaires – and a donation is appropriate to cover the expenses of your food, accommodation and the running costs of the ashram. Most ashrams accept new residents without advance notice, but call ahead to make sure. Some gurus move around frequently so ensure the guru will be in attendance when you visit. Even if you lack spiritual conviction, it's interesting to visit an ashram for the day to see the workings of a modern-day spiritual movement.

Tamil Nadu Sri Aurobindo Ashram (Puducherry; p1074), founded by the famous Sri Aurobindo, has branches around India. The rural Isha Yoga Center (Coimbatore; p1111) offers residential courses and retreats. Sri Ramana Ashram (Tiruvannamalai; p1070) is the ashram founded by Sri Ramana Maharishi.

Uttarakhand There are various ashrams in Rishikesh (p477) and Haridwar (p473). The Rishikesh ashrams are generally more foreigner-orientated and less austere.

West Bengal International Society for Krishna Consciousness (Iskcon; Mayapur; p539) is the global headquarters of the Hare Krishna movement, with branches nationwide.

AYURVEDA

Ayurveda is the ancient science of Indian herbal medicine and holistic healing, which uses natural treatments, massage and other therapies. There are clinics, resorts and colleges across India where you can learn ayurvedic techniques and receive treatments, including the places listed below.

Goa Therapies and courses in ayurveda, reflexology, aromatherapy, acupressure and yoga are run at almost every beach resort on a seasonally changing basis.

Gujarat Ayurvedic therapy and professional courses in ayurvedic medicine are conducted at the famous Ayurvedic University in Jamnagar (p767).

Karnataka Naturopathy classes and ayurvedic therapies are offered in Bengaluru (p906), Mysore (p917) and Gokarna (p936).

Kerala You can undergo ayurvedic treatment at most towns and villages in Kerala, including around Kovalam (p988), in Varkala (p994), Kollam (p997), Alappuzha (Alleppey; p999), Kochi (p1017), Periya (p1008) and Kalpetta (p1032).

Tamil Nadu Courses in ayurvedic massage are available in Puducherry (p1074) and Mamallapuram (p1062).

Kerala is ayurveda paradise: read the boxed texts on p993 and p1033.

BUDDHIST MEDITATION

India has popular courses, classes and retreats in *vipassana* or mindfulness meditation and Buddhist philosophy. Be aware that some courses require students to abide by a vow of silence and many also ban smoking, alcohol and sex. The centre for Tibetan Buddhist teaching in India is McLeod Ganj (p369) – the home of the Dalai Lama. Public teachings are given by the Dalai Lama and 17th Karmapa at certain times of year – visit www.dalailama .com/page.60.htm for the schedule.

Andhra Pradesh *Vipassana* meditation courses are held in Hyderabad (p963) and Vijayawada (p975).

Bihar & Jharkhand Various classes and longer courses are available in Buddhist philosophy and *vipassana* meditation in Bodhgaya (p578).

Gujarat Meditation courses are held at Kutch Vipassana Centre (p773) in Bada village.

Himachal Pradesh There are courses in Tibetan massage and Buddhist meditation and philosophy in McLeod Ganj (p374).

Jammu & Kashmir Courses in *vipassana* meditation and Buddhist philosophy in Leh (p307) and residential retreats in Choglamsar.

Maharashtra Courses of various durations are held here at the world's largest *vipassana* meditation centre at Igatpuri (p817).

Tamil Nadu Various *vipassana* courses in Chennai (p1050).

> Over 2000 plant species are described in ancient ayurvedic texts with at least 550 frequently used in India.

SPA TREATMENTS

If you just want to enjoy the restorative effects without the study, there are scores of spas all over India, from ayurvedic hospitals to luxurious health centres at five-star resorts (see regional chapters for top-end hotel recommendations). However, be cautious of dodgy one-on-one massages by private (often unqualified) operators, particularly in tourist towns – seek advice from fellow travellers and trust your instincts.

This is just a sprinkling of recommended options:

> For details (including branches) about *vipassana* meditation taught by SN Goenka, visit www.dhamma.org.

Delhi Get the full ayurvedic treatment at Ashtaang and Kerala Ayurveda (p138).

Goa Numerous beach resorts offer massages and other spa services at Calangute and Baga (p879), Anjuna (p882), Colva and Benaulim (p891), Arambol (p887) and other locations.

Himachal Pradesh Massages and other healing therapies are available in Vashisht (p366), McLeod Ganj (p373) and Bhagsu (p380).

Karnataka Enjoy herbal rubs and scrubs in Bengaluru (p906), Mysore (p917) and Gokarna (p936).

Kerala Massages and herbal treatments at Varkala (p994) and Kochi (p1017), and therapeutic breaks at Janakanthi Panchakarma Centre (p997) and Thapovan Heritage Home (p992).

Madhya Pradesh & Chhattisgarh Usha Kiran Palace (p675) in Gwalior has a luxurious health spa, as does Jehan Numa Palace Hotel (p692) in Bhopal, and Amar Mahal and Orchha Resort (p679) in Orchha. Ayur Arogyam (p686), run by a Keralan couple, is a recommended massage therapy centre in Khajuraho.

Maharashtra Massages, saunas and spa treatments at the Osho Meditation Resort (p846).

Mumbai The pampering of pamperings at one of Mumbai's finest spas – inside the ITC Maratha hotel (p798).

Orissa There are plush resort spas in Bhubaneswar (p650) and Puri (p656).

Rajasthan Ayurvedic massage clinics in Jaipur (p173), Udaipur (p218) and Jaisalmer (p241).

Tamil Nadu Try the posh hotel spas in Thanjavur (p1085) and Kodaikanal (p1107), and the massage sessions in Mamallapuram (p1062) and Puducherry (p1074).

Uttarakhand Get the works at the Ananda Spa (p482) near Rishikesh, and Haveli Hari Ganga (p472) in Haridwar.

Uttar Pradesh Various hotels in Varanasi offer fine Keralan massage treatments. See p445.

YOGA

Many places in India offer short classes and long courses in various types of yoga, often with meditation sessions on the side. The most common yoga forms are hatha (following the *shatkarma*, or purification, system of postures and meditation), *ashtanga* (following the 'eight limbs' system of postures and meditation), pranayama (controlled yogic breathing)

AMCHI

Tibetan Buddhist areas have their own herbal-medicine tradition – amchi – based on a mixture of astrology and treatments with herbs from the Himalaya. Despite the arrival of Western medicine, amchi is still a popular form of treatment in parts of Ladakh and Himachal Pradesh; see p375 and p393.

---

and Iyengar (a variation of ashtanga yoga that uses physical aids for advanced postures).

Yoga Courses

There are hundreds of yoga courses on offer and some outfits are more reputable than others (especially in tourist towns). Seek advice from tourist offices and other travellers, and visit several to find one that suits your needs. Many ashrams (spiritual retreats) also offer yoga courses, though be aware that some centres require a minimum time commitment and stipulate that residents adhere to strict rules on silence, diet and behaviour – see the boxed text, p116.

The following are some of the numerous possibilities; for those that have no fees, donations are appreciated.

Delhi Courses in various forms of meditation and yoga (p139).

Goa A huge range of yoga courses are offered at hotels, spiritual centres and retreats all around Goa, on a seasonally changing basis.

Gujarat The Ayurvedic University in Jamnagar (p767) offers hatha yoga courses.

Himachal Pradesh Courses in hatha yoga, reiki, and other healing arts are offered in Vashisht (p366) and McLeod Ganj (p373).

Jammu & Kashmir Yoga and meditation classes in Leh (p307).

Karnataka World-renowned courses in ashtanga, hatha and Iyengar yoga and meditation are held in Mysore (p918), and yoga classes held in Bengaluru (p906) and Gokarna (p936).

Kerala Hatha yoga courses are available at Sivananda Yoga Vedanta Dhanwantari Ashram (p988) near Thiruvananthapuram (Trivandrum), as are yoga classes in Varkala (p994) and Kochi (p1017).

Kolkata Yoga courses and meditation in Kolkata (p518).

Madhya Pradesh & Chhattisgarh Yogi Sudarshan Dwiveda (p686) is the most revered of a number of yogis in Khajuraho. In Orchha, Amar Mahal and Orchha Resort (p679) both run daily classes.

Maharashtra Yogic healing is held at the Kaivalyadhama Yoga Hospital (p836) in Lonavla, and advanced Iyengar yoga courses (for experienced practitioners only) are offered at Ramamani Iyengar Memorial Yoga Institute (p849) in Pune.

Mumbai Classes in various styles of yoga are held in Mumbai (p793).

Rajasthan There are yoga, reiki, shiatsu and naturopathy courses in Pushkar (p197), and hatha yoga courses in Jaipur (p174) and Mt Abu (p227).

Tamil Nadu Hatha yoga classes in Chennai (p1050). Various yoga classes and courses in Mamallapuram (p1062) and Puducherry (p1074).

Uttarakhand Classes in hatha, pranayama, Kriya and spiritual yoga are conducted in Rishikesh (p477) and Haridwar (p469).

Uttar Pradesh Recommended yoga courses in Varanasi include those at the Yoga Training Centre and at Benares Hindu University (p446).

Yoga is one of the oldest therapies in human history, dating back 4000 years. Light On Yoga is by one of the world's foremost authorities, BKS Iyengar.

Delhi

Medieval mayhem, opulent metropolis, stately maiden aunt: give it a chance, and this unruly capital will capture your heart. Yes, it's crowded, aggravating, polluted, extreme, and hectic, but hey – nobody's perfect.

This is a city of different worlds. Old Delhi, all fabulous frenzy and crumbling splendour, was once the capital of Islamic India. The British built spacious, gracious New Delhi as their imperial capital. And even-newer Delhi endlessly throws up shops, offices and apartment blocks, chunks of could-be-anywhere modernity.

Recent years have seen impressive developments in preparation for the 2010 Commonwealth Games. Epic new infrastructure includes a 160-acre games village and the gleaming new Metro.

But look past Delhi's less-loveable elements, and you'll find it littered with glittering jewels. Like a subcontinental Rome, India's capital is punctuated by ruins and monuments, vestiges of lost empires. There are magnificent museums, temples and mosques, and a cultural life to satisfy the hungriest vulture. Plus, shopaholics – you are home: all the riches of India twinkle in Delhi's emporiums, from exquisite Kashmiri shawls to jootis from Jaipur.

That's by no means the end of Delhi's sensory extravaganza. Prepare yourself to tuck into some of the subcontinent's finest food, from piled-high pizzas to sublime South Indian dosas (savoury crepes). And the famous *Dilli-ka-chaat* (Delhi street food) – which, rather like the city itself – jumbles up every flavour in one bite.

HIGHLIGHTS

- Let your imagination run riot at the Mughal **Red Fort** (p129)
- Revel in tranquillity at splendid **Humayun's tomb** (p135)
- Hear Sufis sing sunset qawwali at **Hazrat Nizam-ud-din Dargah** (p136)
- Be awestruck by India's largest mosque, the mighty **Jama Masjid** (p134)
- Be bedazzled and bamboozled in **Old Delhi's bazaars** (p129)
- **Shop** (p153) like a fool at the capital's amazing emporiums
- Sample Delhi's famous **street food** (p147), sup **cocktails** (p152) and relish ravishing **restaurants** (p146)

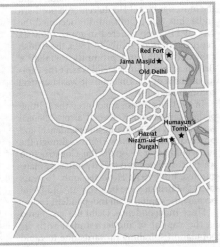

DELHI

FAST FACTS

Population 12.8 million
Area 1483 sq km
Telephone code ☎ 011
Main languages Hindi and English
When to go November to March

HISTORY

Delhi hasn't always been India's capital, but, as a gateway city, it has long played a pivotal part in Indian history, built on the plains near a fording point on the Yamuna River, and on the route between western and Central Asia and Southeast Asia. It's also believed to be the site of the fabled city of Indraprastha, which featured in the Mahabharata over 3000 years ago, but historical evidence suggests that the area has been settled for a mere 2500 years.

At least eight known cities have been founded here, the last of which was the British Raj's New Delhi. The first four cities of Delhi were to the south, around the area where the Qutb Minar now stands. The fifth Delhi, Firozabad, was at Firoz Shah Kotla in present-day New Delhi, while Emperor Sher Shah created the sixth at Purana Qila, also in New Delhi. The Mughal emperor, Shah Jahan, constructed the seventh Delhi in the 17th century, thus shifting the Mughal capital from Agra to Delhi; his Shahjahanabad roughly corresponds to Old Delhi today and is largely preserved. The Chauhans seized control in the 12th century and made Delhi the most significant Hindu centre in northern India, but when Qutb-ud-din occupied the city in 1193, he ushered in more than six centuries of Islamic rule. In 1803, the British captured Delhi and promptly installed a British administrator. Delhi wasn't the capital of India at the time, but it was a critical commercial centre.

In 1911, the British announced the shifting of their capital from Kolkata (Calcutta; Bengal was ardently championing independence) and proceeded to build New Delhi as though the sun would never set on the Raj. Construction wasn't completed and the city officially inaugurated, until 1931. However, only 16 years later, the British were booted out, and Delhi became the capital of an independent India.

Since Independence, Delhi has prospered as the capital of modern India, with its population spiralling upwards due to rapid economic expansion and increased job opportunities. The city is also looking smarter than it has for centuries, with the urban overhaul in time for the 2010 Commonwealth Games (www.cwgdelhi2010.org). The downside of this boom – apart from growing pressure on the city's groaning infrastructure – is chronic overcrowding, traffic congestion, housing shortages, pollution, and ever more extreme contrasts between rich and poor.

ORIENTATION

Delhi is a sprawling city, but the areas of interest to travellers are easy to navigate. To the north of Old Delhi there's the main Inter State Bus Terminal (ISBT) and, to the south, the New Delhi train station. Near this station, between the old and new cities, is Paharganj, jam-packed with cheap accommodation.

New Delhi contains the business and residential areas around Connaught Place (the city's core) and the government areas around Rajpath to the south. Running south from Connaught Place is Janpath, which has the tourist office, some hotels and a shopping strip. Urban sprawl – consisting of both posh residential enclaves and ramshackle shacks – goes on for kilometres; the prosperous satellite city of Gurgaon, around 25km south of the centre, is characterised by ultramodern office blocks and snazzy shopping malls.

The domestic terminals of the Indira Gandhi International Airport are 15km southwest of the centre, and the international terminal is a farther 8km away.

Maps

India Tourism Delhi (p125) has a free foldaway Delhi map, though the free AA City Map (www.delhimapindia.com) available at the office and in many hotels is better. For accurate detail, most newsstands sell the excellent 245-page *Eicher City Map* (Rs290); Eicher also produces a *Delhi Road Map* (Rs75).

INFORMATION
Bookshops

Delhi's many brilliant bookshops sell a great array of fiction, nonfiction, travel, magazines and maps at prices usually much lower than you'll find back home.

CONNAUGHT PLACE AREA
New Book Depot (Map p130; ☎ 23320020; 18 B-Block, Inner Circle; ⊙ 11am-8pm Mon-Sat)

Oxford Bookstore (Map p130; ☎ 23766083; www
.oxfordbookstore.com; Statesman House, 148 Barakhamba
Rd; ⏰ 10am-8pm Mon-Sat, noon-8pm Sun) Attached is
the Cha Bar (p151).
People Tree (Map p130; ☎ 23744877; www.people
treeonline.com; 8 Regal Bldg, Sansad Marg; ⏰ 10.30am-
7pm Mon-Sat) As well as fiction, stocks cerebral nonfiction
(human rights, environmental matters etc).

KHAN MARKET
Bahri Sons (Map pp126-7; ☎ 24694610; ⏰ 10.30am-
7.30pm Mon-Sat)
Faqir-Chand & Sons (Map pp126-7; ☎ 24618810;
⏰ 10am-8pm Mon-Sat)
Full Circle Bookstore (Map pp126-7; ☎ 24655641;
⏰ 9.30am-9.30pm) Café Turtle (p151) is upstairs.

SOUTH EXTENSION
Teksons (Map pp122-3; ☎ 24617030; G4, Part I;
⏰ 10am-8pm) Other branches include Connaught Place.
Timeless (Map pp122-3; ☎ 24693257; 46 Housing
Society, Part I; ⏰ 10am-7pm) Hidden in a back lane (ask
around), Timeless has a devoted following for its quality
coffee-table books, from Indian textiles to architecture.

Cultural Centres & Libraries
Cultural centres often host exhibitions and
seminars plus dance, music and theatrical
performances. Check local listings (see Media
right) for current happenings.
Alliance Française (Map pp126-7; ☎ 43500200; www
.afindia.org; 72 Lodi Estate)
American Center (Map p130; ☎ 23316841;
24 Kasturba Gandhi Marg)
British Council (Map p130; ☎ 23717306; www
.britishcouncil.org; 17 Kasturba Gandhi Marg)
Delhi Public Library (Map p132; ☎ 23962682;
SP Mukherjee Marg)
India International Centre (Map pp126-7;
☎ 24619431; www.iicdelhi.nic.in; 40 Max Mueller Marg)
Max Mueller Bhavan (Map pp126-7; ☎ 23329506;
www.goethe.de/delhi; 3 Kasturba Gandhi Marg)
Rabindra Bhavan (Map pp126-7; Copernicus Marg)
Lalit Kala Akademi (Academy of Contemporary Art;
☎ 23387241); Sangeet Natak Akademi (Academy of
Performing Arts; ☎ 23382975); Sahitya Akademi (Academy
of Literature; ☎ 23386626)

Internet Access
Internet cafes are mushrooming, with centres
in Khan Market, Paharganj, and Connaught
Place, among others, usually charging around
Rs35 per hour, Rs5 to print a page and Rs25
to scan/write a CD. Most top-end hotels have
wi-fi.

Media
To check out what's on, grab the *Delhi City
Guide* (Rs20) and *Delhi Diary* (Rs10). Fab
monthly magazine *First City* (Rs30) has comprehensive listings/reviews, ranging from
theatre to so-now bars, while *Time Out Delhi*
(Rs30) is a hip take on the city. Delhi'ed out?
Grab Outlook Traveller's *Weekend Breaks
from Delhi* (Rs225). Publications are available at newsstands and bookshops.

Medical Services
Pharmacies are ubiquitous in most markets.
All India Institute of Medical Sciences (Aiims; Map
pp122-3; ☎ 26588700; Ansari Nagar)
Apollo Hospital (off Map pp122-3; ☎ 26925858;
Mathura Rd, Sarita Vihar)
Apollo Pharmacy (Map p130; ☎ 32604579;
8 G-Block, Connaught Place; ⏰ 24hr)
Dr Ram Manohar Lohia Hospital (Map pp126-7;
☎ 23365525; Baba Kharak Singh Marg)
East West Medical Centre (Map pp122-3;
☎ 24623738; B-28 Greater Kailash Part I) Opposite
N-Block Market.
Max Medcentre (Map pp122-3; ☎ 26499870; www
.maxindia.com; N110 Panchsheel Park)

Money
ATMS
There are ATMs all over the place, including:
Citibank Basant Lok complex (Map pp122-3; Vasant Vihar);
Khan Market (Map pp126-7)
HDFC Paharganj (Map p142; Main Bazaar, Paharganj);
Connaught Place (Map p130; cnr C- & K-Blocks)
ICICI Connaught Place (Map p130; 9A Phelps Bldg); Pahar-
ganj (Map p142; Rajguru Rd)
UTI (Map p142; Rajguru Rd)

FOREIGN CURRENCY & TRAVELLERS
CHEQUES
American Express (Amex; Map p130; ☎ 23719506;
A-Block, Connaught Place; ⏰ 9.30am-6.30pm Mon-Fri,
to 2.30pm Sat)
Baluja Forex (Map p142; ☎ 41541523; 4596 Main
Bazaar, Paharganj; ⏰ 10am-5.30pm) Does cash advances
on MasterCard and Visa.
Central Bank of India (Map pp126-7; ☎ 26110101;
Ashok Hotel, Chanakyapuri; ⏰ 24hr)
**Delhi Tourism & Transport Development Corpo-
ration** (Map p130; ☎ 23315322; N-36, Middle Circle,
Connaught Place; ⏰ 10am-6pm Mon-Sat) Has a foreign-
exchange counter.
Thomas Cook International airport (☎ 25653439;
⏰ 24hr); Janpath (Map pp126-7; ☎ 23342171; Hotel
Janpath, Janpath; ⏰ 9.30am-7pm Mon-Sat);

DELHI

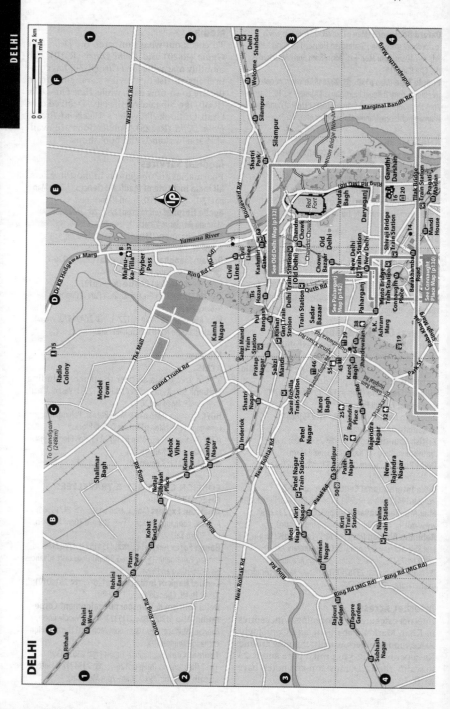

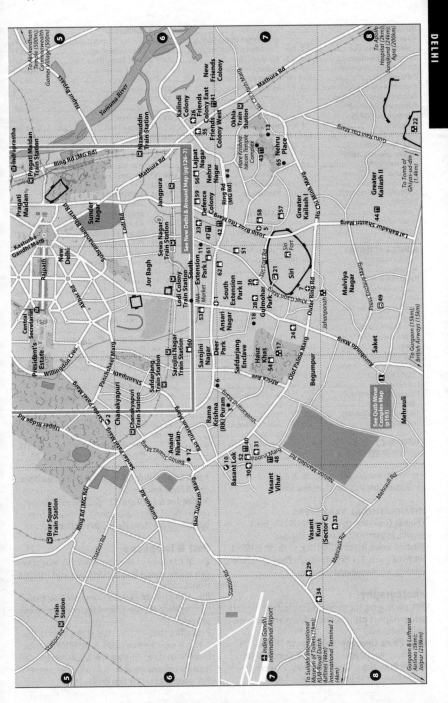

New Delhi train station (Map p142; ☎ 23211819; ☺ 9.30am-6pm Mon-Sat, 11am-6pm Sun)

INTERNATIONAL TRANSFERS
Thomas Cook (Map pp126–7; ☎ 23342171; Hotel Janpath, Janpath; ☺ 9.30am-7pm Mon-Sat)
Western Union (Head Office) (Map p130; ☎ 23355061; Sita World Travels, 12 F-Block, Connaught Place; ☺ 9.30am-7pm Mon-Sat) Many branches citywide.

Photography

For photographic services (including digital) and passport photos, these are some dependable options:
Delhi Photo Company (Map p130; ☎ 23320577; 78 Janpath, Connaught Place; ☺ 10am-7.30pm Mon-Sat)
Kinsey Bros (Map p130; ☎ 23324446; 2 A-Block, Connaught Place; ☺ 10.30am-7.30pm Mon-Sat)

Rama Color (Map pp126–7; ☎ 24628890; Khan Market; ☺ 10.30am-8pm Mon-Sat)
Madan Jee & Co (Map p132; ☎ 23276958; Chandni Chowk; ☺ 10.30am-7.30pm Mon-Sat) Has it all, from 4x5, 120mm and 35mm film to lights and tripods.

Post & Telephone

Delhi has tons of telephone kiosks where you can make cheap local, interstate and international calls.
DHL (Map p130; ☎ 23737587; Mercantile Bldg, ground fl Tolstoy Marg; ☺ 8am-8.30pm) Organises international air freight.
Post office Connaught Place (Map p130; 6 A-Block); New Delhi main post office (Map pp126–7; ☎ 23364111; Baba Kharak Singh Marg; ☺ 10am-1pm & 1.30-4pm Mon-Sat) Poste restante available at the main post office; ensure mail is addressed to GPO, New Delhi – 110001.

FESTIVALS IN DELHI

Delhi's festival dates and venues can vary – for this year's details, contact India Tourism Delhi (below).

Delhi celebrates Diwali (p27) and Dussehra (p27) with particular verve.

Republic Day (26 Jan; Rajpath, p134) Incorporates a spectacular military parade.

Beating of the Retreat (29 Jan; Rajpath, p134) The closing of the Republic Day celebrations is marked by the Beating of the Retreat – more military pageantry. Tickets are essential for both events and are available at India Tourism Delhi (below).

Delhi Flower Show (Jan/Feb) This colourful event lasts several days.

Mango Festival (Jul; Talkatora Gardens) A juicy three-day festival showcasing hundreds of mango varieties.

Independence Day (15 Aug; Red Fort, p129) India celebrates its Independence from Britain in 1947, and the prime minister addresses the nation from the Red Fort ramparts.

Qutb Festival (Oct/Nov; Qutb Minar, p163) Held over several days, featuring Sufi singing and classical dance performances.

Delhi International Arts Festival (DIAF; Dec; www.diaf.in) Three weeks of exhibitions, performing arts, films, literature, and culinary events at Delhi-wide venues.

Tourist Information

Beware Delhi's many dodgy travel agencies and 'tourist information centres'. Do *not* be fooled – the only official tourist information centre is India Tourism Delhi, listed below. Touts may (falsely) claim to be associated with this office.

For Indian regional tourist offices' contact details ask at India Tourism Delhi, or dial directory enquiries on ☎ 197.

India Tourism Delhi (Government of India; www .incredibleindia.org); Janpath (Map p130; ☎ 23320008/5; 88 Janpath ☯ 9am-6pm Mon-Fri, to 2pm Sat); domestic airport (☎ 25675296; ☯ 8am-last flight); international airport (☎ 25656144; ☯ 24hr) Gives tourist-related advice as well as a free Delhi map and brochures. Their special branch investigates tourism-related complaints.

DANGERS & ANNOYANCES

First-time visitors especially should be on their guard against Delhi's touts and tricksters, who are remarkably inventive in their schemes to part tourists from their cash.

Touts buzz around tourist honeypots such as Connaught Place, Paharganj and the New Delhi train station. These oh-so-helpful fellows will try to cart you off to shops, travel agencies or 'official' tourist offices, where they earn commission at your expense.

However, you will probably find the scammers pretty innocuous if you follow a policy of ignoring them or calling their bluff. If you do have problems, you should seek out the 'tourist police', who have marked jeeps stationed at tourist centres, including the international airport, New Delhi train station and Janpath.

For shopping scams, see p1145. Women should take care in Delhi, as in any big city; read p1171.

Hotel Touts

Taxi-wallahs at the international airport frequently act as touts. These sneaky drivers will try to persuade you that your hotel is full, poor value, overbooked, dangerous, burned down or closed, or even that there are riots in Delhi. Their intention is to take you to a hotel where they'll get some commission. Some will even 'kindly' take you to a 'tourist office' where a colleague will phone your hotel on your behalf, and corroborate the driver's story. In reality, of course, he's talking to his mate in the next room. Alternatively, the driver may claim that he's lost and stop at a travel agency for directions. The agent supposedly dials your hotel and informs you that your room is double-booked, and helpfully finds you another hotel. The taxi-wallah, when he delivers you, gets commission and you get a high room rate.

Tell persistent taxi drivers that you've paid for your hotel in advance, have recently confirmed the booking, or have friends/relatives waiting for you there. If they continue, ask that they stop the car so that you can write down the registration plate number. Just to be sure, call or email to confirm your hotel booking, if possible, 24 hours before check-in.

Travel Agent Touts

Be cautious with travel agencies, as many travellers every year report being overcharged and underwhelmed by unscrupulous agents.

NEW DELHI & AROUND

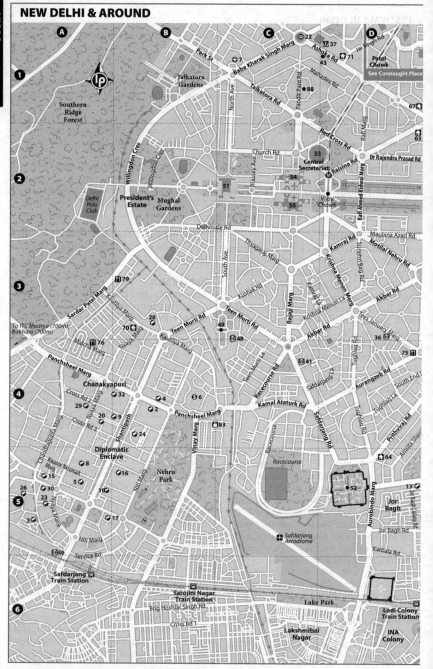

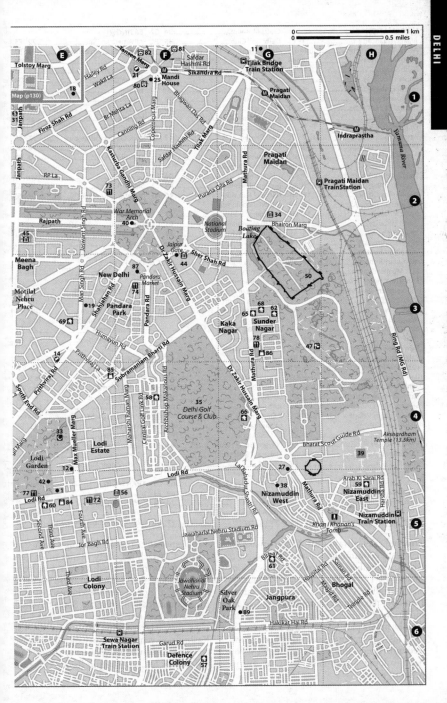

To avoid grief, always shop around or ask for traveller recommendations. Choose agents who are members of accredited associations such as the Travel Agents Association of India and the Indian Association of Tour Operators. Don't get talked into something you had no intention of doing prior to the conversation. Finally, before parting with your hard-earned cash, insist on getting what you've been promised in *writing* – this will be invaluable if you need to lodge a complaint with the tourist office or police.

Be especially careful if booking a multistop trip out of Delhi. Lonely Planet often gets letters from travellers who've paid upfront for a trip and then found out there are extra expenses, they've been overcharged, or that the accommodation is terrible. Some travellers have arranged 'northern mountains' or 'lake' trips, then later find that they are headed for Kashmir. Given the number of letters we've received from unhappy travellers, it's also best not to book tours to Kashmir from Delhi; read p283 and p292.

Two Days
Acclimatise gently at tranquil sites, such as the **National Museum** (p136), **Gandhi Smriti** (p135) and **Humayun's tomb** (p135). In the evening head to **Hazrat Nizam-ud-din Dargah** (p136) to hear the Sufis sing qawwaalis.

On day two, ramble around Old Delhi's **Red Fort** (below), then scoff *jalebis* (fried sweet 'squiggles'), launch into the old city's action-packed **bazaars** (below) and visit the mighty **Jama Masjid** (p134). Afterwards, grab an autorickshaw south to **Connaught Place** (p137) for a bite to **eat** (p148) and to explore the hassle-free, treasure-trove **government emporiums** (p154).

Four Days
Follow the itinerary above, then on the third day wander around **Qutb Minar** (p163) before indulging in some quiet meditation at the **Bahai House of Worship** (p137). In the evening, watch the mesmerising **Dances of India** (p153), then kick back at a **bar** (p152).

On day four, wonder at the glories in the laid-back **Crafts Museum** (p135) and nearby **Purana Qila** (p135). Then head to **Hauz Khas** (p138) to wander around the forgotten tank and mausoleum, and browse in its boutiques.

Train Station Touts

These touts are at their worst at New Delhi Station. Here they may try to prevent you reaching the upstairs International Tourist Bureau and divert you to a local (overpriced and often unreliable) travel agency. Make the assumption that the office is *never* closed (outside the official opening hours; see p159), is not being renovated and has not shifted.

Other swindlers may insist that your ticket needs to be stamped or checked (for a hefty fee) before it is considered valid. Some may try to convince wait-listed passengers that there is a charge to check their reservation status – don't fall for it. Try not to get embroiled in discussion, just politely and firmly make your way to the office. If you are encountering real problems, threaten to fetch the tourist police. Once you are out of the station, avoid overpriced conveyance by heading for the car park's prepaid autorickshaw booth.

SIGHTS

Delhi's major sights are mainly in Old Delhi and in the vicinity of New Delhi's Connaught Place.

There's less traffic on Sundays, rendering travel between sights much quicker, while arriving as close to opening times as possible, is another way to beat the crowds. Note that many sites are shut on Monday.

Behave and dress conservatively whenever visiting places of worship.

Old Delhi

Medieval-like Old Delhi is a crazy hubbub that bombards the senses, and is a different world compared with the rest of the city. Set aside at least half a day to do this fascinating area justice. All of the following attractions feature on Map p132.

The old walled city of Shahjahanabad stretches west from the Red Fort. It was at one time surrounded by a sturdy defensive wall, only fragments of which now exist. The **Kashmiri Gate**, to the north, was the scene of desperate fighting when the British retook Delhi during the 1857 First War of Independence (Indian Uprising). West of here is the British-erected **Mutiny Memorial**, dedicated to the soldiers who died during the Uprising. Near the monument is an **Ashoka Pillar**; like the one in Firoz Shah Kotla, it was brought here by Firoz Shah.

RED FORT (LAL QILA)

This massive **fort** (Indian/foreigner Rs10/250, video Rs25, combined museum ticket Rs5; ⊙ 9am-6pm Tue-Sun) is a sandstone carcass of its former self; but it's the best place in Delhi to imagine the Mughal city's sometime splendour. It dates from the peak of the dynasty's power, a time of unparalleled pomp: of eunuchs, ceremonial elephants, palanquins, and buildings lined in precious stones.

The walls of the fort extend for 2km and vary in height from 18m on the river side to 33m on the city side. Shah Jahan constructed the fort between 1638 and 1648, but never

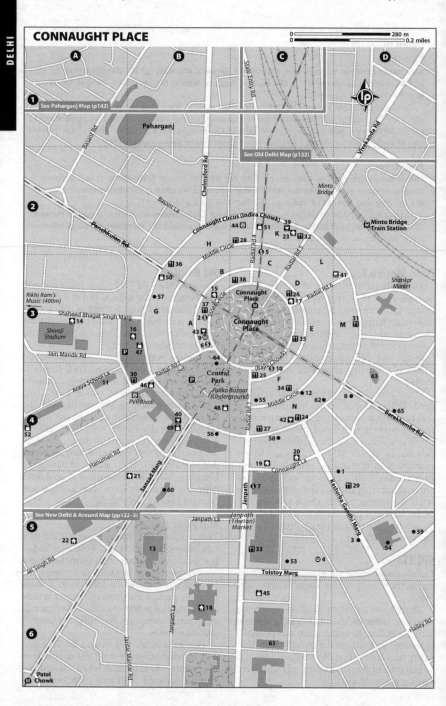

CONNAUGHT PLACE

See Paharganj Map (p142)

See Old Delhi Map (p132)

See New Delhi & Around Map (pp122–3)

completely moved his capital from Agra to his new city of Shahjahanabad, because he was deposed and imprisoned in Agra Fort by his son Aurangzeb.

Mughal reign from Delhi was short; Aurangzeb was the first and last great Mughal emperor to rule from here. Subsequent rulers, sapped by civil war, were unable to maintain the fort properly, and slums within the walls were thronged with impoverished imperial descendants. By the 19th century, it was already much dilapidated. Following the 1857 First War of Independence (Indian Uprising), the British cleared all but the most important buildings to make way for ugly barracks and army offices.

The 10m-deep moat, which has been bone-dry since 1857, was originally crossed on creaky wooden drawbridges, replaced with stone bridges in 1811.

You can buy tickets to the fort and its interior museums from the **ticket kiosk** opposite Lahore Gate (the main gate).

Since Independence, many landmark political speeches have taken place at the fort and every year on Independence Day (15 August) it hosts the prime minister's address to the nation.

Lahore Gate

The fort's **main gate** is so named because it faces towards Lahore, now in Pakistan. Aurangzeb added the external protective bastions, further displeasing his imprisoned father. The gate is a potent symbol of modern India: during the fight for Independence, there was a nationalist aspiration to see the Indian flag flying over the gate – a dream that became reality in 1947.

You enter the fort through here and immediately find yourself in the vaulted arcade known as the **Chatta Chowk** (Covered Bazaar). The tourist-trap arcade once sold rather more exclusive items to the royal household – silks, jewellery and gold.

The arcade leads to the **Naubat Khana** (Drum House), where musicians used to

OLD DELHI

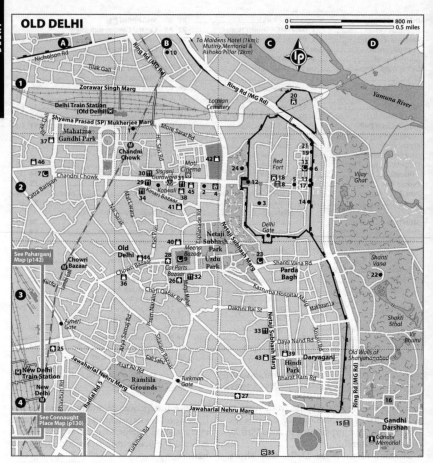

perform, and where visitors were obliged to dismount. There's an **Indian War Memorial Museum** upstairs.

Diwan-i-Am

In the **Hall of Public Audiences** the emperor would hear disputes from his subjects. The emperor's alcove is intricately decorated with exquisite *pietra dura* (marble inlay; partly imported from Italy), set with precious stones, many of which were looted following the First War of Independence (Indian Uprising). The hall was restored following a directive by Lord Curzon, the viceroy of India between 1898 and 1905.

Diwan-i-Khas

The white marble **Hall of Private Audiences** was the luxurious chamber where the emperor would hold private meetings. Centrepiece was once the magnificent solid-gold and jewel-studded Peacock Throne, looted from India by Nadir Shah in 1739. In 1760 the Marathas also removed the hall's silver ceiling. A Persian couplet inscribed above the building's arches reads: 'If there is paradise on the earth – this is it, this is it, this is it.'

Royal Baths

Next to the Diwan-i-Khas are the **hammams** (baths) – three large rooms surmounted by domes, with a fountain in the centre – one of which was set up as a sauna. The floors were once inlaid with more *pietra dura,* and the rooms were illuminated through stained-glass roof panels.

Shahi Burj

This modest, three-storey, octagonal **tower** to the northeastern edge of the fort was once Shah Jahan's private working area. From here, cooling water, known as the *nahr-i-bihisht* (river of paradise), used to flow south through the Royal Baths, the Diwan-i-Khas, the Khas Mahal and on to the Rang Mahal.

Moti Masjid

Built in 1659 by Aurangzeb for his personal use, the small, enclosed, marble **Pearl Mosque** is next to the baths. One curious feature of the mosque is that its outer walls are oriented exactly in symmetry with the rest of the fort, while the inner walls are slightly askew, so that the mosque has the correct orientation with Mecca.

Other Features

The **Khas Mahal**, south of the Diwan-i-Khas, was the emperor's private palace. It was divided into rooms for worship, sleeping and living, with carved walls and painted ceilings.

The **Rang Mahal** (Palace of Colour), farther south again, took its name from its vividly painted interior, now long gone. This was the residence of the emperor's chief wife and is where he dined. On the floor in the centre there's an exquisitely carved marble lotus; the water flowing along the channel from the Shahi Burj would end up here.

Relics from the Mughal era are displayed at the **Museum of Archaeology** in the **Mumtaz Mahal**, once the women's quarters, still further south along the eastern wall.

DODGING THE DODGY

- Decline offers from taxi or auto drivers that you should visit hotels or shops of their choice.
- Double-check that your driver has taken you to the hotel/shop/tourist office you requested, as some try to offload passengers at places where they receive commission – don't pay the fare until you are sure you're at the right destination.
- Ignore touts who surreptitiously dirty your shoe then offer to shine it for you at a price, or offer you a free trial ear-cleaning of one ear.
- Steer clear of chatty young men lurking about (often around Connaught Place), some of whom humbly claim they're students wanting to improve their English – 99.9% are not.
- Don't believe helpful chaps who try to direct you to the many 'tourist offices' around Connaught Place. There is only one official central tourist office, at 88 Janpath.
- Carry small denominations (ie anything below Rs50 notes), as drivers seem to have a perpetual lack of small change.

From Lal Qila you can cross via a bridge to the impressive, much-restored fortifications of **Salimgarh** (1540–55), occupied by the Indian Army until recently. This earlier fort was built by Salim Shah.

Sound-&-Light Show

Each evening (except Monday) this one-hour **show** (admission Rs60; ⏲ in English 7.30pm Nov-Jan, 8.30pm Feb-Apr, Sep & Oct, 9pm May-Aug) gives Red Fort history the coloured-spotlight and portentous-voice-over treatment. It's great, if only to see the fort by night. Tickets are available from the fort's ticket kiosk. Bring mosquito repellent.

CHANDNI CHOWK

Old Delhi's backbone is the madcap **Chandni Chowk** ('moonlight place'), a wide avenue thronged by crowds, hawkers and rickshaws. In the time of Shah Jahan, a canal ran down its centre – at night it reflected the moon in its water, hence the name. Tiny bazaar-crammed lanes snake off the broadway like clogged arteries. At the eastern (Red Fort) end of Chandni Chowk, there's the 16th-century **Digambara Jain Temple** (remove shoes and leather before entering). The fascinating **bird hospital** (donations appreciated; ⏲ 10am to 5pm) here is run by the Jains, who believe in the preservation of all life.

The western end of Chandni Chowk is marked by the mid-17th-century **Fatehpuri Masjid**, named after one of Shah Jahan's wives. After the 1857 First War of Independence (Indian Uprising) the mosque was sold to a Hindu merchant, who used it as a warehouse, but it was later returned to local Muslims.

There's a CNG shuttle service (small green buses) between Digambara Jain Temple and Fatehpuri Mosque (Rs5).

SUNEHRI MASJID

South of the Red Fort is the 18th-century **Sunehri Masjid**. In 1739 Nadir Shah, the Persian invader, stood on its roof and macabrely watched his soldiers conduct a bloody massacre of Delhi's inhabitants.

JAMA MASJID

India's largest **mosque** (camera, video each Rs200; ⏲ non-Muslims 8.30am-12.30pm & 2-4.30pm, 8-11am & 2-4.30pm Fri) can hold a mind-blowing 25,000 people. Towering over Old Delhi, the 'Friday Mosque' was Shah Jahan's final architectural opus, built between 1644 and 1658. It has three gateways, four angle towers and two minarets standing 40m high, and is constructed of alternating vertical strips of red sandstone and white marble. The main entry point is Gate 3.

For Rs50 it's possible to climb the southern minaret (women must be accompanied by a male), for superb views. From the top of the minaret, you can see one of the features that architect Edwin Lutyens incorporated into his design of New Delhi – the Jama Masjid, Connaught Place and Sansad Bhavan (Parliament House) are in a direct line.

Visitors should remove their shoes at the top of the stairs (pay the shoe minder Rs5 upon collection). Beware of fake guides insisting there's a charge to enter the mosque (admission is free). If you wish to hire a guide, ask to see accreditation.

RAJ GHAT

South of the Red Fort, on the banks of the Yamuna River, a simple square **platform** of black marble marks the spot where Mahatma Gandhi was cremated following his assassination in 1948. It's inscribed with what are said to have been his final words 'Hai Ram' (Oh, God), and has a hushed, peaceful atmosphere, set amid tranquil lawns.

Jawaharlal Nehru, the first Indian prime minister, was cremated just to the north, at **Shanti Vana** (Forest of Peace), in 1964. Nehru's daughter, Indira Gandhi, who was assassinated in 1984, and grandsons Sanjay (who died in 1980) and Rajiv (assassinated 1991) were also cremated in this vicinity.

The **National Gandhi Museum** (☎ 23311793; admission free; ⏲ 9.30am-5.30pm Tue-Sun) contains photos and some of Gandhi's belongings.

New Delhi & Around

All of the attractions in this section feature on Map pp126–7.

RAJPATH

Rajpath (Kingsway) is the imposing approach to New Delhi. It hosts the huge Republic Day parade every 26 January and the Beating of the Retreat on 29 January.

Raj-appointed English architect Edwin Lutyens constructed New Delhi between 1914 and 1931, when the British moved their capital here from Calcutta. His designs were intended to spell out in stone the might of the British empire – but a mere 16 years later, the British were out on their ear. New Delhi became the powerhouse of the new Republic.

At the western end of Rajpath is the official residence of the president of India, the **Rashtrapati Bhavan** (President's House), built in 1929. Pre-Independence, this 340-room palace was the viceroy's residence. At the time of Mountbatten, India's last viceroy, the number of servants employed here was staggering. There were 418 gardeners alone, 50 of whom were boys employed to chase away birds. To its west, the **Mughal gardens** occupy 130 hectares; it's only open (admission free; photography prohibited) to the public for several days in February/March – for dates contact India Tourism Delhi (p125).

Rashtrapati Bhavan is flanked by the mirror-image, dome-crowned **North** and **South Secretariat** buildings, housing government ministries, which have over 1000 rooms between them. The three buildings sit upon a small rise, known as Raisina Hill.

At Rajpath's eastern end is **India Gate**. This 42m-high stone memorial arch, designed by Lutyens, pays tribute to around 90,000 Indian army soldiers who died in WWI, the Northwest Frontier operations of the same time and the 1919 Anglo-Afghan War.

Sansad Bhavan (Parliament House), a circular, colonnaded structure 171m in diameter, stands at the end of Sansad Marg.

HUMAYUN'S TOMB

Don't miss this, Delhi's most sublime sight. A beautiful example of early Mughal architecture, this **tomb** (Indian/foreigner Rs10/250, video Rs25; ☾ dawn-dusk) was built in the mid-16th century by Haji Begum, the Persian-born senior wife of the second Mughal emperor Humayun. The tomb brought Persian style to Delhi, but the two-tone combination of red sandstone and white marble is entirely local, showing the complementary merging of the cultures. Elements in its design – a squat building with high arched entrances that let in light, topped by a bulbous dome and surrounded by 30 acres of formal gardens – were to be refined over the years to eventually create the magnificence of Agra's Taj Mahal.

Other beautiful tombs dot the complex, including that of the emperor's favourite barber, Haji Begum herself, and of Isa Khan, a fine example of Lodi architecture through a gate to the left of the entrance. The magnificent Mughal gardens are a magical place to wander, particularly towards sunset.

PURANA QILA

With its massive walls and impressive gateways, **Purana Qila** (Old Fort; ☎ 24353178; Mathura Rd; Indian/foreigner Rs5/100, video Rs25; ☾ dawn-dusk) was built by Afghan ruler Sher Shah during his reign (1538–45), before the emperor Humayun (whom he had previously defeated) regained control of India.

Entering from the south gate you'll see the graceful octagonal, red-sandstone tower, the **Sher Mandal**, later used by Humayun as a library. It was while hurriedly descending the stairs of this tower in 1556 that he slipped and sustained injuries from which he later died. Just beyond it is the 1541 **Qila-i-Kuhran Mosque**, or Mosque of Sher Shah, which delicately combines black-and-white marble to the more easily available deep red sandstone.

A popular, picturesque boating lake has been created from the former moat, with pedaloes for hire (Rs50 per 30 minutes).

The site is thought to be that of ancient Indraprastha (p226).

GANDHI SMRITI

This poignant **memorial** (☎ 23012843; 5 Tees January Marg; admission free, camera/video free/prohibited; ☾ 10am-1.30pm & 2-5pm Tue-Sun, closed every 2nd Sat of month) is where Mahatma Gandhi was shot dead by a Hindu zealot on 30 January 1948. Concrete footsteps represent Gandhi's final steps and lead to the spot where he died, which is marked by a small pavilion known as the Martyr's Column.

The impressive indoor museum has photographs, paintings, and dioramas depicting scenes from Gandhi's life.

Gandhi had been staying in the house as a guest, and spent the last 144 days of his life here. In the room he occupied, his meagre possessions are on display, such as his walking stick, spectacles, spinning wheel, and chappals (sandals).

CRAFTS MUSEUM

Opposite Purana Qila lies this tree-shaded treasure trove of a **museum** (☎ 23371641; Bhairon Marg; admission free; ☾ 10am-5pm Tue-Sun).

The galleries contain more than 20,000 exhibits from around India, including metalware, woodwork, old silver jewellery, tribal masks, paintings, terracotta figurines, and

DELHI

rich-coloured textiles. The fascinating items display the application of art to everyday life, from village toys to a huge 18th-century wooden Gujarati *jharokha* (elaborate balcony). Artisans on-site demonstrate their skills and sell their products. The on-site shop is particularly good.

Photography is only allowed with prior permission.

NATIONAL MUSEUM

An overview of India's last 5000 years, this is a splendid **museum** (☎ 23019272; www.nationalmuseum india.gov.in; Janpath; Indian/foreigner Rs10/300, foreigner price includes audio-guides in English/Hindi/French/Japanese/ German; camera Indian/foreigner Rs20/300; ⏱ 10am-5pm Tue-Sun). Exhibits include rare relics from the Harappan Civilisation, Central Asian antiquities (including silk paintings from the 1st century AD), sacred Buddhist objects, jewel-bright miniature paintings, old coins (including Portuguese, Dutch and Danish), woodcarving, textiles, musical instruments, fearsome Mughal weaponry, Persian manuscripts, and Indus jewellery made from shells and bones. Give yourself at least a few hours – preferably a half-day – to explore this museum, one of India's finest.

You'll need some identification to obtain an audio-guide. Video cameras are prohibited.

Next door is the **Archaeological Survey of India** (☎ 23010822; asi.nic.in; Janpath; ⏱ 9.30am-1pm & 2-6pm Mon-Fri) which stocks publications about India's main sites.

GURDWARA BANGLA SAHIB

The **Gurdwara Bangla Sahib** (Ashoka Rd; ⏱ 4am-9pm) is an important Sikh shrine and a constant hive of activity. Topped with gold onion domes, it was constructed at the site where the eighth Sikh guru, Harkrishan Dev, spent several months in 1664. This guru dedicated most of his time to helping the destitute and sick and was revered for his healing powers. At the back of the gurdwara (Sikh temple) is a huge tank, surrounded by a graceful colonnade. The water is said to have curative properties. Devotional songs are sung throughout the day.

SAFDARJANG'S TOMB

Built by the Nawab of Avadh for his father, Safdarjang, this grandiose mid-18th-century **tomb** (Aurobindo Marg; Indian/foreigner Rs5/US$2, video Rs25; ⏱ dawn-dusk) is one of the last examples of Mughal architecture. Its overwrought mannerism might reflect the final throes of the great empire, but it's still a charming spot.

INDIRA GANDHI SMRITI

The former residence of Indira Gandhi is now a fascinating **museum** (☎ 23010094; 1 Safdarjang Rd; admission free; ⏱ 9.30am-4.45pm Tue-Sun), displaying artefacts, photos and newspaper clippings, as well as personal belongings, including the blood-stained sari she was wearing when she was assassinated in 1984. Some of the rooms are preserved as they were, an interesting window into the understated elegance of her life. Another section is devoted to her son Rajiv, also assassinated in 1991 by a suicide bomber. Fragments of the clothes he was wearing and, even more poignantly, his trainers, are on display. On the way out, you'll pass an enclosed crystal pathway that marks Gandhi's final footsteps before her murder.

HAZRAT NIZAM-UD-DIN DARGAH

Amid a tangle of alleys, attracting hoards of devotees, is the vibrant marble **shrine** (⏱ 24hr) of the Muslim Sufi saint, Nizam-ud-din Chishti. He died in 1325, aged 92, but the mausoleum has been revamped several times, and dates from 1562. Other tombs include the later grave of Jahanara (daughter of Shah Jahan), and the renowned Urdu poet, Amir Khusru. It's one of Delhi's most atmospheric pleasures to hear Sufis sing qawwali, at around sunset after evening prayers, on Thursdays and feast days.

LODI GARDEN

Lovely Lodi **garden** (Lodi Rd; ⏱ 6am-8pm) is a popular place for a morning/evening stroll or jog, and it is especially pretty at dusk. The gardens encompass the crumbling **tombs** of the Sayyid and Lodi rulers, including the impressive 15th-century **Bara Gumbad**.

If you're in search of serenity, avoid Sundays – the garden's most social day.

NATIONAL GALLERY OF MODERN ART

This **gallery** (☎ 23382835; ngmaindia.gov.in; Jaipur House; Indian/foreigner Rs10/150; ⏱ 10am-5pm Tue-Sun) occupies the maharaja of Jaipur's former place, and includes all the great modern Indian masters, with beautiful works by Amrita Sher-Gil, the Tagore family, and India's most famous contemporary artist, MF Husain. Photography isn't allowed.

DELHI

NEHRU MEMORIAL MUSEUM & PLANETARIUM

Teen Murti Bhavan is the former residence of Jawaharlal Nehru (India's first prime minister), and was previously Flagstaff House, home to the British commander-in-chief. Just off Teen Murti Rd, it has been converted into a **museum** (☎ 23016734; admission free; ◷ 9am-5.15pm Tue-Sun), a must-see for those interested in the Independence movement. Some rooms have been preserved as Nehru left them, and there's a wealth of photographs, though some contextualisation would come in handy.

In the grounds is a **planetarium** (☎ 23014504; 45min show Rs15; ◷ in English 11.30am & 3pm).

TIBET HOUSE

Tibet House has a small **museum** (☎ 24611515; 1 Lodi Rd; admission Rs10; ◷ 9.30am-1pm & 2-5.30pm Mon-Fri) displaying ceremonial items, including sacred manuscripts, sculptures and old *thangkas* (Tibetan paintings on cloth). All were brought out of Tibet when the Dalai Lama fled following Chinese occupation. Photography prohibited.

The bookshop sells Buddhist books, chanting CDs, prayer flags and *katas* (sacred Tibetan scarves).

NATIONAL ZOOLOGICAL GARDENS

Popular with families and courting couples, this is India's biggest **zoo** (☎ 24359825; Mathura Rd; Indian/foreigner Rs10/50, video Rs50; ◷ 8am-6pm Sat-Thu summer, 9am-5pm Sat-Thu winter). It's a bit forlorn, in the way of zoos, but there are white Bengal tigers, Himalayan black bears, rhinos, hippos, wolves, elephants, giraffes, and some spectacular birds.

Connaught Place Area
CONNAUGHT PLACE

New Delhi's colonnaded heart is commercial centre **Connaught Place** (CP; Map p130), named after George V's uncle who visited in 1921. Its streets radiate from the central circle, divided into blocks and devoted to shops, banks, restaurants, hotels and offices.

Often creating confusion, the outer circle is technically called 'Connaught Circus' (divided into blocks from G to N) and the inner circle 'Connaught Place' (divided into blocks from A to F). There's also a 'Middle Circle'. In 1995 the inner and outer circles were renamed Rajiv Chowk and Indira Chowk respectively, but these names are rarely used.

Touts are especially rampant in Connaught Place (see p125).

JANTAR MANTAR

Comprised of curious terracotta-red structures, **Jantar Mantar** (Map p130; Sansad Marg; Indian/foreigner Rs5/US$2; ◷ 9am-dusk) is the earliest of Maharaja Jai Singh II's five observatories, constructed in 1725. It's dominated by a huge sundial and houses other instruments plotting the course of heavenly bodies.

Other Areas
BAHAI HOUSE OF WORSHIP (LOTUS TEMPLE)

This extraordinary **temple** (Map pp122-3; ☎ 26444029; Kalkaji; ◷ 9.30am-5.30pm Tue-Sun Oct-Mar, 9am-7pm Apr-Sep) is shaped like the sacred lotus flower. Designed by Iranian-Canadian architect Fariburz Sahba in 1986, it has 27 immaculate white-marble petals. The Bahai philosophy revolves around universal peace and the elimination of prejudice, and adherents of all faiths are welcome to pray or meditate silently according to their own religion.

Refrain from speaking in the temple; photography inside is prohibited.

AKSHARDHAM TEMPLE

Don't miss the Hindu Swaminarayan Group's lavish **Akshardham Temple** (off Map pp122-3; www.akshardham.com; Noida turning, National Hwy 24; ◷ 9am-6pm Tue-Sun Oct-Mar, 10am-7pm Tue-Sun Apr-Sep), on Delhi's outskirts. Inaugurated in 2005, it's made of salmon-coloured sandstone and white marble, contains around 20,000 carved deities, and reflects traditional Orissan, Gujarati, Mughal and Rajasthani architectural elements.

Allow at least half a day to do it justice (weekdays are less crowded) as there's lots to see, including a boat ride through Indian history, and a musical fountain.

LAKSHMI NARAYAN TEMPLE (BIRLA MANDIR)

West of Connaught Place, the Orissan-style **Lakshmi Narayan Temple** (Map pp122-3; Mandir Marg; ◷ 6am-9pm), an overexcited red-and-cream confection, was erected in 1938 by the wealthy industrialist BD Birla. It was inaugurated by Gandhi as a temple for all castes; a sign on the gate says 'Everyone is Welcome'.

NATIONAL RAIL MUSEUM

Trainspotters will adore this **museum** (Map pp126-7; ☎ 26881816; www.nationalrailmuseum.org; Chanakyapuri; admission Rs10, video Rs100; ☒ 9.30am-5pm Tue-Sun Oct-Mar, to 7pm Apr-Sep), with around 30 locomotives and old carriages. Exhibits include an 1855 steam engine, still in working order, and various oddities including the skull of an elephant that charged a train in 1894, and lost.

Kids will love the 'Joy Train' ride (adult/child Rs10/5), and on Sunday you can ride the **Steam Mono Rail** (Rs20; ☒ 2.30-4.30pm).

HAUZ KHAS

Hauz Khas means 'royal tank', named after a 13th-century reservoir built by Allauddin Khilji. The artificial lake was once the water source for Siri Fort – the second city of Delhi – but is now a grassy garden. Nearby lie Firoz Shah's 14th-century domed madrasa (religious school), his **tomb** (Map pp122–3) and some Lodi and Tughlak tombs. This is a fascinating, secluded place to explore, and neighbouring Hauz Khas village (Map pp122–3) is filled with upmarket boutiques and curio shops (see p153).

SHANKAR'S INTERNATIONAL DOLLS MUSEUM

From Spanish bullfighting figurines to Indian bridal dolls, this remarkable **museum** (Map pp122-3; ☎ 23316970; www.childrensbooktrust.com; Nehru House, Bahadur Shah Zafar Marg; admission Rs10; ☒ 10am-5.30pm Tue-Sun) has 6500 dolls from 85 countries.

CORONATION DURBAR SITE

North of Old Delhi, in a desolate field, stands a lone **obelisk** (Map pp122–3). Here, in 1877 and 1903, the great durbars, featuring Indian nobility, paid homage to the British monarch. In 1911, King George V was declared emperor of India here.

FIROZ SHAH KOTLA

Firozabad (the fifth city of Delhi) was built by Firoz Shah in 1354. Its ruins can be found at **Firoz Shah Kotla** (Map pp122-3; Indian/foreigner Rs5/US$2, video Rs25; ☒ dawn-dusk), off Bahadur Shah Zafar Marg. Visit on a Thursday afternoon when crowds come to pray, light candles and leave bowls of milk to appease Delhi's djinns (invisible spirits or genies) that are reputed to inhabit the kotla. In the fortress/palace is a 13m-high sandstone **Ashoka Pillar** inscribed with Ashoka's edicts (and a later inscription).

SULABH INTERNATIONAL MUSEUM OF TOILETS

This quirky **museum** (off Map pp122-3; ☎ 25053646; www.sulabhtoiletmuseum.org; Sulabh Complex, Mahavir Enclave, Palam Dabri Rd; admission free; ☒ 10am-5pm Mon-Sat) houses toilet-related paraphernalia dating from 2500 BC to modern times. It's not just a curiosity: Sulabh International has done extraordinary work in the field of sanitation, developing pour-flush toilets, bio-gas plants and educating the children of 'manual scavengers' (whose job is to remove the crap from dry toilets) for other work. A guided tour (free) brings the loos to life.

ACTIVITIES
Golf

Delhi Golf Club (Map pp126-7; ☎ 24362768; www.delhigolfclub.org; Dr Zakir Hussain Marg; weekdays/weekends US$45/60; ☒ sunrise-sunset) dates from 1931 and has beautiful, well-tended fairways; weekends are busy.

Massage & Ayurvedic Treatments

Ashtaang (Map pp122-3; ☎ 24111802; www.ashtaang.in; E-2 Anand Niketan; ☒ 9.30am-4.30pm) is located opposite Delhi University (South Campus), It offers authentic Ayurvedic treatments such as *sirodhara* (warm oil drizzled on forehead; 40 minutes Rs1600) and *abyangam* (synchronised massage; Rs1100 for 45 minutes).

Kerala Ayurveda (Map pp122-3; ☎ 41754888; www.keralaayurveda.biz; E-2 Green Park Extn; ☒ 8am-8pm) For *abyangam* (Rs900 for 45 minutes), plus other Ayurvedic therapies, try this place.

Swimming

Deluxe hotels have the best pools – most are exclusively for guests, but some do allow outsiders, at a price (taxes extra).

Hotel Samrat (Map pp126-7; ☎ 26110606; Chanakyapuri; per person Rs450)

Jaypee Vasant Continental Hotel (Map pp122-3; ☎ 26148800; Basant Lok complex, Vasant Vihar; per person Rs600)

Radisson Hotel (Map pp122-3; ☎ 26779191; Gurgaon Rd; per person Rs1000)

Siri Fort Sports Complex (Map pp122-3; ☎ 26496657; day membership Indian/foreigner Rs40/100) Olympic-sized swimming pool (Apr-Sep) plus a toddler pool.

COURSES

See p121 for local publications that will contain up-to-the-minute details about various courses.

DELHI

Cooking

Parul Puri (Map pp126-7; ☎ 9810793322; www.koneone.com) At K-One One (p144) runs two-hour classes with a focus on cuisine from North India regions. The charge is Rs1200 per person; book at least two days in advance.

Tannie Baig (☎ 9868217288; baig.murad@gmail.com) The elegant Tannie who is based in Hauz Khas, has written 16 cookery books. A two-hour cooking lesson costs Rs3200, which sounds pricey, but it's a flat rate for up to five people.

Hindi

The **Central Hindi Directorate** (☎ 26103160; West Block VII, RK Puram) runs basic Hindi courses (minimum numbers apply) which cost Rs6000 for 60 hours (two hours daily, thrice weekly).

Meditation & Yoga

The following places are top spots to stretch the body and nourish the soul. Telephone for session timings and, if not stated below, venues. Where no charges are mentioned, donations are appreciated.

Dhyan Foundation (☎ 26253374; www.dhyanfoundation.com) Various yoga and meditation options.

Morarji Desai National Institute of Yoga (Map pp126-7; ☎ 23721472; www.yogamdniy.com; 68 Ashoka Rd) Includes pranayama and hatha yoga as well as meditation. Diploma courses are possible and there's yoga for kids.

Sri Aurobindo Ashram (☎ 26567863) Yoga and meditation, morning and evening, three days a week.

Studio Abhyas (☎ 26962757) Yoga classes combining *asanas* (fixed body positions) and pranayama; meditation classes, and Vedic chanting classes (evenings or by appointment)

Tushita Meditation Centre (☎ 26513400) Twice-weekly Tibetan/Buddhist meditation sessions.

Vedic Wisdom Ashram (☎ 9213204094) Meditation and Raja yoga classes by appointment.

Spa

For a thorough pampering, try **Lambency Spa** (Map pp122-3; ☎ 40587983; www.chandansparsh.com; M-24 Greater Kailash II; 9am-9pm), where you can have a top-of-the-range manicure and pedicure (Rs599) or massage (from Rs999). Prices don't include tax.

TOURS

Delhi is a spread-out city so taking a tour makes sense, although you can feel rushed at some sites. Avoid Monday when many sites are shut. Admission fees and camera/video charges aren't included in tour prices below, and rates are per person. Book several days in advance as minimum numbers may be required.

India Tourism Delhi (p125) can arrange multilingual, government-approved guides (from Rs600/1350 per half-/full-day).

Ashok Travels & Tours (Map pp126-7; ☎ 23340070; www.attindiatourism.com; Hotel Janpath, Janpath) Tours (by coach, Rs200, 8am to 1pm) of Old Delhi or New Delhi, or both (Rs300, 8am to 5.15pm). A day trip to Agra costs Rs950, including breakfast.

Delhi Tourism & Transport Development Corporation (DTTDC; delhitourism.nic.in) Baba Kharak Singh Marg (Map p130; ☎ 23363607; 7am-9pm); international airport (☎ 25675609; 24hr); N-Block (Map p130; ☎ 23315322; 10am-6pm Mon-Sat) New Delhi (9am to 1.30pm) and Old Delhi (2.15pm to 5.45pm) tours cost Rs150 (Rs250 AC) each. Same-day trips to Agra (Rs850, Rs950 AC) run thrice-weekly while three-day tours of Agra and Jaipur (Rs4200 AC) operate twice-weekly.

Hotel Broadway (Map p132; ☎ 43603600; 4/15 Asaf Ali Rd; Rs750) Two-hour walking tours of Old Delhi, starting at 9.30am or 1pm, which include lunch at Chor Bizarre (p147).

Old Delhi Walks (Intach; ☎ 24641304; intachdelhi@rediffmail.com; Rs50) Intach run a walking tour (approximately two hours) every month with an expert guide, exploring different areas, such as Chandhi Chowk, Nizamuddin, Hauz Khas, and Lodhi Gardens. Customised tours are also possible. Book at least a week in advance.

Salaam Baalak Trust (Map p142; ☎ 23584164; www.salaambaalaktrust.com; Gali Chandiwali, Paharganj; suggested donation Rs200) This charitable organisation (p1166) offers 'street walks' with a twist – your guide is a former (Trust-trained) street child, who will show you first-hand what life is like for inner-city homeless kids. The walk takes around two hours and the money goes to the Trust to further assist children on the streets. For details call ☎ 9910099348.

SLEEPING

It's wise to book in advance, as Delhi's most salubrious places can fill up in a flash, leaving new arrivals easy prey for commission sharks (read p125). Most hotels offer pick-up from the airport (p160) with advance notice.

Be warned that street din can be diabolical – request a quiet room and keep earplugs handy. Also, room quality within budget and midrange hotels can radically vary so try to inspect a few rooms first.

Midrange prices have rocketed upwards over recent years, so homestays are becoming

DELHI

an attractive alternative, and a great deal of excellent B&B accommodation has been developed in preparation for the 2010 Commonwealth Games. For details about staying with an Indian family, contact India Tourism Delhi (p125), who categorise properties as either silver (Rs1500 to Rs3000) or gold (Rs2500 to Rs5000). Or check www.incredibleindianhomes.com and (www.mahindra homestays.com).

Long-term stayers could consider renting a furnished apartment – check ads in the latest *Delhi City Guide*, *Delhi Diary* (p121) and local newspapers. Two good websites are www.speciality-apartments.com and www.delhiescape.net.

Hotels with a minimum tariff of Rs500 charge 12.5% luxury tax and some also whack on a service charge (5% to 10%). Taxes aren't included in this chapter unless indicated and all rooms have private bathrooms unless otherwise stated. Most hotels have a noon checkout and luggage storage is usually possible (sometimes for a small charge).

It's a good idea to call or email ahead to confirm your booking 24 hours before you arrive.

Budget

Delhi's budget bunch tend to offer dreary rooms and patchy service. Typically rooms are small, screaming for a fresh lick of paint and a bathroom blitz. Some are even windowless. Your room might be dark, but look on the bright side: accommodation isn't as expensive as many capital cities.

Most backpackers head for hyperactive Paharganj, a touristy pocket near the New Delhi train station that has some of the city's cheapest beds.

In the following budget listings, only the cheapest, non-AC room rates have been provided; AC rooms, where available, will be several hundred rupees higher.

NORTH DELHI
Old Delhi

Few foreign tourists stay in teeming Old Delhi – those who do will probably attract a bit of innocuous attention.

Hotel New City Palace (Map p132; ☎ 23279548; www.hotelnewcitypalace.in; d/q Rs400/650; ✿) A palace it's not, though the rooms are reasonably clean. The position is good, overlooking the Jama Masjid, and the reception friendly.

Hotel Bombay Orient (Map p132; ☎ 23242691; s/d Rs490/580; ✿) Set on the busy bazaar leading from the Jama Masjid's south gate, you'll need to book ahead here. It's one of the old city's best budget bets, but even so, don't expect too much and request one of its newer rooms.

Paharganj Area

Bumper-to-bumper budget lodgings, Paharganj – with its seedy reputation for drugs and dodgy characters – isn't everyone's cup of *chai*. On the plus side, it's walking distance from New Delhi train station – and it's *the* place to tap into the backpacker grapevine. Paharganj also has some of Delhi's cheapest places to sleep, but sun-starved, grimy cells are depressingly common, and hot water erratic.

Most hotels are on or around the main drag of Main Bazaar, with many freckling the numerous (nameless) alleys that tentacle off it. Since Main Bazaar is overwhelmingly congested, taxiwallahs may (understandably) refuse to drop you at your hotel's doorstep; however, most are a short walk away. The following accommodation features on Map p142.

Hotel Downtown (☎ 41541529; 4583 Main Bazaar; s/d Rs250/300) Rooms are smallish and stark, but this hotel is still in better shape than many of its budget brothers.

Hotel Namaskar (☎ 23583456; www.hotelnamaskar.com; 917 Chandiwalan, Main Bazaar; d/tr/q Rs300/400/480; ✿) This old favourite is run by two amiable, helpful brothers. Rooms are spartan, but the colour scheme is bound to tickle you pink. Car hire can be arranged.

Hotel Rak International (☎ 23562478; Tooti Chowk, Main Bazaar; s/d Rs350/450; ✿) Tucked off the main bazaar on a messy corner, the modest rooms at this popular hotel have marble floors, TVs, wardrobes, small dressing tables and…windows!

Major's Den (☎ 23589010; s/d Rs350/500; ✿) In a quietish sidestreet, the friendly Den has no-frills, bearably clean rooms, with cleanish walls; not all have windows.

Hotel Amax Inn (☎ 23543813; www.hotelamax.com; 8145/6 Arakashan Rd; s/d Rs400/450; ✿) Away from the main bazaar, this chilled place is tucked away in a lane off Arakashan Rd, and is good value, with clean rooms and a small roof terrace.

Lord's Hotel (☎ 23588303; 51 Main Bazaar; s/d Rs450/550; ✿) A relatively appealing low-key place, with cool marble floors and TVs, though some rooms are rather gloomy.

A STREET CHILD'S STORY

Danish is 18. Once a child runaway, he was helped by the Salaam Baalak Trust (see p1166). The number of street children in Delhi is estimated to be upwards of 100,000. Most are runaways; some are orphans, some are just lost – often being separated by accident from their families during religious pilgrimages.

When did you come to Delhi?
When I was seven, I ran away from home (Danish is from Arrah in Bihar, over 800km from Delhi).

Why did you run away?
There were problems about food and not enough to eat. My family is really poor.

Weren't you scared?
Not really. I had run away for shorter times, maybe stayed one night away. I stayed first at Allahabad and some other places.

How did you get here, and how did you manage to survive?
I came by train. At first I didn't have anything to eat for two or three days. I saw another child collecting leftover food from luxury train coaches, so I copied him. If people left food, I ate. I shined shoes, I sold water. I started ragpicking. I watched other children ragpicking and I did the same. I sold to the ragpicker and I got money. I was so excited to have Rs10. I spent Rs5 on food, Rs2 on games and the rest on smoking *beedis* (cigarettes).

Where did you live?
I lived in the station roof for eight years. But sometimes I slept in the park, or in a shelter near Kashmiri Gate.

Did you miss your family?
I cried a lot, but always alone. I didn't let other people see.

When did you get involved with Salaam Baalak?
Four years ago, when I was 14. Salaam Baalak came to counsel me. It took a long time to persuade me to leave.

Why? And then what happened?
There's lots of freedom in the station. Life is very bad but you are free. Then, when I joined Salaam Baalak, I had a timetable in my life. I talked to the children in the station saying, why waste your life here? I know the kind of problems they have. It's illegal to live there, so there are problems with the police. Several times I was put into a lock up.

Now I am doing my first year of college. Children living on the street are not able to read anything, not Hindi or English. I want to become a businessman, selling arts. Salaam Balaak really changed my life.

Have you been back to see your family?
Yes, several times. They thought Danish had died. Now they are very happy. Danish creates handcrafted products, using techniques including macramé. For more information on his work and that of other young people helped by the Salaam Balaak Trust, or on ways you can help, contact the **Trust** (Map p142; ☎ 23584164; www.salaambaalaktrust.com; Gali Chandiwali, Paharganj).

Ajay Guest House (☎ 23583125; www.anupam hoteliersltd.com; 5084 Main Bazaar; s/d Rs500/600; 🆒 🖳) Ajay's had a makeover: gleaming white rooms are decorated with colourful geometric detailing; some even have funky blue ceiling lighting. Bathrooms are fresh and colourfully tiled.

Cottage Ganga Inn (☎ 23561516; cottageganga inn@yahoo.co.in; 1562 Bazar Sangtrashan; s/d/tr/q Rs650/750/850/1000; 🆒) Popular with overlanders, this hotel is tucked away off the Main Bazaar in a courtyard, located next to a nursery school. It is clean, comfortable, and a great deal for Paharganj.

Cottage Crown Plaza (☎ 23561800; cottagecrown plaza@yahoo.co.in; 5136 Main Bazaar; d Rs900; 🆒) Tip top for the price, this has pretty comfortable beds, clean sheets and bathrooms, and TVs.

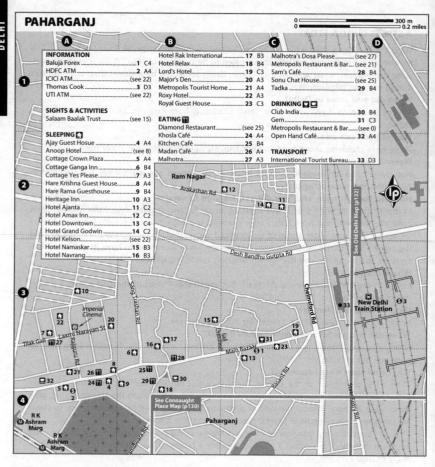

PAHARGANJ

INFORMATION
Baluja Forex	**1** C4
HDFC ATM	**2** A4
ICICI ATM	(see 22)
Thomas Cook	**3** D3
UTI ATM	(see 22)

SIGHTS & ACTIVITIES
Salaam Baalak Trust	(see 15)

SLEEPING
Ajay Guest Hosue	**4** A4
Anoop Hotel	(see 8)
Cottage Crown Plaza	**5** A4
Cottage Ganga Inn	**6** B4
Cottage Yes Please	**7** A3
Hare Krishna Guest House	**8** A4
Hare Rama Guesthouse	**9** A4
Heritage Inn	**10** A3
Hotel Ajanta	**11** C2
Hotel Amax Inn	**12** C2
Hotel Downtown	**13** C4
Hotel Grand Godwin	**14** C2
Hotel Kelson	(see 22)
Hotel Namaskar	**15** B3
Hotel Navrang	**16** B3

Hotel Rak International	**17** B3
Hotel Relax	**18** B4
Lord's Hotel	**19** C3
Major's Den	**20** A3
Metropolis Tourist Home	**21** A4
Roxy Hotel	**22** A3
Royal Guest House	**23** C3

EATING
Diamond Restaurant	(see 25)
Khosla Café	**24** A4
Kitchen Café	**25** B4
Madan Café	**26** A4
Malhotra	**27** A3

Malhotra's Dosa Please	(see 27)
Metropolis Restaurant & Bar	(see 21)
Sam's Café	**28** B4
Sonu Chat House	(see 25)
Tadka	**29** B4

DRINKING
Club India	**30** B4
Gem	**31** B4
Metropolis Restaurant & Bar	(see 0)
Open Hand Café	**32** A4

TRANSPORT
International Tourist Bureau	**33** D3

Cottage Yes Please (☎ 23562300; cottageyesplease@ yahoo.co.in; 1843 Laxmi Narayan St; d Rs900; ✄) Around the corner from Cottage Crown Plaza is this place, its sibling, with a range of glitzy, clean rooms, with TVs, fridges, brassware fans and stained glass.

Other possibilities:

Hotel Navrang (☎ 23561922; 644-C Mohalla Baoli, 6 Tooti Chowk, Main Bazaar; s/d Rs120/150) The card reads: 'A home away from home'. If your home is a cell, sure. But you're paying peanuts!

Hare Rama Guest House (☎ 23561301; www.hare ramaguesthouse.com; off Main Bazaar; s/d from Rs300/400; ✄) Grotty but bearable rooms, tucked in behind the bazaar.

Heritage Inn (☎ 23588222; Rajguru Rd; s/d Rs330/440; ✄) You won't be able to rumba in the poky rooms, but you get a TV and bearable bathroom.

Anoop Hotel (☎ 41541390; 1566 Main Bazaar; d Rs450) Cleanish, light rooms.

Hare Krishna Guest House (☎ 41541341; 1572 Main Bazaar; s/d Rs450/495) Scuffed but bearable rooms.

Royal Guest House (☎ 23586176; royalguesthouse@ yahoo.com; Main Bazaar; s/d Rs490/590; ✄) They might not be regal, but the small rooms do have clean sheets, TVs, and fridges.

Hotel Kelson (☎ 41541020; narang_kelson@hotmail .com; Rajguru Rd; s/d Rs500/600; ✄) Reasonable rooms with marble floors. Adjoining is its (similar) sister property, the Roxy Hotel, which has some useful family rooms.

Majnu-ka-Tilla

The antidote for anyone who's got the big-city blues, this mellow enclave (aka Tibetan Colony), a block intercut by narrow lanes, isn't as central as Paharganj but has better-value rooms. It's packed with travel agents, cyber cafes and trinket markets, and you'll rub shoulders with maroon-clad Buddhist monks, curio vendors and local residents. It's tricky to find though, north of the ISBT (bus station). From the centre, take the Metro to Vidhan Sabha, then take a rickshaw.

Peace House (Map pp122-3; ☎ 23939415; d 4th/3rd/2nd/1st fl Rs300/380/450/450) Plain, neat rooms are clean, though with slightly grubby walls. There's room service and the kitchen makes yummy *momos* (stuffed dumplings).

Wongdhen House (Map pp122-3; ☎ 23816689; wongdhenhouse@hotmail.com; s/d Rs475/550; ✘) The pick of the Majnu-ka-Tilla bunch, this place has basic but good-sized, clean rooms. The rooftop has views over the Yamuna and the tasty restaurant rustles up everything from banana pancakes to Tibetan noodles (and does room service).

NEW DELHI & AROUND
Connaught Place Area
The following accommodation options are featured on Map p130 and they are crusty to the core, but still quite cheap for Connaught Place:

Ringo Guest House (☎ 23310605; ringo_guest _house@yahoo.co.in; 17 Scindia House, Connaught Lane; dm Rs100, s/d Rs350/450, without bathroom Rs150/250)

Sunny Guest House (☎ 23312909; sunnyguesthouse 1234@hotmail.com; 152 Scindia House, Connaught Lane; s/d Rs300/400, without bathroom Rs150/200)

Chanakyapuri & Ashoka Road
Youth Hostel (Map pp126-7; ☎ 26871969; www.yhaindia .org; 5 Nyaya Marg, Chanakyapuri; dm without/with AC Rs150/350, d without/with AC Rs500/1000; ✘ 🖵) The dormitory is good value (membership costs Rs100 per year), pretty clean, basic and handily located.

AIRPORT AREA
Hotel Eurostar (Map pp122-3; ☎ 46062300; www.hotel eurostar.in; A-27/1, Rd No. 1, Mahipalpur Extn, National Hwy 8; s/d Rs695/750; ✘) This is a smartish option, clean, if occasionally musty – a good choice for budget travellers who want to snuggle down close to the airport.

Midrange
NORTH DELHI
Old Delhi
Ginger (Map p132; ☎ 1800 209 3333; www.ginger hotels.com; Rail Yatri Niwas; r Rs1199; ✘ 🖵) The Taj Group's 'Smart Basic' hotel: dapper rooms that are equipped with nice beds and smart bathrooms at a bargain price – ideal for business travel on-the-cheap. It is in an ugly building that is located a few minutes' walk from New Delhi train station. There's a 24-hour restaurant.

Hotel Broadway (Map p132; ☎ 43663600; www .oldworldhospitality.com; 4/15 Asaf Ali Rd; s/d incl breakfast Rs2095/4495; ✘) Semiluxurious Broadway, between the old and new cities, has some rooms with views over Old Delhi. Room standards vary (some are sleek and smart), so look at a few. Nos 44 and 46 have been kitschly kitted out by French designer Catherine Lévy, as has the Chor Bizarre (see p147) restaurant. Broadway runs popular walking tours (p139).

Paharganj Area
For an overview of the Paharganj area, see p140. Grot aside, Paharganj is close to (and cheaper than) Connaught Place and conveniently located for New Delhi train station. The following listings are featured on Map p142.

Metropolis Tourist Home (☎ 23561794; www .metropolistravels.com; 1634 Main Bazaar; s/d incl tax Rs1000/1200; ✘) Rooms (some with tight balconies) here are simple and characterless but come with smooth tiled floors, TVs as well as fridges. The rooftop restaurant is an added bonus.

Hotel Relax (☎ 23562811; vidur109@hotmail.com; Nehru Bazaar; d Rs1200; ✘) This white-fronted, blousy building has lots of artefacts strewn over the hallways and a pretty plant-lined terrace, but dowdy rooms, all with TVs and fridges. You should be able to bargain down the price.

Hotel Ajanta (☎ 29562097; www.ajantahotel.com; 36 Arakashan Rd, Ram Nagar; s/d from Rs1400/1600; ✘ 🖵) Reasonably clean, plain rooms: more money buys you an extra degree of comfort and glitz. There's a pleasant rooftop and a good restaurant. Service, however, receives extremely mixed reports.

Hotel Grand Godwin (☎ 23546891; www.god winhotels.com; 8502, 41 Arakashan Rd, Ram Nagar; s/d Rs1600/1900; ✘ 🖵) Located north of Main Bazaar in Ram Nagar, the Grand Godwin has a snazzy lobby, glass-capsule lift, and clean-and-tidy rooms, but off-hand reception staff. Facilities include wi-fi and room service.

DELHI

NEW DELHI & AROUND
Connaught Place Area
CP properties are unbeatably central, but you pay a premium for the location. These listings feature on Map p130.

YMCA Tourist Hostel (☎ 23361915; ymcath@ndf .vsnl.net.in; Jai Singh Rd; s/d Rs2380/3350, without bathroom Rs1090/1825; ☒ ▢ ☀) Is it fun to stay at this YMCA (men and women)? Perhaps not, with its whiff of a boarding house and lemon-lipped staff, but it has reasonable, functional rooms. The large pool (April to September) sparkles, but the Rs200 charge to get wet is uncool. Rates include tax, breakfast and dinner.

Prem Sagar Guest House (☎ 23345263; premsagar delhi@hotmail.com; 1st fl, 11 P-Block; s/d from Rs2500/3000; ☒) This is a reliable choice. The 12 snug rooms aren't flash, but they're clean, with TV, fridge and wardrobe. There's a pot-plant filled outdoor area.

Hotel Alka (☎ 23344328; www.hotelalka.com; P-Block; s/d from Rs2850/4800; ☒) Alka's cramped standard rooms are comfortable and contemporary, some with wood-panelled walls. More money buys more pizazz, including grrrrooovy leopard-skin-themed rooms. There's a good vegetarian restaurant.

York Hotel (☎ 23415769; www.hotelyorkindia.com; K-Block; s/d Rs3800/4300; ☒) York's rooms are good sized, and smartly refurbished in neutral colours, with wood-panelled floors and satiny bedcovers. Try to avoid the noisy, street-facing rooms.

Hotel Palace Heights (☎ 43582610; www.hotelpal aceheights.com; 26-28 D-Block; s/d Rs5500/6000; ☒ ▢) A smashing choice, this boutique hotel is a rare find: 12 stylish rooms in the heart of the city.

Corus (☎ 43652222; www.hotelcorus.com; 49 B-Block; d Rs6000-8000; ☒) A new, smart kid on the block, the Corus has clean, swish, compact rooms, with dazzling white sheets. More money buys you a lot more space. But readers report mixed service and occasional problems with hot water. There's an attractive restaurant, Bonsai, good for a drink (Kingfisher Rs90), with outdoor seating in a white-pebbled courtyard.

West of Connaught Place
If you like home-style lodgings you will love these hassle-free places (on Map pp122–3), but be aware that they fill up fast – so you should book ahead.

Ess Gee's (☎ 5725403; www.essgees.net; 12/9 East Patel Nagar; d incl breakfast Rs1100; ☒ ▢) A mellow guest house (no signboard), with shrines in the hallways, this may bring back fond memories of grandma's place – the plain rooms have TVs, writing desks and wardrobes. Ask to look at a few as some are better than others.

Master Guest House (☎ 28741089; www.master -guesthouse.com; R-500 New Rajendra Nagar; d Rs2500; ☒) Run by an obliging couple, this suburban residence has five thoughtfully furnished, characterful, if rather overpriced rooms with smart, spotless bathrooms. Guests share a leafy rooftop terrace.

Yatri House (☎ 23625563; www.yatrihouse.com; 3/4 Panchkuian Marg; s/d from Rs2500/3000, newer r Rs5000-5500; ☒ ▢ ☎) Central yet serene, Yatri is fronted by a small garden and backed by a courtyard with wrought-iron furniture. Rooms are large, uncluttered and clean. Price includes an airport pickup/drop, free internet, local calls, tea and coffee and afternoon snack. New rooms upstairs have bigger bathrooms with tubs.

Bajaj Indian Home Stay (☎ 25736509; www.bajajin dianhomestay.com; 8A/34 WEA Karol Bagh; s/d incl tax & breakfast Rs4400/5500; ☒ ▢) This highly professional place has 10 immaculate, well-decorated rooms, with safes, fridges and hairdryers. The tariff includes complimentary tea/coffee, local telephone calls and airport transfers. There's a rooftop restaurant.

Chanakyapuri & Ashoka Road
YWCA Blue Triangle Family Hostel (Map pp126-7; ☎ 23360133; www.ywcaofdelhi.org; Ashoka Rd; s/d incl tax & breakfast Rs1136/1975; ☒ ▢) Despite having an institutional vibe and hint of eau de mothball, this Y (men and women) is central and has reasonable rooms.

SOUTH DELHI
Home Away from Home (Map pp122-3; ☎ 26560289; permkamte@sify.com; 1st fl, D-8 Gulmohar Park; s/d incl breakfast from Rs1800/2200; ☒) This stylish apartment, in a classy suburb, is home to Mrs Kamte and she keeps the place in gleaming condition. There are just two rooms, each tasteful, antique-decorated and with small balconies.

K-One One (Map pp126-7; ☎ 43592583; www.parigold .com; K-11 Jangpura Extn; s/d incl breakfast Rs3500/4000; ☒ ▢ ☎) Set in a peaceful enclave, rooms are spacious and bright, with good bathrooms and LCD TVs, and there's a cool roof terrace. The owner offers cooking lessons (see p139).

Jorbagh 27 (Map pp126-7; ☎ 24698647; www.jorbagh27.com; 27 Jorbagh; s/d Rs3500/4300; ✷ ▯) In a leafy suburb, this unassuming place has 18 rooms in an old-style building. Standard rooms are sterile but clean, while the deluxe offer more space.

our pick Delhi Bed & Breakfast (Map pp122-3; ☎ 9811057103; www.delhibedandbreakfast.com; A6 Friends Colony East; d Rs3550; ✷ ▯) A find (once you've found it) in a leafy corner suburb, Delhi B&B is a homey homestay. Its three nicely decorated rooms have big beds and lots of individual touches, plus there's a plant-filled roof terrace. Book ahead.

Thikana (Map pp122-3; ☎ 46041569; www.thikanadelhi.com; A-7 Gulmohar Park; s/d Rs4000/4500; ✷ ▯) A boutique, luxurious, highly professional and chic homestay that's worth every rupee, with comfortable rooms decorated in warm earth colours, and attractive communal seating areas.

Ahuja Residency Golf Links (Map pp126-7; ☎ 246222555; www.ahujaresidency.com; 193 Golf Links; s/d incl breakfast Rs5063/5738; ✷ ▯); Defence Colony (Map pp126-7; C-83 Defence Colony; s/d Rs4050/4613) Reasonably priced for this swanky area, long-running Ahuja overlooks immaculate green lawns, and has comfortable rooms, many with little terraces. The Defence Colony has a less-smart branch.

Lutyens Guest House (Map pp126-7; ☎ 24625716; www.lutyensguesthouse.com; 39 Prithviraj Rd; s/d incl tax & breakfast Rs5500/6000; ✷ ▯ ☒) This great old rambling house is an atmospheric green oasis, and it even has its own (splendid) swimming pool. The garden is great – lawns, flowers and fluttering parrots – while rooms are rather basic considering the price. Rates have sky-rocketed in recent years, but the garden makes it possibly worth it. Look for '39 Amar Nath'.

Icon Villa (Map pp122-3; ☎ 41669766; www.icon-ysf.com; F-75 Poorvi Marg, Vasant Vihar; d incl breakfast Rs6000; ✷ ▯) Especially good for long-term stayers, Icon is in an elite suburb, southwest of the centre, and has 15 well-presented rooms, with writing desks, TVs, and marble floors. Ask for one with a balcony.

Amarya Haveli (Map pp122-3; ☎ 41759267; www.amaryagroup.com; P5 Hauz Khas Enclave; s/d Rs6100/6500; ✷ ▯) The French owners of Amarya Haveli have created a haven in Hauz Khas, a boutique place that is funkily furnished with Indian artefacts and textiles. Chef on duty 24 hours.

Bnineteen (Map pp126-7; ☎ 41825500; www.bnineteen.com; B-19 Nizamuddin East; d from Rs6750; ✷ ▯) Secluded, and located in fascinating Nizamuddin East, with fabulous views over Humayun's tomb from the rooftop, this place shows an architect's touch. The rooms are spacious and cool, and great for long stayers, with a state-of-the-art shared kitchen on each floor. But what promises to be spectacular is the (pricier) rooftop suite, with views over the tomb, including from the steam bath.

The Manor (Map pp122-3; ☎ 26925151; www.themanordelhi.com; 77 Friends Colony (West); d incl breakfast from Rs7500; ✷ ▯) If you're looking for a more intimate alternative to Delhi's opulent five stars, this 16-room boutique hotel is it. Off Mathura Rd, set amid manicured lawns, the renovated bungalow combines contemporary luxury with caramel-hued elegance that seems from another era. A classy restaurant, lush lawns and a sun-warmed terrace complete the picture.

Amarya Garden (Map pp122-3; ☎ 41759267; D-179 Defence Colony; s/d from Rs7750/8200) Owned by Amarya Haveli, this is a more minimalist, even-more-chic, four-room option. Chef on duty 24 hours.

Icon Towers (Map pp122-3; ☎ 46016611; www.icon-ysf.com; 46 Paschimi Marg, Vasant Vihar; s/d incl breakfast Rs8500/9000, ste Rs9000; ✷ ▯) Close to Icon Villa, sister-property Icon Towers is popular with business travellers for its swish, masculine rooms, with gleaming white linen, and all mod cons.

Connaught (Map p130; ☎ 23742842; www.theconnaughtnewdelhi.com; 37 Shaheed Bhagat Singh Marg; d incl breakfast Rs9000; ✷ ▯) This 79-room hotel has had a thorough revamp: rooms are decorated in designer oriental style, featuring white with strong colours, Chinese silks, and genuine flair. A couple of extra Rs1000s buys you a lot more space.

Sunder Nagar

Posh Sunder Nagar has a clutch of comfortable guest houses, all on Map pp126–7.

Maharani Guest House (☎ 24359521; www.mymaharani.com; 3 Sunder Nagar; s/d Rs3000/3600; ✷) Maharani's 24 rooms are comfortable enough, but a bit tired and drab. However, the price is competitive for this area.

La Sagrita (☎ 24358572; www.lasagrita.com; 14 Sunder Nagar; s/d Rs3690/4090; ✂ 🖳) The soothing garden gets kudos, but the standard rooms won't warrant a postcard home.

our pick Devna (☎ 24355047; www.newdelhiboutique inns.com; 10 Sunder Nagar; d Rs6500; ✂) Fronted by a pretty garden, Devna is one of Delhi's most charismatic choices, with four, pretty, curio- and antique-furnished rooms. Those opening onto the terrace upstairs are the best.

Shervani (☎ 42501000; www.shervanihotels.com; 11 Sunder Nagar; s/d incl breakfast Rs8000/9000; ✂ 🖳) Sleek Shervani is Sunder Nagar's smartest place to stay. The rooms have parquet wooden floors, LCD TVs, cocoa-brown furniture, electronic safes, tea-and-coffee-making facilities and fridges. A 20% discount is offered fairly readily.

AIRPORT AREA

New Delhi Bed & Breakfast (Map pp122-3; ☎ 2689 4812; www.newdelhibedandbreakfast.com; C8/8225 Vasant Kunj; s/d Rs3000/3500; 🖳) Renu Dayal's welcoming homestay has two cosy double rooms (one ensuite) in her elegant house in a leafy enclave, only 10 minutes drive from the airport. Beds are big and comfy, and there's a welcoming, homey atmosphere, plus Dougie the dog.

Top End

Maidens Hotel (off Map p132; ☎ 23975464; www.maidens hotel.com; Sham Nath Marg; d from US$245; ✂ 🖳 🍴) Set in a 3.2-hectare garden, Maidens is a graceful wedding cake, built in 1903. Lutyens stayed here while supervising the building of New Delhi. The high-ceilinged rooms are traditional, old-fashioned, well-equipped and some have good views.

ITC Maurya (off Map pp126-7; ☎ 26112233; www .starwoodhotels.com; Sardar Patel Marg; s/d US$340/370; ✂ 🖳 🍴) In the diplomatic enclave, this offers all creature comforts, and excellent service. There's an exclusive ladies'-only floor. Luxuriate in high thread counts, consult the in-house astrologer and dine at a clutch of sterling restaurants including award-winning Bukhara (see p149).

Le Meridien (Map pp126-7; ☎ 23710101; www.star woodhotels.com; Janpath; s/d US$360/380; ✂ 🖳 🍴) This glassy monolith has contemporary, comfort-packed rooms, styled in pale ochres and pearl-greys, kitted out with the usual five-star trappings: stuffed minibars, fluffy bathrobes and bathroom goodies.

Taj Mahal Hotel (Map pp126-7; ☎ 23026162; www .tajhotels.com; Man Singh Rd; s/d US$365/390; ✂ 🖳 🍴) The Taj pulls out all the stops, with highbrow Indian artwork, Persian rugs, glossy silk furnishings and manicured lawns. The luxuriously appointed rooms have all the five-star frills.

Shangri-La Hotel (Map pp126-7; ☎ 41191919; www .shangri-la.com; Ashoka Rd; s/d US$380/400; ✂ 🖳 🍴) This skyscraping Shangri-La is a place of sumptuous comfort and restrained design. Rooms are dark and masculine, with Oriental touches, cushion-laden beds covered in sugar-white sheets, and LCD TVs.

our pick Imperial (Map p130; ☎ 23341234; www.the imperialindia.com; Janpath; s/d US$425/480; ✂ 🖳 🍴) The inimitable, Raj-era Imperial marries Victorian colonial classicism with gilded art deco, houses an impressive collection of 17th- and 18th-century paintings, and has hosted everyone from princesses to pop stars. The high-ceilinged rooms have it all, from French linen and puffy pillows, to marble baths and finely-crafted furniture. The Spice Route restaurant has real wow-factor – with a wooden temple-style interior – though the Thai food isn't quite as stunning.

Other five-star beauties:

Park (Map p130; ☎ 23744000; www.theparkhotels .com; 15 Parliament St; s/d US$300/340; ✂ 🖳 🍴) Conran-designed, large-scale boutique hotel that has a smashing spa.

Oberoi (Map pp126-7; ☎ 24363030; www.oberoi hotels.com; Dr Zakir Hussain Marg; s/d US$380/410; ✂ 🖳 🍴) Superlative, contemporary rooms with views over Humayun's tomb, the pool or golf course.

AIRPORT AREA

Radisson Hotel (Map pp122-3; ☎ 26779191; www .radisson.com/newdelhiin; National Hwy 8; s/d US$345/365; ✂ 🖳 🍴) Radisson's rooms are business-hotel comfortable. But oh, what a joy to lie down on soft linen and orthopaedic beds after a long-haul flight. On site are Chinese, kebab and Italian restaurants.

EATING

Delhiites love to eat, and visitors will find plenty of delicious options, ranging from ramshackle stalls serving delicious kebabs to top-of-the-range temples of excellence.

Travellers pining for the familiar will find ever-multiplying fast-food chains.

Most midrange and all upmarket restaurants charge a service tax of around 10%,

---

MMMM... DILLI KI CHAAT!

Dilli ki chaat is the catch-all term for Delhi's epicurean street food – snacks that manage to combine a symphony of flavours in one bite. The word *chaat* is thought to come from the Hindi *chatpata* ('tangy') or from *chat* ('to lick'). For more on *chaat*, check out fabulous foodie **Culiblog** (http://culiblog.org/?s=chaat).

We asked *chaat*-loving local entrepreneur Srishti Bajaj for her top tips:

'My favourites are the crispy *chaat papdi* (fried wafers loaded with potatoes, chickpeas, yoghurt and chilli), hot *aloo chaat* (spicy potatoes), spicy *bhel puri* (rice with onion) and the delectable *golgappas* (fried hollow dough filled with spicy potatoes and chickpeas). Not all of them originate from Delhi, but they're very popular. Green mint and tamarind sauces are a must!'

Chaat central is Old Delhi (try **Haldiram's**, below), but also try the **Bengali Sweet House** (Map p149) at Bengali Market near Connaught Place, **Angam** (Map pp122–3), in Karol Bagh, or **Nathu's** (see p150) at Bengali Market and Sunder Nagar.

---

while drinks taxes can suck a further 20% (alcoholic) or 12.5% (nonalcoholic) from your moneybelt. Taxes haven't been included in this chapter unless indicated.

Telephone numbers have been provided for restaurants where reservations are recommended, especially at weekends.

North Delhi

OLD DELHI

The following eateries are featured on Map p132.

Restaurants

Al-Jawahar (mains Rs35-120; ☯ 7am-midnight) Next door to Karim's (see below) and serves similar, cheaper, if less-legendary fare. You can watch the naans being deftly made at the front of the shop.

Haldiram's (Chandni Chowk; mains Rs42-94; ☯ 9.30am-10.30pm) With a clean, bright cafe-restaurant upstairs, this is a handy spot for a top-notch thali (Rs98) or some tasty South Indian cuisine. Downstairs is great for *namkin* (savouries) and *mithai* (sweets) on the dash. Try the *soan papadi* (flaky sweet with almond and pistachio).

Karim's Old Delhi (mains Rs45-180; ☯ 7am-midnight); Nizamuddin West (168/2 Jha House Basti) Down a lane across from the Jama Masjid's south gate (No 1), legendary Karim's has been delighting Delhiites with divine Mughlai cuisine since 1913. The chefs prepare brutally good (predominantly nonveg) fare: try the *burrah* (marinated mutton) kebab. During Ramadan it only opens after sunset.

Moti Mahal (☎ 23273661; 3704 Netaji Subhash Marg, Daryaganj; mains Rs110-235; ☯ noon-midnight) This faded, family-oriented restaurant has been wooing diners with its Indian food for some

six decades. It's famed for its butter chicken and dhal Makhani. There's live qawwali Wednesday to Monday (from 8pm).

Chor Bizarre (☎ 23273821; Hotel Broadway, 4/15 Asaf Ali Rd; mains Rs225-495; ☯ 7.30-10.30am, noon-3.30pm & 7.30-11.30pm) A dim-lit, atmospheric place, filled with eccentric clutter, Chor Bizarre (meaning 'thieves market') offers particularly delicious Kashmiri cuisine. It caters mainly to tourists, and also has folk dance displays from 7pm (Rs115 per person).

Quick Eats

Paratha Wali Gali (parathas Rs15-35) Head to this foodstall-lined (some with seating) lane off Chandni Chowk for delectable *parathas* (traditional flat bread) fresh off the *tawa* (hotplate). Stuffed varieties include *aloo* (potato), *mooli* (white radish), smashed pappadams and crushed *badam* (almond), all served with a splodge of tangy pickles.

Jalebiwala (Dariba Corner, Chandni Chowk; jalebis per kg Rs200) Calories schmalories! Century-old Jalebiwala does Delhi's – if not India's – finest *jalebis* (deep-fried 'squiggles'), so pig out and worry about your waistline tomorrow. Luring everyone from taxi-wallahs to Bollywood stars, you'll quickly see what all the fuss is about once you've taken your first crunchy-yet-oh-so-syrupy bite.

Ghantewala (Chandni Chowk; mithai per kg from Rs220) Delhi's most famous sweetery, 'the bell ringer' has been churning out *mithai* (Indian sweets) since 1790. Try some *sohan halwa* (ghee-dipped gram flour biscuits).

PAHARGANJ AREA

Yielding wobbly results, Paharganj's menus are of the mix-it-up variety, serving anything from Israeli to Italian, Mughlai to Mexican. The eateries are nothing fancy but are they cheap and always abuzz with chattering travellers.

The following places are along, or just off, Main Bazaar (Map p142).

Madan Café (Main Bazaar; mains Rs20-45; 🕚 7am-11pm) Cash crisis? Tuck into a tasty thali for just Rs30 at this basic veg cafe; outside tables are ideal for watching the human traffic. Facing is the similar Khosla Café.

Sonu Chat House (Main Bazaar; mains Rs20-70; 🕚 8am-1am) A dhaba-style, basic dive, this serves reasonable South Indian fare – as well as thalis, Chinese and continental dishes.

Kitchen Café (Hotel Shelton, 5043 Main Bazaar; mains Rs35-120; 🕚 8am-11.30pm) This cane-furnished, plant-strewn rooftop restaurant is a relaxing place to kill time over the usual world-ranging menu.

Malhotra (1833 Laxmi Narayan St; mains Rs35-360; 🕚 7am-11pm) Snug, smartish Malhotra offers tasty Indian, continental and Chinese food that keeps it busy with a mix of locals and backpackers. Next door is Malhotra's southern sister, Malhotra's Dosa Please, with dosas from Rs35.

Diamond Restaurant (Main Bazaar; mains Rs50-260; 🕚 7.30am-11.30pm) Candy-striped Diamond has a huge menu for such a pint-sized locale, with some good pasta dishes.

Tadka (4986 Ram Dwara Rd; mains Rs65-120; 🕚 noon-11pm) Nothing flash, but good for Paharganj: a simple, clean and tasty pure veg restaurant. Try the *saag paneer* (spinach and cottage cheese) and Tadka dhal.

Sam's Café (Vivek Hotel, 1534-1550 Main Bazaar; mains Rs70-165; 🕚 8am-11pm) On Vivek Hotel's ground floor and (more atmospheric) rooftop, Sam's does cracking breakfasts and is a tranquil place to hang; usually packed with travellers. The pizzas are a good bet.

Metropolis Restaurant & Bar (Metropolis Tourist Home, 1634 Main Bazaar; mains Rs125-390; 🕚 8am-11pm) On a rooftop, this crammed, humming travellers' haunt has a more adventurous menu than many in Paharganj, and is the most upmarket in the area, with dishes ranging from chicken wrapped in bacon to sushi (!).

KAROL BAGH
Quick Eats
Angan (Map pp122-3; Chowk Gurudwara Rd; mains Rs60-125) A small but buzzing canteen-style pitstop for Indian and South Indian food, plus yummy

snacks (try the *chana bhatura* – spicy chickpeas with fried Indian bread).

Roshan di Kulfi (Map pp122-3; Gafal Market, Ajmal Khan Rd; kulfi Rs42) This little place is a Delhi institution for its scrumptious *kulfi* (pistachio, cardamom or saffron-flavoured frozen milk dessert). Also has good *golgappas* and lassi.

New Delhi & Around
CONNAUGHT PLACE AREA
The following eateries appear on Map p130 unless otherwise stated.

Restaurants
our pick **Saravana Bhavan** Janpath (46 Janpath; mains Rs47-82; 🕚 8am-11pm); Connaught Place (15 P-Block); Karol Bagh (Map pp122-3; 8/54 Desh Bandhu Gupta Rd; mains Rs47-82; 🕚 8am-11pm) Massively popular, Tamil Saravana has a fast-food feel, but food is by no means junk: dosas, *idlis* and other southern specialities, accompanied by lovely fresh chutneys. Inventive sweets include cucumber-seed *ladoos* (sweet balls). Finish with a South Indian coffee. Arrive early or queue!

Sagar Ratna (15 K-Block; dosas Rs55-75; 🕚 8am-11pm) Another dosa dreamland, with expertly prepared dosas, *idlis*, *uttapams* (savoury rice pancakes) and other smashing southern goodies, plus thalis.

Andhra Bhawan Canteen (Map pp126-7; 1 Ashoka Rd; veg thalis Rs60; 🕚 8.30-10.30am, noon-3pm & 7.30-10.30pm) A bargain: tasty unlimited South Indian thalis at cheap-as-chips prices; non veg is also available. It's canteen-style and hugely popular.

Berco's (26 G-Block; mains Rs125-395; 🕚 12.30-11pm) With white and black booths, and moody lighting, Berco's buzzes with Delhiites digging into its flavoursome Indianised Chinese cuisine. There's a lounge bar upstairs, which should be licensed by the time you read this.

Parikrama (23721616; 22 Kasturba Gandhi Marg; mains Rs150-470; 🕚 12.30-11pm) Identify landmarks through the haze from this fun revolving 24th-floor restaurant, where you can dine on Indian and Chinese food while spinning oh-so-slowly (one revolution takes 1½ hours).

Rajdhani (1/90 P-Block; thalis Rs215, Sat & Sun Rs253 unlimited; 🕚 noon-3.30pm & 7-11pm) Opposite PVR Rivoli Cinema, this pristine, nicely decorated place serves up excellent-value delicious vegetarian Gujarati thalis, including some Rajasthani dishes, to grateful local and foreign punters.

The Chinese (65398888; 14/15 F-Block; mains Rs235-1195; 🕚 12.30-11.30pm) Popular with Chinese diplomats, here the Hunan chef serves up authentic cuisine, such as Hunan smoked lamb or *gong boa ji ding* (chicken with onion, chilli, peanut and hot garlic sauce) in a wow-factor tentlike interior, decorated with calligraphy.

United Coffee House (15 E-Block; mains Rs245-475; 🕚 11am-11pm) Oozing old-world charm, this classic 1940s restaurant – all chandeliers and flock – is a splendid spot to slow the pace. Popular with travellers and Delhi denizens alike, it has a long menu covering everything from pizza to *paneer* (cottage cheese). Try the butter chicken. It's great for an afternoon drink too.

Zen (25 B-Block; mains Rs269-595; 🕚 11am-11.30pm) A high-ceilinged place with a dash of old-style glitz – walls quilted like a Chanel handbag – this has a venerable Chinese menu, including tasty dishes such as crispy sesame lamb and Szechwan prawns, with a few Japanese and Thai cameos.

Véda (☎ 41513535; 27 H-Block; mains Rs291-651; 🕚 noon-midnight) Head here for atmosphere: fashion designer Rohi Bal created this sumptuous interior – dim red lighting, neo-Murano chandeliers, and twisted gold-a-go-go. Mughlai and North-West Frontier specialities are on the menu (try the tandoori grilled lamb chops or the Parsi sea bass). It's popular with foreign tourists, and a DJ plays (loudly) in the lounge bar. They also do a mean margharita.

Legends of India (55 N-Block; mains Rs325-645; 🕚 11am-11.45pm) A smart restaurant selling upmarket *chaat* (try the delectable *aloo chaat*), and tasty Mughlai cuisine. Upstairs is its lounge bar, the Tea Cup, good for a smart cuppa (Assam Golden Tips, etc, is prepared on a tea trolley in front of you) or a Kingfisher beer (Rs109). There's a small terrace.

Also recommended:

Banana Leaf (12 N-Block; dosas Rs55-95; thalis Rs105; 🕚 11am-11pm) Reasonable South Indian standards in this popular low-lit basement.

Embassy (11 D-Block; mains Rs90-300; 🕚 11am-midnight) A long-time favourite, gracious and old-fashioned, featuring Indian and continental creations.

Ruby Tuesday (48 M-Block; mains Rs235-695; 🕚 11am-midnight) American and Tex-Mex food served in a comfy bistro-style setting. Try the awesome ribs and the chocolate tallcake.

Zâffran (☎ 43582610; Hotel Palace Heights , 26-28 D-Block; Rs100-700; 🕚 noon-3.30pm & 7pm-midnight) An excellent restaurant serving Mughlai cuisine and designed to feel like an airy terrace.

Quick Eats

Nirula's (14 K-Block Connaught Place) Drop into Nirula's for its hot chocolate fudge icecream, every Delhiite's favoured flavour.

Wenger's (16 A-Block; cakes/sandwiches Rs33/50) Legendary Wenger's has been baking since 1926 – its convoluted purchasing procedure certainly harks back to ye olde days! But the rigmarole is worth it, with a great array of sweet and savoury treats, including perfect patties.

Bengali Sweet House (Map pp122-3; 27-37 Bengali Market) Bengali Market is famous for its sweets and *chaat* (try the *golgappas*), but this Delhi landmark offers dosas and thalis too.

our pick **Nizam's Kathi Kabab** (5 H-Block; kebabs Rs50-150) This takeaway eatery has some seating and creates masterful kebabs and *kathi* rolls (kebab wrapped in paratha bread).

DIPLOMATIC ENCLAVE & CHANAKYAPURI AREA

Fujiya (Map pp126-7; 12/48 Malcha Marg Market; mains Rs110-360; 🕚 noon-midnight) Reliable, intimate Fujiya, decorated by Japanese paintings, has a Chinese menu laced with Japanese dishes, featuring everything from Peking lamb to Sukiyaki pork.

Bukhara (off Map pp126-7; ☎ 26112233; ITC Maurya, Sadar Patel Marg; mains Rs495-695; 🕚 12.30-2.45pm & 7-11.45pm; 🗙) Considered Delhi's best restaurant, serving Northwest Frontier–style cuisine. Its tandoor and dhal are particularly renowned. Apparently Bill Clinton ate here four times in a row. Reservations are essential (taken between 7pm and 8pm).

Olive Beach (Map pp126-7; Hotel Diplomat, 9 Sardar Patel Marg, Chanakyapuri; mains Rs495-1050; 🕚 noon-12.30pm) Uber-chic, this is decorated in rustic beach-house style, and is one of Delhi's dining hotspots. The Italian chef cooks handmade pasta and pizzas – as tasty as the clientele.

Dhaba (The Claridges, Chanakyapuri, 12 Aurangzeb Rd; mains around Rs500; 🕚 12.30-2.45pm & 7.30-11.30pm) If you prefer something more Indian than Sevilla, Claridge's also has this fun place, with kitsch 'roadside' decor and upmarket highway Punjabi cuisine (try the balti meat and fish or chicken tikka).

Sevilla (Map pp126-7; ☎ 41335082; The Claridges, Chanakyapuri, 12 Aurangzeb Rd; mains Rs625-1550; 🕚 7.30pm-12.30am) Planning to propose? Sevilla brings on the romance, with tables (some in AC huts) shaded by gauzey curtains, set in a landscaped candlelit garden. Food is Spanish-Italian, with delectable tapas.

LODI COLONY & PANDARA MARKET

The eateries below feature on Map pp126–7.

All American Diner (India Habitat Centre, Lodi Rd; mains Rs110-265; 7am-midnight) Make like it's 1950s USA and head down to the cherry-red booths and bar stools of the All American, to eat stars-and-stripes classics, from buttermilk pancakes to hot dogs, and work the jukebox. Or try the Habitat's cheap-and-cheerful food court Eatopia, with good *chaat*, Chinese and Indian food.

Lodi Garden Restaurant (Lodi Rd; mains Rs325-825; 11.30am-3.30pm & 6-11.30pm) A greenery-shaded haven beside lovely Lodi Garden: the menu and clientele are remarkably non-Indian, but it's good for Mediterranean and Lebanese cuisine (think steamed octopus, sesame prawns and mezze). They do brunch at weekends, and there's regular live music.

Pandara Market has a little horseshoe of restaurants, most open daily from noon to midnight, they include:

Pindi (mains Rs120-350) Serving tasty Punjabi food since 1948 – try the butter chicken, kashmiri kebab and *shahi paneer* (cottage cheese in rich cashew sauce).

Gulati (mains Rs140-450) A North Indian focus amid beige-and-mirrored decor; try the *tangri kebab* (charcoal-grilled chicken drumsticks) and *dum aloo* (stuffed potatoes).

Chicken Inn (mains Rs150-410) Flasher than the name suggests, and a popular choice for Indian and Chinese.

Havemore (mains Rs160-380) A snug, smartish spot, serving Indian food with a venerable veg selection.

South Delhi

KHAN & SUNDER NAGAR MARKETS

If you're shopping at the Khan or Sunder Nagar Markets, there are some great places to top up your tank.

The Kitchen (Map pp126-7; 41757960; Khan Market; mains Rs160-385; 11am-11pm) A buzzing, small, backstreet all-rounder, simply and chicly decorated, this offers tasty dishes such as Thai red curry with rice, yummy *pad thai* and fine fish and chips.

Baci (Map pp126-7; 41507445; Sunder Nagar Market; mains Rs175-450; 12.30-11.45pm, to 1am Thu, to 2am Sat) Reasonable Italian cuisine and good coffee is served up here in grown-up surroundings, either at the informal cafe or in the sleek upstairs restaurant. On Thursday and Saturday evenings, there's a DJ and even dancing.

Sidewok (Map pp126-7; 46068122; Khan Market; mains Rs175-595; noon-11.30pm) Sleek Sidewok (slowly) serves up tasty pan-Asian cuisine,

amid dark slatted wood and Japanese minimalism. Try the delicious Vietnamese spring rolls.

Quick Eats

Khan Chacha (Map pp126-7; Khan Market; snacks Rs30-70; noon-10pm Sat-Thu) This backstreet hole-in-the-wall kebab joint is so popular you'll probably have to queue – the roti-wrapped mutton/chicken/paneer is worth the wait.

Nathu's Sunder Nagar (Map pp126-7; Sunder Nagar Market; mains Rs35-70; 8.30am-11pm); Connaught Place (Map pp122-3; 23-25 Bengali Market) Famous sweeterie serving up yummy *chaat* (snacks), *namkin* (savouries) and *mithai* (sweets), plus good thalis (Rs58 to Rs85). Has a fairylit outdoor terrace.

HAUZ KHAS AREA

Naivedyam (Map pp122-3; 26960426; 1 Hauz Khas Village; dishes Rs30-80; 11am-11pm) A smashing South Indian restaurant with a temple-like feel, lined in dark wood with gold trimmings. The food's good too; king of them all is the *tangam paper masala dosai* (pancake stuffed with spiced potatoes). Finish with divine filter coffee.

Park Baluchi (Map pp122-3; 26859369; Hauz Khas Village; mains Rs150-550; noon-midnight) Although service gets the thumbs down, this enchanting, greenery-surrounded restaurant, set in the Deer Park, offers unusual barbecue dishes, such as *banarasi seekh kabab* (minced vegetables and cheese) or *murg potli* (flambéed marinated chicken breast and minced mutton). Avoid weekends if squealing kiddies get your goat.

VASANT VIHAR

Restaurants

Tamura (Map pp122-3; 26154082; D-Block Market; mains Rs300-640; noon-3pm & 6.30-10pm) Curried out? Tamura – armed with a Japanese chef – creates an authentic yet affordable repertoire in serene, bamboo-decorated surroundings, from prawn tempura to sashimi. Reserve a downstairs table.

Punjabi by Nature (Map pp122-3; 41516666; Basant Lok complex; mains Rs425-645; 12.30pm-midnight) Served amid glass raindrops and murals of turbaned men, this place offers ravishingly delicious Punjabi food; mop up flavour-packed sauces with *rumali roti* (paper-thin chapatis) or thick garlic naan. Go on, try the vodka *golgappas*!

Quick Eats

Sugar & Spice Vasant Vihar (Map pp122-3; Basant Lok complex; sandwiches/cakes Rs60/30); Khan Market (Map pp126-7). Takeaway cakes and savoury snacks: the apple strudel, tandoori chicken sandwiches and walnut tarts are recommended, but the desert-dry croissants and doughnuts are not.

Arabian Nites (Map pp122-3; 59 Basant Lok complex; snacks Rs60-295; ☽ 10.30am-11pm) This teeny takeaway (there are a few inside seats) does mighty good chicken shawarma.

EAST OF KAILASH

Govinda's (Map pp122-3; Hare Krishna Iskcon temple complex, East of Kailash; buffet Rs270; ☽ 12.30-3.30pm & 7-10pm) Govinda's pure-veg (no onion or garlic) buffet includes choices of soup, drinks, four veg dishes, two dhals, breads, rice, condiments and deserts; the menu changes daily.

GREATER KAILASH I

Moti Mahal (Map pp122-3; 30 M-Block; mains Rs130-410; ☽ 12.15-3.15pm & 7pm-midnight Wed-Mon) Over at M-Block, there's this place, smarter than the Old Delhi original (see p147), and popular with well-off families for its North Indian and Mughlai cooking.

Kasbah (Map pp122-3; 2 N-Block; ☽ 12.30-3.30pm & 7.30-11pm) This complex is a popular expat and local haunt. Zäffrän (mains Rs160 to Rs300) is enclosed, but feels like an open-air terrace shaded by slatted blinds, and is popular for its tasty Mughlai food. Then, for impressive French cuisine try the serene Café de Paris (mains Rs350 to Rs800), or, if you feel more like some Italian tucker there's decent, palely elegant Spago (mains Rs300 to Rs750).

GREATER KAILASH II

Not Just Parathas (Map pp122-3; 84 M-Block; parathas Rs54-265; ☽ noon-midnight) Yes, this cheery place offers not just parathas, but with 120 types, you have gotta go for the speciality, be they Tawa-fried, roasted tandoori, or low-calorie (wholemeal, olive-oil smothered). Stuffings include *palak* (spinach), chicken tikka and *aloo gobi* (potato and cauliflower), to name a few.

China Garden (Map pp122-3; ☎ 29223456; 73 M-Block; mains Rs250-700; ☽ 12.30-3.30pm & 7.30-11.30pm) Spread over three levels, this slinky, ornate (think jade and waterfalls) Chinese restaurant does sensational garlicky prawns. There's a champagne bar at ground level, where Indian champagne (Kingfisher) costs Rs200.

Diva (Map pp122-3; ☎ 29215673; M-Block; mains Rs390-925; ☽ 12.30-3.30pm & 7.30pm-1am) Chef Ritu Dalmia's *molto chic* Italian restaurant is an intimate space on two levels, with white tablecloths, plateglass windows, and a wood-fired oven behind glass. Cooking is superlative, imaginative and delicious. *Avanti!*

ourpick Smokehouse Grill (Map pp122-3; ☎ 41435530; 2 VIPPS Center, LSC Masjid Moth; mains around Rs590; ☽ 6pm-midnight) Another uber-hip hangout, suffused in minimalist chic, with lots of good, smoked(!) food on the menu. From smoked melon mojitos to smoked tomato and lemongrass broth, it's all excellent. Leave room for the divine chocolate soufflé.

DEFENCE COLONY AREA

Sagar (Map pp122-3; 18 Defence Colony Market; dosas Rs48-75; ☽ 8am-10.30pm) You might have to queue for Sagar's delectable dosas, irresistible *idlis* and other authentic South Indian specialities.

Flavors (Map pp122-3; 49-54C Moolchand Flyover Market, Ring Rd; mains Rs230-450; ☽ 12.30am-11.30pm) Italian-run Flavors is a chic little haven, fronted by lawns and greenery, with some outdoor wrought-iron chairs and tables. Inside is simply decorated, with diners gleefully tucking into pasta, risotto, and wood-fired pizzas. Desserts are good too.

Ego Thai (Map pp122-3; Community Centre, New Friends Colony; mains Rs275-500; ☽ 12.30-3.30pm & 7.30-11.30pm) Lined in carved, painted wood, this is one of Delhi's tastiest Thai restaurants (upstairs has the most atmosphere). Curries are good, as is the *pad thai*. Adjoining is the loungey Ego Lounge bar.

Swagath (Map pp122-3; Defence Colony Market; mains Rs185-725; ☽ 11am-11.45pm) Supremely scrumptious Indian fare with a focus on Mangalorean and Chettinad cuisine (especially seafood), this smart six-floor restaurant swarms with well-heeled locals, here for the excellent *dhal-e-Swagath* (lentil curry), chicken *gassi* (coconut-based curry) and similarly satiating dishes.

DRINKING

Whether it's espresso and croissants for breakfast, or beer and burgers for supper, Delhi's cool cafes and buzzing bars deliver.

Cafes

Caffeine addicts won't lack for a *real* cup of coffee, thanks to Delhi's cafe scene, where cappuccinos and lattes are all the rage. And tea lovers panic not: menus flaunt everything from Earl Grey to Russian Caravan.

Barista Connaught Place (Map p130; 16 N-Block; coffee Rs50-80; ☺ 9pm-1am); Khan Market (Map pp126-7; South Extension Part I (Map pp122-3); Defence Colony Market (Map pp122-3). Barista is a sleek coffee bar chain, with tip-top coffee and tea, though the snacks are unexciting.

Costa (Map p130; L-Block, Connaught Place, Greater Kailash II; coffee Rs25-119; ☺ 9am-11.30pm) One of the best of the coffee chains, a dapper downtown cafe, with strong coffee, delicate teas, English-toffee milkshakes, and good cakes.

Cha Bar (Map p130; Oxford Bookstore, Statesman House, 148 Barakhamba Rd; snacks Rs50-120; ☺ 10am-7.30pm Mon-Sat, noon-7.30pm Sun) After browsing at the Oxford, pop into Cha for a tea with a view (over CP). There are over 75 flavours to choose from, and the blueberry muffins are fab too.

Open Hand Cafe (Map p142; Main Bazaar; snacks Rs45-105; ☺ 7.30am-11.30pm) Bringing a rare touch of class to Paharganj, this South African–owned cafe has a chic, arty feel, sculptural chairs, good coffee and yummy cheesecake.

Club India (Map p142; 2nd fl, 6 Toothi Chowk; mains Rs50-275; ☺ 8am-11pm) With plate-glass windows overlooking the mayhem of the chowk, plus a little roof terrace upstairs it's perfect for lingering over a drink or a snack, including Japanese tempura and noodles.

Café Coffee Day Connaught Place (Map p130; 11 N-Block, Connaught Place; coffee Rs50-112; ☺ 9am-midnight); Khan Market (Map pp126-7). A fine place to loll and natter over endless cups of hot brew and brownies. The icy granitas will quench even the most savage summer thirst. There are citywide branches galore.

Café Turtle Greater Kailash Part I (Map pp122-3; 8 N-Block); Khan Market (Map pp126-7; 2nd fl, Full Circle Bookstore, Khan Market; mains Rs165-300; ☺ 10am-9.30pm) The Turtle is expat heaven for its fine fare, slinky background jazz and little terrace. This bookish, boho cafe ticks all the boxes when you're in the mood for coffee and gateau (the 'gooey chocolate cake' is a triumph). Food ranges from Lucknow mint wraps to bucatini with arrabiata.

Big Chill (Map pp126-7; Khan Market; mains Rs160-450; ☺ noon-11.30pm) Khan Market has two film-poster-lined branches of BC, packed with chattering, well-manicured folk. The menu is a telephone directory of continental, Indian and other dishes. Have you ever seen so much cheesecake on a menu? Who's to quibble when it's this good?

Bars & Nightclubs

Most Delhi bars double up as both restaurants and nightclubs. The scene might not be huge, but it's happening, and as the sun goes down, the party starts, particularly from Wednesday to Saturday night. Be warned that most bars seriously pump up the music anytime after 8pm. A smart-casual dress code (no shorts, singlet tops or flip-flops) applies at most places.

The fancier bars are overflowing with domestic and foreign booze, but the taxes can pack a nasty punch (alcoholic/nonalcoholic 20%/12.5%; taxes aren't included here unless stated).

Many bars, particularly around Connaught Place, have two-for-one happy hours from around noon till 8pm.

PAHARGANJ

The following are on Map p142.

Gem (De Gem; Main Bazaar) In this dark, wood-panelled dive, a Kingfisher costs a bargain Rs78 (including tax). Downstairs you can catch a cricket match on the wide-screen TV, while upstairs has more atmosphere. The snacks are good too.

Metropolis Restaurant & Bar (Metropolis Tourist Home, 1634 Main Bazaar) This hotel's rooftop restaurant (p147) is pricier than the above, but it has more choice and pizzazz.

CONNAUGHT PLACE AREA

The following venues are located on Map p130, and most have happy hours during the daytime.

All Sports Bar (Regal Bldg; ☺ noon-1am) An ideal hangout for the 2010 Commonwealth Games. The only way you could be sportier is by competing. There are disorienting multiscreens, table football (Rs50), a pool table (Rs100), a canoe, and shiny trophies. It's all cheery and bright, with a cheesy soundtrack, and possibly CP's cheapest beers (Kingfisher Rs125).

Regent's Blues (18 N-Block; ☺ noon-midnight) A dark den with reasonably priced beers (Kingfisher Rs155). With brick walls plastered with the likes of Jimi Hendrix and other less-recognisable figures, and a cheerily unhip soundtrack (think Sonny and Cher) gritty RB is a lively, snob-free zone.

Rodeo (12 A-Block; ☺ noon-midnight) In the mood for saloon doors, tequila (Rs225), saddle barstools and staff in cowboy hats? Then easygoing Rodeo is for you, partner. But give the nachos a miss.

our pick @live (12 K-Block; mains Rs175-450; ☽ noon-1am) Intimate and smart without being formal, @live has a cool gimmick: a live jukebox. The Malaysian band plays from 8.30pm, and there's a song menu, so you choose the songs, from a list including the Beejees, Bob Dylan and Sir Cliff. The band mightn't be the most dynamic you've seen, but they're great, and it's a fun, chilled night out (food's good too). A Kingfisher costs Rs175.

Q'BA (1st fl, 42 E-Block; mains Rs135-1100; ☽ noon-midnight) Connaught Place's swishest watering hole has a Q-shaped bar, dim lighting, leather chairs and inviting Chesterfield sofas. Upstairs is the fine dining restaurant (from 7pm), and there's a roof terrace, ideal on sultry evenings. Cocktails cost around Rs350.

1911 (Imperial Hotel, Janpath; ☽ noon-12.45am) Named after the year in which Delhi was proclaimed British India's capital, this is the ultimate neo-colonial treat. Sip cocktails overlooked by oil-painted Maharajas (drinks Rs600 plus).

DIPLOMATIC ENCLAVE & CHANAKYAPURI AREA

F Bar & Lounge (Map pp126-7; Ashok Hotel, 50-B Chanakyapuri; ☽ 10am-3am) All black, with a light-studded bar: if you've cash to splash, dust off your Manolos and get in with the fash-pack – this of-the-moment place is owned by Fashion TV (ubiquitous on the LCD screens).

SOUTH DELHI

The following drinking venues are on Map pp122-3.

Shalom Greater Kailash I (18 N-Block; ☽ noon-1am); Vasant Vihar (4 D-Block) This loungey bar-restaurant, with wooden furniture and whitewashed walls, is one of the doyennes of the Delhi loungebar scene. As well as wine, beers, cocktails (around Rs400), and nightly DJs, there's top-notch Mediterranean fare.

Urban Pind (4 N-Block, Greater Kailash I; ☽ noon-1am) Three-floored, this has cushy flocked sofas, mock-Khajuraho carvings, and nightly DJs (Kingfisher Rs200). Nab a roof-terrace table. Tuesday is Salsa night, with free lessons from 9pm, while expats and diplomats flock here on a Thursday.

Lizard Lounge (1st fl, E5 South Extension Part II; ☽ noon-midnight) If you're in South Extension, slither down to Lizard for a revitalising drink and an apple-scented sheesha. There's hip hop, Bollywood, rock and retro on the decks.

our pick Haze (8 Basant Lok, Visant Vihar; ☽ 3pm-1am) A hip yet unpretentious haunt, this moody, intimate, inexpensive jazz bar has real soul and is *the* place to see live Indian blues and jazz at weekends.

ENTERTAINMENT
Cultural Programs

To access Delhi's dynamic arts scene, check local listings – *First City* (p121) is especially recommended. October and March is the 'season', with happenings (often free) nightly.

Dances of India (Map p132; ☎ 26234689; Parsi Anjuman Hall, Bahadur Shah Zafar Marg; Rs200; ☽ 7.30pm) A one-hour performance of regional dances that includes Bharata Natyam (Tamil dance), Kathakali, bhangra and Manipuri.

Habitat World (Map pp126-7; ☎ 43663333; www.habitatworld.com; India Habitat Centre, Lodi Rd) Check out the Visual Arts Gallery's excellent temporary exhibitions.

India International Centre (Map pp126-7; ☎ 24619431; 40 Max Mueller Marg)

Kamani Auditorium (Map pp126-7; ☎ 23388084; www.kamaniauditorium.org; Mandi House, Copernicus Marg)

Sangeet Natak Akademi (Map pp126-7; ☎ 23387246; www.sangeetnatak.org; Rabindra Bhavan, Copernicus Marg)

Shri Ram Centre (Map pp126-7; ☎ 23714307; www.shriramcenterart.org; 4 Safdar Hashmi Rd)

Triveni Kala Sangam (Map pp126-7; ☎ 23718833; 205 Tansen Marg)

Cinemas

Newspapers supply current movie listings; the following have online booking available at www.pvrcinemas.com and www.satyamcineplexes.com.

PVR Plaza Cinema (Map p130; ☎ 41516787; H-Block, Connaught Place)

PVR Priya Cinema (Map pp122-3; ☎ 41000461; Basant Lok complex, Vasant Vihar)

PVR Saket (Anupam 4) (Map pp122-3; ☎ 41671787; Saket Community Centre, Saket)

Satyam Cineplex (Map pp122-3; ☎ 25893322; Patel Rd, Patel Nagar)

SHOPPING

From bamboozling bazaars to bijiou boutiques, Delhi is a fantastic place to shop. There's an astounding array of wonderful stuff: handicrafts, textiles, clothing, carpets, jewellery, and a kaleidoscope of saris.

Away from the emporiums and other fixed-price shops, put on your haggle hat. Many taxi and autorickshaw drivers earn commissions (via your inflated purchase price), and may not take you to the most reputable stores either, making it best to decline their shopping suggestions.

For dependable art gallery recommendations (many of which sell exhibits), check *First City*.

Government & State Emporiums

Browse hassle-free at these fixed-price emporiums, which stock items from across the country. Although prices can be higher than elsewhere, you're assured of quality. It's sensible to scout here to get an idea of prices before hitting the markets.

Central Cottage Industries Emporium (Map p130; ☎ 23326790; Janpath; ☼ 10am-7pm) A multilevel Aladdin's cave of India-wide handicrafts: woodcarvings, silverware, jewellery, pottery, papier mâché, brassware, textiles (including shawls), beauty products and heaps more.

State Emporiums (Map p130; Baba Kharak Singh Marg; ☼ 10am-6.30pm Mon-Sat, may close for lunch 1.30-2.30pm) These neighbouring state government emporiums showcase products from different states, from Rajasthan to Kashmir. Set aside several hours for these fabulous shops.

Markets, Complexes & Shops

NORTH DELHI

Chandni Chowk (Map p132; Old Delhi; ☼ Mon-Sat) Pure pandemonium, this is the old city's famed shopping strip. Some stores open from around 10am to 7pm, others from noon to 9pm. Winding your way through the jumble of frenzied bazaars is a veritable assault on the senses (see the boxed text, p156).

New Gramophone House (Map p132; ☎ 23271524; Pleasure Garden Market, Chandni Chowk; ☼ 10am-9pm Mon-Sat) Look out for this place situated on Chandni Chowk, opposite Moti Cinema. It's a 1st-floor wonderland of vintage Bollywood records (Rs50 to Rs200) and even older gramophones.

Main Bazaar (Map p142; Paharganj; ☼ around 10am-9pm Tue-Sun) The backpacker-oriented spine of Paharganj is a great place to pick up bargain T-shirts, shawls, leatherware, costume jewellery, essential oil, incense, bindis and even bongs. Although officially closed on Monday, many shops remain open during the tourist season.

Karol Bagh Market (Map pp122-3; ☼ around 10am-7pm Tue-Sun) This middle-class market shimmers with all things sparkly, from dressy *lehanga*

choli (skirt and blouse sets) to princess-style shoes. Get spice-happy at Roopak's (6/9 Ajmal Khan Rd) two neighbouring shops with similar spices (around Rs60 to Rs100 per 100g and well packed). Their *namkin* (savoury nibbles) are ideal for long train journeys – the roasted green lentils are a healthy alternative to the mostly fried varieties.

CONNAUGHT PLACE

Janpath Market (Map p130; Janpath; ☼ 10.30am-7.30pm Mon-Sat) Aka the Tibetan Market, this touristy strip sells the usual trinkets: shimmering mirrorwork textiles, colourful shawls, brass oms, and dangly earrings and trinkets galore. It has some good finds if you rummage through the junk. Haggle hard.

Khadi Gramodyog Bhawan (Map p130; Regal Bldg, Sansad Marg; ☼ 10.30am-7.15pm Mon-Sat) Best known for its excellent *khadi* (homespun cloth) clothing, but also worth a visit for its handmade paper, incense, spices, henna and natural soaps.

Palika Bazaar (Map p130; Connaught Place; ☼ 11am-7.30pm Mon-Sat) A trashy bustling underground bazaar with all sorts of consumer goods (clothing, electronics, fake wristwatches, CDs etc) that are aimed at Delhi's middle class. Bargain hard.

People Tree (Map p130; Regal Bldg, Sansad Marg; ☼ 10.30am-7pm Mon-Sat) The blink-and-you'll-miss-it People Tree sells cool, etching-style T-shirts, many featuring Indian gods, as well as skirts, dresses, shirts (for men and women), shoulder bags, costume jewellery and books.

Soma (Map p130; 1st fl, 44 K-Block, Connaught Place; ☼ 10am-8pm) Opposite PVR Plaza Cinema, 1st-floor Soma has brilliant block-printed textiles: anything from scarves to pyjamas, cushion covers to children's clothing.

SOUTH DELHI

Ansal Plaza (Map pp122-3; Khel Gaon Marg; ☼ 11am-8.30pm) A modern shopping mall geared towards well-to-do locals, with shops selling the usual designer-clothes suspects, and some costume jewellery and upper-end saris. It contains Geoffreys, an appealing English-style pub.

Dilli Haat (Map pp122-3; Aurobindo Marg; admission Rs15; ☼ 10.30am-10pm) Located opposite the colourful INA Market, this open-air food-and-crafts market sells regional handicrafts; bargain hard. Tasty on-site food stalls cook up regionally diverse cuisine. Avoid the busy weekends.

Greater Kailash I: M-Block & N-Block Markets (Map pp122-3; Greater Kailash I; Wed-Mon) A two-part upmarket shopping enclave best known for the awesome mothership of Fabindia (see below). Also check out clothes store Anokhi (N-Block).

Fabindia GKI (Map pp122-3; www.fabindia.com; 7 N-Block Market; 10am to 7.30pm); Khan Market (Map pp126-7; Above shop 20 & 21); Connaught Place (Map p130; Upper Ground fl, 28 B-Block) Readymade clothes that won't look odd back home, plus great home furnishings.

Nalli Silk Sarees Greater Kailash (Map pp122-3; 24629926; Greater Kailash II; 10am-8.30pm); Connaught Place (Map p130; 7/90 P-Block) In GK, this venerable sari emporium has four floors of silk varieties, specialising in those from South India. Prices range from Rs1000 to Rs30,000. CP has two floors.

Hauz Khas Village (Map pp122-3; 11am-7pm Mon-Sat) This arty little enclave is packed with designer Indian-clothing boutiques, art galleries and furniture shops. It's a great place to find superb old Bollywood posters. Try Country Collection for antique and new furniture (they'll post overseas), and Cotton Curios for handprinted kameez, and soft furnishings.

C.Lal & Sons (Map pp126-7; 9/172 Jor Bagh Market; 10.30am-7.30pm) After sightseeing at Safdarjang's tomb, drop into kindly Mr Lal's 'curiosity shop'. Much loved by Delhi-based diplomats for its dazzling Christmas-tree decorations, it also sells competitively priced handicrafts such as papier mâché, tiles, and carvings.

Khan Market (Map pp126-7; around 10.45am-7.30pm Mon-Sat) Favoured by expats and Delhi's elite, the boutiques in this enclave are devoted to fashion (including tailoring), books, sunglasses, homeware and accessories. This is the place to find gourmet groceries, from Australian grapefruit to Italian pesto. Avoid Saturday when the crowds can be exasperating. For handmade paperware (cards, diaries, photo albums etc) check out Anand Stationers. There's a tardis-like branch of Fabindia (above), Anokhi and the excellent Silverline, which does attractive, reasonably priced silver and gold jewellery.

Lajpat Nagar Central Market (Map pp122-3; around 11am-8pm Tue-Sun) This market attracts bargain-hunting locals on the prowl for household goods, clothing and jewellery.

Look out for the local *mehndiwalas* who paint beautiful henna designs.

Sarojini Nagar Market (Map pp122-3; around 11am-8pm Tue-Sun) Go wild rummaging here for good-value Western-style clothes (seek out the lanes lined exclusively with clothing stalls), that have been dumped here either because they were an export surplus or from a cancelled line. Check for holes, faulty zips, crooked seams, stains and missing buttons. Bargain hard. Avoid Sunday afternoons or sharpen your elbows.

Sunder Nagar Market (Map pp126-7; around 10.30am-7.30pm Mon-Sat) Just south of Purana Qila, this genteel enclave specialises in Indian and Nepali handicrafts and 'antiques' (most are replicas). There are two outstanding teashops here: Regalía Tea House (open 10am to 7.30pm Monday to Saturday, 11am to 4pm Sunday); and its neighbour Mittal Tea House (open 10am to 7.30pm Monday to Saturday, 10am to 4.30pm Sunday). They stock similar products and offer complimentary tea tastings. There's plenty on offer, from fragrant Kashmiri *kahwa* (green tea with cardamom; Rs110 per 100g), to the finest of teas, Vintage Musk (Rs700 per 100g). The white tea (Rs600/350 per 100g organic/non-organic) is said to contain even more antioxidants than green tea, while dragon balls (Rs80 each) are a visual thrill when brewed.

Music
MUSICAL INSTRUMENTS
These reputable outlets stock a wide range of Indian and non-Indian musical instruments:

Delhi Musical Stores (Map p132; 23276909; www.indianmusicalinstruments.com; 1070 Paiwalan, Old Delhi; 10am-7pm Mon-Sat) Opposite Jama Masjid's Gate No 3. The website details what's on offer.

Rangarsons Music Depot (Map pp122-3; 41677881; B-100 Lajpat Nagar Part 1; 10am-5.30pm Mon-Sat) Tablas/Indian trumpets/sitars/guitars from Rs2500/3200/4000/2000.

Rikhi Ram (Map p130; 23327685; www.rikhiram.com; 8A G-Block, Connaught Place; 11.30am-8pm Mon-Sat) A beautiful old shop, selling professional classic (Rs35,000-45,000) and electric (Rs38,000) sitars, tablas (Rs7500-11,500) and more.

Rikhi Ram's Music (Map p130; 23340496; www.rikhiram.org; 144 Bhagat Singh Market; 11am-7.30pm Mon-Sat) Near Gole Market. See the excellent website for comprehensive details.

OLD DELHI'S BAZAARS

Old Delhi's bazaars (Map p132) are a headspinning assault on the senses: an aromatic muddle of flowers, urine, incense, chai, fumes and frying food, and a mindbending array of things to see. They're busiest (and best avoided) on Monday and Friday and during other afternoons. Come at around 11.30am when most shops have opened and the jostling is bearable.

For silver jewellery (some gold) head for Dariba Kalan, near the Sisganj Gurdwara. Nearby Kinari Bazaar is famous for *zari* (gold thread weaving) and *zardozi* (gold embroidery), and is the place to head for your bridal trousseau. The cloth market sells swathes of uncut material and linen, while electrical gadgets are the speciality of Lajpat Rai Market. Chowri Bazaar is the wholesale paper and greeting-card market. Nearby, Nai Sarak deals in wholesale stationery, books, and saris.

Near the Fatehpuri Masjid, on Khari Baoli, is the nose-numbing Spice Market, ablaze with powdery piles of scarlet-red chilli powder, brown masala blends and burnt-orange turmeric, as well as pickles, tea and nuts. Being a wholesale market, spices here rarely come hermetically sealed – for these, go to Roopak's (p154) in Karol Bagh.

The Daryaganj Sunday Book Market, north of Delhi Gate, is a bookworm's delight (Sunday afternoons only).

For competitively priced instruments, inspect the **musical instrument shops** (Map p132; 🕑 Mon-Sat) along Netaji Subhash Marg in Daryaganj.

RECORDS, CASSETTES & CDS

Music retailers stock stacks of CDs (including East-meets-West fusion) and a limited range of cassettes – handy if you're hiring a car as most only have cassette decks. There are numerous small music shops in Connaught Place and Paharganj. The excellent Planet M stocks everything from Bollywood to raga, and has citywide branches, including at Connaught Place, Greater Kailash II, and Karol Bagh.

Tailors

Allow a week for tailoring, although some places will sew at lightening speed.

Delhi Cloth House (Map pp126-7; ☎ 24618937; Khan Market; 🕑 11am-7.30pm Mon-Sat) Men's wool suits from Rs5000 to Rs20,000 (including material); ankle-length skirts from Rs400 (excluding material).

M Ram & Sons (Map p130; ☎ 23416558; 21 E-Block, Connaught Place; 🕑 10am-8pm Mon-Sat) Men's suits from Rs3500 (excluding material), ladies long skirts from Rs500 (excluding material). Tailoring is possible in 24 hours.

New Prominent Tailors (Map p130; ☎ 23418007; 25 K-Block, Connaught Place; 🕑 11.30am-7.30pm Mon-Sat) Men's trousers (excluding material) cost Rs300, women's skirts (with lining) cost Rs250.

GETTING THERE & AWAY

Delhi is a major international gateway. It's also a centre for domestic travel, with extensive bus, rail and air connections. Delhi's airport can be prone to thick fog in December and January (often disrupting airline schedules), making it wise not to book back-to-back flights during this period.

Air

The domestic terminals (Terminal 1) of the Indira Gandhi International Airport (Map pp122–3) are around 15km southwest of Connaught Place, and the international terminal (Terminal 2) is a further 8km away. There's a (free) shuttle bus between the two terminals: catch it from within the Arrivals area of the International Airport and allow lots of time for the transfer.

For flight inquiries, call the **international airport** (☎ 25661000; www.newdelhiairport.in) or the **domestic airport** (☎ 25675126).

DOMESTIC
Arrivals & Departures

Check-in at the airport for domestic flights is one hour before departure. Note that if you've just arrived and have an onward connection to another city in India, sometimes Air India flights depart from the international terminal, not the domestic terminal.

Airlines

The most convenient **Air India office** (Map p130; ☎ 23313317; F-Block, Malhotra Bldg, Connaught Place; 🕑 10am-1pm & 2-5pm Mon-Sat) is at Connaught Place. For Air India recorded flight arrival and departure details, dial ☎ 1407.

DOMESTIC FLIGHTS FROM DELHI

These are a sample of domestic air routes – for comprehensive and current details, see *Excel's Timetable of Air Services Within India* (Rs55), available at newsstands. When making reservations request the most direct (quickest) route. Note that airline prices fluctuate and website bookings with some carriers can be markedly cheaper. Fares quoted here are non-refundable singles.

Destination	Airline code	Fare (US$)	Duration (hr)	Frequency
Ahmedabad	IC	25	1¾	1 daily
	9W	35		2 daily
	SG	10		2 daily
	IT	20		1 daily
Amritsar	IC	70	1	1 daily
	IT	10		1 daily
Bengaluru	IC	50	2½	4 daily
	9W	70		3 daily
	SG	30		3 daily
	IT	60		6 daily
Chennai	9W	70	23/4	4 daily
	IC	55		5 daily
Dharamsala	IT	75	1½	1 daily
Goa	SG	60	2½	3 daily
	G8	40		1 daily
	IT	60		1 daily
	6E	40		1 daily
Hyderabad	IC	35	2	3 daily
	9W	55		2 daily
	SG	15		3 daily
Jaipur	9W	30	45min	1 daily
	IC	10		1 daily
Jodhpur	JA	80	1½	3 weekly
	9W	40		3 weekly
Khajuraho	IT	80	1¾	1 daily
	JA	110		1 daily
Kolkata	IC	35	2	2 daily
	9W	50		3 daily
	IT	40		3 daily
	6E	10		3 daily
Kullu	IT	35	1¾	1 daily
Leh	9W	80	1¼	4 weekly
Mumbai	6E	25	2	10 daily
	IC	35		10 daily
	9W	40		11 daily
	IT	45		11 daily
	SG	15		6 daily
Shimla	IT	251	1	1 daily
Trivandrum	IC	100	4½	1 daily
	6E	80		1 daily
	9W	110		1 daily
Udaipur	JA	100	2½-3	2 daily
	9W	45		1 or 2 daily
	IT	45		1 daily
Varanasi	IC	20	1¾	1 daily
	9W	55		1 daily
	SG	10		1 daily

IC – Air India; 9W – Jet Airways/Jetlite; JA – Jagson Airlines; SG – Spicejet; IT – Kingfisher Airlines; G8 – Go Airlines; 6E – IndiGo

DELHI

Other domestic airlines:

Jagson Airlines (Map p130; ☎ 23721593; Vandana Bldg, 11 Tolstoy Marg; ☺ 9am-6pm Mon-Sat)

Jet Airways (Map p130; ☎ 39841111; 40 N-Block, Connaught Place; ☺ 9am-8pm Mon-Fri, to 6pm Sat & Sun) Also has information on Jetlite flights.

Kingfisher Airlines (Map p130; ☎ 23730238; 42 N-Block, Connaught Place; ☺ 9am-7pm Mon-Fri, 10am-5pm Sat & Sun)

INTERNATIONAL
Arrivals

The international airport's arrivals hall has 24-hour money-exchange facilities, an ICICI ATM, prepaid taxi counters, a tourist information counter and a train reservation counter.

Departures

At the check-in counter, ensure you collect tags to attach to hand luggage (mandatory to clear security later).

Airlines

Aeroflot (Map p130; ☎ 23723241; 15-17 Tolstoy Marg)

Air Canada (Map p130; ☎ 41528181; Rm 202, 2nd fl, Ansal Bvn, Kasturba Gandhi Marg)

Air France (Map pp122-3; ☎ /fax 25652274; Departures, Terminal 2, Airport)

Air India (Map p130; ☎ 23731225; Jeevan Bharati Bldg, 124 Connaught Place)

Austrian Airlines (Map p130; ☎ 23350125; 11/12 G-Block, Connaught Place)

British Airways (off Map pp122-3; ☎ 01244120747; DLF Plaza Tower, DLF Phase 1, Qutb Enclave, Gurgaon)

El Al Israel Airlines (Map p130; ☎ 23357965; 303 Prakash Deep Bldg, 7 Tolstoy Marg)

Emirates (Map p130; ☎ 66314444; 7th fl, DLF Centre, Sansad Marg, Connaught Place)

Gulf Air (Map p130; ☎ 25652981; 2nd fl Ansal Bhawan, 16 Kasturba Gandhi Marg)

Japan Airlines (Map p130; ☎ 23324922; Chandralok Bldg, 36 Janpath)

KLM-Royal Dutch Airlines (off Map pp122-3; ☎ 23357747; Departures, Terminal 2)

Lufthansa Airlines (☎ 23724200; 12th fl, Tower B, DLF City, Phase 2 Gurgaon)

Malaysian Airlines (Map p130; ☎ 41512121; Gopal Das Bhavan, 28 Barakhamba Rd)

Pakistan International Airlines (Map p130; ☎ 23737791; 23 Barakhamba Rd)

Royal Nepal Airlines Corporation (RNAC; Map p130; ☎ 23321164; 44 Janpath)

Scandinavian Airlines (Map p130; ☎ 43513201; Thapar House, 124 Janpath)

Singapore Airlines (Map p130; ☎ 23326373; Ashoka Estate Bldg, 24 Barakhamba Rd)

Thai Airways International (Map pp122-3; ☎ 41497777; Park Royal Intercontinental Hotel, America Plaza, Nehru Pl)

Bus

Bikaner House (Map pp126-7; ☎ 23383469; Pandara Rd), near India Gate, operates good state-run buses. There are services to Jaipur (non AC/AC/deluxe Rs300/400/600, six hours, several services daily between 6am and midnight); Udaipur (Rs810, 15 hours, daily at 7pm); Ajmer (Rs531, nine hours, daily at 7pm, 10pm and 11.30pm); and Jodhpur (Rs718, 11 hours, daily at 10pm).

PUBLIC BUSES

Apart from public buses, there are comfortable private bus services (including sleepers), leaving from central locations, but their schedules vary (inquire at travel agencies). Note there are buses to Agra, but the train is much easier and quicker.

Destination	One-way fare (Rs)	Duration (hr)	Departures
Amritsar	255 (A)	10	5.30am-9.30pm (hourly)
Chandigarh	140/400 (A/B)	5	6am-1.50am (half-hourly)
Dehra Dun	145 (A)	7	5am-11pm (hourly)
Dharamsala	325/830 (A/B)	12	4.30am-11pm (hourly)
Jammu	300/400 (A/B)	12	5.15am-11pm (hourly)
Kullu	400/990 (A/B)	13	9am
Manali	410/990 (A/B)	15	1-10pm (hourly)
McLeod Ganj	350 (A)	14	7.40pm
Shimla	240/650 (A/B)	10	5am-10.30pm (hourly)

A – ordinary, B – deluxe AC

MAJOR TRAINS FROM DELHI

Destination	Train No & name	Fare (Rs)	Duration (hr)	Frequency	Departures & train station
Agra	2280 Taj Exp	76/266 (A)	3	daily	7.10am HN
	2002/A Bhopal Shatabdi	370/700 (B)	2	daily	6.15am ND
Amritsar	2013 Shatabdi Exp	645/1200 (B)	5½	daily	4.30pm ND
	2029/2031 Swarna/ Amritsar Shatabdi	600/1145 (B)	5½	daily	7.20am ND
Bengaluru	2430 Bangalore Rajdhani	2120/2765/4625 (C)	34	4 weekly	8.50pm HN
Chennai	2434 Chennai Rajdhani	2075/2700/4500 (C)	28	2 weekly	4pm HN
	2622 Tamil Nadu Exp	537/1455/1997/3386 (D)	33	daily	10.30pm ND
Goa (Margaon)	2432 Trivndrm Rajdhani	2035/2615/4370 (C)	25½	2 weekly	11am HN
Haridwar	2017 Dehradun Shatabdi	435/825 (B)	4½	daily	6.50am ND
Jaipur	2958 ADI SJ Rajdani	605/775/1285 (C)	5	6 weekly	7.55pm ND
	2916 Ashram Exp	441/590/986 (C)	5¾	daily	3pm OD
	2015 Shatabdi Exp	465/885 (B)	4¾	6 weekly	6.05am ND
Khajuraho	2447A Nizamuddin– Khajuraho Exp	273/713 (E)	10¼	3 weekly	9.35 HN
Lucknow	2004 Lko Swran Shatabdi	700/1360 (B)	6¼	daily	6.15am ND
Mumbai	2952 Mumbai Rajdhani	1495/1975/3305 (C)	16	daily	4.30pm ND
	2954 Ag Kranti Rajdani Exp	1495/1975/3305 (C)	17¼	daily	4.55pm HN
Udaipur	2963 Mewar Exp	309/814/1106/1854 (D)	12	daily	6.30pm HN
Varanasi	2560 Shivganga Exp	311/820/1114/1868 (D)	13	daily	6.30pm ND

Train stations: ND – New Delhi, OD – Old Delhi, HN – Hazrat Nizamuddin
Fares: A – 2nd class/chair car; B – chair car/1st-class AC; C – 3AC/2AC/1st-class AC; D – sleeper/3AC/2AC/1st-class AC; E – sleeper/3AC

Delhi's main bus station is the **Inter State Bus Terminal** (ISBT; Map pp122-3; ☎ 23860290; Kashmiri Gate; ⏱ 24hr), north of the (Old) Delhi train station. It has a 24-hour left-luggage facility (Rs15 per bag). This station is chaotic so arrive at least 30 minutes ahead of your departure time. State-government bus companies (and their counters) at the ISBT include (timetables are online):

Delhi Transport Corporation (☎ 23865181; dtc.nic. in; Counter 34)

Haryana Roadways (☎ 23861262; hartrans.gov.in; Counter 35)

Himachal Roadways (☎ 23868654; Counter 40)

Punjab Roadways (☎ 23867842; www.punjabroadways.gov.in; Counter 37)

Rajasthan Roadways (☎ 23386658, 23864470; Counter 36)

Uttar Pradesh Roadways (☎ 23868709; Counter 33)

Train

For foreigners, it's easiest to make ticket bookings at the helpful **International Tourist Bureau** (Map p142; ☎ 23405156; 1st fl, New Delhi train station; ⏱ 8am-8pm Mon-Sat, to 2pm Sun). Do *not* believe anyone who tells you it has shifted, closed or burnt down –

this is a scam to divert you elsewhere (see the boxed text, p133). There are reportedly railway porters involved in scams, so stay on your toes and don't let anyone stop you from going to the 1st floor of the *main* building for bookings.

When making reservations at the International Tourist Bureau, tickets must be paid for in rupees backed up by money-exchange certificates (or ATM receipts) or in US dollars, euros or pounds sterling; any change is given in rupees. Bring your passport. There's a train booking counter at the airport (opposite).

There are two main stations in Delhi – (Old) Delhi train station (Map p132) in Old Delhi, and New Delhi train station (Map p142) at Paharganj; make sure you know which station serves your destination (New Delhi train station is closer to Connaught Place). If you're departing from the Delhi train station, allow adequate time to meander through Old Delhi's snail-paced traffic.

There's also the Nizamuddin train station (Map pp126-7), south of Sunder Nagar, where various trains (usually for south-bound destinations) start or finish.

Railway porters should charge around Rs20 to Rs30 per bag.

There are many more destinations and trains than those listed in the boxed text, p159 – consult *Trains at a Glance* (Rs35), available at most newsstands, or ask tourist office staff.

GETTING AROUND

Local buses can get horrendously crowded so autorickshaws and taxis are desirable alternatives. Keep small change handy for fares.

Women should read Taxis & Public Transport in the Women Travellers section (see p1171).

To/From the Airport

Airport-to-city transport is not as straightforward as it should be, due to predatory taxi drivers – see p125.

Many international flights arrive at ghastly hours, so it pays to book a hotel in advance and notify it of your arrival time.

PREARRANGED PICK-UPS

There's nothing more comforting after a long-haul flight than seeing someone holding a placard with your name on it. Be aware that if you arrange an airport pick-up through a travel agency or hotel, it's more expensive than a prepaid taxi from the airport due to the airport parking fee (up to Rs120) and Rs60 charge for the person collecting you to enter the airport arrivals hall. Sometimes drivers are barred from arrivals for security reasons, in which case, most will wait outside Gate 1.

BUS

Local bus 780, from Super Bazaar, near Connaught Place, goes to the IGI airport (Rs10), but is not all that regular. There's also a half-hourly non-AC deluxe bus from ISBT to the airport, via Super Bazaar (Rs50, luggage Rs25).

TAXI & AUTORICKSHAW

There are two Delhi Traffic Police Prepaid Taxi Booths, one inside the arrivals building, and one outside. It costs about Rs225 to Paharganj; there's a 25% surcharge between 11pm and 5am.

You'll be given a voucher with the destination on it – insist that the driver honours it. Never surrender your voucher until you get

AUTORICKSHAW RATES	
To gauge fares vis-à-vis distances, the following list shows one-way (official) rates departing from Janpath's prepaid autorickshaw booth. Taxis charge around double.	
Destination	**Cost (Rs)**
Ansal Plaza	70
Bahai House of Worship	80
Humayun's tomb	50
Karol Bagh	30
Old Delhi train station	50
Paharganj	30
Purana Qila	30
Red Fort	50
South Extension	60

to your destination; without that docket the driver won't get paid.

You can also book a prepaid taxi at the **Easycabs** counter inside the arrivals building at both the international and domestic airports. This is also prepay: it costs around Rs400 to the centre, but you get a cleaner, AC car, and you can pay by credit card.

At the domestic airport, the prepaid taxi-booking counter is inside the terminal.

For a cheap but boneshaking ride, a prepaid autorickshaw to the airport from New Delhi train station will cost around Rs130.

AIRPORT EXPRESS

The new, high-speed (20 minutes, Rs150) Metro line that runs to/from Rajiv Chowk (Connaught Place) should be finished in time for the Commonwealth Games in 2010. There will also be check-in facilities at Rajiv Chowk.

Bus

The Delhi Transport Corporation runs some buses, and others are privately owned, but they all operate along the same routes. Tickets cost a maximum of Rs15 for travel within the city precincts. If you must use these heinously crowded monsters, try to board at a starting point, as there's more chance of a seat. But the red-and-white AC buses are better, but not that prevalent.

Useful buses include:

Bus 590 Krishi Bhawan to Qutb Minar.

Bus 604 or 620 Connaught Place (on Sansad Marg) to Chanakyapuri (the 620 goes on to Hauz Khas).

Car

HIRING A CAR & DRIVER

Numerous operators offer chauffeur-driven cars. The following companies get positive reports from travellers. Each has an eight-hour, 80km limit per day. All offer tours beyond Delhi (including Rajasthan) but higher charges apply for these. The rates below are only for travel within Delhi.

Kumar Tourist Taxi Service (Map p130; ☎ 23415930; kumartaxi@rediffmail.com; 14/1 K-Block, Connaught Place; non-AC/AC per day Rs700/800; ☼ 9am-9pm) Near the York Hotel is this tiny office run by two brothers, Bittoo and Titoo. Their rates are among Delhi's lowest – beware of frauds/touts claiming association with this company or insisting it has closed.

Metropole Tourist Service (Map p126-7; ☎ 24310313; www.metrovista.co.in; 224 Defence Colony Flyover Market; non-AC/AC per day Rs800/1100; ☼ 7am-7pm) Under the Defence Flyover Bridge (on the Jangpura side), this is another reliable choice.

Cycle-Rickshaw & Bicycle

Cycle rickshaws are still in use in parts of Old Delhi, though they have been banned in Chandni Chowk to reduce congestion (now authorities just need to ban autorickshaws, cars and people, and the traffic problem should be sorted). Let's hope they're not banned in other areas, as they're the best way to get around Old Delhi – the drivers are wizards at weaving through the crowds. Tips are appreciated for this gruelling work.

Cycle-rickshaws are also banned from the Connaught Place area and New Delhi, but they're handy for commuting between Connaught Place and Paharganj (about Rs25).

To purchase a pushbike, the largest range of new and second-hand bicycles can be found at Jhandewalan Cycle Market (Map pp122–3).

Metro

Delhi's marvellous Metro (open 6am to 11pm) has efficient services with arrival/departure announcements in Hindi and English.

At the time of writing, three sections of the Metro system were operational: the Shahdara–Dilshad Garden phase (21 stations), the Vishwa Vidalaya–Central Secretariat route (10 stations) and the Dwarka–Indraprastha line (31 stations). The Metro is scheduled for completion in time for the Commonwealth Games in 2010.

Tokens (Rs6 to Rs22) are sold at Metro stations; there are also one-/three-day (Rs70/200) 'tourist cards' for unlimited short-distance travel. If you're staying longer, buy a Smart Card (Rs50, plus Rs50 refundable deposit). You can recharge the card in denominations from Rs50 to Rs800.

For the latest developments (plus route maps) see www.delhimetrorail.com or call ☎ 24365204.

Motorcycle

For motorcycle rental details, see p1184.

Radiocab

If you have a local mobile number, you can call a radiocab. These AC cars are clean, efficient, and use reliable meters. They charge around Rs15 per km (with 25% surcharge from 11pm to 5am). After calling the operator, you'll receive a text with your driver's registration number, then another to confirm arrival time. To avoid waiting, it's best to call them around 20 to 30 minutes in advance. You can also book online.

Numbers include:

Easycabs (☎ 43434343; www.easycabs.com)
Megacabs (☎ 41414141; www.megacabs.com)
Quickcabs (☎ 45333333; www.quickcabs.in)

Taxi & Autorickshaw

All taxis and autorickshaws are metered but usually the meters are 'not working' or drivers refuse to use them (so they can overcharge). If the meter isn't an option, agree on a fare before setting off. If the driver disagrees, look for one who will. From 11pm to 5am, there's a 25% surcharge for autorickshaws and taxis.

Otherwise, to avoid shenanigans, catch an autorickshaw from a prepaid booth:

Janpath (Map p130; 88 Janpath; ☼ 11am-7pm Mon-Sat, to 2pm Sun) Outside the India Tourism Delhi office.
New Delhi train station car park (Map p142; ☼ 24hr)
Palika Bazaar's Gate No 2 (Map p130; Connaught Place; ☼ 11am-7pm)

GREATER DELHI

For details about possible day trips from Delhi to neighbouring Haryana, see p265.

TUGHLAQABAD

Crumbling **Tughlaqabad** (Map pp122-3; Indian/foreigner Rs5/100, video Rs25; ☼ 8.30am-5.30pm) was the

DELHI METRO MAP

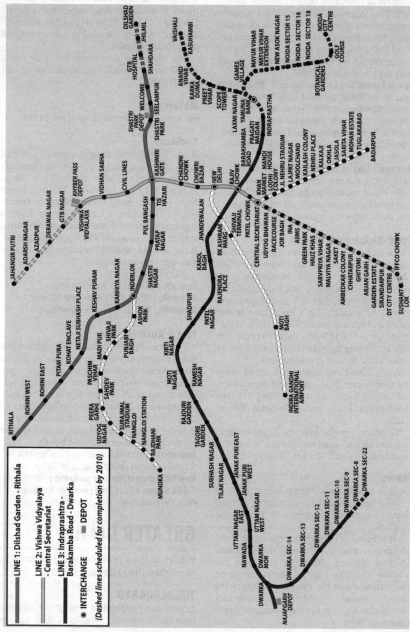

LINE 1: Dilshad Garden - Rithala

LINE 2: Vishwa Vidyalaya - Central Secretariat

LINE 3: Indraprashtra - Barakamba Road - Dwarka

● INTERCHANGE   ■ DEPOT

(Dashed lines scheduled for completion by 2010)

third city of Delhi. This mammoth fort, with 6.5km of walls and 13 gateways, was built by Ghiyas-ud-din Tughlaq. Its construction was said to have sparked a quarrel with the saint Nizam-ud-din: when the Tughlaq ruler refused the workers whom Nizam-ud-din wanted for work on his shrine, the saint cursed the king, warning that his city would be inhabited only by shepherds. Later, this was indeed the case.

Later, when Ghiyas-ud-din was returning from a military campaign, Nizam-ud-din again prophesised doom for him, telling his followers, 'Delhi is a long way off'. Indeed it was, for the king was killed on his way towards Delhi in 1325.

From Janpath an autorickshaw costs around Rs100 one way (Rs250 for one-hour wait and return). The Metro should extend to Tughlaqabad by 2010.

QUTB MINAR

The beautiful religious buildings of the **Qutb Minar complex** (Map p163; ☎ 26643856; Indian/foreigner Rs10/250, video Rs25; ☉ dawn-dusk) date from the onset of Islamic rule in India. Today on Delhi's outskirts, once these constructions were in the heart of the Muslim city.

The Qutb Minar itself is a Babel-like tower of victory, which closely resembles similar Afghan towers, and was also used as a minaret. Muslim sultan Qutb-ud-din began its construction in 1193, immediately after the defeat of the last Hindu kingdom in Delhi. It's nearly 73m high and tapers from a 15m-diameter base to just 2.5m at the top.

The tower has five distinct storeys, each marked by a projecting balcony. The first three storeys are made of red sandstone, the 4th and 5th storeys are of marble and sandstone. Qutb-ud-din built only to the 1st storey. His successors completed it and, in 1368, Firoz Shah rebuilt the top storeys and added a cupola. An earthquake brought the cupola crashing down in 1803 and an Englishman replaced it with another in 1829, which was later removed.

The Qutb Festival takes place here every October/November (see p125).

Avoid visiting Qutb Minar on weekends, as it can get crowded.

Quwwat-ul-Islam Masjid

At the foot of the Qutb Minar stands the first mosque to be built in India, popularly known as the Might of Islam Mosque. This was also

QUTB MINAR COMPLEX

0 — 200 m
0 — 0.1 miles

- Alai Minar
- Tomb of Altamish
- Altamish Extension
- Entrance
- Iron Pillar
- Quwwat-ul-Islam Masjid
- Qutb Minar
- Madrasa of Ala-ud-din
- Alai Darwaza
- Tomb of Imam Zamin

constructed in 1193, with various additions over the centuries. The original mosque was built on the foundations of a Hindu temple, and an inscription over the east gate states that it was built with materials obtained from demolishing '27 idolatrous temples'. Many elements in the mosque's construction indicate their Hindu or Jain origins.

Altamish, Qutb-ud-din's son-in-law, surrounded the original mosque with a cloistered court between 1210 and 1220.

Iron Pillar

This 7m-high pillar stands in the courtyard of the mosque and it was here long before the mosque's construction. A six-line Sanskrit inscription indicates that it was initially erected outside a Vishnu temple, possibly in Bihar, and was raised in memory of Chandragupta II, who ruled from AD 375 to 413.

What the inscription does not tell is how it was made, for the iron in the pillar is of exceptional purity. Scientists have never discovered how the iron, which has not rusted after some 2000 years, could be cast using the technology of the time.

It is said that if you can stand with your back to the pillar and encircle it with your arms your wish will be granted; however, there's no hope of this as the pillar is now protected by a fence.

Alai Minar

When Ala-ud-din made his additions to the mosque, he also conceived a far more ambitious construction program. He aimed to build a second tower of victory, exactly like the Qutb Minar, but twice as high! By the time of his death the tower had reached 27m and no-one was willing to continue his overambitious project. The incomplete tower stands to the north of the Qutb Minar and the mosque.

Other Features

Ala-ud-din's exquisite **Alai Darwaza** gateway is the main entrance to the whole complex. It was built of red sandstone in 1310 and is just southwest of the Qutb Minar. The **tomb of Imam Zamin** is beside the gateway, while the **tomb of Altamish**, who died in 1235, is by the northwestern corner of the mosque. The largely ruined **madrasa of Ala-ud-din** stands at the rear of the complex.

There are some **summer palaces** in the area and also the **tombs** of the last kings of Delhi, who succeeded the Mughals. An empty space between two of the tombs was intended for the last king of Delhi, who died in exile in Yangon, Burma (Myanmar), in 1862, following his implication in the 1857 First War of Independence (Indian Uprising).

Getting There & Away

Catch bus 590 (Rs15) from Krish Bhawan, or from Janpath an autorickshaw costs around Rs100 one way (Rs250 for one-hour wait and return). The Metro should extend to Qutb Minar by 2010.

Rajasthan

Rajasthan, the Land of Kings, is aptly named. It is indeed a fabulous realm of maharajas and their majestic forts and lavish palaces. The remnants of a rich and romantic past, either in evocative ruins or restored to former splendour, have earned Rajasthan a place on most travellers' wish lists. Yet there is much more to this iconic region of the subcontinent. It is a land of deserts and jungle, camel trains and tigers, glittering jewels, vivid art and vibrant culture. There are enough festivals here to fill a calendar and an artist's palette, and the shopping and cuisine are nothing short of spectacular. In short, Rajasthan just about has it all; it is the must-see state of India, brimming with varied, startling and incredible attractions.

Rajasthan's popularity has generated a formidable tourism industry that permits travellers on any budget to experience all its magic and sights. While its colour-charged cities throb with the crowds and chaos of emerging India, the treasures of the past hold pride of place in mind and spirit. There's magnificent Mehrangarh looming large over sea-blue Jodhpur, the golden sandcastle at Jaisalmer, the palaces of Udaipur, Pushkar's reverent yet carnival charm, the storybook whimsy of Bundi and the painted *havelis* (ornately decorated residences) sprinkled through Shekhawati. Rajasthanis are rightly proud of their rich and turbulent history and there's a recognisable acknowledgment of the economy's dependency on tourism.

The state is diagonally divided into the hilly southeastern region and the arid northwestern Great Thar Desert, which extends across the border into Pakistan. The highest point is reached at the pleasant hill station of Mt Abu.

HIGHLIGHTS

- Be mesmerised by the magnificence of **Mehrangarh** (p231), the cliff-top fort watching over the blue city of Jodhpur
- Cross the desert on a camel and explore the sandstone fort at **Jaisalmer** (p240)
- Be seduced by the lake and palaces of **Udaipur** (p213), where fairy-tale views combine with romantic fine dining
- Wander through the colourful bazaars and imperial palaces of the always pink, always chaotic capital of **Jaipur** (p168)
- Join the party in **Pushkar** (p195), a mystical small town around a holy lake, hosting one of India's most famous fairs
- Take it slow in **Bundi** (p203), a relaxed, hassle-free town with a rambling storybook palace
- Explore the forgotten towns and discover the crumbling frescoed *havelis* of **Shekhawati** (p189)

RAJASTHAN

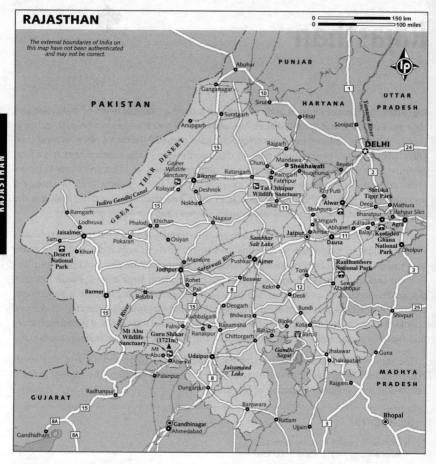

RAJASTHAN

The external boundaries of India on this map have not been authenticated and may not be correct.

History

Rajasthan is home to the Rajputs, warrior clans who claim to originate from the sun, moon and fire, and who have controlled this part of India for more than 1000 years. While they forged marriages of convenience and temporary alliances, pride and independence were always paramount; consequently much

FAST FACTS

Population 56.5 million
Area 342,239 sq km
Capital Jaipur
Main languages Hindi and Rajasthani
When to go mid-October to mid-March

of their energy was spent squabbling among themselves. The resultant weakness eventually led to the Rajputs becoming vassals of the Mughal empire.

Nevertheless, the Rajputs' bravery and sense of honour were unparalleled. Rajput warriors would fight against all odds and, when no hope was left, chivalry demanded *jauhar* (ritual mass suicide). The men donned saffron robes and rode out to face the enemy and certain death, while the women and children perished in the flames of a funeral pyre. It's not surprising that Mughal emperors had such difficulty controlling this part of their empire.

With the Mughal empire declining, the Rajputs gradually clawed back independence – at least until the British arrived. As the British

RAJASTHAN (vertical side tab)

FESTIVALS IN RAJASTHAN

Jaipur Literature Festival (Jan; Jaipur, p168; www.jaipurliteraturefestival.org) Featuring international and Indian authors and a program of talks, films, debates and theatre. See the website for exact dates.

Camel Festival (Jan-Feb; Bikaner, p249) Best-of-breed competitions, races and decorated camels.

Nagaur Camel Fair (Jan/Feb; Nagaur, p239) Camel and cattle fair that focuses on livestock trading but still colours the town with festivities.

Desert Festival (Feb; Jaisalmer, p240) A chance for moustache-twirlers to compete in the 'Mr Desert' contest, and a host of other desert delights.

Elephant Festival (Mar; Jaipur, p168) Parades, polo and human-versus-elephant tugs-of-war.

Thar Festival (Mar; Barmer, p248) Just after the Jaisalmer Desert Festival, this features cultural shows, dancing and puppetry.

Gangaur (Mar/Apr; Jaipur, p168) A statewide festival honouring Shiva and Parvati's love; it's celebrated with particular fervour in Jaipur.

Cattle Fair (Mar/Apr; Barmer, p248) One of Rajasthan's biggest cattle fairs.

Mewar Festival (Mar-Apr; Udaipur, p213) Udaipur's version of Gangaur, with free cultural events and a colourful procession down to the lake. Local women step out in their finest.

Summer Festival (May; Mt Abu, p226) If, like a mad dog, you are travelling through Rajasthan in summer, check out the Summer Festival, dedicated to Rajasthani music.

Teej (Aug; Jaipur, p168, & Bundi, p203) Honours the arrival of the monsoon, and Shiva and Parvati's marriage.

Dussehra Mela (Oct; Kota, p207) Commemorates Rama's victory over Ravana (the demon king of Lanka). It's a spectacular time to visit Kota – the huge fair features 22.5m-tall firecracker-stuffed effigies.

Marwar Festival (Oct; Jodhpur, p230, & Osiyan, p239) Celebrates Rajasthan heroes through music and dance; one day is held in Jodhpur and one in Osiyan.

Bundi Ustav (Oct/Nov; Bundi, p203) Cultural programs, fireworks and processions.

Kashavrai Patan (Oct/Nov; Bundi, p203, & Kota, p207) Held between Bundi and Kota, this festival sees thousands of pilgrims descend for the month of Kartika.

Pushkar Mela (Nov; Pushkar, p199) The Pushkar Camel Fair is the most famous festival in the state; it's a massive congregation of camels, horses and cattle, traders, pilgrims and tourists.

Kolayat Mela (Nov; Kolayat, p253) Held at the same time as Pushkar Mela, but with sadhus rather than camels.

Chandrabhaga Mela (Nov; Jhalrapatan, p209) A cattle fair and a chance for thousands of pilgrims to bathe in the holy Chandrabhaga River.

Winter Festival (Dec; Mt Abu, p226) Focuses on music and folk dance.

Raj inexorably expanded, most Rajput states allied with the British, which allowed them to continue as independent states, subject to certain political and economic constraints.

These alliances proved to be the beginning of the end for the Rajput rulers. Consumption took over from chivalry so that, by the early 20th century, many of the maharajas spent much of their time travelling the world with scores of retainers, playing polo and occupying entire floors of expensive hotels. While it suited the British to indulge them, the maharajas' profligacy was economically and socially detrimental. When India gained its independence, Rajasthan had one of the subcontinent's lowest rates of life expectancy and literacy.

At Independence, India's ruling Congress Party was forced to make a deal with the nominally independent Rajput states to secure their agreement to join the new India.

The rulers were allowed to keep their titles and their property holdings, and they were paid an annual stipend commensurate with their status. It couldn't last forever, though, and in the early 1970s Indira Gandhi abolished the titles and the stipends, and severely sequestered rulers' property rights.

In their absence Rajasthan has made headway, but the state remains poor. The strength of tradition here means that women have a particularly tough time in rural areas. However, literacy stands at 60% in 2008 (males 76%, females 44%), a massive rise from 18% in 1961 and 39% in 1991, although the gender gap remains India's widest, and the literacy rate is still below the national average of around 65%.

Information

Accommodation in Rajasthan is among the best in India for range and value. Here you

RAJASTHAN

RAJASTHANI TRIBES

Groups of Adivasis (tribal people) were the first inhabitants of this region, and today they form 12% of the population – the national average is 8%. The main tribes are the Bhils and the Minas. The Bhils inhabited the southwestern part of the state, and were regarded as fearsome warriors, helping the Rajputs combat the Marathas and Mughals. The Minas live in eastern Rajasthan. Originally a ruling tribe, their downfall began with the rise of the Rajputs, and in 1924 the British declared the Minas to be criminals, a label only removed after Independence. Smaller tribes include the Sahariyas, Damariyas, and the Rajput Garasias and Gaduliya Lohars.

---

can luxuriate in a palace or bed down in a basic hotel. Homestays are a great way of immersing yourself in the local lifestyle, and most Rajasthan cities have a paying guest-house scheme – ask at the tourist office. Taxes (usually 10% on rooms costing Rs1000 or more) are not included in prices in this chapter. While options are plentiful, it's wise to book ahead from October till March.

EASTERN RAJASTHAN

JAIPUR

☎ 0141 / pop 2.63 million

Jaipur, the City of Victory, is chaotic and congested, though it still has a habit of tickling travellers pink. As a modern capital, Jaipur has burst well beyond its old defensive walls, and now shiny chrome-and-glass shopping malls march along its new thoroughfares. As the gateway to Rajasthan, it welcomes and farewells tourists triangulating between Delhi and Agra, as well as those embarking on an extended exploration of the desert state.

Here you'll find a well-preserved and living past – stunning hilltop forts, glorious palaces and humming, bargain-filled bazaars – as well as a wealth of accommodation and dining options. However, Jaipur is also a city permanently under siege by its exploding population and stretched-to-the-limit infrastructure. There are water shortages, beggars, eye-watering pollution and rampaging rickshaw drivers.

There's the **Literature Festival** in January, the **Elephant Festival** in March, **Gangaur** in March/April and **Teej** celebrations in August; see p167 for details.

History

The city owes its name, founding and planning to the great warrior-astronomer Maharaja Jai Singh II (1693–1743). In 1727, with Mughal power on the wane, Jai Singh decided the time was right to move from his cramped hillside fort at nearby Amber. He laid out the city, with its surrounding walls and rectangular blocks, according to principles set down in the Shilpa-Shastra, an ancient Hindu architectural treatise. In 1728 he built Jantar Mantar, Jaipur's remarkable observatory.

In 1876 Maharaja Ram Singh had the entire old city painted pink, a colour associated with hospitality, to welcome the Prince of Wales (later King Edward VII), and the tradition has been maintained.

Orientation

Once the initial shock has subsided, travellers find Jaipur relatively easy to negotiate. The bazaar-lined old city is in the northeast, the newer parts spread to the south and west.

There are three main interconnecting roads in the new part of town: Mirza Ismail (MI) Rd – where the majority of restaurants are found – Station Rd and Sansar Chandra Marg. Many tourist facilities are along or just off these roads.

Information
BOOKSHOPS

Bookwise (✆ 11am-8.30pm Mon-Sat) Mall 21 (Shop 110, Mall 21 Bhagwan Das Rd); Marwari Bazaar (Shop 17 Marwari Bazaar, Hotel Rajputana Palace Sheraton) A great selection of books on Rajasthan and India. You can also arrange to have your purchases posted home.

Books Corner (MI Rd; ✆ 10am-8pm) A wide range of English-language books and magazines; sells the informative Jaipur Vision (Rs20) and Jaipur City Guide (Rs30).

Crossword (1st fl KK Sq, C11, Prithviraj Marg; ✆ 10.30am-9pm Mon-Sat) A vast selection of pictorial and fiction books plus DVDs, CDs and maps.

INTERNET ACCESS

Internet access is available throughout the city, and most hotels offer terminals and/or wi-fi.

Mewar Cyber Cafe & Communication (Station Rd; per hr Rs25; ✆ 24hr) Near the main bus station.

MEDICAL SERVICES
Some good hospitals and clinics:

Galundia Clinic (☎ 2361040; MI Rd; ☎ 24hr) Dr Chandra Sen is the doctor here.

Santokba Durlabhji Hospital (☎ 2566251; Bhawan Singh Marg; ☎ 24hr)

Sawai Mansingh Hospital (☎ 2560291; Sawai Ram Singh Rd; ☎ 24hr) Opposite the hospital are numerous pharmacies where you can replenish your first-aid kit.

MONEY
There are many 24-hour ATMs, including those listed here.

Bank of Rajasthan (Rambagh Palace Hotel; ☒ 7am-8pm)

HDFC ATM (Ashoka Marg)

ICICI ATM (Ganpati Plaza, MI Rd)

IDBI ATM (Sawai Jai Singh Hwy, Bani Park)

SBBJ ATM Bani Park (Sawai Jai Singh Hwy, Bani Park); Church Rd (Om Tower, Church Rd)

Standard Chartered (Bhagwat Bhavan, MI Rd)

Thomas Cook Jaipur Towers (Jaipur Towers, MI Rd); Sunil Sadan (Sunil Sadan 2, MI Rd; ☒ 9.30am-6pm Mon-Sat) Two central locations; changes cash and travellers cheques.

PHOTOGRAPHY
The following photo shops stock memory cards and can save your digital photos onto CD for around Rs100.

Goyal Colour Lab (☎ 221887; MI Rd; ☒ 10.30am-8.30pm Mon-Sat, 10am-4pm Sun)

Sentosa Colour Lab (☎ 2388748; Ganpati Plaza, MI Rd; ☒ 10am-8.30pm Mon-Sat)

POST
DHL Worldwide Express (☎ 2362826; G8 Geeta Enclave, Vinobha Marg) A reliable international courier.

Main post office (☎ 2368740; MI Rd; ☒ 8am-7.45pm Mon-Fri, 10am-5.45pm Sat) A parcel stitcher works between 10am and 4pm Monday to Saturday.

TOURIST INFORMATION
There's a tourism helpline on ☎ 1363. The Tourism Assistance Force (tourist police) is stationed at major tourist traps. The *Pink City Map & Guide* (Rs20), *Jaipur Vision* (Rs20) and *Jaipur City Guide* (Rs30) have maps and listings of restaurants and shops. They are available free from many hotels and shops.

Government of India Tourist Office (GITO; ☎ 2372200; off MI Rd; ☒ 9am-6pm Mon-Fri) Beyond the gated entrance to Hotel Khasa Kothi, provides brochures on all of India.

Rajasthan Tourism Development Corporation Central Reservations Office (RTDC; ☎ 2202586; Station Rd; ☒ 10am-5pm Mon-Sat) Behind RTDC Hotel Swagatam, this office handles bookings for RTDC hotels throughout Rajasthan, including the RTDC Tourist Village at the Pushkar Mela.

RTDC Tourist office airport (☎ 2722647; ☒ flight arrivals); main bus station (☎ 5064102; Platform 3, main bus station; ☒ 10am-5pm); RTDC Tourist Hotel (☎ 2375466; MI Rd; ☒ 8am-8pm Mon-Sat); train station (☎ 2315714; Platform 1, Jaipur train station; ☒ 24hr) For a map and ticketing services.

Sights
OLD CITY (PINK CITY)
The old city is partially encircled by a crenellated wall punctuated by gates *(pols)* including the major gates of Chandpol, Ajmer and Sanganeri. It may not feel like it in today's chaotic mechanised traffic, but the Old City is a masterpiece of town planning. Wide avenues divide the city into neat rectangles, each one specialising in different crafts (see p179), as ordained by the ancient treatise of Shilpa-Shastra. The main **bazaars** include Johari, Tripolia, Bapu and Chandpol. At sunset, the buildings take on a timeless glow.

A handy landmark among the chaos is **Iswari Minar Swarga Sal** (Heaven Piercing Minaret; Indian/foreigner Rs5/10, camera/video Rs10/20; ☒ 9am-4.30pm) near Tripolia Gate. The minaret was erected by Jai Singh's son, Iswari, who later killed himself rather than face the advancing Maratha army. As the ultimate act of Rajput loyalty, 21 wives and concubines committed *jauhar* on his funeral pyre. You can spiral to the top of the minaret for excellent views over the old city. The entrance is around the back of the row of shops lining Chandpol Bazaar. To get there take the alley that's 50m west of the minaret along Chandpol Bazaar, or go via the entrance to the City Palace, which is 50m west of Tripolia Gate and 200m east of the minaret.

Hawa Mahal
Jaipur's most distinctive landmark, the **Hawa Mahal** (Palace of the Winds; Indian/foreigner Rs10/50, video Rs20/70; ☒ 9am-4.30pm Sat-Thu) is a remarkable, five-storey, delicately honeycombed, pink sandstone structure. It was constructed in 1799 by Maharaja Sawaj Pratap Singh to enable ladies of the royal household to watch the life and processions of the city. It's an amazing example of Rajput artistry, and remains a great place for people-watching from behind the small shutters. The top offers stunning views over the Jantar Mantar and the City

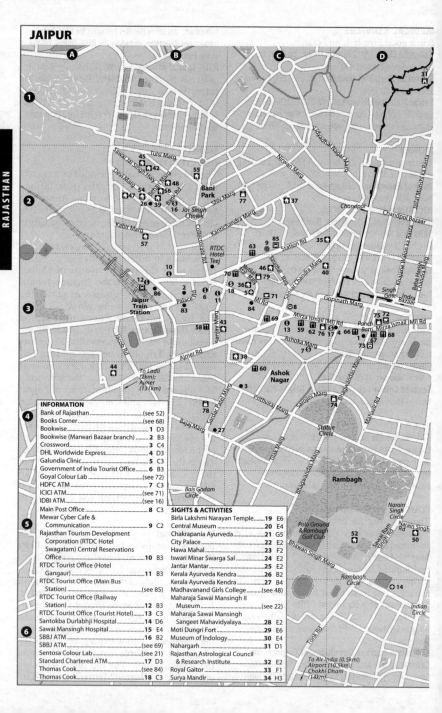

JAIPUR

INFORMATION
Bank of Rajasthan	(see 52)
Books Corner	(see 68)
Bookwise	**1** D3
Bookwise (Marwari Bazaar branch)	**2** B3
Crossword	**3** C4
DHL Worldwide Express	**4** D3
Galundia Clinic	**5** C3
Government of India Tourist Office	**6** B3
Goyal Colour Lab	(see 72)
HDFC ATM	**7** C3
ICICI ATM	(see 71)
IDBI ATM	(see 16)
Main Post Office	**8** C3
Mewar Cyber Cafe & Communication	**9** C2
Rajasthan Tourism Development Corporation (RTDC Hotel Swagatam) Central Reservations Office	**10** B3
RTDC Tourist Office (Hotel Gangaur)	**11** B3
RTDC Tourist Office (Main Bus Station)	(see 85)
RTDC Tourist Office (Railway Station)	**12** B3
RTDC Tourist Office (Tourist Hotel)	**13** C3
Santokba Durlabhji Hospital	**14** D6
Sawai Mansingh Hospital	**15** B2
SBBJ ATM	**16** B2
SBBJ ATM	(see 69)
Sentosa Colour Lab	(see 21)
Standard Chartered ATM	**17** D3
Thomas Cook	(see 84)
Thomas Cook	**18** C3

SIGHTS & ACTIVITIES
Birla Lakshmi Narayan Temple	**19** E6
Central Museum	**20** E4
Chakrapania Ayurveda	**21** G5
City Palace	**22** E2
Hawa Mahal	**23** F2
Iswari Minar Swarga Sal	**24** E2
Jantar Mantar	**25** E2
Kerala Ayurveda Kendra	**26** B2
Kerala Ayurveda Kendra	**27** B4
Madhavanand Girls College	(see 48)
Maharaja Sawai Mansingh II Museum	(see 22)
Maharaja Sawai Mansingh Sangeet Mahavidyalaya	**28** E2
Moti Dungri Fort	**29** E6
Museum of Indology	**30** E4
Nahargarh	**31** D1
Rajasthan Astrological Council & Research Institute	**32** E2
Royal Gaitor	**33** F1
Surya Mandir	**34** H3

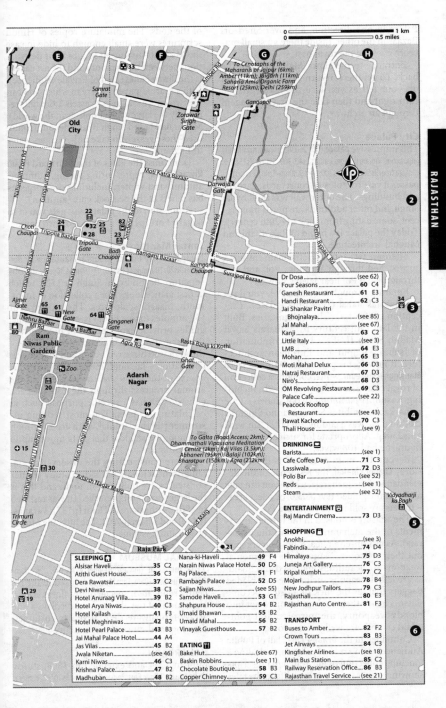

RAJASTHAN

Dr Dosa ....(see 62)
Four Seasons **60** C4
Ganesh Restaurant **61** E3
Handi Restaurant **62** C3
Jai Shankar Pavitri
  Bhojnalaya ....(see 85)
Jal Mahal ....(see 67)
Kanji **63** C2
Little Italy ....(see 3)
LMB **64** E3
Mohan **65** E3
Moti Mahal Delux **66** D3
Natraj Restaurant **67** D3
Niro's **68** D3
OM Revolving Restaurant **69** C3
Palace Cafe ....(see 22)
Peacock Rooftop
  Restaurant ....(see 43)
Rawat Kachori **70** C3
Thali House ....(see 9)

DRINKING 🍷
Barista ....(see 1)
Cafe Coffee Day **71** C3
Lassiwala **72** D3
Polo Bar ....(see 52)
Reds ....(see 1)
Steam ....(see 52)

ENTERTAINMENT 🎭
Raj Mandir Cinema **73** D3

SHOPPING 🛍
Anokhi ....(see 3)
Fabindia **74** D4
Himalaya **75** D3
Juneja Art Gallery **76** C3
Kripal Kumbh **77** C2
Mojari **78** B4
New Jodhpur Tailors **79** B2
Rajasthali **80** E3
Rajasthan Auto Centre **81** F3

TRANSPORT
Buses to Amber **82** F2
Crown Tours **83** B3
Jet Airways **84** C3
Kingfisher Airlines ....(see 18)
Main Bus Station **85** C2
Railway Reservation Office **86** B3
Rajasthan Travel Service ....(see 21)

SLEEPING 🏠
Alsisar Haveli **35** C2
Atithi Guest House **36** C3
Dera Rawatsar **37** C2
Devi Niwas **38** C3
Hotel Anuraag Villa **39** B2
Hotel Arya Niwas **40** C3
Hotel Kailash **41** F3
Hotel Meghniwas **42** B2
Hotel Pearl Palace **43** B3
Jai Mahal Palace Hotel **44** A4
Jas Vilas **45** B2
Jwala Niketan ....(see 46)
Karni Niwas **46** B2
Krishna Palace **47** B2
Madhuban **48** B2
Nana-ki-Haveli **49** F4
Narain Niwas Palace Hotel **50** D5
Raj Palace **51** F1
Rambagh Palace **52** D5
Sajjan Niwas ....(see 55)
Samode Haveli **53** G1
Shahpura House **54** B2
Umaid Bhawan **55** B2
Umaid Mahal **56** B2
Vinayak Guesthouse **57** B2

EATING 🍴
Bake Hut ....(see 67)
Baskin Robbins ....(see 11)
Chocolate Boutique **58** B3
Copper Chimney **59** C3

Palace in one direction, and over Siredeori Bazaar in the other. Inside there's a small museum evoking the royal past.

Entrance to the Hawa Mahal is from the back. To get there, return to the intersection on your left as you face the Hawa Mahal, turn right and then take the first right again through an archway.

City Palace

This impressive **palace** (☎ 2608055; www.royalfamily jaipur.com; Indian/foreigner adult Rs40/300, 5-12yr Rs25/200, camera free/Rs50, video Rs200; ⏰ 9.30am-5pm) encompasses a vast complex of courtyards, gardens and buildings. The outer wall was built by Jai Singh, but other additions are much more recent, some dating from the early 20th century. Today the palace is a blend of Rajasthani and Mughal architecture.

There are two entrances: the main entrance, approached through Virendra Pol, and one through Udai Pol near Jaleb Chowk.

Entering through Virendra Pol, you'll see the **Mubarak Mahal** (Welcome Palace), a reception centre for visiting dignitaries. Built in the late 19th century by Maharaja Sawai Madho Singh II, it's a heady combination of Islamic, Rajput and European architecture. It now forms part of the **Maharaja Sawai Mansingh II Museum**, which contains a collection of royal costumes and superb shawls, including Kashmiri *pashmina* (wool shawls). One remarkable exhibit is Sawai Madho Singh I's clothing. He was a cuddly 2m tall, 1.2m wide and 250kg. Appropriate for such an excessive figure, he had 108 wives.

Beyond the main courtyard is the seven-storey **Chandra Mahal**, the residence of the descendants of the maharaja, where you can take a 45-minute guided **tour** (Rs2500) of select areas – tickets are sold inside Rajendra Pol.

The **armoury** is housed in the former apartments of the maharanis (wives of the maharaja). As visitors enter, fearsome daggers spell out their welcome. Many of the ceremonial weapons are beautifully engraved and inlaid, as are lethal weapons such as the two-bladed daggers that, at the flick of a catch, become scissors inside their victims. If you're not into bloody weaponry, the mirrored and gold-inlaid ceilings are well worth a look.

Contained in the **Diwan-i-Am** (Hall of Public Audience) is an array of exhibits, including a touching collection of illustrated manuscripts showing scenes from everyday life to the tales

of the gods. The miniature copies of Hindu scriptures were small enough to hide in case the Mughal Aurangzeb sought their destruction. Between the armoury and the art gallery is the **Diwan-i-Khas** (Hall of Private Audience), with a marble-paved gallery in which you can see two enormous silver vessels 1.6m tall (reputedly the largest silver objects in the world); Maharaja Madho Singh II, as a devout Hindu, used these vessels to take holy Ganges water to England.

Don't miss the gates of the courtyard **Pitam Niwas Chowk**, representing spring, summer, autumn and winter, including the gorgeous bas reliefs of the peacock gate (autumn).

Admission to the palace also gets you in to Jaigarh Fort (p183); it's valid for two days.

Jantar Mantar

Near the City Palace is **Jantar Mantar** (Indian/foreigner Rs20/100, guides Rs100; ⏰ 9am-4.30pm), an observatory begun by Jai Singh in 1728, which at first glance looks like a collection of mammoth, bizarre sculptures. The guided tour (30 minutes to one hour) is well worthwhile; guides provide explanations of how each of the fascinating instruments work, and how – through watching, recording and meticulous calculation – Jai Singh measured time by the course of the sun's shadow and charted the annual progress through the zodiac. Each construction has a specific purpose, such as calculating eclipses. The most striking instrument is the sundial, with its 27m-high gnomon; the shadow this casts moves up to 4m per hour.

Before constructing the observatory, Jai Singh sent scholars abroad to study similar constructs. He built five in total, and this is the largest and best preserved (it was restored in 1901). Others are in Delhi (p137), Varanasi (p440) and Ujjain (p703). The fifth, the Muttra observatory, is gone.

CENTRAL MUSEUM

This **museum** (Indian/foreigner Rs15/100; ⏰ 10am-4.30pm Tue-Sun, 10am-1pm Mon) is housed in the recently renovated, spectacularly florid Albert Hall, south of the old city, and displays a fine array of tribalware, decorative arts, costumes, drawings and musical instruments.

NAHARGARH

Built in 1734 and extended in 1868, sturdy **Nahargarh** (Tiger Fort; Indian/foreigner Rs10/30, camera/

video Rs20/70; ⊙ 10am-5pm) overlooks the city from a sheer ridge to the north. An 8km road runs up to the fort through the hills from Jaipur, or it can be reached along a zigzagging 2km footpath. There are some interesting furnished rooms in the fort and glorious views – it's a popular picnic spot on weekends, and the perfect place to catch the sunset.

ROYAL GAITOR

The site of the royal **cenotaphs** (admission free, Indian/foreigner camera Rs10/20; ⊙ 9am-4.30pm), just beyond the city walls, is an appropriately restful place to visit. Surrounded by a straggling village, the monuments bear much beautiful, intricate carving. The marble cenotaph of Maharaja Jai Singh II is particularly impressive.

The **cenotaphs of the maharanis of Jaipur** (Amber Rd; admission free, Indian/foreigner camera Rs10/30; ⊙ 9am-4.30pm) are less impressive and less well maintained but OK for a stroll. They are found midway between Jaipur and Amber, opposite the Holiday Inn.

GALTA & SURYA MANDIR

The temple complex at **Galta** is also appropriately known as the Monkey Temple. Hundreds of monkeys live here – graceful langurs and aggressive macaques. You can buy peanuts at the gate to feed them, but be prepared to be mobbed by up to 50 teeth-baring primates. On arrival, it's a steady 200m climb up to the bathing tanks, and it's often packed with pilgrims. Donations are sometimes insisted upon, and women travellers have reported feeling uncomfortable walking up here alone.

On the ridge above Galta is the **Surya Mandir** (Temple of the Sun God), which overlooks Jaipur. The temple can also be accessed by a steep 200m walking trail from Surajpol Bazaar.

The beautiful **Dhammathali Vipassana Meditation Centre** (see p174) is about 3km from Jaipur city centre on the Sisodiarani Baug–Galtaji road. A rickshaw will cost around Rs150 return.

OTHER SIGHTS

The ramshackle, dusty treasure-trove of the **SRC Museum of Indology** (Prachyavidya Path, 24 Gangwell park; Indian/foreigner incl guide Rs20/40; ⊙ 8am-6pm) is an extraordinary private collection of folk-art objects – there's everything from a manuscript written by Aurangzeb to a glass bed. The museum is signposted off J Nehru Marg, south of the Central Museum.

Further south is the small fort of **Moti Dungri** (J Nehru Marg), which is closed to the public. At its foot is the modern **Birla Lakshmi Narayan Temple** (J Nehru Marg; ⊙ 6am-noon & 3-8.30pm), with splendid marble carving. Free guides explain aspects of the temple. Next to the temple there's a small **museum** (admission free; ⊙ 8am-noon & 4-8pm), which houses everyday objects from the industrially renowned Birla family.

Activities
AYURVEDIC MASSAGE

A sure-fire cure for the big-city blues can be found at the swanky **Kerala Ayurveda Kendra** (☎ 5106743; www.keralaayurvedakendra; Bajaj Marg; ⊙ 8am-8.30pm), where an hour-long massage starts at Rs500. Or try **Chakrapania Ayurveda** (☎ 2624003; www.chakrapaniayurveda.com; 8 Diamond Hill, Tulsi Circle, Shanti Path; ⊙ 9am-2pm & 3-7pm Mon-Sat, 9am-1pm Sun).

ASTROLOGY

Dr Vinod Shastri is the medal-laden general secretary of the **Rajasthan Astrological Council & Research Institute** (☎ 2663338; Chandani Chowk, Tripolia Gate; ⊙ consultations 9am-8pm). He will prepare a computerised horoscope if you have your exact time and place of birth, or will read your palm. Although he should know when you're arriving, it's best to make an appointment.

Walking Tour

Start at Panch Batti, beneath the statue of Maharaja Sawai Jai Singh.

Head north along MI Rd, then turn left at Gopinath Marg and enter the walled city. Once inside, walk straight towards **Khajane Walon ka Rasta (1)**, where you'll see fine marble craftsmanship. Turn right at Chandpol Bazaar and continue until you reach the intersection of Choti Chaupar and **Kishanpol Bazaar (2)**, where textile artisans design their *bandhani* (tie-dye) and *loharia* (literally 'waves'; tie-dye technique creating a striped or zigzagged effect).

After crossing Choti Chaupar, you'll reach **Tripolia Bazaar (3)**, home to an array of metal trinkets and kitchen utensils. Tucked away to the right is **Maniharon ka Rasta (4)**, the domain of the lac (resin) bangle makers. To the north of the bazaar is the soaring **Iswari Minar Swarga Sal (5; p169)**. About 50m from the minaret is **Tripolia Gate (6)**, the three-arched main entrance to the City

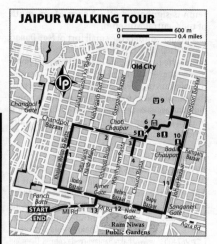

JAIPUR WALKING TOUR

WALK FACTS

Start: Panch Batti
Finish: Panch Batti
Distance: 4km
Duration: 1.5–2.5 hours

Palace, though only the royal descendants are permitted to enter via its portals. The public entrance is to the left, via Atishpol (Stable Gate). From here, you can visit the **City Palace** (**7**; p172), the **Jantar Mantar** (**8**; p172) and, to the north of the City Palace, the impressive **Govind Devji Temple** (**9**), surrounded by gardens.

Come out of the complex through the Jaleb Chowk (you may need to ask). To your right is the **Hawa Mahal** (**10**; p169), and bustling Siredeori Bazaar. A few metres away is the large square Badi Chaupar and further south is **Johari Bazaar** (**11**), known for its gold and silversmiths. Many of the grand *havelis* shading the street belong to wealthy cotton merchants. Of particular interest here is the meenakari. This highly glazed and intricate enamelwork in shades of ruby, bottle green and royal blue is a speciality of Jaipur.

If you turn right before Sanganeri Gate, you'll reach Bapu Bazaar, then further west is **Nehru Bazaar** (**12**), which extends between Chaura Rasta and Kishanpol Bazaar on the inside of the southern wall. Brightly coloured fabrics, camel-skin shoes and perfumes make this area hugely popular with local women. At the end of Nehru Bazaar, to your left, is Ajmer

Gate. Come out of the gate and the road you see is **MI Rd** (**13**) – great for restaurants and for general Jaipur hubbub. Turn right from here, and walk straight ahead and you will come back to Panch Batti.

Courses

Chakrapania Ayurveda (☎ 2624003; www.learn ayurveda.com; 8 Diamond Hill, Tulsi Circle, Shanti Path; ☻ 9am-2pm & 3-7pm Mon-Sat, 9am-1pm Sun). Chakrapani also offers courses in Ayurveda for students (beginners and experienced alike) and regularly takes international students.

Dhammathali Vipassana Meditation Centre (☎ 2680220; Galta) This beautifully located centre runs 10-day meditation courses for a donation.

Madhavanand Girls College (☎ 2200317; C19 Behari Marg, Bani Park) There are free hatha yoga classes here from 6am to 7am.

Maharaja Sawai Mansingh Sangeet Mahavidyalaya (☎ 2611397; ☻ music lessons 8am-11am, dance 4-8pm Mon-Sat) This is an excellent music school located behind Tripolia Gate. Tuition (per month from Rs500) is given in dance and in Indian instruments such as tabla (pair of drums) and *bakhawas* (double-sided drum).

Tours

The RTDC offers half-/full-day tours of Jaipur and around. The **full-day tours** (per person Rs200; ☻ 9am to 6pm) take in all the major sites (including Amber Fort), with a lunch break at Nahargarh. The lunch break can be as late as 3pm, so have a big breakfast. AC bus tours (10am to 5pm) cost Rs135/180; they don't include Nahargarh. Rushed **half-day tours** (Rs150; ☻ 8am to 1pm, 11.30am-4.30pm, 1.30-6.30pm) are confined to the city limits – some travellers recommend these, as you avoid the long lunch break. Fees don't include admission charges. Tours depart from the train station (depending on demand), and pick up from the RTDC tourist offices at the RTDC Hotels Gangaur and Tourist. You're not immune to prolonged stops at emporiums along the way. The **Pink City by Night tour** (Rs250; ☻ 6.30-10.30pm) explores several well-known sights and includes a vegetarian dinner at Nahargarh Fort.

Book all tours at the RTDC Tourist Hotel and the RTDC tourist offices at the RTDC Hotels Gangaur and Tourist where there is a tour office just behind reception.

Sleeping

Autorickshaw drivers besiege travellers who arrive by train or bus. If you take their suggestions, chances are you'll pay a commission to the hotel owner. To avoid such shenanigans, go straight to the prepaid autorickshaw stands at the bus and train stations. Alternatively, most hotels will pick you up if you ring ahead.

From May to September, most midrange and top-end places will offer bargain rates, dropping prices by 25% to 50%.

BUDGET

Jwala Niketan (☎ 5108303; www.jwala-niketan.com; C6 Motilal Atal Marg; r Rs200-700;) This quiet yet centrally located guesthouse has a range of inexpensive, clean but bland rooms. The host family lives on the premises and the atmosphere is decidedly noncommercial – free of any form of decoration or ambience. There is no restaurant but the family's vegetarian food is available.

Hotel Kailash (☎ 2577372; Johari Bazaar; s/d Rs500/575, without bathroom Rs330/360) This hotel, opposite the Jama Masjid, is one of the few places to stay within the old city. It's nothing fancy and the undersized rooms are basic and stuffy despite the central air-cooling. Rooms at the back are quieter and management is buoyant and welcoming.

Hotel Pearl Palace (☎ 2373700; www.hotelpearl palace.com; s Rs300-850, d Rs350-900;) A popular choice in a quiet location off Ajmer Rd. Mr and Mrs Singh put much effort into maintaining the brightly decorated rooms and the outstanding Peacock Rooftop Restaurant. Guests have access to money-changing, travel services and free pick-up and drop-off. By the time you read this, the Pearl Palace Heritage hotel being constructed nearby should be up and running under the same energetic team. Book ahead.

Devi Niwas (☎ 2363727; singh_kd@hotmail.com; Dhuleshwar Bagh, Sadar Patel Marg, C-Scheme; r Rs400, with AC Rs700;) A relaxed and simple homestay featuring genuine family hospitality. There are just five rooms, so it is wise to book ahead. Food is home cooked and tasty, and there's a small garden.

Krishna Palace (☎ 2201395; www.krishnapalace.com; E26 Durga Marg, Bani Park; r Rs450, with AC Rs850;) Krishna Palace is an overly managed hotel with some boisterous staff; however, there are some quiet corners to retreat to with a book. It's convenient for the train station and the rooms are maintained to an adequate standard.

Vinayak Guesthouse (☎ 3249963; vinayaguesthouse@ yahoo.co.in; 4 Kabir Marg, Bani Park; s/d Rs500/600;)

This simple guesthouse in a neighbourhood of similar establishments has none of the trappings to lure foreign guests. The rooms are functional and bare and on the drab side, but the host is welcoming and it's close to the train station.

Karni Niwas (2365433; www.hotelkarniniwas.com; C5 Motilal Atal Marg; s Rs550-950, d Rs650-1200;) Tucked behind Hotel Neelam in a quiet back road, this friendly hotel has spacious, comfortable rooms – many with balconies or relaxing plant-filled terraces. Offers free pick-up from the train and bus stations.

Atithi Guest House (☎ 2378679; atithijaipur@hotmail .com; 1 Park House Scheme Rd; r Rs750-1200;) This unassuming guesthouse with a helpful owner offers clean, simple rooms in a central (though quiet) location between MI and Station Rds. Rooms were being refurbished when we visited and most have balconies. There's a rooftop restaurant and room service.

Hotel Arya Niwas (☎ 2372456; www.aryaniwas.com; r Rs800, with AC s/d Rs990/1500;) Just off Sansar Chandra Marg, this reliable hotel attracts a broad spectrum of short- and long-term clientele. There's a long soothing terrace facing a peaceful grassy lawn, and it has a high-quality self-service veg restaurant. Rooms vary in layout and size so check out a few.

MIDRANGE
Bani Park

The Bani Park area is *relatively* green and peaceful, about 2km from the old city, and home to many midrange, family-owned hotels.

Hotel Anuraag Villa (☎ 2201679; www.anuraagvilla .com; D249 Devi Marg; r Rs800-1900;) This quiet and comfortable option has no-fuss, spacious rooms and an extensive lawn where you find some quiet respite from the hassles of sightseeing. It has a restaurant and efficient, helpful staff.

Sajjan Niwas (☎ 2311544; www.sajjanniwas.com; via Behari Marg, Bani Park; s/d from Rs1200/1400, with AC Rs850;) Sajjan Niwas is a heritage building with some lovely spacious rooms, antique furnishings and delightful coloured glass and old-world charm. So far so good but the tariffs are a little high for what is on offer. There's a delightful rooftop restaurant.

Dera Rawatsar (☎ 2200770; www.derarawatsar .com; D194, Vijay Path; r Rs1400-2800, ste Rs4500;) Situated off the main drag, this quiet hotel is managed by a gracious Bikaner noble family.

It has nicely decorated rooms, sunny court-yards, fantastic home-style Indian meals and a story-telling matriarch.

Madhuban (☎ 2200033; www.madhuban.net; D237 Behari Marg; s Rs1500-2000, d Rs1600-3200; ✗ ☐ 🏊) Madhuban is a popular hassle-free midrange hotel, run by the charming Dicky and his family. Surrounded by walls and greenery, privacy is ensured and the rooms are fully decked out. The restaurant is smart and versatile, and there's a small private pool, though most guests quickly gravitate to the serene, relaxing lawn.

Umaid Bhawan (☎ 2206426; www.umaidbhawan .com; D1-2A, via Behari Marg; r Rs1600-2400, ste Rs3500; ✗ ☐ 🏊) Stepping into this hotel is like entering an Indian painting, with zigzagging stairways, cosy alcoves and scalloped arches, all brightly coloured. The rooftop restaurant has a wonderful setting. The comfortable, decorated rooms come with breakfast.

Umaid Mahal (☎ 2201952; reservation@umaidmahal .com; C20B/2, Behari Marg; s/d from Rs1600/1800; ✗ ☐ 🏊) This lofty, sparkling 'castle' in a quiet back-street is run by the same family as Umaid Bhawan. Rooms are spotless and lavishly decorated, and the indoor pool and rooftop restaurant are delightful. Both hotels offer free pick-up from the train and bus stations.

Hotel Meghniwas (☎ 2202034; www.meghniwas.com; C9 Sawai Jai Singh Hwy; s/d from Rs2000/2200; ste Rs3800; ✗ ☐ 🏊) In a 1950s building constructed in 1948 by Brigadier Singh and run by his friendly descendants, this place has modern rooms with traditional carved furniture and leafy outlooks. Nos 201 and 209 are like mini-apartments – good for long-termers. The pool is in a pleasant lawn area.

Jas Vilas (☎ 2204638; www.jasvilas.com; C9 Sawai Jai Singh Hwy; s/d Rs2800/3200; ✗ ☐ 🏊) Built by a military man in 1950, this excellent choice is run by a charming family, and offers welcoming, eager-to-please service. There are 11 classy rooms, most of which face the romantic courtyard with its sparkling pool. There's a secluded lawn and a cosy dining room.

Shahpura House (☎ 2203069; www.shahpurahouse .com; D257 Devi Marg; s/d/ste Rs3000/3500/4500; ✗ ☐ 🏊) Owned by the Shekhawat Rajput clan, this is a sumptuous option, although it lacks a family-run feel. It's built in elaborate traditional style, and offers immaculate rooms, some with balconies, and even a durbar (royal court) hall with a huge chandelier. The swimming pool is superb.

Elsewhere

Nana-ki-Haveli (☎ 2615502; www.nanakihaveli.com; Fateh Tiba; r Rs1500-3000) A tranquil, tucked-away place with attractive rooms decorated in traditional style, this place is run by a lovely family for whom nothing is too much trouble. It's off Moti Dungri Rd and has a relaxing front garden and home-style cooking.

Narain Niwas Palace Hotel (☎ 2561291; www.hotel narainniwas.com; Narain Singh Rd; s/d/ste Rs3000/4200/5500; ✗ ☐ 🏊) This sprawling palace has a wonderful ramshackle splendour with liveried staff, a formal dining room and a deep verandah where you can settle into the wicker with a book and a cup of tea. There is also a variety of charm-filled heritage rooms, so check out a few (particularly the bathrooms). The good-sized pool is secluded in the vast, lush garden.

Alsisar Haveli (☎ 2368290; www.alsisarhaveli.com; Sansar Chandra Marg; s/d/ste Rs3025/3900/4550; ✗ ☐ 🏊) Set in beautiful grounds, this gracious 19th-century mansion has quaintly furnished, elegant rooms featuring arches and antique furnishings. It's popular with tour groups and lacks a family atmosphere but is still a nice refuge.

TOP END

Samode Haveli (☎ 2632370; www.samode.com; s/d €170/195, ste €225-285; ✗ ☐ 🏊) This classic heritage hotel was once the town house of the Rawal of Samode, the prime minister of Jaipur. The suites get high romance points, with big beds, private terraces and intricate mirror work. The standard rooms are more ordinary but still have charm. The tariff, which includes breakfast, drops remarkably from May to September.

Jai Mahal Palace Hotel (☎ 2223636; www.tajhotels .com; Jacob Rd; d/ste Rs12,500/22,000; ✗ ☐ 🏊) Once the residence of Jaipur's prime minister, this gracious 18th-century building is now a grand, luxurious hotel run by the Taj Group. It is set in 7 hectares of manicured Mughal gardens, which most of the swish, comfortable rooms overlook.

Raj Palace (☎ 2634077; www.rajpalace.com; d/ste US$375-500, ste US$750-40,000; Zorawar Singh Gate, Amber Rd; ✗ ☐) This stunning palace is almost over-the-top-end, with an antique-crockery museum, an enormous crystal chandelier and a stellar list of royal guests. The standard rooms are properly palatial, the numerous suites are all heavenly, and the US$40,000 Shahi Mahal (Presidential suite) is surely astronomical.

Rambagh Palace (☎ 2211919; www.tajhotels.com; Bhawani Singh Marg; d Rs24,000-37,000, ste Rs69,000-199,000; ⊠ ▣ ▨) The former residence of the maharaja, this beautiful palace is now a luxury hotel set in 19 hectares of serene gardens with sweeping views across immaculate lawns. Even nonguests can (and should) treat themselves tea on the verandah, a pick-me-up in the Polo Bar, or a lavish meal in one of the restaurants.

Raj Vilas (☎ 2680101; www.oberoihotels.com; Goner Rd; r US$675, luxury tents US$800, villas US$3400; ⊠ ▣ ▨) About 8km from the centre, Oberoi's Raj Vilas is Jaipur's last word in cost-is-no-option sophistication. Its terracotta domed rooms are set in more than 13 fountain-filled hectares, and each villa has its own pool.

Eating
RESTAURANTS
MI Road

Handi Restaurant (MI Rd; mains Rs60-180; ☯ noon-3.30pm & 6.30-11.30pm) This old favourite is opposite the main post office, at the back of Maya Mansions, and offers scrumptious barbecue dishes and Mughlai cuisine in a village atmosphere. In the evenings a deliciously tempting smoky kebab stall sets up at the entrance to the restaurant.

Natraj Restaurant (MI Rd; mains Rs80-200; ☯ 11am-11pm) This classy vegetarian restaurant has an extensive menu featuring North Indian, continental and Chinese cuisine. The stuffed tomato is divine, and the potato bomb curry will blow you away. There's also a good selection of thalis, and South Indian fans will find scrumptious dosas.

Copper Chimney (Maya Mansions; mains Rs100-220; ☯ noon-3.30pm & 6.30-11.30pm) Near Handi Restaurant, Copper Chimney is a chic, elegant place with a friendly waiter army and a rollicking horse mural. It offers veg and nonveg Indian as well as a small selection of Continental and Chinese food. Indian wines are available to accompany the generous portions.

Dr Dosa (☎ 4038468; Gaurav Tower, MI Rd; mains Rs120-195; ☯ 11am-11pm) Though it has a quirky name and a cartoon sign, this classy all-veg restaurant is worth a visit. Enter through the defensive wooden door, and inside you'll find a feature fish tank, dim lighting and white linen tables with silver service – including goblets. As the name suggests there are traditional dosas, but there are also multicuisine versions

of this South Indian classic. And it's not all dosas: North Indian, Chinese and continental dishes are also offered.

Niro's (☎ 2374493; MI Rd; mains Rs140-370; ☯ 11am-11pm) Niro's has been on duty for more than 50 years, and still pumps out classic Indian fare and piped muzak. Under a mirrored roof, masses tuck into the extensive range of veg and nonveg dishes. The *lal maans* (mutton in spicy red gravy), and *began bharta* (aubergine) were delicious.

Moti Mahal Delux (☎ 4017733; MI Rd; mains Rs140-380; ☯ 11am-4pm, 7-11pm) The famous Delhi restaurant now has franchises all over India delivering its world-famous butter chicken to the masses. The tantalising menu features a vast range of veg and nonveg, including seafood and succulent tandoori dishes. Snuggle into a comfortable booth and enjoy the ambience, spicy food, and last but not least, a delicious *pista kulfi* (pistachio-flavoured sweet similar to ice cream).

Old City

Mohan (144-5 Nehru Bazaar; mains Rs10-60; ☯ 9.30am-10pm) This popular chow pit is grubby on the outside, but prepares freshly cooked food on the inside. The name is in Hindi and it's on the corner of the street, a few steps down from the pavement.

Ganesh Restaurant (☎ 2312380; Nehru Bazaar; mains Rs35-85; ☯ 9.30am-11pm) This pocket-sized outdoor restaurant is in a fantastic location *on* the old city wall. There's not much English spoken, but if you're looking for a local eatery with fresh tasty food you'll love it. It's near New Gate, with a narrow, hidden stairway between two tailors – you'll no doubt be helped to find the stairs.

LMB (Lakshmi Misthan Bandar; ☎ 2560845; Johari Bazaar; mains Rs55-210; ☯ 8am-11pm) LMB is an Art Deco–meets-disco, sattvik (pure vegetarian) restaurant that's been going strong since 1954. The menu includes a warning from Krishna about people who like putrid and polluted food *(tamasic)*. All meals are made with pure ghee (clarified butter), and the *puri* (deep-fried bread) snacks are the best in town. Recommended is the Rajasthani thali, the paneer tikka stuffed with fennel, and the signature *kulfi*.

Palace Cafe (☎ 2616449; City Palace; mains Rs80-350; ☯ 9.30am-5pm) Tucked inside the City Palace, this is a quiet place to break the sightseeing with a cool drink. It has a bar and pleasant outdoor tables where you can snack on Indian and continental snacks and main dishes.

Elsewhere

Jai Shankar Pavitra Bhojnalaya (☎ 25102541; 12 Sindhi Camp Bus Stand, Station Rd; mains Rs10-50; ⏰ 7am-10pm) Convenient to the main bus station, this popular, simple veg place does especially good Indian breakfasts. There is limited English, but the food is fast, fresh and delicious.

Thali House (☎ 5115522; Station Rd; thalis Rs50-80; ⏰ 9am-11pm) This frenetic restaurant is a favourite with thali connoisseurs. There's a fast-service area under cyclonic fans and a more relaxed air-con section where you can savour the very popular veg thali.

Four Seasons (☎ 2373700; D43A Subhas Marg; mains Rs75-170; ⏰ noon-3.30pm & 6.30-11pm) This smart, hugely popular place is on two levels, with a glass wall to the kitchen. It's an alcohol-free, pure vegetarian place with a mouthwatering menu featuring Rajasthani, North Indian and South Indian specialities, thalis, dosas and pizzas.

Little Italy (☎ 4022444; 3rd fl, KK Sq, C-11, Prithviraj Marg; mains Rs165-200; ⏰ noon-3.30pm & 6.30-11pm) The best Italian restaurant in town, Little Italy is part of a small chain that dishes up excellent vegetarian pasta, risotto and wood-fired pizza in cool, contemporary surroundings. The menu is extensive and includes some first-rate Italian desserts. There is a lounge bar attached so your vegetarian dining can be accompanied with wine or beer.

Peacock Rooftop Restaurant (☎ 2373700; Hotel Pearl Palace; Hari Kishan Somani Marg; mains Rs35-120; ⏰ 7am-11pm) Overlooking Hathroi Fort – and most of Jaipur – this multilevel rooftop restaurant with an extraordinary peacock canopy has excellent views and food to match. Sit in the quirky iron furniture or upstairs in the romantic nook to enjoy superb Indian and Chinese dishes, or even a pizza. There are great value thalis (veg and nonveg starting at Rs50) and Western breakfasts.

OM Revolving Restaurant (☎ 2366683; Church Rd; mains Rs110-300; ⏰ noon-3.30pm & 7-11pm) The rocket-shaped tower of Jaipur houses a revolving restaurant 56m above the glittering city. The surrounds are almost glitzy, and the alcohol-free vegetarian menu features several Rajasthani specialities as well as many multi-cuisine variations. The central stage occasionally hosts live *ghazal* singing (Urdu songs derived from poetry; sad love themes).

QUICK EATS

Chocolate Boutique (68 Gopal Bari Rd; cakes Rs20-90; ⏰ 10.30am-8.30pm Mon-Sat) This tiny shop of tempting treats has a small range of fresh cakes, brownies, tarts and pies, as well as quality homemade chocolates, which you can buy separately (Rs10 to Rs12 each) or gift boxed.

Bake Hut (Arvind Marg, off MI Rd; cakes Rs25-100; ⏰ 9am-8pm Mon-Sat) An extremely busy bakery that does a roaring trade in sweet cakes and various breads. It's attached to the back of the Surya Mahal restaurant.

Jal Mahal (MI Rd; ice creams Rs12-110; ⏰ 10am-midnight) This packed little takeaway ice-cream parlour has some inventive concoctions, from the earthquake to the after ate.

Baskin Robbins (Sanjay Marg; ice creams Rs15-140; ⏰ noon-11.30pm) Tucked into the edge of the Hotel Gangaur's compound is this pint-sized ice-cream pit stop.

For great Indian sweets – including Jaipur's own sticky *ghevar* (a honeycomb-shaped cake covered in ghee and milk) topped with flaked almonds – head to the mobbed **Rawat Kachori** (Station Rd; sweets Rs5-10, lassis Rs22); a delicious milk crown should fill you up for the afternoon. Across the road is **Kanji** (Station Rd; sweets per kg Rs110-300), with a similarly fabulous array.

Drinking

CAFES

Barista (Mall 21, Bhagwandas Marg; coffees Rs50-70; ⏰ 9am-11pm) For excellent espresso coffee and iced concoctions, as well as muffins, snacks and sandwiches, head to this branch opposite the Raj Mandir cinema.

Cafe Coffee Day (Ganpati Plaza, MI Rd; coffee Rs35-90; ⏰ 9am-11pm) India's premier coffee chain has the best value espresso and cold coffees in town; you'll find this air-con escape with cakes and snacks hidden downstairs.

Lassiwala (Shop 312, MI Rd; small/large lassi Rs12/24; ⏰ 7.30am-till sold out) This milky institution is a simple little place that whips up fabulous, creamy lassis (yoghurt and filtered iced-water drink) served in clay cups. Will the real Lassiwala please stand up? It's the one that says 'Shop 312', directly next to the alleyway; imitators spread to the right as you face it.

BARS

Reds (☎ 4007710; 5th fl, Mall 21, Bhagwandas Marg; ⏰ 11am-11pm) Overlooking the Raj Mandir cinema and MI Rd with views to Tiger Fort, Reds is a slick place to kick back with a drink or take a meal. Settle down into a couch with a beer (bottled or draught), cocktail or mocktail.

Polo Bar (Rambagh Palace Hotel, Bhawan Singh Marg; ⏱ 11am-11pm) A spiffing watering hole adorned with polo memorabilia and arched, scalloped windows framing the neatly clipped lawns. A bottle of beer costs Rs250 to Rs300 and cocktails around Rs450.

Steam (Rambagh Palace Hotel, Bhawan Singh Rd; ⏱ 7pm-late Wed-Mon) The Rambagh's lounge bar is a relaxed and stylish haven with a steam engine and a DJ. Sip a cocktail, sample a pizza and lighten your wallet.

Entertainment

Raj Mandir Cinema (☎ 2379372; Rs50-110; Bhagwandas Marg; ⏱ reservations 10am-6pm, sessions 12.30pm, 3.30pm, 6.30pm & 9.30pm) The number-one Hindi cinema in India, Raj Mandir is an icon of Jaipur. Opened in 1976, this creamy meringue construction looks good enough to eat. It's usually full, despite its immense size, but bookings can be made one hour to seven days in advance at Windows 7 and 8. Alternatively, sharpen your elbows and join the queue when the current booking office opens 45 minutes before the curtain goes up.

Chokhi Dhani (☎ 2225001; adult/3-9yr incl meal Rs300/150; ⏱ 6pm-11pm) Located 15km from Jaipur, this virtual village provides a fantastical, magical evening. It's pretend ethnicity, but don't let that put you off. Stroll through gardens lit by glimmering lamps and dine on traditional Rajasthani thalis. Then take in some offbeat entertainment: traditional tribal dancers setting fire to their hats, small children balancing on poles, and dancers dressed in lion costumes. It's hugely popular with Delhi-based families.

Shopping

Jaipur is addicted to shopping, and shopaholics will be in heaven. From the timeless bazaars of the old city to the towering malls of glass and chrome, which seem to be sprouting everywhere, there is an amazing array of items for sale – Rajasthani crafts, textiles, art and, of course, gems. Bargaining is the name of the game. Tourist traps around the City Palace and Hawa Mahal have higher starting prices. At some shops, such as the government emporiums, prices are fixed, but often on the high side. For useful tips on bargaining, see p1161.

Most of the larger shops can pack and send your parcels home for you – although it'll be cheaper if you do it yourself (see p169 for postal services).

Jaipur is famous for precious and semiprecious stones. Many shops offer bargain prices, but you do need to be able to recognise both your gems and your charlatans. The main gem-dealing area is around the Muslim area of Pahar Ganj, near Surajpol. Here, in the narrow lanes, you can see stones being cut and polished. Johari and Siredeori Bazaars are where you'll find jewellery shops selling gold, silver and fine, highly glazed enamelwork known as meenakari.

The old city is still loosely divided into traditional artisans' quarters. Bapu Bazaar is lined with saris and fabrics, though you might find better deals along Johari Bazaar, where merchants specialise in cotton. Kishanpol Bazaar is famous for textiles, particularly *bandhani* (tie-dye). Nehru Bazaar has jootis (traditional pointy-toed shoes), trinkets and perfume. MI Rd is another good place to buy

RAJASTHAN

WARNING – GEM SCAMS

A disturbingly large number of travellers continue to get bedazzled by gem deals. These too-good-to-be-true con tricks might involve buying gems for resale at a supposedly huge profit, or getting paid by wealthy dealers to cart gems then suddenly coming up against 'customs problems' that mean you have to shell out huge amounts, or some other cunning ploy.

The con artists are invariably charming, often taking travellers to their homes and insisting on paying for meals. Mistaking a smooth operator for someone showing genuine Indian hospitality, the unsuspecting traveller begins to trust his or her new-found friend. The proposed moneymaking scheme a few days later seems too good to be true – and it is. If you buy gems for resale, they are usually worth a fraction of the price paid (or, if you agreed to have them sent, they may never arrive, even if you see them posted in front of you). Hard-luck stories about an inability to obtain an export licence or having to pay huge taxes are not your problem. Testimonials from other happy gem-dealing punters are easy to fake. Don't let the promise of easy money cloud your judgment.

jootis. The best place for bangles is Maniharon ka Rasta.

Factories and showrooms are strung along the length of Amber Rd between Zorawar Singh Gate and the Holiday Inn to catch tourist traffic. Here you'll find block prints, blue pottery, carpets and antiques, but the emporia are used to busloads swinging in to blow their cash, so you'll need to wear your bargaining hat.

Rickshaw-wallahs, hotels and travel agents will be getting a hefty cut from any shop they take you to. Steer clear of friendly young men on the street trying to take you to their uncle's/brother's/cousin's shop – commission is the name of their game too.

Rajasthali (MI Rd; ☺ 11am-8pm Mon-Sat) This state-government emporium, opposite Ajmer Gate, is packed with good-quality Rajasthani artefacts and crafts on four floors. A good reason to visit is to scout out prices before diving into the bazaars.

Anokhi (www. anokhi.com; 2nd fl, KK Sq, C-11, Prithviraj Marg; ☺ 9.30am-8pm Mon-Sat, 11am-7pm Sun) This classy boutique is well worth visiting, with high-quality textiles including block-printed fabrics and clothes. The pieces are produced just outside Jaipur at an unusually ethical factory built on the grounds of an organic farm. There's also a neat little cafe on the premises.

Fabindia (☎ 5115997; 2nd fl, 22 Godown Circle, Bhawani Singh Road; www.fabindia.com; Sarojini Marg) A great place to coordinate colours with reams of rich fabrics plus furniture and home accessories. As well, you can find organically certified garments, beauty products and condiments.

Kripal Kumbh (☎ 2201127; B18A Shiv Marg, Bani Park; ☺ 9am-5pm) This showroom, in a private home, is a great place to buy Jaipur blue pottery produced with lead-free glaze by Kumud and Manakshi Rathore, daughters of renowned potter and painter, the late Mr Kripal Singh. Ceramics are sold from Rs100 (for a paperweight) to Rs20,000 (for a large vase).

Mojari (Bhawani Villa, Gulab Path, Chomu House; ☺ 11am-6pm Mon-Sat) Mojari sells fabulous footwear. Named after the traditional decorated shoes of Rajasthan, Mojari is a UN-supported project that helps 3500 rural leatherworkers' households. It's fit for shoe fetishists, but not for large feet.

Juneja Art Gallery (www.artchill.com; 6-7 Laksmi Complex, MI Rd; ☺ 10am-8pm Mon-Sat) Has some striking pieces of contemporary art by Rajasthani artists (prices from Rs500 to Rs50,000). There is another branch of the gallery, Artchill, at Amber Fort (p182).

MAJOR TRAINS FROM JAIPUR				
Destination	**Train number & name**	**Fare (Rs)**	**Duration (hr)**	**Departure**
Agra	2308 *Howrah Jodhpur Exp*	157/385/512 (A)	4¾	2am
	2966 *Udaipur-Gwalior Exp*	157/385/512 (A)	4¼	6.10am
Ahmedabad	2958 *Ahmedabad SJ Radhani Exp*	890/1195/1990 (B)	9¼	12.45am (Wed-Mon)
	2916 *Ahmedabad Ashram Exp*	278/727/987/1648 (C)	11	8.45pm
Ajmer	2015 *Shatabdi*	270/530 (D)	2	10.50pm (Thu-Tue)
	9708 *Aravalli Exp*	121/246/331 (A)	2½	8.45am
Bikaner	4737 *Bikaner Exp*	178/643/1080 (E)	8½	10.55pm
	2468 *Intercity Exp*	114/406 (F)	5¼	3.30pm
Delhi	2016 *Shatabdi*	535/1015 (D)	4¼	5.45pm
	4060 *Jaisalmer-Delhi Exp*	91/157/411/560 (G)	6	5am
	2413 *Jaipur-Delhi Exp*	100/177/441/590 (G)	5½	4.35pm
Jaisalmer	4059 *Jaisalmer-Delhi Exp*	143/256/690/946 (G)	12¾	11.55pm
Jodhpur	2465 *Ranthambore Exp*	101/173/359/450 (H)	5½	5.05pm
	4059 *Delhi-Jaisalmer Exp*	92/160/420/573 (I)	5½	11.55am
Sawai Madhopur	2956 *Jaipur-Mumbai Exp*	141/276/361/592 (C)	2	2.10pm
	2466 *Ranthambore Exp*	66/141/224/276 (H)	2¼	10.55am
Sikar	9711 *Jaipur-Sri Ganga Exp*	150/297 (J)	2	8.40pm
Udaipur	2965 *Gwalior-Udaipur Exp*	217/553/745/1252 (C)	7½	10.40pm

Fares: A – sleeper/3AC/2AC; B – 3AC/2AC/1AC; C – sleeper/3AC/2AC/1AC; D – AC chair/executive chair; E – sleeper/2AC/1AC; F – 2nd class/AC chair; G – 2nd class/sleeper/3AC/2AC; H – 2nd class/sleeper/AC chair/3AC; I – 2nd class/sleeper/3AC/1AC; J – sleeper/2AC.

MAJOR BUSES FROM JAIPUR

Destination	Fare (Rs)	Duration (hr)	Frequency
Agra	195, AC 316	5½	11 daily
Ajmer	95, AC 135	2½	13 daily
Bharatpur	120	4½	5 daily
Bikaner	182	8	hourly
Bundi	140, AC 205	5	7 daily
Chittorgarh	200, AC 315	7	6 daily
Delhi	300, AC 400-500	5½	at least hourly
Jaisalmer	390	15	9.45pm daily
Jhunjhunu	105	5	4 daily
Jodhpur	220, AC 325	7	10 daily
Kota	160, AC 240	5	4 daily
Mt Abu	AC 495	13	daily
Nawalgarh	95	4	4 daily
Sawai Madhopur	105	6	2 daily
Udaipur	270, AC 419	10	6 daily

RAJASTHAN

Himalaya (MI Rd; ☉ 10am-8pm Mon-Sat) For ayurvedic preparations, try this place near panch Batti, which has been selling herbal products and remedies for over 70 years. Staff can help you with a wide variety of ailments, including poor memory and hangovers, and even treatments for your pet.

New Jodhpur Tailors (☎ 2365461; www.jodhpurtailors .com; 9 Ksheer Sagar Hotel, Motilal Atal Marg; ☉ 9am-8.30pm Mon-Sat, 9am-5pm Sun) This small tailor shop can make you a pair of jodhpurs (Rs1800) in preparation for a visit to the Blue City. Or you try a made-to-measure suit (Rs7000 to Rs15000) or shirt (Rs700 to Rs900).

Getting There & Away
AIR
Some airlines flying in and out of Jaipur:

Air India (☎ 2743500; www.airindia.com; Nehru Place, Tonk Rd)

Indigo (☎ 1800 1803838; www.goindigo.in; airport)

Jet Airways (☎ 2360450; www.jetairways.com; 1st fl, Umaid Nagar House, MI Rd; ☉ 9.30am-5.30pm Mon-Sat, 10am-3pm Sun)

Kingfisher Airlines (☎ 4030372; www.flykingfisher .com; Usha Plaza, MI Rd; ☉ 9.30am-5.30pm Mon-Sat, 10am-3pm Sun)

Most of these airlines schedule daily flights to Delhi (Rs3200), Mumbai (Rs6800), Udaipur (Rs3600) and Ahmedabad (Rs4400).

You can also book flights at **Rajasthan Travel Service** (☎ 2365408; Ganpati Plaza, MI Rd) or **Crown Tours** (☎ 2363310; www.crowntourslimited.com; Palace Rd), which is opposite the Hotel Rajputana Palace Sheraton.

BUS
Rajasthan State Road Transport Corporation (RSRTC) buses all leave from the **main bus station** (Station Rd), also picking up passengers at Narain Singh Circle. There is a left-luggage office here (Rs10 per bag for 24 hours), as well as a prepaid autorickshaw stand. Deluxe buses all depart from Platform 3, tucked away in the right-hand corner of the bus station, and they may be booked in advance at the **reservation office** (☎ 5116032) at the bus station.

There are regular buses to many destinations, including those in the table above. For long journeys, private buses can be more comfortable, though the RSRTC Silver Line services are pretty good, and the Gold Line and Volvo services are excellent. Private buses (and RSRTC Gray Line) provide sleeper buses (at extra cost) over long distances.

CAR
The RTDC charges Rs4.75 per kilometre in an Ambassador (non-AC), with a daily minimum of 250km; the overnight charge starts at Rs125 and there will be a 12.4% service tax on the total bill. Private taxis charge from Rs5 per kilometre for a non-AC car, with the same minimum and similar night halt charges. Remember you'll have to pay for the driver's return journey.

TRAIN
The efficient **railway reservation office** (☎ 135; ☉ 8am-2pm & 2.15-8pm Mon-Sat, 8am-2pm Sun) is to your right as you exit the main train station.

It's open for advance reservations only. Join the queue for Freedom Fighters, Foreign Tourists etc (Counter 769). For same-day travel, buy your ticket at the train station. For enquiries call ☎ 131. See p180 for details of routes and fares.

Getting Around
TO/FROM THE AIRPORT
There are no bus services from the airport, which is 12km southeast of the city. An auto-rickshaw/taxi costs at least Rs180/280 for the journey into the centre.

AUTORICKSHAW
There are prepaid autorickshaw stands at the bus and train stations. If you want to hire an autorickshaw for local sightseeing, it should cost around Rs200/400 for a half-/full day (including a visit to Amber but not Nahargarh); be prepared to bargain.

CYCLE-RICKSHAW
You can do your bit for the environment by flagging down a lean-limbed cycle-rickshaw rider. A short trip costs about Rs20.

MOTORCYCLE
You can hire, buy or fix a Royal Enfield Bullet (and lesser motorbikes) at **Rajasthan Auto Centre** (☎ 2568074; www.rac.co.in; Sanjay Bazaar, Sanganeri Gate), the cleanest little motorcycle workshop in India. To hire a 350cc Bullet costs Rs400 per day (including helmet).

AROUND JAIPUR
Amber
Situated among rugged hills 11km north of Jaipur, the magnificent honey-hued fort-palace of Amber (pronounced amer) used to be the ancient capital of Jaipur state. It beautifully illustrates Rajput architecture in all its artistic and defensive grandeur; the surrounding hills bristle with battlements while the township lies peacefully in the valley below.

Construction of **Amber Fort** (Indian/foreigner Rs25/150; ☺ 9am-5.30pm) was begun in 1592 by Maharaja Man Singh, the Rajput commander of Akbar's army. It was later extended by the Jai Singhs before the move to Jaipur.

You can climb up to the fort from the road in about 10 minutes (cold drinks are available at the top). A seat in a jeep up to the fort costs Rs150 return. Riding by elephant is popular at Rs550 per elephant one way (elephants carry two people up and return empty), but it's probably more comfortable to walk, and the well-being of the elephants is suspect. Help in Suffering (see p1169) is an organisation lobbying on behalf of the elephants' welfare.

If you don't take the audio guide (Rs150), then hiring a guide (Rs200 for 1½ hours, maximum four people) at the entrance is an asset, as there are few signs.

Otherwise, after leaving the ticket office keep to the right of the main stairs, and take the narrower stairs to the small **Siladevi Temple** (☺ 6am-noon & 4-8pm). From the 16th century to 1980 (when it was banned) a goat was sacrificed here daily. Photography is not permitted.

To the left of the temple the main stairway leads to the **Diwan-i-Am** (Hall of Public Audience), with a double row of columns and latticed galleries above.

The maharaja's apartments are on the higher terrace; you enter through a gateway decorated with mosaics and sculptures. The **Jai Mandir** (Hall of Victory) is noted for its inlaid panels and mirrored ceiling. Carved marble relief panels around the hall are fascinatingly delicate and quirky, with cartoon-like insects and sinuous flowers.

Opposite the Jai Mandir is the **Sukh Niwas** (Hall of Pleasure), with an ivory-inlaid sandalwood door, and a channel that once carried cooling water right through the room. From the Jai Mandir you can take in the fine views from the palace ramparts over the lake below. The **zenana** (women's quarters) surrounds the fourth courtyard, linked by a common passageway for the maharaja's discreet nocturnal visits.

Continuing past Amber Fort into the ancient town, you'll find the **Anokhi Museum of Handprinting** (Anokhi Haveli, Kheri Gate; ☺ 10.30am-5pm Tue-Sat, 11am-5pm Sun), which superbly documents the resurgence in hand-block printing, and runs hands-on demonstrations. The *haveli,* reached up cobblestone pathways, is itself worth the visit, and you can buy a T-shirt and block-print it yourself. A cafe serves excellent coffee and there's also a gift shop.

There are frequent buses to Amber from near the Hawa Mahal in Jaipur (Rs8, 25 minutes). An autorickshaw/taxi will cost at least Rs150/450 for the return trip.

Jaigarh

A scrubby green hill rises above Amber and is topped by the imposing **Jaigarh** (Indian/foreigner Rs25/75, camera or video Rs50; ⊙ 9am-5pm), built in 1726 by Jai Singh. The stern fort, punctuated by whimsical-hatted lookout towers, was never captured and has survived intact through the centuries. It's an uphill walk (about 1km) from Amber and offers great views from the Diwa Burj watchtower. The fort has reservoirs, residential areas, a puppet theatre and the world's largest wheeled cannon, Jaya Vana. Admission is free with a valid ticket from the Jaipur City Palace that is less than two days old.

Abhaneri

About 100km from Jaipur on the Agra road, this remote village, surrounded by wheat fields, is the unlikely location for one of Rajasthan's most awe-inspiring *baoris* (stepwells). An incredible geometric sight, **Chand Baori** (admission free; ⊙ dawn-dusk) has around 11 visible levels of zigzagging steps and is 20m deep. The well, the crumbling palace and the Harshat Mata Temple are believed to have been built by King Chand, ruler of Abhaneri and a Rajput from the Chahamana dynasty.

From Jaipur, catch a bus to Sikandra (Rs45, 1½ hours), from where you can hop into a crowded share vehicle (Rs5) for the 5km trip to Gular. Here you can catch another passenger jeep or minibus to Abhaneri (another 5km and Rs5). If you have your own transport, this is a very easy and worthwhile detour between Jaipur and Bharatpur.

Balaji

The extraordinary Hindu **exorcism temple** of Balaji is about 3km off the Jaipur–Agra road. People bring their possessed loved ones here to have bad spirits exorcised through prayer and rituals. Most exorcisms take place on Tuesday and Saturday, and the only people who can get inside the temple are the holy men and the victims – services are relayed to the crowds outside on video screens. The possessed scream, shout, dance and shake their heads. The often disturbing scenes at this temple may upset some.

If you wait until the service has finished, you will be able to look inside the temple. No photography is permitted.

From Jaipur there are numerous buses to Balaji (Rs55, two to 2½ hours).

BHARATPUR

☎ 05644 / pop 205,104

Bharatpur is home to the World Heritage–listed Keoladeo Ghana National Park, one of the world's prime bird-watching grounds. This peaceful sanctuary is hard-core twitcher territory, and boasts 364 species within its 29-sq-km marshlands, including many threatened aquatic birds on migratory routes from Central Asia.

In the 17th and 18th centuries Bharatpur was an important stronghold of the Jats, who retained their autonomy through their prowess in battle and marriage alliances with Rajput nobility. They successfully opposed the Mughals on several occasions, and their 18th-century fort here withstood an attack by the British in 1805 and a long siege in 1825. This siege led to the signing of the first treaty of friendship between the northwest Indian states and the East India Company. The Jat influence and the town's position next to the border with Uttar Pradesh mean that it resembles the towns in the neighbouring state rather than those in Rajasthan.

Although the fort's sturdy defences remain, Bharatpur itself has lost its charm – but not its mosquitoes.

Sights

Lohagarh, the early 18th-century 'Iron Fort', occupies the entire man-made island in the town centre. Maharaja Suraj Mahl built two towers within the ramparts – the **Jawahar Burj** and Fateh Burj – to commemorate his victories over the Mughals and the British. The austere structure contains three decaying palaces. One of them, centred on a tranquil courtyard, houses a dusty, little-visited **museum** (Indian/foreigner Rs5/10, camera/video free/Rs20; ⊙ 10am-4.30pm Tue-Sun) with Jain sculptures, paintings, weapons and dusty animal trophies. Most noteworthy is the palace's original *hammam* (Turkish bath).

Sleeping

For accommodation options convenient to the park, see p185.

Shagun Guest House (☎ 232455; sites.google.com/site/shagungh; r Rs100, s/d without bathroom Rs80/90) Down a lane inside Mathura Gate, this hideaway place is the friendliest choice in town. Rooms are extremely basic, cell-like and dusty, but it's dirt cheap and fronted by a little tree-shaded garden with hammock. The friendly

RAJASTHAN

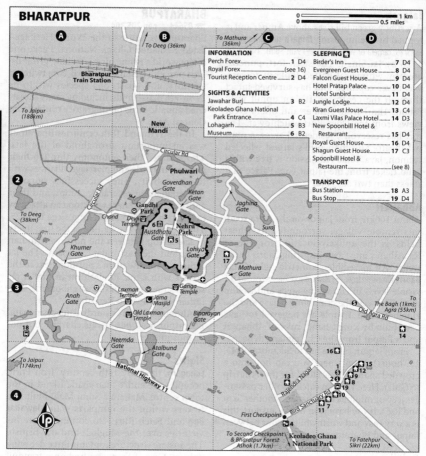

BHARATPUR

INFORMATION	
Perch Forex	**1** D4
Royal Forex	(see 16)
Tourist Reception Centre	**2** D4

SIGHTS & ACTIVITIES	
Jawahar Burj	**3** B2
Keoladeo Ghana National	
Park Entrance	**4** C4
Lohagarh	**5** B3
Museum	**6** B2

SLEEPING	
Birder's Inn	**7** D4
Evergreen Guest House	**8** D4
Falcon Guest House	**9** D4
Hotel Pratap Palace	**10** D4
Hotel Sunbird	**11** D4
Jungle Lodge	**12** D4
Kiran Guest House	**13** C4
Laxmi Vilas Palace Hotel	**14** D3
New Spoonbill Hotel &	
Restaurant	**15** D4
Royal Guest House	**16** D4
Shagun Guest House	**17** C3
Spoonbill Hotel &	
Restaurant	(see 8)

TRANSPORT	
Bus Station	**18** A3
Bus Stop	**19** D4

owner, Rajeev, is knowledgeable about the park, and offers village tours.

Getting There & Away

BUS

There are regular buses heading to destinations including Agra (Rs36, 1½ to two hours), Fatehpur Sikri in Uttar Pradesh (Rs16, one hour), Jaipur (Rs100, five hours), Deeg (Rs22, one hour) and Alwar (Rs56, four hours). Buses depart from the bus station but they'll also stop at the crossroads beside the Tourist Reception Centre (opposite).

TRAIN

The 9023/4 *Janata Express* leaves New Delhi (2nd class/sleeper Rs66/121) at 1.15pm and

arrives in Bharatpur at 5.35pm. It leaves Bharatpur at 8.05am, arriving in the capital at 12.50pm. The 2925/6 *Paschim Express* leaves New Delhi (sleeper/3AC/2AC/1AC Rs141/316/416/686) at 4.55pm and arrives in Bharatpur at 7.40pm. It leaves Bharatpur at 6.35am, arriving in the capital at 10.50pm.

There are several trains daily to Sawai Madhopur (sleeper/3AC/2AC/1AC Rs141/326/430/710) including the 2094 *Golden Temple Mail*, which departs at 10.45am and arrives at Sawai Madhopur at 1.05pm and then continues to Kota and Mumbai.

To Agra (sleeper/3AC/2AC/1AC Rs141/243/313/509), the 2966 *Udaipur–Gwalior Express* departs at 9.05am, arriving at Agra Fort at 10.15am.

Getting Around

Auto- or cycle-rickshaws from the bus station to the tourist office and most hotels should be about Rs30; from the train station it's Rs35.

KEOLADEO GHANA NATIONAL PARK

By far the best time to visit this **park** (Indian/foreigner Rs25/200, video Rs200; ☼ 6am-6pm Apr-Sep, 6.30am-5pm Oct-Mar) is October to February, when you should see many migratory birds. At other times, or even after poor monsoon conditions, it can be dry and relatively bird-free.

The best times for bird-watching are early morning and the evening. Expect to see painted storks, Sarus cranes, herons, egrets, owls, cormorants and kingfishers. Pythons are most commonly seen in the winter, when they come out from underground to sunbathe.

The sanctuary was once a semi-arid region, filling with water during the monsoon season and drying up afterwards. To extend the wetland and prolong its seasonal existence, the Maharaja of Bharatpur diverted water from a nearby irrigation canal and soon birds began to settle in vast numbers.

Admission entitles you to one entrance per day; if you want to spend the day inside, get your hotel to provide a packed lunch. Carry drinking water, as bird-watching is thirsty work.

One narrow road (no motorised vehicles permitted past checkpost 2) runs through the park, with countless embankments leading off into the greenery. Only the government-authorised cycle-rickshaws (recognisable by their yellow licence plates) are allowed beyond checkpost 2. You don't pay admission for the drivers, but they charge Rs50 per hour. A guide costs Rs150 per hour.

An excellent way to see the park is to hire a bike (Rs25 per day), at the entrance.

Orientation & Information

Keoladeo Ghana National Park is 3km south of Bharatpur's centre. For the location of reviewed park facilities, refer to Map p184.

The **Tourist Reception Centre** (☎ 05644-222542; ☼ 9.30am-6pm Mon-Fri), 700m from the park entrance, has an old map of Bharatpur (Rs10). Inside the park, you'll find the Salim Ali Interpretation Centre and a bookshop with bird books.

You can cash travellers cheques, get credit-card advances, change money and surf the internet at **Royal Forex** (☎ 05644-230293; Royal Guest House; New Civil Lines; per hr Rs40; ☼ 6am-10pm). You can also exchange money at **Perch Forex** (☎ 05644-233477; B6 New Civil Lines; ☼ 5am-11pm).

Sleeping & Eating

The following places are all within easy walking distance of the national park entrance. All hire binoculars and bicycles and will arrange park guides. Tariffs fluctuate according to the season, and most guesthouse restaurants will provide a tasty thali for somewhere between Rs70 and Rs160.

Kiran Guest House (☎ 05644-223845; www.kiran guesthouse.com; 364 Rajendra Nagar; s without bathroom Rs80, d Rs150-300, d with AC Rs750; ✖) This is a friendly place with simple rooms and a pleasant rooftop run by eager-to-please brothers, one of whom is a naturalist. It's away from the highway and only a short walk from the park, and they offer free pick-up from the bus and train stations.

Evergreen Guest House (☎ 05644-225917; s/d Rs150/250) This is a very basic, relaxed option, with just five plain rooms separate from the family dwelling. The rooms and beds are spartan, but all have private bathrooms.

Jungle Lodge (☎ 05644-225622; Gori Shankar; r Rs200-400) This place is indeed jungley, even a little bit messy in places. Nevertheless, it has relatively clean, plain, rooms – the more private and brighter ones are upstairs.

Royal Guest House (☎ 05644-230283; www.royal guesthousebharatpur.com; r Rs250-750; ✖ ▯) This busy little one-stop shop offers rooms, meals, foreign exchange and internet. The friendly family also lives on the premises and nothing, it seems, is too much trouble. The rooms are clean and good value. As an added bonus, house guests receive free internet access.

Falcon Guest House (☎ 05644-223815; falconguest house@hotmail.com; r Rs300-1200; ✖) The Falcon is well kept, with a smiling owner and sizable rooms, some with private balcony and some that can be linked into family rooms. Ask for a soft mattress. A tasty veg thali can be had in the garden restaurant.

Spoonbill Hotel & Restaurant (☎ 05644-223571; www.hotelspoonbill.com; r Rs400-1300; ✖) The original Spoonbill has a variety of rooms – the best is super-spacious and has a balcony. The hotel has excellent food, with curd from the family cow and Rajasthani delicacies. There's often a campfire in winter.

Hotel Pratap Palace (☎ 05644-224245; www.hotel pratappalace.net.in; Bird Sanctuary Rd; s/d Rs450/550, deluxe

---

REPLENISHING THE WETLANDS

In 2003 the Panchana Dam on the Gambhir River became operational and the famous wetlands of Keoladeo could no longer rely on their traditional source of monsoonal water. In 2004 the park lodged an appeal for a higher allocation of water from the dam, but came up against fierce opposition from landholders. In 2006 Unesco urged that a permanent backup source of water for the park be established, as drought (along with unchecked cattle grazing) had caused serious damage. In 2007, following another poor monsoon, the park was a dismal echo of its former glory, mostly dry, invaded by thousands of cattle and devoid of the huge flocks of migratory birds. It seemed the politicians were listening but there was little evidence of action on the ground.

In mid-2008 the heavens opened, and vital flows of water arrived from the local Chiksana Canal, partially refilling the wetland. Furthermore, the Panchana Dam completely filled and authorities simply had to release water. And so the sanctuary sprang to life and once again the migratory birds arrived and the reputation of the park was safe for another year. However, because of the ongoing impediments to securing water from the Chambal River, there is now an approved plan to channel monsoon flood water from the Yamuna River in Uttar Pradesh to the reserve, via the Goverdhan drain. Because the Yamuna, with its vast catchment, regularly floods in the monsoon, this should guarantee monsoonal flows even when local rains are insubstantial.

Rs850/1050, with AC Rs1300/1450; 🍴 💻 🛜) This grand-seeming hotel, built in traditional style, offers faded but spacious, comfortable rooms; the standard is variable so look at a few. It has a decent restaurant.

New Spoonbill Hotel & Restaurant (☎ 05644-223571; www.hotelspoonbill.com; r Rs550-1500; 🍴) This place is associated with the original Spoonbill Hotel and has almost modern rooms, each with a small terrace and an individual tariff. There's a restaurant which looks onto the garden.

Hotel Sunbird (☎ 05644-225701; www.hotelsunbird .com; Bird Sanctuary Rd; s/d Rs1150/1350, deluxe Rs1650/1950; 🍴) The Sunbird is a well-run place with a leafy seating area and a reasonable restaurant. Rooms are clean and attractive, although some are a little gloomy. The tariff includes breakfast.

Birder's Inn (☎ 05644-227346; brdinn@yahoo.com; Bird Sanctuary Rd; s/d Rs1450/1900; 🍴 💻) A popular hotel, this inn is set back from the road, with a lovely stone-and-thatch restaurant and a pleasant garden. The spacious, well-appointed and nicely decorated rooms are very appealing and airy and have decent bathrooms.

Bharatpur Forest Ashok (☎ 05644-222760; www .bharatpurashok.com; s/d Rs2990/3300; 🍴) This lodge, run by the Indian Tourism Development Corporation (ITDC), is 1km inside the park. Comfortable, quiet rooms have balconies with swing seats and are surrounded by greenery. It has a restaurant and bar and an air of torpor.

Laxmi Vilas Palace Hotel (☎ 05644-223523; www.laxmivilas.com; Kakaji-ki-Kothi, Old Agra Rd; s/d/ste Rs3650/3950/5050; 🍴 💻 🛜) Once owned by the younger son of Maharaja Jaswant Singh, Laxmi Vilas is divine. Arched ceilings and heavy furniture make for atmospheric rooms, which are set around a courtyard. The pool is splendid.

Bagh (☎ 05644-225415; Agra-Achmera Rd; www.the bagh.com; r Rs6000-7500; 🍴 💻 🛜) The beautiful Bagh hotel is in the former royal orchard, 2km from town. It has 14 elegant rooms with antique furnishings but a contemporary feel, and the 200-year-old 4-hectare garden has masses of birds.

Getting There & Around

For transport information, see p184.

DEEG
☎ 0564

Built by Suraj Mahl in the mid-18th century as a summer resort for the Bharatpur rulers, Deeg was also the second capital of Bharatpur state. The town witnessed a famous battle in which the maharaja's forces withstood a combined Mughal and Maratha army of 80,000 men.

Deeg is famous for the **Suraj Mahl's Palace** (Indian/foreigner Rs5/100; ⏰ 9.30am-5.30pm Sat-Thu), one of India's most beautiful palace complexes, made up of delicately proportioned buildings (bhavans) set in geometric gardens. The main building, **Gopal Bhavan** was used by the maharajas until the early 1950s, and rooms contain their original furnishings, from faded, spilling sofas to huge swing fans. Built in a combination of Rajput and Mughal architectural styles, the 18th-century palace sits in front of a large tank (reservoir), the **Gopal Sagar**, and is flanked by two exquisite pavilions. Outside, the gardens continue the extravagant theme; the **Keshav Bhavan** (Summer Pavilion) is engineered to mimic the sound of thunder when it rains and has hundreds of fountains, which spout coloured water during local festivities.

Deeg's massive walls (up to 28m high) and 12 vast bastions, some with their cannons still in place, are also worth exploring – you can walk up to the top of the walls from the palace.

Frequent buses run to/from Alwar (Rs35, 2½ hours) and Bharatpur (Rs25, one hour, half-hourly). There is one direct bus to Agra (Rs60).

ALWAR
☎ 0144 / pop 260,245

The city of Alwar has a hilltop fort, a sprawling palace with a quaint museum, leafy avenues and some colourful bazaars. It was once an important Rajput state, emerging in the 18th century under Pratap Singh, who pushed back the rulers of Jaipur to the south and the Jats of Bharatpur to the east, and who successfully resisted the Marathas. It was one of the first Rajput states to ally itself with the fledgling British empire, although British interference in Alwar's internal affairs meant that this partnership was not always amicable.

It's the nearest town to Sariska Reserve.

Sights

BALA QUILA

This imposing fort, with its 5km of ramparts, stands 300m above the city. Pre-dating the time of Pratap Singh, it's one of the few forts in Rajasthan built before the rise of the Mughals. Unfortunately, the fort is in ruins and houses a radio transmitter station, and can only be visited with permission from the superintendent of police (SP). However, this is easy to obtain from the SP office in the City Palace complex.

CITY PALACE

Below the fort sprawls the convoluted City Palace complex, its massive gates and tank lined by a beautifully symmetrical procession of ghats and pavilions. Hidden upstairs in the former City Palace is the interesting **Alwar Museum** (Indian/foreigner Rs5/10; ☉ 10am-5pm Sat-Thu). The museum's exhibits evoke the extravagance of the maharajas' lifestyle, with stunning weapons, royal ivory slippers, fascinating and unexpected miniatures, and old musical instruments.

Not far from the museum (take the steps on the far left when facing the palace) is the beautiful **Cenotaph of Maharajah Bakhtawar Singh** with its outlook over the palace's peaceful ghats.

Sleeping & Eating

Several hotels, owned by brothers and aimed at businessmen, ring a courtyard set back from Manu Marg, about 500m east of the bus stand. Single women might not feel comfortable in those places and only one, Ashoka, is reviewed here.

Ashoka (☎ 2346780; off Manu Marg; r Rs400-950; ❄) This place has reasonable rooms in the above-mentioned enclave. The cheaper rooms are less appealing; the priciest have groovy geometric murals and clean-tiled bathrooms.

Alwar Hotel (☎ 2700012; www.hotelalwar.com; 26 Manu Marg; s/d from Rs1225/1650; ❄) Alwar's best and brightest rooms are found at this midrange hotel set back from the road in a carefully clipped garden. The professional staff can help with vehicle hire and local tours and the Dawat restaurant serves complimentary breakfasts and multicuisine dishes in the garden.

Neemrana Fort Palace (☎ 246007; www.neemrana hotels.com; s/d/ste from Rs2000/3000/6000; ❄ 🖳 🏊) If you have your own transport, treat yourself and stay 75km north of Alwar in this magnificent parchment-coloured fort-palace mounted on a fortified plateau. The fort rises to an amazing 10 levels and is in a setting of 10 hectares, among the Aravalli hills.

Prem Pavitra Bhojnalaya (Old Bus Stand; mains Rs30-50; ☉ 10am-10pm) Alwar's best restaurant is in the heart of the old town, and has been serving up inexpensive, fresh, tasty pure-veg food since 1957. You have to pay Rs10 per person to eat in the air-con section – but it is worth it. Try the special *kheer* (creamy rice pudding).

Getting There & Away

From Alwar there are buses to Sariska (Rs20, one to 1½ hours, half-hourly from 5.15am to 8.30pm), which go on to Jaipur (Rs80, four to five hours). There are also frequent (bumpy) services to Bharatpur (Rs50, four hours), and Deeg (Rs35, 2½ hours). Buses to Delhi (Rs90, half-hourly), travel via Tijara (four hours to Delhi) or Ramgarh (five hours to Delhi).

RAJASTHAN

RAJASTHAN

RE-ESTABLISHING TIGERS AT SARISKA

Sariska Tiger Reaserve has taken centre stage in one of India's most publicised wildlife dramas. Although the last Sariska tiger was probably sent in pieces to the Chinese medicine market in 2004, it wasn't until 2005 that it was finally revealed that the tiger population at one of India's leading wildlife reserves had been eliminated. Three years later the story was all about the helicopter transfer of tigers from Ranthambore national Park to Sariska.

An enquiry into the crisis recommended fundamental management changes before tigers could be reintroduced to the reserve. Extra funding was proposed to cover relocation of villages within the park as well as increasing the protection force. While poaching is the most likely cause of the extinction of the last of Sariska's tigers, a WWF (World Wide Fund for Nature) report highlighted the issues of widespread woodcutting and grazing within park boundaries and the low morale among park staff. Action on the recommendations has been slow and incomplete.

Nevertheless, in November 2008 two tigers (a male and a female) were transferred from Ranthambore to Sariska, with an additional female due to be introduced soon after, and another two tigers to follow after some time. Only time will tell if this reintroduction is successful but, as things stand, Sariska remains a sad indictment of tiger conservation in India, from the top government officials down to the underpaid forest guard.

For train travel, the 2015/6 *Shatabdi* departs Alwar Thursday to Tuesday at 8.35am heading to Ajmer (AC chair/1AC Rs435/830, four hours) via Jaipur (Rs320/605, two hours). For Delhi it departs at 7.36pm (Rs365/680, 2½ hours).

The daily 2461 *Mandore Express* leaves at 11.43pm, arriving in Jodhpur (sleeper/3AC/2AC Rs216/554/780) at 8am. The 4059 *Jaisalmer Express,* leaving at 8.56pm, goes all the way to Jaisalmer (sleeper/3AC/2AC Rs293/796/1092, 16 hours).

A return taxi to Sariska Tiger Reserve (with a stop at Siliserh) will cost around Rs750.

SARISKA TIGER RESERVE
☎ 0144

Lying in a wooded valley between Alwar and Jaipur, **Sariska Tiger Reserve** (Indian/foreigner Rs25/200, jeep or car Rs125, video Rs200; ⊙ 7am-4pm Oct-Mar, 6am-4.30pm Apr-Sep) has been at the centre of controversy since 2005 when it was revealed that there were no tigers living in the park. In late 2008 the big cats were once more roaming the reserve, having been relocated from Ranthambore National Park. It is hoped that this reintroduction, coupled with the relocation of villages within the park, will result in a sustainable tiger population.

The sanctuary is still worth visiting with or without the lure of the tiger, however. The 800 sq km (including a core area of 498 sq km) is also home to nilgai, sambar, chital (spotted deer), wild boar and numerous species of bird. It also has some fascinating sights within and around its boundaries, including the spectacular hilltop **Kankwari Fort** (22km from the Forest Reception Office), and **Bhangarh**, a deserted, well-preserved 17th-century city that's famously haunted. If you take a longer tour then you can ask to visit one of these sights, or Bhangarh can be reached by a bus that runs through the sanctuary to nearby Golaka village (Rs35).

Unlike most national parks, Sariska opens year-round, although the best time to spot wildlife is November to March. You'll see most wildlife in the evening.

It's possible to go by private car into the park, but these are only allowed on sealed roads. The best way to visit is by jeep, which costs Rs900/1400 for three/four hours, or Rs2700 for a full day. Jeeps take a maximum of five people. Guides can also be hired for Rs150/300 for three/four hours or Rs500 for a day. Bookings can be made at the **Forest Reception Office** (☎ 2841333). Note that you'll also have to pay an admission charge (Rs1215) for the jeep. Admission to the park is free for Indians visiting the Hanuman temple on Tuesday and Saturday (8am to 3pm). Though this policy is under review, chances are it will still be busy on these days.

Sleeping & Eating
RTDC Hotel Tiger Den (☎ 2841342; s/d from Rs850/1075; ✦) Situated on a long, verandah-shaded block backed by a green, rambling garden and fronted by a neat lawn. It has a bar and restaurant. Rooms are bland but comfortable

and equipped with a TV. A mosquito net or repellent is recommended.

Alwar Bagh (☎ 2885231; www.alwarbagh.com; r or tent Rs2800, ste Rs3500; ❄ ▨) A relaxing option, Alwar bagh is located in the village of Dhawala, between Alwar (14km) and Sariska (19km). The hotel can arrange pick-up and drop-off from Alwar and can also arrange tours of Sariska. The bright, spacious rooms boast traditional styling, and there's an organic orchard and a garden restaurant (breakfast/lunch/dinner Rs150/340/340).

Sariska Tiger Heaven (☎ 224815; r with full board Rs4500; ❄ ▨) This is an isolated place about 3km west of the bus stop at Thanagazi village; free pick-up is on offer. Rooms are set in stone-and-tile cottages and have big beds and window alcoves. It's a tranquil, if overpriced, place to stay. Staff can arrange jeeps and guides to the park.

Getting There & Away
Sariska is 35km from Alwar, a convenient town from which to approach the sanctuary. There are frequent buses from Alwar (Rs18, one to 1½ hours, at least hourly) and on to Jaipur (Rs67). Buses stop in front of the Forest Reception Office.

SHEKHAWATI
Shekhawati is a semiarid region crisscrossed by roads that lead to half-forgotten villages and concealed *havelis* (traditional, ornately decorated residences).

Shekhawati was formerly a wealthy but lawless land on the trade route between the ports of the Arabian Sea and the fertile Ganges Valley. The Shekhawati *thakurs* (noblemen), who were noted for their indulgence in quarrelling among themselves, began to flourish in the mid-18th century when the British East India Company imposed order. A century later the British used the skills of local merchants, Marwaris (they'd long since left Marwar, today's Jodhpur) to improve trade. While the Marwaris settled in the new coastal cities, they built *havelis* for their families back home.

Until 1947 these mansions were symbols of their success and homes in which their families could live the good life; these days they remain one of Rajasthan's better-kept secrets.

GETTING THERE & AWAY
Access to Shekhawati is easiest from Jaipur or Bikaner. Sikar (gateway to the region, but

with no notable *havelis*) and Fatehpur are on the main Jaipur–Bikaner road. RSRTC buses ply regularly between Mandawa and Bikaner (Rs100, 3½ hours). Private buses (Rs90) are also available.

Churu is on the main Delhi–Bikaner railway line, while Sikar, Nawalgarh and Jhunjhunu have slow passenger-train links with Jaipur and Delhi.

GETTING AROUND
Shekhawati towns are well served by government and private buses. The local services can get very crowded and riding 'upper class' (on the roof!) is often necessary. A great option is to hire a taxi (or even an autorickshaw) to tour the area. Prices start from about Rs1000 per day.

Ramgarh
The town of Ramgarh was founded in 1791 by the powerful Poddar merchant family, who had left the village of Churu following a disagreement with the *thakur*. Ramgarh boomed in the mid-19th century and was one of the richest towns of the area.

Ram Gopal Poddar Chhatri, near the bus stand, has brilliantly coloured paintings inside its dome. The **Poddar Havelis**, near Churu Gate, are also densely frescoed, with subjects ranging from soldiers to fish.

Fatehpur
☎ 01571 / pop 78,462
Established in 1451 as a capital for Muslim nawabs (ruling princes), Fatehpur was taken

RAJASTHAN

AN OUTDOOR GALLERY

Most *havelis* are entered through an archway into an outer courtyard where there is often a meeting room, complete with punkahs (swing fans), where the men may do business; opposite is a stable and coach house. Another arch leads via a dogleg passage (to ensure privacy) to one or more inner courtyards – the private domain of the family and run by the women. Galleries around the upper floors provide access to the individual rooms, and there is usually a roof terrace. This is a common arrangement far outside Shekhawati, where it serves male-dominated families and sets a premium on female privacy. Together with the thick walls, it provides deep shade to cool the inner rooms.

The unique feature of the Shekhawatis *havelis* is their painted decorations. The artists belonged to the caste of *kumhars* (potters), and were both the builders and painters, and they used the fresco technique (applying natural pigment to the wet top layer of plaster) to remarkable effect. After about 1900 the artists began to paint on to dry plaster, allowing greater intricacy but losing the original urgency of the work. The outside walls, particularly around the entrance, the outer and inner courtyards and sometimes some of the rooms are painted from the ground to the eaves. Typically the paintings mix depictions of the gods with everyday scenes, often featuring modern inventions such as telephones, trains and aeroplanes. The two worlds often merge, so Krishna and Radha are seen in flying motorcars.

Some *havelis* are open to the public, but most are inhabited by families or caretakers. Take your chance: stand close by and look hopeful. You will often be invited in, either freely or for a small tip. Photography is generally allowed.

One detrimental aspect of the tourist trade is the desire for antiques. A few towns have antique shops chock-a-block with items ripped from the *havelis*, particularly doors and window frames. Investing in these antiques perpetuates this desecration.

---

over by the Shekhawati Rajputs in the 18th century. It's a busy little town, with masses of *havelis*, many in a sad state of disrepair, but with a few notable exceptions.

Haveli Nadine Prince (☎ 231479; www.cultural-centre.com; adult/child Rs100/50; ☻ 9am-6pm) has been restored to its former dazzling glory and the admission includes a detailed guided tour. The 1802 building is owned by French artist Nadine Le Prince, who has turned it into an art gallery and cultural centre and has done much to publicise the plight of Shekhawati. Long-term artist residencies are available, There's a cafe as well as the contemporary art gallery.

Some other Fatehpur highlights include the nearby **Jaganath Sanghania Haveli** (adult/child Rs100/50; ☻ 9am-6pm), the **Mahavir Prasad Goenka Haveli** (often locked, but with superb paintings); **Geori Shankar Haveli**, with mirrored mosaics on the antechamber ceiling; **Nand Lal Devra Haveli**, with red and blue paintings; **Harikrishnan Das Sarogi Haveli**, with a colourful facade and iron lacework; and **Vishnunath Keria Haveli**, which depicts Radha and Krishna in flying gondolas.

Fatehpur makes a convenient base for visits to nearby Ramgarh and Mahansar, but accommodation here is pretty ordinary. **RTDC Hotel Haveli** (☎ 230293; s/d Rs500/600, with AC Rs750/850; ☻)

has nothing-special rooms and a gloomy dining hall. It's about 500m south of the bus stand. About 200m north of Haveli Nadine Prince is the basic and very friendly **Rendezvous**, where you can ask about long-term paying guesthouse accommodation and feast on a veg thali (Rs100).

Mandawa
☎ 01592 / pop 20,830
Mandawa is the preferred base for travellers to Shekhawati. Settled in the 18th century and fortified by the dominant merchant families, it remains a relatively subdued market town, though the very young, very persistent touts are surprisingly forceful.

Binsidhar Newatia Haveli (now the State Bank of Bikaner & Jaipur) has curious paintings on its outer eastern wall – a boy using a telephone, a European woman in a chauffeur-driven car, and the Wright brothers in flight. The **Gulab Rai Ladia Haveli**, southwest of the fort, has some defaced erotic images. The unused half of **Castle Mandawa** has some interesting frescoes.

SLEEPING & EATING
Hotel Shekhawati (☎ 223036; hotelshekwati@sify.com; near Mukungarh Rd; r Rs350-1500; ☻ 🖵) Mandawa's great

budget option is run by a retired bank manager and his hard-working son, Pramod Pareek (a registered tourist guide). Bright, comically lewd murals give the pleasant, clean rooms a lift of colour. Tasty meals are served on the roof.

Hotel Mandawa Haveli (☎ 223088; s/d Rs1250/1950, ste sRs3250; 🈂) Set in a glorious 19th-century restored *haveli* close to Sonathia Gate, highly individual rooms surround a painted courtyard. It's worth splashing out on a romantic suite filled with arches, window seats and numerous small windows, though even some standard rooms feature romantic balconies. There is a rooftop for dinners, another restaurant for lunch, and you can breakfast in the garden.

Hotel Heritage Mandawa (☎ 223742; www.hotel heritagemandawa.com; r Rs1500, deluxe r Rs2200, ste Rs4000; 🈂) This attractive old *haveli* is close to the main bus stand, through Sonathia Gate. There is a mixture of rooms, some gloomy, others brightly decorated and more stylish. Some have a mezzanine with extra beds. The courtyard is relaxing and the restaurant is decent.

Hotel Castle Mandawa (☎ 223124; www.castlemand awa.com; s/d from Rs3300/3800; 🈂 🖳 🐾) With 85 rooms, this is easily Mandawa's biggest hotel. Located in a converted castle, it is easy to get lost in, and even the standard rooms are huge and extravagant. In addition to restaurants, bars and coffee shops, there is an exquisite pool and an ayurvedic spa.

Bungli Restaurant (☎ 200084; Goenka Chowk; mains Rs80-175; ☸ 7am-11pm) A popular outdoor travellers' eatery near the main bus stand, Bungli serves piping-hot tandoori and cold beer. Service can seem a little slow, though the food is cooked fresh.

Nawalgarh
☎ 01594

Being almost in the centre of the region, this is another great base. The town has been disfigured somewhat by modern additions, but it still retains genuine charm, especially in and around the 250-year-old fort. *Havelis* of interest include the **Aath Haveli, Hem Raj Kulwal Haveli, Bhagton-ki-Haveli, Khedwal Bhavan** and **Morarka Haveli Museum** (admission Rs50).

The **Dr Ramnath A Podar Haveli Museum** (Indian/ foreigner Rs75/100, camera Rs30; ☸ 8am-6pm), built in the 1920s on the eastern side of town, has been colourfully restored with vibrant murals. Several rooms feature galleries on Rajasthani

culture, from turbans and tablas to mini polystyrene forts.

SLEEPING & EATING
Hotels arrange all meals and can also arrange bike hire, treks, tours and lessons in cooking Hindi and music.

Ramesh Jangid's Tourist Pension (☎ 224060; www .touristpension.com; s/d from Rs350/380, with AC Rs900/950; 🈂) Run by genial Rajesh (son of Ramesh, owner of Apani Dhani ecoresort), this guesthouse offers homestyle accommodation in spacious rooms with big beds. It has a real family atmosphere with delicious meals made with organic ingredients.

Shekhawati Guest House (☎ 2224658; www.shek hawatiguesthouse.com s/d Rs400/500, with AC Rs799/899, cottages s/d Rs700/800; 🈂 🖳) This splendid option is run by a friendly couple. They have six decorated rooms with private bathrooms and hot showers plus five mud-walled, thatched cottages in the organic garden. The garden supplies most of the hotel's needs and you can learn cooking here for free. It's 4km east of the bus stand (follow the signs to Roop Vilas Palace Hotel).

Apani Dhani (☎ 01594-222239; www.apanidhani .com; s/d Rs600/995) Run by ecotourism pioneer Ramesh Jangid, this award-winning resort is a relaxing place to stay. Rooms are in traditional mud huts with comfortable beds, set around a bougainvillea-shaded courtyard. The adjoining organic farm supplies ingredients for meals, and alternative energy is used wherever possible. It's near the TV tower on the west side of the Jaipur road. Multilingual Ramesh is also president of Les Amis du Shekhawati, an organisation aiming to preserve the *havelis*.

About 4km east of the town are the partitioned siblings, **Roop Niwas Kothi** (☎ 01594-222008; www.roopniwaskothi.com; s/d Rs2400/2700; 🈂 🖳 🐾), and **Roop Vilas Palace Hotel** (☎ 9828199991; www .roopvilas.com s/d from Rs3000/3500; 🈂 🖳 🐾) in a single palace converted into two hotels. Both have a back-to-the-Raj feel, lovely grand grounds and old-fashioned rooms. Roop Vilas has the brighter, restored rooms, while Roop Niwas is more your dusty Raj. Both organise horse riding.

Parsurampura
This little village, 20km southeast of Nawalgarh, has some of the best-preserved and oldest paintings in Shekhawati. The detailed paintings inside the **Chhatri of Thakur**

Sardul Singh dome date from the mid-18th century. There is also the **Shamji Sharaf Haveli**, decorated with a mixture of Hindu gods and Europeans, and the small **Gopinathji Mandir**, a finely painted temple constructed in 1742 by Sardul Singh.

Jhunjhunu
☎ 01592 / pop 100,485

Shekhawati's district headquarters, Jhunjhunu is bigger and busier than other places in the region. Founded by the Kaimkhani nawabs in the mid-15th century, it was taken over by the Rajput ruler Sardul Singh in 1730.

It was in Jhunjhunu that the British based their Shekhawati Brigade, a troop formed in the 1830s to try to halt the activities of the dacoits (bandits), who were largely local petty rulers not above a little part-time thieving.

The **Tourist Reception Centre** (☎ 232909; Mandawa Circle; 🕑 9am-6pm Mon-Fri) is just out of the town centre, on the Churu bypass, and has a basic map of the town and region.

SIGHTS & ACTIVITIES

The **Khetri Mahal** (admission Rs20) is a minor palace dating from around 1770. Although run down, it's one of Shekhawati's most sophisticated buildings, with sensational views. The **Bihariji Temple** is from a similar period and contains some fine, though worn, murals.

Jhunjhunu is famous for the wealthy, ostentatious **Rani Sati Temple** – it's dedicated to the patron goddess of the merchant class, a woman who committed *sati* (ritual suicide of a widow on her husband's funeral pyre) in 1595.

The frescoed **Modi Havelis** and the **Kaniram Narsinghdas Tibrewala Haveli** are both in the main bazaar.

COURSES

Laxmi Kant Jangid at the Hotel Jamuna Resort (below) runs courses in Indian cooking and 'fresco' painting. The cooking courses include field visits and cost around €1000 for two weeks – see www.jamunaresorthotel.com for details.

SLEEPING & EATING

Hotel Shiv Shekhawati (☎ 01592-232651; www.shiv shekhawati.com; d Rs600-1000; 🗶) Just 1km or so east of the bazaar (about 600m east of the private bus stand) is this modern hotel arranged around a central inner courtyard. It has squeaky-clean, plain rooms and helpful management. Good value.

Hotel Shekhawati Heritage (☎ 237134; www.hotel shekhawatihertage.com; off Station Rd; shekhawati_herit age@yahoo.com; s/d Rs800/1000; 🗶) Southwest of the RSRTC bus stand, Shekhawati Heritage is tucked away down a laneway. The bright rooms are well kept with leafy outlooks but seem overpriced.

Hotel Fresco Palace (☎ 325233; off Station Rd; fresco _palace@yahoo.com; r Rs1100/1500; 🗶) Next door to Hotel Shekhawati Heritage, this little hotel has glass cabinets full of knick-knacks and clean, colourful rooms; but like it's close neighbour, it seems overpriced for what is on offer.

Hotel Jamuna Resort (☎ 232871; www.jamuna resorthotel.com; s/d from Rs700/800, ste from Rs2200; 🗶 🖳 🗶) Perched on a hilltop overlooking the eastern edge of town, the hotel is run by Laxmi Kant Jangid, who also runs Hotel Shiv Shekhawati. It has rooms decorated with paintings and mirrors and traditional mud walls. You can stay here for free if you study painting and help with the decorative upkeep; recommended cooking courses are also offered (left).

Mahansar
☎ 01595 / pop 4426

This slow-moving, untouristy village contains the mid-19th-century *haveli*-like **Raghunath Temple**, the gold paintings of **Sona-ki-Dukan Haveli** (admission Rs100) and the **Sahaj Ram Poddar Chhatri**. Mahansar is also famous for homemade liquor that resembles ouzo.

Narayan Niwas Castle (☎ 264322; www.mehansar castle.com; s/d Rs1200/1600) is in the old fort, dating from 1768, and feels evocatively uncommercial. Rooms are dusty but atmospheric, some with paintings covering the walls. The food gets excellent reports and the hotel offers local guides.

AJMER
☎ 0145 / pop 485,197

Surrounded by serrated hills, the city of Ajmer is a noisy, bustling city encircling the calm waters of Ana Sagar. The fascinating Muslim pilgrimage shrine of Khwaja Muin-ud-din Chishti is often overlooked by tourists, due largely to the pull of nearby Pushkar.

Ajmer once had considerable strategic importance. It was sacked by Mohammed of Ghori on one of his forays from Afghanistan, and was later favoured by the mighty Mughals. One of the first contacts between the Mughals and the British occurred in Ajmer, when Sir

Thomas Roe met Jehangir here in 1616. Later the Scindias took the city, and in 1818 it was handed over to the British, becoming one of the few places in Rajasthan that they directly controlled. In 1875 the British set up Mayo College as a prestigious school exclusively for Indian nobility. Today it's open to all boys (whose parents can afford the fees).

Orientation & Information

The main bus stand is to the northeast, and the train station and many hotels are to the east of the Dargah.

Bank of Baroda (Prithviraj Marg; ☾ 10am-3pm Mon-Fri, 10am-12.30pm Sat) Changes travellers cheques and does credit-card advances.

Bank of Baroda ATM (Station Rd) By the entrance to Honeydew restaurant.

HDFC ATM (Sadar Patel Marg)

Satguru's Internet (60-61 Kutchery Rd; per hr Rs20; ☾ 9am-10pm)

State Bank of India (☎ 2627048; ☾ 10am-2pm & 2.30-4pm Mon-Fri, 10am-1pm Sat) Changes travellers cheques and foreign currency.

Tourist office RTDC Hotel Khadim compound (☎ 2627426; ☾ 8am-noon & 3-6pm Mon-Fri); train station (☾ 8am-noon & 3-6pm daily)

Sights & Activities

ANA SAGAR

This large lake, created in the 12th century by damming the River Luni, is set against a blue grey hilly spine that merges into its surface. On its bank are two delightful parks, **Dault Bagh** and **Subash Bagh**, containing a series of marble pavilions erected in 1637 by Shah Jahan.

DARGAH

Located in the old part of town is one of India's most important Muslim pilgrimage sites. The **dargah** (☾ 5am-9pm Jul-Mar, 4am-9pm Apr-Jun) is the tomb of a Sufi saint, Khwaja Muin-ud-din Chishti, who came to Ajmer from Persia in 1192 and lived here until 1233. Construction of the shrine was completed by Humayun and the gate was added by the Nizam of Hyderabad. Akbar used to make the pilgrimage to the dargah from Agra every year.

You must cover your head in certain areas, so don't forget a scarf or cap – you can buy one in the bazaar leading to the shrine.

The first gate is the **Nizam Gate**, up some steps to protect it from the rains; it was built in 1915. The green and white mosque, **Akbari Masjid**, on the right was constructed by Akbar in 1571.

In the second courtyard is a mosque built by Shah Jahan. Beyond this, in the inner courtyard, the large iron cauldrons (one donated by Akbar in 1567, the other by Jehangir in 1631) are for offerings for the poor, and are called the *degs*.

The saint's tomb is in the inner courtyard. It has a marble dome and the tomb inside is surrounded by a silver platform. Pilgrims believe that the saint's spirit will intercede in matters on their behalf, so the notes and holy string attached to the railings are often personal requests.

At the entrance *khadims* (servants of god) wielding donation books will ask you for cash. It's likely you'll be asked for still more money inside, where you might be blessed with the edge of the tomb blanket. It's good to visit in the evening, when there are Qawwali singers (singers of devotional songs) and twinkling lights.

Pilgrims and Sufis come from all over the world on the anniversary of the saint's death, the *urs*, in the seventh month of the lunar calendar. The saint retired to his cloister for a long meditation, and when it was opened six days later he was dead (hence the festival lasts six days). It's an interesting time but the crowds can be suffocating. Many pilgrims also come here in the month of Ramadan.

ADHAI-DIN-KA-JHONPRA & TARAGARH

Beyond the dargah, on the town's outskirts, are the extraordinary ruins of the Adhai-din-ka-Jhonpra (Two-and-a-Half Days) mosque. According to legend, its construction in 1153 took 2½ days. Others say it was named after a festival lasting 2½ days. It was built as a Sanskrit college, but in 1198 Mohammed of Ghori seized Ajmer and converted the building into a mosque by adding a seven-arched wall in front of the pillared hall.

It's a grand building with soaring domes, pillars and arched screens, largely built from pieces of Jain and Hindu temples.

About 3km from the town, and a steep 1½-hour climb beyond the mosque (it's also accessible by car), the ancient **Taragarh** (Star Fort; admission free; ☾ dawn-dusk) commands a superb view over the city. It was built by Ajaipal Chauhan, the town's founder, and saw lots of military action during Mughal times. It was later used as a British sanatorium.

AKBAR'S PALACE

Akbar built this imposing palace in 1570 – partly as a pleasure retreat, but mainly to keep

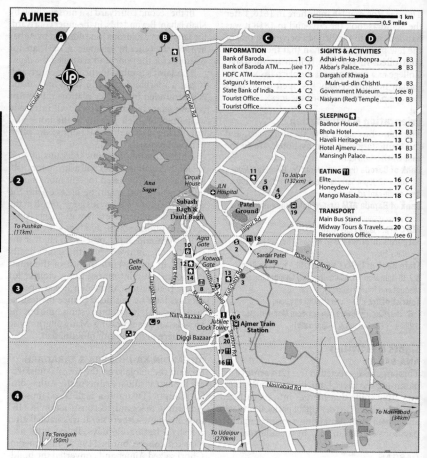

AJMER

a watchful eye on local rulers. It was here, on 10 January, 1616, that Sir Thomas Roe, ambassador of King James 1 of England, was given the first official audience by the Emperor Jehangir. It houses the **government museum** (admission Rs5, camera Rs20; ☿ 10am-4.30pm Sat-Thu), which has a small collection of stone sculptures, weapons and miniature paintings.

NASIYAN (RED) TEMPLE

This amazing **Jain Red Temple** (Prithviraj Marg; admission Rs5; ☿ 8am-5pm) was built in 1865. Its double-storey hall is filled with a colossal golden diorama depicting the Jain concept of the ancient world, with 13 continents and oceans, the golden city of Ajodhya and flying-swan and flying-elephant gondolas.

Sleeping

Bhola Hotel (☎ 2432844; Prithviraj Marg; s Rs250, d Rs350-400) Southeast of Agra Gate, this friendly hotel has five bare and pokey, but tolerably clean, rooms with basic attached bathrooms and ancient air coolers. Tasty thalis cost Rs50.

Hotel Ajmeru (☎ 2431103; www.hotelajmeru.com; Khailand Market; s/d from Rs450/550, with AC Rs800/1100; ✿) About 600m from the train station, through Kotwali Gate, this nondescript business hotel is the best of the bunch in this location – that's not saying much.

Haveli Heritage Inn (☎ 2621607; haveliheritageinn@ hotmail.com; Kutchery Rd; r Rs650-1800; ▣) Set in a 140-plus-year-old *haveli*, this is a good choice in the city centre. The high-ceilinged rooms are spacious, air-cooled and set well back from the busy road. The spotless rooms are beautifully if simply decorated and boast large bathrooms. There's a pleasant, grassy courtyard and a warm, family atmosphere, complete with delicious home-cooked meals.

Badnor House (☎ 2627579; ssbadnor@rediffmail.com; Civil Lines; d incl breakfast Rs2000; ✖) This guesthouse provides an excellent opportunity to stay with a delightful family. The down-to-earth hospitality includes a room in the main house and a spacious and comfortable self-contained room with a private courtyard.

Mansingh Palace (☎ 2425956; Circular Rd; s/d from Rs7000/8000; ✖ 🖳 🖧) Overlooking Ana Sagar, Mansingh Palace is Ajmer's only top-end hotel. It's a modern place, rather out of the way, but has attractive, comfortable rooms, some with views and balconies. There's a pleasant garden as well as a bar and restaurant.

Eating

Mango Masala (☎ 2422100; Sadar Patel Marg; mains Rs40-145; ✖ 11am-11pm) With dim, bar-like lighting and crèche-style decor, this no-alcohol, veg cafe is where Ajmer's teens hang out. There's an extensive menu of pizzas, Chinese, and North and South Indian, as well as cakes, ice cream and sundaes.

Elite (☎ 2429544; Station Rd; mains Rs40-80; ✖ 11am-11pm) Elite has a welcoming ambience attracting families to feast on the town's best thali (Rs54).

Honeydew (☎ 2622498; Station Rd; mains Rs55-120) This dimly lit, staid place has long been Ajmer's best, and it's still the restaurant of choice for Mayo College students. There's a good selection of veg and nonveg Indian, Chinese and continental food (including pizzas).

Getting There & Away
BUS
The main bus stand has regular **RSRTC buses** (☎ 2429398) to/from locations listed in the table above. Private buses serve many destinations; lining Kutchery Rd are numerous agents, where it is definitely buyer beware!

TRAIN
There are no tourist quotas for many Ajmer trains, so book early; go to Booth 5 at the **train station's reservations office** (✖ 8am-2pm & 2.15-8pm Mon-Sat, 8am-2pm Sun). **Midway Tours & Travels** (☎ 2628744; Station Rd; ✖ 8am-8pm) can book sleeper/upper-class berths for a small fee.

RAJASTHAN

BUSES FROM AJMER		
Destination	**Fare (Rs)**	**Duration (hr)**
Agra	210	10
Ahmedabad	270	13
Bharatpur	180	8
Bikaner	150	8
Bundi	105	5
Chittor	110	5
Delhi	265/550 AC	9
Indore	250	12
Jaipur	80	2½
Jaisalmer	280	10
Jodhpur	125	6
Pushkar	10	½
Udaipur	140	8

Ajmer is a regular stop on the Delhi–Jaipur–Ahmedabad–Mumbai line. The 2016/5 *Shatabdi* runs Thursday to Tuesday between Ajmer and Delhi (AC chair/1st class Rs660/1250) via Jaipur (Rs300/575). It leaves Delhi at 6.05am and arrives in Ajmer at 1pm. The other way, it leaves Ajmer at 3.50pm, arriving in Jaipur at 5.45pm and Delhi at 10.40pm. The 2957 *Rajdhani Express* to Delhi (3AC/2AC/1AC Rs660/895/1530, seven hours) leaves Ajmer at 12.35am.

The 9105/6 *Delhi–Ahmedabad Mail* departs Ajmer at 8.40pm and arrives in Delhi (sleeper/3AC/2AC Rs200/531/753) at 5.25am. Heading for Gujarat, the train leaves Ajmer at 7.40am and arrives in Ahmedabad (sleeper/3AC/2AC Rs215/574/800) at 6.40pm.

The 2992 *Ajmer–Udaipur City Express* leaves at 3.55pm, arriving in Udaipur (2nd class/AC chair Rs103/346) at 9.20pm, via Chittor (Rs80/266, 7pm).

Getting Around
There are plenty of autorickshaws (anywhere in town should cost around Rs30) as well as cycle-rickshaws and tongas (two-wheeled horse carriages).

PUSHKAR
☎ 0145 / pop 14,789
Brahma dropped a lotus flower on the earth – so say the epics – and Pushkar appeared. This compact Hindu pilgrimage town, with one of the world's few Brahma temples, curls around a sacred lake. Rows of ghats march down to the mystically placid lake from hundreds of milky-blue temples.

It's a magical though touristy place attracting a mixed bag of tourists and pilgrims. And dodgy operators abound in this low-rent paradise. As well as nimble pickpockets, there are priests trying to outwit pious pilgrims intoxicated by God or bhang (marijuana). Try to play the part in Pushkar – no booze, meat, eggs or kissing – or risk offending what you came here to admire.

Pushkar is 11km from Ajmer, separated from it by the winding Nag Pahar (Snake Mountain).

Orientation & Information

The town clusters around Pushkar Lake, with a maze of streets spreading out from Sadar Bazaar. It's small and tourist-friendly, and easy to find your way around. Cash and travellers cheques can be easily changed, and internet cafes (charging around Rs25 per hour) are everywhere.

Post office (off Heloj Rd; 9.30am-5pm) Near the Marwar bus stand.

Punjab National Bank ATM (Sadar Bazaar; 9.30am-5pm Mon-Fri, 9.30am-4pm Sat) ATM inside branch accepts Cirrus and MasterCard but not Visa cards.

State Bank of Bikaner & Jaipur (Sadar Bazaar; 10am-4pm Mon-Fri, 10am-12.30pm Sat) Changes travellers cheques and cash. The SBBJ ATM (north of the Brahma temple) accepts international cards.

Tourist Information Centre (☎ 2772040; 10am-5pm) In the grounds of Hotel Sarovar; staff will give out a free map.

Sights

TEMPLES

Pushkar has hundreds of temples, though few are particularly ancient, as they were mostly desecrated by Aurangzeb and rebuilt. Most famous is the **Brahma Temple**, said to be one of only a few such temples in the world. Apparently Brahma wanted to perform a *yagna* (self-mortification) at the lake, and when his wife Savitri didn't attend, he married another woman on a whim. Savitri, understandably annoyed, vowed that Brahma would not be worshipped anywhere else. It's marked by a red spire, and over the entrance gateway is the *hans* (goose symbol) of Brahma.

The one-hour trek up to the hilltop **Savitri Temple** overlooking the lake is best made before dawn, though the views are fantastic at any time of day. The views from the closer **Pap Mochani (Gayatri) Temple**, reached by a track behind the Marwar bus stand, are also worth the 30-minute climb.

Approximately 8km southwest of the town (past the turn-off to Savitri Temple) is a collection of **Shiva temples**. They make for a great trip by motorbike (or bicycle if you're fit and start early in the day) through the peaceful hills and villages. Be warned – the track is hilly and rocky. Another Shiva temple is about 8km north, tucked down inside a cave.

GHATS

The lake is surrounded by 52 bathing ghats, where pilgrims bathe in the sacred waters. Some have particular importance: Vishnu appeared at **Varah Ghat** in the form of a boar, Brahma bathed at **Brahma Ghat**, and some of Gandhi's ashes were sprinkled at **Gandhi Ghat** (formerly Gau Ghat). If you wish to join the pilgrims, do it with respect; remove your shoes and don't smoke, kid around or take photographs.

Activities

CAMEL TREKS & HORSE RIDING

For longer camel treks, Pushkar makes a convenient starting point. Trips start at around Rs500 per day, and head out to Jodhpur (six to seven days) and Jaisalmer (10 to 12 days). See p246 for general details about camel treks. Numerous operators line Panch Kund Marg.

PUSHKAR PASSPORTS & PUSHY PRIESTS

Priests, some genuine, some not, will approach you near the ghats and offer to do a *puja* (prayer), for which you'll receive a 'Pushkar passport' (a red ribbon around the wrist). Others proffer flowers. In either case you'll be asked to tot up your family members whose happiness is *surely* worth multiple hundreds of rupees. You could always try denying your family, or you may choose to avoid encouraging these pushy, unprincipled 'priests' altogether. At least don't be bullied and always agree on a price beforehand.

On the other hand, you can head to the Brahma Temple, where there are donation boxes. Here you can offer flowers and sacred sweets for the happiness of friends, family, everyone you've ever known – and still have change for a masala chai.

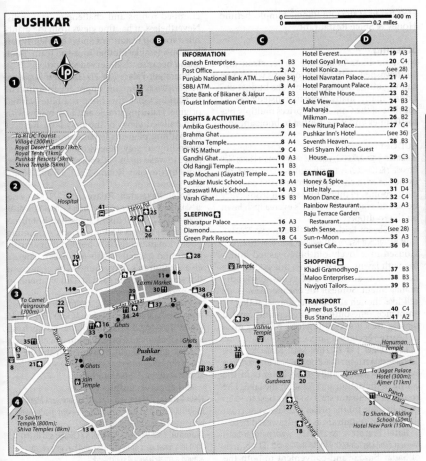

PUSHKAR

INFORMATION
Ganesh Enterprises	1	B3
Post Office	2	A2
Punjab National Bank ATM	(see 34)	
SBBJ ATM	3	A4
State Bank of Bikaner & Jaipur	4	B3
Tourist Information Centre	5	C4

SIGHTS & ACTIVITIES
Ambika Guesthouse	6	B3
Brahma Ghat	7	A4
Brahma Temple	8	A4
Dr NS Mathur	9	C4
Gandhi Ghat	10	A3
Old Rangji Temple	11	B3
Pap Mochani (Gayatri) Temple	12	B1
Pushkar Music School	13	A4
Saraswati Music School	14	A3
Varah Ghat	15	B3

SLEEPING
Bharatpur Palace	16	A3
Diamond	17	B3
Green Park Resort	18	C4

EATING
Honey & Spice	30	B3
Little Italy	31	D4
Moon Dance	32	C4
Rainbow Restaurant	33	A3
Raju Terrace Garden Restaurant	34	B3
Sixth Sense	(see 28)	
Sun-n-Moon	35	A3
Sunset Cafe	36	B4

Hotel Everest	19	A3
Hotel Goyal Inn	20	C4
Hotel Konica	(see 28)	
Hotel Navratan Palace	21	A4
Hotel Paramount Palace	22	A3
Hotel White House	23	B2
Lake View	24	B3
Maharaja	25	B2
Milkman	26	B2
New Rituraj Palace	27	C4
Pushkar Inn's Hotel	(see 36)	
Seventh Heaven	28	B3
Shri Shyam Krishna Guest House	29	C3

SHOPPING
Khadi Gramodhyog	37	B3
Maloo Enterprises	38	B3
Navjyoti Tailors	39	B3

TRANSPORT
Ajmer Bus Stand	40	C4
Bus Stand	41	A2

At **Shannu's Riding School** (☎ 2772043; www .pushkar.bravehost.com; Panch Kund Marg; lessons per hr Rs250) long-time Pushkar resident Marco can organise riding lessons and horse safaris on his graceful Marwari steeds.

REFLEXOLOGY

Dr NS Mathur (☎ 2622777, 9828103031; Ajmer Rd; 10.30am-6.30pm) provides a toe-challenging re-flexology session (Rs250), which will certainly take your mind off the rest of your body. He also teaches reiki (courses I/II Rs1500/3000).

Courses

MUSIC

The **Pushkar Music School** (☎ 5121277; Pushkar Lake Palace hotel; Parakrama Marg) teaches classical sitar,

tabla, harmonium, dancing and more, for Rs150 per hour in a peaceful lakeside location. The **Saraswati Music School** (☎ 2773124; Malniyon ka Chowk, Badi Basti; 10am-10pm) teaches classical tabla, flute, singing and *kathak* (classical dance). Fees start from Rs350 for two hours. There are instruments for sale and often evening performances (8pm to 9.30pm).

YOGA & HEALING

For a fix of reiki, yoga and shiatsu, Reiki Master Roshi Hiralal Verma is based at **Ambika Guesthouse** (☎ 2773154). Prices are charged according to the duration and nature of your session.

Dr Kamel Pandey offers recommended yoga classes and naturopathic consultations.

He's based at the Old Rangji Temple, behind Honey & Spice Restaurant.

Sleeping

Most Pushkar hotels are basic, clean and whitewashed, with lovely rooftops where you can veg out. There are numerous budget options – many, many more than listed here. At the time of the Camel Fair, prices multiply five to 10 times and it's essential to book ahead.

BUDGET

Milkman (☎ 2773452; vinodmilkman@hotmail.com; Mali Mohalla; r Rs100-500) A terrifically welcoming family house with cheeky frescoes in the cosy but clean rooms. Plants galore sprout from every nook and cranny and there's even a lush lawn on the rooftop.

Shri Shyam Krishna Guesthouse (☎ 2772461; Sadar Bazaar; s/d Rs225/300, without bathroom Rs125/225) Housed in a lovely old blue-washed building with lawns and gardens, this guesthouse has ashram austerity and genuine friendly management. Some of the cheaper rooms are cell-like, though all share the simple, authentic ambience. The outdoor kitchen and garden seating are a good setting for a relaxing meal of hearty vegetarian fare.

Lake View (☎ 2772106; Sadar Bazaar Rd; www .lakeviewpushkar.com; r from Rs400, without bathroom from Rs200) This wonderfully sited hotel is in the centre of the action and right on the lake. The rooms are drab but staff do their best to keep them liveable for the price. The lake view from the rooftop restaurant is the drawcard here.

Hotel Everest (☎ 2773417; www.pushkar-hotel -everest.com; r Rs200-600, with AC Rs700; ⬛ ▢) North of Sadar Bazaar and convenient to both the bazaar and the mela ground, this is the pick of the budget hotels, with bright clean rooms and obliging hosts. There's a nice view from the rooftop restaurant. It is run by a friendly father-and-son team who can't do enough for their appreciative guests.

Hotel Paramount Palace (☎ 2772428; hotelpara mountpalace@hotmail.com; Bari Basti; r Rs200-850) This tower of a hotel has bird's-eye views over the town and lake, and formidable stairs. It also has a long-standing reputation for value and friendly service. The rooms vary so find a favourite. The food is good and there's a small garden should you tire of the view.

Hotel White House (☎ 2772147; www.pushkar whitehouse.com; r Rs250-650, with AC Rs650-1350) White House is a spotless place with somewhat cramped rooms and challenging stairwells. Nevertheless, it has fine views from the plant-filled rooftop restaurant and is efficiently run by a businesslike mother-and-son team. Book ahead because it's deservedly popular.

Bharatpur Palace (☎ 2772320; Sadar Bazaar; s/d from Rs300/600) On the upper levels adjacent to Gandhi Ghat, this hotel is a blue-washed original featuring simple and bare rooms with unparalleled views of the holy lake. Respect for bathing pilgrims is paramount for those intending to stay here. Room 1 is the best place to wake up in – it's surrounded on three sides by the lake. Rooms 9, 12, 13 and 16 are also good.

Hotel Navaratan Palace (☎ 2772981; www .pushkarnavaratanpalace.com; s/d from Rs300/400, with AC Rs600/700; ⬛ ▢) This businesslike hotel has functional rooms and a glorious swimming pool (nonguests Rs100), bordered by terrific lawns and gardens (with tortoises). There's also a children's playground. The restaurant delivers meals to the garden. Did we mention the pool?

Pushkar Inn's Hotel (☎ 2772010; hotelpushkarinns@ yahoo.com; Pushkar Lake; s/d without AC Rs500/700, with AC Rs1000/1200; ⬛) A charming hotel comprising a row of clean and bright rooms, backed by a garden and orchard, which catch the breeze from the lake, and that is mostly good, though some wafts are less than holy.

Other good cheapies:

New Rituraj Palace (☎ 2772875; Gurdwara Marg; r Rs80-100) About as basic as it gets. Pleasant garden with home-cooked food in a peaceful nook.

Diamond (☎ 9828462343; Holi Ka Chowk; s/d Rs100-300) In a quiet part of town, Diamond has tiny rooms around a small tranquil courtyard.

Maharaja (☎ 2773527; Mali Mohalta; r Rs120) Popular, tucked-away spot with a restful rooftop.

MIDRANGE

Green Park Resort (☎ 2773532; www.greenparkpushkar .in; Gurdwara Marg; r Rs750-1600; ⬛ ▢) This welcoming place has 18 spiffy rooms all with marble floors, comfy beds and cable TV. The swimming pool is big and inviting and there's a relaxing rooftop restaurant. It's only a 10-minute stroll to town along a dusty country lane.

our pick Seventh Heaven (☎ 5105455; www.inn -seventh-heaven.com; Chotti Basti; r Rs450-2000; ⬛) This lovingly converted *haveli* is the perfect place to chill out, with traditionally crafted furniture, galleries and a central fountain. The cool tiled

PUSHKAR CAMEL FAIR

Come the month of Kartika, the eighth lunar month of the Hindu calendar and one of the holiest, camel drivers spruce up their ships of the desert and start the long walk to Pushkar in time for Kartik Purnima (full moon). Each year around 200,000 people converge here, bringing with them some 50,000 camels, horses and cattle. The place becomes an extraordinary swirl of colour, sound and movement, thronged with musicians, mystics, tourists, traders, animals and devotees.

Trading begins a week before the official fair (a good time to see the serious business), but by the time the RTDC mela (fair) starts, business takes a back seat and the bizarre aspects of the fair jostle into life (musicians, snake charmers, children balancing on poles etc). Even the tourist board's cultural program is bizarre: turban-tying and moustache contests, or seeing how many people can balance on a camel.

It's hard to believe, but this seething mass is all just a sideshow; Kartik Purnima is when Hindu pilgrims come to bathe in Pushkar's sacred waters. The religious event builds in tandem with the Camel Fair in a wild, magical crescendo of incense, chanting and processions to dousing day, the last night of the fair, when thousands of devotees wash away their sins and set candles afloat on the holy lake.

It's crowded, touristy, noisy (light sleepers should bring earplugs) and tacky. Those affected by dust and/or animal hair should bring appropriate medication. However, it's a grand epic, and not to be missed if you're anywhere within camel-spitting distance. It usually takes place in October or November (25 October to 2 November 2009, 13 to 21 November 2010, 2 to 10 November 2011).

rooms have gorgeously individual touches, and blissfully comfy beds. The rooftop Sixth Sense restaurant has a wonderful vibe and delicious food. If it's full, the tiny Hotel Konica has a few very basic rooms (Rs250) in the same building.

Hotel New Park (☎ 2772464; www.newparkpushkar .com; Panch Kund Rd; s/d Rs1050/1200, with AC Rs1050/1200; 🗙 🔊) This quiet hotel is blissfully rural but still an easy walk to/from the lake. The older air-con rooms aren't great value, with questionable plumbing and an air of neglect. Management is aware of this and a discount is offered readily. Balconies overlook an inviting pool, rose gardens and a backdrop of hills.

Hotel Goyal Inn (☎ 2773991; www.hotelgoyalinn.com; Ajmer Rd; s/d Rs800/1000, with AC Rs1200/1500; 🗙 🖳 🔊) Very convenient to the Ajmer bus stand, but the back rooms don't suffer from too much noise. The central courtyard is almost an oasis. Noon check-out is a plus, but unfortunately you will need to check the plumbing, especially in the non-AC rooms.

Pushkar Resorts (☎ 2772944; www.pushkarresorts .com; Motisar Marg; s/d from Rs3495/3945; 🗙 🔊) This sprawling resort, about 5km out of town, is set in an orchard and has a pool shaded by palms. There are four clusters of 10 modern and comfortable cottages, and some have been renovated beautifully. One aspect of its popularity is that it is outside the city limits and so has meat and booze on the menu.

Jagat Palace Hotel (☎ 2772953; www.hotelpush karpalace.com; Ajmer Rd; s/d Rs2662/3267; 🗙 🔊) A gorgeous heritage-style hotel designed to resemble a palace. It offers romantic bedrooms with carved furniture and lovely bathrooms. Balconies overlook lush large gardens and a pool (Rs300 for nonguests). There are tempting packages and low-season discounts.

Eating

Pushkar has plenty of atmospheric restaurants, many with lake views and international traveller fare, though hygiene standards are sometimes wanting. Strict vegetarianism, forbidding even eggs, limits ingredients.

Sunset Cafe (☎ 2772382; mains Rs10–110; ⏰ 7.30am–midnight) Right on the eastern ghats, this cafe has sublime lake views, decent breakfasts and Indian and Italian cuisine. There are also bakery items, and the lakeside setting is picture perfect at sunset.

Sun-n-Moon (☎ 2772883; Bari Basti; mains Rs25–180; ⏰ 7.30am–11pm) This neohippy haunt attracts all kinds for its Italian menu and friendly staff. The courtyard is home to a bodhi tree, a shrine and hungry tortoises. Breakfast includes lassis and masala chai, while for the homesick there are hash browns.

Honey & Spice (☎ 5105505; Laxmi Market off Sadar Bazaar; mains Rs30–85; ⏰ 7.30am–6.30pm) A tiny breakfast-and-lunch place that delivers homemade banana cakes, sandwiches, tofu steak and hearty concoctions served on a bed of brown rice. It is run by a friendly man who is a mine of local information. Oh, and the South Indian coffee is the real deal.

Raju Terrace Garden Restaurant (Sadar Bazaar; mains Rs30-75; ☎ 7.30am-10.30pm) This long-standing rooftopper has fairy lights, potted plants and tremendous views, plus reasonable 'homesick food' such as baked potatoes and pizza. The Indian fare is middling though.

Sixth Sense (☎ 5105455; Seventh Heaven, Chotti Basti; mains Rs40-90; ☎ 8am-11pm) This chilled rooftop restaurant is a great place to head even if you didn't score a room in its popular hotel. Its ambience is immediately relaxing and the pulley apparatus that delivers the delicious food from the ground-floor kitchen is enthralling. Save room for the desserts, such as the excellent homemade tarts.

Rainbow Restaurant (☎ 51210771; mains Rs45-100; ☎ 11am-11pm) Set on a small rooftop with a view over the lake, the Rainbow hums with satisfied customers. The pasta is excellent, and the ice-cream sundaes overflow with sugary goodness. The hummus with fresh pita is pretty darn authentic.

Moon Dance (☎ 2772606; mains Rs60-160; ☎ 7.30am-10.30pm) The attraction here is the neatly manicured garden setting, which puts you at ease as soon as you take a seat. Perhaps there's positive energy emanating from the Vishnu temple opposite. The Indian and Italian are good and there's a small range of Mexican dishes.

Little Italy (☎ 2772366; Panch Kund Marg; mains Rs80-120; ☎ 7.30am-11pm) A delightful garden restaurant with wood-fired pizzas and excellent pasta, pita and hummus. The pesto is made with home-grown basil, and the coffee is good by Pushkar standards.

Shopping

Pushkar's narrow Sadar Bazaar is lined with absorbing little shops selling silver and costume jewellery, glass lamps, embroidery and wall hangings, CDs and Indo-Western clothes. Much of the textile handiwork comes from the Barmer district south of Jaisalmer. As you're in a touristy town, you'll have to haggle.

Pushkar is also a good place to get clothes made. Two reliable options are **Navjyoti Tailors** (Sadar Bazaar) and **Maloo Enterprises** (Varah Ghat Chowk). **Khadi Gramodhyog** (Sadar Bazaar), almost hidden on the main drag, is a fixed-price shop selling traditional hand-woven shirts, scarves and shawls.

Getting There & Away

Frequent buses to/from Ajmer (Rs10, 30 minutes) stop on the road heading eastwards out of town; other buses leave from the station to the north.

Local travel agencies sell tickets for private buses – you should shop around. These buses generally leave from Ajmer, but the agencies should provide you with free connecting transport. Those that leave from Pushkar usually stop for an hour or more in Ajmer anyway. Be warned that some buses (particularly those via Jodhpur) don't go all the way; in spite of promises, they'll involve a change of bus *and* an extra fare. Some destinations and fares from Pushkar are listed in the table opposite.

The post office will book train tickets for services out of Ajmer for about Rs15 commission. For around Rs50 private agencies do the same, including transfer to Ajmer. See p195 for details of trains from Ajmer.

CAMEL FAIR TOURIST VILLAGE

During the Camel Fair, the RTDC and several private operators set up a sea of tents near the fairground. These are usually filled up with tour groups. It gets cold at night, so bring something warm; a torch (flashlight) is also useful. You need to book well ahead.

RTDC Tourist Village (☎ 2772074; s/d huts from Rs700/800, tents s/d from Rs6000/6500) has various permanent huts and semi-permanent tents that are usually booked out by tour groups well in advance. Full payment must be received two months in advance. Rates include all meals.

Further away from the fairground than Royal Tents, **Royal Desert Camp** (☎ 2772957; www .hotelpushkarpalace.com; tents s/d Rs2420/2662) is still a good option. Book at Hotel Pushkar Palace (☎ 2773001).

Royal Tents (www.jodhpurheritage.com; tents US$250) Owned by the descendant of the Maharaja of Jodhpur, these are the most luxurious and expensive tents. Rates include all meals. Reservations should be made through **Jodhpur's Balsamand Palace** (☎ 0291-2571991).

BUSES FROM PUSHKAR		
Destination	**Fare (Rs)**	**Duration (hr)**
Agra	ordinary/sleeper 180/230	9
Bundi	110	6
Delhi	ordinary/sleeper 180/230	10½
Jaipur	100	4
Jaisalmer	ordinary/sleeper 240/340	10½
Jodhpur	120	5
Udaipur	ordinary/sleeper 160/230	8

When entering Pushkar by car there is a toll of Rs35. (Buses also pay a toll which is included in your ticket.)

Getting Around

There are no autorickshaws, but Pushkar's a breeze to get around on foot. Another good option is to hire a bicycle (Rs10/30 per hour/day) or a scooter/motorbike (Rs200/350 per day) from one of the numerous outlets. A wallah can carry your luggage on a hand-drawn cart to/from the bus stand for around Rs15.

RANTHAMBORE NATIONAL PARK

☎ 07462

This **national park** (Oct-Jun) is 1334 sq km of wild jungle scrub hemmed in by rocky ridges. At its centre is the 10th-century **Ranthambore Fort** (admission free, 6am-6pm), and scattered nearby are ancient temples and mosques, crocodile-filled lakes, *chhatris* (cenotaphs) and hides. The park was a maharajas' hunting ground till 1970 – a curious 15 years after it had become a sanctuary.

Ranthambore is the best place to spot wild tigers in Rajasthan. Project Tiger has been in charge of the animals' welfare since 1979, but the project's difficulties were thrown into sharp relief when government officials were implicated in poaching in 2005. Getting an accurate figure on the number of tigers comes down to who you believe – a nongovernment report estimated the figure to be 23 in mid-2008 just prior to two tigers being moved to Sariska Tiger Reserve (see p188 for more information on this relocation).

Aside from the enormous Ganesh Mela (fair) every August, traffic into the park is restricted to organised safaris. Still, the remaining tigers are so used to being observed that they're not scared away by jeeps and canters (large, open-topped trucks seating 20); and sometimes they even seem intrigued by visitors.

Seeing a tiger is just a matter of luck, but the park is also worth visiting for the scenery and other wildlife, particularly if you walk up to the fort. There are also more than 300 species of birds in the park.

Orientation

It's 10km from the town of **Sawai Madhopur** to the first gate and another 3km to the main gate and Ranthambore Fort. Accommodation is stretched out along the road from the town to the park. The train station is in the heart of Sawai Madhopur, just south of the main bazaar.

Information

Bank of Baroda ATM (Bazariya Market, Sawai Madhopur) It's 200m northwest of the train station.
Project Tiger office (☎ 223402; Ranthambore Rd) Only 500m from the train station.
State Bank of Bikaner & Jaipur (Sawai Madhopur, 10am-2pm Mon-Fri, 10am-noon Sat) Will change cash or travellers cheques and has an ATM. It's a couple of blocks north of the train station. There's another SBBJ ATM at the train station.
Tiger Track (Ranthambore Rd; internet per hr Rs60; 7am-10.30pm) Internet access.
Tourist Reception Centre (☎ 2220808; Sawai Madhopur train station; 10am-5pm Mon-Sat)

Activities

The best time to take a **wildlife safari** is between October and April (book on www.rajasthanwildlife.in). The mornings can be cold, so bring warm clothes.

The best option is to travel by gypsy, a small, open-topped 4WD that takes five passengers. You still have a good chance of seeing a tiger from the large, open-topped, 20-seater canter, though sometimes other passengers can be rowdy. Guides will lead you into one of five zones. Each zone hosts four jeeps and four canters per morning and evening session.

Half-day safaris (Indian/foreigner per person in gypsy Rs436/647, in canter Rs340/547) take three hours. From October to February, canters and gypsies leave at 7am and 2.30pm. From March to June they leave at 6.30am and 3.30pm. **Full-day safaris** (Indian/foreigner per person, gypsy only Rs871/1293) take lunch at Bhilai Sagar.

Seats in gypsies and canters can be reserved on the website, though a single gypsy and five

RAJASTHAN

canters are also kept for direct booking at the **Forest Office** (Ranthambore Rd; � 5am-7am & noon-2pm). Direct bookings are best done through your hotel, which will incur a small fee. Demand often outstrips supply during holiday seasons.

A guide is compulsory and is included in the canter ticket price, but will cost an extra Rs200 if you go by gypsy.

Sleeping & Eating

Ranthambore Rd is lined with numerous accommodation options and most offer free pick-up and drop-off from the train and bus stations. Budget travellers will find the cheapest (grimiest and noisiest) lodgings in uninspiring Sawai Madhopur.

RANTHAMBORE ROAD

Hotel Aditya Resort (☎ 9414728468; Ranthambore Rd; r from Rs350, with AC Rs600, without bathroom from Rs250; ❄) This friendly place is way ahead of similarly priced accommodation in the town. The keen young staff will organise safari bookings and allow use of the big air-con room without air-con for a hefty discount.

RTDC Vinayak Tourist Complex (☎ 221333; s/d Rs700/800, with AC Rs1100/1300; ❄) This RTDC complex is close to the park entrance and, although institutional, has relatively bright and spacious rooms with appealing little sitting areas. There's a nice lawn area and a campfire is lit in the winter.

Hotel Tiger Safari Resort (☎ 221137; www.tigersafari resort.com; d from Rs800, cottages from Rs1300; ❄ 💻 🛀) Some 4km from the train station, this is one of the better-value options where the helpful management is adept at organising safaris, and waking and feeding you for the morning safari. There's a decent restaurant, and the spacious doubles and so-called 'cottages' (larger rooms with bigger bathrooms) face a well-kept garden and small pool.

Hotel Anurag Resort (☎ 220751; www.anuragresort .com; s/d Rs1400/1600, cottages Rs2300/2500; ❄ 💻 🛀) Another old hand at organising safaris, this established hotel offers decent, though small, midrange rooms a good restaurant and the gardens are ruler-edge perfect.

Hotel Ankur Resort (☎ 220792; ankurswm@san charnet.in; s/d Rs2200/2640, cottages Rs2640/3080, deluxe Rs3080/3520; ❄ 🛀) Located 3km from the train station, this is a popular choice with clean and bright rooms surrounded by greenery.

RTDC Castle Jhoomar Baori (☎ 220495; s/d Rs2500/3500, ste Rs4000/5000; ❄) This former royal hunting lodge is in a stunning hilltop setting about 7km from the station. Although not exactly luxurious, rooms possess a degree of character and the rooftop is a nice escape.

Hotel Ranthambore Regency (☎ 221176; www.ran thambhor.com; s/d incl full board Rs5670/6930; ❄ 💻 🛀) This is a large and efficiently run place with enormous and beautiful luxury rooms set around an attractive garden with an impressive pool. Not surprisingly, it gets booked by tour groups.

Nahargarh Ranthambore (☎ 252146; www.nahar garhranthambore.com; Village Khilchipur, Ranthambore Rd; s/d/ste incl full board Rs6700/7700/9900; ❄ 💻 🛀) This Alsisar hotel is a palace fit for a king, with impressively spacious rooms; a long, gold-inlaid dining area; and a monstrous courtyard that feels like an abandoned film set. Even management appears awestruck. It's opposite the park entrance, 1km off Ranthambore Rd.

our pick Khem Villas (☎ 252099; www.khemvillas .com; Ranthambore Rd; s/d homestead Rs7000/8000, tents Rs9500/12,000, cottage Rs12,000/15,000; ❄) This splendid option has been created by the Singh Rathore family. The patriarch, Fateh Singh Rathore, is lauded as the driving force behind the conservation of tigers at Ranthambore. His son Goverdhan and his daughter-in-law Usha run this impressive ecolodge. The accommodation ranges from rooms in the colonial-style bungalow to luxury tents and sumptuous stone cottages. Privacy is guaranteed (you can even bathe under the stars) and socialising is relaxed – join the tiger talk at sunset drinks. Prices include all meals and taxes.

SAWAI MADHOPUR

Sawai Madhopur has grotty, inexpensive options convenient to the train station, but not always convenient when it comes to getting assistance with safari bookings.

Hotel Chinkara (☎ 220340; 13 Indira Colony, Civil Lines; s/d Rs200/300) A quiet place run by a welcoming family. It has large, dusty rooms and simple home-cooked meals.

Ganesh Ranthambhore (☎ 220230; 58 Bal Mandir Colony, Civil Lines; r from Rs400; ❄) On the western side of the overpass, this hotel has basic but clean rooms. Higher tariffs get you bigger, brighter rooms with TVs and AC.

Shopping

Dastkar Craft Centre (☎ 252051; Ranthambore Rd; � 10am-8pm) This place, 3km from the station, is worth a visit. The organisation empowers low-caste village women, who produce the attractive handicrafts on sale, including saris, scarves, bags and bedspreads. You can visit the workshop located beyond the park entrance near Khem Villas.

Getting There & Away
BUS
Buses from Sawai Madhopur include services to Jaipur (Rs100, six hours) and Kota (Rs70, four hours). Buses to these destinations via Tonk leave from the small bus stand near the petrol station close to the overpass. To go via Dausa (on the Jaipur–Bharatpur road), buses leave from the roundabout near the main post office. The enquiries number is ☎ 2451020. The train is preferable for most routes.

TRAIN
At Sawai Madhopur train station there's a computerised **reservation office** (🕑 8am-8pm Mon-Sat, 8am-2pm Sun).

The 2903/4 *Golden Temple Mail* leaves Sawai Madhopur at 12.40pm, stopping at Bharatpur (sleeper/3AC Rs141/316) at 3.08pm, arriving in Delhi (Rs192/484) at 7pm. From Delhi, it leaves at 7.45am, stopping at Bharatpur at 10.40am and arriving at 1.05pm. The same train (2904) departs at 1.10pm and arrives at Kota (Rs141/268) at 2.30pm. Another convenient train to Kota is the 9037/8 *Avadh Express*. It leaves Sawai Madhopur at 9.15am and arrives in Kota (sleeper/3AC Rs121/238) on Tuesday, Wednesday, Friday and Saturday at 11am. Going the other way, it departs from Sawai Madhopur at 4.25pm, arriving in Agra (Rs132/340) at 9.50pm on Tuesday, Friday and Sunday.

Getting Around
Bicycle hire is available in Sawai Madhopur's main bazaar (Rs30 per day). Autorickshaws are available at the train station; the journey to Ranthambore Rd will cost Rs30.

SOUTHERN RAJASTHAN

BUNDI
☎ 0747 / pop 88,312
Bundi is an effortlessly captivating town, with narrow lanes of Brahmin-blue houses, assorted temples and a picturesque palace. This – or at least the old town beneath the palace – is the Rajasthan of the travel bro-

chures, virtually free from noisy polluting engines and choking crowds. It still has an atmosphere of past wonders (as Kipling appreciated while he lived and wrote here), most readily felt around the cupola-clad fairy-tale palace that spills down the hillside. From January to March, delicate pink poppies fill surrounding fields.

Here you will find a welcome break from the customary tourist trail. Bundi is still the place to explore laneways or just sit and soak up the history or gaze at contemporary life.

It was the capital of a major princely state during the Rajputs' heyday. Although its importance dwindled with the rise of Kota during Mughal times, it remained independent until incorporation into Rajasthan in 1947.

Information
The very helpful **tourist office** (☎ 2443697; Kota Rd; 🕑 10am-5pm Mon-Fri), south of the bus stand, offers free maps, books buses to Udaipur and can provide the latest on bus and train timings. This is also a good place to ask about organising a visit to Bundi's ancient rock-art sites and picturesque waterfalls. Mukesh Mehta, at the Haveli Braj Bhushanjee (p205) is also a terrific source of information; his brother's website (www.kiplingsbundi.com) is also useful.

There are SBBJ ATMs on Kota Rd and at the town branch near Azad Park, and money-changers south of the palace with highly variable office hours. You'll find numerous places to check your email for Rs60 per hour; all are cramped and the advertised AC just happens to have stopped working at the time you visit.

Sights
TARAGARH
The vine-strewn **Taragarh** (Star Fort; admission free) was built in 1354, and is great to ramble around – but take a stick to battle the overgrown vegetation, help the knees on the steep climb, and provide confidence when surrounded by testosterone-charged macaques. Take the path up behind the Chitrasala, east along the inside of the ramparts, then left up the steep stone ramp just before the **Dudha Mahal**, a small disused building 200m from the palace. Inside the ramparts are massive reservoirs carved into the rock and the **Bhim Burj**, the largest of the battlements, which supports a famous cannon. Views over the town

RAJASTHAN

and surrounding countryside are magical, especially at sunset.

BUNDI PALACE

The **palace** (Indian/foreigner Rs10/60, camera/video Rs50/100; ☷ 8am-5.30pm) is an extraordinary decaying edifice with fabulous though fading turquoise-and-gold murals. It's reached from the bazaar's northwestern end. It was previously shut up and left to the bats, but the erstwhile royal family have leased it to a private company to clean it up and it's now open to the public. Knowledgeable guides (Rs250) hang around the ticket office.

You enter through the huge elephant gate, built in 1607. From here you can visit the Chhatra Mahal, built in 1644, which has some of Bundi's finest murals; one room features well-preserved paintings of Krishna – one for each month. The Phool Mahal was built in 1607 and has a mural of an immense royal procession. Dating from the same period, the Badal Mahal has a wonderful Chinese-inspired ceiling, divided into petal shapes and decorated with peacocks and Krishna.

To get to the **Chitrasala** (Umed Mahal; admission free; ☷ 7am-6pm), built by Rao Umed Singh in the 18th century, you exit the elephant gate and walk (left) further uphill to the entrance. Above the garden courtyard are several rooms covered in beautiful paintings. The back room on the right is the Sheesh Mahal; it's badly damaged, but has beautiful inlaid glass. The morning sun lights up the interiors quite well, but bring a torch (flashlight) if visiting in the afternoon.

MAHARAO RAJA BAHADUR SINGH MUSEUM

This **museum** (admission Rs100, camera Rs50; ☷ 9am-1pm, 2-5pm) is housed in the Moti Mahal, where the current royal descendents live. It is an extraordinary celebration of the lives of the more recent royal members. The first hall is stuffed with stuffed wildlife, chiefly tigers shot by Indian, British and American luminaries. Most visitors are dumbstruck by the tigress with two cubs – all shot by 'Mr Milton Reynolds, inventor of the ball point pen, in 1953 at Bhimlat'. Other halls contain royal portraits and arrays of weapons.

BAORIS & WATER TANKS

There are many impressive *baoris* in Bundi. **Raniji-ki-Baori** (Queen's Baori) is 46m deep and

is decorated with beautiful carvings. Built in 1699 by Rani Nathavatji, it is one of the largest of its kind, though neglect and numerous bats and pigeons make it an odorous excursion. The **Nagar Sagar Kund** is a pair of matching step-wells just outside Chogan Gate.

Visible from the fort is the square artificial lake of **Nawal Sagar**, which tends to dry up if the monsoon is poor. In the centre is a temple to Varuna, the Aryan god of water. Other tanks which would be well worth a look if they didn't happen to double as public toilets are the 16th-century **Bhora-ji-ka-Kund** and the imposing **Dhabhai Kund**.

OTHER SIGHTS

It's great to amble around the old city. Just outside the walls, the **sabzi (vegetable) market**, between Raniji-ki-Baori and Nagar Sagar Kund, is particularly vibrant. There are more than 200 temples here and more than 100 step-wells. Self-guided heritage-walk maps are available at Haveli Braj Bhushanjee (opposite).

Bundi's other attractions are out of town, and best visited by bike, rickshaw or taxi. Several kilometres out of town on the Ajmer road, the modern palace, known as the **Phool Sagar Palace**, has a beautiful artificial tank and gardens. The stately **Sukh Mahal** (☷ 10am-5pm) is a smaller palace, where Rudyard Kipling once stayed and wrote part of *Kim*. It's closer to town, on the edge of the beautiful Jait Sagar. The nearby, neglected **Sar Bagh** has several royal cenotaphs, some with intricate carvings. **Shikar Burj** is a small former royal hunting lodge, next to a water tank, on the road that runs along the north side of Jait Sagar. South of town is the **84-Pillared Cenotaph**, which is particularly stunning when lit up at night.

The countryside around Bundi is ideal for excursions by bicycle. North of Bundi you can visit **Akoda**, a merchant's village, and **Thikarda**, with potteries, around 6km from Bundi. About 20km north is a Shiva cave temple and a waterfall at **Rameshwar**. West of Bundi is rural **Borkhandi** village, around 7km distant. Twenty-two kilometres towards Jaipur is **Hindoli**, with a huge lake and a ruined hilltop fort.

About 33km from Bundi at the village of Garardha you can see ancient **rock paintings** flanking the river, believed to be about 15,000 years old. There's a curious depiction of a man riding a huge bird, as well as some hunting scenes. Ask at the Tourist Information Centre or your hotel about hiring a guide. A half-

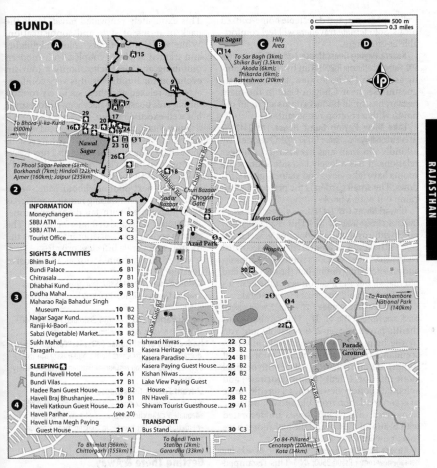

BUNDI

INFORMATION
Moneychangers	1 B2
SBBJ ATM	2 C3
SBBJ ATM	3 C2
Tourist Office	4 C3

SIGHTS & ACTIVITIES
Bhim Burj	5 B1
Bundi Palace	6 B1
Chitrasala	7 B1
Dhabhai Kund	8 B3
Dudha Mahal	9 B1
Maharao Raja Bahadur Singh Museum	10 B2
Nagar Sagar Kund	11 B2
Ranjii-ki-Baori	12 B3
Sabzi (Vegetable) Market	13 B2
Sukh Mahal	14 C1
Taragarh	15 B1

SLEEPING
Bundi Haveli Hotel	16 A1
Bundi Vilas	17 B1
Hadee Rani Guest House	18 B2
Haveli Braj Bhushanjee	19 B1
Haveli Katkoun Guest House	20 A1
Haveli Parihar	(see 20)
Haveli Uma Megh Paying Guest House	21 A1
Ishwari Niwas	22 C3
Kasera Heritage View	23 B2
Kasera Paradise	24 B1
Kasera Paying Guest House	25 B2
Kishan Niwas	26 B2
Lake View Paying Guest House	27 A1
RN Haveli	28 B2
Shivam Tourist Guesthouse	29 A1

TRANSPORT
Bus Stand	30 C3

day trip in a jeep would cost around Rs800 return. On the road to Chittor, about 36km from Bundi is another impressive waterfall and picnic area at **Bhimlat** (Rs600 return by taxi).

Festivals & Events

In October/November the festivals of **Bundi Ustav** and **Kashavrai Patan** inject some evening energy into an otherwise daydreamy town. In August, the town hosts celebrations for **Teej**. See p167 for details of the festivals.

Sleeping & Eating

Bundi's paying guesthouses are excellent value, providing budget accommodation and home-cooked meals. Bundi was once a dry town, so it's not a place for evening revelry; however, a cold beer can usually be arranged. Most guest-houses will also pick you up from the train station or bus stand if you call ahead.

Haveli Uma Megh Paying Guest House (☎ 2442191; haveliumamegh@yahoo.com; r Rs100-550) This bona fide cheapie run by friendly brothers has plenty of dilapidated charm, wall paintings, alcoves, lake views and some really low doorways. The pricier rooms are spacious. It's peaceful and has an overgrown lakeside garden for candlelit dinners (dishes Rs30 to 55).

RN Haveli (☎ 5120098, rnhavelibundi@yahoo.co.in; Rawle ka Chowk; r Rs250, without bathroom Rs150) The dynamic mother-and-two-daughters team who run this guesthouse often lead guests on all kinds of cross-town excursions. It's an old, ramshackle place with a shady garden,

RAJASTHAN

RAJASTHAN

well-kept rooms, and delectable home-cooked meals. Solo female travellers will feel comfortable at once here.

Kasera Paying Guest House (☎ 2446630; d Rs300-500, without bathroom Rs200) Run by the same family as Kasera Heritage View, this small-scale guesthouse, near Chogan Gate in the main bazaar, has small budget rooms set in an old *haveli* with a rooftop restaurant.

Lake View Paying Guest House (☎ 2442326; lakeviewbundi@yahoo.com; r Rs250-500) Overseen by a kindly old man and his assorted younger relations, it has a lovely lakeside spot. Some rooms have lake views and stained-glass windows. The small garden is the perfect place to camp out with a book.

Ishwari Niwas (☎ 2442414; www.ishwariniwas.com; 1 Civil Lines; r Rs500-1800; ☒ ▢) This is a family-run hotel with royal associations in a graceful old colonial building set around an oddly decorated courtyard. It has spacious rooms with murals, and an interesting dining hall (heads, skins and old maps), but the location is not the best: it's away from the old city, past the bus stand.

Haveli Braj Bhushanjee (☎ 2442322; www.kiplings bundi.com; r Rs500-2450; ☒ ▢) This rambling, authentic *haveli* is over 250 years old and run by the helpful Braj Bhushanjee family (descendants of the former prime ministers of Bundi). It's an enchanting place with original stone interiors (plenty of low doorways) and splendid rooftop views. It has a terrific range of accommodation from old and atmospheric to modern with views. Rooms are decorated with beautiful murals and the bathrooms have solar-powered hot water.

Kasera Heritage View (☎ 2444679; www.kasera heritageview.com; r Rs500-3500; ☒) This revamped *haveli* has an incongruously modern lobby but offers a range of slightly more authentic rooms. The rooftop restaurant sits precariously high, but is nevertheless well placed for gazing at its over-the-top sister hotel, Kasera Paradise (www.kaseraparadise.com) in front of the palace, which shares the same phone number and room rates.

Haveli Katkoun Guest House (☎ 2444311; http://haveli katkoun.free.fr; Balchand Para; r Rs600-1800; ☒) Just outside the town's west gate, this totally revamped *haveli* boasts large, spotless rooms with superb views of the lake or the palace. Under renovation at the time we visited, the freshened rooms and rooftop restaurant are sure to please.

our pick **Bundi Haveli Hotel** (☎ 2447861; info@hotel bundihaveli.com; r Rs1350, with AC Rs2500, ste Rs4000; ☒) This exquisitely renovated *haveli* leads the pack in terms of style and sophistication. White walls, stone floors, colour highlights and framed artefacts coupled with modern plumbing and electricity signify a tourism evolution for Bundi. Yes, it is very comfortable and relaxed and there's a lovely rooftop dining area boasting palace views and a small but well-executed menu.

Bundi Vilas (☎ 9414175280; info@bundivilas.com; Balhand Para; r Rs2500, ste Rs5500; ☒ ▢) Access to this delightful heritage *haveli* is up a tiny weaving lane, and many visitors mistake the hotel's grand archway for the entrance to the City Palace – its next-door neighbour. Much of the charming heritage building remains, and it has been augmented with Jaisalmer sandstone, earth-toned walls and deft interior design. The elegant rooms won't disappoint, whereas the rooftop suites are a little less private.

Other family homes run as inexpensive guesthouses:

Kishan Niwas (☎ 2445807; jain_jp@hotmail.com; Nahar ka Chohtta; r Rs100-250) Very basic, bucket hot water.

Haveli Parihar (☎ 2446675; Balchand Para; r Rs150-500) Keen owners with cooking course on offer.

Hadee Rani Guest House (☎ 2442903; hadeeranip .g@yahoo.com; Boari Khera House, Sadar Bazaar; r Rs200-600) A superb rooftop restaurant with an energetic family in charge.

Shivam Tourist Guesthouse (☎ 9214911113; shivam_pg@yahoo.com; Balchand Para; r Rs200-800) An adequately clean cheapie in need of some decoration. The energetic hosts offer courses in cooking, henna design and Hindi.

Getting There & Away
BUS

Bus journeys in and out of Bundi are bone rattlers; however the National Hwy from Kota to Udaipur has been improved so it might be worth a visit to Kota (but not before considering the rail option). See opposite for some destinations and fares.

Private buses launch from Bundi for Udaipur (seat/sleeper Rs130/200) at around 10pm, but are for thrill seekers and sadomasochists only.

TRAIN
The station (2km south of the old city) has several trains, which make for a smoother, if slower, journey. There are two trains daily to Chittor. There is often no need for res-

BUSES FROM BUNDI

Destination	Fare (Rs)	Duration (hr)	Frequency
Ajmer	105	4	half-hourly
Bikaner	235	10	3 daily
Chittor	96	4	4 daily
Indore	200	12	4 daily
Jaipur	120	5	half-hourly
Jodhpur	220	10	7 daily
Kota	25	1	half-hourly
Pushkar	110	5	1 daily (8.30am)
Sawai Madhopur	54	4½	5 daily
Udaipur	160	8½	4 daily

ervations and you can change in Chittor for Udaipur. Usually you can take a tour of Chittor between trains. Work is rapidly proceeding on the conversion to broad-gauge between Chittor and Udaipur. When that is complete (by the time you read this) faster services should run from Agra through Bundi and Chittor to Udaipur.

The 1771/2 *Haldighati Passenger* departs at 7.21am and goes to Chittor (sleeper Rs80, 3¼ hours), having arrived from Agra (sleeper Rs111), from where it departs at 7.10pm. The 9020A *Dehradun Express* departs at 9.38am and goes to Chittor (sleeper/2AC Rs121/331, 2½ hours), having arrived from Delhi (Rs194/786, 11½ hours).

Getting Around

A rickshaw to the train station costs Rs40, a half-day city/outside city tour Rs90/150 and out to Akoda and Rameshwar around Rs250 return. Bike hire (all Hero clunkers at Rs30 per day) and motorcycle hire is available at several outlets in the Old City – your guesthouse should be able to help you.

KOTA

☎ 0744 / pop 695,899

Historically a city of strategic importance, Kota still boasts a huge army base but its contemporary guise is that of a modern industrial centre. For history buffs it has the prerequisite spectacular palace with an eclectic museum and lovely murals. The revitalising Chambal River, populated by crocodiles and plied by boats of all sizes, is the state's only permanent river. Kota is famous for *kota doria*, exquisite saris woven with golden thread in the nearby village of Kaithoon.

Building of the city began in 1264 following the defeat of the Bhils, but Kota didn't reach its present size until the 17th century, when Rao Madho Singh, a son of the Bundi ruler, was handed Kota by the Mughal emperor Jehangir. In 1624 Kota became a separate state, remaining so until it was integrated into Rajasthan after Independence.

Accommodation and dining in Kota is pretty lacklustre, so consider it as a day trip from Bundi or a place to spend a few hours when making a transport connection.

RAJASTHAN

Orientation & Information

Kota is strung out along the Chambal River's east bank. The train station is well to the north; a number of hotels and the bus stand are in the centre. There are HDFC and SBBJ ATMs at the train station, and ICICI and SBBJ ATMs near the Hotel Phul Plaza.

Shiv Shakti Enterprises (Rampura Rd; internet per hr Rs50; 🕑 10am-10pm) Internet access.
State Bank of Bikaner & Jaipur (Industrial Estate) Changes travellers cheques and cash.
State Bank of India (Chawni Circle) Changes currency and Amex travellers cheques.
Tourist Reception Centre (☎ 2327695; 🕑 9.30am-6pm Mon-Fri) In the grounds of the RTDC Hotel Chambal.

Sights & Activities

CITY PALACE & FORT

Beside the Kota Barrage, overlooking the river, is the complex housing the **City Palace** (Garh Palace; 🕑 9am-5pm) and **fort**; it's one of Rajasthan's largest. Entry is from the south side through the **Naya Darwaza** (New Gate).

The palace houses the excellent **Rao Madho Singh Museum** (Indian/foreigner Rs10/100, camera Rs50; 🕑 10am-4.30pm). You'll find all the stuff necessary for a respectable royal existence – silver furniture, ingenious weapons and a stable of palanquins. The oldest part of the palace dates from 1624. Amazing mirror work and some of Rajasthan's best-preserved miniatures decorate the small-scale apartments – the upstairs rooms dance with exquisite paintings of hunting and court scenes.

JAGMANDIR

Between the City Palace and the Tourist Reception Centre is the picturesque (at a distance) lake of **Kishore Sagar**, constructed in 1346. In the middle of the lake, on a small

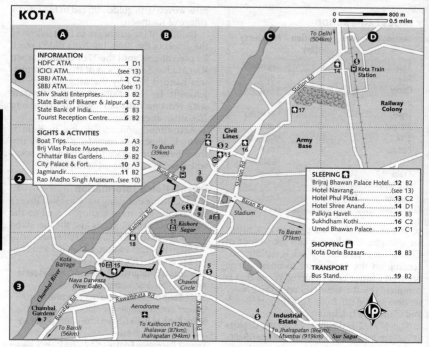

KOTA

0 — 800 m
0 — 0.5 miles

INFORMATION
HDFC ATM.................................**1** D1
ICICI ATM.............................(see 13)
SBBJ ATM................................**2** C2
SBBJ ATM.............................(see 1)
Shiv Shakti Enterprises..........**3** B2
State Bank of Bikaner & Jaipur..**4** C3
State Bank of India.................**5** B3
Tourist Reception Centre........**6** B2

SIGHTS & ACTIVITIES
Boat Trips...............................**7** A3
Brij Vilas Palace Museum........**8** B2
Chhattar Bilas Gardens...........**9** B2
City Palace & Fort.................**10** A3
Jagmandir..............................**11** B2
Rao Madho Singh Museum..(see 10)

SLEEPING
Brijraj Bhawan Palace Hotel...**12** B2
Hotel Navrang........................(see 13)
Hotel Phul Plaza....................**13** C2
Hotel Shree Anand..................**14** D1
Palkiya Haveli.........................**15** B3
Sukhdham Kothi......................**16** C2
Umed Bhawan Palace............**17** C1

SHOPPING
Kota Doria Bazaars.................**18** B3

TRANSPORT
Bus Stand...............................**19** B2

To Delhi (504km)
Kota Train Station
Station Rd
Railway Colony
Civil Lines
Army Base
To Bundi (39km)
Bund Rd
Baran Rd
Stadium
To Baran (71km)
Kishore Sagar
Rampura Rd
Barrage Rd
Kota Barrage
Naya Darwaza (New Gate)
Chambal River
Chambal Gardens
Chawni Circle
Rawatbhata Rd
Aerodrome
To Kaithoon (12km); Jhalawar (87km); Jhalrapatan (94km)
Jhalawar Rd
Industrial Estate
To Jhalrapatan (86km); Mumbai (919km)
Sur Sagar
To Baroli (56km)

island amid palm trees, is the enchanting palace of **Jagmandir**, built in 1740 by one of the maharanis of Kota.

BRIJ VILAS PALACE MUSEUM
Near Kishore Sagar, this small, run-down **government museum** (Indian/foreigner Rs5/10; 10am-4.30pm Sat-Thu) has a collection of 9th-to 12th-century stone idols, a 3rd-century inscription and Copper Age sculptural fragments, as well as some miniature paintings. It is not worth a visit unless you are truly archaeologically bent.

BOAT TRIPS
For an interesting angle on the city take a Chambal River boat trip. Once you escape the industry near the town, it's beautiful, with lush vegetation and craggy cliffs either side, and opportunities to spot birds, gharials (those thin-snouted, fish-eating crocodiles) and muggers (those keep-your-limbs-in-side-the-boat crocodiles). It costs Rs20 for a hardly worth it 10-minute jaunt and Rs400 per person for an 8km trip. Trips start from Chambal Gardens.

GARDENS
Kota is surprisingly blessed with gardens. **Chambal Gardens** (admission Rs2) are on the riverbank south of the fort. Luckily, crocodiles no longer reside in the murky cement ponds, so to see the crocs you need to take a boat ride.

Next to the Tourist Reception Centre are the **Chhattar Bilas Gardens**, a collection of overgrown but impressive royal cenotaphs interspersed with carved elephants.

Festivals & Events
In October, the town hosts a huge **Dussehra Mela**, and thousands of pilgrims descend in the month of Kartika (October/November) for **Kashavrai Patan**. See p167 for details of the festivals and the Tourist Reception Centre for festival programs.

Sleeping & Eating
Hotel Shree Anand (2462473; s/d from Rs150/200, with AC Rs400/500;) As it's along the street opposite the train station, this pink hotel is useful if you're catching an early-morning train. The cells are tiny and dingy but all feature attached bathrooms.

Hotel Phul Plaza (☎ 2329351; Collectorate Circle, Civil Lines; s/d from Rs325/425, with AC Rs550/750; ✷) The Phul Plaza is a clean, no-nonsense business hotel. Rooms at the front are a bit noisy. There's a good veg restaurant with a wide range of dishes.

Hotel Navrang (☎ 2323294; Collectorate Circle, Civil Lines; s/d Rs350/450, with AC Rs650/850; ✷) Navrang is unimpressive from the outside, but it has a conversation starter in the internal courtyard and obliging staff. Its veg restaurant (mains Rs40–85), where art deco gets a muted salute, is a cut above the ordinary.

Palkiya Haveli (☎ 2387497; www.alisar.com; Mokha Para; s/d/ste Rs1600/2000/2400; ✷) A traditional *haveli* that has been owned by the same family for more than 200 years, this is the pick of Kota's accommodation options. It is a lovely, relaxing place to stay, with welcoming hosts, a high-walled garden and a courtyard with a graceful neem tree. There are impressive murals and appealing heritage rooms, and the food is top notch.

Brijraj Bhawan Palace Hotel (☎ 2450529, brijraj@ datainfosys.net; s/d/ste Rs1700/2350/2900; ✷) High above the Chambal River, this charismatic hotel has drawn exclusive guests since 1830. It was built to house the British Residency and is named after the current maharao of Kota, Brijraj Singh (who still lives here). The enormous, classically presented rooms, admittedly a little worn, open onto lofty verandahs and manicured riverside terraces.

Sukhdham Kothi (☎ 2320081; www.sukhdhamkothi .com; Station Rd, Civil Lines; s/d Rs2000/2300; ✷) Set among leafy grounds, this century-old building is filled with foliated arches, cool arcades and terraces. The staid but charming rooms are furnished with heavy antique furniture and the whole place feels lost in a gentler time. The tariff includes breakfast.

Umed Bhawan Palace (☎ 2325262; off Station Rd; deluxe s/d Rs3000/3500, ste Rs4000-6500; ✷ ▢) Surrounded by sprawling gardens, this gracious palace is stuffily Edwardian. It's grander than the Brijraj Bhawan, with voluminous rooms, but they are darker and the overall feel is impersonal.

Shopping

The bazaars around Rampura Rd sell a wide range of *kota doria*, or you can hunt them at their source in nearby Kaithoon, 12km from Kota; it's Rs6 by bus or Rs150 return in a rickshaw.

BUSES FROM KOTA			
Destination	Fare (Rs)	Duration (hr)	Frequency
Ajmer	125	6	half-hourly
Bikaner	300	12	3 daily
Bundi	25	1	half-hourly
Chittor	105	6	5 daily
Jaipur	140	6	half-hourly
	(240 AC)		
Jodhpur	225	11	3 daily
Udaipur	170	6	6 daily

Getting There & Away
BUS
There are plenty of express bus connections. See table above for details.

TRAIN
Kota is on the main Mumbai–Delhi train route via Sawai Madhopur, so there are plenty of trains to choose from (see the table, p210), though departure times are not always convenient.

Getting Around
Minibuses link the train station and bus stand (Rs6). An autorickshaw costs Rs30 for this journey; there's a prepay place at the station.

AROUND KOTA
Baroli
A 9th-century temple complex, Baroli is 56km southwest of Kota. Much was vandalised by Muslim armies, but some fantastic carving remains. Kota's Brij Vilas Palace Museum (opposite) displays some statuary from here.

There are buses from Kota (Rs25, 1½ hours, hourly); tell the driver you want to be dropped off at Baroli.

Jhalawar
A small town 87km south of Kota, Jhalawar has some amazing, seldom-visited sights in its vicinity. Seven kilometres south is **Jhalrapatan** (the City of Temple Bells), which has a huge 10th-century Surya temple with impressive sculptures and one of India's best-preserved idols of Surya (sun god). The 12th-century **Shantinath Jain Temple** is also worth visiting. Jhalrapatan hosts the **Chandrabhaga Mela** (p167) in November. Around 3km from Jhalrapatan is the lovely **Chandrabagha Temple**. **Gagron Fort**, 10km from Jhalawar, is also spectacular: a

MAJOR TRAINS FROM KOTA

Destination	Train Number & Name	Fare (Rs)	Duration (hr)	Departure
Agra	9037 Avadh Exp	166/437/596 (A)	7	2.55pm (Mon, Wed, Thu, Sat)
Chittor	1772 Haldighati Pass	80 (B)	4	6.35am
	9020A Dehradun Exp	121/386/636 (C)	3	9.05am
Delhi	2059 Shatabdi	142/475 (D)	6½	6am
	2903 Golden Temple Mail	223/570/768/1292 (E)	7	11.25am
	2964 Mewar Exp	223/570/768/1292 (E)	6	11.55pm
Jaipur	2181 Dayodaya Exp	149/380/505 (A)	4	8.35am
	2955 Mumbai-Jaipur Exp	155/380/505/841 (E)	4	8.55am
Mumbai	2956 Jaipur-Mumbai Exp	344/913/1244/2091 (E)	14	5.35pm
	2952 Mumbai Rajdhani	1190/1570/2615 (F)	11½	9.05pm
Sawai Madhopur	2059 Shatabdi	72/220 (D)	1	6am
	2903 Golden Temple Mail	141/268/327/533 (E)	1	11.25am
Udaipur	2963 Mewar Exp	171/424/567/946 (E)	6	1.10am

Fares: A – sleeper/3AC/2AC; B – sleeper; C – sleeper/2AC/1AC; D – 2nd class/AC chair; E – sleeper/3AC/2AC/1AC; F – 3AC/2AC/1AC.

well-preserved, middle-of-nowhere fortress set high above the junction of two rivers. Jhalawar has several reasonable hotels and there are regular buses between Jhalawar and Kota (Rs55, two hours).

CHITTORGARH (CHITTOR)
☎ 01472 / pop 96,028

Chittorgarh, the fort (garh) at Chittor, is the greatest in Rajasthan, and is well worth reshuffling an itinerary to explore. The town itself is unspectacular, but the fort complex, occupying a rocky mountain plateau, is an impressive edifice with massive crenellated walls, arched gateways, deserted palaces, peaceful temples and the exquisite Jaya Stambha, Tower of Victory.

Chittor is best explored as a stopover between Udaipur and Bundi (or Kota), a couple of hours will cover the fort, and it can also be a long day excursion from these towns.

History
Chittor is mentioned in the Mahabharata – Bhima, one of the Pandava heroes, struck the ground here so hard that water gushed out to form a large reservoir. But the fort dates from the 8th century, founded by Bappa Rawal of Sisodia. Chittor's first defeat occurred in 1303 when Ala-ud-din Khilji, the Pathan king of Delhi, besieged the fort, apparently to capture the beautiful Padmini, wife of the rana's (king's) uncle, Bhim Singh. When defeat was inevitable, the men rode out to die and the Rajput noblewomen, including Padmini, committed jauhar.

In 1535 it was Bahadur Shah, the sultan of Gujarat, who besieged the fort and, once again, the medieval dictates of chivalry determined the outcome. It's thought that 13,000 Rajput women and 32,000 Rajput warriors died following the declaration of jauhar.

The final sacking of Chittor came just 33 years later, in 1568, when the Mughal emperor Akbar took the fort. Once again, the odds were overwhelming, and the women performed jauhar while 8000 orange-robed warriors rode out to certain death. On this occasion, Maharana Udai Singh II fled to Udaipur, where he re-established his capital. In 1616, Jehangir returned Chittor to the Rajputs. There was no attempt at resettlement, though it was restored in 1905.

Orientation & Information
The fort is roughly fish shaped, and stands on a 28-sq-km site on top of a 180m-high hill that rises abruptly from the surrounding plain. Until 1568 the town of Chittor was within the fort walls, but today's modern town clatters to the west of the hill. The Gambheri River separates the Old Town from the bus stand, railway line and the rest of the town.

There's a **Tourist Reception Centre** (☎ 241089; ◷ 10am-1pm & 2-5pm Mon-Fri) near the train station. You can access an ATM and change money at the **State Bank of Bikaner & Jaipur** (Bhilwara Rd), and there's an ATM at the **State Bank of India** (Gandhi Rd). To check email climb the stairway to **Maharir Cyber Cafe** (Collectorate Circle; per hr Rs25; ☙ 8am-10.30pm).

Sights

All of Chittor's attractions are in the **fort** (Indian/foreigner Rs5/100; ☙ dawn-dusk). A zigzag ascent of more than 1km leads through seven gateways to the main gate on the western side, the **Rampol** (the former back entrance).

On the climb you pass two **chhatris**, memorials marking spots where Jaimal and Kalla fell during the struggle against Akbar – Jaimal was already fatally wounded but was carried out to fight by Kalla. The main gate on the eastern side of the fort is known as the **Surajpol**, and has fantastic views across the plains. Within the fort, a circular road runs around the ruins.

Today the fort is a deserted collection of ruined palaces and around 130 temples. The main sites can all be seen in a few hours (if you're not walking). Guides are available, usually at the Rana Kumbha Palace; they charge around Rs150. There is a **Sound & Light Show** (adult/child Rs50/25; ☙ 7pm daily in Hindi, 8pm Sun in English) at the Rana Kumbha Palace. The Sunday performance coincides with the arrival of the *Palace on Wheels* (see p1188) in Chittor.

RANA KUMBHA PALACE

After entering the fort and turning right, you come to the ruins of this **palace**, which includes elephant and horse stables and a Shiva temple. Padmini's *jauhar* is said to have taken place in a now blocked cellar. Across from the palace are the **museum** and **archaeological office**, and the **treasury building** (Nau Lakha Bhandar). The **Singa Chowri Temple** is nearby.

FATEH PRAKASH PALACE

Just beyond Rana Kumbha Palace, this **palace** is more modern and houses a small, poorly labelled **museum** (Indian/foreigner Rs5/10; ☙ 9.30am-5.30pm) and a school.

JAYA STAMBHA

Heading south, you come to the glorious **Jaya Stambha** (Tower of Victory) – the symbol of Chittor and a particularly masculine expression of triumph. Erected by Rana Kumbha between 1458 and 1468, it rises 37m in nine exquisitely carved storeys; you can climb the narrow, and at times precarious, stairs (the interior is also carved) to the 8th floor, from where there's a good view.

Close to the tower is the **Mahasati**, an area where the ranas were cremated during Chittor's period as the capital of Mewar, the area encompassing Chittor and Udaipur. There are many *sati* stones here – 13,000 women committed *jauhar* close by in 1535. The intensely carved **Sammidheshwar Temple**, built in the 6th century and restored in 1427, is nearby.

GAUMUKH RESERVOIR

Walk down beyond the temple and, at the edge of the cliff, you'll see this deep tank. A spring feeds the tank from a carved cow's mouth (*gaumukh*) in the cliff.

PADMINI'S PALACE

Continuing south, you reach Padmini's Palace, set beside a large pool with a central pavilion. Legend relates that, as Padmini sat in this pavilion, Ala-ud-din saw her reflection in the lake. This glimpse convinced him to destroy Chittor in order to possess her. The bronze gates to this pavilion were carried off by Akbar and can be seen in the fort at Agra.

Continuing around the circular road, you pass a deer park, the **Bhimlat Tank**, the Surajpol and the **Neelkanth Mahadev Jain temple**, before reaching the Kirti Stambha.

KIRTI STAMBHA

The 22m-high Kirti Stambha (Tower of Fame) is older (probably 12th century) and smaller than the Tower of Victory. Built by a Jain merchant, it is dedicated to Adinath, the first Jain *tirthankar* (revered Jain teacher), and is decorated with naked figures of the various *tirthankars*, indicating that it is a monument of the Digambara (sky-clad) order. A narrow stairway, usually locked, leads through the seven storeys to the top.

OTHER SIGHTS

Close to Kirti Stambha is the **Meera Temple**. Built during the reign of Rana Kumbha, it's in the ornate Indo-Aryan style and is associated with the mystic poet Meerabai – she consumed poison sent by an enemy but survived due to the blessings of Krishna. The larger temple in this same compound is the **Kumbha Shyam Temple** (Temple of Varah).

Across from Padmini's Palace is the **Kalika Mata Temple**, an 8th-century sun temple. It was damaged during the first sack of Chittor, and

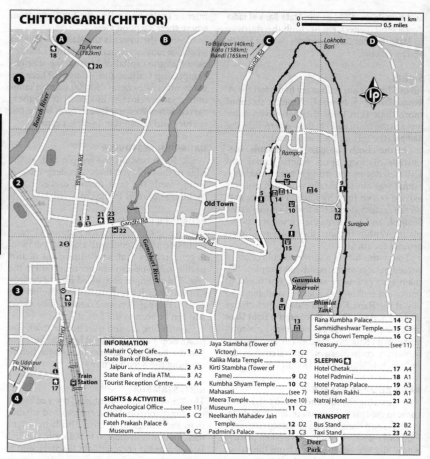

CHITTORGARH (CHITTOR)

INFORMATION		
Maharir Cyber Cafe	1	A2
State Bank of Bikaner & Jaipur	2	A3
State Bank of India ATM	3	A2
Tourist Reception Centre	4	A4

SIGHTS & ACTIVITIES		
Archaeological Office	(see 11)	
Chhatris	5	C2
Fateh Prakash Palace & Museum	6	C2
Jaya Stambha (Tower of Victory)	7	C2
Kalika Mata Temple	8	C3
Kirti Stambha (Tower of Fame)	9	D2
Kumbha Shyam Temple	10	C2
Mahasati	(see 7)	
Meera Temple	(see 10)	
Museum	11	C2
Neelkanth Mahadev Jain Temple	12	D2
Padmini's Palace	13	C3

Rana Kumbha Palace	14	C2
Sammidheshwar Temple	15	C3
Singa Chowri Temple	16	C2
Treasury	(see 11)	

SLEEPING		
Hotel Chetak	17	A4
Hotel Padmini	18	A1
Hotel Pratap Palace	19	A3
Hotel Ram Rakhi	20	A1
Natraj Hotel	21	A2

TRANSPORT		
Bus Stand	22	B2
Taxi Stand	23	A2

then converted to a temple to the goddess Kali in the 14th century. At the fort's northern tip is another gate, the **Lokhota Bari**; at the southern end is a small opening used for hurling criminals into the abyss.

Sleeping & Eating

Hotels in Chittor are mainly dreadful and noisy. Some of those near the train and bus stations are places where lone women will almost certainly feel uncomfortable.

Natraj Tourist Hotel (☎ 241009; reservations@hotel natraj.info; Gandhi Rd; s/d from Rs150/225, with AC from Rs700/850; 🅿 🛜) Probably the best option near the bus stand, Natraj has a quite range of rooms behind its leafy front garden. The better rooms are tolerably clean and have TVs.

Hotel Ram Rakhi (☎ 249558; Bhilwara Rd, r Rs450, with AC Rs750; 🅿) This is a lonely-looking hotel near the Bearch River bridge, incongruously set among the fields. Rooms are colourful, clean and spacious, and management is eager to assist.

Hotel Chetak (☎ 241589; s/d from Rs500/650, with AC Rs900/1000; 🅿) The pick of the train-station lodgings, Chetak has run-of-the-mill rooms with TVs and hot water, and a veg restaurant with North and South Indian and Chinese.

Hotel Padmini (☎ 241718; hotel_padmini@rediffmail .com; s/d Rs800/1000, with AC Rs1800/2000; 🅿) This option, just over the Bearch River, has a huge garden and horses (riding is available, with prior notice), and an elaborate lobby. Some rooms have balconies with views of the distant fort, but rooms are overpriced and run down.

Hotel Pratap Palace (☎ 243563; hpratap@hot mail.com; s Rs1600-2400, d Rs1850-2700; ✵). This is Chittor's best and friendliest option, with a wide range of rooms, a convenient location and travel-savvy staff. The more expensive rooms have window seats and leafy outlooks, and even a big mural (Room 209). There's a garden side restaurant with good food – drop in for lunch and they'll let you stash your luggage while you visit the fort. Village safaris and visits to the hotel's castle in Bijaipur (below) can be arranged.

Getting There & Away
BUS
Express buses serve Delhi (Rs340, 14 hours), and travel regularly to Ajmer (Rs120, five hours), Jaipur (Rs185, eight hours), Udaipur (Rs65, 2½ hours) and Bundi (Rs75, five hours), among other places.

TRAIN
The 2966 *Udaipur–Gwalior Express* leaves Chittor at 12.35am, arriving in Jaipur (sleeper/ 3AC/2AC/1AC Rs183/459/614/1028) at 6am. The 2991 *Udaipur–Ajmer Express* leaves at 9.20am, arriving in Ajmer (2nd class/AC chair Rs76/266) at 12.30pm. To Bundi, the 1771 *Haldighati Passenger* leaves at 2pm and arrives in Bundi (sleeper Rs80) at 5.48pm; and the 9019A *Neemach–Kota Express* leaves at 2.55pm and arrives in Bundi (sleeper/2AC/ 1AC Rs121/331/542) at 5.10pm.

To Udaipur, the 9657 *Udaipur City Express* leaves on Wednesday, Friday and Saturday at 4.40pm, arriving at Udaipur (sleeper/ 3AC/2AC Rs121/238/303) at 7.15pm. The 2963 *Mewar Express* leaves at 4.55am and arrives at Udaipur (sleeper/3AC/2AC/1AC Rs141/268/333/544) at 7am.

Getting Around
Autorickshaws charge around Rs200 to take you from the bus or train station, around the fort, and back (including waiting time). A rickshaw between the bus and train stations should cost Rs25.

AROUND CHITTORGARH
Bijaipur
Forty kilometres from Chittor, **Castle Bijaipur** (www.castlebijaipur.com; s Rs3000-5500; d Rs3400-5500; ste Rs9200-15,000; ✵ ⚐) is a fantastically set

16th-century palace. Rooms are romantic and luxurious. Reservations should be made through the website or Chittor's **Hotel Pratap Palace** (☎ 01472-240099; hpratap@hotmail.com). The owners organise transfer from Chittor as well as horse and jeep safaris, cooking classes and yoga.

UDAIPUR
☎ 0294 / pop 389,317
Udaipur is Rajasthan's, maybe India's, most romantic city. The romantic tag was first applied in 1829 by Colonel James Tod in his *Annals & Antiquities of Rajasthan,* and though modern Udaipur suffers from rampant commercialism and hotel construction the label still applies.

Framed by the ancient Aravalli hills, the old city is dominated by the cupola-crowned City Palace, which rises abruptly from the glassy waters of Lake Pichola. The palace's balconies gaze over the lake towards the city's other famous landmark – the Lake Palace – a reflective, fairy-tale confection gleaming by day and spotlit by night.

Formerly known as Mewar, Udaipur was founded in 1559 when Maharana Udai Singh II took flight from the final sacking of Chittorgarh by the Mughal emperor Akbar. As Udai Singh and his contemporaries resisted Muslim might, the city grew a reputation for patriotic fervour and an aching love of independence.

Orientation
The old city, bounded by the remains of a city wall, is on the east side of Lake Pichola. The train station and bus stand are both just outside the city wall to the southeast.

Information
BOOKSHOPS
Udaipur has numerous shops around Lal Ghat selling and exchanging books in various languages.

EMERGENCY
Police (☎ 2412693; Surajpol)

INTERNET ACCESS
You can surf the internet at loads of places, particularly around Lal Ghat. The following places are reasonably quick:
BA Photo N Book Store (69 Durga Sadan; per hr Rs30; ☾ 9.15am-11pm)

RAJASTHAN

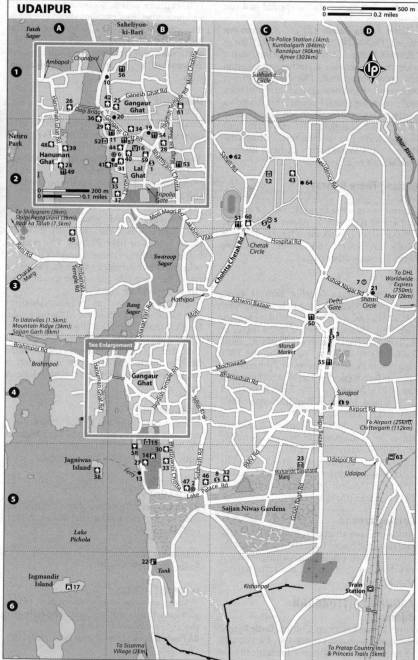

Mewar International (35 Lal Ghat; per hr Rs30;
8am-11pm)

MEDIA

Go Udaipur is a useful publication that has
many of the ins and outs of the city covered.
Although listed as costing Rs15, it's available at
many hotel and shop counters for free.

MONEY

There are lots of ATMs around, including an
HDFC ATM near the main post office; ICICI,
HDFC, SBBJ and IDBI have ATMs near the
bus stand (surely one will be working!) and
there's an Axis Bank ATM near Jagdish
Temple. You can change money and get
credit-card advances at numerous places.

Bank of Baroda (10am-2.30pm Mon-Fri, 10am-
12.30pm Sat) About 200m southeast of Delhi Gate;
changes cash and does credit-card advances.

Thomas Cook (Lake Palace Rd; 9.30am-7pm Mon-
Sat) Next to the Rang Niwas Palace Hotel; changes cash
and travellers cheques.

POST

DHL Worldwide Express (/fax 2412979; 380 Ashok
Nagar Rd; 9.30am-7.30pm Mon-Sat) Has a free collection service within Udaipur.

Main post office (Chetak Circle; 10am-1pm & 1.30-
7pm) North of the old city.

Post office (City Palace Complex; 10.30am-1pm
& 1.30-4.30pm Mon-Sat) Just outside the City Palace
Museum adjacent to the ticket office.

Poste Restante office (Shastri Circle; 10.30am-
1pm & 1.30-4.30pm Mon-Sat)

TOURIST INFORMATION

Tourist Reception Centre (2411535; Fateh Memorial Bldg; 9.30am-6pm Mon-Fri) Near Surajpol. Offers
maps, brochures and guided tours.

Sights
LAKE PICHOLA

Placid Lake Pichola was enlarged by Maharana
Udai Singh II after the city was founded – he
flooded nearby Pichola village by building
a masonry dam, known as the Badipol. The

lake is now 4km long and 3km wide, but it remains shallow and can dry up in severe droughts. The City Palace decorates the east bank of the lake. North of the palace you can wander along the lake shore, where there are some interesting bathing and dhobi (clothes-washing) ghats. South of the palace there is a pot-holed road which winds through woods to Sisarma village on the west bank of the lake. There are plans to upgrade and continue it as a ring road around the lake, which would make for an excellent bike ride.

The lake has two islands: Jagniwas and Jagmandir. **Boat rides** (adult/child 30min Rs200/100, 1hr Rs300/150; ☉ 9.30am-5pm) leave half-hourly from the City Palace jetty (Bansi Ghat) when the lake is deep enough. The longer trip includes a visit to Jagmandir Island. Other craft leave from Lal Ghat (near Jagat Niwas Hotel). **MM Travels** (☎ 2525265) has a variety of dubious-looking craft, including paddle boats (Rs75 per 20 minutes) and motor boats (from Rs450 per 20 minutes).

Jagniwas Island

Completely covered by the palace built by Maharaja Jagat Singh II in 1754, Jagniwas, the Lake Palace Hotel island, is about 1.5 hectares in size. Formerly the royal summer palace, today it is the ultimate in luxury hotels, with shady courtyards, lotus ponds and a pool shaded by a mango tree. Hotel launches cross to the island from the City Palace jetty.

The Lake Palace, along with the Shiv Niwas Palace and Monsoon Palace, was used in the James Bond movie *Octopussy*.

Jagmandir Island

The **palace** on Jagmandir Island was built by Maharaja Karan Singh in 1620, and added to by Maharaja Jagat Singh (1628–52). It is said that the Mughal emperor Shah Jahan derived some of his inspiration for the Taj Mahal from this palace after staying here in 1623–24 while leading a revolt against his father, Jehangir. Europeans were sheltered here by Maharaja Swarup Singh during the uprising of 1857.

Flanked by a row of enormous stone elephants, the island has an impressive *chhatri* carved from grey-blue stone, and fantastic views across the lake to the city and its golden palace.

CITY PALACE & MUSEUMS

The imposing **City Palace** (admission adult/child Rs25/15; ☉ 9am-8pm), surmounted by balconies, towers and cupolas, and towering over the lake, is Rajasthan's largest palace, with a facade 244m long and 30.4m high. A conglomeration of buildings created by various maharajas, it almost manages to retain a uniformity of design. Construction was started by Maharana Udai Singh II, the city's founder. There are fine views over the lake and the city from the upper terraces.

The palace complex and museum is entered from the northern end through the Baripol (built in 1600) and the three-arched Tripolia Gate (1725). To the left, seven arches commemorate the seven times maharajas were weighed here and their weight in gold or silver distributed to the lucky locals. This is where you'll find the ticket office and can pick up audioguides (Rs200), or a personal guide (Hindi/other language Rs100/150).

The main part of the palace is preserved as the **City Palace museum** (adult/child Rs50/30, camera & video Rs200; ☉ 9.30am-4.30pm), which includes the **Mor Chowk**, with its lavish mosaics of peacocks. The **Manak (Ruby) Mahal** has glass and mirror work, while **Krishna Vilas** has a remarkable collection of miniatures (no photography allowed). In the **Bari Mahal** there is a pleasant central garden. The **Moti Mahal** has beautiful mirror work and the **Chini Mahal** is covered in ornamental tiles. More wall paintings can be seen in the **Zenana Mahal**. There's a large tiger-catching cage near the Zenana Mahal entrance.

There's also a **government museum** (admission Indian/foreigner Rs5/10; ☉ 10am-4.30pm) within the complex. Exhibits include a freaky monkey holding a lamp, as well as sculptures, and maharaja portraits with a spectacular array of moustaches.

In the large Manak Chowk (courtyard) outside the City Palace museum are pricey handicraft shops, and a **World Wide Fund for Nature** (☉ 9.30am-5.30pm) shop. Outside Badipol, beside the ticket office, is a post office.

The rest of the palace fronts the lake and has been partly converted into two luxury hotels: Shiv Niwas Palace and the Fateh Prakash Palace. This section of the palace can be entered from the south end of Badi Chowk or from Lake Palace Rd, south of the complex. There's a stunning **crystal gallery** (adult/child incl soft drink Rs500/300; ☉ 9am-7pm) at the Fateh Prakash

Palace Hotel, though the admission charge is rather expensive. Maharaja Sajjan Singh ordered this rare crystal from F&C Osler & Co in England in 1877; he died before it arrived, and all the items stayed packed up in boxes for 110 years. The extravagant, unused collection includes crystal chairs, sofas, tables and even beds. Photography is prohibited.

Palace ladies once used the crystal gallery to observe the grandiose **durbar hall**, which was used for official occasions such as state banquets and meetings. This durbar hall, built in 1909, is undoubtedly one of India's most impressive, with outrageously huge chandeliers. The illustrious Mewar rulers who deck the walls supposedly come from the oldest ruling dynasty in the world, spanning 76 generations. The durbar hall holds hundreds of people and can be hired for special functions.

JAGDISH TEMPLE

Only 150m north of the City Palace entrance, this fantastically carved Indo-Aryan **temple** (☾ darshan 5am-2pm & 4-10.30pm) was built by Maharaja Jagat Singh in 1651. It enshrines a black stone image of Vishnu as Jagannath, Lord of the Universe. A brass image of Garuda is in a shrine in front of the temple.

BAGORE-KI-HAVELI

This gracious 18th-century **haveli museum** (admission Rs25; ☾ 10am-5.30pm), on the water's edge near Gangaur Ghat, was built by a former prime minister and has been carefully restored. There are 138 rooms set around courtyards. Some recreate the times when the house was inhabited, others have cultural displays, including the world's (rather saggy) biggest turban! The *haveli* also houses an interesting art gallery, with contemporary and folk art, and world-famous monuments lovingly carved out of polystyrene. The upper courtyard makes an atmospheric setting for fabulous Rajasthani dance performances at 7pm (p223).

FATEH SAGAR

North of Lake Pichola, this lake – which dries up if the monsoon has been poor – is ringed by hills and is a hang-out for love-struck locals. It was originally built in 1678 by Maharaja Jai Singh but, after heavy rains destroyed the dam, it was reconstructed by Maharaja Fateh Singh. At its centre is **Nehru Park**, a garden island. An autorickshaw from the old city costs Rs35 (one way).

BHARTIYA LOK KALA MUSEUM

This small, private **museum** (Indian/foreigner Rs20/35, camera/video Rs10/50; ☾ 9am-5.30pm) exhibits tribal jewellery, musical instruments, paintings and puppets and stages a daily **puppet show** (Indian/foreigner Rs30/50; ☾ 6-7pm).

SAHELIYON-KI-BARI

In the north of the city is the **Saheliyon-ki-Bari** (Garden of the Maids of Honour; admission Rs5; ☾ 8am-7pm). This small, quaint, ornamental garden was laid out for 48 women attendants who came as part of a princess's dowry, and has fountains (water permitting), kiosks, marble elephants and a delightful lotus pool.

SHILPGRAM

Three km west of town, **Shilpgram** (Indian/foreigner Rs15/25, camera/video Rs10/50; ☾ 11am-7pm) is a crafts village that hosts the Shilpgram festival each December – check with the Tourist Reception Centre for details. The rest of the year sees demonstrations by traditional performers and artisans from Rajasthan, Gujarat, Goa and Maharashtra.

Shilpi Resort Restaurant is next to the village and has a **swimming pool** (admission Rs100; ☾ 11am-8pm).

A return autorickshaw (including a 30-minute stop) from the old city to Shilpgram costs Rs250.

AHAR

About 2km east of Udaipur are over 250 restored **cenotaphs** of the maharajas of Mewar; it's a spectacular city of domes built over a period of 350 years. Nearby you can visit the patchy remains of the Sisodias' ancient capital, and a **museum** (admission Rs5; ☾ 10am-5pm) housing artefacts, some over 5000 years old.

SAJJAN GARH (MONSOON PALACE)

Perched on the top of a distant mountain range like a fairy-tale castle, this neglected late-19th-century **palace** (Indian/foreigner Rs10/80, autorickshaw/car Rs20/65, camera/video free/Rs20; ☾ 9am-6pm) was constructed by Maharaja Sajjan Singh. Originally an astronomical centre, it later became a monsoon palace and hunting lodge. Now government-owned, it's open to the public, but there is not much to see inside, apart from a dreary nature interpretation centre and empty rooms screaming potential. Come for the breathtaking sunset views.

You pay entry per person plus per cost of your vehicle at the foot of the hill to enter the Sajjan Garh Wildlife Sanctuary, from where it is a 4km climb to the palace. At the top, you will find the very basic **Grand Sajjangarh Restaurant** (snacks Rs50) can supply snacks and drinks. Autorickshaw return costs Rs250 (including waiting).

OTHER SIGHTS

The maharajas' **Vintage & Classic Car Collection** (Garden Hotel; admission incl soft drink/veg thali Rs100/150; ☽ 9-6pm) is fascinating for car buffs, with 22 splendid vehicles, including a 1938 Cadillac with modifications for purdah and the beautiful 1934 Rolls Royce Phantom used in *Octopussy*. If you enjoy a vegetarian thali, it's not a bad lunch option (lunch 11am to 3pm, dinner 7pm to 10pm).

Sunset Point is a lovely sunset spot with a musical fountain (water permitting).

Almost 5km beyond Shilpgram is **Badi ka Talab** (Tiger Lake), a mammoth artificial lake, flanked by hills, which makes a pleasant picnic spot. Crocodiles lurk in parts of the lake, so swimmers beware!

Activities

HORSE RIDING

Several operators organise horse rides from a couple of hours to multiday safaris. Costs vary greatly depending on the number of riders, duration of the ride and necessary support (tents, cooks etc). Expect to pay about Rs1000 for a half-day ride, including lunch and transport to/from your hotel.

Krishna Ranch (Hotel Kumbha Palace; ☎ 2422702; www.krishnaranch.com) Arranges riding excursions around Udaipur.

Pratap Country Inn (☎ 2583138; www.horseridingindia.com; Jaisamand Rd; Titardia Village) Run by the pioneer of horse safaris in Rajasthan, Maharaj Narendra Singh; this inn can organise riding lessons, day rides and extensive safaris.

Princess Trails (☎ 242012; www.princesstrails.com; Familie Shaktawat, Jaisamand Rd, Titardia Village) An Indian–German company offering extended horse safaris and half-day nature rides on the famed Marwari horses.

MASSAGE

Ayurvedic Body Care (☎ 5132802; 39 Lal Ghat; ☽ 10.30am-9pm) offers ayurvedic massage, including a head massage (Rs250), back massage (Rs250) and full-body massage (Rs700). It also has ayurvedic products for sale.

TREKKING

Exploring the surrounding countryside and villages on foot is a fantastic way to see rural and tribal life while taking in some beautiful scenery. Piers at **Udaipur Outback** (☎ 3291478; www.udaipuroutback.com; Sisarma) can arrange all kinds of hikes, or will put you in touch with an excellent local guide.

Courses

Ashoka Arts (Hotel Gangaur Palace, Gangaur Ghat Rd) Runs classes in classic miniature painting (Rs100 per hr).

Ashtang Yoga Ashram (☎ 2524872; Raiba House) The teacher here of hatha yoga has upwards of 20 years' experience; payment is by donation (proceeds go to the local animal hospital).

Hotel Krishna Niwas (☎ 2420163; jairaj34@yahoo .com; 35 Lal Ghat; 2hr class incl meal Rs850; ☽ 4.30-6.30pm) Sushma runs cooking classes in a bright purpose-built kitchen, while Jairaj is a renowned artist who teaches miniature and classical painting (Rs600 for a two-hour basic lesson).

Krishna's Musical Instruments (☎ 9950906001; 37 Lal Ghat) Krishna belongs to a caste of musicians and provides sitar, tabla, singing and flute lessons (Rs100 per hour) among others.

Noble Indian Cooking Classes (☎ 2415100; nicc_indya@yahoo.co.in; Nani Gali, Jagdish Chowk) Ruchi and Swati, and proud mum Rajni, run these popular classes where you can tackle a chapati (Rs150 per person) from whoa to go, or an eight-course extravaganza (Rs1000), with plenty of other tasty options in between.

Prem Musical Instruments (☎ 2430599; Gangaur Ghat Rd) Bablu gives sitar, tabla and flute lessons (Rs250 per hour).

Shashi Cooking Classes (☎ 9929303511; www .shashicookingclasses.blogspot.com; 18 Gangaur Ghat Rd; 4hr class Rs400; ☽ 10am-2pm, 5.30-9.30pm) Readers have raved about Shashi's high-spirited classes (maximum four students) beneath Sunrise restaurant.

Spice Box (☎ 9414235252; spicebox2001@yahoo.co.in; Lal Ghat Rd; 3hr class Rs650) Offers recommended cookery lessons with Shakti Singh.

Tours

Five-hour city tours (five people minimum; per person excluding admission charges Rs90) leave at 8am from the RTDC Hotel Kajri. There are also excursions to Ranakpur and Kumbalgarh (Rs330per person including lunch, excluding admission charges).

Festivals & Events

Udaipur celebrates the **Mewar Festival** (p167) in April.

COLOURS THAT SPEAK

The colours of everyday Rajasthani life dazzle against the desert – top-heavy turbans (safas, paags or pagris); fluttering scarlet, yellow and saffron saris; glittering traditional Rajasthani skirts (lehangas or ghagharas); and headscarves (odnis or dupattas).

These are not just decorative, but speak a language of their own, tied up with the strictures of society. Turban colour may signify caste, religion and occasion. Rajputs traditionally wear saffron, signifying chivalry. Brahmins wear pink, Dalits brown and nomads black. Jubilantly multicoloured turbans are for festivals. White, grey, black or blue turbans are worn by Hindus to signify sadness, but these colours are also worn by Muslims. The way a turban is tied further indicates the wearer's social class and origin.

As Hindus believe some shades of blue, green and white to be mournful colours, they tend to be worn by widows, while wives and single women wear more cheery pinks, reds and yellows. These embody more signs: one red-and-yellow combination may only be worn by women who've borne a son. Hindu married women are carefully marked off limits by chudas (arm bangles), bichiyas (toe rings) and a dash of vermillion in their hair parting.

Sleeping

Staying close to the lake shore is most romantic. You can either head west of the Jagdish Temple or to the quieter and less touristy Hanuman Ghat on the other side of the lake. Ask for a lake-facing room (usually more expensive). Most places offer low-season discounts.

To bypass rapacious rickshaw drivers working on commission, use the prepaid autorickshaw stands outside the train and bus stations. If you do have any complaints about rickshaw drivers (note the registration number) or hotels, contact the police or the Tourist Reception Centre.

BUDGET
Lal Ghat

Lalghat Guest House (☎ 2525301; lalghat@hotmail .com; 33 Lal Ghat; dm/s without bathroom Rs100/150, d Rs400-600, with AC Rs1200-2100; ✗ 🖳) This was one of the first guesthouses in Udaipur, and it's still going strong with an amazing variety of rooms. Accommodation starts with spruce dorm beds – two beds to an alcove with curtains for privacy and a secure locker. The cheapest rooms are mere cells, but management plans changes for these rooms. Middle-range rooms have mosquito nets and the best rooms are traditionally decorated and have lake views.

Lehar Paying Guest House (☎ 2417651; 87 Gangaur Ghat Rd; s/d from Rs150/200) Run by a redoubtable matriarch and her son, this homestay stalwart has old, pokey, rather nondescript rooms, which are nevertheless clean. Check out a few before deciding. There's also a basic rooftop restaurant.

Lake Corner Soni Paying Guest House (☎ 2525712; 27 Navghat; s/d Rs200/250, without bathroom from Rs150/200) This exceptionally modest place – nothing ritzy here – has a sleepy family atmosphere and rather shabby rooms and unfortunate bathrooms. How long can it last like this on such prime real estate! The home cooking is good and the rooftop views unexpectedly pretty.

Nukkad Guest House (☎ 2411403; Ganesh Ghat Rd; s Rs150-200, d Rs250-700) Friendly Raju has opened up his traditionally decorated family house with clean simple rooms. The cheapest single has no private bathroom but the other rooms do. There's a basic rooftop restaurant and a very relaxed atmosphere.

Lake View Guest House (☎ 2420527; Lal Ghat; r Rs200-700, with AC Rs800-1000; ✗) Mind-boggling renovations have made Lake View a soaring budget accommodation option. Rooms are minimally maintained with dodgy plumbing so check a few. Some have reach-out-and-touch-it temple views. The cheapest rooms in the older building are small and odd-shaped.

Hotel Ganguar Palace (☎ 2422303; www.ashoka haveli.com; Gangaur Ghat Rd; r Rs250-2000; ✗ 🖳) This classic heritage haveli has oodles of charm and is consistently moving upmarket and adding extras. Set around a stone-pillared courtyard, the Ashoka art school (opposite) is where you can create your own masterpiece; a palm reader; a German bakery; and a rooftop restaurant.

Hotel Udai Niwas (☎ 5120789; www.hoteludai niwas.com; Gangaur Ghat Rd; r Rs300-700, with AC Rs800-1200; ✗ 🖳) A central hotel that has spotless, brightly painted rooms, individually decorated with puppets and wall hangings – the cheapest rooms are a real bargain. On top is the three-tiered Sun & Moon rooftop restaurant where you can watch movies.

Hotel Lake Ghat Palace (☎ 2521636; lakeghatanis@ hotmail.com; Lal Ghat; r Rs300-1000, with AC Rs1200; ☒) This travellers' hot spot has smart, spacious rooms, some with views, some with balconies, all with stained glass. There are splendid views from the rooftop, and a good restaurant.

Jheel Guest House (☎ 2421352; Gangaur Ghat Rd; r Rs450-550) Jheel Guest House is in an old *haveli*. Accommodation ranges from basic back rooms to a room with a small balcony and three lakefacing windows. The owners have plans to renovate along the lines of their other hotel, Jheel Palace Paying Guesthouse (right).

Hanuman Ghat

Dream Heaven Guest House (☎ 2431038; deep_rg@ yahoo.co.uk; Hanuman Ghat; r Rs150-550, with AC Rs650; ☒) This place is deservedly popular, with notably clean, good-value budget rooms decorated with wall hangings and paintings. Bathrooms are smallish, though some rooms have a decent balcony.

Elsewhere

Hotel Kumbha Palace (☎ 2422702; kumbha01@hot mail.com; Bhattiyanni Chohtta; s Rs100, d Rs350-400, with AC Rs900; ☒) Just inside the City Palace retainers' quarters, this place backs on to a lovely lush lawn. The double rooms are comfortable, and the restaurant knows how to satisfy homesick travellers. The Dutch–Indian management team run Krishna Ranch (p218), a recommended horse-riding outfit.

Shambhu Vilas (☎ 2421921; paratour@hotmail.com; Lake Palace Rd; r Rs600, with AC Rs800-1200; ☒) This tired-looking hotel has moved from a good-value cheapie to a somewhat overpriced option for what is on offer. Rooms are OK but could do with an overhaul. There's a rooftop restaurant that allows guests to try their hand in the kitchen.

MIDRANGE
Lal Ghat

Jaiwana Haveli (☎ 2411103; www.jaiwanahaveli.com; 14 Lal Ghat; r Rs400-1950; ☒ ▣) Young professional staff oversee this smart midrange op-

tion where spotless rooms are decorated with block-printed fabrics, and have LCD TVs and decent beds. The Rs400 rooms are very tiny singles; most other rooms are comfortable doubles. Book corner room 21 or 31 for the view.

Poonam Haveli (☎ 2410303; poonamhaveli@hotmail .com; 39 Lal Ghat; r Rs700-1300, ste Rs1800; ☒) Poonam has spacious rooms with big beds – the best have lake views. The 007 room has arches elegant as a raised eyebrow, while the suite has a spa and room to spare. The rooftop restaurant boasts 'real Italian' pizzas among the usual Indian and traveller fare.

Hotel Baba Palace (☎ 2427126; www.hotelbabapalace .com; Jagdish Temple Rd; s Rs750-1800; d Rs1200-2600; ☒) This slick hotel has spotless, fresh rooms with decent beds behind solid doors. All rooms have AC and TVs, and breakfast is included in the tariff. It is eye-to-eye with Jagdish Temple – so many rooms have interesting views – and on top there's the first-rate Mayur Rooftop Cafe.

Kankarwa Haveli (☎ 2411457; www.indianheritage hotels.com; 26 Lal Ghat; r Rs850, with AC Rs1250-2850; ☒ ▣) This option, in an old *haveli*, has a lovely simplicity, with whitewashed rooms, traditional low doorways, original frescos and magical alcoves. Pricier rooms overlook Lake Pichola.

Mewar Haveli (☎ 2521140; www.mewarhaveli.com; 34-35 Lal Ghat; r Rs990-1500; ☒ ▣) Mewar is a great midranger with excellent staff who oversee clean, sun-filled and richly decorated rooms with good beds. Upstairs rooms are divine (and there's a lift!) plus there's the requisite rooftop restaurant. The owners also run Jagat Niwas Palace Hotel.

Hotel Krishna Niwas (☎ 2420163; www.hotelkrishna niwas.com; 35 Lal Ghat; d Rs1100-1400; ☒) A travellers' hot spot with smart clean rooms; those with views are smaller, and some come with balconies. There are splendid views from the rooftop, and a decent restaurant. Or you can eat your own cooking after taking a lesson (p218).

Jheel Palace Paying Guest House (☎ 98298275355; 56 Gangaur Ghat; d Rs1250, with AC Rs2050) Across the road from Jheel Guesthouse, this place sits right on the lake edge (when the lake is full). It has breezy rooms and accommodating, hands-off staff. Room 201 is the best, with windows on three sides. The rooftop restaurant is Brahmin pure veg, so no beer.

Anjani Hotel (☎ 2421770; www.anjanihotel.com; 77 Gangaur Ghat Rd; r Rs1350-2700; 🍴 🖵 🖭) A well-run hotel with numerous rooms, varying widely in size and comfort. The top-floor rooms have fantastic city views. Other salient features include a lift for those tired of stairs, a tiny pool, an art shop and a rooftop restaurant.

Jagat Niwas Palace Hotel (☎ 2420133; www.jagat niwaspalace.com; 23-25 Lal Ghat; r Rs1450, deluxe Rs1950-3450, ste Rs5550; 🍴 🖵) This leading midrange hotel takes the location cake. Set in two converted *havelis*, deluxe rooms are charming, with carved wooden furniture and cushioned window seats. The more expensive rooms face the lake. Standard rooms are smallish and comfortable enough, but you are really paying for the location. And on the roof they make the most of it with a picture-perfect romantic restaurant.

Around Lake Palace Rd

Rang Niwas Palace Hotel (☎ 2523890; www.rang niwaspalace.com; Lake Palace Rd; s Rs770-1800, d Rs900-2100, ste s/d Rs2500/3000; 🍴 🖵 🖭) This delightful 19th-century palace boasts plenty of heritage character and a peaceful central garden with a small pool (nonguests Rs125). It's a real oasis. The rooms in the older section are the most appealing, while the suites – full of carved wooden furniture and balconies with swing seats – are divine.

Hotel Mahendra Prakash (☎ 2419811; www.hotel mahendraprakash.com; Lake Palace Rd; r Rs1000-3500; 🍴 🖵 🖭) This hotel has leafy gardens, spacious, well-furnished rooms, and a cheery atmosphere. Rooms with air-con start at Rs1500. The restaurant overlooks an interesting stepwell; there's a fabulous pool (nonguests Rs100) and a lawn with tortoises. Rooms at the top have private balconies and City Palace views – see if you can secure room 25.

Hotel Raj Palace (☎ 2410364; rajpalaeudr@yahoo .com; Bhattiyani Chohtta; r Rs950, with AC from Rs1500, ste Rs2500; 🍴 🖵) Occupying a grand 300-year-old *haveli* with an imposing entrance, this rambling hotel has a variety of rooms – so inspect a few. A bonus is the quiet yet convenient location and the helpful staff. There is a garden restaurant with a tomato-eating tortoise and a pleasant rooftop restaurant where you can see the cupolas of the city palace.

Hanuman Ghat

Lake Pichola Hotel (☎ 2431197; www.lakepicholahotel .com; s/d from Rs1500/1700; 🍴 🖵) This large and

not very personal hotel has a good position and spacious though rather tired rooms – ask for a discount. Those facing the lake have oddly public balconies whereby you can scan the lake view or, alternatively, observe the other guests sitting on their balcony.

Amet Haveli (☎ 2431085; amethaveli@sify.com; s/d/ste Rs3000/3500/4500; 🍴 🖵 🖭) This 350-year-old heritage building on the lake shore has delightful rooms with cushioned window seats and coloured glass with little shutters. Splurge on one with a balcony or giant bathtub. One of Udaipur's most romantic restaurants, Ambrai, is part of the hotel.

Udai Kothi (☎ 2432810; www.udaikothi.com; r/deluxe/ ste Rs3000/6000/7000; 🍴 🖵 🖭) The highlight at this glitzy concoction of a hotel is the wonderful rooftop terrace, where you can dine well or swim in Udaipur's only rooftop pool (nonguest Rs300); there's even a Jacuzzi with a view. Rooms are comfortable, spotless and well appointed.

Elsewhere

Mountain Ridge (☎ 3291478; www.mountainridge .in; Sisarma; d incl breakfast Rs1700 ste Rs3500; 🖭) This country homestay makes a wonderful base for trips into rural Udaipur. Perched high above Sisarma village, just 10 minutes' drive from Lake Pichola, it has three stylish rooms plus a suite, a fabulous pool and a deck.

Pahuna Haveli (☎ 2526617; www.pahunahaveli.com; 211 Sardarpura; d/ste Rs2000/3000) A fantastic homestay in the Udaipur suburbs, presided over by the charming Hanwant Singh and Hemant Kumari. There are five beautifully presented Mewari-style rooms, lovely gardens and delicious meals (lunch or dinner Rs250).

Ram Pratap Palace Hotel (☎ 2431701; www .hotelrampratap.com; Fateh Sagar Lake; s/d/ste from Rs2400/2800/5000; 🍴 🖵) This delightful hotel appeals for its peaceful location away from the tourist epicentre (it's still within 10 minutes' walking distance of the old city but feels a world away), its creature comforts (including a well-being spa) and friendly service. Many rooms have a terrific view of Fateh Sagar through large windows, though not the standard rooms on the ground floor.

TOP END
City Palace

Shiv Niwas Palace Hotel (☎ 2528016; www.hrhindia.com; d Rs12,000, ste Rs24,000-80,000; 🍴 🖵 🖭) This hotel, in the former guest quarters of the maharaja, has lavishly furnished rooms, some filled with fountains and silver. The standard rooms are not great value; go for a terrace suite, or just go for a swim in the gorgeous marble pool (nonguests Rs500).

Fateh Prakash Palace Hotel (☎ 2528008; www .hrhindia.com; d & ste from Rs15,000; ✗ ☐ ☲) An early-20th-century stomping ground for Maharaja Fateh Singh, this is palatial and classy. The cheapest double rooms are not in the main palace wing, but all have an exquisite lake view.

Lake Palace Hotel (☎ 2528800; www.tajhotels .com; d/ste from Rs18,000/69,000; ✗ ☐ ☲) The icon of Udaipur, this romantic palace seemingly floating on the lake is extraordinary, with open-air courtyards, lotus ponds and a small, tree-shaded pool. Rooms are hung with breezy silks and filled with carved furniture. The cheapest overlook the lily pond or terrace, rather than the lake.

Elsewhere

Garden Hotel (☎ 2418 881; www. hrhindia.com; standard/ superior r Rs4500/5500) This hotel, opposite the Sajjan Niwas Gardens, is more relaxed than many in this price category. Rooms are elegant rather than luxurious, and the family suite, with two levels and two bathrooms, is good value.

Udaivilas (☎ 2433300; www.oberoihotels.com; r Rs22,500-28,000, ste Rs130,500; ✗ ☐ ☲) Udaivilas' butter-sculpture domes are breathtaking. It's a luxury boutique hotel that doesn't spare the glitz and gold leaf. Suites also have their own pools, and there are two excellent and opulent restaurants.

Eating

Udaipur has scores of sun-kissed rooftop cafes, many with lake views, as well as fine dining at the top-end hotels. If you like a drink, the local liquor, *duru* – a heady mixture of saffron, cardamom and aniseed – may appeal. Otherwise, beer is plentiful.

Many budget restaurants screen contemporary movies or endless reruns of *Octopussy*.

RESTAURANTS

Maxim's Cafe (☎ 9414239762; Jagdish Chowk; mains Rs35-90; ☺ 8am-10.30pm) Maxim's has a small, two-tiered roof-top terrace overlooking the Jagdish Temple. The fresh, pure-vegetarian food includes Indian staples plus Chinese, continental and pizza.

Sunrise (☎ 9928580882; cnr Lal Ghat & Gangaur Ghat Rd; mains Rs40-60; ☺ 8am-10pm) Sunrise does a breakfast of champions, plus home-cooked Indian and several Italian and Swiss dishes for the homesick traveller. There are only six tables so arrive early. The delightful Shashi runs spicy cooking lessons (p218) in the downstairs kitchen.

Lotus Cafe (☎ 5103099; Bhattiyani Chohtta; mains Rs40-110; ☺ 8.30am-11.30pm) This funky little restaurant plucks out fabulous chicken dishes (predominantly Indian) and is ideal for meeting and greeting other travellers. There are board games available, a mezzanine to loll about on, and plenty of cool background sounds.

Parkview Restaurant (☎ 2528098; mains Rs50-190; ☺ 9am-11pm) A celebrated local restaurant (since 1968) with a surprisingly low tourist quota, Parkview does a solid spread of Indian staples in a 90-seater elongated room with fuzzy red seats and well-dressed waiters.

Whistling Teal (☎ 24220167; Bhattiyani Chohtta; mains Rs50-180; ☺ 8.30am-10.30pm) This restaurant with superlative curries and exemplary service is entered through the foyer of the Raj Palace Hotel. Set well back from the street in a putting-green-perfect garden, here you can drink cocktails or smoke a hookah in saddles at the bar. The espresso coffee is the real thing – there is also a small coffee bar fronting Bhattiyani Chohtta.

Bawarchi Restaurant (☎ 2414955; 6 Delhi Gate; thalis Rs55) A jumping local thali joint where you can eat Jain, Gujarati or Rajasthani versions for not a lot of money.

Mayur Rooftop Cafe (☎ 2427126; Jagdish Temple Rd; mains Rs80-220; ☺ 8am-11pm) This breezy rooftop restaurant has a great view of the multihued light show on the Jagdish Temple. The usual multicuisine themes fill out the menu, while the Rs55 thali is good value.

Berry's (☎ 2429027; Chetak Circle; mains Rs90-150; ☺ noon-4pm, 7-11pm) A cosy and cool restaurant with a shiny brass door and a swirling fish tank, Berry's is a good bet in the evening, when the trade is busy and the white-table-cloth service comes to the fore. The cooking is classy veg and nonveg, with quality Indian plus Chinese and continental.

our pick Ambrai (☎ 2431085; near Hanuman Ghat; mains Rs95-190; ☺ 12.30-3pm & 7.30-10.30pm) The Indian cuisine at this scenic restaurant – at lake-shore level, looking across to Lake Palace Hotel, Lal Ghat and the City Palace – does justice to its fabulous position. Ambrai feels like a French park, with its wrought-iron furniture, dusty ground and large shady trees, and there's a terrific bar to complement the dining.

Jagat Niwas Palace Hotel (☎ 2420133; 23-25 Lal Ghat; mains Rs115-315; ⏲ 7-11am, noon-3pm & 6.30-10.15pm) A wonderful, classy restaurant with superb lake views, delicious Indian cuisine and good service. Choose from an extensive selection of rich curries (tempered for Western tastes) – mutton, chicken, fish, veg – as well as the tandoori classics. There's a tempting bar menu of cocktails and the beer is icy. It's wise to book ahead for dinner.

Savage Garden (☎ 9414296958; inside Chandpol; mains Rs150-550; ⏲ 11am-10pm) This place, near Chandpol, is very atmospheric, with indigo walls and tables in alcoves or in a pleasant courtyard. The food is Mediterranean with Italian and Middle Eastern influences – try the three meze: babaganoush, hummus and tabouli. The bar is slick, with red, white and sparkling Indian wines from Nasik, Maharashtra.

QUICK EATS

Cafe Namaste (Hotel Gangaur Palace; Gangaur Ghat Rd; cakes Rs15-70; ⏲ 7.30am-7.30pm) A European-themed bakery that delivers the goods with scrumptious muffins, apple pies, cinnamon rolls, brownies, etc. And to wash it down there is coffee from a shiny silver espresso machine (Rs40 to Rs70) taking pride of place.

Cafe Edelweiss (Gangaur Ghat Rd; snacks Rs30-50; ⏲ 7.30am-7.30pm) The Savage Garden folks run this itsy piece of Europe that appeals to homesick and discerning travellers. The cake tray, including cinnamon rolls, apple pies and chocolate cake, disappears quickly, and it's tough to get a seat. The coffee (Rs30 to Rs40) is pretty good.

Drinking

There are plenty of places for a relaxing drink with views over the lazy waters of Lake Pichola, but for a real treat try the top-end hotels. The **Paanera Bar** (Shiv Niwas Palace Hotel; ⏲ 11am-11pm) is a plush poolside spot with soft sofas. The **Pichola Bar** (Jagmandir Island Palace; ⏲ 11am-11pm) is in a former palace in the middle of the lake. And the **Sunset View Terrace** (City Palace complex; ⏲ 11am-10pm) is on a sun-drenched terrace overlooking the lake – perfect for a sunset gin-and-tonic.

Entertainment

Dharohar (Gangaur Ghat; adult/child Rs60/30, camera/video Rs10/50; ⏲ show 7pm) The beautiful Bagore-ki-Haveli hosts the best (and most convenient) opportunity to see Rajasthani folk dancing.

Mewar Sound & Light Show (Manak Chowk, City Palace; adult/child Rs50/25, raised seating Rs100/50; ⏲ 8-9pm) Fifteen centuries of intriguing Mewar history are squeezed into one atmospheric hour of commentary and light switching.

Shopping

Udaipur is known for its local crafts, particularly its miniature paintings in the Rajput-Mughal style; there are shops along Lake Palace Rd and around Jagdish Temple, but finding an authentic artist takes a collector's eye. Numerous 'art schools' certainly teach the craft to youngsters, but they also cheaply generate the bulk of the mass-produced miniatures flogged on the streets. Textiles, silver jewellery, wooden sculptures, leather-bound books and handmade paper (from Jaipur) are other popular buys in this area.

Interesting, less tourist-focused bazaars radiate from the clock tower, east of Gangaur Ghat, and buzz loudest in the evening. Bara Bazaar sells silver and gold, as well as saris and fabrics. Traditional shoes are sold on Mochiwada, more silver is on Bhattiyani Chohtta, and Mandi Market is great for spices.

Be prepared to bargain hard, as most places have inflated prices for tourists.

Rajasthali Chetak Circle (Chetak Circle; ⏲ 10.30am-7pm Mon-Sat); near Lal Ghat (Jagdish Temple; ⏲ 10am-6.30pm) The government fixed-price emporium is worth dropping into to gauge handicraft prices.

Sadhna (☎ 2417454; www.sadhna.org; Jagdish Temple Rd; ⏲ 10am-7pm) This is the outlet for Seva Mandir, an NGO set up in 1969 to help rural women. The small shop sells attractive fixed-price textiles; profits go to the artisans and towards community development work.

Getting There & Away
AIR

Air India (☎ 2410999; www.airindia.com; 1st fl Mumal Towers, Saheli Rd; ⏲ 10am-1pm & 2-5pm Mon-Sat, 10am-2pm Sun) flies to Delhi (from Rs2400 one way) via Jodhpur (Rs1400), Jaipur (Rs1500) and Mumbai (Rs3100). **Jet Airways** (☎ 2561105; www .jetairways.com; Blue Circle Business Centre, Madhuban), near the main post office, has similar flights for similar prices. **Kingfisher Airlines** (☎ 2429428; www.flykingfisher.com; Chetak Circle) has daily flights to Delhi (Rs5300).

BUS

Destinations served by **RSRTC buses** (☎ 2484191) include Agra (express Rs250, 13 hours), Jaipur (express/deluxe Rs170/220, nine hours), Ajmer (express/deluxe Rs120/150, eight hours), Jodhpur (express/deluxe Rs115/145, eight hours), Chittor (local/express Rs50/75, three/2½ hours), Delhi (express/deluxe Rs300/450, 14 hours), and Mumbai (Rs350, 16 hours).

Private bus companies operate services to Mt Abu (Rs100, five hours), Ahmedabad (ordinary/AC Rs150/200, six hours), Jodhpur (seat/sleeper Rs100/150, seven hours), Delhi (seat/sleeper Rs200/350, 14 hours) and Mumbai (seat/sleeper Rs400/600, 16 hours). **Haveli Tours & Travels** (☎ 9828787872; 61 Jagdish Temple Rd) has a daily coach departing for Jodhpur (Rs450) at 8am, which stops at their resort in Ghanerao village for lunch and visits Ranakpur on the way.

TAXI

Many drivers will show you a list of 'official' rates to places like Mt Abu, Chittor and Jodhpur. Shop around (Rs5 per kilometre for non-AC is a good starting point). Remember taxis charge return fares and for an overnight driver's halt even if you're only going one way.

TRAIN

Lines into Udaipur are slowly being converted to broad gauge, and though train services via Chittor are presently slow and limited, they are usually preferable to catching a bus. And by the time you read this, there should be more of the faster services. The enquiries number is ☎ 2527390.

The 2964 *Mewar Express* departs Udaipur at 6.30pm and arrives in Delhi (sleeper/3AC/ 2AC/1AC Rs309/814/1106/1854) at 6.15am, via Chittor (Rs141/268/333/544, two hours) and Kota (Rs171/424/567/946, four hours). In the opposite direction (2963) it leaves Delhi at 7pm and arrives in Udaipur at 7am.

The 2966 *Udaipur–Gwalior Express* departs Udaipur at 10.20pm and arrives in Agra

(sleeper/3AC/2AC/1AC Rs291/763/1036/1734) at 10.15am, via Chittor, Ajmer and Jaipur (Rs217/553/745/1252, 7½ hours).

The 2991 *Udaipur–Ajmer Express* departs at 7.05am and arrives in Ajmer (2nd class/ AC Chair Rs98/346) at 12.30pm, via Chittor (Rs61/210, two hours).

The 9943 *Ahmedabad Express* departs at 7.45pm and arrives in Ahmedabad (sleeper/ 2AC Rs154/548) at 4.30am.

Getting Around
TO/FROM THE AIRPORT

The airport is 25km from the city. A taxi will cost at least Rs350; there's no airport bus.

AUTORICKSHAW

These are not metered, so you should agree on a fare before setting off – the standard fare anywhere in town is around Rs30. There are prepaid autorickshaw stands at the bus and train stations. It costs around Rs300 to hire an autorickshaw for a day of local sightseeing.

The commission system is in place, so tenaciously pursue your first choice of accommodation. Unless your rickshaw is prepaid, ask for the Jagdish Temple when arriving, as it's a good place to start looking for accommodation.

BICYCLE & MOTORCYCLE

You can hire clunky Hero bicycles for around Rs25 per day (plus US$50 deposit) or better mountain bikes for Rs50 per day (US$100 deposit) at **Heera Cycle Store** (☎ 5130625; ⏰ 7.30am-9pm), near Hotel Udai Niwas. It also hires out mopeds/motorcycles/Bullets for Rs70/300/400 per day (with deposit of US$200/400/500).

AROUND UDAIPUR
Kumbalgarh

An incredible stone fort, **Kumbalgarh** (Indian/foreigner Rs5/100; ⏰ 9am-6pm) is situated 84km north of Udaipur, 1100m skyward in the Aravalli hills. Built by Maharana Kumba in the 15th century, the colossal structure fulfils romantic expectations of Rajput grandeur.

It was the most important Mewar fort after Chittor, and rulers used to retreat here in times of danger. It was taken only once in its history, and even then it needed the combined armies of Mughal emperor Akbar and of Amber and Marwar to breach its defences, and they only managed to hang on to it for two days.

The fort walls stretch some 36km and enclose around 360 temples, as well as palaces, gardens, *baoris* and 700 cannon bunkers.

If you stay in Kumbalgarh, you can trek from your hotel to the fort, a dramatic way to approach and reinforce the sense of its impenetrability.

The **Kumbalgarh Wildlife Sanctuary** (Indian/foreigner Rs10/100; ☼ dawn-dusk) is known for its leopards and wolves. Other wildlife includes chowsinghas (four-horned antelope) and sloth bears. The period from March to June, when water is scarce, is the best time to see animals. You need permission from the forest department in nearby Kelwara to enter. All hotels can arrange permits and three-hour horse or jeep safaris. **Shivika Lake Hotel** (☎ 02934-285078; www.shivikalakehotel.com) in Ranakpur arranges jeep tours at a cost of Rs700 per person, which covers admission.

Karni Palace Hotel (☎ 02594-242033; Bus Stand Rd, Kelwara; s/d from Rs600/750, with AC Rs1200/1500, ste Rs3000; ✎) backs onto lovely cornfields. This not-so-attractive hotel has slopped on the paint, but it's squeaky clean and popular with groups.

Kumbhal Castle (☎ 02594-242171; www.thekumbhalcastle.com; s/d from Rs1800/2000; ✎ ⎚), 3km from the fort, is a modern 'castle' with plain, bright rooms with window seats, shared balconies and good views.

Aodhi Hotel (☎ 02594-242341; www.hrhindia.com; r Rs6000, ste Rs7000; ✎ ⎚ ⎚), about 5km from the fort, is an appealing, blissfully tranquil hotel, with an inviting pool and winter campfires.

There are several RSRTC buses to/from Udaipur (Rs40, 3½ hours). Some stop in Kelwara, 7km away, some at the Aodhi Hotel, from where it's a 5km walk to the fort. Hiring a taxi from Udaipur means you can visit both Ranakpur and Kumbalgarh in a day – many travellers ask around to fill the car and share the expense (Rs1400).

Ranakpur

Ninety kilometres north of Udaipur, **Ranakpur** (admission free, camera/video Rs50/100; ☼ Jains 6am-7pm, non-Jains 11am-5pm) is another incredible feat of Jain devotion. Carved from milk-white marble, the complicated series of 29 halls, supported by a forest of 1444 pillars (no two alike), is the finest in Rajasthan, and one the most important in India. The devotion of its builders is encapsulated in the intricate carving.

The main temple is called the **Chaumukha Mandir** (Four-Faced Temple); it's dedicated to Adinath and was built in 1439. Within the complex are two other Jain temples to **Neminath** and **Parasnath**, and a **Sun Temple**. About 1km from the main complex is **Amba Mata Temple**.

Shoes, cigarettes and all leather articles must be left at the entrance.

With small, cosy cottages set amid leafy gardens, **Shivika Lake Hotel** (☎ 02934-285078; www.shivikalake.com; r Rs600-160; ✎ ⎚ ⎚) is an undisturbed, rustic place to stay. The knowledgeable family arranges forest safaris and guides for treks.

Situated deep in mango country, **Ranakpur Hill Resort** (☎ 02934-286411; www.ranakpurhillresort.com; Ranakpur Rd, Post Sadri; s/d from Rs1800/2200; ✎ ⎚ ⎚) has an inviting pool and enormous restaurant. Rooms are generously proportioned with shiny bathrooms.

Eleven kilometres from Ranakpur, **Aranyawas** (☎ 9829699413; www.aranyawas.com; Maga Village; r from Rs1800/2500; ✎ ⎚) is a secluded chalet deep among fruit trees and forests. Most rooms overlook a stream.

The **Maharani Bagh Orchard Retreat** (☎ 02934-285105; balsamand@sify.com; s/d Rs3900/4900; ✎ ⎚), 4km from Ranakpur and set within a lush mango orchard, offers accommodation in wood-furnished cottages with terraces surrounded by green lawns.

Lots of buses run to and from Udaipur to Ranakpur (Rs45, three hours), but it's hard to visit both Ranakpur and Kumbalgarh by public transport in a day, and the accommodation listed here is too far to walk from the bus stop. A taxi from Udaipur taking in Ranakpur and Kumbalgarh costs around Rs1400.

Jaisamand Lake

Located 48km southeast of Udaipur, this startling artificial lake (88 sq km) is one of Asia's largest. Created by damming the Gomti River, it was built by Maharaja Jai Singh in the 17th century. There are beautiful marble *chhatris* around the 330m-long, 35m-high embankment, and Udaipur maharanis' summer palaces are dotted on surrounding hilltops.

Jaisamand Island Resort (☎ 0294-2431401; www.jaisamand.co.in; r from Rs3300; ✎ ⎚ ⎚) is a modern stylish hotel in a wonderful, secluded location 20 minutes by boat across the lake. The pool has a brilliant setting but isn't always full and there can be an air of neglect. Discounts are often available.

There are frequent buses from Udaipur (Rs27, 1½ hours).

Dungarpur

About 110km south of Udaipur, splendid Dungarpur, the City of Hills, was founded in the 13th century. You can visit the wonderful deserted old palace, **Juna Mahal** (admission Rs100; �9am-5pm), with its murals, including the Kama Sutra secreted in a cupboard. The former royal hunting lodge, on a nearby hilltop, has sensational views. Buy tickets from Udai Bilas Palace (above).

The beautiful **Deo Somnath Temple**, about 25km out of town, dates back to the 12th century.

Hotel Pratibha Palace (☎ 02964-230775; Shastri Colony; d Rs150-200) has tiny, adequate rooms that are the best budget digs in town.

Udai Bilas Palace (☎ 02964-230808; www.udaibilas-palace.com; s/d/ste Rs4050/5100/6300; 🆇 💻 🏊), set on sparkling Gaib Sagar, is a fantastic lakeside palace partly converted into a hotel. It's built around the extraordinary Ek Thambia Mahal (One-Pillared Palace), and rooms retain their original Art Deco and 1940s furnishings; some have a lake-view balcony.

Frequent RSRTC buses travel to and from Udaipur (Rs60, three hours). Trains from Udaipur include the 431 *Udaipur–Ahmedabad Passenger,* which departs Udaipur at 9.20am, arriving in Dungarpur (sleeper Rs80) at 1.30pm; and the 9943 *Udaipur–Ahmedabad Express,* which departs Udaipur at 7.45pm, arriving in Dungarpur (sleeper/2AC Rs121/303) at 11pm.

MT ABU

☎ 02974 / pop 22,045 / elev 1200m

Mt Abu, Rajasthan's only hill station, rises high above the baking plains and makes a welcome retreat from the deserts; several maharajas built their summer holiday palaces here. Now it attracts hordes of holidaymakers from neighbouring (and sweltering) Gujarat. The wooded slopes that line the winding climb to the town are home to bears, wild boars, monkeys and other wildlife. There are also plenty of botanical delights on offer, most notably a number of rare orchids, and excellent trekking opportunities for all levels of fitness.

Mt Abu is also known for its extraordinary Jain Dilwara temples, and the presence of Brahma Kumaris followers. Prices skyrocket around Diwali, when the whole place is best avoided. Note that evening temperatures can catch you cold, so pack something warm.

Orientation & Information

Mt Abu is on a hilly plateau about 22km long by 6km wide, 27km from the nearest train station (Abu Road). The main part of the town extends along the road from Abu Road down to Nakki Lake.

There's a **Tourist Reception Centre** (☎ 235151; � 9.30am-6pm Mon-Sat), opposite the bus stand, that has a free map. The **Union Bank of India** (Main Market; � 10am-3pm Mon-Fri, 10am-12.30pm Sat) was the only bank changing travellers cheques and currency at the time of research. It is tucked away behind Yani-Ya Cyber Zone. There's an SBBJ ATM near Cafe Coffee Day and an SBI ATM beside the Tourist Reception Centre. For internet try **Yani-Ya Cyber Zone** (Main Market; per hr Rs30; � 8am-10pm) or **Shree Krishna Telecommunications** (Main Market; per hr Rs30; � 8am-10pm).

Sights & Activities

NAKKI LAKE

Scenic Nakki Lake is a big attraction and the town's focus. It's so named because, according to legend, it was scooped out by a god using his *nakh* (nails). It's a pleasant stroll around the perimeter – look for the strange **rock formations**. The best known, **Toad Rock**, looks just like it's about to hop into the lake. The 14th-century **Raghunath Temple** (☉ dawn-dusk) stands beside the lake. You can hire boats – a **pedalo** or a more romantic **shikara** (gondola-like boat) – at the edge of the lake near the temple; a two-person *shikara* costs Rs100 for 30 minutes, while a two-/four-person pedalo costs Rs50/100.

VIEWPOINTS

Sunset Point is a popular and lovely place to watch the setting sun. Other viewpoints include **Honeymoon Point** and the **Crags**. With a guide you can follow the often obscured path to the summit of **Shanti Shikhar**, west of Adhar Devi Temple, where there are panoramic views. None of these places should be visited alone, especially at times other than sunset when there is likely to be no-one else around. Unfortunately, muggings (and worse) have occurred in recent years.

The best view over the lake is from the terrace of the Maharaja of Jaipur's former summer palace, now **Jaipur House** (see p229).

DILWARA TEMPLES

These **temples** (☉ Jains dawn-dusk, non-Jains noon-6pm) rank among India's finest temple architecture. Note, no photography is allowed (though photographs are sold outside). As at other Jain temples, leather articles (belts as well as shoes) have to be left at the entrance and menstruating women are warned away.

The artisans were paid according to the amount of dust they collected, encouraging them to carve ever more intricately. Whatever their inducement, there are two temples in which the work is dazzling in its intensity.

The older of the temples is the **Vimal Vasahi**, started in 1031 and dedicated to the first *tirthankar*, Adinath. It took 14 years to build and cost Rs180.5 million. The central shrine has an image of Adinath, while around the courtyard are 52 identical cells, each enclosing a cross-legged open-eyed *tirthankar*. Forty-eight pillars form the courtyard entrance. In front of the temple stands the **House of Elephants**, with a procession of elephants marching to the temple entrance, some damaged by marauding Mughals.

The later **Luna Vasahi** is dedicated to Neminath, the 22nd *tirthankar*, and was built in 1230 by the brothers Tejpal and Vastupal for a mere Rs125.9 million. Like Vimal, they were government ministers. Here the marble carving took 2500 workers 15 years to create. The filigree is so fine that, in places, the marble becomes almost transparent. In particular, the many-layered lotus flower that dangles from the centre of the dome is an astonishing piece of work carved from a single block.

The temple is remarkably well preserved, employing several full-time carvers to maintain the work.

There are another three temples in the enclosure: **Bhimashah Pittalhar** (built 1315–1433), with a 4-ton, five-metal statue; **Mahaveerswami** (1582), a small shrine flanked by painted elephants; and the three-storey **Khartar Vasahi**.

You can stroll out to Dilwara from the town in less than an hour, or take a shared taxi (p230).

BRAHMA KUMARIS SPIRITUAL UNIVERSITY & MUSEUM

The white-clad people around town are studying at **Brahma Kumaris Spiritual University** (www .bkwsu.com). This organisation teaches that all religions lead to God and that the principles of each should be studied. The university's aim is the establishment of universal peace through 'the impartation of spiritual knowledge and training of easy raja yoga meditation'. For many, the teachings are intensely powerful; there are over 4500 branches in 70 countries. For others, it gives off a spooky New Age–sect vibe. There's a **Brahma Kumaris museum** (admission free; ☉ 8am-8pm) in town, the entrance labelled Gateway to Paradise!

TREKKING

As well as being the local snake-catcher, Charles from **Mt Abu Treks** (☎ 9414154854; Hotel Lake Palace) arranges tailor-made treks ranging from gentle village visits to longer, wilder expeditions into Mt Abu Wildlife Sanctuary. He's passionate and knowledgeable about the local flora and fauna. Treks include a three- to four-hour trek (Rs280 per person); a half-day (Rs380); a full day including lunch (Rs610); and an overnight village trek including all meals (Rs1250). The sanctuary entrance fee is included in the prices, but if you want to delve deeper into the jungle and require a taxi to the trail head, this will be an additional cost.

The staff at **Shri Ganesh Hotel** (☎ 235062; lalit _ganesh@yahoo.co.in) also organise excellent short treks (Rs200 per person) into the hills. There's a trek in the morning at 9am, and one to see the sunset starting at 3pm. The routes vary and the level of difficulty depends on the fitness of the group. It's common to spot bears and other wildlife.

A final warning from the locals: it's very unsafe to wander unguided in these hills. Travellers have been mauled by bears, and even more disturbing, have been mugged (and worse) by other people.

Tours

The RTDC has five-hour tours of the main sites around town, leaving from the bus stand at 8.30am and 1.30pm (later in summer). Tours cost Rs65 excluding admission and camera fees. The afternoon tour finishes at Sunset Point. Reserve at the **enquiries counter** (☎ 235434) at the bus stand.

Festivals & Events

Mt Abu is crowded for **Diwali** (see p27) in October/November. May sees the **Summer Festival** (p167), while December is the time of the **Winter Festival** (p167).

Sleeping

Mt Abu mostly consists of hotels. The high season lasts from mid-April to June, during and after Diwali (when you need to book

RAJASTHAN

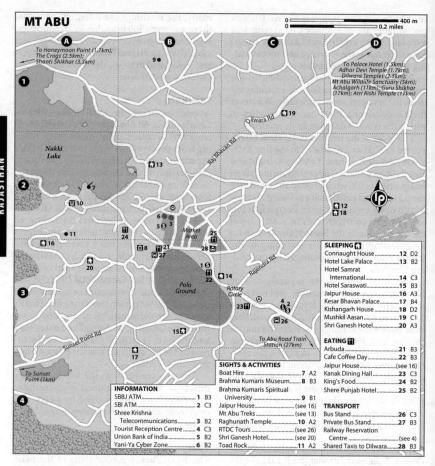

ahead, prices become ridiculous, and you cannot move for crowds), and from Christmas to New Year. Many midrange and top-end places offer off-season discounts and most hotels have an ungenerous 9am check-out time.

Usually there are touts working the bus and taxi stands. In the low season ignore them, but at peak times they can save you legwork, as they'll know where to find the last available room.

Shri Ganesh Hotel (☎ 235062; lalit_ganesh@yahoo .co.in; dm from Rs50, with shower Rs100, r Rs250-600, s/d without bathroom from Rs80/150; 🖥) This serene place has a variety of good-value rooms, loads of helpful local information, a guest kitchen and good breakfasts. It offers early-morning yoga on the roof, cookery lessons (Rs150) where

you eat the food and keep the recipe, and trekking every morning and evening (see p227).

Hotel Saraswati (☎ 238887; r Rs490-890; 🕸) Popular, clean and efficient, this is an appealing place in a peaceful setting behind the polo ground and with a good range of well-kept rooms. Air-con costs an additional Rs400. Room prices can rise by Rs200 at the weekend, though there's an inexpensive Gujarati thali restaurant here where you can save a few rupees.

Mushkil Aasan (☎ 235150; Dilwara Rd; r Rs750) A lovely paying guesthouse nestled in a vale, with nine homely decorated rooms. It's on the road to the Dilwara temples, in a tranquil location with a small lawn. Tariff is room only, though meals are available.

Hotel Samrat International (☎ 235153; Lake Rd; s/d from Rs1000/1250, s without bathroom from Rs170) This honeymoon hotel has a hotchpotch of rooms, from tight-fit doubles to attractive, spacious suites with sheltered balconies overlooking the polo ground. The traffic below is hectic by Mt Abu standards, and the honeymoon suites are 'individual'; however, the tariffs fall by 40% at the drop of a hat outside peak periods.

Hotel Lake Palace (☎ 237154; www.savshantihotels .com; r Rs1800-2800; ✹) A spacious, friendly place overlooking a small garden; it has unfussy, appealing rooms, some with semiprivate lake-view terraces. These rates drop by at least 30% outside weekends and peak season. Charles from Mt Abu Treks (p227) is based here.

Kishangarh House (☎ 238092; www.royalkishangarh .com; Rajendra Marg; s/d cottages Rs2000/2500, s/d deluxe Rs3500/4000) The former summer residence of the Maharaja of Kishangarh has been lovingly converted into a top-notch heritage hotel. It has impressive rooms – probably the best value in this league – with the cottages being cosier and the main rooms boasting extravagantly high ceilings. There is a delightful sun-filled drawing room and the gardens are devotedly tended.

Kesar Bhavan Palace (☎ 235219; www.kesarpalace .com; Sunset Point Rd; r Rs2400; ste Rs4000 ✹) This heritage property is perched up among trees and has appealing leafy views, but also feels a little austere. The comfortable, marble-floored rooms all have balconies, and the suites are on two levels. Check the bathrooms as some are in pretty bad shape for these prices.

Palace Hotel (☎ 238673; www.palacehotelbikaner house.com; Bikaner House, Dilwara Rd; s/d from Rs3800/4000, ste from Rs5500; ✹) Near the Dilwara temples, this cavernous palace built in 1893 by Sir Swinton Jacob, with gardens, a lake and tennis courts, resembles a stately Scottish manor. Rooms are tasteful and massive.

Connaught House (☎ 238560; www.welcomeheritage hotels.com; terrace room/cottage Rs4000/5000; ✹) Connaught House is a stuck-in-time colonial bungalow that looks like an English cottage, with lots of sepia photographs, dark wood, angled ceilings and a gorgeous shady garden. Suite 28 is the best pick for privacy, though the 'cottages' in the main bungalow have oodles of character. It's owned by the descendants of the Maharaja of Jodhpur.

Jaipur House (☎ 235176; www.royalfamilyjaipur.com; d cottage 2 nights Rs6444, d Rs8666, ste Rs10,666-11,777) Perched on a hilltop overlooking the lake, this was built by the Maharaja of Jaipur in 1897. Opulent suites overlook the town from a suitably lofty height. If you're not really a suite person, the cottages (the former servants' quarters) verge on the simple. The tariff includes breakfast and dinner.

Eating & Drinking

Most holidaymakers here are Gujarati – hence the profusion of sweet veg thali restaurants.

Cafe Coffee Day (Rotary Circle; coffee Rs35-90; ⌚ 9am-midnight) Another life-saving branch of the popular caffeine-supply chain. And the tea and cakes aren't bad either.

Shere Punjab Hotel (main market; mains Rs35-200; ⌚ 8am-11pm) This place in the market has bargain Punjabi and Chinese food. There are plenty of regular veg and nonveg curries that won't stretch the budget.

King's Food (☎ 2328478; Nakki Lake; mains Rs40-75; ⌚ 8am-10pm) A busy, open-to-the-street fast-food joint. It has the usual have-a-go menu and offers Chinese, Punjabi and South Indian food, and delicious lassis.

Arbuda (☎ 238358; Arbuda Circle; mains Rs40-90; ⌚ 8am-11pm) This big restaurant is set on a sweeping open terrace filled with chrome chairs. It's very popular for its Gujarati, Punjabi and South Indian food, and does fine continental breakfasts and fresh juices.

Kanak Dining Hall (☎ 238305; Abu Rd; Gujarati/Rajasthani thali Rs70/100; ⌚ 11am-3pm, 7-11pm) The excellent all-you-can-eat thalis are contenders for Mt Abu's best; there's seating indoors in the busy dining hall or outside under a canopy.

Jaipur House (☎ 235176; mains Rs135-300; ⌚ 11.30-3.30pm & 7.30-11pm) This place has divine views over the hills, lake and the town's twinkling lights from a lovely open terrace, with Indian and continental nonveg food fit for a aharaja. It is also a dreamy place for a tipple (beer Rs180, cocktails Rs200).

Getting There & Away

As you enter Mt Abu there's a tollgate; bus and car passengers are charged Rs10, plus Rs10 for a car.

BUS

From 6am to 9pm buses make the 27km climb from Abu Road train station up to Mt Abu (Rs22, one hour, half-hourly). They leave from outside the bus stand, next to the ticket booth.

A direct bus from Mt Abu is usually faster and more convenient than a train from Abu Road station. **RSRTC buses** (☎ enquiries 235434) go to Jaipur (express/deluxe Rs288/495, 12 hours, three daily), Udaipur (Rs106/115, 4½ hours, six daily), Ahmedabad (Rs121, 6½ hours), Jodhpur (Rs165, seven hours, one daily), Ajmer (express/deluxe Rs212/373, 10 hours, three daily), and Jaisalmer (Rs245, 11 hours, one daily). Some RSRTC buses go all the way to Mt Abu, while others terminate at Abu Road train station.

Buses belonging to private bus companies leave from the private bus stand, north of the polo ground, and serve similar destinations and cost about the same.

TAXI
A taxi for up to six people into town from Abu Road train station costs about Rs250. Some taxi drivers claim that this price is only for as far as the bus stand and ask an extra fee (as much as Rs50) to take you to your hotel. A taxi to/from Udaipur will cost about Rs2500.

TRAIN
Abu Road, the railhead for Mt Abu, is on the broad-gauge line between Delhi and Mumbai via Ahmedabad. In Mt Abu, above the Tourist Reception Centre, there's a **railway reservation centre** (◷ 8am-2pm), which has quotas on most of the express trains.

The 9106 *Ahmedabad–Haridwar Mail* leaves Abu Road at 12.45pm and reaches Ahmedabad (sleeper/3AC/2AC/1AC Rs125/321/434/719) at 6.40pm. The 9224 *Jammu Tawai–Ahmedabad Express* leaves at 10.50am and arrives at Ahmedabad (sleeper/2AC Rs121/406) at 3.30pm. To get to Bhuj and the Kathiawar Peninsula in Gujarat, change trains at Palanpur, 53km south of Abu Road.

The 9105 *Haridwar–Ahmedabad Mail* leaves at 2.06pm, arriving in Delhi (sleeper/3AC/2AC/1AC Rs289/784/1076/1804) at 5.25am, via Ajmer (Rs157/411/560/936, 6½ hours) and Jaipur (Rs197/523/715/1202, 8½ hours). The 9707 *Aravalli Express* leaves at 9.58am, reaches Ajmer (sleeper/3AC/2AC Rs157/411/560) at 4.05pm and terminates at Jaipur (Rs197/523/715) at 6.45pm

The 9223 *Ahmedabad–Jammu Tawai Express* leaves at 3.17pm and arrives at Jodhpur (sleeper/2AC Rs145/512) at 8pm.

Getting Around
Local buses go to various sites around Mt Abu, but it's easier to take the five-hour tour (p227). To hire a jeep for local sightseeing costs around Rs600/1000 per half-/full day. For Dilwara you can take a shared taxi (jeep). These leave when full from near the market area (Rs5 per person, or Rs50 all to yourself and Rs150 for waiting an hour).

There are no autorickshaws in Mt Abu, but it's easy to get around on foot. Unique to the town is the *baba-gari*, a porter-pulled handcart. They cart your luggage or even one or two (small) people.

AROUND MT ABU
Guru Shikhar
At the end of the plateau, 15km from Mt Abu, is Guru Shikhar, Rajasthan's highest point, at 1721m. A road goes almost all the way to the summit and the **Atri Rishi Temple**, complete with a priest and fantastic views. It can be visited as part of the RDTC tour, or a jeep will cost Rs500 return.

Achalgarh
A handful of hilltop Jain temples and an ancient Shiva temple 11km north of Mt Abu, perched above a rural village, offer spectacular views of the countryside and are well worth a visit.

Mt Abu Wildlife Sanctuary
This 290-sq-km **sanctuary** (Indian/foreigner Rs10/80, jeep Rs100; ◷ 8am-5pm), 5.5km northeast of Mt Abu, on a large plateau, is home to leopards, deer, foxes and bears. It's about a 3km walk from the Dilwara temples. Contact Mt Abu Treks (p227) to arrange an overnight stay.

WESTERN RAJASTHAN

JODHPUR
☎ 0291 / pop 846,408
Mighty Mehrangarh, the muscular fort that towers over the blue city of Jodhpur, is a magnificent spectacle and an architectural masterpiece. The formidable walls appear to grow organically from its rocky perch. Down below, the old town, a jumble of Brahmin-blue cubes, sprawls into the haze. The 'blue city' really is blue! Jodhpur proper stretches well beyond the 16th-century border, but it's the immediacy and buzz of the old blue city and the larger-than-life fort that capture travellers' imaginations.

Today, Jodhpur is crowded and dirty (though in 2008 there were noises that something would be done about the open sewers); be prepared for some hassle, particularly around the clock tower. You can escape this by delving into the tangle of medieval bazaars of the old city (west of the clock tower), where you'll find everything from boxes of snuff to baggy trousers (oh yes, the city gave its name to those pants favoured by horse riders).

Jodhpur was founded in 1459 by Rao Jodha, a chief of the Rajput clan known as the Rathores, and the city grew out of the profits of opium, sandalwood, dates and copper. Rathore kingdom was once cheerily known as Marwar (the Land of Death).

In October, Jodhpur holds the **Marwar Festival** (p167).

Orientation

The Tourist Reception Centre, train stations and bus stand are all outside the old city. High Court Rd runs from the Raika Bagh train station, past the Umaid gardens, and along the city wall towards the Jodhpur train station.

Information

There's an Axis Bank ATM opposite Sojati Gate; there are also Bank of Baroda ATMs on Nai Sarak and Residency Rd. SBBJ and IDBI also have ATMs on Nai Sarak and there's another IDBI ATM on Airport Rd.

For internet access, there are loads of cheap places around town, usually charging Rs30 per hour.

Gucci's (Killikhana; internet per hr Rs30) The fastest internet speed we found, with cold drinks and chilled chocolates.

iWay (per hr Rs20) In front of the clock tower.

Krishna Book Depot (Sardar Market) Stocks an impressive range of secondhand and new books.

Main post office (Station Rd)

Net Hut (Fort Rd, Makrana Mohalla; per hr Rs30) Broadband, but not blistering, among the budget digs.

Sarvodaya Book Stall (Station Rd) Near the train station, stocks a small range of English-language magazines and books, including Lonely Planet.

State Bank of India (☎ 2543649; High Court Rd; ☺ 10am-4pm Mon-Fri, 10am-1pm Sat) Changes currencies and travellers cheques.

Thomas Cook (☎ 2512064; Shop 1, Mahareer Palace) Changes currencies and travellers cheques.

Tourist Reception Centre (☎ 2545083; ☺ 9.30am-6pm Mon-Fri) In the RTDC Hotel Ghoomar compound. Will grudgingly give you a free map and has a list of paying guesthouses, but it seems tourists are to be endured rather than served well here.

Sights
MEHRANGARH

Still run by the descendants of the Maharaja of Jodhpur, **Mehrangarh** (Indian/foreigner Rs30/250, Indian camera/audio guide Rs50/150; ☺ 9am-5pm Oct-Mar, 8.30am-5.30pm Apr-Sep) is captivating. As you approach, the walls soar overhead in a mesmerising demonstration of the skills of the builders. Cast off your audio-tour prejudices, as this tour, covered by the foreign-visitor admission charge (which also includes camera fees), is terrific, with a mix of history, information and dramatically narrated anecdotes. It's a real treat to wander around at your leisure, taking a fix of information when you feel like it. Personal guides are available for Rs150.

The fort's seven gates include **Jayapol**, built by Maharaja Man Singh in 1806 following his victory over Jaipur and Bikaner, and **Fatehpol** (Victory Gate), erected by Maharaja Ajit Singh to commemorate his defeat of the Mughals. The second gate in the fort behind Jayapol (the main entrance) is still scarred by cannonball hits: this was a fort that earned its keep. The final gate is the **Lohapol** (Iron Gate), beside which are numerous tragic tiny hand prints, the *sati* marks of Maharaja Man Singh's widows, who threw themselves upon his funeral pyre in 1843. They still attract devotional attention and are usually covered in red powder.

Inside the fort walls is a deep-terracotta-coloured, latticed **palace complex** and network of courtyards, beautiful examples of the asymmetry and symmetry that mark Rajput buildings. They house a **museum**, with a splendid collection of the trappings of Indian royalty, including some amazing howdahs, miniatures, armoury and ephemera – from 19th-century ivory-inlaid ladies' dumbbells to camel-bone carpet weights.

The palaces have evocative names, such as the **Moti Mahal** (Pearl Palace), **Sukh Mahal** (Pleasure Palace) and **Phool Mahal** (Flower Palace) – the latter is beautifully decorated, using a curious concoction of gold leaf, glue and cow's urine. The inner courtyard, **Holi Chowk**, was used for the Holi festival; the women were able to view the festivities from above. The small marble seat here was used for coronations from the 17th century.

At the southern end of the fort, old cannons look out from the ramparts over the sheer

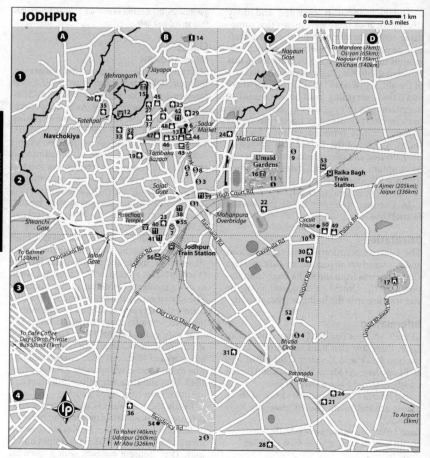

drop to the old town beneath. There are magical views, and you can clearly hear voices and city sounds swept up by the air currents. The **Chamunda Devi Temple**, dedicated to Durga, and the scene of a tragic stampede by devotees in 2008, stands at this end of the fort.

There is a lift to whisk disabled or weary travellers up to the palace level. There's even a fort **astrologer** (☎ 2514614; ⏰ 9am-1pm & 2-5pm); Mr Sharma charges Rs200/300 for a 15-/30-minute (basic/detailed) consultation.

JASWANT THADA

This milky white marble **memorial** (Indian/foreigner Rs15/30, camera Rs25; ⏰ 9am-5pm) to Maharaja Jaswant Singh II is an array of whimsical domes – it's a welcome, peaceful spot after

the hubbub of the city, and the view across to the fort is superb. The cenotaph, built in 1899, was followed by the royal crematorium and three other cenotaphs that stand nearby. Look out for the memorial to a peacock that flew into the funeral pyre. There are some beautiful *jalis* (carved marble lattice screens), and it's the definitive tomb with a view.

CLOCK TOWER & MARKETS

The **clock tower** is an old city landmark, surrounded by the vibrant sounds, sights and smells of Sardar Market. Heading westwards from here, you get deep into the old city's commercial heart, with alleys leading to **bazaars** selling vegetables, spices, sweets, silver and handicrafts.

RAJASTHAN

UMAID BHAWAN PALACE

Sometimes called the Chittar Palace because of the local Chittar sandstone used, this immense edifice was begun in 1929. It was designed by the president of the British Royal Institute of Architects for Maharaja Umaid Singh, and took 3000 workers 15 years to complete. This was apparently a philanthropic job-creation program during a time of severe drought.

Maharaja Umaid Singh died in 1947; his successor still lives in part of the building. The rest has been turned into a luxury hotel and a small **museum** (admission Rs50; 9am-5pm). Most interesting are the photos showing the elegant Art Deco design of the palace interior. Attendants will ensure that you don't stray into the hotel, but you can peer at the soaring domed central hall. Alternatively, you can visit the hotel to eat at one of its restaurants. Look out for some of the Maharaja's highly polished classic cars displayed on the lawn in front of the museum.

UMAID GARDENS & SADAR GOVERNMENT MUSEUM

The Umaid Gardens are home to the **Sadar Government Museum** (admission Rs3; 10am-4.30pm Sat-Thu), which feels frozen in time. The poorly labelled exhibits include weapons and 6th- to 10th-century sculptures.

Tours

The RTDC travel desk within the Hotel Ghoomer (adjacent to the Tourist Reception Centre) runs four-hour city tours (Rs100, excluding admission fees, minimum four persons) from 9am to 1pm and 2pm to 6pm. The tours take in the Umaid Bhawan Palace, Mehrangarh, Jaswant Thada and Mandore gardens.

Jodhpur is renowned for its village safaris – jeep trips to local Bishnoi villages, potters and *dhurrie* (rug) weavers. The Bishnoi are a tribal sect who believe in the sanctity of the environment. Their desire to protect trees and animals dates from the 15th century. It's a well-worn trail, so it can feel touristy – your enjoyment depends on how good your guide is. Just about every hotel organises these excursions; all are fairly similar, and charge around Rs500 to Rs600 per person for a half-day trip, including lunch. **Marwar Eco Cultural Tours & Travels** (5123095; www.marwarecocultural-tours.com) is a recommended private operator.

Alternatively, friendly **Chhota Ram Prajapat** (2696744; chhotaramprajapat@rediffmail.com) offers simple hut accommodation (per person including dinner Rs800) for up to eight guests in nearby Salawas, the main artisan village.

Gemar Singh (☎ 02922-272313, 9460585154; www .hacra.org) arranges homestays, camping, desert walks and camel safaris around his home in Osiyan and surrounding Rajput and Bishnoi villages. The cost is around Rs800 per person per day (minimum two people) and includes bus transfer from Jodhpur, camel ride, guide, food and accommodation (village hut).

Sleeping

If a rickshaw driver is clamouring to take you somewhere, it's probably because he is aiming to receive a commission. You can avoid this by getting dropped at the clock tower and walking (note: there's only one clock tower). As many travellers arrive by train or bus late at night, it helps to arrange a pick-up service with your hotel.

The Tourist Reception Centre has an up-to-date list of paying-guest houses in and around the city – nearly 60 participants with prices ranging from Rs100 to Rs1200 per night. This is an excellent way to get under the skin of this city, which, with pollution, noise and activity, can be as formidable to new visitors as Mehrangarh was to invading armies.

BUDGET

Cosy Guest House (☎ 2612066; www.cosyguesthouse .com; Navchokiya Rd, Brahmpuri; rooftop Rs75, tents Rs150, d Rs350-750, s/d without bathroom Rs175/200; 🗶 🖳) Filled with fellow travellers, this is a peaceful place in the heart of the old blue city. It's a 500-year-old glowing blue house with several levels of higgledy-piggledy rooftops and a mix of rooms, some monastic, others decked. Ask the rickshaw for Navchokiya Rd, from where the guesthouse is signposted, or call genial Mr Joshi.

Hare Krishna Guest House (☎ 2654367; harekrishnaguesthouse@hotmail.com; r Rs100-600; 🗶 🖳) This is another old house that has been extended upwards and squeezes in rooms and stairs wherever possible. The range of rooms is impressive – from the cave-like cheapie to the spacious fort-view rooms. Of course, there's a rooftop restaurant.

Govind Hotel (☎ 2622758; www.govindhotel.com; Station Rd; dm Rs110; s Rs350; d Rs400-1100; 🗶 🖳 🛜) Well set up for travellers, with helpful management (who refuse to pay commission), an internet cafe, and a location convenient to the Jodhpur train station. All rooms are clean and

tiled, with fairly smart bathrooms. There's a rooftop restaurant and coffee shop with excellent espresso coffee and cakes.

Shivam Paying Guest House (☎ 2610 688; shivam gh@hotmail.com; Makrana Mohalla; r Rs200-650, without bathroom Rs150; 🗶) Near the clock tower, this quiet, hassle-free option run by a gentle, helpful family has cosy rooms and a lovely little rooftop restaurant.

Sunrise Guest House (☎ 2623790; anilsunriseguest house@yahoo.com; Makrana Mohalla; s/d from Rs150/250, with air cooler Rs250/350) Sunrise is a simple guesthouse with friendly, helpful management, a terrace restaurant, and basic but clean rooms. Its solution to the great East–West toilet dichotomy? Install both sets so guests get to choose.

Durag Villas Guest House (☎ 2512298; www.durag villas.com; 1 Old Public Park; r Rs250-900; 🗶) Next door to Durag Niwas Guest House, this has simple, good-value rooms – the more expensive rooms have AC and are worth the investment. It's a quiet, relaxed place set around a leafy courtyard.

Durag Niwas Guest House (☎ 2512385; www.durag -niwas.com; 1 Old Public Park; r Rs350-750; 🗶) A friendly place set away from the hustle of the old city. Good home-cooked veg dishes are available, and there's a cushion-floored, sari-curtained area on the roof for relaxing. There are deals for long-termers: a double room with full board for Rs6000 per month. Management offer cultural tours and the opportunity to do volunteer work with the Sambhali Trust (www.sambhali-trust.org), helping to empower disadvantaged women and girls.

Hotel Haveli (☎ 2614615; Makrana Mohalla; s/d from Rs500/650; 🗶 🖳) This 250-year-old building inside the walled city is a popular place. Rooms are individually decorated with colour themes and paintings and many have semibalconies and fort views. The rooftop vegetarian restaurant, Jharokha, has excellent views and nightly entertainment.

Singhvi's Haveli (☎ 2624293; www.singhvihaveli.com; Ramdevji ka Chowk, Navchokiya; r Rs200-1800) This red-sandstone, family-run *haveli* with exquisitely carved *jalis* is an understated gem. There are 11 individual rooms, ranging from the simple to the magnificent maharani suite with 10 windows and a fort view. The relaxing and romantic vegetarian restaurant is decorated with sari curtains and floor cushions.

Some other budget hotels in the old city: **Blue House** (☎ 2621396; Moti Chowk; bluehouse36@ hotmail.com; s Rs150, d Rs250-1500; 🗶) Certainly blue, this rambling old house has a variety of individually decorated rooms and some very steep stairs. Beware of competitors with similarly named hotels.

Yogi's Guest House (☎ 2643436; r Rs350-850, s/d without bathroom Rs200/250) This classic travellers' hangout, situated at the base of the fort walls, boasts numerous highly variable rooms and a rooftop restaurant.

Saji Sanwri Guest House (☎ 2440305; www.saji sanwri.com; Gandhi St, City Police; s Rs350, d Rs350-1700; 🔀) This 350-year-old *haveli* has several flowery rooms with private bathrooms. The family still lives here, and was scooping out a swimming pool in the sitting-room when we visited.

MIDRANGE

Krishna Prakash Heritage Haveli (KP Haveli; ☎ 2633448; www.kpheritage.com; Nayabas, Killikhana; s/d standard Rs850/1050, deluxe Rs1550/1750, ste from Rs2450; 🔀 🖳) This multilevel heritage hotel is a good-value choice; it's close to the clock tower but filled with peace. The rooms are well proportioned and nicely decorated with good-sized bathrooms. To escape the heat of the day there is an undercover swimming pool, and for the cool of the night a relaxing terrace restaurant.

Shahi Guest House (☎ 2623802; wwwshahiguesthouse .com; r from Rs900-1800; 🔀) Shahi is an interesting guesthouse developed from a 350-year-old zenana (women's quarters). There's lots of cool stone, and narrow walkways surrounding a petite courtyard. The rooms are individual and cosy and the family are charming. There is a delightful rooftop restaurant with views.

our pick Devi Bhawan (☎ 2511067; www.devi bhawan.com; Ratanada Circle; r standard/semideluxe/deluxe Rs950/1200/1500; 🔀 🖳 📶 🍽) A charming hotel surrounding a verdant oasis shaded by majestic neem trees. As well as being the most peaceful place in Jodhpur it is also excellent value. There's a superb pool and a good restaurant. The three categories of rooms range from simple to sumptuous, though all are spacious, clean and comfortable and decorated with colourful textiles and traditional furnishings.

Newtons Manor (☎ 2430686; www.newtonsmanor .com; 86 Jawahar Colony, Ratanada; r Rs1095-2195; 🔀 🖳) Strictly Victorian in manner, Newtons Manor has eight elegant rooms fussily decorated with lots of antique furniture. It offers excellent home cooking, though pride of place goes to the good-sized billiard table. There's an eternally ungrateful tiger in the sitting room. Internet access and pick-up are complimentary.

Heritage Kuchaman Haveli (☎ 2547787; www .kuchamanhaveli.com; inside Merti Gate; r Rs1200-3500; 🔀 🍽) This recently renovated *haveli* has a maze of different-sized rooms in a well-proportioned building a short walk from the clock tower. Furnishings are heavy and the decorations are closer to kitsch than traditional. With some of the rough edges yet to be smoothed out, it seems a little overpriced.

Ratan Vilas (☎ /fax 2614418; www.ratanvilas.com; Old Loco Shed Rd, Ratanada; r standard/deluxe/super deluxe Rs1500/2000/2500; 🔀) Built in 1920 by the great polo player Maharaja Ratan Singhji of Raoti, this beauty from a bygone era is the real deal. It's quintessential colonial India, with manicured lawns, spacious, spotless rooms and exceptional staff who prepare wonderful meals.

Haveli Inn Pal (☎ 2612519 www.haveliinnpal.com; Gulab Sagar; r Rs1800-2350; 🔀) This smaller sibling of Pal Haveli is accessed through the same grand entrance, but it exists around to the right in one wing of this grand *haveli*. It's a simpler, more dollar-friendly heritage experience, with 12 comfortable rooms and its own rooftop restaurant – a mere chapati toss from Indique at Pal Haveli. The tariff includes breakfast and taxes.

Karni Bhawan (☎ 2512101; www.karnihotels.com; Palace Rd; s/d Rs2200/2750, ste Rs4000; 🔀 🖳 🍽) A remodelled colonial bungalow that feels eerily motel-like and is popular with groups. It is still good for families, thanks to the peaceful lawns, village-theme restaurant and large, though unshaded, pool. Rooms are heavy with traditional furnishings, but are clean and spacious.

Pal Haveli (☎ 3293328 www.palhaveli.com; Gulab Sagar; standard r Rs2500, royal heritage r Rs4000; 🔀 🖳) Set around a courtyard and built by the *thakur* (nobleman) of Pal in 1847, this is the best and most attractive original *haveli* in the old city. There are 21 charming, individual rooms, mostly large and decorated in tasteful, traditional heritage style. Plus there is an excellent rooftop restaurant, Indique.

TOP END

Ranbanka Palace (☎ 2512801; Airport Rd; r Rs5000-12,500; 🔀 🖳 🍽) This museum-like edifice next to Ajit Bhawan is cheaper than its Siam sibling, but a lot less polished. Still, rooms are cavernous, with Persian rugs and four-poster beds.

Ajit Bhawan (☎ 2513333; www.ajitbhawan.com; Airport Rd; r Rs9000-15,000; 🔀 🖳 🍽) Ajit Bhawan is set back from dusty Airport Rd in splendid gardens. Behind the gracious main heritage building, the accommodation is a series of comfortable thatched stone cottages with traditional furnishings. There's a sensational swimming pool (nonguests Rs562), a fine-dining restaurant and a gift shop.

Taj Hari Mahal Palace (☎ 2439700; www.tajhotels .com; 5 Residency Rd; r garden view/pool view Rs12,000/14,000; ❂ ▣ ▨) This modern Taj Group hotel uses traditional flourishes to good effect. It is centred on a courtyard featuring a huge swimming pool, and the luxurious rooms can be had for hefty discounts when occupancy is low.

Umaid Bhawan Palace (☎ 2510101; www.tajhotels .com; Umaid Bhawan Rd; r Rs25,000-42,000; ste Rs85,000-144,000; ❂ ▣ ▨) This colossal honey-coloured art deco palace looks a little too like a parliament building, but is well worth a visit, if not a night of luxury in a remote palace wing. It has a tennis court, an indoor swimming pool, lush lawns and several restaurants.

Eating
RESTAURANTS

Hotel Priya & Restaurant (☎ 2547463; 181-2 Nai Sarak, Sojati Gate; mains Rs25-60; ❂ 6am-midnight) If you can handle the traffic fumes, this street-facing place has a certain cheerful clamour, and serves up reliable North and South Indian cuisine. The thalis (Rs50) are good and there are sweets, too.

Mid Town (☎ 2637001; Station Rd; mains Rs40-100; ❂ 7am-11pm) Mid Town is fine dining with a choice of seating, live folk music and great veg food. It serves Rajasthani specialities, including some particular to Jodhpur, such as *chakki-ka-sagh* (wheat dumpling cooked in rich gravy) and *kabuli* (vegetables with rice, milk, bread and fruit). The Rajasthani thali costs Rs100.

Jharokha (☎ 2614615; Hotel Haveli, Makrana Mohalla; mains Rs60-80; ❂ 7.30am-10.30pm) The rooftop terraces of the Hotel Haveli host one of the best vegetarian restaurants in Jodhpur. As well as the excellent food and views there's nightly entertainment of traditional music and dance. The dishes include Rajasthani specialities and traditional North Indian favourites, as well as pizza, pasta and pancakes for the homesick.

Kalinga Restaurant (☎ 2615871; Station Rd; mains Rs85-180; ❂ 8am-11pm) This restaurant near the train station is smart and popular, with a bright, classy ambience and AC. It has a well-stocked bar, and tasty veg and nonveg North Indian dishes – tandoori and curries. Try the *lal maans*, a mouthwatering Rajasthani mutton curry.

our pick **Indique** (☎ 3293328; Pal Haveli, Gulab Sagar; mains Rs85-200; ❂ 7am-11pm) This refined candle-lit rooftop terrace is the perfect place for a romantic dinner. Even murky Gulab Sagar glistens at night and the views to the fort, clock tower and Umaid Bhawan are superb. The food is traditional tandoori and North Indian curries and you won't be disappointed by the old favourites – butter chicken and *rogan josh*. On your way, drop into the delightful 18th Century Bar with saddle bar stools and enough heritage paraphernalia to have you ordering pink gins.

On the Rocks (☎ 5102701; mains Rs75-270; ❂ lunch 12.30-3.30pm, dinner 7-11pm) This leafy garden restaurant (candle-lit in the evening) is frequented by families and tour groups. It has tasty Indian cuisine, including lots of barbecue options, a small playground and a cave-like bar, Rocktails (open 7.30pm to 11pm), with a dance floor (couples only).

Mehran Terrace (☎ 2549790; Mehrangarh; veg/non-veg thali Rs540/600; ❂ 7.30-10.30pm) Dining on one of the fort's lofty terraces is unsurpassably romantic and, while the service won't win any awards, the thali is rich and constantly refilled. The candle-lit, well-spaced tables, live music and traditional dancing, all 140m above the city, make for an unforgettable occasion. Don't forget to book.

Umaid Bhawan Palace (Umaid Bhawan Rd; ☎ 2510101; mains Rs650-1750) There is a selection of elegant eateries here. Risala (open 1pm to 3pm and 7.30pm to 11pm), celebrating the famous Jodhpur Lancers (Risala means cavalry), is a relaxed fine-dining experience with Indian and continental dishes, including Rajasthani specialities. Behind Risala on the colonnaded western verandah is Pillars (6.30am to 11pm) a breezy coffee shop and informal à la carte eatery sharing the same menu. There are sublime views across the lawn towards Mehrangarh.

QUICK EATS
Omelette Shop (Sadar Market; mains Rs10-15) Just through the gate (by the inner arch – surrounded by imitators) on the northern side of the square, the Omelette Shop claims to go through several thousand eggs a day – the egg man has been doing his thing for over 30 years. Two tasty, spicy boiled eggs cost Rs10,

and an oily two-egg omelette with chilli, coriander and four pieces of bread Rs15.

Agra Sweets (MG Rd; sweets Rs10, lassis Rs12) This sweet shop, opposite Sojati Gate, sells good lassis, as well as delectable Jodhpur specialities such as *mawa ladoo* (a milk sweet made with sugar, cardamom and pistachios, wrapped in silver leaf) and the baklava-like *mawa kachori*.

Drinking

While you're in Jodhpur, try a glass of *makhania* lassi, a filling saffron-flavoured variety of that milky goodness.

Shri Mishrilal Hotel (Clock Tower, Sadar Market; lassis Rs15; 8am-10pm) At the clock tower, this place is nothing fancy,but whips up the most superb creamy *makhania* lassis. These are the best in town, probably in all of Rajasthan, possibly in all of India.

Five Star Fruit Juice (112 Nai Sarak; small/large fruit juice Rs25/30; 9am-10pm) The pick of the fruit-juice bunch, this hole-in-the-wall juice shop serves superfresh combinations in a traveller-friendly atmosphere.

Coffee drinkers will find the precious beans and espresso machines at **Cafe Sheesh Mahal** (Pal Haveli, Clock tower; 10am-11pm); the rooftop Coffee Bar at the **Govind Hotel** (Station Rd); and, for those who need their dose of double-shot espresso, a branch of **Cafe Coffee Day** (Jaljog Circle, Sardapura; 10am-11pm).

For other forms of liquid refreshment, pull up an elephant-foot stool at the **Trophy Bar** (Umaid Bhawan Palace; Umaid Bhawan Rd; 11am-3pm & 6-11pm).

Shopping

The usual Rajasthani handicrafts are available here, and Jodhpur is famous for antiques. However, we recommend that you do not buy genuine antiques as the trade in antique architectural fixtures is contributing to the desecration of India's cultural heritage (beautiful old *havelis* are often ripped apart for their doors and window frames). Most places can make you a piece of antique-style furniture and prices aren't bad. The greatest concentration of showrooms is along Palace Rd.

The best bets for quality replica antiques are **Ajay Art Emporium** (2510269; Palace Rd), **Rani Handicrafts** (2638785; www.ranihandicrafts. com; Palace Rd), **Maharani Art Exporters** (2639226; Tambaku Bazaar) or **Rajasthan Arts & Crafts House** (2653926; Palace Rd).

Around the clock tower are various spice shops, but these are mainly for tourists, with prices to match, and there have been complaints about quality; however, the hugely successful **MV Spices** (5109347; www.mvspices .com; Vegetable Market, Clock tower; 10am-9pm) does have genuine spices and excellent service. If you would like to buy spices at local prices, head westwards from the clock tower along Tambaku Bazaar towards Navchokiya in the old city. You will pass a small square, past which you will find some small spice shops. Authentic Kashmiri saffron costs around Rs250 per gram, though there's plenty of the cheaper central European stuff around, so be on guard.

Other recommended shops:

Kaman Art (www.kamanart.blogspot.com; Old Fort Rd, Killikhana; 10am-8pm) This tiny contemporary art gallery features the work of about 40 painters from all over India.

Krishna Art & Crafts (1st fl, Tija Mata ka Mandir) A good place to gain knowledge of traditional garments. It also has a large range of carpets and shawls.

Shri Rani Sati Cloth Store (117 Sardar Market) This small store to the left of the clock tower as you enter the market is good for block-printed fabrics.

Getting There & Away
AIR

Air India (2510757; Airport Rd; 10am-1.15pm & 2-4.30pm) has flights to Delhi (Rs5200) via Jaipur (Rs3600), and to Mumbai (Rs6400) via Udaipur (Rs3600). **Jet Airways** (5102222; Room 4, Osho Apartments, Residency Rd) also flies to Delhi (via Jaipur) and Mumbai (via Udaipur). **Kingfisher** (1800 2333131; www.flykingfisher.com) flies daily to Jaipur (Rs4000), Jaisalmer (Rs3300) and Udaipur (Rs3200).

BUS

There are **RSRTC buses** (enquiries 2544686) to Mt Abu (express Rs165, seven hours), Jaisalmer (express/deluxe Rs105/175, 5½ hours, half-hourly), Ahmedabad (Rs240/266, 10/12 hours, six daily), Udaipur (Rs147/157, 6½ hours, seven daily), Jaipur (express/deluxe/AC Rs188/200/322, 7½ hours, half-hourly), Ajmer (Rs115/121/200, 4½ hours, half-hourly), Bikaner (Rs136/146, 5½ hours), Delhi (deluxe/AC Rs388/731, 12½–14 hours, five daily).

Numerous private bus companies, including **Mahadev Travels** (2633927; Station Rd), have offices opposite the train station and in the

RAJASTHANI SOUND & MOVEMENT

From rustic resonators to thunderous kettledrums, Rajasthani instruments are fascinating devices often handcrafted by the musicians themselves. They include the *morchang*, a hand-held trumpet that plays fast in-and-out sounds; the *sarangi*, a popular bowed instrument; and the *kamayacha*, a 16-stringed *langa* speciality that is played with a long bow of horse-tail hair. The *kharta* (a metal castanet) is a favourite with saints and seers, while the *algoza* of the Ajmer region is the South Asian equivalent of a bagpipe.

Rajasthan is a living study in ethno-musicology. Songs are often inspired by daily life – the drawing of water or the preparation of a meal – though Rajasthanis will at times turn to the haunting ballads of Moomal Mahendra, Dhola-Maru and other legendary lovers and heroes. There are two traditional classes of musicians in Rajasthan: the *langas* of western Rajasthan, who are favoured mostly by Muslim audiences and have a distinct Sufi flavour, and the *manganiars*, whose breaks possess a more Hindustani bent.

Then there are the *sapera* snake charmers who blow into two-tubed *poongas*, and the *bhopas*, priestlike singers who play the village circuit in times of sickness or poor harvest. The *mirasis* and *jogis* of Mewar are famed for their gurgling voices – *jogis* sing without accompaniment – while the *maand* are highly sophisticated folk singers, once heard only in royal courts.

Where there is song, there is also dance, and Rajasthanis are never backward in shuffling forward. Aside from the Holi festival staple, the *ghooma gait* – a series of gentle, graceful pirouettes – there is the *teerah taali* of the Kamad community in Pokaran, a boisterous dance in honour of the theft deity Baba Ramdeo. It's an unusual spectacle in which men play a four-stringed instrument called a *chau-tara* while the women move with dozens of *manjeeras* (small cymbals) tied to their bodies.

In Shekhawati the *kacchi ghodi* is skilfully performed on horses. Holding swords aloft, riders move to the beating of drums, while a singer narrates the exploits of notorious bandits. In Bikaner, Jasnathis, revered for their tantric powers, dance on flaming coals until the music peaks and the dancers fall into a trance, while the drum dance of Jalore sees five men with huge drums strapped around their necks accompany a sword-swallower who simultaneously juggles.

Concerts and dances are held regularly for tourists in all major cities, usually in upmarket hotels. Tour operators can arrange a visit to the villages – particularly in the west – and an unforgettable backstage pass to rhythmic Rajasthan.

street leading to the Ranchodji Temple. They serve destinations such as Jaisalmer (seat/sleeper Rs130/200), Udaipur (Rs140/200), Bikaner (Rs130/180), Jaipur (Rs150/220) and Ajmer (Rs110/180). Private buses leave next to Sardarpura cinema, though you can go to the ticket offices and be transferred from there.

Haveli Tours & Travels (☎ 9414295539; Hotel Haveli, Makrana Mohalla) has a daily coach departing for Udaipur (Rs450) at 8am, which stops at the company's resort in Ghanerao village for lunch and visits Ranakpur on the way.

TRAIN

The computerised **railway booking office** (Station Rd; ☺ 8am-8pm Mon-Sat, 8am-1.45pm Sun) is between Jodhpur train station and Sojati Gate. There's a tourist quota (Window 788).

To Jaisalmer, the 4059/60 *Delhi–Jaisalmer Express* departs at 6.10am, arriving in Jaisalmer (sleeper/3AC Rs157/411) at 1pm. The 4809/10 *Jodhpur–Jaisalmer Express* departs every night

at 11.25pm, arriving in Jaisalmer at 5.30am. The latter originates in Jodhpur so the departure time is more reliable.

To Delhi, the 2461/2 *Mandore Express* leaves Jodhpur at 7.30pm, stops at Jaipur (sleeper/3AC Rs180/450) at 1am, arriving in Delhi (Rs276/720) at 6.30am. The 2466 *Ranthambhore Express* departs at 5.55am and arrives in Jaipur (sleeper/3AC Rs180/450) at 10.35am, and Sawai Madhopur (Rs220/561) at 1.15pm. There are several daily trains to Bikaner, including the 4708 *Ranakpur Express* departing at 10.05am and arriving in Bikaner (sleeper/3AC Rs148/386) at 4pm.

The weekly 4889 *Thar Express* (aka *JU MBF Link Express*, see p1178) runs from Jodhpur to Karachi, Pakistan. In Jodhpur it leaves from Raikabad station every Saturday at 1am and reaches Munabao on the border at 7am. From Munabao you change to a Pakistan train (assuming you have a Pakistan visa).

Getting Around

The airport is only 5km from the centre. It costs about Rs70 in an autorickshaw or Rs180 in a taxi.

There's a taxi stand near the main train station. Most autorickshaw/taxi journeys around town should cost around Rs50/90 and a day's sightseeing in a taxi around Rs300.

AROUND JODHPUR
Mandore

Situated 9km north of Jodhpur, Mandore was the capital of Marwar prior to the foundation of Jodhpur. Today, its **gardens** with rock terraces make it a popular local attraction. The gardens also contain a mixture of dark-red stupas and cenotaphs of Jodhpur rulers, including the soaring memorial to Maharaja Dhiraj Ajit Singh.

The 18th-century **Hall of Heroes** contains 15 solemn Hindu deities and local heroes carved out of a rock wall, coated with fine plaster and luridly painted.

Mandore Guest House (☎ 0291-2545210; www.mandore.com; s/d Rs500/100, with AC Rs950/1250; 🕸) has delightful rounded mud-walled cottages set in a leafy garden. There's good home-cooked food. It's also connected with a local NGO working to address drug addiction and provide medical services; there are short-term volunteer programs.

Rohet

A heritage hotel in the small village of Rohet, about 40km south of Jodhpur, **Rohet Garh** (☎ 02936-268231; www.rohetgarh.com; s/d from Rs4000/5000, ste Rs7500; 🕸 🖳 🐾) is where Bruce Chatwin wrote *The Songlines* and William Dalrymple began *City of Djinns*. The heritage rooms are indeed inspirational but, for those who want to escape the desk, there's a gorgeous pool, extensive shaded lawns and the chance to ride a proud Marwari steed. Even better, you can ride your way to the luxury tented desert camp (Rs9000 per person) and see wildlife and visit villages on the way.

Osiyan

This ancient Great Thar Desert town, 65km north of Jodhpur, was an important trading centre between the 8th and 12th centuries. It was dominated by the Jains, who left a legacy of exquisitely sculptured, well-preserved temples. **Sachiya Mata Temple** (🕑 6am-7.15pm) is an impressive walled complex. The **Mahavira Temple** (admission Rs5, camera/video Rs40/100;

🕑 6am-8.30pm) surrounds an image of the 24th *tirthankar*, said to be over 2000 years old and formed from sand and milk.

In October, Osiyan hosts the **Marwar Festival** (p167).

Prakash Bhanu Sharma, a personable Brahmin priest, has an echoing **guesthouse** (☎ 02922-274331; s/d Rs250/300), geared towards pilgrims, near Mahavira Temple.

Gemar Singh (p233) lives near Osiyan and arranges homestays, camping, desert walks and camel safaris in the area.

There are regular buses from Jodhpur (Rs30, 1½ hours, half-hourly). The 4059 *Delhi–Jaisalmer Express* departs Jodhpur at 6.20am and arrives at Osiyan (2nd class/sleeper/3AC/2AC Rs41/121/213/283) at 7.14am and then departs for Jaisalmer (Rs78/135/350/475). On the return journey, the 4060 departs Jaisalmer at 4pm, stops in Osiyan at 9pm and arrives in Jodhpur at 10pm. A return taxi from Jodhpur costs Rs800.

Nagaur

Nagaur, 135km northeast of Jodhpur, has the massive, 12th-century restored ruins of **Ahhichatragarh** (Fort of the Hooded Cobra; Indian/foreigner Rs15/50, camera Rs25/100, guide Rs100; 🕑 9am-1pm & 2-5pm), which has a unique water-recycling system. At the ruins' heart is a richly painted Rajput–Mughal palace complex.

The town hosts the **Nagaur Camel Fair** (p167) in January/February.

Hotel Bhaskar (☎ 01582-240100; Station Rd; s/d from Rs200/300) is friendly, close to the train station and bearable.

About 1km from the fort, **Hotel Mahaveer International** (☎ 243158; Vijai Vallabh Chowk; r Rs350-550, with AC Rs95011500; 🕸) has uninspiring but comfortable rooms aimed at business travellers. Inspect rooms in the old and new wings before deciding. There's a relatively clean and cool vegetarian restaurant (mains Rs85 to Rs175) and a bar.

At fair time, **Royal Tents** (Rs11,500) are available in the fort grounds. These must be booked in advance through **Balsamand Lake Palace** (☎ 0291-2572321; www.jodhpurheritage.com). The **RTDC** (s/d Rs6500/7500) also has tents.

There are hourly buses from Jodhpur (Rs70, three hours).

Khichan

This small village, 140km northwest of Jodhpur, is a twitcher's dream, and a regular stop on long-range camel safaris. From late August/early September to the end of March, you can witness masses of demoiselle cranes circling noisily and then descending on the surrounding lakes and fields at around 7am and 5pm to feed on grain spread around by the villagers. Ten kilometres further west is **Phalodi**, an old caravan centre with beautiful *havelis* and some reasonable places to stay, including the recommended **Lal Niwas** (☎ 02925-223813; www.welcomeheritagehotels.com; Dadha's Mohalla, Phalodi; s/d Rs2400/2650; 🐱 🗩).

There are regular bus services between Phalodi and both Jodhpur (Rs86, 3½ hours) and Jaisalmer (Rs72, 3½ hours). There are daily buses between Phalodi and Khichan (Rs5, 15 minutes). A return autorickshaw to Khichan will cost Rs70.

JAISALMER
☎ 02992 / pop 58,286

The fort of Jaisalmer is a breathtaking sight: a massive sandcastle rising from the sandy plains like a mirage from a bygone era. No place better evokes exotic camel-train trade routes and desert mystery. However, the armies of wind turbines marching across the desert and laying siege are making it harder for visitors to take that imaginary leap back in time.

Ninety-nine colossal bastions encircle the still-inhabited narrow streets. Inside are shops swaddled in bright embroideries, a royal palace and numerous businesses looking for your tourist rupee. Despite the commercialism it's hard not to be enchanted by this desert citadel. Beneath the ramparts the twisting lanes of the old city conceal magnificent *havelis* of crumbling beauty. The *havelis*, the fort and its enclosed palace are all carved from the same golden honey sandstone, hence the city's designation as the Golden City.

But Jaisalmer is in trouble. Overcrowding and poor drainage have seen the fort sinking into Trikuta hill. Add to that the high hassle factor for camel safaris and your money, and the atmosphere can be a touch strained.

The town hosts the **Desert Festival** (p167) in February.

History
Founded in 1156, Jaisalmer's strategic position on the camel-train routes between India and Central Asia brought it great wealth. The merchants and townspeople built magnificent houses and mansions, exquisitely carved from wood and sandstone.

Jaisalmer experienced its share of sieges and sackings, with an inevitable Rajput *jauhar* in the 13th century after a siege that lasted eight years. However, it escaped too much harm from the Mughals. On good terms with Delhi, the 17th-century city saw another golden age and the construction of more grand buildings.

The rise of shipping and the port of Bombay (Mumbai) saw Jaisalmer's decline. Partition and the cutting of the trade routes through to Pakistan seemingly sealed the city's fate, and water shortages could have pronounced its death sentence. However, the India–Pakistan Wars of 1965 and 1971 revealed Jaisalmer's great strategic importance.

Today it's an important stop on another lucrative trade route – tourism rivals the military base as the city's economic mainstay.

Orientation
The fort is entered via the First Fort Gate. Within the fort walls is a warren of narrow, paved streets, replete with Jain temples and the old palace of the former ruler – it's small enough that you'll never get lost for long.

The main market, Bhatia Market, and most of the city's attractions and important offices surround the fort to the north.

Information
There are plenty of places to check email, both inside and outside the fort. Cost is around Rs40 per hour.

Bhatia Newsagency (Bhatia Market; 🕙 9am-9pm) Stocks newspapers (try after 11am for the latest copy), magazines, and new and secondhand books in various languages.

Byas & Co (Bhatia Market; 🕙 9am-9pm) Has photographic supplies and flash cards and develops pictures.

Dr Dube (☎ 9414149500; consultation Rs500) A recommended doctor who will visit your hotel.

Thomas Cook (☎ 253679; Gandhi Chowk; 🕙 9.30am-7.30pm Mon-Sat) Changes cash and travellers cheques.

Main post office (Hanuman Circle Rd; 🕙 10am-5pm Mon-Fri, 10am-1pm Sat) West of the fort.

Police station (☎ 252233; Hanuman Circle Rd)

Post office (🕙 10am-5pm Mon-Fri, 10am-1pm Sat) Just outside the fort gate; sells stamps and you can post postcards.

SBBJ ATM (Shiv Rd)

Tourist Reception Centre (☎ 252406; Gadi Sagar Rd; 🕙 9am-6pm Mon-Fri) One kilometre southeast of the First Fort Gate; this friendly office has a free maps, the latest bus and train timings, and a small list of paying-guest houses.

Sights

JAISALMER FORT

The fort is a warren of narrow streets paved with sandstone, harbouring a palace, temples, and hundreds of deceptively simple-looking *havelis*. Built in 1156 by the Rajput ruler Jaisala, and reinforced by subsequent rulers, the fort crowns the 80m-high Trikuta hill. A significant proportion of the old city's population resides within the fort walls, which have 99 bastions around their circumference. It's an extraordinary, resonant experience to wander around the lanes inside this living museum.

Maharaja's Palace

The fort is entered through a forbidding series of massive gates leading to a large courtyard fronted by the elegant seven-storey palace. The square was formerly used to review troops, hear petitions and present extravagant entertainment for travelling dignitaries. Part of the palace is open to the public as the **Fort Palace Museum** (Indian/foreigner Rs30/250, Indian camera/video Rs50/150, foreigner video Rs150; ☾ 8am-6pm Mar-Jul, 9am-6pm Aug-Feb). The foreigner admission includes an audio guide and camera fee. With floor upon floor of fascinating rooms that peep creepily on the outside world, the highlights are the mirrored and painted Rang Mahal, a small gallery of finely wrought 15th-century sculptures and the spectacular 360-degree views from the top.

Jain Temples

Within the fort walls is a mazelike, interconnecting complex of seven beautiful yellow sandstone **Jain temples** (admission Rs20, camera/video Rs50/100), dating from the 12th to the 16th centuries. Opening times have a habit of changing, so check with the caretakers. The intricate carving rivals that in Ranakpur or Mt Abu, and has an extraordinary quality because of the soft, mellow stone. **Chandraprabhu** (☾ 7am-noon) is the first temple you come to and is dedicated to the eighth *tirthankar*, whose symbol is the moon. Around the upper gallery are 108 marble images of Parasnath, the 22nd *tirthankar*. To the right of this temple is **Rikhabdev Temple** (☾ 7am-noon).

Behind Chandraprabhu is **Parasnath Temple** (☾ 11am-noon), which you enter through a

beautifully carved *torana* (architrave); it has a lovely, brightly painted ceiling. A door to the south leads to the **Shitalnath Temple** (☾ 11am-noon), dedicated to the 10th *tirthankar*, with an eight-metal image. A door in the north wall leads to the beautiful **Sambhavanth Temple** (☾ 11am-noon) – in the front courtyard, Jain priests grind sandalwood for devotional use. Steps lead down to the **Gyan Bhandar** (☾ 10-11am), a fascinating, tiny library of ancient manuscripts, founded in 1500. The remaining two temples are **Shantinath** (☾ 11am-noon), and **Kunthunath** (☾ 11am-noon), below it, both built in 1536, and with plenty of sensual carving.

Laxminath Temple

This Hindu temple is simpler than the Jain temples, with a brightly decorated dome. Devotees offer grain, which is distributed before the temple. There is a repoussé silver architrave around the entrance to the inner sanctum, and a heavily garlanded image enshrined within.

HAVELIS
Patwa-ki-Haveli

Most magnificent of all the *havelis*, its stonework like honey-coloured lace, Patwa-ki-Haveli towers over a narrow lane. It was built between 1800 and 1860 by five Jain brothers who were brocade and jewellery merchants. It's most impressive from the outside. The first of the five sections is opened as the privately owned **Kothari's Patwa Haveli Museum** (Indian/foreigner Rs40/100, camera/video Rs30/40; ☾ 9am-6pm), which richly evokes 19th-century life. Next door is the forlorn and empty (apart from pigeons and bats) government-owned **haveli** (Indian/foreigner Rs10/50).

Salim Singh-ki-Haveli

This private **haveli** (admission Rs15, camera/video Rs15/50; ☾ 8am-6pm Oct-Apr, 8am-7pm May-Sep) has an amazing, distinctive shape – the top storey mushrooms out into a mass of carving, with graceful arched balconies surmounted by pale blue cupolas. It was built about 300 years ago; part of it is still occupied. Salim Singh was a fearsome prime minister when Jaisalmer was the capital of a princely state.

Nathmal-ki-Haveli

This late-19th-century **haveli** (admission free; ☾ 8am-7pm) was also a Jaisalmer prime minister's house and is still partly inhabited. It drips

RAJASTHAN

JAISALMER

0   500 m
0   0.2 miles

To Vyas
Chhattris (200m);
Bada Bagh (7km);
Ramgarh (70km)

To Gorbandh Palace
Hotel (1km);
Rang Mahal (7km);
Amar Sagar (7km);
Mool Sagar (9km);
Lodhruva (15km);
Sam Sand Dunes (42km)

To Airport
(2.5km)

To Fort Rajwada (2km);
Khuri (1.50km);
Khichan (160km);
Jodhpur (285km);
Bikaner (330km)

To Khuri (40km);
Barmer (153km)

Gadi Sagar

To Efe Guest
House (100m)

INFORMATION

Bhatia Newsagency	1 F4
Byas & Co.	2 F4
Main Post Office.	3 B2
Police Station	4 B2
Post Office	(see 34)
SBBJ ATM.	5 C3
Thomas Cook.	6 F4
Tourist Reception Centre.	7 D3

SIGHTS & ACTIVITIES

Boat Hire.	(see 21)
Desert Culture Centre &	
Museum.	8 D3
Fort Palace Museum.	(see 14)
Ganesh Travels.	9 C3
Government Museum.	10 A2
Jain Temples.	11 C3
Jaisalmer Folklore	
Museum	12 E3
Laxminath Temple	13 C2
Maharaja's Palace.	14 C2
Nathmal-ki-Haveli.	15 C2
Patwa-ki-Haveli.	16 D2
Sahara Travels.	17 D2
Salim Singh-ki-Haveli.	18 D2
Satyam Tours.	19 F4
Thar Safari.	20 F4
Tilon-ki-Pol.	21 E3
Trotters.	(see 34)

SLEEPING

Artist's Hotel.	22 C1
Desert Moon.	23 B1
Hotel Fort View.	24 D2
Hotel Golden City.	25 D3
Hotel Jaisal Palace.	26 C2
Hotel Nachana Haveli.	27 F4
Hotel Ratan Palace.	(see 29)
Hotel Renuka.	28 C1
Hotel Swastika.	29 F4
Hotel The Royale	
Jaisalmer.	30 D3
Jawahar Niwas Palace.	31 A1
Mandir Palace Hotel.	32 C2
Residency Centrepoint	
Paying Guest House.	33 C2
Shahi Palace.	34 C3
Shree Giriraj Palace.	35 C2

EATING

Bhang Shop.	(see 40)
Chandan Shree Restaurant.	36 B2
Desert Boy's Dhani.	37 C3
Dhanraj Bhatia Sweets.	38 C2
Kanchan Shree Ice Cream.	39 D2
Little Italy.	40 C2
Mohan Juice Bar.	41 C2
Natraj Restaurant.	(see 18)
Saffron.	42 F4
Trio.	43 F4

SHOPPING

Gandhi Darshan Emporium.	44 B2
Hari Om Jewellers.	45 C2

Khadi Gramodyog Bhavan.	46 C3
Zila Khadi Gramodan	
Parishad.	47 C1

TRANSPORT

Bicycle Hire.	48 F4
Bus Stand.	49 C3
Crown Tours.	50 B2
Jeep Stand.	51 B2
Private Bus Stand.	52 C3
RSRTC Bus Stand.	53 F3
Train Reservation Office.	54 F2

with carving, and the 1st floor has some beautiful paintings that used 1.5kg of gold. A doorway is surrounded by 19th-century British postcards from the prime minister's time, and there's also a picture of Queen Victoria. The left and right wings were the work of two brothers, whose competitive spirit apparently produced this virtuoso work – the two sides are similar, but not identical. Sandstone elephants welcome visitors/shoppers.

GADI SAGAR

This stately tank, south of the city walls, was once the water supply of the city, and there are many small temples and shrines around it. Waterfowl flock here in winter. **Boat hire** (☿ 8am-9pm) costs Rs50 to Rs100 for 30 minutes.

The attractive **Tilon-ki-Pol** that straddles the road down to the tank is said to have been built by a famous prostitute. When she offered to pay to have this gateway constructed, the maharaja refused permission on the grounds that he would have to pass under it to go down to the tank, and he felt that this would be beneath his dignity. While he was away, she built the gate anyway, adding a Krishna temple on top so the king could not tear it down.

MUSEUMS

Next to the Tourist Reception Centre is the **Desert Culture Centre & Museum** (☎ 252188; admission Rs50; ☿ 10am-8pm), which has interesting information on Rajasthani culture, as well as textiles and traditional instruments. A new addition is the interactive mini-DVD presentation which helps bring the static exhibits to life. There's a nightly one-hour **puppet show** (admission Rs50, camera/video Rs20/50) at 6.30pm. Admission to the Desert Culture Centre includes entry to the small **Jaisalmer Folklore Museum** (admission Rs20, camera/video Rs20/50; ☿ 8am-6pm), which has traditional everyday items, ranging from camel ornaments to opium bottles.

The small **government museum** (Indian/foreigner Rs5/10, Mon free; ☿ 10am-4.30pm Sat-Thu) has a limited but well-captioned collection of fossils, puppets and textiles.

Tours

Few travellers visit Jaisalmer without venturing into the desert on a camel. For details see p246.

The Tourist Reception Centre runs sunset tours to the Sam sand dunes (Rs150 per person) at 3pm, returning after sunset. On request, the tours to Sam may stop at Kanoi, 5km before the dunes, from where it's possible to get a camel to the dunes in time for sunset (around Rs250).

Sleeping

Staying within the fort is no longer a sustainable practice, as overdevelopment and increased water consumption has put excessive strain on the fort's structure. For this reason Lonely Planet has taken the decision not to list *any* hotels or restaurants within the fort. We encourage travellers to make an ethical decision when visiting Jaisalmer.

Unfortunately, a few hotels are really into the high-pressure selling of camel safaris. To avoid any drama, be clear from the outset if you are not interested. Many hotels have a stingy 9am check-out time.

BUDGET

You'll find a cluster of places north of Gandhi Chowk.

Hotel Shree Giriraj Palace (☎ 252268; r Rs150-200, without bathroom Rs80) This hotel has cheerful and simple rooms with tiny bathrooms in an old building. There's a delightful rooftop restaurant.

Hotel Swastika (☎ 252483; swastikahotel@yahoo.com; Chainpura St, Ghandi Chowk; s/d from Rs150/200; r with AC Rs600, s without bathroom Rs100; ☒) In this well-run and clean place the only thing you'll be hassled about is to relax. Rooms are simple and unfussy; some have balconies, and there are plenty of restaurants nearby.

Hotel Renuka (☎ 252757; hotelrenuka@rediffmail.com; s/d Rs300/350, with AC Rs600/650, without bathroom Rs100/150; ☒ 🖳) Spread over three floors, Renuka has squeaky clean rooms – the best rooms have balconies and bathrooms. It's been warmly accommodating guests since 1988, so management knows its stuff. The roof terrace has great fort views and a restaurant, and the hotel offers free pick-up from the bus and train stations.

Hotel Ratan Palace (☎ 253615; s/d Rs300/350, with AC Rs600/650, without bathroom Rs100/150; ☒) Run by the same family as Hotel Renuka, and with the same friendly approach, it has a similar range of bright rooms.

Hotel Golden City (☎ 251664; www.hotelgoldencity.com; s/d Rs150/200, s/d with air cooler Rs200/300, r with AC Rs600; ☒ 🖳) Off Gadi Sagar Rd, this busy hotel feels like a mini-budget resort, with a wide range of rooms, satellite TV, two restaurants and a pool (nonguests Rs100).

GOLDEN CITY BLUES

One of the world's most endangered monuments has witnessed rapid deterioration in recent years owing to unprecedented pressure on the fort's porous drainage system. Since 1993, three of the 12th-century bastions have collapsed. Thanks to the actions of concerned people, in particular the British-registered charity **Jaisalmer in Jeopardy** (☎ /fax 020-73524336; www.jaisalmer-in-jeopardy .org; 3 Brickbarn Close, London SW10 0TP), great gains have been made in sealing many of the porous drains over recent years. However, another enemy is the thoughtless building work and disposal of building rubble and waste. While awareness is improving, ironically some of the fort's inhabitants may be harming their own livelihood by not taking conservation measures seriously.

For information on saving Jaisalmer, contact the **Jaisalmer Conservation Initiative** (☎ 011-24631818; www.intach.org; 71 Lodi Estate, New Delhi 110 003), run by the Indian National Trust for Art and Cultural Heritage (INTACH), or Jaisalmer in Jeopardy.

Artist's Hotel (☎ 252082; artisthotel@yahoo.com; Artist Colony, Suly Dungri; s Rs180, d Rs300-450) This Austrian-owned establishment, which helps local musicians, offers simple rooms above a bustling artists' colony. There are regular concerts and views of the fort from the roof.

Hotel Fort View (☎ 252214; r Rs200-600) A stalwart of the budget scene. It was undergoing much-needed renovations when we visited. The final result remains to be seen, but access and views to the fort are hard to beat.

MIDRANGE

Shahi Palace (☎ 255920; www.shahipalacehotel.com; off Shiv Rd; r Rs300-750, with AC Rs750-1750; ✖ 🖳) Shahi Palace is a warm and friendly option with lovely decorated rooms featuring window seats, sandstone walls, and carved stone or wooden beds. The relaxing rooftop has a fantastic fort view and excellent food.

Residency Centrepoint Paying Guest House (☎ / fax 252883; residency_guesthouse@yahoo.com; s/d Rs400/450) Near the Patwa-ki-Haveli, this friendly, family-run, heritage guesthouse has clean, spacious doubles. Room 101 has a lovely balcony, and the rooftop has superb fort views.

Desert Moon (☎ 250116, 9414149350; www.desert moonguesthouse.com; Achalvansi Colony; s Rs500-800, d Rs700-1200; ✖) Beneath the Vyas Chhatris sunset point, Desert Moon is in a peaceful location, about a 10-minute walk from Gandhi Chowk. The guesthouse is run by a friendly Indian–Kiwi couple who can organise camel safaris and pick-up from the train and bus stations. The rooms are cool, clean and comfortable with polished stone floors and sparkling bathrooms.

Hotel Jaisal Palace (☎ 252717; www.hoteljaisalpalace .com; s/d Rs600/750, with AC Rs900/1100; ✖ 🖳) Behind the Mandir Palace Hotel is this clean, well-run place, though the rooms tend to be rather small and characterless. Those on the south side have fort-facing balconies.

Fifu Guest House (☎ 252656; www.fifuguesthouse .com; Bera Rd; r Rs1050-1650; ✖ 🖳 🛜) This hotel is a little out of the way though the beautiful, colour-themed sandstone rooms afford a peaceful and pleasant stay, and the rooftop has tremendous fort views and a great vegetarian restaurant. It's down a dusty lane, so carry a torch if walking home at night.

Hotel The Royale Jaisalmer (☎ 9252808707; www .hotelroyalejaisalmer.com; Dhibba Para; s/d Rs1250/1500, ste Rs2200-2500; ✖ 🖳) South of the fort gate, this bright new hotel has made a good first impression with its spacious, colourful, traditionally decorated rooms and its multicuisine rooftop veg restaurant. The tariff includes breakfast.

Hotel Nachana Haveli (☎ 252538; www.nach anahaveli.com; Ghandi Chowk; s/d Rs2250/2500, ste s/d Rs3250/3500; ✖ 🖳) This 280-year-old sandstone *haveli* is a fascinating hotel. The raw sandstone rooms have arched stone ceilings, and the ambience of a medieval castle. They are beautifully, sumptuously and romantically decorated, though some are a little on the dark side, lacking much in the way of natural light. The courtyard and common rooms come with all the Rajput trimmings, including swing chairs and bearskin rugs.

Jawahar Niwas Palace (☎ 252208; jawaharniwas@ yahoo.co.in; s/d Rs3000/3900; ste Rs4800; ✖ 🖳 🏊) Like a desert mirage, this forlorn beauty stands 1km west of the fort in a barren desert garden. Rooms are elegant and spacious with soaring ceilings and generous bathrooms. Those upstairs at the front have the best fort views. There's a fabulous pool sunk into a walled garden.

Rang Mahal (☎ 250907; www.hotelrangmahal.com; r/ste from Rs3500/Rs8100; ✖ 🖳 🏊) Heading west along Sam Rd, you'll find this impressive hotel with big bastions and divine suites. There's an excellent restaurant and a spectacular pool (nonguests Rs200, or swim with lunch or dinner included for Rs500). Rooms with a fort-facing verandah are the best.

TOP END

Mandir Palace Hotel (☎ 252788; www.welcomheritage hotels.com; Gandhi Chowk; s/d Rs3800/4200; ⊠) Just inside the town walls is this sprawling royal palace with divine stonework. The restored rooms are atmospheric and fabulous, though it's best to avoid the new additions. It's a rather big place that lacks a friendly atmosphere and the staff can be distant.

Gorbandh Palace Hotel (☎ 253801; crs@udaipur .hrhindia.com; Sam Rd; d/ste Rs6000/7000; ⊠ 🖳 🖳) This grandiose modern hotel is blissfully quiet and particularly good for families. It's constructed from local sandstone, and the friezes around the hotel were sculpted by local artisans. There's a superb pool (nonguests Rs200) and restaurant.

Fort Rajwada (☎ 2786835; sales@fortrajwada.com; s/d Rs4750/6300, ste Rs11,000-13,000; ⊠ 🖳 🖳) This is a modern place built according to the ancient Indian design principles of *vaastu* – something like feng shui. All materials in the hotel are natural. An opera designer created the traditional interior, so it's suitably dramatic.

Eating
RESTAURANTS

Chandan Shree Restaurant (Hanuman Chowk; mains Rs20-100; thalis Rs40-100) Always busy, and rightfully so, this is a popular dining hall churning out tasty, spicy all-you-can-eat Gujarati, Rajasthani, Punjabi and Bengali thalis.

Desert Boy's Dhani (Seemagram Campus; mains Rs50-100; ⊙ 9am-11pm) This is a popular garden restaurant in an enclosed setting, with a choice of floor seating or tables. It serves yummy, good-value veg dishes.

Trio (☎ 252733; Gandhi Chowk; mains Rs55-200; ⊙ 6.30-10.30am, noon-3pm & 6-11pm) This casual Indian and continental restaurant, with its romantic setting under a tented roof, is a good, relaxing eating option. There are reliably good vegetarian and nonvegetarian dishes, musicians playing in the evening, and a great fort view. Barbecue fans will enjoy the tandoori thali.

Natraj Restaurant (☎ 252667; mains Rs75-160; ⊙ 8am-11pm) This is an excellent place to sample veg and nonveg in multicuisine forms, and the rooftop has a satisfying view of the upper part of the Salim Singh-ki-Haveli next door.

Saffron (☎ 252538; mains Rs80-140; ⊙ 7am-3pm & 7-10.30pm) Run by the folks in charge of Nanchana Haveli, the veg and nonveg food here is superb, plus it has a great setting on a sandstone terrace overlooking Gandhi Chowk. Evening time is especially atmospheric. The Indian dishes are hard to beat, though the Italian comes a close second.

Little Italy (☎ 253397; First Fort Gate; mains Rs95-130; ⊙ 8.30am-11pm) Though it's run by the same family in charge of the Bhang Shop, you won't have to worry about bhang pizzas. But if the munchies strike, pizza is a logical choice, and here you'll find superb all-veg antipasti, pasta, pizza, salad and dessert served in a cosy indoor restaurant or on a delightful terrace with cinemascopic fort views.

QUICK EATS

Dhanraj Bhatia Sweets (Sadar Bazaar; sweets per 100g Rs13) This place in Bhatia Market has been churning out traditional sweet treats for 10 generations. It is renowned in Jaisalmer and beyond for its local specialities, such as *ghotua ladoos* (sweetmeat balls made with gram flour) and *panchadhari ladoos* (made with wheat flour).

Kanchan Shree Ice Cream (Gadisagar Rd; lassis Rs15-30; ⊙ 9am-10pm) This friendly little dairy whips up homemade ice cream (Rs10) and delicious *makhania* lassis, as well as numerous other flavours. You can also order lassis with a dollop of ice cream or fizzy ice-cream sodas.

Bhang Shop (First Fort Gate; medium/strong lassis Rs50/60) As well as lassis, bhang cookies, cakes and sweets are sold here; camel safari packs are a speciality. Bhang can be deceptively strong and does not agree with everyone – see p1151.

Shopping

Jaisalmer is famous for stunning embroidery, bedspreads, mirror-work wall hangings, oil lamps, stonework and antiques. Watch out when buying silver items: the metal is sometimes adulterated with bronze.

There are several good *khadi* (homespun cloth) shops around town selling fixed-price carpets, shawls and woven garments, including **Zila Khadi Gramodan Parishad**, **Khadi Gramodyog Bhavan** (Seemagram) and **Gandhi Darshan Emporium** (Gandhi Chowk).

JAISALMER CAMEL SAFARIS

Trekking around Jaisalmer by camel is the most evocative and fun way to sample desert life. The best time to go is from October to February.

Before You Go

Competition between safari organisers is cut-throat and standards vary. Hotels don't have their own camels – they're independently owned – so hoteliers and travel agencies are just go-betweens.

Beware of operators who claim they run (and charge for) three-day safaris, when you actually return after breakfast on the third day – hardly value for money.

The realistic minimum price for a safari is about Rs450 to Rs750 per person per day. For this you can expect breakfast of porridge, tea and toast, and lunch and dinner of rice, dhal and chapati. Blankets are also supplied. You may have to bring your own mineral water. Of course, you can pay for greater levels of comfort: tents, stretcher beds, better food, beer etc – but take care, because some travellers have paid extra for promised upgrades only to find out afterwards their safari was much the same as that of people who paid less.

Take care of your possessions, particularly on the return journey. Any complaints you do have should be reported, either to the **Superintendent of Police** (☎ 252233) or the **Tourist Reception Centre** (☎ 252406; Gadi Sagar Rd; ☽ 9am-6pm Mon-Fri).

What to Take

Women should consider wearing a sports bra, as a trotting camel is a bumpy ride. A wide-brimmed hat (or Lawrence of Arabia turban), long trousers, toilet paper, sunscreen and a water bottle (with a strap) are also recommended. It can get cold at night, so if you have a sleeping bag bring it along, even if you're told that lots of blankets will be supplied.

Which Safari?

Several independent agencies have been recommended. **Ganesh Travels** (☎ 250138; ganesh travel45@hotmail.com), inside the fort, is owned by camel drivers and gets good reports. **Sahara Travels** (Map p242; ☎ 252609; sahara_travels@yahoo.com), by the first fort gate, gets good reviews, and is run by Mr Bissa, alias Mr Desert. **Trotters** (☎ 9414469292; www.trotterscamelsafarijaisalmer.com; Gopa Chowk) prides itself on going further off the beaten trail. Their half-day to 21-day trips start with a jeep ride out of town.

Hari Om Jewellers (☎ 9982032342; 101 Valmiki Colony, Murgi Farm ki Gali) Following the famous footsteps of Hari Om, Roop Kishore Soni is a silversmith who makes delicate silver rings and bracelets. Visitors have commissioned personalised wedding rings here. There's a shop inside the fort, or you can visit the home address listed here.

Getting There & Away

AIR

The airport has been recently reopened though services have been disrupted. Political tension with nearby Pakistan is the usual reason for closure to domestic flights. At the time of writing **Kingfisher Airlines** (www.flykingfisher.com) had a direct service to/from Jodhpur (Rs3300 one way) with various connections from there. **Crown Tours** (☎ /fax 251912), about 350m west of Amar Sagar Gate can handle ticketing.

BUS

The main **RSRTC bus stand** (Map p242; ☎ 251541) is near the train station. Fortunately, all buses start at a more convenient bus stand southwest of the fort. Private buses leave from Air Force Circle.

There are regular buses to Jodhpur (express/deluxe Rs137/176, 5½ hours), Bikaner (express Rs140, seven hours), and Jaipur (deluxe Rs391, 12 hours) via Ajmer (Rs308, 12 hours).

You can book private buses through most travel agencies (many congregate around Hanuman Chowk) – if you can't get a ticket, check with a few agencies, as sometimes people will tell you a bus is full when it's not. Destinations include Bikaner (seat/sleeper Rs150/200, seven hours), Jaipur (Rs200/300, 12 hours), Jodhpur (Rs120/180, 5½ hours), Ajmer (Rs180/300, 12 hours) and Ahmedabad

Satyam Tours (☎ 250773; ummedsatyam@yahoo.com; Gandhi Chowk) and Thar Safari (☎ 250227; tharsafari@yahoo.com; Gandhi Chowk) offer variations on the circuit.

Remember that no place is perfect – recommendations here should not be a substitute for doing your own research.

Whoever you go for, insist that all rubbish is carried back to Jaisalmer.

In the Desert

Don't expect dune seas: the Great Thar Desert is mostly arid scrubland that is sprinkled with villages. You will often come across fields of millet, and children herding flocks of sheep or goats, whose neck-bells tinkle in the desert silence – a welcome change from the sound of farting camels.

Camping out at night, huddling around a tiny fire beneath the stars and listening to the camel drivers' songs is magically romantic.

The reins are fastened to the camel's nose peg, so the animals are easily steered. Stirrups make the journey a lot more comfortable. At resting points the camels are unsaddled and hobbled; they limp away to browse on nearby shrubs while the camel drivers brew chai or prepare food. The whole crew rests in the shade of thorn trees.

Most safaris last three to four days and, if you want to get to the most interesting places, this is a bare minimum unless a significant jeep component is included.

Many travellers opt for 'nontouristic' safaris. You are driven in a jeep for around 30km or so and then head off on your steed, shunning the major sights and avoiding encountering other groups.

The traditional circuit takes in **Amar Sagar** (admission Rs20, camera/video Rs50/100), where there's a garden, dried-up step-wells and a Jain Temple; the deserted ruins of **Lodhruva** (p248); **Bada Bagh** (admission Rs50, camera/video Rs20/50), a fertile oasis with an old dam and sandstone-sculpted royal *chhatris* now surrounded by a forest of wind turbines; the dunes of **Sam** (p248); and various abandoned villages.

If you're really pressed for time you could opt for a half-day camel safari (which involves jeep transfers).

The camel drivers will expect a tip or gift at the end of the trip; don't neglect to give them one.

(Rs200/300). These prices are for direct buses; be aware that some private buses (except those going to Bikaner) require a change at Jodhpur. Some travellers have found themselves in Jodhpur with a useless onward ticket, so make sure you clarify what you're getting.

TRAIN

There's a **train reservation office** (⊗ 8am-8pm Mon-Sat, 8am-2pm Sun) at the station.

There are numerous trains to/from Jodhpur, including the 4809 *Jodhpur–Jaisalmer Express*, which leaves Jaisalmer at 11.15pm, arriving in Jodhpur (sleeper/3AC Rs157/411) at 5.20am. On the return trip, the 4810 leaves Jodhpur at 11pm and arrives in Jaisalmer at 5am. The 4060 *Jaisalmer–Delhi Express* leaves at 4pm and calls at Jodhpur (sleeper/3AC Rs157/411) at 10pm, Jaipur (Rs256/690) at 5am, and Delhi (Rs322/877) at 11.05am. The other way, the

4059 leaves Delhi at 5.40pm and arrives in Jaisalmer 19 hours later.

The 4701 *Jaisalmer–Bikaner Express* leaves Jaisalmer at 10.45pm, arriving in Bikaner (sleeper/AC chair Rs163/336) at 4.05am. On the return trip, the 4702 leaves Bikaner at 11.25pm and arrives in Jaisalmer at 5.30am.

Getting Around

BICYCLE

A good way to get around is by bicycle. There are a number of hire places, including one near Gandhi Chowk (Rs5/30 per hour/day).

JEEP

It's possible to hire jeeps (maximum of five people per jeep) from the stand on Gandhi Chowk. To Khuri or the Sam sand dunes expect to pay Rs550 per jeep return with a one-hour wait.

RAJASTHAN

RAJASTHAN

AROUND JAISALMER
Lodhruva
About 15km northwest of Jaisalmer are the deserted ruins of Lodhruva, the ancient capital before the move to Jaisalmer. The **Jain temples**, rebuilt in the late 1970s, are sole reminders of the city's former magnificence. The **main temple** (admission Rs20, camera/video Rs50/100; ☾ dawn-dusk) enshrines a finely wrought silver image of Parasnath, the 23rd *tirthankar*. Apparently a cobra lives in the complex. A taxi will cost about Rs700 and will include a visit to Amar Sagar.

Sam Sand Dunes
The **Desert National Park** (Indian/foreigner Rs5/10, vehicle Rs100) has been established in the Great Thar Desert near Sam village. One of the most popular excursions is to the sand dunes on the edge of the park, 42km from Jaisalmer.

This is Jaisalmer's Sahara-like desert, with huge, silky, undulating folds of sand. It's best to be here at sunrise or sunset, and many camel safaris spend a night at the **dunes**. This place has become a massive tourist attraction, so don't count on a solitary desert sunset experience. Nonetheless, it's still possible to frame pictures of solitary camels against lonely dunes.

One tragic consequence of dune-hungry hordes is the debris and rubbish lying around. Please don't contribute to this problem.

There are three daily buses from Jaisalmer to Sam (Rs25, 1½ hours). The Jaisalmer Tourist Reception Centre runs sunset tours to the dunes (see p240).

Khuri
☎ 03014
A small village located 40km southwest of Jaisalmer, Khuri is an hour and a world away from the fort's swarming trade. It has its own desert sand dunes, and remains a peaceful place (apart from holiday periods), with houses of mud and straw decorated like Persian carpets. There are plenty of camps of mud huts, and camel drivers eager to take you on the dunes, but no shop-lined streets or pancake restaurants. Once the excitement of sunset is over, you have desert solitude and the brilliant star-studded sky at night to look forward to.

Places to stay in Khuri are basic, fanless thatched mud huts with wall paintings, set around a campfire area. All places listed here provide meals and arrange camel safaris.

At **Badal House** (☎ 274120; per person huts/r without bathroom incl full board Rs150/300) you can stay in a spotless family compound with a few charming huts and freshly painted rooms. Badal Singh is a gentle man who charges Rs500 for a camel safari with a night on the dunes. Don't let touts warn you off, and if you arrive by car ask your driver not to demand a commission as this is not included in the above prices.

Mama's Guest House (☎ 274042; gajendra_sodha2003@yahoo.com; huts per person without bathroom incl half-board Rs500) is a long-running place with a circle of whitewashed, cosy huts. A basic/luxurious overnight camel safari costs Rs650/900. **Gangaur Guest House** (☎ 274056; hameersingh@yahoo.com; huts per person Rs750, without bathroom Rs500) is yet another circle of snug huts. It offers packages including a camel ride, dinner with traditional dance entertainment, and breakfast for Rs750.

There are several buses to Khuri from Jaisalmer (Rs22, one hour).

Barmer
☎ 02982 / pop 83,517
Situated 153km south of Jaisalmer, Barmer is famed for woodcarving, carpets, embroidery, block printing and other handicrafts. The small shops in the colourful Sadar Bazaar are a good place to start – in the narrow backstreets you'll find artisans at work. Otherwise, this desert town has little for the visitor.

In March, Barmer holds the **Thar Festival**; there's also a large **cattle fair** around the same time (see p167).

Hotel Krishna (☎ 220785; r Rs300, with AC Rs700; ✸), on the main street leading from the train station, is friendly and has acceptably clean rooms.

From Barmer there are frequent buses to/from Jaisalmer (Rs66, 2½ hours) and Jodhpur (Rs95, four hours).

Trains to/from Barmer include the 4059 *Delhi–Jaisalmer–Barmer Express,* which bifurcates and departs Jodhpur at 6.10am to arrive at Barmer (sleeper/3AC Rs125/321) four hours later. The return train (4060A) departs Barmer at 6.30pm and arrives at Jodhpur at 10pm, where it joins up with the 4060 from Jaisalmer and continues to Delhi. The weekly *Thar Express* (p238) runs from Jodhpur to Pakistan via this line.

Pokaran
At the junction of the Jaisalmer, Jodhpur and Bikaner roads, 110km from Jaisalmer, **Pokaran**

Fort (admission Rs50, camera or video Rs30; ☺ 7am-7pm) is a dusty berry-coloured sandstone strong-hold that overlooks a tangle of narrow streets lined by balconied houses. It dates from the 14th to 17th centuries and once had charge of 108 villages; part of it is now the hotel **Fort Pokaran** (☎ 02994-222274; www.fortpokaran.com; d from Rs3500/7000; ❄ ⚖). There's not much to see here, but a stop breaks the journey between Jodhpur and Jaisalmer.

It was near Pokaran in May 1998 that India detonated five nuclear devices, leaving a huge crater that's strictly off-limits.

Buses run frequently to/from Jaisalmer (Rs40, 2½ hours,). There are also buses to Bikaner (Rs98, five hours) and to Jodhpur (Rs65, three hours).

BIKANER
☎ 0151 / pop 529,007

Bikaner is a vibrant, dust-swirling desert town with a fabulous fort and an energising out-post feel. Close to the fort lies the old walled city, a medieval maze of narrow, irregular streets decorated with rubbish heaps, dark-red sandstone *havelis* and exquisitely painted Jain temples.

Bikaner was founded in 1488 by Rao Bika, a descendant of Jodha, Jodhpur's founder, and was another important staging post on the great caravan trade routes.

Camel safaris continue to grow in popular-ity here, as travellers chase the silken dark-ness of a desert dawn without the hassle of Jaisalmer. People also come here to visit the Karni Mata Temple in Deshnok, 30km south, where pilgrims worship thousands of holy rats, or Kolayat, 54km south, a temple town where sadhus float in tyre tubes.

There's a **camel festival** (p167) in January.

Orientation & Information

The old city is encircled by a 7km-long, 18th-century city wall with five entrance gates. The fort is northeast, outside the walls.

Most hotels now have internet access; oth-erwise there are plenty of cafes with rates of Rs20 per hour. There are numerous ATMs, including a Corporation Bank ATM opposite the fort, and Bank of Baroda, Axis Bank and SBBJ ATMs near the train station.

Try www.realbikaner.com for information about the city.

Bank of Baroda (opp train station; ☺ 10am-2pm Mon-Fri, 10am-12.30pm Sat) Changes travellers cheques only.

Modi Cyber Cafe (Station Rd; internet per hr Rs20; ☺ 9am-10pm) It looks a little grotty, but there's internet access, ice cream, a place to sit, secure left-luggage facility (Rs30) and even the chance to have a shower between trains.

State Bank of Bikaner & Jaipur Ambedkar Circle (☺ noon-4pm Mon-Sat); Public Park (☺ 10am-2pm Mon-Fri, 10am-noon Sat) Changes cash and travellers cheques.

Tourist Reception Centre (☎ 2226701; RTDC Hotel Dhola Maru; ☺ 10am-5pm Mon-Sat) Hands out a free map.

Sights
JUNAGARH

Constructed between 1588 and 1593 by Raja Rai Singh – a general in the army of the Mughal emperor Akbar – this most im-pressive **fort** (admission incl audio guide & camera fee Rs250, Indian/foreigner incl guide Rs20/100, camera/video Rs30/100; ☺ 10am-4.30pm) has a 986m-long wall with 37 bastions, a moat and two entrances. The **Surajpol** (Sun Gate) is the main entrance to the fort. Here you will be accosted by pri-vate guides, even though your ticket includes either the audio guide or an official fort guide (leaving every 15 minutes or so from the ticket office). The palaces within the fort are on the southern side, and make a picturesque ensem-ble of courtyards, balconies, kiosks, towers and windows.

It's the interiors that make the fort stand out. Highlights include the **Diwan-i-Khas**, the **Phool Mahal** (Flower Palace), which is deco-rated with paintings and carved marble pan-els, the **Hawa Mahal**, the **Badal Mahal** and the **Anup Mahal**.

To visit at a leisurely pace, choose the audio guide or ask for your own guide – the larger groups rush around. The nearby **Prachina Bikaner Cultural Centre & Museum** (Indian/foreigner Rs10/50, camera Rs20; ☺ 9am-6pm) is a well-labelled museum featuring over-the-top costumes, jewellery and a rare glimpse of everyday paraphernalia.

LALGARH PALACE

Set about 3km north of the centre, the red-sandstone **Lalgarh Palace** was built by Maharaja Ganga Singh (1881–1942) in memory of his father, Maharaja Lal Singh. It's out-and-out grandeur, with overhanging balconies and delicate latticework. The **Sri Sadul Museum** (Indian/foreigner Rs10/20, camera/video Rs20/50; ☺ 10am-5pm Mon-Sat) features lots of fascinating old

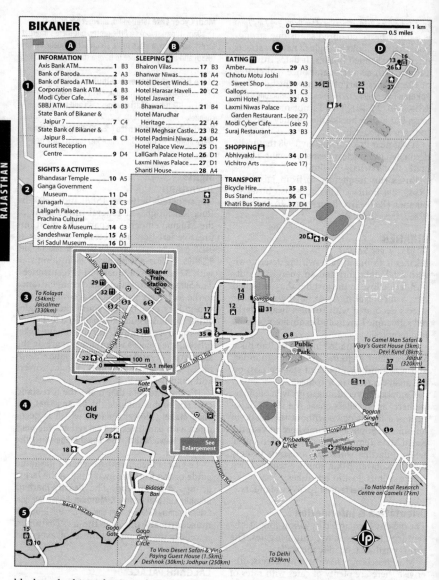

BIKANER

black-and-white photographs and some evocative maharaja accessories. You can stay in the palace (see p252 for details).

OTHER SIGHTS

The narrow streets of the old city conceal a number of old *havelis* and a couple of notable **Jain temples**. The temples date from around the

15th century. **Bhandasar Temple** is particularly beautiful, with yellow-stone carving and dizzyingly vibrant paintings. It's said the foundations contain 40,000kg of ghee, and the floor still gets greasy in summer. **Sandeshwar Temple** is smaller, but has some fine carving.

The **Ganga Government Museum** (Indian/foreigner Rs5/10; 10am-4.30pm Tue-Sun) houses a small, well-displayed collection of sculptures, handicrafts, musical instruments and gold paintings. Entrance is to the back left of the building.

The **National Research Centre on Camels** (admission Rs10, camera Rs20, rides Rs30, guides Rs100; 🕒 2-6pm) is about 8km east of the town centre. Here you can visit baby camels, go for a ride and look around the small museum. The on-site Camel Milk Parlour doesn't look much but can whip up a lassi for Rs5. The round trip, including a half-hour wait at the camel farm, is around Rs150 for an autorickshaw or Rs300 for a taxi.

Sleeping
BUDGET
The cheapest budget options are along horrendously noisy Station Rd. The better budget options are to the north, east or south of town.

Vino Guest House (☎ 2270445; www.vinodesert safari.com; Gangasharhar Rd; s/d from Rs100/200, huts Rs300; 🖳 🐾) Three kilometres south of town, this is a great choice in the family house of a recommended camel-safari operator. Air-cooled rooms are great value, the garden huts are simple and comfy, and there is a plunge pool (Rs50 for nonguests) to cool off in. The home-cooked food is excellent and cooking classes are free.

Shanti House (☎ 2543306, inoldcity@yahoo.com; New Well; r Rs200-350) This is a tiny *haveli* inside the old city, behind the Jain school, with just four bargain rooms (minimum two-night stay) and a narrow staircase, all brightly decorated, and with the bustle of Bikaner at your doorstep. Owner Gouri is a knowledgeable guide who can walk you around the old city (Rs30 per hour) and organise tours to Deshnok (Rs450).

Vijay's Guest House (☎ 2231244; www.camelman .com; Jaipur Rd; r Rs300-800; 🐾) About 3km south of town, this is a home away from home with 10 spacious, light-filled rooms and a garrulous host. Vijay is a camel expert and another recommended safari operator. His family home and guesthouse is an ideal base for taking a safari, with a comfortable common room and garden restaurant. Vijay offers free pick-up and drop-off from the train and bus stations.

Hotel Marudhar Heritage (☎ 2522524; hmheritage 2000@yahoo.co.in; Ganga Shahar Rd; s Rs250-900, d Rs350-999; 🐾 🖳) A short walk from the train station, this friendly choice is well kept and well run, with rooms to suit most budgets. Rooms are plain, comfortable and good value, and are popular with locals. There are nice views from the roof, but meals are served in your room.

Hotel Harasar Haveli (☎ 2209891; www.harasar .com; Harasar House, Near Karni Singh Stadium; r Rs300-2000) Harasar is a popular budget (and midrange) choice, and a great place to meet other travellers. There are 33 rooms covering a huge range in prices. The deluxe rooms are probably worth the added expense, but check that everything is working before deciding on one. There's a great rooftop restaurant, or you can retreat to the tented courtyard dining area during the heat of the day.

MIDRANGE
Hotel Meghsar Castle (☎ 2527315; www.hotelmegh sarcastle.com; 9 Gajner Rd; r Rs350-1050; 🐾 🖳) North of town, this hotel has clean, old-fashioned rooms, with surfaces of terrazzo and tiles, some echoingly large. It's a well-run place, with meals available in the garden, though the front rooms can cop a bit of traffic noise.

Hotel Padmini Niwas (☎ 2522794; padmini_hotel@ rediffmail.com; 148 Sadul Ganj; s/d Rs450/550, with AC Rs750/850; 🐾 🖳 🐾) A fabulous place to unwind from the rush of the city. Has clean (though carpeted) rooms, and a chilled-out, helpful owner. The lawn area is a revelation, boasting one of the town's few outdoor pools (nonguests Rs100).

Hotel Palace View (☎ 2543625; hotelpalaceview@ gmail.com; Lalgarh Palace Campus; s Rs500-900, d Rs600-1000; 🐾) This hotel near Lalgarh Palace is extraordinarily spotless, and the hosts take great pride in accommodating their guests. The decoration is spare and the ambience subdued, but this place still makes for a wise midrange choice for those looking for a little peace.

Hotel Jaswant Bhawan (☎ 2548848; www.hotel jaswantbhawan.com; Alakhsagar Rd; s Rs550-1650, d Rs700-1800; 🐾 🖳) An agreeable heritage house, though it appears to be slowly decaying, with a peaceful small garden. The pricier rooms are clean, and spacious, and the food is first rate.

ourpick **Bhairon Vilas** (☎ /fax 2544751; hbhairon@ rediffmail.com; s Rs800-1600, d Rs900-1800; 🐾 🖳) This hotel is run by the former Bikaner prime minister's great-grandson Harsh Singh, and his grandfather's stately residence is an atmospheric place to stay. Rooms are eclectically decorated with antiques and old family photographs. There's a garden restaurant, a bar straight out of the Addams Family, a very tasteful clothing and art shop, as well as village tours, safaris etc on offer.

Hotel Desert Winds (☎ 2542202; www.hoteldesert winds.in; s/d Rs900/1100, deluxe Rs1100/1300; ✖ ▢) Next door to Harasar Haveli, this venture has spotless and spacious but rather bland rooms, and a friendly, relaxed atmosphere. It's run by a retired director of Rajasthan Tourism.

TOP END

Bhanwar Niwas (☎ 2529323; www.bhanwarniwas.com; Rampuria St; s/d from Rs3500/4500; ✖ ▢) This superb heritage hotel has been developed out of the beautiful Rampuri Haveli – a gem in the old city. It has a range of individual, usually spacious, and always delightfully decorated rooms. Comfortable common rooms drip with antiques and are arranged around a large internal courtyard, which doubles as a venue for cultural programs.

Lallgarh Palace Hotel (☎ 2540201; www.lallgarh palace.com; s/d from Rs4500/5000; ✖ ▢ ▣) Part of the maharaja's palace (p249), dating from 1902, it has well-appointed, old-fashioned rooms around a courtyard – pricier ones are huge, with high ceilings. There's an indoor pool.

Laxmi Niwas Palace (☎ 2202777; www.laxminiwas palace.com; s/d/ste Rs6000/7000/15,000; ✖ ▢ ▣) Also part of the Lalgarh Palace, this hotel is roundly regarded as the more beautiful sibling, boasting exquisite stone carving and plush furnishings. Guest rooms are enormous, elegant and evocative. Of the three internal restaurants the Gulab Mahal, the former royal library, is the most striking. There's also a charming garden restaurant (see below).

Eating

RESTAURANTS

Laxmi Hotel (Station Rd; mains Rs20-30) A simple place, Laxmi is open to the street, with tasty, fresh vegetarian thalis – you can see the roti being flipped in front of you.

Amber (☎ 2220333; Station Rd; mains Rs40-100; Station Rd; ☯ 6am-10pm) With russet walls and mirrors, and a staid, no-nonsense look, Amber is well thought of and popular for veg fare.

Suraj Restaurant (☎ 2542740; Rani Bazaar off Station Rd; mains Rs45-65; ☯ 6am-10.30pm) Situated beneath the Suraj Hotel, this is Bikaner's best-value thali joint. Choose between the 'mini', 'deluxe' and the highly recommended 'special', which can be shared between two people.

Laxmi Niwas Palace Garden Restaurant (☎ 2202777; mains Rs80-150; ☯ noon-3pm & 7.30-10.30pm) A lovely place to eat, this is an excellent garden restaurant, with music in the evenings. It has two menus – a less pricy and spicier one (with Chinese, South Indian, veg and nonveg North Indian) geared for local tastes, and a pricer one from the hotel's swish interior restaurants. Prices shown here are for cheaper menu.

Gallops (☎ 3200833; opp Junagadh Fort; mains Rs150-200; ☯ 10am-10.30pm) This is a spiffy air-conditioned cafe with a camel leather–clad lounge area with big windows. There is real, and very good, espresso coffee, but at Rs100 a cappuccino, you would have to be keen. The menu also features pricey Indian and Chinese veg and nonveg, including tandoori specials.

QUICK EATS

Bikaner is noted for the *namkin* (spicy nibbles) sold along Station Rd, among other places.

Chhotu Motu Joshi Sweet Shop (Station Rd; sweets Rs5-30) Bikaner's most-loved sweet stop has an assortment of Indian treats. Try the milk sweet *rasmalai* (cottage cheese dumplings; Rs16) and saffron *kesar cham cham* (milk, sugar and saffron-flavoured sweet; Rs6).

Modi Cyber Cafe (Station Rd; ice creams Rs10-15; ☯ 9am-10pm) Here you'll find quality ice cream, as well as a place to sit, check your email, leave your luggage and even take a shower.

Shopping

Abhivyakti (Ganganagar Rd; ☯ 8.30am-6.30pm) Run by the Urmul Trust, a local NGO supported by Urmul Dairy (which has an outlet next door), Abhivyakti sells textiles produced by skilled artisans from local villages. The profits of Urmul Trust labelled items go to the producers to help fund a girls' college. The Urmul Trust welcomes volunteers (see p1169).

Vichitra Arts Based at Bhairon Vilas (p251), this shop sells beautiful, individual clothes. There's an adjoining workshop with a resident artist painting miniatures.

Getting There & Away

BUS

The bus stand is 3km north of the centre, almost opposite the road leading to Lalgarh Palace. If your bus is coming from the south, ask the driver to let you out closer to the centre. There are numerous private and RSRTC buses to Udaipur (express Rs293, 12 hours), Ajmer (Rs147, seven hours), Jaipur via Fatehpur and Sikar (Rs182, seven hours), Jodhpur (Rs135, 5½ hours), Jaisalmer (Rs174, eight hours) and Agra (Rs300, 12 hours). There are also buses to Delhi (Rs253, 10 hours),

BIKANER CAMEL SAFARIS

Bikaner is an excellent alternative to the Jaisalmer safari scene and is becoming increasingly popular with travellers. There are fewer organisations running safaris here, so the hassle factor is quite low. There are fewer sights than around Jaisalmer, but it's great if you want to ride in empty desert scrub, sleep on dunes and see life in desert villages. Longer safaris (to Jaisalmer or Jodhpur) are highly recommended. A simple day and one night on the dunes costs around Rs1300 per person including meals and transfers. The daily rate gets lower the more days you take.

Recommended operators are **Vino Desert Safari** (☎ 2270445; vino_desertsafari@yahoo.com), which offers half-day to 13-day trips (Rs500 to 1500 per day, depending on how much luxury you require and how much you use a jeep); and the **Camel Man** (☎ 2231244; www.camelman.com), run by Vijay Singh Rathore, which operates safaris ranging from a half-day trip to 14 days (all the way to Jaisalmer), with basic safaris costing Rs650 per day, and more upmarket excursions (beds with sheets are provided) costing from Rs800 to 1600 per day.

some of which run via Jhunjhunu (Rs122, five hours). Private buses to Nawarlgarh (Rs80, four hours) leave from an intersection near the Ganga Government Museum, known as the Khatri bus stand.

TRAIN
To Jaipur, the 2308A *Bikaner–Howrah Superfast* leaves at 6.30pm (sleeper/3AC Rs201/510, seven hours); the 4738 *Bikaner–Jaipur Express* leaves at 9.20pm (sleeper/2AC/1AC Rs178/643/1080, 8½ hours); and the 2467 *Intercity Express* leaves at 5am (2nd class/AC chair Rs114/406, 6½ hours). The 4707 *Ranakpur Express* leaves for Jodhpur (sleeper/3AC/2AC Rs148/386/525, five hours) at 9.45am. The 2464A *Sampark Kranti Express* leaves at 5.20pm (Tuesday, Thursday and Saturday) and arrives at Delhi Sarai Rohilla station (sleeper/3AC Rs293/771) at 5.30am. The 4702 *Bikaner-Jaisalmer Express,* leaves at 11.25pm and arrives in Jaisalmer (sleeper/AC chair Rs160/329) at 5.30am.

Getting Around
An autorickshaw from the train station to the palace should cost Rs30, but you'll probably be asked for more. Bicycles can be hired near Bhairon Vilas (p251) for Rs30 a day.

AROUND BIKANER
Devi Kund
The marble and red-sandstone royal cenotaphs of the Bika dynasty rulers, with some fine frescoes, are 8km east of Bikaner. This peaceful spot is Rs150 return by rickshaw.

Deshnok
The extraordinary **Karni Mata Temple** (www.karni-mata.com; admission free, camera/video Rs20/50; ◷ 4am-10pm) at Deshnok, 30km south of Bikaner, is one of India's weirder attractions. According to legend, Karni Mata, a 14th-century incarnation of Durga, asked the god of death, Yama, to restore to life the son of a grieving storyteller. When Yama refused, Karni Mata reincarnated all dead storytellers as rats, depriving Yama of human souls.

The mass of *kabas* (holy rodents) is not for the squeamish. It's considered auspicious if the rats scamper over your feet. Keep your eyes peeled for a rare white rat – it's good luck if you spot one.

The temple is an important pilgrimage site, so remove your shoes and be respectful. There are at least two buses hourly from Bikaner's Gogo Gate bus stand to Deshnok (Rs20, 40 minutes). A return taxi with a one-hour wait costs Rs500.

Kolayat
Set around a temple-ringed lake 54km south of Bikaner, Kolayat is a small, untouristed town. Adding to its sleepy air are stoned sadhus emerging from the temples who occasionally take to the waters riding tyre tubes. The **Kolayat Mela** (p167) is held in November.

There are a number of inexpensive *dharamsalas* (pilgrims' guesthouses), but most won't accept tourists. It's best visited as a day trip from Bikaner.

There are regular buses from Bikaner (Rs30, 1½ hours).

254

Haryana & Punjab

Welcome to Punjab, the land of the Sikhs. In this compact but luminous pocket of northwest India, *Sat Sri Akal* replaces *Namaste* as the preferred greeting, gurdwaras outnumber temples as places of worship, and turbans have a cheery attitude when it comes to colour: from candyfloss pink and fire-engine red to buttercup yellow and jellybean green.

Punjab (translating to 'Five Waters') is named after the five rivers of the region: the Beas, Jhelum, Chenab, Ravi and Sutlej. With water making such a big splash, it's little wonder that other states turn green with (agricultural) envy. Indeed, fertile Punjab has been affectionately dubbed as India's bread-basket, due to its phenomenal production of wheat (providing roughly 20% of the nation's output). Its well-nourished soils also deliver a bounty of rice, pearl millet, barley, sugarcane, maize, veggies and fruit, as well as almost 15% of India's cotton. And then there are home-grown products of the human variety, with Prime Minister Manmohan Singh and cricketing superstar Harbhajan Singh being two recent sources of Punjabi pride.

From butter chicken to bhangra (music/dance), the work-hard, party-hard Punjabis have carried their vibrant culture far and wide, with more expatriates per capita than any other Indian state. Another spin-off of this globe-trotting population is the sizeable foreign remittances, which have fast-tracked Punjab's economic development. But amid all the modernisation, there's a formidable sense of tradition, witnessed at sites such as Amritsar's Golden Temple – Sikhism's most sacred shrine and one of India's most breathtaking buildings.

Less-visited Haryana split from Punjab in 1966 but shares its capital, Chandigarh. It's best known for the Hindu holy site of Kurukshetra, where good triumphed over evil.

HIGHLIGHTS

- Immerse yourself in the soul-soothing splendour of Amritsar's divine **Golden Temple** (p270), Sikhism's holiest site
- Cheer with pumped-up patriots as they watch Indian and Pakistani soldiers try to out-stomp, out-scowl and out-salute each other at Attari's fantastical **border-closing ceremony** (p275)
- Explore Le Corbusier's uberstructured modernist metropolis before tumbling into the alternate reality of **Nek Chand Fantasy Rock Garden** (p257)
- Pause at **Pinjore Gardens** (p265), one of India's finest Mughal walled gardens, before trundling up to **Morni Hills** (p265) for some green serenity

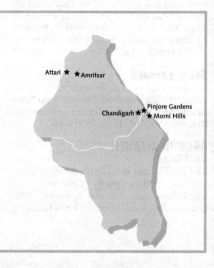

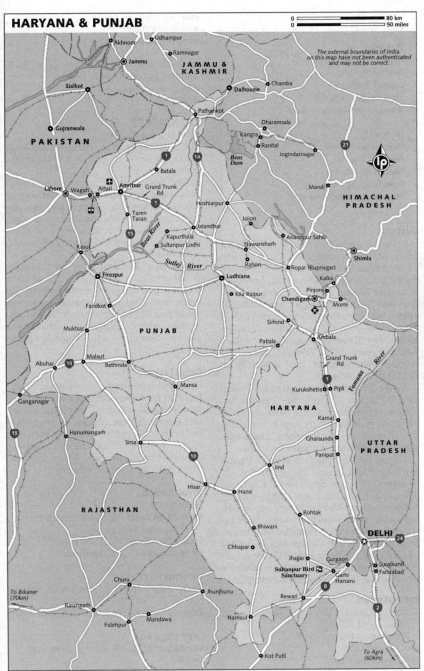

HARYANA & PUNJAB

The external boundaries of India on this map have not been authenticated and may not be correct.

FAST FACTS

Punjab
Population 24.3 million
Area 50,362 sq km
Capital Chandigarh
Main language Punjabi
When to go November to March

Haryana
Population 21.1 million
Area 44,212 sq km
Capital Chandigarh
Main language Hindi
When to go November to March

History

Architectural excavations have revealed that more than 4000 years ago this region was part of the Indus Valley civilisation established by the Harappans. Buddhist relics have been excavated at sites associated with the later Mauryan dynasty in Sanghol, near Ludhiana (p268), while the Kurukshetra district (p265) contains 360 historical sites within a 92-sq-km radius. The Mahabharata mentions Punjab's land and people, while Valmiki is said to have worked on the Ramayana (p69) at Ram Tirath (p271) near Amritsar.

While the Indian campaigns of the Persian king Darius and Alexander the Great reached Punjab before faltering, the more successful Mughal invaders regularly surged through the area. Panipat was where regional domination was won or lost over the next six centuries.

During the 1947 partition of India, Punjab saw horrendous carnage that left hundreds of thousands of people dead (see p52). Later, in 1984, Prime Minister Indira Gandhi's highly controversial decision to militantly remove Sikh separatists – who were championing for an independent Sikh state (to be called Khalistan) – from Amritsar's holy Golden Temple, ignited bloody Hindu–Sikh clashes. In the same year Gandhi was assassinated at her Delhi residence by two of her (Sikh) bodyguards (see p56).

Information

Hotels can quickly fill during weekends and festivals (book ahead).

Read up on the region at:
www.punjabgovt.nic.in
www.haryana-online.com

www.haryanatourism.com
www.citcochandigarh.com
www.chandigarh.nic.in

Websites that may be of interest to Non-Resident Indians (NRIs) include:
www.nrisabhapunjab.in
www.nrizone.in

CHANDIGARH

☎ 0172 / pop 900,914

The capital of Punjab and Haryana, Chandigarh is a Union Territory controlled by the central government.

The modernist architect Le Corbusier's radical design for Chandigarh polarises critics, and this anomaly among Indian cities also splits travellers. Some dislike its grid-esque, rather soulless design, while others relish the city's broad, tree-lined roads and angular sense of order.

Although Chandigarh may lack the razzle-dazzle of its subcontinental (urban) siblings, it offers clean and green respite from life out on the dusty road; is home to the wonderfully wacky Nek Chand Fantasy Rock Garden (one of the country's most visited attractions); and has some of the state's yummiest places to eat.

Orientation

Chandigarh is divided into a series of sectors that are numbered. The main shopping area is located in Sector 17 while most hotels and restaurants are situated in neighbouring Sectors 22 and 35. The train station is 8km from the city centre. The similar-looking streets in Chandigarh's grid design can sometimes make navigation confusing.

Information

BOOKSHOPS

Capital Book Depot (☎ 2702260; Sector 17 E; ◷ 10.30am-2pm & 3.15-8.45pm)
English Book Shop (☎ 2702542; Sector 17 E; ◷ 10.30am-2pm & 3.30-8.30pm Mon-Sat)

INTERNET ACCESS

Each of the central sectors has an internet cafe.
Cyber-22 (Sector 22-C; per hr Rs20; ◷ 9.30am-10pm)

LEFT LUGGAGE

Bus station (☎ 6577050; Sector 43; per day Rs25; ◷ 24hr)

FESTIVALS IN HARYANA & PUNJAB

Kila Raipur Sports Festival (Rural Olympics; www.ruralolympics.net; Feb; Kila Raipur, near Ludhiana, p268)
Three days of sports: bullock-cart races, kabaddi (see p82), strongmen contests, folk dancing and more.

Surajkund Crafts Mela (1-15 Feb; Surajkund, p266) Wildly popular, visiting artisans showcase/sell colourful handicrafts. Delicious food stalls and vibrant cultural performances.

Basant (Feb/Mar; Patiala, p267) Kite-flying, singing and dancing to welcome Spring.

Holla Mohalla (Mar; Anandpur Sahib, p266) Three-day celebration of the Khalsa (Sikh brotherhood): *kirtan* (Sikh hymns), martial-arts demonstrations and re-enactments of past battles.

Baisakhi Festival (www.baisakhifestival.com; 13 or 14 Apr; statewide) Celebrates the onset of the Solar Year and first crop harvest. Festivities include folk dancing.

Baba Sheikh Farid Aagman Purb Festival (Sep; Faridkot, p268) Five days; commemorates this Sufi saint. Cultural performances.

Pinjore Heritage Festival (early Oct; Pinjore Gardens, p265) Three-day festival with music/dance performances, handicraft and food stalls.

Harballabh Sangeet Sammelan (www.harballabh.org; late Dec; Jalandhar, p268) Four-day music festival (in existence for over 130 years) showcasing Indian classical instrumentalists and vocalists.

Gita Jayanti (Nov/Dec; Kurukshetra, p265) Week-long, with cultural events celebrating the Bhagavad Gita's anniversary.

MEDICAL SERVICES

PGI Hospital (☎ 2746018; Post Graduate Institute, Sector 12-A)

Silver Oaks Hospital (☎ 5094125; Phase 9, Mohali) Reputable private hospital.

MONEY

ATMs are plentiful and easy to find.

Thomas Cook (☎ 2745629; Sector 9-D; ⏰ 9.30am-6pm Mon-Sat) Changes foreign currency and travellers cheques. International transfers.

PHOTOGRAPHY

Shri Gurudev (☎ 2704534; Sector 17-D; ⏰ 9.30am-6pm) Good reputation.

POST

Main post office (☎ 2702170; Sector 17; ⏰ 9.30am-4pm Mon-Sat)

TOURIST INFORMATION

Chandigarh Tourism (☎ 2703839; 1st fl, Sector 17-B bus station; ⏰ 9.30am-6pm)

Haryana Tourism (☎ 2702957; Sector 17-B; ⏰ 9am-5pm Mon-Fri)

Himachal Tourism (☎ 2708569; 1st fl, Sector 17-B bus station; ⏰ 10am-5pm Mon-Sat, closed 2nd Sat of month)

Uttar Pradesh Tourism & Uttarakhand (Uttaranchal) Tourism (☎ 2707649; 2nd fl, Sector 17-B bus station; ⏰ 10am-5pm Mon-Sat, closed 2nd Sat of month)

Sights & Activities

CAPITAL COMPLEX

The imposing concrete **High Court**, **Secretariat** and **Vidhan Sabha** (Legislative Assembly), all in Sector 1 and shared by Punjab and Haryana, were designed by Le Corbusier.

The architecturally impressive High Court opened in 1955. A visit inside may be possible from Monday to Friday with prior permission from the Chandigarh Tourism office (left); bring your passport. The internal ramp, the wavy overhanging roof and the colourful supporting slabs are the main features. Courtrooms contain an abstract woollen tapestry designed by Le Corbusier. You can also walk around to the famous **Open Hand** sculpture, another creation of the workaholic Le Corbusier. It symbolises an 'open to give, open to receive' message of peace.

You must enter the High Court via the car park. On the way is a small, well-kept **museum** (☎ 2740071; admission free; ⏰ 10am-5pm Mon-Sat) containing assorted memorabilia including original Le Corbusier sketches and the handcuffs worn by Godse, Mahatma Gandhi's assassin (see boxed text, p54). Most exhibits are on the 1st floor. On request, there's an interesting (free) guided tour.

To visit the huge Secretariat and the silo-like Vidhan Sabha, obtain a permit from the Architecture Department in the **UT Secretariat** (☎ 2741620; Sector 9-D).

NEK CHAND FANTASY ROCK GARDEN

Entering this Chandigarh icon, a 25-acre **garden** (www.nekchand.com; adult/child Rs10/5; ⏰ 9am-6pm Oct-Mar, to 7pm Apr-Sep), is like falling down a rabbit-hole into the labyrinthine interior of one man's mind. Created by Nek Chand (see

HARYANA & PUNJAB

CHANDIGARH

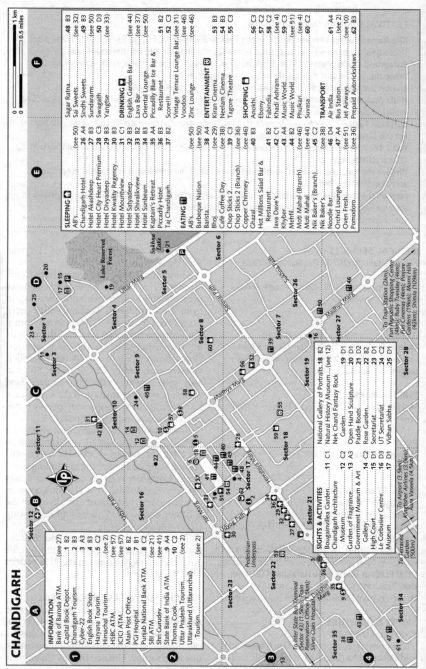

INFORMATION
Bank of Baroda ATM.....................(see 27)
Capital Book Depot..............................1 B2
Chandigarh Tourism.............................2 B3
Cyber-22...3 A3
English Book Shop................................4 B3
Himachal Tourism...............................5 C2
Haryana Tourism..............................(see 2)
HSBC ATM.......................................(see 57)
ICICI ATM.......................................(see 57)
Main Post Office..................................6 B2
PGI Hospital.......................................7 B1
Punjab National Bank ATM...................8 C2
SBI ATM...(see 21)
Shri Gurudev....................................(see 41)
State Bank of India ATM.......................9 A4
Thomas Cook...................................10 C2
Uttar Pradesh Tourism.......................(see 2)
Uttarakhand (Uttaranchal)
  Tourism......................................(see 2)

SIGHTS & ACTIVITIES
Bougainvillea Garden..........................11 C1
Chandigarh Architecture
  Museum.......................................12 C2
Garden of Fragrance..........................13 A3
Government Museum & Art
  Gallery...14 C2
High Court..15 D1
Le Corbusier Centre............................16 D3
Museum...17 D1
National Gallery of Portraits................18 B2
Natural History Museum...................(see 12)
Nek Chand Fantasy Rock
  Garden...19 D1
Open Hand Sculpture.........................20 D1
Paddle Boats....................................21 D2
Rose Garden.....................................22 B2
Secretariat..23 D1
UT Secretariat...................................24 C2
Vidhan Sabha....................................25 D1

SLEEPING
AB's..(see 50)
Chandigarh Hotel...............................26 A4
Hotel Akashdeep................................27 B3
Hotel City Heart Premium....................28 C3
Hotel Divyadeep.................................29 B3
Hotel Kwality Regency........................30 D3
Hotel Mountview................................31 C1
Hotel Satyadeep.................................32 B3
Hotel Shivalikview..............................33 B2
Hotel Sunbeam..................................34 B3
Kaptain's Retreat................................35 A4
Piccadily Hotel...................................36 B3
Taj Chandigarh..................................37 B2

EATING
AB's..(see 50)
Barbeque Nation................................38 A4
Bhoj...(see 29)
Barista...(see 38)
Café Coffee Day...............................(see 38)
Chop Sticks 2....................................39 C3
Chop Sticks 2 (Branch)....................(see 36)
Copper Chimney..............................(see 46)
Ghazal...40 B3
Hot Millions Salad Bar &
  Restaurant.....................................41 B2
Java Dave's.......................................42 C1
Khyber...43 A4
Mehfil..44 B2
Moti Mahal (Branch).......................(see 46)
Moti Mahal.....................................(see 44)
Nik Baker's (Branch)........................45 C2
Nik Baker's.....................................(see 38)
Noodle Bar.......................................46 D4
Orchid Lounge..................................47 A4
Oven Fresh.....................................(see 51)
Pomodoro.......................................(see 36)

Sagar Ratna......................................48 B3
Sai Sweets.....................................(see 32)
Sindhi Sweets....................................49 B3
Sundarams.....................................(see 50)
Swagath...50 D3
Yangtse...(see 33)

DRINKING
English Garden Bar..........................(see 44)
Lava Bar..(see 37)
Oriental Lounge...............................(see 50)
Piccadilly Blue Ice Bar &
  Restaurant.....................................51 B2
Scorelli...52 C3
Vintage Terrace Lounge Bar...........(see 31)
Voodoo...(see 46)
Zinc Lounge....................................(see 46)

ENTERTAINMENT
Kiran Cinema.....................................53 B3
Neelam Cinema.................................54 B3
Tagore Theatre..................................55 C3

SHOPPING
Anokhi...56 C3
Ebony...57 C2
Fabindia..58 C2
Khadi Ashram..................................(see 4)
Music World.......................................59 C3
Music World....................................(see 51)
Phulkari..(see 4)
Suvasa...60 C2

TRANSPORT
Air India..61 A4
Bus Station.....................................(see 2)
Jet Airways.....................................(see 51)
Prepaid Autorickshaws.......................62 B3

Sector 12 · Sector 1 · Sector 2 · Sector 3 · Sector 4 · Sector 5 · Sector 6 · Sector 7 · Sector 8 · Sector 9 · Sector 10 · Sector 11 · Sector 16 · Sector 17 · Sector 18 · Sector 19 · Sector 21 · Sector 22 · Sector 23 · Sector 26 · Sector 28 · Sector 34 · Sector 35

Sukhna Lake
Lake Reserved Forest
Uttar Marg
Madhya Marg
Udyan Path
Jan Marg
Vidya Path
Dakshin Marg
Pedestrian Underpass

To Train Station (2km);
Fun Republic Shopping Centre
(4km); Rallis (3.5km); Nada (4km);
Piri Cinemas (4km); Pinjore
Gardens (19km); Morni Hills
(42km); Shimla (109km)

To Inter State Bus Terminal
(Sector 43) (1.5km); Train
Reservation Office (1.5km);
Silver Oaks Hospital (4.5km)

To Airport (3.5km);
Kingfisher Airlines (3.5km);
Aura Vaxeela (4.5km)

To Terraced
Garden (500m)

0   1 km
0   0.5 miles

CITY OF ANGLES

Chandigarh was built as the new capital of Punjab following Partition (p52) and, in the words of Jawaharlal Nehru (independent India's first prime minister), as 'an expression of the nation's faith in the future'.

It was always going to be radically modern, but it could have turned out very differently. Two pioneering American architects were originally assigned the task: Matthew Nowicki and Albert Mayer, the latter influenced by the 'romantic picturesque' seen in England's Garden Cities movement.

When Nowicki died in a plane crash, Mayer resigned and Le Corbusier was recruited to finish the job. The Swiss-born architect envisaged a modernist utopia where 'arithmetic, texturique and geometrics' would replace the 'oxen, cows and goats driven by peasants, crossing the sun-scorched fields'. However, Chandigarh was meant to be a city of people – more democratic than Delhi – and this called for pedestrian piazzas, tree-lined avenues, houses facing traffic-quiet roads, public gardens, and the artificial Sukhna Lake.

Le Corbusier's master-plan pursued low-density, low-rise housing divided into 1-sq-km neighbourhood sectors, each with their own shops, schools and places of worship.

Nehru approved. 'It is the biggest example in India of experimental architecture. It hits you on the head, and makes you think. You may squirm at the impact but it has made you think and imbibe new ideas.'

the boxed text, p260), cleverly using recycled junk and organic materials, the garden is a curious maze of interlinking courtyards, twisting walkways and staircases suddenly emerging into valleys with crashing waterfalls or amphitheatres overrun by figures made of china shards. No material is wasted, from electrical sockets to colourful wire, glass and even broken bangles, in the legions of men, animals, archways and walls, with broken-art faces around almost every corner.

Wear comfortable shoes and arrive early on weekends to beat the crowds.

SUKHNA LAKE

Another aspect of Le Corbusier's masterplan is this landmark artificial lake (8am-10pm) replete with **paddle boats** (8am-6pm; 2-seaters per 30min Rs40, 4-seaters per 30min Rs80). Ornamental gardens, a playground and the **Mermaid Pub & Restaurant** (meals Rs70-150; 11am-11pm) complete the fun. Sunday afternoons can get crowded.

MUSEUMS

The **Chandigarh Architecture Museum** (City Museum; 2743626; Sector 10-C; admission/camera free/Rs5; 9.45am-5pm Tue-Sun) uses photos, letters, models, newspaper reports and architectural drawings to provide revealing insights into the city's planning and development. There's an outdoor **sound-&-light show** (admission free; 7.30-8.30pm Fri-Sun).

Next door, the **Natural History Museum** (2740261; Sector 10-C; admission/camera Rs10/5; 10am-4.30pm Tue-Sun) is less interesting for its fossilised animal skulls than for its manuscript section, which includes 16th-century Sanskrit texts.

Le Corbusier Centre (2777077; www.lecorbusiercentrechd.org; Sector 19-B; admission free; 10am-1pm & 2.15-5pm Tue-Sun) will especially appeal to those interested in urban planning. Through old documents, sketches and photos it chronicles the work of Chandigarh's chief architect, Le Corbusier (see above). There's a black-and-white photo of a suit and bow tie–attired Le Corbusier on a paddle boat, as well as some fascinating letters, including one from Jawaharlal Nehru to the Chief Minister of Punjab dated November 4 1960, part of which states 'I do hope that you will not overrule Corbusier. His opinion is of value.'

GALLERIES

The **Government Museum & Art Gallery** (2740261; Sector 10-C; admission Rs10, camera Rs5; 10am-4.30pm Tue-Sun, free guided tours 11am & 3pm Tue-Sun, films 11am & 3pm Sun) has a sizeable collection, including *phulkari* (embroidery work) wraps made by Punjabi village women, metalwork, Indian miniature paintings, contemporary art and Buddhist sculptures.

The **National Gallery of Portraits** (2720261; Sector 17-B; admission free; 10am-5pm Tue-Sun), behind the State Library, displays photos and

HARYANA & PUNJAB

JUNK ART GENIUS

Following Independence, as refugees flooded across the Pakistan border and a newly liberated India made the bold statement that was Chandigarh, one of the new city's road inspectors, a diminutive arrival from Pakistan called Nek Chand, was struck by the amount of waste generated as villages were cleared in the construction of Chandigarh. Chand hauled this matter back to his jungle home and gave it a second life as sculptural material.

Eventually he had tens of thousands of forms made of urban and industrial waste, as well as local stone, created by his own hand and the slow forces of nature. His battalions of water women, pipers, chai drinkers, monkeys, cheeky stick men wearing tea-cup hats, dancing women and other characters steadily multiplied in secretly sculpted spaces.

Chand's efforts weren't officially discovered until some 15 years after they began, when a government survey crew stumbled upon them in 1973. The unauthorised garden was illegally occupying government land and should technically have been demolished, but fortunately the local council recognised the garden as a cultural asset. Chand was given 50 labourers and paid a salary so he could devote himself to the project.

Today, the garden is said to receive an average 5000 visitors a day. It's one of Asia's most significant recycling programs. There's a **Nek Chand Foundation** (www.nekchand.com), raising funds and recruiting volunteers.

Now in his mid-80s, asked whether it's true that the garden is India's most visited tourist attraction after the Taj Mahal, Nek Chand humbly replies, 'It is said'.

Chand had no formal education beyond high school. 'In my childhood I used to build mud houses and other toys.' He is said to be influenced by modernist masters such as Le Corbusier and Gaudi, but he is clear on the main source of his ideas: 'they are a gift from God.'

paintings illustrating the country's independence movements.

PARKS & GARDENS

In line with Le Corbusier's vision of a garden city, Chandigarh is dotted with verdant parks. These include the **Rose Garden** (Sector 16), which has over 1500 rose varieties, and **Bougainvillea Garden** (Sector 3). Less central are the **Terraced Garden** (Sector 33) and the **Garden of Fragrance** (Sector 36), the latter with sweet-scented varieties such as jasmine and damask rose.

Tours

A double-decker **tourist bus** (☎ 2703839, 4644484; ticket Rs50; ⌚ 10am-6.30pm) runs two daily half-day trips from Hotel Shivalikview (buy ticket here; opposite) to the Rose Garden, Government Museum & Art Gallery, Nek Chand Fantasy Rock Garden and Sukhna Lake. Schedules can be inconsistent, so check ahead.

Sleeping

Let's be clear: Chandigarh fails to excite on the accommodation front, especially when it comes to value for money. Although lodgings lack the 'wow' factor, the upside is that there are choices to suit all pockets.

To stay with a family, contact the Chandigarh Tourism office (p257) for details about its Bed & Breakfast scheme (rooms from Rs700).

BUDGET

Chandigarh is starved of decent budget possibilities and the best of the (lacklustre) bunch can fill up fast. Expect threadbare rooms and patchy service. Before unpacking your toothbrush, ensure the plumbing works and that any external traffic noise is bearable.

Hotel Satyadeep (☎ 2703103; Sector 22-B; s Rs400-800, d Rs500-900; 🅿 🖳) Upstairs from the affiliated Sai Sweets (p263), this is the most traveller-friendly option, run by the courteous Vikramjit. The rooms aren't fancy but are adequately comfortable, and it's a sound choice for solo women.

Hotel Divyadeep (☎ 2705191; Sector 22-B; s/d Rs600/700; 🅿) Satyadeep's sister hotel, the similar Divyadeep is another reliable choice.

Chandigarh Hotel (☎ 2703690; Sector 22-C; s/d Rs700/900; 🅿) Basic, tired-looking rooms but a fall-back option if you can't get a bed at the above two hotels.

Hotel Akashdeep (☎ 5074086; Sector 22-D; s/d Rs1395/1595; 🅿) Its modernish rooms don't meet the expectations of the price tag, but you can negotiate a 30% discount during low occupancy, making this a budget possibility. The rooms are fair though unimaginatively furnished.

MIDRANGE & TOP END

Hotel Kwality Regency (☎ /fax 2720204; Sector 22-A; s/d Rs1495/1695; ✂) The 14 agreeable rooms have individual character although the cheapest can be on the small, sun-starved side (consider upgrading). Nevertheless, Kwality is good value (for Chandigarh), all rooms with TV, scatter rugs, writing desk and electronic safe. There's a bar and multicuisine restaurant.

Hotel Sunbeam (☎ 2708100; www.hotelsunbeam.com; Sector 22-B; s/d Rs1995/2395; ✂) Sunbeam's rooms adequately shine, despite being a little dowdily decorated. They're reasonably furnished and have 24-hour news channels, including BBC and CNN. Quaff cocktails in the lounge-bar.

Kaptain's Retreat (☎ 5005599; www.kaptainsretreat.com; Sector 35-B; s/d Rs2190/2490; ✂) Owned by cricketing icon Kapil Dev, this 10-room hotel is filled with cricket paraphernalia including signed cricket bats. For unenthusiastic pace-bowlers, there's a relaxing bar-restaurant. The rooms aren't superluxe but are comfy, cosy and with an individual charm.

Hotel City Heart Premium (☎ 2724203; city heartchd@yahoo.com; Sector 17-C; s/d Rs2195/2495; ✂) A possibility if other hotels are full, with kitschy but otherwise OK rooms.

AB's (☎ 6577888; Sector 26; r Rs2500; ✂) Above its namesake restaurant (right), rooms are clean and modern although the cheaper ones are a bit space-frugal. Rooms have flat-screen TVs, tea and coffee–making facilities and guests are just a dash away from the stylish subterranean Oriental Lounge (p263).

Aura Vaseela (☎ 01762-287575; www.auravaseela .com; Nadiali village; r from Rs2599, cottages from Rs3299; ✂ ▯ ▨) Run by a dynamic duo, Gags and Jeeva, this stress-banishing 'ethnic countryside resort' may be tricky to find (pick-ups possible with advance notice) given its secluded location (around 4.5km from the centre), but the effort is well rewarded. Tastefully-appointed accommodation is in traditional Punjabi-style (modern) cottages or rooms in the classy main complex. Amenities include a small gym, craft gallery, restaurant and bar. Did we mention the serenity?

Hotel Shivalikview (☎ 4672222; www.citcochandi garh.com/shivalikview; Sector 17-E; s/d incl breakfast & dinner Rs3500/4000; ✂ ▯) Thoughtful, if somewhat humdrum rooms, each with TV, writing desk and cool tiled floors. There's a business centre, beauty salon and the popular Chinese restaurant, Yangtse (below).

Piccadily Hotel (☎ 2707571; www.thepiccadily.com; Sector 22-B; s/d Rs3990/4990; ✂ ▯) This appealing four-star property offers contemporary wi-fi enabled rooms with plasma TV, mini-bar, sofa, writing desk, tea-and-coffee-making facilities, safe, hair-dryer and satiny bedcovers. Graze on Italian faves at Pomodoro (below).

Hotel Mountview (☎ 4671111; www.citcochandigarh .com/mountview; Sector 10-B; s/d incl breakfast Rs5500/6200; ✂ ▯ ☍ ▨) Well-presented rooms (some carpeted, some wood-floored) have flat-screen TVs, tea-&-coffee-making facilities, minibars, safes and easy-on-the-eye interiors. There's a health club, good restaurants (including 24-hour cafe) and the slick Vintage Terrace Lounge Bar (p263).

Taj Chandigarh (☎ 6613000; www.tajhotels.com; Sector 17-A; s/d Rs9000/10,000; ✂ ☍ ▨) Although not as uberluxurious as we've come to expect of the Taj, TC is still suitably svelte. Plush, big-windowed rooms boast ergonomic furniture, minibars, plasma TVs, electronic safes and round-the-clock concierge services. There are several restaurants, a bar (p263), spa (dare to try the 'warrior massage') and 24-hour business centre. Cosmic quandary? Fear not, there's an astrologer on call.

Eating

Thanks to the locals' love of food, the hungry traveller is well catered for in Chandigarh, with new eateries ever-sprouting. Apart from splendid home-grown offerings, there are familiar fast-food chains.

You'll find a particularly impressive knot of restaurants in Sectors 17, 26 and 35. Telephone numbers are given for places where reservations are advisable (especially weekends).

Restaurants

Sagar Ratna (Sector 17-E; mains Rs65-115; ☉ 8am-11pm; ✂) This all-veg chain-restaurant does South Indian specialities with aplomb, from first-rate dosas (savoury crepes) to satiating thalis. The cool *dahi idli* (spongy rice cake) is a tummy-soothing yoghurty elixir.

Sundarams (Sector 26; dosas from Rs68; ☉ 9.30am-10.30pm; ✂) For superauthentic South Indian dishes, this cute, family-run place can't be beat. Home-style dosas, *idlis* and *uttapams* (savoury rice pancakes) are served with lovely fresh chutneys.

Bhoj (Sector 22-B; thali Rs110; ☺ 7.30am-10.30pm; ☒) A travellers' favourite, this is an unpretentious spot to fuel up on a hearty North Indian veg thali.

Khyber (☎ 2607728; Sector 35-B; mains Rs115-265; ☒) Drink beer at the cowboy-themed basement bar, before diving into flavoursome northwest Frontier-style cuisine at the restaurant. They do startlingly good *dhal Khyber* (slow-simmered curried lentils) and *pathar kebab* (lava stone–roasted lamb).

Mehfil (Sector 17-C; mains Rs120-290; ☺ 11am-midnight; ☒) Indian, Chinese and Continental food served in comfortable surrounds, with the *murg tawa* (Punjabi-style chicken) and *methi murg* (chicken with fenugreek) among the standouts. Spice aficionados may find some dishes too tame.

Ghazal (☎ 2704448; Sector 17-C; meals Rs140-210; ☺ 8am-11.30pm; ☒) A Chandigarh stalwart, grand Ghazal has an admirable Indian, Continental and Chinese menu. *Ghazal special murg* (cream-based chicken) is nicely washed down with draught beer (Rs45 per mug).

Noodle Bar (Sector 26; mains Rs140-240; ☺ 11am-4.30pm & 7.30-11pm; ☒) Oodles of noodles. And when you're all noodled-out there are ample other Asian creations: dim sums, wontons, Singapore chicken satays, lemon coriander broth and an inventive Thai chicken penne.

Chop Sticks 2 (☎ 4642000; Sector 7-C; mains Rs140-240; ☺ 11.30am-4pm & 7-11.30pm; ☒) Moodily lit, this pleasing Chinese restaurant has locals coming back again and again, especially for the sliced chicken in hot garlic sauce. Smaller branch at Sector 22-B.

Moti Mahal (☎ 5073333; Sector 17-C; mains Rs145-250; ☺ 10.30am-11.30pm; ☒) Scrummy North Indian favourites; the butter chicken, *jeera aloo* (spiced potatoes), chicken masala and *palak paneer* (unfermented cheese chunks in spiced pureed spinach) get the thumbs up. Good variety of piping-hot Indian breads. Branch at Sector 26.

Copper Chimney (☎ 5087373; Sector 26; mains Rs145-280; ☺ 11am-3.30pm & 7pm-midnight; ☒) The *boti kebab* (charcoal-grilled marinated mutton) is spicy, succulent goodness, the tandoori *gobi* (cauliflower) is clay-oven magic, and the 'sizzling brownie' is chocolatey bliss. Chic interior.

Barbeque Nation (☎ 4666900; Sector 26; mains Rs145-280; ☺ 12.30-3.30pm & 7.30-11.30pm; ☒) The novelty at this wood-esque restaurant is small grills embedded in each table, allowing diners to partake in the cooking of their meals. The food, however, isn't quite as sexy. There's a good veg/nonveg buffet (lunch Monday to Saturday/Sunday per person Rs309/450; dinner daily Rs450) which includes BBQ Indian, Chinese and Mediterranean fare.

AB's (☎ 2795666; Sector 26; mains Rs155-425; ☺ 11am-midnight; ☒) Settle back at suave AB's (specialising in Punjabi, Kashmiri and Mughlai cuisine) and savour the likes of *tabakh maaz* (spicy, marinated mutton ribs), *paneer achari* (slow flame–cooked, spice and pickle–marinated unfermented cheese) and *jungli gosht* (spicy tomato–based mutton).

Hot Millions Salad Bar & Restaurant (Sector 17-D, 1st fl; mains Rs175-380; ☺ 10am-midnight; ☒) Best of its city-wide branches and popular for its salad buffet (soups, veg/nonveg salads and desserts, Rs201 per person). The higgledy-piggledy à la carte menu has everything from Tex-Mex and Chinese to Indian and Italian. Laid-back vibe.

Swagath (☎ 5000444; Sector 26; mains Rs175-575; ☺ 11am-midnight; ☒) Stellar Indian food with a focus on Mangalorean and Chettinad recipes. Seafood – prawns, squid, crab and a tasty fish *gassi* (coconut-based curry) – is artfully prepared, and the *murgh malai tikka* (clay oven–cooked marinated chicken) isn't bad either.

Yangtse (☎ 4672222; Hotel Shivalikview, Sector 17-E; mains Rs185-275; ☺ 12.30-3pm & 7.30-11.30pm; ☒) Sporting panoramic city views from its lofty heights, this is one of Chandigarh's best Chinese restaurants. Chicken Sichuan, eggplant in garlic sauce, spicy honey chicken, chilli garlic noodles…decisions, decisions! Choosing dessert, however, is a no-brainer: date pancakes with ice-cream, please.

Ruby Tuesday (Fun Republic shopping centre, 1st fl, Mani Majra; mains Rs210-425; ☺ 11am-11pm; ☒) If you're cinema'ing at Fun Republic (see p264), grab a pre- or post-movie bite at this easygoing American-style diner known for its fat burgers, cheesy pizza and finger licking–good ribs. There's also a food court on Fun Republic's top floor.

Orchid Lounge (☎ 2624991; Sector 34-A; mains Rs225-550; ☺ 11.30am-midnight; ☒) This elegant lounge-bar-restaurant is a fancy place to dilly-dally over a bottle of Grover's Sauvignon Blanc

(Rs800) while perusing the 'Oriental' menu. Tempting choices include the sweet-and-sour fish with lemongrass and kafir-lime leaves, pad Thai, and broccoli, baby corn and cashew nuts in chilli plum sauce.

Pomodoro (☎ 2707571; Piccadilly Hotel, Sector 22-B; mains Rs245-345; ☽ 11.30am-3.30pm & 7pm-midnight; ⊠) Traditional Italian food courteously served in a sleek setting makes Pomodoro a *numero uno* choice. Authentic minestrone, pastas, pizzas, risottos, grilled meats and to-die-for desserts like tiramisu and panacotta. Impressive wine list.

Quick Eats

Sai Sweets (Sector 22-B; snacks Rs13-30) Apart from an awesome array of *mithai* (Indian sweets), humble SS has *namkin* (savoury nibbles) and more substantial snacks like plump samosas (deep-fried pastry triangles) and *channa bhatura* (fried Indian-style bread with spiced chickpeas).

Sindhi Sweets (Sector 17-C; snacks/thalis Rs35/90) Indian snacks like *aloo tikki* (potato) burgers as well as an eye-popping mix of *mithai*. Perpetually busy, especially around Diwali.

Nik Baker's (Sector 35-C; snacks & muffins from Rs 40; ⊠) Chandigarh's top bakery, with fresh bread (multigrain, linseed, ciabatta, sunflower, rye etc), snacks (quiche, mushroom panini, chicken croissants) and pastries (lemon tarts, blueberry cheesecake, brownies). There's also gelato ice cream (the brownie-fudge is mmmmmagical). Birthday cakes (from Rs390) can be baked with at least a day's notice. Smaller branch at Sector 9-D.

Java Dave's (Sector 10-D; cakes from Rs50; ⊠) Opposite Hotel Mountview, this is a cheery little coffee-and-cake stop if you're in the area. The 'toasted coconut coffee' sounds interesting.

Oven Fresh (Sector 17-E; snacks Rs75-120; ⊠) Quality bakery: think mushroom pies, fluffy muffins, hot peppermint tea, peach iced tea, latte and the like.

Coffee-chain rivals, **Café Coffee Day** (Sector 35-C; snacks from Rs35; ⊠) and **Barista** (Sector 35-C; snacks from Rs40; ⊠) continue trying to out-froth and out-bake each other on the cappuccino and cake fronts.

Drinking

Watering holes range from the seedy to the swish, the better ones flaunting a great selection of domestic and foreign booze. Women

are less likely to get hassled if they're with a male companion.

Score!!! (Sector 8-C; ☽ 11am-midnight; ⊠) An 'in' place when we were in town, this sleek sports bar – with dim lighting, soft leather couches and an extensive beverage menu – is good for a wind-down Kingfisher (Rs100 per pint) or pick-me-up tequila (Rs225). Shake your groove thing on Wednesday, Friday, Saturday and Sunday nights (DJ from 9pm).

Voodoo (Sector 26; ☽ 11am-midnight; ⊠) A squeezy, dark drinking den with dance floor (DJ on Wednesday and Saturday from 9pm), where the city's 20-somethings switch into top gear with BMW shooters (Baileys, Malibu and whisky; Rs225) and savour Sex on the Beach (vodka, peach schnapps, cranberry and orange juice; Rs200).

Zinc Lounge (Sector 26; ☽ 11am-4.30pm & 7.30-11pm; ⊠) Attached to the Noodle Bar (p261), steely-suave Zinc attracts Chandigarh's pretty people. There's a show-off wine list that includes Indian, Australian, Spanish and French labels (house wine Rs250 per glass). Cocktailers can sup mint juleps, Cosmopolitans, margueritas and 'Indian sangria' (ginger-infused; Rs250).

Vintage Terrace Lounge Bar (Hotel Mountview; Sector 10-B; ☽ 11am-11pm; ⊠) One of the best in the hotel-bar category, with comfy chairs, a big-screen TV and plenty of choice: wine, beer, cocktails, mocktails, spirits and liqueurs (a shot of cointreau is Rs225). The peckish can nibble fish fingers (Rs400).

Lava Bar (Taj Chandigarh Hotel, Sector 17-A; ☽ 11am-11.30pm; ⊠) With lava lamps and a retro vibe, this small bar celebrates an 'amoebic ambiance in a hot modern way.' Rejoice this fact with expensive bubbles (Dom Perignon; Rs22,000)…or, maybe not…thank heaven there's plenty of (affordable) pale ale (Corona beer; Rs300). DJ from 7pm on Wednesday, Thursday, Friday and Saturday.

Oriental Lounge (Sector 26; ☽ 11am-midnight; ⊠) Below AB's restaurant (p261), this chi-chi lounge-bar is a most civilised spot to slow the pace. There's Heineken (Rs180 per can) and mint tequilas (Rs250), among other things, while the impressive pan-Asian food menu has glass noodle soup (Rs75), crab cakes (Rs240) and 'Tickle Me Honey' (Thai honey-marinated pork chops; Rs190). Happy hour is from noon to 6pm.

Piccadilly Blue Ice Bar & Restaurant (Sector 17-E; ☽ 11am-11pm; ⊠) A contemporary, split-level bar-restaurant which is nice for an unhurried drink and bite to eat. A Kingfisher is Rs85/140 per 330/650ml and there's also Long Island Iced Tea (Rs250) and Bacardi Breezers (Rs100). Menu items range from barbecued prawns and Thai fish curry to burgers and chicken stroganoff.

English Garden Bar (Sector 17-C; ☯ 11am-midnight; ☒) A basement bar below Mehfil restaurant (p261), it doesn't exactly bring an English garden to mind, but is OK for a draught beer (Rs55). A tad gloomy it may be, but snooty it is not.

Also recommended for a tipple is the Orchid Lounge (see p261).

Entertainment

Tagore Theatre (☎ 2724278; Sector 18-B) hosts music, dance and theatrical performances.

Movies (mainly Hindi) are screened at the **Kiran Cinema** (☎ 2705082; Sector 22-D) and **Neelam Cinema** (☎ 2703600; Sector 17-D), while a mix of Bollywood and Hollywood is shown at the multiplex **Fun Cinemas** (☎ 9888997806; Fun Republic shopping centre, Mani Majra).

Shopping

The central section of Sector 17 is the main shopping and entertainment area.

Anokhi (www.anokhi.com; Sector 7-C, Inner Market; ☯ 10.30am-7pm Mon-Sat) Beautiful block-printed textiles.

Ebony (Sector 9-D; ☯ 10.30am-7.30pm Mon-Sat) Modern department store with brand-name goods.

Fabindia (www.fabindia.com; Sector 9-C; ☯ 10am-8pm) Gorgeous garments (Indian-meets-Western style) and homewares.

Khadi Ashram (Sector 17-C; ☯ 10.30am-2pm & 3.30-8pm Mon-Sat) Homespun textiles and herbal beauty products (soaps include water-lily, aloe-vera and mint).

Music World (Sectors 17-E & 18-D; ☯ 10am-9.30pm) CDs (from Rs40) and DVDs (from Rs60).

Phulkari (Sector 17-C; ☯ 10.30am-2pm & 3.30-8pm Mon-Sat) Government of Punjab emporium with everything from handicrafts to jootis.

Suvasa (Sector 8-B, Inner Market; ☯ 10.30am-7.45pm) Quality block-printed fabrics that include toiletry bags and *salwar kameez* (traditional dresslike tunic and trouser combination for women).

Getting There & Away

AIR

An international airport is scheduled for completion around 2010.

Air India (Indian Airlines) (☎ 1800227722; Sector 34-A; ☯ 9.30am-1pm & 2-5.30pm Mon-Fri) Daily flights to Delhi (Rs3675) and Mumbai (Rs6875).

Jet Airways (☎ 2741465; Sector 9-D; ☯ 9am-6pm Mon-Sat) Daily flight to Delhi (Rs3945).

Kingfisher Airlines (☎ 9302795005; airport; ☯ 9am-6pm) Daily flights to Delhi (US$100) and Mumbai (US$155).

BUS

Half a dozen companies operate buses with most leaving from the Inter State Bus Terminal (ISBT) in Sector 43.

Regular buses run to Patiala (Rs50, three hours), Sirhind (Rs50, two hours), Anandpur Sahib (Rs45, 2½ hours), Amritsar (Rs125, seven hours), Dharamsala (ordinary/deluxe Rs200/350, eight hours), Manali (ordinary/deluxe Rs290/400, 11 hours), Haridwar (Rs125, six hours), Delhi (Rs145, 5½ hours) and Shimla (Rs100, four hours).

TRAIN

A **reservation office** (☎ 2720242; ☯ 8am-8pm Mon-Sat, to 2pm Sun) is on the 1st floor of the bus terminal at Sector 43. Prepaid autorickshaws from there to the train station cost around Rs55.

Two fast trains connect Delhi and Chandigarh: the daily *Shatabdi Express* (chair car/1AC Rs440/960, three hours) and the *Jan Shatabdi Express* (Rs107/345, four hours).

Half a dozen trains go to Kalka (chair car/executive Rs238/430, one hour) from where four daily trains (chair car/1AC Rs168/250, five hours) rattle up the mountain to Shimla.

Getting Around

Chandigarh is spread out but, with its cycle paths and parks, was built for cycling. The Chandigarh Tourism office (p257) hires out bicycles (Rs100 per eight hours); cycles are also available for hire at Sukhna Lake (p259) for the same cost but with a (refundable) Rs500 deposit.

Cycle-rickshaw rates within town vary from around Rs20 to Rs50, depending on the distance travelled. Fares from the prepaid autorickshaw booth behind the bus station include Rs40 to Sukhna Lake.

Taxis charge around Rs160 to the airport. Two reputable taxi companies are **Indus Cab** (☎ 4646464) and **Mega Cab** (☎ 4141414), with both charging around Rs15 per kilometre. For local sightseeing (including Pinjore Gardens), the Chandigarh Tourism office (p257) can ar-

BHANGRA MANIA

Rhythmic bhangra (music and dance) emerged as part of Punjab's harvest-festival celebrations (dating back to around the 14th century).

This joyful, spirited dance most famously entails the arms being thrust high in the air coupled with the feisty shaking of the shoulders. The predominant musical instrument is the heart-thumping *dhol* (double-sided drum).

In the 1980s and '90s, inventive fusion versions of traditional bhangra (which include elements of hip-hop, disco, techno, rap, House and reggae) exploded onto the international arena, especially in the UK, rocking dance floors across the world.

range taxis (Rs900 per eight hours, 80km limit).

For car (with driver) hire, expect to pay around Rs800/950 for non-AC/AC per eight hours with an 80km limit (after 80km non-AC/AC Rs5/6 per km).

A taxi from Chandigarh to Delhi or Amritsar costs around Rs4500.

AROUND CHANDIGARH
Pinjore (Yadavindra) Gardens

These reconstructed 17th-century Mughal walled **gardens** (☎ 01733-230759; admission Rs20; ⏰ 7am-10pm) are built on seven levels with water features (that sometimes operate) and enjoy panoramic views of the Shivalik hills.

Founded and designed by Nawab Fidai Khan, who also designed Badshahi Mosque in Lahore (Pakistan), the gardens served as a retreat for the Mughal kings and their harems.

There's an annual **heritage festival** (see the boxed text, p257) here.

At the gardens is the pleasant Mughal-style **Budgerigar Motel** (☎ 01733-231877; dm/s/d Rs300/1200/1400; ❄) which has two tidy four-bed dorms, comfy private rooms and free garden entry for its guests. All are welcome at the motel's restaurant, **Golden Oriel** (veg/non-veg thali Rs100/120; ⏰ 7am-11pm).

Jal Mahal (meals Rs60-275; ⏰ 1-10pm) is a cafe-bar in the middle of one of the gardens' green ponds.

To get here from Chandigarh, catch a bus (Rs20, one hour, frequent).

Morni Hills

Haryana's only hill station gazes across the hazy plains to the Shivalik and Kasauli hills in nearby Himachal Pradesh. Morni's leafy heights are a great escape from the rat race, however weekends can get busy.

Located 10km from Morni village, **Hosh & Josh Hills 'n' Thrills** (☎ 01733-201150; Tikka Tal; adult/child Rs50/30; ⏰ 9am-7pm) amusement park promises to keep the kids entertained.

Mountain Quail Tourist Resort (☎ 01733-250166; r from Rs900) was being briskly renovated when we sneaked a peek but should be shipshape by now, along with its restaurant.

Lake View Camping Complex (☎ 01733-250166; Tikka Tal; dm Rs150, r Rs1500, camping per person per night Rs600) has a picturesque lakeside location and very good rooms with water-facing balconies. Tents include sleeping bags and shared bathrooms. Overlooking the lake is a terrace **restaurant** (mains Rs50-230). Four-seat boats can be hired (Rs100 per 30 minutes).

There are daily buses to Morni (Rs45, two hours). Mountain Quail is 2km before the village, from where there is transport to Tikka Tal.

HARYANA

Haryana's name means either 'Abode of God' or 'green home' depending on whether you believe its first syllable refers to Hari, one of Lord Vishnu's aliases, or *hara*, Hindi for green.

The Haryana state government has motel-restaurants along the main roads; **Haryana Tourism** (www.haryanatourism.gov.in) Chandigarh (☎ 0172-2702957; Sector 17-B; ⏰ 9am-5pm Mon-Fri); Delhi (☎ 011-23324910; Chanderlok Bldg, 36 Janpath; ⏰ 9am-5pm Mon-Fri, to 1pm Sat) can supply further details.

KURUKSHETRA
☎ 01744 / pop 154,000

Kurukshetra will appeal to tourists with a specific historical/religious interest. According to Hindu teachings, Brahma created the universe here, and Krishna delivered his epic Bhagavad Gita sermon, offered as advice to Arjuna (p69) before he fought the 18-day Mahabharata battle in which good triumphed over evil. The town takes its name from its founder Kuru, the Aryan king who offered his limbs to Vishnu in order to establish a land of ethics and values.

The **Sri Krishna Museum** (Pehowa Rd; admission Rs15; ☉ 10am-5pm) has ancient and modern representations of this heroic incarnation of Vishnu.

Next door is the **Kurukshetra Panorama & Science Centre** (Pehowa Rd; admission Rs15, camera Rs20; ☉ 10am-5.30pm). Upstairs, an air-brushed sky flares behind vultures picking at severed heads in the diorama relaying the Mahabharata battle. The ground floor has interactive science exhibits.

Just 500m away is India's largest water tank, the ghat-flanked **Bhramasarovar**, which was, according to Hindu holy texts, created by Lord Brahma. It attracts throngs during solar eclipses and **Gita Jayanti**, anniversary of the Bhagavad Gita (see p257).

Another 6km away is Jyotisar, where the **banyan tree** is said to be an offshoot of the one under which Krishna delivered the Bhagavad Gita. There's a one-hour Hindi (English on request) **sound-&-light show** (admission Rs20; ☉ sunset Tue-Sun).

Sheikh Chaheli's tomb (Indian/foreigner Rs5/100; ☉ 9am-5pm Tue-Sun), 2.3km from the Sri Krishna Museum, is where this Sufi saint is buried with his family in sandstone-and-marble mausoleums.

Neelkanthi Krishna Dham Yatri Niwas (☎ 291615; Pehowa Rd; r Rs600; ✕) offers the best accommodation option, with charmless but otherwise fine rooms; the attached **tourist office** (☎ 293570; ☉ 9.30am-5pm Tue-Sat) is of limited help.

There are daily buses to Delhi (Rs95, three hours) and Patiala (Rs37, 1½ hours).

SOUTH & WEST OF DELHI
Surajkund
Some 30km south of downtown Delhi, this sleepy village bursts to life during the two-week **Surajkund Crafts Mela** (see p257).

Surajkund is named after the 10th-century **sun pool** built by Raja Surajpal, leader of the sun-worshipping Tomars.

Most visitors are Delhi day-trippers, but if you wish to stay here Haryana Tourism has three hotels, the best being **Hotel Rajhans** (☎ 0129-2512843; r Rs2800; ✕ ⚲). The midrange options are **Hermitage** (☎ 0129-25112313; r Rs1500; ✕) and, better, **Sunbird Motel** (☎ 0129-2511357; r Rs1500; ✕).

During the mela there are several daily buses from Delhi (Rs40, two hours). A taxi charges around Rs700 (return).

Sultanpur Bird Sanctuary
This 145-hectare **sanctuary** (Indian/foreigner Rs5/40, camera/video Rs25/500; ☉ 6.30am-6pm Apr-Sep, to 4.30pm Oct-Mar) plays host to over 250 bird species, including painted storks, Demoiselle cranes, cormorants, spotted sandpipers, mallards and plovers. Its fluctuating population of woodland, shallow-water and deep-water birds includes an estimated 150 resident species and roughly 100 visiting species from Europe, Afghanistan, Siberia and elsewhere. The best time to visit is October to March.

Unfortunately accommodation is limited to the **Rosy Pelican Complex** (☎ 0124-2375242; r Rs1000-2200; ✕) which has passable, but neglected, rooms. The hotel's restaurant is open to everyone.

Sultanpur is 46km southwest of Delhi and getting there is tougher than spotting a red-crested pochard! There are irregular, bone-shaking buses (Rs40, one hour). It's better to hire a taxi (return Rs1100).

PUNJAB

ANANDPUR SAHIB
☎ 01887 / pop 14,700
The Sikhs' holiest site after the Golden Temple has several historical gurdwaras. An important pilgrimage site for more than 300 years, it was founded by ninth Sikh guru Tegh Bahadur in 1664, before the Mughal emperor Aurangzeb beheaded him for refusing to convert to Islam. His son, Guru Gobind Singh, founded the Khalsa (Sikh brotherhood) here in 1699, and **Holla Mohalla** (see the boxed text, p257) celebrates the anniversary.

The **Kesgarh Sahib** is the largest gurdwara and has a number of holy weapons on display, some of them in the hands of the guards. The smaller gurdwara Sis Ganj marks the spot where Guru Tegh Bahadur's head was cremated after it was brought back from Delhi. Some 500m from town is **Anandgarh Sahib**, where a flight of steps leads to a fort on the roof. From here you can see the five-petal form (inspired by the five warrior-saints in the Khalsa) of the **Khalsa Heritage Complex**, which was undergoing massive renovations when we visited. When completed (around mid to late 2009) it promises to be a must-see, with informative exhibits showcasing Sikhism's vibrant history and culture. For further details click www.khalsaheritagecomplex.org.

Kishan Haveli (☎ 01887-232650; Academy Rd; r Rs400-1000; 🔀) is set in spacious grounds and has an uncommercial, ramshackle charm. This mellow countryside retreat, around 1.5km from town, has comfortable rooms and a simple restaurant (meals Rs80).

Gurdwaras also provide accommodation and meals (donations appreciated), though they are often full.

The bus and train stations are 300m apart on the main road outside town. Buses leave frequently for Chandigarh (Rs50, two hours) and every hour to Amritsar (Rs100, five hours).

The overnight *Delhi-Una Himachal Express* connects Anandpur Sahib with Delhi (sleeper/3AC/2AC/1AC Rs160/400/600/1000, eight hours).

SIRHIND
☎ 01763 / pop 53,800

If you happen to be passing through this small town, sites of interest include the **Aam Khas Bagh**, a Mughal-era walled garden, and the **Gurdwara Fatehgarh Sahib**, which commemorates the 1704 martyrdom of the two youngest sons of the 10th Sikh guru, Gobind Singh. Entombed alive by the Mughals for refusing to convert to Islam, they are honoured at the three-day **Shaheedi Jor Mela** held here every December. There's also **Rauza Sharif**, the marble mausoleum of Muslim saint Shaikh Ahmad Faruqi Sirhindi, which draws pilgrims during the **Urs festival** (August).

If you have to stay overnight, the **Sahil Motel** (☎ 01763-228392; d Rs1250; 🔀) is your best bet.

Buses connect Sirhind with Patiala (Rs20, one hour) and Chandigarh (Rs50, two hours).

PATIALA
☎ 0175 / pop 238,000

Once the capital of an independent Sikh state that was established by Baba Ala Singh as the Mughals weakened (see p44), Patiala is today a modest town that sees just a trickle of travellers. It's well known for the **Basant festival** (see the boxed text, p257) and, of course, the Patiala peg (see the box, below).

The crumbling **Qila Mubarak** fort looks like it could have been transported from the desert to its position in the bazaar area. There's an **arms gallery** (admission Rs10; 🕑 10.30am-5pm Tue-Sun) in its 1859 Durbar Hall which displays antique weapons.

Moti Bagh Palace (Sheesh Mahal; admission Rs10; 🕑 10.30am-5pm Tue-Sun) has a gallery containing ivory figurines, stuffed animals, musical instruments and more. Nearby, the Old Moti Bagh Palace houses a **sports museum** (admission free but ID required; 🕑 10.30am-1pm & 2-5.30pm Mon-Fri) with exhibits that include memorabilia relating to Punjabi sprinting hero Milkha Singh, 'the Flying Sikh'.

It is said that those who pray at the **Dukh Niwaran Gurdwara** (🕑 dawn-dusk), located near the bus stand, are relieved of suffering.

our pick **Baradari Palace** (Rajinder Kothi; ☎ 2304433; www.neemranahotels.com; Baradari Garden area; r Rs3000; 🔀) This sublime heritage-hotel is Punjab's most graceful place to stay and a perfect stop-over for anyone belting out the Delhi–Amritsar road trip. Dripping with old-world charm, the carefully restored property boasts high ceilings, beautiful period furnishings and relaxing terraces that overlook lovely gardens. The airy rooms are elegantly appointed. A swimming pool is planned.

Patiala's other hotel options are grungy, and solo women may feel uncomfortable.

A PATIALA PEG

In the early 1900s a tent-pegging contest took place in Patiala between the teams of the viceroy and the sports-mad maharaja of Patiala. Tent-pegging is the curious sport of spearing tent pegs out of the ground with a lance from the back of a galloping horse.

Desperate to win and fearful of the wrath of their maharaja, the Patialan team invited their opponents to drinks the night before the match. The British were plied with larger-than-usual measures (or pegs) of whisky, while the tent pegs were changed – smaller ones for the viceroy's team and larger ones for the Patialans. The maharaja's team won but the viceroy's team complained about the size of the pegs. The maharaja (not realising that the complaint referred to the tent pegs) replied that in Patiala, well known for its hospitality, the pegs (of whisky) were always larger than elsewhere. Even today an extra-large measure of whisky is known all over India as a Patiala peg.

HARYANA & PUNJAB

The best of the bunch are the midrange **Hotel Narain Continental** (☎ 2212846; Mall; r Rs1375; 🔀) and cheaper **Green's Hotel** (☎ 2213071; Mall; r Rs500; 🔀), both of which have furniture-scarred rooms and matter-of-fact service.

Daily buses connect Patiala and Sirhind (Rs20, one hour).

NORTHERN PUNJAB

A major textile centre, **Ludhiana** is also the headquarters of Hero Cycles, which manufactures upwards of four million bicycles annually. This big city is a convenient base from which to attend the **Kila Raipur Sports Festival** (see the boxed text, p257).

Jalandhar survived sacking by Mahmud of Ghazni nearly 1000 years ago and later became an important Mughal city. Nowadays it's a commercial hub and the venue for the **Harballabh Sangeet Sammelan** (see the boxed text, p257). It's also a good base from which to visit **Kapurthala**, which was the home of the young Spanish flamenco dancer, Anita Delgado, who married the wealthy maharaja (a story that inspired the Javier Moro novel, *Passion India*).

Faridkot was once capital of a Sikh state of the same name and has a 700-year-old fortress. The 13th-century poet and Sufi (Muslim mystic) Baba Sheikh Farid lived here, and he is honoured by a festival (see p257). His belief in equality influenced Guru Nanak (see the boxed text, p71) and some of his poems are in the Sikh holy book, the Guru Granth Sahib.

AMRITSAR

☎ 0183 / pop 1.01 million

Founded in 1577 by the fourth guru Ram Das, Amritsar is home to Sikhism's holiest shrine, the spectacular Golden Temple. The gold-plated gurdwara glitters in the middle of its holy pool near a giant bullion bar and draws millions of pilgrims from all over the world. A welcome escape from the frenetic bazaars, this majestic temple is rated by many tourists as a glowing highlight of their visit to India. Regrettably, the same can't be said for the hyperactive streets! Indeed, Amritsar's crush of mechanical and human traffic, especially in the people-packed old city, can be downright frazzling.

The original site for the city was granted by the Mughal emperor Akbar, but another Mughal, Ahmad Shah Durani, sacked

Amritsar in 1761 and destroyed the temple. It was rebuilt in 1764, and in 1802 was roofed with gilded copper plates by Maharaja Ranjit Singh and became known as the Golden Temple.

During unrest in Punjab in the early 1980s, the Golden Temple was occupied by separatists seeking to create an independent Sikh homeland. They were flushed out by the army in 1984 in a controversial military action that damaged the temple and fuelled violent Sikh–Hindu clashes in Punjab and beyond that left thousands (predominantly Sikhs) dead.

Orientation

The old city, which includes the Golden Temple and bazaars, is located to the southeast of the train station and is surrounded by a circular road, once the site of the city's massive walls. Modern Amritsar, north of the train station, contains the majority of the upmarket hotels and Lawrence Rd, which is a popular eating and shopping street. The bus station is located 2km east of the train station.

Information

BOOKSHOPS

Book Cafe (☎ 5002082; Ranjit Ave; 🕙 9am-11pm Mon-Sat) Small cafe attached.

Booklovers Retreat (☎ 2545666; Hall Bazaar; 🕙 9am-8pm Mon-Sat) Best selection in the old city.

Oxford Bookstore (☎ 6548884; www.oxfordbookstore .com; New Sadak, Lawrence Rd; 🕙 10am-9pm Mon-Sat, noon-9pm Sun) Sip liquorice tea at its little Cha Bar.

INTERNET ACCESS

Cyber Swing (Old city; per hr Rs40; 🕙 9.30am-10pm) Upstairs from Punjabi Rasoi restaurant.

Reliance World (the Mall; joining fee Rs200; 🕙 9am-10pm Mon-Sat, to 9pm Sun) Opposite Hotel Ritz Plaza. The joining fee entitles users to nine hours' use.

MEDICAL SERVICES

Fortis Escort Hospital (☎ 2573901; Majitha Verka Bypass)

MONEY

Amritsar has an ever-mushrooming supply of ATMs.

HDFC (Golden Temple branch; 🕙 9.30am-3.30pm Mon-Sat) Exchanges travellers cheques and currencies; ATM.

ICICI ATM (Lawrence Rd) Also has an ATM in the old city.

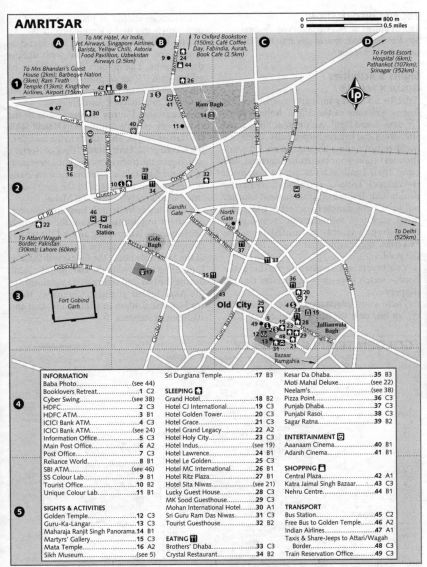

AMRITSAR

PHOTOGRAPHY

The following studios sell memory cards (with prices starting from Rs500 for a 1GB card).

Baba Photo (☎ 5052714; 12 Nehru Centre, Lawrence Rd; ☻ 10.30am-9.30pm Mon-Sat, 4.30-9.30pm Sun)

SS Colour Lab (☎ 2401515; 104 Lawrence Rd; ☻ 10am-9pm Mon-Sat)

Unique Colour Lab (☎ 2223263; MMM Rd; ☻ 10am-9.30pm Mon-Sat, 2-8.30pm Sun) Next door to the Indian Academy of Fine Arts.

POST

Main post office (☎ 2566032; Court Rd; ☻ 9am-3pm Mon-Fri, to 2pm Sat)

Post office (Phawara Chowk; ☻ 9am-7pm Mon-Sat)

TOURIST INFORMATION

Tourist office (☎ 2402452; Queen's Rd; ⏱ 9am–5pm Mon-Sat) Hidden down an alley in the Hotel Palace compound. Limited help.

Sights & Activities

GOLDEN TEMPLE

True to Sikhism's inclusive nature, everyone is welcome at the Sikhs' holiest **shrine** (⏱ dawn–around 10pm). As when at any sacred site, dress and behave respectfully. Everyone must remove their shoes and socks, wash their feet (take your cue from pilgrims), and cover their head; scarves can be borrowed (no charge). Tobacco and alcohol are strictly prohibited. Temple officials request tourists not to casually dangle their feet in the (holy) water tank but, rather, to sit cross-legged. Photography is only permitted from the **Parkarma**, the marble walkway surrounding the pool.

Volunteers are constantly washing the floor – watch your step, as surfaces can get slippery.

There's an **information office** (☎ 2553954; ⏱ 7am-8pm) near the main entrance.

Donations should be placed in one of the donation boxes in the temple precincts.

The temple's architecture is a blend of Hindu and Islamic styles but with unique distinctions. The golden dome (said to be gilded with 750kg of pure gold) represents an inverted lotus flower, a symbol of Sikh devotees' aim to live a pure life.

A causeway (Gurus' Bridge) leads to the two-storey marble temple, **Hari Mandir Sahib** (or Darbar Sahib). This stands in the middle of the sacred pool, **Amrit Sarovar** (Pool of Nectar), which gave the town its name. The lower parts of the marble walls are decorated with inlaid flower and animal motifs in the pietra dura (marble inlay) style of the Taj Mahal.

Priests inside the temple keep up a continuous chant in Gurmukhi from the Sikh holy book and this is broadcast around the temple complex by loudspeakers. The original copy of the Sikh holy book, the **Guru Granth Sahib**, is kept under a shroud in the Hari Mandir Sahib during the day and returns ceremoniously to the Akal Takhat at night. Ceremony times are 5am and 9.40pm in winter, and 4am and 10.30pm in summer.

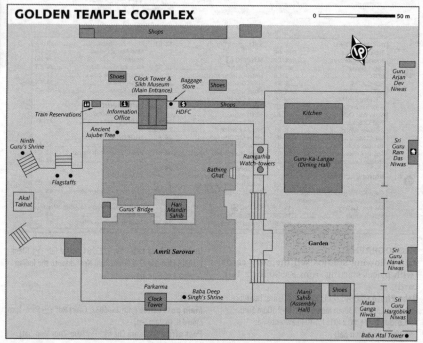

GOLDEN TEMPLE COMPLEX

0 ————— 50 m

Upstairs, in the main entrance clock tower, the **Sikh Museum** (admission free; ⏱ 7am-7pm) vividly shows the grisly history of those Sikhs martyred by the Mughals, the British and Mrs Gandhi.

The **Akal Takhat**, where the Shiromani Gurdwara Parbandhak Committee (SGPC), or Sikh Parliament, traditionally meets, was heavily damaged when it was stormed by the Indian army in 1984 (see p56). The Indian government later repaired it, however the Sikhs, appalled by the army's actions in the first place, pulled it down and rebuilt it themselves.

Completed in 1784, the octagonal **Baba Atal Tower** commemorates Atal Rai, the son of sixth Sikh guru Har Gobind. After Atal performed a miracle, bringing back to life a playmate who had died of a snake bite, his father scolded him for interfering with the ways of god. The repentant youngster committed suicide on this spot in return for the life he had saved. The nine storeys each represent one year of Atal's short life.

Guru-Ka-Langar is the free (donations appreciated) community dining room, a feature of all Sikh temples as a mark of unity among people of all religions, creeds and nationalities. The massive kitchens (one has a chapati machine) prepare vegetarian meals for an estimated 60,000 to 80,000 pilgrims (more during holy festivals) a day. A truly incredible feat! All are welcome to join the masses eating on the floor and we highly recommend the experience (feel free to help volunteers with the washing up).

Try to visit the Golden Temple several times, particularly around dawn and dusk, to fully appreciate the varying light cast upon it at different times of the day.

To learn more about Sikhism, read p71.

JALLIANWALA BAGH

Near the Golden Temple, this poignant **park** (⏱ 6am-9pm summer, 7am-8pm winter) commemorates those Indians killed or wounded here by the British authorities in 1919 – see the boxed text, p272. Some of the bullet marks are still visible, as is the well into which hundreds desperately leapt to avoid the bullets. There's an eternal (24-hour) flame of remembrance. The park also contains the **Martyrs' Gallery** (⏱ 6am-9pm summer, 7am-8pm winter); a sound-and-light show was being planned at the time of research.

MAHARAJA RANJIT SINGH PANORAMA (RAM BAGH)

Within the grounds of the Ram Bagh park is the impressive **Maharaja Ranjit Singh Panorama** (admission Rs10; ⏱ 9am-9pm Tue-Sun), dedicated to the 'Lion of Punjab' (1780–1839). Upstairs is the larger-than-life panorama, replete with booming sound effects, depicting various battle scenes including the maharaja's 1818 conquest of the fort at Multan. Kids, especially, will love it. Exhibits downstairs include colour paintings and dioramas.

Shoes must be removed and cameras aren't permitted inside.

MATA TEMPLE

This labyrinthine Hindu **cave temple** (Model Town, Rani-ka-Bagh; ⏱ dawn-dusk) commemorates the bespectacled 20th-century female saint, Lal Devi. Women wishing to become pregnant come here to pray. The circuitous route to the main shrine passes through ankle-deep waterways, low tunnels, staircases, walkways and caves, the last of which turns out to be the inside of a divine mouth.

SRI DURGIANA TEMPLE

Dedicated to the goddess Durga, this 16th-century **temple** (⏱ dawn-dusk), surrounded by a holy water tank, is a Hindu version of the Golden Temple, sometimes known as the Silver Temple for its carved silver doors. Try to visit when there are soothing bhajans (devotional songs); held daily from around 7.30am to 9.30am and 6.30pm to 8.30pm.

RAM TIRATH TEMPLE

Around 13km west of Amritsar, it's in the vicinity of this **Hindu temple** (⏱ 6am-8pm) that Valmiki is believed to have worked on the Ramayana (p70). It's also said to be the area where Lord Rama's two sons, Luv and Kush, were born.

Near the massive statue of Hanuman (Hindu monkey god) is a temple with tunnels leading to caved deities. Don't miss the temple's small water tank with a floating stone – legend says it was one of the many (similar) stones that Rama's army used to cross an ocean.

A return taxi (including one hour's waiting time) costs around Rs550.

Sleeping

Overall, Amritsar's hotel rooms and service are decidedly ho-hum. Nevertheless, during

---

THE JALLIANWALA BAGH MASSACRE

Unrest in Amritsar was sparked by the controversial Rowlatt Act (1919), which gave British authorities 'emergency' powers to imprison without trial Indians suspected of sedition. Hartals (general strikes) were organised in protest, and escalated into rioting and looting. Three British bank managers were murdered in reprisal attacks following the killing of Indian protestors by the British.

Brigadier-General Dyer was called upon to return order to the city. On 13 April 1919 (Baisakhi day), over 5,000 Indians were holding a peaceful demonstration in Jallianwala Bagh, an open space surrounded by high walls. Dyer arrived with 150 troops and without warning ordered his soldiers to open fire. Some six minutes later, more than 400 people were dead, and a further 1500 were wounded.

The exact number of final fatalities is unknown, but estimated to be upwards of 1500, including many women and children.

Dyer's action was supported by some of his British colleagues but described as 'a savage and inappropriate folly' by Sir Edwin Montague, the Secretary of State for India. It galvanised Indian nationalism – Gandhi responded with his program of civil disobedience, announcing that 'cooperation in any shape or form with this satanic government is sinful'.

Richard Attenborough's acclaimed film *Gandhi* dramatically re-enacts the massacre and subsequent inquiry.

---

low occupancy periods discounts are negotiable. Try to see several rooms before snuggling down, as standards *within* properties can radically vary.

Taxes (not included below) of around 10% often apply.

BUDGET

One word: underwhelming. The upside is that Amritsar's budget-eers won't wound the wallet. Most cheapies are in the old city's boisterous bazaar, not far from the Golden Temple. Bring earplugs!

Golden Temple (dm free but donations appreciated, r without/with AC Rs100/300; 🕸) To stay in the huge accommodation blocks for pilgrims and visitors, check in at Guru Arjan Dev Niwas. Foreigners are generally accommodated in Sri Guru Ram Das Niwas next door. Rooms and dorms are basic, with shared bathrooms. Please respect the requested three-day stay limit.

Tourist Guesthouse (☎ 2553830; bubblesgoolry@yahoo.com; 1355 GT Rd; dm/s/d Rs100/150/300; 🖳) A backpacker institution (especially with overlanders), the rooms may be scuffed and bare but you are paying peanuts! There is a go-with-the-flow vibe, secure parking, small garden and simple restaurant. All rooms are equipped with TVs, hot water and air-coolers.

Hotel Sita Niwas (☎ 2543092; d Rs350, without bathroom Rs250) The basic rooms are oversized shoeboxes but with hard-to-beat prices. More dosh buys bigger rooms.

Lucky Guest House (☎ 2542175) Lucky was being vigorously renovated when we dropped by, so should be spanking new by the time you read this. Tariffs are expected to hover somewhere around Rs400.

Hotel Grace (☎ 2559355; hotelgraceasr@yahoo.com; d Rs550; 🕸) Rooms could do with a lick of paint but are fair at this price, all with TVs and straightforward furnishings. Temple views from the rooftop.

MK Sood Guesthouse (☎ 5093376; r Rs650; 🕸) MKs rooms are mundane but good-sized and comfortable enough for a night or two.

Hotel Golden Tower (☎ 2534446; www.hotelgoldentower.com; Phawara Chowk; r Rs800; 🕸) Another hotel with location at the top of its list of charms, this no-frills option has sparsely decorated but reasonable rooms with TVs and fridges.

Hotel Holy City (☎ 5068111; mail@hotelholycity.co.in; r Rs850; 🕸) Not far from the Golden Temple, with modest rooms and a rooftop terrace.

MIDRANGE

Grand Hotel (☎ 2562424; www.hotelgrand.in; Queen's Rd; s/d Rs1000/1200; 🕸 🖳) This three-star hotel, close to the train station, is deservedly popular. The rooms aren't exactly grand but are certainly comfortably appointed. They, along with a cafe, the Bottoms Up Pub and a breezy veranda with tables and chairs (perfect at beer o'clock) fringe a leafy garden. The amiable owner, Sanjay, is a reliable source of information and can arrange sightseeing trips (including to the India–Pakistan border ceremony; see the boxed text, p276).

Hotel Le Golden (☎ 5028000; www.hotellegolden .com; s/d Rs1200/1350; 🔀) A good choice near the Golden Temple, rooms are tidy (if somewhat squishy) and the rooftop cafe has temple views.

Mrs Bhandari's Guest House (☎ 2228509; http:// bhandari_guesthouse.tripod.com; 10 Cantonment; s/d from Rs1300/1600; 🔀 🖳 🐾) Legacy of the much-loved Mrs Bhandari (1906–2007), this earthy, ecoconscious guest house is set on spacious green grounds. The unfussy, comfy rooms bring back memories of grandma's place and will appeal to those seeking a calm, uncommercial atmosphere. Overlanders with their own tents can camp here for a modest charge. The main house is filled with charming old treasures like the century-old wood stove. Ask about past celebrity guests.

Hotel CJ International (☎ 2543478; www.cjhotel .net; r Rs1450; 🔀 🖳) The rooms are blandly comfortable and the staff can be brusque, but the draw is its proximity to the Golden Temple (prebook one of the five temple-facing rooms).

Hotel Indus (☎ 2535900; www.hotelindus.com; r Rs1550; 🔀) The dramatic million-dollar views of the Golden Temple from the rooftop is reason alone to stay at this modern-style hotel. Apart from being smallish, rooms are otherwise fine with two (303 and 304; Rs2035) boasting spectacular temple vistas – book ahead!

Hotel Lawrence (☎ 2400105; www.lawrenceamritsar .com; 6 Lawrence Rd; s/d Rs2500/3000; 🔀) Don't let the facade put you off. This upper-midranger is a welcome retreat from the bustle outside, with contemporary rooms that have either marble or carpeted floors. Multicuisine restaurant.

TOP END

Amritsar had no five-star hotels at the time of research but several are in the pipeline, including the **Radisson** (www.radisson.com) and **Ista** (www.istahotels.com); both expected to open mid to late 2009, and each promise all creature comforts.

The following hotels aren't superluxe, but rather of the four (ish)-star ilk.

Hotel MC International (☎ 2222901; www.hotel mcinternational.com; the Mall; s/d incl breakfast Rs2800/3200; 🔀 🖳 🐾) So new that we could smell the paint drying when we visited, this looks set to be a terrific choice, with contemporary rooms and a host of facilities including gym, beauty parlour, restaurant, bar, 24-hour coffee shop and business centre.

Mohan International Hotel (☎ 2227801; www .mohaninternationalhotel.com; Albert Rd; s/d Rs3000/4000; 🔀 🐾) The ageing Mohan has seen better days, but is an option if you can't get a bed elsewhere. Rooms are a mixed bag (some in better shape than others), all adequately comfortable. Ensure the AC works in summer!

Hotel Grand Legacy (☎ 5069991; www.grand legacy.net; GT Rd, Model Town; s/d incl breakfast Rs2850/4400 🔀 🖳) Fifty-two attractive rooms: leather chairs, writing desk, LCD TV, minibar, tea and coffee–making facilities and electronic safe. There's a gym, round-the-clock coffee shop, travel desk, business centre, the Moti Mahal Deluxe restaurant (below) and, for a cocktaily escapade, Behind Bars, with its zebra-print chairs and icy Kingfisher beer.

MK Hotel (☎ 2504610; www.mkhotel.com; Ranjit Ave; s/d incl breakfast Rs3000/4600; 🔀 🖳 🐾) The best of Amritsar's four-star batch, elegant MK has all the in-room comforts of the Grand Legacy (see above) as well as a business centre, multi-cuisine restaurant, 24-hour coffee shop, health club and bar.

Hotel Ritz Plaza (☎ 2562836; www.ritzhotel.in; the Mall; s/d incl breakfast Rs3500/4700; 🔀 🖳 🐾) Particularly popular with business travellers and tour groups, the well-furnished rooms (either marble or timber flooring) come with TVs, tea and coffee–making facilities, sofas and minibars. Some rooms are bigger than others. On site is a relaxing bar, round-the-clock cafe and multicuisine restaurant.

Eating

The city is famous for its 'Amritsari' deep-fried fish with lemon, chilli, garlic and ginger; sniff out the stalls frying it up (especially prevalent in the old city).

Hotels and restaurants in the (holy) Golden Temple locale don't serve alcohol.

RESTAURANTS

Neelam's (mains Rs30-90; 🕘 9am-10.30pm) Not far from the Golden Temple, this unassuming eatery is a convenient spot to cool your heels over a banana lassi. The have-a-go-at-anything menu includes pizzas, burgers, soups, dosas, *aloo paratha* and, for breakfast, honey muesli.

HARYANA & PUNJAB

Punjabi Rasoi (mains Rs45-85; 9am-11.30pm) A stone's throw away from the Golden Temple, this unpretentious all-veg restaurant rustles up reasonable Indian, Continental and Chinese fare.

Sagar Ratna (Queen's Rd; dosas from Rs45; 9am-11pm;) An easygoing South Indian veg restaurant with fresh lime sodas that will quench the most savage summer thirst. Excellent southern specialities (*idlis*, dosas, *uttapams* etc) and a sprinkling of North Indian and Chinese dishes.

Pizza Point (Phawara Chowk; mains Rs60-110; 9.30am-11pm;) More memorable for being a cool retreat from the congested old city than for its (ordinary) pizzas. Other possibilities include grilled sandwiches, dosas, soups and stuffed *paratha* with yoghurt and pickle.

Crystal Restaurant (2225555; Cooper Rd; mains Rs110-210; 11am-11.30pm;) Rated by many as Amritsar's classiest restaurant, Crystal boasts all sorts of yummy global favourites, from lasagne to fish curry. Book ahead, especially on weekends. There are two side-by-side 'Crystals', apparently due to a family split...we're equally divided when it comes to judging which is best. Guess you'll just have to try both!

Astoria Food Pavillion (mains Rs125-325; noon-11pm;) A pleasant multicuisine restaurant near the MK Hotel cooking up a mishmash of dishes, from chicken *patiala* and veg biryani to poached fish and spinach cannelloni.

Moti Mahal Deluxe (5069991; Hotel Grand Legacy, GT Rd, Model Town; mains Rs125-350; 9am-11.30pm;) Wolf down expertly prepared North Indian cuisine (especially tandoori) in style. Consider the tasty *murgh makhani* (butter chicken) and *diwani handi* (mixed veggies in a roulette of fenugreek and mint). A bottle of Kingfisher is Rs120.

Yellow Chilli (5005504; District Shopping Centre, B-Block, Ranjit Ave; mains Rs145-295; 11am-4pm & 7-11.30pm;) A stylish chain-restaurant conceived by celebrity chef, Sanjeev Kapoor, locals flock here to tuck into delights like the *hariyali machchi* (charcoal-grilled, mint-flavoured fish), rogan josh (slow-cooked mutton in yoghurt and fennel gravy) and blackcurrant *kulfi* (firm-textured ice cream). There's a good veg buffet (Rs165; lunch only). Dinner reservations wise.

Aurah (B-Block, Ranjit Ave; mains Rs150-250; 11.30am-11.30pm;) Above Subway is this chilled-out cafe-style haven, delighting diners with global goodies: glass-noodle salad, lemongrass chicken skewers, risotto, crispy lotus stems, lettuce wraps with sweet chilly dressing, pasta, Caesar salad and, for the mother of all sugar fixes, the 'chocolate trip'.

Barbeque Nation (MK Towers) Not yet open when we stopped by, this new addition to Amritsar's dining scene will mirror its Chandigarh namesake (see p261).

QUICK EATS

Café Coffee Day (Lawrence Rd; snacks from Rs35;) Part of a hip coffee-chain conglomerate, with savoury and sweet munchies, killer coffee and brain-freezing cold granitas.

Barista (Ranjit Ave; snacks from Rs40;) Part of another trendy chain with real-deal coffee, toffee cinnamon frappes and a very summery watermelon mojito freeze.

Amritsar is famous for its *dhabas* (snack bars) such as **Punjab Dhaba** (Goal Hatti Chowk), **Kesar Da Dhaba** (Passian Chowk) and **Brothers' Dhaba** (Town Hall Chowk), all with (mainly Indian) meals averaging Rs80, and open early to late. Brothers' is the current sweetheart, but only by a whisker.

Entertainment

The **Aaanaam** (2210949; Taylor Rd) and **Adarsh** (2565249; MMM Rd) cinemas screen Hindi (and occasionally English) movies. Consult newspapers for session details.

Shopping

Wandering around the skinny alleys of the old city bazaars is an utterly head-spinning assault on all the senses. There are shops selling everything from devotional ornaments to jootis; a good place to buy jootis is around Gandhi Gate (Hall Gate), where they start at Rs200.

Katra Jaimal Singh Bazaar is full of *salwar kameez* and saris, while the city's more modern shops can be found along Lawrence and Mall Rds.

Fabindia (2503102; www.fabindia.com; 30 Ranjit Ave; 10am-8pm) Contemporary-meets-traditional Indian textiles and homewares store.

Getting There & Away

AIR

Amritsar services domestic and international flights.

Air India (2508122; MK Hotel, Ranjit Ave; 9.30am-5.30pm)

Indian Airlines (☎ 2213392; 39A Court Rd; ◷ 10am-5pm Mon-Fri, to 1pm Sat)

Jet Airways (☎ 2508003; Ranjit Ave; ◷ 9am-6pm Mon-Sat)

Kingfisher Airlines (☎ 080-39008888; airport; ◷ 9am-6pm)

Singapore Airlines (☎ 2500330; Nagpal Tower-II, Ranjit Ave; ◷ 9.30am-5.30pm Mon-Sat)

Uzbekistan Airways (☎ 2507744; Ranjit Ave; ◷ 9.30am-5.30pm Mon-Fri, to 1pm Sat)

BUS
Frequent buses leave for Delhi (Rs255, 10 hours), Chandigarh (Rs145, seven hours), Pathankot (Rs54, three hours) and Jammu (Rs130, six hours).

To Himachal Pradesh, at least one bus travels daily to Dalhousie (Rs135, six hours), Dharamsala (Rs125, six hours), Shimla (Rs250, 10 hours) and Manali (Rs300, 14 hours).

Private buses to Delhi (with/without AC Rs450/300, 8½ hours) leave daily from near the train station at 10pm. Other private buses, including to Chandigarh (Rs250) and Jammu (Rs250) depart from Gandhi Gate.

TRAIN
Apart from the train station, a less busy **train reservation office** (◷ 8am-8pm, to 2pm Sun) is at the Golden Temple.

The fastest train to Delhi is the twice-daily *Shatabdi Express* (5.10am service chair car/executive Rs570/1095, 5pm service Rs675/1260, 5¾ hours). A daily *Amritsar-Howrah Mail* run links Amritsar with Lucknow (sleeper/3AC/2AC Rs310/825/1158, 16½ hours), Varanasi (Rs365/998/1373, 22 hours) and Howrah (Rs489/1346/1857, 37 hours).

Getting Around
A free bus service runs from the train station and the bus stand to the Golden Temple every 45 minutes from 4.30am to 9.30pm. Otherwise, from the train station to the Golden Temple a cycle-rickshaw costs around Rs30, an autorickshaw Rs50 and a taxi Rs100. To the airport, an autorickshaw costs Rs200 and a taxi Rs500.

INDIA–PAKISTAN BORDER AT ATTARI/WAGAH
People come to the border, 30km west of Amritsar, for two reasons: to enjoy the late afternoon border-closing ceremony (see the boxed text, p276) or to use the crossing between India and Pakistan (see the boxed text, below).

Return taxis (official ones have yellow numberplates) from Amritsar to the border cost around Rs600 and take about one hour (price includes waiting time). Shared taxis (return per person Rs80) also run to the border-closing ceremony from the dining-hall

HARYANA & PUNJAB

CROSSING INTO PAKISTAN

Border Hours
The border is open from 10am to 4pm daily, but get there at least half an hour before it closes.

Foreign Exchange
There's a **State Bank of India** (◷ 10am-5pm Mon-Sat) which exchanges currency, but it's a tiny branch so play it safe and change money in Amritsar.

Onward Transport
From Wagah (Pakistan) there are buses and taxis to Lahore, 30km away.

Sleeping & Eating
If you have to stay overnight, there's the **Aman Umeed Tourist Complex** (Attari border; r Rs1000; 🛁), which also has a restaurant (mains Rs75 to Rs190).
    There are small stalls selling snacks and cold drinks.

Visas
Visas are theoretically available at the Pakistan embassy in Delhi, however travellers are strongly urged to apply for a visa in their home country, where the process is usually more straightforward (see also p1177).

BORDER BRAVADO

Every late afternoon, just before sunset, members of the Indian and Pakistani military meet at the border to engage in a 30-minute display of pure theatre. The flag-lowering, closing-of-the-border ceremony is a fusion of orderly colonial-style pomp, comical goose-stepping and, considering the two countries' rocky relationship, stunning demonstration of harmony. So popular is this event, that grandstands have been specially constructed to accommodate the patriotic throngs.

The ceremony starts at around 4.15pm in winter and 5.15pm in summer (but double check, given that timings vary according to sunset). Cameras are permitted (free) but large-ish bags are banned (although this is haphazardly enforced).

It's worth getting here early to avoid the stampede when the crowd charges along the chicken run leading to the grandstands. It's about a 10-minute walk from where vehicles drop you to the seating area. Foreigners are allowed to sit at the front stalls (behind the VIP area, which is closest to the border).

Prior to the ceremony, the stony-faced soldiers mill about with the air of self-conscious debutantes and the real action is that of the spectators, some parading the Indian flag. Loud music and a compere pump up the crowd's patriotic fervour. The Pakistanis are equally vociferous, except during Ramadan, when their stands are noticeably quieter.

Then, with a bellow from the guardroom, a squad stomps out, shoulders square, moustaches twirled and eyes bulging. The drill is to parade up and down as dramatically as possible, preceded by a kick so high the soldier looks in danger of concussing himself. The high-octane march to the border, vaguely reminiscent of Monty Python's Ministry of Silly Walks sketch, rouses thunderous applause from the audience and repetitive chants of 'Hindustan zindabad!' (Long live India!).

The gates are flung open and commanding officers of both countries shake hands and salute (blink and you'll miss it). Then, the flags of both countries are simultaneously lowered and folded and the gates slammed shut. The border is now closed for the night.

entrance to the Golden Temple. They leave about two hours before the ceremony starts.

You can travel to the border by autorickshaw but you run the risk of being stopped by the police, as it's illegal for autos to travel beyond Amritsar's city precincts.

Most hotels can arrange trips to the border; one reliable option is the Grand Hotel (p272) which also takes nonguests with advance notice (prices on application).

PATHANKOT

☎ 0186 / pop 168,000

For travellers, the dusty frontier town of Pathankot is a transport hub for neighbouring Himachal Pradesh and Jammu.

Hotel Venice (☎ 2225061; www.venicehotelindia .com; Dhangu Rd; r Rs980;) has the best accommodation (request a renovated room) and several restaurants. There are also hotels on Railway Rd and for those with ongoing rail

tickets, there's the train station retiring rooms (double Rs200).

The **bus station** (☎ 2254435; Gurdaspur Rd) is 500m from the Pathankot Junction train station and 3km from Chakki Bank train station.

Buses go to Amritsar (Rs70, 2½ hours), Jammu (Rs70, 2½ hours), Chamba (Rs80, 3½ hours), Dalhousie (Rs65, 2½ hours), Dharamsala (Rs65, 2½ hours), Manali (Rs280, 10½ hours), Chandigarh (Rs136, six hours) and Delhi (Rs280, 11 hours).

Several daily express trains leave for Delhi (sleeper/3AC/2AC Rs230/540/1000, 11 hours), Amritsar (chair Rs34, three hours) and Jammu (chair Rs40, three hours). The Kangra Valley narrow-gauge line leaves from Pathankot Junction train station (see the boxed text, p383).

Taxis to Amritsar/Dharamsala cost around Rs1300/1400.

Jammu & Kashmir

Welcome to three incredibly different worlds in one state. For most foreign travellers Jammu and Kashmir's great attraction is Ladakh, an unforgettable Himalayan land predominantly populated by disarmingly friendly Tibetan Buddhist people. A world away from anything else in India, Ladakh is a magical patchwork of monasteries, canyons and arid rocky mountainscapes. When the access roads are open (summer only), Ladakh's appealing little 'capital', Leh, is well set up for travellers' needs and ideal for finding trekking buddies or jeep sharers while you nibble on falafels, tandoori pizzas or *momos* (Tibetan dumplings). And if Leh starts to feel a bit too touristy, there's always the much less visited Ladakhi area of Zanskar, hemmed by dazzling snow-topped peaks soaring to over 7000m.

For Indian tourists, Jammu and Kashmir's top attractions are altogether different. Millions of Hindu pilgrims pour into Armanath and Vaishno Devi near Jammu. Other domestic visitors love Muslim Kashmir for its refreshingly cool summer air, its stunning Austrian-style scenery and the winter skiing at Gulmarg. Although long known as the 'Valley of Paradise', Kashmir's political volatility has put off most Western travellers since the late 1980s. Some do stop to glimpse Jammu's curious Hindu temples and to savour Srinagar's magical lakes from a classic houseboat. However, disputes over Kashmir have caused three wars between India and Pakistan, and intercommunal strife closed the Jammu–Srinagar road almost entirely during summer 2008, so it's essential to check the security situation before travelling to either Jammu or Srinagar. If the situation looks too dodgy, play safe and head to Ladakh by air or via the rough but utterly gorgeous Manali road.

JAMMU & KASHMIR

HIGHLIGHTS

- Murmur meditative mantras in the mural-decked gompas (Tibetan Buddhist monasteries) of the **Indus Valley** (p326)

- Escape India's summer heat in entrancing **Leh** (p301), Ladakh's refreshingly human capital, a low-key traveller hub with dusty medieval backstreets, a Potala-style palace and a deep sense of ecological awareness

- Experience the stark magnificence of **Ladakh** (p315) or **Zanskar** (p298) on an unforgettable high-altitude trek

- Enjoy an amusingly caricatured Raj experience relaxing on a deluxe Dal Lake houseboat in **Srinagar** (p291)

- Gawp at the magnificent mountain-valley scenery backing surreally blue **Pangong Tso** (p328) or the splendid **Nubra Valley** (p323)

Srinagar ★   Ladakh ★ ★ Nubra Valley

Indus Valley ★

★ Leh

Zanskar ★   Pangong Tso ★

FAST FACTS

Population 10.1 million
Area 222,236 sq km
Capitals Srinagar (summer), Jammu (winter), Leh (Ladakh)
Main languages Kashmiri, Urdu, Ladakhi, Hindi, Purig, Balti, Dogri, Punjabi and Pahari
When to go May to October (Srinagar), July to early September (Ladakh), December to March (skiing at Gulmarg)

JAMMU & THE KASHMIR VALLEY

Predominantly Hindu, Jammu swealters at the edge of the plains, north of which seemingly endless layers of Alpine peaks start unfolding. Hemmed deep within those mountains on the bed of what was once a vast lake, the Muslim Kashmir Valley is altogether different both visually and culturally. Here tin-roofed villages guard pretty, terraced ricefields delineated by orchards and pin-straight poplar trees. Proudly independent-minded Kashmiris mostly follow a Sufi-based Islamic faith. Many have distinctive green eyes and in winter keep warm by clutching a *kangri* (wicker fire-pot holder) beneath their flowing grey-brown *pheran* (woollen capes).

Once the very vision of tranquility, the Kashmir Valley has been scarred by violence ever since Indian Independence. Three wars with Pakistan have left greater Kashmir painfully divided. The crippled tourist industry had been significantly recovering until July 2008 when renewed Hindu-Muslim intercommunal disturbances exploded over a seemingly minor land issue. Many locals believe this was blown out of proportion for a variety of somewhat self-serving political reasons. Nonetheless events snowballed rapidly, with a prominent Kashmiri nationalist leader shot and the Jammu–Srinagar road blockaded for much of the summer. Although tempers had cooled by September 2008, the underlying problems remain and it would be foolish to visit Kashmir without triple-checking the political situation first (see boxed text, p283).

History

Geologists and Hindu mystics agree that the 140km-long Kashmir Valley was once a vast lake. Where they disagree is whether it was drained by a post–Ice Age earthquake or by Lord Vishnu and friends to kill a lake demon.

In the 3rd-century BC the Hindu kingdom of Kashmir was transformed into a major centre of Buddhist learning under Emperor Ashoka. For centuries Kashmir's Buddhist artists travelled across the Himalaya, creating fabulous monastery murals like those that still exist at Alchi (p321).

In the 13th- and 14th-centuries AD Islam arrived in Kashmir through the inspiration of peaceable Sufi mystics. Later some Muslim rulers, like the iconaclastic Sultan Sikander (1389–1413), set about the destruction of Hindu temples and Buddhist monasteries. However, others like the great Zeinalab'din (ruled 1423–74) encouraged such religious and cultural tolerance that medieval visitors reported finding it hard to tell Kashmiri Hindus and Muslims apart. Relative open-mindedness continued under Mughal emperor Akbar (1556–1605), whose troops took Kashmir in 1586. The Mughals saw Kashmir as their Xanadu and developed a series of magnificent gardens around Srinagar that partially survive today.

When the British arrived in India, Jammu and Kashmir was a loose affiliation of independent kingdoms, nominally controlled by the Sikh rulers of Jammu. In 1846, after the British had defeated the Sikhs, they handed Kashmir to Maharaja Gulab Singh in return for a yearly tribute of six shawls, 12 goats and a horse. Singh's autocratic Hindu-Dogra dynasty ruled on until Independence, showing an infamous disregard for the welfare of the Muslim majority. Many citizens were little better than slaves and subject to the *begar* system in which serfs were liable for service as unpaid porters or labourers at the whim of local pandit landowners.

As Partition approached in 1947, Kashmir was in an odd situation. Although Jammu and Kashmir's population was majority Muslim, the (jailed) popular leader of the predominantly Islamic opposition favoured joining India. The autocratic Hindu Maharaja Hari Singh favoured Kashmiri independence but proved unable to make a definitive decision. Months passed. Finally, to force the issue, Pashtun tribesmen, backed by the new government in Pakistan, attempted to simply grab the state by force. They almost succeeded. In a nail-biting climax worthy of a Hollywood blockbuster, the tribesmen were within a day or so of reaching virtually unprotected Srinagar. In the nick of time, Nehru, himself a Kashmiri Hindu and independent India's first Prime Minister, airlifted in Indian troops sparking the first India–Pakistani war. Srinagar was held. The invaders were pushed out of the Kashmir Valley, but Pakistan retained control of Baltistan, Muzaffarabad and the valley's main access routes. Kashmir has remained divided ever since along a tenuous UN-demarkated border, known as the Line of Control. A proposed referendum to let Kashmir's people decide (for Pakistan or India) never materialised and Pakistan invaded again in 1965, triggering another protracted conflict.

Although many Indian Kashmiris would rather be independent of both India *and* Pakistan, the conflict became a cause célèbre for pro-Pakistani Islamic radicals. A militant fringe turned to armed rebellion, countered with brutal force from the Indian Army, stoking a cycle of increasing resentment. By 1990 the state was awash with fighters, some from Kashmir but rather more from Afghanistan and Pakistan, whose brand of fundamentalist Sunni Islam jarred significantly with Kashmir's native Sufi-based forms of broadminded spirituality. Groups founded by Afghan mujahedin claimed to be fighting for Kashmiri rights, but terrorised inhabitants of areas they controlled for perceived transgressions against Islam and for failing to support the insurgency.

Kashmir was placed under direct rule from Delhi in 1990, triggering the bloodiest years of unrest. Massacres and bomb attacks by militants were matched by human rights abuses by the Indian army, including the unexplained disappearance of approximately 4000 people. Nuclear tests by the Indian government in 1998 brought tensions almost to breaking point. Pakistan responded with its own tests, then mounted an incursion across the Line of Control near Kargil. Nuclear war seemed possible and US president Bill Clinton described Kashmir as the most dangerous place in the world. Fortunately the UN talked the two countries back from the brink. After a 2003 ceasefire, increasing autonomy for Kashmir was matched by a significant reduction in tensions, while a controversial 2.5m-high double-fenced minefield barrier built parallel to the Line of Control helped India to reduce cross-border attacks. A tragic October 2005 earthquake killed over 75,000 people, mostly in Pakistani-controlled Kashmir, but helped bring the two governments closer together as some aid was allowed to cross the Line of Control.

With militant attacks dwindling, domestic tourist numbers had been increasing dramatically over recent years. However, summer 2008 saw widespread violence and strikes. These were provoked by a seemingly minor dispute over whether a Hindu charity should own a 39-acre plot of land at Amarnath, underlining how sensitive intercommunal relations remain. Disturbances spiralled into a two-month cascade of strikes, violence and curfews. Things calmed significantly in September 2008, but the situation remains extremely tense, with some in Jammu demanding a separate state.

Meanwhile ever-peaceful Ladakh is angling for Union status (like Chandigarh) so that it can finally divorce itself from Jammu and Kashmir's troubles, with which it has no real connection.

Climate

Heavy rains, sweltering heat and high humidity afflict Jammu from June to August, but summers in the mountainous Kashmir Valley are contrastingly cool and fresh. December to March is the ski season at Gulmarg, but while the Jammu–Srinagar road is usually kept open through winter, smaller roads, including the Sonamarg–Kargil route, are blocked by snow and closed until late spring.

Dangers & Annoyances

Political violence is a worry (see boxed text, p283) and you should be wary of dodgy houseboat packages, especially those booked outside Kashmir (see boxed text, p292). Always keep you passport handy when travelling: many police checkpoints will examine and annotate it. All roads to Ladakh become impassable in winter, when most tourist infrastructure closes down from October to May.

Getting There & Around

Numerous domestic airlines fly to Srinagar and Jammu. Buses and shared jeeps connect to Ladakh, but only in summer. Jammu has rail connections to Delhi and Amritsar, but engineering problems have delayed the building of the new Jammu–Srinagar railway. Hitchhiking

JAMMU & KASHMIR

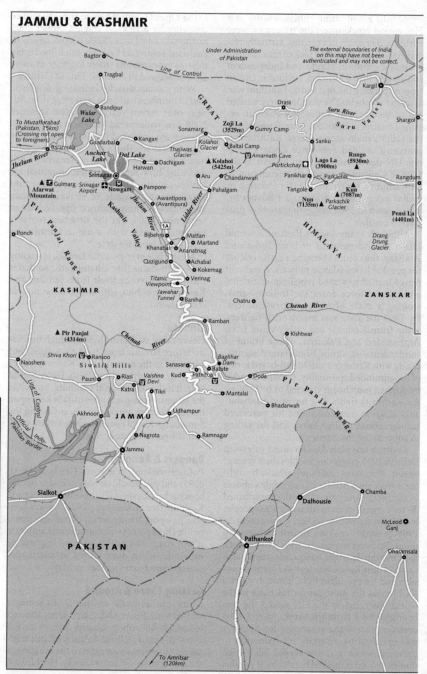

Under Administration of Pakistan

The external boundaries of India on this map have not been authenticated and may not be correct.

Bagtor
Tragbal
Line of Control
GREAT
Kargil
Bandipur
Drass
Suru River
Shargol
Wular Lake
Zoji La (3529m)
Gumry Camp
Suru Valley
To Muzaffarabad (Pakistan, 75km) (Crossing not open to foreigners)
Sonamarg
Sanku
Lago La (3900m)
Rungo (5930m)
Baramulla
Gandarbal
Kangan
Kolahoi Glacier
Baltal Camp
Rangdum
Anchar Lake
Thajiwas Glacier
Amarnath Cave
Purtickchay
Panikhar
Parkachik
Jhelum River
Srinagar
Dal Lake
Harwan
Dachigam
Kolahoi (5425m)
Kun (7087m)
Gulmarg
Srinagar Airport
Nowgam
Pampore
Aru
Chandanwari
Tangole
Nun (7135m)
Parkachik Glacier
Afarwat Mountain
Awantipora (Avantipura)
Pahalgam
HIMALAYA
Pensi La (4401m)
Ponch
Kashmir Valley
Jhelum River
Lidder River
ZANSKAR
Pir Panjal Range
1A
Bijbehra
Mattan
Martand
Drang Drung Glacier
KASHMIR
Khanabal
Ananantag
Qazigund
Achabal
Kokernag
Titanic Viewpoint
Verinag
Chatru
Chenab River
Jawahar Tunnel
Banihal
Pir Panjal (4314m)
Ramban
Kishtwar
Shiva Khori
Ransoo
Chenab River
Baglihar Dam
Naoshera
Siwalik Hills
Sanasar
Batote
Doda
Pir Panjal Range
Pauni
Riasi
Vaishno Devi
Kud
Pathitop
Line of Control
Katra
Tikri
Mantalai
Bhadarwah
Akhnoor
JAMMU
Udhampur
Official Indo-Pakistan Border
Nagrota
Ramnagar
Jammu
Sialkot
Chamba
Dalhousie
McLeod Ganj
Pathankot
PAKISTAN
Dharamsala
To Amritsar (120km)

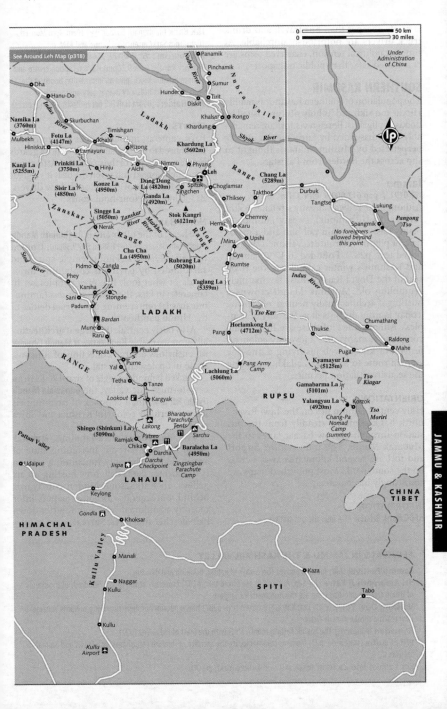

is rarely cheaper than bus travel, and drunk truck drivers are notoriously unreliable. At times of political tension, chartered jeeps are considered safer than public transport.

SOUTHERN KASHMIR

The population of southern Kashmir is mainly Hindu and Sikh and its holy sites are visited by floods of pilgrims. Foreign visitors are remarkably rare, dissuaded by fairly regular attacks perpetrated by Muslim militants thought to slip across the border from Pakistan.

Jammu

☎ 0191 / pop 612,000 / elev 327m

Although the railway already stretches 65km further (to Udhampur), sweaty Jammu remains Kashmir's main rail hub and a major halt for pilgrims en route to Vaishno Devi (see boxed text, p287). Founded in 1730, Jammu and Kashmir's winter capital was the royal seat of the Dogra Rajas, whose fascinatingly crumbling old Mubarak Mandi crowns a bustling if architecturally neutral 'old town'. Today Jammu dubs itself as the 'city of temples'. Although few of these are historically compulsive, many offer a joyously colourful festival of kitsch, well justifying a one-day stop en route to Srinagar/Ladakh, assuming the security situation permits.

ORIENTATION

Hilly central Jammu lies on the Tawi River's north bank climbing steadily from the bus station through narrow bazaar lanes to the Mubarak Mandi. The train station, airport and fort are several kilometres away across on the south bank. Most published maps are confusingly inaccurate.

INFORMATION

HFDC Bank Reliable ATM near the bus station.

J&K Bank (Raghunath Bazaar; ⏰ 10am-4pm Mon-Fri, 10am-1pm Sat) Currency exchange and ATM.

J&K Tourism (☎ 2548172, 2544527; www.jktdc.org; Regency Rd; ⏰ 6am-9.30pm) Has a reception centre and accommodation block, plus an information booth at the train station. Its Rs10 city map is very approximate.

Web Raiders (Dogra Hall Rd; per hr Rs40) Internet access.

SIGHTS

Bags, cameras, mobile phones and even pens might need to be deposited with security guards before visiting any of the main sites. Attractions are widely spread and given the heat it's a great idea to take one of the autorickshaw drivers' Rs300 inclusive four-hour 'tours'.

North Bank

The heart of the older city is **Raghunath Mandir** (Raghunath Bazaar; ⏰ 6-11.30am & 6-9.30pm), fronted by a gilded *sikhara* (Hindu temple-spire) and surrounded by pavilions containing thousands of what look like grey pebbles set in concrete; in fact, these are *saligrams* (ammonite fossils) representing the myriad deities of the Hindu pantheon.

Also fairly central, the large if architecturally unremarkable **Ranbireshwar Mandir** (Shalimar Rd) enshrines a large collection of lingams, some in opalescent crystal.

Tucked behind a gaggle of shawl stalls in an easy-to-miss side valley, the **Gupawala Mandir** (Pinkho Rd) is a small complex of cave-tunnels with glitteringly colourful Krishna and Shiva caves.

The imposing, once-fabulous **Mubarak Mandi** lies in a sorry if intriguing state of semicollapse. The only functioning section is the former **Durba Hall**, now hosting an art gallery. In Kafkaesque hidden courtyards behind, bureaucrats' forgotten papers litter recently abandoned rooms and flutter down half-derelict stairways. Surreal.

FESTIVALS IN JAMMU & THE KASHMIR VALLEY

Jammu Festival (Apr; Jammu, above) Three days of eating, drinking and dancing.

Sri Amarnath Ji Yatra (Jul-Sep; Armanath, see boxed text, p287) Especially at full moon, hundreds of thousands of Hindu trekker-pilgrims venerate the Armanath ice lingam.

Vaishno Devi Yatra (early Oct; Katra, see boxed text, p287) Hindu pilgrim numbers swarming towards Vaishno Devi reach a climax in early October.

Ramadan (statewide) The Islamic fasting month ends with the feast of Eid al-Fitr (p27).

Eid al-Adha (statewide, p27) Muslims commemorate the sacrifice of Ibrahim (Abraham) with feasts and animal sacrifices.

For Ladakh and Zanskar festivals, see boxed text, p300.

IS IT SAFE?

When things are calm, Kashmir is no more dangerous than anywhere else in India, but army presence at banks, offices and religious sites can feel intrusive (don't take photos of anything military without express permission). The problem is that attacks can occur without warning and with intercommunal tempers ever raw, it only takes a firebrand speech or a controversial arrest for the conflict to flare up again.

Before arriving read a wide range of sources to get a feel of the situation, keeping in mind that within the Kashmir debate every viewpoint sounds 'biased' to someone. Compare the following:

■ *Daily Excelsior* (www.dailyexcelsior.com)

■ *Greater Kashmir* (www.greaterkashmir.com)

■ *Kashmir Herald* (www.kashmirherald.com)

■ *Kashmir Times* (www.kashmirtimes.com)

■ *IndiaMike* (www.indiamike.com/india/jammu-and-kashmir-f30)

Be aware that travel insurance policies might be voided if your home government has issued specific advice against travel here. Use common sense and avoid public demonstrations, political rallies and military installations. Buses, bus stations and pilgrim groups have all been targeted in the past.

The **Amar Mahal Palace** (☎ 2546783; Indian/foreigner Rs10/45, camera Rs10; ⊗ 9am-12.50pm & 2-5.50pm Oct-Mar, to 4.50pm Apr-Sep) was the last official residence of the Dogra Rajas. It's a very European brick-and-stone mansion with fine wooden balconies and a token castle tower. The watercolour collection is less impressive than the building's clifftop setting with sweeping valley views.

South Bank

Across the Tawi River the low but completely renovated walls of the 19th-century hilltop **Bahu Fort** now enclose a Kali temple, while the lawn outside covers a subterranean **aquarium** (adult/child Rs20/10; ⊗ 11am-9pm Tue-Sat, to 8pm Sun) entered through the gaping mouth of a giant carp.

The merrily gaudy **Har-ki-Paori Mandir** is a family of giant, concrete gods in a modern, Disneyesque style. They survey a swimming point where young lads dive into the fast-flowing Tawi, egged on by their colourfully dressed families. Viewed across the river, the vast scale of the clifftop Mubarak Mandi becomes apparent.

Some tours wind up the southeast bypass by visiting the very weird **Mahamaya Mandir**. This is half construction site and half army-crow's nest – it is entirely unattractive, but the views are great and the avocado orchards that you will drive through en route will be full of monkeys, goats and even the odd camel.

SLEEPING

Hotels are spread all over town, but many have been comprehensively trashed by less than careful pilgrims who fill virtually every bed during the Vaishno Devi *yatra* (pilgrimage) season (early October). There's a major concentration of basic budget options around Vinaik Bazaar, a block south and east of the bus station, but many rooms here are windowless boxes. Names like Hotel Touch Wood give a premonition of their chancy nature.

Vaishnavi Dham (☎ 2473275; www.maavaishnodevi .org; Railway Rd; dm/d Rs60/650; ✷) Designed specifically for *yatra* devotees but open to all, this big, airy white hostel building is a bargain if you don't mind bedding down in a room of 20 pilgrims. You'll find it by turning right immediately on exiting the train station's large forecourt square.

Green View Hotel (☎ 2573906; 69 Chand Nagar; s from Rs125, d Rs250-350) A little cleaner, quieter and more professionally managed than most Vinaik Bazaar options, the Green View's cheap singles are tiny boxes, but most doubles come with cold shower, air-cooler, TV, clean squat toilet and even windows. There's a bare concrete rooftop terrace. Access is down the lane opposite the gharishly repainted if

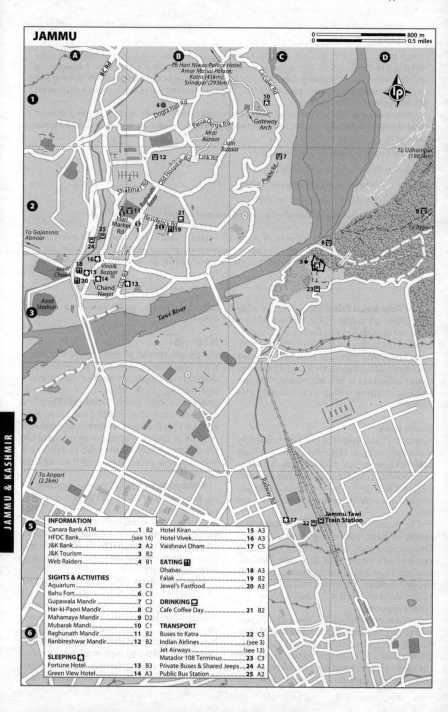

JAMMU

0 — 800 m
0 — 0.5 miles

To Hari Niwas Palace Hotel;
Amar Mahal Palace;
Katra (45km);
Srinagar (293km)

To Udhampur (1983km)

To Gajansoo;
Abnoor

To Bypass

To Airport
(2.2km)

Tawi River

Jammu Tawi
Train Station

Railway Rd

JAMMU & KASHMIR

far from lovely Hotel Kiran, a block east of Jewel Chowk.

Hotel Vivek (☎ 2547545; Below Gumat; s/d from Rs700/900; 🗙) A decent midrange choice very near the bus station. Warm lighting and decent AC make up for windowless back rooms and somewhat noisy front ones.

Fortune Hotel (☎ 2561415; www.fortunehotels.in; GSS Rd; s/d from Rs3300/3600; 🗙 🛜) Apart from minor housekeeping glitches, this stylish, modern business hotel is all you would hope for, with hints of oriental minimalism in the atrium lobby, complimentary coffee, a bar, a disco and an appealing rooftop restaurant. Rates are cheaper if booked online.

Hari Niwas Palace Hotel (☎ 2543303; www.hariniwas palace.com; s/d from Rs3300/6600, deluxe s/d Rs6600/8250; 🗙 🏊) With Maharaja connections and elements of princely style, this all-white 20th-century palace has a fine clifftop setting beside the Amar Mahal Palace. Deluxe rooms are fine but cheaper rooms are below ground level and upkeep is a little flawed. Good indoor pool.

EATING

The one-block link road connecting Jewel Chowk to Vinaik Bazaar has several inexpensive *dhabas* (snack bars) serving *chana puri* (spiced chickpeas served on a *puri*, Rs11) breakfasts and delicious 'chicken fry' dinners (Rs65) that come heaped with splendidly caramelised onions. Nearby are wine shops and two bars.

Jewel's Fastfood (Rs45-100; ⏲ 9am-10.30pm) For a range of burgers, good-value dosas, curries and thalis (veg/nonveg Rs80/100) you might forgive this place's blandly Western atmosphere in return for the air-con and a menu.

Falak (☎ 2520770; KC Residency Hotel, Residency Rd; mains Rs130-275 plus 22.5%; ⏲ 12.30-11pm) This jerkily revolving hotel restaurant serves a faultless if slightly pricey range of enticing Indian food.

Cafe Coffee Day (Residency Rd; ⏲ 10am-11pm) Stop in for Jammu's best coffee in a reliably air-conditioned branch of the Coffee Day chain.

GETTING THERE & AWAY
Air
The airlines **GoAir** (www.goair.in), **Indian Airlines** (☎ 2456086; J&K Tourism complex; ⏲ 10am-4.45pm Mon-Sat), **Jet Airways** (☎ 2574312; KC Residency Hotel), **JetLite** (www.jetlite.com) and **SpiceJet** (www.spicejet.com) all fly to Delhi (from Rs3150, one hour) and Srinagar (from Rs3150, 35 minutes). JetLite and GoAir also fly to Mumbai, while Indian

Airlines also flies to Leh (Rs7345, Monday and Friday).

Bus & Jeep
Private buses and shared jeeps depart from a chaotic strip in the shadow of the BC Rd overpass, while public buses use the big, rotting concrete bus station complex immediately east. Public buses to Delhi leave at 4.30am, 5.45am, 7.40am, 10am, 12.05pm and 1.45pm, with a wide range of private services departing between 6.30pm and 10.30pm, including several sleeper buses (Rs500). Other public bus services include Chamba (p386; Rs170, seven hours, 8.05am), Dalhousie (p383; Rs145, six hours, 8am) and Dharamsala (p368; Rs220, five hours, 8.30am), along with some 30 daily services to Amritsar (p268; Rs102, six hours) via Pathankot (p276; Rs50, 2½ hours). Changing in Pathankot gives you further options.

For Srinagar, bus services are currently suspended, so public transport means sharing/chartering a jeep (from Rs250/3000). There's plenty of choice in the mornings around both bus and train stations. To Katra, buses/minibuses/taxis (Rs29/53/710) depart from the train station.

Train
Jammu Tawi, Jammu's main train station, is 5km from the bus station. Useful overnight trains to Delhi include the *Jammu Mail* (4034) at 4.15pm (13 hours) and the *Shalimar Express* (4646) at 9pm (14 hours). For Amritsar the best train departs at 2.30pm (from Rs125, four hours). The Indore-bound *Malwa Express* (2920) leaves at 9am, reaching Agra at 10.40pm. Departing at 10.45pm on Monday, Thursday and Sunday, the *Himgri Express* (2332) to Howrah (Kolkata, 60 hours) runs via Varanasi (22½ hours).

Enginering and terrorist problems have seriously delayed sections on the Udhampur–Katra–Qazigund sector of the new Jammu–Srinagar railway, but by 2012 the line should cross the Chenab River on what will be one of the world's highest bridges.

GETTING AROUND
Autorickshaws charge Rs30 for short hops, Rs70 between the train and bus stations, and Rs100 to the airport. Overloaded minibuses and curious Matador stretch minibuses operate all over town for Rs5 a ride: take route

108 to the fort or route 117 between the bus and train stations. Satwari minibuses pass the airport.

JAMMU TO SRINAGAR

The well-paved Jammu–Srinagar road laboriously crosses two passes and has many scenic points, but it's also exceedingly busy, a continuously thundering conveyerbelt of trucks and army convoys. The conveyerbelt jams up at landslides and stops altogether during hartals, which rendered the road virtually impassable during summer 2008, paralysing Kashmir's trade and leaving travellers stranded. Be prepared to fly should the route close again.

Leaving Jammu, the road climbs through a bizarre landscape of wooded hilly chunks that seem to have been diced by an overenthusiastic divine sous-chef preparing a never-finished geological recipe. Approaching **Tikri**, a hulking, multishouldered mountain looms ahead like a phantom, climbed by the precarious hairpins of the pilgrim trail to **Vaishno Devi Shrine** (see boxed text, opposite) sitting high on its flank (access from nearby Katra).

Viewed across the Tawi River at Km72.3 (6km beyond sprawling **Udhampur**), an impressive ribbon of **waterfall** pours right out of the wooded mountainside. Hereafter the road winds up a vertical kilometre into mature coniferous woodlands to **Kud** and **Panitop** (Km110), between which lie a sprinkling of somewhat faded **resort hotels** (d off season/rack rate from Rs150/2000). **Sanasar** (http://campsanasar.com), an 18km detour along the mountaintops from Panitop, was once popular for paragliding.

The main road zigzags back down almost as far as the controversial billion-dollar **Baglihar Dam** before winding back up to the 2531m **Jawahar Tunnel**, where foreigners must fill overlong forms for entering/leaving Kashmir (politically curious given that you're supposedly already within Jammu and Kashmir state). The **Titanic Viewpoint** (Km208), 2km beyond the tunnel, provides sweeping views across the vast mountain-rimmed **Kashmir Valley**, with its beautiful poplar-edged rice terraces. Another viewpoint at Km213 surveys **Verinag**, one of three local villages to sport Mughal Gardens. Most traffic makes a tea stop in **Qazigund**, full of saffron sellers and shops selling locally produced cricket bats.

At **Khanabal**, the **Ananatnag** side road leads up the Lidder Valley towards the pine-framed pilgrim-tourist resort of **Pahalgam** (right)

At the roadside in **Awantipora** (Avantipura; Km266.5), 29km before Srinagar, is the chunky ruin of 9th-century **Awantiswarmi Vishnu Temple** (Indian/foreigner Rs5/100; ☾ dawn-dusk), with stylistic similarities to the Hindu temples of Southeast Asia. A smaller, similarly ancient **Shiva Temple**, 1km west, can be visited on the same ticket.

Dusty, sprawling **Pampore**, 14km before central Srinagar, is India's saffron capital and rolling roadside fields directly south are attractively dappled with violet crocus blooms in October (it's the flowers' stamens that produce saffron's yellow pigment, not their purple petals).

Pahalgam

pop 6000 / elev 2740m

During the pilgrimage season (June to August; see boxed text, opposite), Pahalgam is jammed full of Amarnath *yatri*, but in early September it makes a fine spot for gentle walks or pony treks, notably to the Baisarn (5km) and Dhabyan (7.5km) viewpoints or to Tulyan Lake (7km). The **Jawahar Institute** (☎ 243129; ☾ 10am-5pm Mon-Sat), 1km south of the town centre, organises fair-value multiday **treks** (☾ Apr-Nov) and **skiing** (☾ Jan-Feb). Up the Aru road, **white-water rafting** (☾ mid-Apr–late-Sep) is offered by **Highland Excursions** (☎ 01942488061; www.highlandoutdoors.com).

Minor Pahalgam attractions include the 11th-century **Mamleshwar Temple** on the west bank, the wooden town **mosque** and the flower-filled **Club Park**.

Most of Pahalgam's dozens of pilgrim hotels shut down in winter.

SRINAGAR

☎ 0194 / pop 988,000 / elev 1730m

Indulgent houseboats on placid Dal Lake, famous Mughal gardens, colourfully historic wooden mosques and Rozabal's curious 'Jesus tomb' all combine with a delightfully mild sum-

---

SRINAGAR'S BUSINESS HOURS

Most shops, banks and offices shut for Muslim prayers around lunchtime on Friday: if you have urgent business, get it done on Thursday to be safe. Even when there is no official curfew, don't rely on being able to find an autorickshaw or boatman after 8pm, when Srinagar becomes eerily silent.

AMARNATH & VAISHNO DEVI

In a cave at **Armanath**, a bizarre natural stone lingam becomes opalescently encrusted with ice between May and August. This divine phenomenon attracts over half a million pious Hindu pilgrims annually, despite regular threats from Kashmiri militants. Tensions have been particularly strained here since a land-ownership dispute spiralled into state-wide violence during 2008. Nonetheless, joining the chaotic swarm of pilgrim trekkers is an unforgettable experience if you're prepared for the risks, the intrusive security and the human-herd reality (don't expect a meditative country hike). All those attempting the *yatra* (pilgrimage) must sign up for a pilgrim's card and be suitably dressed for the potentially sub-zero conditions before being allowed to start the walk.

There are two approaches. Starting from Pahalgam (opposite), a 16km taxi ride leads to Chandanwari, from where Armanath is accessed by a 36km, three-day hike. Alternatively, shared jeeps departing from Somamarg (p294; 9am) run to Baltal Camp, from where it's possible to reach the cave and return in a long day hike. Wealthier pilgrims complete the journey by pony, helicopter or *dandy* (palanquin).

Throughout summer, hotels in the feeder towns charge virtually any price they want for lacklustre rooms given the crush of pilgrims, with demand peaking during the Shivrani Festival in July.

Every bit as popular is the *yatra* to the cave abode of **Vaishno Devi** (www.maavaishnodevi.org), where Hindu pilgrims pay respect to the goddess' three forms, creative Saraswati, persevering Lakshmi and destructive Kali. The final approach is by wading through icy water after a 13.5km mountain climb from **Katra**, itself 45km from Jammu. Peak seasons here are May, June and early October. As in Armanath, there are serious security concerns.

mer climate to make Srinagar one of India's top domestic tourist attractions. Except, that is, when intercommunal tensions erupt. Sadly, at the time of research one such eruption was in full swing with paralysing strikes and 24-hour curfews. Expect details to change considerably as the situation normalises (or deteriorates further). Visiting Srinagar without thoroughly checking the latest security situation would be foolhardy (see boxed text, p283).

Orientation

Srinagar's three main areas converge around Dalgate, where the southwestern nose of Dal Lake passes through a lock gate. The Old City is northwest, the main commercial centre southwest around Lal Chowk and the main concentration of houseboats faces the Boulevard (aka Boulevard Rd) directly east. Mughal gardens are strung out over several kilometres further east.

Information

INTERNET ACCESS

Cafe Robusta (CRL Lounge, MA Rd; Rs45; ☽ 9.30am-9pm) There's no time limit for wi-fi access at this cafe (p293).

Euphoria (Old Gagribal Rd; per 30min/hr Rs30/50; ☽ 8am-midnight summer, 9am-10pm winter)

Skybiz Internet (Dalgate; per hr Rs40; ☽ 9am-8pm)

Zee Digital Arts (Munawarabad Rd; per hr Rs30; ☽ 9am-7pm)

MONEY

HFDC (Court Rd) Reliable ATM.

J&K Bank (MA Rd; ☽ 10am-4pm Mon-Fri, to 12.30pm Sat) Changes cash and travellers cheques. There's another branch on the Boulevard.

POST

Main post office (Bund; ☽ 10am-5pm Mon-Sat) Intimidatingly fortified, with customers searched on entry.

TOURIST INFORMATION

Tourism Reception Centre (☎ 2456291; www.jk tourism.org, www.jktdc.org; ☽ 24hr) With perseverance you might actually find answers to your questions at this unhelpful centre.

Sights

DAL LAKE

Whether or not you sleep on one of its wonderful time-warp **houseboats**, beautifully serene Dal Lake is likely to be your main memory of Srinagar. In open sections the mirror-flat waters beautifully reflect the misty peaks of the Pir Panjal mountains. From over a dozen boat jetties, hand-paddled, gaily painted *shikaras* (gondola-like boats) transport goods to market, children to school, and visitors on explorative tours of the lake's floating communities, gardens and markets. Apart from the persistant (if usually very polite) waterborn salesmen, it's a truly idyllic scene.

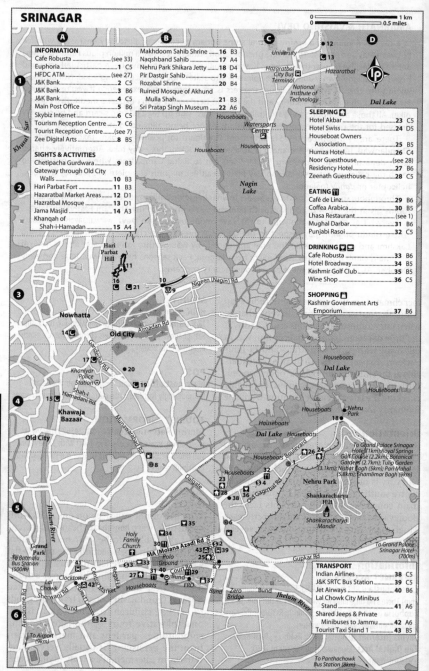

SRINAGAR

INFORMATION
Cafe Robusta	(see 33)
Euphoria	1 C5
HDFC ATM	(see 27)
J&K Bank	2 C5
J&K Bank	3 B6
J&K Bank	4 C5
Main Post Office	5 B6
Skybiz Internet	6 C6
Tourism Reception Centre	7 C5
Tourist Reception Centre	(see 7)
Zee Digital Arts	8 B5

SIGHTS & ACTIVITIES
Chetipacha Gurdwara	9 B3
Gateway through Old City Walls	10 B3
Hari Parbat Fort	11 B3
Hazaratbal Market Areas	12 D1
Hazratbal Mosque	13 D1
Jama Masjid	14 A3
Khanqah of Shah-i-Hamadan	15 A4

Makhdoom Sahib Shrine	16 B3
Naqshband Sahib	17 A4
Nehru Park Shikara Jetty	18 D4
Pir Dastgir Sahib	19 B4
Rozabal Shrine	20 B4
Ruined Mosque of Akhund Mulla Shah	21 B3
Sri Pratap Singh Museum	22 A6

SLEEPING
Hotel Akbar	23 C5
Hotel Swiss	24 D5
Houseboat Owners Association	25 B5
Humza Hotel	26 C4
Noor Guesthouse	(see 28)
Residency Hotel	27 B6
Zeenath Guesthouse	28 C5

EATING
Café de Linz	29 B6
Coffea Arabica	30 B5
Lhasa Restaurant	(see 1)
Mughal Darbar	31 B6
Punjabi Rasoi	32 C5

DRINKING
Cafe Robusta	33 B6
Hotel Broadway	34 B5
Kashmir Golf Club	35 B5
Wine Shop	36 C5

SHOPPING
Kashmir Government Arts Emporium	37 B6

TRANSPORT
Indian Airlines	38 C5
J&K SRTC Bus Station	39 C5
Jet Airways	40 B6
Lal Chowk City Minibus Stand	41 A6
Shared Jeeps & Private Minibuses to Jammu	42 A6
Tourist Taxi Stand 1	43 B5

JAMMU & KASHMIR

A handy jetty for hiring tour *shikaras* faces Nehru Park.

PARKS & GARDENS

Srinagar is famed as a city of delightful gardens, many dating back to the Mughal era. Most have a fundamentally similar design, with terraced lawns, fountain pools and carefully manicured flower beds interspersed with mighty *chinar* trees (national tree of Kashmir) leading back to pavilions or mock fortress facades.

Built for Nur Jahan by her husband Jehangir, **Shalimar Bagh** (adult/child Rs10/5; ☺ 9am-dusk Apr-Oct, 10am-dusk Nov-Mar) is the most famous garden. However, with steeper terracing and a lovely lake-facing panorama, **Nishat Bagh** (adult/child Rs10/5; ☺ 9am-dusk Sat-Thu) is more immediately impressive.

Pari Mahal (admission free; ☺ dawn-dusk) is set amid palace ruins high above the lakeshore. Viewed from afar the ensemble looks especially intriguing when floodlit at night. By day it's worth the long, steep autorickshaw ride for the fabulous lake views more than for the gardens themselves. Bring ID for serious police checks on your way. En route you'll pass the more modest **Cheshmashahi Garden** (adult/child Rs10/5; ☺ 8am-8pm) and the extensive, less formal **Botanical Garden** (adult/child Rs10/5; ☺ 8am-dusk Sat-Thu). Just behind that, Asia's biggest **Tulip Garden** (admission Rs50; ☺ dawn-dusk Apr) attracts crowds in April. Its long, straight rows of blooming tulips would look like a typical Dutch flower farm but for the backdrop of mountains.

OLD CITY
Khanqah of Shah-i-Hamadan

With frontage and interiors covered in elaborately coloured wood carvings and papiermâché reliefs, this distinctively spired 1730s **Khanqah of Shah-i-Hamadan** (Muslim Meeting Hall; Khawaja Bazaar area) is Srinagar's most beautiful historic building. Non-Muslim visitors can peek through the door but may not enter. The building stands on the site of one of Kashmir's first mosques, founded by Persian saint Mir Sayed Ali Hamadani. Nicknamed 'Shah', Hamadani had arrived in 1372, one of 700 refugees fleeing Timur's conquest of Iran. He is said to have converted 37,000 people to Sufi Islam, and it's also likely that his retinue introduced Kashmiris to the Persian art of fine carpet-making.

Jama Masjid

Srinagar's principal mosque, the mighty 1672 **Jama Masjid** (Nowhatta) has room for 33,000 devotees. Each of the 378 roof-support columns was fashioned from the trunk of a single deodar tree. Monumental brick gatehouses mark the four cardinal directions. Bags and cameras are prohibited.

Pir Dastgir Sahib

The large, fanciful green-and-white Sufi shrine **Pir Dastgir Sahib** (Khanyar Chowk area; ☺ 4am-10pm) has a spired tower and wooden filigree work outside. The colourfully faceted interior has some beautiful papier-mâché work around a series of graves that flash gaudily with fairy lights.

Rozabal

The small, green **Rozabal Shrine** (Ziyarat Hazrati Youza Asouph) is a minute's stroll northwest from Pir Dastgir Sahib facing the four-level brick tower of Rozabal Mosque. Although very modest, a highly controversial theory claims that the shrine's crypt holds the grave of Jesus Christ (see boxed text, p290). This claim is at the core of Shawn Haigns' 2007 *The Da Vinci Code*–style thriller *The Rozabal Line*. Supposedly a sarcophagus here features carved feet distinctively punctured by half-moon 'crucifixion marks'. The grave chamber is hidden beneath a spangled black canopy so visitors can't check. Nonetheless the very act of visiting this little place is highly thought-provoking and might inspire you to read more deeply about the fascinating subject of Jesus' historical career.

KASHMIRI MOSQUES

Unique Kashmiri mosques are generally square buildings, topped by multilevel roofs and a modest central spire. Minarets are rarely seen. For visitors, the highlights are the interior walls covered in papiermâché or *khatamband* (faceted wood panelling) painted in vivid geometric and floral patterns. Follow normal Islamic formalities (dress modestly, remove shoes) and ask permission before entering or taking photos inside. As in any mosque, women will usually be expected to cover their hair and use the women's entrance.

JESUS IN KASHMIR?

To many the theory sounds crackpot or even blasphemous, but several authors have claimed that Jesus' 'lost years' (between his youth and the start of his ministry aged 30) were spent in India, where he was inspired by Buddhism. This idea gained a lot of publicity in the 1890s when Russian traveller Nicolas Notovitch 'discovered' since missing but supposedly corroborating documents at Hemis Gompa (p327), described in his book *Unknown Life of Jesus Christ*.

The Koran (surah 4, verses 156–157) suggests that Jesus' death on the cross was a 'grievous calumny' and that 'they slew him not'. Khwaja Nazir Ahmad's *Jesus in Heaven & Earth* further postulates that Jesus (as Isa, Yuz Asaf or Youza Asouph) retired to Kashmir postcrucifixion and was buried in Srinagar. Holger Kersten's *Jesus lived in India*, widely sold in Indian traveller bookshops, agrees and even gives a floorplan of that tomb at Rozabal (p289).

Naqshband Sahib

The beautifully proportioned but uncoloured 17th-century shrine **Naqshband Sahib** (Khanyar Chowk area) was built in Himachal Pradesh style with alternating layers of wood and brick to dissipate the force of earthquakes.

HARI PARBAT

Crowning a prominent hill, the imposing 18th-century **Hari Parbat Fort** is visible from virtually anywhere in Srinagar, but closed to the public for military use. Hindus believe that Hari Parbat was originally the island from which Vishnu and Sharika (Durga) defeated Jalodabhava, Kashmir's mythical lake demon (see History, p278). Meanwhile Muslims pay homage at the large **Makhdoom Sahib Shrine**, reached by beggar-lined steps that pass the ruined 1649 stone mosque of **Akhund Mullah Shah**. The steps start a few hundred metres beyond the scant remains of Srinagar's **Old City walls** (built by Akbar in the 1590s) and the large **Chetipacha Gurdwara** (Sikh Temple).

SRI PRATAP SINGH MUSEUM

You'll need your passport to get into **Sri Pratap Singh Museum** (☎ 2312859; Indian/foreigner Rs10/50; ☺ 10am-4pm Tue-Sun), accessed by a footbridge across the Jhelum River. Mughal papier-mâché work, weaponry and traditional Kashmiri costumes are among the highlights, but the stuffed animals look like they died of fright.

SHANKARACHARYA HILL

The forested **Shankaracharya Hill** (☺ 7.30am-5pm), also known as Takht-i-Sulaiman (Throne of Solomon), has been considered sacred since at least 250 BC. Accessed by a winding 5.5km road, the hill is topped by the 11th-century **Shankaracharya Mandir**, a tiny Shiva temple.

Short-cut hikes lead up from the west end of the Boulevard.

HAZRATBAL

Several kilometres north of the Old City, Srinagar's main university area extends around the large, white-domed **Hazratbal Mosque**. This 20th-century building enshrines Kashmir's holiest relic, the Moi-e-Muqqadas, supposedly a beard hair of the Prophet Mohammed. Hazaratbal's original mosque was specially built to house it when the Nashqband Sahib (left) proved too small for the many pilgrims. In December 1963 the hair briefly disappeared in still-unexplained circumstances, nearly sparking civil war.

The mosque backs onto Dal Lake through heavily guarded prayer lawns. Atmospheric surrounding **market areas** sell lotus pods and vast Kashmiri fried *puris* (flat dough that puffs up when deep fried).

Activities

GOLF

There are several upmarket golf clubs. Green fees are Rs400/Us$20 for Indians/foreigners at the **Royal Springs Golf Course** (☎ 2482582) near the Botanical Gardens.

Organised Tours

When tourist numbers are sufficient the **Tourism Reception Centre** (☎ 2456291; www.jktourism.org, www.jktdc.org) runs useful day-return excursion buses to Sonamarg (Rs170), Gulmarg (Rs160) and Pahalgam (Rs170), all departing at 8.30am.

Sleeping

Staying on a houseboat is one of the city's main attractions, but some visitors prefer to sleep the first night in a hotel while carefully selecting a suitable boat. Touts abound. Most touts will take a cut and might push you towards isolated or less friendly houseboats. However, a few apparent 'touts' are actually genuine hotel or houseboat owners seeking business. Trust your instincts.

HOUSEBOATS

Srinagar's signature houseboats first started appearing back in colonial times when the British were prohibited from owning land. Although most houseboats you'll see are less than 30 years old, the best deluxe ones are still palatial, with chandeliers, carved walnut panels and chintzy sitting rooms redolent of the 1930s Raj era. Just sitting and watching waterborne life go by from a boat's carved wooden veranda is one of Srinagar's great pleasures. Category A boats are comfy but often lack interior sitting areas. Category D boats hopefully stay afloat. Typical houseboats come with three double bedrooms, but in the current political climate you're likely to get the whole boat to yourself, chef and all.

Prices

Officially prices are 'set'. However, when occupancy is low (as at the time of research) most owners ask for your budget: with a little bargaining you're likely to find a houseboat for whatever that might be. For an approximate, unscientific snapshot of current prices for a double room, including transfers, tea and meals, see the boxed table, right.

Always double-check what food and drink is to be provided (only dhal-and-rice? tea extra?) and whether heating will cost extra, and insist on having *shikara* transfers (and/or use of a canoe) included. Ideally get things in writing and double-check prices for whatever isn't included to avoid nasty surprises later.

Selecting a Houseboat

Choosing from the 1400 possible boats is challenging. Always check out any houseboat before paying and under no circumstances prebook in Delhi (see boxed text, p292).

First choose the area. The classic location is Dal Lake where an extraordinary concentration of boats line up facing the Boulevard, backed by a marshy area of partly floating subtown. This area offers a good variety of standards and houseboats are close together, so you can conveniently visit a wide selection by *shikara* before choosing definitively.

Proximity to shore makes it relatively easy to hail a *shikara* should you need to 'escape'. Other houseboats much further out onto the lake sound appealing for the solitude, but getting away is harder, leaving you more prey to boat owners' sob-story charity requests or to trekking-package sales pressure. Nagin Lake houseboats also suffer from that feeling of isolation. Jhelum riverbank houseboats have a boardwalk directly to shore making access easier, but you lose all the romance of the waterbound *shikara* access. Many such boats are getting rather run-down.

In almost any location, visits from *shikara*-bound souvenir sellers are an unavoidable irritation.

To tour a selection of Dal Lake options engage a *shikara* or visit the **Houseboat Owners Association** (☎ /fax 2450326; Residency Rd; ⏰ 8am-6pm), which can organise free *shikara* tours for you. Either option might nudge you gently towards deluxe choices, but especially at current bargain price levels that's not a bad idea for savouring the full-on Srinagar experience.

HOTELS

Dozens of large but unremarkable hotels stand side by side all along the Boulevard, while numerous lower midrange options are dotted along Old Gagribal Rd, a block back. Many budget places lie directly north of Dalgate. Prices vary vastly according to season and the political situation.

Humza Hotel (☎ 2500857; www.incrediblekashmir.net; Old Gagribal Rd; dm/d/q from Rs100/400/600) Unmarked in a back lane, this friendly family homestay cum guesthouse offers carpeted floorspace for budget backpackers plus well-kept rooms with private bathroom. 'Check-in' at the co-owned Handloom House.

Noor Guesthouse (☎ 2450872; off Dalgate; d low/peak season from Rs200/500, without bathroom from Rs100/250) Cheaper rooms are in a creaky but characterful old wooden house, newer ones have

JAMMU & KASHMIR

HOUSEBOAT PRICES

Category	Official cost (Rs)	Typical cost in summer
Deluxe	Rs3600	Rs1200
A	Rs2500	Rs800
B	Rs1500	Rs600
C	Rs1000	Rs500
D	Rs700	Rs400

HOUSEBOAT HASSLES

Staying on a Srinagar houseboat is usually a charming, relaxing experience. But for decades we've been hearing from travellers who come away feeling seriously cheated. The vast majority of complaints relate to prepurchased packages organised outside Kashmir, especially in Delhi. Typical problems include the following:

■ Getting a houseboat that's lower grade than agreed.

■ Hidden charges (sometimes amounting to hundreds of dollars).

■ A boat that's far from shore making 'escape' very awkward.

■ Being held virtual hostage through exaggerated claims of dangers in Srinagar or by simply holding your passport (don't hand it over!).

■ Being pressured to give 'charity' donations or to sign up for ludicrously overpriced treks (typically US$200 per day, almost five times what you'd pay in Ladakh).

■ Being scammed on exchange by note-switching money changers.

■ Single women suffering inappropriate advances from houseboat staff.

The easiest way to avoid most of this criminal behaviour is to arrange your houseboat after you arrive in Srinagar. Inspect the boat thoroughly. Get a clear agreement to say that the fee covers everything promised. If meals, tea, mineral water, transfers etc are not included, be sure to double-check what they will cost.

Don't leave your passport and other valuables unattended on the boat, and consider letting the **Houseboat Owners Association** (☎ /fax 2450326; Residency Rd; ◷ 8am-6pm) know where you're staying. It might be able to arbitrate in any subsequent disputes over fees.

---

thin hardboard divider walls, but all are impressively clean. There's free laundry, electric blankets in some rooms and a sweet little rose garden for relaxed breakfasts.

Zeenath Guesthouse (☎ 2474070; off Dalgate; s Rs150-300, d Rs200-400) Compact, but sparklingly clean, new tile-floored rooms above a doctors' clinic, with quiet minilawn behind.

Hotel Swiss (☎ 2472766; www.swisshotelkashmir.com; Old Gagribal Rd; d Rs400-650; ❏ P) With a peaceful lawn and garden, good-value accommodation (especially rooms 401 to 404) and a charmingly helpful Sufi-spiritual manager, the Swiss remains a justifiably popular travellers' favourite…when there are any travellers. Also available are bicycle hire, free internet and complimentary tea.

Hotel Akbar (☎ 2500507; hotelakbar.com; d old Rs800-2500, new Rs1000-3000) The trump cards of this otherwise fairly standard midrange hotel is its delightfully large garden with blooming vines trained on trellises, and a location that's central yet very quiet. Geysers in newer rooms only. Cobwebs in the stairwell's giant chandelier are surreally thick.

Residency Hotel (☎ 2473702; www.hotelresidency kashmir.com; Court Rd; s/d Rs3500/4500, off season Rs1800/2300; ◉) A glass elevator whisks you up through a shopping-mall atrium to this unusually professional business hotel, with stylishly oversized washing facilities and fine linens.

Lalit Grand Palace (☎ 2501001; www.thelalit.com/Srinagar; ste walk-in/rack rate Rs10,000/20,000) This immaculate Intercontinental hotel offers vast suites in the Maharaja's 1910 palace, beautifully set above acres of manicured lawns. The Durbar Hall features royal portraits and one of the world's largest handmade carpets. Standard 'palace deluxe' rooms (Rs14,000) and the swimming pool are currently under reconstruction.

Eating

Punjabi Rasoi (Boulevard; roti Rs3, curries Rs25-70, mains Rs25-70; ◷ 8am-10pm) Several very basic *dhabas* along the Boulevard serve cheap, filling veggie meals till relatively late.

Mughal Darbar (☎ 2476998; Residency Rd; dishes Rs35-240 plus 22.5%; ◷ 10am-10pm) Mughal-style wall murals contrast with Alpine-scene windows in this reliable restaurant above a popular bakery. Dishes range from inexpensive veggie curries (Rs35 to Rs50) to indulgent Kashmiri specialities (Rs120 to Rs240).

Cafe de Linz (Court Rd; dishes Rs40-140 plus 12.5%; ◷ noon-10.30pm) This somewhat unusual dark-walled, semicircular restaurant serves a typical range of Indian and pseudo-Chinese food, with the family's Austrian connection reduced to a single poster of Linz.

Lhasa Restaurant (Boulevard Lane 2; dishes Rs60-180 plus 12.5%; 🕙 10am-9pm) Dine in a convivial walled garden or a low-ceilinged oriental dining room with elements of Buddhist design. The spicy boneless chicken balls are excellent, but some Chinese and Tibetan dishes are rather lacklustre.

Coffea Arabica (MA Rd; pizzas Rs150-200, pastas Rs120-180, fish & chips Rs200; 🕙 9am-10pm) Inviting, modern multicuisine eatery with a slight TGI Fridays feel offering various fast-food style serving stations, a little bookshop and a lounge area for coffee and cakes up in the wooden rafters.

Drinking

Srinagar's Muslim mores mean that alcohol isn't served in restaurants, but alcohol is available in four wine shops throughout the city and at bars within some hotels.

Wine Shop (Heemal Hotel Shopping Complex, Boulevard) One of the four wine shops throughout the city.

Dar Bar (cocktails Rs300, wine per bottle from Rs2200; 🕙 10am-10pm) The Grand Palace Srinagar's little Dar Bar has fine lawn views towards Dal Lake.

Cafe Robusta (CRL Lounge, MA Rd; coffees Rs35-80; 🕙 9.30am-9pm; 🛜) Serves a selection of great coffees in a pseudo-Western upstairs lounge with a dartboard.

There are upmarket bars at Hotel Broadway and the Kashmir Golf Club.

Shopping

The Boulevard has several emporia flogging Kashmiri souvenirs, including elegantly painted papier-mâché boxes and carved walnut woodwork, plus cashmere and pashmina shawls, originally popularised in Europe by Napoleon's wife Joesphine. Saffron, cricket bats and dried fruits are widely sold around Lal Chowk. Carpet-selling 'factories' line the road to Shalimar Bagh targeting tour groups. Unless you know how to assess carpet values, consider erring instead towards much cheaper chain-stitched *gabbas* (Kashmiri rugs with appliqué) or floral *namda*s (felted wool carpets). Beware that some fur products incorporate skins of endangered species (see boxed text, p1158).

Kashmir Government Arts Emporium (☎ 2452783; Bund; 🕙 10am-5.30pm Mon-Sat) To browse fixed-price souvenirs, including hand-knotted rugs and salwar suits, without sales pressure, visit this surreal, army-guarded arts emporium in a half-timbered mansion flanked by curious gatehouses that seem transported from a dilapidated Oxford College.

Getting There & Away

AIR

Most flights continued operating even during 2008's curfews (a valid air ticket theoretically doubling as a curfew pass). The following flights operate daily unless noted:

GoAir (www.goair.in) Mumbai (Thursday, Saturday), Delhi (Tuesday, Saturday), Delhi via Jammu (Monday, Wednesday, Friday, Sunday)

Indian Airlines (☎ 2450247; Shahenshah Palace Hotel, Boulevard) Leh (Wednesday; Rs6710), Delhi, Jammu

Jet Airways (☎ 2480801; Court Rd) Delhi, Jammu

JetLite (☎ 2106750; www.jetlite.com) Delhi, Mumbai

Kingfisher (www.flykingfisher.com) Delhi, Mumbai

SpiceJet (www.spicejet.com) Delhi, Jammu

Very high airport security means you should allow plenty of check-in time.

BUS & JEEP

The **J&K SRTC bus station** (☎ 2455107; Residency Rd) was paralysed by long-term strikes when we visited, but should offer buses to Kargil (Rs335, 10 hours) and Leh (Rs600, two days) at 7.30am. Shared jeeps to Kargil (Rs600) leave around 7am from **Tourist Taxi Stand 1** (Residency Rd) across the road. Select your vehicle and seat the night before. When the road is open, numerous shared jeeps (Rs250 to Rs300) and private minibuses (Rs220 to Rs270) to Jammu leave from near the clocktower at Lal Chowk, most departing between 6.30am and 9am (sometimes with a change of vehicle at Ramban when Hindu-Muslim tensions flare). From Batmalu bus station, local services run to Uri, Sonamarg (three daily) and Gulmarg (with a change in Tangmarg). From Panthachowk bus station, 8km south of the city centre, buses run to Pampore and Ananatnag (change for Pahalgam).

For excursion buses to Sonamarg, Gulmarg and Pahalgam, see Organised Tours (p290).

The symbolic Srinagar–Muzaffarabad international bus service (twice monthly) carries locals and Pakistani-Kashmiris only.

Getting Around

BUS & TAXI

Enjoyable *shikara* trips on Dal Lake (p287) should cost Rs100 per hour according to the Tourist Reception Centre, though posted rates say Rs200. Be firm when the *shikara* pilot tries to detour to commission-paying souvenir shops. Short houseboat-to-shore rides cost Rs20. There are numerous *shikara* jetties, but finding a boatman after dark can be tough and/or potentially expensive.

BOAT

To the airport, a J&K SRTC coach departs from the Tourist Reception Centre at 8.30am and 11.30am (Rs35). From the airport pre-purchase the bus tickets or taxi vouchers (Rs380) in the arrivals hall. Around town, it takes some courage to use the overcrowded city minibuses, whose destination boards are only written in Urdu: the most useful routes run from Lal Chowk to Hazaratbal or to Shalimar Bagh via Dal Lake's south bank and Nishat Bagh. Autorickshaws charge Rs20 for the cheapest city hops. Reckon on around Rs800 for a full-day tour including the Mughal gardens, Old City and Hazaratbal.

AROUND SRINAGAR

The most popular excusions from Srinagar are **Sonamarg** (right), **Pahalgam** (p286) and **Gulmarg**, 52km west, where a pine-fringed meadow golf retreat transforms in winter into India's top **ski-centre** (⏱ mid-Dec–mid-Apr). A two-stage **Gondola Cable Car** (⏱ 10am-4pm), 1km west of Gulmarg's bus stand, whisks you up Afarwat Mountain to 3930m, then 4390m for outstanding views. In summer forest hikes could bring you back down to Gulmarg in a few hours passing turf-roofed winter houses of the nomadic Gujar people.

Day trips from Srinagar cost Rs160/Rs1200 by J&K SRTC excursion bus/taxi (for details, see Organised Tours, p290).

SRINAGAR TO KARGIL

☎ 0194

This truly beautiful 200km drive takes you from Kashmir's very alpine valleys over the remarkable double loops of the 3529m Zoji La. Beyond you descend into a series of high-sided valleys like Scottish glens that have been stretched vertically for added effect. Windows located on the south side offer the best views.

Sonamarg

☎ 0194

The jerry-built one-street strip settlement of Sonamarg undoubtedly occupies a delightful mountain-valley setting, but in July and August its poorly maintained hotels ratchet up their prices by 500% to milk an endless supply of Indian pilgrim tourists. Many Indians get their first taste of snow here by walking or pony riding two hours to the **Thajiwas Glacier**: the 5km access road leads south near the upper-market Snowland Hotel, 1.5km west of Sonamarg. Pilgrim hikers heading to Armanath's famous ice lingam (see boxed text, p287) depart in a big herd at around 9am from **Baltal Camp** (a Rs400 share-taxi hop east of Sonamarg) for the 15km each-way trek.

By far Sonamarg's best-value accommodation is the central **J&KTDC Tourist Bungalows** (☎ 2417208; d Rs500, 2-bed hut Rs1800) set in attractively manicured lawns that contrast distinctly with the surrounding detritus. It also has Rs100 dorm beds en route to Thajiwas Glacier.

Slightly set back, **Hotel Glacier Heights** (☎ 2417215; d Rs2000) looks like a suburban English brick house. Its rooms are decent value (if icy cold) off season when discounted to around Rs600, and it has a decent restaurant.

Buses to Srinagar depart from Sonamarg at 7.30am, 9.30am and 12.30pm (Rs75, 2½ hours). Alternatively take shared/private jeeps (Rs100/1000), possibly changing en route at Kangan (Rs60/500, one hour). Eastbound buses are often full by the time they reach Sonamarg, so for Kargil consider chartering a taxi/jeep (Rs2500/3500) or returning to Srinagar to get a seat.

Drass

Muslim Drass is a miserable parade of shophouses that, along with several army bases, mars an otherwise attractive, wide valley that would make a good hiking base were it not so close to the Line of Control. On January 9 2005 Drass meterologists recorded a freak temperature of -60°C and ever since the town has touted itself as the world's second coldest place (after Oymyakon in Sakha-Yakutia, Russia). Local tourists stop to visit various battlefields made famous in the 1999 war with Pakistan. Several unappetising if survivable hotels cluster around the bus stand. Women travelling alone might feel uncomfortable here.

KARGIL & ZANSKAR

Ladakh's majestic but less visited 'second half' comprises remote, sparsely populated Buddhist Zanskar and the slightly greener Suru Valley, where villagers predominantly follow Shia-Islam, as they do in the regional capital Kargil. Scenery reaches some truly majestic mountain climaxes.

KARGIL

☎ 01985 / pop 10,700 / elev 2817m

Most travellers only stop in Ladakh's second 'city' to change transport between Leh and Srinagar or Zanskar. After the idyllic calm and charm of Buddhist Ladakh, Muslim Kargil feels grimy and mildly hassled, though the feeling's only very relative. Almost everything travellers might need is conveniently found within three short blocks of the bustling Main Bazaar, with its public call offices (PCOs) and slow **internet cafes** (per hr Rs80). The bus/share-taxi stand is 100m towards the river, past the useful State Bank of India ATM. Tucked behind the bus stand is a friendly **Tourist Reception Centre** (☎ 232721; ☿ 10am-4pm).

Most hotels are cheap (around Rs300 for doubles) and central, but rather down at heel. A good deal is the **J&KTDC Tourist Bungalow** (☎ 232328; d Rs200), which has rooms with geysers above the tourist office. **Hotel Kargil Continental** (☎ 232300; s/d Rs200/300 with bargaining; ℗) looks rather upmarket from the outside and provides towels and clean topsheets, though the interior decor is pretty worn. Get there by the lane signposted for dreary Hotel Greenland next door.

The lane directly north accesses much pricier **Hotel Siachen** (☎ 232221; hotel_siachen_kargil@rediffmail.com; d Rs1200-1800). It has attractive vine-trailed common balconies, but chintzy rooms overdo the dark fake-wood veneer and those thick-pile carpets are hard to clean. Discounts are probable.

Numerous simple restaurants and cheap *dhabas* line the Main Bazaar. However, finding nonmeat options is challenging and apart from bakeries only **Pasgo** (Main Bazaar; meals Rs70-120) opens by day during Ramadan.

Getting There & Away

Leh buses (from Rs250, 10 hours) depart at 4.30am, driving via Mulbekh (1½ hours) and Lamayuru (around five hours). Shared jeeps (Rs500) leave around 7am. When curfews and strikes permit, Srinagar buses (from Rs300, 10 hours) and share taxis (Rs600) usually leave around 1am. Rent your own jeep (Rs3500 to Rs4500) if you want to leave at a much more sociable hour and enjoy the beautiful if occasionally nail-biting scenery. Kargil–Mulbekh minibuses (Rs30) leave at 2pm, 3pm and 4pm from a separate stand 300m along the riverbank, returning next morning.

Getting to Zanskar is Kargil's great traveller conundrum. The Kargil–Padum bus has been cancelled. A Leh–Kargil–Padum bus leaves around thrice weekly, supposedly departing from Kargil around 1am but timetables are infamously idiosyncratic. The best choice is to rent a jeep. Driving at a steady rate takes seven/14 hours to Rangdum/Padum (around Rs10,000 per vehicle), but allow plenty more time for photo stops. Annoyingly, friction between Zanskar and Kargil taxi unions effectively makes it impossible to engage a return-trip ride. And double-check that your driver has Zanskar-endorsed permits! To gather a group of fellow travellers to spread the jeep costs try leaving notes at the Tourist Reception Centre or at Hotel Kargil Continental.

Kargil's only operative petrol pump is 2.5km up the Leh road from the main river bridge.

AROUND KARGIL

☎ 01985

Mulbekh

For one of India's most symphonic views, gaze open mouthed from the top of Mulbekh's medieval **castle site**. Across the gently terraced barley fields of the green Wakha Valley, the Zanskar Mountains rise with Grand Canyon majesty in a series of angular cliffs and craggs. Only two mudbrick towers remain of the castle defences, but the impregnable Mt Athos–style site now hosts a pair of two-monk gompas. **Serdung Gompa** replaced an old one that mostly collapsed in 2003, but the **Gandentse Gompa** is original. Seen from below, the pyrimdal crag on which they sit seems unclimbable; however, a zigzag path behind leads up in 45 sweaty minutes. Alternatively, drive up the 2.8km spaghetti of asphalt lane starting 100m west of **Chamba Gompa** (admission Rs10) on the main road. That tiny 1975 shrine wraps around a tooth of rock on which is inscribed a superb 8m-high Maitreya-Buddha relief that's over 1000 years old. Get the key from the unremarkable **Paradise Hotel and Restaurant**

(☎ 270010; d Rs500, without bathroom Rs300), one of two basic roadhouses opposite. For much more atmospheric accommodation stay at the imposing-looking **Karzoo Guesthouse** (☎ 270027; per person Rs200). Right at the base of the castle crag its three guest rooms share squat toilets, but there's also a beautiful olde-Ladakh dining hall and kitchen.

Unsigned nearby where the main road turns is the new but traditionally styled **Otosnang Guesthouse** (☎ 270028; per person Rs150). Owner Sonam speaks English and his sister-in-law trains student weavers at Wakha's interesting low-tech carpet-making workshop, 4km east (visits possible).

Maitreya Guesthouse (☎ 270035; d room only/full board Rs800/1000), Mulbekh's smartest accommodation, is 1km further west, with modern tiled floors and turned wooden bannisters (hot water Rs20 per bucket).

Shargol

Small but unique **Shargol Gompa** is set almost entirely into a cliffside. The site is distantly visible from the Leh–Kargil road around 5km west of Mulbekh, but accessed by a 1.6km unpaved road that branches off near Km236. Before climbing the short, steep approach path request the key from the new Dukhang (Lower Monastery).

SURU VALLEY

The main road towards Zanskar winds prettily through the fertile Suru Valley, where several rustic Muslim stone-built villages sit beneath a panorama of high valley walls and mountains that reach a thrilling climax with views of spiky, ever snow-capped **Nun** (7135m) and **Kun** (7087m). Perhaps the best panorama is approaching **Panikhar**. A steep but satisfying day trek crosses from the Panikhar bypass road over the 3900m Lago La then descends to **Parkachik**, from where a bus returns to Kargil at 7am. Just beyond Parkachik a large, dust-blackened glacier crumbles into the Suru River as the road starts to wind up to the splendid **Pensi La** (Panzila; 4401m).

SLEEPING & EATING

Assuming you can find the *chowkidar* (caretaker) to open the doors, there are unpretentious but decently maintained **J&K Tourist Bungalows** (d Rs200) at Sanku, lonely Purtickchay (with perfectly framed Nun–Kun views), Panikhar, Tangole (a possible mountaineering

base), Parkachik and Rangdum. Sanku and Rangdum have very simple tea-stall shops.

GETTING THERE & AWAY

From Kargil buses to Panikhar (Rs50, two hours) depart at 6.30am and 2pm, returning around 5am and 11am. Parkachik buses leave Kargil at 11am, returning next morning at 7am. Continuing towards Zanskar transport is limited to very uncertain hitchhiking.

Most jeep drivers refuse to take the very rough Sanku–Drass track.

ZANSKAR

Famed for its splendid isolation, the greatest attraction of this majestically mountain-hemmed, rugged Ladakhi-Buddhist valley is the week-long trek in or out (p298). Indeed, when snow blocks Zanskar's one precarious road from Kargil (via the Suru Valley), the only access is on foot along the frozen Zanskar River (p298).

Beware that Zanskar has no money-changing banks nor any official petrol stations (though Padum's taxi union has its own supply). If camping, be prepared for very cold nights even in summer.

Rangdum

pop 280 / elev 3670m

Set in a wild, big-sky valley, wind-scoured Rangdum is the first Buddhist village heading for Zanskar. The tiny cluster of low-rise Ladakhi houses and communications masts isn't attractive in itself but the setting is awe-inspiring. To the west the mountains Nun and Kun rise spectacularly white-capped. And eastwards the horizon is an arid pastiche of oddly contorted strata fronted by the dot of **Rangdum Gompa** (admission Rs50), 5km away, looking like a tiny island floating above the valley floor. The gompa's 25 yellow-hatted monks are outnumbered by monastery donkeys, who sleep inside at night.

Rangdum's rather misnamed **Zanskar Express Guesthouse** is actually one of three basic **tea-houses** (dahl & rice thali Rs35) beside the slightly hidden police checkpost. They can organise beds in a village home for a negotiable Rs250. There's also a fairly priced **J&K Tourism Bungalow** (d Rs200). Or, 2km beyond the village in marvellously scenic isolation, there's the pricey **Nun-Kun Deluxe Camp** (☎ 1982322153; lakpale@yahoo.co.in; c/o Zanskar Trek, Leh; d bedded tent with full board Rs2500), whose shared outside toilets provide soft paper. Drop-in guests can sometimes bargain prices down to Rs600/1000 without/with meals.

Rangdum to Padum

About 1km after **Pensi La** (4401m), the rugged pass that divides the Suru and Zanskar Valleys, there are spectacular views down onto the long, glistening white **Drang Drung glacier**. Further down, the Zanskar Valley broadens with several small villages in grassy parcels of farmland hemmed by sheer mountain walls. **Phey** has a small gompa and homestay. At **Sani**, Zanskar's oldest gompa, is a small, two-storey prayer hall ringed by a tunnelled cloister and a whitewashed stone wall studded with stupas.

Padum

☎ 01983 / pop 1500 / elev 3505m

After the rigours and beauty of the dramatic drive to get here, Zanskar's dusty little capital comes as rather an anticlimax. Despite an awesome mountain backdrop, central Padum is a characterless (if usefully compact) crossroads, within a block of which you'll find the bus/share-taxi stand, phone offices, a chaotic internet cafe, a **Tourist Office** (☎ 245017; ☺ 10am-4pm Mon-Sat) and most of Padum's dozen hotel-guesthouses. The main road then straggles 700m south past a sizeable 1991 **mosque** to the crumbling little 'old town', where large stupas and a chaos of water-eroded rocks lead up a modest hill. More traditional **Pibiting** village, 2km north, has a small gompa dwarfed by a large hilltop stupa topped with a beacon lamp.

ACTIVITIES

You can often find **horsemen** ready to guide/porter **treks** (per horse per day Rs250-350) at the simple camping ground opposite the Tourist Office. Alternatively ask agencies like **Zanskar Trek** (☎ 245136), which has offices along the road to the mosque. See p298 for popular routes.

SLEEPING & EATING

Most hotels close from late October to June, except when prebooked for winter trekking groups. There's a simple camping ground opposite the Tourist Office, which has an acceptable **Tourist Bungalow** (d Rs200).

Mont-Blanc Guesthouse (☎ 245183; r Rs350, without bathroom Rs250) Friendly, family guesthouse with four traditionally furnished rooms and possibly a free glass or three of *chhang* (barley beer).

Phukthar Guesthouse (☎ 245226; d Rs200-400) The best of three old-town guesthouses, the Phukthar is above a small ethnobotanical museum and an unfinished row of shops. Good-value rooms, some with tiny private bathrooms, share a restaurant counterpointing Tibet and Bob Marley.

Hotel Ibex (☎ 245214; d Rs350-550) Room standards vary, but the pleasant setting around a sheltered garden courtyard plus a convivial restaurant (mains Rs45 to Rs100) makes the Ibex a justifiably popular choice. Similarly priced Kailash and Changthang Hotels nearby look outwardly smarter, but lack the traveller vibe.

Gakyi Hotel (s/d from Rs700/900) Good-looking, well-furnished new rooms seem oddly forgotten beneath Padum's most glitzy restaurant (mains Rs40 to Rs85, beer Rs120). Some smell musty.

GETTING THERE & AWAY

Zanskar's days of isolation will end abruptly when a new Darcha–Padum–Chiling road is completed, but that could take years. Until then public transport remains very limited. The unpredictable Padum–Kargil–Leh bus takes around 18 hours to Kargil (Rs300) and only runs a few times weekly (keep asking!). Jeeps to Kargil cost Rs8000 (yes, 20% cheaper than FROM Kargil) whether done in one gruelling 14-hour drive or with an overnight stop en route. For official Zanskar taxi rates, see the boxed table below.

Around Padum

KARSHA

About 7km across the valley from Padum, Karsha has an appealing patchwork of barley fields and threshing circles worked by dzos (cow-yak half-breed). These are overlooked by old-fashioned homes and the remarkable

TAXIS FROM PADUM		
Destination	**One way (Rs)**	**Return (Rs)**
Pishu	1800	2400
Rangdum	4000	6000
Raru	1300	2500
Zangla	2000	3000

Karsha Gompa, Zanskar's largest Buddhist monastery, which dates back to at least the 10th century. It's a jumble of whitewashed blocks rising almost vertically up the red rock of a mountain cliff. Concrete steps lead to the upper cloister and prayer hall with cracked old murals and wobbly wooden columns. French charity **Solidarijeune** (www.solidarijeune.org) helps with its upkeep.

Karsha has three homestay-style 'guesthouses'. Unmarked **Chetan Guesthouse** (tr Rs300) and garden-set **Thieur Guesthouse** (tent Rs100, d/q Rs300/350) both offer dragon-patterned mattresses on the floor amid low Ladakhi tables. **Tinkuling Guesthouse** (d Rs300) has actual beds in two slightly dusty twin rooms. Local toilets are shared.

The Karsha bus (Rs15) leaves Padum at 4pm, returning next morning at 8am. A taxi from Padum costs Rs520/690 one way/return. Walking takes around two hours across the exposed plain.

ZANGLA & STONGDE

The wonderful drive to Zangla makes a fine half-day excursion from Padum. Especially above **Rinam** and **Shilingskit** villages, notice the astonishingly curled, contorted strata. A highlight of the trip is **Stongde Gompa** crowning a bird's-eye perch 300m above the valley, 12km from Padum. It's accessed by a 3km winding detour or a steep vertical climb on foot. A footbridge 6.5km before Zangla allows trekkers to trek between Karsha and Zangla (around seven hours), but despite lovely views, the terrain is rather bare and sunblasted. The entrance to **Zangla** is guarded by a small hilltop **fortress ruin**. At the far end of the village there's a small, friendly Buddhist **nunnery**. In central Zangla, the conspicuous pink-framed house offers a village homestay.

RARU & BARDAN

Those trekking between Zanskar and Darcha generally start by driving to the little village of **Raru**, where there are two tiny eateries and the possibility of a very basic homestay. The route from Padum passes the **Bardan Gompa** sitting spectacularly above the valley on a rocky outcrop.

TREKKING IN ZANSKAR

Trekking in or out of Zanskar is the area's top activity. The few hamlets en route are tiny, so carrying tents and provisions is essential.

Summer Routes

Many people make arrangements through Leh agencies (per person per day all-inclusive €35 to €55; from June to October), but if you have patience and your own camping equipment you could also organise guides, horses and porters in Padum (p297), Lamayuru (p322) or even Darcha (p329), though you'd be wise to prepurchase key provisions in Leh or Kargil. Going without a guide is not recommended. Storms occasionally interrupt itineraries, snow is possible from early September and proper acclimatisation is essential to avoid Acute Mountain Sickness (AMS, p112). For detailed trekking notes see Lonely Planet's *Trekking in the Indian Himalaya*.

ZANSKAR TO DARCHA

Hiking between Raru and Darcha (on the Manali–Leh road) takes six days via Pepula and Purne, seven if you add a (recommended) second night at Purne before the sustained two-day climb to Shinkun La (5090m). Use the extra day to detour (around five hours return) to dramatic Gelukpa **Phuktal Gompa**, a cave monastery clinging to the side of the near-vertical Shadi gorge. It contains a sacred spring and some 700-year-old murals in the Alchi style. Darcha is tiny, but there are roadside *dhaba*s where traffic, including daily Manali–Leh buses, stop for a passport check.

ZANSKAR TO LAMAYURU

The seven-day core of this classic trek crosses three passes of over 4800m connecting Zangla (left) to Wanla (p322) via **Lingshet Gompa**, one of Zanskar's most important monasteries. Starting/finishing in Padum/Lamayuru adds at least two days.

Winter Route
CHADAR TREK

Every February intrepid travellers and Zanskar's teachers (returning from their winter break) take the unique winter-only Chadar Trek (best in February) in Chiling (p319) or Padum (seven days). The route follows a surreal canyon landscape, much of it along the ice of the frozen Zanskar River. Camping stops are in rock caves along the riverbank as well as at Nerak, one of India's most isolated villages. While there are no high-altitude stages, you'll need serious winter equipment and an experienced local guide who can 'read' the ice.

JAMMU & KASHMIR

LADAKH

Spectacularly jagged, arid mountains enfold this magical, Buddhist ex-kingdom. In summer hikers trek between archetypal gompas that dramatically crown rocky outcrops amid whitewashed stupas and meditational *mani* walls (Tibetan stone walls with sacred inscriptions). Colourful fluttering prayer flags send their spiritual messages metaphorically off into the mountain breeze. Prayer wheels spun clockwise release more merit-making mantras. Gompa interiors are colourfully awash with murals and statuary of numerous bodhisattvas.

Ladakh's remarkably well-balanced traditional society has so much to teach the West in terms of ecological awareness, as you'll learn from a visit to Leh's Women's Alliance (p306) and LEDeG (p306). While most Ladakhis are cash poor, traditional mudbrick homesteads are large, comfortable and self-sufficient in fuel and food, notably dairy products, vegetables and barley used to make *tsampa* (Tibetan staple of roast barley flour) and *chhang*. That is an incredible achievment given the short growing season and very limited arable land in this upland desert, where precious water supplies must be laboriously channelled from glacier-melt mountain streams (so please don't waste water!).

In summer people pile their flat roofs with distinctive twists of *chuchump* (alfalfa grass) sufficient to feed stabled livestock through the harsh winters. Frigid temperatures mean that all work stops in winter, which is thus festival time. Few tourists see Ladakh during this period, however, as access roads cross some of the world's highest road passes, closing entirely between November and May (sometimes earlier) and leaving only peak-dodging flights to Leh as the region's link to the world outside.

History

Ladakh's (now-deposed) royal family traces its dynasty back 39 generations to 975AD. They took the name Namgyal ('Victorious') in 1470 when their progenitor, Lhachen Bhagan, ruling from Basgo (p320), conquered a competing Ladakhi kingdom based at Leh/Shey (p326). Although Ladakh had been culturally 'Tibetanised' in the 9th century, Buddhism originally arrived in an Indian form that's visible in ancient temple craftsmanship at Alchi (p321). Over time, however, different Buddhist sects struggled for prominence, with the Tibetan Gelukpa order eventually becoming the majority philosophy after its introduction in the 14th century by Tibetan pilgrim Tsongkhapa (who left a curious relic at Spituk, p319).

In the 16th century Ladakh launched a disastrously unsuccessful attack on Muslim Skardu. Curiously, rather than killing the Ladakhi king, the victors demanded that he marry one of their princesses. Despite the substantial Muslim immigration into Ladakh that followed, Buddhism bounced back under Ladakh's greatest king, Senge Namgyal (reigned 1616–42), who gained riches by plundering gold reserves from western Tibet and re-established a capital at Leh. Ladakh remained an independent kingdom until 1846 when the Nyamgals lost power and the region was annexed into the Jammu-based kingdom of the Dogra Rajas.

Since Independence Ladakh has been ruled as a (now semi-autonomous) subdistrict of Jammu and Kashmir. That's a culturally odd situation for this 'little Tibet' – which is now one of the last undisturbed Tantric Buddhist societies on earth. When tourism was first permitted in 1974, pessimists predicted that Ladakh's inspirationally balanced traditional lifestyle would be swept away by the arrival of 'modernism'. Globalised economics and climate change have certainly caused many problems, including dangerous population shifts, but so far traditional society has proved unexpectedly robust, while useful, locally relevant technologies, such as solar energy and Trombe walls, are starting to improve rural living standards.

Climate

Ladakh is a high-altitude desert famous for the inspirational purity of its crystal-blue skies. With low precipitation and sunshine for an average 300 days a year, Leh's short tourist season (July to early September) typically sees pleasantly mild T-shirt weather by day, with slightly crisp, chilly nights. However, storms can suddenly brew up any time. And even in August, when clouds cover the sun, you'll need a sweater. On higher treks night-time temperatures can dip below -5°C even in midsummer. By September snow is

---

FESTIVALS IN LADAKH & ZANSKAR

Losar (17 Dec 2009, 6 Dec 2010, 25 Dec 2011) Ladakhi New Year, celebrated in Buddhist homes and gompas with feasts, rituals and dances.

Gu-Stor (times vary) Rituals and masked dances celebrating the victory of good over evil are celebrated in gompas, including those at the following:

- **Spituk** (12-13 Jan 2010, 2-3 Jan 2011; p319)
- **Karsha** (8-9 Jul 2010, 27-28 Jul 2011; p297)
- **Korzok** (14-15 Jul 2010, 2-3 Aug 2011; p327)
- **Thiksey** (5-6 Nov 2009, 25-26 Oct 2010, 13-14 Nov 2011; p326)

Dosmoche (11-12 Feb 2010, 2-3 Mar 2011; widespread incl Leh, opposite, Likir, p320 & Diskit, p324) Buddhist New Year. Masked dances; effigies representing the evil spirits of the old year are burnt or cast into the desert.

Guru Tse-Chu (23-24 Feb 2010, 14-15 Mar 2011; Stok Gompa, p318) Masked dances and predictions of the future from the oracles.

Matho Nagrang (27-28 Feb 2010, 17-18 Mar 2011; Matho, p319) Monastery oracles perform blindfolded acrobatics and ritual mutilations.

Yuru Kabgyat (9 Jun 2010, 28 Jun 2011; Lamayuru, p322) Monastic masked dances.

Tse-Chu (21-23 Jun 2010, 10-12 Jul 2011; Hemis, p327) Birthday of Padmasambhava (p72) cele-brated with three days of masked dancing. Hemis' famous three-storey-high, pearl-encrusted *thangka* (rectangular Tibetan painting on cloth) is unfurled every twelfth year (next 2016).

Phyang Tsedup (13-14 Jul 2010, 1-2 Aug 2011; Phyang Gompa, p319) Ritual masked *chaam* dances celebrate the victory of good over evil and of Buddhism over preexisting religions. Phyang's giant *thangka* is unfurled every third year (next in 2010).

Ladakh Festival (1-15 Sep) Unrepentantly touristy but entertaining cycle of events starting with a colourful, carnivalesque parade through Leh (opposite), then a repeating programme of Buddhist dances (at Spituk, p319), polo (Leh), archery (Alchi, p321) and music.

Chemrey Thekchhok Festival (14-15 Nov 2009, 4-5 Nov 2010, 23-24 Nov 2011; Chemrey's Thekchhok Gompa, p328) Masked dances and mystic rituals.

---

likely on higher ground and, although major passes usually stay open till October, in some years they can be (temporarily) blocked much earlier. In winter temperatures fall below -20°C and most hotels close. Those guesthouses that stay open charge extra for winter heating and offer only bucket water since pipes freeze.

Language

Though Ladakh's Bodyik script uses Tibetan letters, Tibetan and Ladakhi languages are quite different. The wonderfully all-purpose word *jule* (pronounced *joo*-lay) means 'hello', 'goodbye', 'please' and 'thanks'. Adding '*lay*' on the end of a name or phrase adds respect. To the greeting *khamzang*, simply reply *khamzang*. If you don't eat meat, say *sha za-amet*. *Zhimpo-rak* means 'It's delicious'. For more phrases buy Rebecca Norman's excellent *Getting Started in Ladakhi* (Rs200), which also has useful cultural tips.

Information

Whether or not a permit is required, always carry your passport when travelling around Ladakh as checkpoints are fairly common.

PERMITS

To visit the Nubra Valley, Pangong Tso, Dha-Hanu, Tso Moriri or the upper Indus beyond Upshi, you need an inner line permit. This is usually easy to obtain within one working day through a Leh travel agent for Rs100 plus Rs20 per day visitor tax. Permits are valid for seven days and unextendable. Theoretically applications require a minimum group of four people. In reality agencies readily get around this with creative paperwork, but if travelling outbound without the listed group, there remains a small but finite chance that you'll be turned back (returning alone is no problem). Make multiple photocopies of your passport and permit to give to police checkpoints en route (if travelling with an agency, this will be arranged for you).

Dangers & Annoyances

Leh and eastern Ladakh don't suffer any of the violence of the Kashmir Valley.

As most of Ladakh lies above 3000m, fly-in visitors invariably suffer some symptoms of Acute Mountain Sickness (AMS, p1198). Avoid any strenuous exertion for at least the first 24 hours after arrival and drink plenty of water (ginger and garlic are also recommended). Thereafter, always consider the effects of altitude when making steep ascents, particularly over mountain passes. Be properly equipped and acclimatised before trekking.

To avoid carbon monoxide poisoning (see boxed text, p1139) don't use charcoal heaters in unventilated rooms.

Activities

In summer Ladakh is an adventure playground for outdoor types. Thanks to Leh's vast range of agents (see p307), making arrangements is very easy for climbing (p307), rafting (p307) and especially high-altitude trekking (p315).

LEH

☎ 01982 / pop 28,640 / elev 3520m

Few places in India are at once so traveller friendly and yet so hassle free as mountain-framed Leh. Certainly the old Ladakhi townscape is draped in a thick veneer of travel agencies, souvenir shops and pizza restaurants, but even the cheaper backpacker guesthouses occupy traditionally styled buildings with ornate wooden window frames. The crumbling Old Town remains dotted with mudbrick houses and stupas. And the 'suburbs' are invitingly green patchworks of irrigated barley fields dotted with pretty old houses and guesthouses with gushing streams. Leh's a place that's all too easy to fall in love with.

Orientation

A dagger of steep rocky ridge plunging towards the main bazaar is topped by a dramatic palace, fort and gompa. Around the ridge's south flank are the crumbling alleyways of the Old Town. Guesthouses spread in all directions, but the main traveller areas are Changspa Rd and slightly less convivial Fort Rd.

Around 10km southeast the scrappy Choglamsar suburb has grown up around a Tibetan refugee camp. The Dalai Lama has a *photang* (ceremonial residence) there for official visits.

MAPS

Henk Thoma's excellent 1:10,000 *Leh Valley Map* (Rs195) accurately marks nearly 200 of Leh's hotels and guesthouses. **Ladakh Bookshop** (Map p304; Main Bazaar) stocks Olizane's excellent three-sheet *Ladakh Trekking Maps* (www .abram.ch/lzmmaps.php) for Rs1300 per sheet. The **Tourist office** (Map p304; ☎ 253482; Ibex Rd; ☼ 10am-4pm Mon-Sat) has a useful if flawed *Jammu & Kashmir* map (Rs10).

Information

BOOKSHOPS

The following are well stocked with postcards, novels, spiritual works and books on Ladakh, Kashmir and Tibet.

Book Worm (Map p304; Old Fort Rd) Buys and sells second-hand books.

A MOUNTAIN TOOLKIT

Given the high altitude you'll need:

■ warm, insulating clothing (even in summer)

■ hat, lip salve, UV-proof sunglasses and sunscreen (sunburn's an ever-present risk)

■ a good-quality head torch (unlit streets and power cuts are common, even in Leh)

■ plenty of paracetamol to relieve symptoms of mild Acute Mountain Sickness (AMS; but if seriously hit by this potentially deadly condition, you must also retreat to lower altitudes; see p1198)

It's also wise to stock a course of antibiotics (available in Leh), dehydration salts for stomach upsets, plasters for blistered feet and cold-sore cream containing aciclovir (wind-chapped lips are particularly vulnerable). Campers need sleeping bags rated to three or four seasons. Photographers will find polarising filters useful to reduce glare.

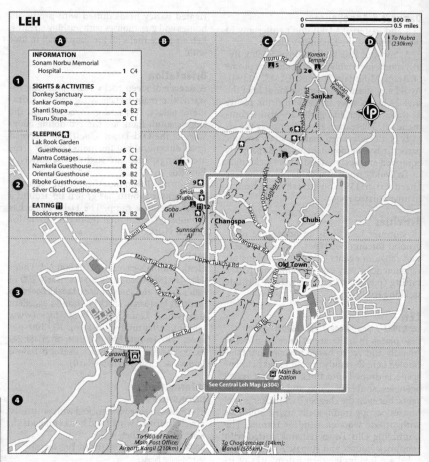

LEH

0 — 800 m
0 — 0.5 miles

To Nubra
(230km)

INFORMATION
Sonam Norbu Memorial
Hospital **1** C4

SIGHTS & ACTIVITIES
Donkey Sanctuary **2** C1
Sankar Gompa **3** C2
Shanti Stupa **4** B2
Tisuru Stupa **5** C1

SLEEPING
Lak Rook Garden
Guesthouse **6** C1
Mantra Cottages **7** C2
Namkela Guesthouse **8** B2
Oriental Guesthouse **9** B2
Riboke Guesthouse **10** B2
Silver Cloud Guesthouse **11** C2

EATING
Booklovers Retreat **12** B2

Tisuru Rd

Korean
Temple

Sankar

Korean
Temple Rd

Khatsal Tisuru Rd

Sankar Rd

Karzoo La

Shanti Rd

Small
Stupas

Goba
Al

Sunnsand
Al

Changspa

Chubi

Changspa Rd

Main Tukcha Rd

Upper Tukcha Rd

Old Town

Lower Tukcha Rd

Old Fort Rd

Old Rd

Fort Rd

Zarawar
Fort

Main Bus
Station

See Central Leh Map (p304)

To Hall of Fame;
Main Post Office;
Airport; Kargil (210km)

To Choglamasar (14km);
Manali (565km)

To Nubra
(230km)

Kangsing Books (Map p304; Changspa Rd)
Ladakh Bookshop (Map p304; Main Bazaar)
Leh Ling Bookshop (Map p304; Main Bazaar)
Otdan Bookshop (Map p304; Zangsti Rd)

EMERGENCY
Police (Map p304; ☎ 252018; Zangsti Rd)

INTERNET ACCESS
Dozens of internet cafes charge Rs90 per hour.
Connection speeds vary randomly even at the
same place. Power cuts can prove annoying.
Get Connected (Map p304; Main Bazaar; ✆ 9am-9pm)
CD burning.
Info Internet (Map p304; Music School Rd; ✆ 9am-
10pm) Good connections, some computers are Skype
enabled. Beside Happy World Cafe.

No-Name Internet (Map p304; Old Fort Rd; ✆ 9am-
11.30pm) Very obliging.
Vista (Map p304; Changspa Lane; ✆ 9am-11.30pm) One
of many internet cafes along this street.

INTERNET RESOURCES
J&K Tourism (www.jktourism.org/ladakh/index.htm)
General info plus accommodation and tour operators.
LAHDC (www.leh.nic.in) Gives open/closed status of the
roads from Srinagar and Manali.
Online Ladakh Map (www.reachladakh.com/
ladakh_map.htm)

LAUNDRY
Star Laundry (Map p304; Ford Rd),
Dzomsa (Map p304; ☎ 250699; per kg Rs70; ✆ 8am-
10.30pm) Offers an environmentally friendly laundry service.

MEDICAL SERVICES

AMS Advice (☎ 253629; ☻ 24hr) AMS questions answered.

Het Ram Vinay Kumar pharmacy (Map p304; ☎ 252160; Main Bazaar; ☻ 9.30am-8pm) Dispenses antibiotics and other essential medicines.

Sonam Norbu Memorial Hospital (Map p302; ☎ 252360/252014)

MONEY

There are numerous moneychangers on Changspa Rd and the Main Bazaar. Compare rates carefully.

J&K Bank ATM (Map p304; Ibex Rd) Seems semipermanently out of service.

J&K Bank Foreign Exchange Office (Map p304; Himalaya Complex, Main Bazaar; ☻ 10am-2pm Mon-Fri, to noon Sat) Decent rates for travellers cheques.

Paul Merchant (Map p304; ☎ 255309; ☻ 9am-9pm) Hassle-free currency exchange (cash and travellers cheques). Western Union transfers available.

State Bank of India (Map p304; Main Bazaar; ☻ 10am-4pm Mon-Fri, to 1pm Sat) The upstairs exchange desk can be chaotic. Queues are common at the 24-hour ATM outside, Leh's only reliable cash machine.

PHOTOGRAPHY & PHOTOCOPIES

Many internet cafes (opposite) download photos to CD for Rs80.

Nirvana Bookstall (Map p304) Photocopies.

RK Exchange (Map p304; Main Bazaar; ☻ variable) Sells flash cards and Sensia slide film (Rs220).

Unique Stationery (Map p304; Old Rd; ☻ 8am-6pm) Photocopies.

World Colour Lab (Map p304; Main Bazaar; ☻ 10am-7pm) Photocopies, digital and print processing, and sells slide film.

POST

Central post office (Map p304; Main Bazaar; ☻ 10am-4.30pm Mon-Sat)

Main post office (Off Map p302; Airport Rd; ☻ 10am-1pm & 2-5pm Mon-Fri, to 1pm Sat)

REPAIRS

Mobile Doctor (Map p304; ☎ 252831; Music School Rd) Claims to fix virtually anything electronic.

Shoe Repairer (Map p304) Usually sits outside Dzomsa (p312) by day.

TELEPHONE

Numerous PCO/STD/ISD offices charge standard Indian rates.

For mobile phone SIM cards (Rs80) provide photocopies of your visa/passport and three photos to **Airtel** (Map p304; Ibex Rd; ☻ 7am-2pm & 3-7pm Mon-Sat). Note that sending SMS texts isn't allowed in Jammu and Kashmir due to terrorism fears.

TOURIST INFORMATION

Noticeboards all over town have adverts for tours, treks and activities.

Tourist office (Map p304; ☎ 253482; Ibex Rd; ☻ 10am-4pm Mon-Sat) Has limited brochures on Ladakh.

Sights
PALACE RIDGE

Leh's major monuments are perched on the stark rocky ridge that forms the town's mesmerising visual focus. Climbing the ridge on your first day in Leh is unwise unless you're already altitude-aclimatised.

Leh Palace

Construction of the nine-storey dun-coloured **Leh Palace** (Map p304; Indian/foreigner Rs5/100; ☻ dawn-dusk) started in 1553. Built by the Buddhist kings of Ladakh, it was once the world's highest building and bears more than a passing similarity to the Potala Palace in Lhasa (Tibet). The very sturdy walls are mostly unadorned and a few interior sections remain in a state of partial collapse; only the palace prayer room gives any sense of former grandeur. Nonetheless it's gently thrilling to weave your way through the maze of dark corridors, hidden stairways and makeshift ladders to reach the rooftop for great views across the city. Carry a torch and watch out for holes in the floor.

Palace Gompas

A trio of photogenic religious structures guard the imposing palace entrance. The courtyard of 1840 **Soma Gompa** (Map p304) is used for traditional dances (admission Rs150; ☻ 5.30pm summer). Behind, the colourfully muralled **Chenrezi Lhakhang** (Map p304; admission Rs20) celebrates the full pantheon of 1000 Buddhas (of which 996 have yet to be born). The main attractions of the red, 1430 **Chamba Lhakhang** (Map p304; admission Rs20) are the partly conserved medieval murals between its inner and outer walls. Its central chamber enthrones a very gaudy three-storey Maitreya statue, reworked in 1957.

Tsemo Fort

A giddying 15-minute climb starting opposite Chenrezi Lakhang zigzags up to the ruinous medieval **Tsemo (Victory) Fort** (Map p304; admission

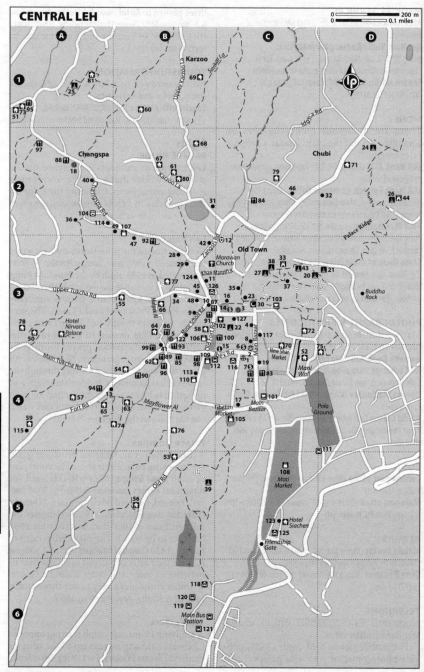

CENTRAL LEH

JAMMU & KASHMIR

Rs10; ⏰ approx 7am-7pm), a structure that's visible from virtually everywhere in Leh. In front of the fort, the **Gonkang Gompa** (Map p304) features protector statues, while the 1430 mud-brick **Namgyal Tsemo Gompa** (Map p304; admission Rs20) enshrines a three-storey-high Buddha.

An alternative descent slithers down to a **forest of stupas** (Map p304) in Chubi.

OLD TOWN
Behind Leh's fanciful Sunni men's mosque **Jama Masjid** (Map p304), the winding alleys and

stairways of Old Town burrow between and beneath a series of eroded chortens (stupas) and traditional mudbrick Ladakhi houses. Belatedly, many finer structures are being restored with help from the **Tibet Heritage Fund** (www.tibetheritagefund.org). A new **library-museum complex** (Map p304) is under construction around the tiny Sunni women's mosque, **Traders' Mosque** (Map p304). Opposite **Datun Sahib** (Map p304) is a sacred tree supposedly planted in 1517 by a Sikh mystic, though others claim it grew magically from a walking staff left here by Staksang Raspa, guru to Ladakh's great king Senge Namgyal.

A tunnel-passage leads up to the 17th-century **Munshi Mansion** (Map p304). Once the residence of the Ladakhi royal secretary, it's now under total reconstruction as the Lamo Arts Centre. Higher up, the squat **Guru Lhakang Shrine** (Map p304) contains newly repainted murals and a fierce-looking Guru Rinpoche statue. A short rocky scramble above, the giant **Namgyal Stupa** (Map p304) is just outside the palace walls.

CHOWKHANG GOMPA
Hidden in a large courtyard behind Main Bazaar, this small, 20th-century **Chowkhang gompa** (Map p304; admission free) has a distinctive gilt-roofed prayer room strung with hundreds of prayer flags. It's the headquarters of the Ladakh Buddhist Association.

SHANTI STUPA
Built by Japanese monks to promote world peace, this large, hilltop **stupa** (Map p302; ⏰ 5am-9pm) has brightly coloured reliefs on its mid-levels and is topped by a spired white hemisphere (smoking is prohibited here). The greatest attraction is the stunning view of Leh. Ideally make the breathless 15-minute climb around 5.30pm when golden afternoon light still illuminates the city, while the steps up from Changspa are in cooling shadow.

STUPAS
The ruined 11th-century **Tisuru Stupa** (Map p302; Tisuru Rd) is a bulky mudbrick structure that looks like a half-built *ziggurat* (stepped pyramid).

The whitewashed 9th-century **Gomang Stupa** (Map p304) rises in concentric serrated layers and is flanked by ancient Buddhist rock carvings and numerous chortens. Its peaceful, shady setting feels genuinely spiritual.

Cloaked in prayer flags the mysterious whitewashed **Nezer Latho** (Map p304) sits atop a rocky outcrop offering superb 360-degree views over Leh. It's a five-minute climb from Hotel Dragon opposite.

LEDEG
The **Ladakh Ecological Development Group** (LEDeG; Map p304; ☎ 253221; www.ledeg.org; ⏰ 10am-4pm Mon-Sat) has a library, a one-room exhibition featuring a typical Ladakhi kitchen scene and a meeting room showing an interesting one-hour DVD documentary (admission by donation), screened at 3pm, about eastern Ladakh's wildlife and nomads. Near the entrance is a display of renewable energy devices and a shop selling competitively priced handicrafts produced by village cooperatives. You can also refill your water bottles here (see boxed text, p312).

WOMEN'S ALLIANCE
A visit to this thought-provoking **community centre** (Map p304; ☎ 250293; www.isec.org.uk/pages/ladakh.html; ⏰ 10am-5pm Mon-Sat) should be compulsory for all visitors to Ladakh! It campaigns to educate locals and foreigners alike about the remarkable balance of traditional Ladakhi society. Screenings of the excellent hour-long documentary *Ancient Futures: Learning from Ladakh* (admission by donation) at 3pm Monday to Saturday are followed by a discussion. Various other films screen at 11am.

SANKAR GOMPA
Walking to the timeless two-storey Gelukpa **Sankar Gompa** (Map p302; admission Rs20) takes you between stone walls and attractive Ladakhi farmhouses following little streamlets and passing a pretty rural stupa. Sankar's small, main prayer room features a portrait of Kushok Bakula Rinpoche (died 2004), Ladakh's former head lama. His recently identified reincarnation will eventually move to the gilt-roofed *photang* (official residence) opposite the monastery.

DONKEY SANCTUARY
Donkeys rescued from mistreatment or end-of-career abandonment retire to this semi-rural **sanctuary** (Map p302; ☎ 9419658777; Korean Temple Rd). Bringing them carrots is a great excuse to wander around lovely, little visited upper Leh. Financial donations are also gratefully received.

HALL OF FAME
About 1km beyond the airport terminal on the Spituk–Kargil road, this small **museum** (Off Map p302; Indian/foreign Rs10/50; ☽ 9am-1pm & 3-7pm) has displays on Ladakhi culture and the war with Pakistan over the disputed Siachen Glacier.

Activities & Courses
YOGA & MEDITATION
The **Mahabodhi Centre** (Map p304; ☎ 253689; www .mahabodhi-ladakh.org; Changspa Lane) runs 1½-hour **yoga classes** (Rs150; ☽ 9.30am Mon-Fri, 4pm Mon-Sat) followed by a meditation session. Book here for three- or 10-day residential courses in *vipassana* meditation at the organisation's much bigger **Meditation Centre** (Map p304; ☎ 264372; dm Rs150, r Rs350-500; ☐), approximately 12km southeast. On Sunday the Meditation Centre runs a one-day discussion and introduction to meditation (Rs400 including lunch and bus transfer from Leh).

Open Ladakh (Map p304; ☎ 9419886135; www.open ladakh.com; Changspa Rd) runs **meditation sessions** (☽ 4pm Mon-Fri), yoga, weekend retreats in Stok (p318) and longer introductory courses.

MASSAGE
Numerous places around town offer massages and rubs, especially on Old Fort Rd. Standards vary enormously, so check the traveller grapevine for recommendations. Rates for Ayurvedic massage start at around Rs500. Charming **Adil** (Map p304; Asia Guesthouse, Changspa) offers €200 multiday courses teaching massage, chakra manipulation and acupressure.

MOUNTAINEERING
Ladakh has many peaks over 6000m. Some like popular Stok Kangri (p317) are 'trekking peaks' accessible to groups with basic equipment but minimal climbing experience. Many more are relatively rarely conquered. Kun (7087m), towering above the Suru Valley (p296), can be attempted by experienced amateur mountaineers with suitable support. Climbing nearby Nun (7135m) requires a world-class expedition. Obviously any climbing at this altitude requires serious acclimatisation and considerable fitness (see p111).

Peak Fees
Per-person peak fees, ranging from US$50 (trekking peaks) to US$400 (summits over 7000m), should be paid directly to **IMF**

(www.indmount.org), whose suavely dapper Ladakh representative, **Sri Sonam Wangyal** (Map p304; ☎ 252992; Changspa Lane), can generally organise things painlessly in under 24 hours. He claims he was the youngest man to climb Everest and has a house-office tucked incongruously into the Mentokling Restaurant yard.

Agencies can also arrange the permits. However, since only Stok Kangri has active IMF permit checks, many agents shamelessly encourage climbers to flout the rules and to climb without paying the fees.

RAFTING & KAYAKING
In summer, agencies including **Splash Adventures** (Map p304; ☎ 254870; gangakayak@yahoo.com; Zangsti Rd) and **Himalayan Journeys** (Map p304; ☎ 250591; stanny104hj@yahoo.co.in; Changspa Rd), offer daily rafting excursions through splendid canyon scenery from Phey to Nimmu (for beginners, grade I/II, Rs650 to Rs850) and from Chiling to Nimmu (grade II/III, Rs1200 to Rs1400). Prepare to get very wet. By prearrangement, more serious multiday rafting trips are possible for experienced rafters on the Indus, climaxing with grade IV sections around Skurbuchan (p322).

TREKKING
For information, see below.

VOLUNTEERING
Experienced TEFL teachers are in demand for volunteer work at local schools and monasteries. Ask directly or apply via agencies like **Beautiful World** (www.beautifulworld.org.uk).

For part-trek, part-volunteering group experiences contact **Around Ladakh with Students** (www.secmol.org/ecotourism) or consider a **rubbish-collecting trek** (www.overlandescape.com/cleaningtrek.php).

Organised Tours
TREKS & JEEP TOURS
For jeep tours, dozens of agencies can arrange a vehicle, driver and permit, but booking a full tour is usually quite unnecessary: simple rural accommodation is generally easy to find on arrival. Prebooking tours in advance can triple costs and since even the busiest tourist usually needs two days in Leh for altitude acclimatisation, you'll normally have long enough to arrange everything in situ. Organising peak-season treks might take somewhat longer if horses are in short supply.

JAMMU & KASHMIR

Choosing an agency is hit and miss. Agents listed below proved competant and/or were warmly recommended by travellers, but there are many, many others. Few seem systematically bad but many are very inconsistent. Seek recent recommendations from other travellers. In reality, a deciding factor is often which agent happens to have a group leaving on the day you need.

Himalayan Journeys (Map p304; ☎ 250591; stanny 104hj@yahoo.co.in; Changspa Rd) Shared jeeps and daily rafting.

Lhasi Karpo Ecological Trek & Tours (Map p304; ☎ 255644; www.eco-ladakh.com; Upper Tukcha Rd; ☻ 5-9pm) The knowledgeable owner is also the guide for Old Town walking tours.

Overland Escape (Map p304; ☎ 250858; www.overland escape.com) Major multiskilled agency whose director is a prominent local travel author. The office is set back above Bon Apetit restaurant.

Snow Leopard Trails (Map p304; ☎ 252074; www .snowleopardtrails.com; Hotel Kanglhachen Complex, Zangsti Rd) Homestay treks.

Splash Adventures (Map p304; ☎ 254870; ganga kayak@yahoo.com; Zangsti Rd) Rafting specialists.

Wild East Adventure (Map p304; ☎ 250505; www .wildeastadventure.com; Upper Tukcha Rd) Good trekking contact.

World Adventure (Map p304; ☎ 251910; gurmetch aru@rediffmail.com; Changspa Rd) Small but obliging.

XploreLadakh (Map p304; ☎ 09906994743; www .xploreladakh.com; Upper Tukcha Rd) Sometimes chaotic, but good at finding jeep shares: if it can't help, a dozen other agents within a minute's walk probably can.

Yama Adventures (Map p304; ☎ 250833; www.yama treks.com; Changspa Rd) Recommended by several reader trekkers.

OLD TOWN WALKING TOURS

Delightfully ponderous small-group **walking tours** (per person Rs300; ☻ 9.30am Tue, Thu & Sat) dawdle around the Old Town starting from Lala's Art Cafe (p312) and visiting partially reconstructed old houses and a selection of temples. Allow five hours.

Sleeping

In most accommodation hot water is available either morning or evening only and can take up to 10 minutes to run warm. Since that's very wasteful of a precious resource, it's wise to request hot water by bucket or to simply shower less often than usual.

A few pricier hotels charge a 10% service fee. If you can forgo a TV and uniformed front

staff, better guesthouses (from around Rs700) are often just as good as tourist-rated hotels (Rs1980). Apart from ubiquitously shabby, ill-fitting corridor carpets, almost all Leh accommodation in each price range has noticeably more charm than equivalents anywhere else in India. And since Leh has dozens and dozens more decent guesthouses than we have space to include, you're likely to find your own gem if you don't stick to this list. Most hotels and many guesthouses close in winter.

Although a few guesthouses are sprinkled about the dusty lanes of the Old Town, the main traveller areas are green yet developed Changspa and busier Fort Rd, which has a greater proportion of upper midrange hotels. Noisier Old Rd has several package-tour hotels. Leafy Karzoo, Upper Karzoo and Tukcha areas are quieter and very appealing, but lack shops or cafes. Chubi and especially Sankar feel distinctly rural.

BUDGET

Room standards within each guesthouse generally vary significantly, so look before you buy. Booking more than 24 hours in advance is often pointless anyway, since cheaper guesthouses only know what space they'll have on the day guests check out.

Changspa

our pick **Zeepata Guesthouse** (Map p304; ☎ 250747; Changspa; s/d Rs100/200) This fairly modern six-room house-hotel 'grows' incongruously out of the ruins of an ancient mudbrick mansion. Clean, shared bathrooms have geysers and the top-floor room has a great little terrace with views. Idyllically calm.

Oriental Guesthouse (Map p302; ☎ 253153; www .oriental-ladakh.com; Changspa; s/d Rs350/850, without bathroom Rs100/200; ☻ year-round; ☐) This large, self-contained if slightly isolated complex has something for most budgets. The lobby-library has internet, there's a sprawling garden, full-scale restaurant, useful noticeboard and free drinking water for guests. Rooms are neat and new; however, the cheapest are underlit off dingy corridors that smell of boiled mutton.

Namkela Guesthouse (Map p302; ☎ 251792; Changspa Rd; d without bathroom Rs200) Simple rooms in an authentic Ladakhi family home.

Riboke Guesthouse (Ribook Guesthouse; Map p302; ☎ 253230; Riboke_gh@yahoo.co.in; Sunnsand Alley; d Rs350, without bathroom Rs200) Bright, sunny rooms, albeit with slightly tatty vinyl floors, in a typical local house, with a relaxed sitting area in a peaceful vegetable garden.

Asia Guesthouse (Map p304; ☎ 253403; ladakhasia@ yahoo.co.in; Changspa Rd; d from Rs500, without bathroom from Rs200) Sprawling traveller institution with garden cafe serenaded by rushing water, and lobby-lounge featuring a stuffed yak. Rs650 rooms have well-tiled bathrooms, but the big, lacklustre annexe (formerly Hotel Sun'n'Sand) needs a lot of work.

Fort Road Area

Jampal Guesthouse (Map p304; ☎ 251272; tse_nain2004@ yahoo.co.in; Mayflower Alley; d without bathroom Rs200-300) Superfriendly family place, with garden and traditional-style sitting room. The rooms without bathroom have hot water morning AND night.

Indus Guesthouse (Map p304; ☎ 252502; masters _adv@yahoo.co.in; Malpak Alley; d Rs200-500, breakfast Rs100) Rooms are good value, especially the bright Rs300 upper ones. There are two shared terraces and a peaceful tree-shaded garden.

Tukcha

Ashoka Guesthouse (Map p304; ☎ 252725; ashokaguest house@gmail.com; Main Tukcha Rd; r Rs300, without bathroom Rs150) Inexpensive, with unusually clean, tidy rooms, but lacks much communal space.

Karzoo

Karzoo Guesthouse (Map p304; ☎ 9906997015; Karzoo Lane; d Rs300, without bathroom Rs200) This Nepali-managed traditional Ladakhi house attracts a laid-back crowd with its congenial garden and great little chill-out zones. Cheaper rooms share bathrooms with rough concrete floors but are more atmospheric than smaller rooms with private bathroom (Rs300).

Magsoon Guesthouse (Map p304; ☎ 919960992683; Sankar Lane; r Rs350) Fairly standard guesthouse made attractive by its flower garden, views of the fortress and traditionally styled dining area.

Old Town

Moonland Guesthouse (Map p304; ☎ 252175; Old Town; s/d without bathroom Rs100/200) Five simple but very clean rooms sharing two bathrooms above a modest family house.

Babu Guesthouse (Map p304; ☎ 252419; Old Town; s/d Rs150/200) Upper rooms have oblique palace views and the shared outside toilets are only a short dash away.

Palace View Guesthouse (Map p304; ☎ 250773; Old Town; d from Rs300, without bathroom from Rs200) This upliftingly lived-in family place has yard seats, two sitting rooms and a basic rooftop with fabulous views of the palace ridge. Bathrooms have geysers. The owner is friendly and conscientious.

Old Ladakh Guesthouse (Map p304; ☎ 252951; Old Town; d from Rs500, without bathroom from Rs200) Despite distinctive semi-oriental crimson timbers, an atmospheric traditional kitchen/breakfast room and phenomenal rooftop views, rooms range from dingily claustrophobic to bright but worn. New annexe rooms, currently under construction, should be better.

Chubi

Spangchenmo Guesthouse (Map p304; ☎ 252257; Idgha Rd; d Rs200) Friendly three-room family guest-house facing the fortress ridge across a field.

Sankar

Lak Rook Garden Guesthouse (Map p302; ☎ 252987; agyal123@yahoo.com; Sankar; r from Rs350, without bathroom from Rs200) This beautiful, ramshackle Ladakhi farmhouse is almost overwhelmed by its fabu-lous organic vegetable garden. With friendly owners, good food, choice of squat or 'local' (composting) toilets and solar-powered show-ers, it's a cult traveller favourite despite sim-ple, sometimes musty, rooms.

MIDRANGE

Travellers' House (Map p304; Karzoo Lane; d from Rs400) Attractive, family-run Karzoo option with black-and-white framed photos and geysers in the bathrooms.

Hotel Yasmin (Map p304; ☎ 255098; www.yasmin ladakh.com; Mayflower Lane; d lower/upper Rs400/500) There's a quiet garden setting and views from the upper-floor room are delightful.

our pick Hotel Saser (Map p304; ☎ 250162; nam _gyal@rediff.com; Karzoo Lane; d Rs400-700) The smartest and calmest of a dozen good-value semitradi-tional guesthouses on Karzoo Lane, the Saser wraps attractively around a flower-hemmed lawn. All rooms have hot water, but the upper-floor (Rs700) versions are more artistic and share an open balcony with palace views. The tastefully appointed cafe is well stocked with locally relevant books.

Jigmet Guesthouse (Map p304; ☎ 253563; jigmet guesthouse@yahoo.com; Upper Tukcha Rd; d Rs500-700; ☼ year-round) Large, clean, if not especially suave rooms overlook a splendid vegetable

THINK GLOBALLY, CRAP LOCALLY

Traditional Ladakhi culture recycles everything, even human waste through special long-drop composting toilets, with earth occasionally sprinkled over the latest 'deposits'. These brilliant inventions prevent sewerage from polluting streams while avoiding the terrible water wastage of flush toilets. Using them when possible is a great idea for ecoconscious visitors. But don't put anything nonbiodegradeable down the hole. Remember whatever goes in will end up on the farmer's field in a year or two.

and flower garden, with tempting book-equipped sitting areas both under the apple trees and indoors.

Saiman Guesthouse (Map p304; ☎ 253161; Saiman _guesthouse@yahoo.com; Malpak Alley; d Rs500-650) Friendly, superclean homestay-style guesthouse, with great garden area, large homey rooms, a little sitting room and lovely views from pricier rooms.

New Moon Guesthouse (Map p304; ☎ 250296; ang chok@india.com; Sankar Rd, Chubi; d Rs600, without bathroom Rs300) Spotlessly clean, with new beds, a Ladakhi sitting room and a decent garden restaurant albeit slightly affected by traffic noise.

Hotel Tso-Kar (Map p304; ☎ 255763; www.lehladakh hotel.com; Fort Rd; d from 600) Rooms aren't as attractive as the seductively collonaded courtyard might imply, but TVs have BBC World and there are day-long hot showers.

Hotel Naro (Map p304; ☎ 255138; www.hotelnaro.com; Karzoo Lane; d Rs950, without bathroom Rs650) Clean, fresh rooms mostly come with solar-heated showers and newly tiled or marble bathrooms. Many have splendid views across a daliah garden towards the Shanti Stupa.

Hotel Lingzi (Map p304; ☎ 252020; www.lingzihotel .com; Old Fort Rd; d lower/mid/upper fl Rs800/1200/1400) Very central, with attentive service, spacious rooftop view areas and 24-hour hot water. The facade and lobby ooze local charm, but the clean rooms are somewhat bland.

TOP END

Hotel Grand Willow (Map p304; ☎ 251835; Fort Rd; s/d Rs1430/1980) Three floors of lavishly carved balconies, neat new bathrooms, silk bedcovers and a small oriental dining room. Off peak, 40% discounts are possible.

Hotel Hilltown (Map p304; ☎ 256451; hilltownleh@ gmail.com; Upper Tuckha Rd; s/d from Rs1430/1980) Bright, fresh rooms with swish new bathrooms in a new-meets-old building with a small beer garden.

Lotus Hotel (Map p304; ☎ 250265; www.hotel-lotus.tk; Upper Karzoo Lane; s/d/ste Rs1430/1980/3300) Designed like a Ladakhi palace, set behind a raised semismart garden-terrace cafe, tasteful rooms have little Tibetan details and thick (if sometimes ill-fitting) carpets.

Pangong Hotel (Map p304; ☎ 254655; www.pan gongladakh.com; Chulung Lane; s/d Rs1400/1980; 💻) About the nearest Leh comes to fashionable modern decor, the Pangong's rooms get more stylish the higher you climb, with good linens, multichannel TV, smart bathrooms and carpets that almost fit. The quiet access lane is unlit.

Snowland Hotel (Map p302; ☎ 253027; snowland tukcha@gmail.com; Main Tukcha Rd; d lower/upper Rs1500/1800) Very peaceful, with mountain views from the little balconies of spick-and-span upper rooms. Check out by 10am.

Mantra Cottages (Map p302; ☎ 253588; www.himalayas -travel.com; Shanti Rd; tw Rs1500, with full board Rs3500) Cramped but cosy and very clean bungalow units arc around a rural barley terrace with lovely views.

Hotel Namgyal Palace (Map p304; ☎ 256356; nam gyalpalace.com; Fort Rd; s/d/ste Rs1570/2180/3630) Less personal but more professional than most Leh hotels, rooms are modern with well-appointed bathrooms, though the silvered windows clash somewhat with the neotraditional Tibetan woodwork. Fabulous mountain panoramas from third-floor rooms.

Hotel Lasermo (Map p304; ☎ 252313; www.hotel lasermo.com; Old Rd; s/d from Rs1600/2200) Packed around a small central garden, pink-marble corridors lead to variable but mostly spacious rooms and two sizeable roof terraces. Obliging service, but some road noise. It's partially open in winter.

Padma Hotel (Map p304; ☎ 252630; www.padma ladakh.com; d Rs1850; 💻) Hidden in a large garden, Padma's attractively appointed new rooms and rooftop restaurant with mountain views keep it constantly popular. The older guesthouse section has some Rs500 rooms with shared bathroom.

our pick **Hotel Lha-Ri-Mo** (Map p304; ☎ 252101; fax 253345; Fort Rd; d Rs1980) This enchanting complex forms a white, black and magenta mini-Potala around an unpretentious central lawn. Newer rooms have hints of trendy minimalism, while the Tibetan-style communal sitting room is an oriental delight. Reliable food. Towels changed daily.

Hotel Dragon (Map p304; ☎ 252139; www.travel ladakh.com; Old Rd; s/d from Rs1994/2026) Pluses include multilevel terraces and an atmospheric dining room. Upper rooms like No 131 have exotic wood-inlay bedheads.

Eating

Traveller cafes abound, Israeli and Chinese options supplementing curries, banana pancakes, tandoori pizzas and Tibetan favourites, like *momos* and *thukpa* (Tibetan noodle soup). Many places, including Changspa's numerous garden and rooftop restaurants, close from mid-September to July, their owners decamping to Goa.

TOWN CENTRE

Amdo Food (Map p304; Main Bazaar; mains Rs45-70) The decor isn't special but the Tibetan food is. Excellent *momos*, great fried cheese wontons and lip-smacking vegetable balls in raspberry-coloured garlic sauce. No alcohol. Enter from the side alley.

Amdo (Map p304; Main Bazaar; mains Rs45-130) Not to be confused with Amdo Food, Amdo is across the road, with a roof terrace and a wider-ranging menu, including stomach-sizzling chilli-garlic Chow Mein (Rs45).

Pumpernickel German Bakery (Map p304; Zangsti Rd; meals Rs50-180) Behind the simple bakery counter is a merrily ramshackle dining room with Ladakhi wooden columns and a full multicuisine menu. Try its tofu curry (Rs80 including rice).

Il Forno (Map p304; Zangsti Rd; pizzas Rs100-170) Unassuming but better than most other lacklustre rooftop restaurants above Main Bazaar, especially for pizza. Beer is also served (Rs130).

FORT ROAD

Lamayuru Restaurant (Map p304; Fort Rd; mains from Rs25) Surrounded by other similar backpacker eateries, this is a plain but very reliable place for good inexpensive Indian, Chinese and international snacks.

Gesmo (Map p304; Fort Rd, curries from Rs35) Loveable old-fashioned traveller haunt, with gingham tablecloths, checkerboard ceilings, and a range of cakes and breakfasts supplementing good-value curries.

Tenzin Dickey Tibetan (Map p304; Fort Rd; mains Rs40-60) Cosy if unpretentious eatery for vegetarian Tibetan food.

Dolphin Bakery (Map p304; Malpak Alley; mains Rs50-110) The Dolphin serves cakes and good vegie burgers (albeit with flourescent yellow fries), on a simple triangle of a streamside, tree-shaded terrace.

Penguin Garden (Map p304; mains Rs50-170) Hidden just off the main drag, this is a peaceful place to read the newspapers while nibbling cake by day, or to sit in the twinkling coloured lamplight over tandoori chicken at night.

Grill-N-Curry (Map p304; Fort Rd; mains Rs50-200, tea Rs20) Climb two flights of metal steps for unusual palace views, then stay for the rich, spicy mushroom *caju masala* (Rs90).

Chopsticks (Map p304; Fort Rd; mains Rs60-180) This third-floor pan-Asian restaurant is Leh's most stylish eatery. The Thai green curry (Rs90) is excellent. The *tom kha kai* (Thai chicken and coconut soup) is much less convincing.

Mona Lisa (Map p304; Fort Rd; mains Rs70-200) Competant multicuisine menu served on a congenial covered terrace.

CHANGSPA

Otsal Restaurant (Map p304; Changspa Lane; mains Rs50-120) Pleasant backpacker retreat serenaded by a gurgling stream.

Booklovers Retreat (Cafe Jeevan; Map p302; Changspa Lane; mains Rs60-120; ☯ 7am-11pm) Comparatively sophisticated yet no pricier than the competition for a wide range of cuisines, including creditable Middle Eastern standards. There's a two-case bookshop and an appealing covered roof terrace.

Sheldon Garden Restaurant (Map p304; Changspa Lane; mains Rs80-140) Calm, candle-lit garden serving brilliantly succulent chicken *malai* tandoori and a vast range of partly successful Mexican, Italian and local options.

our pick **La Pizzeria** (Map p304; Changspa Lane; pizzas Rs130-290, pasta Rs130-205, mains Rs60-500) Leh's most attractively appointed garden restaurant is considerably pricier than most other eateries, but well worth the extra for thin-crust pizzas, excellent pumpkin soup (Rs90), tajines, tandoori dishes or even trout in brandy sauce. Beer is also served (Rs 150).

CHUBI

Local Food Restaurant (Map p304; Women's Alliance; meals Rs40; ☯ 11am-4pm Mon-Sat) Regionally sourced produce and traditional recipes live up to the

Women's Alliance's think-local philosophy. Garden seating. Very limited choice.

Amigo Korean Cafe (Map p304; mains Rs85-300; ☽ 9am-10pm Mon-Sat) Seoul with soul, this delightfully shady garden cafe offers a wide range of Korean specialities, with menus in English and Hangul, along with green tea (Rs20).

SELF-CATERING

Buy fresh produce from the **vegetable market** (Map p304; Old Fort Rd) or from colourfully dressed women along Main Bazaar (Map p304). Fresh-baked bread rounds (Rs3) are sold hot from traditional wood-fired Ladakhi tandoor behind Jama Masjid.

Eco-aware travellers are encouraged to buy locally sourced foods, eg apricots rather than imported chocolate and *tsestalulu* (sea buckthorn) juice instead of packaged soft drinks. Get these and other local fruit products at **Ladag Apricot Store** (Map p304; ☽ 9am-6pm) or at three branches of **Dzomsa** (Map p304; ☎ 250699; ☽ 8am-10.30pm), which also offers safe water-bottle refills (Rs7; see boxed text, right).

Drinking

Many garden and rooftop restaurants serve beer, but it's never on the menu so ask the waiter.

La Pizzeria (Map p304; Changspa Lane) Serves basic cocktails (Rs180).

Indus Wine Shop (Map p304; Ibex Rd; ☽ 10am-9pm, closed full moon days) Sells takeaway alcohol and cold beers but not wine.

La Terrasse (Map p304; Main Bazaar; beers Rs100) Open relatively late with a popular roof terrace and (less appealing) indoor dining room for cold nights.

CAFES

Desert Rain (Map p304; ☎ 256426; New Shar Market; coffees Rs25-40; ☽ 8am-8.30pm Mon-Sat) Good coffee served in a relaxed Western atmosphere, with plenty of books to read. Film nights on Saturdays at 5.30pm.

our pick Lala's Art Cafe (Map p304; Old Town; coffee Rs25) This tiny, brilliantly restored mudbrick Old Town house has trip-you-up stone steps, artistic black-and-white photography and great Italian coffee. Check out the ancient carvings downstairs at the rear.

Entertainment

KC Garden Restaurant (Map p304; ☎ 254499; Changspa Rd) One of Changspa's liveliest evening spots,

---

FILL UP!

To save Leh from vanishing under a sea of plastic bottles, refills of pressure-boiled, purified water are provided by environmental organisations **Dzomsa** (Map p304; ☎ 250699; refill Rs7; ☽ 8am-10.30pm) and **LeDEG** (Map p304; ☎ 253221; www.ledeg.org; refill Rs5; ☽ 10am-4pm Mon-Sat). Both also offer recycling and disposal services for paper, bottles and batteries.

KC's is the pickup point for all-night full-moon parties (Rs400 including transport; full-moon night May to August). Movies are projected at 8pm several nights weekly.

CULTURAL PERFORMANCES

Traditional Ladakhi Song-&-Dance Shows (Map p304; admission R150; ☽ 5.30pm) Tourist-oriented performances on summer evenings outside Soma Gompa.

Shopping

Many souvenir shops and Tibetan Refugee Markets (Map p304) sell wonderful selections of *thangkas*, Ladakhi hats, 'antiques' and heavy turquoise jewellery, as well as Kashmiri shawls and various Nepali, Tibetan and Chinese knick-knacks.

Crafts and clothes sold at **LeDEG** (Map p304; ☎ 253221; www.ledeg.org; ☽ 10am-4pm Mon-Sat) and the **Women's Alliance** (Map p304; ☎ 250293; www.isec.org .uk/pages/ladakh.html; ☽ 10am-5pm Mon-Sat) are locally produced and generally very fair value. Wooden *choktse* tables carved with images of mythical beasts are available from the **Handicrafts Industrial Cooperative Shop** (Map p304; Old Fort Rd; ☽ 9am-6pm) and **Wamda Wood Carving** (Map p304; Old Fort Rd; ☽ 9am-6pm). **Harish** (Map p304; Changspa Rd) sells local and Western musical instruments.

For more prosaic items of cheap clothing plus bags and limited camping supplies, a good first place to look is **Gol Market** (Map p304; Old Rd; ☽ 9am-5.30pm). Moti Market (Map p304) is bigger.

Getting There & Away

AIR

Flights are dramatically scenic, but can be cancelled at short notice when the weather is bad. Rearranging flights can take days, so build flexibility into your plans. Although flying in means you're likely to suffer mild

AMS, taking the road directly from Delhi via Manali is arguably worse as you'll have 5000m passes to cross. Flying is the only way to reach Ladakh once roads close in winter.

Indian Airlines (Map p304; ☎ 252076; Fort Rd; ☼ 10am-1pm & 2-4.30pm) flies to Delhi (Rs10,625, Monday, Wednesday, Friday), Srinagar (Rs6710, Wednesday) and Jammu (Rs7345, Monday and Friday), the easiest connection for reaching Dharamsala (p368) from Leh.

Jet Airways (Map p304; ☎ 250999; Main Bazaar; ☼ 10am-1pm & 2-5pm) flies to Delhi at least daily in August. Frequency drops gradually to twice weekly in February.

Kingfisher (www.flykingfisher.com) flies Leh–Deli–Pune in summer.

BUS & SHARED JEEP
There are a variety of departure points for Manali, Kargil and Srinagar. However, most other local and long-distance public buses leave from several stands within the main bus station (Map p304), 700m south of the town centre.

To Kargil
For Kargil, buses (ordinary/deluxe R250/340, 10 hours) depart around 4am from the Polo

BUSES TO/FROM LEH

Destination	Fare (Rs)	Duration	Departures
Alchi	50	3hr	6am, 8am, noon (return 8am, 11am, 3pm)
Chemrey	30	1hr	see Shakti buses
Choglamsar	7	15min	frequent
Chiling	55	3½hr	9am Wed & Sun (return 1pm)
Chitkan*	144	8hr	8am Tue, Fri, Sun (return Wed, Sat, Mon)
Dha*	146	7hr	9am both directions
Diskit/Hunder**	102	6hr	6am Tue, Thu, Sat (return Sun, Wed, Fri) see Thersey/Skurubu buses
Hemis	32	2hr	9.30am (return noon)
Hemis Skupachan*	74	4hr	2pm (return 8.30am) via Yangthang
Khalsi*	78	4½hr	3pm each way
Korzok		variable	10th, 20th & 30th of each month
Lamayaru	101	5½hr	see Chitkan or Kargil buses
Likir Gompa	33	2hr	4pm (return 6.30am)
Matho	20	40min	9am, 2pm, 5pm
Phey	10	30min	noon, 4.30pm (return 8am, 1pm)
Phyang	18	40min	four daily
Shakti	35	1¼hr	8.15am, noon, then half-hourly till 5pm (return frequent 7am-9am, 12.30pm, 3.30pm)
Shey	12	25min	see Thiksey or Shakti buses
Skurbuchan*	113	6hr	10am
Spituk	7	15min	six daily
Srinagar**	650	1½ days	temporarily suspended
Stakna	15	40min	Thiksey buses terminate nearby
Stok	15	30min	8am, 2pm, 4.30pm (return 9am, 3pm, 5.30pm)
Sumur*	105	7hr	6am Thu, Sat (return Fri, Sun)
Thiksey	15	30min	half-hourly 7.30am-6pm
Tia*	92	4½hr	noon
Timishgang*	87	4hr	11am
Wanla*	105	5hr	8.30am Tue, Thu, Sun

* LBOC Bus (☎ 252792), ** J&K SRTC (☎ 252085), others minibus (☎ 253262)

Ground. Shared jeeps (per seat/vehicle Rs500/3500, 12 hours) leave around 7am from outside Hotel Siachen ('Old Bus Station'). Look for JK07 number plates and ideally make arrangements the day before.

To Srinagar

Srinagar buses are currently suspended, but many tour agencies offer overnight shared jeeps (Rs1000/1300 assuming 10/seven in a jeep) departing around noon, arriving the next morning. The road closes altogether from early November to late May.

To Manali

The beautiful if jarringly bumpy Leh–Manali road (p329) officially opens mid-July to mid-September, though if the road is clear (not guaranteed) private vehicles run until mid-October. The trip (22 to 25 hours) is much more enjoyable with an overnight stop en route. Stopping at Sarchu handily breaks the journey into two roughly equal sections, but you'll be sleeping at 4200m, risking AMS. If you haven't acclimatised, stopping at Keylong (p391) is wiser.

The two-day J&K SRTC bus (ordinary/deluxe Rs585/850) departs from the main bus station (Map p304) around 4.30am, overnighting at Keylong (Rs475, 17 hours). Northbound it departs from Manali/Keylong at 9am/5am. More comfortable HPTDC buses leave outside Leh's J&K Bank HQ, on Ibex Rd, at 5am on alternate days (Rs1250, or Rs1600 including tented accommodation at Keylong). Prebook at the upstairs **HPTDC booking office** (Map p304; ☎ 094518460071; Fort Rd; ☼ 9.30am-1pm & 2-7pm).

Other private buses include relatively rare services overnighting at Sarchu, sold through **Vajra Voyages** (Map p304; ☎ 252043; Main Bazaar) and **Tiger Eye Adventure** (Map p358; ☎ 01902252718; www.tigereyeadventure.com; Old Manali).

Ladakh Taxi Operators Cooperative (Map p304; ☎ 252723; ☼ 6am-7.30pm), overlooking Leh bus station, operates daily packed-full shared jeeps (back/middle Rs900/1500). Virtually every Manali and Leh travel agency offers slightly less crowded jeeps (from Rs1200). All depart between 1am and 2am and do the whole Manali–Leh trip in one exhausting, spine-jangling go. It's far more comfy to gather a group of five travellers and hire an agency jeep with an overnight stop. Expect to pay around Rs12,000 per vehicle southbound, but as little as Rs8500 ex-Manali if you can find a Ladakhi driver.

Southbound, with permits, you could alternatively do Leh–Manali via Tso Moriri (p327) in three days. Northbound that's impossible because permits are only granted in Leh.

Other Destinations

Other buses and minibuses use the 'new' main bus station. To walk there from town there's a toilet-scented footpath shortcut starting opposite Hotel Dragon, or cut through the stepped bazaar from Friendship Gate. Double-check latest departure schedules before traipsing down here with heavy bags.

For details of some of the other bus departures to/from Leh, see the boxed table, p313.

TAXI & CHARTER JEEPS

Annually fixed taxi and charter jeep fares are published in a booklet widely used by drivers and agencies, though modest discounts (around 15%) are often possible. For details of some of the taxi and charter jeep departures from Leh, see the boxed table, opposite.

HOMESTAYS

In small Ladakh villages there's a blurred line between guesthouses and homestays. Either provide a fascinating window into the Ladakhi way of life. Typically you'll eat with the family in a traditional kitchen with pots and pans proudly displayed above the Aga-style winter stove, which partly burns fuel ingeniously made from straw and dried cowpats. You might even be able to help harvesting or planting the family fields. Modest mudbrick rooms generally offer a pile of rugs and blankets for bedding, but many are surprisingly cosy, some with solar-battery electric lamps.

In some areas **Himalayan Homestays** (www.himalayan-homestays.com) has standardised prices (per single/double Rs350/600) and certain Leh agencies can theoretically prebook for you (Rs50 extra), though given the lack of telephones, such 'bookings' are generally just notes in Ladakhi telling a host to look after you. Especially in Rumbak (p316) it's generally easy enough to turn up unannounced and find accommodation.

For Indus Valley day trips, engaging a driver is simple at the three main taxi-van stands. For longer jeep trips, tour agencies can help by putting together a fare-sharing group. Five per jeep is optimal for comfort versus expense. Don't be shy to ask the driver to make photo stops.

Combining destinations makes things much cheaper, eg Leh–Stok–Matho–Stakna–Leh costs only Rs1120.

For extra overnight stops en route add Rs350 for your driver's expenses plus Rs630/1235 per half-/full-day vehicle hire.

MOTORCYCLE
Discover Himalaya Adventure (Map p304; ☎ 250353; Main Bazaar), plus several other companies notably along Music School Rd, hire scooters/125cc motorcycles for Rs400/500 per day. Double-check insurance. Beware that petrol stations are limited (at Leh, Choglamsar, Karu, Diksit, Spituk, Phyang junction, Khaltse and Kargil) and don't always have any petrol to sell!

Getting Around
TO/FROM THE AIRPORT
Taxi transfers to central Leh should cost Rs100. From the highway outside the airport passing (packed-full) public minibuses to central Leh cost Rs5.

TAXI
Leh's taxis are almost all little microvans in which hops cost from Rs70. You'll usually need to go to a taxi stand to find or prearrange a ride. Prebook the night before if requiring an early morning departure.

BICYCLE
Agents including **Himalayan Bikers** (Map p304; ☎ 250937; www.thehimalayanbikers.com; Changspa Lane) and **Summer Holidays** (Map p304; ☎ 252651; standoore@gmail.com; Zangsti Rd) hire mountain bikes (per day from Rs400) and organise daily cycle-back tours to Khardung La (p323), where jeeps take you up but gravity brings you back down. The Rs900 per person fee includes bike hire, permit and support vehicle.

TREKKING IN LADAKH
The mountains of Ladakh provide some inspirational summer trekking. As most routes start at around 3500m and often climb above 5000m, proper acclimatisation is essential to avoid AMS (p1198).

TAXI & CHARTER JEEPS FROM LEH		
Destination	One way (Rs)	Return (Rs)
Alchi	1276	1690
Basgo	780	1040
Chiling	1683	2019
Hemis	903	1204
Kargil	4485	6552
Keylong	11,000	16,076
Lamayuru	2457	3276
Likir	1072	1430
Matho	632	821
Nimmu	702	936
Phey	312	416
Phyang	487	650
Shey	266	335
Spituk	195	260
Srinagar	8463	11,284
Stakna	654	805
Stok Palace	361	514
Thiksey	421	509

If you don't want the trouble of carrying a heavy pack, tent or supplies, the Sham (p316), Zingchen–Rumbak–Stok (p316) or Zingchen–Chiling (p316) routes are ideal choices thanks to homestays/guesthouses and simple parachute cafes along the routes. Several travel agencies including Snow Leopard Trails (p307) can book homestays and arrange a guide (per day Rs800), but they also sell the Rs150 Himalayan Homestays topographic map. This covers the latter two treks in enough detail to hike alone, assuming you're confident at reading the contours; use common sense and local advice rather than slavishly following the map's sometimes inaccurately marked footpaths.

For longer, tougher treks you'll generally need full camping equipment. Carrying heavy packs at Ladakh's elevated altitudes is much more exhausting than many experienced walkers anticipate, so engaging packhorses is very wise, with the bonus that the accompanying horseman can double as a guide. Costs start at Rs250 per horse, but can rise considerably when horses are in short supply (notably during the August harvest), so you might need a couple of day's patience to find a willing horseman. The best places to look are where popular treks end, notably Lamayuru (p322) and Padum (p297).

Many visitors use Leh agencies to sort out everything in advance. Inclusive agency treks typically start from around €35 per person per day assuming a group of four walkers, but costs vary greatly according to numerous factors. The fee usually includes a guide, cook, packhorses, food and tents, but carefully clarify what you'll get and try to check the equipment before departing. Ideally use your own tent and sleeping bag because many agency tents are heavy, old, damaged and/or lacking sufficient pegs.

Route Suggestions

The following is a very basic overview of options. For much more practical detail get Lonely Planet's *Trekking in the Indian Himalaya* or Charlie Loram's *Trekking in Ladakh*. For blogger travelogues, see www .myhimalayas.com/travelogues/ladakh.htm. For Zanskar treks, see p298.

ZINGCHEN–RUMBAK–STOK

- two days
- homestay trek, possible without equipment or guide
- one 4900m pass

In dry weather the delightful three-hour riverside climb from Zingchen to Rumbak is easy to follow. If you're in doubt over the routing, follow donkey droppings and cross any bridge you see (the trail criss-crosses the river much more than maps suggest). Delightful Rumbak (4050m) is an intriguing place to overnight and allows some acclimatisation. Next morning, before deciding to start the seven-hour Rumbak–Stok section, see if clouds are covering the 4900m Stok La (Namling La) pass. If so, consider waiting a day (or returning to Zingchen) as the crossing would be risky in low visibility without a guide. However, in good weather, the steep two-hour climb to the pass is obvious and offers some dramatic scenery of spiky upturned strata. When descending from Stok La turn left and descend after the second minipass (around 25 minutes). Otherwise, follow the majority of hikers across the third minipass, and end up heading towards Stok Kangri base camp (opposite).

Around two hours beyond the pass you will find a parachute cafe offering sustanance. Thereafter keep to the west bank of the river when descending unless the river is very low. There's only one short scramble section, up over a low ridge topped by a mini castle tower.

ZINGCHEN–CHILING

- three to five days
- homestay trek, possible without equipment or guide
- one 4900m pass

On the first day visit attractive Rumbak (three hours; see left), backtrack for half an hour to an obvious parachute cafe, then continue for an hour up to eerie Yurutse (4200m), possibly the world's smallest village. Its one and only house (also a homestay) is flanked by little stupas, has a dribbling fresh-water spring and enjoys a perfectly framed view of Stok Kangri (6121m) through a cleft valley opposite. Next day is a strenuous traverse of the 4900m Ganda La (around four hours from Yurutse), then a two-hour descent past a parachute cafe to two-house Shingo village. Shingo's first house is the homestay. Next day descending to the Markha Valley takes around 2½ hours. There are homestays at Kaya (two) and Skiu (one), or if you're brimming with energy, continuing to Chiling (p319) takes around four more hours.

Important: In 2008 the *trolley* (wire-basket bridge) across the Zanskar River was removed from Chiling and a new one constructed 4km further south near the Zanskar–Markham Rivers junction. A part-built bridge here should be finished by this book's publication, eventually allowing a jeep road to reach Kaya.

To fit in with the twice-weekly Leh–Chiling bus service (Wednesday and Sunday) consider doing this trek in reverse, possibly tacking on a Rumbak–Stok trek for the last day.

SHAM TREK

- one to four days
- guesthouses en route
- no high passes

More a rural stroll than a trek, the full route links Likir (p320) and Nurla (p322) via Yangthang (p320). All but the one-day Hemis Skupachan–Timishgang section follows (very quiet) roads and jeep tracks, though there are several shortcuts (slightly tough to spot near the river just west of Yangthang). The trek's appeal are the homestay-style guesthouses in each intervening rustic hamlet and the fact that bus connections mean you could do any section as a one-day hike, then give up as you please. Hike during early morning as long sections lack any shade whatsoever.

ASCENT OF STOK KANGRI

- typically five days from Stok (p318) or Zingchen (p319)
- climbs to 6120m
- requires tents, mountaineering gear and a guide
- IMF permit US$50 per person

Stok Kangri (6120m) is the dramatic, snow-capped peak visible across the valley from Leh. Scaling its uppermost slopes requires ice axes, crampons and considerable fitness. Groups are roped together for safety, departing from base camp at around 2am to cross the ice-blanketed summit before sunshine renders it too slippery. Expeditions stop at 4400m, 4800m and 5300m to aid acclimatisation but AMS can still be a serious worry.

MARKHA VALLEY TREK

- six to seven days from Chiling to Hemis
- seasonal parachute cafes or homestays most of the way but bring tent and supplies
- one 5030m pass

This very popular trek could alternatively start from Stok or from Zingchen (one day extra) using the Zingchen–Chiling route (opposite) as far as Skiu (two days extra). Overnight in villages Skiu, Markha and then Hankar, dominated by a spectacular shattered fortress tower on a rocky pinnacle. From Hankar it's a longish day's climb through yak pastures at Nimaling (camp) before crossing Kongmaru La (5030m), a lofty eyrie with knee-trembling

---

LITTERBUGS

While trekking, some spiritually impoverished philistines seem to think it's OK to hide juice cartons in bushes, leave cigarette butts on trail rocks or pop chocolate wrappers under stones. Rather than getting exasperated with this littering insensitivity, consider taking an empty bag with you and, on the last day of a trek, collect some of the rubbish you find. You might even inspire others to follow suit. Also remember that trekside parachute cafes have no means of rubbish disposal: if you buy *maggi* (instant noodles) or soft drinks, the wrappers and cans will probably end up in the river if you don't ask for them and carry them out.

---

views. Descend a narrow gorge via pretty Shang Sumdo village.

LAMAYURU TREKS

There are several treks starting from delightful Lamayuru (p322), all requiring tents and best undertaken with a guide and/or horseman. The five-day Lamayuru–Chiling trek can be conveniently added on to Markha Valley (left) or Zingchen–Chiling (opposite) treks. Starting from Wanla (p322) saves one day, but finding horses might prove tough if you're not using an agency. Consider adding an acclimatisation day before crossing the 4950m Konze La. For the Lamayuru–Zanskar route, see p298.

TSO KAR–TSO MORIRI

- four to five days (eight days if starting from Rumtse)
- subzero nights, bring all equipment
- guides essential
- four passes over 4700m (seven if starting from Rumtse)
- lonely, no permanent villages en route

This testing trek crosses broad upland pasture valleys rolling up to high but smooth-topped mountains quite unlike Ladakh's archetypal arid spike peaks. The long final day is rewarded by spectacular views of Tso Moriri and, usually, encountering Chang-Pa nomads near Korzok (p327). If starting from Tso Kar (p329), allow a few lag days for your agency's packhorses to walk in from Rumtse.

AROUND LEH

☎ 01982

Indus Valley villages form green oases amid dun-coloured semideserts backed by craggy dry mountains. Several superb medieval monasteries make interesting day trips by hired motorcycle, jeep or public bus. Many can be easily added as en-route stops to destinations further afield. In some, you might need to ask monks to open certain doors for you.

A few route sectors are marred by unaesthetic army bases.

South of Leh

To visit Stok, Matho and Stakna and then return to Leh via Thiksey and Shey, you'll need a vehicle that's small enough to cross the very narrow Indus River bridge at Stakna.

JAMMU & KASHMIR

AROUND LEH

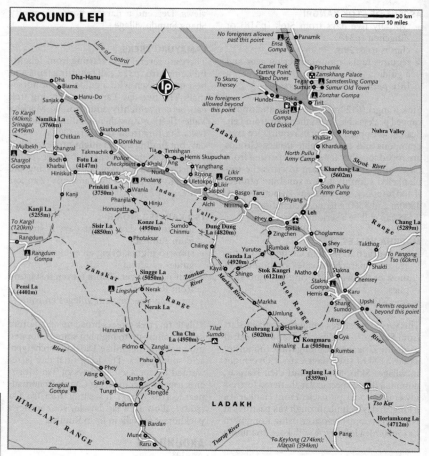

STOK

Ladakh's former royal family (see p299) were stripped of their power in 1846 and now live a comparatively modest life, dividing their time between a private mansion in Manali and the stately **Stok Palace** (admission Rs50; 9am-1pm & 2-7pm May-Oct). Vaguely potala-like and with wobbly, colourful window frames, the palace is photogenic despite a giant telecommunication tower that looms directly behind. The stylish **palace cafeteria** (tea Rs10-20, sandwiches Rs25-30) has a great open terrace. Above, several rooms on two levels form the **palace museum** (admission Rs50, no photography) displaying family treasures, including the queen's ancient turquoise-and-gold *yub-jhur* (crown) and a photo of the young king in sneakers.

Across from the palace, a short alley leads to the 350-year-old **Stok Abagon** (suggested donation Rs20; 8am-7pm), once home to the royal physician. Today the part-furnished mudbrick house is very decrepit, but caretaker-guide Jigmet offers interesting short tours by the light of his mobile phone (better to bring a torch).

Stok's peaceful main lane winds up past whitewashed farmhouses, crumbling old stupas and, after 1km, bypasses the modest **Stok Gompa**, where royal oracles make predictions about the future during Stok's important **Guru Tse-Chu festival** (held in February/March; see boxed text, p300). Another kilometre north, buses from Leh terminate at a trio of simple restaurant-camping areas known as the **trek-**

king point. Five minutes' walk upstream from here on the path to Rumbak, the village's last house is the very basic **Hotel Kangri** (☎ 201009; per person half-board Rs200), a parachute cafe backed by a highly rustic homestay offering floor space in a single tatty room.

At the foot of the palace, **Kalden Guesthouse** (☎ 242057; d Rs300-400) has an attractive Ladakhi facade and vegetable garden, where the traditionally costumed old owners quaff *chhang* from *chapskyan* (brass decanters). Variable-quality rooms share a tiled bathroom, *puja* (literally 'respect'; offering or prayers) room and a somewhat chintzy Ladakhi dining room.

Downhill, 400m towards Leh from the palace, 12-room **Hotel Highland** (☎ 242005; d Rs1500) is cosier and slightly better appointed than the outwardly grander **Hotel Skittsal** (☎ 242051; www .skittsal.com; s/d Rs1430/1980), which is 1.2km further down, commanding a fine valley panorama.

MATHO

Sakya-Buddhist **Matho Gompa** (☎ 246085; admission Rs20) is perched on a colourfully stratified ridge above Matho village. Most of the early-15th-century monastery has been replaced by more modern structures in recent years, but it's still worth the trip for the stupendous valley views. During the monastery's famous **Matho Nagrang festival** (see boxed text, p300), blindfolded monk-oracles perform acrobatics, engage in ritual acts of self-mutilation and make predictions for the coming year.

SPITUK, PHEY & ZINGCHEN

Founded in the late 14th century as See-Thub ('Exemplary') Monastery, the extensive Gelukpa-order **Spituk Gompa** (admission Rs30) is incongruously perched overlooking the end of Leh airport (don't photograph the militarily sensitive runway, soldiers are watching). The gompa's multiple mudbrick buildings tumble appealingly down a steep hillock towards Spituk village on the Indus riverbank. Behind its central, gilt-roofed **Skodong Lakhang** shrine, the very colourful **Chikang** hosts a yellow-hatted statue of Tsongkhapa (1357–1419), who inspired Gelukpa Buddhism. The Buddha statue beside supposedly incorporates an odd relic: Tsongkhapa's nose bleed. On the very top of the gompa hill is a distinctive three-tiered **latho** and the tiny but very atmospheric **Palden Lama temple** hiding veiled deities in an eerie gloom.

For treks, the pretty, two-house oasis of **Zingchen** (Zinchan, Jingchian) makes a much better starting point than Spituk village, as the first 10km of the Spituk–Zingchen road is a sun-blistered masochistic slog. A Leh–Zingchen taxi ride (Rs1300) should allow stops at Spituk Gompa and at photogenic spots along the splendidly stark canyonlands that start 6km before Zingchen.

Zingchen has a homestay, campsite and parachute cafe. With a little patience, finding a ride back to Leh is usually possible for a token fee with empty jeeps that arrive to drop off trekkers. Should you get stranded in Zingchen, you could alternatively walk 11km (via a rather hidden Indus footbridge) to the green oasis of **Phey**, which is the put-in point for popular rafting excursions (p307).

West of Leh
PHYANG

Pretty Phyang is an emerald splash of tree-hemmed barley fields layered for miles up a side valley. There are stupendous views back towards the snow-topped pyramid of Stok Kangri. The white-and-ochre **Phyang Gompa** (admission Rs25) photogenically dominates the village centre despite some earthquake damage. Behind, dzos graze on idyllic meadowland and a beautiful lane follows a rock escarpment past traditional homes to Phyang's only accommodation (1.5km), the delightful **Hidden North Guesthouse** (☎ 226007; www.hiddennorth.com; rented/own tent Rs100/60, d Rs350, without bathroom Rs250). Set in a lovely mountain-facing sunflower garden, unfussy rooms are immaculately maintained and the bathrooms are possibly the cleanest in Ladakh. Room 8 has windows with views of Stok Kangri. You might be tempted to stay awhile. Lunch/dinner is served for Rs70/90.

CHILING

For a feast of colourful geology take the dramatic riverside ledge road up the deep Zanskar canyon from Km400. At first glance tiny Chiling (28km south) seems limited to a single roadhouse, shop-teahouse and camping ground but the village proper hides a fertile plateau above which homestays are possible. It was founded by the families of Nepali copper craftsmen who had originally arrived to build Shey Palace's big Buddha statue (p326) but never went home. Today Chiling is a key trekking point between Lamayuru and the

Markha Valley (p317). For the latter, cross the Zanskar River ropeway 4km further south.

NIMMU (NIMO)

Although Nimmu has a pretty area of timeless, classic Ladakhi houses, the main road is marred at the western end by a sprawling army camp. There's a central strip of truckers' teahouses plus two roadside guesthouse-restaurants.

BASGO

Capital of lower Ladakh until the Ladakhi kingdoms united in 1470, Basgo's ancient chortens whisper hints of its antiquity. Rising above the village on a surreal collection of eroded earthen pinnacles are remnant stubs of once-great **citadel walls**, along with a largely derelict mud-walled **palace** and two brilliant temples, recently stabilised with help from Unesco. The upper **Chamba Gompa** (admission Rs20) has spectacularly restored mural work covering walls and ceilings around a cartoon-like two-storey statue of Maitreya, whose expression embodies the spirit of detachment. Slightly downhill, behind the palace remnants, darker and even more atmospheric **Sar-Zung Temple** (admission Rs20) hosts another outsized Maitreya statue and a library of wrapped scriptures.

The citadel access footpath starts almost opposite Basgo's only accommodation, the pleasant two-room **ToGo Guesthouse** (☎ 225104). Alternatively a vehicular road winds up from Basgo's western end.

LIKIR

Surveying a grand section of mountain ridge, likeable Likir is a possible starting point for the so-called Sham trek (p316). Around 4km above the main village, 15th-century **Likir Gompa** (admission Rs20) very photogenically covers a hillside with archetypal Tibetan structures. The first prayer hall to the right on entry has seats allocated for both the Dalai Lama and his brother, Likir's honourary head lama. After two more colourful prayer halls you climb to the cute, one-room **museum** (☼ 8am-1pm & 2-6pm summer, 10am-1pm & 2-4pm winter). The gompa is backed by a giant gilded 20th-century **Maitreya statue** that looks great from afar, though it's peeling and looks rather gaudy closer up.

For great photos of the gompa complex framed between barley fields and old chortens, decend for 10 minutes on the rocky footpath towards the very basic **Old Likir Guesthouse** (☎ 227505; per person Rs250). Directly above the gompa the equally rustic **Chhuma Guesthouse** (per person Rs200) has superb views from two perfectly located if tatty mattress-on-floor rooms. Great local food is served (to guests only) in the very authentic traditional kitchen.

Back down in Likir village, looking remarkably grand in its well-tended garden, super-friendly **Norboo Spon Guesthouse** (☎ 227137; s/d without bathroom Rs200/400) has attractive rooms with Tibetan motifs and beds draped with colourful quilts. Shared bathrooms come in Western or Ladakhi forms. If you want private bathrooms and 24-hour hot water (in summer), choose the co-owned **Hotel Lhukhil** (www.hotellhukhil.com; s/d Rs1230/1780), five minutes' walk away across the fields. Designed like a Chinese temple, most rooms have views and there's oodles of outdoor sitting space.

Five other guesthouses are dotted about the diffuse village.

SHAM

A spectacular 30-minute detour from Likir winds through grand Nevada-style scenery on a newly asphalted lane to the idyllic little village of **Yangthang**. Designed like an architect's brain-teaser puzzle, its sturdy old houses fit together perfectly forming a neat square around a tiny shrine. It's set in timeless barley fields backed by a jagged horizon of saw-toothed mountains. Three village 'guesthouses' offer Rs250 homestay-style accommodation, with floor mattresses and meals included: a great way to glimpse village life. A steep trail descends to Rizong (opposite) in around 1½ hours.

A painfully bumpy jeep track leads 10km further west, dead ending at bigger **Hemis Skupachan**, where a curiously medieval little knot of houses cluster around a central rocky hillock. Here **Toro Guesthouse** (per person Rs250) has a traditional kitchen and its little communal balcony surveys the beautiful snow-speckled knife-edge mountain horizon. Nearby, beyond the village gompa, **Lungchay Guesthouse** (☎ 240024; per person Rs300-350) has more comfortable accommodation on its new upper floor, but toilets are outside. There are around a dozen more widely scattered guesthouses and homestays.

Hemis Skupachan's famous grove of ancient juniper trees is 1km up the Sham footpath that leads in around six hours via Ang to **Timishgan** (Tingmosgang, Temisgam). This walk is the core section of the Sham trek.

Timishgan, a former co-capital of the 14th-century kingdom of lower Ladakh, is a sizeable monastery-village, where an 1864 treaty was signed with Tibet. There's a 9am shared pickup to Khaltse (Rs20), and several homestays both here and in attractive **Tia**. From both villages there are 8am buses to Leh.

ALCHI

Popular Alchi strikes an agreeable balance between rural gompa village and low-key tourist getaway. Flanked by various guesthouses and eateries, its centre is the dead end of Alchi's 4km spur lane (which leaves the Leh–Kargil road at Km370). From the village centre an obvious footpath descends past souvenir peddlers and a German Bakery to Alchi's main sight, the unmissable Chhoskhor Temple Complex.

Chhoskhor Temple Complex

These 11th-century **temples** (admission Rs30, no photography; 8am-1pm & 2-6pm), founded by 'Great Translator' Lotsava Ringchen Zangpo, are considered the crowning glory of Ladakh's Indo-Tibetan art.

First comes **Sumrtsek Temple**, fronted by a wooden porch with very Indian-style carvings. Inside, murals cover all three levels with hundreds of little *dayani* Buddhas. Oversized wooden statues of Maitreya, Manjushri and Avalokitesvara burst their heads through into the inaccessible upper storey.

Next along, **Vairocana Temple** has a rear chamber full of impressive mandalas.

In the **Lotsa Temple**, Lotsava Ringchen Zangpo himself appears as the slightly reptilian figure to the left behind the central Buddha cabinet. Beneath him, a row of comical-faced figures underline the importance of taking nothing too seriously.

The **Manjushri Temple** enshrines a joyfully gaudy four-sided statue of Manjushri (Buddha of Wisdom).

Directly outside on exiting the temple complex, burrow within the hollow-passage chortens and look up!

Other Sights

Near the school, 700m before Alchi's main centre, there's a timeless, mud-walled manor-house ruin between a pond and rocky knob outcrop.

Alchi's potentially picturesque riverfront is slightly marred by distant hydroelectric engineering works.

Sleeping & Eating

In summer Alchi has nearly a dozen accommodation choices, including overpriced 'luxury' tent-resorts that give the word luxury a bad name. Many close from mid-September.

Lotsava (227129; dorjeystanzin@yahoo.com; r from Rs300, without bathroom from Rs150) The Lotsava is a somewhat austere-looking three-storey cube of traditional Ladakhi farmhouse in a dark, flowerless garden. Downstairs rooms are simple. Upper rooms are brighter and pleasant albeit with plywood ceilings. Take the alley beside Alchi Resort.

Lungpa Guesthouse (227125; d Rs400-600, without bathroom Rs250-300) Right at the exit of the monastery complex, the Lungpa's misleadingly impressive facade leads through to what feels like a half-built interior. Nonetheless the rooms with private bathroom are good value.

Zimskhang Guesthouse (227085; zimskhang@yahoo.com; d Rs800, without bathroom Rs300) Simpler rooms overlook Alchi's best garden restaurant and share its well-cleaned outdoor toilets. The best rooms with private bathroom are on the top floor of an altogether more suave, Ladakhi-styled building across the monastery footpath. The latter has some decent if viewless communal sitting areas.

Alchi Resort (252520; alchi_resort@hotmail.com; s/d Rs2640/3300) A little bridge leads back from an orientally painted restaurant to a garden around which two-unit wood-roofed bungalows are arranged around a central gazebo. Rooms are gently attractive, but very pricey by local standards.

RIZONG

Clinging to the walls of a steep, arid amphitheatre, the two old prayer halls of intriguing **Rizong Gompa** (admission Rs20) have soot-darkened but highly regarded murals and gilded statues. Set in orchards downhill from the gompa, the **Chullichan Nunnery** (donation appreciated) provides an education for local girls.

The 5km link road (entirely washed away in 2008) climbs a narrow gorge from pretty **Uletokpo** village, where there are three upmarket camp resorts but no guesthouses. **Uley Adventure Resort** (227208; ulecamp@sancharnet.in; www.reachladakh.com/uleethnicresort.htm; s/d Rs1300/1800,

JAMMU & KASHMIR

d with full board Rs2800; ⊗ Jun–early Sep) has older tent-hut hybrids hidden in an attractive orchard and newer if less scenic huts that look like bizarre half-timbered lunar landers. All share bathrooms.

A footpath leads up to Yangthang (p320).

NURLA & KHALSI

After the Sham trek (p316), some hikers walk down from Timishgan to the NH1D Leh–Kargil road emerging 2km west of **Nurla** (itself 14km west of Uletokpo). Nurla has no guesthouse, only the overpriced **Faryork Resort** (☎ 229526; tent Rs2800) sitting beside the Indus footbridge where treks start to Taru. Its former Faryork Restaurant (now closed) behind Nurla's village shop sometimes rents better-value **rooms** (d Rs500-600) above a thundering stream.

Khalsi, the comparatively bustling regional centre, has shops, downmarket eateries and phone offices. If you're unavoidably stuck here, the **Khababs Hotel** (☎ 9469291513; main strip; d Rs300) has three unexciting guest rooms. Hitch-hiking westbound is generally easier from the check post 2km west of Khalsi.

DHA-HANU
Permit required

Foreigners with prearranged permits (apply in Leh) may take the lovely, increasingly dramatic Indus Valley road northwest of Khalsi as far as Dha. Views across the river to terraced **Takmachik** are delightful just before reaching the walnut-growing village of **Domkhar**. Picturesque **Skurbuchan** village is topped by a rickety gompa-fort overlooking the Indus canyon. Scattered ancient **petroglyphs** are inscribed on brown, time-polished roadside rocks (eg at Km55.9) but they're small and some are latter-day imitations. From **Sanjak** a side road cuts through a sharp gorge to Chitkan. Kargil-bound shared jeeps (Rs150) heading that way depart at 6.30am from near Sanjak's bridge, teahouses and single guesthouse.

The Indus gorge below **Biama** is crossed by two photogenically wobbly bridges. Intriguing **Dha** (pop 250), 3km beyond, has an unexpectedly warm microclimate and is a centre of the Brokpa (Dard) people (see boxed text, opposite). Though outnumbered by 'one pen' kids, a few Brokpa people still wear pearly button ear decorations and traditional hats, with older women tying their hair in long triple-stranded semidreadlock braids.

The bus from Leh sputters to an unexpected halt at a middle-of-nowhere layby, from where Dha village is a 10-minute walk via the small footpath immediately opposite. Amid Dha's tomato gardens, apricot orchards and huddles of rough stone barns you'll pass mud-floored **Skybapa Guesthouse** (dm/d Rs200/400). Its shared squat toilets are across the yard, but rooms have beds and there's an appealing dining area beneath a vast grapevine.

The yellow house perched above the village's huddled heart is guesthouse-homestay **Siringlamo Bangpa** (per person Rs200). Its *namkin chai* (butter tea) tastes of Roquefort and its ragged rooms have saggy camp beds, but the charming elderly owners are archetypal costumed Brokpas who still offer animist prayers to a curious little black stone kept in a locked, messy side room.

Given linguistic help, other homestays can be arranged in Dha or in less striking Biama, where the overpriced, roadside **Aryan Valley Tent-Camp** (☎ 228543; full board Rs2800) has an attached **guesthouse** (d without bathroom Rs500).

WANLA

Above Wanla village, tiny medieval **Wanla Gompa** (www.achiassociation.org; admission Rs20; ⊗ dawn-dusk) is dramatically perched on a towering knife-edge ridge flanked by two shattered tower remnants of a now-destroyed 14th-century fortress. Its carved porch is reminiscent of Alchi's and a single, spookily dark chamber contains three large statues backed by ancient smoke-blackened murals. If you're driving to Lamayuru, Wanla is an easy 7km detour off the NH1D road: turn south at the colourful new *photong* (ceremonial residence).

The central, misnamed **Wamda Guesthouse** (d Rs200) offers just one dark, bare room above the Dorjay Craft House. **Tarchit Camp** (☎ 254866; camping Rs100, per person incl meals Rs350), 2km beyond Wanla on the Fanjila road, is building two guest rooms and offers homestay mattress spaces in the traditional family dining room.

There are two campsites directly across the bridge from central Wanla on the road that leads (after 4km) to some hot springs.

LAMAYURU
☎ 01982 / elev 3390m

Set among dramatic mountain-backed moonscape badlands, delightful little Lamayuru is

LOST TRIBES

The facial features of the Brokpa (aka Drokpa or Dard) 'people of the pastures' have led to speculation that the tribe was descended from Alexander the Great's invasion force or even a lost tribe of Israel. Based on their dialect, they are thought to have immigrated to Dha-Hanu from Gilgit/Baltistan around a millenium ago. Some Brokpas still follow an animist faith that incorporates elements of the ancient Bon religion, precursor of Tibetan Buddhism.

one of Ladakh's most memorable villages. Homes huddle around a crumbling hilltop that's pitted with caves and topped by the very photogenic **Yungdrung Gompa** (admission Rs20). Behind glass within the gompa's main prayer hall is a tiny cave in which 11th-century mystic Naropa meditated. Before that, legend claims, this whole area was the bottom of a deep lake whose waters receded miraculously thanks to the powerful prayers of Buddhist saint Arahat Nimagung. Lamayuru is a great, low-paced place to break the Kargil–Leh journey, and is also the starting point for several popular treks (p317). Many guesthouses can help you organise packhorses.

Sleeping & Eating
Lamayuru only gets electricity from 7pm to 11pm and some guesthouse rooms lack power points. Prices will probably rise once Kashmir stabilises and transit tourist numbers recover.

Siachen Guesthouse (☎ 224538; d without bathroom Rs150-250) Four good rooms share an unusually clean toilet with free hot-bucket 'showers'. Best rooms 1 and 3 have wraparound windows. There's a delightful garden restaurant.

Tharpaling Guesthouse (☎ 224516; d Rs500, d/tr without bathroom Rs250/300) Ever-smiling matriarch Tsiring Yandol gives this place a jolly, family atmosphere, serving dinner at a big communal table. Upper rooms are airy and bright, the best one with private bathroom.

Dragon Guesthouse (☎ 224501; d Rs600, without bathroom Rs300) The rooms with private bathroom are good value and the garden restaurant is pleasant.

Hotel Niranjana (☎ 224555; s/d without bathroom Rs500/700) Above a cavernous restaurant and reception area, the Niranjana is right beside

the monastery complex, so ideal for those attending 5.30am prayers. Rooms are comfy enough, many with fine views. Shared bathrooms are clean with geysers.

Hotel Moonland (☎ 224551; d Rs600-800) Set in a garden 400m beyond the bus stop at Lamayuru's first hairpin, all eight rooms come with tiled bathrooms and hot showers. Both indoor and outdoor dining areas have postcard-perfect views back towards the monastery complex.

Getting There & Away
Daily Kargil–Leh buses stop in Lamayuru between 9am and 10am in both directions. Leh–Chitkan buses stop eastbound around 10.30am Monday, Wednesday and Saturday, westbound around 1pm Sunday, Tuesday and Friday.

WEST OF LAMAYURU
From Lamayuru, the NH1D road zigzags up towards remarkable Iguanadon-back spires that tower impressively over the **Fotu La** (4147m). From that pass the road descends to **Hansukot**, where there's a tourist bungalow and vague fortress ruins. A comparatively wide, fertile valley extends as far as **Khangral**, where passports are checked. The road then crosses the **Namika La** (3760m pass) and descends into the glorious **Wakha Valley** continuing to Kargil via **Mulbekh** (p295) and **Shargol** (p296).

NUBRA VALLEY
☎ 01982 / permit required
The deep valleys of the Shyok and Nubra Rivers offer stupendous yet accessible scenery with green oasis villages surrounded by thrillingly stark scree slopes, boulder fields and harsh arid mountains. By chartered jeep from Leh, a three-day trip including all places listed in this section costs Rs6931 per vehicle. Two-day trips (Rs5542) are overly hectic considering that lengthy view stops en route are every bit as appealing as the destinations themselves. Beware of attempting this route before you're properly acclimatised.

Khardung La
elev 5602m
Zigzagging up a stark bare-rock mountain via South Pullu Army Camp (permits checked) takes around 1½ hours from Leh to 5602m **Khardung La**, the world's highest motorable

pass. Celebrate by sipping a cuppa at the pass-top canteen, buying T-shirts at the souvenir shop or clambering for five minutes up the dizzy chaos of prayer flag–draped boulders to a viewpoint above.

Descending northbound alongside a gurgling stream, watch for loveable Himalayan marmots and consider stopping where dzo graze on golf-green turf around a delightful **alpine pond**, 3km before North Pullu Army Camp.

Khardung

The journey's most awesome panoramas open up as you enter the yak-herding village of Khardung, a two-centred shelf of barley fields and scattered Ladakhi buildings set within a jaw-dropping bowl of stark dry mountain crags and giant tiger-paw bluffs, with distantly glimpsed teeth of snow mountains poking inbetween. Tiny roadside shop-cafes offer delicious dhal and rice lunches served by traditionally dressed village folk.

Beyond, Grand Canyon scenery descends towards the impressively wide **Shyok Valley**, where soaring red-brown cliff mountains rise from the gleaming grey-white sand of the floodplain.

Diskit
elev 3144m

Schizophrenic Diskit has two very different centres. The Nubra region's biggest settlement, **Diskit** is a comparatively unattractive place by Ladakh's very high standards, but it has a useful bazaar, a tourist reception centre, a power-cut prone **NI Internet cafe** (per hr Rs100) and the region's only petrol pump (1km north).

Altogether more satisfying is the tiny, atmospheric hamlet of **Old Diskit** 1.5km south. From a pair of large prayer wheels, **mani walls** lead down through clusters of **old stupas**, past a collapsing little **old temple** and a derelict Ladakhi mansion-palace (opposite the turn-off for the Sunrise Guesthouse).

Directly above Old Diskit, a 2km spaghetti of hairpins winds up to the fabulous 17th-century **Diskit Gompa** (admission Rs20), a brilliant jumble of Tibetan-style box buildings piled higgledy-piggledy up a steep rocky peak that ends in a toe-curlingly vertical chasm. The access road passes the *photang* of Nubra's head lama, with a six-storey, half-finished **Chamba (Maitreya-Buddha) seated statue** on an intermediate hill.

SLEEPING & EATING
Old Diskit

Karakoram Guesthouse (☎ 220024; d without bathroom Rs150) One block downhill from the Sunrise Guesthouse turn-off, this family farmhouse is run by a traditionally costumed lady who seems older than the surrounding stupas. Beds are brand new, but rooms are somewhat tatty and bathrooms are shared. No English spoken.

Sunrise Guesthouse (☎ 220025; r Rs500, without bathroom Rs250; ☯ year-round) Reached through a 'tunnel stupa', this ageing but loveably authentic guesthouse sits in a peaceful sunflower garden amid scattered Buddhist ruins. Room 1 has perfectly framed gompa views. Two newer rooms have private bathrooms.

Olthang Guesthouse (☎ 220067; dm Rs100, bedded tent Rs300, d Rs400-800; ☯ year-round) By far the biggest and most Western of Old Diskit's four guesthouses, the Olthang is easy to spot on the main road. Its newer 16-room hotel section has semismart Rs800 doubles and less-polished Rs600 ones. The unshaded outdoor sitting area has gompa views.

Diskit Town

Three decent options in quiet lanes conveniently close to the south end of the bazaar.

Sand Dune Guesthouse (☎ 220022; d Rs500, without bathroom Rs200) Set around a pleasant garden courtyard, the rustic, acceptable cheapies share squat toilets. Brighter, newer rooms have less character but enjoy spotlessly clean tiled bathrooms. Friendly English-speaking staff.

Eagle Guesthouse (☎ 220089; r Rs300, without bathroom Rs250) Curiously hidden amid cow pens, the main house has a cute garden and simple, bright rooms. Those with bathroom are contrastingly dark in the annexe opposite.

Zambala Guesthouse (☎ 220418; d from Rs500, without bathroom from Rs350; ☯ year-round) This new, two-storey house-hotel has smart marble-tiled floors, an appealing semitraditional dining room and geysers in the shared bathrooms.

GETTING THERE & AWAY

From Diskit buses to Sumur (Rs30, two hours) depart Monday to Saturday at around 8am and 3pm (returning same hours), sometimes continuing to Panamik. Leh–Hunder buses (see opposite) pass through Diskit thrice weekly.

Jeeps can be chartered from Diskit to Hunder (Rs250), Sumur (Rs1120) and Leh (around Rs3500).

Around Diskit

HUNDER

Lost in greenery 10km from Diskit, pleasant if very 'discovered' **Hunder village** is the furthest west foreigners may go. Some 3km before the village (500m before the army camp), a photogenic series of **sand dunes** and marshy pools are magnificently framed by soaring valley cliffs. Explore them by touristy **Bactrian camel ride** (per 15min Rs150) or on foot. If attempting to walk all the way back to Diskit, bring lots of water, stick relatively near the road and beware not to follow dead-end camel tracks into impenetrable thorn thickets.

In Hunder village, **Hunder Gompa** contains a large gilded Chamba statue, a crude trail that climbs to ruined pilgrims' quarters, and a precarious ridgetop **fort**.

Sleeping & Eating

Hunder has over a dozen garden guesthouses (most allowing camping for Rs100) plus two overpriced deluxe camps.

Moonland Guesthouse (☎ 221048; d Rs200, without bathroom Rs150) Three simple, rustic homestay-style rooms in an austere farmhouse down a signposted streamside footpath. Friendly family.

Goba Guesthouse (☎ 221083; d from Rs200) Choose upper options with private bathroom; notably room 8 (Rs500) for wraparound windows and terrace with wonderful views. Staff are remarkably obliging, the setting is lovely and the food is reliably good.

Himalayan Guesthouse (☎ 221131; r Rs450, without bathroom Rs300) The rooms are fairly standard, but Gulam is disarmingly helpful and the quiet, garden location is so hidden in the warren of village footpaths that there's likely to be a room when all else is full.

Karma Inn (☎ 221042; karmaleh@yahoo.co.in; d lower/ upper Rs1000/1500) Good new rooms have firm-mattressed beds and little sitting areas in bay windows overlooking a splendid panorama of mountains. Coming from Diskit, follow signs towards the 'Organic Camp', 2km before central Hunder.

Getting There & Away

Leh-bound buses (around 6.15am on Wednesday, Friday and Sunday) and several morning services to Diskit travel along the bypass road, picking up from a short walk behind Hunder Gompa. From Hunder village there's a single 9am bus to Diksit.

Sumur to Panamik

The Nubra River proper descends towards the Shyok from the heavily disputed Siachen Glacier, the world's highest battleground (between India and Pakistan). With standard Nubra permits foreigners can take the recently asphalted road as far as Panamik.

At Km12 the road bypasses **Tirit village**, with views across to a long **waterfall** spurting out of the bare rockface. Spooky **Zonzhar Gompa** is a small ruin atop a roadside knoll at Km16.5. The largest of several intriguing villages, **Sumur** (Km22.5) is overlooked by colourful if extensively rebuilt **Samstemling Gompa**. Get up there by a pleasant streamside walk or by driving via the 2km asphalted spur road from **Tegar** (Tiger) village starting at Km25. Directly overlooking that junction, the eerie rubble of Nubra's former royal citadel leads up to the largely intact three-storey ruin of the **Zamskhang Palace**. Cautiously climb to the roof for stunning valley views.

There's a small roadside gompa at **Pinchamik** (Km29), a timeless hamlet full of prayer wheels, chortens and costumed old folk carrying baskets full of greens on their backs.

Panamik (Km50) is a diffuse low-rise hamlet known for two unexciting hot springs that dribble out of iron-orange rock clefts above the main road. Still, if you're driving, it's worth coming here for the surrounding scenery and to squint across the valley towards inaccessible little **Ensa Gompa**, which somehow clings to a foliage-covered ledge on the raw red rock of the cliff face.

SLEEPING

Most guesthouses allow camping (Rs100) in their gardens.

Sumur Centre

AO Guesthouse (☎ 223506; r Rs250) With neat rooms set back from the main junction beyond J&K Bank, AO is convenient for buses and for Sumur's (lacklustre) shack restaurants, but is less scenic than other Sumur options.

Sumur Old Town

Nearly a dozen other guesthouses are accessed from Sumur Link Rd, which winds 2km into the orchards from AO Guesthouse, passing several large prayer wheels.

K,Sar Guesthouse (☎ 223574; dm/d Rs100/300) The cutest of several newer mini guesthouses, each with peaceful and attractive gardens. The two double rooms have decent bathrooms.

Namgyal Guesthouse (☎ 223505; d Rs400, without bathroom Rs200) Lacks atmosphere, but has some fine views through the daliahs towards the mountains.

Largyal Guesthouse (☎ 223537; per person without bathroom Rs250) Furthest from town, this old-style guesthouse has rustic rooms sharing a single basic bathroom, but the family-farm atmosphere is delightful. One bedroom has lovely Tibetan-style furniture, while others are plain.

Tegar

Tegar's two upper-market hotels are on the main road 500m south of the palace. Both have extensive grounds.

Hotel Yarabtso (☎ 223544; norzum@usa.net; s/d Rs800/1200, full board Rs1427/2600) Behind impressive traditional-style facades, mediocre rooms have decent bathrooms, while the sweet sitting room sports 1970s family photos.

Hotel Rimo (☎ 9419340747; hotelrimonubra@rediffmail.com; s/d Rs1500/2500, full board Rs2500/3300) Modern with stylised pseudo-Ladakhi flourishes and very white starched sheets, but somewhat let down by uneven, fake-wood vinyl flooring.

Panamik

Panamik's four modest **guesthouses** (d Rs200-300) are strung along the main road starting around 1km north of the hot springs. All have their charms: **Hot Springs Guesthouse** (☎ 247043) and **Bangka Guesthouse** (☎ 247044) for their flower-filled gardens, **Nebula Guesthouse** (☎ 247013) and **Saser Restaurant** (☎ 247021) for their slightly smarter rooms.

EAST OF LEH
Indus Valley

The Indus Valley road is smoothly asphalted to Karu, where side lanes branch off to Pangong Tso (opposite) via Chemrey (p328) and Hemis (7km; opposite). Permits are required to continue east of Upshi.

SHEY

Once Ladakh's summer capital, Shey is an attractively green, pond-dappled oasis from which rises a central dry rocky ridge, inscribed

with roadside **Buddha carvings** (Km459). The ridge is topped by decrepit **fortress ruins** and by the small if photogenic **Naropa Royal Palace** (admission Rs20; ⊙ 8am-7pm May-Oct). This mini-potala structure is undergoing considerable reconstruction, but its central shrine remains a very holy place, containing an inscrutably smirking two-storey gilded copper **Buddha**, originally installed in 1645.

A kilometre further east is the gold-roofed *photang* of the local lama and, 200m beyond, the **Druk White Lotus School** (www.dwls.org) welcomes suitably skilled volunteer teachers. Its modern buildings elegantly combine traditional design elements with the latest in sustainable technological engineering.

The **Besthang Guesthouse** (☎ 267556; d Rs450, without bathroom Rs300) has three homestay-style rooms, one of which has a private bathroom and kitchen. Guests can use the family's delightful Ladakhi dining room. Fine views look back towards the palace from the dead-end access track.

THIKSEY

At Km454, a steep climb or a 1.5km looping drive leads up to glorious **Thiksey Gompa** (☎ 267011; www.thiksey.com; festival Oct/Nov) covering a large rocky outcrop with layered, whitewashed Tibetan-style buildings. It's one of Ladakh's biggest and most recognisable monasteries, a veritable monastic village incorporating shops, a school, restaurant and hotel. Near the upper car park, the well-labelled **monastery museum** (admission Rs30; ⊙ 8am-1pm & 2-7pm) displays Tantric artefacts, some carved from human bones. Notice the 10 weapons symbolically used to combat evil spirits.

Above, the **main gompa** (admission/video Rs30/100; ⊙ 6am-1pm & 2-6pm) starts with a prayer chamber containing a 14m-high Buddha in an ornately detailed headdress, his expression simultaneously peaceful, smirking and vaguely menacing. Smaller but much more atmospherically ancient is the **Gonkhang** (Protectors' Temple) and a charming little rooftop **library**.

Thiksey's interesting dawn *puja* has become so popular that tourists often outnumber the monks in summer.

Monastery-run **Chamba Hotel** (☎ 267004; kthiksey@vsnl.com; d Rs300-1500, without bathroom Rs300) has two sites, both with restaurants (mains Rs50 to Rs100). The one beneath the gompa's museum building has decent rooms. The second site lies at the main road junction, with good-value if unexotic older courtyard rooms and newer, plusher rooms within a traditionally styled two-storey building.

STAKNA
Small but visually impressive, the 1618 **Stakna Gompa** (admission Rs20) crowns a rocky outcrop just 800m across the Indus from Km449 (where Leh–Thiksey buses terminate), though the gompa's winding access road adds another 900m. The narrow suspension bridge is just wide enough for small taxi-vans. Off the gompa's small central courtyard, four rooms with vivid new Tantric murals can be visited. Behind the main prayer hall, smaller subshrines retain 400-year-old sandalwood statues, original frescoes and statuettes of the Bhutanese lamas who founded the monastery.

HEMIS
A 7km detour from Karu, timelessly pretty Hemis village spills out of a craggy, red-rock canyon beyond astonishingly long *mani* walls. Hidden behind the village in soothingly green foliage, the famous 1672 **Hemis gompa** (admission Rs30; 8am-1pm & 2-6pm) is the spiritual centre of Ladakh's Drukpa Buddhists (www.drukpa .org). Documents supposedly found here support Jesus in India conspiracists' notion that Christ visited Kashmir (see boxed text, p290). For others, Hemis' fame rests primarily on its annual **Tse-Chu festival** (see boxed text, p300).

From outside, the gompa's large rectilinear form is not especially photogenic. However, its superb central courtyard has plenty of colourfully detailed timbers and soaring masts that flutter with prayer flags (best photographed in morning light). The splendid main prayer hall is supported by vast tree trunks that were laboriously lugged all the way from Kashmir. The side shrine features an 8m-high statue of Padmasambhava in all his Popeyed glory.

Across the courtyard, the extensive **monastery museum** (admission Rs100) has some very precious religious treasures mixed in with spurious tiger skins, a gramophone and some banjo-like *damnyan* musical instruments. Labelling is less informative than at Thiksey.

Fairly rudimentary **rooms** (per bed Rs150) sharing Western or Ladakhi toilets are available in the gloomy concrete bowels of the outer gompa wall. Request the key from **Hemis Restaurant & Camping** (camping per tent Rs100) just outside, which serves simple meals (Rs35 to Rs80) and has a basic camping plot.

Village homestays are sometimes available.

Tso Moriri
elev 4595m / permit required
Around this vast, mildly brackish **lake**, wide grassy valleys roll up to rounded yet super-high mountains giving landscapes a very Tibetan feel. You stand a good chance of seeing kiang (wild ass), foxes and marmots, and of meeting nomadic Chang-Pa (Khampa) people herding their goats and yaks. Visiting the major **Chang-Pa summer camp**, just five minutes' drive behind tiny Korzok village, is fascinating when it's in use. Korzok is Tso Moriri's only significant settlement, with a 19th-century **gompa** and an intriguing **festival** (see boxed text, p300), but the strange Wild West ambience isn't entirely pleasant. Virtually every house doubles as a makeshift (if rarely salubrious) homestay.

Goose Homestay (d Rs200) has decent-sized upstairs rooms (accessed by ladder) with floor mattresses, lake views and an outside toilet.

Lake View GH & Restaurant (9419345362; d without bathroom Rs500) does indeed have nice views of the lake (across a foreground of rubbish-strewn roofs), but its very basic rooms aren't always clean.

Nomadic Life Camp (d tent Rs1300) is the best of three, bedded-tent campsites. Its tents are small but very clean, sharing an open-air sink/toilet unit and an enclosed hot-shower room.

A popular way to visit Tso Moriri is on a three-day Leh–Manali jeep charter (around Rs19,000 per vehicle) starting down the Indus through spectacular canyonlands to Mahe, overnighting at Korzok and then using rough tracks to reach the main Manali road via Tso Kar (p329). This is only possible southbound as permits must be issued in Leh.

Towards Pangong Tso
From Leh you can visit Chemrey and Takhtog independently, but a permit is required to proceed to serene Pangong Tso, arguably Ladakh's loveliest lake. Anywhere beyond Spangmik is out of bounds to foreigners.

Many locals pack the Pangong Tso experience into an exhaustingly long day trip from Leh. It's vastly more pleasurable to spend the night at Spangmik.

Note that in certain weathers, melt-water fords beyond Tangtse become impassable in the afternoon.

As you'll cross towering Chang La (5289m), pre-acclimatisation is wise.

CHEMREY

Spectacularly viewed across barley fields and buckthorn bushes, Chemrey village is dominated by the beautifully proportioned **Thekchhok Gompa** (admission Rs20; festival November, p300). A maze of pathways leads up to the main complex where the central 17th-century prayer hall has wonderfully wobbly wooden pillars. The **Lamalakhang** above has murals atmospherically blackened to semi-invisibility by butter-lamp smoke. On the penultimate floor the **Gurulakhang** has contrastingly vivid murals and a 3m-high golden Padmasambhava statue encrusted with turquoise ornamentation.

SHAKTI & TAKTHOG

Just before **Shakti** the road divides. The Pangong Tso road bypasses Shakti, passing just above Shakti village's **fortress** ruins at Km14. Alternatively a dead-end road leads 7km north to **Takthog Gompa** (admission Rs20), the region's only Nyingmapa monastery. Its prayer chamber is set in a highly revered cave where the great sage Padmasambhava supposedly meditated in the 8th century.

TANGTSE

The **Chang La** (5289m) is the world's third-highest motorable pass and probably the only one offering free cups of tea (courtesy of the Indian Army). Descending northbound, the impressively stark road-valley has a breathtakingly serrated mountain backdrop. Should you get stranded in Tangtse, 40km before

Pangong Tso, **Dothguling Guesthouse** (Main St; d Rs500, tr without bathroom Rs300) is the best of five guesthouse-restaurants. However, two-room **Chang Queen Eco Camp** (tr/q Rs300/400) has a nicer riverside setting and serves Rs30 dhal and rice. Just beyond Tangtse a ruined fortress-gompa on a rocky outcrop guards a magnificently arid valley with mountain walls streaked in a palate of beige and red-brown, its white-sand floor occasionally marked by opal-blue ponds.

Pangong Tso
Permit required

If the sun is shining, this giant lake's surreal palate of vivid blues can't fail to impress, set against the swirling mineral colours of the backdrop mountains whose peaks remain snow brushed even in August. The first view is near minuscule **Lukung**, an army checkpoint just beyond which is a trio of very simple mini **guesthouses** (tr Rs500-700) and a pair of **parachute cafes** (bed space Rs100). Seven bumpy kilometres' drive along the lovely lakeside, **Spangmik** is a tiny village of picturesque green-gold barley fields and dry-stone walls. It's a wonderful place to unwind, meet 'part-time' nomads and do gentle lake-view walks, like the 30-minute stroll above the village to the very modest but lovingly maintained **Gontserboom Temple**.

Virtually every Spangmik house offers a **homestay** (tr/q Rs300/400). Most have atmospheric Ladakhi kitchens, solar furnaces and passable food (extra charge). All share composting toilets and none have showers. The best have beds rather than simple floor space. A recommended choice is the well-signed **Gongma Homestay**, where you might be lucky enough to meet delightful, knowledgeable English-speaking guide Stobgais (☎ 9419372322; Stoblha@

THE WOOL MAN

Hip in his *The Matrix*–style shades, Stobgais is a tour guide in summer. The rest of the year he's secretary of the region's Pashmina Cooperative Society. 'Before, traders used to barter grain and other basics for our wool so the farmers were cheated. Now things are better. We get a fixed price, Rs2600 per *bakti* (2kg), and a bonus is shared among everyone if there's a profit from the spinning factory.'

Stobgais' family are Chang-Pa nomads who leave their low-slung homes on the banks of Pangong Tso when December comes around, driving their yak and goat herds three days east to winter pastures around Chushul. 'Cold winters are good because the goats' wool grows longer!' Then in February when the lake is suitably frozen, the whole party crosses the ice to the lake's northern shore. 'When the signs are right we make an earth 'road' so the animals are comfortable. It has to be done fast and before dawn so that the ice doesn't melt!'

yahoomail.com) for better insights into Chang-Pa nomad life (see boxed text, opposite). Also recommended is Dorje & Diskit's, the unmarked two-storey house to the right when entering Spangmik.

If you need a sit-down toilet, central **Pangong Tso Resort** (☎ in Leh 9419179907; 2chhaleh@India.com; d full board Rs2850, bedded tent without bathroom Rs2700) has six rooms, but while very friendly, the dowdy little concrete complex seems blatantly overpriced, especially for its bedded tents.

Towards Manali

The coccyx-crunching Leh–Manali road crosses four passes over 4900m and is closed from late October to June. Even in summer vehicles average less than 20km per hour, but the views are fabulous.

UPSHI TO TAGLANG LA

At a gaggle of teahouses called **Upshi** (Km425), the southbound Manali road leaves the Indus Valley towards **Miru** (Km410), with its shattered fortress and numerous stupas. Beyond is a beautiful, narrow and increasingly dramatic valley edged with serrated vertical mineral strata in alternating layers of vivid red-purple and ferrous green. Across the river from picturesque **Gya** (Km398) village is another crumbling crag-top fortress. Beyond **Rumtse** (Km394) the road becomes painfully rough and climbs seemingly endless hairpins to the dizzying 5359m pass **Taglang La**.

TSO KAR

Around 30km further (signed to 'Pastureland Camp') from Taglang La an off-road diversion leads in 20 minutes' drive to two utterly isolated seasonal **camps** (bedded tent with full board d Rs2000-2800) in an uninhabited meadow from where there are mid-distance views of **Tso Kar** majestically ringed by round-topped, snow-speckled mountains. East of the lake, ornithologists swoon at the chance to observe rare, black-necked cranes, which arrive from Siberia to mate in late spring.

PANG TO KEYLONG

In the stark scenic wonderland between Rumtse and Darcha there are no villages, but simple snacks are available from seasonal parachute cafes at **Pang** (where the army camp has emergency oxygen for those suffering AMS), **Bharatpur** (where tents also allow you sleeping space for Rs50 per person in a lovely high-altitude valley) and **Zingzingbar**. At the base of dramatic switchbacks known as the **Gata Loops** lies **Sarchu**, a photogenic 4200m valley where several comparatively upmarket **bedded tent camps** (per person from Rs500) straggle for several kilometres. While Sarchu is well situated around halfway between Leh and Manali, sleeping at this altitude can cause AMS if you're not well acclimatised. Passports are checked at **Darcha**, whose *dhabas* serve basic food and can offer very simple shelter (not ideal for single women). Many treks from Zanskar finish here, so with lots of patience it's occasionally possible to find horsemen returning 'empty' to Padum. Buses are generally full by the time they reach Darcha, but if heading south, standing for the two hours to Keylong (p391) isn't too bad.

Himachal Pradesh

From forested valleys to mountain passes, and Buddhist monasteries to the Dalai Lama's residence, few Indian states match Himachal Pradesh for diversity and mind-blowing scenery.

Many regard this as India's premier mountain state: awesome but accessible, a place where you can trek for days over high-altitude passes but then relax with a beer at one of the busy traveller towns. The mighty peaks of the Dhauladhar, Pir Panjal and western Himalaya ranges rise above Himachal, providing a setting for a host of adventure activities. Many are drawn here purely for the Tibetan Buddhist culture and head straight to the traveller centre of McLeod Ganj, home to the Dalai Lama and the Tibetan government in exile.

Even before you reach the Himalaya you'll pass British-era hill stations, serene pine forests, endless apple orchards and beautiful valleys. Shimla is India's most enduring hill station, and further north is Kinnaur, the apple capital and eastern gateway to Spiti.

In central Himachal, Manali and the Kullu and Parvati Valleys are a base for hippies, honeymooners and thrill seekers. Across Himachal, the lower hills hold forts, temples and palaces.

Manali, famous in recent decades for its charas (marijuana) and backpacker/hippie scene, is the start of the main overland route to Ladakh. The Great Himalayan Circuit starts in Kashmir, slices through the mountain valleys of Ladakh, Lahaul and Spiti to Kinnaur and ends in Shimla. Here, even the beaten track is a dirt road cut into the side of a mountain wall.

Travel around Himachal can be slow and arduous, but there are plenty of places to relax and enjoy the views. It's a wonderful place to be.

HIGHLIGHTS

- Take the toy train up to **Shimla** (p334), and enjoy the Englishness of India's favourite hill station
- Accumulate karma credits by volunteering with the Tibetan refugees of **McLeod Ganj** (p369)
- Ski, trek, climb, paraglide, raft or zorb in the backpacker playground of **Manali** (p357), Himachal's adventure-sport capital
- Hang out in the **Parvati Valley** (p350) and trek to the mountain village of **Malana** (p350)
- Get off the tourist trail and visit centuries-old temples in little-visited **Chamba** (p386) and **Bharmour** (p388)
- Cross the spectacular mountain passes of Rohtang La and Kunzum La to **Tabo Monastery** (p395) and the incredibly remote **Spiti Valley** (p392)

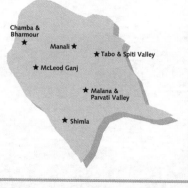

Chamba & Bharmour ★

Manali ★

★ Tabo & Spiti Valley

★ McLeod Ganj

★ Malana & Parvati Valley

★ Shimla

History

Ancient trade routes dominate the history of Himachal Pradesh. Large parts of northern Himachal were conquered by Tibet in the 10th century, and Buddhist culture still dominates the mountain deserts of Lahaul and Spiti. The more accessible areas in the south of the state were divvied up between a host of rajas, ranas and *thakurs* (noblemen), creating a patchwork of tiny states, with Kangra, Kullu and Chamba at the top.

Sikh rajas came to dominate the region by the early 19th century, signing treaties with the British to consolidate their power. The first Westerners to visit were Jesuit missionaries in search of the legendary kingdom of Prester John – a mythical Christian kingdom lost in the middle of Asia. Interestingly, there are several Aryan tribes in North India to this day, including the Kinnauris of eastern Himachal, most following a mixture of Hinduism and Buddhism.

During the 19th century the British started creating little bits of England in the hills of Shimla, Dalhousie and Dharamsala. Shimla later became the British Raj's summer capital, and narrow-gauge railways were pushed through to Shimla and the Kangra Valley. The British slowly extended their influence until most of the region was under the thrall of Shimla.

The state of Himachal Pradesh was formed after Independence in 1948, liberating many villages from the feudal system. In 1966 the districts administered from Punjab – including Kangra, Kullu, Lahaul and Spiti – were added and full statehood was achieved in 1971. Initially neglected by central government, Himachal has reinvented itself as the powerhouse of India, with huge hydroelectric plants providing power for half the country.

Climate

The main seasons for visitors are May to July and September to early November – advance reservations for accommodation are recommended at this time. During the monsoon the middle hills can be chilly and damp. Snow closes many mountainous areas from November to April, including the mountain valleys of Lahaul and Spiti and the Manali–Leh road – however, this is also the peak skiing season at the modest resorts near Manali and Shimla.

Information
PERMITS

The border between India and Tibet is politically sensitive, and foreigners need an inner line permit to travel between Rekong Peo in Kinnaur and Tabo in Spiti. You can obtain the permit easily, with two passport photographs and photocopies of the identity and visa pages from your passport, in Shimla (see boxed text, p337), Kaza (see boxed text, p395) and Rekong Peo (p345).

Activities

Manali is India's adventure capital, with a host of wild summer and winter activities on offer – see boxed text, p362.

PARAGLIDING

The soaring thermals over the Himalayan foothills provide perfect conditions for paragliding, particularly at Solang Nullah (p367) and Billing (p383).

RAFTING

The Beas River near Kullu churns up some impressive white water for kayaking and rafting, best organised out of Manali – see boxed text, p362.

SKIING

From January to March, skiers and snowboarders congregate at Solang Nullah (p367) near Manali, and Narkanda (p342) near Shimla.

TREKKING

Himachal Pradesh is a trekkers' paradise, and dozens of agencies in Manali, McLeod Ganj and other towns offer organised treks to remote valleys and mountain passes. Daily rates for all-inclusive treks start at Rs2000 per person, including guides, tent, food and porters.

The main trekking season runs from May to October, but monsoon rains affect some

HIMACHAL PRADESH

HIMACHAL PRADESH

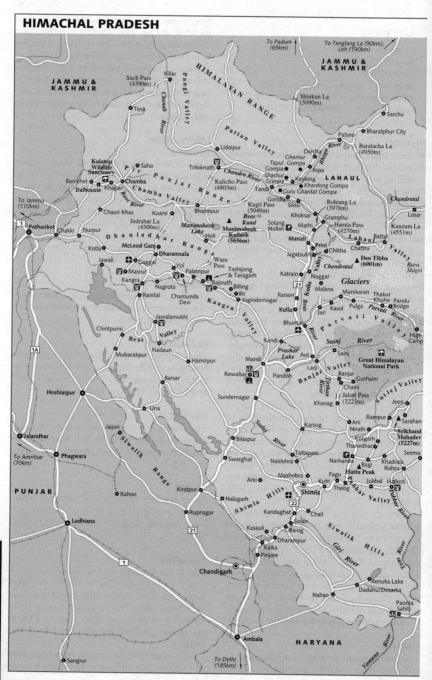

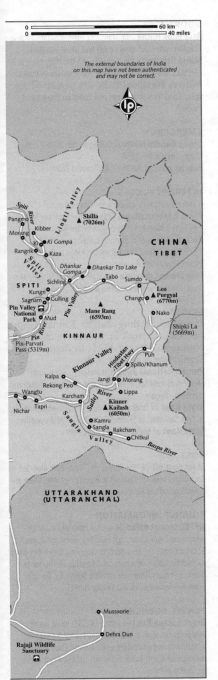

The external boundaries of India on this map have not been authenticated and may not be correct.

routes in July and August. Solo trekking is not advised – a number of accidents and 'disappearances' have occurred in Himachal Pradesh (see boxed text, p350).

Popular treks include the trek from Parvati Valley to Pin Valley in Spiti (see boxed text, p352); the Hamta Pass trek from Manali to Lahaul (p367), and the trek from McLeod Ganj to the Chamba Valley (see p381). Another possible trekking destination is the Great Himalayan National Park (p349) near Bhuntar.

Getting There & Away

The main routes into Himachal are by bus, but there are small airstrips near Shimla (Jubbarhatti), Kullu (Bhuntar) and Dharamsala (Gaggal airport, Kangra) that receive flights from Delhi with **Kingfisher Airlines** (www.flykingfisher.com) and **Jagson Airlines** (www.jagsonairline.com). A common route for travellers is to fly into Leh and make the two-day bus journey from there to Manali.

You can get part-way into Himachal by train via the old metre-gauge lines from Kalka to Shimla and from Pathankot to Jogindarnagar.

Getting Around

Clunky old government buses provide most of the local transport around Himachal Pradesh, though there are a few internal flights and a few private 'deluxe' buses on popular routes to Manali, Shimla and Dharamsala. Many people hire a car and driver for local sightseeing, and, if you're prepared to pay, any taxi will happily take you on an eight-hour journey (over mountain passes, if necessary) to your next destination. Crowded share 4WDs (minimum 10 people) join the buses on the trip from Manali to Lahaul and Spiti.

EASTERN HIMACHAL PRADESH

Eastern Himachal Pradesh is dominated by Shimla, the state capital, and the mountainous district of Kinnaur, which spreads east to the Tibetan border then loops north to Spiti. The official district website is http://hpshimla.nic.in.

HIMACHAL PRADESH

SHIMLA

☎ 0177 / pop 144,900 / elev 2205m

Until the British arrived, there was nothing at Shimla but a sleepy forest glade known as Shyamala (a local name for Kali – the Hindu goddess who is the destroyer of evil). Then a Scottish civil servant named Charles Kennedy built a summer home in Shimla in 1822 and nothing was ever the same again. By 1864 Shimla had developed into the official summer capital of the Raj. Every summer until 1939, the entire government of India fled here from the sweltering heat of the plains, with all their clerks' books and forms filled out in triplicate. When the Kalka–Shimla railway line was constructed in 1903, Shimla's status as India's premier hill station was assured, and a number of prestigious schools are now based here. The city was even briefly the capital of Punjab until the map was redrawn in 1966.

Strung out along a 12km ridge, Shimla is now an overgrown holiday town that seems on the verge of sliding into the valley. The centre has some quaint English-era buildings and there are some good forest walks nearby. A jagged line of snow-covered peaks is clearly visible from April to June, and in October and November, which coincides with the main tourist season. Honeymooners also come here to frolic in the snow in December and January.

Orientation

Shimla sprawls for miles, but the official centre of town is Scandal Point. From here, the flat open area known as the Ridge stretches east to Christ Church, where trails lead uphill towards the Jakhu Temple.

The long, winding, pedestrian-only Mall runs west and east from Scandal Point. Downhill is Cart Rd, with the train station, the Inter State Bus Terminal (ISBT) and taxi stands. A passenger lift provides a quick route between the Mall and Cart Rd, or you can go via the maze of alleyways of the Middle Bazar and Lower Bazar.

At the bus or train stations you will be besieged by porters offering to carry your luggage uphill for Rs30 to Rs50. Most double as touts, and hotels will increase your room tariff to cover their commission.

Information

Laws exist banning plastic bags, littering, smoking and spitting in public places; police can hit offenders with a Rs500 fine.

BOOKSHOPS

Asia Book House (the Mall; ☉ 10am-8.30pm) English-language titles including novels and travel literature.

Maria Brothers (☎ 2565388; 78A the Mall; ☉ 10.30am-8pm) Secondhand and antiquarian books.

Minerva Bookshop (☎ 2803078; the Mall; ☉ 9am-6pm) Good for novels, maps and books on Himachal Pradesh.

EMERGENCY

Indira Gandhi Medical College (☎ 2803073; the Ridge, Circular Rd; 24hr)

Tourist police (☎ 2812344; Scandal Point)

INTERNET ACCESS

There are only a few internet places:

Asian & International Travels (the Mall; per hr Rs30; ☉ 9am-9.30pm) Cramped place on the Mall.

Escape Cafe (6 Andi Bhavan, Jakhu; per hr Rs30; ☉ 9.30am-10pm) Uphill from the Ridge at the Great Escape Routes travel agency.

Play World Cybercafe (the Mall; per hr Rs30; ☉ 9am-9pm) The best of the bunch on the Mall.

MONEY

If you're heading out to Kinnaur, Spiti and Lahaul, stock up on rupees in Shimla. Numerous 24-hour ATMs are dotted around Scandal Point and the Mall.

Punjab National Bank (the Mall; ☉ 10am-4pm Mon-Fri, to 1pm Sat) Changes major currencies in cash and travellers cheques.

State Bank of India (the Mall; ☉ 10am-4pm Mon-Fri, to 1pm Sat) West of Scandal Point; has an ATM opposite.

State Bank of India ATM (Scandal Point)

POST

Main post office (the Ridge; ☉ 10am-8pm Mon-Sat, to 4pm Sun) Looks after parcels and poste restante. There are several suboffices west along the Mall.

TOURIST INFORMATION

HPTDC tourist office (Himachal Pradesh Tourist Development Corporation; ☎ 2652561; www.hptdc.gov.in; Scandal Point; ☉ 9am-8pm, to 6pm Aug, Sep & Dec-Mar) Helpful for advice, brochures and booking HPTDC buses, hotels and tours. There are satellite booths by the Inter State Bus Terminal and the Victory Tunnel.

TRAVEL AGENCIES

Great Escape Routes (☎ 5533037; www.great escaperoutes.com; 6 Andi Bhavan, Jakhu) Specialises in trekking and adventure tours around Shimla and throughout North India. Hires out Enfield motorcycles for Rs500 per day.

HIMACHAL PRADESH

Sights & Activities

HIMACHAL STATE MUSEUM & LIBRARY

About 2.5km west of Scandal Point and a stiff walk up to the telecommunications mast, the **state museum** (Indian/foreigner Rs10/50, camera/video Rs100/1500; ⏲ 10am-1.30pm & 2-5pm Tue-Fri, Sun & 2nd Sat each month) is home to an impressive collection of miniatures from Kangra and Rajasthan, as well as Chamba embroidery, coins and jewellery, temple carvings, paintings of Shimla, and weapons – including some massive and unwieldy-looking blunderbusses. There is also a gallery devoted to the visits that were made by Gandhi to Shimla.

VICEREGAL LODGE & BOTANICAL GARDENS

Built as an official residence for the British viceroys, the **Viceregal Lodge** (Indian/foreigner Rs20/50; ⏲ 9.15am-1pm & 2-5pm, to 7pm May-Jul, tours every 30min) looks like a cross between Harry Potter's Hogwarts School and the Tower of London. Every brick used in its construction was hauled up here by mule. Today it houses the Indian Institute of Advanced Study, but you can take a guided tour of the buildings. Photography is not permitted inside. Tickets cost Rs20 if you just want to look around the gardens.

Opposite the lodge entrance is the **Himalayan Bird Park** (admission Rs5; ⏲ 10am-5pm), with a small

---

FESTIVALS IN HIMACHAL PRADESH

Losar Lahaul & Spiti (Jan/Feb; p389) McLeod Ganj (Dec/Jan; p375) Tibetans across Himachal celebrate the Tibetan New Year with processions, music and dancing, and masked *chaams* (ritual masked dances performed by Buddhist monks in gompas (Tibetan Buddhist monasteries) to celebrate the victory of good over evil and of Buddhism over pre-existing religions). The Dalai Lama holds open teaching sessions in Dharamsala.

Shivaratri Festival (Feb/Mar; Mandi, p347; Baijnath, p383) Villagers march idols of local gods to the temples in Mandi and Baijnath as a tribute to Lord Shiva.

Sui Mata Mela (Apr; Chamba, p387) Four days of singing and dancing to honour Sui Mata, who gave her life to save the people of Chamba.

Dhungri Mela (May; Manali, p359) Animal sacrifices in honour of Hadimba at Manali's ancient Hadimba Temple.

Himalayan Hang-Gliding Rally (May; Billing, p383) Hang-gliders across the world gather on the slopes above Billing for competitions and record flight challenges.

Ki Chaam Festival (Jun/Jul; Ki, p394) The monastery at Ki holds whirling masked dances at this time, attended by villagers from across Spiti.

Lahaul Festival (Jul; Keylong, p391) A big trade and culture festival in Lahaul with market stalls, dancing and music.

Minjar Festival (Jul/Aug; Chamba, p386) A harvest festival, held on the banks of the Ravi. Minjar – shoots of maize – are offered to Varuna, god of rains, in a weeklong celebration, and idols of gods such as Raghuvira (a reincarnation of Rama) are paraded through the streets.

Ladarcha Fair (Aug; Kaza, p393) An ancient trade fair celebrated in Spiti, with Buddhist dances, mountain sports and bustling rural markets.

Pauri Festival (Aug; Triloknath, p391) Buddhists and Hindus gather at the temple of Triloknath and light giant butter lamps in honour of Lord Shiva (Hindu) or Avalokitesvara (Buddhist).

Manimahesh Yatra (Aug/Sep; near Bharmour, p389) Shaivites trek for three days to bathe in Manimahesh Lake, one of Shiva's mythical abodes.

Phulech Festival (Sep/Oct; Kalpa, p346; Sangla, p344) Villagers throughout Kinnaur fill temple courtyards with flowers of intoxicating fragrance, and oracles carry out sacrifices and make predictions for the coming year.

Dussehra or **Durga Puja** (Oct; Kullu, p353; Sarahan, p344) Kullu celebrates the defeat of the demon Ravana with a huge fair and parade, led by the chariot of Raghunath (Rama). Sarahan celebrates Durga's victory over the demon Mahishasura with animal sacrifices in honour of Bhimakali.

Lavi Fair (Nov; Rampur, p343) An ancient trade fair in Rampur on the old trade route to Tibet, marked by three days of haggling and high spirits.

Guktor Festival (Nov; Dhankar, p395) Masked Buddhist dances and processions at Spiti's Dhankar Gompa.

Renuka Mela (Nov; Renuka Lake, p343) A six-day festival culminating in the ritual immersion of idols of Parsasurama (Vishnu).

International Himalayan Festival (10-12 Dec; McLeod Ganj, p375) Celebrating the Dalai Lama's Nobel Peace Prize, this festival promotes peace and cultural understanding with Buddhist dances and music.

HIMACHAL PRADESH

SHIMLA

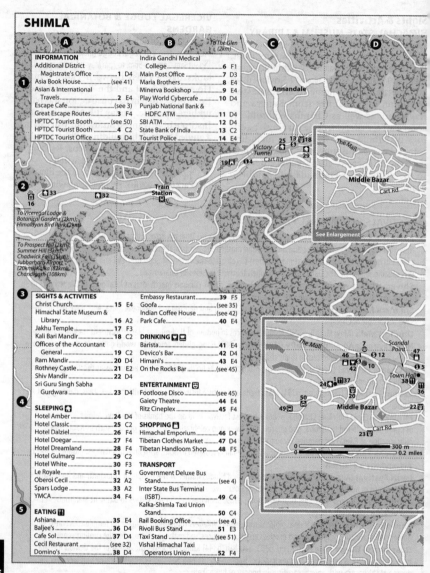

INFORMATION
Additional District
  Magistrate's Office 1 D4
Asia Book House .... (see 41)
Asian & International
  Travels 2 E4
Escape Cafe .... (see 3)
Great Escape Routes 3 F4
HPTDC Tourist Booth .... (see 50)
HPTDC Tourist Booth 4 C2
HPTDC Tourist Office 5 D4
Indira Gandhi Medical
  College 6 F1
Main Post Office 7 D3
Maria Brothers 8 E4
Minerva Bookshop 9 E4
Play World Cybercafe 10 D4
Punjab National Bank &
  HDFC ATM 11 D4
SBI ATM 12 D4
State Bank of India 13 C2
Tourist Police 14 E4

SIGHTS & ACTIVITIES
Christ Church 15 E4
Himachal State Museum &
  Library 16 A2
Jakhu Temple 17 F3
Kali Bari Mandir 18 C2
Offices of the Accountant
  General 19 C2
Ram Mandir 20 D4
Rothney Castle 21 E2
Shiv Mandir 22 D4
Sri Guru Singh Sabha
  Gurdwara 23 D4

SLEEPING
Hotel Amber 24 D4
Hotel Classic 25 C2
Hotel Dalziel 26 F4
Hotel Doegar 27 F4
Hotel Dreamland 28 F4
Hotel Gulmarg 29 C2
Hotel White 30 F3
Le Royale 31 F4
Oberoi Cecil 32 A2
Spars Lodge 33 A2
YMCA 34 F4

EATING
Ashiana 35 E4
Baljee's 36 D4
Cafe Sol 37 D4
Cecil Restaurant .... (see 32)
Domino's 38 D4
Embassy Restaurant 39 F5
Goofa .... (see 35)
Indian Coffee House .... (see 42)
Park Cafe 40 E4

DRINKING
Barista 41 E4
Devico's Bar 42 D4
Himani's 43 E4
On the Rocks Bar .... (see 45)

ENTERTAINMENT
Footloose Disco .... (see 45)
Gaiety Theatre 44 E4
Ritz Cineplex 45 F4

SHOPPING
Himachal Emporium 46 D4
Tibetan Clothes Market 47 D4
Tibetan Handloom Shop 48 F5

TRANSPORT
Government Deluxe Bus
  Stand .... (see 4)
Inter State Bus Terminal
  (ISBT) 49 C4
Kalka-Shimla Taxi Union
  Stand 50 C4
Rail Booking Office .... (see 4)
Rivoli Bus Stand 51 E3
Taxi Stand .... (see 51)
Vishal Himachal Taxi
  Operators Union 52 F4

collection of exotic pheasant, including the iridescent monal pheasant, which is Himachal's state bird.

The lodge is a 4.5km walk west from Scandal Point along the Mall, but it is poorly signposted, so you should try to aim for the telecommunications mast, then stick to the largest road.

CHRIST CHURCH

This very English **church** (☎ 2652953; the Ridge; ☼ services in English 9am Sun) dominates the top of the ridge and is the second-oldest church in northern India (the oldest is in Ambala in Haryana). Built between 1846 and 1857, it contains Raj-era memorials and fine stained glass. There's still a small Sunday service held here.

HIMACHAL PRADESH

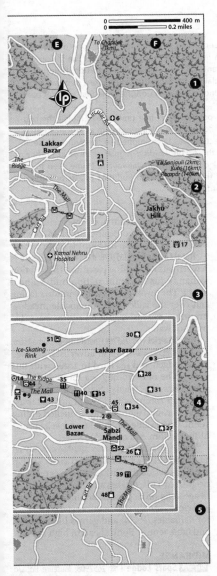

JAKHU TEMPLE

Shimla's most famous temple is dedicated to the Hindu monkey god, Hanuman, and appropriately, hundreds of rhesus macaques loiter around harassing devotees for *prasad* (temple-blessed food offerings). Getting here involves a pleasant but steep 30-minute hike through the forest, starting at the east end of the Ridge; however, the monkeys on this route are, quite frankly, a menace. Consider buying a walking stick at the start of the walk (from Rs25) to discourage them. Taxis from either stand charge around Rs280 return.

OTHER TEMPLES

The most popular temple for locals is the small **Shiv Mandir**, just below the Ridge – crowds of school children drop in before and after school, and sadhus (holy people) wait on the steps, soliciting donations.

About 1km west of the Ridge is the Bengali hut-style **Kali Bari Mandir** (temple), enshrining an image of Kali as Shyamala. Vaishnavites gather at the modernist **Ram Mandir**, just above the bus stand in Middle Bazar, while Sikhs attend the huge white **Sri Guru Singh Sabha Gurdwara** near the ISBT.

HISTORIC BUILDINGS

The Ridge is lined with grand examples of British architecture, including the **Town Hall**, oddly reminiscent of the mansion in Hammer Horror films, and the mock-Tudor folly housing the **post office**. At the west end of the Mall are the grand mock-Gothic **Offices of the Accountant General**. Above Shimla on the way to the Jakhu Temple, you can peek through the gates of **Rothney Castle**, former home of Allan Octavian Hume – see boxed text, p338.

WALKING

About 4km northwest of Scandal Point is **The Glen**, a former playground of rich British colonialists, selected for its similarity to the Scottish highlands. The road here passes through the flat green meadow at **Annandale**, once the site of a famous racecourse, and a popular venue for cricket and polo matches.

INNER LINE PERMITS

Free permits for travel from Rekong Peo to Tabo in Spiti are issued by the office of the **Additional District Magistrate** (☎ 2657005; ⏱ 10am-1.30pm & 2-5pm Mon-Sat, closed 2nd Sat each month), in the Collectorate Building just off the Mall. Permits are issued while you wait. Although not officially required, take along two passport photos and copies of the identity and visa pages from your passport, just in case. Permits are also available in Rekong Peo and Kaza.

HIMACHAL PRADESH

A REMARKABLE CIVIL SERVANT

Regarded as an eccentric reactionary by his peers, Allan Octavian Hume was one of the most colourful characters of the British empire. Born in Kent, England, Hume joined the Indian civil service in 1849 and quickly rose through the ranks of the colonial administration. Horrified by the shameful treatment of the indigenous population, he became an outspoken campaigner for social reform and eventually helped found the Indian National Congress, the first political party run for and by Indians, which still exists today.

Hume was even more remarkable outside of politics. In his free time he assembled the largest collection of stuffed birds in Asia, which he housed in a private museum at Rothney Castle, his palatial mansion in Shimla. The whole collection was later shipped to the British Museum in London. Hume was also an avid student of the occult, holding regular seances at Rothney Castle with such luminaries as Madame Blavatsky, the Ukrainian clairvoyant. Hume even toyed with the idea of becoming a chela (student) of the lamas (Tibetan Buddhist priests or monks), before devoting his energies to self-government for India.

There's an interesting temple and excellent views at **Prospect Hill**, about 4km west of Shimla. About 5km away on the Shimla–Kalka railway line, **Summer Hill** has pleasant, shady walks. Pretty **Chadwick Falls** (67m high) are 2km further west, best visited just after the monsoon. About 3km east of Lakkar Bazar, the village of **Sanjauli** has a Durga temple and a small Buddhist monastery run by Gelugpa monks.

Tours

The HPTDC tourist office organises daily sightseeing bus tours of villages around Shimla. The tours leave from the Rivoli bus stand at around 10.30am. Seats cost Rs160 to Rs250. Contact the office for the current itineraries.

The taxi unions also offer one-day sightseeing tours to Kufri, Naldehra, Fagu and Mashobra (Rs900), and to Mashobra, Naldehra and Tattapani (Rs1200).

Sleeping

Hotels in Shimla charge steep rates during the peak tourist season (April to June, October, November and Christmas). At all other times, ask about discounts. In winter, heating can usually be provided for an extra charge. Touts abound in Shimla – claims that hotels are full or closed should be taken with a pinch of salt.

BUDGET

Hotel Gulmarg (☎ 2653168; gulmarghotel@yahoo.com; s Rs300-450, d Rs500-1450; ✗) Found below the Mall, and spread over several buildings and annexes below the Computer College, this huge honeymoon hotel offers a mixed bag,

from gloriously chintzy doubles with round beds and mirrored ceilings to plain, boxlike singles. Low-season discount is up to 50%.

Hotel Classic (☎ 2653078; d Rs440-950) Classic is a worn but welcoming place and the location is handy for the train station and Scandal Point. The lower rooms with windows facing out over the valley and Annandale meadow are more expensive, but all rooms have TV and hot water.

Hotel Dalziel (☎ 2652691; hoteldalziel@hotmail.com; the Mall; d Rs550-880) Dalziel advertises heritage on a budget, and it's hard to argue with this claim. The old building – a former colonial bungalow – has plenty of character and faded but clean rooms with TV and hot water arranged around a huge wood-panelled dining room. Good value for Shimla, and well located at the bottom end of the Mall.

YMCA (☎ 2650021; ymcashimla@yahoo.co.in; s/d incl breakfast Rs660/850, without bathroom Rs310/410; ☐) Up the steps beside the Ritz Cineplex, expansive, bright-red YMCA takes all comers, regardless of age, religion or gender. Rooms are pleasant and clean, and there's an internet cafe, lockers for valuables (Rs30) and games like snooker and table tennis. Book ahead in high season.

MIDRANGE

our pick **Spars Lodge** (☎ 2657908; Museum Rd; s/d Rs660/990; ☐) On the little road up to the museum, Spars is a real travellers' hotel. It's bright, clean and airy with a lovely sunny dining room upstairs, and the owners are very welcoming. The cafe serves great food, including local trout.

Hotel White (☎ 2656136; www.hotelwhiteshimla.com; Lakkar Bazar; r Rs700-1200, ste from Rs1450) Northeast of

Scandal Point through the bustling bazaar, this place is well run and well priced – rates are fixed all year. It's worth shelling out for one of the 2nd-floor rooms with views over Shimla.

Hotel Amber (☎ 2654774; Middle Bazar; r Rs750-2000) If you want to be in the thick of the bazaar, this noisy but cheerful hotel near Ram Mandir has small but agreeable rooms (more ceiling mirrors and wood panelling) with TVs and shared balconies overlooking the market.

Hotel Dreamland (☎ 2806897; d Rs800-1650; 🖳) A steep climb behind the pavilion at the west end of the Ridge, Dreamland is a big place with a range of reasonably tidy rooms with TVs and modest valley views. Touts may lead you here, and prices are often heavily discounted, so ask before you see the rooms.

Hotel Doegar (☎ 2811927; www.hoteldoegar.com; the Ridge; d Rs1000-2500) Many of Shimla's hotels turn on the chintzy honeymoon charm, but Doegar does it with aplomb. The disco decor features mirrored ceilings, '70s timber panelling and harem-style curtains, though all rooms are different. Great views from the roof terrace, and worth upgrading to a deluxe room with balcony when prices halve in the off season.

TOP END

Le Royale (☎ 2651002; le_royale@hotmail.com; Jakhu Rd; r Rs1700-2950) Perched on the track up to Jakhu Temple, this boutique hotel has plenty of charm, with tastefully furnished rooms. It's close to the Ridge but tucked away enough to feel private. The Green Leaf restaurant is good and there are mountain views from the garden.

Oberoi Cecil (☎ 2804848; www.oberoicecil.com; the Mall; s/d from Rs11,000/12,500, ste from Rs21,000; 🖳 🖳 🖳) This grand high-rise is Shimla's glitziest five-star hotel. Colonial grandeur outside gives way to modern comforts within, and the cavernous central atrium has a gorgeous bar and restaurant, open to nonguests. There's wifi throughout.

Chapslee (☎ 2802542; www.chapslee.com; d with full board Rs10,000-13,000; 🖳) For the full Raj treatment, the outrageously ostentatious former home of Raja Charanjit Singh of Kapurthala is perched atop Elysium Hill, about 4km north of Shimla. The exclusive mountain retreat is crammed with chandeliers, tapestries, Afghan carpets, big-game trophies, Mughal ceramics, baroque furniture and pieces of Victoriana. There are just six sumptuous bedrooms, all with completely original fittings, plus a library, card room, sun lounge, tennis courts and – of course – a croquet lawn. Advance payment by credit card is required.

Eating

Befitting a holiday town and state capital, Shimla has plenty of places to eat, especially along the Mall and the Ridge. As well as the formal restaurants, there are dozens of Indian fast-food places in Middle Bazar serving samosas, potato cakes, *channa puri* (chickpeas and fried bread) and other snacks. Unless otherwise stated, the following eateries are open from 10am to 10pm.

Baljee's (the Mall; dishes Rs15-100) Opposite the Town Hall, Baljee's is a great place to breakfast on omelettes, toast and dosas (lentil-flour pancakes), and there's a popular counter selling Indian sweets.

Indian Coffee House (the Mall; dishes Rs20-35; ⌚ 8.30am-10pm) A Shimla institution, the Indian Coffee House is like an old boys' club with its old-school furniture, uniformed waiters and blackboard menu. Good place for breakfast, cheap dosas and coffee.

Park Cafe (the Ridge; meals Rs30-140) Up some steps from the Mall, this laid-back, studenty cafe is a cool spot for veg snacks such as pizzas and sandwiches, and drinks.

Ashiana (the Ridge; dishes Rs40-170; ⌚ 9am-10pm) In a fanciful circular building on the Ridge (you almost expect it to start revolving!), Ashiana is an elegant restaurant and a good people-watching spot. As well as Indian dishes there are sizzlers, Chinese and a few Thai favourites. Head downstairs to try Goofa restaurant (above).

Goofa (the Ridge; dishes Rs40-100; ⌚ 9am-10pm) Found down below Ashiana (above), Goofa is a cheaper subterranean restaurant and bar serving Indian and continental dishes.

Domino's (the Mall; pizzas Rs60-300) Sure, it's a Western fast-food chain, but travellers flock here for deep-dish pizza after weeks of dhal and rice in the hills, and Indian families queue up for a slice of Americana.

Embassy Restaurant (the Mall; dishes Rs80-190; ⌚ 9am-10pm) It doesn't look like much from the outside but Embassy is a cosy timber-lined restaurant with fabulous views over Shimla, especially at night when the city lights are on. The menu runs to Indian, Chinese and continental, with good biryanis and a tasty chicken curry.

Cafe Sol (the Mall; dishes Rs120-400; ☉ 11am-10pm) In the atrium on the roof of Hotel Combermere, but entered straight off the Mall, Sol serves an interesting blend of Mexican, Italian and Mediterranean dishes. Try the crispy prawn with cornflakes, or filling enchiladas.

Cecil Restaurant (☎ 2804848; the Mall; mains from Rs400, breakfast/dinner buffet Rs580/990) For a formal night out, look no further than the colonial elegance of the Cecil Restaurant. An à la carte menu is available but there are sumptuous buffets for breakfast and dinner. Book ahead. There's also a casual garden restaurant, or you can opt for a drink in the atrium lobby bar.

Drinking

Barista (the Mall; ☉ 9am-10pm) India's version of Starbucks is a popular spot for the trendy young set to meet over cappuccinos or milkshakes.

Himani's (the Mall; dishes Rs45-125; 10am-10pm) The neon and marble decor is straight out of the 1980s, but Himani's is a good place for a casual drink or plate of chicken tikka. On two levels, the top-floor terrace overlooking the Mall is perfect on a sunny afternoon.

Devico's Bar (the Mall; dishes Rs30-100; 10am-10pm) Head downstairs below Cafe Coffee Day for a beer or cocktail in this casual bar.

Entertainment

The most popular entertainment is to stroll along the Mall and the Ridge and watch everyone watching everyone else.

Gaiety Theatre (☎ 2805639; the Mall) Although closed for renovations at the time of writing, the Shimla Amateur Dramatic Club usually puts on shows here. Even if there's no show on, it's worth taking a peek at the fabulous auditorium.

Ritz Cineplex (☎ 2652413; Christ Church; tickets Rs35-75) This modern multiplex cinema has occasional imported blockbusters among the standard Bollywood fare.

Footloose Disco (☎ 2652413; Christ Church; s/couples Rs200/300; ☉ 7.30-11pm) In the Ritz Cineplex building, Shimla's only nightclub rocks to Bollywood soundtracks till late on weekends.

Shopping

Local holidaymakers head to the bustling Lakkar Bazar to haggle for wood and handloom souvenirs, but foreigners probably will find more of interest in the crowded and at-mospheric Middle Bazar, on the way down to the bus station. You can buy everything here from tin pots and peacock feathers to henna kits and bangles. Fruit and veg are sold at the heaving Sabzi Mandi at the bottom of the hill. For well-made, knock-off brand-name clothes, head to the Tibetan Clothes Market, behind the tourist office.

Carpets, shawls and other Himachal souvenirs are sold at **Himachal Emporium** (☎ 2011234; the Mall; ☉ 9am-6pm Mon-Sat), while Tibetan souvenirs are sold at the **Tibetan Handloom Shop** (☎ 2808163; the Mall; ☉ 9am-6pm), aiding Tibetan refugees.

Getting There & Away

AIR

Jubbarhatti airport, 23km south of Shimla, is served by **Kingfisher Airlines** (☎ 1800 2093030; www.flykingfisher.com). Weather permitting, there are daily flights from Shimla to Delhi. **Jagson Airlines** (☎ 2625177; www.jagsonairline.com) has a Delhi–Shimla–Kullu flight on Monday, Wednesday and Friday. A taxi to the airport costs Rs720.

BUS

The HPTDC and private travel agencies offer private overnight deluxe buses (two-by-two seating) to Delhi (Rs650, 10 hours), and morning and evening buses to Manali (from Rs450, 10 hours) in season (April to June, October and November), both from the Government Deluxe Bus Stand near the Victory Tunnel. Regular buses to Chail (Rs34, 2½ hours), Naldehra (Rs24, 1½ hours) and Tattapani (Rs50, three hours) leave from the small Rivoli (Lakkar Bazar) bus stand, north of the Ridge.

Other government buses leave from the large and chaotic **Inter State Bus Terminal** (☎ 2656326; Cart Rd). The computerised booking counter takes reservations up to a month in advance. Reservations are made at Counter 9 and information is at Counter 8. See the table, opposite, for services.

TAXI

The **Kalka-Shimla Taxi Union** (☎ 2658225) has its stand near the ISBT, while **Vishal Himachal Taxi Operators Union** (☎ 2805164) operates from the bottom of the passenger lift. Share taxis are available to Kalka between noon and 2pm (Rs275). Taxis from the train station or the ISBT to the passenger lift cost around Rs70. There's another taxi stand next to the Rivoli bus stand.

BUSES FROM SHIMLA

Destination	Fare (Rs)	Duration (hr)	Frequency
Chamba	375	14	4 daily
Chandigarh	100/145 (ordinary/deluxe)	4	every 15 minutes
Dehra Dun	174	9	5 daily
Delhi	243/450 (ordinary/deluxe)	9	hourly
Dharampur (for Kasauli)	85	2½	regularly
Dharamsala	232	10	5 daily
Jammu	245	12	2 daily (check locally for time)
Kullu	222	8½	5 daily
Manali	257	10	5 daily
Mandi	145	6	hourly
Nahan	127	5	4 daily
Narkanda	60	2	regularly
Paonta Sahib	170	7	5 daily
Rampur	125	5	hourly
Rekong Peo	220	10	hourly
Rohru	120	6	regularly
Sangla	220	10	daily
Sarahan	165	8	3 daily

TRAIN

One of the little joys of Shimla is getting to or from it by the narrow-gauge toy train from Kalka, just north of Chandigarh. Although the steam trains are long gone, it's a scenic four- to six-hour trip, passing through 103 tunnels as it creeps up through the hills. Tiny Shimla train station is 1.5km west of Scandal Point on Cart Rd – about a 15-minute uphill walk. The left-luggage office is open 9am to 5pm.

Ordinary trains (1st/2nd class Rs227/34) run downhill to Kalka at 2.25pm and 6.15pm, returning at 4am and 6am. To travel in style, catch the posh *Shivalik Express* at 5.40pm (returning at 5.15am; Rs280, 1st class only) or the *Himalayan Queen* at 10.30am (returning at 4pm; Rs167, chair car only). All 1st-class prices include food.

The *Himalayan Queen* service connects with the *Himalayan Queen* trains to and from Delhi (chair car/2nd class Rs284/75). The train from Delhi's Nizammudin station leaves at 5.25am, departing from New Delhi station at 5.50am.

There's a rail booking office next to the tourist office on the Ridge, or you can book at the train station.

TAXIS FROM SHIMLA

Destination	One-Way Fare (Rs)
Airport	720
Chail	1200
Chandigarh	1420
Dehra Dun	3500
Dharamsala/McLeod Ganj	3200/3500
Kasauli	920
Kullu	3000
Manali	3200
Naldehra	520
Narkanda	1200
Rekong Peo	3200
Sarahan	2800
Tattapani	1200

Getting Around

The only way to get around central Shimla is on foot. Fortunately, there's a two-part **lift** (per person Rs7; ☻ 8am-10pm, to 9pm low season) connecting the east end of the Mall with Cart Rd, a 15-minute walk above the ISBT. Taxis from the train station to the bottom of the lift cost about Rs80.

AROUND SHIMLA
Shimla to Tattapani

About 12km north of Shimla, the small village of **Mashobra** has an old colonial church and some pleasant walks among deodar trees.

About 15km north of Mashobra, **Naldehra** is famous chiefly for the **Naldehra Golf Course**

HIMACHAL PRADESH

(☎ 0177-2747739; www.naldehragolf.com; green fees Indian/ foreigner Rs250/500, club hire Rs250; ☉ 7am-6pm), established in 1905 by British viceroy Lord Curzon. Set among tall cedars – some of which stand directly between the tee and green – it's a challenging course. Hire a caddy (Rs40/70 for 9/18 holes) or you won't know where you're going. Ponies can be hired for treks along the ridge and there are pine-scented walks.

At the golf course, **Hotel Golf Glade** (☎ 0177-2747739; d Rs1000-1200) is an upmarket HPTDC property offering smart hotel rooms around an inviting restaurant and bar.

Tattapani
☎ 01907 / elev 656m

About 30km below Naldehra on the banks of the Sutlej River, sleepy Tattapani is known for its steaming sulphurous springs, which spill out onto a sandy river beach. But changes are afoot at Tattapani. A proposed hydroelectric project and dam about 35km downstream will flood the lower parts of the village by 2010.

The village has several temples linked to the cult of Rishi Jamdagam, and you can walk to holy Shiva caves and former palaces. Ask directions locally or at New Spring View Guest House.

New Spring View Guest House (☎ 9816341911; www.newspringview.com; d Rs500-750) is an excellent new guest house that replaces the original Spring View Guest House down by the river. Rooms are spacious, bright and airy and there's a good restaurant and hot sulphur baths. Helpful owners can organise activities such as rafting and trekking, and have Enfield motorcycles for rent.

Kasauli
☎ 01792 / elev 1850m

Perched on a hillside 75km southwest of Shimla, Kasauli is another former Raj retreat set among the pines. It has several Raj-era buildings and numerous peaceful walks through the forest, offering grand views over the Punjabi plains.

There is no direct bus to Kasauli from Shimla; instead, catch a southbound bus from Shimla and change to a local bus at Dharampur.

Hotel Ros Common (☎ 272005; d Rs1800-3000) is a charming HPTDC heritage hotel in a small colonial bungalow, set in lovely gardens. There's a slightly cheaper annexe nearby.

Chail
☎ 01792 / elev 2150m

The hilltop village of Chail, 65km south of Shimla, was created by the maharaja of Patiala as his summer capital, after he was expelled from Shimla for getting a little too friendly with the daughter of the British military commander. If you fancy a few overs, Chail lays claim to the 'world's highest cricket ground', a 3km walk from the village. As well as forest strolls, there's a **wildlife park** with deer and birds.

Hotel Pineview (☎ 248349; r from Rs200) is the only reasonable budget accommodation in town. Shared rooms have bucket hot water.

Palace Hotel (☎ 248141; palace@hptdc.in; log huts Rs1300-1600, r Rs2500-6000, ste from Rs8000; ☒) is a former maharaja's palace that's now run by the HPTDC. The grand grey-stone mansion, set in 28 hectares of immaculate lawns, is luxurious in a Raj-era way, and accommodation ranges from log huts to sumptuous suites.

Narkanda
☎ 01782 / elev 2708m

About 65km northeast of Shimla, Narkanda is a nondescript truck-stop town for most of the year, but from January to March it transforms into a modest ski resort. The HPTDC offers three-/five-/seven-day skiing packages from Rs2739/4565/6391, including accommodation, meals, equipment and tuition, but not transport – see www.hptdc.nic.in for dates.

On the busy main road in the village centre, **Hotel Mahamaya Palace** (☎ 242448; r Rs500-900) has a suitably alpine mood, an inviting, dark-wood restaurant and large, worn rooms, some with mountain views.

HPTDC Hotel Hatu (☎ 242430; hotelhatu.tripod.com; d Rs900-1500), off the main road just east of the centre, is a government-run place with pleasant gardens, snug rooms and a restaurant and bar.

Pabbar Valley
☎ 01781 / elev 1400m

Running northeast to Kinnaur, the calm Pabbar Valley is easily accessible from Shimla by public bus. Set in rolling fields at the mouth of the valley, the Durga temple at **Hatkoti** was founded in the 8th century AD. Built in classic Kinnauri style, the slate-roofed temples attract large numbers of Shaivite pilgrims during the Chaitra Navratra and Asvin Navratra festivals in April and October. Pilgrims' quarters are available at the temple or you can stay at the **HPTDC Hotel Chanshal** (☎ 240661; dm Rs100, d Rs800, d with AC Rs900-1000), 10km north of Hatkoti towards Rohru.

Local buses connect Hatkoti to **Jubbal**, 29km west, which has a fanciful slate-roofed palace built by the former Rana of Jubbal.

Nahan
☎ 01702

Most tourists flash through Nahan on the bus between Shimla and Dehra Dun, but the cobbled streets of the old town are crammed with crumbling temples and buildings from the days of the rajas. During the **Bhawan Dwadshi** at the end of the monsoon, idols of Hindu gods are led through the streets and ceremonially bathed in Ranital (Rani Lake) in the town centre.

About an hour by bus from Nahan, **Renukaji** (Renuka Lake) is Himachal's largest lake and a popular picnic spot for Indian families. The week-long **Renuka Mela** festival (see boxed text, p335) is held here in November to honour the goddess Renukaji.

Hotel Regency (☎ 223302; d Rs350-500) is near the maidan (open grassed area) in the town centre in Nahan. At Renukaji, **Hotel Renuka** (☎ 01783-267339; dm Rs100, d Rs700-1000; 🏊) is a large HPTDC place on the lakeshore, with a restaurant and activities such as boating.

There are frequent buses to Paonta Sahib (Rs43, two hours) and Dadahu/Dosarka (Rs35, 45 minutes), the starting point of the 30-minute walk to Renukaji. Taxis charge around Rs500 to Renukaji or Paonta Sahib.

Paonta Sahib
☎ 01704

Well off the tourist track near the Uttarakhand border, Paonta Sahib is famous as the childhood home of Guru Gobind Singh, the 10th Sikh guru. Sikh pilgrims flock here to pay their respects at the sprawling **Paonta Sahib Gurdwara** on the banks of the holy Yamuna River. The town overflows during the **Holi festival** in March, when it can be difficult to find a room anywhere in the area.

On the riverside about 100m from the temple, **Hotel Yamuna** (☎ 222341; d Rs500-700, with AC Rs1100-1700; 🏊) is a standard HPTDC hotel with a good restaurant and bar.

There are hourly morning buses to Shimla (Rs170, seven hours) and several daily services to Dehra Dun (Rs40, two hours).

KINNAUR VALLEY

Blooming with apple orchards, and blessed with the finest mountain views in Eastern Himachal Pradesh, the Kinnaur Valley is an intriguing corner of the state. The old Hindustan–Tibet Hwy (built by the British as a sneaky invasion route into Tibet) runs northeast from Shimla through Kinnaur, providing access to mountain villages with slate-roofed temples and vast orchards of apple trees that provide Himachal's most famous export. The Kinnauris, or Kinners, are proud Aryan people who mainly survive from farming and apple growing. You can recognise Kinners all over India by their green felt *thepang* hats.

With an easy-to-obtain inner line permit (see boxed text, p337) you can travel north to the mountain deserts of Spiti (p392). For most of the last decade, the road between Rekong Peo and Spiti has been blocked, forcing travellers to change buses and cross the river on precarious ropeways to complete their journey. Heavy rains and flooding still wash away parts of the road: at the time of writing it was open all the way to Tabo – check locally before travelling north of Rekong Peo.

For much of the year, Kinnaur is a relaxed oasis of mountains and valleys, but that all changes during the Durga Puja celebrations in September/October when Bengali holidaymakers flood into Kinnaur from the plains. Simultaneously, the annual apple harvest lures hundreds of fruit wholesalers from across India. It can be impossible to find a room anywhere in Kinnaur, especially in popular spots such as Kalpa and the Sangla Valley.

For more information on the Kinnaur Valley, visit the local government website at http://hpkinnaur.nic.in.

Rampur
☎ 01782 / elev 1005m

The gateway to Kinnaur, this nondescript town was once the capital of the Bushahr rajas. Today, Rampur is mainly a place to change buses, but if you decide to stick around, the delightful, terraced and turreted **Padam Palace** was built in 1925 for the maharaja of Bushahr; only the garden is open to visitors. There are several ancient temples, including the stone **Raghunath Temple** on the highway and the **Purohit Mandir** and **Sri Sat Narain Temple** down in the riverside bazaar. The gaudy modern **Dumgir Budh Temple** on the main road recalls Kinnaur's Buddhist past.

The huge **Lavi Fair** (see boxed text, p335) is held yearly in the second week of November, attracting traders and pilgrims from remote villages.

SLEEPING & EATING

There are many better places to stay in Kinnaur than in Rampur, but there are cheap hotels, if you get stuck. Most places to stay are below the bus stand, in the bazaar that cascades downhill from the highway.

Satluj View Guesthouse (☎ 233924; dm Rs50, r Rs200-300) Down some concrete steps, just uphill from the bus station, this place has tatty but cheap rooms on several levels.

Hotel Bushahr Regency (☎ 234103; d Rs900-1300, with AC Rs1300-1500; ✴) This standard HPTDC property on the western edge of Rampur has spacious rooms and a decent restaurant.

GETTING THERE & AWAY

Rampur's chaotic bus station has frequent services to Rekong Peo (Rs100, five hours) and Shimla (Rs125, five hours) via Narkanda. Buses to Sarahan (Rs40, two hours) leave every two hours. Three daily buses run to Sangla (Rs105, five hours).

Sarahan

☎ 01782 / elev 1920m

The former summer capital of the Bushahr kingdom, Sarahan is dominated by the fabulous **Bhimakali Temple** (donation required; ☾ 7am-8pm), built from layers of stone and timber to absorb the force of earthquakes. There are two towers here, one built in the 12th century, and a newer tower from the 1920s containing a highly revered shrine to Bhimakali (the local version of Kali) beneath a beautiful silver-filigree canopy.

There are some strict entry rules. Male visitors must wear a cap (caps can be borrowed inside the temple), shoes must be removed, smoking is banned, and cameras and leather goods like belts and wallets must be left with the guards. Behind the temple is a small display of ancient ceremonial horns, lamps and weaponry, and across the courtyard is the squat **Lankra Vir Temple**, where human sacrifices were carried out right up to the 18th century. The tradition lives on in a tamer form in the Astomi ritual during October's **Dussehra** (see boxed text, p335), when a menagerie of animals is sacrificed to Bhimakali, including goats, chickens and buffalo.

There are peaceful walks in the surrounding hills – stroll downhill to the **Buddhist gompa** in Gharat village, or gird yourself for the treks on the slopes of **Bashal Peak**. The flamboyant **palace** of the last maharaja of Bushahr is just behind the Bhimakali Temple.

SLEEPING & EATING

For such a tiny village, Sarahan has some good places to stay. Apart from the temple guest house, all hotels offer significant discounts out of season (August and December to March).

ourpick Temple Guesthouse (☎ 274248; dm Rs25, r Rs150-300) The obvious place to stay is within the ancient temple precinct and, unlike most temple accommodation, rooms here are far from gloomy and austere. Dorm rooms are basic, but the upper-story rooms are bright and airy, with hot water.

Trehan's Guesthouse (☎ 274205; r Rs500-880) Trehan's has friendly owners and a range of compact rooms with TVs. The more-expensive rooms have fine valley views.

Hotel Srikhand (☎ 274234; dm Rs100, r Rs900-1600) Classier than most HPTDC properties, this stone and timber hotel is styled on the temple and enjoys panoramic views over the valley. Rooms are tastefully decorated and the restaurant serves decent food.

GETTING THERE & AWAY

Three direct buses run to Shimla from Sarahan (Rs165, eight hours) via Rampur (Rs40, two hours). For other destinations take a local bus to Jeori (Rs18, 45 minutes) and change there. Taxis from Jeori to Sarahan cost Rs300.

Sangla Valley

☎ 01786 / elev 2680m

The Sangla, or Baspa, Valley used to be described as 'the most beautiful valley in the Himalaya,' but today the valley is marred by the dams and barrages of the Baspa Hydroelectric Project. It's still a pretty spot and a good place to see traditional Kinnauri architecture, but avoid it during the busy Dussehra (Durga Puja) season. The hair-raising road to the valley begins at Karcham on the Rekong Peo–Shimla highway, passing the gushing outflow pipes from the hydroelectric plant.

SANGLA

The largest village in the valley, Sangla was once a fairy-tale village of low wooden houses and slate-roofed temples looking out over a pristine valley, but hydroelectricity is changing Sangla beyond all recognition. Wooden houses are being rebuilt in concrete and new hotels are springing up on every corner. You'll have to head into the hills to find the peace and quiet that the valley was once famous for. Walk down to the lower village to admire the old stone houses and Hindu and Buddhist temples. The **Bering Nag Temple** forms the centrepiece of the annual **Phulech Festival** (see boxed text, p335) in September.

Sleeping & Eating

All hotels are booked solid during Durga Puja, but ask about discounts outside of September and October, which comprise the main tourist season.

Baspa Guesthouse (☎ 242206; d Rs400-660) Run by a genial Kinnauri family with an obvious love for the colour green, Baspa offers a range of carpeted rooms with hot water and good views from the upper floors.

Sangla Resort (☎ 242201; d Rs650-900) One of Sangla's most appealing places, this cute stone chalet is set in peaceful gardens and surrounded by orchards. Rooms are spotless and the shared terrace and balconies have great valley views.

Banjara Camps (☎ 242536; www.banjaracamps.com; s/d tents Rs5000/5500) These all-inclusive tented camps set up along the Baspa River between April and October. Deluxe tents have attached bathroom and the price includes meals and activities.

The bus stand has half a dozen identical 'Tibetan restaurants' serving *momos* (Tibetan dumplings), *thukpa* (Tibetan noodle soup), chow mein, fried rice and Indian snacks.

Getting There & Away

Buses run in the morning to Rampur (Rs90, five hours) and there are two daily buses to Rekong Peo (Rs40, three hours). Local buses run up the valley to Chitkul (Rs35, two hours) twice a day.

Share 4WDs can take you to Karcham (Rs35, two hours), on the main Shimla–Rekong Peo bus route. A taxi to Rekong costs Rs1000.

AROUND SANGLA

Clinging to a rocky spur 2km above Sangla, the village of **Kamru** was the former capital of the kingdom of Bushahr. The village is modernising rapidly but there are some impressive slate and stone houses and temples. The village is dominated by the tower-style **Kamakhya Devi Fort**, the former home of the *thakurs* of Bushahr (shoes and leather items should be removed and heads must be covered). Kamru is reached by a sealed road through apple and walnut orchards, starting just west of the bridge into Sangla.

Further up the valley from Sangla are the smaller villages of **Rakcham** (3050m), 14km from Sangla, and **Chitkul** (3450m), the last stops on the old trade route to Tibet. Although quieter than Sangla, both are being developed as resorts.

Rekong Peo

☎ 01786 / elev 2290m

Rekong Peo is the main administrative centre for Kinnaur and an important transport hub, but the main reason to visit is as a stepping stone to the pretty village of Kalpa, or to obtain the permit for onward travel to Tabo in Spiti. A steep walk above town near the radio mast is the **Kinnaur Kalachakra Celestial Palace** (Mahabodhi Gompa), with a 10m-high statue of Sakyamuni and great views across to Kinner Kailash (6050m).

Known to locals as 'Peo', the town is spread out along a looping road about 10km above the Hindustan–Tibet Hwy. Most hotels are around the main bazaar at the bottom of town or uphill from the bus stand. A set of concrete steps connects the bus stand and bazaar.

There is nowhere to change money, but the State Bank of India ATM in the main bazaar accepts international cards.

The **Tourist Information Centre** (☎ 222897; ☒ 10am-5pm Mon-Sat) below the bazaar provides some local information but is mainly kept busy as a rail reservation office. It's also the place to arrange inner line permits for onward travel to Tabo in Spiti. The office issues permits (Rs150) within a few hours. Take a passport photo and photocopies of your passport and visa.

In the main bazaar, **Sap Computer** (per hr Rs50; ☒ 10am-7pm) has internet access.

SLEEPING & EATING

Ridang Hotel (☎ 222767; d Rs300-800) The best of several hotels lining the main bazaar, Ridang has a range of tidy rooms, some carpeted and all with TV. There's also a good restaurant.

Hotel Mehfil (ITBP Rd; mains Rs40-200) Uphill from the bazaar, near the start of the steps up to the

HIMACHAL PRADESH

WHAT PRICE HYDROELECTRICITY?

Until 2002, Kinnaur was one of the quietest corners of Himachal Pradesh. Then hydroelectricity took the state by storm. A series of vast concrete dams and turbine stations now harnesses the mighty force of the Sutlej River, providing power to Himachal Pradesh and most of the surrounding states. The Nathpa Jhakri power station is India's largest power plant, capable of generating 1500 megawatts – equivalent to two nuclear power stations – and there are half a dozen similar facilities strung out along the Sutlej and Baspa Rivers.

Although hydroelectricity is one of the cleanest sources of energy, the effect on the landscape of Kinnaur has been dramatic. Whole valleys have been sacrificed to create giant coffer dams, and water that once flowed serenely past forested mountains now surges out of enormous concrete pipes. The projects have flooded Kinnaur with money, leading many villages to demolish their traditional wood and stone houses and rebuild in concrete and steel. Other villages have vanished completely beneath reservoirs, and displaced villagers have been offered minimal compensation. While hydroelectricity is undeniably improving the quality of life for Kinnauris, the loss of natural habitats and cultural heritage will be felt for generations.

---

bus stand, Mehfil serves some of the coldest beer in North India, and a big range of veg and nonveg food.

GETTING THERE & AWAY

The bus stand is 2km from the main bazaar by road or 500m by the steps that start by the police compound at the top of ITBP Rd.

Buses run roughly hourly to Shimla (Rs220, 10 hours) from 4am to 7pm, via Jeori (for Sarahan; Rs150, four hours) and Rampur (Rs100, five hours). To Sangla there are direct buses at 9.30am and 4pm (Rs40, three hours) or you can take any bus heading south and change at Karcham (Rs20, one hour).

For Spiti, there's a 7.30am bus to Kaza (Rs150, 12 hours) via Nako (Rs95, five hours) and Tabo (Rs130, 10 hours). A second bus leaves for Tabo at 4pm. You need an inner line permit to travel on this route – see boxed text, p337. Also see p396 for more on this route.

Local buses run frequently from the main bazaar to Kalpa (Rs10, 30 minutes), or you can take a chartered taxi (Rs200) or shared taxi (Rs30). Taxis charge Rs1000 to Sangla and Rs4000 to Shimla or Kaza.

Kalpa
☎ 01786 / elev 2960m

Reached by a winding road above Rekong Peo, Kalpa is one of the most peaceful villages in Kinnaur, and the views across to Kinner Kailash are nothing short of uplifting. The surrounding orchards and forest provide easy walks but you can easily just while away a few hours wandering the narrow cobbled streets and watching the villagers go about

their business. There are several simple but good-value guest houses in the village, plus a growing number of modern hotels on the ridge above town.

According to legend, this was the winter home of Shiva, and there are some impressive Kinnauri-style temples in the **Narayan-Nagini** temple complex, plus a colourful **Buddhist temple** at the top of the village. In September/October villagers pile wildflowers in the centre of the village as part of the annual **Phulech Festival** (see boxed text, p335).

SLEEPING & EATING

The following hotels are booked solid during the Durga Puja holiday season (September/October) and offer discounts at other times.

Hotel Blue Lotus (☎ 226001; dm Rs150, d Rs300-900) On the main road through the village, this neat place has a big range of rooms and a wide, sunny terrace facing directly across to the mountains – ideal for an early breakfast.

our pick Chini Bungalow (☎ 226385; r Rs300-650; closed Nov-Mar) Signposted up the lane branching right past Hotel Blue Lotus, this cute lemon yellow cottage has a flowery garden facing the mountains, simple but clean and comfy rooms, and friendly owners.

Kailash View Guesthouse (☎ 226026; d Rs550-750, without bathroom Rs 150) Further along from Chini Bungalow up the same path through fields above the village, Kailash View looks out over orchards and mountains. It's a modern building but the simple rooms have a villagey feel.

Hotel Kinner Villa (☎ 226006; r Rs1200-1800) Reached via a steep 1km walk through orchards and farmland beyond the village, Kinner Villa is the pick of Kalpa's guest houses. Rooms have superb mountain views and there are heated lounges with big windows facing the valley for winter.

For meals, try the restaurant at the Blue Lotus or the string of *dhabas* (snack bars) on the road down to the Buddhist temple.

GETTING THERE & AWAY
Local minibuses run throughout the day between Kalpa and Rekong Peo (Rs10, 30 minutes), or you can take a taxi (Rs30/200 shared/chartered) or walk – follow the well-worn stepped path rather than the winding road.

CENTRAL HIMACHAL PRADESH

Central Himachal is dominated by the Kullu and Parvati Valleys – famous for the production of woollen shawls and charas. The area is popular with hippies, honeymooners, trekkers and adrenaline junkies, and is home to Manali, one of the state's main travellers' centres. This is also the main route northwards, and many people continue from Manali over Rohtang La (3978m) to Lahaul, Spiti and Ladakh.

For more information on Kullu district, see the websites www.kullu.net and http://hpkullu.nic.in.

MANDI
☎ 01905 / pop 27,400 / elev 800m
Formerly a trading stop on the salt route to Tibet, Mandi is the gateway to the Kullu Valley and the junction of the main roads from Kullu, Chandigarh and Pathankot. It's certainly no tourist town, and it feels more Punjabi than Himalayan, with a large Sikh community and a sticky air reminiscent of the plains. Sprawling around the confluence of the Beas River and the Suketi Khad stream, the town is dotted with ancient Shaivite temples – at least 81, according to official figures – and you can do a day trip into the hills to visit the holy lakes at Rewalsar and Prashar.

Orientation & Information
Mandi is centred on an interesting sunken shopping complex called Indira Market, arranged around a pretty garden square, with the steps leading to the Raj Mahal Palace on one side. The bus stand is on the east side of the Beas River, a Rs15 autorickshaw ride away.

There isn't anywhere to change travellers cheques, but there are international ATMs at the State Bank of India and HDFC around the market square, while Evening Plaza Hotel can change US dollars (cash). There are several internet cafes around the square.

Sights & Activities
Mandi is crammed with stone temples, most of them spread out along the river. The brightly painted **Bhutnath Mandir**, dating from the 7th century AD, is the focal point for the animated **Shivaratri Festival** (see boxed text, p335) in February, honouring Lord Shiva.

If you follow Bhutnath Bazar to the river, you'll find bathing ghats (steps or landings) with a giant statue of **Hanuman** and a long avenue of carved stone *sikharas* (Hindu temple-spires). Most impressive are the **Panch Bahktar** and **Triloknath** mandirs, facing each other across the river. Also worth seeking out is the **Akardash Rudar** mandir, near the British-built bridge over the Beas.

Perched at the top of Tarna Hill is **Rani Amrit Kaur Park**, with superb views and the colourful **Syamakali Temple**, decorated with paintings of the various bloodthirsty incarnations of Kali. You can walk the 5km from town or take an autorickshaw (Rs50).

Sleeping & Eating
There are several hotels and places to eat conveniently lining Indira Market.

Shiva Hotel (☎ 224221; r Rs300-400) Above the market opposite the palace, Shiva is a modest but inexpensive hotel. There's a small restaurant and bar, and the more-expensive front rooms overlook the orderly bustle in the central market square.

Evening Plaza Hotel (☎ 225123; d Rs250-660, with AC Rs880; ✷) A few doors up from Shiva Hotel, this is a reliable cheapie offering clean rooms with TVs and a resident moneychanger. Front-facing rooms are best.

our pick **Raj Mahal Palace Hotel** (☎ 222401; www.rajmahalpalace.com; r from Rs600, with AC Rs1540, ste Rs1650-2300; ✷) Mandi's most romantic hotel, this refurbished heritage place occupies part of the palace of Mandi's royal family. Tucked in behind the dilapidated main palace buildings, the rooms are bright, cosy and clean, some with the air of a colonial hunting lodge, some with a modern chalet design. The Garden Restaurant here (mains Rs60 to Rs160, open 7am to 11pm) is the best in town, set under trees, with a choice of indoor and outdoor dining, excellent veg and nonveg food and the Copacabana Bar.

Treat Restaurant (Indira Market; dishes Rs30-130) On the lower level of the market square, this small but swish restaurant is a popular meeting spot and serves up Chinese and South Indian food in air-conditioned comfort.

Getting There & Away
BUS
The bus station is across the river in the eastern part of town. Local buses run to Rewalsar (Rs20, 1½ hours, hourly) until early evening.

TAXI
Taxis at the bus station charge Rs800 to Kullu, Rs700 to Bhuntar airport and Rs600 for a return trip to Rewalsar. Expect to pay around Rs1500 per day for longer trips to the Banjar Valley and Great Himalayan National Park.

REWALSAR LAKE
☎ 01905 / elev 1350m
High in the hills about 24km southwest of Mandi, the sacred lake of Rewalsar is revered by Buddhists, Hindus and Sikhs. The Indian scholar Padmasambhava departed from Rewalsar in the 8th century AD to spread Buddhism to Tibet, and Hindus, Buddhists and Sikhs came together here in the 17th century to plan their resistance against ethnic cleansing by the Mughals.

A scenic country road winds up to the village, which clings to the side of the small lake. Here you'll find the ochre-red **Drikung Kagyu Gompa**, with an active *thangka* (Tibetan cloth painting) school, academy of Buddhist studies and a large, central Sakyamuni statue. Just beyond is the pale blue **gurdwara** (Sikh temple) built in honour of Gobind Singh in the 1930s. In the other direction, the **Tso-Pema Ogyen Herukai Nyingmapa Gompa** has artful murals and atmospheric *pujas* (offerings or prayers) in the morning and afternoon. Uphill from the lake is the towering white **Zigar Drukpa Kagyud Institute**, with outsized statues of tantric deities. A 12m-high statue of Padmasambhava on the hill above the lake is easily seen from the village. On the far side of the lake are a number of small **Hindu temples** dedicated to

BUSES FROM MANDI			
Destination	Fare (Rs)	Duration (hr)	Frequency
Aut	38	1	half-hourly
Bhuntar airport	58	2	half-hourly
Chandigarh	140	6	10 daily
Delhi	230/560 (ordinary/deluxe)	12	10 daily
Dharamsala	125	6	6 daily
Kullu	68	2½	half-hourly
Manali	105	4	half-hourly
Shimla	140	6	hourly

the sage Rishi Lomas, who was forced to do penance here as a dedication to Shiva.

Local taxi drivers can arrange tours to other temples and viewpoints around the lake, including the **Padmasambhava Cave** on the ridge, where Padmasambhava allegedly meditated (you can also walk here from the lakeshore).

At the ghats on the northwestern side of the lake is a remarkable fish-feeding frenzy where hundreds of fish practically jump out of the water to get to the puffed rice being thrown in by pilgrims.

Sleeping & Eating
Drikung Kagyu Gompa Guesthouse (☎ 240364; www.dk-petsek.org; r without bathroom Rs100-200) The guest house at the red gompa has simple but cosy quarters for pilgrims and nonpilgrims. Bucket hot water is included.

Nyingmapa Gompa Guesthouse (☎ 240226; r Rs200-300) These austere but clean rooms are provided for Buddhist pilgrims; however, anyone is welcome to stay.

Hotel Lotus Lake (☎ 240239; hlotuslake@yahoo.com; r Rs300-550) Facing the lake, this spotless modern place is Buddhist-run and the bright rooms, with TV and hot water, are a bargain.

There are several *dhabas* and simple Buddhist restaurants. **Topchen Restaurant** (Rs25-50), opposite the Nyingmapa gompa, does good *momos* and *thukpa* from its balcony location. **Kora Community Cafe** (Rs30-80), near Hotel Lotus Lake, is good for coffee, Tibetan snacks and a veg thali.

Getting There & Away
Frequent buses go to Rewalsar from Mandi (Rs20, 1½ hours), making for an easy day

trip. A taxi from Mandi costs Rs 450/600 one way/return.

MANDI TO KULLU

About 15km south of Kullu near the village of Bajaura is **Basheshar Mahadev**, the largest stone temple in the Kullu Valley. Built in the 8th century AD and intricately carved, the temple is a larger version of the classic hut-style *sikhara* seen all over the Kullu Valley.

Hidden away in the hills between Mandi and Bajaura is scenic **Prashar Lake** (2730m), home to the striking, pagoda-style **Prashara Temple**, built in the 14th century in honour of the sage Prashar Rishi. Prashar is an 8km walk from the village of Kandi on the Mandi–Bajaura road, accessible by local bus (ask for times at the bus stand).

Southeast of Mandi is the little-visited **Banjar Valley**, offering peaceful walks and trips to unspoiled villages. The town of **Banjar** has a few simple hotels, and you can hike the steep 6km to the village of **Chaini** to see one of the tallest temple towers in Himachal – damaged by the 1905 earthquake but still impressive at seven storeys. A popular longer walk is the trek to the 3223m **Jalori Pass**.

GREAT HIMALAYAN NATIONAL PARK

This 750-sq-km **national park** (☎ 01902-265320; www.greathimalayannationalpark.com; per day Indian/foreigner Rs10/200, camera Rs50/150, video camera Rs2500/5000) was established in 1984 to preserve a home to 180 species of birds and rare mammals, such as black bears, brown bears, musk deer and the ever-elusive snow leopard. As well as conserving wildlife, the park runs programs that provide a sustainable income for people living on the periphery of the conservation area.

Wildlife is best spotted on a five- to eight-day organised trek, accompanied by a park ranger. Arrangements can be made through the park rangers at the Sai Ropa Tourist Centre, 5km before Gushaini, or with private companies in Manali. You need travel insurance that covers emergency helicopter evacuations.

To get here, catch any bus on the Mandi–Manali route to Aut, then take a taxi to the park entrance.

BHUNTAR

☎ 01902

Bhuntar is a highway town with the main airport for the Kullu Valley (the airport is smack in the centre of town, by the Beas River) and a handful of hotels catering to airline passengers. This is also the junction town for buses to the beautiful Parvati Valley. Most travellers merely pass through on the road to or from Manali or Kasol, or stay at Kullu, 10km down the road.

Bhuntar has a State Bank of India ATM, which is the last place you're able to get cash with the plastic if you're headed to the Parvati Valley.

Sleeping & Eating

There are a few choices opposite the airport, and 500m north in the main bazaar.

Hotel SunBeam (☎ 265790; d Rs250-700) A decent budget choice with dependable rooms and the Yamini Restaurant.

Hotel Amit (☎ 265123; d Rs400-1900) Next door to Hotel Sunbeam, Amit offers smarter rooms with welcome mod cons – TV, phones, carpets and a reliable restaurant.

There are several *dhabas* at the bus stand, or more-substantial meals are available at **Malabar Restaurant** (mains Rs40-120), opposite the airport.

Getting There & Away

AIR

The airport is next to the bus stand. **Kingfisher Air** (www.flykingfisher.com) has a daily flight to Delhi (US$95, one hour and 20 minutes).

Jagson Airlines (☎ 265222; www.jagsonairlines.com; Bhuntar airport; ☒ 8am-5pm) has short-hop flights from Delhi to Bhuntar and on to Dharamsala on Tuesday, Thursday and Saturday, and from Delhi to Bhuntar via Shimla on Monday, Wednesday and Friday. Baggage limit is a measly 10kg.

BUS

There are very regular services to Manali (Rs48, three hours), Kullu (Rs11, 30 minutes) and Mandi (Rs58, two hours). Buses to other destinations pass through three hours after leaving Manali. For the Parvati Valley, there are regular services to Manikaran (Rs32, three hours) via Kasol (Rs25, 2½ hours) and Jari (Rs20, one hour).

TAXI

The taxi stand is in front of the airport. Fares include Jari (Rs450); Kasol (Rs600); Kullu (Rs250); Manali (Rs1000); Mandi (Rs650) and Manikaran (Rs800)

HIMACHAL PRADESH

PARVATI VALLEY

☎ 01902

The Parvati River winds from the highway at Bhuntar to the hot springs at Manikaran and beyond, and the sublime surrounding valley is a popular traveller hang-out. Over the years the Parvati Valley has developed a well-deserved reputation for its wild and cultivated crops of charas (marijuana) – as well as its natural beauty. A couple of villages along the river have been transformed into hippie resorts, offering cheap accommodation, international food and a nonstop reggae soundtrack to crowds of dreadlocked and taffeta-skirted travellers. There are some excellent treks in the area – including the trek to the intriguing mountain village of Malana, over the Chandrakani Pass to Naggar, or across the Pin-Parvati Pass to Spiti. For safety reasons, solo trekking is not recommended – see boxed text, below.

Jari & Malana

About halfway along the Parvati Valley, **Jari** is a busy little village straddling the highway, but it's the quietest of the traveller hang-outs in the valley. Most travellers stay above the village in the peaceful hamlet of Mateura Jari.

Jari is the starting point for the trek to the mountain village of **Malana**, though a road now goes most of the way there – you can arrange a taxi in Jari, Kasol or Manikaran. Malana is an isolated sprawl of traditional wood and stone houses, and the villagers, said to be descended from Greek soldiers, have their own unique caste system and parliament. Visitors must wait on the outskirts of the village to be invited in and it is forbidden to touch any of the villagers or their belongings – including homes, temples or buildings (there's a Rs1000 fine for breaking this rule).

There are a few guest houses above the village proper, where foreigners are welcome to stay overnight for around Rs100. A taxi (Rs450 one way from Jari) will take you to the end of the road, from where it's a steep 1½-hour walk up to the village. Carry your passport as you must show it to security at the hydroelectric plant. It's possible to walk the 17km all the way to Malana, both from Jari and from Kasol. **Negi's Himalayan Adventure** (☎ 276119; www.negis-himalayan-adventure.com) in Jari can organise local treks, including the trip to Malana.

SLEEPING & EATING

Most guest houses are a steep 1.5km walk above Jari through cornfields to the little hamlet of Mateura Jari – follow the guest house signs from the main road.

Village Guest House (☎ 276070; s/d without bathroom Rs50/100; 🖳) This large, welcoming guest house is the first place you come to in Mateura Jari, with a big walled garden and rooms in several old village houses. The owners are very welcoming and the spotless rooms are a bargain. Meals are available.

Just uphill from Village Guest House, near some ornate wooden temples, are the laid-back **Chandra Place Guesthouse** (☎ 276049; r Rs100) and **Rooftop Guesthouse** (☎ 275434; r Rs100), both offering a pleasant, villagey vibe.

GETTING THERE & AWAY

Buses from Bhuntar to Manikaran stop in Jari (Rs20, one hour). A one-way taxi between Bhuntar and Jari is around Rs450.

WARNING – FATAL VACATIONS

Since the mid-1990s more than two dozen foreign tourists have 'disappeared' from the Kullu and Parvati Valleys – killed in accidents while trekking alone or murdered by local drug gangs. With this in mind, it makes sense to be very careful around the local drug scene. Manali charas (marijuana) has an international reputation, but dealing is a high-stakes game and, somewhere out there, there are at least a dozen bodies belonging to travellers who have fallen foul of the criminal underworld.

If you plan to head into the hills, especially around the Parvati Valley, we recommend joining an organised trek. As well as providing safety in numbers, guides can steer you around dangerous terrain and communicate with locals if you get into trouble. Avoid walking alone and always let your hotel know where you are going and when you plan to be back. Be extremely cautious about befriending sadhus (holy people) and others wandering in the hills. Though no recent disappearances have been reported, 'better safe than sorry' is the motto to live by!

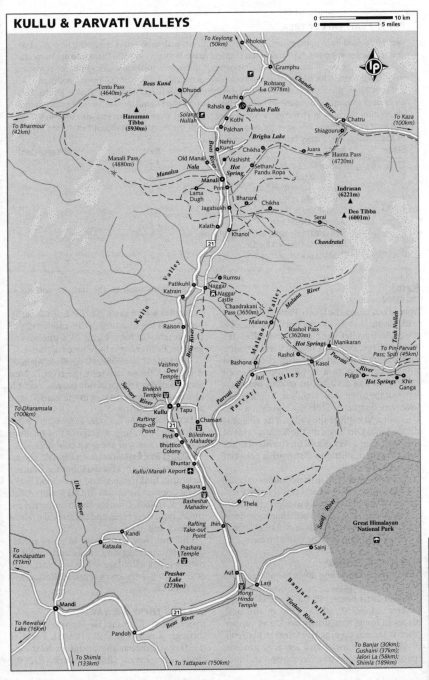

KULLU & PARVATI VALLEYS

PIN-PARVATI VALLEY TREK

Best attempted from mid-September to mid-October, this strenuous but rewarding nine-day trek crosses the snow-bound Pin-Parvati Pass (5319m) to the Pin Valley in Spiti. There's no accommodation en route so you'll have to make arrangements through a trekking agency in Kasol or Manali (see Tours, p359). The trailhead at Pulga is easily accessible by bus or taxi from Manikaran.

From Pulga, the route ascends for two days through forest and pasture to Thakur Khuha. Two more days through arid mountain country takes you to High Camp, for an overnight stop before attempting the pass. A challenging tramp over snow and scree will take you into the Pin Valley. The final stage follows the river for two days through the Pin Valley National Park to the village of Mud, which has a daily bus connection to Kaza.

Stage	Route	Duration (hr)	Distance (km)
1	Pulga to Khir Ganga	4-5	10
2	Khir Ganga to Tunda Bhuj	7-8	18
3	Tunda Bhuj to Thakur Khuha	5-6	16
4	Thakur Khuha to Pandu Bridge	6-7	12
5	Pandu Bridge to Mantalai	6-7	15
6	Mantalai to High Camp	7-8	12
7	High Camp to Pin Valley via Pin-Parvati Pass	5-6	12
8	Pin Valley to Chinpatta Maidan	6-7	14
9	Chinpatta Maidan to Mud	6-7	15

Kasol

☎ 01902

Spread out along the lovely Parvati River and with mountain views to the northeast, Kasol is the main traveller hang-out in the valley. It's a tiny village, but with reggae bars, traveller restaurants, internet cafes and cheap guest houses catering to a largely hippie/Israeli crowd, it's like a Vashaisht or Old Manali – without the large town attached. You'll either love it or loathe it. Still, it's a great base to chill out and explore the valley. The village is divided into Old Kasol on the Bhuntar side of the bridge, and New Kasol on the Manikaran side, but there's little to distinguish between the two sides.

Kasol has plenty of internet cafes charging Rs40 per hour, and several travel agents will happily change cash and travellers cheques.

From Kasol, it's a demanding four-hour walk to the mountain village of **Rashol**, where there are a couple of basic guest houses.

SLEEPING & EATING

Most guest houses close down for winter from November to April.

Alpine Guest House (☎ 273710; alpinehimachal@gmail.com; d Rs350-500, q Rs700) One of the best places in town, this sturdy brick and timber place is set among pine trees next to the river in Old Kasol. Lawns and terraces provide space for swapping traveller stories, and spacious rooms bask in the natural sounds of river and forest.

Panchali Holiday Home (☎ 273095; r Rs300-500) Set back from the main road, this modern hotel has presentable rooms with TVs, phones and geysers. Front rooms have nice balconies.

Taji Place (☎ 9816461684; d Rs150-300, cottage Rs600) A big pink house down by the river in New Kasol, Taji has a range of tidy rooms, a couple of well-equipped cottages in the garden, and a private hot spring.

Little Italy (mains Rs40-120) Pizzas and pasta dishes are better than average at this 1st-floor restaurant, and you can get a cold beer.

our pick Bhoj Restaurant (mains Rs50-150) The atmosphere inside is a bit dark, but the loungey furniture, funky music and great food make this a popular hang-out in Old Kasol. A full menu of Indian, Chinese and continental includes local river trout and desserts like 'Hello to the Queen'.

Old and New Kasol have loads of traveller restaurants serving cakes and identical menus of traveller fare – Moon Dance Cafe & German Bakery and Evergreen Restaurant are good choices.

GETTING THERE & AWAY

Buses from Bhuntar to Manikaran pass through Kasol (Rs25, 2½ hours). Fares at the taxi stand near the bridge in Kasol include Manikaran (Rs100), Jari (Rs200),

Bhuntar (Rs600), Kullu (Rs800) and Manali (Rs1600).

Manikaran

☎ 01902 / elev 1737m

With steam rising from the enormous temple beside the Parvati River, Manikaran is famous for its hot springs and is an important place of pilgrimage for Sikhs and Hindus. The name means 'Jewel from the Ear' – according to local legend, a giant snake stole earrings from Parvati while she was bathing, then snorted them out into the ground. This released the hot springs that bubble beneath. The water emerging from the ground is hot enough to boil rice (as high as 94°C) and it has to be cooled with river water for bathing. Locals claim it can cure everything from rheumatism to bronchitis.

The town is centred on the enormous multistorey **Sri Guru Nanak Ji Gurdwara**, which was built in 1940 by Sant Baba Narain Har Ji and lurks behind a veil of steam on the north side of the river. The shrine inside is revered by both Hindus and Sikhs, and the road through the village receives a steady stream of pilgrims. The shops in the bazaar peddle *prasad* and Guru Nanak souvenirs. To enter you need to remove your shoes and cover your head.

There are baths with separate facilities for men and women in the gurdwara and the village, with water diluted to a bearable temperature. The village also has several temples, including the stone hut–style **Raghunath Mandir**, and the ornate wooden **Naini Devi Temple**. Keep an eye out for pots of rice and bags of potatoes boiling in the vents, fumaroles and springs around the village and gurdwara.

SLEEPING

Manikaran is much less traveller-oriented than Kasol, but there are several budget guest houses near the gurdwara. Most hotels are on the north side of the river in the main village, reached by a suspension bridge from the bus stand.

Moon Guesthouse (☎ 273002; r Rs100-150) Close to Padha Family Guest House, Moon offers a bright, inviting bathing pool. The best rooms face the river.

Padha Family Guest House (☎ 9418408073; d Rs100-250) In the bazaar just before the gurdwara, this recommended budget place has a range of simple rooms with shared and attached bath-

rooms, a good restaurant and a square plunge pool full of spring water at ground level.

Fateh Paying Guesthouse (☎ 273767; r Rs150) Signposted down a rather dirty alley in the old part of the village, this big green house has nice rooms, welcoming owners and a cool vibe.

Country Charm (☎ 273703; d Rs500-600) On the south side of the river near the bus stand, Country Charm has good views across to the village and gurdwara, and decent rooms. The upstairs balconies practically hang out over the river.

EATING

There are several restaurants in the bazaar, but alcohol is banned on the gurdwara side of the river.

Holy Palace Restaurant (dishes Rs35-135) Travellers and pilgrims are lured here by the cosy surroundings, pop soundtrack, and a broad menu of Indian, Chinese and continental veg and nonveg food.

GETTING THERE & AWAY

Buses run regularly between Manikaran and Bhuntar (Rs32, 2½ hours), via Kasol (Rs4, 15 minutes). For Manali, change in Kullu or Bhuntar. Day trips by taxi can be arranged in Manali, Kullu or Bhuntar.

From Manikaran, taxis charge Rs100 to Kasol, Rs750 to Bhuntar, Rs950 to Kullu and Rs1500 to Manali.

KULLU

☎ 01902 / pop 18,300 / elev 1220m

Kullu is the administrative capital of the Kullu Valley and marks the beginning of the ascent to Manali. Although there's not a great deal of interest in the town itself, Kullu makes a gritty change from the hippie holiday resorts found elsewhere in the valley. In October, Kullu hosts one of the largest and loudest **Dussehra** festivals in India (see boxed text, p335). Over 200 idols are paraded into town from surrounding temples, led by a huge rath (chariot) holding the statue of Lord Raghunath from the Raghunath Temple in Sultanpur. Simultaneously, a week-long carnival and market is held on the maidan (parade ground), with entertainment such as acrobats and musicians. With some 30,000 devotees hitting town, accommodation is scarce, but it's an easy day trip from Manali or even Kasol.

Orientation & Information

Kullu is divided in two by the Sarvari River. The southern part of town has the taxi stand, tourist office and most restaurants and hotels. The bus station and Raghunath Temple are north of the river – take the short cut down through the bazaar below the Hotel Shobla International.

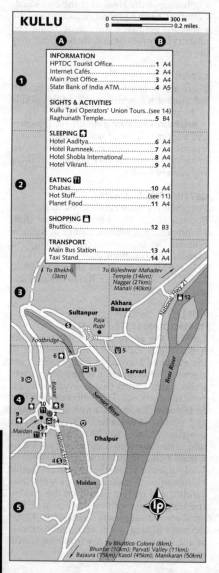

KULLU

0   300 m
0   0.2 miles

INFORMATION
HPTDC Tourist Office.......................1 A4
Internet Cafés.................................2 A4
Main Post Office.............................3 A4
State Bank of India ATM..................4 A5

SIGHTS & ACTIVITIES
Kullu Taxi Operators' Union Tours..(see 14)
Raghunath Temple...........................5 B4

SLEEPING 🛏
Hotel Aaditya..................................6 A4
Hotel Ramneek................................7 A4
Hotel Shobla International.................8 A4
Hotel Vikrant..................................9 A4

EATING 🍴
Dhabas..10 A4
Hot Stuff...................................(see 11)
Planet Food...................................11 A4

SHOPPING 🛍
Bhuttico...12 B3

TRANSPORT
Main Bus Station............................13 A4
Taxi Stand.....................................14 A4

To Bhekhli (3km)
To Bijleshwar Mahadev Temple (14km); Naggar (21km); Manali (40km)
National Hwy 21
Akhara Bazaar
Sultanpur
Raja Rupi
Footbridge
Bees River
Sarvari
Bazaar
Sarvari River
Dhalpur
Maidan
National Hwy 21
Maidan
To Bhuttico Colony (8km); Bhuntar (10km); Parvati Valley (11km); Bajaura (15km); Kasol (45km); Manikaran (50km)

The **HPTDC tourist office** (☎ 222349; 🕑 10am-5pm Mon-Sat) is near the taxi stand on the maidan. It's useful for booking deluxe HPTDC buses, which leave from outside.

The main post office is uphill from the taxi stand. There are internet cafes on the main road in Dhalpur charging Rs30 per hour.

There's an international ATM at the State Bank of India, south of the maidan.

Sights & Activities

The pre-eminent temple in Kullu is the **Raghunath Temple**, just north of the centre in Sultanpur. There are several shrines devoted to Raghunath (Rama), and the revered idol is paraded through town during Dussehra. To get there, take either of the two tracks leading uphill opposite the bus station and look for the gateway near the imposing **Raja Rupi**, the former palace of the rajas of Kullu.

There are several important temples in the surrounding hills, accessible by taxi or local bus (ask for times at the bus stand). About 3km from Kullu, in the village of Bhekhli, the **Bhekhli Temple** (Jagannathi Devi Temple) offers an impressive vista over Kullu and the valley.

Reached via a 3km trek from Chansari, 11km southeast of Kullu on the east bank of the Beas, the hilltop temple of **Bijleshwar Mahadev** (Bijli Mahadev) is surmounted by a 20m wooden pole that attracts divine blessings in the form of lightning. The surge of power shatters the stone Shiva lingam inside the temple, which is then glued back together with butter.

Tours

The **Kullu Taxi Operators' Union** (☎ 222332) offers sightseeing tours from the taxi stand for around Rs800.

Sleeping

Hotel Vikrant (☎ 222756; d Rs300-600) Centrally located down a quiet alley behind the maidan, Vikrant is a good budget choice. The upper-floor rooms are bigger and brighter than those on the ground floor, but all have TVs and hot showers.

Hotel Aaditya (☎ 222713; d Rs380-770) Just across the footbridge from the bus station at the southern end of the bazaar, Aaditya is a lurid multistorey hotel with a good range of rooms – best are the top-floor rooms with balconies overlooking the river.

Hotel Ramneek (☎ 222558; hotel_ramneek@yahoo .co.in; d Rs500-650) Up behind the maidan, Ramneek is a big pink-and-purple place spread over three levels with decent-sized rooms opening onto common balconies.

Hotel Shobla International (☎ 222800; www.shobla international.com; r Rs1320-1650, ste Rs2200-3300; ⌘) Although this is the best of the business hotels in Kullu's centre, rooms in this modern hotel near the bazaar don't really live up to the price tag. There's a good restaurant and bar.

Eating
There are numerous *dhabas* clustered around the taxi stand and bus station, and plenty of cheap eats in the narrow bazaar. The restaurant at Hotel Shobla International is also worth trying.

Hot Stuff (mains Rs50-250; ☻ 7am-9.30pm) A brightly lit fast-food place near the tourist office, Hot Stuff has a good cheap menu of Indian, Chinese and international favourites including pizzas and tandoori chicken. There's a small terrace with tables out the front.

Planet Food (mains from Rs50-250; ☻ 9am-11pm) Apart from the dirty tablecloths and naff name, this multilevel restaurant next to Hot Stuff has a similar menu of Indian veg and nonveg, Chinese, pizzas and burgers. Upstairs is a bar with pool hall at the front and a small, male-oriented drinking den at the back.

Shopping
Kullu has several outlets selling the valley's famous shawls, or you can buy at the source at the huge Bhuttico hand-loom centre just south of Kullu – see boxed text, p356. There's another Bhuttico Store in Akhara Bazaar.

Getting There & Away
AIR
The airport for Kullu is 10km south at Bhuntar – see p349.

BUSES FROM KULLU			
Destination	Fare (Rs)	Duration	Frequency
Aut	30	1½hr	every 15min
Bhuntar Airport	12	30min	every 10min
Manali	38	1½hr	every 10min
Mandi	68	2½hr	every 10min
Manikaran	48	3hr	hourly

TAXIS FROM KULLU	
Destination	Fare (Rs)
Bhuntar	250
Jari	600
Kasol	750
Manali	750
Mandi	1150
Manikaran	800
Naggar	550

BUS
On the north side of the Sarvari River, the bus station has frequent services around the valley. Buses from Manali to destinations outside the Kullu Valley arrive in Kullu about 1½ hours after departure – see p365 for more details.

See the table, left, for useful buses around the valley.

TAXI
The taxi stand on the maidan books tours and charter trips – a day of sightseeing costs Rs800.

Getting Around
Autorickshaws provide services around Kullu; trips in town should cost around Rs30.

NAGGAR
☎ 01902 / elev 1760m
Centred on imposing Naggar Castle, the slumbering village of Naggar was the capital of Kullu for 1500 years. Russian painter Nikolai Roerich set up home here in the early 20th century, ensuring a steady stream of Russian tourists. The village lies on the back road between Kullu and Manali but everything of interest is around the castle, 2km uphill. You can check your email at several small internet cafes and, although it's an easy day trip from Manali, there are some decent guest houses and restaurants around the castle.

Sights & Activities
NAGGAR CASTLE
Built by the Sikh rajas of Kullu in 1460, this beautiful fort (foreigner Rs15; ☻ 7am-10pm) is a fine example of the alternating stone and timber style of Himachali architecture. It was converted into a hotel in 1978 when the last raja fell on hard times. There's a tiny one-room **museum** downstairs, and the **Jagtipath Temple** in the courtyard houses a slab of stone said to

HIMACHAL PRADESH

SHOPPING FOR SHAWLS

The Kullu Valley is famous for its shawls, and the highway between Bhuntar and Manali is lined with scores of shops, showrooms and emporiums dedicated to selling traditional Kullu shawls. The shawls are woven on wooden hand-looms using wool from sheep, pashmina goats or angora rabbits. This is one of the main industries in the Kullu Valley and it provides an income for thousands of local women, many of whom have organised themselves into shawl-weaving cooperatives. You can tour several of these around Kullu and buy shawls directly from the women who make them.

With so much competition, the sales pressure in touristy places can be fairly overbearing and you'll have to haggle hard for a bargain. For high quality without the hard sell, head to the nearest branch of **Bhuttico** (www.bhutticoshawls.com), the Bhutti Weavers' Cooperative, which has showrooms in Manali, Kullu, Bhuntar and other major towns around the state. Established in 1944 by a group of village women, Bhuttico charges fixed prices, so it's a good place to gauge price and quality. Expect to pay upwards of Rs300 for lambswool, from Rs1000 for angora, from Rs3000 for pashmina and Rs6500 for the exquisitely embroidered shawls worn by village women.

have been carried here by wild bees. The best way to experience the castle is to stay here, and there's also a restaurant – see right.

ROERICH GALLERY & URUSVATI MUSEUM

The main road through the village continues for 2km to **Roerich Gallery** (☎ 248290; www .roerichtrust.org; adult/child combined admission to folk & art museum Rs30/20, camera/video Rs25/60; ❧ 10am-1pm & 1.30-6pm Tue-Sun, to 5pm Nov-Mar), the former home of eccentric Russian painter Nikolai Roerich, who died in Naggar in 1947. The lower floors display some of Roerich's surreally colourful paintings of Kullu, Spiti and Lahaul, while the upper floors preserve the artist's private rooms. Roerich was also the brains behind the Roerich Pact, a treaty signed by more than 60 countries guaranteeing the preservation of cultural monuments around the world.

A five-minute walk uphill from the gallery is the **Urusvati Himalayan Folk & Art Museum** (admission with the gallery ticket), which houses the painter's personal collection of ethnological artefacts and photos of the Roerich family.

TEMPLES

Heading down the track beside the castle, you'll pass the handsome 11th-century **Vishnu Mandir**, covered in ornate carvings. Downhill past the tiny post office is the **Gauri Shankar Temple**, dedicated to Shiva and surrounded by smaller temples devoted to Narayan (an incarnation of Vishnu). Just below Roerich Gallery is the pagodalike **Tripura Sundari Devi Temple**, surrounded by carved wooden out-

buildings. High up on the ridge above Naggar, the **Murlidhar Krishna Temple** is reached by a woodland path beyond the Roerich Gallery.

TREKKING

Naggar is the starting point for the excellent three-day trek to Malana village and Jari via Chandrakhani Pass (3660m). Ravi Sharma at Poonam Mountain Lodge (see below) is an experienced operator who can organise this trek, as well as all-inclusive longer treks around the Kullu Valley to Manikaran, Lahaul and Spiti and Ladakh for around Rs1700 per day. Four-wheel-drive safaris cost around Rs2500 per day.

Sleeping & Eating

Hotels are clustered around the castle or there's a village-style guest house downhill in the small hamlet of Chanalti Naggar.

Chanderlok Guesthouse (☎ 248213; d Rs200-300) About five minutes' walk downhill on the path below the castle, this peaceful, family-run village guest house has a few neat, sun-filled rooms and a blooming garden full of old Hindu shrines.

Poonam Mountain Lodge (☎ 248248; www.poonam lodge.com; s Rs250, d Rs300-350; ▢) Just below the castle, the wood-panelled rooms at this well-kept lodge are cosy and comfortable, and the owner, Ravi Sharma, is a mine of local trekking information. For longer stays you can rent his traditional stone-and-timber two-storey house in the nearby village for Rs5000 a month.

Hotel Ragini (☎ 248185; raginihotel@hotmail.com; r Rs800-1200; ▢) Ragini is a clean, modern hotel that's popular with tour groups for its bright rooms with parquet floors and balconies, and a garden used for yoga and other holistic activities. The rooftop restaurant serves great food.

Castle Hotel (☎ 248316; www.hptdc.gov.in; d Rs1050-2650) The most atmospheric place to stay is the castle itself, but with all rooms recently refurbished, there are no longer any budget opportunities. Wood and stone corridors open onto a wide variety of rooms, some original and decked out in colonial finery, others completely refurbished. The views from valley side rooms are superb. Even if the hotel isn't within your budget, there's a good restaurant and terrace overlooking the valley.

La Purezza (meals Rs50-120; ⏱ 11am-10pm, closed winter) On the road to Roerich Gallery, this rooftop cafe serves decent pizza and pasta.

Getting There & Away

Local buses run regularly between Manali and Naggar from 6am to 6pm (Rs20, one hour). A return taxi from Manali to Naggar costs Rs650, and from Kullu it's Rs750.

MANALI

☎ 01902 / pop 4400 / elev 2050m
With super views of the Dhauladhar and Pir Panjal Ranges, and the fast-flowing Beas River running through the town, Manali is a year-round magnet for tourists. Backpackers come to hang out in the hippie villages around the main town; adventure tourists come for trekking, paragliding, rafting and skiing; and Indian honeymoon couples or families come for the cool mountain air and their first taste of snow on a day trip to Rohtang La. Over the years, many tourists have been lured here by the famous Manali charas, but be warned – it's still illegal and local police do arrest people for possession (or sting them for bribes).

Until the 1960s there was nothing much to Manali but a few old stone houses and temples, but today the main town is crammed with concrete hotels and tacky resorts, especially on the highway south of town – most travellers stay in the villages of Vashisht or Old Manali, which still have a relaxed vibe and plenty of traveller services.

As the main jumping-off point for Ladakh, Spiti and Lahaul, it makes sense to unwind here for a few days before continuing the long journey into the mountains. Daily buses and 4WDs to Leh, Keylong and Kaza leave from approximately June to October.

According to legend, Manu, the Hindu equivalent of Noah, alighted his boat here to recreate human life after floods destroyed the world. Indeed, from April to June and September to late October it can feel as if all of humanity has returned to Manali. There's another surge in visitors for Christmas and New Year. Prices for rooms can more than triple at these times. Old Manali and Vashisht close for winter from around October to May.

Orientation

Manali's main street is the Mall, part of the highway that runs into town. The bus and taxi stands are here and most hotels and restaurants are on alleys to the west. Two roads run north from Manali along the Beas River – one to Old Manali on the west bank and one to Vashisht and the Rohtang La on the east bank.

Information

BOOKSHOPS

Bookworm (Map p360; ☎ 252920; ⏱ 10am-6pm) For novels and travel literature. There's also a branch in the NAC Market.

INTERNET ACCESS

Many travel agencies offer internet access, and there are numerous internet cafes in Old Manali and Vashisht charging Rs30 to Rs40 per hour. The following places are in town.
Cafe Digital (Map p360; Manu Market; per hr Rs50; ⏱ 8am-11pm)
Email Cafe (Map p360; Model Town; per hr Rs50; ⏱ 10am-8pm)

MEDICAL SERVICES

Manali Civil Hospital (Off Map p360; ☎ 253385) Just south of town.

MONEY

Banks in Manali don't offer foreign exchange but there are private moneychangers, and the State Bank of India has two international ATMs – the one at the bank branch south of the pedestrian mall has shorter queues. If you are heading north to Ladakh, Lahaul or Spiti, change some extra money here.
HDFC Forex (Map p360; The Mall; ⏱ 9.30am-7.30pm) Changes cash and cheques.

POST

Manali sub-post office (Map p360; Model Town; ⏱ 9.30am-5.30pm Mon-Sat) For poste restante and parcels (before 2pm only).

MANALI & VASHISHT

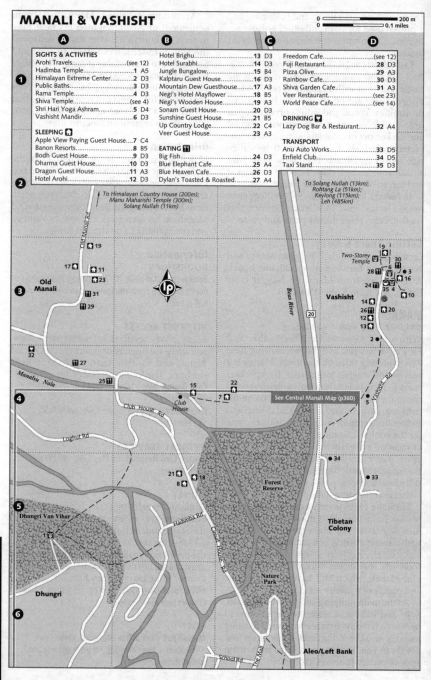

SIGHTS & ACTIVITIES
Arohi Travels....................................(see 12)
Hadimba Temple...............................**1** A5
Himalayan Extreme Center..............**2** D3
Public Baths......................................**3** D3
Rama Temple....................................**4** D3
Shiva Temple..................................(see 4)
Shri Hari Yoga Ashram.....................**5** D4
Vashisht Mandir................................**6** D3

SLEEPING
Apple View Paying Guest House....**7** C4
Banon Resorts...................................**8** B5
Bodh Guest House.............................**9** D3
Dharma Guest House.......................**10** D3
Dragon Guest House........................**11** A3
Hotel Arohi.......................................**12** D3

Hotel Brighu....................................**13** D3
Hotel Surabhi...................................**14** D3
Jungle Bungalow.............................**15** B4
Kalptaru Guest House......................**16** D3
Mountain Dew Guesthouse............**17** A3
Negi's Hotel Mayflower..................**18** B5
Negi's Wooden House......................**19** A3
Sonam Guest House.........................**20** D3
Sunshine Guest House.....................**21** B5
Up Country Lodge............................**22** C4
Veer Guest House.............................**23** A3

EATING
Big Fish...**24** D3
Blue Elephant Cafe..........................**25** A4
Blue Heaven Cafe............................**26** D3
Dylan's Toasted & Roasted.............**27** A4

Freedom Cafe................................(see 12)
Fuji Restaurant.................................**28** D3
Pizza Olive.......................................**29** A3
Rainbow Cafe...................................**30** D3
Shiva Garden Cafe...........................**31** A3
Veer Restaurant............................(see 23)
World Peace Cafe..........................(see 14)

DRINKING
Lazy Dog Bar & Restaurant............**32** A4

TRANSPORT
Anu Auto Works...............................**33** D5
Enfield Club......................................**34** D5
Taxi Stand..**35** D3

TOURIST INFORMATION

HPTDC booking office (Map p360; ☎ 252116; the Mall; ⏰ 7am-8pm, 9am-5pm in winter) Can book seats on HPTDC buses, and rooms in HPTDC hotels.

Tourist office (Map p360; ☎ 253531; the Mall; ⏰ 8am-9pm, 10am-5pm Mon-Sat in winter) Helpful for brochures and local information. You can book train tickets at the railway booking office (open 8am to 1.30pm Monday to Saturday) next door.

Sights & Activities
HADIMBA TEMPLE

Also known as the Dhungri Temple, this ancient wood and stone **mandir** (Map p358) was erected in 1553. Pilgrims come here from across India to honour Hadimba, the wife of Bhima from the Mahabharata. The walls of the temple are covered in woodcarvings of dancers, and horns of bulls and ibex adorn the walls. Grisly animal sacrifices are carried out in May for the three-day **Dhungri Mela** (p335). Photo-wallahs loiter around the temple offering souvenir photos in traditional costume, with your arm around a yak or angora rabbit.

Ghatotkach, the son of Hadimba and Bhima, is worshipped in the form of a **sacred tree** near the temple. Villagers make offerings of knives, goat horns, and tin effigies of animals, people and houses.

Hadimba is a 20-minute walk northwest of Manali, or you can take an autorickshaw (Rs40).

MANALI MUSEUM

Opposite Hadimba Temple, the interesting **Museum of Himachal Culture & Folk Art** (Map p360; ☎ 253846; admission Rs10; ⏰ 8am-8pm) has religious relics, household objects, instruments, weapons, architectural woodcarvings and scale models of Himachal temples.

BUDDHIST MONASTERIES

There's a small Tibetan colony just south of the town centre. The **Himalayan Nyinmapa Buddhist Temple** (Map p360; ⏰ 6am-6pm) contains a two-storey statue of Sakyamuni, the historical Buddha.

Further along the same lane is the more-traditional **Gelukpa Cultural Society Gompa** (Map p360; ⏰ 6am-6pm), with an atmospheric prayer room crammed with statues of bodhisattvas (enlightened beings), revered lamas and Buddhist deities. There's also a small workshop producing Tibetan carpets.

NATURE PARKS

A large grove of deodars (cedars) on the banks of the Beas has been set aside as a **nature park** (Map p360; admission Rs5; ⏰ 9am-7pm), with a small aviary of Himalayan birds, including the monal pheasant, Himachal's state bird. South of the centre is the similar **Van Vihar Park** (Map p360; admission Rs5; ⏰ 8am-7pm, to 5pm in winter), with a children's park.

OLD MANALI

About 2.5km above the Mall on the far side of the Manalsu Nala stream, Old Manali still has some of the feel of an Indian mountain village. There are some beautiful old houses, and the wood and stone **Manu Maharishi Temple** (Off Map p358) is built on the site where Manu is said to have meditated after landing the boat that saved humanity. A trail to Solang Nullah (11km) runs north from here through the village of Goshal (2km).

DIRECTORATE OF MOUNTAINEERING & ALLIED SPORTS

This **adventure sports centre** (Off Map p360; ☎ 250337; www.dmas.gov.in; ⏰ 10am-5pm Mon-Sat, closed 2nd Sat each month) has its headquarters at Aleo, 3km south of Manali on the east bank of the Beas. A huge range of activities can be arranged, from rafting and treks to skiing and mountaineering courses – see the website for details.

Tours

In season, the HPTDC offers day tours by bus to Naggar (Rs200), Rohtang La (Rs250) and Manikaran and the Parvati Valley (Rs275), if there are enough takers. Private travel agencies offer similar bus tours.

The **Him-Anchal Taxi Operators Union** (Map p360; ☎ 252120; the Mall) has fixed-price tours, including Rohtang La (Rs1200), Solang Nullah (Rs600) and Naggar (Rs600).

ADVENTURE TOUR OPERATORS

The following places are reliable and well established and can arrange treks, tours and adventure activities – see boxed text, p362, for popular options.

Antrek Tours & Travel (Map p360; ☎ 252292; www.antrek.co.in; 1 Rambagh, the Mall)

Arohi Travels (Map p360; ☎ 254421; www.arohiecoadventures) Located off the mall, and also has an office at Hotel Arohi in Vashisht (Map p358).

Himalayan Adventurers (Map p360; ☎ 252750; www.himalayanadventurersindia.com; 44 the Mall)

HIMACHAL PRADESH

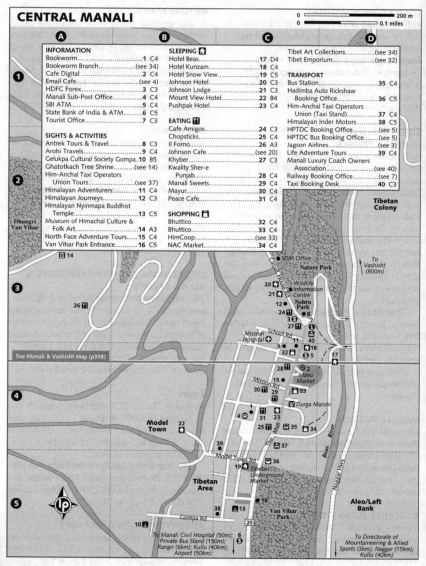

CENTRAL MANALI

INFORMATION	
Bookworm	1 C4
Bookworm Branch	(see 20)
Cafe Digital	2 C4
Email Cafe	(see 4)
HDFC Forex	3 C3
Manali Sub-Post Office	4 C4
SBI ATM	5 C4
State Bank of India & ATM	6 C5
Tourist Office	7 C3

SIGHTS & ACTIVITIES	
Antrek Tours & Travel	8 C3
Arohi Travels	9 C4
Gelukpa Cultural Society Gompa	10 B5
Ghatotkach Tree Shrine	(see 14)
Him-Anchal Taxi Operators	
Union Tours	(see 37)
Himalayan Adventurers	11 C3
Himalayan Journeys	12 C3
Himalayan Nyinmapa Buddhist	
Temple	13 C5
Museum of Himachal Culture &	
Folk Art	14 A3
North Face Adventure Tours	15 C4
Van Vihar Park Entrance	16 C5

SLEEPING 🏠	
Hotel Beas	17 D4
Hotel Kunzam	18 C3
Hotel Snow View	19 C5
Johnson Hotel	20 C3
Johnson Lodge	21 C3
Mount View Hotel	22 B4
Pushpak Hotel	23 C4

EATING 🍴	
Cafe Amigos	24 C4
Chopsticks	25 C4
Il Forno	26 A3
Johnson Cafe	(see 20)
Khyber	27 C4
Kwality Sher-e	
Punjab	28 C4
Manali Sweets	29 C4
Mayur	30 C4
Peace Cafe	31 C4

SHOPPING 🛍	
Bhuttico	32 C4
Bhuttico	33 C4
HimCoop	(see 33)
NAC Market	34 C4

Tibet Art Collections	(see 34)
Tibet Emporium	(see 32)

TRANSPORT	
Bus Station	35 C4
Hadimba Auto Rickshaw	
Booking Office	36 C5
Him-Anchal Taxi Operators	
Union (Taxi Stand)	37 C4
Himalayan Inder Motors	38 C5
HPTDC Booking Office	(see 5)
HPTDC Bus Booking Office	(see 5)
Jagson Airlines	(see 3)
Life Adventure Tours	39 C4
Manali Luxury Coach Owners	
Association	(see 40)
Railway Booking Office	(see 7)
Taxi Booking Desk	40 C3

Himalayan Extreme Center (Map p358; ☎ 9816174164; www.himalayan-extreme-center.com; Vashisht)

Himalayan Journeys (Map p360; ☎ 252365; www.himalayanjourneysindia.com; the Mall) Opposite Nehru Park.

North Face Adventure Tours (Map p360; ☎ 254041; www.northfaceindia.com; the Mall)

Sleeping

Manali has some of the best-value accommodation in the state, though prices are highest during the peak seasons of April to June, September, October and Christmas. At other times, discounts are standard, but bargain anyway. Heating is rare in Manali so be prepared to dive under a blanket to stay warm.

BUDGET

Few backpackers choose to stay in central Manali unless planning to catch an early bus – the best budget places, by far, are a short distance north in the villages of Old Manali and Vashisht (p366).

Manali

Pushpak Hotel (Map p360; ☎ 253656; d Rs300) Down an alley opposite the bus station, this is one of the better budget places along the Mall. Rooms at the back are quieter.

Mount View Hotel (Map p360; ☎ 252465; Model Town; d Rs350-750) A covering of ivy welcomes you to this slightly eccentric place that's in a quiet area a short walk off the Mall. Low-ceilinged rooms are old-style but comfortable, with TV and hot water. Mountain views are wishful thinking.

Sunshine Guest House (Map p358; ☎ 252320; Circuit House Rd; r Rs350) This rambling, creaky Raj-era property will appeal to lovers of unfussy colonial cool rather than modern comforts. Enormous rooms with fireplaces (firewood is extra) and equally giant bathrooms are a bit draughty, but the balconies, sunrooms and overgrown garden are all quaint.

Old Manali

Uphill from Manali on the far side of the Manaslu Nala stream, Old Manali is a well-established traveller centre and has Manali's best budget accommodation. Hotels are spread over a kilometre or more from the stream northwards to the village proper, but most are in an enclave about halfway along. Most places close down in late October when many locals head to Goa for the winter.

Jungle Bungalow (Map p358; ☎ 252278; s/d without bathroom Rs100/150) One of several basic backpacker places across the stream, this rickety but inexpensive guest house has sparsely furnished rooms and big communal balconies. It's on the path above the Club House.

Apple View Paying Guest House (Map p358; ☎ 253899; r without bathroom Rs150) Further east along the path from Jungle Bungalow (above), through orchard groves, this delightful village guest house is run by a friendly family.

Negi's Wooden House (Map p358; ☎ 9816319390; d Rs150-200) The simple backpacker rooms here are set back from the road and the owner offers Tibetan massage.

our pick Veer Guest House (Map p358; ☎ 252710; veerguesthouse@rediffmail.com; s Rs150, d Rs300-500) Set in a pretty garden, long-running Veer is one of Old Manali's best-value places. Rooms in the quaint lime-green original section have plenty of character, while new rooms at the front are bright and slick, with TV and private balconies. There are three singles without bathroom, and there's a chilled-out cafe and a pool table.

Up Country Lodge (Map p358; ☎ 252257; d Rs200-400) Next door to Apple View (left), this is another family-run place but the bright rooms are a step up from those at Apple View, with attached bathroom.

Mountain Dew Guesthouse (Map p358; ☎ 9816446366; d Rs250-300) This solid three-storey house on the main road has nice balconies and a garden full of fruit trees, vines and roses. Get a room up top for the best views.

MIDRANGE

Dragon Guest House (Map p358; ☎ 252290; www .dragontreks.com; Old Manali; r Rs350-850, ste Rs1800-2200; ❄ 🖳) A one-time backpackers' place moving upmarket, Dragon still has a few budget rooms on the ground floor, but the refurbished upper-floor rooms are certainly midrange and the spacious suites at the top are 'honeymoon' standard. There's also a good restaurant, an internet cafe, and a reliable travel agency for treks and tours.

Hotel Beas (Map p360; ☎ 252832; d Rs500-800, ste Rs1000-1100) This massive HPTDC-run hotel has a good location on the riverbank below the main town and clean, comfortable rooms, but it's predictably bland. Still, it's popular with coach tours so book in advance in season.

Himalayan Country House (Off Map p358; ☎ 252294; www.himalayancountryhouse.com; Old Manali; s Rs600, d Rs1200-1600) Ensconced at the end of the road in Old Manali, this four-storey stone and timber hotel overlooks the slate roofs of village homes and across to the mountains. It's beautifully designed, with traditional carved doors and compact wood-panelled rooms opening on to shared balconies.

Hotel Snow View (Map p360; ☎ 252684; www .snowviewhotelmanali.com; d Rs1100-1200, f Rs1600-1800; ❄) Right in the centre of town, Snow View is a comfortable, if nondescript, business hotel with all the mod cons you would expect for the price, as well as a bar and restaurant.

Hotel Kunzam (Map p360; ☎ 253197; the Mall; d Rs1450-1850; ❄) HPTDC has several deluxe hotels in Manali, but this one is the most central. Rooms are spacious and reasonably stylish

OUTDOOR ACTIVITIES IN MANALI

Manali is the adventure sports capital of Himachal Pradesh, and all sorts of outdoor activities can be organised through tour operators in town (see Tours, p359).

Fishing

The rivers of the Kullu and Parvati Valleys are rich in trout and mahseer. The season runs from March to June and October to November, and rods and tackle can be hired from agencies in Manali; daily fishing licences from HPTDC cost Rs100. Top spots include the upper tributaries of the Beas and Parvati Rivers at Kasol.

Jeep Safaris

Jeep safaris can be arranged to Ladakh, Lahaul and Spiti for around Rs2500 per day, visiting monasteries, mountain passes and glacial lakes, with accommodation in tents or village guesthouses.

Mountain Biking

The steep slopes around Manali offer some prime country for mountain biking. Agencies offer bike hire for Rs400 per day, or you can organise tours to Ladakh, Spiti and Lahaul. One audacious day trip is the descent from the Rohtang La – buses and taxis can transport you and your bike to the pass, then you can freewheel down. On all high-altitude routes, take time to acclimatise.

Mountaineering

Mountaineering training can be arranged through the **Directorate of Mountaineering & Allied Sports** (☎ 250337; www.dmas.gov.in). Basic 26-day mountaineering courses run on fixed dates from May to October for Rs4500/US$455 (Indian/foreigner), including food, accommodation, guides and training (minimum age 17 years). The courses cover essential mountain techniques and a series of local ascents. Local agencies can arrange expeditions to Hanuman Tibba (5930m) and Deo Tibba (6001m).

Paragliding

Paragliding is popular at Solang Nullah from April to October. Short flights start at Rs600 for a two-minute flight, but adventure tour operators can organise longer flights from surrounding take-off points for Rs1500 to Rs2500.

Rafting

White-water rafting trips on the Beas River can be arranged in Manali, starting from Pirdi, 3km downriver from Kullu. There is 14km of Grade II and III white water between Pirdi and the take-out point at Jhiri; trips cost around Rs600 per person. Book through travel agents or directly at Pirdi.

and there's a good restaurant and bar. Ask for one of the quieter rooms at the back.

TOP END

Manali has some fine upmarket hotels and all are found along Circuit House Rd, heading uphill to Old Manali.

Johnson Hotel (Map p360; ☎ 253764; www.johnson hotel.in; Circuit House Rd; d Rs1800-4500; ⊠ 🖳) This is one of several places named in honour of the Raj-era landowner Jimmy Johnson. This is a classy wood and stone hotel that has snug heritage rooms, a century-old lodge and lovely gardens, as well as an excellent restaurant.

Negi's Hotel Mayflower (Map p358; ☎ 252104; www .negismayflower.com; Club House Rd; s/d from Rs2200/2500; ⊠ 🖳) Mayflower is a stately wooden lodge with cascading balconies and spacious but cosy, wood-panelled rooms, some with open fireplaces (firewood costs extra). The lawns and gardens are a good place to relax in the afternoon.

Johnson Lodge (Map p360; ☎ 251523; www.johnsons lodge.com; Circuit House Rd; d Rs2650, cottage Rs6350; ⊠ 🖳) Built in wood and timber in the traditional Himachal style, but slick and contemporary inside, this towering hotel boasts bright, designer rooms with king beds, as well as luxurious two- and three-bedroom cottages.

Rock Climbing

The cliffs at Solang, Aleo and Vashisht have a good range of bolted and traditional routes ranging from French 6a to 6c (British 5a to 6a). Himalayan Extreme Center (p359) in Vashisht offers day trips for Rs900/700 per full-/half-day, including all equipment. Independent climbers should bring a selection of slings, nuts and cams (particularly in the smaller sizes) and a 30m or 60m rope.

Skiing & Snowboarding

From January to March, the village of Solang Nullah transforms into Himachal's main ski and snowboarding resort – see p367 for details. Skiing and showboarding equipment can be hired through tour operators in Manali or accommodation places in Solang Nullah for Rs500 per day. Year-round high-altitude skiing expeditions can be arranged on virgin powder (experienced skiers only) through Himalayan Extreme Center (p359) for around Rs2500 per day (trips last three to five days). Costly heli-skiing trips to high-altitude powder can be arranged through **Himachal Heli Adventures** (☎ 9816025899; www.himachal.com).

Walking & Trekking

Manali is a popular starting point for organised mountain treks. Most agencies offer multiday treks for around Rs2500 per day, all-inclusive. Popular options include Beas Kund (three days), the Pin-Parvati Trek from the Parvati Valley to Spiti (eight days) and the Hamta Pass (4270m) to Lahaul (five days).

Plenty of shorter walks are possible from Manali, though the usual rules on safe trekking apply – ie tell someone where you are going and never walk alone. The 13km hike up the western side of the Beas River to Solang Nullah is a pleasing alternative to the bus, or you can trek 6km to the snowline above Lama Dugh meadow along the Manalsu Nala stream.

Zorbing

During summer, the ski slope at Solang Nullah is a popular place for zorbing – basically, rolling downhill inside a giant inflatable ball. You can make arrangements in Manali or in Solang Nullah – expect to pay Rs250 for a roll down the hill.

Other Activities

Other activities available in the area include horse riding (Rs900 per day) and canyoning (Rs900 per day). Quad bike rides around Solang Nullah cost Rs500 for a quick 4km round or Rs1500 per hour. Short hot-air balloon rides are sometimes organised from Solang Nullah during summer.

Banon Resorts (Map p358; ☎ 253026; www.banon resortsmanali.com; d Rs3500, cottages from Rs8800; ⊠) The Banon family opened the first guest house in Manali, but that would have been a far cry from the luxury hotel that now hosts well-heeled tourists. Centrally heated rooms in the main hotel are spacious but plain and don't quite live up to the flashy lobby area, while the two-bedroom cottages are the last word in luxurious peace and privacy.

Eating

Manali has some fine Indian and international restaurants, and there are lots of cheap travellers' cafes in Old Manali and Vashisht.

Most restaurants serve trout sourced from local farms. The following places are open between 8am and 10pm, unless otherwise stated.

MANALI

Manali Sweets (Map p360; snacks from Rs8; ⊗ from 7am) Manali's favourite *dhaba*, serving Indian sticky sweets, hot chai, samosas and hot veg snacks from early morning to late at night.

Cafe Amigos (Map p360; Circuit House Rd; dishes Rs40-150) This reliable little traveller cafe does a good line of enchiladas, burritos and nachos, as well Tibetan, Chinese and pizzas. Good desserts, too.

Kwality Sher-e-Punjab (Map p360; the Mall; dishes Rs30-70) A bright, fast-food-style cafeteria serving pure-veg Punjabi and South Indian food.

Peace Cafe (Map p360; Siyali Mahadev Market; mains Rs45-200) Down an alley near the post office, this cosy 1st-floor Tibetan-run restaurant serves possibly Manali's biggest range of global food, from *momos* to Japanese noodles, and local river trout to Hong Kong lamb. Friendly and efficient service.

Chopsticks (Map p360; the Mall; dishes Rs60-180) The most popular traveller choice along the Mall in Manali town, this intimate Tibetan-Chinese-Japanese place is always busy. Naturally there are Indian dishes here, too, along with local trout. Cold beers and fruit wines are also served. Arrive early to secure a table in the evening.

Mayur (Map p360; Mission Rd; dishes Rs70-250) Locals rate Mayur highly for its well-prepared North and South Indian specialities. Downstairs is traditional Indian, while the contemporary upstairs bistro serves dishes such as croquettes, chicken stroganoff and, oddly, Marmite toast.

ourpick **Il Forno** (Map p360; Hadimba Rd; mains Rs80-200; 12.30-10.30pm) Perched on a hillside near Hadimba Temple, Il Forno is a genuine Italian restaurant in a superb Himachal stone and timber building. The wood-fired pizzas, calzone, lasagne and pasta dishes are prepared by a Veronese chef and you can enjoy an espresso or beer with wonderful valley views from the garden terrace.

Khyber (Map p360; the Mall; dishes Rs80-250; 8am-midnight) Upstairs by the main junction, this darkened bar and restaurant is central Manali's best place for a cold beer or bottle of fruit wine or cider. The food is also good – the speciality is meat-heavy Punjabi and Afghani cuisine but there's also Chinese, continental, and tandoori trout. Drinks are reasonably priced, and the booths are a good place to huddle.

Johnson's Cafe (Map p360; Circuit House Rd; dishes Rs120-350; 8am-10.30pm) The restaurant at Johnson Hotel is one of the best in town for European food, with dishes like lamb and mint gravy, smoked chicken, and fig and apple crumble. The restaurant-bar is cosy, but on warm evenings or sunny afternoons, the garden terrace is the place to be.

OLD MANALI

There are numerous garden restaurants serving all the usual suspects – pizzas, pita-bread wraps, *momos*, banana pancakes, apple pie – from early morning to late evening. All these places close by the start of November.

Pizza Olive (Map p358; mains Rs80-160; 9am-10pm) The aromas wafting from the pizza oven give this place an authentic Italian feel and the pizzas and pasta dishes don't disappoint. You can eat indoors or out in the garden.

Veer Restaurant (Map p358; 252710; mains Rs40-120) Located at Veer Guest House, this chilled restaurant has a big-screen TV, a library and cushions on the floor.

ourpick **Dylan's Toasted & Roasted** (Map p358; www .dylanscoffee.com; drinks & snacks Rs20-70; 8am-8pm) Manali's mellowest hang-out, this hole-in-the-wall cabin-style coffeeshop in Old Manali serves the best espresso coffee in town, cinnamon tea, hearty breakfasts, garlic cheese toast and wicked desserts like chocolate-chip cookies and 'Hello to the Queen'. DVD movies are shown in an adjoining room.

Popular backpacker restaurants include Shiva Garden Cafe and Blue Elephant Cafe near the river, both serving decent traveller fare for Rs30 to Rs120.

Drinking

Restaurants double as bars to form the centre of nightlife in Manali, and most serve alcohol. Himachal's bounteous orchards produce huge quantities of apples, pears, plums and apricots, some of which are fermented locally and made into alcoholic cider and perry (pear cider) and a wide range of strong fruit wines, from apple to plum. In Manali town, the best places for a beer or fruit wine are Khyber (p363) and Chopsticks (p363). The upmarket Johnson Hotel (p362), Johnson Lodge (p362) and Banon Resort (p362) also have good bars.

In Old Manali, most traveller cafes serve beer, including the riverside Lazy Dog Bar & Restaurant. In Vashisht, Rainbow Cafe (p367) is the place to be.

Shopping

Manali is crammed with souvenir shops selling souvenirs from Himachal, Tibet and Ladakh – most are open from 10am to 7pm. **Tibet Art Collections** (Map p360; 252974; NAC Market) has a good choice, while **Tibet Emporium** (Map p360; 252431; the Mall) stocks Tibetan knick-knacks and funky T-shirts with Tibetan messages.

Shawls are sold all over Manali. A good place to start is at the cooperative **Bhuttico** (Map p360; ☎ 260079; the Mall), which charges fair, fixed prices and has another store located in Manu Market. Several other cooperatives have shops around the Mall.

HimCoop (Map p360; the Mall) sells a wide range of locally produced organic juices, jams, dried fruit and pickles.

Getting There & Away

AIR
Manali's closest airport is 50km south at Bhuntar – see p349. You can book seats at local travel agencies or at **Jagson Airlines** (Map p360; ☎ 252843; www.jagsonairlines.com; the Mall).

BUS
The bus station has a **booth** (Map p360; ☎ 252323; ☾ 5am-7pm) for advance bookings.

Luxury buses are run by the **HPTDC** (Map p360; ☎ 252116; the Mall) and **Manali Luxury Coach Owners Association** (Map p360; ☎ 253816; the Mall). Tickets can be bought from their offices or from travel agencies thronging the Mall.

Kullu & Parvati Valleys
Buses go to Kullu every 30 minutes (Rs37, 1½ hours), continuing to Mandi (Rs110, four hours) via the airport at Bhuntar (Rs50, two hours). Regular local services run to Naggar (Rs20, one hour) from 6am to 6pm. For the Parvati Valley, change at Bhuntar.

Leh
From 15 July to 15 September, buses make the bone-shaking ascent to Leh in two exhausting but spectacular days, with a stopover en route at Keylong or Sarchu. Bring a shawl or warm clothing and be alert to the symptoms of Acute Mountain Sickness (AMS; see p1198).

Government buses (Rs585) leave at 1pm, with an overnight stop in Keylong. Private buses run till around mid-October, charging about Rs1500 and stopping at Keylong or Sarchu.

Lahaul & Spiti
The Rohtang La, on the road between Manali and Keylong, is normally open from June to late October and the Kunzum La, between Manali and Spiti, is open from July to mid-October (exact dates depend on snow conditions).

In season, there are regular buses to Keylong between 4am and 1pm (Rs110, six hours). For Spiti, buses leave for Kaza (Rs192, 10 hours) at 5.30am and 6am; the 5.30am service continues to Tabo (Rs230, 13 hours).

Delhi & Chandigarh
The most comfortable options for Delhi are the daily HPTDC buses to the Himachal Tourism office on Janpath in Delhi. The deluxe bus leaves at 5pm (Rs615, 14 hours), while the AC Volvo coach leaves at 6.30pm (Rs815 to Rs990). All buses run via Chandigarh (Rs385, 10 hours). Book at the HPTDC booking office.

Private travel agencies run similar services to Delhi's Paharganj, but make sure you're getting a deluxe bus all the way through to Delhi.

Government buses run regularly from the bus stand till mid-afternoon; the fare to Delhi is Rs405/500/700 (ordinary/deluxe/AC).

Other Destinations
In season, HPTDC and private companies run buses to Shimla (Rs415, 10 hours) and Dharamsala/McLeod Ganj (Rs450, 10 hours).

For details of public buses see the table, left.

TAXI
The **Him-Anchal Taxi Operators Union** (Map p360; ☎ 252120; the Mall) has share 4WDs to Leh (Rs1000 to Rs1500, 14 hours) at 2am from July to mid-October; book a day in advance. In season, travel agents can usually help organise share 4WDs. Seats cost the same if you disembark at Keylong. Share 4WDs to Kaza leave from around 5am and cost about

PUBLIC BUSES FROM MANALI

Destination	Fare (Rs)	Duration (hr)	Frequency
Amritsar	290-355	17	2pm & 3.30pm
Dehra Dun	360	16	6.30pm
Dharamsala	235	10	8am, 6pm & 7pm
Haridwar	390	17	10am & 12.40pm
Jammu	260-350	12	2.30pm & 4pm
Shimla (ordinary/ deluxe)	210/ 280	10	5 daily

HIMACHAL PRADESH

Rs500. Sightseeing trips to the Rohtang La cost Rs1200.

Other one-way fares:

Destination	Fare (Rs)
Bhuntar airport	800
Dharamsala	3400
Kaza	5000
Keylong	3500
Kullu	600 (900 via Naggar)
Leh	10,000
Manikaran	1200
Naggar	400
Solang Nullah	400

Getting Around

AUTORICKSHAW

Autos run to Old Manali and Vashisht for Rs50. If you can't find an auto in the street, head to the **Hadimba Auto Rickshaw Booking Office** (Map p360; ☎ 253366; the Mall).

MOTORCYCLE

Many people tackle the mountain passes to Ladakh or Spiti on bought or rented bikes. The **Enfield Club** (Map p358; ☎ 251094; Vashisht Rd), by the turn-off to Vashisht, does Enfield repairs and sells secondhand machines.

Several places rent out motorbikes, but make sure the price includes third-party insurance. The going rate per day is Rs600 for a 500cc Enfield, Rs400 for a 350cc Enfield and Rs350 for a 100cc to 150cc Yamaha, Honda or Bajaj. Reliable rental places:

Anu Auto Works (Map p358; ☎ 9816163378; Vashisht Rd)

Himalayan Inder Motors (Map p360; ☎ 9816113973; Gompa Rd)

Life Adventure Tours (Map p360; ☎ 253825; Diamond Hotel, Model Town Rd)

AROUND MANALI
Vashisht
☎ 01902

About 3km north of Manali on the slopes east of the Beas River, Vashisht (Map p358) is a village in its own right, but, much like Old Manali on the other side of the river, it's a satellite of Manali and is a popular travellers' hang-out. Indian tourists mostly come here to bathe in the hot springs and tour the temples, while foreign tourists largely come here for the cheap accommodation, chilled atmosphere and charas. Most guest houses close down for the winter from late October.

There are some interesting old wood and stone houses with ornate carving beyond the public baths, and a number of typically Himachali temples in the middle of the village. Vashisht is far more compact than Old Manali – travel agencies, moneychangers, traveller restaurants and internet cafes, including **Anand Internet Cafe** (Vashisht Rd; per hr Rs 30; ⏰ 8am-10pm), line the single street, all within a few minutes' walk.

SIGHTS & ACTIVITIES

Dedicated to the sage Vashisht, the ancient stone **Vashisht Mandir** has **public baths** (admission free; ⏰ 5am-9pm) with separate areas for men and women, or there are open-air baths just uphill. The hot springs area is always busy with locals doing their laundry or washing dishes. Nearby are similar temples to **Shiva** and **Rama**, and there's a second Vashisht mandir at the back of the village, built in the two-storey Kinnauri style.

Travel agencies can arrange treks and other adventure activities around the valley (see p362). **Himalayan Extreme Center** (☎ 9816174164; www.himalayan-extreme-center.com) is an enthusiastic young outfit offering rock climbing at Vashisht, Solang and Aleo (Rs900 per day, with all equipment), canyoning (Rs900) and three- to five-day high-altitude skiing and snowboarding tours.

Along the walking track down to the Beas, orange-roofed **Shri Hari Yoga Ashram** (☎ 250493; ⏰ closed winter) offers daily yoga classes for beginners at 10am, and advanced classes at 8am and 4.30pm (Rs100 to Rs150).

SLEEPING

Most places close from late October to April. Prices listed here can double in the peak season (April to June, September and October).

Bodh Guest House (☎ 254165; s/d without bathroom Rs100/150) This basic, but clean, three-storey place is hidden away in the old village, overlooking the Vashisht Mandir.

Kalptaru Guest House (☎ 253433; d Rs100-150) This big old village house above the temple has loads of character, and the basic rooms draw a hippie crowd. Upstairs rooms have views over the village, and hot water comes straight from the mineral springs.

Dharma Guest House (☎ 252354; budget r Rs150-350, d Rs500-1500; 🖥) Up a steep path above Rama Temple, this huge and expanding place has rooms in all budgets, and the hike up is rewarded with big valley views. The older wing has basic but clean rooms that get more expensive as you get higher, while the new section has spacious deluxe rooms with TV, hot water and balconies.

Sonam Guest House (☎ 251783; r with/without bathroom Rs200/150) This friendly, family-run guest house on the main street has an atticlike wood and stone charm, and the walls are decorated with paintings by the owner. The five rooms are simple but clean. A big selection of world movies can be booked and watched in the 'Inward Arc' lounge.

Hotel Brighu (☎ 253414; d Rs300-450) This big old-fashioned wood and stone place has some interesting rooms with velour bedheads, and huge timber balconies with valley views. Although faded, rooms are carpeted and clean, with TV and hot water.

Hotel Surabhi (☎ 252796; www.surabhihotel.com; d Rs350-1000) One of several big modern places on the main road but facing out over the valley, Surabhi is excellent value. Spacious, clean rooms have balconies with great mountain and river views and all have TVs and hot water. This is one place where you don't really need to spring for the more-expensive rooms.

Hotel Arohi (☎ 254421; www.arohiecoadventures.com; d Rs400-900; ✗) Run by experienced mountaineer, trekker and tour operator, Mr Thakur, Arohi has midrange standard rooms with TVs and geysers and views from everywhere, including the restaurant.

EATING
Vashisht has several good traveller cafes and hotel restaurants. Most close down for the winter by November.

our pick **Rainbow Cafe** (mains Rs40-110; ☺ 8am-10pm) Most people end up at this rooftop Vashisht institution at the end of an evening. Come here for decent traveller fare – breakfast, Tibetan *momos*, yak cheese pasta, pizzas and thalis, as well as cold beers and an endless reggae soundtrack. There's an internet cafe downstairs.

World Peace Cafe (mains Rs40-100) On the rooftop at Hotel Surabhi, this popular choice has cushions on the floor, a menu of Italian, Mexican and Israeli food, and views across to the Dhaulardhar range.

Fuji Restaurant (mains Rs45-60; ☺ 11am-10pm Mon-Sat) On the rooftop of Negi's Paying Guesthouse, past the temple, this authentic Japanese veg place specialises in noodles and miso soup.

Freedom Cafe (mains Rs50-120) A simple dirt-floor tent restaurant with valley views serving good traveller food, including clay-oven pizzas and Thai, Mexican and Israeli dishes.

Other good traveller restaurants include the Blue Heaven Cafe and Big Fish, both with Indian, Chinese and continental favourites from Rs40.

GETTING THERE & AWAY
Autorickshaws charge Rs50 for the journey between Vashisht and Manali; don't rely on being able to get a lift back to Manali later than 7pm. On foot, take the trail near the Himalayan Extreme Center past the Shri Hari Yoga Ashram and down to the banks of the Beas River. Coming uphill, the trail begins about 200m north of the Vashisht turn-off.

Hamta Pass Trek
Easily accessible from Manali, this four- or five-day trek crosses the 4270m Hamta Pass over the Pir Panjal. The trailhead is the village of Prini, accessible by bus on the Manali–Naggar road, but it's camping all the way so it's best to take an organised trek.

From Prini, the route climbs through pine forests to Sethan, then open meadows to Chikha. A waterfall camp site gives time to acclimatise before reaching the foot of the pass at Juara. The climb to the pass is steep and tiring but there are sublime snow-peak views from the top. On the descent, you can possibly push on to Chatru or break the journey with a riverside camp at Shiagouru. From Chatru, road transport runs north to Ladakh, east to Spiti and south to Manali.

Stage	Route	Duration (hr)	Distance (km)
1	Prini to Sethan/Pandu Ropa	5-6	8
2	Sethan/Pandu Ropa to Juara	4-5	10
3	Juara to Shiagouru via Hamta Pass	7-8	10
4	Shiagouru to Chatru	3-4	8

Solang Nullah
☎ 01902
Sitting at the bottom of a long, green meadow about 13km north of Manali, Solang Nullah is Himachal's favourite winter ski resort. With

the impressive backdrop of snowcapped Friendship Peak, it's also a year-round 'beauty spot': in summer the meadow is used for paragliding, hiking, horse-riding and zorbing. From January to March, skiers and snowboarders can enjoy 1.5km of alpine-style runs. A new ropeway (ski-lift) was nearing completion at the time of research. A small drag-lift operates on the beginners' slopes above the village.

Adventure-tour companies in Manali and hotels in Solang Nullah run ski and snow-board courses and rent out equipment – expect to pay Rs500 per day, plus Rs300 for use of the ski lifts. Mangy winter clothing, and slightly tired ski gear, can be rented at dozens of wooden huts on the road between Solang Nullah and Manali. Advanced skiers can join expeditions to high-altitude slopes in Manali and Vashisht.

In summer, Solang Nullah meadow is booming with day-trippers taking pony rides (from Rs150), quad-bike rides (from Rs500), zorbing (from Rs250) and, most popular of the lot, paragliding flights from Rs600 for a tame flight down the slope. The surrounding hills are also good for walking – the **Shiva temple** 3km above the village is a popular destination. See boxed text, p362, for more on all of these activities.

SLEEPING & EATING

Solang Nullah village has quite an alpine feel in the winter months: there are a few chalet-style guest houses with gas heaters or wood-burning stoves (Rs150 extra) and hot showers (book ahead). At other times it's a peaceful base for local trekking.

Friendship Hotel (☎ 256010; r Rs400-500) Just downhill from the ski slope, this cheerful budget place has carpeted rooms with geysers and a stove-warmed lounge downstairs.

Snow View Hotel (☎ 256181; r Rs500) Further downhill from Friendship Hotel, Snow View is similar, with plain but comfortable rooms, ski rental and enthusiastic staff.

Hotel Iceland (☎ 256008; www.icelandsolang.com; r Rs800-1500; 🖵) Solang's best hotel, Iceland is a genuine ski lodge, run by experienced skiers and mountaineers. Although rooms in the original hotel are cosy enough, a completely new wing was nearing completion when we visited, with spacious wood-panelled rooms and a cosy bar and restaurant. Ski and snow-board rental costs Rs450 per day for guests.

GETTING THERE & AWAY

Buses leave Manali at 8am, 9.30am, 2pm and 4pm for Solang Nullah (Rs13, one hour), heading back immediately on arrival. A taxi from Manali is Rs400; it's a two-hour walk from Old Manali. Snow may make the road impassable in January and February, which usually means walking the 3km from the village of Palchan on the highway.

WESTERN HIMACHAL PRADESH

Western Himachal Pradesh is most famous as the home of the Tibetan government in exile, near Dharamsala, but consider travelling further afield to the fascinating Chamba Valley. The official website for Kangra district is http://hpkangra.nic.in, while the official Chamba Valley site is http://hpchamba.nic.in.

DHARAMSALA

☎ 01892 / pop 19,800 / elev 1219m

Dharamsala is best known as the home of the Dalai Lama, but the slightly grubby market town where the buses pull in is actually Lower Dharamsala. The Tibetan government in exile is based just uphill in Gangchen Kyishong, and travellers make a beeline further uphill to the remarkably busy little traveller town of McLeod Ganj, also known as Upper Dharamsala. The bus station, a good museum and the bustling Kotwali Bazar can be found in Dharamsala, but otherwise it's just a place to pass through on your way to McLeod or Bhagsu.

The **State Bank of India** (🕑 10am-4pm Mon-Fri, to 1pm Sat) accepts travellers cheques and changes cash, and there's a nearby ATM in the main bazaar.

Sights

The **Museum of Kangra Art** (☎ 224214; Indian/foreigner Rs10/50; 🕑 10am-1.30pm & 2-5pm Tue-Sun) near the bus station displays some fine miniature paintings from the Kangra school, along with temple carvings, fabrics and embroidery, weapons, and palanquins belonging to local rajas.

Sleeping & Eating

There are a few sleeping options if you have an early bus in the morning.

Hotel Paradise (☎ 224207; Kotwali Bazar; r Rs150-300) A short walk uphill from the bus stand, it may

BUSES FROM DHARAMSALA

Destination	Fare (Rs)	Duration (hr)	Frequency
Amritsar	150	7	5am
Chamba	150-175	8	six daily
Dalhousie	140	6	8.40am & 12.15pm
Dehra Dun	325	13	9pm
Delhi	290-785	12	11 daily
Gaggal	12	30min	frequently
Jammu	135	5	9.45am
Jawalamukhi	50	1½	hourly
Kangra	20	1	frequently
Kullu	210	9	6pm
Manali	250	10	6pm
Mandi	125	6	5 daily
Palampur	35	2	frequently
Pathankot	83	3½	hourly
Shimla	225	10	9 daily

not be paradise but it's pretty good for this price, with spacious, clean rooms with TV – the pricier rooms have hot water. Ask for a front room with some natural light.

Kashmir House (☎ 222977; d Rs900-1000) Come to this HPTDC hotel not so much for the quiet location – it's a hike up the hill towards Gangchen Kyishong – but for the ambience. It once belonged to the maharaja of Jammu and Kashmir. Huge rooms have all mod cons.

Hotel Dhauladhar (☎ 224926; r Rs1200-2000) Although comfortable, rooms here are pricey for what you get. Nevertheless, it's handy for the bus station and there are good views from some rooms. There's also a restaurant and the High Spirits Bar with a terrace overlooking the valley.

Andey's Midtown Restaurant (☎ 222810; mains Rs40-200; ⏰ 9.30am-10.30pm) Dharamsala's best restaurant is a busy family place serving a big range of Indian, Chinese and continental veg and nonveg fare. Come for kebabs, rich curries, burgers and a fine veg or nonveg thali. The bar at the back has horse saddles for seats, so you know they take their drinking seriously.

Getting There & Away
AIR
See p379 for details of air services to the area.

BUS
Minivans run a regular shuttle service from Dharamsala bus station to McLeod Ganj (Rs9, 45 minutes) till about 7pm. For Delhi there's

a deluxe Volvo bus at 8pm (Rs785, 12 hours). See the table, above, for other services.

TAXI
The **taxi stand** (☎ 222105) is up some steep steps from the bus stand. Shared taxis to McLeod Ganj leave when full for Rs9 (30 minutes). Day tours covering less than 80km can be arranged for Rs800 per day, or Rs1500 if roaming further afield.

Fixed one-way fares:

Destination	Fare (Rs)
Gaggal airport	250
Jawalamukhi	700
Kangra	350
Masrur	900
McLeod Ganj	130
Palampur	600

TRAIN
The nearest train station is Kangra Mandir, on the slow narrow-gauge line from Pathankot to Jogindarnagar – see p382 and the boxed text, p383. Reservations for other services from Pathankot can be made at the **Rail Reservation Centre** (☎ 226711; Hotel Dhauladhar; ⏰ 8am-2pm Mon-Sat).

MCLEOD GANJ
☎ 01892 / elev 1770m
When travellers talk of heading up to Dharamsala (to see the Dalai Lama…), this is where they mean. Around 4km above Dharamsala town – or 10km via the main bus route – McLeod Ganj is the headquarters of

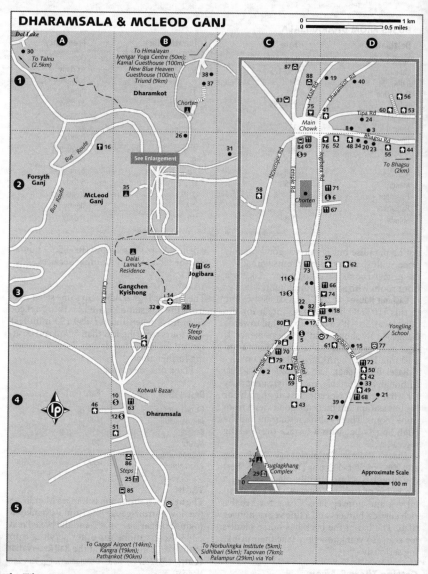

DHARAMSALA & MCLEOD GANJ

the Tibetan government in exile and the residence of His Holiness the 14th Dalai Lama. Along with Manali, it's the big traveller hangout in Himachal Pradesh, with many budget hotels, trekking companies, internet cafes, restaurants, and shops selling Tibetan souvenirs. Naturally, there's a large Tibetan population here, many of whom are refugees, so you'll see plenty of maroon robes about, especially when the Dalai Lama is in residence.

McLeod (named after David McLeod, Lieutenant-Governor of Punjab) was established in the mid-1850s as a British garrison and it served as an administration centre for the colonial government until the earthquake of 1905. It was a backwater until 1960, when the Dalai Lama claimed asylum here following the Chinese invasion of Tibet (see p378).

Since then, McLeod has become a centre for the study of Buddhism and Tibetan culture. There are all sorts of holistic activities and courses on offer, and lots of travellers come here to volunteer on community projects that focus on the refugee community.

Waterproof clothing is handy for McLeod Ganj: it rains a lot here. Many shops and businesses are closed on Monday.

Orientation

From the central bus stand, Jogibara Rd runs south to Gangchen Kyishong and Dharamsala;

Temple Rd runs south to the Tsuglagkhang Complex; Bhagsu Rd runs east to Bhagsu, Tipa Rd runs northeast to the Tibetan Institute of Performing Arts; and Dharamkot Rd runs north to Dharamkot.

The taxi stand is located on Mall Rd, and autorickshaws and share jeeps stop off on the lower northern road that heads out to the Church of St John in the Wilderness and Dal Lake.

Information
BOOKSHOPS
Bookworm (☎ 221465; Hotel Bhagsu Rd; ⊙ 9am-6.30pm Tue-Sun) The best all-round bookshop.

HIMACHAL PRADESH

Hills Bookshop (☎ 220008; Bhagsu Rd; ☺ 9am-9pm) Well stocked with novels and guidebooks.

Namgyal Bookshop (☎ 221492; Tsuglagkhang Complex; ☺ 9.30am-noon & 1-6pm Tue-Sun) Specialises in Buddhist texts.

INTERNET ACCESS

McLeod Ganj has loads of internet cafes, all charging Rs30 an hour.

Green Cyber Cafe (Bhagsu Rd; ☺ 6am-9.30pm) At Green Hotel, with fast connections and wifi access.

Mandala Wifi Coffee House (Temple Rd; ☺ 7am-8pm) Bring your own laptop and use the wifi over a coffee.

MEDIA

Contact (www.contactmag.org) is an informative, free local magazine that contains some useful listings, as well as details regarding courses and volunteer work. It's also a useful website.

Tibetan Review provides coverage of Tibetan issues, as does the *Tibetan Bulletin*, the official journal of the government in exile.

MEDICAL SERVICES

Traditional Tibetan medicine known as *amchi* is a popular form of treatment in McLeod Ganj – see p375.

Tibetan Delek Hospital (☎ 222053; Gangchen Kyishong; consultations Rs10; ☺ outpatient clinic 9am-1pm & 2-5pm).

MONEY

Several places around town offer Western Union money transfers.

Punjab National Bank (Temple Rd; ☺ 10am-2pm & 3-4pm Mon-Fri, 10am-1pm Sat)

State Bank of India (Temple Rd; ☺ 10am-4pm Mon-Fri, to 1pm Sat) Has a busy international ATM.

Thomas Cook (Temple Rd; ☺ 9.30am-6.30pm)

POST

Post office (Jogibara Rd; ☺ 9.30am-5pm Mon-Fri & to noon Sat, parcel post to 1pm Mon-Fri) Poste restante and parcels.

TOURIST INFORMATION

HPTDC tourist office (☎ 221205; Hotel Bhagsu Rd; ☺ 10am-5pm, closed Sun in Jul-Aug & Dec-Mar) Offers maps and guides, and can also make bookings for HPTDC hotels and buses around Himachal.

Information Office of Central Tibetan Administration (☎ 222457; www.tibet.net; Jogibara Rd; ☺ 9am-5.30pm Tue-Sun) For information on Tibetan issues.

TRAVEL AGENCIES

Numerous travel agencies can book train and bus tickets, and can also arrange tours and treks.

Destination Travels (☎ 220012; www.destination travels.co.in; Temple Rd) Reliable agent for international and domestic flights, as well as local transport and tours.

Himachal Travels (☎ 221428; himachaltravels@ sancharnet.in; Jogibara Rd)

Potala Tours & Travels (☎ 221378; Bhagsu Rd)

Sights

TSUGLAGKHANG COMPLEX

The main focus of visiting pilgrims, monks and many tourists is the **Tsuglagkhang** (Temple Rd; Central Chapel; ☺ nonresidents 10am-6pm), comprising the *photang* (official residence) of the Dalai Lama, the Namgyal Gompa, Tibet Museum and the Tsuglagkhang itself.

The revered Tsuglagkhang is the exiles' equivalent of the Jokhang Temple in Lhasa. Sacred to Avalokitesvara (Chenrezi in Tibet), the Tibetan deity of compassion, it enshrines a 3m-high gilded statue of the Sakyamuni Buddha, flanked by Avalokitesvara and Padmasambhava, the Indian scholar who introduced Buddhism to Tibet. The Avalokitesvara statue contains several relics rescued from the Jokhang Temple during the Cultural Revolution.

Next to the Tsuglagkhang is the **Kalachakra Temple**, built in 1992, which contains mesmerising murals of the Kalachakra (Wheel of Time) mandala, specifically linked to Avalokitesvara, currently represented on earth by the Dalai Lama. Sand mandalas are created here annually on the fifth day of the third Tibetan month. Photography is allowed in the Tsuglagkhang, but not in the Kalachakra Temple. Note that during teachings, cameras, mobile phones, cigarettes and lighters are not permitted in the temple.

The remaining buildings form the **Namgyal Gompa**, where you can watch monks debate most afternoons, sealing points of argument with great flourish, a foot stamp and a theatrical clap of the hands. The monastery bookshop has a good selection of Buddhist texts, and you can enjoy cakes and vegetarian food at Namgyal Cafe (p377).

Just inside the main entry gate is the **Tibet Museum** (www.thetibetmuseum.org; admission Rs5; ☺ 9am-5pm), telling the tragic story of the Chinese occupation and the subsequent Tibetan exodus through photographs, interviews and video clips. A visit here is a must for anyone staying in McLeod Ganj.

Most Tibetan pilgrims make a *kora* (ritual circuit) of the Tsuglagkhang Complex, which must be carried out in a clockwise direction. Take the downhill road to the left at the entrance to the temple and follow the winding path leading off to the right. It passes through forest strewn with prayer flags before emerging back on Temple Rd.

SECRETARIAT OF THE TIBETAN GOVERNMENT IN EXILE

Inside the government compound at Gangchen Kyishong, the **Library of Tibetan Works & Archives** (Secretariat Complex; www.ltwa.net; 9am-1pm & 2-5pm Mon-Sat, closed 2nd & 4th Sat of month) preserves the Tibetan texts saved from the Cultural Revolution. Many have since been translated into English and other European languages. Regular visitors can become temporary members (Rs50 per month; passport needed for ID) to access the collection.

Upstairs is a fascinating **cultural museum** (admission Rs10; 9am-1pm & 2-5pm Mon-Sat, closed 2nd & 4th Sat each month) with statues, old Tibetan artefacts and books, and some astonishing three-dimensional mandalas in wood and sand. Also worth a visit is the **Nechung Gompa**, home to the Tibetan state oracle.

TIBETAN MEDICAL & ASTROLOGICAL INSTITUTE (MEN-TSEE-KHANG)

Established to preserve the ancient arts of *amchi* (traditional Tibetan medicine) and astrology, the **Men-Tsee-Khang** (223113; www.men-tsee-khang.org; Gangchen Kyishong) is a five-minute walk below the Secretariat. There's a library and training college, and if you know the exact time you were born, you can have a whole life horoscope prepared in English.

The **Men-Tsee-Khang Museum** (admission Rs5; 9am-1pm & 2-5pm Mon-Sat) has fascinating displays on traditional Tibetan medicine, told via preserved specimens and illustrative *thangkas*.

TSECHOKLING GOMPA

At the base of a long flight of steps below the bus stand, this peaceful gompa was built in 1987 to replace the original Dip Tse Chokling Gompa in Tibet, destroyed in the Cultural Revolution. Home to a small order of Gelukpa monks, the prayer hall enshrines a statue of Sakyamuni in a magnificent jewelled headdress.

OTHER ATTRACTIONS

Run by a local charity that works with former political prisoners, the **Gu Chu Sum Movement Gallery** (Jogibara Rd; admission free; 2-5pm Mon, Wed & Fri) has an exhibition of photos telling the story of political oppression in Chinese-occupied Tibet.

Established by the Tibetan Welfare Office, the **Environmental Education Centre** (Bhagsu Rd; 8.30am-7pm Mon-Sat) provides education on environmental issues. You can refill your water bottle, and the adjacent Green Shop (p379) sells handmade paper and other organic products.

Just off the main road into McLeod, the **Church of St John in the Wilderness** has handsome stained-glass windows dating from the British era. It's open on Sunday mornings for the weekly service. The cemetery contains the graves of many victims of the 1905 earthquake.

Activities

ALTERNATIVE THERAPIES, YOGA & MASSAGE

McLeod Ganj has dozens of practitioners of holistic and alternative therapies, some legitimate and some making a fast buck at the expense of gullible travellers. Adverts for courses and sessions are posted on noticeboards all over McLeod Ganj and in *Contact* magazine, but talking to other travellers is a better way to find the good practitioners.

Lha (220992; Temple Rd; 10am-5pm Mon-Fri) runs yoga classes at 7.30am and 5.30pm (Rs100 per session) and also runs reliable Tibetan massage sessions.

Universal Yoga Centre (9418291929; www.vijaypoweryoga; Yongling School, Jogibara Rd) gets good reports for drop-in yoga classes and longer courses.

WALKS

Interesting short walks around McLeod include the 2km stroll to **Bhagsu** and the 3km walk northeast to **Dharamkot** for uplifting views south over the valley and north towards the Dhauladhar Ridge. You can do a loop to Bhagsu, across to Dharamkot and back down to McLeod in a few hours.

About 4km northwest of McLeod Ganj on Mall Rd, peaceful **Dal Lake** is home to the **Tibetan Children's Village** (221348; www.tcv.org.in; 9.30am-5pm Mon-Fri), which provides free education for some 2000 refugee children. Visitors are welcome and there may be

MEETING THE DALAI LAMA

Meeting face to face with the Dalai Lama is a lifelong dream for many travellers and certainly for Buddhists, but private audiences are rarely granted. Put simply, the Dalai Lama is too busy with spiritual duties and running the government in exile to meet everyone who comes to Dharamsala. Tibetan refugees are automatically guaranteed an audience, but travellers must make do with the occasional public teachings held at Gangchen Kyishong during the monsoon (July/August), after Losar (Tibetan New Year) in February/March and on other occasions, depending on his schedule. For annual schedules and just about everything you need to know about His Holiness, check out www.dalailama.com. To attend, you usually have to register, with your passport and two passport photographs, at the **Branch Security Office** (☎ 221560; www.tibet.com; Bhagsu Rd; ☒ 9am-1pm & 2-5pm Mon-Sat, closed 2nd & 4th Sat each month).

opportunities for volunteers. The lake itself has a small Hindu temple and there are great views from **Naddi** just uphill.

A popular longer walk is the one- or two-day return trip through boulder fields and rhododendron forests to **Triund** (2900m), a 9km walk past Dharamkot. Triund has a simple rest house and you can stop overnight and stroll up to the glacier at Laka Got (3350m) before turning back to McLeod Ganj. There's a scenic route along the gorge from the waterfall at Bhagsu. From Triund, you can trek to **Indrahar La** (4300m) and the Chamba Valley (p383).

TREKKING

It's possible to trek from McLeod Ganj to the Kullu, Chamba, Lahaul and Spiti Valleys, and there are several agencies in town that can make the necessary arrangements. The most popular route crosses the 4300m Indrahar La over the Dhauladhar to Bharmour (p388). All-inclusive treks costs around Rs1500 to Rs2000 per person, per day.

Uphill from the bus stand on the road to Dharamkot, the **Regional Mountaineering Centre** (☎ 221787; ☒ 10am-5pm Mon-Sat) can arrange treks and adventure activities and offers courses and expeditions on set dates. It can also provide a list of registered guides and porters.

Other reliable trekking operators:

Eagle's Height Trekkers (☎ 221097; www.trekking .123himachal.com; Mall Rd) Also runs birdwatching tours and 4WD safaris.

High Point Adventure (☎ 220718; www.trek .123himachal.com; Hotel Bhagsu Rd)

Yeti Trekking (☎ 221060; Dharamkot Rd)

Courses

YOGA, MEDITATION & PHILOSOPHY

Several organisations offer long-term courses in Buddhist philosophy and meditation.

However, they have strict rules on silence, alcohol and smoking.

Himalayan Iyengar Yoga Centre (☎ 221312; www .hiyogacentre.com; Dharamkot Rd; ☒ Apr-Oct) Five-day courses start every Thursday (Rs2500).

Tushita Meditation Centre (☎ 221866; www .tushita.info; ☒ registration 9.30-11.30am & 12.30-4pm Mon-Sat) Near Dharamkot, Tushita offers eight-day nonresidential courses and 10-day residential retreats in Buddhist philosophy, plus courses for advanced students – see the website for course dates.

Vipassana Meditation Centre (☎ 221309; www .sikhara.dhamma.org; ☒ registration 4-5pm Mon-Sat) Located in Dharamkot, this centre runs strict 10-day retreats on *vipassana* (mindfulness meditation) from April to November.

Library of Tibetan Works & Archives (☎ 222467; itwa@gov.tibet.net) At the Gangchen Kyishong complex, there are Buddhist philosophy courses for Rs200 per month, plus Rs50 registration.

COOKING

Cooking courses in McLeod Ganj cover everything from South Indian dosas to chocolate *momos*. Book the following courses one day in advance:

Bhimsen's Cooking Class (Jogibara Rd; classes Rs200; ☒ 11am-1pm & 4-6pm) Courses in North and South Indian cooking.

Lhamo's Kitchen (☎ 9816468719; Bhagsu Rd; classes Rs250, 3-day courses Rs550; ☒ 10am-noon, 5-7pm) Recommended courses in vegetarian Tibetan cooking.

Sangye's Kitchen (☎ 9816164540; Jogibara Rd; classes Rs250; ☒ 11am-1pm & 5-7pm Sun-Fri) Tibetan treats, with a different menu daily. Next to Tashi Choeling Monastery.

Nisha's Indian Cooking Course (☎ 9318877674; www.indiancookingcourse.com; Taste of India Restaurant, Jogibara Rd; courses Rs700; ☒ 3 afternoons weekly) Veg and nonveg North Indian courses.

Tibetan Cooking School (☎ 220992; Lha, Temple Rd; ☒ registration 9am-11am) Hosts three-day courses.

LANGUAGE

Inside the Gangchen Kyishong complex, the **Library of Tibetan Works & Archives** (☎ 222467; www.ltwa.net; ☯ classes Mon-Sat) runs long-term Tibetan-language courses for beginners and experienced students for Rs250 per month, plus a Rs50 registration fee.

Lha (☎ 220992; Temple Rd; ☯ 10am-5pm Mon-Fri) offers private Tibetan-language tuition for Rs100 per hour.

There are several independent Tibetan teachers – check *Contact* magazine for details. Classes run by **Pema Youton** (☎ 9418603523) get good reports.

MASSAGE

The recommended **Tibetan Universal Massage** (☎ 9816378307; www.tibetanmassage.com; Jogibara Rd) offers training in traditional Tibetan massage. Courses run for five afternoons on set dates and cost Rs1500.

Festivals & Events

Performances of traditional lhamo (Tibetan opera) and musical theatre are held on special occasions at the **Tibetan Institute of Performing Arts** (TIPA; ☎ 221478; www.tibetanarts .org), east of Main Chowk. The annual **Opera Festival** runs from 27 March to 4 April and the **TIPA Anniversary Festival** runs from 27 to 30 May.

In December or January, McLeod celebrates **Losar** (Tibetan New Year; see boxed text, p335) with processions and masked dances at local monasteries. The Dalai Lama often gives public teachings at this time. The Dalai Lama's birthday on 6 July is also celebrated with aplomb.

From 10 to 12 December, McLeod Ganj hosts the **International Himalayan Festival** (see boxed text, p335) to commemorate the Dalai Lama's Nobel Peace Prize, featuring cultural troupes from all the Himalayan nations.

Sleeping

Popular places fill up quickly; there are many more places available than are listed here, but advance bookings are strongly advised from April to June, October and November.

BUDGET

Loseling Guest House (☎ 221087; d Rs190-250) Down the same alley as Tibetan Ashoka Guest House (above), Loseling is run by a Tibetan monastery based in Karnataka. It's a good cheapie and all rooms have a hot shower; cheaper ones have squat toilets.

Hotel Ladies Venture (☎ 221559; shantiazad@ yahoo.co.in; Jogibara Rd; s Rs200, d Rs250-500) Named by the two previous lady owners, this peaceful green-and-yellow hotel welcomes all with wraparound balconies, flower pots, a range of tidy rooms and lovely mountain views from the rooftop terrace.

Om Hotel (☎ 221313; omhotel@hotmail.com; Nowrojee Rd; d Rs275-300, without bathroom Rs170-200) A short walk down a lane below the bus stand, the friendly family-run Om has a good range of pleasing rooms and a great little terrace restaurant that catches the sunset over the valley.

Hotel Mount View (☎ 221382; Jogibara Rd; Rs300-500) A tidy Kashmiri-run hotel offering a range of good rooms that extend well back from the street to reveal valley views from the rear balconies. The owners run a trekking outfit

---

AMCHI

Amchi (traditional Tibetan medicine) is a centuries-old holistic healing practice and a popular treatment for all kinds of minor and persistent ailments. There are several clinics around town, including **Men-Tsee-Khang Clinic** (☎ 221484; Tipa Rd; ☯ 9am-1pm & 2-5pm Mon-Sat, closed 2nd & 4th Sat each month) and **Dr Lobsang Khangkar Memorial Clinic** (☎ 220811; ☯ 9am-noon & 2-5pm Mon-Sat), near the post office.

The most popular practitioner in town is the former physician to the Dalai Lama, **Dr Yeshi Dhonden** (☯ 8am-1pm), whose tiny clinic is squirreled away off Jogibara Rd, down an alley past Ashoka Restaurant. No appointment is necessary: you arrive at 8am and collect a token and approximate consultation time. You come back with a sample of urine, which, along with a quick examination, is all the doctor needs to prescribe the appropriate herbal pills. Many locals and expats swear by his treatments.

For an insight into *amchi*, visit the Tibetan Medical & Astrological Institute (Men-Tsee Khang; p373).

VOLUNTEERING IN MCLEOD GANJ

McLeod Ganj has more volunteering opportunities than anywhere else in Himachal Pradesh. It's hard not to feel the need to do something here, whether it be helping newly arrived Tibetan refugees or cleaning up the environment. Travellers can get involved in short-term volunteering such as English-language conversation classes or cleaning up litter, but for longer-term placements always look for a position that matches your existing skills. The following places can match you to a suitable placement. Volunteers generally make their own arrangements for accommodation and meals. Many organisations seeking volunteers also advertise in the free magazine *Contact*. The magazine also looks for volunteers to help with writing, proofreading or design.

One of the best places to start is **VolunteerTibet** (☎ 220894; www.volunteertibet.org.in; Jogibara Rd; ☒ 10am-1.30pm & 2-5pm Mon-Fri), a community organisation that arranges placements in areas of need – eg teaching, computer training, and social services. Volunteers with two months or more to spare are preferred, but short-term placements can also be arranged.

Lha (☎ 220992; www.lhaindia.org; Temple Rd; ☒ 10am-5pm Mon-Fri) also arranges placements at a variety of local community projects, including placements for computer teachers and English- and French-language teachers. You need a minimum of two weeks for teaching placements and one month or more for serious vocational programs.

Hope Education Centre (☎ 9218947689), off Jogibara Rd, runs conversational English classes for Tibetan refugees from 4.30pm to 6pm Monday to Friday, often held informally over coffee at Cafe Oasis. Anyone is welcome to turn up.

Gu Chu Sum (☎ 220680; Jogibara Rd; ☒ 9am-5pm) has similar English-language classes from 6pm Monday to Friday above Lung Ta restaurant.

The **Tibetan Welfare Office** (☎ 221059; Bhagsu Rd; ☒ 9am-1pm & 2-5pm Mon-Sat, closed 2nd & 4th Sat each month) can provide advice on other opportunities for volunteers around McLeod Ganj, including environmental efforts such as the Clean Upper Dharamsala Project.

---

and tours to Pahalgam in Kashmir, but be sure to check that conditions in the area are safe before signing up.

Green Hotel (☎ 221200; www.greenhotel.biz; Bhagsu Rd; r Rs300-800, without bathroom Rs100; ▣) A long-time traveller favourite and still one of the better budget places in McLeod, Green has a diverse range of sunny rooms in two buildings, some with valley and mountain views. The restaurant and internet cafe here are very popular and wifi is available.

Tibetan Ashoka Guest House (☎ 221763; d with/without bathroom Rs350/100) Off Jogibara Rd, down an alley near the chorten (Tibetan for stupa), this big place looks out on the valley and catches plenty of sunlight. There are lots of clean, simple rooms, but it books out in season.

Kunga Guesthouse (☎ 221180; Bhagsu Rd; d Rs400) Above Nick's Italian Kitchen, Kunga's clean rooms are popular and offer reasonable value.

Takhyil Hotel (☎ 221152; Jogibara Rd; r Rs400-500) A calm vibe and tidy rooms with TVs and hot showers add up to a good package at this Tibetan-run hotel that's just downhill from the chorten.

Up some steps off Tipa Rd, Tibetan-run **Kalsang Guest House** (☎ 221709; Tipa Rd; s/d without bathroom Rs100/150, d Rs250-400) has a large, pot-plant-filled front terrace that's perfect for reading and relaxing. The rooms are spartan but clean. The same steps lead to the very similar **Loling Guest House** (☎ 221072; Tipa Rd; r with/without bathroom Rs200/100). Facing Tipa Rd, **Seven Hills Guest House** (☎ 221949; d Rs300) is slightly swankier, with an internet cafe and restaurant.

MIDRANGE & TOP END

Most midrange hotels sit along Hotel Bhagsu Rd, offering sweeping views over the valley, though there are a couple near the bus stand.

Kareri Lodge (☎ 221132; karerihl@hotmail.com; Hotel Bhagsu Rd; r Rs400-900; ☒) Squeezed in among a string of more-upmarket hotels, Kareri has just five clean rooms at varying rates but all have TV and balcony. There's a good vibe here, helped by the friendly manager who offers a reliable trekking service.

Hotel Tibet (☎ 221587; htdshala@sancharnet.in; Bhagsu Rd; r Rs550-990; ☒) A short walk from the bus stand, this place has the feel of an upmarket hotel yet it's at almost budget prices. It's run by the Tibetan government, and has a good restaurant and bar. All rooms have TV and hot water; credit cards accepted.

our pick **Cheryton Cottage Guest House** (☎ 425857; cherytoncottage@yahoo.com; Jogibara Rd; d Rs700, apt Rs1500) In the garden behind Chocolate Log, Cheryton has four peaceful rooms with a relaxing outdoor space. The four-room apartment next door is fully self-contained. Book ahead.

Pema Thang Guest House (☎ 221871; www .pemathang.net; Hotel Bhagsu Rd; r Rs825-1155; ✷) A tasteful Tibetan-style guest house, with a great restaurant and spacious, well-lit rooms with comforting, homey furnishings. Advance booking is recommended.

Hotel Him Queen (☎ 221861; www.himqueenhotel .com; Hotel Bhagsu Rd; d Rs800-1600, ste from Rs1800; ✷) Near Hotel Bhagsu, this is a towering, white-washed, business-style hotel with tidy rooms and valley views. Rooms are also available at the slightly cheaper annexe.

Hotel Bhagsu (☎ 221091; Hotel Bhagsu Rd; d Rs900-2000; ✷) On the road above the bazaar and Tsuglagkhang, this popular HPTDC hotel has a solid Raj-era feel and attractively decorated rooms, some with valley views. Book ahead in season.

Hotel India House (☎ 221457; www.hotelindiahouse .com; Bhagsu Rd; r Rs1320-2200; ✷) In the thick of the action near the bus stand, India House is bright and modern, if a little overpriced. Deluxe rooms come with a tub and balcony.

Asian Plaza Hotel (☎ 220655; www.asianplazahotel .com; Main Chowk; d Rs1600-2200, ste Rs3200) Opposite the noisy bus stand, this is an ostentatious business-type hotel with all the conveniences you would expect for the price but little in the way of charm.

Chonor House Hotel (☎ 221006; www.norbulingka .org; s/d from Rs1900/2300, ste Rs2800/3500; 🖳) Hidden down an anonymous track off Hotel Bhagsu Rd, Chonor House is a real gem. It's run by the Norbulingka Institute (p381), and rooms are decked out with its wonderful handicrafts and fabrics. Each room has a Tibetan theme that runs from the bedspreads to the murals on the walls. There's also a lovely garden, shop, restaurant and net cafe. Advance booking is essential.

Eating
RESTAURANTS

McLeod Ganj is crammed with backpacker restaurants serving identical traveller menus –

> ### LET'S DRINK TO A PLASTIC-FREE PLANET
>
> The hills around McLeod Ganj are scarred by piles of abandoned plastic bottles that will persist in the environment for hundreds of years before breaking down into a polluting chemical dust. Plastic bags are banned in Himachal Pradesh but bottles are not. Give the countryside a chance and refill your drinking water bottle for around Rs10 at one of the filtered-water stations around McLeod Ganj. There's one at Lha (p373), one at the Environmental Education Centre (p373) and one at Green Hotel (p375).

pizzas, pasta, omelettes, Indian and Chinese staples – and commendable attempts at European and Mexican food. For a quick snack, local women sell *momos* and *tingmo* (steamed Tibetan bread) around the chorten and at the entrance to the Tsuglagkhang.

Tsongkha (Jogibara Rd; dishes Rs20-80; ☽ from 8am) A simple but popular Tibetan restaurant with a great rooftop terrace looking out over the chorten and valley, plus an indoor dining room for chilly days.

Snow Lion Restaurant (Jogibara Rd; dishes Rs20-80; ☽ 7.30am-9.30pm) Behind the Snow Lion guest house, this is another good place to come for *momos*, *thukpa* and *tingmo*.

Green Hotel (Bhagsu Rd; dishes Rs25-80; ☽ from 6am) This traveller-oriented hotel-restaurant serves good vegetarian food and the earliest breakfasts in town. The internet cafe and wifi are a bonus.

Peace Cafe (Jogibara Rd; dishes Rs30-40) This cosy little cafe is always full of monks chatting and dining, and tasty Tibetan *momos*, chow chow (stir-fried noodles with vegetables or meat) and *thukpa*.

Lung Ta (Jogibara Rd; dishes Rs30-50; ☽ noon-8.30pm Mon-Sat) The set menu changes daily at this popular, nonprofit, vegetarian Japanese restaurant. Food and ambience are authentic and many Japanese travellers come here for a taste of home.

Namgyal Cafe (snacks Rs30-80; ☽ 10am-10pm Tue-Sun) Located at Namgyal Gompa (part of the Tsuglagkhang Complex; p372), and this cafe serves cakes and vegetarian food. It also provides vocational training for refugees.

Gakyi Restaurant (Jogibara Rd; dishes Rs30-100) A popular traveller hang-out, with good

---

TIBETAN EXILES

The traditional rulers of Tibet are a Buddhist dynasty of Dalai Lamas. For centuries Mongols then the Chinese have challenged their autonomy, acting intermittently as rulers or 'protectors'. From 1949, the Chinese communist takeover exacted a heavy toll. Rebellions were brutally repressed, temples ransacked, and farms replanted with inappropriate crops, resulting in mass starvation. The Central Tibetan Administration estimates 1.2 million died, though the Chinese Communist Party disputes this.

More than 250,000 Tibetan refugees have made the decision to flee their homeland, on foot over the Himalaya, to seek sanctuary in India. They are led by His Holiness the 14th Dalai Lama, Tenzin Gyatso, who was granted asylum in Dharamsala in 1959. The village of Gangchen Kyishong below McLeod Ganj is now the headquarters for the official Tibetan government in exile, with a dedicated team of politicians and legal experts fighting for liberation and the rights of those still oppressed in Tibet.

The Beijing Olympics provided a catalyst for world-wide protests against Chinese rule and an uprising from within Tibet in 2008, but the plight of India's Tibetan refugees remains bleak.

Meanwhile, the refugees continue to eke out a living from farming, manufacturing, and selling carpets and other traditional crafts. Tibetan refugee schools and other charitable projects are in desperate need of long-term volunteers across the region – see boxed text, p376, for more information.

---

breakfasts and a familiar Tibetan-meets-European menu.

Oogo's Cafe Italiano (Jogibara Rd; mains Rs35-150) This cute hole-in-the-wall place serves up mainly Italian fare, but with a few surprises – waffles, baked potatoes, intriguing pasta dishes like 'chicken vodka' and even grilled lamb chops. The atmosphere is warm and busy and there are tempting desserts, as well as a bookshelf full of reading material.

Taste of India (Jogibara Rd; dishes Rs50-100) This tiny place has just five tables and is often full with diners savouring North Indian veg and nonveg curries and tandoori chicken.

Nick's Italian Kitchen (Bhagsu Rd; meals Rs50-100; ☻7am-9pm) At Kunga Guesthouse, Nick's has been serving up tasty vegetarian pizzas, pasta and gnocchi for years. Follow up with heavenly desserts like chocolate brownies with hot chocolate sauce. Eat inside by candlelight or out on the terrace.

Jimmy's Italian Kitchen (Jogibara Rd; dishes Rs60-130) Jimmy's is a well-established Italian place with a new location upstairs opposite the chorten. Authentic pizzas with real pepperoni, and a good range of pasta dishes.

Ashoka Restaurant (Jogibara Rd; dishes Rs60-150; ☻noon-10.30pm) This stylish timber-lined restaurant serves reliable Indian veg and nonveg dishes such as mutton korma and chicken masala. Upstairs is a rather cramped roof terrace.

our pick **McLlo Restaurant** (Bus Stand; dishes Rs65-175; ☻10am-10pm) Crowded nightly and justifiably popular, this big place above the noisy bus stand area serves a mind-boggling menu of Indian, Chinese and international fare, including pizzas and pasta. It's also one of the best places to enjoy an icy cold beer (Rs100), and it has cider and wines.

CAFES

Thanks in part to its expat community, McLeod has some of the best cafes in North India, with several places serving good espresso coffee, cappuccino and English-style tea.

Chocolate Log (Jogibara Rd; Rs25-50; ☻9.30am-7pm Wed-Mon) One of McLeod's original cake shops and still setting a high standard for sweets, coffee and freshly baked cakes.

Mandala Wifi Coffee House (Temple Rd; snacks Rs25-90; ☻7am-8pm) Next to Moonpeak, Mandala has an even more inviting terrace and serves tasty wraps, sandwiches and coffee with the advantage of free wifi (if you spend Rs100).

Moonpeak Espresso (Temple Rd; coffees & snacks Rs30-60; ☻7am-8pm) A little bit of Seattle, transported to India. Come for excellent coffee, cakes, imaginative sandwiches and dishes like poached chicken with mango, lime and coriander sauce.

Khana Nirvana (www.khananirvana.org; Temple Rd; meals Rs35-85) Above Stitches of Tibet, this community cafe is a relaxed hang-out serving healthy vegetarian breakfasts, soups and salad, pita sandwiches, burritos and organic tea. There's local entertainment most nights.

HIMACHAL PRADESH

our pick Cafe Boom Boom (Jogibara Rd; dishes Rs70-250; ☯ 8am-8.30pm Tue-Sun) Although a bit of a hike below McLeod, this remarkable cafe is well worth a visit. Beautifully designed, it boasts a mosaic tile floor, elaborate carved furniture, huge balcony with views and a mellow, slightly eccentric atmosphere. Gourmet pizza, focaccia and delicious cakes and coffee.

Drinking & Entertainment

McLeod's bars are mostly clustered around the main *chowk* (town square) and charge Rs100 for a big bottle of beer. The best choices for a drink are McLlo Restaurant (p377) and X-cite, both in the bus stand area. Hotel Tibet (p376), Hotel India House (p376), Aroma and Hotel Mount View also have bars. Takeaway beer (Rs60) and spirits (from Rs50) are available from several small liquor stores, including one right opposite the bus stand.

Khana Nirvana (www.khananirvana.org; Temple Rd) Cool community cafe with a program of arts and entertainment most nights. There's an open-mic night on Monday, documentary films about Tibet on Tuesday, and Tibetan speakers on Sunday.

Tibetan Music Trust (☎ 9805661031; www.tibetan musictrust.org; admission by donation; ☯ 6pm Thu & Sun) Performances of Tibetan folk music are held twice a week at Yonglings School, off Jogibara Rd. The live shows feature demonstrations of traditional regional Tibetan instruments and song. It's a great cultural and educational experience.

For details of performances of traditional lhamo and musical theatre, see Festivals & Events (p375).

Shopping

Dozens of shops and stalls sell Tibetan artefacts, including *thangkas*, bronze statues, metal prayer wheels, bundles of prayer flags, Tibetan horns and gemstone rosary beads. Some are Tibetan-run, but many are run by Kashmiri traders who apply a fair amount of sales pressure. Several local cooperatives offer the same goods without the hassle.

Tibetan Handicrafts Cooperative Centre (☎ 221415; Jogibara Rd; ☯ 8.30am-5pm Mon-Sat) employs newly arrived refugees in the weaving of Tibetan carpets. You'll pay around Rs6000 for a 0.9m by 1.8m wool carpet in traditional Tibetan colours and you can watch the weavers in action. For made-to-order clothing, head over the road to the Tailoring Section.

Stitches of Tibet (☎ 221527; www.tibetanwomen .org; Temple Rd; ☯ 10am-5pm Tue-Sun) This organisation offers a similar tailoring service to that of the Tibetan Handicrafts Centre of Tibet, providing work for newly arrived women refugees.

TCV Handicraft Centre (☎ 221592; www.tcvcraft.com; Temple Rd; ☯ 10am-5pm Tue-Sun) Has a huge range of Tibetan souvenirs at fixed prices. Sales benefit the Tibetan Children's Village.

Other interesting souvenir outlets include **Green Shop** (Bhagsu Rd; ☯ 10am-5pm Tue-Sun), selling products made from handmade Tibetan paper, and **Norling Designs** (Temple Rd; ☯ 10am-5pm Mon-Sat), selling products from the Norbulingka Institute (p381).

Getting There & Around

Many travel agencies in McLeod Ganj will book train tickets for services out of Pathankot (p276) for a fee. See p369 for train services in the Kangra Valley.

AIR

McLeod Ganj's nearest airport is at Gaggal, 15km southwest of Dharamsala. **Kingfisher** (www.flykingfisher.com) flies to Delhi (from Rs4000, 2½ hours) daily at 4pm. Book at Destination Travels (see Travel Agencies, p372). A taxi to Gaggal costs Rs450 (one hour).

AUTORICKSHAW

Autorickshaws are useful for getting around the immediate area – the autorickshaw stand is just north of the bus stand. Sample fares include Bhagsu (Rs30), Tsuglagkhang (Rs40) and Dharamkot (Rs 50).

BUS

All roads radiate from the bus stand at McLeod's main square, where you can book Himachal Roadways Transport Corporation (HRTC) buses up to a month in advance. Travel agencies can book seats on deluxe private buses to Delhi (Rs450, 12 hours, 6pm), Manali (Rs450, 11 hours, 8.30pm) and other destinations, and there are regular long-haul buses from Dharamsala. For more details on buses from McLeod Ganj see the table, p380.

TAXI

McLeod's **taxi stand** (☎ 221034) is on Mall Rd, north of the bus station. To hire a taxi for the day, for a journey of less than 80km, expect to pay Rs1000.

BUSES FROM MCLEOD GANJ			
Destination	Fare (Rs)	Duration (hr)	Frequency
Dehra Dun	325	13	8pm
Delhi	325	12	4am, 6pm, 7pm (ordinary); 4.30pm, 7.45pm (deluxe); 7.30pm (AC)
Manali	255	11	6am, 6.30am, 5pm
Pathankot	65	4	5 daily

Fares for short hops include Gangchen Kyishong (Rs60), Dharamkot (Rs70), Dharamsala's Kotwali Bazaar (Rs140), Dharamsala bus station (Rs150), Norbulingka Institute (Rs300) and the airport (Rs550). Return fares are about a third more, while longer fares are similar to those charged by the taxi stand in Dharamsala – see p369.

AROUND MCLEOD GANJ
Bhagsu & Dharamkot
☎ 01892

Through pine trees to the north and east of McLeod lie the villages of Dharamkot and Bhagsu, which can both be visited on a pleasant half-day hike, or as an alternative accommodation base. Bhagsu (Bhagsunag) in particular is developing into a busy summer resort. At the back of the village there's a traveller enclave that's popular with the hippie/Israeli crowd, but more-upmarket concrete hotels are making their mark. The village has a cold spring with **baths**, a small **Shiva temple** built by the raja of Kangra in the 16th century, and a gaudy **temple** with stairways passing through the open mouths of a cement crocodile and lion. Continuing through Bhagsu, you can walk on to Dharamkot and back to McLeod, or climb up to Triund via a gushing **waterfall**.

Various alternative therapies are available in the backpacker enclave. The **Buddha Hall** (☎ 221171; www.buddhahall.com) has courses in reiki, yoga and Indian classical music. Bhagsu has half a dozen internet cafes and travel agencies.

SLEEPING
Bhagsu
Oak View Guesthouse (☎ 221530; d Rs200-300) Clean guest house on the path to Upper Baghsu. All rooms have hot water and TV, and the buzzing traveller restaurant at the front serves Thai and Israeli food along with the usual fare.

Sky Pye Guesthouse (☎ 220497; d Rs250; 🖳) A little further up the hill from Oak View, Sky Pye is another good-value traveller hang-out that's often full. There are views from the terrace and from some rooms, an there's an internet cafe and a cute little restaurant with low tables and cushions on the floor.

At the entrance to Bhagsu are half a dozen nondescript midrange hotels. The **Sangam Guesthouse** (☎ 221013; www.hotelsangambhagsunag.com; d Rs600-1000) is a good choice, with clean rooms (some with balconies) and a restaurant.

Dharamkot
Dharamkot is much more low-key than Bhagsu, but has a small knot of guest houses near the Himalayan Iyengar Yoga Centre.

Kamal Guesthouse (☎ 226920; d with/without bathroom Rs200/75) Friendly five-room guest house with roof terrace.

New Blue Heaven Guesthouse (☎ 221005; www.hotelnewblueheaven.com; d Rs 350-880; 🖳) Spotless carpeted rooms with TV, hot water and balconies overlooking the valley make this a solid choice. Upper-floor rooms have the best views.

EATING
Bhagsu is full of busy German bakeries and backpacker cafes serving falafel, hummus and Tibetan food.

Ashoka International Restaurant (dishes Rs30-140) Bhagsu's best Indian and Chinese food is served in a smart dining room with a choice of floor cushions or normal tables.

Unity Bistro & Pizza House (mains Rs35-75) Further up the hill from Ashoka in Upper Bhagsu, this busy cafe serves tasty wood-fired pizzas and pasta dishes.

Sidhibari & Tapovan
About 6km from Dharamsala, the little village of Sidhibari is the adopted home of Ogyen Trinley Dorje, the 17th Karmapa of Tibetan Buddhism, who fled to India in 2000. Although his official seat is Rumtek Monastery in Sikkim, the young leader of the Kagyu (Black Hat) sect has been banned from taking up his seat for fear this would upset the Chinese government.

The temporary seat of the Karmapa is the large **Gyuto Tantric Gompa** (☎ 01892-236637; www

.kagyuoffice.org) in Sidhibari. Public audiences take place here on Wednesday and Saturday at 2.30pm; foreign visitors are welcome but security is tight and bags, phones and cameras are not allowed inside the auditorium.

Nearby is the **Tapovan Ashram**, a popular spiritual retreat for devotees of Rama, with a colourful Ram Mandir, a giant black Shiva lingam and a 6m-high statue of Hanuman.

Regular local buses run from Dharamsala to Sidhibari (Rs5, 15 minutes) or you can take a taxi for Rs250 return. Tapovan is a 2km walk south along a quiet country road.

Norbulingka Institute
☎ 01892

About 6km from Dharamsala, the wonderful **Norbulingka Institute** (☎ 246405; www.norbulingka.org; ☿ 8am-6pm) was established in 1988 to teach and preserve traditional Tibetan art forms, including woodcarving, statue-making, *thangka* painting and embroidery. The centre produces expensive but exquisite souvenirs, including embroidered clothes, cushions and wall hangings, and sales benefit refugee artists. Also here are delightful Japanese-influenced **gardens** and a central **Buddhist temple** with a 4m-high gilded statue of Sakyamuni. Next to the shop is the **Losel Doll Museum** (Indian/foreigner Rs5/20;

☿ 9am-5.30pm), with quaint puppet dioramas of Tibetan life. A short walk behind the complex is the large **Dolma Ling** Buddhist nunnery.

Set in the gorgeous Norbulingka gardens, **Norling Guest House** (☎ 246406; normail@norbulingka.org; s/d from Rs1200/1500) offers fairy-tale rooms decked out with Buddhist murals and handicrafts from the institute, and arranged around a sunny atrium. Meals are available at the institute's Norling Cafe.

To get here, catch a Yol-bound bus from Dharamsala and ask to be let off at Sidhpur (Rs5, 15 minutes), near the Sacred Heart School, from where it's a 15-minute walk. A taxi from Dharamsala will cost Rs280 return.

SOUTHWEST OF DHARAMSALA
Kangra
☎ 01892 / elev 734m

The former capital of the princely state of Kangra, this bustling pilgrim town is an easy day trip from McLeod Ganj. Hindus visit to pay homage at the **Brajeshwari Devi Temple**, one of the 51 *Shakti peeths*, the famous temples marking the sites where body parts from Shiva's first wife, Sati, fell after the goddess was consumed by flames. The Brajeshwari temple marks the final resting place of Sati's left breast (see History, p502, for more on the legend).

MCLEOD GANJ TO BHARMOUR TREK

This popular six- to seven-day route crosses over the Indrahar La (4300m) to the ancient village of Bharmour in the Chamba Valley. The pass is open from September to early November and you can start this trek, and make all arrangements, in McLeod Ganj or Bharmour.

From McLeod, take an autorickshaw along the Dharamkot road, then walk on through pine and rhododendron forests to Triund, where there's a simple rest house. The next stage climbs to the glacier at Laka Got (3350m) and continues to the rocky shelter known as Lahes Cave. With an early start the next day, you can cross the Indrahar La – and be rewarded with astounding views – before descending to the meadow campground at Chata Parao.

The stages on to Bharmour can be tricky without a local guide. From Chata Parao, the path moves back into the forest, descending over three days to Kuarsi, Garola and finally to Bharmour, where you can catch buses on to Chamba. Alternatively, you can bail out and catch a bus at several places along the route.

Stage	Route	Duration (hr)	Distance (km)
1	McLeod Ganj to Triund	4-5	9
2	Triund to Lahes Cave	4-5	6
3	Lahes Cave to Chata Parao over Indrahar La	6-7	11
4	Chata Parao to Kuarsi	5-6	14
5	Kuarsi to Chanauta	6-7	16
6	Chanauta to Garola	5-6	12
7	Garola to Bharmour	5-6	14

Famous for its wealth, the temple was looted by a string of invaders, from Mahmud of Ghazni to Jehangir, before collapsing in the 1905 earthquake. Rebuilt in the original style, the temple is reached through an atmospheric bazaar winding uphill from the main road, lined with shops selling *prasad* and religious trinkets.

On the far side of town, an Rs80 autorickshaw ride from the bus stand, the impregnable-looking **Kangra Fort** (Nagar Kot; Indian/foreigner Rs5/100; ☺ dawn-dusk) soars above the confluence of the Manjhi and Banganga Rivers. The fort was used by Hindu rajas, Mughal warlords and even the British before it was finally toppled by the earthquake of 1905. On clear days, head to the battlements for views north to the mountains and south to the plains. A small **museum** at the fort has stone carvings from temples inside the compound and miniature paintings from the Kangra School.

Royal Hotel & Restaurant (☎ 265013; royalhotel@rediffmail.com; r Rs400-500), on the main road between the steps of the main temple and the bus stand, has neat, tiled rooms with hot showers, plus a decent restaurant.

For meals, eat at your hotel or try one of the many *dhabas* in the centre of town and along the bazaar that runs up to Brajeshwari Devi.

GETTING THERE & AWAY

Kangra's bus stand is 1.5km north of the temple bazaar, a Rs25 autorickshaw ride from the centre. There are frequent buses to Dharamsala (Rs20, one hour), Palampur (Rs35, 1½ hours), Pathankot (Rs70, three hours) and Jawalamukhi (Rs30, 1½ hours).

Trains pull into Kangra Mandir station, 3km east of town, and Kangra station, 5km south. Travellers have reported problems getting an autorickshaw from the stations into town.

Taxis in Kangra charge Rs200 to Gaggal airport, Rs350 to Dharamsala, and Rs500 to McLeod Ganj, Jawalamukhi or Masrur.

Masrur

A winding road runs southwest from Gaggal through pleasant green hills to the 10th century **temples** (Indian/foreigner Rs5/100; ☺ dawn-dusk) at Masrur. Although badly damaged by the 1905 earthquake, the *sikharas* owe more than a passing resemblance to the Hindu temples at Angkor Wat in Cambodia. You can climb to the upper level for mountain views.

The easiest way to get here is by taxi from Dharamsala (Rs900 return), or you can get as far as Lunj (Rs20, 1½ hours) from Dharamsala by public bus and take a local taxi for the last few kilometres.

Jawalamukhi
☎ 01970

About 34km south of Kangra is the town and **temple** of Jawalamukhi, the goddess of light, worshipped in the form of a natural-gas eternal flame issuing from the rocks. The temple is one of the 51 *Shakti peeths*, marking the spot where the tongue of Shiva's first wife, Sati, fell after her body was consumed by flames (see History, p502, for more on the legend). The gold dome and spire were installed by Maharaja Ranjit Singh, the 'Lion of Punjab', who never went into battle without seeking a blessing from the temple.

Hotel Jawalaji (☎ 222280; d Rs600-800, with AC Rs1300-2000; ✗) is a superior HPTDC property, with well-loved rooms, conveniently located for walks to the temple and outlying countryside.

Buses to Dharamsala (Rs50, 1½ hours) and Kangra (Rs30, 1½ hours) leave all day from the stand below the road leading up to the temple. Taxis charge Rs700/1000 one way/return from McLeod Ganj.

DHARAMSALA TO MANDI
Palampur
☎ 01894 / elev 1249m

About 30km southeast of Dharamsala, Palampur is a small junction town surrounded by tea plantations and rice fields. A short trek from town takes you to the pretty waterfall in **Bundla Chasm**, or you can pass a few hours observing the tea-making process at the **Palampur Tea Cooperative** (☎ 230220; ☺ 10.30am-12.30pm & 1.30-4.30pm Tue-Fri), about 2km from town on the road to Mandi.

HPTDC Hotel Tea-Bud (☎ 231298; d Rs900-2000), 1km north of Main Bazar on the edge of town, has large grounds and a good restaurant; rooms are spacious and well kept. The more-expensive rooms are in a new block but the old ones aren't bad.

The bus station is 1km south of Main Bazar; an autorickshaw from the centre costs Rs20. Buses leave all day for Dharamsala (Rs35, two hours). A taxi from Dharamsala costs Rs600. Palampur is a stop on the Pathankot-Jogindarnagar rail line.

THE KANGRA VALLEY TOY TRAIN

A lumbering narrow-gauge train runs east from Pathankot, providing a scenic, if slow, back route to Kangra (2½ hours), Palampur (four hours), Baijnath (6½ hours) and Jogindarnagar (nine hours). There are seven trains a day – two as far as Jogindarnagar and five as far as Baijnath. Ordinary trains cost Rs 27 or less to any destination on the route, but carriages are crammed with passengers and seats cannot be booked in advance. Board early to grab a window seat and enjoy the views en route.

Baijnath

☎ 01894 / elev 1010m

The small town of Baijnath, set on a mountain-facing ridge 46km southeast of Dharamsala, is an important pilgrimage destination. In the middle of the village is the exquisitely carved **Baidyanath Temple**, sacred to Shiva in his incarnation as Vaidyanath, Lord of the Physicians, dating from the 8th century. Thousands of pilgrims make their way here for the **Shivaratri Festival** (see boxed text, p335) in late February and early March.

Most people visit on a day trip, or a stop on the journey from Mandi to Dharamsala. The Pathankot–Jogindarnagar rail line passes through Paprola, about 1km west of the main bus stand.

Tashijong & Taragarh

About 5km west of Baijnath, and 2km north from the Palampur road, the village of Tashijong is home to a small community of Drukpa Kagyud monks and refugees. The focus of life here is the impressive **Tashijong Gompa**, with several mural-filled prayer halls and a carpet-making, *thangka*-painting and woodcarving cooperative.

About 2km south of Tashijong, at Taragarh, is the extraordinary **Taragarh Palace** (☎ 01894-242034, ☎ in Delhi 011-24692317; www.taragarh.com; r Rs4000-5500; 🏊 🎾), the summer palace of the last maharaja of Jammu and Kashmir. Now a luxury hotel, this elegant country seat is full of portraits of the Dogra royal family, Italian marble, crystal chandeliers, tiger skins and other ostentatious furnishings. It's set in beautiful grounds with a pool and tennis courts. The restaurant serves lavish buffet meals (Rs300 to Rs500).

Both villages can be reached on the buses that run along the Mandi–Palampur highway – just tell the bus driver where you want to get off.

Bir & Billing

About 9km east of Baijnath, a road winds uphill to the village of Bir (1300m), a small Tibetan colony with three peaceful **gompas** that welcome passing visitors, and Billing (2600m), a famous launch pad for paragliding and hang-gliding. In 1992 the world record of 135km for an out-and-return flight was set here. International teams come to challenge the record every May for the **Himalayan Hang-Gliding Rally** (see boxed text, p335). You need your own gear to enjoy the thermals, but enquire locally about tandem flights.

A taxi from McLeod Ganj to Billing will cost Rs750. Alternatively, travel by bus or train to Jogindarnagar (on the route to Mandi) and take a taxi there for Rs350 return.

CHAMBA VALLEY

The Chamba Valley is a splendidly isolated valley system, cut off from the Kangra Valley by the Dhauladhar Range and from Kashmir by the Pir Panjal. This area was ruled for centuries as the princely state of Chamba, the most ancient state in North India. Even though good roads connect Chamba with Pathankot and Kangra, surprisingly few travellers make it out here, with even fewer continuing down the valley beyond the old hill station of Dalhousie – which is an attraction in itself.

Dalhousie

☎ 01899 / pop 10,500 / elev 2036m

With its plunging pine-clad valleys and distant mountain views, Dalhousie is another of those cool mountain retreats that the British left behind. Since Independence, the colonial mansions have been joined by the posh Dalhousie Public School and numerous modern hotels catering to honeymooners from the plains, along with obligatory army cantonment. There isn't much to do but stroll and admire the views, which is really the point of coming here.

Quite a few Tibetan refugees have made a home in Dalhousie and there are painted **rock carvings** of Buddhist deities along the south side of the ridge. You can also visit the British-era churches of **St John** and **St Francis**, set among the pines at opposite ends of the ridge.

ORIENTATION

Unusually for a hill station there are few truly steep roads, but Dalhousie is spread far enough to be exhausting. The market areas at Subhash Chowk and Gandhi Chowk are linked by lanes – Thandi Sarak (Cold Rd), and Garam Sarak (Hot Rd). The latter lane receives more sunshine. The bus stand area, with several good hotels, is about 2km north.

Street lighting is limited so carry a torch.

INFORMATION

At the Tibetan Market and near Gandhi Chowk there are internet cafes charging Rs40 an hour.

HPTDC tourist office (☎ 242225; ☿ 10am-5pm Apr-Jul, closed Sun Aug-Mar) Opposite the bus stand; helpful staff can advise on bus times.

Punjab National Bank (Hospital Rd; ☿ 10am-4pm Mon-Fri, to 1pm Sat) About 300m south of Subhash Chowk; travellers cheques are preferred to cash.

State Bank of India (☿ 24hr) International ATM, near the bus stand.

Trek-n-Travels (☎ 242160; Tibetan Market) Near the bus stand; can arrange treks around Chamba Valley from Rs700 per day.

SLEEPING

Dalhousie has more than 100 hotels spread across various ridges and lanes. Most are either old or just look old. High season – when room prices double and availability dwindles – runs from April to July, and Christmas to New Year, and there's a mid-season from September to late October; expect at least 50% off at other times.

Budget

Youth Hostel Dalhousie (☎ 242189; yh_dalhousie@rediff mail.com; dm Rs60, r Rs200; 🖳) A 200m walk down a back lane opposite the bus stand, Dalhousie's hostel is spotless and run with military precision. Dorms are single sex, showers are hot, and facilities include internet access, free wifi and a dining hall. YHA rules include a 10pm curfew, no alcohol, and vacating of rooms from 10am to 12.30pm for cleaning. There can also be noisy school groups – but it's a welcoming place with fixed rates all year.

Hotel Aarti (☎ 242433; d Rs350-500) Down a lane off Garam Sarak, Aarti is a friendly place with simple but clean rooms that have TVs, tiled bathrooms and views across the valley.

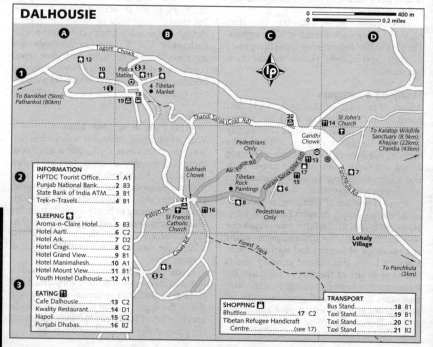

DALHOUSIE

INFORMATION
HPTDC Tourist Office..........1 A1
Punjab National Bank..........2 B3
State Bank of India ATM.....3 B1
Trek-n-Travels..................4 B1

SLEEPING
Aroma-n-Claire Hotel.........5 B3
Hotel Aarti......................6 C2
Hotel Ark.......................7 D2
Hotel Crags....................8 C2
Hotel Grand View..............9 B1
Hotel Manimahesh.............10 A1
Hotel Mount View.............11 A1
Youth Hostel Dalhousie.....12 A1

EATING
Cafe Dalhousie................13 C2
Kwality Restaurant............14 D1
Napoli..........................15 C2
Punjabi Dhabas................16 B2

SHOPPING
Bhuttico........................17 C2
Tibetan Refugee Handicraft
Centre......................(see 17)

TRANSPORT
Bus Stand......................18 B1
Taxi Stand......................19 B1
Taxi Stand......................20 C1
Taxi Stand......................21 B2

HIMACHAL PRADESH

Hotel Crags (☎ 242124; Garam Sarak; r Rs400-700, cottage Rs800) For colonial character and valley views, Crags is the pick of the budget places – listed rates are half this price most of the year. Down some steps from the Subhash Chowk end of Garam Sarak, this big old house has huge rooms and a large front terrace offering spectacular views of the valley – the upper-floor rooms with front sitting room are easily the best and there's a self-contained cottage.

Midrange & Top End

Hotel Ark (☎ 240605; www.hotelarkdalhousie.com; Panchkula Rd; r Rs700-1600) A whimsical colonial folly, built in 1941 in the style of a Mughal mausoleum. Spiral staircases wind up the mock minarets to large, modern rooms. Upper floors are carpeted and a bit threadbare; tiled rooms are better.

Aroma-n-Claire Hotel (☎ 242199; Court Rd; r Rs900-1350) Like a mini-museum, this colourful 1939 hotel just down the road from Subash Chowk is filled with paintings, sculptures and collected bric-a-brac. Rooms with TV and fridge are ageing but spacious and open out to a garden and valley views. It also has a good restaurant.

Hotel Manimahesh (☎ 242793; r Rs1500-2400) The better of the two HPTDC hotels, Manimahesh feels a bit forlorn, but all of the spacious rooms face out to sublime Pir Panjal views, and it's an easy walk from the bus stand.

our pick **Hotel Grand View** (☎ 240760; www.grandviewdalhousie.in; d Rs1800-2000, ste Rs2500-4500) Although not as slick as Mount View, Grand has bags of colonial character and more than lives up to its name. The stately 1920s hotel is surrounded by gardens gazing across to views of the Pir Panjal peaks, and the spacious Raj-inspired rooms open out to sunny glass-panelled hallways.

Hotel Mount View (☎ 242120; www.hotelmountview.com; Club Rd; r Rs2000-2200, ste Rs2800-3800) There's an undeniable Raj-era charm to this delightful hotel, full of dark-wood finishes and period furnishings. Rooms are chintzy but cosy – the suite room has an attic bedroom – and there are good valley views.

EATING

Both Subhash Chowk and Gandhi Chowk have places to eat. Most restaurants are open from 9am to 10pm. None of Dalhousie's hotels are licensed to serve alcohol.

Cafe Dalhousie (Gandhi Chowk; mains Rs35-120; ⏱ from 8am) This little cafe beneath Hotel Dalhousie has a blackboard menu with everything from cheap dosas and other South Indian snacks, to Indian and Chinese dishes.

Kwality Restaurant (Gandhi Chowk; dishes Rs40-160) Regarded as Dalhousie's best independent restaurant, Kwality shows some style in its decor, with solid wooden furniture and comfy cream chairs. The extensive veg and nonveg menu covers Indian and Chinese as well as burgers, pizza and sizzlers.

Napoli (Garam Sarak; dishes Rs45-200) Situated a short walk down from Gandhi Chowk, Napoli has no Italian food but there are well-prepared Indian and Chinese favourites here, as well as offbeat dishes such as 'chicken Mexican'.

For cheap eats, there are several Punjabi *dhabas* on the south side of Subhash Chowk. All are called Sher-E-*something* and all serve good food for Rs70 or less.

The restaurants at Hotel Grand View (left) and Mount View (left) near the bus stand offer a charming colonial dining experience and multicuisine menus.

SHOPPING

Close to Gandhi Chowk on Garam Sarak, you'll find fair-priced Kullu shawls and hats at **Bhuttico** (☎ 240440; ⏱ 10am-6pm Mon-Sat) and a good selection of Tibetan carpets and handicrafts at the **Tibetan Refugee Handicraft Centre** (☎ 240607; ⏱ 10am-6pm Wed-Mon). Just up from the bus stand, the **Tibetan Market** sells textiles, clothing and trinkets for the holiday crowd.

GETTING THERE & AWAY

Bus

The booking office at the bus stand is invariably closed, but the tourist office next door can

BUSES FROM DALHOUSIE			
Destination	Fare (Rs)	Duration (hr)	Frequency
Amritsar	120	6	6am
Delhi	335	12	3pm
Dharamsala	130	6	7am, 11.50am & 2pm
Jammu	120	6	10am
Pathankot	60	3	10 daily
Shimla	350	12	12.45pm

help with bus information; for long-distance services, take any south-bound bus to the larger bus station in Banikhet (Rs5, 10 minutes). Buses run in the morning to Chamba (Rs50, two hours); two go via Khajjiar (Rs20, one hour). For more-frequent Chamba buses, head to Banikhet first. See the table, p385, for direct services.

Taxi

There are unionised taxi stands with fixed fares at Subhash Chowk, Gandhi Chowk and the bus stand. From the bus stand, you'll pay Rs50 to Subhash Chowk and Rs70 to Gandhi Chowk. Other one-way fares:

Destination	Fare (Rs)
Bharmour	2050
Chamba	1020 (1250 return)
Dharamsala	1750
Kalatop	510
Khajjiar	620
Pathankot	1150

Around Dalhousie
KALATOP WILDLIFE SANCTUARY

Midway between Dalhousie and Chamba, accessible by taxi or public bus, the forested hills around Khajjiar are preserved as the **Kalatop Wildlife Sanctuary**. The pine forests provide excellent walking country and you have a chance of spotting langur monkeys, barking deer and black bears. Buses between Dalhousie and Khajjiar pass the park entrance at **Lakkar Mandi**.

KHAJJIAR

India's so-called 'Mini Switzerland', this grassy bowl-shaped *marg* (meadow), 22km from Dalhousie, is ringed by pines and thronged by holidaymakers. In among the *dhabas* on one side is the **Khajjinag Temple**, with fine woodcarvings and crude effigies of the five Pandavas, installed here in the 16th century.

In season, **pony rides** around the meadow and its small central lake cost from Rs100, and **zorbing** in giant inflatable balls costs from Rs100 for a quick roll. Since there are no big slopes, as such, you get pushed along – not exactly high adrenaline!

There are a handful of fast-food restaurants and several hotels, but most travellers make a day trip here by bus from Chamba (Rs25, 1½ hours) or Dalhousie (Rs20, one hour). Buses run on this route about five times a day.

If you do decide to stay, the best option is the **HPTDC Hotel Davdar** (☎ 236333; Rs1100-2000), from where the large front rooms overlook the meadow. Better still are its quaint cottages across the road, with wide verandahs that are perfect for kicking back.

Chamba

☎ 01899 / pop 20,700 / elev 996m

Ensconced in the valley of the fast-flowing Ravi River, the charming capital of Chamba district is dominated by the former palaces of the local maharajas. The princely state of Chamba was founded in AD 920 by Raja Sahil Varman and it survived for 1000 years until it finally fell to the British in 1845. Every year since 935, Chamba has celebrated the annual harvest with the **Minjar Festival** (p335) in July/August in honour of Raghuvira (an incarnation of Rama).

Although en route to Bharmour and popular trekking country, Chamba is well off the tourist radar, giving it an everyday Indian feel. The de facto centre of town is the open grassy sports field known as the Chowgan, the focus for festivals, impromptu cricket matches, picnics and promenades. Most places of interest are tucked away in the alleyways of Dogra Bazar, which runs uphill past the maharaja's palace.

INFORMATION

There's an international ATM at the State Bank of India, near the court house.

Cyberia (per hr Rs30; ☼ 9am-8pm Mon-Sat) Near Hotel Aroma Palace; has broadband connection and helpful staff.

Himachal Tourist Office (☎ 224002; Court Rd; ☼ 10am-5pm Mon-Sat) In the yellow building in the courtyard of Hotel Iravati. Has limited local information but lots of brochures.

Post office (Museum Rd; ☼ 9.30am-5.30pm Mon-Sat)

SIGHTS & ACTIVITIES
Lakshmi Narayan Temple Complex

Opposite the Akhand Chandi Palace are six **sikharas** dating from the 10th to the 19th centuries, built in the Himachal stone-hut style and covered in carvings. The largest (and oldest) is dedicated to Lakshmi Narayan (Vishnu). In front is a distinctive Nepali-style pillar topped by a statue of Vishnu's faithful servant, the man-bird Garuda. The remaining temples are sacred to Radha Krishna, Shiva, Gauri Shankar, Triambkeshwar Mahdev and Lakshmi Damodar. The compound has a

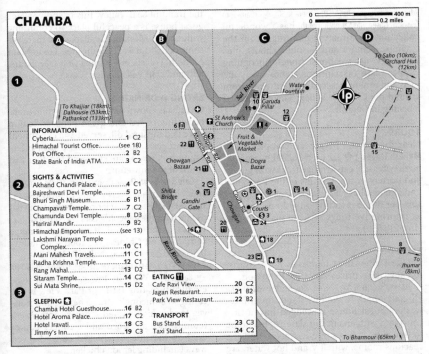

CHAMBA

INFORMATION
Cyberia...1 C2
Himachal Tourist Office............(see 18)
Post Office..2 B2
State Bank of India ATM....................3 C2

SIGHTS & ACTIVITIES
Akhand Chandi Palace 4 C1
Bajreshwari Devi Temple....................5 D1
Bhuri Singh Museum...........................6 B1
Champavati Temple............................7 C2
Chamunda Devi Temple......................8 D3
Harirai Mandir....................................9 B2
Himachal Emporium......................(see 13)
Lakshmi Narayan Temple
    Complex.......................................10 C1
Mani Mahesh Travels........................11 C1
Radha Krishna Temple......................12 C1
Rang Mahal.......................................13 D2
Sitaram Temple.................................14 C3
Sui Mata Shrine................................15 D2

SLEEPING
Chamba Hotel Guesthouse...............16 B2
Hotel Aroma Palace..........................17 C2
Hotel Iravati.....................................18 C3
Jimmy's Inn......................................19 C3

EATING
Cafe Ravi View.................................20 C2
Jagan Restaurant.............................21 B2
Park View Restaurant.......................22 B2

TRANSPORT
Bus Stand...23 C3
Taxi Stand..24 C2

small **museum** (admission free; 11am-5pm Mon-Sat) displaying religious artefacts.

Other Temples

On the hilltop above the Rang Mahal, reached via a set of steps near the bus stand, or by taxi along the road to Jhumar, the stone **Chamunda Devi Temple** features impressive carvings of Chamunda Devi (Durga in her wrathful aspect) and superior views of Chamba and the Dhauladhar. About 500m north along the road to Saho, the **Bajreshwari Devi Temple** is a handsome hut-style mandir with exquisite effigies of Bajreshwari (an incarnation of Durga) set into plinths around the walls.

Between the two is a small shrine to **Sui Mata**, a local princess who gave her life to appease a water spirit that was causing a terrible drought in Chamba. The goddess is highly venerated by local women and the four-day **Sui Mata Mela** (p335) is celebrated each April on the Chowgan in her honour.

By the Chowgan is the 11th-century **Harirai Mandir**, sacred to Vishnu. Dotted nearby Akhand Chandi Palace are similar stone temples to **Radha Krishna**, **Sitaram** (Rama) and **Champavati**,

daughter of Raja Sahil Varman, worshipped locally as an incarnation of Durga.

Historic Buildings

Uphill from the Chowgan and lording over the town is the unmissable stately white **Akhand Chandi Palace**, the former home of the Chamba raja. Built in 1764, the central Darbar Hall is reminiscent of many civic buildings in Kathmandu. It now houses a postgraduate college; you can peek inside during school hours.

A few blocks southeast is the fortresslike, rusty-coloured **Rang Mahal** (Old Palace), which once housed the royal granary and treasury. It now houses the **Himachal Emporium** (222333; 10am-5pm Mon-Sat), which sells Chamba's famous *rumals* – pieces of cloth finely embroidered in silk, with a perfect mirror image of the same pattern on the reverse side and no evidence of knots or loose threads. Prices start at Rs300.

Bhuri Singh Museum

Founded in 1908 and named after the Chamba ruler of that time, this **museum** (222590; Museum

Rd; Indian/foreigner Rs10/50, camera Rs50; 10am-5pm Tue-Sun, closed 2nd Sat each month) has a wonderful collection of miniature paintings from the Chamba, Kangra and Basohli schools, plus woodcarvings, weapons, *rumals*, intriguing copper-plate inscriptions, relics from the rajas and ornately carved fountain slabs from around the Chamba Valley. There's detailed labelling in English.

TOURS

Near the Lakshmi Narayan complex, **Mani Mahesh Travels** (222507, 9816620401; manimahesh-travels@yahoo.com) can arrange treks with guides and porters in the foothills of the Pir Panjal and Dhauladhar (Rs1200 to Rs1800 per person, per day, depending on altitude), as well as informative tours of Chamba's temples (from Rs550).

SLEEPING

Unlike Dalhousie, Chamba is not a tourist town, so hotel prices vary little by season.

Jimmy's Inn (224748; dm Rs50, r Rs200-400) Directly opposite the bus stand, this white-washed guest house is wedged into a tiny courtyard with an ancient slate-roofed home to one side. It has some character, and the spacious rooms, with TV and hot water, are decent for the price.

Chamba House Guesthouse (222564; Gopal Nivas; d Rs550) With fine views over the Ravi River from its balcony, this creaky heritage building near Gandhi Gate is Chamba's best budget bolthole. Rooms are quaint, if a little poky, and the manager speaks little English, but it's very welcoming.

Hotel Aroma Palace (225177; www.hotelaromapalace chamba.com; dm Rs100, s/d from Rs400/500, deluxe r Rs800-3000;) Uphill from the taxi stand and past the courthouse, this modern place has a range of tidy rooms, an internet cafe, a restaurant and a sunny terrace with views over Chowgan. The cheaper rooms are disappointing – you can't swing a cat in the single rooms and others have their own bathroom outside off the hall – but if you pay a bit more you get the real deal.

Hotel Iravati (222671; Court Rd; d Rs700-1500) For a government-run hotel, the HPTDC Iravati punches above its weight – the rooms are spotless, bright and roomy and don't seem at all neglected. Even the in-house restaurant is better than average.

Orchard Hut (9418020401; orchardhut@hotmail .com; r Rs500-850) About 12km from Chamba in

the tranquil Saal Valley, this friendly village guest house is a peaceful place to commune with nature. Meals are available and there are some delightful walks in the area. Go to Mani Mahesh Travels in Chamba first (see Tours, left) and staff will arrange transfers.

EATING & DRINKING

Chamba is known for its *chukh* – a chilli sauce consisting of red and green peppers, lemon juice and mustard oil, served as a condiment in most restaurants. Chamba's most interesting restaurants are clustered together just south of the museum.

Cafe Ravi View (Chowgan; snacks Rs20-45; 9am-9pm) In a circular hut overlooking the Ravi River, this HPTDC-run snack house is worth a visit as much for the icy-cold beers and outdoor terrace as for the food. Still, it serves a good range of Indian and Chinese veg food – including dosas and bargain veg thalis (Rs40).

Park View Restaurant (Museum Rd; dishes Rs30-110; 8am-11pm) With its low ceiling and rickety furniture, tiny 1st-floor Park View is like eating in someone's attic. The veg and non-veg food is highly rated – order some *jheera* (cumin) rice and curd and a copper pail of dhal on the side, or chicken cooked seven ways (including lemon chicken).

Jagan Restaurant (Museum Rd; dishes Rs30-180) It's nothing flash but Jagan offers the tasty Chamba speciality *chamba madhra* (kidney beans with curd and ghee) for Rs65, plus a good selection of veg curries and chicken dishes. The top-floor Madhusala Bar is a no-frills place to have a beer and gaze over the town through glassless windows.

GETTING THERE & AWAY

Six daily buses make the hair-raising run to Bharmour (Rs65, three hours), though the road can be temporarily blocked by rockfalls. Buses for Dalhousie run every two hours (Rs50, 2½ hours), some going via Khajjiar (Rs25, 1½ hours). There are also buses to Dharamsala (Rs160, eight hours).

Official taxi fares include Khajjiar (Rs800 return), Bharmour (Rs1100/1250 one way/return), Dalhousie (Rs900) and Dharamsala (Rs2000).

Bharmour

01895 / elev 2195m

Hovering on the edge of a seemingly bottomless valley, the charming mountain village of

Bharmour is reached by a perilous mountain road winding 65km east of Chamba. This ancient slate-roofed settlement was the capital of the princely state of Chamba until AD 920, and there are fascinating temples and treks to surrounding mountain passes. In fact, you can trek from here all the way to McLeod Ganj. The villages around Bharmour are home to the seminomadic Gaddis, pastoralists who move their flocks up to alpine pastures during the summer, and descend to Kangra, Mandi and Bilaspur in winter.

SIGHTS & ACTIVITIES

Reached through the bazaar leading uphill from the 4WD stand, the **Chaurasi temples** are some of Himachal's finest. Built in the classic stone-*sikhara* style, with wide slate canopies, the Shaivite temples are spread over a flagstone courtyard that doubles as an outdoor classroom for local schools. Highlights of the compound are the towering **Manimahesh Temple**, built in the 6th century AD, and the squat **Lakshna Devi Temple**, featuring an eroded but wildly carved wooden doorway.

Treks from Bharmour can be arranged through the **Himalayan Travelling Agency** (☎ 225059), by the HP State Coop Bank in the bazaar, and the **Directorate of Mountaineering & Allied Sports** (☎ 225036), on the track above the 4WD stand. Expect to pay around Rs1200 a day, for food, tents, guides and porters. The trekking season lasts from May to late October.

Trekking destinations include Keylong and Udaipur in Lahaul, Baijnath and McLeod Ganj in the Kangra Valley, and the popular trek to the sacred lake at **Manimahesh**, a three-day, 35km hike above Bharmour. In August/September, pilgrims take a freezing dip in Manimahesh Lake as part of the **Manimahesh Yatra** (p335) in honour of Lord Shiva.

SLEEPING & EATING

Chamunda Guest House (☎ 225056; r with/without bathroom Rs300/200) The least appealing of Bharmour's guest houses, this lemon yellow village house has bare concrete rooms with bucket hot water. There's definitely room for bargaining. It's on the lower road from the 4WD stand.

Soma Sapan Guesthouse (☎ 225337; r from Rs200) On the track leading away from the temples above the 4WD stand, this bright yellow-and-mauve guest house has a range of rooms that are decent for the price. The cascading stream

outside will either lull you to sleep or drive you mad, but the views over the town and mountain peaks are great.

Chaurasi Hotel & Restaurant (☎ 225615; r Rs300-500, dishes Rs35-160) The derelict-looking timber-and-brick place teetering on the temple road is actually a good-value hotel with generous-sized rooms offering soaring views over the valley, especially from the top-floor room with balcony. The multicuisine restaurant here is Bharmour's best.

As well as hotel restaurants, there are several *dhabas* on the path to the Chaurasi temples.

GETTING THERE & AWAY

Buses leave every few hours for the rugged trip to Chamba (Rs65, three hours), but expect delays due to landslides. Taxis charge Rs1100 but you can bargain at the 4WD stand.

LAHAUL & SPITI

This vast, desolate corner of Himachal Pradesh is also one of the most sparsely populated regions on earth. Lahaul is a relatively green valley north of the Rohtang La, but as you travel east to Spiti the landscape transforms into a rugged network of interlocking river valleys hidden in the rain shadow of the Himalaya. It's 12,000 sq km of snow-topped mountains and high-altitude desert, punctuated by tiny patches of greenery and villages of whitewashed mud-brick houses clinging to the sides of rivers and melt-water streams.

As in Zanskar and Ladakh, Buddhism is the dominant religion, though there are small pockets of Hinduism in Lahaul, where many temples are sacred to Buddhist and Hindu deities. According to legend, some monasteries in Lahaul were founded personally by Padmasambhava, the Indian monk who converted Tibet to Buddhism in the 8th century AD.

Manali is the main gateway to Lahaul and Spiti. A seasonal highway runs north over the Rohtang La (3978m) to Keylong, the capital of Lahaul, continuing to Ladakh over the mighty Baralacha La (4950m) and Tanglang La (5328m). Side roads branch west to the little-visited Pattan Valley and east to Spiti over the 4551m Kunzum La. Growing numbers of travellers are visiting Lahaul and Spiti as part of the Great Himalayan Circuit from Kashmir to

Kinnaur. Snow closes all the mountain passes in winter. The Rohtang La, Baralacha La and Tanglang La are normally open from June to late October, while the Kunzum La to Spiti is accessible from July to October. Exact dates depend on snow conditions. At other times, the entire region is virtually cut off from the outside world, except for the rugged Hindustan–Tibet Hwy from Kinnaur.

For more information on Lahaul and Spiti, visit the local government website at http://hplahaulspiti.gov.in.

Losar, the Tibetan New Year, is celebrated in villages throughout Lahaul and Spiti in January or February, depending on the lunar calendar.

History

Buddhism arrived in Lahaul and Spiti during the 8th century AD with the Indian missionary Padmasambhava. By the 10th century, upper Lahaul, Spiti and Zanskar had been incorporated into the vast Guge kingdom of western Tibet. The Great Translator, Ringchen Zangpo, founded a series of centres of Buddhist learning along the Spiti Valley, including Tabo, one of the most remarkable Buddhist monasteries in North India.

After the kings of Ladakh were defeated by Mongol-Tibetan armies in the 18th century, the region was divided up by the surrounding powers. Lower Lahaul fell to the rajas of Chamba, Upper Lahaul came under the sway of the rajas of Kullu, and geographically isolated Spiti became part of Ladakh.

In 1847 Ladakh and Spiti were conquered by the Dogra Rajas of Kashmir, and Kullu and Lahaul came under British administration as a subdivision of the kingdom of Kangra; Spiti was added two years later. Despite the change of regimes, the region maintained strong links with Tibet right up until the Chinese occupation in 1949.

Since then, there has been a major resurgence in the cultural and religious life of Spiti, aided by the work of the Tibetan government in exile in Dharamsala. The gompas of Lahaul and Spiti are being restored, and money from tourism and hydroelectricity is improving living conditions for the farming communities who get snowed in here each winter.

Climate

Lahaul and Spiti have a markedly different climate from the rest of Himachal Pradesh.

The limited rainfall and high altitude – mostly above 3000m – ensures desperately cold conditions in winter. Even in summer, temperatures rarely rise above 15°C, and winter temperatures can plummet below –30°C!

Realistically, the region is only open to travellers when the mountain passes are open, from early June/July to late October. Whenever you travel, bring plenty of clothing for cold weather. See boxed text, p301, for more tips on high-altitude travel.

LAHAUL

Separated from the Kullu Valley by the 3978m Rohtang La and from Spiti by 4551m Kunzum La, Lahaul is greener and more developed than Ladakh and Spiti, but most travellers whistle straight through on the road between Manali and Leh, missing most of what Lahaul has to offer. The capital, Keylong, is an easy stop on the popular Leh–Manali bus trip and you can detour to a number of mountain villages and medieval monasteries that are blissfully untouched by mass tourism.

Government buses between Manali and Leh run from mid-July to mid-September, and private buses and share 4WDs run till mid-October. Services as far as Keylong continue until the Rohtang La closes in November, and buses east to Kaza stop when the Kunzum La closes in October. Check the status of the passes before visiting late in the season – once the snows arrive, you might be stuck for the winter.

Manali to Keylong

From Manali the road to Leh strikes north along the Beas River valley and climbs slowly through pine forests and switchbacks to the bare rocky slopes below snow-clad **Rohtang La** (3978m). The name literally translates as 'pile of dead bodies' – a reference to the hundreds of travellers who have frozen to death here over the centuries. Many Indian tourists make a day trip to Rohtang La from Manali for their first taste of snow, stopping at the *dhabas* in **Marhi**, and at the pass itself, to warm up with hot chai and *aloo paratha* (potato flat-bread). At the pass, look out for the small, dome-shaped temple that marks the source of the Beas River.

On the far side of the pass, the road plunges spectacularly down into the green **Lahaul Valley**, a soothing landscape of rocky buttresses and green alpine meadows. About 66km northwest of Manali, the tiny hamlet of **Gramphu** marks the turn-off to Spiti. There is only one building in Gramphu – a rustic stone *dhaba* beside a stream where you'll have to wait for the bus if you're heading to Kaza from Keylong.

Khoksar, 5km northwest of Gramphu, has several *dhabas* and a police checkpoint where foreigners must show their passports. The road passes through a sheer-sided valley, hemmed in by rock walls and the white tips of mountain glaciers. There's a spectacular hanging waterfall opposite the tiny village of **Sissu**; you may be able to stay at the PWD Rest House here.

About 18km before Keylong, **Gondla** is famous for its eight-storey tower fort, built from alternating layers of stone and timber. Once the home of the local *thakur*, the fort is no longer occupied, but it's still an impressive sight. Try to visit during the lively **Gondla Fair** in July. From Gondla, you can hike 4km to the village of **Tupchiling** to visit historic **Guru Ghantal Gompa**, allegedly founded by Padmasambhava. Although crumbling, the gompa contains ancient murals and wooden statues of bodhisattvas (Buddhist enlightened beings). Gondla has a basic hotel and a PWD Rest House that may accept travellers.

Pattan Valley

About 8km south of Keylong at Tandi, a side road branches northwest along the Pattan Valley towards **Udaipur**. Overlooking the Chenab River, it's a peaceful spot with a few basic hotels and the plain-looking **Markula Devi Temple**, which hides fabulous wooden panels depicting scenes from the Mahabharata and Ramayana, carved in the 12th century.

From Udaipur, you can backtrack 9km along the valley to the squat stone temple at **Triloknath**, founded as a Shiva temple but converted into a Buddhist shrine by the sage Padmasambhava. Hindus worship the idol inside as Shiva while Buddhists venerate it as Avalokitesvara. Triloknath is a major pilgrimage site for both religions during the **Pauri Festival** (see boxed text, p335) in August.

Keylong

☎ 01900 / elev 3350m

The capital of Lahaul sprawls along one side of the green Bhaga Valley just below the Manali–Leh highway. Although isolated, its position on the overland route between Manali and Ladakh (this is the last town of any size before Leh) has made it a major travellers' stop.

All buses stop for the night here and many travellers leave early the next morning. This means they see only the Keylong bus standing in the dark, but a longer stay reveals some grand mountain views, interesting walks and a laid-back village lifestyle.

The bus stand is off the highway, about a five-minute walk from the main bazaar. At the south end of town is the moderately interesting **Lahaul & Spiti Tribal Museum** (☼ 10am-5pm Tue-Sun), with traditional costumes, old dance masks and treasures from local gompas.

Keylong celebrates the annual **Lahaul Festival** (p335) in July with a big, bustling market and various cultural activities.

SLEEPING & EATING

Hotel Dupchen (☎ 222205; d Rs250) A popular local restaurant, serving Indian and Tibetan staples (Rs20 to Rs80), with a few spick-and-span rooms upstairs.

Hotel Tashi Deleg (☎ 222450; r Rs650-1200) Through the main bazaar, this big white place is Keylong's best-value hotel. Rooms get more expensive the higher you go, but all open out onto a balcony with mountain and valley views. The restaurant serves good Indian-Chinese and Tibetan food (meals Rs40 to Rs100), as well as cold beers.

There are a couple of guest houses around the bus stand, including **Drabla Guesthouse** (Rs250-450), which are convenient for an early exit, but the better hotels are a five-minute walk through the bazaar.

Aside from the hotel restaurants, there are plenty of *dhabas* on the highway and along the bazaar.

GETTING THERE & AWAY

Keylong is the official overnight stop for government buses travelling between Manali and Leh, so there are regular services in both directions when the mountain passes are open – typically June to October. Through bookings are only taken in Manali, so arrange a seat the day before, if you break the journey.

Buses to Leh (Rs475, 15 hours) leave at 5am, arriving at about 8pm the same evening.

There around five daily buses to Manali (Rs108, six hours). There's no direct bus to Kaza in Spiti – take the 5.30am bus and change at Gramphu (Rs45, two hours); the bus from Manali to Kaza pulls in around 8.30am.

For the Pattan Valley, there are four daily buses to Udaipur (Rs52, two hours).

Around Keylong

SHASHUR GOMPA

About 3km above Keylong is Shashur Gompa, dedicated to the Zanskari lama Deva Gyatsho. The original 16th-century gompa is now enshrined inside a modern gompa, with fine views over the valley. Frenetic masked *chaams* (ritual masked dances performed by Buddhist monks in gompas to celebrate the victory of good over evil and of Buddhism over pre-existing religions) are held here every June or July, depending on the Tibetan calendar. The path to the gompa cuts uphill behind the old bus stand – stick to the rough dirt path until you see the white chortens visible on the ridge.

KHARDONG GOMPA

Propped up on stilts on the far side of the valley, the 900-year-old gompa at Khardong is a steep three-hour walk from Keylong. Maintained by an order of Drukpa Kagyud monks and nuns, the monastery enshrines a mighty prayer wheel said to contain a million strips of paper bearing the mantra 'om mani padme hum' (hail to the jewel in the lotus). The surrounding scenery is magnificent and there are excellent frescoes, but you'll have to track down a monk or nun to open the doors. To get to the monastery, head through the bazaar, follow the stepped path down to the hospital and take the bridge over the Bhaga River, from where it's a 4km slog uphill.

TAYUL GOMPA

Perched on the side of the valley above the village of Satingri, the ancient Tayul Gompa has elegant mural work and a 4m-high statue of Padmasambhava, flanked by his two manifestations, Sighmukha and Vijravarashi. Tayul is about 6km from Keylong, reached by a fairly long day-hike.

JISPA

About 20km northeast of Keylong, the pretty village of Jispa is a popular overnight stop for mountain bikers and motorcyclists. There's a small and interesting folk museum (admission Rs25; 9am-6pm) on the main road and a 2km walk south is the 16th-century Ghemur Gompa, where a famous masked 'devil dance' is held in July.

For accommodation, there's the extremely inviting Hotel Ibex Jispa (01900-233203; s/d Rs1600/1800) on the main road.

SPITI

Separated from the fertile Lahaul Valley by the soaring 4551m Kunzum La, Spiti is another piece of Tibet transported to India. Villages are few and far between in this lunar landscape and they arrive like mirages – clusters of whitewashed homes nestled on the arid valley floor. Even more impressive are the Buddhist monasteries built high up on the sides of the valley and dwarfed by the sheer scale of the surrounding landscape. Local farmers eke out a living on the small strip of greenery that hugs the banks of the Spiti River.

In places, the landscape resembles a mini–Grand Canyon, while in others the strange rock formations look like melted candlewax. In any case, the scale is enormous. In many ways Spiti is even more rugged and remote than Ladakh, but buses run over the Kunzum La from Manali from July to October, and the Hindustan–Tibet Hwy to Tabo is theoretically open all year. A steady stream of motorcyclists and mountain bikers pit their machines against some of the most challenging roads in India. Most people start in Manali or Keylong and exit the valley at Rekong Peo in Kinnaur, but a few travellers go against the flow and travel west to Keylong or Ladakh. Sections of the road are frequently washed away by floods and landslides, especially between Nako and Rekong Peo, and teams of road-builders work throughout the year to keep it open.

In either direction, an inner line permit is required for the stretch from Tabo to Rekong Peo – see boxed text, p337.

Gramphu to Kaza

From the *dhaba* at Gramphu, the road to Spiti follows the gorge of the Chandra River, which was carved by glaciers as the Himalaya thrust upwards 50 million years ago. There are few permanent settlements, but buses stop for chai at Chattru, a small cluster of *dhabas* around the first bridge over the Chandra.

There's a second bridge and a single stone-hut *dhaba* at Battal, where a rough track runs 14km north to lovely Chandratal (Moon Lake), a tranquil glacial pool set among snow peaks at 4270m. From June to September you can stay in comfortable tents on the lakeshore at the Dewachen EcoCamp (per person inc meals Rs550) – book through Ecosphere in Kaza (01906-222724). This is also the starting point for treks to nearby Bara Shigri (Big Glacier), one of the longest glaciers in the Himalaya, but the route is treacherous and it's best to travel with an experienced guide.

From Battal, the road leaves the river and creeps up to **Kunzum La** (4551m), the watershed between the Spiti and Lahaul Valleys. Buses perform a respectful circuit of the stupas strewn with fluttering prayer flags at the top before continuing down into the Spiti Valley. An alternative 10.5km trail to Chandratal starts at the pass, continuing to Baralacha La on the Manali–Leh road in three strenuous days.

The first village of any size is **Losar**, a cluster of concrete and mud-brick houses in scrubby vegetation on the valley floor. Buses stop for lunch at the *dhabas* on the highway and there's a passport check. You should have time for the ethnological displays at the one-room **rural museum** (9am-6pm or by request) before the bus heads on to Gramphu or Kaza. A couple of basic guest houses allow you to break the journey here; the friendly **Samsong Cafe & Guesthouse** (s/d without bathroom Rs100/200) has simple but clean rooms, and hot meals.

The final stretch to Kaza follows the edge of the Spiti River, passing the large **Yangchen Choling** nunnery at Pangmo, which provides an education for girls from around the valley. A few kilometres further along is the **Sherab Choling** monastery school at Morang. Experienced teachers may be able to arrange volunteer teaching placements at these schools through the US-based **Jamyang Foundation** (www.jamyang.org).

At **Rangrik**, just before the bridge across the river to Kaza, there's a Buddhist temple with a 5m-high sitting Buddha statue.

Kaza

 01906 / elev 3640m

With its multicoloured rooftops, Kaza looks a bit like a toy town as you descend on the long route from Kunzum La. The capital of Spiti, Kaza sprawls over the eroded flood plain of the Spiti River and is the biggest settlement you'll encounter in this empty corner of the state. The setting is wonderfully rugged – jagged mountains rise on either side and the river coils across the flat valley floor like a python with indigestion. The original, whitewashed village is separated from the modern administrative compound at New Kaza by a stream. The colourful new **Sakya Gompa** dominates the high road in New Kaza, while the ramshackle bazaar of Old Kaza spreads out on the other side of the stream that divides the town.

Most people stay at least one night to arrange the inner line permit for travel beyond Tabo. Kaza is also the starting point for trips to Ki Gompa (p394) and Kibber (p394) and treks into the mountains. The well-organised bus and 4WD stand is below the bazaar in the old village.

In August, villagers from across Spiti descend on Kaza for the **Ladarcha Fair** (p335). All sorts of goods are bought and sold and traders wear their finest clothes.

INFORMATION

There is nowhere to change money, but you can check emails at a couple of internet cafes in the bazaar in Old Kaza. The post office is just below the gompa in New Kaza. Inner line permits for travel to Kinnaur are easy to arrange – see the boxed text, p395.

Ecosphere (222724; www.spitiecosphere.com) Arranges village homestays, tours and accommodation at the Dewachen EcoCamp at Chandratal.

Spiti Holiday Adventure (222711; www.spiti holidayadventure.com; Main Bazar) Organises all-inclusive mountain treks from two to nine days for around Rs2500 per person per day, as well as 4WD safaris and monastery tours.

SLEEPING & EATING

There are a surprising number of guest houses squirreled away in Old Kaza close to the bus and taxi stands, as well as a few places along the highway and across the stream in New Kaza. Most places close down by November.

Mahabudha Guest House (222232; r without bathroom Rs200-300) Just below the main road at the top of the old village, this bright, welcoming village home has big rooms with thick blankets. The shared bathroom has a geyser, meals are served in the traditional kitchen and there's an *amchi* clinic on site.

Hotel Mandala (222757; d Rs500) Right next to the taxi stand, Mandala is a spotless two-storey place run by a friendly family. There's a good restaurant, and the location is handy.

Snow Lion Hotel (222525; r Rs500-800) On the highway at the top of the old village, this modern hotel has six rooms on two floors with balconies overlooking the stream, and another eight new rooms were being built when we visited. It's a reliable choice with a reasonable restaurant.

Banjara Kunphen Retreat (222236; www.banjaracamps.com; s/d with meals Rs3900/4400; May-Oct) This modern set-up near the police station in

New Kaza will appeal to travellers looking for extra comfort. Rooms are bright and tastefully furnished, but, ultimately, are overpriced.

Yak Cafe (Old Kaza; r Rs 40-100) Just uphill from the bazaar, Yak is a friendly little restaurant serving the usual *momos*, pizza and Chinese, along with chicken Kiev and buffalo steak.

Mahabudha Restaurant (dishes Rs30-100) Near Yak Cafe, this is another traveller-oriented place with a big range of dishes and a happy vibe.

As well as the hotel restaurants, there are several traveller-friendly restaurants in the old bazaar.

GETTING THERE & AWAY
Bus
The bus station is at the bottom of the old town, just off the main road or reached on foot through the bazaar. There are buses to Manali (Rs190, 10 hours) at 4.30am and 7am. For Keylong, (Rs150, eight hours) change at Gramphu. A bus leaves for Rekong Peo (Rs205, 12 hours) at 9am, passing through Sichling (for Dhankar; Rs25, one hour) and Tabo (Rs45, two hours). There's a second Tabo bus at 2pm.

There's a single daily bus to Kibber (Rs20, 50 minutes) via Ki (Rs15, 30 minutes) at 5pm, returning at 7.30pm. This gives you time to visit Ki Monastery while the bus goes on to Kibber, but it's worth making a day trip by taxi to visit both places, or staying overnight in Kibber.

For the Pin Valley, buses to Mud (Rs50, two hours) leave at 4pm.

Taxi
The local taxi union is based a few metres from the bus stand, or you can make arrangements at your hotel. Fixed rates include Tabo (Rs1250, 1½ hours), Keylong (Rs5500, seven hours), Manali (Rs6000, nine hours) and Rekong Peo (Rs5000, 10 hours). Day trips include Ki and Kibber (Rs700) and Dhankar and the Pin Valley (Rs1500). A seat in a shared 4WD to Manali is usually easy to arrange, but not so easy going the other way; enquire at the taxi stand and turn up early.

Ki
On the road up to the village of Kibber, about 12km from Kaza, the tiny village of Ki is dominated by the whitewashed buildings of **Ki Gompa** (⏱ 6am-7pm). Set atop a 4116m-high hillock, this is the largest gompa in Spiti and

the views from the top are extremely photogenic. Around 300 monks, including many students from surrounding villages, live here. An atmospheric *puja* is held in the new prayer hall every morning at around 7am (8am in winter). On request, the monks will open up the original medieval prayer rooms, full of *thangkas,* Buddhist texts printed on cloth, and the bed slept in by the Dalai Lama on his visits in 1960 and 2000. Dance masks are brought out for the annual **Ki chaam** festival (June/July) and again in February/March for **Losar**.

The monks offer some basic four-bed **rooms** (☎ 01906-262201; dm without bathroom Rs150); the price includes meals and cold water.

Kibber
☎ 01906
A further 8km above Ki, this charming village of traditional whitewashed homes was once a stop on the overland salt trade. Catch your breath because at 4205m, Kibber once laid claim to being the highest village in the world with a drivable road and electricity, but tiny Gada village, a few hundred metres higher up the gorge, now has both power and a road – and the title belongs to a Tibetan village anyway. The surrounding snow-covered landscape is incredibly beautiful and desolate and you can walk to even remoter, roadless villages along the edge of the gorge.

The villagers (and local children in particular) are friendly but passing tour groups have created a small amount of child begging in the village. Resist the urge to hand out sweets, pens and cash; if you want to help, donate to the village school instead.

SLEEPING & EATING
There are several village guest houses offering rooms and meals. Bucket hot water costs Rs10 to Rs15 and most places close down for the winter in early October.

Rainbow Guest House (☎ 226309; r without bathroom Rs200) Close to the village school, Rainbow offers plain rooms and hearty village meals.

Serkong Guesthouse (☎ 226222; r Rs150-200) Rooms here are neat and clean, and the bohemian front terrace has easy chairs and old photos of Spiti.

Norling Guest House (☎ 226242; d Rs200-300) On the road into the village, this friendly place has the best rooms and the best restaurant in town. Proper furniture and little murals make guests feel at home.

INNER LINE PERMITS

To travel between Tabo in Spiti and Rekong Peo in Kinnaur, travellers need an inner line permit. This is easily arranged in Kaza – free permits are issued in around two hours by the **Assistant District Commissioner's Office** (☎ 222202; ◷ 10.30am-5pm Mon-Sat, closed 2nd Sat each month) in New Kaza – look for the big green-roofed building behind the hospital. There are several forms to fill out and you need two passport photos and photocopies of the identity and visa pages from your passport – both can be arranged in the old village bazaar. Officially, travellers should be in a group of four, but this office routinely issues permits for individual travellers as well as groups. Permits can also be obtained in Rekong Peo and Shimla.

Spittian Guest House (☎ 262264; r Rs 150-200) At the far end of the village, this traditional homestay has just four large furnished rooms and a common room with a log fire.

Dhankar

Southeast of Kaza, the snaking Spiti River merges with the Pin River, creating a single braid of blue in the midst of dust-coloured badlands. Perched high above the confluence is the tiny village of Dhankar, the former capital of the Nono kings of Spiti.

The 1200-year-old **Dhankar Gompa** (admission Rs25; 8am-6pm) is wedged between rocky spurs at the top of the village, with views that inspire euphoria. The lower monastery building has a silver statue of Vajradhara (the Diamond Being), and there's a second prayer hall on the hilltop, with exquisite medieval murals of Sakyamuni, Tsongkhapa and Lama Chodrag.

Just downhill is a small **museum** (admission Rs25; 8am-6pm) with costumes, instruments, old saddles and Buddhist devotional objects. In November, Dhankar monks celebrate the **Guktor Festival** (p335) with energetic masked dances.

Above the gompa are the ruins of the mud-brick **fort** that sheltered the entire population of the Nono kingdom during times of war, and an hour's climb uphill is the scenic lake of **Dhankar Tso**, offering epic views towards the twin peaks of **Mane Rang** (6593m).

Dhankar is a steep 10km walk or drive from the village of Sichling on the Kaza–Tabo highway. You can stay at the monastery in simple **monks' rooms** (dm without bathroom Rs100, r Rs300-400).

Buses from Kaza to Tabo pass through Sichling (Rs25, one hour) or you can do a day trip by taxi from Kaza for Rs800.

Pin Valley National Park

Running south from the Spiti Valley, the wind-scoured Pin Valley National Park (1875 sq km) is famous as the 'land of ibex and snow leopards', though sightings of either species are rare. From July to October, a popular eight-day trek runs from here over the 5319m Pin-Parvati Pass to the Parvati Valley near Kullu (p353).

The road to the Pin Valley branches off the Kaza–Tabo highway about 10km before Sichling, climbing through winter meadows to the cluster of whitewashed farmhouses at **Gulling**. About 2km above Gulling at Kungri, the 600-year-old **Ugyen Sanag Choling Gompa** has old prayer rooms and a huge new monastery with vivid murals of protector deities, including the many-eyed archer Rahula and one-eyed Ekajati, the Guardian of Mantras. There's also a small **museum** (admission Rs25; ◷ 10am-6pm) with ethnological and religious displays and plain, clean **rooms** (r without bathroom Rs250).

Southwest of Gulling, **Sagnam** marks the turn-off to the village of Mud, trailhead for the trek over the Pin-Parvati Pass. The wind moans between the whitewashed houses and there are some uplifting short walks around the valley. There are a couple of cheap guest houses by the main road, or the modern **PWD Resthouse** (r without bathroom Rs150-300), below the hospital.

Buses run daily from Kaza to Mud (Rs50, two hours), stopping in Gulling (Rs30, 1¼ hours) and Sagnam (Rs38, 1½ hours). Taxis in Kaza charge Rs900 to Sagnam and Rs1500 to Mud.

Tabo
☎ 01906

About 47km east of Kaza, tiny Tabo is the only other town in the Spiti Valley. The setting, hemmed in by scree slopes, is wind-blown and dramatic, and the ridge above town is riddled with **caves** used as meditation cells by local lamas. The village is completely dominated by **Tabo Gompa** (admission by donation; 6am-10pm), a

World Heritage Site preserving some of the finest Indo-Tibetan art in the world – see the boxed text, below.

You may be able to check your email and make calls at **Tabo Cyber Cafe** (internet access per hr Rs60; 7am-9pm) near the bus stand, though connections are dodgy.

SLEEPING & EATING

Guest houses in Tabo are clustered around the gompa, or strung out along the main road.

Millennium Monastery Guesthouse (223315; dm Rs50, r with/without bathroom from Rs300/200) Run by the monastery, this ageing but popular place has decent rooms around a bright central courtyard. Rooms have piped hot water for washing, but guests are asked to refrain from smoking, drinking alcohol and other activities that might offend monastic sensibilities.

our pick Zion Cafe (223419; meals Rs40-70) Run by the effusive Angel, Zion is a Rasta cafe with an infectious reggae vibe, good food and four comfortable rooms (Rs250 to Rs300 for a double).

Maitreya Guesthouse (223329; d Rs400-500) Down a lane to the side of the monastery guest house, Maitreya is a comfortable, well-run place with a small garden, a sunny front terrace and the good Third Eye Restaurant.

Banjara Tabo Retreat (233381; www.banjara camps.com; s/d with meals Rs3900/4400; May-Oct)

Tabo's most upmarket accommodation rents its tasteful rooms to passing travellers when it isn't booked out by groups. It also has a good restaurant that's open to nonguests.

Cafe Kunzum Top (dishes Rs25-80) Run by the energetic and widely travelled Sonam, this cheerful Spitian cafe serves tasty *momos*, espresso coffee and compote made with local apples.

GETTING THERE & AWAY

At the time of writing, the road was open from Tabo through to Rekong Peo, with the odd landslide and washout holding up traffic. There are morning and afternoon buses to Kaza (Rs45, two hours). There's a daily bus to Rekong Peo (Rs160, 10 hours) at 11am but since this originates in Kaza it can be overfull. It may also be possible to get a seat on a share 4WD coming through from Kaza in season (June to October). Taxis charge Rs1250 to Kaza (1½ hours) and Rs4000 to Rekong Peo (nine hours).

Tabo to Rekong Peo

One of India's scariest but most sublime mountain roads, the Tabo–Rekong Peo highway in Kinnaur is an adventure. In theory, this highway is open year-round, providing the only winter access to the Spiti Valley; however, the Sutlej River frequently floods, washing away parts of the precarious road,

---

TABO GOMPA

The mud-brick and timber *choskhor* (sacred compound) at Tabo was founded in AD 996 by the Great Translator, Ringchen Zangpo, who hired the best Buddhist mural painters from Kashmir to decorate the interior walls. If you want to view the murals, you must arrange a time with the monks at the modern monastery next door.

The compound is centred on the huge **Tsug Lha-Khang** (Assembly Hall), a dark and atmospheric chamber ringed by exquisite murals and suspended life-sized stucco statues of 33 bodhisattvas. Together with the four-sided effigy of Vairocana at the rear of the chamber, the statues create a three-dimensional mandala.

To the left of the main temple is the **Large Brom-Ston Lha-Khang**, with more Kashmiri-style murals, reached through an intricately carved wooden doorway. Left again is the **Ser-Khang** (Golden Temple), with a large seated Buddha and detailed paintings of celestial deities on the roof and walls. Behind the Ser-Khang is the **Kyil-Khar-Khang** (Mystic Mandala Temple) containing a giant frieze of Vairocana surrounded by giant mandalas.

To the right of the Tsug Lha-Khang are the smaller **Byams-pa Chenpo Lha-Khang**, containing a 6m-high Maitreya statue and murals of the Tashi-Chunpo Temple and Potala Palace in Tibet, and the **Brom-Ston Lha-Khang**, with murals of Sakyamuni and his disciples.

The modern gompa outside the compound has a well-attended morning *puja* (prayer ceremony) at 6.30am, and the monastery guesthouse contains a **Buddhist library** (admission free; 10-noon & 2-4pm Jun-Sep) and a small religious **museum** (admission Rs20, camera/video Rs25/50; 8.30am-5pm Mon-Sat).

and snowfalls can occasionally cut off this route in winter. A number of hydroelectric projects are helping to tame the destructive power of the river, but it's worth checking the road is intact before heading east of Tabo. You will need to show your passport and inner line permit at Sumdo and Jangi. Some of the following places are technically in Kinnaur, but they are covered here because they form part of the Spiti circuit.

From Tabo, the road follows the narrowing Spiti Valley, passing villages full of apple orchards, before soaring over the ridge into the valley of the Sutlej River. If you're on a bus, this may well be the most dangerous and knee-trembling road in India – even die-hard travellers have been known to finger their rosaries as the bus skids around hairpin bends with millimetres to spare. The views of the Spiti River flashing hundreds of metres below and the road ahead zigzagging across the mountainside are mesmerising.

Overnight stops used to be forbidden, but travellers now have seven days to complete the trip. **Sumdo** has a permit checkpost and the road starts its ascent into the hills at **Chango**, which has several Buddhist temples.

The first settlement with accommodation is **Nako**, a pretty village of white mud-brick houses about 1km off the main road and a popular stop for motorcyclists. Even if you're on the bus, this is an interesting place to break the journey. The landscape here is vaguely Central Asian and the village is centred on a small sacred lake, surrounded by the 11th-century buildings of **Nako Gompa**, containing some fine Tabo-style murals and sculptures.

There are several simple guest houses offering rooms without bathroom for around Rs200, or there's the posher **Reo Purgil Hotel** (☎ 01785-236339; d Rs600-800). Better still is the bright **Lake View Guest House** (r Rs400-500), a short walk through the village overlooking the lake.

The final stage of the journey passes through greener country in the narrow gorge of the Sutlej River. The village of **Puh** marks the official crossing into Kinnaur and there are two colourful gompas belonging to the Drukpa sect.

There are more monasteries and temples at **Khanum**, near Spillo, founded by Ringchen Zangpo in the 10th century. **Jangi** marks the end of the permit zone and the starting point of the *parikrama* (ceremonial circumnavigation) around Kinner Kailash (6050m). The village has a number of Kinnauri-style temples and you can continue 14km uphill to visit the Buddhist monastery at **Lippa**. An inner line permit is required, even if you just do a day trip here from Rekong Peo.

Uttar Pradesh

Thanks to a certain white-marble building you may have heard of, Uttar Pradesh is on almost everyone's Indian itinerary. As magical as the Taj Mahal is, though, it's unlikely to fill more than a day or two of your time. Luckily India's most populous state boasts plenty more besides.

Another standout destination is the enthralling city of Varanasi on the banks of India's holiest river, the Ganges. This is one of the world's oldest continually inhabited cities, and the intense spirituality that emanates from its temples and riverside ghats provides one of the most rewarding experiences of a trip to India.

Religion plays an intrinsic role in this vast state. There are more sacred bathing ghats at Chitrakut, the 'mini Varanasi'; Mathura, birthplace of Krishna; and Allahabad, the most revered of India's four Kumbh Mela sites. Ayodhya, the birthplace of Lord Rama, also attracts floods of Hindu pilgrims. Devotees of a different kind visit Sarnath, where Buddha preached his first sermon of the middle way, and Kushinagar, where he died.

But nothing draws tourists like India's most famous icon, the Taj Mahal in Agra. Those who don't shoot straight off to Jaipur, or back to Delhi, also get the chance to see one of India's finest forts, Agra Fort, and the fascinating nearby ruins of Fatehpur Sikri, while the remnants of more recent rulers, the Nawabs, and the British Raj, can be found in stately Lucknow.

HIGHLIGHTS

- Take a pre-dawn boat ride along the River Ganges to witness **Varanasi** and its bathing ghats at their spiritual best (p445)

- Be inspired as the sunrise illuminates the milky white marble of the **Taj Mahal** (p404) before returning for the oh-so romantic sunset view

- Stand in awe beside immense Mughal monuments in the ruined city of **Fatehpur Sikri** (p423)

- Be rowed out to the confluence of two of India's holiest rivers at Sangam, in **Allahabad** (p434), and imagine 70 million people doing the same during Kumbh Mela

- Take time out from the chaos of the cities and relax in the Buddhist pilgrimage centres of **Kushinagar** (p455) or **Sarnath** (p453)

- Experience the spirituality of Varanasi, without the hassle, at the more chilled-out riverside ghats of **Chitrakut** (p438)

- Escape the exhaust fumes by taking a traffic-free temple tour around the narrow lanes of **Ayodhya** (p433), birthplace of Lord Rama

FAST FACTS

Population 166.1 million
Area 231,254 sq km
Capital Lucknow
Main language Hindi
When to go October to March

History

Over 2000 years ago this region was part of Ashoka's great Buddhist empire, remnants of which can be found in the ruins at the pilgrimage centre of Sarnath near Varanasi. Muslim raids from the northwest began in the 11th century, and by the 16th century the region was part of the Mughal empire, with its capital in Agra, then Delhi, and for a brief time, Fatehpur Sikri.

Following the decline of the Mughal empire, Persian invaders stepped in briefly before the nawabs of Avadh rose to prominence in the central part of the region. The nawabs were responsible for turning Lucknow into a flourishing centre for the arts, but their empire came to a dramatic end when the British East India Company deposed the last nawab, triggering the First War of Independence (Indian Uprising) of 1857. Agra was later merged with Avadh and the state became known as United Province. It was renamed Uttar Pradesh after Independence and has since been the most dominant state in Indian politics, producing half of the country's prime ministers, most of them from Allahabad. The local population doesn't seem to have benefited much from this, though, as poor governance, a high birth rate, a low literacy rate and an erratic electricity supply have held back economic progress in UP in the past 60 years.

In 2000 the mountainous northwestern part of the state was carved off to create the new state of Uttaranchal.

AGRA

☎ 0562 / pop 1,321,410

The magical allure of the Taj Mahal draws tourists like moths to a wondrous flame. And despite the hype, it's every bit as good as you've heard. But the Taj is not a stand-alone attraction. The legacy of the Mughal empire has left a magnificent fort and a liberal sprinkling of fascinating tombs and mausoleums. There's also fun to be had in the bustling *chowks* (marketplaces), some of which border on the chaotic.

The downside comes in the form of hordes of rickshaw-wallahs, touts, unofficial guides and souvenir vendors, whose persistence can be infuriating at times.

Many tourists choose to visit Agra on a whistle-stop day trip from Delhi. This is a shame. There is much more of interest here than can be seen in that time. In fact, you can enjoy several days' sightseeing with side trips to the superb ruined city of Fatehpur Sikri and the Hindu pilgrimage centre of Mathura.

History

In 1501 Sultan Sikander Lodi established his capital here, but the city fell into Mughal hands in 1526, when Emperor Babur defeated the last Lodi sultan at Panipat. Agra reached the peak of its magnificence between the mid-16th and mid-17th centuries during the reigns of Akbar, Jehangir and Shah Jahan. During this period the fort, the Taj Mahal and other major mausoleums were built. In 1638 Shah Jahan built a new city in Delhi, and his son Aurangzeb moved the capital there 10 years later.

In 1761 Agra fell to the Jats, a warrior class who looted its monuments, including the Taj Mahal. The Marathas took over in 1770, but were replaced by the British in 1803. Following the First War of Independence of 1857, the British shifted the administration of the province to Allahabad. Deprived of its administrative role, Agra developed as a centre for heavy industry, quickly becoming famous for its chemicals industry and air pollution, before the Taj and tourism became a major source of income.

Orientation

Agra sits on a large bend in the holy Yamuna River. The fort and the Taj, 2km apart, both overlook the river on different parts of the bend. The main train and bus stations are a few kilometres southwest.

The labourers and artisans who toiled on the Taj set up home immediately south of the mausoleum, creating the congested network of alleys known as Taj Ganj, now a popular area for budget travellers.

Information

For an online guide to the city, see www.agra-india.net.

UTTAR PRADESH

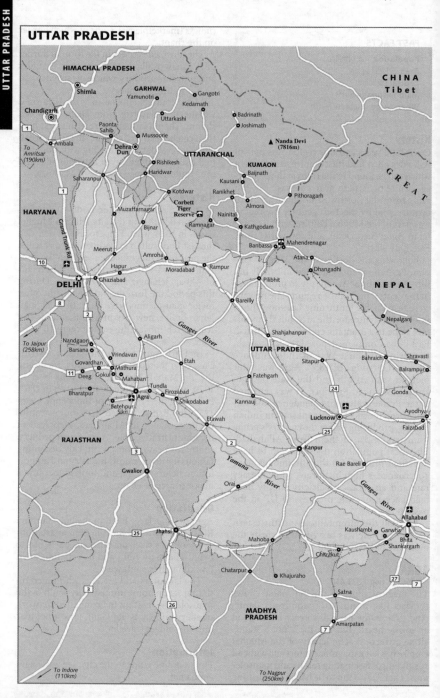

The external boundaries of India on this map have not been authenticated and may not be correct.

HIMALAYA RANGE

Pokhara

Lumbini
Bhairawa
Naugarh
Sunauli
Nautanwa

Gorakhpur
Kushinagar

28

Ghaghara River

29

Jaunpur
Gazipur
Sarnath
Varanasi
Zamania
Mughal
Serai
Mirzapur
Chunar

BIHAR

2

To Kolkata
(450km)

BOOKSHOPS

Imran Internet & Bookshop (Map p404; Taj South Gate; ☷ 8am-10pm) Books and city maps, internet (per hr Rs30) and CD burning (per disk Rs75).

Modern Book Depot (Map p402; Sadar Bazaar; ☎ 2225695; ☷ 10.30am-9.30pm, closed Tue) Great selection of novels at this 60-year-old establishment.

EMERGENCY

Tourist police (Map p402; ☎ 2421204; Agra Cantonment train station; ☷ 24hr) The guys in sky-blue uniforms are based just outside the train station, but it's easier to go through the tourism office inside.

INTERNET ACCESS

The following branches of iway have Skype facilities:

iway Internet Fatehbad Rd (Map p402; per hr Rs50; ☷ 6am-11pm); Sadar Bazaar (Map p402; per hr Rs40; ☷ 24hr); Shahjahan Hotel (Map p404; per hr Rs30; ☷ 24hr)

LEFT LUGGAGE

Agra Cantonment train station (Map p402; Platform 1; per kg per day Rs10; ☷ 24hr)

Yash Cafe (Map p404; Taj South Gate) Storage space and showers are offered to day-trippers for Rs50 per day for both.

MEDICAL SERVICES

District Hospital (Map p402; ☎ 2466099; Mahatma Gandhi (MG) Rd)

SN Medical College (Map p402; ☎ 2463318; Hospital Rd)

MONEY

ATMs are all over the city. There is a handy one in Sadar Bazaar, one by the hotels on Fatehabad Rd, one on Chhipi Tola Rd and one by the east gate of the Taj. There are several private money changers around Taj Ganj.

State Bank of India (Map p402; ☷ 10am-4pm Mon-Fri, to 1pm Sat) Off Chhipi Tola Rd. Changes cash and travellers cheques.

POST

Main post office (Map p402; ☎ 2463886; The Mall; ☷ 10am-5pm Mon-Fri, 10am-3pm Sat)

TOURIST INFORMATION

Government of India Tourism (Map p402; ☎ 2226378; www.incredibleindia.org; 191 The Mall; ☷ 9am-5.30pm Mon-Fri, to 2pm Sat) Very helpful branch; has brochures on local and India-wide attractions and can arrange guides (half/full day Rs450/600).

UTTAR PRADESH

AGRA

0 ————— 1 km
0 ————— 0.5 miles

INFORMATION

Archaeological Survey of
  India 1 C6
District Hospital 2 B5
Government of India
  Tourism 3 B6
iway Internet 4 B6
iway Internet 5 D6
Main Post Office 6 B6
Modern Book Depot 7 B6
SN Medical College 8 B4
State Bank of India 9 B5
Tourist Police 10 A6
UP Tourism 11 C6

SIGHTS & ACTIVITIES

Chini-ka-Rauza 12 D3
Clarks Shiraz Hotel .... (see 17)
Hotel Amar .... (see 18)
Hotel Atithi .... (see 20)
Hotel Yamuna View .... (see 22)
Itimad-ud-Daulah 13 D4
Jama Masjid 14 C4
Mansingh Palace .... (see 24)
Samadhi Swamiji Maharaj
  Bagh 15 B1

To ISBT Bus Stand (5km);
Sikandra (7km); Sur Sarovar
Bird Sanctuary (17km); Mathura
(56km); Delhi (200km)

SLEEPING

Amar Yatri Niwas 16 D6
Clarks Shiraz Hotel 17 C6
Hotel Amar 18 D6
Hotel Ashish Palace 19 D6
Hotel Atithi 20 D6
Hotel Sakura 21 A5
Hotel Yamuna View 22 D6
Howard Park Plaza 23 D6
Mansingh Palace 24 D6
Tourists Rest House 25 B5

EATING

Brijwasi 26 B6
Dasaprakash 27 B6
Lakshmi Vilas 28 B6
Mehfil Restaurant .... (see 16)

SLEEPING (cont)

Mughal Room .... (see 17)
Tourists Rest House .... (see 25)
Zorba the Buddha 29 B6

DRINKING

Jaiwal Bar 30 B6

SHOPPING

Khadi Gramodyog 31 B6
Kinari Bazaar 32 C4
Subhash Emporium 33 B6

TRANSPORT

Idgah Bus Stand 34 A5
Prepaid Autorickshaw
  Booth .... (see 35)
Prepaid Taxi Booth 35 A6

Dayalbagh

Bhagwan

National Hwy 2 Bypass

Ram
Bagh

To Aligarh
(79km)

Yamuna River

Karbala Rd

Parikrama Kalicharan Tiwari Rd

Balkeshwari Rd

Aligarh Rd

Belanganj
Train
Station

Kanpur Rd

Yamuna Bridge
Train Station

Raja ki
Mandi Train
Station

To Bharatpur (60km)

Chhipi Rd

Agra City
Train
Station

Belan Ganj

Ramratan Marg

Bhagat Singh Marg

Capt Naresh Rd

Panchkuiyan Rd

Old Town
Area

Agra Fort
Train
Station

Daresi Rd

Agra
Fort

Kinari Bazaar Rd

Ghalibpura Rd
Mantola Rd

Saiyad Ali Nabi Marg

Mahatma Gandhi (MG) Rd

Mehtab
Bagh

Taj
Mahal

See Agra Fort Map (p408)

Fatehpur Sikri Rd

To Fatehpur
Sikri (40km)

Chhipi Tola Rd

Field Marshal

Yamuna Kinara Rd

Shahjahan
Park

Golf
Course

See Taj Ganj
Map (p404)

Bazaar

Shahjahan Gate

Idgah
Train
Station

Nanner Rd

Kutchery Rd

Swaalor Rd

Lawhapura Rd

To Kheria
Airport (3km)

Ajmer Rd

Station Rd

Fatehpur Sikri Rd

Mahatma Gandhi (MG) Rd

Sadar
Bazaar

The Mall

Gough Rd

Taj Rd

Fatehbad Rd

To Fatehbad
(3.5km)

Agra
Cantonment
Train Station

Station Rd

Taj Rd

Police
Station

To Gwalior
(118km)

To Fatehpur
Sikri

FESTIVALS IN UTTAR PRADESH

Magh Mela (Jan/Feb; Allahabad, (p434)) This religious fair is held at Sangam on the banks of the Ganges at Allahabad. Hindu pilgrims from all over India camp out and take a soul-cleansing dip at auspicious times. Every 12 years the fair is replaced by the massive Kumbh Mela (next in 2013), and every six years with the Ardh (Half) Mela (next in 2019).

Taj Mahotsav (18-27 Feb; Agra, p399) Held in Shilpgram, an otherwise tacky souvenir market about 1km east of the Taj Mahal's east gate, this features live music and dance, food tasting and a Mughal procession.

Holi (Feb/Mar; Barsana, near Vrindavan, p427) This national festival is celebrated with particular fervour around Mathura and Vrindavan, spiritual home of Krishna.

Purnima (Apr/May; Sarnath, p453) Also known as Vesak, Buddha Jayanti or, informally, Buddha's birthday, Purnima actually celebrates the birth, enlightenment and death of Buddha. Sarnath, just outside Varanasi, takes on a particularly festive air on this day, when Buddhists from many countries take part in a procession and a fair is held.

Janmastami (Aug/Sep; Mathura, p425) You can barely move here during Krishna's birthday, when the Dwarka-dhish temple is swathed in decorations and musical dramas about Krishna are performed.

Ram Lila (Sep/Oct; Varanasi, p440) Every year since the early 1800s, the Ram Lila, a lengthy version of the Ramayana, has been performed beside Ramnagar fort in Varanasi. The epic saga of Rama's marriage to Sita and his battle against the demon king, Ravana, is performed mainly by Brahmin youths aided by masks, music, dancing and giant papier-mâché figures.

Lucknow Mahotsav (late Nov-Dec; Lucknow, p428) The spirit of the nawabs comes back to life during this 10-day festival. Events include processions, plays, Kathak (North Indian classical dance), *ghazals* (Urdu songs), sitar recitals, kite flying and tonga (horse-drawn carriage) races.

Eid al-Fitr (Dec/Jan; Fatehpur Sikri, p423) Join the happy crowds in the bazaar and mosque at Fatehpur Sikri, near Agra, for the end-of-Ramadan celebrations.

UP Tourism Agra Cantonment train station (Map p402; ☎ 2421204; ☒ 24hr); Taj Rd (Map p402; ☎ 2226431; agrauptourism@gmail.com; 64 Taj Rd; ☒ 10am-5pm Mon-Sat) The friendly train station branch has round-the-clock help and advice, and is the place to contact the tourist police. Either branch can arrange guides (half/full day Rs600/800).

Dangers & Annoyances

Touts, vendors and rickshaw-wallahs can be pretty draining in Agra, particularly around the Taj, but it's certainly more of an annoyance than a danger. Many hotels, tourist shops and money changers pay hefty commissions to taxi drivers and rickshaw-wallahs who bring in customers. When booking a hotel, try to arrange for a pick-up from the train or bus station or use the prepaid stand. Cheap or free rickshaw rides always lead to a gem or souvenir shop. Lots of 'marble' souvenirs are actually alabaster, or even just soapstone. Avoid hole-in-the-corner travel agents.

When taking an auto or cycle rickshaw to the Taj, make sure you are clear which gate you want to go to when negotiating the price. Otherwise, almost without fail, drivers will take you to the roundabout at the south end of Shahjahan Gardens Rd – where expensive tongas (horse-drawn carriage) or camels wait to take tour groups to the west gate – and claim that's where they thought you meant. Autos cannot go right up to the Taj because of pollution rules, but they can get a lot closer than this.

SCAMS

Don't fall for the gem import scam that has been conning naive tourists in Agra for more than a decade. Travellers are convinced to help a shop avoid import duty by carrying gems back to their home country, where a company representative will reimburse them for their costs plus a tidy profit. The travellers are asked to make a small credit-card payment 'as a sign of good faith'. Without exception, the gems are worthless, the representative never materialises and travellers are lumped with a credit-card bill of US$1000 or more. Keep your credit card firmly sheathed!

Sights & Activities

The entrance fee for Agra's five main sights – the Taj, the Fort, Fatehpur Sikri, Akbar's Tomb and the Baby Taj – is made up of charges from two different bodies, the Archaeological Survey of India (ASI) and the Agra Development Association (ADA). Of the Rs750 ticket for the Taj Mahal, Rs500 is a special ADA ticket, which gives you small savings on the other four sights if visited in the same day. You'll save Rs50 at Agra Fort and Rs10 each at Fatehpur Sikri, Akbar's Tomb and the Baby Taj. You can buy this Rs500 ADA ticket at any of the five sights. Just say you intend to visit the Taj later that day.

All the other sights in Agra are either free or have ASI tickets only which aren't affected by the ADA one-day offer.

Admission to all sights is free for children under 15.

TAJ MAHAL

Rabindranath Tagore described it as 'a teardrop on the cheek of eternity', Rudyard Kipling as 'the embodiment of all things pure', while its creator, Emperor Shah Jahan, said it made 'the sun and the moon shed tears from their eyes'. Every year, tourists numbering almost twice the population of Agra pass through its gates to catch a once-in-a-lifetime glimpse of what is widely considered the most beautiful building in the world. Few leave disappointed.

The Taj was built by Shah Jahan as a memorial for his second wife, Mumtaz Mahal, who died giving birth to their 14th child in 1631. The death of Mumtaz left the emperor so heartbroken that his hair is said to have turned grey virtually overnight. Construction of the Taj began in the same year and, although the main building is thought to have been built in eight years, the whole complex was not completed until 1653. Not long after it was finished Shah Jahan was overthrown by his son Aurangzeb and imprisoned in Agra Fort where, for the rest of his days, he could only gaze out at his creation through a window. Following his death in 1666, Shah Jahan was buried here alongside Mumtaz.

In total, some 20,000 people from India and Central Asia worked on the building. Specialists were brought in from as far away as Europe to produce the exquisite marble screens and pietra dura (marble inlay work) made with thousands of semiprecious stones.

The Taj was designated a World Heritage Site in 1983 and looks as immaculate today as when it was first constructed – though it underwent a huge restoration project in the early 20th century. In 2002, having been gradually discoloured by city pollution, it was spruced up with an ancient face-pack recipe known as *multani mitti* – a blend of

soil, cereal, milk and lime once used by Indian women to beautify their skin. Now only non-polluting vehicles are allowed within a few hundred metres of the Taj.

Entry & Information

The **Taj** (Map p404; ☎ 2330498; Indian/foreigner Rs20/750, video Rs25; ☼ dawn-dusk Sat-Thu) can be accessed

---

TAJ GANJ

0 — 200 m
0 — 0.1 miles

INFORMATION		EATING
Imran Internet &		Gulshan Restaurant........**14** A5
Bookshop.............**1** B5		Hotel Sheela...............(see 10)
iway Internet..........(see 9)		Joney's Place.............**15** A5
		Saniya Palace Hotel......(see 12)
SIGHTS &		Shankara Vegis
ACTIVITIES		Restaurant.............**16** B5
East Gate Ticket		Shanti Lodge
Office...............**2** B4		Restaurant............(see 13)
Jawab...............**3** B3		Stuff Makers.............(see 8)
Mosque...............**4** A3		Taj Cafe................(see 16)
Museum...............**5** A4		Yash Cafe...............**17** B5
South Gate Ticket		
Office...............**6** B5		**DRINKING**
West Gate Ticket		Beer Shop..............**18** A5
Office...............**7** A4		Wine Shop.............(see 16)
SLEEPING		**TRANSPORT**
Hotel Kamal...........**8** B5		Cycle-rickshaw &
Hotel Shahjahan.......**9** A5		Autorickshaw
Hotel Sheela..........**10** B4		Stand.................**19** A5
Hotel Sidartha........**11** A5		Raja Bicycle Store......**20** A5
Saniya Palace Hotel...**12** B5		
Shanti Lodge.........**13** B5		

Yamuna River

Taj Mahal

To Agra Fort (2km)

To Agra Fort (2km)

West Gate

Gateway

East Gate

Shahjahan Park

Shahjahan Gardens Rd

South Gate

Taj East Gate Rd

To Oberoi Amar Vilas (500m); Bellevue (500m); Amar Vilas Bar (500m); Taj Plaza (500m); Shilpgram (1km)

Bazaar

TAJ MAHAL MYTHS

The Taj is a Hindu temple

The well-publicised theory that the Taj was in fact a Shiva temple built in the 12th century and only later converted into Mumtaz Mahal's famous mausoleum was developed by Purushottam Nagesh Oak. In 2000 India's Supreme Court dismissed his petition to have the sealed basement rooms of the Taj opened to prove his theory. Oak also claims that the Kaaba, Stonehenge and the Papacy all have Hindu origins.

The Black Taj Mahal

The story goes that Shah Jahan planned to build a negative image of the Taj Mahal in black marble on the opposite side of the river as his own mausoleum, and that work began before he was imprisoned by his son Aurangzeb in Agra Fort. Extensive excavations at Mehtab Bagh have found no trace of any such construction.

Craftsmen Mutilations

Legend has it that on completion of the Taj, Shah Jahan ordered that the hands of the project's craftsmen be chopped off to prevent them from ever building anything as beautiful again. Some even say he went so far as to have their eyes gouged out. Thankfully, no historical evidence supports either story.

Sinking Taj

Some experts believe there is evidence to show that the Taj is slowly tilting towards, and sinking into, the riverbed due to the changing nature of the soil beside an increasingly dry Yamuna River. The Archaeological Survey of India has dismissed any marginal change in the elevation of the building as statistically insignificant, adding that it has not detected any structural damage at its base in the seven decades since its first scientific study of the Taj was carried out in 1941.

through the west, south and east gates, which all lead to an outer courtyard. The south gate is the main access and is easiest to reach from Taj Ganj, while the east gate generally has the shortest queues. The west gate gets very crowded with tour groups, but they don't normally arrive until after 9am. There are separate queues for men and women. Prohibited items such as food, tobacco, matches, mobile phones and camera tripods can be left without charge in cloakrooms. Don't forget to visit the cloakroom first to avoid queuing twice.

Cameras and videos are permitted but you cannot take photographs of the tombs inside the mausoleum, and the areas into which you can take your video camera are limited. Some readers have complained of being prevented from taking books into the Taj. This, however, is not official policy.

If you keep your Taj ticket you get small entry-fee reductions when visiting Agra Fort, Fatehpur Sikri, Akbar's Tomb or the Baby Taj on the same day.

Note: the Taj is closed every Friday to anyone not attending prayers at the mosque.

From the south gate, entry to the inner compound is through a very impressive, 30m red sandstone **gateway** on the south side of the forecourt, which is inscribed with verses from the Quran.

The Taj is arguably at its most atmospheric at sunrise. This is certainly the most comfortable time to visit, with far fewer crowds. Sunset is another magical viewing time. You can also view the Taj for five nights around full moon. Entry numbers are limited, though, and tickets must be bought a day in advance from the **Archaeological Survey of India office** (Map p402; ☎ 2227263; www.asi.nic.in; 22 The Mall; Indian/foreigner Rs510/750). See its website for details.

Inside the Grounds

Once inside, the **ornamental gardens** are set out along classical Mughal *charbagh* (formal Persian garden) lines – a square quartered by watercourses, with an ornamental marble plinth at its centre. When the fountains are not flowing, the Taj is beautifully reflected in the watercourses.

TOP TAJ VIEWS

Inside the Taj grounds

Your whole life you see pictures of the Taj, but it isn't until you step up onto its platform that you realise how glorious it really is. It's far bigger than I ever imagined. From a distance it wasn't quite as magnificent as when I was up close and able to touch it. I guess, from a distance the Taj was how I expected it to be. But up close, I was blown away.
Brady, Canada

From the north bank of the Yamuna River, in front of Mehtab Bagh

The contrast of looking at one of the most famous and touristy monuments in the world while standing on wasteland among buffalo was amazing. In fact, we felt closer to the Taj Mahal because we were out of the crowds and in amongst nature. It was windy that day so the reflection of the Taj in the Yamuna River was not as smooth as it can be, but it was different from all the pictures we had seen. It was our moment – unique.
Marion & Geoffroy, France

Looking up from the south bank

I was lucky enough to be on the riverbank at sunset one evening, far removed from the tourist crowds. I watched the Taj slowly surrender itself to the climbing shadows of the mosque beside it, and it was one of the most calming moments of my whole time in India. The next day I visited the park on the opposite side of the river but for me, after that view the previous day, it wasn't worth the trip.
Greg, Canada

On a rooftop cafe in Taj Ganj

There can't be many more memorable places to sip a lassi than this, especially at sunset. Pleasantly removed from all that ground-level bustle, and yet the Taj is just a stone's throw away, so you can watch its outline melt into the dusk.
Stuart, UK

From Agra Fort

The best photograph I have of the Taj is from the fort, from the tower where Shah Jahan was held captive for the last eight years of his life. I got to the fort when it opened. In fact, I pounded on the door until they opened it (they said 6am and it was 6.01am!). I ran straight to the tower. The sun rose directly between two of the minarets, almost over the dome. Through the fog and haze, it rose orange, lighting up the Yamuna. Magical. Without the 200mm lens I was using the picture would have been great, but with it, it was awesome.
Scott, USA

The Taj Mahal itself stands on a raised marble platform at the northern end of the ornamental gardens, with its back to the Yamuna River. Its raised position means that the backdrop is only sky – a master stroke of design. Purely decorative 40m-high white **minarets** grace each corner of the platform. After more than three centuries they are not quite perpendicular, but they may have been designed to lean slightly outwards so that in the event of an earthquake, they would fall away from the precious Taj. The red sandstone **mosque** to the west is an important gathering place for Agra's Muslims. The identical building to the east, the **jawab**, was built for symmetry.

The central Taj structure is made of semitranslucent white marble, carved with flowers and inlaid with thousands of semiprecious stones in beautiful patterns. A perfect exercise in symmetry, the four identical faces of the Taj feature impressive vaulted arches embellished with pietra dura scrollwork and quotations from the Quran in a style of calligraphy using inlaid jasper. The whole structure is topped off by four small domes surrounding the famous bulbous central dome.

THE KING OF THRONES

The Taj Mahal, with its exquisite carvings and jewel-encrusted white marble, may be the most famous thing Emperor Shah Jahan ever had built, but it wasn't the most expensive. That record is claimed by the legendary Peacock Throne, once housed in Agra Fort.

Standing nearly 2m tall, the throne was ascended by silver steps and stood on golden feet set with jewels. It was backed by representations of two open peacocks' tails, gilded, enamelled and inset with diamonds, rubies and other precious stones said to weigh 230kg in total. Among the celebrated stones used was the 191-carat Koh-i-noor Diamond. Once the world's largest known diamond, the Koh-i-noor was later acquired by the British (in 1849) before being recut to 109 carats and placed among the Crown Jewels of Queen Victoria.

According to some records, Shah Jahan spent almost twice as much on the Peacock Throne as he did on the Taj Mahal, and some experts believe the throne would be worth as much as US$1billion if it were still around today. Sadly it isn't. Shah Jahan's son Aurangzeb moved it to Delhi from where it was taken to Iran in 1739 by the Persian plunderer Nadir Shah before being dismantled after his assassination in 1747.

Below the main dome is the **Cenotaph of Mumtaz Mahal**, an elaborate false tomb surrounded by an exquisite perforated marble screen inlaid with 43 different types of semiprecious stones. Beside it, offsetting the symmetry of the Taj, is the **Cenotaph of Shah Jahan**, who was interred here with little ceremony by his usurping son Aurangzeb in 1666. Light is admitted into the central chamber by finely cut marble screens. The real **tombs** of Mumtaz Mahal and Shah Jahan are in a locked basement room below the main chamber and cannot be viewed.

On the western side of the gardens is a very small **museum** (admission Rs5; ⏲ 10am-5pm Sat-Thu), housing original architectural drawings of the Taj and some nifty celadon plates, said to split into pieces or change colour if the food served on them contains poison.

AGRA FORT

With the Taj Mahal overshadowing it, one can easily forget that Agra has one of the finest Mughal forts in India. By visiting the fort and Taj on the same day you get a Rs50 reduction in ticket price. Construction of the massive red-sandstone **fort** (Map p402 & Map p408; ☎ 2364512; Indian/foreigner Rs20/300, video Rs25; ⏲ dawn-dusk), on the bank of the Yamuna River, was begun by Emperor Akbar in 1565. Further additions were made, particularly by his grandson Shah Jahan, using his favourite building material – white marble. The fort was built primarily as a military structure, but Shah Jahan transformed it into a palace, and later it became his gilded prison for eight years after his son Aurangzeb seized power in 1658.

The ear-shaped fort's colossal double walls rise over 20m in height and measure 2.5km in circumference. The Yamuna River originally flowed along the straight eastern edge of the fort, and the emperors had their own bathing ghats here. It contains a maze of buildings, forming a city within a city, including vast underground sections, though many of the structures were destroyed over the years by Nadir Shah, the Marathas, the Jats and finally the British, who used the fort as a garrison.

The **Amar Singh Gate** to the south is the sole entry point to the fort and where you buy your entrance ticket. Its dogleg design was meant to confuse attackers who made it past the first line of defence – the crocodile-infested moat.

Diwan-i-Am (Hall of Public Audiences) was used by Shah Jahan for domestic government business, and features a throne room where the emperor listened to petitioners. In

RICKSHAW BREAK

If it's not ridiculously hot, give the rickshaw wallahs a miss one morning and take this mostly peaceful, 2km walk from the Taj to Agra Fort. From the west gate of the Taj, ignore the path immediately on your right, but keep to the right after that, walking through the park, past a riverside temple and some burning ghats before following the river past a small cemetery. Once at the main road, go straight over the roundabout and follow the road for the final few hundred metres up to the fort's south gate.

UTTAR PRADESH

AGRA FORT

SIGHTS & ACTIVITIES		
Anguri Bagh	1	B4
Diwan-i-Am	2	B4
Diwan-i-Khas	3	B3
Hauz-i-Jehangir	4	B4
Jehangir's Palace	5	B4
John Colvin's Grave	6	B4
Khas Mahal	7	B4
Ladies' Bazaar	8	B3
Mina Masjid	9	B4
Moti Masjid	10	B3
Musamman Burj	11	B4
Nagina Masjid	12	B3
Shish Mahal	13	B4
Takht-i-Jehangir	14	B3
Ticket Office	15	B4

Mahal is **Takhti-i-Jehangir**, a huge slab of black rock with an inscription around the edge. The throne that stood here was made for Jehangir when he was Prince Salim. An interesting optical illusion occurs when the Taj is viewed from here and then from the other side of the courtyard – though further away, it appears much larger.

The **Shish Mahal** (Mirror Palace) has walls inlaid with tiny mirrors. At the time of research it had been closed for some time due to restoration, although you could peek through cracks in the doors at the sparkling mirrors inside.

Musamman Burj and **Khas Mahal** are the wonderful white-marble octagonal tower and palace where Shah Jahan was imprisoned for eight years until his death in 1666, and from where he could gaze out at the Taj Mahal, the tomb of his wife. When he died, Shah Jahan's body was taken from here by boat to the Taj. The **Mina Masjid** was his private mosque.

In the courtyard of the large harem quarters is **Anguri Bagh**, a garden that has been brought back to life in recent years. In the courtyard is an innocuous-looking entrance – now locked – that leads down a flight of stairs into a two-storey labyrinth of underground rooms and passageways where Akbar used to keep his 500-strong harem.

The huge red-sandstone **Jehangir's Palace** was probably built by Akbar for his son Jehangir. It blends Indian and Central Asian architectural styles, a reminder of the Mughals' Afghani cultural roots. In front of the palace is **Hauz-i-Jehangir**, a huge bowl carved out of a single block of stone, which was used for bathing.

AKBAR'S MAUSOLEUM

This outstanding sandstone and marble **tomb** (☎ 2641230; Indian/foreigner Rs10/110, video Rs25; ☼ dawn-dusk) commemorates the greatest of the Mughal emperors. The huge courtyard is entered through a stunning gateway. It has three-storey minarets at each corner and is built of red sandstone strikingly inlaid with white-marble geometric patterns.

The mausoleum is at Sikandra, 10km northwest of Agra Fort. Buses (Rs10, 45 minutes) heading to Mathura from Idgah bus stand go past the mausoleum. An autorickshaw should cost Rs150 return from the centre, including waiting time and a quick side trip to nearby Swami Bagh (p410).

front of it is the small and rather incongruous **grave of John Colvin**, a lieutenant-governor of the northwest provinces who died of an illness in the fort during the 1857 First War of Independence. The **Moti Masjid** (Pearl Mosque) was under renovation at the time of research, and is usually closed to visitors. However, don't miss the tiny but exquisite **Nagina Masjid** (Gem Mosque), built in 1635 by Shah Jahan for the ladies of the court. Down below was the **Ladies' bazaar**, where the court ladies bought goods.

Diwan-i-Khas (Hall of Private Audiences) was reserved for important dignitaries or foreign representatives. The legendary Peacock Throne (p407) was originally housed here. Overlooking the river and the distant Taj

ITIMAD-UD-DAULAH

Nicknamed the **Baby Taj** (Map p402; ☎ 2080030; Indian/foreigner Rs10/110, video Rs25; ☼ dawn-dusk), the exquisite tomb of Mizra Ghiyas Beg should not be missed. This Persian nobleman was Mumtaz Mahal's grandfather and Emperor Jehangir's *wazir* (chief minister). His daughter Nur Jahan, who married Jehangir, built the tomb between 1622 and 1628 in a style similar to the tomb she built for Jehangir near Lahore in Pakistan.

It doesn't have the same awesome beauty as the Taj, but it's arguably more delicate in appearance thanks to its particularly finely carved *jali* (marble lattice screens). This was the first Mughal structure built completely from marble, the first to make extensive use of pietra dura and the first tomb to be built on the banks of the Yamuna, which until then had been a sequence of beautiful pleasure gardens.

You can combine a trip here with Chini-ka-Rauza, Mehtab Bagh and Ram Bagh, all on the east bank. A cycle rickshaw covering all four should cost just over Rs100 return from the Taj, including waiting time. An auto will be at least double.

CHINI-KA-RAUZA

This Persian-style riverside **tomb** (Map p402; ☼ dawn-dusk) of Afzal Khan, a poet who served as Shah Jahan's chief minister, was built between 1628 and 1639. Rarely visited, it is hidden away down a shady avenue of trees on the east bank of the Yamuna. Bright blue tiles, which once covered the whole mausoleum, can still be seen on part of the exterior, while the interior is painted in floral designs.

MEHTAB BAGH

This **park** (Map p402; Indian/foreigner Rs5/100; ☼ dawn-dusk), originally built by Emperor Babur as the last in a series of 11 parks on the Yamuna's east bank, long before the Taj was conceived, fell into disrepair until it was little more than a huge mound of sand. To protect the Taj from the erosive effects of the sand blown across the river, the park was reconstructed in recent years and is now one the best places from which to view the great mausoleum. The

---

SAVING THE BEARS

Not so long ago, tourists on the road between Agra and Fatehpur Sikri would have seen performing sloth bears by the roadside, forced to dance like circus animals for money. Thanks to the sterling efforts of one local wildlife group in particular, you won't see them here any more, but sadly this barbaric practice has yet to be completely stamped out. Despite being illegal in India since 1972 the industry still enslaves an estimated 160 bears.

India's first, and now the world's largest sanctuary for 'dancing' bears, the Agra Bear Rescue Facility, was established by **Wildlife SOS** (☎ 9917190666, 9837790369; www.wildlifesos.org) in 2002 and extends for nearly 65 hectares within the Sur Sarovar Bird Sanctuary, 17km west of Agra. The facility provides refuge, rehabilitation and veterinary care for more than 283 sloth bears and has other sanctuaries in Bengaluru (Bangalore), Bhopal and West Bengal.

Bears are poached from the forests as cubs and sold in illegal markets to Qalander tribespeople, who have used dancing bears as a source of income for centuries. A red-hot iron rod is inserted through their muzzle so that a rope or nose ring can be attached and they spend much of their lives chained to a stake. Their canine teeth are knocked out, without anaesthesia, and the bears are beaten into submission to teach them to 'perform'.

Because the bears have been captive most of their lives, it's unlikely they can ever be released into the wild, but the goal of Wildlife SOS is to stamp out the practice of dancing bears and thus stop the poaching of cubs. An important part of this is finding an alternative source of income for the Qalanders, a number of whom are now trained and employed at the sanctuaries helping to care for the bears.

The Agra Bear Rescue Facility welcomes small groups of visitors interested in seeing firsthand this important rehabilitation and conservation work. To arrange a visit, first contact Wildlife SOS by phone or email. To get there you first need to enter the Sur Sarovar Bird Sanctuary (taxi drivers know the sanctuary as Keetham Jheel or Bhalu Park). Note that the Rs350 entry fee is for the forestry department and does not go towards the bear sanctuary. Donations should be made separately. See the website for more information.

gardens in the Taj are perfectly aligned with the ones here, and the view of the Taj from the fountain directly in front of the entrance gate is a special one.

One of Agra's worst-kept secrets is that you can sneak down the side of this park to the riverbank and view the Taj for free in a peaceful, natural ambience of buffaloes and wading birds. For safety reasons, it's best to leave before dusk.

SAMADHI SWAMIJI MAHARAJ BAGH

Known simply as Swami Bagh, this huge white marble **mausoleum** (8am-5pm), which houses the tomb of Sri Shiv Dayal Singh Seth, the founder of the Radhasoami Faith, is of particular interest because it is still being built – more than 80 years after it was started. Inside there's a 1904 painting of what it should look like when finished, complete with a gold-latticed dome. For now it's a work-in-progress project being undertaken by devotees. The design incorporates building styles from other major religions and includes some fabulously delicate floral carvings.

Swami Bagh is in Dayalbagh district. To get here, take a shared auto from Idgah bus stand to Bhagwan (Rs10) then a cycle rickshaw (Rs10). An auto from Taj Ganj and back, including a trip to Akbar's Mausoleum, will cost at least Rs150.

JAMA MASJID

This fine **mosque** (Map p402), built in the Kinari Bazaar by Shah Jahan's daughter in 1648, and once connected to Agra Fort, features striking marble patterning on its domes.

KINARI BAZAAR

The narrow streets behind Jama Masjid are a crazy maze of overcrowded lanes bursting with colourful **markets** (Map p402). There are a number of different bazaars here, each specialising in different wares, but the area is generally known as Kinari Bazaar as many of the lanes fan out from Kinari Bazaar Rd. You'll find clothing, shoes, fabrics, jewellery, spices, marble work, snack stalls and what seems like 20 million other people. Amazingly, there is somehow room for buffaloes and even the odd working elephant to squeeze their way through the crowds. Even if you're not buying anything, just walking the streets is an experience in itself. Don't forget to look up from time to time at the old wooden balco-

nies above some of the shop fronts. As with all crowded markets, take extra care of your belongings here.

SWIMMING

Nonguests can swim in Hotel Amar (Rs250) – with slide! – Hotel Atithi (Rs250), Hotel Yamuna View (Rs350), Mansingh Palace (adult/child Rs300/50), Clarks Shiraz Hotel (Rs450) and Howard Park Plaza (Rs500).

Tours

UP Tourism runs **daily tours** (incl entry fees Indian/foreigner Rs400/1700) that leave Agra Cantonment train station at 10.30am, after picking up passengers arriving from Delhi on the *Taj Express*. The AC coach tour includes the Taj Mahal, Agra Fort and Fatehpur Sikri with a 1¼-hour stop in each place. Tours return to the station so that day trippers can catch the *Taj Express* back to Delhi at 6.55pm. Contact either of the UP Tourism offices (p401) to book a seat.

Sleeping

The main place for budget accommodation is the bustling area of Taj Ganj, immediately south of the Taj, while there's a high concentration of midrange hotels further south, along Fatehabad Rd.

Ask at the UP Tourism office for the latest list of recommended homestays.

BUDGET
Taj Ganj Area

Hotel Shahjahan (Map p404; 3200240; Taj South Gate; s Rs80, s with bathroom Rs100, d Rs150-200, with AC Rs500-600) Clean, spacious rooms, some of which are accessed via a narrow marble staircase, overlook a small inner courtyard. A couple have Taj views, as does the rooftop restaurant. As the prices suggest, the two singles are pretty grim.

Hotel Sidhartha (Map p404; 22309011; www.hotelsidhartha.com; Taj West Gate; s Rs120-150, d Rs300, with cooler/AC Rs450/600;) First opened its doors in 1986 and still going strong. The 18 very smart double rooms (and two decidedly grotty singles) are set around a small, leafy courtyard. The rooftop seating area is a bit exposed, but has a Taj view and is a good spot from which to watch the area's troop of resident monkeys getting up to mischief.

Shanti Lodge (Map p404; 2231973; shantilodge2000@yahoo.co.in; Taj South Gate; s Rs200, d Rs250-300, r with AC Rs500; 🔀) Too many shoddy rooms with dodgy bathrooms stop this from being a top choice, but there are more spacious, cleaner rooms in the newer section behind the old block, and its restaurant still has arguably the best rooftop view of the Taj in all of Agra.

Hotel Kamal (Map p404; ☎ 2330126; hotelkamal@ hotmail.com; Taj South Gate; s/d from Rs300/400, with AC from Rs600/700; 🔀) Rooms here are simple but clean, most come with TV and the pricier ones have a sofa. The rooftop restaurant has a decent Taj view, albeit slightly obscured by a tree.

Saniya Palace Hotel (Map p404; ☎ 3270199; Taj South Gate; d Rs300-600) Set back from the main strip down a tiny alleyway, this place has more character than its rivals, with marble floors and Mughal-style framed carpets hung on the walls. The rooms are clean and big enough, although the bathrooms are miniscule. Along with Shanti's, the rooftop restaurant is a contender for the best view of the Taj in town.

our pick **Hotel Sheela** (Map p404; ☎ 2331194; www .hotelsheelaagra.com; Taj East Gate Rd; s Rs350-550, d Rs400-600; 🔀) If you're not fussed about looking at the Taj Mahal 24 hours a day, this superb budget option could be just the ticket. Rooms are simple (no TVs here), but spotless and come with towel, soap and loo roll – a nice touch for a cheapie. Best of all they're set around a beautifully landscaped garden with singing birds, plenty of shade and a pleasant restaurant area (p412).

Other Areas

Tourists Rest House (Map p402; ☎ 2463961; dontworry chickencurry@hotmail.com; Kutchery Rd; d Rs200-300, with AC Rs450; 🔀 🖳) An Agra institution, this is away from the bustle of Taj Ganj. The shady central courtyard garden is an oasis of peace and a great place to meet other travellers. Its trustworthy owners are helpful and knowledgeable and rooms are spotless, with tiled floors, TV and hot water. There are small discounts on room prices for single occupancy. Free pick-up and free transport reservations. A top choice.

Hotel Sakura (Map p402; ☎ 2420169; www.hotelsakura agra.com; 49 Ajmer Rd; d Rs250-550; 🖳) Rooms are clean, with high ceilings and marble floors, and the management is friendly and very knowledgeable. Even if you don't stay here, it's a decent place to grab a bite to eat (meals Rs50 to Rs100) while waiting for a bus from the Idgah bus stand. Jaipur deluxe buses leave from the hotel's driveway.

MIDRANGE

Taj Plaza (off Map p404; ☎ 2232515; www.hoteltajplaza .com; Taj East Gate Rd; d Rs800, with AC Rs1200, with Taj view Rs1600, ste Rs4000; 🔀 🖳) Good-quality budget hotel stretched into a midrange price bracket. You won't be disappointed if you stay here – rooms are clean, have TV and some come with Taj views – but you won't write home about it. Still, it's a whole lot closer to the Taj than most hotels in the same price range.

Amar Yatri Niwas (Map p402; ☎ 2233030; www.amar yatriniwas.com; Fatehabad Rd; s Rs1200-2500, d Rs1500-2800; 🔀) It's marble galore here – floors, wall panels, tabletops – but narrow corridors and teeny bathrooms may leave you feeling slightly claustrophobic. It has a good restaurant, Mehfil (p421).

Hotel Ashish Palace (Map p402; ☎ 2230032; www .hotelashishpalace.com; Fatehabad Rd; s Rs1200-1700, d Rs1500-2000, ste Rs2500-3500; 🔀) Spacious rooms – some are cavernous – but not enough furniture to fill them, so far from cosy. Marble floors extend into the bathrooms. All rooms have table and chairs, TV and fridge.

Hotel Atithi (Map p402; ☎ 2330880; www.hotel atithiagra.com; Fatehabad Rd; s Rs1750-2100, d Rs2100-2750; 🔀 🏊) Rooms are clean with white-tiled bathrooms, but the green and blue decor leaves a lot to be desired. Guests can use the lovely pool next door for free.

Hotel Amar (Map p402; ☎ 4008402; www.hotel amar.com; Fatehabad Rd; s Rs3000-4500, d Rs3400-4500, ste Rs6000-8000; 🔀 🖳 🏊) Again the decor raises eyebrows – a patchwork of random, non-matching items of furniture – but all rooms are well maintained and large. The real treat is the pool area, complete with a lush green lawn and a 3.5m-tall water slide. Has a branch of Costa Coffee in the lobby.

Hotel Yamuna View (Map p402; ☎ 2462989; www .hotelyamunaviewagra.com; 6B The Mall; s Rs3000-3900, d Rs3795-4995; 🔀 🏊) A pool in the garden, a water feature in the sunken, grand lobby, a plush Chinese restaurant and some spacious rooms with gleaming bathrooms make this friendly hotel in a quiet part of Sadar Bazaar worth the splurge. It also has a 24-hour cafe.

TOP END

Clarks Shiraz Hotel (Map p402; ☎ 2226121; www.hotel-clarksshiraz.com; 54 Taj Rd; s Rs4000-5500, d Rs4500-5800, Taj-facing s/d Rs6200/6500; 🔀 🖳 📶 🏊) One of Agra's original five-star hotels has seen some recent renovation. The standard doubles are still nothing special, but marble-floored deluxe versions are excellent and all bathrooms have been retiled so are spotless. There are two very good restaurants, three bars, a gym, a shady garden pool area and ayurvedic massages. Some rooms have distant Taj views.

Mansingh Palace (Map p402; ☎ 2331771; www.man singhhotels.com; Fatehabad Rd; s Rs5000-5500, d Rs6000-6500, r with Taj view Rs7500, ste Rs12500; ✗ ▣ ▣) This stylish hotel has plush rooms and is crammed with Mughal design themes, along with cool green marble, wood panelling and exotic furnishings. The garden has an interestingly shaped pool and outdoor BBQ area. There's a gym and the quality Sheesh Mahal restaurant has live *ghazals* (Urdu songs) nightly.

Howard Park Plaza (Map p402; ☎ 2331870; www .sarovarhotels.com; Fatehabad Rd; s/d/ste Rs6000/7000/12,000; ✗ ▣ ▣) Rooms in this very welcoming hotel are decked out in elegant dark-wood furniture and stylish decorative tiling. Bathrooms are a little on the compact side for this price, but still very smart. There's an unusual splash-shaped pool out the back, a small gym and a spa offering a whole range of ayurvedic treatments.

Oberoi Amar Vilas (off Map p404; ☎ 2231515; www .oberoihotels.com; Taj East Gate Rd; d Rs29,500-32,000, ste Rs53,000-93,500, presidential Rs136,000; ✗ ▣ ▣) If money is no object, look no further. By far the best hotel in Agra – some say the best in India – this place oozes style and luxury. Elegant interior design is suffused with Mughal themes, a composition carried over into the exterior fountain courtyard and swimming pool, both of which are set in a delightful water garden. All rooms (and even some bathtubs!) have wonderful views of the Taj, as do the excellent restaurant (p421)and classy cocktail bar, both of which are open to nonguests.

Eating

Dalmoth is Agra's famous version of *namkin* (spicy nibbles). *Peitha* is a square sweet made from pumpkin and glucose that is flavoured with rosewater, coconut or saffron. From October to March look out for *gajak*, a slightly spicy sesame-seed biscuit strip.

TAJ GANJ AREA

This lively area directly south of the Taj has plenty of budget rooftop restaurants, where the meals and menus appear to be carbon copies. None are licensed but it's often possible to order in a clandestine beer, which may arrive wrapped in newspaper or even in a teapot. You'll find cheaper restaurants with more of a local feel by the cycle and autorickshaw stand, although many do not have English menus.

Joney's Place (Map p404; mains Rs20-80; ⏰ 5am-10.30pm) Open at the crack of dawn, this pocket-sized, brightly painted, travellers' institution whipped up its first creamy lassi in 1978 and continues to serve visitors veg snacks, pancakes, toasted sandwiches and the like.

Gulshan Restaurant (Map p404; mains Rs25-80; ⏰ 6am-11pm) Cash crisis? Head straight to the roof terrace here and tuck in to the Rs25 veg thali. There's a smaller Rs15 version for breakfast.

Taj Cafe (Map p404; mains Rs35-190; ⏰ 6.30am-11pm) Up a flight of steps and overlooking Taj Ganj's busy street scene, this friendly, family-run restaurant is a nice choice if you're not fussed about Taj views. There's everything from south Indian and meat curries to pizza and Korean. And the thalis here are better value than at its rooftop rivals.

Shankara Vegis Restaurant (Map p404; meals Rs40-90; ⏰ 8am-10.30pm) Another Taj Ganj old-timer, this rooftop vegetarian restaurant does a shockingly good thali (Rs90) and comes with a laid-back atmosphere, a view of the Taj (just about) and games like chess and carrom (a table-top game in which fingers are used to flick playing pieces across a powered board and into corner pockets).

Stuff Makers (Map p404; meals Rs40-100; ⏰ 6am-10.30pm) Hotel Kamal's rooftop terrace, complete with fairy lights, has an excellent view of the Taj from some tables, and of a tree from others. The menu has the usual unimaginative mix of Indian, Western and Chinese dishes.

Yash Cafe (Map p404; mains Rs40-110; ⏰ 7am-10pm) This chilled-out 1st-floor cafe has wicker chairs, sports channels on TV, movies in the evening and a good range of meals, from thalis to pizzas. It also offers a shower and storage space (Rs50 for both) to day visitors.

Shanti Lodge Restaurant (Map p404; mains Rs40-100; ⏰ 7am-10pm) The rooftop Taj view here is superb so this is a great place for breakfast and it packs in the punters at sunset. There's also some shade for hot afternoons. The only letdown is the menu which, although not bad, lacks invention. Banana pancakes, anyone?

Saniya Palace Hotel (Map p404; mains Rs40-100) The rooftop view of the Taj is as good as, if not better than at Shanti, but again it's the usual mix of Western dishes and Western-friendly Indian dishes on offer.

(Continued on page 421)

Delicious
India

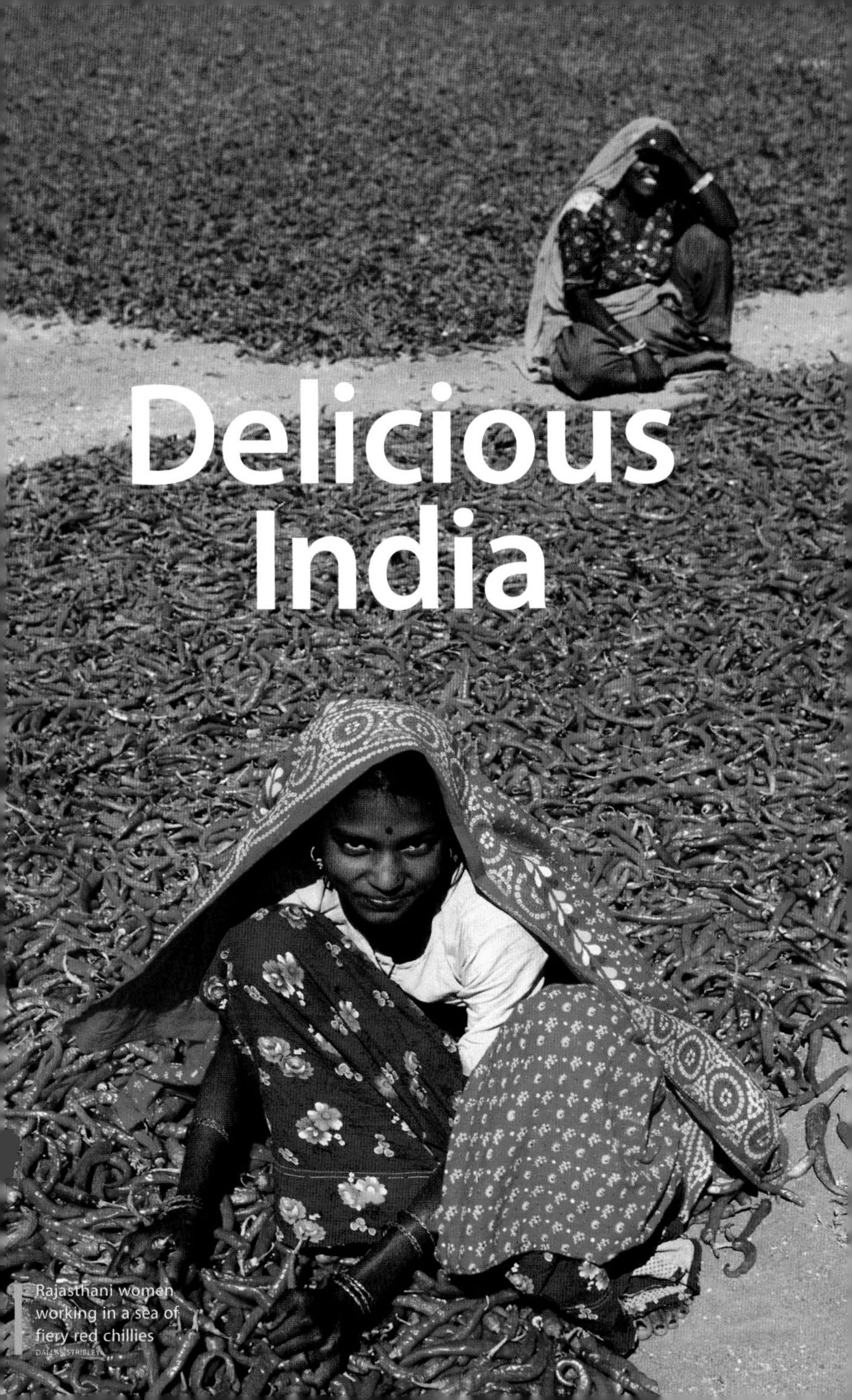

Rajasthani women
working in a sea of
fiery red chillies
DALLAS STRIBLEY

Brace yourself – you're about to jump on board one of the wildest culinary trips of your life! Frying, simmering, sizzling, kneading and flipping a deliciously diverse array of regional dishes, India's talented chefs ensure that feasting your way through the subcontinent promises to be one hell of a ride. Indeed, the hungry traveller can look forward to a seemingly endless smorgasbord of scrummy delights, thanks to the staggering assortment of traditional and contemporary fare on offer. From the spicy succulent goodness of masterfully marinated chicken drumsticks in North India, to the hushed splendour of squidgy rice dumplings in the steamy south, dining out certainly fires the imagination, piques the tastebuds and satiates the belly. So what are you waiting for? Roll up your sleeves, put on your munch-munch hat, and rumble your way down India's superlicious gastronomic highway!

PUNJAB

You are probably familiar with the hearty food of the Punjab region because many of its staple dishes have come to represent Indian food on an international scale. A paste made from onions, garlic and ginger forms the basis of most dishes. Chillies, tomatoes, cumin, garam masala, dried fenugreek leaves and *kalonji* (a black seed that is similar to caraway seed; also called onion seed) are added in varying combinations. The main meal of the day might consist of hot rotis with dollops of unsalted butter, a bowl of dhal and a vegetable dish, such as the favourite *saag* (leafy greens), or *aloo gobi* (cauliflower and potato curry), *baigan bharta* (roasted eggplant that has been fried with onions and tomatoes) or *aloo mattar* (a curry made with potatoes and green peas). An integral part of Punjabi cooking is the tandoor (clay oven), open at the top and fired by charcoal below, that turns out piping-hot naan and a gamut of kebabs: *sheekh* (mincemeat on iron skewers), *tangri* (plump chicken drumsticks), *boti* (spicy bite-sized bits of boneless lamb), chicken tikka (melt-in-your-mouth chunks of chicken) and, of course, the ubiquitous tandoori chicken.

Succulent tandoori chicken from Punjab
GREG ELMS

RAJASTHAN

The largely arid landscape of Rajasthan has led to a spicy cuisine inventively derived from meagre resources. Boosted with limited fresh vegetables, fruits or fish, Rajasthanis make the most of cereals, pulses, spices and milk products to produce a surprisingly elaborate cuisine. Wheat flour is used to make rotis, *puris, parathas* and the state's most remarkable dish, *bati* (baked balls of wholemeal flour). Along with *bati* goes *churma* (fried whole-wheat flour balls pounded with sugar and nuts) to make the

Decadent delights in a sweet shop window, Rajasthan

KAREN TRIST

classic Rajasthani combination, *dhal bati churma*. Besan (gram or chickpea flour) is another staple, and is used to make salted snacks. In the parched deserts of Jaisalmer, Jodhpur and Bikaner, meats are often cooked without water, using milk, curd, buttermilk and plenty of ghee. *Murg ko khaato* (chicken cooked in a curd gravy), *achar murg* (pickled chicken) and *kacher maas* (dry lamb cooked in spices) are classic Rajasthani desert dishes.

KASHMIR

Many migrants from Kashmir have moved to Delhi and other urban hubs, where you can try their unique cuisine, identified by its spice mixes and meats usually cooked in curd or milk, which gives them a whitish colour and smooth texture. Chilli is sometimes added to give curries a fiery red tinge. There is an enticing selection of vegetarian and meat recipes in the Kashmiri kitchen, with mutton dishes being especially popular – don't miss the delicious rogan josh.

UTTAR PRADESH & UTTARAKHAND

Uttar Pradesh and Uttarakhand showcase a variety of cuisines, including pure Hindu vegetarian, majestic Nawabi and simple hill fare. Places of pilgrimage such as Varanasi are predominantly vegetarian; a standard meal comprises *phulkas* (small puffed chapatis), *dhal chawal* (dhal and rice) and seasonal vegetable dishes. Lucknow, Varanasi's Islamic counterpart, is associated with the most majestic Nawabi cuisine and is famous for its kebabs made with mincemeat or meat paste. The *shami* kebab (boiled mincemeat, ground with chickpeas and spices) is particularly loved in Uttar Pradesh homes.

DOSA ME UP!

Dosas (also spelt dosais), a family of large savoury rice-flour crepes, usually served with a bowl of hot *sambar* (soupy lentil dish with cubed vegetables) and another bowl of cooling coconut *chatni* (chutney), are a South Indian breakfast speciality that can be eaten at any time of day. The most popular is the masala dosa (stuffed with spiced potatoes), but there are also other dosa varieties – the *rava* dosa (batter made with semolina), the Mysore dosa (like masala dosa but with more vegetables and chilli in the filling), and the *pessarettu* dosa (batter made with mung-bean dhal) from Andhra Pradesh. Nowadays, dosas are readily found far beyond South India, thanks to their widespread yum-appeal.

Shopping for fresh produce, Sikkim
STAEVEN VALLAK

WEST BENGAL

The food-loving folk of West Bengal are fiercely proud of their cuisine, which they assert to be the epitome of refined taste. A plethora of fish is found in the rivers and ponds of Bengal and it is fried, curried in onions, stewed lightly with vegetables or made into spicy *jhaal* (fish with ground mustard seeds and chillies). Bengali sweets are among the finest in the subcontinent; one of the best known is the luscious *rasgulla* (cream-cheese balls flavoured with rose water). Read more about Bengali cuisine in the boxed text on p523.

BIHAR

Bihar's cuisine is wonderfully rustic and wholesome. *Sattu* (roasted chickpea flour) is the unifying theme; it's cheap, filling and nutritious. Its preparation ranges from the absolutely coarse to the subtly refined – a labourer carries it knotted in his *gamchha* (handloom towel) and mixes it with onion and chilli for a makeshift meal, while a middle-class housewife may dip Bihar's most well-known food, *littis* (balls of spiced *sattu* covered in dough and baked on coals), in a bowl of warm ghee before serving them.

SIKKIM

Like much of Sikkimese culture, local cuisine is reminiscent of that from Tibet and Nepal. *Thukpa* (nourishing noodle soup), *momos* (steamed or fried dumplings stuffed with vegetables or meat) and *gyakho* (stew) are ubiquitous foods. On the liquid side, salt-butter tea is fun to make using the traditional *sudah* plunger-churn, while no trip to Sikkim is truly complete without supping *tongba*, a uniquely Himalayan millet beer.

NORTHEAST STATES

The variety of the Northeast States' cuisines is phenomenal, with each tribe or community developing its own signature dishes. In Assam they're particularly fond of sour tastes and, like the Thais, use lots of lime and lime leaves in their cooking. *Tenga*, the favourite Assamese fish stew, is made of pieces of sweet-tasting *rohu* (a type of carp), lightly sautéed with onions and simmered in a watery gravy that's zested with lemon juice. The major community in Meghalaya, the Khasis, specialises in rice-based dishes such as *putharo* (rice-batter crepe), *pukhen* (sweet fried rice cakes) and *pusla* (steamed rice cakes wrapped in leaves). In Tripura, the locals are passionately fond of both fresh and dried-fish dishes, such as *nona ilish paturi* (salted pieces of hilsa fish, wrapped in an edible leaf and fried)

A tempting thali of Assamese flavours from Guwahati in the Northeast States

GREG ELMS

and *pithali* (dried-fish stew). *Shidol* (a fermented preserve made of tiny freshwater fish) is quintessentially Tripuri and a mainstay of every kitchen. Fish is equally important in Manipur, and the fish preserve made here is known as *ngari*. Nagas have a taste for pork, and several other similarities exist with Chinese food such as the use of spring onions, garlic, ginger and monosodium glutamate (MSG). You'll come across many typical Tibetan dishes in Arunachal Pradesh, including *momos, churpee* (chewy bits of dried yak cheese) and *thukpa* (hearty noodle soup).

MADHYA PRADESH

The food of Madhya Pradesh is typically North Indian, with broad divisions between 'non-tribal' and 'tribal' styles. The food in the dry belt that runs from Gwalior to Indore, known as the Malwa cuisine, is grain- and dhal-based, with few vegetables and a lot of oil and ghee. The capital Bhopal, however, has a long tradition of Islamic rule, and korma, *rizala* (a chilli-flavoured, greenish-white mutton dish), *ishtu* (spicy stew), *achar gosht* (a famous pickle-like meat dish of Hyderabad) and kebabs are cooked in most Muslim homes.

GUJARAT

Vegetarians constitute almost 90% of Gujarat's population, largely due to the number of Jains (see p72) who call this state home. A typical Gujarati thali would have to be one of the most balanced and nutritious meals in India. The meal generally consists of rice, chapati, a salad (could be finely diced tomatoes and cucumbers) or

MANGALORE MAGIC

The fiery cuisine of the Karnatakan coastal city of Mangalore deserves special mention because it has carved a name for itself across India, particularly for its flavour-packed seafood dishes. Mangalorean cuisine is diverse, distinct and especially characterised by its liberal use of chilli and fresh coconut – find out more in the boxed text on p933.

Mumbai's must-try street snack, *bhelpuri* (crisp dough, puffed rice, lentils, lemon juice, herbs and chutr
ORIEN

vegetable relish (shredded cabbage or bean sprouts with grated coconut), raita, a dry vegetable (such as stir-fried beans), a curried vegetable (such as potatoes and eggplant), dhal,
kadhi (a sour dhal-like dish made of curd and besan), pickle and *mithai* (sweets). All the
items are served at once and savoured a little at a time.

MAHARASHTRA

Much of the Deccan Plateau, the heart of Maharashtra, is arid and barren, giving rise to a
simple diet based on pulses and grains. Marathi Brahmin food is the epitome of minimalist cuisine; probably nowhere else in India is dhal quite so simple – it's boiled with salt
and turmeric and then flavoured with a hint of ghee, asafoetida and jaggery. Vegetables,
too, are just tossed with mustard seeds, curry leaves and grated coconut. Fish is the staple
of nonvegetarian Marathi food; Maharashtra's favourite fish is *bombil* (Bombay duck), a
misnomer for this slimy, pikelike fish, which is eaten fresh or sun-dried. The snack most
synonymous with Maharashtra, particularly Mumbai, is *bhelpuri,* a riotous mix of sweet,
sour, hot, soft and crunchy sensations. Tossed up on a leaf plate or a square of newspaper
are puffed rice, slivers of boiled potatoes, chopped onions, peanuts, fine hairlike besan
sticks, sweet tamarind *chatni,* a piquant green-coriander-and-chilli *chatni* and a generous
squeeze of lime. Another all-time Maharasthrian fave is *vada pao,* an Indian-style veg-
burger of sorts.

ANDHRA PRADESH

In Andhra Pradesh, you'll find most of India's Muslim-created specialities, with a unique
Andhra twist, often in the form of heat or spice. Hyderabad's oven-baked biryani, with
layers of vegetables, meat, nuts and spices, is quite different from North Indian biryanis –

a must-try! Andhra Pradesh's other major cuisine – that of the Andhras – comprises a wide variety of lentil, vegetable, meat and fish preparations. A sour touch, provided by tamarind, is added to most dishes.

ORISSA

In Orissa, fish is given pride of place and prepared in many ways – it can be fried, curried with onions or cooked with a mustard-and-curd paste. *Ambul* is a popular mustard fish preparation that derives its tang from the inclusion of dried mangoes. Meanwhile, tamarind adds a cheeky sour touch to dishes, with okra often cooked in a delectable sour gravy of tamarind and tomatoes.

GOA

The deliciously unique cuisine of coast-hugging Goa largely evolved from the intermingling of the highly developed Goan culture, coupled with over four centuries of Portuguese rule. It's little wonder that seafood is the Goan staple, which includes many varieties of freshwater and saltwater fish, as well as a tempting cache of shellfish. A typical Goan lunch may kick off with a mildly spicy side dish such as *caldeen* (fish simmered in coconut milk, ginger and cumin), while the Portuguese influence usually emerges more prominently in the evening meal, when the main course might be *assado de bife* (roast beef) or a hot pork vindaloo (spicy pork curry). Goans specialise in mouth-wateringly good puddings, cakes and sweet snacks; don't leave without trying the famous *bebinca* (the layered 40-egg sweet, rich with ghee and coconut milk) – pure bliss. The cuisine of the western coast of Karnataka, the Konkan Coast, is notably reminiscent of Goan fare, with oodles of fish and coconut.

Bebinca, the delicious Goan dessert made with only 40 eggs!

GREG ELMS

KERALA

Like Goa, seafood is also a favourite in tropical Kerala, and virtually every meal will include it in a fried or curried form – favourites include *meen pollichathu* (fish cooked in banana leaves) and *molee* (fish or seafood cooked in coconut milk and spices). Most food is cooked in coconut oil, and dishes are often abundantly garnished with freshly scraped coconut or coconut milk. Vegetables are rarely overcooked, and are simply steamed or stir-fried to retain their natural flavours and nutrients.

IDYLLIC IDLIS

The humble *idli* is a traditional South Indian snack that can be found around India; low-cal and nutritious, it provides a welcome alternative to oil, spice and chilli. *Idlis* are spongy, round, white fermented rice cakes that you dip in *sambar* and coconut *chatni*. *Dahi idli* is an idli dunked in very lightly spiced yoghurt – terrific for tender tummies. Other top southern snacks, which are also popular throughout the country, include *vadas* (doughnut-shaped deep-fried lentil savouries) and *appams* or *uttappams* (crisp-collared rice-flour and coconut-milk savoury pancakes).

TAMIL NADU

The Tamils are some of the most dedicated vegetarians in India and serve some of the country's tastiest vegetarian fare, but there's meat on offer in the form of spicy curries courtesy of the Chettiar community, an extended clan of bankers and merchants from the driest part of the state. The word 'curry' derives from the Tamil *kari* (sauce), while mango comes from the Tamil *maangaai*. Ironically, the former does not factor hugely into Tamil cuisine; in place of 'wet' dishes, the Tamils love the many varieties of rice flour: *idli* (steamed rice cakes), *appam* (rice pancakes), *idiyappam* (rice noodles, which can be fashioned into bowls for curry or soup) and, of course, the legendary dosa; all of the above are usually served with side dishes of *sambar*, chutney and *rasam* (thin lentil soup).

A serving of *appam* (rice pancakes) and coconut *sambar* (soupy lentil dish), Tamil Nadu

(Continued from page 412)

Hotel Sheela (Map p404; mains Rs50-180; ☯ 7am-10pm) Another unimaginative crack at the same Indian and Western dishes found elsewhere in Taj Ganj. What you do get, though, is a wonderfully peaceful garden retreat that makes it hard to believe you're so close to the Taj.

SADAR BAZAAR

Brijwasi (Map p402; Sadar Bazaar; meals Rs30-90; ☯ 7.30am-11pm; ✗) Mouth-watering selection of traditional Indian sweets, nuts and biscuits on the ground floor, with a good-value restaurant upstairs.

our pick **Lakshmi Vilas** (Map p402; Taj Rd; meals Rs35-70; ☯ 9am-10pm; ✗ ✗) This no-nonsense, plainly decorated restaurant is *the* place in Agra to come for affordable South Indian fare. Treats include *idli* (spongy, round, fermented rice cake), *vada* (doughnut-shaped, deep-fried lentil savoury), *uttapam* (thick, savoury rice pancake) and more than 20 varieties of dosa (large savoury crepe, Rs46 to Rs250), including a family special that is 1.2m long!

Tourists Rest House (Map p402; ☎ 2363961; Kutchery Rd; meals Rs40-75) The courtyard garden restaurant here is often full of chattering travellers enjoying the candle-lit atmosphere around the small fountain, and the all-veg menu is decent.

Zorba the Buddha (Map p402; Gopi Chand Shivhare Rd; meals Rs90-120; ☯ noon-10pm, closed Jun; ✗) Neat little tables are set around a central, marble pillar in this fun veg restaurant. Specialities include kofta (giant mashed potato balls) and paneer (unfermented cheese).

Dasaprakash (Map p402; ☎ 2363535; 1 Gwalior Rd; meals Rs80-190; ☯ 11am-10.45pm) Highly recommended by locals for consistently good South Indian veg food, Dasaprakash whips up spectacular thalis (with bottomless refills), dosa, and a few token continental dishes. The dessert sundaes are tempting but pricey (from Rs90). Comfortable booth seating and wood-lattice screens make for intimate dining.

OTHER AREAS

Mehfil Restaurant (Map p402; ☎ 2233030; mains Rs60-200; ☯ 6am-11pm; ✗) The hotel restaurant at Amar Yatri Niwas serves Chinese and Western dishes as well as rich, reader-recommended Indian cuisine.

Mughal Room (Map p402; ☎ 2226121; 54 Taj Rd; mains Rs175-700; ☯ 6-10am, 12.30-2.30pm & 7.30-11pm) On the top floor of Clarks Shiraz Hotel, you can dine in style with a distant view of the Taj and Agra Fort, although you won't see anything at night. There's live classical music here every evening and the food is thoughtfully prepared Indian, Chinese and continental.

Bellevue (off Map p404; ☎ 2231515; Taj East Gate Rd; mains Rs800-1950; ☯ 6.30am-10.30pm) The only one of the two restaurants in Oberoi Amar Vilas open to nonguests, Bellevue is all class and a majestic place in which to enjoy a sumptuous lunch – soups, salads, grilled meats, pasta – with a Taj view through the large windows.

Drinking & Entertainment

Beer shop (Map p404; ☯ 10am-11pm) In Taj Ganj, this is the handiest place to pick up a bottle of Kingfisher (Rs75) to enjoy on a rooftop.

Wine Shop (Map p404; ☯ 9am-11pm) If you fancy something stronger, this place sells a host of different whiskies from around Rs150 for a small bottle.

Jaiwal Bar (Map p402; 3 Taj Rd, ☯ 10am-11pm) A pleasant change from soulless hotel bars, pocket-sized Jaiwal has a small outdoor seating area with an even smaller AC room indoors. Beers start from Rs80 and snacks are available.

Amar Vilas Bar (Taj East Gate Rd; ☯ 12am-12pm) For a beer (Rs200) or cocktail (Rs450) in sheer opulence, look no further than the bar at Agra's best hotel. A terrace opens out to views of the Taj.

Catch live Indian classical music and *ghazal*s at several restaurants and top-end hotels.

Shopping

Agra is well known for its marble items inlaid with coloured stones, similar to the pietra dura work on the Taj. **Sadar Bazaar** (Map p402), the old town and the area around the Taj are full of emporiums. Taj models are mostly made of soapstone, which scratches easily, rather than marble.

Other popular buys include rugs, leather and gemstones, though the latter are imported from Rajasthan and are cheaper in Jaipur.

Kinari Bazaar (p410) This is just one market of many in a crowded tangle of streets in the old town, selling everything from textiles and handicrafts to fruit and produce.

Subhash Bazaar Skirts the northern edge of Agra's Jama Masjid and is particularly good for silks and saris.

Subhash Emporium (Map p402; ☎ 2850749; 18/1 Gwalior Rd; ⏰ 10am-6.30pm) This expensive but honest marble-carving shop has been knocking up quality pieces for more than 35 years. Watch artisans at work in the entranceway before delving into the stock out the back.

Khadi Gramodyog (Map p402; ☎ 2421481; MG Rd; ⏰ 10.30am-7pm) Stocks simple, good-quality Indian clothing made from the homespun *khadi* fabric famously recommended by Mahatma Gandhi (see box text, p451).

Getting There & Away
AIR
Agra's Kheria airport is 5km southwest of the city centre. **Kingfisher Airlines** (☎ 2400693; airport; ⏰ incoming flights) has daily flights to Delhi and Jaipur, both from Rs4500.

BUS
Agra authorities are trying to shift long-distance buses to the Inter State Bus Terminal (ISBT), but most leave from **Idgah Bus Stand** (Map p402; ☎ 2603536). Services from Idgah include frequent buses to Fatehpur Sikri (Rs22, one hour) between 6am and 4pm; Gwalior (Rs75, three hours) 5am to 11.30pm; Jaipur (Rs137, six hours) 4.30am to 10pm; and Delhi (Rs117, 4½ hours) 4am to 11.30pm, via Mathura (Rs37, 1½ hours). Two buses to Khajuraho (Rs230, 10 hours) run at 5am and 6am.

From **ISBT** (☎ 2603536; off National Hwy 2, near Sikandra) buses run to Lucknow (Rs200, 10 hours) from 4.30am to 10.30pm, and Dehra Dun (Rs250, 12 hours) from 6am to 10pm, via Haridwar for Rishikesh (Rs225, 10 hours). Delhi buses should stop at ISBT on their way out of the city.

To get from Idgah to ISBT take a shared auto to Bhagwan (Rs10) then another (Rs5) along Hwy 2. Private autos cost Rs70.

TRAIN
The train is easily the quickest way to travel to/from Delhi, Varanasi, Jaipur and now Khajuraho too (see Delhi–Agra train table, opposite). Most trains leave from **Agra Cantonment (Cantt) train station** (Map p402; ☎ 2421204), although some east–west trains leave from Agra Fort station. Express trains are well set up for day trippers to/from Delhi (see table, below) but trains run to Delhi all day. If you can't reserve a seat, just buy a 'general ticket' for the next train (about Rs60) then upgrade once on the train. For some reason, seats are almost always available this way.

The long-awaited train service to Khajuraho should be up and running by the time you read this. If so, the 2448 *Nizamuddin–Khajuraho Express* will leave Agra Cantonment at around midnight every Tuesday, Friday and Sunday, and arrive in Khajuraho at around 8am.

Getting Around
AUTORICKSHAW
Just outside Agra Cantonment train station is the **prepaid autorickshaw booth** (Map p402; ⏰ 24hr) which gives you a good guide for haggling elsewhere. Prices here are Taj Mahal Rs50, Fatehbad Rd Rs50, Sadar Bazaar Rs40 and Sikandra Rs140 return. A full-day eight-hour tour costs Rs300. Autos aren't allowed to go to Fatehpur Sikri.

Agra's green-and-yellow autorickshaws run on CNG (compressed natural gas) rather than petrol, and so are less environmentally destructive.

BICYCLE
Bicycles can be rented from **Raja Bicycle Store** (Map p404; per hr/day Rs10/80; ⏰ 8am-8.30pm) in Taj Ganj.

CYCLE-RICKSHAW
Prices include Agra Cantonment to Taj Ganj Rs40, Taj Ganj to Sadar Bazaar Rs30, Taj Ganj to Agra Fort Rs20. Hiring one for half a day costs around Rs150, but it does depend on how far you want to go.

DELHI–AGRA TRAINS – DAY TRIPPERS

Trip	Train no & name	Fare (Rs)	Duration (hr)	Departures
New Delhi–Agra	2001 *Shatabdi Exp*	370/700*	2	6.15am
Agra–New Delhi	2002 *Shatabdi Exp*	400/745*	2	8.30pm
Hazrat Nizamuddin–Agra	2080 *Taj Exp*	76/266**	3	7.10am
Agra–Hazrat Nizamuddin	2079 *Taj Exp*	76/266**	3	6.55pm

*chair/1AC; **2nd/chair

MORE HANDY TRAINS FROM AGRA

Destination	Train no & name	Fare (Rs)	Duration (hr)	Departures
Jaipur*	4853/4863 *Marudhar Exp*	131/355/482	5	6.15am
Kolkata (Howrah)**	3008 *UA Toofan Exp*	401/1009	31	12.10pm
Mumbai (CST)	2134 *Punjab Mail*	417/1118/1528	23	8.55am
Varanasi*	4854/4864 *Marudhar Exp*	250/712/976	12/11	9.15pm

*leaves from Agra Fort station; **sleeper/3AC only

TAXI

Just outside Agra Cantonment train station the **prepaid taxi booth** (⊗24hr) gives a good idea of what taxis should cost. Prepaid taxi fees include Taj Mahal Rs150 and Fatehpur Sikri Rs700 return. It's Rs300 for a four-hour half-day tour. An eight-hour tour, including Fatehpur Sikri, costs Rs950.

FATEHPUR SIKRI

☎ 05613 / pop 28,750

This magnificent fortified ancient city, 40km west of Agra, was the short-lived capital of the Mughal empire between 1571 and 1585, during the reign of Emperor Akbar. Akbar visited the village of Sikri to consult the Sufi saint Shaikh Salim Chishti, who predicted the birth of an heir to the Mughal throne. When the prophecy came true, Akbar built his new capital here, including a stunning mosque – still in use today – and three palaces for each of his favourite wives, one a Hindu, one a Muslim and one a Christian. The city was an Indo-Islamic masterpiece, but erected in an area that suffered from water shortages and so was abandoned shortly after Akbar's death.

It's possible to visit this World Heritage Site as a day trip from Agra, but there are a couple of decent places to stay, and the colourful bazaar in the village of Fatehpur, just below the ruins, as well as the small village of Sikri, a few kilometres north, are worth exploring. Also, the red sandstone palace walls are at their most atmospheric, and photogenic, at sunset.

Orientation & Information

The palace buildings, for which you have to pay an entrance fee, lie beside the Jama Masjid mosque (no fee). Both sit on top of a ridge that runs between the small villages of Fatehpur (immediately south) and Sikri (a couple of kilometres to the north). Official guides (Rs125) are available from the ticket office. There are other ruins scattered all over this area, all of which can be viewed for free. Colourful Fatehpur Bazaar also deserves some of your time.

The bus stand, with services to Agra and Bharatpur, is at the eastern end of the bazaar. A short walk further northeast will bring you to Agra Gate and the junction with the main Agra–Jaipur road, from where you can catch buses, 24 hours a day, to either city.

Dangers & Annoyances

Take no notice of anyone who gets on the Fatehpur Sikri–Agra bus before the final stop at Idgah bus stand, telling you that you have arrived at the city centre or the Taj Mahal. You haven't. You're still a long rickshaw ride away, and the man trying to tease you off the bus is, surprise surprise, a rickshaw driver.

Sights

JAMA MASJID

This beautiful, immense mosque was completed in 1571 and contains elements of Persian and Indian design. The main entrance, at the top of a flight of stone steps, is through the spectacular 54m-high **Buland Darwaza** (Victory Gate), built to commemorate Akbar's military victory in Gujarat.

Inside the courtyard of the mosque is the stunning white-marble **tomb of Shaikh Salim Chishti**, which was completed in 1581 and is entered through a door made of ebony. Inside it are brightly coloured flower murals while the canopy is decorated with mother-of-pearl shell. Just as Akbar came to the saint four centuries ago hoping for a son, childless women visit his tomb today and tie a thread to the *jali*, which are among the finest in India. To the right of the tomb lie the gravestones of family members of Shaikh Salim Chishti and nearby is the entrance to an underground tunnel (barred by a locked gate) that reputedly goes all the way to Agra Fort! Behind

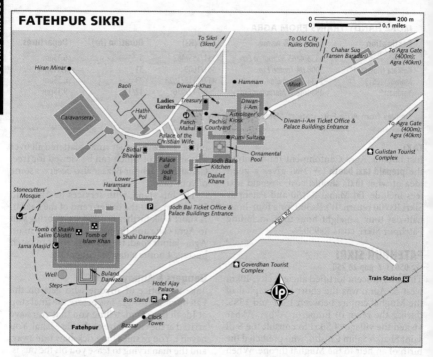

FATEHPUR SIKRI

the entrance to the tunnel, on the far wall, are three holes, part of the ancient ventilation system. You can still feel the rush of cool air forcing its way through them. Just east of Shaikh Salim Chisti's tomb is the red sandstone tomb of Islam Khan, the final resting place of Shaikh Salim Chisti's grandson and one-time governor of Bengal.

On the east wall of the courtyard is a smaller entrance to the mosque – the Shahi Darwaza (King's Gate), which leads to the palace complex.

PALACES & PAVILIONS
The first of the **palace buildings** (Indian/foreigner Rs20/260, video Rs25; ⊙ dawn-dusk) you enter from the south is the largest, the **Palace of Jodh Bai**, and the one-time home of Akbar's Hindu wife, said to be his favourite. Set around an enormous courtyard, it blends traditional Indian columns, Islamic cupolas and turquoise-blue Persian roof tiles.

Just outside, to the left of Jodh Bai's former kitchen, is the **Palace of the Christian Wife**. This was used by Akbar's Goan wife Mariam, who gave birth to Jehangir here in 1569. Like many of the buildings in the palace complex, it contains elements of different religions, as befitted Akbar's tolerant religious beliefs. The domed ceiling is Islamic in style, while remnants of a wall painting of the Hindu god Shiva can also be found.

Continuing anticlockwise will bring you to the **Ornamental Pool**. Here, singers and musicians would perform on the platform above the water while Akbar watched from the pavilion in his private quarters, known as **Daulat Khana** (Abode of Fortune). Behind the pavilion is the **Khwabgah** (Dream House), a sleeping area with a huge stone bunk bed. Nowadays the only sleeping done here is by bats, hanging from the ceiling. The small room in the far corner is full of them!

Heading north from the Ornamental Pool brings you to the most intricately carved structure in the whole complex, the tiny, but elegant **Rumi Sultana**, the palace built for Akbar's Turkish Muslim wife.

Just past Rumi Sultana is **Pachisi Courtyard** where Akbar is said to have played the game *pachisi* (an ancient version of ludo) using slave girls as pieces.

From here you can step down into **Diwan-i-Am** (Hall of Public Audiences), a large courtyard (which is now a garden) where Akbar dispensed justice by orchestrating public executions, said to have been carried out by elephants trampling to death convicted criminals.

The Hall of Private Audiences, or **Diwan-i-Khas**, found at the northern end of the Pachisi Courtyard, looks nothing special from the outside, but the interior is dominated by a magnificently carved stone central column. This pillar flares to create a flat-topped plinth linked to the four corners of the room by narrow stone bridges. From this plinth Akbar is believed to have debated with scholars and ministers who stood at the ends of the four bridges.

Next to Diwan-i-Khas is the **Treasury**, which houses secret stone safes in some corners (one has been left with its stone lid open for visitors to see). Sea monsters carved on the ceiling struts were there to protect the fabulous wealth once stored here. The so-called **Astrologer's Kiosk** in front has roof supports carved in a serpentine Jain style.

On one corner of the **Ladies Garden** is the impressive **Panch Mahal**, a pavilion whose five storeys decrease in size until the top one consists of only a tiny kiosk. The lower floor has 84 columns, all different.

Walking past the Palace of the Christian Wife once more will take you west to **Birbal Bhavan**, ornately carved inside and out, and thought to have been the living quarters of one of Akbar's most senior ministers. The **Lower Haramsara**, just to the south, housed the royal stables.

Plenty of ruins are scattered behind the whole complex, including the **Caravanserai**, a vast courtyard surrounded by rooms where visiting merchants stayed, and the bizarre 21m-tall **Hiran Minar**, a tower decorated with hundreds of stone representations of elephant tusks, which is said to be the place where Akbar's favourite execution elephant died. Badly defaced carvings of elephants still guard **Hathi Pol** (Elephant Gate), while the remains of the small **Stonecutters' Mosque** and a **hammam** (bath) are also a short stroll away. Other unnamed ruins can be explored north of what is known as the Mint but is thought to have in fact been stables, including some in the interesting village of Sikri to the north.

Sleeping & Eating

Hotel Ajay Palace (☎ 282950; Agra Rd; d Rs200) This popular lunch stop (meals from Rs50) has had a makeover, now making it a decent place to stay, too. Rooms are still basic, but now have marble floors and sit-down toilets. A huge, elongated marble table stands on the rooftop so meals can be enjoyed with a view of the Jama Masjid towering above. Nonguests can store luggage here while they visit the ruins.

Goverdhan Tourist Complex (☎ 282643; www.hotel fatehpursikriviews.com; Agra Rd; d Rs300, with cooler/AC Rs400/800; 🏊 🖳) About 200m from the Jama Masjid, Goverdhan has fun, brightly painted rooms set around a very well-kept garden. There's communal balcony and terrace seating and the internet is free for guests for the first 20 minutes. The restaurant is decent (meals Rs40 to Rs80) and the owners use filtered water for cooking.

Gulistan Tourist Complex (☎ 282490; s/d Rs325/400, with cooler Rs525/575, with AC Rs775/900 🏊) The first hotel you come to after Agra Gate, about 500m east of Fatehpur Bazaar, this red sandstone UP Tourism place has rooms with high, dome ceilings set around a large garden courtyard. There's a restaurant, a bar and even a pool table, although you'll be lucky to find another guest to have a game with if there are no tour groups staying at the time.

Fatehpur Sikri's culinary speciality is *khataie*, the biscuits you can see piled high in the bazaar.

Getting There & Away

The last bus back to Agra from the bazaar leaves at 5.30pm. If you miss that, walk to Agra Gate and wave down a Jaipur–Agra bus on the main road. They run regularly, day and night.

Buses from the bazaar leave regularly for Bharatpur (Rs15, 40 minutes) from 10am to 5pm. For Jaipur (Rs100 to Rs150, 4½ hours), either change at Bharatpur or take a direct bus from the main road by Agra Gate.

MATHURA

☎ 0565 / pop 319,235

Famed for being the birthplace of the much-loved Hindu god Krishna, Mathura is one of India's seven sacred cities and attracts floods of pilgrims, particularly during **Janmastami** (Krishna's birthday) in August/September. The town is dotted with temples from various ages and the stretch of the sacred Yamuna River which flows past here is lined with 25 ghats, best seen at dawn, when many people take their holy dip, and just after sunset, when hundreds of candles are sent floating out onto the river during the evening *aarti* ceremony.

Mathura was once a Buddhist centre with 20 monasteries that housed 3000 monks but, after the rise of Hinduism, and later sackings by Afghan and Mughal invaders, today all that's left of the oldest sights are the beautiful sculptures recovered from ruins, now on display in the archaeological museum.

Information

Near New Bus Stand is a friendly but not very useful **UP Tourism office** (☎ 2505351; Station Rd; ☺ 10am-5pm Mon-Sat, closed 2nd Sat of month) and a **State Bank of India** (Station Rd; ☺ 10am-5pm Mon-Sat, closed for lunch) which exchanges travellers cheques and cash and has an ATM. There's a small **internet cafe** (per hr Rs25; ☺ 9am-9pm) opposite the main entrance to Sri Krishna Janmbhoomi.

Sights

SRI KRISHNA JANMBHOOMI

Among the foundations of the mural-filled **Kesava Deo Temple** (☺ 5am-9.30pm, winter 5.30am-8.30pm) is a small, bare room with a slab of rock on which Krishna is said to have been born, some 3500 years ago.

Surrounding the temple are gardens and Krishna souvenir shops. Next door is **Katra Masjid**, a mosque built by Aurangzeb in 1661 on the site of a temple he ordered to be destroyed. The mosque is now guarded round the clock by soldiers to prevent a repeat of the tragic events at Ayodhya in 1992 (p432).

ARCHAEOLOGICAL MUSEUM

The rooms that aren't empty in this large **museum** (☎ 2500847; Museum Rd; Indian/foreigner Rs5/25, camera Rs20; ☺ 10.30am-4.30pm Tue-Sun) house superb collections of religious sculptures by the Mathura school, which flourished from the 3rd century BC to the 12th century AD.

VISHRAM GHAT & AROUND

A string of ghats and temples lines the Yamuna River north of the main road bridge. The most central and most popular is **Vishram Ghat**, where Krishna is said to have rested after killing the tyrannical King Kansa. Boats gather along the banks here to take tourists along the

Yamuna (Rs 50 per half hour). Beside the ghat is the 17m **Sati Burj**, a four-storey tower built by the son of Behari Mal of Jaipur in 1570 to commemorate his mother's *sati* (self-immolation on her husband's funeral pyre).

GITA TEMPLE

This serene marble **temple** (☺ dawn-dusk), on the road to Vrindavan, has the entire Bhagavad Gita written on a red pillar in the garden.

Sleeping, Eating & Drinking

International Guest House (☎ 2423888; d Rs75-150) Clean rooms can be found at this basic guesthouse on the east side of Sri Krishna Janmbhoomi, although it is often full because of Krishna devotees staying here.

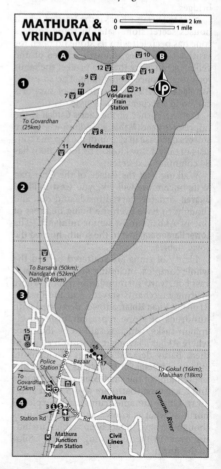

Agra Hotel (☎ 2403318; Bengali Ghat; s Rs150-200, d Rs250-350, with AC Rs650, tr Rs350-400; ✗) This area, with narrow lanes winding their way down to the ghats and temples that line the Yamuna River, is easily the most interesting place to stay. Rooms here are basic but have character and some overlook the river, while staff members are very welcoming. Simple meals are available (thalis Rs50).

Hotel Brijwasi Royal (☎ 2401224; www.brijwasi royal.com; Station Rd; s/d/ste from Rs1500/1700/3600; ✗ 🖳) Rooms that have been recently renovated come with either marble floors or carpets. All have TV, fridge and bathtub, while some overlook a buffalo pond out the back. The multicuisine veg restaurant (meals Rs75 to Rs110) has a striking Krishna mural and is deservedly popular. There's also a bar (beer from Rs110).

Getting There & Around

Long-distance buses may drop you at the crossroads on the main Delhi–Agra highway, 3km west of Mathura, where cycle rickshaws (Rs10) wait to take you into town.

The so-called New Bus Stand has regular buses to Delhi (Rs82, four hours), Agra (Rs37, 90 minutes) and Vrindavan (Rs10, 15 minutes). Tempos (large autorickshaws) also charge Rs10 for the 10km Mathura–Vrindavan run.

Regular trains go to Delhi (2nd class/chair Rs53/68, 2½ hours) between 7am and 7.40pm, Agra (Rs35/50, one hour), 6.10am to 12.49am, and Bharatpur (Rs25/40, 45 minutes), 5.30am to 12.30am. The Bharatpur trains continue to Sawai Madhopur (for Ranthambore National Park, two hours) and Kota (5½ hours).

VRINDAVAN

☎ 0565 / pop 56,618

The village of Vrindavan is where the young Krishna is said to have grown up. Pilgrims flock here from all over India and, in the case of the Hare Krishna community, from all over the world. Dozens of temples, old and modern, dot the area. They come in all shapes and sizes and many have their own unique peculiarities, making a visit here more than just your average temple hop.

There is an **information office** (⏰ 10am-1pm & 5-8.30pm) in the Krishna Balaram temple complex which has lists of places to stay in Vrindavan and can help with booking Gita (studies in the Bhagavad Gita, an ancient Hindu scripture)classes. Nearby is a bank, an ATM, a post office and an internet cafe.

Most temples are open from dawn to dusk and admission is free, but they are well spread out so a cycle-rickshaw tour is a good way to see them. Expect to pay Rs80 for a half-day tour.

The **International Society for Krishna Consciousness** (Iskcon; ☎ 2540343; www.iskcon.com), also known as the Hare Krishnas, is based at the Krishna Balaram temple complex, accessed through a beautiful white-marble gate, which houses the tomb of Swami Prabhupada (1896–1977), the founder of the Hare Krishna organisation. Several hundred foreigners attend courses and seminars here annually. It's possible to stay at the **guesthouse** (d Rs350, with AC Rs600) at the back of the temple complex. There's also a restaurant and food stalls nearby.

The cavernous, red sandstone **Govind Dev Temple**, built in 1590 by Raja Man Singh of Amber, has cute bells carved on its pillars. Resident monkeys here are as cheeky as any in India. During our few minutes inside the temple we saw one running off with a lady's purse and another sitting in the rafters wearing a pair of sunglasses!

The 10-storey **Pagal Baba Temple** (admission Rs2), a fairy-tale-castle lookalike, has an amusing succession of animated puppets and dioramas behind glass cases on the ground floor, which depict scenes from the lives of Rama and Krishna.

The glittery **Krishna Temple**, at the town's entrance, is modern and adorned with mirrors, enamel art and chandeliers. On the right is a fake **cave passageway** (admission Rs3) where you walk past a long line of slightly moving tableaux depicting scenes from Krishna's life.

Rangaji Temple, dating from 1851, **Radha Ballabh Temple**, built in 1626, **Madan Mohan Temple** and **Nidhivan Temple** are also worth a visit.

Tempos and buses both charge Rs10 from Vrindavan to Mathura.

LUCKNOW
☎ 0522 / pop 2.27 million

Liberally sprinkled with British Raj–era buildings – including the famous Residency – and boasting two superb mausoleums, the capital of Uttar Pradesh has enough to keep history buffs interested without attracting the hordes of tourists that sometimes make sightseeing tiresome.

The city rose to prominence as the home of the nawabs of Avadh (Oudh) who were great patrons of the culinary and other arts, particularly dance and music. Lucknow's reputation as a city of culture, gracious living and rich cuisine has continued to this day.

In 1856 the British annexed Avadh, exiling Nawab Wajid Ali Shah to a palace in Kolkata (Calcutta). The disruption this caused was a factor behind the First War of Independence of 1857, culminating in the dramatic Siege of Lucknow at the Residency.

Orientation
Lucknow's commercial centre, known as Hazratganj, contains much of the city's accommodation and restaurants and is centred on Mahatma Gandhi (MG) Rd.

Dangers & Annoyances
Street beggars on Mahatma Gandhi (MG) Rd are incredibly persistent. Sadly, many of them are young children.

Information
BOOKSHOPS
Ram Advani Bookshop (☎ 2223511; Mayfair Bldg, MG Rd; ◷ 10am-7.30pm Mon-Sat) A Lucknow institution, it's worth visiting just to meet the knowledgable Mr Advani, who owns the place. Be aware, though, that he takes his siestas very seriously and is rarely seen between noon and 4pm.

INTERNET ACCESS
Cyber Cafe (Buddha Rd; per hr Rs20; ◷ 8am-10pm)
Cyber City (per hr Rs25; ◷ 10am-10pm) At the end of an alley off MG Rd.

MEDICAL SERVICES
Balrampur District Hospital (☎ 2224040; Hospital Rd) The emergency department is to the right as you enter the complex.

MONEY
ATMs are marked on the map. There is also one at Charbagh train station.
ICICI (MG Rd, Hazratganj; ◷ 10am-5pm Mon-Sat) Changes travellers cheques (Monday to Friday only) and cash and has an ATM.

POST
Hazratganj post office (☎ 2222887; ◷ 9am-6pm Mon- Sat) Off MG Rd.
Main post office (☎ 2253165; MG Rd; ◷ 10am-6pm Mon-Sat) Grand Raj–era architecture.

TOURIST INFORMATION
UP Tours (☎ 2615005; Hotel Gomti, 6 Sapru Marg; ◷ 9.30am-7pm Mon-Sat) Government-run travel agency with brochures, city tours and information.

Sights
THE RESIDENCY
The large collection of gardens and ruins that makes up the **Residency** (Indian/foreigner Rs5/100, video Rs25; ◷ dawn-dusk) offers a fascinating historical glimpse of the beginning of the end for the British Raj. Built in 1800, the Residency became the stage for the most dramatic events of the 1857 First War of Independence, the Siege of Lucknow, a 147-day siege that claimed the lives of thousands. The compound has been left as it was at the time of the final relief and the walls are still pockmarked from bullets and cannon balls.

The focus is the well-designed **museum** (Rs5; ◷ 10am-4.30pm Tue-Sun) in the main Residency building, which includes a scale model of the original buildings. Downstairs are the huge

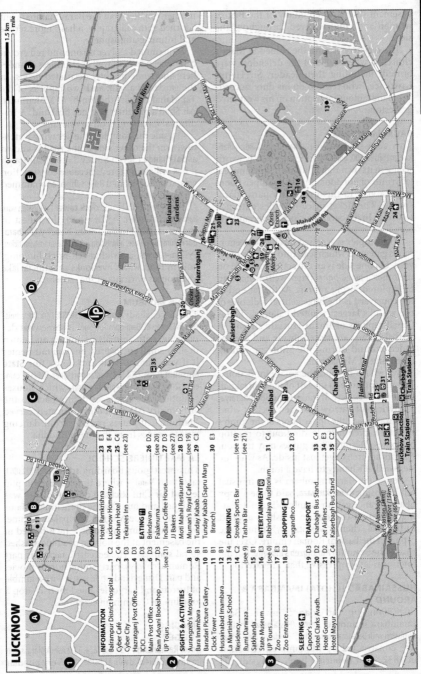

LUCKNOW

0 — 1.5 km
0 — 1 mile

INFORMATION	
Balrampur District Hospital	1 C2
Cyber Café	2 C4
Cyber City	3 D3
Hazratganj Post Office	4 D3
ICICI	5 D3
Main Post Office	6 D3
Ram Advani Bookshop	7 D3
UP Tours	(see 21)

SIGHTS & ACTIVITIES	
Aurangzeb's Mosque	8 B1
Bara Imambara	9 B1
Baradari Picture Gallery	10 B1
Clock Tower	11 B1
Hussainabad Imambara	12 B1
La Martinière School	13 F4
Residency	14 C2
Rumi Darwaza	(see 9)
Satkhanda	15 B1
State Museum	16 B1
UP Tours	17 E3
Zoo	18 E3
Zoo Entrance	19 D3

SLEEPING	
Capoor's	19 D3
Hotel Clarks Avadh	20 D2
Hotel Gomti	21 D2
Hotel Mayur	22 C4

EATING	
Hotel Ramkrishna	23 E3
Lucknow Homestay	24 E4
Mohan Hotel	25 C4
Tekarees Inn	(see 23)
Brindavan	26 D2
Falaknuma	(see 20)
Indian Coffee House	27 D3
JJ Bakers	(see 27)
Moti Mahal Restaurant	28 D3
Muman's Royal Cafe	(see 19)
Tunday Kabab	29 C3
Tunday Kabab (Sapru Marg Branch)	30 E3

DRINKING	
Strokes Sports Bar	(see 19)
Tashna Bar	(see 21)

ENTERTAINMENT	
Rabindralaya Auditorium	31 C4

SHOPPING	
Sugandhco	32 D3

TRANSPORT	
Charbagh Bus Stand	33 C4
Jet Airlines	34 E3
Kaiserbagh Bus Stand	35 C2

UTTAR PRADESH

basement rooms where many of the British women and children lived throughout the siege.

The **cemetery** around the ruined St Mary's church is where 2000 of the defenders were buried, including their leader, Sir Henry Lawrence, 'who tried to do his duty' according to the famous inscription on his weathered gravestone.

BARA IMAMBARA

This colossal **tomb** (Hussainabad Trust Rd; Indian/foreigner Rs20/300; guide Rs75; ☼ dawn-dusk) is worth seeing in its own right, but the highly unusual labyrinth of corridors inside its upper floors make a visit to this imambara particularly special. The ticket price includes entrance to Chota Imambara, the clock tower and the baradari.

The complex is accessed through two enormous gateways which lead into a huge courtyard. On one side is an attractive mosque, on the other a large *baori* (step-well) which can be explored. Bring a torch. At the far end of the courtyard is the huge central hall, one of the world's largest vaulted galleries. *Tazias* (small replicas of Imam Hussain's tomb in Karbala, Iraq) are stored inside and are paraded around during the Shiite mourning ceremony of Muharram.

But what's beyond the small, innocuous-looking entrance to the left of the central hall steals the show here. It leads to the **Bhulbhulaiya**, a labyrinth of narrow passageways that wind their way inside the upper floors of the tomb's structure, eventually leading out to rooftop balconies. Despite what guides may tell you, visitors are free to get lost inside. As with the step-well, it's handy to have a torch.

Beside the Bara Imambara is the unusual but imposing **Rumi Darwaza**, said to be a copy of an entrance gate in Istanbul. 'Rumi' (relating to Rome) is the term Muslims applied to Istanbul when it was still Byzantium, the capital of the Eastern Roman empire. Over the road is the beautiful **Aurangzeb's mosque**, but the interior is less impressive than the exterior.

HUSSAINABAD (CHOTA) IMAMBARA & AROUND

Just 500m up the road from the Bara Imambara is another **tomb** (Hussainabad Trust Rd; admission with Bara Imambara ticket; ☼ dawn-dusk) that was constructed by Mohammed Ali Shah in 1832, who is buried here, alongside his mother. Smaller than the Bara Imambara but adorned with calligraphy, it has a more serene and intimate atmosphere.

Mohammed's silver throne and red crown can be seen here as well as countless chandeliers and some brightly decorated *tazias*. In the garden is a tank and two replicas of the Taj Mahal that are the tombs of Mohammed Ali Shah's daughter and her husband. A traditional *hammam* is off to one side.

Outside the complex, the decaying watchtower on the other side of the road is known as **Satkhanda** (Seven Storey Tower), although it has only four storeys because construction was abandoned in 1840 when Mohammed Ali Shah died.

The 67m red-brick **clock tower** (admission with Bara Imambara ticket; ☼ dawn-dusk), the tallest in India, was built in the 1880s. Nearby is a **baradari** (summer palace; admission with Bara Imambara ticket; ☼ 7am-6.30pm), a striking red-brick building, built in 1842, which overlooks an artificial lake and houses portraits of the nawabs.

ZOO & MUSEUM

The large, shady **zoo** (☎ 2239588; Park Rd; admission Rs15; ☼ 8.30am-6pm Tue-Sun) is somewhat depressing, with animals pacing up and down in their small enclosures, but you must enter it if you want to visit Lucknow's fine **State Museum** (☎ 2206158; Indian/foreigner Rs5/50, camera Rs20; ☼ 10.30am-4pm Tue-Sun), which houses sculptural masterpieces dating back to the 3rd century AD, including intricately carved Mathura sculptures ranging from dancing girls to scenes from the life of Buddha.

LA MARTINIÈRE SCHOOL

This prestigious boarding **school** (☎ 2223863; La Martiniere Marg) – where timeless British pop legend Sir Cliff Richard once studied – was designed and built by the Frenchman Major General Claude Martin as a palatial home. In 1800 it became his tomb – he is buried in the basement at the bottom of a blue-washed spiral staircase. The eccentric facade is part Roman archways, part Gothic horror movie, and part Disneyland-style castle with a jumble of turrets and gargoyles piled merrily atop a long line of Corinthian columns.

Sleeping
BUDGET
Hotel Ramkrishna (☎ 2451824; 17/2 Ashok Marg; s/d/tr from Rs250/300/400, d with AC Rs700; ▨) Very popular

with Indian customers, this well-located hotel is often full. If you do get inside you'll find tidy AC rooms and good-value non-ACs.

Hotel Mayur (☎ 2451824; Subhash Marg; s/d Rs275-350/350-450, without bathroom Rs225/300, with AC Rs550/650; ❄) Bit shabby, but all rooms come with TV and some have huge bathrooms. Definitely one of the better cheapies near the train station.

ourpick Lucknow Homestay (☎ 2235460; naheed 2k@gmail.com; 110D Mall Ave; r Rs400; ☎) This delightful family homestay in a leafy neighbourhood is run by the very welcoming Naheed and her family. The 11 rooms are simple but large and comfortable, and two have private bathrooms. Prices include breakfast, dinner and laundry. You may need to call for directions as Mall Ave is a bit of a maze.

Hotel Gomti (☎ 2611463; hotelgomti@up-tourism.com; 6 Sapru Marg; s/d Rs550/650, s with AC Rs1000-1700, d with AC Rs1100-1800; ❄) Sadly the pristine condition of Gomti's marble lobby doesn't extend into its rooms, which, although big, are somewhat dark and musty. They are all well equipped, however, with TV, sofa, table and chairs.

MIDRANGE

Capoor's (☎ 2623958; www.hotelcapoors.com; 52 MG Rd; s Rs1000-1300, d Rs1200-1500, ste Rs2200; ❄) Although perfectly located in the heart of Hazratganj, Capoor's is in need of a refit. Rooms have a homely feel, and there's an old-fashioned ambience about the place, but the carpets are dirty and the bathrooms underwhelming. The restaurant (mains Rs80 to Rs240) is very popular, however, and you won't forget the neon-tastic Strokes Sports Bar in a hurry.

Mohan Hotel (☎ 4035555; www.mohanhotel.com; Buddha Rd; s/d Rs1050/1250; ❄) Best choice near the train station, this smart outfit has marble corridors and large, tidy rooms with AC, TV and fridge. There's a good restaurant (mains Rs70 to Rs140) and bar (beers from Rs70) and 24-hour checkout.

Tekarees Inn (☎ 4016241; www.tekareesinn.com; 17/3 Ashok Marg; s/d/ste Rs1450/1900/2400; ❄) Smart, clean rooms have TV and fridge and come with big bathrooms, but this is clearly aimed at the business market so lacks character.

TOP END

Hotel Clarks Avadh (☎ 2620131; www.clarksavadh.com; 8 MG Rd; d/ste Rs7000-8000/12000; ❄ ▯ ❄) Lucknow's top hotel displays a cool elegance and re-strained decor. Slick rooms have bathtubs and

views of either the Gomti River or the cricket stadium. The elevated outdoor pool is superb, and there's a gym, a jazzy bar and an excellent top-floor restaurant, Falaknuma.

Eating

The refined palates of the nawabs left Lucknow with a reputation for rich Mughlai cuisine. The city is famous for its wide range of kebabs and for *dum pukht* – the 'art' of steam pressure cooking, in which meat and vegetables are cooked in a sealed clay pot. Huge *rumali roti* (paper-thin chapatis) are served in many small Muslim-style restaurants in the old city. They arrive folded up and should be eaten with a goat or lamb curry like *bhuna ghosht* or rogan josh.

The popular dessert *kulfi faluda* (ice cream with long chickpea flour noodles) is served in several places in Aminabad. The sweet orange-coloured rice dish known as *zarda* is also popular.

JJ Bakers (☎ 2288284; Ashok Marg; snacks from Rs5; ☿ 9.15am-10pm) Recommended by readers, this little bakery sells cakes, cookies and a small selection of sandwiches.

Indian Coffee House (Ashok Marg; coffee from Rs15; ☎ 8am-10pm) Very popular with the locals. There's a touch of the Raj about this place, which also serves snacks and a few mains, including thalis (Rs40).

ourpick Tunday Kabab (☎ 5524046; Aminabad Rd; dishes Rs15-40) Tucked away down a small street in the bustling Aminabad district, this renowned local kabab shop serves up delicious plates of mutton biryani, kebabs and tandoori chicken. The mutton kebab here is fantastic. Consider coming along early to give yourself time for a wander around the bazaar here, a prime location for picking up *chikan* (delicately embroidered muslin cloth). Rickshaw drivers know how to find this place. There's a more centrally located branch in Sapru Marg with the same menu at slightly higher prices, but it's nowhere near as popular.

Moti Mahal Restaurant (MG Rd; meals Rs50-150; ☎ 11am-11pm; ❄) Downstairs is a sweet and snack shop, upstairs is a low-lit AC restaurant serving up tasty, well-presented food. Try the Lucknow *dum aloo* (potatoes stuffed with nuts and paneer in a tomato-based sauce) followed by *kulfi faluda*.

Muman's Royal Cafe (MG Rd; chaat Rs10-40, mains Rs70-150) Even if you don't step inside this popular family restaurant, don't miss its excellent *chaat* (spicy snack) stand at the front

UTTAR PRADESH

where mixed *chaats* are served in an *aloo* (potato) basket. Inside you can dine on chicken Mughlai, tandoor kebabs and pizza.

Brindavan (☎ 3918418; Sapru Marg; mains Rs40-75; ☯ 11am-11pm) Don't be put off by the filthy shared stairwell: this 1st-floor place is smart and clean and has a huge window along the far wall allowing you to eat overlooking the street scenes below. The excellent-value south Indian menu includes more than 20 varieties of *dosa*.

Falaknuma (Hotel Clarks Avadh, 8 MG Rd; mains Rs200-450) Lucknow's best hotel also lays claim to having its best restaurant. The stylish rooftop dining room has bird's-eye views and serves up sumptuous nawab cuisine, such as kakori (minced mutton) and *galawat* (minced goat) kebabs.

Drinking & Entertainment

Strokes Sports Bar (Capoor's, MG Rd; beers from Rs125; ☯ noon-11pm, till 3am Sat) With metallic decor, zebra-print chairs, ultraviolet lights and a backlit bar, this must be one of the strangest places in India to come to watch the latest cricket match on TV.

Tashna Bar (Hotel Gomti; Sapru Marg; beers from Rs100; ☯ 11am-11pm) Has the usual AC bar with no atmosphere found in many hotels, but the added attraction of a beer garden on a well-tended lawn.

Rabindralaya Auditorium (☎ 2635670; Kanpur Rd) Opposite the two train stations, this auditorium hosts a variety of cultural shows, including classical music, dance and theatrical performances, all free of charge. It's often used by schools, however, so is not always open to the public. Call ahead.

Shopping

Lucknow is famous for *chikan*, an embroidered cloth worn by men and women. It is sold in a number of shops in the bazaars near Tunday Kebab (p431) and in the relatively traffic-free Janpath Market, just south of MG Rd in Hazratganj.

Also in Janpath Market is the sweet-scented **Sugandhco** (☎ 9335248633; www.sugandhco.com; D-4 Janpath Market), a family business since 1850 that sells attar – pure essence oil extracted from flowers by a traditional method.

Getting There & Away

AIR

Amausi airport is 15km southwest of Lucknow. **Jet Airlines** (☎ 2239612; Park Rd; ☯ 9.30am-6pm Mon-Sat) has daily flights to Delhi (from Rs3000), Kolkata (from Rs5000) and Mumbai (Bombay; from Rs5000).

BUS

Long-distance buses leave from the excellent new **Alambagh Bus Station** (☎ 2453096; Alambagh), 4km southwest of the town centre, rather than from Charbagh bus stand near the train station. Services include Faizabad (Rs75, three hours), Allahabad (Rs110, five hours), Gorakhpur (Rs150, 8½ hours), Varanasi (Rs165, 8½ hours) and Agra (Rs200, 10 hours).

Regular buses (Rs5) run between Charbagh bus stand and Alambagh Bus Station.

Kaiserbagh bus stand (☎ 2222503; J Narain Rd), near the Residency, is still the place to go for buses to Delhi (non-AC/AC Rs277/465, 14 hours). You can also get to Faizabad and Gorakhpur from here.

TRAIN

The two main stations, **Charbagh** (☎ 2635841; Kanpur Rd) and **Lucknow Junction** (☎ 2635877), are side by side. Services for most major destinations leave from Charbagh, including several daily to Agra, Varanasi, Faizabad, Gorakhpur and New Delhi. Lucknow Junction handles the one daily train to Mumbai. See the table, opposite.

Getting Around

TO/FROM THE AIRPORT

Taxis charge around Rs300, and autorickshaws Rs150, for the 15km trip to Amausi airport.

LOCAL TRANSPORT

A short cycle-rickshaw ride is Rs10. From the train station to the Residency costs Rs30. An autorickshaw from the train station to the Bara Imambara is about Rs60. A half-day (four-hour) autorickshaw tour covering all the main sights costs Rs205 from the prepaid taxi stand at the train station. A full-day tour is Rs405.

FAIZABAD & AYODHYA

☎ 05278 / pop 208,164 & 49,593

The quiet, charming town of Ayodhya is the birthplace of Rama, and as such is one of Hinduism's seven holy cities. It is also where five of Jainism's 24 *tirthankars* (religious teachers) were born.

The town became tragically synonymous with Hindu extremism when, in 1992, riot-

HANDY TRAINS FROM LUCKNOW

Destination	Train no & name	Fare (Rs)	Duration (hr)	Departures
Agra	3237/4201 PNBE-MTJ Exp	166/437/596	6	11.50pm
Allahabad*	4210 Intercity Exp	248	4	7.30am
Faizabad	3010 Doon Exp	121/241/324	2½	8.35am
Gorakhpur	5708 ASR-KIR Exp	146/382/518	5	12.55am
Jhansi	1016 Kushinagar Exp	152/399/543	6½	12.35am
Kolkata (Howrah)	ASR-HWH Exp	353/964/1326	21	10.55am
Mumbai (CST)**	2533 Pushpak Exp	429/1151/1575	24	7.45pm
New Delhi	2229 Lucknow Mail	224/604/816	9	10am
Varanasi	0141 JAT-BSB Exp	169/420/561	5½	7.25am

All fares are sleeper/3AC/2AC; *chair class only; **leaves from Lucknow Junction

ing Hindus tore down the Babri Masjid, a mosque built by the Mughals in the 15th century, which they claimed stood on the site of an earlier Rama temple, marking Lord Rama's birthplace. They put up Ram Janam Bhumi in its place. Following tit-for-tat reprisals, the problem has not been resolved and the Supreme Court has ordered archaeological investigations at the site to verify the Hindu claims.

The slightly larger town of Faizabad, 7km away, is the jumping-off point for Ayodhya and where you'll find more accommodation.

Orientation

From the Faizabad bus stand, turn left onto the main road where you'll find tempos (Rs8) to Ayodhya. From this main road, take the first right for the train station or continue straight on for Hotel Shan-e-Avadh, Cyber Zone internet cafe and signs for Hotel Krishna Palace.

Ayodhya is much smaller and has one main road with traffic-free alleys leading off it, where you'll find all the temples.

Information

There's a **UP Tourism** (☎ 05278-223214; ⏰ 10am-5pm Mon-Sat) and two ATMs beside Hotel Krishna Palace. **Cyber Zone** (per hr Rs20; ⏰ 10am-5pm), just off the main road past Hotel Shan-e-Avadh, has a slow connection.

Sights

In Faizabad, take a cycle-rickshaw to the **Bahu Begum ka Maquabara** (⏰ dawn-dusk), the Begum's unique mausoleum. It has three domes built above each other with wonderfully ornate decoration on the walls and ceilings.

A 20-minute tempo ride (Rs8) brings you to Ayodhya, where you can start your temple tour at the town's most popular one, **Hanumangarhi** (⏰ dawn-dusk), set back off the main street on your left. Walk up the 76 steps to the ornate carved gateway and the fortress-like outer walls, and join the throng inside offering *prasad* (food offerings).

A further 100m up the road is **Dashrath Bhavan** (⏰ dawn-dusk), a temple approached through a colourful entranceway. The atmosphere inside is peaceful, with musicians playing and orange-clad sadhus reading scriptures.

A few minutes' walk further on is the impressive **Kanak Bhavan** (Palace of Gold; ⏰ 8.30-11.30am & 4.30-7pm), an ancient but often rebuilt palace-cum-temple.

Another 300m away is **Ram Janam Bhumi** (⏰ 7-11am & 2-6pm), the contentious temple that marks the birthplace of Rama. Security here is staggering. You must first show your passport then leave all belongings apart from your passport and money in nearby lockers. You are then searched several times before being accompanied through a caged corridor that leads to a spot 20m away from a makeshift tent of a shrine, which marks Rama's birthplace.

A five-minute walk on the other side of the main road brings you to **Ramkatha Museum** (admission free; ⏰ 10am-4.30pm Tue-Sun), a large yellow-and-red building with ancient sculptures and grand images of Rama and Sita. Every evening except Monday the museum hosts free performances of the Ram Lila (a dramatic re-enactment of the battle between Lord Ram and Ravan, as described in the Hindu epic, the Ramayana).

Sleeping & Eating

Ramdhan Guest House (☎ 232791; Ayodhya; s without bathroom Rs150, d Rs200-300, with AC Rs700; ✷) This pink hotel, with green-and-blue pastel interior, is the nicest place to stay in Ayodhya. Rooms are basic (tap-and-bucket showers, squat loos) but are a good size and clean. There's no restaurant but friendly staff will whip up a thali (Rs30 to Rs70) and some chai. From the path leading up to Hanumangarhi, walk about 200m back towards Faizabad then follow the signs.

Hotel Shan-e-Avadh (☎ 223586; shane_avadh@ yahoo.com; Faizabad; s Rs180-300, d Rs200-350, s/d with AC Rs600/700; ✷) For something more comfortable, you need to stay in Faizabad rather than Ayodhya. This popular, good-value hotel has a range of tidy rooms, but is often full.

Hotel Krishna Palace (☎ 221367; hotelkrishna palace@gmail.com; Faizabad; s Rs500-600, with AC Rs990-1200, d Rs700-850, with AC Rs1250-1600; s/d ste Rs2400/3000; ✷) Clean and comfortable rooms come with TV and decent furniture, while staff is helpful and friendly. There's a good restaurant (mains Rs50 to Rs150; open 7am to 10.30pm) and a bar (beer Rs70; open 1pm to 10.30pm).

Getting There & Away

From Faizabad bus stand, buses run to Ayodhya (Rs10, 20 minutes), Lucknow (Rs74, four hours), Gorakhpur (Rs84, four hours) and Allahabad (Rs170, six hours).

Daily trains include Lucknow (3307 *Gangasutlej Express*, sleeper/2AC Rs121/324, four hours, 11am), Varanasi (3010 *Doon Express*, sleeper/3AC/2AC Rs121/311/420, five hours, 11.15am) and Delhi (4205 *Faizabad–Delhi Express*, Rs244/690/946, 12 hours, 6.30pm).

ALLAHABAD

☎ 0532 / pop 1,049,579

For all its importance in Hindu mythology, Indian history and modern politics, Allahabad is a surprisingly relaxed city that offers plenty in terms of sights, but little in the way of in-yer-face hassle.

Brahma, the Hindu god of creation, is believed to have landed on earth in Allahabad, or Prayag as it was originally known, and to have called it the king of all pilgrimage centres. Indeed, Sangam, a river confluence on the outskirts of the city, is the most celebrated of India's four Kumbh Mela locations (see p838). The vast river banks here attract tens of millions of pilgrims every six years for either the Kumbh Mela or the Ardh (Half) Mela, but every year there is a smaller Magh Mela.

Of more immediate interest to casual visitors, perhaps, are Allahabad's grand Raj-era buildings, its Mughal fort and tombs and the historic legacy of the Nehru family.

Orientation

Allahabad's Civil Lines is a district of broad avenues, Raj-era bungalows, hotels, restaurants and coffee shops. The Civil Lines bus stand – the main bus terminal – is also here. This area is divided from Chowk, the crowded, older part of town, by the railway line. Sangam is 4km southeast of the city centre.

Information

There are several ATMs in the Civil Lines area, including one beside Apollo Clinic.

Apollo Clinic (☎ 3290507; MG Marg; ☼ 8am-8pm) A modern private medical facility with 24-hour pharmacy.

i-way Internet MG Marg (1st fl above shops on MG Marg; per hr Rs26; ☼ 10am-9pm); Sardar Patel Marg (per hr Rs50; ☼ 8am-8pm); Hotel Prayag (per hr Rs26; ☼ 8am-10pm)

Post office (Sarojini Naidu Marg; ☼ 10am-4pm Mon-Sat)

UP Tourism (☎ 2601873; rtoalld_upt@yahoo.co.in; 35 MG Marg; ☼ 10am-5pm Mon-Sat) At the Rahi Ilawart Tourist Bungalow. Very helpful.

Sights & Activities
SANGAM

This is the particularly auspicious point where two of India's holiest rivers, the Ganges and the Yamuna, meet one of Hinduism's mythical rivers, the Saraswati. All year round, pilgrims row boats out to this holy spot, but their numbers increase dramatically during the annual **Magh Mela**, a six-week festival held between January and March, which culminates in six communal 'holy dips' (p436). Every 12 years the massive **Kumbh Mela** (p838) takes place here, attracting millions of people, while the **Ardh Mela** (Half Mela) is held here every six years.

In the early 1950s, 350 pilgrims were killed in a stampede to the soul-cleansing water (an incident recreated vividly in Vikram Seth's novel *A Suitable Boy*). The last Ardh Mela, in 2007, attracted more than 70 million people – the largest-ever human gathering. The next Kumbh Mela will take place in 2013. Expect a big one.

ALLAHABAD

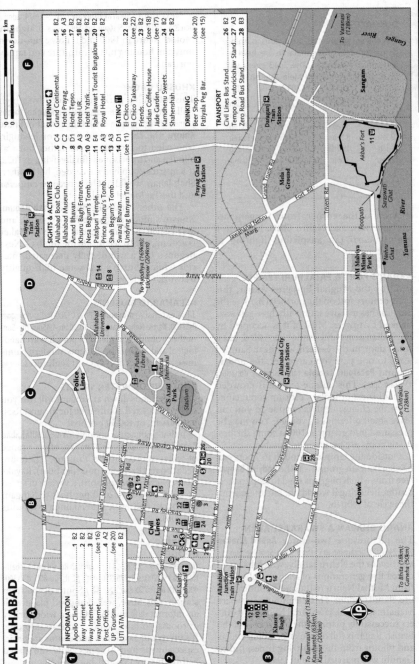

INFORMATION
Apollo Clinic.................................	**1** B2
iway Internet...............................	**2** B2
iway Internet...............................	**3** B2
iway Internet...............................	(see 16)
Post Office..................................	**4** A2
UP Tourism.................................	(see 20)
UTI ATM....................................	**5** B2

SIGHTS & ACTIVITIES
Allahabad Boat Club.......................	**6** C4
Allahabad Museum..........................	**7** C2
Anand Bhavan...............................	**8** D1
Khusru Bagh Entrance......................	**9** A3
Nesa Begum's Tomb.........................	**10** A3
Patalpuri Temple............................	**11** E4
Prince Khusru's Tomb.......................	**12** A3
Shah Begum's Tomb.........................	**13** A3
Swaraj Bhavan..............................	**14** D1
Undying Banyan Tree.......................	(see 11)

SLEEPING
Grand Continental..........................	**15** B2
Hotel Prayag...............................	**16** A3
Hotel Tepso.................................	**17** B2
Hotel UR....................................	**18** D1
Hotel Yatrik................................	**19** B2
Rahi Ilawart Tourist Bungalow..............	**20** B2
Royal Hotel................................	**21** B2

EATING
El Chico.....................................	**22** B2
El Chico Takeaway...........................	**23** B2
Friends.....................................	(see 22)
Indian Coffee House.........................	(see 18)
Jade Garden................................	(see 17)
Kamdhenu Sweets............................	**24** B2
Shahenshah.................................	**25** B2

DRINKING
Beer Shop..................................	(see 20)
Patiyala Peg Bar............................	(see 15)

TRANSPORT
Civil Lines Bus Stand........................	**26** B2
Tempo & Autorickshaw Stand...............	**27** A3
Zero Road Bus Stand........................	**28** B3

DIP DATES

The following are the auspicious bathing dates for upcoming mela to be held at Sangam in Allahabad. The 2013 event will be a full-blown Kumbh Mela (see p838).

2010	2011	2012	2013
31 Dec*	19 Jan	9 Jan	27 Jan
14 Jan	14 Jan	14 Jan	14 Jan
15 Jan	3 Feb	23 Jan	10 Feb
20 Jan	8 Feb	28 Jan	15 Feb
30 Jan	18 Feb	7 Feb	25 Feb
12 Feb	3 Mar	20 Feb	10 Mar

*2009

Around the corner from Sangam are the Saraswati and Nehru **Ghats**, home to a nightly *aarti* (an auspicious lighting of lamps/candles).

AKBAR'S FORT & PATALPURI TEMPLE
Built by the Mughal Emperor Akbar, this 16th-century fort on the northern bank of the Yamuna has massive walls with three gateways flanked by towers. Most of it is occupied by the Indian army and cannot be visited, but a small door in the eastern wall near Sangam leads to one part you can enter, the underground **Patalpuri temple** (admission by donation; 7am-5pm). This unique temple is crowded with all sorts of idols – pick up some coins from the change dealers outside so you can leave small offerings as you go. You may be pressured into giving Rs100 at some shrines. A few coins are perfectly acceptable.

Outside the temple – though its roots can be seen beneath ground – is the **Undying Banyan Tree** from which pilgrims used to leap to their deaths, believing it would liberate them from the cycle of rebirth.

ANAND BHAVAN & SWARAJ BHAVAN
The picturesque two-storey **Anand Bhavan** (2467071; admission Rs5; 9.30am-5pm Tue-Sun) is a shrine to the Nehru family, which has produced five generations of leading politicians from Motilal Nehru to the latest political figure, Rahul Gandhi. This stately home is where Mahatma Gandhi, Jawaharlal Nehru and others successfully planned the overthrow of the British Raj. It is full of books, personal effects and photos from those stirring times. Indira Gandhi was married here in 1942.

Next door, **Swaraj Bhavan** (2467674; admission Rs5; 9.30am-5.30pm Tue-Sun) was bought by Motilal Nehru in 1900 and is now a run-down museum housing bits of furniture and family portraits.

KHUSRU BAGH
This intriguing park, surrounded by a high wall, contains three contrasting **Mughal tombs** (admission free; dawn-dusk). One is that of **Prince Khusru**, the eldest son of Emperor Jehangir, who tried to assassinate his father but was blinded and imprisoned, finally dying in 1622. If Khusru's coup had succeeded, his brother, Shah Jahan, would not have become emperor and the Taj Mahal would not exist.

The other tombs belong to **Shah Begum**, Khusru's mother (Jehangir's first wife), and **Nesa Begum**, Khusru's sister. If the caretaker is around, ask to see inside the tombs – Nesa Begum's has a wonderfully decorated interior while Khusru's has some high-quality fretwork windows.

ALLAHABAD MUSEUM
This extensive **museum** (2601200; Indian/foreigner Rs5/100; Kamla Nehru Marg; 10.30am-4.45pm Tue-Sun) in the grounds of a pleasant park has archaeological and Nehru family items, modern paintings, miniatures and ancient sculptures.

BOAT TRIPS & WATER SPORTS
Old boat hands down at Sangam will row you out to the sacred confluence for around Rs50 per person, or Rs250 per boat.

If that's not active enough for you, **Allahabad Boat Club** (6598277; 11am-5pm) offers a range of water sports on the Yamuna. There are pedal boats (Rs 40 per hour per boat), kayaks (Rs20 per hour per person), a variety of speed boats (Rs500 to Rs2000 per boat to Sangam and back) and even waterskiing (two hours Rs1000).

Sleeping
BUDGET
Hotel Prayag (2656416; Noorullah Rd; s/d without bathroom Rs150/200, s Rs275-350, with AC Rs700-800, d Rs300-400, with AC Rs750-850;) South of the train station, this huge, well-equipped place with an internet cafe and ATM has a wide variety of rooms, so look before you leap into one. It's pretty old-fashioned and rooms are basic, especially the non-AC ones. Note: the shared bathrooms are tap-and-bucket jobs.

Royal Hotel (☎ 2427201; Nawab Yusuf Rd; r Rs250-450) This wonderful old building, also near the train station, used to be royal stables but was converted into a hotel by the King of Kalakankar, a former princely state, after he was refused entry into a British-run hotel nearby. It's also basic, and very run down, but has bags of character and the rooms, and their bathrooms, are absolutely enormous.

Hotel Tepso (☎ 2561409; MG Marg; r Rs600/700; ✹) Rooms arranged around a tatty central garden all have AC and TV, and are a decent size. The important things are clean – bed sheets, floor tiles – but generally this place is a bit grubby. The attached Jade Garden Restaurant is spotless, though.

Rahi Ilawart Tourist Bungalow (☎ 2601440; 35 MG Marg; dm Rs120, q Rs900, s Rs600-650, with AC Rs1000-1600, d Rs650-750, with AC Rs1100-1800; ✹) Rooms here are huge but not very clean considering the price. Renovation was going on at the time of research so improvements should come. The restaurant is good, though, and the bar is bright and busy.

MIDRANGE & TOP END

Hotel UR (☎ 2427334; mj1874@gmail.com; cnr MG Marg & Clive Rd; d Rs795-995) Not a bad choice with a good location and clean, comfortable rooms. All have AC, TV and clean bathrooms.

Grand Continental (☎ 2260631; www.birhotel .com; Sardar Patel Marg; s Rs1900-2500, d Rs2200-2800, ste Rs3500; ✹ ▣) Despite the elegant lobby and one beautiful marble courtyard with swimming pool, this place is a bit old fashioned, with carpeted rooms and non-matching furniture. There's a good restaurant and bar, though, where there are evening *ghazal* performances.

Hotel Yatrik (☎ 2260921; hotelyatrik.com; 33 Sardar Patel Marg; s Rs2200, d Rs2400-3010, ste Rs4000; ✹ ▣) The best-value top-end hotel in Allahabad, Yatrik's marble lobby, corridors and stairways are dotted with heritage furniture and delightful artwork. The tastefully decorated rooms, with olive-green tiled bathrooms, are immaculate. The unusual L-shaped pool behind a beautiful lawn, where you can eat in the evening, is also a big draw.

Eating

Allahabadians have a sweet tooth and MG Marg is lined with shops selling ice creams, shakes, cakes and sweets. Outdoor eating is all the rage, with many stalls along MG Marg setting up tables and chairs on the footpath in the evening.

Kamdhenu Sweets (MG Marg; snacks Rs5-25) Very popular snack shop selling delicious home-made sweets, cakes, samosas, sandwiches and ice cream.

Indian Coffee House (MG Marg; mains Rs15-30; ✹ 8am-10pm) This large, airy, 50-year-old coffee hall is a top choice for breakfast with waiters in fan-tailed headgear serving up delicious south Indian fare – dosa, *idli*, *uttapam* – as well as eggs, omelettes and toast.

Shahenshah (MG Marg; mains Rs20-80; ✹ 11am-10.30pm) Watch young chefs frying up their creations from a couple of stalls set around a half open-air seating area with plastic tables and chairs and a high corrugated iron roof. This is no-nonsense, cheap eating, but it's popular with the locals so there's a nice atmosphere. The menu includes *uttapam*, *paratha* (flaky bread made with ghee and cooked on a hotplate), a few Chinese dishes, pizza and some absolutely cracking dosa.

Friends (Sadar Patel Marg; mains Rs70-195; ✹ 10am-11pm; ✹) This bright, slimline cafe-restaurant is very popular with Allahabad's 20-somethings. An extensive veg and nonveg multi-cuisine menu includes tandoori, sizzlers, pizza and a range of oh-so tempting desserts. Fresh coffee (from Rs25) is also available.

Jade Garden (☎ 2561408; Hotel Tepso, MG Marg; mains Rs100-200; ✹ 7am-11pm; ✹) Spotless hotel restaurant with attentive black-tie staff serving Indian, Chinese, non-veg sizzlers, salads and tandoori.

El Chico (MG Marg; mains Rs90-280; ✹ 9am-11pm; ✹) A swish restaurant with a reliable Indian, Chinese and continental menu, including fish dishes and sizzlers. Next door, El Chico Takeaway (snacks Rs15 to Rs45) tempts diners with ice creams, cakes, cheesecake and savoury snacks.

Drinking

The Patiyala Peg Bar at the Grand Continental has live *ghazal* music nightly from 7.30pm. There are a few beer shops around town. One is on MG Marg near the Rahi Ilawart Tourist Bungalow, which also has a bar.

Getting There & Away

AIR

Bamrauli airport is 15km west of Allahabad on the road to Kanpur. **Air India** (☎ 2581370; ✹ incoming flights), at the airport, has daily flights

HANDY TRAINS FROM ALLAHABAD

Destination	Train no & name	Fare (Rs)	Duration (hr)	Departures
Kolkata (Howrah)	2312 Kalka Mail	323/855/1162	14	5.30pm
Lucknow*	4307 Ald-Be Pass	84	7½	11.05pm
New Delhi	2559 Shiv Ganga Exp	281/735/996	9	10.30pm
Satna**	152 Gorakhpur-Dadar Spec	121/291	3	7.20am
Varanasi	1107 Bundelkhand Exp	121/251/378	3½	7.10am

All fares are sleeper/3AC/2AC; *sleeper only; **sleeper/3AC only

to Delhi from Rs4500, except on Sunday. An autorickshaw to the airport costs Rs150 to Rs200, a taxi around Rs350.

BUS

From the **Civil Lines Bus Stand** (☎ 2601257; MG Marg) regular buses run to Varanasi (non-AC/AC Rs70/110, three hours), Lucknow (non-AC/AC Rs110/210, five hours), Faizabad (non-AC/AC Rs110/210, five hours) and Gorakhpur (Rs240, 10 hours). To get to Delhi or Agra, change in Lucknow, or take a train.

For hourly buses to Chitrakut (Rs75, four hours, 3am to 7pm), head to **Zero Road Bus Stand**.

TRAIN

Allahabad Junction is the main station. Regular trains runs to Lucknow, Varanasi, Delhi and Kolkata, and one daily express goes to Agra (2403 Ald–Mtg Exp; sleeper/3AC/2AC Rs223/570/768; 11.30pm; 7½hrs). Frequent trains also run to Satna from where you can catch buses to Khajuraho. Also see table, above.

Getting Around

Cycle-rickshaws (Rs10 for a short trip) are plentiful. The train station is your best bet for autos. A return auto to Sangam should cost around Rs150. Consider hiring one for half a day (Rs300, four hours) to take in more of the sights.

CHITRAKUT

☎ 05198 / pop 22,294

Known as a mini Varanasi because of its many temples and ghats, this small, peaceful town on the banks of the River Mandakini is the stuff of Hindu legends. It is here that Hinduism's principal trinity – Brahma, Vishnu and Shiva – took on their incarnations. It is also the place where Lord Rama is believed to have spent

11½ years of his 14-year exile after being banished from his birthplace in Ayodhya at the behest of a jealous stepmother.

Today Chitrakut attracts throngs of pilgrims, giving the area a strong religious quality, particularly by Ram Ghat, the town's centre of activity, and at the holy hill of Kamadgiri, 2km away.

Dozens, sometimes hundreds, of devotees descend onto **Ram Ghat** to take holy dips at dawn before returning at the end of the day for the evening *aarti*. **Rowboats** wait here to take you across to the opposite bank (Rs5), which is actually in Madhya Pradesh, or to scenic spots along the river. The trip to **Janaki Kund** (Rs100 return) is popular. During the day, many people make their way to **Kamadgiri** (Rs5 by tempo), a hill revered as the holy embodiment of Lord Rama. A 5km-circuit (90 minutes) around the base of the hill takes you past prostrating pilgrims, innumerable monkeys and temples galore.

The most enjoyable place to stay in Chitrakut is **Pitra Smiviti Vishramgrah** (☎ 9450223214; Ram Ghat; r Rs150, with bathroom Rs200). Rooms built just in front of Bada Math, a 300-year-old red-stone palace, are very basic, but lead out onto a huge shared balcony overlooking Ram Ghat. There are more comfortable rooms at **UP Tourist Bungalow** (☎ 224219; dm Rs100, with AC Rs250, s/d/tr with AC Rs700/750/925; ❄), which also has an OK restaurant (mains Rs25 to Rs50).

Shared minivans and tempos ply the 10km route from the train station to Ram Ghat (Rs8), passing the bus stand (2km from the train station) and the UP Tourist Bungalow (1km before Ram Ghat).

Bus destinations include Khajuraho (Rs76, four hours, 7am to 1pm) via Satna, and Allahabad (Rs75, four hours, 7am to 6.30pm). Train destinations include

Allahabad (sleeper/3AC/2AC Rs141/286/375, three hours), Gwalior (Rs192/484/650, seven hours), Agra (Rs229/587/793, nine hours) and a 3.46am train to Varanasi (Rs145/377/512, seven hours).

JHANSI
☎ 0510 / pop 420,665
Jhansi is mostly used by travellers on their way to Orchha, Gwalior or Khajuraho, all in Madhya Pradesh. The fort here is of some interest, but otherwise there's little reason to linger.

History
When the raja here died in 1853, his widow and successor, Rani Lakshmibai, was forcibly retired by the British (a controversial law allowed them to take over any princely state under their patronage if the ruler died without a male heir). During the First War of Independence four years later, Rani Lakshmibai was at the forefront of Jhansi's rebellion. The British contingent here was massacred, but the following year the British retook Jhansi. The rani fled to Gwalior. In a fatal last stand she rode out against the British disguised as a man and subsequently became a heroine of Indian Independence.

Orientation
The east–west-running Shivpuri–Khajuraho road is the spine of the town. The fort is 1km to the north, the train station 2km southwest and the bus station 3km east.

Information
Madhya Pradesh Tourism (☎ 2442622; ☼ 10am-6pm) On Platform 1 at the train station; has information about Orchha and Khajuraho.
Bunty Cyber Cafe (Elite Rd; per hr Rs20; ☼ 10am-10pm) Below National Bakery.
State Bank of India (☎ 2330319; Elite Rd; ☼ 10am-4pm Mon-Fri, 10am-1pm Sat) Changes money and travellers cheques; there's an ATM outside the train station.
Uttar Pradesh Tourism (☎ 2442622; ☼ 10am-5pm Mon-Sat, closed every 2nd Sat) Next to the Madhya Pradesh Tourism office.

Sights
Built in 1613 by Maharaja Bir Singh Deo of Orchha, **Jhansi Fort** (☎ 2442325; Indian/foreigner Rs5/100, video Rs25; ☼ dawn-dusk) still bears signs of the blood-letting that took place within

its double walls and moat, once inhabited by crocodiles. These days its shaded lawns make for pleasant strolls and there are some good views of the city and surrounding rocky outcrops.

Near the flag turret is a parapet, over which the fleeing Rani Lakshmibai, with her adopted son mounted behind her, rode her horse. The horse is said to have died, but the story still seems incredible looking at the steep, rocky slope 15m below.

Sleeping & Eating
Hotel Samrat (☎ 2444943; Elite Rd; s Rs300-400, with AC Rs625-875, d Rs350-450, with AC Rs675-925; ☒) This well-run hotel, about 2km from the train station, has decent rooms, all with TV and private bathroom, although the cheaper ones have squat loos. Some travellers have complained about grubby bed sheets, so check first.

National Bakery (Shivpuri Rd; mains Rs30-120; ☼ 9am-11pm) A well-stocked cafe-restaurant offering coffee, juices and snacks – pasties, cakes, ice creams – as well as a seemingly random selection of main dishes from around the world: *dosa*, noodles, pizza, burgers.

Red Tomato (Hotel Samrat; Elite Rd; mains Rs45-135; ☼ 7am-10.30pm; ☒) A smart, clean restaurant newly opened at Hotel Samrat offering veg and meat dishes, including juicy kebabs.

Getting There & Away
BUS
Express buses for Khajuraho leave from the bus station (Rs110, four hours) at 5.30am, 8.30am, 11.30am and 2.30pm. There are a few more local buses (Rs100), although not many more, the last one leaving at 3.30pm.

Regular buses leave throughout the day and night to Gwalior (Rs60, three hours).

Buses go to Orchha (Rs10) all day, but start to thin out in the afternoon. Tempos cost the same and run later.

TRAIN
Several daily trains run to Gwalior, Agra and Delhi. See table, p440.

Getting Around
Tempos run all the main routes in Jhansi. Prices include train station to bus station Rs5, train station to Hotel Samrat Rs2, bus station to Jhansi Fort Rs5 and bus station to Orchha Rs10. Autos cost up to 10 times more.

HANDY TRAINS FROM JHANSI

Destination	Train no & name	Fare (Rs)	Duration (hr)	Departure
Agra	2137 Punjab Mail	148/360/478	3½	2.30pm
Delhi	2614 Grand trunk Exp	207/527/709	7	11.37pm
Gwalior	2137 Punjab Mail	141/243/313	1½	2.30pm
Mumbai	2138 Punjab Mail	385/1028/1403	19	12.35pm
Varanasi	1107 Bundelkhand Exp	232/625/857	12	10.30pm

All fares are sleeper/3AC/2AC

VARANASI

☎ 0542 / pop 1,211,749

Brace yourself. You're about to enter one of the most blindingly colourful, unrelentingly chaotic and unapologetically indiscreet places on earth. Varanasi takes no prisoners. But if you're ready for it, this may just turn out to be your favourite stop of all.

Also known at various times in history as Kashi (City of Life) or Benares, this is one of the world's oldest continually inhabited cities, and one of the holiest places in India. Hindu pilgrims come to the ghats lining the River Ganges here to wash away a lifetime of sins in the sacred waters or to cremate their loved ones. It's a particularly auspicious place to die, since expiring here offers moksha (liberation from the cycle of birth and death), making Varanasi the beating heart of the Hindu universe. Most visitors agree it's a magical place, but it's not for the faint-hearted. Here the most intimate rituals of life and death take place in public and the sights and sounds in and around the ghats – not to mention the almost constant attention from touts – can be overwhelming. Persevere. Varanasi is unique, and a walk along the ghats or a boat ride on the river will live long in the memory.

History

Thought to date back to around 1200 BC, it was in the 8th century AD that Varanasi – also known over the years as Kashi or Benares – really rose to prominence when Shankaracharya, a reformer of Hinduism, established Shiva worship as the principal sect. The Afghans destroyed Varanasi around AD 1300, after laying waste to nearby Sarnath, but the fanatical Mughal emperor Aurangzeb was the most destructive, looting and destroying almost all of the temples. The old city of Varanasi may look antique, but few buildings are more than a couple of hundred years old.

Orientation

The old city of Varanasi is situated along the western bank of the Ganges and extends back from the riverbank ghats in a labyrinth of alleys called galis that are too narrow for traffic. They can be disorienting, but the popular hotels and restaurants are usually signposted and, however lost you become, you will eventually land up at a ghat where you can get your bearings. You can walk all the way along the ghats, apart from during and immediately after the monsoon, when the river level is too high.

Most places of interest, and much of the accommodation, are in the old city, but immediately south of the train station are the less congested areas of Lahurabir and Chetganj, where you'll find other places to stay. Behind the station is the peaceful Cantonment area, home to most of the top-end hotels.

Information

For an online guide to the city, visit the websites www.varanasi.nic.in or www.visit varanasi.com.

BOOKSHOPS

The following bookshops stock books on yoga, meditation and spirituality, Indian literature, travel guides and maps.

Indica Books (Map p444; ☎ 2450818; www.indica books.com; Mandapur Rd; Godaulia; ⏱ 9am-8pm Mon-Sat) There's a second branch of this excellent bookshop at Assi Ghat (Map p442).

Universal Book Company (Map p444; ☎ 2450042; universalvns@sify.com; Mandapur Rd; ⏱ 10am-8.30pm) Also stocks art and photography books.

EMERGENCY

Tourist Police (Map p442; ☎ 2506670; UP Tourism office, Varanasi Junction train station; ⏱ 6am-7pm) Tourist police wear sky-blue uniforms.

INTERNET ACCESS
iway Internet Assi Ghat (Map p442; per hr Rs20; ⏰ 8.30am-10pm); Hotel Surya (Map p442; per 45min Rs25; ⏰ 7.30am-10pm); Vidyapeeth Rd (Map p442; per hr Rs30; ⏰ 9am-9pm)
Messenger (Map p444; per hr Rs20; ⏰ 8am-10pm) Next to Mona Lisa Restaurant.

LEFT LUGGAGE
Varanasi Junction train station (Map p442; per bag per day Rs10; ⏰ 24hr)

MEDICAL SERVICES
Heritage Hospital (Map p442; ☎ 2368888; www .heritagehospital.in; Lanka) Modern, private hospital with a 24-hour pharmacy in reception and an International Travellers Clinic on the 1st floor.

MONEY
There are several ATMs scattered around town.
State Bank of India (Map p442; ☎ 2343742; The Mall; ⏰ 10am-2pm & 2.30-4pm Mon-Fri, 10am-1pm Sat) Changes travellers cheques and cash.

POST
There are post offices in the Cantonment (Map p442), near Dasaswamedh Ghat (Map p444) and south of Vishwanath temple (Map p444). The **main post office** (Map p442; ☎ 2331398; Kabir Chaura Rd; ⏰ 10am-7pm Mon-Sat, parcels 10am-4pm), known as GPO by rickshaw drivers, is the place to go to send parcels.

TOURIST INFORMATION
GITO (Map p442; ☎ 43744; indtourvns@sify.com; 15B The Mall; ⏰ 9am-5.30pm Mon-Fri, 9am-2pm Sat) Helpful staff have all-India information and brochures.
UP Tourism Tourist Bungalow (Map p442; ☎ 2206638; Parade Kothi; ⏰ 9am-5pm Mon-Sat); Varanasi Junction train station (Map p442; ☎ 2506670; ⏰ 9am-5pm) The patient Mr Umashankar at the office inside the train station has been dishing out reasonably impartial information to arriving travellers for years; he's a mine of knowledge, so take advantage of it if you arrive here by train.

Sights
GHATS
Spiritually enlightening and fantastically photogenic, Varanasi is at its brilliant best by the ghats, the long stretch of steps leading down to the water on the western bank of the Ganges. Most are used for bathing but there are also several 'burning ghats' where bodies are cremated in public. The main one is Manikarnika: you'll often see funeral processions threading their way through the backstreets to this ghat. The best time to visit

---

THE VARANASI SHAKEDOWN

If you thought the touts and rickshaw-wallahs were annoying in Agra, wait till you get to Varanasi. The attention here, particularly around the ghats and old city, is incredible, but with a bit of mental preparation it needn't spoil your enjoyment of this unique city.

The first issue is getting to your accommodation when you arrive – and not the one your rickshaw or taxi driver wants to take you to. Arrange a hotel pick-up if you can, or tell your driver that you have arranged to meet friends at a nearby landmark, then walk from there. Don't tell drivers the name of the hotel you want to go to, even if they guess. It just invites them to spin yarns about that place being closed, full, burnt down or full of gangsters.

While wandering the ghats and *galis* (lanes/alleyways) you will have to put up with persistent offers from touts and drivers of 'cheapest and best' boat trips, guides, tour operators, travel agents, silk shops and money changers (to name a few). Take it in good humour but resist all offers. Authorised guides can be organised through the India Tourism or UP Tourism offices. It's safer – and cheaper – to arrange boat trips in groups. And it's certainly cheaper to arrange them directly with the boat hand. Don't take photos at the 'burning' ghats and resist offers to 'follow me for a better view', where you'll be pressured for money and possibly be placed in an uncomfortable situation.

While most of this is little more than a mild irritation, Varanasi, like all cities, does have a darker side and a criminal element operates mainly around the train and bus stations, so take extra care with your valuables in these places, and be cautious when walking alone at night.

But, of course, not everyone is out to fleece you, and meeting the locals is a valuable part of every travel experience. Visitors who display confidence, patience and humour and take sensible precautions usually avoid catastrophe.

UTTAR PRADESH

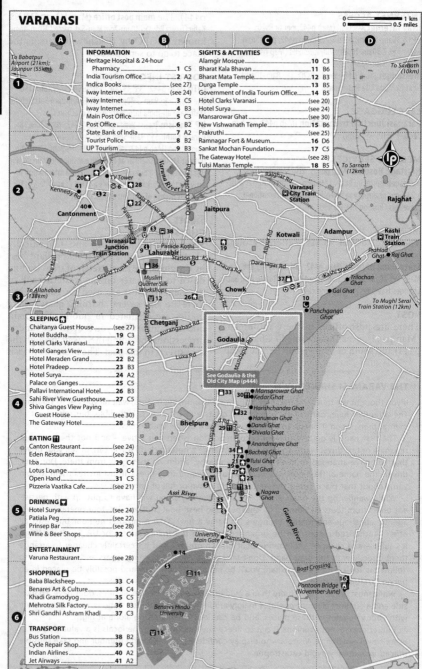

VARANASI

0 ———— 1 km
0 ———— 0.5 miles

INFORMATION
Heritage Hospital & 24-hour
  Pharmacy..............................1 C5
India Tourism Office................2 A2
Indica Books......................(see 27)
iway Internet......................(see 24)
iway Internet..........................3 C5
iway Internet..........................4 B3
Main Post Office......................5 C3
Post Office..............................6 B2
State Bank of India..................7 A2
Tourist Police..........................8 B2
UP Tourism..............................9 B3

SIGHTS & ACTIVITIES
Alamgir Mosque.....................10 C3
Bharat Kala Bhavan................11 B6
Bharat Mata Temple...............12 B3
Durga Temple.........................13 B5
Government of India Tourism Office...14 B5
Hotel Clarks Varanasi..........(see 20)
Hotel Surya........................(see 24)
Mansarowar Ghat................(see 30)
New Vishwanath Temple........15 B6
Prakruthi............................(see 25)
Ramnagar Fort & Museum.......16 D6
Sankat Mochan Foundation.....17 C5
The Gateway Hotel.............(see 28)
Tulsi Manas Temple...............18 B5

SLEEPING
Chaitanya Guest House........(see 27)
Hotel Buddha.........................19 C3
Hotel Clarks Varanasi.............20 A2
Hotel Ganges View.................21 C5
Hotel Meraden Grand.............22 B2
Hotel Pradeep........................23 B3
Hotel Surya............................24 A2
Palace on Ganges...................25 C5
Pallavi International Hotel........26 B3
Sahi River View Guesthouse....27 C5
Shiva Ganges View Paying
  Guest House......................(see 30)
The Gateway Hotel.................28 B2

EATING
Canton Restaurant...............(see 24)
Eden Restaurant...................(see 23)
I:ba.......................................29 C4
Lotus Lounge.........................30 C4
Open Hand.............................31 C5
Pizzeria Vaatika Cafe...........(see 21)

DRINKING
Hotel Surya.........................(see 24)
Patiala Peg..........................(see 22)
Prinsep Bar.........................(see 28)
Wine & Beer Shops................32 C4

ENTERTAINMENT
Varuna Restaurant...............(see 28)

SHOPPING
Baba Blacksheep....................33 C4
Benares Art & Culture............34 C4
Khadi Gramodyog..................35 C5
Mehrotra Silk Factory.............36 B3
Shri Gandhi Ashram Khadi......37 C3

TRANSPORT
Bus Station............................38 B2
Cycle Repair Shop..................39 C5
Indian Airlines.......................40 A2
Jet Airways............................41 A2

To Babatpur
Airport (21km);
Jaunpur (55km)

To Sarnath
(10km)

To Sarnath
(12km)

Rajghat

Kashi
Train
Station

Prahlad
Ghat •Raj Ghat

Trilochan
Ghat

•Gai Ghat

To Mughl Serai
Train Station (12km)

Panchganga
Ghat

Kennedy Rd

Cantonment

Varanasi
Junction
Train Station

The Mall

To Allahabad
(138km)

Grand Trunk Rd

Raja Bazar Rd

Patel Nagar

Queen's College Rd

Varuna River

Raighat Rd

Jaitpura

Parade Kothi
Station Rd
Kabir Chaura Rd

Lahurabir

Muslim
Quarter Silk
Workshops

Kotwali

Nation Rd

Daranagar Rd

Chetganj

Aurangabad Rd

Luxa Rd

Godaulia

See Godaulia & the
Old City Map (p444)

Chowk

Kashi Station Rd

Varanasi
City Train
Station

Adampur

Bhelpura

Durgakund Rd

Assi River

Assi Rd

Ramnagar Rd

University
Main Gate

Benares Hindu
University

Mansarowar Ghat
•Kedar Ghat
•Harishchandra Ghat
•Hanuman Ghat
•Dandi Ghat
•Shivala Ghat
•Anandmayee Ghat
•Bachraj Ghat
•Tulsi Ghat
•Assi Ghat
•Nagwa
  Ghat

Ganges River

Boat Crossing

Pontoon Bridge
(November-June)

TV Tower

the ghats is at dawn when the river is bathed in a mellow light as pilgrims come to perform *puja* (literally 'respect'; offering or prayers) to the rising sun, and at sunset when the main *ganga aarti* (river worship ceremony) takes place at Dasaswamedh Ghat.

About 80 ghats border the river, but the main group extends from Assi Ghat, near the university, northwards to Raj Ghat, near the road and rail bridge.

A boat trip along the river provides the perfect introduction, although for most of the year the water level is low enough for you to walk freely along the whole length of the ghats. It's a world-class 'people-watching' stroll as you mingle with the fascinating mixture of people who come to the Ganges not only for a ritual bath but also to wash clothes, do yoga, offer blessings, sell flowers, get a massage, play cricket, wash their buffaloes, improve their karma by giving to beggars or simply hang around.

Assi Ghat (Map p442), the furthest south of the main ghats, and one of the biggest, is particularly important as the River Assi meets the Ganges near here and pilgrims come to worship a Shiva lingam (phallic image of Shiva) beneath a peepul tree. Evenings are particularly lively, as the ghat's vast concreted area fills up with hawkers and entertainers. It's a popular starting point for boat trips and there are some excellent hotels here. Nearby **Tulsi Ghat** (Map p442), named after a 16th-century Hindu poet, has fallen down towards the river but in the month of Kartika (October/November) a festival devoted to Krishna is celebrated here. The NGO campaigning for a cleaner Ganges also has its research laboratory here (see the boxed text, p446). Next along, **Bachraj Ghat** (Map p442) has three Jain temples. A small Shiva temple and a 19th-century mansion built by Nepalese royalty, sit back from **Shivala Ghat** (Map p442), built by the local maharaja of Benares. The **Dandi Ghat** (Map p442) is used by ascetics known as Dandi Panths, and nearby is the very popular **Hanuman Ghat** (Map p442).

Harishchandra Ghat (Map p442) is a cremation ghat – smaller and secondary in importance to Manikarnika, but one of the oldest ghats in Varanasi. Above it, **Kedar Ghat** (Map p442) has a shrine popular with Bengalis and South Indians. **Mansarowar Ghat** was built by Raja Man Singh of Amber and named after the Tibetan lake at the foot of Mt Kailash, Shiva's Himalayan home. **Someswar Ghat** (Map p442; Lord of the Moon Ghat) is said to be able to heal diseases. The **Munshi Ghat** (Map p444) is very photogenic, while **Ahalya Bai's Ghat** (Map p444) is named after the female Maratha ruler of Indore.

Varanasi's liveliest and most colourful ghat is **Dasaswamedh Ghat** (Map p444), easily reached at the end of the main road from Godaulia Crossing. The name indicates that Brahma sacrificed *(medh)* 10 *(das)* horses *(aswa)* here. In spite of the oppressive boat owners, flower sellers and touts trying to drag you off to a silk shop, it's a wonderful place to linger and people-watch while soaking up the atmosphere. Every evening at 7pm an elaborate *ganga aarti* ceremony with *puja*, fire and dance is staged here.

A little further north, Raja Man Singh's **Man Mandir Ghat** (Map p444) was built in 1600, but was poorly restored in the 19th century. The northern corner of the ghat has a fine stone balcony.

Meer Ghat (Map p444) leads to a Nepali temple, which has erotic sculptures. **Manikarnika Ghat** (Map p444), the main burning ghat, is the most auspicious place for a Hindu to be cremated. Dead bodies are handled by outcasts known as *doms*, and are carried through the alleyways of the old city to the holy Ganges on a bamboo stretcher swathed in cloth. The corpse is doused in the Ganges prior to cremation. Huge piles of firewood are stacked along the top of the ghat; every log is carefully weighed on giant scales so that the price of cremation can be calculated. Each type of wood has its own price, sandalwood being the most expensive. There is an art to using just enough wood to completely incinerate a corpse. You can watch cremations but always show reverence by behaving respectfully. Photography is strictly prohibited. You're almost guaranteed to be led by a priest, or more likely a guide, to the upper floor of a nearby building from where you can watch cremations taking place, and then asked for a donation (in dollars) towards the cost of wood. If you don't want to make a donation, don't follow them.

Above the steps here is a tank known as the **Manikarnika Well**. Parvati is said to have dropped her earring here and Shiva dug the tank to recover it, filling the depression with his sweat. The **Charanpaduka**, a slab of stone between the well and the ghat, bears footprints

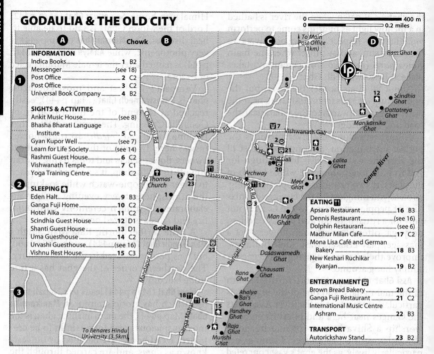

GODAULIA & THE OLD CITY

INFORMATION	
Indica Books	1 B2
Messenger	(see 18)
Post Office	2 C2
Post Office	3 C2
Universal Book Company	4 B2

SIGHTS & ACTIVITIES	
Ankit Music House	(see 8)
Bhasha Bharati Language Institute	5 C1
Gyan Kupor Well	(see 7)
Learn for Life Society	(see 14)
Rashmi Guest House	6 C2
Vishwanath Temple	7 C1
Yoga Training Centre	8 C2

SLEEPING	
Eden Halt	9 B3
Ganga Fuji Home	10 C2
Hotel Alka	11 C2
Scindhia Guest House	12 D1
Shanti Guest House	13 D1
Uma Guesthouse	14 C2
Urvashi Guesthouse	(see 16)
Vishnu Rest House	15 C3

EATING	
Apsara Restaurant	16 B3
Dennis Restaurant	(see 16)
Dolphin Restaurant	(see 6)
Madhur Milan Cafe	17 C2
Mona Lisa Café and German Bakery	18 B3
New Keshari Ruchikar Byanjan	19 B2

ENTERTAINMENT	
Brown Bread Bakery	20 C2
Ganga Fuji Restaurant	21 C2
International Music Centre Ashram	22 B3

TRANSPORT	
Autorickshaw Stand	23 B2

made by Vishnu. Privileged VIPs are cremated at the Charanpaduka, which also has a temple dedicated to Ganesh.

Dattatreya Ghat (Map p444) bears the footprint of the Brahmin saint of that name in a small temple nearby. **Scindhia Ghat** (Map p444) was originally built in 1830, but was so huge and magnificent that it collapsed into the river and had to be rebuilt. **Ram Ghat** (Map p444) was built by a maharaja of Jaipur.

Panchganga Ghat (Map p442), as its name indicates, is where five rivers are supposed to meet. Dominating the ghat is Aurangzeb's smaller mosque, also known as the **Alamgir Mosque** (Map p442), which he built on the site of a large Vishnu temple. **Gai Ghat** (Map p442) has a figure of a cow made of stone. **Trilochan Ghat** (Map p442) has two turrets emerging from the river, and the water between them is especially holy. **Raj Ghat** (Map p442) was the ferry pier until the road and rail bridge was completed here.

VISHWANATH TEMPLE
Also called the Golden Temple (Map p444), this is the most popular Hindu temple in

Varanasi and is dedicated to Vishveswara – Shiva as lord of the universe. The current temple was built in 1776 by Ahalya Bai of Indore; the 800kg of gold plating on the tower and dome was supplied by Maharaja Ranjit Singh of Lahore 50 years later.

The area is full of soldiers because of security issues and communal tensions. Bags, cameras and mobile phones must be deposited in lockers (Rs10) before you enter the alleyway it's in. However, non-Hindus are not allowed inside the temple itself so most travellers find it pointless to go through the security rigmarole.

Next to Vishwanath Temple is the **Gyan Kupor Well** (Well of Knowledge; Map p444). The faithful believe drinking its water leads to a higher spiritual plane, though they are prevented from doing so by a strong security screen.

BENARES HINDU UNIVERSITY
Long regarded as a centre of learning, Varanasi's tradition of top-quality education continues today at **Benares Hindu University** (BHU; Map p442; www.bhu.ac.in), established in 1916. If

you're interested in studying here, contact the **International Centre** (Map p442; ☎ 2307639; internationalcentrebhu@gmail.com).

The wide tree-lined streets and parkland of the 5-sq-km campus offer a peaceful atmosphere a world away from the city outside. On campus is **Bharat Kala Bhavan** (Map p442; ☎ 316337; Indian/foreigner Rs10/100, camera Rs50; ⏲ 10.30am-4.30pm Mon-Sat, 7.30am-1pm May-Jun), a roomy museum with a wonderful collection of miniature paintings, as well as 12th-century palm-leaf manuscripts, sculptures and local history displays.

The attractive **New Vishwanath Temple** (Map p442; ⏲ 4am-noon & 1-9pm), unlike most temples in Varanasi, is open to all, irrespective of religion.

RAMNAGAR FORT & MUSEUM

This crumbling but impressive 17th-century fort and palace (Map p442), on the eastern bank of the Ganges, is a beautiful place to watch the sun set over the river. It also houses an eccentric **museum** (Map p442; ☎ 2339322; admission Rs7; ⏲ 9am-noon & 2-5.30pm). There are vintage American cars, jewel-encrusted sedan chairs, a superb weaponry section and an extremely unusual astrological clock. The current maharaja, Anant Narayan Singh – still known in these parts as the Maharaja of Benares despite such royal titles being officially abolished in 1971 – continues his family tradition of attending the annual month-long **Ram Lila drama festival** (p403) held in the streets behind the fort.

Boats operate a shuttle service across the river (Rs10 return, 10 minutes) between 5am and 8pm, but from November to June you can also cross on the somewhat unsteady pontoon bridge. A boat all the way back to Dasaswamedh Ghat is about Rs200.

OTHER SIGHTS

The small **Durga Temple** (Map p442; Durgakund Rd; ⏲ dawn-dusk) was built in the 18th century by a Bengali maharani and is stained red with ochre. Nearby is the modern marble, *sikhara*-style **Tulsi Manas Temple** (Map p442; Durgakund Rd; ⏲ 5am-noon & 4-9pm) whose walls are engraved with verses and scenes from the Ram Charit Manas, the Hindi version of the Ramayana.

The **Bharat Mata Temple** (Map p442; Vidyapeeth Rd; camera/video Rs10/20; ⏲ dawn-dusk), built in 1918, has an unusual marble relief map of the Indian subcontinent inside.

Activities

RIVER TRIPS

A dawn rowing boat ride along the Ganges is a quintessential Varanasi experience. The early morning light is particularly inspiring, and all the colour and clamour of pilgrims bathing and performing *puja* unfolds before you. An hour-long trip south from Dasaswamedh Ghat to Harishchandra Ghat and back is popular, but be prepared to see a burning corpse at Harishchandra. Early evening is also a good time to be on the river, when you can light a lotus flower candle (Rs10) and set it adrift on the water before watching the nightly *ganga aarti* ceremony (7pm) at Dasaswamedh Ghat directly from the boat.

Boats, available at most ghats, cost about Rs50 per person per hour, but be prepared for some hard bargaining.

Another trip worth considering is the lazy one-hour journey to Ramnagar Fort which should cost around Rs200 from Dasaswamedh Ghat.

Many guesthouses offer boat trips, although all are more expensive than dealing with the boatmen directly.

SWIMMING & HEALTH TREATMENTS

Hotel Surya (Map p442; ☎ 2508466; www.hotelsuryavns.com; The Mall; ⏲ 9am-11pm) offers perhaps the best-value massage treatments in Varanasi. Full-body massages start from Rs500. More expensive Keralan massage therapies are available at **Prakruthi** (Map p442; Palace on the Ganges; ☎ 2315050; Assi Ghat; ⏲ 8am-7pm) and at Rashmi Guesthouse (p448).

Nonguests can use the outdoor swimming pools at Hotel Surya (Rs150), Hotel Clarks Varanasi (Rs200) and Gateway Hotel Ganges (Rs350).

VOLUNTEERING

Learn for Life Society (Map p444; ☎ 2403566; www.learn-for-life.org), which can be contacted through the nearby Brown Bread Bakery (p449) has established a small school for disadvantaged children, and travellers are welcome to turn up and help out. The charity also recently started a women's empowerment group, offering fair-paid work to local women, some of whom are mothers of the school's students. The women make produce such as jams and pickles which travellers can buy from Brown Bread Bakery. See the website for more details.

CLEANING UP THE GANGES

Looking at it now, it's hard to believe Varanasi's sewage-filled stretch of the River Ganges could ever be clean. But, thanks to one man's 40-year mission, that could very soon be the case.

Professor Veer Bhadra Mishra, who has been campaigning to clean up the Ganges since the 1970s, says that, assuming the government doesn't make another U-turn, this famous stretch of India's holiest river could be clean by 2014.

It's an incredible statement to make, given current pollution levels. Water that is safe for bathing should have less than 500 faecal coliform bacteria in every litre of water. Samples show this part of the Ganges has 1.5 million! And the river is so heavily polluted in parts that the water is actually septic – no dissolved oxygen exists.

But, after years of indecision, the state government has decided to fund a sewage-treatment system specifically designed by Professor Mishra's **Sankat Mochan Foundation** (SMF; Map p442; ☎ 2313884; vbmganga@satyam.net.in; Tulsi Ghat) to deal with Varanasi's special needs.

'I was very happy, of course,' he said, describing the moment in July 2008 when he opened the letter from the government outlining its full support for the plan. 'But I'm still sceptical because of the problems we've had before. I just hope they keep their promise.

'I am a practising Hindu so I believe the Ganga is Mother. She is divine. She delivers happiness to our world, and salvation when we leave it. I take holy dips in the river. In fact, I cannot live without her, and many of the users of the Ganga in Varanasi are like this. For them she is a way of life. And because of these people, the traditions associated with the Ganga continue to this day. What is the meaning of traditions if they can't be practised?'

But they can't be, at least not without endangering people's health. Devotees believe these holy waters should be looked at, touched, bathed in and even sipped. These days it's simply not safe to do so.

Some say it's their own fault. People frequently bathe in the river, place innumerable offerings into it and every day cremate bodies that can be seen floating away downstream. No

---

The **Sankat Mochan Foundation** (Map p442; ☎ 2313884; vmbganga@satyam.net.in; Tulsi Ghat), a charity dedicated to cleaning up the Varanasi stretch of the River Ganges (above) is always looking for extra volunteers to help with research and administration.

Courses

HINDI LANGUAGE

The long-running **Bhasha Bharati Language Institute** (Map p444; ☎ 9839076805; www.bhashabharati.com; 19/8 Thatheri Bazaar, Chowk), near Chowk police station, offers small classes costing Rs250 per hour, run in one-week blocks of 30 hours. All-inclusive family homestays can be arranged for Rs1350. Students should book courses two weeks in advance. In any case, phoning ahead is helpful as this place is hard to find.

Readers recommend Rajeswar Mukherjee at **Pragati Hindi** (☎ 9335376488; pragatihindi@yahoo.co.in; B-7/176 Kedar Ghat). Private classes start from Rs200 per hour.

Foreigners wanting to study at **Benares Hindu University** (Map p442; ☎ 2307639; internationalcentrebhu@gmail.com; International Centre, BHU) must enrol for at least one year. Courses cost just over Rs13,000 per academic year (July to June). Applications should be received by March.

MUSIC & DANCE

The family-run **International Music Centre Ashram** (Map p444; ☎ 2452303; keshavaraonayak@hotmail.com) is hidden in the tangle of backstreets near Rana Ghat but worth seeking out. Sitar, tabla, flute and classical dance tuition is Rs150 per hour, and concerts are held every Saturday and Wednesday evening at 8pm (Rs50).

Ankit Music House (Map p444; ☎ 9336567134; ankitmusichouse@hotmail.com; Sakarkand Gali), in the same building as the Yoga Training Centre, in the alleys near Meer Ghat, also offers classical music tuition, for Rs100 an hour. Instructors Bablu and Vijay can give advice on buying musical instruments.

YOGA & MEDITATION

Beware of 'fake' yoga teachers who are mainly interested in hands-on lessons with young females. The following are bona fide.

Yoga master Sunil Kumar runs two-hour classes three times a day (8am, 10am and 4pm; Rs200) at the **Yoga Training Centre** (Map

wonder the Ganges is polluted!' That's a common misunderstanding,' says Professor Mishra. 'Our research has shown that just 5% of the river's pollution is from direct users. The other 95% is caused by sewage. Not one of the 116 cities on the Ganga stops raw sewage from flowing into the river.'

In Varanasi alone there are 32 point sources of raw sewage. 'These flow directly into the parts of the river where people take their holy dips,' says Professor Mishra.

The government sat up and took notice for a while, launching its own Ganga Action Plan (GAP) in 1986, but then politics began to take over. GAP stopped listening to Mishra's advice and formulated its own solution. 'A lust for power,' Mishra thinks.

GAP's aims were spot on, he says, but its solutions were flawed. Despite there being 32 point sources in Varanasi, the government installed just five sewage pumps. And despite Varanasi's frequent power cuts, the pumps were electric.

'They prescribed medicines without diagnosing the disease,' said Mishra, whose foundation has, with the help of experts in America, designed a purpose-built, gravity-collection sewage system which would intercept sewage as it falls into the river and divert it through pipes to a nonelectric treatment centre 7km downstream.

At one stage the council agreed on the plan, only for the state government to veto it (litigations are still with the High Court), but finally Professor Mishra got that letter telling the Sankat Mocha Foundation to go ahead with a trial unit, which should be finished by 2010. Then four years after that Varanasi should have an all-new, singing-and-dancing sewage-treatment system, by which time Professor Mishra will be 75 years old. That would be time to hang up his campaigning boots, surely?

'Absolutely not,' he insists. 'Our aim is not just to clean up Varanasi, but the whole of the Ganga. We want this to be a model for the whole river.'

SMF warmly welcomes volunteers and donations. Contact the office at Tulsi Ghat.

p444; ☎ 9919857895; yoga_sunil@hotmail.com; Sakarkand Gali), on the 3rd floor of a small backstreet building near Meer Ghat. He teaches an integrated blend of hatha, Iyengar, pranayama and ashtanga, and serious students can continue on certificate and diploma courses. This place is highly recommended by travellers.

At **Benares Hindu University** (Map p442; ☎ 2307639; internationalcentrebhu@gmail.com; International Centre, BHU) four-week physical yoga certificate courses cost Rs2500, while a four-month diploma course costs Rs5500. Email the International Centre for enrolment details.

Tours

If time is short, contact the **UP Tourism office** (Map p442; ☎ 2506670; Varanasi Junction train station; ☽ 7am-7pm) for details of a full-day guided tour by taxi of the major sites, including a 5.30am boat ride and an afternoon trip to Sarnath. It costs Rs1400 per person, Rs900 for half a day.

Sleeping

The majority of Varanasi's budget hotels – and some midrange gems – are concentrated in

the most interesting part of the city – the tangle of narrow streets back from the ghats along the River Ganges. There's a concentration around Assi Ghat, while others are in the crazy, bustling northern stretch of alleys between Scindhia and Meer Ghat.

Varanasi has an active paying-guest house scheme with more than 100 family homes available for accommodation from Rs200 to Rs2000 a night. UP Tourism has a full list.

BUDGET
Old City & the Ghats
Uma Guesthouse (Map p444; ☎ 2403566; brownbread bakery@yahoo.co.in; dm/s Rs50/100, d Rs150-200) Part of the Learn for Life Society (p445) run by the excellent Brown Bread Bakery; 20% of your bill goes to the charity that runs the school behind the guesthouse. Rooms are basic but clean. Bookings should be made through the bakery, where you can also ask about volunteering or donating.

Vishnu Rest House (Map p444; ☎ 2455238; Pandhey Ghat; dm Rs60, s without bathroom Rs70-120, d Rs150-800) Accessed through a small courtyard with family homes coming off it, or directly from

Pandhey Ghat itself, this simple guesthouse has bags of character. Rooms are poky, and not the cleanest, but the atmosphere is friendly and the communal terrace overlooking the ghat is a winner.

Shanti Guest House (Map p444; ☎ 392568; varanasi shanti@yahoo.com; Manikarnika Ghat; s without bathroom Rs70-100, s/d Rs150/200, r with AC Rs500-1000; ✖ ▣) Big, bold and bright yellow, Shanti is as popular as ever. Rooms are nothing special, but it's the very high, 24-hour rooftop restaurant with fabulous views of the Ganges that pulls in the punters.

Urvashi Guesthouse (Map p444; ☎ 3258534; Ganga Mahal; s without bathroom Rs100, d Rs200-250) Run by the same management as the popular Apsara Restaurant below it, Urvashi's doubles are large, clean and homely. A good-value option.

Ganga Fuji Home (Map p444; ☎ 3093949; raj327333@ yahoo.com; Sakarkand Gali; s/d without bathroom from Rs150/400, s/d from Rs300/350, d with AC from Rs700; ✖) Back from the ghats in a relatively quiet location, Ganga Fuji's best and brightest rooms are near the top. The cheaper ones are a bit cramped and gloomy. The top-floor restaurant – not to be confused with nearby Ganga Fuji Restaurant – offers panoramic city views and live entertainment in the evenings.

Eden Halt (Map p444; ☎ 2454612; Raja Ghat; r Rs160-200) This pocket-sized guesthouse only has four rooms. Two have private bathrooms, two have river views. All are very basic, but spacious and come with interesting alcoves and built-in shelving, just in case you bring along your favourite ornaments. A simple roof terrace overlooks peaceful Raja Ghat.

Sahi River View Guesthouse (Map p442; ☎ 2366730; sahi_rvgh@sify.com; Assi Ghat; d Rs200-1000, with AC Rs800-1200; ✖) There's a huge variety of rooms at this friendly place, but most are good quality and clean, and some have interesting private balconies. Each floor has a pleasant communal seating area with river view, creating a great feeling of space throughout.

Scindhia Guest House (Map p444; ☎ 2420319; www .scindhiaguesthouse.com; Scindhia Ghat; r without bathroom Rs250-350, r Rs450-550, with AC Rs900; ✖ ▣) Rooms aren't the biggest in this well-run, ghat-side guesthouse, but they're clean and some – the much pricier AC rooms – have balconies with river views.

Hotel Alka (Map p444; ☎ 2401681; www.hotelalkavns .com; Meer Ghat; r without bathroom Rs300, r Rs350-1100, with AC Rs700-1500; ✖ ▣) An excellent ghat-side budget option, Alka has pretty much spotless rooms that open onto or overlook a large, plant-filled courtyard. In the far corner, a terrace juts out over Meer Ghat for arguably the best view in all of Varanasi, a view shared from the balconies of the pricier rooms. Some travellers have complained about the food here, but this is still a great choice.

Chaitanya Guest House (Map p442; ☎ 2313686; Assi Ghat; s/d Rs350/400, d with AC Rs800; ✖) In complete contrast to next door Sahi River View Guesthouse, Chaitanya has just four rooms: a single, two doubles and a double with AC. All are comfortable, with high ceilings and clean bathrooms, and are well looked after by friendly staff.

Other Areas
Hotel Buddha (Map p442; ☎ 2203686; www.visitvara nasi.com/hotelbuddha; s/d without bathroom Rs250/350, s/d Rs450-500/550-600, s/d with AC Rs770-880/880-990, ste Rs1650; ✖) Friendly enough, but lacking in character, especially now that a huge marriage hall has been added. What you do get, though, is space. Rooms off an open central courtyard are large and come with bright, modern bathrooms. Steer clear of the two minuscule cheapies, though.

MIDRANGE
Old City & the Ghats
our pick **Hotel Ganges View** (Map p442; ☎ 2313218; www.hotelgangesview.com; Assi Ghat; r Rs1500, with AC Rs2500-3500; ✖) Simply gorgeous, this beautifully restored and maintained colonial-style house overlooking Assi Ghat is crammed with books, artwork and antiques. Rooms are spacious and immaculate and there are some charming communal areas in which to sit and relax. Home-cooked meals are another great feature. Booking ahead is essential.

Rashmi Guest House (Map p444; ☎ 2402778; rashmiguesthouse@sify.com; Man Mandir Ghat; d Rs1575, river view Rs2625-4420; ✖ ▣) Sparkling white-tiled corridors and marble staircases lead to clean and modern rooms, which are small but smart. Many have views of Man Mandir Ghat, although the excellent rooftop Dolphin Restaurant offers the best views of all. Ayurvedic massage (Rs1250) is also available.

Shiva Ganges View Paying Guest House (Map p442; ☎ 2450063; www.varanasiguesthouse.com; Mansarowar Ghat; r Rs2000-2500, with AC Rs3000; ste Rs5000 ✖) Next to Lotus Lounge Restaurant, this delightful, bright-red brick building is part of the city's paying-guest house scheme. Rooms here ooze character, with central double beds, high ceilings, chunky door and window shutters, and some attractive ornaments on shelves. All have river views and spotlessly clean bathrooms. Home-cooked food is also available.

Other Areas

Hotel Surya (Map p442; ☎ 2508465; www.hotelsurya vns.com; 20/51 The Mall; s/d Rs550/750, with AC from Rs900/1200; ✕ ▢ ▣) A big price hike in recent years puts some travellers off, but this is still an excellent choice if you don't mind being away from the ghats. Rooms are built around a huge lawn area that now includes a laid-back Middle Eastern–style cafe where you can smoke sheesha pipes while sipping a beer. The hotel has modern rooms, a beautiful swimming pool, a quality restaurant and a recommended massage centre (p445).

Hotel Pradeep (Map p442; ☎ 2204963; www.hotelpra deep.com; Kabir Chaura Rd; s Rs1100-2100, d Rs1400-2600; ✕) Decorated in tasteful browns and creams, AC rooms here are smart and comfortable. Some have balconies. The standout feature, though, is the rooftop garden restaurant, Eden.

Pallavi International Hotel (Map p442; ☎ 2393012; www.pallavinternationalhotel.com; Hathwa Pl; r Rs1700-2000, ste Rs2500/4000; ✕ ▣) The antique-filled former palace of the maharaja of Bahadur is now a slightly eccentric heritage hotel. Some rooms are reasonably modern, but others are tatty for this price. The garden, interior courtyard with fountain and small pool help create a tranquil atmosphere, though.

TOP END

Hotel Meraden Grand (Map p442; ☎ 2509952; www.mera dengrand.com; 57 Patel Nagar; s Rs3000-3900 d Rs3500-4500, ste Rs6200-8000; ✕) The beautifully designed central atrium garden and restaurant make for a grand entrance, but rooms here are smart and comfortable rather than luxurious. The suite, with private bar and butler service, though, is superb. There's also a rooftop restaurant and a bar. No pool, though.

Palace on Ganges (Map p442; ☎ 2315050; palace onganges@indiatimes.com; Assi Ghat; d Rs3500; ✕ ▢) Each room in this immaculate heritage accommodation costs the same, but is individually themed on a regional Indian style, using antique furnishings and colourful design themes. The colonial, Rajasthan and Jodhpur rooms are among the best.

Hotel Clarks Varanasi (Map p442; ☎ 2501011; www .clarkshotels.com; The Mall; s Rs5000-6500 d Rs5500-7000, ste Rs8500-9500; ✕ ▢ ▣ ▣) The executive-category rooms are enormous, with their own private dining areas, but standard rooms are run-of-the-mill for this price range. Wonderful restaurant, though, and a delightful teardrop-shaped pool shaded by bamboo and palm trees. There's also a 24-hour cafe.

Gateway Hotel Ganges (Map p442; ☎ 2503001; www. tajhotels.com; Raja Bazaar Rd; r Rs8500-9500, ste Rs11000-13000; ✕ ▢ ▣) Varanasi's best hotel is set in five hectares of beautiful gardens with fruit trees, a tennis court, a pool, an outdoor yoga centre and the old maharaja's guesthouse. You can walk, cycle or take a ride in a maharaja's buggy around the grounds. Inside, rooms are luxurious, service is top class and there are two fine restaurants and two bars.

Eating

In the old city look out for locally grown *langda aam* (mangoes) in summer or *sitafal* (custard apples) in autumn. *Singhara* is a blackish root that tastes like water chestnut.

OLD CITY & THE GHATS

Mona Lisa Cafe and German Bakery (Map p444; mains Rs20-100; ⏱ 7am-10.30pm; ▢) A pint-sized cafe with fresh coffee and bread as well as the usual multicuisine menu.

Madhur Milan Cafe (Map p444; Dasaswamedh Ghat Rd; mains Rs25-60; ⏱ 4am-11pm) Popular with locals, this no-nonsense restaurant serves up a range of good-value, mostly south Indian dishes, including dosa, *idli* and *uttapam*, and *paratha*. Thalis start from Rs25, and they have lassis.

Apsara Restaurant (Map p444; ☎ 3258554; 24/42 Ganga Mahal; mains Rs25-60) This cosy AC restaurant has cushioned seats, good music and friendly staff. The multicuisine menu includes Indian, Chinese, continental, Japanese, Israeli and Korean food, and there's a small rooftop area.

Open Hand (Map p442; ☎ 2369751; www.openhand online.com; coffee Rs30-50; ⏱ 8am-8pm Mon-Sat; ▣) A cafe-cum-gift shop with fresh coffee and a range of cakes and snacks plus good-quality clothing and textiles at fixed prices.

Lotus Lounge (Map p442; Mansarowar Ghat; mains Rs40-140; ⏱ 8am-10pm) A great place to chill, this laid-back, half–open-air restaurant, with broken-tile mosaic flooring and wicker chairs, has a terrace that juts out over Mansarowar Ghat. The menu's a mixed bag, with fresh coffee, salads, pasta, curry and even Tibetan *momos* (dumplings).

Dennis Restaurant (Map p444; 25/49 Ganga Mahal; pizza Rs45-70; ☻ midday-10pm) Funky, bright-red restaurant specialising in pizza, but with Indian and Chinese too.

New Keshari Ruchikar Byanjan (Map p444; Dasaswamedh Ghat Rd; mains Rs50-100; ☻ 8.30am-10.30pm) This 1st-floor veg restaurant, specialising in both North and South Indian cuisine, is the nicest place to eat along this busy market street and is popular with local families.

Ganga Fuji Restaurant (Map p444; Kalika Gali; ☻ 7.30am-11pm; mains Rs50-120) Free live Indian classical music is played every evening at 7.30pm, which makes this otherwise ordinary multicuisine restaurant worth considering for dinner. Not to be confused with the nearby hotel, Ganga Fuji Home, which also has a restaurant.

Dolphin Restaurant (Map p444; Rashmi Guest House, Man Mandir Ghat; mains Rs50-170; ☻ 7am-10.30pm) Perched high above Man Mandir Ghat, this rooftop restaurant at Rashmi Guest House is a fine place for breakfast or an evening meal. Watch food being prepared through the glass-walled kitchen or sit out on the breezy balcony.

Pizzeria Vaatika Cafe (Map p442; Assi Ghat; pizza Rs65-100; ☻ 7am-10pm) Sit in the shady garden terrace overlooking Assi Ghat while you munch your way through top-notch pizza baked in a wood-fired oven. None of that thick-crust nonsense here – it's all thin and crispy, as every pizza should be. Don't forget to leave some room for the delicious apple pie.

our pick Brown Bread Bakery (Map p444; 17 Tripura Bhairavi; mains Rs75-230; ▯) Not only does this place lead the way socially and environmentally – it supports a local school, runs a women's empowerment group, uses organic produce wherever possible, and refills your water bottles for you (Rs5) – but the food is also terrific. The fabulous menu includes more than 20 varieties of cheese and more than 30 types of bread, cookies and cakes as well as main courses from around the world. The ambience is spot on too, with seating on cushions around low tables and live classical music performances in the evenings. Admittedly, it's pricier than most, but part of the profits go to the charity Learn for Life (p445).

I:ba (p442; mains Rs75-200; ☻ 7am-11pm) Slick decor and lounge-style furniture make this place – specialising in Japanese and Thai

food – a fashionable choice. The menu also includes a range of pasta dishes and some tasty wraps.

OTHER AREAS

Eden Restaurant (Map p442; Hotel Pradeep, Kabir Chaura Rd; mains Rs100-195) Hotel Pradeep's rooftop restaurant, complete with garden, manicured lawn and wrought-iron furniture, is a lovely place for a candlelit evening meal. Note that staircase-weary waiters will be very appreciative if you order at the ground-floor restaurant behind the lobby before heading up to the roof. The good-quality Indian menu is the same in both restaurants.

Canton Restaurant (Map p442; Hotel Surya, The Mall; mains Rs110-240) The AC dining room of Hotel Surya's excellent restaurant has a colonial elegance, and on warm evenings you can eat out in the garden. The menu is probably a bit ambitious – there are Indian, Chinese, continental, Korean and even Mexican dishes – but the food is good, with some unusual offerings, such as fish Portuguese.

Varuna Restaurant (Map p442; Gateway Hotel Ganges, Raja Bazaar Rd; mains Rs185-845; ☻ lunch & 7-10.30pm) As you'd expect from Varanasi's best hotel, this is one of the city's top restaurants. Elegant without being stuffy, Varuna's specialities include classic North Indian and Afghan dishes, the sumptuous maharaja thali and tandoor kebabs. There's live sitar and tabla music every evening.

Drinking & Entertainment

Side-by-side **wine and beer shops** (Map p442; ☻ 10am-10pm) lie discreetly on Shivala Rd and others are dotted around the city away from the river. Note that it is frowned upon to drink alcohol on or near the holy Ganges. For bars, head to midrange and top-end hotels away from the ghats.

Prinsep Bar (Map p442; Gateway Hotel Ganges, Raja Bazaar Rd) For a quiet drink with a dash of history try this tiny bar, named after James Prinsep, who drew wonderful illustrations of Varanasi's ghats and temples. A Kingfisher is Rs185, cocktails Rs200.

The more reasonably priced and very laid-back cafe in the garden at Hotel Surya (p449) is another relaxing place for a drink. Another hotel bar is the Patiala Peg at Hotel Meraden Grand (p449).

The Ganga Fuji Restaurant has nightly live **classical music**, as does Brown Bread Bakery and

Varuna Restaurant at Gateway Hotel Ganges (p449).

The International Music Centre Ashram (Map p444; p446) has **concerts** (Rs50) on Wednesday and Saturday evenings.

Shopping

Varanasi is justifiably famous for silk brocades and beautiful Benares saris, but being led by touts and rickshaw drivers to a silk shop is all part of the Varanasi shuffle and virtually everyone involved will try to rip you off. Don't believe much of what the silk salesmen tell you about the relative quality of products, even in government emporiums. Instead, shop around and judge for yourself.

Varanasi is also a good place to shop for sitars (starting from Rs3000) and tablas (from Rs2500), but talk to musicians first, for example at Ganga Fuji Restaurant or Ankit Music House. The cost depends primarily on the type of wood used. Mango is cheapest, while teak and vijaysar (a wild Indian herb, the bark of which is used in ayurvedic medicine) are of the highest quality.

Ingenious locally made toys, Bhadohi carpets, brass ornaments, perfumes and textiles are other popular purchases.

Mehrotra Silk Factory (Map p442; ☎ 2200189; www .mehrotrasilk.com; ☯ 10am-8pm) Tucked away down a tiny alleyway near the Varanasi Junction train station, this pocket-sized, fixed-priced shop is a fun place to buy good-quality silk scarves (from Rs250), saris (from Rs1500) and

bedspread sets (from Rs5000). Turn right out of the station, take the first major left turn, then turn left just before the iway Internet cafe and it's down a small alleyway on your left.

Baba Blacksheep (Map p442; ☎ 2454342; Bhelpura) Another reasonable option for silk shopping, with similar prices to Mehrotra Silk Factory.

Shri Gandhi Ashram Khadi (Map p442; Khabir Chaura Rd; ☯ 10.30am-7pm) On the 1st floor of the row of shops opposite the post office, this unassuming branch stocks shirts, kurta pyjamas, saris and head scarves, all made from the famous khadi fabric (below), and offers a tailoring service. There's another branch (called Khadi Gramodyog) near the university.

Benares Art & Culture (Map p442; Shivala Rd; ☯ 10am-8pm Mon-Sat) This centuries-old haveli (traditional, ornately decorated residence) stocks quality carvings, sculptures and art, all made by local artists. Prices are fixed.

Getting There & Away

AIR

From Varanasi's Babatpur airport, **Indian Airlines** (Map p442; ☎ 2502527; ☯ 9.30am-5pm Mon-Sat) has daily flights to Delhi (from Rs3675), Mumbai (from Rs7705) and Kathmandu (from Rs7275). **Jet Airways** (Map p442; ☎ 2506444; Krishnayatan Bldg, Kennedy Rd, Cantonment; ☯ 9.30am-6pm Mon-Sat) flies to Delhi (from Rs3885) and Khajuraho (from Rs4765).

BUS

Varanasi's small but chaotic **bus station** (Map p442; ☎ 2203476) is a few hundred metres east

---

GANDHI'S CLOTH

More than 80 years ago Mahatma Gandhi sat by his spinning wheel and urged Indians to support the freedom movement by ditching their foreign-made clothing and turning to khadi – homespun cloth. Like the spinning wheel itself, khadi became a symbol of the struggle for freedom and of Indian independence, and the fabric is still closely associated with politics. The government-run, nonprofit group Khadi and Village Industries Commission (☎ 022-26714320; www.kvic.org.in; Gramodaya, 3 Irla Rd, Vile Parle (West), Mumbai) serves to promote khadi, most politicians still wear it and the Indian flag is only supposed to be made from khadi cloth. In recent years the fashion world too has taken a growing interest in this simple fabric, which is usually cotton, but can also be silk or wool.

We list khadi outlets in Varanasi (above), Agra (p421), Bhopal (p693) and Delhi (p154), but you'll find them all over India. They are simple, no-nonsense places from which to pick up genuine Indian clothing such as kurta (long, collarless shirt), pyjamas, headscarves and saris, and branches like the excellent one in Delhi's Connaught Place also sell handicrafts made from khadi. Prices are reasonable – expect to pay Rs150 for a full-length kurta – and for the 90 days following Gandhi's birthday (2 October) all khadi is discounted, usually by 30%. Most outlets also have a tailoring service.

of Varanasi Junction train station. Frequent express buses run to Allahabad (non-AC/AC Rs76/112, three hours), Gorakhpur (Rs121/191, seven hours) and Lucknow (Rs165/272, 8½ hours). Four daily buses go to Faizabad (Rs132, seven hours) between 6.30am and 1.30pm, and one early-morning bus runs direct to Khajuraho (Rs259, 12 hours, 5am).

Buses to Sarnath (Rs10, 40 minutes) leave from outside the Varanasi Junction train station (although you'll need a great deal of patience to catch one), as do shared jeeps to Mughal Serai train station (Rs20).

TRAIN
Luggage theft has been reported on trains to and from Varanasi so you should take extra care. A few years ago there were reports of drugged food and drink, so it's probably still best to politely decline any offers from strangers.

Varanasi Junction train station (Map p442; ☎ 132), also known as Varanasi Cantonment (Cantt) train station, is the main station. Foreign tourist quota tickets (p1189) must be purchased at the **Foreign Tourist Centre** (⏱ 8am-8pm Mon-Sat, 8am-2pm Sun), a ticket counter just past the UP Tourism office, on your right as you exit the station.

There are several daily trains to Allahabad (although, apart from the 5am, all are afternoon trains), Gorakhpur and Lucknow. A few daily trains leave for New Delhi and Kolkata, but only one daily train goes to Agra. Only the night train to Satna (11.20pm) connects with the direct buses to Khajuraho. See table, below.

Note that some of the faster trains between Delhi and Kolkata, as well as trains from Darjeeling, go to **Mughal Serai train station** (☎ 255703), 12km southeast of Varanasi. Shared jeeps (Rs20, 40 minutes) are the easiest way to travel between the two stations.

TO/FROM NEPAL
From Varanasi's bus station there are regular services to Sunauli (non-AC/AC Rs172/215, 10 hours) until 8pm.

By train, go to Gorakhpur then transfer to a Sunauli bus.

Indian Airlines has direct flights to Kathmandu (Rs7275). Nepali visas are available on arrival.

Getting Around
TO/FROM THE AIRPORT
Babatpur Airport (☎ 2622081) is 22km northwest of the city. An autorickshaw costs Rs150, a taxi Rs350.

BICYCLE
You can hire bikes (per day Rs20) from a small cycle repair shop (Map p442) near Assi Ghat.

CYCLE-RICKSHAW
Rough prices from Godaulia Crossing include Assi Ghat Rs20, Benares Hindu University Rs30 and Varanasi Junction train station Rs20. Be prepared for hard bargaining.

TAXI & AUTORICKSHAW
Prepaid booths for taxis and autos are outside Varanasi Junction train station. Prices from here will give you a marker for bargaining elsewhere. Prices include Assi Ghat auto/taxi Rs60/200, Benares Hindu University Rs90/250, Sarnath Rs80/200, Mughal Serai train station Rs200/360, or a half-day tour Rs300/500 or full-day tour Rs500/800.

HANDY TRAINS FROM VARANASI

Destination	Train no & name	Fare (Rs)	Duration (hr)	Departures
Agra	4853/4863 Marudhar Exp	250/712/976	13	5.20pm
Allahabad	4005 Lichchavi Exp	121/241/317	3¼	3.45pm
Gorakhpur	5003 Chaurichaura Exp	134/345/468	6½	12.30am
Jabalpur	1062/1066 MFP/DBG-LTT Exp	215/574/786	10	11.20pm
Kolkata (Howrah)*	2334 Vibhuti Exp	315/831	14	6pm
Lucknow**	4235 BSB-BE Exp	163/429/481	7½	11.45pm
New Delhi	2559 Shiv Ganga Exp	311/820/1114	12	7.15pm
Satna	1062/1066 MFP/DBG-LTT Exp	157/411/560	7	11.20pm

All fares are sleeper/3AC/2AC; *sleeper/3AC/1st class; **sleeper/3AC

SARNATH
☎ 0542

Buddha came to Sarnath to preach his message of the middle way to nirvana after he achieved enlightenment at Bodhgaya and gave his famous first sermon here. In the 3rd century BC Ashoka had magnificent stupas and monasteries erected as well as an engraved pillar. When Chinese traveller Xuan Zang dropped by in AD 640, Sarnath boasted a 100m-high stupa and 1500 monks living in large monasteries. However, soon after, Buddhism went into decline and, when Muslim invaders destroyed and desecrated the city's buildings, Sarnath disappeared altogether. It was rediscovered by British archaeologists in 1835.

Today it's one of the four important sites on the Buddhist circuit (along with Bodhgaya, Kushinagar and Lumbini in Nepal), and attracts followers from around the world. An easy day trip from Varanasi, Sarnath is also a peaceful place to stay.

Information

iway Internet (per hr Rs25; ⊙ 7.30am-9pm)
Modern Reception Centre (MRC; Ashoka Marg; ⊙ 10am-5pm Mon-Sat) Tourist information; opposite the museum.
Post office (⊙ 8am-4pm Mon-Sat)

Sights

DHAMEKH STUPA & MONASTERY RUINS

Set in a peaceful **park** (Indian/foreigner Rs5/100, video Rs25; ⊙ dawn-dusk) of monastery ruins is the impressive 34m **Dhamekh Stupa**, which marks the spot where the Buddha preached his first sermon. The floral and geometric carvings are 5th century AD, but some of the brickwork dates back as far as 200 BC.

Nearby is a 3rd-century BC **Ashoka Pillar** with an edict engraved on it. It once stood 15m tall and had the famous four-lion capital (now in the museum) perched on top of it, but all that remains are five fragments of its base.

CHAUKHANDI STUPA

This large ruined **stupa** (⊙ dawn-dusk) dates back to the 5th century AD, and marks the spot where Buddha met his first disciples. The incongruous tower on top of the stupa is Mughal and was constructed here in the

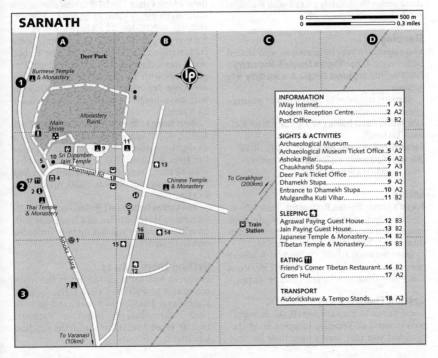

SARNATH

0 _____ 500 m
0 _____ 0.3 miles

Deer Park

Burmese Temple & Monastery

Monastery Ruins

Main Shrine

Sri Digamber Jain Temple

Dharmapal Rd

Chinese Temple & Monastery

To Gorakhpur (200km)

Thai Temple & Monastery

Ashoka Marg

Train Station

To Varanasi (10km)

INFORMATION
iWay Internet.................................1 A3
Modern Reception Centre.................2 A2
Post Office....................................3 B2

SIGHTS & ACTIVITIES
Archaeological Museum.....................4 A2
Archaeological Museum Ticket Office..5 A2
Ashoka Pillar.................................6 A2
Chaukhandi Stupa..........................7 A3
Deer Park Ticket Office....................8 B1
Dhamekh Stupa.............................9 A2
Entrance to Dhamekh Stupa............10 A2
Mulgandha Kuti Vihar....................11 B2

SLEEPING 🛏
Agrawal Paying Guest House..........12 B3
Jain Paying Guest House...............13 B2
Japanese Temple & Monastery........14 B2
Tibetan Temple & Monastery..........15 B3

EATING 🍴
Friend's Corner Tibetan Restaurant...16 B2
Green Hut...................................17 A2

TRANSPORT
Autorickshaw & Tempo Stands........18 A2

16th century to commemorate the visit of Emperor Humayun.

MULGANDHA KUTI VIHAR & DEER PARK

This modern **temple** (☎ 2585595; ⏱ 4-11.30am & 1.30-8pm; photo Rs20, video Rs50) was completed in 1931 by the Mahabodhi Society. Buddha's first sermon is chanted daily, starting between 6pm and 7pm depending on the season. A **bodhi tree** growing outside was transplanted in 1931 from the tree in Anuradhapura, Sri Lanka, which in turn is said to be the offspring of the original tree in Bodhgaya under which Buddha attained enlightenment.

Behind the temple is a large **deer park** (admission Rs2; ⏱ dawn-dusk) together with some aviaries and a crocodile pool.

ARCHAEOLOGICAL MUSEUM

This fully modernised, 100-year-old sandstone **museum** (admission Rs2; ⏱ 10am-5pm Sat-Thu) houses wonderfully displayed ancient treasures such as the very well preserved 3rd-century BC lion capital from the Ashoka pillar, which has been adopted as India's national emblem, and a huge, 2000-year-old stone umbrella, ornately carved with Buddhist symbols.

Sleeping

You can stay in very basic rooms, with shared bathrooms, at the **Tibetan Temple & Monastery** (r Rs100) or the **Japanese Temple & Monastery** (r by donation).

Sarnath has several places in the paying–guest house scheme, including:

Jain Paying Guest House (☎ 2595621; d Rs100-350) Simple but friendly.

Agrawal Paying Guest House (☎ 221007; r Rs400-500) Magical place with a refined owner and spotless rooms overlooking a beautiful garden.

Eating

Friend's Corner Tibetan Restaurant (mains Rs25-40; ⏱ 7am-8.30pm) A cute restaurant-cafe with smiley staff that does a great *momo* (Tibetan dumpling). Near Agrawal guest house.

Green Hut (meals Rs15-60; ⏱ 7am-9pm) A breezy open-sided restaurant opposite the museum that offers dosa, snacks and chicken dishes.

Getting There & Away

Local buses to Sarnath (Rs10, 40 minutes) pass in front of Varanasi Junction train station, but you may wait a long time for one.

An autorickshaw costs about Rs70 from the train station.

GORAKHPUR

☎ 0551 / pop 624,570

There's little to see in Gorakhpur itself, but this well-connected transport hub is a short hop from the pilgrimage centre of Kushinagar – the place where Buddha died – making it a possible stopover on the road between Varanasi and Nepal.

Information & Orientation

Gorakhpur's train station is a convenient one-stop place for information. Inside is the helpful **UP Tourism office** (☎ 2335450; ⏱ 10am-5pm Mon-Sat) and just outside on the concourse is a State Bank of India ATM and the **Railtel Cyber Express** (per hr Rs23; ⏱ 9am-9pm).

For the main bus stand, come out of the train station and keep walking straight for about 300m. For Varanasi buses you need the Katchari bus stand, about 3km further south.

Sleeping & Eating

Hotel Adarsh Palace (☎ 2201912; hotel.adarshpalace@ rediffmail.com; Railway Station Rd; dm Rs150, s Rs300-400, d500, with AC Rs700-800; ▨) There's something for everyone at this smart place opposite the train station and to the left a bit. The 10-bed dorm has lockers above each bed, cheap singles come with TV and bathroom and there are some decent-quality AC rooms too. As with most hotels here, checkout is available 24 hours.

Hotel Sunrise (☎ 2209076; s Rs200, d Rs300-350, with AC Rs550; ▨) If Adarsh is full, you'll find a host of slightly shabbier hotels directly opposite the train station. This is the least shabby, with cleaner rooms than most and a rooftop restaurant (mains Rs30 to Rs70; open 11am to 11pm).

New Varden Restaurant (⏱ 8am-10pm; mains Rs25-60) Next to Hotel Sunrise, this is popular with travellers and they will box up your order for onward journeys.

Getting There & Away

Frequent bus services run from the main bus stand to Faizabad (Rs84, five hours), Kushinagar (Rs30, two hours) and Sunauli (Rs56, three hours). Buses to Varanasi (Rs120, seven hours) leave from the Katchari bus stand.

There are six daily trains to Varanasi (sleeper/3AC, Rs134/345, 5½ hours), including one slower, cheaper night train (No 549, seven hours, 11.10pm). A number of daily trains also leave for Lucknow (sleeper/3AC Rs166/412, six hours) and Delhi (Rs317/837, 14 hours) and one for Kolkata (No 3020, Rs312/848, 1pm, 24 hours). Counter 811 serves foreigners.

KUSHINAGAR
☎ 05564 / pop 17,982

One of the four main pilgrimage sites marking Buddha's life – the others being Lumbini (Nepal), Bodhgaya and Sarnath – Kushinagar is where Buddha died. There are several peaceful, modern temples where you can stay, chat with monks or simply contemplate your place in the world, and there are three main historical sights, including the simple but wonderfully serene stupa where Buddha is said to have been cremated.

Plans to build the world's tallest statue here – a 152m-tall bronze Buddha, complete with education centre, hospital, temples, museum and library – were still in the pipeline when we visited. See www.maitreyaproject.org for the latest.

Information

The tiny **UP Tourism** (10am-5pm Mon-Sat) is opposite the Mahasukhamdadachan Thargyi Pagoda. You'll find a couple of private money changers here, but no ATMs.

Sights

In recent years all the major Buddhist communities of the world have built temples here and they are peaceful places to visit. There are also three main sights of historical interest, all free and open from dawn to dusk.

RAMABHAR STUPA

Architecturally, this half-ruined, 15m-high stupa is little more than a large, dome-shaped clump of red bricks, but there is an unmistakable aura about this place which is hard to ignore. This is where Buddha's body is said to have been cremated and monks and pilgrims can often be seen meditating by the palm-lined path that leads around the stupa.

MAHAPARINIRVANA TEMPLE

The highlight of this modest temple set among extensive lawns with a circumambulatory path, is its serene 5th-century reclining Buddha, unearthed in 1876. Six metres long, it depicts Buddha on his ancient death-bed and is one of the world's most moving Buddhist icons. Behind the temple is an ancient 19m-tall stupa, and in the surrounding park is a large bell erected by the Dalai Lama.

MATHAKUAR TEMPLE

This small shrine, set among monastery ruins, marks the spot where Buddha is said to have made his final sermon and now houses a 3m-tall blue-stone Buddha statue, thought to date from the 10th century AD.

Walking Tour

The main places of interest in Kushinagar can be seen on a 2.5km L-shaped walk along Buddha Marg, starting at the triple archway where buses drop you off and ending at Kushinagar's most auspicious spot, Ramabhar Stupa.

The first temple you come across on the left is the Chinese **Linh Son Temple**, an impressive complex that includes a meditation hall and gardens.

Just past Yama Cafe on your left and the UP tourism office on your right is the Burmese temple complex, with its unmistakable golden **Mahasukhamdadachan Thargyi Pagoda**. The pagoda itself contains four Buddha images and the complex includes a school for local children.

Next on your left is the huge grounds of the fifth-century **Mahaparinirvana Temple** (left), opposite which you'll find the Pathik Niwas hotel.

Where the road turns left, you'll see **Mathakuar Temple** (left) in front of you, diagonally opposite which is the small **Tibetan Temple**.

Next door to the Tibetan Temple is the **Buddha Museum** (10.30am-4.30pm Tue-Sun), which exhibits Buddhist relics, sculptures and terracottas unearthed from the Kushinagar region, as well as some Tibetan *thangkas* (rectangular painting on cloth) and Mughal miniature paintings.

Opposite the museum, the **Japan–Sri Lanka Buddhist Centre** has a beautiful meditation centre in the red-brick stupa at the front.

Continue on, past three flash hotels, to the impressive **Wat Thai complex** (9-11.30am & 1.30-4pm), which features an elaborate temple, beautifully maintained gardens with bonsai-style trees, a monastery and a temple containing a gilded Buddha. There's also a Sunday school and health clinic, each of which welcomes visitors.

From here it's a lovely 10-minute walk past villagers' homes set among rice and sugarcane fields until you reach Kushinagar's most auspicious site – the ruins of the **Ramabhar Stupa** (p455). Cycle-rickshaws (Rs10) can take you back to the main road.

Activities

Yama Cafe organises a so-called **Holy Hike** (incl guide, food, water & return transport Rs750), a 13km-walk that takes in some of the area's historical sights as well as local villages and a school in the surrounding farmland.

Sleeping & Eating

All three top-end hotels are closed from 1 April to 1 October.

Pathik Niwas (☎ 273045; s Rs500-600, with AC Rs1400-1500, d Rs 600-700, with AC Rs1700-1800); 🕸) Opposite the Mahasukhamdadachan Thargyi Pagoda, this UP Tourism hotel has rooms set around pleasant gardens. Be aware that the pricey AC rooms are the same as the cheaper rooms, only with AC. Offers meals (Rs40 to Rs125).

Lotus Nikko Hotel (☎ 274403; s/d Rs3800/4500; 🕸) The best value of Kushinagar's three top-end hotels, Lotus Nikko has huge rooms with din-ing table, sofa and chairs. There's a restaurant (meals Rs500) and a Japanese bath house.

Yama Cafe (🕙 7am-8pm, mains Rs25-50) Run by the welcoming Mr and Mrs Roy, this Kushinagar institution has a traveller-friendly menu which includes toast, omelettes, fried rice and *thukpa* (Tibetan noodle soup) and is the best place to come for information about the area.

Many of the temples which have basic accommodation for pilgrims also welcome tourists, including the following:

Tibetan Temple (r without bathroom by donation) Rooms are run down, but the place is welcoming.

Linh Son Temple (r Rs250) Has simple, clean triples with private bathroom and hot water.

Japan-Sri Lanka Buddhist Centre (☎ 273044; tr/q Rs375/500) Set up for tour groups but has decent quality, clean rooms.

Getting There & Away

Frequent buses to Gorakhpur (Rs30, two hours) will pick you up at the triple archway.

SUNAULI & THE NEPAL BORDER
☎ 05522

Sunauli is a dusty town that offers little more than a bus stop, a couple of hotels, a few shops and a border post. The border is open 24 hours and the crossing is straightforward (below) so most travellers carry on into Nepal without stopping here. There are more facilities in the

---

CROSSING INTO NEPAL

Border Hours

The border is open 24 hours but closes to vehicles at 10pm, and if you arrive in the middle of the night you may have to wake someone to get stamped out of India.

Foreign Exchange

There's a **State Bank of India** (🕙 10am-4pm Mon-Fri, 10am-1pm Sat) in Sunauli and there are foreign-exchange places just across the border on the Nepal side. Note, this will be the last place in Nepal you will be able to change Rs500 or Rs1000 notes. Small denominations of Indian currency are accepted for bus fares on the Nepal side.

Onward Transport

Buses leave all day until around 8pm from the Nepal side of the border for Kathmandu (NRs600, six hours) and Pokhara (NRs500, six hours). A taxi to Kathmandu costs around NRs15,000. Rickshaws (NRs50) can take you from the border to Bhairawa, 4km away, where you can also catch buses to Kathmandu and Pokhara, for the same prices, as well as to Buddha's birthplace, Lumbini (NRs20, 30 minutes).

Visas

Multiple-entry visas (15-/30-/90-day US$25/40/100 – cash, not rupees) are available at the immigration post just across the border. You will need two recent passport photos.

Nepali part of Sunauli; Bhairawa, a further 4km north, is a more substantial town.

Buses drop you 200m from the Indian immigration office, so you can ignore the cycle-rickshaws.

If you're coming from Nepal but miss the last bus to Gorakhpur, then **Hotel Indo-Nepal** (☎ 238142; r without bathroom Rs250, r Rs315-425) has very basic rooms but a more homely atmosphere than the ghost-like **Rahi Tourist Bungalow** (☎ 238201; rahiniranjana@up-tourism.com; dm Rs75, s/d from Rs250/300, with AC Rs550/650; 🌀) a couple of doors down. Rahi, though, has a restaurant. Both are just past the bus stand.

If you're leaving India, the very helpful **Nepal Tourism Board information centre** (☎ 0977 1520197; 🕙 10am-5pm Sun-Fri) is on your right, in no-man's land.

The Nepali side of Sunauli has a few cheap hotels, outdoor restaurants and a more upbeat atmosphere, but most travellers prefer to stay in Bhairawa, or get straight on a bus to Kathmandu or Pokhara.

Regular buses run from Sunauli to Gorakhpur (Rs56, three hours, until 9pm) from where you can catch trains to Varanasi. A couple of early morning (6am and 6.30am) and afternoon (3.30pm to 6.30pm) buses run direct to Varanasi (Rs172, 11 hours).

Be wary of buying 'through' tickets from Kathmandu or Pokhara to Varanasi. Some travellers report being intimidated into buying another ticket once over the border. Travelling in either direction, it's better to take a local bus to the border, walk across and take another onward bus (pay the conductor on board).

Uttarakhand

High mountains, holy rivers, remnants of the British Raj (British rule) and renowned ashrams: for a small state, Uttarakhand packs in an incredible amount. You can take yoga classes at an ashram in Rishikesh and white-water raft down the Ganges one day, and trek in the shadow of the Himalaya the next. Walk with pilgrims to ancient temples near the source of the Ganges and Yamuna Rivers, or take *puja* (offerings or prayers) with thousands of devotees on the ghats (steps or landings on a river) at Haridwar. Put up your feet and relax in Raj-era hill stations, or ride an elephant and take your camera on a hunt for tigers at Corbett Tiger Reserve or Rajaji National Park. If you get your timing right, it's all possible in Uttarakhand.

This is a region where nature reigns – rolling forest-clad hills, snow-topped 6000m peaks, rivers, waterfalls, lakes and glaciers. The state is 90% hills and 80% forest. The sacred Ganges River, which rises at Gaumukh Glacier in the far north, winds its way down to the plains via the significant pilgrimage centres of Gangotri, Rishikesh and Haridwar.

The high Himalaya attracts trekkers, mountaineers and skiers as well as pilgrims on the Char Dham and Hem Kund routes. But it's Rishikesh that draws most foreign tourists for its ashrams, yoga, meditation and all-round spirituality. Whatever your interest, square for square, this is one of India's richest regions for travellers.

HIGHLIGHTS

- Grab a backpack and **trek** (opposite) to remote, pristine glaciers and passes, that are surrounded by the mightiest mountain range on the planet

- Join the stream of pilgrims on the **Char Dham** (p483) and **Hem Kund** (p485) treks to remote temples, holy rivers and sacred lakes

- Scout for rare Bengal tigers and ride an elephant in **Corbett Tiger Reserve** (p487)

- Get your asanas and chakras sorted at **Rishikesh** (p475), the yoga and ashram capital of the universe

- Cool off in a scenic Raj-era hill station in **Mussoorie** (p465) or **Nainital** (p489), in the Himalayan foothills

- Trek into the sublime **Valley of Flowers** (p485), then visit charming **Mana village** (p486), in the shadow of the Himalaya

Mana village ★
Hem Kund & Valley of the Flowers ★
★ Mussoorie
★ Rishikesh
Corbett Tiger Reserve ★
★ Nainital

FAST FACTS

Population 8,479,562

Area 51,125 sq km

Capital Dehra Dun

Main languages Hindi, Garhwali and Kumaoni

When to go May to July and September to November; in lowlands (ie Rishikesh, Corbett Tiger Reserve and Rajaji National Park) October to March

---

History

Uttarakhand consists of the culturally distinct Garhwal (in the west) and Kumaon (east) districts. Over the centuries various dynasties have dominated the region, including the Guptas, Kuturyi and Chand rajas (kings). In the 18th century the Nepalese Gurkhas attacked first the kingdom of Kumaon, then Garhwal, prompting the British to step in and take most of the region as part of the Treaty of Sigauli in 1817.

After Independence the region was merged with Uttar Pradesh, but following a vocal separatist movement, the present-day state of Uttaranchal was formed in 2000. In 2007 the state was officially renamed Uttarakhand, a traditional name meaning 'northern country'.

Climate

The hill stations can be visited all year, although winters (December to February) are freezing cold. Further north, the main trekking and pilgrim season runs between April and late October or early November, with a break in July and August when the monsoon rains arrive and landslides block roads. As in all mountainous regions the weather is fickle and can vary greatly during any season. Look at the altitude to get an idea of likely temperatures. Rishikesh and Haridwar can be visited year-round (but it's best from October to March), while the main season at Corbett Tiger Reserve and Rajaji National Park is November to May.

Information

Most towns in the region have an Uttarakhand Tourism office, however the main responsibility for the region's tourism rests with the **Garhwal Mandal Vikas Nigam** (GMVN; www.gmvnl. com), which covers the western Garhwal district; and **Kumaon Mandal Vikas Nigam** (KMVN; www .kmvn.org), which covers the eastern Kumaon district.

Activities

TREKKING

Whether walking through the hills and forests of Kumaon or tackling a 3500m mountain pass, Uttarakhand provides some of India's finest and most accessible trekking country. In the Garhwal district, the Char Dham pilgrim routes mean that public transport to many treks is excellent. But you can also get away from the crowds and head to spectacularly remote places like Har ki Dun Valley in Uttarakhand's north, or the magical Nanda Devi Sanctuary, in the northeast. In the eastern Kumaon region, nudging up against the Tibetan border, you can tackle challenging Pindari or Milam Glacier treks. Note that there are certain restrictions on trekking in Garhwhal and in most cases treks must be organised through a registered trekking outfit.

The best (safest) time to trek is either the premonsoon period (mid-May until the end of June), or the postmonsoon season (mid-September to mid-October). In July and August the major problem is landslides that cut roads to the trailheads and cause long delays. The Char Dham temples and other high-altitude treks close in winter (late November to March).

Government-run **GMVN** (www.gmvnl.com) and **KMVN** (www.kmvn.org) organise all-inclusive treks for Rs1000 to Rs3000 per person per day. There are plenty of reliable private trekking companies offering much the same thing for Rs1000 to Rs4000 a day, depending on group numbers and the level of food and service required. Depending on the region you can organise your own trek: guides costs around Rs500 a day, cooks Rs500 and porters Rs300. Ponies may also be available for hire on some treks. On *yatra* (pilgrimage) trails and on popular treks a guide is not necessary, but on more-remote treks it is recommended for safety and to support the local economy. Trekking maps are available from the **Survey of India** (www .surveyofindia.gov.in).

RAFTING & KAYAKING

White-water rafting on the fast-flowing Ganges and Alaknanda Rivers is fast growing in popularity, with a dozen or more companies setting up riverside rafting camps from October to May. Rishikesh is the main place to organise rafting trips (p478) but agencies in Joshimath also arrange trips, usually starting from Rudraprayag. Kayaking is also gaining popularity and there's a recommended outfit in Rishikesh.

SKIING

India's premier ski resort is Auli, near Joshimath in the northern Garhwal district. Although it's a small resort with only one chairlift and one rope tow, the snow is reliable from January to March.

YOGA & MEDITATION

Yoga and meditation are big business in Rishikesh (p477), where you can stay in an ashram or just turn up to classes at one of dozens of yoga centres. Haridwar also has some less-touristed ashrams.

Getting There & Away

Uttarakhand's main airport is Jolly Grant, near Dehra Dun, though there are only a handful of flights from Delhi. Dehra Dun, Haridwar, Ramnagar and Haldwani (for Nainital) can be reached by train from Delhi, and there are rail connections to other cities such as Varanasi and Amritsar. To reach most other towns in Uttarakhand requires long bus rides.

Getting Around

Although Dehra Dun, Haridwar, Rishikesh and Ramnagar are accessible by train, tough old government buses are the main means of travelling around Uttarakhand. Because of the popular pilgrim routes, they run to very remote areas deep in the Garhwal Himalaya

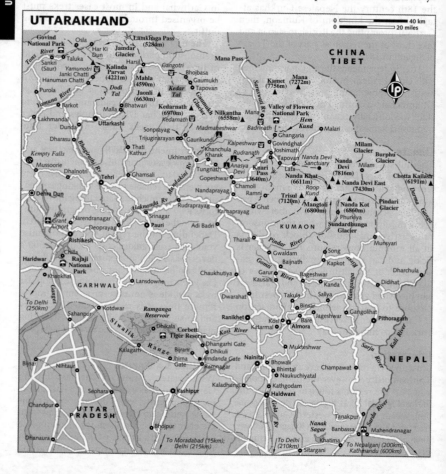

FESTIVALS IN UTTARAKHAND

Makar Sakranti day (Jan; Uttarkashi, p482) Religious images are borne aloft on palanquins and carried into town from outlying villages.

Magh Mela (Jan & Feb; Haridwar, p469) Hundreds of thousands more pilgrims than usual come to bathe in the soul-cleansing Ganges during this huge annual religious fair; every six years the Ardh Kumbh Mela is held; and millions of pilgrims attend the mega Kumbh Mela every 12 years – the next is 2010.

International Yoga Festival (Feb/Mar; Rishikesh, p479) Yoga and meditation masters from around the world converge and give demonstrations and lectures.

Shivaratri (usually Mar; Tapkeshwar Temple, p463) A festival celebrated in style with carnival rides and stalls at a picturesque riverside cave temple on the outskirts of Dehra Dun.

Nanda Devi Fair (Sep; Almora, p495) During this five-day fair, thousands of devotees parade the image of the goddess around and watch dancing and other cultural shows.

---

for much of the year. In addition, a network of crowded share 4WDs criss-crosses the state, linking remote towns and villages in the hills to important road junctions and bus routes. They tout for customers on the highway in the direction of the next town or transport hub, but usually don't leave until full. Although they're supposed to carry 10 passengers, a few more will often squeeze in. Drivers charge slightly more than the equivalent bus ride. Pay 10 times the share-taxi rate and you can hire the whole vehicle and travel in comfort.

Some of the hairpin mountain roads are frightening to travel on – especially when you're on a bus being driven by a particularly impatient and insane driver – and are subject to landslides (often after the monsoon). On most roads don't expect to cover more than 25km in an hour.

DEHRA DUN
☎ 0135 / pop 527,859 / elev 700m

Best known for the institutions the British left behind – the huge Forest Research Institute Museum, the Indian Military Academy, the Wildlife Institute of India and the Survey of India – the capital of Uttarakhand is a hectic, congested city sprawling in the Doon Valley between the Himalayan foothills and the Shivalik Range.

A once green and pleasant town of rice and tea gardens, Dehra Dun has lost much of its charm, but you don't have to go far out of the city centre to find relief from the traffic. Rishikesh and Mussoorie are both just over an hour away, so most travellers merely pass through, but Dehra Dun is worth a stop for its lively Paltan bazaar and vibrant Tibetan community south of the city in Clement Town. It's also a transit point for Himachal Pradesh.

Information

BOOKSHOPS

English Book Depot (☎ 2655192; www.english bookdepot.com; 15 Rajpur Rd; ⊕ 9.30am-8.30pm) CDs, trekking books and maps are available, and there is a Barista cafe attached.

Natraj Booksellers (17 Rajpur Rd; ⊕ 10.30am-1.30pm & 3-8pm Mon-Sat) Specialises in ecology, spirituality, local books and local author Ruskin Bond.

EMERGENCY

Ambulance ☎ 2650102
Police ☎ 2653333

INTERNET ACCESS

Cyber Park (per hr Rs15; ⊕ 10.30am-8pm) Located near the clock tower.

iWay (Hotel Grand, Shri Laxmi Plaza, 64 Gandhi Rd; per hr Rs30; ⊕ 10am-8pm)

MEDICAL SERVICES

Doon College Hospital (☎ 2760330; General Mahadev Singh Rd)

MONEY

The banks that are located on Rajpur Rd exchange travellers cheques and currency, and there are numerous ATMs that accept foreign credit cards.

POST

Main post office (Rajpur Rd; ⊕ 10am-6pm Mon-Fri, 10am-1pm Sat)

TOURIST INFORMATION

Uttarakhand Tourism office (☎ 2653217; 45 Gandhi Rd; ⊕ 10am-5pm Mon-Sat) This is the local tourist office – you will find it attached to the Hotel Drona. It also has a tourist-information counter located at the train station.

UTTARAKHAND

DEHRA DUN

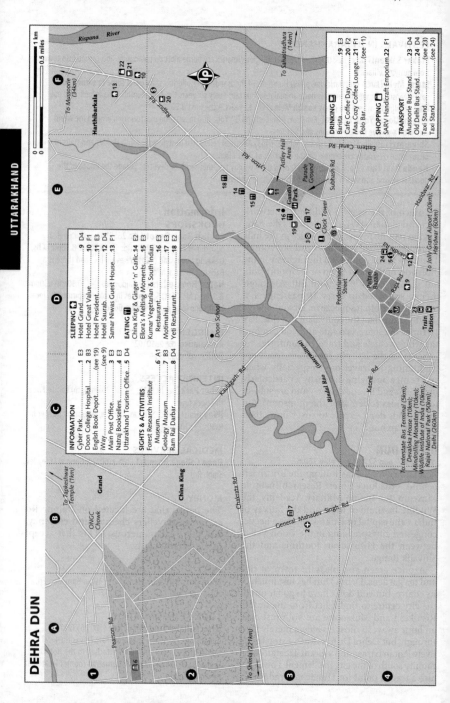

INFORMATION

Cyber Park...........................	1 E3
Doon College Hospital...........	2 B3
English Book Depot...............	(see 19)
iWay..................................	(see 9)
Main Post Office..................	3 E3
Natraj Booksellers................	4 E3
Uttarakhand Tourism Office.....	5 D4

SIGHTS & ACTIVITIES

Forest Research Institute	
Museum..........................	6 A1
Geology Museum..................	7 B3
Ram Rai Darbar....................	8 D4

SLEEPING

Hotel Grand.......................	9 D4
Hotel Great Value.................	10 F1
Hotel President...................	11 E3
Hotel Saurab.......................	12 D4
Samar Niwas Guest House......	13 F1

EATING

China King & Ginger 'n' Garlic.	14 E2
Ellora's Melting Moments........	15 E3
Kumar Vegetarian & South Indian	
Restaurant.......................	16 E3
Motimahal..........................	17 B3
Yeti Restaurant....................	18 E2

DRINKING

Barista..............................	19 E3
Cafe Coffee Day..................	20 F2
Maa Cozy Coffee Lounge.......	21 F1
Polo Bar............................	(see 11)

SHOPPING

SARV Handicraft Emporium......	22 F1

TRANSPORT

Mussoorie Bus Stand............	23 D4
Old Delhi Bus Stand..............	24 D4
Taxi Stand.........................	(see 23)
Taxi Stand.........................	(see 24)

Sights & Activities

FOREST RESEARCH INSTITUTE MUSEUM

The prime attraction of this **museum** (☎ 2759382; www.icfre.org; admission Rs10, guide Rs50; ☺ 9.30am-1pm & 1.30-5.30pm) is the building itself. Set in a 500-hectare park, the institute – where most of India's forest officers are trained – is larger than Buckingham Palace and is one of the Raj's grandest buildings. Built between 1924 and 1929, designed by CG Blomfield, this red-brick colossus has Mughal towers, perfectly formed arches and Roman columns in a series of quadrangles edged by elegant cloisters. Six huge halls have rather old-fashioned and dry displays on every aspect of forestry in India. Highlights include beautiful animal, bird and plant paintings by Afshan Zaidi, exhibits on the medicinal uses of trees, and a cross-section of a 700-year-old deodar tree. A return autorickshaw from the city centre, including waiting time, costs around Rs150.

RAM RAI DARBAR

This unique **mausoleum** (Paltan Bazaar; admission free; ☺ dawn-dusk) is made of white marble, and the four smaller tombs in the garden courtyard are those of Ram Rai's four wives. The entrance gate is adorned with colourful murals. Ram Rai, the errant son of the seventh Sikh guru, Har Rai, was excommunicated by his father. He formed his own Udasi sect, which still runs schools and hospitals. When Ram Rai died in 1687, one of his supporters, Mughal emperor Aurangzeb, ordered the building of the mausoleum. As in other gurdwaras (Sikh temples), a free communal lunch of dhal, rice and chapatis is offered to anyone who wants it, although a donation is appreciated.

GEOLOGY MUSEUM

The Wadia Institute of Himalayan Geology has a small **museum** (☎ 2627387; 37 General Mahadev Singh Rd; admission free; ☺ 9.30am-1pm & 2.15-5.15pm Mon-Fri) that covers local rocks, glaciers and earthquakes. Fossils include a dinosaur egg and stacks of teeth.

GREAT STUPA & BUDDHA STATUE

The region around Dehra Dun is home to a thriving Tibetan Buddhist community, mainly focused on the **Mindrolling Monastery** (☎ 2640556; www.mindrolling.org), about 10km south of the centre in Clement Town. Everything about the monastery is on a grand scale: it boasts a large college, manicured gardens and the

five-storey **Great Stupa** (admission free; ☺ 5am-9pm). At over 60m tall, it's believed to be the world's tallest stupa and contains a series of shrine rooms displaying relics, murals and Tibetan art. Presiding over the monastery is the impressive 35m-high gold **Buddha Statue**, dedicated to the Dalai Lama.

The streets around the monastery have several Tibetan-run guest houses and cafes. Take *vikram* (large tempo) 5 from the city centre (Rs5). An autorickshaw costs about Rs150.

TAPKESHWAR TEMPLE

In a scenic setting on the banks of the Tons Nadi River, you'll find an unusual and popular Shiva **shrine** (☺ dawn-dusk) inside a small, dripping cave. The shrine is the site of the popular annual **Shivaratri** festival (see the boxed text, p461). Turn left at the bottom of the steps for the main shrine, and cross the bridge over the river to visit another cave shrine where you have to squeeze through a narrow cave to see an image of Mata Vaishno Devi. The temple is about 5km north of the centre.

Sleeping

There are plenty of cheapies along the Haridwar road outside the train station, some charging as little as Rs150 a double, but the better places can be found along Gandhi Rd and Rajpur Rd. There are also some cheap guest houses in the Tibetan colony at Clement Town.

Hotel Grand (☎ 2726563; Shri Laxmi Plaza, 64 Gandhi Rd; dm Rs80, s/d Rs300/550) Not so grand but handy to the train station, rooms in this acceptable place have TV and bucket hot water.

Devaloka House (☎ 9759862769; Clement Town; s/d/tr Rs250/350/450) Part of the Mindrolling Monastery complex, the spotless white rooms here are above the semicircular arcade looking across to the monumental Great Stupa and gardens. Rooms have TV, hot water, a small balcony and tile floors. Check in at Norjin Restaurant.

Hotel Saurab (☎ 2728042; hotelsaurab@hotmail.com; 1 Raja Rd; s/d from Rs550/660, with AC from Rs1200/1550; ☒) With midrange quality at a near-budget price, this neatly furnished, comfortable hotel just off Gandhi Rd is a great deal. All rooms have hot water and TV, and there's a multicuisine restaurant.

our pick **Samar Niwas Guest House** (☎ 2740299; M-16 Chanderlok Colony; d Rs800-1000, with AC Rs1000-1500; ☒) This charming four-room guest house is as cosy and welcoming as it gets. The owners

UTTARAKHAND

are descendants of the Tehri royal family and their home is stuffed full of antiques, artworks and collectibles. Rooms are modern and beautifully presented, and meals, massage and yoga can be arranged. It's in a peaceful residential area just off Rajpur Rd.

Hotel President (☎ 2657082; www.hotelpresident dehradun.com; 6 Astley Hall, Rajpur Rd; s Rs1650-1950, d Rs1900-2200; 🔀) Modern hotel in the popular complex of shops, restaurants and fast-food places known as Astley Hall. Rooms are compact but well appointed. There are two good restaurants and the Polo Bar.

Hotel Great Value (☎ 2744086; www.greatvaluehotel .com; 74C Rajpur Rd; s Rs1750-2750, d Rs2500-3500, ste Rs5700; 🔀 💻) Don't be put off by the silly name: Great Value is an elegant and stylish hotel with marble decor, antique furniture and greenery spicing up the lobby, lounge and garden areas. Rooms have TV, fridge and wi-fi access. Good restaurant, bar and coffee shop.

Eating

Dehra Dun has an eclectic range of restaurants, but by far the best hunting ground is along Rajpur Rd, northeast of the clock tower. The Astley Hall precinct is popular for fast food and has a couple of upmarket bars.

Ellora's Melting Moments (29 Rajpur Rd; mains Rs15-70) Often packed with local families, Ellora's is a fast-food institution serving up pizza, sandwiches, burgers, sweets and lassis (yoghurt-and-iced-water beverages).

Kumar Vegetarian & South Indian Restaurant (15B Rajpur Rd; meals Rs25-75; 🕒 lunch & dinner) Super South Indian dosas (lentil-flour pancakes) and thalis ('all-you-can-eat' meals) are served in this clean, busy restaurant.

China King & Ginger 'n' Garlic (☎ 2655773; 33 Rajpur Rd; mains Rs35-180; 🕒 11.30am-11.30pm; 🔀) Two restaurants in one, this bright, spotless fast-food place specialises in all things Chinese, from dim sum and chicken wings to chow mein. Upstairs, Ginger 'n' Garlic has a more Indian flavour with North Indian veg and nonveg standards. Down below is a branch of New Zealand Natural Ice-cream.

Yeti Restaurant (☎ 2652256; 55A Rajpur Rd; mains Rs55-260; 🕒 lunch & dinner) This intimate little restaurant specialises in spicy Thai and Chinese cuisine with tasty tom yum, green curry and stir-fried prawns. There's a nice little courtyard terrace at the front.

Motimahal (7 Rajpur Rd; mains Rs65-225; 🕒 10am-11pm; 🔀) Locals consistently rate Motimahal

as one of the best midrange diners along Rajpur Rd. An interesting range of veg and nonveg includes Goan fish curry and Afghani *murg* (chicken), along with traditional South Indian fare and Chinese food.

Drinking

Maa Cozy Coffee Lounge (76 Rajpur Rd; 🕒 11am-11pm) Dehra Dun's coolest hang-out, Maa Cozy is an Arabian-style lounge where you can smoke a fruit sheesha (water pipe; Rs150 to Rs185) while reclining on Middle Eastern cushions and rugs. Has a big range of tea, coffee and cold drinks, and the sheesha flavours range from cola to jasmine.

Polo Bar (6 Astley Hall, Rajpur Rd; 🕒 11am-11pm) One of the more salubrious of Dehra Dun's many hotel bars, this one is at Hotel President.

Barista (Rajpur Rd; drinks & snacks Rs10-50; 🕒 9am-10pm) is a popular modern café with board games and an excellent bookshop next door. **Cafe Coffee Day** (Rajpur Rd; 🕒 9am-10pm) is another chain place that does great coffee, shakes and snacks.

Shopping

SARV Handicraft Emporium (☎ 2742141; 78 Rajpur Rd; 🕒 10am-7pm Mon-Sat) This small store has a great range of crafts and clothes with striking designs at reasonable prices. Money raised here benefits women working in Himalayan villages who have few employment opportunities.

The congested but virtually traffic-free street through Paltan Bazaar, running south from the clock tower, is a popular spot for an evening stroll. Here you can pick up everything from cheap clothing and souvenirs to camping and trekking gear.

Getting There & Away

AIR

Kingfisher Airlines (www.flykingfisher.com) flies from Delhi to Dehra Dun's Jolly Grant airport, about 20km east of the city on the Haridwar road. There's one daily morning flight and an additional afternoon flight from Wednesday to Saturday. Internet fares for the one-hour flight start at Rs980. A taxi from the airport costs around Rs500.

BUS

Although a few buses still leave from the Old Delhi bus stand, almost all long-distance buses arrive and depart from the huge, modern Interstate Bus Terminal (ISBT) at Majra,

Destination	Fare (Rs)	Duration (hr)	Frequency
BUSES FROM DEHRA DUN			
Chandigarh	130	6	hourly btwn 5.30am & 5pm
Delhi (deluxe)	240/300AC	7	hourly btwn 6.15am & 12.15am
Delhi (standard)	160	7	hourly btwn 6.30am & 10.30pm
Dharamsala	295	14	12.30pm & 5pm
Haridwar	38	2	half-hourly
Manali	395	14	3pm
Mussoorie (A)	33	1½	half-hourly btwn 6am & 8pm
Nainital	270	12	8 per day
Ramnagar	160	7	4.30am, 5.30am, 12.30pm, 5.30pm & 8.30pm
Rishikesh	29	1½	half-hourly
Shimla	202	10	6am, 8am, 10am, 11.30pm
Uttarkashi	135	8	5.30am

A – buses departing from Mussoorie bus stand. Some go to the Picture Palace bus stand at one end of Mussoorie while others go to the Library bus stand at the other end.

5km south of the city centre. To get there take a local bus (Rs4), *vikram* 5 (Rs4) or an auto-rickshaw (Rs50). A few Mussoorie buses leave from here but most go from the Mussoorie bus stand next to the train station. For more bus details, see the table, above.

TAXI
A taxi to Mussoorie costs Rs450, while a share taxi should cost Rs90 per person; both can be found in front of the train station. Taxis charge Rs700 to Rishikesh and Rs860 to Haridwar.

TRAIN
Dehra Dun is well connected by train to Delhi, and there are a handful of services to Lucknow, Varanasi, Chennai (Madras) and Kolkata (Calcutta). The quickest service linking Dehra Dun and Delhi is the daily *Shatabdi Express* (chair/executive Rs390/780), which leaves New Delhi train station at 6.50am and reaches Dehra Dun at 12.40pm. The return trip leaves Dehra Dun at 5pm.

The daily *Mussoorie Express* (sleeper/3AC/2AC Rs130/365/508, 11 hours) is an overnight service that leaves Delhi Sarai Rohilla station at 9.05pm, arriving at Dehra Dun at 8am. The return trip leaves Dehra Dun at 9.30pm.

The overnight *Dehradun-Amritsar Express* (sleeper/3A Rs127/356, 12 hours) to Amritsar departs daily at 7.40pm.

Getting Around
Hundreds of eight-seater *vikrams* (Rs3 to Rs5 per trip) race along five fixed routes (look at the front for the number). Most useful is

vikram 5, which runs between the ISBT stand, the train station and Rajpur Rd, and as far south as the Tibetan colony at Clement Town. Autorickshaws cost Rs30 for a short distance, Rs80 from ISBT to the city centre or Rs120 per hour for touring around the city.

MUSSOORIE
☎ 0135 / pop 29,319 / elev 2000m
Perched on a ridge 2km high, the 'Queen of Hill Stations' vies with Nainital as Uttarakhand's favourite holiday destination. When the mist clears, views of the green Doon Valley and the distant white-capped Himalayan peaks are superb, and in the hot months the cooler temperatures and fresh mountain air make a welcome break from the plains below. Although Mussoorie's main bazaars can at first seem like a tacky holiday camp for families and honeymooners, there are plenty of walks in the area, interesting Raj-era buildings, and an upbeat atmosphere.

Established by the British in 1823, Mussoorie became hugely popular with the Raj set. The ghosts of that era linger on in the architecture of the churches, libraries, hotels and summer palaces. The town is swamped with visitors between May and July, but at other times many of the 300 hotels have vacancies and their prices drop dramatically.

Orientation
Central Mussoorie consists of two developed areas: Gandhi Chowk (also called Library Bazaar) at the western end and the livelier Kulri Bazaar (Picture Palace) at the eastern

UTTARAKHAND

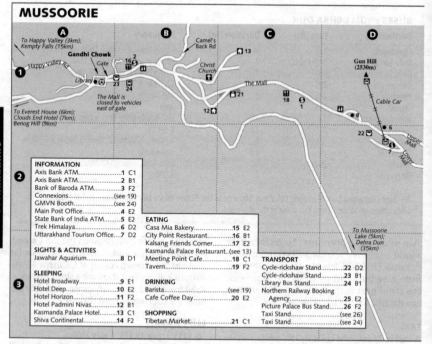

MUSSOORIE

INFORMATION	
Axis Bank ATM	1 C1
Axis Bank ATM	2 B1
Bank of Baroda ATM	3 F2
Connexions	(see 19)
GMVN Booth	(see 24)
Main Post Office	4 E2
State Bank of India ATM	5 E2
Trek Himalaya	6 D2
Uttarakhand Tourism Office	7 D2

SIGHTS & ACTIVITIES	
Jawahar Aquarium	8 D1

SLEEPING	
Hotel Broadway	9 E1
Hotel Deep	10 E2
Hotel Horizon	11 F2
Hotel Padmini Nivas	12 B1
Kasmanda Palace Hotel	13 C1
Shiva Continental	14 F2

EATING	
Casa Mia Bakery	15 E2
City Point Restaurant	16 B1
Kalsang Friends Corner	17 E2
Kasmanda Palace Restaurant	(see 13)
Meeting Point Cafe	18 C1
Tavern	19 F2

DRINKING	
Barista	(see 19)
Cafe Coffee Day	20 E2

SHOPPING	
Tibetan Market	21 C1

TRANSPORT	
Cycle-rickshaw Stand	22 D2
Cycle-rickshaw Stand	23 B1
Library Bus Stand	24 B1
Northern Railway Booking Agency	25 E2
Picture Palace Bus Stand	26 F2
Taxi Stand	(see 26)
Taxi Stand	(see 24)

end, and the two are linked by the (almost) traffic-free 2km Mall. Beyond Kulri Bazaar a narrow road leads 5km to the settlement of Landour.

Information

INTERNET ACCESS
Connexions (the Mall, Kulri Bazaar; per hr Rs60; ☒ 10.30am-10.30pm) Above the Tavern.

MONEY
Axis Bank ATM Along the Mall and at Gandhi Chowk.
Bank of Baroda ATM (Kulri Bazaar)
State Bank of India ATM (the Mall, Kulri Bazaar)
Trek Himalaya (☎ 2630491; Upper Mall; ☒ 9.30am-8pm) Exchanges major currencies and travellers cheques at a fair rate.

POST
Main post office (☎ 2632206; the Mall, Kulri Bazaar; ☒ 9am-5pm Mon-Sat)

TOURIST INFORMATION
GMVN booth (☎ 2631281; Library bus stand; ☒ 10am-5pm Mon-Sat) Can book local tours, treks and far-flung rest houses.

Uttarakhand Tourism office (☎ 2632863; Lower Mall; ☒ 10am-5pm Mon-Sat) Near the cable-car station.

Sights & Activities

GUN HILL
From midway along the Mall, a **cable car** (return Rs55; ☒ 8am-9pm May-Jul & Oct, 10am-6.30pm Aug-Sep & late Nov-Apr) runs up to Gun Hill (2530m), which, on a clear day, has views of several peaks, including Bandarpunch. A steep path also winds up to the viewpoint. The most popular time to go up is an hour or so before sunset and there's a minicarnival atmosphere in season with kids' rides, food stalls, magic shops and honeymooners having their photos taken dressed up in Garhwali costumes.

JAWAHAR AQUARIUM
Just up from the cable-car station, this **aquarium** (the Mall; admission Rs10; ☒ 9am-9pm) is Mussoorie's newest attraction. What may be Uttarakhand's only escalator takes you to eight modest but well-presented tanks containing tropical fish, tiny sharks and red piranha.

UTTARAKHAND

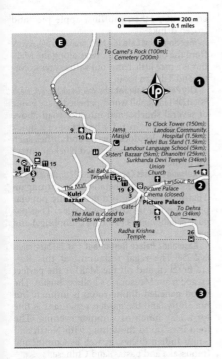

WALKS
When the clouds don't get in the way, the walks around Mussoorie offer great views. **Camel's Back Rd** is a popular 3km promenade from Kulri Bazaar to Gandhi Chowk, and passes a rock formation that looks like a camel. There are a couple of good mountain viewpoints along the way, and you can ride a horse (one way/return Rs120/150) along the trail if you start from the Gandhi Chowk end. An enjoyable, longer walk (5km one way) starts at the Picture Palace Cinema, goes past Union Church and the clock tower to Landour and the Sisters' Bazaar area.

West of Gandhi Chowk, a more demanding walk is to the Jwalaji Temple on **Benog Hill** (about 18km return) via Clouds End Hotel. The walk passes through thick forest and offers some fine views. A slightly shorter walk is to the abandoned **Everest House** (12km return), former residence of Sir George Everest, first surveyor-general of India and namesake of the world's highest mountain. **Trek Himalaya** (☎ 2630491; Upper Mall; ☼ 9.30am-8pm) can organise guides for around Rs650 a day.

Courses
Mussoorie is home to many schools and colleges, including the **Landour Language School** (☎ 2631487; www.landourlanguageschool.com; Landour; ☼ 1st Mon in Feb-2nd Fri in Dec). One of India's leading schools for teaching conversational Hindi at beginner, intermediate and advanced levels, group classes are Rs175 per hour, and private tutorials are Rs275 per hour. There's an enrolment fee of Rs250, and course books are an extra Rs2000.

Tours
GMVN booth (☎ 2631281; Library bus stand; ☼ 10am-5pm Mon-Sat) GMVN organises a number of local bus tours, including Kempty Falls (three-hour tour Rs70), and Dhanoltri, Surkhanda Devi Temple and Mussoorie Lake (full-day tour Rs160). Tours can also be booked at the tourist office on Mall Rd.

Trek Himalaya (☎ 2630491; www.trekhimalaya.com; Upper Mall; ☼ 9.30am-8pm) For around Rs2500 per day, long-time local trekker Neelambar Badoni organises three-day treks to unspoilt Nagtibba as well as customised treks to Dodital, Har ki Dun and Gaumukh Glacier and safaris as far as Ladakh.

Sleeping
The absolute peak season is summer (May to July) when hotel prices shoot to ridiculous heights. There's a mid-season during the honeymoon season around October and November, and over Christmas and New Year. At other times you should be able to get a bargain. The following prices are for the mid-season, unless otherwise specified.

BUDGET
Budget places are few, but most hotels drop their rates to almost budget levels out of season.

Hotel Broadway (☎ 2632243; Camel's Back Rd, Kulri Bazaar; d Rs600-1200, low-season discount 50%) The best of the budget places by a country mile, this historic 1880s wooden hotel with colourful flowerboxes in the windows oozes character without sacrificing comfort. It's in a quiet location but close to the Mall. Room 1 has good views and lovely sunlit bay windows.

Hotel Deep (☎ 2632470; deephotel@hotmail.com; Camel's Back Rd; r from Rs990, low season Rs300-900) Conveniently located next door to Broadway, this candy-striped warren of a place has a huge range of rooms. In the low season, rooms here are pretty good value (not so in peak season), and there's a pleasant terrace with views.

UTTARAKHAND

MIDRANGE & TOP END

Shiva Continental (☎ 2632174; www.shivacon.com; Landour Rd; r Rs1800-3500, low season Rs1250-2500) This slightly eccentric hotel on the road up to Landour has marble decor, sculptures, a shady terrace and so many pot plants that they threaten to take over the place. Carpeted rooms are bright and comfortable, and most have views.

Hotel Horizon (☎ 2632899; Picture Palace; d Rs2000-2200, low-season discount 40%) A touch of style with hand-painted murals in all the rooms. You descend below the street-level reception to the rooms, most of which have valley views as well as TV and heating.

Hotel Padmini Nivas (☎ 2631093; www.hotelpadmininivas.com; the Mall; d Rs2000-2700, ste Rs3300-3700, off-season discount 50%; 🖳) Built in 1840 by a British colonel and then bought by the Maharaja of Rajpipla, this green-roofed heritage hotel looks a bit ramshackle but has a real old-fashioned charm. Large rooms with quaint sun rooms, suites and even a private cottage are well appointed and beautifully furnished. The dining room, with its antique furniture, is an outstanding feature, and the whole place is set on 5 acres of landscaped gardens.

our pick **Kasmanda Palace Hotel** (☎ 2632424; www.kasmandapalace.com; d Rs4000-6000, low-season discount 20%) Located off the Mall, this is Mussoorie's most romantic hotel. The white Romanesque castle was built in 1836 for a British officer and was bought by the Maharaja of Kasmanda in 1915. The red-carpeted hall has a superb staircase flanked by moth-eaten hunting trophies (the tiger and leopard skins are a sad anachronism). All of the rooms have charm but the wood-panelled and antique-filled Maharaja Room is the royal best. There's also a separate cottage with six renovated contemporary-style rooms. The formal dining room and pretty garden area complete the picture.

Eating

Mussoorie's best eating places are at the Kulri Bazaar and Picture Palace end of town. True to the holiday feel there are lots of fast-food places, and most hotels have their own restaurants. Branches of the popular Barista coffee shops are at Picture Palace and Gandhi Chowk and there's a Cafe Coffee Day in Kulri Bazaar.

Casa Mia Bakery (the Mall, Kulri Bazaar; snacks Rs15-50) The best of the many hole-in-the-wall bakeries, Casa Mia has a dazzling range of croissants, cakes, muffins, apple pies and frozen drinks.

Meeting Point Cafe (the Mall; meals Rs25-50) Away from the bazaars and halfway along the Mall, this is a nice little hang-out with espresso coffee and Tibetan food.

City Point Restaurant (the Mall, Gandhi Chowk; meals Rs30-120) This small wood-panelled place is one of several shoehorned into the road above the bus stand. Great for breakfast or a quick snack, but also does curries and dishes such as *kadhai* chicken (wok-fried chicken curry) for dinner.

Kalsang Friends Corner (☎ 2633710; the Mall, Kulri Bazaar; meals Rs45-130) Tibetan-run but strong on Thai food, Kalsang is a deservedly popular place serving up coconut curries, Thai papaya salad, *momos* (Tibetan dumplings) and noodles.

Kasmanda Palace Restaurant (☎ 2632424; meals Rs60-250) The regal restaurant at this Raj-era hotel (found off the Mall) is the perfect escape from Mussoorie's holiday bustle. The wood-panelled dining room is intimate but not stuffy, and the garden restaurant is fine for a lazy lunch or summer evening. The food lives up to the setting with North and South Indian dishes, as well as Continental (moussaka and pastas) and Chinese.

Tavern (☎ 2632829; the Mall, Picture Palace; meals Rs90-250) A favourite place to dine and hang out, the Tavern boasts a global range of food from crispy roast lamb to Goan fish curry and just about everything in between. The decor is a bit British pub, but staff are welcoming and there's live music in the evening. Beer (Rs120) and cocktails are available at the bar.

Shopping

There's a **Tibetan Market** (the Mall; 🕐 from 9am) with cheap clothing and other goods. Mussoorie has a wonderful collection of magic shops, where you can buy cheap but baffling magic tricks and whacky toys – great gifts for kids – these shops are scattered mainly along the Mall and at Gun Hill.

Getting There & Away
BUS

Frequent buses leave from Dehra Dun's Mussoorie bus stand (next to the train station) for Mussoorie (Rs31, 1½ hours). Some go to the **Picture Palace bus stand** (☎ 2632259) while others go to the **Library bus stand** (☎ 2632258) at the other end of town – if you know where you're staying it helps to be on the right bus. The return trip takes an hour. There are no direct buses to Rishikesh or Haridwar – change at Dehra Dun.

Mussoorie provides access to the mountain towns of the western Garhwal, but direct buses are not frequent. Head to the Library bus stand for buses and 4WDs heading north. For Yamunotri, take a local bus to Barkot (Rs90, 3½ hours), then another to Hanuman Chatti (Rs40, 2½ hours), from where there are 4WDs. The trip to Sankri for the Har ki Dun trek also requires a combination of buses and share 4WDs. Local buses, such as those to Tehri Dam, leave from the Tehri bus stand on the way to Landour. Take the same buses to Chamba and change for the trip to Uttarkashi.

TAXI
From taxi stands at both bus stands you can hire taxis to Dehra Dun (Rs450) and Rishikesh (Rs1200), or 4WDs to Uttarkashi (Rs2500). A shared taxi to Dehra Dun should cost Rs70 per person.

TRAIN
The **Northern Railway booking agency** (☎ 2632846; the Mall, Kulri Bazaar; ☼ 8-11am & noon-3pm Mon-Sat, 8am-2pm Sun) books tickets for trains from Dehra Dun and Haridwar.

Getting Around
Central Mussoorie is very walkable – for a hill station, the Mall and Camel's Back Rd are surprisingly flat. Cycle-rickshaws along the Mall cost Rs20, but can only go between Gandhi Chowk and the cable-car station. A full day of sightseeing around Mussoorie by taxi, including Kempty Falls and Dhanoltri, costs around Rs1800.

AROUND MUSSOORIE
The most popular sight around Mussoorie is 15km northwest at **Kempty Falls**, although the natural beauty is dulled by the trinket stalls, *dhabas* (snack bars) and thumping music. A rather pointless **cable car** (Rs70; ☼ 10am-5pm) runs the short distance down to the base of the falls, or you can just walk down the steps from the main road. In summer you can take a refreshing dip in the crowded natural waterhole.

A trip to **Dhanoltri** offers panoramic snow-capped Himalayan views and is a lovely picnic spot set among deodar forests 25km northeast

of Mussoorie. About 9km further north is **Surkhanda Devi Temple**, at a height of 3030m above sea level, which is a 2km walk from the road.

HARIDWAR
☎ 01334 / pop 220,433 / elev 249m
Propitiously located at the point where the Ganges emerges from the Himalaya, Haridwar (also called Hardwar) is Uttarakhand's holiest Hindu city, and pilgrims arrive here in droves to bathe in the often fast-flowing Ganges. The sheer numbers of people gathering around Har-ki-Pairi Ghat give Haridwar a chaotic but reverent feel – as in Varanasi, it's easy to get caught up in the spiritual clamour here. Within the religious architecture of India, Haridwar is much more significant than Rishikesh, an hour further north, and every evening the river comes alive with flickering flames as floating offerings are released onto the Ganges.

Dotted around the city are impressive temples, both ancient and modern, *dharamsalas* (pilgrims' guest houses) and ashrams, some of which are the size of small villages. Haridwar is busy during the *yatra* season from April to November, and is the site of the annual Magh Mela religious festival (see the boxed text, p461). However, in 2010 Haridwar will host the mega Kumbh Mela, attracting literally millions of pilgrims in March and April.

Orientation
Haridwar's main street is Railway Rd, becoming Upper Rd, and runs parallel to the Ganges canal (the river proper runs further to the east). Generally only cycle-rickshaws are allowed between Laltarao bridge and Bhimgoda Jhula (Bhimgoda Bridge), so vehicles travel around the opposite bank of the river. The alleyways of Bara Bazaar run south of Har-ki-Pairi Ghat.

Information
INTERNET ACCESS
Internet Zone iWay (Upper Rd; per hr Rs30; ☼ 10am-9pm)
Mohan's Adventure Tours (Railway Rd; per hr Rs40; ☼ 8am-10.30pm)

MEDICAL SERVICES
Rishikul Ayurvedic Hospital (☎ 221003; Railway Rd) A long-established medical college and hospital with a good reputation.

UTTARAKHAND

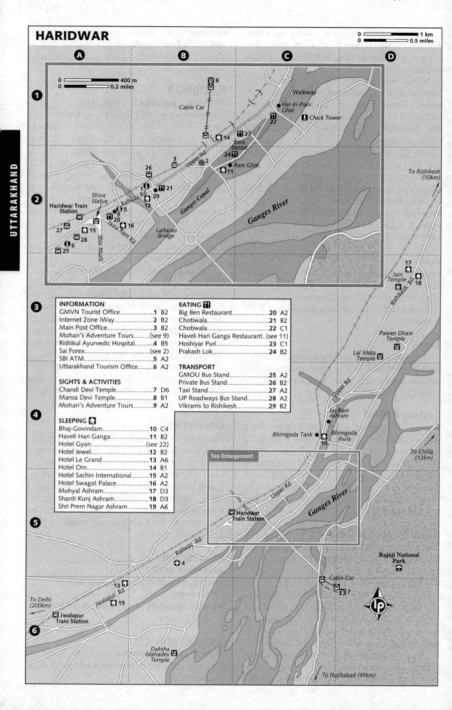

HARIDWAR

0 ———— 1 km
0 ———— 0.5 miles

0 ———— 400 m
0 ———— 0.2 miles

Cable Car

Walkway

Har-ki-Pairi Ghat

Clock Tower

Bara Bazaar

Ram Ghat

Upper Rd

Ganges Canal

Ganges River

To Rishikesh (10km)

Shiva Statue

Haridwar Train Station

Railway Rd

Jassa Ram Rd

Shiv Murti

Lalfarao Bridge

Jain Temple

Pawan Dham Temple

Lal Mata Temple

INFORMATION
GMVN Tourist Office..................**1** B2
Internet Zone iWay...................**2** B2
Main Post Office........................**3** B2
Mohan's Adventure Tours.........(see 9)
Rishikul Ayurvedic Hospital.......**4** B5
Sai Forex...................................(see 2)
SBI ATM....................................**5** A2
Uttarakhand Tourism Office.......**6** A2

SIGHTS & ACTIVITIES
Chandi Devi Temple...................**7** D6
Mansa Devi Temple....................**8** B1
Mohan's Adventure Tours..........**9** A2

SLEEPING
Bhaj-Govindam.........................**10** C4
Haveli Hari Ganga......................**11** B2
Hotel Gyan...............................(see 22)
Hotel Jewel..............................**12** B2
Hotel Le Grand.........................**13** A6
Hotel Om.................................**14** B1
Hotel Sachin International.........**15** A2
Hotel Swagat Palace.................**16** A2
Mohyal Ashram........................**17** D3
Shanti Kunj Ashram..................**18** D3
Shri Prem Nagar Ashram...........**19** A6

EATING
Big Ben Restaurant...................**20** A2
Chotiwala.................................**21** B2
Chotiwala.................................**22** C1
Haveli Hari Ganga Restaurant...(see 11)
Hoshiyar Puri............................**23** C1
Prakash Lok..............................**24** B2

TRANSPORT
GMOU Bus Stand......................**25** A2
Private Bus Stand......................**26** B2
Taxi Stand................................**27** A2
UP Roadways Bus Stand...........**28** A2
Vikrams to Rishikesh.................**29** B2

See Enlargement

Upper Rd

Haridwar Train Station

Ganges River

Jai Ram Ashram

Bhimgoda Tank

Bhimgoda Jhula

To Chilla (13km)

Rajaji National Park

Railway Rd

Cable Car

To Delhi (200km)

Jwalapur Rd

Jwalapur Train Station

Daksha Mahadev Temple

To Najibabad (49km)

PRIESTLY PANDAS

'Where can I find my family panda?' This is a common question from Hindu pilgrims visiting Haridwar. Pandas (priests and pilgrim guides) also maintain accurate records of a family's history, which can date back hundreds of years. You can see them not only at the ghats (steps or landings on a river) but also at the train station. Pilgrims give a panda the name of their clan, caste, village, district and state and are then directed to their specific family panda.

Once found, their panda will record their visit and any births, marriages and deaths that have taken place since the last pilgrimage of a family member. In the past, pilgrims stayed with their trusted panda, who acted as banker, minder and cook. Today, this is not so common, but pandas still help with the many cremation rituals. Pandas can become wealthy as pilgrims donate not just generous sums of money, but also valuable items belonging to their deceased relatives.

MONEY

Sai Forex (Upper Rd; ☽ 10am-9pm) Changes cash and travellers cheques for 1% commission.

State Bank of India ATM (Railway Rd)

POST

Main post office (Upper Rd; ☽ 10am-6pm Mon-Sat)

TOURIST INFORMATION

GMVN tourist office (☎ 2244240; Railway Rd; ☽ 10am-5pm Mon-Sat)

Uttarakhand Tourism office (☎ 265304; Rahi Motel, Railway Rd; ☽ 10am-5pm Mon-Sat)

Sights & Activities

HAR-KI-PAIRI GHAT

Har-ki-Pairi (The Footstep of God) is where Vishnu is said to have dropped some heavenly nectar and left behind a footprint. As such, it is very sacred to Hindus, and is the place to wash away your sins. Pilgrims bathe here in its often fast currents and donate money to the priests and shrines.

The ghat sits on the western bank of the Ganges canal, and every evening hundreds of worshippers gather for the *ganga aarti* (river worship ceremony). Officials in blue uniforms collect donations (and give out receipts), and as the sun sets, bells ring out a rhythm, torches are lit, and leaf baskets with flower petals inside and a candle on top (Rs5) are lit and put on the river to drift away downstream.

Tourists can mingle with the crowd to experience the rituals of an ancient religion that still retains its power in the modern age. Someone may claim to be a priest and help you with your *puja* before asking for Rs200 or more. If you want to make a donation, give it to a genuine priest or uniformed collector or put money in a charity box.

The best times to visit the ghat are early morning or just before dusk.

MANSA DEVI & CHANDI DEVI TEMPLES

Take the **cable car** (return Rs48; ☽ 7.30am-7pm Apr-Oct, 8.30am-6pm Nov-Mar) to the crowded hilltop temple of **Mansa Devi**, a wish-fulfilling goddess. The path to the cable car is lined with stalls selling packages of *prasad* (food offering used in religious ceremonies) to take up to the goddess on the hill. You can walk up (1.5km) but beware of *prasad*-stealing monkeys. Photography is forbidden in the temple.

Many visitors and pilgrims combine this with a **cable car** (return Rs70; ☽ 8am-6pm) up Neel Hill, 4km southeast of Haridwar, to **Chandi Devi Temple**. The temple was built by Raja Suchet Singh of Kashmir in 1929. Pay Rs155 at Mansa Devi and you can ride on both cable cars and take an AC coach between the two temples.

Tours

From his office next to Chitra Talkies cinema, Sanjeev Mehta of **Mohan's Adventure Tours** (☎ 220910, 9837100215; www.mohansadventure.in; Railway Rd; ☽ 8am-10.30pm) can organise any kind of tour, including trekking, fishing, birdwatching, cycling, motorcycling and rafting. An accomplished wildlife photographer, he specialises in five-hour safaris (Rs1750 per person) around Rajaji National Park. Sanjeev also runs three-day trips to Corbett Tiger Reserve – these tours operate year-round.

Sleeping

Haridwar has loads of hotels catering to Hindu pilgrims. The busiest time of year is the *yatra* season from April to November – outside this time you should have no problem finding a room at discounts of 20% to 50%. For details on staying at an ashram, see the boxed text, p473.

Accommodation is hard to find during the Kumbh Mela, but most of the pilgrims stay at vast camps set up around the city, so with advance booking (at least three months) you might get a room. Contact Sanjeev at Mohan's Adventure Tours (see Tours, p471) – he can make hotel bookings and also operates a private camp for foreigners during the Kumbh Mela season.

BUDGET

Jassa Ram Rd and the other alleys running off Railway Rd have plenty of budget hotels and although some of the fancy foyers and neon signs may raise your hopes, none are very good. Rishikesh has far superior budget accommodation.

Hotel Om (☎ 226639; Upper Rd; d with/without AC Rs850/400; ❄) The central location near the cable car to Mansa Devi Temple is a bonus at this otherwise nondescript hotel. Rooms are clean enough, some with balcony.

Hotel Swagat Palace (☎ 221581; Jassa Ram Rd; d/tr Rs450/550, d with AC Rs950; ❄) Represents reasonable value, as the better rooms are spacious with TV and clean tiled floors.

Hotel Jewel (☎ 266500; www.hoteljewel.in; Railway Rd; d/tr from Rs850/1100; ❄) On busy Railway Rd, Jewel is well run and friendly, with a range of tidy, modern rooms with TV. Discounts bring this into budget range.

MIDRANGE & TOP END

Down by the ghats are a number of similar high-rise hotels that are recommended mainly for the location and views, and are popular with middle-class pilgrims.

Hotel Gyan (☎ 225348; Subhash Ghat; d Rs700-1000, with AC Rs1400; ❄) Above Chotiwala and convenient for Har-ki-Pairi Ghat, Gyan is one of the better-value places along the river. Rooms are well kept – those facing the river are harder to get.

Hotel Sachin International (☎ 222655; starhotel@ rediffmail.com; Railway Rd; s/d Rs750/950, with AC Rs1600/1800; ❄) Opposite the train station, Sachin is a large, nondescript but clean hotel with rooms around a central car park and a restaurant reached over a causeway. Rooms at the back are quieter.

Bhaj-Govindam (☎ 261682; haridwar@usnl.com; near Bhimgoda Jhula; huts with/without AC Rs1200/800; ❄) With a wonderful location and absolute river frontage on the bank of the Ganges, these comfortable bamboo huts are set in a pleasant garden and are equipped with fans, air cooler or AC, and tiled private bathrooms. It's a bit hard to find – ask to be dropped at 'Bhimgoda Jhula', take the first alleyway in from the bridge and look for the signs.

Hotel Le Grand (☎ 2429250; www.hotellegrand .com; Jwalapur Rd; d Rs1600-2000; ❄) An enormous echoing central foyer greets you at this stylish, upmarket hotel 2km southeast of the train station. Comfortable rooms have balconies and mod cons, and there's a veg restaurant.

our pick Haveli Hari Ganga (☎ 226443; www .havelihariganga.com; 21 Ram Ghat; r US$100-125; ❄ ▯) Hidden away in Bara Bazaar, but right on the Ganges, this superb 1918 *haveli* (traditional, ornately decorated residence) is Haridwar's finest hotel. Airy courtyards, marble floors, hanging flower baskets and balconies overlooking the river give it a regal charm. Room rates include breakfast, steam bath, yoga and the hotel's own *ganga aarti* on its private ghat. The Ganges laps one terrace, and downstairs an ayurvedic health spa offers treatments as well as yoga classes. It's hard to find, so call ahead for a pick-up.

Eating & Drinking

Being a holy city, only vegetarian food and nonalcoholic drinks are available.

Chotiwala (meals Rs20-60) There are a couple of outlets for this popular veg restaurant – one on Upper Rd and another down on the river at Subhash Ghat. You may find the forlorn mascot (the chotiwallah) sitting out the front. The veg snacks and Chinese dishes are simple but tasty.

Hoshiyar Puri (Upper Rd; meals Rs20-70; ⏰ 11am-4pm & 7pm-4am) Established in 1937 and still with a loyal following – the kidney beans, *lacha paratha* (stuffed fried bread), *aloo gobi* (potato-and-cauliflower curry) and *kheer* (rice pudding) are lip-smackingly good.

Big Ben Restaurant (Hotel Ganga Azure, Railway Rd; meals Rs45-125; ⏰ 8.30am-10.30pm) Watch the passing parade through the big windows and enjoy some of Haridwar's best comfort food in this restaurant of mirrors, soft music and polite staff. It's especially good for breakfast, soups or the gourmet special thali (Rs120).

Haveli Hari Ganga Restaurant (☎ 226443; 21 Ram Ghat; dinner buffet Rs350; ⏰ 8.30-11pm) The evening Indian vegetarian buffet at this lovely heritage hotel is the classiest in Haridwar.

Don't miss a creamy lassi at **Prakash Lok** (Bara Bazaar; lassis Rs20), a Haridwar institution for

---

HARIDWAR'S ASHRAM STAYS

While most travellers make a beeline for Rishikesh to partake in yoga and spirituality and to stay in an ashram, Haridwar has several serious ashrams where you'll be surrounded by long-term ashramites, fewer foreigners and a less commercial feel. Everything – lodging, meals, religious practice – is usually free, but a donation is expected.

Shanti Kunj Ashram (☎ 260602; www.awgp.org; Rishikesh Rd) A large ashram set in beautiful gardens on the road to Rishikesh, this is an inspirational community (founded in 1971) that offers simple accommodation. It suits serious students of sadhana (spiritual achievement), as meditation and mantras start at 5am, followed by yagyar (fire ceremony) and meditation in a hall dominated by a model of the Himalaya. Contact the foreigners office (the 'Abroad Cell') for further information. The ashram has established its own university and runs 'spiritual camps' (in Hindi and English) running from nine days to one month.

Shri Prem Nagar Ashram (☎ 226345; www.manavdharam.com; Jwalapur Rd) This large ashram was founded by Hansji Maharaj, who died in 1966. His extraordinary mausoleum features a pyramidical blue ceiling with eight steps representing the seven holy rivers and the sea. Meditation and singing take place daily at 5am and the ashram has its own cows, ayurvedic medicine factory and bookshop, as well as a huge, pillarless meeting hall and a ghat facing the Ganges. Plain accommodation has fans, private bathrooms and hot water.

Mohyal Ashram (☎ 261337; mohans_india@yahoo.com; Rishikesh Rd; d Rs600-1050, with AC Rs1100; 🔲) More a yoga retreat than an ashram, Mohyal has peaceful lawns, marble floors and a meditation and yoga hall with wonderful acoustics. The spotless midrange accommodation includes meals and classes. This is not a usual strict ashram (although smoking, alcohol and meat are prohibited), and casual guests are welcome.

---

its ice-cold lassis and almond milk served in tin cups. It's not signed in English but locals know where to find it.

Getting There & Away
Haridwar is well connected by bus and train, but book ahead for trains during the pilgrimage season.

BUS
For details of major bus routes from Haridwar, see the table, p474.

Private deluxe buses and sleeper buses run to Delhi (deluxe/Volvo Rs175/400), Agra (seat/sleeper Rs240/295), Jaipur (Rs375/475) and Pushkar (Rs400/500). They leave from a stand around the corner from the GMVN tourist office by the gurdwara (Sikh temple), and any travel agent in town can make a booking.

TAXI & VIKRAM
The main taxi stand is outside the train station on Railway Rd. Official rates include Chilla (for Rajaji National Park, Rs410), Rishikesh (Rs600, one hour) and Dehra Dun (Rs800), but it's usually possible to arrange a taxi for less than these rates.

Shared vikrams run to Rishikesh (Rs20, one hour) from Upper Rd at Laltarao Bridge, but buses are more comfortable. You can hire the whole thing to Rishikesh's Lakshman Jhula for Rs350.

TRAIN
Numerous trains run between Haridwar and Delhi, but the only overnight service is the Mussoorie Express (sleeper/3AC/2AC Rs130/365/508, 8½ hours), which departs at 11.20pm and gets in to Old Delhi station at 7.45am. The fastest service is the Shatabdi Express (chair car/executive Rs390/780, 4½ hours). The overnight Doon Express runs daily to Kolkata/Howrah (sleeper/3AC/2AC Rs405/1138/1581, 32 hours) via Lucknow (Rs195/548/761, 10 hours) and Varanasi (Rs282/792/1101, 18 hours). Two trains run to Amritsar, which is the easiest way to get to Dharamsala – there's the Jan Shatabdi (daily except Thursday, 2nd class/chair car Rs120/385, seven hours), and the overnight Amritsar Passenger (sleeper/3AC Rs139/391, 12 hours).

Getting Around
Cycle-rickshaws cost Rs10 for a short distance and Rs25 for longer hauls such as from the train station to Har-ki-Pairi. To hire a taxi for three hours to tour the local temples and

UTTARAKHAND

BUSES FROM HARIDWAR

The following buses depart from the UP Roadways bus stand.

Destination	Fare (Rs)	Duration (hr)	Frequency
Agra	193	12	early morning
Almora	250	10	early morning & afternoon
Chandigarh	120	10	early morning
Dehra Dun	38	2	half-hourly
Delhi	116	6	half-hourly
Dharamsala	275	15	2pm
Jaipur	275-300	12	early morning
Nainital	186	8	early morning & evening
Ranikhet	190	10	6am & 5pm
Rishikesh	19	1	half-hourly
Shimla	215	14	early morning & evening
Uttarkashi	184	10	7.30am & 9.30am

In the *yatra* (pilgrimage) season from April to October, buses from the GMOU bus stand run as follows:

Destination	Fare (Rs)	Duration (hr)	Frequency
Badrinath (via Joshimath)	300	15	btwn 3.30am & 7am
Gangotri	280	10	btwn 3am & 5am
Hanuman Chatti	220	10	btwn 3am & 5am
Kedarnath	225	10	btwn 3am & 5am

ashrams costs around Rs500; an autorickshaw costs Rs250.

RAJAJI NATIONAL PARK
elev 300-1000m

This unspoilt **park** (admission Indian/foreigner per day Rs40/350, camera free/Rs50, video 2500/5000; ☉ 15 Nov-15 Jun), covering 820 sq km in the forested foothills near Haridwar, is best known for its wild elephants, numbering around 450 to 500 at last count.

As well as elephants, the park contains some 32 tigers and 250 leopards, although they're not easily seen. They have thousands of chital (spotted deer) and hundreds of sambars (India's largest species of deer) to feed on. A handful of rarely seen sloth bears are hidden away. Over 300 species of birds also add interest.

The village of **Chilla**, 13km northeast of Haridwar, is the base for visiting the park. **Elephant rides** (Rs400), which can take up to four passengers, are available on a first-come-first-served basis at sunrise and 3pm, but there are currently only two elephants. Contact the Forest Ranger's office, close to the tourist guesthouse at Chilla, where you can also pick up a brochure, pay entry fees and organise a 4WD. These take up to eight people and

cost Rs700 for the standard safari (plus Rs100 entry fee for the vehicle).

Before visiting, contact the **GMVN tourist office** (Map p470; ☎ 2244240; Railway Rd, Haridwar; ☉ 10am-5pm Mon-Sat) and **Mohan's Adventure Tours** (Map p470; ☎ 220910; www.mohansadventure.in; Railway Rd, Haridwar; ☉ 8am-10.30pm), which offers Rajaji safaris even when the park is officially closed. These are five-hour trips (Rs1750 per person) that include being taken on a short safari, watching a parade of wild elephants, and visiting a tribal village of Gujjar buffalo herders. If you're lucky, Sanjeev may take you to visit his legally adopted orphaned elephant.

Sleeping & Eating

Chilla Guesthouse (☎ 0138-226678; dm Rs200, huts 500-650, r with AC Rs1200-1600; ☒) This is the GMVN rest house and the most comfortable place to stay in Chilla. There's a good restaurant here and a pleasant garden.

Within the park there are nine historical but basic forest **rest houses** (Indian/foreigner Rs500/1000) at Asarohi, Beribara, Chilla, Kansrao, Kunnao, Motichur, Phandowala, Ranipur and Satyanarayan. If you're staying at one of the rest houses, the park entry fee is valid for three days. The 1883 forest rest house in Chilla has three rooms downstairs and a suite upstairs with a balcony. The rest house at Satyanarayan is also recommended, while the one at Kansrao has retained all its original features. No food is available (except in Chilla) and if you don't have your own transport you will have to make a special arrangement with a 4WD driver. To book a forest rest house, contact the director at the **Rajaji National Park Office** (☎ /fax 0135-2621669; 5/1 Ansari Marg, Dehra Dun). Mohan's Adventure Tours (see Tours, p471) can also make bookings for forest lodges.

Getting There & Away

Buses to Chilla (Rs15, one hour) leave the GMOU bus stand in Haridwar every hour from 7am to 2pm. The last return trip leaves Chilla at 5.30pm. Taxis charge Rs410 one way for the 13km journey.

RISHIKESH

☎ 0135 / pop 79,591 / elev 356m

Ever since the Beatles rocked up at the ashram of the Maharishi Mahesh Yogi in the late '60s, Rishikesh has been a magnet for spiritual seekers. Today it styles itself as the 'Yoga Capital of the World', with masses of ashrams and all kinds of yoga and meditation classes. Most of this action is north of the main town, where the exquisite setting on the fast-flowing Ganges, surrounded by forested hills, is conducive to meditation and mind expansion. In the evening, the breeze blows down the valley, setting temple bells ringing as sadhus (spiritual men), pilgrims and tourists prepare for the nightly ganga aarti.

Rishikesh is very New Age: you can learn to play the sitar or tabla on your hotel roof; try laughing yoga; practise humming or gong meditation; experience crystal healing and all styles of massage; have a go at chanting mantras; and listen to spiritually uplifting CDs as you sip ayurvedic tea with your vegetarian meal.

But it's not all spirituality and contorted limbs. Rishikesh is now a popular white-water rafting centre, backpacker hang-out, and gateway to treks in the Himalaya.

Orientation

Rishikesh is divided into two main areas: the crowded, unattractive downtown area (Rishikesh town), where you'll find the bus and train stations as well as the Triveni Ghat; and the riverside communities 2km upstream around Ram Jhula and Lakshman Jhula, where most of the accommodation, ashrams, restaurants and travellers are ensconced. The two *jhula* (suspension bridges) that cross the river are pedestrian-only. Swarg Ashram, located on the eastern bank, is the traffic-free 'spiritual centre' of Rishikesh, while High Bank, west of Lakshman Jhula, is a small enclave popular with backpackers.

Information

INTERNET ACCESS

Internet access is available all over town, usually for Rs20 or Rs30 per hour.

Blue Hills Travels (Swarg Ashram; per hr Rs30)

Lucky Internet (Lakshman Jhula; per hr Rs30; ☽ 8.30am-10pm) Wi-fi access.

Red Chilli Adventure (Lakshman Jhula Rd; per hr Rs30; ☽ 9am-9pm) Surf with a view.

MEDICAL SERVICES

Himalayan Institute Hospital (☎ 2471133; ☽ 24hr) The nearest large hospital, 17km along the road to Dehra Dun and 1km beyond Jolly Grant airport.

Shivananda Ashram (☎ 2430040; www.sivanandaonline.org; Lakshman Jhula Rd) Provides free medical services and a pharmacy.

MONEY

Several travel agents around Lakshman Jhula and Swarg Ashram will exchange travellers cheques and cash.

Bank of Baroda ATM (Dehra Dun Rd)

State Bank of India ATM (Swarg Ashram & Dehra Dun Rd)

Axis ATM (Swarg Ashram)

POST

Main post office (Ghat Rd; ☽ 10am-4pm Mon-Fri, 10am-1pm Sat) Near Triveni Ghat.

Post office (Swarg Ashram; ☽ 10am-4pm Mon-Fri, 10am-1pm Sat)

TOURIST INFORMATION

Uttarakhand Tourism office (☎ 2430209; Dhalwala Bypass Rd; ☽ 10am-5pm Mon-Sat) Inconveniently located out on the road to Haridwar, it's in the same building as the GMVN Yatra office. It has a few brochures and can book tours.

Dangers & Annoyances

Travellers should be cautious of being befriended by sadhus – while many sadhus are on genuine spiritual journeys, the orange robes have been used as a disguise by fugitives from the law since medieval times. In

UTTARAKHAND

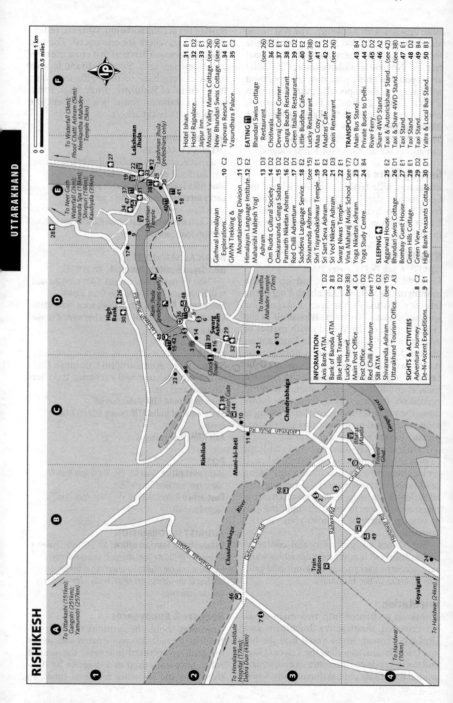

RISHIKESH

Hotel Ishan	31	E1
Hotel Rajpalace	32	D2
Jaipur Inn	33	E1
Mount Valley Mama Cottage	(see 26)	
New Bhandari Swiss Cottage	34	E1
Tapovan Resort	(see 26)	
Vasundhara Palace	35	C2

EATING 🍴
Bhandari Swiss Cottage Restaurant	(see 26)	
Chotiwala	36	D2
Devraj Coffee Corner	37	E1
Ganga Beach Restaurant	38	E2
Green Italian Restaurant	39	D2
Little Buddha Cafe	40	E2
Lucky Restaurant	(see 15)	
Maa Cozy	41	E2
Madras Cafe	42	D2
Oasis Restaurant	(see 26)	

TRANSPORT
Main Bus Stand	43	B4
Private Buses to Delhi	44	C2
River Ferry	45	D2
Share 4WD Stand	46	A2
Taxi & Autorickshaw Stand	(see 42)	
Taxi & Share 4WD Stand	(see 38)	
Taxi Stand	47	E1
Taxi Stand	48	D2
Taxi Stand	49	B4
Yatra & Local Bus Stand	50	D1

Garhwal Himalayan Explorations	10	C2
GMVN Trekking & Mountaineering Division	11	C3
Himalayan Language Institute	12	E2
Maharishi Mahesh Yogi Ashram	13	D3
Om Rudra Cultural Society	14	D2
Omkarananda Ganga Sadan	15	D2
Parmarth Niketan Ashram	16	D2
Red Chilli Adventure	17	D1
Sachdeva Language Service	18	E2
Shivananda Ashram	(see 15)	
Shri Trayanbakshwar Temple	19	E1
Sri Sant Seva Ashram	20	E2
Sri Ved Niketan Ashram	21	D3
Swarg Niwas Temple	22	E1
Vina Maharaj Music School	(see 17)	
Yoga Niketan Ashram	23	C2
Yoga Study Centre	24	B4

INFORMATION
Axis Bank ATM	1	D2
Bank of Baroda ATM	2	B3
Blue Hills Travels	3	D2
Lucky Internet	(see 38)	
Main Post Office	4	C4
Post Office	5	D2
Red Chilli Adventure	(see 17)	
SBI ATM	6	D2
Shivananda Ashram	(see 15)	
Uttaranjal Tourism Office	7	A3

SIGHTS & ACTIVITIES
Adventure Journey	8	C2
De-N-Ascent Expeditions	9	E1

modern times, females walking alone may be at risk.

The current in some parts of the Ganges is very strong, and as inviting as a dip from one of the beaches may seem, people drown here every year. Don't swim out of your depth.

Sights & Activities

LAKSHMAN JHULA & AROUND

The defining image of Rishikesh is the view across the Lakshman Jhula hanging bridge to the huge 13-storey wedding-cake temples of **Swarg Niwas** and **Shri Trayanbakshwar**. Built by the organisation of the guru Kailashanand, they resemble fairyland castles and have dozens of shrines to Hindu deities on each level, interspersed with jewellery and textile shops – spiritual commercialism. Sunset is an especially good time to photograph the temples from the bridge itself, and you'll hear the bell-clanging and chanting of devotees in the morning and evening. Shops selling devotional CDs add to the cacophony of noise on this side of the river. Markets, restaurants, ashrams and guest houses sprawl on both sides of the river, and in recent years the area has grown into the busiest and liveliest part of upper Rishikesh.

SWARG ASHRAM

A pleasant 2km walk south of Lakshman Jhula along the path skirting the east bank of the Ganges leads to the spiritual community of **Swarg Ashram**, made up of temples, ashrams, a crowded bazaar, sadhus and the bathing ghats where religious ceremonies are performed at sunrise and sunset. The colourful, though rather touristy, *ganga aarti* is held at the riverside temple of the Parmarth Niketan Ashram every evening at sunset, with singing, chanting, musicians and the lighting of candles.

WALKS & BEACHES

An easy walk to two small **waterfalls** starts 3km north of Lakshman Jhula bridge on the south side of the river. The start of the 15-minute walk is marked by drink stalls and a roadside shrine, and the path is easy to find. Four-wheel-drive taxis cost Rs100 from Lakshman Jhula. Between here and Lakshman Jhula are several sandy **beaches**, sheltered from the road and popular with travellers escaping the crowds. Resist the temptation to swim in the Ganges here as the current can be deceptively strong. On the other side of the river, it's about 2km

north to the signposted walk to lovely **Neer Garh Waterfall** (admission Rs30), from where it's a 20-minute uphill walk.

For a longer hike, follow the dedicated pilgrims who take water from the Ganges to offer at **Neelkantha Mahadev Temple**, a 7km, approximately three-hour walk along a forest path from Swarg Ashram. Neelkanth (Blue Throat) is another name for Shiva, who once drank poison churned up from the sea by gods and demons, which turned his throat blue. A much longer road (17km) via Lakshman Jhula also goes to the temple. A 4WD taxi costs Rs600 return.

MAHARISHI ASHRAM

Just south of Swarg Ashram, slowly being consumed by the forest undergrowth, is what's left of the original **Maharishi Mahesh Yogi Ashram**. It was abandoned in 1997 and is now back under the control of the forest department. However, the shells of many buildings, meditation cells and lecture halls can still be seen, including Maharishi's own house and the guest house where the Beatles stayed and apparently wrote much of the *White Album*.

YOGA, MEDITATION & ASHRAMS

Rishikesh styles itself as the yoga capital of the world, and yoga and meditation are the buzzwords here. Lots of people are cashing in, and teaching and yoga styles vary tremendously, so check out a few classes before committing yourself to a course. If you want to get started, virtually every hotel offers one-hour yoga sessions for around Rs100, but ashram stays are the best way to truly immerse yourself in the spiritual vibe. Many place also offer ayurvedic massage.

Recommended:

Sri Sant Seva Ashram (☎ 2430465; www.santse waashram.com; d Rs150-600, with AC Rs1000; 🖳) Overlooking the Ganges in Lakshman Jhula, the large rooms here are popular, so book ahead. The more-expensive rooms have balconies with river views. The yoga classes are mixed styles and are open to all. Beginner (Rs100) and intermediate and advanced (Rs200) sessions run daily. There are also courses in reiki, ayurvedic massage and cooking.

Omkarananda Ganga Sadan (☎ 2430763; www .iyengaryoga.in; Lakshman Jhula Rd; r with/without AC Rs850/280, minimum 3-day stay) Also on the river, at Muni-ki-Reti, this ashram has comfortable rooms and specialises in Iyengar yoga classes at the Patanjala Yoga Kendra centre. There are daily classes (except Sunday; Rs250) and intensive seven- to 10-day courses (Rs800) on

UTTARAKHAND

THE MAHARISHI & THE BEATLES

In February 1968 Rishikesh hit world headlines when the four Beatles and their partners stayed at Maharishi Mahesh Yogi's ashram in Swarg Ashram, following an interest and earlier visit by George Harrison. Ringo and his wife didn't like the vegetarian food, missed their children and left after a couple of weeks, but the others stayed for a month or two. They relaxed and wrote tons of songs, many of which ended up on their double album *White Album*. But rumours of the Maharishi's demands for money and his behaviour towards some female disciples eventually disillusioned all of them. 'You made a fool of everyone,' John Lennon sang about the Maharishi. In later years, Harrison and McCartney went on record as saying the rumours were unfounded. The original ashram is now abandoned, but nearly 40 years on, idealistic foreigners still swarm into Rishikesh seeking spiritual enlightenment from the teachers and healers in their tranquil ashrams scattered along the Ganges River.

offer from October to May. The ashram has its own ghat and evening *ganga aarti*.

Shivananda Ashram (☎ 2430040; www.sivanandaon line.org; Lakshman Jhula Rd) Founded by Swami Shivananda, this ashram is run by the Divine Life Society. Free yoga and meditation classes are available every morning, but two months' advance notice is required if you want to stay – email the ashram through its website.

Yoga Niketan Ashram (☎ 2430227; www.yoganike tanashram.org; Lakshman Jhula Rd; r Rs500-750; 🕸) Stays at this rather austere ashram include comfortable rooms, all meals, hatha yoga classes, meditation sessions, lectures and the use of the library. But it's only for serious students – the minimum stay is 15 days, with each day beginning at 4.30am sharp.

Yoga Study Centre (☎ 2433837; Koyalgati) According to locals, this one of Rishikesh's most highly regarded yoga schools and runs two- and three-week Iyengar yoga courses for all levels (payment by donation). It's a small ashram on the river south of the town, off Haridwar Rd.

Parmarth Niketan Ashram (☎ 244008; www .parmarth.com; Swarg Ashram; r Rs600) Dominating the centre of Swarg Ashram and drawing visitors to its evening *ganga aarti* on the riverbank, Parmarth has a wonderfully ornate and serene garden courtyard. The price includes a room with a private bathroom, all meals and hatha yoga lessons.

Sri Ved Niketan Ashram (☎ 2430279; viedniketan@ gmail.com; s/d Rs150/250) Also called the International Vishwaguru Meditation and Yoga Institute, this place in Swarg Ashram has a large inner courtyard, a spacious meditation and yoga hall offering hatha, pranayama, meditation and philosophy classes, and spartan rooms with private bathrooms. Minimum three-day stay.

Phool Chatti Ashram (☎ 2440022; www.phoolchat tiyoga.com; s per person Rs5000, d per person Rs5500) This modern yoga retreat 5km upstream from Lakshman Jhula offers seven-day beginner and intermediate yoga courses in a very peaceful, rural environment. Includes accommodation and meals.

MOTORCYCLING

Motorcycles (Enfields and Yamahas) and mopeds can be hired for Rs200 to Rs350 a day around the Lakshman Jhula area. There are no specific shops – you just hire from private owners, so there's no insurance; ask around at guest houses or look for rental signs.

MUSIC, DANCE & LANGUAGE CLASSES

Look out for flyers around Lakshman Jhula, Swarg Ashram and High Bank advertising music tuition and concerts.

Om Rudra Cultural Society (☎ 2434425; rudradance@ rediffmail.com; Swarg Ashram; 🕙 Sep-May) is run by an enterprising couple and offers *kathak* (classical) dance, flute, tabla or Hindi lessons.

In Lakshman Jhula, **Vina Maharaj Music School** (☎ 9412029817) offers sitar, tabla, harmonium and flute lessons at Rs200 per hour, and organises concerts.

Himalayan Language Institute (☎ 9917892959; www.himalayanlanguageinstitute.com; Lakshman Jhula) offers Hindi language classes for groups (Rs80 to Rs150 per hour) or individuals (Rs250 per hour). For casual one-on-one Hindi classes, try **Sachdeva Language Service** (☎ 9897103808; Lakshman Jhula; per hr Rs100).

RAFTING, KAYAKING & TREKKING

A number of companies offer full- and half-day rafting trips, putting in upstream and paddling back to Rishikesh. Some also offer multiday rafting trips, staying at rafting camps along the river bank. The official rafting season runs from 15 September to 30 June. A half-day trip starts at about Rs700 per person, while a full day costs from Rs1300. Most companies also offer all-inclusive Himalayan treks to places such as Kuari Pass, Har ki Dun and Gangotri from around Rs2000 per day.

Recommended rafting and trekking companies are:

Adventure Journey (☎ 6537951; www.theadventure journey.com; Ram Jhula) Rafting trips and a private rafting river camp.

De-N-Ascent Expeditions (☎ 2442354; www.kayak himalaya.com; Tapovan Sarai, Lakshman Jhula) Specialist in kayaking lessons and expeditions. Paddle and eskimo roll with an experienced instructor from Rs1000 per day; kayaking expeditions cost from Rs2400 per day. Also organises rafting and trekking trips.

Garhwal Himalayan Explorations (☎ 2433478; www.thegarhwalhimalayas.com; Lakshman Jhula Rd, Muni-ki-Reti; ☾ 8am-8pm) Himalayan trekking and rafting trips. The company runs three river camps – Ganga Nature Camp, the Himalayan Retreat and Himalayan Heights.

GMVN Trekking & Mountaineering Division (☎ 2430799; www.gmvnl.com; Lakshman Jhula Rd; ☾ 10am-5pm) Can arrange high-altitude treks in the Garhwal Himalaya and hires out trekking equipment, guides and porters.

Red Chilli Adventure (☎ 2434021; www.redchil liadventure.com; Lakshman Jhula Rd; ☾ 9am-9pm) Reliable outfit offering Himalayan trekking and rafting trips throughout Uttarakhand and to Himachal Pradesh and Ladakh.

Festivals & Events

In the first week of March, Rishikesh hosts the **International Yoga Festival** (www.internationalyo gafestival.com), attracting swamis and yoga masters from around the world for discourses and lectures. Most of the action is centred on the Parmarth Niketan Ashram (p477) in Swarg Ashram. Check the festival website for dates.

Sleeping

Most of the accommodation is spread on both sides of the river around Lakshman Jhula; there are a handful of hotels among the ashrams at Swarg Ashram and directly across the river around Ram Jhula, and some good budget places at High Bank. For ashram stays, see p477.

BUDGET
High Bank

This leafy travellers' enclave is a 20-minute walk up the hill from Lakshman Jhula and has some of the best backpacker accommodation in Rishikesh. All of the following places are clean, relaxed and good value. It gets pretty rowdy during peak season from November to March, with backpackers staying up late and enjoying deep conversations.

Bhandari Swiss Cottage (☎ 2432939; www.bhanda riswisscottage.com; r Rs150-600, ste with AC Rs1500; ☒ ▣) The first place you come to, this is a well-run backpacker favourite with rooms in several budgets – the higher up you stay, the higher the price. Rooms with big balconies have expansive views of the river backed by green mountains. Excellent little restaurant, internet cafe and yoga classes.

Mount Valley Mama Cottage (☎ 2432817; d Rs250-400, without bathroom Rs150) The price is right at this small and simple guest house and it feels like someone's home – which is pretty much what it is. Mama will look after you and cook up her famous thalis.

New Bhandari Swiss Cottage (☎ 2431322; d Rs300-800, AC cottages Rs1200-1500; ☒ ▣) Further up the hill from Bhandari Swiss Cottage, this is another large, popular place with a range of tidy accommodation, a massage centre and a good restaurant.

High Bank Peasants Cottage (☎ 2431167; d Rs600-800, with AC Rs1500-2000; ☒ ▣) A High Bank original, this is the most upmarket accommodation here (it's closer to midrange than budget). Lovely gardens feature flowering trees and giant cacti, there are wicker chairs on the balconies, and the spacious rooms are neatly furnished.

Lakshman Jhula

There are several good budget options on both sides of the river here, and this is one of the liveliest parts of Rishikesh.

Bombay Guest House (☎ 3250038; s/d Rs100/130) Just north of the bridge, rooms in this big red Mughal-style house are very basic but it has old-school backpacker character.

Aggarwal House (☎ 2433435; s Rs150, d Rs200-350) This small family-run guest house overlooks the river and a sandy beach. The upper terrace and riverside rooms have fine sunset views.

Green Hills Cottage (☎ 2433060; Badrinath Rd; d Rs200-250, with AC Rs800; ☒) On the north side of the river, Green Hills welcomes you with a manicured garden and a laid-back vibe. Rooms are plain but good value.

Hotel Ishan (☎ 2431534; narendra_u@hotmail.com; r Rs250-700; ▣) This long-running riverfront place near Lakshman Jhula looks a bit rough, but has a wide range of clean rooms, some with balconies overlooking the river. The top-floor room with TV and balcony has a prime view.

UTTARAKHAND

Swarg Ashram

If you're serious about yoga and introspection, stay at one of Swarg's numerous ashrams. Otherwise, there's a knot of guest houses a block back from the river towards the southern end of Swarg.

Hotel Rajpalace (☎ 2440079; rajholidays@hotmail .com; d Rs450-650, with AC from Rs1050; ❄) Small but well-run hotel with clean rooms. The rooftop terrace has views, and facilities include a yoga hall and a travel agent offering tours and activities.

MIDRANGE & TOP END

Midrange and top-end hotels are in relatively short supply in budget-minded Rishikesh.

Lakshman Jhula

Jaipur Inn (☎ 2440221; www.jaipur-inn.com; d Rs990; ❄) In a good location close to the bridge, the clean and smart rooms with pastel decor, TVs and balcony views make this a good choice, especially in summer when the air-con makes it worth the price – go for the upper-floor front rooms.

Tapovan Resort (☎ 2442091; www.tapovanresort.com; s/d from Rs1350/1850, ste Rs3000; ❄ ▣) This tidy hotel on the western side of Lakshman Jhula lacks much in the way of character with its resort feel, but the rooms are plush, and the more-expensive rooms have balconies with river views. There's a pleasant terrace, a garden, yoga classes, and an unusual circular restaurant.

Swarg Ashram & Ram Jhula

Green View (☎ 2434948; www.hotelgreen.com; Swarg Ashram; d with/without AC Rs1650/1100) In a small enclave of hotels down an alleyway, Green View has bright rooms with hot showers and TVs. Rates halve in the low-season (April to May and August to September). The sibling Green Hotel was closed for a full renovation at the time of research.

Vasundhara Palace (☎ 2442345; www.vasundharapal ace.com; Muni-ki-Reti; s/d Rs2950/3550, ste Rs5500; ❄ ▣) Rishikesh's top riverside hotel, this modern high-rise has luxurious, tastefully designed rooms, an elegant restaurant, and a rooftop pool and health spa with river views – unfortunately, views from the rooms are blocked by apartments.

Eating

Virtually every restaurant in Rishikesh serves only vegetarian food, but there are lots of travellers' restaurants whipping up various interpretations of Continental and Israeli food, as well as Indian and Chinese.

LAKSHMAN JHULA

our pick Devraj Coffee Corner (meals Rs30-100; ☺ 8am-9pm) Perched above the bridge and looking across the river to Shri Trayanbakshwar temple, this German bakery is a sublime spot for an early breakfast and is usually busy all day. Fresh brown bread with yak cheese, croissants and apple strudel sit comfortably alongside soups, pizzas, enchiladas and veg sizzlers. There's a good bookshop next door and free filtered water is available.

On the east bank of the river is a string of restaurants with global menus catering to travellers. There's no real beach at **Ganga Beach Restaurant** (meals Rs30-100), but the riverside location, spacious terrace and cushioned chill-out area make this a relaxing spot. The big menu includes wood-fired pizzas and crepes, and the lassis are ice-cold. At **Maa Cozy** (mains Rs30-110), Persian rugs and cushions on the floor go some way to giving this modern 1st-floor place an Arabian feel. The speciality is the sheesha pipes (from Rs130), with fruit-, mint- or cola-flavoured tobacco. Good coffee and smoothies.

Other places:

Lucky Restaurant (mains Rs20-80) An awesome riverside garden shaded by a huge tree and a cushioned area.

Little Buddha Cafe (mains Rs40-100) Funky treehouse-style restaurant with an ultraloungey top floor and good food.

SWARG ASHRAM & RAM JHULA

Chotiwala (Swarg Ashram; meals Rs20-80, thalis Rs65-120) There are two open-fronted and fiercely competitive Chotiwalas side by side here, both serving up thalis, South Indian food, ice creams and sweet lime sodas. There's little to distinguish between them and they're easy to spot by the rotund (but not very jolly) mascots with the pointy hairdo (a *choti*) sitting out the front.

Green Italian Restaurant (Swarg Ashram; mains Rs40-110) Wood-fired veg pizzas and imported pastas including gnocchi and cannelloni keep the customers coming back to this spotless, glass-fronted restaurant in the heart of Swarg.

Madras Cafe (Ram Jhula; meals Rs50-100) This local institution dishes up tasty South and North Indian veg food, thalis, a mean mushroom curry, whole-wheat pancakes and the intriguing Himalayan health pilau, as well as super-thick lassis.

UTTARAKHAND

HIGH BANK

Backpackers gather at the popular restaurants on High Bank, and this is the only area in town where you'll find meat on the menu.

Bhandari Swiss Cottage Restaurant (meals Rs40-100) The relaxed garden restaurant here serves bakery items, pizzas (including nonveg), ayurvedic tea, big breakfasts and a global range of dishes.

Oasis Restaurant (meals Rs40-130) At New Bhandari Swiss Cottage, this restaurant is more refined, with candlelit tables in the garden and hanging lanterns inside. The menu ransacks oodles of world cuisines from Mexican and Thai to Israeli and Tibetan, and features a number of chicken dishes including a delicious chilli chicken. Great desserts include apple crumble.

Shopping

Swarg Ashram is the place to go for bookshops, ayurvedic herbal medicines, clothing, handicrafts and tourist trinkets such as jewellery and Tibetan singing bowls, though there are also plenty of stalls around Lakshman Jhula. Many stalls sell *rudraksh mala* (the strings of beads used in *puja*), made from the nuts of the rudraksh tree, which originally grew where Shiva's tears fell. Beads with *mukhi* (different faces) confer various blessings on the wearer.

Getting There & Away

BUS

There are regular buses to Haridwar and Dehra Dun; for Mussoorie change at Dehra Dun. During the *yatra* season (April to November), buses run north to pilgrimage

centres, and to Joshimath and Uttarkashi year-round. See the table, below, for details of buses from Rishikesh.

Private deluxe buses to Delhi (Rs250, seven hours) leave from Kailash Gate, just south of Ram Jhula, at 1.30pm and 9.30pm. Private night buses to Jaipur (seat/sleeper Rs375/475, 13 hours), Agra (Rs240/295, 12 hours) and Pushkar (Rs400/500, 16 hours) can be booked at travel agents in Lakshman Jhula, Swarg Ashram and High Bank, but they leave from Haridwar (see p473).

SHARE 4WDS & TAXI

Share 4WDs leave when overfull from the corner of Dehra Dun Rd and Dhalwala Bypass Rd to Uttarkashi (Rs180, five hours) and Joshimath (Rs250, eight hours), mostly early in the morning, starting from 4am.

From the taxi stand near the bus stand, official taxi rates include Haridwar (Rs500), Dehra Dun (Rs650, 1½ hours) and Uttarkashi (for Gangotri; Rs2000, seven hours).

There are also taxi stands at Ram Jhula and Lakshman Jhula (west bank), charging Rs550 to Haridwar, Rs800 to Dehra Dun, Rs2300 to Uttarkarshi and Rs3500 to Joshimath. Although these rates are fixed, on long distance trips you can usually get a cheaper rate by asking around at travel agents and guest houses.

Vikrams charge Rs300 to make the trip to Haridwar.

TRAIN

Bookings can be made at the **reservation office** (⌚ 8am-6pm Mon-Sat, to 2pm Sun) at the train station, or at travel agents around Lakshman

BUSES FROM RISHIKESH			
Destination	Fare (Rs)	Duration (hr)	Frequency
Dehra Dun (A)	29	1½	half-hourly
Delhi (A)	135/210 ordinary/deluxe	7	half-hourly
Gangotri (B)	235	12	btwn 3am & 7am or 9am
Haridwar (A)	19	1	half-hourly
Joshimath (B)	220	10	btwn 3am & 7am or 9am
Kedarnath (B)	190	12	btwn 3am & 7am or 9am
Nainital (A)	175	11	9.30am (continuing from Ramnagar)
Uttarkashi (B)	150	7	btwn 3am & 7am or 9am

(A) buses departing from the main bus stand
(B) buses departing from the *yatra* (pilgrimage) bus stand leave when full

Jhula and Swarg Ashram (for a fee). Only a handful of slow trains run from Rishikesh to Haridwar, so it's usually better go by bus or taxi.

Getting Around

Shared *vikrams* run from the downtown Ghat Rd junction up past Ram Jhula (Rs8 per person) and the High Bank turn-off to Lakshman Jhula. To hire the entire *vikram* from downtown to Ram Jhula should cost Rs80, and from Ram Jhula to High Bank or Laksham Jhula is Rs40.

To get to the eastern bank of the Ganges you either need to walk across one of the suspension bridges or take the **ferry** (one way/return Rs10/15; ⏰ 7.30am-6.45pm) from Ram Jhula.

On the eastern bank of the Ganges, taxis and share 4WDs hang around to take passengers to waterfalls and Neelkantha temple, but it's a 16km trip by road to get from one side of the river to the other.

AROUND RISHIKESH

Part palace, part exclusive, luxury spa resort, the prize-winning **Ananda Spa** (☎ 01378-227500; www.anandaspa.com; Badrinath Rd; s/d from US$525/575, ste US$920-1440, villa US$1440-2025; ✖ 🖥 🏊) is the last word in indulgent pampering, and plays host to the rich and famous from India and abroad. Perched high up in the hills 18km north of Rishikesh, Ananda Spa occupies part of the palace of the Maharaja of Tehri-Garhwal and spreads out over a manicured estate that includes luxury accommodation, a six-hole golf course, a jogging track, garden restaurants, an amphitheatre and a swimming pool.

Spa facilities include steam baths, ayurvedic treatments, yoga sessions and beauty therapy, but the resort is exclusive – you need to be a guest to indulge here.

UTTARKASHI

☎ 01374 / pop 16,220 / elev 1158m

Uttarkashi, 155km from Rishikesh and the largest town in northern Garhwal, is a major stop on the road to Gangotri Temple and the Gaumukh Glacier trek, so it's an obvious place to break your journey and stock up on supplies at the local market. Guides and porters can also be arranged here.

There's a State Bank of India ATM at the bus stand.

The town is probably best known for the **Nehru Institute of Mountaineering** (☎ 222123; www

.nimindia.org), which trains many of the guides running trekking and mountaineering outfits in India. The centre has a museum and outdoor climbing wall. Basic and advanced mountaineering and adventure courses are open to all – check the website for details and admission information.

Uttarkashi also hosts the annual **Makar Sakranti day** festival (see the boxed text, p461), in January.

Uttarkashi has plenty of cheap *dhabas*, but the best eating is in the hotels.

Monal Guest House (☎ 222270; d from Rs600), on the Gangotri road 3km north of town, is a small homely place run by a keen mountaineer.

Mahima Resort (☎ 222252; s/d Rs700/850) is an excellent choice, 7km north of Uttarkashi on the road to Gangotri. Spotless rooms are very comfortable.

Buses depart in the morning for Gangotri (Rs110, six hours) and Rishikesh (Rs150, seven hours).

GARHWAL TEMPLE TREKS
Gangotri Temple & Gaumukh Glacier Trek

☎ 01377 / elev 3042m

In a grand, remote setting at an altitude of 3042m, Gangotri temple was originally constructed by Gorkha commander Amar Singh Thapa in the 18th century. The brave and devout take a dip in the freezing flow of an embryonic Ganges River. Nearby is the rock on which Shiva is said to have received the Ganga (Ganges) in his matted locks. Gangotri village has guest houses, ashrams, *dharamsalas* and a **GMVN Tourist Bungalow** (☎ 22221; dm Rs150, d Rs400-900).

As the source of the Ganges (known as the Bhagirathi until it reaches Deoprayag), Gangotri is one of the holiest places in India. The trek (38km return) from Gangotri to the source of the river at Gaumukh (the Cow's Mouth) now requires a permit from the **District Forest Officer** (☎ 222444) in Uttarkashi. The permit costs Rs50/350 per Indian/foreigner, valid for two days, and the trek is restricted to 150 people per day. From Gangotri temple, it's 14km (six hours) to **Bhojbasa** (3790m), which has basic accommodation including a **GMVN Tourist Bungalow** (dm 250), then 5km (three hours) to the dramatic **Gaumukh Glacier**, which has a 500m exclusion zone.

Buses run from Gangotri to Uttarkashi (Rs110, six hours) and Rishikesh (Rs250, 12

THE CHAR DHAM

The Char Dham of Garhwal refers to the four ancient temples that mark the spiritual sources of four sacred rivers, the Yamuna (Yamunotri), the Ganges (Gangotri), the Mandakini (Kedarnath) and the Alaknanda (Badrinath). Every year during the *yatra* (pilgrimage) season from April to November, hundreds of thousands of dedicated Hindu pilgrims make these important treks – the exact dates that the temples are open are announced each year by local priests.

Religious tourism is big business and numerous buses, share 4WDs, porters, ponies and palanquins are on hand for transport, along with a well-established network of budget guest houses, ashrams and government rest houses. As a result, getting to these temples is easy enough without the need for a guide or carrying supplies. For more information see Yamunotri Temple Trek (below), Gangotri Temple & Gaumukh Glacier Trek (opposite), Kedarnath Temple Trek (below) and Badrinath Temple & Mana Village (p486). Only Gangotri and Badrinath temples can be visited without having to undertake a trek.

hours). Share 4WDs (Rs150) also run between Gangotri and Uttarkashi.

Yamunotri Temple Trek
elev 3185m

Yamunotri Temple nestles in a valley close to the source of the Yamuna, Hinduism's second-most-sacred river after the Ganges. For pilgrims Yamunotri is the least visited and so least developed of the Char Dham temples, but once you get to the trailhead it's an easy trek in.

The trek begins where the road ends at Janki Chatti, 7km beyond the village of Hanuman Chatti (2400m). There are hot springs and 1km away is a pretty village, Kharsali. From here it's a 5km, two-hour trek to Yamunotri Temple (3185m). High mountains close in around the temple and there are several hot springs where you can take a dip, and others where pilgrims cook potatoes and rice as *prasad*. The Yamuna River emerges from a frozen lake of ice and glaciers on the Kalinda Parvat mountain at an altitude of 4421m, 1km beyond the temple, but this is a very tough climb that requires mountaineering skills.

Accommodation is available in basic pilgrims' guest houses or at the **GMVN tourist lodges** (www.gmvnl.com) at Yamunotri, Janki Chatti and Hanuman Chatti.

Buses run from Dehra Dun, Mussoorie and Rishikesh to Hanuman Chatti during the *yatra* season. Buses also run to Uttarkashi (Rs70, six hours) for those heading to the next Char Dham stop, Gangotri.

Har ki Dun Valley Trek

The wonderfully remote Har ki Dun (3510m) is a botanical paradise criss-crossed by glacial streams and surrounded by pristine forests and snowy peaks. The area is preserved as **Govind Wildlife Sanctuary & National Park** (Indian/ foreigner up to 3 days Rs50/350, subsequent days Rs20/175). You might be lucky enough to glimpse the elusive snow leopard above 3500m.

The trail begins at Sankri (also called Saur), and there are **GMVN Tourist Bungalows** (dm/d Rs150/450) at Sankri, Taluka and Osla, but you have to stay in a Forest Department rest house or else camp in the valley itself. It's a 38km hike to Har ki Dun, which takes three days – or two days if you take a share 4WD to Taluka. A side trip to Jamdar Glacier takes another day. The trek can be busy during June and October.

To get to Sankri, take a bus or a share 4WD from Gandhi Chowk in Mussoorie. If you cannot find a bus or share 4WD going all the way, go as far as you can and then catch other buses or share 4WDs.

Kedarnath Temple Trek
☎ 01364 / elev 3584m

Kedarnath is revered as the source of the Mandakini River, but this magnificent temple is primarily dedicated to the hump that Shiva (who had taken the form of a bull) left behind when he dove into the ground to escape the Pandavas. Other portions of Shiva's body are worshipped at the other four Panch Kedar shrines, which are hard to reach but can be visited: the arms at Tungnath; the face at Rudranath; the navel at Madmaheshwar; and the hair at Kalpeshwar. The actual source of the Mandakini River is 12km past Kedarnath.

The temple was originally built in the 8th century by Guru Shankara, who is buried

UTTARAKHAND

behind the shrine. The surrounding scenery is superb, but Kedarnath attracts 100,000 pilgrims every year, which means plenty of people, noise and litter. The site is so auspicious that pilgrims used to throw themselves from one of the cliffs behind the temple in the hope of instantly attaining *moksha* (liberation).

The tough 14km uphill trek to the temple (3584m) takes six hours on foot (five hours on a pony) and begins at Gaurikund, which has basic accommodation and a **GMVN Tourist Bungalow** (☎ 269202; dm Rs150, d Rs600-990). Stalls store luggage, and porters and ponies can be hired. The wide, paved trail to the temple is lined with *dhabas* and chai stalls.

The whole area is a wildlife sanctuary, and a **musk deer breeding farm** has been established at Khanchula Kharak, 32km from Gopeshwar on the road to Ukhimath. These tiny deer with big ears have been hunted to the brink of extinction.

There is more pilgrims' accommodation available near the temple, including the **GMVN Tourist Bungalow** (☎ 263218; dm Rs150, d Rs400-950).

Buses run from Gaurikund to Rishikesh (Rs190, 12 hours), or you can use share 4WDs to make the same journey. Get off at Rudraprayag for connections to Joshimath, Badrinath and the eastern Kumaon district.

JOSHIMATH
☎ 01389 / pop 13,202 / elev 1845m

As the gateway to Badrinath Temple, Valley of the Flowers and Hem Kund, Joshimath sees a steady stream of Hindu and Sikh pilgrims from April to October. And as the base for the excellent Kuari Pass and Nanda Devi treks and Auli ski resort, adventure travellers are drawn here year-round.

Reached from Rishikesh by a hair-raising mountain road that hugs steep-sided valleys for the final few hours, Joshimath is a ramshackle two-street town and a rather ugly administrative centre full of rusting rooftops, erratic power supply and limited places to eat. Although the mountain views are lost from the town itself, it's only a short cable-car ride from here to magnificent views of Nanda Devi.

Information
There's a **GMVN Tourist Office** (☎ 222181; ⏲ 10am-5pm Mon-Sat) located just above the town (follow the Tourist Rest House sign off Upper Bazar Rd), and there's a State Bank of India ATM that accepts foreign cards.

Activities
TREKKING
Kuari Pass and Nanda Devi are two of the most popular treks from Joshimath. You need a permit and a registered guide to undertake these treks and there are three excellent operators in town who can organise all-inclusive treks:

Adventure Trekking (☎ 222446; www.adventuretrek king.org; Main Bazar)
Treks of anything from two to 10 days can be arranged here for around US$45 per person per day, as well as white-water rafting, skiing and mountain climbing. The owner, Santosh, is helpful and runs a guest house on the way up to Auli (r Rs1000 to Rs2000).

Eskimo Adventures (☎ 222630; eskimoadventures@ rediffmail.com) Offers treks and rock-climbing expeditions from Rs1500 per day, and equipment rental (for trekking and skiing), as well as white-water rafting trips on the Ganges.

Himalayan Snow Runner (☎ 222252; www.hima layansnowrunner.com; Main Bazar) Recommended outfit for trekking (from Rs1900 per day), skiing and adventure activities. The owner, Ajay, also takes cultural tours to Bhotia and Garhwali villages in the region, and runs a guest house in his home in the village of Mawari, 5km from Josimath (d Rs1060).

Sleeping & Eating
There are lots of cheap lodgings and a few hotels scattered around town. Joshimath's trekking outfits also operate upmarket homestay-style guesthouses that are worth considering.

Hotel Snow Crest (☎ 222344; dm Rs200, d Rs1450-1650) Right behind Kamet (see above), the rooms here are clean and cosy but grossly overpriced. The front rooms are brightest. There's a good restaurant serving a vegetarian menu of North and South Indian and Chinese. Rates are usually reduced by 40% (except in May and June), and there's a 10-bed dorm.

Hotel Kamet (☎ 222155; Main Bazar; d Rs250-900) Good central budget option. Slightly worn rooms have TV and bucket hot water and, at the time of research, the owners were building a new annexe.

There are several *dhabas* in the main bazaar, all serving similar veg thalis and dosas from Rs20 to Rs90.

Getting There & Away

Although the main road up to Joshimath is maintained by the Indian army, and a hydroelectric plant on the way to Badrinath has improved that road, the area around Joshimath is inevitably prone to landslides, particularly in the rainy season from mid-June to the end of August.

Buses run to Badrinath (Rs45, two hours) at 6.30am, 9am, 11.30am, 2pm and 4.30pm, departing from near the Narsingh Temple on Lower Bazar Rd. Take the same buses to Govindghat (Rs20, one hour), which is the start of the treks to the wonderful Valley of Flowers and dramatic Hem Kund. Share 4WDs (Rs60) do the same trip, departing from the 4WD stand at the top end of Upper Bazar Rd when full – your best chance of a ride is in the morning. To hire the whole 4WD is Rs600.

Buses run from Joshimath to Rishikesh (Rs230, 10 hours) and Haridwar (Rs250, 11½ hours) about every hour between 4am and 7am. They leave from outside the tiny **GMOU booth** (Upper Bazar Rd; ☾ 4am-8pm), where you can also book tickets. To get to the eastern Kumaon region take any Rishikesh bus to Karnaprayag (Rs75, 3½ hours), from where local buses and share 4WDs can take you along the slow-going route towards Kausani, Bageshwar and Almora. There are direct buses from Karnaprayag to Gwaldam (Rs60, 3½ hours), where you can pick up another bus or shared 4WD.

AROUND JOSHIMATH
Auli
☎ 01389 / elev 3019m

Rising above Joshimath, 14km by road – and only 4km by the gondola-style cable car – Auli is India's premier ski resort. But you don't have to visit in winter to do some hiking and enjoy the awesome views of Nanda Devi (India's highest peak) from the top of the cable-car station.

As a ski resort, Auli is hardly spectacular, with gentle 5km-long slopes, one 500m rope tow (Rs100 per trip) that runs beside the main slope, and an 800m chairlift (Rs200) that connects the upper and lower slopes. The snow is consistently good, though, and the setting is superb. The season runs from January to March and equipment hire and instruction can be arranged here or in Joshimath.

The state-of-the-art **cable car** (return Rs500; ☾ every 20min 8am-6.50pm), India's longest, links Joshimath to the upper slopes above Auli. There's a cafe, of sorts, at the top, serving hot chai and tomato soup.

There are just two places to stay at Auli and both hire out ski equipment and provide ski lessons.

GMVN Tourist Rest House (☎ 223208; www.gmvnl .com; dm Rs150-200, huts Rs900, d Rs1500-1700) Located at the start of the chairlift, there are no views from the rooms but the four-person dorms are certainly cheap and the flimsy huts are cosy inside. There's a restaurant and bar.

Cliff Top Club Resort (☎ 223217, in Delhi 011-25616679; www.nivalink.com/clifftop; studio Rs4500, ste Rs7500, f Rs9500) This hotel wouldn't look out of place in the Swiss Alps with its solid timber interior finish, cosy atmosphere and spacious rooms, some with views of Nanda Devi. Meals and all-inclusive ski packages are available.

VALLEY OF FLOWERS & HEM KUND TREK

British mountaineer Frank Smythe stumbled upon the Valley of Flowers in 1931. 'In all my mountain wandering,' he wrote, 'I have not seen a more beautiful valley where the human spirit may find repose.' The *bugyal* (high-altitude meadows) of tall wildflowers are a glorious sight on a sunny day, rippling in the breeze, and framed by mighty 6000m mountains that have glaciers and snow decorating their peaks all year.

The 300 species of flowers make the valley a unique and valuable pharmaceutical resource that may soon be a World Heritage Site. Unfortunately most flowers bloom during the monsoon season in July and August, when the rains make access difficult and hazardous. But the peace and beauty that Smythe found here can be experienced at any season, and there's still a good chance of seeing a carpet of flowers in September.

To reach the 87-sq-km **Valley of Flowers National Park** (Indian/foreigner up to 3 days Rs40/350, subsequent days Rs20/175; ☾ 6am-6pm May-Oct, last entry 3pm) requires a full-day trek from Govindghat to the village of Ghangaria, less than 1km from the park. Just 2km from the ticket office, the fabled valley begins and continues for another 5km. Tracks are easy to follow. No overnight stay is permitted here (or at Hem Kund) so you must stay in Ghangaria.

A tougher trek from Ghangaria is to join the hundreds of Sikh pilgrims toiling up to the 4300m **Hem Kund**, the sacred lake where Sikh guru Gobind Singh is believed to have meditated in a previous life. The pilgrim season runs from around 1 June to 1 October. Ponies (Rs350) are available if you prefer to ride up the 6km zigzag track.

Also called Govinddham, **Ghangaria** is a one-street village in a wonderful deodar forest with a busy market, a handful of budget hotels and restaurants, hundreds of ponies, a pharmacy and a doctor. Water and electricity supplies are erratic. The **Nature Interpretation Centre** (3-8pm 1 Jun-5 Oct) shows a film on the Valley of Flowers nightly at 7pm.

Hotel Priya (d from Rs250) is one of the better budget places to stay, or try **Nanda Lokpal Palace** (9412909307; d from Rs200).

Ghangaria is a scenic but strenuous 14km, seven-hour uphill trek from Govindghat, but you can help the local economy by hiring a porter (Rs350) or a pony (Rs450). The return trip takes four to five hours. You don't need to carry food because there are *dhabas* and drink stalls along the way serving the army of pilgrims heading to Hem Kund.

At **Govindghat** you can stay at the huge **gurdwara** (payment by donation), where VIP rooms are basic, or the new **Hotel Bhagat** (01381-225226; d Rs600), with very clean rooms and meals available.

All buses and share 4WDs between Joshimath and Badrinath stop in Govindghat, so you can easily find transport travelling in either direction.

BADRINATH & MANA VILLAGE

 01381 / elev 3133m

Basking in a superb setting in the shadow of snow-topped Nilkantha, **Badrinath Temple** appears almost lost in the tatty village that surrounds it. Sacred to Lord Vishnu, this vividly painted temple is the most easily accessible and most popular of the Char Dham temples. It was founded by Guru Shankara in the 8th century, but the current structure is much more recent. Below the temple are hot springs that reach a scalding 40°C and serve as a laundry for locals.

A very scenic 3km walk beyond Badrinath along the Alaknanda River (cross over to the temple side to pick up the path), past fields divided by dry-stone walls, leads to tiny but charismatic **Mana village**. The village is

crammed with narrow stone laneways and traditional houses of varying designs – some have slate walls and roofs while others are wooden with cute balconies. You can wander around and watch the village ladies knitting colourful jerseys or weaving blankets or carpets while the men tend the sheep or play cards or carom. Carpets (Rs150 for a small square, Rs2000 for bigger ones), blankets, jerseys, hats and gloves are all on sale.

Just outside the village in a small cave is the tiny, 5000-year-old **Vyas Temple**. Nearby is **Bhima's Rock**, a natural rock arch over a river that is said to have been made by Bhima, strongest of the Pandava brothers, whose tale is told in the Mahabharata. The 145m **Vasudhara Waterfall** can be seen from the village and is a 4km hike along the river. The villagers migrate to somewhere warmer and less remote – usually Joshimath – between November and April.

From the large bus station at the entrance to Badrinath, buses run to Govindghat and Joshimath during *yatra* season, but check scheduled departure times or you may end up stranded.

Sleeping & Eating

Badrinath can easily be visited in a day from Joshimath, but it's a serene place to spend the night and there are plenty of places to stay and eat here during the pilgrimage season. Budget guest houses are generally discounted to Rs100 a room outside the short peak season of May and June.

Jagirdar Guest House (9412935549; r Rs400) In a stone building across the river about 100m from the temple, this is a good budget place accustomed to travellers.

Brahma Kamal (meals Rs30-80) Directly opposite the temple, overlooking the river, this is a popular restaurant.

KUARI PASS TREK

Also known as the Curzon Trail (though Lord Curzon's party abandoned its attempt on the pass following an attack of wild bees), the trek over the Kuari Pass (3640m) was popular in the Raj era. It's still one of Uttarakhand's finest and most accessible treks, affording magnificent views of the snow-clad peaks around Nanda Devi. The trailhead is at Auli and the 75km trek to Ghat past lakes, waterfalls, forests, meadows and small villages takes five days, though it's possible to do a shorter version that finishes in Tapovan in three days. A tent, guide, permit and your own food supplies are necessary, all of which can be organised easily in Joshimath.

Auli can be reached by bus or cable car from Joshimath. From Ghat share 4WDs (Rs40, 1½ hours) go to Nandaprayag, from where buses run to Joshimath or southwest to Rishikesh and Haridwar.

NANDA DEVI SANCTUARY TREK

The 630 sq km of breathtaking World Heritage scenery that makes up this sanctuary was closed to all visitors in 1983, but small-group treks are now permitted within the inner sanctuary. Only 20 visitors a week are allowed inside this fabled Himalayan wonder between 1 May and 31 October. Check details with the GMVN or trekking outfits in Joshimath. Some 27km of the outer sanctuary is open, but you still need to arrange it through registered trekking agencies. Access is via Lata village, near Joshimath.

CORBETT TIGER RESERVE

☎ 05947 / elev 400-1210m

This famous **reserve** (☼ 15 Nov-15 Jun) was established in 1936 as India's first national park. Originally called Hailey National Park, then Ramganga National Park, it was renamed in 1957 after legendary tiger hunter Jim Corbett (1875–1955), who put Kumaon on the map with his book *The Man-Eaters of Kumaon*. The British hunter was greatly revered by local people for shooting tigers that had developed a taste for human flesh, but he eventually shot more wildlife with his camera than with his gun.

The reserve Jim Corbett established inspired the India-wide Project Tiger program, which started in 1973 and saw the creation of 22 other reserves. Tiger sightings are down to chance as the 168 or so tigers in the reserve are neither baited nor tracked, but if you spend a bit of time in the park, there's a good chance you'll see one of these magnificent endangered animals in the wild. Your best chance of spotting a tiger is late in the season (April to mid-June), when the forest cover is low and animals come out in search of water.

Notwithstanding tiger sightings, few serious wildlife enthusiasts will leave disappointed, as the 1318-sq-km park has a variety of wildlife and birdlife in grassland, sal forest and river habitats, and a beautiful location in the foothills of the Himalaya on the Ramganga River. Commonly seen wildlife include wild elephants (200 to 300 live in the reserve), sloth bears, langur monkeys (black face, long tail), rhesus macaques (red face and backside), peacocks, schools of otters and several types of deer including chital (spotted deer), sambars, hog deer and barking deer. You might also see leopards, mugger crocodiles, gharials, monitor lizards, wild boars and jackals. The Ramganga Reservoir attracts large numbers of migrating birds, especially from mid-December to the end of March, and over 600 species have been spotted here.

While the core park area (Dhikala Zone) is closed between 15 June and 15 November, parts of the reserve are open year-round. The jungle around Jhirna Gate, 25km from Ramnagar in the southern part of the reserve, remains open all year, and short 4WD safaris and elephant rides can be organised in Ramnagar. In 2004, the park started opening for day safaris (a maximum of 60 vehicles per day) a month early on 15 October from Amdanda Gate, although this date was moved forward to 1 October in 2008, and the Durga Devi Gate in the northeast of the park was also opened from 1 November – check with the reception centre!

Be sure to bring binoculars (you can hire them at park gates) and plenty of mosquito repellent and mineral water. If you're interested in the life of Jim Corbett, his former house at Kaladhungi, 26km southeast of Ramnagar, is now a **museum** (admission Rs10; ☼ 8am-5pm).

Orientation & Information

The main **reception centre** (☎ 251489; Ranikhet Rd; ☼ 6am-4pm) is located on the main road in Ramnagar, almost opposite the bus stand. This is the main place to organise 4WD safaris and entry into the park.

The main entry points for the park are Amdanda Gate (for Bijrani visitor centre), 2km north of Ramnagar, Dhangarhi Gate (for Dhikala), 18km north of Ramnagar, and Durga Devi Gate (for Domunda zone), 26km north of Ramnagar, as well as Jhirna Gate (also called Khara Gate), 25km west of Ramnagar.

Dhikala, 49km northwest of Ramnagar and deep inside the reserve, is the main accommodation centre within the park's core area, but it is only open to overnight guests, or as part of a tour booked through the reception centre at Ramnagar. Dhikala has a library and wildlife films are shown here for free at 7pm. Day trippers are restricted to the Bijrani visitor centre (11km from Ramnagar), which has an interpretative centre and a restaurant and is close to the reserve entrance.

Two-hour **elephant safaris** (Indian/foreigner 4 passengers per elephant Rs150/250) are available at Dhikala, Khinnanauli, Gairal and Jhirna Gate at 6am and 4pm on a first-come, first-served basis.

Located at the southeast corner of the park, Ramnagar is the main service town, and while it has plenty of facilities, hotels, restaurants, internet cafes (Rs30 per hr), ATMs (State Bank of India ATM at the train station, and a Bank of Baroda ATM on Ranikhet Rd) and transport connections – mostly along Ranikhet Rd – it's a busy, unappealing place.

PERMITS, COSTS & 4WD TRANSPORT

All entry permits are organised at the reception centre. In the low season (15 June to 15 November) you can only enter through Jhirna (Khara) Gate. However, from 15 October to 15 November, day visits are also permitted through Amdanda Gate and Durga Devi Gate (Rs200 plus 4WD and guide fees, open 6.30am to 11am and 3pm to 5.30pm).

From 15 November to 15 June the entry fee (Indian/foreigner Rs50/450) covers three days. The 4WD fee is Rs100 at Bijrani and Rs150 at Dhikala, and a compulsory guide fee (Rs200) must also be paid.

Four-wheel drives or the smaller Maruti Gypsies can be hired at the reception centre in Ramnagar, or through your accommodation or a tour agency. The 4WD owners have formed a union, so in theory the rates are fixed (on a per 4WD basis, carrying up to six people). Half-day safaris (leaving in the morning and afternoon) should cost Rs800 to Bijrani, Rs900 to Jhirna or Rs1200 to Durga Devi, excluding the entry fees. Full-day safaris cost double. Transport to Dhikala is Rs1500. Check prices at the reception centre and at your hotel before hiring a 4WD.

Fishing permits (along the Ramnagar River outside the park) can be obtained at the reception centre.

Tours

The reception centre in Ramnagar runs a daily **bus tour** (Indian/foreigner Rs600/1200) to Dhikala at 8.30am.

Sleeping & Eating

For serious wildlife viewing, Dhikala – deep inside the reserve – is the best place to stay, though the prices for foreigners are exorbitant. Book through the reception centre in Ramnagar except where indicated. Book ahead as space is limited and you must have accommodation arranged to stay within the park. The town of Ramnagar has budget accommodation, while upmarket resorts are strung out along the road skirting the eastern side of the park between Dhikuli and Dhangarhi Gate.

DHIKALA

Easily the cheapest beds in the park are at **Log Huts** (dm Indian/foreigner Rs100/200), resembling 3AC train sleepers, with 24 basic beds (no bedding supplied). **Tourist Hutments** (Indian/foreigner Rs800/1800) offer the best value accommodation in Dhikala and sleep up to six people. Dhikala has a couple of restaurants serving vegetarian food. No alcohol is allowed in the park.

If you're after VIP accommodation, the **Old Forest Rest House** (r Rs800/2000 or Rs1300/2800), the **New Forest Rest House** (r Rs800/1800) and three **cabins** (Rs800/1800) can all be booked at the reception centre in Ramnagar. **Annexe** (r Rs600/1400) can be booked through the **Uttarakhand Tourism Development Board** (UTDB; ☎ 011-23319835) in Delhi.

ELSEWHERE IN THE RESERVE

Small rest houses in the park are at Kanda, Sultan Mailini and Jhirna (Indian/foreigner Rs600/1400), Lohachaur, Halduparao, Morghatti, Sendhikal, Mudiapani, Rathuadhab, Pakhro and Dhela (Rs400/800). Other places:

Bijrani Rest House (s/d Indian Rs400/600, foreigner Rs800/1400) The first place in from Amdanda Gate; meals and elephant rides available.

Gairal Rest House (r Indian/foreigner Rs600/1400) On the Ramnagar River, accessed from Dhangarhi Gate; meals available.

Sarapduli Rest House (r Indian/foreigner Rs1300/2800) Also has a good location in the reserve's core area.

Khinnanauli Rest House (r Indian/foreigner Rs1300/2800) Near Dhikala, deep in the reserve.

RAMNAGAR

Hotel Anand (☎ 254385; Ranikhet Rd; s/d Rs250/450) A noisy budget option located about 100m from the bus stand, Anand has average rooms with bucket hot water and TV – however many of the rooms only have windows onto a corridor.

Corbett Motel (☎ 9837468933; karansafaris@yahoo.co.in; tent Rs400, d/tr Rs500/600) Set in a beautiful mango orchard only a few hundred metres from the train station, this is Ramnagar's best budget accommodation and a world away from the traffic-clogged centre. You can stay in sturdy tents or basic but spotless rooms, and the restaurant serves fine Kumaon food. The owner, Karan, is a well-known local naturalist and can organise 4WD safaris into the park. Call ahead for a pick-up.

Krishna Nidhi Corbett Inn (☎ 251755; Ranikhet Rd; d with/without AC Rs990/590; 🅿) Clean, spacious rooms with balconies or verandas make this a good midrange option at the northern end of Ramnagar's main street. The manager can help organise safaris.

Govind Restaurant (Ranikhet Rd; meals Rs45-160) Although a bit gloomy inside, the food is good and the menu huge with monster thalis, biryani, chicken tikka, tasty stuffed tomatoes and mushroom curry. There's a pastry and sweet shop at the front.

NORTH OF RAMNAGAR

Half a dozen upmarket African-style safari resorts are strung along the Ramnagar–Ranikhet road that runs along the reserve's eastern boundary, and given the cost of accommodation at Dhikala, these are well worth considering. Most are around a settlement called Dhikuli – not to be confused with Dhikala! When most of the reserve is closed (15 June to 15 November), discounts of up to 50% are offered. Rates given here are for room only, but most have packages that include meals and safaris. All places have resident naturalists, recreational facilities, restaurants and bars.

Tiger Camp (☎ 2551963; www.tiger-camp.com; r Rs2050/2500, cottages Rs3050; 🅿) This intimate, excellent-value resort is nestled in shady jungle-style garden by the Kosi River 8km from Ramnagar. Modern, cosy cottages and bungalows have all the facilities, and nature walks and village tours are offered.

Corbett Hideaway (☎ 284132; www.corbetthideaway.com; Dhikuli; cottages Rs6750-8250; 🅿 🅰) The luxurious ochre cottages offer privacy, the riverside garden is relaxing, and there's a poolside bar and thatched restaurant at this quality resort, 12km north of Ramnagar.

Infinity Resorts (☎ 251279; www.infinityresorts.com; Dhikuli; s/d incl breakfast from Rs7000/9000; 🅿 🅰) The most impressive of the resorts in this area, Infinity has luxurious rooms, a roundhouse

with restaurant and bar, and a swimming pool in a lovely garden backing onto the Kosi River (where you can see hordes of golden mahseer fish).

Getting There & Away

Buses run almost hourly to Delhi (Rs150, seven hours), Haridwar (Rs113, six hours) and Dehra Dun (Rs150, seven hours). For Nainital (Rs71, 3½ hours) there are four direct buses, or take one to Kaladhungi and change there. Buses to Ranikhet (Rs77, 4½ hours) leave every couple of hours in the morning, and some continue to Almora. Frequent buses run to Haldwani (Rs35, two hours).

Ramnagar train station is 1.5km south of the main reception centre. The nightly *Corbett Park Link Express* (sleeper/2AC Rs107/417) leaves Delhi at 10.40pm, arriving in Ramnagar at 4.55am. The return trip leaves Ramnagar at 9.40pm, arriving in Old Delhi at 4.15am. For other destinations, change at Moradabad.

NAINITAL

☎ 05942 / pop 39,840 / elev 1938m

Crowded around a deep, green volcanic lake, Nainital is Kumaon's largest town and favourite hill resort. It occupies a steep forested valley around the namesake lake Naini and was founded by homesick Brits reminded of the Cumbrian Lake District. Disaster struck here in December 1880 when a major landslide buried a hotel and 150 people, creating the memorial recreation ground now known as the Flats.

Plenty of hotels are set in the forested hills around the lake, there's a busy bazaar, and a spider's web of walking tracks covers the forested hillsides to viewpoints overlooking the distant Himalayan peaks. For travellers it's a good place to kick back and relax, eat well, go horse riding or go paddling on the lake, but avoid peak seasons – roughly May to mid-July and October – when Nainital is packed to the gills with holidaying families and honeymooners, and hotel prices skyrocket.

Orientation

Tallital (Lake's Foot) is at the southeastern end of the lake where you'll find the bus stand and the main road heading east towards Bhowali. The 1.5km promenade known as the Mall leads to Mallital (Lake's Head) at the northwestern end of the lake. Most hotels, guest houses and restaurants are strung out along the Mall between Mallital and Tallital.

Information

Bank of Baroda ATM (The Mall, Tallital) Accepts international cards.

BD Pandey Government Hospital (☎ 235012; Mallital) Located off the Mall.

Cyberia (Mallital; per hr Rs20; ☽ 9.30am-9pm) Nainital's best internet cafe offers CD burning, printing and wi-fi access. Found off the Mall.

HDFC Bank (the Mall; ☽ 10am-4pm Mon-Fri, to 1pm Sat) Forex desk exchanges cash and travellers cheques; 24-hour ATM.

Main post office (Mallital; ☽ 10am-5pm Mon-Sat)

Narains (the Mall, Mallital; ☽ 10am-7.30pm) Good selection of books including plenty relating to local hero Jim Corbett, who used to patronise this bookshop.

Post office (the Mall, Tallital; ☽ 10am-5pm Mon-Sat)

State Bank of India (the Mall, Mallital; ☽ 10am-4pm Mon-Fri, to 1pm Sat) Exchanges major foreign currencies and travellers cheques. The ATM accepts international cards.

Uttarakhand Tourism office (☎ 235337; the Mall; ☽ 10am-5pm Mon-Sat) Ask for the Nainital brochure.

Sights & Activities

NAINI LAKE

This pretty lake is Nainital's centrepiece and is said to be one of the emerald green eyes of Shiva's wife, Sati (*naina* is Sanskrit for eye). **Naina Devi Temple**, rebuilt after the 1880 landslide, is on the precise spot where the eye is believed to have fallen. Nearby is the **Jama Masjid** and a **gurdwara**. You can walk around the lake in about an hour – the southern side is more peaceful and has good views back to the town.

Boatmen will row you around the lake for Rs125 (Rs85 one way) in the brightly painted gondolalike boats, or the **Nainital Boat Club** (Mallital; ☽ 10am-4pm) will sail you round for Rs130. Pedal and rowing boats can also be hired for Rs60 to Rs80 per hour.

SNOW VIEW & CABLE CAR

A **cable car** (adult/child return Rs100/60; ☽ 8am-7pm May & Jun, 10.30am-6pm Jul-Nov, 10.30am-4pm Dec-Apr) runs up to the popular Snow View at 2270m, which (on clear days) has panoramic Himalayan views, including of Nanda Devi. At the top you'll find the usual food, souvenir and carnival stalls, as well as **Mountain Magic** (rides Rs30-100), an amusement park with kids' entertainment including bumper cars, trampolines and a flying fox.

A highlight of the trip to Snow View is hiking to viewpoints such as **Cheena/Naina Peak**, 4km away. Local guides may offer to lead you on walks. One such guide, Sunil Kumar (☎ 9411196837), has plenty of experience as a trekker and birdwatcher and can take you on day walks (Rs375), or overnight walks where you stay in local villages (Rs950).

If you want to get up to Snow View for sunrise, taxis charge Rs150.

RAJ BHAVAN & GOLF COURSE

About 4km south of Tallital, **Raj Bhavan** (adult/child Rs50/20; ☽ 11am-1pm & 2-4pm Mon-Sat) is the official residence of the Governor of Uttarakhand. Styled on Buckingham Palace, it's an impressive castlelike building set in extensive grounds. Tours of the grounds are available but the residence is only open when the governor is out. In the grounds is a lovely 18-hole **golf course** (foreigners Rs800). Club hire and caddies are available.

TIFFIN TOP & LAND'S END

A 4km walk west of the lake brings you to Tiffin Top (2292m), also called Dorothy's Seat, from where it's a lovely 30-minute walk to Land's End (2118m) through a forest of oak, deodar and pine. Mangy horses gather west of town on the road to Ramnagar to take you on rides to these spots. A three-hour ride costs about Rs450, but you can take shorter rides (eg Tiffin Top for Rs70). Touts for these rides will no doubt accost you in Mallital near the ropeway.

NAINITAL ZOO

This high-altitude hillside **zoo** (☎ 236536; admission Rs25, camera Rs25; ☽ 10am-5pm Tue-Sun) has some large enclosures containing Himalayan animals, Siberian tigers, leopards and lots of pheasant species. It's a steep 20-minute walk from the Mall or a Rs50 taxi ride.

ROCK CLIMBING & TREKKING

The enthusiasts at **Nainital Mountaineering Club** (☎ 235051; Mallital) offer rock-climbing courses at the rock-climbing area, a 15m-high rock outcrop to the west of the town.

Snout Adventures (☎ 231749; www.snoutadventure.com; Ashok Cinema Bldg, Mallital) is a recommended outfit offering treks in the Kumaon and Garhwal mountains (from Rs2200 per day, all inclusive), rock-climbing courses (Rs400 per day) and adventure camps.

For information on KMVN's rest houses and trekking packages, visit **KMVN Parvat Tours** (☎ 235656; www.kmvn.org; Tallital).

NAINITAL

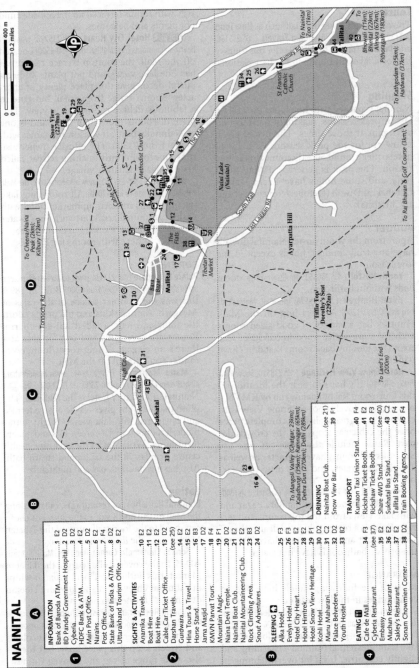

UTTARAKHAND

UTTARAKHAND

Tours

Travel agencies along the Mall such as **Hina Tours & Travel** (☎ 237126), **Anamika Travels** (☎ 235186) and **Darshan Travels** (☎ 235035) offer bus tours of the local lakes and tours to Corbett National Park.

Sleeping

Nainital is packed with hotels but they fill up fast in peak seasons, making it hard to find a bargain at those times. The prices given below are for the peak season; virtually all hotels offer around 50% discounts in the low season. The peak is generally 1 May to 30 June, and some hotels have a semipeak in October, at Diwali (October/November) and at Christmas.

BUDGET

Apart from the youth hostel, Nainital doesn't have any truly 'budget' hotels except in the low season.

Youth Hostel (☎ 236353; dm Rs60) Has dorm beds without bathroom.

Hotel Himtrek (☎ 235578; the Mall, Mallital; d/tr/q Rs500/800/1200) A short hop off the Mall, Himtrek has a variety of good-sized rooms with TV, some with a wood-lined 'chalet' feel. Avoid the gloomy back rooms that don't have windows.

Hotel Snow View Heritage (☎ 238570; Snow View Peak; d Rs990) It's hard to beat the location of this four-room Raj bungalow run by KMVN – perched in a lovely spot on Snow View with easy access to great walks and complete peace once the cable car stops and the crowds depart. Rates include the cable-car ride up. Spacious old rooms have character as well as TV and hot water, and rates drop to Rs600 out of season.

Kohli Hotel (☎ 236368; the Mall, Mallital; d Rs1000-1200, q Rs1800) Through bustling Bara Bazar and with lake views from the top rooms and terrace, Kohli is a reasonably good deal in the off season. Light and clean rooms have TV and the private bathrooms have hot water.

MIDRANGE

Most of the following hotels have budget range prices in the low season.

Evelyn Hotel (☎ 235457; www.hotelevelynnainital .com; the Mall, Tallital; d Rs1200-2100, ste Rs2400-5000) This large Victorian-looking hotel overlooking the lake is quintessential Nainital – charming and slightly eccentric. It's a bit overwhelming in

size, with rooms terraced up the hillside amid pot plants and balconies.

our pick **Hotel City Heart** (☎ 235228; www.city hearthotel.netfirms.com; Mallital; d Rs1450-3500) Located off the Mall, the rooftop terrace restaurant has fine lake views, and pot plants and colourful decor give this place plenty of character. Rooms range from small but cute to a fabulous deluxe room with a view. This place discounts more than most and is one of Nainital's best off-season bargains, with rooms from Rs500. The effusive owner also runs an eco and birdwatching retreat called Wild Ridzz in Ghatgar village.

Alka Hotel (☎ 235220; www.alkahotel.com; the Mall; d Rs2800-3800, ste Rs5000-7000) All rooms are lake-facing at this modern, upmarket hotel with flashy communal areas, artworks and water features. Rooms are small but neat. Nearby is a 'budget' annexe with rooms for Rs990.

TOP END

Palace Belvedere (☎ 237434; www.palacebelvedere.com; Mallital; s/d/ste from Rs4000/4700/6000) Built in 1897, this was the summer palace of the rajas of Awagarh. Animal skins and old prints adorn the walls and lend a faded Raj-era charm. Rooms are cavernous and comfortable and there's an elegant dining room/lounge/veranda. You'll find it off the Mall.

Manu Maharani (☎ 237341; www.manumahara nihotel.com; Mallital; r Rs6000-7500, ste Rs11,000; ⊠ 🖳) Nainital's top luxury hotel is the real deal. The plush marble lobby gives way to a large terrace and lawn area with lake views. Bright, ultramodern rooms have flat-screen TVs and quality furnishings. Work out in the exclusive health centre or relax in the sauna and steam bath. Also has a restaurant, bar and nightclub.

Eating

Nainital has a host of restaurants, mostly along the Mall on the north side of the lake. For cheap eats, head to the food stalls around the Tibetan Market or to the *dhabas* in Bara Bazar.

Sonam Chowmein Corner (the Flats, Mallital; meals Rs10-25) In the covered alley part of the Tibetan Market, this authentic Tibetan *dhaba* whips up fabulous chow mein and *momos* (Tibetan dumplings) for next to nothing.

Cyberia Restaurant & Pastry Shop (Mallital; meals Rs40-140, pastries & chocolates from Rs15) Thalis, *momos* and mouth-watering homemade chocolates and sweets keep this place busy, but there's also a big range of veg and nonveg Chinese,

Indian and Continental dishes. Wi-fi available. Located off the Mall.

Embassy (☎ 235597; the Mall, Mallital; meals Rs45-195; ✆ 10.30am-11pm) With a wood-lined chalet interior and snappily dressed staff, Embassy has been serving up five pages of menu items for over 40 years. For drinks try 'dancing coffee' or a rosewater lassi. Good people-watching terrace.

Machan Restaurant (☎ 237672; the Mall, Mallital; meals Rs45-110; ✆ 10am-11pm) The jungle-themed decor and bamboo facade here represent Corbett's wildlife-spotting towers, while the menu offers some of Nainital's best comfort food in the form of pizzas and burgers, along with Indian fare. Watch the chefs at work in the open kitchen.

Cafe de Mall (☎ 235527; the Mall, Tallital; meals Rs80-135; ✆ 9am-4pm & 5.30-10.30pm) This open-fronted lakeside cafe halfway along the Mall is a great place for breakfast or a cappuccino on the terrace, but the menu ranges from fish curry and kali mirch chicken to pizzas and impressive veg sizzlers.

Sakley's Restaurant (☎ 235086; Mallital; mains Rs85-375; ✆ 9am-10pm) A spotless restaurant found off the Mall, serving up a range of unusual global items such as Thai curries, honey chicken, roast lamb, pepper steaks, and plenty of Chinese dishes, pizzas and sizzlers. Desserts include pastries and Black Forest cake.

Drinking

Nainital Boat Club (The Mall, Mallital; temp membership men/women/couples Rs340/170/340; ✆ 10am-10pm) This lakeside club is a classic remnant of the Raj. The atmospheric bar is all timber beams, wicker chairs and buttoned-up barmen with handlebar moustaches, and the outdoor decking is perfect for an afternoon drink overlooking the lake. Temporary membership is steep but facilities include card-playing rooms, snooker tables (Rs40), table tennis and a library. The dress code specifies no shorts or thongs, and signs warn that 'decorum should be maintained'.

Snow View Bar (Snow View; ✆ 10am-7pm) Although there are no views from the rustic bar, it's worth dropping in for a beer and a snack after walking around the viewpoint. It's below the cable-car station.

Shopping

Nainital is crowded with souvenir shops and emporiums selling textiles, clothing and handicrafts from different regions of India. Intricately carved multicoloured candles are a local speciality. On the southwest side of the lake near the flats is a busy Tibetan Market with cheap clothing and crafts.

Getting There & Away

BUS

For details of buses leaving from the Tallital bus stand, see the table, below.

Although there are direct buses from Nainital, many more services leave from the transport hubs of Haldwani and Bhowali. From Haldwani, regular buses head to Ramnagar, Delhi and the Nepal border at Banbassa. Haldwani is also a major train terminus. To go north, take a bus or share 4WD to Bhowali (Rs10, 20 minutes) and catch one of the regular onward buses to Almora, Kausani and Ranikhet.

From the Sukhatal bus stand there are three daily buses to Ramnagar (Rs71, 3½ hours) via Kaladhungi.

Travel agencies sell tickets on private overnight deluxe coaches (with reclining seats) to Delhi (Rs250, nine hours), which leave around 9.30pm.

TAXI & SHARE 4WD

From the Kumaon Taxi Union stand in Tallital, taxi drivers charge Rs300 to Kathgodam (1½ hours), Rs700 to Ramnagar (three hours) and Rs800 to Almora (three hours) or Ranikhet.

Share 4WDs leave when full, and go to Bhowali (Rs10, 20 minutes) and Kathgodam/Haldwani (Rs60, 1½ hours).

BUSES FROM NAINITAL

The following buses leave from the Tallital bus stand.

Destination	Fare (Rs)	Duration (hr)	Frequency
Almora	60	3	7am
Dehra Dun	220	10	6 daily; early morning & evening
Delhi	191	9	3 daily
Haldwani	35	2	half-hourly
Haridwar	180	8	several early morning
Kathgodam (A)	31	1½	half-hourly
Rishikesh	195	9	5am
A – take the Haldwani bus			

UTTARAKHAND

TRAIN

Kathgodam (35km south of Nainital) is the nearest train station, but Haldwani, one stop further south, is the regional transport hub. The **train booking agency** (9am-noon & 2-5pm Mon-Fri, 9am-2pm Sat), next to the Tallital bus stand, has a quota for trains to Dehra Dun, Delhi, Moradabad, Lucknow, Gorakhpur and Kolkata. The daily *Ranikhet Express* (sleeper/ 3AC/2AC Rs121/339/472) departs Kathgodam at 8.40pm and arrives at Old Delhi station at 4.15am. In the other direction, it departs Delhi at 10.15pm, arriving at 5.45am.

Getting Around

Cycle-rickshaws charge a fixed Rs10 along the Mall, but can only pick up and drop off at the ticket booths at either end. Taxi rides within town cost Rs80 to Rs200.

RANIKHET

☎ 05966 / pop 19,049 / elev 1829m

Ranikhet, home to the Kumaon Regiment and bristling with good, old-fashioned military atmosphere, spreads over rolling green hills with some lovely views over the distant Himalaya. The focus of the town is a busy single-street bazaar area, but you don't have to walk far along the winding Mall Rd to be immersed in forest and tall English trees. Apart from a military museum, some peaceful walks and views of snowcapped peaks, there's not much to do in Ranikhet – it's much more of a retreat than some other hill stations and in the off season (December to March and August to September) accommodation is good value.

Information

Main post office (the Mall; 9am-5pm Mon-Fri)
Post office (Sadar Bazaar; 9am-5pm Mon-Fri)
Ranikhet Cyber Cafe (Gandhi Chowk; per hr Rs25; 9.30am-6.30pm) Ranikhet's best internet cafe is next to Ranikhet Inn.
State Bank of India (Sadar Bazaar; 10am-4pm Mon-Fri, to 1pm Sat) Exchanges travellers cheques but not cash.
State Bank of India ATM Found next to Ranikhet Inn, this ATM accepts foreign cards.
Uttarakhand Tourism office (220227; 10am-5pm Mon-Sat) Located above UP Roadways bus stand.

Sights & Activities

The **Kumaon Regimental Centre Museum** (admission Rs10; 9am-5pm Mon-Sat, to 12.30pm Sun), located off the Mall, is stuffed full of photos and military memorabilia relating to the Kumaon regiment. These include weapons captured in various battles, and the coffin of General TN Raina.

The **KRC Community Centre** (220567; the Mall; admission free; 8am-6.30pm, factory closed Wed & Sun), run by a welfare organisation for army widows, is in a converted church. One half is a factory where you can see workers at handlooms producing shawls and tweed, while the other half is a modern shop selling the finished products, along with candles, condiments and shoes.

From Sadar Bazar, the Mall winds 3km south to the army headquarters. A walking path starting by the sports ground provides a pleasant short-cut, passing a small pond and the stone Catholic church. From the southern end of the Mall it's a 1km walk to **Jhula Devi Temple**, which is festooned with bells.

Sleeping & Eating

Outside the two peak seasons (generally mid-April to mid-July and 1 October to early November), the prices given below are reduced by 30% to 50%.

Hotel Rajdeep (220017; Sadar Bazar; d Rs500-1800) The best of a gloomy bunch of hotels in the bazaar, Rajdeep has a big range of old-fashioned rooms from poky budget ones at the back to spacious rooms with veranda and view at the front.

Hotel Meghdoot (220475; the Mall; s Rs600-900, d Rs1100-1300, ste Rs1600) This big old hotel, just past the army headquarters 3km from the bazaar, has some quaint historical touches, a range of clean, spacious rooms, and a veranda packed with pot plants and greenery. Off-season rates are a bargain here.

Ranikhet Inn (221929; ranikhetinn@gmail.com; Gandhi Chowk; d Rs1800, ste Rs2400) This stylish boutique hotel with a castlelike facade is the pick of the midrange hotels in the Sadar Bazar area. Although showing a little wear, rooms are spotless with tiled floors, TV and hot water. The best rooms have balconies commanding good views. The terrace restaurant (mains Rs35 to Rs120) has a fine view and a good range of dishes, from pizza to chicken tikka to biryani.

Ranikhet Club (226011; the Mall; d year-round Rs2400-3000, ste Rs4200) For a taste of Raj nostalgia, look no further than the four classic rooms at this 1860 heritage wooden bungalow. The gentrified army ambience is typified by the members' bar, billiard room, card-playing rooms, tennis court and stylish restaurant.

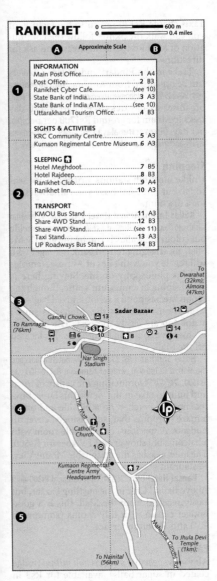

RANIKHET	0 _____ 600 m
	0 _____ 0.4 miles
Approximate Scale	

INFORMATION
Main Post Office..............................**1** A4
Post Office.......................................**2** B3
Ranikhet Cyber Cafe...................(see **10**)
State Bank of India...........................**3** A3
State Bank of India ATM..............(see **10**)
Uttarakhand Tourism Office...........**4** B3

SIGHTS & ACTIVITIES
KRC Community Centre....................**5** A3
Kumaon Regimental Centre Museum.**6** A3

SLEEPING 🏠
Hotel Meghdoot.................................**7** B5
Hotel Rajdeep...................................**8** B3
Ranikhet Club...................................**9** A4
Ranikhet Inn...................................**10** A3

TRANSPORT
KMOU Bus Stand.............................**11** A3
Share 4WD Stand............................**12** B3
Share 4WD Stand.........................(see **11**)
Taxi Stand.....................................**13** A3
UP Roadways Bus Stand.................**14** B3

UTTARAKHAND

hours) at 8.30am, and to Haridwar (Rs265, 10 hours) at 8.30am. Frequent buses run to Haldwani and Kathgodam via Bhowali (Rs40, two hours), which is only a short ride from Nainital. For the Garhwal region, buses go to Karnaprayag (Rs190, six hours) at 11.30am.

From the KMOU bus stand, at Gandhi Chowk, regular buses run to Almora (Rs45, two hours), and to Ramnagar (Rs77, 4½ hours) hourly from 6.30am to 2pm. One bus goes to Nainital at 9.30am (Rs77, 2½ hours).

Share 4WDs leave when full for Dwarahat (Rs50, 1½ hours), Almora (Rs80, two hours), Nainital (Rs100, 1½ hours) and Haldwani (Rs80, two hours) from near either of the two bus stands.

ALMORA
☎ 05962 / pop 32,357 / elev 1650m
Clinging to a steep-sided valley, Almora is the sprawling regional capital of Kumaon, first established as a summer capital by the Chand rajas of Kumaon in 1560. A cool climate and mountain views are attractions, but don't be put off by the ugly, shambolic main street when you're first deposited at the bus stand – head one block south to the pedestrian-only cobbled Lalal Bazaar, lined with intricately carved and painted traditional wooden shop facades. It's a fascinating place to stroll, people-watch and shop. While otherwise not bursting with interest, Almora has some colonial-era buildings, reliable trekking outfits and a couple of community-based weaving enterprises. You'll often see Westerners floating around, thanks to a hippy subculture of travellers living up around Kasar Devi temple.

Information
Internet access is available at several places in Lalal Bazaar and the Mall, usually from Rs25 per hour.
Post office (the Mall; 🕙 10am-5pm Mon-Fri, to 1pm Sat)
State Bank of India (the Mall; 🕙 10am-4pm Mon-Fri, to 1pm Sat) An ATM here accepts foreign cards.
State Bank of India ATM (Hotel Shikhar, the Mall) This ATM is located in front of the hotel. Accepts foreign cards.
Uttarakhand Tourism office (☎ 230180; Upper Mall Rd; 🕙 10am-5pm Mon-Sat)
Web Zone (The Mall; per hr Rs25; 🕙 9am-8.30pm) Internet access and train reservations.

Sights & Activities
The stone **Nanda Devi Temple** in Lalal Bazaar dates back to the Chand raja era, and is

The Seven Peaks Bar has a colonial feel – dress smartly after 7pm.

Getting There & Away
From the UP Roadways bus stand at the eastern end of the bazaar, buses run to Delhi (ordinary/deluxe Rs235/430, 12 hours) at 4pm, 4.30pm and 5pm, to Ramnagar (Rs80, 4½

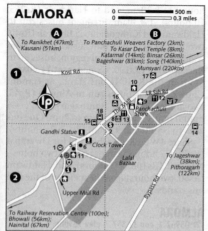

ALMORA

INFORMATION
Post Office	**1** A2
State Bank of India	**2** B2
State Bank of India ATM	(see 10)
Uttarakhand Tourism Office	**3** A2
Web Zone	**4** A2

SIGHTS & ACTIVITIES
Discover Himalaya	**5** A2
High Adventure	**6** A2
Nanda Devi Temple	**7** B1
Pt GB Pant Museum	**8** B1

SLEEPING
Bansal Hotel	**9** B1
Hotel Shikhar	**10** B1
Kailas International Hotel	**11** A2

EATING
Bansal Cafe	(see 9)
Glory Restaurant	**12** B1
New Soni Restaurant	**13** B1

TRANSPORT
Dharanaula Bus Stand	**14** B2
KMOU Bus Stand	**15** A1
Taxi & Share 4WD Stand	**16** B1
Taxi Stand	**17** B1
UP Roadways Bus Stand	**18** A1

covered in folk-art carvings, some erotic. Every September, the temple plays host to a **fair** (see the boxed text, p461).

The small **Pt GB Pant Museum** (the Mall; admission free; 10.30am-4.30pm Tue-Sun) houses local folk art and ancient Hindu sculptures.

The **Panchachuli Weavers Factory** (232310; admission free; 10am-5pm Mon-Sat), off Bageshwar Rd, employs some 300 women to weave woollen shawls. The shop here has a wider range of products than at the small shop in the Mall.

Taxis charge Rs120 return to the factory, or you can walk the 3km – follow the continuation of Mall Rd to the northeast and ask for directions.

Treks to the Pindari and Milam Glaciers can be organised from Almora. **High Adventure** (9012354501; highadventure@rediffmail.com; the Mall) organises six-day treks to Pindari and 10-day treks to Milam for around Rs1700 per person, per day. **Discover Himalaya** (236890; discoverhima laya@sancharnet.in; the Mall) runs similar trips.

Sleeping

Unlike most hill stations, prices are not seasonal, but if it's not busy you can always try for a discount.

Kailas International Hotel (230624; jawahar lalsah@india.com; dm Rs80, d Rs120-360) Ramshackle but colourful, Kailas is run by the elderly Mr Shah, an engaging retired bank manager who will regale you with tales of Almora, temples and his philosophy on life. Staying here is like sleeping in a museum's attic, though the rooms are basic and a serious mixed bag – the large rooms (such as the 'Maharaja suite') at the top are easily the best. The cheapest rooms have common bathrooms. It's located off the Mall.

Hotel Shikhar (230253; www.hotelshikhar.com; the Mall; d Rs300-990, without bathroom Rs150-300, ste Rs1500;) Dominating the centre of town and built to take in the views, this large, box-like hotel is perched on a hillside and offers a maze of rooms that, surprisingly, cover all budgets. A spacious, comfortable room with a balcony, hot shower and TV goes for Rs600. The hotel also has the reasonable Mount View Restaurant.

Bansal Hotel (230864; Lalal Bazaar; d Rs300-400) Above Bansal Cafe in the bustling bazaar, but easily reached from the Mall, this is a good budget choice with tidy rooms (some with TV) and a rooftop terrace.

Eating

Almora's speciality sweet is *ball mithai* (fudge coated in sugar balls), available for Rs3 in sweet shops all along the Mall and bazaar.

Bansal Cafe (Lalal Bazaar; drinks & snacks Rs15-30) This simple cafe in a lane between the Mall and Lalal Bazaar serves up a range of drinks and veg snacks, including good coffee, lassis, *chaat* (snack served with chutney) and samosas.

New Soni Restaurant (the Mall; mains Rs25-100) A popular Sikh *dhaba* serving tasty *paneer* (unfermented cheese), chicken and mutton dishes, and egg curry.

Glory Restaurant (☎ 230279; LR Sah Rd; mains Rs30-110) This long-running family eatery on two floors is clean and modern and serves up popular South and North Indian veg and nonveg dishes, including biryanis and lemon chicken.

Getting There & Away

Buses run from the adjacent UP Roadways and KMOU bus stands on the Mall roughly hourly until 3pm to Ranikhet (Rs40, two hours), Kausani (Rs42, 2½ hours) and Bhowali (Rs45, two hours). From Bhowali it's only a short bus or share-4WD ride to Nainital. Hourly buses run to Bageshwar (Rs67, two hours), from where you can pick up buses or share 4WDs to Song and Munsyari for the Pindari and Milam Glacier treks. There are early morning buses to Pithoragarh (Rs96, five hours) and more run from the Dharanaula bus stand on the Bypass Rd. For Banbassa on the Nepal border, take a bus to Haldwani and change there. Buses to Delhi (Rs300, 12 hours) leave in the morning and evening.

There's a **Railway Reservation Centre** (☉ 9am-noon & 2-5pm Mon-Sat) at the KMVN Tourist Holiday Home.

Taxis or 4WDs can be picked up from the Mall to Ranikhet (Rs700, two hours), Kausani (Rs800, 2½ hours), Bageshwar (Rs1000, two hours), Nainital (Rs1000), Pithoragah (Rs1500, five hours) and Munsyari (Rs3500, 10 hours).

AROUND ALMORA

The hilltop **Kasar Devi Temple**, where Swami Vivekananda meditated, is 8km north of Almora and can be reached by share 4WD (Rs15) or taxi (Rs400). The 800-year-old **Surya (Sun) temple** at Katarmal, 14km from Almora and a 2km walk from the main road, can be visited by getting on any share 4WD (Rs20, 30 minutes) going to Ranikhet. Picturesque **Binsar** (2420m), 26km from Almora, was once the summer capital of the Chand rajas and is now a popular beauty spot for forest trekking, with panoramic views of the Himalayan peaks. There's a Rs100 fee to enter the sanctuary. A return taxi from Almora costs Rs800.

A large temple complex is set in a forest of deodars at **Jageshwar**, 38km northeast of Almora. The 124 temples and shrines date back to the 7th century AD and vary from waist-high linga shrines to large *sikhara* (Hindu temples). They are a 4km walk from Jageshwar, which can be reached by taxi (Rs800 return).

KAUSANI

☎ 05962 / pop 4000 / elev 1890m

Perched high on a forest-covered ridge, this tiny village has lovely panoramic views of distant snowcapped peaks, fresh air, a cool climate and as relaxed an atmosphere as you'll find in northern India. Mahatma Gandhi found Kausani an inspirational place to retreat and write his Bhagavad Gita treatise *Anasakti Yoga* and there is still an ashram devoted to him here.

Information

Kausani has a State Bank of India ATM in the main bazaar, but no foreign currency exchange.

Hill Queen Cyber Cafe (Anasakti Ashram Rd; per hr Rs40; ☉ 6am-9.30pm)

Uttarakhand Tourism office (☎ 258067; the Mall; ☉ 10am-5pm)

Sights & Activities

At **Kausani Tea Estate** (☎ 258330; www.uttaranchaltea .com; admission free; ☉ 9am-6pm mid-Mar–mid-Nov), a tea plantation that involves private enterprise, the government and local farmers, you can look around and sample and buy its products, which are exported around the world. It's 3.5km north of the village on the road to Baijnath, an easy and scenic walk.

About 1km uphill from the bus stand, **Anasakti Ashram** is where Mahatma Gandhi spent two weeks pondering and writing *Anasakti Yoga* in 1929. It has a small **museum** (admission free; ☉ 5.30am-noon & 4-7pm) that tells the story of Gandhi's life through photographs and words. Visit at 6pm to attend nightly prayers in his memory.

Just up from Hill Queen Restaurant, there's a nightly **stargazing show** (admission Rs20; ☉ 7.30pm & 8.30pm May, Jun & Oct/Nov, 6.15pm winter) where you can see various stars and planets through a high-powered telescope.

Sleeping & Eating

Outside the two short peak seasons (May, June and October/November) the accommodation prices listed below are discounted by 50%.

Kausani Village Resort (☎ 258353; Bajnath Rd; r Rs300, d/tr huts Rs500/700) Overlooking the tea garden 3km north of Kausani village, these round, machan-style huts are a quirky and peaceful place to stay. Inside, they're a lot more comfy than they appear, with clean tiled bathrooms and views across the gardens to the mountains.

ourpick Hotel Uttarakhand (☎ 258012; www .uttarakhandkausani.zoomshare.com; d Rs750-1550; 🖳) Up some steps from the bus stand but in a quiet location with a panoramic view of the Himalaya from your veranda, this is Kausani's best-value accommodation. The cheaper rooms are small, but upper-floor rooms are spacious and all have hot showers and TV. The manager is helpful and friendly, and credit cards are accepted.

Krishna Mountview (☎ 258008; www.kumaonin dia.com; Anasakti Ashram Rd; d Rs2200-4500, ste Rs5500) Just past Anasakti Ashram, this is one of Kausani's smartest hotels, with clipped formal gardens (perfect for mountain views), the good Vaibhav restaurant, a gym and a pool table. All rooms are well kept and comfy, but the spacious upstairs rooms with balcony, bay windows and even rocking chairs are the pick.

You can stay at the **Anasakti Ashram** (☎ 258028; Anasakti Ashram Rd) for a donation but you must respect ashram rules, including attending evening prayers. Meals cost Rs30.

There a lots of cheap *dhabas* around the main bazaar and the road leading uphill from the bus stand.

Garden Restaurant (Hotel Uttarakhand; meals Rs40-300; 🕙 24hr) In front of Hotel Uttarkhand and enjoying fine Himalayan views, this bamboo and thatch-roofed restaurant is Kausani's coolest. The food comprises first class dishes from Swiss rösti to chicken tikka and imported pasta, as well as some Kumaon specialities, using fresh ingredients.

Getting There & Away

Buses and share 4WDs stop in the village centre. Buses (Rs42, 2½ hours) run about hourly to Almora, but afternoon buses generally stop at Karbala on the bypass road, from where you need to take a share 4WD (Rs5). Heading north, buses run every two hours to Bageshwar via Baijnath (Rs40, 1½ hours). Share 4WDs (Rs25, 30 minutes) run to Garur, 16km north of Kausani, from where other share 4WDs go to Gwaldam for onward buses and 4WDs to Garhwal (via Karnaprayag). A taxi to Almora costs around Rs800.

AROUND KAUSANI

About 19km north of Kausani, **Baijnath village** is known for its small 12th-century *sikhara*-style temples. The main group is devoted to Shiva and his consort Parvati and has a lovely location shaded by trees alongside the Gomti River. Several other Shaivite shrines are in the old village, a 10-minute walk north of Baijnath.

Take a Bageshwar bus from Kausani, or a share 4WD (Rs25) to Garur and then another (Rs25) to Baijnath. A return taxi from Kausani is Rs400.

You can trek to **Rudradhari Falls** and a small Shiva temple in the hills about 10km from Kausani. The easiest way is to take a taxi (Rs300 return) to the start of the path, from where it's a 1.5km walk along a marked trail to the temple.

BAGESHWAR

☎ 05963 / pop 7803 / elev 975m

At the confluence of the Gomti and Sarju Rivers, Bageshwar is a bustling pilgrimage town – Hindu pilgrims file in throughout the year to worship at the ancient stone **Bagnath Temple**. Dedicated to Shiva, this important temple is festooned with bells of all sizes and features impressive carvings. Both rivers are lined with bathing ghats. Bageshwar can be used as a jumping-off point for the Pindari Glacier trek – there's a **KMVN office** (☎ 220034; www.kmvn.org; Tarcula Rd) at Bageshwar Tourist Rest House, where the trekking manager can arrange all-inclusive six-day treks. At the bus stand, **Annapurna Communication & Cafe** (per hr Rs50; 🕙 8.30am-9.30pm) has internet access, and there's a State Bank of India ATM in the main bazaar.

Hotel Annapurna (☎ 220109; r Rs200-400, s/d without bathroom Rs70/150) is conveniently located next to the bus stand. It has a pleasant riverside terrace at the back and simple, functional rooms.

Across the river about 1km from the bus stand, the large KMVN **Bageshwar Tourist Rest House** (☎ 220034; Tarcula Rd; dm Rs100, d Rs250-600) is a bit institutional but has reasonable, spacious rooms and dorms.

Several daily buses go to Almora (Rs67, three hours) and Ranikhet (Rs81, three hours) via Kausani (Rs32, 1½ hours). Frequent buses run to Bhowali (Rs105, six hours) and Haldwani (Rs140, 7½ hours). For connections to Garhwal, take a bus (Rs40, two hours) or share 4WD (Rs60) to Gwaldam and change there. For Pindari Glacier trek, there are two daily buses to Song (Rs33, two hours). For Milam Glacier, there's a 9am bus to Munsyari (Rs125, six hours). The 4WD stand is close to the bus stand: share 4WDs go to Garur (Rs20, 30 minutes), Kausani (Rs50, 1½ hours) and Gwaldam (Rs60, two hours). A taxi to Song costs Rs800 (two hours).

PITHORAGARH

☎ 05964 / pop 41,157 / elev 1815m

Pithoragarh is the main town of a little-visited region that borders Tibet and Nepal and has several Chand-era temples and an old fort. The town sits in a small valley that has been dubbed 'Little Kashmir', and picturesque hikes in the area include the rewarding climb up to **Chandak** (7km) for views of the Panchachuli (Five Chimneys) massif.

The town has a **tourist office** (☎ 225527) that can help with trekking guides and information, and a **KMVN Rest House** (☎ 225434; dm Rs100, d Rs500-990).

Several buses leave in the morning for Almora (Rs96, five hours). Regular buses go to the transport hub of Haldwani and on to Delhi. Buses run north to Munsyari (Rs110, eight hours), the trailhead for Milam Glacier, as do the ubiquitous share 4WDs.

PINDARI GLACIER TREK

This six-day, 94km trek passes through truly virgin country that's inhabited by only a few shepherds, and it offers wonderful views of Nanda Kot (6860m) and Nanda Khat (6611m) on the southern rim of Nanda Devi Sanctuary. The 3km-long, 365m-wide Pindari Glacier is at 3353m, so take it easy to avoid altitude sickness. Permits aren't needed but bring your passport.

The trek begins and finishes at **Song** (1140m), a village 36km north of Bageshwar. Guides and porters can be organised easily in Song, or you can organise package treks through companies in Bageshwar or Almora. KMVN operates all-inclusive six-day treks out of Bageshwar for Rs5000 per person, staying at government rest houses. KMVN dorms (mattresses on the floor for Rs150), basic guest houses or *dhaba* huts (Rs50 to Rs200) are dotted along the route, and food is available.

Buses (Rs33, two hours) or share 4WDs (Rs50, 1½ hours) run between Song and Bageshwar.

MILAM GLACIER TREK

A challenging eight-day, 118km trek to this massive glacier at 3450m is reached along an ancient trade route to Tibet that was closed in 1962 following the war between India and China. It passes through magnificent rugged country to the east of Nanda Devi (7816m) and along the sometimes spectacular gorges of the Gori Ganga River. A popular but tough side trip to Nanda Devi East base camp adds another 30km or two days.

Permits (free; passport required) are available from the District Magistrate in Munsyari. You

UTTARAKHAND

CROSSING INTO NEPAL

Border Hours

The border is open 24 hours, but before 7am and after 5pm you're unlikely to find any officials to stamp you in and out of the respective countries. The border is officially manned from 9am to 5pm.

Foreign Exchange

Banks in Banbassa and Mahendranagar will change Indian currency to Nepali rupees but there is no foreign currency exchange and there are no ATMs.

Onward Transport

From the border, take a rickshaw to Mahendranagar. The bus station is about 1km from the centre on the Mahendra Hwy, from where buses leave for Kathmandu (Rs800, 16 hours) three times a day. There's also a single Pokhara service at 10.30am (Rs750, 16 hours).

Visas

Visas are available for US$30 (cash only) at the Nepali side of the border between 9am and 5pm.

will also need a tent and your own food supplies as villages on the route may be deserted.

KMVN organises all-inclusive eight-day treks out of Munsyari for Rs8000.

The trailhead is the spectacularly located village of **Munsyari** (2290m), where a guide, cook and porters can be hired. The plentiful accommodation in Munsyari includes **KMVN Rest House** (☎ 05961-222339; dm Rs100, d Rs600-900).

A daily bus runs to Munsyari (Rs190, 11 hours) from Almora; a 4WD taxi costs around Rs3000 (10 hours). Buses and share 4WDs run to and from Pithoragarh (Rs140, eight hours) and Bageshwar (Rs125, six hours).

BANBASSA
pop 7138

Banbassa is the closest Indian village to the Nepal border post of Mahendranagar, 5km

away. Although a remote and little-used crossing compared with Sunauli in Uttar Pradesh, a trickle of travellers enters Nepal here and makes the long trip to Pokhara or Kathmandu. Check the current situation in western Nepal – although considered safe at the time of writing, Maoist trouble can flare up. It certainly should not be attempted in the monsoon or immediate postmonsoon season because the roads in western Nepal are often impassable due to landslides and washed-out bridges.

Although Banbassa has a train station, only metre-gauge local trains run to the main railhead at Bareilly. A better option is the bus service that runs to Almora and Delhi. Alternatively, you can take a train from Delhi to Bareilly and then a bus from there to Banbassa.

Kolkata (Calcutta)

India's second-biggest city is a daily festival of human existence, simultaneously noble and squalid, cultured and desperate. And everything plays out before your very eyes on teeming streets where not an inch of space is wasted. By its old spelling, Calcutta conjures up images of human suffering to most Westerners. But Bengalis have long been infuriated by one-sided depictions of their vibrant capital. Kolkata is locally regarded as the intellectual and cultural capital of the nation. Several of India's great 19th- and 20th-century heroes were Kolkatans, including guru-philosopher Ramakrishna, Nobel Prize-winning poet Rabindranath Tagore and celebrated film director Satyajit Ray. Dozens of venues showcase Bengali dance, poetry, art, music, film and theatre. And while poverty is certainly in your face, the dapper Bengali gentry continue to frequent grand old gentlemen's clubs, back horses at the Calcutta Racetrack and play soothing rounds of golf at some of India's finest courses.

As the former capital of British India, Kolkata retains a feast of colonial architecture, with more than a few fine buildings in photogenic states of semicollapse. The city still has many slums but is developing dynamic new-town suburbs and a rash of air-conditioned shopping malls. Kolkata's also a fabulous place to sample the mild, fruity tang of Bengali cuisine.

Friendlier than India's other megacities, Kolkata is really a city you 'feel' more than just visit. But don't come between May and September unless you're prepared for a very serious drenching.

KOLKATA (CALCUTTA)

HIGHLIGHTS

- Watch goddesses coming to life in the curious lanes of **Kumartuli** (p517) or **Kalighat Rd** (p515)

- Ponder the contradictions of the magnificent **Victoria Memorial** (p508) which remains Kolkata's most splendid building 60 years after the end of the colonial era

- Venture into **Bhojohari Manna** (p523) to sample the best of lipsmackingly authentic Bengali cuisine

- Discover the enlightened universalist idealism of **Ramakrishna** (p518) and **Tagore** (p517) of which Kolkatans are understandably proud

- **Volunteer** (p1167) to help the destitute

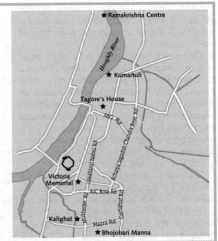
★ Ramakrishna Centre
Hooghly River
★ Kumartuli
Tagore's House ★
JL Nehru Rd
Acharya Jagadish Chandra Bose Rd
Victoria Memorial ★
AJC Bose Rd
Gariahat Rd
Kalighat ★
Hazra Rd
★ Bhojohari Manna

FAST FACTS

Population 14.7 million
Area 185 sq km
Telephone code ☎ 033
Main language Bengali
When to go October to March

HISTORY

In the Hindu epics, the God Shiva was understandably dismayed to happen upon the charred corpse of Sati, his newly wed wife (an incarnation of Kali). However, his decision to destroy the world in retribution was considered somewhat of an over-reaction by fellow deities. Vishnu interceded to stop Shiva's 'dance of destruction', but in so doing dismembered Sati's cadaver into 51 pieces. These gory chunks landed at widely disbursed points across India. One of her toes fell at Kalikata (now Kalighat, p515), where the site became honoured by a much revered temple.

Famed as Kalikata/Kalighat might have been, the place was still a fairly typical rural backwater when British merchant Job Charnock showed up in 1686. Charnock reckoned the Hooghly River bend would make an ideal settlement, and by 1698 the villages of Sutanuti, Gobindapur and Kalikata had been formally signed over to the British East India Company. The British thereupon created a miniature version of London-on-Hooghly, with stately buildings, wide boulevards, English churches and grand formal gardens. The grand illusion vanished abruptly at Calcutta's frayed edges where Indians servicing the Raj lived in cramped, overcrowded bastis (slums).

The most notable hiccup in the city's meteoric rise came in 1756, when Siraj-ud-daula, the nawab of nearby Murshidabad, recaptured the city. Dozens of members of the colonial aristocracy were imprisoned in a cramped room beneath Fort William. By morning, around 40 of them were dead from suffocation. The British press exaggerated numbers, drumming up moral outrage back home: the legend of the 'Black Hole of Calcutta' was born.

The following year, Clive of India retook Calcutta for Britain. The nawab sought aid from the French but was soundly defeated at the Battle of Plassey (now Palashi), thanks mainly to the treachery of former allies. A stronger fort was built and the town became British India's official capital, though well into the late 18th century one could still hunt tigers in the bamboo forests around where Sudder St lies today.

The late 19th century Bengali Renaissance movement saw a great cultural reawakening among middle-class Calcuttans. This was further galvanised by the massively unpopular 1905 division of Bengal, sowing the seeds of the Indian Independence movement. Bengal was reunited in 1911, but the British promptly transferred their colonial capital to less troublesome Delhi.

Initially loss of political power had little effect on Calcutta's economic status. However, the impact of partition was devastating. While West Pakistan and Punjab saw a fairly equal (if bloody) exchange of populations, migration in Bengal was almost entirely one way. Around four million Hindu refugees from East Bengal arrived, choking Calcutta's already overpopulated bastis. For a period, people really were dying of hunger in the streets, creating Calcutta's abiding image of abject poverty. No sooner had these refugees been absorbed than a second vast wave arrived during the 1971 India-Pakistan War.

After India's partition, the port of Calcutta was hit very hard by the loss of its main natural hinterland, now behind closed Pakistan–Bangladesh borders. Labour unrest spiralled out of control, while the city's dominant party (Communist Party of India) spent most of its efforts attacking the feudal system of land ownership. Well-intentioned attempts to set strict rent controls have since backfired: where tenants still pay as little as Rs1 a month, landlords have no interest in maintaining or upgrading properties so many fine old buildings are crumbling before one's eyes.

Since 2001 Calcutta has officially adopted the more phonetic spelling, Kolkata. Around the same time the city administration implemented a new business-friendly attitude that is has encouraged a noticeable economic resurgence.

ORIENTATION

Administrative Kolkata takes up several blocks of colonial-era buildings around BBD Bagh. North of here lanes are narrow and intriguingly vibrant. Well south in Alipore and around Rabindra Sarovar are wealthier suburbs. Budget travellers head for the Sudder St area where you'll find travel agencies, moneychangers and Kolkata's only sprinkling of backpacker cafes. Upmarket dining and boutiques are prevalent around Elgin, Camac and Park Sts. The central business district is around Shakespeare Sarani though corporate offices are increasingly relocating to Sector 5 of Salt Lake City, a large new-town area northeast of the centre.

Maps

Various commercially sold city maps verge on fiction. The *Inside India Series: Kolkata* (Rs90 from Crossword, see below) is better than most, if lacking detail. More comprehensive online maps based on Google Earth images include **Maplandia** (www.maplandia .com/india/west-bengal/Calcutta/).

INFORMATION
Bookshops

Classic Books/Earthcare Books (Map p510; ☎ 22296551; www.earthcarebooks.com; 10 Middleton St; ⏱ 11am-7pm Mon-Sat, 11am-3pm Sun) Charming family publisher-bookshop with strengths in development, environmentalism, politics, spirituality and women's issues. Located behind Drive-Inn.

Crossword (Map p510; ☎ 22836502; www.crossword bookstores.com; 8 Elgin Rd; ⏱ 10.30am-8.30pm) Spacious three-storey chain bookshop with cafe (coffee Rs18 to Rs44). Sells *Times Food Guide* (Rs100).

Oxford Bookstore (Map p510; ☎ 22297662; www .oxfordbookstore.com; 17 Park St; ⏱ 10am-9pm Mon-Sat, 11am-8pm Sun; ⏼) Excellent full-range bookshop with browse-seating and cafe.

Seagull Bookstore (Map pp504-5; ☎ 24765869; www .seagullindia.com; 31A SP Mukherjee Rd; ⏱ 10.30am-7.30pm) Academic bookshop with strengths on humanities, regional politics and social sciences.

Huddled around the Sudder–Mirza Ghalib St junction (Map p510) are several small traveller-oriented bookstalls including Bookland and Cosmos Books.

Internet Access

Most internet centres charge at least 30-minutes' minimum usage.

Cyber Indya (Map p510; 6 Ballygunge Circular Rd; per hr Rs15-20; ⏱ 9am-10pm; ⏼)

Cyber Zoom (Map p510; 27B Park St; per hr Rs15; ⏱ 9am-11pm; ⏼)

E-Merge (iWay) (Map p510; 59B Park St; per hr Rs30; ⏱ 10am-10pm Mon-Sat, 11.30am-10pm Sun; ⏼) Dated booths but good air-con and fast connection.

Enternet (Map p510; Chowringhee Lane; per hr Rs20; ⏱ 10am-9.30pm) Decent connection.

Hotline/Saree Palace (Map p510; 7 Sudder St; per hr Rs15; ⏱ 8.30am-11.30pm) New flat-screens, pleasant owners and long hours. Fabrics for sale too.

Nav-Softyn (Map p512; 3 Khetra Das Rd; per half/full hr Rs20/30; ⏱ 11am-8pm Mon-Sat; ⏼) Cramped but refreshingly air-conditioned down a narrow alley.

Sky@ber (Airport, International Terminal; per half-hr Rs60; ⏱ 24hr)

Internet Resources

Useful websites:
http://kolkata.clickindia.com
www.calcuttaweb.com
www.wbtourism.com/kolkata/index.htm

Left Luggage

Many Sudder St hotels will store bags for a small fee. At the airport, a useful **baggage store** (small/large bag per 24hrs Rs5/10; ⏱ 24hr) is diagonally across the carpark from the international terminal. At Howrah and Sealdah train stations, **cloakrooms** (bags per day Rs10-15; ⏱ 24hr) require users to show valid long-distance train tickets.

Medical Services

Apollo Gleneagles Clinic (Map pp504-5; ☎ 24618028; www.apollogleneagles.in; 48/1F Lila Roy Sarani, Gariahat Rd; ⏱ 8am-8pm) Health checks and dental work; its hospital (Map pp504-5; ☎ 23203040; EM Bypass) offers 24-hour ambulance service.

KOLKATA (CALCUTTA)

FESTIVALS IN KOLKATA

Dover Lane Music Conference (www.thedoverlanemusicconference.org/schedule.php; late Jan) Indian classical music at Rabindra Sarovar.

Kolkata Boi Mela (www.kolkatabookfaironline.com; late Jan/early Feb) Asia's biggest book fair.

Saraswati Puja (early Feb) Prayers for educational success, all dressed in yellow.

Rath Yatra (Jun/Jul) Major Krishna chariot festival similar to the Puri equivalent (p652).

Durga Puja (www.durga-puja.org; Oct) Kolkata's biggest festival, see p507.

Lakshmi Puja (Oct) on the full moon after Durga Puja and **Kali Puja** (Diwali; Nov) feature more idol dunking.

Kolkata Film Festival (www.kff.in; mid-Nov) Week-long festival of Bengali and international movies.

KOLKATA

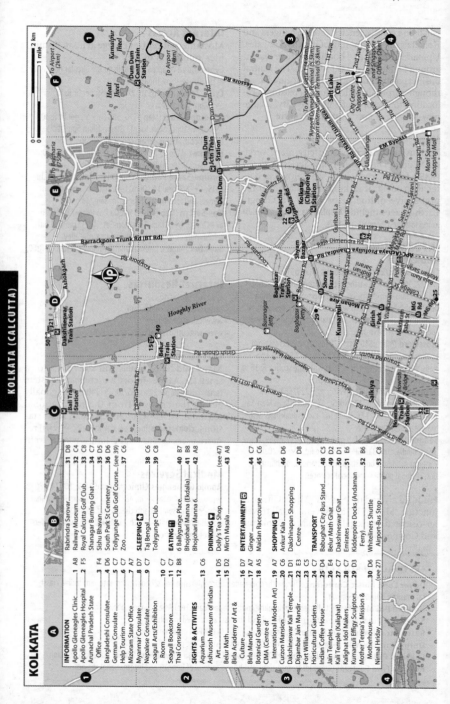

INFORMATION
Apollo Gleneagles Clinic	1	A8
Apollo Gleneagles Hospital	2	F5
Arunachal Pradesh State Office	3	F4
Bangladeshi Consulate	4	D6
German Consulate	5	C7
Help Tourism	6	C7
Mizoram State Office	7	A7
Myanmar Consulate	8	D7
Nepalese Consulate	9	C7
Seagull Arts/Exhibition Room	10	C7
Seagull Bookstore	11	C7
Thai Consulate	12	B8

SIGHTS & ACTIVITIES
Aquarium	13	C6
Ashutosh Museum of Indian Art	14	D5
Belur Math	15	D2
Birla Academy of Art & Culture	16	D7
Birla Mandir	17	A7
Botanical Gardens	18	A5
CIMA (Centre of International Modern Art)	19	A7
Curzon Mansion	20	C6
Dakshineswar Kali Temple	21	D1
Digambar Jain Mandir	22	E3
Fort William	23	C5
Horticultural Gardens	24	C7
Indian Coffee House	25	D4
Jain Temples	26	E4
Kali Temple (Kalighat)	27	C7
Kalighat Idol Makers	28	C7
Kumartuli Effigy Sculptors	29	D3
Mother Teresa's Mission & Motherhouse	30	D6
Nirmal Hriday	(see 27)	
Rabindra Sarovar	31	D8
Railway Museum	32	C4
Royal Calcutta Golf Club	33	C8
Shanagar Burning Ghat	34	C7
Sishu Bhavan	35	D5
South Park St Cemetery	36	D6
Tollygunge Club Golf Course	(see 39)	
Zoo	37	C6

SLEEPING
Taj Bengal	38	C6
Tollygunge Club	39	C8

EATING
6 Ballygunge Place	40	B7
Bhojohari Manna (Ekdalia)	41	B8
Bhojohari Manna 6	42	A8

DRINKING
Dolly's Tea Shop	(see 47)	
Mirch Masala	43	A8

ENTERTAINMENT
Ginger	44	C7
Maidan Racecourse	45	C6

SHOPPING
Ankur Kala	46	D6
Dakshinapan Shopping Centre	47	D8

TRANSPORT
Babughat City Bus Stand	48	C5
Belur Math Ghat	49	D2
Dakshineswar Ghat	50	D1
Emirates	51	E6
Kidderpore Docks (Andaman Ferry)	52	B6
Whiteliners Shuttle	53	C8
Airport-Bus Stop		

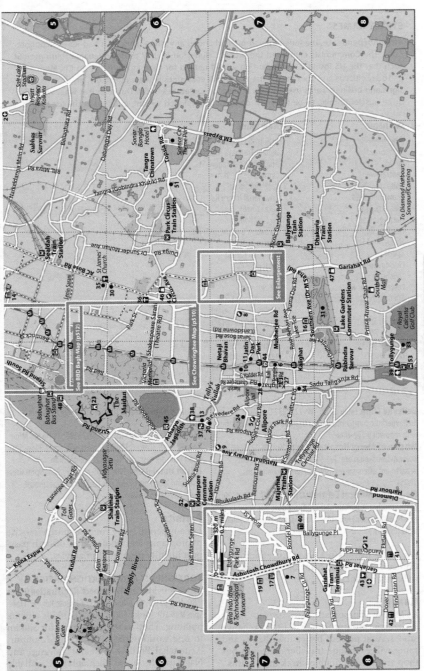

STREET NAMES

After Independence, the Indian government changed any street name that had Raj-era connotations. The Communists continued the process. Humorously they chose to rename Harrington St such that the US found its consulate on a road named for then arch-enemy, Ho Chi Minh.

Today citizens and taxis mostly use the British-era names while, confusingly, most maps, street signs and business cards use the new names (or sometimes both). This text uses what we found, quite unscientifically, to be the most commonly employed variant, *italicised* in the list below:

Old name	New name
Ballygunge Rd	Ashutosh Chowdhury Ave (AC Rd)
Brabourne Rd	Biplabi Trailokya Maharaja Rd
Camac St	Abinindranath Tagore St
Central Ave	*Chittaranjan (CR) Ave*
Chitpore Rd	*Rabindra Sarani*
Chowringhee Rd	Jawaharlal Nehru Rd
Free School St	*Mirza Ghalib St*
Harrington St	*Ho Chi Minh Sarani*
Harrison Rd	Mahatma Gandhi (MG) Rd
Hungerford St	Picasso Bithi
Kyd St	Dr M Ishaque Rd
Lansdowne Rd	*Sarat Bose Rd*
Loudon St	Dr UM Bramhchari St
Lower Circular Rd	*AJC Bose Rd*
Old Courthouse St	Hemant Basu Sarani
Park St	Mother Teresa Sarani
Rowden St	Sarojini Naidu Sarani
Theatre Rd	*Shakespeare Sarani*
Victoria Terrace	*Gorky Terrace*
Waterloo St	Nawab Siraj-ud-Daula Sarani
Wellesley St	*RAK (Rafi Ahmed Kidwai) Rd*
Wood St	Dr Martin Luther King Sarani

Bellevue Clinic (Map p510; ☎ 22872321; www .bellevueclinic.com; 9 Loudon St) Upmarket central hospital with renowned eye-clinic.

Mission of Mercy Hospital (Map p510; ☎ 22296666; www.momhospital.org; 2/7 Sarat Bose Rd) Outpatients' department offers inexpensive doctors' consultations (Rs75).

Wockhardt Medical Centre (Map p510; ☎ 24754320; www.wockhardhospitals.net; 2/7 Sarat Bose Rd; ⏳ 10.30am-noon) Reliably modern for doctor's consultations (Rs300).

For fuller listings see www.kolkatainforma tion.com/diagnostic.html or www.calcutta web.com/doctor.php.

Money

ATMs are widespread. Many private moneychangers around Sudder St offer exchange rates several percent better than banks and some will exchange travellers cheques but shop around and double-check their maths.

Camara Bank (Map p510; Kyd St) Handy ATM near Sudder St.

Globe Forex (Map p510; ☎ 22828780; 11 Ho Chi Minh Sarani; ⏳ 9.30am-6.30pm Mon-Fri, 9.30am-2.30pm Sat) Good rates for cash and TCs; Rs25 commission.

Hilson Hotel (Map p510; Sudder St; ⏳ 9am-9pm) Great rates and long hours from this backpacker guesthouse foyer; Rs20 commission.

Permits

For any permit bring your passport, visa-style photographs and photocopies of both passport identity page and Indian visa.

FOREIGNERS' REGISTRATION OFFICE

From outside, the **Foreigners' Registration Office** (FRO; Map p510; ☎ 22837034; 237 AJC Bose Rd; ⏳ 11am-5pm Mon-Fri) looks like a grand 1930s cinema building. They issue free permits for Sikkim in one working day. Permits for Manipur, Arunachal Pradesh (but not Tawang) and Nagaland (Mon and Phek only) are available to groups of four applicants at Rs1350 per person per permit in one working day if you arrived in India via Kolkata airport, but will take much longer if you arrived elsewhere (they track down your entry papers). The FRO won't issue Mizoram permits.

STATE OFFICES

Indian nationals can get state-specific Inner Line permits at the following state offices but, except for Sikkim, foreigners shouldn't expect any permit help whatsoever.

Arunachal Pradesh (Map pp504-5; ☎ 23341243; Arunachal Bhawan, Block CE 109, Sector 1, Salt Lake City)

Manipur (Map p510; ☎ 24758163; Manipur Bhawan, 26 Rowland Rd)

Mizoram (Map pp504-5; ☎ 24617887; Mizoram Bhawan, 24 Old Ballygunge Rd) Take the lane beside 23 AC.

Nagaland (Map p510; ☎ 22825247; Nagaland House, 11 Shakespeare Sarani)

Sikkim (Map p510; ☎ 22817905; Sikkim House, 4/1 Middleton St; ☉ 10.30am-4pm Mon-Fri, 10.30am-2pm Sat) Permits usually issued within 24 hours.

Photography

Electro Photo-Lab (Map p510; ☎ 22498743; 14 Sudder St; ☉ 10.30am-9.30pm Mon-Sat, noon-7pm Sun) Instant passport photos (eight mugshots Rs60), film-developing, digi-prints and camera-to-CD (Rs60 per disk).

Summer Photographic (Map p512; Moti Lal Market; ☉ 10am-9pm) Stocks Sensia 100 slide film (Rs180).

Post

Kolkata's imposing **General Post Office** (GPO; Map p512; BBD Bagh; ☉ 6am-8pm Mon-Sat, 10am-3.30pm Sun, parcel service from 10am) is a worthy attraction in itself (see p514). Convenient branch post offices include locations at Park St (Map p510), CR Ave (Map p512) and Mirza Ghalib St (Map p510).

Telephone

The **Central Telegraph Office** (Map p512; ☉ 24hr) is under reconstruction but calls are cheap from ubiquitous PCO/STD/ISD booths throughout the city. Numerous stalls around Sudder St sell Vodafone SIM cards (Rs200 including Rs10 credit) if you provide a visa-style photograph and passport photocopies. SIM procurement for foreigners seems much harder elsewhere in Kolkata.

Tourist Information

Cal Calling (Rs45) Very useful monthly info-booklet sold at Oxford Bookstore (p503).

CityInfo (www.exploicity.com) Advertisement-led listings pamphlet available free from better hotels.

India Tourism (Map p510; ☎ 22825813; 4 Shakespeare Sarani; ☉ 10am-6pm Mon-Fri, 10am-1pm Sat) Helpful young staff, free Kolkata maps.

West Bengal Tourism (Map p512; ☎ 22437260; www.wbtourism.com; 3/2 BBD Bagh; ☉ 10.30am-1.30pm & 2-5.30pm Mon-Fri, 10.30am-1pm Sat) Comfortable, recently redecorated office mostly set up to sell tours (last sales 4.30pm).

Travel Agencies

For city tour agents see p518.

Help Tourism (Map pp504-5; ☎ 24549682; www .helptourism.com; 67A Kali Temple Rd, Kalighat) Personalised ecotours.

DURGA PUJA

Much as Carnival transforms Rio or New Orleans, Durga Puja brings Kolkata to chaotically colourful life. For five days people venerate gaudily painted idols of 10-armed goddess Durga and her entourage (see p517). These are displayed in *pandals* (marquees) that dominate yards, block roads or fill little parks. In the last 30 years, design competitions and increasing corporate sponsorship have seen *pandals* growing ever more ornate and complex. Some have topical or political messages, such as the 2008 *pandal* shaped like a car factory (at the time West Bengal was still arguing with Tata over the controversial Nano car plant, see p534).

West Bengal Tourism (above) takes tourists around a selection of the best *pandals* but getting anywhere close can take hours given their popularity. After five days the festival's climax comes when myriad Durga idols are thrown into the sacred Hooghly River amid singing, water throwing, fireworks and indescribable traffic congestion. If you just want *pandal* photos and not the festival aspect, consider visiting just after Durga Puja when the idol has gone but *pandals* have yet to be deconstructed.

Many diaspora Bengalis return to Kolkata for Durga Puja so hotels fill up. Then afterwards so many go away on holiday that getting rail- or air-tickets out can be virtually impossible for weeks.

KOLKATA IN...

Two Days

First day, tour the **Indian Museum** (opposite), admire the **Victoria Memorial** (below) and surrounding attractions then grab a Marble Palace permit for tomorrow at India Tourism (p507) before dining and dancing on Park or Camac Sts. Next day wander from the **Maidan** (p511) through the crumbling colonial wonderland of **BBD Bagh** (p513) then use tram 6 to chug up Rabindra Sarani to fascinating **Kumartuli** (p517). Return by metro to the bizarre **Marble Palace** (p517) or by ferry to Howrah then cross the famous bridge to colourful **Mullik Ghat flower market** (p515).

Two Weeks

Consider approaching the city thematically.

- **Traditional Kolkata** Hand-drawn rickshaws (p531), effigy-makers in Kumartuli (p517) and goats sacrifices at Kalighat (p515).
- **Colonial Kolkata** The General Post Office (p513), golf at the Tollygunge Club (p518), a flutter at the Maidan racecourse (p527) and garden beers at the Fairlawn Hotel (p526).
- **Modern Kolkata** Dancing at Tantra nightclub (p527), coffee at Barista (p526), cocktails at Roxy (p526) and browsing at Oxford Bookstore (p503).
- **Squalid Kolkata** Street kids on Howrah train station (p515), Old Chinatown (p515) and volunteering (p518) to help the destitute.
- **Multicultural Kolkata** Synagogues, mosques and churches of Barabazaar (p514), Belur Math (p518), meditation evenings (p518), reading Tagore (p517) and laughing-yoga at Rabindra Sarovar (p516).

STIC Travel (Map p510; ☎ 22265989; www.stictravel .com; 3C Camac St; ☻ 9am-1pm & 2-5.30pm Mon-Fri, 9am-2pm Sat)
Super Travel (Map p510; Super Guesthouse) One of numerous agencies on Sudder St and Chowringhee Lane.
Thomas Cook (Map p510; ☎ 22830473; www.thomas cook.in; 19B Shakespeare Sarani; ☻ 9.30am-6pm)

DANGERS & ANNOYANCES

Kolkata feels remarkably unthreatening. Predictable beggar-hassle around the Sudder St traveller ghetto is a minor irritant. Crossing the road is a more day-to-day worry: the mad traffic takes no prisoners. *Bandhs* (strikes) occur with monotonous regularity, closing shops and stopping all land transport (including taxis to the airport). Monsoon-season flooding is highly inconvenient but rickshaw-wallahs somehow manage to ferry passengers through knee-deep, waterlogged streets.

SIGHTS

Most attractions that don't charge for photography forbid it.

Chowringhee Area

Sites appear on Map p510, except where otherwise noted.

VICTORIA MEMORIAL

Set in an attractive, well-tended **park** (admission Rs4; ☻ 5.30am-7pm), the incredible **Victoria Memorial** (VM; ☎ 22235142; Indian/foreigner Rs10/150; ☻ 10am-5pm Tue-Sun, last tickets 4.30pm) is a vast, beautifully proportioned confection of white marble domes: think US Capitol meets Taj Mahal. Built to commemorate Queen Victoria's 1901 diamond jubilee, the structure was finally finished nearly 20 years after her death. Had it been built for a beautiful Indian princess rather than a dead colonial queen, it would surely rate as one of India's greatest buildings.

The VM is magnificently photogenic when viewed across reflecting ponds from the northeast. Inside there's an impressively soaring central chamber but the ground floor galleries of prints and paintings are displayed on thoughtlessly insensitive whitewashed hardboard hoardings that clash with the original splendour. Nonetheless the Kolkata Gallery traces an impressively even-handed history of the city and there is an upstairs gallery of manuscripts and portraits that is better presented. Don't miss the statues in the main (northern) entrance hall: King George V faces his wife Mary but looks more a queen himself in his camp posing britches. No wonder interior photography is forbidden.

By day, entrance is from the park's north or south gates (though you can exit to the east). For the informative English-language **sound-and-light show** (Indian/foreigner Rs10/20; ☉ 7.15pm Tue-Sun Nov-Feb, 7.45pm Tue-Sun Mar-Jun, no shows in summer), enter from the east gate.

AROUND THE VM

Loosely styled on the Buddhist stupa located at Sarnath (p453), the **Birla Planetarium** (☎ 22231516; Chowringhee Rd) is one of the world's largest. Its exterior looks impressive when floodlit. Inside, its outer circle forms a small but well-presented, tomb-like gallery featuring astronomer busts and fading star-gazer pictures. The **star shows** (admission Rs30; ☉ 1.30pm & 6.30pm in English) are slow moving, thickly accented introductions to the night sky.

With its central crenellated tower, the 1847 **St Paul's Cathedral** (☎ 22230127; Cathedral Rd; ☉ 9am-noon & 3-6pm) would look quite at home in Cambridgeshire. Inside, its extraordinarily broad, unbutressed nave twitters with birdsong and retains the original hardwood pews. Don't miss the stained-glass west window by pre-Raphaelite maestro Sir Edward Burne-Jones.

The bright, ground-floor galley of the **Academy of Fine Arts** (☎ 22234302; 2 Cathedral Rd; admission free; ☉ 3-8pm) has changing exhibitions featuring local contemporary artists but the upstairs **museum** section is under reconstruction.

THE MAIDAN

After the 'Black Hole' fiasco, a moated 'second' **Fort William** (Map pp504-5; closed to public) was constructed in octagonal, Vaubanesque form (1758). The whole village of Gobindapur was flattened to give the new fort's cannons a clear line of fire. Though sad for then-residents, this created the **Maidan** (pronounced moi-dan), a vast 3km-long park that is today as fundamental to Kolkata as Central Park is to New York City. Fort William remains hidden within a walled military zone, but for an amusingly far-fetched tale of someone who managed to get in, read *Simon Winchester's Calcutta*.

INDIAN MUSEUM

Kolkata's old-fashioned main **museum** (☎ 22499979; Chowringhee Rd; Indian/foreigner/cam-era Rs10/150/50; ☉ 10am-4.30pm Tue-Sun, guided tours 10.30am, 12.30pm & 3.15pm, last entry 4pm) fills a glorious colonnaded palace around a central lawn. Extensive exhibits include fabulous 1000-year-old Hindu sculptures, lumpy minerals, a whole dangling whale skeleton and endless pinned insects. Gag at the pickled human embryos (gallery 19), notice the surreal Glyptodon dinosaur-armadillo (gallery 11) and don't miss the impressive life-size reproduction of the 2nd-century BC Barhut Gateway. No bags are allowed inside. Handbags can be checked in at the entrance but don't arrive with a backpack.

PARK STREET

Today Park St is one of Kolkata's top commercial avenues. But when it was constructed in the 1760s, it was a simple causeway across uninhabited marshlands built to allow mourners to access the then-new **South Park Street Cemetery** (Map pp504-5; cnr Park St & AJC Bose Rd; donation expected; ☉ 7.30am-4.30pm Mon-Fri, 7.30am-11am Sat). These days that cemetery remains a wonderful oasis of calm with mossy Raj-era graves – from rotundas to soaring pyramids – jostling for space in a lightly manicured jungle. To support the cemetery's maintenance, a Rs30 donation is appropriate, or buy the guidebook (Rs100) from the gatekeeper.

If strolling south from Park St, check out the latest modern art in the bright, calm **Aakriti Gallery** (Map p510; 1st fl, 12/3 Hungerford St; admission free; ☉ 11am-7pm Mon-Sat).

MOTHER TERESA'S MISSION

The Missionaries of Charity's **Motherhouse** (Map pp504-5; ☎ 22172277; www.motherteresa.org; 54A AJC Bose Rd; ☉ visits 8am-noon & 3-6pm Fri-Wed) can be entered from the first alley north of Ripon St. Pilgrims arrive here regularly to pay homage at Mother Teresa's large, sober **tomb**. Exhibits in a small adjacent **museum** include Teresa's worn sandals and battered enamel dinnerbowl. Located upstairs, the **'Mother's room'** where she worked and slept from 1953 to 1997, is preserved in all its simplicity with a crown-of-thorns placed above her modest camp bed.

The charity's numerous Kolkata sites welcome short-term volunteers, qualified or not. Start by attending a briefing two blocks north at **Sishu Bhavan** (Map pp504-5; 78 AJC Bose Rd; ☉ 3pm Mon, Wed & Fri).

KOLKATA (CALCUTTA)

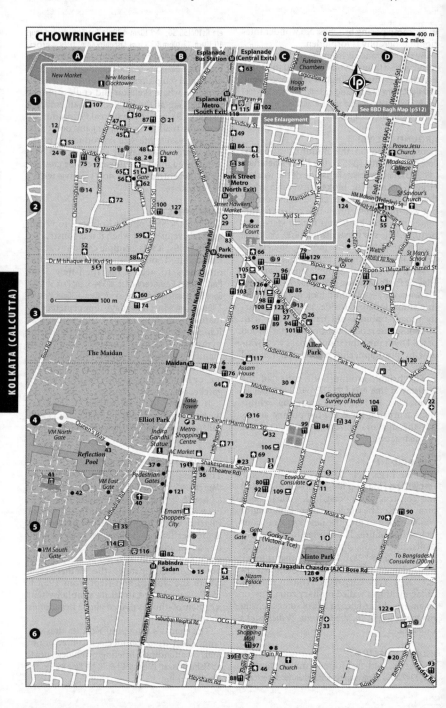

KOLKATA (CALCUTTA)

BBD Bagh Area

Sites appear on Map p512, except where otherwise noted.

NORTH OF THE MAIDAN

Curiosities around New Market (see p527) include the fascinatingly crumbling **Futani**

Chambers, the perfect '50s-style facade of **Elite Cinema**, the brilliant colonial-era **Metropolitan Building** and the fanciful **Tipu Sultan's Mosque**, hidden behind an almost impenetrable ring of market stalls.

Rising above Esplanade bus station, the 1828 **Sahid Minar** is a 48m-tall round-topped

KOLKATA (CALCUTTA)

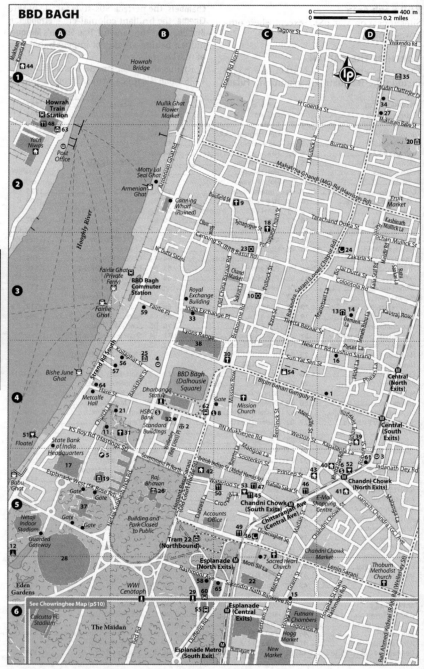

BBD BAGH

obelisk originally celebrating an 1814 British military victory over Nepal. Somewhat resembling the US White House, the grand **Raj Bhavan** (http://rajbhavankolkata.nic.in/) was designed in 1799 along the lines of Kedleston Hall, the Derbyshire home of the Curzon family. By strange coincidence, one of its most famous masters a century later would be none other than Lord Curzon. Today the building is the official residence of the West Bengal governor and visitors may only peep through the ornate giant gates.

The vast **Ranji Stadium** hosting Kolkata cricket matches is commonly nicknamed for the **Eden Gardens** (admission free; ☺ 1-6pm) that lie behind. Those gardens feature a lake and picturesque **Burmese pagoda**. Entry is usually limited to the south gate, but a small, more convenient north portal near Gate 12 of Ranji Stadium is occasionally open. Bring ID.

The resplendent 1872 **High Court** building is a wonderful architectural confection reputedly modelled on the Cloth Hall in Ypres (Flanders). For the best view, approach from the south walking past the western end of the low-domed **West Bengal Assembly building**. Beside it is the imposing colonnaded cube of the former **Town Hall Building** (4 Esplanade West) where

Kolkata Panorama (☎ 22483085; weekdays/weekends Rs10/15; ☺ 11am-6pm Tue-Sun) introduces the city's heritage through a lively collection of working models and interactive exhibits. It's well designed, though historically selective, and many foreigners will struggle to appreciate fully the detailed sections on Bengali popular culture. The accompanying guide makes it awkward to 'escape' quickly.

ST JOHN'S CHURCH

More colonnades buttress the stone-spired 1787 **St John's Church** (☎ 22436098; KS Roy Rd; ☺ 8am-5pm). The small, portrait-draped room on the right as you enter was once used as an office by Warren Hastings, Bengal's first British governor-general.

In the church's somewhat overgrown **graveyard** (admission Rs10) are two curious octagonal monuments. The **mausoleum of Job Charnock** celebrates Kolkata's disputed 'founder'. A 1902 **Black Hole Memorial** was hidden away here in 1940.

AROUND BBD BAGH

Arranged around BBD Bagh is much of the finest colonial architecture in Kolkata. Originally called Tank Sq, its palm-lined

MOTHER TERESA

For many people, Mother Teresa (1910–97) was the living image of human sacrifice. Born Agnes Gonxha Bojaxhiu to Albanian parents in then-Ottoman Üsküp (now Skopje in Macedonia), she joined the Irish Order of Loreto nuns and worked for over a decade teaching in Calcutta's **St Mary's High School** (☎ 22298451; 92 Ripon St). Horrified by the city's spiralling poverty she established a new order, the **Missionaries of Charity** (www.motherteresa.org) and, in 1952, opened Nirmal Hriday (Sacred Heart; see opposite). This was the first of many refuges offering free shelter and a little human dignity to the destitute and dying. Although the order expanded into an international charity, Mother Teresa herself continued to live in absolute simplicity. She was awarded the Nobel Peace Prize in 1979 and beatified by the Vatican in October 2003, the first official step towards being made a saint.

But this 'Saint of the Gutters' is not universally beloved. For some Kolkatans it's slightly galling to find their cultured, predominantly Hindu city popularly linked in the world's mind with a Catholic heroine whose work underlined the city's least appealing facet. Meanwhile Germaine Greer has accused Mother Teresa of religious imperialism, while Christopher Hitchens' book, *The Missionary Position,* decries the donations from dictators and corrupt tycoons. Many have questioned the Missionaries of Charity's minimal medical background and Teresa's staunchly Catholic position against contraception, which seems particularly untenable given Kolkata's growing AIDS and hepatitis epidemic. Of course, the organisation was never primarily focused on saving lives, simply offering a little love to the dying. Before Mother Teresa, even that was an unknown luxury for the truly destitute.

central reservoir-lake ('tank') once supplied the young city's water. Some locals still use its later-colonial name **Dalhousie Sq**, commemorating British Lieutenant-Governor Lord Dalhousie. But with delicious irony, the square is now re-renamed after the nationalists who tried to assassinate him. In fact the BBD trio (Binoy, Badal and Dinesh) bungled their 1930 raid, killing instead an unlucky prisons inspector. Nonetheless the attack was a highly symbolic moment in the self-determination struggle. The assassination took place within the photogenic 1780 **Writers' Building**, whose glorious south facade looks something like a French provincial city hall. Originally built for clerks ('writers') of the East India Company, it's still a haven of pen-pushing bureaucracy.

There are many other imposing colonial edifices. The red-brick **Standard Buildings** (32 BBD Bagh) have carved nymphs and wonderful wrought-iron balconies at the rear. The former **Standard Chartered Building** (Netaji Subhash Rd) has a vaguely Moorish feel, while **St Andrews Church** has a fine Wren-style spire. The 1866 General Post Office (see p507) was built on the ruins of the original Fort William, site of the infamous 'Black Hole of Calcutta' (see p502). Beneath its vast central cupola occasional mini-exhibitions are held around a

statue of a traditional Bengali mail-runner. In a nearby building there's a loveable little **philatelic museum** (☎ 22437331; Koilaghat St; admission free; ⊗ 11am-4pm Mon-Sat).

BARABAZAAR

Scattered north and northeast of BBD Bagh lies a wide scattering of religious buildings. Alone none warrants a special trip, but weaving between them is a great excuse to explore some of Kolkata's most vibrantly chaotic alleys. Looking like a tall-spired church, **Moghan David Synagogue** (Canning St) is somewhat more impressive than **BethEl Synagogue** (Pollock St). The 1797 Portuguese-Catholic **Holy Rosary Cathedral** (Brabourne Rd; ⊗ 6-11am) has eye-catching crown-topped side towers. Hidden away amid the bustle of Old China Bazaar St, the 1707 **Armenian Church** (Armenian St; ⊗ 9-11am Sun) is claimed to be Kolkata's oldest place of Christian worship. It has a low but finely proportioned, whitewashed spire that can be best spied from Bonfield Lane. Located to the east, the 1926 red-sandstone **Nakhoda Mosque** (1 Zakaria St) rises impressively above the bustling shop fronts of ever-fascinating Rabindra Sarani. Its roof, which is bristling with domes and minarets, was loosely modelled on Akbar's Mausoleum at Sikandra (p408).

OLD CHINATOWN
On ragged little Damzen lane there's a former **Chinese Church** and an old **Chinese Temple** (now used as a local school) along with a bright turquoise home whose oversized **gateway** (10 Damzen Lane) was built to allow passage for the family's domestic elephants. For nearly two centuries this area was home to a predominantly Christianised Chinese community, many of whom fled or were interned during a fit of anti-Chinese fervour during the 1962 war. These days, Kolkata's unexotic newer Chinatown is in Tangra and the old Chinatown area is pretty run down. Beside the ruined but once-grand 1924 **Nangking Restaurant**, a rubbish heap (due for eventual removal) supports a community of destitute scavengers who scrape together a miserable existence living in tent-and-box shacks on neighbouring pavements. Very humbling.

Hooghly Riverbank
The Hooghly River's chocolate sludge might look unappealing, but it's holy to Hindu Kolkatans whose main festivals involve plunging divine images into its waters (see p503). Riverside **ghats** are interesting any dawn or dusk when die-hard devotees bathe and make offerings. A photogenic if distinctly seedy vantage point is **Babu Ghat** (Map pp504–5), hidden behind a grubby, pseudo-Greek gateway near Eden Gardens.

HOWRAH (HAORA)
Kolkata's 705m-long architectural icon, **Howrah bridge** (Rabindra Setu; Map p512) is a vibrating abstraction of steel cantilevers, traffic fumes and sweat. Although built back in WWII, it remains one of the world's busiest bridges. Beneath the east end, **Mullik Ghat flower market** is a sensory overload of sights and smells. It's very photogenic but beware that photography of the bridge itself is strictly prohibited. You might be able to sneak a discreet shot from one of the various river-ferries that ply across the Hooghly to the vast **Howrah train station**. That 1906 edifice has clusters of towers topped in terracotta tiles giving it a look reminiscent of a Spanish desert citadel. The station serves millions daily, emptying trains picked clean by legions of destitute street children who are the subject of much charity work and plenty of moving prose.

Some 500m south, the open-air **Railway Museum** (admission Rs5; ☼ 1-8pm Fri-Wed) has a two-storey model of Howrah train station, several 19th-century steam locos and a toy-train ride (Rs10).

West Kolkata
BOTANICAL GARDENS
Founded in 1786, the 109-hectare **Botanical Gardens** (Map pp504-5; ☎ 26685357; Indian/foreigner Rs5/50; ☼ 5.30am-5pm Oct-Feb, 5am-5.30pm Mar-Sep) played an important role in cultivating tea long before it became a household commodity. Today there's a cactus house, palm collection, river-overlook and a boating-lake with splendid Giant Amazon Lily pads but the biggest draw is a 250-year-old **banyan tree**, 140m across. It's reputedly the world's largest but the central trunk rotted away in the 1920s leaving a curious 'forest' of cross-branches and linked aerial roots that have become virtual trees of their own.

The banyan is five minutes' walk from the park's Bicentenary Gate (Andul Rd) or 25 minutes' walk from the gardens' main gate where bus 55 and minibus 6 from Howrah/Esplanade (Rs7) terminate. Taxis from Shakespeare Sarani charge around Rs90 via the elegant **Vidyasagar Setu** (Hooghly Suspension Bridge).

South Kolkata
KALIGHAT
Kalighat's ancient **Kali Temple** (Map pp504-5; ☎ 22231516; ☼ 5am-2pm & 4-10pm Nov-Feb, 4am-2pm & 3-10.30pm Apr-Oct) is Kolkata's holiest spot for Hindus and possibly the source of its name (p502). Today's version, a 1809 rebuild, has floral- and peacock-motif tiles that look more Victorian than Hindu. The double-stage roof is painted silver-grey with rainbow highlights. More interesting than the architecture are the jostling pilgrim queues that snake into the main hall to fling hibiscus flowers at a crowned, three-eyed Kali image. Priests loitering around the temple might whisk you to the front of the queue for an obligatory 'donation' (significant money). Behind the bell pavilion but still within the mandir complex, goats are ritually beheaded to honour the ever-demanding goddess, or, as a local guide described it, to buy 'God power'.

The temple is somewhat hidden in a maze of alleys jammed with market stalls selling votive flowers, brassware, religious artefacts and pictures of Kali. From Kalighat metro station (with its four-storey Mother Teresa mosaic)

SUBHAS CHANDRA BOSE

In the early 1940s the two most prominent figures in the Indian anticolonial campaign were Gandhi (who favoured nonviolence) and Subhas Chandra Bose (who certainly didn't). Eminently intelligent, Cambridge-educated Bose managed to become Chief Executive of Calcutta despite periods in jail after accusations of assault and terrorism. During WWII he fled first to Germany, then Japan. Along with Rash Behari Bose, he developed the Indian National Army (INA), mostly by recruiting Indian soldiers from Japanese POW camps and armed by Hitler. The INA then marched with Japan's invading force towards northeastern India, getting bogged down, and eventually defeated in Manipur and Nagaland. Bose fled but later died in a mysterious plane crash.

Today his image is somewhat ambivalent in much of India, but in Bengal, Bose remains a hero nicknamed Netaji (revered leader). Patriotic songs are intoned before his many statues and Kolkata's airport is named after him.

walk towards the putrid Tolisnala Stream where **Shanagar Burning Ghat** hosts an impressive gaggle of monuments celebrating those cremated here. Turn north up Tollygunge Rd which becomes vibrant Kalighat Rd after one block. The temple is to the right down the footpath immediately before **Nirmal Hriday** (251 Kalighat Rd). That's Mother Teresa's world famous, if surprisingly small, home for the dying (see p514), its roof-corners pimpled with neo-Mughal minidomes.

If you walk further north up lively Kalighat Rd, you will notice unsophisticated pot-painter artisans at work in the west-leading lane just before **Kalighat Market**. After curving across Hazra Rd, upper Kalighat Rd hosts numerous image makers: less famous but almost as intriguing as those in Kumartuli (opposite).

ALIPORE

Kolkata's 16-hectare **zoo** (Map pp504-5; ☎ 24791152; Alipore Rd; admission Rs10; ◷ 9am-5pm Fri-Wed) first opened in 1875. The spacious lawns and lakeside promenades are very popular with weekend picnickers (hence all the rubbish). Grass is so high in the moated Bengal Tiger enclosure that it's hard to spot the animals but it's better than several more confining cages and the aviaries whose thick rusty-black wire-mesh rather obscures viewing. Across the road an **aquarium** (Rs3; ◷ 10.30am-5pm Fri-Wed) displays a few sorry tankfuls of fish. Get here by bus 230 from Rabindra Sadan.

Located directly south of the entrance to the zoo, the (private) access road to the **National Library** (www.nlindia.org), India's biggest, loops around the very regal **Curzon Mansion**, once the colonial Viceroy's residence. It's not (yet) a museum.

Around 1km southeast, the lawn, tropical trees and flowering shrubs of the delightful **Horticultural Gardens** (Map pp504-5; admission Rs10; ◷ 6-10am & 2-7pm) offer some respite from the traffic rumble.

ELGIN ROAD & GARIAHAT

Netaji Bhawan (Map p510; ☎ 24756139; www.netaji.org; 38/2 Elgin Rd; adult/child Rs5/2; ◷ 11am-4.15pm Tue-Sun), an interesting museum celebrating the life and vision of controversial independence radical Subhas Chandra Bose (above), maintains several rooms decorated in 1940s style. It was Bose's brother's residence from which Subhas made his famous 'Great Escape' from British-imposed house arrest in January 1941. The veteran getaway car is parked in the drive.

For cutting-edge contemporary Bengali art visit **CIMA** (Centre for International Modern Art; Map pp504-5; ☎ 24858509; Sunny Towers, 2nd fl, 43 Ashutosh Chowdhury Rd; admission free; ◷ 11am-7pm Tue-Sat, 3-7pm Mon) a well-lit, six-room gallery with an eclectic giftshop.

Nearby, the 20th-century **Birla Mandir** (Map pp504-5; Gariahat Rd; ◷ 6-11.30am & 4.30-9pm Nov-Mar, 5.30-11am & 4.30-9pm Apr-Oct) is a large Lakshmi Narayan temple complex in cream-coloured sandstone whose three corn-cob shaped towers are more impressive for their size than their carvings.

RABINDRA SAROVAR

Around dawn, middle-class Kolkatans arrive en masse to exercise in the parkland surrounding **Rabrindra Sarovar** (Map pp504–5), a lake that prettily reflects the hazy sunrise. As well as jogging, rowing and meditation, some people form circles to do group-yoga routines culminating in ho-ho ha-ha-ha laugh-ins. These are the informal **Laughing Clubs** (◷ 6-7am), engagingly described by Tony Hawks in *The Weekenders: Adventures in Calcutta*. Even if forced, a good giggle can be refreshingly therapeutic.

In the manicured lawns of the **Birla Academy of Art & Culture** (Map pp504-5; ☎ 24666802; 109 Southern Ave; admission Rs2; ⏰ 4-7pm Tue-Sun) stands an androgynous three-storey **Krishna Statue**, a flute dangling from his stone cod-piece. Next-door, **Lake Kalibari** is a small but revered Kali shrine.

North Kolkata

These sights appear on Map pp504–5.

KOLKATA UNIVERSITY AREA

Tucked behind Kolkata University's Central Library, the **Ashutosh Museum of Indian Art** (☎ 22410071; www.caluniv.ac.in; Centenary Bldg, 87/1 College St; admission Rs10; ⏰ 11.30am-4.30pm Mon-Fri) displays priceless if slightly dry displays of fabulous antique Indian sculpture, brasswork and Bengali terracotta. It's down the first lane off College St as you walk north from Coloottola Rd.

Nearby, the mythic **Indian Coffee House** (1st fl, 15 Bankim Chatterjee St; coffee Rs8, snack meals Rs20-35; ⏰ 9am-9pm Mon-Sat, 9am-12.30pm & 5-9pm Sun) was once a meeting place of freedom fighters, bohemians and revolutionaries. Today its crusty high ceilings and grimy walls ring with deafening student conversation but despite the dishwater coffee, it's perversely fascinating. One block south of MG Rd, walk 20m east off College St and it's upstairs on the left.

The section of MG Rd between here and Sealdah Station is an inspiring chaos of mouldering generations-old box shops, potion sellers and card-makers beneath dishevelled occasionally grand old facades.

MARBLE PALACE

This grand 1853 **mansion** (☎ 22393310; 46 Muktaram Babu St; ⏰ 10am-4pm Tue, Wed & Fri-Sun) is indulgently overstuffed with statues, Victoriana, Belgian glassware and fine paintings – there's even a reputedly original Rubens. The music room is lavishly floored with marble inlay but much of the antique furniture remains haphazardly draped in torn old dust-sheets. It's an odd place where admission is technically free, but guards, guides and even the toilet monitor all expect tips. Before visiting you need to get a permission note from either West Bengal Tourism or India Tourism (see p507).

From MG Rd metro, walk two blocks north and turn west at 171 Chittaranjan Ave. To continue to Tagore's House, continue west down Muktaram Babu St, turn right on Rabindra Sarani, and walk two blocks north passing the wonderful olde-worlde **Ram Prasad apothecary shop** (Map p512; 204 Rabindra Sarani; ⏰ 8.30am-8.30pm Mon-Sat) and several **stone-carving workshops**.

TAGORE'S HOUSE

Within Rabindra Bharati University, the comfortable 1784 family mansion of Rabindranath Tagore (p78) has become an extensive, shrine-like **museum** (Rabindra Bharati Museum; Map p512; ☎ 22181744; 246D Rabindra Sarani; Indian/foreigner Rs10/50, student Rs5/25; ⏰ 10.30am-4.30pm Tue-Sun) to India's greatest modern poet. Even if his personal effects don't inspire you, some of the well-chosen quotations might spark an interest in Tagore's deeply universalist philosophy. There's also a decent gallery of paintings by his family and contemporaries. The 1930 photo of Tagore taken with Einstein could win a 'World's Wildest Hair' competition.

Tram 6 connects to Kumartuli.

KUMARTULI

This fascinating district is named for the *kumar* (sculptors) who fashion giant **puja effigies** of the gods that will eventually to be ritually immersed in the holy Hooghly (p507). Different workshops specialise in creating the straw frames, adding clay coatings or painting the divine features. Craftsmen are busiest from August till November for the Durga and Kali festivals (p507).

To explore, take the narrow lane west from 499 Rabindra Sorani then turn north on Banamali Sakar St. A short walk west down Charan Banerjee St brings you to a ghat where the clay-mud is brought in, and a pleasant five-minute stroll north up the riverbank past Kashi Mitra Burning Ghat leads to Bagbazar Jetty whence ferries (Rs4) cross to Howrah (four hourly) and Baranagar (twice hourly) or shared tuk-tuks run along Bagbazar Rd towards Shova Bazaar metro.

JAIN TEMPLES

Three eye-catching **Jain temples** (Badridas Temple St; donation appropriate; ⏰ 6am-noon & 3-7pm) are grouped together two short blocks east of Raja Dinendra Rd (1.6km from Shyam Bazaar metro, two big blocks south of Aurobindo Sarani). The best known is 1867-built **Sheetalnathji Jain Mandir**.

Its dazzling if somewhat unrefined pastiche of colourful mosaics, spires, columns and slivered figurines looks like a work of Gaudi. Directly south, the quieter **Sri Sri Channa Probhuji Mandir** has a fine gateway arch and plenty of greenery. The sedate 1810 **Dadaji Jain Mandir** has a central marble tomb-temple patterned with silver studs.

In bird-filled gardens 250km west of Belgachia metro is the **Digambar Jain Mandir** (🕙 6am–noon & 5-7pm), with a tall lighthouse style tower encasing a meditating statuette.

DAKSHINESWAR KALI TEMPLE

The heart of this vibrant complex of 14 temples is a red-and-yellow 1847 **Kali Temple** (☎ 25645222; 🕙 6.30am–noon & 3-8.30pm) shaped like an Indian Sacré-Coeur. This was where Ramakrishna started his remarkable spiritual journey and his small room in the outer northwest corner of the temple precinct is now a place of special meditative reverence. On Sundays the extensive complex is thronged with devotees.

Bus DN9/1 from Dum Dum metro (Rs5) terminates at the start of the temple's 400m hawker-jammed access lane. To continue to Belur Math take one of the leave-when-full river boats (Rs7, 20 minutes). Bring a hat as they're uncovered.

BELUR MATH

This attractively landscaped riverside **religious centre** (☎ 26545892; www.sriramakrishna.org/belur.htm; Grand Trunk Rd; 🕙 6.30am–noon & 3.30-8.30pm) is the headquarters of the Ramakrishna Mission. Amid the palms and manicured lawns, its centrepiece is the unique 1938 **Ramakrishna Mandir** (🕙 6.30am-12.30 & 3.30-8pm), which somehow manages to look like a cathedral, Indian palace and Istanbul's Aya Sofya all at the same time. That's deliberate and perfectly in keeping with the message of 19th-century Indian sage Ramakrishna Paramahamsa who preached the unity of all religions.

Behind the main mandir near the Hooghly riverbank, several smaller **shrines** (🕙 6.30-11.30am & 3.30-5.15pm) include the **Sri Sarada Devi Temple** entombing the guru's wife.

Accessed from the car park, the beautifully presented, dual-level **museum** (admission Rs3; 🕙 8.30-11.30am & 3.30-5.30pm Tue-Sun) charts Ramakrishna's life and travels, with mock-ups of buildings in which he stayed from Rajasthan to New York.

Take minibus 10 or bus 54/1 from Esplanade, or bus 56 from Howrah train station. Boats to Dakshineswar go against the current so it's better to arrive that way. Weekends only, boats run eight times daily to Bagbazar near Kumartuli (p517).

ACTIVITIES
Cooking Courses

Several times weekly Kali Travel Home (below) arranges highly recommended three-hour Bengali **cooking courses** (www.traveleastindia.com/cooking_classes/cooking_classes.html; Rs500-700) led by local housewives in their homes. Costs include food.

Golf

The beautiful golf course at the **Tollygunge Club** (Map pp504-5; ☎ 24732316 ext 142; www.thetollygungeclub.com/home.htm; SP Mukherjee Rd) charges Rs1740 green fees for visitors but only Rs175 if you're staying here. Renting clubs costs around Rs300.

The magnificent **Royal Calcutta Golf Club** (Map pp504-5; ☎ 24731288; www.royalCalcuttagolfclub.com/history.htm; 18 Golf Club Rd) was established in 1829, making it the oldest golf club in the world outside Britain. Foreign guests pay US$50 plus Rs300 for club-rental and Rs125 for caddy fees.

Meditation, Yoga & Dance

The **Aurobindo Bhawan** (Map p510; ☎ 22822162; 8 Shakespeare Sarani; 🕙 8am-8pm) has a city centre garden-oasis with open-air meditation space to sit as you wish or to join half-hour group **meditations** (🕙 7pm Thu & Sun). Enquire about **meditation lessons** (free; 🕙 5pm Tue) and **classical Indian dance lessons** in various styles: **Odissi** (Rs100; 🕙 5pm Mon), **Bharatnatyam** (Rs100; 🕙 4.30pm Thu), **Kathak** (Rs150; 🕙 5pm Fri & Sat). Tailor-made yoga-exercise programmes are available by arrangement.

Art of Living (www.artofliving.org; aolkol@vsnl.net) runs five-day yoga courses at varying locations.

Volunteering

Several organisations welcome foreign volunteers (see p1170).

TOURS

West Bengal Tourism's full-day sightseeing **bus tour** (Rs200; 🕙 8.30am) is a relative bargain but gives only sweaty, drive-by glimpses of most sights and rushes round Belur Math and

Dakshineswar in barely half an hour apiece. Their office (BBD Bagh, p507) opens at 7am to sell last-minute tickets but trips are cancelled when there are less than 15 customers (cancellations least likely on Sundays).

Blue Sky Cafe (p522) organises five-hour **van tours** (per person Rs550; ☺ 8.30am Thu, Sat & Sun) including Kalighat and the Marble Palace (minimum three guests).

Enthusiastic expats at **Kali Travel Home** (☎ /fax 25587980; www.traveleastindia.com) offer very personal accompanied city-walks and longer customised tours around Bengal, Darjeeling and Sikkim.

For excursions to the Sunderbans Tiger Reserve, see p534.

SLEEPING

In summer big off-season discounts are possible but AC will be virtually essential. In winter fan rooms are fine but demand is high, so you might have to take whatever's available. Things rot rapidly in this climate and renovations are cyclical so ideally look before you book.

Although there are numerous cheap hotels in other areas (notably around Sealdah station), the Sudder St area is the only one where most budget hotels accept foreigners. Standards vary considerably but even in many of the better cheapies, peeling paint and damp patches come as standard and putting a mat on the bed to guard against bed-bugs is generally wise. Be prepared for furniture scars even in upper midrange places. Many lock their gates by midnight so if planning to be late, forewarn the staff.

Top-end hotels are very pricey but internet discounters (eg www.yatra.com) can shave up to 50% off rack-rates.

Most hotels add luxury tax (5%) but some tack on further service charges (up to 25%). For fairness we quote total prices.

Sudder & Park St Areas

Looks can be deceptive. Some eye-catchingly smart facades mask lacklustre, mustily disappointing rooms. Other very survivable places are hidden within buildings that look like crumbling wrecks. The following options appear on Map p510.

BUDGET

If you want to pay under Rs400 a room it can be done. But don't expect to enjoy the experience.

The one-eyed manager limped up the stairs to show us this miserable pit of a room. Over the bed someone had scribbled 'This is the worst night of my life'. Unable to keep up with us as we fled, the hobbling manager shouted out ever-lower prices. But zero rupees wouldn't have been cheap enough. We realised then that in Kolkata 'budget' accommodation represented a whole new league of nastiness.
Maud Hennessy, Sudder St Backpacker

One positive point for the ultracheap hotels Paragon, Maria and Modern Lodge is that each has a roof terrace with plastic seats (albeit utterly decrepit) where you can sit and hang out with fellow slummers. Don't assume that the cheapest rooms listed below will have power points or windows.

Hotel Maria (☎ 22520860, 22224444; 5/1 Stuart Lane; d/q Rs300/450, dm/s/d without bathroom Rs70/150/200; ☐) Mouldering but peaceful old mansion whose dorm offers zero privacy but plenty of air. It's pleasantly set in a green courtyard and has on-site internet for Rs15 per hour.

Paragon Hotel (☎ 22522445; 2 Stuart Lane; dm Rs90, r without bathroom Rs150-330) Coffin-box rooms are as spirit-crushing as you'd expect for the price and the jam-packed dorms are windowless. Bring your own padlock.

Modern Lodge (☎ 22524960; 1 Stuart Lane; r Rs250, without bathroom from Rs100) Although not modern at all, Modern Lodge probably offers the best value of all the ultrabudget dives. High-ceilinged rooms are as ragged as ever but there's a somewhat atmospheric old 1st-floor sitting room and a peaceful roof terrace.

Centrepoint Guest House (☎ 22520953; ian_rashid@ yahoo.com; 20 Mirza Ghalib St; dm Rs100, s/d without bathroom from Rs300/350, with AC s/d Rs500/600) Rooms are bare-bones boxes but repainted and with less damp than many competitors. Three large 4th-floor bunk-dorms are nominally sex-segregated and have under-bed safe-boxes (bring a padlock). Their shared showers and toilets are on the open terrace.

Continental Guesthouse (☎ 22520663; Sudder St; s/d without bathroom from Rs150/200, d with toilet Rs350) Aesthetically rooms are much nicer than most other cheapies, but low ceilings mean a tendency to over-heat and there's only one shared toilet for over a dozen rooms.

Timestar Hotel (☎ 22528028; 2 Tottie Lane; s/d from Rs200/325) This chunky-walled colonial mansion house has tatty walls but newly tiled floors and high enough ceilings in the upstairs rooms that they don't overheat so badly.

Hotel Pioneer International (☎ 22520557; 1st fl, 1 Marquis St; d without/with AC Rs450/650) Wobbly wooden stairs within an unpromisingly aged house lead to a hotel whose six rooms are neat with new tiled floors and multilingual TV. Friendly, helpful staff. Some readers found the mattresses rather itchy.

ourpick Hotel Aafreen (☎ 22654146; afreen-cal@ yahoo.co.in; Nawab Abdur Rahman St; d with fan/AC Rs450/700; 🖾) Offering midrange quality at budget prices, the Aafreen's paintwork is mostly intact, staff are obliging, the lift works and freshly tiled bathrooms have hot water.

Ashreen Guest House (☎ 22520889; ashreen_guest house@yahoo.com; 2 Cowie Lane; d Rs495, d/tr with AC Rs840/960; 🖾) Still one of Kolkata's best value minihotels, the rooms are small but sparkling clean with geysers and playful interior touches. Service is caring and proactive but there's often a waiting list. If the Ashreen is full they may send you across the road to the co-managed Afridi International in which six rooms (so far) are fully upgraded but the rest are typical Sudder St cheapies.

Aafreen Tower (☎ 22293280; aafreen_tower@yahoo .co.in; 9A Kyd St; d with fan/AC Rs600/900; 🖾) A glass elevator and bright orange-and-gold corridors lead to decent-sized, well-ventilated rooms which remain an excellent deal, although some of the glossily ornate fittings show a little wear.

Super Guesthouse (☎ 22520995; super_guesthouse@ hotmail.com; Sudder St 6; d Rs660-2500; 🖾) This all-AC guesthouse occupies three separate but very close-by buildings and runs a restaurant, bar and helpful travel agency. The Rs660 double rooms were suffering damp when we visited but the new Rs1100 ones were great value for money. Some lack natural light.

Chowringhee YMCA (☎ 22492192; 25 Chowringhee Rd; s/d Rs600/900 plus Rs50 'membership', with AC Rs250-300 extra; 🖾) Asia's oldest YMCA looks pretty run-down as you climb the once-grand steps to the little reception box (open from 8am to 8pm only) but above the Corinthian-columned badminton court lies an open courtyard surrounded by very reasonably priced en-suite rooms with optional air-con. Breakfast is included.

Hotel Pushpak (☎ 22265841; www.hotelpushpak international.com; 10 Kyd St; s/d with fan Rs700/900, with AC Rs1050/1260, deluxe Rs1400/1600; 🖾) Retro touches

in the corridors don't quite create 'style' but the paintings and statuary give a human touch and the pleasant beige-cream rooms have neat little geyser bathrooms. Two deluxe rooms come with king bed and fridge.

Sunflower Guest House (☎ 22299401; 5th fl, 7 Royd St; d/tr from Rs750/850, with AC Rs950/1000) In a venerable old apartment block, assiduously cleaned if largely unadorned, high-ceilinged rooms have freshly tiled bathrooms with geysers. Take the original 1940s lift (with 2006 workings) to the top of the 1865 Solomon Mansions building and seek out staff behind the little roof garden.

CKT Inn (☎ 22520130; cktinn_kolkata@yahoo.com; 3rd fl, 12/1 Lindsay St; s/d Rs825/1100; 🖾) CKT's furniture has some art-deco touches, south-facing rooms are peaceful, central air-con is effective but carpets are slightly rucked. Enter from the side of an unlikely office building and take the cramped cage-lift.

MIDRANGE

Hotel VIP InterContinental (☎ 22520150; vipinter continental@rediffmail.com; 44 Mirza Ghalib St; s/d from Rs1150/1205, super-deluxe r Rs1790; 🖾) Behind the very narrow, one-desk reception hall, the friendly little VIP InterContinental has small but well air-conditioned rooms in varying styles, all with stone floors and hot water in presentable little bathrooms. The Super Deluxe rooms are unexpectedly hip. Don't confuse with the nearby Hotel VIP Continental whose dashing foyer hides sad corridors and seriously overpriced rooms.

Fairlawn Hotel (☎ 22521510; www.fairlawnhotel.com; 13A Sudder St; s/d Rs2215/2658; 🖾) Taking guests since 1936, the Fairlawn is a characterful 1783 Raj-era home fronted by tropical greenery. The stairs and sitting room are smothered with photos, family mementos and articles celebrating the hotel's nonagenarian owner. While not luxurious, most rooms have been recently freshened up. Most sport kettles, fridges and a sitting area, though bathtubs are painted rather than enamelled. Breakfast and tea are included.

Dee Empressa Hotel (☎ 40021888; www.deeempresa .com; 12/2A Kyd St; s/d/ste Rs3780/4410/4830; 🖾) The two-storey atrium, flat-screen TVs and silk bed-sashes give this new 48-room tower a mild chic, though the elaborately uniformed doormen seem a touch too much and the lift is overworked. The marble-floored rooms are very clean but not large.

Housez 43 (☎ 22276020; www.housez43.com; 43 Mirza Ghalib St; s/d from Rs4000/4500; ⊠) Bright colours, funky lamps and odd-shaped mirrors bring character to this handily central boutique hotel. Some rooms are trendier than others.

Lytton Hotel (☎ 22491872/3; www.lyttonhotelindia .com; 14 Sudder St; standard s/d/ste Rs4350/5550/6825; ⊠) This slightly old-fashioned but well-maintained hotel has Tiffany-style panels in the stairwells, period touches in the bedrooms and arty sinks in the modest-sized bathrooms. Room sizes vary significantly.

TOP END

Park Hotel (☎ 22499000; www.theparkhotels.com; 17 Park St; d Rs12,600-17,850; ⊠ 🖳 🖳) Perfectly central and hosting much of the city's nightlife, one of the Park's pricier floors uses stylish black-on-black decor, though some of the contemporary goldfish-bowl wash basins already look tired. Live music buffets the small, overworked lobby till 4am at weekends and on Wednesdays with noise carrying through especially to the rather disappointing cheaper rooms.

Oberoi Grand (☎ 22492323; www.oberoikolk ata.com; 15 Chowringhee Rd; s/d/ste Rs19,950/21,525/36,750; ⊠ 🖳 🖳) This marvellous oasis of genteel calm deserves every point of its five stars. A vast antique chandelier, gilt-capitalled columns, classical music and the scent of fresh lilies welcome you to the sumptuous lobby. Immaculate accommodation oozes atmosphere with a fresh rose on arrival and four-poster beds in upper-category rooms. The limpid swimming pool is ringed with palms, staff anticipate your needs and a Banyan Tree spa massages away any cares.

Southern Chowringhee

Most Southern Chowringhee hotels (Map p510) are comparatively upmarket catering for business clientele.

Sikkim House (☎ 22815328; 4/1 Middleton St; d/ste Rs1200/1500; ⊙ reception 8am-10pm; ⊠) Sikkimese guests get first call on these large, clean if fairly functional all-AC rooms but tourists may stay if there's a vacancy.

Old Kenilworth Hotel (Purdey's Inn; ☎ 22825325; 7 Little Russell St; d without/with AC Rs2250/2940; ⊠) Run by the Anglo-Armenian Purdey family since 1948, this is more of a spacious homestay than a hotel. Rooms are very large if sparse with items of '50s-style furniture and unique Heath Robinson–style rope-drag fans on some

high ceilings. There's a private lawn, but no restaurant nor lift.

Allenby Inn (☎ 24869984; allenbyinn@vsnl.net; 1/2 Allenby Rd; s/d/ste Rs3150/3675/4200; ⊠) Spread over several floors of an apartment block with fashionable trimmings and lashings of abstract art, some of the 25 rooms are very large, though towels could be softer. Two 5th-floor 'suites' share a very spacious dining area and small kitchen.

The Astor (☎ 22829950; http://astorkolkata.com; 15 Shakespeare Sarani; s/d/ste Rs5250/5775/8925; ⊠) Artful floodlighting brings out the best of the Astor's solid 1905 architecture, while some floors are quaintly uneven and stairways have original wrought-iron banisters. Rooms have some attractive three-colour woodwork though the floral bedspreads maintain that nursing-home feel. A few of the cheaper singles (Rs4725) are windowless.

The Bigboss (☎ 22901111; www.bigbosspalace.com; 11/1A Rowden St; s/d/ste/deluxe Rs5775/6300/7140/7875; ⊠) Above a 24-hour restaurant-coffeeshop, most rooms are no-nonsense new business affairs, though deluxe suites have unusual two-person Jacuzzi baths.

The Kenilworth (☎ 22823939; www.kenilworth hotels.com/kolkata/index_g.htm; 1 Little Russell St; s/d Rs10,500/11,550; ⊠) The deep lobby of cream marble, dark wood and chandeliers contrasts successfully with a more contemporary cafe that spills out onto a pleasant lawn dining-area. Pleasing fully equipped rooms have sensitive lighting, restrained sunny colour schemes and large mirrors. Suites are in an old mansion opposite.

The HHI (Hotel Hindusthan International; ☎ 40018000; www.hhihotels.com; 235/1 AJC Bose Rd; d walk-in/internet-rate from Rs11,550/6786; ⊠ 🖳 🖳) This vast 1960s-style concrete tower has been elegantly remodelled inside, especially the exclusive Colony business floor (8th floor, doubles Rs18,900). Standard 3rd-floor rooms are also well renovated but some corridors have damp-patches, dated decor and low ceilings. North-facing rooms suffer some road noise.

BBD Bagh Area

Most options are handy for Chandni Chowk metro and appear on Map p512. There's no traveller scene here but hotels are fair value by Kolkata standards.

Bengal Buddhist Association (Bauddha Dharmankur Sabha; ☎ 22117138; bds1892@dataone.in; Buddhist Temple Rd; tw without/with AC Rs250/600; ⊠) Although intended for Buddhist students, anyone can rent these clean, simple rooms. Shared bathrooms have geysers and the three en-suite rooms have air-con (but are otherwise just as Spartan). The courtyard location is quiet but gates lock from 10.30pm to 5am.

Broadway Hotel (☎ 22363930; http://business .vsnl.com/broadway; 27A Ganesh Chandra Ave; s/d/tr from Rs475/575/730) This excellent value, well-maintained old hotel has a vaguely 1950s feel. Most rooms are generously large with high ceilings. Corner rooms offer plenty of light and the free newspaper under the door is a nice touch.

Esplanade Chambers (☎ 22127101; GC Ave; s/tw/d from Rs880/1210/1430; ✹) Two floors up off a narrow alley, rooms here vary from unadorned narrow singles to sweet little mini-suites complete with ornaments and brassware on the bookshelves (once the apartment of the hotel's congenial owner). Air-con works well and showers run hot.

Hotel Embassy (☎ 22129702; ssspareworld@hotmail .com; 27 Princep St; s/d from Rs1000/1100; ✹) Most rooms are competently if unexotically renovated in Kolkata's answer to New York's Flatiron Building. The attached bar-restaurant is noisy at night.

Howrah

Howrah Hotel (Map p512; ☎ 26413878; www .thehowrahhotel.com; 1 Mukhram Kanoria Rd; s/d/tr/q from Rs250/355/445/585, s/d/tr without bathroom from Rs165/280/400) Though pretty run-down, this characterful 1890 mansion retains elements of original tile-work and Italian chequer-board marble flooring. The inner courtyard is an unexpected oasis of birdsong and the brilliantly antiquated reception has featured in three movies. The small, tatty rooms are as survivable as Sudder St equivalents. It's only two minutes' walk from Howrah train station's northern exit. Enter around the corner from the outwardly neater but actually less appealing Hotel Bhimsain. Reception stays open 24 hours.

Outer Kolkata

The following appear on Map pp504–5.

our pick Tollygunge Club (☎ 24732316; www.tolly gungeclub.org; d/ste Rs3090/3764; ✹) Set in idyllic calm amongst mature trees and golf greens, this otherwise exclusive colonial-era club rents good, motel-standard guest rooms. Guests get temporary club membership allowing access to the wonderful Raj-era Wills Lounge bar

(dress-code enforced) and, except Monday, use of many sporting facilities including especially reasonable rates for the wonderful golf course (p518). Book ahead.

Hyatt Regency (☎ 23351235; http://kolkata.regency .hyatt.com; EM Bypass; d weekend/weekday from Rs11,025/ 12,075; ✹ ▣ ✹) Preening itself above a palm-slope entry drive, Kolkata's most impressive modern hotel uses vast windows to great effect in its inviting open-plan restaurants and has guest rooms with inspired marble-sweep bathrooms.

Taj Bengal (☎ 22233939; www.tajhotels.com/Luxury /taj%20bengal,Kolkata; 34B Belvedere Rd, Alipore; s/d from Rs18,961/20,597, Taj Club s/d Rs23,686/25,322; ✹ ▣ ✹) This vast, international-standard hotel has an eight-storey atrium in which cellists serenade and painters sketch. The 1990s architecture is softened by numerous local antiques, carved panels and terracotta reliefs. The self-sufficient Taj Club level has 24-hour butler service, free laundry, private restaurant and exclusive bar with leather-padded sofas and free-drink happy hours.

Airport Area

An accommodation booth in the airport's domestic terminal suggests numerous 'airport area' hotels but most are over 2km away down VIP Rd. The following suggestions are walkably close to the terminals, such that you're well placed should a strike paralyse city road transport.

Hotel Airways (☎ 25127280; www.hotelairways .com; Jessore Rd; s/d/tr/q from Rs300/450/550/650, with AC Rs650/750/900/1000; ✹ ▣) Fan rooms are sweltering claustrophobic boxes and road rumble can be annoying but the AC rooms are refreshingly cool and decor is gently pleasant. The small, covered rooftop restaurant (mains Rs40 to Rs70) overlooks the airport. It's 100m northeast of (pedestrian-only) Airport Gate 2 and easy to spot at night, festooned with fairy lights.

Sheela's Guesthouse (☎ 25129381; 1/1 Jessore Rd; s/d from Rs500/700, with AC Rs987/1523; ✹) The pink-and-turquoise colour-scheme lacks taste and carpets are ragged but air-con rooms have decent wrought-iron furniture and hot water. It's located 200m northeast of Hotel Airways.

EATING
Traveller Cafes

Half a dozen cafes around Sudder St serve backpacker-favourites like banana pancakes, muesli and toasted sandwiches complimented by fresh fruit juices and a range of good-value Indian dishes. However, none has any special vibe.

Blue Sky Cafe (Map p510; Chowringhee Lane; mains Rs22-165; ⏱ 6.30am-10.30pm; ❄) Reasonable air-con, reliable food, witty waiters and almost stylish with high-backed zinc chairs at long glass tables.

Fresh & Juicy (Map p510; Chowringhee Lane; mains Rs25-60; ⏱ 6.30am-10pm) Good, inexpensive food and excellent banana lassis (Rs20) make up for a total lack of decor in this simple five-table cafe.

Super Chicken (Map p510; Sudder St; mains Rs35-100; ⏱ 8-11pm; ❄) Succulent chicken tikka and a full menu of tempting alternatives in a small new, well–air conditioned room.

Restaurants

Most restaurants add 12.5% tax to bills. A few posher places add further 'service charges'. Tips are welcome at cheaper places and expected at most expensive restaurants. The *Times Food Guide* (Rs100) covers hundreds of restaurants, though reviews are suspiciously uncritical.

BENGALI

Bengali cuisine is a wonderful discovery, with a whole new vocabulary of names and flavours (see below). Portion sizes are often tapas-sized so in cheaper places order two or three dishes along with rice/*luchi* and sweet tomato-*khejur* (date) chutney.

Radhuni (Map p510; 17G Mirza Ghalib St; dishes Rs15-90, rice Rs10; ⏱ 7.30am-11pm; ❄) Unpretentious place for local breakfasts and surprisingly credit-able, pre-prepared Bengali food.

Flamez (Map p510; ☎ 22264251; Mirza Ghalib St; dishes Rs40-130, rice Rs45; ⏱ noon-11pm; ❄) Confuse your taste-buds with *sukto*, a vegetarian curry that blurs the sweet-savoury divide. Indian and non-Bengali 'coastal' cuisines are also available.

our pick **Bhojohari Manna (Ekdalia)** (Map pp504-5; ☎ 24401933; www.bhojohorimanna.org; 9/18 Ekdalia Rd/ PC Sorcan Sarani; dishes Rs20-190; ⏱ noon-9pm; ❄) Serving sublime Bengali food, it was this tiny restaurant-cum-takeaway that launched the now-growing chain. Pick items ticked on the daily-changing white-board. There's no better place to splurge on coconut-tempered *chingri malaikari*, featuring prawns so big they speak lobster. Sketches on the walls are by the father of celebrated film-director Satyajit Ray.

Bhojohari Manna 6 (Map pp504-5; ☎ 24663941; www.bhojohorimanna.org; 18/1 Hindustan Rd; dishes Rs45-190, rice Rs30, thalis Rs145-170; ⏱ noon-9pm; ❄) Bhojohari Manna's latest and most spacious branch is less daunting for non-Bengali speakers, has gently stylish decor and serves complete thalis.

Kewpies (Map p510; ☎ 24861600; 2 Elgin Lane; dishes Rs58-125, prawn dishes Rs325, rice Rs30, thalis Rs195-415; ⏱ 12.30-3pm & 7.30-11pm Tue-Sun; ❄) Dining at Kewpies feels like being invited to a dinner party in the chef's eclectic, gently old-fashioned home. First-rate Bengali food comes in small but fairly-priced portions. Minimum spend is Rs220 per person.

6 Ballygunge Place (Map pp504-5; ☎ 24603922; 6 Ballygunge Pl; dishes Rs95-245, prawn dishes Rs255-355, rice Rs65; ⏱ 12.30-3.30pm & 7.30-10.30pm Tue-Sun; ❄) This sturdy but not over-formal Raj-era mansion offers lunch-time buffets with six main courses plus deserts, chutneys and rice allowing a good all-round introduction to Bengali food. Minibus 118 from Jatin Das Park metro stops a block north on Bondel Rd.

BENGALI CUISINE

Fruity and mildly spiced, Bengali food favours the sweet, rich notes of jaggery (palm sugar), *daab* (young coconut), *malaikari* (coconut milk) and *posto* (poppy seed). Typical Bengali curry types include the light, coriander-scented *jhol*, drier spicier *jhal* and richer, ginger-based *kalia*. Mustard notes feature in *shorshe* curries and *paturi* dishes which come steamed in a banana leaf. *Chingri* (river prawns) and excellent fish (particularly *bhekti*, *ilish* and swordfish-like *aier*) are more characteristic than meat or chicken (*murgir*). Excellent vegetarian choices include *mochar ghonto* (mashed banana-flower, potato and coconut) and *doi begun* (eggplant in creamy sauce). *Gobindobhog bhaat* (steamed rice) or *luchi* (small puris) are the usual accompaniment.

Bengali desserts and sweets are legendary. Most characteristic is *mishti dhoi* (curd deliciously sweetened with jaggery).

For recipes and a great Bengali menu decoder visit http://sutapa.com.

Oh! Calcutta (Map p510; ☎ 22837161; 4th fl, Forum Mall, Elgin Rd; mains Rs180-625, rice Rs120, beer Rs216; ⏱ 12.30-3pm & 7-11pm; ✗) Shutter-edged mirror 'windows', bookshelves and B&W photography create a casually up-market atmosphere in this appealing Bengali-fusion restaurant. *Luchi* are feather-light and fresh lime brings out the subtleties of *koraishatir dhokar dalna* (pea-cakes in ginger).

INDIAN REGIONAL

As well as the following, there are many cheaper stalwarts around Hogg market (Map p510).

Anand (Map p512; ☎ 22129757; 19 CR Ave; dosas Rs30-73; ⏱ 9am-9.30pm Thu-Tue; ✗) Prize-winning pure-veg dosas served in a well-kept if somewhat old-fashioned family restaurant with bamboo and mirror-tiled ceilings.

Dustarkhwan (Map p510; ☎ 22275596; 6 Ripon St; mains Rs35-110; ⏱ noon-11.30pm; ✗) Reliable curries, piled-high biriyanis (Rs100) and vampire-repelling garlic chicken-balls served inexpensively in a well air-conditioned if none-too stylish local restaurant. Cheaper options next door.

Crystal Chimney (Map p510; CR Ave; ⏱ noon-10pm Tue-Sun) Located next door to Anand, this tiny place serves good momos and chilli-chicken.

Jarokha (Map p510; www.guptabros.com; 1st fl, Gupta Brothers, Mirza Ghalib St; mains Rs75-110, rice Rs60, thalis Rs110; ⏱ 12.30-4pm & 7-10.30pm) The thali is a good deal in this cosy, attractively vegetarian dining room with Indian historical-fantasy decor, reached via a spiral stairway from within Gupta Brothers (opposite).

our pick **Teej** (Map p510; ☎ 22170730; www.teej.in; 1st fl, 2 Russell St; mains Rs110-175, rice Rs120, thalis Rs265-350, beers Rs140; ⏱ noon-3.30pm & 7-10.30pm; ✗) Superbly painted with Mughal-style murals the wonderfully atmospheric interior feels like a Rajasthani *haveli* (traditional, often ornately decorated, residences). The excellent, 100% vegetarian food is predominantly Rajasthani, too.

Riviera (Map p510; ☎ 22274974; 1st fl, 24 Park St; mains Rs165-320, rice Rs60; ⏱ noon-3pm & 7-11.30pm) 'Coastal' cuisine picks the best from a variety of Indian regions: Puducherry stuffed prawns, Mangalore *bhekti* curry, coconut-flavoured Keralan dishes and Chettinad chicken. Vegetarians can order from the menu of attached Angaar Restaurant.

INDO-CHINESE

Gypsy Restaurant (Map p512; GC Ave; mains Rs25-55, rice Rs15; ⏱ noon-10pm) Unusually bright, clean and well appointed for such an inexpensive, open-sided diner.

The Heritage (Map p510; ☎ 22900940; 9A Short St; mains Rs45-75, rice Rs30, breakfast snacks Rs30-60; ⏱ noon-11pm) The decor isn't memorable and party-wrapped chairs will prove hard to clean but staff are obliging and the very reasonable 100%-veg food is packed with marvellously complex flavours. A former gallery behind hosts a rare hookah parlour (water-pipe Rs160 to Rs 230, mocktails Rs45 to Rs75) to have survived the October 2008 smoking ban.

Midway (Map p510; ☎ 22290487; 2C Middleton Row; mains Rs55-145, momos Rs20, rice Rs40; ⏱ noon-11pm; ✗) Incredibly good value thalis (veg/non-veg Rs55/65) are served in this attractively designed new chrome and lime-green modernist restaurant.

Bar-B-Q (Map p510; ☎ 22299078; 1st fl, 43 Park St; mains Rs115-160, rice Rs70, beers Rs120; ⏱ noon-4pm & 7-10.45pm) Three interconnected dining rooms offer different but similar menus in this enduring family favourite. Decor is comfortably unpretentious.

EAST ASIAN

Song Hay (Map p512; ☎ 22480974; 3 Waterloo St; lunch mains Rs21-75, dinner mains Rs44-160, rice Rs16, beer Rs75; ⏱ 11am-10.30pm; ✗) This modest but prize-winning restaurant cooks authentic Chinese food at prices that are especially reasonable before 5pm when half-priced, half-size portions are available.

Bayleaf (Map p512; ☎ 64542244; Waterloo St; mains Rs50-85, prawn mains Rs120-150, rice Rs30; ⏱ 11.30am-11pm; ✗) Tibetan, Burmese and semi-Thai options bolster some imaginative Chinese cuisine like the delicious mushroom delights (half mushrooms stuffed with paneer, deep-fried and served in mild sauce). The decor is black seats at black-glass tables.

Mainland China (Map p510; ☎ 22837964; www.mainlandchinaindia.com/contact_kolkata.html; 3A Gurusaday Rd; mains Rs210-675, rice Rs120, beer Rs216; ⏱ 12.30-3.30pm & 7-11.30pm) Consistent, upmarket Chinese food in sophisticated surroundings. Reservations advised.

Jong's (Map p510; ☎ 22490369; Sudder St; mains Rs290-590, rice Rs125, beer Rs160; ⏱ 12.30-3pm & 7.30-11pm Wed-Mon) This double-character restaurant is magnificently wooden-panelled like a Raj-oriental gentleman's club with silver-plated cutlery, antique-style umbrellas and lazy wind chimes dangling overhead. Free nibbles precede the meal, but the Thai and

Korean options lack 'kick' and teppanyaki isn't done at the table.

MULTICUISINE

The following offer selections of European and Indian fare.

Food First (Map p510; 5 Camac St; mains Rs35-110; ⏰ 11am-10.30pm; ⊗) Looking like an upmarket fast-food place but waiter-served, widely varying cuisines are prepared at in-view cooking stations.

Drive Inn (Map p510; 10 Middleton St; mains Rs46-82, rice Rs31, juices Rs18-25; ⏰ 11.15am-10pm) Sandwiches, *chaats* (snacks) and plate-lickingly good vegetarian food are served in a modest open-air 'garden' with simple fan-pavilion tables. Try the stuffed capsicum.

Mocambo (Map p510; ☎ 22290095; Mirza Ghalib St; mains Rs83-210, beer Rs108; ⏰ 11am-11pm; ⊗) Despite somewhat old-fashioned red leather scoop-seats and benches, Mocambo has a very loyal following for its mixed grills (Rs189), fish Wellington (Rs192), chicken Kiev (Rs181) and *bhekti* meuniere (well they don't have trout).

Peter Cat (Map p510; ☎ 22298841; Middleton Row; mains Rs85-250, rice Rs89, beers/cocktails from Rs108/81; ⏰ 11am-11pm; ⊗) Opposite KFC, this phenomenally popular Kolkata institution offers fizzing sizzlers, great *chelo*-kebabs (barbequed fingers of spiced, ground-lamb) and beers quaffed from pewter tankards. Waiters wear Rajasthani costumes in an atmosphere redolent of a mood-lit 1970s steakhouse.

Amber/Essence (Map p512; ☎ 22483477; 2nd fl, 11 Waterloo St; mains Rs102-193, beer Rs110; ⏰ 1.30-11pm; ⊗) This pleasantly semitrendy middle-class restaurant has back-lit panels and triangular lamp niches, though their signature brain curry isn't to everyone's taste.

Marco Polo (Map p510; ☎ 22273939; 24 Park St; mains Rs170-395, rice Rs125, beer Rs120, wine Rs1100; ⏰ 1.30-11pm; ⊗) This invitingly modern, spacious split-level restaurant takes diners on a tempting culinary world tour from Bengal to Italy via Goa, China and even Hungary.

ITALIAN & TEX-MEX

Jalapenos (Map p510; ☎ 22820204; 10 Wood St; mains Rs85-250; ⏰ 11.30am-10.15pm; ⊗) In a pleasant, high-ceilinged room with mock wooden beams and little alcoves decorated with spice bottles, the food is enjoyable as long as you don't expect much resemblance to the Tex-Mex and Mediterranean names on the menu.

Pizza Hut (Map p510; ☎ 22814343; 22 Camac St; pizzas Rs75-485; ⏰ 11am-11pm) Popular with travellers seeking a taste of home.

Fire and Ice (Map p510; ☎ 22884073; www.fireand icepizzeria.com; Kanak Bldg, Middleton St; pizzas Rs210-320, pastas Rs240-300, beers Rs130; ⏰ 11am-11.30pm; ⊗) Self-consciously handsome wait-staff sporting black shirts and bandanas bring forth real Italian pastas and pizzas whose fresh-baked thin crusts are Kolkata's best, though the home-made mozzarella melts in a rather odd fashion.

Little Italy (Map p510; ☎ 22825152; 8th fl, Fort Knox Tower, Camac St; pizzas Rs230-465, pastas Rs315-435, small beers Rs145; ⏰ 12.15-3.30pm & 7-10.45pm) À la mode but charmingly relaxed, Little Italy manages a remarkable range of great Italian food considering it's 100% vegetarian. Reservations recommended.

Quick Eats
FAST FOOD

Beef Hotel (Map p510; Tegiya Darbar Hotel, Collin Ln; mains Rs5-20; ⏰ 7-11.45pm) If your stomach's stronger than your wallet you can fill up on rice and veg curry for just Rs8 at this entirely unlovely, rubbish-strewn eatery. We didn't get sick.

Haldiram (Map p510; 58 Chowringhee Rd; Rs30-85; ⏰ 7am-10pm) Excellent value pay-then-queue vegetarian thalis (Rs60 to Rs66), *dosas* (Rs30 to Rs42), burgers (Rs28 to Rs48) and Bengalis sweets.

Snack stalls (Map; p510; Humayan Pl; ⏰ 10am-9pm) Pastry stalls, KFC, Dominos Pizza and Barista Coffee front the New Empire cinema while over the road a colourful series of local stall-shops serve cheap *dosas*, chow mein and great fresh juices. More stalls line Bertram St and nearby Madge Lane.

ROLL HOUSES

Bengal's trademark fast food is the *kati roll*: take a *paratha* roti, fry it with a one-sided coating of egg then fill with sliced onions, chilli and your choice of stuffing (curried chicken, grilled meat or paneer). Roll it up in a twist of paper and it's ready to eat, generally on the street. Typical hole-in-the-wall serveries include **Hot Kati Rolls** (Map p510; 1/1 Park St; rolls Rs12-50; ⏰ 11am-10.30pm) and **Kuzums** (Map p510; 27 Park St; rolls Rs12-45; ⏰ noon-11.30pm).

SWEETS, CAKES & PASTRIES

The following offer only take-away unless otherwise noted.

KC Das (Map p512; Lenin Sarani; sweets Rs3-16; ⏰7.30am-9.30pm) This historic, if not especially atmospheric, Bengali sweet shop invented *rasgulla* (syrupy sponge balls) in 1868. Seating available.

Gupta Brothers (Map p510; www.guptabros.com; Mirza Ghalib St; sweets Rs3-10; ⏰7.30am-10.30pm; 🐾) Classic sweetshop that's now a local snack chain. Their Rs6 veg cutlet balls burst with flavour.

Kathleen Confectioners (Map p510; 12 Mirza Ghalib St; snacks Rs9-30; ⏰8am-8pm; 🐾) Their sickly-sweet cakes aren't exactly the promised 'Taste of Hapinezz' but their savoury pastries are delicious. Stand-and-eat tables offer free filter water if you dare to use the shared metal cup. There are many other branches, including one on AJC Bose Rd.

Kookie Jar (Map p510; Rowden St; pastries Rs20-60; ⏰8am-10pm; 🐾) Kolkata's most heavenly take-away cakes and fudge brownies (Rs32) along with multigrain bread (Rs50), Mexican chicken wraps (Rs55) and fluffy pastries.

Gangaur (Map p510; http://gangaur.org; 2 Russell St; sweets Rs9-25; ⏰7.30am-8pm; 🐾) Upper-market Bengali sweetshop.

DRINKING
Cafes

Ashalayam (Map p510; www.ashalayam.org; 1st fl, 44 Mirza Ghalib St; coffee Rs6-15; ⏰10.30am-7pm Mon-Fri, 10.30am-3.30pm Sat; 🐾) Play chess at low wicker tables while sipping cheap machine-frothed Nescafe in this calm, bright charity craft-shop cafe (see p528).

Flury's (Map p510; Park St; coffees Rs60-145; sandwiches Rs40; ⏰7.30am-9.45pm; 🐾) Great espressos (Rs60) and iced-tea (Rs60) layered like a tequila sunrise in an enticing art deco palace-cafe.

Cafe Coffee Day (Map p510; Wood St; coffees Rs40-75; ⏰10.30am-11pm; 🐾) is the most appealing branch of the Starbucks-style chain thanks to its garden terrace. Along with **Barista** (Map p510; Humayun Pl; coffees Rs24-50; ⏰9am-10pm; 🐾) there are numerous alternative branches (see maps), some cheaper, in which to linger in air-conditioned comfort.

Teashops

Dolly's Tea Shop (Map pp504-5; ☎24237838, mobile 9830115787; Unit G62, Dakshinapan Shopping Centre; teas Rs15-100, snacks Rs20-70; ⏰10.30am-7.30pm Mon-Sat) Teak-panels, rattan chairs, tea-crate tables and the regal presence of matriarch Dolly transform what would otherwise be just another unit in the dreary Dakshinapan Shopping Centre into a charming little oasis that attracts a wonderfully eclectic clientele. Toasted sandwiches or apple pie accompany over 50 choices of tea.

ChaBar (Map p510; Oxford Bookshop, Park St; teas Rs25-75, coffees Rs40-120; ⏰6.30am-11.30pm) A full menu of teas to taste while you book-browse.

Bars

While most better bars are in hotels or restaurants, cheaper places are usually dingy and overwhelmingly male-dominated with a penchant for over-loud music.

Broadway Bar (Map p512; Broadway Hotel; beers Rs70; ⏰11am-10.30pm) Back-street Paris? Chicago 1930s? Prague 1980s? This cavernous, unpretentious old-men's pub defies easy parallels but has a compulsive left-bank fascination with cheap booze, 20 ceiling fans, grimy walls, marble floors and, thankfully, no music.

Fairlawn Hotel (Map p510; 13A Sudder St; beers Rs90; ⏰11.30am-2pm & 2.30-9pm) Half rainforest, half Santa-grotto the small tropical garden of the historic Fairlawn is strung with fairy lights and plastic fruit creating a unique and rather loveable place for a cold brew (no spirits).

Mirch Masala (Map pp504-5; ☎24618900; Monoronjan Roy Sarani; mains Rs75-220, beers Rs95, cocktails Rs110; ⏰noon-3pm & 7am-10.30pm) Old clocks, fake trees, half a taxi-chassis and a north Indian menu presented like a gossip magazine combine to create an amusing ambience that feels like a Bollywood Tex-Mex joint. Take the lane beside Pantaloons department store.

Rocks (Map p512; 9 Waterloo St; beers from Rs100; ⏰ground fl 11am-midnight, 2nd fl 7pm-midnight) Different floors offer different experiences of local drinking culture. The ground floor is a musty old-boys' dive while the 2nd floor has proficient, if ear-splittingly loud, live Bengali music.

Blue & Beyond Restaurant (Map p510; ☎22521039; 9th fl, Lindsay Hotel, Lindsay St; beers Rs110, mains Rs95-175; ⏰11am-11pm) The open-air rooftop terrace offers unusual views over New Market.

Floatel (Map p512; www.floatelhotel.com; Strand Rd; buffet lunch/dinner Rs399/499, beers Rs150; ⏰bar noon-midnight; 🐾) Although primarily a restaurant, wide river views make the Floatel a fine place for a sunset drink.

Roxy (Map p510; Park Hotel; small beers Rs175; ⏰6pm-midnight Sun-Tue, 6pm-4am Wed, Fri & Sat; 🐾) With unusually mellow music and a *Clockwork Orange* retro-futuristic atmosphere, Roxy is the most poised of several fun pub-bars around and within the Park Hotel.

Several wine shops, such as **Scotts, National Stores** and **Republic Stores** (☯ typically 10am-10pm; beer Rs47) are marked on Map p510 and Map p512.

ENTERTAINMENT

Events and cultural happenings are announced in the *Telegraph* newspaper's *Metro* section and the various listings brochures (p507).

Nightclubs

Kolkata's party nights are Wednesday, Friday and Saturday when clubs open till 4am. On other nights most are half empty and close at midnight. Note the difference between entry charge and cover charge: the latter can be recouped in drinks or food to the same value. Either is charged *per couple* and single men (known as stags) are generally excluded.

Tantra (Map p510; Park Hotel; entry Rs500-1000, small beers Rs225) Considered Kolkata's top club, contemporary sounds throb through the single dance floor and not-so-chilled chill-out zone around a central-island bar with an overhead observation bridge.

Marrakech (Map p510; Cinnamon Restaurant, 1st fl, 24 Park St; cover Rs500, beers Rs135) Moroccan-themed bar-club with octagonal tables and low, cushion-seated alcoves around a small, pulsating dance floor.

Venom (Map p510; 8th fl, Fort Knox, 6 Camac St; cover Rs500, Rs1000 Sat) Oscillating bars of vertical red light makes it feel like you're dancing in a giant 1970s amplifier. Musical styles vary.

Ginger (Map pp504-5; ☎ 24863052; 104 SP Mukherjee Rd; no cover, small beers Rs120; ☯ 9pm-late Wed, Fri & Sat) Kolkata's best hope for stags, Ginger can be fun with a group watching the majority-male clientele whoop to 1990s dance hits.

Cultural Programmes

Kolkata's famous poetry, music, art, film and dance are regularly showcased at the **Nandan Complex** (Map p510; 1/1A AJC Bose Rd) comprising theatre halls **Rabindra Sadan** (☎ 22239936) and **Sisir Mancha** (☎ 22235317), plus art-house **Nandan Cinema** (☎ 22231210).

Cinemas

Cinemas are ubiquitous. Of at least nine around New Market, **New Empire Cinema** (Map p510; ☎ 22491299; 1-2 Humayan Pl; tickets Rs50-150) is the most comfortable. **Inox Elgin Rd** (Map p510;

☎ 23584499; www.inoxmovies.com; 4th fl, Forum Shopping Mall, 10/3 Elgin Rd; tickets Rs140-230) is a modern multiplex, bookable online.

Live Music

Bars like Rocks (opposite) have local bands squealing high-volume Indian music. Others feature all-female singers for the delectation of drooling all-male drinkers. Western rock and heavy-rock cover bands play nightly at the Anglo-pub **Someplace Else** (Map p510; Park Hotel; beers Rs200; ☯ from 9.30pm). No cover charges.

Spectator Sports

Dozens of sports clubs on the Maidan practise everything from cricket to kabaddi. Even if you don't know Ganguly from a googly, the electric atmosphere of a **cricket** match at Ranji Stadium (p511) is an unforgettable experience. Pre-book **ICL** (http://indiancricketleague.in/tickets .html) tickets online.

The Victoria Memorial provides a beautiful backdrop to **Maidan racecourse** (☎ 22291104; www.rctconline.com; Acharya Jagdish Rd; admission from Rs14) from whose 19th-century grandstands you can watch some of India's best horse racing at over 40 annual meets.

SHOPPING

New Market is a pestilential nest of handicraft touts. Come before 8am, while touts are sleeping, to admire the grand colonial clocktower and to calmly appreciate the nearby, atmospheric Hogg Market (selling fresh food and live chickens). Traditional, ultracrowded shopping alleys spread in confusing profusion north of BBD Bagh. Rabindra Sarani offers intriguing thematic groupings of trades at different points.

Crafts & Souvenirs
GOVERNMENTAL EMPORIA

State-government emporia sell good-quality souvenirs at decent fixed prices. A large number are gathered together at the **Dakshinapan Shopping Centre** (Map pp504-5; Gariahat Rd; ☯ 11am-7pm Mon-Fri, to 2pm Sat), whose soul-crushing 1970s architecture is slightly softened by the presence of Dolly's Tea Shop (opposite). Fabrics here are good value and **Purbasha** (Unit F4/5 upstairs) has great deals on bamboo- and cane-ware from Tripura.

Similar cane-ware along with pearls, fabrics and Assam tea is available more centrally at **Assam Craft Emporium** (Map p510; ☎ 22298331; Assam

House, 8 Russell St; 10.30am-6pm Mon-Fri, 10.30am-2.30pm Sat). **Nagaland Emporium** (Map p510; 11 Shakespeare Sarani; 10am-6pm Mon-Fri, 10am-2pm Sat) sells Naga crafts, such as shawls and double-face necklaces for wannabe head-hunters.

The impressive, if comparatively pricey, **Central Cottage Industries Emporium** (Map p512; www.cottageemporiumindia.com; Metropolitan Bldg, 7 Chowringhee Rd; 10am-7pm Mon-Fri, to 2pm Sat) showcases handicrafts from right across India.

CHARITY COOPERATIVES

Buy gifts and support these causes:

Ankur Kala (Map pp504-5; 22878476; www.ankurkala.org; 3 Meher Ali Rd) This cooperative training-centre empowers women from the slums. The small shop sells batik, stitch-work, attractive greetings cards and leather-ware. From Park Street walk two blocks east from AJC Bose Rd, turn south passing Tiger Inn and crossing Shakespeare Sarani then look for a big '3' on the alley-gate.

Ashalayam (Map p510; www.ashalayam.org; Mirza Ghalib St) Buying cards, handmade paper and fabrics funds the (ex)street kids who made them (see p526).

Women's Friendly Society (Map p510; 22295285; 29 Park Lane; 8am-1pm & 2-5pm Mon-Fri, 8am-1pm Sat) This 120-year-old charity for destitute women sells somewhat twee hand-embroidered tableware, fabrics and children's clothes from a fine, if ageing, Raj-era mansion.

Clothing

Kolkata is great value for tailored or off-the-rack clothing. Smart shirts cost just Rs100 from Chowringhee Rd **Hawkers Market** (Map p510). Choice around Newmarket is endless while **local tailors** (Map p510) on Elliot Rd are less tourist-oriented.

Musical Instruments

Shops and workshops along Rabindra Sarani sell a great range of musical instruments. For tablas and other percussion try numbers 248, 264 and 268B near Tagore's House (p517). For sitars (from Rs4000) or violins (from Rs2000) visit **Mondal & Sons** (Map p512; 22349658; 8 Rabindra Sarani; 10am-6pm Mon-Fri, 10am-2.30pm Sat). Family run since the 1850s, the Mondals count Yehudi Menuhin among their satisfied customers.

GETTING THERE & AWAY
Air

Kolkata's **Netaji Subhash Bose International Airport** (NSBIA; 25118787) offers direct connections to London and Frankfurt plus several Asian cities.

INTERNATIONAL

Air India (Map p510; 22822356/59; 50 Chowringhee Rd)

Air India Express (www.airindiaexpress.in) Budget flights to Bangkok, Dhaka & Singapore.

Biman Bangladesh Airlines (Map p510; 22491879; www.bimanair.com; Room 126, Lytton Hotel, Sudder St) Flies to Dhaka.

British Airways (98-31377470) Flies to London.

China Eastern Airlines (Map p510; 40448887; c/o InterGlobe, Ground fl, Landmark Bldg, 228A AJC Bose Rd) Flies to Kunming (Yunnan).

Druk Air (Map p510; 22902429; 51 Tivoli Court, 1A Ballygunge Circular Rd) Flies to Bhutan and Bangkok.

Emirates (Map pp504-5; 40099555; Trinity Tower, 83 Topsia Rd) Flies to Dubai.

GMG Airlines (Map p510; 30283030; www.gmgairlines.com; 20H Park St) Flies to Chittagong (Rs5930) and Dhaka (Rs4580), Bangladesh.

Gulf Air (Map p510; 22901522; 3rd fl, Landmark Bldg, 228A AJC Bose Rd) Flies to Bahrain.

Indian Airlines (below) Flies to Kathmandu (Nepal) and Yangon (Burma).

JET Airways (below) Flies to Bangkok and Dhaka.

Lufthansa (off Map pp504-5; 22299365; 8th fl, IT Park Tower, DN62, Sector 5, Salt Lake City) Flies to Frankfurt.

Singapore Airlines (off Map pp504-5; 23675422; 9th fl, IT Park Tower, DN62, Sector 5, Salt Lake City)

Thai Airways International (Map p510; 22838865; 8th fl, Crescent Towers, 229 AJC Bose Rd) Flies to Bangkok.

United Airways Bangladesh (Map p510; 93-3999 8587; www.uabdl.com; 55B Mirza Ghalib St) Flies to Dhaka, Chittagong and Barisal.

DOMESTIC

Indian Airlines (Map p512; 22114433; 39 Chittaranjan Ave; 9am-8pm)

IndiGo (Map p510; http://book.goindigo.in)

Jet Airways (Map p510; 39840000; www.jetairways.com; 18D Park St; 8am-8pm Mon-Sat, 9am-5.30pm Sun)

JetLite (www.jetlite.com)

Kingfisher (www.flykingfisher.com)

spiceJet (www.spicejet.com)

Boat

Sporadic ferries to Port Blair (Andaman Islands, p1125) depart from **Kidderpore Docks** (Map pp504-5; Karl Marx Sarani), entered from Gate 3 opposite Kidderpore commuter train station. Tickets (Rs1700 to Rs7640) go on sale 10 days before departure at the **Shipping Corporation of India** (Map p512; 22484921; Hare St; 10am-1pm & 2.30-5pm Mon-Fri).

DOMESTIC FLIGHTS FROM KOLKATA

Destination	Airlines (& days if less than daily)	Duration
Agartala	IC, IT, 6E, 9W	55min
Ahmedabad	6E daily, IC Thu & Sun	2¾hr
Aizawl	IC, IT	1½hr
Bagdogra (Siliguri)	IT, SG, 9W daily, IC Tue, Thu &Sat	55min
Bengaluru (Bangalore)	IC, IT, SG, S2, 9W	2hr
Bhubaneswar	IT, 9W	55min
Chennai	IC, IT, SG, 6E, 9W	2hr
Delhi	IC, IT, SG, S2, 6E, 9W	2hr
Dibrugarh	IC Tue, Wed, Thu, Sat & Sun, S2/9W Mon-Sat	1½hr
	IT Mon, Wed, Fri & Sun via Guwahati	3hr
Dimapur	IC, usually indirect	1-2hr
Gaya	IC Fri	1hr
Goa	6E via Bangalore	6hr
	IT via Mumbai	4½hr
Guwahati	IC, IT, SG, S2, 6E, 9W,	1¼hr
Hyderabad	IT, 6E, 9W daily, IC Tue, Wed, Thu, Sat & Sun	2hr
Imphal	IC, IT, 6E	1¼hr
	S2/9W Mon, Tue, Wed, Fri & Sat via Guwahati	2¾
Indore via Raipur	IT	4½
Jaipur	6E, IC	2½hr
Jammu via Delhi	IT	4hr
Jamshedpur (Jharkand)	IT	55min
Jorhat	9W Mon, Wed & Fri	1½hr
	IC Tue, Thu & Sat via Shillong	3hr
	via Guwahati IT Tue, Thu & Sat, S2 Thu & Sun	2¾
Lilabari (North Lakhimpur)	IT Tue & Thu via Guwahati	3hr
Lucknow	S2	1½hr
Mumbai	IC, IT, SG, S2, 9W	2½hr
Nagpur	6E, S2	1¾
Patna	IT, S2	1hr
Port Blair	IC, IT, S2	2hr
Raipur	IT	2hr
Ranchi	IT, S2	1¼hr
Shillong	IC Tue, Thu & Sat	1¾hr
Silchar	IC, IT	1½hr
Visakhapatnam (Vizag)	IT, S2	1½hr

Bus

INTERNATIONAL

Several Marquis St agencies run Bangladesh-bound services involving a change of vehicle at the Benapol border. **Shohagh Paribahan** (Map p510; ☎ 22520757; 21A Marquis St; ◷ 5am-9.30pm) runs six daily bus services to Dhaka (Rs660, 13 hours). **GreenLine** (Map p510; ☎ 22520757; 12B Marquis St; ◷ 4am-11pm) has 5am and 6am Dhaka bus services (Rs700) and buses that travel to Chittagong (Rs1080, 22 hours) at 10am and 1pm.

A **Bhutan Postbus** departs 7am to Phuentsholing from Esplanade bus station where there's a special **ticket booth** (◷ 9.30am-1pm & 2-6pm Mon-Sat).

DOMESTIC

From Esplanade

For Darjeeling or Sikkim take one of many night buses to Siliguri (Rs325 to Rs650, 12 hours), departing between 6pm and 8pm from **Esplanade bus stand** (Map p512). For Malda, CSTC buses leave at 7am, 8.30am, 9.30am and 10.45am with LNB overnighters at 9.45pm (Rs120, 9 hours).

From Babughat

Babughat bus stand (Map pp504–5) is beside Eden Gardens train station. Numerous companies including **Whiteliners** (☎ 40195000; www.whiteliners.in) run overnight services to Ranchi (Rs210, 10 hours) and to Puri (Rs330, 12 hours) via Bhubaneswar (Rs295, 9½ hours). Arrive by 5pm if you have any baggage.

Train
INTERNATIONAL
For Dhaka, Bangladesh, the **Maitree Express** (Rs368 to Rs920, 12 hours) runs Saturday and Sunday from Kolkata Station at 7.20am, returning from Dhaka Cantt at 8.30am. You must have Darsana marked on your Bangladesh visa. Buy tickets at a **special desk** (◷ 10am-5pm Mon-Thu, 10am-3pm Fri & Sat, 10am-2pm Sun) within Eastern Railways' Foreign Tourist Bureau (right).

DOMESTIC
Check whether your long-distance train departs from Howrah (Haora; HWH, Map pp504–5), Sealdah (SDAH, Map pp504–5) or 'Kolkata' (Chitpore) Station (CP, pp504–5).

BOOKINGS
Buying tickets is usually easiest by internet or through Sudder St agencies. **Eastern Railways' Foreign Tourist Bureau** (Map p512; ☎ 22224206; 6 Fairlie Pl; ◷ 10am-5pm Mon-Sat, 10am-2pm Sun) has a tourist quota for most trains ex-Kolkata, but you must show foreign-exchange receipts or pay in US dollars or euros. **Computerised booking offices** (Map

MAJOR TRAINS FROM KOLKATA

Departures daily unless otherwise stated.

Useful for	Train no & name	Duration (hr)	Departures	Fares
Bhubaneswar	2073 *Shatabdi*	7	1.40pm Mon-Sat (HWH)	2S/CC Rs142/460
Chennai	2841 *Coromandal*	26½	2.50pm (HWH)	SL/3A/2A Rs469/1264/1731
	2839 *Chennai Mail* via Bhubaneswar	28 6¾	11.45pm (HWH)	Rs217/553/745
Delhi	2381 *Poorva* via Gaya	23	8.05am/8.20am (HWH)	SL/3A/2A Rs433/1163/1590
	0231	22½	11.45am Tue, Wed & Sat (HWH)	
	2329 *Sam. Kranti*	23	1pm Mon & Fri (SDAH)	
Gorakhpur	5047 *Purbanchal*	17¾	2.30pm Mon, Tue, Thu & Sat (CP)	SL/3A/2A Rs312/848/1165
Guwahati	2345 *Saraighat*	17½	4pm (HWH)	SL/3A/2A Rs365/971/1325
	5657 *Kanchenjunga* via Malda	22 7	6.45am (SDAH)	
Jammu	3151 *Tawi Exp* via Lucknow	45½	11.45am (CP)	SL/3A/2A Rs501/1380/1904
		23		Rs345/941/1295
Malda	3465 *Howrah-Malda*	5	3.15pm Mon-Sat (HWH)	2S/CC Rs96/342
Mumbai CST	2810 *Mumbai Mail*	33	8.15pm (HWH)	SL/3A/2A Rs490/1399/1918
New Jalpaiguri	2343 *Darjeeling Mail*	10	10.05pm (SDAH)	SL/3A/2A Rs263/684/926
	3147 *CoochBehar*	12	7.35pm Mon, Wed & Sat (SDAH)	
Patna	3111 *Delhi Lal Quila*	10½	8.10pm (CP)	SL/3A Rs235/633
Puri	2837 *Howrah-Puri*	9¼	10.35pm (HWH)	SL/3A/2A Rs247/641/866
	8409 *SriJagannath*	9½	7pm daily (HWH)	
Siliguri Jctn	3149 *Kanchankaya*	12	7.35pm Tue, Thu & Fri & Sun (SDAH)	SL/3A/2A Rs245/684/926
Varanasi	3005 *Amritsar Mail*	15	7.10pm (HWH)	SL/3A/2A Rs293/796/1092

2S=seat, CC=AC chair-car, 2AC=AC two-tier, 3AC=AC three-tier, SL=non-AC sleeper, HWH=ex-Howrah, SDAH=ex-Sealdah, CP=ex-Chitpur

KOLKATA (CALCUTTA)

p512; 14 Strand Rd South & Koilaghat St; ⏰ 8am-8pm Mon-Sat, 8am-2pm Sun) offer tickets on the wider train network but have no tourist quota.

GETTING AROUND

Tickets on most public transport cost Rs4 to Rs8. Men shouldn't sit in assigned 'Ladies' seats'.

To/From the Airport

NSBIA Airport is 5km east of Dum Dum, itself 20 minutes by metro (Rs6) from central Kolkata.

SUBURBAN TRAIN

From Biman Bandar, the airport train station, trains run to Sealdah at 10.45pm, to Majerhat (Map pp504–5) via BBD Bagh Commuter Station (Map p512) at 7.40am and 1.54pm, and to Majerhat via Ballygunge (Map pp504–5) at 10.40am and 6.45pm. These, plus a 6.30am train, stop at Dum Dum Junction metro. Don't mistakenly alight at Dum Dum Cantt.

TAXI

Fixed-price taxis to Dum Dum metro/Sudder St/Howrah cost Rs140/230/255. Prepay in the terminal then cross over to the rank of yellow cabs ignoring touts in between.

BUS

Crowded city-buses run regularly but are hard to use with luggage. From Airport Gate 1 (900m southwest of the terminals) minibus 151 runs to BBD Bagh, bus 46 to Esplanade via VIP Rd and Whiteliners Shuttle to Tollygunge Metro.

Buses DN9/1 and 30B (bound eventually for Babughat) pick up along Jessore Rd and run via Dum Dum metro (25 minutes). From the international terminal, Jessore Rd is just 400m northwest: walk straight out of the terminal keeping the Hindu temple to your direct left and exit the walled airport zone through the pedestrian-only Airport Gate 2½ (opposite a sweet-shop just east of Ankur Travel).

Alternatively from the domestic terminal, walk 700m northwest exiting via Airport Gate 2 (opposite Ahaar Restaurant).

Bus

Passenger-crammed mechanical sweat boxes hurtle along at frightening speeds wherever the chronic congestion abates. Most buses' route-numbers are written in Western script even when signboards aren't. Pay aboard.

Ferry

The fastest way from central Kolkata to Howrah train station is generally by **river ferry** (Rs4; ⏰ 8am-8pm Mon-Sat) departing every 15 minutes from Bagbazar, Armenian, Fairlie, Bishe June and Babu Ghats.

Metro

Kolkata's one-line **metro** (Rs4-8; ⏰ 7am-9.45pm Mon-Sat, 2-9.45pm Sun) is the city's most stress-free form of public transport. For BBD Bagh use Central or Chandni Chowk stations, for Sudder St area use Esplanade or Park St.

Rickshaw

Kolkata is the last bastion of human-powered '*tana* rickshaws', especially around New Market. During monsoon, high-wheeled rickshaws are the transport most able to cope in the worst-flooded streets. Although rickshaw pullers sometimes charge foreigners disproportionate fares, many are virtually destitute, sleeping on the pavements beneath their rented chariots at night so tips are heartily appreciated.

Autorickshaws squeeze aboard five passengers to operate as share-taxis on fixed routes.

Taxi

Kolkata's ubiquitous yellow Ambassador cabs charge around Rs10 per kilometre (minimum Rs22). To calculate short-trip fares, double the taxi-meter reading and add two rupees. That will be a couple of rupees under for longer trips when you can consult the driver's conversion chart. Just make sure the meter's switched on. That's usually easier when flagging down a passing cab than if approaching a parked one.

Beware that around 1pm, the one-way system that applies on many major roads reverses direction! Not surprisingly many taxis are reluctant to make journeys around this chaotic time.

There are prepaid taxi booths at Howrah Station, Sealdah Station and both airport terminals.

Tram

Routes 20 and 26 link Sealdah train station, Mother Teresa's Motherhouse and Park Circle, with the 26 continuing south to Gariahat terminus. Route 6 links Kumartuli and the sights of upper Rabindra Sarani.

KOLKATA (CALCUTTA)

West Bengal

Stretching from the jagged northern hills down to the paddy fields of the Gangetic plains and into the sultry mangrove delta of the Bay of Bengal, few states offer such a rich range of destinations and experiences as West Bengal.

The 'toy train' of the Darjeeling Himalayan Railway chugs up the hills through British-era hill stations, looping its way to Darjeeling, still a summer retreat and a quintessential remnant of the Raj. Here, amid Himalayan giants and renowned tea estates, lies a network of mountain treks and gushing rivers ripe for white-water rafting. These mountain retreats offer a glimpse into the Himalayan peoples and cultures of Sikkim, Bhutan, Nepal and Tibet.

As you head to the plains, brilliant green fields of rice surround bustling trading towns, mud-and-thatch villages, and vestiges of Bengal's glorious history: ornate, terracotta-tiled Hindu temples and monumental ruins of the Muslim nawabs (ruling princes). Further south, the delta rivers of the Sunderbans run through the world's most extensive mangrove forest; inside are darting kingfishers, spotted deer and the elusive Royal Bengal tiger.

West Bengal was the cradle of the Indian Renaissance and national freedom movement, and has long been considered the country's cultural heartland, famous for its eminent writers, artists, spiritualists and revolutionaries. Overshadowed perhaps by the reputation of its capital Kolkata (Calcutta), the rest of West Bengal sees surprisingly few foreign tourists. Perhaps visitors should learn from the Bengalis themselves, enthusiastic travellers who never tire of exploring their own fascinating and diverse region.

HIGHLIGHTS

- Enjoy 360-degree views over Nepal, Sikkim and West Bengal from mountaintop ridges on the **Singalila Ridge Trek** (p559)

- Ride (or walk alongside) the **toy train** (p552) between the tea towns of Kurseong and Darjeeling

- Meander up the wide **Hooghly River** (p537) to uncover colonial and Mughal relics in Serampore, Chandarnagar and Hooghly

- Ride the rapids in a white-water rafting trip down the Teesta River from **Teesta Bazaar** (p565)

- Admire intricate scenes from the Hindu epics carved on the medieval terracotta temples of **Bishnupur** (p537)

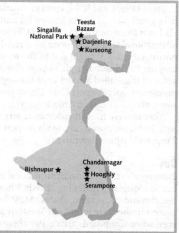

Teesta Bazaar
Singalila National Park ★ ★
★ Darjeeling
★ Kurseong
Chandarnagar
Bishnupur ★
★ Hooghly
Serampore

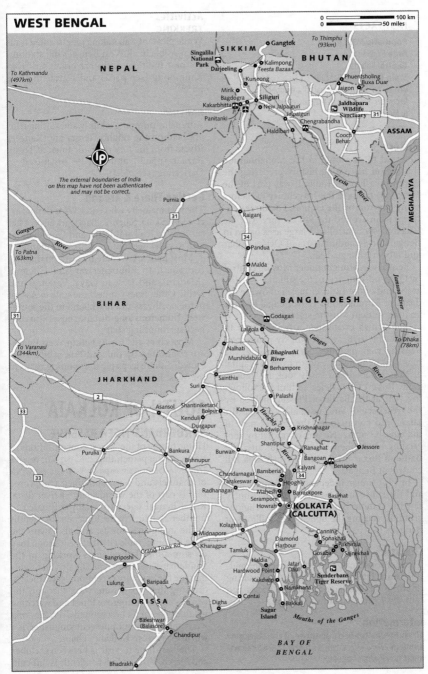

WEST BENGAL

FAST FACTS

Population 80.2 million
Area 87,853 sq km
Capital Kolkata
Main language Bengali
When to go West Bengal hills, October to December and March to May; lower plains, October to March

---

History

Referred to as Vanga in the Mahabharata, this region has a long history predating the Aryan invasions of India. It was part of the Mauryan empire in the 3rd century BC before being overrun by the Guptas. For three centuries from around the 9th century AD, the Pala dynasty controlled a large area based in Bengal and including parts of Orissa, Bihar and modern Bangladesh.

Bengal was brought under Muslim control by Qutb-ud-din, first of the sultans of Delhi, at the end of the 12th century. Following the death of Aurangzeb in 1707, Bengal became an independent Muslim state.

The British established a trading post in Kolkata in 1698, which quickly prospered. Sensing rich pickings, Siraj-ud-daula, the nawab of Bengal, came down from his capital at Murshidabad and easily took Kolkata in 1756. Robert Clive defeated him the following year at the Battle of Plassey, helped by the treachery of Siraj-ud-daula's uncle, Mir Jafar, who commanded the greater part of the nawab's army. He was rewarded by succeeding his nephew as nawab, but after the Battle of Buxar in 1764 the British took full control of Bengal.

In 1947 Indian independence from Britain and the subsequent partition of the country saw the state of Bengal divided on religious grounds, causing the upheaval of millions of Bengalis (see p227).

Climate

The monsoon deluges West Bengal from mid-June until late September and the resulting flooding wreaks havoc with the roads and railways from the plains to the hills.

Information

Useful websites include those of the **state government** (www.wbgov.com) and the **tourist department** (www.wbtourism.com).

Activities
TREKKING

While pleasant walks along pine-scented trails are possible in all West Bengal's hill stations, the best multiday treks are organised from Kalimpong (see p562) and Darjeeling (see p559).

RAFTING

Adrenalin-pumping white-water rafting trips are held on the mighty Teesta and Rangeet Rivers from the tiny riverside town of Teesta Bazaar (p565), and can be organised in Darjeeling (see p554).

Getting There & Around

The vast majority who enter West Bengal arrive in Kolkata. Siliguri's Bagdogra airport has services to Kolkata, Delhi and Guwahati, as well as daily helicopter flights to Gangtok.

Most land arrivals are by train: main lines run south to Bhubaneswar and Chennai (Madras), and west to Gaya, Varanasi and Delhi. Other lines connect the state to Assam in the northeast and Jharkhand in the southwest. Numerous long-distance buses also connect surrounding states.

Most cities and towns within West Bengal are connected by rail and bus, while overcrowded share jeeps ply the winding roads of the West Bengal hills.

SOUTH OF KOLKATA

SUNDERBANS TIGER RESERVE

Home to one of the largest concentrations of tigers on the planet, this 2585-sq-km **reserve** (☎ 03218-55280; admission per day Rs15) is a network of channels and semisubmerged mangroves that is part of the world's largest river delta. Royal Bengal tigers (officially estimated to number 289) lurk in the impenetrable depths of the mangrove forests, and also swim the delta's innumerable channels. Although they do sometimes kill villagers working in the Sunderbans, tigers are typically shy, and sightings are the very rare exception. Nevertheless, cruising the broad waterways through the world's biggest mangrove forest and watching wildlife, whether it be a spotted deer, 2m-long water monitor or luminescent kingfisher, is a world away from Kolkata's chaos.

The best time to visit is between October and March. Visiting independently is difficult,

---

FESTIVALS IN WEST BENGAL

Lepcha & Bhutia New Year (Jan; West Bengal hills, p540) Colourful fairs and traditional dances in and around Darjeeling.

Gangasagar Mela (mid-Jan; Sagar Island, p536) The most intense West Bengal festival; hundreds of thousands of Hindu pilgrims converge where the Ganges meets the sea, to bathe en masse.

Magh Mela (6-8 Feb; Shantiniketan, p538) Crafts take centre stage at this festival.

Bengali New Year (Naba Barsha; mid-Apr; statewide) A statewide holiday celebrates the first day in the Bengali calendar.

Rath Yatra (Car Festival; Jun & Jul; Mahesh) Celebrated by pulling Lord Jagannath's chariot in Mahesh, 3km from Serampore (p537).

Jhapan Festival (mid-Aug; Bishnupur, p537) Draws snake charmers to honour the goddess Manasa, the central figure of snake worship.

Fulpati (Sep & Oct; Darjeeling, p547) Linked to Durga Puja, this predominantly Nepali festival is also celebrated by Lepchas and others with processions and dancing from Ghoom to Darjeeling.

Durga Puja (Oct; statewide) Across the state, especially in Kolkata, temporary *pandals* (castles) are raised and intense celebrations take place to worship Durga. After four colourful days, beautiful images of the 10-armed goddess are immersed in the rivers.

Darjeeling Carnival (7-16 Nov; Darjeeling, p547) Celebrating the region's unity with cultural shows, activities, children's festivals, jazz music and even a contest for *momo* (Tibetan dumpling) eating.

Jagaddhatri Puja (Nov; Chandarnagar, p537) Honours the goddess Jagaddhatri.

Rash Mela (Nov; Cooch Behar & the Sunderbans) Immortalises the union of Lord Krishna and Radha.

Teesta Tea & Tourism Festival (Nov; West Bengal hills, p540) Features cultural events.

Paush Mela (Dec; Shantiniketan, p538) Folk music, dance, theatre and Baul songs radiate over town.

Bishnupur Festival (late Dec; Bishnupur, p537) Highlights handicrafts and local music.

---

with tricky transport connections (and possibly permits) to organise, and it's not cheap; you'll have to bear the cost of boat rentals alone. Organised tours (see below) are the easy and comfortable alternative.

At Sajnekhali, the official gateway into the reserve, you'll find the **Mangrove Interpretation Centre** (8.30am-5pm) with a small turtle and crocodile hatchery, a collection of pickled wildlife and a blackboard with the date of the last tiger-spotting chalked up. **Boats** (3hr from Rs700, guide Indian/foreigner Rs150/200, permit Rs100) are available for hire.

Permits

The permit requirement for foreigners visiting the reserve has been dropped temporarily: for the latest news check with the West Bengal Tourism centre (p507) in Kolkata, or your tour operator.

Tours

Tours prices vary widely. They typically include return transport from Kolkata, as well as all the fees, but do check what is and isn't included.

West Bengal Tourism (p507) can organise weekly boat cruises that are run during the high season (from September through to January), costing from Rs2150 per person for one night and two half-days, including food and on-board accommodation. Trips that include a worthwhile extra day start from Rs3000.

Sunderban Tiger Camp (033-32935749; www.sunder bantigercamp.com;) provides expert guides and quality accommodation (on dry land) with good food and even a bar. Tiger-spotting excursions are on-board comfortable river boats with ample shade. Traditional entertainment is arranged for the evenings. All-inclusive prices range from Rs2750/4440 per person for one-/two-night trips staying in comfortable tents to Rs3500/5650 for fan-cooled huts and Rs4050/7450 for more luxurious AC cottages.

The following agencies run recommended Sunderbans tours for smaller groups, with an emphasis on environmental and cultural sensitivity. They include hotel transfers in Kolkata.

Help Tourism (p507; 1/2 nights for 2 people all-inclusive from Rs11,400/18,900) Longer trips also available.

Kali Travel Home (/fax 25587980; www.travel eastindia.com; 1/2 nights for 2 people all-inclusive from Rs14,000/18,500)

SURVIVING THE TIGER *Niranjan Raptan*

My village here in Sunderbans is Jamespur. Another village is called Annpur; they're named after the children of Daniel Hamilton (an English trader who developed the Sunderbans area in the late 19th century).

When I was 18, I was in the mangroves, collecting honey with my uncle. Suddenly a tiger jumped out at us. My uncle threw himself over me. The tiger ran away, but my uncle died from his wounds. That was 42 years ago, he died saving me.

Over the next years I kept going out and collecting honey and fishing, and I saw many more tigers. One day I met the forest field director Mr Sandal and he asked me about when I had seen tigers, and then he asked me 'Do you want to be a guide?' – and you know, I said 'What's a guide?'.

I came from a poor family, I had no education, I didn't speak English, but now it's 28 years later and I know all the scientific names of the mangrove plants and animals, all the English and Bengali names, and tourists have been my teachers of English.

I'll tell you about the Sunderbans tiger. He's very clever, he will always attack from behind. The tiger isn't naturally a man-eater, but lack of adequate prey has caused him to take anything he can eat – wild pigs, even crabs, and man. Old tigers that are starving, they swim across the river and take the goat, or the man.

I've seen many tigers. You know, if you close your eyes you can picture your home in your country? I can close my eyes and see the tigers. I don't need a camera. When you see the mother with her cubs, they want to play, but they have no cricket ball, no doll! So the mother says 'Look behind me' and she moves her tail and the cubs chase it and play. Of course she's training them for hunting too.

Niranjan Raptan is a guide in the Sunderbans Tiger Reserve

Sleeping & Eating

Sajnekhali Tourist Lodge (☎ 03218-214960; dm/d incl half-board Rs250/700) This place is perfectly located in Sajnekhali, but its rooms are dark and dank. Some private tour operators use this accommodation option so bookings are essential. Dorms can't be booked in advance.

Getting There & Away

From Babu Ghat in Kolkata get a bus to Sonakhali (Rs40, hourly, three hours); aim for the first departure at 6.30am. Then go by boat to Gosaba (Rs11, 1½ hours, hourly), where there are shared cycle-rickshaws to Pakhirala (Rs8, 40 minutes). From there, take another boat across the river to Sajnekhali (Rs4, 10 minutes). The last Kolkata bus leaves Sonakhali at 4.30pm.

DIAMOND HARBOUR

☎ 03174 / pop 37,238

Diamond Harbour, once the main port of the East India Company, rests 51km south of Kolkata, where the Hooghly turns south and flows into open sea. It's a good staging area for points in the south.

While Diamond Harbour is a popular picnic spot, there isn't much to see. Across the

water are the smoking chimneys of industrial Haldia Island.

Diamond Harbour Tourist Centre (Sagarika Tourist Lodge; ☎ /fax 255246; dm Rs150, d from Rs300, with AC from Rs700; ✷) is a rather dank but feasible overnight stop with a cavernous cafeteria-style restaurant. The better rooms back onto the ocean.

Buses from Kolkata's Esplanade (Rs27, 1½ hours) come and go every 30 minutes.

SAGAR ISLAND

According to legend, after the sage Kapil reduced King Sagar's 60,000 sons to ashes, it was at Sagar Island that the Ganges revived their souls by flowing over their dusty remains. Each year the **Gangasagar Mela** (see boxed text, p535) is held here, near the Kapil Muni Temple, honouring the legend. Accommodation on the island is always booked out a long way ahead of the mela; a better way to see the festival is the two-day, one-night boat tour run from Kolkata by West Bengal Tourism (p507), with accommodation on board (per person in berth/cabin Rs6500/8000).

From Diamond Harbour, take a bus to Hardwood Point (Rs20, one hour), where a ferry (Rs8, 25 minutes) crosses the Hooghly to Sagar Island. Buses run the 30km from the ferry landing to the temple (Rs25, 45 minutes).

BAKKALI
☎ 03210

Bakkali is a beach town 132km south of Kolkata. The white-sand beach is rather desolate and exposed, but OK for a stroll. An hour north is the photogenic fishing village of Namkhana; your vehicle will have to cross the river by ferry here, which may involve a wait of up to two hours.

A few minutes' walk from Bakkali's beach is the government-run **Bakkali Tourist Lodge** (☎ 225260; dm/d/tr Rs126/499/790, d with AC Rs893; 🕸). It's rather neglected (an impression not helped by monsoon muds that engulfed the grounds when we were there), but comfortable and friendly enough. There's a decent restaurant here.

A couple of kilometres out of Bakkali is **Henry Island** (d Rs600-1200; 🕸), an aquaculture project with some clean rooms and cottages. Some rooms have balconies and there's a rooftop terrace with views of the mangroves and across to the Sunderbans. There's no restaurant but you can order food (and even beer) in advance. Booking is strictly in advance through the **fisheries department** (☎ 033-23376470; sfdcltd@yahoo.com) in Kolkata. An autorickshaw van will bring you here from Bakkali for Rs60.

A government bus departs Kolkata's Esplanade for Bakkali daily at 7am (Rs75, 4½ hours).

NORTH OF KOLKATA

UP THE HOOGHLY
On the Hooghly River, 25km north of Kolkata, Serampore was a Danish trading centre until Denmark's holdings in India were transferred to the East India Company in 1845. **Serampore College** was founded by the first Baptist missionary to India, William Carey, and houses a library that was once one of the largest in the country.

Further upriver is the former French outpost of **Chandarnagar**, where you can visit the **Eglise du Sacre Coeur** (Sacred Heart Church) and the nearby 18th-century mansion now housing the **Cultural Institut de Chandarnagar** (admission free; 🕙 11am-5.30pm, closed Thu & Sat), with collections documenting this colonial outpost. A few blocks north is the atmospheric, decaying **Sacred Heart Cemetery**.

In 1537 the Portuguese set up a factory in **Hooghly**, 41km north of Kolkata, which became an important trading port long before Kolkata rose to prominence. Climb the lofty clocktower of the romantically crumbling **Imambara** (admission Rs5; 🕙 8am-6pm Dec-Jul, to 5.30pm Aug-Nov), where the view over the river (not to mention the climb) will take your breath away. The building was constructed in 1806 to host the Shiite procession of Muharram. Only 1km south of Hooghly, **Chinsura** was exchanged by the Dutch for the British possessions on the (Indonesian) island of Sumatra in 1825. There is a fort and a Dutch cemetery, 1km to the west.

About 6km north of Hooghly, **Bansberia** has two interesting temples. The 13 *sikharas* (spires) at **Hansewari** look like something you'd expect to see in St Petersburg, while the ornate terracotta tiles covering the **Vasudev Temple** resemble those seen in Bishnupur.

BISHNUPUR
☎ 03244 / pop 61,943

Known for its beautiful terracotta temples, Bishnupur flourished as the capital of the Malla kings from the 16th to the early 19th centuries. The architecture of these intriguing **temples** (Indian/foreigner Rs5/100; 🕙 dawn-dusk) is a bold mix of Bengali, Islamic and Orissan styles. Intricately detailed facades of numerous temples play out scenes of the Hindu epics Ramayana and Mahabharata. The most striking temples are the Jor Bangla, Madan Mohan, the multi-arched Ras Mancha and the elaborate Shyam Rai. You need to pay for your ticket at Ras Mancha, and show it at the other temples. Cycle-rickshaw-wallahs offer tours (the best way to negotiate the labyrinth of lanes) for Rs150.

There's a small **museum** (admission Rs10; 🕙 11am-7pm Tue-Sun) that's worth a look for its painted manuscript covers, stone friezes, musical instruments and folk-art gallery.

Bishnupur is in Bankura district, famous for its pottery, particularly the stylised Bankura horse, and Baluchari silk saris. Reproductions of detailed terracotta tiles from the temples are sold everywhere.

Bishnupur Tourist Lodge (☎ 252013; College Rd; d from Rs300, with AC from Rs600; 🕸) is a typically sleepy government-run hotel with adequate, unremarkable rooms and a restaurant. It's

WEST BENGAL

UP ON THE FARM, DOWN ON THE FARM

If you want to get off the tourist track and enjoy views and solitude, we recommend two (very different) farm homestays in West Bengal. Both need to be booked in advance.

Perched on an idyllic mountainside three hours' bumpy jeep ride from Darjeeling (p547) or two hours' drive from Rimbik, at the end of the Singalila Ridge Trek (p559; it's a great place to kick back if you've just finished the trek), **Karmi Farm** (☎ in the UK 0208 903 3411; www.karmifarm .com; karmifarm@yahoo.co.uk; per person incl full board Rs1500) overlooks Sikkim in one direction and Nepal in another. It's managed by Andrew Pulger, whose Sikkimese grandparents once ran an estate from the main house here, where delicious home-cooked (and often home-grown) meals are now served up to visitors on the old kitchen table. The simple but very comfortable double and family rooms are attractively decorated with colourful local fabrics, and bathrooms have 24-hour hot water. A small clinic for villagers is run from the farm, providing a volunteer opportunity for medical students and doctors. Treks and other activities can be organised, but you may not be able to drag yourself from the rooftop deck; it would be easy to sit here for a week with a book and a pot of tea, overlooking the bird- and flower-filled gardens in the foreground and towering peaks in the distance. Highly recommended.

Back down on the plains and halfway across the state, endless miles of brilliant-green paddy fields stretch out from the simple adobe farmhouse at **Basudha Farm** (☎ in Kolkata 033-25928109, 9434062891; www.cintdis.org/basudha.html; per person incl full board Rs300), less than an hours' drive from Bishnupur (p537). Basudha was founded by ecologist Dr Debal Deb, who operates a seed bank of indigenous rice strains. At Basudha he grows and experiments with rices, using organic methods, and teaches these methods to other farmers as an alternative to using genetically modified rice varieties. Visitors to the farm are assumed to be interested in the work and the local culture; members of WWOOF (Willing Workers on Organic Farms) get free board in exchange for farm work. Accommodation is basic, with limited (solar) power, and all water needs to be pumped from the well (men are encouraged to piss on the garden to add nitrates to the soil). The all-veg food is mostly grown on the farm, and is cooked in the local style. The strictly vegetarian Dr Deb assured us that the snakes in jars (decorating the guest room) died of natural causes.

---

close to the museum, and a Rs40 rickshaw ride from the train station. It's often full – book ahead.

Regular buses run to Kolkata (Rs70, five hours). For Shantiniketan (Rs65, five hours) you may have to change in Durgapur (see opposite). Two trains run daily to Howrah (2nd class/chair Rs81/285, four hours); the *Rupashi Bangla Express* 2884 departs at 5.23pm and the *Howrah Express* 2828 departs at 7.33am.

SHANTINIKETAN
☎ 03463

Shantiniketan is the epitome of its Bengali name, which means peaceful *(shanti)* abode *(niketan)*. The mystic, poet and artist Rabindranath Tagore (1861–1941) founded a school here in 1901, which later developed into the Visva-Bharati University, with an emphasis on humanity's relationship with nature. It's a relaxed place with students from all over India and overseas.

The **post office** (Santiniketan Rd; ◷ 9am-5pm Mon-Sat) is on the main road, opposite the turn-off to the university entrance. The **State Bank of India** (Santiniketan Rd; ◷ 10am-3pm Mon-Fri), on the same road, has an ATM and changes foreign currency and Amex travellers cheques.

Spread throughout the leafy university grounds are eclectic **statues**, the celebrated **Shantiniketan Murals** and the **Tagore Prayer Hall**. The **museum and art gallery** (adult/student Rs5/3; ◷ 10.30am-1pm & 2-4.30pm Thu-Mon, 10.30am-1pm Tue) within the Uttarayan complex (Tagore's former home) are worth a peek if you are an aficionado of Tagore. Reproductions of his sketches and paintings are sold here. The bookshop at the main gate has plenty of Tagore's titles (Rs80 to Rs250) in English.

Sleeping & Eating
Hotel Santiniketan (☎ 254434; Bhubandanga; s/d from Rs250/300, d with AC Rs700; ❄) This salmon-coloured (inside and out) balconied hotel provides good value, with clean rooms (though the sheets and towels have seen much better days). The ground-floor rooms are cool and there's a pleasant garden. The restaurant (mains Rs35

WEST BENGAL

to Rs80) dishes up a limited range of Indian standards.

Hotel Rangamati (☎ 252305; Hwy 31, Bhubandanga; s/d from Rs550/700, with AC from Rs650/850) A fun 'jungle hut' theme with faux branches, wooden fittings and lots of fish tanks at the entrance. Rooms are clean with big bathrooms and dark wood furniture. There's a basic restaurant.

Camellia Hotel & Resort (☎ 262042; Prantik; d Rs1150, with AC from Rs1450; 🔀 🖵) The Camellia has a pleasant country setting about 1km from the university, with leafy gardens and green lawns. Tasteful art and furniture make the rooms especially comfortable; the suites have fridge and bathtub. Pick-up from the train station is available.

Green Chilli (☎ 9832277095; Bhubandanga; mains Rs20-55, thali Rs30) Good Indian breakfasts and a range of tasty curries and Chinese. Stylishly done up with bright colours, it's a pleasant spot to grab a bite. It's just off the highway on the way to Hotel Santiniketan.

Getting There & Away

Several trains ply between Bolpur station, 2km south of the university, and Kolkata daily. The best is *Shantiniketan Express* 2337/8 (2nd class/chair Rs69/235, 2½ hours) departing at 10.10am from Howrah and 1.10pm from Bolpur. To New Jalpaiguri choose between *Kanchenjunga Express* 5657 (sleeper/3AC Rs190/505, eight hours) departing at 9.40am or *Kolkata Haldibari Superfast Express* 2563 (2nd class/chair Rs126/425) departing at 11.31am on Tuesday, Thursday and Saturday. There's a **train booking office** (Santiniketan Rd; 🕑 8am-noon, 12.30-2pm Thu-Tue) near the post office.

The Jambuni bus stand is in Bolpur. Buses go to Berhampore/Murshidabad (Rs55, four hours) and Bishnupur (Rs65, five hours) but direct buses can be hard to find: you may need to change in Durgapur for Bishnupur and Suri for Berhampore.

NABADWIP & MAYAPUR
☎ 03472 / pop 115,036

Nabadwip, 114km northwest of Kolkata, is an important Krishna pilgrimage centre, attracting throngs of devotees, and is an ancient centre of Sanskrit culture. The last Hindu king of Bengal, Lakshman Sen, moved his capital here from Gaur.

Across the river from Nabadwip, Mayapur is a centre for the Iskcon (Hare Krishna) movement. There's a large, colourful temple and the basic but clean **Iskcon Guest Houses** (☎ 245620; mghb@pamho.net; d/tr/q from Rs300/350/450, d without bathroom from Rs100). Iskcon runs a private bus to Kolkata (Rs200, five hours) early on Friday, Saturday and Sunday mornings, returning in the evening; for details or to make a booking call **Iskcon Kolkata** (☎ 033-30289258, 30280865).

MURSHIDABAD & BERHAMPORE
☎ 03482 / pop 36,894

In Murshidabad, rural Bengali life and 18th-century architecture meld on the verdant shores of the Bhagirathi River. When Siraj-ud-daula was nawab of Bengal, Murshidabad was his capital, and he was assassinated here after the defeat at Plassey (now Palashi).

The main draw here is the **Hazarduari** (Indian/foreigner Rs5/100; 🕑 10am-4.30pm Sat-Thu), a palace famous for its 1000 doors (real and false), built here for the nawabs in 1837. It houses an astonishing collection of antiquities from the 18th and 19th centuries. The Great Imambara on the palace grounds is being renovated and may be closed; have a peek through the gates.

Murshid Quli Khan, who moved the capital here in 1705, is buried beneath the stairs at the impressive ruins of the **Katra Mosque**. Siraj-ud-daula was assassinated at the **Nimak Haram Deohri** (Traitor's Gate). Within the **Kathgola Gardens** (admission Rs7; 🕑 6.30am-5.30pm) is an interesting Jain Parswanath Temple and a museum.

Berhampore is 11km south of Murshidabad and acts as its bus and railway hub.

Sleeping & Eating

Hotel Samrat (☎ 251147; fax 253091; NH34 Panchanantala; s/d from Rs175/250, with AC from Rs600/700; 🔀) We'd recommend Samrat even if it wasn't pretty much the only hotel in Berhampore: it's excellent value, with fresh, brightly painted rooms with new furnishings, and helpful staff who can organise sightseeing for you. The fancy-pants new restaurant (mains Rs30 to Rs80), all faux marble and low lighting, has a bar and a big range of dishes, mainly Indian.

Hotel Manjusha (☎ 270321; Murshidabad; d Rs300-400) A wonderful setting on the bank of the Bhagirathi, behind the Great Imambara. Downstairs rooms are cheapest, while rooms 201 to 203 have both river and Hazarduari views. It's all about the location and period charm (check out the pictures of

King Edward!) – the rooms themselves are threadbare and fading, and some are slightly whiffy.

Getting There & Around

There's a daily express train *Bhagirati Express* 3103/4 to/from Kolkata (2nd class/chair Rs67/236, four hours), departing Sealdah station, Kolkata at 6.25pm and Berhampore at 6.34am. Regular buses leave for Kolkata (Rs65, six hours) and Malda (Rs55, four hours). To Shantiniketan/Bolpur (Rs55, four hours) there are occasional direct buses but you may need to change in Suri.

Shared autorickshaws (Rs10) whiz between Murshidabad and Berhampore. Cycle-rickshaws/taxis offer guided half-day tours to see the spread-out sites for Rs150/400.

MALDA
☎ 03512 / pop 161,448

Malda, 347km north of Kolkata, is a convenient base for visiting the ruins of Bengal's former capitals in nearby Gaur and Pandua. Malda is also famed for its Fajli mangoes ripening in spring; even if it's not mango season, you'll probably get mango pickle on the side with any food you order here.

State Bank of India and ICICI ATMs are on the highway, near the turn-off to the bus station. **i-Zone** (per hr Rs20; ⏱ 8am-7pm), behind the bus station on the way to the museum, has fast internet connections. **Malda Museum** (admission Rs2; ⏱ 10.30am-5pm Thu-Tue) is next to the library and has a small collection of sculpture and coins from Gaur and Pandua.

Continental Lodge (☎ 252388; fax 251505; 22 KJ Sanyal Rd; s/d from Rs150/250, d with AC from Rs650; ❄) is a friendly lodge almost directly opposite the bus station; it offers fairly clean, oddly furnished rooms for every budget.

Hotel Kalinga (☎ 284503; www.hotelkalingamalda .com; NH34, Ram Krishna Pally; d without/with AC from Rs425/800; ❄ 🖳) is a big place on the highway, about halfway between the bus and train stations. The AC rooms are fine, but the cheaper ones are grubby and bare. The restaurant on the top floor has an Indian/Chinese/continental menu (mains Rs40 to Rs90) and great views over the town.

The best train from Kolkata (Sealdah station) is *Kolkata Haldibari Superfast Express* 2563 (2nd class/chair Rs111/372, six hours), departing 9.05am Tuesday, Thursday and Sunday. It continues to New Jalpaiguri

(Rs91/301, four hours), departing at 3.20pm. If returning to Kolkata take the *Intercity Express* 3466 to Howrah (2nd class/chair Rs96/342, seven hours), departing 6.10am Monday to Saturday. Buses depart regularly for Siliguri (Rs120, six hours), Berhampore/Murshidabad (Rs55, four hours) and Kolkata (from Rs140, 10 hours).

GAUR & PANDUA

Rising from the flooded paddy fields of Gaur (16km south of Malda) are mosques and other vestiges of the 13th- to 16th-century capital of the Muslim nawabs. Little remains from the 7th- to 12th-century pre-Muslim period, when Gaur was the capital of the successive Buddhist Pala and Hindu Sena dynasties.

Wander through the ruins of the impressive **Baradwari Mosque** and the intact arcaded aisle of its corridor, or beneath the fortresslike gateway of **Dakhil Darwaza** (1425). The **Qadam Rasul Mosque** enshrines the flat footprint of the Prophet Mohammed. The adjacent **tomb of Fath Khan** (1707) startlingly informs you that he 'vomited blood and died on this spot'. Lotus-flower motifs grace the terracotta facade of the **Tantipara Mosque** (1480), while remnants of colourful enamel cling to the **Lattan** and **Chamkati** mosques.

North of Pandua (18km north of Malda) are the vast ruins of the 14th-century **Adina Masjid**, once India's largest mosque. Within an intact section of arched and domed bays sits the tomb of Sikander Shah (1364–79), the builder of this mosque. About 2km away is the **Eklakhi mausoleum**, so-called because it cost Rs1 lakh (Rs100,000) to build.

The monuments are spread throughout Gaur and Pandua along some of the worst roads in India; it's worth hiring a taxi from Malda for half a day (Rs600).

WEST BENGAL HILLS

SILIGURI & NEW JALPAIGURI
☎ 0353 / pop 655,935 / elev 119m

The crowded trading hub encompassing the twin towns of Siliguri and New Jalpaiguri (NJP) is the jumping-off point for Darjeeling, Kalimpong, Sikkim, the northeast states, eastern Nepal and Bhutan. There's not a lot to see here: for most travellers, Siliguri is an overnight transit point where you can catch a glimpse of snowy peaks.

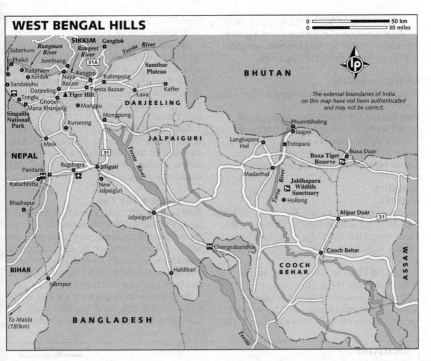

Orientation

Most of Siliguri's hotels, restaurants and services are spread along Tenzing Norgay Rd, better known by its old moniker, Hill Cart Rd. NJP Station Rd leads southward to NJP station, while branching eastward off Hill Cart Rd are Siliguri's other main streets, Sevoke and Bidhan Rds.

Information

INTERNET ACCESS

Cyber Space (Hotel Vinayak, Hill Cart Rd; ☉ 10am-8pm) Internet (Rs30), USB connection and CD burning (Rs25). Down behind a shop.

iWay (Hill Cart Rd; per hr Rs30; ☉ 9am-9pm) A tangerine dream, with bright-orange interior.

Netcafe (☎ 9434020017; Hospital Rd; per hr Rs15; ☉ 10am-10pm) Small, hot, crowded and half the price of anywhere else.

MEDICAL SERVICES

Sadar Hospital (☎ 2436526, 2585224; Hospital Rd)

MONEY

There are ATMS for Standard Chartered Bank, State Bank of India and UBI Bank on Hill Cart Rd.

Delhi Hotel (☎ 2516918; Hill Cart Rd; ☉ 9am-8pm) Currency and travellers cheques exchanged.

Multi Money (☎ 2535321; 143 Hill Cart Rd; ☉ 9.30am-7pm Mon-Sat) Exchanges currency and Amex travellers cheques. Western Union agent.

POST

General post office (☎ 2538850; Hospital Rd; ☉ 7am-7pm Mon-Sat, 10am-3pm Sun) No parcel service late afternoon or Sunday.

TOURIST INFORMATION

Darjeeling Gorkha Hill Council Tourist Office (DGHC; ☎ 2518680; Hill Cart Rd; ☉ 8am-5pm Mon-Fri, 8am-1pm Sat & Sun) A friendly office that offers helpful service and brochures on Darjeeling, Kalimpong, Kurseong and Mirik.

Government of Assam Tourist Office (Pradhan Nagar Rd; ☉ 10am-4pm Mon-Fri) No phone, six pamphlets, and you have to sign in triplicate to confirm you took a pamphlet.

Sikkim Tourist Office (☎ 2512646; SNT Terminal, Hill Cart Rd; ☉ 10am-4pm Mon-Sat) Issues permits for Sikkim. If you apply in the morning, your permit should be ready by the afternoon; bring your passport and one passport-sized photo.

West Bengal Tourist Office (☎ 2511979; Hill Cart Rd; ⏲ 10am-5pm Mon-Fri) Can also book accommodation for the Jaldhapara Wildlife Sanctuary. Less helpful information desks are also at the airport and NJP train station.

TRAVEL AGENCIES
Private transport booking agencies line Hill Cart Rd.

Help Tourism (☎ 2433683; www.helptourism.com; 143 Hill Cart Rd) A recommended agency with a strong environmental and community-development focus. It has links to homestays and lodges around the hills, and can organise tour and trekking packages that get rave reviews.

Sleeping
BUDGET
Conclave Lodge (☎ 2514102; Hill Cart Rd; s/d from Rs200/350) Tucked away behind the more visible Hotel Conclave, this lodge is the best budget option, with clean, quiet whitewashed rooms with TV.

Hotel Hill View (☎ 2519951; Hill Cart Rd; d 400, s/tr without bathroom Rs200/350) This vintage 1951 accommodation has the tiniest vestiges of colonial charm left (mainly on the exterior), but the rooms are basic and run down. The friendly manager doesn't try to oversell his 'very simple rooms'.

Hotel Chancellor (☎ 2432372; cnr Sevoke & Hill Cart Rds; d Rs285, with TV Rs335) A no-frills but friendly Tibetan-run place that gets a fair bit of traffic noise. Rooms are clean, but ongoing renovations mean you might have to pick your way through exposed concrete and piles of junk to get there.

Hotel Mount View (☎ 2512919; Hill Cart Rd; d from Rs500) Rooms contain an odd mix of cheap and quality furniture. Take a look at a few rooms as some (mainly upstairs) are much nicer than others.

MIDRANGE & TOP END
Hotel Conclave (☎ 2516144; www.hotelconclave.com; Hill Cart Rd; s/d from Rs500/600, with AC from Rs750/900; ❄) A recommended contemporary hotel with fine woodwork and artwork, quality mattresses and an unexpected external glass elevator. The rooms are spotless and downstairs is the excellent Eminent Restaurant.

Hotel Himalayan Regency (☎ 650 2955; Hill Cart Rd; s/d from Rs500/600, with AC from Rs1100/1200; ❄) Comfortable rooms with big clean bathrooms.

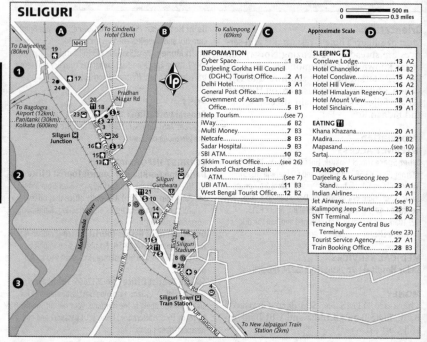

SILIGURI

0 ──── 500 m
0 ──── 0.3 miles

Approximate Scale

To Cindrella Hotel (3km)
To Kalimpong (69km)
To Darjeeling (80km)
NH31
To Darjeeling (80km)
Pradhan Nagar Rd
To Bagdogra Airport (12km); Panitanki (30km); Kolkata (600km)
Siliguri Junction
Mahananda River
Siliguri Gurdwara
Sevoke Rd
Hill Cart (Tenzing Norgay) Rd
Bidhan Rd
Kachari Rd
Tilak Rd
Siliguri Stadium
Hospital Rd
NJP Station Rd
Siliguri Town Train Station
To New Jalpaiguri Train Station (2km)

INFORMATION	
Cyber Space	1 B2
Darjeeling Gorkha Hill Council (DGHC) Tourist Office	2 A1
Delhi Hotel	3 A1
General Post Office	4 B3
Government of Assam Tourist Office	5 B1
Help Tourism	(see 7)
iWay	6 B2
Multi Money	7 B3
Netcafe	8 B3
Sadar Hospital	9 B3
SBI ATM	10 B2
Sikkim Tourist Office	(see 26)
Standard Chartered Bank ATM	(see 7)
UBI ATM	11 B3
West Bengal Tourist Office	12 B2

SLEEPING 🏠	
Conclave Lodge	13 A2
Hotel Chancellor	14 B2
Hotel Conclave	15 A2
Hotel Hill View	16 A2
Hotel Himalayan Regency	17 A1
Hotel Mount View	18 A1
Hotel Sinclairs	19 A1

EATING 🍴	
Khana Khazana	20 A1
Madira	21 B2
Mapasand	(see 10)
Sartaj	22 B3

TRANSPORT	
Darjeeling & Kurseong Jeep Stand	23 A1
Indian Airlines	24 A1
Jet Airways	(see 1)
Kalimpong Jeep Stand	25 B2
SNT Terminal	26 A2
Tenzing Norgay Central Bus Terminal	(see 23)
Tourist Service Agency	27 A1
Train Booking Office	28 B3

A lot of thought has obviously gone into the design and colour scheme here (not necessarily by someone with good taste).

Hotel Sinclairs (☎ 2517674; www.sinclairshotels.com; off NH31; d from Rs2900; 🅿 🅿) This comfortable three-star hotel escapes the noise of Hill Cart Rd, about 2km north of the bus terminal. The rooms are spacious, if a little tired, but there's an excellent restaurant-cum-bar and the chance to dive into a cool, clean pool.

Cindrella Hotel (☎ 2544130; 3rd Mile, Sevoke Rd; www .cindrellahotels.com; s/d from Rs3300/3500; 🅿 🖥 🅿) The top place in town is very luxurious; rooms have polished floorboards, comfy couches, huge beds, minibar and stylish lighting. There's a small pool and gym, and free wi-fi throughout.

Eating

Mapasand (☎ 2778704; Mangaldeep Blg, Hill Cart Rd; sweets from Rs5; 🕙 8am-9pm) While other bakeries embrace the trend towards lurid Western-style cakes, this clean shop presents tray upon enticing tray of classic Indian sweets like *barfi* (a fudgelike sweet; complete with real silver) and *ladoo* (sweetmeat balls made with gram flour).

Madira (☎ 2435980; Hill Cart Rd; mains Rs25-150) A small bar-restaurant, reached via a tunnel beside Airview Lodge. Decorated in cute bright colours it serves a range of North Indian dishes and snacks, along with some Chinese of the 'American Chopsuey' variety.

Khana Khazana (☎ 2517516; Hill Cart Rd; mains Rs40-90) The secluded outdoor area here makes a nice lunch spot. The extensive menu ranges from pizzas and Chinese and South Indian specials to Mumbai street snacks, and includes plenty of vegetarian options.

Sartaj (☎ 2431759; Hill Cart Rd, mains Rs45-180; 🅿) A sophisticated and cool (literally – it's heaven when the AC hits you) restaurant with a huge range: first-rate North Indian tandooris and curries, good Chinese and top-notch service. There's a bar, and alcohol is served to your table.

Getting There & Away

AIR

Bagdogra airport is 12km west of Siliguri. **Indian Airlines** (☎ 2511495; www.indianairlines.in; Hill Cart Rd; 🕙 10am-1pm & 1.45-4.30pm Mon-Sat) has three flights a week to Kolkata (one hour), five to Delhi (four hours), and two to Guwahati (50 minutes). **Jet Airways** (☎ 2538001; www.jetairways

---

> ### PRODUCING THE PERFECT CUPPA
>
> Live-in training courses for aspiring tea experts are popular in the West Bengal hills. The following estates have good reputations and use organic methods.
>
> **Lochan Tea Limited** (www.lochantea.com, www.doketea.com; Siliguri) Offers a three-month course in international tea trading that includes tea tasting and practical experience in buying tea at auction. Students live at the company guest house in Siliguri.
>
> **Makaibari Tea Estate** (www.makaibari.com; Kurseong) Courses include five-day intensives (Rs10,000) in tea manufacturing and biodynamics; accommodation is available on the estate or at nearby Cochrane Place (p546). For more about Makaibari see the boxed text, p547.

.com; Hill Cart Rd; 🕙 9am-5.30pm Mon-Sat) flies to Kolkata (daily), Delhi (daily; some flights via Guwahati) and Guwahati (four per week). **Kingfisher Airlines** (☎ 39008888; www.flykingfisher .com) has daily flights to Kolkata and Delhi, and three flights a week to Guwahati. Check websites for fares, which can vary widely.

Daily helicopter flights (Rs3000, 30 minutes, 10kg luggage limit) travel from Bagdogra to Gangtok at 2pm. You can buy tickets from the **Tourist Service Agency** (TSA; ☎ 2531959; tsaslg@sanchar net.in; Pradhan Nagar Rd), which is close to the Delhi Hotel.

BUS

Most North Bengal State Transport Corporation (NBSTC) buses leave from **Tenzing Norgay central bus terminal** (Hill Cart Rd), as do many private buses plying the same routes.

Sikkim Nationalised Transport (SNT) buses to Gangtok (Rs96, 4½ hours) leave at 9.30am, 11.30am, 12.30pm and 1.30pm from the **SNT terminal** (Hill Cart Rd). There is also a deluxe bus (Rs110) that departs here at 12.30pm. If travelling to Sikkim, you'll require a permit available in Siliguri at the adjacent Sikkim Tourist Office (p541).

JEEP

A faster and more comfortable way of getting around the hills is by share jeep. There are a number of jeep stands: for Darjeeling (Rs120, 2½ hours) and Kurseong (Rs60, 1½ hours), look around and opposite the bus terminal; for Kalimpong (Rs80, 2½ hours) there's a

NBSTC BUSES FROM SILIGURI			
Destination	Fare (Rs)	Duration (hr)	Frequency
Darjeeling	80	3½	every 30min
Guwahati	280	12	5pm only
Kalimpong	50	3	every 2hr
Kolkata	266	12-16	5 daily
Kurseong	42	2	every 30min
Madarihat	65	3	hourly
Malda	115	6½	every 30min
Mirik	50	2½	every 2hr

stand on Sevoke Rd; and for Gangtok (Rs140, four hours) jeeps leave from next to the SNT terminal. Share and charter jeeps for all these destinations also leave straight from the NJP train station.

Chartering a jeep privately costs roughly 10 times that of a shared ticket. An option for XL-sized Westerners is to pay for and occupy all the front three seats next to the driver.

TRAIN
The fastest of the four daily services to Kolkata is the *Darjeeling Mail* 2344 (sleeper/3AC Rs263/684, 13 hours, departs 5.25pm), which stops in Malda. A better option for Malda is the *New Jalpaiguri Sealdah Express* 2504 (2nd class/chair Rs111/372, four hours, departing 9.45am Monday, Wednesday and Saturday). The *North East Express* 2505 is the fastest to Delhi (sleeper/3AC Rs437/1174, 27 hours, departs 5.05pm), travelling via Patna (Rs229/587, 11 hours). Eastward, train 2506 reaches Guwahati (sleeper/3AC Rs207/527, eight hours, departs 8.40am).

There's a **train booking office** (☎ 2537333; cnr Hospital & Bidhan Rds; ☺ 8-11.30am & noon-8pm Mon-Sat, to 2pm Sun) in Siliguri.

Toy Train
The diesel toy train climbs the 88km from New Jalpaiguri to Darjeeling in eight long hours (2nd/1st class Rs42/247, departs 9am). It's wise to make reservations (booking fee Rs15/30) two to three days in advance at NJP station or the train booking office. If steam is your passion, you can catch the steam version to Darjeeling from Kurseong (p547).

Getting Around
From the bus terminal to NJP train station a taxi/autorickshaw costs Rs200/90, while cycle-

rickshaws charge Rs50 for the 35-minute trip. Taxis between Bagdogra airport and Siliguri cost Rs300.

JALDHAPARA WILDLIFE SANCTUARY
☎ 03563 / elev 61m
This rarely visited **sanctuary** (☎ 262239; Indian/foreigner Rs25/100, camera/video Rs5/2500; ☺ mid-Sep–mid-Jul) protects 114 sq km of lush forests and grasslands along the Torsa River and is a refuge for over 50 Indian one-horned rhinoceros (Rhinoceros unicornis).

The best time to visit is mid-October to May, particularly March and April when wild elephants, deer and tigers (rarely seen) are attracted by new grass growth. Your best chance of spotting a rhino is aboard an elephant (Indian/foreigner Rs120/200 per hour); these lumbering safaris are booked by the tourist lodges, and if staying elsewhere, you'll be last in line. You can't book ahead for elephant rides, so if an elephant falls sick or a VIP wants a ride, you might miss out.

The West Bengal tourist offices in Kolkata (p507) and Siliguri (p542) organise overnight **tours** (per person Rs2050; ☺ departs 10am Sat, returns 5pm Sun) from Siliguri to Jaldhapara, which include an elephant ride, transport, accommodation at the Hollong Tourist Lodge and all meals.

Sleeping & Eating
The two lodges should be booked well in advance through the West Bengal Tourist Office in Siliguri, Darjeeling or Kolkata; they won't take direct bookings.

Jaldhapara Tourist Lodge (☎ 262230; dm Rs300, cottage Rs650, d Rs1000) This WBTDC hotel is outside the park precincts near Madarihat. All meals are included in the room rates. Check out rooms in both blocks.

Hotel Relax (☎ 262304; Madarihat; d Rs350) A very basic option opposite the Jaldhapara Tourist Lodge, with OK beds, cement floors and squat toilets. Expect some odd smells.

Hollong Tourist Lodge (☎ 262228; d Rs1000, plus compulsory Rs175 per person for breakfast & dinner) This is a smaller and more comfortable option within the park itself. Lunch is available for an additional Rs75.

Getting There & Away
Jaldhapara is 124km east of Siliguri. Buses frequent the route from Siliguri to Madarihat (Rs65, three hours, hourly 6am to 4pm), 9km

from Jaldhapara. A taxi from Madarihat to Hollong inside the park is Rs150.

MIRIK

☎ 0354 / pop 9179 / elev 1767m

Nestled near the Nepal border, halfway between Siliguri and Darjeeling, is this low-profile hill station. Mirik is surrounded by an undulating carpet of tea estates, orange orchards, cardamom plantations and forests of tall, dark Japanese cedars. It has a quiet charm and relaxed vibe that make it quite different from Darjeeling or Kalimpong. Some of Mirik's higher hilltops offer wonderful views of morning's first light striking Khangchendzonga (8598m).

Information

Krishnanagar Cyber Cafe (Main Rd, Krishnanagar; per hr Rs30), opposite Hotel Jagjeet, has a slow dial-up connection. There are no money-changing facilities but there's a reliable State Bank of India ATM next to Hotel Jagjeet.

Foreigners should register (just show your passport) at the **Frontier Check Post** (Main Rd, Krishnanagar) if staying overnight. The check post is on your right on the way down to lake, near the bottom of the hill; staff are relaxed and keen to chat.

Sights & Activities

Mirik is centred on the artificial murky-coloured **Sumendu Lake** and there's a walk around its 3.5km circumference. On the west side of the lake, climb the steps to the diminutive Hindu **Devi Sthan temple complex**. Perched high above Mirik, the richly painted **Bokar Gompa** has bright murals; take a bracing walk up Monastery Rd if you don't want to be gouged Rs80 for a taxi.

Pedal boats (per 30min Rs60) can be hired near the bridge and **pony rides** (half/full round-the-lake trips Rs80/160) are offered for various trips around Mirik.

Sleeping & Eating

Prices can drop by up to 50% outside of the high season (October to November and March to May).

Lodge Ashirvad (☎ 2243272; s Rs180, d Rs250-350) A friendly family-run budget hotel down a lane just off the main road. The rooms are clean

---

CROSSING INTO BANGLADESH, BHUTAN & NEPAL

To/From Bangladesh

A number of private agencies in Siliguri, including **Shyamoli** (☎ 9932627647; Hotel Central Plaza complex, Hill Cart Rd) run regular AC buses direct to Dhaka (Rs650) – you'll need to get on and off at the border at Chengrabandha.

Regular buses go from the Tenzing Norgay central bus terminal to Chengrabandha (Rs42) starting from 7.30am. The border post is open from 8am to 6pm daily. From near the border post you can catch buses on to Rangpur, Bogra and Dhaka. Visas for Bangladesh can be obtained in Kolkata and New Delhi (see p1176).

To/From Bhutan

Bhutan Transport Services have a counter inside Tenzing Norgay central bus terminal. Two buses leave daily for Phuentsholling (Rs75, departs 7am and 2pm). Indian immigration is in Jaigon, between the police station and Hotel Kasturi. Non-Indian nationals need a valid visa authority from a Bhutanese tour operator to enter Bhutan. See www.tourism.gov.bt and Lonely Planet's *Bhutan* for details.

To/From Nepal

For Nepal, local buses pass the Tenzing Norgay central bus terminal every 15 minutes for the border town of Panitanki (Rs20, one hour). Share jeeps to Kakarbhitta (Rs70) are readily available in Siliguri. The Indian border post in Panitanki is officially open 24 hours and the Nepal post in Kakarbhitta is open from 7am to 7pm. See p558 for information on buses from Darjeeling to Kathmandu. Onward from Kakarbhitta there are numerous buses to Kathmandu (17 hours) and other destinations. Bhadrapur airport, 23km southwest of Kakarbhitta, has regular flights to Kathmandu. Visas for Nepal can be obtained at the border, or in Kolkata or New Delhi (see p1177).

and there's a rooftop terrace with a great view across to the monastery. Hot-water buckets cost Rs10. Home-cooked food is served in a slightly dank basement set up in the high season.

Buddha Lodge (☎ 2243515; d Rs300-400) Spotless, charming rooms with TV and nice furniture; upstairs rooms have especially appealing wood panelling.

Hotel Ratnagiri (☎ 2243243; www.hotelratnagiri.com; d Rs600-800) Warm, wood-panelled doubles upstairs (with cute sloping ceilings) plus larger family suites. Some rooms have balconies and views of Sumendu Lake; all have TV and geyser. There's a good garden restaurant out back (mains Rs30 to Rs90).

Hotel Jagjeet (☎ 2243231; www.jagjeethotel.com; d from Rs1000) The best hotel in town, with a variety of clean and comfy rooms, most with balconies, and attentive service. The restaurant (mains Rs30 to Rs115) is deservedly popular, serving excellent Indian, Chinese and continental dishes. Toothsome sweets, including *barfi*, are sold at a separate counter here.

Sukh Sagar Restaurant (mains Rs15-60) At the bottom of the hill near the lake, a pure-veg cafeteria-type place catering to lakeside day trippers with good snacks and South Indian favourites. A thali with the works is Rs70.

Getting There & Away

Buses leave for Darjeeling and Siliguri (both Rs50, three hours). Share jeeps depart regularly to Darjeeling and Siliguri (both Rs55, 2½ hours) and Kurseong (Rs60, three hours).

Mirik Out Agency (Main Rd, Krishnanagar; ☉ 9am-noon, 1-4pm), opposite Hotel Ratnagiri, sells a quota of tickets for trains from NJP.

KURSEONG

☎ 0354 / pop 40,067 / elev 1458m

Kurseong, 32km south of Darjeeling, is the little sister of (and quiet alternative to) the Queen of the Hills further up the track. Its name derives from the Lepcha word *kur-son-rip*, a reference to the small white orchid prolific in this area. Surrounded by tea estates, it is the southern terminus for the steam-powered toy trains of the Darjeeling Himalayan Railway.

Hill Cart Rd (Tenzing Norgay Rd) – the shop-lined main thoroughfare from Siliguri to Darjeeling – and its remarkably close shadow, the railway line, wind through town.

There are numerous good walks in the area, including one to Eagle's Crag (2km return) that affords splendid views down the Teesta and the plains to the south. Along Pankhabari Rd, the lushly overgrown old graveyard at St Andrews has poignant reminders of the tea-planter era, while the organic Makaibari Tea Estate (see the boxed text, opposite) and **Ambootia Tea Estate** (☎ 9434045602) welcome visitors to their aromatic factories. The **Kunsamnamdoling Gompa** is a lovely monastery run by Red Hat *ani* (Buddhist nuns).

Check email at **Kashyup Computers & Systems** (Hill Cart Rd; per hr Rs30) and **Kay Deez** (per hr Rs25), off Hill Cart on your left as you walk into town from the train station.

Sleeping & Eating

A number of hotels near the station have grotty, overpriced rooms, but it's well worth going the extra few steps to these places.

Hotel Delhi Darbar (☎ 2345862; delhidarbarinn@ yahoo.com; Hill Cart Rd; d/tr Rs300/400) A budget option a few blocks from the train station. It's friendly but only just clean (go for the rooms with new lino rather than icky old carpet), hot water comes by the bucket and there's TV. You can order in good cheap food from the restaurant below (mains Rs20 to Rs45) – we had the world's best *aloo paratha* (potato-filled bread) here.

Kurseong Tourist Lodge (☎ 2344409; Hill Cart Rd; d Rs800-900) The staff don't care a whole lot but the building is very inviting, with warm, wood-lined rooms that feature stunning views. The toy train whistles past the cafe where you can snack on *momos* (dumplings), or you can enjoy an Indian, Chinese or continental meal at its scenic restaurant (mains Rs30 to Rs80).

ourpick **Cochrane Place** (☎ 2330703; www.imperial chai.com; 132 Pankhabari Rd; s/d from Rs2250/2650) With 360-degree views around tea plantations, the Himalaya and the lights of Siliguri, this quirky, charming boutique hotel is a destination in its own right. Rooms are individually decorated with antiques and have either a view or a balcony. Delicious meals and a range of teas are available. The hotel is wheelchair-friendly, provides airport (Siliguri's Bagdogra airport) and train station pick-up, and staff can point you towards trails and sights in the region. Also on offer are tea tastings, and massage and beauty treatments. Significant discounts available in the low season.

THUNDERBOLT RAJAH

One of the most recognisable figures in the Darjeeling region and a guru in the tea industry, Rajah Banerjee is the fourth generation of the Banerjee family to own and manage the **Makaibari Tea Estate** (Pankhabari Rd; www.makaibari.com) near Kurseong. A patrician man in a self-designed safari suit, he's usually found astride a horse that takes him through the winding forest paths of the estate. The first person to bring organic and biodynamic tea farming to the region, he's also one of the very few estate owners to actually live and work in the hills.

Banerjee came to visit his father at the estate more than 30 years ago, after studying in the UK. 'I had no intention of living in Makaibari, I came for a holiday, but man proposes, God disposes', he says. Riding through the estate one day, he was thrown from his horse; as he fell, he says, he had a vision of the trees calling out to be saved. 'I knew then that I had to spend the rest of my life at Makaibari.'

Permaculture, the taste of tea, the welfare of estate workers, biodiversity and the biodynamics philosophy of Rudolf Steiner are just some of the passions that drive the 'Thunderbolt Rajah' (the nickname comes from the Tibetan meaning of Darjeeling, 'land of the thunderbolt'). The factory at Makaibari is open to visitors (as well as volunteers and students, and in between the huge sorting and drying machines and the fields of green bushes, you may just run into the tea guru himself.

Zimba's (Hill Cart Rd; dishes Rs10-20) This outdoor place in a bus and jeep depot at the Darjeeling end of town is the unlikely setting for shockingly cheap, fresh and tasty Indian and Tibetan snack foods – try the *momos* (Rs10).

Getting There & Away

Numerous share jeeps run to Darjeeling (Rs40, 1½ hours), Siliguri (Rs60, 1½ hours), Kalimpong (Rs100, 3½ to four hours) and Mirik (Rs60, 2½ hours). Buses leave from near the train station for Darjeeling (Rs25, two hours) and Siliguri (Rs40, 2½ hours).

The Darjeeling Himalayan Railway's steam toy train for Darjeeling (2nd/1st class Rs18/159, four hours) leaves at 3pm, weather permitting, while the diesel version (originating at New Jalpaiguri) departs around 1.35pm. A diesel train (originating in Darjeeling) to Siliguri (2nd/1st class Rs27/182, four hours) departs at 12.05pm.

Kurseong station has a limited quota of tickets for major departures from NJP that can be booked between 9am and 11am. The available services are on display at the station.

DARJEELING

☏ 0354 / pop 109,160 / elev 2134m

Spread over a steep mountain ridge, surrounded by tea plantations, with a backdrop of jagged white Himalayan peaks floating over distant clouds, the archetypal hill station of Darjeeling is rightly West Bengal's premier attraction. When you aren't gazing at Khangchendzonga (8598m), you can explore colonial-buildings, Buddhist and Hindu temples, botanical gardens and a zoo for Himalayan fauna. The steep narrow streets are crowded with colourful souvenir and handicraft shops, and a good steaming brew and excellent Indian and Tibetan fare are never far away. Walkers can enjoy superb treks that trace ancient trade routes and provide magnificent viewpoints.

Most tourists visit after the monsoon (October and November) and during spring (mid-March to the end of May) when skies are dry, panoramas are clear and temperatures are pleasant. Tourist attractions and other establishments will often extend their hours during these periods (specified as 'high season' in the following reviews), although they are not set in stone, so it is worth checking ahead rather than relying on those extended hours.

History

This area belonged to the Buddhist chogyals (kings) of Sikkim until 1780, when it was annexed by the invading Gurkhas from Nepal. The East India Company gained control of the region in 1816 then returned most of the lands back to Sikkim in exchange for British control over any future border disputes.

During one such dispute in 1828, two British officers stumbled across the Dorje Ling monastery, on a tranquil forested ridge, and passed word to Calcutta that it would be a perfect site for a sanatorium; they were

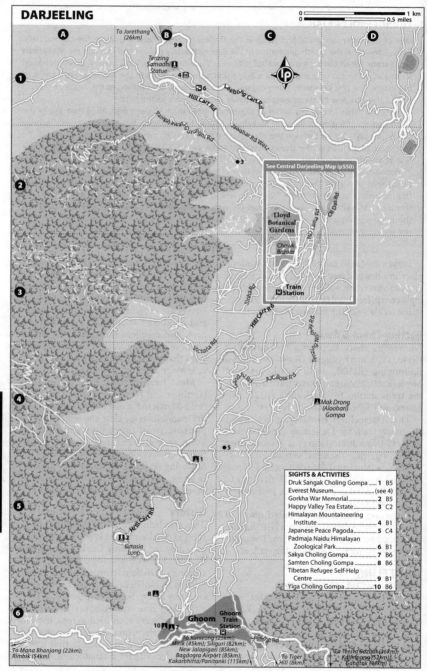

DARJEELING

0 — 1 km
0 — 0.5 miles

To Jorethang (26km)

Tenzing Samadhi Statue

Hill Cart Rd

Leebong Cart Rd

Jawahar Rd West

Pamohawa-Gurung-ni Rd

See Central Darjeeling Map (p550)

Lloyd Botanical Gardens

Ch Das Rd

H D Lama Rd

Chowk Bazaar

Train Station

Sinhta Rd

Hill Cart Rd

Victoria Rd

Tenzing Rd

Bay Rd

Gandhi Rd

AJC Bose Rd

Mak Drong (Aloobari) Gompa

Batasia Loop

Ghoom

Ghoom Train Station

RDC Rai Rd

To Kurseong (25km);
Mirik (45km); Siliguri (82km);
New Jalalpigari (85km);
Bagdogra Airport (85km);
Kakarbhitta/Panitanki (115km)

To Mana Bhanjang (22km);
Rimbik (54km)

To Tiger Hill (8km)

To Teesta Bazaar (36km);
Kalimpong (52km);
Gangtok (94km)

SIGHTS & ACTIVITIES

Druk Sangak Choling Gompa	**1**	B5
Everest Museum	(see 4)	
Gorkha War Memorial	**2**	B5
Happy Valley Tea Estate	**3**	C2
Himalayan Mountaineering Institute	**4**	B1
Japanese Peace Pagoda	**5**	C4
Padmaja Naidu Himalayan Zoological Park	**6**	B1
Sakya Choling Gompa	**7**	B6
Samten Choling Gompa	**8**	B6
Tibetan Refugee Self-Help Centre	**9**	B1
Yiga Choling Gompa	**10**	B6

WEST BENGAL

sure to have also mentioned its strategic military importance in the region. The Chogyal of Sikkim (still grateful for the return of his kingdom) happily leased the uninhabited land to the East India Company in 1835 and a hill station was born.

Forest gradually made way for colonial houses and tea plantations, and by 1857 the population of Darjeeling reached 10,000, mainly because of a massive influx of Gurkha labourers from Nepal.

After Independence, the Gurkhas became the main political force in Darjeeling and friction with the state government led to calls for a separate state of Gorkhaland in the 1980s. In 1986, violence and riots orchestrated by the Gurkha National Liberation Front (GNLF) brought Darjeeling to a standstill, leading to the Darjeeling Gorkha Hill Council (DGHC) being given a large measure of autonomy from the state government.

Calls for full secession have continued, and in 2007 the political party Gorkha Janmukti Morcha (GJM), headed by Bimal Gurung, was formed out of the GNLF. It has encouraged people to agitate for a separate state of Gorkhaland by 2010 by using tactics ranging from strikes (see p552) and nonpayment of bills and taxes to active support for the Gurkha contestant on *Indian Idol* (who eventually won season three).

Orientation

Darjeeling sprawls over a west-facing slope in a web of interconnecting roads and steep flights of steps. Near the top of town is the square known as Chowrasta. Further north is the forested Observatory Hill and skirting the hill is Bhanu Bhakta Sarani. The zoo lies to the northwest.

Hill Cart Rd (aka Tenzing Norgay Rd), which runs the length of town, is Darjeeling's major vehicle thoroughfare. From Chowk Bazaar it leads north towards the zoo and Himalayan Mountaineering Institute, and heads south past the train station en route to Ghoom. Nehru Rd (aka the Mall), the main shopping street, heads south from Chowrasta, meeting Laden La Rd (which leads to Hill Cart Rd) and Gandhi Rd at a junction called Clubside.

Information
BOOKSHOPS
Oxford Book & Stationery Company (Map p550; ☎ 2254325; Chowrasta; ☺ 9.30am-7.30pm Mon-Sat, daily high season) The best bookshop in Darjeeling, selling a vast selection of books and maps on Tibet, Nepal, Sikkim, Bhutan and the Himalaya. They will mail worldwide.

EMERGENCY
Police assistance booth (Map p550; Chowrasta)
Sadar Police Station (Map p550; ☎ 2254422; Market Rd)

INTERNET ACCESS
There are dozens of internet cafes around the town, all charging about Rs30 per hour with a minimum of Rs10 to Rs15. The outlet at Glenary's (p556) is the most convenient to the Mall.
Compuset Centre (Map p550; Gandhi Rd; per hr Rs30; ☺ 8am-8pm) Digital-camera friendly. Does printing and photocopying.
Loyang Cyber Zone (Map p550; Gandhi Rd; per 30min Rs10; ☺ 9am-7.30pm) Does scanning and colour printing, and has Skype set up.
Pineridge Cybercafe (Map p550; Dr Zakir Hussain Rd; per 30min Rs15; ☺ 9.30am-8pm) Small, friendly place up on the ridge near the budget accommodation.

MEDICAL SERVICES
Planter's Hospital (D&DMA Nursing Home; Map p550; ☎ 2254327; Nehru Rd) The best private hospital.
Yuma Nursing Home (Map p550; ☎ 2257651; Ballen Villa Rd)

MONEY
A number of shops and hotels around Darjeeling can change cash and travellers cheques at fairly good rates; shop around.
ICICI Bank ATM (Map p550; Laden La Rd) Accepts most international bank and credit cards. There's another ATM on HD Lama Rd.
Poddar's (Map p550; Laden La Rd; ☺ 8.30am-9pm, later high season) Inside a clothing store next to the State Bank. Better rates than the State Bank, and changes most currencies and travellers cheques. It accepts credit cards and is a Western Union agent.
State Bank of India (Map p550; Laden La Rd; ☺ 10am-4pm Mon-Fri, to 1pm Sat) Changes US dollars, euros and pounds sterling, and travellers cheques issued by Amex (in US dollars) and Thomas Cook (in US dollars, euros and pounds sterling). The commission rate is Rs100 per transaction. It has an adjacent ATM, another in the bazaar and another in Chowrasta; all accept Visa cards.

PHOTOGRAPHY
Das Studios (Map p550; ☎ 2254004; Nehru Rd; ☺ 9.30am-6.30pm Mon-Fri, to 2.30pm Sat, daily in high season) Film and printing, lots of camera gear, passport pics (six for Rs50), burns two CDs for Rs75.

WEST BENGAL

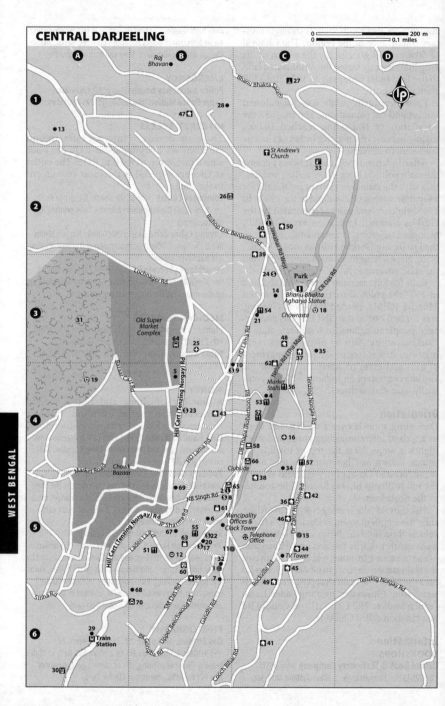

CENTRAL DARJEELING

Joshi Studio (Map p550; ☎ 9832346413; HD Lama Rd;
☻ 9am-7pm Mon-Sat) Passport photos, film developing and processing, CD burning (Rs50) and DVD burning
(Rs100).

POST
Main post office (Map p550; ☎ 2252076; Laden La Rd;
☻ 9am-5pm) Reliable parcel service and poste restante.

TOURIST INFORMATION
**Darjeeling Gorkha Hill Council Tourist Reception
Centre** (DGHC; Map p550; ☎ 2255351; Jawahar Rd
West; ☻ 9am-6pm Mon-Fri, 9am-1pm every 2nd Sat,
9am-1pm Sun high season) The staff are friendly, well
organised and the best source of information in Darjeeling.
The centre also has counters at the train station and on
Laden La Rd.

West Bengal Tourist Bureau (Map p550;
☎ 2254102; Chowrasta; ☻ 10am-5pm Mon-Fri) Little
useful information but sells a basic map of the town
(Rs3) and can book accommodation at government
lodges, including those at Jaldhapara Wildlife Sanctuary
(p544).

TRAVEL AGENCIES
Most of the travel agencies here can arrange
local tours and some can also arrange treks,
rafting trips and other activities. Agencies
that take you to Sikkim usually help with
permits. The DGHC (left) and Darjeeling
Transport Corporation (p558) also do local
tours. Reliable agencies and their specialities
include the following:

Diamond Tours & Travels (Map p550;
☎ 9832094275; Old Super Market Complex; ☻ 8am-
7pm) Books buses to various destinations from Siliguri. Can
organise airport transfers.

Himalayan Travels (Map p550; ☎ 2252254; kkgurung@
cal.vsnl.net.in; 18 Gandhi Rd; ☻ 8.30am-7pm) Experienced company arranging treks and mountaineering
expeditions in Darjeeling and Sikkim. Can supply tents and
other equipment.

Kasturi Tours & Travels (Map p550; ☎ 2254430; Old
Super Market Complex; ☻ 8am-7pm) Sells bus tickets to
various destinations from Siliguri.

Samsara Tours, Travels & Treks (Map p550;
☎ 2252874; samsara1@sancharnet.in; 7 Laden La Rd)

Helpful and knowledgeable agency offering good-value rafting and trekking trips. Recommended.

Somewhere Over the Rainbow Treks & Tours (Map p550; ☎ 9832025739, 9775955105; kanadhi@yahoo.com; HD Lama Rd; ☻ 8am-6pm, later in high season) Organises some off-the-beaten track walks around Darjeeling, as well as rafting, climbing, and trekking in Sikkim, with a particular interest in West Sikkim.

Dangers & Annoyances

General strikes in support of the GJM's call for a separate Gurkha state were semiregular at the time of research. While there has been little violence and tourists have not been targeted, everything simply shuts down, including all banks and transport.

Sights & Activities

See p559 for information on trekking around Darjeeling.

MOUNTAIN VIEWS

Himalayan views are a big attraction in Darjeeling. The skyline is dominated by Khangchendzonga, India's highest peak and the world's third-highest mountain. The name 'Khangchendzonga' is derived from the Tibetan words for 'big five-peaked snow fortress'. Views from lookouts along Bhanu Bhakta Sarani, which runs from Chowrasta around the north side of Observatory Hill, can be stunning in clear weather.

TIGER HILL

To set your eyes on a spectacular 250km stretch of Himalayan horizon, including Everest (8848m), Lhotse (8501m), Makalu (8475m), Khangchendzonga, Kabru (6691m) and Janu (7710m), rise early and get to **Tiger Hill** (off Map p548; 2590m), 11km south of Darjeeling, above Ghoom.

The sunrise over the Himalaya from here can be spectacular if the weather is clear, and has become a major tourist attraction, with convoys of jeeps leaving Darjeeling for Tiger Hill every morning around 4.30am. At the summit, you can either pay Rs10 to stand in the pavilion grounds, or buy a ticket for one of the heated lounges in the pavilion (Rs20 to Rs40). It can be a real bunfight, even outside of the high season, with crowds jostling for the best viewing spots.

Organised sunrise trips (usually with a detour to Batasia Loop on the way back) can be booked through a travel agency (see p551) or

directly with jeep drivers at the Clubside taxi stand. It's also possible to jump on a jeep going to Tiger Hill from along Gandhi or Laden La Rds between 4am and 4.30am, allowing you to check whether skies are clear before you go. Return trips cost around Rs70/600 per person/jeep.

Some people take the jeep one way to Tiger Hill and then spend their day wandering back to Darjeeling, visiting the gompas (Tibetan Buddhist monasteries) in Ghoom along the way.

TOY TRAIN

The **Darjeeling Himalayan Railway** (Map p550), known affectionately as the toy train, made its first journey along its precipice-topping, 2ft-wide tracks in September 1881 and is one of the few hill railways still operating in India. Besides its regular diesel service to/from New Jalpaiguri and steam service to/from Kurseong (see p558), there are joy rides (Rs250) during the high season that leave Darjeeling at 10.40am and 1.20pm for a two-hour steam-powered return trip to Ghoom. It's wise to book at least a day ahead at the **train station** (Map p550; Hill Cart Rd).

TEA PLANTATIONS

Happy Valley Tea Estate (Map p548; Pamphawati Gurungni Rd; ☻ 8am-4pm Mon-Sat), below Hill Cart Rd, is worth visiting when the plucking and processing are in progress. March to May is the busiest time, but occasional plucking also occurs from June to November. Outside of high season there's no plucking on Sunday, which means most of the machinery isn't working on Monday. An employee will whisk you through the aromatic factory and its various processes before politely demanding a tip – Rs20 from each visitor is appropriate. Take the turn-off 500m northwest of the Office of the District Magistrate, or take Lochnager Rd from Chowk Bazaar.

OBSERVATORY HILL

Sacred to both Buddhists and Hindus, this **hill** (Map p550) was the site of the Dorje Ling monastery, the gompa that gave the city its name. Today, devotees come to a temple in a small cave, below the crest of the hill, to honour Mahakala, a Buddhist deity and an angry form of the Hindu god Shiva. The summit is marked by several shrines, a flurry of colourful prayer flags and the notes from numerous devotional bells. A path leading up to the hill through giant Japanese cedars starts about 300m along Bhanu Bhakta Sarani from Chowrasta. Be careful of the marauding monkeys.

GOMPAS & PAGODAS

Darjeeling and Ghoom are home to a number of fascinating Buddhist monasteries. The most scenic is **Bhutia Busty Gompa** (Map p550), with Khangchendzonga providing a spectacular backdrop. Originally on Observatory Hill, it was rebuilt in its present location by the chogyals of Sikkim in the 19th century. It houses a fine gold-accented mural and the original copy of the Tibetan Book of the Dead, but permission is required to see it. To get here, follow CR Das Rd downhill for 400m from Chowrasta and take the right fork where the road branches.

Yiga Choling Gompa (Old Monastery; Map p548; camera per photo Rs10), the region's most famous monastery, has wonderful old murals and is home to monks of the yellow-hat sect. Built in 1850, it enshrines a 5m-high statue of the Maitreya Buddha (Future Buddha) and 300 beautifully bound Tibetan texts. It's just west of Ghoom, about a 10-minute walk off Hill Cart Rd. Other gompas of interest in this area include the fortresslike **Sakya Choling Gompa** (Map p548) and the **Samten Choling Gompa** (New Monastery; Map p548), with the protector Garuda atop the ornate backdrop to the Buddha; it has a festive air, with tour groups and souvenir stalls. These gompas are on Hill Cart Rd and can be reached by share jeep from Darjeeling (Rs12); some people organise to visit on the way back from Tiger Hill (opposite).

About halfway between Ghoom and Darjeeling is the vast **Druk Sangak Choling Gompa** (Map p548), inaugurated by the Dalai Lama in 1993. Known for its vibrant frescoes, it houses 300 Himalayan monks who study philosophy, literature, astronomy, meditation, dance and music.

Perched on a hillside at the end of AJC Bose Rd is the gleaming white **Japanese Peace Pagoda** (Map p548; pujas 4.30-6am & 4.30-6.30pm), one of more than 70 pagodas built by the Japanese Buddhist Nipponzan Myohoji organisation around the world. Drumming resonates through the forested grounds during their daily *pujas* (prayers). It's about a 35-minute walk from Clubside along Gandhi and AJC Bose Rds.

PADMAJA NAIDU HIMALAYAN ZOOLOGICAL PARK

This **zoo** (Map p548; admission incl Himalayan Mountaineering Institute Indian/foreigner Rs30/100; 8.30am-4.30pm Fri-Wed, ticket counter closes 4pm), one of India's best, was established in 1958 to study, conserve and preserve Himalayan fauna. Housed within the rocky and forested environment is India's only collection of Siberian tigers, as well as Himalayan black bears, red pandas, snow leopards and Tibetan wolves.

The zoo is a pleasant 30-minute walk down from Chowrasta along Jawahar Rd West; alternatively, take a share jeep from the Chowk Bazaar bus/jeep station (Rs10, about 10 minutes) or a private taxi (Rs70).

HIMALAYAN MOUNTAINEERING INSTITUTE

Tucked away within the grounds of the zoological park, this prestigious **mountaineering institute** (HMI; Map p548; 2254087; www.exploredarjeeling.com/hmidarj.htm; admission incl zoo Indian/foreigner Rs30/100; 8.30am-4.30pm Fri-Wed) was founded in 1954 and has provided training for some of India's leading mountaineers. Within the complex is the fascinating **Everest Museum**, which traces the history of attempts on the world's highest peak.

On a nearby hilltop, where Tenzing Norgay was cremated, stands the **Tenzing Samadhi statue**. The intrepid mountaineer lived in Darjeeling for most of his life and was the director of the institute for many years.

Various mountaineering courses are offered here; see p554 for more information.

TIBETAN REFUGEE SELF-HELP CENTRE

Established in 1959, this **refugee centre** (Map p548; Lebong Cart Rd; dawn-dusk Mon-Sat) comprises a home for the aged, school, orphanage, clinic, **gompa** and **craft workshops** that produce carpets, woodcarvings, leatherwork and woollen items. There's also an interesting, politically charged **photographic exhibition** (you might have to ask for the hall to be opened) portraying the establishment and workings of the centre.

The refugees are welcoming, so wander through the workshops. The handicrafts are for sale in the **showroom** (2252552; 8am-4.30pm), which doesn't have as many knick-knacks as the souvenir shops in town, but the proceeds go straight back into the Tibetan community. See p557 for details regarding Tibetan carpets.

Share jeeps from the Chowk Bazaar bus/jeep station run along Lebong Cart Rd and pass the turn-off to the centre (Rs20, about 20 minutes). A chartered taxi costs around Rs300 return.

LLOYD BOTANICAL GARDENS

These pleasant **gardens** (Map p550; ☎ 2252358; admission free; ❤ 8am-4.30pm) contain an impressive collection of Himalayan plants, most famously orchids and rhododendrons, as well as temperate trees from around the world. Follow the signs along Lochnager Rd from the Chowk Bazaar bus/jeep station. A map and guide is available from the park office.

OTHER ATTRACTIONS

The most conspicuous Hindu temple in Darjeeling, **Dhirdham Mandir** (Map p550), is a replica of the famous Pashupatinath Temple in Kathmandu. It's easy to find – just below the Darjeeling train station. There's a great view over Darjeeling from its grounds.

If you're travelling on the toy train, or walking back from Tiger Hill, look out for the scenic and sobering **Gorkha war memorial** (Map p548; admission Rs5; ❤ dawn-dusk) where the train makes its famous **Batasia Loop**. Some tours come here after the sunrise trip at Tiger Hill; the views are almost as good, and the atmosphere much more serene.

The **Bengal Natural History Museum** (Map p550; Bishop Eric Benjamin Rd; adult/child Rs5/2; ❤ 9am-5pm), established in 1903, houses a mildewed and moth-eaten collection of Himalayan and Bengali species. Hidden away in a compound just off Bishop Eric Benjamin Rd, it's well signed, and remarkably popular. The enormous leeches in jars will provoke a shudder.

WHITE-WATER RAFTING

Darjeeling is the easiest place to organise white-water rafting trips along the Rangeet and Teesta Rivers. Rafting trips leave from Teesta Bazaar (p565), along the road to Kalimpong. The rapids are graded from Grade II to Grade IV, and the best times for rafting are September to November and March to June.

The DGHC (p551) runs trips for minimums of four to six people (moderate rapids 11/18/25km trip Rs350/450/700, challenging rapids Rs500/600/800) and can also arrange transport to Teesta Bazaar (Rs350) and accommodation at its Chitrey Wayside Inn (p565). Private companies, such as Samsara

Tours, Travels & Treks (p551), offer similar routes for a minimum of four people, and prices include lunch and transport.

OTHER ACTIVITIES

The **Darjeeling Gymkhana Club** (Map p550; ☎ 2254341; Jawahar Rd West; membership per day/week/month Rs50/250/600) offers tennis, squash, badminton, roller skating and table tennis; call to check the schedules.

Be an aristocrat for the day and join the **Planters' Club Darjeeling** (Map p550; ☎ 2254348; per day Rs100). Lounge in style or rack them up in the billiards room (Rs100 per person per hour).

From Chowrasta, children can take a **pony ride** around Observatory Hill for Rs50, or through tea estates to visit a monastery for Rs90 per hour.

Courses

LANGUAGE

Beginner and advanced lessons in written and spoken Tibetan are offered at the **Manjushree Centre of Tibetan Culture** (Map p550; ☎ 2256714; www.manjushree-culture.org; 12 Ghandi Rd; 3-/6-/9-month courses Rs9030/13,760/18,490 plus Rs1350 registration; ❤ Mar-Dec). It also supplies discounted guest-house accommodation for students.

MOUNTAINEERING

The Himalayan Mountaineering Institute (p553) runs 15-day adventure courses (Indian/foreigner Rs2000/US$325), which include climbing, jungle survival and canoeing, and 28-day basic and advanced mountaineering courses (Indian/foreigner Rs4000/US$650), between March and December. Some courses are women-only. Foreigners should apply directly to the centre at least three months in advance.

Tours

During the high season the DGHC and other travel agencies offer a variety of tours around Darjeeling, usually including the zoo, Himalayan Mountaineering Institute, Tibetan Refugee Self-Help Centre and several viewpoints. See p552 for Tiger Hill sunrise-tour information.

Taxis can be hired for custom tours for around Rs750 per half-day.

Sleeping

Darjeeling has some excellent-value accommodation; only a small selection is mentioned here. Prices given are for the high season (October to early December and mid-March to June), when it's wise to book ahead. In the low season prices can drop by 50%.

BUDGET

Hotel Tower View (Map p550; ☎ 2254452; Dr Zakir Hussain Rd; dm Rs70, d with/without shower Rs350/250) Rooms are basic but clean (go for one upstairs, as downstairs can be cold and damp), but the real draw at this friendly, Tibetan-run place is the cosy restaurant area that doubles as the family kitchen and lounge, complete with books and games. The food (mains Rs20 to Rs40) is wholesome and delicious (try the veg soup if you're feeling a bit off – instant wellness) and there are fab views over the mountains.

Hotel New Galaxy (Hotel Kanika; Map p550; ☎ 5520771; Dr Zakir Hussain Rd; s Rs150, d Rs250-400, tr Rs500) A clean, acceptable budget option almost opposite Andy's, with wood-panelled walls, smallish rooms and hot-water buckets for Rs10. Try for room 104, with the best views across to the mountains.

Hotel Aliment (Map p550; ☎ 2255068; alimentwe@sify.com; 40 Dr Zakir Hussain Rd; d Rs250-400; 💻) A travellers' favourite with good food (and cold beer), books, rooftop patio, helpful owners and cosy wood-lined rooms. The upstairs rooms have a TV and valley views. All rooms have geysers, but they only operate for an hour in the evening.

Andy's Guesthouse (Map p550; ☎ 2253125; Dr Zakir Hussain Rd; s/d from Rs250/300) This simple, spotless, stone-walled place has airy, carpeted rooms, a comfy common area and a rooftop terrace with a great view. Andy's has especially friendly owners, and we think it's the best value for money in town.

Hotel Tranquility (Map p550; ☎ 2257678; hoteltranquility@yahoo.co.in; Dr Zakir Hussain Rd; s Rs300, d from Rs400) This good-value new place is sparkling clean, with 24-hour hot water and uniformly duck-egg-blue walls and fittings. A rooftop garden restaurant was being built at the time of research, which should make it even homier. The helpful owners are local schoolteachers, and can provide all kinds of info about the area; ask about the tragic story of the burned-out mansion you can see from the roof.

MIDRANGE

our pick **Dekeling Hotel** (Map p550; ☎ 2254159; www.dekeling.com; 51 Gandhi Rd; d Rs650-1400; 💻) Dekeling is spotless and full of charming touches like coloured diamond-pane windows, a traditional *bukhari* (wood-burning heater) in the lounge, wood panelling and sloping ceilings. Then there's the cosy common areas, very comfy rooms, wi-fi and possibly the best views in town. Good deals are available in the low season, and the whole place is a perfect combination of clean and homey, right down to the well-bathed and adorable dog.

Pineridge Hotel (Map p550; ☎ 2254074; pineridgehotel@yahoo.com; Nehru Rd; s/d/tr from Rs700/850/950) The location is great and the Raj-era building has renovation potential to make a decorator weep, but for now the reality is echoing corridors and draughty, dilapidated rooms. There are still some touches of period charm, and with a bucket of coal (Rs200) glowing in the fireplace maybe you can forget the broken window.

Hotel Alice Villa (Map p550; ☎ 2254181; hotelalicevilla@yahoo.com; 41 HD Lama Rd; d/tr from Rs750/850) This well-cared-for old bungalow close to Chowrasta provides inexpensive heritage accommodation. The rooms are spacious and the high ceilings in the older rooms can make them a bit chilly. A mezzanine floor has been built into one, making it a cosy and good-value option for families.

Hotel Valentino (Map p550; ☎ 2252228; 6 Rockville Rd; d Rs800-1500, q Rs1200) Everything except the name is Chinese – the decor in the comfortable rooms tends toward Chinese fans, vases and paintings, and the menu at the restaurant-bar has a big range of regional Chinese dishes (mains Rs60 to Rs80).

Bellevue Hotel (Map p550; ☎ 2254075; pulger@rediffmail.com; Chowrasta; d Rs800-1600) This rambling Tibetan-run complex has a variety of wood-panelled rooms. Most are spacious with grass-mat floors and a *bukhari*. The affable staff, communal breakfast/lounge area and location, not to mention the outlook over Chowrasta towards Khangchendzonga, all make this a popular choice. Don't confuse it with the Olde Bellevue Hotel up the road.

Travellers Inn (Map p550; ☎ 2258497; Dr Zakir Hussain Rd; travellersinn2000@gmail.com; s/d/ste Rs1100/1500/2600) This is a beautifully decorated boutique hotel, which comes complete with stone fireplace, polished wood panelling, framed old photos of Darjeeling, and a terrace restaurant with stunning views (mains Rs40 to Rs80). Mountain-lodge-style rooms are stylish and comfy. On Sunday there's loud gospel music from the church next door.

Hotel Seven Seventeen (Map p550; ☎ 2252017; www.hotel717.com; 26 HD Lama Rd; s/d/ste from Rs1300/1500/2000) An inviting Tibetan-themed place with friendly service and clean rooms. Don't confuse it with the older Hotel Heritage Seven Seventeen, which is up the street. The colourful restaurant and bar (mains Rs50 to Rs90) has a big range of Indian, Chinese, Tibetan and continental dishes.

TOP END

These hotels offer rooms on the so-called 'American Plan', with breakfast, lunch and dinner included; taxes and service charges usually add 15% to 20% to the bill.

Windamere Hotel (Map p550; ☎ 2254041; www.win damerehotel.com; Jawahar Rd West; s/d from Rs6650/7750) The liveried staff at this quaint, old-fashioned place really look after you, and won't leave you hungry. This hotel on Observatory Hill is a rambling relic of the Raj, and while some rooms are getting a little tired they are comfortable, clean and spacious. High tea will be a joy for aficionados of things colonial.

Elgin (Map p550; ☎ 2257226; elgin@elginhotels.com; HD Lama Rd; s/d/ste Rs6800/5800/6800) A grand yet friendly heritage hotel full of colonial ambience. Most of the elegantly furnished rooms have separate sitting areas, open fireplaces and marble bathrooms with old clawfoot baths; the cosy 'attic room' is especially charming. The restaurant is pukka (proper) and the lovely gardens are the perfect place to relax and enjoy high tea.

Mayfair Darjeeling (Map p550; ☎ 2256376; www .mayfairhotels.com; Jawahar Rd West; d from Rs9000) Originally a maharaja's summer palace but renovated within an inch of its life, this plush choice sits among lovingly manicured gardens and a bizarre collection of kitschy sculptures. Soft carpets and coal fires add to the warm welcome; there's choice of DVDs and a comfortable bar. The outside and common areas don't have quite the cosy charm of the Elgin, but inside the rooms are beautifully decorated in warm colours with fine art.

Eating

Most restaurants close their doors by 8pm or 9pm.

Danfay Munal (Map p550; ☎ 9434380444; Clubside Motor Stand; mains Rs20-70) A classic Darjeeling restaurant – simple set-up, great views, a range of cheap and tasty Indian, Chinese and Tibetan food (great *momos*), and it's right in the centre. They do takeaway picnic packs.

Frank Ross Café (Map p550; ☎ 2258194; 14 Nehru Rd; mains Rs20-105, full breakfast Rs85) Strictly vegetarian with a global menu, including pizzas, burgers, South Indian snacks and even enchiladas, tacos and nachos. The attached Frank Ross Pharmacy has groceries for self-caterers.

Big Bite (Laden La Rd; mains Rs30-80, thali Rs80) We don't know who copied whom, but Darjeeling has a few good 'pure veg' places that offer South Indian classics such as dosa (lentil-flour pancake) and *idli* (rice cake), alongside vegie burgers, pizza and other fast food. You'll know this one by the hot-pink entrance.

Hot Pizza Place (La Casse Croute; Map p550; ☎ 2257594; HD Lama Rd; mains Rs35-120) A one-table pizza joint with excellent pizza, pasta, panini, salads and sandwiches. Come here also for breakfast, pancakes and good coffee, as well as that hard-to-find bacon fix. Service is friendly but slow.

our pick Sonam's Kitchen (Map p550; Dr Zakir Hussein Rd; mains Rs40-90; ☿ from 7.30am) Providing an island of real brewed coffee in a sea of tea, Sonam and her Nepali family serve up lovely breakfasts, pancakes, soups and pasta; the deliciously chunky wholemeal sandwiches can be packed to go for picnics. Mains need to be pre-ordered at least an hour and a half early, so someone can dash up the street to the nearby fruit and veg stalls to get just what you want. If you miss your mama's cooking, Sonam offers the next best thing.

Park Restaurant (Map p550; ☎ 2255270; Laden La Rd; mains Rs40-140) The Park is very popular with local tourists and fills up quickly. It has tasty North Indian curries or there's a good range of mainly fish and chicken Thai dishes from the Lemon Grass menu. The new bar has been a real hit, with snacks, cocktails (Rs90 to Rs100) and impressive mocktails (Rs25 to Rs80).

Shangrila (Map p550; ☎ 2254149; Nehru Rd; mains Rs45-145) This comfy bar-restaurant near the top of the Mall offers an upmarket version of the usual Indian/Chinese/continental food mix in appealing surrounds, with wooden floors, clean tablecloths and friendly service. Take a closer look at that painting of the Last Supper on the wall – yes, those apostles are Buddhist monks.

Glenary's (Map p550; Nehru Rd; starters Rs35-120, mains Rs50-155; ☿ 11.30am-9pm, later high season) This elegant restaurant atop the famous bakery and cafe receives mainly rave reviews: of note are the continental sizzlers, Chinese dishes, tan-

WEST BENGAL

doori specials and the highly recommended veg gratin (especially if you're off spicy food). We've heard a few grumbles that it's coasting on its reputation, but most people love it.

Drinking

Where in the world is a better place to sip a cup of Darjeeling tea? If a cool pint is your idea of drinking, there are a couple of good choices.

TEA

Glenary's (Map p550; Nehru Rd; small pot Rs25, cakes & biscuits Rs10-20; ☺ 7.30am-8pm, to 9pm in high season) Below the restaurant, this cafe has massive windows and good views – order your tea, select a cake, grab your book and sink into some wicker. Internet is available too (Rs30 per hour). There's a takeaway branch in the bazaar.

Goodricke, the House of Tea (Map p550; Nehru Rd) Sit and sip a range of brewed teas from local estates before purchasing packaged tea.

Classic high teas with local brews are served up at **Elgin** (opposite; Rs460) and **Windamere Hotel** (opposite; Rs426).

BARS

Joey's Pub (Map p550; SM Das Rd; ☎ 2258216; beer Rs80; ☺ noon-10pm) This classic pub, near the post office, is a great place to meet other travellers. It has sports on TV, warm rum and cold beer, and was expanding its premises at the time of research. Generally very friendly, though lone women have experienced some not entirely good-natured teasing from staff.

Buzz (Map p550; ☺ 11am-9pm) A very kitsch Hollywood-themed bar in the basement at Glenary's.

The top-end hotels all have bars; the Windamere is the most atmospheric place to kick back with an early-evening G&T.

Entertainment

Inox Theatre (Map p550; ☎ 2257226; www.inoxmovies.com; Rink Mall, cnr Laden La & SM Das Rds; tickets Rs80-180) Three cinemas and several classes of seating. Shows Hindi blockbusters and fairly recent Hollywood fare.

Shopping

DARJEELING TEA

This is some of the finest tea in the world and is a very popular and portable souvenir. The best supplier, with over 50 varieties, is

Nathmull's Tea Room (Map p550; ☎ 2256437; www.nathmulltea.com; Laden La Rd; ☺ 9am-7.30pm Mon-Sat, daily high season). Expect to pay Rs80 to Rs150 per 100g for a decent tea and up to Rs1400 per 100g for the finest brews. You can ask for a tasting, which will be expertly brewed, and you can also buy attractive teapots and cosies. The family has run the business for 80 years, and is very knowledgable. (The Nathmull's in the Rink Mall is a recent start-up, and no connection to this long-established business.)

Try before you buy at Goodricke, The House of Tea (left).

Cheaper tea is available in Chowk Bazaar, but the packaging isn't particularly sturdy. Avoid the tea in fancy boxes, because it's usually blended and packaged in Kolkata.

TIBETAN CARPETS

The Tibetan Refugee Self-Help Centre (p553) makes gorgeous carpets to order and can ship the finished carpet to your home address (US$370/200 with/without shipping). **Hayden Hall** (Map p550; ☎ 2253228; Laden La Rd; ☺ 9am-6pm Mon-Sat) sells carpets as part of its charitable work (Rs5000 for a 3ft by 6ft carpet). There are carpets in most of the souvenir shops, but they're not likely to be locally made.

TREKKING GEAR

The **Trekking Shop** (Map p550; Singalila Market, Nehru Rd; ☺ 10.30am-6pm) sells satisfactory Nepali counterfeit clothing, and waterproofs and jackets, as well as Chinese- and Russian-made boots (larger sizes are rare).

OTHER SOUVENIRS

There are numerous souvenir shops at Chowrasta and along Gandhi and Nehru Rds selling Nepali woodcarvings (including masks), *thangkas* (Tibetan cloth paintings), religious objects and jewellery.

You'll be spoiled for choice if you're feeling the cold – quality woollens, particularly shawls, are available everywhere, so you can afford to bargain. Woollens stalls stretch down Nehru Rd in season.

There are a couple of good fair-trade shops selling locally made clothes and handicrafts. Hayden Hall (above) has good knitwear and bags made by local women. **Life & Leaf Fair Trade Shop** (Map p550; ☎ 93333551831; 19 Nehru Rd) supports local artisans and environmental projects, and sells stylish and cute bags, scarves, toys and organic tea.

WEST BENGAL

PERMITS FOR SIKKIM

Forms for Sikkim permits (p587) are available at the **Foreigners' Regional Registration Office** (Map p550; ☎ 2254203; Laden La Rd; ⏰ 10am-7pm), and must then be taken to the **Office of the District Magistrate** (ODM; Map p550; ☎ 2254233; Hill Cart Rd; ⏰ 11am-1pm & 2.30-4pm Mon-Fri), downhill from the Chowk Bazaar bus/jeep station. The whole process takes about 1½ hours and there's no fee – bring your passport. Note that if you're crossing at Rangpo you don't have to go through this process – you can get a free 15-day permit on the spot at the border, though you'll need three passport photos. These rules looked likely to change again at the time of research, so you had best check with the Foreigners' Regional Registration Office.

Getting There & Away

AIR

The nearest airport is 90km away at Bagdogra, about 12km from Siliguri. See p543 for details about flights to/from Bagdogra.

Indian Airlines (Map p550; ☎ 2254230; ⏰ 10am-5.30pm Mon-Sat) is at Chowrasta. **Clubside Tours & Travels** (Map p550; ☎ 2254646; www.clubside.in; JP Sharma Rd; ⏰ 9.30am-6pm) does domestic airline bookings. **Pineridge Travels** (Map p550; ☎ 2253912, 2253036; pineridge@mail.com; ⏰ 10am-5pm Mon-Sat) is an agent for a number of domestic airlines, and is the only agency in Darjeeling licensed for international-flight booking.

BUS

From the Chowk Bazaar bus/jeep station (Map p550), regular buses depart for Mirik (Rs40, three hours) and Siliguri (Rs60, three hours). Tickets can be bought from the ground-floor counter at the Old Super Market Complex that backs on to the station.

Kasturi Tours & Travels (p551) and Diamond Treks, Tours & Travels (p551) can book 'luxury' buses from Siliguri to destinations such as Kolkata (Rs900, 12 hours). Samsara Tours, Travels & Treks (p551) offers similar services. These tickets don't include transfers to Siliguri.

JEEP & TAXI

Numerous share jeeps and taxis leave the crowded south end of the Chowk Bazaar bus/jeep station for Siliguri (Rs80, three hours) and Kurseong (Rs40, 1½ hours). Jeeps leave for Mirik (Rs50, 2½ hours) about every 1½ hours. Ticket offices on the ground floor of the Old Super Market Complex sell advance tickets for the frequent jeeps to Kalimpong (Rs90, two hours) and Gangtok (Rs130, four hours).

At the northern end of the station, three to four jeeps a day leave for Jorenthang (Rs80,

two hours). You must already have a permit to enter Sikkim (see the boxed text, above) via this route.

Darjeeling Transport Corporation (Map p550; ☎ 9832081338; Laden La Rd) has jeeps to Gangtok (share/charter Rs130/1300, four hours, share jeeps depart hourly) and Siliguri (share/charter Rs90/900, three hours, hourly).

To New Jalpaiguri or Bagdogra, get a connection in Siliguri, or charter a jeep or taxi from Darjeeling (Rs1000 to NJP, Rs1200 to Bagdogra).

TRAIN

The nearest major train station is at New Jalpaiguri (NJP), near Siliguri. Tickets can be bought for major services out of NJP at the **Darjeeling train station** (Map p550; ☎ 2252555; ⏰ 8am-2pm).

Darjeeling Himalayan Railway

The diesel toy train (Map p550) leaves Darjeeling at 9.15am for NJP (2nd/1st class Rs42/247, seven hours), stopping at Ghoom (Rs21/96, 50 minutes), Kurseong (Rs37/159, three hours) and Siliguri (Rs48/232, 6½ hours). It's an exhausting haul to NJP, so if you simply want to experience the train, take the steam train to/from Kurseong or the joy ride (p552).

TO/FROM NEPAL

Foreigners can only cross the border into Nepal at Kakarbhitta/Panitanki (not at Pasupati).

Kasturi Tours & Travels (p551) and Diamond Treks, Tours & Travels (p551) sell tickets for buses from Darjeeling to Kathmandu (Rs800). These are not direct buses and involve transfers in Siliguri and at the border – leaving room for problems. However, it's not difficult to do this yourself and you'll save some money. See the boxed text, p545 for Siliguri–Panitanki transport, as well as border and Nepali bus details.

Getting Around

There are several taxi stands around town, but rates are absurd for short hops. You can hire a porter to carry your bags up to Chowrasta from Chowk Bazaar for around Rs60.

Share jeeps to anywhere north of the city centre (eg North Point for Rs7) leave from the northern end of the Chowk Bazaar bus/jeep station. To Ghoom, get a share jeep (Rs15) from the Hill Cart Rd jeep stand at Chowk Bazaar (Map p550).

TREKKING AROUND DARJEELING

A number of rewarding and picturesque treks are accessible from Darjeeling. October and November's clear skies and warm temperatures make it an ideal time to trek, as do the long days and rhododendron blooms of May and early June. The Darjeeling Gorkha Hill Council (DGHC; p551) produces the excellent *Himalayan Treks* leaflet (Rs25), which includes a map and descriptions of major trekking routes.

Most popular is the **Singalila Ridge Trek** from Sandakphu to Phalut, which passes through the scenic **Singalila National Park** (admission Rs100, camera/video Rs25/250) and offers fantastic views of the Himalaya. Guides (about Rs350 per day) are mandatory within the park (the park entrance is near Tumling) and can be hired privately through the DGHC, travel agencies or at the trek's starting point in Mana Bhanjang, 26km from Darjeeling; you're more likely to get a good guide if you line it up beforehand. Mana Bhanjang is served by regular shared jeeps as well as a 7am bus from Darjeeling's Chowk Bazaar bus/jeep station (Rs30, three hours). The usual trekking itinerary is described in the boxed text, p560. Some travellers have enjoyed doing just the first stage; the route is easy to follow and a guide isn't required (although you may be strongly encouraged to hire one anyway).

From Rimbik, there are two connecting morning buses to Darjeeling (Rs80, five hours, 6am and 12.30pm) and regular jeeps. If you don't have five days, there are short cuts available at Sandakphu and Sabarkum. At the time of research the basic trekkers' huts along the

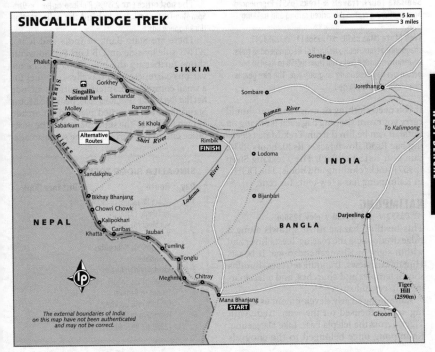

SINGALILA RIDGE TREK

0 — 5 km
0 — 3 miles

Phalut
Soreng
SIKKIM
Gorkhey
Singalila National Park
Samandar
Sombare
Jorethang
Molley
Ramam
Raman River
Sabarkum
Sri Khola
To Kalimpong
Alternative Routes
Shiri River
Rimbik **FINISH**
Lodoma
INDIA
Sandakphu
Lodoma River
Bikhay Bhanjang
Bijanbari
Chowri Chowk
Kalipokhari
Darjeeling
Khatta — Garibas
Jaubari
NEPAL
Tumling
BANGLA
Tonglu
Meghma
Chitray
Tiger Hill (2590m)
Mana Bhanjang **START**
Ghoom

The external boundaries of India on this map have not been authenticated and may not be correct.

WEST BENGAL

route were closed for renovation; check with the DGHC (p551). Better private accommodation options in small family 'guest houses' are available; Shikhara Lodge in Tumling has been especially recommended by trekkers. All-inclusive guided treks on this route, including porters, meals and accommodation, are offered by Darjeeling travel agencies (p551) for Rs1200 to Rs2000 per day depending on the level of service and number of people.

Nearer to Kalimpong is the Rochela Trek, which gives you a taste of the stunning Samthar Plateau. You can trek for four to eight days through dense forests, visiting remote villages and crossing a pass at 3000m. Note that it takes four days, with camping, to reach the highpoint of Rochela from Kalimpong.

Recommended trekking agencies include the following:

Darjeeling Gorkha Hill Council Tourist Reception Centre (Darjeeling p551; Kalimpong right) Charges about Rs2000 per day (all-inclusive) for Singalila Ridge, and organises guides/porters (Rs350 per day) for Rochela.

Gurudongma Tours & Travels (p562) Offering customised all-inclusive treks in this region, with knowledgeable guides and accommodation.

Samsara Tours, Travels & Treks (p551) Experienced agency offering reasonably priced rafting and trekking trips.

Trek Mate (Map p550; ☎ 2256611, 9832083241; chagpori@satyam.net.in; Nehru Rd) Recommended treks: all-inclusive guided treks run from Rs950 to Rs1450 per person per day depending on group size. The hire gear is clean and well maintained.

If you need clothing or gear (and you should carry your own sleeping bag even if relying on huts), it can be hired from Trek Mate (sleeping bag Rs30, down jacket Rs20, boots Rs30, rain gear Rs15 per day). The Trekking Shop (p557) stocks clothing and boots. The DGHC in Kalimpong has a few tents for rent.

KALIMPONG

☎ 03552 / pop 42,980 / elev 1250m

This bustling bazaar town sprawls along a ridge overlooking the roaring Teesta River and within sight of Khangchendzonga. It boasts Himalayan views, tranquil retreats, Buddha shops, temples and churches, and a fascinating nursery industry.

Kalimpong's early development as a trading centre focused on the wool trade with Tibet, across the Jelepla Pass. Like Darjeeling, Kalimpong once belonged to the chogyals

of Sikkim, but it fell into the hands of the Bhutanese in the 18th century and later passed to the British, before becoming part of India at Independence. Scottish missionaries, particularly the Jesuits, made great efforts to win over the local Buddhists in the late 19th century and Dr Graham's famous orphanage and school is still running today.

The Gorkhaland movement is active in Kalimpong. The Gurkha leader CK Pradhan was assassinated here in October 2002, and is commemorated by a small shrine on the spot where he was gunned down.

Orientation & Information

Kalimpong is centred on its chaotic Motor Stand. Nearby are restaurants, cheap hotels and shopping, while most sights and quality accommodation are a few kilometres from town, accessed via DB Giri and Rinkingpong Rds.

The staff at the **Darjeeling Gorkha Hill Council Tourist Reception Centre** (DGHC; ☎ 257992; DB Giri Rd; ⏰ 9.30am-5pm) can help organise tours of the area. The private website www.kalimpong .org is a good resource.

The **post office** (☎ 255990; Rinkingpong Rd; ⏰ 9am-5pm Mon-Fri, to 4pm Sat) is behind the **police station** (Rinkingpong Rd).

There are State Bank of India and ICICI ATMs side by side on DB Giri Rd. Souvenir shops further up the hill offer to exchange various currencies and travellers cheques for a small commission. Internet options include **Net Hut** (per hr Rs30; ⏰ 9.30am-8pm), near the Motor Stand, and an unnamed place in an arcade known locally as 'the supermarket' at the post-office end of DB Giri Rd. In the same arcade,

SINGALILA RIDGE TREK

Day	Route	Distance (km)
1	Mana Bhanjang (2130m) to Tonglu (3100m) via Meghma Gompa	14
2	Tonglu to Sandakphu (3636m) via Kalipokhri & Garibas	17
3	Sandakphu to Phalut (3600m) via Sabarkum	17
4	Phalut to Ramam (2530m) via Gorkhey	16
5	Rammam to Rimbik (2290m) via Srikhola	19

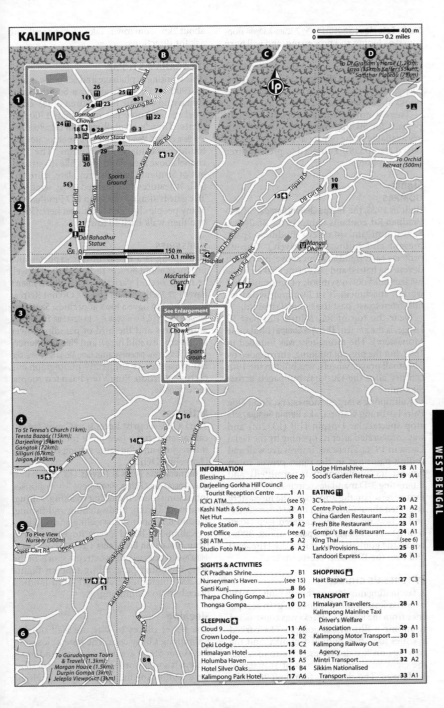

INFORMATION

Blessings	(see 2)
Darjeeling Gorkha Hill Council	
Tourist Reception Centre	**1** A1
ICICI ATM	(see 5)
Kashi Nath & Sons	**2** A1
Net Hut	**3** B1
Police Station	**4** A2
Post Office	(see 4)
SBI ATM	**5** A2
Studio Foto Max	**6** A2

SIGHTS & ACTIVITIES

CK Pradhan Shrine	**7** B1
Nurseryman's Haven	(see 15)
Santi Kunj	**8** B6
Tharpa Choling Gompa	**9** D1
Thongsa Gompa	**10** D2

SLEEPING

Cloud 9	**11** A6
Crown Lodge	**12** B2
Deki Lodge	**13** C2
Himalayan Hotel	**14** B4
Holumba Haven	**15** A5
Hotel Silver Oaks	**16** B4
Kalimpong Park Hotel	**17** A6
Lodge Himalshree	**18** A1
Sood's Garden Retreat	**19** A4

EATING

3C's	**20** A2
Centre Point	**21** A2
China Garden Restaurant	**22** B1
Fresh Bite Restaurant	**23** A1
Gompu's Bar & Restaurant	**24** A1
King Thai	(see 6)
Lark's Provisions	**25** B1
Tandoori Express	**26** A1

SHOPPING

Haat Bazaar	**27** C3

TRANSPORT

Himalayan Travellers	**28** A1
Kalimpong Mainline Taxi	
Driver's Welfare	
Association	**29** A1
Kalimpong Motor Transport	**30** B1
Kalimpong Railway Out	
Agency	**31** B1
Mintri Transport	**32** A2
Sikkim Nationalised	
Transport	**33** A1

Studio Foto Max (☎ 260113; ☯ 7.30am-7.30pm) does film developing and processing, and will burn pictures to a CD for Rs50.

Two small adjoining bookshops – **Kashi Nath & Sons** (DB Giri Rd) and **Blessings** (DB Giri Rd; ☯ 10am-6.30pm) – have a good range on Buddhism, and books about Nepal and Tibet.

There is nowhere in Kalimpong to obtain permits for Sikkim, but free 15-day permits are available at the border at Rangpo (see the boxed text, p558). You need to present three passport photos.

Sights

GOMPAS

Built in 1926, the **Tharpa Choling Gompa**, off KD Pradhan Rd, contains statues of the Bhaisajya, Sakyamuni and Maitreya Buddhas (past, present and future, respectively). Garuda protects each Buddha from above, his mouth devouring hatred and anger (the snake), while his feet hold down symbols of ignorance and worldly attachment. It's a 30-minute walk (uphill) from town, past the top of Tripai Rd.

Near the top of RC Mintri Rd, past JP Lodge, is the ancient **Thongsa Gompa** (Bhutanese Monastery). The monastery was founded in 1692, but the present building, surrounded by 219 small prayer wheels, was built in the 19th century after the Gurkhas rampaged across Sikkim.

Kalimpong's largest monastery, Zong Dog Palri Fo-Brang Gompa, aka **Durpin Gompa**, sits atop spectacular Durpin Hill (1372m) and was consecrated after its opening by the Dalai Lama in 1976. There are impressive wall and ceiling paintings in the main prayer room downstairs (photography is permitted), and interesting 3-D mandalas (circles symbolising the universe) on the 2nd floor. The monastery is located about 5km south of the town centre, and is best reached by chartered jeep (Rs80 return). The **Jelepla Viewpoint**, about 300m below the gompa, looks out to the Himalaya and over the Relli and Teesta Rivers.

ST TERESA'S CHURCH

A fascinating missionary church built in 1929 by Swiss Jesuits and designed to gain acceptance from the locals, St Teresa was constructed to mimic a Bhutanese gompa. The carved apostles look like Buddhist monks, and the carvings on the doors resemble *tashi tagye*, the eight auspicious symbols of Himalayan Buddhism. The church is found off 9th Mile,

about 2km from town. Take a taxi or walk and ask for directions.

DR GRAHAM'S HOME

This working orphanage and school was built in 1900 by Dr JA Graham, a Scottish missionary, to educate the children of tea-estate workers, and now has more than 1300 students. There's a small **museum** (admission free; ☯ 9am-3.30pm Mon-Fri) that commemorates the founder and his wife Katherine. The 1925 chapel above the school looks like it's straight out of Scotland, with its grey slate, spire and bell. It features fine stained-glass windows. The gate is 4km up the steep KD Pradhan Rd. Many people charter a taxi to get here (Rs90) and then walk back to town.

NURSERIES

Kalimpong is a major flower exporter and produces about 80% of India's gladioli as well as many orchid varieties. Visit **Nurseryman's Haven** (☎ 256936; 9th Mile) and the Orchid Retreat (opposite) to have a look at orchids; **Santi Kunj** (BL Dixit Rd; ☯ 8.30am-noon & 1.30-4pm Sun-Fri) to see anthuriums and the bird of paradise flower (bulbs are also sold here); and **Pine View Nursery** (☎ 255843; www.pineviewcactus.com; Atisha Rd; admission Rs5) to gaze at its eminently photographable cactus collection. Pine View has a few rooms; see opposite.

Activities

The DGHC Tourist Reception Centre (p560) can arrange treks (see p559 for trekking in this region) and the same rafting trips as the Darjeeling DGHC.

Gurudongma Tours & Travels (☎ 255204; www.gurudongma.com; Hilltop, Rinkingpong Rd) organises interesting tours, including trekking, rafting, mountain-biking, birdwatching and fishing, around Kalimpong, Darjeeling and Sikkim.

Kalimpong-based Swede Roger Lenngren from **Himalayan Bike Tours** (☎ 9635116911; www.himalayanbiketours.se) offers extreme sports in the area, including paragliding tandem flights (Rs2000 including transport from landing place back to Kalimpong).

Sleeping

The better places to stay are well outside Kalimpong's busy core. The hotels closest to the Motor Stand are mainly grotty and overpriced; it's well worth going a few extra steps for a significant increase in quality. High-season rates (October to early December and mid-March to early June) are given here.

BUDGET

Lodge Himalshree (☎ 255070; Ongden Rd; dm/d without bathroom Rs100/200, tr Rs250) This extremely basic little place with an affable owner is on the top floor of a tall building right in the busiest part of town. The stairs are steep and the rooms are plain and passably clean. The dorm is pretty much the hotel lobby. Bathrooms are dank, and hot-water buckets cost Rs10.

Deki Lodge (☎ 255095; www.geocities.com/dekilodge; Tripai Rd; s/d/tr Rs250/550/900, deluxe d Rs950) This lovely Tibetan-owned lodge is close to the Thongsa and Tharpa Choling monasteries and still handy to town. It's a friendly, family-run place set in a garden with a pleasant cafe and rooftop viewing area. Rooms are spotless and appealing and the fluffy dogs will make you feel right at home. It's well worth the steepish walk to get up here – it's light years better than anything near the Motor Stand.

Crown Lodge (☎ 255846; off Baghdara Rd; s/d Rs350/600) This big place has large rooms with TVs and geyser, but furnishings are on the shabby side, and it's very noisy at night. Nonetheless it's probably the best of the Motor Stand–adjacent hotels.

Pine View Nursery (☎ 255843; pineviewnursery@yahoo.co.in; Atisha Rd; d/tr Rs550/750) A few passably clean, simple and spacious rooms for those who have always wanted to sleep in a cactus nursery (not recommended for sleepwalkers).

MIDRANGE & TOP END

our pick **Holumba Haven** (☎ 256936; www.holumba.com; 9th Mile; s/d from Rs700/1600, cottage from Rs4500) Described by its welcoming owners as 'more of a homestay than a hotel', this family-run guest house is situated in a splendid orchid nursery just 1km out of town. The spotless, comfy rooms are arranged in beautifully decorated cottages spread around the lush garden, and spring water is piped directly into the rooms. Good home-style meals (guests only) are available in the dining room. You'll want to be keen on animals – dogs, ducks and rabbits are just some of the beasts you'll bump into.

Cloud 9 (☎ 259554; cloud9kpg@yahoo.com; Rinkingpong Rd; d Rs800-1000) A very friendly place with wood-panelled rooms, a cosy TV lounge and a good restaurant, serving Bhutanese, Tibetan and Chinese food. Guitars in the lounge attest to many late-night jams.

Sood's Garden Retreat (☎ 260321; www.soodsgardenretreat.com; 9th Mile; s/d from Rs900/1200) The eager-to-help owners at this new hotel can organise tours and trips, including rafting expeditions. The clean, inviting rooms are decorated with wood panelling and warm colours, but make sure you get one with a view.

Orchid Retreat (☎ 274489; www.theorchidretreat.com; Ganesh Villa; s/d from Rs1400/2000; 🖳) An attractive family-run getaway, with tastefully decorated cottages scattered through the grounds of a large orchid nursery that's heaven for birders. In line with the 'getting away from it all' theme there are no phones or TVs in rooms. Home-cooked, fixed-menu food is available in the airy dining room. Prior bookings are preferred.

Kalimpong Park Hotel (☎ 255304; www.kalimpongparkhotel.com; s/d from Rs1500/2000) This former maharaja's home has oodles of Raj-era charm. Wicker chairs and flowers line the verandah and there's a super-cute bar and restaurant. Rooms in the new wing lack some of the period charm of the old house but are still very appealing (and the big new slate-floor bathrooms are by far the best in town).

Himalayan Hotel (☎ 254043; www.himalayanhotel.co.in; Upper Cart Rd; s/d from Rs1700/2700, with full board Rs2600/4500) This hotel was opened by the revered David MacDonald, an interpreter from Francis Younghusband's mission to Lhasa in 1904 and one of those who helped the 13th Dalai Lama escape Tibet in 1910. The original rooms have loads of Raj-era appeal beneath a sloping Himalayan-oak ceiling, while the new suites mesh old-world charm with modern comfort; their terraces gaze upon Khangchendzonga. It's a triumph of sympathetic renovation; comfortable but full of lovely original fittings.

Hotel Silver Oaks (☎ 255296; silveroaks@sanchernet.in; Rinkingpong Rd; s/d Rs4800/5100) This centrally located Raj-era homestead has been renovated into a modern and very comfortable hotel. The rooms are plushly furnished (love the puffy satin bed-heads) and offer grand views down the valley. The tariff includes all meals in the excellent restaurant and there's a sociable bar.

Eating

RESTAURANTS

Fresh Bite Restaurant (☎ 274042; DB Giri Rd; mains Rs30-140) Upstairs, across the road from the DGHC, this place has a huge range of almost uniformly good food including some hard-to-find dishes that you might just have been craving, like miso soup and bacon sandwiches.

China Garden Restaurant (☎ 257456; Lal Gulli, mains Rs35-90) In the China Garden Hotel near the Motor Stand, this is Kalimpong's best Chinese restaurant. The authentic soups, noodles and the spicy ginger chicken attract aficionados, though several Indian curries have snuck onto the menu.

Tandoori Express (DB Giri Rd; mains Rs40-90) A clean new place filling a gap in Kalimpong's food market by offering a good range of North Indian curries and tandoori dishes.

Gompu's Bar & Restaurant (☎ 257456; off DB Giri Rd; mains Rs45-90) Gompu's is famous for its massive *momos* (pork, chicken and veg), and has been pleasing locals and travellers with Tibetan, Bhutanese, Indian, Chinese and continental fare for ages. It's found within the hotel of the same name.

our pick **King Thai** (3rd fl 'supermarket', DB Giri Rd; mains Rs50-170) A multicultural hang out with a Thai name, Chinese food, Bob Marley posters and British soccer banners for decoration, and Hindi/Nepali live music for entertainment. The excellent food is mainly Chinese with some Thai and Indian dishes: four different versions of chop suey are offered, along with wantons as a change from *momos*. There's a bar with comfy chairs and a disco ball, and a regular crowd that mixes expats, monks, businessmen and Tibetan cool kids.

QUICK EATS

Kalimpong cheese has been produced in Kalimpong since the Jesuits established a dairy here in the 19th century, and Kalimpong lollipops are made at the dairy from milk, sugar and butter.

3C's (DB Giri Rd; cakes & snacks Rs10-30) A popular bakery and restaurant offering a variety of mouth-watering pastries and cakes.

Lark's Provisions (DB Giri Rd) The best place to pick up Kalimpong cheese (Rs180 per kg) and a packet of Kalimpong lollipops (Rs25). Also sells groceries and yummy home-made pickles.

Shopping

Along RC Mintri Rd there's a profusion of fabric shops selling Tibetan cloth and Indian or Chinese silk brocade – both higher in quality and lower in cost than those seen in Darjeeling.

Haat Bazaar (btwn Relli & RC Mintri Rds) On Wednesday and Saturday, this normally quiet bazaar roars to life.

Getting There & Away

All the bus and jeep options, and their offices mentioned here, are found at the chaotic Motor Stand.

BUS & JEEP

Bengal government buses run regularly to Siliguri (Rs55, 2½ hours), and there's also a single Sikkim Nationalised Transport (SNT) bus to Gangtok (Rs70, 3½ hours) at 1pm.

Himalayan Travellers (☎ 9434166498) runs minibuses or share jeeps to Gangtok (Rs90, three hours, four daily) and Lava (Rs50, 1½ hours, regular departures).

Kalimpong Mainline Taxi Driver's Welfare Association (KMTDWA; ☎ 257979) has regular share jeeps to Siliguri (Rs70, 2½ hours), Gangtok (Rs80, 2½ hours), Lava (Rs50, 1½ hours) and Kaffer (Rs60, 2½ hours), and one daily to Jorenthang (Rs60, two hours, departs 7.15am). **KS & AH Taxi Driver's Welfare Association** (☎ 259544) has regular jeeps to Ravangla in Sikkim (Rs100, 3½ hours). **Kalimpong Motor Transport** (☎ 255719) has a regular share-jeep service to Darjeeling (Rs80, 2½ hours).

Jeeps can also be chartered for Darjeeling (Rs900), Siliguri (Rs800) and Gangtok (Rs850).

TRAIN

The **Kalimpong Railway Out Agency** (☎ 259954; Mani Rd; ⌚ 10am-4pm Mon-Sat, to 1pm Sun) and **Mintri Transport** (☎ 2556997; DB Giri Rd; ⌚ 10.30am-6pm) sell a small quota of tickets from New Jalpaiguri train station.

TO/FROM BHUTAN & NEPAL

A government bus travels to the Bhutan border, Jaigon (Rs95, 5½ hours) at 8.40am, and KMTDWA has a 7.30am shared jeep (Rs130, five hours). The KMTDWA has regular jeeps to the Nepal border at Panitanki (Rs90, three hours), and Himalayan Travellers has a 7.30am jeep for Pashupati (Rs100, 3½ hours).

Border information can be found in the boxed text, p545.

Getting Around

Taxis can be chartered for local trips from along DB Giri Rd. A half-day rental to see most of the sights should cost Rs700.

AROUND KALIMPONG
Teesta Bazaar
☎ 03552

About 16km west of Kalimpong, Teesta Bazaar is an important centre for white-water rafting. Most people book at travel agencies in Darjeeling (see p551) or at the DGHC office in Kalimpong, but you can also book here with the **DGHC** (☎ 268261; Chitrey Wayside Inn, NH-31A), about 1.5km from Teesta Bazaar along the road to Kalimpong.

The friendly **Chitrey Wayside Inn** (☎ 213520; dm Rs100, d/ste Rs450/600) has a bar, restaurant and balcony overlooking the jungle banks of the Teesta River. The spacious rooms have hot water and are clean, if spartan, and meals are good.

Teesta Bazaar is about 30 minutes by road from Kalimpong; take any bus or share jeep (Rs25) in the direction of Darjeeling.

Lava & Kaffer

About 35km east of Kalimpong, Lava (2353m) is a small village with a Kagyupa **gompa** and a bustling **market** on Tuesday. The summit of Khangchendzonga can be seen from **Kaffer** (1555m), also known as Lolaygoan, about 30km further east. Both villages see few tourists and make peaceful and scenic getaways. The picturesque drive from Kalimpong passes through mist and moss-laden old-growth forests.

Daffey Munal Tourist Lodge (☎ 03552-277218; Kaffer; dm Rs100, d/tr Rs600/700) has huge, clean rooms with hot water and fireplaces. It's a rambling old DGHC place.

Jeeps and a daily bus serve Kalimpong from both Lava (Rs50, 1½ hours) and Kaffer (Rs60, 2½ hours).

Samthar Plateau

This remote plateau offers awesome views of Bhutan's Himalaya range and a chance to visit traditional villages. **Gurudongma Tours & Travels** (☎ 255204; www.gurudongma.com; Hilltop, Rinkingpong Rd, Kalimpong; s/d full board from Rs3800/4800) runs the cosy Farm House at Samthar. It'll arrange transport for its customers from Kalimpong.

Bihar & Jharkhand

As the birthplace of Buddhism, Bihar holds great significance in India's cultural and spiritual heritage. Siddhartha Gautama – Buddha – spent much of his life here and attained enlightenment underneath a bodhi tree in Bodhgaya, making it the most important pilgrimage site in the world for Buddhists. Following a trail of ancient and modern Buddhist sites, you can visit the extensive ruins of Nalanda, the largest university in the ancient world, the many shrines and temples at nearby Rajgir, and the great Ashokan pillar at Vaishali.

In August 2000, Bihar was split along tribal lines, creating the new state of Jharkhand. Home to numerous waterfalls and lush forests, Jharkhand is notable as the most significant Jain pilgrimage site in north-central India, although the state's best-kept secret is Betla (Palamau) National Park, where you can take an elephant ride into the forest's depths in search of an elusive tiger.

Bihar and Jharkhand are perhaps more representative of traditional India than any other northern states. Outside the big cities most signage is in Hindi and men are more likely to be wearing the kurta and dhoti rather than Western-style shirt and trousers.

This has been one of India's poorest and most troubled regions. Bihar has a reputation for endemic government corruption and ineptitude, kidnappings, extortion, banditry and Naxalite violence. The lot of Biharis has been a sorry one, causing many to escape the state and seek work elsewhere. But it's improving: a new government is controlling corruption and lawlessness, and new infrastructure developments are being built.

All this keeps it well out of most visitors' comfort zone, but don't be put off; this is pioneer travelling territory, barely diluted by tourism and the more intriguing for it.

HIGHLIGHTS

- Absorb the dawn atmosphere at the serene **Mahabodhi Temple** (p576) in Bodhgaya, and observe the monks and nuns at *puja* (prayer)
- Imagine the ancient university at **Nalanda** (p581) with its 10,000 pupils from all over Asia
- Wade into India's largest livestock fair at the **Sonepur Mela** (p570) – an event that makes Pushkar's camel fair look like a Sunday market
- Ride an elephant through the forest of **Betla (Palamau) National Park** (p583) and hopefully spy a tiger

★ Sonepur Mela

★ Nalanda

★ Bodhgaya

★ Betla (Palamau) National Park

BIHAR & JHARKHAND

0 ____ 100 km
0 ____ 50 miles

To Pokhara (47km)

Mugling

Naubise ◆ **KATHMANDU**

Narayanghat

The external boundaries of India on this map have not been authenticated and may not be correct.

SIKKIM

Amlekhganj

NEPAL

Valmiki Nagar Wildlife Sanctuary

Bayaha

Raxaul

Birganj

Lalbiti

Dharan Bazaar

Kakarbhitta

Bettiah

Kushinagar

28

To Gorakhpur (10km)

Sagauli

Motihari

Sitamarhi

Jaleshwar

Jaynagar

Jogbani

Biratnagar

Gopalganj

Chakia

Madhubani

Kesariya

Siwan

Muzaffarpur

Darbhanga

Saharsa

Purnia

31

34

UTTAR PRADESH

Vaishali

Lalganj

Samastipur

Katihar

Chapra

Sonepur

Hajipur

28

Ghaghara River

Maner

Patna

Ganges River

Arrah

30

Ganges

Munger

Bhagalpur

River

Buxar

Katihar

Nalanda

Bihar Sharif

To Varanasi (44km)

River Son

Barabar Caves

Rajgir

Pawapuri

BIHAR

Godda

Sasaram

Dehri

Bela

Hot Springs

Gaya

Dungeshwari Cave Temples

Bodhgaya

31

Deoghar

Grand Trunk Rd (GTR)

Hazaribagh Road Train Station

Giridih

Sikayi

Madhuban

Daltonganj

Hazaribagh National Park

2

Parasnath

Dhanbad

Betla (Palamau) National Park

Hazaribagh

33

JHARKHAND

Asansol

Macluskiganj

Hundru Falls

Netarhat

Lohardaga

Ranchi

Bankura

To Kolkata (113km)

23

CHHATTISGARH

Khunti

33

WEST BENGAL

Jamshedpur

Chaibasa

Kharagpur

Rourkela

ORISSA

23

Kendujhargarh

6

Baleshwar

Bay of Bengal

> **FAST FACTS**
>
> **Population** 82.9 million (Bihar), 26.9 million (Jharkhand)
> **Area** 173,877 sq km
> **Capital** Patna (Bihar), Ranchi (Jharkhand)
> **Main language** Hindi
> **When to go** October to March

History

Prince Siddhartha Gautama arrived in Bihar during the 6th century BC and spent many years here before leaving enlightened as Buddha. The life of Mahavira, a contemporary of Buddha and the founder of Jainism, was also entwined with Bihar. In the 4th century BC, after Chandragupta Maurya conquered the Magadha kingdom and its capital Pataliputra (now Patna), he expanded into the Indus Valley and created the first great Indian empire. His grandson and successor, Ashoka, ruled the Mauryan empire from Pataliputra, which could have been the largest city in the world at that time. Emperor Ashoka embraced Buddhism (see p41), erecting stupas, monuments and his famous Ashokan pillars throughout northern India – notably at Sarnath (Uttar Pradesh) and Sanchi (Madhya Pradesh). In Bihar, Ashoka built the original shrine on the site of today's Mahabodhi Temple in Bodhgaya (p576) and the lion-topped pillar at Vaishali (p573).

Bihar continued to be coveted by a succession of major empires until the Magadha dynasty rose to glory again during the reign of the Guptas (7th and 8th centuries AD).

In 1193, Muhammad Khilji, a general of Qutbuddin, invaded Bihar, destroyed the university at Nalanda (p581) and massacred the monks. Bihar declined into being an inconsequential province ruled from Delhi until the time of Sher Shah. Based in Sasaram in western Bihar, he was not only a warrior emperor but also an able administrator. He built the Grand Trunk Rd from east of Calcutta (Kolkata) up to Peshawar (in present-day Pakistan) and introduced a tax-collection system that is still in use today. With the decline of the Mughal empire, Bihar came under the control of Bengal until 1912, when a separate state was formed. Part of this state later became Orissa and, more recently in 2000, Jharkhand.

Information

State tourism offices exist in every major town but are of little use beyond handing out leaflets. A more helpful place for practical information is the India tourism office in Patna (p570). Also try the following websites:

Bihar State Tourism Development Corporation (BSTDC; http://bstdc.bih.nic.in)
Bihar Tourism (http://discoverbihar.bih.nic.in)
Jharkhand Tourism (http://jharkhand.nic.in)

Dangers & Annoyances

Conditions have improved in Bihar and Jharkhand, with a reduction in lawlessness since the Nitish Kumar government came into power. Dacoit (bandit) activity in holding up cars and buses is still a possibility and Maoist and Naxalite groups are still active (but outside the tourist areas) so precautions are wise. Although foreign and domestic tourists are not specific targets and chances are you won't encounter any trouble, it's a good idea to split up your valuables on long journeys and always avoid travelling after dusk. Check the security situation before arriving: *Bihar Times* (www.bihartimes.com) and *Patna Daily* (www.patnadaily.com) present local news in English. For more information on security issues, see p1144.

BIHAR

PATNA

☎ 0612 / pop 1,285,470

Bihar's busy capital sprawls out over the south bank of the polluted Ganges, just east of the river's confluence with three major tributar-

> **RIVER OF SORROW**
>
> Flooding is a curse of Bihar and many roads, especially those on the northern flood plains, become impassable during the monsoon (usually June to September). In August 2008, a barrage controlling the flow of the Kosi River in Nepal broke. The resulting enormous surge of water within Bihar caused the river to shift its course eastwards more than 150km, flooding much of eastern part of the state, killing hundreds and making tens of thousands homeless. Not for nothing is the Kosi called the 'River of Sorrow'.

ies. Unlike Varanasi, there's nothing along the river itself and Patna has only a handful of worthwhile sights, but it's the major transport hub for the state and a base for visiting the Buddhist sites of Vaishali and Kesariya. The 5.7km-long Mahatma Gandhi Setu, the longest bridge in mainland Asia, connects Patna with Hajipur.

Patna was once a powerful city. Early in the 5th century BC, Ajatasatru shifted the capital of his Magadha kingdom from Rajgir to Pataliputra (Patna), fulfilling Buddha's prophecy that a great city would arise here. Emperors Chandragupta Maurya and Ashoka also called Pataliputra home and it remained one of India's most important cities for almost 1000 years.

Orientation

The old and newer parts of Patna stretch along the southern bank of the Ganges for about 15km. The main train station, airport and hotels are in the western half, known as Bankipur, while most of the historic sites are in the teeming older Chowk area to the east.

Although Fraser, Exhibition and Boring Rds have been renamed Muzharul Haque Path, Braj Kishore Path and Jal Prakash Rd respectively, the old names are still in common use.

Information
BOOKSHOPS
Tricel Bookshop (☎ 2221412; Ajanta Bldg, Fraser Rd; ☺ 10am-8.30pm Mon-Sat) Friendly bookshop with literature, maps, music and film DVDs.

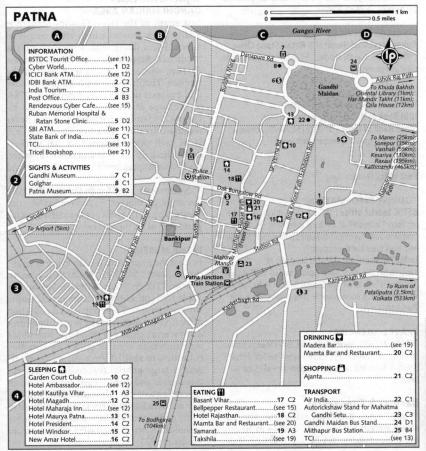

PATNA

INFORMATION
BSTDC Tourist Office..............(see 11)
Cyber World.................................**1** D2
ICICI Bank ATM........................(see 12)
IDBI Bank ATM..........................**2** C2
India Tourism.............................**3** C3
Post Office................................**4** B3
Rendezvous Cyber Cafe.........(see 15)
Ruban Memorial Hospital &
Ratan Stone Clinic.................**5** D2
SBI ATM....................................(see 11)
State Bank of India..................**6** C1
TCI...(see 13)
Tricel Bookshop......................(see 21)

SIGHTS & ACTIVITIES
Gandhi Museum........................**7** C1
Golghar......................................**8** C1
Patna Museum..........................**9** B2

SLEEPING
Garden Court Club..................**10** C2
Hotel Ambassador...................(see 12)
Hotel Kautilya Vihar................**11** A3
Hotel Magadh...........................**12** C2
Hotel Maharaja Inn.................(see 12)
Hotel Maurya Patna................**13** C1
Hotel President........................**14** C2
Hotel Windsor..........................**15** C2
New Amar Hotel.......................**16** C2

EATING
Basant Vihar............................**17** C2
Bellpepper Restaurant............(see 15)
Hotel Rajasthan.......................**18** C2
Mamta Bar and Restaurant....(see 20)
Samarat....................................**19** A3
Takshila...................................(see 19)

DRINKING
Madera Bar..............................(see 19)
Mamta Bar and Restaurant.....**20** C2

SHOPPING
Ajanta.....................................**21** C2

TRANSPORT
Air India...................................**22** C1
Autorickshaw Stand for Mahatma
Gandhi Setu............................**23** C3
Gandhi Maidan Bus Stand......**24** D1
Mithapur Bus Station..............**25** B4
TCI...(see 13)

Ganges River

Danapure Rd

Gandhi Maidan

Ashok Raj Path

To Khuda Bakhsh
Oriental Library (1km);
Har Mandir Takht (11km);
Qila House (12km)

To Maner (25km);
Sonepur (35km);
Vaishali (55km);
Kesariya (110km);
Raxaul (195km);
Kathmandu (465km)

Police
Station

Dak Bungalow Rd

Bankipur

Mahavir
Mandir

Patna Junction
Train Station

Circular Rd

To Airport (5km)

Birchand Patel Path (Gardiner Rd)

Buddha Marg

Muzharul Haque Path
(Fraser Rd)

SP Verma Rd

Braj Kishore Path (Exhibition Rd)

Rajendra Path

Station Rd

Kankerbagh Rd

Kankerbagh Rd

Mithapur Khagaul Rd

To Ruins of
Pataliputra (3.5km);
Kolkata (533km)

To Bodhgaya
(104km)

0   1 km
0   0.5 miles

BIHAR & JHARKHAND

FESTIVALS IN BIHAR & JHARKHAND

Pataliputra Mahotsava (Mar; Patna, opposite) Patna celebrates its historic past with parades, sports, dancing and music.

Rajgir Mahotsava (Oct; Rajgir, p580) A classical performing arts festival with folk dances, devotional songs and instrumental music.

Chhath Festival (Oct/Nov; Bihar & Jharkhand statewide) People line the banks of rivers and water bodies to celebrate this festival, which honours Surya, the Sun God. At sunset on the sixth day after Diwali, married women, having fasted for 36 hours, immerse themselves in the water and offer fruits and flowers to the deity. The following sunrise, devotees return to the water and offer prayers and traditional music.

Sonepur Mela (Nov/Dec; Sonepur, p574) With 700,000 attendees and countless thousands of animals taking part, this three-week festival is four times the size of Pushkar's camel fair.

INTERNET ACCESS

Cyber World (Rajendra Path; per hr Rs20; 🕑 9.30am-9pm)

Rendezvous Cyber Cafe (Hotel Windsor, Exhibition Rd; per hr Rs25; 🕑 9am-10pm)

MEDICAL SERVICES

Ruban Memorial Hospital & Ratan Stone Clinic (☎ 2320446; Gandhi Maidan; 🕑 24hr) Emergency room, clinic and pharmacy.

MONEY

ICICI Bank ATM (Station Rd; 🕑 24hr)
IDBI Bank ATM (Dak Bungalow Rd; 🕑 24hr)
State Bank of India (☎ 2226134; Gandhi Maidan) Currency and travellers cheques exchanged.

POST

Post office (Buddha Marg)

TOURIST INFORMATION

BSTDC tourist office (☎ 2225411; bstdc@sancharnet .in; Hotel Kautilya Vihar, Birchand Patel Path; 🕑 10am-5pm Mon-Sat) This office has limited information, but can help book tours and their hotels.

India Tourism (☎ 2348558; Sundama Pl, Kankerbagh Rd; 🕑 9.30am-6pm Mon-Fri) Staff at this 3rd-floor office, above the Central Bank of India, are very helpful and knowledgable about Patna, Bihar and Jharkhand.

TRAVEL AGENCIES

TCI (☎ 2221699; www.tcindia.com; Hotel Maurya Patna, South Gandhi Maidan; 🕑 9.30am-6pm Mon-Sat) Airline ticketing agent and car rental company (see p573 for details).

Dangers & Annoyances

While Patna's streets are safe during the day, avoid walking alone after dark – as in any big city, robbery can be a possibility. Take all the usual precautions of not displaying valuables.

Sights & Activities

GANDHI MAIDAN AREA

Just south of the river, Gandhi Maidan is a large park around which are a couple of sights. For a dome with a view, climb the landmark **Golghar** (Danapure Rd; admission free; 🕑 24hr), which is a short walk west of the maidan. The British army built this massive and bulbous beehive of a granary in 1786, in the hope of avoiding a repeat of the vicious 1770 famine. Fortunately it was never required. Its dual spiralling staircases (250 steps each side), designed so that workers could climb up one side and down the other, lead to an unparalleled view of the city and Ganges.

Nearby is the small **Gandhi Museum** (☎ 2225339; Danapure Rd; admission free; 🕑 10am-6pm Sun-Fri), containing a pictorial history of the Mahatma's life plus some of his meagre belongings.

PATNA MUSEUM

Behind the impressive but decaying exterior, this **museum** (☎ 2235731; Buddha Marg; Indian/foreigner Rs10/250; 🕑 10.30am-4.30pm Tue-Sun) houses a splendid collection of Mauryan and Gupta stone sculptures. There's the usual collection of period weapons, including Humayun's dagger, and a gallery of wonderful Rajasthani miniatures. In another gallery is a motley collection of stuffed animals, including tigers, a large gharial (crocodile), a bizarre three-eared and eight-legged goat kid and an Australian wombat! Upstairs in a locked gallery an extra Rs500 permits you a glimpse of a tiny casket that's believed to contain some of Buddha's ashes which were retrieved from Vaishali (p573).

BIHAR & JHARKHAND

HAR MANDIR TAKHT

Behind a grand gate and sheltered from the mayhem of Patna's Chowk area is an important **Sikh shrine** (☎ 2642000). Its miniature marble domes, sweeping staircases and fine latticework mark the spot where Guru Gobind Singh, last of the 10 Sikh gurus, was born in 1666. It's 11km east of Gandhi Maidan. There is a free guide to show you around and you can show your appreciation of his services by putting a contribution in the temple donations box.

QILA HOUSE (JALAN MUSEUM)

This intriguing and eclectic private **museum** (☎ 2641121; Jalan Ave; admission free; ☼ by appointment only) overflows with antiques ranging from elaborate Mughal-period silverware and weaponry to the wooden bed of Napoleon III. Look for Marie Antoinette's Sèvres porcelain and the Crown Derby dinner service printed bold and garish for the failing eyes of King George III. To visit, telephone ahead and provide a photocopy of your passport identity and visa pages.

RUINS OF PATALIPUTRA

These historic **ruins** (Kankerbagh Rd; Indian/foreigner Rs5/100; ☼ 9am-sunset) are unfortunately often flooded, but excavations of this ancient capital have found evidence from the periods of Ajatasatru (491–459 BC), Chandragupta (321–297 BC) and Ashoka (274–237 BC). The ruins/ponds are surrounded by well cared for gardens and a **museum** that details the site's historic past.

KHUDA BAKHSH ORIENTAL LIBRARY

This fascinating **library** (☎ 2300209; Ashok Raj Path; admission free; ☼ 9.30am-5pm Sat-Thu), founded in 1900, contains a renowned collection of Arabic and Persian manuscripts, Mughal and Rajput paintings, and even the Quran inscribed in a book just 25mm wide. A significant exhibit is Nadir Shah's sword – perhaps this was the one he raised at Sunehri Mosque, Delhi, in 1739 to order the massacre of the city's residents.

Festivals & Events

Patna honours its historic past every March with **Pataliputra Mahotsava**, a celebration featuring parades, sports, dancing and music.

Sleeping

Most accommodation choices are around Fraser and Station Rds. Rooms below Rs1000 have a 5% tax, those above 10%.

BUDGET

Hotel Kautilya Vihar (☎ 2225411; bstdc@sancharnet.in; Birchand Patel Path; dm Rs100, d Rs600-1000, with AC Rs800-1200; ☒) The state tourism's sprawling hotel has clean and spacious rooms although it's well overdue for a paint job. It lacks atmosphere, but there's a restaurant, a bar and eager staff. The six-bed dorms are cramped.

LALU – LORD OF BIHAR

No chapter on Bihar would be complete without mention of India's most loathed and loved politician, Lalu Prasad Yadav. Although born into a low-caste family of cattle-herders, in a state where high-caste landowners have traditionally had a stranglehold on power, Lalu managed to mobilise the masses of his low-caste brethren and astonish all by rising to become chief minister of Bihar in 1990. Despite Lalu being a self-proclaimed champion of the poor, it is generally regarded little improved for them under his rule. Money was creamed off and just enough allowed to trickle down to keep his vote-bank happy. Bihar descended into the chaos that it struggles to escape today.

Lalu remained in power until 1997, when he was arrested and accused of milking millions out of an animal-husbandry program. He stepped aside, and in a move that shocked the nation, appointed his illiterate wife, Rabri Devi, as chief minister. He served little time behind bars and is now back and popular as ever. Although his wife was replaced as chief minister by Nitish Kumar in 2005, Lalu continued to lead a high profile life when in 2004 he was appointed Minister of Railways in the Congress-led Indian government. In a peculiar twist of fate he replaced Nitish Kumar, the previous railways minister in the BJP (Bharatiya Janata Party) government, and both have been lauded for the improvements they have made in their new jobs. Lalu still maintains a palatial mansion in Patna where he continues to meddle in state politics.

New Amar Hotel (☎ 2224157; s/d Rs260/400) The bright-green New Amar is the best of several budget hotels (some don't take foreigners because of the paperwork) down a small lane off Fraser Rd. Rooms are simple, fan-cooled and without hot water.

The following three, good, adjacent hotels in Station Rd are suspiciously alike in rooms, paint style, furniture and prices. All have 24-hour checkouts, lifts and room service instead of restaurants.

Hotel Magadh (☎ 2321278; s/d Rs550/700, with AC Rs800/995; 🞂) Non-AC rooms are the best value.

Hotel Ambassador (☎ 2321903; s/d Rs550/700, with AC Rs800/1050; 🞂) Smallish but cosy singles; the AC doubles are very good with clean carpets.

Hotel Maharaja Inn (☎ 2321292; s/d Rs550/700, with AC Rs950/1050; 🞂) Some bathrooms have squat toilets, so choose according to your skill in balancing with knees bent.

MIDRANGE & TOP END

Garden Court Club (☎ 3202279; www.gardencourtclub .com; SP Verma Rd; s/d Rs400/500, with AC from Rs700/900; 🞂) Take the lift within a small shopping complex up to the intimate 13-room Garden Court Club. Rooms differ; some have views, some have squat toilets, 11 have AC and we reckon the carpet-less deluxe rooms are the best value. The lovely faux-forest open-air rooftop restaurant is a big attraction.

Hotel President (☎ 2209203; s/d from Rs450/500, with AC Rs750/900; 🞂) This family-run hotel is in a relatively quiet location off Fraser Rd and close to Patna Museum. Rooms are simple, clean and reasonable value with TV and bucket hot water. We liked room 103.

our pick Hotel Windsor (☎ 2203250; www.hotel windsorpatna.com; Exhibition Rd; s/d/ste Rs1000/1200/1500; 🖥🞂) This is Patna's best midrange hotel, with well-designed rooms, spotless bathrooms, cheery and prompt service, good restaurant and internet centre. With a bar it'd be perfect.

Hotel Maurya Patna (☎ 2203040; www.maurya.com; South Gandhi Maidan; s/d from Rs4500/5000; 🖥🞂🞂) Fine appointments and luxurious surroundings distinguish Patna's top business hotel. The large gardens host a tempting pool (Rs350 for nonguests), and there are two good restaurants and a bar. Rooms are tastefully furnished, centrally air-conditioned and have wi-fi.

Eating & Drinking

Animated Fraser Rd is the main shopping street, with a buzz of restaurants and bars.

Basant Vihar (Fraser Rd; mains Rs30-70) There's nothing like a delicious dosa (paper-thin lentil-flour pancake) to tide over a lunch-hungry stomach. It's the 1st-floor restaurant you need, not the ground-floor one.

Hotel Rajasthan (Fraser Rd; ice creams Rs35-115, mains Rs50-105) Children drag their parents here for 16 types of ice cream and single/double/triple sundaes. Good food but typically North Indian rather than Rajasthani. Try the almond soup.

Mamta Bar and Restaurant (cnr Fraser & Dak Bungalow Rds; mains Rs50-120) A pleasant place for a few beers and meal chaser. The food and service excel.

Bellpepper Restaurant (Hotel Windsor, Exhibition Rd; mains Rs55-220; 🕑 noon-3.30pm & 7-11pm; 🞂) The Bellpepper is an intimate, contemporary restaurant popular for its tandoori dishes. The *murg tikka lababdar* (tandoori chicken basted with garlic, ginger, green chillies, and pistachio- and cashew-nut paste) is divine and shares the menu with Afghani dishes and Hyderabadi biryanis. No booze available.

Hotel Chanakya in Birchand Patel Path has two good restaurants. The downstairs **Samarat** (mains Rs130-225; 🕑 noon-11pm; 🞂) has a multicuisine family restaurant. The upstairs **Takshila** (mains Rs125-375; 🕑 noon-3.30pm & 7.30-11pm; 🞂) exudes the ambience of the North-West Frontier with its solid furniture and exposed brick decor. The speciality is meat-heavy Mughlai, Afghan and tandoori dishes. Vegetarians, try the Diwan-i-Handi, a creamy mixed-vegetable masala with fluffy butter naan (only a half portion is needed). You can order beer from the Madera Bar, or drink a well-cooled Kingfisher there with a ready supply of pappad and masala peanuts.

Shopping

Ajanta (Hotel Satka Arcade, Fraser Rd; 🕑 10.30am-8pm Mon-Sat) Come here for Patna's best selection of Mithila paintings (see opposite). Although most of the stock on display appears to be bronzes, the owner can show you a wide range of unmounted paintings starting from Rs300.

Getting There & Away
AIR

Air India (☎ 2222554; Gandhi Maidan) and **Jet Airways** (☎ 3298224; Patna airport) both fly daily to Delhi, from Rs4425 and Rs5496 respectively. **Kingfisher Red** (☎ 18002093030; Patna airport) flies daily to Delhi (from Rs4584) and Kolkata (from Rs4232).

BUS

The new Mithapur bus station occupies a large, dusty space about 1km south of the train station. Services include buses to Gaya (Rs50, three hours, hourly), Ranchi (Rs182, eight hours, 9pm) and Raxaul (Rs110, eight hours, 9.15am, 9.30pm).

From the Gandhi Maidan bus stand, government bus services travel to Ranchi (Rs184, 10 hours, 6am, 7am, 7.30pm, 9pm, 9.30pm, 10pm) and Raxaul (Rs114, eight hours, 10pm).

CAR

Hiring a car and driver is the best way for day trips from Patna. Most hotels and the BSTDC tourist office (p570) can arrange this service, starting from Rs6.5 per km (minimum 200km). Arrange an early start, as few drivers operate after dark.

TCI (☎ 2221699; www.tcindia.com; Hotel Maurya Patna, South Gandhi Maidan; ☽ 9.30am-6pm Mon-Sat) is a travel agency offering car rental. Local charges for four/eight/12 hours are Rs370/670/870; outstation is from Rs6.5 per km plus Rs225 per day.

TRAIN

Patna Junction is a chaotic station, but there's a **foreign-tourist ticket counter** (window No 7; ☽ 8am-8pm) at the 1st-floor reservation office, in the right-hand wing of the station.

There are four daily trains that run to Howrah station in Kolkata (sleeper/3AC/2AC Rs173/485/673, eight to 13 hours), 10 to Delhi (sleeper/3AC/2AC Rs301/845/1174, 12 to 28 hours) and three daily trains to Silguri/New Jalpaiguri for Darjeeling and Sikkim (sleeper/3AC/2AC Rs203/569/791, 10 to 14 hours).

Daily trains serve Varanasi (2nd class/sleeper/3AC Rs59/102/285, five hours, 11.50am), Gaya (sleeper/chair Rs54/122, 2½ hours, 11.40am, 9.25pm) and Ranchi (sleeper/chair/3A/2A Rs160/350/450/626, 10 to 12 hours, 11.40am, 3.30pm, 9.15pm).

Getting Around

The airport is located 7km west of the city centre. Autorickshaws to/from the city cost Rs80, while prepaid taxis cost around Rs200.

Shared autorickshaws shuttle between the train station and Gandhi Maidan bus stand (Rs5). For short trips, cycle-rickshaws are best.

AROUND PATNA

As the sights of Vaishali are well dispersed and transport to both Vaishali and Kesariya sporadic, it is far better to organise a car and driver (see left) for a longish day.

Vaishali

☎ 06225

Most sites in Vaishali surround a large tank. Dominating the skyline is a gleaming, modern **Japanese Peace Pagoda**, while opposite is a small **museum** (☎ 229404; admission Rs2; ☽ 10am-5pm Sat-Thu) presenting a collection of clay and terracotta figures plus an intriguing 1st- to 2nd-century AD toilet pan with appropriately sized exit holes. Nearby are the ground-floor remains of a **stupa** that contained Buddha's ashes that now reside in Patna Museum (p570).

Lord Mahavira, the 24th and final Jain *tirthankar* (teacher), was born about 3km away. An engraved stone marks the spot in a flower-decorated plot while an impressive Jain temple is being erected alongside.

A similar distance are the ruins of the **Kolhua Complex** (Indian/foreigner Rs5/100; ☽ 7am-5pm), comprising a hemispherical brick stupa guarded by a dignified lion squatting atop a 2300-year-old Ashoka pillar. The pillar is plain and contains no Ashokan edicts that were usually carved onto Ashoka pillars. Attending are the ruins of smaller stupas and monastic buildings. According to legend, Buddha was given a bowl of honey here by monkeys who

---

MITHILA PAINTINGS

Bihar's unique and most famous folk art is its Mithila (or Madhubani) paintings. Traditionally, wives from Madhubani and surrounding villages started creating strong line drawings on the walls of their homes from the first day of their marriage. Using pigments from spices, minerals, charcoal and vegetable matter, the women painted local deities and scenes from mythology, often intermingled with special events and aspects of everyday life.

These paintings, in both black and white and strong primary colours, are now professionally produced onto paper, canvas and textiles and are for sale. Original wall paintings can still be seen in homes around Madhubani, 160km northeast of Patna.

also dug out a rainwater tank for his water supply.

Hotel Amrapali Vihar (☎ 9431441655; r Rs350), a BSTDC hotel with rudimentary rooms, squat toilets and no hot water, is in a peaceful location overlooking the tank. As it's the only hotel you need to book ahead in season.

Kesariya

Rising high out of the earth from where the dying Buddha donated his begging bowl, this **stupa** (☉ 24hr) is an enthralling example how nature reclaimed a deserted monument. Excavated and half revealed from under a grassy and wooded veil, is what's likely to be the world's second-tallest (38m) Buddhist stupa dating from the Pala period. Above the 425m-circumference pedestal are five uniquely shaped terraces that form a gargantuan Buddhist tantric mandala. Each terrace has a number of niches containing mutilated Buddha statues whose heads were lopped off by Muslim invaders.

Sonepur
☎ 06654

According to the Gajendra Moksha legend, Sonepur is where Vishnu ended the prehistoric battle between the lords of the forest (elephants) and the lords of the water (crocodiles). Each November/December, during the full moon of Kartik Purnima, the three-week **Sonepur Mela** (p570) celebrates this infamous tale. During this auspicious time devotees bathe where the Ganges joins with the Gandak and Mehi Rivers while Asia's largest cattle fair takes place nearby at Hathi Bazaar. More than mere bovines are on sale – camels, birds, and probably the odd elephant change hands although trade in the latter is illegal. Mark Shand found his Tara here, the star of his book *Travels on my Elephant*. Tara is now resident at Kipling Lodge in Kanha National Park (p717).

BSTDC in Patna erects temporary straw huts prosaically called **Swiss Cottages** (☎ 2225411; d Rs2000) during the fair. They come with twin beds and plumbed-in private bathrooms.

Sonepur is 25km north of Patna across Mahatma Gandhi Setu. An autorickshaw direct to Sonepur should cost around Rs250.

Maner

Worth visiting 30km west of Patna is **Chhoti Dargah** (☉ 24hr), an architecturally elegant

three-storey mausoleum fronted by a large tank. The venerable Muslim saint Makhdum Shah Daulat was buried here in 1619 under a canopied tomb. As it is auspicious to be buried close to a saint, several cloth-covered graves in front of the mausoleum keep the saint company. The large body of water is a favourite swimming playground for local children and its steps provide a good laundry site.

Maner is well known for its sweets, so stop off on the way back for a chai and *ladoo* (yellow sweet made from flour and sugar) or *jalebi* (circular, deep-fried squiggly sweet).

RAXAUL
☎ 06255 / pop 41,347

Raxaul is a grim, dirty and crowded border town. Through it, and its twin Birganj over the border, pass most of the goods imported into Nepal. Consequently the road into Raxaul has been macerated by millions of heavy truck movements and is now no more than a dirt road. Raxaul, as you'd guess, is not a place to hang around. If you must spend the night, head to **Hotel Kaveri** (☎ 221148; Main Rd; d from Rs300), which has the cleanest rooms.

The Karai Tala bus stand is 200m down a western side road about 2km south of the border. There are three night buses to Patna (Rs110, six hours, 9pm). The *Mithila Express* train runs daily to Kolkata (train No 3022, SL/3AC/2AC Rs210/591/821, 18 hours, 10am).

GAYA

☎ 0631 / pop 383,197

Gaya is a raucous town 100km south of Patna. Although a centre for Hindu pilgrims, its primary interest to travellers is for transport to Bodhgaya, 13km away. Pilgrims come here to offer *pinda* (funeral cake) at the ghats along the river, and perform a lengthy circuit of the holy places around Gaya to free their ancestors from bondage to the earth.

Information

There's a **Bihar state tourist office** (☎ 2155420; ☽ 10am-8pm Mon-Sat) and a State Bank of India ATM at the train station. Next to the Hotel Heritage Inn is an ICICI Bank ATM. Bodhgaya has the nearest foreign exchange. Several **internet cafes** (per hr Rs30) line Swarajayapur Rd.

Sights & Activities

Close to the banks of the Falgu River south of town, the *sikhara* (spired) **Vishnupad Temple** was constructed in 1787 by Queen Ahilyabai of Maheshwar, Madhya Pradesh, and houses a 40cm 'footprint' of Vishnu imprinted into solid rock. Non-Hindus are not permitted to enter, but you can get a look from the pink platform near the entrance. Along the ghats on the river's edge, Hindus bathe and light funeral pyres, so be discreet in your visiting. Most likely you'll be approached by pandits offering prayers (Rs500) for your deceased ancestors.

One thousand stone steps lead to the top of the **Brahmajuni Hill**, 1km southwest of the Vishnupad Temple, where Buddha is said to have preached the fire sermon.

Sleeping & Eating

If you arrive late or have an early departure, staying here might be more convenient than Bodhgaya.

Hotel Akash (☎ 2222205; Laxman Sahay Rd; s/d Rs200/250) Pick of the budget places. The turquoise timber facade leads to an inner courtyard surrounded by clean, basic rooms with TV, and there's a relaxing open-air area upstairs. An air cooler costs an extra Rs150.

Hotel Vishnu International (☎ 2431146; Swarajayapur Rd; s Rs300, d Rs400-700, with AC Rs1000; ⊠)

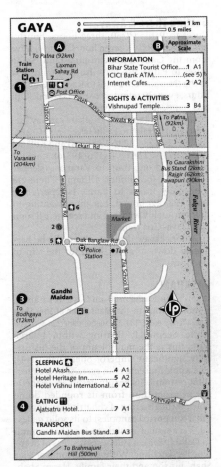

While the attention lavished on the French castle–like facade does not extend to the rooms of this hotel, this is still the best-value option in town. Clean and well kept, most rooms have TV, but hot water comes by bucket (Rs10).

Hotel Heritage Inn (☎ 2431009; Swarajayapur Rd; r Rs600, with AC Rs1200-1500) Located at the junction with Dak Bungalow Rd, this friendly place has a range of clean rooms. Only the more expensive rooms have top sheets, and some of the cheaper rooms don't have an external window.

Ajatsatru Hotel (Station Rd; mains Rs35-70) This hotel has a multicuisine restaurant that is a useful place for a bite while waiting for a train.

BIHAR & JHARKHAND

Getting There & Away

Buses to Patna (Rs50, three hours, hourly) and Ranchi (Rs101, seven hours, hourly) leave from the Gandhi Maidan bus stand. Some buses to Patna also leave from a stand next to the train station. Buses to Rajgir (Rs40, 2½ hours, every 30 minutes) use the Gaurakshini bus stand, across the river.

Gaya is on the Delhi–Kolkata railway line with regular trains to Delhi (sleeper/3AC/2AC Rs329/924/1284, 12 to 13 hours) and Kolkata (sleeper/3AC/2AC Rs176/493/685, eight hours), and one train to Varanasi (sleeper Rs102/310, four hours, 4.15am). There are four daily trains to Patna (sleeper/chair Rs54/122, 2½ hours). For those wanting to link spirituality with sun and sea there'll soon be a Gaya–Goa train.

Autorickshaw drivers can usually be bargained down to about Rs80 for the trip to Bodhgaya.

SASARAM

If you're motoring on from Gaya to Varanasi, a short detour to the **Mausoleum of Sher Shah** (Indian/foreigner Rs5/100; ☿ sunrise-sunset) is worthwhile. Seemingly floating within a large tank, this is the mausoleum of the historically significant emperor Sher Shah (p44). The whole museum is an exercise in architectural restraint. Its beauty lies in an aesthetic use of proportion from its rounded dome down through a ring of chhatris (pavilions or pillar-supported canopies) to its solid pedestal. Very similar in style to Isa Khan's tomb in Delhi (p135), it still bears vestiges of deep-blue Persian tiling. Within is the tomb of Sher Shah, his son and their family. Hasan Shah, father of Sher Shah, has his own less spectacular tomb minus a watery setting 200m away.

BODHGAYA

☎ 0631 / pop 30,883

This serene and spiritually important town attracts Buddhist pilgrims from around the world who journey here for prayer, study and meditation. It was here 2600 years ago that Prince Siddhartha Gautama attained enlightenment beneath a bodhi tree and became Buddha. A beautiful temple in a garden setting marks the spot and a descendent of that original bodhi tree flourishes here, its roots embedded in the same soil as its celebrated ancestor.

Many monasteries and temples dot the bucolic landscape, built in their national style by foreign Buddhist communities. Naturally Bodhgaya has the best range of accommodation and eating in Bihar, and all the attendant tourist paraphernalia and souvenir stalls.

The best time is October to March when Tibetan pilgrims come down from McLeod Ganj in Dharamsala and Bodhgaya becomes a sea of maroon and yellow robes. The Dalai Lama often visits in December and January. High season is mid-November to February.

Information

BOOKSHOPS

Kundan Bazaar (Bodhgaya Rd; www.kundanbazar.com; ☿ 7.30am-10pm) Novels and Buddhist literature. Book swap or hire.

Mahabodhi Bookshop (Mahabodhi Temple; ☿ 5am-9pm) Within the temple complex entrance. Range of Buddhist literature.

INTERNET ACCESS

Magadh Internet Dhaba (Bodhgaya Rd; per hr Rs40; ☿ 8am-9pm)

Vishnu Cyber Cafe (Bodhgaya Rd; per hr Rs30; ☿ 8am-9.30pm)

MEDICAL SERVICES

Verma Health Care Centre (☎ 2201101; ☿ 24hr) Emergency room and clinic.

MONEY

State Bank of India (☎ 2200852; Bodhgaya Rd) Best rates for cash and travellers cheques; has an ATM.

POST

Main post office (☎ 2200472; cnr Bodhgaya & Godam Rds)

TOURIST INFORMATION

BSTDC Tourist Complex (☎ 2200672; cnr Bodhgaya Rd & Temple St; ☿ 10.30am-5pm Tue-Sat) Little more than dusty brochures.

TRAVEL AGENCIES

Middle Way Travels (☎ 2200648; Bodhgaya Rd; ☿ 9am-10pm) A sign of success is when others open businesses with similar names. This is the one to deal with. Almost opposite the temple entrance, the agency exchanges currency and travellers cheques, sells or swaps books, and deals with ticketing and car hire.

Sights & Activities

MAHABODHI TEMPLE

The magnificent World Heritage–listed **Mahabodhi Temple** (admission free, camera/video Rs20/500;

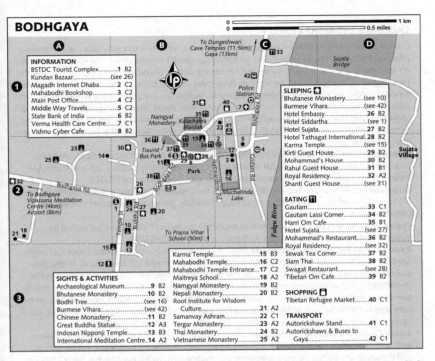

5am-9pm), where Buddha attained enlightenment and formulated his philosophy of life, forms the spiritual heart of Bodhgaya.

The Mahabodhi Temple was built in the 6th century AD atop the site of a temple erected by Emperor Ashoka almost 800 years earlier. After being razed by 11th-century Muslim invaders, the temple underwent major restorations, the last in 1882. Topped by a 50m pyramidal spire, the ornate structure houses a 2m-high gilded image of a seated Buddha. Amazingly, four of the original sculpted stone railings surrounding the temple, dating from the Sunga period (184–72 BC), have survived amid the replicas.

Thankfully, before Ashoka's wife killed the original **Bodhi Tree** (she was jealous of Ashoka's attention towards it), one of its saplings was carried off to Anuradhapura, in Sri Lanka, by Sanghamitta (Ashoka's daughter). That tree continues to flourish and provided a cutting that was carried back to Bodhgaya and planted where the original had stood. The red sandstone slab between the tree and the temple was placed there by Ashoka and marks the spot of Buddha's enlightenment – it's referred to as the Vajrasan (Diamond Throne).

Pilgrims and visitors from all walks of life and religions come to worship or just soak up the ambience of this sacred place. An enthralling way to start or finish the day is to stroll around the perimeter of the temple compound and watch a sea of maroon and yellow dip and rise as monks perform endless prostrations on their prayer boards.

MONASTERIES & TEMPLES

The different monasteries offer visitors a unique opportunity to peek into different Buddhist cultures and compare architectural styles. For example, the **Indosan Nipponji Temple** (☻ 5am-noon & 2-6pm) is an exercise in quiet Japanese understatement compared to its richly presented **Bhutan** neighbour. The most impressive is the **Thai Monastery**, a brightly coloured *wat* with shimmering gold leaf and manicured gardens. Meditation sessions are held here in the morning. The Tibetan **Karma Temple** and **Namgyal Monastery** each contain large prayer wheels, and the brand new **Tergar Monastery** of the Karmapa (Black Hat sect) is a glory of Tibetan decorative arts. Other noteworthy monasteries include those from

BIHAR & JHARKHAND

CHOOSING THE RIGHT CHARITY

Central Bihar is one of the poorest parts of India and with its influx of visitors and Buddhist pilgrims, Bodhgaya has become home to numerous charity organisations and schools that rely on donations and volunteers. Some are set up by dodgy characters jumping on the charity bandwagon to fleece tourists. Be wary of those who approach you in the street for donations, especially children who besiege tourists asking for money for everything from school books and educational sponsorship to new cricket bats – they may speak several languages but are most likely illiterate. Genuine charities advise that you never give money directly to children. It's far better to help by donating to legitimate institutions or volunteering. The following are some local organisations:

Maitreya School (☎ 2200620; www.maitreyaeducation.org) One of the largest and best-established school projects in Bodhgaya, Maitreya has over 500 students attending day and evening classes. As well as education, free uniforms, books, meals and health care are provided. You can sponsor a child for a year (US$240).

Niranjana Public Welfare School (☎ 9934057511; www.npws.org) This school provides education for some 270 local children and runs an orphanage in Sujata Village. Donations, sponsorships and volunteers are welcome. Contact the curator Siddhartha Kumar.

Prajna Vihar School Volunteers are sometimes required for this nonprofit village school just south of the Mahabodhi Temple. For information, contact the **Burmese Vihar** (☎ 2200721).

Root Institute for Wisdom Culture (☎ 2200714; www.rootinstitute.com) This Buddhist meditation centre (see below) runs an established charitable health program, providing free health care to villagers via an onsite hospital and mobile clinic. Visitors are welcome to call in to see the health program at work. Skilled volunteers (nurses, physiotherapists etc) are occasionally needed to train local health workers – see the volunteer section of the website.

Samanvay Ashram (☎ 09934463202; samanvayashram@hotmail.com) This Gandhian ashram has been run for many years by Dwarko Sundrani, and works with disadvantaged village children, providing education, clothing and medicine. It is now also providing free eye operations. Volunteers are welcome to come and learn.

Sujata Children's Welfare Foundation (☎ 9934145989, 9431207949; www.sujatachildren.dk) Sujata works with local orphans and poor children, providing free education, clothing and medical care. You can sponsor a child through the organisation's website, or volunteer with teaching skills and building projects at Sujata Village just outside Bodhgaya.

China, **Burma**, **Vietnam** and **Nepal**. Monasteries are open sunrise to sunset.

OTHER ATTRACTIONS

A 25m-high **Great Buddha Statue** (☯ 7am–noon & 2–5pm) towers above a pleasant garden at the end of Temple St. The impressive monument was unveiled by the Dalai Lama in 1989, and is surrounded by 10 smaller sculptures of Buddha's disciples. The statue is partially hollow and is said to contain some 20,000 bronze Buddhas.

The **archaeological museum** (☎ 2200739; admission Rs2; ☯ 10am–5pm Sat–Thu) contains a small collection of local Buddha figures, but pride of place goes to part of the original granite railings and pillars rescued from the Mahabodhi Temple.

Courses

The **Root Institute for Wisdom Culture** (☎ 2200714; www.rootinstitute.com; ☯ office 8.30–11.30am & 1.30–4.30pm) holds popular introductory 10-day meditation courses from late October to March that are useful for beginners. A requested donation of Rs7020 covers the course, accommodation and meals. Intermediate-level courses are also scheduled from December to February. The 6.45am 45-minute meditation session is open to all, and for a donation visitors are welcome to stay on for breakfast. Visit the website for other events.

Bodhgaya Vipassana Meditation Centre (Dhamma Bodhi; ☎ 220437; www.dhamma.org) runs intensive 10-day vipassana courses twice each month throughout the year. The small compound is 4km west of town and runs on donations.

The courses at the **International Meditation Centre** (☎ 2200707; per day Rs100) are more informal and students can start and finish any time they choose, all year-round.

Tergar Monastery (☎ 2201256; www.tergar.org) runs a variety of courses on Tibetan Buddhism and welcomes long-term qualified volunteer English teachers.

Other courses are sometimes advertised at local restaurants and the Burmese Vihara.

Sleeping

Prices listed are for November through March and can fall by 50% in the low season, so it pays to negotiate.

BUDGET

Mohammad's House (☎ 9934022691, 9431085251; s/d Mar-Sep from Rs100/150, Oct-Feb from Rs200/300) A wonderful opportunity to live within a village. Rooms are basic but popular with long-term stayers and Mohammad is a mine of useful information and advice. A rooftop terrace gives commanding views of rice paddies, sunsets and monasteries, and during November to February has a kitchen for residents to use.

Several guest houses back onto the Kalachakra Maidan. At **Rahul Guest House** (☎ 2200709; s/d Rs150/250) the upstairs rooms with whitewashed walls, nice breezes and simple furnishings are better than those on the ground floor. **Shanti Guest House** (☎ 2200129; www.shanti-guesthouse.com; s/d from Rs200/250, with AC Rs450/650; ☒ ▣) has similar rooms, the cheaper having shared bathrooms.

If you don't mind some simple rules, it's possible to stay at some of the monasteries. The **Bhutanese Monastery** (☎ 2200710; Buddha Rd; d Rs250, with bathroom Rs300) is a tranquil place typified by colourful surroundings, gardens and big rooms. The Tibetan **Karma Temple** (☎ 2200795; Temple St; d with shared bathroom Rs250) has a similar feel. The **Burmese Vihara** (☎ 2200721, 06112-696464; Bodhgaya Rd; r Rs50) is popular with foreigners; there's a maximum stay of three days unless you're engaged in dharma studies.

MIDRANGE

Hotel Siddartha (☎ 2200127; Bodhgaya Rd; d Rs400, with AC Rs600) The best of the BSTDC accommodation though it's still a bit austere. Rooms are in an unusual circular building overlooking a quiet garden area.

Kirti Guest House (☎ 2200744; kirtihouse744@yahoo.com; Bodhgaya Rd; s/d Rs800/1100) Run by the Tibetan Monastery and one of the best of the midrange places, Kirti has clean, bright rooms behind a monastery-like facade. Go for one of the front rooms opening out onto the balcony. All rooms have TV and (eventual) hot water.

Hotel Embassy (☎ 2200711; embassyhotelbodhgaya@yahoo.com; Bodhgaya Rd; s/d Rs1050/1350, with AC Rs1200/1500; ☒) This central, no-frills hotel is looking a bit old and dated, though all rooms have TV and hot water and the management is welcoming. Prices tumble for February to October.

Hotel Tathagat International (☎ 2200106; www.hoteltathagatbodhgaya.net; Bodhgaya Rd; s/d Rs1400/1700, with AC Rs1700/2000; ☒) This place has simple and conservatively furnished rooms, but is clean and efficiently run. Some rooms have balconies and all have TV and hot water. Avoid the Mahabodhi Temple–end rooms above the generator.

TOP END

Hotel Sujata (☎ 2200761; www.hotelsujata.com; Buddha Rd; s/d/ste Rs3200/3600/4800; ☒ ▣) Swish, spacious rooms with soft beds, an excellent restaurant, and his and hers *o-furo* (communal Japanese baths) make this hotel, opposite the Thai Monastery, the most interesting in the top-end range. The Japanese bath is only available to groups of 10 or more, so find some friends.

Royal Residency (☎ 2200124; www.theroyalresidency.net/bodhgaya; Bodhgaya Rd; s/d/tr/ste Rs6000/6500/7500/8500; ☒ ▣) Bodhgaya's most luxurious hotel stands in a quiet location about 1.5km west of the centre. Fine woodwork, rich marble, pleasant gardens and comfy rooms await those who are not too concerned about value for money.

Eating & Drinking

During the peak season, when Tibetan pilgrims pour into Bodhgaya, temporary tent restaurants are set up next to the Tibetan refugee market and serve a range of Tibetan dishes and sweets.

Unfortunately eating places sometimes decline once they've established themselves in our guides, so if you find one boldly advertising its Lonely Planet credentials but absent from the following listings, there's a chance that this is the case.

The first two places reviewed here stand above the rest.

Mohammad's Restaurant (Kalachakra Maidan; mains Rs20-60) A small tent restaurant behind the well-lit Fujia Green. OK, it's not a flash joint, but it has some of the town's best Indian food and those in the know flock to it. Mohammad also runs one of the temporary tent restaurants.

Tibetan Om Cafe (dishes Rs20-60; ☽ 7am-9pm) Lies within the western courtyard of Namgyal Monastery. It's run by friendly Tibetans who know all about traveller hunger for *momos* (dumplings), pancakes, brown bread, pies and cakes. The food is cheap and superb, and you can loiter for as long as you like. For just Rs5

BIHAR & JHARKHAND

you can refill your water bottle with 'well-boiled filter water'. A small shop here sells Tibetan items and clothing.

Gautam (Bodhgaya Rd; mains Rs20-80) Opposite the Burmese Vihara is this basic semi-tent affair with a sit-out garden. It offers a standard travellers menu and the banana pancakes are the best in town.

Swagat Restaurant (Hotel Tathagat International, Bodhgaya Rd; mains Rs50-150) A really good choice with an innovative menu of veg and non-veg dishes, such as *mutton badam pasanda* (mutton stuffed with almonds and cooked in an almond gravy), Portuguese-style fish and a creamy *malai kofta* (fried cottage-cheese dumplings served in a spicy tomato and onion based gravy).

Harri Om Cafe (mains Rs80-150) At the northern end of the Kalachakra Maidan, this is the only place in Bodhgaya for real coffee. It also does good pasta and has Korean items on the menu, and while you wait you can get a body work-over in the massage centre.

Siam Thai (Bodhgaya Rd; mains Rs80-400) A new restaurant serving some authentic Thai dishes. The walls are decorated with all the menu items you might consider, while an inscrutable and plump Buddha observes everything. Service is friendly and helpful.

The **Royal Residency** (Bodhgaya Rd; mains Rs70-150) and **Hotel Sujata** (Buddha Rd; mains Rs65-200) are similar high-class restaurants in two of Bodhgaya's upmarket hotels. They are the only ones in town to officially serve alcohol (Rs240 for a beer).

Other suggestions:

Gautam Lassi Corner (Bodhgaya Rd) Opposite Mahabodhi Temple, serves up creamy lassis and juices.

Sewak Tea Corner (snacks Rs10-30) On the edge of the bus parking lot, has Indian sweets, thalis, lassis and chai.

Shopping

Tibetan refugee market (🕐 8am-8pm Oct-Jan) The place to pick up winter woollens or textiles, and you'll be helping the Tibetan community in exile. Elsewhere there are scores of souvenir stalls.

Getting There & Away

Overcrowded shared autorickshaws (Rs20) and occasional buses (Rs5) leave outside the Burmese Vihara for the 13km to Gaya. A private autorickshaw to Gaya should cost Rs80.

Gaya airport is 8km west of town. **Air India** (☎ 2201155; airport) flies once a week to Kolkata;

during the high season there are direct international flights from Bangkok (Thailand), Thimphu (Bhutan) and Yangon (Myanmar).

DUNGESHWARI CAVE TEMPLES

The hillside Dungeshwari cave where Buddha underwent years of penance before descending to Bodhgaya is 12km northeast of Bodhgaya. As the site is not signposted in English, it's best to hire an autorickshaw in Bodhgaya (Rs200) that'll take you to the base of a concrete path wending up the hillside. Expect plenty of begging children and men selling biscuits for you to give to them. It's either a scam or bad diet option.

RAJGIR
☎ 06112 / pop 33,691

Surrounded by five semiarid rocky hills, each lined with vestiges of ancient 'cyclopean' walls, is the ancient capital of Magadha, known today as Rajgir. Thanks to both Buddha and Mahavira spending some serious time here, Rajgir is an important pilgrimage site for Buddhists and Jains. A mention in the Mahabharata also ensures that Rajgir has a good supply of Hindu pilgrims who come to bathe in the hot springs at the Lakshmi Narayan Temple.

For travellers, a couple of days spent exploring the many historic Buddhist sites around Rajgir and the ancient university site of Nalanda (opposite), 12km south of town, provides the perfect complement to Bodhgaya, 80km away.

Rajgir Mahotsava, held in October, is the town's three-day cultural festival featuring Indian classical and folk music and dance.

Information

The centre lies 500m east of the main road, on which you'll find the train station, bus stand and a number of hotels. There's a BSTDC tourist office at the Hotel Gautam Vihar, about 1km south of the train station, and a **State Bank of India ATM** (Bank Rd) about 200m west of the bus stand.

Sights & Activities

About 5km south of town, a wobbly, single-person **ropeway** (chairlift; return ticket Rs30; 🕐 8.15am-1pm & 2-5pm) runs to the top of Ratnagiri Hill and its blazing white 40m-high **Vishwashanti Stupa**. Recesses in the stupa feature golden statues of Buddha in the four stages of his life –

AJATASATRU: THE UNBORN ENEMY

According to legend, in the 6th century BC Bimbisara, the elderly ruler of the Magadha kingdom, was without an heir. He called on a seer who told him that there was an old hermit three years from death in the distant hills and when the hermit died his spirit would impregnate Bimbisara's wife, Vaidehi. The impatient Bimbisara ordered the hermit killed and soon Vaidehi was expecting.

However, the news was not all good for Bimbisara, as the hermit had cursed the future heir in his last breath. This led to numerous bad omens and prophecies that Bimbisara's heir would grow up to murder him and usurp the throne. Bimbisara grew fearful and named his son Ajatasatru, which translates as 'he whose enemy is not born'.

Bimbisara may have tried to have Ajatasatru killed on a few occasions, but the boy always eluded death. He grew up to seize the crown and starve his father to death in prison.

---

birth, enlightenment, preaching and death. Expansive views reveal some of the 26 Jain shrines dotting the distant hilltops. If you walk back down, you can detour to the remains of a stupa and **Griddhakuta** (Vulture's Peak), where Buddha preached to his disciples.

Spread around town are relics of the ancient city, caves and places associated with Ajatasatru and Bimbisara (see the boxed text, above). Hindu pilgrims are drawn to the rowdy and very pink **Lakshmi Narayan Temple complex**, about 2km south of town, to enjoy the health benefits of the hot springs. Brahmakund, the hottest spring, is a scalding 45°C. Temple priests will show you around, pour hot water on you and ask for generous donations (Rs100 to Rs200 would be appropriate).

The easiest way to see Rajgir's scattered sites is to rent a tonga, which should cost about Rs400 for a half-day.

Sleeping & Eating

Hotel Gautam Vihar (☎ 255273; Nalanda Rd; dm Rs75, d Rs450, with AC Rs700; ✗) One of three Bihar Tourism (BSTDC) hotels in town, this is well located between the bus and train stations, and the spacious, clean rooms have lounge chairs, TV and hot water.

Hotel Siddharth (☎ 255616; s/d Rs450/650, d with AC Rs750; ✗) A bit of a hike south of the bus and train stations, and near the hot springs, Siddharth has a pleasant walled courtyard, good-sized rooms and an enjoyable restaurant.

Rajgir Residency (☎ 255404; www.rajgir-residency.com; s/d US$95/115) A top-end choice offering expensive luxury for tour guests.

Centaur Hokke Hotel (☎ 255245; centaur@dte.vsnl.net.in; s/d Rs6000/6500; ✗ 🖵 ☎) Surrounded by lovely manicured gardens, this is Bihar's unique sleeping experience. Most of the rooms are furnished Japanese-style with tatami mats instead of beds, teak furniture and Eastern decor. Soak in the Japanese bathhouse and meditate in the towering cylindrical Buddhist prayer hall.

Green Restaurant (mains Rs24-68) Opposite the temple complex and hot springs just south of town, this simple restaurant offers some of the best Indian meals in town.

Lotus Restaurant (meals US$2-22) At the Centaur Hokke Hotel, this elegant restaurant with high-backed chairs and long tables is part Japanese, part Indian. The Japanese menu features soba noodles, teriyaki and tempura with authentic flavours and fresh ingredients. A memorable dining experience.

While the beloved puff-pastry sweet known as *khaja* is sold throughout Bihar, its origins lay in the tiny village of Silao, just north of Rajgir.

Getting There & Around

Frequent buses run to Gaya (Rs50, 2½ hours) and Patna (Rs70, three hours) from the bus stand on the Nalanda road. Ridiculously crowded shared jeeps shuttle between Rajgir and Nalanda (Rs12). Three daily trains connect Rajgir (SL/CC/3AC/2AC Rs30/122/158/218, 2½ hours, 8.10am, 2.50pm, 11pm) with Patna.

AROUND RAJGIR
Nalanda
☎ 061194

Founded in the 5th century AD, Nalanda was the ancient world's great university and an important Buddhist centre. When Chinese scholar and traveller Xuan Zang visited sometime between 685 and 762 AD, 10,000 monks and students lived here, studying theology, astronomy, metaphysics, medicine and philosophy. It's said that Nalanda's three libraries were so extensive they burnt for six months when invaders sacked the university in the 12th century.

Allow an hour or two for wandering the extensive **ruins** (Indian/foreigner Rs5/100; 9am-5.30pm) – they're peaceful and well-maintained with a park-like atmosphere of clipped lawns, shrubs and roses. A guide (Rs50 per hour) is a worthwhile investment in unravelling the labyrinthine buildings and their history. The red-brick ruins consist of nine monasteries and four main temples. Most impressive is the **Great Stupa**, with steps, terraces, a few intact votive stupas, and monks' cells.

Across from the entrance is the **archaeological museum** (admission Rs2; 10am-4.45pm Sat-Thu), a small but fascinating museum housing the Nalanda University seal and a host of sculptures and bronzes unearthed from Nalanda and Rajgir. Along with the many Buddha figures and Picasso-like 9th-century Kirtimukha (gargoyle), look out for the bizarre many-spouted pot.

About 2km further on is the huge **Xuan Zang Memorial Hall** (admission free; 9am-5pm), built by the Chinese as a peace pagoda in honour of the famous Chinese traveller who studied and taught for some years at Nalanda. Modern-day backpackers will appreciate the statue of Xuan Zang at the front.

Regular shared jeeps run between Rajgir and Nalanda village (Rs15), and from there you can take a shared tonga (Rs20) for the final 3km to the site.

Pawapuri

Mahavira, the final *tirthankar* and founder of Jainism, died and was cremated here about 500 BC, making Pawapuri a major Jain pilgrimage centre. Legend has it that the demand for Mahavira's sacred ashes was so great that copious amounts of soil were removed from around his funeral pyre, creating a massive, often lotus-filled, tank. Simmering in the middle of the tank is the beautifully proportioned, white marble temple of Jalmandir, which shelters Mahavira's cremation place.

JHARKHAND

Jharkhand was hewn out of neighbouring Bihar in 2000 to meet the autonomy demands of the Adivasi (tribal) population. Despite the fledgling state having a jaw-dropping 40% of the country's mineral wealth (mostly coal, copper and iron ore), rich forests, several major industrial centres and the healthy budget of a newly formed state, it still suffers thanks to poverty, incompetence, corruption, and outbursts of Maoist and Naxalite violence. For travellers, Jharkhand's prime attractions are its national parks, the waterfalls around the capital Ranchi, and the chance to explore a tourist-free northern India.

RANCHI

 0651 / pop 846,454

Set on a plateau at 700m and marginally cooler than the plains, Jharkhand's capital, Ranchi, was the summer capital of Bihar under the British. There's little of interest in the city and it's not really on the way to anywhere except Betla (Palamau) National Park (opposite).

Information

There's a **tourist office** (2332179; samridhi travels@rediffmail.com; Main Rd; 8am-8pm) at the Birsa Vihar tourist complex that will also make railway reservations and accommodation bookings. The **State Bank of India** (Main Rd; 10am-3.30pm Mon-Fri) changes cash and travellers cheques, and has an ATM. **Simmer Broadband Cafe** (Gurunanak Market, Station Rd; per hr Rs20; 8am-11pm), within a small shopping centre next to Hotel Embassy, has internet access.

In the same shopping centre is **Suhana Tour and Travels** (3293808, 9431171394; suhana_jharkhand tour@yahoo.co.in; 10am-8pm), which organises day trips to local waterfalls (from Rs175), three-day trips to Betla National Park (from Rs4200 for four people), and other transport ticketing.

Sights & Activities

The **Jagannath Temple**, about 12km southwest of town (Rs100 by autorickshaw), is a smaller version of the great Jagannath Mandir at Puri (p654), and is open to non-Hindus. Every year, at the same time and in the same manner as in Puri, Jagannath and his brother and sister gods are charioted to their holiday home, a smaller temple some 500m away.

The **Tribal Research Institute Museum** (2541824; Murabadi; admission free; 8am-6pm Mon-Fri, 8am-1pm Sat) is also worth a visit to delve into the history of Jharkhand's many tribal groups, including the Asurs, Mundas and Gonds. The museum is not signed in English and is about 200m from Murabadi stadium.

There are several pretty waterfalls that can be visited on day trips from Ranchi. The most spectacular, especially after the monsoon, is the **Hundru Falls**, 45km northeast of the city.

Sleeping & Eating

Station Rd, running between the train and bus stations, is lined with hotels of varying quality, though few are interested in checking in foreigners because of the paperwork required. Other hotels and restaurants can be found on the seemingly endless Main Rd, running at right angles to Station Rd.

Hotel Birsa Vihar (☎ 2331828; Main Rd) Jharkhand Tourism's hotel was undergoing badly needed renovation at the time of research.

Hotel Amrit (☎ 2461952; Station Rd; s/d from Rs300/300, with AC Rs900/1150; ✷) A cheap option close to the embassy but with unremarkable rooms. Checkout is 24 hours.

Hotel Embassy (☎ 2460449; embassyhotel@rediffmail .com; Station Rd; s/d Rs600/700, with AC from Rs700/850; ✷) One of the few budget places along Station Rd to accept foreigners; the comfortable AC rooms are refreshingly contemporary and decently clean. It's a goodie.

our pick **BNR Guesthouse** (☎ 2461481; Station Rd; chanakyabnrranchi@hotmail.com; r Rs2000; ✷) The best-value hotel in Ranchi. Almost opposite the train station, this red-tiled terracotta-roofed Raj relic is a most pleasant haven. The large rooms and bathrooms have been pleasantly renovated with modern furniture and equipment, and the service is very friendly. Additional rooms are being built, and the older rooms opening out onto a verandah and the well-tended lawns are being kept.

Hotel Capitol Hill (☎ 2331330; www.hotelcapitol hill.com; Main Rd; s/d Rs4000/4500; ✷ ▯) A classy upmarket hotel in the Capitol Hill shopping complex. The ultramodern 3rd-floor lobby with cream leather chairs complements equally modern rooms with a Scandinavian touch and wi-fi. The restaurant and bar are also Ranchi's most stylish.

Planet Masala (☎ 3291765; 56C Main Rd; mains Rs50-85) Spotless and with a funky interior – high ceilings and a glassed-in upper AC level – this modern cafe is a great escape from Main Rd. Along with a full menu of dosas, thalis, veg pizzas and Chinese dishes, there's proper coffee, sundaes and chocolate biscuits.

The Nook (☎ 2460128; Station Rd; mains Rs55-140) The best restaurant in the train station area; the dining room in Hotel Kwality Inns is comfortable and the service attentive without being obsequious. The food is good – plenty of taste without over-relying on chillies – and beer is available.

Getting There & Away

Kingfisher Red (☎ 18002093030; airport) flies daily to Kolkata (from Rs2828), Delhi (from Rs5087) and Patna (from Rs2828). **Air India** (☎ 2331342; Main Rd) has daily flights to Delhi (from Rs4925) and Mumbai (from Rs5825).

Buses to Gaya (Rs130, seven hours, hourly) and Patna (Rs200, eight hours, hourly) leave the main bus stand from 6am, while buses to Daltonganj (for Betla National Park) leave from the Ratu Rd bus stand (Rs95, six hours, hourly). From the Birsa Vihar tourist complex on Main Rd there are two deluxe buses to Patna at 8am (Rs170, nine hours) and 8pm (Rs200).

The *Hatia-Patna Express* (train No 8626, 06.25am) calls at Gaya (CC Rs291, 6½ hours) and Patna (CC Rs476, 10 hours). For Kolkata you can take the *Shatabdi* (train No 2020, CC Rs474, 7½ hours, 1.45pm) or the overnight *Howrah-Hatia Express* (train No 8616, SL/3AC/2AC Rs164/459/638, eight hours, 10.45pm).

BETLA (PALAMAU) NATIONAL PARK
☎ 06562

This undisputed natural gem is 140km west of Ranchi and one of the better places in India to see wild elephants. Tiger sightings are comparatively rare. The park covers around 1026 sq km, while the core area of 232 sq km was declared as Betla National Park in 1989. Stands of sal forest, rich evergreens, teak trees and bamboo thickets are home to some 17 tigers, 52 leopards, 216 elephants and four lonely nilgai (antelope) according to a 2007 census. There are several rickety observation towers for the brave to climb and lie low while watching wildlife in silence. This area was the seat of power of the Adivasi kings of the Chero dynasty and the ruins of its 16th-century forts and 10km of walls still exist in the jungle.

The **park** (☎ 222650, 9973819242; admission per vehicle Rs100, camera/video Rs60/80; ✷ 5am-7pm) is open year-round, but the best time to visit is October to April. If you can stand the heat, May is prime time for tiger spotting as forest cover is reduced and animals venture out in search of waterholes. **Jeep safaris** (per hr Rs200) can be arranged privately at the park gate. You must also hire a local **guide** (per hr Rs25) to accompany you.

The park has **elephant safaris** (per hr Rs100, up to 4 people) that plod into the jungle for an unparalleled look at the flora and fauna.

The government-run **Van Vihar** (☎ 06567-226513; dm Rs100, d from Rs400, with AC Rs900; ✷) is the best of limited accommodation around the park entrance and is open all year. The decrepit but spacious rooms are being renovated. More interesting accommodation is the **Tree House** (☎ park office 9973819242; r Rs500), with two elevated sets of rooms built out of teak and containing two bedrooms, a bathroom and an observation deck. Alternatively, there is the nearby **Forest Lodge** (☎ 222282; r Rs250) with smallish but adequate rooms, shared bathrooms and no hot water.

The nearest town to the park entrance is Daltonganj, 25km away. There are five daily buses between Betla and Daltonganj (Rs18, one hour) or you can arrange a taxi for around Rs300. Daltonganj is connected to Ranchi by bus (Rs98, six hours, hourly). Alternatively, organise a tour through a Ranchi travel agency that will take you directly to the park. Suhana Tour and Travels (p582) has two-day trips, or longer, from Rs3200 per person, including transport, accommodation and safari. This is probably the best option considering the inadequate transport and safety issues in this isolated and sometimes lawless part of the state. In any case, call the park for security advice before leaving.

PARASNATH
☎ 06532

Parasnath, a dusty town in eastern Jharkhand, is the railhead for the major Jain pilgrimage centre in east India. The site and its many temples blanket the top of **Parasnath Hill** – Jharkhand's highest point. At the summit (1366m), where the Parasnath Temple now stands, 23 of the 24 Jain *tirthankars* reached salvation, including Parasnath at the age of 100.

The southern approach is from Isri Bazar, with the first 2km accessible by transport and thereafter 8km of climbing. The easier approach is from Madhuban, 13km northeast of Parasnath, from where about the first 9km can be covered by transport. The walk up through lush forest is as rewarding as the grand view from the top. If you don't want to walk you can hire a *dandi* – a cart carried by two men.

The whole mountain circuit is 29km, taking about eight hours, so a start before dawn is essential. You must carry all the water you'll need.

If you're staying the night, there are some *dharamsalas* (pilgrims guest houses) in Madhuban and a **tourist lodge** (☎ 0658232378). In Isri Bazar there's the Hotel Bhavan and more *dharamsalas*.

Parasnath is on the Kolkata–Gaya–Delhi train line. A few daily trains run to Gaya (SL/3AC/2AC Rs75/211/293, three hours) and Kolkata (SL/3AC/2AC Rs176/493/685, six hours). Regular minibuses run from Parasnath's bus stand to Madhuban.

Sikkim

If you're suffering from too much heat, city dust and dirt, or just crowd overload, then a spell in the little, former kingdom of Sikkim is the perfect antidote. Clean, fresh mountain air sweeps the state; there's room to move and even feel alone, but the people are among India's most friendly, with a charming manner that's unobtrusive and slightly shy.

Plunging mountain valleys are lushly forested, interspersed with rice terraces and flowering rhododendrons. Tibetan-style Buddhist monasteries (gompas) add splashes of white, gold and vermilion to the green ridges and are approached through avenues of colourful prayer flags.

Sikkim's big-ticket item is the majesty of Khangchendzonga (Kanchenjunga, 8598m), the world's third-highest mountain straddling the border between Sikkim and Nepal. Khangchendzonga's guardian spirit is worshipped in a series of spectacular autumn festivals and its magnificent white peaks and ridges can be spied from many points around the state. Dawn is its best show, when the sun lights up the eastern face.

An independent kingdom until 1975, Sikkim has long been considered one of the last Himalayan Shangri Las. But hurry. In the last few years a tourist boom has seen an increase in domestic visitors escaping the lowlands' heat. Every year more concrete hotels appear in once -idyllic villages, and most towns are already lacklustre huddles of multistorey box-homes.

Sikkim is tiny, only approximately 80km from east to west and 100km north to south but, due to the terrain, it is slow to traverse. Your next destination, over the valley, looks so close but it may be three or four hours away.

HIGHLIGHTS

- Wonder at the might of nature carving out different landscapes on a trip from **Lachung** to **Yumthang Valley** (p606)
- Be enthralled by a *chaam* dance at **Rumtek gompa** (p594)
- Wake up in **Pelling** (p598) to watch the dawn Khangchendzonga show from the comfort of your hotel
- Join the locals in some tongba (Himalayan millet beer) drinking, in mountain-edge villages like **Thanggu** (p608)
- Wander through the prayer flag–bannered chorten compound of ancient **Tashiding Gompa** (p605) and have your sins washed away by gazing on the chorten of Thong-Wa-Rang-Dol

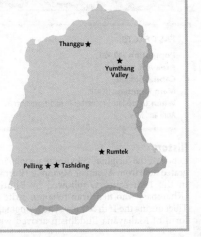

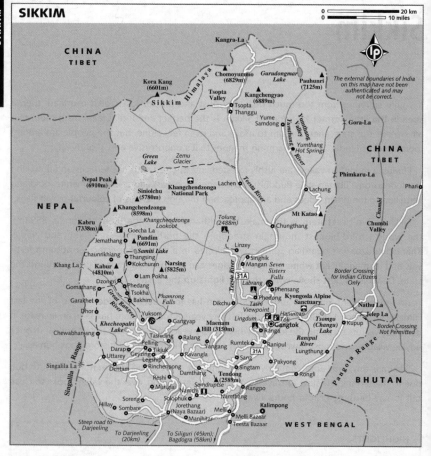

SIKKIM

The external boundaries of India
on this map have not been
authenticated and may
not be correct.

FAST FACTS

Population 540,490
Area 7096 sq km
Capital Gangtok
Main language Nepali
When to go late September to mid-November;
April and May

History

Lepchas, the 'original' Sikkimese people, migrated here from Assam or Myanmar (Burma) in the 13th century, followed by Bhutias (Khambas) who fled from religious strife in Tibet during the 15th century. The Nyingmapa form of Mahayana Buddhism arrived with three refugee Tibetan lamas who encountered each other at the site of modern-day Yuksom. Here in 1641 they crowned Phuntsog Namgyal as first chogyal (king) of Sikkim. The capital later moved to Rabdentse (near Pelling), then to Tumlong (now hidden ruins behind Phodong) before finally settling in Gangtok.

At their most powerful the chogyals' rule encompassed eastern Nepal, upper Bengal and Darjeeling. However, much territory was later lost during wars with Bhutan and Nepal, and throughout the 19th century large numbers of Hindu Nepali migrants arrived, eventually coming to form a majority of Sikkim's population.

In 1835 the British bribed Sikkim's chogyal to cede Darjeeling to the East India

Company. Tibet, which regarded Sikkim as a vassal state, raised strong objections. In 1849, amid rising tensions, the British annexed the entire area between the present Sikkim border and the Ganges plains, repulsing a counterinvasion by Tibet in 1886. In 1903–04, Britain's real-life James Bond character Francis Younghusband twice trekked up to the Sikkim–Tibet border. There, with a small contingent of soldiers, he deliberately set about inciting a fracas that would 'justify' an invasion of Tibet.

Sikkim's last chogyal ruled from 1963 to 1975, when the Indian government deposed him after a revolt by Sikkim's Nepali population. China never recognised India's claim to Sikkim until 2005, so prior to this, to bolster pro-Delhi sentiment, the Indian government made Sikkim a tax-free zone, pouring crores (tens of millions) of rupees into road building, electricity, water supplies and local industry. As a result Sikkim is surprisingly affluent by Himalayan standards.

Climate
Timing is crucial when visiting Sikkim. Summer's monsoonal rains hide the main attraction, those soaring mountains. The Yumthang and Tsopta Valleys are very cold by October and become really fingertip-numbing between December and February.

Information
The best times of year to visit Sikkim are late September to mid-November and March to May. These are the high seasons for domestic tourists: prices shoot up and normally serene monasteries get overrun. Crowd pressure is highest for Durga Puja celebrations (early October) and just after, but immediately before the celebrations Sikkim is contrastingly very quiet.

PERMITS
Standard Permits
Foreigners require a permit to enter Sikkim. Happily, these are free and a mere formality, although you need photos and passport photocopies to apply. Permits are most easily obtainable at the following places:
- Indian embassies abroad when getting your Indian visa (the best solution)
- Rangpo border post on arrival
- **Sikkim House** (☎ 1126883026; 12-14 Panchsheel Marg, Chankyapuri, Delhi) in Delhi

- Sikkim House (p507) in Kolkata
- Sikkim Tourist Office (p541) in Siliguri, West Bengal
- Major Foreigners' Regional Registration Offices (FRROs), including those in Kolkata (p506), Delhi (p1164), Mumbai (p783) or Darjeeling (p558).

Extensions
Permits are valid for 15 days from the date of entry. One or two days before expiry they can be extended for a further 15 days and then twice again, giving a maximum of 60 days. For the extension try:
- Gangtok Foreigners' Registration Office (p589)
- Tikjuk District Administration Centre, Superintendent of Police, (p598), 5km from Pelling.

Once you leave Sikkim, you must wait three months before applying for another permit. However, if you're on Sikkim-to-Sikkim public transport cutting through a corner of West Bengal (between Rangpo and Melli), your permit remains valid.

Permit Validity
The standard permit is valid for visits to the following areas:
- Gangtok, Rumtek and Lingdum
- South Sikkim
- anywhere on the Gangtok–Singhik road
- most of West Sikkim to which paved roads extend.

Foreigners need additional permits beyond Singhik up to Yumthang north of Lachung,

---

NO BAGS PLEASE

The Sikkim Democratic Front (SDF) state government has earned a reputation as the most environmentally aware in India, banning plastic bags and fining people who pollute streams. But, as so many commodities – such as snacks and *paan* (betel nut and leaf mixture for chewing) – now come in plastic sachets, the banning of plastic bags only solves one part of the problem. Getting manufacturers to change their packaging, encouraging proper rubbish disposal and changing public attitudes to littering are the real answers.

FESTIVALS IN SIKKIM

Sikkim has dozens of festivals; see www.sikkiminfo.net/fairs&festivals.htm. The most distinctive events feature colourful masked dances known as *chaams*, retelling stories from Buddhist mythology. Dates generally follow the Tibetan lunar calendar, which is handily listed under 'Government Holiday' on www.sikkim.gov.in.

Bumchu (Jan/Feb; Tashiding Gompa, p605) *Bum* means pot or vase and *chu* means water. The lamas open a pot of holy water to foretell the year's fortunes.

Losar (Feb/Mar; Pemayangtse, p600, Rumtek, p594) Sikkim's biggest *chaam* dances take place just before Tibetan New Year.

Khachoedpalri Mela (Mar/Apr; Khecheopalri Lake, p601) Butter candles float across the lake.

Drupchen (May/Jun; Rumtek, p594) *Chaam* dances form part of the annual group-meditation ceremony, with dances every second year honouring Padmasambhava.

Saga Dawa (May/Jun; all monastery towns) Buddhist scriptures paraded through the streets.

Diwali (Oct/Nov; widespread) Festival of lights and lots of fireworks.

Mahakala Dance (Nov; Ralang, p598)

Losoong (Dec/Jan; widespread incl Old Rumtek, p595, Lingdum, p595, Phodong, p606) Sikkimese New Year, preceded by *chaam* dances in many locations.

---

and the Tsopta Valley north of Lachen. Areas nearest to the Chinese border are out of bounds entirely. Indian citizens do not need a permit except north of Singhik, where they are subject to the same restrictions as foreigners. Indian citizens can also travel further, to Yume Samdong north of Yumthang, and Gurudongmar north of Thangu. They can also travel east past Tsomgo Lake to the Tibetan border at Nathu La.

Special Permits

High-altitude treks, including the main Goecha La and Singalila Ridge routes, require trekking permits valid for up to 15 days and organised by trekking agents.

Restricted area permits for Tsomgo (Changu) Lake (day trips) and visits anywhere north of Singhik are issued locally through approved tour agencies. You'll have to join the agent's 'tour', but this simply means a rental jeep, guide and agreed itinerary. Virtually any Gangtok agency can arrange this within 24 hours. You'll need a minimum group of two; so single travellers have every excuse to make friends. You'll need a passport photo and copies of your existing permit, visa and passport details page.

Dangers & Annoyances

Sikkim is generally a very safe place; the only annoyance are the famous little leeches. They aren't dangerous, just a nuisance. They're ubiquitous in damp grass so stick to dry, wide paths.

Activities

Sikkim offers considerable **trekking** potential. Day hikes between villages follow age-old footpaths and normally don't require extra permits: the best-known options are along the Monastery Loop, notably between Yuksam and Tashiding (p604). Nepal-style multiday group treks head into the really high mountains to Goecha La at the base of Khangchendzonga. For this, permits and guides are required and, although there are variants, most groups tend to follow pretty much the same route (p603).

Tour agencies (p591) are striving to open new trekking areas, notably the fabulous route across Zemu Glacier to Green Lake in Khangchendzonga National Park. However, these permits still remain very expensive and take months to arrange, while other tempting routes close to the Tibetan border remain off limits.

EAST SIKKIM

GANGTOK
☎ 03592 / pop 31,100 / elev 1400-1700m

Sikkim's capital is mostly a functional sprawl of multistorey concrete boxes. But, true to its name (meaning 'hill top'), these are steeply tiered along a precipitous mountain ridge. When clouds clear, typically at dawn, views are inspiring with Khangchendzonga soaring above the western horizon. While Gangtok's manmade attractions are minor, it's a reasonable place to spend a day or two organising trekking permits or trips to the north.

Orientation

Gangtok's crooked spine is the Rangpo–Mangan road, National Hwy 31A, cryptically referred to as 31ANHWay. The tourist office, banks and many shops line the central pedestrianised Mahatma Gandhi (MG) Marg. Nearby Tibet Rd is the nearest Gangtok gets to a travellers' enclave.

Information

BOOKSHOPS

Jainco Booksellers (☎ 203774; 31ANHWay; ⌚ 9am-8pm Mon-Sat) Small but central.
Rachna Bookshop (☎ 204336; www.rachnabooks.com; Development Area) Gangtok's best-stocked and most convivial bookshop. Occasional film (Small Town Film Club) and music events are held on the upstairs terrace.

EMERGENCY

Police station (☎ 202033; 31ANHWay)
STNM hospital (☎ 222059; 31ANHWay)

INTERNET ACCESS

Connections are slow and erratic.
Big Byte (Tibet Rd; per hr Rs30; ⌚ 8.30am-8pm)
ComShop (Tibet Rd; per hr Rs30; ⌚ 9am-8pm)
New Light (Tibet Rd; per hr Rs30; ⌚ 9am-7pm)

LAUNDRY

Deepak Dry Cleaners (☎ 227073; Tibet Rd; ⌚ 7am-8pm Fri-Tue) Next-day laundry service.

MONEY

Stock up with rupees in Gangtok: exchange is virtually impossible elsewhere in Sikkim. ATMs accepting foreign cards include SBI, UTI Bank and HDFC, all on MG Marg.
State Bank of India (SBI; ☎ 202666; MG Marg) Changes cash and major travellers cheques.

PERMIT EXTENSION

Foreigners' Registration Office (☎ 223041; Kazi Rd; ⌚ 10am-4pm, 10am-noon public hols) In the lane beside Indian Overseas Bank.

POST

Main post office (☎ 203085; PS Rd, Gangtok 737101) Poste-restante service.

TOURIST INFORMATION

There are plenty of basic pamphlets and books available. One of the best is the lavishly illustrated *Sikkim* by Arundhati Ray (not to be confused with the author of *The God of Small Things*) available at Rachna Bookshop (left) and Golden Tips (p593). Maps, however, approach pure fiction.

Sikkim Tourist Information Centre (☎ 221634, toll free 204408; www.sikkimtourism.travel; MG Marg; ⌚ 8am-4pm Dec-Feb & Jun-Aug, 10am-8pm Sep-Nov & Mar-May) has some useful free booklets, sells helicopter tours and can advise on the latest permit requirements. For more specific queries regarding trekking and permit-area travel, deal with a travel agent.

Sights

NAMGYAL INSTITUTE OF TIBETOLOGY & AROUND

Housed in traditionally styled Tibetan architecture, this unique **institute** (☎ 281642; www.tibetology .net; admission Rs10; ⌚ 10am-4pm Mon-Sat, closed 2nd Sat of month) was established in 1958 to promote research into Mahayana Buddhism and Tibetan culture. It contains one of the world's largest collections of Buddhist books and manuscripts, plus statuettes, *thangkas* (Tibetan cloth paintings) and sacred objects, such as a *kapali* (sacred bowl made from a human skull) and human thighbone trumpets. There are plenty of useful explanatory captions.

Further along the same road is the **Do-Drul Chorten**, a large white Tibetan pagoda surrounded by dormitories for young monks.

The institute sits in an **Orchid Sanctuary** and is conveniently close to the lower station of **Damovar Ropeway** (☎ 280587; per person Rs60; ⌚ 9.30am-4.30pm), a cable car running from just below the Tashi Ling offices on the ridge. Views are stupendous.

THE RIDGE

With views east and west, it's very pleasant to stroll through shady parks and gardens on the city's central ridge. Sadly its focal point, the **Raj Bhawan (Royal Palace)** is closed to visitors. When the orchids bloom (March) it's worth peeping inside the **Flower Exhibition Centre** (admission Rs10; ⌚ 9am-5pm), a modestly sized tropical greenhouse full of exotic plants.

ENCHEY GOMPA & VIEWPOINTS

Approached through gently rustling conifers high above Gangtok, this **monastery** (⌚ 6am-4pm Mon-Sat), dating back to 1909, is Gangtok's most attractive, with some decent murals and statues of Tantric deities. It comes alive for

lonelyplanet.com

GANGTOK

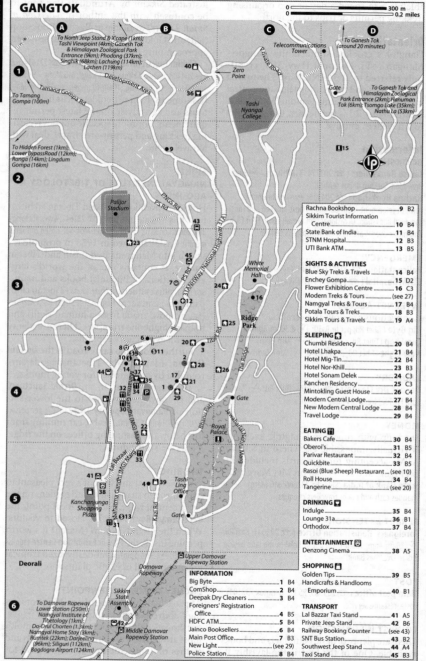

0 — 300 m
0 — 0.2 miles

INFORMATION

Big Byte	1	B4
ComShop	2	B4
Deepak Dry Cleaners	3	B4
Foreigners' Registration Office	4	B5
HDFC ATM	5	B4
Jainco Booksellers	6	B4
Main Post Office	7	B3
New Light	(see 29)	
Police Station	8	B4
Rachna Bookshop	9	B2
Sikkim Tourist Information Centre	10	B4
State Bank of India	11	B4
STNM Hospital	12	B3
UTI Bank ATM	13	B5

SIGHTS & ACTIVITIES

Blue Sky Treks & Travels	14	B4
Enchey Gompa	15	D2
Flower Exhibition Centre	16	C3
Modern Treks & Tours	(see 27)	
Namgyal Treks & Tours	17	B3
Potala Tours & Treks	18	B3
Sikkim Tours & Travels	19	A4

SLEEPING

Chumbi Residency	20	B4
Hotel Lhakpa	21	B4
Hotel Mig-Tin	22	B4
Hotel Nor-Khill	23	B3
Hotel Sonam Delek	24	C3
Kanchen Residency	25	C3
Mintokling Guest House	26	C4
Modern Central Lodge	27	B4
New Modern Central Lodge	28	B4
Travel Lodge	29	B4

EATING

Bakers Cafe	30	B4
Oberoi's	31	B5
Parivar Restaurant	32	B4
Quickbite	33	B5
Rasoi (Blue Sheep) Restaurant	(see 10)	
Roll House	34	B4
Tangerine	(see 20)	

DRINKING

Indulge	35	B4
Lounge 31a	36	B1
Orthodox	37	B4

ENTERTAINMENT

Denzong Cinema	38	A5

SHOPPING

Golden Tips	39	B5
Handicrafts & Handlooms Emporium	40	B1

TRANSPORT

Lal Bazzar Taxi Stand	41	A5
Private Jeep Stand	42	B6
Railway Booking Counter	(see 43)	
SNT Bus Station	43	B2
Southwest Jeep Stand	44	A4
Taxi Stand	45	B3

the colourful **Detor Chaam** (December/January) masked dances.

From the gompa, follow the access road northeast around the base of an unmissable telecommunications tower. An initially obvious path scrambles up in around 15 minutes to **Ganesh Tok viewpoint**. Festooned in colourful prayer flags, Ganesh Tok offers superb city views and its minicafe serves hot teas. Across the road, a lane leads into the **Himalayan Zoological Park** (☎ 223191; admission Rs10, vehicles Rs25, video Rs500; ☒ 9am-4pm). Red pandas, Himalayan bears and snow leopards roam around in extensive wooded enclosures so large that you'll really value a car to shuttle between them.

Hanuman Tok, another impressive viewpoint, sits on a hilltop around 4km drive beyond Ganesh Tok, though there are shortcuts for walkers.

Considered perhaps Gangtok's best view of Khangchendzonga can be found from the **Tashi viewpoint** at the northwest edge of town beside the main route to Phodong.

Tours

Classic 'three-point tours' show you Ganesh Tok, Hanuman Tok and Tashi viewpoints (Rs500). Almost any travel agent, hotel or taxi driver offers variants, including a 'five-point tour' adding Enchey Gompa and Namgyal Institute (Rs700), or 'seven-point tours' tacking on old-and-new Rumtek (Rs900) or Rumtek plus Lingdum (Rs1200). Prices are per vehicle holding three or four passengers.

TOUR AGENCIES

For high-altitude treks, visits to Tsomgo Lake or tours to northern Sikkim you'll need a tour agency. There are more than 180 agencies but only 10% of those work with foreigners; check with fellow travellers for the latest recommendations. Choose a government-registered agency, as it has to conform to certain guidelines including ecologically and culturally responsible travel. Look for a company that belongs to TAAS (Travel Agents Association of Sikkim) as all their members are registered. Try these:

Blue Sky Treks & Travels (☎ 205113; blueskytourism@yahoo.com; Tourism Bldg, MG Marg) Trekking and trips to Tsomgo Lake (Rs1600 per person).

Modern Treks & Tours (☎ 204670; www.modernresidency.com; Modern Central Lodge, MG Marg) For trekking.

Namgyal Treks & Tours (☎ 203701; www.namgyaltreks.net; Tibet Rd) Trekking, tours to northern Sikkim.

Potala Tours & Treks (☎ 200043; www.sikkimhimalayas.com; PS Rd)

Sikkim Tours & Travels (☎ 202188; www.sikkimtours.com; Church Rd) Specialises in trekking, birdwatching and botanical tours.

SCENIC FLIGHTS

For eagle-eye mountain views, **Sikkim Tourist Information Centre** (☎ 281372; stdcsikkim@yahoo.co.in) arranges scenic helicopter flights. Book at least three days ahead. Prices are for up to five passengers (four for Khangchendzonga ridge): buzz over Gangtok (Rs7590, 15 minutes); circuit of West Sikkim (Rs82,500, 55 minutes); circuit of North Sikkim (Rs97,500, 65 minutes); Khangchendzonga ridge (Rs112,500, 75 minutes).

Sleeping

Rates typically drop by 15% to 30% in the low season (November to February and June to August), much more if demand is very low and you're good at bargaining. The high seasons, which influence accommodation prices, are March to May and September to November.

BUDGET

Many cheaper hotels quote walk-in rates of around Rs500. Some are worth it. Others are just waiting for you to bargain them down to Rs200. Check rooms carefully as standards can vary widely even within the same hotel. Foreigners generally flock around central Tibet Rd, the only area where a Rs200 room is likely to be habitable.

New Modern Central Lodge (☎ 201361; Tibet Rd; d Rs300, without bathroom s Rs100, d Rs150-250) A traveller's favourite for so long that people still come here despite somewhat ill-kept rooms and reports of falling standards. With plenty of cheap rooms and a useful meeting-point cafe-bar, it will probably remain a backpacker standby.

Modern Central Lodge (☎ 221081; info@modernhospitality.com; 31 ANHWay; dm Rs100, d Rs250-500) More rupees buy you a larger room at the top of the building away from the traffic noise below. All doubles have private bathrooms; the dorms share separate facilities. Great home-cooked food on the roof garden.

Hotel Mig-Tin (☎ 204101; Tibet Rd; d Rs300-600) Above a lobby with naive Tibetan-style murals and a great little meet-up cafe, most rooms are worn but become good value out of high

SIKKIM

season with some bargaining. The cheapest rooms are damp and airless.

MIDRANGE & TOP END

All places listed here have cable TV and private bathroom with hot showers. Most add 10% tax and some a 10% service charge.

Kanchen Residency (☎ 9732072614; kanchen residency@indiatimes.com; Tibet Rd; d back/side/front Rs450/600/700) Above the dismal (unrelated) Hotel Prince, this sparklingly airy discovery is spacious, light and well run. Front rooms have great views.

Namgyal Home Stay (☎ 203701; www.namgyaltreks .net; s/d Rs800/1200) Parading space, simplicity and friendliness, this homestay is 3km south on the 31ANHWay. Full board is available. Book through Namgyal Treks & Tours (p591).

Mintokling Guest House (☎ 204226; www.mintok ling.com; Bhanu Path; s/d from Rs950/1250) Set within secluded gardens, this expanded family home is a real oasis with Bhutanese fabrics, timber ceilings and local design features. Very friendly.

Travel Lodge (☎ 203858; Tibet Rd; d Rs1000-1200) Popularity has caused high-season prices to shoot up but discounts of 50% to 60% are available at other times. Unusually good-value rooms have BBC World TV and well-heated showers with towels and soap provided, though the ground-floor cheapies have thin walls and upstairs a few smell musty.

Hotel Sonam Delek (☎ 202566; www.hotelsonam delek.com; Tibet Rd; d Rs1100-1500) This is a long-standing favourite offering good service and reliable food; the best-value deluxe rooms come with soft mattresses and decent views. Bigger super-deluxe rooms have better views and balconies, but the standard rooms are a very noticeable step down – in the basement.

ourpick Hidden Forest(☎ 205197; www.hiddenfor estretreat.com; Middle Sichey; s/d Rs1500/1700) A wonderful, friendly family-run hide-away on the edge of town secluded on more than a hectare of orchid, fruit tree and flower nursery that's also home to birds and butterflies. The self-contained cottages are marvellously furnished with Tibetan motifs, polished wood floors and a real orchid adding a little touch of colour. Hidden Forest does its bit to help the environment: superb food comes from the solar-powered kitchen, a resident cow provides dairy produce and all vegetable matter is composted.

Chumbi Residency (☎ 226618; www.thechumbiresi dency.com; Tibet Rd; s/d from Rs2250/2950) This wonderfully central three-star hotel has comfortable but smallish rooms with fresh white walls, good furniture and tea-and-coffee–making equipment. There's little difference between the two grades of rooms but go for one with a view. The relaxed Tangerine bar-restaurant is firmly recommended.

Hotel Nor-Khill (☎ 205637; norkhill@elginhotels.com; PS Rd; s/d incl full board Rs5600/5900) Oozing 1930s elegance, this sumptuous 'house of jewels' was originally the King of Sikkim's royal guest house. Historical photos and artwork feature throughout, and the lobby has antique furniture and imperial-sized mirrors. The spaciously luxurious old-building rooms attract film stars and Dalai Lamas.

Eating

RESTAURANTS & CAFES

Most budget hotels have cheap cafe-restaurants serving standard Chinese/Tibetan dishes, basic Indian meals and Western breakfasts.

Parivar Restaurant (MG Marg; dishes Rs25-70) Eat here for good-value South Indian vegetarian food; try the various *masala dosas* for breakfast or the all-inclusive thali for Rs70. The restaurant's downstairs from the HDFC Bank.

Bakers Cafe (MG Marg; mains Rs50-125; ☙ 8am-8pm) The perfect breakfast escape, this cosy Western-style cafe has great coffee (Rs35), scrunchy pastries and squidgy cakes.

ourpick Tangerine (ground fl, Chumbi Residency, Tibet Rd; mains Rs50-150) Descend five floors for sublime cuisine, tasty Western snacks or cocktails in the brilliant Japanese-style floor-cushioned bar area. Try the stuffed-tomato curry or sample Sikkimese specialities like *sochhya* (nettle stew). Stylishly relaxed decor with a waiter/origami-ist who turns napkins into birds.

Rasoi (Blue Sheep) Restaurant (MG Marg; mains Rs50-110; ☙ 8.30am-9.30pm) Still looking brand new, this well-patronised family restaurant serves good food, hot and fast. No booze.

QUICK EATS

Roll House (MG Marg; rolls Rs15-30; ☙ 8am-8pm) In an alley just off MG Marg this hole-in-the-wall serves delicious *kati* rolls (see p525) that upstage even the Kolkata originals.

Quickbite (MG Marg; snacks Rs20-40; ☙ 8am-8pm) Takeaway snacks from dosas to pizzas to Indian sweets.

Oberoi's (MG Marg; snacks Rs25-60; ☻ 7.30am-8.30pm) *Momos* (Tibetan dumplings), chow mein, sandwiches, Indian snacks and pizzas.

Drinking

Lounge 31a (Zero Point; beers Rs70; ☻ 10am-9.30pm) Swooping glass architecture offers Zen aesthetics and light-suffused sunset views from four storeys high, above the Sikkim State Bank.

Indulge (Tibet Rd; beers Rs70; ☻ 11am-11pm) Big windows overlooking MG Marg add to the airiness of this bar-cafe (snacks Rs40 to Rs120) with its white decor and curvy designs.

Orthodox (MG Marg; beers Rs55; ☻ 7am-10pm) Tables are squished together as tightly as lovers in this cosy bar. An intrusive ultraviolet light annoys at night but it's a bar for companionable beers with friends (or lovers). Solve the picture puzzles on the wall before too many beers. Meals Rs60 to Rs170, early-morning breakfasts until 10am.

Entertainment

Denzong Cinema (☎ 202692; Lal Bazaar; tickets from Rs25) Screens the latest Bollywood blockbusters in Hindi.

X'cape (☎ 228636; Vagra Cinema Hall; entry Rs400; ☻ 7.30pm-11.30pm Thu-Sun) Gangtok's leading nightclub.

Shopping

Several souvenir shops on MG Marg and PS Rd sell pricier Tibetan and Sikkimese handicrafts. Bustling Lal Bazaar has several stalls selling wooden tongba (Himalayan millet beer) pots, prayer flags and Nepali-style knives.

A few Sikkimese liquors are available in novelty souvenir containers. Opening a 1L monk-shaped bottle of Old Monk Rum (Rs220) means screwing off the monk's head! Fireball comes in a bowling ball–style red sphere.

Handicrafts & Handloom Emporium (☎ 9434137131; Zero Point; ☻ 10am-4pm Mon-Sat, daily Jul-Mar) Teaches traditional crafts to local students and sells their produce, which make good gifts – including purses (Rs75), handwoven carpets (from Rs4200), *thangkas* (Rs125 to Rs6800) and traditional women's dresses (Rs2000).

Golden Tips (www.goldentipstea.com; Kazi Rd; teas from Rs25; ☻ 12.30-9.30pm) An inviting tea showroom with a wide selection of blends to buy and taste.

Getting There & Away

Landslides and route changes mean road journeys can take vastly longer than expected. If flying out of Bagdogra, play safe by making the Gangtok–Siliguri trip a full day ahead.

AIR

The nearest airport to Sikkim is Bagdogra (p543), 124km from Gangtok, near Siliguri in West Bengal, which has flights to Kolkata, Delhi and Guwahati. **TSA Helicopters** (☎ 0353-2531959; www.mountainflightindia.com) shuttles from Gangtok to Bagdogra (Rs3000, 35 minutes), departing at 11am and returning at 2.30pm, but services can be cancelled in adverse weather and if bookings are insufficient. In Gangtok, **Sikkim Tourist Information Centre** (☎ 221634) sells the tickets.

Fixed-price Maruti vans/sumos (jeeps) go from Bagdogra direct to Gangtok (Rs1500/1700, 4½ hours). You might be able to find slightly better prices from jeeps in the car park: look for Sikkim (SK) number plates.

BUS

Buses listed in the table, above, leave from the government **SNT bus station** (☎ 202016; PS Rd).

SHARE JEEPS & MINIBUSES

By regulation there are fixed departures for various destinations; in practice these are augmented by as many jeeps as passenger numbers require. Departures usually start at 6.30am for the more distant destinations and continue up to about 3pm.

From the hectic but relatively well-organised **private jeep stand** (31ANHWay), share jeeps/minibuses depart to Darjeeling (Rs125, five hours), Kalimpong (Rs90, three hours) and Siliguri (Rs125, four hours), some continuing to New Jalpaiguri train station (Rs135, 4½

BUSES FROM GANGTOK			
Destination	**Cost (Rs)**	**Duration (hr)**	**Departures**
Jorethang	70	4	7am
Kalimpong	70	4	7.15am
Namchi	68	3	7.30am
Pelling	90	5½	7am
Siliguri (via Rangpo)	85-110	5	hourly 6.30am-1.30pm

hours). There are one-off jeeps to Kakarbhitta (Rs140, 4½ hours, 6.30am) on the Nepali border and Phuentsholing (Bhutan border; Rs220, six hours, 8.30am). Purchase tickets in advance.

West Sikkim vehicles depart from **Southwest jeep stand** (☎ 203862; Church Rd) for Geyzing (Rs120, 4½ hours), Ravangla (Rs80, three hours), Namchi (Rs90, three hours) and Jorethang (Rs100, three hours). Jeeps for Yuksom, Tashiding and Pelling (Rs120 to Rs150, five hours) depart around 7am and again around 12.30pm. For independent travel, small groups can charter a vehicle.

Sumos to North Sikkim use the **North jeep stand** (31ANHWay), about 3km north of the centre. From here vehicles go to Mangan (Rs80), Singhik (Rs100) and Phodong (Rs50).

TRAIN
The nearest major train station is over 120km away at New Jalpaiguri (NJP). There's a computerised **railway booking counter** (☎ 220201; ⏱ 8am-2pm Mon-Sat, 8am-11am Sun & public hols) at the SNT bus stand.

Getting Around
Hail a taxi on the street or pick one up at the various taxi stands around the city. There's a taxi stand in Lal Bazaar opposite the Denzong Cinema, and another in PS Rd just north of the post office.

AROUND GANGTOK
Rumtek and Lingdum Gompa are most easily visited on a 'seven-point tour' (see p591). Viewing the temples takes perhaps half an hour each, but the infinitely winding country lane that links them is a big part of the attraction, curving through mossy forests high above river valleys and artistically terraced rice-slopes.

Rumtek
☎ 03592 / elev 1690m
Facing Gangtok distantly across a vast green valley, Rumtek village is entirely dominated by its very extensive gompa complex. Spiritually the monastery is hugely significant as the surrogate home of Buddhism's Kagyu (Black Hat) sect. Visually it is not Sikkim's most spectacular and by day it can get annoyingly crowded in the high season. To experience Rumtek at its most serene, stay the night and hike around the delightful nearby hilltops at dawn.

FLYING BLACK HATS

The Black Hat sect is so named because of the priceless ruby-topped headgear used to crown the Karmapa (spiritual leader) during key ceremonies. Being woven from the hair of angels, the hat must be kept locked in a box to prevent it from flying back to heaven. But maybe that's just what it has done. Nobody has seen it since 1993 when the 16th Karmapa died. Only when the 17th Karmapa is finally crowned will anyone dare to unlock the box and check.

SIGHTS
Rumtek Gompa Complex
This rambling and walled **complex** (☎ 252329; www.rumtek.org) is a village within a village, containing religious buildings, schools and several small lodge-hotels. To enter, foreigners must show both passport and Sikkim permit. Unusually for a monastery, this place is guarded by armed police, as there have been violent altercations, and an invasion, by monks who dispute the Karmapa's accession.

The main **monastery building** (admission Rs5; ⏱ 6am-5pm) was constructed between 1961 and 1966 to replace the Tsurphu Monastery in Tibet, which had been destroyed during China's Cultural Revolution. The giant throne within awaits the crowning of Kagyu's current spiritual leader, the (disputed) **17th Karmapa** (Ogyen Trinley Dorje; www.kagyuoffice.org). This young lama fled from Tibet in 2000 but currently remains based at Dharamsala: Indian authorities are believed to have prevented him from officially taking up his Rumtek seat for fear of upsetting Chinese government sensibilities. Those who want to learn more about the 17th Karmapa might wish to read *Dance of 17 Lives* by Mick Brown.

Rear stairs lead up to the **Golden Stupa**. It's not really a stupa at all, just a smallish concrete room, but it holds the ashes of the 16th Karmapa in a jewel-studded reliquary to which pilgrims pay their deepest respects. If locked, someone from the colourful Karma Shri Naland Institute of Buddhist Studies opposite can usually open it for you.

Rumtek holds impressive masked *chaam* dances during the annual **Drupchen** (group meditation) in May/June, and two days before Losar (Tibetan New Year) when you might also catch traditional *lhamo* (Tibetan opera) performances.

Old Rumtek Gompa

About 1.5km beyond the gompa towards Sang, a long avenue of white prayer flags leads attractively down to the powder-blue **Old Rumtek Gompa**. Despite the name, the main prayer hall has been so thoroughly renovated that it looks virtually new. However, the interior is a riotous festival of colour and the lonely location is idyllic with some wonderful west-facing views. Two days before Losoong (Sikkimese New Year), Old Rumtek holds the celebrated **Kagyed Chaam** dance.

Lingdum Gompa

Only completed in 1998, peaceful Lingdum Gompa is visually more exciting than Rumtek. Its structure grows out of the forest in grand layers with photogenic side buildings, though the exterior paintings are not especially accomplished. The extensively muralled main prayer hall enshrines a large Sakyamuni (historic) Buddha wreathed in an expansive gilded aura. Sonorous chanting at the 7.30am and 3.30pm *puja* (prayers/offerings) adds to the magical atmosphere.

SLEEPING & EATING

Currently the **Sungay Guesthouse** (☎ 252221; dechenb@dte.vsnl.net.in; d/tr Rs400/250) is the only accommodation option open. The comfortable if rather Spartan rooms have faux wood-veneer walls and private bathrooms with geyser. Doubles have great balcony views, hence the higher price.

Further up, where the monastery access road bends, is the **Sangay Hotel**, which was being rebuilt when we visited. Outside the gompa walls and 300m back towards Gangtok, the **Shambhala Mountain Resort** (☎ 252240; resort_sham bhala@sify.com) is also being renovated and may be open again by the time you read this.

At Lingdum Gompa, the complex has a cafe and its **Zurmang Tara Hotel** (☎ 9933008818; s Rs600, d Rs1000) offers full board and lodging in reasonable rooms with parquet floors and private bathrooms.

GETTING THERE & AWAY

Rumtek is 26km from Gangtok by a very winding road. Lingdum Gompa is a 2km walk from Ranga or Ranka village, reached by rough back-lanes from Gangtok. Share

jeeps are too sporadic to rely on for a day out here so linking the two sites requires private transport or a tour.

TOWARDS TIBET

Tsomgo (Changu, Tsangu) Lake
elev 3780m

Pronounced Changu, this scenic lake is an established tour stop for Indian visitors, but permits are necessary. To get one, sign up for a 'tour' by 2pm and most Gangtok agents can get the permit for next-day departure (two photos required). Tours (ie guided shared taxis) typically cost Rs700/450 per person for groups of two/three. Individual travellers usually can't get the permit.

At the lakeside, food stalls sell hot chai, chow mein and *momos,* while short **yak rides** (about Rs100) potter along the shore. If you can muster the puff, the main attraction is clambering up a nearby hilltop for inspiring views.

Nathu La

Indian citizens are permitted to continue 18km along the spectacular road from Tsomgo Lake to the 4130m **Nathu La** (Listening Ears Pass). Here the border post to southeastern Tibet 'opened' with much fanfare in 2006. Only local villagers are eligible to cross, and only to travel 8km to the first Tibetan market. Maybe one day it will be possible to reach Yatung (52km) in Tibet's fabled **Chumbi Valley**, where the Sikkimese kings once had their summer palace. From there, the road towards Lhasa (525km) winds up onto the Tibetan plateau via the old fortress town of **Phari**, one of the world's highest settlements (4350m).

A few kilometres southeast of Nathu La, **Jelep La** was the pass used by Francis Younghusband in the British Great Game-era attack on Tibet (1904). Until 1962 Jelep La was the main trade route between Kalimpong and Lhasa, but it shows no signs whatsoever of reopening.

SOUTH SIKKIM

The main sights in South Sikkim are Namchi's gigantic statues. The region has plenty of other great viewpoints, too, but visitors generally hurry to Pelling leaving much of the region comparatively unvisited. Ravangla (p597) falls administratively within South Sikkim, but we cover it in the Gangtok to Pelling section (p597), where it fits more logically.

SIKKIM

NAMCHI
☎ 03595 / elev 1524m

When Shiva on Solophuk Hill is completed, two utterly vast statues will be facing each other from opposite hillsides across this quietly prosperous market town. The Buddhist one at Samdruptse is already finished. **Super Computer Point** (Main Bazaar; per hr Rs30; ☽ 8am-8pm) has internet on the first floor of the block containing the well-signed Anapurna Restaurant. An Axis Bank ATM is opposite the entrance to Main Bazaar.

Sights
SAMDRUPTSE

Painted in shimmering copper and bronze, the impressively vast 45m-high **Padmasambhava statue** (Indian/foreigner Rs10/100; ☽ 7am-5pm) dominates its hilltop. Completed in 2004 on a foundation stone laid by the Dalai Lama, it's visible from miles around, shining like a golden cone amid the forests of Samdruptse Hill. Reputedly it can be seen from Darjeeling and most certainly by its rival, Shiva, on Solophuk Hill opposite. The site is 7km from Namchi, 2km off the Damthang road.

Taxis want you to pay around Rs300 return. Alternatively you could walk back to Namchi, shortcutting via steps down to and through a **rock garden** (admission Rs10). Or, more interestingly, follow the nose of the Samdruptse Hill down to **Ngadak Gompa**. Ngadak's ruined **old dzong**, dating back to 1717, is delightfully 'real' despite the unsightly steel buttressing that stops it from falling down. Its unpainted stone exterior incorporates ancient carved door pillars and upstairs intriguing but very decrepit fragments of painting remain on the peeling old cloth wallpaper.

SOLOPHUK

A massive 33m **Shiva statue** is being raised on the memorably named Solophuk hilltop surrounded by a complex of temples representing many of India's Hindu temple styles. This will become a huge pilgrimage complex and the Namchi authorities are joining in by building a shopping mall and remodelling the Main Bazaar down in the town. Intended completion dates have come and gone and the latest we were given at the time of research was mid-2009. So by the time you read this it may be open; ask down in Namchi town.

Sleeping & Eating

Dungmali Guest House (☎ 263272, 9434126992; Solophuk Rd, Km4; d Rs500, without bathroom Rs350-400) For now, this family homestay offers just three rooms, the best having a private bathroom and a fabulous view window. The inspired owner Bimuka Dungmali will be adding three cottages, one each in Nepali, Lepcha and Bhutia style, plus another storey onto the house. The family already grows its own organic vegetables, offers bird-watching walks in 2.4 hectares of private jungle and can take you to meet a traditional healer.

Hotel Samdruptse (☎ 264708; Jorethang Rd; d Rs100-1000) Scuffed paint and damp patches shouldn't deter you from staying here except in the cheap dingy downstairs rooms. The higher the room rate the better the view from the Khangchendzonga-facing rooms. The hotel, including Namchi's finest restaurant, is 300m west of the centre facing the Solophuk-bound road junction.

Hotel Mayel (☎ 9434127322; Jorethang Rd; d Rs500-1500) Opposite the Samdruptse, it lacks the views but is an option if the latter is full.

There are several hotels within the Main Bazaar that was under massive reconstruction in association with the Solophuk Hill development. Consequently many of the hotels and businesses were closed when we visited. **Hotel Zimkhang** (☎ 263625) could be a good option once they put the bazaar back together.

Getting There & Around

Around 200m east in descending layers off the Rangpo road are the main market, the jeep stand and the **SNT bus stand** (☎ 263847). Buses go to Jorethang (Rs26, one hour, 7am, 11.30am and 1pm), Ravangla (Rs26, two hours, 11.30am and 2pm).

Share jeeps leave when full to Jorethang (Rs25, one hour) and Ravangla (Rs30, one hour) plus to Gangtok (Rs90, 3½ hours, 6.30am, 7am, 7.30am, 8.30am and 3pm), Darjeeling (Rs110, four hours, 7.30am) and Siliguri (Rs100, four hours, 6.30am, 7am, 7.30am, 8am and 3pm). For Geyzing there are frequent jeeps (Rs70, three hours).

JORETHANG (NAYA BAZAAR)
☎ 03595 / elev 518m

This useful transport hub between West Sikkim, Namchi and Darjeeling/Siliguri could make a launching point for visits to interesting but lesser-known Sikkimese villages like

BUSES FROM JORETHANG			
Destination	**Cost (Rs)**	**Duration (hr)**	**Departure**
Gangtok	72	4	12.30pm
Namchi	20	1	8.30am, noon, 4.30pm
Pelling (via Geyzing)	50	3	3pm
Ravangla (via Namchi)	45	2½	noon
Siliguri	71	3½	9.30am

Rinchenpong (country getaways) or **Reishi** (hot springs and holy cave).

At its westernmost edge, Jorethang's most striking feature is the **Akar Suspension Bridge**, 400m north of which are the passingly photogenic roadside Shiva niches of **Sisne Mandir** (Legship Rd).

The brightest, friendliest accommodation option remains **Hotel Namgyal** (☎ 276852; d Rs450), on the main drag 70m east of the bridge just before the SNT bus station. Rooms are clean, the ones at the back overlook the river and room 101's toilet has a commanding view. Across the road beside the Darjeeling jeep stand there's a particularly helpful **tourist office** (◷ 8am-4pm Mon-Sat Dec-Feb & Jun-Aug, 10am-8pm Sep-Nov & Mar-May) and several other back-up hotels.

Useful services from the SNT bus station are listed in the table, above.

From the main jeep stand, sumos leave regularly for Darjeeling (Rs90, two hours), Gangtok jeeps (Rs100 via Melli, Rs112 via Namchi), Geyzing (Rs55, two hours), Namchi (Rs30, one hour), Siliguri (Rs100, three hours), Tashiding (Rs100, 1½ hours) and Yuksom (Rs150, three hours). For Nepal there's a 7am jeep to Kakarbhitta (Rs150, four hours). Buy tickets before boarding.

WEST SIKKIM

Sikkim's greatest tourist draw is simply staring at Khangchendzonga's white-peaked magnificence from Pelling. Most visitors then add excursions to nearby waterfalls and monasteries, plus perhaps a spot of walking. Some lovely one-day hikes start from the charming village of Yuksom. That's also the trailhead for serious multiday group-trek expeditions to Dzongri (group trekking permits required).

GANGTOK TO PELLING

There are three main routes from the capital to Sikkim's main tourist hub. The longest and least interesting loops a long way south to Rangpo, then back via Melli, Jorethang and Legship. Fortunately this is normally only used by public sumos when landslides block the two possible routes via Singtam and Ravangla. Both of these are highly attractive, especially the longer, little-used route via Yangyang (hired jeep only), which approaches Ravangla along an extremely dramatic cliff-edge drive around the precipitous base of Maenam Hill.

Ravangla (Rabongla)
☎ 03595 / elev 2009m

Rapidly expanding Ravangla is spectacularly perched overlooking a wide sweep of western Sikkim, the gompas of Old Ralang, Tashiding, Pemayangtse and Sangachoeling all distantly visible against a horizon that's sawtoothed with snow-capped peaks.

The town is a modern creation with little aesthetic distinction, but useful as a hub to visit Ralang. Joining the main highway is the Main Bazaar, a concentration of shops, small eateries, plentiful hotels, the jeep stand and **Cyber Cafe** (☎ 9933003225; per hr Rs30; ◷ 8.15am-7pm).

At the junction is **Hotel 10-Zing** (☎ 260705; d Rs150-500), open all year. All rooms have private bathrooms and those in the Rs300 to Rs500 range have geysers; otherwise it's free bucket hot water. Good English is spoken here.

Hotel Snow White (☎ 9434864915; d Rs600-800) has small but clean rooms with private bathrooms and geysers. Some of the cheaper rooms have smelly carpets. There are good, if partially obscured, views from the rear. The restaurant (mains Rs20 to Rs60) is quite cheery with curtained alcoves for private liaisons.

Several more hotels, many with views, line the main road for about a kilometre.

Lonely **Mt Narsing Resort** (☎ 226822; www.yuksom-tours.com; bungalows s/d Rs600/700, cottages from Rs1400/1600) is a rustic bungalow place 5km out of Ravangla with fabulous tree-framed views towards the mountains.

The bus booking office is part of Hotel 10-Zing. Buses run to Namchi (Rs25, one hour, 9am and 2pm) and Siliguri (Rs89, five hours, 6.30am). From 8am to noon share jeeps run to Gangtok (Rs80, three hours), Namchi (Rs40, one hour), Pelling (Rs80, three hours) and

Legship (Rs30, one hour); for Yuksom, change at Legship.

Around Ravangla

RALANG

At Ralang, 13km below Ravangla, the splendid 1995 **Palchen Choeling Monastic Institute** (New Ralang Gompa) is home to about 200 Kagyu-order monks. Arrive early morning or around 3pm to hear them chanting in mesmerising unison. There's a 9m-high golden statue of the historical Buddha in the main hall, and locally the gompa is famous for elaborate butter sculptures. At November's very impressive **Mahakala dance**, the dancers wear masks representing the Great Protector and chase away negative energy. If you're interested, ask to peek inside the room where the amazing costumes are stored.

About 1.5km downhill on the same road is peaceful **Old Ralang Gompa**, established in 1768.

A chartered taxi to Ralang costs around Rs350 from Ravangla (return with two hours' wait).

BON MONASTERY

Beside the main Legship road, 5.5km from central Ravangla, small but fascinating **Yung Drung Kundrak Lingbon** is the only Bon monastery in Sikkim. The Bon faith preceded Buddhism in Tibet. Unusually for Sikkim, non-flash photography is allowed inside, but check first. Daily *pujas* are at 5am and 4pm.

MAENAM HILL

A steep three- to four-hour hiking trail leads from the Ravangla–Ralang road to the top of **Maenam Hill** (3150m) through the rhododendrons and magnolia blooms of the **Maenam Wildlife Sanctuary**. The views are wonderful and you just might see rare red pandas and monal pheasants (Sikkim's state bird). A guide is useful to avoid getting lost in the forest on your return. Longer treks continue to **Borong** village.

GEYZING, TIKJUK & LEGSHIP
☎ 03595

The following three towns have little to offer a visitor apart from a permit extension at Tikjuk and transport changes at Geyzing. Geyzing is West Sikkim's capital, but for permit extensions you need Tikjuk, half way to Pelling.

Tikjuk

This is the District Administrative Centre for West Sikkim. Permits can be extended at the **Superintendent of Police office** (☎ 250763; side wing 3rd fl; ☷ 10am-4pm Mon-Sat, closed 2nd Sat of month).

Geyzing (Gyashaling)
elev 1552m

Apart from its vaguely interesting Sunday market, Geyzing is most useful as West Sikkim's transport hub.

SNT buses go to Jorethang (Rs50, two hours, 8am) and Siliguri (Rs105, five hours, 8am). Frequent shared jeeps go to Jorethang (Rs55, 1½ hours), Legship (Rs25, 30 minutes), Pelling (Rs20, 20 minutes), Tashiding (Rs55, 1½ hours) and Yuksom (Rs60, 2½ hours). Several serve Gangtok (Rs120, seven to nine hours, 6.15am), Ravangla (Rs60, one hour, 11.30am) and Siliguri (Rs135, four hours, 7am and 12.30pm).

Legship

When no other transport is available, especially to or from Tashiding, try connecting here. Should you get stranded, **Hotel Trishna** (☎ 250887; d/tr Rs200/300) is simple, with private bathrooms, bucket hot water, plenty of greenery and a rooftop terrace.

PELLING
☎ 03595 / elev 2083m

Pelling's raison d'être is its stride-stopping view of Khangchendzonga at dawn. It's not so much a town as a 2km string of tourist hotels, but don't be put off. The view *is* worth it. Despite hordes of visitors, locals remain surprisingly unjaded, and the best budget hotels are great for meeting fellow travellers. The helipad gives magnificent panoramic views.

Orientation & Information

Pelling is nominally divided into Upper, Middle and Lower areas, though these effectively merge. A focal point of Upper Pelling is a small roundabout where the main road from Geyzing turns 180 degrees in front of Hotel Garuda. At the same point, minor roads branch south to Dentam and southwest to the helipad and **tourist office** (☎ 9434630876; ☷ 9am-5pm Dec-Feb & Jun-Aug, 8am-8pm Sep-Nov & Mar-May). A useful website is www.gopelling.com. Opposite the Hotel Garuda is an ATM and a few doors down an **internet cafe** (per hr Rs30; ☷ 7am-7pm).

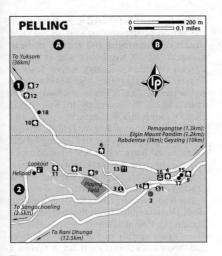

PELLING

Tours

Hotel Garuda (below; tours per day per 8-10 person jeep Rs1500-1600), **Simvo Tours & Travels** (☎ 258549; day tour per person/jeep Rs175/1600), **Dolphin Tours** (☎ 250621; Hotel Parodzong; jeep trips Dec-Feb & Jun-Aug/Sep-Nov & Mar-May Rs1200/2000) and many hotels plus several other agencies offer one-day tours. A popular choice visits Yuksom via Khecheopalri Lake and three waterfalls.

Sleeping
Budget

The Garuda and Kabur are backpacker specialists. Others are just cheap local hotels.

Hotel Garuda (☎ 258319; dm Rs60, d Rs250-350) A backpacker favourite with clean, unsophisticated rooms, unbeatable Khangchendzonga views from the roof and a cosy Tibetan-style bar-restaurant ideal for meeting other travellers. Tours (above) are good value and guests receive a handy schematic guide map.

our pick **Hotel Kabur** (☎ 9735945598, 258504; r Rs150-600) Entry is via the top floor, which is a delightful restaurant fronted by a wooden balcony crowded with potted plants while, several floors down, a veranda and sun beds look out onto the mountains. Great-value rooms have cute wicker lamps, towels, soap, toilet paper and heaters in winter – all usually absent in rooms of this price. Rooms have TV with CNN, BBC and Star Movies. If you need to know something, do something or go somewhere, the owner, Deepen, is the person to ask. Local tours for up to six people cost Rs1800 per vehicle.

Hotel Parodzong (☎ 258239; r Rs400-1000) No nonsense, good-value rooms have clean squat toilets and water heaters. From those facing north you can see Khangchendzonga from your bed, albeit across a communal walkway terrace. Out of season prices drop by 50%.

Midrange & Top End

Most of Pelling's hotels are midrangers catering primarily to domestic tourists. Rates typically drop 30% in low season and are highly negotiable during low occupancy. Midrange hotels charge a 10% service charge.

Hotel Simvo (☎ 258347; d Rs500-1400) Down steps beside the Hotel Sonamchen and with similar fine views. The Simvo's upper, and more expensive, rooms are its best; the acceptable cheapies on the bottom floors aren't as dingy as the corridors might suggest.

Hotel Sonamchen (☎ 258606; www.sikkiminfo .net/sonamchen; s/d from Rs750/1000) A magnificently decorated lobby greets you but that's the best you get. Nonetheless, most rooms – even on the cheapest bottom floor – have truly superb Khangchendzonga views, but the upstairs rooms are overpriced.

Newa Regency (☎ 258596; www.hotelnewaregency .com; s/d from Rs2000/2150) Pelling's most stylish choice is a triangular slice of modern architecture decorated with Sikkimese touches, notably in the charming 1st-floor sitting room. The bar has an outside terrace. Front rooms, like 201, have balconies and the best views.

Norbu Ghang Resort (☎ 258272; www.norbughang resort.com; s/d from Rs2500/2700; 🕸) A spread of pretty, self-contained cottages dots the hillside of this resort. All have Khangchendzonga views; lie in bed at dawn with a cup of tea and watch the sun wash the mountain in gold.

Elgin Mount Pandim (☎ 250756; mtpandim@elgin hotels.com; s/d from Rs4800/5100; 🕸 🖳) Pelling's most aristocratic hotel is a 10-minute stroll from Pemayangtse gompa, with arguably the best mountainscape viewpoint in all of Sikkim. The fairy godmother of renovation has waved her wand over the property and this former state-owned hotel now twinkles. Be prepared for serious cosseting.

Other options:

Touristo Hotel (☎ 258206; s Rs350-700, d Rs475-900) The best rooms have good Khangchendzonga views.

Hotel Rabdentse Residency (☎ 258612; rabdentse .pelling@yahoo.co.in; s/d from Rs750/850) Downstairs behind the Touristo. Obliging staff and a great attention to detail.

Eating & Drinking

Pelling's best dining is in the hotels. The Norbu Ghang, Kabur and Rabdentse Residency serve particularly good food, while the Garuda's a great place for a beer and a travel chat.

Taatopani Bar and Restaurant (Middle Pelling; mains Rs50-90; 🕙 10am-10pm Dec-Feb & Jun-Aug, to 12.30am Sep-Nov & Mar-May) has a long, thin terrace bar tacked onto its restaurant. Mocktails are Rs90, cocktails Rs165 and beer Rs70 to Rs80; a band entertains during the high season.

Shopping

Rural Artisan Marketing Centre (🕙 8am-7pm) just downhill from the tourist office sells local crafts, traditional costumes and organic produce such as tea, cardamom and walnuts.

Getting There & Away

SNT buses run to Gangtok (Rs85, 5½ hours, 7am and 12.30pm) via Ravangla (Rs70, two hours), and Siliguri (Rs150, 4½ hours, 7am) via Jorethang (Rs40, 2½ hours). Booking ahead is advised; go to the **SNT counter** (☎ 250707; Hotel Pelling; 🕙 7am-6pm Dec-Feb & Jun-Aug, 7am-9pm Sep-Nov & Mar-May) in Lower Pelling from where the buses depart.

The frequency of shared jeeps increases as the season progresses but year-round rides depart early morning and around noon to Gangtok (Rs160, five hours) and at 8am to Siliguri (Rs155, 4½ hours). Simvo Tours & Travels (p599) also offers high-season sumos to Darjeeling (Rs175, five hours, 8am). **Father Tours** (☎ 258219) has jeeps to Kalimpong (Rs135, four hours, 6.15am).

If nothing is available ex-Pelling, change in Geyzing. Share jeeps to Geyzing (Rs20, 20 minutes) leave when full (around twice an hour) from near Hotel Garuda. They pass close to Pemayangtse, Rabdentse and Tikjuk District Administrative Centre.

For Khecheopalri Lake (Rs60) or Yuksom (Rs60) jeeps start from Geyzing and, although booking ex-Pelling is sometimes possible, it's often easier simply to join a day-trip tour and throw away the return ticket. A taxi for a day trip to Khecheopalri Lake, Pemayangtse Gompa and Rabdentse will cost Rs1200.

AROUND PELLING
Pemayangtse Gompa
elev 2105m

Literally translated as 'Perfect Sublime Lotus', the 1705 **Pemayangtse** (Indian/foreigner Rs10/20; 🕙 7am-4pm Dec-Feb & Jun-Aug, 7am-6pm Sep-Nov & Mar-May) is one of Sikkim's oldest and most significant Nyingmapa gompas. Magnificently set on a hilltop overlooking the Rabdentse ruins, the atmospheric compound is ringed by gardens and traditional monks' cottages walled in unpainted stone. The contrastingly colourful prayer hall is beautifully proportioned, its doors and windows painted with Tibetan motifs. The statue is of Padmasambhava in his awful form as Dorje Bhurpa Vajrakila with multiple heads and arms. Upstairs, fierce-looking statues depict all eight of Padmasambhava's incarnations. On the top floor, **Zandog Palri** is an astounding seven-tiered model of Padmasambhava's heavenly abode, handmade over five laborious years by a single dedicated lama.

During February/March impressive *chaam* dances celebrating Losar culminate with the unfurling of a giant embroidered scroll and the zapping of evil demons with a great fireball.

Pemayangtse is 25 minutes' walk (1.3km) from Upper Pelling. The signposted turnoff from the Pelling–Geyzing road is near an obvious stupa.

PADMASAMBHAVA

Known as Guru Rinpoche in Tibetan, Sibaji in Nepali/Hindi or Padmasambhava in Sanskrit, this 8th-century 'second Buddha' is credited with introducing Tantric Buddhism to Tibet. Padmasambhava statues and murals are common throughout Sikkim. In his most classic form, he's usually shown sitting cross-legged with wild, staring eyes and a *tirsul* (a trident-headed staff) tucked into the folds of his left sleeve. This spears a trio of heads in progressive stages of decomposition representing the three *kayas* (aspects of enlightenment). Meanwhile Padmasambhava's right hand surreptitiously gives a two-fingered salute from behind a *dorje* (mini sceptre).

Padmasambhava has seven other alternative manifestations. The most striking of these, Dorje Bhurpa Vajrakila, shows him with three frightful heads and a lusty wench gyrating on his groin.

Rabdentse

The royal capital of Sikkim from 1670 to 1814, the now-ruined **Rabdentse** (admission free; dawn-dusk) consists of chunky wall-stubs with a few inset inscription stones. These would look fairly unremarkable were they not situated on such an utterly fabulous viewpoint ridge. The entrance to the site is around 3km from Upper Pelling. From the site's ornate yellow gateway, the ruins are a further 15-minutes' hike around a pond then across a forested hill.

Sangachoeling Gompa

The second-oldest gompa in all of Sikkim, **Sangachoeling** has some beautiful murals and a magnificent ridgetop setting. It's a steep 3km walk from Pelling starting along the track that veers left where the asphalted road rises to Pelling's new helipad.

A jungle trek continues 10km beyond Sangachoeling to **Rani Dhunga** (Queen's Rock), supposedly the scene of an epic Ramayana battle between Rama and 10-headed demon king Ravana. Take a guide.

Darap

For a relaxing day trip from Pelling, walk down to gently pleasant **Darap village** using the web of village footpaths through small rural hamlets. Khangchendzonga should be visible to your right most of the way, at least if the clouds are magnanimous. Hotel Garuda (p599) offers guided walks with a ride home afterwards.

THE MONASTERY LOOP
☎ 03595

The three-day 'Monastic Trek' from Pelling to Tashiding via Khecheopalri Lake remains possible; however, improvements to the Pelling–Yuksom road means dust clouds get stirred up by ever-more frequent tourist jeeps, diminishing the appeal of hiking the trek's on-road sections. Consider catching a ride to wonderful Yuksom (via Khecheopalri Lake using tour jeeps) and hiking from there to Tashiding (one day, no permit required). Even if you don't trek further than the Yak Restaurant, Yuksom is a delightful place to unwind.

Pelling to Yuksom

Tourist jeeps stop at several relatively lacklustre time-filler sites. **Rimbi** and **Khangchendzonga Falls** are best after rains while **Phamrong Falls** are impressive any time. Although it's several kilometres up a dead-end spur road, virtually all Yuksom-bound tours visit Khecheopalri, dropping you for about half an hour at a car park that's a five-minute stroll from the little lake.

KHECHEOPALRI LAKE
elev 1951m

Pronounced catch-a-perry, this holy lake is highly revered by Sikkimese Buddhists who believe that birds assiduously remove any leaves from its surface. During **Khachoedpalri Mela** (March/April), butter lamps are floated out across the lake. Prayer wheels line the lake's jetty, which is backed by fluttering prayer flags and Tibetan inscriptions, but the setting, ringed with forested hills, is serene rather than dramatic. To appreciate this you could stay overnight and visit once the tourists have left. If you trek up to the **Dupok** viewpoint (ask at the Trekkers Hut) you'll see the outline of the lake as a footprint.

Trekkers Hut Guest House (☎ 9733076995; dm/tw without bathroom Rs50/150) is an isolated pale-green building about 300m back down the access road from the car park. The government owns the hut and doesn't invest enough in its upkeep, but the tenant, the helpful Mr Teng, does what he can. So the rooms are basic but clean and share several bathrooms. You can get tongba (Rs30), filling meals (Rs50) ,trekking information and sometimes bird-watching or culturally-themed guided hikes. If sleeping over, you'll have time to trek up to **Khecheopalri Gompa** above the lake.

Around the car park is a Buddhist nunnery (behind a shrine-style gateway), a small shop, and the very basic **Jigme Restaurant** serving tea, *momos* and chow mein. There's no village. We've heard, subsequent to our research, that the gompa operates the **Palas Guest House** (☎ 9832471253) where meditation is also taught. Facing the end of the car park take the small path wending upwards from the left-hand side.

Share jeeps to Geyzing (Rs70, two hours) leave the lake at about 6am travelling via Pelling (23km).

The trail to Yuksom (9km, three to five hours) descends to the main road, emerging near the Khangchendzonga Falls. After a suspension bridge, follow the shortcut trail uphill to meet the Yuksom road, about 2km below Yuksom village. Ask at the Trekkers Hut for detailed directions.

Yuksom

☎ 03595 / elev 1780m

Loveable little Yuksom is historic, charming and unspoilt. Domestic tourists avoid it as it lacks the mountain views and it hasn't become a travellers' ghetto like Hampi or Manali. The town is the main trailhead for the Khangchendzonga Trek (opposite); otherwise it's an ideal place for day walks. The **Community Information Centre** (per hr Rs50; ☽ 10am-1pm & 3-5pm) offers internet connections in an unlikely hut near Kathok Lake. Opposite is a small shop selling souvenirs and Tibetan-style woolly socks.

A number of trekking agencies in Yuksom, such as **Mountain Tours and Treks** (☎ 241248; www .sherpatreks.in), operate on the Khangchendzonga trek. Prices are around US$40 per person per day assuming a group of four.

SIGHTS

Yuksom means 'meeting place of the three lamas', referring to the trio of Tibetan holy men who crowned the first chogyal of Sikkim here in 1641. The site is now **Norbugang Park**, which contains a prayer house, big prayer wheel, chorten (stupa) and the supposedly original **Coronation Throne** (Norbugang). Standing beneath a vast cryptomeria pine, it looks something like an ancient Olympic medal podium made of whitewashed stone. Just in front of the throne is a spooky footprint fused into the stone, believed to that of one of the crowning lamas: lift the little wooden guard-plank and you can see a distinct impression of sole and toes.

Walking to Norbugang Park past Hotel Tashi Gang you'll pass the murky **Kathok Lake**, from which anointing waters were taken for the original coronation.

When Yuksom was Sikkim's capital, a royal palace complex known as **Tashi Tenka** sat on a slight ridge to the south with superb almost 360-degree views. Today barely a stone remains but the views are still superb. To find the site take the small path marked by two crumbling little whitewashed stupas near the village school. The site is less than five minutes' walk away through tiny **Gupha Dara**, a sub-hamlet of around a dozen semi-traditional houses.

High on the ridge above Yuksom, **Dubdi Gompa** is set in beautifully tended gardens behind three coarsely hewn stupas. Established in 1701, it's likely to be Sikkim's oldest monastery but the prayer house looks vastly newer. There's no resident monk but there should be a caretaker on site during the daytime. Start the steep 45-minute climb from Yuksom's village clinic; the way rises through thickets of trumpet lilies and some lovely mature forest. Beware of leeches.

Yuksom has two photogenic new gompas. **Kathok Wodsallin Gompa**, near Hotel Tashi Gang, has an impressively stern statue of Guru Padmasambhava surrounded by a collection of yogis, gurus and lamas in glass-fronted compartments. Similarly colourful is **Ngadhak Changchub Choling**, accessed through an ornate gateway opposite Hotel Yangri Gang. A many-handed and -headed Buddha gazes benignly at the monks, who perform *puja* here at 6am and 7pm.

The trail to Dzongri and Goecha La passes the police post where trekking permits are carefully checked, and then continues uphill past the driveway to the Hotel Tashi Gang.

SLEEPING & EATING

Many small hotels are dotted all along the short but meandering main street.

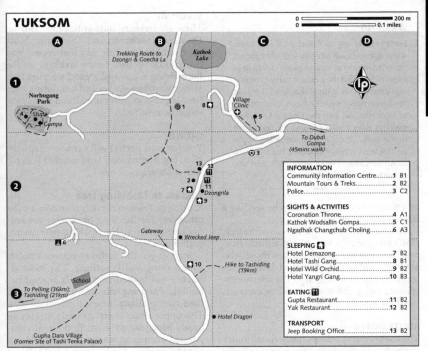

YUKSOM

0 | 200 m
0 | 0.1 miles

Trekking Route to Dzongri & Goecha La

Kathok Lake

Norbugang Park

Stupa Gompa

Village Clinic

To Dubdi Gompa (45mins walk)

Dzongrila

Gateway

Wrecked Jeep

Hike to Tashiding (19km)

School

To Pelling (36km); Tashiding (21km)

Hotel Dragon

Gupha Dara Village (Former Site of Tashi Tenka Palace)

INFORMATION

Community Information Centre	**1**	B1
Mountain Tours & Treks	**2**	B2
Police	**3**	C2

SIGHTS & ACTIVITIES

Coronation Throne	**4**	A1
Kathok Wodsallin Gompa	**5**	C1
Ngadhak Changchub Choling	**6**	A3

SLEEPING

Hotel Demazong	**7**	B2
Hotel Tashi Gang	**8**	B1
Hotel Wild Orchid	**9**	B2
Hotel Yangri Gang	**10**	B3

EATING

Gupta Restaurant	**11**	B2
Yak Restaurant	**12**	B2

TRANSPORT

Jeep Booking Office	**13**	B2

Hotel Demazong (☎ 241215, 9775473687; dm Rs100, r without bathroom Rs200-500) A budget option with shared bathrooms and off-season discounts.

Hotel Wild Orchid (☎ 241212; tw/tr without bathroom Rs150/225) This neat, clean half-timbered house is rather ragged but the most charming budget option. Bathrooms are shared, bucket hot water costs Rs10.

Hotel Yangri Gang (☎ 241217; d Rs350-800, without bathroom Rs200) Basement rooms are functional concrete cubes, but the upstairs options are airy with clean wooden floors, wooden half-panelling and good hot showers.

Hotel Tashi Gang (☎ 241202; s/d from Rs850/1100) The colours of the bedspreads, frilly yellow and red ceiling curtains in the restaurant, and *thangkas* in some bedrooms all show a reference to Sikkimese monastic art. Rooms are large with clean wooden floors and well fitted-out bathrooms. Out of season, bargaining can make this the most appealing option in town.

Beers, chow mein, curries, breakfast cornflakes and *thukpa* are cheaply available from a pair of atmospheric restaurants, Yak and Gupta, side by side at the bus/jeep stand. Both have an outside get-around-and-be-friendly table with thatched roof, but the Gupta has the more pleasant interior. Mains are Rs35 to Rs70. Eat early as doors close by 8pm.

GETTING THERE & AWAY

Around 6.30am, several shared jeeps leave for Jorethang (Rs90, four hours) via Tashiding (Rs40, 1½ hours), Gangtok (Rs150, six hours) and Geyzing via Pelling (Rs60, approximately 2½ hours). Best to book at the hut opposite the Yak restaurant the day before.

Dzongri & Goecha La – The Khangchendzonga Trek

For guided groups with permits, Yuksom is the starting point of Sikkim's classic trek to Goecha La, a 4940m pass with quite fabulous views of Khangchendzonga.

Taking seven to 10 days, trek costs start at US$40 to US$55 per person per day (assuming a group of four), including food, guides, porters and yaks. For more information, see the route notes and boxed text on p604.

Trekking agencies will sort out the permits. Paperwork must be done in Gangtok, but given two or three days, agents in Pelling

WARNING

For the final leg to Goecha La and back, some agencies will have their groups depart from Thangsing at 1am to avoid camping at Lamuni because they do not carry camping equipment. This is unadvisable as it makes for a very long day (12 hours plus stops), at high altitude, and the first part involves walking over rocky ground by torchlight in the dark, where a sprained ankle might be the least of your troubles. Far better to camp at Lamuni, take your time and see everything in daylight.

or Yuksom can organise things by sending a fixer to the capital for you.

Don't underestimate the rigours of the trek. Don't hike too high too quickly: altitude sickness (see p1198) usually strikes those who are fittest and fastest. Starting at dawn makes sense, as rain is common in the afternoons, spoiling views and making trail sections annoyingly muddy.

ROUTE NOTES

The route initially follows the Rathong Valley through unspoilt forests then ascends steeply to **Bakhim** (2740m) and the rustic village of **Tsokha** (3050m), where spending two nights helps with acclimatisation.

The next stage climbs to pleasant meadows around **Dzongri** (4025m). Consider another acclimatisation day here spent strolling up to **Dablakang** or **Dzongri La** (4550m, four-hour round trip) for fabulous views of Mt Pandim (6691m).

From Dzongri, the trail drops steeply to **Kokchuran** then follows the river to **Thangsing** (3840m). Next day takes you to camping at **Lamuni**, 15 minutes before **Samiti Lake** (4200m) from where a next-morning assault takes you to head-spinning **Goecha La** (4940m) for those incredible views of Khangchendzonga. Readers have recommended an alternative viewpoint reached by climbing an hour up from the left side of Samiti Lake.

The return is by essentially the same route but with shortcuts that are sometimes a little overgrown. Alternatively at Dzongri you could cut south for about a week following the **Singalila Ridge** along the Nepal–Sikkim border to emerge at **Uttarey**, from where public transport runs to Jorethang.

SLEEPING

There are trekkers' huts at Bakhim, Tsokha, Dzongri, Kokchuran and Thangsing. Most have neither furniture nor mattresses; you just cuddle up with fellow trekkers on the floor. Bring a mat and a good sleeping bag. Huts sometimes get booked out during high trekking season, so some additional camping might be involved.

EATING

You (or your porter) will need to carry supplies, but limited food (and tongba) is available at Dzongri.

Yuksom to Tashiding Trek

Starting in Yuksom is easier than coming the other way for this long but highly rewarding one-day trek. No trekking permits are required.

Start down the pathway between hotels Yangri Gang and Penathang. The most attractive but longest route leads around behind the **Phamrong Falls** (heard but not seen), then rises to **Tsong**, where the trail divides. The upper route leads up fairly steeply to lonely **Hongri Gompa**, a small, unusually unpainted ancient monastery building with a superlative ridge-top location. Local folklore claims the gompa was moved here from a higher spot where monks kept being ravaged by yeti.

KHANGCHENDZONGA TREK SCHEDULE		
Stage	**Route**	**Duration (hr)**
1	Yuksom to Tsokha, via Bakhim	6-7
2	Acclimatisation day at Tsokha	1 day
3	Tsokha to Dzongri	4-5
4	Acclimatisation day at Dzongri, or continue to Kokchuran	1 day
5	Dzongri (or Kokchuran) to Lamuni, via Thangsing	6-7
6	Lamuni to Goecha La, then down to Thangsing	8-9
7	Thangsing to Tsokha	6-7
8	Tsokha to Yuksom	5-6

To this point the route is relatively easy to follow, with stone grips. But descending from Hongri there are slippery patches with lurking leeches. At **Nessa** hamlet, finding the way can be mildly confusing. A few minutes beyond in attractive **Pokhari Dara** the trail divides again beside the village shop. Descending takes you the more direct way to Tashiding. Continuing along the ridge brings you to **Sinon Gompa** very high above Tashiding. The final approach to that monastery has some fascinating, ancient *mani* walls (stone walls with sacred inscriptions) but the descent to Tashiding is long and steep by the shortcut paths or almost 10km of long switchbacks by road.

Tashiding
elev 1490m
Little Tashiding is just a single, sloping spur-street forking north off the Yuksom–Legship road, but its south-facing views are wide and impressive. Walking 400m south from the junction towards Legship takes you down past a series of **mani walls** with bright Tibetan inscriptions to a colourful **gateway**. A 2.4km uphill driveable track leads to a car park from where a sometimes-slippery footpath leads up steeply between an avenue of prayer flags to the ancient **Tashiding Gompa**, about 15 minutes' walk away.

Founded in 1641 by one of the three Yuksom lamas (see p602), the monastery's five colourful religious buildings are strung out between more functional monks' quarters. Notice the giant-sized prayer wheel with Tibetan script picked out in gilt. Beautifully proportioned, the four-storey **main prayer hall** has a delicate filigree topknot and looks noble from a distance. On closer inspection most of the exterior decor is rather coarse, but wonderfully wide views from here across a semi-wild flower garden encompass the whole valley towards Ravangla.

Beyond the last monastic building, a curious compound contains dozens of white chortens, including the **Thong-Wa-Rang-Dol**, said to wash away the sins of anyone who gazes upon it. Smaller but more visually exciting is the golden **Kench Chorgi Lorde** stupa. Propped up all around are engraved stones bearing Buddhist prayers; at the back of the compound is the engraver's lean-to.

In January or February, the monastery celebrates the **Bumchu festival** during which lamas gingerly open a sacred pot. Then, judging from the level of holy water within, they make all-important predictions about the coming year.

Tashiding village's three basic, friendly hotels all have shared bathrooms. **Hotel Blue Bird** (☎ 243248; r without bathroom Rs100) at the bottom of the street is the cheapest but most decrepit. The neater **Mt Siniolchu Guest House** (☎ 243211, 9733092480; r without bathroom Rs100-200) is a better option. **New Tashiding Lodge** (☎ 243249; Legship Rd; tr without bathroom Rs200), 300m south of the market, has fine views from Rooms 3, 4 and 5 and even better ones from the shared bathroom.

Share jeeps to Gangtok (Rs120, four hours) via Legship (Rs30, one hour) pass the main junction, mostly between 6.30am and 8am. A few jeeps to Yuksom pass through during early afternoon but if you want an early start it's better to go via Legship or Geyzing.

NORTH SIKKIM
☎ 03592
The biggest attractions in North Sikkim are the idyllic Yumthang and Tsopta Valleys. Reaching them and anywhere north of Singhik requires a special permit, that's easy to obtain (see p587), although foreign visitors are only allowed to travel in North Sikkim in groups of two or more. It's perfectly possible to visit Phodong and Mangan/Singhik independently using public jeeps but they can also be conveniently seen during brief stops on any Yumthang tour and at no extra cost.

GANGTOK TO SINGHIK
The narrow but mostly well-paved 31ANHWay clings to steep wooded slopes above the Teesta River, occasionally descending in long coils of hairpins to a bridge photogenically draped in prayer flags, only to coil right back up again on the other side. If driving, consider brief stops at Tashi Viewpoint (p589), Kabi Lunchok, Phensang and the Seven Sisters waterfall

Kabi Lunchok
This atmospheric glade, 17km north of Gangtok, decorated with memorial stones is the site of a 13th-century peace treaty between the chiefs of the Lepcha and Bhutia peoples. They swore a blood brotherhood until the River Rangit ran dry and Khangchendzonga ceased to exist.

Phensang

This small 240-year-old monastery belonging to the Nyingmapa sect has lower and upper floor prayer halls that are beautifully decorated. It's all recent, though, as the monastery was rebuilt after a 1957 fire. The **Chaam festival** is celebrated here on the 28th and 29th days of the Tibetan 10th month, usually December.

Seven Sisters Waterfall

A multistage cascade cuts a chasm here above a roadside cardamom grove and plummets into a rocky pool and then a ravine. An ancient girder bridge spans the ravine, 30km north of Gangtok, while on the south side there's a welcome chai shop.

Phodong

elev 1814m

The little strip of roadside restaurants at Phodong make it a popular lunch stop. Simple rooms are available at the **Hotel Yak and Yeti** (☎ 9434357905; dm Rs100, d without bathroom Rs200-250), where English is spoken.

About 1km southeast near the Km39 post, a 15-minute walk along a very degraded former road leads to the **Phodong Gompa** (established in 1740), belonging to the Kagupa sect. The beautiful two-storey prayer hall contains extensive murals and a large statue of the 9th Karmapa. A rear room contains a hidden statue of Mahakla, a protective deity of the monastery.

Walk on another 30 minutes to the much more atmospheric and peaceful **Labrang Gompa** (established in 1884). Its prayer hall murals repeat the same Padmasambhava pose 1022 times. Upstairs a fearsome depiction of Guru Padmasambhava sports a necklace of severed heads. *Chaam* dances take place in early December.

Phodong to Singhik

North Sikkim's district headquarters, **Mangan** (Km67 post) proudly declares itself to be the 'Large Cardamom Capital of the World'. Some 1.5km beyond, weather-blackened stupas on a sharp bend mark a small footpath; a three-minute descent leads to a panoramic **viewpoint**.

Apart from the stunningly magnificent scenery there's nothing specific to stop for between Mangan and Lachen or Lachung, which are the places where visitors stop for the night.

BEYOND SINGHIK

With relevant permits and an organised tour you can continue north beyond Singhik. At Chungthang, the next settlement, the Teesta divides into the Lachung Chu (valley) and the Lachen Chu.

Accommodation is available in Lachung and Lachen, with two more basic options in Thanggu. We have listed a few favourites but normally your tour agencies will preselect for you. Some family places stay open on the off chance of passing Indian tourists, but most lodges close up when there's no prebooked group due.

Cheaper hotels tend to have a mixed bag of rooms whose prices are the same whether or not the room has geyser, shower, heating, window or balcony. It's pot luck, so try to see a few different rooms even if you can't choose your hotel.

Lachen and Lachung are both Lepcha villages with a unique form of local democracy in which the *pipon* (headman) is elected every year.

Lachung Chu

LACHUNG

elev 3000m

Soaring rock-pinnacled valley walls embroidered with long ribbons of waterfall surround the scattered village of Lachung. To appreciate the full drama of its setting, take the metal cantilever bridge across the wild Yumthang River to the Sanchok side then climb 1.5km along the Katao road for great views from the **Lachung Gompa** (established 1880). The gompa's refined murals include one section of original paintings (inner left wall as you enter) and its twin giant prayer wheels chime periodically. Two large dragons keep guard above the entrance. **Internet** (per hr Rs30; ⏰ 10am-4pm Mon-Sat) is available in a room across the other side of the football field of the local secondary school.

Mt Katao, nearly 30km beyond, is popular with Indian tourists, who drive up to the top to play in the snow. However, it remains off-limits to foreign tourists.

Many hotels are dotted around Lachung, with the most convenient concentration around Faka Bazaar just over the bridge. Rates start at Rs300 for the most basic, but will double in high season. Many outwardly modern places maintain traditional Tibetan-style wood-fire stoves and can churn salt-butter tea for you in a traditional churn-plunger device.

NORTH SIKKIM TOUR TIPS

- A group size of four or five people is ideal for sharing costs while not overfilling the jeep.
- To find jeep-share partners, try hanging out in the cafe at New Modern Central Lodge (Gangtok; p591) around 6pm a few days before you plan to travel. There's no fixed system, just ask other travellers.
- Less than four days is too rushed to comfortably visit both Yumthang/Lachung and Lachen. Three-night/four-day tours start at Rs2500 per person for groups of five, depending on accommodation standards.
- Leave Gangtok early on the first day: it's a shame to arrive in the dark.
- Your (obligatory) 'guide' is actually more of a translator. Don't assume he'll stop at all potential points of interest without prodding.
- Bring a torch for inevitable power cuts.
- Don't miss tasting tongba (tiny extra cost).

Open year-round, the family-run and friendly **Sila Inn Lodge** (☎ 214808; r without bathroom Rs300-500) has a typically mixed bag of rooms above a friendly hostelry-restaurant. Best rooms are on the top floor.

Nearby hotels **Le Coxy** (www.nivalink.com/lecoxy resort) and **Sonam Palgey** are more upmarket.

In a side lane around 3km south of Lachung, a brilliantly colourful flight of fancy rises like a fairy-tale Tibetan monastery. Staying at the **Modern Residency** (Tagsing Retreat; ☎ 214888; Singring Village; d Rs2500) is one great advantage of taking a tour with Modern Treks & Tours (p591). Rooms have local design features and are comfortable, though walk-in prices are very steep. Even if you don't stay, the building is well worth visiting. One upper floor has a veritable mini-museum and the top-floor roof, above the prayer room, offers magnificent views across the valley.

YUMTHANG VALLEY

The main point of coming to Lachung is continuing 23km further north to admire the majestic Yumthang Valley, which starts some 10km after leaving Lachung. This point is also the entry to the **Singba Rhododendron Sanctuary** where both vegetation and landscape change from the preceding steep-sided Lachung Chu. The valley widens and flattens, and is spotted with stands of conifers festooned with woollen strands of lichen. Stumps of trees from indiscriminate felling flank the roadway and mosses cover the bare rocks in green, while everywhere rhododendron bushes flourish. From March to early May this valley lives up to its other name, the Valley of Flowers,

as primulas, rhododendrons and a host of other plants burst into flower and carpet the valley floor.

At the 23km point there are a number of snack shacks that open up in the high season and where the Sikkim tourism authority is building a guest house. On the other side of the river, a grimy, unlit, 2-sq-metre pool in a rubbish-ringed hut presents itself as **hot springs**. The real drama starts about 1km north of here down by the riverbank. Weather permitting, you should have 360-degree views of an utterly magnificent Himalayan scene: glaciers, spiky peaks and a veritable candelabra of white jagged mountains rising towards Tibet. Lucky Indian tourists are allowed to venture a further 23km to Yume Samdong.

Lachen Chu

LACHEN
elev 2750m

Until recently Lachen was an untouched, traditional Lepcha village. That's changing fast with pretty roadside houses being progressively replaced by concrete house-hotels. Nonetheless, alleyways remain sprinkled with old wooden homes on sturdy stone bases, and Tibetan-style constructions with colourful, faceted window frames. Logs are stacked everywhere for winter fuel.

Lachen Gompa is about 15 minutes' walk above the town. While the grey brick exterior is unappealing no interior surface has been left uncovered. All display different manifestations of Guru Padmasambhava.

Lachen is the trailhead for expeditionary treks to **Green Lake** along the Yeti-infested **Zemu**

Glacier towards Khangchendzonga's northeast face. These require long advance planning and very expensive permits.

Sinolchu Lodge (☎ 9434356189; d Rs300-400) has the advantage of being open all year. Rooms are small but cosy and the beds are piled with thick blankets. It's here that you relish bringing along a sleeping sheet, as there are no bed sheets. Rooms have attached bathrooms but only the dearer rooms have geysers. Otherwise it's bucket hot water.

If you can choose your accommodation, a great budget option is super-friendly **Bayul Lodge** (tw without bathroom Rs250), whose upper facade is colourfully carved with Tibetan motifs. It's above the tiny video-cinema, beside the post office.

THANGGU & TSOPTA
elev 4267m

Beyond a sprawling army camp 32km north of Lachen, **Thanggu** has an appealing end-of-the-world feel. It's too high for leeches, there are no phones (mobile or otherwise), the Chinese are only 15km away and the only electricity is solar-generated.

Misleadingly named **Thanggu Resort** (d & tr without bathroom Rs500) is outwardly an ordinary family house incorporating a traditional-styled kitchen, dining area and tongba-drinking den (tongba Rs10). Rooms are simple but two have attached squat toilet and views of the river. Open May to November.

A boulder-strewn moorland stream leads on 2km to tiny **Tsopta**. Just above the tree line, the scenery feels rather like Glencoe (Scotland) but the valley's western horizon has the added drama of a glacier-toothed mountain wall. Yak, dzho (cattle/yak crossbreed) and donkey convoys wander through on missions to supply some of the Indian military's more far-flung outposts way beyond. Indian visitors can continue 30km north to **Gurudongmar Lake** up the Tsopta Valley, but for foreigners the only option is to park by the army post at the bend leading into the valley. Still there's plenty to appreciate. Below is a verdant dried lakebed and to its left a long ridge of high land forested with rhododendrons and conifers. This moraine, left by a glacier, is responsible for damming the Tsopte River and creating the lake. As you return towards Thanggu you'll notice that at one place the dammed river has broken through and descends the moraine in a series of scintillating cascades.

Northeast States

India's 1947 partition left the Northeast States dangling like a fragile appendage to the main body of the country, way out on the edge of the map and national perception.

The Northeast States only figure in the national consciousness when something dramatic happens. Likewise the region is off the tourist map for most foreign visitors, perhaps because of its lack of a 'Taj Mahal–style, must-see' place. Despite this, the region has many attractions worth seeking out.

The great, flat Brahmaputra valley and its wide, muddy river is a traditional Hindu heartland, and is the backdrop to several Krishna tales. Lying mostly within Assam, the valley is home to beautiful tea plantations and national parks with rhinoceroses, elephants and tigers.

In contrast, the mountainous surrounding states are home to tribal peoples whose varied cultures and faces have more in common with Burma, China and Tibet than mainstream India.

Despite the region's attractions, infuriating permits (not required for Assam, Meghalaya or Tripura) and safety worries deter most travellers from visiting the northeast. This makes it a place for adventurers who want something different from their India experience. You'll meet very few foreigners in the region's national parks. And you'll get vast tracts of fabulous rice, tea and mountain scenery all to yourself. A few insurgency campaigns do rumble on (for safety advice, see p611), but generally the people here are among the friendliest in the whole subcontinent.

For extended coverage of this region consult Lonely Planet's *Northeast India* guidebook.

HIGHLIGHTS

- Ride atop a lumbering elephant through boggy grassland visiting rhinos in **Kaziranga National Park** (p618)

- Touch the clouds at the 4176m pass of Se La before descending to **Tawang Valley** (p626), Arunachal Pradesh's 'little Tibet'

- Visit intriguing tribal villages around **Ziro** (p623) and meet the last of the bizarrely adorned Apatani women

- Gaze down on the plains of Bangladesh from the lofty escarpment around **Cherrapunjee** (Sohra; p640), incised by waterfalls and burrowed into by caves

- Feel as if you've stepped out of India into a different culture and country in Nagaland's **Mon** (p629)

★ Ziro

★ Tawang Valley

Mon ★

★ Kaziranga National Park

★ Cherrapunjee (Sohra)

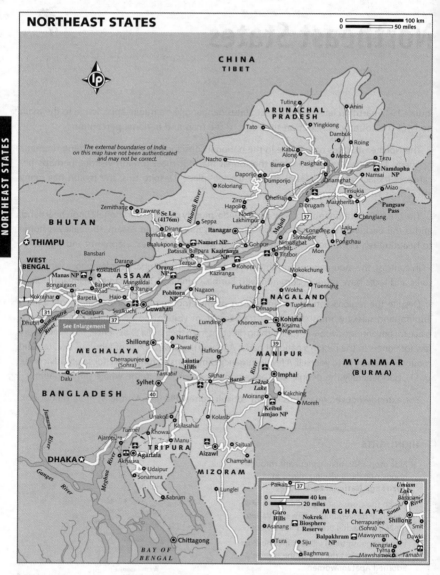

NORTHEAST STATES

The external boundaries of India on this map have not been authenticated and may not be correct.

Information

PERMITS

Permits are a pain, being too bureaucratically involved for many foreigners. However those who take the trouble will be rewarded. Permits are mandatory for Nagaland, Arunachal Pradesh, Mizoram and Manipur, and entry without one is a serious matter. Indian citizens just need

an inner line permit, issued with little fuss in Guwahati or Kolkata (Calcutta; p507). The rest of this section applies to foreigners who'll require a Restricted Area Permit (RAP).

Minimum Group Size

Permit applications need a four-person minimum group. Exceptions are Nagaland, for a

TRAVELLING SAFELY IN THE NORTHEAST STATES

In recent decades many ethno-linguistic groups have jostled – often violently – to assert themselves in the face of illegal Bangladeshi immigration, governmental neglect and a heavy-handed defence policy. Some want independence from India, others autonomy, yet more are effectively fighting clan or turf wars. Although many Western governments currently advise against travel in Manipur, Tripura, Nagaland and Assam (it might affect your travel insurance), it's worth noting that not all of these states are equally affected. At the time of writing Arunachal Pradesh, most of Assam, Meghalaya, Mizoram, and the tourist areas of Nagaland and Tripura seem the most peaceful.

The problem is that trouble can flare up suddenly and unpredictably. Bombings have hit the normally safe cities of Guwahati (2008), Agartala (2008) and Dimapur (2004) just as they have struck London and Madrid, so the level of danger to travellers is hard to quantify. Communal violence surged in 2008 in northern Assam between the Bodo people and Bangladeshi immigrants, but as most of the tourist sites are south of the Brahmaputra, visitors were not affected.

Still it's wise to keep abreast of latest news with the *Assam Tribune* (www.assamtribune.com) and if you're with a tour group, ensure your guide is up to date with the latest situation.

legally married couple with marriage certificate; and Arunachal Pradesh for a minimum of two people.

In Nagaland and Manipur, authorities may refuse you entry if some people listed on your permit are 'missing', Mizoram doesn't seem to bother and Arunachal Pradesh is now much more relaxed.

Validity & Registration
Permits are valid for 10 days from a specified starting date, but Arunachal now allows 30 days. You *might* be able to extend your permit, but only in state capitals at the Secretariat, Home Department. Be aware that permits only allow you to visit specified districts, so plan carefully as changing routes might be problematic.

Be sure to make multiple photocopies of your permit to hand in at each checkpoint, police station and hotel.

Where to Apply
Applications through the **Ministry of Home Affairs** (Map pp122-3; ☎ 011-23385748; Jaisalmer House, 26 Man Singh Rd, Delhi; ⏲ inquiries 9-11am Mon-Fri) or the appropriate State House in Delhi can take weeks and end in frustration. Kolkata's **Foreigners' Registration Office** (FRO; Map p510; ☎ 22837034; 237 AJC Bose Rd; ⏲ 11am-5pm Mon-Fri) can issue permits but it seems to want to exclude Tawang from Arunachal, restrict access to Nagaland and not allow you into Mizoram.

The easiest and most reliable way to get permits is through a reputable agency; see the Information section for each state.

CLIMATE
Decent AC rooms will be preferable for anywhere not well up a mountain until early October. But by December even sweaty Guwahati can feel chilly at night. Warm clothes will be useful at any time in Tawang where temperatures can dip to -15°C in January.

WHEN TO GO
Tourist season is October to April. However, most national parks only open from November and you'll see many more of the big animals if you wait till February.

ASSAM

Fascinating Assam (also known as Asom and Axom) straddles the fertile Brahmaputra valley, making it the most accessible of India's Northeast States. The archetypal Assamese landscape offers golden-green vistas over seemingly endless rice fields that are patched with palm and bamboo groves, and framed in the distance by the hazy-blue mountains of Arunachal. In between lie manicured tea estates.

ASSAM FAST FACTS

Population 26.6 million
Area 78,438 sq km
Capital Guwahati
Main languages Assamese, Bengali, Bodo
When to go October to March

FESTIVALS IN THE NORTHEAST

Tribal dances linked to the crop cycle take place year-round.

Torgya (Jan) and **Losar** (Jan/Feb) Tibetan-Buddhist *chaam* (ritual masked dances performed by some Buddhist monks in gompas to celebrate the victory of good over evil and of Buddhism over pre-existing religions) held most spectacularly at Tawang Gompa (p626).

Chapchar Kut (Mar; Mizoram statewide; http://mizotourism.nic.in/festival.htm) Spring festival, song and dance.

Rongali Bihu (late Apr; Assam statewide) Springtime celebrated with song and dance.

Ambubachi Mela (Jun; Kamakhya Mandir, Guwahati; p614) Tantric rituals and even more animal sacrifices than usual.

Kang (Rath Yatra; Jul; Manipur & Assam statewide) Chariot fest for Krishna's birthday.

Durga Puja (Oct; all Hindu areas) The region's biggest festival.

Buddha Mahotsava (variable; Tawang; http://tawang.nic.in/tawangbm/main.html) Government-sponsored Buddhist cultural festival.

Diwali (Oct/Nov; all Hindu areas) Lamps lit on banana-stem posts outside homes, Kali images dunked in rivers, general good humour.

Kwak Tenba (Oct/Nov; Imphal; p630) Fourth day of Durga Puja, religious ceremonies and re-enactments of past battles.

Wangala (Oct/Nov; Meghalaya statewide) Four-day Garo harvest festival with impressive dancing.

Nongkrem (Nov; Smit, p640) Five-day Khasi royal festival.

Ras Mahotsav Festival (3rd week of Nov; Majuli Island, p620) Major Vishnu festival with plenty of Krishna-epic recitations and dance-theatre.

Pawl Kut (Nov/Dec; Mizoram statewide) Mizoram's harvest festival.

Hornbill Festival (Dec; Kohima, p629) Nagaland's biggest event with wildly costumed dance performances by all main Naga tribes.

Assamese people might look Indian, but Assamese culture is proudly distinct: their Vishnu-worshipping faith is virtually a regional religion (see boxed text, p621) and the *gamosa* (a red-and-white scarf worn by most men) is a subtle mark of regional costume.

However, by no means is all of Assam ethnically Assamese. Before the Ahom invasions of the 13th and 15th centuries much of today's Assam was ruled from Dimapur (now Nagaland) by a Kachari-Dimasa dynasty. The Chutiaya (Deori-Bodo) kingdom was an important force further west. The Dimasa and Bodo peoples didn't just disappear; during the 20th century increasing ethnic consciousness led their descendents to resent the Assamese in much the same way as the Assamese have resented Bangladeshi immigration and greater India. The result was a major Bodo insurgency that was only settled in 2004–05 with the creation of an autonomous 'Bodoland' in northwestern Assam.

Don't let this put you off. Assam is a delightful, hospitable and deeply civilised place that you can easily grow to love. Its national parks protect a remarkable range of wildlife.

For more information, visit www.assamtourism.org. Rongali Bihu is a spring festival marking the beginning of the sowing season happening around the spring equinox or mid-April. Assamese wear new and colourful clothes, visit neighbours, friends and family and distribute sweets. Grand feasts may also be held to celebrate the occasion.

GUWAHATI

☎ 0361 / pop 964,000

A casual glance might place Guwahati alongside any other Indian city but wander the back alleys around Jorpulkuri Ponds, away from the central business district concrete jungle, and you might think yourself in a village made up of ponds, palm trees, small single-storey traditional houses and old colonial-era mansions. Come here to arrange tours to the Northeast States.

History

Guwahati is considered the site of Pragjyotishpura, a semimythical town founded by Asura King Naraka who was later killed by Lord Krishna for a pair of magical earrings. The city was a vibrant cultural centre well before the Ahoms arrived, and later it was the theatre of intense Ahom-Mughal fighting, changing hands eight times in 50 years before

1681. A huge 1897 earthquake followed by a series of devastating floods wiped out most of the old city.

Orientation

Hectic commercial bustle animates the central Fancy and Panbazaar areas, and stretches 10km southeast down Guwahati Shillong (GS) Rd from Paltan Bazaar (the bus station area).

Information

EMERGENCY

Police station (☎ 2540126) On Hem Barua (HB) Rd.

INTERNET ACCESS

i-way (Lamb Rd; per hr Rs25; ☺ 9am-last customer)

MEDICAL SERVICES

Downtown Hospital (☎ 2331003; GS Rd, Dispur) The area's best.

MONEY

ATMs abound. Change foreign currency and travellers cheques here (as limited elsewhere).
State Bank of India (SBI; ☎ 2544264; 3rd fl, MG Rd) ATM, changes major currencies and travellers cheques.
Thomas Cook (☎ 2664450; J Borooah Rd; ☺ 9.30am-6pm Mon-Sat) Shop behind Jet Airways. Changes 26 currencies and travellers cheques, no Bangladeshi taka though.

PERMITS

Indian citizens can obtain inner line permits (see list) but foreigners shouldn't expect any assistance (for foreigner permits, see p610).

NORTHEAST STATES

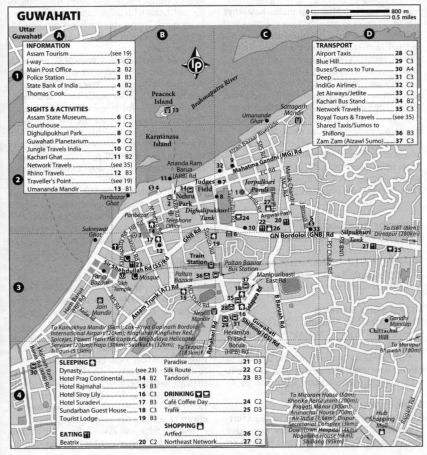

GUWAHATI

INFORMATION	
Assam Tourism	(see 19)
i-way	**1** C2
Main Post Office	**2** B2
Police Station	**3** B3
State Bank of India	**4** B2
Thomas Cook	**5** C2

SIGHTS & ACTIVITIES	
Assam State Museum	**6** C3
Courthouse	**7** C2
Dighulipukhuri Park	**8** C2
Guwahati Planetarium	**9** C2
Jungle Travels India	**10** C2
Kachari Ghat	**11** B2
Network Travels	(see 35)
Rhino Travels	**12** B3
Traveller's Point	(see 19)
Umananda Mandir	**13** B1

TRANSPORT	
Airport Taxis	**28** C3
Blue Hill	**29** C3
Buses/Sumos to Tura	**30** A4
Deep	**31** C3
IndiGo Airlines	**32** C2
Jet Airways/Jetlite	**33** C2
Kachari Bus Stand	**34** B2
Network Travels	**35** C3
Royal Tours & Travels	(see 35)
Shared Taxis/Sumos to Shillong	**36** B3
Zam Zam (Aizawl Sumo)	**37** C3

SLEEPING	
Dynasty	(see 23)
Hotel Prag Continental	**14** B2
Hotel Rajmahal	**15** B3
Hotel Siroy Lily	**16** C3
Hotel Suradevi	**17** B3
Sundarban Guest House	**18** B3
Tourist Lodge	**19** B3

EATING	
Beatrix	**20** C2
Paradise	**21** D3
Silk Route	**22** C2
Tandoori	**23** B3

DRINKING	
Café Coffee Day	**24** C2
Trafik	**25** D3

SHOPPING	
Artfed	**26** C2
Northeast Network	**27** C2

Uttar Guwahati

Peacock Island **13**

Brahmaputra River

Umananda Ghat

Sattagarh Mandir

Karmanasa Island

Ujan Bazaar Riverside

Mahatma Gandhi (MG) Rd

Ananda Ram Barua (ARB) Rd

Judges Field **7**

Nehru Park **2**

Dighalipukhuri Tank

Jorpulkuri Ponds

Argwal Path

Telephone Office

GNB Rd

GN Bordoloi (GNB) Rd

Silpukhuri Tank

To ISBT (8km); Dimapur (280km)

Panbazar Ghat

Sukreswar Ghat

Sir Shahadullah Rd (SS) Rd

Train Station

Paltan Bazaar Bus Station

Manipuribasti East Rd

Fancy Bazaar

Sikh Temple

Mosque

Paltan Bazaar **36**

Assam Trunk (AT) Rd

Jain Mandir

Nepali Mandir

Shillong (GS) Rd

B Baruah Rd

Gandhi Mandap

Chitrachal Hill

Heramba Prasad Borua (HPB) Rd

To Tezpur (181km)

To Manipur Bhawan (100m)

Hem Barua (HB) Rd

To Kamakhya Mandir (5km); Lok-Priya Gopinath Bordoloi International Airport (20km); Kingfisher/Kingfisher Red; Spicejet, Pawan Hans Helicopters, Meghalaya Helicopter Services (20km); Hajo (30km); Sualkuchi (32km); Siliguri (513km)

To Mizoram House (50m); Khorika Restaurant (200m); Pragati Manor (300m); Arunachal House (700m); Air India (1.6km); Dispur Secretariat Complex (3km); Downtown Hospital (4km); Nagaland House (6km); Shillong (95km)

Hub Shopping Mall

0   800 m
0   0.5 miles

Arunachal House (☎ 2229506; Rukmini Gao, GS Rd)
Manipur Bhawan (☎ 2540707; Rajgarh Rd)
Mizoram House (☎ 2529411; GS Rd, Christian Basti)
Nagaland House (☎ 2332158; Sachel Rd, Sixth Mile, Khanapara)

POST

Main post office Chaotic. On Ananda Ram Barua (ARB) Rd.

TOURIST INFORMATION

Assam Tourism (☎ 2547102; www.assamtourism.org; Station Rd) Informal help desk within the Tourist Lodge and a tour booth just outside.

Sights

KAMAKHYA MANDIR

While Sati's disintegrated body parts rained toes on Kolkata (see p502), her yoni (genitalia) fell on Kamakhya Hill. This makes **Kamakhya Mandir** (admission for queue/short queue/no queue free/Rs100/500; ☺ 8am-1pm & 3pm-dusk) important for sensual tantric worship of female spiritual power (shakti). Goats, pigeons and the occasional buffalo are ritually beheaded in a gory pavilion and the hot, dark inner womblike sanctum is painted red to signify sacrificial blood. The huge June/July **Ambubachi Mela** festival celebrates the end of the mother goddess' menstrual cycle with even more blood.

Kamakhya is 7km west of central Guwahati and 3km up a spiralling side road. Occasional buses from Guwahati's Kachari bus stand run all the way up (Rs5, 20 minutes). Continue 1km further for sweeping Brahmaputra views.

RIVERSIDE GUWAHATI

Umananda Mandir complex sits on a pretty forested river island, accessed by a 15-minute ride on a ferry (Rs10 return, half-hourly 8am to 4.30pm) from **Kachari Ghat**, which itself offers attractive afternoon river views.

ASSAM STATE MUSEUM

This worthwhile **museum** (☎ 2540651; adult/camera/video Rs5/10/100; ☺ 10am-4pm Tue-Sun), on GN Bordoloi (GNB) Rd, has a large sculpture collection, while the upper floors are devoted to informative tribal culture displays. You get to walk through reconstructed tribal homes.

OLD GUWAHATI

The distinctive beehive dome of the **Courthouse** (MG Rd) rises above mildly attractive **Dighulipukhuri Park** (HB Rd; admission Rs5, boats per adult/child Rs25/15; ☺ 9.30am-8pm) tank. The nearby **Guwahati Planetarium** (☎ 2548962; MG Rd; shows Rs15; ☺ noon & 4pm, closed 1st & 15th of the month) looks somewhere between a mosque and a landed UFO.

Tours

Traveller's Point (☎ 2604018; www.assamtourism.org; Tourist Lodge, Station Rd) Assam Tourism's commercial booth runs day excursions to Hajo via the silk-weaving centre of Sualkuchi (adult/child Rs450/375, minimum five people). It also offers two-day all-inclusive packages to Kaziranga National Park (Indian/foreigner from Rs1280/2280).

Network Travels (☎ 2605335; www.networktravels india.net; GS Rd; ☺ 5am-9pm) A highly experienced agency whose operations cover the whole of the northeast with tailor-made and fixed itinerary tours. It operates the Eco-Camp (p618) in Nameri National Park. Organising permits is a speciality.

Jungle Travels India (☎ 2660890; www.jungle travelsindia.com; 1st fl, Mandovi Apt, GNB Rd) Another experienced agency covering the entire northeast with tailor-made tours and fixed-date departures for Nagaland and Arunachal Pradesh. It organises all the permits. With two boats, it runs Brahmaputra cruises (see www.assambengalnavigation.com) for four to 10 nights at US$320 per person per night, and also runs the Bansbari Lodge in Manas National Park (p617).

Rhino Travels (☎ 2540666) Located on M Nehru (MN) Rd, this agency offers tours in Assam and Arunachal Pradesh, from Rs52,000 for two for seven days/six nights. It also runs Mou Chapori River Resort (p620).

Sleeping

BUDGET

Hotel Suradevi (☎ 2545050; MN Rd; s/d Rs250/350, without bathroom Rs100/250) Well-organised warren of spartan rooms but check in early to get a room.

Sundarban Guest House (☎ 2730722; s/d from Rs200/300, d with AC Rs700-800; 🍴) A cheery, colourful hotel that's the best budget option in town. Rooms are atypically clean and tidy, and management is helpful. Non-AC Rs500 rooms are the best value. It's off Manipuribasti East (ME) Rd, in the first side lane. Many nastier, cheap hotels line the surrounding lanes.

Tourist Lodge (☎ 2544475; Station Rd; s/d from Rs330/440; 🍴) Convenient for the train station, the rooms are OK but the staff could do with a brush up in hospitality management. It's a genuine bargain, though, but be prepared for some train noise and up to five-storeys of stairs.

MIDRANGE & TOP END

All the hotels listed here offer cable TV and private bathrooms with hot water. Many add a 15% tax and 10% service charge.

Hotel Siroy Lily (☎ 2608492; Solapara Rd; s/d Rs700/900, with AC Rs1100/1300; ✱) Professionally run, well-maintained hotel with a lift, a pleasantly air-conditioned foyer, complimentary breakfast and free newspapers delivered to your door.

Hotel Prag Continental (☎ 2540850; M Nehru Rd; s Rs850-1600, d Rs1200-2000; ✱) A pleasantly run popular hotel in a quiet central street. Accommodating its mainly business clientele, it has a gents' beauty parlour and a good restaurant.

Hotel Rajmahal (☎ 2549141; www.rajmahalhotel.com; s/d with fan from Rs1200/1800, with AC from Rs1900/2500; ✱ ▯ ⚇ ⚇) On Assam Trunk (AT) Rd. A long lobby with an appealing cakes stand leads you into this 10-storey semi-international tower-hotel. There's a cool and enticing rooftop swimming pool with a poolside cafe.

Dynasty (☎ 2516021; www.hoteldynastyindia.com; s/d from Rs3400/3800, ste Rs6000-15,000; ✱ ▯) Guwahati's top hotel with all the luxury and services that you'd expect although from its location in crowded Fancy Bazaar and unappealing exterior you'd think otherwise. On Sir Shahdullah (SS) Rd.

Eating

Beatrix (dishes Rs30-70) Upbeat and cartoon-walled, Beatrix is just a peg above a student-style hangout. Its eclectic menu offers fish and chips, *momos* (Tibetan dumplings), Hakka Chow and a mysterious 'con est soir'. It's on Manik Chandra (MC) Rd.

Silk Route (GNB Rd; mains Rs30-80; ✆ 11am-9pm) Good-value Indian, Chinese and Thai food served in a cosy, two-storey place. Its cold fruit beer (nonalcoholic) is an absolute thirst-killer.

Khorika Restaurant (GS Rd; dishes Rs50-120; ✆ 10.30am-4pm & 6-10.30pm) Named after the Assamese *khorika* (barbecued dishes), this restaurant may be canteen-style but it has authentic Assamese cuisine. For the whole hog share the sample-everything *khorika* (Rs500) with friends.

Tandoori (☎ 2516021; Dynasty, SS Rd; mains Rs100-300; ✆ noon-3pm & 7-11pm) Majestic North Indian cuisine served at stylish low tables by waiters in Mughal uniforms accompanied by gentle live tabla music. The prawn dishes, yes a little expensive, are delightful.

Paradise (1st fl, GNB Rd; mains Rs110-280) Well known for its authentic Assamese cuisine, its thali is the best way to get a lot of small tasters. Assamese food is not a lip tingler like typical Indian food and for some this cuisine can seem rather bland, but it's the subtleties you're after rather than the heat.

Drinking

Café Coffee Day (Taybullah Rd; espresso Rs23; ✆ 10am-10pm) Guwahati's central coffee shop, pumping out contemporary music, attracts the city's student and nouveau-riche youth with perfect (if very slow) macchiatos. It also has a branch at the airport.

Trafik (GNB Rd; beers Rs60; ✆ 10am-10pm) This under-lit bar has a vast screen for cricket matches or *filmi* (slang term describing anything to do with Indian movies; in this case, Bollywood music) clips.

Shopping

Northeast Network (☎ 2631582; www.northeastnetwork.org; JN Borooah Lane; ✆ 11am-4pm Mon-Fri) This NGO seeds self-help projects in rural villages including several handloom-weaving cooperatives. Buying beautiful (and good-value) cottons here supports this fine work.

Artfed (GNB Rd; ✆ 10am-8pm) Well stocked with bargain bamboo crafts, wickerwork and many a carved rhino. Several nearby shops specialise in Assam's famous golden-toned silks.

Getting There & Away

AIR

Guwahati's orderly Lok-Priya Gopinath Bordoloi International Airport is occasionally international when Air India schedules Bangkok flights. Getting into town costs Rs450/100/70 for taxi/shared taxi/airport bus. The following airlines fly from Guwahati:

Air India (Indian Airlines, IC; ☎ 2264425, Ganeshguri)

IndiGo Airlines (6E; ☎ 9954890345; Brahmaputra Ashok Hotel, MG Rd)

Jet Airways/Jetlite (9W; ☎ 2668255; GNB Rd)

Kingfisher/Kingfisher Red (IT; ☎ toll free 18001800101; airport)

SpiceJet (SG; ☎ toll free 18001803333; airport)

NORTHEAST STATES

FLIGHTS FROM GUWAHATI

Destination	Airlines
Agartala	IC, 9W, IT
Aizawl	IC
Bagdogra	IC, 9W, IT, SG
Delhi	IC, 6E, 9W, IT, SG
Dibrugarh	IC, IT
Dimapur	IC, IT
Imphal	IC, 6E, 9W, IT
Jorhat	IC, IT
Kolkata (Calcutta)	IC, 6E, 9W, IT, SG
Lilabari	IC
Silchar	IC

Helicopter

Pawan Hans Helicopters (☎ 2229501; www.pawanhans.nic.in; airport) shuttles to Shillong (Rs945, 45 minutes, twice daily), Tura (Garo Hills, Rs1750, 50 minutes, thrice weekly), Naharlagun near Itanagar (Rs3400, 1¼ hours, six times weekly) and Lumla (Rs3400, twice weekly) for Tawang. Phone your booking then pay at the airport if the service flies (weather and passenger numbers permitting). **Meghalaya Helicopter Service** (☎ 09435145033; airport) has two daily flights to Shillong (Rs945, 20 minutes, 9am and 12.30pm); return trips are at 9.40am and 1.10pm.

Helicopter travel in India has a poor safety record.

BUS & SUMO

Distance buses leave from the new Interstate Bus Terminal (ISBT) 8km east of Guwahati. Private bus operators run shuttle services from their offices to the ISBT. With exten-

BUSES FROM GUWAHATI

Destination	Fare (Rs)	Duration (hr)
Agartala (Tripura)	480-500	24-26
Dibrugarh	300-350	12
Dimapur via Numaligarh	250	10
Imphal (Manipur) via Mao	600	18-20
Jorhat	210-250	8
Kaziranga	150-210	6
Kohima (Nagaland)	330	13
Shillong (Meghalaya)	100	3½
Silchar	310	12-15
Siliguri (West Bengal)	350	13
Sivasagar	250	9½
Tezpur	110	5

sive networks are **Network Travels** (☎ 2739634; GS Rd), **Royal Tours & Travels** (☎ 2739768; GS Rd), **Deep** (☎ 2152937) on Heramba Prasad Borua (HPB) Rd and **Blue Hill** (☎ 2607145; HPB Rd). All companies charge the same regulated fares.

For Shillong shared taxis and sumos (jeeps; known after the Tata Sumo, a popular 4WD) leave from outside Hotel Tibet (taxi/sumo Rs110/150). For Aizawl (Mizoram), **Zam Zam** (☎ 2639617; ME Rd, 2nd side lane) runs several daily sumos (Rs650, 16 hours) via Silchar (Rs350, 11 hours). Buses/sumos to Tura (Rs175/230, six/10 hours), in western Meghalaya depart from Kaliram Ram Barua (KRB) Rd.

TRAIN

Of the four daily trains to Delhi, the *Guwahati New Delhi Rajdhani* (Nos 2423/35; 3AC/2AC Rs1481/2079, 31 hours, 7.05am) is the fastest; others take up to 43 hours. The best daily train to Kolkata (Sealdah) is the *Kanchenjunga Express* (No 5658; sleeper/3AC/2AC Rs301/845/1174, 21 hours, 10.30pm). The same train is also best for New Jalpaiguri (for Darjeeling and Sikkim; sleeper/3AC/2AC Rs164/459/638, nine hours).

Several trains serve Dimapur (sleeper/ 3AC/2AC Rs109/305/425, five hours), Jorhat (sleeper/3AC/2AC Rs148/416/578, seven to 11 hours) and Dibrugarh (sleeper/3AC/2AC Rs203/569/791, 14 hours). Trains to Jorhat and Dibrugarh cut through Nagaland, but you don't need a Nagaland permit as long as you stay on the train (the same rule doesn't apply for buses however).

Getting Around

Shared taxis to the airport (per person/car Rs100/500, 23km) leave from outside the poorly-run Hotel Mahalaxmi on GS Rd. From the Kachari bus stand city buses run to Kamakhya Mandir, Hajo (bus 25; Rs20, one hour) and Sualkuchi (bus 22; Rs18, one hour). Autorickshaws charge Rs25 to Rs50 for shorter hops.

AROUND GUWAHATI
Hajo

Some 30km northwest of Guwahati, the pleasant little town of Hajo attracts Hindu and Buddhist pilgrims to its five ancient temples topping assorted hillocks. Haigriv Madhav temple is the main one accessed by a long flight of steps through an ornate quasi-Mughal gateway. The images inside of

Madhav, an avatar of Krishna, are alleged to be 6000 years old.

POA Mecca

Two kilometres east of Hajo is a **mosque** (🕐 24hr) sheltering the tomb of the multi-named Hazarat Shah Sultan Giasuddin Aulia Rahmatullah Alike who died some 800 years ago. Muslims need to walk (the less pious may drive) 4km up a spiral road to reach the mosque, which is architecturally unremarkable.

Pobitora National Park

Only 40km from Guwahati, this small national park has the highest concentration of rhinoceroses in the world. Entrance fees are the same as Kaziranga National Park, p619. Getting into the park involves a boat ride over the river boundary to the elephant-mounting station. From there it's a one-hour trip atop an elephant lumbering through boggy grassland and stirring up petulant rhinos. An armed guard rides with you in case a rhino gets too close up and personal although a trumpeting, head-shaking elephant seems to do the job just as well.

NORTHWESTERN ASSAM (BODOLAND)
Manas National Park
☎ 03666

Bodoland's Unesco-listed **Manas National Park** (www.manas100.com; 🕐 Oct-Mar) has two 'ranges' – Bansbari and Koklabari – with different access points. National park fees are as for Kaziranga (p619).

BANSBARI RANGE

Famous for tigers (though you'll probably only see their pug marks), this range is comparatively accessible and can be appreciated in delightful comfort from **Bansbari Lodge** (☎ 3612602223; www.assambengalnavigation.com/bansbari.htm; d Rs1250, jungle package Rs6000). Jungle packages cover full board, early morning elephant safari, jeep safari, guide and park entry fee. Ask about river rafting. For guests staying two or more days the lodge runs trips to Koklabari range. Contact Jungle Travels India in Guwahati (p614) for bookings. Access is from Barpeta Road.

MOTHANGURI LODGE

Staying at Mothanguri is Manas' top highlight. Two simple, lonely **lodges** (per person Rs200)

are 20km north of Bansbari besides an unguarded Bhutan border crossing. Choose the seven-room upper lodge with its enchanting views across the Beki River and a man-eating tiger (stuffed) in the lounge. Bring food for the *chowkidar* (caretaker) to cook for you and diesel fuel for the generator. Book weeks ahead through the **Manas Field Director's Office** (☎ 260289, 9435080508; abhijitrabha@hotmail.com; Main Rd, Barpeta Road).

GETTING THERE & AWAY

Guwahati–Kokrajhar buses serve Pathsala junction and pass within 3km of Barpeta Rd. Two buses run Pathsala to Koklabari (Rs15, two hours, 1.30pm and 2.30pm). Barpeta Rd–Bansbari buses (Rs15, 1½ hours) leave twice hourly until 5pm just north of the railway line.

The *Kamrup Express* (No 5960, sleeper Rs121, 2¼ hours, 7.45am) and *Brahmaputra Mail* (No 4055, sleeper Rs121, 2¼ hours, 12.15pm) connect Guwahati and Barpeta Rd.

Jeep rental is available at Koklabari, Barpeta Rd and (for guests) at Bansbari Lodge to reach Mothanguri.

TEZPUR
☎ 03712 / pop 59,000

Tezpur is probably Assam's most attractive city thanks to beautifully kept parks, attractive lakes and the enchanting views of the mighty Brahmaputra River as it laps the town's edge. **Cinex Computers** (Santa Plaza; per hr Rs20; 🕐 10am-9pm) on Shyama Charan (SC) Rd, 250m north of the Baliram Building restaurants has internet.

Sights

Chitralekha Udyan (Cole Park; Jenkins Rd; adult/child/camera/video Rs10/5/10/100; 🕐 9am-7pm) has a U-shaped pond wrapped around pretty manicured lawns, dotted with fine **ancient sculptures**. The bearded chap in Mesopotamian-style costume is Banasura. A block east, then south, stands **Ganeshgarh temple** backing onto a ghat overlooking the surging river, a good place for Brahmaputra sunsets. Nearly 1km east along the narrow, winding riverside lane is **Agnigarh Hill** (Padma Park; adult/child/camera/video Rs10/5/20/100; 🕐 8.30am-7.30pm) that might have been Banasura's fire fortress site. River views are lovely from the top and there's a snacks bar; statues-in-action all around it vividly illustrate the Usha legend.

BLOODY TEZPUR

Banasura, the thousand-armed demon-king was so overprotective of his beautiful daughter Usha that he locked her into an impregnable 'fire fortress' (Agnigarh) to keep away unwanted suitors. The ploy failed. A dashing prince, Aniruddha, magically found his way in and secretly married her. Banasura was not a happy demon. He considered feeding Aniruddha to his pet snakes, but the lad turned out to be Lord Krishna's grandson. Krishna sent in his troops and an almighty battle ensued. The resulting carnage was so appalling that the site has been known ever since as Tezpur (or Sonitpur), the City of Blood.

Across town is a boulder-strewn **Bhamuni Hill**, location for a set of demolished Vishnu temples that were only revealed after the 1889 earthquake.

Sleeping & Eating

Hotel Luit (☎ 222083; luit@rediffmail.com; Ranu Singh Rd; s/d old wing Rs200/300, new wing Rs600/700, with AC Rs1000/1200; ✷) Close to the bus station, the Luit is on a small lane linking Jenkins Rd with Main Rd. Reception is professional and budget rooms are remarkably reasonable, while a lift whisks you up to the 5th-floor AC offerings. The very tired 'old wing' rooms are to be renovated in 2009.

Indralay Hotel (☎ 232918; s Rs250, d Rs450-800) On Naren Chandra (NC) Rd. The wonders of fresh white paint make this an airy and pleasant hotel. Cheap rooms are a little small but good, consider room 102.

Tourist Lodge (☎ 221016; Jenkins Rd; dm Rs100, r with/without AC Rs550/330; ✷) Facing Chitralekha Udyan, two blocks south of the bus station, the Tourist Lodge offers good-value spacious rooms with bathrooms (some squat toilets) and mosquito nets. The dorm is for the desperate.

The modern glass tower Baliram Building, on the corner of Naren Bose (NB) and NC/SC Rds, contains several floors of good dining. The ground-floor stand-up-and-eat **dosa house** (snacks from Rs25; ✷ 6am-9pm) serves South Indian fare and cheap breakfasts. Semismart **China Villa** (meals from Rs275; ✷ 10am-10.30pm) offers Indian and Chinese food in AC comfort, while the rooftop **Chat House** (snacks from Rs20; ✷ 8am-9.30pm) has an open-sided, but roofed, terrace for cooling breezes, good views, Indian snacks, noodles, pizzas and *momos*.

Getting There & Away

Air India's agent is **Anand Travels** (☎ 220083; Jenkins Rd) near the Tourist Lodge. Tezpur airport was being rebuilt at the time of research.

Sumos have their booking counters in Jenkins Rd. Bargain for a taxi in the same street for Guwahati (Rs1700), Eco-Camp at Potasali (Rs400) and Kaziranga (Rs1300). A little further on is the **bus station** (☎ 225140; Jenkins Rd) with frequent services to Guwahati (Rs115, five hours), Jorhat (Rs115, four hours) and Kohora for Kaziranga (Rs80, two hours).

Tezpur's delightfully parochial train station has a computerised **booking office** (☎ 2737155; ✷ 8am-2pm & 2.30-8pm).

AROUND TEZPUR

Picturesque **Nameri National Park** (Indian/foreigner Rs20/250; ✷ Nov-Apr) specialises in low-key, walk-in birdwatching treks. Access is from **Potasali**, 2km off the Tezpur–Bhalukpong road (turn east at one-house hamlet Gamani, 12km north of Balipara).

Potasali's delightful **Eco-Camp** (☎ 9435250052; dm/d Rs100/1250, plus membership per person Rs60) organises all Nameri visits, including two-hour ornithological rafting trips (Rs1305 per boat). Accommodation is in 'tents', but colourful fabrics, private bathrooms, sturdy beds and thatched-roof shelters make the experience relatively luxurious. A bigger 'tent' offers great-value dorm beds and there's an atmospheric open-sided restaurant. At dawn, walk 1.3km to the idyllic Bharali riverbank, above which rise horizons of forested foothills crowned by a line of white-topped horizon peaks.

KAZIRANGA NATIONAL PARK
☎ 03776

Assam's must-do attraction is a rhinoceros-spotting safari through the expansive flat grasslands of this **national park** (✷ 1 Nov-30 Apr, elephant rides 5.30-8.30am, jeep access 7.30am-noon & 2.30pm-dusk). Kaziranga's population of around 1900 Indian one-horned rhinos (just 200 in 1904) represents two-thirds of the world's total. There is a western, central and an eastern range. The central is the most accessible giving the best viewing chances for rhinos, elephants and swamp deer plus plenty of bird life (take binoculars). One-hour elephant-back rides, central range only for foreign visitors, are especially satisfying when a 'team' of elephants makes pincer movements, surrounding rhinos without frightening them off.

Information

Kohora village is closest for Kaziranga's central range with an obvious Rhino Gate leading to the Kaziranga Tourist complex 800m south. Here you'll find the **range office** (☎ 262428; ⏰ 24 hr), **elephant-ride booking office** (⏰ 6-7pm, book the previous night) and **jeep rental stand** (rental from Rs600). Pay your fees at the range office before entering the park, 2km north.

Better hotels in the Tourist Complex organise everything.

Fees for Indians/foreigners are: entry fees Rs20/250 per day; cameras Rs50/500; videos Rs500/1000; elephant rides Rs280/750; and vehicle toll fee Rs150/150 (including an armed escort – a Rs50 tip is customary).

Sleeping & Eating

Prices drop at least 30% when Kaziranga National Park closes.

TOURIST COMPLEX

All of the following are within a five-minute walk of the range office. Booking ahead is wise and advance payment is often required.

Aranya Lodge (☎ 262429; r Rs690, with AC Rs863, AC cottages Rs863; 🎱) This a could-be-anywhere concrete but garden-fronted lodge with a bar and decent restaurant.

Prashanti Cottage (d Rs863) This fine place has six modern split-level units overlooking a small river, the workplace of women dhobis and net fishermen. It's run by the Aranya Lodge.

Jupuri Ghar (☎ 9435196377, 9435843681; per cottage Rs1600; 🎱) A new resort with traditional-style cabins around a grassy area and an open-air restaurant.

The following are run by and booked through **Bonani Lodge** (☎ 262423). **Kunjaban Lodge** (dm Rs50, r Rs150) has passable three- and 12-bed dorms, and double rooms. **Bonoshree Lodge** (r Rs260) offers ageing but acceptable rooms fronting onto a long shady verandah. **Bonani Lodge** (r ground/upper fl Rs380/410) has cool and airy rooms in a two-storey building with wicker furniture.

BEYOND THE COMPLEX

Uninspiring lodgings dot the road around Rhino Gate. None compare with those in the Tourist Complex. However, there is one good option outside the complex.

Wild Grass Resort (☎ 262085; www.oldassam.com; s May-Oct/Nov-Apr negotiable/Rs900, d May-Oct/Nov-Apr Rs1250/1850; 🎱) This delightful, eco-friendly resort is so justifiably popular that it doesn't bother with a sign but carefully labels all the trees instead. Raj-inspired decor makes you feel that the clock has slowed for you. The atmospheric dining room serves tasty Assamese food and there's a jungle-edged summer-only swimming pool. Wild Grass entrance is opposite the Km373 marker on National Highway (NH) 37. In season, bookings are essential.

Getting There & Away

Network Travel buses travel to Guwahati (Rs230 to Rs300, five hours, hourly 7.30am to 4.30pm), Dibrugarh (Rs230 to Rs300, five hours, 11.30am, 12.30pm and 2pm), Tezpur (Rs60, two hours, hourly 7.30am to 3pm) and Shillong (Rs400, nine hours, 9pm). Many Network buses divert the 800m up to the Tourist Complex for a lunch stop. A small **public call office** (PCO; ☎ 09864779028) west of Rhino Gate books bus seats.

UPPER ASSAM
Jorhat
☎ 0376 / pop 70,000

Bustling Jorhat is the junction for Majuli Island. Jorhat's commercial street (Gar-Ali) meets the main east–west thoroughfare – Assam Trunk (AT) Rd or NH37 – in front of a lively **central market** area. Head 200m west for a tall shopping complex, Unnayan Bhawan, with an **internet cafe** (per hr Rs20; ⏰ 9am-10pm). Opposite is the SBI Bank with an ATM.

Journey another 200m west along AT Rd, then south to find a small **museum** (☎ 9435247058; admission free; Postgraduate Training College, MG Rd; ⏰ 10am-4.30pm Tue-Sun) with Ahom artefacts and nearby **Assam Tourism** (⏰ 10am-5pm Mon-Sat, closed 2nd & 4th Sat) in the good-value **Tourist Lodge** (☎ 2321579; MG Rd; s/d Rs210/330), which has tiled floors and mosquito nets.

Tucked conveniently behind the Assam State Transport Corporation (ASTC) Bus Station (AT Rd), Solicitor Rd has half-a-dozen reasonable hotels. **Hotel Janata Paradise** (☎ 2320610; Solicitor Rd; d Rs280-450) has budget fan rooms. Maybe it's the chintzy rugs and paintings in the rooms plus the corridor-housed chair collections but this quirky place has a soul. Its **lobby-restaurant** (11am-4pm & 8-9pm) serves excellent-value 10-dish Assamese thalis (Rs40).

The wedding-cake-exterior **Hotel Heritage** (☎ 2327393; Solicitor Rd; s/d from Rs250/425, d with AC Rs800;), with lift, is a friendly midrange choice, with the non-AC rooms the best value.

Next door in the faded Hotel Paradise you'll find **Air India** (☎ 2320011), and **Jet Airways** (☎ 2325652). Both fly to Kolkata and Air India also to Guwahati. **Kingfisher Red** (☎ 2310854; airport) also flies to Guwahati and Kolkata. **ASTC bus station** (☎ 2301896; AT Rd) has very frequent services to Sivasagar (Rs30, 1½ hours) and Tezpur (Rs70 to Rs115, four hours). Guwahati buses (Rs210, eight hours, eight buses 6am to noon) pass Kaziranga en route.

The *Jorhat Guwahati Jan Shatabdi* (No 2068, CC Rs209, 6¾ hours, 1.55pm Monday to Saturday) goes to Guwahati.

Around Jorhat

TEA ESTATE GETAWAYS

Colonial-era heritage bungalows offer relaxing, do-nothing stately getaways. Bookings are essential.

Sangsua (☎ 2385075, bookings 9954451548; www .heritagetourismindia.com/sangsua.html; s/d Rs2400/2700) dates from the 1870s and has wonderful lawns and verandahs overlooking a tea estate. There's antique furniture including two Bombay fornicators – chairs with reclining backs and extending arms for putting your legs up on... get the picture? The site is 7km down rural tracks from Km442 on NH37 (Jorhat–Deragaon road).

With a classical portico and wide, immaculate lawns, **Thengal Manor** (☎ 2339519, bookings 2304267; Jalukanburi; s/d Rs2700/3300) oozes grandeur. Old photos, four-post beds and medal certificates from King George VI add atmosphere to this stately mansion. Thengal is 15km south of Jorhat down MG Rd, towards Titabor.

NIMATIGHAT

This windswept sandbank pockmarked with chai shacks is the departure point for photogenically overcrowded ferries to Majuli Island.

An otherwise deserted river-island reached by private launch (Rs50) accommodates the

Mou Chapori River Resort (☎ 9435357171; camprhino@ gmail.com; 2 days/1 night ex-Guwahati per person Rs5500) with traditionally styled hut accommodation. The one-day group tours (Rs800 per person) from here are a particularly convivial way to visit Majuli Island. Book with Rhino Travels (p614).

Nimatighat is a jarring 12km-ride from Jorhat by shared autorickshaw (Rs70, 40 minutes). With your own transport, stop 2km before the ferry at Green View Resort restaurant for fish freshly caught through a hole in the floor.

Majuli Island

☎ 03775 / pop 54,000

The great muddy-brown Brahmaputra River's ever-shifting puzzle of sandbanks includes **Majuli**, the world's largest river island. Here you can contemplate landscapes of rice fields and water meadows with fish traps, and meet the local Mising people; or learn about the neo-Vaishnavite philosophy at one of Majuli's 22 ancient *satras* (Hindu Vaishnavite monasteries and centres for art; see opposite).

Ferries arrive 3km south of **Kamalabari**; the main village **Garamur** is 5km further north. The most interesting, accessible *satras* are the large, beautifully peaceful **Uttar Kamalabari** (1km north, then 600m east of Kamalabari) and **Auniati** (5km west of Kamalabari), where monks are keen to show you their little **museum** of Ahom royal artefacts. The best chances of observing chanting, dances or drama recitations are around dawn and dusk or during the big **Ras Mahotsav Festival** (third week of November).

Contact **Jyoti Naryan Sarma** (☎ 9435657282; jyoti24365@gmail.com, majulitourism@rediffmail.com; per day Rs500) for local guiding, accommodation or bicycle hire. **Danny Gam** (☎ 9435205539) provides similar services.

SLEEPING & EATING

Accommodation is very basic: bring a sleeping sheet or bag.

Donipolo (☎ 9435205539; dm Rs120) In the same lane as La Maison de Ananda is this similar house, with four beds.

Hotel Island (☎ 274712; s/d/tr without bathroom Rs120/240/350) At the crossroads in Garamur. A less-than-exciting dive with shared bathrooms, squat toilets and no hot water; mosquito nets, though, are a plus.

SATRAS

A *satra* is a monastery for Vishnu worship, Assam's distinctive form of everyman-Hinduism. Formulated by 15th-century Assamese philosopher Sankardev, the faith eschews the caste system and idol worship, focussing on Vishnu as God, especially in his Krishna incarnation. Much of the worship is based around dance and melodramatic play-acting of scenes from the holy Bhagavad Gita. The heart of any *satra* is its *namghar*, a large, simple, prayer hall usually open sided and shaped like an upside down oil tanker. Beneath the eastern end, an inner sanctum hosts an eternal flame, the Gita and possibly a horde of instructive (but not divine) images. *Satras* are highly spiritual, but don't expect anything especially photogenic.

La Maison de Ananda (☎ 9435205539; dm Rs200) On a Garamur back lane, this is a traditionally styled thatched house on bamboo stilts with three bamboo beds and locally made fabrics. It's run by local guide/fixer Danny Gam.

Seuj Bilas (☎ 27345; r Rs600-750) Opposite the police station, this is Kamalabari's only option. Rooms are utilitarian and the more expensive comes with a sitting room. The basic restaurant is also the only eating place in the village.

Those actively interested in neo-Vaishnavite philosophy can usually arrange space at a *satra* guest house.

GETTING THERE & AWAY

Crowded passenger ferries (adult/jeep Rs15/550, 2½ hours) leave Nimatighat at 10.30am, 1.15pm and 3pm; return trips are at 7.15am, 10am and 2pm. The ferry schedule makes day trips pointless unless you charter your own boat (Rs5000); ask the **harbour manager** (☎ 9854022724).

GETTING AROUND

Jam-packed buses meet arriving ferries then drive to Garamur (Rs10) via Kamalabari where three-wheelers are easier to rent. For a few days consider arranging a bicycle through Jyoti, Danny or by asking around.

Sivasagar

☎ 03772 / pop 64,000

Despite being an oil-service town Sivasagar exudes a residual elegance from its time as the capital of the Ahom dynasty that ruled Assam for more than 600 years. The name comes from 'waters of Shiva', the graceful central feature of a rectangular reservoir dug in 1734 by Ahom Queen Ambika. Three typical Ahom **temple towers** rise proudly above the tank's partly wooded southern banks – to the west **Devidol**, to the east **Vishnudol** and in the centre, the 33m-high **Shivadol Mandir**, India's tallest Shiva temple. Its uppermost trident balances upon an egg-shaped feature whose golden covering the British reputedly tried (but failed) to pilfer in 1823. Sadhus line the temple approach path; the interior is eerie and the floor slippery. Unusually the lingam is inverted being just a hole in the ground rather than proud-standing stone.

At the tank's southwest corner, Assam Tourism is within the great-value, garden-sited **Tourist Lodge** (☎ 222394; s/d Rs210/260), whose six large rooms have clean tiled floors and tidy beds.

Around 500m from Shivadol a gaggle of hotels line AT Rd, the most appealing of which is the surprisingly swish **Hotel Shiva Palace** (☎ 222629; hotelshivapalace@rediffmail.com; s/d economy Rs450/550, with AC Rs850/950; 🍴), incorporating a decent restaurant (mains Rs50 to Rs180).

Hotel Siddhartha (☎ 222276; e7safari@rediffmail.com; s/d from Rs174/200, r with AC from Rs620; 🍴) is a worthy midrange option with rooms better than the corridors suggest. The owner is a talented multi-instrumentalist who composes and plays his own Indian fusion music.

The **ASTC bus station** (☎ 222944; cnr AT & Temple Rds) has frequent services to Jorhat (Rs30, one hour) and Dibrugarh (Rs40, two hours) plus buses to Tezpur (Rs150, five hours, 9.30am and 10.30am) and Guwahati (Rs249, eight hours, frequent 7am to 9.30am). Many private buses have ticket counters on nearby AT Rd. For Kareng Ghar, use Gargaon buses (Rs12, 45 minutes), which depart from an unmarked stop on Bhuban Gogoi (BG) Rd, 300m north up AT Rd then 50m right.

Around Sivasagar

Dotted around Sivasagar are many lemon-squeezer–shaped temples and ochre-brick ruins built by the Ahom monarchs during their 17th- and 18th-century heyday.

TALATALGHAR

This famous (but not spectacular) Ahom ruin is 4km down AT Rd from central Sivasagar.

Some 2km beyond a WWII-era metal lift-bridge, look right to see the rather beautiful **Rang Ghar** (Indian/foreigner Rs5/100; ☽ dawn-dusk). From this two-storey oval-shaped 'pavilion', Ahom monarchs once watched buffalo and elephant fights.

Just beyond, a left turning passes the **Golaghar** or Ahom ammunition store, the stonework of which is held together with a mix of dhal, lime and egg. Beyond are the two-storey ruins of **Talatalghar** (Indian/foreigner Rs5/100; ☽ dawn-dusk), the extensive, two-storey Ahom palace built by Ahom King Rajeswar Singha in the mid-18th century.

KARENGHAR

Dramatic if largely unadorned, this 1752 brick **palace** (Indian/foreigner Rs5/100; ☽ dawn-dusk) is the last remnant of the Ahom's pre-Sivasagar capital. The unique four-storey structure rises like a sharpened, stepped pyramid above an attractive forest-and-paddy setting spoilt by nearby electricity substations. It's 900m north of the Sivasagar–Sonari road: turn just before Gargaon (14km) from Sonari.

GAURISAGAR

Like a practice run for Sivasagar, Gaurisagar has an attractive tank and a trio of distinctive 1720s temples – **Vishnudol**, **Shivadol** and **Devidol** – built by 'dancing girl queen' Phuleswari. The more impressive is Vishnudol, not as tall as Sivasagar's Shivadol but sporting finer, but eroded carvings. Gaurisagar is on the main NH37 at Km501.5.

Dibrugarh

☎ 0373 / pop 122,000

Travelling to Dibrugarh ('tea-city') usefully closes a loop between Kaziranga and the Ziro–Along–Pasighat route. It's a rapidly growing city with a new road and rail bridge being built at Bogibeel Ghat (opening 2010) that will extend the railway system to north of the Brahmaputra.

From Dibrugarh Town train station, Radha Kanta Borgohain (RKB) Path follows the rail tracks northeast passing Hanuman Singhania Road (HS) Rd that leads to market area. After 800m RKB Path intersects Mancotta Rd at Thana Charali. Around this junction are many places to eat, hotels and internet cafes such as **Ajmera** (Sachit Studio, Mancotta Rd; per hr Rs20; ☽ 9am-9pm), and **Internet Cafe** (HS Rd; ☽ 9am-7.30pm Mon-Sat, 9am-2pm Sun) down an alley next to the Grand Hotel. **SBI Bank** (☎ 2321999; RKB Path) changes travellers cheques and foreign currency. Its ATM (on RKB Path) is next to the City Regency hotel.

Purvi Discovery (☎ 2301120; www.purviweb.com; Medical College Rd, Jalan Nagar) organises regional tours, kayaking days (Rs3000) and horse-riding trips (Rs 7800 per day including meals). Given three days' notice it can organise two-hour **tea estate visits** (admission Rs400; ☽ Tue-Sat Apr-Nov). Purvi also handles bookings for two colonial-era tea bungalow retreats: the delightful 1849 **Mancotta Chang Bungalow** (Mancotta Rd, Mancotta; s/d main bldg Rs2600/5200; ✗), 4km from town, and **Jalannagar South Bungalow** (Convoy Rd; s/d Rs1500/2600, with AC Rs3200/3700; ✗), 700m from the bus station. In both cases choose the upper rooms that have polished hardwood floorboards and a wonderful heritage feel.

The conveniently central **Hotel East End** (☎ 2322698; New Market; s/d from Rs375/550, with AC Rs625/780; ✗), just off HS Rd, has basic but clean budget rooms and attached cold showers. The standard deluxe specials are worth the extra Rs75 to Rs100.

City Regency (☎ 2326805; city_regency@sify.com; RKB Path; s/d from Rs1350/1600; ✗) is a good-priced midrange hotel, well (but not lavishly) furnished, and with a lift. A few rooms have no view. El Dorado is its suave, under-lit lounge bar.

H2O (Mancotta Rd; mains Rs50-110, beers Rs65) is an upstairs bar-restaurant with elements of spaceship decor. Upbeat little **Flavours** (Mancotta Rd; mains Rs30-70; ☽ 10am-10pm) before the railway bridge serves snacks and the most refreshing Soda Sikanji (Rs20) – just the thing for a sultry day.

GETTING THERE & AWAY

JetLite (☎ 0361-39893333; airport) flies to Kolkata, **Kingfisher Red** (☎ toll free 18002093030; airport) to Guwahati and **Air India** (☎ 2300658; Paltan Bazaar, Circuit House Rd) to Guwahati, Imphal and Kolkata from Mohanbari airport, 16km northeast of Dibrugarh and 4km off the Tinsukia road.

From the main **bus station** (Mancotta Rd) ASTC buses depart for Sivasagar (Rs60, two hours, frequent 6am to 9am), Jorhat (Rs90, three hours, frequent 6am to 9am), Tezpur (Rs207, six hours, 7.45am and 8.15am) and Guwahati (Rs355, 10 hours, 9am). Various private overnight services to Guwahati (Rs310 to Rs355, 12 hours, 6pm to 10pm) leave from Mancotta Rd or from outside the train station.

The *Kamrup Express* is the best-timed overnight train for Guwahati (No 5960; sleeper/3AC/2AC Rs203/569/791, 14 hours, 6pm).

Kusum Hotel (☎ 2320143; Talkiehouse Rd) sells a jeep-ferry-jeep combination ticket to Pasighat (Rs280) in Arunachal Pradesh. Hotel departure is 7.30am, boat departure 8.15am, boat arrival at Majibari Ghat 10.30am and Pasighat arrival 1.30pm.

The rough-and-ready **DKO Ferry** (passenger Rs67, vehicle Rs2500-3100) cruises daily to Oriamghat where it's met by a bus to Pasighat. It can carry just two jeeps. There's little shelter and the journey takes around eight hours (5½ hours downstream), so bring an umbrella, water and sunscreen. Brief stops en route give scenic glimpses of isolated riverside hamlets. Exact departure points depend on the Brahmaputra's water level.

ARUNACHAL PRADESH

The 'Land of Dawn-lit Mountains' abruptly rises from the Assam plains as a mass of densely forested hills. These in turn rise to fabulous snow-capped peaks along the China border. At least 25 tribal groups with traditional settlements live in Arunachal's valleys. High in the dramatic Tawang Valley are several splendid Monpa monastery villages. China has never formally recognised Indian sovereignty here and it took their surprise invasion of 1962 before Delhi really started funding significant infrastructure. The Chinese voluntarily withdrew. Now border passes are heavily guarded by the Indian military and the atmosphere is extremely calm.

Arunachal Tourism (www.arunachaltourism.com) has additional information.

ITANAGAR

☎ 0360 / pop 38,000

Built since 1972, Arunachal's pleasantly green, tailor-made capital is named for the mysterious **Ita Fort** whose residual brick ruins crown a hilltop above town. Itanagar is useful for on-

ward transport to central Arunachal. There's a stack of ATMs in Mahatma Gandhi Marg along with several internet cafes. **Abor Country Travels** (☎ 2211722; B Sector) runs trekking, rafting, tribal visits and angling in western and central Arunachal.

With an oversized foyer better suited as a car showroom, **Hotel Arun Subansiri** (☎ 2212806; Zero Point; s/d Rs900/1000) has comfortably large rooms with soft beds. It's within walking distance of the decent **State Museum** (☎ 2222518; Indian/foreigner Rs10/75; ☻ 9.30am-4pm Sun-Thu) and the gorgeously decorated **Centre for Buddhist Culture** gompa set in gardens on the hill above. The **Poong Nest** (VIP Rd, mains Rs30-100; ☻ 8am-9pm; ☻) is a friendly place for refreshing beers and meals; it serves local tribal dishes – boiled chicken or pork, with bamboo shoots and veggies.

Some 3km west on Mahatma Gandhi Marg is **Ganga Market**, landmarked by a red, triple-spired temple and nearby clock tower. The especially good-value **Hotel Blue Pine** (☎ 2211118; dm Rs100, s Rs200-300, d Rs300-450, with AC Rs750; ☻) is here with well-maintained rooms and private bathrooms with squat toilets. Don't mind the caged receptionist, he's quite tame and helpful.

The **APST bus station** (☎ 2212338; Ganga Market) has services to Along (Rs230, eight hours, 5.30am Tuesday to Sunday), Tezpur (Rs110, four hours, 5.30am), Pasighat (Rs170, eight hours, 6.30am Thursday to Tuesday), Lilabari, for the airport (Rs80, 1½ hours, 7.15am Monday to Saturday) and Guwahati (Rs190, 11 hours, 6am).

Over the road **Royal Sumo Counter** (☎ 2290455) has daily services to Ziro (Rs250, four hours, 5.30am and 2.50pm), Daporijo (Rs480, 14 hours, 5.30am), Along (Rs400, 12 hours, 5.30am), Pasighat (Rs300, eight hours, 5.30am), Lilabari (Rs250, 3½ hours, 6.30am) and Bhalukpong (Rs250, four hours, 6.30am).

Helicopter tickets are only sold at **Naharlagun Helipad** (☎ 2243262; ☻ 7.30am-4pm Mon-Sat), 16km east of Itanagar's Zero-Point. Flights run daily (except Sunday) to Guwahati (Rs3400) and weekly to many destinations, including Along (Rs3400), Ziro (Rs1500), Daporijo (Rs1700) and Pasighat (Rs2700).

CENTRAL ARUNACHAL PRADESH
Ziro Valley

☎ 03788

More vale than valley, the district's rice fields and fenced bamboo groves are attractively

---

ARUNACHAL PRADESH FAST FACTS

Population 1.1 million
Area 83,743 sq km
Capital Itanagar
Main languages Hindi and Assamese
When to go October to March

NORTHEAST STATES

cupped by hills dotted with pine trees. Tall *babo* (poles) and traditional *lapang* (meeting platforms) add interest to the tight-packed villages of the utterly intriguing **Apatani tribe**.

The voyeuristic main attraction here is meeting older Apatani women who sport alarming **facial tattoos** and bizarre **nose plugs** (see below). Most people work in the fields so a good time to see village activity is late afternoon. The most authentic Apatani villages are **Hong** (the biggest and best known), **Hijo** (more atmospheric), **Hari**, **Bamin** and **Dutta**. None are more than 10km apart.

Sprawling **Hapoli** (New Ziro), starting 7km further south than **Ziro**, has hotels and road transport. Just below the Commissioner's office on a bend in MG Rd, is an SBI ATM. In an alley under Hotel Pine Ridge is **Mom & Dot's Cyber Cafe** (Hapoli; per hr Rs50; ⏰ 9am-9pm). The **Emporium Crafts Centre**, a government organisation teaching the indigenous crafts of weaving, carpet making and bell-metal casting, sells its work in its **shop** (☎ 225327; Hapoli; ⏰ 9.30am-1pm & 2.30-4pm Mon-Fri).

The warrenlike **Hotel Pine Ridge** (☎ 224725; MG Rd; s Rs350, d Rs500-700), in a courtyard off the main road, is a good option with the Rs500 rooms the best value. The helpful receptionist speaks good English.

Hotel Blue Pine (☎ 224812; s/d Rs300/450), is its best lodging, albeit a slightly long walk from town (unlit at night). The restaurant is worthy of a visit but service can be slow; if staying, order your meals in advance.

FACIAL TATTOOING

Historically famous for their beauty, Apatani women were all too often kidnapped by warriors of the neighbouring Nishi tribes. As a 'defence', Apatani girls were deliberately defaced. They were given facial tattoos, like graffitied beards scribbled onto living Mona Lisa paintings, and extraordinary nose plugs known as *dat* fitted into holes cut in their upper nostrils. Some men also have tattoos.

Peace with the Nishis in the 1960s meant the end to that brutal practice, but many older women still wear *dat*. Photography is an understandably sensitive issue, so ask first. Some Apatani women have had cosmetic surgery to remove their tattoos.

Sumos depart from MG Rd, Hapoli (near SBI ATM), for Itanagar (Rs250, five hours, 5.30am, 6am, 10.30am, 11am and 11.30am) and Lakhimpur (Rs170, four hours); prebook. The journey has some particularly beautiful forest sections. A jeep from Itanagar continues to Daporijo (Rs250, around 9.30am) leaving from outside the Nefa Hotel, opposite the high school on the Hapoli–Ziro road.

Ziro to Pasighat

A peaceful lane winding on and on through forested hills and tribal settlements links Ziro to Pasighat via Along. Highlights are dizzying suspension footbridges and thatched Adi villages around Along.

DAPORIJO
☎ 03792 / pop 14,000 / elev 699m

This is probably the dirtiest and most unsophisticated town in Arunachal Pradesh, but it's a necessary stopover. You have little choice in places to sleep. The four-room **Circuit House** (☎ 223250; d Rs320) is scenically plonked on a hilltop overlooking the town but requires a visit to the *babus* (clerks) in the District Commissioner's office to get the required *chit* (permission to stay). The other option is **Hotel Santanu** (☎ 223531; New Market; s/d from Rs300/400), setting new standards of basicness, but serving good local delicacies in its cheerless restaurant.

Sumos leave New Market at 6am for Itanagar (Rs480, 12 hours) and Ziro (Rs300, six hours). The **bus station** (☎ 223107) has a lackadaisical 6am service to Along (Rs110, six hours) on alternate days – depending on when the bus returns from Along.

ALONG
☎ 03783 / pop 20,000 / elev 302m

This friendly, nondescript market town has an **internet cafe** (☎ 9436632430; Abu-Tani Centre, Nehru Chowk; per hr Rs40; ⏰ 7am-7pm) opposite the APST bus station, an SBI ATM in Main Rd just below the Circuit House that's adjacent to an informative little **district museum** (☎ 222214; admission free; ⏰ 9am-4pm Mon-Fri), 300m east selling Adi-related books. The **Crafts Centre** (☎ 222145; ⏰ 9am-4.30pm), 1km south on Main Rd teaches weaving, carpet making, blacksmithing and bamboo work. Buy your Adi-style hat here.

The best accommodation option here is **Hotel Holiday Cottage** (☎ 222463; Hospital Hill; r Rs400-500) southwest of the helipad. Pay the extra

Rs100 for a deluxe room and preferably take room 104.

There are sumos to Itanagar (Rs370, 12 hours, 5.30am and 5pm) and Pasighat (Rs200, five hours, 5.30am and 11pm) but not to Daporijo.

Kabu is an easily accessible Adi village 2km north of Along. Dare to cross the river on a cable-trussed but bamboo-decked wobbly suspension bridge over the river.

Pasighat
☎ 0368 / pop 22,000

Nestled before a curtain of luxuriantly forested foothills, Pasighat holds the Minyong-Adi tribe's **Solung Festival** (1–5 September). The **internet cafe** (per hr Rs60; ☷ 7.30am-8pm) is 50m from the Hotel Aane and there's an SBI ATM just along from the sumo stand in the central market area.

Sleep at the friendly, central **Hotel Oman** (☎ 2224464; Main Market; s Rs250-300, d Rs400-500) or plusher **Hotel Aane** (☎ 2223333; d Rs1000, d with AC Rs1500; ☒), which has hot showers and an appealing rooftop terrace.

GETTING THERE & AWAY

Helicopters from **Pasighat Aerodrome** (☎ 2222088; ☷ 8am-noon Mon-Sat), 3km northeast, serve Naharlagun (Itanagar) via Mohanbari (Dibrugarh) on Monday, Wednesday and Friday; Guwahati via Naharlagun on Tuesday; and Along on Friday.

The inconveniently located APST bus station (take an autorickshaw) has services to Along (Rs100, 5½ hours, 7am Wednesday to Monday) and Itanagar (Rs170, 10 hours, 6am Tuesday to Sunday). Sumos run to Along (Rs220, five hours, 6am and noon) and Itanagar (Rs300, six hours, 6am). **Hotel Siang** (☎ 2224559; central market area) sells jeep-boat-jeep combination tickets (Rs250, 5½ hours, 5.30am) to Dibrugarh (Assam) via Majerbari Ghat.

WESTERN ARUNACHAL PRADESH

Culturally magical and scenically spectacular, a mountain-hopping journey to Tawang through lands inhabited by Monpa (a people of Buddhist-Tibetan origin) is one of the northeast's greatest attractions. Ideally budget at least five days return from Guwahati (or Tezpur), breaking the journey each way at Dirang or less interesting Bomdila. Be prepared for intense cold in winter. Come cashed up: there are no ATMs.

CENTRAL ARUNACHAL'S TRIBAL GROUPS

Adi (Abor), Nishi, Tajin, Hill Miri and various other Tibeto-Burman tribes of central Arunachal Pradesh consider themselves very self-consciously different from one another. But most are at least distantly related. Most traditionally practise Donyi-Polo (sun and moon) worship. For ceremonial occasions, village chiefs typically wear scarlet shawls and a bamboo wicker hat spiked with porcupine quill or hornbill feather. A few old men still wear their hair long, tied around to form a topknot above their foreheads. Women favour hand-woven wraparounds like Southeast Asian sarongs. House designs vary somewhat. Traditional Adi villages are generally the most photogenic with luxuriant palmyra-leaf thatching and boxlike granaries stilted to deter rodents.

Bhalukpong to Dirang

Permits are checked in Bhalukpong. The road then winds endlessly up on the very edge of heavily forested slopes before descending into wider valleys pockmarked with military camps, and then ascending again to mountaintop Bomdila.

BOMDILA
03782 / elev 2682m

The town is an alternative sleeping place to Dirang with the traditionally decorated, newly furnished **Doe-Gu-Khill guest house** (☎ 223643; sonchuki@yahoo.com; r/ste Rs700/1500) just below the monastery providing fabulous views. The reliable tour-agency **Himalayan Holidays** (☎ 222017; www.himalayan-holidays.com; ABC Bldg, Main Market; ☷ 8am-6pm) organises tours and treks in Arunachal, arranges permits, sells sumo tickets and has internet (Rs50 per hour).

Dirang
☎ 03780 / elev 1621m

Fabulous **Old Dirang**, 5km south of Dirang, is a picture-perfect Monpa stone village. The main road separates its rocky **minicitadel** from a huddle of picturesque streamside houses above which rises a steep ridge topped with a timeless **gompa**.

All Dirang's commercial services are in **New Dirang** with a strip of cheap hotels, eateries and sumo counters around the central crossroads.

Dirang Resort (☎ 242352; d Rs750), on Inspection Bungalow (IB) Rd, is a basic, rather overpriced, but friendly family hotel in an old-style hill house with a wooden wraparound balcony crowded with colourful potted plants. Nicest is the homely **Hotel Pemaling** (☎ 242615; s/ste Rs750/3000, d Rs1000-2000), 1km south overlooking New Dirang. The food is superb, try the paneer masala (cottage cheese in a creamy spicy saucy); the front garden and suites have sit-down-and-watch views towards the sometimes snow-bound Se La.

Dirang to Tawang Valley

The road endlessly zigzags sharply upward, eventually leaving the forest behind. **Se La**, a 4176m pass, breaches the mountains and provides access to Tawang Valley. Beyond could be a Scottish glen were it not for the yaks. From here the road plummets down the mountainside into the belly of Tawang Valley.

Tawang Valley

☎ 03794 / elev 3048m

Calling the Tawang Valley a valley just doesn't do justice to its incredible scale; it's more a mighty gash in the earth ringed by immense mountains. Patchworking the sloping ridges of the lower hills is a vast sweep of fields dotted with Buddhist monasteries and Monpa villages.

The biggest attraction is magical **Tawang Gompa** (☎ 222243; admission free, camera/video Rs20/100; ☽ dawn-dusk) backdropped by snow-speckled peaks. Founded in 1681, this medieval citadel is reputedly the world's second-largest Buddhist monastery complex and famed in Buddhist circles for its library. Within its fortified walls, narrow alleys lead up to the majestic and magnificently decorated **prayer hall** containing an 8m-high statue of **Buddha Shakyamuni**. Across the central square is a small but interesting **museum** (Rs20; ☽ 8am-5pm) containing images, robes, telescopic trumpets and some personal items of the sixth Dalai Lama. Spectacular *chaam* (ritual masked dances performed by some Buddhist monks in gompas to celebrate the victory of good over evil and of Buddhism over pre-existing religions) are held during the Torgya, Losar and Buddha Mahotsava festivals.

Other enchanting gompas and anigompas (nunneries) offer great day hikes from Tawang, including ancient if modest **Urgelling Gompa** where the sixth Dalai Lama was born. By road, it's 6km from Tawang town but closer on foot downhill from Tawang Gompa.

TAWANG TOWN
☎ 03794 / elev 3048m

Tawang town is a transport hub and service centre for the valley's villages; its setting is more beautiful than the town itself. Nonetheless, colourful **prayer wheels** add interest to the central old market area. These are turned by apple-cheeked Monpa pilgrims, many of whom sport traditional black yak-wool *gurdam* (skullcaps that look like giant Rastafarian spiders). Just 50m east is **Monyul Cyber Café** (per hr Rs50; ☽ 8.30am-8pm). **PL Traders** (☎ 222987; Old Market; ☽ 7am-7.30pm) opposite the turning up to the Tourist Lodge, sells handicrafts and traditional clothing (including *gurdam*).

Tawang has a number of small hotels. **Tourist Lodge** (☎ 222359; tw Rs300-1050) is exceedingly tatty, the only good-value reasonable-quality rooms happen to be the cheapest. It's 150m above the main drag. The **tourist office** (☎ 222359; ☽ 5am-8pm) is also here with a rather fine illustrated brochure on Tawang.

Outwardly smart, pseudo-Tibetan, **Hotel Gorichen** (☎ 224151; hotelgorichen@indiatimes.com; s Rs600, d Rs500-1800) in the upper old market area has traditional wood-lined rooms. The cheaper rooms are perfectly acceptable if you like to be cosy. Prices drop June to September.

Tawang Inn (☎ 224096; d from Rs1000-1200, ste Rs1500), which you enter from a back lane 400m southeast of the market, is central Tawang's most polished choice.

While each of these hotels have good restaurants, the cosy 14-seater **Chinese Restaurant** (Old Market; mains Rs35-80) is the town's best eatery with freshly made food (Indian as well as Chinese) that you may have to wait a while for.

Getting There & Away

From Lumla, 42km towards Zemithang, helicopters (Rs3400, two hours) fly Monday and Wednesday to Guwahati. APST buses leave Tawang 5.30am Monday and Friday for Tezpur (Rs290, 12 hours), calling at Dirang (Rs130 six hours), Bomdila (Rs170, seven hours) and Bhalukpong (Rs240, 10 hours) and return the next day. More frequent public sumos to Tezpur depart at dawn from Tawang for Dirang, Bomdila and Bhalukpong.

NAGALAND

The Naga peoples originated in Southeast Asia and are distributed all along the India–Myanmar border, but in Nagaland they form a majority. For centuries some 20 headhunting Naga tribes valiantly fought off any intruders. In between they kept busy by fighting each other and developing mutually unintelligible languages. Today intertribe communication uses a 'neutral' lingua franca, Nagamese. Major Naga groups include the developed Angami and Rengma of Kohima district, the Lotha of Wokha district and the Konyak of Mon district, whose villages have the most striking traditional architecture. For festivals, Naga women wear a hand-woven shawl that's distinctive for each tribe, while the men dust off their old warrior wear, loincloth and all.

It's festival Nagaland that most tourists imagine when booking a Nagaland tour. And Kohima's December Hornbill Festival easily justifies the trip. At other times some visitors may find the lack of spectacle disappointing. But if you lower your *National Geographic* image expectations, there's still lots of interest in meeting peoples whose cultures, in the words of one Indian journalist, have been through '1000 years in a lifetime'.

Dangers & Annoyances

Since 1947 Naga insurgents have battled for an independent Nagaland and some remote areas are partially under rebel control. A truce exists, most major Nagaland towns are stable, though can't be considered totally safe. Always check the current security situation before visiting anywhere in the region. Even in Kohima virtually everything closes by 5pm and travel by night is highly discouraged.

DIMAPUR

☎ 03862 / pop 308,000 / elev 260m

Nagaland's flat, uninspiring commercial centre was the capital of a big Kachari kingdom

---

NAGALAND FAST FACTS

Population Two million
Area 16,579 sq km
Capital Kohima
Main languages Nagamese, various Naga languages, Hindi, English
When to go October to March

---

that ruled much of Assam before the Ahoms showed up. All that remains are some curious, strangely phallic pillars of a former palace complex dotted about scraggy **Rajbari Park** (admission free) near an interesting **market**. The only reason tourists visit Dimapur is to transfer to Kohima. Right beside the NST bus station, the **Tourist Lodge** (☎ 226355; Kohima Rd; s/d Rs250/300) is a basic but acceptable option.

Air India (☎ 229366, 242441) flies to Kolkata, Guwahati and Imphal. The airport is 400m off the Kohima road, 3km out of town. The **NST bus station** (☎ 227579; Kohima Rd) runs services to Kohima (Rs65, three hours, hourly) and Imphal (Rs190, seven hours, 6am).

KOHIMA

☎ 0370 / pop 96,000 / elev 1444m

Nagaland's agreeable capital is scattered across a series of forested ridges and hilltops. Avoid Kohima on Sunday as apart from hotels, places are closed; for security reasons, the town shuts down by 5pm.

Information

Alder Tours & Travels (☎ 9436011266; kevi_alder toursntravels@rediffmail.com; AG Colony) Nagaland cultural tours, birdwatching trips and permits.
Amizone (cnr Dimapur & Imphal Rds; per hr Rs30; 10am-5.30pm Mon-Sat) Internet downstairs from Dream Café.
Axis Bank (Stadium Approach, Razhu Point) One of several ATMs.
Secretariat, Home Department (☎ 2221406; Secretariat Bldg) Permit extensions.
Tribal Discovery (☎ 9436000759, 9856474767; yiese _neitho@rediffmail.com; Science College Rd) Neithonuo Yeise ('Nitono') is an eloquent guide to local sites and can arrange permits.

Sights & Activities

An immaculate **War Cemetery** (dawn-dusk Mon-Sat) contains graves of 1200 British, Commonwealth and Indian soldiers. It stands at the crucially strategic junction of the Dimapur and Imphal roads, the site of intense fighting against the Japanese during a 64-day WWII battle. This reached its climax on the deputy commissioner's tennis court (marked out) with seven days of incredibly short-range grenade-lobbing across the net. Deuce!

The superbly presented **State Museum** (☎ 2220749; admission Rs5; 9.30am-3.30pm Tue-Sun), 3km north, includes plenty of tableaus with

NORTHEAST STATES

NAGA CULTURE

Naga villages are perched defensively on top of impregnable ridgetops. Many are still subdivided into *khel*s (neighbourhoods) guarded by ceremonial *kharu* (gates) with some still retaining their massively heavy, strikingly carved, wooden or stone doors. Although exact designs vary considerably, the central motif is usually a Naga warrior between the horns of a *mithun* (distinctive local bovine), with sun, moon, breasts (for fertility) and weaponry all depicted. *Kharu* also provide an ornamental entranceway into villages and usually behind them is a dedicated head-hanging tree where once the tribe's collection of heads would have been displayed.

As a sign of wealth, *mithun* skulls also adorn traditional Naga houses, especially around Mon, whose designs typically have rounded prow-fronts. Conversion to Christianity has meant a loss of Naga tradition. Fortunately headhunting has ended, but Christian villages no longer retain *morungs* (bachelor dormitories) where young men lived communally while learning traditional skills.

Headhunting was officially outlawed in 1935, with the last recorded occurrence in 1963. Nonetheless, severed heads are still an archetypal artistic motif found notably on *yanra* (pendants) that originally denoted the number of human heads a warrior had taken. Some villages, such as Shingha Changyuo in Mon district, still retain their 'hidden' collection. Some intervillage wars continued into the 1980s, and a curious feature of many outwardly modern settlements is their 'treaty stones' recording peace settlements between neighbouring communities.

Visiting a Naga village without a local guide is unproductive, there will be language difficulties and you'll be unaware of local cultural expectations. The guide will also know the local security situation.

---

mannequins-in-action depicting different traditional Naga lifestyles plus everyday tools.

At the fascinating if tiny **central market** (Stadium Approach; ☾ 6am-4pm), tribal people sell such 'edible' delicacies as *borol* (wriggling hornet grubs).

Sleeping & Eating

Accommodation becomes extremely scarce for kilometres around during the Hornbill Festival, book well in advance.

Hotel Pine (☎ 2243129; d Rs400-800) Down a side lane off Phool Bari this small hotel is suitable for a night's stay, being centrally located, well kept and in reasonable condition. Top sheets only come with the more expensive rooms, but you could ask for one.

Viewpoint Lodge (☎ 2241826, 9436002096; 3rd fl, Keditsu Bldg, PR Hill; s/d Rs700/1000) Perched above two handy internet cafes at Police Station Junction (1km south of the bus station), Viewpoint Lodge offers sparklingly clean rooms with neatly tiled floors. Singles are at the front so choose a double for the good rearside views.

Hotel Japfü (☎ 2240211; hoteljapfu@yahoo.co.in; PR Hill; s/d from Rs1000/1400) This high-service hotel on a small hill directly above Police Station Junction has glassed-in balconies, hot showers and only slightly worn decor. The restaurant food is superb but service is woeful – best to order meals well in advance.

Popular Bakery (PR Hill; from Rs5; ☾ 5.30am-8.30pm) Stroll two minutes down the hill from Viewpoint Lodge for delicious breakfast pastries or Indian sweets.

Dream Café (☎ 2290756; cnr Dimapur & Imphal Rds; instant coffee Rs10; ☾ 10am-6pm) Beneath UCO Bank is Kohima's youth meeting point, with twice-monthly live minigigs and CDs of Naga music for sale. Great views from the back windows, a bunch of magazines to read and homemade cakes make this is a good lingering place.

Flaming Wok (Rs40-90; ☾ 10am-7pm Mon-Sat) On Nagaland State Transport (NST) Rd; upstairs overlooking the taxi stand. The fare is mainly Chinese but with some Indian dishes. A guitar is available if you wish to serenade your fellow diners.

Getting There & Away

The **NST bus station** (☎ 2291018; Main Rd) has services to Dimapur (Rs65, three hours, hourly Monday to Saturday, 7am Sun), Mokokchung (Rs132, seven hours, 6.30am Monday to Saturday) and Imphal (Rs123, six hours, 7.30am Monday, Wednesday and Friday). The taxi stand opposite has share taxis to Dimapur (Rs150, 2½ hours). A car for a day out to Kisama and Khonoma costs Rs600 to Rs1000. A railway line is being built from Dimapur to Kohima.

AROUND KOHIMA
Kisama Heritage Village

This **open-air museum** (admission Rs10; ☾ 8am-6pm May-Sep, 8am-4.30pm Oct-Apr) has a representative selection of traditional Naga houses and *morungs* (bachelor dormitories) with full-size log drums. Nagaland's biggest annual festival, the Hornbill Festival (1–7 December) is celebrated here with various Naga tribes converging for a weeklong cultural, dance and sporting bash, much of it in full warrior costume. Simultaneously Kohima also hosts a **rock festival** (www.hornbillmusic.com). Kisama is 10km from central Kohima along the well-surfaced Imphal road.

KIGWEMA

Kigwema village, 3km south of Kisama, has Angami-Naga homes with traditional-style *kikeh* (crossed-horn gables). There's a sign on a building in the main square announcing that Japanese troops arrived in Kigwema on '4-4-44 at 3pm'. Some houses are still roofed with corrugated metal sheets donated by the British army after the village was burnt out in a battle to take it back from the Japanese.

Khonoma

This historic **Angami-Naga village** was the site of two major British-Angami siege battles in 1847 and 1879. Built on an easily defended ridge (very necessary back in headhunting days), Khonoma looks beautifully traditional. Amid flowers and pomelo trees, squash gourd vines and megaliths, the houses range from corrugated shacks to sturdy concrete homes still decorated with *mithun* (distinctive local bovine) skulls. Basket weavers work quietly at their open doors, public rubbish bins are regularly emptied and graves are dotted everywhere along the neatly laid stone stairways that form the main thoroughfares. From the ridge there are panoramic views of splendid rice terraces nestled in an arc of surrounding forested mountains. A heritage museum is being built and will open in 2009.

Of three simple homestay–guest houses the best option is **Via Meru's House** (☎ 943619378, 9436011266; s/d Rs400/700, meals extra). The three wooden-floored twin rooms are well kept and one room has a delightful balcony from where the top section of the village is perfectly framed. The place exudes character and the aroma of polished wood pervades the house.

KOHIMA TO MON

Road conditions require you to travel some of the way through Assam and the journey is usually broken with a night's stay at the friendly and well-run **Tourist Lodge** (☎ 0369-2229343; touristlodgemkg@yahoo.com; dm Rs200, r Rs600-1000; 🖳) in unexceptional **Mokokchung**. An alternative is **Tuophema Tourist Village** (☎ 0370-2270786; s/d/tr Rs800/1200/1200), where you sleep in comfortable but traditionally styled Naga thatched bungalows set in a delightful flower garden giving great sunset views.

NORTHERN NAGALAND

This is the most unspoiled part of the state with many tribes living in villages of thatched longhouses. However, it's rugged country and only a few villages are easily accessible by road.

The most accessible villages are the Konyak settlements around Mon. Traditional houses abound, and some villages have *morungs* and religious relics from pre-Christian times. Village elders may wear traditional costume and Konyak of all ages carry the fearsome-looking *dao* – a crude machete used for headhunting right up until the mid-20th century.

The impoverished hill town of **Mon** is in a gorgeous setting but feels like a frontier town. Accommodation is at the delightful **Helsa Cottage** (☎ 9436433782, 9436657434; r Rs800) run by Aunty who can organise transport and local guides. Talk to Aunty and she'll tell you how much Mon and Nagaland have changed. She relates the time she came to Mon in the early 1960s when there were no roads and she was carried up from the plains, aged seven, on the back of a porter to be greeted by a population that wore no clothes.

Shingha Chingyuo village (20km; population 5900) has a huge longhouse decorated with *mithun* and deer skulls, three stuffed tiger carcases, and a store of old human skulls. There used to be 10 *morungs* in this village. **Longwoa** (35km) is on the India–Burma border with one longhouse actually straddling the border. **Chui** (8km) includes an elephant skull in its longhouse collection. **Shangnyu** village has a shrine full of fertility references such as tumescent warriors, a crowing cock, a large snake, a man and woman enjoying sex and, to complete the picture, a double rainbow.

NORTHEAST STATES

MANIPUR

This 'Jewelled Land' is home to Thadou, Tangkhul, Kabul, Mao Naga and many other tribal peoples, but the main grouping is the predominantly neo-Vaishnavite Meitei who are battling to have Meitei script used in local schools. Manipuris are famed for traditional dances, spicy multidish thalis and the sport of polo that they claim to have invented. Manipur's forested hills provide cover for rare birds, drug traffickers and guerrilla armies making it by far the Northeast's most dangerous state.

Permit conditions usually restrict foreigners to Greater Imphal although this represents more a zone of safety rather than a geographical area. Most foreigners fly into Imphal; however, with a guide, driving in from Kohima (Nagaland) or Silchar (Assam) to Imphal is possible. Travelling east of Kakching towards the Burma border is not permitted.

IMPHAL
Orientation
Major highways, including Airport Rd, intersect at Kanglapat, which skirts Kangla, the former fortified centre of Imphal. MG Ave runs off Kanglapat north of NC Rd. The airport is 9km to the southwest.

Information
Click Communication (☎ 9862241707; MG Ave; per hr Rs20; ✆ 8am-7pm Mon-Sat, 11am-2pm Sun) Internet.
SBI ATM (MG Ave) About 100m from Hotel Nirmala.
Tourist office (☎ 224603; Jail Rd; http://manipur.nic.in/tourism.htm) For brochures.

Sights
Fortified **Kangla** (admission free; ✆ 9am-4pm Nov-Feb, 9am-5pm Mar-Oct) was the off-and-on-again regal capital of Manipur until the Anglo-Manipuri War of 1891 saw the defeat of the Manipuri maharaja and a British takeover. A previous 1869 earthquake destroyed many of the earlier

---

MANIPUR FAST FACTS

Population 2.4 million
Area 22,327 sq km
Capital Imphal
Main languages Manipuri (Meitei), Assamese, Bengali
When to go October to March

---

buildings that were replaced and strengthened by Chandrakriti, the last but one reigning maharaja. Entrance is by way of an exceedingly tall gate on Kanglapat. The interesting, older, buildings are at the rear of the citadel guarded by three recently restored large white *kangla sha* (dragons).

Manipur State Museum (☎ 2450709; off Kangla Rd; Indian/foreigner Rs3/20; ✆ 10am-4pm Tue-Sun) has a marvellous collection of historical, cultural and natural history ephemera. Tribal costumes, royal clothing, historical polo equipment, stuffed carnivores in action and pickled snakes compete with a two-headed calf for the visitor's attention.

The 1776-built **Shri Govindajee Mandir**, with two rather suggestive domes, is a neo-Vaishnavite temple with Radha and Govinda the presiding deities. Guarding the outside of the temple are Garuda (the vehicle of Vishnu) and the monkey god Hanuman. Afternoon *puja* (offerings, prayers) is for one hour at 4pm in winter and 5pm in summer.

Adjacent to the mandir is the **Royal Palace**, closed to visitors except for the annual **Kwak Tenba festival**. Then a colourful procession in traditional costume and headed by the titular maharaja walk to the Polo Ground for religious ceremonies and cultural festivities. The festival takes place on the fourth day of Durga Puja.

Khwairamband Bazaar (Ima Market; ✆ 7am-5pm) is a photogenic all-women's market run by some 3000 *ima* (mothers). Divided by a road, one side sells vegetables, fruit, fish and groceries while the other deals in household items, fabrics and pottery.

Imphal War Cemetery (Imphal Rd; ✆ 8am-5pm) contains the graves of more than 1600 British and Commonwealth soldiers killed in the battles that raged around Imphal in 1944. It's a peaceful and well-kept memorial. Off Hapta Minuthong Rd is a separate **Indian War Cemetery** (✆ 8am-5pm).

Sleeping & Eating
The state tax that is in place, disappointingly, adds 20% to your bill.

Hotel White Palace (☎ 2452322; 113 MG Ave; s/d Rs160/280, VIP Rs200/310, ste Rs450-700) A fairly standard hotel that despite its abuse of the terms 'VIP' and 'suite' has some good budget rooms, although a few have no external windows. They all come with mosquito nets and some sort of TV; we felt that room 14 was the best.

Hotel Nirmala (☎ 2459014; MG Ave; s/d from Rs250/400, with AC from Rs600/800; ❄) A friendly place with an ultra quick-service restaurant although it doesn't open until 10am so breakfast has to be by room service. The rooms are nothing special but you do feel a sense of belonging when staying here.

Anand Continental (☎ 2449422; Khoyathong Rd; hotel_anand@rediff.com; s/d from Rs425/800, with AC Rs675/1000; ❄) Smallish rooms, a little too much furniture, friendly management and possession of a vacuum cleaner characterise this acceptable hotel. Hot water flows 6am to 11am, thereafter by a free bucket-load.

Getting There & Away
Private buses to Guwahati (Rs600, 20 hours, 10am) and Dimapur (Rs330, 10 hours, frequent between 6am and 10.30am) via Kohima (Rs240, six hours) are run by **Manipur Golden Travels** (☎ 9856247872; MG Ave; ☼ 5.30am-7pm). Next door, Royal Tours has buses to Shillong (Rs660, 20 hours, 10am). A train line to Imphal is being planned.

Air India (☎ 2450999; airport) flies to Aizawl, Dimapur, Guwahati, Kolkata and Silchar. **IndiGo** (☎ toll free 18001803838; airport) flies to Agartala, Kolkata and Delhi. **Jetlite** (☎ 2455054; airport) flies to Guwahati and Kolkata. **Kingfisher Red** (☎ toll free 18002093030; airport) flies to Dimapur, Guwahati, Kolkata and Silchar.

AROUND IMPHAL
One area allowed on a foreigner's permit is along 48km of NH150, south to Loktak Lake. If you're part of a guided tour there are several tourist sites that you'll be taken to. **Lokpaching battlefield** (Red Hill), 16km south of Imphal, has a rather uninspiring Japanese war memorial on a site that marks the last battle on Indian soil.

Conjure up an image of a shimmering blue lake broken up into small lakelets by floating 'islands' of thick matted weeds. Add bamboo bridges, tribal people in dugout canoes and thatched hut-villages anchored on to the floating islands, and you have **Loktak Lake**. This, apart from being India's largest freshwater lake, is a beautiful spot and well worth the drive from Imphal. More peculiar than floating villages are the large, perfectly circular fishing ponds created out of floating rings of weeds. The best view is atop Sendra Island, more a promontory than island.

Moirang's **INA Museum** (Indian National Army; ☎ 0385-262186; admission Rs2; ☼ 10am-4pm Tue-Sun) celebrates the town's small but symbolic role in the Indian Independence movement. It was here on 14 April 1944 that the anticolonial INA first unfurled the Azad Hind (Free India) flag while advancing with Japanese WWII forces against British-held Imphal. The INA Museum is mostly dedicated to Netaji (dear leader) Subhash Chandra Bose, the head of the INA.

MIZORAM

Mizoram is slashed by north–south–running valleys, the remainder of the Himalaya foothills flung to the side as the Indian subcontinent collided with Asia all those millions of years ago. Mizoram is tidy and almost entirely Christian, and you'll see very few Indian faces among the local Thai- and Chinese-style features.

Mizoram runs to its own rhythm. Most businesses open early and shut by 6pm; virtually everything closes tight on Sunday. Mizos traditionally have two main meals, *zingchaw* (morning meal, 9am to 10am) and *tlaichaw* (afternoon meal, 4pm to 6pm).

Mizo culture has no caste distinctions and women appear liberated; in Aizawl girls smoke openly, wear jeans and hang out in unchaperoned posses meeting up with their beaus at rock concerts on the central field.

Two main Mizo festivals, Chapchar Kut (Kut is Mizo for festival) and Pawl Kut celebrate elements in the agricultural cycle. Chapchar Kut takes place towards the end of February and signals the start of the spring sowing season. Participants don national costume and celebrate in folk dancing and singing traditional songs as they do also for Pawl Kut held at the end of November. This time though it is to celebrate the harvest.

Information
PERMITS
Agencies, notably Serow Travels and Omega Travels (p632), can arrange and fax you a

NORTHEAST STATES

MIZORAM FAST FACTS

Population 895,000
Area 21,081 sq km
Capital Aizawl
Main languages Mizo, English
When to go October to March

10-day permit. Mizoram permit restrictions are perhaps the most lax of the Northeast States. Be sure that all places you wish to visit are on your permit and you should be allowed to go anywhere in the state. Visit the Superintendent of Police, Criminal Investigation Department (SP-CID; below) for 10-day permit extensions. Note though that the Kolkata FRO doesn't grant Mizoram permits.

AIZAWL

☎ 0389 / pop 275,000

From a distance Aizawl (pronounced eye-zole) seems a painted backdrop to an Italian opera, such is the steepness of the ridge on which it's perched. Backs of homes at road level might be held there with stilts three times higher than their roofs.

Addresses refer to areas and junctions ('points' or 'squares'). The unnamed spaghetti of roads and steep linking stairways is confusing, but the central ridge road is reasonably flat joining Zodin Sq (old bus station), Upper Bazaar (shops), Zarkawt (hotels and long-distance sumos) and Chandmari (east Mizoram sumos).

Information

Directorate of Tourism (☎ 2333475; www.mizo tourism.nic.in; PA-AW Bldg, Bungkawn)
Omega Travels (☎ 2322283; Zodin Sq; ✆ 9am-5pm Mon-Fri, 9am-3pm Sat) Arranges tourist permits and tours. Zova (☎ 9436142938) speaks good English.
SBI ATM (Raj Bhawan Junction)
Serow Travels (☎ 2301509, 9436150484; D/74 Millennium Centre, Dawrpui; www.serowtours.com; ✆ 9.30am-6pm Mon-Sat) Arranges permits, Mizoram tours and village homestays. Helpful Ruati speaks excellent English.
Serps Connection (Zarkawt; per hr Rs30; ✆ 9am-10.30pm)
SP-CID (☎ 2333980; Maubawk Bungkawn; ✆ 10am-4pm Mon-Fri) Permit extensions.

Sights

Mizoram State Museum (☎ 2340936; Macdonald Hill, Zarkawt; admission Rs5; ✆ 9.30am-5pm Mon-Fri) has interesting exhibits on Mizo culture. It's up a steep lane from Sumkuma Point past Aizawl's most distinctive **church**, whose modernist bell-tower spire is pierced by arched 'windows'.

The **Salvation Army Temple** (Zodin Sq) has bell chimes that are endearingly complex and can be heard throughout the city, especially on a bible-quiet Sunday morning.

The **KV Paradise** (Durtlang; admission Rs5; ✆ 10am-9pm Mon-Sat) site is 8km from Zarkawt, 1km off the Aizawl–Silchar road via an improbably narrow dirt lane. V is for Varte who died in a 2001 motor accident. K is for her husband Khawlhring who has since lavished his entire savings and energy creating a three-storey mausoleum to her memory. The marble fountain-patio has wonderful panoramic views. Inside and downstairs is Varte's grave and upstairs an odd collection displays her wardrobe and shoe collection, including the clothes (neatly laundered) she died in.

A Saturday **street market** (Mission Veng St) sprawls along the street with village women offering fruit, vegetables, maybe a dead pig, fish and live hens in individualised wickerwork carry-away baskets.

Sleeping

ZARKAWT

There's a convenient concentration of lower midrange hotels around Zarkawt's Sumkuma Point. Hotels typically add a 10% service charge.

Hotel Tropicana (☎ 2346156; hotel_tropicana@rediff mail.com; s Rs200-400, d Rs550-650) Resplendently green but with its name painted over, Hotel Tropicana is right at Sumkuma Point roundabout. The better double rooms are quite cosy but look at a few before deciding as some have no views and smell musty.

Hotel Clover (☎ 2305736; www.davids-hotel-clover .com; G-16 Chanmari; s/d from Rs750/1500; 🛜) The accommodation side of David's Kitchen with impressively decorated and furnished rooms, but without external windows. Bonus is free wi-fi and a 30% discount at David's Kitchen.

UPPER KHATLA

Hotel Arini (☎ 2301557; Upper Khatla; s/d from Rs460/720) Only a small red sign announces the new semiboutique Hotel Arini, named after the owner's precocious three-year-old daughter. The rooms are cheerily bright and fresh-looking, and the staff pleasant and obliging. Choose a backside room with a stupendous down-valley view.

ZEMABAWK

Tourist Home (☎ 2352067; Berawtlang; d Rs350-500) High above Zemabawk, some 11km from Zarkawt, the peaceful Tourist Home has great new rooms and older, mustier cottages. However the hilltop setting is idyllic and

NORTHEAST STATES

Aizawl's best viewpoint is just a 10-minute stroll away. It's worth the Rs250 taxi ride for the views and a snack at the cafeteria.

Eating

David's Kitchen (☎ 2305736; Zarkawt; mains Rs65-210; ⏰ 10am-9.30pm Mon-Sat, noon-9.30pm Sun) David's fine Mizo, Thai, Indian, Chinese and continental food, mocktails, friendly staff and pleasant decor will please everyone. It's 200m south of Hotel Chief.

Curry Pot (Upper Khatla; meals Rs50-120; ⏰ 10am-9pm Mon-Sat) Next door to Hotel Arini, this place has tasty Indian and Chinese dishes on the menu with a rather good, well-portioned biryani on offer.

On Sunday only hotels and David's Kitchen will save you from starving.

Getting There & Away

Taxis charge Rs500 and shared sumos charge Rs45 to efficient little Lengpui airport, 35km west of Aizawl. **Air India** (☎ 344733) flies to Guwahati, Kolkata and Imphal, while Kingfisher Red goes to Kolkata.

Counters for long-distance sumos are conveniently clustered around Zarkawt's Sumkuma Point. For Saitual the most central are **RKV** (☎ 2305452) and Nazareth in Chandmari. For details, see the boxed table, right.

Getting Around

Frequent city buses run Zodin Sq–Upper Bazaar–Zarkawt–Chandmari–Lower Chatlang–Zasanga Point, then either climb to Durtlang or curl right round past the new Chunga Bus Station (6km) to Zemabawk. Maruti-Suzuki taxis are ubiquitous and reasonably priced.

RURAL MIZORAM

Mizoram's pretty, green hills get higher as you head east. **Champhai** is widely considered the most attractive district. But for a more accessible taste of small-town Mizo life, visit **Saitual**. An incredibly good-value **Tourist Lodge** (☎ 2562395; d Rs250) in a hilltop garden, 700m north of Saitual market, offers extensive views. There's little to do but meet the locals and find some biscuits for dinner. However, a very bumpy 10km side trip to **Tamdil Lake** is mildly memorable. This local beauty spot is ringed by lush mountains, patches of poinsettia and a few musty if pleasantly situated

SUMO SERVICES FROM AIZAWL

Destination	Cost (Rs)	Duration (hr)	Departure
Guwahati	550	14-18	4pm
Saitual	75	3	1pm, 3pm
Shillong	435	15	4pm
Silchar	265	5½	6.30am, 10am, 1pm

cottages (☎ 94361449479; d Rs400). There are boats to rent (Rs10), but there's no cafe.

TRIPURA

Tripura is culturally and politically fascinating, and the state's royal palaces and temples draw a growing flow of domestic tourists. However, if you're expecting the exotic grandeur of Rajasthani castles, Tripura might seem a long detour for relatively little.

History

Before joining India in 1949, Tripura (Twipra) was ruled for centuries by its own royal family (the Manikyas), based first at Udaipur, then Old Agartala (Kayerpur) and finally Agartala. In the 1880s Tripura's maharaja became a benefactor of Bengali poet-philosopher Rabindranath Tagore. Indian partition flooded Tripura with Bengali refugees, leaving the local Borok-Tripuri people a minority in their own state.

Dangers & Annoyances

The Agartala, Udaipur and Kailasahar areas are generally safe. However, there is serious instability in north-central Tripura. All vehicles must travel in armed convoys through two sections of the Agartala–Kailasahar road. While attacks are rare, they do happen.

AGARTALA

☎ 0381 / pop 189,330

Tripura's low-key capital is centred on Ujjayanta Palace. If you've come from the early

TRIPURA FAST FACTS

Population 3.2 million
Area 10,486 sq km
Capital Agartala
Main languages Bengali, Kokborok
When to go November to February

closures of Manipur, Nagaland or Mizoram, it's delightful to find that life continues after 6pm. If you've arrived from Bangladesh, whose border is just 3km east, the town feels refreshingly organised and manageable. **Durga puja** is ecelebrated with huge *pandals* (temporary temples built from wood and cloth).

Information

BOOKSHOP

Jnan Bichitra Bookzone (11 JB Rd; 9am-9pm;) Welcoming, well-stocked bookshop selling postcards and music.

INTERNET ACCESS

Netzone (6 Sakuntala Rd; per hr Rs20; 8am-10pm) Best of several closely grouped options.

MONEY

Axis ATM (Hotel Welcome Palace, HGB Rd)

SBI (2311364; top fl, SBI Bldg, HGB Rd) Changes cash and travellers cheques, but allow at least an hour. ATM also. On Hari Ganga Basak (HGB) Rd.

TOURIST INFORMATION

Tripura Tourism (2225930; http://tripura.nic.in /ttourism1.htm; Swet Mahal, Palace Complex; 10am-5pm Mon-Sat, 3-5pm Sun) Helpful and enthusiastic with many great-value tours.

TripuraInfo (2380566; www.tripurainfo.com) Useful news and tourism website.

Sights

Agartala's indisputable centrepiece is the striking, dome-capped **Ujjayanta Palace**. Flanked by

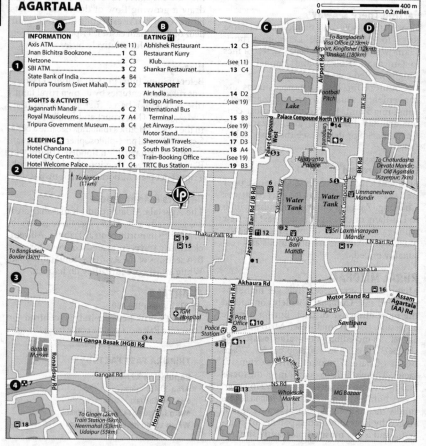

AGARTALA

0 — 400 m
0 — 0.2 miles

INFORMATION	
Axis ATM	(see 11)
Jnan Bichitra Bookzone	1 C3
Netzone	2 C3
SBI ATM	3 C2
State Bank of India	4 B4
Tripura Tourism (Swet Mahal)	5 D2

SIGHTS & ACTIVITIES	
Jagannath Mandir	6 C2
Royal Mausoleums	7 A4
Tripura Government Museum	8 C4

SLEEPING	
Hotel Chandana	9 D2
Hotel City Centre	10 C3
Hotel Welcome Palace	11 C4

EATING	
Abhishek Restaurant	12 C3
Restaurant Kurry Klub	(see 11)
Shankar Restaurant	13 C4

TRANSPORT	
Air India	14 D2
Indigo Airlines	(see 19)
International Bus Terminal	15 B3
Jet Airways	(see 19)
Motor Stand	16 D3
Sherowali Travels	17 D3
South Bus Station	18 A4
Train-Booking Office	(see 19)
TRTC Bus Station	19 B3

To Bangladesh Visa Office (2.5km); Airport, Kingfisher (12km); Unakoti (180km)

Football Pitch

Lake

Airport Rd

BK Rd

Palace Compound North (VIP Rd)

Palace Compound West

Palace Compound East

Ujjayanta Palace

BK Rd

To Chaturdasha Devata Mandir; Old Agartala (Kayerpur; 7km)

Ummaneshwar Mandir

Sri Laxminarayan Mandir

LN Bari Rd

To Airport (11km)

Water Tank

Water Tank

Jagannath Bari Rd (JB Rd)

Sakuntala Rd

Old Pretrum

Thakur Palli Rd

Durga Bari Mandir

To Bangladesh Border (3km)

Akhaura Rd

Mantri Bari Rd

Central Rd

Old Thana La

Motor Stand Rd

Assam Agartala (AA) Rd

IGM Hospital

Post Office

Police Station

Hari Ganga Basak (HGB) Rd

Masjid Rd

Santipara

Ronaldsay Rd

Batala Market

Gangail Rd

Old Guenthorpe Rd

NS Rd

Wholesale Market

MG Bazaar

CRB Rd

Hospital Rd

To Ginger (2km); Train Station (5km); Neermahal (53km); Udaipur (55km)

two large reflecting ponds, the whitewashed 1901 edifice was built by Tripura's 182nd maharaja. It looks particularly impressive floodlit at night, but for security reasons the grounds and interior are not open to the public.

Of four Hindu temples around the palace compound, the most fanciful is **Jagannath Mandir** (4am-2pm & 4-9pm). Its massive sculptured portico leads into a complex with wedding-cake architecture painted in ice-cream sundae colours. The small **Tripura Government Museum** (2326444; http://tripura.nic .in/museum/welcome.html; Post Office Circle; admission Rs2; 10am-1.30pm & 2-5pm Mon-Fri) has a variety of tribal displays plus some interesting musical instruments made from bamboo. Several **royal mausoleums** are decaying quietly on the riverbank behind Batala market. Be discreet as it's also the burning ghats (crematorium).

OLD AGARTALA

Chaturdasha Devata Mandir (Temple of Fourteen Deities) hosts a big seven-day July **Kharchi Puja** festival in Old Agartala, 7km east down Assam Agartala (AA) Rd (NH44) at Kayerpur.

Sleeping

State taxes add 10% to your bill.

Hotel Chandana (2311216; Palace Compound Lane; s/d/tr Rs95/210/285) Lacklustre but cheap and bearable, the Chandana's simple rooms have mosquito nets and cold showers. Peaceful yet central.

Hotel City Centre (2385092; www.hotelcitycentre .co.in; 39 HGB Rd; s/d from Rs350/450, AC from Rs650/1000;) Choose from a variety of different rooms depending on your requirements for fridges, fancy carpets or plush sofas. The mid-priced rooms are the better value. There's internet at the friendly reception.

Hotel Welcome Palace (2384940; HGB Rd; s from Rs500, d Rs700-1800;) This hard-to-beat option has helpful English-speaking staff, eager room service and superb food. Rooms are neat if not huge; some may not have external windows.

Ginger (toll free 18002093333, 2303333; www.ginger hotels.com; Airport Rd; s/d Rs1499/1999;) Part of the new Tata-owned Ginger chain of hotels, this brand-spanking place has superb rooms with wi-fi, real coffee and a small gym. There's even a room for someone with disabilities.

Eating

Eating out in Tripura is disappointing and despite the state not being dry, no restaurant serves alcohol. Better restaurants to be found include:

Shankar Restaurant (mains Rs30-70) Provides some of Agartala's best food; nothing fancy just straightforward rice and veg in an AC street cafe. On Netaji Subhash (NS) Rd.

Restaurant Kurry Klub (Hotel Welcome Palace, HGB Rd; mains Rs40-150; 10am-10pm) Very tasty food served in a small dining room whose decor would be rather striking if only the lighting was improved. If you're staying in the hotel, room service is faster and beers can be acquired.

Abhishek Restaurant (LN Bari Rd; mains Rs60-100) Reliable food served either on an inviting outdoor terrace or in a marine-themed dining room with good AC. A prawn curry comes with one large prawn. 'Very expensive, sah', the waiter explained.

Getting There & Around

Air India (2325470; VIP Rd) flies to Kolkata, Guwahati and Silchar; **Indigo Airlines** (2325602; TRTC bus station) to Kolkata and Imphal; and **Jet Airways** (2325602; TRTC bus station) to Guwahati and Kolkata. **Kingfisher** (18002093030; airport) flies to Kolkata and Guwahati. Agartala's airport is 12km north, Rs70/90/100 by bus/autorickshaw/share taxi and Rs400 to Rs500 by taxi.

Private bus operators clustered on LN Bari Rd include **Sherowali Travels** (2216608); others leave from the **TRTC bus station** (2325685; Thakur Palli Rd). Sumos use the **Motor Stand** (Motor Stand Rd) and **South Bus Station** (SBS; 2376717; Ronaldsay Rd). Destinations for bus and sumo trips are:

Guwahati bus (Rs530, 20 hours, 6am and noon); sumo (Rs500, 24 hours, 11.30am)

Kailasahar bus (Rs73, eight hours, 6am); sumo (Rs120, seven hours, 7am, 10am and noon)

Melagarh (for Neermahal) bus (Rs24, 1½ hours)

Shillong bus (Rs530, 18 hours, 6am and noon); sumo (Rs410, 20 hours, 11.30am)

Silchar bus (Rs250, 12 hours, 6am); sumo (Rs136, 12 hours, 6am)

Udaipur bus (Rs25, 1¾ hours)

Opposite the TRTC is the **International Bus Terminal** (9863045083) where Bangladesh Road Transport Corporation's daily bus departs for Dhaka (Rs232, six hours, 1pm).

Agartala's brand-new, palace-style train station is 5km south on the Udaipur road. Currently there are only two trains a day, to

NORTHEAST STATES

Silchar (No 863; Rs67, eight hours, 2pm) and Lumding (No 5696; Rs95, 18 hours, 1.15pm). At the time of research trains were still such a novelty that people were turning up at the station to see the two daily departures.

There's a computerised **train-booking office** (☏ 8am-7.30pm Mon-Fri, 8-11.30am Sun) at Agartala's TRTC bus station.

AROUND AGARTALA

Southern Tripura's best known sights can be combined into a long day trip from Agartala, though sleeping at Neermahal is worthwhile. Any of Agartala's hotels can arrange a taxi or engage **Banti Bhattacharjee** (☏ 9856877883) for about Rs1800 per day trip for three people in an AC car. All transport passes the gates of **Sepahijala Wildlife Sanctuary** (☏ 2361225; Km23, NH44 extension; admission/camera/video Rs5/10/500; ☏ 8am-4pm Sat-Thu), a local picnic and boating spot famous for its spectacled monkeys.

Udaipur
☏ 03821

Udaipur was Tripura's historic capital and remains dotted with ancient temples and a patchwork of tanks. Ruined but still massive, **Jagannath Mandir** is a most curious temple, overgrown with creepers Angkor Wat–style. It sits at the southwest corner of the huge **Jagannath Digthi tank**, around 1km from Udaipur bus stand, and behind a more modern temple. The famous Jagannath statue of Puri once resided

here, but has been replaced by another idol that, like the original, still takes an annual chariot ride to its holiday home.

MATABARI

When Sati's toes fell on Kolkata (see p502), her divine right leg dropped on Matabari. This gruesome legend is piously celebrated at the **Tripura Sundari Mandir** (☏ 4.30am-1.30pm & 3.30-9.30pm), a 1501 Kali temple where a steady stream of pilgrims make almost endless animal sacrifices that leave the grounds as bloody as the temple's vivid-red *shikhara* (Buddhist monastery). Even more people come here at the big **Diwali festival** (October/November) to bathe in the fish-filled tank by the temple. The temple is 100m east of the NH44, 4km south of Udaipur.

GETTING THERE & AROUND

Udaipur's bus stand has quarter-hourly departures to Agartala (Rs23, 1¼ hours) and Melagarh (Rs13, 45 minutes). An autorickshaw for an around-Udaipur tour will cost Rs300.

Neermahal & Melagarh
☏ 0381 / pop 21,750

Tripura's most iconic building, the 1930 Neermahal, is a long, red-and-white **water palace** (admission Rs3; ☏ 9am-4pm), empty, but shimmering on its own boggy island in the lake of Rudra Sagar. Like its counterpart in

---

CROSSING INTO BANGLADESH AT AGARTALA

Border Hours

The border at Agartala is open from 7am to 6pm.

Foreign Exchange

There's no exchange booth and Agartala banks don't sell Bangladeshi taka, so changing money is hit and miss; ask local traders or border officials.

Onward Transport

From central Agartala the border is just 3km along Akhaura Rd (Rs25 by rickshaw). On the Bangladesh side the nearest town is Akhaura, 5km beyond reached by 'baby taxi' (autorickshaw). Akhaura train station is on the Dacca–Comilla line. However for Dacca–Sylhet trains, continue 3km further north to Ajampur train station. Coming eastbound be sure to pay your Bangladeshi departure tax at a Sonali bank before heading for the border.

Visas

Unhelpful, but the northeast's only **Bangladesh visa office** (☏ 2324807; Airport Rd, Kunjaban; ☏ application 9am-1pm Mon-Thu, 9am-noon Fri, collection same day 4pm) hides down a small lane in Agartala, about 2km north of the Ujjayanta Palace.

Rajasthan's Udaipur, this was a princely exercise in aesthetics; the finest craftsmen building a summer palace of luxury in a blend of Hindu and Islamic architectural styles. The delightful waterborne approach by speed boat (passenger/boat Rs15/300) or fancy rowboat (passenger/boat Rs15/75) is the most enjoyable part of visiting.

Boats leave from near the remarkably decent **Sagarmahal Tourist Lodge** (☎ 2524418; dm Rs60, d from Rs160, d with AC Rs300-400; 🖭), where most rooms have lake-facing balconies and a good restaurant presides downstairs. Non-AC rooms take the ground floor while the advantages of AC also bring upstairs lakeside views. The lodge is 1km off the Agartala–Sonamura road, 1.3km from Melagarh bus stand.

NORTH TRIPURA
☎ 03824

Around 180km from Agartala, North Tripura's regional centre is **Kailasahar**, where the excellent **Unakoti Tourist Lodge** (☎ 223635; d with/without AC Rs330/165) is a real bargain. **Unakoti** itself, around 10km away, is an ancient pilgrimage centre famous for 8th-century bas-relief rock carvings, including a 10m-high Shiva. Reaching Kailasahar from Agartala requires transiting Tripura's most sensitive areas. Foreign tourists are very rare and will turn heads.

MEGHALAYA

Carved out of Assam in 1972, hilly Meghalaya (The Abode of Clouds) is a cool, pine-fresh contrast to the sweaty Assam plains. Set on dramatic horseshoes of rocky cliff above the Bengal plains, Cherrapunjee and Mawsynram are statistically the wettest places on earth. Most rain falls April to September creating very impressive waterfalls and carving out some of Asia's longest caves. Important in Garo culture are the Wangala dances held at harvest time to honour Saljong, the sun-god

---

MEGHALAYA FAST FACTS

Population 2.3 million
Area 22,429 sq km
Capital Shillong
Main languages Khasi, Garo, Assamese, Bengali
When to go October to March

---

of fertility. These have been formalised into the 100-drum festival held at Asanang 18km north of Tura.

Eastern and central Meghalaya are mainly populated by the closely related Jaintia, Pnar and Khasi peoples (see p640), originally migrants from Southeast Asia. Western Meghalaya is home to the unrelated Garo tribe. Despite their different ethnic backgrounds, these two groups still use a matrilineal system of inheritance with children taking the mother's family name.

SHILLONG
☎ 0364 / pop 268,000

This sprawling hill station was the capital of British-created Assam from 1874 until 1972. Since becoming the state capital it has rapidly developed into a typical modern Indian town and in doing so some of its older building have been demolished. In parts it still retains its charm, the air is refreshingly cool and it has become a favourite holiday destination for domestic tourists.

Information
BOOKSHOPS
National Book Agency (OB Shopping Mall, Jail Rd) Stocks Lonely Planet guides, Indian and English-language fiction.

INTERNET ACCESS
Techweb (basement Zara's Arcade, Keating Rd; per hr Rs20; 🕘 9am-8.30pm) Bright and relatively comfy.

MONEY
Purchase of Bangladeshi taka is not possible. There are many ATMs.
SBI (☎ 2211439; Kacheri Rd) Exchange of foreign currency and travellers cheques; ATM outside.

POST
Post office (Kacheri Rd; 🕘 10am-5pm Mon-Sat)

TOURIST INFORMATION
Cultural Pursuits Adventures (☎ 9436303978; www.culturalpursuits.com; Hotel Alpine Continental, Thana Rd) Experienced agency for caving, trekking, village stays and off-the-beaten-track stuff.
Government of India tourist office (☎ 2225632; Tirat Singh Syiem Rd; 🕘 9.30am-5.30pm Mon-Fri, 10am-2pm Sat) Free basic maps and brochures.
Meghalaya Tourism (☎ 2226220; Jail Rd; 🕘 7am-8.30pm Sep-Nov, 7am-7.30pm Dec-Aug) Sells good-value tours.

Sights & Activities
COLONIAL SHILLONG

Colonial-era Shillong was planned around the ever-attractive **Ward's Lake** (admission/camera Rs5/10; ⏰ 8.30am-5.30pm Nov-Feb, 8.30am-7pm Mar-Oct) with its pretty **ornamental bridge**. The city's half-timbered architecture has been rather swamped by lots of drab Indian concrete, but areas such as Oakland retain many older houses and even in the centre a few gems remain.

The **Pinewood Hotel** (Rita Rd), a 1920s tea-growers retreat, is particularly representative and looks great at night. The 1902 **All Saints' Cathedral** (Kacheri Rd) would look perfect pictured on a biscuit tin. Located nearby, the turreted **Das-Roy House** (closed to the public) lurks be-

hind a traffic circle that harbours five forgotten **Khasi monoliths** as well as a mini Soviet-style **globe monument**.

MUSEUMS

The very professional **Don Bosco Museum of Indigenous Cultures** (www.dbcic.org; Sacred Heart Theological College; Indian/foreigner Rs50/150, student Rs30/90; ⏰ 9.30am-4.30pm Mon-Sat, 1.30-4.30pm Sun) displays a truly vast, very well laid-out collection of tribal artefacts interspersed just occasionally with gratuitous galleries on Christian missionary work. The hexagonal museum building is an impressive, symbolic tower, seven storeys high for the seven states of the northeast. Tours (compulsory) last over an hour, departing on the half-hour. For an

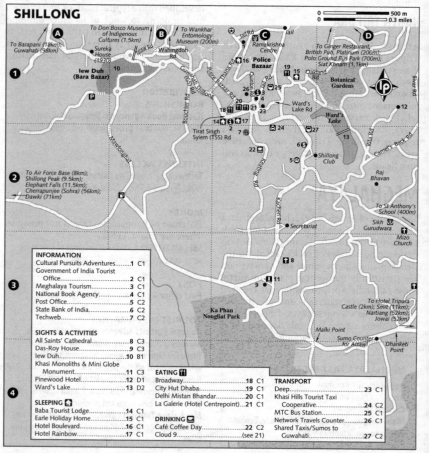

SHILLONG

extra Rs50, a video explains the Nongkrem festival (p640) or you could choose from various film alternatives.

The memorably named **Wankhar Entomology Museum** (☎ 2544473; Riatsamthiah; admission Rs25; ⊙ 11am-4pm Mon-Fri or by arrangement) is a remarkable one-room display of pinned butterflies, gruesome rhinoceros beetles and incredible stick-insects in the home of the original collector.

IEW DUH

This vast **market** (Bara Bazaar; ⊙ Mon-Sat) is one of the most animated in the northeast. Thousands of Khasi tribespeople flock in from their villages, selling everything from tribal baskets to fish traps and edible frogs.

SIAT KHNAM

All around Shillong gambling booths offer 'Forecast' odds on Siat Khnam. This is a unique 'sport'. A semicircle of weather-beaten Khasi men fire hundreds of arrows at a drum-shaped straw target for a set time before a canvas curtain is raised to keep further arrows off the target. Those that stick in are counted and bets predict the last two digits of this total. It's effectively a lottery but the shooting is a gently fascinating spectacle. Shoots are usually scheduled at 4pm and 5pm every day, timings can vary somewhat by season. The easy-to-miss Siat Khnam site is a small grassy area approximately opposite the big Nehru Stadium on the south river bank.

Sleeping

Tariffs are seasonal and highly negotiable in the low season. During peak periods hotels fill fast, but there are dozens of choices around the Police Bazaar area so just keep looking. Taxes are a discouraging 20%.

Earle Holiday Home (☎ 2228614; Oakland Rd; r from Rs350-1500) The cheapest rooms are original half-timbered affairs within a classic 1920 Shillong hill house adorned with sweet little turrets. Pricier rooms in the concrete annexe are less atmospheric but more comfortable. The Rs750 rooms are the best. There's also a good, inexpensive restaurant (City Hut Dhaba, see right).

Baba Tourist Lodge (☎ 2211285; GS Rd; d/tr Rs500/700) Ageing but clean and popular with backpackers, Baba hides behind a deceptively small PCO shop. The best rooms have windows and views out onto greenery. Bucket showers and bucket hot water.

Hotel Rainbow (☎ 2222534; TSS Rd; s/d/tr Rs500/875/975) Nine pleasantly styled rooms with wood panelling decor (but no geyser) are managed by a friendly man called Vicky. The best is room 103 with a little balcony.

ourpick Hotel Boulevard (☎ 2229823; Thana Rd; s/d from Rs890/1190) Among dozens of similarly priced hotels, the Boulevard stands out for its modernist chic and unusually luxurious standards, even in the cheapest rooms. Don't miss the view from the stylish top-floor bar-cafe where you'll take your free breakfast.

Hotel Tripura Castle (☎ 2501111; Cleve Colony; s/d from Rs1680/2160) Tucked away on a wooded hillside is the distinctively turreted summer villa of the former Tripura maharajas. It's this private 'castle' that features in hotel brochures, but accommodation is actually in a mostly new, if pseudo-heritage building behind. Pine-framed rooms have a gently stylish, slightly Balinese vibe with some period furniture and a level of service that's hard to beat.

Eating & Drinking

City Hut Dhaba (Oakland Rd; mains Rs50-140) Tucked behind Earle Holiday Home, modestly priced City Hut serves a variety of Indian, Chinese, barbecue and ice creams in four different eating rooms, including a family-only room and an attractive, flower-decked straw pavilion.

Broadway (GS Rd; mains Rs60-130) A no-nonsense restaurant serving the usual mix of Indian and Chinese meals, although staff here have taken that literally with bicultural offerings such as paneer Szechwan (unfermented cheese in a Chinese chilli sauce).

La Galerie (☎ 2220480; Hotel Centrepoint, TSS Rd; mains Rs60-170) A suave restaurant compartmentalised into booths by photographs of local scenes offering excellent Indian food. Booking is advisable. Cloud 9 is the top-floor bar-restaurant serving dainty Thai dishes, cold beers and cocktails.

Sink into cream-leather seating and enjoy a break from Indian fare with pasta, crepes, cannelloni, stroganoff or just a fruit sundae at **Ginger Restaurant** (☎ 2222341; Hotel Polo Towers, Polo Bazaar; mains Rs65-200; ⊙ 11am-10pm). Attached is the futuristic, metal-panelled bar **Platinum** (beers Rs120; ⊙ 1-9pm), and a faux–**British pub** (⊙ 1-9pm). PS: Early closing is a government restriction.

NORTHEAST STATES

Cheap street stalls abound around Police Bazaar with many dreary but inexpensive eateries along Thana Rd. There's real coffee and good cakes at **Café Coffee Day** (Keating Rd; from Rs5; ⊗ 9am-10pm). **Delhi Mistan Bhandar** (Police Bazaar Rd; from Rs5) is a popular sit-down sweet shop with lassis, snacks and gorgeous *gulab jamun* (deep-fried balls of dough soaked in rose-flavoured syrup).

Getting There & Away

From an air force base 8km towards Cherrapunjee, **Meghalaya Transport Corporation** (☎ 2223129) offers helicopter flights to Guwahati (Rs725, 30 minutes, twice daily except Sunday) and Tura (Rs1525, 1½ hours, thrice weekly). Book at the MTC bus station.

The **MTC bus station** (☎ 2540330; Jail Rd) also has a computerised railway-reservation counter (nearest station is Guwahati), frequent minibuses to Guwahati (Rs85, 3½ hours), Tura (Rs268, 12 hours via Guwahati, 7.15am and 4pm), and overnight buses to Silchar (Rs199, 10 hours, 7pm) and Siliguri (Rs393, 16 hours, 3pm).

More comfortable private buses for Agartala (Rs480, 20 hours, 5pm), Silchar (Rs280, 10 hours, 9pm), Dimapur (Rs350, 14 hours, 3.30pm), Siliguri (Rs390, 14 hours, 3pm) and Aizawl (Rs460, 15 hours, 7.30pm) depart from Dhanketi Point; book tickets from counters around Police Bazaar, including **Network Travels** (☎ 9863060458; Shop 44, MUDA Complex, Police Bazaar) and **Deep** (☎ 9836047198; Ward's Lake Rd).

From a Kacheri Rd parking area, shared taxis/sumos leave frequently to Guwahati (Rs190/140, 3½ hours). Some shared taxis continue to Guwahati airport (Rs220).

The **Khasi Hills Tourist Taxi Cooperative** (☎ 2223895; Kacheri Rd) charges Rs190/300 for a shared taxi to Guwahati/Guwahati airport or Rs760/1200 for the whole vehicle. For a day trip to Cherrapunjee the cost is Rs1600, to drop at the Bangladesh border near Dawki it's Rs1500 and a day about town is Rs1000.

AROUND SHILLONG
Smit

Framing itself as the Khasi cultural centre, Smit hosts the major five-day **Nongkrem Festival** (October). This features animal sacrifices and a curious slow-motion shuffling dance performed in full costume in front of the thatched bamboo '**palace**' of the local *syiem* (traditional

---

KHASI CULTURE

Meghalaya is dotted with timeless stone monoliths erected as memorials for tribal chieftains. Local Khasi 'monarchies' are still nominally ruled by a *syiem* (traditional ruler). Although they might lack political power, the Syiem of Mylliem remains a considerable economic force effectively controlling Shillong's vast Iew Duh market, while the Syiem of Khrim is elaborately feted at Smit's annual Nongkrem festival (left).

Many Khasi women wear a *jaiñkyrsha* (pinafore) in gingham-checked cotton, fastened on one shoulder and overlaid with a tartan shawl. Most Khasis consider *kwai* (betel) chewing a semireligious habit. Khasi markets work on an eight-day rotation and some fairs feature *yaturmasi* (bull versus bull fights). 'Thank you' in Khasi is '*kublei*'.

---

ruler). Smit is 11km from Shillong, 4km off the Jowai road.

Cherrapunjee (Sohra)
☎ 03637 / pop 11,000

Once you leave the outskirts of Shillong the road to Cherrapunjee passes through pretty scenery that becomes dramatic at **Dympep viewpoint**, where a photogenic V-shape valley slit deeply into the plateau attracts numerous domestic tourists and their cameras. There are several chai and snacks shops here.

Although straggling for several kilometres, Cherrapunjee (known locally as Sohra) has a compact centre. Huddling beside the marketplace are the sumo stand and a one-computer internet place.

SIGHTS & ACTIVITIES

The surrounding grassy moors do justify Meghalaya's over-played 'Scotland of the East' tourist-office soubriquet, although they're dotted with Khasi monoliths and scarred by quarrying. Much more impressive is the series of 'grand canyon' valleys that plunge into deep lush chasms of tropical forest sprayed by a succession of seasonally inspiring waterfalls. The **Nohkalikai Falls**, fourth highest in the world, are particularly dramatic, especially in the monsoon when their capacity increases 20-fold. You can see them easily enough without quite entering the official **viewpoint** (admission/camera

Rs5/200; ⊙ 8am-5pm), 4.4km southwest of Sohra market.

Cherrapunjee's **Ramakrishna Mission** (admission free; ⊙ 9.30am-3.30pm) has an interesting one-room collection of everyday tribal artefacts plus a discordant display of 78rpm records.

Nothing could seem more incongruous than sari-clad women stooping through the low passages of the 150m-long **Mawsmai Cave** (admission/camera/video Rs5/15/50; ⊙ 9.30am-5.30pm) but the cave is immensely popular with domestic tourists. Mawsmai's tall row of roadside **monoliths** is as impressive as the cave but don't receive the same attention.

Better than any of this is descending the narrow 14km-road to **Mawshamok** for views back up to the falls and an escarpment sliding down to the plains of Bangladesh. Few places in the northeast can better these views.

The most fascinating visit is to the incredible **root bridges**, living rubber fig-tree roots that ingenious Khasi villagers have trained across streams to form natural pathways. Three of these root bridges (including an amazing 'double-decker') are near **Nongriat**. Access involves a two-hour very steep trek down from **Tyrna**, a pretty, palm-clad village that's 2km from Mawshamok. This hike is highly strenuous and en route there's a truly hairraising wire bridge to cross, but the scenery is magnificent and there's a natural swimming pool in which to cool off. The Cherrapunjee Holiday Resort (below) provides maps.

SLEEPING & EATING

Sohra Plaza Hotel (☎ 235762; s/d Rs450/550) This convivially run two-room place is by the market. The hotel is basic but colourful and with an extension planned. Its restaurant (mains Rs35 to Rs100; open 8am to 9pm Monday to Saturday) has the best-ever *momos*.

our pick **Cherrapunjee Holiday Resort** (☎ 244218; www.cherrapunjee.com; Laitkynsew village; d Rs1300-1400; ▣) Eco-friendly, with six eminently comfortable rooms, this resort is run by truly delightful hosts. They offer a selection of hikes, either self-orientated (using their hand-drawn maps) or with a local guide (Rs150 to Rs300). Built on a ridge, rooms either look down to Bangladesh or up to the escarpment. During peak times tent accommodation (Rs500) is available with shared bathrooms but no hot water. A taxi from Cherrapunjee costs Rs250 to Rs 300.

Dawki

☎ 03653 / pop 5500

You'll probably only go to Dawki for the Bangladesh border crossing, but the journey from Shillong includes a dramatic 10km section along the lip of the vast green **Pamshutia Canyon**. It then descends through mildly picturesque Khasi villages amid waving betel-nut palms, finally crossing a suspension bridge over the surreally blue-green **Umngot Creek** where waters are dotted with flimsy local fishing boats.

If coming northbound from Bangladesh, sleep in Sylhet and start very early as Dawki's only property, the Inspection Bungalow, usually refuses tourists. Shillong–Dawki–Sylhet is considerably easier southbound.

GARO HILLS

Although it is still part of Meghalaya, the lush green Garo Hills are easier to visit from Guwahati than from Shillong. The landscape's undulations vary from charming patchworks of rice fields, cassava-patch and orange orchard to sad slash-and-burn hillsides of depleted jungle. The towns are not visually distinctive, but most houses in small hamlets remain traditionally fashioned from bamboo-weave matting and neatly cropped palm thatch.

NORTHEAST STATES

CROSSING INTO BANGLADESH

Border Hours

The border is open from 6am to 5pm.

Foreign Exchange

There's no official exchange booth but ask at the Bangladesh customs office.

Onward Transport

The border post is at Tamabil, 1.7km from Dawki market. That's Rs40 by taxi (southbound) but northbound expect to walk. Northbound beware that Tamabil has no Sonali bank, so prepay your Tk300 Bangladeshi departure tax in Sylhet or in Jaintiapura. Frequent Tamabil–Sylhet minibuses pick up from a triangular junction 350m from the checkpoint.

Visas

The nearest Bangladeshi visa offices are in Kolkata (Calcutta), or Agartala in Tripura.

Tura

☎ 03651 / pop 58,400

Sprawling Tura is the western Garo Hills' regional centre and an unhurried transport hub. Most key facilities are within two minutes' walk of the central market area around which Circular Rd makes a convoluted one-way loop. An SBI ATM can be found in Tura Bazaar opposite the Tura Dala (TD) Rd Evening district branch of the bank. The **tourist office** (☎ 242394; ⏱ 10am-5pm Mon-Fri) is 4km away towards Nazing Bazaar. Friendly staff offer brochures and sketchy maps, and arrange guides for anywhere in the Garo Hills, including a three-day hike to **Nokrek Biosphere Reserve**. There it's possible to watch for Hoolock Gibbons from a traditional-style *borang* (Garo tree house). By road the reserve is around 50km from Tura.

SLEEPING & EATING

Rikman Continental (☎ 220744; Circular Rd; s/d from Rs455/546, with AC Rs1364/1582; ✉ 🖳) Just seconds from the central market and transport booths is this ultra-friendly place. Although some cheaper rooms are small and worn, the more expensive ones have huge windows, bathtubs with hot water and AC. Rikman's restaurant is probably the best place to taste Garo cuisine; breakfast is complimentary and there's a bar. Internet is available in the lobby (per hour Rs50).

One block from the Rikman, **Hotel Sundare** (☎ 224610; Circular Rd; dm Rs250, s/d from Rs450/600, d with AC Rs900; ✉) is a reasonable alternative with similar rooms.

GETTING THERE & AWAY

On Monday, Wednesday and Friday, triangular **helicopter flights** (☎ 0364-2223206) run to Guwahati.

Booths selling bus and sumo tickets are dotted around the central market. For Guwahati, most sumos (Rs250, six hours) depart at 6.30am and 2pm. They're faster than buses (Rs175, eight to 10 hours), which mostly leave at 6.30am and 7.30pm. Buses to Shillong (Rs230, nine hours, around 8pm) pass close to Guwahati airport. **Aashirwad** (☎ 9436322845) runs a handy but grindingly slow overnight bus to Siliguri (Rs280, 15 to 17 hours, 4pm).

A chartered/shared autorickshaw to the tourist office costs Rs60/20 from outside Dura Travels by the Hotel Sundare.

Baghmara & Siju

☎ 03639

Almost on the Bangladesh border, **Baghmara** is the southern Garo Hills' district centre. Sitting above the town is the pleasantly quiet **Tourist Lodge** (☎ 222141; dm Rs200, r Rs400-500) commanding outstanding views.

From Baghmara you can visit the **Balpakhram National Park** (admission Rs50, camera/video Rs50/500), 45km away, but jeep (from Rs1200) and guide (from Rs500) hire will have to be organised in Tura. Traditionally Balpakhram is considered by Garo people as the 'abode of souls' where people temporarily go after they die. The park is thick with wild flowers and butterflies in spring, and its little 'grand canyon' separates the Garo and Khasi Hills.

Speleologists can visit **Siju Cave** (34km from Baghmara), reputedly the third-longest cave in the Indian subcontinent with 5km explored and more to go. Bring your own equipment and follow the golden rules of caving, never go alone and don't touch the formations. Curious noncavers will be able to penetrate about 100m into the gaping entrance.

Orissa

A captivating state with diverse, vibrant living cultures and an unrivalled architectural legacy, Orissa has nonetheless slipped under the radar of mass tourism and is refreshingly laid back.

Medieval temples are dotted through the streets of the capital, Bhubaneswar, and stone carvings of exquisite beauty continue to be excavated from early Buddhist sites. The World Heritage–listed Sun Temple in Konark bursts with brilliantly worked scenes of Orissan life, while stone carving, painting, silverwork and textiles are produced by modern artists across the state.

Wonderful national parks and wildlife sanctuaries are another highlight: elephants and tigers crash and prowl through the mountainous Similipal National Park, a key tiger reserve. Chilika Lake, Asia's largest lagoon, hosts the rare Irrawaddy dolphin as well as millions of migratory birds, including pink flamingos. Bhitarkanika Wildlife Sanctuary has dolphins, a surfeit of birdlife and monster crocodiles. In January masses of olive ridley marine turtles pull themselves up onto Orissa's long beaches to lay their eggs.

Inexpensive seaside retreats are dotted along Orissa's coast, making it a draw for weary travellers ready to kick back at the beach. Inland there's a different India, where Adivasis (tribal people) live precariously on the edge of mainstream society, yet manage to retain their colourful, fascinating traditions.

Travellers are waking up to Orissa's charm, so it's worth seeing now. Tourist infrastructure is still unsophisticated, but the flip side of this is relaxed and genuine friendliness and an almost entire lack of tourist-industry touting and harassment.

ORISSA

HIGHLIGHTS

- Chill out in a beachside thatched restaurant in traveller favourite **Puri** (p652)
- Spy on the herons, cranes and flashy flamingos nesting around **Chilika Lake** (p659)
- Get away from it all in a hot bath or treetop cottage in the tiny hot-springs hamlet of **Taptapani** (p662)
- Barter in the colourful tribal marketplaces of **Onkadelli** (p664) and **Chatikona** (p662)
- Watch carved scenes of the everyday, the erotic and the exotic unfold at the stunning Sun Temple in **Konark** (p657)
- Hire a boat and explore the wildlife-rich mangroves of **Bhitarkanika Wildlife Sanctuary** (p667)

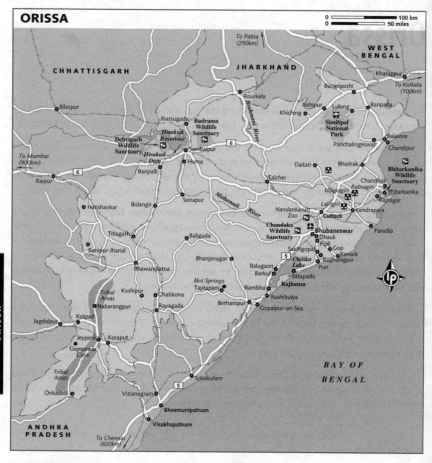

FAST FACTS

Population 36.7 million
Area 155,707 sq km
Capital Bhubaneswar
Main language Oriya
When to go November to March

History

Orissa (formerly known as Kalinga) was once a formidable maritime empire that had trading routes leading down into Indonesia, but its history is somewhat hazy until the demise of the Kalinga dynasty in 260 BC at the hands of the great emperor Ashoka. Appalled at the carnage he had caused, the emperor Ashoka forswore violence and converted to Buddhism.

Around the 1st century BC Buddhism declined and Jainism was restored as the faith of the people. During this period the monastery caves of Udayagiri and Khandagiri (in Bhubaneswar) were excavated as important Jain centres.

By the 7th century AD, Hinduism had supplanted Jainism. Under the Kesari and Ganga kings, trade and commerce increased and Orissan culture flourished – countless temples from that classical period still stand. The Orissans defied the Muslim rulers in Delhi until finally falling to the Mughals during the 16th century, when many of Bhubaneswar's temples were destroyed.

Until Independence, Orissa was ruled by Afghans, Marathas and the British.

Since the 1990s a Hindu fundamentalist group, Bajrang Dal, has undertaken a violent campaign against Christians in Orissa in response to missionary activity. The often illiterate and dispossessed tribal people have suffered the most from the resulting communal violence, which has been as much about power, politics and land as religious belief.

Violence flared up again in 2008 after the killing of a Hindu leader in Kandhamal district, and thousands of Christians were moved to government relief camps outside the district after their homes were torched.

The creation of the neighbouring states of Jharkhand and Chhattisgarh has prompted calls for the formation of a separate, tribal-oriented state, Koshal, in the northwest of Orissa, with Sambalpur as the capital. A separatist political party, the Kosal Kranti Dal (KKD), fielded candidates in the 2009 state election.

The last few years have seen something of an industrial boom in Orissa, with an influx of big steel plants.

Climate

Monsoon time is July to October, when cyclones are likely. Cyclones and severe monsoonal rains can have a substantial impact on transport. A particularly devastating cyclone struck Orissa in 1999 causing significant damage and the loss of thousands of lives, and in 2008 serious flooding destroyed crops and villages and led to mass evacuations.

National Parks

The admission fee for foreigners to visit any of Orissa's national parks and wildlife sanctuaries is Rs1000 per day, a hefty cost that Orissa's private tour operators have protested against.

Information

Orissa Tourism (www.orissatourism.gov.in) has a presence in most towns, with offices for information and tour/hotel booking. It also maintains a list of approved guides for tribal-area visits. **Orissa Tourism Development Corporation** (OTDC; www.panthanivas.com), the commercial arm of Orissa Tourism, runs tours and hotels throughout the state. OTDC-run hotels, which often house an Orissa Tourism desk or office, are usually called Panthanivas.

Dangers & Annoyances

Mosquitoes here have a record of being dengue and malaria carriers. See p1195 for advice, and consider bringing a mosquito net.

Getting There & Away

Air routes connect Bhubaneswar with Delhi, Mumbai (Bombay) and Kolkata (Calcutta). There were no flights to Chennai (Madras) at the time of research, but they may start up again. Major road and rail routes between Kolkata and Chennai pass through coastal Orissa and Bhubaneswar with spur connections to Puri. Road and rail connect Sambalpur with Kolkata, Chhattisgarh and Madhya Pradesh.

Getting Around

Public transport in the coastal region is good with ample long-distance buses and trains. For touring around the interior hiring a car is the best option, although buses and trains are available if you're not in a hurry.

BHUBANESWAR

☎ 0674 / pop 647,310

On its edges, Bhubaneswar has wide avenues, green belts and public artwork that reflects its temple-town heritage, but its centre is typically noisy, polluted and congested. The old city's spiritual centre is around Bindu Sagar where, from the thousands that once stood here, 50-odd stone temples remain, survivors from the heyday of Orissan medieval temple architecture.

Orientation

Cheaper lodgings, restaurants, banks and transport are within an area bounded by Cuttack Rd, Rajpath, Sachivajaya Marg and the train station.

Information
BOOKSHOPS

Modern Book Depot (☎ 2502373; Station Sq; ☺ 9.30am-2pm & 4.30-9pm) Maps, English-language novels, coffee-table books, postcards and books on Orissa. If you're interested in learning some Oriya, ask the owner about the well-regarded *Oriya in Small Bites*.

EMERGENCY

Police (☎ 2533732; Capitol Police Station, Rajpath)

INTERNET ACCESS

Cyber World (cnr Janpath & Rajpath; per hr Rs20; ☺ 9am-9.30pm Mon-Sat, 10am-6pm Sun)

FESTIVALS IN ORISSA

Makar Mela (2nd week of Jan; Kalijai Island, Chilika Lake, p659) Celebrates the sun entering the orbit of Capricorn. Surya, the sun god, is the attention of worship.

Adivasi Mela (26-31 Jan; Bhubaneswar, p645) Features art, dance and handicrafts of Orissa's tribal groups.

Magha Mela (Jan/Feb; Konark, p657) Sun festival, with pilgrims bathing en masse at the beach before sunrise then worshipping at the temple.

Maha Shivaratri (Feb/Mar; Bhubaneswar, p645) Devotees fast and perform *pujas* (prayers or offerings) throughout the night ready to witness the priest placing a sacred lamp on the top of Lingaraj Mandir.

Ashokastami (Apr/May; Bhubaneswar, p645) The idol of Lord Lingaraj is taken by chariot to Bindu Sagar for ritual bathing and then to Rameswaram Temple for a four-day stay.

Rath Yatra (Jun/Jul; Puri, p652) Immense chariots containing Lord Jagannath, brother Balbhadra and sister Subhadra are hauled from Jagannath Temple to Gundicha Mandir.

Beach Festival (Nov; Puri, p652) Song, dance, food and cultural activities, including sand artists, on the beach.

Tribal Festival (16-18 Nov; location varies) An exposition of Orissan tribal dances and music. Contact Orissa Tourism (below) as the location changes yearly.

Baliyatra (Nov/Dec; Cuttack, p666) Four days commemorating past trading links with Indonesia. A huge fair is held on the river bank.

Konark Festival (1-5 Dec; Konark, p657) Features traditional music and dance and a seductive temple ritual. Festivities are in the open-air auditorium with the Sun Temple as the backdrop.

Ganpati Travel & Communication (Kalpana Sq; per hr Rs30; ☽ 8.30am-9.30pm)

Sify Iway (cnr Janpath & Rajpath; per hr Rs17; ☽ 8.30am-9.30pm)

MEDICAL SERVICES

Capital Hospital (☎ 2401983; Sachivajaya Marg) Has a 24-hour pharmacy on site.

MONEY

Indian Overseas Bank (Station Sq; ☽ 10am-4pm Mon-Fri, 10am-1pm Sat) Currency exchange and travellers cheques.

State Bank of India (☎ 2533671; Rajpath; ☽ 10am-4pm Mon-Fri, 10am-2pm Sat, closed 2nd Sat in month) Cashes travellers cheques and exchanges foreign currency. ATMs around town, including Lewis Rd and Kalpana Sq.

Thomas Cook (☎ 2539892; 130 Ashok Nagar, Janpath; ☽ 10am-2pm Sat) Cashes travellers cheques, including Amex, and exchanges foreign currency.

POST

Post office (☎ 2402132; cnr Mahatma Gandhi & Sachivajaya Margs; ☽ 9am-7pm Mon-Sat)

TOURIST INFORMATION

Orissa Tourism (www.orissatourism.gov.in) airport (☎ 2534006); main office (☎ 2431299; Paryatan Bhavan, behind State Museum, Lewis Rd; ☽ 10am-5pm Mon-Sat, closed 2nd Sat in month); train station (☎ 2530715; ☽ 24hr) Tourist information, maps and lists of recommended guides.

Orissa Tourism Development Corporation (OTDC; ☎ 2432382; behind Panthanivas Bhubaneswar, Lewis Rd; ☽ 8am-8pm Mon-Sat) Commercial arm of Orissa Tourism. Books sightseeing tours and hotels.

Sandpebbles Tour N Travels (☎ 2541452, 25545868; www.sandpebblestours.com; NH5) Bookings for forest rest houses in Dangmal (p668).

Sights

BINDU SAGAR

Bindu Sagar (Ocean Drop Tank) reputedly contains water from every holy stream, pool and tank in India. During the Ashokastami festival (see boxed text, above), the Lingaraj Mandir's deity is brought here for ritual bathing.

TEMPLES

Bhubaneswar's medieval temples are a mix of 'live' (still in use as places of worship) and 'dead' (archaeological sites); a live temple will always have a red flag fluttering above it.

Unless you're on an organised tour, a priest will probably approach you and expect a donation; Rs20 is reasonable. Consider it a guiding fee as undoubtedly the priest will reveal something about his temple.

To see all the major temples, charter an autorickshaw for two to three hours (about Rs300).

Lingaraj Mandir

The 54m-high Lingaraj Mandir is dedicated to Tribhuvaneswar (Lord of Three Worlds).

BHUBANESWAR

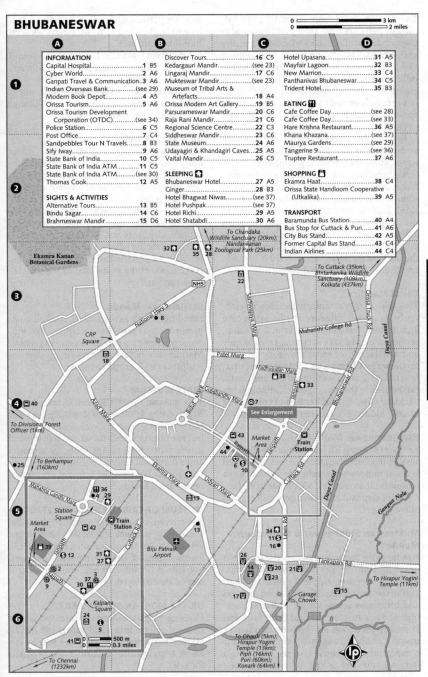

| 0 | 3 km |
| 0 | 2 miles |

INFORMATION
Capital Hospital..............................**1** B5
Cyber World..................................**2** A6
Ganpati Travel & Communication.**3** A6
Indian Overseas Bank................(see 29)
Modern Book Depot......................**4** A5
Orissa Tourism.............................**5** A6
Orissa Tourism Development
  Corporation (OTDC)................(see 34)
Police Station................................**6** C5
Post Office...................................**7** C4
Sandpebbles Tour N Travels........**8** B3
Sify Iway......................................**9** A6
State Bank of India.....................**10** C5
State Bank of India ATM............**11** C5
State Bank of India ATM............(see 30)
Thomas Cook..............................**12** A5

SIGHTS & ACTIVITIES
Alternative Tours........................**13** B5
Bindu Sagar................................**14** C6
Brahmeswar Mandir...................**15** D6

Discover Tours............................**16** C5
Kedargauri Mandir.....................(see 23)
Lingaraj Mandir..........................**17** C6
Mukteswar Mandir....................(see 23)
Museum of Tribal Arts &
  Artefacts.................................**18** A4
Orissa Modern Art Gallery.........**19** B5
Parsurameswar Mandir...............**20** C6
Raja Rani Mandir........................**21** C6
Regional Science Centre.............**22** C3
Siddheswar Mandir.....................**23** C6
State Museum.............................**24** A6
Udayagiri & Khandagiri Caves....**25** A5
Vaital Mandir..............................**26** C5

SLEEPING 🏠
Bhubaneswar Hotel.....................**27** A5
Ginger...**28** B3
Hotel Bhagwat Niwas.................(see 37)
Hotel Pushpak............................(see 37)
Hotel Richi..................................**29** A5
Hotel Shatabdi...........................**30** A6

Hotel Upasana............................**31** A5
Mayfair Lagoon...........................**32** B3
New Marrion................................**33** C4
Panthanivas Bhubaneswar...........**34** C5
Trident Hotel..............................**35** B3

EATING 🍴
Cafe Coffee Day.........................(see 28)
Cafe Coffee Day.........................(see 33)
Hare Krishna Restaurant.............**36** A5
Khana Khazana..........................(see 37)
Maurya Gardens.........................(see 29)
Tangerine 9.................................(see 36)
Truptee Restaurant.....................**37** A6

SHOPPING 🛍
Ekamra Haat...............................**38** C4
Orissa State Handloom Cooperative
  (Utkalika).................................**39** A5

TRANSPORT
Baramunda Bus Station...............**40** A4
Bus Stop for Cuttack & Puri........**41** A6
City Bus Stand............................**42** A5
Former Capital Bus Stand............**43** C4
Indian Airlines............................**44** C4

ORISSA

The temple dates from 1090 to 1104 (although parts are over 1400 years old) and is surrounded by more than 50 smaller temples and shrines. The granite block, representing Tribhuvaneswar, is bathed daily with water, milk and bhang (marijuana). The main gate, guarded by two moustachioed yellow lions, is a spectacle in itself as lines of pilgrims approach, *prasad* (temple-blessed food offering) in hand.

Because the temple is surrounded by a wall, and closed to non-Hindus (Indira Gandhi wasn't allowed in, as her husband was a Parsi), foreigners can see it only from a viewing platform (this can also include foreign Hindus, as some Indian Hindus do not believe in conversion). Face the main entrance, walk around to the right and find the viewing platform down a short laneway to the left. There have been reports of aggressive hassling for 'donations' at the viewing platform; again, Rs20 is enough, and there's no fee to stand there.

Vaital Mandir

This 8th-century temple, with a double-storey 'wagon roof' influenced by Buddhist cave architecture, was a centre of Tantric worship, eroticism and bloody sacrifice. Look closely and you'll see some very early erotic carvings on the walls. Chamunda (a fearsome incarnation of Devi), representing old age and death, can be seen in the dingy interior, although her necklace of skulls and her bed of corpses are usually hidden beneath her temple robes.

Parsurameswar Mandir

Just west of Lewis Rd lies a cluster of about 20 smaller but important temples. Best preserved is Parsurameswar Mandir, an ornate Shiva temple built around AD 650. It has lively bas-reliefs of elephant and horse processions, and Shiva images.

Mukteswar, Siddheswar & Kedargauri Mandirs

Not far from Parsurameswar is the small but beautiful 10th-century **Mukteswar Mandir**, one of the most ornate temples in Bhubaneswar; you'll see representations of it on posters and brochures across Orissa. Intricate carvings show a mixture of Buddhist, Jain and Hindu styles – look for the Nagarani (snake queen), easily mistaken by Westerners for a mermaid, who you'll also see at the Raja Rani Mandir. The ceiling carvings and stone arch are particularly striking as is the arched *torana* (architrave) in front, clearly showing Buddhist influence.

Siddheswar Mandir, in the same compound, is a later but plainer temple with a fine red-painted Ganesh.

Over the road is **Kedargauri Mandir**, one of the oldest temples in Bhubaneswar, although it has been substantially rebuilt.

Raja Rani Mandir

This **temple** (Indian/foreigner Rs5/100, video Rs25; ☉ dawn-dusk), built around 1100 and surrounded by manicured gardens, is famous for its ornate *deul* (temple sanctuary) and tower. Around the compass points are pairs of statues representing eight *dikpalas* (guardians) who protect the temple. Between them, nymphs, embracing couples, elephants and lions peer from niches and decorate the pillars. The name of the temple isn't for a particular king and queen, but is the name of the stone used in the temple's construction.

Brahmeswar Mandir

Standing in well-kept gardens, flanked on its plinth by four smaller structures, this 9th-century temple is a smaller version of Lingaraj Mandir. It's notable for its finely detailed sculptures with erotic elements.

STATE MUSEUM

This **museum** (☎ 2431797; Lewis Rd; Indian/foreigner Rs5/50, camera Rs10/100; ☉ 10am-4.30pm Tue-Sun) boasts Orissa's best collection of rare palm-leaf manuscripts, traditional and folk musical instruments, Bronze Age tools, an armoury and a display of Orissan tribal anthropology. Don't miss the salvaged colonial gravestone on the front lawn.

MUSEUM OF TRIBAL ARTS & ARTEFACTS

For anyone considering a visit to the tribal areas, this **museum** (☎ 2563649; admission free; ☉ 10am-5pm Mon-Sat), off National Hwy 5 (NH5), is recommended. Dress, ornaments, weapons, household implements and musical instruments are displayed.

ORISSA MODERN ART GALLERY

Housing a high standard of contemporary art by local artists, this small **gallery** (☎ 2595765; 132 Forest Park; admission free; ☉ 11am-1.30pm & 4-8pm Tue-Sat, 4-8pm Sun) also has prints and originals for sale.

UDAYAGIRI & KHANDAGIRI CAVES

Six kilometres west of the city centre are two hills riddled with **rock-cut shelters** (admission both sites Indian/foreigner Rs5/100, video Rs25; ☉ dawn-dusk). Many are ornately carved and thought to have been chiselled out for Jain ascetics in the 1st century BC.

Ascending the ramp at Udayagiri (Sunrise Hill), note **Swargapuri** (Cave 9) to the right with its devotional figures. **Hathi Gumpha** (Cave 14) at the top has a 117-line inscription relating the exploits of its builder, King Kharavela of Kalinga, who ruled from 168 to 153 BC.

Around to the left you'll see **Bagh Gumpha** (Tiger Cave; Cave 12), with its entrance carved as a tiger mouth. Nearby are **Pavana Gumpha** (Cave of Purification) and small **Sarpa Gumpha** (Serpent Cave), where the tiny door is surmounted by a three-headed cobra. On the summit are the remains of a defensive position. Around to the southeast is the single-storey elephant-guarded **Ganesh Gumpha** (Cave 10), almost directly above the two-storey **Rani ka Naur** (Queen's Palace Cave; Cave 1), carved with Jain symbols and battle scenes.

Continue back to the entrance via **Chota Hathi Gumpha** (Cave 3), with its carvings of elephants, and the double-storey **Jaya Vijaya Cave** (Cave 5) with a bodhi tree carved in the central area.

Across the road, Khandagiri offers fine views over Bhubaneswar from its summit. The steep path splits about one-third of the way up the hill. The right path goes to **Ananta Cave** (Cave 3), with its carved figures of athletes, women, elephants and geese carrying flowers. Further along is a series of **Jain temples**; at the top is another (18th-century) Jain temple.

Buses don't go to the caves, but plenty pass nearby on NH5, or take an autorickshaw (about Rs80 one way).

REGIONAL SCIENCE CENTRE

Kids will love this parkland **museum** (Prehistoric Life Park; ☎ 2542795; Sachivajaya Marg; admission Rs7; ☉ 10.30am-7pm Tue-Sun, 10am-5.30pm Mon) with its giant dinosaurs. Included in the admission is a 30-minute movie screened hourly. Other treats are hands-on demonstrations of the laws of physics and displays on astronomy and insects. You may have the whole place to yourself if a school group isn't there.

Tours

Orissa Tourism runs a hop-on, hop-off **bus service** (per day Rs250) starting at the OTDC (p646). The AC buses do a loop of the city's temples every hour.

The OTDC runs a **city tour** (non-AC/AC Rs150/200) every day except Monday, covering the Nandankanan Zoo (p651), Dhauli, the Lingaraj and Mukteswar temples, the State Museum and Udayagiri and Khandagiri Caves. Another tour goes to Pipli, Konark and Puri (non-AC/AC Rs180/250, daily). Both tours leave from the Panthanivas Bhubaneswar hotel. These prices don't include entry fees, which can add up to more than Rs300 for foreigners.

Private tour operators organise customised tours into Orissa's tribal areas; these can also include visits to handicraft villages, and Similipal National Park (p665) and Bhitarkanika Wildlife Sanctuary (p667). Prices will depend on number of people, transport and hotel standards, but expect to pay at least US$60 per person per day for tours that include transport, accommodation and a professional guide. Tribal tours usually start on a Sunday or Monday to synchronise with village markets.

Alternative Tours (☎ 2593463; www.travelclubindia .com; Room 5 BDA Market Complex, Palaspalli) Operates tribal and wildlife tours.

Discover Tours (☎ 2430477; www.orissadiscover.com; 463 Lewis Rd) A helpful, recommended agency specialising in tribal and textile village tours as well as Bhitarkanika and Similipal.

Sleeping

Bhubaneswar has plenty of accommodation, but a real dearth of anything in the way of clean or appealing family-run places or traveller dens in the budget and lower mid ranges. Conversely, it has a great selection of top-end hotels and one excellent midrange place. Rates drop substantially during the monsoon season, June to September, and most places will negotiate.

BUDGET

Hotel Bhagwat Niwas (☎ 2313708; Kalpana Sq; s Rs180-250, d Rs300-450, d with AC Rs750-1000; ✍) Behind the Hotel Padma and signed down a small lane, the friendly Bhagwat has simple, relatively clean rooms with TV, some with a balcony. Checkout is 24 hours, and it pays to book ahead.

Bhubaneswar Hotel (☎ 2313245; Cuttack Rd; s/d from Rs200/260, with AC Rs700/800; ✍) A friendly enough hotel with rooms that are par for the course in their price range: just clean enough, a tad threadbare, with dank bathrooms. The hierarchy of room rates is determined by your TV choice.

Hotel Richi (☎ 2534619; fax 2539418; 122A Station Sq; s/d from Rs300/500, d with AC from Rs900; ✴) Proximity to the train station and decent rooms make this place (very) popular. Booking ahead is advised. Rates include bed, tea and breakfast. Checkout and the coffee shop are open 24 hours.

Hotel Shatabdi (☎ 2314202; 71 Buddhanagar, Kalpana Sq; d Rs400-600) A cleanish, acceptable budget choice; rooms are small and fittings a bit shabby, but the more expensive rooms have been brightly painted, giving a cheerful feel.

MIDRANGE & TOP END

Hotel Upasana (☎ 2310044; upasana_bbsr@rediffmail .com; off Cuttack Rd; d from Rs700, with AC from Rs850; ✴) Behind the Bhubaneswar Hotel. The rooms are not dissimilar to the pricier rooms at the Bhubaneswar, though it's marginally more clean and welcoming, plus it's off the main road so it's less noisy.

Hotel Pushpak (☎ 2310185; Kalpana Sq; s/d from Rs800/900, with AC Rs1400/1700; ✴ 🖳) A recent refit has seen this hotel go upmarket, with not-quite-justifiable price increases for cheerful renovated rooms with bright-coloured walls. The non-AC rooms are about as good as you'll get for this price, and the veg restaurant is popular.

Panthanivas Bhubaneswar (☎ 2432314; Lewis Rd; d Rs1500; ✴) Well located in pleasant grounds, Panthanivas is quiet and is the closest hotel to the temples. The rooms were tired for the price, though renovations were under way at research time, and the restaurant is decidedly ordinary. Staff are less than enthusiastic.

our pick **Ginger** (☎ 2303933; www.gingerhotels .com; Jayadev Vihar, Nayapalli; s/d Rs1799/2299; ✴ 🖳 🛜) Young friendly staff, clean modern lines, and a self-service philosophy that means you're not constantly surrounded by tip-demanding bag-carriers, laundry peons etc. The fresh, spotless rooms have LCD TVs, tea and coffee, minifridge and silent AC. Meals are served buffet style in the restaurant and there's a 24-hour branch of Cafe Coffee Day that will deliver to your room. Save Rs300 or more if you book online. It's a Rs60 auto ride out of town in an upmarket area, next to (and dwarfed by) the Swosti Plaza hotel.

New Marrion (☎ 2380850; www.hotelnewmarrion .com; 6 Janpath; s/d from Rs6100/6500; ✴ 🖳 🛜) A cen-

trally located hotel where rooms have contemporary, classy design – LCD TVs, dark-wood panelling and extraordinarily stylish bathroom sinks – and you can negotiate the price. Great restaurants here include south Indian, Italian-Mexican combo and Chinese, and a cafe with real coffee.

Mayfair Lagoon (☎ 2360101; www.mayfairhotels .com; Jaydev Vihar; d cottages from Rs8000, d villas Rs28,000; ✴ 🖳 🛜) Quirky, colourful, even kitschy, but thoroughly luxurious at the same time. In the jungle-like grounds you'll find static tigers, an elephant, even a twin-prop 1942 aircraft. The cottages are scattered around a lagoon and facilities run to a complimentary breakfast, a British-style pub, and Chinese and Indian restaurants. There's a spa and gym, as well as a hairdresser.

Trident Hotel (☎ 2301010; www.tridenthotels .com; CB-1, Nayapalli; s/d/ste from Rs10,000/11,000/14,000; ✴ 🖳 🛜) The cool, high-ceilinged lobby of the Trident, inspired by Konark's temple architecture, will take your breath away. The restrained whitewash-and-sandstone colour scheme extends into the very comfortable rooms, which feature sketches of Konark temples and inset terracotta tiles replicated from local temples. As distinctive and charming an ambience as the Mayfair's, but very different.

Eating & Drinking

Cafe Coffee Day (drinks Rs22-80, snacks Rs10-65) Janpath (New Marrion Hotel); Nayapalli (Ginger, Jayadev Vihar) Yes it's a chain but you'll appreciate the real coffee beans, the refreshing iced drinks and the chilly AC on any typically sweltering day.

Khana Khazana (outside Hotel Padma, Kalpana Sq; snacks & mains Rs20-70; ⏰ from 5.30pm) A popular street stall with a few chairs and tables scattered outside. Alfresco diners savour tandoori chicken, chicken biryani or large serves of delicious chow mein featuring chicken, vegetables and prawns. Traditional Bengali hot rolls (try the tandoori chicken) are the cheapest and tastiest snack in town for Rs20.

Truptee Restaurant (☎ 231565; under Hotel Padma; mains Rs30-60; ✴) This clean and cool basement restaurant has all the South Indian favourites (and it opens at 7.30am, so it's ideal for an *idli* – spongy, round, fermented rice cake – and *vada* breakfast) plus a range of northern curries, including a few good paneer (unfermented cheese) dishes.

Maurya Gardens (☎ 2534619; Hotel Richi, Station Sq; mains Rs40-150) A darkened restaurant where you may have trouble reading the menu of Indian, Chinese and continental dishes. The curries are nice and hot, but if you want a beer to cool it down you'll have to eat (same menu) in the bar next door. Nearest to the train station, it's suitable for pre- or post-travel drinks.

Hare Krishna Restaurant (☎ 2534188; Station Sq; mains Rs60-120; 🍽) The menu says 'Surrender to the pleasure of being vegetarian', and it's not difficult at this excellent veg restaurant. In dimly lit, upmarket surrounds you can enjoy mainly Indian dishes, including a wide range of tasty biryanis and pilaus, along with a good selection of soups and desserts. The lassi is outstanding. It's upstairs; enter though a shopping arcade.

our pick Tangerine 9 (☎ 2533009; Station Sq; mains Rs69-249; 🍽) If you're not ready to surrender to vegetarianism, step next door to Tangerine 9, also upstairs, where there's all the meat you can handle and all the dishes burst with the flavour of fresh herbs and spices. There's a big range of Indian (especially tandoori) and Chinese, plus some nicely executed Thai dishes. Pan-Asian starters include *momos* (Tibetan dumplings) and salt-and-pepper prawns. Decor is blonde wood and signature tangerine.

Shopping

A wide-ranging exposition of Orissan handicrafts (and snack stalls) can be found at **Ekamra Haat** (☎ 2403169; Madhusudan Marg; 🕙 10am-10pm), a permanent market in a large garden space. While the gates open at 10am, many stalls don't get going until later.

Orissan textiles, including appliqué and *ikat* (a technique involving tie-dyeing the thread before it's woven) works, can be bought at the **Orissa State Handloom Cooperative** (Utkalika; Eastern Tower, Market Bldg; 🕙 10am-1.30pm & 4.30-9pm Mon-Sat) and a number of shops nearby on Rajpath.

Getting There & Away
AIR
Indian Airlines (☎ 2530544; www.indianairlines.in; Rajpath; 🕙 10am-1.15pm & 2-4.45pm Mon-Sat) flies daily to Delhi, Mumbai, Bengaluru (Bangalore) and Kolkata. **Jet Lite** (☎ 2596180; www.jetlite.com; airport) flies direct to Delhi and Kolkata daily, with connections on to Mumbai, Hyderabad and Bengaluru. Check the websites for schedules and latest fares.

BUS
Baramunda bus station (☎ 2400540; NH5) has frequent buses to Cuttack (Rs13, one hour), Puri (Rs31, 1¼ hours) and Konark (Rs35, two hours). Less frequent services go to Berhampur (Rs98, five hours), Sambalpur (Rs200, nine hours) and Baripada (Rs200, seven hours). There are several daily services to Kolkata (Rs300 to Rs600, 12 hours) where price relates to comfort.

Cuttack buses also go from the city bus stand, just off Station Sq, and the bus stop at the top end of Lewis Rd, from where buses also go to Puri.

TRAIN
The *Coromandal Express* 2841 travels daily to Chennai (sleeper/3AC/2AC Rs377/1014/1450, 20 hours, 9.40pm). The *Purushotlam Express* 2801 goes to Delhi (Rs493/1331/1825, 31 hours, 11.25pm) and the *Konark Express* 1020 to Mumbai (Rs493/1358/1873, 37 hours, 3.15pm).

Howrah is connected to Bhubaneswar by the *Jan Shatabdi* 2074 (2nd class/chair Rs142/439, seven hours, 6.20am daily except Sunday) and the daily *Howrah Dhauli Express* 2822 (Rs123/439, seven hours, 1.15pm). To Sambalpur, the *Bhubaneswar–Sambalpur Express* 2893 (chair Rs339, five hours, 6.45am) is quick, comfortable and convenient.

Getting Around
No buses go to the airport; a taxi costs about Rs150 from the centre. An autorickshaw to the airport costs about Rs80, but you'll have to walk the last 500m from the airport entrance. Prepaid taxis from the airport to central Bhubaneswar cost Rs100, and to Puri or Konark Rs700. Another way to get to Puri or Konark in relative comfort is to go one-way on an OTDC tour (p649; let the guide know you won't be returning).

AROUND BHUBANESWAR
Nandankanan Zoological Park
Famous for its blue-eyed white tigers, the **zoo** (☎ 2466075; Indian/foreigner Rs10/100, camera/video Rs5/500; 🕙 8am-5pm Tue-Sun) also boasts rare Asiatic lions, rhinoceroses, copious reptiles, monkeys and deer. Don't get food out of your bag in front of any of the monkeys that roam free around the zoo; trust us.

The highlight is the **lion and tiger safari** (Rs30) which leaves on the hour from 10am to noon and 2pm to 4pm. Other attractions include a toy train and boat rides. A **cable car** (Rs30; ☺ 8am-4pm) crosses a lake, allowing passengers to get off halfway and walk down (300m) to the State Botanical Garden. Early or late in the day you might catch the elephants having a bath in the lake.

OTDC tours stop here for an (insufficient) hour or so. From Bhubaneswar, frequent public buses (Rs6, one hour) leave from Kalpana Sq (near Hotel Padma) and outside the former Capital bus stand for Nandankanan village, about 400m from the entrance to the zoo. By taxi, a one-way trip costs about Rs350.

Dhauli

In about 260 BC one of Ashoka's famous edicts was carved onto a large rock at Dhauli, 8km south of Bhubaneswar. The rock is now protected by a grill-fronted building and above, on top of a hillock, is a carved elephant.

On a nearby hill is the huge, white **Shanti Stupa** (Peace Pagoda), built by the Japanese in 1972. Older Buddhist reliefs are set into the modern structure. You have to climb the hot stairs barefoot (ow! ow! ow!) but it's worth it for the four lovely images of the Buddha and great views of the surrounding countryside.

You'll find the turn-off to Dhauli along the Bhubaneswar–Puri road, accessible by any Puri or Konark bus (Rs8). From the turn-off, it's a flat 3km walk to the rock, and then a short, steep walk to the stupa. By autorickshaw/taxi, a one-way trip costs about Rs100/250.

Chandaka

Chandaka Wildlife Sanctuary (City Sanctuary; Indian/foreigner Rs10/1000; ☺ 8am-5pm Tue-Sun) was declared primarily to preserve wild elephants and elephant habitat. If you're lucky you might also see leopard, deer, mugger crocodiles and over 100 species of birds.

Facilities include five watchtowers, two of which contain rest houses for overnight stays. Before you visit you must pay for and collect an entry permit, gain permission for photography and reserve a rest house, all at the office of the **divisional forest officer** (☎ 2472040; Chandaka Wildlife Division, SFTRI campus, Ghatika; ☺ 10am-5pm Mon-Fri) in Bhubaneswar. Chandaka is about 20km by road from Bhubaneswar, and visits and transport are best organised through a travel agent in Bhubaneswar.

Hirapur

Among iridescent-green paddies, 15km from Bhubaneswar, is a small village with an important **Yogini Temple**, one of only four in India. The low, circular structure, open to the sky, has 64 niches within, each with a black chlorite goddess. Getting here requires hired transport or coming on an OTDC tour (p649).

Pipli

This town, 16km southeast of Bhubaneswar, is notable for its brilliant appliqué craft, which incorporates small mirrors and is used for door and wall hangings and the more traditional canopies hung over Lord Jagannath and family during festival time. Lampshades and parasols hanging outside the shops turn the main road into an avenue of rainbow colours. The work is still done by local families in workshops behind the shops; you may be able to go back and have a look. Pipli is easily accessible by any bus between Bhubaneswar and Puri or Konark.

SOUTHEASTERN ORISSA

PURI

☎ 06752 / pop 157,610

Hindu pilgrims, Indian holidaymakers and foreign travellers all make their way to Puri, setting up camp in different parts of town. For Hindus, Puri is one of the holiest pilgrimage places in India, with religious life revolving around the great Jagannath Mandir and its famous Rath Yatra (Car Festival).

Puri's other attraction is its long, sandy beach and esplanade. Backing this, in Marine Pde, is a long ribbon of hotels, resorts and company holiday homes that become instantly full when Kolkata rejoices in a holiday.

In the 1970s Puri became a scene on the hippie trail through Southeast Asia, travellers attracted here by the sea and bhang, legal in Shiva's Puri. There's little trace of that scene today; travellers come just to hang out, gorge on good food and recharge their backpacking spirit.

Orientation

The action is along a few kilometres of coast, with the backpacker village clustered around Chakra Tirtha (CT) Rd to the east, busy Marine Pde to the west and resorts in the middle. A few blocks inland is the holy

ORISSA

lonelyplanet.com

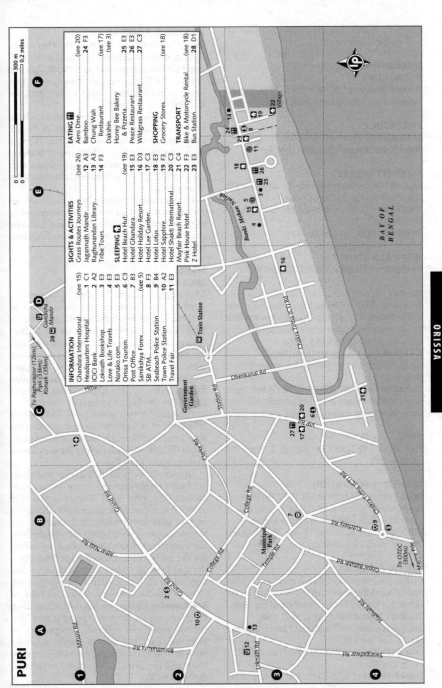

ORISSA

PURI

INFORMATION
Chandara International............(see 15)
Headquarters Hospital.....................1 C1
ICICI Bank.......................................2 A2
Loknath Bookshop............................3 E3
Love & Life Travels.........................4 E3
Nanako.com....................................5 E3
Orissa Tourism.................................6 C3
Post Office.......................................7 B3
Samikshya Forex..........................(see 5)
SBI ATM..8 F3
Seabeach Police Station..................9 B4
Town Police Station.......................10 A2
Travel Fair......................................11 E3

SIGHTS & ACTIVITIES
Grass Routes Journeys.................(see 26)
Jagannath Mandir..........................12 A3
Raghunandan Library.....................13 A3
Tribe Tours....................................14 F3

SLEEPING
Hotel Beach Hut..........................(see 19)
Hotel Ghandara.............................15 E3
Hotel Holiday Resort......................16 D3
Hotel Lee Garden..........................17 C3
Hotel Lotus....................................18 C3
Hotel Sapphire...............................19 F3
Hotel Shakti International................20 F3
Mayfair Beach Resort.....................21 C4
Pink House Hotel...........................22 F3
Z Hotel..23 E3

EATING
Aero Dine...................................(see 20)
Bamboo...24 F3
Chung Wah Restaurant................(see 17)
Dakshin.......................................(see 3)
Honey Bee Bakery & Pizzeria.........25 E3
Peace Restaurant...........................26 E3
Wildgrass Restaurant.....................27 C3

SHOPPING
Grocery Stores............................(see 18)

TRANSPORT
Bike & Motorcycle Rental............(see 18)
Bus Station....................................28 D1

BAY OF
BENGAL

quarter's chaotic jumble of streets. Buses arrive in the centre of town.

Information
BOOKSHOPS
Loknath Bookshop (☎ 9861332493; CT Rd; ⦿ 9am-10pm) Sells and exchanges secondhand books.

EMERGENCY
Seabeach Police Station (☎ 222025; CT Rd)
Town Police Station (☎ 222039; Grand Rd)

INTERNET ACCESS
Internet places have sprung up all along CT Rd; most charge Rs20 per hour.
Nanako.com (CT Rd; ⦿ 8am-10.30pm) CD burning Rs30, DVDs Rs60.
Travel Fair (CT Rd; ⦿ 7am-10pm)

MEDICAL SERVICES
Headquarters Hospital (☎ 223742; Grand Rd)

MONEY
The State Bank of India has a number of reliable MasterCard and Visa ATMs around town, including a convenient one in the main traveller-hotel stretch of CT Rd.
ICICI Bank (Grand Rd; ⦿ 8am-8pm) MasterCard and Visa ATM; does foreign exchange but not travellers cheques.
Samikshya Forex (☎ 2225369; CT Rd; ⦿ 6am-10pm) Cashes travellers cheques and foreign currencies and does credit-card advances. Thomas Cook agent.

POST
Post office (☎ 222051; cnr Kutchery & Temple Rd; ⦿ 10am-5pm)

TOURIST INFORMATION
Orissa Tourism CT Rd (☎ 222664; CT Rd; ⦿ 10am-5pm Mon-Sat); train station (☎ 223536; ⦿ 7am-9pm) Tourist information, hotel, vehicle and tour booking.
OTDC (☎ 223526; Marine Pde; ⦿ 6am-10pm) Booking office and start/finish point for day tours.

TRAVEL AGENCIES
There are numerous travel agencies within and around the hotels on CT Rd that can arrange air, bus and train tickets and car hire.
Gandhara International (☎ 2224623; www .hotelgandhara.com; Hotel Gandhara; CT Rd; ⦿ 8am-7pm Mon-Fri, 8am-1pm Sun)
Love & Life Travels (☎ 224433; Hotel Love & Life, CT Rd; ⦿ 7am-10pm)
Samikshya Forex (☎ 2225369; CT Rd; ⦿ 6am-10pm)

Dangers & Annoyances
Ocean currents can become treacherous in Puri, and drownings are not uncommon, so don't venture out beyond your depth. Ask one of the *nolias* (fishermen/lifeguards), with their white-painted, cone-shaped wicker hats, for the best spots.

Muggings and attacks on women have been reported along isolated stretches of beach, even during the day, so take care. Foreign men may be approached by young boys on the beach; Puri has an ongoing problem with paedophiles giving gifts to, and abusing, local youngsters.

Hassle from persistent hotel touts, souvenir sellers and so on is low-key compared to most tourist hot spots in India, but it can be frustrating if you've been elsewhere in Orissa, where such hassle is nonexistent.

Sights
JAGANNATH MANDIR
This mighty temple belongs to Jagannath, Lord of the Universe and incarnation of Vishnu. The jet-black deity with large, round, white eyes is hugely popular across Orissa; figures of Jagannath are tended and regularly dressed in new clothes at shrines across the state. Built in its present form in 1198, the temple (closed to non-Hindus) is surrounded by two walls; its 58m-high *sikhara* (spire) is topped by the flag and wheel of Vishnu.

Guarded by two stone lions and a pillar crowned by the Garuda that once stood at the Sun Temple at Konark, the eastern entrance (Lion Gate) is the passageway for the chariot procession of Rath Yatra.

Jagannath, brother Balbhadra and sister Subhadra reside supreme in the central *jagamohan* (assembly hall). Priests continually garland and dress the three throughout the day for different ceremonies. Incredibly, the temple employs about 6000 men to perform the complicated rituals involved in caring for the gods. An estimated 20,000 people – divided into 36 orders and 97 classes – are dependent on Jagannath for their livelihood.

Non-Hindus can spy from the roof of **Raghunandan Library** (cnr Temple Rd & Swargadwar Rd; ⦿ 9am-1pm & 4-7pm Mon-Sat) opposite; a 'donation', while not officially compulsory, is expected (Rs10 is fine). On Sunday a nearby hotel (whose touts will find you) takes over the scam and demands Rs50 – easily negotiated down to Rs20.

ORISSA

BEACH

Puri is no palm-fringed paradise – the beach is wide, shelves quickly with a nasty shore break and is shadeless; but it is the seaside. To the east it's a public toilet for the fishing village.

By Marine Pde the beach is healthier (although still not particularly pleasant for swimming) and often crowded with energetic holidaymakers, especially at night. Be on the look out for artists constructing **sand sculptures**, a local art form.

It's worth getting up before sunrise to watch the fishermen head out through the surf.

Tours

OTDC (☎ 223526; Marine Pde; ⏲ 6am-10pm) runs a series of day trips. Tour 1 (Rs170, departs 6.30am Tuesday to Sunday) skips through Konark, Dhauli, Bhubaneswar's temples, Udayagiri and Khandagiri Caves plus Nandankanan Zoo. Tour 2 (Rs130, departs 7am daily) goes for a boat jaunt on Chilika Lake. Tour 3 (Rs100, departs 7am daily) goes to Konark. Various admission fees are additional to the tour cost.

Several tour operators organise tours into Orissa's tribal areas that can include visits to handicraft villages plus Similipal National Park (p665) and Bhitarkanika Wildlife Sanctuary (p667). Tribal tours have to be approached cautiously as not all agencies have the necessary local contacts to conduct a responsible tour. For recommended options in Bhubaneswar see p649 and for more details see the boxed text, p663.

Grass Routes Journeys (Adventure Odyssey; ☎ 2226642, 9437022663; www.grassroutesjourneys.com; CT Rd) This recommended agency works from a philosophy of environmental and cultural sustainability, with contacts in the tribal communities and policies about appropriate ways to photograph people and contribute to the welfare of the community. It plans to offer filtered-water refills from the office, as Orissa has no plastic recycling facility. Its recently opened 'travellers lounge' offers a resource library of books and maps.

Tribe Tours (☎ 2224323; tribetours@hotmail.com; CT Rd; ⏲ 7.30am-9pm) Organises Chilika Lake day tours (Rs600 to Rs2100 per person depending on group size, stops, food and transport) and overnight camping trips (about Rs6000 for two people all-inclusive).

Festivals

A four-year calendar of festivals and events can be consulted at www.orissatourism.gov.in. Highlights of the festival-packed year include the celebrated festival of **Rath Yatra** (see the boxed text, p646) and the **Puri Beach Festival** (23–27 November; p646) featuring magnificent sand art, food stalls, traditional dance and other cultural programs.

Sleeping

For Rath Yatra, Durga Puja (Dussehra), Diwali or the end of December and New Year, book well in advance.

Prices given are for October to February. Significant discounts can be negotiated during the monsoon, while prices can triple during a festival. Many hotels have early checkout times – often 8am.

BUDGET

Hotel Gandhara (☎ 224117; www.hotelgandhara.com; CT Rd; dm Rs75, s/d from Rs450/650, without bathroom Rs175/250, with AC Rs750/950; ✷ ☐) A wide range of rooms for different budgets. The rear five-storey block has rooftop AC rooms catching breezes and views; other rooms are arrayed around a tree-shaded garden and have balconies. There's a rooftop restaurant and a travel agency that does foreign exchange.

ourpick Z Hotel (☎ 222554; www.zhotelindia.com; CT Rd; dm women only Rs100, r Rs700, s/d without bathroom Rs250/500) This former maharaja's home has huge, clean, airy rooms, many of them facing the sea. Great common areas include a TV room with movies screened nightly, and a 'restaurant' (table on a verandah) with a friendly cook who will chat with you, gauge your tastes and bring you something fantastic that isn't on the menu. Shared bathrooms are spotless.

Pink House Hotel (☎ 222253; off CT Rd; r Rs250, without bathroom Rs150-200) Right on the beach with sand drifting to your front door, the Pink House is an almost-romantic remnant of 1970s Puri. The very basic rooms, either on the beach side with little verandas, or round at the back, are only just clean. Mozzie nets are provided and the toilets are all squat.

Hotel Lotus (☎ 227033; CT Rd; d Rs300-450, with AC Rs950; ✷) The Lotus has a range of inexpensive rooms that are clean and comfortable and even feature some tasteful artwork. The non-AC rooms are some of the best value for money in Puri, though the front rooms may suffer a bit of street noise. The friendly owner, who also runs the vegetarian Harry's Cafe downstairs, will point out various landmark temples from the hotel roof.

ORISSA

Also recommended:

Hotel Sapphire (☎ 226488; off CT Rd; d Rs200-600, with AC Rs850-1850; ⊠) A wide range of clean rooms with sea views, bright-coloured walls and noisy AC.

Hotel Beach Hut (☎ 225704; hotel_beachhut2001@ yahoo.co.in; off CT Rd; d Rs350-650, with AC Rs950; ⊠) Similar to the Sapphire: clean, with sea views, cool tiled floors and not much character.

MIDRANGE & TOP END

Hotel Lee Garden (☎ 223647, leegarden@rediffmail.com; VIP Rd; d from Rs650, with AC from Rs1100; ⊠) This welcoming hotel has a range of spacious, spotless good-value rooms with balconies (but not particularly good views). The pricier rooms are quite stylish. A bonus of staying here is the excellent Chinese restaurant, Chung Wah (right). Checkout is 7am!

Hotel Holiday Resort (☎ 222440; www.holidayresort puri.com; CT Rd; r Rs1330-4000, d cottages Rs1800; ⊠ ⊠) Yes it's a blight on the landscape, a huge white edifice with a neon sign that probably guides the fishermen home at night. But inside are sea views from clean and welcoming rooms with warm colour schemes and Mughal reproductions on the walls. Cottages have pleasant lawn areas out front and there's a pool (nonguests Rs100 for two hours) full of roughhousing Bengali men.

Hotel Shakti International (☎ 222388; www.shak tiinternational.in; VIP Rd; s/d incl breakfast from Rs2500/3000; ⊠) A sparkling new modern place with requisite conference hall, aimed mostly at business travellers. Rooms have comfy and stylish furniture, plasma TV and all the mod cons, plus two restaurants, one of which, Aero Dine (right), will blow your mind.

Mayfair Beach Resort (☎ 227800; www.mayfair hotels.com; r from Rs6000; ⊠ ⊠) The benchmark for Puri luxury features spacious units nestled into idyllic gardens dotted with carved statues. The guests-only swimming pool comes with a swim-up bar, and there's a semiprivate beach, a gym and a spa. Some rave about the restaurants (mains Rs105 to Rs575), but we found the seafood a bit hit-and-miss and the staff somewhat snooty. The white-wicker charm of the Verandah deck restaurant makes it a lovely setting for a drink or two.

Eating

There's excellent fresh seafood to be enjoyed almost anywhere in Puri, and in CT Rd homesick travellers can find muesli, pancakes and puddings. Low-season opening times can be a bit random.

Dakshin (☎ 9937552252; CT Rd; dosas Rs25-35, thali Rs50) Standing out in CT Rd's string of ageing sand-floor banana-pancake joints, this clean new place has a simple menu of well-prepared South Indian dishes. The excellent thali includes *puri* (flat dough that puffs up when deep fried) and dessert. There are nice touches like lime-scented finger bowls.

Bamboo (CT Rd; mains Rs30-90) A traveller-oriented place with muesli, pancakes and other usual suspects, all in the open air with thatched umbrellas and friendly staff who'll give you a game of chess when things are quiet. Ask the price of off-menu seafood suggestions before you order; they can cost three times more than anything on the menu.

Peace Restaurant (CT Rd; mains Rs30-150) 'Peace Restaurant world famous in Puri but never heard of anywhere else.' So reads the menu, which features curries, macaroni, the best muesli in town and tasty fish dishes; the fish *dopiaza* is fab. This simple row of tables with thatch canopies is deservedly popular. Your food might take a while to arrive but it will be worth it, and you can enjoy a cold beer while you wait.

Honey Bee Bakery & Pizzeria (☎ 320479; CT Rd; mains Rs40-140; ◷ 8.30am-2pm & 6-10pm) The pizzas aren't bad, the pancakes are great, the real coffee, toasted sandwiches and fry-up brekkies (including bacon!) might be just what you've been craving, and the lassis are excellent.

Wildgrass Restaurant (☎ 9437023656; VIP Rd; mains Rs45-140; ⊠) With mismatched sculptures and precarious tree-huts scattered through its grounds, Wildgrass is a secret garden gone wild. The garden surrounds a small restaurant with an Indian and continental menu enlivened with excellent seafood dishes and Orissan specialties.

our pick Chung Wah Restaurant (☎ 223647; VIP Rd; mains Rs55-135) The Chung Wah is a first-rate Chinese restaurant serving the real thing. Favourites on the menu include spring rolls, sweet-and-sours and a commendable Sichuan chicken.

Aero Dine (☎ 222388; Hotel Shakti International, VIP Rd; mains Rs70-250; ⊠) Are you in Puri or are you in a 1960s movie set in a futuristic spaceship? This very surprising place has white modular furniture, random flashing lights and monitors, and there's even a 'cockpit' area for kids to play. The menu brings you back down to

ORISSA

earth a little with Indian, Chinese and continental standards, but there are a few wildcards thrown in: Waldorf salad, crêpes Suzette or Tom Yam soup anyone?

Shopping

Shops along Marine Pde sell fabric, beads, shells and bamboo work, while shops on CT Rd sell Kashmiri and Tibetan souvenirs.

Near Jagannath Mandir, many places sell Jagannath images, palm-leaf paintings, handicrafts and Orissan hand-woven *ikat*, which you can buy in lengths or as ready-made garments.

A couple of general grocery stores on CT Rd (mainly around the Hotel Lotus) stock a good range of toiletries that might be hard to find elsewhere in Orissa, eg women's deodorant.

Getting There & Away

BUS

From the sprawling **bus station** (☎ 224461) near Gundicha Mandir, frequent buses serve Konark (Rs20, one hour), Satapada (Rs39, three hours) and Bhubaneswar (Rs25, two hours). For Pipli and Raghurajpur, take the Bhubaneswar bus. For other destinations change at Bhubaneswar.

TRAIN

Book well ahead if travelling during holiday and festival times. The booking counter at the train station can become incredibly crowded, but CT Rd agencies will book tickets for a small fee.

The *Purushottam Express* 2801 travels to Delhi (sleeper/3AC/2AC Rs501/1354/1856, 32 hours, 9.45pm), while Howrah can be reached on the *Puri–Howrah Express* 2838 (Rs236/641/866, nine hours, 8.05pm) and the *Sri Jagannath Express* 8410 (Rs227/611/836, 10 hours, 10.30pm). The *Neelachal Express* 2875 goes to Varanasi (Rs377/1005/1372, 21 hours, 10.55am), continuing to Delhi, on Tuesday, Friday and Sunday. To Sambalpur, the *Puri–Sambalpur Express* 8304 (2nd class/chair Rs100/356, six hours, 3.45pm), running every day except Sunday, is best.

Getting Around

Several places along CT Rd (mainly around the Hotel Lotus) rent bicycles from Rs20 per day and both mopeds and motorcycles from Rs250. From CT Rd, cycle-rickshaws charge about Rs10 to the train station and Rs20 to the bus station or Jagannath Mandir.

RAGHURAJPUR

The artists' village of **Raghurajpur**, 14km north of Puri, is two streets and 120 thatched brick houses adorned with murals of geometric patterns and mythological scenes – a traditional art form that has almost died out in Orissa.

The village is most famous for its *patachitra* – work made using a cotton cloth coated with a mixture of gum and chalk and then polished. With eye-aching attention and a very fine brush, artists mark out animals, flowers, gods and demons, which are then illuminated with bright colours.

Take the Bhubaneswar bus and look for the 'Raghurajpur The Craft Village' signpost 11km north of Puri, then walk or take an autorickshaw for the last 1km.

KONARK

☎ 06758 / pop 15,020

The majestic Sun Temple at Konark – a Unesco World Heritage Site – is one of India's signature buildings and Konark's raison d'être. Most visitors are day-trippers from Bhubaneswar or Puri, and accommodation is limited, but it's possible to stay overnight.

Originally nearer the coast (the sea has receded 3km), Konark was visible from far out at sea and known as the 'Black Pagoda' by sailors, in contrast to the whitewashed Jagannath of Puri.

Orientation & Information

The road from Bhubaneswar swings around the temple and past a couple of hotels and eateries before continuing to meet the coastal road to Puri. To the north and east of the temple is the **post office** (☒ 10am-5pm Mon-Sat), a State Bank of India ATM, the bus station and numerous souvenir shops. The **tourist office** (☎ 236821; Panthanivas Konark hotel; ☒ 10am-5pm Mon-Sat) can line up a registered guide to meet you at the temple.

Sights

SUN TEMPLE

The massive **Sun Temple** (Indian/foreigner Rs10/250, video Rs25, guides per hr Rs100; ☒ dawn-dusk) was constructed in the mid-13th century, probably by Orissan king Narashimhadev I to celebrate his military victory over the Muslims, and was in use for maybe only three centuries. In the late

ORISSA

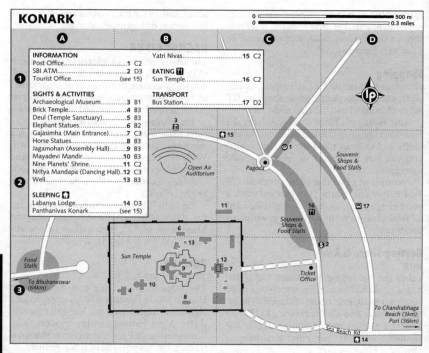

KONARK

0   500 m
0   0.3 miles

ORISSA

16th century marauding Mughals removed the copper over the cupola; this may have led to the partial collapse of the 40m-high *sikhara* (spire), and subsequent cyclones probably compounded the damage.

The entire temple was conceived as the cosmic chariot of the sun god, Surya. Seven mighty prancing horses (representing the days of the week) rear at the strain of moving this leviathan of stone on 24 stone cartwheels (representing the hours of the day) that stand around the base. The temple was positioned so that dawn light would illuminate the *deul* interior and the presiding deity, which may have been moved to Jagannath Mandir in Puri in the 17th century.

The **gajasimha** (main entrance) is guarded by two stone lions crushing elephants and leads to the intricately carved **nritya mandapa** (dancing hall). Steps, flanked by straining horses, rise to the still-standing **jagamohan**. Behind is the spireless **deul** with its three impressive chlorite images of Surya aligned to catch the sun at dawn, noon and sunset.

The base and walls present a chronicle in stone of Kalinga life; you'll see women cooking and men hunting. Many are in the erotic style for which Konark is famous and include entwined couples as well as solitary exhibitionists.

Around the grounds are a small shrine called **Mayadevi Mandir**; a deep, covered **well**; and the ruins of a **brick temple**. To the north are a couple of **elephant statues**, to the south a couple of **horse statues**, both trampling soldiers.

If there's anywhere worth hiring a guide, it's here. The temple's history is a complicated amalgam of fact and legend, and religious and secular imagery, and the guides' explanations are thought-provoking. They'll also show you features you might otherwise overlook – the woman with Japanese sandals, a giraffe (proving this area once traded with Africa) and even a man treating himself for venereal disease! Be sure your guide is registered. There are only 29 registered guides in Konark, listed on the name board by the entrance.

NINE PLANETS' SHRINE

This 6m-chlorite slab, once the architrave above the *jagamohan*, is now the centrepiece of a small shrine just outside the temple walls.

Carved seated figures represent the Hindu nine planets – Surya (the sun), Chandra (moon), Mars, Mercury, Jupiter, Venus, Saturn, Rahu and Ketu.

ARCHAEOLOGICAL MUSEUM

This interesting (and refreshingly cool and quiet) **museum** (☎ 236822; admission Rs5; ◷ 10am-5pm Sat-Thu), just west of Yatri Nivas, contains many impressive sculptures and carvings found during excavations of the Sun Temple. Highlights include the full-bellied Agni (the fire god) and the larger-than-life, voluptuous Bina Badini. Check out the carved *Lady with a Bird* – it's pecking her in a place that can't be comfortable.

CHANDRABHAGA BEACH

The local beach at Chandrabhaga is 3km from the temple down the Puri road. Walk, cycle or take an autorickshaw (Rs60 return), or use the Konark-Puri bus. The beach is quieter and cleaner than Puri's, but beware of strong currents; there have also been reports of thefts on the beach. To the east is a fishing village with plenty of boating activity at sunrise.

Sleeping & Eating

Labanya Lodge (☎ 236824; Sea Beach Rd; s from Rs75, d Rs150-350; 🖳) The best budget choice, this friendly place has a garden and a fresh coconut drink to welcome guests. The bright-coloured rooms come in different sizes, and there's a rooftop terrace. This is the only internet facility (per hour Rs60) in town and there's bike hire (per day Rs25). The roll-out of geysers to all rooms should be complete by now.

Panthanivas Konark (☎ 236831; d with/without AC Rs750/450; 🍴) One of two adjoining OTDC properties; this one has tired rooms that can get mosquito-ridden. The restaurant (mains Rs30 to Rs80) has a small and lacklustre range, though the set breakfasts aren't bad and there are sometimes seafood specials.

Yatri Nivas (☎ 236830; d Rs1500; 🍴) Set in a large garden next to the museum, the Yatri Nivas has new, clean, unremarkable rooms with silent AC systems. You may need to go through reception next door at the Panthanivas.

Sun Temple (mains Rs30-180) A busy, friendly place with a big range of Indian veg and non-vegetarian dishes, including recommended seafood dishes. It also has a decent stab at traveller favourites like chips and banana pancakes.

Getting There & Away

Overcrowded minibuses regularly run along the coastal road between Puri and Konark (Rs20, one hour). There are also regular departures to Bhubaneswar (Rs40, two hours). Konark is included in OTDC tours from Bhubaneswar (p649) and Puri (p649). An autorickshaw will take you to Puri, with a beach stop along the way, for between Rs200 and Rs300, depending on the season and your bargaining skills. Because the Puri–Konark road is flat, some diehards even cycle the 36km from Puri.

CHILIKA LAKE

Chilika Lake is Asia's largest brackish lagoon. Swelling from 600 sq km in April/May to 1100 sq km in the monsoon, the shallow lake is separated from the Bay of Bengal by a 60km-long sand bar called Rajhansa.

The lake is noted for the million-plus migratory birds – including grey-legged geese, herons, cranes and pink flamingos – that flock here in winter (from November to mid-January) from as far away as Siberia and Iran and concentrate in a 3-sq-km area within the bird sanctuary on Nalabana Island.

Other attractions are rare Irrawaddy dolphins near Satapada, the pristine beach along Rajhansa, and Kalijai Island temple where Hindu pilgrims flock for the Makar Mela festival (p646) in January.

Satapada

☎ 06752

This small village, on a headland jutting southwestwards into the lake, is the starting point for most boat trips. There's an **Orissa Tourism office** (☎ 262077; Yatri Nivas hotel) here.

Boat trips from Satapada usually cruise towards the new sea mouth for a paddle in the sea and some dolphin and bird spotting en route. Travellers have reported dolphins being (illegally) herded and otherwise harassed; make it clear you don't want this.

OTDC (☎ 262077; Yatri Nivas hotel) has boats for hire (for large groups) or a three-hour tour (per person Rs80) at 10.30am, with another at 2pm if there's enough interest.

Dolphin Motor Boat Association (☎ 262038; Satapada jetty; 1-8hr trips per boat Rs400-1300), a cooperative of local boat owners, has set-price trips mixing in dolphin sightseeing, Nalabana Bird Sanctuary and Kalijai Island temple.

ORISSA

Chilika Visitor Centre (☎ 262013; admission Rs10; ☒ 10am-5pm) is an exhibition on the lake, its wildlife and its human inhabitants. The centre has an upstairs observatory with a telescope and bird identification charts.

A regular ferry (Rs30, four hours) plies between Satapada and Balugaon just north of Barkul, departing at 1pm and returning at 6.30am the next day. Tour operators and travel agents lining CT Rd in Puri can organise return trips on comfortable buses for around Rs100, including about four hours in Satapada where you can organise your own boat.

Yatri Nivas (☎ 262077; d Rs250, with AC Rs650; ☒) is a government-run hotel whose best rooms have balconies with lake views. The restaurant (mains Rs30 to Rs80) has a small selection of standard Indian fare and a couple of seafood dishes.

Several shops and food stalls line the road to the jetty. Don't forget to take water on your boat trip.

Barkul
☎ 06756
On the northern shore of Chilika, Barkul is just a scatter of houses, basic 'lodges' and food stalls on a lane off NH5. From here boats go to Nalabana and Kalijai Island. Nalabana is best visited in early morning and late afternoon, November to late February.

With a minimum of seven people, the **OTDC** (Panthanivas Barkul) runs tours to Kalijia (Rs50), and Nalabana and Kalijia (Rs150). Otherwise, a boat with a quiet engine (that doesn't scare birds) can be hired from Rs450 to Rs1150 per hour. Private boat owners (with no insurance and often no safety gear) charge around Rs350 an hour; a recommended operator is fisherman **Babu Behera** (☎ 9937226378).

Panthanivas Barkul (☎ 220488, 211078; r Rs650, with AC Rs1500; ☒) has a great setting, with comfortable rooms overlooking the garden to the lake. The new cottages are clean and inviting, with lake views. The very AC restaurant (mains Rs30 to Rs100) is good, with seafood specials such as crab masala always available. We found this and the nearby hotel at Rambha (right) to be the best of the government-run hotels in Orissa.

Frequent buses dash along NH5 between Bhubaneswar (Rs40) and Berhampur (Rs70). You can get off anywhere en route.

A ferry (Rs30) goes to Satapada at 6.30am from Balugaon, a couple of kilometres north of Barkul – autos and taxis whiz up and down the route.

Rambha
☎ 06810
The small town of Rambha is the nearest place to stay for turtle watching on Rushikulya beach. Not as commercial as Barkul, Rambha is a very pleasant little backwater. Boat hire costs Rs500 for a three-hour trip around the lake.

Panthanivas Rambha (☎ 278346; dm Rs150, d Rs550, d/d cottage with AC Rs990/2000; ☒), about 200m off the main road, and 1km west of Rambha centre, looks a tad battered outside but has fine rooms (the AC rooms are better) with big clean bathrooms and balconies overlooking the lake. The new cottages with terracotta-tile ceilings have charm and views, and all beds have mozzie nets. The restaurant (mains Rs30 to Rs100) is very good, especially the seafood.

There are regular bus services to/from Bhubaneswar (Rs70) and Berhampur (Rs60).

Rushikulya
The nesting beach for olive ridley marine turtles is on the northern side of Rushikulya River, near the villages of Purunabandh and Gokharkuda. The nearest accommodation is in Rambha, 20km away; taxis and autos run between the two towns.

During nesting and hatching there will be conservationists on the beaches and activity takes place throughout the night. Don't use lights during hatching as they distract the turtles away from the sea; see the boxed text, opposite, for more on olive ridley marine turtles.

GOPALPUR-ON-SEA
☎ 0680 / pop 6660
Gopalpur-on-Sea is a seaside town the British left to slide into history until Bengali holidaymakers discovered its attractions in the 1980s. Prior to this, it had a noble history as a seaport with connections to Southeast Asia, the evidence of which is still scattered through the town in the form of romantically crumbling old buildings.

It's no paradise, but the peaceful and relatively clean beach is great for a stroll and a paddle, or you can just relax and watch the fishing boats come and go. A recent cleanup of the beachfront saw a series of tacky statues added: look for the mermaid about to snog a fish.

ORISSA'S OLIVE RIDLEY TURTLES

One of the smallest of the sea turtles and a threatened species, the olive ridley marine turtle swims up from deeper waters beyond Sri Lanka to mate and lay eggs en masse on Orissa's beaches. The main nesting sites are Gahirmatha within the Bhitarkanika National Park, Devi near Konark and Rushikulya.

Turtle deaths due to fishing practices are unfortunately common. Although there are regulations, such as requiring the use of turtle exclusion devices (TEDs) on nets and banning fishing from certain areas, these laws are routinely flouted in Orissa. Another threat has been afforestation of the Devi beach-nesting site with casuarina trees. While preserving the beaches, the trees occupy areas of soft sand that are necessary for a turtle hatchery. Other potential threats include oil exploration off Gahirmatha and seaport development near Rushikulya.

Turtles mass at sea between late October and early December. Then in January they congregate near nesting beaches and, if conditions are right, they come ashore over four to five days. If conditions aren't right, they reabsorb their eggs.

Hatching takes place 50 to 55 days later. Hatchlings are guided to the sea by the luminescence of the ocean and can be easily distracted by bright lights; unfortunately NH5 runs within 2km of Rushikulya beach, so many turtles crawl the wrong way. However, villagers in the Sea Turtle Protection Committee gather up errant turtles and take them to the sea.

The best place to see nesting and hatching is at Rushikulya (opposite). Ask at Panthanivas Rambha (opposite) – staff can tell you what conditions are like. Autos and taxis can take you between Rambha and Rushikulya.

Orientation & Information

The approach road from NH5 runs straight through town and terminates in front of the sea, where you'll find most of the hotels and restaurants. There's a PCO (Public Call Office) by Krishna's restaurant; the bus stand is 500m before the beach.

A modern new **post office** (NH5; internet access per hr Rs20; ☽ 9am-5pm Mon-Sat) is near the bus stand, on your left on the way down to the beach.

Dangers & Annoyances

Foreigners, especially women, are always an attraction for the curious; it can be incredibly annoying. Cover up, and if you go for a walk, find a fellow traveller for company or just attach yourself to an obliging Indian family and bask under their general protection.

Swimming in the nasty shore break at Gopalpur, where there are undercurrents, is an untested activity; most visitors are content with a paddle.

Sights

Peering over the town is the **lighthouse** (Indian/foreigner/child Rs10/25/3, camera Rs20; ☽ 3.30-5.30pm), with its immaculate gardens and petite staff cottages. It's a late-afternoon draw card and after puffing up the spiral staircase you're rewarded with expansive views and welcome cooling breezes.

Sleeping & Eating

Gopalpur-on-Sea can be booked out during holiday and festival time. Prices here are for the high season (November to January); discounts are available at other times.

Hotel Green Park (☎ 2242016; greenpark016@yahoo.com; d Rs350-500, d/tr with AC Rs700/900; 🗷) One street back from the beach, Green Park is a clean, friendly and good-value option (with no bar or restaurant). Some rooms have front-facing balconies and there's a 24-hour checkout.

Holiday World Plaza (☎ 9338859489; s/d Rs350/650, d with AC Rs750; 🗷) Clean, spacious and right on the beach, with big windows for views and breezes. The singles are small and simple, but be warned that all doubles have bright-coloured cartoon murals on the walls – kids will like it.

Hotel Sea Pearl (☎ 2242556; d Rs600-750, with AC Rs950-1200; 🗷) Any nearer the sea and it'd be in it; the big and popular Sea Pearl has some great rooms, especially the upper-storey, beach-facing, non-AC rooms, and a little private entrance to the beach. Look at a few rooms; price doesn't necessarily reflect quality here. There are two restaurants, with standard multicuisine menus (mains Rs40 to Rs120); one is on the roof.

Swosti Palm Resort (☎ 2243718; www.swosti.com; Main Rd; s/d Rs2600/3200; 🗷) Further back in town, and an unfortunate walk past a rubbish tip, the

Swosti has the best accommodation in town with comfortable, well-appointed rooms. The excellent multicuisine restaurant, Chilika, serves good seafood including authentic local dishes (mains Rs50 to Rs260).

Krishna's (mains Rs20-100) Mainly Indian and Chinese standards (nicely executed) and excellent *kati rolls* (see p525) in the quiet season but, if you ask, the kitchen can produce good pancakes, pasta and fried calamari or fish and chips. Expect to pay Rs100 and up, though, for some of the seafood. Naz Cafe, next door, is similar.

Beach restaurants don't serve alcohol, but there's a liquor shop on the road between the beach and Hotel Green Park where you can pick up a Kingfisher or two to enjoy on your balcony.

Getting There & Away

Frequent, crowded minibuses travel to Berhampur (Rs8, one hour), where you can catch onward transport by rail or bus. Alternatively, an autorickshaw will cost you about Rs150.

WESTERN ORISSA

Although permits aren't usually needed, there are tribal areas in western and central Orissa where foreigners have to register their details with the police. This is all done for you if you are on a tour but independent visitors should check their plans with the police in the nearest city.

TAPTAPANI
☎ 06816

Apart from the small **hot springs** in this attractive and peaceful village in the Eastern Ghats, there's not much else to see. The public baths (free; and full of soapy scunge) next to the springs are particularly popular with people with skin diseases and other disorders. It's a sacred place, considered a manifestation of the goddess, and as such has various temple trappings set up around it, including some truly gory statuary.

For a great winter treat (December nights plunge to zero) book one of the hot-springs rooms at **Panthanivas Taptapani** (☎ 255031; d from Rs750, with AC Rs2000, with hot bath Rs2500, tree house Rs2000; 🖭). Hot spring water is channelled directly to vast tubs in the Roman-style bathrooms; these hot-tub rooms can be rented for

the day (up to 4pm) for Rs1500. Other options on the leafy property include an appealing 'tree house' with charming rattan furniture that puts you right up in the treetops (it's reportedly best avoided in windy weather, though it's noisily creaky rather than dangerous) and less interesting cabins (overpriced, though perfectly clean and comfortable). The cool, clean restaurant (mains Rs30 to Rs100) has the standard Panthanivas menu and fabulous views over the ghats.

Buses go regularly to Berhampur (Rs25, two hours).

BALIGUDA
☎ 06846

This tiny one-street town is the base for visits to the Belghar region, home to fascinating and friendly Desia Kondh and Kutia Kondh villages. At the time of research it was closed to visitors following an outbreak of communal violence in the area; for the latest news, check with tour operators in Bhubaneswar or Puri.

The State Bank of India ATM accepts Visa, and you can check email at **Mahakali Communication** (Main Rd). The only place to stay in Baliguda is the **Hotel Santosh Bhavan** (☎ 243409; s Rs150-300, d Rs250-500), and food is confined to a few *dhaba*-style (cheap and basic) restaurants.

RAYAGADA
☎ 06856

Rayagada is the base for visiting the weekly Wednesday market at **Chatikona** (about 40km north). Here, highly ornamented Dongria Kondh and Desia Kondh villagers from the surrounding Niayamgiri Hills bring their produce and wares to sell. Alongside piles of chillies and dried fish are bronze animal sculptures made locally using the lost wax method.

The friendly **Hotel Rajbhavan** (☎ 223777; Main Rd; d incl breakfast from Rs500, with AC from Rs950; 🖭) has bright and airy rooms and a good multicuisine restaurant (mains Rs40 to Rs80). Breakfast is an *idli*. It's just across the main road from the train station. **Hotel Sai International** (☎ 225554; JK Rd; d Rs600-1500; 🖭) has spotless, comfortable rooms, hot water and a good restaurant (mains Rs50 to Rs200).

There's a regular local bus from Rayagada to Chatikona (Rs17, two hours), as well as shared jeeps (Rs20). The *Hirakhand Express* 8447 leaves Bhubaneswar daily at 8pm and

ORISSA'S INDIGENOUS TRIBES

Sixty-two tribal (Adivasi) groups live an area that encompasses Orissa, Chhattisgarh and Andhra Pradesh. In Orissa they account for one-quarter of the state's population and mostly inhabit the jungles and hilly regions of the centre and southwest. Regardless of their economic poverty, they have highly developed social organisations and distinctive cultures expressed in music, dance and arts.

Most Adivasis were originally animists but over the last 30 years have been targeted (with varying degrees of success and cultural sensitivity) by both Christian missionaries and Hindu activists. Naxalites (members of an ultra-leftist political movement) have used Adivasis as foot soldiers while claiming to defend them.

The tribes have become something of a tourist attraction. Visits are possible to some villages and *haats* (village markets) that Adivasis attend on a weekly basis. There are arguments regarding the morality of visiting Adivasi areas. Usually you need to gain permission to visit the villages, whereas at the *haats* you are free to interact with and buy directly from the villagers. However, it remains the case that tourism still brings very little income to the tribes.

Of the more populous tribes, the Kondh number about one million and are based around Koraput in the southwest and near Sambalpur in the northwest. The Santal, with a population above 500,000, live around Baripada and Khiching in the far north. The 300,000 Saura live near Bolangir in the west. The Bonda, known as the 'Naked People' for wearing minimal clothing, have a population of about 5000 and live in the hills near Koraput.

It is important to visit these areas on an organised tour for the following reasons:

- Some areas are prohibited and others require permits, which are much more easily obtained by a tour operator.
- Some tribal areas are hard to find and often not accessible by public transport.
- Adivasis often speak little Hindi or Oriya, and usually no English.
- Some tribes can get angry, even violent, if foreigners visit their villages uninvited and without official permission.

Some operators are more sensitive to the issues than others; it's worth asking about the size of your group and attitudes to photography (some people do not allow themselves to be photographed), and trying to get a feel for how interactions will be handled. Communal violence involving tribal people can flare up (see p644) and, while tourists haven't been targeted, a good operator should be honest and careful about avoiding areas experiencing trouble. Try to meet the guide who will be travelling with you rather than just speaking with the boss in the office. See p655 and p649 for details of recommended agencies.

Most tours start from Bhubaneswar or Puri, take in the more accessible areas in the southwest and can then go on to visit Similipal National Park. Options can include jungle trekking, staying at a village (tents and cooking supplied by the tour operator) and visiting one or more of the *haats*.

reaches Rayagada at 5.10am on its way to Koraput.

JEYPORE

☎ 06854 / pop 77,000

Jeypore is the base for visiting the amazingly colourful Onkadelli market (p664). The derelict palace, with heavy decorated gates, was built in 1936 and is off limits. There's a State Bank of India ATM on Main Rd and another near the bus stand. There's little in the way of budget accommodation for independent travellers; you're better off in temple accommodation in Koraput.

Hotel Mani Krishna (☎ 321139; MG Rd; www.hotel manikrishna.com; s/d Rs500/600, with AC from Rs800/900; ✦) has spotless rooms that are tastefully decorated with interesting old photos of tribal people. The downstairs restaurant offers a good selection of tasty Indian and Chinese food (mains Rs40 to Rs90, thalis from Rs35). The menu has tourist information and terrible jokes for you to read while you wait.

Until recently, **Hello Jeypore** (☎ 231127; www.hoteljeypore.com; NH Rd; s/d from Rs795/995, with AC Rs995/1195; ✗ ▢) was pretty much the only player in town and didn't have to try too hard. Happily, it has lifted its game and is still the best place to stay, with clean, comfortable rooms with contemporary design and an excellent restaurant (mains Rs35 to Rs120) serving fresh produce. There's an eerily lit bar and a pleasant garden.

The main bus station is 2km out of town but buses also stop in town to pick up passengers. An auto between the centre of town and the station will cost about Rs30. Frequent buses go to Koraput (Rs15, 45 minutes); others go to Berhampur (Rs200, 12 hours), Bhubaneswar (Rs300, 14 to 16 hours) and Rayagada (Rs70, three hours).

Slow passenger trains Nos 1VK and 2VK connect Jeypore with Visakhapatnam daily.

AROUND JEYPORE

Onkadelli and Kotpad are best accessed by hired car and Onkadelli should only be visited with a professional guide. You'll get much more out of the experience with a guide, who will usually be able to take you to visit craftspeople. This doesn't mean you have to come all the way from Bhubaneswar or Puri with a group or guide – it's feasible to come to Jeypore independently and organise a guide at your hotel.

Koraput
☎ 06852

Koraput is just a few kilometres from Jeypore and is an attractive town that's emerging as an alternative base for tribal visits. The temple is fascinating, especially for those non-Hindus who couldn't enter the Jagannath temple (p654) in Puri.

The **tourist office** (☎ 250318; Jeypore Rd; ☺ 10am-5pm Mon-Sat, closed 2nd Sat in month) has information and can arrange car hire. It's housed in the new, bright-blue Panthanivas Koraput, which had yet to open its rooms at the time of research; expect simple non-AC doubles for about Rs200.

The **Tribal Museum** (admission free; ☺ 10am-5pm) has an extensive exhibition of tribal culture including utensils, tools and clothes, as well as some paintings for sale. The museum will open out of hours if you can find the friendly caretaker. The open-air Jungle Restaurant here does Indian and Chinese dishes in a cool, leafy setting.

The **Jagannath temple** has an exhibition of gods of the different states of India. There's also a selection of local forms of *ossa* (also known as *rangoli*), traditional patterns made with white and coloured powders on doorsteps. At the back of the temple is a series of apses containing statuettes of Jagannath in his various guises and costumes.

The temple operates two budget hotels just outside its grounds. **Atithi Bhaban** (☎ 250610; atithibhaban@hotmail.com; d without/with AC Rs200/400; ✗) is the older building, with 'pure veg' restaurant and simple, clean-enough rooms. **Yatri Nivas** (☎ 9337622637; d Rs150) was only two months old when we visited, and had simple but very clean rooms. It has become popular fast; don't count on the 'very clean' lasting for long. Food can be ordered in from Atithi Bhaban.

The *Hirakhand Express* 8447/8 plies daily between Bhubaneswar and Koraput, and there are regular buses to Jeypore (Rs15, 45 minutes).

Onkadelli

This small village, 65km from Jeypore, has a most remarkable and vibrant Thursday **market** (best time 10am to 1pm) that throngs with Bonda, Gadaba, Mali and Didai villagers.

The market is popular with tour groups; if you stand back and watch Westerners photographing tribal people, you may well see Indian tourists taking photos of the equally exotic Westerners. Photographs should only be taken with the consent of the subject and will often come with a request for Rs10 or more; carry small denomination notes. Souvenir shopping is pretty much limited to jewellery sold by Bonda women.

Alcohol is an important ingredient in this social event; combined with the hunting bows and arrows it's a further incentive to make use of a professional guide. Police may shoo you away from the designated drinking areas.

Kotpad

This town, 40km north of Jeypore on the road to Sambalpur, has a thriving home-based fabric-dyeing and weaving industry. Along the lanes you'll see ropes of thread in a rich range of colours from reds and burgundies to browns laid out to dry. You can buy scarves and shawls (Rs600 to Rs3000) in silk and cotton direct from artisans – the distinctive local animal designs are especially appealing.

SAMBALPUR

☎ 0663 / pop 154,170

Sambalpur is the centre for the textile industry spread over western Orissa, and Gole Bazaar is the place to buy *ikat* or *sambalpuri* weaving. The town is a base for nearby Badrama National Park, and Debrigarh Wildlife Sanctuary on the edge of Hirakud Dam.

Orientation & Information

NH6 passes through Sambalpur to become VSS Marg. Laxmi Talkies Rd crosses VSS Marg and leads down to the government bus stand and Gole Bazaar.

Orissa Tourism (☎ 2411118; Panthanivas Sambalpur, Brooks Hill; ☺ 10am-5pm Mon-Sat, closed 2nd Sat in month)

Police station (☎ 403224; Laxmi Talkies Rd)

sify e-port (VSS Marg; per hr Rs20; ☺ 8.30am-10pm; ☒) Cool, clean, reliable internet access and friendly. Upstairs above a row of shops.

State Bank of India (VSS Marg; ☺ 10.30am-4.30pm Mon-Fri, 10.30am-1.30pm Sat) Next to Sheela Towers. Does currency exchange and has a MasterCard and Visa ATM. There's another ATM in the bazaar.

Sleeping & Eating

Hotel Uphar Palace (☎ 2400519; fax 2522668; VSS Marg; s/d from Rs450/500, with AC from Rs750/850; ☒) The sparkling cleanliness of the lobby doesn't quite carry into the bathrooms, though the rooms themselves are clean enough and it's the friendliest place in town. The Sharda restaurant has an Indian and Chinese menu (mains Rs45 to Rs130).

Sheela Towers (☎ 2403111; www.sheelatowers.com; VSS Marg; s/d from Rs995/1095; ☒) Staff can be unhelpful to the point of rudeness and the AC is arctic, but this is still Sambalpur's top hotel, with a range of comfortable rooms. The restaurant (mains Rs50 to Rs185) has a good range of tasty food and erratic opening hours.

New Hong Kong Restaurant (☎ 2532429; VSS Marg; mains Rs40-180; ☺ closed Mon) For 18 years the Chen family has been providing authentic Chinese in Sambalpur; we met expats who'd driven 60km cross-country to eat here. The menu also includes several Thai dishes and some tasty Indian-Chinese fusion dishes like Sichuan paneer. Ultraviolet light and doof music at night give it a clubby feel.

Getting There & Away

The government bus stand has buses running to Jeypore (Rs215, 14 hours), Bhubaneswar (Rs190, eight hours) and Berhampur (Rs207, 12 hours). Travel agencies in the street between the government bus station and Laxmi Talkies Rd book (usually more comfortable) buses leaving from the private **Ainthapali bus stand** (☎ 2540601), 3km from city centre (Rs10 by cycle-rickshaw). Several buses go to Bhubaneswar (Rs195), Raipur (Rs180, eight hours) and Jashipur for Similipal (Rs200, 10 hours).

The *Tapaswini Express* 8451 goes to Puri (sleeper/3AC/2AC Rs178/471/643, nine hours, 10.50pm) via Bhubaneswar (Rs160/420/573, seven hours). The *Koraput–Howrah Express* 8006 goes to Howrah (Rs243/654/896, 10 hours, 6.15pm).

DEBRIGARH & BADRAMA WILDLIFE SANCTUARIES

The 347-sq-km **Debrigarh Wildlife Sanctuary** (☎ 0663-2402741; per day Indian/foreigner Rs20/1000; ☺ 8am-5pm 15 Nov-1 Jun), 40km from Sambalpur, is an easy day out. Mainly dry deciduous forest blankets the Barapahad Hills down to the shores of the vast Hirakud reservoir, a home for migratory birds in winter. Wildlife here includes deer, antelopes, sloth bears, langur monkeys and the ever-elusive tigers and leopards. **Badrama Wildlife Sanctuary** (per day Indian/foreigner Rs20/1000), 37km from Sambalpur, shelters elephants, tigers, panthers and bears. It can be closed with no notice in the event of bad weather.

Access to the sanctuaries usually requires a 4WD, which can be arranged through Orissa Tourism, a private tour agency, or your hotel in Sambalpur for about Rs1000 for a half day.

NORTHEASTERN ORISSA

SIMILIPAL NATIONAL PARK

☎ 06792

The 2750-sq-km **Similipal National Park** (per day Indian/foreigner Rs40/1000, camera per 3 days Rs50/100; ☺ 6am-noon day visitor, to 2pm 15 Nov-15 Jun with accommodation reservation) is Orissa's prime wildlife sanctuary.

The scenery is remarkable: a massif of prominent hills creased by valleys and gorges, and made dramatic by plunging waterfalls, including the spectacular 400m-high **Barheipani Waterfall** and the 150m-high **Joranda Waterfall**. The jungle is an atmospheric mix of dense sal forest and rolling open savannah. The core area is only 850 sq km and much of the southern part is closed to visitors.

There's a huge range of reptile, bird and mammal species. The tigers aren't tracked; the best chance to spot them will be at the **Joranda salt lick**. What you're more likely to see is your first wild elephant (there are over 400 in the park), most probably at the **Chahala salt lick**. The best time to visit is early in the season before high visitor numbers affect animal behaviour.

There are two entrances, **Tulsibani**, 15km from Jashipur, on the northwestern side, and **Pithabata**, near Lulung, 25km west of Baripada. Options are a day visit or an overnight stay within the park. Overnight accommodation needs to be booked 30 days in advance, and remember you'll have to pay the Rs1000 entry fee for both days you're here.

Entry permits can be obtained in advance from the **assistant conservator of forests** (☎ 06797-232474; National Park, Jashipur, Mayurbhanj District, 757091), or the **field director, Similipal Tiger Reserve Project** (☎ 06792-252593; Bhanjpur, Baripada, Mayurbhanj District, 757002). Alternatively a day permit can be purchased from either gate.

Visitors either come on an organised tour or charter a vehicle (Rs1200 to Rs2000 per day for 4WD); hiring a guide (around Rs500) is advisable.

If you want to avoid the hassles of arranging permits, transport, food and accommodation, an organised tour from Bhubaneswar, Puri or Baripada is the answer.

Forest Department bungalows (d Indian/foreigner from Rs600/800) has seven sets of bungalows; Chahala, Joranda and Newana are best for animal spotting and Barheipani for views. The very basic accommodation has to be booked well in advance with the field director at Baripada – see above. You have to bring your own food (no meat or alcohol allowed) and water.

In March 2009 Maoist rebels blew up three forest offices inside the park and raided the Chahala bungalow, robbing tourists who were staying there. At the time of going to print the park had been completely shut off to tourists. The situation should be resolved by the time the park is due to re-open in November 2009, but check with tour operators or the field director.

JASHIPUR
☎ 06797

This is an entry point for Similipal Park and a place to collect an entry permit and organise

a guide and transport. Accommodation is very limited.

Sairam Holiday Home (☎ 232827; NH6; s Rs80, d with/without AC from Rs550/250; 🅿) has basic, clean rooms with mosquito nets. The owner can help arrange Similipal trips.

There are regular buses between Jashipur and Sambalpur (Rs200, 10 hours).

BARIPADA
☎ 06792 / pop 95,000

This town is the best place to organise a Similipal visit; if you're planning an independent trip, see **Orissa Tourism** (☎ 252710; Baghra Rd; 🕙 10am-5pm Mon-Sat, closed 2nd Sat in month). Recommended agency **Mayur Tours & Travels** (☎ 253567; mayur_tour@rediffmail.com; Lal Bazaar) can also organise tours and has capable guides.

Hotel Sibapriya (☎ 255138; Traffic Sq; s/d Rs130/250, d with AC from Rs600; 🅿) has a restaurant and tackily decorated rooms. The cheaper ones are a bit grubby but the AC rooms are fine. The clean and comfortable **Hotel Ambika** (☎ 252557; hotel_ambika@yahoo.com; s/d from Rs300/350, with AC from Rs900/950; 🅿) has a good bar and restaurant. It can organise Similipal trips.

Regular buses go to Kolkata (Rs140, three hours) and frequently to Bhubaneswar (Rs170, five hours) and Balasore (Rs35, one hour). The 2892 *Bhubaneswar–Baripada Express* (BBS-BPO Express, Rs70, second-class seats only, five hours, 5.10pm) runs from Bhubaneswar every day except Saturday, and returns as the 2891 at 5.00am every day except Sunday.

CUTTACK
☎ 0671 / pop 535,140

Cuttack, one of Orissa's oldest cities, was the state capital until 1950; today it's a chaotic, crowded city. The **tourist office** (☎ 2309616; Panthanivas, Buxi Bazaar; 🕙 10am-5pm Mon-Sat) is a little way out of town on a congested road, and not very helpful.

The 14th-century **Barabati Fort**, about 3km north of the city centre, once boasted nine storeys, but only some foundations and moat remain. The 18th-century **Qadam-i-Rasool shrine**, in the city centre, is sacred to Hindus as well as Muslims (who believe it contains footprints of the Prophet Mohammed).

Shopping is great in Cuttack: handloom saris, horn and brassware are crafted here, along with the famed, lacelike, silver filigree work *(tarakasi)*. The best jewellers are on

Naya Sarak and Chowdary Bazaar, while you can see pieces being crafted in Mohammedia Bazaar.

Express buses whiz back and forth between Cuttack and Bhubaneswar every 10 minutes (Rs13, one hour).

BALASORE
pop 106,000

Balasore, the first major town in northern Orissa, was once an important trading centre. Now it's a staging post for Chandipur or Similipal National Park.

The office of **Orissa Tourism** (☎ 262048; ☻ 10am-5pm Mon-Sat) is located in **Panthanivas Balasore** (☎ 240697; Police Line; d with/without AC Rs700/400; ✸), where you'll find friendlier-than-average staff and worn but clean rooms; they're fine for a night.

Several buses leave from Remuna Golai at around 10pm for Kolkata (Rs200, seven to eight hours) and more frequently for Bhubaneswar (Rs100, five hours). The infrequent bus service to Chandipur makes an autorickshaw (Rs200) a better option.

CHANDIPUR
☎ 06782

This cute and laid-back seaside village ambles down to the ocean through a short avenue of casuarina and palm trees. It amounts to a couple of hotels, snack places and some souvenir shops. It has a huge beach at low tide when the sea is some 5km away; it's safe to swim here when there's enough water.

There's a bustling fishing village 2km further up the coast at a river mouth; in the early morning, walk up and watch the boats unloading fish and prawns.

Panthanivas Chandipur (☎ 270051; dm Rs150, d with/without AC from Rs990/650; ✸) has a great location overlooking the beach, but is otherwise not the best value in town. Best of the bunch is **Hotel Shubham** (☎ 270025; d with/without AC from Rs900/480; ✸), with spotless and comfortable rooms, a pleasant garden and a good restaurant. **Hotel Golden** (☎ 270021; mains Rs20-100), on the main drag, does a limited selection of mainly veg Indian food, plus recommended local seafood; crab masala (Rs100) is the house speciality.

Regular buses ply the NH5 between Bhubaneswar and Balasore. From Balasore, taxis and autorickshaws can take you the 15km to Chandipur.

BHITARKANIKA WILDLIFE SANCTUARY

Three rivers flow out to sea at Bhitarkanika forming a tidal maze of muddy creeks and mangroves. Most of this 672-sq-km delta forms **Bhitarkanika Wildlife Sanctuary** (☎ 272460; Indian/foreigner per day Rs20/1000), a significant ecosystem containing hundreds of estuarine crocodiles that bask on mud flats waiting for the next meal to swim by. Dangmal Island contains a successful breeding and conservation program for these crocodiles. Pythons, water monitors, wild boar and timid spotted deer can also be seen. The best time to visit is from December to February.

Bird-watchers will find eight species of brilliantly coloured kingfishers, plus 190 other bird species. A large heronry on Bagagahan Island is home for herons that arrive in early June and nest until early December, when they move on to Chilika Lake (p659). Raucous open-billed storks have set up a permanent rookery here.

The only way to get around the sanctuary is by boat. Many boats are a little battered, with old tyres on ropes acting as life preservers: this definitely adds piquancy to the thrill of boating on waters where enormous crocodiles can suddenly surface rather close to you.

Orientation & Information

Permits, accommodation and boat transport can all be organised in the small port of **Chandbali**. Organise a boat (per day Rs2000, negotiable) with one of the private operators, such as the recommended **Sanjog Travels** (☎ 06786-220495; Chandbali Jetty), which can also help with obtaining the permit from the **divisional forest officer** (☎ 06729-272460; Rajnagar).

Sights

First stop is a permit check at Khola jetty before chugging on to **Dangmal Island** for the crocodile conservation program (and accommodation).

The heronry at **Bagagahan Island** is reached by a narrow pathway leading to a watchtower, where you can spy on a solid mass of herons and storks nesting in the treetops.

Back at Khola, a 2km walk leads to Rigagada with its interesting 18th-century **Jagannath temple**, built with some erotica in Kalinga style. While there, take an amble through this typical Orissan village.

ORISSA

ORISSA

Sleeping & Eating

Forest rest houses (r per person Indian/foreigner from Rs434/574) This comfortable accommodation at Dangmal has solar lights, mosquito nets and shared bathrooms. The restaurant has a limited menu of mainly veg food along with fresh seafood (thalis Rs50 to Rs80). At the time of research the only way of booking was in advance through Sandpebbles Tour N Travels (p646) in Bhubaneswar.

Aranya Nivas (☎ 06786-220397; Chandbali; d with/ without AC Rs1000/500; ✷) Within 50m of the Chandbali jetty, it has somewhat threadbare and less-than-spotless rooms with lots of mozzies; the restaurant serves up a limited menu that has to be ordered in advance (mains Rs30 to Rs80). Boats can be organised here.

Getting There & Away

Chandbali is 55km and two hours southeast of Bhadrak on NH5. Buses go from Chandbali bazaar to Bhadrak (Rs25), Bhubaneswar (Rs75) and Kolkata (Rs150). The *Howrah–Bhubaneswar Dhauli Express* 2821/2 stops in Bhadrak at 10.27am going south to Bhubaneswar (2nd class/chair Rs71/232, two hours); and at 3.30pm going north to Howrah (2nd class/chair Rs104/346, five hours).

RATNAGIRI, UDAYAGIRI & LALITGIRI

These Buddhist ruins are about 60km northeast of Cuttack. Currently there's no accommodation and inadequate transport, so the only feasible way to visit is by hired car organised in Bhubaneswar or Puri. The OTDC is building a Panthanivas hotel opposite the museum in Ratnagiri.

Ratnagiri

Ratnagiri has the most interesting and extensive **ruins** (Indian/foreigner Rs5/100, video Rs25; ✷ dawn-dusk). Two large monasteries flourished here from the 6th to 12th centuries. Noteworthy are an exquisitely carved doorway and the remains of a 10m-high stupa. The excellent **museum** (admission Rs2; ✷ 10am-5pm Sat-Thu) contains beautiful sculptures from the three sites; look for the exquisite miniature bronze images of the Buddha and Tara in gallery 4.

Udayagiri

Another **monastery complex** is being excavated here. There's a large pyramidal brick stupa with a seated Buddha and some beautiful doorjamb carvings. There's no entry fee, but unhelpful guides may attach themselves to you then ask for a donation (not compulsory).

Lalitgiri

Several **monastery ruins** (Indian/foreigner Rs5/100, video Rs25; ✷ dawn-dusk) are scattered up a hillside leading to a small museum and a hillock crowned with a shallow stupa. During excavations of the stupa in the 1970s, a casket containing gold and silver relics was found.

Madhya Pradesh & Chhattisgarh

The vast state of Madhya Pradesh (MP) doesn't roar for attention like its neighbours. Instead it growls deeply, offering something big and beautiful to those who will prowl the plains.

Tiger parks are the star attraction, with Kanha, Pench and Bandhavgarh offering excellent chances to see India's most treasured animal. In fact, at Bandhavgarh you'd have to be pretty unlucky *not* to see one. Outdoor enthusiasts can also head to the hill station of Pachmarhi for more jeep safaris and trekking, while river rafting can be done around Orchha.

Rivers play a more spiritual role elsewhere. The ghats at Ujjain are one of the four locations for Hinduism's Kumbh Mela, the world's largest festival. A similarly reverent aura envelopes the temples and ghats at Omkareshwar and Maheshwar. Mosques and bazaars abound in Muslim-dominated Bhopal, while those interested in Buddhism shouldn't miss Sanchi's stupas.

The erotic carvings at Khajuraho are among India's finest examples of temple art, but they don't stand alone, either architecturally or artistically. There are splendid Afghan monuments at the ruined hilltop city of Mandu and wonderfully imposing palaces towering over the laid-back village of Orchha, while Bhimbetka offers 12,000-year-old rock paintings.

The more adventurous will love a foray into tribal Chhattisgarh, which split from Madhya Pradesh in 2000. Poor infrastructure leaves much of this densely forested state out of bounds for the average tourist, but for the intrepid it offers a fascinating glimpse into the life of tribespeople in central India, a world still far removed from mainstream Indian culture.

HIGHLIGHTS

- Ride elephant-back through the tiger parks of **Bandhavgarh** (p719), **Kanha** (p717) or **Pench** (p716)
- Stay with a tribal family in the villages around **Jagdalpur** (p723)
- Blush at erotic carvings on the World Heritage temples at **Khajuraho** (p682)
- Raft the Betwa River in **Orchha** (p677) before drying off with a stroll around the village's magnificent palaces
- See 12,000-year-old rock paintings at **Bhimbetka** (p695), a short bus ride from the mosques and bazaars of **Bhopal** (p689)
- Escape the heat of the plains at the ruined city of **Mandu** (p709) or the picturesque hill station of **Pachmarhi** (p699)

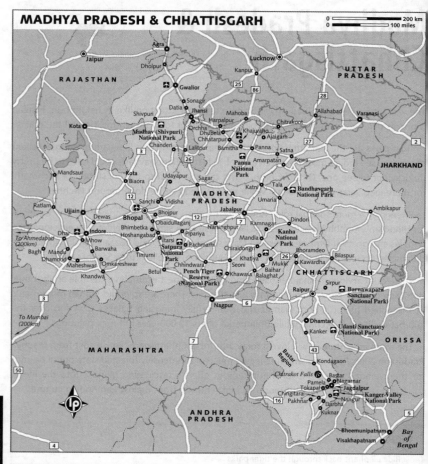

MADHYA PRADESH & CHHATTISGARH

FAST FACTS

Madhya Pradesh
Population 60.4 million
Area 308,000 sq km
Capital Bhopal
Main language Hindi
When to go October to March

Chhattisgarh
Population 20.8 million
Area 135,000 sq km
Capital Raipur
Main language Hindi
When to go October to March

History

Virtually all phases of Indian history made their mark on the region historically known as Malwa, starting with the rock paintings at Bhimbetka (p695) and Pachmarhi (p699), which date back more than 10,000 years. They tell of a cultural succession through the late Stone Age to the start of recorded history in the 3rd century BC, when the Buddhist emperor Ashoka (see boxed text, p41) controlled the Mauryan empire from Malwa and built Sanchi's Great Stupa (p696).

The Mauryas were followed by the Sungas and the Guptas (see p40) – Chandragupta II ruled from Ujjain and had the caves cut at Udaigiri (p699) – before the Huns rampaged across the state. Around 1000 years ago the Parmaras reigned in southwest Madhya Pradesh – notably Raja Bhoj, who ruled over Indore, Mandu and Bhopal.

From AD 950 to 1050 the Chandelas' nimble-fingered sculptors enlivened the facades of some 85 temples in Khajuraho (p680) with erotic scenes. Between the 12th and 16th centuries, the region experienced continuing struggles between Hindu and Muslim rulers (p42), and Mandu was the scene of some decisive clashes. The Mughals were eventually superseded by the Marathas (p46), who enjoyed most power in Malwa before they fell to the British, for who the Scindia maharajas of Gwalior were powerful allies.

With the States Reorganisation Act of 1956, several former states were combined to form Madhya Pradesh. In 2000, Chhattisgarh became an independent state.

Climate

The plains of Madhya Pradesh sweat for much of the year, with temperature highs of 48°C in summer (March to May), although there are hill-station getaways, such as Pachmarhi, to cool off in. Winter (November to February) is much more pleasant, but the north sees some rain in December and January. The main wildlife reserves, including the big tiger parks, close during the rainy season (June to September).

Getting There & Away

AIR
Domestic flights serve Gwalior, Khajuraho, Bhopal, Indore, Jabalpur and Raipur.

TRAIN
Madhya Pradesh has excellent train connections. The most significant line arrives from northwest India via Delhi and Agra, and passes through Jhansi and Bhopal before forking at Itarsi, from where it heads to Mumbai (Bombay) and to Hyderabad and Chennai (Madras).

Coming from Mumbai, the state's other major line passes through Itarsi, Jabalpur, Katni and Satna en route to Allahabad, Varanasi and Kolkata (Calcutta). From Katni, lines run into Chhattisgarh, Orissa and Jharkhand.

Two lines run from Indore to Jaipur in Rajasthan, one via Ujjain, but there is only one direct train a day; the other option is to go via Agra.

Unless otherwise mentioned, fares in this chapter are sleeper/3AC/2AC.

Getting Around

Madhya Pradesh's roads are pretty shoddy, and Chhattisgarh's are worse, but to get to many locations – the tiger parks, Pachmarhi, the Mandu area and most of Chhattisgarh – you

---

FESTIVALS IN MADHYA PRADESH & CHHATTISGARH

Festival of Dance (Feb/Mar; Khajuraho, p680) Week-long event with the cream of Indian classical dancers performing amid floodlit temples in the western enclosure.

Shivaratri Mela (Feb/Mar; Pachmarhi, p699) Up to 100,000 Shaivite pilgrims, sadhu (spiritual men) and Adivasis (tribal people) attend celebrations at Mahadeo Temple. Participants bring symbolic tridents and hike up Chauragarh Hill to plant them by the Shiva shrine.

Magh Mela (Apr/May; Ujjain, p702) This religious fair is held on the banks of the Shipra River at Ujjain. Hindu pilgrims from all over India take a soul-cleansing dip at auspicious times over the course of about six weeks. Every 12 years the fair is replaced by the massive Kumbh Mela (next in 2016), and every six years with the Ardh (Half) Mela (next in 2010).

Ahilyabai Holkar's Birthday (Apr/May; Maheshwar, p708) The birthday of Ahilyabai Holkar (b 1725) is celebrated with palanquin (enclosed seats carried on poles on four men's shoulders) processions through the town and cultural activities including music and dance.

Navratri (Festival of Nine Nights; Sep/Oct; Ujjain, p703) This Hindu festival leading up to Dussehra is celebrated with particular fervour. Lamps on the large pillars in Harsiddhi Mandir are lit.

Dussehra (Oct; Jagdalpur, p721) Nothing to do with Ramayana, but this 75-day festival is dedicated to local goddess Danteshwari. It culminates with eight days of (immense) chariot-pulling around the streets.

Chethiyagiri Vihara Festival (Nov; Sanchi, p695) Buddhist monks and pilgrims flock to see relics of two of Buddha's early disciples, Sari Puttha and Maha Moggallana (discovered in Stupa 3 in 1853).

Tansen Music Festival (Nov/Dec; Gwalior, p672) Four-day music festival attracting classical musicians and singers from all over India; free performances are usually staged at the tomb of Tansen, one of the most revered composer-musicians of Hindustani classical music.

have no choice. Off the main highways, work on a basis of around 25km/h.

NORTHERN MADHYA PRADESH

GWALIOR

☎ 0751 / pop 865,548

Famous for its medieval hilltop fort, Gwalior makes an interesting stop en route to some of the better-known destinations in this part of India. The city also houses the eccentric Jai Vilas Palace, home of the Scindia Museum and the historic seat of the Scindias, one of the country's most revered families.

The Tansen Music Festival – a four-day classical music event attracting performers from all over India – comes to town in November/December (see boxed text p671).

History

Gwalior's legendary beginning stems from the hermit Gwalipa who cured the Rajput chieftain Suraj Sen of leprosy using water from Suraj Kund tank (which still remains in Gwalior fort). Renaming him Suhan Pal, he foretold that Suhan's descendants would remain in power as long they retained the name Pal. Suhan's next 83 descendants did just that, but number 84 changed his name to Tej Karan and, naturally, lost his kingdom.

In 1398 the Tomar dynasty came to power. Gwalior Fort became the focus of continual clashes with neighbouring powers and reached its ascendancy under Raja Man Singh (1486–1516). Two centuries of Mughal possession followed, ending with its capture by the Marathas in 1754.

Over the next 50 years the fort changed hands several times, including twice to the British before finally passing to the Scindias.

During the First War of Independence (Indian Uprising) in 1857, Maharaja Jayajirao remained loyal to the British but his troops rebelled, and in mid-1858 the fort was the scene of some of the uprising's final events. Near here the British defeated rebel leader Tantia Topi and it was in the final assault on the fort that the rani (wife) of Jhansi was killed (see p439).

Orientation

Gwalior sprawls beneath its fort, which crowns the massive ridge to the west. The old town clings to the northeast base of the fort.

To the south is the new town, Lashkar, with its market area, Jayaji Chowk. The Station Rd area has the main concentration of hotels and restaurants.

Information

Fun Stop Cyber Zone (MLB Rd; per hr Rs30; ☀ 9am-10pm) Internet access and webcams for Skype use.

MP Tourism Tansen Residency (☎ 2340370; 6A Gandhi Rd; ☀ 10am-5pm); train station (☎ 4070777; ☀ 9am-7.30pm) Books MP Tourism hotels and cars.

Post office (☎ 4010555; Station Rd; ☀ 9am-5pm Mon-Fri, 9am-1.30pm Sat)

State Bank of India (☎ 2336291; Bada Chowk; ☀ 10.30am-4pm Mon-Fri, 10.30am-1.30pm Sat) Cashes travellers cheques; also has an ATM in the train station foyer.

Sights

GWALIOR FORT

Perched majestically on top of a 3km-long plateau overlooking Gwalior, this hilltop **fort** (☀ dawn-dusk) is an imposing yet eye-catching sight, with the circular towers of the dominating Man Singh Palace ringed with turquoise tiles.

There are two approaches to the fort, both steep treks. Rickshaws can drive you up to Urvai, the western gate, so it's tempting to go that way. But the western entrance is an anticlimax compared with the formidable view of the fort from the eastern approach, which makes entering from the east well worth the climb. Don't, however, miss the rock sculptures part of the way down the western side. The upper set in particular are far more impressive than those on the eastern approach and make a rewarding detour during your stroll around the fort.

A **ticket counter** (☎ 2480011; Indian/foreigner Rs5/100, video Rs25; ☀ dawn-dusk) near Man Singh Palace sells tickets for the monuments, and another ticket (Rs2) for a small, adjacent museum.

An atmospheric **sound-and-light show** (Indian/foreigner Rs40/100; ☀ Hindi 7.30pm Mar-Oct, 6.30pm Nov-Feb, English 8.30pm Mar-Oct, 7.30pm Nov-Feb) is held nightly in the open-air amphitheatre.

Much of the fort is now occupied by the prestigious private Scindia School, established by Maharaja Madhavrao Scindia in 1897 for the education of Indian nobility.

Man Singh Palace

This imperial palace is one of the more unusually decorated monuments you'll see in

MADHYA PRADESH & CHHATTISGARH

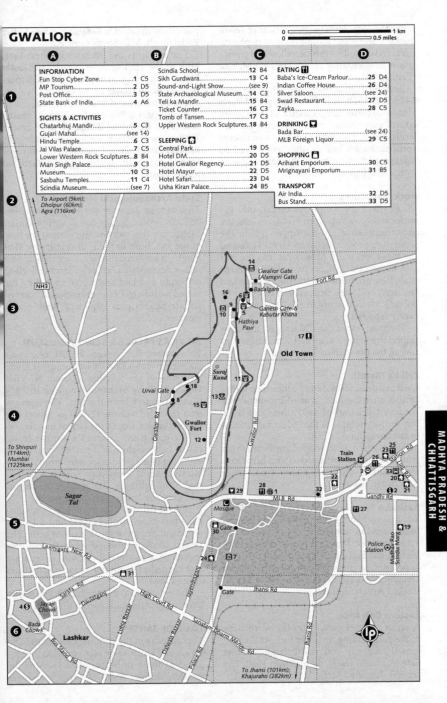

GWALIOR

INFORMATION
Fun Stop Cyber Zone.................1 C5
MP Tourism.................................2 D5
Post Office.................................3 D5
State Bank of India....................4 A6

SIGHTS & ACTIVITIES
Chatarbhuj Mandir.....................5 C3
Gujari Mahal..........................(see 14)
Hindu Temple............................6 C3
Jai Vilas Palace...........................7 C5
Lower Western Rock Sculptures..8 B4
Man Singh Palace.......................9 C3
Museum.....................................10 C3
Sasbahu Temples.......................11 C4
Scindia Museum....................(see 7)

Scindia School............................12 B4
Sikh Gurdwara............................13 C4
Sound-and-Light Show..........(see 9)
State Archaeological Museum...14 C3
Teli ka Mandir............................15 B4
Ticket Counter...........................16 C3
Tomb of Tansen..........................17 C3
Upper Western Rock Sculptures.18 B4

SLEEPING
Central Park...............................19 D5
Hotel DM....................................20 D5
Hotel Gwalior Regency...............21 D5
Hotel Mayur...............................22 D5
Hotel Safari................................23 D4
Usha Kiran Palace......................24 B5

EATING
Baba's Ice-Cream Parlour..........25 D4
Indian Coffee House..................26 D4
Silver Saloon.........................(see 24)
Swad Restaurant.......................27 D5
Zayka..28 C5

DRINKING
Bada Bar...............................(see 24)
MLB Foreign Liquor...................29 C5

SHOPPING
Arihant Emporium.....................30 C5
Mrignayani Emporium...............31 B5

TRANSPORT
Air India...................................32 D5
Bus Stand.................................33 D5

To Airport (9km);
Dholpur (60km);
Agra (116km)

NH3

Gwalior Gate
(Alamgiri Gate)

Fort Rd

Badalgarh

Ganesh Gate &
Kabutar Khana

Hathiya
Paur

Old Town

Suraj
Kund

Urvai Gate

Gwalior
Fort

Gwalior Rd

Gwalior Rd

To Shivpuri
(114km);
Mumbai
(1225km)

Train
Station

Station Rd

Sagar
Tal

Mosque

MLB Rd

Gandhi Rd

Gate

Police
Station

Laxmiganj New Rd

Madhav Rao Scindia Marg

Jayati
Chowk

Bada
Chowk

Lashkar

Bus Stand Rd

Sarafa Rd

Daulatganj

Lohia Bazaar

Datwala Bazaar

High Court Rd

Jayendraganj

Sanatam Dharm Mandir Rd

Palace Rd

Gate

Jhansi Rd

Jhansi Rd

To Jhansi (101km);
Khajuraho (282km)

0 .... 1 km
0 .... 0.5 miles

India: the outer walls include a frieze of yellow ducks! These – and mosaic tiling of elephants, tigers and crocodiles in blue, yellow and green – give it its alternative identity of Chit Mandir (Painted Palace).

Built by Tomar ruler Man Singh between 1486 and 1516, this fine example of early Hindu architecture consists of two open courts surrounded by apartments on two levels. Below ground lie another two storeys constructed for hot weather, connected by 'speaking tubes' built into the walls and used by the Mughals as prison cells.

Rock Sculptures

While there are sculptures carved into the rock on the way up from Gwalior Gate, the most impressive are the upper set on the western approach, between Urvai Gate and the inner fort walls. Mostly cut into the cliff face in the mid-15th century, they represent nude figures of *tirthankars* (the 24 great Jain teachers) and were defaced and castrated by Babur's Muslim army in 1527 but more recently repaired.

There are more than 30 images, the most impressive being a 17m-high standing sculpture of the first *tirthankar*, Adinath.

Teli ka Mandir

Used as a drinks factory and coffee shop by the British after the First War of Independence (Indian Uprising) of 1857, this 30m-high, 8th-century temple is the oldest monument in the compound.

The modern, gold-topped gurdwara (Sikh temple) nearby is dedicated to Sikh hero Guru Har Gobind, who Nur Jahan imprisoned in Man Singh Palace.

Sasbahu Temples

The Mayan-like Sasbahu, or **Mother-in-Law** and **Daughter-in-Law** temples, date from the 9th to 11th centuries. Mother-in-Law, dedicated to Vishnu, has four gigantic pillars supporting its heavy roof, layered with carvings. The smaller Daughter-in-Law, dedicated to Shiva, is also stacked with sculptures.

Eastern Entrance

A series of gates punctuates the worn steps of the path leading up to the fort. At the bottom, the first gate you pass through is **Gwalior Gate** (Alamgiri Gate), dating from 1660. The second, Bansur (Archer's Gate), has disap-

peared, so the next is **Badalgarh**, named after Badal Singh, Man Singh's uncle.

Further up is the interesting **Ganesh Gate**, built in the 15th century. Nearby is **Kabutar Khana**, a small pigeon house, and a small four-pillared **Hindu temple** to the hermit Gwalipa, after whom fort and town are named.

You'll pass a 9th-century Vishnu shrine known as **Chatarbhuj Mandir** (Temple of the Four-Armed) before reaching the fifth gate, **Hathiya Paur** (Elephant Gate), now the entrance to the palace as the sixth gate, Hawa Gate, no longer exists.

State Archaeological Museum

This **museum** (Indian/foreigner Rs10/100, camera/video Rs50/200; 🕙 10am-5pm Tue-Sun) is within Gujari Mahal, just through Gwalior Gate at the base of the fort. Built in the 15th century by Man Singh for his favourite rani, the palace is now rather deteriorated. There's a large collection of Hindu and Jain sculptures, including the famed Salabhanjika (an exceptionally carved female figure) plus copies of Bagh Caves frescoes.

JAI VILAS PALACE & SCINDIA MUSEUM

This **museum** (Indian/foreigner Rs30/200, camera/video Rs30/80; 🕙 10am-5.30pm Thu-Tue) occupies about 35 rooms of the Scindias' opulent Jai Vilas Palace, built by Maharaja Jayajirao in 1874 using prisoners from the fort. The convicts were rewarded with the 12-year job of weaving the hall carpet, one of the largest in Asia.

The gold paint around the durbar (royal court) hall weighs half a tonne. Supposedly, eight elephants were suspended from its ceiling to check it could cope with two 12.5m-high, 250-lightbulb, 3.5-tonne chandeliers, said to be the largest pair in the world.

Bizarre items fill the rooms: Belgian cut-glass furniture, stuffed tigers and a ladies-only swimming pool with its own boat. The cavernous dining room displays the pièce de résistance, a model railway with silver train that carried after-dinner brandy and cigars around the table.

Note: the gate to the north is locked so you have to enter the palace from the west.

TOMB OF TANSEN

Tucked away in the winding lanes of the Old Town, and in the same compound as the resplendent tomb of Mohammed Gaus, is the smaller, simpler tomb of Tansen, a singer much admired by Akbar and held to be the father of Hindustani classical music. Chewing the leaves of the tamarind tree here supposedly enriches your voice. Free performances are staged here during the four-day Tansen Music Festival in November/December (see boxed text p671).

Sleeping

BUDGET

Hotel Safari (☎ 2340638; Station Rd; s/d Rs225/325, with AC Rs600/675; ❄) Couldn't be handier for trains (with 24-hour checkout), and the bar-restaurant is an OK place for a beer (Rs100), but rooms are generally pretty shabby and should only be considered if nearby Hotel DM is full.

Hotel Mayur (☎ 2325559; Padav; s Rs240-450, d Rs300-540, with AC Rs480-920; ❄) Spacious rooms around a courtyard, extending up three floors. The cheapies are a bit gloomy, but the AC options come with marble floors, sit-down flush toilets and bathtubs. Sadly, the dirt-cheap dorm beds are not available to foreign tourists. Offers 24-hour checkout.

Hotel DM (☎ 2342083; Link Rd; r Rs300-Rs400) The best budget choice, Hotel DM has cute little rooms (the Rs400 rooms are slightly larger), some with their own wooden bench outside, leading to a small lawn at the back of the building. Rooms come with clean bathrooms and a TV locked securely inside a special cabinet. When was the last time you stole a hotel TV?

MIDRANGE & TOP END

Hotel Gwalior Regency (☎ 2340670; Link Rd; s/d incl breakfast Rs1650-2200/2200-2750, ste s/d Rs2900/3500; ❄) The marble lobby is perhaps a bit too grand for this modest but friendly hotel. Understated rooms decorated in soft colours do, however, come with goodies such as fridge, kettle, mini-bar and bathtub.

Central Park (☎ 2232440; www.thecentralpark.net; Madhav Rao Scindia Marg; s Rs2700-4000, d Rs3200-4500, ste Rs7500; ❄ 🖥 🛜 📶) Rooms at Gwalior's top business hotel are big on space but somewhat lacking in furniture. The facilities are excellent, however. There's currency exchange, a doctor on call, a health club, a visiting palm-reader and a chic, low-lit bar. Rates include breakfast.

Usha Kiran Palace (☎ 2444000; www.tajhotels.com; Jayendraganj; r Rs9500-11,500, ste Rs13,000-15,500, villa Rs23,000-30,000; ❄ 🖥 📶) Live like royalty

in this 120-year-old building, which once accommodated the visit of King George V. Every room has its own unique touches – mosaic-tiled bathtubs, silk-cushioned lounging areas – while the luxury villas come with their own private pool. The main pool can be used by nonguests (Rs500) as can the health spa (treatments from Rs1000), restaurant (Silver Saloon; below) and bar (Bada Bar; below).

Eating & Drinking

Baba's Ice-Cream Parlour (Station Rd; ice cream Rs40-150, mains Rs30-110; ❂ 11am-midnight) Brightly lit, spotlessly clean and a great place for a snack while you're waiting for a train. Menu includes South Indian, Chinese, pizza and, of course, ice cream.

Indian Coffee House (Station Rd; mains Rs35-95; ❂ 7.30am-11pm) It's hard not to love Indian Coffee House, and Gwalior's branch (handily located between train and bus stations) is no exception. It does all the usual breakfast favourites – real coffee, dosa (large savoury crepes), scrambled eggs – but also has a proper main-course menu, including a killer thali (all-you-can-eat meal; Rs70), in its separate first-floor area.

Zayka (MLB Rd; mains Rs40-110; ❂ 10am-10pm) This trendy, cafe-style restaurant with glass table-tops and brightly painted walls pulls in young local punters with its foreign menu – noodles, burgers, pizza – but the Indian veg dishes are still very good. Try the stuffed capsicum.

Swad Restaurant (Hotel Landmark, 47 Manik Vilas Colony; mains Rs90-230; ❂ 7am-11pm) Rooms in this midrange hotel may be overpriced, but the restaurant is top-notch, offering a dizzying range of Indian, Chinese and Continental dishes in contemporary surroundings. Save some space for the lip-smacking *gulab jamuns* (deep-fried balls of dough soaked in rose-flavoured syrup).

Silver Saloon (☎ 2444000; Usha Kiran Palace, Jayendraganj; mains Rs325-750; ❂ 11am-11pm) Mouth-watering Indian, Nepali and Continental dishes are served either in the tangerine-and-magenta restaurant or the palm-shaded courtyard of this exquisite hotel (left).

MLB Foreign Liquor (MLB Rd; beer Rs100; ❂ 10am-11pm) Like most of the bottle shops around town, this one serves beers and spirits and comes with a seedy drinking den out the back.

Bada Bar (☎ 2444000; Usha Kiran Palace, Jayendraganj; beer Rs250; ❂ 5-11pm) Take a peek inside Gwalior's most luxurious hotel (p675), order a beer or a glass of French wine, then rack up for a frame or two on the 120-year-old snooker table.

Shopping

Arihant Emporium (Moti Mahal Rd; ☒ 10am-7pm Mon-Sat) Near Jai Vilas Palace, Arihant Emporium specialises in a Gwalior favourite – silver boxes decorated with images from the tile work on Man Singh Palace (from Rs1200).

Mrignayani Emporium (High Court Rd; ☒ 11am-8pm Mon-Sat) State-owned chain selling handicrafts and fabrics, including Chanderi and Maheshwar saris.

Getting There & Away

AIR
Air India (☎ 2376872; MLB Rd; ☒ 10am-5pm Mon-Sat) has flights to Delhi (from Rs4515) and Jabalpur (from Rs4625) every Monday, Tuesday, Thursday and Saturday.

BUS
Regular buses go to Agra (Rs74 to Rs103, 3½ hours, from 5am to 9pm), Shivpuri (Rs67 to Rs74, two hours, from 5am to 10pm) and Jhansi (Rs60, three hours, day and night). There are three daily buses to Orchha (Rs75, 3½ hours, 5.30am, 12.30pm, 10pm) and Khajuraho (Rs160, seven hours, 7.15am, 8.30am, 11.40am) and four to Jaipur (Rs220, 10 hours, 6.30am, 7.15am, 6.30pm, 7.30pm). Only one daily government bus goes to Indore (Rs250, 12 hours, 7.15am) and one sleeper to Bhopal (Rs230, 12 hours, 8.15pm), although private firms run regular evening services.

TRAIN
More than 20 daily trains go to Agra's Cantonment station and to Jhansi for Orchha or Khajuraho, while more than 10 go to Delhi and Bhopal. See the boxed text (below) for details.

The new train service to Khajuraho should be running by the time you read this, although trains will pass through Gwalior at an unearthly time of the morning and only on Wednesdays, Saturdays and Mondays.

Getting Around
Cycle- (Rs5 to Rs10) and autorickshaws (Rs10 to Rs30) are plentiful. Brutish-looking tempos (large autorickshaws; Rs2 to Rs6) chug along fixed routes. An auto to the airport will cost Rs100 to Rs150.

AROUND GWALIOR
Shivpuri
☎ 07492 / pop 146,892
A possible day trip from Gwalior, the old Scindia summer capital is the site of the family's *chhatris* (cenotaphs), appropriately grand memorials to the maharajas and maharanis. It is also home to Madhav National Park, the Scindia's former hunting estate, now a protected wildlife zone.

There's an HDFC ATM near the bus stand. Turn right, towards the town centre, and you'll see it from the roundabout.

Two kilometres in the other direction from the bus stand, and set in formal gardens, the **chhatris** (admission Rs40; camera/video Rs10/40; ☒ 8am-noon & 3-8pm) are magnificent walk-in marble structures with Mughal-style pavilions and *sikharas* (Hindu temple-spires), facing each other across a pool with a criss-cross of walkways. The *chhatri* to Madhorao Scindia, built between 1926 and 1932, is exquisitely inlaid with intricate pietra dura (marble inlay work).

A further 4km beyond the *chhatris*, **Madhav National Park** (☎ 280422; entrance per vehicle Indian/foreigner Rs400/1500, camera/video Rs40/300, guide Rs150; ☒ 7am-4.30pm) is scattered with relics from the Scindias' hunting days – a shooting box, hunting lodge and sailing club. The last tiger was shot many years ago, but the 355-sq-km park

HANDY TRAINS FROM GWALIOR				
Destination	**Train no & name**	**Fare (Rs)**	**Duration (hr)**	**Departure**
Agra	2617 *Mangala Ldweep*	141/268/340	2	8.23am
Bhopal	2138 *Punjab Mail*	201/510/685	6	10.40am
Delhi	2625 *Kerala Exp*	180/450/603	5	8.08am
Indore	2920 *Malwa Exp*	286/749/1016	13	12.40am
Jhansi	2138 *Punjab Mail*	141/243/313	2	10.40am
Mumbai	2138 *Punjab Mail*	401/1073/1466	21	10.40am

s still home to leopards, antelope, deer, wild boar, wild dogs and mugger crocodiles. A 20km circuit of the park takes about two hours.

In between the *chhatris* and Madhav National Park, **Tourist Village** (☎ 223760; tvshiv puri@mptourism.com; q Rs1190, d with AC Rs1490; ⛱ 🖫) has lovely cottages in well-kept gardens overlooking a huge lake that borders the national park. There's a swimming pool, table tennis, a pool table and pedal boats on the lake (per person per 30 minutes Rs25), as well as a bar (beer Rs110) and restaurant (mains Rs45 to Rs130, open 8am to 10.30pm).

Buses leave regularly for Gwalior (Rs68, two hours) and Jhansi (Rs60, three hours). An auto from the bus stand costs Rs15 to the *chhatris* and Rs30 to the Tourist Village. You need a jeep to enter the park. You can hire them for Rs500 per vehicle (including a two-hour circuit of the park and a stop at the *chhatris*), but you'll have to ask around at the bus stand yourself as neither the park nor the Tourist Village arranges park transport.

JHANSI

This nondescript town is commonly used as a gateway to Orchha, Khajuraho and Gwalior, but is in fact in Uttar Pradesh. See p439 for details.

ORCHHA
☎ 07680 / pop 8501

Like nearby Khajuraho, this tranquil village getaway on the banks of the boulder-strewn Betwa River showcases some fabulous architecture – albeit without such high-quality carvings – but the atmosphere here is far more laid-back and hassle-free, making for a more relaxing stay. There are also good opportunities to enjoy the surrounding countryside, with walking, cycling, swimming and rafting all on the agenda.

History
Orchha was the capital of the Bundela rajas from the 16th century to 1783, when they decamped to nearby Tikamgarh. Bir Singh Deo ruled from Orchha from 1605 to 1627 and built Jhansi fort. A favourite of Mughal prince Salim, he feuded with Akbar, who all but ruined his kingdom. In 1605 Prince Salim became Emperor Jehangir, making Bir Singh a powerful figure. The Jehangir Mahal was built for his visit the following year. When Shah Jahan became emperor in 1627, Bir Singh

was once again out of favour; his revolt was crushed by 13-year-old Aurangzeb.

Orientation
Activity centres on the crossroads at the small street market where you'll find a scattering of shops and souvenir stalls as well as some guesthouses and restaurants. Tempos will drop you here. To the east is the main palace complex, elevated and surrounded by the Betwa River on one side and the seasonal offshoot of the Betwa on the other.

Information
Two or three travel agents just south of the crossroads offer internet use for Rs30 per hour.

Canara Bank (☎ 252689; Jhansi Rd; ⏰ 10.30am-2.30pm & 3-4pm Mon-Fri, 10.30am-1pm Sat) Changes travellers cheques and cash.

MP Tourism (☎ 252624; Hotel Sheesh Mahal, Jehangir Mahal; ⏰ 7am-10pm)

Post office (☎ 252631; Jhansi Rd; ⏰ 9am-5pm Mon-Fri, 9am-noon Sat)

Sights
The ticket for Orchha's **sites** (Indian/foreigner Rs10/250, camera Rs25) covers seven monuments – Jehangir Mahal, Raj Mahal, Raj Praveen Mahal, the camel stables, the *chhatris*, Chaturbhuj Temple and Lakshmi Narayan Temple. You can only buy it at the **ticket office** (⏰ 8am-6pm). You can walk around the palace grounds for free.

PALACES
Crossing the granite bridge over the mostly dry river channel brings you to a fortified complex dominated by two wonderfully imposing 17th-century palaces – Jehangir Mahal and Raj Mahal. Langurs play by the ruins here, while vultures perch on the rooftops.

Jehangir Mahal, an assault course of steep staircases and precipitous walkways, represents a zenith of medieval Islamic architecture. There's a small **archaeological museum** on the ground floor and behind the palace sturdy **camel stables** overlook a green landscape dotted with monuments.

In the nearby **Raj Mahal**, the caretaker will open the painted rooms where Rama, Krishna and Orchha royalty wrestle, hunt, fight and dance across the walls and ceilings.

Downhill from the palace compound are the smaller **Raj Praveen Mahal**, a pavilion and formal Mughal garden, and **Khana Hammam** (Turkish Bath), with some fine vaulted ceilings.

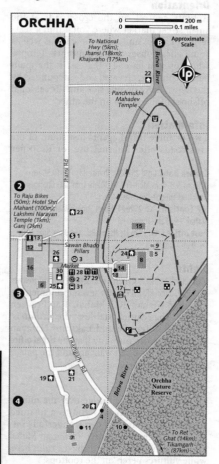

ORCHHA

On the other side of the village, **Palki Mahal** was the palace of Dinman Hardol (the son of Bir Singh Deo), who committed suicide to 'prove his innocence' over an affair with his brother's wife. His memorial, two cloth-covered stone beds in a pavilion, is in the adjacent **Phool Bagh**, a traditional *charbagh* (formal Persian garden, divided into quarters). Prince Hardol is venerated as a hero in Bundelkhand culture. Women sing songs about him, tie threads onto the *jali* (carved marble lattice screen) of his memorial and walk around it five times, clockwise, to make wishes they hope he'll grant.

MUSEUM
More of an art gallery than a museum, the **Saaket Museum** (admission free; ⏲ 10am-5pm Tue-Sun) showcases some beautiful folk paintings from different states of India. The Madhubani paintings from Bihar are particularly striking.

TEMPLES
Orchha's impressive 16th-century temples still receive thousands of Hindu pilgrims. At the centre of a lively square is the pink and gold-domed **Ram Raja Temple** (⏲ 8am-noon & 8-10pm), the only temple where Rama is worshipped as a king. Built as a palace for Madhukar Shah's wife, it became a temple when an image of Rama, temporarily installed by the rani, proved impossible to move.

Ram Raja is overlooked by the spectacular towers of **Chaturbhuj Temple**, an immensely solid building on a cruciform plan. Buy a cheap torch from the bazaar and climb the internal stairs to the roof where, from among the mossy spires and domes, you get the best view in town.

Lakshmi Narayan Temple, on the road out to Ganj village, has fine rooftop views and well-

MADHYA PRADESH & CHHATTISGARH

reserved murals on the ceilings of its domed towers.

CHHATRIS

Cenotaphs to Orchha's rulers, including Bir Singh Deo, the *chhatris* rise from the rubble and undergrowth 500m south of the village. They're best seen at dusk, when the birds reel above the children splashing at the river ghats.

VILLAGES

Consider renting a bicycle (see p680) and getting out into the smaller surrounding villages. The oldest is the half-ruined, half-lived-in village of **Ganj**, about 1km beyond Lakshmi Narayan Temple, which ends at a 16th-century archway marking the far western edge of the old city of Orchha. You can clamber along the city's outer wall here for some distance. We've heard the villages of **Gundrai**, **Nakta** and **Aajadbura** are also worth a visit. Let us know what they're like.

Activities
HIKING

You can wander the vast palace grounds. Some paths lead down to the river through gates in the wall. Another option is the 12km-long **nature trail** in Orchha Nature Reserve, a 44-sq-km island surrounded by the Betwa and Jamni Rivers. You need to buy a ticket (Rs150) from the ticket office (open 8am to 6pm) to enter the reserve, then you are free to explore, although guides (Rs200) are available. The nature trail is well marked and the roads are signposted, making this a nice place to cycle. Wildlife you're likely to see on the walking trail includes monkeys, deer, monitor lizards and peacocks. For a chance to spot one of four types of turtles found here, cycle to Ret Ghat, 14km south of the ticket office, on the Jamni River.

MASSAGE & YOGA

Amar Mahal (right) and **Orchha Resort** (☎ 252222; www.orchharesort.com) both offer good-quality ayurvedic massage treatments (Rs500 to Rs2000, from 8.30am to 8.30pm) and hold yoga classes (Rs800) every morning and evening.

RAFTING

River-rafting (per raft per 1½/3hr Rs1200/2500) trips start from the boat club, but tickets must be bought through MP Tourism at Hotel Sheesh Mahal or Betwa Retreat. Rafts take one to six people.

SWIMMING

Locals swim in the **Betwa River** every day. A popular spot is in front of the boat club by the bridge that leads into the Orchha Nature Reserve. Another option is the boulder-strewn section beside Bundelkhand Riverside hotel. Follow the track to the hotel but instead of turning left into the hotel itself, carry on down to the river.

Nonguests can use the **swimming pools** at the following hotels: Bundelkhand Riverside (Rs100), Amar Mahal (Rs300) and Orchha Resort (Rs300).

Sleeping
BUDGET

Shri Mahant Guest House (☎ 252715; r Rs150-350, with AC Rs600; ⚡) Overlooking the souvenir market at the entrance to Ram Raja Temple and overlooked itself by the wonderful Chaturbhuj Temple, this excellent budget choice has a superb location, clean rooms – some with TV, others with balconies – and friendly staff.

Shiva Guesthouse (☎ 252626; Tikamgarh Rd; r Rs200) Simple, well-looked-after double rooms with bedside tables and clean bathrooms. Most have palace views.

Hotel Shri Mahant (☎ 252341; Lakshmi Narayan Temple Rd; r Rs300-600, with AC Rs700-1200; ⚡) Sri Mahant Guest House's laid-back sister property has a chilled-out location with good views from the rooftop.

Fort View Guest House (☎ 252701; Jhansi Rd; r Rs300-600, with AC Rs1000; ⚡) Smart but basic rooms off a cute courtyard. The three AC rooms have huge windows with palace views. One has a marble bed.

Bhandari Guesthouse (☎ 252745; off Tikamgarh Rd; r Rs400, without bathroom Rs200) Newly opened at the time of research, this place has clean rooms (with spacious bathrooms) set around a simple courtyard. The shared bathroom is a squat toilet and bucket shower.

MIDRANGE & TOP END

Betwa Retreat (☎ 252618; www.mptourism.com; tents Rs990, cottages Rs1690, ste Rs4990; ⚡) Set in a peaceful, well-tended garden, this MP Tourism property overlooks the river and has views of the *chhatris*. Rooms come in Mughal-style cottages or Swiss tents and have nice touches such as iron bed frames. There's a new restaurant (below), a bar and an outdoor terrace, and it's only a five-minute walk from the main drag.

our pick Hotel Sheesh Mahal (☎ 252624; smorchha@ mptourism.com; Jehangir Mahal; r Rs1190-1490, ste Rs3990-4990;) Literally palatial, this hotel is actually located in a wing of Jehangir Mahal. As you'd expect, the architecture is stunning – arches, columns, lattice windows, decorative wooden door frames – but the rooms themselves are gorgeous too, and each is unique, some with regal touches such as thronelike toilets. Even if you don't stay here, pretend you want to and have a look around.

Amar Mahal (☎ 252102; www.amarmahal.com; s Rs1900-2700, d Rs3150-4050, ste Rs5000;) Grand rooms containing lovely wood-carved furniture, such as four-poster beds, are set around a courtyard with white pillars supporting a covered walkway. There's an ayurvedic massage and yoga centre (see p679) beside the large, but slightly exposed, pool.

Bundelkhand Riverside (☎ 252612; s Rs2600-3600, d Rs3000-5000;) The granddaddy of Orchha hotels is owned by the grandson of Orchha's last king, Vir Singh, who sold his palaces to the state after India's Independence. Some of the maharaja's personal art collection is displayed in the corridors. Exquisite rooms overlook either the river or the hotel's beautiful gardens which contain some 16th-century monuments as well as a small swimming pool.

Eating & Drinking

Don't make the same religious faux pas one Lonely Planet author made by eating the fudgelike sweets on sale on the approach to the Ram Raja Temple. Tasty though they are, they're supposed to be given as offerings to Lord Rama.

Bhola Restaurant (cnr Jehangir Mahal & Tikamgarh Rds; mains Rs20-60; 7am-11.30pm) A great spot for people-watching, this street-side restaurant does mostly Indian fare – dhal, pakora, paneer – but also some Korean and Dutch dishes as well as pizza.

Ram Raja (Jehangir Mahal Rd; mains Rs20-60) A friendly, family-run street-side restaurant offering reasonable vegetarian fare under the shade of a large tree.

Betwa Tarang (Jehangir Mahal Rd; mains Rs25-70) Sit on the rooftops overlooking the market, with the old palace to your right and Chaturbhuj Temple to your left, as you sip beer (Rs100) or tuck into the well-priced veg menu.

Betwa Retreat Restaurant (Betwa Retreat; mains Rs50-150; 7am-10pm) Sit in the new AC room or out on the terrace overlooking the river. It's the usual MP tourist menu, plus fish tikka. There's also a bar (beer Rs150) and live classical Indian music every evening.

Hotel Sheesh Mahal (☎ 252624; Jehangir Mahal; mains Rs75-200; 7.30am-10pm) Indian tandoori, Chinese and Continental are all on the menu but it's the historic surroundings that are the attraction here.

Turquoise Diner (☎ 252612; Bundelkhand Riverside; mains Rs145-230; 7am-10pm) Fabulous green and blue–tiled AC restaurant inside the sumptuous grounds of this top-notch hotel with good-quality Indian food.

Shopping

Largely hassle-free souvenir stalls set up around the crossroads.

Rajasthan Emporium & Indian Art Gallery (Shops 12 & 13, Tikamgarh Rd; 7am-9.30pm) Embroidery is the speciality at this small, friendly shop.

Getting There & Around

Regular buses (Rs10) go between Jhansi bus stand and Orchha, although they start to thin out in the afternoon. Tempos ply the same 18km route for the same price all day, while autorickshaws charge Rs150. Coming from Khajuraho, you can ask the bus driver to drop you off at the Orchha turn-off on the National Hwy, 9km east of Jhansi, where you should be able to wave down a tempo or bus to Orchha.

There are no buses between Khajuraho and Orchha. You need to go to Jhansi first then catch a bus (Rs100, from 5.30am to 3.30pm) from there as Jhansi–Khajuraho buses tend not to stop for you if you wait on the side of the highway. Taxis to Khajuraho cost at least Rs1500.

Raju Bikes (Lakshmi Narayan Temple Rd) hires out rickety bicycles at unbeatable prices (per hour/day Rs5/25).

KHAJURAHO

☎ 07686 / pop 19,286

The Kama Sutra carvings that swathe Khajuraho's three groups of World Heritage–listed temples are among the finest temple art in the world, and the new railway line means getting to see them doesn't have to be the cross-country mission it once was. Many travellers complain about the tiring persistence of touts

KHAJURAHO

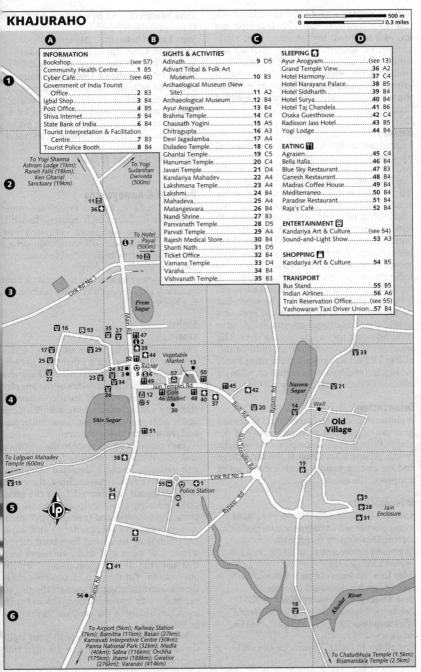

0 ————————— 500 m
0 ————————— 0.3 miles

INFORMATION
Bookshop.............................(see 57)
Community Health Centre..........**1** B5
Cyber Café..........................(see 46)
Government of India Tourist
  Office.............................**2** B3
Iqbal Shop..........................**3** B4
Post Office.........................**4** B5
Shiva Internet......................**5** B4
State Bank of India.................**6** B4
Tourist Interpretation & Facilitation
  Centre.............................**7** B3
Tourist Police Booth................**8** B4

SIGHTS & ACTIVITIES
Adinath...............................**9** D5
Adivart Tribal & Folk Art
  Museum.............................**10** B3
Archaeological Museum (New
  Site)..............................**11** A2
Archaeological Museum..............**12** B4
Ayur Arogyam.......................**13** B4
Brahma Temple......................**14** C4
Chausath Yogini....................**15** A5
Chitragupta........................**16** A3
Devi Jagadamba.....................**17** A4
Duladeo Temple.....................**18** C6
Ghantai Temple.....................**19** C5
Hanuman Temple....................**20** C4
Javari Temple......................**21** D4
Kandariya Mahadev.................**22** A4
Lakshmana Temple..................**23** A4
Lakshmi............................**24** A4
Mahadeva..........................**25** A4
Matangesvara......................**26** A4
Nandi Shrine.......................**27** B3
Parsvanath Temple.................**28** D5
Parvati Temple.....................**29** A4
Rajesh Medical Store...............**30** B4
Shanti Nath........................**31** D5
Ticket Office......................**32** B4
Vamana Temple.....................**33** D4
Varaha.............................**34** B4
Vishvanath Temple.................**35** B3

SLEEPING 🏠
Ayur Arogyam.......................(see 13)
Grand Temple View.................**36** A2
Hotel Harmony.....................**37** C4
Hotel Narayana Palace.............**38** B5
Hotel Siddharth...................**39** B4
Hotel Surya.......................**40** B4
Hotel Taj Chandela................**41** B6
Osaka Guesthouse.................**42** C4
Radisson Jass Hotel...............**43** B5
Yogi Lodge........................**44** B4

EATING 🍴
Agrasen...........................**45** C4
Bella Italia......................**46** B4
Blue Sky Restaurant..............**47** B3
Ganesh Restaurant................**48** B4
Madras Coffee House..............**49** B4
Mediterraneo.....................**50** B4
Paradise Restaurant..............**51** B4
Raja's Café......................**52** B4

ENTERTAINMENT 🎭
Kandariya Art & Culture..........(see 54)
Sound-and-Light Show.............**53** A3

SHOPPING 🛍
Kandariya Art & Culture..........**54** B5

TRANSPORT
Bus Stand.........................**55** B5
Indian Airlines...................**56** A6
Train Reservation Office..........(see 55)
Yashoworan Taxi Driver Union.....**57** B4

To Yogi Sharma
Ashram Lodge (1km);
Raneh Falls (18km);
Ken Gharial
Sanctuary (19km)

To Yogi
Sudarshan
Dwiveda
(500m)

To Hotel
Payal
(500m)

Link Rd No 1

Prem
Sagar

Main Rd

Vegetable
Market

Bazaar

Jain Temples Rd

Gole
Market

Shiv Sagar

To Lalguan Mahadev
Temple (600m)

Narora
Sagar

Well

Old
Village

Basti Rd

Bypass Rd

Jain Temple Rd

Link Rd No 2

Police Station

Bypass Rd

Jain
Enclosure

Jhansi Rd

Khodar River

To Airport (5km); Railway Station
(7km); Bamitha (11km); Basari (27km);
Karnavati Interpretive Centre (30km);
Panna National Park (32km); Madla
(40km); Satna (116km); Orchha
(175km); Jhansi (188km); Gwalior
(276km); Varanasi (414km)

To Chaturbhuja Temple (1.5km);
Bijamandala Temple (2.5km)

MADHYA PRADESH & CHHATTISGARH

here, preferring instead the more laid-back charms of nearby Orchha. Their complaints are well founded, but be aware that missing out on Khajuraho means missing out on some of the most beautiful temples in India. Come February/March, the western group of temples here becomes the stage for the week-long Festival of Dance (see boxed text, p671).

History

Legend has it that Khajuraho was founded by Chardravarman, the son of the moon god Chandra, who descended on a beautiful maiden as she bathed in a stream. Historians tell us that the Chandela dynasty built the temples, many of which originally rose from a lake. Most of the 85 temples – of which 25 remain – were built during a century-long burst of creative genius from AD 950 to 1050 and remained active long after the Chandelas moved their capital to Mahoba.

Khajuraho's isolation helped preserve it from the desecration Muslim invaders inflicted on 'idolatrous' temples elsewhere, but perhaps for the same reason the area was slowly abandoned and eventually fell into ruin, allowing the jungle to take over. The wider world remained ignorant until British officer TS Burt was guided to the ruins by his palanquin (enclosed seats carried on poles on four men's shoulders) bearers in 1838.

Orientation

A cluster of hotels, restaurants and shops lies near the biggest and most impressive of the town's three groups of temples – the western group. About 1.5km east is the old village and the eastern temples, with another set of temples to the south.

Information

Bookshop (Jain Temples Rd; ⏰ 8.30am-8.30pm) All-purpose bookshop with internet (per hr Rs40), handicrafts and films. CD burning costs per disk Rs100.
Community health centre (☎ 272498; Link Rd No 2; ⏰ 9am-1.30pm & 2-4pm)
Cyber Café (Jain Temples Rd; per hr Rs30, Skype per hr Rs40; ⏰ 9am-9pm) Underneath Bella Italia.
Government of India tourist office (☎ 272347; Main Rd; ⏰ 9.30am-6pm Mon-Sat) Extremely helpful.
Iqbal Shop (Main Rd; ⏰ 7am-10.30pm) Camera film and memory cards.
Post office (☎ 274022; ⏰ 10am-5pm Mon-Sat, for parcels 10am-2pm)

Shiva Internet (Main Rd; per hr Rs30; ⏰ 8am-10pm) CD burning costs Rs40 per disk.
State Bank of India (☎ 272373; Main Rd; ⏰ 10.30am-4.30pm Mon-Fri, 10.30am-1.30pm Sat) Changes cash and travellers cheques and has an ATM.
Tourist Interpretation & Facilitation Centre (☎ 274051; khajuraho@mptourism.com; Main Rd; ⏰ 10am-6pm Mon-Sat, closed every 2nd & 3rd Sat) Still just a not-particularly-helpful tourist office, but extra facilities such as a train reservation office and a foreign exchange counter were promised at the time of research.
Tourist police booth (☎ 272690; Main Rd; ⏰ 6am-10pm)

Dangers & Annoyances

Most of the hassle tourists experience comes in the form of seemingly endless demands for money, pens and photo fees, often from children. Also be wary of commission-driven operations such as guides offering to take you to a local school or charity.

Many yogis and massage therapists are not qualified. That doesn't mean they're not good, but be aware of it.

Sights

TEMPLES

The temples are superb examples of Indo-Aryan architecture, but it's their liberally embellished carvings that have made Khajuraho famous. Around the outsides of the temples are bands of exceedingly artistic stonework showing a storyboard of life a millennium ago – gods, goddesses, warriors, musicians and real and mythological animals.

Two elements appear repeatedly – women and sex. While the *mithuna* (pairs of men and women, usually depicted in erotic poses) are certainly eye-catching, the erotic content should not distract from the great skill underlying the sculptures. Sensuous, posturing *surasundaris* (heavenly nymphs), *apsaras* (dancing *surasundaris*) and *nayikas* (mortal *surasundaris*) have been carved with a half-twist and slight sideways lean that make the playful figures dance and swirl out from the flat stone. A classic example is the washerwoman with a wet sari clinging to her body – an image imbued with as much eroticism as any of the couples, threesomes or foursomes.

Walk round the temples with your right shoulder facing the building – the right side is considered divine.

KNOW YOUR TEMPLES

Khajuraho's temples follow a fairly consistent design, but you might need this quick-look guide to help you get your head around some of the temple terminology.

Exterior

■ *torana* – finely carved entrance gate to the temple

■ *adisthana* – high terrace which the whole temple sits on

■ *urusringas* – lower towers over the temple halls, often pyramid-shaped

■ *sikhara* – taller, curvilinear spire which tops the sanctum

Vertical towers are balanced by equally ornate bands of sculptures that run around the temple.

Interior

■ *ardhamandapa* – entrance porch

■ *mandapa* – initial hall

■ *mahamandapa* – main hall, which is supported with pillars and has a corridor around it

■ *garbhagriha* – inner sanctum, where the resident deity is displayed. A small *antarala* (vestibule) leads into the inner sanctum.

■ *pradakshina* – enclosed corridor running around the inner sanctum

Simpler three-part temples lack the *mandapa* and *pradakshina*.

Sculptures

■ *mithuna* – Khajuraho's most famous image; sensuously carved figures of couples in erotic poses

■ *apsara* – heavenly nymph, shown dancing in various postures

■ *salabhanjika* – female figure with tree which acts as a supporting bracket within the temple; *apsaras* also perform this bracket function

■ *surasundari* – when a *surasundari* is dancing she is an *apsara;* otherwise she attends the gods and goddesses by carrying flowers, mirrors or other offerings

■ *nayika* – the only difference between a *surasundari* and a *nayika* is that the *surasundari* is supposed to be a heavenly creature while the *nayika* is human

■ *sardula* – mythical beast, part lion, part some other animal or even human; *sardulas* usually carry armed men on their backs

Western Group

The main temples are in the **western group** (Indian/foreigner Rs10/250, video Rs25; ☾ dawn–dusk), the most interesting and the only group you have to pay to see. An Archaeological Survey of India (ASI) guidebook to Khajuraho (Rs99) and a two-hour audio guide (Rs50) are available at the ticket office.

The temples are described here in a clockwise direction. For temple terminology, see the boxed text above.

Varaha, dedicated to Vishnu's boar incarnation, and the locked **Lakshmi** are two small shrines facing the large Lakshmana Temple. Inside Varaha is a wonderful, 1.5m-high sandstone boar, dating from AD 900 and meticulously carved with a pantheon of gods.

The large **Lakshmana Temple** took 20 years to build and was completed in about 954 during the reign of Dhanga according to an inscribed slab in the *mandapa* (pillared pavilion in front of a temple). You'll see carvings of battalions of soldiers here – the Chandelas were generally at war when they weren't inventing new sexual positions. On the south side is a highly gymnastic orgy, including one gentleman

MADHYA PRADESH & CHHATTISGARH

proving that a horse can be a man's best friend, while a shocked figure peeks out from behind her hands. More sensuous figures intertwine between the elephants in the frieze ringing the basement, while some superb carvings can be found around the *garbhagriha* (inner sanctum).

One of the earliest and best-preserved monuments in this group, Lakshmana is dedicated to Vishnu, although in design it is similar to the Shiva temples Vishvanath and Kandariya-Mahadev.

The 30.5m-long **Kandariya-Mahadev**, built between 1025 and 1050, is the largest temple in town and represents the highpoint of Chandelan architecture. It also has the most representations of female beauty and sexual aerobics, all crammed into three central bands. There are 872 acrobatic statues, most nearly 1m high – taller than on the other temples. One particularly well-photographed sculpture illustrates the feasibility of the handstand position. The 31m-high *sikhara* here is, like linga, a phallic Shiva symbol, worshipped by Hindus hoping to seek deliverance from the cycle of reincarnation. It's decorated with 84 subsidiary spires – replicas of itself.

Mahadeva, a small, ruined temple on the same platform as Kandariya-Mahadev and Devi Jagadamba, is dedicated to Shiva, who is carved on the lintel of its doorway. It houses one of Khajuraho's finest sculptures – a *sardula* (mythical beast, part lion, part some other animal or even human) caressing a 1m-high lion.

Devi Jagadamba was originally dedicated to Vishnu, but later to Parvati and then Kali. The carvings include *sardulas* accompanied by Vishnu, *surasundaris,* and *mithunas* frolicking in the third uppermost band. Its three-part design is simpler than Kandariya-Mahadev and Chitragupta. It has more in common with Chitragupta, but is less embellished with carvings so is likely a little older.

North of Devi Jagadamba, **Chitragupta** (1000–25) is unique in Khajuraho – and rare among North Indian temples – in being dedicated to the sun god Surya. While not in as good a condition as the other temples, it has some fine carvings of *apsaras* and *surasundaris*, elephant fights and hunting scenes, *mithuna* and a procession of stone-carriers. In the inner sanctum, Surya drives his seven-horse chariot, while in the central niche on the south facade is an 11-headed statue of Vishnu, representing the god and 10 of his 22 incarnations.

Continuing around the enclosure, the closed-up **Parvati Temple** is on your right, a small temple originally dedicated to Vishnu and now with an image of Gauri riding a *godha* (iguana).

Believed to have been built in 1002, the **Vishvanath Temple** and **Nandi Shrine** are reached by steps on the northern and southern side. Elephants flank the southern steps. Vishvanath anticipates Kandariya-Mahadev, with which it shares *saptamattrikas* (seven mothers) flanked by Ganesh and Virabhandra, and is another superlative example of Chandelan architecture. Its sculptures include sensuous *surasundari* writing letters, cuddling babies and playing music while languishing more provocatively than at other temples.

At the other end of the platform, a 2.2m-long statue of Nandi, Shiva's bull vehicle, faces the temple. The basement of the 12-pillared shrine is decorated with an elephant frieze that recalls similar work on Lakshmana's facade.

Matangesvara, outside the fenced enclosure, is the only temple in Khajuraho still in everyday use. It may be the plainest temple here (suggesting an early construction), but inside it sports a polished 2.5m-high lingam (phallic image of Shiva). From its platform you can peer into an open-air storage facility scattered with temple finds but not open to the public.

The ruins of **Chausath Yogini**, beyond Shiv Sagar, date to the late 9th century and are probably the oldest at Khajuraho. Constructed entirely of granite, it's the only temple not aligned east to west. The temple's name means 64 – it once had 64 cells for the *yoginis* (female attendants) of Kali, while the 65th sheltered the goddess herself. It is reputedly India's oldest *yogini* temple.

A further 600m west, down a track and across a couple of fields (just ask the locals), is the sandstone-and-granite **Lalguan Mahadev Temple** (AD 900), a small ruined shrine to Shiva.

Eastern Group

The eastern group includes three Hindu temples scattered around the old village and four Jain temples further south, three of which are in a walled enclosure.

The **Hanuman Temple**, on Basti Rd, contains a 2.5m-tall statue of the Hindu monkey god. It's little more than a bright orange shrine, but the interest is in the pedestal inscription dating to AD 922, the oldest dateable inscription in Khajuraho.

The granite **Brahma Temple**, with its sandstone *sikhara* overlooking Narora Sagar, is one of the oldest in Khajuraho (about AD 900). The four-faced lingam in the sanctum led to it being incorrectly named, but the image of Vishnu above the sanctum doorway reveals its original dedication to Vishnu.

Resembling Chaturbhuja Temple in the southern group, **Javari Temple** (1075–1100) stands outside the old village. It's dedicated to Vishnu and is a good example of small-scale Khajuraho architecture for its crocodile-covered entrance and slender *sikhara*.

Vamana Temple (1050–75), 200m further north, is dedicated to the dwarf incarnation of Vishnu. It has quirky touches such as elephants protruding from the walls, but its *sikhara* is devoid of subsidiary spires and there are few erotic scenes. Its roofed *mahamandapa* (main hall) is an anomaly in Khajuraho but typical among medieval west Indian temples.

Located between the old village and the Jain group, the small **Ghantai Temple** is named after the *ghanta* (chain and bell) decorations on its pillars. It was once similar to nearby Parsvanath, but only its pillared shell remains and it's normally locked.

While not competing in size and erotica with the western-enclosure temples, **Parsvanath Temple**, the largest of the Jain temples in the walled enclosure, is notable for the exceptional skill and precision of its construction, and for its sculptural beauty. Some of Khajuraho's best-known figures can be seen here, including the woman removing a thorn from her foot and another applying eye make-up, both on the south side. Although the temple was originally dedicated to Adinath, a jet-black image of Parsvanath was substituted about a century ago. Both an inscription on the *mahamandapa* doorway and its similarities with the slightly simpler Lakshmana Temple date it to 950–70.

The adjacent, smaller **Adinath** has been partially restored over the centuries. With fine carvings on its three bands of sculptures it's similar to Khajuraho's Hindu temples, particularly Vamana. Only the striking black image in the inner sanctum triggers a Jain reminder.

Shanti Nath, built about a century ago, houses components from older temples, including a 4.5m-high Adinath statue with a plastered-over inscription on the pedestal dating to about 1027.

Southern Group

A dirt track runs to the isolated **Duladeo Temple**, about 1km south of the Jain enclosure. This is the youngest temple, dating to 1100–1150. Its relatively wooden, repetitious sculptures, such as those of Shiva, suggest that Khajuraho's temple builders had passed their artistic peak by this point, although they had certainly lost none of their zeal for the Kama Sutra.

Anticipating Duladeo and its flaws, the ruined **Chaturbhuja Temple** (c 1100) has a fine 2.7m-high, four-armed statue of Vishnu in the sanctum. It is Khajuraho's only developed temple without erotic sculptures.

Just before Chaturbhuja there's a signed track leading to **Bijamandala Temple**. This is the excavated mound of an 11th-century temple, dedicated to Shiva judging by the white marble lingam at the apex of the mound. Although there are some exquisitely carved figures, unfinished carvings were also excavated, suggesting that what would have been Khajuraho's largest temple was abandoned as resources flagged.

MUSEUMS

The **Archaeological Museum** (☎ 272320; Main Rd; admission Rs5; ☼ 10am-5pm Sat-Thu), announced by a wonderful 11th-century statue of Ganesh dancing sensuously for an elephant-headed deity, has a small but well-presented collection of sculptures from around Khajuraho. It was about to move to a larger site north of the western temples at the time of research.

Adivart Tribal & Folk Art Museum (☎ 272721; Chandela Cultural Centre, Link Rd No 1; Indian/foreigner Rs10/50; ☼ 10am-5pm Tue-Sun) makes a colourful change from the temples. It gives a taste of Madhya Pradesh's vibrant tribal culture through pointillist Bhili paintings, terracotta Jhoomar sculptures, masks, statues and bamboo flutes. Original signed paintings are for sale from around Rs5500.

OLD VILLAGE

If you can put up with the persistent requests from local children for pens and money then a stroll or cycle around the dusty narrow streets of the old village can be very rewarding. Homes here are whitewashed or painted in colourful pastels and the lanes are dotted with small shrines, old wells and water pumps.

Activities
MASSAGE

Many hotels offer cheap ayurvedic massage treatments of varying levels of authenticity. For the real deal, head to **Ayur Arogyam** (☎ 272572; treatment US$15-35; ☽ 24hr). The lovely Keralan couple who run the place also have two simple doubles rooms to rent (Rs100). There were plans to move to larger premises on Basti Rd at the time of research.

Barbers in Gole Market offer simple but rejuvenating head massages for Rs20.

YOGA

Apart from the hotels offering yoga, the inspiring **Yogi Sudarshan Dwiveda** (☎ 9993284940; Vidhya Colony; fee by donation; ☽ 6am) runs sessions at his home. Accommodation can be arranged. There is no English sign. If you have trouble contacting him, go through **Rajesh Medical Store** (☽ 9am-9pm) in Gole Market.

VOLUNTEERING

The NGO **Global Village** (☎ 272819; ajay.awasthi@gmail.com), based outside Khajuraho, principally targets environmental problems such as the plastic bags littering the town, but also supports local education as well as working towards curbing more disturbing problems such as child prostitution by running local awareness campaigns.

Volunteers are very welcome, particularly those with health and environment backgrounds, but must make prior arrangements by email or telephone.

SWIMMING

Nonguests can use the pools at Radisson Jass Hotel (Rs300) and Hotel Taj Chandela (Rs500).

Sleeping

Hefty discounts (20% to 50%) are available out of season (April to September). The **Government of India tourist office** (☎ 272348; Main Rd; ☽ 9.30am-6pm Mon-Sat) can organise homestays in Basari, a tribal village 27km east of Khajuraho.

BUDGET

Ayur Arogyam (☎ 272572; r Rs100) There are two basic double rooms beside the treatment rooms at this simple ayurvedic massage lodge (see left). Both have attached bathrooms with squat toilets.

Yogi Lodge (☎ 274158; r Rs150-250) Rooms are basic – some with tap-and-bucket showers – but small courtyards, narrow corridors and the cute stone tables in the rooftop restaurant give this place character. As at Yogi Sharma's other hotel, Ashram Lodge (above) there are yoga classes (7.30am to 8.30am). At the time of research Yogi Sharma was opening another guesthouse by the new train station. Expect similar, dependable budget lodgings.

Osaka Guesthouse (☎ 272839; off Basti Rd; r Rs150-350, with AC Rs500; ☒) If you don't mind lino flooring and plastic furniture then Osaka is a good-value option. Quietly tucked away down a small lane, it comes with large, clean rooms.

Yogi Sharma Ashram Lodge (☎ 272273; Main Rd; r Rs200-400) This gorgeous two-storey whitewashed house, 1.5km north of town, is set in a lush garden thick with flowers, banana plants and mango trees. Rooms are simple, but clean and spacious, the menu (mains Rs25 to Rs45) uses vegetables from the garden whenever possible, and the atmosphere is very peaceful. Yogi Sharma runs yoga classes (7.30am to 8.30am), which nonguests can attend for a small donation.

Hotel Surya (☎ 274145; www.hotelsuryakhajuraho.com; Jain Temples Rd; r Rs300-700, with AC Rs800-900; ☒ ▣) Decent rooms set among whitewashed corridors, marble staircases and a huge, underused garden. Some have TV and balconies. There's yoga (7am to 8am) and massage, and the atmosphere is generally laid-back.

Hotel Harmony (☎ 244135; Jain Temples Rd; r Rs350-550, with AC Rs850-950; ☒ ▣) Excellent-value rooms off marble corridors are tastefully decorated with green and brown furnishings and come with BBC World News on the box. Yoga and massage available.

MIDRANGE

Hotel Narayana Palace (☎ 272832; govindgautam@rediffmail.com; Jhansi Rd; s/d basement rooms Rs450/550, s/d Rs700/800, with AC Rs1000/1100; ☒) This new, kitsch-tastic hotel with orange-and-white facade will dazzle you with the pinks, purples, reds and greens of its interior paintwork, decor and ornaments. Rooms are clean, large and come

MADHYA PRADESH & CHHATTISGARH

with TV. The only let-downs are the two cheap basement rooms around the back which are musty.

Hotel Siddharth (☎ 274627; hotelsiddharth@rediff mail.com; Main Rd; d/q Rs490/890, d with AC Rs990-1500; ❄) The more expensive AC rooms at this old-fashioned hotel have great views of the western temples and come with bathtubs. The cheaper rooms don't, and are a little gloomy. All rooms, though, are huge, and there's a terrace restaurant.

Hotel Payal (☎ 274064; payal@mptourism.com; Link Rd No 1; r Rs690, with AC Rs1190; ❄ ✉) This MP Tourism hotel has smart rooms with dark-wood furniture set around unkempt garden courtyards. There's a small pool and bike hire (per day Rs50).

TOP END

Hotel Taj Chandela (☎ 272355; www.tajhotels.com; Jhansi Rd; d Rs5000-6000, ste Rs7000-9000; ❄ ▢ ✉) Set in luscious gardens with areas for tennis, volleyball and crazy golf, this high-quality hotel sports modern rooms with traditional artwork and ornaments. There's a lovely pool and discounts are common.

Radisson Jass Hotel (☎ 272344; www.radisson.com; Bypass Rd; r Rs6000; ❄ ▢ ✉) A marble spiral staircase winds its way up from the fountain in the lobby to modern, stylish first-floor rooms. There's a comfortable bar area (with pool table), a restaurant and a fine swimming pool.

Lalit Temple View (☎ 272111; www.thelalit.com /Khajuraho; Main Rd; r Rs15,000, with temple view Rs17,000, ste Rs35,000-50,000; ❄ ▢ ✉) Sweeps aside all other five-star pretenders with supreme luxury, impeccable service and astonishingly high prices. Rooms are immaculate with large plasma-screen TV, wood-carved furniture and tasteful artwork. Guests who don't have temple-view rooms can see the western group from the delightful lotus-shaped pool.

Eating

Madras Coffee House (cnr of Main and Jain Temples Rds; mains Rs30-60; ❧ 8am-9.30pm) Good, honest South Indian fare – dosa, *idli* (spongy round fermented rice cakes), *uttapam* (thick savoury rice pancakes), thali – as well as coffee and chai, served in a simple, slimline cafe-restaurant.

ourpick Raja's Café (Main Rd; mains Rs30-140; ❧ 8am-10.30pm) The central location is great, as is the restaurant design, with a delight-

ful wrought-iron spiral staircase linking a shaded courtyard with a temple-view terrace. But it's the food that steals the show. The Indian dishes are superb – the paneer *kofta* (unfermented cheese and vegetable balls) and chicken *kababi* (barbecued chicken pieces marinated in yoghurt), in particular – and not too expensive, and there's good-quality Italian and Chinese too.

Ganesh Restaurant (Jain Temples Rd; mains Rs40-100; ❧ 8am-10.30pm) Run by friendly staff, this no-nonsense restaurant – minimal decor, plastic chairs – serves good-quality Indian and Chinese, with vegetarian and meat dishes, as well as the usual curd and banana–based breakfasts.

Blue Sky Restaurant (Main Rd; mains Rs40-150; ❧ 6am-10pm) A rickety wooden platform, three storeys up, leads out to the most unusual place to eat in the whole of Khajuraho – a one-table tree house with an unrivalled view of the western temples. The view from the ordinary, terraced balcony is good too, while the menu is the usual Indian and Chinese, plus Western breakfasts. The grumpy service is perhaps understandable. Would you like to serve food to customers in a tree?

Paradise Restaurant (Main Rd; mains Rs45-200; ❧ 7am-9.30pm) Nothing flash about this place with plastic chairs, but the food's good – the *mulai kofta* (mashed potato balls with onion, spices and curry sauce) particularly so – and it serves booze (beer Rs130, cocktails from Rs95).

Agrasen (Jain Temples Rd; mains Rs50-200; ❧ 6.30am-10.30pm) This smart place with gingham table-cloths and a first-floor terrace serves up safe-to-eat salads, pasta and pizza as well as a variety of Indian veg and meat dishes.

Bella Italia (Jain Temples Rd; mains Rs70-195; ❧ 7am-10.30pm) A cheaper version of Mediterraneo, this rooftop restaurant overlooks Gole Market and sits beside a couple of huge trees which every day from around 6pm stage remarkable parrot-squawking contests.

Mediterraneo (Jain Temples Rd; pizza Rs190-280; ❧ 7.30am-10pm) Food served on a lovely terrace overlooking the street includes chicken, salads and organic whole-wheat pasta, but it's all about the pizza here, baked in the wood-fired oven. There's also beer (Rs130) and Maharastran wine (bottle Rs750).

Entertainment

Admittedly, the temples do look magical illuminated with technicolour floodlights, but the one-hour **sound-and-light show** (Indian/foreigner Rs50/300; ☾ Hindi 8.20pm Nov-Feb & 8.40pm Mar-Oct, English 7.10pm Nov-Feb & 7.30pm Mar-Oct) chronicling the history of Khajuraho is still about 45 minutes too long.

Folk dancing can be seen at the comfortable indoor theatre at **Kandariya Art & Culture** (☎ 274031; Jhansi Rd; admission Rs350; ☾ 7-8pm & 8.45-9.45pm).

Shopping

Kandariya Art & Culture (☎ 274031; Jhansi Rd; ☾ 9am-9pm) Full-size replicas of some of Khajuraho's temple carvings can be bought, if you have a spare Rs100,000. Smaller, more affordable versions, along with textiles, wood carvings and marble inlay can be found indoors.

Getting There & Away

AIR

Reserve in advance, as seats can be booked solid for days by tour groups.

Jet Airways (☎ 274406; ☾ 9.30am-4.30pm), at the airport, flies daily to Delhi (from Rs6615, 3½ hours) via Varanasi (from Rs4765, 40 minutes). **Indian Airlines** (☎ 274035; Jhansi Rd; ☾ 10am-5pm Mon-Sat), closer to town, has cheaper flights (Varanasi/Delhi from Rs3975/4755) but they only leave on Monday, Wednesday and Friday.

BUS

If the bus stand **ticket office** (☾ 7am-noon & 1-3pm) is closed, the owner of the Agrawal coffee stand nearby is very helpful and trustworthy.

There are regular buses to Jhansi (Rs100 to Rs120, five hours, 8am to 3.45pm), Mahoba (Rs40 to Rs50, four hours) and Madla (for Panna National Park; Rs30, 1½ hours). There's one daily bus to Agra (Rs270, nine hours, 8am) and one to Varanasi (Rs250, 15 hours, 6am) via Mahoba, Chitrakut and Allahabad.

Three buses run to Satna (Rs80 to Rs85, 3½ hours, 8am, 2pm, 3pm) from where you can catch trains to Varanasi.

Regular buses can be caught at the Bamitha crossroads, 11km away on Hwy 75 where buses between Gwalior, Jhansi and Satna shuttle through all day. Catch a shared jeep (Rs10, 7am to 7pm) to Bamitha from the bus stand.

TAXI

Yashowaran Taxi Driver Union (☎ 9425143774) is opposite Gole Market. Fares include: Raneh Falls (Rs400 return), Panna National Park (Rs1000), Mahoba (Rs1100), Satna (Rs1500), Orchha (Rs2200), Allahabad (Rs4000) and Varanasi (Rs5500) and Agra (Rs5500).

TRAIN

Khajuraho's long-awaited train station – 7km out of town – should be up and running by the time you read this. One train – the 2447 *Khajuraho-Nizamuddin Express* – will leave Khajuraho at 6.15pm every Monday, Wednesday and Saturday and will stop at Mahoba (where you can change for a 1am train to Varanasi), Harpalpur, Jhansi, Gwalior and Agra before arriving in New Delhi at 5.25am. The return service, the 2448 *Nizamuddin-Khajuraho Express,* will leave Delhi at 9.35pm every Tuesday, Friday and Sunday, and arrive in Khajuraho at 7.50am the following morning.

Train tickets can be bought from the **train reservation office** (☎ 274416; ☾ 8am-noon & 1-4pm Mon-Sat) at the bus stand. Note, at the time of research, a new train reservation office was due to open at the Tourist Interpretation & Facilitation Centre, just north of town.

Getting Around

Bicycle is a great way to get around. Several places along Jain Temples Rd rent them (per day Rs20).

Cycle-rickshaws should cost Rs10 to Rs20 wherever you go in Khajuraho, and around Rs100/200 for a half-/whole-day tour. Autorickshaws are about double the price.

PANNA'S TIGERS – THE PAINFUL TRUTH

Tiger sightings used to be a common occurrence at Panna National Park, but when we visited none had been seen for almost two years.

'The official number is 35 tigers here,' said one park guide who didn't want to be named. 'But really I think there are only four or five now. A few years ago, every time we went into the park we could see a tiger. Now none.'

And the reason for their decline? 'Hunting and bad park management,' he explained. 'Security is much better now. We have fencing all round the park and watchtowers with a 24-hour watch. But it's too late.'

Taxis to and from the airport charge Rs150, autorickshaws Rs50.

AROUND KHAJURAHO
Raneh Falls

These 30m-high **waterfalls** (☎ 07686-272622; Indian/foreigner Rs15/150, motorbike Rs40/200, autorickshaw Rs80/400, car Rs200/1000, compulsory guide Rs40; ◷ 6am-6pm), 18km from Khajuraho, tumble as a churning mass over black and red rocks. The ticket office is 2km before the falls so if you don't want to pay the high fees for vehicle entry be prepared for a bit of a walk. When you get to the falls there are boats for hire (from Rs50) and it's possible to view gharials – a critically endangered species of crocodile – at nearby **Ken Gharial Sanctuary** (◷ 9am-5pm, closed during monsoon). The road is signposted if you fancy cycling from Khajuraho, or else its Rs300/400 return in an autorickshaw/taxi.

Panna National Park

Sadly, the tigers in this **reserve** (☎ 07732-252135; for park fees see p716; boat ride per hr Rs150; ◷ dawn-dusk Oct-Jun) have all but disappeared (see boxed text, opposite), but this is a great place to see crocodiles and you have a better than average chance of spotting a leopard. In any case, with the Ken River flowing through it, Panna is a peaceful, picturesque place to spend a day on your way to or from Khajuraho.

If you're coming from Khajuraho, about 300m before the Ken River bridge on your left is the **Karnavati Interpretive Centre** (☎ 07732-275231; Indian/foreigner Rs5/50; ◷ 6am-6pm), with a useful introduction to the history and ecology of the area. You can stay here in spacious riverside cottages (Rs1200) with AC, TV, dining area and veranda, or if you have your own gear you can camp (Rs100). There's a restaurant (mains Rs30 to Rs80) and you can arrange your safari here.

Crossing over the bridge, Madla Gate, the most used entrance to the park, is on the edge of Madla village. If you're not staying overnight, you can simply arrange your safari here. A few hundred metres into the village is the **Panna Tiger Reserve Tourist Hut** (☎ 09424791243; r Rs500), which has two large but basic rooms with fans.

Regular buses run between Madla and Khajuraho (Rs25, one hour). For Satna, take either a direct bus (Rs45, 2½ hours) or change at the nearby town of Panna (Rs10, 30 minutes).

PARK LIFE

Name Deepak
Home Panna National Park
Job Naturalist at Karnavati Interpretive Centre
Favourite sighting Sitting with three tourists under the shade of a tree by the Ken River, looking for crocodiles, when blood started dripping onto his shirt sleeve. Looked up to see a leopard sitting in the branches above, devouring a langur monkey.

SATNA
☎ 07672 / pop 229,307

Satna is of no interest to tourists but is a transport link between Khajuraho and the three big tiger parks – Bandhavgarh, Kanha and Pench – around the Jabalpur area.

The bus and train stations are 3km apart (cycle-/autorickshaw Rs10/25). There is an ATM opposite the bus stand and one at the train station, where you'll also find **MP Tourism** (☎ 225471), which is occasionally open.

Hotel Savera (☎ 407777; Rewa Rd; s/d from Rs950/1050, with AC from Rs1350/1650; 🍴) is 500m from the bus stand. **Maheshwari Bhoj** (mains Rs40-100), opposite, does good food.

Four buses go to Khajuraho (Rs75, four hours, 6am, 6.30am, 9am, 2.30pm). At other times you can go via Panna (Rs42, two hours, last bus 6pm). There are also morning buses to Chitrakut (Rs50, three hours, 6am to 10.30am).

Four daily trains go to Varanasi (Rs160/420/573, seven hours), frequent daily trains go to Jabalpur (Rs141/331/436, three hours) and two to Umaria, for Bandhavgarh National Park (Rs121/271/365; three hours, 7pm; four hours, 10.15pm).

CENTRAL MADHYA PRADESH

BHOPAL
☎ 0755 / pop 1.46 million

Split by a pair of central lakes, Bhopal offers two starkly contrasting cityscapes. In the north is the Muslim-dominated old city, a fascinating area of mosques and crowded bazaars. Bhopal's population is 40% Muslim – one of India's highest concentration of Muslims – and the women in black *niqabs* (veils) are reminders of the female Islamic rulers who

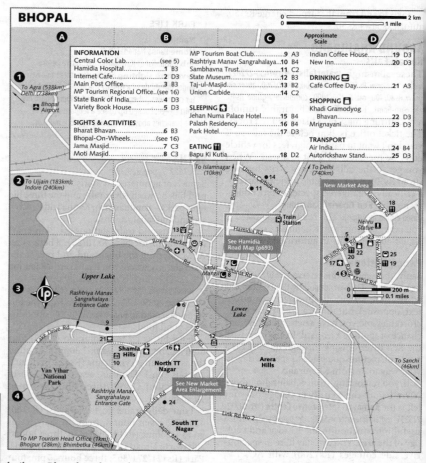

BHOPAL

INFORMATION
Central Color Lab..................(see 5)
Hamidia Hospital.........................**1** B3
Internet Cafe...............................**2** D3
Main Post Office..........................**3** B3
MP Tourism Regional Office..(see 16)
State Bank of India.....................**4** D3
Variety Book House.....................**5** D3

SIGHTS & ACTIVITIES
Bharat Bhavan............................**6** B3
Bhopal-On-Wheels..................(see 16)
Jama Masjid.................................**7** C3
Moti Masjid.................................**8** C3

MP Tourism Boat Club..................**9** A3
Rashtriya Manav Sangrahalaya...**10** B4
Sambhavna Trust........................**11** C2
State Museum.............................**12** B3
Taj-ul-Masjid..............................**13** B2
Union Carbide.............................**14** C2

SLEEPING
Jehan Numa Palace Hotel..........**15** B4
Palash Residency........................**16** B4
Park Hotel..................................**17** D3

EATING
Bapu Ki Kutia.............................**18** D2

Indian Coffee House...................**19** D3
New Inn.....................................**20** D3

DRINKING
Café Coffee Day.........................**21** A3

SHOPPING
Khadi Gramodyog
   Bhavan....................................**22** D3
Mrignayani.................................**23** D3

TRANSPORT
Air India.....................................**24** B4
Autorickshaw Stand...................**25** D3

MADHYA PRADESH & CHHATTISGARH

built up Bhopal in the 19th century. North of here is a reminder of a more recent, tragic history – the Union Carbide plant, site of the world's worst industrial disaster (see boxed text, opposite).

South of the two lakes, Bhopal is more modern, with wide roads, shopping complexes and upmarket hotels and restaurants nestled comfortably in the Arera and Shamla Hills which overlook the lakes and the old city beyond.

Orientation

The train and bus stations are just off Hamidia Rd – the main hotel area – with the bustling *chowk* (marketplace; Map p693) slightly further southeast. Hamidia Rd is accessed via

the Platform 5 end of the train station. The Platform 1 end is where you'll find left luggage (you need your own padlock), MP Tourism, the post office and an ATM.

The 6-sq-km Upper Lake (Map p690) is separated from the smaller Lower Lake (Map p690) by a causeway, which links the old city's maze-like streets with the broad, leafy avenues of the new city, also known as TT Nagar or just New Market. Most of the city's modern shops, banks and facilities are in New Market, Bhopal's central shopping area.

Information

Central Color Lab (Map p690; ☎ 4234000; GTB Complex, Bhadbhada Rd; per disk Rs50; ☂ 10.30am-9pm) CD burning and film processing.

Hamidia Hospital (Map p690; ☎ 2540222; Royal Market Rd)

Internet cafe (Map p690; Rang Mahal Rd; per hr Rs10; ☺ 10am-10pm) There's a cheap internet cafe in New Market.

Main post office (Map p690; ☎ 2531266; Sultania Rd; ☺ 10am-7pm Mon-Sat) Also a counter at the train station.

MP Tourism airport (☺ incoming flights); head office (off Map p690; ☎ 2774340; Bhadbhada Rd; ☺ 10am-5pm); regional office (Map p690; ☎ 3295040; Palash Residency, TT Nagar; ☺ 10am-5.30pm); train station (p690; ☎ 2746827; ☺ 9.30am-5.30pm) Books accommodation and is able to organise guides and transportation.

Raj Medical Store (Map p693; ☎ 2744728; Hamidia Rd; ☺ 9am-9.30pm)

Sainath Internet Cafe (Map p693; per hr Rs15; ☺ 9am-10pm) Off Hamidia Rd.

State Bank of India (Map p690; Rang Mahal Rd; ☺ 10.30am-4.30pm Mon-Fri, 10.30am-1.30pm Sat) Changes travellers cheques and cash. Other ATMs are marked on the maps; there's also an ATM at the train station.

Variety Book House (Map p690; 14-15 GTB Complex, Bhadbhada Rd; ☺ 10am-9.30pm) Stationery, maps and Lonely Planet titles are available here. It also has a wonderful selection of novels.

Dangers & Annoyances
Beware of pickpockets working around the train station and the bus stand, and along Hamidia Rd.

Sights & Activities
MOSQUES
Bhopal's third female ruler, Shah Jahan Begum wanted to create the largest mosque in the world, so in 1877 set about building **Taj-ul-Masjid** (Map p690; ☺ closed to non-Muslims Fri). It was still incomplete at her death in 1901, after funds had been diverted to other projects, and construction did not resume until 1971. Fortresslike terracotta walls surround three gleaming white onion domes and a pair of towering pink minarets with white domes. If you can make the dawn azan (Muslim call to prayer), you won't regret it.

The gold spikes crowning the squat minarets of the **Jama Masjid** (Map p690), built in 1837 by Bhopal's first female ruler, Qudsia Begum, glint serenely above the skull caps and veils swirling through the fascinating bazaar below.

The **Moti Masjid** (Map p690) near Sadar Manzil was built by Qudsia Begum's daughter and Bhopal's second female ruler, Sikander

---

THE BHOPAL DISASTER – A CONTINUING TRAGEDY

At five minutes past midnight on 3 December, 1984, 40 tonnes of deadly methyl isocyanate (MIC) gas leaked out over Bhopal from the US-owned Union Carbide chemical plant (Map p690). Blown by the wind, rivers of the heavy gas coursed through the city. In the ensuing panic, people were trampled trying to escape while others were so disorientated that they ran into the gas.

There were 3828 initial fatalities according to official figures, but the continuing death toll stands at over 20,000, while more than 120,000 people suffer from a catalogue of illnesses from hypertension and diabetes to premature menopause and skin disorders. Their children experience growth disorders, such as shrunken rib cages.

The leak at the plant resulted from a saga of untested technology, negligent maintenance and cost-cutting measures. Damages of US$3 billion were demanded, and in 1989 Union Carbide paid the Indian government US$470 million, but winning compensation for the victims has been a tortuous process slowed by the Indian government's wrangling over who was a victim and Dow Chemical's acquisition of Union Carbide in 2001. Both buyer and seller deny ongoing liability.

Union Carbide also financed the building of a multimillion dollar hospital, while charity **Sambhavna Trust** (Map p690; ☎ 2730914; sambavna@sancharnet.in; Bafna Colony, Berasia Rd; ☺ 8.30am-3pm) treats more than 200 people a day using yoga, allopathic (conventional Western) and Panchakarmic (an ayurvedic procedure for detoxification through medicated oil massage, steam bath and medicinal enema) treatments, and ayurvedic remedies prepared using herbs from its medicinal garden. Volunteers can work in a range of areas from administration and water-testing to medical research and internet communications. They are hugely appreciated and are offered board and lodgings in the charity's excellent centre. Visitors and, of course, donations are also always welcome.

For more information, visit www.bhopal.org or read *Five Past Midnight in Bhopal*, the royalties of which go to disaster victims.

Jahan Begum, in 1860. Similar in style to the Jama Masjid in Delhi, this smaller marble-faced mosque has two dark-red minarets and gold-spiked cupolas. Inside, the kiblah has 11 white arches. The five central-most are marble.

RASHTRIYA MANAV SANGRAHALAYA
A kind of tribal safari park, only without the tribes, the open-air, hillside complex **Rashtriya Manav Sangrahalaya** (Museum of Man; Map p690; ☎ 2661319; Shamla Hills; admission Rs10, vehicle Rs10, video Rs50; 🕑 10am-5.30pm Tue-Sun Sep-Feb, 11am-6.30pm Tue-Sun Mar-Aug) is possibly your best chance to get a taste of India's 450-plus tribes without actually visiting an Adivasi village. Authentic-looking dwellings – built and maintained by Adivasis using traditional tools and materials – dot the hillside. There's a mythological trail and a more conventional museum on the hilltop.

STATE MUSEUM
This first-class **archaeological museum** (Map p690; ☎ 2661856; Shamla Hills; Indian/foreigner Rs10/100, camera/video Rs50/200; 🕑 10.30am-5.30pm Tue-Sun) includes some wonderful temple sculptures as well as 87 Jain bronzes unearthed by a surprised farmer in western Madhya Pradesh. Keep an eye out for the tiny, but remarkably animated, metal carpet seller in the Royal Collections Gallery.

BHARAT BHAVAN
This **cultural centre** (Map p690; ☎ 2660239; admission galleries/performances Rs10/20, galleries free on Fri; 🕑 2-8pm Tue-Sun Feb-Oct, 1-7pm Tue-Sun Nov-Jan) is a serene place to take in modern Indian art, tribal carvings and paintings, a library and private contemporary art galleries. There is a cafe, and regular evening performances (7pm) of poetry, music and theatre.

UPPER LAKE
The **MP Tourism Boat Club** (Map p690; ☎ 3295043; Lake Drive Rd; 🕑 9am-6.30pm winter, 9am-7.30pm summer) offers motorboat rides (per person Rs40, five minutes, minimum three people), pedal boats (per boat Rs30, 30 minutes) and kayaking (per kayak Rs30, 30 minutes).

Tours
Bhopal-On-Wheels (3hr tour adult/child Rs60/30; 🕑 11am) is a guided tour on a toy-train lookalike open bus, departing from **Palash Residency** (Map p690; ☎ 2553066; TT Nagar) and winding through the

hills and the old city. Stops include Lakshmi Narayan Temple, MP Tourism Boat Club and Rashtriya Manav Sangrahalaya. Minimum five passengers.

Provided water levels are high enough, **Lake Princess** (upper deck/AC lower deck Rs75/100; 🕑 6.30pm) cruises Upper Lake for 45 minutes, leaving from MP Tourism Boat Club (left).

Sleeping
All hotels here, including budget ones, add 10% to 15% tax to their listed rates.

HAMIDIA ROAD
Hotel Rama International (Map p693; ☎ 2740542; 2 Hamidia Rd; s/d Rs275/325, with AC Rs550/600; 🏠) Big, airy rooms in this old-school Indian hotel come with clean, tiled flooring and quality wooden furniture. Much better value than its foreign-friendly neighbours, but you may face language problems.

Hotel Richa (Map p693; ☎ 4231980; 1 Hamidia Rd; s Rs320-370, d Rs400-450, s/d with AC Rs570/700, ste Rs900; 🏠) The cheapest rooms are good value with Hollywood films on the TV and decent furniture. Grubby carpets are the only let-down.

Hotel Ranjit (Map p693; ☎ 2740500; ranjeethotels@sancharnet.in; 3 Hamidia Rd; s Rs350-500, d Rs500-650, with AC s Rs550-650, d Rs700-800; 🏠) Rooms are quite small but even the cheapies are clean and smart and come with TV, some artwork and attractive bedspreads. The bar-restaurant (mains Rs72 to Rs126, beer Rs99) is very popular.

Hotel Sonali (Map p693; ☎ 2740880; sonalinn@sancharnet.in; Radha Talkies Rd; s/d from Rs450/495, with AC incl breakfast s Rs600-750, d Rs750-850, ste from Rs1000; 🏠 💻) Excellent service and shiny tiled floors in big rooms make this the best quality option near Hamidia Rd. Some non-AC rooms come with slightly shabby carpets, but all have TV and there's 24-hour internet in the lobby.

NEW CITY
Park Hotel (Map p690; ☎ 4057711; Rang Mahal Rd; s Rs500-650, d Rs600-750, with AC s Rs700-800, d Rs900-1000, ste Rs1100/1400; 🏠) Smart rooms with marble floors, dark-wood furniture, TV and balcony, right in the heart of New Market.

Palash Residency (Map p690; ☎ 2553066; palash@mptourism.com; TT Nagar; s Rs1790-2690, d Rs2090-2990; 🏠) Whitewashed walkways lead to 33 clean and spacious AC rooms, all of which are comfortable albeit lacking character. Bathrooms are cramped for this price range. Has a bar and restaurant.

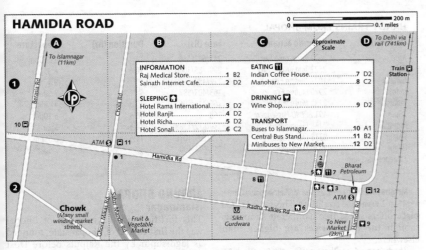

HAMIDIA ROAD

INFORMATION
Raj Medical Store.....................1 B2
Sainath Internet Cafe...............2 D2

SLEEPING
Hotel Rama International.........3 D2
Hotel Ranjit............................4 D2
Hotel Richa.............................5 D2
Hotel Sonali...........................6 C2

EATING
Indian Coffee House................7 D2
Manohar................................8 C2

DRINKING
Wine Shop..............................9 D2

TRANSPORT
Buses to Islamnagar...............10 A1
Central Bus Stand...................11 B2
Minibuses to New Market........12 D2

Jehan Numa Palace Hotel (Map p690; ☎ 2661100; www.hoteljehanumapalace.com; 157 Shamla Hill; incl breakfast, cottage s/d Rs2950/3550, s Rs3950-5950, d Rs4850-6850, ste Rs9550-12000; ⚡ 🖥 🛜 🏊) This former 19th-century palace lost none of its colonial charm through conversion into a top-class hotel. Arched walkways and immaculate lawns lead you to beautifully decorated rooms. There's a palm-lined pool, an excellent health spa and three restaurants including one under the shade of an enormous mango tree.

Eating & Drinking

Manohar (Map p693; 6 Hamidia Rd; mains Rs24-74; ⏰ 6am-11pm) There's only *chhole* (masala chickpeas, served with *puri*, a flat savoury dough that puffs up when deep fried) to go with your tea or coffee in the morning, but mains – pizza, Chinese, South Indian – are served from midday onwards. Has an impressive range of Indian confectionary at a side counter.

Bapu Ki Kutia (Map p690; Sultania Rd; mains Rs35-70; ⏰ 10am-11pm) Papa's Shack has been serving up delicious Indian veg dishes since the '60s and is so popular you may have to share a table. There's an English menu, but no English sign. Look for the picture of a beach hut and palm tree above the door.

Indian Coffee House (Map p693; Hamidia Rd; mains Rs35-85; ⏰ 7am-10.30pm) Not as salubrious as the New Market branch (Map p690), but nonetheless a top spot for a breakfast of filter coffee and scrambled eggs. The usual South Indian favourites – dosa, *idli* and *vada* (doughnut-shaped deep-fried lentil savoury) – are all

here too, as are the waiters with the white fan-tailed hats.

New Inn (Map p690; Bhadbhada Rd; mains Rs40-110; ⏰ 8am-10.30pm) Clean and colourful split-level restaurant with a well-priced menu served by staff in waistcoats and bow ties. There are good breakfast choices, including filter coffee (Rs10), but it's the delicious main courses that hit the spot. If you like a bit of spice, don't leave this place without trying the *mattar paneer* (unfermented cheese and pea curry).

Café Coffee Day (Map p690; Lake Drive Rd; coffee from Rs28; ⏰ 8.30am-10.30pm) Quality fresh coffee and overpriced snacks come with the best view in town. Very popular with Bhopal's young crowd.

Wine Shop (Map p693; Hamidia Rd; draft beer Rs30; ⏰ 9.30am-midnight) One of a number of bottle shops on this stretch of Hamidia Rd, this one has the added attraction of beer on tap. You'll have to drink it standing on the pavement, however, as there are no tables or chairs.

Shopping

Bhopal's two main shopping areas are the small shops and stalls around New Market and the labyrinthine alleys of the *chowk* that weave their way towards the Jama Masjid (p691). Both areas stock delicate gold and silver jewellery, fancifully woven saris, hand-embroidered appliqué skirts and *jari* (glittering embroidery, often including shards of mirror or glass) shoulder bags, a speciality of Bhopal.

MADHYA PRADESH &
CHHATTISGARH

HANDY TRAINS FROM BHOPAL

Destination	Train No & name	Fare (Rs)	Duration (hr)	Departure
Agra	2627 Karnataka Exp	247/641/866	7	11.50pm
Delhi	2621 Tamil Nadu Exp	299/785/1066	10½	8.35pm
Gwalior	1077 Jhelum Exp	172/480/655	6	9.15am
Indore	2920 Malwa Exp	163/403/537	5	7.50am
Jabalpur	8233 Narmada Exp	166/418/596	7	11.35pm
Jaipur*	491 BPL JU Passenger	168	16½	5.10pm
Mumbai	2138 Punjab Mail	330/872/1188	14½	5pm
Raipur	8238 Chhattisgarh Exp	273/709/1016	14½	6.55pm
Ujjain	2920 Malwa Exp	141/326/430	3½	7.50am

*Sleeper class only

Mrignayani (Map p690; 23 New Market Shopping Centre; 11am-2.30pm & 3.30-8pm Tue-Sun) This state-owned place offers stress-free handicraft shopping, though the fixed prices are higher than elsewhere.

Khadi Gramodyog Bhavan (Map p690; Bhadbhada Rd; 11am-8pm) Pyjamas, head scarves and shirts made from *khadi* cotton, plus some quality *khadi* silk garments. Next-day tailoring service available.

Getting There & Away

AIR

Air India (Map p690; ☎ 2770480; Bhadbhada Rd; 10am-5pm Mon-Sat) flies daily to Delhi (from Rs4755, one hour) and Mumbai (from Rs4955, two hours) via Indore (Rs4000, 20 minutes).

BUS

From the **central bus stand** (Map p693; ☎ 4257602; Hamidia Rd), buses go to Bhimbetka (Rs30, one hour), Sanchi (Rs25, 1½ hours), Vidisha (Rs35, two hours), Indore (Rs110, five hours) and Ujjain (Rs110, five hours). Five daily buses go to Pachmarhi (Rs113, six hours, 5.15am, 6.15am, 8.15am, 10.15am, 3pm) while regular private buses go to Jabalpur (Rs180, nine hours).

TRAIN

There are more than 20 daily trains to Gwalior and Agra and more than 10 to Ujjain and Delhi. See boxed text, above.

Getting Around

Minibuses and buses (both Rs5) for New Market leave almost constantly from the corner of Hamidia Rd, while an autorickshaw costs about Rs40. The airport is 16km northwest of central Bhopal. Expect to pay Rs100/200 for an autorickshaw/taxi.

AROUND BHOPAL
Islamnagar

This fortified city 11km north of Bhopal was the first capital of Bhopal state, founded as Jagdishpur by the Rajputs before Dost Mohammed Khan occupied and renamed it in the early 18th century. The still-standing walls enclose two villages and remains including two **palaces** (Indian/foreigner Rs10/250; dawn-dusk), Chaman Mahal and Rani Mahal.

The 18th-century **Chaman Mahal** is a synthesis of traditional Indian and Islamic architecture with Bengali-influenced drooping eaves. The main attraction is the Mughal water garden. There is also an interpretation centre, giving a fragmented view of local history, and a *hammam* (Turkish bath) with changing rooms and water troughs in the dark, cool interior.

Adjacent is the dusty 19th-century **Rani Mahal** with a colonnaded Diwan-i-Am. Outside stand eight massive iron treasure chests, presumably delivered by outsized porters from the nearby *hathi khana* (elephant stables).

Catch a tempo or bus (both Rs10) up Berasia Rd (Map p693), though you may have to change, or take an autorickshaw (Rs100).

Bhojpur

Built by the founder of Bhopal, Raja Bhoj (1010–53), Bhojpur used to be home to a 400-sq-km manmade lake, which was destroyed in the 15th century by the dam-busting Mandu ruler Hoshang Shah. Thankfully, the magnificent **Bhojeshwar Temple** survived the attack.

Square in shape and simple in design, this 1000-year-old Hindu temple doesn't look much from the outside, but the interior of the sanctum, supported by four gargantuan pillars and housing the world's tallest Shiva lingam

(22ft), is very powerful indeed. Beautifully carved figures now share space with beehive honeycombs on the part-restored ceiling.

Round the back, a large stony ramp illustrates how such huge pieces of rock would have been moved into position onto the temple's 17ft-tall platform. Off to the side, fenced-off areas of rocky slopes show etchings of grander plans for a temple complex which was never in fact finished.

Take the Bhimbetka bus to the turn-off for Bhojpur (Rs10, 30 minutes), where tempos (Rs10) ply the 11km-road to the temple.

Bhimbetka

Secreted in a forest of teak and sal in craggy cliffs 46km south of Bhopal are more than 700 **rock shelters** (Indian/foreigner Rs10/100, vehicle Rs50/200; ☉ dawn-dusk). Around 500 of them contain some of the world's oldest prehistoric paintings.

Thanks to their natural red and white pigments, the colours are remarkably well preserved and, in certain caves, paintings of different eras adorn the same rock surface. A gamut of figures and scenes spill across the rocks: gaurs (Indian bison), rhinoceroses, bears and tigers, and scenes of hunting, initiation ceremonies, childbirth, communal dancing and drinking, religious rites and burials.

The oldest paintings (Upper Palaeolithic) in red, often of huge animals, are thought to be 12,000 years old. Successive periods depict hunting tools, trade with the agricultural communities on the Malwa plains, and, still later, religious scenes involving tree gods. The latest are crude geometric figures probably dating from the medieval period, when much of the artistry was lost.

The rock shelters are easy to find. The 15 most accessible are numbered, signposted and linked by a concrete path. **Zoo Rock Shelter** (Shelter 4), famous for its variety of animal paintings, is one of the first you come to; **Shelter 15** features a magnificent red bison attacking a helpless stick figure. There are no facilities here, so bring water.

Highway Treat Bhimbetka (☎ 07480-281558; r Rs890; ❄), with a pleasant restaurant-cafe (mains Rs60 to Rs100), a children's playground and five comfortable AC rooms, is by the Bhimbetka turning, 3km from the rock shelters. The ticket office is halfway up the road to the rocks from here.

Ask your bus driver to drop you at the turning for Bhimbetka, about 6.5km beyond Obaidullaganj. It's a 45-minute, 3km walk from here. Alternatively, take an autorickshaw from Obaidullaganj.

On the return journey, flag down anything that moves (buses often won't stop for you) and go as far as Obaidullaganj (Rs5), where you'll find buses to Bhopal (Rs20) via the Bhojpur turning (Rs10).

SANCHI
☎ 07482 / pop 6784

Rising from the plains, 46km northeast of Bhopal, is a rounded hill topped with some of India's oldest Buddhist structures.

In 262 BC, repentant of the horrors he had inflicted on Kalinga in present-day Orissa, the Mauryan emperor Ashoka (see boxed text, p41) embraced Buddhism. As a penance he built the Great Stupa at Sanchi, near the birthplace of his wife. A domed edifice used to house religious relics, it was the first Buddhist monument in the region and many other religious structures followed.

As Hinduism gradually reabsorbed Buddhism, the site decayed and was forgotten,

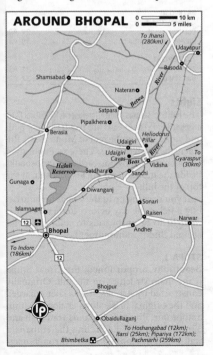

AROUND BHOPAL

0   10 km
0   5 miles

To Jhansi (280km)
Udaypur
Shamsabad
Basoda
Nateran
Betwa River
Satpara
Pipalkhera
Berasia
Heliodorus Pillar
Udaigiri
Udaigiri Caves
Beas River
To Gyaraspur (30km)
Halali Reservoir
Satdhara
Vidisha
Sanchi
Gunaga
Diwanganj
Sonari
Islamnagar
Raisen
Narwar
12
Bhopal
Andher
To Indore (186km)
12
Bhojpur
Obaidullaganj
To Hoshangabad (12km); Itarsi (25km); Pipariya (172km); Pachmarhi (259km)
Bhimbetka

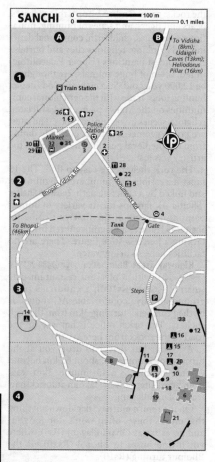

until being rediscovered in 1818 by a British army officer.

Although Sanchi can be visited from Bhopal, this crossroads village is a relaxing spot to spend the night, and a number of side trips can be taken from here.

Orientation & Information

The Bhopal–Vidisha road intersects Monuments Rd, which leads from the train station to the hill with the stupas.

Canara Bank (Monuments Rd; 10.30am-4pm Mon-Fri, 10.30am-1pm Sat) Changes travellers cheques and cash.

Health centre (266724; Monuments Rd; consultation Rs100; 9am-1pm Mon-Sat)

Internet (per hr Rs40; 8am-10.30pm) At the market

Post office (Monuments Rd; 9am-3pm Mon-Sat)

Sights

The hilltop **stupas** (Indian/foreigner Rs10/250, car Rs10, museum Rs5; dawn-dusk) are reached via a path and stone steps at the end of Monuments Rd, where the ticket office is. There's a Publication Sale Counter selling postcards and guidebooks inside the monuments enclosure itself, at the top of the hill.

If you're going up to the stupas for sunrise, buy a ticket the day before. Remember, it is thought to be auspicious to walk clockwise around Buddhist monuments.

STUPA 1

Beautifully proportioned, the Great Stupa is the main structure on the hill. Originally constructed by Ashoka, it was later enlarged and the original brick stupa enclosed within a stone one. Presently it stands 16m high and 37m in diameter. Encircling the stupa is a wall which has four entrances through magnificently carved *toranas* (gateways) that are the finest Buddhist works of art in Sanchi, if not India.

TORANAS

Four gateways were erected around 35 BC and had all completely fallen down when the site was rediscovered. Scenes carved onto the pillars and their triple architraves are mainly tales from the Jatakas, episodes from Buddha's various lives. At this stage in Buddhist art he was never represented directly – his presence was alluded to through symbols. The lotus stands for his birth, the bodhi tree his enlightenment, the wheel his teachings, and the footprint and throne his presence. The stupa itself also symbolises Buddha.

Northern Gateway

Topped by a broken wheel of law, this is the best preserved of the *toranas*. Scenes include a monkey offering a bowl of honey to Buddha, represented by a bodhi tree. Another panel depicts the Miracle of Sravasti – one of several miracles represented here – in which Buddha, again in the form of a bodhi tree, ascends a road into the air. Elephants support the architraves above the columns, while delicately carved *yakshis* (maidens) hang nonchalantly on each side.

Eastern Gateway

This gateway's breathtakingly carved figure of a *yakshi*, hanging from an architrave, is one of Sanchi's best-known images. One of the pillars, supported by elephants, features scenes from Buddha's entry to nirvana. Another shows Buddha's mother Maya's dream of an elephant standing on the moon, which she had when he was conceived. Across the front of the middle architrave is the Great Departure, when Buddha (a riderless horse) renounced the sensual life and set out to find enlightenment.

Southern Gateway

The back-to-back lions supporting the oldest gateway form the state emblem of India and can be seen on every banknote. The gateway narrates Ashoka's life as a Buddhist, with scenes of Buddha's birth and another representation of the Great Departure. Also featured is the Chhaddanta Jataka, a story in which Bodhisattva (Buddha before he had reached enlightenment) took on the form of

an elephant king who had six tusks. The less favoured of the elephant king's two wives was so jealous of the other that she decided to starve herself to death, vowing to come back to life as the queen of Benares in order to have the power to avenge her husband's favouritism. Her wish came true and as queen she ordered hunters to track down and kill the elephant king. A hunter found the great elephant but before he could kill it, the elephant handed over his tusks, an act so noble it led to the queen dying of remorse.

Western Gateway

Potbellied dwarfs support the architraves of this gateway, which has some of the site's most interesting scenes. The top architrave shows Buddha in seven different incarnations, manifested three times as a stupa and four times as a tree. The rear of one pillar shows Buddha resisting the Temptation of Mara (the Buddhist personification of evil, often called the Buddhist devil), while demons flee and angels cheer.

OTHER STUPAS

Stupa 2 is halfway down the hill to the west. If you come from the town by the main route you can walk back down via Stupa 2. Instead of gateways, 'medallions' decorate the surrounding wall – naive in design, but full of energy and imagination. Flowers, animals and people – some mythological – ring the stupa.

Stupa 3 is northeast of the main stupa and similar in design, though smaller, with a single, rather fine gateway. It once contained relics of two important disciples of Buddha, Sari Puttha and Maha Moggallana. They were moved to London in 1853 but returned in 1953 and are now kept in the modern *vihara* (resting place). The Chethiyagiri Vihara Festival is held here every November (see boxed text, p671).

Only the base is left of the 2nd-century-BC **Stupa 4**, which stands behind Stupa 3. Between Stupas 1 and 3 is the small **Stupa 5**, unusual in that it once had an image of Buddha, now displayed in the museum.

PILLARS

Of the scattered remains of pillars, the most important is **Pillar 10**, erected by Ashoka but later broken. Two upper sections of this beautifully proportioned and executed shaft lie side by side under a shelter 20m away; the capital (head of the pillar, usually sculpted) is in the museum (below). **Pillar 25**, dating from the Sunga period (2nd century BC), and the 5th-century-AD **Pillar 35** are less impressive.

TEMPLES

Temple 18 is a *chaitya* (prayer room or assembly hall) remarkably similar in style to classical Greek-columned buildings. It dates from around the 7th century AD, but traces of earlier wooden buildings have been discovered beneath it. Nearby is the small **Temple 17**, also Greek-like. The large **Temple 40**, slightly southeast, in part dates back to the Ashokan period.

The rectangular **Temple 31** was built in the 6th or 7th century but reconstructed during the 10th or 11th century. It contains a well-executed image of Buddha.

MONASTERIES

The earliest monasteries were made of wood and are long gone. The usual plan is of a central courtyard surrounded by monastic cells. **Monasteries 45** and **47**, standing on the eastern ridge, date from the transition from Buddhism to Hinduism, with strong Hindu elements in their design. The former has two sitting Buddhas. The one housed inside is exceptional.

Behind **Monastery 51**, partway down the hill towards Stupa 2, is the **Great Bowl**, carved from a boulder, into which food and offerings were placed for distribution to the monks. The **vihara** (9am-5pm) was built to house the returned relics from Stupa 3. They can be viewed on the last Sunday of the month.

ARCHAEOLOGICAL MUSEUM

This **museum** (10am-5pm Sat-Thu; admission Rs5) has a small collection of sculptures from the site. The centrepiece is the lion capital from the Ashoka Pillar 10. Other highlights include a *yakshi* hanging from a mango tree, and beautifully serene Buddha figures in red sandstone – some of the earliest found anywhere.

Sleeping & Eating

Sri Lanka Mahabodhi Society Guest House (☎ 2266699; Monuments Rd; d & tr Rs100-150, with AC & bathroom Rs350; ﹢) Visiting Buddhists stay here in cloistered rooms around a peaceful garden quadrangle – there's even a prayer room. The monks are friendly and it's great value

if you don't mind basic rooms with shared bathrooms.

Krishna Hotel (☎ 266610; Bhopal-Vidisha Rd; dm Rs100, d Rs200-250) Simple rooftop rooms, some with sit-down flush toilets, are slightly more expensive than the darker, noisier rooms at the front. A large hall is sometimes used as a dorm. It's above Jaiswal Medical Store.

New Jaiswal Lodge (☎ 266508; Monuments Rd; d/tr Rs200/300) Right outside the train station, this friendly place, set around a colourful courtyard, has basic rooms with sit-down flush toilets.

Gateway Retreat (☎ 266723; www.mptourism .com; Bhopal–Vidisha Rd; s/d with breakfast Rs1490/1690, ste Rs1990; ﹢) The smartest hotel in Sanchi, this MP Tourism property has good-quality AC rooms around well-kept gardens, plus a bar (beer Rs120) and restaurant (mains Rs45 to Rs125, open 7am to 11pm).

Gateway Cafeteria (☎ 266743; Monuments Rd; mains Rs35-110; 7am-10.30pm) MP Tourism also runs this place, which has two four-bed, air-cooled rooms (per bed Rs150).

By the bus stand, **Pal Restaurant** (9am-10pm) and next-door Pathak Restaurant will whip you up a veg thali for Rs30.

Getting There & Around

Frequent local buses connect Sanchi with Bhopal (Rs25, 1½ hours, 6am to 8pm) and Vidisha (Rs5, 20 minutes, 6am to 7.30pm). It's better to wait at the crossroads for buses as some don't bother going into the bus stand.

Four daily trains go from Bhopal to Sanchi (sleeper Rs121, 40 minutes) at 8am, 3.15pm, 5.10pm and 6pm. Only three go in the other direction (8am, 8.40am and 4.30pm) and they take almost twice as long.

You can rent bicycles at the market for Rs4 per hour (from 8am to 7pm).

AROUND SANCHI
Vidisha
☎ 07592 / pop 125,453

This small but thriving market town, 8km northeast of Sanchi, was a commercial centre in the 5th and 6th centuries BC. These days it's a great place for a wander or a chai break en route to the Udaigiri Caves (opposite).

Many of the attractive whitewashed or painted buildings still have old wooden balconies that overlook the market streets where horse-drawn carts share space with scooters and rickshaws. There are also a number of brightly coloured temples dotted around the old town, which is located to the left of the main road from Sanchi.

Past the town, and over the railway line, is the dusty **District Museum** (Sagar-Vidisha Rd; Indian/foreigner Rs5/50, camera Rs50; ☼ 10am-5pm Tue-Sun), which houses some beautiful sculptures recovered from local sites, the most impressive of which is a 3m-high, 2nd-century-BC stone statue of Kuber Yaksha, treasurer of the gods, on display as you enter.

It's a straightforward 30-minute cycle from Sanchi or else there are frequent buses (Rs5, 20 minutes, until 7.30pm).

Udaigiri Caves

Cut into a sandstone hill, about 5km northwest of Vidisha, are some 20 Gupta **cave shrines** (☼ dawn-dusk) dating from the reign of Chandragupta II (AD 382–401). Most are Hindu but two, near the top of the hill, are Jain (Caves 1 and 20) – unfortunately both are closed due to unsafe roofs.

In Cave 4 is a lingam bearing Shiva's face complete with a third eye. Cave 5 contains the finest carving – a superb image of Vishnu in his boar incarnation topped with a frieze of gods, who also flank the entrance to Cave 6. Lotus-ceilinged Cave 7 was cut out for the personal use of Chandragupta II. On the top of the hill are ruins of a 6th-century Gupta temple dedicated to the sun god.

To get here by bike from Sanchi, head to Vidisha and 50m past the bus stand (still on the main road from Sanchi), turn left past a small white temple and carry on into the fascinating old town. Continue straight all the way through the centre and out of town until you cross the Betwa River where you'll see a sign for the caves on your left. A rickshaw from Vidisha will cost Rs50 return, Rs100 from Sanchi.

Heliodorus Pillar

The Heliodorus Pillar (Khamb Baba), 3km beyond the Udaigiri Caves turning, was erected by a Greek ambassador, Heliodorus, from Taxila (now in Pakistan), in about 140 BC, and dedicated to Vasudeva. The pillar is worshipped by local fishermen. On full-moon nights one is chained to the pillar, becomes possessed and is able to drive evil spirits from other locals. When someone has been exorcised, they drive a nail into the tamarind tree nearby, fixing to it a lime, a piece of coconut,

a red thread and supposedly the spirit. The large tree is bristling with old nails.

PACHMARHI

☎ 07578 / pop 11,370 / elev 1067m

This small mountain town surrounded by waterfalls, cave temples and the forested ranges of the Satpura National Park offers a perfect escape from steamy central India.

Even if you don't go on an organised trek or jeep safari, you can easily spend a couple of days here cycling or hiking to the numerous sights before taking a dip in one of the natural pools that dot the area.

Explorer Captain J Forsyth 'discovered' Pachmarhi as late as 1857 and set up India's first Forestry Department at Bison Lodge in 1862. Soon after, the British army set up regional headquarters here, starting an association with the military that remains today.

Orientation

The main road into Pachmarhi passes the bus stand at the northwest end of the village, which has a bazaar, several hotels and some delightful whitewashed buildings with original wooden features such as beams and balconies. The road continues southwest for about 2km to the seven-way junction called Jaistambha, where more accommodation is found.

Information

Bagri Internet Cafe (Patel Rd; per hr Rs30; ☼ 11am-11pm)

MP Tourism (☎ 252100; ☼ 10am-5pm Mon-Sat) Near Jaistambha; also has a small kiosk at the bus stand.

Post office (☎ 252050; ☼ 10am-6pm Mon-Sat) Near Jaistambha.

State Bank of India ATM (cnr main road & Patel Rd)

Sights & Activities

A ticket for **Satpura National Park** (Indian/foreigner per day Rs20/200, jeep entry Indian/foreigner Rs250/1500; ☼ dawn-dusk) must be bought at the **ticket office** (☼ 8am-8pm) outside Bison Lodge. It includes entry to Bison Lodge Museum, Bee Falls, Duchess Falls, Reechgarh, Astachal, Ramykund and Rajat Prapat (including Panchuli Kund and Apsara Vihar). Other sights are free. Most decent-length treks, and all wildlife safaris, will also require a park ticket.

Captain Forsyth named **Bison Lodge** (☎ 225130; ☼ 8am-noon & 4-7pm Tue-Sun Apr-Oct, 9am-1pm & 3-7pm Tue-Sun Nov-Mar) after a herd of bison

MADHYA PRADESH & CHHATTISGARH

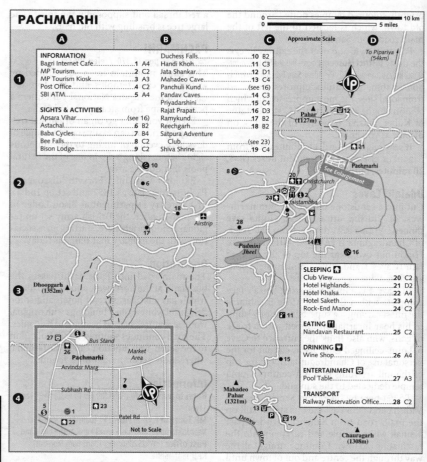

PACHMARHI

0 — 10 km
0 — 5 miles
Approximate Scale

INFORMATION
Bagri Internet Cafe.............................**1** A4
MP Tourism..**2** C2
MP Tourism Kiosk................................**3** A3
Post Office...**4** C2
SBI ATM...**5** A4

SIGHTS & ACTIVITIES
Apsara Vihar...................................(see 16)
Astachal...**6** B2
Baba Cycles...**7** B4
Bee Falls..**8** C2
Bison Lodge...**9** C2
Duchess Falls.....................................**10** B2
Handi Khoh..**11** C3
Jata Shankar......................................**12** D1
Mahadeo Cave...................................**13** C4
Panchuli Kund..............................(see 16)
Pandav Caves.....................................**14** C3
Priyadarshini......................................**15** C4
Rajat Prapat.......................................**16** D3
Ramykund...**17** B2
Reechgarh...**18** B2
Satpura Adventure
  Club...(see 23)
Shiva Shrine.......................................**19** C4

To Pipariya
(54km)

Pahar
(1127m)

Pachmarhi

See Enlargement

Christchurch

Jaistamba

Dhoopgarh
(1352m)

Airstrip

Padmini
Jheel

SLEEPING
Club View..**20** C2
Hotel Highlands.................................**21** D2
Hotel Khalsa......................................**22** A4
Hotel Saketh......................................**23** A4
Rock-End Manor................................**24** C2

EATING
Nandavan Restaurant.......................**25** C2

DRINKING
Wine Shop...**26** A4

ENTERTAINMENT
Pool Table...**27** A3

TRANSPORT
Railway Reservation Office...............**28** C2

Bus Stand

Pachmarhi

Arvindar Marg

Market
Area

Subhash Rd

Patel Rd

Not to Scale

Mahadeo
Pahar
(1321m)

Denwa
River

Chauragarh
(1308m)

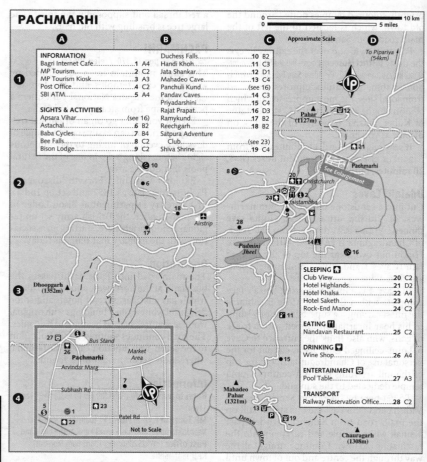

he spotted here. It's now an interesting museum focusing on the history, flora and fauna of the Satpura region.

The nearest sight to Pachmarhi village is **Jata Shankar**, a cave temple in a beautiful gorge about 2.5km along a good track that's signed just north of the town limits. The small Shiva shrine is hidden under a huge overhanging rock.

Just south of town, past Christchurch, **Bee Falls** are also easy to reach by bike. There are chai and snack stalls on the way down to the bottom.

On the same road west of Christchurch are the access roads for **Duchess Falls**, the two beauty points known as **Reechgarh** and **Astachal**, and a small, crystal-clear pool called **Ramykund**.

Just southeast of Jaistamba, you'll find **Pandav Caves**. The foundations of a brick Buddhist stupa have been excavated on top of the caves, which are believed to have been carved by Buddhists as early as the 4th century. About 1km past the caves is the trailhead for **Rajat Prapat** (Big Fall), where a waterfall cascades down a gully in a sheer cliff. In the forest nearby are **Panchuli Kund**, five descending rock pools leading to **Apsara Vihar** (Fairy Pool).

Directly south of Jaistamba is the road that leads towards **Chauragarh** (1308m), Madhya Pradesh's third-highest peak. The Shiva shrine at the top attracts tens of thousands of pilgrims during Shivaratri Mela (see boxed text, p671). On the way, stop at **Handi Khoh**, also known as Suicide Point, to gawk down the 100m canyon into the dense forest. You'll spy Chauragarh in the distance from here as well as **Priyadarshini** (Forsyth Point).

About 3km beyond Priyadarshini the road ends at **Mahadeo Cave**, where a path 30m into the damp gloom reveals a lingam with attendant priest. This is the beginning of the 1365-step pilgrim trail to Chauragarh (five hours' return hike). A kilometre further on, another **Shiva shrine** is at the back of a terrifyingly narrow passage created by sticks holding open a fissure in the cliff.

CYCLING
All the sights mentioned here can be cycled to, although bikes have to be left at the trailheads from where the hiking begins. **Baba Cycles** (Subhash Rd; hr/day Rs5/40; ☯ 10am-9pm) rents bikes.

PARASAILING
Vinay Sahu of **Satpura Adventure Club** (☎ 252256, 09425367365; per person Rs250, minimum 2 people; ☯ 9am-5pm), based at Hotel Saketh, arranges parasailing at the airstrip near Reechgarh.

SWIMMING
Locals paddle at the bottom of Bee Falls and Duchess Falls, and Ramykund is good for an invigorating plunge, but for a proper swim, try Apsara Vihar.

TREKKING
Again, contact Vinay of Satpura Adventure Club (above). His guides (per day Rs250; Hindi-speaking only) can also take you on a two-day trip deep into the forest with an overnight stay in a tribal village (per person all inclusive Rs600, minimum two people). Alternatively, arrange a forestry commission guide (per day Rs350) at Bison Lodge ticket office. Some speak English.

WILDLIFE SAFARIS
The national park has tigers and leopards, although you're almost as likely to see a dodo. What you will get, though, is virgin forests without another tourist jeep in sight, plus plenty of monkeys, deer and birds of all types. A two-day, one-night stay inside the reserve can be arranged at Bison Lodge ticket office. Jeep hire is Rs4000 per jeep for two days. Park entrance is Rs1500 per jeep per day, while accommodation at a forest rest house is Rs600

for a double room. Food costs are on top of this.

Sleeping & Eating
High seasons are from April to July and December/January, when places fill up and room rates rocket. The same applies during national holidays and major festivals. Hotel Saketh and Hotel Khalsa have decent restaurants. Hotel Khalsa's is particularly good.

PACHMARHI VILLAGE
Hotel Saketh (☎ 252165; hotelsaket2003@yahoo.com; r Rs200-500, with AC Rs700; ☒) There is a wide range of rooms in this friendly hotel on a quiet side street off Patel Rd, from budget classics to midrange options with AC and bathtub. The restaurant Raj Bhoj (mains Rs30 to Rs90) produces Gujarati, Bengali Chinese and South Indian dishes, including delicious breakfast dosa.

Hotel Khalsa (☎ 252991; Patel Rd; r Rs350-400) Portraits of gurus decorate this Sikh-run hotel. Some rooms have mattresses on concrete beds. Others have incredibly kitsch bed-cabinet combos in one corner. All have TV, bathroom and small balcony. The restaurant (mains Rs38 to Rs100) is very good here and serves a tremendous veg Punjabi thali (Rs60).

Hotel Highlands (☎ 252099; highland@mptourism .com; Pipariya Rd; r Rs890, with AC Rs1290; ☒) A number of five-room bungalows with green, corrugated-iron roofs dot well-tended gardens with a children's play area. Rooms have high ceilings, dressing rooms, modern bathrooms and verandas. There's also a restaurant.

JAISTAMBA AREA
our pick Club View (☎ 252801; r Rs1200) This spearmint-coloured colonial building near Christchurch has six charming rooms, all different. Some are in a small outhouse, but try to nab one in the main building, with wonderfully high wood-beam ceilings, stone fireplaces and period furniture. Big clean bathrooms have sit-down flush toilet and modern shower.

Rock-End Manor (☎ 252079; mptremph@sancharnet .in; r Rs4190; ☒) A gorgeous, whitewashed heritage building, Rock-End is perched above the parched fairways of the army golf course. Like Club View, spacious rooms have wonderfully high ceilings, but here the furnishings are more luxurious with quality upholstery and framed paintings. There are also great views to be had from seating areas around the covered walkway.

Nandavan Restaurant (mains Rs30-90; ☺ 8am-11pm) An outdoor restaurant with an interesting take on the concept of a zoo, as monkeys sit outside watching humans eating in a cage. South Indian, Gujarati and thalis.

Drinking & Entertainment

The **Wine Shop** (Pipariya Rd; ☺ 8am-11pm) near the bus stand sells beer (Rs90) and spirits. Opposite is an open-sided *paan* kiosk which has a **pool table** (per hr Rs80; ☺ 8am-9pm).

Getting There & Away

Nine buses go to Bhopal (Rs115, six hours, 7am, 8am, 9am, 1pm, 1.30pm, 3pm, 3.30pm, 6.30pm, 8pm). The two evening ones are sleepers and carry on to Indore (seat/bed Rs270/320, 12 hours). There are three buses – all nonsleeper – to Nagpur (Rs190, eight hours, 8am, 10am, 9pm). The friendly guys at the bus-ticket counter are around from 7am to 9pm.

All Bhopal buses, plus some extra local ones (6.30am, 10.45am, 12.30pm, 3.30pm, 5pm) go via Pipariya (Rs40, two hours) from where you can catch trains to onward destinations such as Jabalpur and Varanasi without having to go all the way to Bhopal. Train tickets can be bought at the **Railway Reservation Office** (☺ 8am-2pm) beside the forlorn Woodlands Adventure Camp. The bus station and train station in Pipariya are next to each other.

Getting Around

A place in a shared jeep costs about Rs150 for a day. Cycling (p701) will give you more freedom.

WESTERN MADHYA PRADESH

UJJAIN

☎ 0734 / pop 431,162

First impressions aren't always as they seem. Give Ujjain a chance. The area around the train and bus stations is a mess, but wander down towards the ghats – exploring the maze of tiny alleys along the way – and you'll discover an older, more spiritual side to the town which has been attracting pilgrims for hundreds of years. An undeniable energy pulses

through the temples here – perhaps because of their Hindu significance or perhaps because the Tropic of Cancer runs through Ujjain.

The city is one of four sites which host the Kumbh Mela (p838), during which millions bathe in the Shipra River. It takes place here every 12 years, normally during April and May (see boxed text, p704).

History

The Guptas, the Mandu sultans, Maharaja Jai Singh (of Jaipur fame), the Marathas and the Scindias have all had a controlling hand in Ujjain's long and chequered past, which stretches back to when the city, originally called Avantika, was an important trade stop. When the Scindias moved their capital to Gwalior in 1810, Ujjain's prominence declined rapidly.

Orientation

The train line divides the city. The newer part is to the southeast, centred on the wedding-cake Clock Tower. The far more interesting old section, including most of the temples, narrow lanes and the ghats, is to the northwest. The alleys here, dotted with wooden buildings and small shrines, wind their way southwest from Gopal Mandir, down towards Ram Ghat.

Information

There are ATMs all over Ujjain, some of which are marked on the map, but the nearest place to change money is Indore.

MP Tourism (☎ 2561544; toujjain@mptourism.com; ☺ 10am-5pm Mon-Sat) In the train station.
Net 2 Net (per hr Rs15; ☺ 10am-11pm) Other, less-comfortable internet cafes can be found by the Clock Tower.

Sights

TEMPLES

Mahakaleshwar Mandir

While this is not the most stunning temple, tagging along behind a conga-line through the underground chambers can be magical. At nonfestival times, the marble walkways are a peaceful preamble to the subterranean chamber containing one of India's 12 sacred Shiva shrines known as *jyoti linga* – naturally occurring lingam believed to derive currents of *shakti* (creative energies) from within themselves rather than being ritually invested with *mantra-shakti* by priests. The

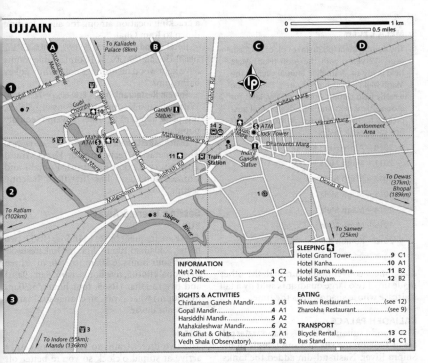

UJJAIN

INFORMATION	
Net 2 Net	1 C2
Post Office	2 C1

SIGHTS & ACTIVITIES	
Chintaman Ganesh Mandir	3 A3
Gopal Mandir	4 A1
Harsiddhi Mandir	5 A2
Mahakaleshwar Mandir	6 A2
Ram Ghat & Ghats	7 A1
Vedh Shala (Observatory)	8 B2

SLEEPING	
Hotel Grand Tower	9 C1
Hotel Kanha	10 A1
Hotel Rama Krishna	11 B2
Hotel Satyam	12 B2

EATING	
Shivam Restaurant	(see 12)
Zharokha Restaurant	(see 9)

TRANSPORT	
Bicycle Rental	13 C2
Bus Stand	14 C1

temple was destroyed by Altamish in 1235 and restored by the Scindias in the 19th century. You may be asked to give a donation, but it's not compulsory.

Gopal Mandir
The Scindias built this magnificent, marble-spired example of Maratha architecture in the 19th century. Muslim pillagers originally stole the sanctum's silver-plated doors from Somnath Temple in Gujarat (p755) and installed them in Ghazni, Afghanistan. Mohammed Shah Abdati later took them to Lahore (in present-day Pakistan), before Mahadji Scindia brought them back here.

Harsiddhi Mandir
Built during the Maratha period, this temple enshrines a famous image of goddess Annapurna. At the entrance, two tall black-ened stone towers bristling with lamps are a special feature of Maratha art. They add to the spectacle of **Navratri** (Festival of Nine Nights; Hindu festival leading up to Dussehra) in September/October when filled with oil and ignited.

Chintaman Ganesh Mandir
This temple is believed to be of considerable antiquity – the assembly hall's artistically carved pillars date to the Parmara period. Worshippers flock here to pray to the deity, whose name means 'assurer of freedom from worldly anxieties'. It's an easy cycle from the centre, mostly through farmland.

GHATS
The best times to visit the ghats, including **Ram Ghat**, the largest, are dawn and dusk when the devout chime cymbals and light candles at the water's edge. People bathe here at all times of the day, though. You can also rent **pedal boats** (Rs5).

VEDH SHALA (OBSERVATORY)
Ujjain has been India's Greenwich since the 4th century BC and this simple but interesting **observatory** (Jantar Mantar; admission Rs5; ☼ 8am-6pm) was built by Maharaja Jai Singh in about 1730. He also built observatories in Jaipur, Delhi, Varanasi and Mathura, but Ujjain's is the only one still in use. Among the instruments in the small garden are two marble-topped sun

MADHYA PRADESH &
CHHATTISGARH

MELA CYCLE

The Kumbh Mela (p838) takes place in Ujjain every 12 years, with the Ardh (Half) Mela held every six. A smaller, annual event – the Magh Mela – is also celebrated. Each mela, usually held during April and May, lasts for around six weeks and includes several auspicious bathing dates. Ask at the tourist office for specific dates.

- 2010 – Ardh (Half) Kumbh Mela
- 2011 – Magh Mela
- 2012 – Magh Mela
- 2013 – Magh Mela
- 2014 – Magh Mela
- 2015 – Magh Mela
- 2016 – Kumbh Mela

dials; one a conventional sun dial, the other made up of two large quadrants split by a tall staircase whose shadow tells the time.

KALIADEH PALACE

The Mandu sultans built this island **water palace** in 1458 on the site of a sun temple on the Shipra River. Nasir-ud-din added the tanks, through which river water is diverted to stir up cooling breezes. The central dome is a good example of Persian architecture. It's another possible bicycle trip.

Sleeping & Eating

You can find budget rooms for as little as Rs150 on Subhash Rd, but they're generally pretty grubby. Thali restaurants line the road here and are good value (from Rs20) but have no English menus and don't open before around 9.30am.

Hotel Rama Krishna (☎ 2553017; Subhash Rd; s/d Rs240/330, with AC Rs540/660; ✹) This cleaner-than-average Subhash Rd hotel has rooms with white-tiled floors, TV and sit-down flush toilet. The restaurant is decent too.

Hotel Satyam (☎ 9425917376; support@enjoyinfo .biz; 125 Mahakal; d/6-bed Rs600/1100, d/6-bed with AC Rs850/1450; ✹) This well-looked-after hotel is extremely popular with Indian tourists due to its close proximity to Mahakaleshwar Temple, so book ahead.

Hotel Kanha (☎ 4041502; Gudri Chouraha or Mahakal Marg; d/q/5-bed Rs650/1100/1300, d with AC Rs900-1200; ✹) New, decent quality midrange hotel with

a cracking location among the alleys leading down to Ram Ghat.

Hotel Grand Tower (☎ 2553699; 1 Vikram Marg; s Rs600-1300, d Rs700-1500; ✹) Comfortable rooms have light wood furnishings but slightly pokey bathrooms.

Shivam Restaurant (mains Rs40-60; ⏱ 7am-11pm) With a great selection of delicious veg dishes, this place adjacent to Hotel Satyam is equally popular.

Zharokha Restaurant (mains Rs45-70; ⏱ 7am-10.30pm) The vegetarian restaurant at Hotel Grand Tower serves good Kashmiri, Punjabi and Chinese food and has first-floor balcony seating.

Getting There & Away
BUS

There are frequent buses to Indore (Rs33, two hours, 5.30am to 10pm), four to Omkareshwar (Rs72, four hours, 6.20am to 3.30pm), three to Bhopal (Rs105, five hours, 6am, 8am, 9am) and five to Dhar (Rs65, four hours, 5.30am to 1.30pm) where you can change for Mandu and Maheshwar.

TRAIN

The two direct trains to Gwalior and Agra arrive at stupid o'clock so you're better off going via Bhopal which, like Indore, is served by more than 10 daily trains. See the boxed text (opposite) for details.

Getting Around

Tempos chug out to the sites from the centre. Alternatively, hire a rickshaw (to Ram Ghat Rs20) at the prepaid counter at the train station. A four-hour trip to all the sights mentioned here will cost Rs300. You can also rent dirt-cheap **bicycles** (per hr/day Rs5/15; ⏱ 7am-11pm) from a place behind the bus stand.

The more romantic can try a tonga (two-wheeled horse-drawn carriage, to Ram Ghat Rs50). You'll find them outside the train station.

INDORE

☎ 0731 / pop 1.52 million

The small old town here is worth a stroll, and the Holkar dynasty has left behind some fine buildings, but Indore – Madhya Pradesh's business powerhouse – is primarily used by tourists as the gateway to Omkareshwar (p707), Maheshwar (p708) or Mandu (p709).

MADHYA PRADESH & CHHATTISGARH

HANDY TRAINS FROM UJJAIN

Destination	Train no & name	Fare (Rs)	Duration (hr)	Departure
Bhopal	9303 Intercity Exp	66*	3½	7.45am
Delhi	2919 Malwa Exp	338/896/1220	15	2.12pm
Indore	8234 Narmada Pas Exp	80/213/283	2	8.35am
Jaipur	2465 Ranthambore Exp	137/239/510/648**	8½	8.15am
Mumbai	2962 Avantika Exp	309/814/1106	13	5.35pm

*2nd class only **2nd class/sleeper/chair car/3AC

Orientation

Mahatma Gandhi (MG) Rd, running east–west, is the city's main artery, with shopping malls and office blocks. The fast-developing RNT Marg leads south from here, linking the modern part of the city with the small old town, south of the Nehru Statue.

Information

ATMs are marked on the map.

007 Cyber Gallery (Silver Mall; per hr Rs10; 8.30am-12.30am) Internet cafe serving drinks and snacks.

Left luggage (per piece per 12hr Rs10; 24hr) At Sarwate bus stand.

Main post office (☎ 2700023; AB Rd; 10am-8.30pm Mon-Sat, 10am-4pm Sun)

MP Tourism (☎ 2521717; RNT Marg; 10am-5pm Mon-Sat, closed 2nd & 3rd Sat of month)

MY Hospital (☎ 2527300, casualty medical officer 4041689; MY Hospital Rd)

Royal Chemist (MY Hospital Rd; 9.15am-10pm)

Rupayana (☎ 2531720; MG Rd; 10.15am-8.15pm) This bookshop has a friendly owner with an unusual selection of books on India.

State Bank of India (AB Rd; 10.30am-4.30pm Mon-Fri, 10.30am-1.30pm Sat) Changes travellers cheques and cash, and has an ATM.

Wintech Cyber (per hr Rs10; 11am-10pm) Internet cafe set back from Ushaganj Main Rd.

Sights

Built between 1886 and 1921, **Lal Bagh Palace** (☎ 2473264; Indian/foreigner Rs5/100, camera/video Rs10/50; 10am-5pm Tue-Sun) is the finest building left by the Holkar dynasty. Replicas of the Buckingham Palace gates creak at the entrance to the 28-hectare garden, where there is a statue of Queen Victoria. The palace is dominated by European styles, with baroque and rococo dining rooms, an English library with leather armchairs, a Renaissance sitting room with ripped sofas and a Palladian queen's bedroom.

The **Central Museum** (☎ 2700374; AB Rd; Indian/foreigner Rs10/100, camera/video Rs20/50; 10am-5pm Tue-Sun), another Holkar building, has one of Madhya Pradesh's best collections of medieval and premedieval Hindu sculptures, along with tools, weaponry and copper-engraved land titles. Skirmishes took place here during the First War of Independence (Indian Uprising) – the well in the garden was poisoned during the struggle.

The Gothic **Gandhi Hall** (Town Hall), built in 1904 and originally called King Edward's Hall, stands incongruously on MG Rd like a ghost of the Independence era.

Sleeping

Hotel Neelam (☎ 2466001; 33/2 Patel Bridge Corner; s Rs200-250, d Rs300-350, with AC Rs475;) One of the few budget places near the train and bus stations that accepts foreigners, friendly Neelam has simple but clean rooms off a central courtyard.

Rama Inn (☎ 4043762; RNT Marg; r Rs350-450, with AC Rs650;) Very friendly, basic accommodation on the edge of the old town. All rooms are essentially the same with the addition of first TV then AC, the more you pay. There's a veg restaurant (mains Rs40 to Rs80) in the fan-cooled lobby, open from 7am to 9pm.

Hotel Chanakya (☎ 2704497; swarup_chanaky@yahoo.com; RNT Marg; s Rs450-550, d Rs550-650, with AC s Rs700-800, d Rs800-900;) The grey stone and tiled interior may be a bit depressing, but great staff makes this place exceptionally welcoming and it's right in the heart of the more interesting old town. Rooms are a decent size and all have TV. The cheapest don't have windows.

Hotel Shreemaya (☎ 2515555; shree@shreemaya.com; RNT Marg; s Rs1400-2400, d Rs1900-2900;) Very well-run hotel with quality throughout. Modern rooms have wide-screen TVs.

Eating & Drinking

Uday Palace Pure Veg Restaurant (Hotel Uday Palace, Kibe Compound Rd; mains Rs35-60; 7am-1am) Cheap and cheerful, as opposed to the hotel it fronts,

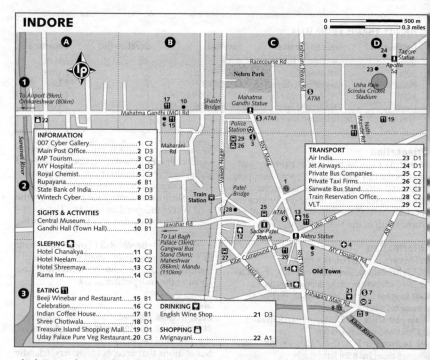

INDORE

0   500 m
0   0.3 miles

INFORMATION
007 Cyber Gallery.....................**1** C2
Main Post Office.......................**2** D3
MP Tourism.............................**3** C2
MY Hospital..............................**4** D3
Royal Chemist..........................**5** C3
Rupayana...............................**6** B1
State Bank of India...................**7** D3
Wintech Cyber.........................**8** D3

SIGHTS & ACTIVITIES
Central Museum........................**9** D3
Gandhi Hall (Town Hall)..........**10** B1

SLEEPING
Hotel Chanakya......................**11** C3
Hotel Neelam.........................**12** C2
Hotel Shreemaya....................**13** C3
Rama Inn...............................**14** C3

EATING
Beeji Winebar and Restaurant......**15** B1
Celebration..............................**16** C2
Indian Coffee House..................**17** B1
Shree Chotiwala.......................**18** D1
Treasure Island Shopping Mall....**19** D1
Uday Palace Pure Veg Restaurant....**20** C3

DRINKING
English Wine Shop.....................**21** D3

SHOPPING
Mrignayani..............................**22** A1

TRANSPORT
Air India.................................**23** D1
Jet Airways.............................**24** D1
Private Bus Companies..............**25** C2
Private Taxi Firms....................**26** C2
Sarwate Bus Stand...................**27** C2
Train Reservation Office............**28** C2
VLT......................................**29** C2

which is just cheap, Uday Palace has a decent range of Indian veg dishes and a good thali.

Indian Coffee House (MG Rd; mains Rs35-85; 7am-10pm) Drink coffee with Indore's judiciary at this branch set inside the grounds of the commissioner's office and near the district court. As always, a top spot for breakfast, with dosa and particularly good *idli* sharing the menu with eggs and toast.

Shree Chotiwala (Nath Mandir Rd; mains Rs40-100; 11am-midnight) This very popular restaurant has comfy booth seating and a family-friendly veg menu that includes Jain dishes and a children's thali.

Treasure Island Shopping Mall (MG Rd; mains Rs40-200; 11am-11pm) Sprinkled among five floors of designer labels is a host of food joints ranging from South Indian specialists to American diners. There are coffee shops, a Baskin-Robbins ice-cream parlour and even a sports bar where, in between courses, you can play pool or go tenpin bowling.

Beeji Winebar and Restaurant (MG Rd; mains Rs45-120; 11am-11pm) Don't be fooled by the 'family restaurant' sign. This is a friendly place, but it's a restaurant for drinkers, not kids.

Celebration (Tuko Ganj; mains Rs60-95; 7.30am-10.30pm) This clean and modern bakery next to Hotel Shreemaya sells pastries, sandwiches, cookies and cakes, as well as a handful of mains, including pizza. Good choice for breakfast if you can't be bothered going to Indian Coffee House.

English Wine Shop (Ushaganj Main Rd; beer Rs70; 8.30am-midnight) A popular drinking den in the old town that serves bottled beers and spirits.

Shopping
Mrignayani (165 MG Rd; 11am-1.30pm & 2.30-8pm Mon-Sat) Fixed-price government emporium with two floors crammed with handicrafts from across the state, including leather toy animals – an Indore speciality.

Getting There & Away
AIR
Air India (2431595; Racecourse Rd; 10am-1pm & 2-5pm Mon-Sat) flies daily to Mumbai (from Rs4675) and Delhi (Rs5205).

Jet Airways (2544590; Racecourse Rd; 9.30am-6pm Mon-Sat) flies daily to Mumbai (Rs3525),

MADHYA PRADESH & CHHATTISGARH

HANDY TRAINS FROM INDORE				
Destination	**Train No & name**	**Fare (Rs)**	**Duration (hr)**	**Departure**
Bhopal	2919 *Malwa Exp*	163/403/537	5	12.25pm
Mumbai	2962 *Avantika Exp*	325/861/1171	15	3.50pm
Delhi	2919 *Malwa Exp*	355/943/1285	16½	12.25pm
Ujjain	9657 *Udaipur City Exp*	121/213/283	2	8.05am

Delhi (Rs5225), Bhopal (Rs4385), Raipur (Rs5245), Ahmedabad (Rs5055) and Hyderabad (Rs5835, except Tuesday).

BUS

Frequent buses from **Sarwate bus stand** (☎ 2465688) serve Omkareshwar (Rs50, three hours, 7.30am to 7pm), Ujjain (Rs35, two hours, 5.30am to 11pm) and Bhopal (Rs110, five hours, day and night). Two buses go to Pachmarhi (seat/sleeper Rs275/320, 12 hours, 8pm, 10.30pm) and three to Gwalior (Rs252, 12 hours, 7.30am, 11am, 9.30pm).

For Mandu, catch a bus from **Gangwal bus stand** (☎ 2380688; Jawahar Rd) to Dhar (Rs35, three hours, frequent), from where buses head to Mandu (Rs23, one hour, frequent). It costs Rs40 to get between the two bus stands in an autorickshaw.

Among the private bus operators on the service road parallel to Valiash Nagar and at Sadar Patel Statue, **VLT** (☎ 2512791) runs buses to Nagpur (Rs350, 14 hours, 6.30pm) for Pench Tiger Reserve, Udaipur (Rs250, 10 hours, 8pm to 9.30pm), Mumbai (Rs400, 13 hours, 5pm to 6.30pm) and Gwalior (Rs250, 11 hours, 6pm to 9.30pm). Sleeper berths cost Rs100 more.

TAXI

Private taxi firms on the service road parallel to Valiash Nagar charge around Rs1200 return to Mandu and the same price for a trip incorporating Omkareshwar and Maheshwar.

TRAIN

There are seven daily trains to Bhopal and more than 10 to Ujjain – see boxed text, above. The **train reservation office** (◷ 8am-8pm Mon-Sat, 8am-2pm Sun) is 200m east of the train station.

Getting Around

The airport is 9km from the city. Autorickshaws charge at least Rs80, taxis around Rs150. Autorickshaw journeys around Indore cost Rs10 to Rs20.

AROUND INDORE
Omkareshwar
☎ 07280 / pop 6616

One of a number of holy places with ghats referred to as a 'mini Varanasi', this Om-shaped island attracts pilgrims in large numbers and has become a popular chill-out destination on the backpacker trail.

The controversial dam (p102) has changed the look of Omkareshwar considerably, but the island has retained at least some of its spiritual vibe and remains a pleasant place to stay.

ORIENTATION & INFORMATION

Most activity takes place off the island, on Mamaleshwar Rd, a 500m-long main drag between the bus stand and main square, Getti Chowk, from where the old bridge crosses to the island. South of the old bridge are the ghats (where you can cross the river on boats for Rs5), the new bridge and the dam.

The path leading from the old bridge to Shri Omkar Mandhata temple is the hub of the island.

Some telephone stalls on Mamaleshwar Rd and on the island have a computer and a stuttering **internet connection** (per hr Rs50-70). The **State Bank of India ATM** (Mamaleshwar Rd) is near the bus stand. There's a **pharmacy** (◷ 9am-9pm) opposite.

SIGHTS & ACTIVITIES

Tourists can rub shoulders with sadhus in the island's narrow lanes, browse the colourful stalls selling chillums and souvenir linga, or join pilgrims attending the thrice daily *puja* (prayer) at **Shri Omkar Mandhata**. This cavelike temple, which houses the only shapeless *jyothi lingam*, is one of many Hindu and Jain monuments on the island.

From the old bridge, instead of turning right to Shri Omkar Mandhata, you can also head left and walk up the 287 steps to the 11th-century **Gaudi Somnath Temple**, from where you can descend the hill to the northern tip of

MADHYA PRADESH & CHHATTISGARH

the island, where sadhus bathe in the confluence of the holy Narmada and Keveri Rivers. You can also climb the narrow, inner staircase of the temple. Nearby, a 30m-tall **Shiva statue** was being built by the Raj Rajeshwari Seva Sahsrhan Trust at the time of research. The path passing in front of this statue can be followed back to the ghats (45 minutes), up and down hills and past a number of temple ruins. Don't miss the beautifully sculpted **Siddhanatha Temple** (left at the T-junction in the pathway) with marvellous elephant carvings around its base.

SLEEPING & EATING

On the island, accommodation is in the form of *dharamsalas* (pilgrim's rest house) only. The friendliest, cleanest and best located is **Manu Guest House** (s/d Rs100/150). There's no sign, but it's perched up above the old bridge. Just keep asking for Manu *dharamsala*. Other accommodation listed below is just off the island.

our pick **Maharaja Guesthouse** (☎ 271237; r Rs150-500, without bathroom Rs70) Like something out of an adventure book, this 600-year-old stone building, accessed via a small path off Getti Chowk, is slowly being swallowed up by the undergrowth on the cliffs overlooking the river. Its nine extremely basic rooms are all in various states of disrepair, and come with tap-and-bucket showers and squat toilets only, but each has its own unique character – a wooden doorway here, a carved alcove there. Room 1, with family portraits on the walls and two doorways that lead out to private clifftop river views, is certainly worth asking for.

Ganesh Guest House (☎ 271370; r Rs150-250, without bathroom Rs100) Off the path leading down to the ghats from Mamaleshwar Rd, friendly Ganesh has spotless budget rooms and a peaceful ambience. Its shaded garden restaurant (mains Rs40 to Rs120) overlooking the ghats is one of the nicest places to eat in town.

Geeta Shree Guest House (☎ 271560; r Rs400, without bathroom Rs200, with AC Rs700; 🅰) The cheapest rooms are dark and dingy, but the AC ones are decent and can be nabbed for Rs500 if you agree not to use the AC.

Om Shiva Restaurant (Getti Chowk; mains Rs30-60; 🕓 8.30am-9.30pm) One of the few *dhabas* (snack bars) with an English sign and English menu, this all-veg place whips up dependable dishes including a tasty thali.

Lassi & Juice Centre (Getti Chowk; drinks Rs6-20; 🕓 8am-9pm) A great place to sit and while away time with some people-watching.

GETTING THERE & AWAY

Regular buses serve Indore (Rs45, two hours, 6am to 6.30pm), Maheshwar (Rs40, three hours, 6am to 6.45pm) and Dhamnod (Rs47, three hours, 6am to 5pm) where you can change for Mandu (Rs33, three hours), via Oonera (see opposite). There are four daily buses to Ujjain (Rs70, four hours, 6am, 11.30am, 2.30pm, 6pm).

Maheshwar

☎ 07283 / pop 19,649

The friendly, peaceful town of Maheshwar has long held spiritual significance – it's mentioned in the Mahabharata and Ramayana (p69) under its old name, Mahishmati, and still draws sadhus and *yatris* (pilgrims) to its ancient ghats and temples on the holy Narmada River. The town enjoyed a golden age in the late 18th century under Holkar queen Ahilyabai, who built the palace in the towering fort and many other monuments. Away from the ghats and historic buildings, Maheshwar's colourful streets house old wooden doorways and overhanging balconies fronting brightly painted local homes.

ORIENTATION & INFORMATION

The river, and the fort which overlooks it, is about 1.5km south of the bus stand. Leaving the bus stand, walk straight over the crossroads and continue past the **internet cafe** (per hr Rs20; 🕓 10am-9pm) and ATM until you reach a floodlit roundabout. Take the left fork to get to the ghats via Akash Deep guesthouse, Labboo's Café and the fort. Take the right fork to head directly to the ghats.

SIGHTS & ACTIVITIES

Apart from the holy river itself, the most treasured part of the town is its 16th-century **fort**. The huge, imposing ramparts were built by Emperor Akbar, while the **Maheshwar Palace** and several **temples** within its grounds were added during the reign of Holkar queen Ahilyabai (r 1767–95). The palace is part public courtyard, part posh hotel. Housed within the courtyard, among a collection of rusty matchlocks and dusty palanquins, is a glass-cased statue of Ahilyabai, treated with the reverence of a shrine. Nearby is a Shiva temple with a golden lingam – the starting point for palanquin processions on Ahilyabai's birthday (see boxed text, p671) and Dussehra.

From the ramparts there's a view of boats (return trip per person/boat Rs10/100) and incense smoke drifting across the water to **Baneshwar Temple**, located on a tiny island in the middle of the river. Descending to the dhobi-wallahs (clothes washers) at the **ghats**, you pass two stone temples. The one on the right, guarded by stone Holkar sentries and a frieze of elephants, houses more images of Ahilyabai and two candle towers, lit during festivals.

Before the temples a small doorway announces the NGO **Rehwa Society** (☎ 273203; www .rehwasociety.org; ☯ 10am-5.30pm Wed-Mon), a craft cooperative where profits are ploughed back into the education, housing and welfare of the weavers. A local school, run entirely by Rehwa, is behind the workshop. Maheshwar saris are famous for their unique weave and simple, geometric patterns, often using stripes. You can watch the weavers at work and buy shawls, saris, scarves and fabrics (from Rs450) made from silk, cotton and wool. Volunteers with some design background are always welcome.

SLEEPING & EATING

Akash Deep (Kila Rd; r Rs200) Clean, spacious rooms in this friendly place are basic, although they do have TV. Three on the roof have fort views – just about. Checkout time is 10am.

our pick **Labboo's Café** (☎ 09229125267; r Rs1000-1500) Not only a delightful cafe in a shaded courtyard (open 8am to 8pm), but also a place with four wonderful rooms to stay in. All are different but each is decorated with care and attention, and two of them actually form part of the fort's outer wall – the upper, more expensive one coming with its own fort-wall veranda. The cafe menu is snacks only (Rs10 to Rs40), but staff will whip up a delicious, unlimited thali (Rs100) if you ask nicely. They also organise river trips (per hour per boat Rs200) here.

Narmada Retreat (☎ 273455; www.mptourism.com; q Rs890, r with AC Rs1290-1590; ☒) About 2km from the centre, Narmada has bungalows set around a huge, well-tended garden overlooking the river. The spacious quads, or 'family rooms' – which come with three toilets! – are great value if you're in a group, while the AC tents have lovely river views. There's also a restaurant

DAWN DIP

For a deeper understanding of the spiritual essence of Maheshwar, get up while it's still dark and wander down to the ghats for an early-morning dip in the holy Narmada River. The water is surprisingly warm, even in winter, and cleaner than at the likes of Varanasi and Omkareshwar. Dive in at first light to give yourself time after drying off to find a good spot from where to watch the sun rise. The scene is wonderfully spiritual with locals and pilgrims alike taking their own holy dips, lighting floating candles, offering flowers and chanting mantras.

(mains Rs45 to Rs125) open from 8am to 10.30pm. Turn right just before the floodlit roundabout and continue over two crossroads before turning left at the end of the road.

Ahilya Fort (☎ 273329, Delhi 011-41551575; www .ahilyafort.com; r €185-240; ☒ ☒) This superior-quality heritage hotel, owned by Prince Shivaji Rao Holka, a direct descendent of Ahilyabai, forms part of Maheshwar Palace and looks magical from the brochure. It's a little snooty, though. We weren't allowed in, even just to look around, as we hadn't booked our visit in advance through the Delhi office. Let us know what it's like.

GETTING THERE & AWAY

There are regular buses to Omkareshwar (Rs40, three hours, 9am to 5.30pm) and Dhamnod (Rs8, 30 minutes, 7am to 11pm) where you can change for Indore (Rs60, three hours). For Mandu, first head to Dhamnod then take a Dhar-bound bus as far as a forked junction in the main road, known as Oonera (Rs23, two hours). From there flag down a bus (Rs10, 30 minutes) or hitch for the final 14km to Mandu.

MANDU

☎ 07292 / pop 8550 / elev 634m

Perched on top of a pleasantly green, thinly forested 20-sq-km plateau, picturesque Mandu is home to some of India's finest examples of Afghan architecture. The area is littered with palaces, tombs, monuments and mosques, all within easy cycling distance of each other. Some cling to the edge of ravines, others are beside lakes, while Rupmati's Pavilion, the most romantic of them all, sits majestically at the far end of the plateau, overlooking the vast plains below.

History

Raja Bhoj, of Bhopal fame, founded Mandu as a fortress retreat in the 10th century before it was conquered by the Muslim rulers of Delhi in 1304. When the Mughals captured Delhi in 1401, the Afghan Dilawar Khan, governor of Malwa, set up his own little kingdom and Mandu's golden age began.

Although Dilawar Khan established Mandu as an independent kingdom, it was his son, Hoshang Shah, who shifted the capital from Dhar to Mandu and raised it to its greatest splendour.

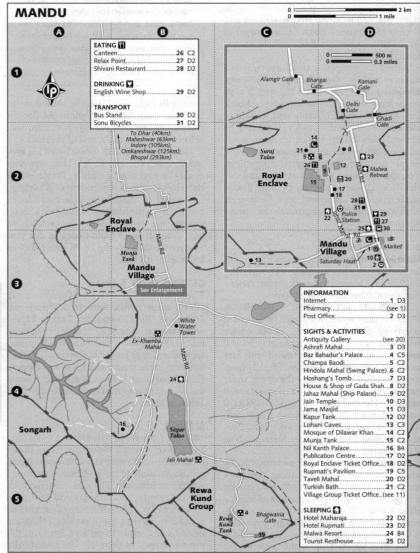

MANDU

EATING 🍴		
Canteen	26	C2
Relax Point	27	D2
Shivani Restaurant	28	D2

DRINKING 🍷		
English Wine Shop	29	D2

TRANSPORT		
Bus Stand	30	D2
Sonu Bicycles	31	D2

To Dhar (40km); Maheshwar (63km); Indore (105km); Omkareshwar (125km); Bhopal (293km)

Royal Enclave
Munja Tank
Mandu Village
See Enlargement

White Water Tower
Ex-Khamba Mahal
Main Rd

Songarh

Jali Mahal

Sagar Talao

Rewa Kund Group
Rewa Kund Tank
Bhagwania Gate

Alamgir Gate
Bhangai Gate
Kamani Gate
Delhi Gate
Ghadi Gate
Suraj Talao
Royal Enclave
Malwa Retreat
Police Station
Mandu Village
Saturday Haat
Market

INFORMATION	
Internet	1 D3
Pharmacy	(see 1)
Post Office	2 D3

SIGHTS & ACTIVITIES	
Antiquity Gallery	(see 20)
Ashrafi Mahal	3 D3
Baz Bahadur's Palace	4 C5
Champa Baodi	5 C2
Hindola Mahal (Swing Palace)	6 C2
Hoshang's Tomb	7 D3
House & Shop of Gada Shah	8 D2
Jahaz Mahal (Ship Palace)	9 D2
Jain Temple	10 D3
Jama Masjid	11 D3
Kapur Tank	12 D2
Lohani Caves	13 C3
Mosque of Dilawar Khan	14 C2
Munja Tank	15 C2
Nil Kanth Palace	16 B4
Publication Centre	17 D2
Royal Enclave Ticket Office	18 D2
Rupmati's Pavilion	19 C5
Taveli Mahal	20 D2
Turkish Bath	21 C2
Village Group Ticket Office	(see 11)

SLEEPING 🛏	
Hotel Maharaja	22 D2
Hotel Rupmati	23 D2
Malwa Resort	24 B4
Tourist Resthouse	25 D2

In 1526, Bahadur Shah of Gujarat conquered Mandu, only to be ousted in 1534 by the Mughal Humayun, who in turn lost the kingdom to Mallu Khan, an officer of the Khalji dynasty. Ten more years of feuds and invasions saw Baz Bahadur eventually emerge in the top spot, but in 1561 he fled Mandu rather than face Akbar's advancing troops.

After Akbar added Mandu to the Mughal empire, it kept a considerable degree of independence, until taken by the Marathas in 1732. The capital of Malwa was then shifted back to Dhar, and the slide in Mandu's fortunes that had begun with the absconding of Baz Bahadur became a plummet.

Orientation & Information

The area around the bus stand, which includes the Village Group of monuments, is where most of the activity takes places. The Royal Enclave, the most impressive of the three main groups of monuments, stands slightly northwest of here. The Rewa Kund Group is 4km south.

The only place with **internet** (Main Rd; per hr Rs80; 8.30am-9.30pm) is painfully slow so best left for emergencies. There's a small **pharmacy** (8am-9.30pm) next door, while the **post office** (263222; Main Rd; 9am-5pm) is further south. There's nowhere to change money. Malwa Retreat can help arrange a guide.

Sights & Activities
ROYAL ENCLAVE

These **ruins** (Indian/foreigner Rs5/100, video Rs25; dawn-dusk Sat-Thu) are the only ones fenced off into one single complex. There's a **Publication Centre** (10am-6pm) selling guidebooks by the entrance and a shaded garden canteen selling snacks and chai by Hindola Mahal.

Jahaz Mahal

Also called the Ship Palace, this is the most famous building in Mandu. Built on a narrow strip of land between Munja and Kapur Tanks, with a small upper storey like a ship's bridge (if you use your imagination), it's far longer (120m) than it is wide (15m). Ghiyas-ud-din, who is said to have had a harem of 15,000 maidens, constructed its lookouts, scalloped arches, airy rooms and beautiful pleasure pools.

Taveli Mahal

These former stables now house the ASI's **Antiquity Gallery** (9am-5pm Sat-Thu), which fea-

tures artefacts found here including stone slabs with Quranic text dating back to the 15th century.

Hindola Mahal

Just north of Ghiyas' stately pleasure dome is Hindola Mahal (Swing Palace), so called because the slope of the walls is supposed to create the impression that they are swaying. It doesn't give that impression, but is an eye-catching design nonetheless.

House & Shop of Gada Shah

The house is within the enclave but the shop is outside on the road to Delhi Gate. As the buildings' size and internal workmanship suggest, their owner was more than a shopkeeper. His name, which means 'beggar master', is thought to identify him as Rajput chief Medini Ray, a powerful minion of the sultans. The 'shop' was a warehouse for saffron and musk, imported and sold at a handsome profit when there were enough wealthy people to shop here.

Mosque of Dilawar Khan

Built by Dilawar Khan in 1405, this mosque is Mandu's earliest Islamic building. Typically for this era, there are many Hindu elements to the architecture, notably the pillars and ceilings inside.

Champa Baodi

So called because its water supposedly smelt as sweet as the champak flower, Champa Baodi is a step-well surrounded by subterranean vaulted chambers, some of which you can explore.

Turkish Bath

Stars and octagons perforate the domed roofs of this tiny *hammam,* which had hot and cold water and a hypocaust sauna.

LOHANI CAVES

Local guides seem unsure as to just how old these sculpted caves are but some insist that a now-blocked tunnel leads from the caves to Dhar, 35km away. One thing is certain, they command a fabulous view of the ravine below which you can hike down to from here.

VILLAGE GROUP

One ticket covers the following three **monuments** (Indian/foreigner Rs5/100, video Rs25; dawn-dusk).

Jama Masjid

Entered by a flight of steps leading to a 17m-high domed porch, this disused red-stone mosque dominates the village of Mandu. Hoshang begun its construction, basing it on the great Omayyad Mosque in Damascus, Syria, and Mohammed Khalji completed it in 1454. Despite its plain design, it's reckoned to be the finest and largest example of Afghan architecture in India.

Hoshang's Tomb

Reputed to be India's oldest marble building, this imposing tomb is crowned with a crescent thought to have been imported from Persia or Mesopotamia. Inside, light filters into the echoing dome through stone *jalis,* intended to cast an appropriately subdued light on the tombs. An inscription records Shah Jahan sending his architects – including Ustad Hamid, who worked on the Taj Mahal – here in 1659 to pay their respects to the tomb's builders.

Ashrafi Mahal

Mohammed Shah originally built his tomb as a madrasa (Islamic college), before converting and extending it. The overambitious design later collapsed – notably the seven-storey circular tower of victory. The building is an empty shell, but intricate Islamic pillarwork can be seen at the top of its great stairway.

JAIN TEMPLE

Entered by a turquoise doorway, this complex is a splash of kitsch among the Islamic monuments. The richly decorated temples feature marble, silver and gold *tirthankars* with jade eyes, and behind them is a themepark-like museum with a walk-on replica of Shatrunjaya (p748), the hilltop temple complex at Palitana in Gujarat. In the colourful murals, bears devour sinners' arms, crocodiles chew their heads, and demons saw one evil character in half, lengthways.

REWA KUND GROUP

A pleasant 4km-cycle south of the village, past Sagar Talao, brings you to two more **ruins** (Indian/foreigner Rs5/100, video Rs25; ☼ dawn-dusk). Tickets for both should be bought from outside Baz Bahadur's Palace.

Baz Bahadur's Palace

Baz Bahadur was the last independent ruler of Mandu. His palace, constructed around 1509, is beside the Rewa Kund Tank where a water lift at the northern end supplied water to the palace. A curious mix of Rajasthani and Mughal styles, it was actually built decades before Baz Bahadur came to power.

Rupmati's Pavilion

Standing at the top of a cliff plunging 366m to the plains, Rupmati's Pavilion has a subtle beauty unmatched by the other monuments – and some of the dinkiest stone staircases you'll ever climb.

According to Malwa legends, the music-loving Baz Bahadur built it to persuade a beautiful Hindu singer, Rupmati, to move here from her home on the plains. From its terrace and domed pavilions Rupmati could gaze down at the distant glint of the sacred Narmada River.

In fact, the pavilion was built in two or three phases and the style of its arches and pillars suggest it was completed 100 years before Rupmati's time. Nonetheless, the love story is a subject of Malwa folk songs – not least because of its tragic ending. Lured by tales of Rupmati's beauty, Akbar marched on the fort and Baz Bahadur fled, leaving his lover to poison herself.

This place is simply gorgeous at sunset, but bring a torch for the ride back.

NIL KANTH PALACE

Leave Main Rd at the white water tower to reach this Mughal palace, which is well worth the 20-minute bike ride. It stands at the head of a ravine, on the site of an earlier Shiva shrine – its name means God with Blue Throat – and is now once again used as a place of worship. A stream built by one of Akbar's governors trickles through a delightful spiral channel and is usually filled with scented water, giving the palace a sweet aroma.

SATURDAY HAAT

This colourful weekly **market** (☼ 10am-dusk), behind Jama Masjid, is similar to ones held all over the Bastar region, a tribal stronghold of Chhattisgarh (p723). Adivasis walk miles to come here to buy and sell goods ranging from mountains of red chillies to dried *mahuwa,* a flower used to make a potent liquor of the same name.

Sleeping & Eating

Tourist Resthouse (☎ 263264; Jahaz Mahal Rd; r Rs150) This row of seven identical and extremely basic rooms with squat toilets and tap-and-bucket showers is the cheapest place in town. Rooms come with small, private verandas and couldn't be more centrally located.

Hotel Maharaja (☎ 9981883767; Jahaz Mahal Rd; s/d Rs200/300) Rooms here are slightly bigger, cleaner and quieter than at Tourist Resthouse, but are basic nonetheless.

Hotel Rupmati (☎ 263270; Main Rd; r Rs650, with air-cooler/AC Rs850/1350; ▓) Clean, colourful cottages, with large bathrooms, are set around gardens on the edge of a cliff. Some come with exceptional views of the valley below. AC rooms can be had for Rs825 if you don't use the AC. Has a restaurant.

Malwa Resort (☎ 263235; tcmandav@sancharnet.in; Main Rd; r Rs1090, with AC Rs1790; ▓ ▓) This family-friendly MP Tourism property, 2km south of the village, has large gardens, children's play areas and a pool. Rooms are in cottages with new furniture and verandas. The pricier ones overlook the lake. Rates include breakfast.

Relax Point (Main Rd; mains Rs20-35; ☉ 8.30am-10pm) A village shop, gathering point and restaurant rolled into one; the menu is very limited, and in the evening it's thali only (Rs50, unlimited refills), but staff is friendly and the snacks they sell – nuts, dried fruit, chocolate, samosas – are ideal for bike rides into the countryside.

Shivani Restaurant (Main Rd; mains Rs25-60; ☉ 8.30am-10pm) No-nonsense diner with plastic tables and chairs and an excellent menu including a range of thalis and local specialities such as *Mandu kofta* (dumplings in a mild sauce).

English Wine Shop (Main Rd; beer Rs70; ☉ 7.30am-10.30pm) By Relax Point, this place sells beer and spirits.

Mandu is one of the few places in India where you'll see the baobab tree, which looks like it has been planted upside down with its roots in the air. Look out for the green, hard-shelled baobab seed – it's a bit like eating sweet-and-sour chalk.

Getting There & Away

There are three direct buses to Indore (Rs70, 3½ hours, 9am, 9.30am, 3.30pm), one to Ujjain (Rs80, four hours, 6am) and regular services to Dhar (Rs25, one hour, 6am to 5pm) where you can change for buses to Dhamnod (Rs23, two hours) then, in turn, for Maheshwar (Rs10, 30 minutes, last bus 11pm) or Omkareshwar (Rs50, three hours, last bus 7pm). If doing this, it's quicker to

get off 14km before Dhar at a junction called Oonera (Rs10, 30 minutes) where you can flag down Dhamnod-bound buses.

Getting Around

Cycling is best, as the terrain is flat, the air clear and the countryside beautiful. **Sonu Bicycles** (Main Rd; per hr/day Rs5/20; ☉ 6am-10pm) is one of a few places that rent bikes.

You can tour the monuments in half a day in an autorickshaw (from Rs200).

EASTERN MADHYA PRADESH

JABALPUR

☎ 0761 / pop 1.1 million

Domestic tourists mostly come here to visit Marble Rocks, an attractive river gorge nearby, but for foreigners this industrial city of *chowks* and working men's taverns is used mainly as a launchpad for the big tiger parks – Kanha (p717), Pench (p716) and Bandhavgarh (p719).

Orientation

Most of the action takes place north of the railway line, in the dusty lanes of the Old Bazaar, along Vined Talkies Road and as far south as Russell Chowk. The Civil Lines district, south of the railway line, is much quieter and of less interest to tourists.

Information

Agrawal (☎ 2411056; Russell Chowk; ☉ 10am-10pm) Film printing, memory cards and CD burning.

City Hospital (☎ 4033111; North Civil Lines; ☉ 24hr) Modern, private healthcare facility.

Jai Medical Store (☎ 2610457; Malviya Chowk; ☉ 10am-10.30pm)

MP Tourism (☎ 2677690; ☉ 7am-8pm) At train station, south entrance. Good advice on national parks and helps book MP Tourism accommodation and cars.

Net Space Cyber Café (Vined Talkies Rd; per hr Rs20; ☉ 10am-10pm) On the first floor.

Post office (Residency Rd; ☉ 10am-5pm Mon-Fri, 10am-2pm Sat) An unusual 1860s, English-made red post box stands outside the entrance.

State Bank of India (☎ 2677777; South Civil Lines; ☉ 10.30am-4.30pm Mon-Fri, to 12.30pm Sat) Changes travellers cheques and currency; there's an ATM at the train station and others around the city.

Universal Book Service (☎ 2310591; Malwaya Marg; ☉ 10am-8.30pm)

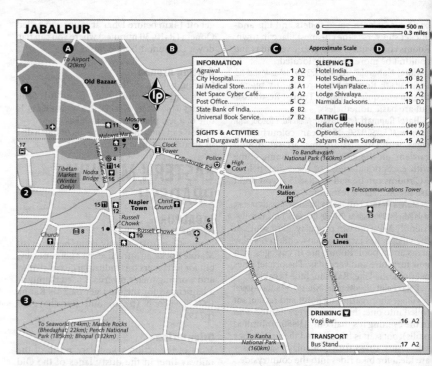

JABALPUR

INFORMATION
Agrawal...................................1 A2
City Hospital...........................2 B2
Jai Medical Store.....................3 A1
Net Space Cyber Café..............4 A2
Post Office..............................5 C2
State Bank of India..................6 B2
Universal Book Service............7 B2

SIGHTS & ACTIVITIES
Rani Durgavati Museum............8 A2

SLEEPING
Hotel India.............................9 A2
Hotel Sidharth.......................10 B2
Hotel Vijan Palace.................11 A1
Lodge Shivalaya.....................12 A2
Narmada Jacksons.................13 D2

EATING
Indian Coffee House.........(see 9)
Options................................14 A2
Satyam Shivam Sundram.......15 A2

DRINKING
Yogi Bar...............................16 A2

TRANSPORT
Bus Stand............................17 A2

Sights & Activities

RANI DURGAVATI MUSEUM

West of Russell Chowk, this **museum** (Indian/for-
eigner Rs5/30, camera/video Rs20/50; ☺ 10am-5pm Tue-Sun)
has a collection of 10th-century sculptures
from local sites such as Chausath Yogini (opposite). Upstairs are letters and photographs
relating to Mahatma Gandhi and an elaborate
gallery exploring Adivasi culture.

SEAWORLD

Some 14km towards Marble Rocks, this child-
friendly **swimming-pool complex** (☎ 4917601;
Bhedaghat Rd; adult/child Rs120/90; ☺ midday-5pm)
has outdoor slides and pools. Take any bus
(Rs5 to Rs10) or shared auto heading for
Bhedaghat.

Sleeping

Lodge Shivalaya (☎ 2625188; Napier Town; s/d Rs185/285)
Simple but spacious-enough rooms with stone
floors are the best value around. Many open
onto a shared balcony overlooking the street.

Hotel Vijan Palace (☎ 4063309; Vijan Market; s Rs375-
475, d Rs425-525, with AC Rs700-1000; ✴) Hiding down
a lane off Vined Talkies Rd, the busy Vijan

spans budget and midrange. Room service,
checkout and hot water are all 24-hour.
Cheaper rooms have squat toilets.

Hotel Sidharth (☎ 4007779; hotel_sidharth@hotmail
.com; Russell Chowk; s/d Rs495/550, with AC Rs675-995, ste
Rs1450-2150; ✴) An old-fashioned lift leads to
comfortable, compact rooms in this no-frills
midrange hotel. AC rooms are no smarter
than non-AC.

Hotel India (☎ 2480093; www.indiancoffeehouse
jabalpur.com; s/d/ste from Rs600/800/1800; ✴) This new
hotel has marble staircases leading to bright,
clean bedrooms with sparkling bathrooms.
There's a branch of the excellent Indian Coffee
House in the lobby.

Narmada Jacksons (☎ 4001122; www.jacksons-hotel
.com; South Civil Lines; s Rs2200-4200, d Rs2500-4800, ste
Rs8300-9500; ✴ ▯ ✴) This Raj-era hotel was
given its modern makeover some time ago,
and rooms have simple but attractive furnishings. The five-star facilities include three
restaurants, a bar and a health club.

Eating & Drinking

Indian Coffee House (Hotel India; coffee from Rs7, mains
Rs30-100; ☺ 7.30am-11pm) As well as good coffee,

the guys in white suits and fan-tailed hats serve up delicious breakfasts – from dosa and *uttapam* to French toast and omelettes – and hearty Indian and Chinese mains.

Satyam Shivam Sundram (Napier Town; mains Rs30-68, thalis Rs50-80; ☽ 9am-11pm) Friendly first-floor veg restaurant with a delicious Indian menu including very generous thalis.

Options (☎ 4006279; Vined Talkies Rd; mains Rs40-75; ☽ 10am-11pm) Popular with families, courting couples and 20-somethings, this child-friendly veg restaurant with funky decor serves up good-quality Indian and Chinese cuisine to a backdrop of Indian pop music and Bollywood soundtracks.

Jabalpur is thick with seedy but harmless drinking dens. One of the more salubrious establishments is **Yogi Bar** (Vined Talkies Rd; beer from Rs75; ☽ 10am-10pm).

Getting There & Away

AIR
Kingfisher Airlines (☎ 2901048, 18001800101) at the airport has direct flights to Delhi (from Rs4700) and Indore (from Rs3200).

BUS
Three daily buses go to Kisli in Kanha National Park (Rs95, 5½ hours, 7am, 11am, midday) and two to Raipur (Rs175, 10 hours, 6am, 9.30am). For Pench Tiger Reserve, take any Nagpur-bound bus as far as Khawasa (Rs150, five hours, 7am to 10pm) then take a shared jeep for the final 11km to Turia Gate.

TRAIN
More than 10 daily trains leave for Satna, but none leave in the morning, meaning direct bus connections to Khajuraho cannot be met.

Take an early afternoon train instead then take a bus to Panna and change again for Khajuraho. For Bandhavgarh National Park, take a train to Umaria. Also see boxed text, below.

Getting Around
To get anywhere in the city in a cycle-rickshaw should cost Rs10 to Rs20, in an auto Rs20 to Rs30.

AROUND JABALPUR
Marble Rocks
Known locally as Bhedaghat, the marblelike magnesium-limestone cliffs at this **gorge** on the holy Narmada River, 22km from Jabalpur, turn different colours in different lights, from pink to black. They're particularly impressive by moonlight, and parts are floodlit at night.

The trip up the 2km-long gorge is made in a shared **rowboat** (per person 30/50min Rs21/31; ☽ 7am-7pm, full moon 8pm-midnight, closed Jun 15–Oct 15 due to monsoon) from the jetty at Panchvati Ghat. Alternatively hire a boat (standard/large Rs200/Rs320) to yourself. There's good **swimming** at the ghat too, but currents can be strong; take your lead from the locals. For a nice post-boating stroll, and a closer look at village life, carry on up the hill past the ghat entrance and turn right just before Motel Marble Rocks, where you'll find a tiny path leading past local homes and down towards the gorge.

Dhuandhar (Smoke Cascade) is a worthwhile 1.5km walk uphill from the ghat. Along the way is the exquisitely carved **Chausath Yogini**, a circular 10th-century temple dedicated to the Hindu goddess Durga. Once at the falls, you can take a short cable-car ride (Rs50 return) to the other side of the gorge.

HANDY TRAINS FROM JABALPUR

Destination	Train No & name	Fare (Rs)	Duration (hr)	Departure
Agra	2189 *Mahakaushal Exp*	315/831/1131	14	6.05pm
Bhopal	1472 *Jbp-Bhopal Exp*	158/437/596	7	11pm
Kolkata (Howrah)	2189 *Kolkata Mail*	393/1050/1434	22	1.40pm
Mumbai (CST) 2321 *Howrah-Mumbai Mail*	361/960/1309	17½	6.05pm	
Delhi	2192 *Jbp-NDLS Exp*	369/983/1340	18	5.45pm
Raipur	2854 *Amarkantak Exp*	250/622/876	9½	9.35pm
Satna*	2322 *Kolkata Mail*	141/331/436	2½	1.40pm
Umaria	8233 *Narmada Exp*	80/251/352	4	6.40am
Varanasi	139 *Dadar-Varanasi Spl*	227/611/836	13	5.30pm

*not Saturday

MADHYA PRADESH & CHHATTISGARH

Just before Chausath Yogini, **Hotel River View** (☎ 6942004; Bhedaghat; r no view/river view Rs500/800, with AC & river view Rs1200; 🍴) has clean, spacious rooms, some with wonderful views of the river; these views are matched from its back-garden restaurant (mains Rs40 to Rs60).

Local buses leave regularly for Bhedaghat (Rs10, 40 minutes) from Jabalpur bus stand. They drop you at a crossroads from where shared autos (Rs5) wait to take you the final 5km. Getting back is just a case of waiting at the crossroads for a passing bus. The impatient might like to try squeezing into a jam-packed, Jabalpur-bound shared auto-rickshaw (also Rs10). See if you can beat 14 passengers!

PENCH TIGER RESERVE
☎ 07695 / tiger pop 33

Your chances of seeing a tiger here aren't great – they're spotted once or twice a week on average – but Pench is much quieter than the likes of Kanha (opposite) and Bandhavgarh (p719) so you're more likely to get the feeling that you have the whole teak-tree forest to yourself. There are also rarely seen leopards here, but what you will see a lot of are deer (chital, samba, nilgiri), birds (some 250 species are found here) and, of course, monkeys. Elephant rides are also available (p718).

TIGER PARK COSTS, AT A GLANCE

The four major tiger parks in Madhya Pradesh have now had their safari costs standardised by the state government. Private resorts will often charge more, usually incorporating safari costs into an accommodation, meals and safari package, known as a Jungle Plan (p718). At the time of research, standard government prices were as follows:

- Jeep hire – Rs1000
- Jeep entrance – Rs2030 (Indian citizen Rs530)
- Compulsory guide – Rs150
- Total cost – Rs3180 (Indian citizen Rs1680)

Prices are per safari, not per day, and per jeep, not per person. Each jeep holds one to six people, but it's normally up to you to arrange jeep groups. Guide prices can rise to Rs400 for a trained naturalist.

Like its bigger, more famous brother, Kanha National Park, Pench also makes false claims about being the place upon which Rudyard Kipling based his *Jungle Book* (see opposite).

For park fees, see the boxed text (left).

Orientation & Information
Buses running between Nagpur and Jabalpur will drop you at Khawasa, which is about 12km from the small crossroads village of Turia near which you'll find accommodation. The main gate to the **park** (☎ 223794; 🕐 dawn-dusk Oct 16–Jun 30) is about 3km beyond Turia. The nearest airport and major train station is in Nagpur.

There's nowhere to change money and no internet.

Sleeping & Eating
All these hotels have restaurants. See the boxed text (p718) for details about American and Jungle Plans.

Kipling's Court (☎ 232830; kiplingc@sancharnet .in; dm/s/d American Plan Rs490/2140/2590, with AC Rs3140/3590; 🍴) Considering prices include all meals, the dorms are a bargain here. There are two with five beds each and a large shared shower area. The tatty-looking private cottages are a bit dated, but are comfortable and clean and come with TV and wardrobe. It's 2km past Turia.

Mriganayanee (☎ 09424633485, Nagpur office 0712-2247987; dm/cottage/tent Rs600/2500/3000; 🍴 🏊) Tent accommodation on the roofs of AC cottages, a huge Shiva statue overlooking the swimming pool, an emu in the gardens and a 40-bed dormitory block surrounded by a moat with pedal boats – this place has to be seen to be believed. Mriganayanee oozes eccentricity, with bright red carpets in the tent rooms and kitsch sofa covers and bedspreads throughout. It's 1km before Turia.

our pick Mowgli's Den (☎ 232832, s/d Rs1300/1900, American Plan Rs1900/3100) Ideal for families; the reception and restaurant are set around a lush lawn with children's playground, tyre swing, duck pond and rabbit hutch. Log cabin-lookalike concrete huts come with delightful wrought-iron furniture and huge circular bathrooms with Jacuzzi-sized sunken baths. There's no TV to spoil the natural sounds of the jungle, and when you turn off the lights to sleep, a fluorescent night sky magically appears on your bedroom ceiling. It's 1km past Turia.

THE MOWGLI MYTH

Both Kanha and Pench National Parks claim to be the place upon which Rudyard Kipling based his *Jungle Book* (1894), the famous tale of Mowgli, a boy raised by wolves. Pench's claim seems the stronger of the two, since places mentioned in the story – the Seeonee Hills, Kanhiwara village and Waingunga River gorge – are all actual locations in the Pench area, albeit with slightly different spellings. In fact, Kipling (1865–1936) never visited either area. He wrote the book in Vermont, in the US, and originally based the story in the Aravalli Hills in Mewar, a region in Rajasthan which he knew very well. For some reason, before publication Kipling switched some of the place names in his story using reference books, including some written by Robert Armitage Sterndale, whose unusual spelling of Seoni (Seonee) Kipling seems to have copied, albeit in later manuscripts adding a fourth 'e'. And so the Aravalli Hills became the Seeonee Hills and the myth of Mowgli's true origins began.

Tuli Tiger Corridor (☎ 09981994119, Nagpur office 0712-2534784; www.tuligroup.com; s/d cottage American Plan US$295/395, Jungle Plan US$445/595, s/d luxury tent Jungle Plan US$800/950; ✄ ▨) Extravagance by the bucket-load in exquisite cottages with verandas and luxury tents with private lawns. There's also a gorgeous pool. It's 500m past Mowgli's Den.

Getting There & Away

Regular buses, day and night, link Khawasa with Nagpur (Rs60, two hours) and Jabalpur (Rs120, 5½ hours). Shared jeeps (Rs10) go between Khawasa and Turia when full. If you're in a rush, a private jeep costs Rs150. You can go to Kanha National Park from Khawasa without going all the way to Jabalpur or Mandla. Flag down any east-bound bus to Seoni (Rs25, one hour) then take a Mandla-bound bus to Chiraidongri (Rs50, 2½ hours) where you can catch buses to Khatiya Gate (Rs25, one hour).

KANHA NATIONAL PARK

☎ 07649 / tiger pop 80

One of the largest national parks in India, Kanha gives you the chance to venture deep into tiger territory. Its sal forests and vast meadows are home to more than 200 tigers and leopards and support huge populations of deer and antelope, including the extremely rare *barasingha*. You'll see plenty of langur monkeys, the odd gaur (Indian bison) and maybe even a family or two of wild boar. The park is also home to more than 300 bird species. Elephant rides are also available (p718).

For park fees, see the boxed text (opposite).

Orientation & Information

The 1945-sq-km **park** (☎ 07642-250760; www .kanhanationalpark.com; ☯ dawn-dusk Oct-Jun) consists of a 900-sq-km core zone surrounded by a 1005-sq-km buffer zone.

Khatiya Gate, the main entrance to the buffer zone, is at the village of Kisli, where you'll find most of the accommodation. Some 4km further into the park, Kisli Gate is the main entrance to the core zone. MP Tourism has a great hostel here. Mukki Gate, 35km southeast on the far side of the park, is more remote.

There's nowhere to change money and only a couple of hotels have internet.

VISITOR CENTRES

There are **visitor centres** (☯ 8-11am & 3.30-5pm 1 Oct–15 Feb, 7.30-10.30am & 4.30-6pm 16 Feb–15 Apr, 7-10am & 5.30-7pm 16 Apr–30 Jun) at Khatiya and Mukki Gates, and within the park itself. The centre in the park, which you will visit on morning safaris from Kisli Gate, is the most impressive, with several galleries.

NATURE TRAILS

A well-marked 7km-trail leads from Khatiya Gate and skirts along the edge of the park before looping back to the village. Mostly you'll see a lot of monkeys and birds, but tigers do venture into this area on occasions. Check with locals before you leave. Raheel, the manager at Pugmark Resort (p718), is well informed. Another, shorter trail starts near Kanha Safari Lodge (p718) in Mukki.

SWIMMING

Mowgli Resorts (p718) has a very inviting pool which is open to nonguests (Rs50).

Sleeping & Eating

All hotels listed here have restaurants. See the boxed text (p718) for details about American and Jungle Plans.

ELEPHANT RIDES

Kanha, Bandhavgarh and Pench National Parks all use elephants to track tigers in the morning. Tourists on jeep safaris are then radioed in, transferred to elephants (per person Rs600) and led out to where the tiger is. You get your money back if the tiger has scarpered by the time you get there.

KISLI

There's a row of small *dhabas* just before Khatiya Gate serving cheap food and chai. The MP Tourism property has the only facilities at Kisli Gate.

Panther Resort (☎ 277233; dm Rs100, r Rs500-700) Only recommendable because of its dirt-cheap dorms; unless you can get serious discounts on the shabby doubles, look elsewhere. It's 500m before Khatiya Gate.

Van Vihar (☎ 277241; r Rs200-500, with AC Rs700; ✷) Uninspiring rooms are basic, but this is the best-value budget option. It's 300m left of Khatiya Gate.

our pick Baghira Log Huts & Tourist Hostel (☎ 277227; Kisli Gate; American Plan dm Rs490, s Rs3140-3840, d Rs3590-4290; ✷) This MP Tourism property is the only hotel actually inside the core zone and is *the* place to stay at Kanha. Good-quality rooms are set amongst the monkey-filled forest with many overlooking a small meadow which attracts deer throughout the day. Large, clean dorms are excellent value as prices include all meals. There's even a bar. Book as far ahead in advance as possible. All buses in and out of Khatiya, apart from the last one at 6pm, swing by here.

Pugmark Resort (☎ 277291; www.pugmarkresort .com; s/d American Plan Rs1200/2400; ✷) Large, clean cottage rooms are bright and airy and set around a lovely, if slightly overgrown, garden. There's a gazebo-covered campfire and a bar, and Raheel, the manager, is very knowledgeable. It's 700m down a track to the right of Khatiya Gate.

Mogli Resorts (☎ 9425156245; www.mogliresorts .com; s Rs1400-2200, d Rs1500-2500, American Plan s Rs2050-2850, d Rs2800-3800; ✷ ▣) Cottages around huge grounds have a lot of space. Non-AC ones come with seating in the bay window, while AC versions have a reception area and a dressing room. There's also a great pool. It's 500m beyond Pugmark Resort.

Tuli Tiger Resort (☎ 277221; www.tuligroup.com; American Plan s/d cottages Rs4000/5500, luxury tents Rs17,500/21,500, Jungle Plan s/d cottages Rs11,000/12,000, tents Rs23,500/25,500; ✷ ▣) Fabulous five-star luxury set in peaceful bamboo grounds located 4km before Khatiya gate, just outside the village of Mocha. Buses to Khatiya all stop here.

MUKKI

There's no direct bus between Kisli and Mukki. The quickest, and most enjoyable way to get here is by hitching a lift on motorbike (Rs300 return, 1½ hours). Unlike at Kisli, there are no facilities in Mukki outside the hotels.

Kanha Safari Lodge (☎ 07637-226029; s/d American Plan Rs1640/2090, with AC Rs2440/2890; ✷) Another MP Tourism gem. Grand, spacious cottages with TV and DVD player are set among trees (one actually has a tree growing up through the roof of the veranda) and face onto a well-kept garden with swing chairs, a lawn and a thatched gazebo. There's a restaurant, a bar and views over the river. It's 1½km before Mukki Gate.

Mehail Hotel & Kanha Meadows Retreat (☎ 07637-290074; www.kanhameadows.com; r American Plan Rs2100, with AC Rs3500; ✷ ▣) Close to Kanha Safari Lodge, this two-property resort has simple, well-kept rooms in the small hotel with larger cottages in the new retreat next door. There's a pool and a massage centre.

Getting There & Away

Buses for Mandla (Rs40, 2½ hours) leave from Kisli Gate at 6am, 8am, 9am, 12.30pm, 1.30pm and 2.30pm. They all go past Khatiya Gate. The 6am, 9am and 1.30pm continue on to Jabalpur (Rs95, 5½ hours). A 6pm bus also leaves Khatiya Gate (it doesn't go to Kisli Gate) for Mandla.

Mandla has regular buses to Jabalpur (Rs55, five hours, last bus 8.30pm), Nagpur (Rs175 to

---

JUNGLE PLAN

Many of the more upmarket resorts at the tiger reserves have part-/all-inclusive packages rather than straight accommodation prices. The so-called American Plan includes accommodation and all meals, while the Jungle Plan includes accommodation and meals plus a morning and an afternoon jeep safari.

Rs240, nine hours, last bus 11pm) and Raipur (Rs170 to Rs190, 10 hours, last bus 11pm).

For Nagpur or Pench Tiger Reserve, it's quicker to get off a Mandla-bound bus at Chiraidongri (45 minutes) from where you can wave down regular buses heading west. Most go all the way to Nagpur (Rs80, six hours), past Khawasa for Pench, although you may have to change at Seoni (Rs50, 2½ hours).

Buses leave from Mukki to Mandla (Rs100, five hours) at 8am, 8.30am, 2pm and 5pm. For Raipur, it's much quicker to change at the village of Baihar (Rs12, 30 minutes) than go all the way to Mandla.

BANDHAVGARH NATIONAL PARK
☎ 07653 / tiger pop 65

If your sole reason for visiting a national park in India is to see a tiger, look no further. One day spent here, including a morning and an afternoon safari, almost guarantees you a tiger sighting in this relatively small park which boasts the highest density of tigers in India. As well as the star attraction, there are also more than 40 leopards (although they are rarely seen) and more commonly sighted animals such as deer, wild boar and langur. Elephant rides are also available (opposite).

The park takes its name from an ancient fort perched on top of 800m-high cliffs. Its ramparts provide a home for vultures, blue rock thrushes and crag martins. You can visit it on special jeep trips during the day, but you'll have to pay all the usual park entry fees (see boxed text, p716).

Orientation & Information
The **park** (☎ 222214; www.bandhavgarhnationalpark .com; ☼ dawn-dusk Oct-Jun) is entered at the small, laid-back village of Tala, 32km from Umaria, the nearest railhead.

There's internet access at **Yadav Cyber Café** (per hr Rs50; ☼ 8am-11pm), but nowhere to change money.

Sleeping & Eating
All accommodation is on, or walking distance from, the main strip. All accommodation listed here has a restaurant. See the boxed text (opposite) for details about American and Jungle Plans.

Kum Kum Home (☎ 265324; r Rs350-400) Best budget option – rooms are basic but comfortable and come with large bathrooms and a veranda.

> **PARK LIFE**
>
> **Name** Sheevendra
>
> **Age** 20
>
> **Home** Bandhavgarh National Park
>
> **Job** Naturalist at Maharaja's Royal Retreat
>
> **Most tigers seen in one safari** Ten: two mothers with cubs, a courting couple and one solitary tiger (one morning in December 2007).
>
> **Favourite sighting** Following a tiger chasing a wild boar along a jeep track before seeing it catch the boar and carry it off into the jungle.

Hotel Bagh Vihar (☎ 265302; s/d Rs400/500) Nothing fancy, but first-floor rooms above the only internet cafe in the village are tidy and spacious.

Maharaja's Royal Retreat (☎ 265306; r Rs2000-2500, with AC Rs3000; ☒) At this former hunting retreat of Maharaja Martan Singh, the buildings – the oldest is 95 years old – house a mixed bag of rooms. The cheapest are very run down, but others are smart with tiled flooring, vases and free-standing wooden towel racks. There's a small museum (Rs50) on the premises, housing some of the maharaja's old hunting guns and a couple of stuffed tigers.

White Tiger Forest Lodge (☎ 265366; s/d American Plan Rs2140/2590, with AC Rs3140/3590; ☒ ☒) The old rooms, linked by elevated walkways, look a little run down, but are smart enough inside. Newer, brighter cottages, for the same price, have been built at the back of the unkempt gardens. There's a restaurant, bar and pool.

Nature Heritage Resort (☎ 265351; shalinidev@eth .net; r American/Jungle Plan Rs3500/11,060; ☒) It's all about bamboo here, with luxury, bamboo-trim cottages, containing bamboo furniture including bamboo bed frames, set around lush gardens shaded by…yep, bamboo.

Tiger's Den (☎ 265353; www.tigerden.com; American Plan r Rs4500, Jungle Plan s Rs9500; ☒) Very smart olive-green bungalows set around a lush, palm-lined garden. Nice touches include decorative mirrors, tiger photos on the bedroom walls and tubs in the bathrooms.

Kolkata Restaurant (mains Rs25-170) does a big range of Indian food, including tasty thalis (from Rs60), plus some Chinese and Italian. It also serves beer (Rs110). Next door, **Priyanka Restaurant** (samosas Rs3) does delicious veg samosas. On the other side of the road, **Al-Mezbaan** (mains Rs30-100) has friendly staff and a roadside terrace with plastic tables and chairs, and serves Indian veg and meat dishes. Near here is the **Wine Shop** (Kingfisher Rs80; ☉ 9am-11pm).

Getting There & Around

You can hire bicycles (per day Rs50) for exploring the surrounding villages from a rental place opposite Yadav Cyber Café.

Tala is connected with Umaria, the nearest railhead, by frequent buses, shared jeeps (Rs15, one hour) and taxis (Rs300).

Trains from Umaria include the 8477 *Utkal Express* to Delhi's Nizamuddin station (Rs316/860/1181, 17 hours, 9pm) via Gwalior (11 hours), Agra (14 hours) and Mathura (15 hours), and the 8234 *Narmada Express* which goes to Jabalpur (Rs80/261/352, 4½ hours, 4.30pm) before continuing to Bhopal (12 hours), Ujjain (16½ hours) and Indore (18½ hours).

There's one daily train to Varanasi, but it's at 4.22am so you might prefer to go via Satna on the 1710 *Chirmiri-Rewa Passenger* (sleeper Rs80, four hours, 12.45am) from where you can also catch buses to Khajuraho (p680) and Panna National Park (p689).

CHHATTISGARH

Chhattisgarh is remote, its public transport system is poor and its tourist infrastructure outside the main cities is almost nonexistent, but for the intrepid traveller, time spent here may well prove to be the highlight of your trip to this part of India. The country's most densely forested state is blessed with natural beauty, and waterfalls and unspoilt nature reserves abound. More interestingly, though, it is home to 42 different tribes whose pointillist paintings and spindly sculptures are as vivid as the colourful *haats* (markets) that take place across the region, particularly around Jagdalpur in Bastar.

Chhattisgarh is one of the eastern states associated with the Naxalite guerrillas (an ultra-leftist political movement that began in Naxal Village, West Bengal), but they rarely stray from their remote hideouts on Chhattisgarh's northern and southern borders.

RAIPUR

☎ 0771 / pop 700,113

Chhattisgarh's ugly capital is a centre for the state's steel industry and, apart from being a day trip away from Sirpur, has little in the way of tourist attractions. The Chhattisgarh Tourism Board is worth visiting here, however, because the office in Jagdalpur is almost useless.

Information

There are ATMs outside the bus and train stations.

Chhattisgarh Tourism Board head office (☎ 4066415; www.chhattisgarhtourism.net; beside Sibbal Palace Hotel, GE Rd; ☉ 10.30am-5.30pm); airport (☉ incoming flights); train station (☎ 6456336; ☉ 10am-5pm) Gives statewide advice and can help organise tribal visits, transport, accommodation and guides.

Internet cafe (per hr Rs15; ☉ 9.30am-9.30pm) Turn left out of the bus station and it's 500m along on your right.

State Bank of India (☎ 2535176; Jaistambh Chowk; ☉ 10.30am-5.30pm Mon-Fri) Opposite Hotel Radhika. Changes travellers cheques and cash, and has an ATM.

Sleeping & Eating

Hotel Radhika (☎ 2233806; Jaistambh Chowk; r Rs240-650, ste Rs900; ☒) A centrally located one-stop point for all your needs – a bank opposite, an ice-cream parlour below, a thali restaurant above and two bars next door. What more could you need? Rooms vary from basic budget jobs to decent AC midrangers. Book ahead – it's popular.

Hotel Jyoti (☎ 2428777; Pandri; s Rs350-650, d Rs450-800; ☒) A tranquil retreat after a long bus journey. Rooms are well looked after and the manager is helpful. Right opposite the bus stand.

Supreet Restaurant (Pandri; mains Rs15-60; ☉ 9am-10pm) Dhal, dosa, *paneer*, *paratha* (flaky unleavened bread) and tandoor flatbreads, as well as three types of thali (from Rs35) are all on offer at this cheap and cheerful place near the bus stand. It also does half portions, handy for lunchtime snacks. Turn left out of the bus stand and it's 500m along on your left.

Girnar Restaurant (☎ 2234776; Hotel Radhika, Jaistambh Chowk; mains Rs60-150; ☉ 10.30am-10.30pm) Good-quality Indian food right opposite Hotel Radhika reception. The thali-speciality restaurant upstairs was being renovated at the time of research, but has a good reputation.

Getting There & Around

AIR

Air India (☎ 4060942; Pandri; ☉ 10am-5pm Mon-Sat) flies daily to Mumbai (Rs4575, 3½ hours) via Bhubaneswar (Rs3375, 50 minutes), and Delhi (Rs5025, 2½ hours) via Nagpur (Rs3375, 40 minutes). Turn left out of the bus stand and the office is 1km along on your left, just past the railway-line level crossing. **Kingfisher** (☎ 2418601; airport; ☉ 7.30am-7pm) flies to Delhi and Mumbai too, and has twice-daily flights to Kolkata (Rs5100, two hours).

BUS
There are frequent buses to Jagdalpur (Rs280 to Rs320, seven hours, 5am to 11.30pm), three to Jabalpur (Rs300, 12 hours, 4am, 6am, 8.30pm) and a few to Nagpur (Rs180, eight hours, 7.30am, 8.30am, then 8pm to 11pm).

RICKSHAWS
A cycle-/autorickshaw between the bus and train stations costs Rs15/30. Shared autos (Rs5) ply the same route as well as the main GE Rd between Jaistambh Chowk and Chhattisgarh Tourism's head office.

TRAIN
Useful trains include the 8237 *Chhattisgarh Express* to Delhi's Nizamuddin station (Rs405/1110/1530, 29½ hours, 3.40pm) via Bhopal (Rs273/741/1016, 15 hours), Gwalior (Rs357/975/1342, 21½ hours) and Agra (Rs373/1020/1404, 24 hours), and the 2859 *Gitanjali Express* to Kolkata's Howrah station (Rs328/867/1179, 13 hours, 11.40pm).

AROUND RAIPUR
A possible day trip from Raipur, **Sirpur** is home to dozens of ruined Hindu temples and Buddhist monasteries, all dotted around the village and surrounding countryside. Many of the excavations are works-in-progress. All are free to see apart from the star of the show, the 7th-century **Laxman Temple** (Indian/foreigner Rs5/100; ☉ dawn-dusk), one of the oldest brick temples in India.

Buses drop you at Sirpur Mudh (Rs40, two hours), a junction 17km from Sirpur where you'll have to wait for a bus or shared jeep (Rs10, 25 minutes) to the village. For Laxman Temple, turn right past the snack stalls and keep walking for 1km. It's on the left, past the petrol pump.

JAGDALPUR
☎ 07782 / pop 103,123
The friendly capital of the Bastar region is an ideal base for exploring tribal Chhattisgarh (see boxed text, p722). The town itself hosts a *haat* every Sunday where you'll see Adisvasis

buying, selling and bartering alongside town traders, but it's only in the surrounding villages where Adivasi life can be fully appreciated. Some villages are extremely remote, and only really accessible with a guide. Others, though, are just a bus ride away and, particularly on market days (see boxed text, p723), can be easily explored independently. For eight particularly lively days in October, Jagdalpur's streets transform into race tracks as immense, homemade chariots are pitted against each other in an unusual climax to the 75-day festival of Dussehra (see boxed text p671).

Orientation & Information
Sanjay Market, which hosts a *haat* every Sunday, is the heartbeat of Jagdalpur. Hotel Rainbow is opposite, while Main Rd, a lively shopping street, is 200m away (turn left out of the market, then first right). The bus and train stations are 3km and 4km south respectively; Rs15 and Rs20 in a cycle-rickshaw.

Internet Garden (Main Rd; per hr Rs20; ☉ 7.30am-11pm) is walking distance from Sanjay Market. Turn left, take the first right (Main Rd) and it's 500m on your left. There's nowhere to change money, but the **State Bank of India** (Main Rd) has one of a few ATMs dotted round town. It's a further 300m past Internet Garden.

At the time of research **Chhattisgarh Tourism Board** (Durgar Mandir; ☉ 10.30am-5.30pm Mon-Sat), above Kidzee School, had neither a telephone nor anyone who could speak English. It's far easier to contact the Raipur office (opposite) or arrange your own guide (p722).

FANCY A BITE?

Red ants are more than just a painful nuisance to the Bastar tribes. Known as *chapura*, they also play an important role in food and medicine. They are often eaten live, served on a leaf with white ant eggs. Alternatively, villagers grind them into a paste and mix them with chilli to make chutney. The bodies of *chapura* contain formic acid believed to have useful medicinal qualities. If suffering from a fever, locals will sometimes put their hand into an ants nest, allowing it to be bitten hundreds of times so that the acid is administered into their bloodstream. Paracetamol for the hardcore, if you like.

THE EIGHT TRIBES OF BASTAR

- Bhatra – Women are distinguished by their particularly colourful saris and an abundance of jewellery, including their distinctive gold, conical nose studs.

- Bhurwa – Men wear simple headscarves wrapped around their foreheads, often coloured red and white.

- Bison-Horn Maria – Famed for their distinctive double-horned headdress worn during festivals.

- Ghadwa – The bell-metal specialists of Bastar.

- Dorla – The only tribe to make their homes not from mud thatch, but from the branches and leaves of trees found in the remote forests of the far south of Chhattisgarh.

- Halba – Excellent farmers, taller in stature than other Adivasi Men often only wear a loin cloth.

- Hill Maria or Abhuj Maria – Extremely remote tribe whose people very rarely venture out from their villages in the dense forests of the Bastar Hills.

- Muria – Known for the huge amount of jewellery worn by men as well as women.

Sights

The **Anthropological Museum** (☎ 229356; Chitrakote Rd; admission free; ☉ 10.30am-5.30pm Mon-Sat), 4km from the town centre, gives a fascinating insight into Bastar's tribes. To get there by cycle-rickshaw costs Rs30.

Sleeping & Eating

Hotel Chetak (☎ 223503; s/d Rs325/425, with AC Rs625/725; ✖) Handy for late-night buses. Tidy rooms are smaller than Rainbow's but clean and with sit-down flush toilets. The low-lit restaurant-bar (mains Rs40 to Rs100), open 10am to 10.30pm, is a decent spot for a beer (Rs100). Turn right out of the bus stand and walk 100m.

Hotel Rainbow (☎ 221684; hotelrainbow@indiatimes .com; s/d with air-cooler Rs380/480, with AC Rs700/825; ✖) Even the cheap, non-AC rooms are huge and well furnished in this excellent-value hotel, while the restaurant (mains Rs50 to Rs130), open 7am to 10.30pm, is the best in town. Try the stuffed capsicum. Opposite Sanjay Market.

Shopping

Shabari (Chandi Chowk; ☉ 11am-8pm Mon-Sat) A fixed-price government emporium selling Adivasi handicrafts from small, spindly iron figures (Rs20) to more expensive, heavy bell-metal statues. From the Sanjay Market end of Main Rd, take the third right and continue for 500m. Opposite the Bank of Baroda ATM.

Getting There & Away

BUS

There are regular services to Raipur (Rs180 to Rs220, seven hours), via Kondagaon (Rs55, 1½ hours), and to Kanger Valley National Park (Rs25, 45 minutes).

Buses to Chitrakote Falls (Rs40, two hours) leave from Anumapa Takij, a local cinema about 2km (cycle-rickshaw, Rs10) from the bus stand.

TRAIN

There's only one train here, but it's a goodie. The 2VK *Kirandul-Visakhapatnam* heads over the scenic Eastern Ghats on India's highest broad gauge line to Visakhapatnam (sleeper/ 1st Rs103/384, 10½ hours) on the Andhra Pradesh coast, via Koraput (Rs80/199, three hours) for connections into Orissa. It leaves Jagdalpur daily at 9.50am. In the opposite direction, the 1VK arrives in Jagdalpur at 4.30pm. **Train reservations** (☉ 8am-noon & 2-4pm Mon-Sat, 8am-noon Sun) can be made at the train station, which is a Rs10 rickshaw ride from the bus stand.

AROUND JAGDALPUR

You can get to many local Adivasi villages by bus – this is certainly an option on market days – but some are pretty inaccessible, and if you want to actually meet the Adivasis, rather than just look at them, a guide is essential as a translator if nothing else. They can also help you arrange homestays. **Awesh**

Ali (☎ 9425244925; per day Rs1000) comes highly recommended. Contact him directly, or go through the Raipur or Jagdalpur tourist offices. A car and driver will cost Rs800 per day plus diesel. At the time of research diesel was Rs40 per 10km.

Haats

These colourful **markets** are the lifeblood of Adivasi Chhattisgarh, and visiting them is an excellent way to get a taste of Bastar's vibrant tribal culture. Different tribes walk up to 20km to trade everything from their distinctive, almost fluorescent, saris to live red ants. Called *chapura* (see boxed text, p721), these ants are sold as food, eaten live (yes, still crawling and biting) off a leaf. Rs2 per leaf, if you're interested. More appetising perhaps are *bobo* (rice and lentil cakes, Rs3) or *bhajiya* (fried lentil powder, Rs3), both eaten with a spicy relish.

The large piles of what look like squashed dates are in fact dried *mahuwa,* a type of flower, either eaten fresh, or dried then boiled to create steam which is fermented to produce a potent liquor, the favourite tipple of many Bastar Adivasis.

For more information on *haats,* see the boxed text (below).

Adivasi Villages

There are more than 3500 villages in Bastar. **Earrakote**, 3.5km beyond Tokapal, is a mixed-tribe village, but made up largely of Ghadwa, specialists in the art of bell-metal craftwork.

The skill has been passed down through generations of many families, in some instances for as long as 300 years. A number of family members take part in the multipart process, from initial clay moulding and the melting of scrap metal to the painstaking job of covering the moulds in wax thread, a part of the process which is unique to Bastar. Awesh Ali (opposite) can put you in touch with families here who will put you up for the night in exchange for scrap metal or wax, which you can buy for them in Jagdalpur.

Every village has a *sirha* (shaman), a wise old man who people come to with their problems. He goes into a trance in order to contact the gods who then, through him, give advice on what action the troubled villager should take.

Chitrakote Falls

India's broadest waterfall (300m), two-thirds the size of Niagara, is at its roaring best just after the rains, but beautiful all year round, particularly at sunset. When the water is low, it's possible to paddle in pools at the top of the drop. Take extreme care.

In the river below the falls you can swim, hire a pedal boat (Rs25) or get a local boathand to row you up to the spray (Rs25). Take the steps that lead down from the garden of the government-only hotel.

Chitrakote Log Huts (☎ 07859-200194; bamboo huts/concrete AC cabins Rs1000/1500; ❄), with basic huts as well as modern cabins (some with fantastic views of the falls), is a peaceful place to stay.

MADHYA PRADESH & CHHATTISGARH

BASTAR HAATS – HOW TO FIND ADIVASI MARKETS

Most *haats* (markets) run from around midday to 5pm. These are just some of the more popular ones; there are many more. Ask at the Raipur tourism office (p720) for details.

When	Where	Distance from Jagdalpur	Bus from Jagdalpur	Why go?
Mon	Tokapal	23km	Rs30, 1hr	To buy bell-metal craftwork from Ghadwa Adivasis
Tue	Pakhnar	70km	No direct bus	Beautiful forest setting
Wed	Darbha	40km	Rs30, 1hr*	Attended by Bhurwa Adivasis
Thu	Bastar	18km	Rs25, 30min	Easy to reach from Jagdalpur
Fri	Nangur	35km	No direct bus	Attended by distant forest Adivasis
	Nagarnar	18km	No direct bus	Chance to see colourful Bhatra Adivasis
Sat	Kuknar	65km	Rs50, 2hr	Bison-Horn Maria stronghold
Sun	Jagdalpur	-	-	Central city location, open late into the evening
	Chingitarai	52km	No direct bus	Open, meadow setting
	Pamela	12km	Rs20, 45min	To see animated crowds bet on cockfighting

*bus goes from Anumapa Takij, not main bus stand

A new restaurant-bar was close to completion at the time of research.

The last bus back to Jagdalpur leaves at 4pm.

Kanger Valley National Park

The 200-sq-km **park** (☎ 07782-227596; Indian/foreigner Rs25/200, camera/video Rs25/200, vehicle entry Rs50; ◷ 8am-4pm Nov-Jun), some 40km southwest of Jagdalpur, consists of ancient forest flanking the Kanger River.

Four kilometres from the park entrance are **Tirathgarh Falls**, where water drops 100m through three sets of cascades. Open all year, they're best visited after the monsoon. Three **caves** (compulsory guide Rs25, lights hire Rs25; ◷ 8am-3pm Nov-Jun) with stunning, pristine formations can also be visited.

Wildlife includes deer, boars, sloths and leopards. Small lake **Bhaimsa Darha** is the habitat of turtles and crocodiles. Although you can get close in a bus from Jagdalpur, you will need private transport to enter and explore the park.

Kondagaon

☎ 07786 / pop 26,898

Some 76km north of Jagdalpur is a craft complex run by NGO **Saathi** (☎ 242852; saathibastar@yahoo.co.in; Kondagaon; training & daily board Rs400, weekly materials Rs500; ◷ 8am-6pm Mon-Sat), encouraging Adivasis in production of terracotta, woodcarving and metalwork. You can visit craftspeople at work, there's a shop and training can be given. Volunteers with design and craft knowledge are welcome. All Raipur–Jagdalpur buses go through Kondagaon.

Gujarat

Gujarat is a dynamic and diverse state with unexpected treasures to reward the traveller who is willing to explore beyond the tourist trail. Although it's easy to slot in a visit to Gujarat between Mumbai (Bombay) and Rajasthan, few people take the time to explore this vast state with a 1600km coastline and a fascinating geography. Of course, the scarcity of foreign tourists is an attraction in its own right, and here you are more likely to enjoy a friendly chat rather than hard sell from a local.

Attractions include the main city of Ahmedabad, a frantic metropolis that is home to Mahatma Gandhi's peaceful ashram as well as one of the world's finest textile museums. There's a florid maharaja's palace to explore in the university town of Vadodara, and pastel Portuguese cultural legacies to experience on the relaxing island of Diu. In the remote northwest, the seasonal island of Kutch barely rises above hardened salt plains and seasonal marshes. Here, local artisans weave and embroider the finest tribal textiles in India. The unforgiving elements of Little Rann are habitat to wild ass and flocks of flamingos; meanwhile the lush forests of Sasan Gir, in Saurashtra, harbour the last wild Asiatic lions.

Gujaratis are renowned for their entrepreneurial nous and austerity and these characteristics have helped make Gujarat one of India's wealthier and most industrialised states. Gujaratis also make up a huge proportion of India's large diaspora. The highly visible Jain community – the devout of whom follow a disciplined path towards *moksha* (liberation from the cycle of birth and death) – are largely responsible for Gujarat's industrious reputation, stunning white-marble temples, and exquisite, ever-so-slightly sweet vegetarian fare (and prohibition laws!).

HIGHLIGHTS

- Change down a gear, and head for the former Portuguese enclave of **Diu** (p749), for a sleepy island sojourn.

- Tackle a thali, explore the Old City mosques, and pay homage to Mahatma Gandhi in bustling **Ahmedabad** (p727)

- Undertake a challenging dawn pilgrimage to the hill-top temples of **Shatrunjaya** (p748) in Palitana and **Girnar Hill** (p760) in Junagadh

- Go looking for Indian wild ass on the flat salt plains of **Little Rann** (p775)

- Explore the colourful tribal villages of **Kutch** (p774) to understand, experience and acquire some of India's best textiles

GUJARAT

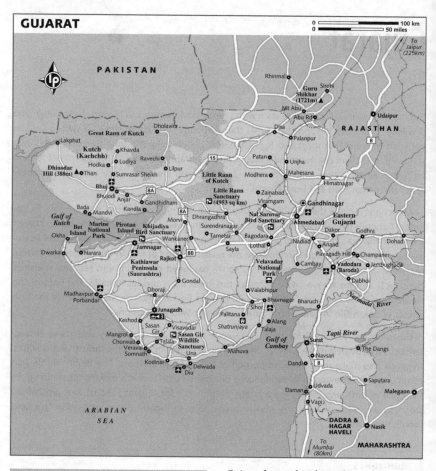

FAST FACTS

Population 50.6 million
Area 196,024 sq km
Capital Gandhinagar
Main language Gujarati
When to go October to March

History

It's said that Gujarat's Temple of Somnath witnessed the creation of the universe, and many significant sites in Krishna's life lie along the state's outh coast.

On a firmer historic footing, Lothal and Dholavira (Kutch) were sites of a Harappan (Indus) civilisation more than 4000 years ago.

Gujarat featured in the exploits of the mighty Buddhist emperor Ashoka, and you can see his rock edict near Junagadh.

Later, Gujarat suffered Muslim incursions by Mahmud of Ghazni and subsequent Mughal rulers, and was a battlefield between the Mughals and the Marathas. It was also an early point of contact with the West; the first British commercial outpost was established at Surat. Daman and Diu survived as Portuguese enclaves within Gujarat borders until 1961.

Saurashtra was never incorporated into British India. Instead it survived as more than 200 princely states until Independence. In 1956, all the states were amalgamated into the state of Mumbai. In 1960, Mumbai was split, on linguistic grounds, into the states of Maharashtra and Gujarat.

Congress was mainly in control of Gujarat after Independence, till 1991 when the Bharatiya Janata Party (BJP) came to power. In 2002, communal violence erupted after a Muslim mob was blamed for an arson attack on a train at Godhra that killed 59 Hindu activists. Hindu gangs then set upon Muslims in revenge. This violence coincided with the beginning of the election campaign, and BJP Chief Minister Najendra Modi followed a policy of fiercely Hindu rhetoric, which may have encouraged immigration in the state, but brought him a landslide victory. Since the 2002 riots, however, the state has been peaceful, and continues to enjoy its reputation as one of India's most prosperous states. In late 2008 this progressive state secured the large and lucrative Tata Motors' Nano car project.

Information
PERMITS
Alcohol permits are easy to get and obtainable at most large hotels with a 'wine shop'; show your passport plus a certificate from your hotel (your 'residence form' in Gujarat) to receive a one-month permit. Although permits for foreigners are 'officially free', local authorities often demand Rs100 from the shops and the shops pass this cost on to the customer. The permit allows you two units over the month and that equates to 20 bottles of standard beer. Cheers.

EASTERN GUJARAT

AHMEDABAD (AMDAVAD)
☎ 079 / pop 4.52 million

Ahmedabad (also called Amdavad) is Gujarat's major city and a startling metropolis which straddles the Sabarmati River. It's a city with a long history and many remarkable buildings, yet the old-world charm is all but swamped by new-world crowding and noise. It's remarkably cosmopolitan, with a fascinating maze of an old city, stunning museums, fine restaurants and fabulous night markets. Many travellers stop off briefly en route to Rajasthan or Mumbai, sneaking in a visit to Sabarmati Ashram (Gandhi's former headquarters).

Each January, the city hosts Makar Sakranti, an international kite festival that's well worth the stiff neck.

History
Over the centuries Ahmedabad has boomed and declined. Founded in 1411 by Ahmed Shah, at the spot where he saw a hare chasing a dog (he was impressed by its bravery), Ahmedabad was thought to be one of the finest cities in India in the 17th century, but by the 18th century its influence had waned. Its industrial strength once again raised the city to prominence, becoming a huge textile centre from the second half of the 19th century, which resulted in much immigration to staff the mills. From 1915 it became famous as the site of Gandhi's ashram. In 1970 the last mills closed and the subsequent economic hardship may have been a contributing factor in the communal unrest that split the city in 2002.

Orientation
On the eastern bank of the Sabarmati River, Mahatma Gandhi (MG) Rd and Relief Rd run east to the train station, about 3km away. The old city spreads north and south of Relief Rd. The busy road flanking the western bank of the Sabarmati is known as Ashram Rd and leads to Sabarmati Ashram. The airport is to the northeast. Most of the old city walls are now demolished, although some formidable gates remain as forlorn traffic islands around which congested traffic swirls.

Information
BOOKSHOPS
Art Book Center (Map p728; ☎ 26582130; www .artbookcenter.net; off Mangaldas Rd; ⏰ 10am-6pm) This specialist treasure trove is found upstairs in a brightly painted building near Ellis Bridge. Indian architecture, miniature painting and textile design are the main topics stocked.

Crossword (Map p728; Shree Krishna Centre, Mithakali Six Rd; ⏰ 10.30am-9pm) This bustling basement bookshop boasts a Cafe Coffee Day cafe.

INTERNET ACCESS
Cyberpoint (Map p728; Shree Krishna Centre, Mithakali Six Rd; per hr Rs15; ⏰ 10am-10pm) Above Crossword bookshop.

Relief Cyber Café (Map p730; Relief Rd; per hr Rs15) Opposite Relief Cinema and it's air-conditioned, what a relief!

MEDICAL SERVICES
Civil Hospital (Map p728; ☎ 27474359) Located 2.5km north of Ahmedabad train station.

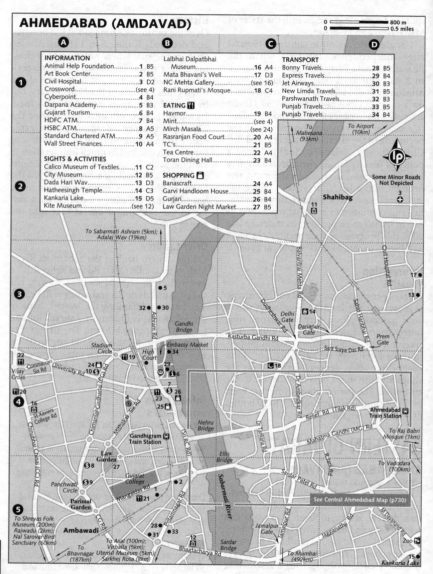

AHMEDABAD (AMDAVAD)

INFORMATION
Animal Help Foundation............1 B5
Art Book Center........................2 B5
Civil Hospital.............................3 D2
Crossword..............................(see 4)
Cyberpoint................................4 B4
Darpana Academy.....................5 B3
Gujarat Tourism........................6 B3
HDFC ATM................................7 B4
HSBC ATM.................................8 A5
Standard Chartered ATM...........9 A5
Wall Street Finances.................10 A4

SIGHTS & ACTIVITIES
Calico Museum of Textiles........11 C2
City Museum............................12 B5
Dada Hari Wav.........................13 D3
Hatheesingh Temple.................14 C3
Kankaria Lake...........................15 D5
Kite Museum..........................(see 12)

Lalbhai Dalpatbhai
  Museum................................16 A4
Mata Bhavani's Well.................17 D3
NC Mehta Gallery...................(see 16)
Rani Rupmati's Mosque............18 C4

EATING 🍴
Havmor...................................19 B4
Mint.......................................(see 4)
Mirch Masala..........................(see 24)
Rasranjan Food Court...............20 A4
TC's..21 B5
Tea Centre...............................22 A4
Toran Dining Hall.....................23 B4

SHOPPING 🛍
Banascraft................................24 A4
Garvi Handloom House.............25 B4
Gurjari....................................26 B4
Law Garden Night Market........27 B5

TRANSPORT
Bonny Travels...........................28 B5
Express Travels.........................29 B4
Jet Airways...............................30 B3
New Limda Travels....................31 B5
Parshwanath Travels.................32 B3
Punjab Travels..........................33 B4
Punjab Travels..........................34 B4

MONEY

For changing travellers cheques and currency, try **State Bank of India** (Map p730; ☎ 25506800) near Lal Darwaja (the local bus stand); and **Wall Street Finances** (Map p728; ☎ 26426682; CG Rd).

There are numerous ATMs:
Bank of Baroda (Map p730; Dr Tankaria Rd)
HDFC (Map p728; Ashram Rd)
HSBC (Map p728; CG Rd)
Standard Chartered (Map p728; CG Rd)
State Bank of India (Map p730; Ramanial Sheth Rd) At the main post office.

POST

Main post office (Map p730; ☎ 23220977; Ramanial Sheth Rd)

FESTIVALS IN GUJARAT

Makar Sakranti (Jan; Ahmedabad, p727) International kite festival when the sky fills with colour.

Modhera Dance Festival (Jan; Modhera, p738) A three-day festival of classical dance.

Bhavnath Fair (Jan/Feb; Junagadh, p759) Held in the month of Magha. Folk music and dancing, and *nagas* (naked sadhus or spiritual men) throng Bhavnath Mahadev Temple, at the foot of Girnar Hill.

Dang Durbar (Feb/Mar; The Dangs, east of Surat, p742) A tribal festival held a week before Holi in the forested region called the Dangs, near the Maharashtra border.

Mahakali (Mar/Apr; Pavagadh, p741) In the month of Chaitra, pilgrims pay tribute to the goddess Mahakali at Pavagadh hill, near Vadodara.

Janmastami (Aug/Sep; Dwarka, p764) This festival celebrates Krishna's birthday.

Tarnetar Fair (Aug/Sep; Tarnetar, northeast of Rajkot, p768) In the month of Bhadra, the Trineteshwar Temple at Tarnetar, 65km northeast of Rajkot, hosts this colourful fair, an opportunity for tribal men and women to find spouses. Gujarat Tourism arranges accommodation for the fair, and special state buses go to/from Rajkot.

Navratri (Sep/Oct; statewide; www.navratrifestival.com) The Festival of Nine Nights is a fantastic time to be in Gujarat. The festival leads up to Dussehra and is devoted to the worship of Durga, the mother goddess. Junctions and market places are filled with nightly *garbas* – where people dress up in sparkling finery to perform entrancing dances till the early hours – and it's a great festival for foreigners to join in.

Dussehra (Sep/Oct; statewide) Dussehra is the culmination of Navratri, and celebrates the victory of Durga and Rama over the demon king Ravana, with more all-night dancing and fireworks.

Kartik Purnima (Nov/Dec; Somnath, p755) A large fair at the full moon of Kartik Purnima.

TOURIST INFORMATION

The very helpful **Gujarat Tourism** (Map p728; ☎ 26589172; www.gujarattourism.com; ⏲ 10.30am-1.30pm & 2-6pm Mon-Sat, closed 2nd & 4th Sat of month) office is off Ashram Rd. Ask autorickshaw drivers for HK House. As well as having all sorts of information at their fingertips there is an associated **Travel service** (☎ 9727723928) that organises air ticketing, car hire and tours.

Fast-paced five-day tours to Saurashtra and northern Gujarat/southern Rajasthan cost around Rs3500. Prices include all transport, accommodation and guide fees. Check out the website for details.

Sights

BHADRA FORT & TEEN DARWAJA

Bhadra Fort (Map p730; Lal Darwaja), built by the city's founder, Ahmed Shah, in 1411, now houses government offices and a Kali temple. Ask for access to the roof, where you can check out the formidable structure, a perfunctory gallows and views of the surrounding streets. Two of the fort bastions partly collapsed in the 2001 earthquake. To the east is the **Teen Darwaja** (Triple Gateway), once the gateway into the Royal Square, or Maidan Shahi, where royal processions and polo games took place.

MOSQUES & MAUSOLEUMS

Jama Masjid (Map p730), built by Ahmed Shah in 1423, is to the east of the Teen Darwaja.

Demolished Hindu and Jain temples provided the building materials. The 260 columns support 15 domes at different elevations. There were once two 'shaking' minarets, but they lost half their height in the great earthquake of 1819 and collapsed after another tremor in 1957. The 2001 earthquake then took its toll, leaving cracks in the masonry and destroying several *jalis* (carved marble lattice screens).

The **Tomb of Ahmed Shah** (Map p730), constructed after his death in 1442, stands outside the Jama Masjid's east gate, and includes the cenotaphs of his son and grandson. Women are not allowed to go into the central chamber. Across the street on a raised platform is his queen's tomb, now engulfed by market stalls, and in poor shape.

Southwest of Bhadra Fort and dating from 1414, **Ahmed Shah's Mosque** (Map p730) was one of the city's earliest mosques. It has an elaborately carved ceiling with a circular symmetry reminiscent of Hindu and Jain temples, and beautiful pillars and *jalis*.

Sidi Saiyad's Mosque (Map p730; Dr Tankaria Rd), close to the river, was once part of the old citadel wall. Constructed in 1573 by Sidi Saiyad, a sometime slave of Ahmed Shah, it is one of Ahmedabad's most stunning buildings, with exquisite *jalis*, spiderweb fine, depicting the intricate intertwining branches of the 'tree of life'.

CENTRAL AHMEDABAD

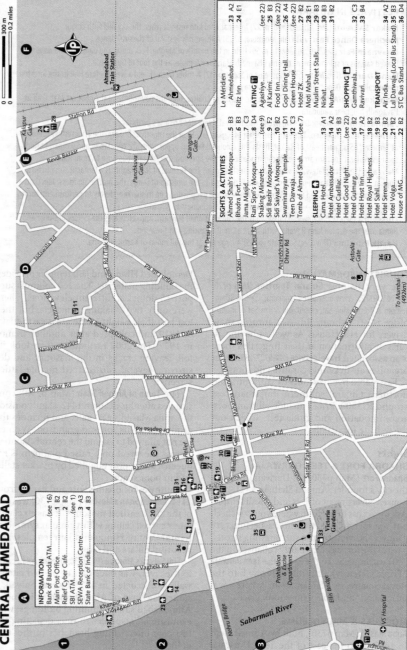

0   300 m
0   0.2 miles

INFORMATION
Bank of Baroda ATM.........	(see 16)
Main Post Office...............	1 B2
Relief Cyber Café.............	2 B2
SBI ATM............................	(see 1)
SEWA Reception Centre.....	3 A3
State Bank of India...........	4 B3

SIGHTS & ACTIVITIES
Ahmed Shah's Mosque........	5 B3
Bhadra Fort........................	6 B3
Jama Masjid.......................	7 C3
Rani Sipri's Mosque............	8 D4
Shaking Minarets................	(see 9)
Sidi Bashir Mosque.............	9 F2
Sidi Salyad's Mosque..........	10 B2
Swaminarayan Temple.........	11 D1
Teen Darwaja......................	12 C3
Tomb of Ahmed Shah..........	(see 7)

SLEEPING
Cama Hotel.........................	13 A1
Hotel Ambassador...............	14 A2
Hotel Cadillac.....................	15 B3
Hotel Good Night................	(see 22)
Hotel Gulmarg....................	16 B2
Hotel Host Inn....................	17 A2
Hotel Royal Highness..........	18 B2
Hotel Sahil.........................	19 B3
Hotel Serena.......................	20 B2
Hotel Volga........................	21 B2
House of MG.......................	22 B2

Le Méridien........................	23 A2
Ritz Inn.............................	24 E1

EATING
Agashiye............................	(see 22)
Al Karimi...........................	25 B3
Food Inn............................	(see 22)
Gopi Dining Hall................	26 A4
Green House.......................	(see 22)
Hotel ZK............................	27 B3
Moti Mahal........................	28 E1
Muslim Street Stalls...........	29 B3
Nishat...............................	30 B3
Nutan................................	31 B2

SHOPPING
Gamthiwala........................	32 C3
Ravivari..............................	33 B4

TRANSPORT
Air India............................	34 A2
Lal Darwaja (Local Bus Stand)	35 B3
STC Bus Stand....................	36 D4

GUJARAT

North of the centre, **Rani Rupmati's Mosque** (Map p728), built between 1430 and 1440, was named after the Hindu wife of the sultan. The minarets were damaged in the great earthquake of 1819. The dome is elevated to allow light in around its base. Like so many of Ahmedabad's early mosques, it combines elements of Hindu and Islamic design.

The small **Rani Sipri's Mosque** (Map p730), southeast of the centre, is also known as the Masjid-e-Nagira (Jewel of a Mosque) because of its graceful construction, with slender minarets. It's said to have been commissioned in 1514 by a wife of Sultan Mahmud Begara after he executed their son for some misdemeanour – she is also buried here.

South of Ahmedabad station, outside Sarangpur Gate, the **Sidi Bashir Mosque** (Map p730) is famed for its 21.3m-high shaking minarets (*jhulta minars*). Built to shake to protect against earthquake damage, this certainly worked in 2001.

The shaking minarets of the **Raj Babri Mosque**, southeast of Ahmedabad station in Gomtipur, were destroyed by their ingenuity, as one was partially dismantled by an inquisitive Englishman in an unsuccessful attempt to find out how it worked. It was never completely repaired, and in 2001 both minarets collapsed. Repairs continue.

TEMPLES

Outside Delhi Gate, north of the old city, the Jain **Hatheesingh Temple** (Map p728; Balvantrai Mehta Rd) is constructed of delicately carved white marble. Built in 1848, it's dedicated to Dharamanath, the 15th Jain *tirthankar* (great teacher).

Dive into the old city's narrow streets to find the glorious, multicoloured, woodcarved **Swaminarayan Temple** (Map p730), a grand *haveli* (traditional, often ornately decorated, residences) dating from 1850, enclosed in a large courtyard.

KANKARIA LAKE

Built in 1451, this polygonal **lake** (Map p728), southeast of the city, is a breath of fresh air, and a popular place for a promenade. There is a grand colonial Dutch tomb nearby, one of Gujarat's oldest.

SARKHEJ ROSA

Located 8km southwest of the city, **Sarkhej Rosa** (☎ 26828675; admission free; ☽ 6am-10pm) is a col-

lection of intriguing Islamic buildings. They cluster around a great tank, constructed by Sultan Mahmud Shah I (1458–1511).

By the entrance is the tomb of Sultan Mahmud Begada, with geometric *jalis* casting patterns of light on the floor. Shaikh Ahmed Khattu (his name means 'bestower of wealth') lived at Sarkhej and built the mosque with a great open space in front of the prayer hall surrounded by domes.

A return rickshaw here will cost around Rs150 and it can be combined with a visit to Vishalla Utensil Museum (p732) and Vishalla Restaurant (p734).

STEP WELLS

Dada Hari Wav (Map p728; admission free; ☽ dawn-dusk), built in 1499 by a woman of Sultan Begara's harem, has steps to lower platforms, terminating at a small, octagonal well. The depths are cool, even on the hottest day. Neglected and often bone dry, it's a fascinating and eerie place. The best time to visit and photograph the well is between 10am and 11am (earlier in the summer, later in the winter); at other times the sun doesn't penetrate to the various levels. Bus 34 and 111 (Rs5) to Asarwa stops nearby.

Mata Bhavani's Well (Map p728) is about 200m north of Dada Hari's. Thought to be several hundred years older, it's less ornate and used as a simple Hindu temple.

CALICO MUSEUM OF TEXTILES

This **museum** (Map p728; ☎ 22868172; Shahibag; admission free; ☽ 10.30am-12.30pm with no entry after 11am, & 2.45-4.45pm with no entry after 3.15pm Thu-Tue) contains one of the world's finest collections of antique and modern Indian textiles – there are some astoundingly beautiful pieces here, displaying incredible virtuosity and extravagance.

There are two parts to the museum: first, the Calico Museum's main textile galleries, which can only be visited in the morning session; and second, Invisible Presence: Images and Abodes of Indian Deities, which explores depictions of Indian gods with indoor and outdoor exhibits, including textile galleries, which can only be visited in the afternoon. Opposite the underbridge, the museum is part of the Sarabhai Foundation, housed in a *haveli* constructed from old village houses, with wonderful woodcarving. It's 4.5km north of the city. Take bus 101, 102 or 105 (Rs5) through Delhi Gate. An autorickshaw should cost Rs40.

DEEP & MEANINGFUL

The profound significance of water in the drought-prone districts of Gujarat and Rajasthan is set in stone in the step well – *wav*, *kuva* or *baoli* (*baori* in Rajasthan). These elaborate constructions are unique to northwestern India. Ancient Hindu scriptures venerate those who build communal wells. With the Indian inclination to turn the functional into works of art, sophisticated water-storage structures were developed, first by Hindus and then under the Mughals. Although the nobility considered it a religious obligation to construct these, the wells were evidently status symbols – the grandeur and artistry reflected the power and sensibility of their patrons. Often attached to temples so that devotees could bathe, the wells were also meeting places, with verandas where people could take refuge from the summer heat, and stopping places on caravan routes. Reliant on rainfall and (dropping) levels of ground water, the wells have been long neglected and are often used as toilets, and so are no longer the cleanest sources of water.

No bags, cameras or mobile phones are allowed to be taken into the museum and there's a maximum of 20 visitors at a time.

OTHER MUSEUMS

The **City Museum** (Map p728; ☎ 26578369; Sanskar Kendra, Sanskar Chendra, Bhagtacharya Rd; admission free; ☉ 10am-6pm Tue-Sun), housed in a Le Corbusier building and reminiscent of a high school under demolition, covers Ahmedabad's history. It has sections that focus on the city's religious communities, Gandhi and the Independence struggle. On the ground floor you will find the **Kite Museum** (Map p728; admission free; ☉ 10am-8pm Tue-Sun) with a selection of patterned tissue-paper kites resembling trapped butterflies.

The **Lalbhai Dalpatbhai Museum** (Map p728; ☎ 26306883; St Xaviers College Rd; admission free; ☉ 11.30am-5pm Tue-Sun), near Gujarat University, houses fine stone, marble and wood carvings from around India, as well as local bronzes, cloth paintings and coins. Among the sculptures is a sandstone carving from Madhya Pradesh dating from the 6th century AD, the oldest-known carved image of the god Rama.

In the same building is the **NC Mehta Gallery** (Map p728; ☎ 26302463; admission free; ☉ 10.30am-5.30pm Tue-Sun Jul-Apr, 8.30am-12.30pm Tue-Sun May-Jun) with an important collection of jewel-like illustrated manuscripts and miniature paintings. Best known is *Chaurapanchasika* (Fifty Love Lyrics of a Thief), written by Vilhana, an 11th-century Kashmiri poet sentenced to be hanged for loving the king's daughter. Just before his execution he composed the poems and so impressed the king that there was a lucky turnaround for Vilhana and the king gave his daughter to him in marriage.

The **Shreyas Folk Museum** (☎ 26601338; Indian/foreigner Rs7/45; ☉ 10am-1.30pm & 2-5.30pm Fri-Tue), about 2.5km west of the river, in the suburb of Ambavadi, displays an impressive range of Gujarati folk arts and crafts, with elaborately decorated everyday items, including textiles, clothing and woodcarving. Take bus 34 or 200 (Rs5), or an autorickshaw costs around Rs50.

The **Utensil Museum** (☎ 26602422; Vishalla; admission Rs10, camera/video Rs50/100; ☉ 11am-3pm & 4.30-10pm), opposite Vasana Tol Naka, displays the graceful practicality of pots and utensils.

SABARMATI ASHRAM

About 5km from the centre, peacefully set on the river's west bank, this **ashram** (☎ 27557277; admission free; ☉ 8.30am-6.30pm) was Gandhi's headquarters during the long struggle for Indian independence. He founded the ashram in 1915 and it moved to its current site a few years later. It was from here on 12 March 1930 that Gandhi set out on his famous Salt March to the Gulf of Cambay in a symbolic protest. Handicrafts, handmade paper and spinning wheels are still produced on the site. There's a **paper factory** (☉ 11am-5pm Mon-Sat) over the road that's worth a look (ask at the ashram for permission). Gandhi's poignant, spartan living quarters are preserved and there's a pictorial record of his life. The library contains the letter sent by Gandhi to Hitler on 23 July 1939 asking him to pull back from war. Gandhi was imprisoned at Sabarmati Jail, just down the road, in 1922.

There's usually a **sound-and-light show**, which was out of action at the time we visited. Telephone for current times. Buses 13/1 and 83 (Rs5) run here. An autorickshaw costs about Rs30.

Tours

The **Municipal Corporation** (☎ 26574335, 9824032866) runs fascinating heritage **walking tours** (Indian/foreigner Rs20/50) through the old city. They start from the Swaminarayan Temple in Kalupur (p731) at 8am and finish near the Jama Masjid around 10.30am. It's advisable to book. The tours, through narrow, confusing streets and past dilapidated, carved wooden houses, are an excellent way to get a feel for the city and its *pols* (gated neighbourhoods). Commentaries are given in English and there's a brief slide show beforehand.

The Municipal Corporation has also collaborated with the House of MG (p734) to develop an ingenious **audio guide walk** (Rs100). Beginning at the famed hotel, this 80-minute MP3-guided walk takes an alternative route through the Old City, ending at the **Bholantah Divetia Haveli**. This carefully restored, finely carved house is now a museum, shop and cafe rolled into one.

Sleeping

As a part of the Walled City Revitalisation project, several heritage homes have been restored with modern facilities. A few have started accommodating guests, and it's a fascinating way to experience Ahmedabad. Contact the **Municipal Corporation** (☎ 9824032866).

Otherwise, many budget hotels are scattered around noisy, polluted Relief Rd. Most hotels have 24-hour check-out, although others will turf you out at 9am.

BUDGET

Hotel Cadillac (Map p730; ☎ 25507558; Advance Cinema Rd; dm Rs70, r without bathroom Rs220, r Rs280) Opposite Electricity House, this very cheerful and cheap option, sporting a wooden balustrade, is a classic from 1934. Management vouch for the comfort of the lumpy cotton mattresses, but we remain dubious. The dorm is male only and while the street noise and bathrooms are not selling features, the people-watching balcony is.

Hotel Gulmarg (Map p730; ☎ 25507202; Dr Tankaria Rd; s/d Rs250/350, without bathroom Rs200/300, with AC Rs400/500; ☒) Near Sidi Sayad's Mosque, this 4th-floor hotel is proud of its range of dull, dishevelled rooms, with usable bathrooms and tough-as-boots mattresses. Most rooms have a TV and telephone. Stretch your calves on the dusty stairwell if the lift isn't working or it frightens you.

Hotel Sahil (Map p730; ☎ 25507351; Advance Cinema Rd; s/d from Rs400/500) The sign is hard to spot from street level but look for the ice cream parlour in the Advance Cinema Mall (the cinema has long since gone). This hotel has small, slipshod rooms, some immeasurably better than others.

Hotel Good Night (Map p730; ☎ 25507181; hotelforyou2002@yahoo.com; Dr Tankaria Rd; s/d from Rs400/500, with AC from Rs700/800; ☒) This tidy hotel has budget rooms better than the average in these parts. There are seven categories of rooms with Rs200 jumps in prices, so it shouldn't be too hard to find one that suits your budget and comfort needs. The attached thali restaurant, Food Inn (p734), is also recommended.

Hotel Serena (Map p730; ☎ 25510136; Dr Tankaria Rd; s/d Rs450/550, with AC from Rs650/750; ☒) Here the rooms are actually better than the lobby would have you believe. The unassuming front desk is friendly and efficient, and the walls and floors are squeaky clean. All in all, Serena represents good value (the rooms at the back will be the quietest).

Hotel Volga (Map p730; ☎ 25509497; www.hotelvolga .com; off Relief Rd; s/d Rs500/650, with AC from Rs700-800; ☒ 🖥) This is a surprisingly good option tucked down a dark alley behind Relief Rd and is worth searching out. Rooms are smart and respectably clean, with a hint of 1970s design in the curved beige walls – some are more dashingly decorated. And the front desk is friendly and efficient.

MIDRANGE

Hotel Ambassador (Map p730; ☎ 26182222; www.ambassadorahmedabad.com; Khanpur Rd; s/d from Rs900/1100; ☒) This hotel doesn't look that much from the outside. And it isn't much. But it's honest value and the rooms are acceptably clean and OK for a quick stay. As usual, check the plumbing before accepting a room – bathroom functionality is highly variable.

Hotel Host Inn (Map p730; ☎ 30226555; www.hotelhostinn.com; Khanpur Rd; s/d from Rs1500/1800; ☒ 🖥) The front of this hotel looks like a 1950s ice-cream parlour – look for the ice-cream cone pillars and caramel colouring. The deeply chilled and glitzy lobby is all front, however, and the rooms, comfortable enough and well appointed, are rather overpriced. Look at a few, negotiate, and choose a back room.

Ritz Inn (Map p730; ☎ 22123842; www.hotelritzinn .com; Station Rd; s/d from Rs2000/2600; ☒ 🖥) Near the railway station, this smart hotel has unusual

GUJARAT

class and is excellent value for money. The art deco lobby, comfortable rooms with superb beds, and unusually slick service make this an outstanding option. There's a good veg restaurant, check-out is a civilised 24 hours, and it offers free airport transfer.

Hotel Royal Highness (Map p730; ☎ 25507450; www.hotelroyalhighness.com; Relief Rd; s/d from Rs2250/2700, ste Rs3750; ✖ 🖵 🛜) This grand edifice is in a convenient, though noisy location. The lobby is very grand, and in comparison the rooms are spacious and clean but a little ordinary. The bathrooms aren't cutting edge, but there is a restaurant, a 24-hour coffee shop, and an airport shuttle service.

TOP END

our pick House of MG (Map p730; ☎ 25506946; www.houseofmg.com; Dr Tankaria Rd; s/d from Rs5000/6000, ste from Rs9000; ✖ 🖵 🛜 🍴) This 1920s building (with two excellent restaurants; see right) was once the home of the industrialist Sheth Mangaldas Girdhardas, converted into a beautiful heritage hotel by his great grandson. All the rooms are vast, verandah-edged and tastefully decorated, with great attention to detail. Included in the tariff are breakfast and first-rate service. It's an icon of the upper classes, and hugely popular with locals and foreigners alike. The indoor swimming pool and health club are divine. If you know your dates, book a couple of months in advance online to receive up to 30% discount.

Cama Hotel (Map p730; ☎ 25601234; www.camahotelsindia.com; Khanpur Rd; s/d from Rs6500/7500; ✖ 🍴) The Cama overall is a little weary; rooms are overpriced so ask for a discount. Although comfortable, the standard rooms (called superior rooms) are small. There are two restaurants, a big outdoor pool (nonguests Rs500), and a lush lawn which runs down to the piles of rubbish on the river bank.

Le Méridien Ahmedabad (Map p730; ☎ 25505505; www.lemeridien.com; Khanpur Rd; s/d from Rs6500/7500, ste Rs20,000; ✖ 🖵 🍴) This is a luxurious option that towers over the fragile shacks scattered along the river bank. All rooms are sumptuous and the suites are palatial. The price includes breakfast, and there's a neat indoor swimming pool (Rs250 nonguests), spa and sauna.

Eating

Ahmedabad is a great place to sample the Gujarati thali – the traditional all-you-can-eat vegetarian meal, with a greater variety of dishes that are sweeter, lighter and less spicy and oily than the Punjabi version.

RESTAURANTS

Nishat (Map p730; ☎ 25507335; Khas Bazaar; mains Rs20-60; 🕑 11am-4pm & 7-11.30pm; ✖) This place gets packed in the evenings with Muslim men devouring hearty veg and, more often, nonveg tandoori dishes.

Green House (Map p730; ☎ 25506946; House of MG, Dr Tankaria Rd; mains Rs30-100; 🕑 7am-11pm) The Green House is the casual front restaurant at the House of MG. Choose the fan-blasted outdoor courtyard or the AC room with a big-screen TV. The selection of Gujarati dishes is superb. Do try the house special *sharbat*; and the delicate and delicious *panki*, a thin crepe cooked between banana leaves; or the divine *malpura*, a sweet, deep-fried pancake in saffron syrup, topped with rose petals. And don't leave without trying the hand-churned ice cream.

Mint (Map p728; G-36 Shree Krishna Centre, Mithakhali Six Rd; mains Rs40-115; 🕑 9am-10pm) This is a cool, mint-coloured retreat with a soothing atmosphere and tasty snacks, such as *pav bhaji* (spiced vegetables with bread) and international comfort food, such as cheese-topped mashed potatoes.

Mirch Masala (Map p728; CG Rd; mains Rs45-170; 🕑 12.30-3pm & 7-11pm) Lively and popular, with lots of bright pictures, puppets and Bollywood posters. Although à la carte is good for dinner, the lunch specials are great value.

Nutan (Map p730; ☎ 25501542; Opposite Dinbai Tower; mains Rs45-75; 🕑 9-11am, 11.30am-4pm, 6.30-11pm) An immensely popular pure veg eatery (no thalis here though) that's packed with businessmen at lunchtime.

Moti Mahal (Map p730; ☎ 22121881; Kapasia Bazaar; mains Rs50-90; 🕑 11am-11pm) Ahmedabad's oldest restaurant boasts a long Indian, Chinese, veg and non-veg menu. You can eat simple fare downstairs in an open-fronted restaurant or upstairs in the AC shiny booths. The mezzanine has private booths for tiny couples with zenana screens for private people-watching.

Hotel ZK (Map p730; ☎ 25506121; Relief Rd; mains Rs50-130; 🕑 11am-4pm, 7am-11pm) A slinky AC, non-veg restaurant, with tinted windows, low lighting and impeccable service. The Chicken Afghani curry is recommended but apparently the most popular dish with the locals is the interesting sounding Chicken Pesto Chinese.

GUJARAT

Gopi Dining Hall (Map p730; ☎ 26576388; off Pritamnagar Rd; mains Rs62-82; ⏰ 10am-3pm & 6-10.30pm) Just off the west end of Ellis Bridge, opposite the Town Hall, this small restaurant is a much-loved thali institution. The standard thali is Rs62, the unlimited is Rs72 and the deluxe is Rs82.

Food Inn (Map p730; ☎ 25509512; Dr Tankaria Rd; mains Rs65-160; ⏰ noon-4pm, 6.30-11pm) A clean, bright and bustling curry house where carnivores can tuck into numerous chicken, mutton and fish dishes, including biryani, sizzlers and Chinese. There are plenty of snacks and deserts on the menu too, which is dominated by spicy Punjabi curries and lip-smackin' tandoori.

Toran Dining Hall (Map p728; Opposite Sales India, Ashram Rd; thali Rs80; ⏰ 11am-3pm & 7-10pm) Gung-ho staff knock up delicious, never-ending Gujarati thalis to a mostly middle-class crowd.

our pick **Agashiye** (Map p730; ☎ 25506946; House of MG, Dr Tankaria Rd; lunch reg/deluxe Rs295/395, dinner reg/deluxe Rs345/495; ⏰ noon-2.30pm & 7-11pm) This is Ahmedabad's best dining experience. On the rooftop of one of the city's finest mansions, the lovely tiled terrace is an oasis of calm and space, candle-lit at night and a world away from the congested streets. The all-veg menu, which changes daily, begins with a rose-and-lemon-flavoured welcoming drink and is a cultural journey around the traditional thali – a multitude of ravishingly tasty vegetable dishes – and finishes with hand-churned ice cream.

Vishalla (☎ 26602422; lunch Rs180, dinner Rs360; ⏰ 11am-3pm & 8-11pm) On the southern edge of town, opposite Vasana Tol Naka, Vishalla is a magical eating experience evoking a traditional Gujarati village. You eat a veg thali seated on the floor in rustic wooden huts, and the complex includes craft stalls and a fascinating Utensil Museum (p732). Dinner is accompanied by puppet or magic shows and traditional music. Bus 150 or 31 will take you nearby; an autorickshaw costs about Rs90 return.

QUICK EATS

Havmor (Map p728; Stadium Complex; ice cream Rs15-70) Ahmedabad is famous for its ice cream and the Havmor ice-cream bar, behind Navrangpura bus stop, has tons of flavours.

Tea Centre (Map p728; Vijay Char Rasta; mains Rs15-80) A calm place to sip chai, above a busy chowk. The iced teas are heavenly – try the *caiparinha*.

Al Karimi (Map p730; Advance Cinema Rd; mains Rs90-20; ice cream Rs15-175) This chilled ice cream parlour is a panel of glass away from the chaos and dirt outside. Guilt trips aside, it also doubles as a non-veg restaurant, though the house speciality described as 'seafood and chicken chunks' had us sticking with the very karimi ice cream.

Rasranjan Food Court (Map p728; Chinubhai Chinai (CC) Rd; mains Rs15-80; ⏰ 11am-11pm) A popular emporium offering fast-food, south Indian and Punjabi dishes, with sweets and *chaat* (snacks) downstairs.

TC's (Map p728; ground fl, Mangaldas Rd; mains Rs35-140; ⏰ 11am-11pm) This trendy little cafe near Gujarat College offers pita and hummus, Chinese noodles and Indian dishes in a bright cafe setting, with bubbling hookahs, big TV screens and bemused waiters. The sweet hookah smoke fills the chilled room and the Red Bull mocktails are about as wild as things get.

Muslim street food is available near Teen Darwaja on Bhathiyar Gali (Map p730), a small street parallel to MG Rd. You can get a good meaty feed for about Rs25 from the evening stalls. The Law Garden Night Market (Map p728) is also good for street food.

Shopping

Law Garden Night Market (Map p728; Law Garden) This evening market is packed with stalls selling glittering wares from Kutch and Saurashtra. It's chock-a-block with cholis (sari blouses) and richly decorated *chaniyas* (long, wide traditional skirts), both traditionally worn at Navratri (see the boxed text, p729); embroidered wall hangings; costume jewellery and more.

Gurjari (Map p728; Ashram Rd; ⏰ 10am-2pm & 3-7pm) South of Gujarat Tourism is this state emporium on several floors, with some fantastic finds if you rummage around, including silk saris.

Garvi Handloom House (Map p728; Ashram Rd; ⏰ 10.30am-8pm) Opposite Gurjari, this place sells a range of textiles.

Gamthiwala (Map p730; Manekchowk; ⏰ 11am-1pm & 2-7pm Mon-Sat) In the old city, this shop sells quality block-printed textiles.

Asal (5 Tejpal Society; ⏰ 10am-8pm) An organic shop that sells utensils, *khadi* fabric, ayurvedic spices, herbal bath soaps, oils and essences.

SEWA

The Self-Employed Women's Association (SEWA) is Gujarat's largest union. Established in 1972, it's based on the notion that poor women need organisation, not aid.

SEWA identifies three types of self-employed workers: hawkers and vendors; home-based workers such as weavers, potters and *bidi* (hand-rolled cigarettes) rollers; and manual labourers and service providers, such as agricultural labourers, construction workers and domestic workers.

SEWA assists self-employed workers to organise into unions and cooperatives, so that they can control the fruits of their labours. SEWA's approach focuses on health and childcare, literacy, appropriate housing and self-sufficiency, and the SEWA Academy conducts leadership courses for its members. SEWA is also active in the campaign for a needs-based minimum wage. SEWA runs a bank, giving many poor women their first access to a savings or reputable lending body, and provides access to legal aid.

The **SEWA Reception Centre** (Map p730; ☎ 5506444; www.sewa.org; ☯ 10.30am-6pm Mon-Sat) is at the eastern end of Ellis Bridge. It has a range of literature and visitors are welcome. SEWA's fixed-price handicrafts are sold at Banascraft (see p735).

Banascraft (Map p728; 8-9 Chandan Complex, CG Rd; ☯ 10.30am-8pm Mon-Sat, to 6.30pm Sun) The retail outlet of the Self-Employed Women's Association (SEWA; see the boxed text, above), Banascraft sells embroidered shawls, clothes and wall hangings.

Ravivari (Map p730; ☯ dawn-dusk Sun) This riverside flea market is a crazy mass of animals, music, crockery, clothing and gadgets that makes for fascinating rummaging.

Getting There & Away

AIR

Several international airlines fly to/from Ahmedabad. Recommended ticketing offices:

Gujarat Tourism Travel Service (Map p728; ☎ 9727723928; www.gujarattourism.com; off Ashram Rd)

Parshwanath Travels (Map p728; ☎ 27544142; parshtrvl@wilnetonline.net; Ashram Rd)

Express Travels (Map p728; ☎ 26588602; express @wilnetonline.net; off Ashram Rd) Around the corner from Gujarat Tourism.

Air India (Map p730; ☎ 26585622, airport office 22867237; www.airindia.com; Relief Rd; ☯ 10am-5pm), near the Nehru Bridge, and **Jet Airways** (Map p728; ☎ 27543304; www.jetairways.com; Ashram Rd; ☯ 10am-6.30pm Mon-Fri, to 4pm Sat & Sun) fly regularly to Mumbai (from Rs3500) and Delhi (Rs4000).

BUS

Private buses from the north may drop you at Naroda Rd, about 7km northwest of the city centre – an autorickshaw will complete the journey for around Rs50.

Leaving from the bus stand near Rani Sipri's Mosque, numerous **State Transport Corporation** (STC; Map p730; ☎ 25463360) buses go to Vadodara (Rs75, two hours), Jamnagar (Rs150, seven hours), Junagadh (Rs120, eight hours), Bhavnagar (Rs100, four hours) and Rajkot (Rs105, 4½ hours).

For long distances, private buses are quicker; some offices are east of the STC bus stand. **Punjab Travels** (Map p728; ☯ 9am-9pm) Embassy Market (☎ 26589200; off Ashram Rd); Shefali Shopping Centre (☎ 26579999; Pritamnagar Rd) offers a number of intercity services, including to Ajmer (seat/sleeper Rs230/360, 11 hours), Aurangabad (Rs360/465, 16½ hours), Jaipur (Rs280/400, 14½ hours), Udaipur (Rs150/245, seven hours), and Jodhpur (seat only Rs235, 11 hours).

New Limda Travels (Map p728; ☎ 26579379; 5 Shroff Chambers) has buses to Palitana (Rs150, 4½ hours), Bhavnagar (Rs135, four hours) and Mumbai (seat/sleeper/deluxe Rs390/560/790, 24 hours). **Bonny Travels** (Map p728; ☎ 26579265; Pritamnagar Rd; ☯ 6am-11pm) serves Jamnagar (Rs250, six hours) and Rajkot (Rs180, four hours) several times daily.

TRAIN

There's a **computerised booking office** (Map p730; ☎ 135; ☯ 8am-8pm Mon-Sat, to 2pm Sun) to the left as you exit Ahmedabad train station. Window 6 handles the foreign-tourist quota, and you could try booking with your credit card at Window 7. Computerised booking is also available at Gandhigram train station and, although there is no window dedicated to foreigners, it is a *relatively* quiet station (Window 1 takes credit cards).

Getting Around

TO/FROM THE AIRPORT

The airport is 10km north of town; a prepaid taxi should cost no more than Rs300 depending on your destination. An autorickshaw costs about Rs150 to the old town. A cheaper option is bus 105 from Lal Darwaja (Rs10).

AUTORICKSHAW

Autorickshaw drivers here are supposed to use the meter and are mostly honest, though the occasional rascal might try to fleece you. Travelling from Ahmedabad train station to Sidi Saiyad's Mosque should cost about Rs30.

AROUND AHMEDABAD

Adalaj Wav

Adalaj Wav, 19km north of Ahmedabad, is among the finest of the Gujarati step wells. Built by Queen Rudabai in 1499, it has three entrances leading to a huge platform that rests on 16 pillars, with corners marked by shrines. The octagonal well is five storeys deep and is decorated with exquisite stone carvings; subjects range from eroticism to buttermilk. The Gandhinagar bus will get you within walking distance (ask the conductor where to get off). An autorickshaw costs Rs300 return.

Nal Sarovar Bird Sanctuary

This 116-sq-km lake, located some 60km southwest of Ahmedabad, is a flood of ceaseless blue dissolving into the sky, surrounded by iron-flat plains. Between November and February, the **sanctuary** (Indian/foreigner Rs10/250, car Rs20, video Rs2500) sees flocks of indigenous and migratory birds with as many as 250 species passing through the park. Ducks, geese, pelicans and flamingos are best seen early in the morning (aim for 5.30am) and in the evening.

The sanctuary is busiest at weekends and on holidays. To see the birds, it's best to hire a boat (Rs100 per person per hour).

Take supplies as there's no cafe. Gujarat Tourism runs a group of podlike **cottages** (☎ 02715-2245083; s/d Rs300/400, with AC Rs450/650) outside the sanctuary boundary.

Buses are infrequent (Rs40, 2½ hours); your best bet may be a taxi from Ahmedabad (return around Rs1300).

Lothal

About 85km southwest of Ahmedabad, this important archaeological site was discovered in 1954. The city that stood here 4500 years ago is related to the Indus Valley cities of Moenjodaro and Harappa, both in Pakistan. It has a similar street layout, mud brickwork, and a drainage system.

Lothal means 'mound of the dead' in Gujarati, as does Moenjodaro in Sindhi. Excavations have revealed a tidal dockyard (with a lock-gate system). At its peak, this was probably one of the more important ports on the subcontinent. The Sabarmati River, which no longer runs past here, connected the dock

MAJOR TRAINS FROM AHMEDABAD

Destination	Train No & Name	Departure	Duration (hr)	Fare (Rs)
Bhavnagar	2971 *Bhavnagar Exp*	5.45am	6	174/433/578 (A)
Bhuj	9115 *Bandra-Bhuj Exp*	11.59pm	7¾	172/454/620 (A)
Delhi	2957 *Rajdhani*	5.25pm (Tue-Sun)	14	1210/1595/2660 (B)
	2915 *Ashram Exp*	5.45pm	16½	348/925/1260/2119 (C)
	9105 *Ahmedabad-Haridwar Mail*	9.25am	20	332/907/1247/2098 (C)
Jamnagar	9005 *Saurashtra Mail*	5.15am	7	166/437/596/998 (C)
Mumbai	2010 *Shatabdi*	2.30pm (Mon-Sat)	7	695/1330 (D)
	2902 *Gujarat Mail*	10pm	8¾	235/604/816/1374 (C)
Porbandar	9215 *Saurashtra Exp*	8.10pm	10	206/548 (E)
Rajkot	1464 *Rajkot Exp*	8.20am (Mon, Wed-Sat)	4¾	133/360/490 (A)
Udaipur	9944 *Ahmedabad-Udaipur Exp*	11pm	8½	154/548 (F)
Vadodara	2010 *Shatabdi*	2.30pm (Mon-Sat)	1¾	285/550 (D)

Fares: A – sleeper/3AC/2AC, B – 3AC/2AC/1AC, C – sleeper/3AC/2AC/1AC, D – AC chair/1AC, E – sleeper/3AC, F – sleeper/2AC

GUJARAT

to the Gulf of Cambay. Seals discovered at the site suggest that trade may have been conducted with the civilisations of Mesopotamia, Egypt and Persia.

The **archaeological museum** (admission Rs2; ☺ 10am-5pm Sat-Thu) at the site displays fragments of this well-ordered civilisation, such as intricate seals, weights and measures, games and jewellery.

Palace Utelia (☎ /fax 079-26445770; r Rs3000), 7km from the archaeological site, by the Bhugavo River, is an imposing palace – complete with aged retainers – that dwarfs the village it oversees. The shabby rooms are overpriced, but it's an unusual place with charm if not comfort.

Lothal is a long day trip from Ahmedabad, and a taxi (Rs1500 return) may be your best bet. There are buses (Rs70, three hours), or you can reach it via a train to Bhurkhi (6km away), from where you can take a bus. There's a train from Ahmedabad at 7.50am (2nd class Rs45, three hours).

Modhera

The beautiful **Sun Temple** (Indian/foreigner Rs 5/200; ☺ 8am-6pm) was built by King Bhimdev I in 1026 and 1027 and resembles the better-known Konark Temple in Orissa, which it predates by 200 years. It was similarly designed so that the dawn sun shone on the image of Surya, the sun god, during the equinox. The main hall and shrine are reached through a pillared pavilion. The temple exterior is intricately carved with demons and deities. As at Somnath, this temple was ruined by Mahmud of Ghazni, but it remains impressive. Fifty-two intricately carved pillars depict scenes from the Ramayana and the Mahabharata. The interior contains a hall with 12 niches representing Surya's different monthly manifestations. Erotic sculpture panels complete the sensual decoration.

It's fronted by the **Surya Kund**, an extraordinary rectangular step-well that contains over 100 shrines, resembling a sunken art gallery. Shrines to Ganesh, Vishnu and an incarnation of Shiva surround the tank on its other three sides.

In January, Modhera is also the scene for a three-day **classical dance festival**.

Modhera is 105km northwest of Ahmedabad. There are direct buses (Rs75, 3½ hours), or you can take the train to Mahesana and then catch a bus to Modhera (26km).

Buses from Zainabad stop at Modhera (Rs30, 1½ hours), and go on to Patan (Rs66, one hour). A taxi from Ahmedabad and back will cost about Rs1250.

Patan
☎ 02766 / pop 112,038

Patan is a dusty, little-visited town with narrow streets lined by elaborate wooden houses and more than 100 Jain temples, the largest of which is **Panchasara Parasvanath**.

About 130km northwest of Ahmedabad, Patan was an ancient Hindu capital before being sacked by Mahmud of Ghazni in 1024 – the only sign of its former glory is **Rani-ki-Vav** (Indian/foreigner Rs5/100; ☺ 8am-6pm), an astoundingly beautiful step well, incongruously grand in this unassuming town. Built in 1050, the step well is the oldest and finest in Gujarat and is remarkably well preserved – it was protected by centuries of silt and restored in the 1980s.

Patan is also famous for its beautiful Patola silk saris produced in a torturously laborious process. Threads are painstakingly tie-dyed to create the pattern *before* the weaving process begins. To see them made visit **VK Salvi** (www.patanpatola.com; Salviwado, Patolawala St).

Neerav Hotel (☎ 222127; r Rs350-500, with AC Rs900; 🔃), near Kohinoor Cinema, is reasonable, while nearby **Anand Restaurant** (Kilachand Shopping Centre; mains Rs30-60) has good thalis and à la carte dishes.

Patan is 25km northwest of Mahesana. Buses from Ahmedabad take 3½ hours and cost Rs60. There are also buses from Zainabad (Rs66, 2½ hours), via Modhera.

GANDHINAGAR
pop 195,891

With broad avenues and greenery, Gandhinagar forms a striking contrast to Ahmedabad. This is where state politicians live in large, fortified houses. Although Ahmedabad became the capital of Gujarat when the old state of Mumbai was split, this new capital was planned 32km northeast on the west bank of the Sabarmati River. Named Gandhinagar after Mahatma Gandhi, it's India's second planned city after Chandigarh. The secretariat was moved here in 1970.

The only reason for visiting is the spectacular **Akshardham Temple** (Ja Rd, Sector 20; ☺ 9.30am-6.30pm Tue-Sun), belonging to the wealthy Hindu Swaminarayan group. Built by nearly 1000 artisans, it is an elaborately carved building constructed out of 6000 tonnes of pink sandstone and surrounded by manicured gardens. Note that cameras and mobile phones are not allowed into the compound.

Getting There & Away

From Ahmedabad, buses to Gandhinagar (Rs18, 45 minutes, every 15 minutes) depart from the back northwest corner of Lal Darwaja and from the numerous stops along Ashram Rd.

VADODARA (BARODA)

☎ 0265 / pop 1.49 million

Vadodara (or Baroda as it's often known) is a cultured university town 100km southeast of Ahmedabad. Prior to Independence, Vadodara was the capital of the princely Gaekwad state. There are some interesting city sights, including the impressive, overwrought Indo-Saracenic palace, city museum and beautiful Tambekar Wada, but the main reason for coming here is the nearby Unesco World Heritage Site Champaner, with its decaying mosques lost in the landscape.

Orientation & Information

The train station, bus stands and hotels are on the west side of the Vishwamitri River, which bisects the city. Tilak Rd connects the station with the main part of town.

There are SBI and ICICI ATMs at the train station, SBI and Standard Chartered ATMs on RC Dutt Rd, and Bank of Baroda and ICICI ATMs in the precinct of Sayajigunj.

Crossword (2/1 Arunoday Society, Alkapuri; ⏰ 10.30am-8.30pm Mon-Fri, to 9pm Sat & Sun) A good bookstore, with CDs, DVDs and a revitalising Coffee Brio cafe.

Gujarat Tourism (☎ 2427489; ground fl, Narmada Bhavan, Jail Rd; ⏰ 10.30am-6pm Mon-Sat, closed 2nd & 4th Sat of month). On the ground floor of the red-and-yellow tower and not well signed. Unless you want to organise a tour or get brochures, this office is rather disappointing.

ICICI Bank (Sayajigunj) As well as the 24-hr ATM, it changes travellers cheques and cash.

Speedy Cyber Cafe (Sayajigunj; per hr Rs15; ⏰ 9am-11pm).

Sights

SAYAJI BAGH

Within this shady park is the **Baroda Museum & Picture Gallery** (admission Rs10; ⏰ 10.30am-5pm),

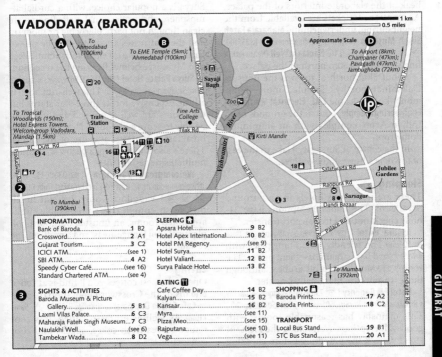

VADODARA (BARODA)

INFORMATION		
Bank of Baroda	1	B2
Crossword	2	A1
Gujarat Tourism	3	C2
ICICI ATM	(see 1)	
SBI ATM	4	B2
Speedy Cyber Café	(see 16)	
Standard Chartered ATM	(see 4)	

SIGHTS & ACTIVITIES		
Baroda Museum & Picture		
Gallery	5	B1
Laxmi Vilas Palace	6	C3
Maharaja Fateh Singh Museum	7	C3
Naulakhi Well	(see 6)	
Tambekar Wada	8	D2

SLEEPING		
Apsara Hotel	9	B2
Hotel Apex International	10	B2
Hotel PM Regency	(see 9)	
Hotel Surya	11	B2
Hotel Valiant	12	B2
Surya Palace Hotel	13	B2

EATING		
Cafe Coffee Day	14	B2
Kalyan	15	B2
Kansaar	16	B2
Myra	(see 11)	
Pizza Meo	(see 15)	
Rajputana	(see 10)	
Vega	(see 11)	

SHOPPING		
Baroda Prints	17	A2
Baroda Prints	18	C2

TRANSPORT		
Local Bus Stand	19	B1
STC Bus Stand	20	A1

GUJARAT

which houses Asian statues and carvings, some rather mangy zoology exhibits and an Egyptian room. The gallery has lovely Mughal miniatures and a motley crew of European masters.

TAMBEKAR WADA

This wooden multi-storeyed **townhouse** (admission free; ◷ 8am-6pm) is a typical Maratha mansion, once the residence of Bhau Tambekar, Diwan of Baroda (1849–54). Inside are some beautiful but decaying 19th-century murals, many featuring Krishna and European subjects.

OTHER SIGHTS

Laxmi Vilas Palace (Nehru Rd; Indian/foreigner Rs25/100; ◷ 10.30am-4pm Tue-Sun) was built in full-throttle 19th-century Indo-Saracenic flourish for Rs6 million. After purchasing your ticket at the Maharaja Fateh Singh Museum head north along Nehru Rd to the second gate (after the entrance to the golf course and before the grand main entrance to the palace). At the palace, pick up an audio guide (included in the admission) and have a leisurely sticky beak at the elaborate interiors of the palace. As mentioned, tickets are available from the neighbouring, underwhelming **Maharaja Fateh Singh Museum** (Nehru Rd; Indian/foreigner Rs25/100; ◷ 10.30am-5.30pm). The **Naulakhi Well** (Nehru Rd), a fine step well, is 50m north of the palace.

About 5km north of town is the unusual Dakshinamoorthy Temple, more commonly known as the **EME (Electrical Mechanical Engineering) Temple**, built in the grounds of an Indian Army complex with an aluminium dome roof.

In the centre of Sursagar, a lake in the east of town, is a huge statue of **Shiva**.

Sleeping

There are numerous hotels in and around Sayajigunj. The midrange options have 24-hour check-out and free airport transfer.

Apsara Hotel (☎ 2225399; Sayajigunj; s/d from Rs150/250) This friendly, welcoming place with a leafy yard has bargain basement prices. The rooms are small and a bit grubby, although those upstairs are marginally brighter.

Hotel PM Regency (☎ 2361616; Sayajigunj; economy s Rs350, s/d from Rs750/950, with AC Rs1050/1250; 🌣) This mainstay has reasonable rooms, with good-value options overlooking the pleasant street. Check the plumbing before checking

in; claustrophobics need not apply for the 'economy' single rooms.

Hotel Valiant (☎ 2363480; 7th fl, BBC Tower, Sayajigunj; s/d Rs475/625, with AC from Rs650/800; 🌣) This hotel has surprisingly fresh rooms on the 7th and 8th floors of this high-rise building. The rooms, reached via a creaky lift, are clean and well presented and all come with TV and fridge.

Hotel Apex International (☎ 2362551; www.hotel apex.com; Sayajigunj; s/d from Rs1050/1350; 🌣) Opposite the statue of Sardar Patel, this hotel has 40 smart rooms divided into five categories. It's worth paying a few hundred rupees more for the executive rooms. Many rooms have balconies with street views.

Hotel Express Towers (☎ 3055000; www.express world.com; RC Dutt Rd; s economy Rs1975, s/d/ste from Rs2800/3200/5500; 🌣 💻) The first government-approved hotel in Gujarat (way back in 1973), this is a good choice, with business-minded rooms, a wine shop and two very good restaurants. It's about 1.5km west of the train station.

Hotel Surya (☎ 2361361; www.hotelsurya.com; Sayajigunj; s/d with breakfast from Rs2500/3000; 🌣 💻) Surya is a popular choice, with a cordial atmosphere and professional staff. Rooms are clean though not particularly big or modern, and the mattresses are on the firmer side of hard. There are two excellent restaurants, Vega and Myra (see below) flanking the reception.

Surya Palace Hotel (☎ 23623366; www.suryapalace .com; Sayajigunj; r from Rs4000) This well-run hotel is a little expensive for its three-star status but the rooms are well appointed and you may be able to score a discount. The rates include breakfast, a massage and use of the sauna. There's also a wine shop, a pastry shop and a multicuisine restaurant.

Welcomgroup Vadodara (☎ 2330033; www .itcwelcomgroup.in; RC Dutt Rd; r incl breakfast from Rs8000; 🌣 💻 🔌) Vadodara's only five-star hotel, this swish complex has predictable, well-appointed rooms, an unusual outdoor pool, plenty of cool lounge areas, and a multicuisine restaurant.

Eating

One of the best coffees you'll find is at **Coffee Brio** inside the Crossword bookshop (p739).

Cafe Coffee Day (Sayajigunj; coffee Rs40-90, ◷ 9am-11pm) As well as espresso coffee, this cool refuge serves fresh cakes, snacks and cool concoctions.

Kalyan (☎ 2362211; Sayajigunj; dishes Rs15-80; 🕙 7.30am-10.30pm) Kalyan is a breezy student hang-out serving healthy portions of south Indian food and less healthy attempts at Western fast food (though all dishes are vegetarian).

Rajputana (☎ 6622799; Sayajigunj; mains Rs65-145; 🕙 11am-3pm & 6.30-11pm) Specialising in Punjabi and Chinese vegetarian, with a few pizzas thrown in, this intimate restaurant is partitioned by feature walls of hanging chains and bells, and window tables have a view over the busy Sadar Patel Chowk.

Kansaar (☎ 2362596; 101 Unique Trade Centre, Sayajigunj; thali Rs100) A classy thali joint on the 2nd floor, with impeccable service and delicious food; the thali is bottomless and you can eat inside or out on the terrace to enjoy the street view.

Tropical Woodlands (☎ 2321495; 139 Windsor Plaza, RC Dutt Rd; mains Rs45-110; 🕙 11am-3pm, 7-10.30pm) This place, tucked into one of those shopping malls bristling with signs, serves delicious North and South Indian and Chinese food behind big plate-glass windows for views of the busy road.

Pizza Meo (☎ 2361361; Sayajigunj; pizza Rs90-160, pasta Rs125-140; 🕙 11am-11pm) This small Italian *ristorante e pizzeria* serves excellent veg pizza, and so-so veg pasta. With a Sistine Chapel ceiling and red-green-and-white aproned waiters, it is an almost-convincing slice of the continent on the subcontinent.

Mandap (Hotel Express Towers, RC Dutt Rd; thali Rs150; 🕙 11am-3pm & 7.30-10.30pm) One the best thalis in town, served in a splendidly decorated room with a desert-tent interior.

Vega (☎ 2361361; Hotel Surya, Sayajigunj; mains Rs90-130; 🕙 7-10.30am, noon-3pm & 7.30-11pm) Comfortable Vega serves decent Chinese and Indian curries.

Myra (☎ 2361361; Hotel Surya, Sayajigunj; thali Rs110, silver thali Rs175; 🕙 11am-3pm & 7-11pm) This hotel restaurant serves up two versions of the ever-popular, ever-filling Gujarati thali. The vegetable dishes comprising the thali change daily.

Shopping

Baroda Prints Salatwada (Salatwada Rd; 🕙 9am-8pm Mon-Sat, 10am-8pm Sun); Aries Complex (GF-2,3 Productivity Rd; 🕙 9.30am-8.30pm Mon-Sat, 10.30am-8.30pm Sun) A shop selling hand-printed textiles. In the Salatwada store you can see the printers at work in the back room.

Getting There & Away

AIR

The airport is 8km northeast of town. **Jet Airways** (☎ 2343441; www.jetairways.com) has daily flights to Mumbai and Delhi starting at around Rs3500. **Air India** (☎ 2794747/8; www.airindia.com) also has daily Mumbai and Delhi connections.

BUS

The STC bus stand is about 300m north of the train station, and there are buses to many destinations in Gujarat, western Madhya Pradesh and northern Maharashtra. Every 10 minutes there are buses to Ahmedabad (local/deluxe Rs60/68, two hours). Regular buses also serve Bhavnagar (Rs110, five hours), Palitana (Rs122, eight hours), Diu (Rs160, 13 hours) and Tararbul (for Lothal; Rs62). Many private bus companies have offices nearby.

TRAIN

To Ahmedabad, the 9011 *Gujarat Express* leaves Vadodara at 12.40pm (2nd class/AC chair/1st class Rs49/167/228, 2¼ hours), and the 2009 *Shatabdi* departs at 11.17am Monday to Saturday (AC chair/1AC Rs315/590, two hours). From Ahmedabad the 2010 *Shatabdi* leaves at 2.30pm, arriving in Vadodara at 4.15pm and going on to Mumbai (AC chair/1AC Rs605/1150), arriving at 9.35pm.

AROUND VADODARA
Champaner & Pavagadh

Spectacular Champaner and Pavagadh are 47km northeast of Vadodara: Champaner is a Unesco World Heritage Site, Gujarat's former capital, scattered on and around Pavagadh, an 800m volcanic hill looking like a chunk of the Himalaya dumped on the plain.

Pavagadh's oldest monument is the 10th- to 11th-century **Lakulisha Temple**, near the top of the hill. On the highest point is the temple of **Kalika Mata** – an important pilgrimage site, and home to a month-long **festival** in honour of the goddess Mahakali, which takes place in the month of Chaitra (March/April). You can walk to the temples at the top of Pavagadh hill, which will take two to three hours, or you can take the cable car (Rs87 return). You'll need to take a bus to the base from Champaner (Rs10).

Champaner (☎ 02676-245631; Indian/foreigner Rs5/100; 🕙 10am-6pm) was established as the Chauhan Rajput capital in about the 8th century. On a strategic trade route, it was besieged by Sultan Mahmud Begara, who succeeded in taking it in 1484 (the Rajputs committed *jauhar* – ritual mass suicide – in the face of defeat) and built many religious structures as well as the impressive fort wall on Pavagadh. But the city began to decline from 1535 when the Mughals, led by Humayun, scaled the fort walls and captured both the fort and its city.

The walls at the base of the hill were once 6km long; they surrounded military, civic and religious buildings and water-harvesting systems. The most stunning features are the mosques, with a blending of Islamic and Hindu decoration styles, including the Jama Masjid. Dating from 1513, it took 125 years to build, and has a wonderful carved entrance and imposing courtyard. Inside, the ruler's prayer hall is divided from the main space by *jalis*. Behind the building is an octagonal *kund* (lake or tank), Hauz-i-Vazu, used for washing before prayer.

Other beautiful mosques include **Kewda Masjid**, where you can walk up the narrow stairs to the rooftop, with the globelike domes, and even further up the minarets for great views. Nearby is **Iteri Masjid**, with minarets that resemble factory chimneys, and even further into the countryside is **Nagina Masjid**, with no minarets but exquisite geometric carving.

Hotel Champaner (☎ 02676-245641; Pavagadh Manchi; dm/s/d Rs75/330/440, s/d with AC Rs550/825; ⌘) has typically state-run rooms that are plain and basic, but all have balconies with superb views.

There are several daily buses from Vadodara (Rs45, two hours); a return taxi costs around Rs650.

Jambughoda

Around 25km from Champaner is the ex-princely state of Jambughoda, turned sanctuary in 1992, encompassing 130 sq km of lush countryside. You can stay at the rambling **Jambughoda Palace** (☎ 241258; www.jambughoda palace.com; r Rs1200-1400), built in 1924 and run by the erstwhile royal family who still live here. Rooms are simple and it's an enchantingly peaceful place.

BHARUCH
pop 148,391

Bharuch appeared in historical records nearly 2000 years ago. It's on the main rail line between Vadodara and Surat, about an hour from each.

The hilltop **fort** overlooks the wide Narmada River and has the **Jama Masjid** at its base. On the river bank, east of the city, is the **Temple of Bhrigu Rishi**, from which the city took its name, Bhrigukachba, later shortened to Bharuch.

The Narmada River is notorious because of the Sardar Sarovar, a hugely controversial dam, upstream of Bharuch near the village of Manibeli.

SURAT
☎ 026 / pop 2.4 million

On the Tapti River, Surat is a busy commercial centre for textiles and diamonds. It has long attracted outsiders: Parsis settled here in the 12th century, it later became a vital Mughal port and transit point for Mecca, and in 1613 was the first English settlement in India.

Once India's chief trading port, it declined when the East India Company shifted to Bombay. In 1994 there was an outbreak of the plague and it was rated as India's filthiest city. Big clean-ups have supposedly left it the second cleanest and healthiest (after Chandigarh). You might be inclined to rate it the noisiest and most exhausting, but travellers with an interest in colonial history might be tempted to stop.

Built in 1546, the riverside **castle** is alongside the Tapti Bridge and now full of offices, but there are good views from its bastions. **Colonial tombs** here date from the 15th to the 18th centuries. Most magnificent is the 17th-century memorial to Baron Adrian Van Reed, a local Dutch company director.

The city has huge textile outlets, including **Bombay Market** (Umarwada) – a big sari retail centre 1km south of the train station.

The nearby Dangs mountains near Maharashtra host a spectacular, largely tourist-free **festival** in the week before Holi.

Getting There & Away

Surat is on the main Mumbai–Ahmedabad railway line. There are many trains to Ahmedabad, including the 9215 *Saurashtra Express*, which departs Surat at 2.20pm and arrives in Ahmedabad (sleeper/3AC Rs132/340) at 7.45pm. Just as many trains arrive from Ahmedabad, including the 9012 *Gujarat Express*, which departs Ahmedabad at 7am and arrives in Surat (2nd class/AC chair/1st class Rs76/267/378) at 11.15am.

AROUND SURAT

Twenty-nine kilometres south of Surat (30 minutes by train), **Navsari** has been a head-quarters for the Parsi community since 1142. Some 13km from Navsari is **Dandi**, the destination of Gandhi's epic Salt March in 1930. It's reached along a pleasant rural road, and by the strikingly empty beach are several monuments to Gandhi, including a small museum. There's another museum at **Karodi**, 3km from Dandi, where he was arrested.

Udvada, 10km north of Vapi, the station for Daman, has India's oldest Parsi sacred fire; it's said to have been brought from Persia to Diu, on the opposite coast of the Gulf of Cambay, in AD 700. **Sanjan**, in the extreme south of the state, is the small port where the Parsis first landed. A pillar marks the spot.

DAMAN

☎ 02602 / pop 35,743

The ex-Portuguese enclave of Daman is an alcohol-infused resort town on a grey sea that ain't no tropical paradise. There is the piquancy of old Portugal here though, in the hulking forts, cow-free avenues of Moti Daman, and the quiet churches (the evening services are charming). Contemporary Nani Daman is a quiet coastal town that suddenly erupts into booze-soaked whimsy on weekends and holidays as thrill seekers from Maharashtra indulge in low-tax booze and thirsty Gujaratis wet their whistle.

Along with Diu and Goa, Daman was taken in 1961 from the Portuguese, who had seized Daman in 1531. The Portuguese had been officially ceded the region by Bahadur Shah, the last major Gujarati sultan, in 1559. For a time Daman and Diu were governed from Goa but both now constitute the Union Territory of Daman and Diu, overseen by Delhi.

You are forbidden to take alcohol out of Daman unless you have a permit; there are police checks as you leave.

Orientation & Information

The two Damans are linked by a condemned bridge, which is only allowed to carry two-wheelers and pedestrians, and a new monsoon-proof bridge 500m to the east, which was nearing the end of construction at the time of writing. An autorickshaw from the old bridge to Jampore beach costs Rs50 one way.

Bank of Baroda ATM (Kavi Khabardar Marg)

Dena Bank ATM (Kavi Khabardar Marg)

Main post office (☎ 2230453; Moti Daman) South of the river.

Net City (Vikas arcade, Devka Rd; per hr Rs20; ☻ 10am-9pm)

Post office (☎ 2254353; Nani Daman) More convenient than the main post office.

Speed Age Cyber Café (Kavi Khabardar Marg; per hr Rs20; ☻ 9.30am-9.30pm)

Tourist office (☎ 2255104; ☻ 9.30am-1.30pm & 2-6pm Mon-Fri) Near the bus stand; gives out a free map. Don't bother going before 11.30am!

World Wide Travels & Tours (☎ 2255734; Devka Rd) In the arcade below Hotel Maharaja, it changes travellers cheques and cash, and does air ticketing.

Sights & Activities

NANI DAMAN

You can walk around Nani Daman's **Fort of St Jerome** ramparts, with views over the colourful fishing fleet. The fort has a magnificent gateway facing the river to impress incoming traffic. The 1901 **Church of Our Lady of the Sea** inside the walls is worth a look for its garish, gilded interior.

To the north is a **Jain temple** that has 18th-century murals depicting the life of Mahavira, who lived around 500 BC.

MOTI DAMAN

Moti Daman's **fort** dates from 1559. The walls, divided by 10 bastions, encircle 30 sq km of land. Inside are incongruously clean, sleepy, leafy streets reminiscent of the Portuguese era, and there are relaxing views across the river to Nani Daman from the ramparts near the lighthouse. Moti Daman once housed the Portuguese gentry, and near the fort gate is the sometime home of 18th-century Portuguese poet Bocage.

Sé (Portuguese for 'cathedral'), or **Church of Bom Jesus**, built in 1603, is a piece of Iberia in India, with elaborate woodcarving.

The **Church of Our Lady of the Rosary**, across the overplanted square, has ancient Portuguese tombstones set into its cool, flagstoned floor. Light filters through the dusty windows, illuminating the altar, a masterpiece of furiously detailed, gold-painted woodcarving. If it's closed, try the Sé for the key.

BEACHES

About 3km north of Nani Daman are the grubby, rocky shores of **Devka Beach** – not an appealing prospect. The ambience of the beachside bars and hotels sways between

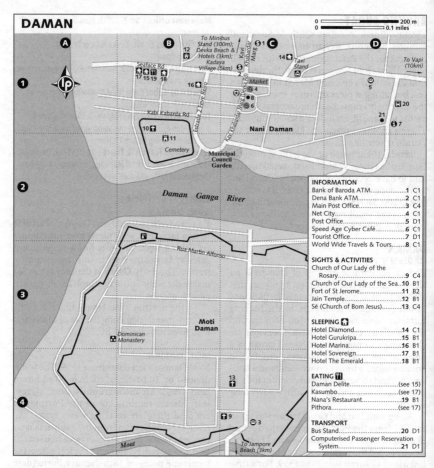

DAMAN

INFORMATION

Bank of Baroda ATM...................**1**	C1
Dena Bank ATM........................**2**	C1
Main Post Office.......................**3**	C4
Net City....................................**4**	C1
Post Office................................**5**	D1
Speed Age Cyber Café...............**6**	C1
Tourist Office...........................**7**	D1
World Wide Travels & Tours.......**8**	C1

SIGHTS & ACTIVITIES

Church of Our Lady of the Rosary....................................**9**	C4
Church of Our Lady of the Sea..**10**	B1
Fort of St Jerome....................**11**	B2
Jain Temple............................**12**	B1
Sé (Church of Bom Jesus).........**13**	C4

SLEEPING

Hotel Diamond.......................**14**	C1
Hotel Gurukripa......................**15**	B1
Hotel Marina..........................**16**	B1
Hotel Sovereign......................**17**	B1
Hotel The Emerald..................**18**	B1

EATING

Daman Delite.......................(see 15)	
Kasumbo.............................(see 17)	
Nana's Restaurant.................**19**	B1
Pithora...............................(see 17)	

TRANSPORT

Bus Stand..............................**20**	D1
Computerised Passenger Reservation System.................................**21**	D1

easygoing and cheap drunk. The palm-shaded beach at **Jampore**, located about 3km south of Moti Daman, is slightly better, but still not very good for swimming. An auto-rickshaw journey from town to Devka will cost Rs30, and from the bridge to Jampore costs Rs50.

Sleeping & Eating

Daman gets packed during holiday periods (particularly Diwali), when it's advisable to book ahead or, even better, avoid altogether.

In February, Daman is noted for *papri*, boiled and salted sweet peas served wrapped in newspaper. Crab and lobster are in season in October. *Tari* palm wine is a popular drink sold in earthenware pots. A Kingfisher beer costs only Rs35 at takeaway shops, but hotel bars charge Rs50 or more.

TOWN AREA

Hotel Marina (☎ 2254420; www.hotelmarinadaman.com; Estrada 2 Feve Reiro; s/d Rs675/765, deluxe Rs765/855; ✦) By far the pick of hotels in Daman, this restored and converted, 150-year-old Portuguese-style house has delightful upstairs rooms opening onto a gable-roofed mezzanine. All rooms are air-conditioned with modern facilities and olde-worlde charm and are excellent value. The restaurant (mains Rs50 to Rs120) has delicious curries, including the requisite local seafood, and cold beer.

Hotel Diamond (☎ 2254235; s/d Rs500/650, with AC Rs750/900; ✦) This is a friendly though overpriced choice, with musty rooms, featuring beds with thin mattresses and one sheet, and shielded TV cabinets (do excited patrons throw things at the TV?). It's off the main drag and near the taxi stand.

Hotel the Emerald (☎ 2255069; www.hotelthe emerald.co.in; Seaface Rd; economy s Rs850, s/d from Rs1050/1400; ☒) This sparkling salmon pink and beige hotel has ultrachic rooms with no obvious reference to the colour green. If you like a shower that really works and you don't need a bathtub, then the cheaper 'deluxe' is a better room than the 'executive'. The lounge bar and restaurant is a class act.

Hotel Gurukripa (☎ 2255046; www.hotelgurukripa .com; Seaface Rd; s/d from Rs1095/1475; ☒ 🖳) This option has OK rooms with renovated bathrooms and double beds with satin-quilted bed covers lending a touch of the boudoir. It also runs yoga classes and boasts a moody bar-restaurant with sparkling stars on the ceiling.

Hotel Sovereign (☎ 2250236; www.hotelgurukripa .com; Seaface Rd; s/d from Rs1095/1475; ☒ 🖳) Very near Hotel Gurukripa, with the same owners, this is the all-veg option with slightly cleaner and more comfortable rooms and a less creaky lift. However, the bathrooms appear older and smaller than those in Gurukripa. There are two veg restaurants.

Pithora (☎ 2250236; Hotel Sovereign, Seaface Rd; mains Rs40-100, Gujarati/Punjabi thali Rs75/90; ⏰ 7-10pm) Serves up tasty thalis in a rooftop restaurant with a sloping bamboo ceiling. Thalis and the Indian and Chinese à la carte are all vegetarian.

Kasumbo (☎ 2250236; Hotel Sovereign, Seaface Rd; mains Rs40-200; ⏰ 11am-3pm, 7-10pm) This chilled AC, all-veg restaurant has a sultry blue domed ceiling and a massive menu featuring North Indian and Chinese delights. And you can grab a sweet, unlimited Gujarati thali for Rs100.

Nana's Restaurant (☎ 2250659; Seaface Rd; mains Rs55-150; ⏰ 8am-10pm) A very polished restaurant with an army of helpful staff, cocktails, icy cold beer and delicious North Indian food. The selection of veg and non-veg curries is impressive – from Afghani to Vindaloo, and there's Chinese, and of course the local seafood: pomfret, *dara*, prawns and *surmai*. A great feature is the family room where families and females can dine in a no-stare zone.

Daman Delite (Hotel Gurukripa, Seaface Rd; mains Rs70-240) This small place with stars on the ceiling and white tablecloths is popular with groups of men on their Daman break and the oc-

casional family. The food is veg and non-veg with some inspired seafood dishes to accompany the chilled beer.

BEACHES

There are several midrange 'beach resorts' at Devka Beach, stretching for 1.5km along the main road. All have a restaurant and a bar and, outside holiday times, will drop prices like a shot. Jampore is more limited, with one beachfront hotel and a few guesthouses in the village.

Sandy Resort (☎ /fax 2254644; www.sandyresort.com; Devka Beach; r Rs1300-2500; ☒ 🏊) This is a comfortable place with spacious rooms ranging from peeling-paint standard to breezy deluxe options with balconies. The swimming pool is old-fashioned and not that inviting.

Hotel Miramar (☎ 2250671; www.miramarmirasol.in; Devka Beach; r with AC from Rs3000; ☒ 🏊) This place, right on the beach 4km from Nani Daman, is one of the better-maintained hotels, with clean rooms, an excellent swimming pool and a cavernous outdoor eating area. There is also an AC restaurant if you don't want to join in the fun. The same owners run Mirasol, a hotel and watersports resort, two kilometres further north.

Hotel China Town (☎ 2230920; Jampore, Moti Daman; r Rs800, with AC from Rs1200; ☒) Nestled among the swaying coconut palms with a hazy westward gaze, this unspectacular option offers typically neglected rooms with questionable plumbing, along with a bar and restaurant.

Getting There & Away

Vapi (3½ hours from Vadodara), on the main railway line, is about 10km from Daman. You can reserve tickets at the **Computerised Passenger Reservation System** (☎ 2254254; ⏰ 9.30am-1.30pm, 4-9pm, Thu-Tue), opposite the tourist office.

Plenty of share-taxis (Rs15 per person, 20 minutes) wait outside the train station and leave frequently for Daman. It costs Rs70 by autorickshaw, but most aren't permitted to enter Daman district. There are also some ramshackle buses (Rs7).

SAURASHTRA

Saurashtra, also known as the Kathiawar Peninsula, was never part of British India. It consisted of 200 princely states up until Independence, during which time the landowners had amassed considerable wealth. The cities are bustling and industrial, but elsewhere, where the cotton fields seem to stretch on forever, there is a timeless feudal feel. Farmers dress head to toe in white, with turbans, pleated jackets and jodhpurs, and golden stud earrings. The rural women are as colourful as their sisters in Rajasthan and wear embroidered backless cholis and heavy jewellery.

Saurashtra has a reputation for being fond of its sleep, and siesta takes place from *at least* 1pm to 3pm.

The peninsula took its name from the Kathi tribes who used to roam the area at night stealing whatever was not locked into the many *kots* (forts). It consists of a central plateau sloping down towards secluded coastal plains, with dense forests on its other side.

BHAVNAGAR
☎ 0278 / pop 510,958

Bhavnagar is a hectic industrial centre that makes a base for journeys to nearby Shatrunjaya and Velavadar National Park. Founded in 1743, Bhavnagar has long been an important cotton trading post, but now supplements its survival on diamonds, plastics and ship parts – Bhavnagar lock gate keeps ships afloat in the port at low tide. Gandhi attended university here, and a small museum displays photos of his life. The tangled bazaars and crumbling wooden houses of the old city feel remarkably untouched by the outside world, but otherwise there's little to see.

Orientation & Information

Bhavnagar is a sprawling city with distinct old and new sections. The STC bus stand is in the new part of town and the train station is at the far end of the old city, around 2.5km away. There are many ATMs: HDFC near the clock tower, SBI beside Hotel Sun 'n' Shine, and Axis Bank beside the Galaxy Cinema.

Post office (☺ 10am-8pm Mon-Fri, to 3pm Sat)

Reliance Cyber Café (188 Madhav Darshan, Waghawadi Rd; min charge for 3½hr Rs100; ☺ 10am-10pm)

State Bank of India (☎ 2439746; ☺ 10.30am-2.30pm & 3-7pm Mon-Fri, 10.30am-4pm Sat) In the old city; changes cash and travellers cheques.

Sights & Activities

Takhteshwar Temple sits on a small hillock high enough to provide splendid views over the city and out into the Gulf of Cambay.

Northeast, by the clock tower, the dusty **Gandhi Smriti Museum** (admission free; ☺ 9am-1pm, 2-6pm Mon-Sat) has a multitude of Gandhi photographs. Downstairs, the equally dusty **Barton Museum** (Indian/foreigner Rs2/50; ☺ 9am-1pm, 2-6pm Mon-Sat, closed 2nd & 4th Sat of month), has religious carvings, betel-nut cutters, and a skeleton in a cupboard.

Near the State Bank of India is the oldest part of the city (worth a wander), busy with small shops and cluttered with dilapidated elaborate wooden buildings leaning over the colourful crowded bazaars.

Sleeping

The budget hotels, mostly found in the old city and near the train station, are fairly grim, but the midrange hotels are reasonable value.

Vrindavan Hotel (☎ 2518928; Darbargadh; d/tr Rs275/350) This place, nestled behind a massive, intricately carved gateway, looks promising. But expectations fall away quickly. This old, rambling place around a courtyard has very basic rooms of various shapes and sizes and none are all that clean.

Hotel Mausam (☎ 2518776; Station Rd; s/d Rs350/600, with AC from Rs600-850; ☒) Close to the train station, this place has a variety of rooms, and while the cheapest are quite basic, they are reasonably clean with OK beds and modern facilities. The staff are genuinely helpful.

Hotel Apollo (☎ 2425251; www.thehotelapollo.com; opposite central bus station; s/d Rs500/700, with AC Rs700/900; ☒) The Apollo, opposite the STC bus stand, has drab but quite spacious rooms with balconies where you can watch the buses have a dust bath. Bathrooms are OK but test the taps. There are also money-changing facilities here.

Bluehill Hotel (☎ 2426951; hotelbluehill@yahoo.com; Pill Garden; s/d from Rs1000/1300, ste Rs2700; ☒ ☐) Down a quiet park-side road, this is a good choice for bird-watchers – overlooking painted storks roosting in the tree-tops in Pill Garden. Rooms are reasonably clean but are looking and smelling very tired and are therefore overpriced.

Narayani Heritage Hotel (☎ 2513535; narayani heritage@gmail.com; s/d Rs1100/1500; ☒ ☒) This hotel occupies one of the administrative buildings of the royal compound of Nilambag Palace Hotel. The bright, spacious rooms are good value, and though they don't have the atmosphere of the palace they do share the pool, gym and tennis court.

GUJARAT

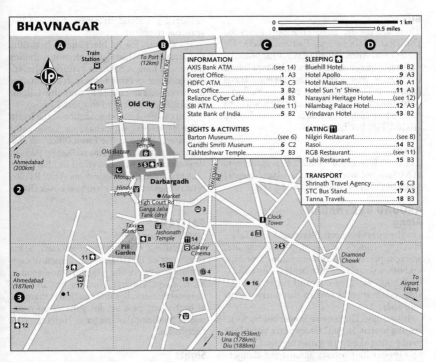

BHAVNAGAR

INFORMATION
AXIS Bank ATM.................................(see 14)
Forest Office...1 A3
HDFC ATM..2 C3
Post Office..3 B2
Reliance Cyber Café.............................4 B3
SBI ATM...(see 11)
State Bank of India...............................5 B2

SIGHTS & ACTIVITIES
Barton Museum..............................(see 6)
Gandhi Smriti Museum.........................6 C2
Takhteshwar Temple............................7 B3

SLEEPING
Bluehill Hotel.......................................8 B2
Hotel Apollo...9 B2
Hotel Mausam....................................10 A1
Hotel Sun 'n' Shine............................11 A3
Narayani Heritage Hotel................(see 12)
Nilambag Palace Hotel.......................12 A3
Vrindavan Hotel.................................13 B2

EATING
Nilgiri Restaurant............................(see 8)
Rasoi..14 B2
RGB Restaurant..............................(see 11)
Tulsi Restaurant.................................15 B3

TRANSPORT
Shrinath Travel Agency......................16 C3
STC Bus Stand....................................17 A3
Tanna Travels.....................................18 B3

Hotel Sun 'n' Shine (☎ 2516131; ST Rd; s/d from Rs1300/1600; ❄ 🖳) This well-run, three-star hotel represents the best value in Bhavnagar. It has a Mediterranean-inspired and vertigo-inducing atrium, a very welcoming front desk, and the recommended RGB restaurant (see below). The standard rooms are fresh and clean with comfortable beds. The more you pay the more windows you get. Breakfast is included, as is the complimentary airport pick-up and drop-off.

Nilambag Palace Hotel (☎ 2424241; nilambag@bsnl .in; s/d Rs2500/4000; ❄ 🖳) On the Ahmedabad road is this former maharaja's palace, a rather stern-looking place (built in 1859) on the outside. Inside it has a more personal feel, with stately rooms, solid wooden furniture, and attractive gardens. There's a circular swimming pool (Rs100 nonguests), a gym and a garden restaurant.

Eating

Rasoi (☎ 2522535; mains Rs50-70; thali Rs100; ❄ 11am-3pm & 7-11pm) This secluded bungalow and garden restaurant – look behind the police post and fig tree beside the Galaxy Cinema – is run

by the folks at Tulsi Restaurant. Here you'll find great unlimited Gujarati thalis, as well as Punjabi and Chinese veg fare.

Nilgiri Restaurant (Bluehill Hotel; mains Rs50-100; ❄ 11am-3pm & 7-11pm) Nice and bright, with big plate-glass windows, this place has reliable Indian and Chinese veg dishes.

Tulsi Restaurant (☎ 2425535; Kalanala Chowk; mains Rs55-75; ❄ noon-3.30pm & 7-11pm) Low-lit with plants and understated decor, this cosy place with Punjabi and Chinese veg dishes is rightly popular.

RGB Restaurant (Hotel Sun 'n' Shine; mains Rs60-115; ❄ 7-11pm) This cool and cosy restaurant on the hotel's 1st floor offers generous serves of veg Jain, North Indian and Chinese. There are partitions for privacy and platoons of eager staff. And that bar at the end? Don't get excited – mocktails only.

Getting There & Away

AIR

Air India (☎ 2426503) and **Jet Airways** (☎ 2433371) have regular Mumbai flights (Rs 3600). An autorickshaw to/from the airport costs Rs150.

GUJARAT

BUS

There are regular State Transport buses for Diu (Rs108, six hours), Palitana (Rs33, 1½ hours) and Ahmedabad (Rs91, four hours).

Private bus companies include **Tanna Travels** (☎ 2425218; Waghawadi Rd) and **Shrinath Travel Agency** (☎ 2427755), on the road to Palitana, with buses to Ahmedabad (with/without AC Rs140/120, four hours) and Vadodara (Rs160/140, five hours).

TRAIN

The 2972 *Bhavnagar–Bandra Express* departs at 6.05am and arrives at Ahmedabad (sleeper/3AC/2AC Rs174/433/578) at 11.17am.

AROUND BHAVNAGAR
Alang

On the coast between Bhavnagar and Talaja is Alang, India's largest ship-breaking site, where supertankers, container ships, warships and other vessels are dismantled – by hand – by 20,000 workers day and night. A huge ship takes around two to three months to pull apart.

It's an epic, Dickensian scene, but tricky to see as a tourist. In 2002 Greenpeace visited the yard posing as buyers, gathering photographs to support its protests against the dangerous working conditions and the toxic waste produced through ship breaking. You can keep up to date with the controversy at www .greenpeace.org. These protests have made it more difficult for foreign tourists to visit the yard, but authorities can be lax. You may find you can wander unobtrusively onto the beach after asking a gatekeeper – it all depends on luck. A few kilometres along the road approaching the shipyard is a curious collection of junk shops selling things pulled off the ships – this is where to come if you want to buy a 1970s 20-seater sofa, a mirrored bar or a few hundred portholes.

For official permission, contact the **Gujarat Port Trust** (☎ 079-23238346) in Ahmedabad. You'll have to send a fax stating the date of the proposed visit, the reason and your passport number, and pay a fee.

Velavadar National Park

This beautiful, off-the-beaten-track, 34-sq-km **park** (Indian/foreigner Rs10/250, car Rs20/250, 4hr guide Rs30/250, camera Rs5/250, video Rs200/2500; ☥ 7.30am-6pm 15 Oct-15 Jun), 65km north of Bhavnagar, encompasses large areas of pale, custard-coloured grassland stretching between two seasonal rivers.

It's famous for its blackbucks, beautiful, fast antelopes, which sport elegant spiralling horns – as long as 65cm in mature males. It's also good for spotting birds such as wintering harriers. You can explore by car or by walking. Local guides don't tend to speak English.

You can book accommodation at the **Tourist Lodge** (d Rs500-1000), which has four rooms at the sanctuary, through the **Forest Office** (☎ 0278-2426425; 1st fl, 10 Annexe Bldg, Bahamali Bhan; ☥ 11am-6pm Mon-Fri) near the STC bus stand in Bhavnagar.

A taxi from Bhavnagar costs about Rs1000 return. However, there are also buses (Rs28) that run here.

PALITANA
☎ 02848 / pop 51,934

The hustling, dusty town of Palitana, 51km southwest of Bhavnagar, has grown uncontrollably to serve the pilgrim trade around Shatrunjaya. Gujarat Tourism has an office at Hotel Sumeru, but information is marginal at best. Your best bet for general information is the helpful manager at Hotel Shravak (opposite).

Sights
SHATRUNJAYA

One of Jainism's holiest pilgrimage sites, **Shatrunjaya** (Place of Victory; camera Rs40; ☥ temples 6.30am-7.45pm) is an incredible hilltop sea of temples, built over 900 years on a plateau dedicated to the gods.

The temples are grouped into nine *tunks* (enclosures), each with a central temple and many minor ones. Some of the earliest were built in the 11th century, but were destroyed by Muslims in the 14th and 15th centuries; the current temples date from the 16th century onwards.

The 600m climb from the base of the hill to the summit is 2.5km, up 3200 steps, and will take about 1½ hours. It's best to start around dawn so you can climb before it gets too hot (or walk up for sunset). You can be carried up the hill in a *dholi* (portable chair with two bearers), which costs about Rs1000.

You should be properly dressed (no shorts etc). Leave behind leather items, including belts and bags, and don't take any food, drinks or mineral water inside the temple. Photo permits must be obtained from the main office before you commence the ascent.

As you near the top of the hill, the road forks. The main entrance, Ram Pol, is reached by taking the left-hand fork. To see the best views over the site first, take the right-hand fork.

There are superb views in all directions; on a clear day you can see the Gulf of Cambay. Approaching from the right, you reach one of the finest temples first, dedicated to Shri Adishwara, one of the most important Jain *tirthankars*. Note the frieze of dragons. Adjacent is the Muslim shrine of **Angar Pir**, where women who want children make offerings of miniature cradles. The Muslim saint protected the temples from a Mughal attack.

Built in 1618 by a wealthy Jain merchant, the **Chaumukh** (Four-Faced Shrine) has images of Adinath facing out in the four cardinal directions. Other important temples are **Kumar Pal**, **Sampriti Raj** and **Vimal Shah**, named after their wealthy Jain patrons.

An autorickshaw from the bus station to the hill costs Rs20, or you can walk in about 30 minutes. Water (not bottled) can be bought at intervals, and you can buy refreshing curd in pottery bowls (Rs5) outside the temple compound.

Sleeping & Eating

Palitana has scores of *dharamsalas* (pilgrim's guesthouses), but for Jains only.

Hotel Shravak (☎ 252428; men-only dm Rs50, s without bathroom Rs100, d/tr/q Rs300/400/500, d with AC Rs700; ✷) Opposite the bus stand is this friendly place where the ultrabasic rooms are the best in town. Doubles are better than singles for cleanliness and are also spacious. Two rooms have AC and a handful have geysers for hot water. Check-out is at 10am.

Hotel Sumeru (☎ 252327; Station Rd; dm Rs75, s/d Rs210/325, with AC Rs425/700; ✷) Run by Gujarat Tourism, this heavily-staffed place is 200m towards the station from the bus stand. Rooms are very rundown, but at the time of research extensive renovations were supposedly underway – there was no evidence of this, but management were insistent. Upstairs rooms have balconies, and there's a restaurant. Prices almost halve from April to September. Check-out is at 9am.

Vijay Vilas Palitana (☎ book through North West Safaris in Ahmedabad 079-26302019; www.northwestsafaris .com; s/d incl meals Rs1800/3600) This lovely, small 1906 palace has plain but nicely decorated rooms, with original furniture. It's family-run,

with great attention to detail and delicious home-cooked food.

Jagruti Restaurant (thali Rs30, mains Rs30-50; ✷ 10am-10pm) Across the laneway from Hotel Shravak, Jagruti is a wildly busy thali house offering Punjabi and Chinese dishes at lunch and dinner.

On the left, as soon as you cross the bridge going southwest, is the **Willingdon Vegetable Market**, where you can stock up on a remarkable variety of fresh fruit and vegetables at very cheap prices.

Getting There & Away

Numerous STC buses go to/from Bhavnagar (Rs25, 1½ hours) and regularly to/from Ahmedabad (Rs120, five hours). A direct bus to Diu (Rs130, seven hours) departs at 1.30pm. Otherwise, regular buses go every hour to Talaja (Rs20, one hour), from where you can catch a bus to Diu (Rs90, six hours). Buses are uncomfortable and the roads are horrendous, but the amount of roadwork in evidence hopefully indicates gradual improvement.

At the time of research, the train from Bhavnagar was undergoing conversion to broad gauge. There were still two slow passenger trains to Bhavnagar, one at 8am and one at 8pm.

DIU

☎ 02875 / pop 21,576

What is Diu? For better or worse, this tiny ex-Portuguese island is the reason most travellers come to Gujarat. And while it may not be the tropical paradise they imagined, it has a quirky charm and serenity.

Diu boasts some reasonable beaches, whitewashed churches, an imposing fort, colourful Lisboa streets, fresh seafood, as well as groups of giggly Gujarati weekenders who flock here for the cheap booze. Plus it's the safest place to ride a scooter in all of India, with minimum traffic and excellent roads.

Like Daman and Goa, Diu was a Portuguese colony until taken over by India in 1961. With Daman, it is still governed from Delhi as a Union Territory. It includes Diu Island, about 11km by 3km, separated from the coast by a narrow channel, and two tiny mainland enclaves. One of these, housing the village of Ghoghla, is the entry point to Diu from Una. The northern side of the island, facing Gujarat, is tidal marsh and salt pans, while the

GUJARAT

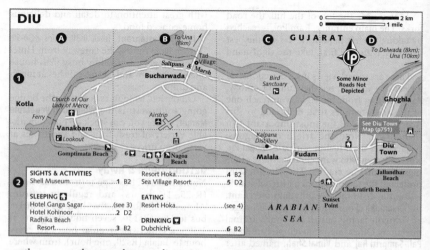

DIU

SIGHTS & ACTIVITIES		
Shell Museum	1	B2

SLEEPING		
Hotel Ganga Sagar	(see 3)	
Hotel Kohinoor	2	D2
Radhika Beach		
Resort	3	B2

Resort Hoka	4	B2
Sea Village Resort	5	D2

EATING		
Resort Hoka	(see 4)	

DRINKING		
Dubchichk	6	B2

southern coast alternates between limestone cliffs, rocky coves and sandy beaches.

The island's main industries are fishing, tourism, alcohol and salt. Kalpana Distillery at Malala produces rum from sugar cane.

Note that one legacy of the Portuguese that is very much respected by many local businesses is that of the siesta.

History
Between the 14th and 16th centuries Diu was an important trading post and naval base from which the Ottomans controlled the northern Arabian Sea shipping routes.

Portugal unsuccessfully attempted to capture the island in 1531, during which the Turkish navy helped Bahadur Shah, Sultan of Gujarat. The Portuguese finally secured control in 1535 by taking advantage of a quarrel between the sultan and the Mughal emperor, Humayun.

Under pressure from the Portuguese and the Mughals, Bahadur signed a peace treaty with the Portuguese, giving them control over Diu Port. The treaty was soon ignored and, although both Bahadur Shah and his successor, Sultan Mahmud III, attempted to contest the issue, the peace treaty that was eventually signed in 1539 ceded the island of Diu and the mainland enclave of Ghoghla to Portugal.

Seven Rajput soldiers and a few civilians were killed in Operation Vijay, which ended Portuguese rule in 1961. After the Indian Air Force unnecessarily bombed the airstrip and terminal near Nagoa, it remained derelict until the late 1980s.

Information
Note that many shops around town change money.

A to Z (Map p751; Vaniya St; per hr Rs30; ☾ 9am-midnight) The best internet cafe is near Panchwati Rd. Others may look like they have better hardware, but here you'll find the necessary speed to get the job done.

Post office (Map p751; ☎ 252122) Overlooks the town square.

SBI ATM (Map p750) On Bunder Rd, the only working ATM at the time of research but there are plans for another ATM at Gomptimata Beach.

State Bank of India (Map p751; ☎ 252492; Main Bazaar; ☾ 10am-4pm Mon-Fri, to 1pm Sat) You can change money here, near the town square.

Super Surfing (Map p751; Super Silver Guest House; per hr Rs30; ☾ 9am-11pm) Good for internet.

Tourist office (Map p751; ☎ 252653; www.diuindia.com; Bunder Rd; ☾ 9am-1.30pm & 2.30-6pm Mon-Sat) This unhelpful office is on Diu Town's main road, parallel to the waterfront. If you find it open, it has simple maps.

Uma Cyber Café (Map p751; Uma Shakti Hotel; per hr Rs30; ☾ 9.15am-2pm & 4-11pm) Good for internet.

Dangers & Annoyances
Much more an annoyance than a danger, drunk male tourists can be tiresome, particularly towards single or pairs of women, and particularly around Nagoa Beach.

Sights & Activities
DIU TOWN
Diu Town was the first landing point for the Parsis when they fled from Persia, although they stayed for only three years.

The town is sandwiched between the massive fort to the east and a huge city wall to the west. The main **Zampa Gateway** (Map p751) has carvings of lions, angels and a priest, while just inside the gate is a chapel with an icon dating from 1702.

Cavernous **St Paul's Church** (Map p751; ☼ 8am-6pm) is a wedding cake of a church, founded by Jesuits in 1600 and then rebuilt in 1807. Inside, it's a great barn, with a small cloister next door, above which is a school. Daily mass is heard here. Nearby is white-walled **St Thomas' Church**, a lovely, simple building housing the **Diu Museum** (Map p751; admission free; ☼ 8am-9pm). There's a spooky, evocative collection of old Catholic saint statues. Once a year, on 1 November, this is used for a packed-out mass. There are also some remnants of a Jain temple. There's a guesthouse upstairs around to the left. The **Church of St Francis of Assisi** (Map p751) has been converted into a hospital, but is also sometimes used for services. The Portuguese-descended population mostly live in this area, still called the 'foreigners' quarter'.

Many Diu buildings show a lingering Portuguese influence. The town is a maze

of narrow, winding streets and many houses are brightly painted, with the most impressive buildings on Panchwati, including decadent **Nagar Sheth Haveli** (Map p751), laden with stucco scrolls and fulsome fruit.

Built in 1535, with additions made in 1541, the massive, well-preserved **Portuguese fort** (Map p751; admission free; ☼ 8am-6pm) with its double moat (one tidal) must once have been impregnable, but sea erosion and neglect are leading to a slow collapse. Cannonballs litter the place and the ramparts have a superb array of cannons. The lighthouse is Diu's highest point, with a beam that reaches 32km. There are several small chapels, one holding engraved tombstone fragments. Part of the fort also serves as the island's jail.

The former jail is **Fortim-do-Mar (Pani Kotha)**, the boat-shaped building that seems to float in the bay. You can take boat trips out around the harbour, which stop at Pani Kotha, when it's calm enough (which is seldom; Rs25 return to Pani Kotha).

Outside the city wall are the **Naida Caves** (Map p751), an intriguing, overgrown network of square-hewn hollows and steps leading off

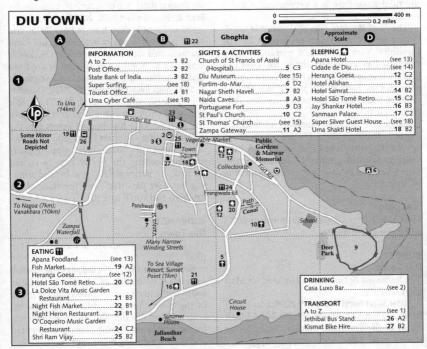

DIU TOWN

Ghoghla

Approximate Scale

0 — 400 m
0 — 0.2 miles

To Una (14km)

Bunder Rd

Some Minor Roads Not Depicted

To Nagoa (7km); Vanakbara (10km)

Zampa Waterfall

Vegetable Market

Town Square

Collectorate

Public Gardens & Marwar Memorial

Fort Rd

Panchwati

Firangiwada Rd

Path

Canal

School

Many Narrow Winding Streets

To Sea Village Resort, Sunset Point (1km)

Deer Park

Circuit House

Summer House

Jallandhar Beach

GUJARAT

into nowhere. This is where the Portuguese hacked out their building materials.

The ferry was undergoing servicing at the time of research, though when running, Diu-by-Night is an evening cruise that departs from the jetty at 7.30pm nightly (weather permitting). It heads to Pani Kotha and Nagoa Beach, and returns around 9pm. Music and snacks are provided.

AROUND THE ISLAND

Nagoa Beach is a long, palm-fringed beach that's safe for swimming but busy, and often with drunk men: foreign women receive a lot of unwanted attention. **Gomptimata**, to the west, is a long, empty, sandy beach that gets big waves – you need to be a strong swimmer here. Beaches within easy reach of Diu Town include **Jallandhar**, **Chakratirth** and the stunning **Sunset Point**, the most popular with foreign tourists, a small, gentle curve that's popular for swimming and relatively hassle free. However, the region around Sunset Point is also the town's dumping ground. Waste is sometimes dumped directly into the sea, and any early morning excursion will reveal that the tidal zone here is a very popular toilet venue.

The **Shell Museum** (Map p750; adult/child Rs10/5; �9am-6pm) is a labour of love. Captain Devjibhai Vira Fulbaria, a merchant navy captain, has collected shells for over 50 years. Close to Diu Town, **Fudam** has a simple church, Our Lady of Remedies, that is now derelict, though a large carved wooden altar remains inside.

At the extreme west, **Vanakbara** is a fascinating little fishing village. It's great to wander around the port, packed with colourful fishing boats and bustling activity – best at 7am to 8am when the fishing fleet returns and sells off its catch.

Sleeping

Most hotels offer a discount (as much as 60%) when things are quiet.

BUDGET
Diu Town

The following options are all located on Map p751.

Super Silver Guest House (☎ 2522020; Super Silver Complex; s/d from Rs200/300, with AC Rs600; 🟦) A block south of the vegetable market, Super Silver is very good value, with simple, tidy, shiny-

tiled rooms, some with views, and helpful management.

Hotel São Tomé Retiro (☎ 253137; georgedesouza 84@hotmail.com; r Rs400-600, without bathroom Rs250) This atmospheric guesthouse, housed in lovely old St Thomas' Church, is definitely the place to stay for the shoes-off, gone fishin' Diu experience. Your host, George D'Souza, is a gentle soul, and his barbecue parties (see opposite) are a treat. Rooms range from small, hot and basic structures on the roof to charming, breezy thick-walled abodes. You can negotiate longer stays. The 360-degree views from the church spire are unrivalled on the island.

Herança Goesa (☎ 253851; 205/3 behind Diu Museum, off Hospital Rd; d Rs350-400) This family (Goan heritage) house has eight absolutely spotless doubles that represent incredible value. Take one of the upstairs rooms that captures the sea breeze and just relax. There are plans for a self-catering barbecue and kitchen which will be ideal for long-term guests. And ask about the proposed Goan cookery classes; of course, they cook up a storm (see opposite).

Around the Island

Jay Shankar Hotel (Map p751; ☎ 252424; near Jalandhar Beach; d Rs200-250, with AC Rs500; 🟦) Here, the cheapest rooms are not that clean, but pay Rs250 and you'll get taken upstairs to a simple, hot foam mattress, cold shower, but otherwise OK double with balcony. Some have sea views. It also has a budget restaurant with veg and non-veg food.

Sea Village Resort (Map p750; ☎ 254345; Chakratirth Beach; s/d Rs250/350, r with AC Rs750; 🟦) Think of a village of shipping containers and you have the picture. This low-budget resort has the prime location at Sunset Point, and has shoe-string guests in plastic chairs, sipping beers and overlooking the pretty bay. Detached 'rooms' are pretty airless, grubby and stinking hot. Get past that (and the state of the kitchen) and you'll love it.

MIDRANGE
Diu Town

The following options are all located on Map p751.

Hotel Samrat (☎ 252354; budget r Rs600, standard/ deluxe with AC Rs1000/1200; 🟦) A couple of blocks south of the town square, Hotel Samrat is one of the town's better middle-range choices, with comfortable doubles, some with street-facing balconies. Credit cards are accepted and there's a decent restaurant and bar.

Sanmaan Palace (☎ 253031; r without/with AC Rs650/1200, ste 2000; ✗) This is an old Portuguese villa in a superb, breezy waterfront location between the town square and fort. The cheap rooms are stuffy converted shipping containers in the garden and best avoided. The original villa rooms are plain and simple, but their high ceilings lend a little charm. There's a pleasant rooftop restaurant – perfect for a beer.

Hotel Alishan (☎ 252340; Fort Rd; d Rs700-2000; ✗ ▯) Alishan has standard, cement-block rooms, some with water views. Cheaper rooms are grubby, while the back and front rooms are overpriced but can be had for a decent discount out of season or during the week.

Uma Shakti Hotel (☎ 252150; d Rs800; ✗) Next door to Super Silver, and near the vegetable market, this has decent, small, overpriced doubles. There's a decent rooftop restaurant.

Cidade de Diu (☎ 254595; s/d from Rs1100/1500; ✗) Behind Hotel Samrat, with the same owners, this lavender dedication to kitsch is worth a look for connoisseurs of certain taste. Rooms, however, are stock standard, small and functional, their best feature being the private balconies. Even in mid-October you may score a 50% discount.

Apana Hotel (☎ 253650; Fort Rd; d Rs1250, with AC Rs1800; ✗) On the seafront, Apana has smallish white-tiled rooms with balconies and breezy sea views. Some female travellers have reported hassles here. There's a bustling garden restaurant (right).

Around the Island

The following options are all located on Map p750.

Hotel Ganga Sagar (☎ 252249; Nagoa Beach; d without AC Rs900, d/t with AC Rs1200/1600; ✗) A classic beachfront hotel, with salty sea-shack ambience and a well-stocked bar. The beach-fronting balcony rooms are the best, though all rooms are clean and simple. A downside can be the weekend clientele.

ourpick Resort Hoka (☎ 253036; www.resorthoka .com; Nagoa Beach; r Rs1150; ✗ ▯ ▣) Hoka is a great place to stay, with colourful, clean and cool rooms in a small, palm-shaded complex with a small swimming pool. Some rooms have terraces over the palm trees. The management here is very helpful, you can hire mopeds, and the food is excellent.

Hotel Kohinoor (☎ 252209; www.htelkohinoordiu .com; r with AC from Rs1950, ste Rs3450; ✗ ▯ ▣) On the

road to Fudam is this very comfortable option. Its well-equipped rooms have balconies and are grouped in villas around a large inviting pool. There's a multicuisine, non-veg restaurant, pastry shop, gym and the Footloose disco and bar.

Radhika Beach Resort (☎ 252553; www.radhika resort.com; Nagoa Beach; d from Rs2250; ✗ ▯) An immaculate, smart, modern place – Diu's best-located upmarket option, with comfortable villas set in grassy grounds around a large central pool. Rooms are spacious, clean and worth the money, and there's a very good multicuisine restaurant.

Eating

Fresh fish is excellent here, and beer and drinks are blissfully cheap – around Rs35 for a Kingfisher, while port costs around Rs120 per bottle.

RESTAURANTS

Herança Goesa (Map p751; ☎ 253851; 205/3 behind Diu Museum, off Hospital Rd; breakfast Rs20-30, dinner Rs30-100, buffet dinner Rs350) Here you eat in the friendly family's front room. For breakfast you can wander in till noon, and the cold coffee is good. For dinner you'll have to book, and it's deservedly popular, with authentic Goan and Portuguese dishes such as delicious baked prawns with piripiri sauce, Goan fish curry, and vindaloo. The buffet spread (three times a week) comprises eight sumptuous courses.

ourpick O'Coqueiro Music Garden Restaurant (Map p751; ☎ 9824681565; Firangiwada Rd; mains Rs30-120; ☉ 7.30am-10.30pm) Here, a dedicated owner has developed a soul-infused garden restaurant celebrating freshness and quality. The small menu offers simple renditions of veg with pasta and excellent seafood. The chef has learnt a handful of Portuguese dishes from a local Diu matriarch. There's also good coffee and cold beer. Near Diu Museum

Night Heron Restaurant (Map p751; ☎ 253166; Jetty, Bunder Chowk; mains Rs40-110; ☉ 9am-3.30pm, 7-11pm) This water-edge open-air restaurant, with upstairs tables, is not bad for an evening meal, ice cream or a beer. During the day it gets a bit hot, though. South Indian breakfasts are a feature while lunch and dinner feature tandoori, Punjabi and Chinese dishes.

La Dolce Vita Music Garden Restaurant (Map p751; ☎ 9824203925; Hospital Rd; mains Rs55-270; ☉ 8am-10pm) This is a simple little roadside restaurant with good breakfasts (homemade muesli, fruit

GUJARAT

salad, lassi) and coffee. Lunch and dinner comprise veg and non-veg curries, pasta and seafood. Near Jallandhar Beach.

Apana Foodland (Map p751; Apana Hotel; mains Rs65-400; ☺ 7am-5pm & 7-11pm) This outdoor, waterfront restaurant does everything: breakfasts, south Indian, Gujarati, Punjabi and Chinese. The fish dishes, including shark tikka, kingfish/prawns with rice, chips and salad can be pre-ordered so you don't miss out. The Gujarati fruit salad is delicious.

Resort Hoka (Map p750; ☎ 253036; resorthoka @travelindia.com; Nagoa Beach; mains Rs70-175; ☺ 8am-10pm) This rooftop restaurant has notably excellent food, with inviting continental breakfasts and delicious choices such as penne with tuna and tomato, fish and chips, and prawn masala. It's relaxed, pleasant and palm-shaded.

Hotel São Tomé Retiro (Map p751; ☎ 253137; all-you-can-eat BBQ Rs150) From around September to April, hospitable George and family hold BBQ parties every other evening. The food offered is fantastic – fresh fish and delicious salads, beer's available and it's an atmospheric place to sit around a blazing campfire and meet other travellers.

There are two fish markets (Map p751), one opposite Jethibai bus stand, and an evening market, lit by flame torches, in Ghoghla. The fresh fish and seafood are delicious; most guesthouses and hotels will cook anything you buy.

QUICK EATS

ourpick Shri Ram Vijay (Map p751; ice creams Rs10-20; ☺ 9am-1.30pm, 3.30-10pm) Forget the alcohol – Diu earns its place on the map for this small, squeaky-clean, old-fashioned ice cream parlour, with delicious handmade ice cream and milkshakes. Going since 1933, this family enterprise started out with soft drinks, and they still make their own brands (Dew and Leo) in Fudam – try the exceptional Dew cream soda and then try all the ice creams!

Drinking

Apart from the restaurants (most of which double as bars), there are some good places for a tipple.

Casa Luxo Bar (Map p751; ☺ 9am-2pm & 4-10pm Tue-Sun) Opened in 1963, it looks like the decor hasn't changed since, with lots of dusty bottles. A Kingfisher costs Rs35.

Dubchichk (Map p750; Nagoa beach; ☺ 11am-3.45pm & 6.30-10.30pm) This drinking platform has a great

vantage point for overlooking drunken antics on the beach from a safe distance.

Getting There & Away

AIR

Jet Airways (☎ 252365; www.jetairways.com) flies to Mumbai (Rs3800). For bookings there are numerous ticketing agents in town.

BUS

From Jethibai bus stand there are buses to Veraval (Rs40, three hours), Rajkot (Rs110, five hours), Jamnagar (Rs120, seven hours) and Bhavnagar (Rs108, five hours). More frequent departure times exist from Una, about 10km away (Rs15, 40 minutes).

Buses depart from Una bus stand for Diu (from 6.30am to 8.15pm). Outside these hours, walk 1km to Tower Chowk in Una, from where shared autorickshaws go to Ghoghla or Diu for about the same fare. An autorickshaw costs Rs200.

Private buses go from Diu to Mumbai at 10am (seat/sleeper Rs450/500, 24 hours) and to Ahmedabad at 7.30pm (Rs200/250, 10½ hours). Book in advance at **A to Z** (Map p751; ☎ 254080; Vaniya St; ☺ 9am-midnight).

TRAIN

Delwada, between Una and Ghoghla, and only about 8km from Diu, is the nearest railhead. A shared autorickshaw from there to Ghoghla costs about Rs10. There's a direct passenger train (313/314) at 8.10am from Delwada to Veraval (2nd class Rs22, 3½ hours), which stops at Gir at 9.50am (Rs20, two hours).

Getting Around

Travelling by autorickshaw anywhere in Diu Town should cost no more than Rs20. To Nagoa beach pay Rs60 and to Sunset Point, Rs40. Shared autorickshaws to Ghoghla cost Rs10 per person. Note that rickshaw-wallahs in Una are unable to proceed further than the bus station (Rs200), so cannot take you all the way to Nagoa Beach (an additional Rs60).

Mopeds are a perfect option for exploring the island – the roads are deserted and in good condition. The going rate per day is Rs150 for a moped (not including fuel). Motorcycles and scooters cost Rs150 to 250. Most hotels arrange mopeds, although quality varies. Try **Kismat** (☎ 252971; ☺ 9am-7pm Mon-Sat, to 1pm Sun), which also rents bicycles (Rs15 per day), or

A to Z (☎ 254080; Vaniya Rd; ⏱ 9am-midnight). A Rs200 to Rs500 deposit is usually required.

Local buses from Diu Town to Nagoa and Vanakbara leave from the Jethibai bus stand at 7am, 11am and 4pm. From Nagoa, they depart for Diu Town from near the police post at 1pm, 5.30pm and 7pm (Rs5).

VERAVAL
☎ 02876 / pop 141,207

Veraval is cluttered, chaotic, and smells strongly of fish – not surprising given that it's one of India's major fishing ports – and its busy harbour is full of bustle and boat building. On the south coast of Saurashtra, Veraval was the major seaport for Mecca pilgrims before the rise of Surat. The main reason to come here is to visit the Temple of Somnath (see right), 6km to the east.

JP Travels International (☎ 20110; Sadar Bazaar) changes travellers cheques and cash, as does the **State Bank of India**. There's an HDFC ATM and an Axis Bank ATM near the municipal gardens. **Om Cyber World** (Chandra-Mauli Complex; per hr Rs15; ⏱ 9.30am-midnight), in the same building as Hotel Ustav, allows you to slowly surf the internet while squeezed into a pod.

Sleeping & Eating
Hotel Kaveri (☎ 220842; 2 Akar Complex, ST Rd; s/d Rs250/400, with AC from Rs550/650; ✴) Kaveri is easily the pick of the town's accommodation, and the most convenient choice, with a range of well-kept rooms and a switched-on manager. Unfortunately, there is no restaurant, just a small canteen for snacks and drinks.

Hotel Utsav (☎ 222306; 3rd fl, Chandramauli Complex, ST Rd; d Rs300, with AC Rs550; ✴) This hotel, opposite the local bus stand, has reasonably clean doubles with views over the dusty town and the bus stand (the main source of the dust).

Toran Tourist Bungalow (☎ 246588; College Rd; s/d Rs325/425, with AC Rs475/700; ✴) Practically a pile of rubble when we visited, the expected three-month renovation of this government-run hotel should deliver brightly painted rooms – at least for a couple of seasons. Near the lighthouse, the location is quiet but rather inconvenient. Deluxe rooms have balconies with sunset and ocean views.

Hotel Park (☎ 242703; Veraval-Junagadh Rd; r without/with AC Rs500/1000; ✴ ✳) About 1.5km out of town, this hotel has passed its prime and appears to be slowly dying. It still has a nice big pool in the palm-shaded grounds, spacious though shabby rooms and a functioning (just) restaurant.

Sagar (ST Rd; mains Rs30-90; ⏱ 9am-3.30pm & 5-11pm) This subdued, friendly vegetarian restaurant serves reasonable Punjabi and Chinese food.

Getting There & Away
BUS
Departures are more frequent if you change at Una. See p757 for details of STC buses from Veraval.

There are private bus agencies opposite the STC bus stand, including **HK Travels** (☎ 221934; ST Rd; ⏱ 7am-11pm), which offer a nightly jaunt to Ahmedabad (seat/sleeper Rs180/300) at 9pm.

TRAIN
The 1465/3 *Veraval–Jabalpur Express* leaves at 10.05am and arrives at Ahmedabad (sleeper/3AC/2AC Rs187/523/715) at 6.25pm, via Rajkot (Rs121/296/400, 3½ hours) on Monday and Saturday only. Trains leave for Sasan (2nd class Rs15, 1½ to two hours) at 9.40am, 2.20pm, 2.40pm and 3.05pm.

A passenger service (313) to Delwada (for Diu) leaves at 4.05pm (2nd class Rs24, 3½ hours).

There's a **reservation office** (☎ 131; ⏱ 8am-8pm Mon-Sat, to 2pm Sun) at the station.

Getting Around
An autorickshaw to Somnath, 6km away, should cost you about Rs40; buses are Rs8 and leave from the local bus stand, near the STC bus stand.

SOMNATH
☎ 02876

Somnath consists of a few dusty streets leading away from its phoenix-like temple. The sea below gives it a wistful charm and the pilgrim trade is relentless. There's a Bank of Baroda ATM on your right as you approach the temple. Somnath celebrates Kartik Purnima (November to December) with a large colourful fair.

Sights
TEMPLE OF SOMNATH
This **temple** (⏱ 6am-9.30pm, light & sound show 7.45pm), 80km from Junagadh, has been razed and rebuilt at least eight times. It's said that Somraj, the moon god, constructed a gold version, rebuilt by Ravana in silver, by Krishna in

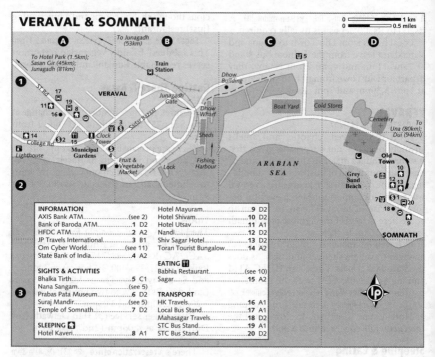

VERAVAL & SOMNATH

INFORMATION	
AXIS Bank ATM	(see 2)
Bank of Baroda ATM	1 D2
HFDC ATM	2 A2
JP Travels International	3 B1
Om Cyber World	(see 11)
State Bank of India	4 A2

SIGHTS & ACTIVITIES	
Bhalka Tirth	5 C1
Nana Sangam	(see 5)
Prabas Pata Museum	6 D2
Suraj Mandir	(see 5)
Temple of Somnath	7 D2

SLEEPING	
Hotel Kaveri	8 A1

Hotel Mayuram	9 D2
Hotel Shivam	10 D2
Hotel Utsav	11 A1
Nandi	12 D2
Shiv Sagar Hotel	13 D2
Toran Tourist Bungalow	14 A2

EATING	
Babhia Restaurant	(see 10)
Sagar	15 A2

TRANSPORT	
HK Travels	16 A1
Local Bus Stand	17 A1
Mahasagar Travels	18 D2
STC Bus Stand	19 A1
STC Bus Stand	20 D2

wood and by Bhimdev in stone. A description of the temple by Al-Biruni, an Arab traveller, was so glowing that it prompted a visit in 1024 by a most unwelcome tourist – Mahmud of Ghazni. At that time, the temple was so wealthy that it had 300 musicians, 500 dancing girls and even 300 barbers.

Mahmud of Ghazni, a legendary looter, descended on Somnath from his Afghan kingdom and, after a two-day battle, took the town and the temple. Having stripped it of its fabulous wealth, he destroyed it. So began a pattern of Muslim destruction and Hindu rebuilding that continued for centuries. The temple was again razed in 1297, 1394 and finally in 1706 by Aurangzeb, the notorious Mughal fundamentalist.

After the 1706 demolition, the temple wasn't rebuilt until 1950. Outside, opposite the entrance, is a statue of SV Patel (1875–1950), responsible for the reconstruction.

The current serene, symmetrical temple was built to traditional designs on the original coastal site. It contains one of the 12 sacred Shiva shrines known as *jyoti linga*. Photography is prohibited.

PRABAS PATA MUSEUM
Nearby, the **Prabas Pata Museum** (☎ 232455; Indian/foreigner Rs2/50; ☷ 10.30am-5.30pm Thu-Tue, closed 2nd & 4th Sat of month) is laid out in courtyard-centred rooms and contains remains of the previous temples, with lots of beautiful fragments, including an elaborate 11th-century ceiling.

OTHER SIGHTS
Halfway between Veraval and Somnath is **Bhalka Tirth**, where Krishna was mistaken for a deer (he was sleeping in a deerskin) and wounded by an arrow. The legendary spot is at the confluence of three rivers. You get to it through the small *sangam* (confluence gate), known simply as the **Nana** (Small Gate). North of this sacred spot is **Suraj Mandir** (Sun Temple), which Mahmud of Ghazni also had a go at knocking down. This ancient temple, with a frieze of lions with elephant trunks, probably dates from the same time as the original Temple of Somnath.

Sleeping & Eating
Hotel Shivam (☎ 231451; s/d without AC Rs200/400, with AC Rs500/750; ☷) Among the lanes opposite the

temple, this is another good, friendly, comfortable hotel with unsurprising, serviceable rooms.

Nandi (☎ 231839; r without/with AC Rs350/550; ✖) The Somnath stalwart, on a market-filled street leading from the temple, has small, cleanish rooms; many come with temple views and a cheery atmosphere.

Shiv Sagar Hotel (☎ 233111; r without/with AC Rs350/600; ✖) Opposite the temple and with a bevy of staff wandering around, this hotel has bright though smallish rooms with simple bathrooms and a veg restaurant.

Hotel Mayuram (☎ 231286; r without/with AC Rs450/800; ✖) Just down the coast road heading away from the temple, this quiet option has clean, plain doubles shining with tiles.

Babhia Restaurant (☎ 9898193130; mains Rs40-70; ☽ 8am-11pm) Tucked away near Shiv Sagar Hotel, this is the best restaurant on the temple side of town. It has black vinyl booth seating and keen staff. The menu features Punjabi, Chinese and Gujarati.

Getting There & Away
BUS
Somnath has fewer departures than Veraval, but buses run to Diu (Rs57, 3½ hours, one bus at 9.45am), Jamnagar (Rs120, seven hours), Porbandar (Rs70, six hours), Dwarka (Rs90, seven hours), Una (Rs45, three hours) and Rajkot (Rs100, five hours).

Mahasagar Travels (☎ 98467817; ☽ 10am-10pm), opposite the STC bus stand, has buses to Ahmedabad (seat/sleeper Rs200/280, 10 hours).

SASAN GIR WILDLIFE SANCTUARY
☎ 02877
The last refuge of the Asiatic lion (*Panthera leo persica*) is 59km from Junagadh via Visavadar. The rugged, hilly, 1400-sq-km sanctuary feels beguilingly uncommercial, and encompasses

BUSES FROM VERAVAL

Destination	Fare (Rs)	Duration (hr)	Frequency
Ahmedabad	175	10	5 daily
Diu	40	3	5 daily
Junagadh	45	2	every 30min
Porbandar	60	3	15 daily
Rajkot	75	5	hourly
Sasan	25	1½	5 daily

some beautiful forested land. It was set up to protect lions and their habitat: since 1980 numbers have increased from fewer than 200 to over 360 today. However, while lions have been lucky, the distinctively dressed local *maaldhari* (herders), a devout, nomadic community, have lost valuable grazing land. In recent years the lions have been wandering outside the limits of the sanctuary in search of easy game – namely calves. One lion ended up on the beaches of Diu! The problem is compounded by the declining areas of forest outside the sanctuary, forcing villagers to forage for fuel within its precincts, reducing the lions' habitat.

Sasan Gir is not big enough for the number of lions, but moves by the Madhya Pradesh government to transfer lions to the Pulpur Kuno Sanctuary in Madhya Pradesh were unceremoniously canned by the Gujarat government, and there are no agreed measures to address the difficulties caused by the competition for land and resources.

As well as lions, there are leopards, hyenas, foxes, wild boars, parrots, peacocks, crocodiles (there's also a crocodile-breeding centre), monkeys, nilgai, gazelles and deer.

The best time to visit is from December to April; it's closed from mid-June to mid-October and possibly even longer if there has been a heavy monsoon.

Information
The **Gir Orientation Centre** (☽ 9am-6pm), next to the Sinh Sadan Forest Lodge, has displays of the park's inhabitants and a replica *maaldhari* hut. A creaking film about the park is screened at 7pm.

Sights & Activities
SAFARIS
The lions are elusive, but you'd be unlucky not to see at least one on a safari. If you're determined to spot one, allow for a couple of trips.

Before you go on safari, you must obtain a **permit** (Indian/foreigner Rs400/US$40). Permits are valid for one vehicle (for four hours) and up to six people and are issued on the spot at the **Sinh Sadan Forest Lodge Office** (☽ 6.30-10.30am & 3-5pm 16 Oct-15 Feb, 6.30-11am & 4-5.30pm 16 Feb-15 Jun). Private vehicles are not allowed into the sanctuary, so you need to hire a vehicle (Rs700) for the roughly 2½-hour trip. The vehicles, petrol Gypsies and larger diesel SUVs wait outside the Forest Lodge Office; advance bookings

GUJARAT

THE LAST WILD ASIATIC LIONS

In the 19th century the territory of the Asiatic lion stretched from its current refuge in Gujarat's Gir Forest as far east as Bihar. Widespread hunting decimated the population, with the last sightings recorded near Delhi in 1834, in Bihar in 1840 and in Rajasthan in 1870. The last lion to die in the Indian wild outside Gujarat's Kathiawar Peninsula was recorded in 1884. Why did they survive in Gujarat? They almost didn't. Hunting pushed Gir lions to the brink of extinction, with as few as 12 remaining in the 1870s. It was not until one of their erstwhile pursuers, the enlightened nawab of Junagadh, decided to set up a protection zone at the beginning of the 20th century, that the lions began slowly to recover. This zone now survives as the Sasan Gir Wildlife Sanctuary.

Separated from their African counterpart (Panthera leo leo) for centuries, Asiatic lions have developed unique characteristics. The mane of Panthera leo persica is less luxuriant and doesn't cover the top of the head or ears, while a prominent fold of skin runs the length of the abdomen. The skin is slightly lighter in colour, too. They are also purely predatory, unlike African lions which sometimes feed off carrion.

---

are recommended. The guide's fee is Rs50. Although prices are quoted in US dollars, payment is in rupees and the exchange is at the official's discretion – usually fair. Be aware that all fees are raised 25% on weekends and festival times, namely Navratri, Diwali and Christmas.

GIR INTERPRETATION ZONE
Twelve kilometres from Sasan village at Devalia, within the sanctuary precincts, is the **Gir Interpretation Zone** (Indian/foreigner Rs75/US$20; ☻ 8-11am & 3-5pm Thu-Tue), better known as simply 'Devalia'. The 4.12-sq-km fenced off compound is home to a cross section of Gir wildlife. Chances of seeing lions here are good but stage-managed, and you're only likely to get 30 to 45 minutes looking for wildlife and only from a bus. Vehicles run here from Sasan Gir's main street for Rs150. Just in case you were thinking about dashing off into the bushes on the way to Devalia, we had a lioness cross the road in front of us, about 1km from the compound.

CROCODILE BREEDING CENTRE
This **centre** (admission free; ☻ 8.30am-6pm), near Sinh Sadan, is a good place to see crocs, from baby to big, bred here to restock the sanctuary.

Sleeping & Eating
It's a good idea to make an advance booking. Sasan Gir has one main street and most accommodation is on it or nearby, with a few upmarket options further away.

Rajeshri Guest House (☎ 285740; r Rs100-200) Opposite the gate to Sinh Sadan, this place has basic, grubby rooms. The young, betel-spitting staff are eager park guides, but are a real put-off. Thalis cost Rs35.

Hotel Umang (☎ 285728; www.hotelumang.com; SBS Bank Rd; dm 300, r Rs950, with AC Rs1650; ⊠) Signposted off the main road 100m west of Rajeshri Guest House, this is a quiet option with serviceable rooms and decent meals. It also offers a two-night package with all meals for Rs3150.

Sinh Sadan Forest Lodge (☎ 285540; dm Indian/foreigner Rs50/US$5, r Rs500/US$30, with AC Rs1000/US$50; ⊠) This is pleasant but outrageously priced for foreigners (meal prices are similarly imbalanced) and the service is lackadaisical.

Amidhara Resort (☎ 285950; www.amidhararesort.com; Talala; r from Rs3300, with AC from Rs3800; ⊠ ▢ ▣) On the road to Veraval, this is easily the best choice in these parts – note that the tariff includes all meals. The rooms are generously decked out, there's a multicuisine restaurant and an inviting pool. It is possible to negotiate a tariff without meals.

Maneland Jungle Lodge (☎ 285690; www.maneland.com; d from Rs3500; ⊠ ▣) Off the road to Junagadh, 3km from Sasan, this place backs on to the reserve and has decent rooms in cottages with alcoves and window seats. The tariff includes all meals. Hopefully the pool water will have been refreshed by the time you visit.

You can also stay at Nitin Ratangayra's **family house** (☎ 285686; d without bathroom Rs200-300). Nitin is also a guide who arranges village tours.

Sasan village is lined with food stalls and nothing-special thali restaurants.

Getting There & Away
STC buses travel regularly between Junagadh and Veraval via Sasan. There are buses to

Veraval (local/express Rs12/20, 1½ hours) and to Junagadh (Rs20/31, two hours).

Trains run to Veraval (Rs15, 1½ hours) and Delwada (for Diu, Rs20, two hours).

JUNAGADH

☎ 0285 / pop 168,686

Junagadh is an interesting small city practically devoid of tourists. It's an ancient, fortified city at the base of holy Girnar Hill. The city is named after the fort that enclosed the old city (*jirna* means old). Dating from 250 BC, the Ashokan Edicts nearby are testament to its earthly age.

At the time of Partition, the nawab of Junagadh opted to take his tiny state into Pakistan – a wildly unpopular decision as the inhabitants were predominantly Hindu, so the nawab departed on his own.

Junagadh makes a good base for chasing lions at Sasan Gir (see p757).

Information

The **tourist information office** is at the Hotel Girnar, but has no useful information or town maps. Travellers will find all the information they need at the Hotel Relief.

Axis Bank ATM in Diwan Chowk.

Bank of Baroda Has an ATM and changes travellers cheques and cash. Next to the local bus stand.

Main post office (☎ 2627116) Inconveniently located south of the centre at Gandhigram.

XS Cyber Café (Lake View Complex, Talav Gate; per hr Rs15; ☒ 10am-midnight)

Post office (☒ 10am-3pm) Off MG Rd, near the local bus stand.

State Bank of India (☒ 11am-2pm) Near Diwan Chowk, has an ATM and changes travellers cheques and cash.

Sights

UPERKOT FORT

This ancient **fort** (admission Rs2; ☒ 6.30am-6.30pm, closed 2nd & 4th Sat of month), on Junagadh's eastern side, is believed to have been built in 319 BC by Chandragupta (ruler of India in the 3rd century BC), though it has been extended many times. An ornate triple gateway forms the entrance, and in places the walls reach 20m high. It's been besieged 16 times, and legend has it that the fort once withstood a 12-year siege. It's also said that the fort was abandoned from the 7th to the 10th centuries and, when rediscovered, was completely overgrown by jungle.

The **Jama Masjid**, the mosque inside the fort, was built from a demolished Hindu palace and has an interior filled with columns.

Close to the mosque are 2nd century AD **Buddhist caves** (Indian/foreigner Rs5/100, video Rs25; ☒ 8am-6pm), an eerie three-storey carved complex – the main hall contains pillars with weathered carvings.

Other points of interest include the **Tomb of Nuri Shah** and two fine step wells. One is **Adi Chadi** (named after two slave girls who used to fetch water from it), built into the narrow leaning walls of a cave, and the other, **Navaghan Kuva**, dramatically deep and reached by a magnificent staircase cut into the rock.

MAHABAT MAQBARA

This stunning **mausoleum** of a nawab of Junagadh seems to bubble up into the sky. One of Gujarat's most glorious examples of Indo-Islamic architecture, its lavish appeal is topped off by its silver doors. Boasting even more flourish is the neighbouring vazir's *maqbara*, sporting storybook minarets encircled by spiralling stairways. Both buildings are generally locked (the exteriors are best anyway) – or you can try to obtain the keys from the adjacent mosque.

DURBAR HALL MUSEUM

This **museum** (Indian/foreigner Rs2/50; ☒ 9am-12.15pm & 2.45-6pm Thu-Tue, closed 2nd & 4th Sat of month) displays weapons, armour, palanquins, chandeliers, and howdahs from the days of the nawabs, as well as a huge carpet woven in Junagadh's jail. There's a royal portrait gallery, including photos of the last nawab with his numerous beloved dogs.

ASHOKAN EDICTS

On the way to the Girnar Hill temples, you pass a huge **boulder** (Indian/foreigner Rs5/100; ☒ 8am-1pm & 2-6pm) on which Emperor Ashoka inscribed 14 edicts in Pali script in about 250 BC instructing people to be kind to women and animals and give to beggars, among other things. Sanskrit inscriptions were added around AD 150 by Emperor Rudradama and in about AD 450 by Skandagupta, the last emperor of the Mauryas, referring mainly to recurring floods destroying the embankments of a nearby lake, the Sudershan, which no longer exists.

The boulder, with its spidery inscriptions, is curiously enclosed in a small building.

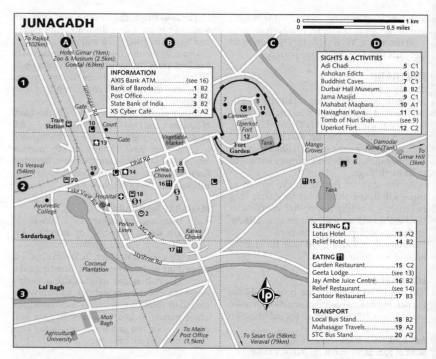

JUNAGADH

INFORMATION
AXIS Bank ATM..............(see 16)
Bank of Baroda........................1 B2
Post Office.............................2 B2
State Bank of India..................3 B2
XS Cyber Café........................4 A2

SIGHTS & ACTIVITIES
Adi Chadi.............................5 C1
Ashokan Edicts......................6 D2
Buddhist Caves......................7 C1
Durbar Hall Museum...............8 B2
Jama Masjid..........................9 B2
Mahabat Maqbara..................10 A1
Navaghan Kuva......................11 C1
Tomb of Nuri Shah...............(see 9)
Uperkot Fort........................12 C2

SLEEPING
Lotus Hotel..........................13 A2
Relief Hotel..........................14 B2

EATING
Garden Restaurant.................15 C2
Geeta Lodge.......................(see 13)
Jay Ambe Juice Centre...........16 B2
Relief Restaurant................(see 14)
Santoor Restaurant................17 B3

TRANSPORT
Local Bus Stand....................18 B2
Mahasagar Travels.................19 A2
STC Bus Stand......................20 A2

GIRNAR HILL

The long climb up 10,000 stone steps to the summit of **Girnar** is best begun at dawn. It is a magical experience in the early morning light, as pilgrims and porters begin to trudge up the well-maintained steps, which were built between 1889 and 1908, through scrubby teak forest and past chai stalls. The start is about 2km beyond Damodar Kund – the road takes you to around the 3000th step – which leaves you *only* 7000 to the top. As you gain height, the views begin to sweep across wooded hills.

The refreshment stalls on the 2½-hour ascent sell chalk, so you can graffiti your name onto the rocks. As you near the top, take a moment to marvel at how the stallholders can rustle up a chilled drink. If you can't face the walk, *dholis* carried by porters can be hired; they are charged by weight so, before setting off, you suffer the indignity of being weighed on a huge beam scale.

Like Palitana, the temple-topped hill is of great significance to the Jains, but several important Hindu temples mean that Hindus make the pilgrimage, too.

The Jain temples, a cluster of mosaic-decorated domes interspersed with elaborate stupas, are about two-thirds of the way up. The largest and oldest is the 12th-century **Temple of Neminath** – dedicated to the 22nd *tirthankar* – go through the first left-hand doorway after the first gate. Many temples are locked from around 11am to 3pm, but this is open all day.

The nearby triple **Temple of Mallinath**, dedicated to the ninth *tirthankar,* was erected in 1177 by two brothers. During festivals this temple is a sadhu magnet.

Further up the steps are various Hindu temples. First is the **Temple of Gorakhnath**, perched on the highest peak at 600m. The next peak is topped by the **Temple of Amba Mata**, where newlyweds worship to ensure a happy marriage. On top of the final outcrop is **Dat Tatraya**, dedicated to three gods.

Bus No 3 or 4 from the local bus stand will take you to Girnar Taleti at the base of the hill. Buses run about once an hour from 6am (Rs5) and pass by the Ashokan Edicts. An autorickshaw journey from town costs about Rs35.

GUJARAT

JUNAGADH ZOO

If you don't make it to Sasan, Junagadh's **zoo** (admission Rs10; 9am-6.30pm Thu-Tue) at Sakar Bagh, 3.5km from the centre, on the Rajkot road, has Gir lions. The nawab set up the zoo in 1863 to save lions from extinction and, though the concrete enclosures at the front rival much of Asia for sheer cruelty, it has a surprisingly good 'safari' park, with an abundance of lions, tigers and leopards. There is also a **museum** (closed 2nd & 4th Sat of month) at the zoo with paintings, manuscripts, archaeological finds and other exhibits, including a natural-history section. Take bus 6 (Rs5) or an autorickshaw (Rs25) to get here.

Sleeping

There are several cheap hotels around Kahra Chowk which, because of the clientele they attract, are best avoided by females – even when travelling with a male partner.

Hotel Girnar (2621201; Majewadi Darwaja; dm Rs75, s/d Rs210/325, with AC Rs425/700;) About 2km out of town, this state-run, charmless cement block has bleak but spacious rooms; try to get one with a balcony. There are big discounts from mid-June to mid-September. The restaurant is privately run and has thalis for Rs50.

Relief Hotel (2620280; www.reliefhotel.com; Dhal Rd; s/d Rs250/300, r with AC Rs660;) Mr Sorathia (Junagadh's unofficial tourist information officer) presides over the pick of the town's accommodation, which has simple, freshly painted rooms and the best setup for travellers. There's also a fabulous restaurant and secure parking is available.

Lotus Hotel (2658500; www.thelotushotel.com; Station Rd; s/d from Rs1500/2500;) This luxurious and comfortable option occupies the totally renovated top floor of a former *dharamsala*. Pilgrims never had it so good, with split-system AC and LCD TVs. Rooms are spacious, the beds are great and everything works. There isn't a restaurant; however, theres room service and Geeta Lodge is in the same building and other restaurants aren't too far away.

Eating

Junagadh is famous for its fruit, especially for *kesar* (mangoes) and *chiku* (sapodilla), which are popular in milkshakes in November and December.

Garden Restaurant (mains Rs35-100; 6.30-10.30pm Thu-Tue) Something different: this restaurant has a lovely garden setting near Jyoti Nursery and beneath Girnar Hill, and reasonable Jain, Punjabi and south Indian food – it's popular with families and is worth the short rickshaw ride.

Santoor Restaurant (MG Rd; mains Rs21-55) Popular Santoor has quick service, good, fresh vegetarian Punjabi and south Indian, delectable mango shakes, booth seating and dim lighting.

Geeta Lodge (2623317; thali Rs55; 10am-3.30pm & 6-11pm) Close to the station, with all-you-can-eat veg Gujarati thalis and an army of waiters. Finish off with sweets, such as fruit salad or pureed mango for Rs15.

Relief Restaurant (2620280; Relief Hotel, Dhal Rd; mains Rs50-90; 11.30am-3.30pm & 6.30-11.30pm) This spotless, relaxed, AC restaurant serves up delicious Punjabi, tandoori and Chinese dishes. Meat-eaters can choose from chicken, mutton, fish or prawns, and there's a good choice of veg and paneer dishes. This is also the best place for continental breakfasts.

Jay Ambe Juice Centre (Diwan Chowk; snacks & drinks Rs25-40; 10am-11pm) Great for a fresh juice, milkshake or ice cream; this is a perfect retreat.

Getting There & Away

BUS

Buses leave regularly for Rajkot (Rs60, two hours), Sasan Gir (Rs40, two hours), Porbandar (Rs60, three hours), Veraval (Rs45, three hours), Diu (Rs90, 5½ hours, one bus at 7am), Una (for Diu; Rs70, five hours), Jamnagar (Rs80, four hours) and Ahmedabad (Rs120, eight hours).

Various private bus offices are on Dhal Rd, near the rail tracks. **Mahasagar Travels** (2629199) serves Mumbai (Rs350), Vadodara (Rs220), Ahmedabad (Rs180, eight hours) and Udaipur (Rs400, 15 hours).

TRAIN

There's a **reservation office** (131; 8am-1pm & 3-8pm Mon-Sat, 8am-2pm Sun) at the station.

The 1465 *Veraval–Jabalpur Express* departs at 11.45am (Monday and Saturday) and arrives in Rajkot (sleeper/3AC/2AC Rs121/232/290) at 1.55pm and Ahmedabad (Rs161/446/608) at 6.25pm.

There's a 7am train to Delwada (near Diu) via Sasan Gir.

GONDAL
☎ 02825 / pop 96,000

Gondal is a small, leafy town, 38km south of Rajkot, that sports a string of palaces on a gentle river. Once capital of a 1000-sq-km princely state, it was run by the Jadeja Rajputs, later overtaken by the Mughals, then recovered in the 1650s. Maharaja Bhagwat Singhji ruled in the 19th century and was a progressive social reformer who, among other things, introduced compulsory education for both sexes.

Sights & Activities

Naulakha Museum (Naulakha Palace; admission Rs20; ⊙ 9am-noon, 3-6pm) is housed in a beautiful, decrepit riverside palace that was built in a mixture of styles, with striking gargoyles. The museum shows royal artefacts, including scales used to weigh the maharaja in 1934 (his weight in silver was distributed to the poor) and dinky toys.

The **Car Museum** (Orchard Palace; admission Rs60; ⊙ 9am-noon, 3-6pm) contains the royal fleet of around 50 impressive vehicles, including a car from 1907, made by the 'New Engine Company Acton'.

The **Shri Bhuvaneshwari Aushadhashram Ayurvedic Pharmacy** (☎ 222445; www.bhuvaneshwari pith.com; Ghanshyam Bhuvan Mahader Wadi) was founded in 1910 by the Royal Physician. The pharmacy manufactures medicines and it's possible to see all the weird machinery involved, as well as buy medicines for treating hair loss, vertigo, insomnia etc. The founding physician here first coined the title 'Mahatma' (Great Soul) for Gandhi.

Swaninarayan Temple (⊙ 7.30am-1pm & 3.30-8.30pm), owned by the wealthy Swaninarayan sect, is a white, 19th-century building built on land donated by the maharaja, with an attached farm.

About 3km off the road to Rajkot is **Veri Lake**, a large reservoir that's good for birdwatching (return rickshaw Rs60).

Udhyog Bharti Khadi Gramodyog (Udhyog Bharti Chowk; ⊙ 8am-1pm & 3-5pm) is a large *khadi* shop where hundreds of women work spinning cotton upstairs, while downstairs embroidered *salwar kamees* (traditional tunic and trousers) and saris are on sale.

Sleeping & Eating

Bhuveneshari Guest House (☎ 222481; r Rs250, with AC Rs450; ✵) A few streets from Orchard Palace, and part of the Bhuveneshari complex, this is a pilgrims' guesthouse that has reasonable rooms.

Orchard Palace (☎ 220002; hghgroup@yahoo.com; Palace Rd; d full-board Rs5600, d bed & breakfast Rs4000, d room only Rs3400; ✵) This small palace, once the royal guesthouse, has six well-kept, though hardly luxurious, high-ceilinged rooms of different sizes, filled with 1930s and '40s furniture. It's rather overpriced, though a peaceful place to stay where guests get free admission to all of Gondal's attractions.

Dreamland (2nd fl, Kailash Complex; mains Rs35-70, thali Rs55; ⊙ 11am-3pm & 7-11pm) Near the bus stand, this has Gondal's best Gujarati thalis, in a bright, clean, busy restaurant, with good veg Punjabi, south Indian and Chinese dishes.

Getting There & Away

Buses run regularly to/from Rajkot (Rs20, one hour), Junagadh (Rs30, two hours) and Porbandar (Rs90, three hours).

Slow passenger trains from Rajkot (Rs15, one hour) to Junagadh (Rs18, 1½ hours) stop at Gondal (they go on to Veraval).

PORBANDAR
☎ 0286 / pop 133,083

The port town of Porbandar, located between Veraval and Dwarka, is famed as the birthplace of Mahatma Gandhi. You can't swim here due to the polluted seas; in fact, you can't do much at all except wander the chaotic streets (while sniffing the drying fish) leading to the former house of the great man, or pay respects at a neighbouring shrine. Back towards Jubilee Bridge you'll find some lovely mangroves with abundant bird life.

In ancient times, the city was called Sudamapuri after Sudama, a compatriot of Krishna, and there was once a flourishing trade from here to Africa and the Gulf. The Africa connection is apparent in the number of African-Indians, known as Siddis, who form a separate caste of Dalits.

Information

There's no tourist office, but you could check out www.porbandaronline.com. There's an Axis Bank ATM on Mahatma Gandhi (MG) Rd and an SBI ATM near the Gandhi Statue on MG Rd.

iWay (Hotel Natraj basement; per hr Rs35) Internet access.
JK Forex & Services (☎ 2242511; MG Rd; ⊙ 9.30am-8pm Mon-Sat) Changes travellers cheques and currency.

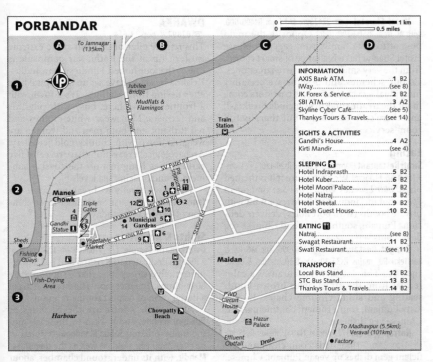

PORBANDAR

Skyline Cyber Café (25 Indraprasth Complex, ST Cross Rd; per hr Rs30; ☯ 9.30am-12.30am)

Thankys Tours & Travels (☎ 2244344; MG Rd; ☯ 9am-8pm Mon-Sat, 10am-1.30pm Sun) Changes travellers cheques and currency.

Sights

KIRTI MANDIR

This **memorial** (admission free; ☯ 7.30am-7pm) to Gandhi was built in 1950. Reflecting Gandhi's age when he died, it's 79ft high and has 79 candle holders; symbols from all the world's major religions are incorporated. There's a small bookshop and photographic exhibition (take the stairs by the entrance). Next door is **Gandhi's birthplace** – a three-storey, 220-year-old house. He was born here on 2 October 1869 (the very spot is marked on the floor by a swastika), and it was his home till the ripe old age of six. The house is an interesting warren of 22 rooms.

Sleeping

Hotel Moon Palace (☎ 2241172; moonpalace@porbandaronline.com; MG Rd; s/d from Rs150/250, deluxe ste Rs600/700) This is a reasonably clean, comfort-

able, friendly option, with some good-value rooms. Pricier rooms are bigger, better and brighter. A thali is Rs35.

Nilesh Guest House (☎ 2249496; MG Rd; r Rs200) A very welcoming, dollar-friendly guesthouse, with passable doubles with attached bathroom.

Hotel Indraprasth (☎ 2242681; ST Cross Rd; s/d from Rs300/500, with AC from Rs400/600; ☒) An unprepossessing mall block holds this beige in colour and beige in character hotel. Nevertheless, rooms are clean enough and not bad value.

Hotel Natraj (☎ 2215658; www.hotelnatrajp.com; MG Rd; s/d from Rs350/500, with AC from Rs550/800) This smart-looking and well-run hotel is the best in town. It's centrally located, most budgets are catered for, and the rooms are squeaky clean with modern facilities, and there's an excellent restaurant.

Hotel Kuber (☎ 2241289; ST Cross Rd; s/d from Rs400/500, with AC from Rs600/800; ☒) Another ugly mall block concealing a hotel. The Kuber has a swish modern lobby (beyond the mall entrance) and the rooms are comfortable and well appointed. Beware the narrow and low doorways, however.

Hotel Sheetal (☎ 2247596; s/d from Rs400/500, with AC from Rs500/700; ❄) Opposite the main post office, the family-run, eager-to-please Hotel Sheetal has a big range of smart rooms, from the very small to the bizarre larger ones. Colour schemes and designs are certainly individual – even the narrow corridors come in for the treatment. Prices include breakfast, and there's no restaurant but there is full room service.

Eating

Swati Restaurant (Ramtekri Rd; mains Rs20-110; ☷ 10am-3.15pm & 6-11.15pm) We aren't sure if it is themed on *20,000 Leagues Under the Sea* or *Lost in Space*, but this individual little restaurant with private booths (with port holes) delivers delicious Punjabi, south Indian and Chinese veg dishes plus veg pizzas.

Swagat Restaurant (☎ 2242996; cnr MG Rd & Ramtekri Rd; mains Rs35-80; ☷ 8.30am-3pm & 5.30-11pm; ❄) This 1st-floor restaurant is a calm retreat from the street, with brown-booth seating and shiny chrome chairs. It sells tasty Punjabi, south Indian, continental and Chinese veg dishes.

Natraj (☎ 2211777; Hotel Natraj; mains Rs45-80; ☷ 11am-3pm, 7-11pm) This cool, clean and efficient gem dishes up veg in Punjabi, Chinese, pizza and pasta styles. The menu is mammoth and a spelling free-for-all, but the food is delicious and the service keen.

Getting There & Away

AIR

Jet Airways offers daily flights to Mumbai (Rs5400). Bookings can be made with **Thankys Tours & Travels** (☎ 2244344; Jeevan Jyot, MG Rd; ☷ 9am-8pm Mon-Sat, 10am-1.30pm Sun).

An autorickshaw to/from the airport costs around Rs40.

BUS

There are regular services along a bumpy road to Dwarka (Rs60, three hours), Jamnagar (Rs65, four hours), Veraval (Rs70, three hours) and Junagadh (Rs45, three hours). Private bus companies have offices on MG Rd.

TRAIN

The 9216 *Saurashtra Express* leaves Porbandar at 8.25pm and arrives at Jamnagar (sleeper/3AC Rs121/246) at 11.13am, Rajkot (Rs128/330) at 12.50am, Ahmedabad (Rs206/548) at 6am, and finally Mumbai (Rs332/907) at 7.15pm.

DWARKA

☎ 02892 / pop 33,614

This remote pilgrimage town at the extreme western tip of the Kathiawar peninsula is one of the four holiest Hindu sites in India – Krishna is said to have set up his capital here after fleeing from Mathura. It's a town with a frontier atmosphere, busy with pilgrims and farmers. Men wear white clothes and red turbans, and both men and women are weighed down with chunky gold jewellery. Archaeological excavations have revealed five earlier cities lying just off the coast – submerged under rising sea levels.

The town swells to breaking point for **Janmastami** in August/September in celebration of Krishna's birthday.

Sights & Activities

Dwarkanath Temple (☷ 7-8am, 9am-12.30pm & 5-9.30pm) is dedicated to Krishna and has a magnificent, five-storey spire that is supported by 60 columns. To enter, non-Hindus must make a declaration of respect for the religion.

Also worth a look are the carvings of **Rukmini Temple**, about 1km to the east, and the many-pillared **Sabha Mandapa**, reputed to be over 2500 years old, as well as the **Nageshwar Mandir**, with its underground chamber, about 16km away.

Dwarka's **lighthouse** (admission Rs10; ☷ 5-6.30pm) affords a beautiful panoramic view, though photography is not allowed (neither are mobile phones).

About 30km north of Dwarka is a ferry service crossing the 3km from Okha to the island of **Bet**, where Vishnu is said to have slain a demon. There are Krishna temples on the island, and a deserted beach on the northern coast. An STC bus goes to Okha (Rs15, every 30 minutes) from Dwarka.

The sights around Dwarka can be visited on a **tour** (Rs50 not incl ferry ticket; ☷ 8am & 2pm), which whips around Nageshwar, Gopi Taleo (a river), Bet and Rukmini Temple. It's run by Dwarka Darshan, which has an office in the vegetable market. You could also see the sights by taxi.

Sleeping & Eating

Most places offer significant discounts, except during festivals.

Kokila Dhiraj Dham (☎ 236746; Hospital Rd; d/tr Rs300/400) This tall, pink Reliance hotel with no sign in English is seriously good value (though no rooms have AC). A lift takes guests to long, wide corridors, which lead to similarly well-proportioned rooms. The whole place is squeaky clean. The communal TV room can get rowdy at night.

Meera Hotel (☎ 234031; meerahotel@yahoo.com; Highway Rd; d/tr Rs350/450, with AC Rs500/750; 🔀) This hotel is on the main approach road, and rather on the outskirts, but it has a good range of rooms – those on the top floor are cheap and cheerless, while the deluxe rooms are more appealing. There's a popular dining hall that does decent thalis.

Hotel Rajdhani (☎ 234070; Hospital Rd; r Rs400, with AC 600; 🔀) A very decent, quiet, and central hotel, with marble floors and basic, clean rooms. There is no restaurant, though breakfast can be provided.

Hotel Darshan (☎ 235034; Jawahar Rd; d Rs500, with AC Rs700; 🔀) Rooms are arranged around a lovely cooling central atrium filled with black vinyl. The rooms are OK, though the bathrooms are tiny. It's near the old bus stand.

Hotel Gurupreena (☎ 234512; opposite Bhadrakali Temple; r without/with AC Rs500/900; 🔀) Almost impressive on the outside, but cavernous and bland on the inside, Gurupreena is still decent value.

Sharanam (mains Rs35-75; 🕑 8am-3pm & 6-11pm) Located at Hotel Gurupreena, this place has Punjabi, Chinese and south Indian food and is one of the better restaurants in town.

Getting There & Away

STC buses serve Jamnagar (Rs60, four hours), Junagadh (Rs105, six hours) and Somnath (Rs110, 6½ hours). As well, there are numerous private companies running pilgrims to Jamnagar (Rs100) and beyond.

There are several trains to Jamnagar, including the 9006 *Saurashtra Mail*, which departs at 1.03pm and arrives at Jamnagar (sleeper/3AC/2AC/1AC Rs121/251/338/553) at 3.28pm, and Rajkot (Rs130/335/445/755) at 5.20pm, before continuing on to Ahmedabad and Mumbai. The station is 3km from town and has a **reservation office** (🕑 8am-2pm & 2.15-8pm Mon-Sat, 8am-2pm Sun).

JAMNAGAR
☎ 0288 / pop 447,734

Jamnagar is another little-visited city, brimming with ornate, decaying buildings and colourful bazaars displaying the town's famous, brilliant-coloured *bandhani* (tie-dye)

– produced through a laborious 5000-year-old process involving thousands of tiny knots in a piece of folded fabric.

Jamnagar is best known for having Gujarat's largest ayurvedic university, where you can learn the techniques of ancient medicine and yoga, and a temple that has hosted nonstop chanting since 1964 (it's in the *Guinness Book of Records*; see below).

Prior to Independence, the town was ruled by the Jadeja Rajputs. It's built around Ranmal Lake, which has a small palace at its centre.

Orientation & Information

The centre of the newer town, with most places to stay, is Teen Batti Chowk. The old town, known as Chandi Bazaar, is to the southeast, with Darbar Gadh, a semicircular gathering place where the maharajas of Nawanagar once held public audiences, at its centre. The bus stand and train station are a long way west and northwest, respectively.

The **Forest Office** (☎ 2679357; 🕑 10.15am-6.15pm Mon-Sat, closed 2nd & 4th Sat of month) provides permits for exploring the Gulf of Kutch, with its marine park, as well as the nearby Khijadiya Bird Sanctuary, however, not much English is spoken and there is very little useful information. Your best bet is to contact Hotel President (p767) for assistance in visiting these two parks.

Precious Money Exchange (☎ 2679701; Teen Batti Chowk) changes money. The Hotel President will change cash US dollars, pounds sterling and euros. There are plenty of ATMs.

Surf the internet at **iWay** (Pancheshwar Tower Rd; per hr Rs25; 🕑 8am-11pm).

Sights & Activities
LAKHOTA PALACE & RANMAL LAKE

This diminutive mid-19th-century palace on Ranmal Lake once belonged to the maharaja of Nawanagar. It houses a small **museum** (Indian/ foreigner Rs2/50; 🕑 10.30am-1.15pm, 2.45-6pm) which, at the time of research, was closed for renovations. It's a striking building with some fine woodcarving and grotesque gargoyles, though the lake itself is a polluted mess.

BALA HANUMAN TEMPLE

At this **temple**, on the southeastern side of Ranmal Lake, there has been continuous chanting of the prayer *Shri Ram, Jai Ram, Jai Jai Ram* since 1 August 1964. This devotion has earned the temple a place in an Indian

GUJARAT

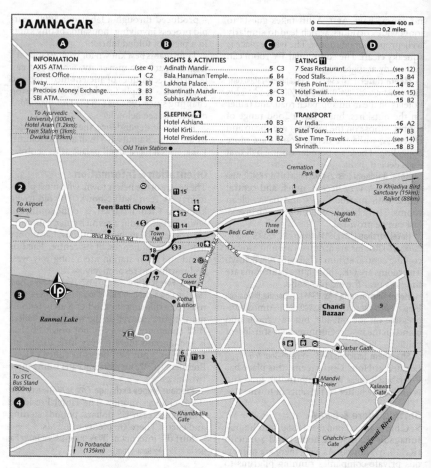

JAMNAGAR

0 ————— 400 m
0 ————— 0.2 miles

To Ayurvedic University (300m);
Hotel Aram (1.2km);
Train Station (3km);
Dwarka (139km)

Old Train Station ●

Cremation Park ●

To Khijadiya Bird Sanctuary (15km);
Rajkot (88km)

To Airport (9km)

Teen Batti Chowk

Nagnath Gate

Bhid Bhanjan Rd

Town Hall

Bedi Gate

Three Gate

KV Rd

Clock Tower

Kotha Bastion

Ranmal Lake

Chandi Bazaar

To STC Bus Stand (800m)

Darbar Gadh

Mandvi Tower

Kalawat Gate

Khambhalia Gate

To Porbandar (135km)

Ghahchi Gate

Ranguali River

---

favourite, the *Guinness Book of Records*. Early evening is a good time to visit as the temple and lakeside area gets busy.

JAIN TEMPLES & OLD CITY

In the thick of Chandi Bazaar are four beautiful Jain temples. The larger two, **Shantinath Mandir** and **Adinath Mandir**, dedicated to the 16th and first *tirthankars,* in front of the post office near Darbar Gadh, explode with fine murals, mirrored domes and elaborate chandeliers. The Shantinath Mandir is particularly beautiful, with coloured columns and a gilt-edged dome of concentric circles. Opening hours vary, but you can usually find someone to let you in.

Around the temples spreads the old city with its lovely buildings of wood and stone,

peeling, pastel-coloured shutters and crumbling wooden balconies. **Subhas market** – the vegetable market – has lots of local colour.

KHIJADIYA BIRD SANCTUARY

This small **sanctuary** (Indian/foreigner Rs10/250; ☼ dawn-dusk) encompasses salt- and freshwater marshlands that host flocks of cranes from September to March. It's best to visit around sunrise. Permits are available from the Forest Office (p765). A return taxi costs around Rs1200, or you can take a bus (Rs10) to nearby Khijadiya, then walk the last 3km.

MARINE NATIONAL PARK

This isolated **park** (Indian/foreigner Rs30/250, Narara car permit Rs35/200; ☼ Oct-Jun) stretches 170km along

GUJARAT

the coast and encompasses 42 islands, 33 of which are ringed by coral reefs. It's rich in marine and bird life. The best time to visit is from December to March. The Forest Office (p765) administers the park, or you can arrange a visit to any of the 42 islands through Hotel President (below). It takes two hours to reach **Pirotan Island** (timings are restricted because of tides – you must spend 12 hours on the island to wait for the tide to turn), which is the only offshore route set up for regular visitors. Note that pilgrim boats to Pirotan Island can be dangerously overloaded.

You can also visit beaches along the coast, such as **Narara**, 60km from Jamnagar off the Dwarka road, where it's possible at low tide to walk among the corals.

GUJARAT AYURVED UNIVERSITY

Gujarat's largest **ayurvedic university** (☎ 2770103; www.ayurveduniversity.com; ☼ 6am–noon & 3-7pm Mon-Sat) runs many courses in ayurvedic medicine, including a full-time, 12-week introductory course (registration US$20, tuition fee per month US$300, accommodation per month without/with AC US$60/80) teaching basic theory and medicine preparation, as well as diploma and degree courses. These courses are set up for foreign nationals with medical qualifications; see the website for more information.

Sleeping

Hotel Ashiana (☎ 2559110; www.ashianahotel.com; s Rs200-400, d Rs300-450, s/d with AC from Rs500/600; ste Rs1500; ✷ 🖵) This vast, rambling top-floor hotel in the heart of the old city has helpful management and a variety of rooms, from simple and cleanish to huge and comfortable, most with eclectic furnishings.

Hotel Kirti (☎ 2558602; Teen Batti Chowk; s Rs350-450, d Rs500, s/d with AC Rs600/700; ✷) Off Teen Batti Chowk is this good-value option, with clean, bright, well-appointed rooms that have a bit of a view.

Hotel President (☎ 2557491; www.hotelpresident.in; Teen Batti Chowk; r Rs650, with AC from Rs1250; ✷) This hotel has helpful management and a range of reasonable, though rather tired, rooms. Many of the rooms have a balcony. There's also a recommended restaurant (see right).

Hotel Aram (☎ 2551701; www.hotelaram.com; Pandit Nehru Marg; r from Rs1300, ste Rs5000; ✷ 🖵 w) This heritage hotel has more potential magnificence than actual opulence. For the money it's a little run down and the furnishings are worn, though it is not without charm, and the rooms are spacious. There's a good multicuisine veg restaurant with garden seating.

Eating

For cheap snack food in the evening try the stalls set up near Bala Hanuman Temple.

Madras Hotel (☎ 2541057; Teen Batti Chowk; mains Rs25-65; ☼ 11am-3pm, 7-11pm) This buzzing eatery, near Hotel Swati, is basic and popular and pumps out vegetarian South Indian, Jain, Punjabi, as well as the odd pizza.

Hotel Swati (☎ 2663223; Teen Batti Chowk; mains Rs25-80; ☼ 10am-3pm & 5-11pm) This upstairs, AC vegetarian restaurant has a faded ambience, but offers a big range of delicious south Indian, Chinese and Punjabi dishes.

Fresh Point (☎ 9426458288; Town Hall Rd; mains Rs30-70; ☼ 10.30am-3pm & 6-11pm) A simple, friendly, bustling restaurant with generous serves of Punjabi, south Indian and Chinese in clean surroundings.

7 Seas Restaurant (Hotel President, Teen Batti Chowk; mains Rs40-90) This hotel restaurant offers tasty Punjabi, Chinese and continental veg and non-veg dishes. The tandoori *bhindi* (okra) is a triumph.

Getting There & Away

AIR

Air India (☎ 2550211; Bhid Bhanjan Rd; ☼ 10am-5pm) has daily flights to Mumbai (Rs5000). Bookings can be made with **Save Time Travels** (☎ 2553137; Town Hall Rd; ☼ 9.30am-8.30pm).

BUS

There are STC buses to Rajkot (Rs62, two hours) and Junagadh (Rs79, four hours); other buses head for Dwarka (Rs80, four hours), Porbandar (Rs68, four hours) and Ahmedabad (Rs155, seven hours).

There are also numerous private companies, many based west of the clock tower. **Patel Travels** (☎ 2552419; Pancheswar Tower Rd) serves Bhuj (seat/sleeper Rs150/200), Mandvi (Rs170/220), Rajkot (Rs80) and Ahmedabad (Rs330).

Shrinath (☎ 2553333; Town Hall Circle) goes to Ahmedabad (Rs230, six hours) via Rajkot (Rs80, two hours), Mt Abu (seat/sleeper Rs310/410, 12 hours) and Udaipur (Rs355/455, 14 hours), and plenty of other destinations.

TRAIN

The 9006 *Saurashtra Mail* departs at 3.30pm and arrives at Rajkot (sleeper/3AC/2AC/1AC

Rs121/213/283/459) at 5.20pm, Ahmedabad (Rs166/437/596/998) at 10.25pm, and Mumbai (Rs305/831/1141/1916) at 7.15am. In the other direction, the 9005 departs at 12.19pm and arrives at Dwarka (Rs121/251/338/553) at 3.07pm.

Getting Around

There's no bus to the airport – it's 10km west and autorickshaw drivers demand at least Rs130. An autorickshaw from the bus stand to Bedi Gate costs Rs20. From Teen Batti Chowk to the train station, about 4km north of the centre, costs around Rs50.

RAJKOT

☎ 0281 / pop 1.137 million

This former capital of the princely state of Saurashtra was once a base for the Western States British government office. The now bustling commercial city has an evocative old city at its heart, where farmers still sell ghee on street corners. Mahatma Gandhi lived here for a while and you can visit his family home.

Information

The State Bank of India, north of Jubilee Gardens, changes money, and there are ATMs all over town, including Axis Bank and HDFC near the Imperial Palace hotel.

Buzz Cyber Café (Alaukik Bldg, Kasturba Rd; per hr Rs15; ☽ 8.30am-9.30pm) Tucked away opposite Lord's Banquet restaurant.

Interlink Cyber Café (off Lakhajiraj Rd; per hr Rs30; ☽ 10am-midnight) Opposite Bapuna Bawala.

Tourist office (☎ 2234507; Jawahar Rd; ☽ 10.30am-1.30pm & 2-6pm Mon-Sat, closed 2nd & 4th Sat of month) Behind the State Bank of India building. Garrulous staff but no town map and little useful information.

Sights

WATSON MUSEUM & LIBRARY

The **Watson Museum & Library** (Jubilee Gardens; Indian/foreigner Rs2/50; ☽ 9am-1pm & 3-6pm Mon-Sat, closed 2nd & 4th Sat of month) commemorates the work of Colonel John Watson, political agent (administrator) from 1886 to 1889. It's a jumbled attic of a collection, featuring 3rd-century inscriptions, arrays of arms and delicate ivory work overseen by an unamused marble statue of Queen Victoria.

KABA GANDHI NO DELO

This is the **house** (Ghee Kanta Rd; admission free; ☽ 9am-noon & 3-5.30pm Mon-Sat) where Gandhi lived from the age of six, and it contains lots of interesting information on his life. The Mahatma's passion for the hand loom is preserved in the form of a small weaving school. The narrow streets surrounding the old city reward a wander.

PATOLA SARI WEAVING

Rajkot has quickly developed a Patola-weaving industry. This skill comes from Patan, and is a torturous process that involves dyeing each thread before it is woven. However, in Patan both the warp and weft threads are dyed (double *ikat*), whereas in Rajkot only the weft is dyed (single *ikat*), so the product is more affordable. You can visit workshops that are located in people's houses in the Sarvoday Society area, including **Mayur Patola Art** (☎ 2464519; ☽ 10am-1pm & 3-6pm), behind Virani High School.

Sleeping

BUDGET

Hotel Yash (☎ 2223574; Dhebar Rd; budget s Rs200, s/d Rs250/400, with AC Rs600/700; ☒) On a very busy street, this place is friendly and reasonably clean with small rooms – those at the back are quieter; however, some have no window.

Hotel Bhakti (☎ 2227744; Karanpara Rd; s/d Rs440/550, with AC from Rs700/1000) This reasonable semi-cheapie has neat and comfortable rooms, but check your bathroom for proper functioning. It's right behind the bus station (but you have to walk round the block as the bus station has no rear entrance).

MIDRANGE & TOP END

Galaxy Hotel (☎ 222904; www.thegalaxyhotelrajkot.com; 3rd fl, Galaxy Commercial Centre, Jawahar Rd; s/d Rs440/660, s with AC Rs675-990, d with AC Rs1010-1485; ☒) This is an oddly classy hotel on the 3rd floor of a very ordinary building. It's worth noting that access is by lift only since they lock the stairwell. Rooms are spacious and incongruously gleaming. Tiny, crummy bathrooms are disappointing, though. There's no restaurant but there is 24-hour room service, and you can eat dinner on the pleasant rooftop terrace.

Silver Palace (☎ 2480008; www.hotelsilverpalace.com; Gondal Rd; budget s Rs1195, s/d from Rs2195/2695; ☒ ▣) This hotel is managed by Rajkot's premier hotel, the Imperial Palace, and is good value. Because it was undergoing extensive redevelopment when we visited, the tariffs may rise

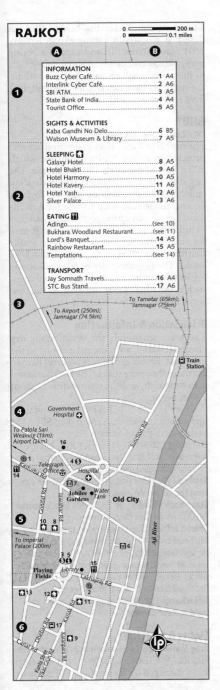

RAJKOT

0 200 m
0 0.1 miles

INFORMATION
Buzz Cyber Café............................**1** A4
Interlink Cyber Café.......................**2** A6
SBI ATM......................................**3** A5
State Bank of India.........................**4** A5
Tourist Office...............................**5** A5

SIGHTS & ACTIVITIES
Kaba Gandhi No Delo.....................**6** B5
Watson Museum & Library................**7** A5

SLEEPING
Galaxy Hotel................................**8** A5
Hotel Bhakti................................**9** A6
Hotel Harmony............................**10** A6
Hotel Kavery...............................**11** A6
Hotel Yash.................................**12** A6
Silver Palace...............................**13** A6

EATING
Adingo....................................(see 10)
Bukhara Woodland Restaurant.........(see 11)
Lord's Banquet...........................**14** A5
Rainbow Restaurant......................**15** A5
Temptations.............................(see 14)

TRANSPORT
Jay Somnath Travels......................**16** A4
STC Bus Stand.............................**17** A6

To Tarnetar (65km);
Jamnagar (75km)

To Airport (250m);
Jamnagar (74.5km)

Train Station

Government Hospital

To Patola Sari Weaving (1km);
Airport (2km)

Telegraph Office

Hospital

Jubilee Gardens

Water Tank

Old City

Aji River

To Imperial Palace (200m)

Playing Fields

Library

Lakhajiraj Rd

Canal Rd

considerably, but it is hoped that it remains a good deal.

Hotel Kavery (☎ 2240950; www.hotelkavery.com; Kanak Rd; s/d from Rs1250/1850; 🍴 🖥) A popular midrange business hotel, the rooms here fill up quickly. Part of the reason is undoubtedly the excellent Bukhara Woodland restaurant (see below).

Hotel Harmony (☎ 2240950; www.hotelharmony rajkot.com; s/d from Rs1795/2195) This modern establishment has reasonable, business-like rooms that are invariably beige and, though overpriced, are certainly comfortable. It is opposite Shastri Maidan, near Limda Chowk.

Imperial Palace (☎ 2480000; www.theimperial palace.biz; Dr Yagnik Rd; s/d from Rs3400/3900, ste Rs5900; 🍴 🖥 w 🍷) The numero uno in town, with a masterful lobby and lavish, well-appointed rooms and real mattresses on the beds. There's a busy little wine shop, and the multicuisine 24-hour coffee shop and restaurant do exquisite veg dishes. Breakfast is complimentary.

Eating

Rainbow Restaurant (Lakhajiraj Rd; mains Rs25-85; 🕙 11am-3.30pm & 7-11pm; 🍴) Rainbow is popular and serves tasty and cheap south Indian cuisine in the open-fronted downstairs, and Punjabi and Chinese dishes upstairs in AC comfort. There's a tantalising ice-cream selection.

Temptations (☎ 2475010; Kasturba Rd; mains Rs30-150; 🕙 11am-12.30am) A few doors down from Lord's Banquet (same management), Temptations has Mexican, pizzas, falafel, sandwiches and south Indian in a brightly decorated cafe.

Adingo (☎ 2227073; mains Rs35-75, thali Rs80; 🕙 11am-3pm, 6.30-11pm) This flashy red-tiled, red-upholstered restaurant does tremendous lunchtime Gujarati thalis for the professional set. The dinner menu features the usual veg multicuisine plus local Kathiyavadi dishes. Opposite Shastri Maidan near Limda Chowk.

Bukhara Woodland Restaurant (Hotel Kavery, Kanak Rd; mains Rs45-140, thali Rs100; 🕙 11am-11pm) Bukhara is smart, cool and calm with good service and quality food, including Gujarati thali for lunch, and south Indian, among others, for dinner.

Lord's Banquet (☎ 2444486; Kasturba Rd; mains Rs50-135; 🕙 12.30-3.30pm & 7.30-11.30pm) This is a long-established place, popular for pure-veg Punjabi, continental and Chinese cuisine.

GUJARAT

Getting There & Away

AIR

There are daily flights to Mumbai (Rs3700) with **Air India** (☎ 2222295).

BUS

Regular STC buses connect Rajkot with Jamnagar (Rs56, 2½ hours), Junagadh (Rs52, two hours), Porbandar (Rs95, five hours), Ahmedabad (Rs110, 3½ hours) and Bhuj (Rs120, seven hours).

Private buses operate to Ahmedabad, Bhavnagar, Una (for Diu), Mt Abu, Udaipur and Mumbai. Several offices are on Kanak Rd, by the bus stand. Head to **Jay Somnath Travels** (☎ 2433315; Umesh Complex) for buses to Bhuj (Rs160, six hours).

TRAIN

The 9006 *Saurashtra Mail* leaves at 5.40pm and arrives in Ahmedabad (sleeper/3AC/2AC/1AC Rs139/360/490/813) at 10.25pm and Mumbai (Rs286/777/1106/1787) at 7.15am. In the other direction, the 9005 departs at 10.33am and arrives at Jamnagar (Rs121/213/283/459) at 12.17pm.

Getting Around

An autorickshaw to the airport from the centre costs Rs80; to the train station, expect to pay Rs30.

KUTCH (KACHCHH)

Kutch, India's wild west, is a geographic phenomenon. The tortoise-shaped land (*kachbo* means tortoise in Gujarati) is flat and dry, and a seasonal island. The villages dotted throughout the dramatic, inhospitable landscape produce some of India's finest folk textiles, glittering with exquisite embroidery and mirror work.

It's edged by the Gulf of Kutch and Great and Little Ranns. During the dry season, the Ranns are vast expanses of hard, dried mud. Then, with the start of the monsoon, they're flooded first by seawater, then by fresh river water. The salt in the soil makes the low-lying marsh area almost completely barren. Only on scattered 'islands' above the salt level is there vegetation – coarse grass – which provides fodder for the region's wildlife.

The Indus River once flowed through Kutch until a massive earthquake in 1819 altered its course, leaving behind this salt desert. A mammoth earthquake in January 2001 again altered the landscape, destroying many villages completely. Although the effects of the tragedy will resonate for generations, the residents have determinedly rebuilt their lives and are welcoming to visitors.

BHUJ

☎ 02832 / pop 136,500

The capital of Kutch is an interesting city resurrected from the 2001 earthquake, which killed 10% of the city's 150,000 people. The city still bears scars, though its revitalisation and that of the surrounding region is obvious. To encourage economic growth the government has opened up the surrounding salt flats to industry and Bhuj is an ideal springboard for visits to the surrounding villages. Textile tourism is attracting visitors from around the world. The beguiling city bazaars sell amazing Kutch handicrafts, and historic buildings, such as the Aina Mahal and Prag Mahal, possess an eerie beauty.

Orientation & Information

The town surrounds the occasionally dry Hamirsar Kund, with the palaces just to the northeast. East of the palaces is Shroff Bazaar, the main shopping street. The STC bus stand is to the south, and the train station is about 2.5km north.

There is a an ICICI ATM on Hospital Rd and a Bank of Baroda ATM and an SBI ATM at the south end of Station Rd.

Crossword (☎ 224141; ST Rd; ☼ 7.30am-2pm & 4-9pm Mon-Sat, 7.30am-2pm Sun) A tiny branch of this franchise with a good selection of books and magazines.

Krishna Cyber Cafe (Station Rd; per hr Rs20; ☼ 9am-9pm) You can surf the internet here.

State Bank of India (☎ 256100; NRI Branch, Hospital Rd) Changes travellers cheques or currency.

Tourist information office (☼ 10.30am-6pm Mon-Sat, closed 2nd & 4th Sat) At the Aina Mahal. PJ Jethi, the knowledgeable curator of the Aina Mahal (see below) knows all there is to know about the city and surrounding villages. He's also written a very useful Kutch guidebook (Rs50), published in both English and French.

UAEchange (☎ 227580; Hospital Rd) Changes travellers cheques or currency.

Sights & Activities

Prag Mahal (New Palace; admission Rs12, camera/video Rs30/100; ☼ 9-11.45am & 3-5.45pm) is in a forlorn state, damaged by the earthquake and dusty,

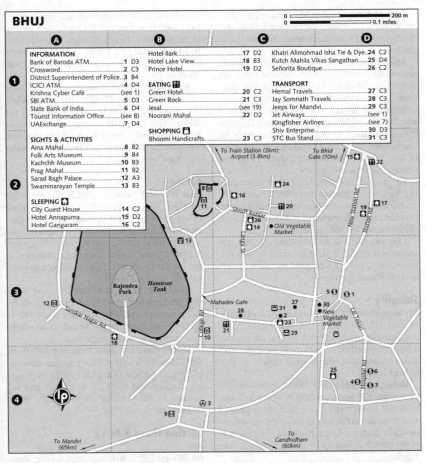

BHUJ

0 — 200 m
0 — 0.1 miles

INFORMATION	
Bank of Baroda ATM	1 D3
Crossword	2 C3
District Superintendent of Police	3 B4
ICICI ATM	4 D4
Krishna Cyber Café	(see 1)
SBI ATM	5 D3
State Bank of India	6 D4
Tourist Information Office	(see 8)
UAExchange	7 D4

SIGHTS & ACTIVITIES	
Aina Mahal	8 B2
Folk Arts Museum	9 B4
Kachchh Museum	10 B3
Prag Mahal	11 B2
Sarad Bagh Palace	12 A3
Swaminarayan Temple	13 B3

SLEEPING	
City Guest House	14 C2
Hotel Annapurna	15 D2
Hotel Gangaram	16 C2

Hotel Ilark	17 D2
Hotel Lake View	18 B3
Prince Hotel	19 D2

EATING	
Green Hotel	20 C2
Green Rock	21 C3
Jesal	(see 19)
Noorani Mahal	22 D2

SHOPPING	
Bhoomi Handicrafts	23 C3

Khatri Alimohmad Isha Tie & Dye	24 C2
Kutch Mahila Vikas Sangathan	25 D4
Señorita Boutique	26 C2

TRANSPORT	
Hemal Travels	27 C3
Jay Somnath Travels	28 C3
Jeeps for Mandvi	29 C3
Jet Airways	(see 1)
Kingfisher Airlines	(see 7)
Shiv Enterprise	30 D3
STC Bus Stand	31 C3

but is worth visiting for its ghostly, exuberant Durbar Hall, with broken chandeliers and gold-skirted classical statues that wouldn't look out of place decorating a gay nightclub. Several scenes from *Lagaan*, the much-acclaimed Bollywood cricket blockbuster, were filmed here.

Next door is the beautiful **Aina Mahal** (Old Palace; ☎ 260094; admission Rs10, camera/video Rs30/100; ☾ 9am-noon, 3-6pm Sun-Fri), built in 1752 at a cost of Rs2 million. It lost its top storey in the earthquake, but the lower floor is open, with a fantastic 15.2m scroll showing a Kutch state procession. The 18th-century elaborately mirrored interior is a demonstration of the fascination with all things European – an inverted mirror of European Orientalism –

with blue-and-white Delphi-style tiling and the Hogarth lithograph series *The Rake's Progress*. In the bedroom is a bed with solid gold legs (the king apparently auctioned his bed annually).

Much of the oldest palace, the **Durbar Gadh**, has collapsed, but many of its latticed windows and elaborate carvings remain. It's estimated that the Aina Mahal will cost Rs2.5 million to repair. Donations are gratefully received – contact PJ Jethi at the museum for details (a fund has been set up through the V&A Museum in London).

Nearby is **Swaminarayan Temple**. This has a garishly painted exterior; however, it's no longer being used – a new temple has been constructed to the south of town.

GUJARAT

Kachchh Museum (College Rd; Indian/foreigner Rs2/50; 10am-1pm, 2.30-5.30pm & Thu-Tue, closed 2nd & 4th Sat of month), Gujarat's oldest museum, houses many ancient artefacts.

Folk Art Museum (Bhartiya Sanscruti Darshan Kachchh; admission Rs10, camera Rs50; 9am-noon & 3-6pm Mon-Sat) displays embroidery, children's toys, beautiful paintings and traditional mud huts.

Sarad Bagh Palace (Indian/foreigner Rs10/50, camera/video Rs20/100; 9am-noon & 3-6pm) was a graceful Italianate palace, built in 1867, in the midst of shady trees full of crows and bats. It lost most of the 3rd floor in the earthquake, and the remaining lower floors are closed. However, nearby is an adjacent building, the former dining hall, which houses this eclectic museum. Standout exhibits are two huge stuffed tigers that the erstwhile maharao of Kutch shot, and the aforementioned maharao's coffin.

Outside Bhuj is its 18th-century **fort**, an impressive edifice built at the same time as the town walls, but it's occupied by the military and off-limits to visitors.

Sleeping

City Guest House (221067; Langa St; r Rs200, s/d without bathroom Rs90/200) Just off the main bazaar, this is unusually bright, ultraclean and cheery for a budget guesthouse, with neat basic rooms. Bathrooms have either squat toilets or the hybrid variety.

Hotel Annapurna (220831; hotelannapurna @yahoo.com; Bhid Gate; s/d Rs200/250, without bathroom Rs100/150) Annapurna has a nice atmosphere, and friendly staff, but is situated on a frenetically busy junction. Rooms are clean and some have balconies so you can overlook the mayhem.

Hotel Gangaram (224231; Darbargarh Chowk; s/d Rs300/500, with AC Rs700/800;) In the old city, near Aina Mahal, this is a great place where nothing is too much trouble, run by kindly Mr Jethi. The rooms vary greatly so it might be worth inspecting a few. The meals here are delicious.

Hotel Lake View (253422; Sanskar Nagar Rd; r budget Rs500, s/d deluxe Rs900/1000, with AC 1050/1150;) This welcoming hotel has a premium lakeside location, and generous, though run-down rooms. The swimming pool looks beyond rescue.

Prince Hotel (220370; www.hotelprinceonline .com; Station Rd; s/d Rs800/1000, with AC from Rs1800/2200;) Rightfully acknowledged as Bhuj's best, the Prince Hotel has slick service, smart rooms and great restaurants. It offers free airport transfers. You can get an alcohol permit from reception (free), though you will need to find the use of a fridge to chill the warm beer (minimum purchase five bottles) from its wine shop.

Hotel Ilark (258999; www.hotelilark.com; Station Rd; s/d from 1800/2000;) This glitzy-looking hotel is a bit disappointing beyond the lobby. The standard rooms are reasonable but overpriced – the deluxe are better value, while all the bathrooms really should be better in such a new hotel.

Eating

Jesal (Prince Hotel, Station Rd; mains Rs25-100; 7am-3pm & 7-11pm) This smart multicuisine restaurant offers good breakfast options, as well as curries and Chinese for lunch and dinner.

Green Hotel (Shroff Bazaar; mains Rs30-55; 9am-10.30pm) A small, multicuisine veg restaurant in the bazaar that's related to – but not as good as – the Green Rock.

Green Rock (253644; Bus Stand Rd; mains Rs30-130; 11am-3pm & 7-10.30pm) This popular, 1st-floor, AC place opposite the STC bus stand serves up tasty lunchtime thalis, as well as an extensive multicuisine, all-veg menu.

Noorani Mahal (226328; Station Rd; mains Rs35-100; 11.30am-3pm & 7-11pm) This popular non-veg place gets packed out with mostly men eating chicken, but there's also mutton and veg cooked in the tandoor or in a spicy north Indian curry.

Getting There & Away

AIR

Jet Airways (253671; www.jetairways.com; Station Rd; 9am-6pm Mon-Sat, to 2pm Sun) and **Kingfisher Airlines** (227385; www.flykingfisher.com; Hospital Rd; 9am-7pm Mon-Sat) have regular flights to Mumbai (Rs 4500).

BUS

Numerous STC buses run to/from Mandvi (Rs22, 1½ hours), Ahmedabad (Rs165, eight hours), Rajkot (Rs130, six hours) and Jamnagar (Rs130, 7½ hours). Book private buses at **Hemal Travels** (252491; STC bus stand; 8am-9pm), which has buses to Ahmedabad (seating/sleeper non-AC Rs200/300, with AC Rs250/350, nine hours) and Jamnagar (seating/sleeper Rs150/200), while **Jay Somnath Travels** (221919; ST Rd; 8am-9pm) has buses to Rajkot (Rs160).

GUJARAT

TRAIN

Bhuj station is 2.5km north of the centre and has a **reservations office** (8am-2pm & 2.15-8pm Mon-Sat, 8am-2pm Sun). The 4312 *Ala Hazrat Express* leaves at 11.05am (Monday, Thursday, Saturday, Sunday) and arrives at Ahmedabad (sleeper/3AC/2AC Rs172/454/703) at 6.50pm. For the same fares, the 9116 *Bhuj–Bandra Express* leaves at 10.15pm and hits Ahmedabad at 5.05am. Going the other way, the 9115 departs Ahmedabad at 11.59pm and arrives at Bhuj at 7.40am.

Getting Around

It's 5km to the airport – a taxi will cost around Rs200, an autorickshaw Rs100. Autorickshaws to the train station cost Rs30. You can hire mopeds and motorbikes at **Shiv Enterprise** (251329; Waniayawad; per day Rs300, deposit Rs1000; 9.30am-9pm Mon-Sat, to 2pm Sun).

AROUND BHUJ

Kutch is one of India's richest areas for handicrafts, particularly famed for its beautiful embroidery work, but it also has many villages specialising in pottery or block printing. The local Jat, Ahir, Harijan and nomadic Rabari communities have distinct, colourful traditions that make their villages fascinating to visit.

The village of **Hodka** – 50km north of Bhuj – is home to a fascinating project in 'endogenous tourism'. In partnership with hospitality professionals from around India, and various NGOs, **Shaam-e-Sarhad Rural Resort** (574124; www.hodka.in; Hodka; tents s/d Rs1600/1800, bhunga s/d Rs2600/2800) is a successful exponent of this burgeoning self-help tourism trend, and a welcome addition to the Kutch countryside. Set in the beautiful Banni grasslands, 'Sunset at the Border' as it's known, consists of three *bhungas* (traditional mud huts) with sloping roofs and neat interiors, and six luxurious tents, all with private bathroom. Owned and operated by the Halepotra people, it's a fascinating opportunity to witness the daily life of an indigenous community, and to witness first-hand the positive impact of thoughtful tourism.

Other interesting villages north of Bhuj include the Jat **Sumrasar Sheikh** (see the boxed text, p774), **Khavda** for pottery, the Ahiri **Danati** and **Ludiya** (mudwork). You can head towards the edge of the Great Rann, with its snow-glare of salt.

Little-visited **Lakhpat**, an ancient port city with some interesting monuments, including a Muslim tomb and Sikh shrine, is about 140km from Bhuj.

Northeast of Bhuj is the Harappan site (pre-2500 BC) of **Dholavira**, which is both fascinating and remote. Excavations are ongoing but demonstrate a complex town. You'll need your own transport as there's no nearby accommodation and the journey's at least seven hours.

You need a permit to visit some villages north of Bhuj, but this is easy to obtain. You have to take a copy of your passport and visa (and the originals) to the **District Superintendent's Office** (11am-2pm & 3-6pm Mon-Sat), 200m south of Hamirsar Tank in Bhuj, and complete a form listing the villages you want to visit – you should get the permit (free of charge; maximum 10 days) straightaway.

About 60km northwest of Bhuj is **Than**, an eerie monastery set in the hills. The holy man Dhoramnath, as a penance for a curse he had made, stood on his head for 12 years. The gods pleaded with him to stop, and he agreed, provided the first place he looked at became barren – hence Little Rann. He then established the Kanphata's (Slit Ears) monastic order at Than. There's one bus daily to Than from Bhuj (Rs28, two hours). This is a laid-back place to explore the surrounding hills, and the architecture ranges from crumbling mud brick to Portuguese-style stucco, blue and white-wash bell towers, with a hint of basil and marigold in the air.

Towns to the east of Bhuj were hardest hit by the earthquake, but many, including **Anjar** and **Rahpar**, have been rebuilt and are handy bases for trips to see artisans at work. To the south, Bada village is the base for the **Kutch Vipassana Centre** (02832-221437, 02834-73303), which runs free 10-day meditation courses.

Bhujodi is a large village about 12km south of Bhuj that specialises in weaving, with many outlets specialising in shawls and blankets. Take a bus towards Ahmedabad and ask the driver to drop you at the turn-off for Bhujodi (Rs6). It's a 2km walk or autorickshaw ride from the highway. A return rickshaw from Bhuj costs Rs250.

Getting Around

PJ Jethi (see p770) arranges customised tours, or you could explore using local buses: for example, there are hourly buses to Sumrasar Sheikh (Rs10, one hour). Otherwise you can

KUTCH CREATIVITY

The crafts of Kutch are beautiful and intricate, with a diversity that reflects the differing traditions of different tribes. Numerous local cooperatives invest in social projects and preserve the area's artistic heritage by ensuring work is not merely market driven.

Kutch Mahila Vikas Sangathan (☎ 256281; 11 Nootan Colony, Bhuj) is a grass-roots organisation, comprising 12,000 rural women (1200 artisans), that pays members a dividend of the profits and invests money to meet social needs. The embroidery and appliqué are exquisite, employing the distinctive styles of eight different communities. Visit the head office in Bhuj, the Qasab outlet at the Prince Hotel in Bhuj, or Khavda, a village north of Bhuj.

Khamir (☎ 271272; www.khamir.org; Lakhond Crosswords, Kukma Rd, Kukma; ☼ 9am-5.30pm), about 5km beyond Bhujodi and 17km from Bhuj, is an umbrella organisation dedicated to preserving and encouraging Kutch handicrafts in all their diversity.

Kala Raksha Trust (☎ 253697; www.kala-raksha.org; ☼ 10am-2pm & 3-6pm), based at Sumrasar Sheikh, 25km north of Bhuj, also aims to preserve and promote Kutch arts, and specialises in Suf, Rabari and Garasia Jat embroidery. The trust has a small museum, works with nearly 600 artisans from seven different communities and can arrange visits to villages to meet artisans and see them at work. There are some beautiful items on sale; 30% goes to the artisans, who also help price the goods.

Shrujan (☎ 240272; Hasta Shilp Kendra; ☼ 9am-5.30pm), in Bhujodi, 12km from Bhuj, works with a network of 80 villages, benefiting nearly 3000 women and artisans.

Parmath (☎ 273453; Ramkrushn Nagar, New Dhaneti; ☼ 8.30-9pm), run by a delightful family, specialises in Ahir embroidery and wallpieces. It's in New Dhaneti, 15km north of Bhuj.

The prestigious **Dr Ismail Mohammad Khatri** in Ajrakhpur, near Bhujodi, heads a block-printing business of real quality. You can stay with the family to learn the craft, or pick up unique, naturally dyed pieces on a passing visit.

In Bhuj, textile dealers line the Shroff Bazaar. However, plenty of so-called block-printed fabric is in fact screen-printed. A good shop is **Señorita Boutique** (☎ 226773; Main Bazaar; ☼ 8.30am-9pm), which sells various regional types of embroidery and tie-dyeing. **Bhoomi Handicrafts** (☎ 225808; ☼ 9am-9pm), opposite the bus station, is popular with locals.

If you're interested in antique embroidery, get in touch with **Mr AA Wazir** (☎ 224187). He has a stunning collection of more than 3000 pieces. Prices range from Rs200 to 20,000.

Other recommended shops:

Kutch Rabari Art (☎ 240005; ☼ 9am-9pm) In Bhujodi, this Rabari family sells fine old Rabari pieces from their home.

Vankar Vishram (☎ 240723; ☼ 8am-8pm) Also Bhujodi-based; sells excellent woven products, with some beautiful woollen shawls.

pick up jeeps from Bhuj, which cost the same as buses and can be quicker – leave in time to get back to town though, as they thin out after 4pm.

MANDVI

Mandvi is an hour down the road from Bhuj and is a busy little place with an amazing ship-building yard. Hundreds of men construct, by hand, these wooden beauties for faraway Arab merchants. The massive timbers apparently come from Malaysian rainforests. There are also some sweeping beaches, the best of which include the long, clean private beach (Rs30) near Vijay Vilas Palace and another, just east of town, by the Toran Beach Resort.

Sights

Vijay Vilas Palace (vehicle admission Rs20, admission Rs25, camera/video Rs50/200; ☼ 9am-6pm) is a nicely proportioned 19th-century palace, 7km west of town in the centre of extensive, overgrown orchards and plantations, and set by a magnificent private beach. The palace was used as a setting for *Lagaan* and many other Bollywood hits. There's not much of interest inside but the view from the rooftop pavilion is worth the climb.

Sleeping & Eating

Rukmavati Guest House (☎ 223557; rukmavati@rediff mail.com; near Bridge Gate; dm Rs150, s/d from Rs300/400, r with AC Rs1050; ⊠) The best Indian hospital to spend the night in, this pleasant former medical centre, just by the bridge as you enter town, doesn't feel institutional. It's light and bright, with solar-water heaters and self-catering facilities. Check-out is 24 hours. Owner Vinod is a gentleman, and the town's unofficial tourist officer, with maps and helpful info.

Jitendra Guest House (☎ 222841; behind Taluka Panchayat, ST Rd; r Rs400, with AC Rs800) A useful option run by a pair of cruisy brothers. Rooms are tidy and spacious, and room service is available.

Hotel Sea View (☎ 224481; www.hotelseaviewindia .com; ST Rd; r Rs450, with AC from Rs945-1785; thalis Rs50; ✷) A small hotel on the waterfront, this has brightly decorated rooms with big windows that make the most of the views of the ship-building. Room 3 has windows on two sides and the hot water is solar heated.

The Beach at Mandvi Palace (☎ 9879013118, 295725, in Ahmedabad 079-28218551; www.mandvibeach .com; d with breakfast Rs6000; ✷) A tented resort on the private 2.5km beach stretching down from Vijay Vilas Palace, this is a fantastic location. The luxurious tents have big beds, white-tiled bathrooms and AC. The Dolphin restaurant is a pavilion with a wonderful beach setting that is open to nonguests. The beach is open to nonguests for Rs100 per person unless you are having a meal at the Dolphin (mains Rs130 to Rs220).

Zoraba the Buddha (☎ 23155; Osho Hotel, Bhid Gate; thali Rs60; ✷ 11am-3pm & 7-10pm) In the heart of the city, Zoraba's (the sign says 'Osho') is a massively popular place for cheap veg Gujarati thalis.

Getting There & Away

Regular buses to/from Bhuj (Rs22) take two hours. Or you can take faster share taxis for Rs30, which run between the road opposite Bhuj bus station and Mandvi.

LITTLE RANN SANCTUARY

This is not a region for the faint-hearted. The barren, blindingly white land of Little Rann is nature at its harshest and most compelling, and home to India's last remaining population of khur (Asiatic wild ass). There's also a huge bird population, and the area is one of the few places in India where flamingos are known to breed naturally. Khurs and flamingos are protected in the 4953-sq-km **Little Rann Sanctuary** (Indian/foreigner Rs5/US$5, camera Rs20/US$5, video Rs2500/ US$200; ✷ dawn-dusk). The area is punctuated by desolate salt farms, where people eke out a living by pumping up ground water and extracting the salt. Heat mirages disturb the vast horizon – bushes and trees seem to hover above the surface.

The approximately 3000 khurs in the sanctuary survive off the flat, grass-covered expanses or islands, known as *bets*, which rise up to around 3m. These remarkable creatures are capable of running at an average speed of 50km/h for long distances.

Rain turns the desert into a sea of mud, and even during the dry season the solid-looking crust is often deceptive, so it's essential you take a local guide when exploring the area, or when running the gauntlet to distant Dholavira – a white-knuckled, white-hot jeep ride.

The small town of **Zainabad**, 105km northwest of Ahmedabad, is very close to the Little Rann. **Desert Coursers** (☎ 02757-241333; www.desert coursers.net) is a family-run tour company that organises interesting safaris and village tours in the Little Rann. It runs **Camp Zainabad** (full-board incl unlimited safaris d Rs4000; ✷ Sep-Apr), offering comfortable and attractive *kooba* (traditional thatch-roofed huts) in a peaceful, remote setting. Advance booking is advised.

To get to Zainabad by road from Ahmedabad, you can take a bus to Dasada, 12km away (Rs50, 2½ hours). From here Desert Coursers does free pick-ups, or there are local buses. There are direct buses to Zainabad from Patan (Rs48, 2½ hours, three daily) via Modhera (Rs12, 1½ hours). Desert Coursers can arrange taxis around the area for Rs4.5 per kilometre.

Rann Riders (www.rannriders.com), near Dasada, 10km from the sanctuary, is also family-run and offers luxurious cottage accommodation and jeep safaris. Book through **North West Safaris** (☎ 079-26302019) in Ahmedabad.

You may also approach from **Dhrangadhra**. The town itself is worth visiting, if only to break up the Bhuj–Ahmedabad hike. The streets and alleys wind around each other, and almost every turn is a mosaic of white-washed and coloured buildings of all periods, description and type. Temple bells ring out, and the locals aren't used to tourists, making for some refreshing dialogue and even a flute concert if you're lucky.

The personable Devji Bhai Dhamecha (☎ 9825548090) is a wildlife photographer who makes a wonderful guide. He is passionate about the sanctuary and welcomes travellers with a special interest in wildlife. You can stay at his appealing **house** (per person incl meals from Rs500), and visit the sanctuary in his jeep (maximum five) for Rs750/1500 per half-/full day. He is planning two campsites within the sanctuary as well, for those who want to get even closer to nature, with similar accommodation prices. If you can't get Devji, try his son Ajai (☎ 985548104).

Permission from the **Deputy Conservator of Forests** (☎ 02754-260716) in Dhrangadhra is required to enter the sanctuary; the guides mentioned will arrange this.

An hour south of Dhrangadhra is **Sayla**, a peaceful, pastoral town that swells during the Tarnetar Fair in August/September. The surrounding countryside is lush, tourist-free yet rich with princely states and skilled artisans (Sayla itself is noted for *ikat* silk weaving).

The nomadic Bharwad shepherds are known for their intricate beadwork, Somasar village for silk and cotton weaving, and Sejathpur is a Kathi village famed for its beadwork. A little further away at Wadhwan you'll find exquisite *bandhani* (tie-dye) and brassware.

Old Bell Guest House (☎ 280017; www.ahmedabadcity.com/sayla; Sayla Circle, Rajkot Hwy; d from Rs2000), presided over by the erstwhile ruling family of Sayla, is a wonderful retreat set in flowery gardens. All rooms are equipped with spacious ensuites; the upstairs corner rooms have two balconies.

Sayla is located on the Ahmedabad–Rajkot highway, while Dhrangadhra is on the Bhuj–Ahmedabad rail route, 230km from Bhuj (2nd class Rs68, 5¼ hours) and 130km from Ahmedabad (2nd class Rs49, three hours). It's well served by buses, for example to and from Ahmedabad (Rs47, 3½ hours) and Bhuj (Rs86, six hours).

Mumbai (Bombay)

Mumbai is big. It's full of dreamers and hard-labourers, actors and gangsters, stray dogs and exotic birds, artists and servants and fisherfolk and *crorepatis* (millionaires) and lots and lots of other people. It has the most prolific film industry, one of Asia's biggest slums and the largest tropical forest in an urban zone. It's India's financial powerhouse, fashion capital and a pulse point of religious tension. It's evolved its own language, Bambaiyya Hindi, which is a mix of…everything. It has some of the world's most expensive real estate and a knack for creating land from water using only determination and garbage.

But wait. Mumbai is not frantic, it's not *overwhelming*. Or at least, it doesn't have to be. Contrary to what you might think, you may not have almost just died in that taxi or been rushed by that station crowd or run over by that guy with the funny outfit and the monkey. The city just has its own rhythm, which takes a little while to hear: it's a complex but playful raga, a gliding, light-footed dance that all of Mumbai seems to know.

So give yourself some time to learn it and appreciate the city's lilting cadences, its harmonies of excess and restraint. The stately and fantastical architecture, the history hanging in the air of the markets, the scent of jasmine in the ladies' car of the train, the gardens and street vendors and balloon-wallahs and intellectuals in old libraries – it will all take you in if you let it. So sit back, develop your equanimity, and let yourself become part of the song.

HIGHLIGHTS

- Eat in one of India's best **restaurants** (p798), then watch – or be one of – the beautiful people at a posh **bar, lounge** (p802) or **club** (p803)

- Stock up on odd and exquisite things at Mumbai's ancient **bazaars** (p805) and outsource your wardrobe to its **boutiques** (p804)

- Admire the grandiose frilliness of Mumbai's colonial-era architecture: **Chhatrapati Shivaji Terminus** (p788), **University of Mumbai** (p787) and **High Court** (p787)

- Resist the urge to bow down before the commanding triple-headed Shiva sculpture at **Elephanta Island** (p809)

- Feel the city's sea breeze among playing kids, big balloons and a hot-pink sunset at **Chowpatty Beach** (p788)

Chowpatty Beach ★

Chor Bazaar ★

Mangaldas Market ★
★Crawford Market

Chhatrapati Shivaji Terminus ★

High Court ★

University of Mumbai ★

Elephanta Island ★

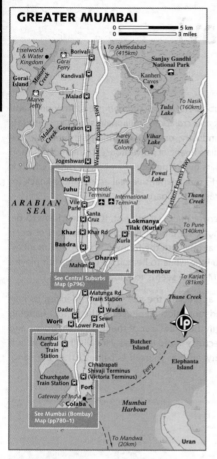

GREATER MUMBAI

FAST FACTS

Population 16.4 million
Area 440 sq km
Telephone code ☎ 022
Languages Marathi, Hindi, Gujarati
When to go October to February

HISTORY

Koli fisherfolk have inhabited the seven islands that form Mumbai as far back as the 2nd century BC. Amazingly, remnants of this culture remain huddled along the city shoreline today. A succession of Hindu dynasties held sway over the islands from the 6th century AD until the Muslim Sultans of Gujarat annexed the area in the 14th century, eventually ceding it to Portugal in 1534. The only memorable contribution the Portuguese made to the area was christening it Bom Bahai, before throwing the islands in with the dowry of Catherine of Braganza when she married England's Charles II in 1661. The British government took possession of the islands in 1665, but leased them three years later to the East India Company for the paltry annual rent of UK£10.

Then called Bombay, the area flourished as a trading port. So much so that within 20 years the presidency of the East India Company was transferred to Bombay from Surat. Bombay's fort was completed in the 1720s, and a century later ambitious land reclamation projects joined the islands into today's single landmass. Although Bombay grew steadily during the 18th century, it remained isolated from its hinterland until the British defeated the Marathas (the central Indian people who controlled much of India at various times) and annexed substantial portions of western India in 1818.

The fort walls were dismantled in 1864 and massive building works transformed the city in grand colonial style. When Bombay took over as the principal supplier of cotton to Britain during the American Civil War, the population soared and trade boomed as money flooded into the city.

A major player in the Independence movement, Bombay hosted the first Indian National Congress in 1885, and the Quit India campaign was launched here in 1942 by frequent visitor Mahatma Gandhi. The city became capital of the Bombay presidency after Independence, but in 1960 Maharashtra and Gujarat were divided along linguistic lines – and Bombay became the capital of Maharashtra.

The rise of the pro-Maratha regionalist movement, spearheaded by the Shiv Sena (Hindu Party; literally 'Shivaji's Army'), shattered the city's multicultural mould by actively discriminating against Muslims and non-Maharashtrans. The Shiv Sena won power in the city's municipal elections in 1985. Communalist tensions increased and the city's cosmopolitan self-image took a battering when nearly 800 people died in riots following the destruction of the Babri Masjid in Ayodhya in December 1992.

The riots were followed by a dozen bombings on 12 March 1993, which killed more than 300 people and damaged the Bombay Stock

---

FESTIVALS IN MUMBAI

Banganga Festival (Jan) A two-day classical-music festival held at the Banganga Tank (p789).

Mumbai Festival (Jan) Based at several stages around the city, it showcases the food, dance and culture of Mumbai.

Elephanta Festival (Feb) Classical music and dance on Elephanta Island (p809).

Kala Ghoda Festival (Feb) Getting bigger and more sophisticated each year, this two-week-long offering has a packed program of arts performances and exhibitions.

Nariyal Poornima (Aug) Festivals in the tourist hub of Colaba kick off with this celebration of the start of the fishing season after the monsoon.

Ganesh Chaturthi (Aug/Sep) Mumbai's biggest annual festival – a 10- to 11-day event in celebration of the elephant-headed deity Ganesh – sweeps up the entire city. On the first, third, fifth, seventh and 10th days of the festival families and communities take their Ganesh statues to the seashore and auspiciously drown them: the 10th day, which sees millions descending on Chowpatty Beach to submerge the largest statues, is particularly ecstatic.

Colaba Festival (Oct) A small arts festival in Colaba that sometimes overlaps with Diwali festivities.

Prithvi Theatre Festival (Nov) A showcase of what's going on in contemporary Indian theatre; also includes performances by international troupes and artists.

Exchange and Air India Building. The more recent train bombings of July 2006, which killed more than 200 people, and November 2008's coordinated attacks on 10 of the city's landmarks, which lasted three days and killed 173 people, are reminders that tensions are never far from the surface.

In 1996 the city's name was officially changed to Mumbai, the original Marathi name derived from the goddess Mumba, who was worshipped by the early Koli residents. The Shiv Sena's influence has since seen the names of many streets and public buildings changed from their colonial names. The airport, Victoria Terminus and Prince of Wales Museum have all been renamed after Chhatrapati Shivaji, the great Maratha leader, although the British names of these and most streets are still in popular local use.

ORIENTATION

Mumbai, the capital of Maharashtra, is an island connected by bridges to the mainland. The island's eastern seaboard is dominated by the city's (off-limits) naval docks. The city's commercial and cultural centre is at the southern, claw-shaped end of the island known as South Mumbai. The southernmost peninsula is Colaba, traditionally the travellers' nerve-centre ,with most of the major attractions, and directly north of Colaba is the busy commercial area known as Fort, where the old British fort once stood. It's bordered on the west by a series of interconnected, fenced grassy areas known as maidans (pronounced may-*dahns*).

Though just as essential a part of the city as South Mumbai, the area north of here is collectively known as 'the suburbs'. The airport (p805) and many of Mumbai's best restaurants, shopping and night spots are here, particularly in the upmarket suburbs of Bandra and Juhu.

Maps

Eicher City Map Mumbai (Rs250) is an excellent street atlas, worth picking up if you'll be spending some time here.

INFORMATION
Bookshops

Vendors lining the footpaths around Flora Fountain, the maidans and Mahatma Gandhi (MG) Rd sell new and secondhand books.

Crossword (Map pp780-1; ☎ 23842001; Mohammedbhai Mansion, NS Patkar Marg, Kemp's Corner; ⏰ 11am-8.30pm) Enormous.

Oxford Bookstore (Map p786; ☎ 66364477/88; www .oxfordbookstore.com; Apeejay House, 3 Dinsha Wachha Marg, Churchgate; ⏰ 10am-10pm) Modern, with a tea bar.

Search Word (Map p784; ☎ 22852521; Metro House, Colaba Causeway, Colaba; ⏰ 10.30am-8.30pm) Small and tidy, with a choice selection of books and magazines.

Strand Book Stall (Map p786; ☎ 22661719; www .strandbookstall.com; Cowasji Patel Rd; ⏰ 10am-8pm Mon-Sat) Old-school and smart, with good discounts.

Internet Access

Portasia (Map p786; ☎ 22032022; Kitab Mahal, Dr Dadabhai Naoroji Rd, Fort; per hr Rs20; ⏰ 9am-9pm Mon-Sat) Entrance is down a little alley; look for the 'cybercafe' sign hanging from a tree.

MUMBAI (BOMBAY)

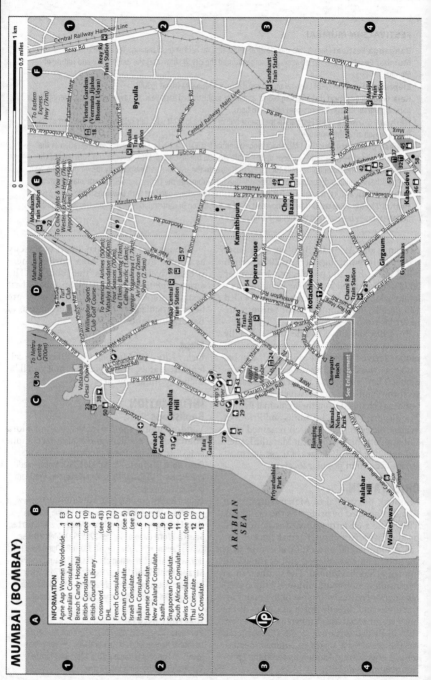

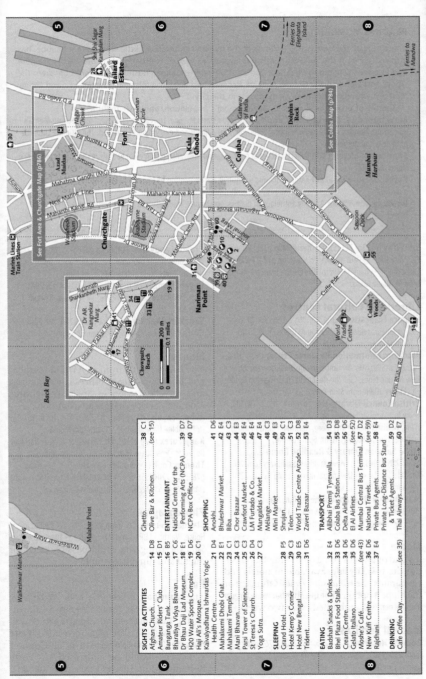

See Fort Area & Churchgate Map (p786)

See Colaba Map (p784)

Ferries to Elephanta Island

Ferries to Mandwa

SIGHTS & ACTIVITIES	
Afghan Church..........................	14 D8
Amateur Riders' Club...............	15 D1
Banganga Tank.........................	16 B5
Bharatiya Vidya Bhavan............	17 C6
Dr Bhau Daji Lad Museum.........	18 E1
H20 Water Sports Complex.......	19 D6
Haji Ali's Mosque.....................	20 C1
Kaivalyadhama Ishwardas Yogic	
Health Centre.......................	21 D4
Mahalaxmi Dhobi Ghat.............	22 E1
Mahalaxmi Temple...................	23 C1
Mani Bhavan............................	24 C3
Parsi Tower of Silence..............	25 C3
St Teresa's Church...................	26 D4
Yoga Sutra..............................	27 C3

SLEEPING	
Grand Hotel............................	28 F5
Hotel Kemp's Corner................	29 C3
Hotel New Bengal....................	30 E5
Trident..................................	31 D6

EATING	
Badshah Snacks & Drinks..........	32 E4
Bhel Plaza Food Stalls..............	33 D6
Cream Centre...........................	34 D6
Gelato Italiano.........................	35 D6
Moshe's Café...........................	(see 43)
New Kulfi Centre......................	36 D6
Rajdhani.................................	37 E4

DRINKING	
Cafe Coffee Day.......................	(see 35)

Ghetto..................................	38 C1
Olive Bar & Kitchen.................	(see 15)

ENTERTAINMENT	
National Centre for the	
Performing Arts (NCPA)..........	39 D7
NCPA Box Office......................	40 D7

SHOPPING	
Anokhi..................................	41 D6
Bhuleshwar Market..................	42 E4
Biba.......................................	43 C3
Chor Bazaar............................	44 E3
Crawford Market.....................	45 E4
LM Furtado & Co.....................	46 E4
Mangaldas Market...................	47 E4
Melange.................................	48 C3
Mini Market............................	49 E3
Shrujan..................................	50 C1
Telon.....................................	51 C3
World Trade Centre Arcade......	52 D8
Zaveri Bazaar..........................	53 E4

TRANSPORT	
Allibhai Premji Tyrewalla..........	54 D3
Colaba Bus Station..................	55 D8
Delta Airlines.........................	56 D6
El Al Airlines..........................	(see 52)
Mumbai Central Bus Terminal...	57 D2
National Travels......................	(see 59)
Private Bus Agents..................	58 E4
Private Long-Distance Bus Stand	
& Ticket Agents.....................	59 D2
Thai Airways...........................	60 E7

MUMBAI (BOMBAY)

READING MUMBAI

Containing all the beauty and ugliness of the human condition, it's little wonder that Mumbai has inspired some of the subcontinent's best writers as well as international scribes like VS Naipaul and Pico Iyer. Leading the field are Booker Prize–winner Salman Rushdie (*Midnight's Children*, *The Moor's Last Sigh* and *The Ground Beneath Her Feet*) and Rohinton Mistry (*A Fine Balance* and *Family Matters*), who have both set many novels in the city.

The list of other good reads is, like Mumbai's population, endlessly multiplying.

Maximum City: Bombay Lost and Found Equal parts memoir, travelogue and journalism, Suketu Mehta's epic covers Mumbai's riots, gang warfare, Bollywood, bar dancers and everything in between. The ultimate chronicle of the city's underbelly.

Shantaram Gregory David Roberts' factional saga about an Australian prison escapee's life on the run in Mumbai's slums and jails.

Rediscovering Dharavi Kalpana Sharma's sensitive and engrossing history of Dharavi's people, culture and industry.

Bombay, Meri Jaan A heady anthology of politics, pop culture, literature and history edited by Jerry Pinto and Naresh Fernandes.

Sify iWay (per 3hr Rs125) Churchgate (Map p786; Prem Ct, J Tata Rd; ☽ 9am-11pm); Colaba (Map p784; Colaba Causeway; ☽ 8am-11.30pm) The Colaba branch entrance is on JA Allana Marg.

Libraries & Cultural Centres

Alliance Française (Map p786; ☎ 22035993; 40 New Marine Lines; annual membership Rs1000; ☽ 9.30am-5.30pm Mon-Fri, to 1pm Sat)

American Information Resource Center (Map p786; ☎ 22624590; http://mumbai.usconsulate.gov/airc.html; 4 New Marine Lines, Churchgate; annual membership Rs400; ☽ library 10am-6pm Mon-Fri)

British Council Library (Map pp780-1; ☎ 22790101; www.britishcouncilonline.org; 1st fl, Mittal Tower A Wing, Barrister Rajni Patel Marg, Nariman Point; monthly membership Rs250; ☽ 10am-6pm Tue-Sat)

David Sassoon Library & Reading Room (Map p786; ☎ 22843703; www.davidsassoonlibrary.com; MG Rd, Kala Ghoda; 45-day/annual membership Rs500/2200; ☽ 8am-9pm)

Max Mueller Bhavan (Goethe Institut; Map p786; ☎ 22027542; www.goethe.de/mumbai; K Dubash Marg, Fort; ☽ library 11am-6pm Mon-Fri)

Media

To find out what's going on in Mumbai, check out the free **City Info**, available in hotels and restaurants, the *Hindustan Times'* **Café** insert or the hippest option, **Time Out Mumbai** (www.timeout mumbai.net; Rs30), published every two weeks.

Medical Services

Bombay Hospital (Map p786; ☎ 22067676, ambulance 22067309; www.bombayhospital.com; 12 New Marine Lines)

Breach Candy Hospital (Map pp780-1; ☎ 23672888; www.breachcandyhospital.org; 60 Bhulabhai Desai Rd, Breach Candy) Best in Mumbai, if not India.

Royal Chemists (Map p786; ☎ 22004041-3; 89A Maharshi Karve Rd, Churchgate; ☽ 8.30am-8.30pm Mon-Sat)

Sahakari Bhandar Chemist (Map p784; ☎ 22022399; Colaba Causeway, Colaba; ☽ 10am-8.30pm)

Money

You'll never be far from an ATM in Mumbai, and foreign-exchange offices changing cash and travellers cheques are also plentiful. Nominal service charges are common.

Akbar Travels (Map p786; ☎ 22633434; 4th fl, 167/169 Dr Dadabhai Naoroji Rd; ☽ 10am-7pm Mon-Sat)

Kanji Forex (Map p786; ☎ 22040206; 40 Veer Nariman Rd, Fort; ☽ 9.30am-6pm Mon-Fri, 9.30am-4pm Sat)

Thomas Cook (☽ 9.30am-6pm Mon-Sat) Fort (Map p786; ☎ 22048556-8; 324 Dr Dadabhai Naoroji Rd) Colaba (Map p784; ☎ 22882517-20; Colaba Causeway)

Photography

Standard Supply Co (Map p786; ☎ 22612468; Image House, Walchand Hirachand Marg, Fort; ☽ 10am-7pm Mon-Sat) Everything you could possibly need for digital and film photography.

Post

The **main post office** (Map p786; ☎ 22620956; ☽ 9am-8pm Mon-Sat, 10am-5.30pm Sun) is an imposing building behind Chhatrapati Shivaji Terminus (CST; Victoria Terminus). **Poste restante** (☽ 9am-8pm Mon-Sat) is at Counter 1. Letters should be addressed c/o Poste Restante, Mumbai GPO, Mumbai 400 001.

Bring your passport to collect mail. The **EMS Speedpost parcel counter** (9am-10pm Mon-Sat, 10am-4.30pm Sun) is across from the stamp counters. Regular parcels can be sent from the parcel office behind the main building. Opposite the post office, under the tree, are parcel-wallahs who will stitch up your parcel for Rs40. The **Colaba post office** (Map p784; Henry Rd) is convenient.

Private express-mail companies:

Blue Dart (Map p786; 22822495; www.bluedart.com; Khetan Bhavan, J Tata Rd; 10am-8pm Mon-Sat)

DHL (Map pp780-1; 22837187; www.dhl.co.in; Embassy Centre, Nariman Point; 9am-8.30pm Mon-Sat).

Telephone

Justdial (69999999; www.justdial.com) and 197 provide Mumbai phone numbers.

Tourist Information

Government of India tourist office (Map p786; 22074333; www.incredibleindia.com; 123 Maharshi Karve Rd; 9am-6pm Mon-Fri, to 2pm Sat) Provides information for the entire country.

Government of India tourist office airport booths domestic (26156920; 7am-9pm); international (26829248; 24hr)

Maharashtra Tourism Development Corporation booth (MTDC; Map p784; 22841877; Apollo Bunder; 8.30am-3.30pm Tue-Sun & 5.30-8pm weekends) For city bus tours (p794).

MTDC reservation office (Map p786; 22845678; www.maharashtratourism.gov.in; Madame Cama Rd, opposite LIC Bldg, Nariman Point; 9.30am-5.30pm Mon-Sat) Information on Maharashtra and bookings for MTDC hotels and the *Deccan Odyssey* train package.

Travel Agencies

Akbar Travels (Map p786; 22633434; Terminus View, Dr Dadabhai Naoroji Rd, Fort; 10am-7pm Mon-Sat)

Magnum International Travel & Tours (Map p784; 22838628; 10 Henry Rd, Colaba; 10am-5.30pm Mon-Fri, to 3.30pm Sat)

Thomas Cook (Map p786; 22048556-8; 324 Dr Dadabhai Naoroji Rd, Fort; 9.30am-6pm Mon-Sat)

Visa Extensions

Foreigners' Regional Registration Office (FRRO; Map p786; 22620446; Annexe Bldg No 2, CID, Bada-ruddin Tyabji Rd, near Special Branch) Does not officially issue extensions on tourist visas; even in emergencies they will direct you to Delhi (p1164). However, some travellers have managed to procure an emergency extension here after much waiting and persuasion.

MUMBAI BY NUMBERS

- Number of black taxis: about 40,000
- Population density: 29,000 people per square kilometre
- Average annual income: Rs48,900 (US$1000, or three times the national average)
- Number of public toilets for every 1 million people: 17
- Number of people passing through Chhatrapati Shivaji Terminus (Victoria Terminus) daily: 2.5 million
- Number of people in an 1800-person-capacity train at rush hour: 7000
- Proportion of Mumbai built on re-claimed land: 60%
- Number of Bollywood movies made since 1931: 68,500

SIGHTS
Colaba

For mapped locations of all the following sights, see p784.

Sprawling down the city's southernmost peninsula, Colaba is a bustling district packed with street stalls, markets, bars and budget to midrange lodgings. **Colaba Causeway** (Shahid Bhagat Singh Marg) dissects the promontory and Colaba's jumble of side streets and gently crumbling mansions.

Sassoon Dock is a scene of intense and pungent activity at dawn (around 5am) when colourfully clad Koli fisherfolk sort the catch unloaded from fishing boats at the quay. The fish drying in the sun are *bombil*, the fish used in the dish Bombay duck. Photography at the dock is forbidden.

While you're here, visit the 1847 Church of St John the Evangelist, known as the **Afghan Church** (Map pp780–1), dedicated to British forces killed in the 1838–43 First Afghan War.

During the more reasonable hours of the day, nearby **Colaba Market** (Lala Nigam St) is lined with jewellery shops and fruit-and-veg stalls.

GATEWAY OF INDIA

This bold basalt arch of colonial triumph faces out to Mumbai Harbour from the tip of Apollo Bunder. Derived from the Islamic styles of 16th-century Gujarat, it was built to commemorate the 1911 royal visit of King George V. It was completed in 1924. Ironically, the gateway's British architects used it just 24 years later to parade off their last British regiment as India marched towards Independence.

These days, the gateway is a favourite gathering spot for locals and a top spot for people-watching. Giant-balloon sellers, photographers,

beggars and touts rub shoulders with Indian and foreign tourists, creating all the hubbub of a bazaar. Boats depart from the gateway's wharfs for Elephanta Island and Mandwa.

The **horse-drawn gilded carriages** that ply their trade along Apollo Bunder are known as Victorias. A whirl around the Oval Maidan at night, when you can admire the illumi-

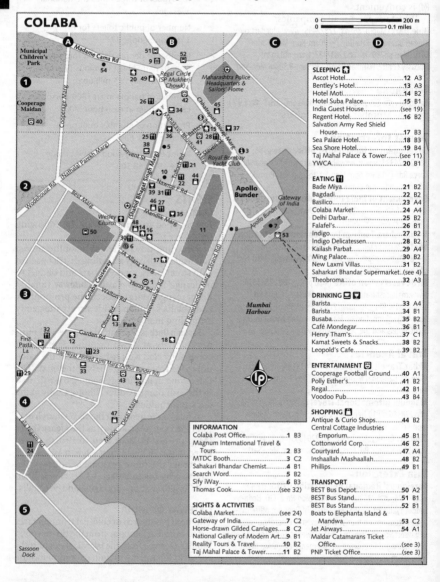

COLABA

SLEEPING
Ascot Hotel	12 A3
Bentley's Hotel	13 A3
Hotel Moti	14 B2
Hotel Suba Palace	15 B1
India Guest House	(see 19)
Regent Hotel	16 B2
Salvation Army Red Shield House	17 B3
Sea Palace Hotel	18 B3
Sea Shore Hotel	19 B4
Taj Mahal Palace & Tower	(see 11)
YWCA	20 B1

EATING
Bade Miya	21 B2
Bagdadi	22 B2
Basilico	23 A4
Colaba Market	24 A4
Delhi Darbar	25 B2
Falafel's	26 B2
Indigo	27 B2
Indigo Delicatessen	28 B2
Kailash Parbat	29 A4
Ming Palace	30 B2
New Laxmi Villas	31 B2
Saharkari Bhandar Supermarket	(see 4)
Theobroma	32 A3

DRINKING
Barista	33 A4
Barista	34 B1
Busaba	35 B2
Café Mondegar	36 B1
Henry Tham's	37 C1
Kamat Sweets & Snacks	38 B2
Leopold's Cafe	39 B2

ENTERTAINMENT
Cooperage Football Ground	40 A1
Polly Esther's	41 B2
Regal	42 B1
Voodoo Pub	43 B4

SHOPPING
Antique & Curio Shops	44 B2
Central Cottage Industries Emporium	45 B1
Cottonworld Corp	46 B2
Courtyard	47 A4
Inshaallah Mashaallah	48 B2
Phillips	49 B1

TRANSPORT
BEST Bus Depot	50 A2
BEST Bus Stand	51 B1
BEST Bus Stand	52 B1
Boats to Elephanta Island & Mandwa	53 C2
Jet Airways	54 A1
Maldar Catamarans Ticket Office	(see 3)
PNP Ticket Office	(see 3)

INFORMATION
Colaba Post Office	1 B3
Magnum International Travel & Tours	2 B3
MTDC Booth	3 C2
Sahakari Bhandar Chemist	4 B1
Search Word	5 B2
Sify iWay	6 B3
Thomas Cook	(see 32)

SIGHTS & ACTIVITIES
Colaba Market	(see 24)
Gateway of India	7 C2
Horse-drawn Gilded Carriages	8 C2
National Gallery of Modern Art	9 B1
Reality Tours & Travel	10 B2
Taj Mahal Palace & Tower	11 B2

MUMBAI IN...

Two Days

Start at the granddaddy of Mumbai's colonial-era giants, the old Victoria Terminus, **Chhatrapati Shivaji Terminus** (CST; p788) and stroll up to **Crawford Market** (p805) and the maze of bazaars here. Lunch at **Rajdhani** (p800), with a juice shake from **Badshah Snacks & Drinks** (p799).

Spend the afternoon at the **Oval Maidan** (p786), checking out the cricket and the grand edifices of the **High Court** (p786) and the **University of Mumbai** (p786). Walk down to the **Gateway of India** (p783) and **Taj Mahal Palace & Tower** (below) and, after the sun sets, eat street-side at **Bade Miya** (p798). Swap tall tales with fellow travellers at **Leopold Café & Bar** (p802).

The next day, soak in the serenity of Malabar Hill's **Banganga Tank** (p789) and head to Kemp's Corner for lunch at **Moshe's Cafe** (p798) and some shopping. Make your way down to **Mani Bhavan** (p789), the museum dedicated to Gandhi, and finish the day with a **Chowpatty Beach** (p788) sunset and *bhelpuri* (crisp fried thin rounds of dough mixed with puffed rice, lentils, lemon juice, onions, herbs and chutney).

Four Days

See **Elephanta Island** (p809) and spend the afternoon visiting the museums and galleries of **Kala Ghoda** (below). In the evening, head to Bandra for a candle-lit dinner at **Sheesha** (p801), followed by some seriously hip bar action at **Zenzi** (p802).

Another day could be spent visiting the **Dhobi Ghat** (p790) and the nearby **Mahalaxmi Temple** and **Haji Ali's Mosque** (p790). Lunch at **Olive Bar & Kitchen** (p803) at Mahalaxmi Racecourse and then spend the afternoon wandering the tiny lanes of **Kotachiwadi** (p789) and finish in style downtown at Indigo (p799).

nated buildings, should cost (after bargaining) around Rs150/250 for 15/30 minutes.

TAJ MAHAL PALACE & TOWER

This sumptuous hotel (p798) is a fairy-tale blend of Islamic and Renaissance styles jostling for prime position among Mumbai's famous landmarks. Facing the harbour, it was built in 1903 by the Parsi industrialist JN Tata, supposedly after he was refused entry to one of the European hotels on account of being 'a native'. The Palace side has a magnificent grand stairway that's well worth a quick peek, even if you can't afford to stay or enjoy a drink or meal at one of its restaurants and bars.

Kala Ghoda

'Black Horse', the area between Colaba and Fort, contains most of Mumbai's main galleries and museums alongside a wealth of colonial-era buildings. The best way to see these buildings is on a guided (p794) or self-guided (p792) walking tour.

CHHATRAPATI SHIVAJI MAHARAJ VASTU SANGRAHALAYA (PRINCE OF WALES MUSEUM)

Mumbai's biggest and best **museum** (Map p786; ☎ 22844484; www.bombaymuseum.org; K Dubash Marg;

Indian/foreigner Rs15/300, camera/video Rs200/1000; ⏲ 10.15am-6pm Tue-Sun), this domed behemoth is an intriguing hodgepodge of Islamic, Hindu and British architecture displaying a mix of dusty exhibits from all over India. Opened in 1923 to commemorate King George V's first visit to India (back in 1905, while he was still Prince of Wales), its flamboyant Indo-Saracenic style was designed by George Wittet – who also did the Gateway of India.

The vast collection inside includes impressive Hindu and Buddhist sculpture, terracotta figurines from the Indus Valley, miniature paintings, porcelain and some particularly vicious weaponry. There's also a natural-history section with suitably stuffed animals. Take advantage of the free, multilanguage audioguides as not everything is labelled.

Students with a valid International Student Identity Card (ISIC) can get in for a bargain Rs10.

GALLERIES

The **National Gallery of Modern Art** (Map p784; ☎ 22881969/70; MG Rd; Indian/foreigner Rs10/150; ⏲ 11am-6pm Tue-Sun) has a bright, spacious and modern exhibition space showcasing changing exhibitions by Indian and international artists. **Jehangir Art Gallery** (Map p786; ☎ 22843989; 161B MG Rd; admission free; ☼ 11am-7pm) hosts interesting shows by local artists; most works are for sale. Rows of hopeful artists often display their work on the pavement outside. Nearby, the museum's contemporary-art annexe, **Museum Gallery** (Map p786; ☎ 22844484; K Dubash Marg; ☼ 11am-7pm) has rotating exhibitions in a beautiful space.

KENESETH ELIYAHOO SYNAGOGUE
Built in 1884, this impossibly sky-blue **synagogue** (Map p786; ☎ 22831502; Dr VB Gandhi Marg) still functions and is tenderly maintained by the city's dwindling Jewish community. One of two built in the city by the Sassoon family (the other is in Byculla), the interior is wonderfully

adorned with colourful pillars, chandeliers and stained-glass windows – best viewed in the afternoons when rainbows of light shaft through.

Fort
For mapped locations of the following sights see p786.

Lined up in a row and vying for your attention with aristocratic pomp, many of Mumbai's majestic Victorian buildings pose on the edge of **Oval Maidan**. This land, and the **Cross** and **Azad Maidans** immediately to the north, was on the oceanfront in those days, and this series of grandiose structures faced west directly out to the Arabian Sea. The reclaimed land along the western edge

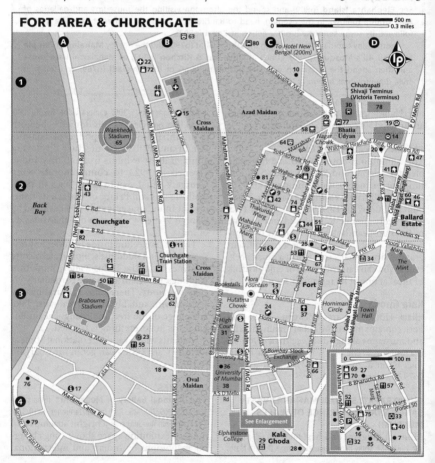

FORT AREA & CHURCHGATE

of the maidans is now lined with a remarkable collection of art deco apartment blocks. Spend some time in the Oval Maidan admiring these structures and enjoying the casual cricket matches.

HIGH COURT

A hive of daily activity, packed with judges, barristers and other cogs in the Indian justice system, the **High Court** (Eldon Rd) is an elegant 1848 neo-Gothic building. The design was inspired by a German castle and was obviously intended to dispel any doubts about the authority of the justice dispensed inside, though local stone carvers presumably saw things differently: they carved a one-eyed monkey fiddling with the scales of justice on one pillar. You are permitted (and it is highly recommended) to walk around inside the building and check out the pandemonium and pageantry of public cases that are in progress.

UNIVERSITY OF MUMBAI (BOMBAY UNIVERSITY)

Looking like a 15th-century French-Gothic masterpiece plopped incongruously among Mumbai's palm trees, this university on Bhaurao Patil Marg was designed by Gilbert Scott of London's St Pancras Station fame. You can go inside both the exquisite **University Library** and **Convocation Hall**, but the 80m-high **Rajabai Clock Tower**, decorated with detailed carvings, is off-limits.

ST THOMAS' CATHEDRAL

Recently restored to its former glory, this charming **cathedral** (Veer Nariman Rd; ⊙ 6.30am-6pm) is the oldest English building standing in Mumbai (construction began in 1672, though it remained unfinished until 1718). The cathedral is an interracial marriage of Byzantine and colonial-era architecture, and its airy, whitewashed interior is full of exhibitionist colonial memorials. A look at some

---

BOLLYWOOD DREAMS

Mumbai is the glittering epicentre of India's gargantuan Hindi-language film industry. From silent beginnings with a cast of all-male actors (some in drag) in the 1913 epic *Raja Harishchandra,* to the first talkie, in 1931, *Lama Ara,* today the industry churns out more than 900 films a year – more than any other industry (yes, Hollywood included). Not surprising considering they have one-sixth of the world's population as a captive audience, as well as a sizable Non-Resident Indian (NRI) following.

Every part of India has its regional film industry, but Bollywood continues to entrance the nation with its winning escapist formula of masala entertainment – where all-singing, all-dancing lovers fight and conquer the forces keeping them apart. These days, Hollywood-inspired thrillers and action extravaganzas vie for moviegoers' attention alongside the more family-oriented saccharine formulas.

Bollywood stars can attain near godlike status in India. Their faces appear in advertisements around the country, and Bollywood star-spotting is a favourite pastime in Mumbai's posher establishments.

Extra, Extra!

Studios often look for extras for background scenes and sometimes want Westerners to add a whiff of international flair (or provocative dress, which locals often won't wear) to a film. It's gotten so common, in fact, that in 2008, 100,000 junior actors nearly went on strike to protest, among other things, losing jobs to foreigners, who will work for less and come with no strings attached.

If you're still game, just hang around Colaba. Scouts, sent by the studios to conscript travellers for the following day's shooting, will usually find you. You receive Rs500 for a day's work, but it can be a long, hot day standing around on the set without promised food and water; others have described the behind-the-scenes peek as a fascinating experience. Before agreeing to anything, always ask for the scout's identification.

---

of the gravestones reveals many colonists died young of malaria.

CHHATRAPATI SHIVAJI TERMINUS (VICTORIA TERMINUS)

Imposing, exuberant and overflowing with people, this is the city's most extravagant Gothic building, the beating heart of its railway network, and an aphorism for colonial India. As historian Christopher London put it, 'the Victoria Terminus is to the British Raj what the Taj Mahal is to the Mughal empire'. It's a meringue of Victorian, Hindu and Islamic styles whipped into an imposing, Daliesque structure of buttresses, domes, turrets, spires and stained-glass windows. Be sure to get close to the jungle-themed facade, particularly around the reservation office: it's adorned with peacocks, gargoyles, cheeky monkeys and lions.

Designed by Frederick Stevens, it was completed in 1887, 34 years after the first train in India left this site. Today it's the busiest train station in Asia. Officially renamed Chhatrapati Shivaji Terminus (CST) in 1998, it's still better known locally as VT. It was added to the Unesco World Heritage list in 2004.

MONETARY MUSEUM

While you're in the area, pop into this tiny and thoughtfully presented **museum** (☎ 22614043; www.rbi.org.in; Amar Bldg, Sir PM Rd; admission Rs10; ☽ 10.45am-5.15pm), run by the Reserve Bank of India. It's an engrossing historical tour of India through coinage: from early concepts of cash to the first coins of 600 BC, through Indo-European influences, right up to today's Gandhi-covered notes. Also on display is the world's smallest coin, probably found in the crack of an ancient couch.

Chowpatty Area

For mapped locations of the following sights see pp780–1.

MARINE DRIVE & CHOWPATTY BEACH

Built on land reclaimed from Back Bay in 1920, **Marine Drive** (Netaji Subhashchandra Bose Rd) arcs along the shore of the Arabian Sea from Nariman Point past Chowpatty Beach (where it's known as Chowpatty Seaface) and continues to the foot of Malabar Hill. Lined with flaking art deco apartments, it's one of Mumbai's most popular promenades and sunset-watching spots. Its twinkling night-time lights earned it the nickname 'the Queen's Necklace'.

Chowpatty Beach (Girgaon Chowpatty) remains a favourite evening spot for courting couples, families, political rallies and anyone out to enjoy what passes for fresh air. Eating an evening time *bhelpuri* (crisp fried thin rounds of dough mixed with puffed rice, lentils, lemon juice, onions, herbs and chutney) at the throng of stalls found here is an essential part of the Mumbai experience. Forget about taking a dip: the water is toxic.

MANI BHAVAN

As poignant as it is tiny, this **museum** (☎ 23805864; www.gandhi-manibhavan.org; 19 Laburnum Rd; admission free; ♥ 9.30am-5.30pm) is in the building where Mahatma Gandhi stayed during visits to Bombay from 1917 to 1934. The museum showcases the room where the leader formulated his philosophy of satyagraha (nonviolent protest popularised by Gandhi) and launched the 1932 Civil Disobedience campaign that led to the end of British rule. Exhibitions include a photographic record of his life, along with dioramas and original documents, such as letters he wrote to Adolf Hitler and Franklin D Roosevelt. Nearby, August Kranti Maidan is where the campaign to persuade the British to 'Quit India' was launched in 1942.

Kotachiwadi

For mapped locations of the following sights see pp780-1.

This *wadi* (hamlet) is a bastion clinging onto Mumbai life as it was before high-rises. A Christian enclave of elegant, two-storey wooden mansions, it's 500m northeast of Chowpatty, lying amid Mumbai's predominantly Hindu and Muslim neighbourhoods. These winding laneways allow a wonderful glimpse into a quiet life free of rickshaws and taxis. To find it, aim for **St Teresa's Church** on the corner of Jagannath Shankarsheth Marg and RR Roy Marg (Charni Rd), then duck into the warren of streets directly opposite.

Malabar Hill

For mapped locations of the following sights see pp780-1.

Mumbai's most exclusive neighbourhood of sky-scratchers and private palaces, **Malabar Hill** is at the northern promontory of Back Bay and signifies the top rung for the city's social and economic climbers.

Surprisingly, one of Mumbai's most sacred and tranquil oases lies concealed among apartment blocks at its southern tip. **Banganga Tank** is a precinct of serene temples, bathing pilgrims, meandering, traffic-free streets and picturesque old *dharamsalas* (pilgrims' rest houses). The wooden pole in the centre of the tank is the centre of the earth: according to legend, Lord Ram created the tank by piercing the earth with his arrow.

THE PARSI CONNECTION

Mumbai has a strong – but diminishing – Parsi community. Descendants of Persian Zoroastrians who fled persecution by Muslims in the 7th century, the Parsis settled in Bombay in the 17th and 18th centuries. They proved astute businesspeople, enjoyed a privileged relationship with the British colonial powers, and became a powerful community in their own right while remaining aloof from politics.

With the departure of the British, the Parsi influence waned in Mumbai, although they continued to own land and established trusts and estates built around their temples, where many of the city's 60,000-plus Parsis still live.

Perhaps the most famous aspect of the Zoroastrian religion is its funerary methods. Parsis hold fire, earth and water sacred and do not cremate or bury their dead. Instead, the corpses are laid out within towers – known as Towers of Silence – to be picked clean by vultures. In Mumbai the **Parsi Tower of Silence** (Map pp780-1) is on Malabar Hill (although it's strictly off-limits to sightseers).

The Parsi population has been declining steadily for decades; in 1940-41, the census counted 115,000 in India, Pakistan and Bangladesh, but the 2001 census recorded only 70,000 in India. (According to one survey, only 99 Parsis were born in 2007.) Their numbers are projected to fall to 23,000 by 2020, at which point they will be counted, officially, as a tribe.

BIRDING IN MUMBAI

Sunjoy Monga has been watching and listening to Mumbai's birds for 40 years.

When did you start bird-watching? My family first stayed downtown, in a congested area full of pigeons, and I would watch them. But then we shifted in 1968 to Kandivali in northwestern Mumbai, where at the time it was all groves, almost a forest and a little river. We could see a lot of birds from my home, and it just took off there.

I'm surprised that birds still like it here. It's so polluted. Actually, in urban areas, there's a featherfolk phenomenon happening. While some species lose out, the concentration of certain birds in the urban context – the numbers, and also the variety – is actually rising in many parts of the world, and especially the tropics.

Why? Well, the warmth of the urban world and the variety of stuff available in a limited area – the amount of garbage, all that filth, as well as, often, a wealth of introduced flowering and fruiting plants. At landfills, you have huge numbers of birds, thousands. Waders, wagtails, raptors... Certain bird species are even expanding. The cattle egret is worldwide now, I think, except for Antarctica. They're common in South Mumbai around railway tracks.

What's the deal with the pink flamingos at the Colgate Factory? At Sewri, the huge numbers of birds could actually be related to the industrialisation – the warm water and food, like algae, that arise from the pollution. The pink flamingos started to be observed in the early 1990s.

What other birds visit Sewri? Waders, gulls, terns, a lot of egrets, herons... The mangroves themselves attract birds, so wherever mangroves are surviving, you'll find a good number of birds. Most of Mumbai's mangroves are along Thane Creek. But probably as much as half of the mangroves across the Mumbai region have disappeared over the last few decades, I would say – especially in northwest Mumbai, in Manori Creek, Malad Creek, in all the small creeks around Mumbai. They're not designated protected areas.

What about the national park? We have approximately 300 species of birds there, the bulk of them woodland birds, but also many aquatic birds because of the freshwater lakes there. It has

---

The lush and well-tended **Hanging Gardens** (Pherozeshah Mehta Gardens) on top of the hill are a pleasant but often crowded place for a stroll. For some of the best views of Chowpatty and the graceful arc of Marine Drive, visit the smaller **Kamala Nehru Park**, opposite. It's popular with couples, and there's a two-storey 'boot house' and colourful animal decorations that the kiddies like.

Mahalaxmi to Worli

For mapped locations of the following sights see pp780–1.

MAHALAXMI DHOBI GHAT

If you've had washing done in Mumbai, chances are your clothes have already visited this 140-year-old **dhobi ghat** (place where clothes are washed; Map pp780–1). The whole hamlet is Mumbai's oldest and biggest human-powered washing machine: every day hundreds of people beat the dirt out of thousands of kilograms of soiled Mumbai clothes and linen in 1026 open-air troughs. The best view, and photo opportunity, is from the bridge across the railway tracks near Mahalaxmi train station.

MAHALAXMI TEMPLE

It is only fitting that in money-mad Mumbai one of the busiest and most colourful temples is dedicated to Mahalaxmi, the goddess of wealth. Perched on a headland, it is the focus for Mumbai's **Navratri** (Festival of Nine Nights) celebrations in September/October. After paying your respects to the goddess, climb down the steps, making your way towards the shore and snack on tasty *gota bhaji* (fried lentil balls) at the cliffside Laxmi Bhajiya House.

HAJI ALI'S MOSQUE

Floating like a sacred mirage off the coast, this mosque is one of Mumbai's most striking shrines. Built in the 19th century on the site of a 15th-century structure, it contains the tomb of the Muslim saint Haji – legend has it that Haji Ali died while on a pilgrimage to Mecca and his casket miraculously floated back to this spot. A long causeway reaches into the Arabian Sea, providing access to the mosque. Thousands of pilgrims, especially on Thursdays and Fridays, cross it to make their visit, many donating to the beggars who

some amazing birds; we've sighted rarities like the great and malabar pied hornbills, and the malabar trogon, among others.

What are some of your favourites? My favourite would have to be the greater racket-tailed drongo. That's an absolute exhibitionist of a bird, a real flamboyant character. In the city, my favourite is the house crow.

Ugh. Really? It's a very colourful character. It's immensely adaptable, good at finding solutions to problems. The nesting material it uses is astounding, from sticks to metal wires, spectacle frames, all kinds of paraphernalia. I've got crow nests made of plastic bags, shells, dice. And we found a nest made completely – completely – of sanitary napkins.

Brilliant! Absolutely! Hugely adaptable! It's a great bird. I love it.

What are some other good bird-watching places? Thane Creek and Sewri, even the other creeks on a good day. Aarey Milk Colony, a 3000-plus-acre grassy wilderness near the park, the Powai Lake area. And little parks and gardens, especially in South Mumbai, are wintering grounds, little stopovers. Elephanta Island has a mix of waders and woodland birds, some raptors also. Overall in Mumbai, almost 400 species of birds have been recorded, just under a third of India's total count.

Wow. What is it about the city? Mumbai is wonderfully cocooned by nature on all sides. On the eastern side is forest, the Sahyadri Hills, the Western Ghats. In the central area, Mumbai lies in the fertile Konkan. Then there are the creeks, the sandy coast and also grass and scrub. Add to that the gardens and parks and all the conditions created by people.

What's your favourite place? I do a lot of good bird-watching just by the roadside. My ears and eyes are really well attuned, I'd say, so I can pick up sounds among traffic and commotion. I'll hear a little snatch of a song and I can find the bird. But the crow remains my favourite. It will always be my favourite.

Sunjoy Monga is the author of Birds of Mumbai, The Mumbai Nature Guide and City Forest, Mumbai's National Park.

line the way; but at high tide, water covers the causeway and the mosque becomes an island.

Erosion has taken its toll on the concrete structure, and at press time, demolition of the building, along with construction of a new mosque in white Rajasthani marble, was under way. The dargah will remain open, but access may be limited.

NEHRU CENTRE

This **cultural complex** (off map pp780–1; ☎ 24964676; www.nehru-centre.org; Dr Annie Besant Rd, Worli) includes a decent **planetarium** (☎ 24920510; adult/child Rs50/25; ✆ English show 3pm Tue-Sun), theatre, gallery (☎ 24963426; ✆ 11am-7pm) and the serpentine but interesting history exhibition **Discovery of India** (admission free; ✆ 11am-5pm). The architecture is striking: the tower looks like a giant cylindrical pineapple, the planetarium a UFO.

ACTIVITIES
Bird-Watching

Mumbai has surprisingly good bird-watching opportunities (see the boxed text opposite).

site). Sanjay Gandhi National Park (p809) is popular for woodland birds, while the marshlands of industrial Sewri (pronounced *shev*-ree) swarm with birds in winter. Contact the **Bombay Natural History Society** (BNHS; map p786; ☎ 22821811; www.bnhs.org; Hornbill House, Dr Salim Ali Chowk, Shaheed Bhagat Singh Rd, Kala Ghoda) or Sunjoy Monga at **Yuhina Eco-Media** (☎ 26341531) for information on upcoming trips.

To visit Sewri on your own, check tide timings and arrive three to four hours before, or two hours after, high tide. Take the Harbour Line train from CST to Sewri, get off on the east side and take an autorickshaw or walk 1km to the Colgate factory. Then turn right for Sewri Bunder. Bring binoculars.

Horse Riding

The **Amateur Riders' Club** (Map pp780–1; ☎ 65005204/5; www.arcmumbai.com; Mahalaxmi Racecourse; ☎ office 9am-5.30pm Mon-Fri, 9am-1pm Sat) has horse rides for those who know how to ride for Rs1000 per 30 minutes; escorts cost Rs250 to Rs500 extra. If you don't, 10-day camps, with a half-hour lesson daily, cost Rs4500. Both require advance booking at the office.

Water Sports

At Chowpatty Beach, **H20 Water Sports Complex** (Map pp780-1; ☎ 23677546/84; www.drishtigroup.com; Marine Dr, Mafatlal Beach; ⏰ 10am-10pm Oct-May) rents out jet skis (per 10 minutes Rs950), kayaks (per half-hour Rs150) and speed boats (per person per 'round' – about five minutes – Rs100) – all weather permitting (it often doesn't). It also operates cruises (p794)

Outbound Adventure (☎ 9820195115, www.out boundadventure.com) runs one-day rafting trips on the Ulhas River near Karjat, 88km southeast of Mumbai, from July to early September (Rs1500 per person). After a good rain, rapids can get up to Grade III+, though usually the rafting is much calmer, with lots of twists and zigzags. OA also organises camping and canoeing trips.

WALKING TOUR

Mumbai's distinctive mix of colonial-era and art deco architecture is one of its defining features. Look for the hard-to-find guidebook *Fort Walks* at local bookshops to learn more.

Starting from the **Gateway of India** (1; p783) walk up Chhatrapati Shivaji Marg past the members-only colonial relic **Royal Bombay Yacht Club** (2) on one side and the art deco residential-commercial complex **Dhunraj Mahal** (3) on the other towards **Regal Circle** (4; SP Mukherji Chowk). Dodge the traffic to reach the car park in the middle of the circle for the best view of the surrounding buildings, including the old **Sailors Home** (5), which dates from 1876 and is now the Maharashtra Police Headquarters, the art deco cinema **Regal** (6; p803) and the old **Majestic Hotel** (7), now the Sahakari Bhandar cooperative store.

Continue up MG Rd, past the beautifully restored facade of the **National Gallery of Modern Art** (8; p785). Opposite is the **Chhatrapati Shivaji Maharaj Vastu Sangrahalaya** (9; Prince of Wales Museum; p785); step into the front gardens to admire this grand building. Back across the road is the 'Romanesque Transitional' **Elphinstone College** (10) and the **David Sassoon Library & Reading Room** (11; p782), where members escape the afternoon heat lazing on planters' chairs on the upper balcony.

Cross back over to Forbes St to visit the **Keneseth Eliyahoo Synagogue** (12; p786) before returning to MG Rd and continuing north along the left-hand side to admire the vertical art deco stylings of the **New India Assurance**

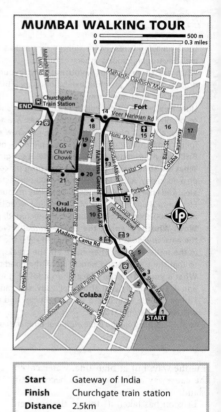

MUMBAI WALKING TOUR

Start	Gateway of India
Finish	Churchgate train station
Distance	2.5km
Duration	3 hours minimum

Company Building (13). In a traffic island ahead lies the pretty **Flora Fountain (14)**, named after the Roman goddess of abundance, and erected in 1869 in honour of Sir Bartle Frere, the Bombay governor responsible for dismantling the fort.

Turn east down Veer Nariman Rd, walking towards **St Thomas' Cathedral (15**; p787). Ahead lies the stately **Horniman Circle (16)**, an arcaded ring of buildings laid out in the 1860s around a circular and beautifully kept botanical garden. The circle is overlooked from the east by the neoclassical **Town Hall (17)**, which contains the regally decorated members-only Asiatic Society of Bombay Library and Mumbai's State Central Library.

Retrace your steps back to Flora Fountain and continue west past the Venetian Gothic–style **State Public Works Department (18)**. Turn south on to Bhaurao Patil Marg to see the august **High Court** (**19**; p787) and the equally venerable and ornately decorated **University of Mumbai** (**20**; p787). The facades of both buildings are best observed from within the **Oval Maidan (21)**. Turn around to compare the colonial edifices with the row of art deco beauties lining Maharshi Karve (MK) Rd, culminating in the wedding cake tower of the **Eros Cinema (22)**. End your walk at Churchgate train station.

COURSES
Yoga
Several yoga classes are held daily at the **Kaivalyadhama Ishwardas Yogic Health Centre** (Map pp780-1; ☎ 22818417; www.kdham.com; 43 Marine Dr, Chowpatty; ☒ 6.30-10am & 3.30-7pm Mon-Sat). Fees include a Rs500 (students/seniors Rs400/300) monthly membership fee and a Rs300 admission fee.

The **Yoga Institute** (Map p796; ☎ 26122185; www .theyogainstitute.org; Shri Yogendra Marg, Prabhat Colony, Santa Cruz East; per 1st/2nd month Rs400/300), near Santa Cruz station, has daily classes as well as weekend and weeklong programs.

Iyengar Yogashraya (off map pp780-1; ☎ 24948416; www.bksiyengar.com; Elmac House, 126 Senapati Bapat Marg, Lower Parel; per class Rs276) has classes in Iyengar yoga, including some for the developmentally disabled. There is a Rs276 admission fee.

Language
Professor Shukla is based at **Bharatiya Vidya Bhavan** (Map pp780-1; ☎ 23871860; cnr KM Munshi Marg & Ramabai Rd, Girgaon) and offers private Hindi, Marathi and Sanskrit classes (Rs500 per hour). Contact this worldly octogenarian directly to arrange a syllabus and class schedule to suit your needs.

Crafts
The **Khatwara Institute** (Shri Khatwari Darbar; Map p796; ☎ 26042670, cnr Linking Rd & Khar Station Rd, Khar West) offers dozens of courses, lasting from three days to one month, for women only (sorry guys!) in Arabic mehendi (decorative henna tattoos), 'basic' mehendi, block printing, embroidery, sewing and cooking, among other things. Call Vanita for details.

MUMBAI FOR CHILDREN
Rina Mehta's www.mustformums.com has the Mumbai Mums' Guide, with info on crèches, health care and even kids' salsa classes in the city. *Time Out Mumbai* (Rs30) often lists fun things to do with kids.

Little tykes with energy to burn will love the Gorai Island amusement parks, **Esselworld** (Map p778; ☎ 28452222; www.esselworld.com; adult/child Rs480/350; ☒ 11am-7pm) and **Water Kingdom** (☎ 28452310; adult/child Rs480/350; ☒ 11am-7pm).

DHARAVI SLUM

Mumbaikers had mixed feelings about the stereotypes in 2008's runaway hit, *Slumdog Millionaire* (released in Hindi as *Slumdog Crorepati*). But slums are very much a part of – some would say the foundation of – Mumbai city life. An astonishing 60% of Mumbai's population live in shantytowns and slums, and the largest slum in Mumbai is Dharavi. Originally inhabited by fisherfolk when the area was still creeks, swamps and islands, it became attractive to migrant workers, from South Mumbai and beyond, when the swamp began to fill in as a result of natural and artificial causes. It now incorporates 1.75 sq km sandwiched between Mumbai's two major railway lines and is home to more than one million people.

While it may look a bit shambled from the outside, the maze of dusty alleys and sewer-lined streets of this city-within-a-city are actually a collection of abutting settlements. Some parts of Dharavi are mixed population, but in others, inhabitants from different parts of India, and with different trades, have set up homes and tiny factories. Potters from Saurashtra live in one area, Muslim tanners in another, embroidery workers from Uttar Pradesh work alongside metalsmiths, while other workers recycle plastics as women dry pappadams in the searing sun. Some of these thriving industries export their wares, and the annual turnover of business from Dharavi is thought to top US$650 million.

Up close, life in the slums is strikingly normal. Residents pay rent, most houses have kitchens and electricity, and building materials range from flimsy corrugated-iron shacks to permanent, multistorey concrete structures. Many families have been here for generations, and some of the younger Dharavi residents even work in white-collar jobs. They often choose to stay, though, in the neighbourhood they grew up in.

Both are well maintained and have lots of rides, slides and shade. Combined tickets are Rs680/550 (adult/child). Off-season weekday ticket prices are lower. It's a Rs35 ferry ride from Borivali jetty.

Several museums have kid-friendly exhibits, including the **Prince of Wales Museum** (p785), with lots of stuffed animals, and **Mani Bhavan** (p789), with fascinating dioramas of Gandhi's life.

Nature trips for kids are often conducted by BNHS (p791) and Yuhina Eco-Media (p791), while **Yoga Sutra** (Map pp780-1; ☎ 32107067; www .yogasutra.co.in; Chinoy Mansions, Bhulabhai Desai Rd, Cumballa Hill; drop-in classes Rs250-500) has kids' yoga classes, taught in English.

TOURS

Fiona Fernandez's *Ten Heritage Walks of Mumbai* (Rs395) contains excellent walking tours in the city, with fascinating historical background.

Bombay Heritage Walks (☎ 23690992; www.bom bayheritagewalks.com), run by two enthusiastic architects, has the best city tours. Private guided tours are Rs1500 for up to three people, Rs500 for each additional person. Email enquiries and bookings are best.

Transway International (☎ 26146854; transwaytours@hathway.com; per 1-/2-/3-person tour Rs2250/3100/4050) runs five-hour day or night tours of South Mumbai's sights. Prices include pick-up and drop-off.

MTDC (p783) runs one-hour open-deck **bus tours** (Rs120, weekends 7pm & 8.15pm) of illuminated heritage buildings. They depart from and can be booked near the Apollo Bunder office. **H2O** (p792) arranges 45-minute day (Rs200 per person, minimum four people) and night (Rs280, 7pm to 11pm) cruises.

Cruises (☎ 22026364; ⏱ 9am-8.30pm) on Mumbai Harbour are a good way to escape the city and offer the chance to see the Gateway of India as it was intended. Ferry rides (Rs50, 30 minutes) depart from the Gateway of India.

For the luxury version, hire the **Taj Yacht** (up to 10 people per 2hr Rs48,000); contact the Taj Mahal Palace & Tower (p798) for details.

The Government of India tourist office (p783) can arrange **multilingual guides** (per half-/ full day Rs600/750). Guides using a foreign language other than English will charge at least Rs200 extra.

Whether or not to visit a slum area on a tour is a delicate question. **Reality Tours & Travel**

(Map p784; ☎ 9820822253; www.realitytoursandtravel.com; Unique Business Centre, 1st fl, Nawroji F Rd, Colaba; short/long tours Rs400/800) runs guided tours of Dharavi (see boxed text p793) and tries to do it right. Photography is strictly forbidden and 80% of post-tax profits go to Dharavi-based NGOs.

SLEEPING

You'll need to recalibrate your budget here: Mumbai has the most expensive accommodation in India. Book ahead at Christmas and in Diwali season.

Colaba is compact, has the liveliest foreigner scene and many of the budget and midrange options. Fort is more spread out and convenient to sights and the main train stations (CST and Churchgate). Most of the top-end places are dotted around the suburbs; hotels in Juhu are convenient for the trendy Bandra district.

To stay with a local family, contact the Government of India tourist office (p783) for a list of homes participating in Mumbai's **paying-guest scheme** (r Rs250-2000; 🅿).

Budget
COLABA
For mapped locations of the following venues see p784.

Salvation Army Red Shield House (☎ 22841824; 30 Mereweather Rd; dm with breakfast Rs195, d/tr/q with full board & without bathroom Rs600/897/1116, d with AC & full board without bathroom Rs891; 🅿 🖳) Salvy's is a Mumbai institution popular with travellers counting every rupee. The large, ascetic dorms are clean, though bed bugs make the odd cameo appearance (they seem to like the women's dorm). Rooms can be reserved in advance, but for dorm beds come just after the 9am kick-out to ensure a spot, as they can't be booked ahead.

Sea Shore Hotel (☎ 22874237; 4th fl, Kamal Mansion, Arthur Bunder Rd; s/d without bathroom Rs400/550) In a building housing several budget guesthouses, the Sea Shore has a clean and friendly atmosphere that makes up for the shoe box–sized rooms and plywood walls. It's worth paying extra for a window and harbour views. On the floor below, India Guest House (☎ 22833769; singles/doubles without bathroom Rs350/450) is a less clean but passable backup, with even shoddier walls.

YWCA (☎ 22025053; www.ywcaic.info; 18 Madame Cama Rd; dm/s from Rs787/896; s/d with AC from Rs1035/1655; 🅿 🖳) The vibe here is very clean and monastic. The frosty-cold lobby has an internet and ISD booth and an overwhelming feeling of orderliness. Renovated rooms, meanwhile, including spacious three- and four-bed dorms, have geysers and immaculate bathrooms. Rooms facing the front can be noisy and/or smelly, but the flip side is that they have pretty balconies. Rates include tax, breakfast, dinner and 'bed tea', and the guesthouse takes men and women.

Hotel Moti (☎ 22025714; hotelmotiinternational @yahoo.co.in; 10 Best Marg; s/d/tr with AC Rs1500/2000/3000; ✖) Occupying the ground floor of a gracefully crumbling, beautiful colonial-era building, rooms are nothing special, really, but they have ghosts of charm and some nice surprises, like ornate stucco ceilings. Some are huge and all have fridges filled with soda and bottled water which is charged at cost – one of the many signs of the pragmatic and friendly management.

FORT

For mapped locations of the following venues see p786, unless otherwise stated.

Hotel New Bengal (Map p786; ☎ 23401951-6; www .hotelnewbengal.com; Sitaram Bldg, Dr Dadabhai Naoroji Rd; s/d incl breakfast from Rs1000/1150, without bathroom Rs495/695; ✖) This well-organised Bengali-run hotel occupies a rambling, mazelike building perennially buzzing with Indian businessmen. They know a good thing when they see it: tidy rooms are an excellent deal. Look at a few, as some have lots of natural light while others flirt with pokiness.

Hotel Lawrence (☎ 22843618; 3rd fl, ITTS House, 33 Sai Baba Marg; s/d/tr without bathroom incl breakfast & tax Rs500/600/800) Modestly tucked away in a little side lane, Lawrence is a pleasant place with basic, clean rooms and affable management (ask them about their meditation practice!). The foyer has fun, original '70s styling and the location can't be beat.

Hotel Outram (☎ 22094937; Marzaban Rd; d with AC Rs1550, s/d without bathroom Rs670/830; ✖) This plain but superfriendly place is in a quiet spot between CST and the maidans. It's definitely rundown and a little dark, with unexciting shared bathrooms, but it has a tiny bit of character, some old-fashioned architectural details and peaceful, green surrounds.

Traveller's Inn (☎ 22644685; 26 Adi Marzban Rd, Ballard Estate; r from Rs780; ✖) On a quiet, tree-lined street, the tiny Traveller's Inn has well-kept rooms and professional, friendly staff. Rooms

have new tiles and geysers and are small but don't feel cramped. Deluxe rooms have kooky decor, eg crown molding, funky colours and a metal locker like from gym class! There are also singles with shared bathroom (Rs364) that are usually unavailable.

Hotel City Palace (☎ 22666666; www.hotelcitypalace .net; 121 City Tce, Walchand Hirachand Marg; s/d with AC from Rs1250/1900, with AC & without bathroom from Rs850/1350,; ✖) City Palace is organised, clean and quiet, despite its location across from CST; the downside is the tininess of the rooms, which seem to increase in height only in higher price brackets. (Standard rooms have oddly low ceilings that are conducive to claustrophobia.) Do-able if you're only in Mumbai for a night or two.

Hotel Oasis (☎ 22697887/8, fax 22697889; 276 Colaba Causeway; r Rs980, s/d with AC Rs930/1340; ✖) Rooms are incredibly small and they need some paint, but they're spick and span and a stone's throw from CST. The kooky pastel design scheme makes you feel like you're inside an ice-cream cone. In a good way.

our pick **Welcome Hotel** (☎ 66314488-90; welcome _hotel@vsnl.com; 257 Colaba Causeway; s/d from Rs2530/2980, without bathroom from Rs1270/1450; ✖) You've never seen anything so clean in your life. Even rooms without bathrooms are fabulous, with segregated bathrooms that are positively spotless. Reception and room staff are cheerful, while the common areas' grey carpeting, grey stone walls, and gleaming black-granite stairs are unintentionally high-fashion. Top-floor rooms are very bright and have awesome views of CST. Rates include breakfast and evening tea.

CST has superexcellent, always full **retiring rooms** (dm from Rs300, s/d with AC from Rs700/1400; ✖) for those on their way in or out. Rooms have high ceilings and tall, old wooden windows and doors set with crazed glass. Check in at the office of the Deputy Station Manager (Commercial), near platform 8/9. They don't take reservations, but you may be able to book one day in advance if you're sweet.

THE SUBURBS

Hotel Kemp's Corner (Map pp780-1; ☎ 23634646; 131 August Kranti Marg; s/d from Rs1500/2000; ✖) With the old-school price and the great spot close to the Kemp's Corner fashion bonanza, you might forgive the occasional carpet bald spot of this old-fashioned place. It's worth forking out a bit more for the deluxe double rooms, but all

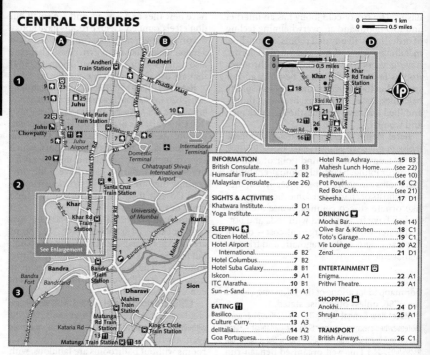

CENTRAL SUBURBS

INFORMATION	
British Consulate	1 B3
Humsafar Trust	2 B2
Malaysian Consulate	(see 26)

SIGHTS & ACTIVITIES	
Khatwara Institute	3 D1
Yoga Institute	4 A2

SLEEPING	
Citizen Hotel	5 A2
Hotel Airport International	6 B2
Hotel Columbus	7 B2
Hotel Suba Galaxy	8 B1
Iskcon	9 A1
ITC Maratha	10 A1
Sun-n-Sand	11 A1

EATING	
Basilico	12 C1
Culture Curry	13 A3
delItalia	14 A2
Goa Portuguesa	(see 13)

Hotel Ram Ashray	15 B3
Mahesh Lunch Home	(see 22)
Peshawri	(see 10)
Pot Pourri	16 C2
Red Box Café	(see 21)
Sheesha	17 D1

DRINKING	
Mocha Bar	(see 14)
Olive Bar & Kitchen	18 C1
Toto's Garage	19 C1
Vie Lounge	20 A2
Zenzi	21 D1

ENTERTAINMENT	
Enigma	22 A1
Prithvi Theatre	23 A1

SHOPPING	
Anokhi	24 D1
Shrujan	25 A1

TRANSPORT	
British Airways	26 C1

rooms have tree views and a bit of old-timey character, eg white-painted furniture.

Midrange
COLABA

For mapped locations of the following venues see p784.

Bentley's Hotel (☎ 22841474; www.bentleyshotel .com; 17 Oliver Rd; s/d incl breakfast & tax from Rs1620/2010; ✖) Bentley's definitely has the most charm of any hotel around, with old-school floor tiles and colonial wooden furniture in some rooms. The hotel is spread out over several buildings on Oliver St and nearby Henry Rd, and all rooms are spotless and come with TV and optional AC (around Rs275 extra). But the welcome is a bit harsh and the service can be indifferent – definitely a weak spot. Rooms come in dozens of sizes and flavours: rooms 31 and 21 have balconies overlooking a garden (you'll have to book months in advance), while the cheaper ones on Henry Rd are a bit noisier.

Sea Palace Hotel (☎ 22854404/10; www.seapalace hotel.com; 26 PJ Ramchandani Marg; s/d with AC from Rs3500/4000; ✖) The standard doubles here are small and the whole place is done in slighly nauseating colour schemes (eg lime yellow), but the gorgeous sea views from the pricier rooms (doubles Rs6250) redeem it. Sort of. The best part is the patio restaurant downstairs, just across from the sea.

Hotel Suba Palace (☎ 22020636; www.hotelsuba palace.com; Battery St; r with AC incl breakfast Rs3700; ✖ ▣) Soothing neutral tones permeate the newly renovated Suba Palace, from the tiny taupe shower tiles in the contemporary bathrooms to the creamy crown molding and beige quilted headboards in the tastefully remodelled rooms. Comfy, quiet and central.

Regent Hotel (☎ 22871853/4; www.regenthotel colaba.com; 8 Best Marg; s/d/tr with AC incl breakfast Rs3700/3900/4200; ✖ ▣ 🛜) This stylish, Arabian-flavoured hotel has marble surfaces and soft pastels aplenty. Comfortable, freshly painted rooms all have fridge, an enclosed balcony, and a prayer mat (just in case!).

Ascot Hotel (☎ 66385566; www.ascothotel.com; 38 Garden Rd; d with AC incl breakfast from Rs5500; ✖ ▣) From the decadent marble bathrooms with bathtubs and soft lighting to the warm beiges and creams in the huge, uncluttered rooms, the Ascot is all class. Rooms have internet connection and DVD players, and front rooms get lots of natural light and tree views. The service seems a bit disorganised, though, for the price.

FORT, CHURCHGATE & MARINE DRIVE

Residency Hotel (Map p786; ☎ 22625525-9; residencyhotel@vsnl.com; 26 Rustom Sidhwa Marg, Fort; s/d from Rs2000/2200; ❇ 🖳 🛜) We love how the Residency bucks the trend and doesn't double its rates every other year. It has good vibes like that. Rooms are very small but tasteful and come with fridges, flat-screen TVs and flip-flops (see what we mean?). The lobby and hallways have lots of marble and plants all around and a skylit atrium. There's free internet access.

West End Hotel (Map p786; ☎ 22039121; www.westendhotelmumbai.com; 45 New Marine Lines; s/d with AC from Rs3200/3600; ❇ 🖳 🛜) You'd half expect Austin Powers to be swinging in this hotel's grey velour–lined bar, Chez Nous. The hotel has a funky, unintentionally retro feel, and the old-fashioned rooms are plain but roomy, with soft beds. The catch is there's a 20% tax is charged on rooms.

Grand Hotel (Map pp780-1; ☎ 66580500; www.grandhotelbombay.com; 17 Shri Shiv Sagar Ramgulam Marg, Ballard Estate; s/d/tr incl breakfast Rs3500/4000/5000; ❇ 🖳 🛜) The Grand is a good deal, with spunk – note the plaques labelling everything in the 1960s-era lobby. The place is superquiet – you can hear a pin drop in the placid, robin's egg–blue hallways – and rooms are well kept and extremely clean. The furniture is so dated that it's coming back around to brilliant. Wi-fi and computer use are free.

Sea Green Hotel (Map p786; ☎ 66336525; www.seagreenhotel.com; 145 Marine Dr; s/d Rs2400/2950; ❇) and **Sea Green South Hotel** (Map p786; ☎ 22821613; www.seagreensouth.com; 145A Marine Dr; s/d Rs2400/2950; ❇) are identical art deco hotels with spacious but spartan AC rooms, originally built in the 1940s to house British soldiers. Ask for one of the sea-view rooms as they're the same price. Both places are great value – even with the 10% service charge.

THE SUBURBS

There are several midrange hotels on Nehru Rd Extension in Vile Parle East near the domestic airport, but rooms are overpriced and only useful for early or late flights. Juhu is

convenient for Juhu Beach and for the restaurants, shops and clubs in Bandra.

For mapped locations of the following venues see p796.

Iskcon (☎ 26206860; guesthouse.mumbai@pamho.net; Hare Krishna Lane, Juhu; s/d incl tax Rs2095/2495, with AC incl tax Rs2395/2995; ❇) Part of Juhu's lively Hare Krishna complex, this very efficiently managed guesthouse is spread out across two buildings – one of which is flamingo-pink. Rooms are big and spick and span – those in the original building have balconies – but don't have TV or fridge. A good vegetarian buffet restaurant, Govinda's, is on site.

Hotel Suba Galaxy (☎ 26821188; www.hotelsubagalaxy.com; NS Phadke Marg, Saiwadi, Andheri East; s/d with AC incl breakfast from Rs2800/5000; ❇) Clean lines, oversized windows and mirrors, and lots of dark-wood laminate and bright white makes for good-looking rooms in this newish tower 4km from the international airport. The standard single is a box, but even that has all the mod cons – flat-screen TV, broadband, etc. Oh, and lots of fluffy pillows.

Hotel Columbus (☎ 26182029; hotel_columbus@rediffmail.com; 344 Nanda Patkar Rd, Vile Parle East; s/d with AC from Rs3000/3500; ❇ 🖳) One of the few decent midrange hotels in the domestic airport area, the Columbus is on a cute, tree-lined street off Nehru Rd (opposite the BP petrol pump), away from the airport chaos. The gussied-up deluxe rooms (Rs4000) have stylised wood-grain accents and flat-screen TVs and aspire to high design.

Hotel Airport International (☎ 26182222; www.hotelairportinternational.com; Nehru Rd, Vile Parle East; s/d with AC incl breakfast from Rs5000/6500; ❇ 🛜) This is the pick of the Nehru Rd hotels, it's so close to the domestic airport you can see the runway from some rooms. Just renovated, rooms are impeccably clean, compact and tastefully done; superdeluxe rooms have bathtubs and fridges.

Citizen Hotel (☎ 66932525; www.citizenhotelmumbai.com; Juhu Tara Rd, Juhu; s/d with AC from Rs7000/7500; ❇ 🖳 🛜) The Citizen's location, right on the beach, is what you're paying for here, but rooms are also well maintained, with marble floors and marble-top furniture, flat-screen TVs, wi-fi access, fridges – and, of course, excellent views. The place also has an AC restaurant and a patio cafe, both overlooking the sea.

Sun-n-Sand (☎ 66938888; www.sunnsandhotel.com; 39, Juhu Beach, Juhu; r with AC from Rs10,500; ❇ 🖳 🍴)

The Sun-n-Sand has been offering up beachfront hospitality for decades. The best rooms here are the sea-facing ones (Rs12,000): lots of silk and shades of tangerine complement the pool, palm-tree and ocean views from the huge window. It's off Juhu Rd, near the old Holiday Inn.

Top End

Trident (Oberoi Hotel; Map pp780-1; ☎ 66324343; www .tridenthotels.com; Marine Dr, Nariman Point; s/d from Rs17,250/18,500; ✵ ☐ ☎) The Trident is, along with the Oberoi, part of the Oberoi Hotel complex. But the Trident wins out both on price and on the spiffy, streamlined design of its restaurants, bars and pool area. Plus, it reopened like a champion less than a month after 2008's three-day terrorist occupation.

InterContinental (Map p786; ☎ 39879999; www.in tercontinental.com; 135 Marine Dr, Churchgate; r incl breakfast from Rs18,500; ✵ ☐ ☎) You'll want to pay a little extra for the splendid sea views at this sophisticated boutique-style hotel. Room decor is cosy but understated, with clean lines and warm tones. The stunning Dome bar and restaurant (p802) elegantly crowns the rooftop and overlooks the sea.

Taj Mahal Palace & Tower (Map p784; ☎ 66653366; www.tajhotels.com; Apollo Bunder, Colaba; tower rooms s/d from Rs18,250/19,750, palace rooms from Rs25,250/26,750; ✵ ☐ ☎) We already loved it, but when it got back on its feet just three weeks after the November 2008 terrorist attacks (following massive construction work and blessings from leaders of seven religions), we were floored. A Mumbai landmark since 1903, this distinguished hotel, with its sweeping arches, staircases and domes, is unstoppably exquisite. Palace rooms are peaceful, heritage and plush, with separate foyer and soothing white-marble bathroom, plasma TV with internet hookup and a separate breakfast nook (some with Gateway views). Tower rooms are gorgeous but not as special. Even if you don't stay here, have a drink or meal in one of its many excellent bars and restaurants.

Fabulous digs in the suburbs:

Four Seasons Hotel (off map pp780-1; ☎ 24818000; www.fourseasons.com; Dr E Moses Rd, Worli; r from Rs17,650; ✵ ☐ ☎) Great sea views and elegance. The service is exceptional, the staff practically psychic.

ITC Maratha (Map p796; ☎ 28303030; www.itcwelcom group.in; Sahar Rd, Andheri East; s/d incl breakfast & tax from Rs22,000/23,500; ✵ ☐ ☎) The five-star with the most luxurious Indian character, from the Jaipur-style

lattice windows around the atrium to the silk pillows on the beds.

EATING

Food options in the metropolis are as diverse as the squillion inhabitants – go on a cultural history tour by sampling Parsi *dhansak* (meat with curried lentils and rice), Gujarati or Keralan thalis ('all-you-can-eat' meals) and everything from Mughlai kebabs and Goan vindaloo to Mangalorean seafood. If you find Bombay duck on a menu, remember it's actually *bombil* fish dried in the sun and deep-fried.

Don't miss Mumbai's famous *bhelpuri*, readily available at Chowpatty Beach (p788). During the Islamic holy month of Ramadan, fantastic night food markets line Mohammed Ali and Merchant Rds in Kalbadevi. Street stalls offering rice plates, samosas, *pav bhaji* (spiced vegetables and bread) and *vada pav* (deep-fried spiced-lentil-ball sandwich) for Rs5 to Rs15 do a brisk trade around the city.

For self-caterers, the **Colaba market** (Map p784; Lala Nigam St) has fresh fruit and vegetables. **Saharkari Bhandar Supermarket** (Map p784; ☎ 22022248; cnr Colaba Causeway & Wodehouse Rd; ☯ 10am-8.30pm) and, even better, **Suryodaya** (Map p786; ☎ 22040979; Veer Nariman Rd; ☯ 7.30am-8.30pm) are well-stocked supermarkets.

Colaba

For mapped locations of the following venues see p784.

Theobroma (Colaba Causeway; confections Rs20-100; ☯ 8.30am-midnight) Theobroma calls its creations 'food of the gods' – and they are. Dozens of perfectly executed cakes, tarts and chocolates, as well as sandwiches and breads, go well with the coffee here. The solo hazelnut mousse cake (Rs80) or the genius pistachio-and-green-cardamom truffle (Rs25) will take you to the next plane.

Bagdadi (11 Tulloch Rd; mains Rs20-70; ☯ 7am-12.30am) Bagdadi is full of everyday guys who come for the traditional Mughlai food and no-nonsense service. There's lots and lots of fish, prawns and meat (including beef brain fry; Rs40) on the menu, cooked up in biryanis and daily-changing specials. The best-deal rotis in town are enormous and cost Rs7. But alas, 'food will not be served to drunken person'.

New Laxmi Vilas (19A Ram Mansion, Nawroji F Rd; light meals Rs18-55, mains Rs40-85) A budget eatery that

DABBA-WALLAHS

A small miracle of logistics, Mumbai's 5000 *dabba* (food container)-wallahs (also called tiffin-wallahs) work tirelessly to deliver hot lunches to office workers throughout the city.

Lunch boxes are picked up each day from restaurants, homes, mothers and wives and carried on heads, bicycles and trains. Taken to a centralised sorting station, a sophisticated system of numbers and colours (many wallahs are illiterate) is then used to determine where every lunch must end up. More than 200,000 meals are delivered in Mumbai in this way – always on time, come (monsoon) rain or (searing) shine.

This same intricate supply-chain system has been used for centuries, and dabba-wallahs are known to take immense pride in their work. Considering that on average only about one mistake is made every six million deliveries, they've certainly earned it.

serves great southern specialities in comfortable, modern, AC surrounds. Dosas are the speciality; one reader even wrote in 'we still dream of the meals we ate there'. The thalis (Rs43) are also high calibre.

Kailash Parbat (5 Sheela Mahal, First Pasta Lane; mains Rs40-78) Nothing fancy, but a Mumbai legend nonetheless thanks to its inexpensive Sindhi-influenced vegetarian snacks, mouth-watering sweets and extra-spicy masala chai. Kailash Parbat Hindu Hotel across the street is its also good, more playful, cousin.

Bade Miya (Tulloch Rd; meals Rs50-80; 7pm-3am) As Mumbai as traffic jams, this street-stall-on-steroids buzzes nightly with punters from all walks of Mumbai life lining up for spicy, fresh grilled treats. Grab a chicken tikka roll to go, or sample the *boti kebab* (lamb kebab) or *paneer masala* (unfermented-cheese and tomato curry) on the footpath.

Falafel's (Wodehouse Rd; sandwiches & salads Rs55-125; 11am-midnight) It's very chain-restaurant-like and a bit too marketing-savvy for our tastes, but there's no denying that the falafel, hummus and Greek salads are delish.

Basilico (66345670; Sentinel House, Arthur Bunder Rd; mains Rs210-375; 7.30am-midnight) A très sleek, Euro-style bistro, Basilico whips up creative fresh pastas, salads and couscous that will make you melt. Veggies will flat out die – from either the wholesome green salad (mixed lettuce, corn, asparagus and sprouts with feta, lime and olive-oil dressing; Rs225) or the homemade mushroom and goat-cheese cannelloni (Rs340). The coup de grâce? It's also a bakery. The Bandra branch is on St John Rd, next to HDFC, Pali Naka (Map p796; 67039999, open noon to midnight).

Indigo Delicatessen (Pheroze Bldg, Chhatrapati Shivaji Marg; mains Rs245-495; 9am-midnight) Indigo's less expensive sister is just as elegant as the original, with good jazz on, warm but sleek decor and massive wooden tables. It has breakfast any time (Rs145 to Rs265), casual meals and desserts, teas, wines (Rs360 to Rs710 per glass) and a selection of breads and imported cheeses.

Indigo (66368980; 4 Mandlik Marg; mains Rs485-985; 12-4pm & 7-11pm) Colaba's finest eating option, Indigo has inventive European cuisine, a long wine list, sleek ambience and an absolutely gorgeous roof deck lit with fairy lights. Daily specials come with wine recommendations. Favourites include the soft basil-crusted Norwegian salmon, with asparagus, beetroot couscous and lemon and orange-caper butter (Rs985). Or lemon ricotta tortellini with fennel spinach sauce, porcini mushrooms and walnuts (Rs585). Bookings are essential.

Also recommended:

Delhi Darbar (Holland House, Colaba Causeway; mains Rs85-175; 11.30am-12.30am) Excellent Mughlai, tandoori and Middle Eastern.

Ming Palace (Colaba Causeway; mains Rs160-680; 11.30am-3.15pm & 6.45-11.30pm) Quality Chinese with gargantuan portions.

Kala Ghoda & Fort

Badshah Snacks & Drinks (Map pp780-1; opposite Crawford market; snacks Rs20-95; 7am-12.30am) Badshah been serving snacks, fruit juices and its famous *falooda* (rose-flavoured drink made with milk, cream, nuts and vermicelli) to hungry bargain-hunters for more than 100 years.

Anubhav (Map p786; 292 Shahid Bhagat Singh Marg; mains Rs40-75; 8am-9.45pm Mon-Sat) This local veg joint, aka the Veg Delite, has good South Indian food, as well as a smattering of Punjabi standbys. There are six – count 'em, six – kinds of vegetarian biryani, and a tasty lunch thali, known simply as 'lunch' (Rs45).

Ideal Corner (Map p786; Gunbow St, Fort; mains Rs40-90; ⏰ 9am-4.30pm Mon-Fri) This classic Parsi cafe has the style to match its odd little spot in the crook of a funky, rounded building, with a royal-blue and mango colour scheme and wooden stairs leading to a loft space. But the most artful thing here is the fresh, homemade dishes on the daily-changing menu. Even a simple *khichdi masoor pappad* (lightly spiced rice and lentils; Thursday) is memorable.

Shivala (Map p786; Walchand Hirachand Marg; mains Rs50-110) Shivala is a working-fellas' joint with excellent North Indian food (and the requisite South Indian and Chinese offerings). The AC room upstairs is way contemporary, with lots of glass, pebbles and blue light, but also views: Shivala is just across from Bhatia Udyan, the pocket of green in front of CST.

Moshe's Cafe (Map p786; Fabindia, 1st fl, Jeroo Bldg, MG Rd, Kala Ghoda; light meals Rs60-135; ⏰ 10am-7.45pm) After shopping downstairs, refuel with Moshe's excellent salads, sandwiches, baked goods, coffees and smoothies. The marinated garlic, mushroom, leek and bell-pepper open-faced sandwich with melted mozzarella on brown bread will make you collapse with pleasure on your bag of new block-printed kurtas. There's also a Moshe's in Kemp's Corner (Map pp780–1, open 11am to 8.30pm).

Mahesh Lunch Home (Map p786; ☎ 22023965; 8B Cowasji Patel St, Fort; mains Rs120-400; ⏰ 11.30am-3.30pm & 6-11.30pm) A great place to try Mangalorean seafood in Mumbai. It's renowned for its lady-fish, pomfret, lobster and crabs, and its *rawas tikka* (marinated white salmon) and tandoori pomfret are outstanding. There's also a branch on Juhu Tara Rd (Map p796, ☎ 26108848).

Trishna (Map p786; ☎ 22703213-5; Sai Baba Marg, Kala Ghoda; mains Rs160-490; ⏰ 12-3.30pm & 6.30pm-midnight) This might just be the best seafood in town. One reader wrote in to describe how a dish here sent her into deliciousness shock ('This was the best fish I have EVER had!'). It specialises in Mangalorean preparations, and the crab with butter, pepper and garlic and various shrimp dishes – all brought to your table for inspection – are outstanding.

Rajdhani (Map pp780–1; 361 Sheikh Memon St, Kalbadevi; thali Rs225; ⏰ 12-4pm & 7-10.30pm) Opposite Mangaldaas Market, Rajdhani is famous for its Gujarati and Rajasthani thalis. It's a great spot to refuel while shopping in the markets. On Sundays, dinner isn't served and lunch prices are slightly higher.

Khyber (Map p786; ☎ 40396666; 145 MG Rd, Fort; mains Rs275-475; ⏰ 12.30-4pm & 7.30pm-midnight) Khyber serves up Punjabi and other North Indian dishes in moody, burnt-orange, Afghan-inspired interiors to a who's who of Mumbai's elite. The food is some of the city's best, with the meat-centric menu wandering from ke-babs and biryanis to its pièce de résistance, *raan* (a whole leg of slow-cooked lamb).

Churchgate

For mapped locations of the following venues, see p786.

Pizzeria (Soona Mahal, 143 Marine Dr; pizza & pasta Rs145-350; ⏰ noon-midnight) Serves up pizzas and pasta dishes along with Indian wines, but the ocean views are the real draw.

Samrat (☎ 42135401; Prem Ct, J Tata Rd; lunch/dinner thalis Rs190/220; ⏰ 12-4pm & 7-10.45pm) A busy traditional Indian pure-veg restaurant, Saurat is part of a family restaurant at the same location. Relish (mains Rs150 to Rs250, open noon to midnight) is the funkier cousin, with dishes ranging from Lebanese platters to Mexican, while 210°C is an outdoor cafe and bakery (coffees and pastries Rs20 to Rs80; open noon to 11pm).

Gaylord (☎ 22821259; Veer Nariman Rd; meals Rs190-650; ⏰ 12.30-3.30pm & 7.30-11.30pm) Great North Indian dishes served with over-the-top, Raj era–style dining complete with tuxedo-wearing waiters hanging on your every gesture. It also serves domestic and imported wines (Rs175 to Rs600 per glass).

Chowpatty

For mapped locations of the following venues see pp780–1.

The evening stalls at Bhel Plaza on Chowpatty Beach are the most atmospheric spots to snack on *bhelpuri* (Rs20) or *panipuri* (small, crisp puffs of dough filled with spicy tamarind water and sprouted gram; Rs15). Mobile chai-wallahs do the rounds.

New Kulfi Centre (cnr Chowpatty Seaface & Sardar V Patel Rd; kulfi per 100gm Rs18-38; ⏰ 9am-1.30am) Serves the best *kulfi* (firm-textured ice cream flavoured, often with pistachio) you'll have anywhere, which means it's the best-tasting thing in the entire world. When you order, the *kulfi* is placed on a betel-nut leaf and then weighed on an ancient scale – which makes it even better.

In fact, there's a lot of serious ice-cream action going on here:

Cream Centre (Chowpatty Seaface; mains Rs100-195; ☯ noon-midnight) An excellent ice-cream parlour in a bright, slick interior. Oh, and real food, too: a pure-veg hodgepodge of Indian, Mexican and Middle Eastern.

Gelato Italiano (Chowpatty Seaface; scoops Rs30-70; ☯ 11am-12.30am) Flavours like custard-apple sorbetto or limoncello – yum.

The Suburbs

North Mumbai's trendy dining joints centre on Bandra West and Juhu, while *bhelpuri*, *panipuri*, et al are served at Juhu Chowpatty. For mapped locations of the following venues see p796.

ourpick Hotel Ram Ashray (Bhandarkar Rd, Matunga East; light meals Rs12-38; ☯ 5.30am-9.30pm) We wouldn't send you to Matunga – on the Central line, no less – if this weren't something special. Tucked away in a Tamil enclave near King's Circle (a stone's throw from the station's east exit), Ram Ashray is popular with southern families for its spectacular dosas, *idli* and *upma* (semolina cooked with onions, spices and coconut). You won't taste a better coconut chutney anywhere (sorry, Chennai).

Culture Curry (Kataria Rd, Matunga West; mains Rs129-459; ☯ 12-3.30pm & 7pm-12.30am) As the Culture Curry folks rightly point out, there's a lot more to southern food than *idli* and dosas. Exquisite dishes from all over the South, ranging from Andhra and Coorg to Kerala, are the specialty here. Veggies are particularly well served: the Kooru Curry (kidney and green beans in coconut gravy; Rs179) is extraordinary. The same owners run Diva Maharashtracha, down the street, and Goa Portuguesa, next door, specialising in fiery Goan dishes. Guitar-strumming musicians and singers wander between the two connected spaces.

Pot Pourri (Carlton Ct, cnr of Turner & Pali Rds, Bandra West; mains Rs150-285; ☯ noon-midnight Mon-Sat, 9am-midnight Sun) In a good spot for watching Bandra streetlife, Pot Pourri serves up sandwiches and Western- and Eastern-style cuisine. It excels with the Asian stuff: the Thai papaya salad (Rs115) and veg or meat *khau suey* (Burmese noodles with a coconut broth; Rs265) are superb.

Sheesha (☏ 66770555; 7th flr, Shoppers Stop, Linking Rd, Bandra West; mains Rs170-250; ☯ 11.30am-1.30am) With maybe the most beautiful ambience in town, Sheesha's alfresco rooftop lair has glass lanterns hanging from wooden beams, comfy couches and coloured-glass lamps high above the city and shopping madness below. You almost forget about the food – good Indian fare (Goan fish curry; Rs245) nestling alongside 386 varieties of kebab (Rs130 to Rs220). Reserve on weekends.

Red Box Cafe (155 Waterfield Rd, Bandra West; mains Rs190-375; ☯ noon-1.30am) Where Bandra's beautiful people go when they want something 'simple'. Red Box does good sandwiches, salads, pizza, fondue and espresso. There's Wham! playing in the background, picture windows and outdoor tables, and a red-and-black goth-meets-McDonald's design scheme. It works, though, on some weird level.

dellitalia (☏ 26284040; Juhu Tara Rd, opposite Juhu Beach; mains Rs280-410; ☯ 11.30am-3pm & 7.30pm-12.30am) The Italian villa decor here – the semialfresco terrace with hanging plants, the faux terracotta walls, the wooden pantry on the 1st floor – is a little theme-y but lovely even so, especially at night. Some of the Italian food here (ahem, pizza) is so-so, but most is sublime, for example, the artichoke and bocconcini salad with sundried tomato. Bottles of Italian wine start at Rs1500.

Peshawri (☏ 28303030; ITC Maratha, Sahar Rd; mains Rs500-1250; ☯ 12.30-2.45pm & 7-11.45pm) Make this Indian north-west frontier restaurant, just outside the international airport, your first or last stop in Mumbai. You won't regret forking out for the leg of spring lamb and amazing dhal Bukhara (a thick black dhal cooked for a day!). The ITC is also home to Dakshin (open 7.30pm to 11.45pm) – better for vegetarians – serving some of Mumbai's finest southern food.

DRINKING

Mumbai's lax attitude to alcohol means that there are loads of places to drink – from hole-in-the-wall beer bars and chichi lounges to brash, multilevel superclubs. You'll pay around Rs80 to Rs130 for a bottle of Kingfisher in a bar or restaurant, a lot more in a club or fashionable watering-hole.

If it's the caffeine buzz you're after, espresso is ubiquitous.

Cafes

Kamat Sweets & Snacks (Map p784; 24 Colaba Causeway; teas & coffees Rs7-38) It's just tea, sweets and snacks and it's small and cramped, but we just can't resist the retro vibe – or the cold coffee with ice cream (Rs38).

Mocha Bar (coffees Rs30-175, light meals Rs95-175; 10am-1:30am) Churchgate (Map p786; 82 Veer Nariman Rd) Juhu (Map p796; 67 Juhu Tara Rd) This atmospheric, Arabian-styled cafe is often filled to the brim with bohemians and students deep in esoteric conversation, or just gossip. Cosy, low-cushioned seating, hookah pipes, exotic coffee varieties and world music add up to longer stays than you expected.

Samovar Café (Map p786; Jehangir Art Gallery, 161B MG Rd, Kala Ghoda; 11am-7.30pm Mon-Sat) This intimate place inside the art gallery overlooks the gardens of the Prince of Wales Museum and is a great spot to chill out over a beer, mango lassi or light meal.

Cha Bar (Map p786; 66364477; Oxford Bookstore, Apeejay House, 3 Dinsha Wachha Marg, Churchgate; 10am-9.30pm) An inspiring range of teas and tasty snacks amid lots of books.

Meanwhile, Barista and Café Coffee Day are still trying to out-Starbucks each other:

Barista (9am-1am; coffees Rs38-85) Colaba (Map p784; Colaba Causeway); Colaba (Map p784; Arthur Bunder Rd); CST (Map p786; Marzaban Rd)

Café Coffee Day (8am-midnight; coffees Rs34-90) Chowpatty (Map pp780-1; Chowpatty Seaface); CST (Map p786; Marzaban Rd)

Bars

SOUTH MUMBAI

For mapped locations of the following venues see Map p784, unless otherwise indicated.

Leopold's Café (cnr Colaba Causeway & Nawroji F Rd; 7.30am-12am) Love it or hate it, most tourists end up at this Mumbai travellers' institution at one time or another. Around since 1871, Leopold's has wobbly ceiling fans, open-plan seating and a rambunctious atmosphere conducive to swapping tales with random strangers. Although there's a huge menu, the lazy evening beers are the real draw.

Café Universal (Map p786; 299 Colaba Causeway; 10am-11pm Mon-Sat, 7-11pm Sun) A little bit of France near CST. The Universal has an art nouveau look to it, with butterscotch-colour walls, a wood-beam ceiling and lots of windows, and is a comfy, pretty place for happy hour.

Busaba (☎ 22043779; 4 Mandlik Marg; noon-3.30pm & 6pm-1am) Red walls and contemporary art of Buddhas give this loungey restaurant-bar a nouveau Tao. It's next to Indigo so gets the same trendy crowd but serves cheaper, more potent cocktails. The upstairs restaurant serves pan-Asian (mains Rs300 to Rs750); its back room feels like a posh treehouse. Reserve ahead.

Café Mondegar (☎ 22020591; Metro House, 5A Colaba Causeway; 8am-12.30am) Like Leopold's, Café Mondegar is usually filled entirely with foreigners, but some readers find it less overwhelmingly foreign somehow. It also has more character. 'Purple Haze' seems to be always playing on the CD jukebox.

Henry Tham's (☎ 22023186; Apollo Bunder; 12.30-3pm & 7.30pm-1.30am) This superswanky bar-cum-restaurant features towering ceilings, gratuitous use of space and strategically placed minimalist decor. It's a darling of the Mumbai jet set and therefore *the* place to see and be seen. The real star here, though, is the Chinese food.

Dome (Map p786; ☎ 39879999, ext 8872; Hotel InterContinental, 135 Marine Dr, Churchgate; 6pm-1.30am) This white-on-white rooftop lounge has awesome views of Mumbai's curving seafront. Cocktails beckon the hip young things of Mumbai nightly – get out your Bollywood star-spotting logbook.

THE SUBURBS

Ghetto (Map pp780-1; ☎ 23538418; 30B Bhulabhai Desai Marg, Mahalaxmi; 7pm-1.30am) This graffiti-covered rocker's hang-out blares rock nightly to a dedicated set of regulars.

Shiro (off map pp780-1; ☎ 66155980; Bombay Dyeing Mills Compound, Worli; 7pm-1.30am) No lounge anywhere has ambience as soothing as Shiro's. Water pours from the hands of towering Balinese stone goddesses into lotus ponds, which reflect shimmering light on the walls. Lighting is soft and dramatic, with lots of candles (and good Japanese food).

Toto's Garage (Map p796; ☎ 26005494; 30 Lourdes Heaven, Pali Naka, Bandra West; 6pm-1am) Forget the beautiful people. Toto's is a local joint where you can go in your dirty clothes, drink beer and listen to '80s music with the locals. Get there early or you won't get a seat.

Vie Lounge (Map p796; ☎ 26603003; Juhu Tara Rd, Juhu; 4.30pm-1.30am) Right on Juhu Beach is this glamorous party spot (opposite Little Italy restaurant). The drinks menu is 18 pages long and includes aged imported whiskies. It's also a nice place for an early-evening coffee and snack. Call before coming to check there isn't a private Bollywood bash on.

Zenzi (Map p796; ☎ 66430670-2; 183 Waterfield Rd, Bandra West; 7pm-1am) This stylish hang-out pad is a favourite among the well-heeled.

Comfy lounges are sheltered by fairy lights and a tree growing out of one wall, and the burnt-orange decor is bathed in soft light. It's at its best when the canopy is open to the stars.

Olive Bar & Kitchen (Map p796; ☎ 26058228; Pali Hill Tourist Hotel, 14 Union Park, Khar West; ⏰ 7.30pm-1.30am) Hip, gorgeous and snooty, this Mediterranean-style restaurant and bar has light and delicious food, soothing DJ sounds and pure Ibiza decor. Thursday and weekends are packed. The opening of a new branch at Mahalaxmi Racecourse (open for lunch and dinner, till 1.30am), next to the Turf Club, made South Mumbai's rich and famous very happy.

ENTERTAINMENT

The daily English-language tabloid *Mid-Day* incorporates the *List*, a guide to Mumbai entertainment. Newspapers and *Time Out Mumbai* (p782) list events and film screenings, while www.gigpad.com has live-music listings.

Nightclubs

The big nights in clubs are Wednesday, Friday and Saturday, when there's usually a cover charge. Dress codes apply so don't rock up in shorts and sandals.

Enigma (Map p796; ☎ 66933288; JW Marriott, Juhu Tara Rd, Juhu; ⏰ 9.30pm-3am Wed-Sun) For Bollywood star-spotting, Enigma is the place to see and be seen. It doesn't get going till after midnight, but then it *really* gets going. The couples cover is Rs1000.

Ra (off Map pp780-1; ☎ 66614343; Phoenix Mills, Senapati Bapat Marg, Lower Parel; ⏰ 9pm-1.30am Wed-Sat) Where the city's beautiful people come to shake their money-makers. Ra's glass roof opens wide to the stars, and your wallet will open even wider to pay for its top-notch cocktails. Cover for couples is Rs1000, but you may be able to call ahead and get on the guest list.

Polly Esther's (Map p784; ☎ 22871122; Gordon House Hotel, Battery St, Colaba; cover per couple Rs800-1500; ⏰ 9pm-2.45am Tue-Sun) Wallowing in a cheesy time-warp of retro pop, rock and disco, this mirror-plated, groovy nightclub still manages to pull a crowd. It comes complete with a *Saturday Night Fever* illuminated dance floor and waiters in Afro wigs. Wednesday is free for the gals.

Voodoo Pub (Map p784; ☎ 22841959; Kamal Mansion, Arthur Bunder Rd, Colaba; cover Rs250; ⏰ 8.30pm-1.30am) Hosting Mumbai's only regular gay night (Saturday; cover Rs300), this dark and sweaty

bar has little going for it on other nights of the week.

Cinema

It would be a crime not to see a movie in India's film capital. Unfortunately, Hindi films aren't shown with English subtitles. The following all show English-language movies, along with some Bollywood numbers.

Eros (Map p786; ☎ 22822335; MK Rd, Churchgate; tickets Rs60-100)

Metro Big (Map p786; ☎ 39844060; MG Rd, New Marine Lines, Fort; tickets Rs250-750) This grand dame of Bombay talkies was just renovated into a multiplex.

Regal (Map p784; ☎ 22021017; Colaba Causeway, Colaba; tickets Rs100-150) Check out the art deco architecture.

Sterling (Map p786; ☎ 66220016; Marzaban Rd, Fort; tickets Rs120-150)

The lesbian and gay organisation **Bombay Dost** (http://bombay-dost.pbwiki.com) organises 'Sunday High', a twice-monthly screening of queer-interest films, usually in the suburbs.

Music, Dance & Theatre

Bluefrog (off map pp780-1; ☎ 40332300; www.bluefrog.co.in; D/2 Mathuradas Mills Compound, NM Joshi Marg, Lower Parel; admission after 9pm Sun & Tue-Thu Rs300, Fri & Sat Rs500; ⏰ 7pm-1am Tue-Sun) The most exciting thing to happen to Mumbai's music scene in a long time, Bluefrog is a concert space, production studio, restaurant and one of Mumbai's most happening spaces. It hosts exceptional local and international acts, and has cool booth seating.

Not Just Jazz By the Bay (Map p786; ☎ 22851876; 143 Marine Dr; admission weekdays/weekends Rs150/200; ⏰ noon-3.30am) This is the best, and frankly the only, jazz club in South Mumbai. True to its name, there are also live pop, blues and rock performers most nights, but Sunday, Monday and Tuesday are reserved for karaoke.

National Centre for the Performing Arts (NCPA; Map pp780-1; ☎ 66223737; www.ncpamumbai.com; cnr Marine Dr & Sri V Saha Rd, Nariman Point; tickets Rs200-500) Spanning 800 sq metres, this cultural centre is the hub of Mumbai's music, theatre and dance scene. In any given week, it might host Marathi theatre, poetry readings and art exhibitions, Bihari dance troupes, ensembles from Europe or Indian classical music. The Experimental Theatre occasionally has English-language plays. Many performances are free. The box office (☎ 22824567; open 9am to 7pm) is at the end of NCPA Marg.

THIEVES BAZAAR

Nobody is sure exactly how Mumbai's Chor Bazaar (literally 'thieves market') earned its moniker. One popular explanation has it that Queen Victoria, upon arrival to Mumbai in her steam ship, discovered that her violin/purse/jewellery went missing while being unloaded off the ship. Having scoured the city, the missing item was supposedly found hanging in Chor Bazaar's Mutton St, and hence the name.

Prithvi Theatre (Map p796; ☎ 26149546; www.prithvi theatre.org; Juhu Church Rd, Juhu) At Juhu Beach, this is a good place to see both Hindi and English-language theatre. It hosts an excellent annual international theatre festival, too.

The **Nehru Centre** (p791) occasionally stages dance, music and English-language theatre performances.

Sport
CRICKET
To prepare for the Cricket World Cup final in February/March 2011, **Wankhede Stadium** (Mumbai Cricket Association; Map p786; ☎ 22795500; www.mumbaicricket.com; D Rd, Churchgate) is closed until the end of 2010 for a massive renovation. When open, test matches and One Day Internationals are played a few times a year in season (October to April). Contact the Cricket Association for ticket information; for a test match you'll probably have to pay for the full five days.

FOOTBALL
The **Cooperage Football Ground** (Map p784; ☎ 22024020; MK Rd, Colaba; tickets Rs20-25) is home to the Mumbai Football Association and hosts national-league and local soccer matches between October and February. Tickets are available at the gate.

SHOPPING
Mumbai is India's great marketplace, with some of the best shopping in the country. Colaba Causeway is lined with hawkers' stalls and shops selling garments, perfumes and knick-knacks. Electronic gear, pirated CDs and DVDs, leather goods and mass-produced gizmos are for sale at stalls on Dr Dadabhai Naoroji Rd between CST and Flora Fountain, and along MG Rd from Flora Fountain to Kala Ghoda.

Antiques & Curios
Small antique and curio shops line Merewether Rd behind the Taj Mahal Palace & Tower (Map p784). They aren't cheap, but the quality is a step up from government emporiums.

If you prefer Raj-era bric-a-brac, head to Chor Bazaar (Map pp780–1); the main area of activity is Mutton St, where you'll find a row of shops specialising in antiques (and many ingenious reproductions, so beware) and miscellaneous junk.

Mini Market (Map pp780-1; ☎ 23472427; 33/31 Mutton St; ⊙ 11am-8pm Sat-Thu) Sells original vintage Bollywood posters and other movie ephemera as well as odd and interesting trinkets.

Phillips (Map p784; ☎ 22020564; www.phillipsantiques .com; Wodehouse Rd, Colaba; ⊙ 10am-7pm Mon-Sat) The 150-year-old Phillips has nizam-era royal silver, wooden ceremonial masks, Victorian glass and various other gorgeous things that you never knew you wanted. It also has high-quality reproductions of old photos, maps and paintings, and a new warehouse shop of big antiques.

Clothes
Snap up a bargain backpacking wardrobe at Fashion Street, the strip of stalls lining MG Rd between Cross and Azad maidans (Map p786), or in Bandra's Linking Rd (Map p796); hone your bargaining skills. Kemp's Corner has many good shops for designer threads.

Fabindia (Map p786; ☎ 22626539; Jeroo Bldg, 137 MG Rd, Kala Ghoda; ⊙ 10am-7.45pm) Founded as a means to get traditional fabric artisans' wares to market, Fabindia has all the vibrant colours of the country in its cotton and silk fashions, materials and homewares. in modern-meets-traditional Indian shop. The Santa Cruz outpost (Map p796) is also good.

Khadi & Village Industries Emporium (Khadi Bhavan; Map p786; ☎ 22073280/8; 286 Dr Dadabhai Naoroji Rd, Fort; ⊙ 10.30am-6.30pm Mon-Sat) All dusty and old school, Khadi Bhavan is 1940s time-warp with ready-made traditional Indian clothing, material, shoes and handicrafts that are so old they're new again.

More good shopping:

Anokhi (⊙ 10am-7.30pm Mon-Sat) Chowpatty (Map pp780-1; ☎ 23685761; AR Rangnekar Marg, off Hughes Rd) Bandra West (Map p796; ☎ 26408261; Waterfield Rd) Gets the East–West balance just right, with men's and women's clothes and bedding in block-printed silk and cotton.

Biba (Map pp780-1; ☎ 23894184; 1 Hughes Rd, Kemp's

Corner; 10.30am-9pm Mon-Sat) Gorgeous salwar kurtas with just the right amount of bling.

Cotton Cottage (Map p786; ☎ 22674026; Agra Bldg, MG Rd, Kala Ghoda; 10am-8.30pm) Stock up on simple cotton kurtas and various pants – salwars, *churidars*, *patiala* – for the road.

Cottonworld Corp (Map p784; ☎ 22850060; Mandlik Marg; 10.30am-8pm Mon-Sat, noon-8pm Sun) Small chain selling stylish Indian–Western-hybrid goods. Entrance is behind the State Bank of India.

Courtyard (Map p784; SP Centre, 41/44 Minoo Desai Marg; 11am-7.30pm) A collection of couture boutiques. Good if you're interested in India's fashion design scene.

Kala Niketan (Map p786; ☎ 22005001; 95 MK Rd; 10am-8pm Mon-Sat) Sari madness on Queens Rd.

Mélange (Map pp780–1; ☎ 23534492; 33 Altamount Rd, Kemp's Corner; 10am-7pm Mon-Sat) High-fashion garments from 70 Indian designers in a chic exposed-brick space. Payal Singhal, next door, is also good.

Telon (Map pp780–1; ☎ 23648174; 149 Warden Rd, Kemp's Corner; 10.30am-8.30pm Mon-Sat) Fine gents tailor. Suits to order start at Rs13,000.

Handicrafts & Gifts
Various state-government emporiums sell handicrafts in the World Trade Centre Arcade (Map pp780–1) near Cuffe Parade.

Bombay Store (Map p786; 40669999; Western India House, Sir PM Rd, Fort; 10.30am-7.30pm Mon-Sat, to 6.30pm Sun) A classy selection of rugs, clothing, teas, stationery, aromatherapy and brass sculptures.

Bombay Paperie (Map p786; ☎ 66358171; 59 Bombay Samachar Marg, Fort; 10.30am-6pm Mon-Sat) Sells handmade, cotton-based paper crafted into charming cards, sculptures and lampshades.

Shrujan Juhu (Map p796; ☎ 26183104; Hatkesh Society, 6th North South Rd, JVPD Scheme; 9.30am-7pm Mon-Sat) Breach Candy (Map pp780–1; ☎ 23521693; Sagar Villa, Warden Rd, opposite Navroze Apts; 10am-7.30pm Mon-Sat) Selling the intricate embroidery work of women in 114 villages in Kutch, Gujarat, the nonprofit Shrujan aims to help women earn a livelihood while preserving the spectacular embroidery traditions of the area. The sophisticated clothing, wall hangings and purses make great gifts.

Other stores worth popping into:

Central Cottage Industries Emporium (Map p784; ☎ 22027537; Chhatrapati Shivaji Marg, Colaba; 10am-7pm) Easy-breezy souvenir shopping.

Chimanlals (Map p786; ☎ 22077717; Dr Dadabhai Naoroji Rd, Fort; 9.30am-6pm Mon-Sat) Writing materials made from traditional Indian paper. Enter from Wallace St.

Inshaallah Mashaallah (Map p784; ☎ 22049495; Best Marg, Colaba; 10.30am-8pm) Local oils and perfumes in antediluvian bottles; the rose is popular (Rs250 for 12ml).

Markets
You can buy just about anything in the dense bazaars north of CST (see Map pp780–1). The main areas are Crawford Market (fruit and veg), Mangaldas Market (silk and cloth), Zaveri Bazaar (jewellery), Bhuleshwar Market (fruit and veg) and Chor Bazaar (antiques and furniture), where Dhabu St is lined with fine leather goods and Mutton St specialises in antiques, reproductions and fine junk.

Crawford Market (Mahatma Phule Market) is the last outpost of British Bombay before the tumult of the central bazaars begins. Bas-reliefs by Rudyard Kipling's father, Lockwood Kipling, adorn the Norman Gothic exterior. The meat market is strictly for the brave.

Music
LM Furtado & Co (Map pp780–1; ☎ 22013163; 540-544 Kalbadevi Rd, Kalbadevi; 10am-8pm Mon-Sat) The best place in Mumbai for musical instruments – sitars, tablas, accordions and local and imported guitars. It also has a branch around the corner on Lokmanya Tilak Rd.

For nonpirated CDs and DVDs, visit **Planet M** (Map p786; ☎ 22071148; Dr Dadabhai Naoroji Rd, Fort; 10.30am-10.30pm) or, our fave, **Rhythm House** (Map p786; 22842835; 40 K Dubash Marg, Fort; 10am-8.30pm Mon-Sat, 11am-8.30pm Sun), which also sells tickets to concerts, plays and festivals.

GETTING THERE & AWAY
Air
AIRPORTS
Mumbai is the main international gateway to South India and has the busiest network

MAJOR NONSTOP DOMESTIC FLIGHTS (ONE WAY) FROM MUMBAI			
Destination	Lowest OW Fare (Rs)	Duration (hr)	Flights per Day
Bengaluru	4700	1½	32
Chennai	5100	1¾	24
Delhi	5000	2	60
Goa	4100	1	21
Hyderabad	3000	1¼	22
Jaipur	4800	1¾	6
Kochi	4800	1¾	18
Kolkata	5700	2¾	22

of domestic flights. The **Chhatrapati Shivaji International Airport** (☎ domestic 26264000, international 26813000; www.csia.in), about 30km from downtown, comprises two domestic and two international terminals. However, the domestic side is accessed via Vile Parle and is known locally as Santa Cruz airport, while the international, with its entrance 4km away in Andheri, goes locally by Sahar. Both terminals have ATMs, foreign-exchange counters and tourist-information booths (p783). A free shuttle bus runs between the two every 30 minutes.

INTERNATIONAL AIRLINES

Travel agencies are often better for booking international flights, while airline offices are increasingly directing customers to their call centres.

Air France (off Map pp780–1; ☎ 1800 180033; Sarjan Plaza, 100 Dr Annie Besant Rd, Worli; ⊗ 9am–1pm & 1.30-5pm Mon-Fri)

Air India (Map p786; ☎ 26818098, airport 26168000; Air India Bldg, cnr Marine Dr & Madame Cama Rd, Nariman Point; ⊗ 9.30am-5.30pm)

American Airlines (off Map pp780–1; ☎ 18002001800; 114 Nirman Kendra, Dr E Moses Rd, Mahalaxmi; ⊗ 9am-6pm Mon-Fri, 10am-2pm Sat)

British Airways (Map p796; ☎ 9892577470, 1800 10235922; Notan Plaza, Turner Rd, Bandra West; ⊗ 9.30am-1pm Mon, Wed, Fri)

Cathay Pacific (off Map pp780–1; ☎ 66572222, airport 66859002/3; 2 Brady Gladys Plaza, Senapati Bapat Marg, Lower Parel; ⊗ 9.30am-6.30pm Mon-Sat)

Delta Airlines (Map pp780–1; ☎ 22839712-5; Interglobe Enterprises Ltd, 12th fl, Bajaj Bhawan, Nariman Point; ⊗ 9am-5.30pm Mon-Sat)

El Al Airlines (Map pp780–1; ☎ 22154701, airport 66859425/6; 57 The Arcade, World Trade Centre, Cuffe Parade; ⊗ 9.30am-5.30pm Mon-Fri, to 1pm Sat)

Qantas (Map p786; ☎ 22007440; Godrej Bhavan, 2nd fl, Home St, Fort; ⊗ 9am-1.15pm & 2.30-5.30pm Mon-Fri)

Thai Airways (Map pp780–1; ☎ 66373737; Mittal Towers A Wing, 2A, Nariman Point; ⊗ 9.30am-5pm Mon-Fri, to 4pm Sat)

Virgin Atlantic (Map p786; ☎ 67523701-5; Poddar House, 10 Marine Dr, Churchgate; ⊗ 9.15am-5.30pm)

DOMESTIC AIRLINES

The following all have ticketing counters at the domestic airport; most open 24 hours.

Go Air (☎ 9223222111)

Indian Airlines (Map p786; ☎ 22023031, call centre 18001801407; Air India Bldg, cnr Marine Dr & Madame Cama Rd, Nariman Point)

IndiGo (☎ call centre 18001803838, airport 26156774)

Jet Airways (Map p784; ☎ 39893333, airport 26266575; Amarchand Mansion, Madame Cama Rd; ⊗ 9am-7pm Mon-Fri, 9am-5.30pm Sat, 9.30am-1.30pm Sun) Also handles JetLite bookings.

JetLite (☎ airport 30302020)

Kingfisher (Map p786; ☎ 40340500, airport 26262605; Nirmal Bldg, Marine Dr, Nariman Point; ⊗ 9am-7pm Mon-Sat, 10am-2pm Sun)

SpiceJet (☎ call centre 9871803333, 18001803333)

Bus

Numerous private operators and state governments run long-distance buses to and from Mumbai.

Private buses are usually more comfortable and simpler to book but can cost significantly more than government buses; they depart from Dr Anadrao Nair Rd near Mumbai Central train station (Map pp780–1). Fares to popular destinations (like Goa) are up to 75% higher during holiday periods. To check on departure times and current prices, try **National Travels** (Map pp780–1; ☎ 23015652; Dr Anadrao Nair Rd; ⊗ 7am-10pm).

More convenient for Goa and southern destinations are the private buses (Map p786) that depart twice a day from in front of Azad Maidan, just south of the Metro cinema. Ticket agents are located near the bus departure point.

Long-distance government-run buses depart from **Mumbai Central bus terminal** (Map pp780–1; ☎ 23074272/1524) by Mumbai Central train station. Buses service major towns in Maharashtra and neighbouring states. They're cheaper and more frequent than private services, but the quality and crowd levels vary.

Fares for popular routes:

Destination	Fare (Rs)	Duration (hr)
Ahmedabad	220/350-400*	13
Aurangabad	200/350	10
Mahabaleshwar	180/300-450	7
Panaji	410/550-800	14-18
Pune	120/220-250	4
Udaipur	390/550-800	16

* Fares are for private/government non-AC buses.

Train

Three train systems operate running out of Mumbai, but the most important services for travellers are Central Railways and Western Railways. Tickets for either system can be

MAJOR TRAINS FROM MUMBAI

Destination	Train No & name	Fare (Rs)	Duration (hr)	Departure
Agra	2137 *Punjab Mail*	417/1118/1528	22	7.40pm CST
Ahmedabad	2901 *Gujarat Mail*	235/604/816	9	9.50pm MC
Aurangabad	7057 *Devagiri Exp*	178/471/643	7	9.05pm CST
	7617 *Tapovan Exp*	103/369*	7	6.10am CST
Bengaluru	6529 *Udyan Exp*	377/1031/1420	25	8.05am CST
Bhopal	2137 *Punjab Mail*	330/872/1188	14	7.40pm CST
Chennai	1041 *Chennai Exp*	389/1095/1467	27	2.00pm CST
Delhi	2951 *Rajdhani Exp*	1495/1975/3305**	16	4.40pm MC
	2137 *Punjab Mail*	449/1208/1653	25½	7.40pm CST
Margao	0103 *Mandavi Exp*	293/796/1092	11½	6.55am CST
	2051 *Shatabdi Exp*	197/680*	9	5.10am CST
Hyderabad	2701 *Hussainsagar Exp*	317/837/1139	14½	9.50pm CST
Indore	2961 *Avantika Exp*	325/861/1171	14½	7.05pm MC
Jaipur	2955 *Jaipur Exp*	389/1039/1419	18	6.50pm MC
Kochi	6345 *Netravati Exp*	441/1211/1670	26½	11.40pm T
Kolkata	2859 *Gitanjali Exp*	517/1399/1918	30½	6.00am CST
	2809 *Howrah Mail*	490/1399/1918	33	8.35pm CST
Pune	2125 *Pragati Exp*	77/270*	3½	5.10pm CST
Varanasi	1093 *Mahanagari Exp*	406/1178/1623	2½	12.10am CST
Trivandrum	6345 *Netravati Exp*	473/1301/1795	30	11.40am T

Station abbreviations: CST (Chhatrapati Shivaji Terminus); MC (Mumbai Central); T (Lokmanya Tilak); D (Dadar).
Note: Fares are for sleeper/3AC/2AC except for: *2nd/CC, **3AC/2AC/1AC.

bought from any station, in South Mumbai or the suburbs, that has computerised ticketing.

Central Railways (☎ 134), handling services to the east, south, plus a few trains to the north, operates from CST. The **reservation centre** (Map p786; ☎ 137; 🕑 8am-8pm Mon-Sat, to 2pm Sun) is around the side of CST where the taxis gather. **Foreign tourist-quota tickets** (Counter 52) can be bought up to 90 days before travel, but must be paid in foreign currency or with rupees backed by an encashment certificate or ATM receipt. Indrail passes (p1190) can also be bought at Counter 52. You can buy nonquota tickets with a Visa or MasterCard at the much faster credit-card counters (10 and 11) for a Rs30 fee.

Some Central Railways trains depart from Dadar (D), a few stations north of CST, or Churchgate/Lokmanya Tilak (T), 16km north of CST.

Western Railways (☎ 131, 132) has services to the north (including Rajasthan and Delhi) from Mumbai Central (MC) train station (☎ 23061763, 23073535), usually called Bombay Central. The **reservation centre** (Map p786; 🕑 8am-8pm Mon-Sat, to 2pm Sun), opposite Churchgate train station, has a **foreign tourist-quota counter** (Counter 28) upstairs next to the Government of India tourist office. The same rules apply as at CST station. The credit-card counter is No 20.

GETTING AROUND
To/From the Airports
INTERNATIONAL
The prepaid-taxi booth that is located at the international airport has set fares for every neighbourhood in the city; Colaba, Fort and Marine Dr are Rs325, Bandra and Juhu Rs200. There's a 25% surcharge between midnight and 5am and, at all times, a Rs10 service charge and a charge of Rs10 per bag. The journey to Colaba takes about 45 minutes at night and 1½ to two hours during the day. Tips are not required.

Autorickshaws queue up at a little distance from Arrivals, but don't try to take one to South Mumbai: they can only go as far as Mahim Creek. You can catch an autorickshaw (around Rs30) to Andheri train station, though, and catch a suburban train (Rs9, 45 minutes) to Churchgate or CST. Only attempt this if you arrive during the day outside of rush 'hour' (6am to 11am) and are not weighed down with luggage. At the very least, buy a 1st-class ticket (Rs86).

Minibuses outside Arrivals offer free shuttle services to the domestic airport and Juhu hotels.

A taxi from South Mumbai to the international airport shouldn't cost more than Rs400 with the meter by negotiating a fixed fare beforehand; official baggage charges are Rs10 per bag. Add 25% to the meter charge between midnight and 5am. We love the old-school black-and-yellows, but there's also **Meru** (☎ 44224422; www.merucabs.com), AC, metered call taxis charging Rs15 for the first km and Rs13 each km thereafter (25% more at night). Colaba to the airport will cost around Rs400, and the route is tracked by GPS, so no rip-offs!

DOMESTIC

Taxis and autorickshaws queue up outside both domestic terminals. There are no prepaid counters, but both queues are controlled by the police – make sure your driver uses the meter and conversion card. A taxi to Colaba costs around Rs350.

If you don't have too much luggage, bus No 2 (limited) stops on nearby Nehru Rd and passes through Colaba Causeway (Rs18). Coming from the city, it stops on the highway opposite the airport.

A better alternative is to catch an autorickshaw between the airport and Vile Parle train station (Rs15), and a train between Vile Parle and Churchgate (Rs9, 45 minutes). Don't attempt this during rush hour (6am to 11am).

Boat

Both **PNP** (☎ 22885220) and **Maldar Catamarans** (☎ 22829695) run regular ferries to Mandwa (Rs110 one-way), useful for access to Murud-Janjira and other parts of the Konkan Coast (p832), avoiding the long bus trip out of Mumbai. Their ticket offices are at Apollo Bunder (near the Gateway of India; Map p784).

Bus

Mumbai's single- and double-decker buses are good for travelling short distances. Fares around South Mumbai cost Rs3 for a section; pay the conductor once you're aboard. The service is run by **BEST** (Map p784; ☎ 22856262; www .bestundertaking.com), which has a depot in Colaba

Destination	Bus No
Breach Candy	132, 133
Chowpatty	103, 106, 107, 123
Churchgate	70, 106, 123, 132
Haji Ali	83, 124, 132, 133
Hanging Gardens	103, 106
Mani Bhavan	123
Mohammed Ali Rd	1, 3, 21
Mumbai Central train station	124, 125
CST & Crawford Market	1, 3, 21, 103, 124

(the website has a useful search facility for bus routes across the city). Just jumping on a double-decker bus (such as No 103) is an inexpensive way to see South Mumbai. Day passes are available for Rs15.

In the table above are some useful bus routes; all of these buses depart from the bus stand at the southern end of Colaba Causeway and pass Flora Fountain.

Car

Cars are generally hired for an eight-hour day and an 80km maximum, with additional charges if you go over. For an AC car, the best going rate is Rs1000.

Agents at the Apollo Bunder ticket booths near the Gateway of India can arrange a non-AC Maruti with driver for a half-day of sightseeing for Rs700 (going as far as Mahalaxmi and Malabar Hill). Regular taxi drivers often accept a similar price.

Motorcycle

Allibhai Premji Tyrewalla (Map pp780-1; ☎ 23099313; www.premjis.com; 205/207 Dr D Bhadkamkar Rd, Opera House; ☉ 10am-7pm Mon-Sat), around for almost 100 years, sells new and used motorcycles with a guaranteed buy-back option. For two- to three-week 'rental' periods you'll still have to pay the full cost of the bike upfront. The company prefers to deal with longer-term schemes of two months or more, which work out cheaper anyway. A used 350cc or 500cc Enfield costs Rs25,000 to 80,000, with a buy-back price of around 60% after three months. A smaller bike (100cc to 180cc) starts at Rs25,000. It can also arrange shipment of bikes overseas (around Rs24,000 to the UK).

Taxi & Autorickshaw

Every second car on Mumbai's streets seems to be a black-and-yellow Premier taxi (India's version of a 1950s Fiat). They're the most convenient way to get around the city, and in South Mumbai drivers almost always use the meter without prompting. Autorickshaws are confined to the suburbs north of Mahim Creek.

Drivers don't always know the names of Mumbai's streets (especially new names) – the best way to find something is by using nearby landmarks. The taxi meters are out of date, so the fare is calculated using a conversion chart, which all drivers must carry. The rate during the day is around 13 times the meter reading, with a minimum fare of Rs13 for the first 1.6km (flag fall) and Rs7 per kilometre after this. Add 30% between midnight and 5am.

If you're north of Mahim Creek and not heading into the city, catch an autorickshaw. They're also metered: the fare is 10 times the meter reading, minus one. Flag fall is Rs9 (the meter will read 1.00). Add 25% between midnight and 5am.

Train

Mumbai has an efficient but overcrowded suburban train network.

There are three main lines, making it easy to navigate. The most useful service operates from Churchgate heading north to stations such as Charni Rd (for Chowpatty), Mumbai Central, Mahalaxmi (for the dhobi ghat; p790), Vile Parle (for the domestic airport), Andheri (for the international airport) and Borivali (for Sanjay Gandhi National Park). Other suburban lines operate from CST to Byculla (for Veermata Jijabai Bhonsle Udyan, formerly Victoria Gardens), Dadar and as far as Neral (for Matheran). Trains run from 4am till 1am. From Churchgate, 2nd-/1st-class fares are Rs6/44 to Mumbai Central, Rs9/78 to Vile Parle or Andheri and Rs11/104 to Borivali.

'Tourist tickets' are available, which permit unlimited travel in 2nd/1st class for one (Rs50/180), three (Rs90/330) or five (Rs105/390) days.

Avoid rush hours when trains are jam-packed, even in 1st class; watch your valuables, and gals, stick to the ladies-only carriages.

GREATER MUMBAI

ELEPHANTA ISLAND

In the middle of Mumbai Harbour, 9km northeast of the Gateway of India, the rock-cut temples on **Elephanta Island** (Map p778; http://asi.nic

.in/; Indian/foreigner Rs10/250; ☺ caves 9am-5pm Tue-Sun) are a Unesco World Heritage Site and worth crossing the waters for. Home to a labyrinth of cave-temples carved into the basalt rock of the island, the artwork represents some of the most impressive temple carving in all of India. The main Shiva-dedicated temple is an intriguing latticework of courtyards, halls, pillars and shrines, with the magnum opus a 6m-tall statue of Sadhashiva – depicting a three-faced Shiva as the destroyer, creator and preserver of the universe. The enormous central bust of Shiva, its eyes closed in eternal contemplation, may be the most serene sight you witness in India.

The temples are thought to have been created between AD 450 and 750, when the island was known as Gharapuri (Place of Caves). The Portuguese renamed it Elephanta because of a large stone elephant near the shore, which collapsed in 1814 and was moved by the British to Mumbai's Veermata Jijabai Bhonsle Udyan.

The English-language guide service (free with deluxe boat tickets) is worthwhile; tours depart every hour on the half-hour from the ticket booth. If you explore independently, pick up Pramod Chandra's *A Guide to the Elephanta Caves* from the stalls lining the stairway. There's also a small **museum** on site, which has some informative pictorial panels on the origin of the caves.

Getting There & Away

Launches (economy/deluxe Rs100/130) head to Elephanta Island from the Gateway of India every half-hour from 9am to 3.30pm Tuesday to Sunday. Buy tickets at the booths lining Apollo Bunder. The voyage takes just over an hour.

The ferries dock at the end of a concrete pier, from where you can walk (around three minutes) or take the miniature train (Rs10) to the stairway (Rs5) leading up to the caves. It's lined with handicraft stalls and patrolled by pesky monkeys. Wear good shoes.

SANJAY GANDHI NATIONAL PARK

It's hard to believe that within 90 minutes of the teeming metropolis you can be surrounded by this 104-sq-km **protected tropical forest** (Map p778; ☎ 28866449; adult/child Rs30/15, 2-/4-wheeler vehicle Rs15/50; ☺ 7.30am-6pm). Here, bright flora, birds, butterflies and elusive wild leopards replace pollution and crowds, all surrounded by forested hills on the city's northern edge.

Urban development and shantytowns try to muscle in on the edges of this wild region, but its status as a national park has allowed it to stay green and calm.

One of the main attractions is the **lion & tiger safari** (adult/child Rs30/15; ☼ every 20min 9.20am-12.40pm & 2-5.30pm Tue-Sun), departing from the tiger orientation centre (about 1km in from the main entrance). Expect a whirlwind 20-minute jaunt by bus through the two separate areas of the park housing the tigers and lions.

Inside the main northern entrance is an information centre with a small exhibition on the park's wildlife. The best time to see birds is October to April and butterflies August to November.

Another big draw is the 109 **Kanheri Caves** (Indian/foreigner Rs5/100; ☼ 9.30am-5pm Tue-Sun) lin-

ing the side of a rocky ravine 5km from the northern park entrance. They were used by Buddhist monks between the 2nd and 9th centuries as *viharas* (monasteries) and *chaityas* (temples), but don't compare to the caves at Ajanta (p825), Ellora (p822) or even Lonavla (p835).

Mumbai's main conservation organisation, the Bombay Natural History Society (p791) can provide more information on the park and occasionally offers trips here.

Getting There & Away

Take the train from Churchgate to Borivali (Rs11, one hour). From there take an autorickshaw (Rs15) or catch any bus to the park entrance. It's a further 10-minute walk from the entrance to the safari park.

Maharashtra

Stretching from the unspoilt greens of the sleepy Konkan Coast, all the way into the parched innards of India's throbbing heartland, Maharashtra packs in enough wonders to satisfy even the pickiest of travellers. Being India's second most populous state (and third largest by area), its gigantic canvas is painted with a smattering of lazy beaches, lofty mountains, virgin forests and historical hot spots, complemented by the famed sights, sounds, tastes and experiences of India.

Up north, there's Nasik, where riotous colours blend with timeless Hindu ritual. Down south, modern India comes of age in Pune, a city as famous for its sex guru as its food-and-beverage circuit. Further south still, in Kolhapur, cameras work overtime to capture overwhelming temples, extravagant palaces and grimy action in the wrestling pits. Deep in the eastern crannies, the adventurous can pitch tent in Nagpur, before setting out to spy tigers hidden in the thickets. Out west, along the shores of the Arabian Sea, the emerald greens conceal a rash of pristine, white sands that give Goa's tropical dreams a run for their money. Within spitting distance, the hills of the Western Ghats await with their stupendous views and quaint hill stations. And located in the midst of it all are the architectural and artistic wonders of the state, topped by the World Heritage–listed cave temples of Ellora and Ajanta. Whichever way you look at it, Maharashtra is truly one of the most vibrant and rewarding corners of India.

HIGHLIGHTS

- Drop your jaws at the awe-inspiring beauty of the monumental Kailasa Temple, the shining jewel of the cave temples at **Ellora** (p822)

- Choose between sipping chardonnay among the vines or losing yourself in a holy confluence of colours, faith and rituals in **Nasik** (p813)

- Gasp in wonder upon being mesmer-ised by antique Buddhist art in the cave galleries of **Ajanta** (p825)

- Bite into a fresh catch of marine good-ies or hunt out serene beaches, ele-phant temples and tumbling fortresses along the **Konkan Coast** (p831)

- Gallop on a horse to Echo Point, or simply outrun the toy train chugging up the slopes in **Matheran** (p833)

- Learn how to make friends with snakes, and pick up the basics of 'zennis' (Zen tennis) in **Pune** (p846)

★Ajanta
★Nasik ★Ellora
★Matheran
★Pune
★Konkan Coast

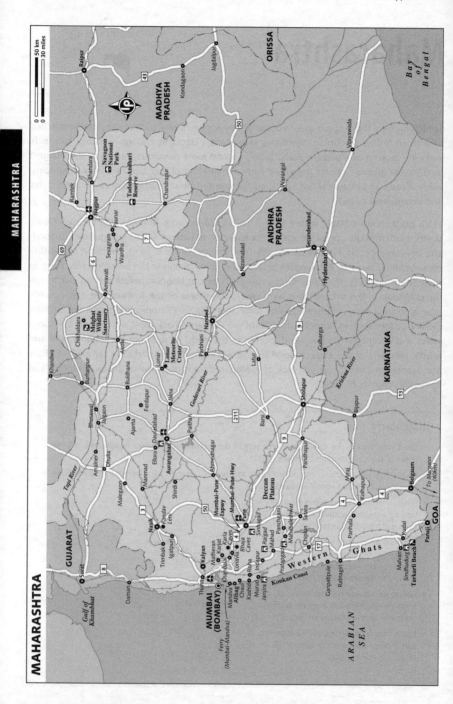

MAHARASHTRA

FAST FACTS

Population 96.8 million
Area 307,690 sq km
Capital Mumbai (Bombay)
Main languages Marathi, Hindi, English
When to go October to March (coast); September to mid-June (hills)

History

Maharashtra was given its political and ethnic identity by Maratha leader Chhatrapati Shivaji (1627–80) who, from his stronghold at Raigad, lorded over the Deccan and much of western India through his reign. Still highly respected among Maharashtrians, Shivaji is credited for instilling a strong, independent spirit among the region's people, apart from establishing Maharashtra as a dominant player in the power equations of medieval India.

From the early 18th century, the state was under the administration of a succession of ministers called the Peshwas who ruled until 1819, ceding thereafter to the British. After Independence, western Maharashtra and Gujarat were joined to form Bombay state, only to be separated again in 1960, when modern Maharashtra, was formed with the exclusion of Gujarati-speaking areas, with Mumbai as its capital.

Climate

Maharashtra is left drenched by the seasonal monsoons from May through September. The rest of the year, you can expect the coastal and interior regions to be hot; for some respite head to the hill stations of the Western Ghats.

Information

The head office of the **Maharashtra Tourism Development Corporation** (MTDC; Map p786; ☎ 022-22845678; www.maharashtratourism.gov.in; Madame Cama Rd, Nariman Point; ☼ 10am-5.30pm Mon-Sat) is in Mumbai. Most major towns throughout the state have offices, too, but they're generally only useful for booking MTDC accommodation and tours. For in-depth information, Mumbai remains the safest bet. While Sunday is the weekly day off, many offices are closed on alternate Saturdays.

ACCOMMODATION

In Maharashtra, rooms costing Rs1199 or less are charged a 4% tax, while those that are Rs1200 and up are slapped a 10% tax. Some hotels also levy an extra expenditure tax (up to 10%). Rates in this chapter do not include taxes unless otherwise indicated. High-season rates are quoted, but prices might rise, sometimes unreasonably, during local holidays such as Diwali and New Year's Eve. Many places in Maharashtra also have government-approved homestays which are listed on the MTDC website www.maharashtratourism.gov.in.

Getting There & Away

Mumbai (p805) is Maharashtra's main transport hub, although Pune (p851), Jalgaon (p828) and Aurangabad (p821) are also major players.

Getting Around

Because the state is so large, internal flights (eg Mumbai to Nagpur) can help speed up your explorations. Airfares vary widely on a daily basis. Prices quoted here exclude taxes, which can sometimes be double the ticket amount. A cheaper and more exciting way to get around is by hopping onto trains or long-distance buses, of which there are plenty. The **Maharashtra State Road Transport Corporation** (MSRTC) has a superb semideluxe bus network spanning all major towns, with the more remote places being served by ordinary buses. Some private operators have luxury Volvo services connecting major cities; **Neeta Volvo** (☎ 022-28902666; www.neetavolvo.com) is highly recommended. AC Indica taxis are readily available too, and charge around Rs7 per kilometre. For long trips, factor in a minimum daily distance of 250km, and a daily driver's allowance of Rs150.

NORTHERN MAHARASHTRA

NASIK

☎ 0253 / pop 1.2 million / elev 565m

Standing on the Godavari, one of India's holiest rivers, Nasik (or Nashik) derives its name from the episode in the Ramayana where Lakshmana, Rama's brother, hacked off the *nasika* (nose) of Ravana's sister, the demon enchantress Surpanakha. True to its name, the town is an absorbing place with many associations with the Hindu epic, where you can't walk more than a few steps without chancing upon an exotic temple or colourful bathing ghat.

Adding to its religious flavour is the fact that Nasik also serves as a base for pilgrims visiting Trimbak (p817) and Shirdi (79km southeast), birthplace of the original Sai Baba. Every 12 years, Nasik plays host to the grand Kumbh Mela, the largest religious gathering on earth that shuttles between four Indian religious hot spots, and is held every three years. The next one in Nasik is due in 2015; see the boxed text, p838.

Orientation

Mahatma Gandhi Rd, better known as MG Rd, a few blocks north of the Old Central bus stand, is Nasik's commercial hub. The temple-strewn Godavari River flows through town just east of here.

Information

Cyber Café (Vakil Wadi Rd; per hr Rs20; ☉ 10am-10pm) Near Panchavati Hotel Complex.

HDFC Bank (MG Rd) Has a 24-hour ATM.

MTDC tourist office (☎ 2570059; T/I, Golf Club, Old Agra Rd; ☉ 10.30am-5.30pm Mon-Sat) About 700m

south of the Old Central bus stand. Sells a useless city map (Rs5).

State Bank of India (☎ 2502436; Old Agra Rd; ☉ 11am-5pm Mon-Fri, 11am-1pm Sat) Opposite the Old Central bus stand. Changes cash and travellers cheques and has an ATM.

Sights

RAMKUND

This **bathing tank** in the heart of Nasik's old quarters sees hundreds of Hindu pilgrims arriving daily to bathe, pray and, because the waters provide moksha (liberation of the soul), to immerse the ashes of departed friends and family. For a tourist, it's an intense cultural experience, which is taken a notch further by the colourful **market** just downstream. It's OK to take photographs, but try not to be intrusive.

TEMPLES

A short walk uphill east of the Ramkund, the **Kala Rama Temple** is the city's holiest shrine. Dating to 1794 and containing unusual black-stone representations of Rama, Sita and Lakshmana, the temple stands on the

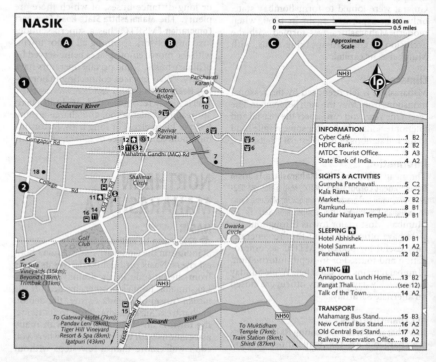

NASIK

0 ——————— 800 m
0 ——————— 0.5 miles

Approximate Scale

Godavari River

Gangapur Rd

To Sula Vineyards (15km); Beyond (18km); Trimbak (31km)

To Gateway Hotel (7km); Pandav Leni (8km); Tiger Hill Vineyard Resort & Spa (8km); Igatpuri (43km)

Panchavati Karanja

Victoria Bridge

Ravivar Karanja

Mahatma Gandhi (MG) Rd

Shalimar Circle

College Rd

Golf Club

Dwarka Circle

NH3

NH3

NH50

Nasardi River

Nasik-Mumbai Rd

To Muktidham Temple (7km); Train Station (8km); Shirdi (87km)

MAHARASHTRA

FESTIVALS IN MAHARASHTRA

Ellora Dance & Music Festival (Mar; Ellora, p822) A popular classical music and dance festival held at the caves.

Naag Panchami (Aug; Pune, p846 & Kolhapur, p855) A slithery snake-worshipping festival.

Ganesh Chaturthi (Aug & Sep; Pune, p846) Ganesh Chaturthi is celebrated with fervour across Maharashtra, but one of the best places to be is Pune, where a host of cultural events accompany the general mayhem for the elephant-headed deity.

Dussehra (Sep & Oct; Nagpur, p829) Being a Hindu festival, this is also when thousands of Buddhists celebrate the anniversary of the famous humanist and Dalit leader Dr BR Ambedkar's conversion to Buddhism.

Kalidas Festival (Nov; Nagpur, p829) A music and dance festival dedicated to the legendary Sanskrit poet Kalidas.

Sawai Gandharva (Dec; Pune, p846) Features night-long sessions of Indian classical music and dance performances.

---

site where Lakshmana sliced off Surpanakha's nose. Nearby is the **Gumpha Panchavati**, where Sita supposedly hid from the evil Ravana.

The ramshackle **Sundar Narayan Temple**, at the western end of Victoria Bridge, contains three black Vishnu deities, while the modern **Muktidham Temple**, about 7km southeast of the city near the train station, has 18 chapters of the Bhagavad Gita lining its interior walls.

All temples listed here are open from 6am to 9pm.

Sleeping & Eating

Hotel Abhishek (☎ 2514201; hotabhi_nsk@sancharnet.in; Panchavati Karanja; s/d from Rs340/435) Boasting value-for-money rooms with hot showers and TV, this budget option scores over its rivals thanks to its location. A few minutes' walk uphill from the Godavari River, it sits amid all the ritualistic action, and is a vantage point from which to be totally overwhelmed by sacred India at its best (and noisiest).

Panchavati (430 Chandak Wadi, Vakil Vadi) To save yourself the hassles of scouting for a comfy bed in town, head straight for this excellent complex, comprising four hotels that cover every pocket from budget to top-end, and deliver each and every penny's worth. Kicking off at the cheaper end is Panchavati Guest House (☎ 2578771; single/double Rs500/600), which has clean but cramped rooms, well enough for a couple of nights' sleep. A more inviting option is Panchavati Yatri (☎ 2578782; single/double from Rs1025/1250; AC), featuring excellent rooms with hot showers, spot-on service and an in-house health club. Hotel Panchavati (☎ 2575771; single/double from Rs1199/1499; AC) is a pricier joint with classier rooms, that caters largely to business trav-

ellers. Last of all is the sumptuous Panchavati Millionaire (☎ 2312318; single/double from Rs1700/2050; AC), a moody affair where the lavish rooms are complemented by private sit-outs, perfect for the steaming morning cuppa.

Hotel Samrat (☎ 2577211; www.hotelsamratnasik .com; Old Agra Rd; s/d from Rs535/770;) The snug rooms here are tastefully done up in brown and beige, with balconies and cable TV thrown in for good measure. Located right next to the bus stands, its spick-and-span vegetarian restaurant is open 24 hours and serves as a popular refuelling stop.

Gateway Hotel (☎ 6603344; www.thegatewayhotels .com; MIDC Ambad; d from Rs4680;) This is Nasik's most luxurious hotel, situated about 8km south of town off the Nasik–Mumbai Rd, close to Pandav Leni and well away from all the urban mayhem. Offering standard five-star comfort, its USPs include the delectable morsels tossed up by its multicuisine restaurant Panchratna (mains Rs150 to Rs300).

Annapoorna Lunch Home (MG Rd; snacks & meals Rs15-70) No surprises on offer here, but it would be hard to find faults with the cheap and pan-fresh eats dished out by the hospitable waiters here. Peak lunch hours are a bad time to walk in; you'd have trouble finding a seat.

Talk of the Town (Old Agra Rd; mains Rs80-250) One of the few classy dining options in Nasik, this restaurant, next to the New Central bus stand, is a nice place to wash down sundry succulent Indian bites with a refreshing pint of lager. Don't get too adventurous with the Chinese section of the menu; your noodles might arrive smelling of raw eggs.

Pangat Thali (Panchavati Hotel Complex; thalis Rs80) A big-eater's delight, this no-frills vegetarian

MAHARASHTRA

GRAPES OF WORTH

So you thought chai was the only drink India churned out with zeal. Surprise, surprise! As it turns out, hilly Nasik, gifted with fertile soils and a cool climate, boasts conditions similar to Bordeaux. And over the past decade, the town has slowly but steadily been emerging as the Grand Crux of India's fledgling wine industry. Sauvignon blanc, chenin blanc, zinfandel, shiraz; Nasik produces them all. What's better, some of the wineries have now thrown their doors open for you to sample their drops, and associated luxuries, first-hand!

Located 15km west of Nasik, industry pioneer **Sula Vineyards** (☎ 09970090010; www.sulawines .com; Govardhan, Gangapur-Savargaon Rd; 11.30am-5.30pm) runs a tasting room where you can round off a vineyard tour with a spirited session of wine-tasting (Rs150) in its wood-and-mosaic balcony bar. For a more lavish experience, head 3km inland to **Beyond** (☎ 09970090010; www.sulawines.com; weekdays/weekends Rs16,000/20,000), a charming three-bedroom bungalow set amid the vines, where you can ride out on bicycles past the rolling hills, picnic beside the nearby lake or skim the still waters on a kayak. Chateau Indage, another of Nasik's wine biggies, has recently joined the tourism race with **Tiger Hill Vineyards Resort & Spa** (☎ 0253-2336274; www.tigerhillvineyards.com; s/d from Rs2800/3500). A serene, stylish getaway located 8km south of town, it's the perfect place to imbibe copious amounts of chardonnay and champagne in the cosy comfort of its snazzy wine bar, and top things off with a relaxing grape seed–oil massage in rustic bamboo huts at the spa.

restaurant cooks up an array of delicious Gujarati dishes, which liveried waiters lovingly heap on your platter quicker than you can tuck them in. Soon, you're fed up to your eyeballs, and dessert isn't served yet!

Getting There & Around
BUS
Nasik is a major player on the road-transport scene, with frequent state buses operating from three different stands.

The **Old Central bus stand** (CBS; ☎ 2309310) is useful mainly for those going to Trimbak (Rs20, 45 minutes). A block south, the **New Central bus station** (☎ 2309308) has services to Aurangabad (semideluxe Rs165, 4½ hours) and Pune (semideluxe/deluxe Rs180/297, 4½ hours). The **Mahamarg bus stand** (☎ 2309309) has services hourly to Mumbai (semideluxe Rs155, four hours) and twice-hourly to Shirdi (Rs75, 2½ hours).

Many private bus agents are based near the CBS and most buses depart from Old Agra Rd. Destinations include Pune, Mumbai, Aurangabad and Ahmedabad, and fares are marginally lower than those charged on state buses. Note that most of the Mumbai-bound buses terminate at Dadar.

TRAIN
The Nasik Rd train station is 8km southeast of the town centre, but a useful **railway reservation office** (☎ 134; 1st fl, Commissioner's Office, Canada Corner; 8am-8pm Mon-Sat, 8am-2pm Sun) is

500m west of the CBS. The 7am *Panchavati Express* is the fastest train to Mumbai (2nd class/chair Rs66/224, 2½ hours), and the 9.35am *Tapovan Express* is the only convenient direct train to Aurangabad (2nd class/chair Rs68/240, 3½ hours). Local buses leave frequently from Shalimar Circle, a few minutes' walk northeast of the CBS, to the train station (Rs7). An autorickshaw ride costs about Rs60.

AROUND NASIK
Pandav Leni
Dating from the 1st century BC to the 2nd century AD, the 24 early Buddhist caves of **Pandav Leni** (Indian/foreigner Rs5/100; 8am-6pm) are located about 8km south of Nasik along the Mumbai road. There's a steep, 20-minute hike separating the caves from the highway. Caves 19 and 23 have some interesting carvings; the rest are virtually empty and of limited interest to the lay person. Some caves bear animal figures and dice boards once engraved into the stone floors by resident monks.

Below the caves is the **Dadasaheb Phalke Memorial** (admission Rs10; 10am-9pm), dedicated to the pioneering Indian movie producer of the same name.

Local buses (Rs10) run past the caves from Shalimar Circle, near the CBS in Nasik, but the easiest way there is by autorickshaw. A return journey including waiting time costs around Rs250.

Trimbak

The moody **Trimbakeshwar Temple** stands in the centre of Trimbak, 33km west of Nasik. It's one of India's most sacred temples, containing a *jyoti linga*, one of the 12 most important shrines of Shiva. Only Hindus are allowed in; non-Hindus can get as far as peeking into the courtyard. Nearby, the waters of the Godavari River flow into the **Gangadwar bathing tank**, where earthly sins are regularly washed away by bathing pilgrims; everyone is welcome. Also try making the four-hour return hike up the **Brahmagiri Hill** behind town to the source of the Godavari. Pilgrims from across the nation clamber up to the flower-encrusted summit where the Godavari dribbles forth from a spring and into a couple of temples soaked in incense. En route you will pass a number of other temples, shrines and caves inhabited by sadhus (spiritual men). Don't attempt the ascent if rain looks imminent, as the trail can quickly become dangerous under a raging torrent.

Regular buses run from the CBS in Nasik to Trimbak (Rs20, 45 minutes).

Igatpuri

Heard of *vipassana*, haven't you? Now head to Igatpuri to see where (and how) it all happens. Located about 44km south of Nasik, this village is home to the world's largest *vipassana* meditation centre, the **Vipassana International Academy** (☎ 02553-244076; www.vri .dhamma.org), which institutionalises this strict form of meditation first taught by Gautama Buddha in the 6th century BC and reintroduced in India by teacher SN Goenka in the 1960s. The centre also serves as the apex body governing the spread of *vipassana* around the world. Ten-day residential courses (advance

bookings compulsory) are held here throughout the year, though authorities warn that it requires rigorous discipline, and dropping out midway isn't encouraged. Basic accommodation, food and meditation instruction are provided free of charge, but candidates are free to make a donation once they have successfully completed their courses.

AURANGABAD

☎ 0240 / pop 892,400 / elev 513m

After lying low through most of the tumultuous history of medieval India, Aurangabad's flash-in-the-pan moment came when the last Mughal emperor, Aurangzeb, made the city his capital from 1653 to 1707. With the emperor's death, it withered away as quickly as it had bloomed, but its brief period of glory gave it some fascinating monuments, including a Taj Mahal replica, that continue to draw a steady trickle of visitors today. Coupled with other historic relics, such as a group of ancient Buddhist caves, Aurangabad makes for a fairly decent weekend excursion. But the real reason for traipsing all the way out here is because the town is an excellent base from which to explore the World Heritage Sites of Ellora and Ajanta.

Silk fabrics were once Aurangabad's chief revenue generator, but the city is now a major industrial centre with beer and bikes being the big earners.

Orientation

The train station, cheap hotels and restaurants are clumped together in the south of the town. The MSRTC bus stand is 1.5km to the north. Northeast of the bus stand is the buzzing old town with its narrow streets and Muslim quarters.

HOLY MAN FROM SHIRDI

His iconic status is confirmed by the millions of posters and souvenirs bearing his calm, smiling face that one finds strewn across India. And his divinity, to some, is unquestionable. But Sai Baba, for all his popularity, remains one of India's most enigmatic figures. No one knows where he came from, what his real name was, or when he was born. His childhood veiled by obscurity, Sai Baba appeared in the town of Shirdi near Nasik around the age of 16. There, he advocated religious tolerance, and practised what he preached by sleeping alternately in a mosque and a Hindu temple and praying in them both equally. The masses took to him like fish to water, and by the time he died in 1918, the many miracles attributed to him had seen him gather a large following. Today, his temple complex in Shirdi draws an average of 40,000 pilgrims a day. Interestingly, in Andhra Pradesh, another widely respected godman called Sathya Sai Baba (born around 1926–27) claims to be the reincarnation of the original Sai Baba (see p979).

MAHARASHTRA

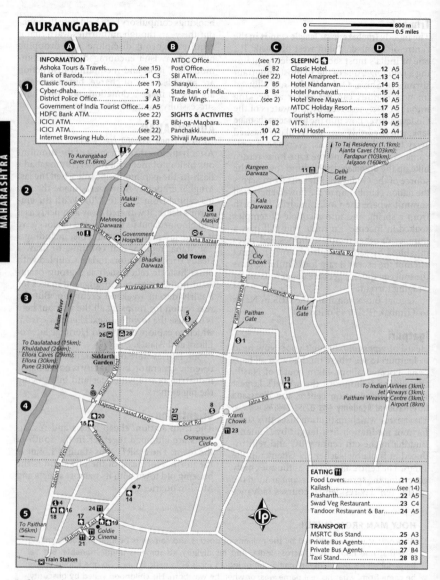

AURANGABAD

INFORMATION
Ashoka Tours & Travels..............(see 15)
Bank of Baroda.................................1 C3
Classic Tours.................................(see 17)
Cyber-dhaba.....................................2 A4
District Police Office.........................3 A3
Government of India Tourist Office....4 A5
HDFC Bank ATM...........................(see 22)
ICICI ATM...5 B3
ICICI ATM.......................................(see 22)
Internet Browsing Hub...................(see 22)

MTDC Office....................................(see 17)
Post Office..6 B2
SBI ATM..(see 22)
Sharayu..7 B5
State Bank of India...........................8 B4
Trade Wings...................................(see 2)

SIGHTS & ACTIVITIES
Bibi-qa-Maqbara..............................9 B2
Panchakki.......................................10 A2
Shivaji Museum..............................11 C2

SLEEPING
Classic Hotel....................................12 A5
Hotel Amarpreet.............................13 C4
Hotel Nandanvan............................14 B5
Hotel Panchavati.............................15 A4
Hotel Shree Maya............................16 A5
MTDC Holiday Resort......................17 A5
Tourist's Home...............................18 A5
VITS..19 A5
YHAI Hostel....................................20 A4

To Aurangabad Caves (1.6km);
To Taj Residency (1.1km); Ajanta Caves (103km); Fardapur (103km); Jalgaon (160km)
Rangeen Darwaza
Delhi Gate
Makai Gate
Ghati Rd
Kala Darwaza
Begumpura Rd
Mehmood Darwaza
Panchakki Rd
Government Hospital
Jama Masjid
Juna Bazaar
Old Town
Bhadkal Darwaza
Dr Ambedkar Rd
City Chowk
Sarafa Rd
Aurangpura Rd
Kham River
Paithan Darwaza Rd
Gulmandi Rd
Jafar Gate
Paithan Gate
To Daulatabad (15km); Khuldabad (26km); Ellora Caves (29km); Ellora (30km); Pune (230km)
Nirala Bazaar
Siddarth Garden
Station Rd West
Dr Rajendra-Prasad Marg
Jalna Rd
To Indian Airlines (3km); Jet Airways (3km); Paithani Weaving Centre (3km); Airport (8km)
Court Rd
Kranti Chowk
Osmanpura Circle
Padampura Rd
To Paithan (56km)
Station Rd East
Goldie Cinema
Train Station

EATING
Food Lovers....................................21 A5
Kailash...(see 14)
Prashanth.......................................22 A5
Swad Veg Restaurant......................23 C4
Tandoor Restaurant & Bar..............24 A5

TRANSPORT
MSRTC Bus Stand...........................25 A3
Private Bus Agents.........................26 A3
Private Bus Agents.........................27 B4
Taxi Stand......................................28 B3

Information
BOOKSHOPS
Sharayu (☎ 2335220; 119A Kailash Market, Station Rd East; ☻ 10.30am-8.30pm) Fine English-language books.

INTERNET ACCESS
Internet Browsing Hub (Station Rd East; per hr Rs20; ☻ 8am-10pm)

Cyber-dhaba (Station Rd West; per hr Rs20; ☻ 8am-11pm) Also changes money.

MONEY
ICICI, State Bank of India (SBI) and HDFC have several ATMs that are located along Station Rd East, Court Rd, Nirala Bazaar and Jalna Rd.

Bank of Baroda (☎ 2337129; Pattan Darwaza Rd; ☉ 10.30am-3pm Mon-Fri, to 12.45pm Sat) Near the Paithan Gate; gives cash advances on Visa and MasterCard.
Trade Wings (☎ 2322677; Station Rd West; ☉ 9am-7pm Mon-Sat, to 1pm Sun) Charges a Rs50 fee on exchanges.

POST
Post office (☎ 2331121; Juna Bazaar; ☉ 10am-6pm Mon-Sat)

TOURIST INFORMATION
Government of India tourist office (☎ 2331217; Krishna Vilas, Station Rd West; ☉ 8.30am-6pm Mon-Sat) A friendly and helpful tourist office with a decent range of brochures.
MTDC office (☎ 2331513, 2343169; MTDC Holiday Resort, Station Rd East; ☉ 10am-5.30pm Mon-Sat)

TRAVEL AGENCIES
Ashoka Tours & Travels (☎ 9890340816; Hotel Panchavati, Station Rd West) City and regional tours, car hire and hotel pick-ups.
Classic Tours (☎ 2335598; www.classictours.info; MTDC Holiday Resort, Station Rd East) Trusty place to book transport and tours.

Sights
BIBI-QA-MAQBARA
Built by Aurangzeb's son Azam Khan in 1679 as a mausoleum for his mother Rabia-ud-Daurani, **Bibi-qa-Maqbara** (☎ 2400620; Indian/foreigner Rs5/100; ☉ dawn-10pm) is widely known as the 'Poor man's Taj'. With its four minarets flanking a central onion-domed mausoleum, the white structure bears striking resemblance to the original Taj Mahal in Agra. However, it is much less grand, and apart from a few marble adornments, most of the structure is finished in lime mortar. Apparently, the prince had conceived the entire mausoleum in white marble like the Taj, but was thwarted by his frugal father who opposed his extravagant idea of draining state coffers for the purpose. Despite the use of cheaper material and the obvious weathering, however, it remains a sight far more impressive than the average gravestone.

AURANGABAD CAVES
Strictly architecturally speaking, the **Aurangabad caves** (☎ 2400620; Indian/foreigner Rs5/100; ☉ dawn-dusk) aren't a patch on Ellora or Ajanta. But they nonetheless throw some light onto early Buddhist architecture and, above all, make

for a quiet and peaceful outing. Carved out of the hillside in the 6th or 7th century AD, the 10 caves – comprising two groups 1km apart (retain your ticket for entry into both sets) – are all Buddhist. Cave 7 with its sculptures of scantily clad lovers in suggestive positions is everyone's favourite. An autorickshaw from Bibi-qa-Maqbara shouldn't cost more than Rs100 including waiting time.

PANCHAKKI
Literally meaning 'water wheel', **Panchakki** (Indian/foreigner Rs5/20; ☉ 6am-8pm) takes its name from the hydro-mill which, in its day, was considered a marvel of engineering. Driven by water carried through earthen pipes from the river 6km away, it once ground grain for pilgrims. You can still see the humble machine at work, but don't expect any grandeur.

Baba Shah Muzaffar, a Sufi saint and spiritual guide to Aurangzeb, is buried here. His **memorial garden** is flanked by a series of fish-filled tanks, near a large shade-giving banyan tree.

SHIVAJI MUSEUM
This dull **museum** (☎ 2334087; Dr Ambedkar Rd; admission Rs5; ☉ 10.30am-6pm Fri-Wed), dedicated to the life of the Maratha hero Shivaji, includes a 500-year-old chain-mail suit and a copy of the Quran handwritten by Aurangzeb.

Tours
Classic Tours (left) and the **Indian Tourism Development Corporation** (ITDC; ☎ 2331143) both run daily tours to the **Ajanta caves** (Rs300; ☉ 8am-5.30pm Tue-Sun) and **Ellora caves** (Rs200; ☉ 9.30am-5.30pm Wed-Mon), which include a guide but no admission fees. The Ellora tour also includes all the other major Aurangabad sites, Daulatabad Fort and Aurangzeb's tomb in Khuldabad, which is a lot to swallow in a day. Tours start and end at the MTDC Holiday Resort.

Sleeping
BUDGET
YHAI Hostel (☎ 2334892; Station Rd West; dm/d Rs70/180) This decrepit old place meets all the usual youth-hostel norms, but the lady who runs the show is a real gem, whose charming personality compensates for any shortfall on the lodging front. Breakfast is available for Rs20 and a thali dinner Rs25.

MAHARASHTRA

Tourist's Home (☎ 2337212; Station Rd West; s/d Rs200/300) Just why would anyone renovate the lobby before giving the rooms a much-needed coat of paint? Well, these guys surely have their own reasons, so for the moment, you're stuck with drab blue walls and squat toilets in the rooms. But it's bright and airy, so not all's lost.

Hotel Nandanvan (☎ 2338916; Station Rd East; s/d Rs350/450; 🔀) This place has spacious rooms the size of mini banquet halls (joking!) and more importantly, toilets that are cleaner than most other budget accommodation options in town. The friendly room-service staff here dresses in pink. Colour therapy, did someone say?

Hotel Panchavati (☎ 2328755; www.hotelpanchavati .com; Station Rd West; s/d from Rs400/650; 🔀) With walls painted in floral hues and matching upholstery in its well-appointed rooms, this place seems to have buried its ghosts and redeemed its status as a premium budget option in town. The managers are efficient and friendly and it sits easily at the top of the value-for-money class.

Hotel Shree Maya (☎ 2333093; shrimaya_agd@ dataone.in; Bharuka Complex; s/d from Rs445/595; 🔀) The inviting aroma of mouth-watering food wafting out of the pantry hangs heavy in the lobby here. Scent-sitive travellers can't help but check-in, and are duly rewarded with a relaxing experience in the hotel's simple but comfortable rooms, with the added advantage of exchanging notes with other travellers on the outdoor terrace, where a sumptuous all-you-can-eat breakfast (Rs40) and other meals are served.

MIDRANGE

Classic Hotel (☎ 5624314; www.aurangabadhotel.com; Station Rd East; s/d from Rs800/1000; 🔀 🖵) Perched atop an automobile showroom, this shiny hotel next to Goldie Cinema is somewhat let down by its inconsistent housekeeping and staff. Its saving grace, however, is its prime location and 24-hour room service.

MTDC Holiday Resort (☎ 2331513; Station Rd East; d from Rs900; 🔀) Set amid shaded grounds, this curiously disorganised hotel is one of the better MTDC operations. The rooms, though characterless, are spacious and tidy, and there's a well-stocked bar, restaurant and a couple of travel agencies on-site. Drop in between March and July, and you pay 20% less.

Hotel Amarpreet (☎ 6621133; www.amarpreethotel .com; Jalna Rd; s/d from Rs2200/3100; 🔀) A glitzy lobby leads to slightly less impressive rooms, but it's much cleaner and more professional than any other hotel in its category. New rooms were being added during research, which hopefully will conform to classier standards when completed.

TOP END

Taj Residency (☎ 2381106; www.tajhotels.com; Ajanta Rd; s/d from Rs3980/4700; 🔀 🖵 🕽) Set in 2 hectares of pleasantly landscaped gardens, this palace-like hotel is a quiet oasis of well-appointed rooms on the northern fringes of Aurangabad. The more expensive rooms have romantic Mughal-style swings on the balconies. For those travelling with infants, there's babysitting service on offer.

VITS (☎ 2350701; www.vitshotels.com; Station Rd East; s/d incl breakfast Rs5500/6500; 🔀 🖵 🕽) This brand-new luxury business option, with chintzy lighting in its lobby and classy interiors (faux waterfalls!), seems to have taken all steps in the right direction. The rooms already in commission boast features such as LCD TVs and wi-fi, with comfort to boot. Other rooms are slated to follow soon.

Eating

Swad Veg Restaurant (Kanchan Chamber, Station Rd East; mains Rs30-60) As well as a pile of cheap-eat Indian staples, this place offers pizzas (Rs40 to Rs50) and lots of ice creams and shakes – all of which are gobbled up under the benevolent gaze of swami Yogiraj Hanstirth. It's quite hard to find, but if and when you do get to it, you'll realise it's worth the effort.

Prashanth (Siddharth Arcade, Station Rd East; mains Rs30-90) Prashanth wins trophies from travellers for its delightful vegetarian-only dishes, epic fruit juices and enjoyable patio setting.

Kailash (Station Rd East; mains Rs30-100) Adjacent to Hotel Nandanvan, this pure-veg restaurant is a classy glass-and-chrome place where you can sit back after a long day out and wolf down a variety of local delicacies brought to your table by smartly dressed waiters.

Food Lovers (Station Rd East; mains Rs60-200) For some lip-smacking Punjabi and Chinese fare, try this restaurant across the road from the MTDC Holiday Resort, where the decor comprises a row of aquariums (sadly dry at the time of research). Locals vouch for its quality, and say it's a reliable place to tuck into the meaty stuff.

Tandoor Restaurant & Bar (☎ 2328481; Shyam Chambers, Station Rd East; mains Rs70-220) Offering fine tandoori dishes and flavoursome North Indian and Chinese vegetarian options in a weirdly Pharaonic atmosphere, this is one of Aurangabad's top restaurants.

Shopping

Hand-woven Himroo material is a traditional Aurangabad speciality (though people have differing opinions regarding its aesthetic appeal). Made from cotton, silk and silver threads, it was developed as a cheaper alternative to Kam Khab, the more lavish brocades of silk and gold thread woven for royalty in the 14th century. Most of today's Himroo shawls and saris are mass-produced using power looms, but some showrooms in the city still run traditional workshops, thus preserving this dying art. One of the best places to come and watch the masters at work is the **Paithani Weaving Centre** (☎ 2482811; Jalna Rd; 11.30am-8pm), behind the Indian Airlines office. It's worth a visit even if you're not buying.

Himroo saris start at Rs1000 (cotton and silk blend). Paithani saris, which are of superior quality, range from Rs5000 to Rs300,000, but before you baulk at the price, bear in mind that some of them take more than a year to make!

Getting There & Away

AIR

The **airport** (☎ 2483392) is 10km east of town. En route are the offices of **Indian Airlines** (☎ 2485241; Jalna Rd) and **Jet Airways** (☎ 2441392; Jalna Rd). Most domestic airlines operate daily flights from Aurangabad to Delhi, with a stopover in Mumbai. Fares start from around Rs1250.

BUS

Local buses head half-hourly to Ellora (Rs20, 45 minutes) and hourly to Jalgaon (Rs113, four hours) via Fardapur (Rs74, two hours). The T-junction near Fardapur is the drop-off point for Ajanta (see p828 for more details).

Buses leave regularly from the **MSRTC bus stand** (☎ 2240164; Station Rd West) to Pune (ordinary/semideluxe Rs156/195, five hours) and Nasik (ordinary/semideluxe Rs95/120, five hours). For longer distances, private luxury buses are more comfortable and better value. The private bus agents congregate around the corner where Dr Rajendra Prasad Marg

becomes Court Rd; a few sit closer to the bus stand on Station Rd West. Deluxe overnight bus destinations include Mumbai (with/without AC Rs250/200, sleeper Rs550, eight hours), Ahmedabad (Rs350, 15 hours) and Nagpur (Rs350, 12 hours).

TRAIN

On the southern edge of town is Aurangabad **train station** (☎ 131; Station Rd East). It's not on a main line, but two direct trains (often heavily booked) run daily to/from Mumbai. There's the 2.40pm *Tapovan Express* (2nd class/chair Rs94/336, six hours), and the 6am *Janshatabdi Express* (2nd class/chair Rs117/385, 5½ hours).

To Hyderabad (Secunderabad), the *Devagiri Express* departs daily at 4.05am (sleeper/2AC Rs227/836, 10 hours). To reach northern or eastern India by train, take a bus up to Jalgaon and board one of the major trains from there.

Getting Around

Autorickshaws are as common as mosquitoes in a summer swamp. The taxi stand is next to the bus stand; share jeeps also depart from here for destinations around Aurangabad, including Ellora and Daulatabad.

Ashok T Kadam (☎ 9890340816) and **Bhima** (☎ 9370246907) are trustworthy rickshaw drivers who won't try and wrangle every rupee they can from you. Bhima carries a notebook bearing recommendations and 'thank you' notes from travellers worldwide, while Kadam owes the fact that he owns his rickshaw to a *Lonely Planet* reader!

AROUND AURANGABAD
Daulatabad

No trip to Aurangabad is complete without a pit-stop at the ruined but truly magnificent hilltop fortress of Daulatabad, about 15km away from town en route to Ellora. A 5km battlement surrounds this ancient **fort** (☎ 2615777; Indian/foreigner Rs5/100; 6am-6pm), a most beguiling structure built by the Yadava kings through the 12th century. In 1328, it was renamed Daulatabad, the City of Fortune, by Delhi sultan Mohammed Tughlaq, who decided to shift his kingdom's capital to this citadel from Delhi. Known for his eccentric ways, Tughlaq even marched the entire population of Delhi 1100km south to populate it. Ironically, Daulatabad soon proved untenable as a capital for strategic reasons, and Tughlaq forced its weary inhabitants to slope all the way back to Delhi, which had by then been reduced to a ghost town!

The central bastion of Daulatabad sits atop a 200m-high craggy outcrop originally known as Devagiri, the Hill of the Gods. The climb to the summit takes about 45 minutes, and leads past an ingenious series of defences, including multiple doorways at odd angles with spike-studded doors to prevent elephant charges. A tower of victory, known as the **Chand Minar** (Tower of the Moon), built in 1435, soars 60m above the ground to the right; it's closed to visitors. Higher up, you can walk into the **Chini Mahal**, where Abul Hasan Tana Shah, king of Golconda, was held captive for 12 years before his death in 1699. It was once coated in blue-and-white tiles, of which only a few fractured fragments remain today. Nearby, there's a 6m **cannon**, cast from five different metals and engraved with Aurangzeb's name.

Part of the ascent to the top goes through a pitch-black, bat-infested, water-seeping, spi-ralling tunnel – down which the fort's defend-ers hurled burning coals and boiling water at invaders. Apparently, these were measures put in place to make the fort impregnable. Nonetheless, history records how the fort was once successfully conquered by simply bribing the guards at the gate!

Guides (Rs450) are available near the ticket counter to show you around, and their flame-bearing assistants will lead you through the dark tunnel for a small tip. But on the way down you'll be left to your own devices. Note that the crumbling staircases and sheer drops can make ascent or descent difficult for the elderly, children and those suffering from vertigo or claustrophobia. If you take an or-ganised tour from Aurangabad to Daulatabad and Ellora, you may not have time to climb to the summit.

Khuldabad

The scruffy walled town of Khuldabad, the Heavenly Abode, is a quaint and cheerful lit-tle Muslim pilgrimage village just 3km from Ellora. A number of historical figures are buried here, including emperor Aurangzeb, the last of the Mughal greats. Despite match-ing the legendary King Solomon in terms of state riches, Aurangzeb was an ascetic in his personal life, and insisted that he be buried in a simple tomb constructed only with the money he had made from sewing Muslim skullcaps. An unfussy affair of modest marble in a courtyard of the **Alamgir Dargah** (7am-8pm) is exactly what he got, which, in stark contrast to the tombs of other Mughal greats, was prudent, to say the least.

Generally a calm place, Khuldabad is swamped with millions of pilgrims every April when a robe said to have been worn by the Prophet Mohammed, and kept within the dargah (shrine), is shown to the public. The shrine across the road from the Alamgir Dargah contains hairs of the Prophet's beard and lumps of silver from a tree of solid silver, which miraculously grew at this site after a saint's death.

ELLORA

☎ 02437

The saga of the hammer and chisel comes full circle at the World Heritage–listed **Ellora cave temples** (☎ 244440; Indian/foreigner Rs10/250; dawn-dusk Wed-Mon), located 30km from Aurangabad. The pinnacle of ancient Indian rock-cut architecture, these caves were chipped out laboriously through five centuries by gen-erations of Buddhist, Hindu and Jain monks. Monasteries, chapels, temples; the caves served every purpose, and style quotient was duly met by embellishing them with a profu-sion of remarkably detailed sculptures. Unlike the caves at Ajanta (p825), which are carved into a sheer rock face, the Ellora caves line a 2km-long escarpment, the gentle slope of which allowed architects to build elaborate courtyards in front of the shrines as well.

Ellora has 34 caves in all: 12 Buddhist (AD 600–800), 17 Hindu (AD 600–900) and five Jain (AD 800–1000). The grandest, however, is the awesome Kailasa Temple (Cave 16), the world's largest monolithic sculpture, hewn top to bottom from the rock by 7000 labourers over a 150-year period. Dedicated to Lord Shiva, it is clearly among the very best that ancient Indian architecture has had to offer.

Historically, the site represents the renais-sance of Hinduism under the Chalukya and Rashtrakuta dynasties, the subsequent decline of Indian Buddhism and a brief resurgence of Jainism under official patronage. An increas-ing influence of Tantric elements in India's three great religions can be seen in the way the sculptures are executed. Their coexistence at one site also indicates a lengthy period of religious tolerance.

Official guides can be hired at the ticket office in front of the Kailasa Temple for Rs600. Most relay an extensive knowledge of the cave architecture, so try not to skimp. And if you only have time to visit either Ellora or Ajanta, Ellora wins hands down.

Sights

KAILASA TEMPLE

Halfway between a cave and a religious shrine, this **rock-cut temple**, built by King Krishna I of the Rashtrakuta dynasty in AD 760, was built to represent Mt Kailasa (Kailash), Shiva's Himalayan abode. To say that the assignment was daring would be an understatement. Three huge trenches were bored into the sheer cliff face with hammer and chisel, following which the shape 'released', a process that entailed removing 200,000 tonnes of rock! All this, while taking care to leave behind those sections of rock which would later be used for sculpting. Covering twice the area of the Parthenon in Athens and being half again as high, Kailasa was an engineering marvel executed straight out of the head; modern draughtsmen can go hang themselves in shame.

Size aside, the temple is remarkable for its prodigious sculptural decoration. The temple houses several intricately carved panels, depicting scenes from the Ramayana, the Mahabharata and the adventures of Krishna. The best one depicts the demon king Ravana flaunting his strength by shaking Mt Kailasa. Unimpressed, Shiva crushes Ravana's pride by simply flexing a toe. Kailasa is a living temple, very much in use; you'll have to remove your shoes to enter the main shrine.

After you're done with the main enclosure, bypass the hordes of chip-munching day trippers to explore the temple's many dank, bat urine-soaked corners with their numerous forgotten carvings. Afterwards take a hike up the path to the south of the complex and walk around the top perimeter of the 'cave', from where you can appreciate its grand scale.

BUDDHIST CAVES

The southernmost 12 caves are Buddhist *viharas* (monasteries), except Cave 10, which is a *chaitya* (assembly hall). While the earliest caves are simple, Caves 11 and 12 are more ambitious, on par with the more impressive Hindu temples.

Cave 1, the simplest *vihara*, may have been a granary. **Cave 2** is notable for its ornate pillars and its imposing seated Buddha figure facing the setting sun. **Cave 3** and **Cave 4** are unfinished and not well-preserved.

Cave 5 is the largest *vihara* in this group, at 18m wide and 36m long; the rows of stone benches hint that it may have once been an assembly hall.

Cave 6 is an ornate *vihara* with wonderful images of Tara, consort of the Bodhisattva Avalokiteshvara, and of the Buddhist goddess of learning, Mahamayuri, looking remarkably similar to Saraswati, her Hindu equivalent. **Cave 7** is an unadorned hall, but from here you can pass through a doorway to **Cave 8**, the first cave in which the sanctum is detached from the rear wall. **Cave 9** is notable for its wonderfully carved fascia.

Cave 10 is the only *chaitya* in the Buddhist group and one of the finest in India. Its ceiling features ribs carved into the stonework; the grooves were once fitted with wooden panels. The balcony and upper gallery offer a closer view of the ceiling and a frieze depicting amorous couples. A decorative window gently illuminates an enormous figure of the teaching Buddha.

Cave 11, the Do Thal (Two Storey) Cave, is entered through its third basement level, not discovered until 1876. Like Cave 12, it probably owes its size to competition with the more impressive Hindu caves of the same period.

Cave 12, the huge Tin Thal (Three Storey) Cave, is entered through a courtyard. The (locked) shrine on the top floor contains a large Buddha figure flanked by his seven previous incarnations. The walls are carved with relief pictures, like those in the Hindu caves.

HINDU CAVES

Where calm and contemplation infuse the Buddhist caves, drama and excitement characterise the Hindu group (Caves 13 to 29). In terms of scale, creative vision and skill of execution, these caves are in a league of their own.

All these temples were cut from the top down, so it was never necessary to use scaffolding – the builders began with the roof and moved down to the floor.

Cave 13 is a simple cave, most likely a granary. **Cave 14**, the Ravana-ki-Khai, is a Buddhist *vihara* converted to a temple dedicated to Shiva sometime in the 7th century.

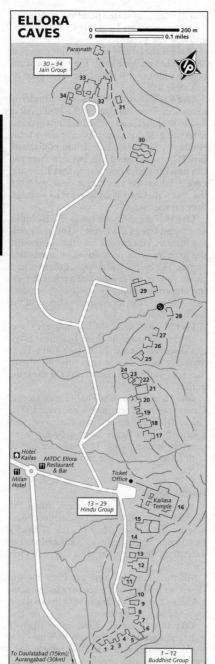

Cave 15, the Das Avatara (Ten Incarnations of Vishnu) Cave, is one of the finest at Ellora. The two-storey temple contains a mesmerising Shiva Nataraja, and Shiva emerging from a lingam (phallic image) while Vishnu and Brahma pay homage.

Caves 17 to **20** and **22** to **28** are simple monasteries.

Cave 21, known as the Ramesvara Cave, features interesting interpretations of familiar Shaivite scenes depicted in the earlier temples. The figure of goddess Ganga, standing on her *makara* (mythical sea creature), is particularly notable.

The large **Cave 29**, the Dumar Lena, is thought to be a transitional model between the simpler hollowed-out caves and the fully developed temples exemplified by the Kailasa. It has views over a nearby waterfall you can walk down to.

JAIN CAVES

The five Jain caves may lack the artistic vigour and ambitious size of the best Hindu temples, but they are exceptionally detailed. The caves are 1km north of the last Hindu temple (Cave 29) at the end of the bitumen road.

Cave 30, the Chhota Kailasa (Little Kailasa), is a poor imitation of the great Kailasa Temple and stands by itself some distance from the other Jain temples.

In contrast, **Cave 32**, the Indra Sabha (Assembly Hall of Indra), is the finest of the Jain temples. Its ground-floor plan is similar to that of the Kailasa, but the upstairs area is as ornate and richly decorated as the downstairs is plain. There are images of the Jain *tirthankars* (great teachers) Parasnath and Gomateshvara, the latter surrounded by wildlife. Inside the shrine is a seated figure of Mahavira, the last *tirthankar* and founder of the Jain religion.

Cave 31 is really an extension of Cave 32. **Cave 33**, the Jagannath Sabha, is similar in plan to 32 and has some well-preserved sculptures. The final temple, the small **Cave 34**, also has interesting sculptures. On the hilltop over the Jain temples, a 5m-high image of Parasnath looks down on Ellora.

Sleeping & Eating

Hotel Kailas (☎ 244446; www.hotelkailas.com; d from Rs900, cottages from Rs1500) The sole decent hotel near the site, this place should be considered only if you can't have enough of Ellora in a single day. The comfy stone cottages here come with warm showers; those with cave views are Rs500 pricier. There's a good restaurant and a lush lawn tailor-made for an evening drink.

Locals say the best food emerges from the kitchens of the **Milan Hotel** (mains Rs25-60), just across the road. Also reliable is the spotless **MTDC Ellora Restaurant & Bar** (dishes Rs40-170), which offers takeaways in case you want to picnic beside the caves.

Getting There & Away

Buses regularly ply the road between Aurangabad and Ellora (Rs20); the last bus returns from Ellora at 8pm. Share jeeps leave when they're full and drop-off outside the bus stand in Aurangabad (Rs30). A full-day autorickshaw tour to Ellora with stops en route costs Rs500; taxis charge around Rs850.

AJANTA
☎ 02438

Being Ellora's venerable twin in the World Heritage listings, the **Buddhist caves of Ajanta** (☎ 244226; Indian/foreigner Rs10/250; ☼ 9am-5.30pm Tue-Sun), 105km northeast of Aurangabad and about 60km south of Jalgaon, are the Louvre of ancient India. Much older than Ellora, these secluded caves date from around the 2nd century BC to the 6th century AD and were among the earliest monastic institutions to come up in the country. Ironically, it was Ellora's rise that brought about Ajanta's downfall. As Buddhism gradually waned in the region, the site was abandoned and the

focus shifted to Ellora. Upon being deserted, the caves were soon reclaimed by the greens and were forgotten until 1819, when a British hunting party led by officer John Smith stumbled upon them purely by chance. Despite their age, the paintings in these caves remain in a fine state of preservation today, and many attribute it to their relative isolation from humanity for centuries.

Information

Flash photography is banned in the caves due to its adverse effect on natural dyes used in the paintings. A video-camera permit costs Rs25. Authorities have recently installed tiny pigment-friendly lights within the dark caves, which cast a faint glow on the paintings, but bring a torch if you want to glimpse minute details.

A cloakroom near the main ticket office is a safe place to leave gear (Rs4 per item for four hours). This makes it possible to visit Ajanta from Aurangabad in the morning, before moving on to Jalgaon in the evening, or vice versa. The caves are a short, steep climb from the ticket office; the elderly can opt for a chair carried by four bearers (Rs400), available at the foot of these steps.

Authorised and experienced tourist guides can be hired at Cave 1 for an approximately two-hour tour (Rs600).

Sights & Activities
THE CAVES

The 30 caves of Ajanta line the steep face of a horseshoe-shaped rock gorge bordering

MAHARASHTRA

CARBON DATING AJANTA'S GOLDEN AGE

Historians worldwide have constantly been reviewing theories on major archaeological sites and their periods of existence. Unsurprisingly, the Ajanta caves are no exception.

One prominent theorist is American professor Dr Walter M Spink. With more than 40 years of research behind him, he suggests that the splendour of the later Mahayana group may have been accomplished in fewer than 20 years, rather than over centuries as previously thought.

Scholars agree that the caves had two periods of patronage: an early group was crafted around the 1st and 2nd centuries BC while a second wave began centuries later. Spink pinpoints the Vakataka emperor Harisena as a reigning sponsor of the incredible renaissance. Soon after his rise to the throne in AD 460, the caves began to realise their present forms, until Harisena's unexpected death in 477. The site was probably deserted in the 480s. The silver lining to the tragedy, according to Spink, is that the sudden downfall of the eminent Vakataka empire at the pinnacle of the caves' energetic crafting is solely responsible for their phenomenally well-preserved state today.

If you're interested, Spink's book *Ajanta: A Brief History and Guide* (1994) can be bought from touts near the site.

the Waghore River flowing below. They are sequentially numbered from one end to the other, baring Caves 29 and 30. The numbering has nothing to do with their chronological order; the oldest caves are actually in the middle and are flanked by newer caves on both sides.

Caves 3, 5, 8, 22 and 28 to 30 are either closed or inaccessible. Other caves, such as Cave 14, might be closed at times because of restoration work. During rush periods, viewers are allotted 15 minutes within each cave. Some have to be entered barefoot (socks allowed).

Five of the caves are *chaityas* while the other 25 are *viharas*. Caves 8, 9, 10, 12, 13 and part of 15 are early Buddhist caves, while the others date from around the 5th century AD (Mahayana period). In the simpler, more austere early Buddhist school, the Buddha was never represented directly – his presence was always alluded to by a symbol such as the footprint or wheel of law.

Of special note are the Ajanta 'frescoes', more correctly temperas, which adorn many of the caves' interiors. It's believed that the pigments for these paintings were mixed with animal glue and vegetable gum, to bind them to the dry surface. Many caves have small, craterlike holes on their floors, which acted as colour palettes during paint jobs.

Cave 1, a Mahayana *vihara,* was one of the latest to be excavated and is the most beautifully decorated. This is where you'll find a rendition of the Bodhisattva Padmapani, the most famous of the Ajanta artworks. A verandah in front leads to a large congregation hall, housing sculptures and narrative murals known for their splendid perspective and elaborate detailing of dress, daily life and facial expressions. The colours in the paintings were created from local minerals, with the exception of the vibrant blue made from Central Asian lapis lazuli. Look up to the ceiling to see the carving of four deer sharing a common head.

Cave 2 is also a late Mahayana *vihara* with deliriously ornamented columns and capitals, and some fine paintings. The ceiling is decorated with geometric and floral patterns. The murals depict scenes from the *Jataka* tales, including Buddha's mother's dream

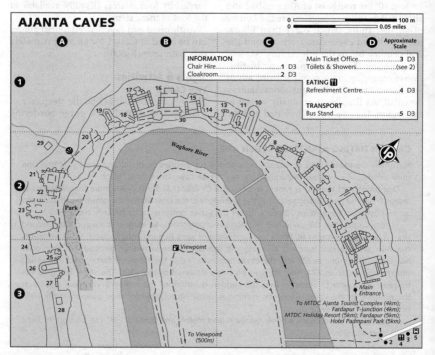

AJANTA CAVES

INFORMATION
Chair Hire.................................**1** D3
Cloakroom................................**2** D3

Main Ticket Office....................**3** D3
Toilets & Showers................(see **2**)

EATING
Refreshment Centre...............**4** D3

TRANSPORT
Bus Stand................................**5** D3

Waghore River

Park

Viewpoint

Main Entrance

To MTDC Ajanta Tourist Complex (4km);
Fardapur T-junction (4km);
MTDC Holiday Resort (5km); Fardapur (5km);
Hotel Padmpani Park (5km)

To Viewpoint (500m)

of a six-tusked elephant, which heralded his conception.

Cave 4 is the largest *vihara* at Ajanta and is supported by 28 pillars. Although never completed, the cave has some impressive sculptures, including scenes of people fleeing from the 'eight great dangers' to the protection of Avalokiteshvara.

Cave 6 is the only two-storey *vihara* at Ajanta, but parts of the lower storey have collapsed. Inside is a seated Buddha figure and an intricately carved door to the shrine. Upstairs the hall is surrounded by cells with fine paintings on the doorways.

Cave 7 has an atypical design, with porches before the verandah, leading directly to the four cells and the elaborately sculptured shrine.

Cave 9 is one of the earliest *chaityas* at Ajanta. Although it dates from the early Buddhist period, the two figures flanking the entrance door were probably later Mahayana additions. Columns run down both sides of the cave and around the 3m-high dagoba at the far end. The vaulted roof has traces of wooden ribs.

Cave 10 is thought to be the oldest cave (200 BC) and was the first one to be spotted by the British hunting party. Similar in design to Cave 9, it is the largest *chaitya*. The facade has collapsed and the paintings inside have been damaged, in some cases by graffiti dating from soon after the rediscovery. One of the pillars bears the engraved name of Smith, who left his mark here for posterity.

Cave 16, a *vihara*, contains some of Ajanta's finest paintings and is thought to have been the original entrance to the entire complex. The best known of these paintings is the 'dying princess' – Sundari, wife of the Buddha's half-brother Nanda, who is said to have fainted at the news that her husband was renouncing the material life (and her) in order to become a monk. Carved figures appear to support the ceiling in imitation of wooden architectural details, and there's a statue of the Buddha seated on a lion throne teaching the Noble Eightfold Path.

Cave 17, with carved dwarfs supporting the pillars, has Ajanta's best-preserved and most varied paintings. Famous images include a princess applying make-up, a seductive prince using the old trick of plying his lover with wine and the Buddha returning home from his enlightenment to beg from his wife and

astonished son. A detailed panel tells of Prince Simhala's expedition to Sri Lanka. With his 500 companions he is shipwrecked on an island where ogresses appear as enchanting women, only to seize and devour their victims. Simhala escapes on a flying horse and returns to conquer the island.

Cave 19, a magnificent *chaitya,* has a remarkably detailed facade; its dominant feature is an impressive horseshoe-shaped window. Two fine standing Buddha figures flank the entrance. Inside is a three-tiered dagoba with a figure of the Buddha on the front. Outside the cave to the west sits a striking image of the Naga king with seven cobra hoods around his head. His wife, hooded by a single cobra, sits by his side.

Cave 24, had it been finished, would be the largest *vihara* at Ajanta. You can see how the caves were constructed – long galleries were cut into the rock and then the rock between them was broken through.

Cave 26, a largely ruined *chaitya*, now dramatically lit, contains some fine sculptures and shouldn't be missed. On the left wall is a huge figure of the 'reclining Buddha', lying back in preparation for nirvana. Other scenes include a lengthy depiction of the Buddha's temptation by Maya.

Cave 27 is virtually a *vihara* connected to the Cave 26 *chaitya*.

VIEWPOINTS
Two lookouts offer picture-perfect views of the whole horseshoe-shaped gorge. The first is a short walk beyond the river, crossed via bridges below Caves 8 and 27. A further 20-minute uphill walk leads to the lookout from where the British party first spotted the caves.

Sleeping & Eating
Accommodation options close to the caves are limited and you're better off using Aurangabad or Jalgaon as a base.

Hotel Padmapani Park (☎ 244280; padmpanipark@yahoo.co.in; Aurangabad-Jalgaon Rd; d with/without AC Rs700/500; 🍴) The small and clean rooms here come with a warm welcome. It's often booked out, so call in advance if you plan to stay over.

MTDC Holiday Resort (☎ 244230; Aurangabad-Jalgaon Rd; d with/without AC from Rs900/550; 🍴) This one's overpriced, and the staff prone to dragging their feet. The rooms, however, are clean and spacious.

MTDC Ajanta Tourist Complex (☎ 09422204326; Fardapur T-junction; cottages Rs1300; 🅿) Located just behind the shopping 'plaza' and the bus stand is this mint-fresh resort, featuring five charming and well-appointed cottages nestled amid grassy lawns overlooking the hills.

As far as tanking up goes, there is a string of cheap, unappetising restaurants in the shopping plaza – you could pack a picnic and enjoy it in the shady park below Caves 22 to 27. There's also a buzzing refreshment centre by the ticket office, which serves an overpriced vegetarian thali (Rs70).

Getting There & Away

Buses from Aurangabad (p821) or Jalgaon (right) will drop you off at the T-junction (where the Aurangabad–Jalgaon Rd meets the road to the caves), 4km from the site. From here, after paying an 'amenities' fee (Rs7), race through the shopping plaza to the departure point for the green-coloured 'pollution-free' buses (Rs7 to Rs12), which zoom up to the caves. Buses return on a regular basis (half-hourly, last bus at 6.15pm) to the T-junction.

All MSRTC buses passing through Fardapur stop at the T-junction. After the caves close you can board buses to either Aurangabad or Jalgaon outside the MTDC Holiday Resort in Fardapur, 1km down the main road towards Jalgaon. Taxis are available in Fardapur; Rs700 should get you to Jalgaon.

JALGAON

☎ 0257 / pop 368,000 / elev 208m

Apart from being a handy base for exploring Ajanta 60km away, Jalgaon is really nothing more than a convenient transit town. A grubby settlement, it stands on the passing rail trade, connecting northern Maharashtra to all major cities across India. Indeed, it's a place to consider if you're moving out of the state towards northern India, or vice versa.

Information

You can find a couple of banks, ATMs and internet cafes along Nehru Rd, which runs along the top of Station Rd.

Sleeping & Eating

Most of the hotels in Jalgaon have 24-hour check out.

ourpick Hotel Plaza (☎ 2227354; hotelplaza_jal@ yahoo.com; Station Rd; dm/s/d from Rs150/250/350; 🅿 🖳)

Staying a night in this hotel is reason enough to visit Jalgaon. Nothing fancy on offer, but this cheapie has been done up with the kind of love and care that goes into building homes. The spotless rooms are simple and clean and come in a pick-and-mix range of styles and sizes. The effusive owner is a mine of useful information.

Hotel Kewal (☎ 2223949; Station Rd; d with/without AC from Rs875/625; 🅿) Another of those drab places to walk into. But it's nonetheless a decent midrange option, with motley interiors and efficient staff, which is perhaps all you need for a decidedly short stay-over.

Hotel Arya (Navi Peth; mains Rs35-70) Opposite Kelkar Market, near the clock tower. This place tosses up a long list of surprisingly tasty and well-tempered Indian fare, including some lip-smacking Punjabi delights. It's so popular you may have to queue for a table.

Silver Palace (Station Rd; mains Rs50-170) Next door to Hotel Plaza, this restaurant's claims of luxury may be stretching things too far. But the food is good, so all is forgiven.

Getting There & Away

Several express trains connecting Mumbai, Delhi and Kolkata (Calcutta) stop briefly at Jalgaon **train station** (☎ 131). Expresses to Mumbai (sleeper/2AC Rs175/632, seven hours) are readily available. The *Sewagram Express*, leaving from Jalgaon at 10.10pm, goes to Nagpur (sleeper/2AC Rs210/721, eight hours).

The first run from the **bus stand** (☎ 2229774) to Fardapur (Rs35, 1½ hours) is at 6am; buses depart every half-hour thereafter. The same bus continues to Aurangabad (Rs109, four hours).

Jalgaon's train station and bus stand are about 2km apart (Rs15 by autorickshaw). Luxury bus offices on Railway Station Rd offer services to Aurangabad (Rs120, 3½ hours), Mumbai (Rs250, nine hours), Pune (Rs250, nine hours) and Nagpur (normal/ sleeper Rs300/350, 10 hours). Rates may vary according to season and load factor.

LONAR METEORITE CRATER

If you have time on your hands, make a trip to Lonar to relive a prehistoric experience. Around 50,000 years ago, a meteorite slammed into the earth at this place, leaving behind a massive crater, some 2km across and 170m deep. In scientific jargon, it's known as the only hypervelocity natural impact crater in basaltic rock in the world. Means nothing to you? Well, then just take faith in the fact that, with a shallow green lake in its base and wilderness all around, it's as tranquil and relaxing a spot as you could hope to find. The lake itself is highly alkaline and its water supposedly excellent for the skin. Scientists suspect that the meteorite is still embedded about 600m below the southeastern rim of the crater.

The crater's edge is home to several **Hindu temples** as well as wildlife, including langurs, peacocks, gazelles and an array of birds. The **Government Rest House**, which is the starting point for the trail down to the bottom, is about 15 minutes' walk from the bus stand.

MTDC Tourist Complex (☎ 07260-221602; dm/d Rs150/550), has a prime location just across the road from the crater, and offers rather good-value rooms in a cluster of freshly painted, red-tiled cottages. Carry some mosquito repellent, and if the electricity fails at night, capitalise on the darkness by counting stars against a pitch-black sky.

Getting There & Away

There are a couple of buses a day between Lonar and Aurangabad (Rs101, 3½ hours). It's also possible to visit Lonar on a day trip from Aurangabad or Jalgaon if you hire a car and driver, and don't mind dishing out about Rs2000.

NAGPUR

☎ 0712 / pop 2.1 million / elev 305m

In the heart of India's orange country, Nagpur is located way off the main tourist routes. Nonetheless, it makes a good base for venturing out to the far eastern corner of Maharashtra. First up, it's close to Ramtek (p830) and the ashrams of Sevagram (p830). Besides, Nagpur is a convenient stop for those heading to the isolated **Tadoba-Andhari Reserve**, 150km south of Nagpur, which has some of India's densest forests teeming with wildlife, including the famed Bengal tigers.

The city, however, is hopelessly devoid of sights, and gets interesting only somewhat during the **Dussehra Festival** (September or October).

Information

Computrek (18 Central Ave; per hr Rs20) Internet access on the main drag.

Cyber Zoo (54 Central Ave; per hr Rs20; 🕙 10am-10pm Mon-Sun) Another central internet cafe.

MTDC (☎ 2533325; near MLA Hostel, Civil Lines; 🕙 10am-5.45pm Mon-Sat)

State Bank of India (☎ 2531099; Kingsway; 🕙 11am-2pm, Mon-Fri) A two-minute walk west of the train station. Deals in foreign exchange.

Sleeping & Eating

The majority of decent hotels are clustered along noisy Central Ave, a 10-minute walk east of the train station. An autorickshaw to Central Ave from the bus stand costs around Rs20. Most hotels cater to businesspeople rather than tourists.

Hotel Blue Diamond (☎ 2727461; www.hotelblue diamondnagpur.com; 113 Central Ave; s/d Rs345/456, with AC Rs800/912; 🗷) The mirrored ceiling in the reception is straight out of a bad '70s nightclub and the rooms are pretty much the type you'd expect above a seedy '70s nightclub. But hey, it's got a Formula One–themed restaurant-cum-disco that plays blaring music and tosses up some wannabe Italian and American dishes, so you could never be bored in the evenings!

Hotel Blue Moon (☎ 2726061; fax 2727591; Central Ave; s/d from Rs450/600, with AC Rs850/950; 🗷) One of the closest hotels to the train station with large, plain and clean rooms that don't win any awards for imagination. But the staff is helpful, and things move at an agreeable pace.

Hotel Skylark (☎ 2724654; fax 2726193; 119 Central Ave; s/d Rs600/700, with AC Rs1150/1225; 🗷) Another of Nagpur's recommended budget options, which has drab rooms but scores on the assistance front, and has a good restaurant with occasional live music, serving diverse Indian and Chinese items (meals Rs70 to Rs150).

Krishnum (Central Ave; mains Rs30-60) One of the popular eateries on the main road, this place dishes out South Indian snacks and fruit juices of reasonable quality.

The dozens of *dhabas* (snack bars), food stalls and fruit stands opposite the train station rouse in the evening. Summer is the best time to sample the famed oranges.

Getting There & Away

AIR

Most domestic airlines, including **Indian Airlines** (☎ 2533962) and **Jet Airways** (☎ 5617888), operate daily flights to Delhi (from Rs1200, 1½ hours), Mumbai (from Rs500, 1½ hours) and Kolkata

MAHARASHTRA

A MAN, A MISSION

Not everybody has the courage and resolve to walk out of a wealthy family and throw away a lucrative career in law, only to stand up for a social cause. But Murlidhar Devidas 'Baba' Amte (1914–2008) was an exception to the norm. Hailing from an upper-class Brahmin family in Wardha near Nagpur, Amte was snugly ensconced in the material world until he saw a leper die unattended on the streets one night.

It was an incident that changed him forever. Amte soon renounced worldly comforts, embracing an austere life through which he actively worked for the benefit of leprosy patients and those belonging to marginalised communities. In the primitive jungles of eastern Maharashtra, he set up his ashram called Anandwan (Forest of Joy). A true Gandhian, Amte believed in self-sufficiency, and his lifelong efforts saw several awards being conferred upon him, including the Ramon Magsaysay Award in 1985.

Amte's work has been carried forward by his sons Vikas and Prakash and their wives – the latter couple also won the Magsaysay Award in 2008. The family now runs three ashrams in these remote parts to care for the needy, both humans and animals. Volunteering opportunities are available; contact the ashram offices on mss@niya.org.

(from Rs1000, 1½ hours), apart from linking Hyderabad, Ahmedabad, Bengaluru, Chennai and Pune. Taxis/autorickshaws from the airport to the city centre cost Rs350/200.

BUS

The main **MSRTC bus stand** (☎ 2726221) is 2km south of the train station and hotel area. Buses head regularly for Wardha (Rs51, two hours) and Ramtek (Rs31, 1½ hours). Two buses roar off daily to Jalgaon (Rs296, 10 hours), and three go to Hyderabad (Rs164, 12 hours).

TRAIN

Nagpur **train station** (☎ 131), on the Mumbai–Howrah line, is an impressive edifice in the centre of town. The overnight *Vidarbha Express* originates in Nagpur and departs at 5.15pm for Mumbai CST (sleeper/2AC Rs328/1165, 14 hours). The same train departs Mumbai at 7.10pm for Nagpur. Heading north to Kolkata the *Mumbai Howrah Mail* departs from Nagpur at 11.25am and arrives in Howrah at 5.50am (sleeper/2AC Rs366/1403, 18½ hours). Several Mumbai-bound expresses stop at Jalgaon (for Ajanta caves; sleeper/2AC Rs210/721, seven hours). There are also connections to Bengaluru, Delhi and Hyderabad.

AROUND NAGPUR
Ramtek

About 40km northeast of Nagpur, Ramtek is believed to be the place where Lord Rama, of the epic Ramayana, spent some time during his exile with his wife Sita and brother Lakshmana. The place is marked by a clus-

ter of **temples** (☉ 6am-9pm), about 600 years old, which sit atop the Hill of Rama and have their own population of resident monkeys. Autorickshaws will cart you the 5km from the bus stand to the temple complex for Rs40; you can return to town via the 700 steps at the back of the complex. On the road to the temples you'll pass the delightful **Ambala Tank**, lined with small temples. If you're interested, you can take a boat ride (Rs20 per head) around the lake.

The **Kalidas Memorial** (admission Rs5; ☉ 8am-8.30pm), on the top of the hill beside the temple complex, is dedicated to the famous classical Sanskrit poet Kalidas. Also worth visiting is a **Jain temple** at the base of the hill and a **mosque** on the opposite hill.

On the hilltop and not far from the temples, **Rajkamal Resort** (☎ 0712-2228401; d with/without AC Rs1300/800; ✵) has large but overpriced rooms that come with TVs. There's a basic restaurant-bar.

Buses run half-hourly between Ramtek and the MSRTC bus stand in Nagpur (Rs31, 1½ hours). The last bus to Nagpur is at 8.30pm.

Sevagram
☎ 07152

Sevagram, or the Village of Service, occupies a prominent place in the history of India's Independence Movement. Chosen by Mahatma Gandhi as his base during the freedom struggle, the village played host to several nationalist leaders, who would regularly come to visit the Mahatma at his **Sevagram Ashram** (☎ 284753; ☉ 6am-5.30pm).

The peaceful ashram, built on 40 hectares of farmland, is a long way from anywhere and would motivate only die-hard Gandhi fans. The highlights of a visit are the original huts that Gandhi lived in, as well as some of his personal effects, including his walking stick. Across the road, the shoddy **Gandhi Picture Exhibition** (admission free; ☿ 10am-5.30pm Wed-Mon) traces his life through old photographs.

Very basic lodging is available in the **Yatri Nivas** (☎ 284753; d Rs100), across the road from the entry gate (advance booking recommended), and vegetarian meals are served in the ashram's dining hall.

Just 3km from Sevagram en route to Nagpur, Paunar village is home to the **Brahmavidya Mandir Ashram** (☎ 288388; ☿ 6am-noon & 2-8pm). Founded by Vinoba Bhave, a nationalist and disciple of Gandhi who participated in the Satyagraha and Quit India Movements, the ashram is now run almost entirely by women. Modelled on *swaraj* (self-sufficiency), it's operated on a social system of consensus with no central management. Basic accommodation and board (Rs100 per person) in two rooms sharing a bathroom is available; call in advance.

Sevagram can be reached by taking a Wardha-bound bus from Nagpur (Rs40, 1½ hours).

Tadoba-Andhari Reserve

Now under India's Project Tiger directorate, this little-explored national park lies 150km south of Nagpur. Less visited than most other forests in India, this is a place where you can get up close with wildlife, which includes gaurs, chitals, nilgais, sloth bears and the showcase Bengal tigers, without having to jostle past truckloads of shutter-happy tourists. The flipside, however, is that comfort levels are drastically low, and modern amenities unavailable. The park remains closed through the monsoons.

The **field director's office** (☎ 0712-2528953) in nearby Chandrapur can arrange for accommodation in forest rest houses and organise jungle safaris in minibuses. A better idea may be to opt for the all-inclusive weekend package trip to the reserve organised by **MTDC** (see p829) in Nagpur (Rs3750 per person), as it takes care of logistical hassles.

Several state buses ply between Nagpur and Chandrapur through the day (Rs101, 3½ hours).

SOUTHERN MAHARASHTRA

KONKAN COAST

A perfect holiday option for the intrepid kind, the Konkan Coast is a narrow strip of little-explored shoreline that runs from south of Mumbai all the way to Goa. Bordered by the Western Ghats to the east and the Arabian Sea to the west, it's a remote and rural area peppered with flawless beaches, tropic-green paddy fields, emerald hills and crumbling forts. Far from being developed, it's not the easiest of places to navigate. Accommodation is scant, the cuisine unsophisticated and monotonous, and the locals unaccustomed to tour groups, especially foreigners. Limited transport makes things more difficult; though the Konkan Railway provides access to the bigger towns, the smaller dots can only be reached by rickety local buses. A good option is to rent a taxi in Mumbai and drift slowly down the coast to Goa. Even better, get off the highway as often as you can, and try meandering your way along the back roads, which take you through uninhabited stretches of pristine mountain folds and virgin forests where few outsiders ever set foot. You may have to ask for directions often, and spend some nights sleeping in villagers' houses – be generous with how much you give. But the reward for your efforts may be an experience of which seasoned explorers would be envious!

Murud

☎ 02144 / pop 12,500

About 165km south of Mumbai, the sleepy fishing hamlet of Murud is your first port of call. Step on to its lazy beaches and feel the white surf rush past your feet, and you'll be happy you came.

More importantly, Murud is home to the commanding island fortress of **Janjira** (admission free; ☿ 7am-5.30pm), built on an island 500m offshore, which might just revoke your childhood memories of Long John Silver and Captain Flint. The citadel was built in 1140 by the Siddis, descendants of sailor-traders from the Horn of Africa, who settled here and allegedly made their living through piracy. Their exploits soon prompted many local kings to wage wars against them, including Shivaji and his son Sambhaji, who even attempted to tunnel to it. However, no outsider ever made it past the fort's 12m-high walls which, when seen during high tide, seem to rise straight from the sea. Unconquered through history, the fort finally fell to the spoils of nature: today, its walls are slowly turning to rubble as the forest reclaims its interiors.

The only way to reach Janjira is by boat (Rs15 return, 10 minutes) from Rajpuri Port. Boats depart from 7am to 5.30pm daily, but require a minimum of 20 passengers. You can also have a boat to yourself (Rs400), and most oarsmen will double as guides (Rs350). To get to Rajpuri from Murud, take an autorickshaw (Rs50) or hire a bicycle (Rs5 per hour) from the shop opposite the mid-road shrine on Darbar Rd.

Back in Murud you can waste away the days on the beach, peer through the gates of the off-limits **Ahmedganj Palace**, estate of the Siddi Nawab of Murud, or scramble around the decaying mosque and tombs on the south side of town.

About 17km north of Murud lies **Kashid Beach**, which boasts a stretch of white sand that would give the Maldives an inferiority complex. Share autorickshaws (Rs10) go to Kashid from Murud all day, and shacks on the beach stock coconuts and basic snacks and have changing facilities (Rs5). However, avoid weekends, when Mumbai inc. comes calling.

SLEEPING & EATING

Several accommodation options are strung out along Murud's beach road. If you want to stay right on the sands, Kashid is a better option, where new hotels and private home-stays are sprouting up by the day. Enquire in Murud.

Mirage Holiday Homes (☎ 276744; hotelmirage@san charnet.in; opposite Kumar Talkies, Darbar Rd; d with/without AC Rs1500/1000; ☒) A small and friendly hotel with a pretty garden and clean, simple rooms. The downside is it's across the road from the beach, so no sea views to wake up to.

Golden Swan Beach Resort (☎ 274078; www.gold enswan.com; Darbar Rd; d with/without AC from Rs3200/1700, cottages from Rs6400; ☒) The first place you come to as the bus enters town is also the smartest. It's an upscale affair with plush rooms, and has a superb promenade to view the distant fishing boats.

On the food front, **Patel Inn** (☎ 274153; mains Rs40-80; ☼ 9am-10.30pm) serves fresh fish dishes that make you drool. Near the boat pier, **New Sea Rock Restaurant** (☼ 9am-10pm) is a nice place

from where you can watch the sun set behind the fort. Just order yourself a cup of chai and snacks and you gain access to its excellent sea-facing sit-out!

GETTING THERE & AWAY

In Mumbai, regular ferries (Rs60, one hour) or hydrofoils (Rs110, 45 minutes) from the Gateway of India cruise to Mandva. If you take the hydrofoil the ticket includes a free shuttle bus to Alibag (30 minutes), otherwise an autorickshaw will be about Rs150. Rickety local buses from Alibag head down the coast to Murud (Rs30, two hours). Alternatively, buses from Mumbai Central bus stand take almost six hours to Murud (Rs150).

Avoid the railways. The nearest rail-head is at Roha, two hours away and badly connected.

Ganpatipule

☎ 02357

Can't make it to Goa? Well, at least you can visit Ganpatipule, on the coast 375km south of Mumbai – and you won't be crying sour grapes. A sleepy but picturesque seaside village, it boasts several kilometres of almost perfect beaches and clean waters. Life generally plods along very slowly here, but heaven help anyone coming for a bit of peace and quiet during holidays such as Diwali or Ganesh Chaturthi. These are times when hordes of raucous 'tourists' turn up to visit the seaside **Ganesha Temple** (☎ 235248; ☼ 6am-9pm) housing a monolithic Ganesha (painted a lurid orange), supposedly discovered 1600 years ago.

There are several places to stay in and around town, the best bet being the **MTDC Resort** (☎ 235248; fax 235328; d with/without AC from Rs1550/1200; ☒), nicely ensconced among the palms on a prime beachside spot. On the pricier end are the sea-view cottages (Rs2650). The resort offers a variety of water sports, has a **Bank of Maharashtra** (☎ 235304) that changes travellers cheques, and the **Tarang Restaurant** (mains Rs40-110), serving local specialities such as Malvani fish curry.

For a quirkier experience, walk up a kilo-metre or so from the beach to **Hotel Shiv Sagar Palace** (☎ 235070; d with/without AC from Rs1800/1500; ☒). This massive pink structure, full of col-onnades, domes and arches looks like a tacky Las Vegas hotel on LSD. Inside the hallowed halls is a kitsch world of orange plastic palm trees and towering chandeliers. Novelty factor apart, it's the stunning sea view, good vegetarian restaurant and a professional attitude that bring an unexpected class to the place.

GETTING THERE & AWAY

One MSRTC bus heads daily to Ganpatipule from Mumbai (semideluxe Rs345, 10½ hours), leaving the Borivali terminal at 9pm. Another bus rumbles back to Mumbai from Ganpatipule at 7pm. Frequent ordinary buses head down to Ratnagiri (ordinary/semideluxe Rs31/40, 1½ hours), from where you can catch an express train to Mumbai or Goa.

Ratnagiri
☎ 02352 / pop 70,300

Around 50km south of Ganpatipule, Ratnagiri is the largest town on the southern Maharashtra coast and the main transport hub (it's on the Konkan Railway). But for a tourist, that's about all that can be said for it. There's little to see and do apart from visiting the former home of freedom fighter Lokmanya Tilak, now a small **museum** (Tilak Alley; admission free; ☽ 9am-7pm), and the remnants of the **Thibaw Palace** (Thibaw Palace Rd; admission free; ☽ 10am-5.30pm Tue-Sun), where the last Burmese king, Thibaw, was interned under the British from 1886 until his death in 1916. A more exciting option is to take an evening stroll along the **Bhatya Beach**, but you certainly wouldn't want to step into the filthy water there.

There is no shortage of ATMs or internet cafes along the main road into town.

Just west of the bus stand, **Hotel Landmark** (☎ 220120; fax 220124; Thibaw Palace Rd; d with/without AC Rs1500/1000; ☒) has clean rooms and a restaurant serving good Indian food.

You could also try **Hotel Vihar Deluxe** (☎ 222944; fax 220544; Main Rd; d with/without AC Rs1500/900; ☒), a gigantic structure with efficient service and rejuvenating coastal food. A hearty South Indian breakfast is complimentary.

Ratnagiri **train station** (☎ 131) is 10km east of town. All express trains stop here, including the 10.45am *Janshatabdi Express* heading south to Margao (2nd class/chair Rs122/390, 3½ hours, daily except Wednesday) and north to Mumbai (Rs132/435, four hours, daily except Wednesday). The **old bus stand** (☎ 222340), in the town centre, has ordinary state buses to Kolhapur (Rs90, four hours) and Ganpatipule (Rs26, one hour). The **new bus stand** (☎ 227882), 1km further west, has a

7.45am ordinary bus to Panaji (Panjim) in Goa (Rs160, seven hours).

Tarkarli & Malvan
☎ 02365

Don't snigger if you come across a government ad parading this place as Tahiti. Two hundred kilometres south of Ratnagiri and within striking distance of Goa, pristine Tarkarli has white sands and sparkling blue waters that any self-respectable beach resort should have, with the addition of forested hills and meandering rivers. What's lacking is a well-oiled tourist industry and urban bounties, but do you care?

There are a few places to stay on the bumpy 7km road in from Malvan, the nearest town, the **MTDC Holiday Resort** (☎ 252390; d with/without AC Rs2100/1500; ☒) being the most obvious. On offer are an array of simple but surprisingly pleasant chalets and an excellent restaurant serving some sinful Malvani seafood. Also enquire at the resort about backwater tours on its houseboats (standard/luxury including full board Rs6050/7150).

The monstrous **Sindhudurg Fort**, dating from 1664, is visible floating on an offshore island and can be reached by frequent ferries (Rs30) from Malvan. It's said that Shivaji helped build this almost impregnable island citadel; his hand- and footprints can be found in one of the turrets above the entrance.

The closest train station is Kudal, 38km west of the coast. Frequent buses (Rs20, one hour) run between here and Malvan **bus stand** (☎ 252034). An autorickshaw from Kudal to Malvan or Tarkarli is about Rs300. Malvan has several buses daily to Panaji (Rs80, four hours) and a couple of services to Ratnagiri (Rs100, five hours). An autorickshaw between Malvan and Tarkarli costs Rs60.

MATHERAN
☎ 02148 / pop 5100 / elev 803m

Within spitting distance from Mumbai's heat and grime, Matheran (Jungle Above), resting atop the craggy Sahyadri Mountains amid a shady forest criss-crossed with foot trails and breathtaking lookouts, is easily the most elegant of Maharashtra's hill stations.

The credit for discovering this little gem goes to Hugh Malet, collector of Thane district, who chanced upon it while climbing the path known as Shivaji's Ladder in 1850. Soon it became a hill station patronised by the

MAHARASHTRA

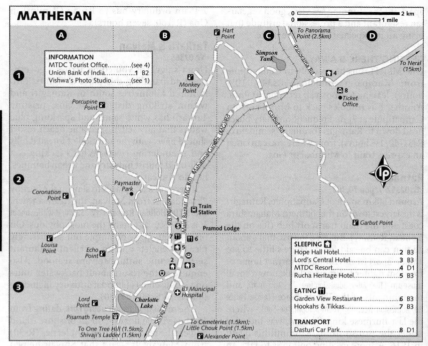

MATHERAN

INFORMATION
MTDC Tourist Office............(see 4)
Union Bank of India................**1** B2
Vishwa's Photo Studio..........(see 1)

SLEEPING
Hope Hall Hotel...............................**2** B3
Lord's Central Hotel.........................**3** B3
MTDC Resort....................................**4** D1
Rucha Heritage Hotel.......................**5** B3

EATING
Garden View Restaurant....................**6** B3
Hookahs & Tikkas.............................**7** B3

TRANSPORT
Dasturi Car Park...............................**8** D1

British. A quaint and hung-over village topped by a canopy of evergreen trees, the place owes its tranquillity to a ban on motor vehicles, making it an ideal place to rest your ears and lungs, and give your feet some exercise.

From around mid-June to early October, the monsoons hit Matheran hard, forcing it to virtually hibernate. During sunnier times, it brims over with cheerful day trippers, especially over weekends. During the true high season (summer months of May and June, Diwali and Christmas) it's nothing short of bursting at its seams with tourists.

Getting to Matheran is really half the fun. While speedier road options are available, nothing beats arriving in town on the narrow-gauge toy train (mini train) that chugs laboriously along a scenic 21km route to the heart of the village.

Information

Entry to Matheran costs Rs25 (Rs15 for children), which you pay on arrival at the train station or the car park.

On the main road into town, Mahatma Gandhi (MG) Rd, **Vishwa's Photo Studio**

(☎ 230354; MG Rd; ☯ 9.30am-10pm) sells useful miniguides (Rs25) and is actually a far better source of information than the so-called **MTDC Tourist Office** (☎ 230540) inside the MTDC Resort next to the car park. The **Union Bank of India** (☎ 230282; MG Rd; ☯ 10am-2pm Mon-Fri, to noon Sat) changes travellers cheques only.

Sights & Activities

You can walk along shady forest paths to most of Matheran's viewpoints in a matter of hours, and it's a place suited to stress-free ambling. If you've got the early morning energy then **Panorama Point** is the most dramatic place to glimpse the sunrise, while **Porcupine Point** (also known as Sunset Point) is the most popular (read: packed!) as the sun drops. **Louisa Point** and **Little Chouk Point** also have stunning views of the Sahyadris and if you're visiting **Echo Point**, do give it a yell. Stop at **Charlotte Lake** on the way back from Echo Point, but don't go for a swim – this is the town's main water supply and stepping in is prohibited. You can reach the valley below **One Tree Hill** down the path known as **Shivaji's Ladder**, supposedly trod upon by the Maratha leader himself.

Horses can be hired along MG Rd – you will certainly be approached – for rides to lookout points; they cost about Rs200 per hour.

Sleeping & Eating

Hotels in Matheran are low on quality and unreasonably high on tariff, so if you're not feeling generous, simply make a day trip from Mumbai. Most decent staying options are a short walk from the train station (1½ hours from the Dasturi car park). Check-out times vary wildly, and can be as early as 7am. Rates quoted here are standard high-season prices, but might just rise further. If you're visiting during the low-season, however, you might get a hefty discount.

MTDC Resort (☎ 230540; fax 230566; d from Rs1100; 🔀) This government-run joint offers spruce, good-value rooms in a charming wooded location. The downside is it's next to Dasturi car park, so you're away from the mid-town action.

Lord's Central Hotel (☎ 230228; www.matheran.com; MG Rd; s/d Rs1600/3200, valley view Rs2300/4600; 🔀 🖳 🛋) This charming colonial affair is one of Matheran's reputed establishments, but could do with the odd nip and tuck. Requisite brownie points are picked up by the stunning views, an inviting swimming pool and a rather hospitable and well-informed management. Note that they charge per person rather than per room.

Hope Hall Hotel (☎ 230253; MG Rd; d from Rs2000) 'Since 1875', says a plaque at the reception, and frankly, the age shows in the quality of the rooms! However, going by the many cheerful 'adieu' notes left by visitors, it seems that few mind the oddities such as squat toilets, hot bucket showers, or the hard-smoking, head-banging entrepreneur and his cowboy ways.

Rucha Heritage Hotel (☎ 230072; MG Rd; d from Rs2200) A grand white-pillared facade leads to less impressive rooms, but the management says they're putting in new rooms which guests are bound to love. And will pay through their noses for, obviously!

Hookahs & Tikkas (☎ 230240; MG Rd; mains Rs50-110) Operating out of a balcony overlooking the main road, this cheerful place serves savoury Indian fare and an assortment of hookahs (Rs150), the ban on public smoking notwithstanding!

Garden View Restaurant (☎ 230550; MG Rd; mains Rs70-110) Locals insist that the tastiest meals in Matheran come from this kitchen, and might get tastier once it's done with the renovation work that was on during research time.

Getting There & Away

TAXI

Taxis run from Neral to Matheran (Rs250, 30 minutes), but might get dearer since the local cabbies have recently started demanding their pound of tourism flesh. Taxis stop at the Dasturi car park, an hour's hike from Matheran's bazaar area. Horses (Rs160) and hand-pulled rickshaws (Rs200) wait here in abundance to whisk you in a cloud of red dust to your hotel of choice. Taxis from Mumbai will take you on a daylong trip for about Rs2000.

TRAIN

The toy train (2nd class/1st class Rs36/210) trundles up to Matheran from Neral Junction five times daily, with an equal number of return journeys. During the monsoons, trains are less frequent. From Mumbai's Chhatrapati Shivaji Terminus (CST), the most convenient express train to Neral Junction is the 7.10am *Deccan Express* (2nd class/chair Rs47/167). The 9am *Koyna Express* gets to Neral Junction at 10.31am. Most expresses from Mumbai stop at Karjat, down the line from Neral, from where you can backtrack on one of the frequent local trains. Alternatively, take a suburban Karjat-bound train from CST and get off at Neral (2nd/1st class Rs20/100, 2½ hours). From Pune, you can get to Karjat by the 6.05am *Sinhagad Express* (2nd class/chair Rs48/147, two hours).

Getting Around

Apart from hand-pulled rickshaws and horses, your feet are the only other transport option in Matheran. Keep walking!

LONAVLA

☎ 02114 / pop 55,600 / elev 625m

Sorry to rain in on the party. But Lonavla, 106km southeast of Mumbai, is a cheeky little scam masquerading under the name of a hill station. Catering to weekenders and conference groups coming in from Mumbai, this overdeveloped (and overpriced) town has no soaring peaks or quaint malls. Besides, it's a long way off from being attractive; Lonavla's main drag consists almost exclusively of garishly lit shops flogging *chikki,* the rock-hard, brittle sweet made in the area.

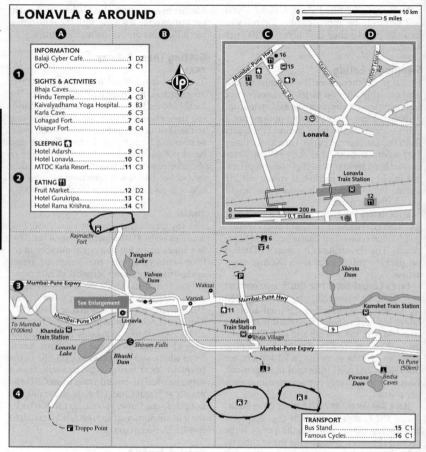

LONAVLA & AROUND

INFORMATION	
Balaji Cyber Café	1 D2
GPO	2 C1

SIGHTS & ACTIVITIES	
Bhaja Caves	3 C4
Hindu Temple	4 C3
Kaivalyadhama Yoga Hospital	5 B3
Karla Cave	6 C3
Lohagad Fort	7 C4
Visapur Fort	8 C4

SLEEPING	
Hotel Adarsh	9 C1
Hotel Lonavla	10 C1
MTDC Karla Resort	11 C3

EATING	
Fruit Market	12 D2
Hotel Gurukripa	13 C1
Hotel Rama Krishna	14 C1

TRANSPORT	
Bus Stand	15 C1
Famous Cycles	16 C1

What saves Lonavla's is its close proximity to the nearby Karla and Bhaja Caves which, after those of Ellora and Ajanta, are the best in Maharashtra.

Hotels, restaurants and the main road to the caves lie north of the train station (exit from platform 1). Most of Lonavla town and its markets are located south of the station.

It's advisable to change money in Mumbai or Pune. Internet access is available at **Balaji Cyber Café** (1st fl, Khandelwal Bldg, New Bazaar; per hr Rs20; ⏰ 12.30-10.30pm), immediately south of the train station.

Activities

Those wishing for a session of yogic healing can head to the **Kaivalyadhama Yoga Hospital**
(☎ 273039; www.kdham.com; Indian/foreigner from Rs9000/US$300), set in neatly kept grounds about 2km from Lonavla en route to the Karla and Bhaja Caves. Founded in 1924 by Swami Kuvalayanandji, it combines yoga courses with naturopathic therapies. Room rates cover full board, yoga sessions, programs and lectures. Rates mentioned are for a seven-day package, though two- and three-week sessions are also offered.

Mumbai-based **Nirvana Adventures** (☎ 022-26493110; www.nirvanaadventures.com) offers paragliding courses (three-day learner course from €250) or short tandem flights (Rs1500) at Kamshet, 25km from Lonavla.

(Continued on page 845)

Festive India

An explosion of colour
in the night sky at
the Thrissur Pooram
Festival (p982)

From larger-than-life extravaganzas replete with merry brass bands, caparisoned elephants and body-twisting acrobats, to pint-sized harvest fairs paying reverence to a much-loved local deity, no other country on earth can throw a festival quite like India. With its extraordinary melange of religious denominations – from Sikhs and Jains to Muslims and Buddhists – the subcontinent is home to a fantastical array of wildly diverse celebrations. And then, of course, there are the Hindu festivals: with a pantheon of around 330 million gods and goddesses, it is little wonder there's a sacred happening almost every other day, each with its own special set of traditional protocols. But no matter what the religious ilk, each and every festival is an essential thread when it comes to weaving the unique and colourful tapestry that is Festive India.

To find out what's happening when and where, see the Events Calendar on p26, the 'Festivals In...' boxed texts in the regional chapters, and, for some of our favourite festivals, the 'Festival & Events' boxed text on p23.

KUMBH MELA

If crowds worry you, stay away. This one's big. Held four times every 12 years at four different locations across central and northern India, the Kumbh Mela is the largest religious congregation on the planet. This vast celebration attracts tens of millions of Hindu pilgrims, including mendicant Naga sadhus (naked spiritual men) from radical Hindu monastic orders. The Kumbh Mela doesn't belong to any particular caste or creed – devotees from all branches of Hinduism come together to experience the electrifying sensation of mass belief and to take a ceremonial dip in the sacred Ganges, Shipra or Godavari Rivers.

Naga sadhus gather at Maha Kumbh Mela, Allahabad

The origins of the festival go back to the battle for supremacy between good and evil. In the Hindu creation myths, the gods and demons fought a great battle for a *kumbh* (pitcher) containing the nectar of immortality. Vishnu got hold of the container and spirited it away, but in flight four drops spilt on the earth – at Allahabad (p434), Haridwar (p469), Nasik (p813) and Ujjain (p702). Celebrations at each of these cities last for around six weeks but are centred on just a handful of auspicious bathing dates, normally six. The Allahabad event, known as the Maha (Great) Kumbh Mela, is even larger with even bigger crowds. Each location also holds an Ardh (Half) Mela every six years and a smaller, annual Magh Mela. For more details, visit www .kumbhamela.net.

Kumbh Mela Schedule

- **2010** Haridwar (March–April)
- **2013** Allahabad (January–February)
- **2015** Nasik (August–September)
- **2016** Ujjain (April–May)

HOLI-MANIA!

Fun-filled Holi would have to be India's most exuberant Hindu festival. Falling on the full moon day in the Hindu month of Phalguna (February/March), it's a time when people join nature in whipping off their winter coats and revelling in the arrival of spring. Folks greet each other with bright colours – everything from a cheeky smearing of pink powder on someone's face to a veritable deluge of multi-coloured-dyed water mercilessly thrown from buckets. A tip: wear old clothes and get ready to duck!

A riot of colour breaks out at Holi, Jaipur
CHRISTER FREDRIKSSON

PONGAL

Tamil Pongal is the major harvest festival of the south which takes place in Magha (January/February). It's all about the community giving thanks to the gods for the gifts of crops, nature, the cow and kinship. Spring cleaning is the focus of the first three days, and worn-out household items – particularly utensils – are flung into community bonfires as a symbol of people starting anew. The outsides of many homes are decorated with pretty, intricate kolams (see the 'Kolams' boxed text on p81). Families may prepare pots of *pongal* (a mixture of rice, sugar, dhal and milk), symbolic of prosperity and abundance, then feed it to adorned cows.

DIWALI

Diwali (Deepavali), popularly known as the Festival of Lights, is the country's most widely celebrated Hindu event (primarily in North India), spanning five days in Kartika (October/November). Homes and shops are illuminated with twinkling fairy lights and flickering candles are set afloat on rivers to guide Lord Rama home from exile. Houses and business premises are cleaned, decorated, and possibly given a fresh lick of paint leading up to the festival. Many homes sport colourful *rangolis,* the northern term for *kolams* (p81), and fireworks and crackers abound. Diwali is a delightfully upbeat

Pilgrims buy marigolds for Diwali, Varanasi
GREG ELMS

festival; moods are buoyant, people are dressed in their 'good' clothes, gifts are cheerfully exchanged and there's plenty of feasting. Sweet-makers do a roaring trade, with this festival particularly characterised by the manic distribution of *mithai* (Indian sweets) among family, friends and business associates.

DUSSEHRA

The Hindu festival of Dussehra, honouring Durga and Rama – who both valiantly conquered evil forces – spans 10 joyous days in Asvina (September/October). The festival takes different forms in different states, but all are united by the underlying theme of good prevailing over evil. According to legend, it is said that Durga, the Eternal Mother, was created when the gods needed an all-powerful being to destroy the Demon King Mahishasura. All of the other gods gave their prized weapons to Durga who subsequently vanquished the wicked demon. In temples across India you'll often see images of Mahishasura cowering at Durga's feet with her mythological vehicle, a lion (or tiger), snarling at him. Durga is portrayed as the ultimate form of feminine beauty and strength – her meditative smile, with large outlined eyes, exudes a protective, maternal glow, but her body, with 10 arms splayed around her, each holding a different weapon, reflects her readiness to battle dark forces.

People from right around India (except West Bengal, where the festival takes a different form, known as Durga Puja) spend Navaratri (the first nine nights) in the worship of Durga. A strict vegetarian diet is followed by the devout, and many people only eat sweets and fruits during this time. Celebrations are largely focused around the home and local neighbourhood. It's a sociable period, with people happily visiting one another and exchanging gifts. Different sweets are made each day with the first offered to the Divine, then eaten by the family and distributed among friends. In states such as Maharashtra and Gujarat, lively community dances called Dandiya take place throughout the night. The 10th day, Dussehra itself, is in fervent honour of Durga. It's considered a most auspicious time among Hindus, who believe that any venture started on this day is destined to succeed.

DURGA PUJA

In West Bengal (p532) Dussehra takes the form of Durga Puja, a jamboree of devotion, merriment and feasting (sweets are the focus in this carnival of calories) that lasts for 10 days in September/October. One of the most typical Durga Puja items is *bhog*, the ceremonial food served to Durga and later consumed as a community meal. It consists of a delicious *khichdi* (lightly spiced rice and lentils), along with eggplant and potato fritters, *labda* (a spicy mixed vegetable) and a sweet tomato *chatni* (chutney). The people of each neighbourhood often get together, pool funds and organise a sculpted idol of Durga for their locality. Artistic licence is known to be pushed to the extreme and there have been Durgas made of coloured glass shards, curly wood shavings, delicate shells and even plastic bottles. After nine

NARIAL PURNIMA

This festival is celebrated by those who rely on the sea for their livelihood, and takes place on the full moon day of the Hindu month of Sravana (July/August). The Vedic Sea God Varuna is worshiped, and coconuts (considered an auspicious offering) are respectfully tossed into the ocean so as to invoke his blessing for fruitful and safe fishing.

days of celebration and worship, the Durga idols are auspiciously submerged in a nearby river or lake, in accordance with tradition. The more upbeat Durga Puja celebrations in Bengal generally start from the sixth day – from then on there are *bhog*-focused community lunches like the one described earlier. Sometimes on the eighth day of worship, *mangsher jhol* (mutton curry) and *luchi* (fried flour puffs) are served. Traditionally on this day a goat was sacrificed to Durga, but these days the symbolic sacrifice tends to be the beheading of a banana tree.

GANESH CHATURTHI

The jolly elephant-headed Hindu god Ganesh is a much-loved deity and this festival is dedicated to him, taking place in Bhadra (August/September). The most spectacular celebrations occur in Mumbai (Bombay; p777), where giant idols are constructed, feted in processions around the city, keenly worshipped for 10 days and then carried by crowds to be ritually immersed in the sea. And because of Ganesh's supposed fondness for sweets – he is rarely depicted without a bowl of *modaks* (dim sum–shaped sweets filled with a scrumptious paste of coconut, condensed milk, sugar and cardamom) – he symbolically gorges on different sugary treats offered by devotees on each day of this festival. These sweets include *modaks,* of course, as well as *karanji* (a sweet, fried pastry with the same filling as *modaks*), *kheer* (Indian-style

A Hindu holy man prepares for *puja* (prayers) during Durga Puja, Kolkata

RICHARD I'ANSON

rice pudding), and a magnificent range of *ladoos* (sweet balls made with gram flour and semolina). Once the pot-bellied Ganesh has 'taken' his spiritual nourishment, the sweets are shared among his mortal devotees.

GANGAUR

One of Rajasthan's (p165) most widely celebrated festivals is Gangaur (March/April), which honours the love between Shiva and his consort Parvati. Parvati symbolises perfection in married life, so it is deemed a wise move for both unmarried and married women to worship her during this festival.

Festive beats at Ganesh Chaturthi, Mumbai
RICHARD I'ANSON

Wives pray for their spouses, and unmarried women pray for good husbands. People make small terracotta and/or wooden figures of the two deities which are then the focus of worship for as long as a month. The last three days are usually the climax of the festival. The terracotta and wooden figures are dressed to impress in beautiful costumes and jewels. In Jaipur (p168), the capital of Rajasthan, an elaborately costumed image of the goddess is carried on a palanquin from Tripolia Gate, at the City Palace, through the streets of the Old City. Meanwhile, in the vicinity of Mt Abu (p226), members of the Garasia tribe carry an image of Parvati from village to village, accompanied by spirited singing and dancing. In Bundi (p203), Kota (p207) and Jhalawar (p209), unmarried women collect poppies from the fields and fashion them into attractive wreaths for the goddess.

Enchanting swirls of colour, Gangaur, Jaipur
JOHN SONES

JANMASTAMI

Celebrated in Bhadra (August/September), this festival commemorates the birth of Lord Krishna, who is popular with Hindus of all castes. He is often depicted as a charming, flute-playing seducer of *gopis* (milkmaids) and is fondly regarded as the God of Song and Dance. Especially in Mathura (Uttar Pradesh; p425) where he was born and raised, this festival is marked with uniquely colourful pageantry and *ras-lila* (the re-enactment of Krishna's dances with the *gopis*). *Naivedya* (a sweet made with puffed rice, milk, curd and sugar) is the most popular offering made to him in temples. Krishna is also known as Makhan Chor

(Thief of Butter) because of his childhood pilfering of butter, milk and curd from earthenware pots hanging outside houses. His mischievous pranks are gleefully recreated today, and have provided some of Bollywood's most popular images. Traditionally, people would hang pots of curd, sweets and coins out high on the streets. Gangs of young men, calling themselves *gopalas* (cowboys, of sorts) would form human pyramids to reach the pots and then smash them with squeals of joy before divvying up their bounty. It is believed to be auspicious if it rains on this day, as folklore purports that Krishna was born during a great deluge. The devout stay awake, fasting until midnight to mark the moment of his birth.

CHRISTMAS

December 25 is the most widely celebrated festival among India's Christian population (see p72). Christmas is celebrated most prolifically in the South Indian states of Kerala (p980) and Goa (p858), but the festivities also occur in other places such as Mumbai. Christmas carols, roast turkey and plum pudding complement regional specialities and, in Kerala, the season is given a unique Indian twist with processions of musicians and brightly decorated elephants.

RAMADAN & EID AL-FITR

Islam is India's biggest minority religion. An important Islamic festival is Ramadan (Ramazan), the Muslim month of dawn-to-dusk fasting that falls in August, September or October (dates vary each year, according to the Islamic lunar calendar). The holy book, the Quran, was revealed to the Prophet Mohammed during this month and Muslims are enjoined to fast so they can understand the suffering of the poor. During the fast, Muslims abstain from eating, smoking or drinking even water during daylight, replenishing themselves only before dawn and after dusk. Eid al-Fitr is the final (30th) day of Ramadan, and follows the appearance of the new moon. Extravagant feasts joyously mark the end of the holy fast.

Desert love at the Pushkar Camel Fair

ANDREW BAIN

GET CAMEL HAPPY

Crazy about camels? You're in luck! Every year (October/November) India hosts the spectacular Pushkar Camel Fair in Rajasthan – for more information trot straight to p199.

Pretty pachyderms
on parade at the
Elephant Festival
(p167), Jaipur
RICHARD I'ANSON

(Continued from page 836)

Sleeping & Eating

Lonavla's hotels suffer from inflated prices and low standards. Most places are packed out during weekends and holidays. All hotels listed here have a 10am check-out time.

Hotel Lonavla (☎ 272914; Mumbai-Pune Hwy; d Rs995) Recently renovated, this place has small fan-only rooms, and seems a hit with corporate trainees coming for interaction programs. They insist that you clear your bills every third day, but who's staying that long, honestly?

Hotel Adarsh (☎ 272353; fax 278052; near Bus Stand; d with/without AC from Rs2000/1600; ⊠) Among the better options in town, this place has rather impressive and well-appointed rooms for the price. The management is smart and friendly, and a swimming pool is on its way to completion.

Hotel Gurukripa (Mumbai-Pune Hwy; mains Rs40-90) The dark interiors may leave you fumbling with your food, but the Punjabi dishes served here are truly worth savouring.

Hotel Rama Krishna (☎ 273600; Mumbai-Pune Hwy; dishes Rs50-120) The sleekest and busiest of the Lonavla lot, this place is famed for its meaty fare, especially the kebab preparations.

The bazaar, south of the train station, has a **fruit market**.

Getting There & Away

Lonavla is serviced by a host of MSRTC buses that depart from the **bus stand** (☎ 273842) to Dadar in Mumbai, (ordinary/semideluxe Rs58/75, two hours) and Pune (ordinary/semideluxe Rs47/60, two hours). You can hop onto luxury AC buses (about Rs100) plying the route to reach either city.

All express trains from Mumbai to Pune (2nd class/chair Rs56/190, 2½ hours) stop at Lonavla **train station** (☎ 273725). From Pune, you can also reach Lonavla by taking an hourly shuttle train (Rs14, two hours).

Bicycles can be hired from **Famous Cycles** (Mumbai-Pune Hwy; per hr Rs5).

KARLA & BHAJA CAVES

While they pale in comparison to Ajanta or Ellora, these rock-cut caves (dating from around the 2nd century BC) are among the better examples of Buddhist cave architecture in India. They are also low on commercial tourism, which make them ideal places for a quiet excursion. Karla has the most impressive single cave, but Bhaja is a quieter site to explore.

Karla Cave

Karla Cave (Indian/foreigner Rs5/100; ☯ 9am-5pm), the largest early Buddhist *chaitya* in India, is reached by a 20-minute climb from a mini-bazaar at the base of the hill. Completed in 80 BC, the *chaitya* is around 40m long and 15m high, and sports similar architectural motifs as *chaityas* in Ajanta and Ellora. Ellora's Kailasa Temple apart, this is probably the most impressive cave temple in the state.

Karla Cave is also the only site in Maharashtra where the original woodwork, more than two centuries old, has managed to survive. A semicircular 'sun window' filters light in towards a dagoba or stupa (the cave's representation of the Buddha), protected by a carved wooden umbrella, the only remaining example of its kind. The cave's roof also retains ancient teak buttresses. The 37 pillars forming the aisles are topped by kneeling elephants. The carved elephant heads on the sides of the vestibule once had ivory tusks.

The beauty of this cave is somewhat marred by the modern **Hindu temple** built in front of the cave mouth. However, the temple is a big draw for the pilgrims and their presence adds some colour to the scene.

Bhaja Caves

Across the expressway, it's a 3km jaunt from the main road to the **Bhaja Caves** (Indian/foreigner Rs5/100; ☯ 8am-6pm), where the setting is lusher, greener and quieter than at Karla Cave. Thought to date from around 200 BC, 10 of the 18 caves here are *viharas*, while Cave 12 is an open *chaitya*, earlier than Karla, containing a simple dagoba. Beyond this is a strange huddle of 14 stupas, five inside and nine outside a cave. From Bhaja Caves, you'll see the ruins of the **Lohagad** and **Visapur Forts**, which local kids will happily lead you to for a tip (not recommended during the rains).

Sleeping & Eating

MTDC Karla Resort (☎ 02114-282230; fax 282370; d from Rs800; ⊠ 💻) Set near the access point to Karla and Bhaja Caves, this is the nicest option around Lonavla, where the silence and lush surroundings can overwhelm you. The rooms and pricier cottages are prim and well-maintained, and there's a little lake where you can go boating. The resort has a restaurant, and is just off the Mumbai–Pune Hwy. Passing buses and autorickshaws can drop you within walking distance of the resort.

MAHARASHTRA

Getting There & Away

Karla and Bhaja can be visited over a single day from Lonavla. You can get to the access point to the caves on the highway by taking a local bus (Rs10, 30 minutes). From there, it's about a 6km return walk on each side to the two sites. A less rigorous option is to take an autorickshaw (Rs400) from Lonavla for a tour of both Karla and Bhaja, including waiting time.

PUNE

☎ 020 / pop 3.7 million / elev 457m

With its healthy mix of small-town wonders and big-city blues, Pune (also pronounced Poona) is a city that epitomises 'New India'. Once little more than a pensioners' town and an army outpost, it is today an unpretentious place with oodles of cosmopolitanism, inhabited by a cheerful and happy population. A thriving centre of academia and business, Pune is also known globally for its numerouno export, the late guru Bhagwan Shree Rajneesh and his ashram, the Osho Meditation Resort (see the boxed text, right).

First given its pride of place by Shivaji and the ruling Peshwas who made it their capital, Pune fell to the British in 1817. Thanks to its cool and dry climate, it soon became the Bombay Presidency's monsoon capital. Globalisation knocked on Pune's doors in the 1990s, and the city went in for an image overhaul. However, the colonial charm was retained by preserving its old buildings and residential areas, bringing about a pleasant coexistence of the old and new which, despite the presence of pollution and hectic traffic, now makes Pune a wonderful place to explore.

Orientation

The city sits at the confluence of the Mutha and Mula Rivers. Mahatma Gandhi (MG) Rd, about 1km south of Pune train station, is the main street lined with banks, restaurants and shops. Koregaon Park, northeast of the train station, is the undisputed chill-out zone, home to some of the best restaurants and coffee shops frequented by travellers, and the city's uberchic crowd, and of course, the Osho Ashram.

MAPS

Destination Finder (Rs60) and *Geo Pune* (Rs200) are the best maps around. The former is more easily available; you can pick it up on platform 1 of the train station.

Information

BOOKSHOPS

Crossword (1st fl, Sohrab Hall, RBM Rd; ☻ 10.30am-9pm) On Raibahadur Motilal (RBM) Rd. Offers a diverse collection of books and magazines.

Manneys Booksellers (7 Moledina Rd; ☻ 10am-8pm)

INTERNET ACCESS

You'll find several internet cafes along Pune's main thoroughfares.

Cyber-Net (North Main Rd, Koregaon Park; per hr Rs20; ☻ 8am-11.30pm) Opposite Citibank ATM; beats the competition with its lightning-fast broadband speed.

MONEY

Citibank has 24-hour ATMs on East St and North Main Rd. HSBC dispenses cash at its main branch on Bund Garden Rd. You'll find ICICI Bank and State Bank of India ATMs at the railway station and an Axis Bank ATM on MG Rd.

Thomas Cook (☎ 26346171; 2418 G Thimmaya Rd; ☻ 9.30am-6pm Mon-Sat)

POST

Main post office (☎ 26125516; Sadhu Vaswani; ☻ 10am-6pm Mon-Sat)

TOURIST INFORMATION

MTDC tourist office (☎ 26126867; I Block, Central Bldg, Dr Annie Besant Rd; ☻ 10am-5.30pm Mon-Sat) Buried in a government complex south of the train station. There's an MTDC desk at the train station (open 9am to 7pm Monday to Saturday, and to 3pm Sunday).

TRAVEL AGENCIES

Rokshan Travels (☎ 26136304; rokshantravels@ hotmail.com; 1st fl, 19 Kumar Pavilion, East St; ☻ 10am-6pm) These guys shine when it comes to getting you on the right bus, train or flight without a glitch. They also book taxis.

Sights & Activities

OSHO MEDITATION RESORT

You'll either like it or hate it. A splurge of an institution, this **ashram** (☎ 66019999; www.osho .com; 17 Koregaon Park), located in a leafy, upscale northern suburb, has been drawing thousands of *sanyasins* (seekers), many of them Westerners, ever since the death of Osho (see the boxed text, p849) in 1990. With its placid swimming pool, sauna, 'zennis' and basketball

PUNE

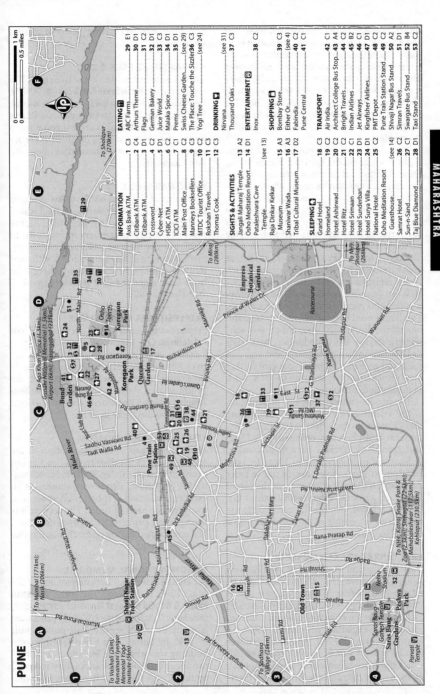

MAHARASHTRA

INFORMATION
Axis Bank ATM................................ 1	C3
Citibank ATM.................................. 2	C4
Citibank ATM.................................. 3	C1
Crossword...................................... 4	C2
Cyber-Net..................................... 5	D1
HSBC ATM..................................... 6	C2
ICICI ATM...................................... 7	C1
Main Post Office............................ 8	C3
Manneys Booksellers....................... 9	C3
MTDC Tourist Office...................... 10	C2
Rokshan Travels............................ 11	C3
Thomas Cook................................ 12	C3

SIGHTS & ACTIVITIES
Jangali Maharaj Temple................... 13	A2
Osho Meditation Resort................. 14	D1
Pataleshvara Cave.................(see 13)	
Raja Dinkar Kelkar	
Museum....................................... 15	A3
Shaniwar Wada.............................. 16	A3
Tribal Cultural Museum................... 17	D2

SLEEPING
Grand Hotel.................................. 18	C3
Homeland..................................... 19	C3
Hotel Ashirwad.............................. 20	C2
Hotel Ritz..................................... 21	C2
Hotel Srimaan............................... 22	B2
Hotel Sunderban............................ 23	D1
Hotel Surya Villa............................ 24	D1
National Hotel............................... 25	C2
Osho Meditation Resort	
Guesthouse.........................(see 14)	
Samrat Hotel................................ 26	C2
Sun-n-Sand.................................. 27	D1
Taj Blue Diamond.......................... 28	C2

EATING
ABC Farms.................................... 29	E1
Arthurs Theme.............................. 30	D1
Flags... 31	C2
German Bakery.............................. 32	D1
Juice World................................... 33	C3
Malaka Spice................................ 34	D1
Prems.. 35	D1
Swiss Cheese Garden..............(see 29)	
The Place: Touche the Sizzler........ 36	C3
Yogi Tree..............................(see 24)	

DRINKING
Nirvana..............................(see 31)	
Thousand Oaks.............................. 37	C3

ENTERTAINMENT
Inox.. 38	C2

SHOPPING
Bombay Store................................ 39	C3
Either Or................................(see 4)	
Fabindia...................................... 40	C2
Pune Central................................ 41	C1

TRANSPORT
Air India....................................... 42	C1
Architect College Bus Stop............ 43	A4
Bright Travels............................... 44	C2
Indian Airlines.............................. 45	B2
Jet Airways................................... 46	C1
Kingfisher Airlines......................... 47	D1
PMT Depot................................... 48	C2
Pune Train Station Stand............... 49	C2
Shivaji Nagar Bus Stand................ 50	A2
Simran Travels.............................. 51	D1
Swargate Bus Stand...................... 52	B4
Taxi Stand................................... 53	C2

courts, massage and beauty parlour, bookshop and a boutique guest house (opposite), it is, to some, the ultimate place to indulge in some stress-busting meditation and rediscover one's lost spiritual self. Alternately, there are many who point fingers at the ashram's blatant commercialisation, calling it nothing short of a clever business ploy, marketing a warped version of the mystic East to gullible Westerners.

The main centre for meditation and the nightly white-robed spiritual dance is the Osho Auditorium (a cough-free and sneeze-free zone!). The Osho Samadhi, where the guru's ashes are kept, is also open for meditation. Pondering sessions apart, the commune is big business. Its 'Multiversity' runs a plethora of courses in meditation as well as New-Age techniques. If you wish to take part, or even just to visit for the day to meditate, you'll have to pay Rs1300/1500 (Indian/foreigner), which covers registration, a mandatory on-the-spot HIV test (sterile needles used), introductory sessions and your first day's meditation pass. You'll also need two robes (one maroon and one white, from Rs200 per robe). For subsequent days, a daily meditation pass costs Rs200/500 (Indian/foreigner), and you can come and go as you please. If you want further involvement, you can also sign up for a 'work as meditation' program.

The curious can watch a video presentation at the visitor centre and take a 10-minute silent tour of the facilities (Rs10; adults only, cameras and phones prohibited) at 9.15am and 2pm daily. Tickets have to be booked at least a day in advance (9.30am to 1pm and 2pm to 4pm). If you decide not to enter the resort, it's worth checking out the placid 5-hectare gardens, **Osho Teerth** (admission free; 6-9am & 3-6pm), behind the commune; the gardens are accessible all day for those with a meditation pass.

RAJA DINKAR KELKAR MUSEUM

This fascinating **museum** (24461556; www .rajakelkarmuseum.com; 1377-1378 Natu Baug, Bajirao Rd; Indian/foreigner Rs50/200; 9.30am-5.30pm) is one of Pune's true delights. Housing only a fraction of the 21,000-odd objects of daily life collected by Dinkar Gangadhar, who died in 1990, it's worth an entire day out. The quirky collection includes a suit of armour made of fish scales and crocodile skin, hundreds of hookah pipes, writing instruments, lamps, toys, betel-

nut cutters and an amazing gallery of musical instruments.

KATRAJ SNAKE PARK & ZOO

There's a mediocre selection of Indian wildlife on show at the **Katraj Snake Park & Zoo** (24367712; Pune-Satara Hwy; adult/child Rs3/2; 10.30am-6pm Thu-Tue). But a trip to this faraway park on Pune's southern outskirts makes sense if you want to know more about snakes, of which there are plenty. Most snakes are housed in open pits; don't lean over!

SHANIWAR WADA

The ruins of this fortresslike **palace** (Shivaji Rd; Indian/foreigner Rs5/100; 8am-6pm) are located in the old part of the city. Built in 1732, the palace of the Peshwa rulers burnt down in 1828, but the massive walls and plinths remain, as do the sturdy palace doors with their daunting spikes. In the evenings there is an hour-long **sound-and-light show** (admission Rs25; 8.15pm Thu-Tue).

PATALESHVARA CAVE TEMPLE

Set across the river is the curious rock-cut **Pataleshvara Cave Temple** (Jangali maharaj Rd; 6am-9.30pm), a small and unfinished (though active) 8th-century temple, similar in style to the grander caves at Elephanta Island off the Mumbai coast. Adjacent is the **Jangali Maharaj Temple** (6am-9.30pm), dedicated to a Hindu ascetic who died here in 1818.

TRIBAL CULTURAL MUSEUM

About 1.5km east of the train station, at the southern end of the flyover, this obscure but excellent **museum** (26362071; Richardson Rd; admission free; 10.30am-5.30pm Mon-Sat) showcases an excellent collection of tribal jewellery sourced from remote parts of India. The section featuring ornate papier-mâché festival masks was being renovated during research, but was due to re-open soon.

GANDHI NATIONAL MEMORIAL

Set amid a sylvan 6.5-hectare plot across the Mula River in Yerwada, the grand **Aga Khan Palace & Gandhi National Memorial** (26680250; Ahmednagar Rd; Indian/foreigner Rs5/100; 9am-5.45pm) is easily Pune's biggest crowd-puller. Built in 1892 by Sultan Aga Khan III, this lofty building was where the Mahatma and other prominent nationalist leaders were interned by the British for about two years following

SEX, SALVATION & THE STYLE GURU

Ever tried mixing spirituality with primal instincts, and garnishing the potent concoction with oodles of panache? Well, Bhagwan Shree Rajneesh (1931–90) certainly did – and how! Osho, as he preferred to be called, was one of India's most flamboyant 'export gurus' to market the mystic East to the world, and undoubtedly the most controversial. Initially based in Pune, he followed no particular religion or philosophy, and outraged many across the world with his advocacy of sex as a path to enlightenment. A darling of the international media, he quickly earned himself the epithet 'sex guru'. In 1981, Rajneesh took his curious blend of Californian pop psychology and Indian mysticism to the USA, where he set up an agricultural commune in Oregon. There, his ashram's notoriety as well as its fleet of (material and thus valueless!) Rolls Royces grew, until raging local paranoia about its activities running amok moved the authorities to charge Osho with immigration fraud. He was fined US$400,000 and deported. An epic journey then began, during which Osho and his followers, in their search for a new base, were deported from or denied entry to 21 countries. By 1987, he was back at his Pune ashram, where thousands of foreigners soon flocked for his nightly discourses and meditation sessions.

They still come in droves. To house them all, the capacious Osho Auditorium was unveiled in 2002, which saw the centre's name being changed from 'Osho Commune International' to 'Osho Meditation Resort'. Such is the demand for the resort's facilities that prices are continually on the rise, with luxury being redefined every day. Interestingly, despite Osho's comments on how nobody should be poor, no money generated by the resort goes into helping the disadvantaged. That, resort authorities maintain, is up to someone else.

Gandhi's Quit India resolution in 1942. Both Kasturba Gandhi, the Mahatma's wife, and Mahadeobhai Desai, his secretary for 35 years, died here in confinement. You'll find their shrines (containing their ashes) in a quiet garden to the rear.

Within the main palace, you can peek into the room where Gandhi used to stay. Photos and paintings exhibit moments in his extraordinary career, but it's poorly presented.

RAMAMANI IYENGAR MEMORIAL YOGA INSTITUTE

To attended classes at this famous **institute** (☎ 25656134; www.bksiyengar.com; 1107 B/1 Hare Krishna Mandir Rd, Model Colony), 7km northwest of the train station, you need to have been practising yoga for at least eight years.

Sleeping

Pune's main accommodation hubs are around the train station and Koregaon Park. Many families rent out rooms to passing travellers, starting at about Rs250 (without bathroom) to about Rs600 (with bathroom). For longer-term stays you can negotiate a room from Rs5000 to 12,000 per month. Rickshaw drivers will know where to look (they get a cut from every deal) But don't go hunting after dark, especially if you're alone. Standards can vary widely.

BUDGET

Grand Hotel (☎ 26360728; grandhotelpune@gmail.com; MG Rd; d Rs770, s without bathroom Rs290) The cheapest beds here (and in all of Pune) are in cabins next to the bar, where you might get that sea-faring feeling! The private rooms are in converted family homes, not the most luxurious of their kind. On the positive side, the patio bar is a good place for a beer.

National Hotel (☎ 26125054; 14 Sasson Rd; s/d/q Rs850/1000/1100, cottages s/d/q Rs650/750/950) It's a toss-up between charm and comfort at this run-down colonial mansion opposite the train station. The rooms in the main building border on suffocating, while the cottages across the garden have tiled sit-outs.

Homeland (☎ 26123203; www.hotelhomeland.net; 18 Wilson Garden; s/d from Rs800/1000; 🖳) A recent touch-up has made this place surprisingly restful. The labyrinthine corridors lead to rooms with fresh enamel-painted walls and clean sheets, and the restaurant downstairs shows movies in the evenings.

MIDRANGE

All hotels listed have a noon check out and accept credit cards.

Hotel Sunderban (☎ 26124949; www.tghotels .com; 19 Koregaon Park; d incl breakfast with/without AC from Rs1500/1000, without bathroom from Rs700; 🖳 🖳) 'Wow' is the word! Located right next to the

Osho Resort, this renovated art deco bungalow effortlessly combines antiquity with style. The snug rooms, sporting a variety of classy furniture, get 30% cheaper if you drop in between April and September. The pricier rooms are across the lawns, in a sleek, glass-fronted building.

Hotel Surya Villa (☎ 26124501; www.hotelsurya villa.com; 294/1 Koregaon Park; s/d Rs1200/1500, with AC Rs1500/2000; ❖ ▣) Clearly the best among Pune's budget options, this cheerful place has bright, airy and spacious rooms and squeaky-clean loos. Managed by a spry lot, it stands just off the Koregaon backpacker hub, so you're always clued in to the coolest developments in town. Overall, a nice place to camp.

Samrat Hotel (☎ 26137964; thesamrathotel@vsnl .net; 17 Wilson Garden; s/d incl breakfast Rs1800/2200, with AC Rs2500/2900; ❖) Every Indian town has one hotel that shines above all the others and in Pune, that honour falls to Samrat. A sparkling modern hotel with excellent rooms opening around a central, top-lit foyer, this place sure knows how to make you feel at home.

Hotel Ritz (☎ 26122995; fax 26136644; 6 Sadhu Vaswani Path; s/d incl breakfast from Rs2550/2750; ❖) Plush, friendly, atmospheric: three words that sum it all up for the Ritz, a Raj-era building that holds its own in town. The pricy rooms are in the main building, while the cheaper ones are located in an annexe next to the garden restaurant, which serves good Gujarati and Maharashtrian food.

ourpick Osho Meditation Resort Guesthouse (☎ 66019900; www.osho.com; Koregaon Park; s/d Rs3000/3500; ❖) This place will allow you in only if you come to meditate at the Osho Meditation Resort (p846). The rooms in this stylish guest house are an exercise in modern aesthetics, as minimalist as they are chic. Add to that other luxe features, such as purified fresh air supply! Be sure to book well in advance; it's perpetually rushed.

Hotel Ashirwad (☎ 26128687; hotelashir@vsnl.net; 16 Connaught Rd; s/d from Rs3500/4000; ❖) A large, smooth-moving joint, this place stands out for its well-kept rooms and the popular Akshaya vegetarian restaurant downstairs, which serves a good range of Punjabi, Mughlai and Chinese fare.

Hotel Srimaan (☎ 26136565; srimaan@vsnl.com; 361/5 Bund Garden Rd; s/d Rs3500/4000; ❖ ▣) Jackson Pollock–inspired paintings lend their colour to the small but luxurious rooms in this hotel. The loos, though smart, are the size of those you'll only find on aeroplanes. A good Italian joint called La Pizzeria available on-site.

TOP END

Taj Blue Diamond (☎ 66025555; www.tajhotels.com; 11 Koregaon Rd; d from Rs12,000; ❖ ▣ ❖) Being an elegant business hotel, this place possibly assumes you work on the move, so you have comfort features such as Aeron chairs at work desks in its wooden-floored rooms! It houses a stylish selection of restaurants, as well as the happening nightclub Polaris.

Sun-n-Sand (☎ 26167777; www.sunnsandhotel .com; 262 Bund Garden Rd; d incl breakfast from US$250; ❖ ▣ ❖) Centrally located on one of Pune's main thoroughfares, this luxury hotel has inviting rooms with large windows, soothing wall hues and classy upholstery. Some of the high-enders are fashionably built on split-levels and have gizmos such as LCD TVs.

Eating

Pune is a place with an adventurous palate. Predictably, there are a host of well-priced, high-quality eateries, many around Koregaon Park. Unless otherwise mentioned, the following are open noon to 3pm and 7pm to 11pm daily; last orders at 10.45pm.

RESTAURANTS

Vaishali (☎ 25531244; FC Rd; mains Rs30-70) Old-timers can't stop raving about this institution, known for its range of delicious snacks and meals. 'Don't miss the SPDP', notes a college student hanging out by the entrance. The scrumptious *sev potato dal puri* (Rs35), a favourite local snack, is what she means. Go find out for yourself!

Yogi Tree (☎ 26124501; 294/1 Koregaon Park; mains Rs50-150; ⏱ 8.30am-11pm) Below Hotel Surya Villa is this cosy little restaurant with rainbow-coloured table linen, specialising in vegetarian organic food. Try the various pizzas or Indian curries that strike a deep chord with passing travellers.

Flags (☎ 26141617; G2 Metropole, Bund Garden Rd; mains Rs75-200) This super-popular global cuisine place was on hibernation mode during research, and should be back with its legendary Lebanese delights and dishes such as Mongolian cauliflower and *yakisoba* (fried Japanese noodles) soon.

Prems (☎ 66012413; North Main Rd, Koregaon Park; mains Rs100-250) In a quiet, leafy courtyard tucked away behind a commercial block, Prems is perfect for those lazy, beer-aided lunch sessions, and is patronised for its Indian, continental and Chinese selection.

The Place: Touche the Sizzler (☎ 26134632; 7 Moledina Rd; mains Rs120-200) As the name suggests, this long-running place specialises in sizzlers, but it also offers Indian, tandoori, seafood and continental dishes.

ourpick Malaka Spice (☎ 26151088; Lane 6, North Main Rd; mains Rs120-350, ☺ 11am-11pm) A chic and happening restaurant that sometimes doubles as a gallery. Admire the artworks while gorging on some excellent Southeast Asian food, and wash it all down with one of the eatery's fine wines or a pint of fresh draught.

Arthur's Theme (☎ 66032710; Lane 6, North Main Rd; mains Rs150-300) A stylish place offering decent French cuisine in a slightly formal atmosphere. The dishes here have wacky names after figures such as Don Quixote. Taste for adventure, eh?

The ABC Farms is a complex of midrange restaurants in Koregaon Park, where healthy, organic food is the order of the day. One of the best restaurants here is the **Swiss Cheese Garden** (☎ 9890911923; mains Rs100-400), which, alongside delicious pastas, offers good old cheese fondues.

CAFES

German Bakery (North Main Rd, Koregaon Park; dishes Rs50-150, cakes Rs25-50; ☺ 6.30am-11.30pm) Pune's melting pot and a compulsory halt on the Koregaon Park backpacker trail, this long-running cafe is known for its light, healthy snacks and a good range of cakes and puddings.

Juice World (2436/B East St; ☺ 8am-11.30pm) As well as producing delicious fresh fruit juices and shakes, this casual cafe with outdoor seating serves inexpensive snacks such as pizza and *pav bhaji* (spiced vegetables and bread) for around Rs40 to Rs50.

Drinking & Entertainment

Pune puts a great deal of effort into nocturnal activities. But somehow, several pubs tend to shut up shop as quickly as they open. So ask around for the latest hotspots. Most are open from 7pm to around 1.30am. Some charge a weekend cover fee, around Rs200.

Nirvana (☎ 66024733; Metropole, Bund Garden Rd) Located in one of Pune's central hang-outs, this roomy, glowing lounge is a nice place to down drinks with gusto.

Thousand Oaks (☎ 26343194; 2417 East St) This one is an old favourite, featuring a cosy and quiet pub-style bar with a charming, moodily lit sit-out.

Inox (Bund Garden Rd) A state-of-the-art multiplex where you can take in the latest blockbuster, either from Hollywood or Mumbai.

Shopping

Pune has some good shopping options.

Bombay Store (322 MG Rd; ☺ 10.30am-8.30pm Mon-Sat) The best spot for general souvenirs.

Pune Central (Bund Garden Rd, Koregaon Park) This glass-fronted mall is full of Western high-street labels and premium Indian tags.

For modern Indian clothing, try **Either Or** (24/25 Sohrab Hall, 21 Sasson Rd; ☺ 10.30am-8pm Fri-Wed) or **Fabindia** (Sakar 10, Sasson Rd; ☺ 10am-8pm).

Getting There & Away

AIR

Airline offices in Pune:

Air India (airline code AI; ☎ 26128190; Hermes Kunj, 4 Mangaldas Rd)

Indian Airlines (airline code IC; ☎ 26052147; 39 Dr B Ambedkar Rd)

Jet Airways (airline code W8; ☎ 26123268; 243 Century Arcade, Narangi Bung Rd)

Kingfisher Airlines (airline code IT; ☎ 26059351; Koregaon Rd)

Indian Airlines, Jet Airways, Kingfisher and IndiGo fly daily from Pune to Delhi (from Rs1200, two hours), Bengaluru (from Rs750, 1½ hours), Kolkata (from Rs2300, three hours) and Goa (from Rs1000, one hour). Spicejet and IndiGo have cheap flights to Chennai (from Rs100, 1½ hours). Kingfisher also flies daily to Ahmedabad, Chennai and Hyderabad.

BUS

Pune has three main bus stands: **Pune train station stand** (☎ 26126218), for Mumbai and destinations south and west, including Goa, Belgaum, Kolhapur, Mahabaleshwar and Lonavla; **Shivaji Nagar bus stand** (☎ 25536970), for points north and northeast, including Aurangabad, Ahmedabad and Nasik; and **Swargate bus stand** (☎ 24441591), for Sinhagad, Bengaluru and Mangalore. Deluxe buses shuttle from the train-station bus stand to Dadar (Mumbai) every hour (Rs230, four hours).

Several private deluxe buses head to Panaji (Panjim) in Goa (ordinary/sleeper

MAHARASHTRA

MAJOR TRAINS FROM PUNE

Destination	Train No & name	Fare (Rs)	Duration (hr)	Departure
Bengaluru	6529 *Udyan Exp*	345/1295	21	11.45am
Chennai	2163 *Chennai Exp*	377/1372	19½	12.10am
Delhi	1077 *Jhelum Exp*	437/1654	27	5.20pm
Hyderabad	7031 *Hyderabad Exp*	250/926	13½	4.35pm
Mumbai CST	2124 *Deccan Queen*	77/270	3¼	7.15am

Express fares are sleeper/2AC; *Deccan Queen* fares are 2nd class/chair. To calculate 1st class and other fares see p1188.

Rs300/400, 12 hours), Nasik (semideluxe/deluxe Rs150/250, five hours) and Aurangabad (Rs150, six hours). Prices can go up during rush periods. Make sure you know where the bus will drop you off (going to Mumbai, for instance, some private buses stop at Borivali). Try **Brright Travels** (☎ 26114222; Connaught Rd); its buses depart from the service station near the roundabout.

TAXI
Long-distance share taxis (four passengers) link up Pune with Dadar in Mumbai around the clock. They leave from the **taxi stand** (☎ 26121090) in front of Pune train station (per seat Rs355, 2½ hours). Several tour operators have an express Mumbai-airport drop-off scheme (Rs1600, 2½ hours). Try **Simran Travels** (☎ 26153222, 26159222; Koregaon Park).

TRAIN
Pune is an important rail hub with connections to many parts of the state. The swarming computerised **booking hall** (☎ 131) is to the left of the station as you face the entrance.

For getting to Mumbai, train is the safest option. The *Deccan Queen, Sinhagad Express* and *Pragati Express* are fast commuter trains to Mumbai (2nd class/chair Rs58/198, 2½ hours).

GETTING AROUND
The airport is 8km northeast of the city. An autorickshaw there costs about Rs80; a taxi is Rs250.

Turtle-paced city buses gather at the PMT depot across the road from the train station. Useful buses include bus 4 to Swargate, bus 5 to Shivaji Nagar, and bus 159 to Koregaon Park.

Autorickshaws can be found everywhere. A ride from the train station to Koregaon Park costs about Rs30 in the daytime and Rs50 at night.

AROUND PUNE
Sinhagad
Now reduced to near-rubble, the scenic **Sinhagad** (admission free; ☼ dawn-dusk) or Lion Fort, about 24km southwest of Pune, is steeped in history. Earlier controlled by Bijapur, the fort was conquered by Shivaji after an epic battle in 1670, in which he lost his son Sambhaji. Legend has it that Shivaji used pet monitor lizards yoked with ropes to scale the craggy walls of the fort. Today, all is forgotten, and the fort's interiors are studded with telecommunication towers and ugly government buildings. However, it's worth a visit for the sweeping views it offers.

If you don't want to walk up 10km to reach the fort from Sinhagad village, jeeps (Rs30) can cart you to the base of the summit. Bus 50 runs frequently to Sinhagad village from 7am until evening, leaving from either Swargate or the Architect College bus stop opposite Nehru Stadium (Rs17, 45 minutes).

MAHABALESHWAR
☎ 02168 / pop 12,700 / elev 1372m
With all due respect to its founders, Mahabaleshwar is one of the most characterless and congested hill stations you can find in India. High up in the Western Ghats, it was founded in 1828 by Sir John 'Boy' Malcolm, a British governor, after which it quickly became the summer capital of the Bombay presidency. But much of the old-world charm that the town once had has been undone today by mindless construction and lousy town planning. Add to that the fact that it's a popular destination for sea-swept Mumbai weekenders, for whom this motor exhaust–belching place is as good as a Himalayan getaway.

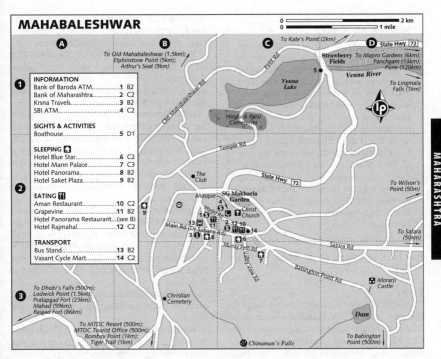

MAHABALESHWAR

What still works in Mahabaleshwar's favour, however, are the delightful views it offers, but they may not be half as good in practice, given that you'll have to combat riotous tourists while appreciating them.

You'll find the hill station virtually shuts down during the monsoon season (June to September), when an unbelievable 6m of rain falls.

Orientation

The action is in the main bazaar (Main Rd, also called Dr Sabane Rd) – a 200m strip of holiday tack. The bus stand is at the western end. You have to cough up Rs15 as 'tourist tax' on arrival.

Information

Mahabaleshwar has no internet facilities. State Bank of India and Bank of Baroda have 24-hour ATMs on Masjid Rd.

Bank of Maharashtra (☎ 260290; Main Rd) Changes cash and travellers cheques.

Krsna Travels (☎ 261035; Subhash Chowk, Main Rd; ⏰ 9am-8pm) Reliable onward travel information, a variety of local tours and ticketing.

MTDC tourist office (☎ 260318; Bombay Point Rd) At the MTDC Resort south of town.

Sights & Activities

The hills are alive with music, though it's usually blasted out of car windows as people race by in an effort to tick off all the viewpoints as quickly as possible. If you can ignore this, or beat them by starting your day early, then fine views can be savoured from **Wilson's Point** (also known as Sunrise Point), within easy walking distance of town, as well as **Elphinstone**, **Babington**, **Kate's** and **Lodwick Points**.

The sunset views at **Bombay Point** are stunning; but you won't be the only one thinking so! Much quieter, thanks to being 9km from town, is **Arthur's Seat**, on the edge of a sheer drop of 600m. Attractive waterfalls around Mahabaleshwar include **Chinaman's**, **Dhobi's** and **Lingmala Falls**. On the edge of Venna Lake, a **boathouse** (Temple Rd; ⏰ 8am-8pm) rents out rowboats (Rs180 per hour) and pedal boats (Rs200 per hour), but the long queues can be off-putting.

A nice walk out of town is the two-hour stroll to Bombay Point, then following **Tiger**

BERRIES, ANYONE?

Fruity Mahabaleshwar is India's berry-growing hub, producing some of the country's finest strawberries, raspberries, mulberries and gooseberries. The best crops come around February, though fruits are harvested from late November through June. If you're visiting during the season, you can buy fresh berries direct from the farms, or get them from the many vendors in Mahabaleshwar's bazaar. In the absence of fresh fruits, you can always pick up fruit drinks, sweets, fudges or jams. One place to shop for farm-fresh stuff is **Mapro Gardens** (☎ 02168-240112; ⏰ 10am-1pm & 2pm-6.30pm), between Mahabaleshwar and Panchgani.

Trail back in (maps are available from the MTDC tourist office).

Tours

The MSRTC conducts sightseeing tours for the very rushed. The Mahabaleshwar round (Rs65, 4½ hours) takes in nine viewpoints plus Old Mahabaleshwar, leaving the bus stand thrice from 2.15pm. Alternatively, taxi drivers will give a three-hour tour for about Rs400. Tours are also available to lookout points south of town (Rs300, 2½ hours), Panchgani (Rs400, three hours) and Pratapgad Fort (Rs450, three hours).

Sleeping & Eating

Hotel prices soar during peak holidays in Mahabaleshwar (November to June); at other times you might get heavy discounts. Most budget places are around the main bazaar, while dozens of resort-style lodges are scattered around the village – check out is usually at 8am or 9am. Single travellers can forget about camping in town; local laws bar hotels from renting out rooms to loners, especially men. Rates quoted here are high-season prices.

MTDC Resort (☎ 260318; fax 260300; d from Rs900) This large-scale operation is situated about 2km southwest from town, and comes with quieter and greener surroundings. Rooms smack of government aesthetics, but that's no deterrent. Taxis can drop you here from the city centre for about Rs50.

Hotel Blue Star (☎ 260678; 114 Main Rd; d Rs1200) These guys offer hefty off-season discounts,

which is just about the right value for the mediocre rooms. It sits on the main thoroughfare, which you might consider a bonus.

Hotel Mann Palace (☎ 261778; Murray Peth Rd; d Rs1500) This place flanks a quiet street below the main market. The neighbourhood is dingy, but the rooms are well cared for, and the staff a professional lot.

Hotel Panorama (☎ 260404; www.panoramaresorts .net; 28 MG Rd; d from Rs3500; 🖳 🖳) A midtown luxury joint, this is where business meets leisure. The rooms have recently been given a facelift, and the food at its vegetarian restaurant is recommended. If you go swimming in its pool, look out for oncoming swan-shaped paddle boats!

Hotel Saket Plaza (☎ 260583; www.saketplaza.com; Old Band Rd; d incl full board from Rs3900) Located pleasantly away from the din, this place is more of a family joint, with associated facilities such as indoor games. The beds are comfy, the food highly palatable and AC available for Rs300 extra.

Hotel Rajmahal (80 Main Rd; meals Rs40-75) A good place to dig into some lip-smacking vegie delights.

Aman Restaurant (Main Rd; kebabs Rs50-100) Little more than a roadside stall, Aman can pull out some amazing meaty bites from the skewers.

Grapevine (Masjid Rd; dishes Rs60-180) Charming wrought-iron table settings topped with Mediterranean-themed placemats topped with the finest Parsi and continental dishes, with a glass of wine for the added effect. Skip this place, and you've missed half the fun in town.

Mahabaleshwar is famous for its berries, which you can buy fresh (in season) or as juice, fruit bars and jams (see the boxed text; left).

Getting There & Away

From the **bus stand** (☎ 260254) state buses leave regularly for Pune (ordinary/semideluxe Rs82/100, 3½ hours), with less frequent buses rolling to Satara (Rs43, two hours), Panchgani (Rs12, 30 minutes) and Mahad (for Raigad Fort; Rs39, two hours). Two buses go daily to Kolhapur (Rs125, five hours), while eight buses ramble off to Mumbai Central Station (ordinary/semideluxe Rs156/200, seven hours).

Private agents in the bazaar book luxury buses to destinations within Maharashtra, and Goa (seat/sleeper Rs550/750, 12 hours, with a changeover at Surur). Remember to ask where they intend to drop you. Buses to Mumbai (Rs400, 6½ hours) generally don't go beyond Borivali, while those bound for Pune (Rs200) will bid you adieu at Swargate.

Getting Around

Taxis and Maruti vans near the bus stand will take you to the main viewpoints or to Panchgani. For trips within town, the minimum charge is Rs30 (for up to 2km).

Cycling around is an option, but be careful of speeding traffic especially on the outskirts. Bikes can be hired from **Vasant Cycle Mart** (Main Rd; ☽ 8am-9pm) for Rs10 per hour or Rs50 per day.

AROUND MAHABALESHWAR
Pratapgad Fort

Closely associated with Deccan's history, the windy **Pratapgad Fort** (maintenance fee Rs5; ☽ 7am-7pm), built by Shivaji in 1656, straddles a high Sahyadri ridge 24km west of Mahabaleshwar. It was here that a cornered Shivaji agreed to meet Bijapuri General Afzal Khan in an attempt to end a stalemate in 1659. Despite a no-arms agreement, Shivaji, upon greeting Khan, disembowelled his enemy with a set of iron *baghnakh* (tiger's claws). Khan's tomb marks the site of this painful encounter at the base of the fort, though it's out of bounds for tourists.

Pratapgad is reached by a 500-step climb, which affords brilliant views. Guides are available for Rs150. To get here from Mahabaleshwar, you can take the 9.30am state bus (Rs72 return, one hour). It waits at the site for an hour before returning. A taxi to Pratapgad and back costs Rs450.

Raigad Fort

Some 80km northwest of Mahabaleshwar, all alone on a remote hilltop, stands **Raigad Fort** (Indian/foreigner Rs5/100; ☽ 8am-5.30pm), a must-see for history buffs. This was Shivaji's capital, from where he held sway over his vast empire, from when he was crowned in 1648 until his death in 1680. Much of the fort was later destroyed by the British, and some colonial structures added. But monuments such as the royal court, plinths of royal chambers, the main marketplace and Shivaji's tomb still remain, and are worth a daylong excursion.

You can hike to the top; it's a 2½-hour steep haul up 1475 steps. For an offbeat experience, take the vertigo-inducing **ropeway** (☎ 02145-274831; ☽ 8.30am-5.30pm), which zooms up the cliff and offers an eagle-eye view of the gorges below. A return ticket costs Rs150. Guides (Rs150) are available within the fort complex.

Raigad is best reached by bus from Mahad (Rs15, 45 minutes) on the Mumbai–Goa highway. Or you can take a taxi tour direct from Mahabaleshwar (Rs1200).

KOLHAPUR
☎ 0231 / pop 505,500 / elev 550m

It's surprising why people rarely visit Kolhapur, even though this historically important town offers a great opportunity to get up close and personal with the vibrant side of India. Its proximity to Goa, a friendly population and an intriguing temple complex are enough reasons why you should go, and chances are that Kolhapur will end up being the most fascinating discovery on your trip. Gastronomes take note: the town is also the birthplace of the famed, spicy Kolhapuri cuisine, especially chicken and mutton dishes.

In August, Kolhapur hosts **Naag Panchami**, a snake-worshipping festival, in tandem with Pune.

Orientation

The old town around the Mahalaxmi Temple is 3km southwest of the bus and train stations, while the 'new' palace is a similar distance to the north. Rankala Lake, a popular spot for evening strolls, is 5km southwest of the stations.

Information

Axis Bank (Station Rd) Has a 24-hour ATM below Hotel Panchsheel.

Internet Zone (Kedar Complex, Station Rd; per hr Rs20; ☽ 8am-11pm) Internet access.

MTDC tourist office (☎ 2652935; Assembly Rd; ☽ 10am-5.30pm Mon-Sat) Opposite the Collector's Office.

State Bank of India (☎ 2660735; Udyamnagar) A short autorickshaw ride southwest of the train station near Hutatma Park. Deals in foreign exchange.

Sights
SHREE CHHATRAPATI SHAHU MUSEUM

'Bizarre' takes on a whole new meaning at this 'new' palace, built by the Kolhapur kings in 1884. Designed by British architect 'Mad' Charles Mant, this Indo-Saracenic behemoth still serves as the royal family's private residence. The ground floor houses a wacky **museum** (☎ 2538060; Indian/foreigner Rs13/30; ⏰ 9.30am-5.30pm), with one of the most peculiar collections of memorabilia in the country. An unconventional sort of an animal-lover, the eponymous king went on several trigger-happy trips into the jungles. The trophies he returned with were then put to some ingenious uses, such as making walking sticks from tiger vertebrae, or fashioning ashtrays out of rhino feet! Then, there's an armoury, which houses enough weapons to stage a mini coup. The horror-house effect is brought full circle by the taxidermy section, where you'll see everything from tigers to African dik-diks! Don't forget to visit the durbar hall, a rather ornate affair, where the king once held court sessions. Photography is strictly prohibited.

OLD TOWN

Kolhapur's atmospheric old town is built around the lively and colourful **Mahalaxmi Temple** (⏰ 5am-10.30pm) dedicated to Amba Bai, or the Mother Goddess. The temple's origins date back to AD 10, but much of the modern structure is from the 18th century. It's one of the most important Amba Bai temples in India and therefore attracts an unceasing tide of humanity. Non-Hindus are welcome and it's a fantastic place for a spot of people-watching. Nearby, past a foyer in the Old Palace, is **Bhavani Mandap** (⏰ 6am-8pm), dedicated to the goddess Bhavani.

Kolhapur is famed for the calibre of its wrestlers and at the **Motibag Thalim**, a courtyard beside the entrance to Bhavani Mandap, young athletes train away in a muddy pit. You are free to walk in and watch, as long as you don't mind the sight of sweaty, seminaked men and the stench of urine emanating from the loos! Professional matches are held between June and December in the **Kasbagh Maidan**, a red-earth arena in a natural sunken stadium a short walk south of Motibag Thalim. Events are announced in local papers.

Finally, for shopaholics, the streets of the old town are crammed with shops where the hard sell of some Indian tourist cities is unheard of. Kolhapur produces the renowned Kolhapuri leather sandals, prized the world over for their intricate needlework. You can drive a good bargain here; most designs come within Rs200 to Rs400. By the way, the sandals are notorious for blistering your feet when new!

CHANDRAKANT MANDARE MUSEUM

Dedicated to actor and artist Chandrakant Mandare (1913–2001), this well-maintained **gallery** (☎ 2525256; Rajarampuri, 7th Lane; admission Rs3; ⏰ 10.30am-1pm & 1.30-5.30pm Tue-Sun) houses stills of his movies as well as his fine paintings and sketches.

Sleeping & Eating

Kolhapur's hotels are of very good value, and most of them line Station Rd, which appropriately enough is the busy main street running west of the train station.

Hotel Tourist (☎ 2650421; Station Rd; s/d incl breakfast from Rs525/675; 🖫) Known for its quality service, this place was undergoing renovation during research, and should emerge an even better place.

Hotel Vrindavan Deluxe (☎ 2664343; Station Rd; s/d from Rs550/650; 🖫) These folks have done a neat job imitating urban business hotels. The rooms sport sleek orange and buff upholstery, and open onto a breezy central vestibule. It's near Shivaji Park, and street noise is a downside.

Hotel Pavillion (☎ 2652751; www.hotelpavillion.co.in; 392E, Assembly Rd; s/d incl breakfast from Rs850/1000; 🖫) Located at the far end of a foliaged park–cum–office area, this wonderful place has large rooms with windows that open out to a splendid view of seasonal blossoms. It's very close to the MTDC office.

Hotel Pearl (☎ 6684451; hotelpearl@hotmail.com; New Shahupuri; s/d incl breakfast from Rs1700/1900; 🖫 💻) It's expensive by Kolhapur's standards, but has an ambience even city hotels would be jealous of. The rooms are large, smart and well-equipped, and service is commendable.

Surabhi (Hotel Sahyadri Bldg; snacks & mains Rs20-50) This bustling eatery is the right place in town to sample some of Kolhapur's legendary snacks such as *misal* (a spicy snack not unlike *bhelpuri*), thalis and lassi.

Getting There & Around

Rickshaws are abundant in Kolhapur and most drivers are honest with their billing. Most carry conversion charts to calculate fares from outdated meters.

From the **bus stand** (☎ 2650620), services head regularly to Pune (ordinary/semideluxe Rs152/195, five hours), Mahabaleshwar (Rs125, five hours) and Ratnagiri (Rs90, four hours). For longer hauls, your body will be happier on a deluxe private bus. Most of the private bus agents are on the western side of the square at Mahalaxmi Chambers, across from the bus stand. Overnight services with AC head to Mumbai (seat/sleeper Rs350/600, nine hours) and non-AC overnighters go to Panaji (Rs180, 5½ hours).

The **train station** (2654389) is 10 minutes' walk west of the bus stand. Three daily expresses, in-cluding the 10.50pm *Sahyadri Express,* zoom to Mumbai (sleeper/2AC Rs206/750, 12½ hours) via Pune (Rs163/584, eight hours). The 2.05pm *Rani Chennamma Express* makes the long voyage to Bengaluru (sleeper/2AC Rs299/1117, 17½ hours). You can also fly cheap between Kolhapur and Mumbai on a daily basis with Kingfisher Red (from Rs450).

Goa

Goa

It's green, it's glistening and it's gorgeous: just three of the reasons why Goa has allured visitors – both of the friendly and invading varieties – for so many hundreds of years. Today, the biggest drawcard to its over two million annual visitors is the silken sand, the cocohut culture and the *sossegado* (clunkily translated as 'laid-backness) of which its residents are justifiably proud.

Nowhere else in India will you find the warmth of a Goan household and hassle-free haggling for goods in bustling marketplaces. Pour in a dash of Portuguese-influenced wine, food and crumbling colonial-era architecture, infuse with a colourful blend of Hinduism, Islam and Catholicism, pepper with parties, and you've got a happy, heady mix that proves just too enticing to long-staying foreigners, who've been clinging to its crystalline shores since the '60s.

But there's far more to discover here than the pleasure of warm sand between your toes. Wander around a vanilla-scented spice plantation, stroll the bird-filled banks of the state's gentle rivers, marvel at centuries-old cathedrals, and venture out to white-water waterfalls.

All is not perfect in paradise, however, and Goa has problems aplenty – the state's environment, in particular, is currently being sorely taxed. Nevertheless, with a slowly growing group of environmentalists and ecofriendly individuals on the scene, the picture remains relatively rosy for this most magical of miniature states. So, come, minimise your impact as much as possible, and unwind to the swaying palms and Portuguese rhythms of Goa's still-irresistible charms.

HIGHLIGHTS

- Wander the Portuguese-flavoured old quarters of **Panaji** (Panjim; p864) and linger over lunch at one of its ravishing restaurants
- Shiver in the shadows of grand cathedrals in **Old Goa** (p870), once the ecclesiastical wonder of the Eastern world
- Indulge in barefoot luxury on quiet white-sand **beaches** (p889) in the state's sleepy southern stretches
- Dream of grand times long gone in the slowly crumbling mansions of **Chandor** (p891)
- Peruse the peppercorns and munch a banana-leaf lunch at an inland spice plantation around **Ponda** (p872)
- Worship or salute the sun away from the northern crowds on **Mandrem's** beautiful beach (p887)

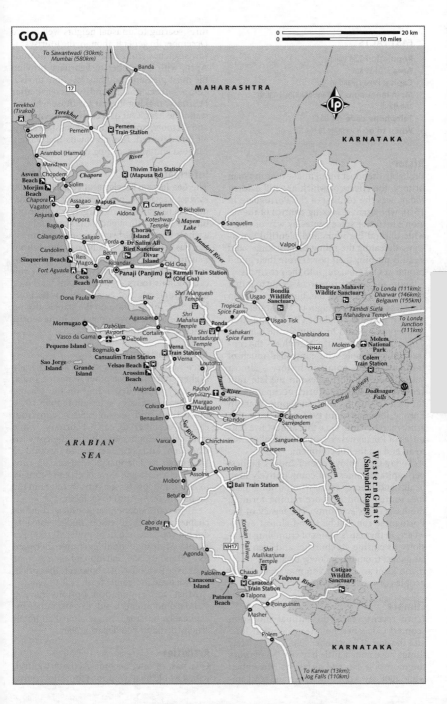

FAST FACTS

Population 1.34 million
Area 3701 sq km
Capital Panaji (Panjim)
Main languages Konkani, Marathi, English and Hindi
Telephone code ☎ 0832
When to go November to March

History

Probably the most influential event in Goan history, the effects of which are still evident today, was the coming of the Portuguese in 1510, who arrived seeking control of the region's lucrative spice routes by way of Goa's wide natural harbours and plentiful waterways, defeating the ruling Bijapur kings, and steadily pushing their power from their grand capital at Old Goa, out into the provinces.

Soon, the conquerors were seeing to it that not only Portuguese rule, but their religion too, was spread throughout the state – by force, if need be – and the Goan Inquisition saw repression and brutality in the name of Christianity. Though the Marathas – the central Indian people who controlled much of India at various points in history – almost vanquished the Portuguese in the late 18th century, and despite a brief occupation by the British during the Napoleonic Wars in Europe, it was not until 1961, when the Indian army marched into Goa, that almost five centuries of Portuguese occupation finally came to an end on the subcontinent.

Today Goa enjoys one of India's highest per-capita incomes and comparatively high health and literacy rates, with farming, fishing, tourism and iron-ore mining forming the basis of its economy. The legacy of the Portuguese can still be found almost everywhere, in the state's scores of crumbling mansions, its cuisine, its churches and even in its language; though it's slowly becoming rarer, if you keep an ear out you may hear elderly people conversing in Portuguese.

Climate

Until recent years, the annual monsoon scoured Goa's beaches clean between June and the end of September reliably, but lately things have gone a little haywire. Sometimes the monsoon can end as late as November, while 2008 saw a poor monsoon and temperatures soaring to unusual heights well before December. In general, though, the tourist season stretches from mid-November to mid-April, with December to February proving the most pleasant (and busiest) time to visit. Temperatures and humidity increase after February, making it great for those who can stand the heat. Out of season, between April and October, you'll find most coastal resorts all but deserted, though towns like Panaji, Mapusa and Margao chug on as usual.

Information

The **Goa Tourism Development Corporation** (GTDC; www.goa-tourism.com), provides maps and information, operates hotels (largely adequate but uncharismatic) throughout the state, and runs a whole host of whirlwind one-day and multi-day bus trips, as well as daily boat cruises from Panaji. Its main branches are in Panaji (p866) and at Dabolim airport (see p862), but you can book its tours, its hotel rooms, and pick up a simple map of Goa at any of its hotel branches. Information on the state is also up for grabs at the Government of India tourist office in Panaji (p866).

ACCOMMODATION

Accommodation prices in Goa are generally higher than in most other states of India, and vary wildly depending on the season. High season prices – often more than 100% more than mid-season rates – run from early December to early February, while prices climb higher still during the crowded Christmas and New Year period (around 22 December to 3 January). Mid-season runs from October to late November, and February to April, and low season runs throughout the monsoon, from April to October.

All accommodation rates indicated in this chapter are for high season. Budget-category double rooms come in at under Rs1000 per night. Midrange doubles range between Rs1000 and Rs2500, and top-end choices come in at over Rs2500. Note, however, that prices can fluctuate incredibly from year to year.

Most accommodation options have a standard noon check out, except, rather inexplicably, in Panaji, where almost all hotels cruelly demand you depart at 9am.

Activities

Goa has, of late, become Activity Central, with a whole host of options for water sports,

---

WHERE TO GOA...

Where to go during your stay in this little beachy paradise depends very much on what you want to do when you get here, though, with enough time and possibly a scooter on which to spend some of it, you should be able to experience a little of everything that takes your fancy in this relatively tiny Indian state.

Very generally, Goa can be split up into three distinct regions: north, south and central. The north, above the Mandovi River, is the place for those seeking action, shopping and activities in equal supply, and for folks looking for the remnants of Goa's fabled trance party scene. In addition, the north boasts some beautiful stretches of almost-empty beach, along with a string of highly developed resorts with lots of choice in restaurants, hotels and water-sports outfits.

Head into central Goa, nestling between the Mandovi and Zuari Rivers, and things get decidedly more cultural. Here sits Panaji, Goa's small and loveable state capital, which slings itself lazily along the broad banks of the Mandovi River, whilst inland lie spice plantations and the glorious remnants of Goa's grand and glittering past in the form of mansions, temples and cathedrals.

Things slow down in the south, where the beaches grow generally quieter and the sun-lounges are spaced further apart. Not the place for partying the night away, the beaches here cater to a quieter, calmer crowd, with lots of homespun charm. This is the place to sit back, unwind, and perhaps spot a hatching turtle or two, before saddling up your scooter and heading back up the twisting National Highway (NH17) to the bright lights and big beaches of the north.

---

alternative therapies and yoga. Many outfits change annually – especially those run by foreigners – so it's best to head to your destination and ask around. There's no shortage of noticeboards and keen individuals on hand to bring you up to speed on current options.

WATER SPORTS

Water sports such as **parasailing** and **jet-skiing** are particularly readily available on the beaches at Baga (p877), Benaulim and Colva (p893).

You can try **paragliding** at Anjuna (p882) and Arambol (p887), where there's also an opportunity for **kite surfing**. Based in Baga, Barracuda Diving (p877), offers a range of **scuba diving** opportunities, including boat dives and PADI (Professional Association of Diving Instructors) courses.

YOGA & ALTERNATIVE THERAPIES

From Ashtanga through to Zen, every imaginable form of **yoga**, along with **reiki**, **ayurvedic massage** and a multitude of other spiritually orientated health regime, is practised, taught and relished in Goa. Palolem and Patnem (p895), in the south of the state, and Arambol (p887), Mandrem (p887) and Anjuna (p882) in the north are great places to take courses in reiki and manifold forms of yoga, t'ai chi and healing, and many also host retreat centres for longer meditation and yoga courses.

Since course locations and contact details change annually, we've only listed the longer-established operations here; for the full gamut of options, it's best to head to your beach of choice and scan hotel and cafe noticeboards.

WILDLIFE-WATCHING

Goa is a nature-lover's paradise, perfect for **wildlife-watching**, with an abundance of brilliant birdlife and a fine (but largely well-concealed) collection of fauna, including sambars, barking deer and the odd leopard. Head to Cotiago Wildlife Sanctuary (p895) to scout out birds and beasts alike, or to the Tropical Spice Plantation (p872) which offers waterborne bird-watching on its lake. Day Tripper in Calangute (p879) offers various nature-related tours, while John's Boat Tours in Candolim (p874) offers bird-watching boat trips, along with sea-based dolphin tours and crocodile-spotting trips up the Mandovi River. At almost any beach, though, and you'll be sure to find someone with a boat and a strong desire to show you (on a no-show, no pay basis) those adorable grey mammals of the waves.

Dangers & Annoyances

One of the greatest – and most deceptive – dangers in Goa is to be found right in front of your beautiful bit of beach. The Arabian Sea, with its strong currents and dangerous undertows, claims dozens of lives per year,

GOA

many of them foreign. Lonely Planet has received one letter from a reader whose adult daughter and her friend both drowned while paddling in the sea in north Goa.

Though some of Goa's beaches are now overseen by lifeguards during daylight hours, it's most important to heed local warnings on the safety of swimming, and don't, whatever you do, venture into the water after drinking or taking drugs.

Other dangers and annoyances are of the rather more universal kind. Be sure to keep your valuables under lock and key – especially if you're renting an easy-to-penetrate coco-hut – and don't walk along empty stretches of beach alone at night. Away from the beaches, it makes sense for visitors of both sexes to adopt the same, more modest forms of dress that they would in other parts of the country. See p1170 for advice specifically for women travellers.

DRUGS

Acid, ecstasy, cocaine, *charas* (cannabis or hashish), marijuana and all other forms of recreational drugs are illegal in India (though still very much available in Goa) and purchasing or carrying drugs is fraught with danger. Goa's Fort Aguada jail is filled with prisoners, including some foreigners, serving lengthy sentences for drug offences, and being caught in possession of even a small quantity of illegal substances can mean a 10-year stay in a cockroach-infested cell.

Getting There & Away

AIR

Goa's sole and diminutive airport, Dabolim, is situated right in the centre of the state, around 29km south of Panaji, and an easy taxi ride (usually two hours, at most) from any of the state's beaches. Few international flights arrive here, and those that do are package-holiday charters, mostly from Russia and Britain: independent travellers from the UK could check Thomson (www.thomsonfly.com) and those flying from Germany can try Condor (www.condor.com) which both offer flight-only fares.

Generally, the quickest way to reach Goa from overseas is to take an international flight into Mumbai, and then a quick 45-minute hop by domestic airline down to Goa.

Numerous domestic airlines fly daily in and out of Goa, most flights taking off and landing throughout the morning and early afternoon, to a number of Indian destinations. Of them, **Indigo** (☎ toll free 18001803838; www.go indigo.in), **GoAir** (☎ toll free 180022211; www.goair.in) and **SpiceJet** (☎ toll free 18001803333; www.spicejet .com) are the cheapest, and **Kingfisher** (☎ toll free 1800180010; www.flykingfisher.com) and **Jet Airways** (☎ toll free 1800225522; www.jetairways.com) by far the most comfortable. It's usually cheapest and easiest to book online as far in advance of your travel as possible, and any enquiries are best made to the airlines' toll-free numbers in India.

Dabolim airport's arrivals hall is equipped with a money exchange office, GTDC branch (see Information p860), Airtel office for purchasing mobile-phone credit, and charter-airline offices. There are two prepaid taxi booths (one in the arrivals hall and the other just outside), for heading by taxi elsewhere in the state.

BUS

Plenty of long-distance interstate buses operate to and from Panaji, Margao, Mapusa and Calangute, and you can also pick up some long-distance services from Chaudi near Palolem. See individual destination sections for detailed information.

TRAIN

The **Konkan Railway** (www.konkanrailway .com), the main train line running through Goa, connects Goa with Mumbai to the north, and with Mangalore to the south. Its main train station in Goa is Madgaon station in Margao, from which there are several useful daily services to Mumbai.

The convenient overnight *Konkan Kanya Express* (KKE; train number 0111; 1AC/2AC/ 3AC/sleeper Rs1832/1092/796/293) departs Mumbai's Dadar station at 11.05pm, arriving at Madgaon the next morning at 10.45am. In the opposite direction, the *KKE* (train number 0112) departs Madgaon at 6pm daily, and arrives at Mumbai's Dadar station at 5.20am.

From Mumbai's Chhatrapati Shivaji Terminus (CST; also known as Victoria Terminus),

---

FESTIVALS IN GOA

Feast of the Three Kings (6 Jan; Chandor, p891) Held in historic Chandor, local boys re-enact the story of the three kings bearing gifts for Christ.

Shigmotsav (Shigmo) of Holi (Feb/Mar; statewide) Goa's version of the Hindu spring festival Holi, this festival sees coloured water and powders thrown about with abandon, and joyous parades held in most towns.

Sabado Gordo (Fat Saturday; Feb/Mar; Panaji, p864) Part of the statewide Carnival, this festival is held on the Saturday before Lent. It's celebrated by a procession of floats and raucous street partying.

Carnival (Mar; statewide) A three-day festival heralding the arrival of spring, the party's particularly raucous in the streets of Panaji.

Procession of All Saints (Mar/Apr; Goa Velha, p870) On the fifth Monday in Lent, this is the only procession of its sort outside Rome, whereby 30 statues of saints are paraded around Old Goa and neighbouring villages.

Fama de Menino Jesus (2nd Mon in Oct; Colva, p891) Colva's biggest feast day, when the Menino Jesus (a statue of the infant Jesus said to perform miracles) is paraded through town.

International Film Festival of India (IFFI; www.iffi.nic.in; over 10 days from the last week of Nov; Panaji, p864) Based in Goa since 2004, this is the largest film festival in India and sees the glitterati of Mumbai arrive in Panaji for premiers and parties aplenty.

Feast of St Francis Xavier (3 Dec; Old Goa, p870) Old Goa's biggest bash, this feast sees lots of festivities, processions and huge crowds. Once every decade, an exposition involves the patron saint's body being paraded through Old Goa's streets. The next is scheduled for 2014.

Feast of Our Lady of the Immaculate Conception (8 Dec; Margao, p889, & Panaji, p864) A large fair and a church service is held at the Church of Our Lady of the Immaculate Conception in Panaji. Around the same time, Margao celebrates with a large fair.

---

the *Mandovi Express* (train number 0103; 1AC/2AC/3AC/2nd class Rs1832/1092/796/165) departs at 6.55am and arrives at 6.45pm. In the opposite direction, the *Mandovi Express* (train number 0104) leaves Madgaon at 9.40am. arriving at CST at 9.45pm.

The fastest train from Mumbai is the *Jan Shatabdi Express* (train number 2051; AC seat/2nd class Rs680/197) which departs Mumbai's CST at 5.10am and arrives in Madgaon at 2.10pm. In the opposite direction, the *Jan Shatabdi Express* (train number 2052) departs Madgaon at 2.30pm and arrives at Mumbai's CST at 11.20pm.

There are plenty of other rail options, too, to other parts of India. The daily *Goa Express* (train number 2780; 16½ hours) and the daily *Rajdhani Express* (train number 2432; 25 hours) both link Madgaon to Delhi's Nizamuddin station. A number of daily services link Madgaon to Trivandrum (around 20 hours); numerous daily options also head south to Mangalore (eight hours). There are also trains to Pune (14 hours) and Hospet Junction (eight hours 20 minutes), which is useful for travellers to Hampi. These services' frequencies and departure times seem to change fairly often, so check at the station or on the website for the most recent information.

Train bookings are best made at Madgaon station (p891), at the train reservation office at Panaji's Kadamba bus stand (p869) or at any travel agent vending train tickets (though you'll probably pay a small commission for the convenience). Make sure you book as far in advance as possible for sleepers, since they fill up quickly.

You can also book *Konkan Kanya Express* tickets online (www.konkanrailway.com), subject to a long list of conditions: you can only book between seven and two days in advance of travel, only in three-tier sleeper AC class for a cost of Rs1500 per ticket, and with no date changes permitted.

Other smaller, useful Goan railway stations include Pernem for Arambol, Thivim for Mapusa and the northern beaches, Karmali (Old Goa) for Panaji and Canacona for Palolem.

Getting Around
BUS

Goa boasts an extensive network of buses, shuttling to and from almost every tiny town and village. There are no timetables, bus numbers, or, it seems, fixed fares, though it would be hard to spend more than Rs20 on any one single journey (and fares are usually far less). Buses range from serviceable to spluttering, and most pack passengers to bursting point, but are a fun and colourful way to experience local life. Head to the nearest bus stand (often called the Kadamba bus stand, after the state's biggest bus company) and scan the signs posted on the bus windscreen to find the service you're after, or ask a driver who'll point you to the right old banger. Check individual destination listings for more detailed information on services.

CAR

It's easy, in most destinations, to organise a private car with a driver if you're planning on taking some long-distance day trips. Prices vary, but you should bank on paying around Rs1500 to Rs2000 for a full day out on the road.

It's also possible, if you've the nerves and the skills, to procure a self-drive car, giving you the (white-knuckled) freedom to explore Goa's highways and byways at your own pace. A small Chevrolet or Maruti will cost around Rs600 to Rs900 per day and a jeep around Rs1000, excluding petrol; there are few organised rental outlets, so ask around for a man with a car willing to rent it to you.

Note the slightly mystifying signposts posted on Goa's major National Highway 17 (NH17), which advise of different speed limits (on the largely single-carriageway road) for different types of vehicles.

MOTORCYCLE

You'll rarely go far on a Goan road without seeing an intrepid tourist whizzing by on a scooter or motorbike, and renting (if not driving) one is a breeze. You'll likely pay around Rs150 to Rs300 per day for a scooter, Rs400 for a smaller Yamaha motorbike, and about Rs500 for that most alluring, roaring symbol of mechanical freedom, the Royal Enfield Bullet. These prices can drop considerably if you're renting for more than one day, or if you've hit Goa during a less than peak period.

If you've never biked or scooted before, however, bear in mind that Goan roads are treacherous, filled with human, bovine, canine, feline, mechanical and avian obstacles, as well as a good sprinkling of potholes and hairpin bends. Take it slowly, try not to drive at night (when black cows can prove a dangerous impediment to your progress), don't attempt a north–south day trip on a 50CC scooter, and the most cautious of riders might even consider donning a helmet or shoes.

TAXI

Taxis are widely available for hopping town-to-town, and, as with a chauffeured car, a full day's sightseeing, depending on the distance, is likely to be around Rs1500 to Rs2000. From the airport to your destination, there are two prepaid taxi stands, one inside and the other just outside the arrivals hall; buy your ticket here and you'll be ushered to a cab.

Motorcycles are also a licensed form of taxi in Goa. They are cheap, easy to find, and can be identified by a yellow front mudguard – and even the heftiest of backpacks seem to be no obstacle.

CENTRAL GOA

PANAJI (PANJIM)
pop 98,915

Panaji (also commonly known as Panjim) is an anomaly among Indian state capitals, as clean, friendly and manageable as many others are chaotic, frustrating and missable. Its Portuguese-era colonial charms make it a perfect place to lull away a day or two, strolling pretty, peaceful streets, taking a decidedly kitsch sunset river cruise, eating vindaloos and *xacutis* (spicy sauces combining coconut milk, freshly ground spices, and red chillies) to your heart's content, and ending the evening in one of dozens of hole-in-the-wall local bars. With a madcap Carnival during Lent, a growing number of 'lifestyle' stores catering to the well-heeled traveller, and a friendly, easygoing riverside vibe, it's a great base for explorations of Goa's historic hinterland, or simply a terrific option for a day trip back from the beach.

Orientation & Information

Panaji is a manageable-sized city, all the more so because only two or three distinct areas have much of interest to visitors. The central, pretty districts of Sao Tomé and Fontainhas are where you're likely to spend most of your time, with 31st January Rd providing the central spine to link them. On this road you'll find plenty of (fairly grim) budget accommodation, tiny thali joints, hole-in-the-wall bars, internet outlets, a supermarket or two, and several places for placing cheap international calls.

PANAJI (PANJIM)

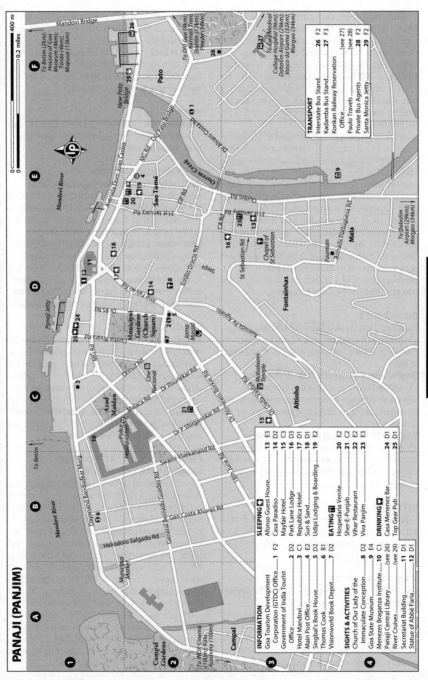

GOA

The wide road that runs riverside (Dayanand Bandodkar Marg to the west, Avenida Dom Joao Castro to the east) is another good destination for eating and bar-hopping, and to the eastern end, just across the New Pato Bridge, you'll find the Santa Monica jetty for river cruises, and the local and long-distance bus stands. Further south, incongruously tucked away on the banks of Ourem Creek, is the Goa State Museum.

Back in the centre of town, clustered around the Municipal Gardens you'll find a range of cheap and cheerful joints for vegetable thalis, fish fry, and fish-curry-rice, the central, impressive Church of Our Lady of the Immaculate Conception, travel agents, shopping opportunities, and a crop of ATMs.

The other area around which you might find yourself spending time is 18th June Rd, which runs southwest from the southeast corner of the Municipal Gardens. Here are more accommodation options, eating places, ATMs, travel agents and the like, heading off down toward the nearby Kala Academy.

BOOKSHOPS

Book Fair (Hotel Mandovi, Dayanand Bahdodkar Marg; ☻ 9am-9pm) A small, well-stocked bookshop in the Hotel Mandovi lobby, with plenty of well-illustrated books on Goa.

Singbal's Book House (☎ 2425747; Church Sq; ☻ 9.30am-1pm & 3.30-7.30pm Mon-Sat) A good selection of international magazines and newspapers, and lots of books on Goa are offered at this slightly grumpy establishment.

Visionworld Book Depot (☎ 2182865; Church Sq; ☻ 9.30am-9pm) Offers a good selection of self-help and spiritual titles, novels and children's books, as well as vending an assortment of locally made snacks to provide sustenance for browsing.

INTERNET ACCESS

You'll find no shortage of internet cafes dotted across town. Most charge Rs30 per hour, have fairly slow connection times, and are open from 9am to 11pm daily.

MEDICAL SERVICES

Goa Medical College Hospital (☎ 2458700; Bambolin) Situated 9km south of Panaji on NH17.

MONEY

As with most places in Goa, you can't walk far without finding an ATM booth, with its usually icy air-conditioning and sleepy security guard. Most take international cards and you'll find a particularly bumper crop on 18th June Rd.

Thomas Cook (☎ 2221312; Dayanand Bandodkar Marg; ☻ 9.30am-6pm Mon-Sat year-round, 10am-5pm Sun Oct-Mar) Changes travellers cheques commission-free and gives cash advances on Visa and MasterCard.

POST

Main post office (MG Rd; ☻ 9.30am-5.30pm Mon-Fri, 9am-5pm Sat) Offers swift parcel services and Western Union money transfers.

TOURIST INFORMATION

Goa Tourism Development Corporation office (GTDC; ☎ 2424001; www.goa-tourism.com; Dr Alvaro Costa Rd; ☻ 9.30am-5.45pm Mon-Fri) This GTDC office, just south of the Old Pato Bridge, is a decent place to pick up maps of Goa and Panaji, and to book GTDC's host of tours.

Government of India tourist office (☎ 2223412; www.incredibleindia.com; Communidade Bldg, Church Sq; ☻ 9.30am-1.30pm & 2.30-6pm Mon-Fri, 10am-1pm Sat) Staff here are extremely helpful, and can provide a list of qualified guides for tours and trips in Goa. A half-day tour (up to four hours) for two people, for example, costs Rs600.

Sights & Activities

Panaji is a city of long, leisurely strolls, through the sleepy Portuguese-era Sao Tomé, Fontainhas and Altinho districts, for a spot of shopping on 18th June Rd, and down along the languid Mandovi River, and if you happen to be here in November, don't miss catching a few flicks at the excellent **International Film Festival of India** (www.iffi.gov.in, www.iffigoa.org), India's largest and most glittering film festival.

CHURCH OF OUR LADY OF THE IMMACULATE CONCEPTION

Panaji's spiritual, as well as geographical, centre is its gleamingly picturesque main **church**, consecrated in 1541 and stacked like a fancy white wedding cake to the southeast of the ragged municipal gardens. When Panaji was little more than a sleepy fishing village, this place was the first port of call for sailors from Lisbon, who would clamber up here to thank their lucky stars for a safe crossing, before continuing to Old Goa, the state's capital until the 19th century, further east up the river.

If your visit coincides with 8 December, be sure to call in for the Feast of Our Lady of the Immaculate Conception, which sees a special church service and a lively fair spilling away from the church to mark the date.

GREEN GOA?

Goa's environment has suffered from an onslaught of tourism over the last 40 years, but equally from the effects of logging, mining and local customs. Rare turtle eggs have traditionally been considered a dining delicacy; plastic bottles lie in vast glaciers (as unreceding as the real kind are the reverse); and vagrant cows feast by roadsides on refuse from unfragrant rubbish bins.

There are, however, a few easy ways to minimise your impact on Goa's environment. Since plastic – in both bag and bottle forms – is a major problem, bring your own nonplastic bag along while shopping, and try to refill water bottles with filtered water wherever possible. The 5L Bisleri water bottles come with a deposit and are returnable to be reused; invest in these, instead of the regular size, when you can. Don't, of course, leave litter on the beaches, and consider – if you're travelling with small children – using washable nappies, instead of the disposable kind (especially since laundry services generally cost so much less than the price of a pack of disposable nappies).

Turtles are currently protected by the Forestry Department, who operate huts on beaches, such as Agonda, where turtles arrive to lay eggs. Drop into these, or go to www.goaforest.com to find out more about the department's work.

The **Goa Foundation** (☎ 2256479; www.goafoundation.org; G-8 Feira Alta, Mapusa) is the state's main environmental pressure group and has been responsible for a number of conservation projects since its inauguration in 1986. Its excellent *Fish Curry & Rice* (Rs400), a rich sourcebook on Goa's environment and lifestyle, is available for sale at the Other India Bookstore (p873) in Mapusa, and online (international order accepted) at www.otherindiabookstore.com. This excellent shop also stocks a host of other environment-related books, pamphlets and publications.

SECRETARIAT BUILDING

Dating from the 16th century, this handsome **colonial-era building** (Avenida Dom Joao Castro) was originally the palace of Muslim ruler Adil Shah, before becoming the viceroy's official residence in 1759. Nowadays it houses rather less exciting government offices, but remains worth a gaze as the oldest building in town. It is currently under renovation and will be for quite some time. Immediately to the west, the strange and compelling **statue** of a man bearing down upon a supine female form depicts one of Goa's most famous home-grown talents, Abbé Faria, an 18th-century Goan priest, 'father of hypnotism' and friend of Napoleon, in full melodramatic throes.

MENEZES BRAGANZA INSTITUTE

Located on the west side of the Azad Maidan, about 1km west of the Secretariat, this beautiful early 20th-century affair houses the **Panaji Central Library** (Malaca Rd; ☺ 9.30am-1.15pm & 2-5.30pm Mon-Fri) and is worth dropping into to see the pretty blue-and-white *azulejos* (glazed ceramic-tile compositions) in the west entrance hall.

GOA STATE MUSEUM

An eclectic collection of items awaits visitors to this large **museum** (☎ 2438006; www.goamuseum .nic.in; EDC Complex, Pato; admission free; ☺ 9.30am-5.30pm Mon-Fri), in a strangely uncentral area southwest of the Kadamba bus stand. As well as Hindu and Jain sculptures and bronzes, and a few nice examples of Portuguese-era furniture, exhibits include an elaborately carved table used by the notoriously brutal Portuguese Inquisition in Goa, and some ancient coins. Though not exactly bursting at the seams, it's a diverting way to while away a couple of hours while waiting for a bus or river trip.

HOUSES OF GOA MUSEUM

A short taxi ride across the river to the north of Panaji, in the little village of Torda, you'll arrive at this highly worthwhile **museum** (☎ 2410711; ☺ 10.30am-7.30pm Sun-Sat). It was created by a well-known local architect, Gerard da Cunha, to illuminate the history of Goan homes, apparent statewide in various states of picturesque decrepitude. Marooned ship-like in the middle of a traffic island, it's hard to miss, and a taxi here from central Panaji should cost around Rs200.

Courses

London-based **Holiday on the Menu** (www.holiday onthemenu.com) offers a range of Goan-cooking holidays, ranging from a Saturday 'Curry Morning' to a whole-week program including trips out to a spice plantation and a local market, based in the picturesque village of Betim, just across the river north of Panaji. Prices start at £59 per person for the 'Curry Morning', and all courses are suitable for vegetarians.

Tours

GTDC (see p860) operates a range of entertaining daily hour-long **cruises** (Rs150; ☼ dusk cruise 6pm & 6.30pm, sundown cruise 7.15pm & 7.45pm) along the Mandovi River aboard the *Santa Monica* and *Shantadurga*. All include a live band – sometimes lively, sometimes lacklustre – performing Goan folk songs and dances. There are also twice-weekly, two-hour **dinner cruises** (Rs400 incl snacks & buffet dinner; ☼ 8.30pm) and regular two-hour **dolphin-watching trips** (Rs250 incl refreshments; ☼ 8.30am Wed, Sat & Sun). All cruises depart from the Santa Monica jetty next to the huge Mandovi Bridge and tickets can be purchased here.

Various other companies offer virtually identical cruises also from Santa Monica jetty. Head down to the jetty to see what's on offer; in general, though, the GTDC cruises are a little more staid, whilst others – perhaps because of the promise of 'free beer' – can get a little rowdier with groups of local male tourists.

GTDC also runs a two-hour daily **Goa By Night bus tour** (Rs200; ☼ 6.30pm), which leaves from the same jetty spot and includes a river cruise. As ever, its breakneck tour packs in as much as possible; in this case, in just two hours you'll experience a river cruise, a long string of churches, a palace, a temple and a panoramic view.

Sleeping

BUDGET

If you're looking for rock-bottom budget accommodation, lots of lodging options run the length of 31st January Rd. Don't, however, expect atmospheric old Portuguese haunts: most consist of nothing much but a cell-like room, no view, and a 9am or earlier check out, with attached doubles going for around Rs500 or less. Wander up and down and check out a few before you decide; there's little to choose between them, though some may let you barter down the price.

Udipi Lodging & Boarding (☎ 228047; Sao Tomé; d without bathroom Rs200) For a really basic stay, without quite so much of a disturbing prison-like feel as some of the budget options along

31st January Rd, check into one of the eight rooms at the Udipi, just around the corner from the main post office. Don't expect any home comforts, but it's dingy rather than dirty and a decent enough place to lay down your backpack for a night or two.

Republica Hotel (☎ 2224630; Jose Falcao Rd; d Rs600) There are some places that promise so much and deliver so little, and the Republica, sadly, is one of them – though its dilapidation is, in part, its charm. You'll not receive a warm welcome or a well-decorated room; indeed, the service is gloomy and the decor grim, but this elderly, ramshackle wooden building is certainly no shoe-box concrete cell. It's not comfy, but it's fairly cheap, and offers a central location and a stay you're unlikely to forget.

Park Lane Lodge (☎ 2227154; St Sebastian Rd; d Rs755-1025; ☒) Set in an old and rambling bungalow near the Chapel of St Sebastian, the Park Lane has been popular with travellers for years, despite its seemingly ever-extending list of rules. Current formidable warnings include 'No Laundry', 'No Internet', 'Gates Closed 10pm' and '8am Checkout'. If you can work with all this, it makes a characterful – if crumbling – place to stay.

Mayfair Hotel (☎ 2223317; Dr Dada Vaidya Rd; s/d/tr from Rs780/980/1300; ☒) With its bright, cheerful balconies, beautiful ground-floor oyster-shell windows and general, slightly musty air of yesteryear, the Mayfair is an atmospheric central option. Note the 'hot-water timings' chart at reception, and be sure to arrange your showers accordingly.

MIDRANGE

Afonso Guest House (☎ 2222359; St Sebastian Rd; d Rs1200) Run by a friendly elderly gentleman, this lovely place set in a pretty old Portuguese town house offers plain but comfortable rooms, and a little rooftop terrace for sunny breakfasting (dishes Rs15 to Rs25). It's a simple, serene stay in the heart of the most atmospheric part of town.

our pick Casa Paradiso (☎ 2420297; www.casaparadisogoa.com; Jose Falcao Rd; d Rs1350-1800; ☒) A new and terrific stay at the heart of the city, just steps away from Panaji's Church of Our Lady of the Immaculate Conception, with friendly staff and modern, well-decorated rooms.

TOP END

Sun & Sand (☎ 240000; www.sunsandhotel.com; Bairo Alto Dos Pilotos, Jose Falcao Rd; d with/without river view

Rs5500/6500, ste Rs12,000; 🍴 💻 🍸) Perched high above Panaji, with lovely views from its terrace and small pool, this is a great option for a little bit of luxury in the midst of the city. The price includes breakfast and pick-up/drop-off at the airport or railway station, for stays of over two nights.

Eating

You'll never go hungry in Panaji, where food is enjoyed fully and frequently. A stroll down 18th June or 31st January Rds will turn up a number of great, cheap canteen-style options, as will a quick circuit of the Municipal Gardens.

Vihar Restaurant (MG Rd; veg thalis Rs30-60) A vast menu of 'pure veg' food, great big thalis and a plethora of fresh juices make this clean, simple canteen a popular place for locals and visitors alike. Sip a hot chai, invent your own juice combination, and dig into an ice cream for afters.

Viva Panjim (31st January Rd; mains Rs50-160; ⏰ 11.30am-3pm, 7-11pm Mon-Sat, 7-11pm Sun) Though it might be more than a touch touristy these days this little side-street eatery, with a couple of tables out on the street itself, nevertheless still delivers tasty Goan staples, as well as the standard range of Indian fare. Keep an eye out in the dim interior for Mrs Linda de Souza, restaurant founder and doughty matriarch.

ourpick **Sher-E-Punjab** (18th June Rd; mains Rs60-150) A cut above the usual lunch joint, Sher-E-Punjab caters to well-dressed locals with its generous, carefully spiced Indian dishes. There's a pleasant garden terrace out back, and an icy AC room if you're feeling sticky. Try the delicious paneer tandoori *tikka* (Indian cheese coated in red spice paste, and baked in a tandoor oven; Rs90) but note, if you're hungering for snacks, that the fish fingers and chicken fingers are 'seasonal only'.

Hospedaria Venite (31st January Rd; mains Rs65-110) Along with Viva Panjim, this is without a doubt the lunch address to which most tourists head, and, though the food isn't exactly excellent, the atmosphere warrants the visit. Its tiny, rickety balcony tables, looking out onto pastel-washed 31st January Rd, make the perfect lunchtime spot, and the Goan *chouriços* (spiced sausages; Rs145) and vegetable vindaloo (Rs95) are actually pretty tasty. Order a cold beer or two, munch on a slightly '70s-style salad (think cold boiled vegetables in vinaigrette) and watch lazy Panaji slip by.

Drinking

Panaji's got pick-me-up pit stops aplenty, and a visit to 31st January Rd or Dayanand Bandodkar Marg will take you hopping in and out of lots of them. Mostly simple little bars with a few plastic tables and chairs and a friendly barman presiding, they're a great way to escape the midday heat and the best place to get chatting to locals on a balmy evening.

Casa Menenez Bar (Dayanand Bandodkar Marg; ⏰ 11am-3pm & 7-10.30pm) A down-to-earth drinking hole on the river road, open to the street and with just a scattering of plastic tables, this place is great for grabbing a cool Kingfisher.

Top Gear Pub (Dayanand Bandodkar Marg; ⏰ 11am-3pm & 6.30pm-midnight) A few doors down from Casa Menenez, there's a tiny, cool, retro bar hidden behind Top Gear's unassuming doors. There's no food here, so don't come hungry, but it's a great place to wet your whistle or whet your appetite.

Entertainment

Casino boats ply the Mandovi waters each night, offering lose-your-savings fun to all who step aboard; most leave from the Panaji jetty, so head there to make preparations for blowing your budget. **Casino Royale** (☎ 6659400; www.casinoroyalegoa.com; ⏰ 6pm-8am; entry Mon-Thu Rs1500, Fri-Sun Rs1800) is the newest and largest; various age and dress restrictions apply.

INOX Cinema (☎ 2420999; www.inoxmovies.com; Old GMC Heritage Precinct; tickets Rs100-170) This comfortable multiplex cinema, which shows Hollywood and Bollywood blockbusters alike, is near the Kala Academy. You can even book online and choose your seats in advance.

Kala Academy (☎ 2420451; www.kalaacademy.org; Dayanand Bandodkar Marg) On the west side of the city at Campal is Goa's premier cultural centre, which features a program of dance, theatre, music and art exhibitions throughout the year. Many shows are in Konkani, but there are occasional English-language productions; call to find out what's on when you're in town.

Getting There & Away

AIR

A taxi from Panaji to Dabolim airport takes 1½ hours, and costs Rs800. See p862 for domestic airline details.

BUS

All local services depart from Panaji's Kadamba bus stand, with frequent local

GOA

services (running to no apparent timetables) heading out all over the state every few minutes. To get to South Goan beaches, take a bus to Margao (Rs15; 45 minutes) and change there. State-run long distance services also depart from the Kadamba bus stand, but since the prices offered by private operators are about the same, and levels of comfort are far greater, it makes sense to go private instead.

Many private operators have booths outside the entrance to the Kadamba bus stand, but most private interstate services depart from the interstate bus stand next to the Mandovi Bridge.

One reliable private operator is **Paulo Travels** (☎ 2438531; www.paulotravels.com; G1, Kardozo Bldg) with offices just north of the Kadamba bus stand. It operates a number of services with varying levels of comfort to Mumbai (Rs350 to Rs700; 11 to 15 hours), Pune (Rs450 to Rs600, 10 to 12 hours), Hampi (Rs450 to Rs650, 10 hours), Begaluru (Rs450 to Rs750, 14 to 15 hours) and various other long distance destinations.

TRAIN

The closest train station to Panaji is Karmali (Old Goa), 12km to the east, at which a number of long-distance services stop. Note, though, that Panaji's **Konkan Railway reservation office** (⏰ 8am-8pm Mon-Sat) is on the 1st floor of the Kadamba bus stand. You can also check times, prices and routes online at www .konkanrailway.com.

Getting Around

It's easy enough to get around Panaji itself on foot, and it's unlikely you'll need even as much as an autorickshaw. To Old Goa, a taxi costs around Rs300, and an autorickshaw should agree to take you there for Rs150 to Rs200. Lots of taxis hang around at the Municipal Gardens, making it a good place to haggle for the best price.

OLD GOA

Gazing at the crumbling cathedral-filled remains of Old Goa today it's hard to believe that it was, from the 16th to the 18th centuries, the 'Rome of the East'. But travel back five centuries, to a time when Old Goa's population exceeded that of Lisbon or London and that's exactly what this fallen city, then capital of Goa, was considered. Its reign, however, was as short as it was glorious, and devastating outbreaks of cholera and malaria finally

forced the abandonment of the city in 1835. By 1843, the capital had been shifted to Panaji, further along the river, and the towering city was inhabited only by ghosts and the occasional grim hanger-on.

These days, Old Goa makes for an interesting outing, particularly if you're there to mill among the weekend crowds, and in the 10 days leading up to the **Feast of St Francis Xavier** on 3 December.

Sights
SÉ CATHEDRAL

The largest church in Old Goa, the **Sé de Santa Catarina**, as it's known by its full name, is also the largest in Asia, standing at over 76m long and 55m wide. Construction here begun in 1562, under orders from King Dom Sebastio of Portugal, and the finishing touches to the altars weren't made until 1652, some 90 years later.

Fairly plain all-round, the cathedral has three especially notable features: the first, up in the belfry, is the **Golden Bell**, the largest bell in Asia; the second is in the little screened chapel inside to the right, known as the **Chapel of the Cross of Miracles**, wherein sits a cross said to have miraculously – and vastly – expanded in size after its creation by a group of local shepherds in 1619. The third point of particular interest is the massive gilded *reredos* (ornamental screen behind the altar) which depicts the life of St Catherine, to whom the cathedral is dedicated, and who came to a sticky end in Alexandria, Egypt, where she was eventually beheaded.

CHURCH OF ST FRANCIS OF ASSISI

A beautifully fading **church** built in 1661 over an earlier 16th century chapel, its lovely interior is filled with gilded and carved woodwork, murals depicting the life of St Francis, 16th-century Portuguese tombstones, and another stunning *reredos*. Note the sign inside that reads 'No Photography of Persons'. Presumably, they've no problem with you clicking pictures of any heavenly hosts that decide to put in an appearance.

Just behind the church, its former convent houses an **archaeological museum** (⏰ 10am-5pm Sat-Thu; admission free), whose small but worthwhile collection includes a portrait gallery of Portuguese viceroys, a couple of bronze statues, fragments of Hindu temple sculpture, and some interesting 'hero stones', carved to

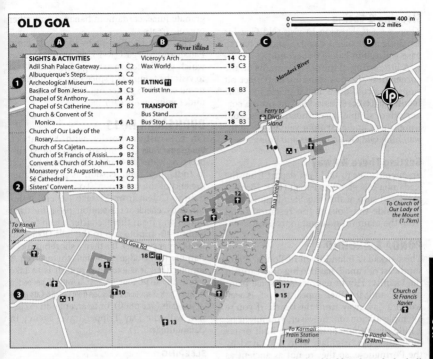

commemorate Hindu warriors who perished in combat.

BASILICA OF BOM JESUS
Famous throughout the Roman Catholic world for its rather grizzled and grizzly long-term resident, the Basilica's vast, gilded interior forms the last resting place of Goa's patron saint, St Francis Xavier (except for his diamond-encrusted fingernail, which sits in Chandor – see p891) who, in 1541, embarked on a mission to put right the sinful, heady lifestyles of Goa's Portuguese colonials.

Construction of the imposing red-stone basilica was completed in 1605; St Francis himself is housed in a **mausoleum** to the right, in a glass-sided coffin amid a shower of gilt stars.

MONASTERY OF ST AUGUSTINE
The melancholy, evocative ruins of this once vast and impressive **Augustinian monastery** are all that remains of a huge structure founded in 1572 and finally abandoned in 1835. The building's facade came tumbling down in 1942; all that remains, amid piles of rubble,

is the towering skeletal belfry, though the bell itself was rescued and now hangs in Panaji's Church of Our Lady of the Immaculate Conception.

WAX WORLD
If you're a fan of kooky representations of obscure historical figures, look no further than this brand new **waxworks** (☎ 9970126202; admission Rs30; ⏰ 9.30am-7pm), which boasts of a host of 'Life-Size Look-Alike Wax Statues' including a full, waxen version of Michelangelo's Last Supper.

OTHER HISTORIC SITES
There are plenty of other monuments, sprinkled throughout Old Goa, to explore, including the **Church & Convent of St Monica**, **Church of St Catejan**, **Viceroy's Arch**, **Adil Shah's Palace Gateway**, **Chapel of St Anthony**, **Chapel of St Catherine**, **Albuquerque's Steps**, the **Convent & Church of St John**, **Sisters' Convent** and the **Church of Our Lady of the Rosary**. For a wonderful view of the city hike up to the hilltop **Church of Our Lady of the Mount**, 2km east of Sé Cathedral, especially worth the trip for a spectacular sunset.

Sleeping & Eating

There's no real reason to visit Old Goa for anything more than a day trip, and it's best to base yourself in Panaji or beyond.

A little string of tourist restaurants on the corner near the bus stand make perfect pit stops for a cold drink and a snack; the basic **Tourist Inn** (Old Goa Rd; mains from Rs90) on the corner offers simple, tasty Indian dishes, cold Kingfishers, and a 1st-floor vantage point for watching Old Goa comings and goings.

Getting There & Away

Frequent buses to Old Goa depart from the Kadamba bus stand at Panaji (Rs7, 25 minutes) and stop at the 'Bus Stand-cum-ATM' just beside the Tourist Inn restaurant and from the main roundabout to the east.

PONDA & AROUND

The workaday inland town of Ponda, 29km southeast of Panaji, has two big drawcards in the vicinity: Hindu temples and spice plantations, and, if either appeal to you, is well worth a day away from the beach. If you're a temple aficionado, however, you might be a little disappointed; most were built or rebuilt after the originals were destroyed by the Portuguese, so they're not as ancient as in other parts of India.

The 18th-century hilltop **Manguesh Temple** at Priol, 5km northwest of Ponda is an architecturally composition dedicated to Manguesh, a god known only in Goa, whilst 1km away at Mardol is the **Mahalsa Temple**, also dedicated to a specifically Goan deity. The 1738 **Shantadurga Temple**, meanwhile, is dedicated to Shantadurga, the goddess of peace, and is one of the most famous shrines in Goa.

One of the best spice plantations to visit is the **Tropical Spice Farm** (☎ 2340329; admission Rs300; ◷ 9am-5pm), 5km northeast of Ponda. An entertaining (especially so if your guide happens to be Martin) 45-minute tour of the spice plantation, followed by a banana-leaf buffet lunch is included in the price, and elephant rides/bathings are available for Rs500/600 extra.

Nearby, the 200-year-old **Savoi Plantation** (☎ 234 0272; www.savoiplantations.com; ◷ daily), whose motto is 'Organic Since Origin', is less touristed and elephant-free, but you'll find a warm welcome from knowledgeable guides keen to walk you through the 100-acre plantation at your own pace. Local crafts are for sale, and you're welcomed with fresh pomegranate juice, cardamom bananas and other organic treats.

There are regular buses to Ponda from Panaji and Margao (Rs15, 45 minutes), after which you'll need to arrange an onward taxi to visit the temples or spice farms. Far better, if you can, is to potter out to this scenic area under your own steam.

DUDHSAGAR FALLS

On the eastern border with Karnataka, **Dudhsagar Falls** (603m) are Goa's most impressive waterfalls, and the second highest in India, best seen as soon as possible after the end of the monsoon. To get here, take a train to Colem from Margao (several trains run daily; check at the station, p891, for train times) and from there, charter a jeep for the bumpy 40-minute trip to the falls (Rs800 to Rs1000 per person). It's then a short but rocky clamber to the edge of the falls themselves. A simpler (but less exciting) option is to take a full-day **GTDC tour** (without AC/with AC per person Rs700/800; ◷ 9am-6pm Wed & Sun from Panaji & Calangute) to the falls (see p860), or to arrange an excursion with the Day Tripper travel agency in Calangute (p879).

SLEEPING

Backwoods Camp (☎ 9822139859; www.backwoodsgoa.com) For bird-watching enthusiasts, this quiet, rustic camp in the village of Matkan near Tamdi Surla offers one of Goa's richest sources of feathered friends, with everything from Ceylon Frogmouths and Asian Fairy Bluebirds, to Puff-throated Babblers and Indian Pittas putting in a regular appearance. Accommodation comes in the form of tents on raised forest platforms, bungalows and farmhouse rooms, and the camp makes valiant attempts to protect this fragile bit of the Goan ecosystem, through measures including waste-recycling, replanting indigenous tree species, and employing local villagers. Three-day bird-watching excursions, including guide, transport, accommodation at the camp and all meals, cost from Rs5500 per person.

NORTH GOA

MAPUSA
pop 40,100

The market town of Mapusa (pronounced 'Mapsa') is the largest town in northern Goa, and is most often visited for its busy **Friday**

Market (8am-6.30pm) which attracts scores of buyers and sellers from neighbouring towns and villages, and a healthy intake of tourists from the northern beaches. It's a good place to pick up the usual slew of embroidered bedsheets and the like, at prices far lower than in the beach resorts.

There's not a lot else to see here, though it's a pleasant, bustling and typically Indian town to wander for a while, and if you're interested in learning more about the admirable work of El Shaddai, International Animal Rescue, (for both, see Getting Involved, p875) or the Goa Foundation (see Green Goa?, p867), which all have their headquarters here or very close by.

Information

There are plenty of ATMs that are scattered about town, and you won't have any trouble locating one. There is a bumper crop that is located around the Municipal Gardens and the market area.

Mapusa Clinic (2263343; Consultations from 10am-noon & 4-6pm daily) A well-run medical clinic, and the place to go in an emergency.

Other India Bookstore (2263306; www.otherindia bookshore.com; Mapusa Clinic Rd; 9am-5pm Mon-Fri, to 1pm Sat) A little hard to find, go up the steps on the right as you walk down Mapusa Clinic Rd, and follow signs: this friendly and rewarding little bookshop is at the end of a highly dingy corridor.

Pink Panther Travel Agency (2250352, 2263180; panther_goa@sancharnet.in) A very helpful agency, selling bus, train and air tickets (both international and domestic) as well as performing currency exchange and property consultancy services.

Softway (2262075; per hr Rs20; Chandranath Apts, opposite Police Station) In a small shopping complex to the left just after the post office, this place has fast internet connections, and vends ice creams to keep you cool whilst surfing.

Sleeping

Sleeping options are pretty grim in Mapusa, and there's little reason to stay the night when the beaches of the north coast are all so close.

Hotel Vilena (2263115; Feira Baixa Rd; d Rs450, without bathroom Rs300) Friendly owners run Mapusa's best budget choice, though don't bring a cat since there won't be room in any of the 14 plain double rooms to swing it. The hotel's quaint Obsession Pub is open for bar-propping each evening.

Eating & Drinking

There are plenty of nice, old-fashioned cafes within the market area, serving simple Indian snacks, dishes and cold drinks to a local clientele. Thalis come in at the Rs40 mark, and chai at Rs5.

Hotel Vrundavan (dishes Rs8-50; 7am-late) An all-veg place bordering the Municipal Gardens, this is a great place for a hot chai and a quick breakfast. Dip your *pau* (fluffy white Portuguese bread roll) or *puri* (flat savoury dough that puffs up when deep fried) into a cashew-nut *bhaji* (small vegetable-based curry) for just Rs10, or try the tomato version for a more modest Rs9.

The Pub (9am-10.30pm; mains from Rs70) Don't be put off by the dingy entrance or stairwell; this place is great for watching the milling market crowds over a cold beer or long glass of *feni* (Goan liquor distilled from coconut milk or cashews). Eclectic daily specials (Rs108) include roast beef and goulash with noodles.

Getting There & Away

If you're coming to Goa by bus from Mumbai, Mapusa's Kadamba bus stand is the jumping-off point for the northern beaches. Private operators vend tickets to Mumbai (normal/AC Rs500/700, 14 hours) and Bengaluru (normal/AC Rs500/700, 12 hours) from just next to the bus stand. There's generally little difference in prices, comfort or duration between services, but shop around for the best fare.

Frequent local services – express and regular – also arrive and depart from the Kadamba bus stand; just look for the correct destination on the sign in the bus windscreen. Express services to Panaji (Rs9, 25 minutes), Calangute (Rs8, 20 minutes) and Anjuna (Rs8, 20 minutes), all depart every 30 minutes or so. For buses to the southern beaches, take a bus to Margao (Rs10, 1½ hours) and change there.

An autorickshaw to Anjuna or Calangute should cost Rs150; a taxi will charge at least Rs250.

Thivim, about 12km northeast of town, is the nearest train station on the Konkan Railway. Local buses meet trains (Rs10); an autorickshaw into Mapusa from Thivim costs around Rs120.

CANDOLIM, SINQUERIM & FORT AGUADA
pop 8600

Candolim's long, clean and narrow beach, which curves round as far as smaller Sinquerim beach in the south, is largely the preserve of slow-roasting package tourists from the UK, Russia and Scandinavia, and is fringed with an unabating line of beach shacks, all offering sun beds and shade in exchange for your custom. There are, however, some great independent budget hotels, which make for great stays in the area if you've got your own transport.

None of the most interesting attractions here, however, are directly beach-related. The most astonishing is the hulking wreck of the *River Princess* tanker, which ran aground in the late 1990s. Nothing can quite prepare you for the surreal sight of this massive industrial creature, marooned just a few dozen metres offshore, with tourists sunbathing in her sullen shadow.

The post office, supermarkets, travel agents, pharmacies and plenty of banks with ATMs are all located on the main road, known as Fort Aguada Rd, which runs parallel to the beach. Ask around for the season's latest internet outfit.

Sights & Activities

Aside from lazing on the beach, the Candolim area boasts a number of noteworthy attractions. First, guarding the mouth of the Mandovi River and hugely popular with Indian tour groups, is **Fort Aguada**, constructed by the Portuguese in 1612 and the most impressive of Goa's remaining forts. It's worth braving the crowds and hawkers at the moated ruins on the hilltop for the views,

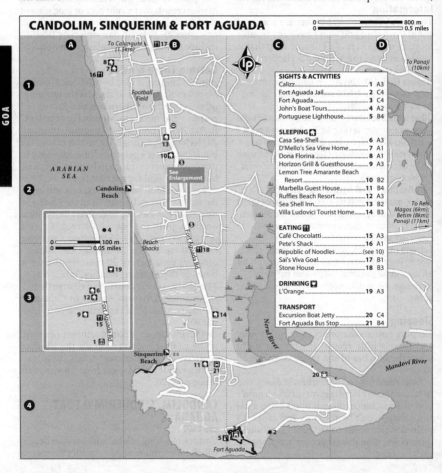

CANDOLIM, SINQUERIM & FORT AGUADA

0 — 800 m
0 — 0.5 miles

SIGHTS & ACTIVITIES	
Calizz...1	A3
Fort Aguada Jail.......................2	C4
Fort Aguada..............................3	C4
John's Boat Tours....................4	A2
Portuguese Lighthouse..........5	B4

SLEEPING	
Casa Sea-Shell.........................6	A3
D'Mello's Sea View Home.......7	A1
Dona Florina............................8	A1
Horizon Grill & Guesthouse....9	A3
Lemon Tree Amarante Beach Resort.......10	B2
Marbella Guest House............11	B4
Ruffles Beach Resort..............12	A3
Sea Shell Inn...........................13	B2
Villa Ludovici Tourist Home...14	B3

EATING	
Café Chocolatti......................15	A3
Pete's Shack...........................16	A1
Republic of Noodles.....(see 10)	
Sai's Viva Goa.........................17	B1
Stone House...........................18	B3

DRINKING	
L'Orange.................................19	A3

TRANSPORT	
Excursion Boat Jetty..............20	C4
Fort Aguada Bus Stop.............21	B4

GET INVOLVED

'Never work with children or animals', so the old thespian adage goes, but for those with the opportunity to volunteer while in the sunny state, three opportunities exist for helping small creatures with two or four – and sometimes even three – legs who need help most.

- **El Shaddai** (☎ 2266520, 6513286, 6513287; www.childrescue.net; El Shaddai House, Socol Vaddo, Assagao) A British-founded charity, El Shaddai aids impoverished and homeless children throughout Goa and beyond, running a number of day and night shelters, an open school and children's homes located throughout the state. Volunteers (who undergo a rigorous vetting process) able to commit to more than four weeks work with El Shaddai are encouraged to contact James d'Souza (☎ 9225901266). This is an undertaking to arrange in advance, since it can take up to six months to complete the vetting process. You can also sponsor a child, and make an difference to a young life, for less than £1 per day: check El Shaddai's website for details.

- **International Animal Rescue** (IAR; ☎ 2268328/272; www.iar.org.uk/india/goa; Animal Tracks, Mandungo Vaddo, Assagao) An internationally active charity, helping Goa's furry and feathered sick, unwanted and strays, IAR runs its Animal Tracks rescue facility in Assagao, near Mapusa, in north Goa. Visitors and volunteers (both short- and long-term) are always welcome, and IAR's website includes a 'Needs List' of things you might be able to fit into your backpack and bring from home, including antiseptic ointment, flea powder and puppy toys. You will also find online moving blogs that are written by current volunteers, and a downloadable PDF of information for willing volunteers. If you find an animal in distress in Goa, you should call the shelter for help.

- **Goa Animal Welfare Trust** (GAWT; ☎ 2653677; www.gawt.org; Old Police Station, Curchorem) Based in South Goa, GAWT operates an animal shelter at Curchorem (situated in the Old Police Station on the main road), helping sick, stray and injured dogs, cats and even a calf or two, and is open daily from 9am to 5pm for visits. GAWT, like IAT, undertakes extensive dog sterilisation projects throughout Goa, offers low-cost veterinary care, deals with animal cruelty cases, and finds homes for stray puppies. Volunteers are welcome, if only for a few hours to walk or play with the dogs, and even your old newspapers (all those you've bought from beach vendors) will be gratefully received for lining kennel floors, as will old sheets, towels and anything else you might not be taking home. GAWT also operates a shop and information centre in Colva (see p893).

---

which are particularly good from the four-storey **Portuguese lighthouse**, built in 1894 and the oldest of its type in Asia. It's a pleasant 2km ride along a hilly, sealed road to the fort, or you can walk via a steep, uphill path past Marbella Guest House. Beneath the fort, facing the Mandovi, is the **Fort Aguada Jail**, whose cells were originally fort storehouses.

A highlight of Candolim for anyone who has an interest in Goan heritage is **Calizz** (☎ 325000; Fort Aguada Rd; admission Rs300; ☒ 10am-7pm), an impressive compound that is filled with traditional Goan houses. Tours, which last for 45 minutes, are conducted by historians to bring the state's cultural history to life, in this National Tourism Award–winning project.

Throughout town there are numerous boat cruises on offer, the best known of which are

John's Boat Tours (☎ 5620190, 9822182814; www.johnsboattours.com), offering a variety of boat and jeep excursions, and arranging wonderful houseboat cruises (Rs4300 per person per day, full board). A dolphin-watching trip costs Rs795; a boat trip to Anjuna Market and backs costs Rs500, and a 'Crocodile Dundee' river trip, to catch a glimpse of the Mandovi's 'muggers' (crocodiles), costs Rs1000. If you're looking to haggle for a dolphin-spotting trip, head up to the **excursion boat jetty** along the Nerul River, from which lots of independent local boatmen operate.

Sleeping

Though Candolim is largely frequented by package tourists bussed straight in from Dabolim airport, there's a great range of accommodation for the independent traveller, with the added bonus that many midrange places include nice little swimming pools. Most of the best value budget choices are situated either in the northern part of Candolim or in the Sinquerim area further south; the little road up to Marbella (see right) has lots of private houses offering double rooms for around Rs500 per night.

BUDGET

Villa Ludovici Tourist Home (☎ 2479684; Fort Aguada Rd; d incl breakfast Rs650) For 30 years, Ludovico's has been welcoming travellers into its well-worn, creaky rooms in a grand old Portuguese villa. This is the place for a four-poster bed on a budget; rooms are vast, if definitely faded, and the hosts (and ghosts) are kind and amiable.

D'Mello's Sea View Home (☎ 2489650; dmellos_seav iew_home@hotmail.com; d small/large Rs700/1200) Lovely breezy rooms are the principle attraction at D'Mello's, which has the advantage of being just a stone's throw from the beach. A great choice for a simple, serene stay, especially when nearby Dona Florina is fully booked.

our pick Dona Florina (☎ 2489051; www.donaflorina .com; Monteiro's Rd; s/d/seaview Rs750/850/1000) It's hard to get better value in Candolim than friendly Dona Florina, just a quick walk from the sea and situated in the quiet northern part of the village. Front-facing rooms have spectacular sea views, there's daily yoga on the roof terrace, and the lack of vehicle access ensures a quiet night's repose.

Sea Shell Inn (☎ 2489131; seashellgoa@hotmail .com; Fort Aguada Rd; d Rs850) You won't miss this beautiful white-painted Portuguese mansion, just opposite the massive Newton's supermarket. Its eight plain rooms might come as a bit of a disappointment, however, after visiting the reception; they're in a '70s-style annexe around the back. Still, they're clean, fan-cooled and reasonable value, and rates include breakfast.

MIDRANGE

Casa Sea-Shell (☎ 2479879; seashellgoa@hotmail.com; Fort Aguada Rd; d without AC/with AC Rs1150/1850; 🐾 🖭 ▣) This modern, rather characterless choice, run by the same people as the Sea Shell Inn, nevertheless represents good value with its efficient service, nice little pool and comfortable rooms.

Horizon Grill & Guesthouse (☎ 2479727; d without AC/with AC Rs1200/1800; www.horizonview.co.in; 🐾 🖭 ▣) One of the few midrange places in town catering solely to independent tourists, this small hotel is a good value new option run by British expats, with simple rooms set around a small swimming pool. Don't expect luxury, but for the price tag, it can't be beat.

Ruffles Beach Resort (☎ 6641039; www.rufflesgoa .com; Fort Aguada Rd; d/tr Rs1500/1800; 🐾 ▣) 'Welcome to your abode in Paradise', declares Ruffles' website; that might be a bit much, but this decent place does have a pleasant courtyard pool and good value, well-equipped rooms.

TOP END

Marbella Guest House (☎ 2479551; www.marbellagoa .com; d from Rs2700; presidential ste Rs4700; 🐾) You might be put off by the name – particularly if you've already noticed the similarities on the sands – but this place has not a touch of Spain's Costa del Sol about it. A stunning Portuguese villa filled with antiques and backed by a peaceful courtyard garden, this place is a romantic, redolent old-world remnant. Its kitchen serves breakfast, lunch and dinner daily, with some imaginative touches, and its penthouse suite is a dream of polished tiles and four-posters. Sadly for kids with a keen sense of style, no guests under 12 are permitted.

Lemon Tree Amarante Beach Resort (☎ 3988188; www.lemontreehotels.com; Fort Aguada Rd; r Rs10,500-21,000; 🐾 🖭 🛜 ▣) Squeezed in on the main strip, this boutiquey, luxey place conjures up a strange mixture of Thai-spa style and medieval motifs, intended to echo, apparently 'the history and romance of 15th-century Portugal'. Whatever the mix, it works, with swish rooms equipped with DVD players, a luxurious spa and a roomy courtyard pool with swim-up bar.

Eating & Drinking

Candolim's drinking scene is largely hotel-based, but its plentiful beach shacks are popular places for a lunchtime beer or a happy-hour sunset cocktail or two. Look out for **Pete's Shack** (mains from Rs80) on the northern end of the strip, which is one of the sleekest, coolest beachfront operations.

Sai's Viva Goa! (Fort Aguada Rd; mains from Rs60; ☽ 11am-midnight) This cheap, locals-oriented little place serves flipping-fresh fish and Goan seafood specialities such as a spicy mussel fry.

our pick Café Chocolatti (Fort Aguada Rd; cakes from Rs80; ☽ 9am-7pm) When you're tired of thalis or simply seeking sanctuary, there's nowhere better to treat yourself in Candolim than this lovely tea room, set in a green garden light years from the bustle of the beach. Though the cafe serves sandwiches and salads, the clue to its speciality is in the name. Order a ginger lime fizz (Rs60) and a slice of double-chocolate cake (Rs80) and sink back into cocoa heaven.

L'Orange (Fort Aguada Rd; mains from Rs90; 🕙 12pm-12am) A cute, and largely orange, bar, restaurant and art gallery just beside John's Boat Tours, head here on Tuesday and Thursday nights for 'live music by Elvis', who's apparently alive and well and living in Candolim.

Stone House (Fort Aguada Rd; mains Rs90-240; 🕙 6pm-midnight) Surf 'n' turf's the thing at this venerable old Candolim venue, inhabiting a stone house and a leafy front courtyard, and the improbable sounding 'Swedish Lobster' tops the list. There's live music most nights of the week, amid the twinkle of fairy lights.

Republic of Noodles (Fort Aguada Rd; appetisers Rs200, mains from Rs425; 🕙 11.30am-3pm, 7-11pm) For a sophisticated dining experience, the RoN delivers with its dark bamboo interior, Buddha heads and floating candles. Delicious, huge noodle plates are the order of the day, and if you're feeling flush there's an exquisite brunch on Sunday mornings: Rs1200 buys you an extensive southeast Asian buffet, along with unlimited Mimosas and Bloody Marys.

Getting There & Away

Buses run about every 10 minutes to and from Panaji (Rs7, 45 minutes), and stop at the central bus stop near John's Boat Tours. Some continue south to the Fort Aguada bus stop at the bottom of Fort Aguada Rd, then head back to Panaji along the Mandovi River road, via the villages of Nerul and Betim.

Frequent buses also run from Candolim to Calangute (Rs3, 15 minutes) and can be flagged down on Fort Aguada Rd.

CALANGUTE & BAGA
pop 15,800

Once the summertime preserve of wealthy Goans escaping the oppressive heat of the premonsoon hinterlands, and later the heady '60s hotspot for naked, revelling hippies, the Calangute of today is India's 'Kiss Me Quick' capital, and, if you're not expecting pristine tropical sands, can prove just the place for fun-in-the-sun akin to a quick trip to Blackpool in a heatwave.

While Calangute's northern beach area is very much bucket-and-spade territory, its southern beach is more relaxed, refined, and upscale. Baga to the north, meanwhile, is the place for drinking and dancing with – unusually these days for Goa – clubs open until 4am, and a younger beach-shack based crowd. To escape the Baga heat, head north across the Baga River to some budget accommodation bargains clinging to the coast.

Orientation & Information

Currency exchange offices, ATMs, supermarkets and pharmacies cluster around Calangute's main market and bus stand area, continue north up to Baga, and head south too along the main road leading to Candolim. Here you'll also find international brand stores such as Levis, Lee and even a Crocs shop.

There are plenty of internet cafes (most charging Rs40 to Rs60 per hour) and prices tend to drop as you go further inland from the beach.

Literati Bookshop & Cafe (☎ 2277740; www.literati-goa.com; 🕙 10am-6.30pm Mon-Sat) Tucked away down a dusty lane leading to the beach at the far southern end of Calangute is this refreshingly different bookshop. Piles of good reads are stacked onto shelves throughout the owners' home, and there's a good line in strong Karnatakan coffee to keep you focussed.

MGM International Travels (☎ 2276249; www.mgmtravels.com; 🕙 9.30am-6.30pm Mon-Sat) A long-established and trusted travel agency near Calangute's central roundabout, this travel agency offers competitive prices on domestic and foreign air tickets.

Mubli Cybercafé (Tito's Rd; per hr Rs60; 🕙 9am til late) Order a simple breakfast or a strong cup of Italian coffee, surf and watch the beach crowds mill by.

Activities

Aside from frolicking in the waves with scores of other holiday makers, there's a host of activities on offer in both Calangute and Baga, including a highly respectable diving school.

WATER SPORTS

You'll find numerous jet-ski and parasailing operators on Baga Beach, and it pays to compare a few to find the most competitive rate. Parasailing usually costs around Rs1500 per ride; jet-skis cost Rs900 per 15 minutes, and water-skiing can be had for about Rs800 per 10 minutes.

Barracuda Diving (☎ 2182402; www.barracudadiving.com; Sun Village Resort, Baga) This longstanding

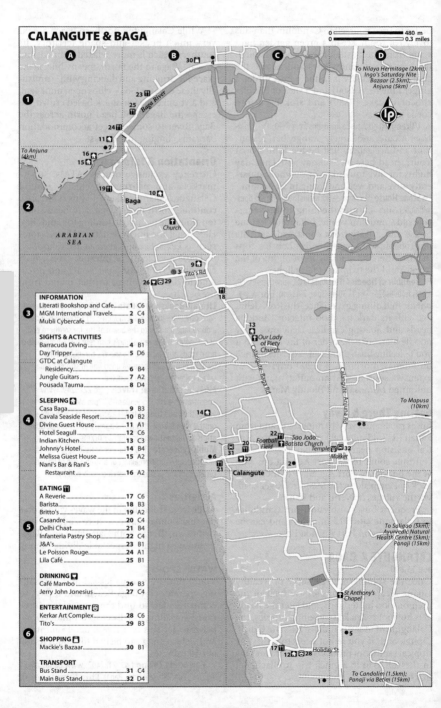

CALANGUTE & BAGA

diving school offers a vast range of classes, dives and courses, including a free 'Try Scuba' family session every Monday. It's also exceptional for its 'Project A.W.A.R.E' which undertakes marine-conservation initiatives and annual underwater and beach clean-ups.

YOGA & AYURVEDA

Ayurvedic Natural Health Centre (☎ 2409275; www .healthandayurveda.com; Chogm Rd, Saligao) This highly respected centre, 5km inland, offers a vast range of courses, in reflexology, aromatherapy, acupressure, yoga and various other regimes. There's also a range of herbal medicines on offer and treatments available by an ayurvedic doctor.

Pousada Tauma (☎ 2279061; www.pousada-tauma .com; d from €225; ❄ 🖳 ☎) If you're looking for luxury with your ayurvedic regime, check right into this gorgeous little boutique hotel in Calangute. Costs for treatments range from €45 for a 1½ hour treatment, up to €495 for a 14-day 'Pizhichil' course to treat complaints such as arthritis and sciatica.

BOAT TRIPS

Local fishermen congregate around the northern end of Baga beach, offering dolphin-spotting trips (Rs350 per person), visits to Anjuna Market (Rs270 per person) and whole-day coastal excursions up to Arambol, Mandrem and back (Rs800 per person). To pre-arrange and negotiate a trip, call friendly fisherman Eugenio (☎ 9226268531).

OTHER ACTIVITIES

Kerkar Art Complex (☎ 2276017; www.subodhkerkar. com; ❄ 10am-11pm) Showcasing the paintings, photographs and sculptures of local artist Dr Subodh Kerkar; the complex is most notable for its weekly open-air Indian music and dancing recitals (per person Rs300; ❄ 6.45-8pm Tue).

Jungle Guitars (☎ 9823565117; www.jungleguitars .com) If you've always been one to strum to your own tune, Jungle Guitars might just be the place for you. Fifteen to 20-day courses will allow you to build your very own steel-string or classical guitar from scratch, overseen by master guitar-builder, Chris. Courses

cost Rs55,000, including all materials and a case for the finished product.

Tours

Day Tripper (☎ 2276726; www.daytrippergoa.com; Calangute–Anjuna Rd; ❄ 9am-6pm end Oct-end Apr), with its head office in south Calangute, is one of Goa's best tour agencies. It runs a wide variety of trips around Goa, including to Dudhsagar Falls (p872), and also interstate to Hampi and the Kali River (for rafting and bird-watching trips) in Karnataka.

GTDC tours (see p860) can be booked at the '70s monstrosity **Calangute Residency** (☎ 2276024) beside the beach.

Sleeping

Calangute and Baga's sleeping options are broad and varied, though most decent budget options are towards the top end of the budget range. Generally, the quietest, most laid-back hotels lie in south Calangute, and across the bridge north of Baga.

BUDGET

Calangute

Johnny's Hotel (☎ 2277458; s/d Rs400/600-900) Twelve basic rooms in this backpacker-popular place make for a sociable stay, with regular classes available in yoga, ayurveda, reiki, and the tantalisingly titled 'metamorphic technique'. A range of apartments and houses are also available for longer-stayers: ask at reception for current prices. Johnny's is also home to a popular cafe: stop in for baked beans on toast for breakfast (Rs100) or spice up lunchtime with a Goan 'veg vindaloo' (Rs60).

our pick The **Indian Kitchen** (☎ 2277555; ikitchen2602@yahoo.co.in; off Calangute–Baga Rd; d Rs880; 🖳 🛜 ☎) If a colourful stay is what you're after, look no further than this family-run guesthouse, which offers basic, rather ramshackle rooms with lots of attempts at individual charm, around a sparkly, spangly central courtyard. Each room has its own terrace or sit-out, but what really tips the budget scales in its favour is the small, sparklingly clean swimming pool out the back. Roomy air-conditioned apartments are also available for long stayers, for Rs15,000 to Rs18,000 per month.

Baga

Melissa Guest House (☎ 2279583; d Rs500) Neat little rooms, all with attached bathrooms and hot-water showers, comprise this quiet, good value little place, pleasantly situated just past Nani's & Rani's.

Divine Guest House (☎ 2279546; www.indivinehome.com; d from Rs800; ✖ 🖳) You'll get the general optimistic air of this place as soon as you see the 'Praise the Lord' gatepost, and the happiness continues indoors with quietly cheerful rooms embellished with the odd individual touch amid a quiet riverside location.

Nani's Bar & Rani's Restaurant (☎ 2276313; www.naniranigoa.com; r Rs1000; 🖳) Situated on the tranquil north side of the Baga River, just a short hop from the Baga beach action, Nani's is as charming as it is well-situated, with simply furnished rooms set around a garden and a gorgeous colonial bungalow. Be sure to try the restaurant's food, cooked, its website claims, by the 'inmates', and look out for the heritage room equipped with such mod cons as an 'inverter'.

MIDRANGE & TOP END
Calangute

Hotel Seagull (☎ 2179969; www.villatheresagoa.com; Holiday St, Calangute; d without AC/with AC Rs2300/2500; ✖ 🖳) Bright, friendly and welcoming, the Seagull's rooms, set in a cheerful orange-painted house in quieter South Calangute, are light and airy, with antique bits and pieces of furniture to give them character, and there's a popular bar-restaurant downstairs with meals served all day.

Nilaya Hermitage (☎ 2276793; www.nilaya.com; Arpora; d incl breakfast & dinner €320; ✖ 🖳 🕾) Ultimate Goan luxury, set 6km inland from the beach at Arpora, a stay here will see you signing the guestbook with the likes of Giorgio Armani, Sean Connery and Kate Moss. Beautiful red-stone laterite structures undulate around a swimming pool, around which are set 11 luxury rooms and four stunning tents. The food is as dreamy as the surroundings, and the spa will see you spoiled rotten.

BAGA

Cavala Seaside Resort (☎ 2276090; www.cavala.com; s/d without AC from Rs850/1100, d with AC from Rs2200; ✖ 🕾) Idiosyncratic, ivy-clad Cavala has been charming Baga-bound travellers for over 25 years, and continues to deliver clean, simple, nicely furnished rooms, ranged about a large

complex with two central swimming pools. Rates include a hearty breakfast, and the bar-restaurant cooks up a storm most evenings.

Casa Baga (☎ 2253205; www.casaboutiquehotels.com; d Rs6000-7000; ✖ 🖳 🕾) Twenty Balinese-style rooms, some with huge four-poster beds, make for a classy and tranquil stay, with all the little stylish touches the Casa boutique team are so adept at providing.

Eating

Calangute and Baga boast probably the greatest concentration of dining options of anywhere in Goa, with everything on offer from the simplest curbside *bhelpuri* (thin fried rounds of dough with rice, lentils, lemon juice, onion, herbs and chutney) to the finest Scottish smoked salmon.

For the best of the area's street food, try the main Calangute beach strip, which is thick with vendors grilling sweetcorn, serving up *bhaji pau* (spicy vegetable curry with a white bread roll for dipping, served for breakfast), and spinning luminescent candyfloss. Dining gets more sophisticated to both the north and south, with a number of Mediterranean stunners, whilst all along the beach, you'll find the usual gamut of beach shack cuisine. The market area, meanwhile, is filled with little local chai-and-thali joints, where an all-veg lunch can be had for a mere Rs30 or so.

CALANGUTE

Delhi Chaat (snacks from Rs20; 🕒 8am-late) In the thick of the seaside action, this highly popular takeaway joint dispenses all manner of spicy, savoury snacks to the milling masses, as well as delicious hot, sweet chai (Rs10). A *bhaji pau* comes in at Rs40; an *aloo fry masala chaat* at Rs20.

Barista (Calangute–Baga Rd; coffee Rs45-79; 🕒 10am-4am) For a cup of Joe around the clock, rest weary feet on the pleasant terrace of this countrywide coffee chain, and kick back with a cappuccino.

Infanteria Pastry Shop (Calangute–Baga Rd; cakes Rs50-100; 🕒 7.30am-midnight) Next to the Sao João Batista church is this scrummy bakery, loaded with homemade cakes, croissants and little flaky pastries. The noticeboard here is a hotbed for all things current and counter-current.

Casandre (mains from Rs100; 🕒 9am-midnight) Housed in an old Portuguese bungalow, this dim and tranquil retreat seems mightily out of place amid the tourist tat of Calangute's main beach drag. With a long and old-fashioned menu encompassing everything from 'sizzlers' to Goan specialities, and a cocktail list featuring the good old gimlet, this is a loveable time warp, with a pool table to boot.

our pick **A Reverie** (Holiday St; mains from Rs320; ✆ 7pm-late) A gorgeous lounge bar, all armchairs, cool jazz and sparkling crystals, this is the place to spoil yourself, with the likes of Serrano ham, grilled asparagus, French wines and Italian cheeses. Try the delectable forest-mushroom soup with truffle oil (Rs255) or go for a bowl of wasabi-flavoured guacamole (Rs215).

BAGA

Lila Café (mains from Rs70; ✆ 8.30am-6pm Wed-Mon) Airy, white and enticing is this semi–open air riverside place, run by German expats and with a great line in home-baked breads and perfect, frothy cappuccinos. The restful river view is somewhat obscured by the cafe's own guest parking places, but it still makes for a soothing place for a quiet cuppa.

Britto's (mains Rs70-250; ✆ 8am-late) Long-running, usually packed-to-the-gills, and sometimes open as late as 3am, this Baga institution tumbles out onto the beach, serving up a healthy mixture of Goan and Continental cuisines, satisfying cakes and desserts, and live music several nights a week.

J&A's (mains from Rs250) A pretty cafe set around a gorgeous little Portuguese villa, this little slice of Italy is a treat even before the sumptuous, if rather pricey, food arrives. Owned by a wonderful couple originally from Mumbai, the jazz-infused garden and twinkling evening lights makes for a place as drenched in romance as a tiramisu is in rum. Add to this triple-filtered water, electric car and composted leftovers, and you've got an experience almost as good for the world as it is for your tastebuds.

Le Poisson Rouge (dishes from Rs250; ✆ 7pm-late) Baga manages to do fine dining with aplomb, and this French-slanted experience is one of the picks of the place. Simple local ingredients are combined into winning dishes such as beetroot carpaccio and red-snapper masala, and served up beneath the stars.

Drinking & Entertainment

Boisterous, brash and booming, Baga's club scene somehow manages to bubble on long after the trance parties of further north have been locked down for good by late-night noise regulations. Just how this little strip of night-owls' nirvana has managed to escape the lockdown is anybody's guess, but escape it has, and if you're up for a night of decadent drinking or dancing on the tables, don your glad rags and hit the hotspots with the best of them.

If you're seeking something lower-key, go for the main Calangute seaside road, where simple bars are populated with a captivating mix of frazzled foreigners, heavy-drinking locals, and tipsy out-of-towners.

Jerry John Jonesius (JJJ; ✆ 7am-10.30pm) Largely the preserve of locals, JJJ is a suitably dingy and atmospheric bar to down a few beers. Snacks and basic Indian meals (from Rs50) are also available, if you need to line your stomach with something more substantial than *feni*.

Tito's (☎ 9822765002; www.titos.in; Tito's Rd; cover charge men/women from Rs300/free; ✆ 8pm-3am) Tito's, the titan on Goa's clubbing scene, is trying its hardest to escape the locals-leering-at-Western-women image of yesteryear, though it's still hardly the place for a hassle-free girls' night out. Thursday's Bollywood Night and Friday's hip-hop are the pick of the bunch, for the closest thing to Ibiza this side of Star TV.

Café Mambo (☎ 9822765002; www.titos.in; before/after 10pm free/Rs200; ✆ 8pm-late) Owned and managed by Tito's, this is a – very slightly – more sophisticated version of the same thing, with nightly DJs pumping out commercial house, Hip Hop and Latino tunes.

Shopping

At the time of writing, the future of both the area's famous night markets – alternatives to Anjuna's weekly Wednesday market – looked uncertain. Both **Mackie's Saturday Nite Bazaar** (Map p878) and **Ingo's Saturday Nite Bazaar** (off Map p878), held each Saturday night from 6pm to midnight, had been cancelled and opinion was divided on whether they might be reinstated. Ask around to make sure.

Getting There & Away

There are frequent buses to Panaji (Rs7, 45 minutes) and Mapusa (Rs6) from the bus stand near the beach, and some services also stop at the bus stop near the temple. A taxi from Calangute or Baga to Panaji costs around Rs350 and takes about 45 minutes. A prepaid

GOA

taxi from Dabolim airport to Calangute costs Rs645.

ANJUNA

Dear old Anjuna, that stalwart on India's hippy scene, still drags out the sarongs and sandalwood each Wednesday for its famous – and once infamous – flea market. Though it continues to pull in droves of backpackers and long-term hippies, midrange tourists are also increasingly making their way here for a dose of hippy-chic without the beach-hut rusticity of Arambol further up the coast. The town itself is might be a bit ragged around the edges these days, but that's all part of its charm, and Anjuna remains a favourite of long-stayers and first-timers alike.

Orientation & Information

Anjuna is spread out over a wide area, its most northerly point being the main Starco cross-roads – where most buses stop and around which many eating options are dotted – and the southernmost being the flea market site, about 2km south. Most accommodation and other useful services are sprinkled along the beach, or down shady inland lanes, in between.

Internet access in Anjuna – away from the midrange hotels – is perilously slow and unreliable and internet joints thus open and close down regularly. Ask around for the best new option on the scene, or head to the German Bakery which offers wireless access for those with their own laptops.

Something important to consider – especially on market day – is that there are no ATMs in Anjuna. The **Bank of Baroda** (9.30am-2.30pm) gives cash advances on Visa and MasterCard, but won't exchange currency. For this, try one of the travel agents below.

There are plenty of reliable travel agents in town. Try **Speedy Travels** (2273266) near the post office, or the excellent **MGM Travels** (2274317; www.mgmtravels.com; Anjuna–Mapusa Rd; 9.30am-6pm Mon-Sat).

Activities

Anjuna's charismatic, rocky beach runs for almost 2km from the northern village area to the flea market. The northern end shrinks to almost nothing when the tide washes in, when it's fun to watch local tourist ladies hopping perilously from rock to rock in strappy sandals and saris, in search of a scenic photo op-portunity. When the tide goes out, it becomes a lovely – and surprisingly quiet – stretch of sand, with lots of room to escape the presence of other sunbathers.

There's lots of yoga, reiki and ayurveda on offer, seasonally, in town; look out for notices posted at Café Diogo and the German Bakery (see Eating p884), while the popular upscale **Purple Valley Yoga Retreat** (www.yogagoa.com) in nearby Assagao village offers one and two-week residential courses in Ashtanga yoga; rates begin at £390 for one week.

For an adrenalin rush, **paragliding** usually takes place off the headland at the southern end of the beach on market days; tandem rides cost Rs1500. And if you're looking to embellish yourself whilst in town, try **Andy's Tattoo Studio** (11am-7pm; www.andys-tattoo-studio-goa.com), attached to San Francisco Restaurant, just where the Anjuna cliffside slides down to meet the beach. Drop in to make an appointment and receive a price quote for your permanent souvenir.

Sleeping

BUDGET

Dozens of rooms of the largely concrete cell variety string themselves along Anjuna's northern clifftop stretch; most come in at Rs250 to Rs500 per night. There are also plenty of small, family-run guesthouses tucked back from the main beach strip, offering nicer double rooms for a similar price; take your pick from the dozens of signs announcing 'Rooms To Let'. Below, though, are three exceptional choices for something a little bit different.

our pick **Peace Land** (2273700; s/d Rs300/500;) You can't get better on a budget than Peace Land, run by a friendly couple and arranged around a tranquil courtyard garden. Rooms are small but spotlessly clean and comfortable, and their little restaurant cooks up some great Indian food. There's internet access for Rs30 per hour, and a small shop selling basic provisions.

Paradise (9922541714; janet_965@hotmail.com; Anjuna–Mapusa Rd; d without AC Rs400-800, with AC Rs1500) A paradise for animal-lovers particularly, since proprietor Janet is a keen collector of all things canine, feline and avian, this friendly place fronted by an old Portuguese home offers good, clean rooms with particularly well-decorated options in the newer annexe. And Janet doesn't stop at accommodation: her enterprising family can service your

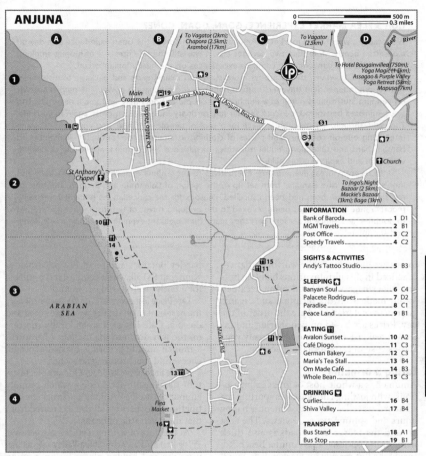

ANJUNA

INFORMATION
Bank of Baroda 1   D1
MGM Travels 2   B1
Post Office 3   C2
Speedy Travels 4   C2

SIGHTS & ACTIVITIES
Andy's Tattoo Studio 5   B3

SLEEPING
Banyan Soul 6   C4
Palacete Rodrigues 7   D2
Paradise 8   C1
Peace Land 9   B1

EATING
Avalon Sunset 10   A2
Café Diogo 11   C3
German Bakery 12   C3
Maria's Tea Stall 13   B4
Om Made Café 14   B3
Whole Bean 15   C3

DRINKING
Curlies 16   B4
Shiva Valley 17   B4

TRANSPORT
Bus Stand 18   A1
Bus Stop 19   B1

GOA

every need, with its pharmacy, general store, restaurant, internet access (Rs40 per hour), Connexions travel agency, money exchange, Western Union services and beauty parlour. You name it and Janet can probably arrange it for you.

Palacete Rodrigues (☎ 273358; www.palacetegoa .com; s/d without AC Rs850/950, d with AC Rs1050; ✼) This beautifully old-fashioned mansion, filled with antiques, odd corners and bags of charm, is as cool and quirky as you could hope Anjuna to come.

MIDRANGE

Banyan Soul (☎ 9820707283; sumityardi@thebanyansoul .com; d Rs1500; ✼) A slinky new 12-room option, tucked just behind Anjuna's scrummy

German bakery, lovingly conceived and run by a young escapee of the Mumbai technology rat race. Rooms are chic and well-equipped, the decor is flawless, and there are plans afoot for a rooftop restaurant. It's without a doubt the best midrange choice in town, and staff are extremely keen to please.

Hotel Bougainvillea (☎ 2273270; www.granpasinn .com; d incl breakfast & tax Rs1950-3250; ✼ ✼) An old-fashioned hotel housed in a centuries-old mansion, this place – also known as Grandpa's Inn – offers charm with a touch of luxury with a lovely pool and well-decorated rooms.

TOP END

Yoga Magic (☎ 6523796; www.yogamagic.net; tent/villa per person Rs2750/3500) Solar lighting and compost

---

GOA'S FLEA MARKET EXPERIENCE: GOAN, GOAN, GONE?

Wednesday's weekly **flea market** at Anjuna is as much part of the Goan experience as a day on a deserted beach. More than two decades ago, it was still the sole preserve of hippies smoking jumbo joints and convening to compare experiences on the heady Indian circuit.

Nowadays, however, things are far more staid and mainstream, and package tourists seem to beat out independent travellers both in numbers and purchasing power. The market sprawls on vending stuff that is much of a muchness: a couple of hours here and you'll never want to see a mirrored bedspread, peacock feather fan, or floaty Indian cotton dress again in your life. That said, though, it's still a great place for a spot of people-watching, and you can find some interesting one-off souvenirs and pieces of clothing in amongst the tourist tat. Remember to bargain hard and take along equal quantities of patience and stamina, applicable to dealing with local and expat vendors alike.

Until recently, great evening-time alternatives to the Anjuna experience were Mackie's and Ingo's Saturday 'Nite Bazaars,' both set up in the region of Calangute and Baga. At the time of research, however, both had been cancelled. Reasons for the cancellations remained unclear – reports range from licenses being revoked to the ongoing threat of terrorism – but ask around to double-check, since in seasons past they made for a pleasant evening mix of live music, food, and shopping.

---

toilets are just some of the worthy initiatives practiced in this ultraluxurious bamboo hut-and-villa village, where hand-printed textiles, locally made ironwork furniture and organic gourmet vegetarian food are the order of the day. Prices are based on two sharing and include breakfast and afternoon tea; daily yoga classes cost an extra Rs300 per session.

Eating & Drinking

Anjuna has a whole host of great eating options, with jostling cliffside cafes sporting the standard traveller-orientated menus, happy hours and stunning coastal views. The area around the Starco crossroads is also thick with dining options, as is Anjuna Beach Rd. Inside the flea market on market days, you'll find a number of boozy bars with stages manned by cover version–singing foreigners. For a quick market shopping stop, look out for teensy **Maria's Tea Stall** (� market day; Flea Market; snacks from Rs10), selling tasty chai and snacks made by colourful elderly local Maria herself.

Avalon Sunset (dishes from Rs60; 奈) Good food, a pool table, a chill-out area, free wi-fi and rooms for rent (from Rs400) make this a great representative of Anjuna's clifftop restaurant parade. There's daily yoga on the roof, too; call in for class times.

German Bakery (dishes from Rs60; 奈) Leafy, filled with prayer flags and jolly lights, this is a perfect place for a huge lunch from its equally huge menu. Tofu balls in mustard sauce with

parsley potatoes and salad is a piled-platter winner at Rs150; wireless internet is available for a fairly steep Rs100 per hour.

Café Diogo (dishes from Rs70; ☉ 9am-4pm) Probably the best fruit salads in the world are sliced and diced at Café Diogo, a small locally run cafe on the way down to the market. Also worth a munch are the generous toasted avocado, cheese and mushroom sandwiches.

Whole Bean (dishes Rs70-130) This simple, tasty, tofu-filled health-food cafe – which proudly announces itself as 'Anjuna's premier soy destination' – focuses on all things created from that most versatile of beans.

At the time of writing, **Curlies** (mains from Rs50; ☉ till late) and nearby **Shiva Valley** (☉ till late) were the best-hidden places for an evening drink, an alternative crowd and the odd impromptu party. Head down to either to find out what's on.

our pick **Om Made Café** (☉ 8.30am-sunset; dishes Rs90-190) A highlight on Anjuna's clifftop strip, this cheery little place offers striped deckchairs from which to enjoy the views and the simple, sophisticated breakfasts, sandwiches and salads. Go for a raw papaya salad with ginger and lemongrass (Rs170), accompanied by a *chickoo* (Sapodilla fruit) and coconut smoothie or a glass of 'perfumed water' (Rs20).

Getting There & Away

There are buses every half-hour or so from Mapusa to Anjuna (Rs6), stopping at end of the road to the beach and continuing on to Vagator and Chapora, while some continue to Arambol. Plenty of motorcycle taxis gather at the main crossroads and you can also hire scooters and motorcycles easily from here.

VAGATOR & CHAPORA

Dramatic red-stone cliffs, dense green forests and a crumbling 17th-century **Portuguese fort** provide Vagator and its diminutive neighbour Chapora with one of the prettiest settings on the north Goan coast. Once known for their wild trance parties and heady, hippy lifestyles, things have slowed down considerably these days, though Chapora – reminiscent of Star Wars' Mos Eisley Cantina – remains a fave for smokers, with the smell of *charas* hanging heavy in the air.

If you're keen to see the remnants of the trance scene, hang around long enough in Vagator and you'll likely be handed a flyer for a party (many with international DJs) which can range from divine to dire. You may also catch wind of something going down in a hidden location – if you're lucky, it won't have been closed down by the time you get there.

Information

In Vagator, the lovely little **Rainbow Bookshop** (☎ 2273613; ☀ 9.30am-10pm), run by a charming elderly gentleman, stocks a good range of secondhand and new books, including this very guide. Plenty of internet places are scattered along the road to Little Vagator beach; **Tanu Communications** (Ozran Beach Rd; ☀ 9am-late; per hr Rs50) just before the Alcove Resort at Little Vagator, is one reliable option.

Sleeping

VAGATOR

Budget accommodation, much of it in private rooms, ranges along Ozran Beach Rd in Vagator; you'll see lots of signs for 'rooms to let' in the side roads, too, in simple private homes and guest houses. Most charge Rs300 to Rs500 per double room.

Paradise on the Earth (☎ 2273591; www.moondance .co.nr; huts without bathroom Rs300) Simple bamboo huts with shared bathrooms clinging to the cliff above Little Vagator Beach offering great value for the beachside location, though the name might be a little overkill. The website boasts, intriguingly, of a 'well-stocked bare', something to certainly bear in mind come sunset.

Bean Me Up Soya Station (☎ 2273479; www.myspace .com/beanmeupindia; d Rs550, without bathroom Rs350) The rooms around a leafy, parachute-silky courtyard might look a bit cell-like from the outside, but step in and you'll be pleased to find that the billowing silks and mellow, earthy shades follow you there. Bicycles (Rs1000 deposit and Rs100 per day) and motorbikes (Rs250 per day) are both available for rent, and there's a nice vegetarian restaurant (see Eating below).

our pick **Shalom** (☎ 2273166; d with/without TV & fridge Rs1500/800, 2-bed apt per month Rs25,000) Arranged around a placid garden not far from the path down to Little Vagator Beach, this place, run by a friendly family (whose home is on-site), offers a variety of well-kept rooms, and a two-bedroom apartment for long-stayers.

Janies (☎ 2273635; janiesricardo@hotmail.com; d Rs800, 1-bed/2-bed bungalow Rs1000/1200) A great choice for long-stayers, run by a very friendly lady and with a simple but homely vibe. The three double rooms each come equipped with small kitchen, bathroom and TV, and there are two large bungalows, the first with one double bedroom and the second with two.

Alcove Resort (☎ 2274491; www.alcovegoa.com; Ozran Beach Rd; d without/with AC Rs1800/2200, cottages without/with AC Rs2000/2500, ste without/with AC Rs3000/3500; ▨ ▧) Attractively furnished rooms, slightly larger cottages, and four suites within easy striking distance of Little Vagator Beach, this place is for those who want a touch of luxury at surprisingly reasonable prices. When you tire of the sands there's a cool central pool.

CHAPORA

Head down the road to the harbour and you'll find lots of rooms – and whole homes – for rent, far nicer than setting yourself up in the congested village centre; be sure to thoroughly trawl what's on offer before you land your catch.

Casa de Olga (☎ 2274355, 9822157145; d from Rs250) This welcoming choice arranged around a nice garden offers clean rooms of a variety of sizes with some better equipped than others. You'll pay more for the best of them, which come with hot showers, kitchenette and balcony.

Eating

VAGATOR

There are a few eating options clustered around the entrance to Little Vagator Beach,

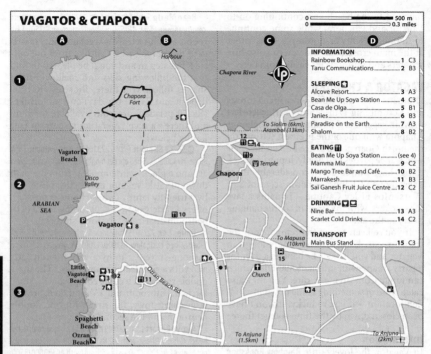

VAGATOR & CHAPORA

along with the usual slew of much-of-a-muchness beach shacks down on the sands themselves.

Mango Tree Bar & Café (mains Rs70-120) An ever-popular place for its big breakfasts and far-ranging menu, with films screened here most nights around 7.30pm.

Marrakesh (mains Rs120-160; ⏰ 11am-11pm) Billing itself as the 'Heart of Moroccan cuisine', this is the place to pick up a tasty tagine or a delectable veg couscous (Rs150), in what seems to be Goa's only Moroccan restaurant.

Bean Me Up Soya Station (Ozran Beach Rd; mains from Rs150) A delicious, all-vegetarian restaurant at this popular place to stay, with lots of carefully washed salads and a wealth of tasty tofu and tempeh.

CHAPORA

our pick **Mamma Mia** (paninis & pizza Rs100; ⏰ 8am-9pm Tue-Sun) The best of the Chapora bunch is Mamma Mia, run by Marco who makes his own focaccia fresh every night ready for the next day. The cappuccinos are perfect, the pizza is simple and filling, and the smoke is strong and heady.

Two long-lived local institutions are **Scarlet Cold Drinks** (drinks & desserts Rs15-50) and the **Sai Ganesh Fruit Juice Centre** (juices Rs15-30), both offering juices, snacks and lassis, in close proximity to the thickest gusts of *charas* smoke. The former has an exceptionally good noticeboard, to keep you abreast of local developments.

Drinking & Entertainment

Aside from secretive parties, there's not too much going on in Vagator and Chapora these days. The once heaving **Nine Bar** (Sunset Point, Little Vagator Beach; ⏰ till 10pm), however, is still thumping on; gone, though, are the all-nighters and the trance is now turned off promptly at 10pm.

Getting There & Away

Fairly frequent buses run to both Chapora and Vagator from Mapusa (Rs12) throughout the day, many via Anjuna. The bus stand is near the road junction in Chapora village. Many people hire a motorcycle to buzz back and forth; enquire wherever you see a man with a scooter. Prices tend to be around Rs150/200 per day for a scooter/motorbike.

WHERE'S THE PARTY?

Though Goa was long legendary amongst Western visitors for its all-night, open-air Goan trance parties, a central government 'noise pollution' ban on loud music in open spaces between 10pm and 6am has largely curbed its often notorious, drug-laden party scene. With a tourist industry to nurture, however, authorities tend to turn a blind eye to parties during the peak Christmas–New Year period, and seem to allow the monster main-stream clubs of Baga to carry on regardless. If you're looking for the remainder of the real party scene, though, you'll need to cross your fingers, keep your ear close to the ground, and wait out for word in Vagator or Anjuna.

MANDREM

Lovely, hidden Mandrem has in recent years become an in-the-know bolt hole for those seeking respite from the relentless traveller scene of Arambol and Anjuna. The beach is beautiful, and there's little to do but laze on it; the narrow lane leading down to the sea is filled with accommodation options to suit most budgets. There are also lots of cocohuts to be had for Rs400 or thereabouts on the beach, and there's a plethora of yoga and ayurveda on offer, mostly taught by foreigners, each season. It's not easy to get here by public transport; the best bet is to rent a scooter at Arambol.

Sleeping & Eating

Oasis on the Beach (huts Rs500-700) One of the many tip-top beach hut options, with the added advantage of an excellent ayurvedic massage parlour, run by Shanti (massages Rs800 to Rs1000), whose claim to fame is having massaged Dawn French. Oasis's beachfront restaurant gets rave reviews, too, especially for its seafood and tandoori dishes.

Cuba Retreat (☎ 2645775; www.cubagoa.com; d without/with AC Rs1050/1500; ❀) Those people from Cuba seem to get everywhere, including to this spick and span set of suites just a few moments walk from the beach. Though it didn't seem too pricey to us, Cuba's website claims it serves up 'exorbitant seafood delicacies' in its great courtyard bar-restaurant.

Villa River Cat (☎ 2247928; www.villarivercat.com; d Rs1700-3600; ❀ 🖳) This fabulously unusual circular guesthouse, filled with art, light and antiques, makes for a wonderful – and extremely popular – stay in Goa. Because of this, the management advises you to book an astonishing eight months ahead during the high season.

Shree Gopal Supreme Pure Juice Centre & Café (juice Rs30-35; ☯ 7am-10pm) On the road down to the beach, thirst-quenching juicy combinations are squeezed and served up in a cute little chill-out area. Lots of notices are posted in the vicinity, with info on the latest yoga class locations.

ARAMBOL (HARMAL)

Arambol first emerged in the 1960s as a mellow paradise for long-haired long-stayers. Today, things are still decidedly cheap and cheerful, with much of the village's mostly budget accommodation ranged in simple little huts along the cliff sides. However, it's a bit more mainstream festivalish than in days gone by and you have a feeling that many of today's 'hippies' shave off their fortnight's beards and take off their tie-dye once they're back to the nine-to-five.

Some people love Arambol for all this; others turn up their pierced noses and move along, leaving today's long-stayers to enjoy the pretty beach and extensive 'alternative' shopping opportunities provided by nonstop stalls all the way down the beach road and along round the cliff. If you're looking for a committed traveller vibe, this is the place to come; if you're seeking laid-back languidness, you might be better heading on down the coast to Mandrem.

Information

Everything you'll need in the way of services – dozens of internet outfits, travel agents, money changers and the like – you'll find in abundance on 'Glastonbury Street', the road leading down to Arambol's beach. Internet access here generally costs Rs30 to Rs40 per hour, and money-changing commission rates are all comparable. There are also several agencies towards the top of the road offering parcel services with Federal Express and DHL deliveries, and by air and sea mail.

Activities

The **Himalayan Iyengar Yoga Centre** (www.hiyoga centre.com) is a popular spot for a spot of yoga, with five-day courses, intensive workshops,

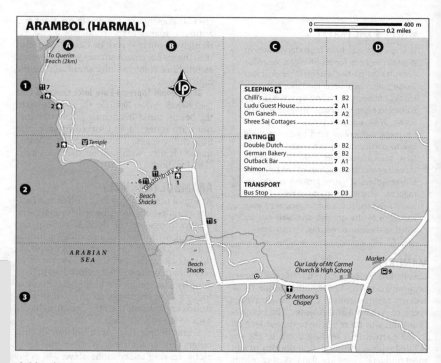

Map legend:

SLEEPING 🛏
Chilli's 1 B2
Ludu Guest House 2 A1
Om Ganesh 3 A2
Shree Sai Cottages 4 A1

EATING 🍴
Double Dutch 5 B2
German Bakery 6 B2
Outback Bar 7 A1
Shimon 8 B2

TRANSPORT
Bus Stop 9 D3

children's classes, and teacher training all available.

Aside from yoga and beach lounging, the most popular pursuits in Arambol these days are **paragliding** and **kite surfing**. Several operators give lessons and rent equipment on the very south of Arambol beach; walk down there, or check out some noticeboards, to find out who's renting what this season.

Sleeping

Accommodation in Arambol is almost all of the budget variety, and it pays to trawl the cliffside to the north of Arambol's main beach stretch for the best hut options. Here you can expect simple accommodation, mostly without private bathrooms but with the benefit of incredible sea views (along with attendant breezes). Most come in at Rs350 to Rs500 in high season, and it's almost impossible to book in advance – simply turn up early in the day to check out who's checking out of your dream-hut.

Chilli's (☎ 9921882424; Glastonbury St; d Rs300) This clean and simple place, owned by friendly and helpful Derek Fernandez, is one of Arambol's best nonbeachside bargains. Chilli's offers 10 nice, no-frills rooms on the beach road, all with attached bathrooms, fan and a hot-water shower, and there's an honour system for buying bottled water, self-service, from the fridge on the landing.

Om Ganesh (☎ 2297675; some without bathroom r Rs350-400) Popular huts, especially those on the sea-side of the coastal path, as well as a great place for lunch or dinner, with almost everything you can think of on the menu (if you can manage to decode entries such as 'Gokomadi' in the Mexican section). Some huts have no attached bathroom.

Shree Sai Cottages (☎ 2262823; shreesai_cottages@ yahoo.com; huts without bathroom Rs400) A good example of what's on offer, Shree Sai has simple sea-facing huts a short walk north from the main Arambol beach, with lovely views out over the water, and a calm, easy going vibe.

Ludu Guest House (☎ 2242734; some without bathroom r Rs700-1000) A cut above many other Arambol options, Ludu offers simply decorated, clean and bright cliffside rooms with attached cold-water showers. Hot water can be ordered by the bucketful. Some huts have no attached bathroom.

Eating & Drinking

Aside from myriad standard shacks lining the sands, plenty of cute, sparkly little places are dotted along the top part of the road curving down towards the beach. Many change annually; stroll along and see which organic and parachute-silk destination takes your fancy. For simpler fare, head up to the village, where chai shops and small local joints will whip you up a chai for Rs4 and a thali for Rs40.

German Bakery (Welcome Inn, Glastonbury St; cakes from Rs40; 7am-late) This rather dim and dingy corner cafe is exceptionally popular, with great cakes including lemon cheese pie (Rs50) and a scrummy chocolate biscuit cake (Rs40), as well as big breakfasts coming in at around the Rs90 mark.

Outback Bar (mains from Rs50) Seafood's a speciality at this nice place tucked away from the Arambol action; it also makes a fantastic spot for a sundown cocktail or two.

Double Dutch (mains from Rs70) An ever-popular option for its steaks, salads and famous apple pies, this is a great place to peruse the noticeboard for current affairs, whilst munching on a plateful of cookies or a huge, tasty sandwich.

Shimon (Glastonbury St; snacks from Rs70; 8am-midnight) If you can navigate the surly service, Israeli-owned Shimon is a good place to fill up on a tasty falafel (Rs70) before hitting the beach. For something more unusual, go for *sabich* (Rs70), crisp slices of aubergine stuffed into pita bread along with boiled egg, boiled potato, salad and spicy relishes.

Getting There & Away

Buses from Mapusa stop on the main road at Arambol (Rs12), where there's a church, a school and a few shops. From here, follow the road about 1.5km through the village to get to the main road down to the beach, or hop into a rickshaw for Rs20. Lots of places in the village advertise scooters and motorbikes to rent, for Rs150 and Rs200 respectively, per day. A prepaid taxi to Arambol from Dabolim Airport costs Rs975.

SOUTH GOA

MARGAO (MADGAON)

pop 94,400

The capital of Salcete province, Margao (also known as Madgaon) is the main population centre of south Goa and is a happy, bustling market town of a manageable size for getting things done. If you're basing yourself in south Goa, it's a useful place for shopping, organising bus and train tickets, checking emails or simply enjoying the busy energy of big-city India in manageable small-town form.

Information

There are lots of banks offering currency exchange and 24-hour ATMs ranged around the municipal gardens, and on the western extension of Luis Miranda Rd. GTDC trips (see p860) can be booked at the front desk of the Margao Residency Hotel.

Golden Heart Emporium (Confidant House, Abade Faria Rd) One of Goa's best bookshops, crammed with fiction, nonfiction and illustrated books on the state's food, architecture and history.

Maharaja Travels (☎ 2732744, Luis Miranda Rd; 9am-1pm, 3-6pm Mon-Sat) A great source of long-distance bus tickets.

Main post office (9am-1.30pm & 2-4pm) On the north side of the municipal gardens, the post office also arranges Western Union money transfers.

The Cyberlink (Caro Centre, Abade Faria Rd; for 20 mins Rs8, per hr Rs20; 8.30am-7pm Mon-Sat) Reasonably swift internet access on the central square; be sure to heed the notice that requests you to 'Register yourself before sitting on the PC'.

Sights

Margao has plenty of workaday, practical shopping opportunities, and the daily **covered market** in the town centre is one of the most colourful and raucous in all of Goa. It's also worth a walk around the lovely, small northern **Largo de Igreja** district, home to lots of atmospherically crumbling old Portuguese homes. Stop in, too, at the quaint and richly decorated 17th-century **Church of the Holy Spirit**, particularly impressive when a Sunday morning service is taking place.

Sleeping

With the southern beaches all so close, there's little, if any, reason to stay in Margao.

Hotel Tanish (☎ 2735656; Reliance Trade Centre, Valaulikar Rd; s/d without AC Rs900/1500, s/d/ste with AC Rs1300/1900/2500) Without doubt the best place to stay in town, this top-floor hotel offers great views of the surrounding countryside, with stylish, well-equipped rooms. Suites come with a bathtub, a big TV and a view all the way to Colva.

GOA

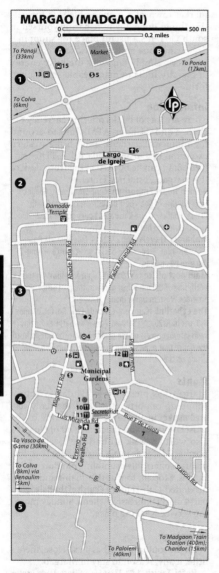

MARGAO (MADGAON)

INFORMATION		
Cyberlink..	**1**	A4
Golden Heart Emporium	**2**	A3
Maharaja Travels...............................	**3**	A4
Main Post Office................................	**4**	A3
UTI Bank ATM....................................	**5**	A1

SIGHTS & ACTIVITIES		
Church of the Holy Spirit...................	**6**	B2
Covered Market.................................	**7**	B4

SLEEPING		
Hotel Tanish.....................................	**8**	B4
Margao Residency..............................	**9**	A4

EATING		
Casa Penguim de Gelados...................	**10**	A4
Longhuino's......................................	**11**	A4
Tato...	**12**	B4

TRANSPORT		
Bus Stand...	**13**	A1
Buses to Palolem, Colva, Benaulim & Betul..	**14**	B4
Kadamba Bus Stand...........................	**15**	A1
Old Bus Stand...................................	**16**	A4

our pick **Longhuino's** (Luis Miranda Rd; mains from Rs40) Since 1950, quaint old Longhuino's has been serving up tasty Indian and Chinese dishes, popular with locals and tourists alike. To thoroughly hark back to the '50s, order the tongue roast for Rs80 (and that doesn't mean a very spicy masala) and follow it up with a rum ball (Rs15).

Tato (Apna Bazaar Complex, Varde Valualikar Rd; veg thali with/without AC Rs45/40; ☺ 7am-10pm Mon-Sat) A favourite local lunch spot, offering tasty vegetarian fare in a bustling backstreet canteen.

Getting There & Around
BUS

Local buses all arrive and depart the busy Kadamba bus stand about 2km north of the Municipal Gardens, though many services also stop at the old bus stand in the centre of town. Buses to Palolem, Colva, Benaulim and Betul stop at the Kadamba bus stand and at the bus stop on the east side of the Municipal Gardens. Services run to no timetable at all, but are cheap and frequent.

Though there are daily public buses to Mumbai (Rs700, 16 hours) and Bengaluru (Rs400, 14 hours), a better bet is to take a long-distance private bus, which is more comfortable, quicker and about the same price. You'll find booking offices all over town; Maharaja Travels (see Information p889) is one helpful choice.

Private buses to Mumbai (with/without AC Rs750/650, 12 hours), Bengaluru (with/without

Eating

Casa Penguim de Gelados (Abade Faria Rd; veg thali Rs30; ☺ 8.30am-8pm Mon-Sat) Tea and ice creams are really their thing, but this clean, fan-cooled place does serve out a decent vegetarian thali as well as an array of dosas and *idlis* (South Indian spongy, round, fermented rice cakes) too.

AC Rs700/350, 12 hours), Pune (with/without AC Rs750/650, 11 hours) and Hampi (sleeper/ luxury Rs750/650, eight hours) all leave from the bus stand opposite Kadamba bus station.

TAXI

Taxis are plentiful around the municipal gardens and Kadamba bus stand, and are a quick and comfortable means to reach any of Goa's beaches, including Palolem (Rs650), Calangute (Rs1000), Anjuna (Rs1000) and Arambol (Rs1700). Be sure to wear your best bargaining cap for negotiating your fare.

TRAIN

Margao's well-organised train station, about 1.5km south of town, serves both the Konkan Railway and local South Central Railways routes. Its **reservation hall** (🕑 8am-2pm & 2.15-8pm Mon-Sat, 8am-2pm Sun) is on the 2nd floor of the main building. See p862 for details of Konkan Railway services.

A taxi or autorickshaw from the town centre to the station should cost Rs50.

CHANDOR

The lush village of Chandor, 15km east of Margao, makes a perfect day away from the south Goan beaches, and it's here, more than anywhere else in the state, that the once opulent lifestyles of Goa's former landowners, who found favour with the Portuguese aristocracy, are still visible in its strings of quietly decaying colonial-era mansions.

A kilometre east past the church and open to the public is the **Fernandes House** (☎ 2784245; 🕑 10am-5pm Mon-Sat), whose original building dates back more than 500 years, whilst the Portuguese section was tacked on by the Fernandes family in 1821. The secret basement hideaway, full of gun holes and with an escape tunnel to the river, was used by the family to flee attackers. A minimum Rs100 per visitor donation is expected.

The best way to reach Chandor is with your own transport, or by taxi from Margao (Rs200 for the round trip). On 6 January, Chandor hosts the colourful **Feast of the Three Kings**, during which local boys re-enact the arrival of the three kings from the Christmas story.

COLVA & BENAULIM
pop 10,200

Colva and Benaulim might between them comprise the biggest resorts on the south

---

CHANDOR'S COLONIAL JEKYLL & HYDE

Braganza House, built in the 17th century and stretching along one whole side of Chandor village square, is possibly the best – and worst – example of what Goa's scores of once grand and glorious mansions have today become. Built on land granted by the King of Portugal, the house was divided from the outset into the east and west wings, to house two sides of the same big family.

The **West Wing** (☎ 2784201; 🕑 10am-5pm) belongs to one set of the family's descendents, the Menezes-Braganças, and is filled with gorgeous chandeliers, Italian marble floors and antique treasures from Macau, Portugal, China and Europe. The elderly, rather frail, Mrs Aida Menezes-Braganza nowadays lives here alone, but will show you around with the help of her formidable lady assistant. Between them, they struggle valiantly with the upkeep of a beautiful but needy house, whose grand history oozes from every inch of wall, floor and furniture.

Next door at the **East Wing** (☎ 2784227; 🕑 10am-5pm), prepare for a shock. Owned by the Pereira-Braganza family, descendents of the other half of the family, it's as shabby and decaying as the other is still grand. Paint peels from windows; ceilings sag; antiques are mixed in willy-nilly with a jumble of cheap knick-knacks and seaside souvenirs. The only high point here is the small family chapel, which contains a carefully hidden fingernail of St Francis Xavier (see p871), and even this – the chapel, not the fingernail – is beginning to show signs of neglect. A starker architectural contrast at such close quarters you're unlikely to see for quite a while, and it's a moving, if melancholy, experience.

Both homes are open daily, and there's almost always someone around to let you in. Though there are no official entry fees, the owners rely on contributions for the hefty costs of maintenance: Rs100 per visitor per house is reasonable, though anything extra would, of course, be welcome.

GOA

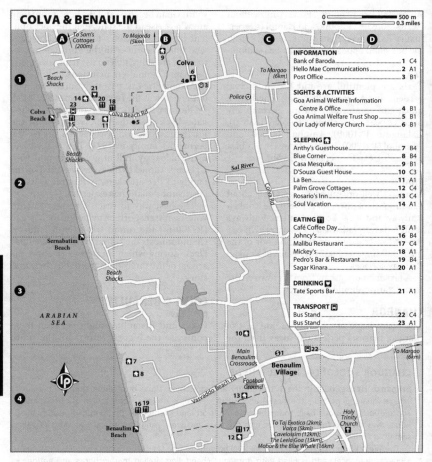

COLVA & BENAULIM

0   500 m
0   0.3 miles

coast, but they're certainly not the first place for backpackers to head, and most tourists here are of the domestic or ageing European varieties. Of the two, Benaulim has the greater charm, though out of superduper high season still gives off the sad sort of feel of a deserted Welsh seaside town, were global warming to get that far. Perhaps the biggest reason to stay at either is if you're keen to explore this part of southern coast (which stretches north as far as Velsao and south as far as the mouth of the Sal River at Mobor), which in many parts is empty and gorgeous. The inland road that runs this length is perfect for gentle scootering, with lots of picturesque Portuguese mansions and white-washed churches along the way.

Information

Colva has plenty of banks and ATM machines strung along Colva Beach Rd, and a post office on the lane that runs past the eastern end of the church. Benaulim has a single Bank of Baroda ATM – which professes to be 24-hour but is sometimes locked – at the top of Vasvaddo Beach Rd, and most of its useful services (pharmacies, supermarkets and travel agents) are clustered around the main crossroads.

Hello Mae Communication (Colva Beach Rd; per 15 min Rs10, per hr Rs30; ☯ 8am-10pm) Internet access and a currency-exchange service are available here. There are weekly Wednesday trips out to Anjuna Market for Rs150 per person. Keep in mind the stern warning: 'No Surfing of Porn Websites'.

Sights & Activities

The beach entrances of Colva and Benaulim throng with young men keen to sell you **parasailing** (per ride Rs500), **jet-skiing** (per 15min Rs700), and **dolphin-watching trips** (per person around Rs250). There's little to choose between operators, which gives you significant leeway in terms of haggling for the best deal.

A worthy place to stop off is at the **Goa Animal Welfare Trust Shop** (www.gawt.org; Colva Beach Rd; ☎ 10am-12.30pm, 5-7pm Mon-Sat) in Colva where you can borrow books from its lending library, or peruse the new and secondhand goods on offer. There's also a newly opened **Information Centre & Office** (Below Infant Jesus Church Hall; ☿ 9.30am-1pm & 3-5pm Mon-Sat), also in Colva, where you can find out more about the work of this wonderful organisation.

Sleeping

It's hard to recommend many budget or midrange options in Colva, since the majority are either horribly overpriced or, more simply, horrible. Indeed, unless you're lying low in one of the town's groovier top-end choices, you're far better off heading down to Benaulim or pushing on further south.

BUDGET
Colva

Casa Mesquita (r Rs300) With just three rooms that go beyond simple and no telephone to book them by, this atmospheric old mansion on the main coast road is certainly the place to go if you thrive on the atmosphere that Colva lacks. Goodness knows when rooms were last cleaned; nevertheless, the elderly inhabitants are friendly, the paint's suitably peeling, and the ghosts of better days linger lovingly in the shadows.

Sam's Cottages (☎ 2788753; r Rs350) Up where the countryside begins you'll find Sam's, painted a cheerful bright orange and with decent, clean rooms. If your name happens to be Sam too, prepare yourself for a particularly ebullient welcome.

La Ben (☎ 2788040; www.laben.net; Colva Beach Rd; with/without AC Rs965/575; ▒) Neat, clean and not entirely devoid of atmosphere, this place is particularly known for its rooftop restaurant, though its rooms represent reasonable value.

Benaulim

There are lots of village homes along the Vasvaddo Beach Rd, and in among the lanes off it, advertising simple rooms to let for tourists. This, combined with a couple of really decent budget options, make Benaulim a far better bet for backpackers than Colva.

Rosario's Inn (☎ 2770636; r Rs300, without bathroom Rs150; ▒) Across a football pitch flitting with young players and dragonflies, Rosario's is a large, motel-like establishment with clean, simple rooms. There's a nice bar-restaurant in the garden, and its two AC rooms go for Rs500 each.

D'Souza Guest House (☎ 2770583; d Rs400) As you'd guess from the name, this traditional blue house is run by a local Goan family and comes with bundles of homey atmosphere, a lovely garden and just three spacious, clean rooms – making it best to book ahead.

Blue Corner (☎ 9850455770; www.blue-cnr-goa.com; huts from Rs600) One of only a handful of truly beachside places on this entire strip of coast, Blue Corner offers simple beach huts, and a nice beachfront restaurant which gains stellar reviews from guests.

MIDRANGE & TOP END
Colva

Soul Vacation (☎ 2788144, 2788147; www.soulvacation .in; d from Rs5500; ▒ ▢ ▒) Thirty restful white rooms arranged around nice gardens and a great pool are the trademarks of sleek Soul Vacation, set 400m back from Colva Beach. Equipped with all the mod cons, it's a great – if slightly pretentious – place to unwind without ever even having to venture out of the resort itself.

Benaulim

Anthy's Guesthouse (☎ 2771680; anthysguesthouse@ rediffmail.com; r Rs1300-1800) One of just a handful of places lining Benaulim's beach itself, Anthy's is a firm favourite with travellers for its warm service (manager Prabot is extremely friendly and helpful), its good restaurant, and its well-kept, chalet-style rooms, which stretch back from the beach surrounded by a pretty garden. Ayurvedic massage is available here for Rs500 per, um, squeeze.

Palm Grove Cottages (☎ 2770059; www.palmgrove goa.com; d without/with AC from Rs1460/1575; ▒) Old-fashioned, secluded charm is to be had amid the dense foliage at Palm Grove Cottages, hidden amongst a thicket of trees on a road winding slowly south out of Benaulim. Guest rooms are atmospheric, and the ever-popular Palm Garden Restaurant graces the garden.

GOA

Taj Exotica (☎ 2771234; www.tajhotels.com; d from US$300; 🍴 🖳 🏊) If your budget runs to it, don't hesitate: here's one of Goa's plushest resorts, set in 56 acres of tropical gardens, and just aching to pander to your every whim. It's probably best to just relinquish the struggle and let it.

Eating & Drinking
COLVA
There are plenty of wooden beach shacks lining the Colvan sands, offering the long, and standard range of fare, and you'll spot this season's best by the crowds already dining within. For simpler eating, head up to the roundabout just before the church, where tourist joints are replaced by simple chai shops and thali places, and there's plenty of fruit, vegetable and fish stalls for self-caterers. At night, *bhelpuri* vendors set up camp here, dishing up big portions of the fried noodle snack for just a few rupees.

Café Coffee Day (cakes & coffees from Rs40; 🕙 8am-midnight) A pleasant enough place to escape the heat, this wannabe sleek joint offers a half-decent cappuccino (Rs44) along with a range of cakes, including the suitably '70s Black Forest Gateau (Rs44), reminiscent of the era when Colva was still cool.

Mickey's (Colva Beach Rd; mains from Rs60) An ever popular place to drink the afternoon away or munch lunch from the extensive Indian/Continental/Chinese menu, Mickey's is usually busy and the food dispensed is fresh and filling.

Sagar Kinara (Colva Beach Rd; mains Rs30-100) A pure-veg restaurant with tastes to please even committed carnivores, this great place is clean, efficient and offers cheap and delicious North and South Indian cuisine all day long.

Tate Sports Bar (🕙 8am-midnight) Hearty English breakfasts, draught Kingfisher on tap and football on TV inhabit a comfier, more cosmopolitan drinking option than Colva is used to.

BENAULIM
Johncy (Vasvaddo Beach Rd; mains Rs60-120) Like Pedro's beside it, Johncy dispenses standard beach shack favourites from its location just back from the sands themselves. Staff are obliging and food, if not exciting, is fresh and filling.

Pedro's Bar & Restaurant (Vasvaddo Beach Rd; mains Rs60-120) Set amid a large, shady garden on the beachfront and popular with local and inter-

---

> ### COLVA'S MENINO JESUS
> If the only miracle you've experienced in Colva is finding a nice budget bed, the village's 18th-century **Our Lady of Mercy Church** has been host to several miracles of its own, of the rather more celestial kind. Inside, closely guarded under lock and key, lives a little statue known as the 'Menino' (Baby) Jesus, which is said to miraculously heal the sick and which only sees the light of day during the **Fama de Menino Jesus festival**, on the second Monday in October. Then, the little image is paraded about town, dipped in the river, and installed in the church's high altar for pilgrims hoping for their own personal miracle to pray to.

---

national tourists alike, Pedro's offers standard Indian, Chinese and Italian dishes, as well as a good line in Goan choices and some super 'sizzlers'.

Malibu Restaurant (mains Rs90-150) With a secluded garden setting, this place, a short walk back from the beach, offers one of Benaulim's more sophisticated dining experiences, with great renditions of Italian favourites and live jazz and blues on Tuesday evenings.

Getting There & Away
Buses run from Colva to Margao roughly every 15 minutes (Rs12, 20 minutes) from 7.30am to about 7pm, departing from the parking area at the end of the beach road.

Buses from Margao to Benaulim are also frequent (Rs8, 15 minutes); some continue on south to Varca and Cavelossim. Buses stop at the crossroads quite a distance from the main action (such as it is) and beach; it's best to hail a rickshaw (Rs20) for the five-minute ride to the sea.

BENAULIM TO PALOLEM
Immediately south of Benaulim are the beach resorts of **Varca** and **Cavelossim**, both boasting wide, pristine sands and a line of roomy five-star hotel complexes set amid extensive landscaped grounds fronting onto the beach. The most luxe of all is **Leela Goa** (☎ 2871234; www.theleela.com; d from Rs8500; 🍴 🖳 🏊) at Mobor, 3km south of Cavelossim. Stray just beyond it, however, to the end of the peninsula, and you'll find one of the most picture-perfect spots in the whole of Goa, at the simple **Blue**

Whale beach shack (mains from Rs50; 🕑 8.30am-late), run by friendly local Roque Coutinho.

If you're heading down this coast under your own steam, you can cross the Sal River, to continue south, at Cavelossim, by taking the rusting tin-tub ferry. To reach it, turn at the sign saying 'Village Panchayat Cavelossim' close to Cavelossim's white-washed church, then continue on for 2km to the river. From here you can ride on to the fishing village of **Betul**; ferries run approximately every half an hour between 8am and 8.30pm. They're free for pedestrians and cost Rs7 for cars; outside those hours, you can charter the ferry for a princely Rs50.

From Betul on south to Agonda, the road winds over gorgeous, undulating hills thick with palm groves. It's worth stopping off at the bleak old Portuguese fort of **Cabo da Rama**, (look for the green, red and white signposts leading the way) which has a small church within the fort walls, stupendous views and several old buildings rapidly becoming one with the trees.

Back on the main road there's a turn-off to **Agonda**, a small village with a wide, empty beach on which rare Olive Ridley turtles sometimes lay their eggs, and which remains the silent, idyllic secret of south Goa. There's plenty of accommodation to choose from, but don't come here looking for any sort of action: the pace is slow and the only bright lights at night are the stars. **Chattai** (☎ 9822481360; www.chattai.co.in; huts Rs1200), at the north end of the beach, offers lovely, simple huts on the sands, while **Praia de Agonda** (☎ 9763129429; praia-deagonda@gmail.com; huts from Rs1200) is a well-run and child-friendly set-up at the south end, with fun jam sessions and live bands several evenings per week.

There's lots of yoga and ayurveda about in Agonda – look out for notices – and plenty of beach restaurants serving up good grub. For a simpler local breakfast, *bhaji pau* and chais are to be had at the cluster of tiny eateries beside the church.

PALOLEM & AROUND

Palolem's stunning crescent beach was, as recently as 10 years ago, another of Goa's undiscovered gems, with few tourists and even fewer facilities to offer them. Nowadays, it's no longer quiet or hidden, but remains one of Goa's most beautiful spots, with a friendly, laid-back pace, and lots of budget accommodation ranged along the sands. Nightlife's still sleepy here –

there are no real clubs or pubs and the place goes to sleep when the music stops at 10pm. But if you're looking for a nice place to lay up, rest a while, swim in calm seas and choose from an infinite range of yoga, massages and therapies on offer, this is the place for you.

If even Palolem's version of action is all too much for you, head south, along the small rocky cove named **Colomb Bay**, which hosts several basic places to stay, to **Patnem Beach** beyond, where a fine selection of beach huts, and a less pretty – but infinitely quieter – stretch of sand awaits.

Information

Palolem's beach road is lined with travel agencies, internet places, and money changers.

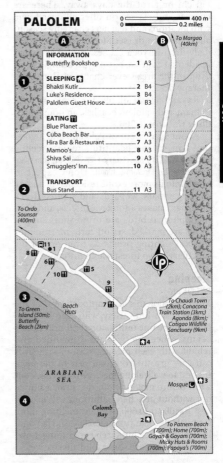

PALOLEM

0 ——— 400 m
0 ——— 0.2 miles

To Margao (40km)

INFORMATION	
Butterfly Bookshop	1 A3

SLEEPING	
Bhakti Kutir	2 B4
Luke's Residence	3 B4
Palolem Guest House	4 B3

EATING	
Blue Planet	5 A3
Cuba Beach Bar	6 A3
Hira Bar & Restaurant	7 A3
Mamoo's	8 A3
Shiva Sai	9 A3
Smugglers' Inn	10 A3

TRANSPORT	
Bus Stand	11 A3

To Ordo Sounsar (400m)

To Green Island (50m); Butterfly Beach (2km)

Beach Huts

To Chaudi Town (2km); Canacona Train Station (3km); Agonda (8km); Cotigao Wildlife Sanctuary (9km)

ARABIAN SEA

Mosque

Colomb Bay

To Patnem Beach (700m); Home (700m); Goyan & Goyam (700m); Micky Huts & Rooms (700m); Papaya's (700m)

GOA

There are no ATM machines in Palolem it-self, but two in the nearby workaday village of Chaudi, which also boasts a supermar-ket, several pharmacies, and all the other amenities you might require. An autorick-shaw from Palolem to Chaudi costs Rs100, or you can walk the flat 2km in a leisurely 45 minutes.

Butterfly Book Shop (☎ 9341738801; ☼ 9am-late) The best of several good bookshops in town, this cute and cosy place with resident cat stocks bestsellers, classics and a good range of books on yoga, meditation and spirituality.

Sights & Activities

Palolem and Patnem are these days the places to be if you're keen to yoga, belly dance, reiki, t'ai chi or tarot the days away. There are courses and classes on offer all over town, with locations and teachers changing season-ally. Bhakti Kutir (see Sleeping below) offers daily drop-in yoga classes, as well as longer residential courses, but it's just a single yogic drop in the area's ever-changing alternative therapy ocean.

Kayaks are available for rent on both Patnem and Palolem beaches; an hour's pad-dling will cost Rs300.

About 9km south of Palolem, and a good day trip, is the beautiful, remote-feeling **Cotigao Wildlife Sanctuary** (☎ 2965601; admission/ camera Rs5/25; ☼ 7am-5.30pm). Don't expect to bump into its more exotic residents (including gaurs, sambars, leopards and spotted deer), but frogs, snakes, monkeys, insects, and blaz-ingly plumed birds are in no short supply. Trails are marked; set off early morning for the best sighting prospects from one of the sanctuary's two forest watch towers.

Sleeping

PALOLEM

Most of Palolem's accommodation is of the simple beach-hut variety, with little to distin-guish where one outfit stops and next door's begins. Since the huts are dismantled and rebuilt with each passing season, standards can vary greatly from one year to the next. It's best to walk along the beach and check out a few before making your decision; a simple hut without attached bathroom will usually cost Rs400 to Rs600, while something more sophisticated can run to Rs2000 and beyond. If bamboo beach huts aren't your thing, how-ever, following are some solid alternatives.

Palolem Guest House (☎ 2644879; www.palolem guesthouse.com; d Rs600-1200; ☒) If you pale at the thought of another night in a basic beach hut, this splendid place a quick walk from the beach offers lots of plain but comfortable rooms with solid, brick walls arranged around a nice leafy garden.

Ordo Sounsar (☎ 9822488769; www.ordosounsar .com; huts Rs2000, without bathroom Rs1500) Beach huts they might be, but set as far north up Palolem beach as it's possible to go, across a rickety bridge spanning a wide creek, this hidden haven makes a cool, quiet alternative to some of the elbow-to-elbow options further on down the sands.

Bhakti Kutir (☎ 2643472; www.bhaktikutir.com; cottages from Rs2500; ☐) Ensconced in a thick wooded grove between Palolem and Patnem Beaches, Bhakti's well-equipped rustic cot-tages are a little on the pricey side these days, but still offer a unique jungle retreat. There are daily drop-in yoga classes, and the out-door restaurant, beneath billowing parachute silks, turns out yummy, imaginative, health-ful stuff.

Luke's Residence (☎ 2643003; www.lukesresi dence.com; d Rs2500) Set in a quiet, green part of Palolem, about 10 minutes' walk from the beach, Luke's is praised by its oft-returning guests for its warm, helpful hospitality and great food. The beds are comfy, most rooms would easily fit three or four beach huts in-side, and rates include a simple breakfast.

PATNEM

Long-stayers will revel in Patnem's choice of village homes and apartments available for rent. A very basic house can cost Rs10,000 per month whilst a fully equipped apartment will go for anything up to Rs50,000.

Micky Huts & Rooms (☎ 9850484884; huts Rs200) If you don't blanche at basic, this is the best bargain on the whole of Patnem beach, run by the friendliest and most obliging local family you could imagine. There's no sign-post: just head for the huge patch of bamboo beside the small stream towards the north-ern end of the beach, and enquire at the restaurant.

Papaya's (☎ 9923079447; www.papayasgoa.com; huts Rs1500) Lovely, rustic huts head back into the palm grove from Papaya's popular restaurant. Each is lovingly tended to, with lots of wood and floating muslin, and the staff are incred-ibly keen to please.

Goyam & Goyam (☎ 9822685138; www.goyam.net; huts with/without sea view Rs3000/2500) Comfortable, cute and well-equipped pastel-shaded huts are the trademark here, with plenty of character and lots of room to breathe between each one.

Eating & Drinking
Both Palolem and Patnem's beaches are lined with beach shacks, offering all-day dining and fresh, fresh seafood as the catch comes in and the sun goes down. As with accommodation, places here change seasonally, but below are a few well-established options.

Hira Bar & Restaurant (breakfast from Rs12; ☻ breakfast & lunch) The best place to start the morning in Palolem with a *bhaji pau* and a glass of chai, along with locals on their way out to work.

our pick **Mamoo's** (mains from Rs40) Don't be put off by the rather dark, cavernous interior: here's where you'll find Palolem's very best Indian food, in delicious and generous portions. For a taste sensation, explore the variety of vegetarian tandoori options; you'll likely be back the following night to continue trawling the extensive menu.

Shiva Sai (vegetable thali Rs40; ☻ breakfast & lunch) A thoroughly local lunch joint, knocking out tasty thalis of the veggie, fish and Gujarati kinds, and a good line, too, in breakfasts such as banana pancakes (Rs40).

Blue Planet (dishes from Rs60) Tasty vegan and organic treats served up with love by a local couple at this shady retreat from the hot Palolem day. Bring your water bottles here to be refilled with safe, filtered drinking water for just Rs3 per litre (free to restaurant patrons), to do your little bit towards reducing Palolem's plastic problem.

Home (☎ 2643916; home.patnem@yahoo.com; mains from Rs80) This hip, relaxed restaurant, run by a lovely British couple, serves up unquestionably the best food in Patnem. Fill up for breakfast with a thick, delicious rosti topped with fried eggs, cheese and tomatoes, or stop in for coffee and the best chocolate brownies in India. Home also rents out nicely decorated, light rooms (Rs1000 to Rs2500): call to book or ask at the restaurant.

Cuba (mains from Rs100) For scrambled eggs, soups and sundowners alike, perennially popular Cuba, down on the beach and with a bar on the beach road, has it all. Its Indian food is tasty and filling, as are its Chinese specialities, and the Cuba experience is enhanced by a great music collection, and a laid-back, lazy vibe.

Smugglers' Inn (mains from Rs120) If you're craving full English breakfasts or Sunday dinner with all the trimmings, the Smugglers' Inn, with its football on TV and weekly quiz nights, provides that little bit of Britain in the midst of beachside India.

Getting There & Away
There are hourly buses to Margao (Rs25, one hour) from the bus stand on the main road down to the beach. There are also regular buses to nearby Chaudi (Rs5), the nearest town, from which you can get frequent buses to Margao and Panaji or south to Karwar and Mangalore. The closest train station is Canacona.

An autorickshaw from Palolem to Patnem costs Rs50; an autorickshaw from Palolem to Chaudi costs Rs100. A prepaid taxi from Dabolim airport to Palolem/Patnem costs Rs1005/1080.

Karnataka

'One state, many worlds', goes the slogan currently peddling Karnataka's tourism wonders to the world. And that's kidding you not! Rounding off the southern extent of the Deccan Plateau, this sprawling south Indian state exemplifies natural and cultural variety. And complemented by its ultra-professional tourism industry and inherent friendliness, Karnataka has, in recent times, surged ahead to redefine itself as a travellers' haven. It's fun, stress-free and thoroughly enjoyable all the way, and you're unlikely to go home disappointed.

The epicurean silicon-capital Bengaluru (Bangalore), overfed with the good life, is your entry-point to the state. Within arm's length is Mysore, the royal jewel in Karnataka's crown, with its spectacular palace and vibrant markets. Dodge the herds of grumpy tuskers in the Nilgiri Biosphere Reserve to arrive at the rock-cut temples of Belur and Halebid, and you've probably already sniffed the heady aroma of coffee and spices from the lush plantations of hilly Kodagu (Coorg). A stone's throw away is the shimmering Karnataka coastline, dotted with beaches and fascinating temple towns. If history is your forte, head to the centre of the state, studded with ancient architectural gems including the World Heritage–listed monuments of Hampi and Pattadakal. Finally, sign off by visiting the forgotten battlements and monuments of Bijapur and Bidar, where you'll be bowled over by a true blast from the state's glorious past.

HIGHLIGHTS

- Be dazzled by the Maharaja's Palace and the technicolour Devaraja Market in **Mysore** (p914)
- Savour aromatic coffee while recharging your spirit in the lush, cool highlands of the **Kodagu region** (p927)
- Drink yourself under the table, or stab into top-notch global cuisine in **Bengaluru** (p909)
- Stride across the deserted ramparts of the romantic 15th-century fort in **Bidar** (p952)
- Marvel at the gravity-defying boulders, and wander amid the melancholic ruins of **Hampi** (p938)
- Survey the sensuous carvings in the ancient caves and temples of **Badami** (p946)
- Play Robinson Crusoe and wave at passing boats along the deserted beaches of **Gokarna** (p935)

★ Bidar

★ Badami

Hampi ★

★ Gokarna

Bengaluru (Bangalore) ★

Kodagu region ★

★ Mysore

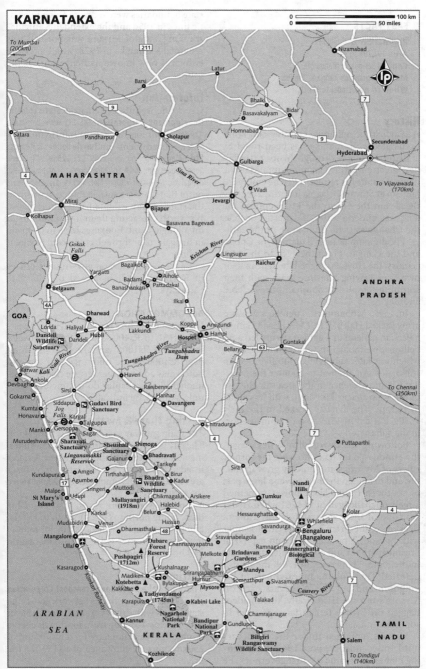

KARNATAKA

History

A playfield of religions, cultures and kingdoms galore, Karnataka has been ruled by a string of rulers through history. India's first great emperor, Chandragupta Maurya, made the state his retreat, when he embraced Jainism at Sravanabelagola in the 3rd century BC. From the 6th to the 11th century, the land was under a series of dynasties such as the Chalukyas (who built some of the earliest Hindu temples near Badami), the Cholas and the Gangas. From the 11th to the 14th century, the Hoysalas shaped the state in their own way, leaving a lasting mark with their stunning temples at Somnathpur, Halebid and Belur.

In 1327, Mohammed Tughlaq's Muslim army sacked Halebid. In 1347, Hasan Gangu, a Persian general in Tughlaq's army led a rebellion to establish the Bahmani kingdom, which was later subdivided into five Deccan sultanates. An attempt to counter the growing Islamic presence in the area saw the rise of the Vijayanagar kingdom, with its capital in Hampi. The dynasty peaked in the early 1550s, but fell in 1565 to a combined effort of the sultanates.

Following the downfall of Vijayanagar, the Hindu Wodeyars (who were the former rulers of Mysore state) quickly grew in stature and extended their rule over a large part of southern India. Their power remained largely unchallenged until 1761 when Hyder Ali (one of their generals) deposed them. Backed by the French, Hyder Ali together with his son, Tipu Sultan, set up capital in Srirangapatnam and consolidated their rule in the region. However, in 1799, the British defeated Tipu Sultan, annexed part of his kingdom and put the Wodeyars back on Mysore's throne. Historically, this incident flagged off British territorial expansion in southern India.

Mysore remained under the Wodeyars until Independence; post-1947, the reigning maharaja became the first governor. The state boundaries were redrawn along linguistic lines in 1956 and the extended Kannada-speaking state of Mysore was born. It was renamed Karnataka in 1972, with Bangalore (which is now known as Bengaluru) as the capital.

Information

Check the website of **Karnataka State Tourism Development Corporation** (KSTDC; www.karnataka tourism.org) for lots of relevant information.

The government-run **Jungle Lodges & Resorts Ltd** (Map p905; ☎ 080-25597021, 25597944; www .junglelodges.com; 2nd fl, Shrungar Shopping Complex, MG Rd, Bengaluru; ⏱ 10am-5.30pm Mon-Sat) is an excellent outfit that manages sustainable ecotourism in the state's many wildlife parks and reserves. It's worth contacting them if you want to go on a jungle jaunt. Bookings have to be made in Bengaluru, or through credit card payment online.

Be aware that several government offices in Karnataka remain closed on alternate Saturdays.

ACCOMMODATION

In Karnataka luxury tax is 4% on rooms costing Rs151 to Rs400, 8% on those between Rs401 and Rs1000, and 12% on anything over Rs1000. Some midrange and top-end hotels may add a further service charge. Rates quoted in this chapter do not include taxes unless otherwise indicated.

Getting There & Away

The main gateway to Karnataka is Bengaluru. The city is serviced by most domestic airlines, including some international carriers. Airfares listed in this chapter are indicative only. Taxes are extra, and can sometimes be almost twice the actual fare.

Coastal Mangalore is a transit point for those going north to Goa, or south to Kerala. Hubli, in central Karnataka, is a major railway junction for routes going into Maharashtra and northern India.

Getting Around

The **Karnataka State Road Transport Corporation** (KSRTC) has a superb bus network across the state. Taxis with drivers are easily available in major towns. For long trips, most taxis charge around Rs7 per kilometre for a minimum of 250km, plus an allowance of Rs150 for the driver.

FESTIVALS IN KARNATAKA

Udupi Paryaya (Jan; Udupi, p934) Held in even-numbered years, with procession and ritual marking the handover of swamis at the town's Krishna Temple.

Classical Dance Festival (Jan/Feb; Pattadakal, p948) Features some of India's best classical dance performances.

Tibetan New Year (Feb; Bylakuppe, p930) Lamas in the Tibetan refugee settlements take shifts leading nonstop prayers that span the week of celebrations, which also include special dances and a fire ceremony.

Vasantahabba (Feb; Nrityagram, p913) The largest free classical dance and music event in India, hosted by the dance village of Nrityagram, featuring traditional and contemporary Indian dance and music.

Mastakabhisheka (Feb; Sravanabelagola, p924) Held once every 12 years, when the 58-foot monolithic statue of Bahubali is swathed in colourful offerings. The next date is in 2018.

Shivaratri Festival (Feb/Mar; Gokarna, p935) Two gargantuan chariots barrel down Gokarna's main street on 'Shiva power' amid much colourful ritual.

Muharram (Feb/Mar; Hospet, p943) This Shi'ia Muslim festival sees fire-walkers in action, to the accompaniment of mass hoopla.

Vairamudi Festival (Mar/Apr; Melkote, p922) Lord Vishnu is adorned with jewels at Cheluvanarayana Temple, including a diamond-studded crown belonging to Mysore's former maharajas.

Ganesh Chaturthi (Aug/Sep; Gokarna, p935) Families quietly march their Ganeshas to the sea at sunset.

Dussehra (Sep/Oct; Mysore, p917) Also spelt 'Dasara' in Mysore. The Maharaja's Palace is lit up in the evenings and a vibrant procession hits town to the delight of thousands.

Vijaya Utsav (Nov; Hampi, p938) Traditional music and dance re-creates Vijayanagar's glory among Hampi's temples and boulders.

Lakshadeepam (Nov; Dharmasthala, p933) A hundred thousand lamps light up this Jain pilgrimage town, offering spectacular photo-ops.

Huthri (Nov/Dec; Madikeri, p927) The Kodava community of Kodagu celebrates the start of the season's rice harvests with ceremony, music, traditional dances and much feasting for a week, beginning on a full-moon night.

SOUTHERN KARNATAKA

BENGALURU (BANGALORE)

☎ 080 / pop 5.7 million / elev 920m

Strategically located at the southern tip of the Deccan and within close range of Kerala and Tamil Nadu, cosmopolitan Bengaluru (formerly Bangalore) makes a great base and starting point for venturing out across southern India. The hub of India's booming IT industry, the city has experienced a mad surge of urban development of late, which shows in terms of its crazy traffic, rising pollution levels and civic congestion. However, it's also a city that has taken care to preserve its green spaces and its colonial heritage. Add to that a benevolent climate, a handful of interesting sights and a progressive dining, drinking and shopping scene, and Bengaluru promises a few great nights on the town.

History

Literally meaning 'Town of Boiled Beans', Bengaluru supposedly derived its name from an ancient incident involving an old village woman, who served cooked pulses to a lost and hungry Hoysala king. Kempegowda, a feudal lord, was the first person to earmark Bengaluru's extents by building a mud fort in 1537. However, the town remained obscure until 1759, when it was gifted to Hyder Ali by the Mysore maharaja.

The British came to town in 1809, and made it their regional administrative base in 1831, thus renaming it Bangalore. During the Raj era, the city played host to many a British officer, including Winston Churchill, who enjoyed life here during his greener years and famously left a debt (still on the books) of Rs13 at the Bangalore Club!

That Bengaluru was a city with a knack for technology became apparent quite early; in 1905, it was the first Indian city to have electric street lighting. Since the 1940s, it has been home to Hindustan Aeronautics Ltd (HAL), India's premier aerospace company. And if you can't do without email today, you owe it all to a Bangalorean too; Sabeer Bhatia, inventor of the pioneering Hotmail service, grew up here!

A nominal step backward was taken when the city's name was changed back to Bengaluru

KARNATAKA

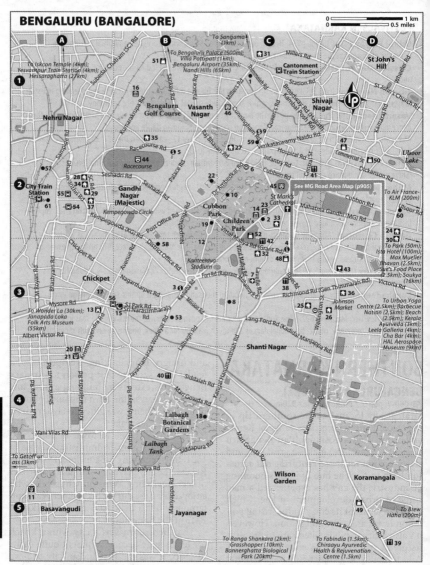

BENGALURU (BANGALORE)

in November 2006, though few care to use it in practice. Home to a swanky new international airport and a rush of software, electronics and business process outsourcing firms, Bengaluru's skyline is increasingly being dotted by skyscrapers today, each of which seem to be reaching for the sky, literally as well as figuratively.

Orientation

Increasing development continues to push Bengaluru's boundaries outward by the day. However, the central part remains more or less unchanged. Of interest to travellers are Gandhi Nagar (the old quarters); Mahatma Gandhi (MG) Rd, the heart of British-era Bangalore; and the Central Business

District (CBD), north of MG Rd, across the greens.

Locally known as Majestic, Gandhi Nagar is a crowded area where Bengaluru's central bus stand and the City train station are located. A few historical relics lie to its south, including Lalbagh Botanical Gardens and Tipu Sultan's palace.

About 4km east are the high streets bounded by Mahatma Gandhi (MG), Brigade, St Mark's and Residency (FM Cariappa) Rds. This is Bengaluru's cosmopolitan hub, with parks, tree-lined streets, churches, grand houses and military establishments. In between are sandwiched the golf club, the racecourse and the cricket stadium.

Finding directions in Bengaluru can be slightly disorienting at times. In certain areas, roads are named after their widths (eg 80ft Rd). The city also follows a system of mains and crosses; 3rd cross, 5th main, Residency Rd, for example, refers to the third lane on the fifth street branching off Residency Rd.

MAPS
The tourist offices (p904) give out decent city maps. The excellent *Eicher City Map* (Rs200) is sold at Bengaluru's many bookshops (right).

Information
BOOKSHOPS
Blossom (Map p905; 84/6 Church St; ⏰ 10.30am-8pm Mon-Sat) The excellent collection here gets even better when you know the books often come at bargain prices!

Crossword (Map p905; ACR Tower, Residency Rd; ⏰ 10.30am-9pm Mon-Sat) Offers a great selection of books, magazines, CDs and DVDs.

Premier Bookshop (Map p905; 46/1 Church St; ⏰ 10am-1.30pm & 3-8pm Mon-Sat) It's tiny but somehow has everything; enter from Museum Rd.

CULTURAL CENTRES
Alliance Française (Map p902; ☎ 41231340; www .afindia.org/bangalore; 108 Thimmaiah Rd; ⏰ 10am-7pm Mon-Sat) French cultural hub offering courses, events, a cafe and a library.

British Library (Map p902; ☎ 22489220; www .library.britishcouncil.org.in; 23 Kasturba Rd Cross; ⏰ 10.30am-6.30pm Mon-Sat) English newspapers, books and magazines, and free internet access for members (annual membership Rs1000).

Max Mueller Bhavan (off Map p902; ☎ 25205305; www.goethe.de; 716 CMH Rd, opp MK Retailers, Indiranagar 1st Stage; ⏰ 9am-5pm Mon-Fri) Has a good cafe and a library of German titles. Also runs exhibitions and courses.

INTERNET ACCESS
For an IT city, internet cafes are plentiful in Bengaluru, as is wi-fi access in hotels.

KARNATAKA

LEFT LUGGAGE

Both the City train station (Map p902) and Central bus stand (Map p902), located either side of Gubbi Thotadappa Rd, have 24-hour cloakrooms (per day Rs10).

MEDIA

City Info (www.explocity.com) is a bimonthly listings booklet that's available free from tourist offices and many hotels. *Ticket Bengaluru* (Rs350) is a great handbook and is available in major bookstores.

MEDICAL SERVICES

Most hotels here have doctors on call.
Chetak Pharma (Map p902; ☎ 22212449; Basement, Devatha Plaza, Residency Rd; ⊙ 9am-9pm Mon-Sat, 9.30am-2pm Sun) Well-stocked pharmacy.
Mallya Hospital (Map p902; ☎ 22277979; www .mallyahospital.net; Vittal Mallya Rd) With a 24-hour pharmacy.

MONEY

ATMs are common.
Monarch (Map p905; ☎ 41123253; 54 Monarch Plaza, Brigade Rd; ⊙ 10am-8pm Mon-Sat) Deals in forex, travellers cheques and ticketing.
TT Forex (Map p902; ☎ 22254337; 33/1 Cunningham Rd; ⊙ 9.30am-6.30pm Mon-Fri, 9.30am-1.30pm Sat) Changes travellers cheques with no commission.

PHOTOGRAPHY

Digital services are easy to come by.
GG Welling (Map p905; 113 MG Rd; ⊙ 9.30am-1pm & 3-7.30pm Mon-Sat)
GK Vale (Map p905; 89 MG Rd; ⊙ 10am-7pm Mon-Sat)

POST

Main post office (Map p902; ☎ 22892211; Cubbon Rd; ⊙ 10am-7pm Mon-Sat, 10am-1pm Sun)

TOURIST INFORMATION

Government of India tourist office (Map p905; ☎ 25585417; 48 Church St; ⊙ 9.30am-6pm Mon-Fri, 9am-1pm Sat)
Karnataka State Tourism Development Corporation (KSTDC; Map p902; Badami House (☎ 22275883; Badami House, Kasturba Rd; ⊙ 10am-7pm Mon-Sat); Karnataka Tourism House (☎ 41329211; 8 Papanna Lane, St Mark's Rd; ⊙ 10am-7pm Mon-Sat) Bookings can be made for KSTDC city and state tours, as well as for luxury holidays such as the Golden Chariot (p1188).
Karnataka Tourism (Map p902; ☎ 22352828; 2nd fl, 49 Khanija Bhavan, Racecourse Rd; ⊙ 10am-5.30pm Mon-Sat)

TRAVEL AGENCIES

Skyway (Map p902; ☎ 22111401; www.skywaytour .com; 8 Papanna Lane, St Mark's Rd; ⊙ 9am-6pm Mon-Sat) A thoroughly professional outfit with satellite offices in Mysore and Madikeri. Reliable for booking long-distance taxis and air tickets.
STIC Travels (Map p902; ☎ 22202408; www .stictravel.com; Imperial Ct, 33/1 Cunningham Rd; ⊙ 9.30am-6pm Mon-Sat)

Dangers & Annoyances

For information about safety on local buses, see p913.

Sights
LALBAGH BOTANICAL GARDENS

Spread over 96 acres of landscaped terrain, **Lalbagh** (Map p902; ☎ 26579231; admission Rs10; ⊙ 5.30am-7.30pm) or the Red Garden was laid out in 1760 by Hyder Ali, and is now one of Bengaluru's most famous greens. Ten-seater ecofriendly buggies (per head Rs100) can take you on a guided tour across the garden, telling you more about the centuries-old trees and collections of plants from around the world. A beautiful glasshouse, modelled on the original Crystal Palace in London, is the venue for flower shows in the weeks preceding Republic Day (26 January) and Independence Day (15 August). Walk in early on Sundays, and you can also hear the police band perform at the Police Bandstand.

BENGALURU PALACE

The private residence of the Wodeyar family, **Bengaluru Palace** (off Map p902; ☎ 23315789; Palace Rd; Indian/foreigner Rs100/200, camera/video Rs500/1000; ⊙ 10am-6pm) preserves a slice of the bygone royal life for you to see. Aged retainers show you around the building, designed to resemble Windsor Castle, and you can marvel at the lavish interiors and galleries featuring family photos and a collection of nude portraits. Ask before you get clicking. The palace grounds, interestingly, are now Bengaluru's hottest concert arena, having hosted everyone from Iron maiden, the Rolling Stones, Aerosmith and Deep Purple in the past!

KARNATAKA CHITRAKALA PARISHATH

This **visual arts gallery** (Map p902; ☎ 22261816; www.chitrakalaparishath.org; Kumarakrupa Rd; admission Rs10; ⊙ 10.30am-5.30pm Mon-Sat) is Bengaluru's definitive art institution. A wide range of Indian and international contemporary art

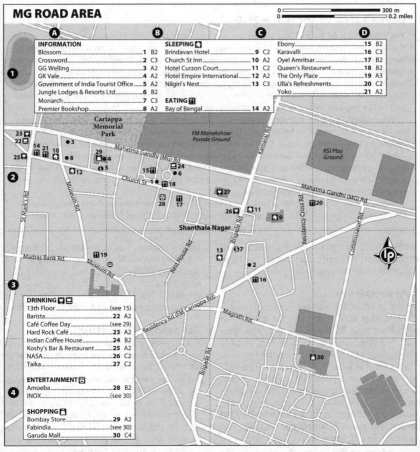

MG ROAD AREA

0   300 m
0   0.2 miles

INFORMATION	
Blossom	**1** B2
Crossword	**2** C3
GG Welling	**3** A2
GK Vale	**4** A2
Government of India Tourist Office	**5** A2
Jungle Lodges & Resorts Ltd	**6** B2
Monarch	**7** C3
Premier Bookshop	**8** A2

SLEEPING 🏠	
Brindavan Hotel	**9** C2
Church St Inn	**10** A2
Hotel Curzon Court	**11** C2
Hotel Empire International	**12** C2
Nilgiri's Nest	**13** C3

EATING 🍴	
Bay of Bengal	**14** A2

Ebony	**15** B2
Karavalli	**16** C3
Oye! Amritsar	**17** B2
Queen's Restaurant	**18** B2
The Only Place	**19** A3
Ulla's Refreshments	**20** C2
Yoko	**21** A2

DRINKING 🍷🖵	
13th Floor	(see 15)
Barista	**22** A2
Café Coffee Day	(see 29)
Hard Rock Café	**23** A2
Indian Coffee House	**24** B2
Koshy's Bar & Restaurant	**25** A2
NASA	**26** C2
Taika	**27** C2

ENTERTAINMENT 🎭	
Amoeba	**28** B2
INOX	(see 30)

SHOPPING 🛍	
Bombay Store	**29** A2
Fabindia	(see 30)
Garuda Mall	**30** C4

is on show at its exhibition galleries (open 10.30am to 7pm), while permanent displays showcase lavish gold-leaf works of Mysore-style paintings and folk and tribal art from across Asia. A section is devoted to the works of Russian master Nicholas Roerich, known for his vivid paintings of the Himalayas, and his son Svetoslav.

CUBBON PARK

Named after former British commissioner Sir Mark Cubbon, the leafy boughs of the 120-hectare **Cubbon Park** (Map p902) provide a few moments' respite to the city's stressed-out residents. On its fringes are the red-painted Gothic-style **State Central Library** and two municipal museums. For the gadget-oriented

kind, there's the **Visvesvaraya Industrial & Technical Museum** (☎ 22864009; Kasturba Rd; admission Rs15; ☽ 10am-6pm Mon-Sat), which showcases a wide range of electrical and engineering displays, from a replica of the Wright brothers' 1903 flyer to 21st-century virtual-reality games. The **Government Museum** (☎ 22864483; Kasturba Rd; admission Rs4; ☽ 10am-5pm Tue-Sun) to the south of Cubbon Park houses a collection of stone carvings and relics, including some good pieces from Halebid. Your ticket also gets you into the attached **Venkatappa Art Gallery** (☽ 10am-5pm Tue-Sun), where you can see several works and personal memorabilia of K Venkatappa (1887–1962), court painter to the Wodeyars.

At the northwestern end of Cubbon Park are the colossal neo-Dravidian-style **Vidhana**

KARNATAKA

GROUND ZERO OF THE FLAT WORLD

You'll be pardoned for mistaking it for the sets of a utopian movie. In reality, however, it's only the lush and modern campus of Indian IT giant Infosys, located on the southeastern edge of Bengaluru. A pioneer in India's booming software industry, the company has almost single-handedly ushered in India's IT revolution through its years of operation. In 2005, it was also responsible for cementing Bengaluru's reputation as the silicon-coated heart of India, when Pulitzer Prize-winning writer Thomas L Friedman wrote *The World Is Flat* after visiting its campus and being inspired by the company's progressive principles.

Established by seven software engineers in 1981, Infosys today has over 100,000 employees and revenues of over US$4 billion – its client list currently includes nearly 100 Fortune 500 companies. Its campus (not open to the public) represents an alternative, enterprising India exists in the form of shiny glass and steel structures sprouting amid rolling lawns. The workforce (average age 26) cycle or use electric golf carts to get around the 32-hectare campus, passing five food courts (serving 14 types of cuisine), banks, a supermarket, basketball courts, putting green and state-of-the-art gyms, and even a hotel!

The point, perhaps, is to prove that Infosys can compete on equal terms with the Western world – thus putting India on a level playing field with other nationalities in Friedman's 'flat world'.

Soudha, built in 1954, and the neoclassical **Attara Kacheri,** opposite, that houses the High Court. Both are closed to the public.

TIPU SULTAN'S PALACE

In the heart of the vibrant Krishnarajendra City Market stands the elegant **palace** (Map p902; Albert Victor Rd; Indian/foreigner Rs5/100, video Rs25; 8.30am-5.30pm) of Tipu Sultan, notable for its teak pillars and ornamental frescoes. Though not as beautiful (or well-maintained) as Tipu's summer palace in Srirangapatnam, it's an interesting monument, and definitely worth an outing when combined with other nearby sights such as the **Krishnarajendra (City) Market,** the massive **Jama Masjid** (Map p902; Silver Jubilee (SJ) Park Rd; admission free), the remains of Kempegowda's **fort** (Map p902) and the ornate **Venkataraman Temple** (Map p902; Krishnarajendra Rd; 8.30am-6pm).

BULL TEMPLE & DODDA GANESHA TEMPLE

Built by Kempegowda in the 16th-century Dravidian style, the **Bull Temple** (Map p902; Bull Temple Rd, Basavangudi; 7am-8.30pm) contains a huge granite monolith of Nandi and is one of Bengaluru's most atmospheric temples. Nearby is the **Dodda Ganesha Temple** (Map p902; Bull Temple Rd, Basavangudi; 7am-8.30pm), with an equally enormous Ganesh idol.

ISKCON TEMPLE

Built by the International Society of Krishna Consciousness (Iskcon), better known as the Hare Krishnas, this shiny **temple** (off Map p902; Hare Krishna Hill, Chord Rd; 7am-1pm & 4-8.30pm), 8km northwest of the town centre, is lavishly decorated in a mix of ultra-contemporary and traditional styles. The Sri Radha Krishna Mandir has a stunning shrine to Krishna and Radha.

HAL AEROSPACE MUSEUM

For a peek into India's aeronautical history, visit this wonderful **museum** (off Map p902; 25228341; Airport-Varthur Rd; admission Rs20; 9am-5pm Tue-Sun) past the old airport, where you can see some of the indigenous aircraft models designed by HAL, sometimes with a little help from other nations. Interesting exhibits include the infamous MIG-21, indigenous models such as the Marut and Kiran, and a vintage Canberra bomber. You can also engage in mock dogfights at the simulator machines (Rs10) on the top-floor.

Activities

AYURVEDA & YOGA

Chiraayu Ayurvedic Health & Rejuvenation Centre (off Map p902; 25500855; 6th block, 17th D Main, Koramangala; 8.30am-6pm) These people take their practice seriously, so don't make vague demands like 'I'd like a massage!'. Take an appointment, discuss your problems, and the resultant therapy could range from a day-long spa session (from Rs700) to long-term programs.

Based in the eastern part of town, **Kerala Ayurveda** (off Map p902; 25262515; 3282 12th Main, HAL 2nd Stage), a veteran in the wellness industry offers holistic ayurvedic treatment through its centres across Bengaluru. Prices kick off from around Rs600. For a more lavish experience, try **Soukya** (off Map p902; ☎ 25318405; www .soukya.com; Soukya Rd, Samethanahalli, Whitefield; ☯ 6am-8.30pm), an internationally renowned place set on a picture-perfect 30-acre organic farm, that offers some of the best programs in ayurvedic therapy and yoga (per hour therapy Indian/foreigner Rs2200/US$55).

Stylish **Urban Yoga Centre** (off Map p902; ☎ 32005720; www.urbanyoga.in; 100ft Rd, Indiranagar; ☯ 6.30am-9pm) has a smart yoga studio offering a range of classes, and sells yoga clothes, accessories and books.

OUTDOOR ADVENTURE

Getoff ur ass (off Map p902; ☎ 26722750; www.getoff urass.com; 858 1D Main Rd, Giri Nagar 2nd Phase) has perfect recipes for outward-bound adventures, including rafting, kayaking, trekking and mountaineering in Karnataka and elsewhere. It also sells and rents outdoor gear.

WATER RIDES

Wonder La (off Map p902; www.wonderla.com; adult/child weekdays Rs450/350, weekends Rs570/420; ☯ 11am-6pm weekdays, 11am-7pm weekends) Located 30km out of town on the Mysore highway, this massive aqua park offers dozens of water rides.

Tours

Bangalore Walks (☎ 9845523660, 9880671192; www .bangalorewalks.com) is a must-do! Choose between a traditional walk, garden walk or Victorian walk to get under Bengaluru's skin. Held on Saturdays and Sundays (7am to 10pm), the walks (Rs495 including breakfast) teach you to love Bengaluru in a way that many locals have forgotten. Book in advance; each walk takes a maximum of 15 people.

KSTDC runs a couple of city bus tours, all of which begin at Badami House. The basic city tour runs twice daily at 7.30am and 2pm (ordinary/deluxe Rs170/190), while a 16-hour tour to Srirangapatnam, Mysore and Brindavan Gardens departs daily at 7.15am (ordinary/deluxe Rs525/675). There are longer tours to other destinations; enquire at the KSTDC offices (see p904).

Sleeping

With demands for a decent bed rising by the day, accommodation in Bengaluru is pricey and in short supply. A decent night's sleep could set you back by at least Rs1000. Anything under Rs500, and you're possibly courting asphyxia. Service apartments are frequently a better deal than many midrange (Rs1500 to Rs5000) and top-end hotels. Most hotels have 24-hour checkout. Book early.

BUDGET

Stacks of hotels line the loud and seedy neighbourhood of Subedar Chatram (SC) Rd, east of the bus stands and City train station. It's an unpleasant area, but convenient if you're in transit. For longer stays, consider moving into town, preferably closer to MG Rd. All hotels listed here have hot water, at least in the mornings.

Hotel Adora (Map p902; ☎ 22200024; 47 SC Rd; s/d from Rs400/600) A largish and popular budget option near the stations, this place has unfussy rooms with clean sheets. Downstairs is a good veg restaurant, Indraprastha.

Hotel Ajantha (Map p902; ☎ 25584321; fax 25584780; 22A MG Rd; s/d from Rs450/700, with AC from Rs999/1050; ✹) Old Indian tourism posters and stacks of potted foliage welcome you into this place that has a range of par-for-the-course rooms in a semi-quiet compound off MG Rd. It's popular with local tourists; book in advance.

Brindavan Hotel (Map p905; ☎ 25584000; 108 MG Rd; s/d from Rs550/850, with AC Rs1250/2550; ✹) Another place where advance booking is recommended. Its central position is a definite advantage, and the rooms are clean, bright and airy (with balconies). There's an in-house astro-palmist, if you're interested.

Sandhya Lodge (Map p902; ☎ 22874071; 70 SC Rd; d from Rs555, with AC Rs1450; ✹) Functionality overrides comfort at this place with somewhat unimaginative rooms, but at least they're tidy and the loos are well-scrubbed. Try for a room on the upper floors; it gets brighter the higher you climb.

Tom's (Map p902; ☎ 25575875; 1/5 Hosur Rd; s/d Rs999/1299, with AC Rs1800/2100; ✹ 🖳) Clearly the best of Bengaluru's low-cost brigade. The spacious modern rooms here come with freshly-painted walls, moody lighting, large windows and spotless linen. Add to that its prime location and a warm, friendly management – need we say more?

MIDRANGE

Hotel Curzon Court (Map p905; ☎ 25582997; 10 Brigade Rd; s/d from Rs1400/1600; ✹) Not too elaborate on the decor front, but this place has well-appointed and neat rooms with AC comfort. A sumptuous range of vegie delights are served at their restaurant, Aathithya.

Hotel Empire International (Map p905; ☎ 25593743; www.hotelempire.in; 36 Church St; s/d incl breakfast from Rs1550/1850; ❄ 🖵) The modern rooms here are spacious and bright, and it's in the heart of all the action and nightlife. The reception desk is manned by a professional lot, and the travel desk does a good job at booking tours.

Nilgiri's Nest (Map p905; ☎ 25588401; www.nilgiris1905.com; 171 Brigade Rd; s/d from Rs1650/2150; ❄) An air of freshness hangs in the snug rooms of this centrally located hotel. Below is an upmarket ration store run by the same company, which stocks some great ready-to-eat delights.

Ashley Inn (Map p902; ☎ 41233415; www.ashleyinn.in; 11 Ashley Park Rd; s/d incl breakfast from Rs1800/2200; ❄ 🖵) Seconds away from the MG Rd mayhem is this charming island of quiet. With eight pleasant rooms done up in soothing colours, this sweet guest house evokes that homey feeling you sometimes desperately yearn for while on the move.

Church Street Inn (Map p905; ☎ 30577190; 46/1/1 Church St; s/d Rs1900/2100; ❄) It's perfect for a longish stay. Guess why? The tariff goes down by 10% with every successive day! The rooms, some with wooden floors and tinted windows looking down on Church St, are comfy. The bookshelf at the reception is worth a thumbing.

Casa Piccola Service Apartments (Map p902; ☎ 22270754; www.casapiccola.com; Wellington Park Apartments, Wellington St; r with/without AC Rs2300/2000; ❄) A wonderful range of two- and three-bedroom apartments are available in this building on a shared basis. Tastefully done up in pastel shades, they're stocked with all amenities. It's owned by the Oberoi family which runs the Casa Piccola Cottage across the lane.

Tricolour Hotel (Map p902; ☎ 41279090; www.ibchotels.co.in; 15 Tank Bund Rd; s/d incl breakfast Rs2000/2500; ❄ 🖵) Built back-to-back against a shopping mall, this place is both classy and contemporary, with lavishly laid-out rooms and cheerful, sky-lit foyers. Convenient for both the bus and train stations.

Hari International (Map p902; ☎ 40214021; www.hotelhariinternational.com; 68/68/1 SC Rd; d incl breakfast Indian/foreigner from Rs2400/US$60; ❄ 🖵) More of a business joint, this place, despite its noisy surroundings, makes for a pleasant stay.

Rooms meet requisite luxury standards, and the amiable staff is always ready to meet your requirements.

our pick Casa Piccola Cottage (Map p902; ☎ 22270754; www.casapiccola.com; 2 Clapham St; r incl breakfast from Rs3000; ❄ 🖵) The rates may have gone up considerably, but this beautifully renovated 1915 cottage still scores on the comfort front. A tranquil sanctuary from the madness of the city, its studio rooms are high on old-world charm, and the gazebo in the garden across the tiny lawn is a nice place to tuck into your complimentary breakfast.

Villa Pottipati (off Map p902; ☎ 23360777; www.neemranahotels.com; 142 8th Cross, 4th Main, Malleswaram; s/d from Rs3500/5000; ❄ 🖵 🏊) Located a little off-centre, this heritage building packs in dollops of quaintness (read antique four-poster beds and arched doorways); adding to its ambience is a garden full of ageless trees, seasonal blossoms and a dunk-sized pool.

Jayamahal Palace (Map p902; ☎ 23331321; www.jayamahalpalace.com; 1 Jayamahal Rd; s/d from Rs5000/6000; ❄ 🖵) Once an Englishman's residence, this heritage structure is now royal property, owned by the former royal family of the Gujarati princely state of Gondal. Thoughtfully renovated, its rooms are stacked with relics from the past; the more expensive suites house things like brass swings and excellent stained glass-work.

The Chevron Hotel (Map p902; ☎ 22356000; www.thechevronhotel.com; 147 Infantry Rd; d Indian/foreigner from Rs5550/US$160; ❄ 🖵) A glitzy player in Bengaluru's midrange scene, this boutique place ups its style quotient with ocean-blue lighting, and serves a host of succulent bites at its multicuisine restaurant, Ground Pepper. The snug rooms are well-appointed, and house everything you require for a good night's sleep.

Also recommended:

Mélange (Map p902; ☎ 22129700; www.melange bangalore.com; 21 Vittal Mallya Rd; apt from Rs3250; ❄) A range of designer service apartments.

Regaalis (Map p902; ☎ 41133111; www.ushalexus hotels.com; 40/2 Lavelle Rd; d incl breakfast from Rs5000; ❄ 🖵) A midrange option in the heart of town.

TOP END

Ista Hotel (off Map p902; ☎ 25558888; www.ista hotels.com; 1/1 Swami Vivekananda Rd, Ulsoor; s/d from Rs6500/13,000; ❄ 🖵 🏊) Its name meaning 'Sacred Space', Ista delivers accommodation happiness in a cool, minimalist style.

The smallish but elegant rooms with king-sized windows offer sweeping vistas across Ulsoor lake and the city; and the bar and restaurant, opening on to the rooftop pool, are heavenly.

Taj West End (Map p902; ☎ 66605660; www.tajhotels.com; 23 Racecourse Rd; s/d from Rs8000/9200; ✖ 🖳 🕿) These guys have done a swell renovation job – the rooms, though new, still look old! A charming property set amid a luscious 8-hectare garden, this place offers rooms that ooze character. Each room comes with a private verandah, and boasts butler service.

Park (off Map p902; ☎ 25594666; www.bangalore.theparkhotels.com; 14/7 MG Rd; s/d from Rs15,000/17,000; ✖ 🖳 🕿) This Terence Conran–styled hotel dares to defy the norms. You have psychedelic red-and-white chairs in its bar, yellow-and-black upholstery in its ultramodern rooms and romantic candle-lit tables in its futuristic poolside club, Aqua. The Italian restaurant i-t.alia is one of the premium dining addresses in town.

Eating

Bengaluru's delicious dining scene keeps pace with the whims and rising standards of its hungry, moneyed masses. Unless mentioned otherwise, all restaurants are open from noon to 3pm, and 7pm to 11pm. If there's a telephone number, it's advisable to book.

MG ROAD AREA

All the following venues appear on Map p905.

Ullas Refreshments (1st fl, Public Utility Bldg, MG Rd; mains Rs40-70; ✷ 9am-10pm) On a quiet terrace overlooking the MG Rd mad-rush, this place serves simple North and South Indian snacks that can fuel your lazy chat-sessions. A hit with students and young executives.

Queen's Restaurant (Church St; mains Rs100-150) The rustic, tribal decor in this cosy restaurant complements its lip-smacking Indian fare, especially the vegie dishes.

Bay of Bengal (☎ 25320332; 48/1 St Mark's Rd; mains Rs100-150) Run by a Kolkata catering heavyweight, this place has some delightful Bengali dishes on offer. Recommended for treats of the fishy kind.

The Only Place (☎ 32718989; 13 Museum Rd; mains Rs100-250) Burgers, steaks, apple pies or the classic shepherd's pie – no one serves them better than this oldie, which boasts semi-alfresco interiors and a relaxed vibe.

Ebony (☎ 41783344; 13th fl, Barton Centre, 84 MG Rd; mains Rs120-300) Rated highly by Bengaluru's foodies, this place high up on a skyscraper serves the best Parsi food in town, along with some delectable Thai and French dishes.

Oye! Amritsar (☎ 41122866; 4th fl, Asha Enclave, Church St; mains Rs200-250) Get a feel and taste of good old Punjab at this place with funky interiors and wacky graffiti. Don't forget to wash down your meals with that frothy glass of yoghurt-based lassi!

Yoko (☎ 41266588; 42 Church St; mains Rs300-400) Walk into this unfussy joint to gorge on sumptuous sizzlers, choosing from one of its many cracking offerings. The downside: you'll miss that cold pint of beer to go along with the meat.

Karavalli (☎ 66604545; 66 Residency Rd; mains Rs400-600) Mangalore's some 500km away, but you'll have to come only as far as this fine-dining spot to savour its famous coastal cuisine. Adorned with dark wood interiors, this classy restaurant at the Gateway Hotel serves some of the best seafood in town.

OTHER AREAS

Mavalli Tiffin Rooms (MTR; Map p902; Lalbagh Rd; dishes Rs20-80; ✷ 6.30-11am, 12.30-2.45pm, 3.30-7.30pm & 8-9.30pm) This legendary joint, commonly called MTR, has been feeding Bengaluru its stock South Indian fare such as *masala dosas* for more than seven decades. The queues can get long during lunch hours.

Gramin (Map p902; ☎ 41104103; 20, 7th Block Raheja Arcade, Koramangala; mains Rs100-150) A wide choice of flavourful and breezy North Indian fare is on offer at this extremely popular all-veg place. Try the excellent range of lentils, best had with oven fresh rotis.

Sue's Food Place (off Map p902; ☎ 25252494; Subedar Garden, Sri Krishna Temple Rd, Indiranagar; mains Rs150-250) Run by the charming proprietor Sue, this Jamaican restaurant has lacy curtains, kitschy plastic creepers and football shirts as part of its decor, and serves Caribbean cuisine to die for. The lunch buffet (Rs225) is not to be missed!

Casa del Sol (Map p902; ☎ 41510101; 3rd fl, Devatha Plaza, 131 Residency Rd; mains Rs200-350; ✷ 11am-11pm) This is a relaxed Mediterranean-style bistro that has a semi-alfresco area. Wednesday is disco night, Thursday has free salsa classes and Sunday has an opulent brunch (Rs600) with unlimited drinks and children's activities.

KARNATAKA

Sunny's (Map p902; ☎ 22120496; 34 Vittal Mallya Rd; mains Rs250-450) Missing those Mediterranean flavours? Well, just head to Sunny's and pamper yourself with a wide range of salads, mains and desserts. It's particularly popular with Bengaluru's expat community, and the food is simply divine.

Barbeque Nation (off Map p902; ☎ 32504455; 100Ft Rd, Indiranagar; per head Rs400) Good news for Kebab lovers! This stylish new place makes your dreams come true by serving a set meal of select barbecues, of which you can have unlimited portions! What's better, you can have them skewered at your table to suit your tastes. Eat till you're beat.

our pick **Grasshopper** (off Map p902; ☎ 26593999; 45 Kalena Agrahara, Bannerghatta Rd; multi-course meal Rs1000) Save this one for a special occasion. Some 15km south of town, this leafy boutique restaurant run by a designer couple has no menu; you just have to go by what it tosses up for the day. Besides, you have to book at least a day in advance and inform them about your food preferences. The upside of all this is a scrumptious, heart-warming meal, which you'll remember for a long time to come.

Also recommended:

Samarkand (Map p902; ☎ 41113364; Gem Plaza, Infantry Rd; mains Rs150-300) For Peshawari food.

Harima (Map p902; ☎ 41325757; 4th fl Devatha Plaza, 131 Residency Rd; mains Rs250-400) For Japanese food.

Drinking

BARS & LOUNGES

Despite Bengaluru's rock-steady reputation of getting sloshed in style, local laws require pubs and discos to shut shop at 11.30pm (opening time is usually 7.30pm). That's the bad news. The good news is that given the wide choice of chic watering holes, you can indulge in a spirited session of pub-hopping in this original beer town of India. The trendiest spots will typically charge you a cover of between Rs500 and Rs1000 per couple, but it's often redeemable against drinks or food.

Beach (off Map p902; 1211 100ft Rd, HAL 2nd Stage, Indiranagar) Feel the sand between your toes – literally – at this fun beach-bums' bar in the happening Indiranagar area. Women drink for free on Wednesday.

Fuga (Map p902; 1 Castle St, Ashoknagar) This eye-poppingly slick bar-club-lounge is where the beautiful people dance the evening away to groovy music, aided by a steady supply of absinthe from the bar.

Koshy's Bar & Restaurant (Map p905; 39 St Mark's Rd; ⏰ 9am-11.30pm) Don't step into the AC section; it's considered a place for wannabes. The seasoned guys gather in its buzzy old wing, where they put away pints of beer and classic British meals (mains Rs50 to Rs250) in between fervent discussions. It's an institution that has a reputation for serving Bengaluru's intelligentsia.

NASA (Map p905; 1A Church St; ⏰ 11am-11pm) This old favourite is decked out like a spaceship, with laser sparks adding to your Spaceman Spiff experience. Three drinks later, you're speeding through the galaxy of faux stars that decorate the pub's walls!

Hard Rock Café (Map p905; 40 St Mark's Rd) Eric Clapton or Jimi Hendrix? The guitar-god debate continues here, and you're free to join in. Or just sit quietly and drink, while the PA system comes alive with your classic rock favourites.

Taika (Map p905; Church St) This one is twice as much fun, and comprises two clubs playing different strains of music. You can fleet from one to the other, and choose the right kind of music to go with your drink.

13th Floor (Map p905; 13th fl, Barton Centre, 84 MG Rd) Come early to grab a spot on the terrace sit-out, with all of Bengaluru glittering at your feet. The atmosphere is that of a relaxed cocktail party, and you can tap your feet to a good selection of retro music.

CAFES & TEAHOUSES

Bengaluru is liberally sprinkled with good chain cafes; those such as **Café Coffee Day** (Map p905; MG Rd; ⏰ 8am-11.30pm) and **Barista** (Map p905; 40 St Mark's Rd; ⏰ 8am-11.30pm) have several outlets across town. For something different, try one of the following.

Indian Coffee House (Map p905; 78 MG Rd; ⏰ 8.30am-8.30pm) On par with Koshy's in terms of heritage value, this charming old-timer churns out the best java, South Indian style, which is brought to your table by noddy waiters in turbans and fabulous buckled belts.

Brew Haha (off Map p902; 5th block Koramangala; ⏰ 11am-11pm) A hit with youngsters, this hip cafe located in Bengaluru's stylish southern quarters has a neat collection of board games and a selection of books to go with your coffee.

Cha Bar (off Map p902; Oxford Bookstore, Leela Galleria, Airport Rd; ⏰ 10am-10pm) Offering more than 20 different types of tea, Cha Bar allows you to hunker down with a book or magazine from the attached bookshop.

Entertainment

BOWLING

Amoeba (Map p905; ☎ 25594631; 22 Church St; ☒ 11am-11pm) A date with the lanes at this state-of-the-art bowling alley costs Rs100 to Rs150 per person, depending on the time of day.

CINEMA

English-language films are popular, and tickets range from Rs80 to Rs250, depending on your theatre of choice and the show-time.

INOX (Map p905; ☎ 41128888; www.inoxmovies.com; 5th fl, Garuda Mall, Magrath Rd) Bollywood movies are shown here.

Nani Cinematheque (Map p902; ☎ 22356262; 5th fl, Sona Tower, 71 Millers Rd) Classic Indian and European films are screened here Friday, Saturday and Sunday.

PVR Cinema (Map p902; ☎ 22067511; www.pvrcinemas.com; Forum, 21 Hosur Rd) A megacinema with 11 screens. Bollywood movies are shown here.

SPORT

Bengaluru's winter horse-racing season runs from November to February; summer season is from May to July. Races are generally held on Friday and Saturday afternoons. Contact the **Bangalore Turf Club** (Map p902; ☎ 22262391; www.bangaloreraces.com; Racecourse Rd) for details.

For a taste of India's sporting passion up close, attend one of the regular cricket matches at **M Chinnaswamy Stadium** (Map p902; ☎ 22869970; MG Rd). Details can be found on the **Karnataka Cricket Association** website www.cricketk arnataka.com.

THEATRE

Ranga Shankara (off Map p902; ☎ 26592777; www.rangashankara.org; 36/2 8th Cross, JP Nagar) All kinds of interesting theatre (in a variety of languages) and dance are held at this cultural centre.

Shopping

Bengaluru's shopping options are abundant, ranging from teeming bazaars to glitzy malls. Some good shopping areas include Commercial St (Map p902), Vittal Mallya Rd (Map p902) and the MG Rd area (Map p905).

Ffolio (Map p902; 5 Vittal Mallya Rd; ☒ 10.30am-8pm) A good place for high Indian fashion. There's also a branch at Leela Galleria (23 Airport Rd, Kodihalli).

Fabindia (off Map p902; 54 17th Main Koramangala; ☒ 10am-8pm); Commercial St branch (Map p902); Garuda mall branch (Map p905; McGrath Rd) This flagship shop contains Fabindia's full range of stylish clothes and homewares in traditional cotton prints and silks.

Raintree (Map p902; 4 Sankey Rd; ☒ 10am-7pm Mon-Sat, 11am-6pm Sun) This early 20th-century villa has been turned into a stylish gift shop, fashion shop and cafe; it includes a branch of ethnic clothes shop Anokhi, which is also found at the Leela Galleria (23 Airport Rd, Kodihalli).

UB City Mall (Map p902; Vittal Mallya Rd; ☒ 11am-9pm) Global haute couture and high Indian fashion comes to roost at this towering new complex in the heart of town.

Bombay Store (Map p905; 99 MG Rd; ☒ 10.30am-8.30pm) A one-stop option for gifts ranging from ecobeauty products to linens.

Mysore Saree Udyog (Map p902; 1st fl, 294 Kamaraj Rd; ☒ 10.30am-8.30pm Mon-Sat) Located close to Commercial St, Mysore Saree Udyog is a great choice for top-quality silks and saris.

Some good malls in town include **Garuda Mall** (Map p905; McGrath Rd), **Forum** (Map p902; Hosur Rd; Koramangala) and **Leela Galleria** (off Map p902; 23 Airport Rd, Kodihalli).

Getting There & Away

AIR

Airline offices are generally open from 9am to 5.30pm Monday to Saturday, with a break for lunch. Domestic carriers serving Bengaluru include the following:

Indian Airlines (Map p902; ☎ 22978406, 22978484; www.indian-airlines.nic.in; Housing Board Bldg, Kempe-gowda Rd)

DAILY FLIGHTS FROM BENGALURU		
Destination	**Starting price (INR)**	**Duration (hr)**
Ahmedabad	2100	3½
Chennai (Madras)	480	¾
Delhi	1330	2½
Goa	480	1
Hyderabad	180	1
Kochi	950	1½
Kolkata (Calcutta)	1850	3
Mangalore	1335	1
Mumbai (Bombay)	1180	2
Pune	480	1½
Trivandrum	800	1½

KARNATAKA

Jet Airways (☎ 39893333, 39899999; www.jetairways .com; Unity Bldg, JC Rd)
Kingfisher Airlines (Map p902; ☎ 41979797; www .flykingfisher.com; 35/2 Cunningham Rd)
Spice Jet (☎ 9871803333; www.spicejet.com)

Some international airline offices and help-lines in Bengaluru:
Air France-KLM (off Map p902; ☎ 66783110, 1800110088, 1800114777; www.airfrance.in, www.klm .com; 21 Ulsoor Rd)
Air India (Map p902; ☎ 22277747, 22277748; www .airindia.in; Unity Bldg, JC Rd)
British Airways (☎ 18001021213; www.britishairways .com)
Lufthansa (Map p902; ☎ 66784050; www .lufthansa.com; 44/2 Dickenson Rd)

BUS

Bengaluru's huge, well-organised **Central bus stand** (Map p902; Gubbi Thotadappa Rd), also known as **Majestic**, is directly in front of the City train station. **Karnataka State Road Transport Corporation** (KSRTC; ☎ 22870099, 22872050) buses run throughout Karnataka and to neighbouring states. Other interstate bus operators:
Andhra Pradesh State Road Transport Corporation (APSRTC; ☎ 22873915)
Kadamba Transport Corporation (☎ 22351958) Goa.
State Express Transport Corporation (SETC; ☎ 22876974) Tamil Nadu.
Computerised advance booking is available for most buses at the station; **KSRTC** (Map p902; Devantha Plaza, Residency Rd) also has convenient booking counters around town, including one at Devantha Plaza. It's wise to book long-distance journeys in advance.

Numerous private bus companies offer comfier and only slightly more expensive services. Private bus operators line the street facing the Central bus stand, or you can book through an agency (see p904).

For major KSRTC bus services from Bengaluru, see below.

TRAIN

Bengaluru's **City train station** (Map p902; Gubbi Thotadappa Rd) is the main train hub and the place to make reservations. **Cantonment train station** (Map p902; Station Rd) is a sensible spot to disembark if you're arriving and headed for the MG Rd area, while **Yesvantpur train station** (off Map p902; Rahman Khan Rd), 8km northwest of downtown, is the starting point for Goa trains.

Rail reservations in Bengaluru are computerised. If the train is fully booked, foreign travellers can get into the emergency quota; first, buy a wait-listed ticket, then fill out a form at the **Divisional Railway Office** (Map p902; Gubbi Thotadappa Rd) building immediately north of the City train station. You'll know about 10 hours before departure whether you've got a seat (a good chance); if not, the ticket is refunded. The **train reservation office** (Map p902; ☎ 139; ☼ 8am-8pm Mon-Sat, 8am-2pm Sun), on the left as you face the station, has separate counters for credit-card purchases (Rs30 fee), for women and foreigners. Luggage can be left at the 24-hour cloakroom on Platform 1 at the City train station (Rs10 per bag per day).

See opposite for information on major train services.

MAJOR BUS SERVICES FROM BENGALURU

Destination	Fare (Rs)	Duration (hr)	Frequency
Chennai	251 (R)/423 (V)	7-8	15 daily
Ernakulam	377 (R)/637 (V)	10-12	6 daily
Hampi	301 (R)	8½	1 daily
Hospet	370 (V)	8	1 daily
Hyderabad	667 (V)	10-12	3 daily
Jog Falls	328 (R)	9	1 daily
Mumbai	1060 (V)	19	4 daily
Mysore	121 (R)/212 (V)	3	Every 30min
Ooty	237 (R)	8	6 daily
Panaji	779 (V)	12-14	3 daily
Puttaparthi	220 (V)	4	3 daily

R – Rajahamsa, V – Airavath Volvo AC

MAJOR TRAINS FROM BENGALURU

Destination	Train No & Name	Fare (Rs)	Duration (hr)	Departures
Chennai	2658 *Chennai Mail*	195/662	6	10.45pm
	2028 *Shatabdi*	510/1105	5	6am Wed-Mon
Delhi	2627 *Karnataka Exp*	559/2083	39	7.20pm
	2649 *Sampark Kranti Exp*	547/2036	35	10.20pm Mon, Wed, Fri, Sat & Sun
Hospet	6592 *Hampi Exp*	203/738	9½	10.30pm
Hubli	6589 *Rani Chennamma Exp*	206/750	8	9pm
Kolkata	2864 *YPR Howrah Exp*	517/1918	35	7.35pm
Mumbai	6530 *Udyan Exp*	369/1389	22	8.10pm
Mysore	2007 *Shatabdi*	305/590	2	11am Wed-Mon
	2614 *Tippu Exp*	67/228	2½	2.15pm
Trivandrum	6526 *Kanyakumari Exp*	312/1165	17	9.45pm

Shatabdi fares are chair/executive; Express (Exp/Mail) fares are 2nd/chair for day trains and sleeper/2AC for night trains.

Getting Around
TO/FROM THE AIRPORT
The swish new **airport** (off Map p902; ☎ 23540000; www.bengaluruairport.com) is in Hebbal, about 40km north from the MG Rd area. Prepaid taxis can take you from the airport to the city-centre (Rs600). You can also take the shuttle AC bus service to Majestic or MG Rd (Rs150).

AUTORICKSHAW
The city's autorickshaw drivers are legally required to use their meters; few comply in reality. After 10pm, 50% is added onto the metered rate. Flag fall is Rs14 for the first 2km and then Rs7 for each extra kilometre.

BUS
Bengaluru has a thorough but somewhat crowded local bus network, operated by the **Bangalore Metropolitan Transport Corporation** (BMTC). Pickpockets abound and locals warn solo women against taking buses after dark. Most local buses (light blue) run from the City bus stand (Map p902), next to Majestic; a few operate from the City Market bus stand (Map p902) to the south.

To get from the City train station to the MG Rd area, catch any bus from Platform 17 or 18 at the City bus stand. For the City market, take bus 31, 31E, 35 or 49 from Platform 8.

CAR
Several places around Bengaluru offer car rental with driver. Standard rates for a long-haul Tata Indica cab are Rs7 per kilometre for a minimum of 250km, plus an allowance of Rs150 for the driver. For an eight-hour day rental, you're looking at around Rs1100. Luxury Renault cabs are also available for around Rs15 per kilometre.

We recommend:
Meru Cabs (☎ 44224422)
Skyway (☎ 22111401)

AROUND BENGALURU
Bannerghatta Biological Park
The attached zoo is a little grim, but it's worth making the 25km trek south of Bengaluru to this **nature reserve** (off Map p902; ☎ 080-27828425; admission weekday/weekend Rs25/30, video Rs100; ☯ 9am-5.30pm Wed-Mon) to take its hour-long **grand safari** (weekday/weekend Rs65/80; ☯ 11am to 4pm) in a mini-bus through an 11,330-hectare enclosure. Here the Karnataka Forest Department rehabilitates tigers, lions and sloth bears rescued from circuses or the wilds. To get here, take bus 366A from City Market (Rs20, one hour).

Hessaraghatta
Located 30km to the northwest of Bengaluru, Hessaraghatta is home to **Nrityagram** (☎ 080-28466313; www.nrityagram.org; ☯ 10am-5.30pm Tue-Sat, 10am-3pm Sun), the living legacy of celebrated dancer Protima Gauri Bedi, who died in a Himalayan avalanche in 1998. Protima established this dance academy in 1990 to revive and popularise Indian classical dance.

Designed in the form of a village by Goa-based architect Gerard da Cunha, the attractive complex offers long-term courses in classical

KARNATAKA

dance within a holistic curriculum. Local children are taught for free on Sundays. Self-guided tours cost Rs20 or you can call ahead to book a tour, lecture-cum-demonstration and vegetarian meal (Rs1250, minimum 10 people). A month-long beginners' workshop is held in July for US$1000. Earmark the first Saturday in February for the free dance festival **Vasantahabba** (p901).

Opposite the dance village, **Taj Kuteeram** (☎ 080-28466326; www.tajhotels.com; d from Rs4000; 🅿) combines comfort with rustic charm. It also offers ayurveda and yoga sessions.

Learn how to drive a bullock cart and how to milk a cow at **Our Native Village** (☎ 080-41140909; www.ournativevillage.com; Survey 72, Kodihalli, Madurai Hobli; s/d incl breakfast Rs7000/8500; 🅿), an ecofriendly organic farm and resort. The resort generates its own power, harvests rainwater, and processes and reuses all its waste.

From Bengaluru's City Market, buses 253, 253D and 253E run to Hessaraghatta (Rs20, one hour), with bus 266 continuing on to Nrityagram.

Nandi Hills

Rising to 1455m, the **Nandi Hills** (admission Rs5; 🕑 6am-10pm), 60km north of Bengaluru, were once the summer retreat of Tipu Sultan. Today, it's Bengaluru's favourite weekend getaway, and is predictably congested on Saturdays and Sundays. It's a good place for hiking, with stellar views and two notable **Chola temples**. A recommended retreat out here is **Silver Oak Farm** (☎ 9342510445; www.silveroakfarm .com; Sultanpet Village; s/d incl full board from Rs3250/4750), which has a beautiful hillside position. Buses head to Nandi Hills (Rs40, two hours) from Bengaluru's Central bus stand.

Janapada Loka Folk Arts Museum

Situated 53km south of Bengaluru, this **museum** (admission Rs10; 🕑 9am-1pm & 2.30-5.30pm Wed-Mon) has a wonderful collection of folk art objects, including 500-year-old shadow puppets, festival costumes and musical instruments. Mysore-bound buses (one hour) can drop you here; get off 3km after Ramnagar.

MYSORE
☎ 0821 / pop 799,200 / elev 707m

The historic headquarters of the Wodeyar maharajas, Mysore is a city that bowls you over with its fascinating regal heritage. That apart, it's one of the most flamboyant places

you could visit in South India, known for its bustling markets, magnificent monuments and a friendly populace. A thriving centre for the production of premium silk, sandalwood and incense, Mysore also flaunts a considerable expertise in yoga and ayurveda, two trades that it has recently begun to market worldwide. So stretch your body in a traditional yoga pose or take a gentle stroll through the city's magnificent palace and bazaars; Mysore is a place that will surely reward your languid pace.

History

Mysore owes its name to the mythical Mahisuru, a place where the demon Mahisasura was slain by the goddess Chamundi. Its regal history began in 1399, when the Wodeyar dynasty of Mysore was founded, though they were to remain in service of the Vijayanagar empire until the mid-16th century. With the fall of Vijayanagar in 1565, the Wodeyars declared their sovereignty, which – apart from a brief period in the late 18th century, when Hyder Ali and Tipu Sultan claimed power – remained unscathed until 1947.

Orientation

The train station is northwest of the city centre, about 1km from the main shopping street, Sayyaji Rao Rd. The Central bus stand is on Bengaluru–Mysore (BM) Rd, on the northeastern edge of the city centre. The Maharaja's Palace sits in the heart of the buzzing quarters southeast of the city centre. Chamundi Hill is an ever-visible landmark to the south.

Information
BOOKSHOPS

Ashok Book Centre (396 Dhanvanthri Rd; 🕑 10am-8pm Mon-Sat, 10am-2pm Sun) Stocks books on religion, ayurveda and yoga.
Geetha Book House (KR Circle; 🕑 10am-1pm & 5-7.30pm Mon-Sat)
Sapna Book House (1433 Narayan Shastry Rd; 🕑 10.30am-8.30pm)

INTERNET ACCESS

Internet cafes are sprinkled around town.
Reliance Webworld (115D Devaraj Urs Rd; per hr Rs30; 🕑 10am-8pm) Has lightning-fast internet connections with webcam facility.

LEFT LUGGAGE

The City bus stand's cloakroom, open from 6am to 11pm, costs Rs10 per bag for 12 hours.

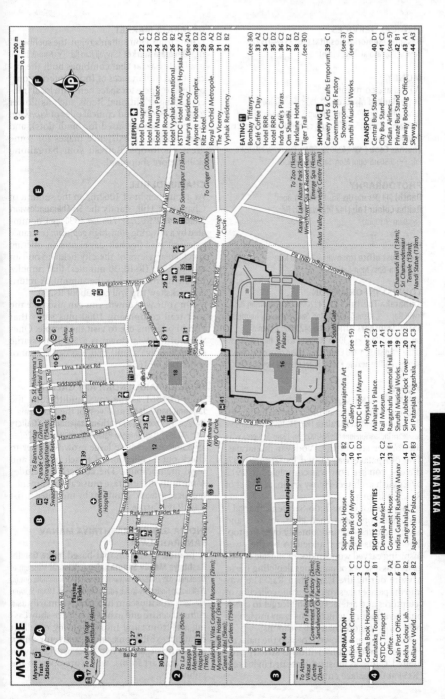

MYSORE

INFORMATION
Ashok Book Centre	1 C1
Danthi	2 C2
Geetha Book House	3 C2
Karnataka Tourism	4 B1
KSTDC Transport Office	5 A2
Main Post Office	6 D1
Rekha Colour Lab	7 B2
Reliance World	8 B2

SIGHTS & ACTIVITIES
Devaraja Market	12 C2
Government House	13 E1
Indira Gandhi Rashtriya Manav	
Sangrahalaya	14 D1
Jaganmohan Palace	15 B3

Sapna Book House	9 B2
State Bank of Mysore	10 C1
Thomas Cook	11 D2

Jayachamarajendra Art Gallery	(see 15)
KSTDC Hotel Mayura Hoysala	(see 27)
Maharaja's Palace	16 C3
Rail Museum	17 A1
Rangacharlu Memorial Hall	18 C2
Shruthi Musical Works	19 C1
Silver Jubilee Clock Tower	20 D2
Sri Patanjala Yogashala	21 C3

SLEEPING
Hotel Dasaprakash	22 C1
Hotel Maurya	23 C2
Hotel Maurya Palace	24 D2
Hotel Roopa	25 D2
Hotel Vyshak International	26 B2
KSTDC Hotel Mayura Hoysala	27 A2
Maurya Residency	(see 24)
Mysore Hotel Complex	28 D2
Ritz Hotel	29 D2
Royal Orchid Metropole	30 A2
The Viceroy	31 D2
Vyshak Residency	32 B2

EATING
Bombay Tiffanys	(see 36)
Café Coffee Day	33 A2
Hotel RRR	34 C2
Hotel RRR	35 D2
Indra Café's Paras	36 C2
Om Shanthi	37 E2
Parklane Hotel	38 D2
Tiger Trail	(see 30)

SHOPPING
Cauvery Arts & Crafts Emporium	39 C1
Government Silk Factory Showroom	(see 3)
Shruthi Musical Works	(see 19)

TRANSPORT
Central Bus Stand	40 D1
City Bus Stand	41 C2
Indian Airlines	(see 5)
Private Bus Stand	42 B1
Railway Booking Office	43 A1
Skyway	44 A3

MEDICAL SERVICES
Basappa Memorial Hospital (☎ 2512401; 22B Vinoba Rd, Jayalakshmipuram)

MONEY
ATMs are common.
State Bank of Mysore (☎ 2538956; cnr Irwin & Ashoka Rds; ☒ 10.30am-2.30pm & 3-4pm Mon-Fri, 10.30am-12.30pm Sat) Changes cash and Amex travellers cheques.
Thomas Cook (☎ 2420090; Silver Tower, 9/2 Ashoka Rd; ☒ 9.30am-6pm Mon-Sat) For forex.

PHOTOGRAPHY
Danthi (44 Devaraj Urs Rd; ☒ 10am-8pm)
Rekha Colour Lab (142 Dhanvanthri Rd; ☒ 9am-9.30pm)

POST
Main post office (cnr Irwin & Ashoka Rds; ☒ 10am-6pm Mon-Sat)

TOURIST INFORMATION
Karnataka Tourism (☎ 2422096; Old Exhibition Bldg, Irwin Rd; ☒ 10am-5.30pm Mon-Sat) Extremely helpful.
KSTDC Transport Office (☎ 2423652; 2 Jhansi Lakshmi Bai Rd; ☒ 8.30am-8.30pm) KSTDC has counters at the train station and Central bus stand, as well as this transport office next to KSTDC Hotel Mayura Hoysala.

Sights
MAHARAJA'S PALACE
Among the grandest of India's royal buildings, the fantastic **Mysore Palace** (☎ 2421051; www.mysorepalace.in; Indian/foreigner Rs20/200; ☒ 10am-5.30pm) was the former seat of the Wodeyar maharajas. The old palace was gutted by fire in 1897; the one you see now was completed in 1912 by English architect Henry Irwin, at a cost of Rs4.5 million.

The interior of this Indo-Saracenic marvel – a kaleidoscope of stained glass, mirrors and gaudy colours – is undoubtedly over the top. The decor is further added to by the awe-inspiring carved wooden doors, mosaic floors, as well as a series of paintings depicting life in Mysore during the Edwardian Raj. The way into the palace takes you past a fine collection of sculptures and artefacts. Don't forget to check out the armoury, which houses an intriguing collection of more than 700 weapons!

While you are allowed to snap the palace's exterior, photography within is strictly prohibited. Cameras must be deposited in lockers (Rs5) at the palace entrance.

DEVARAJA MARKET
Dating from Tipu Sultan's reign, the spellbinding **Devaraja Market** (Sayyaji Rao Rd; ☒ 6am-8.30pm) is a lively bazaar that combines both the ancient and Indian faces of India. International brands compete for space here with local traders selling traditional items such as flower garlands, spices and conical piles of *kumkum* (coloured powder used for bindi dots), and their unique co-existence makes for some great photo-ops. Refresh your bargaining skills before shopping!

CHAMUNDI HILL
At a lofty height of 1062m, on the summit of Chamundi Hill, stands the **Sri Chamundeswari Temple** (☎ 2590027; ☒ 7am-2pm & 3.30-9pm), dominated by a towering 40m-high *gopuram* (entrance gateway). It's a fine half-day excursion, offering spectacular views of the city below; you can take bus 201 (Rs10, 30 minutes) that rumbles up the narrow road to the summit. A return autorickshaw trip will cost about Rs250.

On your way down, you can also take the foot trail comprising 1000-plus steps that Hindu pilgrims use to visit the temple. One-third of the way down is a 5m-high statue of **Nandi** (Shiva's bull) that was carved out of solid rock in 1659.

JAYACHAMARAJENDRA ART GALLERY
Built in 1861 as the royal auditorium, the **Jaganmohan Palace**, just west of the Maharaja's Palace, houses the **Jayachamarajendra Art Gallery** (☎ 2423693; Jaganmohan Palace Rd; adult/child Rs20/10; ☒ 8.30am-5pm), where large crowds gather to check out a collection of kitsch objects and regal memorabilia. The collection includes some fantastic and rare musical instruments, Japanese art, and paintings by the noted artist Raja Ravi Varma.

INDIRA GANDHI RASHTRIYA MANAV SANGRAHALAYA
A branch of the Bhopal-based **Indira Gandhi Rashtriya Manav Sangrahalaya** (National Museum of Mankind; ☎ 2448231; www.museumofmankindindia.gov.in; Wellington House, Irwin Rd; admission free; ☒ 10am-5.30pm Tue-Sun), this museum functions primarily as a cultural centre and exhibition space showcasing arts from rural India. Housing excellent rotating exhibitions and a souvenir shop, the centre organises two-week workshops in traditional art forms, which are open to the public.

KARNATAKA

DUSSEHRA JAMBOREE

Mysore is at its carnivalesque best during the 10-day Dussehra (locally spelt 'Dasara') festival. During this period, the Maharaja's Palace lights up in the collective glow of more than 96,000 light bulbs every evening (7pm to 9pm), while the town is transformed into a gigantic fairground, with concerts, dance performances, sporting demonstrations and cultural events running to packed houses. On the last day, the celebrations are capped off in grand style. A dazzling procession of richly costumed elephants, garlanded idols, liveried retainers and cavalry kicks off around 1pm, marching through the streets to the rhythms of clanging brass bands, all the way from the palace to the Bannimantap parade ground. A torchlight parade at Bannimantap and a spectacular session of fireworks then closes the festival for the year.

Mysore is choc-a-bloc with tourists during the festival, especially on the final day. To bypass the suffocating crowds, consider buying a Dasara VIP Gold Card (Rs6000 for two). Though expensive, it assures you good seats at the final day gala and helps you beat the entry queues at all the other events and performances, while providing discounts on accommodation, dining and shopping. It's also possible to buy tickets (Rs250 to Rs1000) just for entering the palace and Bannimantap for the final day's parades. Contact the local KSTDC office or the **Dasara Information Centre** (☎ 2418888; www.mysoredasara.com) for more details.

JAYALAKSHMI VILAS COMPLEX MUSEUM

This **museum** (☎ 2419348; Mysore University Campus; admission free; ☯ 10am-5.30pm Mon-Sat, closed alternate Sat), housed in a grand mansion, specialises in folklore. A wooden puppet of the 10-headed demon Ravana, leather shadow puppets, rural costumes and a 300-year-old temple cart are part of its curious collection.

RAIL MUSEUM

A must-see. Located behind the train station, this **museum** (KRS Rd; adult/child Rs5/2, camera/video Rs10/25; ☯ 9.30am-6.30pm Tue-Sun) bears testimony to the stylish way in which the royals rode the railways in the past. The chief exhibit is the Mysore maharani's saloon, a wood-panelled beauty dating from 1899. There are also five steam engines, each with its own story, and a sprinkling of instruments and memorabilia from the Indian Railways' chequered past.

OTHER SIGHTS

For architecture buffs, Mysore has quite a handful of charming buildings. Dating from 1805, **Government House** (Irwin Rd), formerly the British Residency, is a Tuscan Doric building set in 20 hectares of **gardens** (admission free; ☯ 5am-9pm). Facing the north gate of the Maharaja's Palace is the 1927 **Silver Jubilee Clock Tower** (Ashoka Rd); nearby stands the imposing **Rangacharlu Memorial Hall**, built in 1884. The beauty of towering **St Philomena's Cathedral** (☎ 2563148; St Philomena St; ☯ 5am-6pm, English mass 7am), built between 1933 and 1941 in neo-Gothic style, is emphasised by beautiful stained-glass windows.

Mysore's **zoo** (☎ 2440752; Indiranagar; adult/child Rs25/10, camera/video Rs10/150; ☯ 8.30am-5.30pm Wed-Mon), set in pretty gardens on the eastern edge of the city, dates from 1892. A range of primates, tigers, elephants, bears, birds and rhinos live here.

Activities

BIRDWATCHING

Karanji Lake Nature Park (Indiranagar; admission Rs10, camera/video Rs10/25; ☯ 8.30am-5.30pm), next to the zoo, is a place to spy on sundry bird species, including great and little cormorants, purple and grey herons, egrets, black ibises, rose-ringed parakeets, green bee-eaters and painted storks, as well as several kinds of butterfly.

AYURVEDA

Mysore's spa operations are spearheaded by the slick **Emerge Spa** (☎ 2522500; www.emergespa .co.in; Windflower Spa & Resort, Maharanapratap Rd, Nazarbad), where you can drop by for an hour's ayurvedic massage starting around Rs750, or choose from a range of Balinese massage, hydrotherapy and beauty treatments.

Set on 16 acres of gardens, the classy **Indus Valley Ayurvedic Centre** (☎ 2473437; www.ayurindus .com; Lalithadripura) is a place that derives its therapies from ancient scriptures and prescriptions. A wide range of treatments are on offer, as well as basic training programs. It's wise to visit with some time on your hands; the best deals are the overnight-stay packages (Indian/foreigner from Rs9300/US$269).

KARNATAKA

For an exceptionally peaceful and refreshing ayurvedic vacation, head about 12km towards Srirangapatnam to the **Swaasthya Ayurveda Retreat Village** (☎ 6557557, 08236-217476; www.swaasthya.com; 69 Bommaru Agrahara; s incl full board Rs1500), where you can spend some time in quiet meditation and feel your senses feast on the lush greenery, the aromatic herb gardens, the simple vegetarian food and the gurgling sounds of the Cauvery River. Daily rates include basic yoga sessions; for specific ayurvedic treatments, there are a range of special packages on offer. Book well in advance.

Courses
YOGA
The following places have put Mysore on the international yoga map. Unlike casual centres, they are all austerely committed to the art, and require at least a month's commitment on your part. You'll also need to register far in advance, since they are often booked out. Call or write to the centres for details.

Ashtanga Yoga Research Institute (AYRI; ☎ 2516756; www.kpjayi.org; 3rd Stage, 235 8th Cross, Gokulam) Founded by the renowned Ashtanga teacher K Pattabhi Jois, who taught Madonna her yoga moves.

Atma Vikasa Centre (☎ 2341978; www.atmavikasa yoga.com; Kuvempunagar Double Rd) 'Backbending expert' Yogacharya Venkatesh offers courses in yoga, Sanskrit and meditation. Opposite State Bank of India.

Sri Patanjala Yogashala (Yoga Research Institute; Sri Brahmatantra Swatantra Parakala Mutt, Jaganmohan Palace Circle; ☼ 6-8am & 5-7pm) The baby of well-respected Ashtanga practitioner BNS Iyengar (not to be confused with BKS Iyengar, famed exponent of Iyengar yoga).

MUSIC
The folks at **Shruthi Musical Works** (☎ 2529551; 1189 3rd Cross, Irwin Rd; ☼ 10.30am-9pm Mon-Sat, 10.30am-2pm Sun) get good reviews for their tabla instruction (Rs200 per hour).

Tours
The **KSTDC** runs a daily Mysore city tour (Rs155), which takes in the entire city, along with Chamundi Hill, Srirangapatnam and Brindavan Gardens. It starts daily at 8.30am, ends at 8.30pm and is likely to leave you breathless!

Other KSTDC tours include one to Belur, Halebid and Sravanabelagola (Rs400) on Tuesdays and Thursdays from 7.30am to 9pm. There's also a three-day tour of Ooty, Kodaikanal, Doddabetta and Coonoor every Monday, Thursday and Saturday (per person including accommodation is Rs2200) that starts off from Bengaluru; you can join at Mysore. These tours generally run during the high season.

All tours leave from the **KSTDC Hotel Mayura Hoysala** (2 Jhansi Lakshmi Bai Rd). Bookings can be made at the nearby KSTDC Transport Office (p916) or at travel agencies around town.

Sleeping
Mysore attracts tourists through the year and can fill up very quickly during Dussehra. Booking early is recommended. Check with the tourist office about the local government-approved homestays, which offer rooms from around Rs400 per person.

BUDGET
The following have hot water (at least in the morning) and 24-hour checkout.

Mysore Youth Hostel (☎ 2544704; www.yhmysore.com; Gangothri Layout; dm from Rs45) Despite the usual rules and regs, including a 10.30pm curfew, this well-run hostel set amid green lawns is exceptionally clean and tidy. Breakfast costs Rs17; dinner is Rs24. Don't forget to bring an age proof and identity document.

Hotel Dasaprakash (☎ 2442444; www.mysore dasaprakashgroup.com; Gandhi Sq; s/d from Rs250/470; ✖) This long-time favourite is a tried and tested sleeping option, popular with local tourists. Rooms are well-maintained; some get a touch of antiquity with old wooden furniture. An inexpensive veg restaurant, an ice-cream parlour and an astro-palmist are available within the complex.

Hotel Maurya (☎ 2426677; Hanumantha Rao St; s/d from Rs350/500) In the process of upgrading its well-kept rooms, this justifiably popular place has obliging staff and a great location among Mysore's winding alleys. There are also a few dirt-cheap beds (singles/doubles Rs140/260) on site, but they're – well – dirty.

Mysore Hotel Complex (☎ 2426217; BM Rd; s/d from Rs350/500; ✖) A giant affair, this place comprises row after row of pleasant, non-fussy rooms, where you'll be made to feel at home by a friendly staff. Scattered across the property is a travel agent and a few souvenir shops.

Ritz Hotel (☎ 2422668; BM Rd; d/q Rs500/900) A quaint, ramshackle place in the heart of town, the Ritz makes little effort to latch on to its heritage. The lack of enthusiasm shows in its mediocre rooms, which are charming but a tad run-down. The shaded restaurant-bar downstairs is a good place for an unhurried evening drink.

MIDRANGE

KSTDC Hotel Mayura Hoysala (☎ 2425349; www.nic .in/kstdc; 2 Jhansi Lakshmi Bai Rd; s/d incl breakfast Rs650/800, with AC Rs800/1000; 🔀) With lace-lined curtains and heavy wooden doors in its rooms, and an assortment of cane furniture and potted plants in the corridors, this place sure brings back the memories. The bar downstairs is popular with Mysore's tipplers.

Hotel Roopa (☎ 2443370; 2724C BM Rd; d from Rs775; 🔀) A surprisingly cheerful hotel, this place boasts spacious modern rooms done up in fresh upholstery, and is often one of the first places to fill up. The pure-veg restaurant Nakshatraa is a good place to start the day, with a sumptuous buffet breakfast (Rs40).

Hotel Vyshak International (☎ 2421777; vyshak international@yahoo.com; 19 Seebaiah Rd; d from Rs800; 🔀) Clean, efficiently run and welcoming – what more could you want? It also runs the Vyshak Residency (doubles from Rs850) across the road, which is equally good.

Maurya Residency (☎ 2523375; www.sangrouphotel .com; Sri Harsha Rd; d from Rs835; 🔀) The best of the Sri Harsha Rd midrange gang, this ultra-friendly place has snug beds, offers a refreshing welcome drink of grape juice and has ecofriendly directives smattered across its rooms. Hotel Maurya Palace (☎ 2435912; doubles from Rs725), its sister property, is next door.

Ginger (☎ 6633333; www.gingerhotels.com; Nazarbad Mohalla; s/d Rs1499/1999; 🔀 🖳) An ultramodern business hotel, Ginger has sleek and comfortable rooms painted in warm orange tones. Features include self check-in, a gymnasium, wi-fi and LCD TVs, and its location away from the city centre makes for a peaceful stay.

The Viceroy (☎ 2424001; www.theviceroygroup.com; Sri Harsha Rd; s/d from Rs1895/2295; 🔀 🖳) Sporting an all-new look with spacious, cosy and warmly-lit rooms, this swish place is worth considering if you desire a combination of both luxury and location. Some of the rooms – and the rooftop restaurant – have million-dollar views of the Maharaja's Palace just across the road!

TOP END

Green Hotel (☎ 4255000; www.greenhotelindia .com; 2270 Vinoba Rd, Jayalakshmipuram; s/d incl breakfast garden from Rs2250/2750, palace from Rs2950/3250) You're largely paying for the quaint ambience here, which is more prominent in the themed and moody palace rooms. The garden rooms, though fronted by blooming antirrhinum beds, are characterless (and a trifle overpriced).

Windflower Spa & Resort (☎ 2522500; www .thewindflower.com; Maharanapratap Rd, Nazarbad; s/d incl breakfast from Rs3900/4500; 🔀 🖳 🛍) Bali comes to Mysore at this stylish and relaxing resort, where the elegant rooms are complemented by the world-class Emerge Spa, and Olive Garden, a top-of-the-line fine-dining restaurant and bar. Other activities at the resort include cycling, trekking and golfing.

our pick Royal Orchid Metropole (☎ 4255566; www.royalorchidhotels.com; 5 Jhansi Lakshmi Bai Rd; s/d incl breakfast from Rs5000/5600; 🔀 🖳 🛍) This recently renovated hotel was originally built by the Wodeyars to serve as the residence of the Maharaja's British guests. A fascinating colonial structure with bona fide old-world charm, it has 30 rooms oozing heritage, and a stay here is spiced up with several add-ons such as occasional magic, music and dance performances. The friendly and efficient management is among the best that Karnataka's hotels have to offer.

Eating

Mysore is well-served by Indian restaurants, but for Western food you're best sticking with the major hotels. Unless otherwise mentioned, restaurants are open from noon to 3pm and 7pm to 11pm.

Bombay Tiffanys (Sayyaji Rao Rd; sweets Rs5-40; 🕒 7.30am-10pm) For traditional Indian sweets, Bombay Tiffanys has a solid reputation. Those with a sweet tooth could try the local delicacy Mysore pak (a sweet made from chickpea flour, sugar and ghee).

Café Coffee Day (Devaraj Urs Rd; snacks Rs30-50; 🕒 10am-11pm) Part of the pan-Indian chain of coffee shops, this is currently where Mysore's young generation hangs out. The open-air terrace is a particularly good spot for that steaming cup of cappuccino.

Indra Café's Paras (1740 Sayyaji Rao Rd; mains Rs30-60; 🕒 7.30am-10pm) Take your pick from South (Rs30) or North (Rs60) Indian-style thalis at this popular joint opposite the main market. It's perpetually crowded.

Parklane Hotel (☎ 2430400; www.parklanemysore .com; 2720 Sri Harsha Rd; mains Rs40-150) Choose from a wide selection of Indian, Continental, Chinese and Mexican dishes at this popular restaurant-bar, where food is served by candlelight at night, with occasional live music. Occasional barbecue nights have a special range of kebabs and grills on offer.

Hotel RRR (Gandhi Sq; mains Rs40-70) Classic Andhra-style food is belted out at this ever-busy eatery, and you might have to queue for a table if you walk in during lunch. One item to try is the piping-hot veg thali (Rs43) served on banana leaves. Some meaty options are available, too. There's a second branch on Sri Harsha Rd.

Om Shanthi (Hotel Siddhartha, Guest House Rd; mains Rs40-100; ☿ 7.30am-10pm) Om Shanthi is a byword for excellent veg food in Mysore. Its special South Indian thali (Rs80) is really quite special, as is the hearty breakfast platter of *puris* and vegetables (Rs25).

La Gardenia (☎ 2426426; Hotel Regaalis, 3-14 Vinoba Rd; mains Rs100-180) This place serves tasty and well-presented food in a sophisticated environment. In case you've tired of the local Indian options, this is a nice place to dig into some tasty Continental fare.

Tiger Trail (☎ 4255566; Royal Orchid Metropole, 5 Jhansi Lakshmi Bai Rd; mains Rs100-250) This delightful restaurant specialising in tandoori dishes serves decent food in a courtyard that twinkles with torches and fairy lights at night. There's often live classical Indian music performances.

Shopping

Mysore is a great place to shop for its famous sandalwood products, silk saris and wooden toys. It is also one of India's major incense-manufacturing centres, peppered with scores of little family-owned *agarbathi* (incense) factories.

Souvenir and handicraft shops are dotted around Jaganmohan Palace and Dhanvanthri Rd, while silk shops line Devaraj Urs Rd.

Cauvery Arts & Crafts Emporium (Sayyaji Rao Rd; ☿ 10am-7.30pm) Not the cheapest place, but the selection is extensive and there's no pressure to buy.

Government Silk Factory (☎ 2481803; Mananthody Rd, Ashokapuram; ☿ 10am-noon & 2-4pm Mon-Sat) It's the best place to shop for Mysore silk, given that the exclusive fabric is made at this very place and thus comes at its cheapest. Behind the showroom is the factory, where you can drop by between 7.30am and 4pm to see how the fabric is made. There's also a factory show-

room on KR Circle, open from 10.30am to 7.30pm, barring Sundays.

Sandalwood Oil Factory (☎ 2483531; Ashokapuram; ☿ 9.30am-11pm & 2-4pm Mon-Sat) Buy authentic incense sticks and pure sandalwood oil (Rs650 for 5ml!) at this factory, located about 2km southeast of the Maharaja's Palace, off Mananthody Rd. Guided tours are also available to show you around the factory, and explain how the products are made.

Fabindia (☎ 4259009; 451 Jhansi Lakshmi Bai Rd, Chamrajpuram; ☿ 10am-8pm) There's a branch of the ever reliable clothing and homewares shop on the way to the silk and sandalwood factories.

Shruthi Musical Works (☎ 2529551; 1189 3rd Cross, Irwin Rd; ☿ 10.30am-9pm Mon-Sat, 10.30am-2pm Sun) Sells a variety of traditional musical instruments; you can view the workshop across the road from the shop.

Getting There & Away

AIR

Mysore's new airport was nearing completion at the time of research and should be ready by the time you visit. **Indian Airlines** (☎ 2421846; Jhansi Lakshmi Bai Rd; ☿ 10am-1.30pm & 2.15-5pm Mon-Sat) has an office next to KSTDC Hotel Mayura Hoysala where you can book tickets for routes starting from Bengaluru, Mangalore or elsewhere. For booking on other carriers, try **Skyway** (☎ 2444444; 370/4 Jhansi Lakshmi Bai Rd; ☿ 10am-6pm Mon-Sat).

BUS

The **Central bus stand** (☎ 2520853; BM Rd) handles all KSRTC long-distance buses. The **City bus stand** (☎ 2425819; Sayyaji Rao Rd) is for city, Srirangapatnam and Chamundi Hill buses. KSRTC bus services from Mysore include those listed on opposite.

For Belur, Halebid or Sravanabelagola, the usual gateway is Hassan. For Hampi, the best transfer point is Hospet.

The **Private bus stand** (Sayyaji Rao Rd) has services to Hubli, Bijapur, Mangalore, Ooty and Ernakulam. You'll find several ticketing agents around the stand.

TRAIN

At the **railway booking office** (☎ 131; ☿ 8am-8pm Mon-Sat, 8am-2pm Sun), located within the train station, you can reserve a seat on the 6.45am *Chamundi Express* or the 11am *Tippu Express* to Bengaluru (2AC/chair Rs67/198, three

BUSES FROM MYSORE

Destination	Fare (Rs)	Duration (hr)	Frequency
Bandipur	47 (O)	2	hourly
Bengaluru	121 (R)/212 (V)	3	every 30min
Channarayapatna	55 (O)	2	hourly
Chennai	742 (V)	12	3 daily
Ernakulam	388 (R)	11	5 daily
Gokarna	290 (O)	12	1 daily
Hassan	68 (O)	3	hourly
Hospet	247 (O)	10	4 daily
Mangalore	147 (O)/224 (R)	7	10 daily
Nagarhole	55 (O)	3	4 daily
Ooty	75 (O)/114 (R)	5	6 daily

O – Ordinary, R – Rajahamsa, V – Airavath Volvo

hours), or on the high-speed *Shatabdi Express* (chair/executive Rs275/550, two hours), departing at 2.20pm daily except Tuesday. The *Shatabdi* continues to Chennai (chair/executive Rs690/1315, seven hours). Several passenger trains also go daily to Bengaluru (Rs30, 3½ hours), stopping at Srirangapatnam (Rs10, 20 minutes). Two passenger and three express trains go daily to Arsikere and Hassan. The 8.10pm *Swarna Jayanthi Express* goes to Hubli (sleeper/2AC Rs457/1684, nine hours).

Getting Around

Agencies at hotels and around town rent cabs for about Rs7 per kilometre for an AC Indica, with a minimum of 250km per day, plus Rs150 for the driver.

Flag fall on autorickshaws is Rs16, and Rs6 per kilometre is charged thereafter. Autorickshaws can also be hired for a day's sightseeing (Rs850). Try the polite and energetic **Ganesh** (☎ 9342201774).

AROUND MYSORE
Srirangapatnam
☎ 08236

Steeped in bloody history, the fort town of Srirangapatnam is built on an island straddling the Cauvery River 16km from Mysore. The seat of Hyder Ali and Tipu Sultan's power, this town was the de facto capital of much of southern India during the 18th century. Srirangapatnam's glory days ended when the British waged an epic war again Tipu Sultan in 1799, when he was defeated and killed. However, the ramparts, battlements

and some of the gates of the fort still stand, as do a clutch of monuments.

Close to the bus station is a handsome twin tower mosque built by the sultan, and within the fort walls you can also find the dungeon where Tipu held British officers captive, and the handsome **Sri Ranganathaswamy Temple** (☺ 7.30am-1pm & 4-8pm). Srirangapatnam's star attraction, however, is Tipu's summer palace, the **Daria Daulat Bagh** (☎ 252023; Indian/foreigner Rs5/100; ☺ 9am-5pm), which lies 1km east of the fort. Built largely out of wood, the palace is notable for the lavish decoration that covers every inch of its interiors. The ceilings are embellished with floral designs, while the walls bear murals depicting courtly life and Tipu's campaigns against the British. There's a small museum within, which houses several artefacts including a portrait of Tipu Sultan aged 30, painted by European artist John Zoffany in 1780.

About 2km further east, the remains of Hyder Ali, his wife and Tipu are housed in the impressive onion-domed **Gumbaz** (☎ 252007; ☺ 8am-8pm), which stands amid serene gardens. Head 500m east of Gumbaz for the river banks to end your trip with a refreshing coracle ride (Rs100 per boat, 15 minutes).

Just three kilometres upstream, the **Ranganathittu Bird Sanctuary** (☎ 0821-2481159; Indian/foreigner Rs25/75, camera/video Rs25/100; ☺ 8.30am-6pm) is on one of three islands in the Cauvery River. The storks, ibises, egrets, spoonbills and cormorants here are best seen in the early morning or late afternoon on a short **boat ride** (per person Rs100). There's also a maze made from herbal plants and a restaurant on site.

SLEEPING & EATING

Royal Retreat New Amblee Holiday Resort (☎ 217474; www.ambleeresort.com; d from Rs1200; ⛄ ⛄) A menagerie of rabbits and ducks, and the owner's (covered) Rolls-Royce greets you at the Amblee, which offers relatively good accommodation, a pleasant riverside setting and a reasonably priced restaurant.

Mayura River View (☎ 217454; d Rs1750; ⛄) Set on a quiet patch of riverbank, this government outfit has a handful of cute bungalows, each well-appointed and comfortable, along with a bug-themed children's park. The restaurant (mains Rs30 to Rs100) has a wonderful sit-out from where you can gaze at the river.

GETTING THERE & AWAY

Take the frequent buses 313 or 316 (Rs10, one hour) from Mysore's City bus stand. Passenger trains travelling from Mysore to Bengaluru (Rs10, 20 minutes) also stop here. The stand for private buses heading to Brindavan Gardens (Rs15, 30 minutes) is just across from Srirangapatnam's main bus stand.

GETTING AROUND

The sights are a little spread out, but walking isn't out of the question. For a quicker tour, tongas (two-wheeled horse carriages) cost about Rs150 for three hours, and an autorickshaw from Mysore is about Rs300 (three hours).

Brindavan Gardens

If you're familiar with Bollywood, these ornamental **gardens** (☎ 08236-257247; adult/child Rs20/15, camera/video Rs50/100; ⌚ 8am-8.30pm) might just give you that sense of déjà vu – they've indeed been the backdrop to many a shimmying musical number. The best time to visit is in the evening, when the fountains are illuminated and made to dance to the accompaniment of popular film tunes!

Within the gardens are two hotels: the no-frills **Hotel Mayura Cauvery** (☎ 08236-215876; d Rs400) and the swanky **Royal Orchid Brindavan Garden** (☎ 08236-257257; www.royalorchidhotels.com; s/d incl breakfast from Rs4500/5000; ⛄), with lavish rooms and the strategically-located Elephant Bar, the best spot from which to view the light-and-sound shows while sipping on your poison.

The gardens are 19km northwest of Mysore. One of the KSTDC tours stops here, and buses 301, 304, 305, 306 and 365 depart

from Mysore's City bus stand hourly (Rs10, 45 minutes).

Melkote

Life in the devout Hindu town of Melkote, about 50km north of Mysore, revolves around the 12th-century **Cheluvanarayana Temple** (☎ 08236-298739; Raja St; ⌚ 8am-1pm & 5-8pm), with its rose-coloured *gopuram* (gateway tower) and ornately carved pillars. Get a work-out on the hike up to the hilltop **Yoganarasimha Temple**, which offers fine views of the surrounding hills. The town comes alive for the **Vairamudi Festival** in March or April (p901).

Three KSRTC buses a day shuttle between Mysore and Melkote (Rs40, 1½ hours).

Somnathpur

The astonishingly beautiful **Keshava Temple** (☎ 08227-270010; Indian/foreigner Rs5/100; ⌚ 9am-5.30pm) is one of the finest examples of Hoysala architecture, on par with the masterpieces of Belur and Halebid. Built in 1268, this star-shaped temple located some 33km from Mysore, is adorned with superb stone sculptures depicting various scenes from the Ramayana, Mahabharata and Bhagavad Gita, and the life and times of the Hoysala kings.

On a tree in the temple grounds there's a red postbox, where prestamped mail posted by you will be collected by the local post office and marked with a special postmark bearing the temple's image – this is a great memento to send back home.

Somnathpur is 7km south of Bannur and 10km north of Tirumakudal Narsipur. Take one of the half-hourly buses from Mysore to either village (Rs12, 30 minutes) and change there.

Sivasamudram

About 60km east of Mysore is Sivasamudram, home to the twin waterfalls of Barachukki and Gaganachukki. The site of the first hydro-electric project in India, in 1902, it's a place where you can spend a quiet time while indulging in natural bounties. The relaxing **Georgia Sunshine Village** (☎ 9448110660; www.georgiasunshine.com; d incl full board from Rs3700; ⛄ ⛄) is a wonderful place to camp; accommodation is in bungalows and the homemade food is delicious. The dog-loving hosts can arrange treks to the waterfalls and fishing trips on request.

Frequent buses run from Mysore (Rs25, one hour) to Malavalli, 14km away. Call ahead and they'll arrange an autorickshaw to pick you up for around Rs100.

HASSAN
☎ 08172 / pop 133,200

With a good range of hotels, a railhead and other conveniences, Hassan is a handy base for exploring Belur (38km), Halebid (33km) and Sravanabelagola (48km). Situated not far from either Mysore or Bengaluru, it's a bustling town with friendly people, and promises a good night's sleep in between hectic days of sightseeing.

Orientation & Information
The train station is 2km east of the town centre on busy Bengaluru–Mangalore (BM) Rd. The Central bus stand is on the corner of AVK College and Bus Stand Rds. The **tourist office** (☎ 268862; AVK College Rd; ⏱ 10am-5.30pm Mon-Sat), 100m east of the bus stand, is one of Karnataka's more helpful. There are plenty of ATMs and internet cafes. It's advisable to change foreign currency in Bengaluru or Mysore.

Sleeping
Vaishnavi Lodging (☎ 263885; Harsha Mahal Rd; s/d Rs190/270) Located across a quiet courtyard in a building close to the bus stands. It's cheap, tidy and the sheets are clean.

Hotel Sri Krishna (☎ 263240; BM Rd; s/d from Rs350/725; ☼) Hugely popular with local tourists, this place has biggish rooms done up in red-black checks. The staff is efficient, and there's a quality veg restaurant downstairs (mains Rs30 to Rs60).

Jewel Rock (☎ 261048; BM Rd; d with/without AC Rs950/600; ☼) Close to the train station, this place is a steal. The spacious rooms, with floral curtains, are comfortable, and the hotel houses two popular eateries, the pure-veg Annapurna and Chalukya, a reliable place for meaty delights.

Hotel Suvarna Regency (☎ 266774; www.hotel suvarnaregency.com; BM Rd; d with/without AC Rs1025/705; ☼ 🖳) This place, just south of Gandhi Sq, is frequented by business people, and is one of Hassan's trusted oldies. Get over the stiff smell of sanitisers that welcomes you into its well-kept rooms, and the rest is a breeze.

Hotel Hassan Ashhok (☎ 268731; www.hassanashok .com; BM Rd; s/d from Rs3000/3350; ☼ 🖳) Clearly the classiest of Hassan's hotels, this superbly renovated place offers you luxe features such as mini bars in its plush rooms and baskets full of herbal toiletries in the showers. The soft, cotton-white beds and stacks of fluffy pillows are simply irresistible!

our pick Hoysala Village Resort (☎ 256764; www .trailsindia.com; Belur Rd; d incl breakfast from Rs4800; ☼ 🖳) Located 6km from town on the road to Belur, this rustic and relaxing place is set amid a patch of manicured gardens. Its cosy rooms have a country feel, with large windows looking out onto the palms and hedges. There's a tree house where you can laze away the evening, beer in hand, or flex your pectorals in the aqua-blue pool. The resort also has an ayurvedic massage centre, where sessions kick off for around Rs400.

Eating
Hotel Sanman (Municipal Office Rd; meals Rs15-20; ⏱ 7am-10pm) Pay upfront and take your pick from *masala dosas* (curried vegetables inside crisp pancakes) or a thali at this busy joint located a block south of the bus station.

Hotel GRR (Bus Stand Rd; meals Rs20-50; ⏱ 11am-11pm) Top-of-the-line Andhra-style thalis (Rs25) are on offer at this busy place, as is the popular chicken biryani (Rs50).

Suvarna Gate (Hotel Suvarna Regency, BM Rd; mains Rs40-120; ⏱ noon-3.30pm & 6.30-11.30pm) You might have to wait a while for your food but it's worth it. The chicken tandoori masala is delicious and the terrace dining room overlooking neatly trimmed hedges has ambience. It's located to the rear of Hotel Suvarna Regency.

Getting There & Away
BUS
Buses leave from the Central bus stand, situated on the corner of AVK College and Bus Stand Rds. Buses to Halebid (Rs15, one hour) run half-hourly starting 6am, with the last bus back leaving Halebid at 7.30pm. Frequent buses connect Hassan and Belur (Rs20, one hour); the first leaves Hassan at 6am, and the last bus from Belur is at 10pm.

To get to Sravanabelagola, you must take one of the many buses to Channarayapatna (Rs20, 45 minutes) and change there.

There are frequent services to Mysore (Rs68, three hours), Bengaluru (semideluxe/deluxe Rs159/190, four hours) and Mangalore (Rs148, five hours).

TAXI
Taxi drivers hang out on AVK College Rd, north of the bus stand. A tour of Belur and

KARNATAKA

Halebid will cost you about Rs800 for the day. A return taxi to Sravanabelagola will cost the same. Firmly set the price before departure.

TRAIN

The well-organised **train station** (☎ 268222) is about 2km east of town (Rs15 by autorickshaw). The main building should be fully renovated by mid-2009; and cloakroom services available again. Three passenger trains head to Mysore daily (2nd class Rs27, three hours). For Bengaluru, take one of the four daily trains to Arsikere (Rs15, one hour) and change there.

BELUR & HALEBID

☎ 08177 / elev 968m

The Hoysala temples at Halebid (also known as Halebeedu) and Belur (also called Beluru), along with the temple at Somnathpur (p922), are the apex of one of the most artistically exuberant periods of ancient Hindu cultural development. Architecturally, they are South India's answer to Khajuraho (see p680) in Madhya Pradesh and Konark (see p657), near Puri in Orissa.

Only 16km lie between Belur and Halebid, and the towns are connected by frequent shuttle buses from 6.30am to 7pm (Rs15, 30 minutes). See p923 for details of buses to/from Hassan. Belur also has ordinary buses to Bengaluru (Rs120, five hours). To get to Hampi, it's best to return to Bengaluru and take an overnight bus to Hospet.

Belur

The **Channakeshava Temple** (Temple Rd; ☉ dawn-dusk) was commissioned in 1116 to commemorate the Hoysalas' victory over the neighbouring Cholas. It took more than a century to build, and is currently the only one among the three major Hoysala sites still in daily use – try to be there for the *puja* (offerings or prayer) ceremonies at 9am, 3pm and 7.30pm. Some parts of the temple, such as the exterior lower friezes, were not sculpted to completion and are thus less elaborate than those of the other Hoysala temples. However, the work higher up is unsurpassed in detail and artistry, and is a glowing tribute to human skill. Particularly intriguing are the angled bracket figures depicting women in ritual dancing poses. While the front of the temple is reserved for images depicting erotic sections from the Kama Sutra, the back is strictly for gods. The roof of the inner sanctum is held up by rows of exquisitely sculpted pillars, no two of which are identical in design.

Scattered around the temple complex are other smaller temples, a marriage hall which is still used and the seven-storey *gopuram*, which has sensual sculptures explicitly portraying the après-temple activities of dancing girls.

Guides can be hired for Rs150; they help to bring some of the sculptural detail to life.

Vishnu Regency (☎ 223011; Kempegowda Rd; d with/without AC Rs1000/500; 🔀 🖳) is clearly the best of Belur's none-too-salubrious hotels. Its simple rooms are clean and fresh, and it has a pleasant **restaurant** (mains Rs30-80; ☉ 11.30am-10.30pm) serving North Indian and Chinese food. From the bus stand, walk up Temple Rd and turn left at the statue of Kempegowda.

Near Kempegowda's statue is **Shankar Hotel** (Temple Rd; meals Rs27; ☉ 7am-9.30pm), a busy place serving fine South Indian thalis, *masala dosas*, Indian sweets, snacks and drinks.

Halebid

Construction of the **Hoysaleswara Temple** (☉ dawn-dusk), Halebid's claim to fame, began around 1121 and went on for more than 80 years. It was never completed, but nonetheless stands today as a masterpiece of Hoysala architecture. The interior of its inner sanctum, chiselled out of black stone, is marvellous. On the outside, the temple's richly-sculpted walls are covered with a flurry of Hindu deities, sages, stylised animals and friezes depicting the life of the Hoysala rulers. A huge statue of Nandi (Shiva's bull) sits to the left of the main temple, facing the inner sanctum.

The temple is set in large, well-tended gardens, adjacent to which is a small **museum** (admission Rs2; ☉ 10am-5pm Sat-Thu) housing a collection of sculptures.

If the pesky touts get on your nerves, take some time out to visit the nearby, smaller **Kedareswara Temple**, or a little-visited enclosure containing three **Jain** temples, which also have fine carvings.

If you're really stuck in Halebid for the night, count away the hours in the drab rooms of the shoddy **KSTDC Mayura Shanthala** (☎ 273224; d/q without bathroom Rs250/350).

SRAVANABELAGOLA

☎ 08176

Atop the bald rock of Vindhyagiri Hill, the 17.5m-high statue of the Jain deity Gomateshvara (Bahubali), said to be the world's tallest monolithic statue, is visible long before you reach the pilgrimage town of Sravanabelagola. Viewing the statue close up is the main reason for heading to this sedate town, whose name means 'the Monk of the White Pond'. Sravanabelagola also played hermitage to emperor Chandragupta Maurya, who came here in the 3rd century BC after renouncing his kingdom.

Information

The defunct **tourist office** (☎ 257254; ☯ 10am-5.30pm) sits in a new complex at the foot of Vindhyagiri Hill. The grand plans to have an audiovisual display, a cafe and a gift store have sadly not materialised. There are no entry fees to the sites in Sravanabelagola, though donations are encouraged.

Sights

GOMATESHVARA STATUE

A steep climb up 614 steps takes you to the top of Vindhyagiri Hill, the summit of which is lorded over by the towering naked statue of **Gomatesvara** (Bahubali; ☯ 6am-6.15pm). Commissioned by a military commander in the service of the Ganga king Rachamalla and carved out of a single piece of granite by the sculptor Aristenemi in AD 981, its serenity and simplicity is in stark contrast to the Hoysala sites at Belur and Halebid.

Bahubali was the son of emperor Vrishabhadeva, who later became the first Jain *tirthankar* (revered teacher) Adinath. Embroiled fiercely with his brother Bharatha to succeed his father, Bahubali realised the futility of material gains and renounced his kingdom. As a recluse, he meditated in complete stillness in the forest until he attained enlightenment. His lengthy meditative spell is denoted by vines curling around his legs and an ant hill at his feet.

Leave shoes at the foot of the hill, but it's fine to wear socks. If you want it easy, you can hire a *dholi* (portable chair) with bearers for Rs150, from 7am to 12.30pm and 3pm to 5.30pm.

Every 12 years, millions flock here to attend the Mastakabhisheka ceremony, when the statue is dowsed in holy waters, pastes, powders, precious metals and stones. The next ceremony is slated for 2018.

TEMPLES

Apart from the Bahubali statue, there are several interesting Jain temples in town.

The **Chandragupta Basti** (Chandragupta Community; ☯ 6am-6pm), on Chandragiri Hill opposite Vindhyagiri, is believed to have been built by Emperor Ashoka. The **Bhandari Basti** (Bhandari Community; ☯ 6am-6pm), in the southeast corner of town, is Sravanabelagola's largest temple. Nearby, **Chandranatha Basti** (Chandranatha Community; ☯ 6am-6pm) has well-preserved paintings depicting Jain tales.

Sleeping & Eating

The local Jain organisation **SDJMI** (☎ 257258; d/tr Rs135/160) handles bookings for its 15 guest houses. The office is behind the Vidyananda Nilaya Dharamsala, past the post office.

Hotel Raghu (☎ 257238; d with/without AC Rs800/500; ✵) It's the only privately owned hotel around, and offers basic but clean rooms. The real bonus is its vegetarian restaurant (mains Rs20-40; ☯ 6am-9pm) downstairs, which works up an awesome thali (Rs40), sometimes served caringly by the owner himself.

Getting There & Away

There are no direct buses from Sravanabelagola to Hassan or Belur – you must go to Channarayapatna (Rs10, 20 minutes) and catch an onward connection there. Three direct buses a day run to both Bengaluru (Rs78, 3½ hours) and Mysore (Rs52, 2½ hours). Long-distance buses clear out before 3pm. If you miss these, catch a local bus to Channarayapatna, which is on the main Bengaluru–Mangalore road and has lots of connections.

NILGIRI BIOSPHERE RESERVE

The pristine forests of the **Nilgiri Biosphere Reserve** are one of India's best-preserved wildernesses, and span about 5500 sq km across the states of Karnataka, Kerala and Tamil Nadu. Human access to the reserve is through a number of national parks, such as Wayanad (see p1031) in Kerala and Mudumalai (see p1118) in Tamil Nadu. In Karnataka, the best access points are the national parks of Bandipur and Nagarhole, and the super-green forested region around the Kabini Lake.

Home to over 100 species of mammals and some 350 species of birds, the reserve is also a natural habitat for the prized but endangered Bengal tigers and Asiatic elephants; more than a fifth of the world's population of jumbos live here.

Bandipur National Park

About 80km south of Mysore on the Ooty road, the **Bandipur National Park** (☎ 08229-236021; Indian/foreigner Rs60/200) covers 880 sq km and was once the Mysore maharajas' private wildlife reserve. The park is noted for its herds of gaurs (Indian bison), chitals (spotted deer), sambars, panthers, sloth bears and langurs, apart from tigers and elephants. Despite its rich wildlife, however, Bandipur isn't the best place for animal sightings; unrestricted traffic hurtling down the busy highway that cuts through the forest has made the animals wary of venturing close to safari areas of late.

Brief **elephant rides** (Indian/foreigner Rs50/150) are available for a minimum of four people. For a **safari** (Indian/foreigner Rs25/175; ◔ 6am, 7am, 8am, 4pm & 5pm) there's the forest department's minibus, the rumbling of which further puts off the shy creatures. Resort vehicles are permitted to go into the forest; they are quieter and thus a better bet.

SLEEPING & EATING

Forest Department Bungalows (d Indian/foreigner from Rs490/840) It's all pretty basic, but you'll love it when the chitals spill onto the grounds at night. Meals are available upon advance notice. Book early with Project Tiger (☎ 0821-2480901, Aranya Bhavan, Ashokapuram) in Mysore.

Tusker Trails (☎ 080-23618024, 09845326467; per person incl full board Indian/foreigner Rs2200/US$80; ▣) A lovely resort located on the eastern edge of the park, this place provides accommodation in simple huts, with good food and an inviting pool to splash about in. Rates include two daily safaris.

GETTING THERE & AWAY

Buses between Mysore and Ooty will drop you at Bandipur (Rs47, three hours). You can also book an overnight taxi from Mysore (about Rs2000).

Nagarhole National Park

West of the Kabini River is the 643-sq-km wildlife sanctuary of **Nagarhole National Park** (Rajiv Gandhi National Park; Indian/foreigner Rs50/150), pronounced *nag-ar-hole-eh*. The lush forests here are home to tigers, leopards, elephants, gaurs, muntjacs (barking deer), wild dogs, bonnet macaques and common langurs. The park can remain closed for long stretches between July and October, when the rains transform the forests into a giant slush-pit.

The park's main entrance is 93km southwest of Mysore. If you're not staying at a resort nearby, the only way to see the park is on the forest department's bus **tour** (per person Rs95; ◔ 6-8am & 3-5.30pm). The best time to view wildlife is during summer (April to May), though winter (November to February) is kinder.

Decent sleeping options are limited in Nagarhole. An OK place to camp is **Jungle Inn** (☎ 08222-246022; www.jungleinnnagarhole.com; Hunsur-Nagarhole Rd; per head incl full board Indian/foreigner from Rs1800/US$60) about 35km from the park reception on the Hunsur road. With a welcoming atmosphere, evening campfires and simple, clean rooms, it also serves good food made from organic produce. Rates for safaris are extra.

Kabini Lake

About 70km south of Mysore lies **Kabini Lake**, a giant forest-edged reservoir formed by the damming of the Kabini River. Endowed with rich and unspoilt vegetation, the area is rapidly growing as one of Karnataka's best wildlife destinations. Positioned midway between the animal corridors of Bandipur and Nagarhole, the Kabini forests are also the habitat for a large variety of wildlife, and give you the chance to view the animals up close.

Tourism around Kabini is managed by a few resorts, most of which are founded on ecofriendly principles. Jungle safaris and other activities such as boat rides and birdwatching are conducted by the resorts, generally between 6.30am to 9.30am, and 4pm to 7pm.

SLEEPING & EATING

our pick **Kabini River Lodge** (☎ 08228-264402; per person tents/r/cottages Indian Rs3000/3750/4250, foreigner US$160) No sooner than you've entered will you be told that Goldie Hawn was here! Rated among the world's best wildlife resorts, this fascinating government-run eco getaway is located on the grounds of the former Mysore maharaja's hunting lodge beside Kabini Lake. Manned by an excellent staff, it offers accommodation in a choice of large canvas tents, regular rooms and cottages. Rates include full board, safaris, boat rides and forest entry fees. Book through Jungle Lodges & Resorts Ltd (Map p905; ☎ 080-25597021, 25597944; www.junglelodges.com).

Cicada Kabini (☎ 080-41152200, 9945602305; www.cicadaresorts.com; s/d from Rs8000/12,000; ▣ ▣ ▣) Another highly recommended ecoresort, this well-conceived luxury option brings a dash of contemporary chic to the lakeside. The rates are for accommodation and meals only; safaris (Rs750) and kayaks and pedal boats (Rs250) are extra.

GETTING THERE & AWAY
A few buses depart daily from Mysore and can drop you at Kabini village. However, it's better to have your own taxi. Enquire with the resorts while making a booking.

KODAGU (COORG) REGION
Nestled amid the verdant, ageless hills that line the southernmost edge of Karnataka is the luscious Kodagu (Coorg) region, gifted with emerald green landscapes and acre after acre of plantations. A major centre for coffee and spice production, this rural expanse is also home to the unique but numbered Kodava race, believed to have descended from migrating Persians and Kurds or perhaps Greeks left behind from Alexander the Great's armies. The uneven terrain and cool climate make it a fantastic area for trekking, birdwatching or lazily ambling down little-trod paths that wind their way around the carpeted hills. All in all, Kodagu is rejuvenation guaranteed.

The best season for trekking is October to March. Guides are available for hire and can arrange food, transport and accommodation; see right for recommendations. Treks can last from two to three days to a week; the most popular routes are to the peaks of Tadiyendamol (1745m) and Pushpagiri (1712m), and to smaller Kotebetta. Adventure activities are conducted between November and May; the rest of the year is too wet for traipsing around.

Kodagu was a state in its own right until 1956, when it merged with Karnataka. The region's chief town and transport hub is Madikeri, but for an authentic Kodagu experience, you have to venture into the plantations. Avoid weekends, when places can quickly get filled up by Bengaluru's IT and call-centre crowd.

Madikeri (Mercara)
☎ 08272 / pop 32,400 / elev 1525m
Also known as Mercara, this congested market town is spread out along a series of ridges. The only reason for coming here is to organise treks or sort out the practicalities of travel. The Huthri festival (see the boxed text, p901),

which falls sometime between November and December, is a nice time to visit.

ORIENTATION & INFORMATION
In the chaotic centre around the KSRTC and private-bus stands, you'll find most of the hotels and restaurants as well as several ATMs.

A semi-functional **KSTDC Office** (☎ 228580; near Raja's Seat; ⊙ 10am-5.30pm Mon-Sat) offers basic tourist information about the region. If you need to change money, cash travellers cheques or get a credit-card advance, try **Canara Bank** (☎ 229302; Main Rd, Gandhi Chowk; ⊙ 10.30am-2.30pm Mon-Fri) or **ICICI Bank** (☎ 645380; College Rd; ⊙ 10am-6pm Mon-Sat). Internet cafes are plentiful.

SIGHTS
Madikeri's **fort**, now in use as the municipal headquarters, was built in 1812 by Raja Lingarajendra II. There's an old church here, housing a quirky **museum** (admission free; ⊙ 10am-5.30pm Tue-Sun) displaying dusty, poorly labelled artefacts. Panoramic views of the hills and valleys can be taken in from **Raja's Seat** (admission free; MG Rd; ⊙ 5.30am-7.30pm). Behind are gardens, a toy train line for kids and a tiny Kodava-style **temple**.

On the way to **Abbi Falls**, a pleasant 7km hike from the town centre, visit the quietly beautiful **Raja's Tombs**, better known as Gaddige. An autorickshaw costs about Rs150 return.

ACTIVITIES
A trekking guide is essential for navigating the labyrinth of forest tracks. Most of the estates in Kodagu also offer trekking programs.

Raja Shekhar and Ganesh at **V-Track** (☎ 229974; Crown Towers, College Rd; ⊙ 10am-2pm & 4.30-8pm Mon-Sat) can arrange one- to 10-day treks including guide, accommodation and food. Rates are around Rs600 per person per day, and can vary depending on the duration and number of people. Short walks take only a day or two to prepare. For long treks, trips on obscure routes or big groups, it's best to give a week's notice.

Coorg Trails (☎ 320578; coorgtrails@yahoo.co.in; Main Rd; ⊙ 9am-8.30pm) can arrange day treks for Rs400 per person, and a 22km trek to Kotebetta, including an overnight stay in a village, for Rs1200 per person. The office is near the town hall.

Located in Kirudale, about 25km from Madikeri, **Coorg Planters' Camp** (☎ 08276-320500; www.coorgplanterscamp.com; d incl full board Rs2400) is a fantastic ecoresort featuring tented accommodation, which treats guests to activities such as a tour of coffee plantations and nature walks through Kodagu's dense forests. Daylong treks to the summits of Pushpagiri and Kotebetta, the region's second and third-highest peaks respectively, require a nominal extra charge.

Ayurjeevan (☎ 224466; Kohinoor Rd; 🕑 9am-6pm), a short walk from ICICI Bank, offers a whole range of rejuvenating ayurvedic packages, with 30-minute sessions kicking off at around Rs400.

SLEEPING

Many hotels reduce their rates in the low season (June to September); all of those listed below have hot water, at least in the morning, and 24-hour checkout.

Hotel Cauvery (☎ 225492; School Rd; s/d Rs250/500) This ageing hotel behind Hotel Capitol opposite the private bus stand is slowly going through a facelift. The decor is a mix of printed upholstery and plastic creepers, which lend a rather kitschy character to the place.

Hilltown Hotel (☎ 223801; www.hilltownhotel.com; Hill Town Rd; s/d from Rs350/700; 🖳) Down the lane running past Hotel Chitra, the Hilltown is a spruce place with fish tanks on the stairs and a pretty garden opposite. Singles are small; some have damp walls. It also has a restaurant (mains Rs30 to Rs60).

Hotel Hill View (☎ 223808; Hill Rd; s/d Rs850/1000) Situated at a far corner of the new town, this cosy place has small but well-kept rooms. The wall shades and the pruned hedges in the tiny sit-outs are perfectly colour coordinated with the green hills that overlook the rooms.

Hotel Mayura Valley View (☎ 228387; near Raja's Seat; d incl breakfast from Rs1200; 🖳) It's recently been renovated, but the lack of maintenance has already begun to tell. However, nothing beats the stunning views that you get from the floor-to-ceiling windows of its rooms. Service is patchy, and the restaurant-bar (mains Rs30 to Rs100, open 7am to 10pm) with a terrace is certainly the best place in town for a drink.

Hotel Coorg International (☎ 228071; www .coorginternational.com; Convent Rd; s/d incl half-board from Rs3200/4000; 🖳 🖳) Madikeri's classiest option isn't a bad deal considering rates include fixed-menu breakfast and dinner, snacks through the day, and facilities such as cable TV, a small pool, a gym and an ayurvedic massage room.

EATING

Popular Guru Prasad (Main Rd; meals Rs25-30; 🕑 7am-10pm) The aptly named Popular Guru Prasad serves a range of vegie options, including a value-for-money veg thali (Rs30) and breakfast snacks.

Athithi (mains Rs30-50; 🕑 7am-10pm) The best vegetarian option in town, Athithi is known for its lip-smacking vegetarian thali (Rs40), an elaborate affair served on banana leaves. Near the police station.

Hotel Capitol (School Rd; mains Rs30-70; 🕑 7am-9.30pm) Don't mind the shabby interiors. This is one of the best places in town to sample the local speciality, the flavourful and spicy *pandhi* (pork) curry (Rs60), best had with a pint of cold beer.

East End Hotel (GT Circle; mains Rs35-80; 🕑 7am-10pm) An assortment of South Indian staples and local chicken and mutton dishes are offered at this eatery, its popularity seconded by the locals who converge here during meals.

GETTING THERE & AWAY

Five deluxe buses a day depart from the KSRTC **bus stand** (☎ 229134) for Bengaluru (Rs279, six hours), stopping in Mysore (Rs140, three hours) on the way. Deluxe buses also go to Mangalore (Rs160, three hours, three daily), while ordinary buses head to Hassan (Rs65, three hours) and Shimoga (Rs151, eight hours).

GETTING AROUND

Madikeri is a small town easy to negotiate on foot. For excursions around the region, several places rent out motorcycles for around Rs300 a day, with an initial refundable deposit of Rs500. Try **Spice's Mall** (☎ 9449275669; opposite KSRTC bus stand) or **Coorg The Guide** (☎ 9448184829; Chethana Complex). Carry your driver's licence, tank up on petrol and off you go!

The Plantations

Spread around Madikeri town are Kodagu's quaint and leafy spice and coffee plantations. Many estates here offer homestays, ranging from basic to quite luxurious, while high-end resorts have begun to spring up recently. The following are our pick of places within easy reach of Madikeri; also see right. Unless otherwise mentioned, rates include meals and trekking guides. Advance bookings should be made. Some options remain closed during the monsoons. Most arrange transport to/from Madikeri; enquire while booking.

our pick **Rainforest Retreat** (☎ 08272-265636; www.rainforestours.com; Gallibeedu; s/d from Rs1750/3000) Located on an organic plantation, these eco-chic cottages are run by the friendly owners Sujata (a botanist) and Anurag (a molecular biologist) who are a fount of regional knowledge. The trekking is excellent, or you can just lie in a hammock and watch the birds. All proceeds go to the couple's NGO, which promotes environmental awareness and sustainable agriculture.

The snug, earth-coloured cottages at the **Alath-Cad Estate Bungalow** (☎ 08274-252190; www.alathcadcoorg.com; Ammathi; d incl breakfast from Rs1900), set on a 26-hectare coffee plantation about 28km southeast of Madikeri, are a good place to give in to unadulterated nature. Activities include plantation tours and picnics, while treks and fishing trips can be arranged upon request. Lunch and dinner cost Rs150 each.

Plantation Trails (☎ 08274-251428; www.tatacoffee .com/plantation_trails; Pollibetta; d incl breakfast Indian/foreigner from Rs3080/US$105) rides on its parent company Tata Coffee's heritage to throw open a number of old planters' bungalows scattered among their plantations, all luxuriously renovated but still sporting antique features such as wooden floors, teak furniture and fireplaces. Guests get to use facilities reserved for company officials, including the minigolf course. Meals are Rs280 each.

A German-owned organic plantation, **Golden Mist** (☎ 08272-265629; www.goldenmist.4t .com; Kaloor village; d Rs3500), is one of the nicest options near Madikeri town, with cottage accommodation for up to six people. Similar

in atmosphere to Rainforest Retreat, it offers nature walks and plantation tours. For larger groups, the price drops to Rs1200 per person per day.

Green Hills Estate (☎ 08274-254790; www.neemrana hotels.com; Virajpet; r incl breakfast Rs5000) is another quaint planter's bungalow that houses stacks of family memorabilia within its rosewood panelled interiors. The rooms have quirky names such as Lord Jim and Lady Madcap, supposedly named after racing thoroughbreds once owned by the planter's family. Lunch and dinner are Rs350 each.

Kadkani (☎ 08274-254186; www.kadkani.com; Ammathi; r from Rs14,500; ✷ ❖), an ultra luxurious retreat nestled in a dale amid silent forests by the Cauvery River, effortlessly matches the best of modern comforts and rustic charm in its classy ecocottages. An excellent place to unwind in style, the sprawling resort also offers activities such as golf, river crossing and river rafting (Rs300 per person). The evenings are reserved for listening to the cicadas.

Kakkabe
☎ 08272

About 40km from Madikeri, the region around the village of Kakkabe is an ideal base if you're planning an assault on Kodagu's highest peak, Tadiyendamol. At the bottom of the summit, 3km from Kakkabe, is the picturesque **Nalakunad Palace** (admission free; ⌚ 9am-5pm), the restored hunting lodge of a Kodagu king dating from 1794. Within walking distance are several excellent places to camp.

our pick **Honey Valley Estate** (☎ 238339; d from Rs700, s without bathroom from Rs300) is a wonderful place 1250m above sea level where you can wake to a chirpy dawn and cool, fresh air. The owners' friendliness, ecomindedness and scrumptious organic food make things even better (meals Rs95). The estate is only accessible by jeep or by a one-hour uphill walk. Advance bookings are essential.

The name of tiny **Misty Woods** (☎ 238561; www .coorgmisty.com; cottages from Rs2799), immediately uphill from Nalakunad Palace, aptly sums up the landscape that surrounds it. The *vastu shastra* (ancient science similar to Feng Shui)–style cottages are both comfortable and stylish. Meals are extra.

Regular buses run to Kakkabe from Madikeri (Rs20, 1½ hours) and from Virajpet (Rs14, one hour).

Dubare Forest Reserve

En route to Kushalnagar, Kodagu's second-largest town, is the Dubare Forest Reserve on the banks of the Cauvery River, where about a dozen elephants retired from forest department work live on pension. Cross the river (Rs25) to participate in an **elephant interaction program** (Indian/foreigner Rs270/550; ☼ 8.45am-noon), when you can bathe, feed and then ride the jumbos.

Bookings can be made through **Jungle Lodges & Resorts Ltd** (Map p905; ☎ 080-25597021, 25597944; www.junglelodges.com), which also runs the reserve's rustic but good **Dubare Elephant Camp** (☎ 9449599755; per person Indian/foreigner Rs2250/US$90). Rates include the elephant-interaction program.

White-water rafting (per person Rs850) is also organised from here, over an 8km stretch that features rapids up to grade 4.

Bylakuppe

☎ 08223

Tiny Bylakuppe, 5km southeast of Kushalnagar, was among the first refugee camps set up in South India to house thousands of Tibetans who fled from Tibet following the 1959 Chinese invasion. Comprising several clusters of settlements amid 1200 hectares of rolling sugarcane fields that rustle in the breeze, it's among the few camps where many Tibetans have been able to return to their agrarian ways of life. That apart, it has all the sights and sounds of a Tibetan colony, with resident maroon-and-yellow-robed monks and locals selling Tibetan food and handicrafts. The atmosphere is heart-warmingly welcoming. The settlement is also home to much festivity during the Tibetan New Year celebrations (see the boxed text, p901).

Foreigners are not allowed to stay overnight in Bylakuppe without a Protected Area Permit (PAP) from the Ministry of Home Affairs in Delhi. Contact the **Tibet Bureau Office** (☎ 26474798, 26439745; 10B Ring Rd, Lajpat Nagar IV, New Delhi) for details.

The area's highlight is the **Namdroling Monastery** (☎ 254036; www.palyul.org/eng_centers), home to the jaw-droppingly spectacular **Golden Temple** (Padmasambhava Buddhist Vihara; ☼ 7am-8pm), presided over by an 18m-high gold-plated Buddha. The temple is at its dramatic best when school is in session and it rings out with gongs, drums and chanting of hundreds of young novices. You're welcome to sit and meditate; look for the small blue guest cushions lying around. The **Zangdogpalri Temple** (☼ 7am-8pm), a similarly ornate affair, is next door.

Opposite the Golden Temple is a shopping centre, where you'll find the simple **Paljor Dhargey Ling Guest House** (☎ 258686; pdguesthouse@yahoo.com; d Rs280). Add Rs100 if you want a TV.

In the same shopping centre is **Shanti Family Restaurant** (mains Rs30-60; ☼ 7am-9.30pm), offering a decent range of Indian meals and Tibetan dishes such as *momos* (dumplings) and *thukpa* (noodle soup).

If you cannot manage a PAP, a good place is the lovely **Shri Kalpa Farm** (☎ 9886776923; per person per day Rs500), just outside the settlement on the approach way, where the friendly Kaveriappa family can accommodate up to four people in the pleasant terrace room of their plantation villa. Meals are extra.

Autorickshaws (shared/alone Rs10/30) ply to Bylakuppe from Kushalanagar. Buses frequently do the 34km run to Kushalnagar from Madikeri (Rs20, 1½ hour) and Hassan (Rs70, four hours); most buses on the Mysore–Madikeri route stop at Kushalnagar.

KARNATAKA COAST

MANGALORE

☎ 0824 / pop 539,300

Situated at the estuaries of the Netravathi and Gurupur Rivers on the Arabian Sea coast, Mangalore has been a major pit stop on international trade routes since the 6th century AD. The largest city on the Karnataka coast, it's a nice place to break long-haul journeys along the western shoreline, go shopping for amenities or move inland.

Once the main port of Hyder Ali's kingdom, Mangalore now ships out a bulk of the region's spice, coffee and cashew crops from the modern port, 10km north of the city. Apart from a few tourist charms, such as the quiet Ullal Beach, 12km south, the city also has a pleasant cosmopolitan air about it and, with a sprinkling of pubs and restaurants, makes for a relaxing stay.

Orientation

Mangalore is hilly, with winding, disorienting streets. Luckily, most hotels and restaurants, the bus stand and the train station are in or around its frenzied centre. The KSRTC bus stand is 3km to the north.

KARNATAKA

Information

ATMs and internet cafes are everywhere, and several banks in town also have facilities for changing foreign currency.

Athree Book Centre (Balmatta Rd; 🕙 8.30am-1pm & 2.30-8pm Mon-Sat)

Bookmark (PM Rao Rd; 🕙 8.30am-8.30pm Mon-Sat, 8.30am-1pm Sun)

KSTDC tourist office (☎ 2453926; Lalbagh Circle; 🕙 10am-5pm Mon-Sat) Kind of useless.

Trade Wings (☎ 2427225; Lighthouse Hill Rd; 🕙 9.30am-5.30pm Mon-Sat) Travel agency. Changes travellers cheques.

Sights

Catholicism's roots in Mangalore date back to the arrival of the Portuguese in the early 1500s, and today the city is liberally dotted with churches. One of the most impressive is the Sistine Chapel-like **St Aloysius College Chapel** (Lighthouse Hill; 🕙 8.30am-6pm Mon-Sat, 10am-noon & 2-6pm Sun), with its walls and ceilings painted with brilliant frescoes. Also worth checking out is the imposing Roman-style **Milagres Church** (Falnir Rd; 🕙 8.30am-6pm) in the city centre.

Sultan's Battery (Sultan Battery Rd; admission free; 🕙 6am-6pm), the only remnant of Tipu Sultan's fort, is 4km from the centre on the headland of the old port; bus 16 will get you there. The Kerala-style **Kadri Manjunatha Temple** (Kadri; 🕙 6am-1pm & 4-8pm) houses a 1000-year-old bronze statue of Lokeshwara, if you're interested.

The real ace up Mangalore's sleeve is serene **Ullal Beach**, which is best enjoyed from Summer Sands Beach Resort (right). If you're not staying there, the resort charges you Rs25 to access its beach, but it's well worth it if you drop by at sunset. You can also use the pool for Rs100. An autorickshaw is Rs170 one way, or the frequent bus 44A (Rs10) from the City bus stand will drop you right outside the gate. Buses 44C or 44D also go to Ullal.

Sleeping

BUDGET

Hotel Surya (☎ 2425736; Balmatta Rd; s/d/tr from Rs225/360/425; 🛎 🖳) The rooms in this basic joint set back from the main road look a little bombed out. But the dirt-cheap rates help it barely make the cut. It's behind Lalith Bar & Restaurant.

Hotel Manorama (☎ 2440306; KS Rao Rd; s/d from Rs250/360; 🛎) A motley collection of sculptures welcomes you into its lobby, and the spartan rooms with squat loos have an air of quaintness to them. It's the best of the budget brigade.

Hotel Srinivas (☎ 2440061; GHS Rd; s/d from Rs450/600; 🛎) It's central and reasonably clean, but characterless and really nothing to write home about.

MIDRANGE & TOP END

Hotel Poonja International (☎ 2440171; www.hotel poonjainternational.com; KS Rao Rd; s/d from Rs750/900; 🛎) This well-managed place has faux sunflowers and creepers lining its lobby, and the rooms offer standard comfort with few frills. It's huge; 154 rooms, for the record!

Nalapad Residency (☎ 2424757; www.nalapad.com; Lighthouse Hill Rd; s/d incl breakfast from Rs800/900; 🛎) It's one of Mangalore's best midrange options. The rooms are spruce, with floor to ceiling windows and heavy red curtains. The rooftop restaurant, Kadal, is a definite bonus.

Moti Mahal (☎ 2441411; www.motimahalmangalore .com; Falnir Rd; d incl breakfast Indian/foreigner from Rs950/US$25; 🛎 🖳 🏊) The rooms here are average, but the selling points include its clean outdoor pool, a gym and three restaurants.

The Gateway Hotel (☎ 6660420; www.thegate wayhotels.com; Old Port Rd; s/d from Rs3500/4000; 🛎 🖳 🏊) Head and shoulders above the rest of Mangalore's hotels, this business hotel offers all the services you would expect in a four-star hotel. Some of the superior rooms have sea views.

Summer Sands Beach Resort (☎ 2467690; www .summersands.in; d from Rs4000; 🛎 🏊) Set amid the greens on a remote patch along Ullal Beach, Summer Sands offers a series of ethno-style bungalows done up in earth and floral shades and is the ideal place for a quiet retreat. Memories of Joanna, its restaurant, sometimes organises food galas with candle-lit dinner on the beach (buffet per person Rs350).

Eating & Drinking

While in town sample some Mangalorean delights such as *kane* (ladyfish) served in a spicy coconut curry, or the spicy deep-fried prawn *koliwada*.

Janatha Deluxe (Hotel Shaan Plaza, KS Rao Rd; mains Rs20-45; 🕙 7am-11pm) This local favourite serves good thalis (Rs30) and a range of North and South Indian veg dishes.

Lalith Bar & Restaurant (Balmatta Rd; mains Rs30-110; 🕙 9am-3pm & 5.30-11pm) Unwind in the Lalith's cool, subterranean interior while enjoying a cocktail combined with prawns, crab or

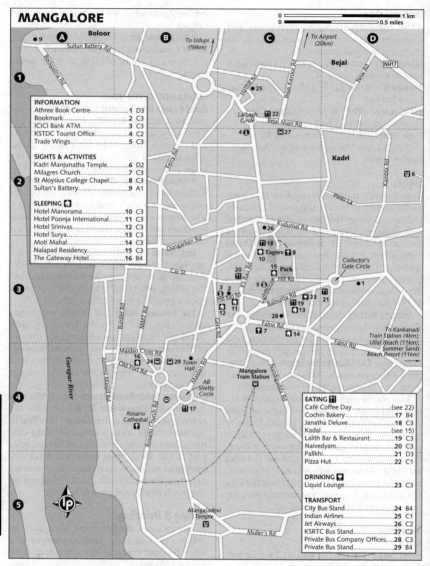

MANGALORE

0 ___ 1 km
0 ___ 0.5 miles

INFORMATION
Athree Book Centre.................1 D3
Bookmark............................2 C3
ICICI Bank ATM......................3 C3
KSTDC Tourist Office...............4 C2
Trade Wings........................5 C3

SIGHTS & ACTIVITIES
Kadri Manjunatha Temple..........6 D2
Milagres Church....................7 C3
St Aloysius College Chapel........8 C3
Sultan's Battery...................9 A1

SLEEPING
Hotel Manorama....................10 C3
Hotel Poonja International........11 C3
Hotel Srinivas....................12 C3
Hotel Surya.......................13 C3
Moti Mahal........................14 C3
Nalapad Residency.................15 C3
The Gateway Hotel.................16 B4

EATING
Café Coffee Day................(see 22)
Cochin Bakery.....................17 B4
Janatha Deluxe....................18 C3
Kadal.........................(see 15)
Lalith Bar & Restaurant...........19 C3
Naivedyam.........................20 C3
Pallkhi...........................21 D3
Pizza Hut.........................22 C1

DRINKING
Liquid Lounge.....................23 C3

TRANSPORT
City Bus Stand....................24 B4
Indian Airlines...................25 C1
Jet Airways.......................26 C2
KSRTC Bus Stand...................27 C2
Private Bus Company Offices.......28 C3
Private Bus Stand.................29 B4

kingfish from its extensive menu. The day's special seafood is usually the best bet.

Naivedyam (Hotel Mangalore International, KS Rao Rd; mains Rs40-90) Probably the best place in town to sample some vegetarian delicacies. It also has an interesting range of tandoori dishes.

Pallkhi (☎ 2444929; 3rd fl, Tej Towers, Balmatta Rd; mains Rs80-180; ☺ noon-3pm & 7-11pm) This rela-

tively smart and easygoing place, with stylish interiors and efficient service, has a good reputation for its seafood.

Kadal (Nalapad Residency, Lighthouse Hill Rd; mains Rs80-250; ☺ noon-3.30pm & 7.30-11pm) This high-rise restaurant has elegant and warmly lit interiors, with sweeping views of town and the sea beyond. Try the spicy chicken *varval*

SAVOURY SOUTH

Apart from all its touristy attractions, what really gives southern Karnataka its pride of place on the national stage is its diverse and distinctive cuisine. The highest-flying of them all are the spicy, tangy non-vegetarian dishes that emerge from the kitchens of the Kodagu region (p927). One delicacy that foodies can't stop raving about is *pandhi* curry, the flavourful signature dish of the Kodavas, made of pork and tempered with a mix of local spices. Mangalore out on the coast, refurbishes its regional identity with fiery Mangalorean cuisine, which features a train of dishes made from fresh marine catches of prawns, fish and crabs. Prawn *koliwada* is one of Mangalore's many dishes to have gathered a pan-Indian following, while typically indigenous delights such as the sinful chicken ghee roast can only be sampled if you happen to be passing through town.

Vegans take heart: southern Karnataka isn't only about exercising the canines. The temple town of Udupi (p934) has been nothing short of trademarked by thousands of restaurateurs peddling its legendary vegetarian thalis across India. Made fresh, these simple but lip-smacking spreads are bound to leave your taste buds tingling for more. *Bon Appetit!*

(a coastal Karnataka style of curry) or the fresh prawn dishes. Also enquire about the day's specials.

Liquid Lounge (☎ 4255175; Balmatta Rd; ☯ 7-11.30pm) The coolest (and loudest) pub in town, this place has funky posters and neon-lit interiors, including a backlit Les Paul guitar replica dangling above the bar! A good selection of beers is on offer, and its staff in floral shirts are a courteous lot.

For Western food, head to **Bharath Mall** (Bejai Main Rd; ☯ 10am-10pm), with branches of Pizza Hut and Café Coffee Day. For desserts, there's **Cochin Bakery** (AB Shetty Circle; cakes Rs10-20; ☯ 9.30am-9pm Mon-Sat), with its delicious puffs and cakes.

Getting There & Away

AIR

The **airport** (☎ 2254252; www.mangaloreairport.com) is in Bajpe, about 20km northeast of town. **Indian Airlines** (☎ 2254254; Hathill Rd) and **Jet Airways** (☎ 2253432; Ram Bhavan Complex, KS Rao Rd) both operate daily flights to Mumbai (from Rs725, 1½ hours). Jet Airways also flies daily to Bengaluru (from Rs725, one hour).

BUS

The **KSRTC bus stand** (☎ 2211243; Bejai Main Rd) is 3km north of the city centre; an autorickshaw there costs about Rs20. Be warned, however, that bus rides in or out of Mangalore can be harsh on your posteriors, as the roads are pot-hole hell, especially during the monsoons.

Several deluxe buses depart daily to Bengaluru (Rs421, eight hours), via Madikeri (Rs139, 3½ hours) and Mysore (Rs305, six hours). Semideluxe buses go daily to Hassan (Rs148, five hours). A 9.30pm semideluxe

bus heads to Panaji (Rs305, 10 hours). Private buses heading to destinations including Udupi, Dharmasthala and Jog Falls run from opposite the City bus stand. Tickets can be purchased at offices near Falnir Rd.

TRAIN

The main **train station** (☎ 2423137) is south of the city centre. The 12.15am *Netravati Express* stops at Margao in Goa (sleeper/2AC Rs197/715, 5½ hours), and continues to Mumbai (sleeper/2AC Rs369/1389, 16 hours). The 6.15pm *Malabar Express* heads to Thiruvananthapuram (Trivandrum; sleeper/2AC Rs261/966, 15 hours). The 9.30pm *West Coast Express* heads to Chennai (sleeper/2AC Rs322/1206, 18 hours).

Several Konkan Railway trains (to Mumbai, Margao, Ernakulam or Trivandrum) use **Kankanadi train station** (☎ 2437824), 5km east of the city.

Getting Around

To get to the airport, take buses 47B or 47C from the City bus stand, or catch a taxi (Rs400). Indian Airlines has a free airport shuttle for its passengers.

The City bus stand is opposite the State Bank of India, close to The Gateway Hotel. Flag fall for autorickshaws is Rs10, and they cost Rs6 per kilometre thereafter. For late-night travel, add on 50%. An autorickshaw to Kankanadi station costs around Rs40, or take bus 9 or 11B.

DHARMASTHALA

Move inland from Mangalore, and you'll come across a string of Jain temple towns, including

Venur, Mudabidri and Karkal. The most interesting is Dharmasthala, 75km east of Mangalore on the banks of the Netravathi River. Some 10,000 pilgrims pass through this town every day; during major holidays and major festivals (see p901), the footfall can go up tenfold.

Three elephants trunk out blessings to pilgrims outside the **Manjunatha Temple** (☎ 08256-277121; ☼ 6.30am-2pm & 5-9pm); men have to enter bare-chested, with legs covered. Simple free meals are available in the temple's **kitchen** (☼ 11.30am-2.15pm & 7.30-10pm), attached to a hall that can seat up to 3000.

If you're passing through town, also check out the 12m-high **statue of Bahubali** at Ratnagiri Hill; the **Manjusha Museum** (admission Rs2; ☼ 10am-1pm & 4.30-7pm Mon-Sat) housing a collection of Indian stone and metal sculptures, jewellery and local craft products; and, best of all, the **Car Museum** (admission Rs3; ☼ 8.30am-1pm & 2-7pm), home to 48 vintage autos, including a 1903 Renault and a monster 1954 Cadillac!

Should you wish to stay, contact the helpful **temple office** (☎ 08256-277121; www.shridharmasthala .org), which can arrange accommodation for Rs50 per person in one of its pilgrim lodges.

There are frequent buses to Dharmasthala from Mangalore (Rs35, two hours).

UDUPI (UDIPI)
☎ 0820

Udupi is home to the atmospheric, 13th-century **Krishna Temple** (☎ 2520598; Car St; ☼ 3.30am-10pm), which draws thousands of Hindu pilgrims through the year. Surrounded by eight *maths* (monasteries), it's a hive of activity, with musicians playing at the entrance, elephants on hand for *puja,* and pilgrims constantly coming and going. Non-Hindus are welcome inside the temple; men must enter bare-chested. Elaborate rituals are also performed in the temple during the Udupi Paryaya festival (see the boxed text, p901).

Near the temple, above the Corp Bank ATM, the **tourist office** (☎ 2529718; Krishna Bldg, Car St; ☼ 10am-5.30pm Mon-Sat) is a useful source of advice on Udupi and the surrounding area.

Udupi is famed for its vegetarian food – it's particularly well-known for its vegetarian thali. A good place to sample the local fair is **Woodlands** (Dr UR Rao Complex; mains Rs30-45; ☼ 8am-9.30pm), a short walk south of the temple.

Udupi is 58km north of Mangalore along the coast; regular buses ply the route (Rs30, 1½ hours).

MALPE
☎ 0820

A laid-back fishing harbour on the west coast 4km from Udupi, Malpe has fabulous beaches ideal for flopping about in the surf. A good place to stay is the **Paradise Isle Beach Resort** (☎ 2538777; www.theparadiseisle.com; s/d from Rs2500/3000; 🅿 🖳 🛜), right on the sands, which has comfortable rooms and offers a host of water sports for guests such as bumpy rides and jet skiing (Rs450 to Rs1600), and scuba-diving on request. Also enquire about its **house boats** (d incl full board Rs4000) in the backwaters of Hoode nearby.

From Malpe pier, you can take a boat (Rs70 per person) at 10.30am and 3.30pm out to tiny **St Mary's Island**, where Vasco da Gama supposedly landed in 1498. Over weekends the island is busy with locals inspecting the curious hexagonal basalt formations that jut out of the sand; during the week you might have it to yourself. An autorickshaw from Udupi to Malpe is around Rs50.

DEVBAGH

About 50km north of Gokarna, on one of the many islands that dot the Arabian Sea near the port town of Karwar, is the heavenly **Devbagh Beach Resort** (☎ 08382-221603; d incl full board Indian/foreigner from Rs2500/US$90; 🅿). It's the perfect place to cosy up with your favourite paperback or stroll aimlessly along the sands, while the roar of the breakers and the rustle of the forests work their sonic magic on you. Accommodation comes in a choice of cute and comfy fishermen's huts, cottages, log huts and houseboats. Water sports such as snorkelling and scooter rides cost extra.

You can reach Karwar by taking a slow bus from Gokarna (Rs29, 1½ hours) or Panaji (Rs42, three hours). Alternatively, take a taxi from either place. Call the resort in advance to arrange for a ferry to the island. Bookings can be made through **Jungle Lodges & Resorts Ltd** (Map p905; ☎ 080-25597021, 25597944; www.jungle lodges.com).

JOG FALLS
☎ 08186

Nominally the highest waterfalls in India, the Jog Falls only come to life during the monsoon. At other times, the Linganamakki Dam further up the Sharavati River limits the water flow. The tallest of the four falls is the Raja, which drops 293m.

BUFFALO SURFING

Call it an Indian take on the ancient Roman chariot race. Kambla, the traditional sport of buffalo racing, is a hugely popular pastime among villagers along the southern Karnataka coast, and indeed worth a watch, time and place permitting. Kambla first became popular in the early part of the 20th century, born out of the local farmers' habit of racing their buffaloes home after a day in the fields. Today the best of the races have hit the big time, with thousands of spectators attending each edition. Valuable racing buffaloes are pampered and prepared like thoroughbreds for the occasion; a good animal can cost more than Rs300,000!

Kambla events are held in the Dakshina Kannada region between November and March, usually on weekends. Parallel tracks are laid out in a paddy field, along which buffaloes hurtle towards the finish line. There are two versions: in one, the man runs alongside the buffalo; in the other, he rides on a board fixed to a ploughshare, literally surfing his way down the track behind the beasts!

Keep your cameras ready, but don't even think of getting in the buffaloes' way to take that prize-winning photo. The faster creatures can cover the 120m-odd distance through water and mud in around 14 seconds!

To get a good view the falls, bypass the scrappy area close to the bus stand and hike to the foot of the falls down a 1200-plus step path. It takes about an hour to get down and two to come up. Watch out for leeches in the wet season.

The **tourist office** (☎ 244732; ⏰ 10am-5pm Mon-Sat) is above the food stalls close to the bus stand. On site is the **KSTDC Hotel Mayura Gerusoppa** (☎ 244732; s/d Rs300/400), about 150m from the car park, with enormous, musty rooms.

Stalls near the bus stand serve omelettes, thalis, noodles and rice dishes, plus hot and cold drinks. KSTDC's mediocre **restaurant** (meals Rs30-50) is just next door.

Jog Falls has buses roughly every hour to Shimoga (Rs45, three hours), and three daily to Karwar via Kumta (Rs43, three hours), where you can change for Gokarna (Rs12, one hour). For Mangalore, change at Shimoga.

GOKARNA
☎ 08386

The quaint village of Gokarna, 50km south of Karwar, provides a fantastic glimpse into vibrant Hindu rituals and a medieval way of life. A low-key settlement on the coast, Gokarna is where hordes of pilgrims gather through the year to pay their respects in the ancient temples. During Hindu festivals such as Shivaratri and Ganesh Chaturthi (see the boxed text, p901), the village is at its dramatic best. While the main village is rather conservative in its outlook, a few out-of-town beaches provide an ideal opportunity for some carefree sunbaking.

Information
There are lots of places to access the internet, including many of the guest houses.
Pai STD Shop (Main St; ⏰ 9am-9pm) Changes cash and travellers cheques and gives advances on Visa.
Shree Radhakrishna Bookstore (Car St; ⏰ 10am-6pm) Good selection of new and secondhand books.
Sub post office (1st fl, cnr Car & Main Sts; 10am-4pm Mon-Sat)

Sights & Activities
TEMPLES
Foreigners and non-Hindus are not allowed inside Gokarna's temples. However, there are plenty of colourful rituals to be witnessed around town. At the western end of Car St is the **Mahabaleshwara Temple**, home to a revered lingam (phallic representation of Shiva). Nearby is the **Ganapati Temple**, while at the other end of the street is the **Venkataraman Temple**. About 100m further south is **Koorti Teertha**, the large temple tank (reservoir) where locals, pilgrims and immaculately dressed Brahmins perform their ablutions next to washermen on the ghats (steps or landings).

BEACHES
Gokarna's 'town beach' is dirty, and not meant for casual bathing. The best sands are due south, and can be reached via a footpath that begins south of the Ganapati Temple and heads down the coast (if you reach the bathing tank – or find yourself clawing up rocks – you're on the wrong path).

A 20-minute hike on the path brings you to the top of a barren headland with expansive

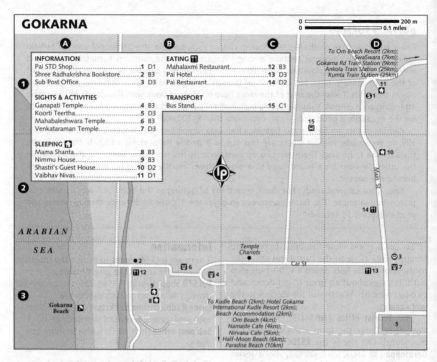

GOKARNA

INFORMATION		
Pai STD Shop	...1	D1
Shree Radhakrishna Bookstore	...2	B3
Sub Post Office	...3	D3
SIGHTS & ACTIVITIES		
Ganapati Temple	...4	B3
Koorti Teertha	...5	D3
Mahabaleshwara Temple	...6	B3
Venkataraman Temple	...7	D3
SLEEPING		
Mama Shanta	...8	B3
Nimmu House	...9	B3
Shastri's Guest House	...10	D2
Vaibhav Nivas	...11	D1
EATING		
Mahalaxmi Restaurant	...12	B3
Pai Hotel	...13	D3
Pai Restaurant	...14	D2
TRANSPORT		
Bus Stand	...15	C1

To Om Beach Resort (2km);
SwaSwara (7km);
Gokarna Rd Train Station (25km);
Ankola Train Station (25km);
Kumta Train Station (25km)

ARABIAN SEA

Gokarna Beach

Temple Chariots

Car St

To Kudle Beach (2km); Hotel Gokarna
International Kudle Resort (2km);
Beach Accommodation (2km);
Om Beach (4km);
Namaste Cafe (4km);
Nirvana Cafe (5km);
Half-Moon Beach (6km);
Paradise Beach (10km)

sea views. On the southern side is **Kudle** (kood-lay), the first of Gokarna's pristine beaches. Basic snacks, drinks and accommodation are available here.

South of Kudle Beach, a track climbs over the next headland, and a further 20-minute walk brings you to **Om Beach**, with a handful of chai shops and shacks. South of Om Beach lie the more isolated **Half-Moon Beach** and **Paradise Beach**, which come to life generally between November and March. They are a 30-minute and one-hour walk, respectively.

Depending on demand, fishing boats can ferry you from Gokarna Beach to Kudle (Rs100) and Om (Rs200). An autorickshaw from town to Om costs around Rs150.

Don't walk around after dark, and not alone at any time – it's easy to slip on the paths or get lost, and muggings have occurred. For a small fee, most lodges in Gokarna will safely store valuables and baggage while you chill out in the beach huts.

AYURVEDA

Quality ayurvedic therapies and packages are available at specialist ayurvedic centres

in SwaSwara (below) and Om Beach Resort (opposite).

Sleeping

With a few exceptions, the choice here is between a rudimentary beach shack or a basic but more comfortable room in town. Some hotels in town cater to pilgrims, and may come with certain rules and regs. Prices quoted here are for the high season (November to March), but may increase depending on demand.

BEACHES

Both Kudle and Om beaches have several shacks offering budget huts and rooms – shop around. Places also open up on Half-Moon and Paradise Beaches from November to March. Most places provide at least a bedroll; bring your own sheets or sleeping bag. Padlocks are provided and huts are secure. Communal washing and toilet facilities are simple.

Namaste Cafe (☎ 257141; Om Beach; deluxe hut Rs600, s without bathroom Rs150) In and out of season, Namaste is the place to hang. Its restaurant-bar cooks up great bites and is the premier

Om chill-out spot. In season it also offers basic huts (Rs50) at Paradise Beach and cottages at Namaste Farm (from Rs400) on the headland.

Nirvana Cafe (☎ 329851; Om Beach; cottage w Rs600, s without bathroom Rs250) Located on the southern end of Om is this pleasant option, with a handful of cute and rustic cottages with little sit-outs, nestled amid shady palms and groves.

Hotel Gokarna International Kudle Resort (☎ 257843; Kudle Beach; d with/without AC Rs1500/1200; 🉐) Run by the same management that owns Hotel Gokarna International in town, this midrange option has smart rooms and a lovely garden in front overlooking the sea. The waves wash up to its gates during high tide!

SwaSwara (☎ 257132, 0484-2668221; www.swaswara.com; Om Beach; d 7 nights Indian/foreigner Rs120,000/US$2300; 🉐 🖳 🖳) No short stays on offer here, but you can chill out at this elegant and superbly designed red laterite resort for a full week, and enjoy a holiday based around yoga and ayurvedic treatments. Rates include full board, transport, leisure activities and daily yoga sessions. Weeklong ayurvedic treatment packages kick off at around US$570.

GOKARNA

Vaibhav Nivas (☎ 256714; off Main St; d Rs200, s/d without bathroom Rs100/150; 🖳) The cell-like rooms at this place tucked away from the main drag come with mosquito nets and hot water in the morning. There's also a rooftop restaurant.

Mama Shanta (☎ 256213; r with/without bathroom Rs150/100) Just past Nimmu House is this rather gloomy and basic homestay, but the kindly old lady of the house does her best to make you feel at home. It's right next to the beach.

Shastri's Guest House (☎ 256220; dr_murti@rediffmail.com; Main St; s/d Rs150/200) This place has a hostel-like feel to it. The singles are tiny; the doubles in the new block out back are bright and airy, with squat loos. Some have balconies and palm-tree views.

Nimmu House (☎ 256730; nimmuhouse@yahoo.com; s/d old block Rs250/500, new block Rs300/1000; 🖳) Just off the foot trail along the beach is this pleasant option run by a friendly family. The rooms in the new block are nice, with tiled floors and balconies.

our pick **Om Beach Resort** (☎ 257052; www.ombeachresort.com; Bangle Gudde; d incl breakfast Indian/foreigner Rs2100/US$80; 🉐 🖳) This little jewel sits on a headland 2km out of Gokarna off the Om

Beach road. Set amid lawns and shady trees, its red-brick cottages are excellently designed, and its restaurant serves some delectable seafood. There's a professional ayurvedic centre on site, offering short sessions (from Rs750) as well as longer treatment packages.

Eating

The chai shops on all of the beaches rustle up basic snacks and meals.

Pai Hotel (Car St; mains Rs20-35; ☯ 6am-9.30pm) A good place for veg food.

Pai Restaurant (Main St; mains Rs25-40; ☯ 6.30am-9.30pm) This place draws in visiting pilgrims with its vegetarian fare.

Mahalaxmi Restaurant (meals Rs30-70) This popular hang-out promises 'all types of world famous dishes' (ie banana pancakes and cornflakes!) in myriad ways. The ambience, however, is relaxing.

Namaste Cafe (meals Rs30-80; ☯ 7am-11pm) Om Beach's social centre serves decent Western stand-bys – pizzas and burgers – and some Israeli specials.

Getting There & Away
BUS

From Gokarna's rudimentary **bus stand**, rickety buses rumble out to Karwar (Rs29, 1½ hours), which has connections to Goa. Direct buses run to Hubli (Rs92, four hours), where you can change for Hospet and Hampi. There are two direct evening buses to Bengaluru (semideluxe/sleeper Rs256/456, 12 hours).

TRAIN

Only slow passenger trains stop at **Gokarna Rd train station** (☎ 279487), 9km from town. A 10.40am train heads daily to Margao in Goa (Rs21, three hours). For Mangalore (Rs42, five hours), a train departs daily at 4.20pm.

A better idea is to head out by local bus to **Kumta station** (☎ 223820) 25km away, to board one of the expresses which stop there. From Kumta, the 2.14am *Matsyagandha Express* goes to Mangalore (sleeper Rs168, four hours); the return train leaves Kumta at 6.38pm for Margao (sleeper Rs141, 3½ hours). Many of the hotels and small travel agencies in Gokarna can book tickets. Ankola Station, 25km south of Gokarna, is also a convenient railhead.

Autorickshaws charge Rs100 to go to Gokarna Rd station. Buses go hourly (Rs7) and also meet arriving passenger trains. A bus to Kumta station is Rs12.

KARNATAKA

CENTRAL KARNATAKA

HAMPI

☎ 08394

Unreal and bewitching, the forlorn ruins of Hampi lie scattered over a landscape that leaves you spellbound the moment you cast your eyes on it. Heaps of giant boulders perch precariously over miles of undulated terrain, their rusty hues offset by jade-green palm groves, banana plantations and paddy fields, while the azure sky painted with fluffy white cirrus only adds to the magical atmosphere. A World Heritage Site, Hampi is a place where you can lose yourself among the ruins that come alive with a fascinating tale, or simply be mesmerised by the vagaries of nature, wondering how millions of years of volcanic activity and erosion could have resulted in a landscape so fascinating.

Hampi is a major pit stop on the traveller circuit, with the cooler months of November to March being the peak season. While it's possible to see the main sites in a day or two, this goes against Hampi's relaxed grain; plan on lingering for a while.

History

Hampi and its neighbouring areas find mention in the Hindu epic Ramayana as Kishkinda (see Anegundi p943), the realm of the monkey gods. In 1336, Telugu prince Harihararaya chose Hampi as the site for his new capital, Vijayanagar, which, over the next couple of centuries, grew into one of the largest Hindu empires in Indian history. By the 16th century, it was a thriving metropolis of about 500,000 people, its busy bazaars dabbling in international commerce, brimming with precious stones and merchants from faraway lands. All this, however, ended in a stroke in 1565, when a confederacy of Deccan sultanates razed Vijayanagar to the ground, striking it a death blow from which it never recovered.

A different battle rages in Hampi today, between conservationists bent on protecting Hampi's architectural heritage and the locals who have settled there. A master-plan is being prepared to notify all of Hampi's ruins as protected monuments, while resettling villagers at a new commercial-cum-residential complex away from the architectural enclosures. However, implementation is bound to take time, given the resistance from the locals who fear their livelihoods might be affected by the relocation process. **Global Heritage Fund** (www.globalheritagefund.org) has more details about Hampi's endangered heritage.

Orientation

Hampi Bazaar and the southern village of Kamalapuram are the two main points of entry to the ruins. Kamalapuram has the KSTDC Hotel and the archaeological museum. But the main travellers' scene is Hampi Bazaar, a village crammed with budget lodges, shops and restaurants, all dominated by the majestic Virupaksha Temple. The ruins are divided into two main areas: the Sacred Centre, around Hampi Bazaar; and the Royal Centre, towards Kamalapuram. To the northeast across the Tungabhadra River is the village of Anegundi (see p943).

Information

Andhra Bank (Map p941) Has an ATM off the entrance to Hampi Bazaar.

Aspiration Stores (Map p941; ☯ 10am-1pm & 4-8pm) For books on the area. Try *Hampi* by John M Fritz and George Michell, a good architectural study.

Canara Bank (Map p941; ☎ 241243; ☯ 11am-2pm Mon-Tue & Thu-Fri, 11am-12.30pm Sat) Changes travellers cheques and gives cash advances on credit cards.

Hampi Heritage Gallery (Map p941; ☯ 10am-1pm & 3-6pm) Sells books and offers half-day walking or cycling tours for Rs200.

Sree Rama Cyber Cafe (Map p941; per hr Rs30; ☯ 7am-11pm) The best of Hampi's internet cafes. It also burns CDs of digital snaps for Rs50.

Tourist office (Map p941; ☎ 241339; ☯ 10am-5.30pm Sat-Thu) Can arrange guides for Rs300/500 for a half/full day.

Dangers & Annoyances

Hampi is generally a safe, peaceful place. However, don't wander around the ruins after dark or alone, as muggings are not unreported. Besides, it's a dangerous terrain to get lost in, especially at night.

Sights & Activities

VIRUPAKSHA TEMPLE

The focal point of Hampi Bazaar is the **Virupaksha Temple** (Map p941; ☎ 241241; admission Rs2; ☯ dawn-dusk), one of the city's oldest structures. The main *gopuram*, almost 50m high, was built in 1442, with a smaller one added in 1510. The main shrine is dedicated to Virupaksha, a form of Shiva.

If Lakshmi (the temple elephant) and her attendant are around, she'll smooch (bless) you for a coin. The adorable Lakshmi gets her morning bath at 8.30am, just down the way by the river ghats.

To the south, overlooking Virupaksha Temple, **Hemakuta Hill** (Map p941) has a few early ruins, including monolithic sculptures of Narasimha (Vishnu in his man-lion incarnation) and Ganesha. It's worth the short walk up for the view over the bazaar. At the east end of Hampi Bazaar is a monolithic **Nandi statue** (Map p941), around which stand some of the colonnaded blocks of the ancient marketplace. This is the main location for **Vijaya Utsav**, the Hampi arts festival held in November (see p901).

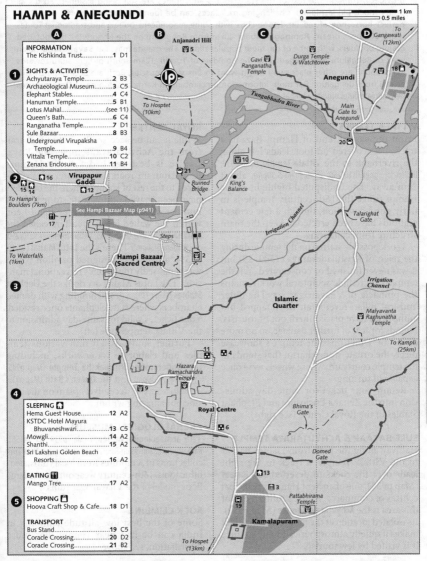

HAMPI & ANEGUNDI

INFORMATION
The Kishkinda Trust.....................**1** D1

SIGHTS & ACTIVITIES
Achyutaraya Temple.................**2** B3
Archaeological Museum.............**3** C5
Elephant Stables.......................**4** C4
Hanuman Temple......................**5** B1
Lotus Mahal.........................(see 11)
Queen's Bath............................**6** C4
Ranganatha Temple..................**7** D1
Sule Bazaar..............................**8** B3
Underground Virupaksha
   Temple.................................**9** B4
Vittala Temple.........................**10** C2
Zenana Enclosure....................**11** B4

SLEEPING
Hema Guest House...................**12** A2
KSTDC Hotel Mayura
   Bhuvaneshwari......................**13** C5
Mowgli....................................**14** A2
Shanthi....................................**15** A2
Sri Lakshmi Golden Beach
   Resorts.................................**16** A2

EATING
Mango Tree..............................**17** A2

SHOPPING
Hoova Craft Shop & Cafe.........**18** D1

TRANSPORT
Bus Stand................................**19** C5
Coracle Crossing.....................**20** D2
Coracle Crossing.....................**21** B2

Anjanadri Hill
To Gangawati (12km)
Gavi Ranganatha Temple
Durga Temple & Watchtower
Anegundi
To Hospet (10km)
Tungabhadra River
Main Gate to Anegundi
Virupapur Gaddi
Ruined Bridge
King's Balance
Irrigation Channel
Talarighat Gate
To Hampi's Boulders (7km)
See Hampi Bazaar Map (p941)
Steps
To Waterfalls (1km)
Hampi Bazaar (Sacred Centre)
Islamic Quarter
Irrigation Channel
Malyavanta Raghunatha Temple
To Kampli (25km)
Hazara Ramachandra Temple
Royal Centre
Bhima's Gate
Domed Gate
Pattabhirama Temple
Kamalapuram
To Hospet (13km)

KARNATAKA

CLIMBING IN KARNATAKA

Karnataka is a place which promises that perfect high, on the rocks! Magnificent bluffs and rounded boulders stand tall all over the state, offering some of India's best rock-climbing opportunities. However, bolting is limited, so bring a decent bouldering mat and plenty of gear from home – see p111.

Hampi is the undisputed bouldering capital of India, and Anegundi (p943), across the Tungabhadra River, is a place to indulge in some hassle-free climbing (rocks are graded and equipment provided). Through the rest of the state, routes and grades are still being assigned, so it's all pretty much old-fashioned. Challenging rock faces can be found in Badami (p946), where the perfect horseshoe of red sandstone cliffs with some magnificent bolted and traditional routes is any climber's dream. Ramnagar, about 40km from Bengaluru on the Mysore Rd, has outsized granite boulders, with some of the more popular climbs. The granite massif at Savandurga, 50km west of Bengaluru near Magadi, and the boulders of Turalli, 12km south of Bengaluru towards Kanakapura, are other places you might want to flex your muscles. Both are accessible by bus or taxi from Bengaluru. For more information on climbing in Karnataka, log on to Dreamroutes (www.dreamroutes.org/etc/allclimbs.html).

VITTALA TEMPLE

From the eastern end of Hampi Bazaar, a track, best covered on foot, leads left along the riverbank to the **Vittala Temple** (Map p939; Indian/foreigner Rs10/250; 8.30am-5.30pm), about 2km away. The undisputed highlight of the Hampi ruins, the 16th-century temple is in fairly good condition, though a few cement scaffolds have been erected to keep the main structure from collapsing.

Work possibly started on the temple during the reign of Krishnadevaraya (1509–29) but it was never finished or consecrated. Yet, the temple's incredible sculptural work remains the pinnacle of Vijayanagar art. The outer 'musical' pillars reverberate when tapped, but authorities have placed them out of tourists' bounds for fear of further damage, so no more do-re-mi. Don't miss the temple's showcase piece, the ornate stone chariot that stands in the temple courtyard, whose wheels were once capable of turning.

Retain your ticket for same-day admission into the Zenana Enclosure and Elephant Stables in the Royal Centre (see right).

SULE BAZAAR & ACHYUTARAYA TEMPLE

Halfway along the path from Hampi Bazaar to the Vittala Temple, a track to the right leads over the rocks to deserted **Sule Bazaar** (Map p939), one of ancient Hampi's principal centres of commerce. At the southern end of this area is the **Achyutaraya Temple** (Map p939). Its isolated location at the foot of Matanga Hill makes it quietly atmospheric, doubly so since it is visited by few tourists.

ROYAL CENTRE

While it can be accessed by a 2km foot trail from the Achyutaraya Temple, the Royal Centre is best reached via the Hampi–Kamalapuram road. It's a flatter area compared to the rest of Hampi, where the boulders have been shaved off to create stone walls. A number of Hampi's major sites stand here, within the walled ladies' quarters called the **Zenana Enclosure** (Map p939; Indian/foreigner Rs10/250; 8.30am-5.30pm). There's the **Lotus Mahal** (Map p939), a delicately designed pavilion which was supposedly the queen's recreational mansion. The Lotus Mahal overlooks the **Elephant Stables** (Map p939), a grand building with domed chambers where state elephants once resided. Your ticket is valid for same-day admission to the Vittala Temple (see left).

Further south, you'll find various temples and elaborate waterworks, including the **Underground Virupaksha Temple** (Map p941; 8.30am-5.30pm) and the **Queen's Bath** (Map p939; 8.30am-5.30pm), deceptively plain on the outside but amazing within.

ARCHAEOLOGICAL MUSEUM

The **archaeological museum** (Map p939; 241561; Kamalapuram; admission Rs5; 10am-5pm Sat-Thu) has collections of sculptures from local ruins, neolithic tools, 16th-century weaponry and a large floor model of the Vijayanagar ruins.

ROCK CLIMBING

Some of the best low-altitude climbing in India can be had near Hampi. For more information, see above.

Sleeping

There's little to choose from between many of the basic rooms in Hampi Bazaar and Virupapur Gaddi. If you need AC and cable TV, stay in Kamalapuram (p942). Prices listed can shoot up by 50% or more during Christmas, and drop just as dramatically in the low season (April to September).

Most guest houses display notices saying use of narcotics and alcohol are strictly prohibited. Trip on nature instead!

HAMPI BAZAAR

All of the following places are shown on Map p941.

Shanthi Guest House (☎ 241568; s/d Rs250/300, without bathroom Rs150/250) An oldie but a goodie, Shanthi offers a peaceful courtyard with a swing chair, and has plastic creepers and divine posters decorating its basic rooms. There's a small shop that operates on an honour system.

Gopi Guest House (☎ 241695; kirangopi2002@yahoo .com; d Rs300; ☐) The Gopi empire has expanded to a renovated block across the road, which contains four pleasant en suite rooms. The rooftop room, equipped with a carom board and guitar, is a nice place to hang out. It also makes a mean cup of espresso (Rs30).

Vicky's (☎ 241694; vikkyhampi@yahoo.co.in; d Rs350; ☐) One of the village's larger operations done up in pop purple and green, with 10 brightly painted and tiled rooms, internet access and the requisite rooftop cafe.

Pushpa Guest House (☎ 241440; d/tr Rs400/500) The fresh new rooms here have pink walls and brightly printed upholstery, with a cordial family playing host. The lovely sit-out on the first floor gives it an edge over its competitors.

Padma Guest House (☎ 241331; d Rs400-800) The astute Padma might have got her spellings wrong ('Recommendation by Lovely Plant', reads her business card!), but the tidy rooms are more than inviting. Try one upstairs for great views of the Virupaksha Temple.

Other good options:

Sudha Guest House (☎ 652752; d from Rs200) Has a good family vibe and a riverside location.

Rama Guest House (☎ 241962; s/d Rs300/400) Some rooms are a little low on light, but the cool rooftop cafe seals the deal.

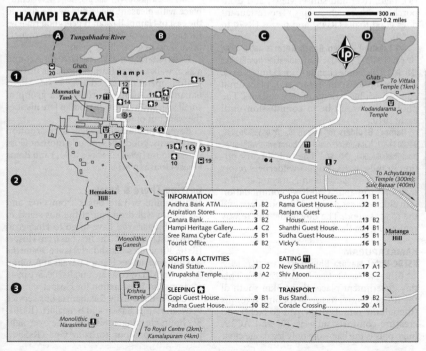

HAMPI BAZAAR

INFORMATION		
Andhra Bank ATM	1	B2
Aspiration Stores	2	B2
Canara Bank	3	B2
Hampi Heritage Gallery	4	C2
Sree Rama Cyber Cafe	5	B1
Tourist Office	6	B2

SIGHTS & ACTIVITIES		
Nandi Statue	7	D2
Virupaksha Temple	8	A2

SLEEPING		
Gopi Guest House	9	B1
Padma Guest House	10	B2
Pushpa Guest House	11	B1
Rama Guest House	12	B1
Ranjana Guest House	13	B2
Shanthi Guest House	14	B1
Sudha Guest House	15	B1
Vicky's	16	B1

EATING		
New Shanthi	17	A1
Shiv Moon	18	C2

TRANSPORT		
Bus Stand	19	B2
Coracle Crossing	20	A1

Tungabhadra River
Ghats
Hampi
Manmatha Tank
Ghats
To Vittala Temple (1km)
Kodandarama Temple
Hemakuta Hill
Monolithic Ganesh
Matanga Hill
To Achyutaraya Temple (300m); Sule Bazaar (400m)
Krishna Temple
Monolithic Narasimha
To Royal Centre (2km); Kamalapuram (4km)

0 300 m
0 0.2 miles

KARNATAKA

Ranjana Guest House (☎ 241696; d Rs400-600) On par with Padma Guest House. The terrace rooms have great views and TV.

VIRUPAPUR GADDI

Many travellers prefer the tranquil atmosphere of Virupapur Gaddi, across the river from Hampi Bazaar. A small boat (Rs10) shuttles frequently across the river from 7am to 6pm. During the monsoon, the river runs high and ferry services may be suspended.

Hema Guest House (Map p939; ☎ 9449103008; dm/bungalows Rs100/500) One of Virupapur Gaddi's most popular spots, this place has rows of cute and comfy cottages laid out in a shady grove, and scores with its informal restaurant in a beautiful wooden belvedere overlooking the river.

Mowgli (Map p939; ☎ 329844; hampimowgli@hotmail.com; d from Rs250; 🖳) With prime views across the rice fields, shady gardens sheltering hammocks, and thatched-roof bungalows, this is a top-class chill-out spot. The rooms with views are the most expensive, around Rs500.

Shanthi (Map p939; ☎ 325352; cottages Rs600, d without bathroom Rs300) Shanthi's bungalows have rice-field, river and sunset views, and front porches with couch swings. The restaurant does good thalis (Rs45) and pizzas (Rs70 to Rs85).

Sri Lakshmi Golden Beach Resorts (Map p939; ☎ 08533-287008, 9448436537; d incl breakfast from Rs2000; 🔀 🖳) A welcome change from Hampi's basic sleeping options, this resort-style place amid paddy fields has a range of cosy cottages. The pool, sadly, won't be in commission until early 2010.

Hampi's Boulders (off Map p939; ☎ 08539-265939, 9448034202; Narayanpet; d incl full board with/without AC from Rs8000/6000; 🔀 🖳) The only luxury option in these parts, this ecowilderness resort sits amid leafy gardens in Narayanpet, 7km west of Virupapur Gaddi. Accommodation is in chic cottages designed like boulders, and the food is good. The downside: you're way removed from the buzz.

KAMALAPURAM

KSTDC Hotel Mayura Bhuvaneshwari (Map p939; ☎ 08394-241574; d/tr from Rs825/1125; 🔀) This tidy government place, about 3km south of the Royal Centre, has well-appointed rooms (though the murals make you go bleh!) and creature comforts such as TV and AC. A huge plus is the bar – the only legal one close to Hampi – and ayurvedic sessions (from Rs1550) on request.

Eating

With one exception, Hampi is not renowned for its restaurants. Due to Hampi's religious significance, meat is usually off the menu, and alcohol is banned. Places are open from 7am to 10pm.

New Shanthi (Map p941; mains Rs30-50) A hippie vibe, complete with trance music and acid-blue lights, hangs over this popular option serving a good selection of juices and shakes. The bakery churns out passable cookies and crumbles.

ourpick Mango Tree (Map p939; mains Rs30-90) Creativity blends with culinary excellence at this rural-themed chill-out joint, spread out under the eponymous mango tree by the riverbanks. The walk out here is through a banana plantation, and the food is delicious – the restaurant does lip-smacking dosas for breakfast and dinner. The ambience is simply overwhelming, and the terraced seating perfect for whiling away a lazy afternoon, book in hand.

Shiv Moon (Map p941; mains Rs35-90) This friendly place with pleasant views sits by the river to the east of Hampi Bazaar. It gets good reviews for the quality of its food, though the owners often tend to get politely pushy.

Waterfalls (off Map p939; mains Rs40-60) Around a 2km walk west of Hampi Bazaar is this appealing operation tucked away beside shady banana plantations en route to a group of small waterfalls. The tasty Indian fare justifies the walk out of town.

Several of Hampi's lodges sport rooftop restaurants; good ones include those at Gopi Guest House (p941), Vicky's (p941) and Rama Guest House (p941).

Getting There & Away

While some private buses from Goa and Bengaluru will drop you at the bus stand in Hampi Bazaar, you have to go to Hospet to catch most buses out. The first bus from Hospet (Rs10, 30 minutes, half-hourly) is at 6.30am; the last one back leaves Hampi Bazaar at 8.30pm. An autorickshaw costs around Rs100. See p944 for transport information for Hospet.

KSRTC has a daily Rajahamsa bus service between Hampi Bazaar and Bengaluru (Rs301, 8½ hours) leaving at 8.45pm. The overnight private sleeper bus to/from Goa (Rs550), which runs November to March, is a popular option – but don't expect a deep sleep. Numerous travel agents in Hampi Bazaar are eager to book onward bus, train and plane tickets, or arrange a car and driver.

Getting Around

Once you've seen the main sights in Hampi, exploring the rest of the ruins by bicycle is the thing to do. The key monuments are haphazardly signposted all over the site; while they're not adequate, you shouldn't get lost. Bicycles cost about Rs30 per day in Hampi Bazaar; mopeds can be hired for around Rs200, plus petrol. You can take your bicycle or motorbike (extra Rs10) across the river on the boat.

Walking is the only way to see all the nooks and crannies, but expect to cover at least 7km just to see the major ruins. Autorickshaws and taxis are available for sightseeing, and will drop you as close to each of the major ruins as they can. A five-hour autorickshaw tour costs Rs300.

Organised tours depart from Hospet; see p944 for details.

AROUND HAMPI
Anegundi

Across the Tungabhadra River, about 5km northeast of Hampi Bazaar, sits Anegundi, an ancient fortified village that's part of the Hampi World Heritage Site but predates Hampi by way of human habitation. Gifted with a landscape similar to Hampi, quainter Anegundi has been spared the blight of commercialisation, which is why it remains a chosen getaway for those who want to soak up the local atmosphere without having to put up with the touristy vibe.

SIGHTS & ACTIVITIES

Mythically referred to as Kishkinda, the kingdom of the monkey gods, Anegundi retains many of its historic monuments, such as sections of its defensive wall and gates, and the **Ranganatha Temple** (Map p939; ☼ dawn-dusk) devoted to Rama. The whitewashed **Hanuman Temple** (Map p939; ☼ dawn-dusk), accessible by a 570-step climb atop the Anjanadri Hill, has fine views of the rugged terrain around. Many believe this is the birthplace of Hanuman, the Hindu monkey god who was Rama's devotee and helped him in his mission against Ravana. The hike up is pleasant, though you'll be courted by impish monkeys, and within the temple you'll find a horde of chillum-puffing resident sadhus!

The **Kishkinda Trust** (TKT; ☎ 08533-267791, 9449284496; www.thekishkindatrust.org), a nonprofit organisation that manages tourism in Anegundi, has a slew of nature and adventure activities that you can indulge in. Events include rock climbing, camping, trekking, rappelling, and zoomering. Equipment and trained instructors are provided. A string of cultural events, such as performing arts sessions and classical and folk music concerts, are also conducted from time to time. For more information on TKT, see the boxed text, p944.

SLEEPING & EATING

Anegundi has several homestays, managed by TKT. Contact the trust for bookings.

Champa Guest House (d incl breakfast Rs600) Champa offers basic but pleasant accommodation in two rooms, and is looked after by an affable village family.

TEMA Guest House (d incl breakfast Rs600; ▢) For an alternative experience try the two rooms here, attached to the trust's information centre, where you can read up on local heritage and sit in during local community interaction programs.

Naidile Guest House (r Rs1000) A charmingly rustic air hangs over this place, a renovated village home in the heart of Anegundi where you can savour all the sights and sounds of the ancient village. It can sleep up to five people.

The **Hoova Craft Shop & Cafe** (dishes Rs20-40; ☼ 9.30am-5pm Mon-Sat, 9.30am-2pm Sun) A lovely place for a laid-back meal or snack. You can also pick up sundry souvenirs made by women's self-help groups of the village here.

Meals are also provided by the guest houses upon prior notice.

GETTING THERE & AWAY

Anegundi can be reached by crossing the river on a coracle (Rs10) from the pier east of the Vittala Temple. If and when the new concrete bridge at the site is completed, you can simply cycle across.

Alternately, you can get to Anegundi by taking a bus (Rs20, one hour) from Hospet.

HOSPET
☎ 08394 / pop 164,200

This busy regional centre is the transport hub for Hampi. There's no reason to linger unless

KARNATAKA

THE KISHKINDA TRUST

Since 1995, the **Kishkinda Trust** (TKT; ☎ 08533-267791, 9449284496; www.thekishkindatrust.org) has been actively involved in promoting rural tourism, sustainable development and women's empowerment in Anegundi, apart from preserving the architectural and living heritage of the Hampi World Heritage Site. The first project in 1997 created a cottage industry of crafts using locally produced cloth, banana fibre and river grass. It now employs over 600 women, and the attractive crafts produced are marketed in ethnic product outlets across India, along with the village outlet at the **Hoova Crafts Shop & Cafe**.

The trust's other projects include holding cottage industry workshops and sensitising the village folk in regard to self-help and sustainable ecotourism. Its home-stay program has met with enormous success, and the revenue generated through tourism now goes into community welfare, training and empowerment of village personnel as well as running interaction programs in village schools. An information and interpretation centre has also been set up, while more self-help projects have recently taken their positions at the starting line.

---

you desire an air-conditioned hotel room and cable TV. The Muslim festival of Muharram (see the boxed text, p901), however, brings things to life in this otherwise mundane place.

Information

Internet joints are common, with connections costing Rs30 per hour. ATMs are common too. The bus-stand cloakroom holds bags for Rs10 per day.

KSTDC tourist office (☎ 228537, 221008; Shanbag Circle; ☺ 10am-5.30pm Mon-Sat) Offers a Hampi tour (Rs175), daily from 9.30am to 5.30pm. The quality of guides varies. Call ahead as tours won't run with fewer than 10 people.

State Bank of India (☎ 228576; Station Rd; ☺ 10.30am-4pm Mon-Sat) Changes currency.

Sleeping & Eating

Hotel Malligi (☎ 228101; www.malligihotels.com; Jabunatha Rd; d with/without AC from Rs1500/650; ✉ 🖳 🕿) Only the more expensive rooms here, some with a vague contemporary look, are worth it. A couple of decent restaurants, a swimming pool (Rs35 for nonguests and guests in the cheapest rooms) and a gym on site.

Hotel Priyadarshini (☎ 228838; www.priyain hampi.com; Station Rd; s/d from Rs1300/1500; ✉ 🖳) Conveniently located between the bus and train stations, the fresh rooms here have balconies and TV. The outdoor nonveg restaurant-bar Manasa (mains Rs60 to Rs120) has a good menu.

Udupi Sri Krishna Bhavan (meals Rs15-45; ☺ 6am-11pm) Opposite the bus stand, this clean spot dishes out Indian vegie fare, including thalis for Rs27.

Getting There & Away

BUS

The **bus stand** (☎ 228802) has services to Hampi from Bay 10 every half-hour (Rs10, 30 minutes). Several express buses run to Bengaluru (ordinary/deluxe Rs320/400, nine hours); two overnight buses head to Panaji (Rs215, 11 hours) via Margao. Two buses go to Badami (Rs130, six hours), or you can take a bus to Gadag (Rs52, 2½ hours) and transfer. There are frequent buses to Bijapur (Rs130, six hours) and overnight services to Hyderabad (Rs340, 10 hours). For Gokarna, take a bus to Hubli (Rs82, 4½ hours) and change. For Mangalore or Hassan, take a morning bus to Shimoga (Rs145, five hours) and change there.

TRAIN

Hospet's **train station** (☎ 228360) is a Rs15 autorickshaw journey from town. The daily *Hampi Express* heads to Hubli at 7.50am (2nd class Rs43, 3½ hours) and then to Bengaluru at 7.50pm (sleeper/2AC Rs193/738, 10 hours). Every Monday, Wednesday, Thursday and Saturday, a 6.30am express train heads to Vasco da Gama (sleeper/2AC Rs178/643, 8½ hours).

To get to Badami, catch a Hubli train to Gadag and change there.

HUBLI

☎ 0836 / pop 786,100

The prosperous city of Hubli is a hub for rail routes from Mumbai to Bengaluru, Goa and northern Karnataka. Several hotels and restaurants sit close to the train station; others surround the old bus stand, a 15-minute walk from the train station. Long-distance buses usually stop here before heading to the new bus stand 2km away, where there are few amenities.

Information

ATMs are easy to find. There are several internet cafes too, charging around Rs20 per hour.

Sleeping & Eating

Hotel Ajanta (☎ 2362216; Jayachamaraj Nagar; s/d from Rs150/210) This well-run place near the train station has basic, functional rooms. Its ground-floor restaurant (thalis Rs27) is packed at lunch.

Hotel Samrat Ashok (☎ 2362380; Lamington Rd; s/d from Rs425/810; 🖳) Above a bookshop on Lamington Rd, this tidy place is handy for both the train station and old bus stand.

Sagar Palace (Jayachamaraj Nagar; mains Rs30-70; 🕙 11am-3.30pm & 7-11.30pm) A pure-veg restaurant and bar serving good food, including rum-spiked ice-cream sundaes!

Getting There & Away

BUS

Long-distance buses depart from the **new bus stand** (☎ 2221085). There are numerous semideluxe services to Bengaluru (Rs370, 10 hours) and Hospet (Rs85, four hours); one bus goes daily to Mangalore (Rs331, 10 hours). Buses also head to Borivali in Mumbai (semideluxe/sleeper Rs484/531, 14 hours, four daily), Mysore (Rs231, 12 hours, one daily), Bijapur (Rs100, six hours, several daily), Gokarna (Rs92, five hours, two daily) and Panaji (Rs113, six hours, six daily), as well as Vasco da Gama and Margao.

Private deluxe buses to Bengaluru (Rs335) run from opposite the **old bus stand** (Lamington Rd), 2km away.

TRAIN

From the train station, which has a **reservation office** (☎ 2345333; 🕙 8am-8pm), three expresses head to Hospet (2nd class Rs47, 3½ hours). Five expresses run daily to Bengaluru (sleeper/2AC Rs241/936, 11 hours); and

---

'THIS PLACE NATURALLY CASTS ITS SPELL ON YOU'

At 36, H Virupaksha, a proud resident of Anegundi, comes across as a personification of enthusiasm. Cross the Tungabhadra River from Hampi and amble down the road towards Anegundi, and there's every chance you'll run into this spry son-of-the-soil patrolling the magical landscape on his motorbike, camera slung across his shoulder, going about his mission to put his native village firmly on the tourism map. He's out to make a difference, and there's simply no stopping him.

Born to a humble family, Virupaksha – like any other aspiring youth – had left his birthplace in 1991 to pursue big city dreams. 'But I just couldn't stay away,' he admits, sitting by the river, his gaze fixed on the boulder-strewn horizon far away. 'I was craving for the sense of peace this place gives you. I realised that this was the only place on earth where I could be truly happy and at peace with myself. It's one of those few places still largely out of mobile phone coverage; no ringtones to disturb the sound of the flowing waters. You know what I mean?' he smiles.

Ever since he returned in 1997, Virupaksha has trained himself in the tourism trade. Fluent in English, he's now a qualified guide, and plans to pursue a further course in front-office management. 'Tourism is our chief source of income, and we have to know how to best make use of our natural and historic resources to draw in people,' he says. Now associated with **The Kishkinda Trust** (see the boxed text, opposite), Virupaksha goes about informing his fellow villagers about the benefits of sustainable ecotourism, and hopes that his village will wake to a new and prosperous dawn very soon. 'This place naturally casts its spell on you,' he says. 'With a little bit of organisation, we can extend its charm to many more people, don't you think?'

A keen nature lover and photographer, Virupaksha also offers professional services related to camping, trekking, birdwatching and documentary filmmaking. He scouted for the 2005 Jackie Chan production The Myth, a part of which was shot in Hampi, and is now making a string of short films on Anegundi to upload on YouTube! So if you touch base at The Kishkinda Trust, get in touch with him for that really memorable excursion in Hampi's magical backyards. 'I'm also a trained snake-catcher; I rescue snakes trapped within the village and release them in the wilds,' he grins. Feeling adventurous, anyone?

there's one direct train to Mumbai (sleeper/ 2AC Rs276/1026, 14 hours). Trains run on Monday, Wednesday, Thursday and Saturday to Vasco de Gama (via Margao; sleeper/2AC Rs134/468, six hours).

NORTHERN KARNATAKA

BADAMI

☎ 08357 / pop 25,800

Now in a shambles, scruffy Badami is a far cry from its glory days, when it was the capital of the mighty Chalukya empire. Its importance lasted from the 6th to the 8th century AD, when the Chalukya kings shifted the capital here from Aihole, with a satellite capital in Pattadakal. The relocation of power saw Badami being scattered with several temples and, most importantly, a group of magnificent rock-cut cave temples, which are the main reason for coming to the village today.

History

Badami was the Chalukyan capital from about AD 540 to 757. At its height, the empire was enormous, stretching from Kanchipuram in Tamil Nadu to the Narmada River in Gujarat. Badami eventually fell to the Rashtrakutas, and changed hands several times thereafter. Everyone from the Chalukyas of Kalyan (a separate branch of the Western Chalukyas), the Kalachuryas, the Yadavas of Devagiri, the Vijayanagar empire, the Adil Shahi kings of Bijapur and the Marathas held sway over Badami in the years to come. The handing-down of Badami is chronicled by the numerous temples, fortifications, carvings and inscriptions that stand around the village, dating not just from the Chalukyan period but also from other times when the site was occupied.

The sculptural legacy left by the Chalukya artisans in Badami includes some of the earliest and finest examples of Dravidian temples and rock-cut caves. During Badami's heydays, Aihole and Pattadakal served as trial grounds for new temple architecture; the latter is now a World Heritage Site.

Orientation & Information

Station Rd, Badami's busy main street, has several hotels and restaurants; the old village is between this road and the hilltop caves. The **tourist office** (☎ 220414; Ramdurg Rd; ☼ 10am-

5.30pm Mon-Sat), in the KSTDC Hotel Mayura Chalukya, is not very useful.

Mookambika Deluxe hotel changes currency for guests, but at a lousy rate.

Internet is available at **Hotel Rajsangam** (Station Rd; per hr Rs60) in the town centre.

State Bank of India has an ATM that is located on Ramdurg Rd.

Sights

CAVES

Badami's highlight is its beautiful **cave temples** (Indian/foreigner Rs5/100; ☼ dawn-dusk). Non-pushy and informed guides ask Rs200 for a tour of the caves, or Rs300 for the whole site. Watch out for pesky monkeys!

Cave One

This cave, just above the entrance to the complex, is dedicated to Shiva. It's the oldest of the four caves, probably carved in the latter half of the 6th century. On the wall to the right of the porch is a captivating image of Nataraja striking 81 dance poses.

On the right of the porch area is a huge figure of Ardhanarishvara. The right half of the figure shows features of Shiva, such as matted hair and a third eye, while the left half has aspects of his wife Parvati. On the opposite wall is a large image of Harihara; the right half represents Shiva and the left half Vishnu.

Cave Two

Dedicated to Vishnu, this cave is simpler in design. As with Caves One and Three, the front edge of the platform is decorated with images of pot-bellied dwarfs in various poses. Four pillars support the verandah, their tops carved with a bracket in the shape of a *yali* (mythical lion creature). On the left wall of the porch is the bull-headed figure of Varaha, an incarnation of Vishnu and the emblem of the Chalukya empire. To his left is Naga, a snake with a human face. On the right wall is a large sculpture of Trivikrama, another incarnation of Vishnu. The ceiling panels contain images of Vishnu riding Garuda, *gandharva* (demi-god) couples, swastikas and 16 fish arranged in a wheel.

Between the second and third caves are two sets of steps to the right. The first leads to a **natural cave**, where resident monkeys laze around. The eastern wall of this cave contains a small image of Padmapani (an incarnation of the Buddha). The second set of steps –

sadly, barred by a gate – leads to the hilltop **South Fort**.

Cave Three

This cave, carved in AD 578 under the orders of Mangalesha, the brother of King Kirtivarma, contains some sculptural highlights.

On the left-hand wall is a carving of Vishnu, to whom the cave is dedicated, sitting on a snake. Nearby is an image of Varaha with four hands. The pillars have carved brackets in the shape of *yalis;* the sides are also carved. The ceiling panels contain images, including Indra riding an elephant, Shiva on a bull and Brahma on a swan.

Cave Four

Dedicated to Jainism, Cave Four is the smallest of the set and was carved between the 7th and 8th centuries. The pillars, with their roaring *yalis,* are of similar design to the other caves. The right wall has an image of Suparshvanatha (the seventh Jain *tirthankar*) surrounded by 24 Jain *tirthankars*. The inner sanctum contains an image of Adinath, the first Jain *tirthankar*.

OTHER SIGHTS

Badami's caves overlook the 5th-century **Agastyatirtha Tank** and the waterside **Bhutanatha temples**. On the other side of the tank is an **archaeological museum** (☎ 220157; admission Rs2; ☯ 10am-5pm Sat-Thu), which houses superb examples of local sculpture, including a remarkably explicit Lajja-Gauri image of a fertility cult that once flourished in the area. The stairway just behind the museum climbs through a dramatic sandstone chasm and fortified gateways to reach the various temples and ruins of the **North Fort**.

It's also worth exploring Badami's **laneways**, where you'll find old houses with brightly painted and carved wooden doorways, the occasional Chalukyan ruin and, of course, flocks of curious children.

Activities

Badami offers some great low-altitude climbing. For more information, see p940.

Sleeping

Many of Badami's hotels offer discounts in the low season.

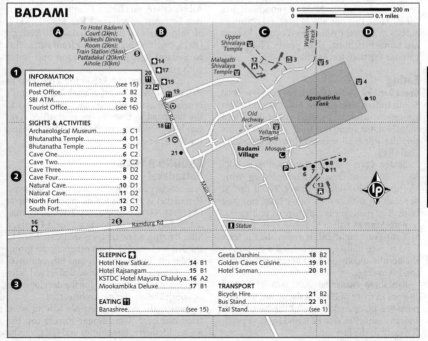

BADAMI

0 — 200 m
0 — 0.1 miles

To Hotel Badami Court (2km); Pulikeshi Dining Room (2km); Train Station (5km); Pattadakal (20km); Aihole (30km)

INFORMATION
Internet..............................(see 15)
Post Office...........................1 B2
SBI ATM...............................2 B2
Tourist Office.......................(see 16)

SIGHTS & ACTIVITIES
Archaeological Museum.......3 C1
Bhutanatha Temple..............4 D1
Bhutanatha Temple..............5 D1
Cave One...............................6 C2
Cave Two...............................7 C2
Cave Three.............................8 D2
Cave Four...............................9 D2
Natural Cave........................10 D1
Natural Cave........................11 D2
North Fort............................12 C1
South Fort............................13 D2

Ramdurg Rd

Statue

SLEEPING
Hotel New Satkar................14 B1
Hotel Rajsangam.................15 B1
KSTDC Hotel Mayura Chalukya..16 A2
Mookambika Deluxe............17 B1

EATING
Banashree..........................(see 15)

Geeta Darshini....................18 B2
Golden Caves Cuisine..........19 B1
Hotel Sanman.....................20 B1

TRANSPORT
Bicycle Hire.........................21 B2
Bus Stand............................22 B1
Taxi Stand.........................(see 1)

Upper Shivalaya Temple

Walking Track

Malagatti Shivalaya Temple

Agastyatirtha Tank

Station Rd

Old Archway

Yellama Temple

Badami Village

Mosque

Main Rd

KARNATAKA

Hotel New Satkar (☎ 220417; Station Rd; s/d from Rs250/350; ✕) Not the best of places, but at least the rooms are clean and the staff efficient. The best holes, painted in beige and cream, are on the 1st floor.

Mookambika Deluxe (☎ 220067; fax 220106; Station Rd; s/d from Rs350/550; ✕) Faux antique lampshades hang in the corridors of this friendly hotel, leading to comfy rooms done up in matte orange and green. It's Badami's de facto tourist office, and can arrange taxis and guides.

KSTDC Hotel Mayura Chalukya (☎ 220046; Ramdurg Rd) This place with large and pleasant rooms, located in a quiet compound away from the bustle, was undergoing renovation at the time of research, and should be open by November 2009.

Hotel Rajsangam (☎ 221991; www.hotelrajsangam .com; Station Rd; d Indian/foreigner from Rs800/US$20; ✕ 🖳 🖳) This midrange place with good rooms (the best are the quieter deluxe ones at the back) is a useful addition to Badami's hotel scene. The defunct plunge pool on the roof should be back in commission by mid-2009 – brilliant views on offer here.

Hotel Badami Court (☎ 220230; Station Rd; s/d incl breakfast from Rs2500/3200; ✕ 🖳) As good as it gets for Badami, this one sits in pastoral countryside 2km from the noisy town centre. Rooms are more functional than plush. Nonguests can use the pool for Rs100.

Eating

Geeta Darshini (Station Rd; snacks Rs6-15; ✕ 7am-9pm) South Indian bites such as *idlis* (South Indian spongy, round, fermented rice cakes) and *masala dosas* come out thick and fast at this popular joint, all washed down with milky chai (Rs5).

Golden Caves Cuisine (Station Rd; mains Rs30-80; ✕ 9am-11pm) Desperately missing your Continental breakfast platter? You'll find it here, along with several other tasty non-veg bites. The manager is a picture of politeness.

Hotel Sanman (Station Rd; mains Rs35-60; ✕ 10am-11.30pm) You might call it ropey, but it feels kind of nice to disappear behind a curtain in the booths and sip on your beer in peace. The food is average.

Banashree (Station Rd; mains Rs40-70; ✕ 7am-10.30pm) In front of Hotel Rajsangam, this tidy pure-veg place makes one of the best North Indian thalis (Rs65) to be found in these parts. It's tasty to the last morsel.

Pulikeshi Dining Room (mains Rs60-150; ✕ 24hr) People rave about the good range of Continental and Indian dishes at this silver-service restaurant in Hotel Badami Court.

Getting There & Away

Direct buses shuffle off from the Badami **bus stand** (Station Rd) to Bijapur (Rs84, four hours, two daily), Hubli (Rs65, three hours, seven daily) and Bengaluru (semideluxe/sleeper Rs276/453, 12 hours, four daily). Three buses go direct to Hospet (Rs130, six hours), or you can catch any of the buses to Gadag (Rs46, two hours) and transfer. The tarmac's rough down this lane; mind your bum!

The medium-gauge train line to Badami was being upgraded to broad-gauge during research. If and when it meets its 2009 deadline, direct trains should begin plying to Hubli and Hospet.

Getting Around

Exploring the surrounding area by local bus is easy, since they're moderately frequent and usually run on time. You can visit both Aihole and Pattadakal in a day from Badami if you get moving early; it's best to start with Aihole (Rs18, one hour). Frequent buses then run between Aihole and Pattadakal (Rs12, 30 minutes), and from Pattadakal to Badami (Rs15, one hour). The last bus from Pattadakal to Badami is at 8pm. Take food and water with you.

Taxis cost around Rs800 for a day trip to Pattadakal, Aihole and Mahakuta. Badami's hotels can arrange taxis; alternatively, go to the **taxi stand** in front of the post office. You can hire bicycles from Station Rd in Badami for Rs10 per day.

AROUND BADAMI
Pattadakal

A secondary capital of the Badami Chalukyas, Pattadakal is known for its group of **temples** (☎ 08357-243118; Indian/foreigner Rs10/250; ✕ 6am-6pm), which are collectively a World Heritage Site. Barring a few temples that date back to the 3rd century AD, most others in the group were built during the 7th and 8th centuries AD. Historians believe Pattadakal served as an important testing ground for the development of South Indian temple architecture.

Two main types of temple towers were tried out here. Curvilinear towers top the Kadasiddeshwra, Jambulinga and Galaganatha temples, while square roofs and receding tiers are used in the Mallikarjuna, Sangameshwara and Virupaksha temples.

The main **Virupaksha Temple** is a massive structure, its columns covered with intricate carvings depicting episodes from the Ramayana and Mahabharata. A giant stone sculpture of Nandi sits to the temple's east. The **Mallikarjuna Temple**, next to the Virupaksha Temple, is almost identical in design. About 500m south of the main enclosure is the Jain **Papanatha Temple**, its entrance flanked by elephant sculptures. The temple complex also serves as the backdrop to the annual Classical Dance Festival (see the boxed text, p901), held sometime between January and February.

Pattadakal is 20km from Badami. See opposite for transport details.

Aihole

Some 100 temples, built between the 4th and 6th centuries AD, dot the ancient Chalukyan regional capital of Aihole (*ay-ho-leh*). However, most of them are either in ruins or have been engulfed by the modern village. Aihole documents the embryonic stage of South Indian Hindu architecture, from the earliest simple shrines, such as the most ancient Lad Khan Temple, to the later and more complex buildings, such as the Meguti Temple.

The most impressive of them all is the 7th-century **Durga Temple** (☎ 08351-284533; Indian/foreigner Rs5/100; ☾ 8am-6pm), notable for its semicircular apse (inspired by Buddhist architecture) and the remains of the curvilinear *sikhara* (temple spire). The interiors house intricate stone carvings. The small **museum** (admission Rs2; ☾ 10am-5pm Sat-Thu) behind the temple contains further examples of Chalukyan sculpture.

To the south of the Durga Temple are several other temple clusters, including early examples such as the Gandar, Ladkhan, Kontigudi and Hucchapaya groups – pavilion type with slightly sloping roofs. About 600m to the southeast, on a low hillock, is the Jain **Meguti Temple**. Watch out for snakes!

The unappealing **KSTDC Tourist Home** (☎ 08351-284541; Amingad Rd; d/tr Rs300/500), 1km from the village centre, is the only accommodation in town. You're better off staying in Badami.

Aihole is about 40km from Badami. See opposite for transport information.

BIJAPUR

☎ 08352 / pop 253,900 / elev 593m

A fascinating open-air museum dating back to the Deccan's Islamic era, dusty and tattered Bijapur tells a faded but glorious tale that dates back some 600 years. Blessed with a heap of mosques, mausoleums, palaces and fortifications, the town is a must-visit on the historical circuit.

The capital of the Adil Shahi kings from 1489 to 1686, Bijapur was one of the five splinter states formed after the Bahmani Muslim kingdom broke up in 1482. Despite its strong Islamic character, Bijapur is also a centre for the Lingayat brand of Shaivism, which emphasises a single personalised god. The **Lingayat Siddeshwara Festival** runs for eight days in January/February.

Orientation

Bijapur's prime attractions, the Golgumbaz and the Ibrahim Rouza, are at opposite ends of town. Between them runs Station Rd (also known as MG Rd), dotted with the town's major hotels and restaurants. The bus stand is a five-minute walk from Station Rd; the train station is 2km east of the centre.

Information

State Bank of India (☎ 251182; Station Rd; ☾ 10.30am-4.30pm Mon-Fri, 10.30am-1.30pm Sat) Changes travellers cheques and is super-efficient.
Cyber Park (MG Rd; per hr Rs20; ☾ 9am-10pm) Internet access.
Tourist office (☎ 250359; Station Rd; ☾ 10am-5.30pm Mon-Sat) A poorly serviced office behind KSTDC Hotel Mayura Adil Shahi Annexe.

Sights

GOLGUMBAZ

Set in tranquil gardens, the magnificent **Golgumbaz** (☎ 240737; Indian/foreigner Rs5/100, video Rs25; ☾ 6am-5.40pm) is big enough to pull an optical illusion on you; despite the perfect engineering, you might just think it's ill-proportioned. Golgumbaz is actually a mausoleum, dating back to 1659, and houses the tombs of emperor Mohammed Adil Shah (r 1627–56), his two wives, his mistress (Rambha), one of his daughters and a grandson.

Octagonal seven-storey towers stand at each corner of the monument, which is capped by an enormous dome, 38m in diameter. In fact, it's said to be the largest dome in the world after St Peter's Basilica in Rome.

KARNATAKA

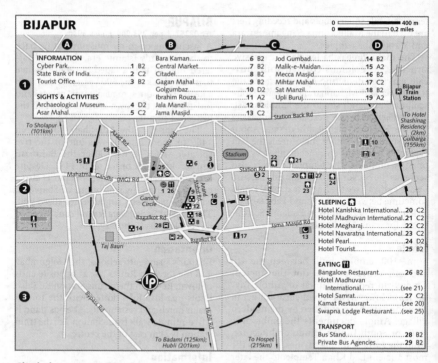

BIJAPUR

0 _____ 400 m
0 _____ 0.2 miles

INFORMATION
Cyber Park..............................1 B2
State Bank of India..................2 C2
Tourist Office..........................3 B2

SIGHTS & ACTIVITIES
Archaeological Museum...........4 D2
Asar Mahal.............................5 C2

Bara Kaman............................6 B2
Central Market........................7 B2
Citadel...................................8 B2
Gagan Mahal..........................9 B2
Golgumbaz............................10 D2
Ibrahim Rouza.......................11 B2
Jala Manzil............................12 A2
Jama Masjid...........................13 C2

Jod Gumbad..........................14 B2
Malik-e-Maidan......................15 A2
Mecca Masjid.........................16 B2
Mihtar Mahal.........................17 C2
Sat Manzil.............................18 B2
Upli Buruj.............................19 A2

Bijapur
Train
Station

To Hotel
Shashinag
Residency
(2km)/
Gulbarga
(155km)

SLEEPING
Hotel Kanishka International....20 C2
Hotel Madhuvan International.21 C2
Hotel Megharaj......................22 B2
Hotel Navaratna International.23 C2
Hotel Pearl............................24 D2
Hotel Tourist.........................25 B2

EATING
Bangalore Restaurant.............26 B2
Hotel Madhuvan
International.....................(see 21)
Hotel Samrat.........................27 C2
Kamat Restaurant...............(see 20)
Swapna Lodge Restaurant.....(see 25)

TRANSPORT
Bus Stand.............................28 B2
Private Bus Agencies..............29 B2

Climb the steep, narrow stairs up one of the towers to reach the 'whispering gallery' within the dome. An engineering marvel, its acoustics are such that if you whisper into the wall, a person on the opposite side of the gallery can hear you clearly. Unfortunately people like to test this out by hollering, so come early in the morning before any school groups or vocal tourists arrive.

Set in the lawns, fronting the monument, is a fantastic **archaeological museum** (admission Rs2; 10am-5pm Sat-Thu). Skip the ground floor and head upstairs; there you'll find an excellent collection of artefacts, such as Persian carpets, china crockery, weapons, armours, scrolls and objects of daily use, dating back to Bijapur's heydays.

IBRAHIM ROUZA

The beautiful **Ibrahim Rouza** (Indian/foreigner Rs5/100, video Rs25; 6am-6pm) is clearly among the most elegant and finely-proportioned Islamic monuments in India. Its tale is rather poignant: the monument was built by emperor Ibrahim Adil Shah II (r 1580–1627) as a future mausoleum for his queen, Taj

Sultana. Ironically, he died before her, and was thus the first person to be rested there. Interred here with Ibrahim Adil Shah and his queen are his daughter, his two sons, and his mother, Haji Badi Sahiba.

Unlike the Golgumbaz, which is impressive for its immensity, the emphasis here is on grace and architectural finery. Its 24m-high minarets are said to have inspired those of the Taj Mahal. For a tip (Rs150 is fine), caretakers will show you around the monument, including the dark labyrinth around the catacomb where the actual graves are located.

CITADEL

Surrounded by fortified walls and a wide moat, the **citadel** once contained the palaces, pleasure gardens and durbar (royal court) of the Adil Shahi kings. Now mainly in ruins, the most impressive of the remaining fragments is the **Gagan Mahal**, built by Ali Adil Shah I around 1561 as a dual-purpose royal residency and durbar hall.

The ruins of Mohammed Adil Shah's seven-storey palace, the **Sat Manzil**, are nearby. Across the road stands the delicate **Jala Manzil**, once a water pavilion surrounded by secluded courts and gardens. On the other side of Station Rd are the graceful arches of **Bara Kaman**, the ruined mausoleum of Ali Roza.

JAMA MASJID

The finely proportioned **Jama Masjid** (Jama Masjid Rd; 9am-5.30pm) has graceful arches, a fine dome and a vast inner courtyard with room for more than 2200 worshippers. It was constructed by Ali Adil Shah I (r 1557–80), also responsible for erecting the fortified city walls and the Gagan Mahal. You can take a silent walk through its assembly hall, which still retains some of the elaborate murals. Women should make sure to cover their heads and not wear revealing clothing.

OTHER SIGHTS

On the eastern side of the citadel is the tiny, walled **Mecca Masjid** (admission free), thought to have been built in the early 17th century. Some speculate that this mosque, with high surrounding walls, may have been for women. Further east, the **Asar Mahal** (admission free), built by Mohammed Adil Shah in about 1646 to serve as a Hall of Justice, once housed two hairs from Prophet Mohammed's beard. The rooms on the upper storey are decorated with frescoes and a square tank graces the front. It's out of bounds for women. The stained but richly decorated **Mihtar Mahal** (admission free) to the south serves as an ornamental gateway to a small mosque.

Upli Buruj (admission free) is a 16th-century, 24m-high watchtower near the western walls of the city. An external flight of stairs leads to the top, where you'll find two hefty cannons and good views of other monuments around town. A short walk west brings you to the **Malik-e-Maidan** (Monarch of the Plains), a huge cannon over 4m long, almost 1.5m in diameter and estimated to weigh 55 tonnes. Cast in 1549, it was supposedly brought to Bijapur as a war trophy thanks to the effort of 10 elephants, 400 oxen and hundreds of men!

In the southwest of the city, off Bagalkot Rd, stand the twin **Jod Gumbad** tombs with handsome bulbous domes; an Adil Shahi general and his spiritual adviser, Abdul Razzaq Qadiri, are buried here. The surrounding gardens are a popular picnic spot.

Don't forget to spend a few hours in Bijapur's colourful **central market**, with its spice sellers, florists and tailors.

Sleeping

Hotel Tourist (250655; MG Rd; d with/without TV Rs250/160) Bang in the middle of the bazaar, with scrawny (but clean) rooms. Service is apathetic, so bring that DIY manual along.

Hotel Megharaj (254458; Station Rd; d with/without AC Rs540/300;) The cost-cutting is evident in the poor quality of the washrooms. But it's a friendly place, and the yellow and pink walls might just cheer you up!

Hotel Navaratna International (222771; fax 222772; Station Rd; d from Rs400;) A touch of class is provided by paintings in the style of Kandinsky and Chagall that hang in the lobby here. Rooms are sparkling clean, with shiny floor tiles.

Hotel Pearl (256002; fax 243606; Station Rd; d Indian/foreigner from Rs450/600;) Across the road from the Golgumbaz is this orderly business hotel, with a central atrium and clean, brightly painted rooms. Ask for one to the rear to avoid street noise.

Hotel Kanishka International (223788; fax 243131; Station Rd; s/d from Rs500/600;) One of Bijapur's trusted options, this place has spacious and clean rooms, some with balconies. There's a small gym for guests' use, and the dealmaker is the excellent vegetarian restaurant downstairs.

Hotel Madhuvan International (255571; fax 256201; Station Rd; d from Rs600;) Freshly renovated, this pleasant hotel boasts lime-green wall shades, tinted windows and an amiable management. The garden restaurant is a hit with locals, but watch out for those boisterous wedding receptions that are often thrown there!

Hotel Shashinag Residency (260344, fax 265544; www.hotelsshashinagresidency.com; Sholapur-Chitradurga Bypass Rd; s/d incl breakfast Indian Rs650/1000, foreigner US$50/60;) The most upmarket choice in Bijapur, this hotel has large rooms with frilly curtains and floral blankets! Bonuses are a small pool (Rs30 per hour for nonguests), a gym and a snooker room.

Eating

Unless otherwise mentioned, all places are open from around 6pm to 10pm.

Kamat Restaurant (Station Rd; mains Rs15-60; 9am-11pm) Below Hotel Kanishka International, this popular vegetarian eatery churns out superb food in clean surroundings. Try the elaborate and delicious Kamat special thali (Rs55).

Hotel Samrat (Station Rd; mains Rs15-60; 🕑 9am-11pm) On par with Kamat Restaurant and located just beside it, Samrat scores with its North Indian (Rs55) and South Indian (Rs44) thalis, which begin with tomato soup and end with ice cream!

Bangalore Restaurant (MG Rd; meals Rs20) This modest little pink-painted place does a decent South Indian veg thali. Don't fuss over its skeletal appearance; just refuel and leave!

Swapna Lodge Restaurant (MG Rd; mains Rs30-110; 🕑 11am-11pm) It's located two floors up a dingy staircase in the building next to Hotel Tourist, and has good grub, cold beer and a 1970s lounge feel. Its open-air terrace is perfect for evening dining, though it does get a little noisy with the maddening traffic below.

Hotel Madhuvan International (Station Rd; mains Rs35-70) Delicious vegie food is served here either in the garden or inside in AC relief. Try the yummy *masala dosa* or the never-ending North Indian thalis dished out by waiters in red turbans. The downside is that you'll sorely miss the booze.

Getting There & Away

BUS

From the **bus stand** (☎ 251344), buses run direct to Bidar (Rs155, seven hours, four daily). Buses head frequently to Gulbarga (Rs85, four hours) and Hubli (Rs100, five hours). Three evening buses go to Bengaluru (Rs372, 12 hours) via Hospet (Rs100, five hours), four buses a day go to Hyderabad (ordinary/semideluxe Rs196/288, 10 hours), while two go to Pune (Rs226, 10 hours).

TRAIN

From **Bijapur train station** (☎ 244888), there are four daily passenger trains to Sholapur (Rs23, 2½ hours), which has connections to Mumbai, Hyderabad and Bengaluru. A daily express to Bengaluru (sleeper/2AC Rs286/1125, 17 hours) also passes through, as do 'fast passenger' trains to Mumbai (chair/sleeper Rs70/143, 12 hours, four weekly) and Hyderabad (sleeper Rs123, 15½ hours, daily).

Getting Around

Autorickshaws are oddly expensive in Bijapur, so be prepared to haggle. Rs60 should get you from the train station to the town centre. Between the Golgumbaz and Ibrahim Rouza they cost about Rs40. Tonga drivers are eager for business but charge around the same.

Autorickshaw drivers ask for about Rs250 for four hours around town.

BIDAR

☎ 08482 / pop 174,200 / elev 664m

Tucked away in Karnataka's far northeastern corner, Bidar is a little gem that most travellers choose to ignore, and no one quite knows why. At most an afterthought on some itineraries, this old walled town – first the capital of the Bahmani kingdom (1428–87) and later the capital of the Barid Shahi dynasty – is drenched in history. That apart, it is home to some amazing ruins and monuments, including the colossal Bidar Fort – the largest fort in South India. Wallowing in neglect, Bidar sure commands more than the cursory attention it gets today.

Orientation & Information

The modern town centre is strung along Udgir Rd, down which you'll also find the bus station. Fast internet access is available at **Arien Computers** (per hr Rs20; 🕑 9.30am-10.30pm) near Hotel Krishna Regency, and at **iWeb World** (per hr Rs20; 🕑 11am-11pm), off Ambedkar Circle. There are several ATMs around town.

Sights

BIDAR FORT

Keep aside a few hours for peacefully wandering around the remnants of the magnificent 15th-century **Bidar Fort** (admission free; 🕑 dawn-dusk). Sprawled across rolling hills 2km east of Udgir Rd, this fort was once the

---

BIDRI: THE ART OF BIDAR

Highly prized for its intricate designs, *bidriware* is a traditional art-form that was invented around the 14th century by the Persian craftsmen of Bidar. Heavily influenced by medieval Islamic decorative motifs, *bidriware* is produced by moulding metals such as zinc, copper, lead and tin, and blackening them by applying a mixture containing dark clay typically found in the region. Then, after being embossed, the objects are overlaid or inlaid with pure silver. Finely crafted pieces, such as hookahs, goblets, and jewellery boxes, are exquisitely embellished with interwoven creepers and flowing floral patterns, occasionally framed by strict geometric lines.

administrative capital of much of southern India. Surrounded by a triple moat hewn out of solid red rock and 5.5km of defensive walls (the second longest in India), the fort has a fairy-tale entrance on a roadway that twists in an elaborate chicane through three gateways.

Inside the fort are many evocative ruins, including the **Rangin Mahal** (Painted Palace) which sports elaborate tilework, woodwork and panels with mother-of-pearl inlay, and the **Solah Khamba Mosque** (Sixteen-Pillared Mosque). There's also a small **museum** (admission free; ◷ 9am-5pm) in the former royal bath. Clerks at the **archaeological office** (☎ 230418) beside the museum often double as guides. It helps to ask one of them to show you around; for a small tip (Rs100 is fine) they can show you many hidden places within the fort which ordinarily remain locked.

BAHMANI TOMBS

The huge domed **tombs** (admission free; ◷ dawn-dusk) of the Bahmani kings, in Ashtur, 3km east of Bidar, have a desolate, moody beauty that strikes a strange harmony with the sunny hills around them. These impressive mausoleums were built to house the remains of the sultans – their graves are still regularly draped with fresh satin and flowers – and are arranged in a long line along the edge of the road. The painted interior of Ahmad Shah Bahman's tomb is the most impressive, and is regularly prayed in.

About 500m prior to reaching the tombs, to the left of the road, is **Choukhandi** (admission free; ◷ dawn-dusk), the serene mausoleum of Sufi saint Syed Kirmani Baba, who travelled here from Persia during the golden age of the Bahmani empire. An uncanny air of calm hangs within the monument, and its polygonal courtyard houses rows of medieval graves, amid which women in hijab sit quietly and murmur inaudible prayers. You are welcome to sit in or walk around, and soak up the ambience.

Both places are best visited during afternoons, as it's difficult to find transport back to Bidar after dark.

OTHER SIGHTS

Dominating the heart of the old town are the ruins of **Khwaja Mahmud Gawan Madrasa** (admission free; ◷ dawn-dusk), a college built in 1492. To get an idea of its former grandeur, check out the remnants of coloured tiles on the front gate and one of the minarets that still stands intact.

Bidri artists (see opposite) still tap away at their craft in the back streets on and around Chowbara Rd, near Basveshwar Circle.

Sleeping & Eating

Don't expect much in the way of pampering – the best you can hope for is a clean room with AC and hot shower. Places listed below are all within a few minutes' walk of the bus stand.

Krishna Regency (☎ 221991; fax 228388; Udgir Rd; s/d from Rs350/450; ✖) A friendly place by the bus stand that you can identify by the glass elevator running up outside. The rooms are tidy though unimaginative. Some lack natural light, and there's no food available.

Sapna International (☎ 220991; fax 226824; Udgir Rd; s/d from Rs400/450; ✖) On a par with the Krishna Regency in terms of rooms – but not as friendly. In its favour are its two restaurants: the pure-veg Kamat and the Atithi, which offers meat dishes and booze. Mains cost Rs25 to Rs70.

Hotel Mayura (☎ 228142; Udgir Rd; d with/without AC Rs550/350; ✖) Across from the bus station and set back from the road is this non-fussy hotel, with rooms decent enough for a comfortable night's stay.

Jyothi Udupi (Udgir Rd; meals Rs20-45; ◷ 6.30am-11pm) This place opposite the bus stand has 21 kinds of dosa (Rs16 to 32), filling South Indian thalis (Rs25) and an ice-cream dessert called Easy Sunday!

Getting There & Away

From the **bus stand** (☎ 228508), frequent services run to Gulbarga (Rs65, three hours), which has good express-train connections to Mumbai and Bengaluru. Buses also run to Hyderabad (Rs70, four hours), Bijapur (Rs180, seven hours) and Bengaluru (semi-deluxe/AC Rs470/700, 12 hours).

The train station, around 1km southwest of the bus stand, has daily services to Hyderabad (2nd class/sleeper Rs27/80, 5½ hours) and Bengaluru (sleeper Rs295, 17 hours).

Getting Around

Rent a bicycle at **Sami Cycle Taxi** (Basveshwar Circle; per day Rs15; ◷ 7am-10pm) against your proof of identity. Or simply arrange a day tour in an autorickshaw for around Rs300.

KARNATAKA

Andhra Pradesh

Andhra Pradesh is not going to hit you over the head with its attractions. It doesn't brag about its temples or talk about its colourful history. It does not name streets after its long roster of enlightened beings. It's forgotten most of its palaces and royal architecture – the extreme wealth of most of the last 500 years is apparently no big deal – and if you don't purposely seek them out, they'll be missed. No, to travellers, Andhra Pradesh is not flirtatious.

Andhra prefers to play hard to get: its charms are subtle. But if you look closely, you'll find a long, fascinating history of arts and culture, spiritual scholarship and religious harmony. In Hyderabad's Old City, Islamic monuments, Persian-inspired architecture and the call of the muezzin speak of the city's unique history, created most notoriously by two wealthy family dynasties that loved Allah, diamonds and, above all, beauty.

Dig a little deeper and you'll find another Andhran history, peopled by the good life's renunciates: the region was an international centre of Buddhist thought for several hundred years from the 3rd century BC. Today ruins of stupas and monasteries defy impermanence at 150 sites around the state.

Meanwhile, deep in the countryside, more than 8 million tribal people practise ancient religious, cultural and farming traditions, writing their own quiet history away from the compulsively modernising cities nearby.

So come, but only if you're prepared to dig: the jewels here have to be earned. But if you keep your eyes open and your curiosity sharp, you're bound to find something that even Andhrans, in their modesty, hadn't thought to mention.

HIGHLIGHTS

- Find out how many bangles and sequined slippers one person can buy at Hyderabad's 400-year-old **Laad Bazaar** (p959)

- Absorb the meditative vibrations of monks past at **Sankaram** (p974), **Bavikonda** and **Thotlakonda** (p974), destinations on a 2300-year-old monastic trail

- Eat cotton candy, drink chai, and ride the kitschy Kailasagiri ropeway with local tourists at Visakhapatnam's **beaches** (p973)

- Get hypnotised by the lush intricacy and rich colours of kalamkari paintings in **Sri Kalahasti** (p978)

- Notice how death doesn't seem so bad before the sublime beauty of Hyderabad's **Paigah tombs** (p962) and **tombs of Qutb Shahi kings** (p962)

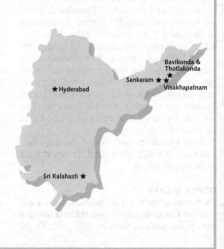

ANDHRA PRADESH

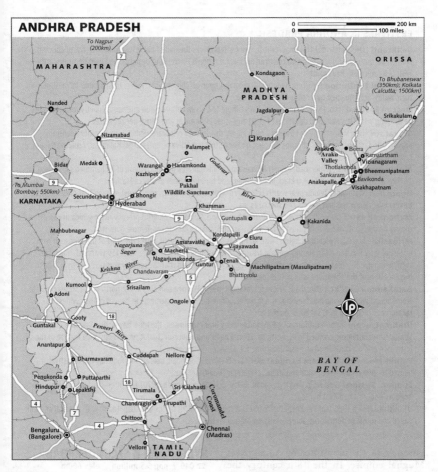

ANDHRA PRADESH

History

From the 2nd century BC, the Satavahana empire, also known as the Andhras, reigned throughout the Deccan plateau. It evolved from the Andhra people, whose presence in southern India may date back to 1000 BC. The Buddha's teaching took root here early on, and in the 3rd century BC the Andhras fully embraced it, building huge edifices in its honour. In the coming centuries, the Andhras would develop a flourishing civilisation that extended from the west to the east coasts of South India.

From the 7th to the 10th century, the Chalukyas ruled the area, establishing their Dravidian style of architecture, especially along the coast. The Chalukya and Chola dynasties merged in the 11th century to be overthrown by the Kakatiyas, who introduced pillared temples into South Indian religious architecture. The Vijayanagars then rose to become one of the most powerful empires in India.

By the 16th century the Islamic Qutb Shahi dynasty held the city of Hyderabad,

FAST FACTS

Population 75.7 million
Area 276,754 sq km
Capital Hyderabad
Main languages Telugu, Urdu, Hindi
When to go September to February

ANDHRA PRADESH

FESTIVALS IN ANDHRA PRADESH

Sankranti (Jan; statewide) This important Telugu festival marks the end of harvest season. Kite-flying abounds, women decorate their doorsteps with colourful *kolams* (or *rangolis* – rice-flour designs), and men decorate cattle with bells and fresh horn paint.

Industrial Exhibition (Jan/Feb; Hyderabad, below) A huge exhibition with traders from around India displaying their wares, accompanied by a colourful, bustling fair.

Deccan Festival (Feb; Hyderabad, below) Pays tribute to Deccan culture. Urdu *mushairas* (poetry readings) are held, along with Qawwali (Sufi devotional music) and other local music and dance performances.

Shivaratri (Feb/Mar; statewide) During a blue moon, this festival celebrates Shiva with all-night chanting, prayers and fasting. Hordes of pilgrims descend on the auspicious Shiva temples at Sri Kalahasti, Amaravathi and Lepakshi.

Muharram (Feb/Mar; Hyderabad, below) Muharram commemorates the martyrdom of Mohammed's grandson for 14 days in Hyderabad. Shiites wear black in mourning, and throngs gather at Mecca Masjid.

Ugadi (Mar; statewide) Telugu new year is celebrated with *pujas* (offerings or prayers), mango-leaf *toranas* (archi-traves) over doorways, and sweets and special foods.

Mahankali Jatra (Jun/Jul; statewide) A festival honouring Kali, with colourful processions in which devotees convey *bonalu* (pots of food offerings) to the deity. Secunderabad's Mahankali Temple goes wild.

Mrigasira (Jun/Jul; Hyderabad, below) Also known as Mrugam, this event marks the start of the monsoon with a feast of local fish and a fascinating medical treatment for asthma sufferers; more than 150 years old, it involves swallowing live fish that have consumed a herbal remedy. It's believed that the remedy was revealed by a sage to the ancestors of the physicians who now dispense it.

Batakamma (Sep/Oct; Hyderabad, below & Warangal, p970) Women and girls in the north of the state celebrate womanhood with dancing and feasting, and make elaborate flower arrangements in honour of the goddess Ba-takamma, which they then set adrift on rivers.

Brahmotsavam (Sep/Oct; Tirumala, p976) Initiated by Brahma himself, the nine-day festival sees the Venkateshwara temple adorned in decorations. Special *pujas* and colourful chariot processions are a feature of the festivities, and it's considered an auspicious time for *darshan* (deity viewing).

Pandit Motiram–Maniram Sangeet Samaroh (Nov; Hyderabad, below) This four-day music festival, named for two renowned classical musicians, celebrates Hindustani music.

Lumbini Festival (2nd Fri in Dec; Hyderabad, below & Nagarjunakonda, p970) The three-day Lumbini Festival honours Andhra's Buddhist heritage.

Visakha Utsav (Dec/Jan; Visakhapatnam, p972) A celebration of all things Visakhapatnam, with classical and folk dance and music performances; some events are staged on the beach.

---

but in 1687 was supplanted by Aurangzeb's Mughal empire. In the 18th century the post-Mughal rulers in Hyderabad, known as nizams, retained relative control as the British and French vied for trade, though their power gradually weakened. The region became part of independent India in 1947, and in 1956 the state of Andhra Pradesh, an amalgamation of Telugu-speaking areas, plus the predominantly Urdu-speaking capital, was created.

Information

ACCOMMODATION

Hotels charge a 5% 'luxury' tax on all rooms over Rs300; it's not included in the prices quoted in this chapter. All hotels listed have 24-hour checkout unless stated otherwise.

HYDERABAD & SECUNDERABAD

☎ 040 / pop 5.5 million / elev 600m

Hyderabad, City of Pearls, is like an elderly, impeccably dressed princess whose time has past. Once the seat of the powerful and wealthy Qutb Shahi and Asaf Jahi dynasties, the city has seen centuries of great prosperity and innovation. Today, the 'Old City' is full of centuries-old Islamic monuments and even older charms. In fact, the whole city is laced with architectural gems: ornate tombs, mosques, palaces and homes from the past are tucked away, faded and enchanting, in corners all over town. Keep your eyes open.

In the last decade, with the rise of Hyderabad's west side – our aged princess's sexy and popular granddaughter – a new decadence has emerged. 'Cyberabad', with Bengaluru (Bangalore) and Pune, is the seat of

India's mighty software dynasty and generates jobs, wealth and posh lounges like she was born to do it. Opulence, it would seem, is in this city's genes.

A sizeable percentage of Hyderabad's population is Muslim, and the city is known for its tolerance. You'll probably be taken aback by the chilled-out kindness of Hyderabadis, and many find the city delightful: lots to see and do with almost no hassle.

History

Hyderabad owes its existence to a water shortage at Golconda in the late 16th century. The reigning Qutb Shahis were forced to relocate, and so Mohammed Quli and the royal family abandoned Golconda Fort for the banks of the Musi River. The new city of Hyderabad was established, with the brand-new Charminar as its centrepiece.

In 1687 the city was overrun by the Mughal emperor Aurangzeb, and subsequent rulers of Hyderabad were viceroys installed by the Mughal administration in Delhi.

In 1724 the Hyderabad viceroy, Asaf Jah, took advantage of waning Mughal power and declared Hyderabad an independent state with himself as leader. The dynasty of the nizams of Hyderabad began, and the traditions of Islam flourished. Hyderabad became a focus for the arts, culture and learning, and the centre of Islamic India. Its abundance of rare gems and minerals – the world-famous Kohinoor diamond is from here – furnished the nizams with enormous wealth. (Get a copy of William Dalrymple's *White Mughals* for a fascinating portrait of the city at this time.)

When Independence came in 1947, the then nizam of Hyderabad, Osman Ali Khan, considered amalgamation with Pakistan – and then opted for sovereignty. Tensions between Muslims and Hindus increased, however, and military intervention saw Hyderabad join the Indian union in 1948.

Orientation

Hyderabad has four distinct areas. The Old City by the Musi River has bustling bazaars and important landmarks, including the Charminar.

North of the river is Mahatma Gandhi (Imlibun) bus station, Hyderabad (Nampally) station and the main post office. Abids Rd runs through the Abids district, a good budget-accommodation area.

Further north, beyond the Hussain Sagar, lies the British-founded Secunderabad. Technically it's Hyderabad's sister city, but it's generally considered part of the Hyderabad metropolitan area. Here you'll find Jubilee bus station and the huge Secunderabad train station.

Jubilee Hills and Banjara Hills, west of Hussain Sagar, are where the well heeled – and their restaurants, shops and lounges – reside, and further west is Cyberabad's capital, Hitec (Hyderabad Information Technology Engineering Consulting) City.

Information

BOOKSHOPS

On Sunday, second-hand books are sold on Abids Rd; a few gems nestle among the computer books.

AA Husain & Co (Map p960; ☎ 23203724; Abids Rd; ⏱ 10am-8.30pm Mon-Sat) Heaps of Indian and foreign authors.

MR Book Centre (Map p960; ☎ 23205684; Abids Rd; ⏱ 10am-9pm) New and secondhand novels; magazines from back home.

Walden (Map p958) Banjara Hills (☎ 23551613; Trendset Towers, Rd No 2; ⏱ 10.30am-9pm); Begumpet (☎ 23413434; Greenlands Rd; ⏱ 9am-9pm) Hyderabad's megastore.

CULTURAL CENTRES & LIBRARIES

Alliance Française (Map p958; ☎ 27700734; www .afindia.org; St No 16, West Marredpally, Secunderabad; ⏱ 9am-1pm & 2-6pm Mon-Fri, 9am-1pm Sat)

British Library (Map p960; ☎ 23483333; www.british councilonline.org; Secretariat Rd; ⏱ 11am-7pm Tue-Sun) Membership costs Rs1200.

Goethe-Zentrum (Map p960; ☎ 65526443; www .goethe.de/hyderabad; Hill Fort Rd; ⏱ 9.30am-5pm Mon-Sat)

State Library (Map p958; ☎ 24600107; Maulvi Allaudin Rd; ⏱ 8am-8pm Fri-Wed) Beautiful old building with 700,000 books.

INTERNET ACCESS

Both Hyderabad (Map p960) and Secunderabad stations (Map p958) have a **Railtel Cyber Express** (per hr Rs23; ⏱ 9am-7pm).

Reliance Web World (Map p960; ☎ 30339991; MPM Mall, Abids Circle; per 3hr Rs100; ⏱ 9am-10pm)

LEFT LUGGAGE

All three train stations, as well as Mahatma Gandhi bus station, have left-luggage facilities, charging Rs10 per bag per day, or Rs15 for a locker.

ANDHRA PRADESH

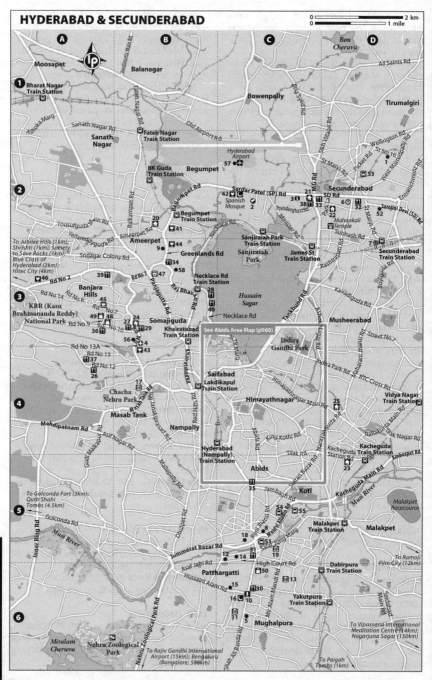

MEDIA

Good 'what's on' guides include *Channel 6*, *GO Hyderabad* and *City Info*. The juiciest is **Wow! Hyderabad** (www.wowhyderabad.com; Rs25). The *Deccan Chronicle* is a good local paper; its *Hyderabad Chronicle* insert has info on happenings.

MEDICAL SERVICES

Apollo Pharmacy (Map p960; ☎ 23431734; Hyderguda Main Rd; ☺ 24hr) Delivers.

Care Hospital Banjara Hills (Map p958; ☎ 30418888; Rd No 1); Nampally (Map p960; ☎ 66517777; Mukarramjahi Rd) Reputable hospital with a 24-hour pharmacy.

Mor Chemists (☎ 23297111; Bashirbagh Rd; ☺ 10am-9pm Mon-Sat) Helpful and well-stocked.

MONEY

The banks offer the best currency-exchange rates here. ATMs are everywhere.

State Bank of India (Map p960; ☎ 23231986; HACA Bhavan, Saifabad; ☺ 10.30am-4pm Mon-Fri)

Thomas Cook (Map p960; ☎ 23296521; Nasir Arcade, Saifabad; ☺ 9.30am-6pm Mon-Sat) Changes travellers cheques with no commission.

POST

Post office (☺ 8am-8.30pm Mon-Sat, 10am-6pm Sun) Secunderabad (Map p958; Rashtrapati Rd); Abids (Map p960; Abids Circle)

TOURIST INFORMATION

Andhra Pradesh Tourism Development Corporation (APTDC; ☎ 24-hr info 23450444; www.aptdc.in; ☺ 7am-8pm) Bashirbagh (Map p960; ☎ 23298456; NSF Shakar Bhavan, opposite Police Control Room); Secunderabad (Map p958; ☎ 27893100; Yatri Nivas Hotel, SP Rd); Tankbund Rd (Map p960; ☎ 65581555) Organises tours.

Indiatourism (Government of India; Map p960; ☎ 23261360, 23260770; Netaji Bhavan, Himayathnagar Rd; ☺ 9.30am-6pm Mon-Fri, to noon Sat) Information for Hyderabad and beyond.

Sights

CHARMINAR & BAZAARS

Hyderabad's principal landmark, the **Charminar** (Four Towers; Map p958; Indian/foreigner Rs5/100; ☺ 9am-5.30pm) was built by Mohammed Quli Qutb Shah in 1591 to commemorate the founding of Hyderabad and the end of epidemics caused by Golconda's water shortage. Standing 56m high and 30m wide, the dramatic four-column structure has four arches facing the cardinal points. Minarets sit atop each column. The 2nd floor, home to Hyderabad's oldest mosque, and upper columns are not usually open to the public, but you can try your luck with the man with the key. The structure is illuminated from 7pm to 9pm.

West of the Charminar, the incredible, crowded **Laad Bazaar** (Map p958) is the perfect place to get lost. It has everything from

ANDHRA PRADESH

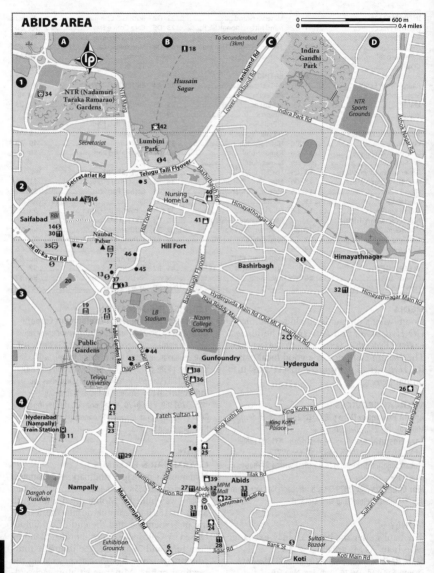

fine perfumes, fabrics and jewels to musical instruments, second-hand saris and kitchen implements. Artisans are tucked away creating jewellery and scented oils, large pots and burkas. The lanes around the Charminar also form the centre of India's pearl trade. Some great deals can be had – if you know your stuff.

SALAR JUNG MUSEUM

The huge collection of the **Salar Jung Museum** (Map p958; ☎ 24523211; Salar Jung Marg; Indian/foreigner Rs10/150; ☑ 10am-5pm Sat-Thu), dating back to the 1st century, was put together by Mir Yusaf Ali Khan (Salar Jung III), the grand vizier of the seventh nizam, Osman Ali Khan (r 1910–49). The 35,000 exhibits from every corner of the world include sculptures, wood carvings, devotional objects, Persian miniature paintings, illuminated manuscripts, weaponry and more than 50,000 books. The impressive nizams' jewellery collection is sometimes on special exhibit. Cameras are not allowed. You should avoid visiting the museum on Sunday when it is bedlam. From any of the bus stands in the Abids area, take bus 7, which stops at Afzal Gunj bus stop on the north side of the nearby Musi River bridge.

Just west of the bridge are the spectacular **Osmania General Hospital** (Map p958), on the north side, and, on the south, the **High Court** (Map p958) and **Government City College** (Map p958) buildings, all built under the seventh nizam in the Indo-Saracenic style.

CHOWMAHALLA PALACE

In their latest act of architectural showmanship, the nizam family has sponsored a restoration of this dazzling **palace** (Khilwat; Map p958; 24522032; www.chowmahalla.com; Indian/ foreigner Rs25/150, camera Rs50; 10am-5pm Sat-Thu) – or, technically, four (*char*) palaces (*mahalla*). Begun in 1750, it was expanded over the next 100 years, absorbing Persian, Indo-Saracenic, Rajasthani and European styles. The southern courtyard has one mahal with period rooms that have been reconstructed with the nizams' over-the-top furniture; another *mahal* with an exhibit on life in the zenana (women's quarters) that includes bejewelled clothes, carpets and a bride palanquin; antique cars (one nizam allegedly used a Rolls Royce as a garbage can); and curiosities like elephant seats, a clock with a miniature dancing band, and a Remington Urdu typewriter.

In the northern courtyard is the Khilwat Mubarak, a magnificent durbar hall where nizams held ceremonies under 19 enormous chandeliers of Belgian crystal. Today the hall houses exhibitions of photos, arms and clothing. Hung with curtains, the balcony over the main hall once served as seating for the family's women, who attended all durbars in purdah.

HEH THE NIZAM'S MUSEUM

The 16th-century Purani Haveli was home of the sixth nizam, Fath Jang Mahbub Ali Khan (r 1869–1911), rumoured to have never worn the same thing twice. His 72m-long, two-storey wardrobe of Burmese teak is on display at this **museum** (Purani Haveli; Map p958; 24521029; adult/student Rs70/15; 10am-5pm Sat-Thu). Also on exhibit, in the palace's former servants' quarters, are personal effects of the seventh nizam and gifts from the Silver Jubilee celebration of his reign. The pieces are unbelievably lavish and include some exquisite artwork. The museum's guides do an excellent job putting it all in context.

The rest of Purani Haveli is now a school, but you can wander around the grounds and peek in the administrative building, the nizam's former residence.

ANDHRA PRADESH

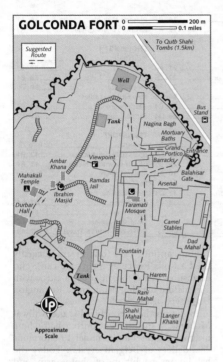

GOLCONDA FORT

GOLCONDA FORT

Although most of this 16th-century **fortress** (off Map p958; ☎ 23513984; Indian/foreigner Rs5/100; ☺ 9am-6pm) dates from the time of the Qutb Shah kings, its origins, as a mud fort, have been traced to the earlier reigns of the Yadavas and Kakatiyas.

Golconda had been the capital of the independent state of Telangana for nearly 80 years when Sultan Quli Qutb Shah abandoned the fort in 1590 and moved to the new city of Hyderabad.

In the 17th century, Mughal armies from Delhi were sent to the Golconda kingdom to enforce payment of tribute. Abul Hasan, last of the Qutb Shahi kings, held out at Golconda for eight months against Emperor Aurangzeb's massive army. The emperor finally succeeded with the aid of a treacherous insider.

It's easy to see how the Mughal army was nearly defeated. The citadel is built on a granite hill, 120m high and surrounded by crenellated ramparts constructed from large masonry blocks. Outside the citadel there stands another crenellated rampart, with a perimeter of 11km, and yet another wall beyond

this. The massive gates were studded with iron spikes to obstruct war elephants.

Survival within the fort was also attributable to water and sound. A series of concealed glazed earthen pipes ensured a reliable water supply, while the acoustics guaranteed that even the smallest sound from the Grand Portico would echo across the fort complex.

Knowledgeable guides around the entrance charge Rs500 for a 1½-hour tour. Check for their shirt badge, or better yet, go through the AP Tourism table in front of the entrance. Small guidebooks to the fort are also sold near the entrance.

An autorickshaw from Abids costs around Rs150. Mornings are best for peace and quiet.

A trippy **sound-and-light show** (admission Rs50; ☺ in English 6.30pm Nov-Feb, 7pm Mar-Oct) is also held here.

QUTB SHAHI TOMBS

These graceful domed **tombs** (off Map p958; admission Rs20, camera/video Rs20/100; ☺ 9am-5pm) sit serenely in landscaped gardens about 1.5km northwest of Golconda Fort's Balahisar Gate. You could easily spend half a day here taking photos and wandering in and out of the mausoleums and various other structures. The upper level of Mohammed Quli's tomb, reached via a narrow staircase, has good views of the area. *The Qutb Shahi Tombs* (Rs20) booklet is sold at the ticket counter.

The tombs are an easy walk from the fort, but an autorickshaw ride shouldn't be more than Rs25. Bus 80S also stops right outside.

PAIGAH TOMBS

The aristocratic Paigah family, purportedly descendents of the second Caliph of Islam, were fierce loyalists of the nizams, serving as statespeople, philanthropists and generals under and alongside them. From 1797, the two families began intermarrying as well, solidifying their close bond. The Paigahs' **necropolis** (off Map p958; Phisalbanda, Santoshnagar; ☺ 9am-5pm), tucked away in a quiet neighbourhood 4km southeast of Charminar, is a small compound of exquisite mausoleums made of marble and lime stucco. The main complex contains 27 tombs with intricate inlay work, surrounded by delicately carved walls and canopies, stunning filigree screens with geometric patterning and, overhead, tall, graceful turrets. The tombs are down a small lane across from Owasi Hospital. Look for the Preston Junior College sign. *The Paigah Tombs* (Rs20) booklet is sold at the AP State Museum, but not here.

BUDDHA STATUE & HUSSAIN SAGAR

Hyderabad has one of the world's largest free-standing stone **Buddha statues** (Map p960), completed in 1990 after five years of work. However, when the 17.5m-high, 350-tonne monolith was being ferried to its place in the **Hussain Sagar** (Map p960), the barge sank. Fortunately, the statue was raised – undamaged – in 1992 and is now on a plinth in the middle of the lake.

Frequent **boats** (adult/child Rs45/25) make the 30-minute return trip to the statue from both **Eat Street** (Map p958; ☎ 9848354440; 2-9pm) and **Lumbini Park** (Map p960; ☎ 65510372; admission Rs5; 9am-9pm), a pleasant place to enjoy sunsets and the popular musical fountain. The Tankbund Rd promenade, on the eastern shore of Hussain Sagar, has great views of the Buddha statue.

AP STATE & HEALTH MUSEUMS

The continually renovated **AP State Museum** (Map p960; ☎ 23232267; Public Gardens Rd, Nampally; admission Rs10, camera/video Rs100/500; 10.30am-5pm Sat-Thu) hosts a collection of important archaeological finds from the area, as well as a Buddhist sculpture gallery, with some relics of the Buddha and an exhibit on Andhra's Buddhist history. The ever-expanding museum also has Jain and bronze sculpture galleries, a decorative-arts gallery, an exhibition of paintings by Lahore painter AR Chughtai, and an Egyptian mummy. The museum, like the gorgeous **Legislative Assembly building** (Map p960) down the road (both commissioned by the seventh nizam), is floodlit at night.

Also in the Public Gardens area is the **Health Museum** (admission free; 10.30am-5pm Sat-Thu), where you'll see a bizarre collection of medical and public-health paraphernalia.

NEHRU CENTENARY TRIBAL MUSEUM

Andhra Pradesh's 33 tribal groups, based mostly in the northeastern part of the state, comprise several million people. This **museum** (Map p958; ☎ 23391270; Masab Tank; admission free; 10.30am-5pm Mon-Sat), run by the government's Tribal Welfare Department, exhibits photographs, dioramas of village life, musical instruments and some exquisite Naikpod masks. It's basic, but you'll get a glimpse into the cultures of these fringe peoples. There's a

small, interesting library here, and next door is the tiny Girijan Sales Depot, selling products made in tribal communities. Both are across from Chacha Nehru Park.

MECCA MASJID

This **mosque** (Map p958; Shah Ali Banda Rd, Patthargatti; 9am-5pm) is one of the world's largest, with space for 10,000 worshippers. Women are not allowed inside.

Construction began in 1614, during Mohammed Quli Qutb Shah's reign, but the mosque wasn't finished until 1687, by which time the Mughal emperor Aurangzeb had annexed the Golconda kingdom. Several bricks embedded above the gate are made with soil from Mecca – hence the name. To the left of the mosque, an enclosure contains the tombs of Nizam Ali Khan and his successors.

Since the 2007 bomb blasts here, security is tight; no bags are allowed inside.

BIRLA MANDIR & PLANETARIUM

The Birla **temple** (Map p960; 7am-noon & 2-9pm), constructed of white Rajasthani marble in 1976, graces Kalabahad (Black Mountain), one of two rocky hills overlooking the Hussain Sagar. Dedicated to Venkateshwara, it's a popular Hindu pilgrimage centre and affords excellent views over the city, especially at sunset. The library here is worth a visit (open 4pm to 8pm).

Next door are the **Birla Planetarium & Science Museum** (Map p960; ☎ 23235081; museum/planetarium Rs20/25; museum 10.30am-8pm, to 3pm Fri, planetarium shows 11.30am, 4pm & 6pm) and the **Birla Modern Art Gallery** (Map p960; admission Rs10; 10.30am-6pm).

RAMOJI FILM CITY

Movie fans can't miss the four-hour tour of **Ramoji Film City** (off Map p958; ☎ 23412262; www.ramojifilmcity.com; adult/child Rs300/250; 9.30am-5.30pm), an 800-hectare movie-making complex for Telugu, Tamil and Hindi films. This place has everything – dance routines, gaudy fountains, flimsy film sets – and the whole thing wraps up with a Wild West song-and-dance number. Buses 205 and 206 from Koti Women's College, northeast of Koti station, take an hour to get here.

Courses

The **Vipassana International Meditation Centre** (off Map p958; Dhamma Khetta; ☎ 24240290; www.khetta.dhamma.org; Nagarjuna Sagar Rd, 12.6km) has intensive 10-day meditation courses at its peaceful grounds 20km outside the city. Apply online or at the Hyderabad **office** (☎ 24732569). A shuttle runs to/from Hyderabad on the first and last day of courses.

Tours

APTDC (see p959) conducts tours of the city (Rs270), Ramoji Film City (Rs500), Nagarjuna Sagar (weekends, Rs450) and Tirupathi (three days, Rs1750). The Sound & Light tour (Rs200) takes in Hitec City, the botanic gardens and Golconda Fort's sound-and-light show, but you may spend much of it in traffic.

Society To Save Rocks (off Map p958; ☎ 23552923; www.saverocks.org; 1236 Rd No 60, Jubilee Hills) organises monthly walks through the Andhran landscape and its surreal-looking boulders.

Sleeping

Rooms tend to fill up, so call ahead.

BUDGET

Youth Hostel Hyderabad (Map p960; ☎ 66758393; www.yhaindia.org; YMCA Circle, Narayanguda; dm/d Rs80/300; ✖) There doesn't seem to be a reception desk here, per se, and the staff may be confused by your presence – all a bit mysterious, really. But it's clean, damn cheap and worth exploring if you don't mind the 10pm curfew and 8am checkout. It's opposite the Shanti Theatre.

Hotel Suhail (Map p960; ☎ 24610299; www.hotelsuhail.in; Troop Bazaar; s/d/tr from Rs375/475/650; ✖) If all budget hotels were like the Suhail, we'd all be much better off. Staff are friendly and on top of it, and rooms are large and quiet and have balconies and constant hot water. It's tucked away on an alley behind the main post office and the Grand Hotel – away from the Hyderabad bustle, but it's also unlit at night; some readers find it sketchy.

Nand International (Map p958; ☎ 24657511; www.nandhotels.com; Kacheguda Station Rd; s/d/tr from Rs450/550/650; ✖) The Nand is a pleasant surprise near Kacheguda Station. It has a roof garden (with chai on order and potted geraniums), sitting areas and water coolers on each floor, and well-looked-after peach rooms hung with weird mixed-media art.

Hotel Jaya International (Map p960; ☎ 24752929-39; hoteljaya2007@yahoo.com; Hanuman Tekdi Rd; s/d from Rs650/750; ✖) The Jaya's capacious, sunny rooms have stained-glass lamps and arched balconies with apple-green trim and tree views. It all blends harmoniously to create a

Brady-Bunch-meets-the-Mughals look. It's also as clean as anything and runs like a champion. But you absolutely must book ahead.

Hotel Rajmata (Map p960; ☎ 66665555; fax 23204133; Public Gardens Rd; s/d Rs690/790; ✖) A recent reno freshened the Rajmata up and added huge and shiny (but overpriced) AC rooms. Since the place is set back from Public Gardens Rd, rooms are quiet – but some are better than others so check out a few. Staff are very professional, and there's a helpful travel desk. The place is popular with families.

If you arrive late at Secunderabad train station, try their good-deal **retiring rooms** (dm/s/d from Rs100/250/450; ✖).

MIDRANGE

APTDC can help arrange rooms from Rs1000 in private homes.

our pick **Taj Mahal Hotel (Himayathnagar)** (Map p958; ☎ 27637836-9; tajcafe@gmail.com; Himayathnagar; s/d from Rs900/1200; ✖) Don't everybody all go here – we don't want them to get cocky – but this Taj is, for now, Hyderabad's best deal. Despite its unfortunate location in front of an overpass on Himayathnagar Rd, it's a peaceful, sunny, stylish place where the staff are warm and welcoming and the hallway floors look like Jaipuri marble. Rooms are surprisingly tasteful, with sleek lamps and chunky, contemporary wooden furniture. Comfy and classy for less than the going rate.

Taj Mahal Hotel (Map p960; ☎ 24758250, 66511122; fax 24758253; cnr Abids & King Kothi Rds; s/d with AC from Rs1050/1475; ✖) This rambling 1924 heritage building has a magnificent exterior, plants peppered about, and some exceedingly charming rooms. Each is different so ask to see a few: the better ones have boudoirs, crystal-knobbed armoires and wood-beam ceilings. The standard singles are small, with less personality, but all rooms are peaceful.

Hotel Harsha (Map p960; ☎ 23201188; www.hotelharsha.net; Public Gardens Rd; s/d incl AC & breakfast from Rs1400/1600; ✖) The formerly budget Harsha now aspires to being high class. Rooms don't have tonnes of character, but they're bright, with fridges, the furniture is in good taste and the art is a step up from the usual schlock. The overall effect is polished but comfy. The lobby smells like success, with lots of glass and marble. One of the city's best deals.

Good deals in Secunderabad:

Hotel Ambassador (Map p958; ☎ 27843760; fax 27899095; SD Rd; s/d from Rs850/1000; ✖)

Yatri Nivas Hotel (Map p958; ☎ 23461855; www .amogh-india.com; SP Rd, Secunderabad; s/d incl AC & breakfast Rs1400/1600; ✕)

TOP END

The following have central AC, wi-fi access, complimentary breakfast and noon checkout.

Green Park (Map p958; ☎ 66515151; www.hotelgreen park.com; Greenlands Rd, Begumpet; s/d from Rs5250/6250; ✕ ▯) Don't bother going beyond the standard rooms here, which are comfy and classy, with flower petals in the bathroom and bamboo flooring. The lobby is a paragon of peace and gentle lighting, while smiley staff look on.

Minerva Grand (Map p958; ☎ 66117474; www.min ervagrand.com; SD Rd, Secunderabad; s/d from Rs4000/4400; ✕ ▯) It's rare to find a hotel that has genuine style; the Minerva Grand has nailed it. Standard rooms (one wheelchair-accessible) have striking deep-fuchsia walls, white furniture, tasselled bedspreads and piles of pillows. More-expensive rooms are similarly bold in design, and all rooms have hardwood floors, gentle lighting and sleek, spacious bathrooms. A diamond in the rough of SD Rd.

Taj Krishna (Map p958; ☎ 66664242; www.tajho tels.com; Rd No 1, Banjara Hills; s/d from Rs22,000/23,500; ✕ ▯ ▨) The gardens of the Taj Krishna are where Hyderabad's beautiful people come to have their fashion shows. But they're likely to be upstaged by the lush, artful gardens. Or the rooms, with their elegant furniture, antique parquet floors, and piles of taffeta pillows. The opulence you expect for the price.

Eating

Andhra Pradesh's cuisine has two major influences. The Mughals brought tasty biryanis, *haleem* (pounded, spiced wheat with mutton; see the box, right) and kebabs. The Andhra style is vegetarian and famous for its spiciness.

Per local usage, we use the term 'meal' instead of 'thali' in this chapter.

CITY CENTRE

Mozamjahi Market (Map p958; cnr Mukarramjahi & Jawaharlal Nehru Rds; ☽ 6am-6pm) A great place to buy fruit and vegies (or ice cream), while enjoying the alluring architecture of the stone building, commissioned by the seventh nizam and named after his son.

G Pulla Reddy (Map p958; Patthargatti; sweets Rs8-25 ☽ 10am-9pm) Sweets so good you'll die. Also has branches in Abids (Map p960) and Begumpet (Map p958).

> **BEATING THE BHATTIS**
>
> If you're travelling around Andhra Pradesh during Ramadan (known locally as Ramzan), look out for the clay ovens called *bhattis*. You'll probably hear them before you see them. Men gather around, taking turns to vigorously pound *haleem* (a mixture of meat, ghee, wheat and spices) inside purpose-built structures. Come nightfall, the serious business of eating begins. The taste is worth the wait.

Karachi's (Map p960; Mahaprabhu House, JN Rd; snacks Rs12-40; ☽ 11.30am-10.30pm) A tacky, fun fast-food joint with good *chaat* (snacks), vegie burgers, pizza and the enigmatic 'Chinese dosa'.

Kamat Hotel (Map p958; SD Rd, Secunderabad; mains Rs45-75; ☽ 7.30am-10pm) How much do we love Kamat Hotel? Words can't say. Each Kamat is slightly different, but they're all cheap and good. There are two branches on SD Rd; the others are in Saifabad and on Nampally Station Rd (Map p960). Meals (from Rs36) are reliably delish.

Kamat Andhra Meals (Map p960; Troop Bazaar; meals Rs45; ☽ noon-3.30pm & 7-10.30pm) Excellent authentic Andhra meals on banana leaves, topped up till you almost faint with pleasure, and finished off with a banana. Its sister restaurants in the same compound – Kamat Jowar Bhakri (Maharashtran), Kamat Restaurant (North and South Indian) and Kamat Coffee Shop – are likewise friendly family joints full of happy diners. No relation to Kamat Hotel.

Sagar Papaji Ka Dhaba (Map p960; Hanuman Tekdi Rd; mains Rs45-110; ☽ noon-4pm & 7-11pm) Always busy, Papaji's has profoundly delicious veg and non-veg biryanis, curries and tikkas. Watch the guys making naan and throwing it in the tandoor while you wait for a table.

Hotel Shadab (Map p958; High Court Rd, Patthargatti; mains Rs60-145; ☽ noon-2am) One meal at Shadab and you'll be forever under its spell. The hopping restaurant is *the* place to get biryani and, during Ramadan, *haleem* (see above). It has even mastered veg biryani (!) and hundreds of other veg and non-veg delights (if you try the chocolate chicken or pineapple mutton, let us know how it goes). Packed with Old City families and good vibes.

Minerva Coffee Shop (Map p960; Himayathnagar Rd; mains Rs105-150; ☽ 7am-10.30pm) You can depend on this old-school cafe with contemporary decor for excellent meals, dosas (thin lentil pancake) and masala chai (Rs27). Both this and the Somajiguda branch (Map p958) are popular with friends catching up for lunch.

our pick **Waterfront** (Map p958; ☎ 65278899; Necklace Rd; mains Rs175-450; ☺ noon-11pm) Just next to Eat Street, the outdoor deck here on the water (dinner service only) may have the best ambience in all of Hyderabad, with soft lighting overhead and the Buddha Statue, the entire Hussain Sagar and the Birla Mandir all twinkling in the distance. Eating indoors, alongside enormous picture windows, isn't bad either. But it's the Chinese, Indian and Thai food that's to die for – their take on *phad kea mou* (noodles with tasty bok choy) is a must-eat.

Eat Street (Map p958; Necklace Rd; ☺ 7am-11pm) The food court has good coffee and fast food, and you'll also find kids' rides, boat launches to the Buddha Statue (see p963) and tables on a waterfront boardwalk. It could be cheesy; instead it's delightful.

Also recommended:

Paradise Persis Restaurant (Map p958; ☎ 27843115; cnr SD & MG Rds, Secunderabad; mains Rs125-200; ☺ 11am-11pm) Ask any Hyderabadi about biryani, and they'll mention Paradise.

Ming's Court (Map p960; ☎ 23298811; Ohri's Cuisine Court, Bashirbagh Rd; mains Rs190-280; ☺ 11.30am-3.30pm & 7pm-midnight)

BANJARA HILLS

Ofen (Map p958; ☎ 23372205; Rd No 10; desserts Rs15-110; ☺ 8am-11pm) Two words: Linzer torte. Scrumptious desserts (even some vegan and sugar-free), fresh-baked bread and comfort food like sandwiches and pasta (Rs90 to Rs195).

Le Café d'Art (Map p958; ☎ 65506661/2; Rd No 1; light meals Rs115-185; ☺ 9am-11pm) Beautiful young people come here come to smoke hookahs (Rs250) in antique-chic surrounds. We like it for the salads, sandwiches and espresso, though the service charge – for slow service – is a downer.

Angeethi (Map p958; ☎ 66255550; 7th fl, Reliance Classic Bldg, Rd No 1; mains Rs150-275; ☺ 12.30-3.30pm & 7-10.30pm) The setting, designed to resemble an old Punjabi *dhaba* (snack bar), is over the top. But Angeethi does outstanding North Indian and Punjabi dishes, such as corn *methi malai* (sweet-corn stew with fenugreek leaves; Rs170).

Fusion 9 (Map p958; ☎ 65577722; Rd No 1; mains Rs325-425; ☺ 12-3.30pm & 7pm-midnight) Soft lighting and cosy decor set off pan-fried Norwegian salmon (Rs750) or Brazilian tenderloin steak (Rs1200). There's also (less expensive)

Mexican, Thai, pizzas and veg dishes, and lots of imported liquor.

Healthy people will appreciate **24-Lettered Mantra** (Map p958; ☎ 23300303; Rd No 12; ☺ 9.30am-9.45pm), a tiny grocery shop with organic produce, snacks and juices.

Other recommendations:

Southern Spice (Map p958; ☎ 23353802; Rd No 2; mains Rs85-260; ☺ 12.15-3.30pm & 7.15-10.30pm) Spicy goodness.

Ohri's Far East (Map p958; ☎ 23302200; Rd No 12; mains Rs185-350; ☺ 12.30-3.30pm & 7-11.30pm) Pan-Asian.

Drinking

CAFES

Mocha (Map p958; Rd No 7, Banjara Hills; coffees Rs30-180, light meals Rs75-150; ☺ 9am-11pm) Full of 20-somethings smoking hookahs, but the decor, the garden and the coffee are fabulous.

Also worth a try for reliable coffee are **Café Coffee Day** (Map p958; Eat Street, Necklace Rd; coffees Rs28-85; ☺ 7.30am-11pm) and **Barista** (Map p958; Rd No 1, Banjara Hills; coffees Rs30-95; ☺ 8am-10pm).

BARS & LOUNGES

Hyderabad's scene is growing, but drinking establishments are limited by a midnight curfew law. Unless stated otherwise, the following are open noon to midnight (but don't get going till 9pm). All serve food and charge covers (Rs500 to Rs1000) on certain nights – for couples, that is: guys usually need a gal to enter. Beer starts at Rs150, cocktails at Rs300.

Liquids Again (Map p958; ☎ 66259907; Bhaskar Plaza, Rd No 1, Banjara Hills) Regularly featured in the papers' Society pages, Liquids is the reigning queen of Hyderabad nightlife.

Touch (Map p958; ☎ 23542422; Trendset Towers, Rd No 2, Banjara Hills) Touch is all about image. It's a stylish, comfy place to watch the beautiful people.

Awana (Map p958; ☎ 23300427; Rd No 12, Banjara Hills) Awana has fun theme nights and a low-key restaurant next door.

Marco Polo Bar (Map p958; ☎ 23400132; ITC Hotel Kakatiya, Ameerpet) With views of the pool and palm trees, stools with antler-esque backrests, and old maps of the world, it's the perfect place for a twilight drink. The ITC also has Dublin, a popular 'Irish' pub.

Begumpet bars club on weekends:

10 Downing Street (Map p958; ☎ 66629323; My Home Tycoon Bldg)

Bottles & Chimney (Map p958; ☎ 27766464; SP Rd)

Entertainment

ARTS

Ravindra Bharati Theatre (Map p960; ☎ 23233672; www
.artistap.com; Public Gardens Rd) Regular music, dance
and drama performances. Check local papers.

Hyderabad has a burgeoning contemporary
art scene:

ICCR Art Gallery (Map p960; ☎ 23236398; Ravindra
Bharati Theatre, Public Gardens Rd; ☽ 11am-7pm)

Kalakriti (Map p958; ☎ 66564466; www.kalakriti.in; Rd
No 10, Banjara Hills; ☽ 11am-7pm)

Shrishti (off Map p958; ☎ 23540023; www.shrishtiart
.com; Rd No 15, Jubilee Hills; ☽ 11am-7pm)

CINEMA

Mega-cinemas have taken over Hyderabad's
English-language movie scene:

Prasad's Multiplex (Map p960; ☎ 23448989, booking
39895050; www.prasadz.com; NTR Marg) A monstrous
Imax theatre.

PVR Cinemas (Map p958; ☎ 66621115; www.pvrcin
emas.com; Hyderabad Central, Panjagutta Rd)

Shopping

The bazaars near the Charminar (see p959)
are the most exciting places to shop: you'll
find exquisite pearls, silks, gold and fabrics
alongside billions of bangles.

Hyderabad Perfumers (Map p958; ☎ 24577294;
Patthargatti; ☽ 10am-8pm Mon-Sat) The family-
run Hyderabad Perfumers, which has been
in business for four generations, can whip
something up for you on the spot.

Meena Bazar (Map p960; ☎ 24753566; Tilak Rd;
☽ 10.30am-8.30pm Mon-Sat) Gorgeous saris, *salwar* (trouser) suits and fabrics at fixed prices.
Even if you're not in the market, come here
to sightsee.

Kalanjali (Map p960; ☎ 23423440; Public Gardens Rd;
☽ 10am-9.30pm Mon-Sat) With a huge range of arts,
crafts, fabrics and clothing, Kalanjali has higher
prices than the bazaar, but you can get a feel for
what things cost in a relaxed environment.

Sangeet Sagar (Map p960; ☎ 23225346; Bashirbagh Rd;
☽ 10.30am-9pm Mon-Sat) Great little music shop.

Nursing Home Lane is a sweet little street
with kurta stores and our favourite bangle shop,
New Fashion Ladies Emporium (Map p960; ☎ 66688867;
Bashirbagh; ☽ 11am-10pm Mon-Sat, 2-10pm Sun).

Other places for crafts and clothes:

Anokhi (Map p958; ☎ 23350271; Rd No 10, Banjara
Hills; ☽ 10.30am-7.30pm Mon-Sat) Sophisticated clothes
in hand-block prints.

Bidri Crafts (Map p960; ☎ 23232657; Gunfoundry;
☽ 11am-9pm Mon-Sat)

Fabindia (Map p958; ☎ 23354526; Rd No 9, Banjara
Hills; ☽ 10am-9pm Tue-Sun) Hip clothes in traditional
artisanal fabrics.

Lepakshi (Map p960; ☎ 23212902; Gunfoundry;
☽ 10am-8pm Mon-Sat) Andhra crafts.

Getting There & Away

Hyderabad's massive newly built **Rajiv Gandhi
International Airport** (☎ 66546370, 1800 4192008;
http://hyderabad.aero) is 22km southwest of the
city in Shamshabad.

AIR

You'll get the best fares online or with a travel
agent. Try **Neo Globe Tours & Travels** (Map p960;
☎ 66751786; Saifabad; ☽ 10am-7.30pm Mon-Sat) beside
the Nizam Club.

Airline offices are usually open from 9.30am
to 5.30pm Monday to Friday, with a one-hour
lunch break, and to 1.30pm Saturday.

Domestic Airlines

GoAir (☎ airport 9223222111, 1800 222111; Rajiv
Gandhi International Airport)

Indian Airlines (Map p960; ☎ 23430334, 1800
1801407, airport 24255161/2; HACA Bhavan, Saifabad)

IndiGo (Map p960; ☎ 23233590, airport 24255052; Interglobe Air Transport, Chapel Rd; ☽ 8.30am-6pm Mon-Sat)

Jet Airways (Map p960; ☎ 39824444, airport
39893322; Hill Fort Rd; ☽ 9am-7pm Mon-Sat) Also
handles bookings for JetLite.

MAJOR DOMESTIC FLIGHTS FROM HYDERABAD			
Destination	**Lowest one-way fare (Rs)**	**Duration (hr)**	**Flights per day**
Bengaluru	3500	1	18
Chennai	3500	1	20
Delhi	5700	2	24
Kolkota	6000	2	16
Mumbai	3500	1¼	22
Tirupathi	3500	1	3
Visakhapatnam	3500	1	10

ANDHRA PRADESH

BUSES FROM HYDERABAD

Destination	Fare (Rs)	Duration (hr)	Departures (daily)
Bengaluru	358/695	12/10	34 (evening)
Bidar	70	4	half-hourly
Chennai	390-660	12	5 (evening)
Hospet	305	12	10
Mumbai	430/810	16/12	8 (evening)
Mysore	480	13	4
Nagarjuna Sagar	63-85	4	8
Tirupathi	255-560	12	12
Vijayawada	160-275	6	half-hourly
Warangal	65	3	half-hourly

JetLite (☎ 30302020, 1800 223020; Rajiv Gandhi International Airport)

Kingfisher Airlines (Map p960; ☎ 23210985/8, 1800 2333131; Summit House, Hill Fort Rd)

Paramount Airways (☎ airport 66605220-2, 1800 1801234; Rajiv Gandhi International Airport)

SpiceJet (Map p958; ☎ 27904796, 1800 1803333; Begumpet)

International Airlines

Air India (Map p960; ☎ 1800 227722, airport 24255161/2; HACA Bhavan, Saifabad)

Cathay Pacific (Map p958; ☎ 27704310; SD Rd, Secunderabad)

Emirates (Map p958; ☎ 66234444; Rd No 1, Banjara Hills)

GSA Transworld Travels (Map p960; ☎ 66102781; Chapel Rd) For Qantas.

Interglobe Air Transport (Map p960; ☎ 23233590; Chapel Rd) For Air New Zealand, Delta, South African, Turkish, United and Virgin Atlantic.

KLM (☎ airport 66605102; Rajiv Gandhi International Airport)

Lufthansa (Map p958; ☎ 44331000; Begumpet) Next to the Lifestyle Building.

Sri Lankan Airlines (Map p958; ☎ 23372429/30; Raj Bhavan Rd, Somajiguda) Opposite the Yashoda Hospital.

Qatar Airways (Map p958; ☎ 0124 4566000; Rd No 1, Banjara Hills)

Thai Airways (Map p958; ☎ 23333030; Rd No 1, Banjara Hills)

BUS

Hyderabad's long-distance bus stations are mind-bogglingly efficient. **Mahatma Gandhi bus station** (Map p958; ☎ 24614406, 23434268/80), better known as Imlibun, has **advance booking offices** (☽ 8am-11pm). For trips to Karnataka, go with **KSRTC** (☎ 24656430).

Secunderabad's **Jubilee bus station** (Map p958; ☎ 27802203) operates Volvo AC buses to Bengaluru (Rs685, 10 hours, three daily), Chennai (Rs700, 12 hours, daily) and Visakhapatnam (Rs701, 13 hours, daily).

Private bus companies with AC services are on Nampally High Rd, near the train station entrance.

TRAIN

Secunderabad (Map p958), Hyderabad (Map p960) – also known as Nampally – and Kacheguda (Map p958) are the three major train stations. Most through trains stop at Secunderabad and Kacheguda, which is convenient for Abids. See the boxed text, opposite, for key routes. You can book at Hyderabad and Secunderabad stations from 8am to 8pm Monday to Saturday (to 2pm Sunday). Both stations have a tourist counter. For general inquiries, phone ☎ 131; for reservation status, ☎ 135.

Getting Around
TO/FROM THE AIRPORT

The new airport is fabulous, but until the express highway is completed, it's a 1½-hour schlep from town. Free shuttle buses run to the airport's Public Transportation Centre (PTC).

Bus

Frequent public buses depart from the PTC for Jubilee and Imlibun stations. More comfy are AC **Aeroexpress** (☎ 1800 4192008; Rs120-150; ☽ 24hr) buses, which run half-hourly to five locations: Charminar, Secunderabad, Begumpet, Mehdipatnam and Hitec City.

Taxi

For prepaid taxis, pay at the counter inside the terminal, then get your cab at the PTC.

Meru (☎ 44224422) and **Easy** (☎ 43434343) 'radio taxis' queue up outside arrivals and charge Rs15 per kilometre, Rs18.75 at night. The trip to Abids or Banjara Hills shouldn't exceed Rs450. Going to the airport, try **Yellow Taxi** (☎ 44004400).

AUTORICKSHAW

Flag fall is Rs12 for the first kilometre, then Rs7 for each additional kilometre. Between 10pm and 5am a 50% surcharge applies. Unfortunately, the new electronic meters often don't work and lots of drivers won't use them: be prepared to negotiate.

BUS

Lots of local buses originate at **Koti bus station** (Map p958; ☎ 23443320; Rani Jhansi Rd), so if you come here you might get a seat. The 'travel as you like' ticket (ordinary/express Rs28/40), available from bus conductors, permits unlimited travel anywhere within the city on the day of purchase. The tiny *City Bus Route Guide* (Rs10) is available at bookshops around Koti.

MAJOR BUS ROUTES FROM HYDERABAD & SECUNDERABAD	
Bus No	**Route**
20D	Jubilee station–Nampally
1P/25	Secunderabad station–Jubilee station
2/2V, 8A/8U,	Charminar–Secunderabad station
1K, 1B, 3SS, 40	Secunderabad station–Koti
20P, 20V, 49, 49P	Secunderabad station–Nampally
65G/66G	Charminar–Golconda, via Abids
87	Charminar–Nampally
1190R, 142M	Nampally–Golconda
142K	Koti–Golconda

CAR

There are several car-rental places around Hyderabad station. **Links Travels** (☎ 9348770007) is reliable for local or long-distance day rental.

TRAIN

MMTS trains are convenient, particularly for the three main train stations. There are two main lines: Hyderabad (Nampally) to

MAJOR TRAINS FROM HYDERABAD & SECUNDERABAD				
Destination	**Train No & Name**	**Fare (Rs)**	**Duration (hr)**	**Departure Time & Station**
Bengaluru	2430 *Rajdhani*	3AC/2AC Rs1065/1410	12	6.50pm Secunderabad (Tue, Wed, Sat & Sun)
	2785 *Secunderabad–Bangalore Exp*	sleeper/3AC/2AC Rs291/731/1036	11	7.05pm Kacheguda
Chennai	2604 *Hyderabad–Chennai Exp*	sleeper/3AC/2AC Rs301/792/1076	13	4.55pm Hyderabad
	2760 *Charminar Exp*	sleeper/3AC/2AC Rs317/837/1139	14	6.30pm Hyderabad
Delhi	2723 *Andhra Pradesh Exp*	sleeper/3AC/2AC Rs473/1275/1747	26	6.25am Hyderabad
	2429 *Rajdhani*	3AC/2AC Rs1725/2245	26	7.50am Secunderabad (Mon, Tue, Thu & Fri)
Kolkata	2704 *Falaknuma Exp*	Rs449/1208/1653	26	4pm Secunderabad
	8646 *East Coast Exp*	sleeper/3AC/2AC Rs437/1200/1654	30	10am Hyderabad
Mumbai	2702 *Hussainsagar Exp*	sleeper/3AC/2AC Rs317/837/1139	15	2.45pm Hyderabad
	7032 *Hyderabad–Mumbai Exp*	sleeper/3AC/2AC Rs297/807/1109	16	8.40pm Hyderabad
Tirupathi	2734 *Narayanadri Exp*	sleeper/3AC/2AC Rs288/756/1026	12	6.05pm Secunderbad
	2797 *Venkatadri Exp*	sleeper/3AC/2AC Rs281/704/996	12	8.05pm Kacheguda
Visakhapatnam	2728 *Godavari Exp*	sleeper/3AC/2AC Rs299/785/1106	13	5.15pm Hyderabad

Lingampalli (northwest of Banjara Hills) has 11 stops, including Lakdikapul, Khairatabad, Necklace Rd, Begumpet and Hitec City; the Falaknuma (south of Old City) to Begumpet line passes by Yakutpura, Dabirpura, Malakpet, Kacheguda and Secunderabad, among others. Trains will be labelled with their start and end point: so, HL is Hyderabad–Lingampalli, FS is Falaknuma–Secunderabad and so on. Trains are efficient but only run every 30 to 40 minutes. Tickets are Rs2 to Rs7.

NAGARJUNAKONDA
☎ 08680

The Hill of Nagarjuna, 150km southeast of Hyderabad, is a peaceful island in the middle of the Nagarjuna dam peppered with ancient Buddhist structures. From the 3rd century BC until the 4th century AD, the Krishna River valley was home to powerful empires that supported the sangha (Buddhist community of monks and nuns), including the Ikshvakus, whose capital was Nagarjunakonda. It's estimated that this area alone had 30 monasteries.

The remains here were actually discovered in 1926 by archaeologist AR Saraswathi in the adjacent valley. In 1953, when it became known that a massive hydroelectric project would soon create the **Nagarjuna Sagar** reservoir, flooding the area, a six-year excavation was launched to unearth the area's many Buddhist ruins: stupas, *viharas, chaitya-grihas* (assembly halls with stupas) and *mandapas* (pillared pavilions), as well as some outstanding examples of white-marble depictions of the Buddha's life. The finds were reassembled on Nagarjunakonda.

AP Tourism (☎ 276634; ☽ 9am-6pm Mon-Sat) has an office at Project House, across from the bus stand.

Sights
The thoughtfully laid-out **Nagarjunakonda Museum** (Indian/foreigner Rs5/100; ☽ 9.30am-3.45pm Sat-Thu) has Stone Age tools on exhibit, but more exciting are its Buddha statues and carved stone slabs that once adorned stupas. Most are from the 3rd century AD and depict scenes from the Buddha's life, interspersed with *mithuna* (paired male and female) figures languorously looking on. The re-assembled **monuments** are spread around the hilltop outside.

Launches (Rs75, one hour) depart from Vijayapuri, on the banks of Nagarjuna Sagar,

at 9.30am and 1.30pm, and stay for one hour. To do the place justice, take the morning launch out and the afternoon one back. Extra morning launches usually run on weekends and holidays.

Sleeping & Eating
Nagarjunakonda is popular, and accommodation can be tight during weekends and holidays. **Nagarjuna Resort** (☎ 08642-242471; r from Rs630; ☒) is the most convenient place to stay, across the road from the boat launch. It has spacious, slightly shabby rooms with geysers, balconies and good views. Two kilometres up the hill from the bus stand is the fancy **Vijay Vihar Complex** (☎ 277362; fax 276633; r with AC from Rs1650; ☒ ☒) overlooking the lake. Room balconies have excellent views. Both hotels have restaurants.

Getting There & Away
The easiest way to visit Nagarjunakonda is with **APTDC** (☎ 040-65581555) in Hyderabad. Tours (Rs450) depart on weekends at 7am from Yatri Nivas Hotel (see p964) and 7.30am from APTDC in Bashirbagh (see p959), returning at 9.30pm.

You can also make your own way there from Hyderabad or Vijayawada. From Hyderabad, take a bus to Nagarjuna Sagar (or to Macherla or Vinukonda, which will stop at Nagarjuna Sagar). From there, it's a Rs10 shared rickshaw to Pylon, and another Rs10 to the boat launch. The nearest train station is 22km away at Macherla, where buses leave regularly for Nagarjuna Sagar.

WARANGAL
☎ 0870 / pop 528,570

Warangal was the capital of the Kakatiya kingdom, which covered the greater part of present-day Andhra Pradesh from the late 12th to early 14th centuries until it was conquered by the Tughlaqs of Delhi. The Hindu Kakatiyas were great builders and patrons of Telugu literature and arts, and it was during their reign that the Chalukyan style of temple architecture reached its pinnacle. If you're interested in Hindu temple development, then it's worth the trip to Warangal and Palampet (see p972). It's possible to visit both places on a long day trip from Hyderabad, 157km away.

Most buses and trains will stop en route at Bhongir, 60km from Hyderabad. It's worth jumping down for a couple of hours to climb

STATE OF GOOD KARMA

In its typically understated way, Andhra Pradesh doesn't make much of its vast archaeological – and karmic – wealth. But in fact, the state is packed with impressive ruins of its rich Buddhist history. Only a few of Andhra's 150 stupas, monasteries, caves and other sites have been excavated, turning up rare relics of the Buddha (usually pearl-like pieces of bone) with offerings like golden flowers. They speak of a time when Andhra Pradesh – or Andhradesa – was a hotbed of Buddhist activity, when monks came from around the world to learn from some of the tradition's most renowned teachers, and when Indian monks set off for Sri Lanka and Southeast Asia via the Krishna and Godavari Rivers and the Bay of Bengal to spread the teaching of the Buddha.

Andhradesa's Buddhist culture, in which sangha (community of monks and nuns), laity and statespeople all took part, lasted around 1500 years from the 6th century BC. There's no historical evidence for it, but some even say that the Buddha himself visited the area.

Andhradesa's first practitioners were likely disciples of Bavari, an ascetic who lived on the banks of the Godavari River and sent his followers north to bring back the Buddha's teachings. But the dharma really took off in the 3rd century BC under Ashoka (see p41), who dispatched monks out across his empire to teach and construct stupas enshrined with relics of the Buddha. (Being near these was thought to help progress on the path to enlightenment.)

Succeeding Ashoka, the Satavahanas and then Ikshvakus were also supportive. At their capital at Amaravathi, the Satavahanas adorned Ashoka's modest stupa with elegant decoration. They built monasteries across the Krishna Valley and exported the dharma through their sophisticated maritime network.

It was also during the Satavahana reign that Nagarjuna lived. Considered by many to be the progenitor of Mahayana Buddhism, the monk was equal parts logician, philosopher and meditator, and he wrote several ground-breaking works that shaped contemporary Buddhist thought. Other important monk-philosophers would emerge from the area in the following centuries, making Andhradesa a sort of Buddhist motherland of the South.

Today, the state's many remains are ripe for exploring; even in ruins, you can get a sense of how large some of the stupas were, how expansive the monastic complexes, and how the monks lived, sleeping in caves and fetching rainwater from stone-cut cisterns. Plus, most of the sites have stunning views across seascapes and countryside. Head to the area around Vijayawada for Chandavaram, Guntupalli or Bhattiprolu, and near Visakhapatnam for Thotlakonda and Bavikonda (p974), Sankaram (p974), and Ramatirtham.

---

the fantastical-looking 12th-century Chalukyan **hill fort** (admission Rs3). Looking like a gargantuan stone egg, the hill is mostly ringed by stairs.

Orientation & Information

Warangal, Hanamkonda and Kazhipet are sister towns. The Warangal train station and bus stand are opposite each other, and the post office and police station are on Station Rd. Main Rd connects Warangal and Hanamkonda.

Lots of ATMs and **Apple Computers** (per hr Rs8) are near Hotel Ratna on JPN Rd. The **Department of Tourism** (☎ 2459201; Hanamkonda-Kazhipet Rd; ☼ 10.30am-5pm Mon-Sat), opposite REC, is helpful.

Sights

Warangal's **fort** (Indian/foreigner Rs5/100; ☼ dawn-dusk) was a massive construction with three distinct circular strongholds surrounded by a moat. Four paths with decorative gateways, set according to the cardinal points, led to the Swayambhava, a huge Shiva temple. The gateways are still obvious, but most of the fort is in ruins. It's easily reached from Warangal by bus or autorickshaw (Rs100 return).

Built in 1163, the **1000-Pillared Temple** (☼ 6am-6pm) on the slopes of Hanamkonda Hill, 400m from Hanamkonda crossroads, is a fine example of Chalukyan architecture in a peaceful, leafy setting. Dedicated to three deities – Shiva, Vishnu and Surya – it has been carefully restored with intricately carved pillars and a central, very impressive Nandi (bull; Shiva's mount) of black basalt.

Down the hill and 3km to the right is the small **Siddheshwara Temple**. The **Bhadrakali Temple**, featuring a stone statue of Kali seated with a weapon in each of her eight hands, is high on a hill between Hanamkonda and Warangal.

Sleeping & Eating

Vijaya Lodge (☎ 2501222; fax 2446864; Station Rd; s/d from Rs150/240) About 100m from the train station, the Vijaya is well organised with helpful staff, but the rooms are becoming a little dreary.

Hotel Ratna (☎ 2500645; fax 2500555; MG Rd; s/d from Rs400/600; ✖) The Ratna has shiny floors, fresh paint and professional staff, and it accepts credit cards. Oh, and it's super-clean. Its veg restaurant, Kavya (open 6.30am to 10pm, mains Rs65 to 100), makes insanely delicious, enormous meals (Rs48) that will leave you feeling fully satisfied and slightly intoxicated.

Hotel Surya (☎ 2441834; fax 2441836; Station Rd; s/d incl breakfast from Rs450/575; ✖) Near the stations, the Surya has smart rooms, which are only just beginning to fade, and constant hot water. The restaurant downstairs, Surabhi (mains Rs75 to Rs140), has good Chinese food and kebabs, and plenty of non-veg fare.

Hotel Ashoka (☎ 2579260; Main Rd, Hanamkonda; s/d from Rs450/600; ✖ ▢) Good-value rooms near the Hanamkonda bus stand and the 1000-Pillared Temple. Also in the compound are a restaurant, a bar-restaurant, a pub and the veg Kanishka (mains Rs40 to Rs110).

The train station has a few **retiring rooms** (r without/with AC Rs100/200; ✖).

Getting There & Around

Buses head to Vijayawada (express/deluxe Rs115/150, seven hours, seven daily) from **Warangal bus stand** (☎ 9959226057). Frequent buses to Hyderabad (express/deluxe/luxury Rs66/74/85, four hours) depart from **Hanamkonda bus stand** (☎ 9959226056), a Rs6 bus ride away.

Warangal is a major rail junction. Trains go regularly to Hyderabad (2nd class/chair Rs68/232, three hours), Vijayawada (2nd class/chair Rs80/282, four hours) and Chennai (sleeper/3AC/2AC Rs281/735/996, 11 hours). Many trains go to Delhi daily.

Shared autorickshaws ply fixed routes around Warangal (including to the fort), Kazhipet and Hanamkonda. A shared autorickshaw ride costs Rs5 to Rs7.

AROUND WARANGAL
Palampet

About 65km northeast of Warangal, the stunning **Ramappa Temple** (☉ 6am-6.30pm), built in 1234, is an attractive example of Kakatiya architecture, although it was clearly influenced by Chalukya and Hoysala styles. Its pillars are ornately carved and its eaves shelter fine statues of female forms.

Just 1km south, the Kakatiyas constructed **Ramappa Cheruvu** to serve as temple tank. The lake, along with nearby Pakhal Lake 20km south, is popular with migrating birds.

The easiest way to get here is by private car (Rs1200), but frequent buses also run from Hanamkonda to Palampet (Rs28). The temple is about 500m from here.

VISAKHAPATNAM
☎ 0891 / pop 1.3 million

Visit Visakhapatnam – also called Vizag (*vie*-zag) – during the holiday season and you'll see domestic tourism in rare form: balloons, cotton candy and, of course, weddings! But the crowds only enhance the area's kitschy coasts. The run-down boardwalk along Ramakrishna Beach has lots of spunk, and the beach at nearby Rushikonda is one of Andhra's best.

The old beach-resort vibe exists despite the fact that Vizag is Andhra Pradesh's second-largest city, famous for shipbuilding, steel manufacturing and now, call centres, software and film production. It's a big, dusty city, but it's surrounded by little gems: sweet beaches, a gorgeous temple and, further out, the Araku Valley (see p974), and several ancient Buddhist sites (p974 and p974).

Orientation

Vizag's train station sits in a hive of shops and hotels on the western edge of town, near the port. Dwarakanagar, Vizag's commercial centre, is 2km east of the train station, and RTC Complex, the bus stand, is just southeast of here. Waltair and its Ramakrishna Beach are about 3km south of RTC.

Information

ATMs are everywhere. RTC Complex has several internet cafes, some open 24 hours.

Apollo Pharmacy (☎ 2788652; Siripuram Junction; ☉ 24hr)

APTDC RTC Complex (☎ 2788820; ☉ 6am-9pm); Train station (☎ 2788821; ☉ 5am-10pm) Information and tours.

Cloak rooms RTC Complex (per day Rs8); Train station (per day Rs10, locker per day Rs15; ☉ 24hr)

Pages Book Shop (☎ 6450555; Old Jail Rd, Daba Gardens; ☉ 9.30am-9.30pm) Opposite State Bank of India. Stocks the English-language what's-on mag, *Yo! Vizag* (Rs40).

Thomas Cook (☎ 2588112; Eswar Plaza, Dwarakanagar; ☉ 9am-6.30pm Mon-Sat) Near ICICI Bank.

Sights & Activities

The long beaches of **Waltair** overlook the Bay of Bengal, with its mammoth ships and brightly painted fishing boats. Its coastal **Beach Rd**, lined with parks and weird sculptures, is great for long walks.

The best beaches for swimming are at **Rushikonda**, 8km north. On the way, **Kailasagiri Hill** has gardens, playgrounds and a gargantuan Shiva and Parvati. The views from the hill and the **Kailasagiri Passenger Ropeway** (☎ 6510334; admission Rs55; ✆ 11am-1pm & 2-8pm) are awesome. Movies or cricket matches are sometimes shown across Beach Rd, at the festive **Tenetti Beach**.

At Simhachalam Hill, 10km northwest of town, is a fine 11th-century **Vishnu Temple** (✆ 6-10am & 4-6pm) in Orissan style. You can give *puja* to the deity, who's covered with sandalwood paste. Bus 6 A/H (Rs13) goes here.

Tours

APTDC operates full-day tours of the city (from Rs300) and Araku Valley (see p974).

Sleeping

Dumpy budget hotels huddle around the train station, which has **retiring rooms** (dm/r from Rs50/250; ✖). Waltair has better vibes, but few inexpensive hotels. Prices rise for Dussehra/Diwali holidays, when Bengalis swarm to Vizag.

Sree Kanya Lodge (☎ 5564881; Bowdara Rd; s/d from Rs200/450; ✖) Near the train station but out of the bustle, Sree Kanya is mostly characterless and a little dirty, but it's the best of the sorry lot. On the flip side, most rooms have balconies and the restaurant downstairs is good. Go for the 'deluxe' singles (Rs250) if you like daylight.

Sai Priya Resort (☎ 2790333; www.saipriya beachresorts.com; cottages/r from Rs700/1300; ✖ ✆) Modern rooms, some with sea views, and cottages of bamboo and cane on Rushikonda beach. The grounds are lush and *almost* really beautiful, but like the rest of the place, they fall short of their potential. Also, checkout's a rude 8am. Nonguests can use the pool for two hours for Rs100.

Haritha Hotel (☎ 2562333; Beach Rd, Appughar; r incl breakfast from Rs850; ✖) This APTDC hotel, formerly Punnami, is near Kailasagiri Hill and right across from the beach. The lowest-priced rooms (with no views) are only so-so; bump yourself up if you can. Checkout is 10am.

Park (☎ 2754488; www.theparkhotels.com; Beach Rd; s/d from Rs7000/9000; ✖ ✆ ✆) Vizag's only five-star is very elegant, very high-design. Even if you don't stay here, visit Bamboo Bay, its beachfront restaurant, for a drink. Checkout is noon.

Other recommendations:

YMCA Tourist Hostel (☎ 2755826; ymca_visakha@ yahoo.com; Beach Rd; dm/s/d from Rs150/550/650; ✖) Best value in town, with superb views, but always full. Call anyway; you might get lucky.

Gateway Hotel (☎ 6623670; www.tajhotels.com/gate way; Beach Rd; s/d from Rs6500/7500; ✖ ✆ ✆) The usual Taj classiness, with great views. Checkout is noon.

Eating & Drinking

At night, the snack stalls on Ramakrishna Beach and the beachfront restaurants at Rushikonda, next to Punnami, are hopping.

New Andhra Hotel (Sree Kanya Lodge, Bowdara Rd; mains Rs25-75; ✆ 11am-3.30pm & 7-10.30pm) An unassuming little place with *really* good, *really* hot Andhra dishes. Meals (Rs40/100 for veg/non-veg) and biryani are top-notch.

our pick **Vaisakhi** (☎ 2564825; Hotel Daspalla, Suryabagh; mains Rs55-100; ✆ 11.30am-3pm & 7-10.30pm) Words don't do justice to the super-deliciousness of the meals (Rs72) at this family veg restaurant. *And* they come with ice cream. Yes, we're still dreaming of them.

Masala (☎ 2750750; Signature Towers, 1st fl, Asilmetta; mains Rs70-130; ✆ 11am-3.30pm & 7-11pm) Near Sampath Vinayaka Temple, Masala does out-of-this-world Andhra, tandoori and Chinese. Try the *chepa pulusu* (Andhra-style fish; Rs100).

Café Coffee Day (coffees Rs20-50; ✆ 9.30am-10.30pm) Up the road from Masala.

Getting There & Around

You'll have to negotiate fares with autorickshaw drivers here. Most in-town rides will be around Rs20. **Guide Tours & Travels** (☎ 2754477), reliable for car rental, is opposite the RTC Complex 'out gate'.

AIR

Take an autorickshaw (Rs150), taxi (Rs225) or bus 38 (Rs6) to Vizag's airport, 13km west of town.

Domestic airlines and their daily services: **Indian Airlines** (☎ 2746501, 1800 1801407; LIC Bldg) Chennai (except Sunday), Delhi (except Sunday), Hyderabad and Mumbai (via Hyderabad).

Jet Airways (☎ airport 2741092) Delhi, Hyderabad, Kolkota and Mumbai.

Kingfisher (☎ 2503285, airport 2517614; Ardee Bldg, Siripuram Junction) Bengaluru, Chennai, Hyderabad, Kolkota and Tirupathi.

Paramount (☎ airport 2010400) Bengaluru, Chennai (via Hyderabad) and Hyderabad.

SpiceJet (☎ airport 2010422) Hyderabad; Delhi and Mumbai via Hyderabad.

BOAT

Boats depart every month-ish for Port Blair in the Andaman Islands (see p1127). Bookings for the 56-hour journey (Rs2000) can be made at the **Shipping Office** (☎ 2565597, 2562661, 9866073407; Av Bhanoji Row; ☒ 9am-5pm Mon-Sat) in the port complex. Bring your passport.

BUS

Vizag's well-organised **RTC Complex** (☎ 2746400) has frequent bus services to Vijayawada (deluxe/Volvo Rs193/402, eight/six hours) and, in the afternoon, Hyderabad ('superluxury'/ Volvo Rs395/700, 14/12 hours).

TRAIN

Visakhapatnam Junction station is on the Kolkata–Chennai line. The overnight *Coromandel Express* (sleeper/3AC/2AC Rs338/896/1220, 13½ hours) is the fastest of the five daily trains running to Kolkata. Heading south, it goes to Chennai (sleeper/3AC/2AC Rs300/796/1131, 12½ hours). Frequent trains head to Vijayawada including 2717, the *Ratnachalam Express* (2nd-class/chair Rs109/386).

AROUND VISAKHAPATNAM
Araku Valley

Andhra's best train ride is through the magnificent Eastern Ghats to the **Araku Valley**, 120km north of Vizag. The area is home to isolated tribal communities, and the tiny **Museum of Habitat** (admission Rs10; ☒ 10am-1pm & 2-5pm) has fascinating exhibits of indigenous life. APTDC runs tours from Vizag (see p972; Rs500), which take in a performance of Dhimsa, a tribal dance, and the million-year-old limestone **Borra Caves** (Rs25; ☒ 10am-5.30pm), 30km from Araku.

The **Punnami Hill Resort** (☎ 958936-249204; cottages from Rs650; ☒), near the museum, has cottages with good views. But it's more fun to stay at the forest retreat of **Jungle Bells** (Tyda; cottages from Rs800; ☒), 45km from Araku, with

cottages tucked away in woods. Book at APTDC (see p972).

The Kirandol passenger train (Rs28, five hours) leaves Vizag at 6.50am and Araku at 3pm. It's a slow, spectacular ride; sit on the right-hand side coming out of Vizag for best views. For Jungle Bells, get off at Tyda station, 500m from the resort.

Bavikonda & Thotlakonda

The Vizag area's natural harbours have long been conducive to dropping anchor, which helped monks from Sri Lanka, China and Tibet come here to learn and practice meditation. **Bavikonda** (☒ 9am-6pm) and **Thotlakonda** (☒ 10am-3pm) were popular hilltop monasteries on the coast that hosted up to 150 monks at a time – with the help of massive rainwater tanks and, at Thotlakonda, a natural spring.

The monasteries flourished during the Theravada period (Bavikonda, from the 3rd century BC to the 3rd century AD, and Thotlakonda, from the 2nd century BC to 2nd century AD) and had votive stupas, congregation halls, *chaitya-grihas* (assembly halls enclosing stupas), *viharas,* and refectories. Today only the ruins of these massive monastic compounds remain, but they're impressive nonetheless, with a placid, almost magical, air and sea views to meditate on. Bavikonda and Thotlakonda are 14km and 16km, respectively, from Vizag on Bheemli Beach Rd. Vizag's autorickshaw drivers charge around Rs400 return to see both.

Sankaram

Forty kilometres southwest of Vizag is this stunning **Buddhist complex** (☒ 9am-6pm), better known by the name of its two hills, Bojjannakonda and Lingalakonda. Used by monks from the 1st to 9th centuries AD (see the boxed text on p971), the hills are covered with rock-cut caves, stupas, ruins of monastery structures, and reliefs of the Buddha that span the Theravada, Mahayana and Vajrayana periods. Bojjannakonda has a two-storey group of rock-cut caves flanked by *dwarapalakas* (doorkeepers) and containing a stupa and gorgeous carvings of the Buddha (some restored). Atop the hill sit the ruins of a huge stupa and a monastery; you can still make out the individual cells where monks meditated. Lingalakonda is piled high with stupas, some of them enormous. Each hill requires some climbing and hiking – better to take in the spectacular views of palms and rice fields below.

A private car from Vizag costs around Rs800. Or, take a bus to Anakapalle (Rs24, one hour, every 20 minutes), 3km away, and then an autorickshaw (Rs150 return including waiting time).

VIJAYAWADA
☎ 0866 / pop 1 million

Vijayawada is a busy, rapidly growing city and an important port at the head of the delta of the mighty Krishna River. It's bustling, but it's also intersected by canals, lined with ghats and ringed by fields of rice and palm. The surrounding area is intensely lush and green.

Vijayawada is considered by many to be the heart of Andhra culture and language and has an important Durga temple. Nearby Amaravathi, meanwhile, was a centre of Buddhist learning and practise for many centuries.

Orientation

The Krishna River cuts across the city's southern end. The bus station is just north of the river, and the train station is in the centre of town, near the Hanumanpet and Governorpet neighbourhoods, which are separated by Eluru Rd. **Om Art Print** (☎ 2578333; JD Hospital Rd, cnr Besant Rd; ✆ 10am-8.30pm Mon-Sat) sells maps.

Information

Apollo Pharmacy (☎ 2432333; Vijaya Talkies Junction, Eluru Rd; ✆ 24hr)

APTDC (☎ 2571393; MG Rd, opposite PWD Grounds; ✆ 8am-8pm) Don't bother, unless you need brochures.

Care Hospital (☎ 2470100; Siddhartha Nagar)

Cloakrooms (per day Rs10; ✆ 24hr) At the train and bus stations.

MagicNet (☎ 2570956; Swarnalok Complex, Eluru Rd; per hr Rs20; ✆ 9.30am-9pm) Internet access.

Department of Tourism (☎ 2577577; train station; ✆ 10am-5pm)

State Bank of Hyderabad (☎ 2574832; 1st fl, Vijaya Commercial Complex, Governorpet; ✆ 10.30am-3pm Mon-Fri) Changes currency and travellers cheques.

Sights
CAVE TEMPLES

Four kilometres southwest of Vijayawada, the stunning **Undavalli cave temples** (Indian/foreigner Rs5/US$2; ✆ 9am-5pm) cut a fine silhouette against the palm trees and rice paddies. Shrines are dedicated to the Trimurti – Brahma, Vishnu and

Shiva – and one cave on the third level houses a huge, beautiful statue of reclining Vishnu while seated deities and animals stand guard out front. The caves, in their Hindu form, date to the 7th century, but they're thought to have been constructed for Buddhist monks 500 years earlier. Bus 301 goes here.

VICTORIA JUBILEE MUSEUM

The best part of this **museum** (☎ 2574299; MG Rd; admission Rs3; ✆ 10.30am-5pm Sat-Thu) is the building itself, built in 1877 to honour Queen Victoria's coronation jubilee. Later, in 1921, it hosted the Congress meeting where a new tricolour flag was introduced: Mahatma Gandhi added a wheel to the design and made it the Indian National Congress's official flag.

The interesting architecture outshines the museum's small collection of art and arms. But the garden, where temple sculptures from around the state line shady paths, is lovely.

GHATS

Vijayawada's Krishna River has 10 ghats running along its shores. The **Krishnaveni ghat**, just across from the bus stand, is a fascinating place to sit and watch the world – and its swimming kids, laundry and prayers – go by.

Courses

Dhamma Vijaya (Vipassana Meditation Centre; ☎ 08812-225522, 9441449044; www.dhamma.org; Eluru-Chintalapudi Rd) offers intensive 10-day *vipassana* meditation courses free of charge in lush palm- and cocoa-forested grounds. Frequent buses (Rs33, 1½ hours, every 15 minutes) and trains (2nd-class/chair Rs52/197, one hour) run from Vijayawada to Eluru. The centre is 15km from Eluru; call for details.

Sleeping

Hotel Sri Ram (☎ 2579377; Hanumanpet; s/d from Rs320/450; ✆) This cheapie has bright, clean, nondescript rooms near the train station. A conveniently located safe bet.

Hotel Raj Towers (☎ 2571311; Eluru Rd, Governorpet; s/d from Rs410/510; ✆) Raj Towers seems to be confused, acting like an expensive hotel when it's not. Staff are super-helpful, rooms are scrubbed daily and have constant hot water, and there are laundry bags and stationery(!). The restaurant downstairs isn't bad, either.

Vijayawada's two best midrange places, **Swarna Palace** (☎ 2577222; fax 2574602; Eluru Rd, Governorpet; s/d with AC from Rs1400/1500; ✆) and

Hotel Ilapuram (☎ 2571282; fax 2575251; Prakasam Rd; s/d with AC from Rs1500/1700; ✷), both fall short of the sleekness they aspire to. But they're professionally run – and a little bit sleek anyway.

The train station's clean and spacious **retiring rooms** (dm/s/d from Rs50/120/250; ✷) are a great option. The bus station has **dorms** (☎ 3097809; from Rs100) for gents.

Eating

Sree Lakshmi Vilas Modern Cafe (Besant Rd, Governorpet; meals Rs30; ✷ 6.30am-10.30pm) With black-and-white-check floors and mismatched wooden chairs, this gritty, down-home veg joint has a heavy 1940s vibe. The meals are great, as are the fresh juices (Rs12).

Cross Roads (Prakasam Rd; mains Rs65-135; ✷ 11am-10.30pm) There's sometimes a wait at this popular family place specialising in quality non-veg kebabs, biryani and North Indian dishes. Save room for ice cream.

ourpick Minerva Coffee Shop (Museum Rd; mains Rs70-105; ✷ 6am-11.30pm) Just around the corner from Big Bazaar, this outpost of the fabulous Minerva chain has great North and South Indian, including top-notch dosas (Rs21 to Rs45). Its rava masala dosa is the best thing *ever*.

Getting There & Around

The bus stand has a helpful **inquiry desk** (☎ 2522200). Frequent services run to Hyderabad (deluxe/Volvo Rs132/273, six hours), Amaravathi (Rs21, two hours), Warangal (deluxe Rs120, four hours) and Visakhapatnam (deluxe/Volvo Rs192/370, 10 hours).

Vijayawada is on the main Chennai–Kolkata and Chennai–Delhi railway lines. The daily *Coromandel Express* (2841) runs to Chennai (sleeper/3AC/2AC Rs205/522/733, seven hours), and the other way, to Kolkata (2842; sleeper/3AC/2AC Rs401/1073/1466, 20 hours). Speedy *Rajdhani* (Thursday and Saturday) and *Jan Shatabdi* (daily except Tuesday) trains also ply the Vijayawada–Chennai route. Trains galore run to Hyderabad (2nd-class/chair Rs109/386, 6½ hours) and Tirupathi (sleeper/3AC/2AC Rs201/510/685, seven hours). The **computerised advance-booking office** (☎ inquiry 2577775; reservations 2578955) is in the basement.

The train station has a prepaid autorickshaw stand marked 'Traffic Police'.

AROUND VIJAYAWADA
Amaravathi

Once the Andhran capital and a significant Buddhist centre, Amaravathi is India's biggest **stupa** (Indian/foreigner Rs5/100; ✷ dawn-dusk), measuring 27m high, was constructed here in the 3rd century BC, when Emperor Ashoka sent monks south to spread the Buddha's teaching. Located 60km west of Vijayawada, all that remains are a mound and some stones, but the nearby **museum** (admission Rs2; ✷ 10am-5pm Sat-Thu) has a small replica of the stupa, with its intricately carved pillars, marble-surfaced dome and carvings of scenes from the Buddha's life. It also has a reconstruction of part of the surrounding gateway, which gives you an idea of the stupa's massive scale. It's worth the trip, but many of Amaravathi's best sculptures are in London's British Museum and Chennai's Government Museum (p1047).

About 1km down the road is the **Dhyana Buddha**, a 20m-high seated Buddha built on the site where the Dalai Lama spoke at the 2006 Kalachakra.

Buses run from Vijayawada to Amaravathi every half-hour or so (Rs21, two hours), but it may be quicker to head to Guntur (Rs9, 45 minutes) and take another bus from there.

Kondapalli

Situated strategically on the old Machilipatnam–Golconda trade route, **Kondapalli fort** (admission Rs5; ✷ 10.30am-5pm) was built in 1360 by the Reddy kings, and was held by the Gajapathis, the Qutb Shahis, the Mughals and the nizams before becoming a British military camp in 1767. Today it's a quiet, lovely ruin. On weekdays, you'll likely have the place to yourself and you can easily spend a few hours hiking around. Kondapalli village, 1km downhill, is famous for its wooden dolls. The fort is 21km from Vijayawada; an autorickshaw costs Rs400 return.

TIRUMALA & TIRUPATHI
☎ 0877 / pop 302,000

The holy hill of Tirumala is, on any given day, filled with tens of thousands of blissed-out devotees, many of whom have endured long journeys to see the powerful Lord Venkateshwara here, at his home. It's one of India's most visited pilgrimage centres: on average, 40,000 pilgrims come each day (the total often exceeds 100,000), and *darshan* (deity-viewing) runs 24/7. Temple staff alone number 12,000, and the efficient **Tirumala Tirupathi Devasthanams** (TTD; ☎ 2277777; www .tirumala.org) brilliantly administers the crowds. As a result, although the throngs can be over-whelming, a sense of order, serenity and ease mostly prevails, and a trip to the Holy Hill can be fulfilling, even if you're not a pilgrim.

'It is believed that Lord Sri Venkateshwara enjoys festivals', according to the TTD. And so do his devotees: *darshan* queues during October's Brahmotsavam can run up to several kilometres.

Orientation & Information

Tirupathi is the service town at the bottom of the hill, with hotels, restaurants, and transport; a fleet of buses constantly ferries pilgrims the 18km up and down. You'll find most of your worldly needs around the Tirupathi bus sta-tion (TP Area) and, about 500m away, the train station. G Car St becomes Tilak Rd fur-ther from the train station.

Apollo Pharmacy (☎ 2252314; G Car St; 24hr)
Anu Internet Centre (☎ 3202119; APSRTC Com-mercial Complex; per hr Rs15; 8am-11pm) Next to the bus stand.
APTDC (☎ 2289120; Sridevi Complex, 2nd fl, Tilak Rd; 9am-7pm)
Cloakrooms (per day Rs10; 24hr) At the train and bus stations.
Police station (☎ 2289006; Railway Station Rd)

Sights
VENKATESHWARA TEMPLE

Devotees flock to Tirumala to see Venkateshwara, an avatar of Vishnu. Among the many powers attributed to him is the granting of any wish made before the idol at Tirumala. Many pilgrims also donate their hair to the deity – in gratitude for a wish fulfilled, or to renounce ego – so hundreds of barbers attend to devotees. Tirumala and Tirupathi are filled with tonsured men, women and children.

Legends about the hill itself and the sur-rounding area appear in the Puranas, and the temple's history may date back 2000 years. The main **temple** is an atmospheric place, though you'll be pressed between hun-dreds of devotees when you see it. The inner sanctum itself is dark and magical; it smells of incense, resonates with chanting and may make you religious. There, Venkateshwara sits gloriously on his throne, inspiring bliss and love among his visitors. You'll have a moment to make a wish and then you'll be shoved out again.

'Ordinary *darshan*' requires a wait of several hours in the claustrophobic metal cages ringing the temple. 'Special *darshan*' tickets (Rs50) can be purchased a day in advance in Tirupathi. These come with a *darshan* time and get you through the queue faster – in theory.

Foreigners are advised to have VIP 'cellar' *darshan,* which involves minimal waiting. Bring your passport, photocopies of your visa and passport, and Rs100 to the Joint Executive Officer's (JEO) office at Tirumala, about 2km from the Tirupathi bus drop-off. The free red buses go here.

Tours

If you're pressed for time, APTDC runs three-day tours (Rs1750) to Tirumala from Hyderabad. KSTDC (see p904) and TTDC (see p1046) offer the same from Bengaluru and Chennai, respectively. APTDC also has a full-day tour (Rs340) of temples in the Tirupathi area.

Sleeping & Eating

The TTD runs *choultries* (guest houses) for pilgrims in Tirumala and Tirupathi, but most non-Hindu visitors stay in one of Tirupathi's many hotels.

TIRUMALA

Vast **dormitories** (beds free) and **guest houses** (Rs100-2500) surround the temple, but these are in-tended for pilgrims. To stay, check in at the Central Reception Office. Huge **dining halls** (meals free) serve thousands of pilgrims daily. Veg restaurants also serve meals for Rs15.

TIRUPATHI

Hotel Mamata Lodge (☎ 2225873; fax 2225797; 1st fl, 170 TP Area; s/d/tr & q Rs150/250/300) A friendly, spick-and-span cheapie. Some of the sheets are stained, but they're tucked in tight and lovingly patched with white squares. Avoid the downstairs lodge of the same name.

Hotel Annapurna (☎ 2250666; 349 G Car St; r from Rs750;) The Annapurna is a wee bit over-priced, but it's convenient and well-organised. Rooms are clean, compact and pink, with con-stant hot water. Since it's on a corner (across from the train station), non-AC front rooms can be noisy. Its veg restaurant has fresh juices and Tirupathi's best food (mains Rs45 to Rs80) in sublime air-conditioning.

TRAINS FROM TIRUPATHI

Destination	Fare (Rs)	Duration (hr)	Daily Departures
Bengaluru	sleeper/3AC/2AC Rs166/437/596	7	2
Chennai	2nd-class/chair Rs61/209	3	2
Hyderabad/Secunderabad	sleeper/3AC/2AC Rs288/756/1026	12	7
Vijayawada	sleeper/3AC/2AC Rs201/510/685	7	11

Hotel Mayura (☎ 2225925; mayurahotels@yahoo.co.in; 209 TP Area; s/d from Rs1000/1150; 🖳) Across from the bus stand, the Mayura is somehow strangely peaceful, with super-tidy, spacious rooms, cool stone floors, and serene views of the surrounding hills from some rooms.

Hotels are clustered around the bus stand and train station, which has super-value **retiring rooms** (dm/r from Rs45/150, with AC Rs400; 🖳). **Hotel Universal Deluxe** (49 G Car St; mains Rs20-50; ⏰ 5.30am-11.30pm), near the train station, and **Hotel Vikram** (☎ 2225433; TP Area; mains Rs35-65; ⏰ 5am-11pm) by the bus stand both serve hearty meals and juices.

Getting There & Away

It's possible to visit Tirupathi on a (very) long day trip from Chennai. If travelling by bus or train, buy a 'link ticket', which includes transport from Tirupathi to Tirumala.

AIR

Indian Airlines (☎ 2283992; Tirumala Bypass Rd; ⏰ 9.30am-5.30pm), 2km from town, has daily flights to Delhi (Rs7840, two hours) via Hyderabad (Rs3675, one hour). **Kingfisher Red** (☎ 9849677008) plies the same route, including Bengaluru and Visakhapatnam. Book with **Mitta Travels** (☎ 2221135; Prakasam Rd; ⏰ 9am-7.30pm Mon-Sat, 9am-12.30pm Sun), next to Manasa Fast Foods, 2km from the train station.

BUS

Tirupathi's **bus station** (☎ 2289900) has buses to Chennai (Rs56, four hours) and Hyderabad (deluxe/Volvo Rs276/560, 12/10 hours). Tonnes of APSRTC and KSTDC buses go to Bengaluru (deluxe/Volvo Rs140/325, six/five hours), and seven buses go to Puttaparthi daily (express/deluxe Rs136/160, eight hours).

Private buses depart from TP Area, opposite the bus stand.

TRAIN

Tirupathi station is well served by express trains. The **reservation office** (☎ 2225850; ⏰ 8am-8pm Mon-Sat, 8am-2pm Sun) is across the street.

Getting Around

BUS

Tirumala Link buses have two bus stands in Tirupathi: next to the main bus stand and outside the train station. The scenic 18km trip to Tirumala takes one hour (Rs44 return); if you don't mind heights, sit on the left side for views. A prepaid taxi is Rs350.

WALKING

TTD has constructed probably the best footpath in India for pilgrims to walk up to Tirumala. It's about 15km and takes four to six hours. Leave your luggage at the toll gate at Alipiri near the Hanuman statue. It will be transported free to the reception centre. It's best to walk in the cool of the evening, but there are shady rest points along the way, and a few canteens.

AROUND TIRUMALA & TIRUPATHI

Chandragiri Fort

Only a couple of buildings remain from this 15th-century **fort** (☎ 2276246; Indian/foreigner Rs7/100; ⏰ dawn-dusk), 14km west of Tirupathi. Both the Rani Mahal and the Raja Mahal, which houses a small **museum** (⏰ 10am-5pm Sat-Thu), were constructed under Vijayanagar rule and resemble structures in Hampi's Royal Centre. There's a nightly **sound-and-light show** (admission Rs30; ⏰ 8pm Mar-Oct, 7.30pm Nov-Feb), narrated by Bollywood great Amitabh Bachchan. Buses for Chandragiri (Rs6) leave Tirupathi train station every half-hour. A prepaid taxi is Rs400 return.

Sri Kalahasti

Around 36km east of Tirupathi, Sri Kalahasti is known for its important **Sri Kalahasteeswara Temple** and for being, along with Machilipatnam near Vijayawada, a centre for the ancient art of *kalamkari*. These paintings are made with natural ingredients: the cotton is primed with *myrabalam* (resin) and cows' milk; figures are drawn with a pointed bamboo stick dipped in fermented jaggery and water; and the dyes are made from cow dung, ground seeds, plants and flowers. You can see the artists at work in the Agraharam neighbourhood, 2.5km from the bus stand. **Sri Vijayalakshmi Fine Kalamkari Arts** (☎ 08578-230701) is an old family business with 40 artists. Studio visits by appointment.

Buses leave Tirupathi for Sri Kalahasti every 10 minutes (Rs18, 45 minutes); a prepaid taxi is Rs650 return.

PUTTAPARTHI
☎ 08555

Prasanthi Nilayam (Abode of Highest Peace) is the main ashram of Sri Sathya Sai Baba, who has a huge following around the globe. He set up this ashram in Puttaparthi, his hometown, 60 years ago and lives here most of the year.

When he was 14, Sai Baba declared himself to be the reincarnation of another Sai Baba, a saintly figure who died in 1918 (p817). Today, millions of devotees regard Sai Baba as a true avatar and believe he performs miracles. They come for the program of *darshan* (here, that means seeing Baba), chanting and prayer.

Everything about Sai Baba is big: the Afro hairdo; the big-name devotees; and the millions of dollars pumped into the nearby hospital, schools and university. And there's the big controversy: serious allegations of sexual misconduct have led some devotees to lose faith. Others, however, regard the controversy as simply another terrestrial test for their avatar.

Sleeping & Eating
Most people stay at the **ashram** (☎ 287390; www .srisathyasai.org.in), a small village with all amenities. Accommodation and food are cheap but basic. Advance bookings aren't taken, and visitors under 25 must be in a family or group.

Non-ashram options include the clean and simple **Sri Pratibha Guest House** (☎ 289599; Gopuram Rd, 1st Cross; r from Rs350), and the excellent-value **Sri Sai Sadan** (Meda's Guest House; ☎ 287507; srisaisadan@gmail.com; Gopuram Rd; s/d from Rs630/810; 🖳), near Venugopalaswamy Temple, with a roof garden, and spacious rooms with fridges and balconies.

The rooftop **World Peace Café** (German Bakery; Main Rd; mains Rs55-115; 🕑 7.30am-9.30pm) is an old favourite for saffron lassis, good filter coffee and healthy food. The Tibetan **Bamboo Nest** (1st fl, Chitravathi Rd; mains Rs55-80; 🕑 9.30am-2pm & 4.30-9pm) has a memorable veg wonton soup (Rs45) and good *momos* (dumplings).

Getting There & Around
Puttaparthi is most easily reached from Bengaluru; nine KSRTC buses (express/

Volvo Rs107/243, four hours) and eight trains (sleeper/3AC/2AC Rs145/351/464, three hours) head here daily. The **KSRTC office** (☎ 288938) is next to the bus station.

From the **APSRTC bus station** (☎ 287313), uncomfortable buses run to/from Tirupathi (express/deluxe Rs136/160, eight hours, seven daily) and Chennai (Rs277, 12 hours, two daily).

The bus station has a **train reservation booth** (🕑 8am-noon & 5-7pm Mon-Sat, 8am-2pm Sun). For Hyderabad, an overnight train goes daily to Kacheguda (7604; sleeper/3AC/2AC Rs230/592/846, 10 hours). Overnight train 8564 runs to Visakhapatnam (sleeper/3AC/2AC Rs330/901/1239, 20 hours), stopping at Vijayawada. The daily *Udyan Express* (6530) heads to Mumbai (sleeper/3AC/2AC Rs341/930/1279, 21 hours).

A free shuttle for ashram visitors runs from the train station. An autorickshaw is Rs50.

LEPAKSHI
About 70km from Puttaparthi is Lepakshi, site of the **Veerbhadra Temple**. The town gets its name from the *Ramayana:* when demon Ravana kidnapped Rama's wife, Sita, the bird Jatayu fought him and fell, injured, at the temple site. Rama then called him to get up; 'Lepakshi' derives from the Sanskrit for 'Get up, bird'.

Look for the 9m-long monolithic Nandi – India's largest – at the town's entrance. From here, you can see the temple's Nagalingam, a lingam (image of Shiva) crowned with a spectacular seven-headed cobra. The temple is known for its unfinished Kalyana Mandapam (Marriage Hall), which depicts the wedding of Parvati and Shiva, and its Natyamandapa (Dance Hall), with its carvings of dancing gods. The temple's most stunning feature, though, are the Natyamandapa's ceiling frescoes.

Ramana, an excellent guide, brings the temple to life (Rs100 is an appreciated offering). Bring change for the friendly priests giving blessings in the inner sanctum.

To get here, take a Puttaparthi–Bengaluru bus and alight at Kodakonda Checkpost. From there, take a Hindupur-bound bus (Rs6) or an autorickshaw (Rs300 return) to Lepakshi. A private car from Puttaparthi is Rs1000.

You can also go from Hindupur, a main stop on the Puttaparthi–Bengaluru train line with a few hotels. It's 11km from the temple.

Kerala

Kerala's deliberate and thoughtful pace of life is as contagious as the Indian head-wobble – just setting foot on this sliver of green will slow your stride to an intoxicatingly slow amble. Consisting of a skinny strip of land running between the Arabian Sea and the Western Ghats, Kerala is, at the same time, one of India's most beautiful and successful states.

The spindly network of rivers, lakes and canals that make up the breathtaking backwaters of Kerala are the region's star attraction. Here, one can meander through an infinite network of rice paddies, coconut groves and bucolic villages, viewed from the comfort of an elegant houseboat. Further south, the golden beaches of Kovalam and Varkala are where Kerala's green interior flirts with the azure shore, making an ideal destination for the sun-worshipping crowd. Higher inland, the mountainous Ghats lie covered in a thick blanket of spices and tea plantations, also home to thousands of species of exotic bird and wildlife.

Adventurers and traders have been exploring this thriving land for aeons. Serene Fort Cochin is a melange of colonial influences, with dozens of buildings paying homage to Chinese visitors, Portuguese traders, Jewish settlers, Syrian Christians and Muslim merchants. Yet even with all these colonial distractions, Kerala still clings to vibrant traditions of its own: Kathakali – a blend of religious play and dance; *kalarippayat* – a gravity-defying martial art and *theyyam* – a trance-induced ritual. Mix that with some of the most taste-bud-tingling cuisine in India and you can imagine how hard it will be to leave before you even get here.

HIGHLIGHTS

- Soak in 500 years of colonial history and stay in a restored heritage home in laid-back **Fort Cochin** (p1015)

- Slowly meander your way through the famed **backwaters** (p1002) of Kerala on a houseboat, handmade in the style of traditional rice barges

- Sneak in some serious R & R time at one of Kerala's beach-side resort towns, **Kovalam** (p988) and **Varkala** (p993)

- Frolic in the tea-plantation–filled green hills of **Munnar** (p1010), high in the lush mountains of Kerala's Western Ghats

- Go elephant spotting at **Wayanad** (p1031) or **Periyar Wildlife Sanctuary** (p1006)

- Get off the beaten track to explore the little-visited beaches of **Kannur** (p1034) and **Bekal** (p1035)

Bekal ★

Kannur ★

Wayanad
Wildlife
Sanctuary

Fort Cochin ★   ★ Munnar

Backwaters ★   ★ Periyar
Wildlife
Sanctuary

Varkala ★

Kovalam
★

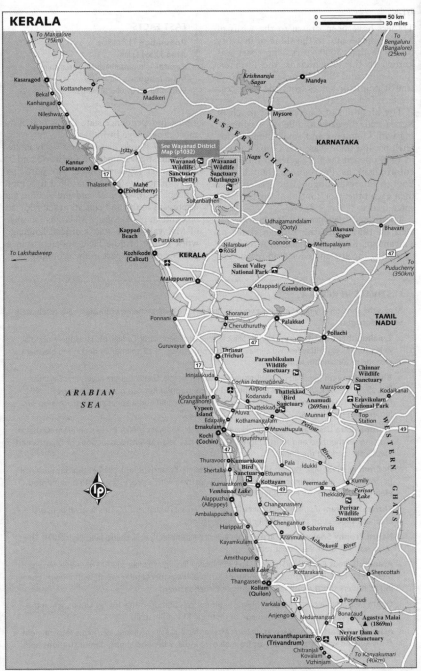

KERALA

0 — 50 km
0 — 30 miles

To Mangalore (15km)
To Bengaluru (Bangalore) (25km)

Kasaragod
Kottancherry
Bekal
Kanhangad
Nileshwar
Valiyaparamba
Madikeri
Krishnaraja Sagar
Mandya

WESTERN GHATS

Mysore
KARNATAKA

Iritty

Kannur (Cannanore)
Thalasseri
Mahé (Pondicherry)

See Wayanad District Map (p1032)
Wayanad Wildlife Sanctuary (Tholpetty)
Wayanad Wildlife Sanctuary (Muthanga)
Nagu

Sultanbatheri

Udhagamandalam (Ooty)
Bhavani Sagar
Bhavani

Kappad Beach
Purakkatri
Coonoor
Mettupalayam

To Lakshadweep

Kozhikode (Calicut)
KERALA
Nilambur Road
47
To Puducherry (350km)

Malappuram
Silent Valley National Park

Ponnani
Shoranur
Cheruthuruthy
Attappadi
Coimbatore

Guruvayur
Thrissur (Trichur)
47
Palakkad
Pollachi
TAMIL NADU

17
Irinjalakuda
Parambikulam Wildlife Sanctuary

Cochin International Airport
Kodanadu
Thattekkad Bird Sanctuary
Chinnar Wildlife Sanctuary

ARABIAN SEA

Kodungallur (Cranganore)
Vypeen Island
Edapally
Aluva
Thattekkad
Kothamangalam
Marayoor
Kodaikanal

Anamudi (2695m)
Eravikulam National Park
Top Station

Ernakulam
Kochi (Cochin)
Tripunithura
Munnar
Periyar River

47
49

Thuravoor
Shertallai
Kumarakom Bird Sanctuary
Pala
Idukki

Kumarakom
Vembanad Lake
Ettumanur
Kottayam
Peermade
Kumily

Alappuzha (Alleppey)
Changanassery
Thekkady
Periyar Lake

Ambalappuzha
Tiruvilla
Periyar Wildlife Sanctuary

Harippad
Chenganur
Sabarimala

Kayamkulam
Aranmula
Achankovil River

Amrithapuri

Ashtamudi Lake
Kottarakara
Shencottah

Thangassen
Kollam (Quilon)
Ponmudi

Varkala
47
Bonacaud
Agastya Malai (1869m)

Anjengo
Nedumangad

Thiruvananthapuram (Trivandrum)
Neyyar Dam & Wildlife Sanctuary

Chitranjali
Kovalam
Vizhinjam
To Kanyakumari (40km)

WESTERN GHATS

History

Traders have been drawn to the whiff of Kerala's spices and to the shine of its ivory for more than 3000 years. The coast was known to the Phoenicians, the Romans, the Arabs and the Chinese, and was a transit point for spices from the Moluccas (eastern Indonesia).

The kingdom of Cheras ruled much of Kerala until the early Middle Ages, competing with kingdoms and small fiefdoms for territory and trade. Vasco da Gama's arrival in 1498 opened the floodgates to European colonialism as Portuguese, Dutch and English interests fought Arab traders, and then each other, for control of the lucrative spice trade.

The present-day state of Kerala was created in 1956 from the former states of Travancore, Kochi and Malabar. A tradition of valuing the arts and education resulted in a post-Independence state that is one of the most progressive in India.

In 1957 Kerala had the first freely elected communist government in the world and it's held power regularly since. The participatory political system has resulted in a more equitable distribution of land and income, and impressive health and education statistics (see boxed text, p991). Many Malayalis (speakers of Malayalam, the state's official language) work in the Middle East, and remittances play a significant part in the economy.

FAST FACTS

Population 31.8 million
Area 38,864 sq km
Capital Thiruvananthapuram (Trivandrum)
Main language Malayalam
When to go October to March

FESTIVALS IN KERALA

Across the state on any night in Kerala you can find temple festivals being enthusiastically celebrated. Some highlights:

- **Ernakulathappan Utsavam** (Jan/Feb; Shiva Temple, Ernakulam, Kochi [Cochin], p1013) Hugely popular in Kochi, this eight-day festival climaxes with a procession of 15 splendidly decorated elephants, ecstatic music and fireworks.

- **Bharni Utsavam** (Feb/Mar; Chettikulangara Bhaghavathy Temple, Chettikulangara village, near Kayamkulam, p999) This one-day festival is dedicated to the popular Keralan goddess Bhagavathy. It's famous for its *kootiattam* (traditional Sanskrit drama) ritual and a spectacular procession of larger-than-life effigies.

- **Thirunakkara Utsavam** (Mar; Thirunakkara Shiva Temple, Kottayam, p1004) There's all-night Kathakali dancing on the third and fourth nights of this 10-day festival; with processions of caparisoned elephants marking the finale.

- **Pooram Festival** (Apr; Asraman Shri Krishna Swami Temple, Kollam [Quilon], p997) Full-night Kathakali performances are common during this 10-day festival; with a procession of 40 ornamented elephants marking the end of festivities.

- **Thrissur Pooram** (Apr/May; Vadakkumnatha Temple, Thrissur [Trichur], p1027) This festival boasts the elephant procession to end all elephant processions.

- **Nehru Trophy Snake Boat Race** (2nd Sat in Aug; Punnamadakalyal, Alappuzha [Alleppey], p1001) The most popular of Kerala's boat races.

- **Aranmula Boat Race** (Aug/Sep; near Shri Parthasarathy Temple, Aranmula, p1006) This water regatta recreates a ritualistic journey in honour of Krishna. It's a spectacular event, with crowds cheering as rowers shout along with the songs of the boatmen.

- **Onam** (Aug/Sep; statewide) Kerala's biggest cultural celebration is the 10-day Onam, when the entire state celebrates the golden age of mythical King Mahabali.

- **Ashtamudi Craft & Art Festival** (Dec/Jan; Asraman Maidan, Kollam [Quilon], p997) This festival, held every second year, features folk art from all over India, with workshops, demonstrations and exhibitions.

Information

Kerala Tourism (☎ 0471-2321132; www.keralatour ism.org) is a government tourism promotion body with information offices – usually called District Tourism Promotion Council (DTPC) or Tourist Facilitation Centres – in most major towns.

ACCOMMODATION

Parts of Kerala – particularly the beach-side towns and backwater hubs – have a distinct high season around November to March. Around the mid-December to mid-January peak season, prices creep up again, though great deals are to be had during the monsoon season (April to September). Homestays are a popular alternative to dowdy hotels in areas like Fort Cochin and Periyar Wildlife Sanctuary.

National Parks

All national parks mentioned in this chapter close for one week for a tiger census during the months of January or February. The dates differ, so check with Kerala Tourism for exact dates.

Getting Around

The Kerala State Road Transport Corporation (KSRTC) runs a network of buses between most Keralan cities. They're not the fastest or most comfortable, but they are reliable and nearly always punctual. Private buses ply the same routes, plus some the KSRTC don't cover, and can be more comfortable – though departure times are more erratic.

SOUTHERN KERALA

THIRUVANANTHAPURAM (TRIVANDRUM)

☎ 0471 / pop 889,191

For obvious reasons, Kerala's capital Thiru-vananthapuram is still often referred to by its colonial name: Trivandrum. Most travellers merely springboard from here to the nearby beachside resorts of Kovalam and Varkala, though laid-back and hill-enclosed Trivandrum can muster enough appeal to keep you entertained for a day or so. All you have to do is get off Trivandrum's racing-drag of a main street to find yourself immersed in old Kerala: surrounded by pagoda-shaped buildings, red-tiled roofs and narrow, winding lanes.

Orientation

Mahatma Gandhi (MG) Rd, the town's main artery and unofficial speedway, runs 4km north–south from the museums and zoo to the Sri Padmanabhaswamy Temple area.

Information

BOOKSHOPS & LIBRARIES

Alliance Française (☎ 2320666; www.afindia.org/ trivandrum; Forest Office Lane, Vazhuthacaud; ☼ 9am-1pm & 2-6pm Mon-Sat) Library and cultural events.

DC Books (☎ 2453379; www.dcbooks.com; Statue Rd; ☼ 9.30am-7.30pm Mon-Sat) Kerala's excellent bookshop chain, with a respectable selection of fiction and nonfiction books.

INTERNET ACCESS

Almikkice (Capital Centre; MG Rd; per hr Rs20; ☼ 7.30am-11.30pm) One of several good internet places in this small mall.

Yahoo Internet City (Manjalikulam Rd; per hr Rs20; ☼ 9am-9.30pm) Fast connections in cartoon-coloured cubicles.

MEDICAL SERVICES

KIMS (Kerala Institute of Medical Sciences; ☎ 2447676; Kumarapuram) With the best medical facilities Trivandrum has to offer, it's about 3km northwest of Trivandrum.

MONEY

There are ATMs that accept foreign cards all along MG Rd.

Thomas Cook (☎ 2338140-2; MG Rd; ☼ 9.30am-5.30pm Mon-Sat) Changes cash and travellers cheques.

POST & TELEPHONE

There are several STD/ISD kiosks around town.

Main post office (☎ 2473071; MG Rd)

TOURIST INFORMATION

Tourist Facilitation Centre (☎ 2321132; Museum Rd; ☼ 24hr) Supplies maps and brochures.

Tourist Reception Centre (KTDC Hotel Chaithram; ☎ 2330031; Central Station Rd; ☼ 6.30am-9.30pm Tue-Sun) Arranges KTDC-run tours (see p985) and car hire.

Sights & Activities

ZOOLOGICAL GARDENS & MUSEUMS

This collection of museums, a gallery and the excellent zoo make a peaceful retreat from the flurry of the city.

The modern **zoological gardens** (☎ 2115122; admission Rs10, camera Rs25; ☼ 9am-6pm Tue-Sun) are among the most impressive in India. There

KERALA

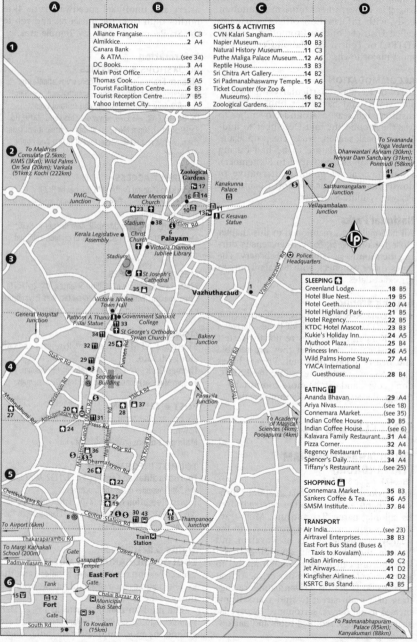

THIRUVANANTHAPURAM (TRIVANDRUM)

0 _____ 500 m
0 _____ 0.3 miles

INFORMATION
Alliance Française...............................1 C3
Almikkice...2 A4
Canara Bank
& ATM...(see 34)
DC Books...3 A4
Main Post Office................................4 A4
Thomas Cook......................................5 A5
Tourist Facilitation Centre................6 B3
Tourist Reception Centre...................7 B5
Yahoo Internet City............................8 A5

SIGHTS & ACTIVITIES
CVN Kalari Sangham...........................9 A6
Napier Museum.................................10 B3
Natural History Museum...................11 C3
Puthe Maliga Palace Museum..........12 A6
Reptile House....................................13 B3
Sri Chitra Art Gallery........................14 B2
Sri Padmanabhaswamy Temple......15 A6
Ticket Counter (for Zoo &
Museums)....................................16 B2
Zoological Gardens...........................17 B2

SLEEPING
Greenland Lodge...............................18 B5
Hotel Blue Nest.................................19 B5
Hotel Geeth......................................20 A4
Hotel Highland Park..........................21 B5
Hotel Regency...................................22 B5
KTDC Hotel Mascot..........................23 B3
Kukie's Holiday Inn...........................24 A5
Muthoot Plaza..................................25 B4
Princess Inn......................................26 A5
Wild Palms Home Stay......................27 A4
YMCA International
Guesthouse..................................28 B4

EATING
Ananda Bhavan.................................29 A4
Ariya Nivas...................................(see 18)
Connemara Market........................(see 35)
Indian Coffee House.........................30 B5
Indian Coffee House.......................(see 6)
Kalavara Family Restaurant..............31 A4
Pizza Corner......................................32 A4
Regency Restaurant..........................33 B4
Spencer's Daily.................................34 A4
Tiffany's Restaurant.....................(see 25)

SHOPPING
Connemara Market...........................35 B3
Sankers Coffee & Tea........................36 A5
SMSM Institute.................................37 B4

TRANSPORT
Air India.......................................(see 23)
Airtravel Enterprises.........................38 B3
East Fort Bus Stand (Buses &
Taxis to Kovalam).......................39 A6
Indian Airlines..................................40 C2
Jet Airways.......................................41 D2
Kingfisher Airlines............................42 D2
KSRTC Bus Stand..............................43 B5

To Maldives
Consulate (2.5km);
KIMS (3km); Wild Palms
On Sea (20km); Varkala
(51km); Kochi (222km)

To Sivananda
Yoga Vedanta
Dhanwantari Ashram (30km);
Neyyar Dam Sanctuary (31km);
Ponmudi (58km)

Zoological
Gardens

Kanakunna
Palace

Sasthamangalam
Junction

PMG
Junction

Mateer Memorial
Church

Vellayambalam
Junction

Kerala Legislative
Assembly

Stadium

Christ
Church

Palayam

C Kesavan
Statue

Museum Rd

Stadium

Victoria Diamond
Jubilee Library

St Joseph's
Cathedral

Police
Headquarters

Vazhuthacaud

General Hospital
Junction

Victoria Jubilee
Town Hall

Pathom A Thanu
Pillai Statue

Government Sanskrit
College

St George's Orthodox
Syrian Church

Bakery
Junction

Statue Rd

Secretariat
Building

Panavila
Junction

YMCA Rd

To Academy
of Magical
Sciences (4km);
Poojapura (4km)

Press Rd

GAK Rd

Dharmasyam Rd

Chettikulangara Rd

Central Station Rd

Thampanoor
Junction

To Airport (6km)

Train
Station

Thakaraparambu Rd

To Margi Kathakali
School (200m)

Padmavilasam Rd

Power House Rd

Tank

Ganapathy
Temple

East Fort

Gate

Fort

Gate

Chalai Bazaar Rd
Municipal
Bus Stand

South Rd

To Kovalam
(15km)

To Padmanabhapuram
Palace (85km);
Kanyakumari (88km)

are shaded paths meandering through woodland and lakes, where animals, such as tigers, macaques and lots of bird-life, happily frolic in massive, open enclosures that mimic their natural habitats. There's a separate **reptile house** (entrance with zoo ticket), where dozens of the slithery things do their thing and cobras frequently flare their hoods – just don't ask what the cute guinea pigs are here for.

A single Rs10 entry ticket, purchased at the **ticket counter** (☉ 9am-5.15pm), covers the **gallery and two museums** (☉ 10am-5pm Tue & Thu-Sun, 1-5pm Wed) in the park. Housed in an fetching Keralan-style wooden building from 1880, the **Napier Museum** has an eclectic display of bronzes, Buddhist sculptures, temple carts and ivory carvings. The brightly painted, carnivalesque interior is stunning and worth a look in its own right. The dusty **Natural History Museum** has hundreds of stuffed animals and birds, a fine skeleton collection and the odd mysteriously empty display case. The **Sri Chitra Art Gallery** has paintings by the Rajput, Mughal and Tanjore schools, and works by Ravi Varma.

SRI PADMANABHASWAMY TEMPLE

This 260-year-old **temple** (☉ 4am-7.30pm) is Trivandrum's spiritual heart. Spilling over 2400 sq metres, its main entrance is the 30m tall, seven-tier eastern *gopuram* (gateway tower). In the inner sanctum, the deity Padmanabha reclines on the sacred serpent and is made from over 10,000 *salagramam* (sacred stones) that were purportedly, and no doubt slowly, transported from Nepal by elephant.

The temple is officially open to Hindus only, but the path around to the right of the gate offers good views of the *gopuram*.

PUTHE MALIGA PALACE MUSEUM

The **Puthe Maliga Palace Museum** (admission Rs20; ☉ 8.30am-1pm & 3-5pm Tue-Sun) is housed in the 200-year-old palace of the Travancore maharajas. The traditional Keralan palace has carved wooden ceilings, marble sculptures and even imported Belgian glass. Inside you'll find Kathakali images, an armoury, portraits of Maharajas, ornate thrones and other artefacts.

The annual **classical music festival** is held here in January/February.

Courses

Margi Kathakali School (☎ 2478806; Fort) conducts courses in *kathakali* (see the boxed text, p1022) and *kootiattam* (traditional Sanskrit drama) for beginner and advanced students. Fees average Rs200 per 1½-hour class. Visitors can peek at uncostumed practice sessions held 10am to noon Monday to Friday. It's in an unmarked building behind the Fort School.

CVN Kalari Sangham (☎ 2474182; South Rd; ☉ 9.30am-12.30pm & 4.30-6.30pm) offers three-month courses (Rs1000 per month) in *kalarippayat* (see boxed text, p1022) for serious students with some experience in martial arts. Contact **Sathyan** (☎ 2474182; sathyacvn@vsnl.net) for details. On Monday to Saturday at 7am to 8.30am, training sessions are open for public viewing.

Tours

KTDC runs several tours, all leaving from the Tourist Reception Centre at the KTDC Hotel Chaithram on Central Station Rd. The **Kanyakumari Day Tour** (per person Rs350; ☉ 7.30am-9pm Tue-Sun) visits Padmanabhapuram Palace (p992), Kanyakumari (p1100) and the nearby Suchindram Temple. The **Thiruvananthapuram City Day Tour** (half-/full-day tours Rs100/175) visits Trivandrum's major sights plus Kovalam beach (half day 8.30am to 1pm and 2pm to 7pm; full day 8.30am to 7pm). Avoid Monday, when some places are closed.

Sleeping

BUDGET

The best hunting ground is along the comparatively quieter Manjalikulam Rd – some streetside rooms at MG Rd hotels are subject to ear-splitting noise.

Kukie's Holiday Inn (☎ 2478530; Lukes Lane; s/d Rs180/300) This meticulously maintained little gem lies enveloped in verdant silence at the end of a small lane. The rooms are very simple but thoughtfully maintained and offer frilly bits, like wicker chairs and bright paintwork. Excellent bang for your buck.

Greenland Lodge (☎ 2328114; Thampanoor Junction; s/d Rs231/296, r with AC Rs805; 🖳) Greenland lays out lots of serenity-inducing pastel colours to greet you. Inside, the spick-and-span rooms are great value, have lots of space and come with hybrid squat/sit-down toilets. It's efficiently run by smiling staff – though expect to pay a hefty two-night deposit upon arrival.

Princess Inn (☎ 2339150; Manjalikulam Rd; s/d Rs250/325, r with AC Rs600; 🖳) In a modern (read: '80s) glass-fronted building, the Princess Inn promises a relatively quiet sleep in spotless surrounds. Satellite TV and immaculate green-tiled bathrooms are thrown in for good measure.

YMCA International Guesthouse (☎ 2330059; YMCA Rd; s/d Rs330/440) On a quiet street well off MG Rd. Our value-ometer went off the scale when we saw this place. The rooms here are spacious, spotless and come with flawless tiled bathrooms and TV as standard. Both men and women accepted.

MIDRANGE

Hotel Regency (☎ 2330377; www.hotelregency.com; Manjalikulam Cross Rd; s/d Rs490/650, with AC Rs800/1000;) With small, cosy rooms boasting satellite TV, a leafy entryway, lots of hush and plenty of smiles, this is a solid choice for a solid night's rest.

Hotel Highland Park (☎ 2338800; Manjalikulam Rd; s/d Rs500/750, with AC Rs950/1150;) Relatively new and in very good nick, only the single rooms here are really cramped. Don't mistake this for its older sister-hotel, Hotel Highland, across the road.

Hotel Blue Nest (☎ 3012800; www.hotelbluenest.com; Manjalikulam Rd; s/d Rs700/800, s/d with AC Rs1000/1150;) Clean and dull, this standard-issue midrange joint has little to differentiate it from the competition, though it still makes for a comfy night's kip.

Wild Palms Home Stay (☎ 2471175; www.wildpalmsonsea.com; Mathrubhumi Rd; s Rs1095-1795, d Rs1395-2195;) Even though this is the only place in town with any real character, recent price hikes are probably not justified. Still, nowhere else has a *Venus de Milo* statue greeting you in the front garden. The ornate, comfortable family home here has several spacious rooms, all handsomely furnished and offering a welcoming vibe. The same owners also have a beachside property, Wild Palms On Sea, a more resorty place 20km from town, that can be booked here.

Hotel Geeth (☎ 2471987; www.geethinternational.in; Ambujarilasam Rd; s/d from Rs1200/1500;) This place will teach you not to judge a hotel by its drab cover. The Geeth comes to you fresh from a round of drastic renovations that have left the rooms decked out in stylish modern furniture, IKEA-inspired wooden panelling, huge bathrooms and flat-screen TVs. Top value.

TOP END

KTDC Hotel Mascot (☎ 2318990; hotelmascot@vsnl.net; Mascot Sq; s/d from Rs3000/3500;) Lots of period touches, massive hallways and an imposing reception area lend this place an aura

of old-world charm. It has a monster pool and ayurvedic spa, and is convenient for visits to the zoo, museums and galleries.

Muthoot Plaza (☎ 2337733; www.themuthootplaza.com; Punnen Rd; s/d from Rs5400/6200, ste from Rs8500;) Even though the arctic-level AC would make penguins shiver, this ultrachic business-focused hotel is still a great place to stay. Expect 3m chandeliers in the lobby, zealous staff and plush rooms stuffed with pillows, couches and all mod cons.

Eating

For some unusual refreshments with your meal, look out for *karikku* (coconut water) and *sambharam* (buttermilk with ginger and chilli).

Ananda Bhavan (☎ 2477646; MG Rd; dishes Rs15-25; lunch & dinner) A classic Keralan sit-down-and-dig-in-with-your-hands type situation.

Indian Coffee House (Maveli Cafe; Central Station Rd; dishes Rs15-45) This branch of the Indian Coffee House chain serves its yummy coffee and snacks in a unique, four-storey, spiralling tower lined inside by bench tables. Equal parts funhouse and Indian diner, it's a must-see. There's also a traditional branch (open 8.30am to 6pm) in Museum Rd, opposite the zoo.

Kalavara Family Restaurant (Press Rd; dishes Rs30-150; lunch & dinner) A bustling favourite of Trivandrum's middle class, this place does commendable lunchtime biryanis (Rs40 to Rs80) and a range of Keralan fish dishes. Our money's on the fish *molee* (fish pieces in coconut sauce, Rs90).

Ariya Nivaas (Manorama Rd; meals Rs42; 7am-9pm) Close to the train station and convenient for a quick feed between trains, this popular thali (traditional 'all-you-can-eat' meal) place gets positive reports from travellers. It's sparking and run with efficiency.

Pizza Corner (MG Rd; small pizzas Rs85-170; lunch & dinner) A bit of East meets West, with tasty pizza's sporting everything from traditional toppings (margarita) to Indian twists on a theme (ie Punjabi chicken tikka).

There's a choice of decent hotel buffets at places like **Tiffany's Restaurant** (Muthoot Plaza; lunch/dinner Rs600/750) and **Regency Restaurant** (South Park Hotel; MG Rd; lunch/dinner Rs325/250). **Spencer's Daily** (MG Rd; 9am-9pm) is a well-stocked supermarket with lots of Western food (and even tampons!). Stock up on fruit and veg at Connemara Market.

BUSES FROM TRIVANDRUM (KSRTC BUS STAND)

Destination	Fare (Rs)	Duration (hr)	Frequency
Alleppey	98	3½	every 15min
Chennai	325	17	8 daily
Ernakulm (Kochi)	135	5	every 20min
Kanyakumari	40	2	6 daily
Kollam	45	1½	every 15min
Kumily (for Periyar)	161	8	2 daily
Madrai	180	7	9 daily
Neyyar Dam	22	1½	every 40min
Puducherry	280	16	1 daily
Thrissur	183	7½	every 30min
Udhagamandalam (Ooty)	305	14	1 daily
Varkala	36	1¼	hourly

Shopping

Wander around **Connemara Market** (MG Rd) to see vendors selling vegetables, fish, live goats, fabric, clothes, spices and more bananas than you can poke a hungry monkey at.

Sankers Coffee & Tea (☎ 2330469; MG Rd; ◷ 9am-9pm Mon-Sat) You'll smell the fresh coffee well before you reach this dainty little shop. It sells Nilgiri Export OP Leaf Tea (Rs250 per kg) and a variety of coffees and nuts.

SMSM Institute (☎ 2330298; YMCA Rd; ◷ 9am-8pm Mon-Sat) No, this place is not dedicated to the study of text messaging, but is a Kerala Government-run handicraft emporium with an Aladdin's cave of goodies that are well-priced.

Getting There & Away

AIR

Some airlines with offices in Trivandrum:
Air India (☎ 2317341; Mascot Sq; ◷ 9am-5.30pm Mon-Sat)
Indian Airlines (☎ 2314781; Museum Rd; ◷ 10am-1pm & 1.45-5.35pm Mon-Sat)
Jet Airways (☎ 2728364; Sasthamangalam Junction; ◷ 9am-5.30pm Mon-Sat)
Kingfisher Airlines (☎ 18002333131; Star Gate Bldg; TC 9/888, Vellayambalam)

Between them these airlines fly daily to Mumbai (from US$150) and several times a day to Kochi (US$85). There are at least four flights a day to Bengaluru (Bangalore, US$74), two to Chennai (Madras, US$75) and one direct flight to Delhi (US$180).

There are regular flights from Trivandrum to Colombo and Male; see p1175.

All airline bookings can be made at the efficient **Airtravel Enterprises** (☎ 3011412; www.ategroup.org; New Corporation Bldg, MG Rd; ◷ 9.30am-6pm Mon-Sat, 9.30am-5pm Sun).

BUS

For buses operating from the **KSRTC bus stand** (☎ 2323886), opposite the train station, see the table, above.

For Tamil Nadu destinations, the State Express Transport Corporation (SETC) buses leave from the eastern end of the KSRTC bus stand.

Buses leave for Kovalam beach (Rs9, 30 minutes, every 20 minutes) between 5.40am and 10pm from the southern end of the East Fort bus stand on MG Rd.

TRAIN

Trains are often heavily booked, so it's worth visiting the **reservation office** (☎ 139; ◷ 8am-8pm Mon-Sat, to 2pm Sun). See the table, p988, for major long-distance services.

Within Kerala, there are frequent trains to Varkala (2nd class/AC chair Rs22/142, one hour), Kollam (Rs26/142, one hour) and Ernakulam (Rs56/238, 4½ hours), with trains passing through either Alleppey (Rs45/180, three hours) or Kottayam (Rs46/188, 3½ hours). There are also a number of daily services to Kanyakumari (sleeper/3AC/2AC Rs101/188/258, 2½ hours).

Getting Around

The **airport** (☎ 2501424) is 6km from the city and 15km from Kovalam; take local bus 14 from the East Fort bus stand (Rs6). Prepaid taxi vouchers from the airport cost Rs206 to the city and Rs313 to Kovalam.

MAJOR TRAINS FROM TRIVANDRUM

The following are some of the major long-distance trains departing from Trivandrum.

Destination	Train no & name	Fare (Rs*)	Duration (hr)	Departures
Bengaluru	6525 *Bangalore Exp*	322/868/1234	18	12.55pm
Chennai	2696 *Chennai Exp*	356/938/1271	16½	5.25pm
Coimbatore	7229 *Sabari Exp*	204/534/722	9¼	7.15am
Delhi	2625 *Kerala Exp*	614/1615/2281	50	11.15am
Mangalore	6347 *Mangalore Exp*	270/724/985	14½	8.45pm
	6347 *Malabar Exp*	270/724/985	15½	6.30pm
Mumbai	6346 *Netravathi Exp*	483/1320/1814	30½	10.00am

*Sleeper/3AC/2AC

Autorickshaws patrol the streets and are the easiest way to get around. Standard rates are Rs10 flag fall, then Rs5 per km, but all rules go out the window at night – 50% over the meter is fair. Agree on a fare beforehand. A cheap way to get around is to hop on and off any of the crowded buses plying the length of MG Rd (Rs4).

AROUND TRIVANDRUM
Neyyar Dam Sanctuary

This **sanctuary** (☎ 2272182; Indian/foreigner Rs10/100; ☻ 9am-4pm Tue-Sun), 32km north of Trivandrum, lies around an idyllic lake created by the 1964 Neyyar Dam. The fertile forest lining the shoreline is home to gaurs, sambar deer, sloth, elephants, lion-tailed macaques and the occasional tiger.

The sanctuary office organises one-hour **lion safaris** (per person Rs250) by boat and bus, though you're more likely to see monkeys than any big cats. For improved spotting opportunities it's better to sneak around on a guided **trek** (per person per hr Rs100). Nearby there's a **Crocodile Protection Centre** (Indian/foreigner Rs5/10). Get here from Trivandrum's KSRTC bus stand by frequent bus (Rs22, 1½ hours). A taxi is Rs700 to Rs800 return (with two hours waiting time), a very bumpy rickshaw about half that.

Sivananda Yoga Vedanta Dhanwantari Ashram

Just before Neyyar Dam, this superbly located **ashram** (☎ /fax 0471-2273093; www.sivananda.org/ndam), established in 1978, is renowned for its hatha yoga courses. Courses start on the 1st and 16th of each month, run for a minimum of two weeks and cost Rs600 per day for accommodation in a double room (Rs450 in dormitories). Low season (May to September) rates

are Rs100 less. There's an exacting schedule (5.30am to 10pm) of yoga practice, meditation and chanting; and students rave about the food (included in the rates). Bookings are required. Month-long yoga-teacher training and ayurvedic massage courses are also available.

KOVALAM
☎ 0471

Holding the dubious title of India's most 'developed' resort, these days Kovalam's sliver of beach plays second fiddle to the bumper-to-bumper development onshore. After it was discovered by backpackers in the '70s, it didn't take long for European package-tour operators, looking for the next Goa goldmine, to descend en masse on this once-calm fishing village. Nevertheless, shreds of charm do remain – particularly outside the peak season, when sky-high prices subside and resident touts and male gawkers seem to go into hibernation.

Orientation

Kovalam consists of two coves (Lighthouse beach and Hawah beach) separated from less-populated beaches north and south by rocky headlands. The town proper is at Kovalam Junction, about 1.5km from the beaches.

Information

Almost every shop and hotel will change money – ask around for the best rate. In Kovalam, near the Leela resort there's a **National Bank of India** (☻ 10.30am-1.30pm Mon-Fri, ☻ 10.30am-noon Sat) that changes cash and, near the hospital, a CBS ATM taking Visa cards. Otherwise, there are Federal Bank and ICICI ATMs at Kovalam Junction. There are lots of small, slow internet places charging Rs30 to Rs50 per hour, as well as numerous STD/ISD facilities around.

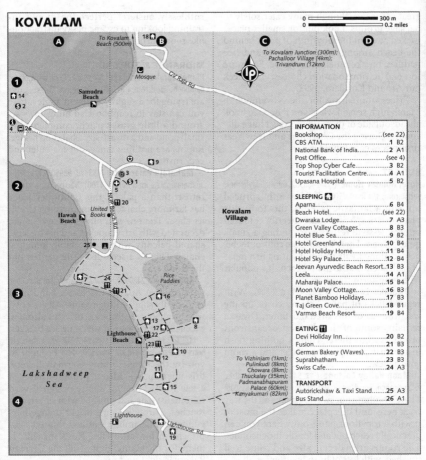

KOVALAM

0 — 300 m
0 — 0.2 miles

INFORMATION

Bookshop	(see 22)
CBS ATM	**1** B2
National Bank of India	**2** A1
Post Office	(see 4)
Top Shop Cyber Cafe	**3** B2
Tourist Facilitation Centre	**4** A1
Upasana Hospital	**5** B2

SLEEPING

Aparna	**6** B4
Beach Hotel	(see 22)
Dwaraka Lodge	**7** A3
Green Valley Cottages	**8** B3
Hotel Blue Sea	**9** B2
Hotel Greenland	**10** B4
Hotel Holiday Home	**11** B4
Hotel Sky Palace	**12** B4
Jeevan Ayurvedic Beach Resort	**13** B3
Leela	**14** A1
Maharaju Palace	**15** B4
Moon Valley Cottage	**16** B3
Planet Bamboo Holidays	**17** B3
Taj Green Cove	**18** B1
Varmas Beach Resort	**19** B4

EATING

Devi Holiday Inn	**20** B2
Fusion	**21** B3
German Bakery (Waves)	**22** B3
Suprabhatham	**23** B3
Swiss Cafe	**24** A3

TRANSPORT

Autorickshaw & Taxi Stand	**25** A3
Bus Stand	**26** A1

Map labels: To Kovalam Beach (500m); Mosque; GV Raja Rd; To Kovalam Junction (300m); Pachalloor Village (4km); Trivandrum (12km); Samudra Beach; Hawah Beach; United Books; NUP Beach Rd; Kovalam Village; Rice Paddies; Lighthouse Beach; Lakshadweep Sea; To Vizhinjam (1km); Pulinkudi (8km); Chowara (8km); Thuckalay (35km); Padmanabhapuram Palace (60km); Kanyakumari (82km); Lighthouse; Lighthouse Rd

Bookshop (7am-11pm) A great range of books to rent/buy/exchange, next to the German Bakery.

Post office (9am-1pm Mon-Sat)

Top Shop Cyber Cafe (per hr Rs30; 9.30am-8.30pm) Off the beach up a steep hill, this is the only dedicated internet joint.

Tourist Facilitation Centre (2480085; 10am-5pm) Very helpful, inside the entrance to the Kovalam Beach Resort.

Upasana Hospital (2480632; 9.30am-1pm & 5-8.30pm) Has two English-speaking doctors who can take care of minor injuries.

Dangers & Annoyances

Women are likely to grow tired of the parade of male Indian day-trippers stalking the beach in hope of glimpsing female flesh – though it's more annoying than dangerous. Theft does occur, both from hotels and the beach – watch your possessions at the beach.

There are strong rips at both ends of Lighthouse beach that carry away several swimmers every year. Swim only between the flags in the area patrolled by lifeguards.

Kovalam has frequent blackouts and the footpaths further back behind Lighthouse beach are unlit, so carry a torch (flashlight) after dark.

Sleeping

Kovalam is chock-a-block with hotels, though budget places here cost more than usual and are becoming a dying breed. Beachfront properties are the most expensive and have

KERALA

great sea views, though many cater solely to package groups. Look out for smaller places tucked away in the labyrinth of paths behind the beach among the palm groves and rice paddies; they're much better value. For more top-end accommodation choices, also check out Around Kovalam, p992.

Prices quoted are for the November to March high season when you'll need to book ahead; outside of these times expect huge discounts. During the Christmas and New Year rush prices can double.

BUDGET

Hotel Holiday Home (☎ 2486382; newholidayhome@ yahoo.com; s/d Rs300/500; 🖳) Recently spruced up with a fantastic face-lift, this top-value place offers spacious and cheerily coloured bungalow-style rooms surrounding a small, quiet garden. There's a tangible chill-out vibe, helped along by its tranquil setting in a maze of paths behind the main beach. It's popular with long-term travellers.

Dwaraka Lodge (☎ 2480411; d Rs500) With regular licks of paint helping cover up the war wounds of this tired old-timer, Dwarka remains some of the cheapest ocean-front properties out there. There's nothing flash inside, just clean sheets, a toilet and a room with a view.

Moon Valley Cottage (☎ 9446100291; sknairkovalam@yahoo.com; d from Rs500, upstairs apt per week Rs5000) There's nothing but swaying palms all the way back here, and this place makes the most of it with a top-floor hang-out where you can practically reach out and fondle the coconuts. The rooms are a decent size and come well finished, with lots of hush on offer for all.

Hotel Sky Palace (☎ 9349083949; s Rs500, d Rs800-1000) This little two-storey place lies sandwiched down a small lane and has just a few lovely rooms – all have small balconies or patios – with a sliver of garden at the front. It's relaxed and central without being too noisy.

Hotel Greenland (☎ 2486442; hotelgreenlandin@ yahoo.com; r Rs600/1200) Family run and as friendly as they come. The well-kept refurbished rooms in this multilevel complex have lots of natural light – some even have small kitchenettes for self-catering. Will cook up yummy food on request.

Green Valley Cottages (☎ 2480636; indira_ravi@ hotmail.com; r Rs800) Also way back in the paddy fields, this serene spot is the place to revel in serious shush time. The rooms are rather

ruthlessly austere, perfect for monks-in-training looking to escape pesky distractions like room furnishings.

MIDRANGE & TOP END

Planet Bamboo Holidays (☎ 9946477929; www.planet bambooholidays.com; r Rs1000) At least these guys are trying for a slightly different angle – here you can stay in bamboo-clad bungalows set around a little grassy patch, complete with small pond and a dwarf-sized bamboo bridge. Rooms are nothing fancy, but it's quiet and very rustic.

Maharaju Palace (☎ 2485320, 9895012129; www .maharajupalace.in; d Rs1500-1700) More of a quiet retreat than a palace, this boutiquey place has far more character than anything else in its class. The few medium-sized rooms are decorated with artsy touches and have a large shared balcony with comfortable lounging chairs. There's a secluded little garden out the front.

Aparna (☎ 2480950; www.aparnahotelkovalam.com; s/d Rs1500/1750) Aparna has just a handful of cute, oddly shaped little rooms. All are cosy, with bright blue bathrooms, private balconies, excellent sea views and welcome sea breezes.

our pick Beach Hotel (☎ 2481937; www.thebeach hotel-kovalam.com; s/d Rs1500/2500; 🔀) Brought to you by the long-running German Bakery, this uberhip beachfront property has just a few rooms, though all are designed with minimalist flair and finished with smart, arty touches. Throw in some bright orange/burgundy tones, bamboo window shutters, and the crown for 'affordable Kovalam chic' is theirs for the taking. Best of all, the German Bakery is right upstairs.

Varmas Beach Resort (☎ 2480478; www.calanguete beach.com; Lighthouse Rd; d Rs1650, with AC Rs2300; 🔀) This is one of the nicest-looking places in Kovalam, with a wood-panelled, Kerala-style facade and rooms adorned with wooden furniture. Throw in comfy sitting areas on private balconies, some exceptional views and access to an isolated beach and, bingo! – we have a winner.

Hotel Blue Sea (☎ 9349991992; www.hotelbluesea .net; r Rs2500, with AC Rs4000; 🔀 🖳) Something different: great rooms inside circular, three-storey towers with polished floors and round verandas. They also offer plain-old square rooms for Rs1000.

Jeevan Ayurvedic Beach Resort (☎ 2480662; www .jeevanresort.com; d Rs3000-4500; 🔀 🖳) This resort

LEADER OF THE PACK

In 1957 Kerala was first in the world to freely elect a communist government. While communism's hammer and sickle hasn't had much luck in running other parts of the world, Kerala's unique blend of democratic-socialist principles has a pretty impressive track record.

Kerala has been labelled 'the most socially advanced state in India' by Nobel prize–winning economist Amartya Sen. Land reform and a focus on infrastructure, health and education have played a large part in Kerala's success. The literacy rate (91%) is the highest of any developing nation in the world, though a strong history of education stretches back centuries to the days of magnanimous rajas and active missionaries. The infant mortality rate in Kerala is one-fifth of the national average, while life expectancy stands at 73 years, 10 years higher than the rest of the country.

The picture is not all rosy, however. Lack of any industrial development or foreign investment means that the ambitions of many educated youth are curtailed. This might explain why Kerala also has the highest suicide rates and liquor consumption statistics in the country. A big hope for the economy's future is the recent boom in tourism, with Kerala emerging as one of India's most popular new tourist hot spots. So, thanks for coming, and congratulations on being a part of the solution.

has a neat colour scheme, ageing, decent-sized rooms with bathtubs and an alluring pool that practically plays footsies with the ocean. Upstairs rooms have balconies with sea views.

Leela (☎ 2480101; www.theleela.com; s/d from US$295/320; ✷ ⊠) The only real top-end option right in Kovalam, the Leela comes jam-packed with a ridiculous amount of facilities. Glamorously located around extensive grounds on the headland north of Hawah beach, there are three (three!) swimming pools, an ayurvedic centre, a gym, two private beaches, several restaurants and more. Rooms aren't huge, but are sumptuously decorated with period touches, colourful textiles and Keralan artwork.

Eating

Each evening, dozens of open-air restaurants line the beach area displaying the catch of the day – just pick a fish, settle on a price (per serve around Rs150, tiger prawns over Rs400) and decide how you want it prepared. Menus and prices are pretty much indistinguishable, so it's more about which ambience takes your fancy.

Devi Holiday Inn (mains Rs40-120) A tiny, family run eatery a little off the beach, this hotel whips up great veg and nonveg Indian food for refreshingly reasonable prices.

Suprabhatham (meals Rs45-80) This cosy little veggie place dishes up excellent, dirt-cheap and truly authentic Keralan cooking in a rustic setting. Out in the palm groves, it's secluded and intimate, with an option to dine under the stars to a nightly orchestra of crickets.

German Bakery (Waves) (mains Rs140-700) In a swanky new location on an airy, sunburnt-orange balcony, this remains the most popular hang-out in town. Finger-licking pastries still take pride of place on the menu, as do a huge range of winning breakfasts, strong coffee and quiches. Nowadays it's easy to spend the entire day relaxing here, with a varied selection of classy main courses featuring curries, seafood, tofu and pizzas taking you into your evening meal.

Swiss Cafe (mains Rs140-230) While the setting here is lovely, with an upstairs balcony and lots of wicker seating, the menu offers pretty much the same choices as everywhere else, with a few token Swiss dishes (ie schnitzel) thrown in to justify the name.

Fusion (mains Rs140-450) This funky eatery has an inventive menu where dishes from the East meet dishes from the West – and it seems like they get along pretty well. You can get regular Indian or Western meals, but the fun part is trying their fusion options where the two cuisines collide to form yummy new taste combinations. Also serves French press coffee and herbal teas.

Entertainment

During the high season, an abridged version of Kathakali is performed most nights somewhere – enquire about locations and times at the Tourist Facilitation Centre (p988).

Hollywood film fodder is shown nightly in some restaurants. Dedicated bars are thin on the ground, but beer is available in most restaurants (around Rs80), with some serving cocktails (Rs80 to Rs120) to a repetitive soundtrack of reggae, trance and classic rock.

Getting There & Away

BUS

There are local buses connecting Kovalam and Trivandrum every 20 minutes between 5.30am and 10.10pm (Rs9, 30 minutes); catch them from the entrance to Leela resort. Buses to Ernakulam leave at 6am and 2.30pm (Rs140, 5½ hours), stopping at Kallambalam (for Varkala, Rs39, 1½ hours), Kollam (Rs44, 2½ hours) and Alleppey (Rs87, four hours). There's another 6.30am bus to Ernakulam via Kottayam that bypasses Varkala.

TAXI & AUTORICKSHAW

A taxi between Trivandrum and Kovalam beach is around Rs300. Autorickshaws should be about Rs120. Prepaid taxis from Trivandrum airport to Lighthouse beach cost Rs313.

Voyager Travels (☎ 9847065093) rents out scooters/Enfields for around Rs450/550 per day. It has no fixed office address.

AROUND KOVALAM

Samudra Beach

Samudra beach, about 4km north of Kovalam by road, has seen a growing number of resorts edge out what was until recently a small fishing village. Although more peaceful, the steep and rough beach here is not as good as Lighthouse beach for swimming.

Taj Green Cove (☎ 2487733; www.tajhotels.com; r from Rs11,000-30000; ❄ 💻 🏊) The Kovalam branch of this swanky Indian hotel chain is set among lolling, green grounds and has direct access to a private beach. The individual chalets here are simply but tastefully adorned, some with private gardens and others with primo sea views. Several restaurants and the usual top-end amenities are all here for the taking.

Pulinkudi & Chowara

Around 8km south of Kovalam are some luxury alternatives to Kovalam's crowded beaches.

For those serious about ayurvedic treatment, **Dr Franklin's Panchakarma Institute** (☎ 2480870; www.dr-franklin.com; Chowara; s €15-38, d €20-55; 💻) is a reputable and less expensive alternative to the flashier resorts. Daily treatment costs €35, with a full meal plan an additional €16. Accommodation is tidy and comfortable but not resort style. There are therapy packages for whatever ails you, including spine problems, purification/detox treatments, as well as general rejuvenation and stress relief. A one-off relaxation or rejuvenation massage costs €12 to €17.

Thapovan Heritage Home (☎ 2480453; www.thapovan.com; s/d Rs3300/4125) is the way to live the simple life (no pool, AC or TV) in complete, understated luxury. The gorgeous Keralan teak cottages here are filled with handcrafted furniture and are set among perfectly manicured grounds overlooking breathtaking swaying palm groves. Ayurvedic treatments available range from one-hour massages to 28-day treatment marathons. It's a few kilometres from the nearest beach.

Bethsaida Hermitage (☎ 2267554; www.bethsaidahermitage.com; Pulinkudi; r €80-140) is a resort with a difference: this is a charitable organisation that helps support a nearby orphanage. As a bonus, it's also a luxurious and remote beachside escape, with sculpted gardens, seductively slung hammocks, putting-green perfect lawns, palms galore and shade in spades. It offers a variety of cottages, from rainbow-painted, half-ovals to spacious, cool Kerala-style huts.

The luscious, small resort of **Surya Samudra Beach Garden** (☎ 2480413; www.suryasamudra.com; Pulinkudi; r incl breakfast €120-350; ❄ 🏊) has several types of cottages, many of which are transplanted traditional Keralan homes, with spectacular carved ceilings and open-air bathrooms. There are private beaches, an infinity pool and ayurvedic treatments – all on 8.5 hectares of wonderfully cultivated grounds. It was closed for extensive renovations at the time of our last visit.

PADMANABHAPURAM PALACE

With dozens of lumberyards worth of intricately carved ceilings and polished-teak beams, this **palace** (☎ 04651-250255; Indian/foreigner Rs25/200, camera/video Rs25/1500; 🕒 9am-5pm Tue-Sun) is considered the best example of traditional Keralan architecture today. Parts of it date back to 1550 though, as the egos of successive rulers left their mark, it expanded into the magnificent conglomeration of 14 palaces it is today.

The largest wooden palace complex in Asia, it was once the seat of the rulers of Travancore, a princely state taking in parts of Tamil Nadu and Kerala. Fetchingly constructed of teak and granite, the exquisite interiors include carved rosewood ceilings, Chinese-style screens, and floors finished to a high black polish.

Padmanabhapuram is about 60km southeast of Kovalam. Catch a local bus from Kovalam (or Trivandrum) to Kanyakumari and get off at Thuckalay, from where it's a short autorickshaw ride or 15-minute walk. Alternatively, take one of the tours organised by the KTDC (see p985), or hire a taxi (about Rs1500 return from Trivandrum or Kovalam).

VARKALA
☎ 0470 / pop 42,273

With a gaggle of guest houses and restaurants perched almost perilously along the edge of breathtaking cliffs, Varkala is a sight to behold. This beachside resort town is considerably more laid back than its Kovalam cousin, valiantly clinging to its backpacker roots in the face of ongoing development. The strand of golden beach here nuzzles Varkala's cliff edge, where restaurants play more Bob Marley music that you can poke a dreadlocked backpacker at. Even though more hotels mushroom every year and prices creep that little bit higher, this is still a great place to while away some time and watch the days slowly turn into weeks.

Orientation & Information

The main beach is accessed from either Beach Rd or by several steep stairways cut into the north cliff. Varkala town and the train station are about 2km from the beach.

A 24-hour SBI ATM at the temple junction takes Visa cards, otherwise there's a State Bank of India ATM in Varkala town. Many of the money changers and travel agents lining the cliff do cash advances on credit cards and change travellers cheques. There are plenty of places to update your Facebook profile along the cliff top (around Rs40 per hour) – save emails often, as power cuts are not uncommon.

Police aid post (☾ Nov-Feb) At the helipad, rarely staffed.

Post office (☾ 10am-2pm Mon-Sat) North of Temple Junction.

Dangers & Annoyances

The beaches at Varkala have strong currents; even experienced swimmers have been swept away. This is one of the most dangerous beaches in Kerala, so be careful and swim between the flags or ask the lifeguards for the best place to swim.

Indian male gawkers are starting to discover the many bikini-clad attractions at Varkala. However, with police patrolling beaches to keep male starers a-walkin' and the hawkers at bay, this is more of a nuisance than a danger. It still pays to dress sensitively, especially if you're going into Varkala town.

AYURVEDA

With its roots in Sanskrit, the word ayurveda is derived from *ayu* (life) and *veda* (knowledge); it is the knowledge or science of life. Principles of ayurvedic medicine were first documented in the Vedas some 2000 years ago, but it may even have been practised centuries earlier.

Ayurveda sees the world as having an intrinsic order and balance. It argues that we possess three *doshas* (humours): *vata* (wind or air); *pitta* (fire); and *kapha* (water/earth), known together as the *tridoshas*. Deficiency or excess in any of them can result in disease: an excess of *vata* may result in dizziness and debility; an increase in *pitta* may lead to fever, inflammation and infection. *Kapha* is essential for hydration.

Ayurvedic treatment aims to restore the balance, and hence good health, principally through two methods: panchakarma (internal purification, see boxed text, p1033) and herbal massage. The herbs used in ayurveda grow in abundance in Kerala's moist climate, and every village has its own ayurvedic pharmacy.

Having an occasional ayurvedic massage, something offered at tourist resorts all over Kerala, is relaxing, but you'll have to go in for the long haul to reap any real benefits – usually 15 days or longer. Expect a thorough examination followed by an appropriate ayurvedic diet, exercises and a range of treatments.

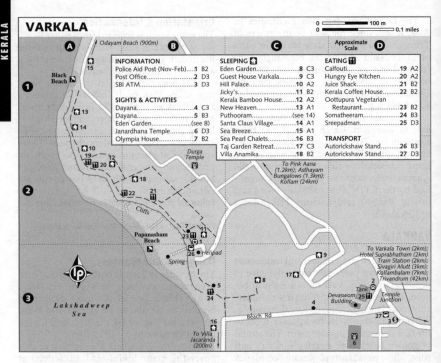

VARKALA

INFORMATION		
Police Aid Post (Nov–Feb).....1	B2	
Post Office.................................2	D3	
SBI ATM..................................3	D3	

SIGHTS & ACTIVITIES

Dayana...................................4	C3	
Dayana...................................5	B3	
Eden Garden....................(see 8)		
Janardhana Temple............6	D3	
Olympia House.....................7	B3	

SLEEPING		
Eden Garden........................8	C3	
Guest House Varkala............9	C3	
Hill Palace..........................10	A2	
Jicky's.................................11	B2	
Kerala Bamboo House........12	A2	
New Heaven.......................13	A1	
Puthooram.....................(see 14)		
Santa Claus Village............14	A1	
Sea Breeze.........................15	A1	
Sea Pearl Chalets...............16	B3	
Taj Garden Retreat.............17	C3	
Villa Anamika.....................18	B3	

EATING		
Calfouti..............................19	A2	
Hungry Eye Kitchen...........20	A2	
Juice Shack.........................21	B2	
Kerala Coffee House...........22	B2	
Oottupura Vegetarian		
Restaurant.......................23	B2	
Somatheeram....................24	B3	
Sreepadman.......................25	D3	

TRANSPORT

Autorickshaw Stand...........26	B3	
Autorickshaw Stand...........27	D3	

Sights & Activities

Varkala is a temple town, and **Janardhana Temple** is the main event – its technicolour Hindu spectacle sits hovering above Beach Rd. It's closed to non-Hindus, but you may be invited into the temple grounds where there is a huge banyan tree and shrines to Ayyappan, Hanuman and other Hindu deities.

Sivagiri Mutt (☎ 2602807; www.sivagiri.org) is the headquarters of the Sree Narayana Dharma Sanghom Trust, the ashram devoted to Shri Narayana Guru (1855–1928), Kerala's most prominent guru. This is a popular pilgrimage site and the resident swami is happy to talk to visitors.

Practically everyone in town offers ayurveda, yoga or massage (see also Dangers & Annoyances, p993). A recommended place for ayurvedic beauty treatments is **Dayana** (☎ 2609464; manicure & pedicure Rs250, facials Rs400-1000; ⊙ 9am-7pm), which has a shack on the beach and a shop on Beach Rd (women only). Mr Omanakuttan at **Olympia House** (☎ 9349439675) is a qualified massage instructor, in both ayurveda and other schools, and has a sound reputation. The excellent **Eden Garden** (☎ 2603910; www.eden-garden.net) is a popular ayurvedic resort offering single treatments and packages; see opposite for accommodation details. Yoga is offered at several guest houses for around Rs200 to Rs300 per hour.

Boogie boards can be hired from places along the beach for Rs100, but be wary of very strong currents.

Sleeping

Most places to stay are crammed in along the north cliff; some open only for the tourist onslaught in November. Slightly quieter places are found either inland, north at Black beach, or along the south cliff. Undeveloped Odayam beach, about 1km further north of Varkala's black beach, is becoming a tranquil alternative to Varkala's bustle.

Prices given are average high-season (November to March) rates, which fluctuate daily with the ebb and flow of demand – expect astronomical prices around the Christmas holidays and bargains in the low season.

The commission racket is alive and well – make sure that your rickshaw takes you to the place you've asked for.

BUDGET

Guest House Varkala (☎ 2602227; s/d Rs165/220) This government-run guest house is probably the best kept secret in Varkala. Located near the Taj hotel, it has several rooms in huge Keralan-styled bungalows that were once part of a palace complex. Though spartan, each bargain-basement abode is finished with lots of polished wood and has high ceilings.

Jicky's (☎ 2606994; www.jickys.com; s Rs350, d Rs500-1000) Way back in the palm groves, family run Jicky's is as friendly as they come. There is a range spotless of rooms available in a large two-storey building here, all surrounded by oodles of by green and piles of hush.

New Heaven (☎ 9846074818; newheavenbeachresort@yahoo.com; r Rs500-700) Just back from the northern cliffs, New Heaven has easy access to Black beach and great top-floor views. Bedrooms are roomy, basic and tidy, with big blue bathrooms and hanging wicker chairs out the front for lazing.

Asthamay Bungalows (☎ 2663613; www.asthamay.com; s/d Rs500/1000) Asthamay crowns a small bluff on the lovely, yet-to-be-discovered Odayam beach, where fishermen still outnumber tourists at least three-to-one. There are just six octagonal duplex bungalows out here, all lying around a grassy coconut grove, lovingly maintained and in immaculate order. Excellent value – book ahead.

Villa Anamika (☎ 2600096; www.villaanamika.com; s Rs600, d Rs1200-1400, with AC Rs2000; ☒) One of the more pleasant stays in Varkala, this Keralan/German-run place offers up spacious rooms, all neatly furnished with homely decorations and art done by owner Chicku. The trim little garden out the back is a bonus.

Kerala Bamboo House (☎ 9895270993; www.keralabamboohouse.com; huts d Rs750-1500) For that bamboo-hut experience, this popular place squishes together dozens of pretty, Balinese-style huts in a massive compound. The bamboo interiors are basic but handsome, and popular cooking classes are run from here (Rs500 for two) as well as regular culture shows and yoga.

MIDRANGE & TOP END

Hill Palace (☎ 2610142; www.hillpalaceresort.com; r Rs750-1000) Chintzy decor will greet you here, but the place is always sparkling clean and freshly painted, with balconies facing the ocean and a decent sea breeze.

Santa Claus Village (☎ 9249121464; www.santaclausvillageresort.com; r Rs800-2000, with AC Rs1800-2500; ☒ ☒) Even though the cheesy name is only apt once a year, this place is surprisingly well designed – with traditional Keralan-themed buildings, fetching bits of furniture and lots of teak-wood flair. The two deluxe rooms at the front are the money shot, with huge bay windows facing out to sea.

Sea Pearl Chalets (☎ 2660105; www.seapearlchalets.com; d Rs1300) Precariously dangling off a bluff at Varkala's southern cliff, these small, basic and charismatic wigwams have unbeatable views. They're definitely worth checking out before they tumble into the ocean.

Eden Garden (☎ 2603910; www.edengarden.in; r €23-33, luxury ste €105) Delightfully situated overlooking peaceful paddy fields, this place has a few small, orderly and well-decorated double rooms set around a lush lily pond. Recently added phantasmagoric luxury suites are organically shaped like white space-mushrooms and decked out with intricate paintwork, curvy windows and an opulent shower room. A recommended ayurvedic resort is based here, with both short- and long-term treatments available.

Sea Breeze (☎ 2603257; www.seabreezevarkala.com; r Rs1500, with AC Rs2000-3000; ☒) The large and orderly rooms in this pink building all offer great sea views and share a large veranda – perfect for nightly sunset adulation. While the rooms here are achingly nondescript, the friendly owners and quiet location give this place a slight edge over the competition.

Puthooram (☎ 3202007; www.puthooram.com; r Rs2000-3000) If garden gnomes were looking for a holiday destination, they'd probably come here. Puthooram has bungalows that are panelled with wood both inside and out, all set around a charming little garden. Budget rooms are also available, though they're not nearly as nice.

Pink Aana (☎ 9746981298; www.pinkaana.at; r €50) On the quiet Odayam beach north of Varkala, there are just four sturdily constructed bungalows at the 'Pink Elephant'. Made of coconut wood and bamboo, they're sparse but very stylish and great value. Each has a private veranda and they're right on the beach, enjoying uninterrupted sunset views.

KERALA

Villa Jacaranda (☎ 2610296; www.villa-jacaranda
.biz; d Rs3600-5000) The ultimate in understated
luxury, this romantic retreat has just a handful of huge, bright rooms in a large house,
each with a balcony and decorated with a
chic blend of minimalist modern and period
touches. It's all kept refreshingly simple, and
the solitude here is all-encompassing. The
delicious complimentary breakfast is served
on your veranda.

Taj Garden Retreat (☎ 2603000; www.tajhotels.com;
r Rs6500-9000; ✉ 🖳 🖳) Luxury, '80s-style: this
ritzy-but-dated resort has big fancy rooms,
an ayurvedic centre, a bar and health club.
The Sunday lunch buffet (12.30pm to 3pm;
Rs600) is deservedly popular – particularly
since you get to use the pool. Poolside cocktails
all round, then?

Eating

Most restaurants in Varkala offer pretty much
the same predictable mix of Indian, Asian and
Western fare. It's best to join in the nightly
Varkala cliff-side saunter till you find a place
that suits your mood. The following places
have stood the test of time and offer reliably
decent victuals.

Oottupura Vegetarian Restaurant (mains from Rs30)
Bucking the trend and serving only veggie
options, this budget eatery has a respectable
range of yummy dishes, including breakfast
puttu (flour with milk, bananas and honey)
and lots of lunch and dinner options.

Sreepadman (meals Rs30-45) For dirt cheap and
authentic Keralan fare – think dosas (paper-
thin lentil-flour pancakes) and thalis – where
you can rub shoulders with rickshaw drivers
rather than tourists, hit Sreepadman. This is a
real hole-in-the-wall with a view: there is neat
seating out the back with temple tank views.

Juice Shack (juices Rs50, snacks Rs30-150; ⏱ 7am-
7.30pm-ish) A funky little health-juice bar that
doubles as Varkala's informal intranet – this
is where long-termers come to gossip and
share the latest news the old way.

Somatheeram (meals Rs60-150) This bare-bones
beachside restaurant whips up consistently
tasty Indian fare. The location, right on the
main beach where you can dig your toes
into the sand, is about as good as it gets.

Hungry Eye Kitchen (meals Rs60-160) We love
the stepped, multilevel design of Hungry
Eye – this way everyone gets uninterrupted
sea views. Very diplomatic. Thai food is a
speciality here, and the kitchen can whip up

red and green curries as well as the usual
suspects of Varkala dishes.

Kerala Coffee House (breakfast/mains around Rs70/100)
With oodles of atmosphere and top service,
this perennially popular hang-out has table-
clothed dining under the swaying palms. It
serves cocktails (around Rs80) and has particularly flavoursome pizzas (Rs70 to Rs90),
all served to a dancy, reggae soundtrack.

Calfouti (meals Rs70-200) The menu here
doesn't look that different from everywhere
else, but the setting is a notch swishier than
most places, with an upper level balcony,
colourful lamps and more than its fair share
of dinner-time fairy lights.

Drinking

Although most of the places along the cliff
aren't licensed, many will serve beer (around
Rs80) in a discreet teapot and with a watchful eye for patrolling police.

Entertainment

Kathakali performances are organised during
December and January; look out for signs
advertising location and times.

Getting There & Away

There are frequent trains to Trivandrum
(2nd class/AC chair Rs22/142, one hour)
and Kollam (Rs18/142, 30 minutes), as well
as three daily services to Alleppey (Rs35/155,
two hours). It's feasible to get to Kollam in
time for the morning backwater boat to
Alleppey (see the boxed text, p1002). From
Temple Junction, four daily buses pass by on
their way to Trivandrum (Rs36, 1½ hours),
with one heading to Kollam at around 11am
(Rs32, one hour). Alternatively you can catch
a bus or autorickshaw to the highway junction at Kollambalam (7km away) for more
frequent express buses rumbling north.

Getting Around

It's about 2.5km from the train station to
Varkala beach, with rickshaws covering the
distance for between Rs30 and Rs50, taxis for
Rs80. Local buses also travel regularly between
the train station and the temple junction (Rs5).
Beware that many drivers will try to shoehorn
you into the hotel that pays them the highest
commission – it's often best to be dropped off
at the helipad and walk to your chosen hotel.

Many places along the cliff hire out
scooters/Enfields for Rs300/450 per day.

KOLLAM (QUILON)

☎ 0474 / pop 380,100

Tiny Kollam (Quilon) is the sleepy southern approach to Kerala's backwaters. One of the oldest ports in the Arabian Sea, it was once a major commercial hub that saw Roman, Arab, Chinese and later Portuguese, Dutch and British traders jostle into port – eager to get their hands on spices and the region's valuable cashew crops. The town's shady streets and antediluvian market are worth a wander, and the calm waterways of the surrounding Ashtamudi Lake are still fringed with coconut palms, cashew plantations and traditional villages.

Information

There are several ATMs around town.

Silver Net (per hr Rs15; ☺ 9.30am-9pm Mon-Sat) The most convenient of numerous internet cafes at the Bishop Jerome Nagar Complex.

DTPC information centre (☎ 2745625; info@dtpc kollam.com; ☺ 7am-7pm) Very helpful; near the KSRTC bus stand and boat jetty.

Post office (☎ 2746607; Alappuzha Rd)

UAE Exchange (☎ 2751240-1; Alapuzha Rd; ☺ 9.30am-6pm Mon-Sat, 9.30am-1pm Sun) For changing cash and travellers cheques.

Sights

If you have the time, it's well worth visiting **Kollam beach** to stroll past picturesque Keralan fishing hamlets and watch fishermen mending nets while their bright fishing boats colour the shoreline. There's a rowdy **fish market** here where customers and fisherfolk alike pontificate on the value of the catch of the day – get there early in the morning. The beach is 2km south of town, a Rs20 rickshaw ride away.

South of Main Rd, the **Mukkada Bazaar** has been a commercial hub of activity for hundreds of years. Here, spice merchants sit atop bags of bright powders, porters ferry goods deftly on their heads and shop fronts are draped in mysterious herbs (many used for ayurvedic treatments).

Activities

Janakanthi Panchakarma Centre (☎ 2763014; www .santhigiri.co.in; Vaidyasala Nagar, Asraman North) is an ayurvedic resort, 5km from Kollam, popular for its seven- to 21-day treatment packages (seven-day packages including basic accommodation start at around Rs9000). You can

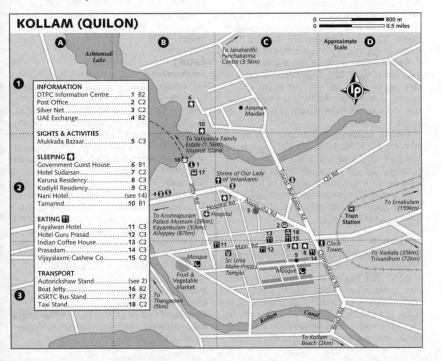

KOLLAM (QUILON)

INFORMATION	
DTPC Information Centre	1 B2
Post Office	2 C2
Silver Net	3 C2
UAE Exchange	4 B2

SIGHTS & ACTIVITIES	
Mukkada Bazaar	5 C3

SLEEPING	
Government Guest House	6 B1
Hotel Sudarsan	7 C2
Karuna Residency	8 C3
Kodiyil Residency	9 C3
Nani Hotel	(see 14)
Tamarind	10 B1

EATING	
Fayalwan Hotel	11 C3
Hotel Guru Prasad	12 C3
Indian Coffee House	13 C2
Prasadam	14 C3
Vijayalaxmi Cashew Co	15 C2

TRANSPORT	
Autorickshaw Stand	(see 2)
Boat Jetty	16 B2
KSRTC Bus Stand	17 B2
Taxi Stand	18 C2

also just visit for a rejuvenation massage and herbal steam bath (Rs750). An autorickshaw from Kollam should cost around Rs100.

Tours

Excellent **Canoe-boat tours** (per person Rs300; ☺ 9am & 2pm) through the canals of Munroe Island and across Ashtamudi Lake are organised by the DTPC. On these excursions (with knowledgable guides) you can observe daily village life, see *kettuvallam* (rice barge) construction, toddy (palm beer) tapping, coir-making (coconut fibre), prawn and fish farming, and do some birdwatching spice-garden visits.

Festivals & Events

The **Pooram festival** (p982) is held in Kollam every April, while the **Ashtamudi Craft & Art festival** (December/January) is every two years.

Sleeping
BUDGET

The DTPC office keeps a list of **homestays** (d Rs200-500) in and around Kollam.

Government Guest House (☎ 2743620; r Rs220, with AC Rs440; ⊠) In a splendid colonial-era relic that still wafts in the remnants of faded grandeur, this guest house offers immense, crumbling rooms with high ceilings and wooden floors. They're a bargain, but isolated 3km north of the centre on Ashtamudi Lake.

Karuna Residency (☎ 3263240; Main Rd; s/d Rs350/450, r with AC Rs600; ⊠) This little budgeter is starting to show its age, but is still maintained in decent condition. The central location close to the train station is probably its single biggest asset.

Kodiylil Residency (☎ 3018030; Main Rd; s/d Rs399/499, with AC Rs699/799; ⊠) This new hotel brings a mild touch of class to the budget category. Bright red walls are lit by mood lighting; rooms come in shades of lime and have stylishly modern furniture and TVs. Shame about the complete lack of windows. Check-out is 24 hours.

MIDRANGE

Valiyavila Family Estate (☎ 2701546, 9847132449; www .kollamlakeviewresort.com; Panamukkom; r Rs750-1500, with AC Rs2500; ⊠) The pick of Kollam's sleeping bunch, this estate crowns a breezy peninsula surrounded by leisurely backwaters on three sides. The enormous rooms are a little sparse, but come with lots of windows to enjoy the views, the morning breeze and the extraor-

dinary sight of large bosoms (belonging to a misshapen sculpture – the *Goddess of Light*). Call ahead for a boat pick-up, catch a public ferry from Kollam (Rs3), or grab an autorickshaw (Rs100) to get here.

Hotel Sudarsan (☎ 2744322; Alappuzha Rd; www .hotelsudarsan.com; s/d with AC from Rs900/1000, executive Rs1500/1750; ⊠) Sudarsan is welcoming enough, but a little institutionally designed for our taste. The non-AC rooms in the front wing are spacious but very noisy, while the executive rooms at the back are smaller, quieter and probably a little overpriced.

Nani Hotel (☎ 2751141; Chinnakada Rd; r Rs1200-3000; ⊠ ▭) This brand spanking new boutique hotel boasts some of the best bang for buck in India. Built by a cashew magnate, it's gorgeously designed and mixes traditional Keralan elements and modern chic like it's not even trying. Even the cheaper rooms have mod cons you'd expect at double these prices, including flat panel TVs, feathery pillows and sumptuous bathrooms.

Tamarind (☎ 2745538; r Rs2000; ⊠) Fresh from a life-changing set of renovations, this once-rusty government guest house has gone all upmarket and now has big, airy, bright orange rooms offering pleasant views over backwaters. An autorickshaw from town is around Rs50.

Eating

Fayalwan Hotel (Main Rd; meals Rs10-40) This is a real Indian working-man's diner, packed to the rafters come lunchtime. There are concrete booths and long benches for sitting and tucking in – try the mutton biryani (Rs45).

Hotel Guru Prasad (Main Rd; meals Rs18) In a neat colonial building still clinging to remnants of a once-cheery paint job, this busy lunchtime place draws the punters with dirt-cheap set meals.

Prasadam (☎ 2751141; Chinnakada Rd; meals Rs60-175) The restaurant at the swish Nani Hotel has a comely setting amid intricate copper-relief artwork depicting Kollam history. The meals are well prepared, and dishes range from Western fare, salads and pastas to lots of typical Indian victuals. The massive thalis are Rs80.

Also recommended:

Indian Coffee House (Main Rd) Reliable for a decent breakfast and strong coffee.

Vijayalaxmi Cashew Co (Main Rd; ☺ 9.30am-8pm) A major exporter of Kollam's famous cashews; quality nuts are around Rs250 per 500g.

Getting There & Away

BOAT

See the boxed text, p1002, for information on cruises to Alleppey. From the main boat jetty, there are frequent public ferry services across Ashtamudi Lake to Guhanandapuram (one hour) and Perumon (two hours). Fares are around Rs10 return.

BUS

Kollam is situated on the well-trodden Trivandrum–Kollam–Alleppey–Ernakulam bus route, with superfast/superexpress (but sadly no super-duper-double-fast-express) buses departing every 10 or 20 minutes to Trivandrum (Rs45, 1½ hours), Alleppey (Rs55, two hours) and Ernakulam (Kochi, Rs91, 3½ hours). Buses depart from the **KSRTC bus stand** (☎ 2752008) near the boat jetty.

TRAIN

There are frequent trains to Ernakulam (2nd class/AC chair Rs46/188, 3½ hours, 12 daily) and Trivandrum (Rs26/142, one hour) via Varkala (Rs18/142, 30 minutes). Four daily trains go to Alleppey (Rs33/142, 1½ hours).

Getting Around

Most autorickshaw trips should cost around Rs20, but drivers will ask for more at night. There's a prepaid stand opposite the post office.

AROUND KOLLAM
Krishnapuram Palace Museum

Two kilometres south of Kayamkulam (between Kollam and Alleppey), this restored **palace** (☎ 0479-2441133; admission Rs10, camera Rs25, video camera Rs250; ⏰ 10am-1pm & 2-5pm Tue-Sun) is a fine example of grand Keralan architecture. Now a museum, inside are paintings, antique furniture, sculptures, and a renowned 3m-high mural depicting the Gajendra Moksha (the liberation of Gajendra, chief of the elephants) as told in the Mahabharata. The **Bharni Utsavam Festival** is held at the nearby Chettikulangara Bhaghavathy Temple in February/March.

Buses (Rs24) leave Kollam every few minutes for Kayamkulam. Get off at the bus stand near the temple gate, 2km before the palace.

ALAPPUZHA (ALLEPPEY)

☎ 0477 / pop 282,700

Almost Venice-like, the shady streets of Alappuzha are set around a grid of canals that spill into the vast watery highways of the region. As the gateway to the famed backwaters, this is the place in Kerala to organise some relaxed houseboat action and is also home to the famous Nehru Trophy Snake Boat Race. It's worth stopping in Alleppey to soak up some tropical village living before making a beeline for the backwaters.

Orientation

The bus stand and boat jetty are close to each other; the hotels spread far and wide. The train station is 4km southwest of the town centre. There's a beach about 2km west of the city centre.

Information

There are several ATMs around town.

Danys Bookshop (Hotel Royale Park; YMCA Rd; ☎ 2237828; ⏰ 10am-9pm, 10am-1pm Sun) Tiny bookshop in the Hotel Royal Park.

DTPC Tourist Reception Centre (☎ 2253308; www .alappuzhatourism.com; ⏰ 8.30am-6pm) Barely offers rudimentary tourist info.

Mailbox (☎ 2339994; Boat Jetty Rd; internet per hr Rs40; ⏰ 9am-8pm)

National Cyber Park (☎ 2238688; YMCA Compound; internet per hr Rs30; ⏰ 10am-10pm Mon-Sat)

Tourist Police (☎ 2251161; ⏰ 24hr)

UAE Exchange (☎ 18004259585; cnr Cullan & Mullackal Rds; ⏰ 9.30am-6pm Mon-Sat, to 1pm Sun) For changing cash and travellers cheques.

Activities

For ayurvedic treatments, **Ayurveda: Sree Krishna** (☎ 3290728, 9847119060; www.krishnayurveda .com), near Fishing Point, does one-hour rejuvenation massages for Rs600. For more serious health issues, the ayurvedic doctor here has over 20 years' experience and will suggest a course of multiday treatment suitable to your ailments. It's near the Nehru race finishing point.

Tours

Any of the dozens of travel agencies in town, or the KTDC, can arrange canoe-boat tours of the backwaters; see also the boxed text, p1002.

Sleeping

Look out for guest house and heritage home accommodation in Alleppey; they're better that the town's uninspiring hotels.

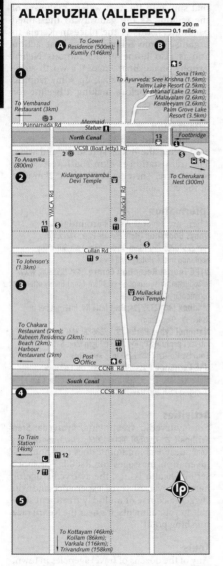

ALAPPUZHA (ALLEPPEY)

look a little sketchy, the fresh lick of yellow paint and spacious rooms at rock-bottom prices are hard to ignore. It's uberbasic – the communal bathrooms have quite a waft about them.

Palmy Residency (☎ 2235938; www.palmyresort.com; r Rs300-500) Run by the friendly folk of Palmy Resort, this central little place has four absurdly neat and quiet rooms of varying size – all with mosquito netting, flyscreens and free bicycles. It's just north of the footbridge.

Johnson's (☎ 2245825; www.johnsonskerala.com; r Rs300-750) On a quiet street just west of town, Johnson's homestay takes up several rooms in a large quirky mansion. Captained by the zealous Johnson Gilbert, this rambling residence is filled with funky furniture and loads of plants. It offers just a few big, bright upstairs rooms with enormous balconies. The cheaper bamboo and thatch huts are a bit dowdy for our tastes.

Gowri Residence (☎ 2236371; www.gowriresidence .com; r Rs500-800, with AC Rs1000-1800; 🖳) What started as a small heritage home has turned into a huge complex of great rooms and bungalows. There's a bewildering selection of abodes here, ranging from traditional wood-panelled rooms in the main house to several types of bungalows made from either stone, wood, bamboo or thatch. Good food is served in gazebos in the garden or on your veranda.

Cherukara Nest (☎ 9947059628; www.cherukara nest.com; d incl breakfast Rs550, with AC Rs1200; 🖳) This commendably maintained heritage home has the sort of welcoming family atmosphere that

There are several relaxed sleeping options on the backwaters a few kilometres north of Alleppey; all can arrange pick-ups and drop offs from town.

BUDGET

St George Lodgings (☎ 2251620; CCNB Rd; s/d Rs105/200, without bathroom Rs75/155) While this place might

---

NEHRU TROPHY SNAKE BOAT RACE

This famous regatta on Vembanad Lake in Alleppey takes place on the second Saturday of August each year, with scores of giant, low-slung *chundan vallam* (snake boats) competing. Each boat is over 30m long with a raised, snaking prow, and is crewed by 100 rowers singing in unison, all shaded by gleaming silk umbrellas. Watched avidly by thousands of cheering spectators, the annual event celebrates the seafaring and martial traditions of ancient Kerala with floats and performing arts.

Tickets entitle you to seats on bamboo terraces, which are erected for the races. Prices range from Rs75 to Rs500 for the best seats in the Tourist Pavilion, which offers views of the finishing point and separates you from gatherings of rowdy men. Take food, drink and an umbrella.

Other less famous but no less spectacular boat races are held around the backwaters between June and September. Ask at any KTDC office for details.

---

makes you miss your grandma. There are four large rooms filled with character, each sporting lots of polished wood touches and antediluvian doors with ornate locks. Great value.

MIDRANGE & TOP END

Palmy Lake Resort (☎ 2235938; www.palmyresorts.com; Punnamada Rd East; cottages d Rs750) With six handsome cottages, some in bamboo and some in concrete, there's loads of charm and peace at this small homestay, 3.5km north of Alleppey. It's set among palm groves near the backwaters, with gracious owner Bigi and his wife Macy providing delicious meals on request.

Sona (☎ 2235211; www.sonahome.com; Shornur Canal Rd; r Rs800, with AC Rs1100) Run by an affable family, this charming old heritage home has cool, spacious rooms with loads of character, high rosewood ceilings, four-poster beds and secluded verandas overlooking a well-kept garden.

Malayalam (☎ 2234591; malayalamresorts@yahoo.com; Punnamada; r Rs1000) With one of best locations in Alleppey, this little family-run pad has a handful of cute cottages that practically play footsies with the backwaters. And if your front porch is still not close enough to the water for you, you can laze on two bamboo sit-outs that jut out over the lake. It lies surrounded by the Keraleeyam resort.

Keraleeyam (☎ 2231468; www.keraleeyam.com; Punnamada; s/d from Rs1140/1425; 🛠) This miniresort is laid out along the backwaters a few kilometres north of Alleppey. There are several comfortable AC rooms inside the main building, which is a traditional Keralan home, but our money's on the charming, two-storey, deluxe thatch bungalows (single/double Rs1425/1710) with porches that practically hang over the backwater lake. Also offers ayurvedic treatments.

Palm Grove Lake Resort (☎ 2235004; www.palmgrovelakeresort.com; Punnamada; cottages d Rs1500-1750) Close to the starting point of the Nehru Trophy Snake Boat Race on Punnamada Lake, this isolated upmarket option has stylish, airy double cottages right on the lake. Made of natural materials, each skilfully finished hut has a secluded veranda, eye-catching outdoor showers and perfect patio views of the lake.

Anamika (☎ 242044; www.anamikahome.com; VCSB (Boat Jetty) Rd; d incl breakfast Rs1800-2200) This elegant Syrian Christian home has four massive, breezy rooms sparsely decorated with traditional furniture and glistening polished floorboards. The simple yet elegant ambiance is helped along by moody lamp lighting.

Raheem Residency (☎ 2239767; www.raheemresidency.com; Beach Rd; s/d from €140/170; 🛠 🛋) This thoughtfully renovated 1860s heritage home is an absolute delight to visit, let alone stay in. All the rooms here have been restored to their former glory and boast bathtubs, dashing antique furniture and period fixtures. The common areas are airy and comfortable, there are pretty indoor courtyards, a well-stocked library and a great little pool. This is the ideal luxury getaway.

Eating

Kream Korner (Mullackal Rd; dishes Rs30-130) This relaxed place is popular with Indian and foreign families and offers a tasty multicuisine menu. The yummy cold coffee with ice cream (Rs25) beats a frappuchino any day. There's another branch on Cullan Rd.

Thaff (YMCA Rd; meals Rs35-110) An absurdly popular joint that has scrumptious Indian bites, with some Arabic flavours mixed in, to boot. It does succulent roast spit-chicken (Rs90), scrumptious *shawarma* (Rs25) and brain-freezing cold ice-cream shakes (Rs25).

THE BACKWATERS

The undisputed main attraction of a trip to Kerala is travelling through the 900km network of waterways that fringe the coast and trickle far inland. Long before the advent of roads, these waters were the slippery highways of Kerala, and many villagers today still use paddle-power as their main form of transport. Trips through the backwaters traverse palm-fringed lakes studded with cantilevered Chinese fishing nets, and wind their way along narrow, shady canals where coir (coconut fibre), copra (dried coconut kernels) and cashews are loaded onto boats. Along the way are isolated villages where farming life continues as it has for eons.

Kerala Tourism (www.keralatourism.org) produces a *Backwater Map*.

Tourist Cruises

The popular tourist cruise between Kollam and Alleppey (Rs400) departs at 10.30am, arriving at 6.30pm, daily from August to March and every second day at other times. Generally, there are two stops: a 1pm lunch stop (with a basic lunch provided) and a brief afternoon chai stop. The crew has an ice box full of fruit, soft drinks and beer to sell. Bring sunscreen and a hat.

It's a scenic and leisurely way to get between the two towns, but as a backwater experience the cruise is limited by the fact that the boat travels along the major highways of the canal system – you won't see much of the close-up village life that makes the backwaters so magical. Travellers have reported getting bored with the eight-hour trip.

Another option is to take the trip halfway (Rs200) and get off at the **Matha Amrithanandamayi Mission** (☎ 0476-2897578; www.amritapuri.org; Amrithapuri), the incongruously pink ashram of Matha Amrithanandamayi. One of India's few female gurus, Amrithanandamayi is also known as Amma (Mother), or 'The Hugging Mother,' because of the *darshan* (blessing) she practises, often hugging thousands of people in marathon all-night sessions. The ashram runs official tours at 5pm each day. It's a huge complex, with about 2000 people living here permanently – monks, nuns, students, Indian families and Westerners. It offers food, ayurvedic treatments, yoga and meditation, as well as souvenirs from the cult of Amma, everything from books to postcards of her toes. Amma travels around for much of the year, so you might be out of luck if you're in need of a cuddle.

Visitors should dress conservatively and there is a strict code of behaviour. With prior arrangement, you can stay at the ashram for Rs150 per day (including simple vegetarian meals) and pick up an onward or return cruise a day or two later. Alternatively, you can take the free ferry to the other side of the canal and grab a rickshaw to Karunagappally 10km away (around Rs100), from where you can catch buses to Alleppey (Rs32, 1½ hours).

Houseboats

Renting a houseboat designed like a *kettuvallam* (rice barge) could be one of your most expensive experiences in India, but it's worth every darned rupee. Drifting through quiet canals lined with coconut palms, eating deliciously authentic Keralan food, meeting local villagers and sleeping on the water under a galaxy of stars – it's a world away from the clamour of India.

Houseboats cater for couples (one or two double bedrooms) and groups (we've seen seven bedroom boats being constructed!). Food (and an onboard chef to cook it) is generally included in the quoted cost. Houseboats can be chartered through a multitude of private operators in

Royal Park Hotel (YMCA Rd; meals Rs70-210) The extensive menu at this swish hotel restaurant is heavily meat-centric, but the food is excellent. You can order from the same menu in the upstairs bar and wash down your meal with a cold Kingfisher.

Harbour Restaurant (☎ 2230767; Beach Rd; meals Rs80-200; ☽ lunch & dinner) This beachside, casual Euro-style eatery is run by the swish Raheem Residency Hotel. It's a little more casual and budget conscious than the hotel's main restaurant, but promises equally well-prepared Indian and Western cuisine.

Chakara Restaurant (☎ 2230767; Beach Rd; 3 courses lunch/dinner €12/17; ☽ lunch & dinner) The restaurant at Raheem Residency is the most expensive, and best, place in town. The menu creatively combines elements of traditional Keralan and European cuisine. Local Indian wine is available by the bottle.

Kollam and Alleppey. Be warned that this is the biggest business in Kerala, and some operators are unscrupulous. The quality of boats varies widely, from veritable rust buckets to floating palaces – try to lay eyes on the boat you'll be travelling in before agreeing on a price. Travel-agency reps will be pushing you to book a boat as soon as you set foot in Kerala, though most of the bad experiences we hear about are from people who booked their trip outside the backwater hub towns. Your choice is greater in Alleppey (500 boats and counting), but it's a ridiculously popular activity there and you're likely to get caught in backwater-gridlock in the high season. It's not possible to travel by houseboat between Alleppey and Kollam, or between Alleppey and Kochi. Prices are hugely variable. Expect a boat for two people for 24 hours to cost anything from Rs4500 to Rs7000, more for larger boats or for AC. Shop around to negotiate a bargain; but in the peak season you'll definitely pay more.

Village Tours & Canoe Boats
Village tours usually involve small groups of five to six people, a knowledgable guide and an open canoe or covered *kettuvallam*. The tours (from Kochi, Kollam or Alleppey) last from 2½ to six hours and cost between Rs300 and Rs650 per person. They include visits to villages to watch coir-making, boat building, toddy (palm beer) tapping and fish farming. On longer trips a traditional Keralan lunch is often provided. The Munroe Island trip from Kollam (see p998) is an excellent tour of this type; and the tourist desk in Ernakulam (p1014) also organises recommended tours.

In Alleppey, rented canoe boats offer a nonguided laze through the canals on a small, covered canoe for up to four people (two people for four hours Rs600) – a great way to spend a relaxing afternoon.

Public Ferries
If you want the local backwater transport experience, there are State Water Transport boats between Alleppey and Kottayam (Rs12, 2½ hours, five boats daily from 7.30am to 5.30pm). The trip crosses Vembanad Lake and has a more varied landscape than the Alleppey cruise.

Environmental Issues
Environmental problems, such as pollution, land reclamation, and industrial and agricultural development, seriously threaten the backwaters and the communities that live on their banks. It's estimated that water levels have dropped by two-thirds since the mid-19th century and many migratory birds no longer visit the area.

Pollution from houseboat motors is becoming a major problem as boat numbers swell every season. The Keralan authorities have introduced an ecofriendly accreditation system for houseboat operators. Among the criteria an operator must meet before being issued with the 'Green Palm Certificate' are the installation of solar panels and sanitary tanks for the disposal of waste. Although the system is still new, you can ask operators whether they have the requisite certification. There's been talk of running boats on cleaner natural gas, though we've yet to see this being implemented. Seriously consider choosing one of the few remaining punting, rather than motorised, boats if possible to reduce pollution.

Others to try:
Vembanad Restaurant (Alleppey Prince Hotel; AS Rd; mains Rs40-170) Fine dining pool-side to nightly live music.
Indian Coffee House (snacks Rs4-12) Branches on Mullackal Rd and YMCA Rd.

Getting There & Away
BOAT
Ferries run to Kottayam from the boat jetty on VCSB (Boat Jetty) Rd; see above.

BUS
From the KSRTC bus stand, frequent buses head to Trivandrum (Rs98, 3½ hours, every 20 minutes), Kollam (Rs55) and Ernakulam (Kochi, Rs39, 1½ hours). Buses to Kottayam (Rs30, 1¼ hours, every 30 minutes) are considerably faster than the ferry. One bus daily leaves for Kumily at 6.30am (Rs90, 5½ hours). For Varkala you can catch certain Trivandrum-bound buses, which will drop

you off at Kollambalam (Rs76, 2½ hours), 7km from Varkala.

TRAIN
There are several trains to Ernakulam (2nd class/AC chair Rs25/135, 1½ hours) and Trivandrum (Rs45/180, three hours) via Kollam (Rs33/142, 1½ hours). Three trains a day stop at Varkala (2nd class/AC chair Rs35/155, two hours). The train station is 4km west of town.

Getting Around
An autorickshaw from the train station to the boat jetty and KSRTC bus stand is around Rs50. Several guest houses around town hire out scooters for Rs200 per day.

AROUND ALLEPPEY
Kerala's backwaters snake in all directions from Alleppey and, while touring on a houseboat is a great experience, taking time to slow down and stay in a village can be just as rewarding.

Just 10km from Alleppey, and run by the erudite and ever-helpful Thomas, **Green Palms Homes** (☎ 0477-2724497, 9495557675; community .greenpalms@gmail.com; Chennamkary; s/d/tr with full board Rs1100/1800/2250) is a series of homestays that seem a universe away, set in a typical, achingly picturesque backwater village, where you will sleep in basic rooms in villagers' homes among the rice paddies. Your host will double as a guide to the village and its traditions, and will prepare three Keralan meals a day. It's splendidly quiet, there are no roads in sight and you can hire bicycles (Rs25 per hour) and canoes (Rs50 per hour) or take cooking classes with your hosts (Rs150). If you have the time, you can stay longer and learn local trades like rice farming, carpentry, coconut collecting and more. Book ahead during the high season.

To get here, call ahead and catch one of the hourly ferries from Alleppey to Chennamkary (Rs5, 1¼ hours). Please remember this is a traditional village; dress appropriately.

KOTTAYAM
☎ 0481 / pop 172,867
Sandwiched between the Western Ghats and the backwaters, Kottayam is more renowned for being Kerala's centre of the spice and rubber trade than for its aesthetic appeal. For most travellers it's a hub town, well connected to both the mountains and the backwaters.

Kottayam has a bookish history: the first Malayalam-language printing press was established here in 1820, and this was the first district in India to achieve 100% literacy. A place of churches and seminaries, Kottayam was a refuge for the Orthodox church when the Portuguese began forcing Keralan Christians to switch to Catholicism in the 16th century.

The **Thirunakkara Utsavam Festival** is held in March at the Thirunakkara Shiva Temple.

Orientation & Information
The KSRTC bus stand is 1km south of the centre, the boat jetty a further 2km (at Kodimatha), while the train station is 1km north of Kottayam. There are a handful of ATMs around.

DTPC office (☎ 2560479; dtpcktm@sancharnet.in; ⏰ 10am-5pm Mon-Sat) At the boat jetty.
Sify iWay (☎ 2563418; KK Rd; per hr Rs25; ⏰ 8.30am-8.30pm Mon-Sat) Internet.
UAE Exchange (☎ 2303865; 1st fl, MC Rd; ⏰ 9.30am-6pm Mon-Sat, ⏰ 9.30am-12.30pm Sun) Changes cash and travellers cheques.

Sleeping
Accommodation options are pretty dire in Kottayam – you're better off heading to Kumarakon for some great top-end hotels. Also try checking for homestays at the **DTPC office** (☎ 2560479), which range from the basic (Rs1000 per person full board) to deluxe (up to US$100).

Ambassador Hotel (☎ 2563293; KK Rd; www.fhrai .com; s/d from Rs250/325, d with AC Rs650; 🛏) A very respectable budget sleeping option, the rooms here are spartan but spotless, spacious and quiet. It has a bakery, an AC bar, an adequate restaurant and a huge painting of the *Last Supper* to greet you in the lobby.

Homestead Hotel (☎ 2560467; KK Rd; s/d from Rs317/502, d with AC Rs1483; 🛏) Easily the pick of the budget litter, this place has painstakingly maintained rooms in a blissfully quiet building off the street. The foyer sports '60s-style decor that's accidentally stumbled into vogue again, and there are two great eateries right out front.

Pearl Regency (☎ 2561123; www.pearlregencyktm .com; MC Rd; s/d from Rs1500/1900; 🛏 🖥) This slick business-focused contender has roomy-but-dull abodes. It's all run very efficiently, and there's an internet centre, coffee shop and restaurant on site. It's decent value.

Windsor Castle (☎ 2363637; www.thewindsorcastle.net; MC Rd; s/d from US$80/100, cottages RsUS$150; ❄ ⬛) This grandiose carbuncle of a building has some of the better rooms in Kottayam – minimally furnished, spacious and with bathtubs, though they're still overpriced by our measure. You may as well go for the deluxe cottages lying strewn around the private backwaters.

Eating

Hotel Suryaas (TB Rd; dishes Rs20-60) It's no surprise this cosy dining room is packed to the rafters with hungry families come mealtime – the North and South Indian food here is excellent. Thalis cost Rs45.

Meenachil (2nd fl, KK Rd; dishes Rs50-110; ❍ lunch & dinner) This is our favourite place in Kottayam to fill up on scrumptious Indian fare. The family atmosphere is friendly, the dining room modern and tidy and the menu expansive – everything from biryanis, veg and nonveg dishes to tandoori.

Thali (1st fl, KK Rd; meals Rs53-63) This place is a slightly swankier version of the typical Keralan set-meal place. Spotlessly kept. The food here is great.

Nalekattu (Windsor Hotel; MC Rd; dishes Rs60-125; ❍ lunch & dinner) The traditional Keralan restaurant at the Windsor Castle is in an open-walled pavilion and serves tasty Keralan specialities like *chemeen* (mango curry) and *tharavu mappas* (duck in coconut gravy).

Indian Coffee House (TB Rd) We just can't get enough of this South Indian institution serving the whole gamut of tasty Indian snacks.

Getting There & Away

BOAT

Ferries run to Alleppey; see p1003.

BUS

The **KSRTC bus stand** has buses to Trivandrum (Rs86, four hours, every 20 minutes), Alleppey (Rs30, 1¼ hours, every 30 minutes) and Ernakulam (Kochi, Rs46, two hours, every 20 minutes). There are also frequent buses to nearby Kumarakom (Rs8.50, 30 minutes, every 15 minutes), to Thrissur (Rs81, four hours), Calicut (Rs162, seven hours, 13 daily), Kumily for Periyar Wildlife Sanctuary (Rs69, four hours, every 30 minutes) and Munnar (Rs101, five hours, five daily). Certain buses to Trivandrum pass by Kollamballam, 7km from Varkala (Rs80, three hours).

TRAIN

Kottayam is well served by frequent trains running between Trivandrum (2nd class/AC chair Rs46/188, 3½ hours) and Ernakulam (Rs26/142, 1½ hours).

Getting Around

An autorickshaw from the jetty to the KSRTC bus stand is around Rs30, and from the bus stand to the train station about Rs20. Most trips around town cost Rs15.

AROUND KOTTAYAM
Kumarakom
☎ 0481

Kumarakom, 16km west of Kottayam and on the shore of Vembanad Lake, is an unhurried backwater town with a smattering of dazzling, top-end sleeping options. You can arrange houseboats through Kumarakom's less-crowded canals, but expect to pay considerably more than in Alleppey.

Arundhati Roy, author of the 1997 Booker Prize–winning *The God of Small Things*, was raised in the nearby Aymanam village.

SIGHTS

Kumarakom Bird Sanctuary (☎ 2525864; Indian/foreigner Rs5/45; ❍ 6am-5.30pm) is on the 5-hectare site of a former rubber plantation and is the haunt of a variety of domestic and migratory birds. October to February is the time for travelling birds like the garganey teal, osprey, marsh harrier and steppey eagle, while May to July is the breeding season for local species like the Indian shag, pond herons, egrets and darters. Early morning is the best viewing time.

Buses between Kottayam's KSRTC stand and Kumarakom (Rs8.50, 30 minutes, every 15 minutes) stop at the entrance to the sanctuary.

SLEEPING

Cruise 'N Lake (☎ 2525804; www.homestaykumarakom.com; Puthenpura Tourist Enclave; r Rs1000-1500, with AC Rs1500-2000; ❄) As any estate agent will tell you, it's all about location, location, location. Crowning the tip of a small peninsula surrounded by backwaters on one side and a lawn of rice paddies on the other, this is the ideal affordable getaway. The rooms are plain, but it's lovely and secluded out here, surrounded by bucolic villages where houseboats are made by hand. To get to it, go several kilometres past the sanctuary and take a left, it's then 2km down a dirt road. Pick-ups from Kottayam cost Rs350.

Tharavadu Heritage Home (☎ 2525230; www .tharavaduheritage.com; r Rs2000, with AC Rs1400; 🐜) Tharavadu means 'large family house', an apt description. Rooms are either in the superbly restored 1870s teak family mansion or in equally comfortable individual creekside cottages. All abodes are excellently crafted and come with arty touches – some have glistening teak beams while others have big bay windows and relaxing patios. It's 4km before the bird sanctuary.

Coconut Lagoon (☎ 2524491, reservations 0484-2668221; coconutlagoon@cghearth.com; cottages €200-380; 🐜 🖴 🐜) Spread languidly over 9 hectares of grounds, this luxurious resort offers the ultimate in seclusion: it's reachable only by private boat. Surrounded by backwaters and with perfect sunsets guaranteed, the different *tharawad* (ancestral home) cottages on offer here are variously filled with polished wood, classy antique-style furnishings and neat open-air bathrooms. This place might be familiar to those who have read Arundhati Roy's *The God of Small Things*.

Ettumanur

The **Shiva Temple** at Ettumanur, 12km north of Kottayam, has inscriptions dating from 1542, but parts of the building may be even older than this. The temple is noted for its exceptional woodcarvings and murals similar to those at Kochi's Mattancherry Palace. The annual **festival**, involving exposition of the idol (Shiva in his fierce form) and elephant processions, is held in February/March.

Sree Vallabha Temple

Devotees make offerings at this temple, 2km from Tiruvilla, in the form of traditional, regular all-night **Kathakali** performances that are open to all. Tiruvilla, 35km south of Kottayam, is on the rail route between Ernakulam and Trivandrum.

Vijnana Kala Vedi Cultural Centre

This French-run **centre** (☎ 0468-2214483; www .vijnanakalavedi.org; Tarayil Mukku) at Aranmula, 10km from Chengannur, offers highly recommended courses in Indian arts with expert teachers. You can choose from a range of 15 subjects to study, including ayurveda, Kathakali, classical dances, Carnatic music,

Keralan cooking, languages (Malayalam, Sanskrit and Hindi) and *kalarippayat*. Classes are generally individual and are held for a minimum of three hours per day, Monday to Friday.

Fees, which include lessons, accommodation in the village and all meals, are Rs10,120/28,600 per week/month – less for longer stays. You can volunteer to teach English to children in the village schools, which will entitle you to a discount on your fees. Short stays of one to three nights are also possible (Rs2000 per night), though you will need to book well ahead.

The **Aranmula Boat Race** is held here in August/September.

THE WESTERN GHATS

PERIYAR WILDLIFE SANCTUARY
☎ 04869

Periyar (☎ 224571; www.periyartigerreserve.org; Indian/foreigner Rs25/300; ☀ 6am-6pm), South India's most popular wildlife sanctuary, encompasses 777 sq km and a 26-sq-km artificial lake created by the British in 1895. The vast region is home to bison, sambar, wild boar, langur, over 1000 elephants and around 46 tigers. Firmly established on both the Indian and foreign tourist trails, the place can sometimes feel a bit like Disneyland-in-the-Ghats, but its mountain scenery and neat jungle walks make for an enjoyable visit. Bring warm and waterproof clothing.

Orientation

Kumily, 4km from the sanctuary, is a growing strip of hotels, spice shops and Kashmiri emporiums. Thekkady is the actual sanctuary centre with the KTDC hotels and boat jetty. Confusingly, when people refer to the sanctuary they tend to use Kumily, Thekkady and Periyar interchangeably.

Information

DC Books (☎ 222548; ☀ 9.30am-8.30pm) Has a small but excellent selection of fiction and nonfiction books.

DTPC office (☎ 222620; ☀ 10am-5pm Mon-Sat) Behind the bus stand, not as useful as the Ecotourism Centre.

Ecotourism Centre (☎ 224571; ☀ 9am-5pm) For park tours and walks.

IR Communications (internet per hr Rs40; ☀ 7am-10pm)

Spider-Net Cafe (per hr Rs30; ☀ 10am-10pm)

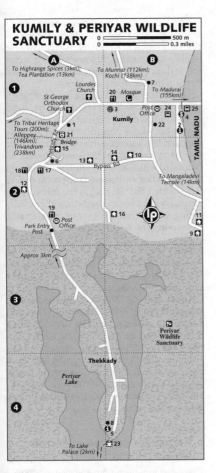

KUMILY & PERIYAR WILDLIFE SANCTUARY

State Bank of Travancore (10am-3.30pm Mon-Fri, to 12.30pm Sat) Changes travellers cheques and currency; has an ATM accepting foreign cards.

Wildlife Information Centre (☎ 222028; 6am-6pm) Above the boat jetty in Thekkady.

Sights & Activities

VISITING THE PARK

Two-hour **KTDC boat trips** (lower/upper deck Rs75/150; departures 7am, 9.30am, 11am, 2pm & 4pm) around the lake are the usual way of touring the sanctuary. The trips can be enjoyable enough, though they are often packed, rowdy, and not an ideal way to spot wildlife. The smaller, more decrepit **Forest Department boats** (per person Rs40; departures 9.30am, 11.30am, 2pm & 4pm) offer a chance to get a bit closer to the animals, and are driven by sanctuary workers who may not offer commentary. Entry to the park doesn't guarantee a place on the boat; get to the **ticket office** (6.30am-4pm) one hour before each trip to buy tickets. The first and last departures offer the best wildlife-spotting prospects, and October to March are generally the best times to see animals.

Guided three-hour **jungle walks** (up to 5 people Rs500; departures 7am, 10.30am & 2pm) cover 4km or 5km and are a better way to experience the park close up, accompanied by a trained tribal guide. Note that leeches are common after rain.

A number of more adventurous explorations of the park can be arranged by the Ecotourism Centre (opposite). These include two-/three-day 'tiger trail' treks (per person Rs3000/5000), full-day hikes (Rs750), three-hour night treks (Rs500), elevated cloud walks (Rs200) and full-day bamboo rafting (Rs1000) on the lake. **Tribal Heritage Tours** (per person Rs50; 8am-4pm) are engaging 45-minute tours

KERALA

through Mannakudy tribal village inside the sanctuary, which include visits to a small village museum. See www.periyartigerreserve.org for more information on what's available.

Most hotels and agencies around town can arrange all-day 4WD **Jungle Safaris** (per person Rs1600-2000; ⏰ 5am-6pm), which cover over 40km of trails in jungle bordering the park. Tours include meals as well as a paddleboat trip.

SPICE GARDENS & PLANTATIONS

Interesting spice tours cost around Rs400/600 by autorickshaw/taxi (two to three hours) and can be arranged by most hotels. If you want to see a tea factory in operation, do it from here – tea-factory visits are not permitted in Munnar.

If you'd rather do a spice tour independently, you can visit a few excellent gardens outside Kumily. **Abraham's Spice Garden** (☎ 222919; ⏰ 6.30am-7.30pm) has been going for 56 years and does tours of its one-hectare garden for Rs100. **Highrange Spices** (☎ 222117; ⏰ 7am-7pm), 3km from Kumily, has 4 hectares of spice garden and you can see ayurvedic herbs and vegetables growing. A one-hour tour is Rs100. A rickshaw to either spice garden and back will be around Rs200 to Rs250. About 13km away from Kumily is a working **tea plantation** (⏰ 8am-5pm) where you can wander around the grounds and see displays of the tea-making process for free.

OTHER ACTIVITIES

You can arrange **elephant rides** (Rs350 per 30 minutes) at most hotels and agents in town. If you want the extended elephant experience, you can pay Rs2000 for a two-hour ride that includes elephant feeding and cleaning. **Cooking classes** are offered by many of the homestays in town and cost around Rs250.

AYURVEDA

One recommended place for the ayurvedic experience is **Santhigiri Ayurveda** (☎ 223979; Vandanmedu Junction), offering both massage (Rs650 to Rs750) and long-term treatments including 21-day panchakarma cleansing (Rs30,000).

Sleeping

INSIDE THE SANCTUARY

The Ecotourism Centre can arrange accommodation in a basic **forest cottage** (d with dinner Rs2000), a one-hour hike in from the forest check-point.

The KTDC runs three steeply priced hotels in the park. It's a good idea to make reservations (at any KTDC office), particularly for weekends. Note that there's effectively a curfew at these places – guests are not permitted to roam the sanctuary after 6pm.

Lake Palace (☎ 222023; aranyanivas@sancharnet.in; r with all meals Rs16,000-20,000) Located on an island in the middle of the Periyar Lake, this is the best value of the government hotels inside the park. It is a stunningly restored old palace that has a handful of charismatic rooms, all decorated with flair using antique furnishings and a selection of modern conveniences (like flat-screen TVs). Staying in the midst of the sanctuary gives you the best chance of actually seeing wildlife, right from your private patio. Transport is by boat across the lake.

KUMILY

The growing homestay scene in Kumily offers far better bang for your rupee than the uninspiring hotels.

Coffee Inn (☎ 222763; coffeeinn@sancharnet.in; Thekkady Rd; huts Rs150-500, r Rs500-1500) While still keeping its original range of rustic bamboo huts, tree houses and cottages, Coffee Inn has recently expanded to include much swankier digs. The deluxe rooms here have great antique features like enormous brass-studded doors and colourful interiors, several offering balconies with sweeping private views of the sanctuary.

THE TEMPLE WITH THE SHORTEST OPENING HOURS

Located just 14km from Kumily, the 2000-year-old **Mangaladevi Temple** lies shrouded deep in the forests bordering Kerala and Tamil Nadu. Built in the Pandya architectural tradition, today there is little to see of this once impressive shrine but foundations and rubble, with stunning views of the Western Ghats thrown in for good measure. The temple site is closed all year, except for one day during the Chithra Pournami festival (around April each year). On this day, tens of thousands of pilgrims hike and jeep for hours through the thick forest to come and worship the deity Kannaki here, only to return home on the very same day. The temple then closes at dusk, not to reopen again for another year.

Mickey Homestay (☎ 223196; www.mickeyhomestay.com; Bypass Rd; r Rs300-750) Mickey has just a handful of intimate rooms in their family house, all with homely touches that make them some of the most comfortable in town. Balconies have rattan furniture and hanging bamboo seats and the whole place is surrounded by greenery.

Green View Homestay (☎ 224617; sureshgreenview@yahoo.com; Bypass Rd; r incl breakfast Rs300-900) Grown from its humble homestay origins to be practically hotel-size today, Greenview manages to retain the friendly family welcome that has made it so popular with travellers over the years. The multistorey buildings house several classes of immaculately maintained rooms with private balconies, bamboo or wood furniture and loads of greenery.

Claus Garden (☎ 222320; www.homestay.in; r Rs700-1000) This lovely big building sports gently curving balconies and has warm, bright colours in spades. The excellent rooms are spacious and have neat touches like colourful blankets, rugs, artwork and funky bathrooms. Top value.

Chrissie's Hotel (☎ 224155; www.chrissies.in; Bypass Rd; r Rs1400-1800) This four-storey building behind the popular expat-run restaurant of the same name somehow manages to blend in with the forest green surrounds. The chic rooms are refreshingly spacious and bright, with cheery furnishings, lamps and colourful pillows. Yoga is held on the rooftop.

Spice Village (☎ 222314; spicevillage@cghearth .com; Thekkady Rd; villas €190-295; ⚑) This place has captivating, spacious cottages in pristinely kept grounds. Its restaurant does lavish buffets (breakfast/lunch/dinner Rs375/675/800) and you can find the Wildlife Interpretation Centre here (open 7.30am to 7.30pm), which has a resident naturalist showing slides and answering questions about the park.

Also recommended:

Benny's Bamboo Village (☎ 321919; www.bamboovillage.in; r Rs300-1000) Six neat rooms flavoured with either rattan walls, concrete or wood panelling.

Tranquilou (☎ 223269; tranquilouhome@hotmail.com; Bypass Rd; r Rs800-1000; 🖥) Friendly family homestay huddled among some hush.

Eating

There are plenty of good cheap veg restaurants in the bazaar area.

Ambadi Restaurant (meals Rs35-100) At the hotel of the same name, the North and South Indian victuals here are expertly prepared and served in an airy indoor dining room.

Periyar Cafe (meals Rs35-110) Painted in blindingly bright colours, this cheery eatery serves up loads of North Indian and local dishes at very sensible prices. Located right near the park entrance, it's perfect for an early breakfast or quick lunch between animal spotting trips.

Chrissie's Cafe (Bypass Rd; snacks Rs40-80, meals Rs110-180) A perennially popular haunt that satisfies travellers with yummy cakes and snacks, excellent coffee, and well-prepared Western faves like pizza and pasta. Try the spinach lasagne (Rs130).

Coffee Inn (meals Rs75-200) This laid-back restaurant, in a peaceful spice-garden setting, serves just a few Indian and Western meals in what might just be the cosiest setting in Kumily. The food is OK, and can take quite a while to arrive, but the relaxing dining room, filled with arty and soulful music, makes it all worthwhile.

Also worth a try:

Sree Krishna (meals Rs35-85) Modern, clean veg place serving several versions of thali.

French Restaurant & Bakery (meals Rs60-120) Friendly and rustic shack with good snacks and brown bread.

Entertainment

For Kathakali performances, visit **Mudra** (☎ 9447157636; admission Rs125; ⊙ shows 4pm & 8pm), which has shows twice a day, with make-up starting 30 minutes before each show. One-hour **Kalaripayattu demonstrations** (admission Rs200) are held in Kumily at 6pm daily, though the location changes so make sure to ask around.

Getting There & Away

Buses originating or terminating at Periyar start and finish at Aranya Nivas, but they also stop at the Kumily bus stand, at the eastern edge of town.

Eight buses daily operate between Ernakulam (Kochi) and Kumily (Rs115, five hours). Buses leave every 30 minutes for Kottayam (Rs69, four hours), with two direct buses to Trivandrum at 8.45am and 11am (Rs161, eight hours) and at least one daily bus to Alleppey (Rs90, 5½ hours). One KSRTC bus goes to Munnar at 8.25am (Rs79, 4½ hours), though several private buses also make this trip throughout the day from the same bus stand.

Tamil Nadu buses leave every 30 minutes to Madurai (Rs42, four hours) from the Tamil Nadu bus stand just over the border.

Getting Around

Kumily is about 4km from Periyar Lake; you can catch the bus (almost as rare as the tigers), take an autorickshaw (Rs40) or set off on foot; it's a pleasant, shady walk into the park. **Bicycle hire** (per hr Rs5; ⊙ 6.30am-8pm) is available from a couple of shacks near the bus stand and many guest houses.

MUNNAR

☎ 04865 / elev 1524m

Scruffy little Munnar town may not be much to look, but wander just a few kilometres outside the city and you'll be engulfed in a sea of stunning green. The lolling hills all around here are covered by a thick carpet of tea-trees, with breathtaking mountain scenery and fresh crisp air aplenty. Once known as the High Range of Travancore, today Munnar is the commercial centre of some of the world's highest tea-growing estates.

Information

There are ATMs near the bridge, south of the bazaar.

DTPC Tourist Information Office (☎ 231516; ⊙ 8.30am-7pm) Marginally helpful.

Forest Information Centre (☎ 231587; enpmunnar@ sify.com; ⊙ 10am-5pm)

Olivia Communications (per hr Rs35; ⊙ 8.30am-10pm) Surprisingly fast internet.

State Bank of Travancore (☎ 230274; ⊙ 10am-3.30pm Mon-Sat, to noon Sun) Has an ATM.

Tourist Information Service (☎ 231136; ⊙ 9am-6pm) Run by local legend Joseph Iype, a walking Swiss-army knife of Munnar information. His office has maps, local history, travel tips and more.

Sights & Activities

The main reason to be in Munnar is to explore the lush, tea-filled hillocks that surround it. Hotels, travel agencies, auto-rickshaw drivers and practically every passer-by will want to organise a day of sightseeing for you: shop around.

The **Tata Tea Museum** (☎ 230561; adult/child Rs75/35; ⊙ 10am-4pm Tue-Sun) is, unfortunately, about as close as you'll get to a working tea factory around Munnar. It's a slightly sanitised version of the real thing, but it still shows the basic process. A collection

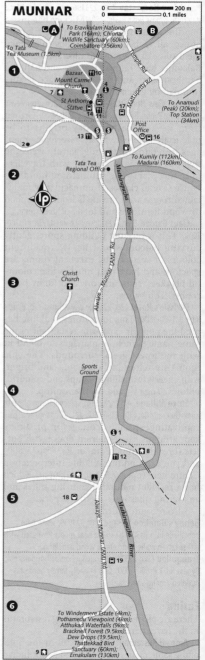

MUNNAR   0 ____ 200 m
          0 ____ 0.1 miles

To Eravikulam National Park (16km); Chinnar Wildlife Sanctuary (60km); Coimbatore (156km)

To Tata Tea Museum (1.5km)

To Anamudi (Peak) (20km); Top Station (34km)

To Kumily (112km); Madurai (160km)

To Windermere Estate (4km); Pothamedu Viewpoint (4km); Atthukad Waterfalls (9km); Bracknell Forest (9.5km); Dew Drops (19.5km); Thattekkad Bird Sanctuary (60km); Ernakulam (130km)

of old bits and pieces from the colonial era, including photographs and a 1905 tea-roller, are also kept here. The short walk to here from town is lovely, passing some of the most accessible tea plantations from Munnar town.

Tours

The DTPC runs a couple of fairly rushed full-day tours to points around Munnar. The **Sandal Valley Tour** (per person Rs300; ☻ 9am-6pm) visits Chinnar Wildlife Sanctuary (p1012), several viewpoints, waterfalls, plantations, a sandal-wood forest and villages. The **Tea Valley tour** (per person Rs250; ☻ 10am-6pm) visits Echo Point, Top Station and Rajamalai (for Eravikulam National Park), among other places.

Sleeping

There are several basic-and-cheap hotels right in Munnar town, but these are best avoided. Prices are a bit higher than in comparable Indian towns and there are several great options outside of Munnar.

AROUND TOWN

Kaippallil Homestay (☎ 230203; www.kaippallil.com; r Rs300-1000) Up the hill and away from (most of) the clatter of the bazaar, Kaippallil is the best place to stay in town, with several unique rooms set in attractively landscaped gardens. There are sitting areas out the front, and the

rooms are eclectically but tastefully decorated, some with balconies and sweeping views. The budget room shares a bathroom and is a bit dingy.

JJ Cottage (☎ 230104; jjcottagemunnar@sancharnet .in; d Rs350-800) The mothering family at this superb homestay will go out of its way to make sure your stay is comfortable. The varied and uncomplicated rooms are ruthlessly clean, bright and have TV and geysers. The one deluxe room has frilly pink curtains and sweeping views.

Zina Cottages (☎ 230349; r incl tax Rs700-900) Just on the outskirts of town but immersed in lush tea plantations, with a cute garden. The cosy rooms in this hospitable homestay are an outstanding deal. Frilly touches in the rooms and stunning vistas come as standard, as do the piles of information provided by gregarious owner Mr Iype from the Tourist Information Service.

Government Guest House (☎ 230385; Colony Rd; r Rs1150) If no visiting dignitaries are in town, travellers are welcome to stay at this Government Guest House trim front garden, perched above the town. The five ageing rooms here are top value: absolutely huge, with high wood-panelled ceilings.

Westwood Riverside Resort (☎ 230884-6; www .westwoodmunnar.com; Always-Munnar (AM) Rd; r Rs2200-3200) You might be forgiven for thinking you'd stumbled onto a lost ski lodge. It has lots of polished wood, heartfelt murals on the walls, and rooms that are refreshingly inviting for a midrange hotel.

MUNNAR HILLS

There are some excellent top-end accommodation options in plantations in the hills around Munnar, where the mountain serenity is unbeatable.

Dew Drops (☎ 0484-231555; wilsonhomes2003@yahoo .co.in; Kallar; r incl breakfast Rs1000-1200) Set in the thick forest far below Munnar, this fantastic guest house lies on 97 hectares of spice plantation and farmland. The resplendent building is expertly constructed, with modern and bright rooms that are finished with finely crafted furnishings and bits of artwork. Each room has a veranda on which you can sit and enjoy the hush and the small restaurant has 280-degree views. It's 20km from Munnar, call for a pick-up (Rs50).

Windermere Estate (☎ 230512; www.windermer emunnar.com; Pothamedu; s incl breakfast Rs3750-7650, d

Rs5000-10,250) Windermere is a boutique-meets-country-retreat and manages to be both luxurious and intimate at the same time. There are farmhouse rooms and newer, swankier cottages with spectacular views, and surrounded by shush and 26 hectares of cardamom and coffee plantations. Book ahead.

Bracknell Forest (☎ 231555; www.bracknellforest munnar.com; Ottamaram; r Rs4500) Located 9.5km from Munnar, this compact two-storey building houses several lovely rooms overlooking a lush valley. It's surrounded by deep forest on all sides and makes for a remote getaway. The rooms are very neat, spacious and handsomely furnished.

Eating

Early-morning food stalls in the bazaar serve breakfast snacks and cheap meals.

SN Restaurant (AM Rd; meals Rs30-80) Serving some of the best-value Indian food in town, SN seems to be perpetually full of people digging into morning dosas (Rs15 to Rs25) and other Indian dishes.

Surya Soma (dishes Rs35-60) Surya Soma is a modern and bright eatery that dishes up cheap North Indian, local and Chinese dishes in a welcoming, modern dining area. Good tunes can usually be heard playing on the crackle-free sound system.

Rapsy Restaurant (Bazaar; dishes Rs35-70) This hole-in-the-wall is packed at lunchtime, with locals lining up for Rapsy's famous *paratha* or biryani (from Rs40). It also makes a decent stab at fancy international dishes like Spanish omelette (Rs25) and Israeli *shakshuka* (scrambled eggs with tomatoes and spices; Rs35).

Silver Spoon (AM Rd; meals Rs50-140; ☾ lunch & dinner) What is probably the swankiest joint in town, this family eatery has tables overlooking the river and whips up a fantastic Keralan fish-curry set meal (Rs75).

Getting There & Away

Roads around Munnar are in poor condition and can be affected by monsoon rains, so bus times may vary. The main **KSRTC bus station** (AM Rd) is south of town, but it's best to catch buses from stands in Munnar town (where more frequent private buses also depart).

There are around 10 buses a day to Ernakulam (Kochi, Rs80, 5½ hours) and a few services to Kottayam (Rs101, five hours), Kumily (Rs79, 4½ hours) and Trivandrum (Rs193, nine hours). There are two daily Tamil

Nadu buses to Coimbatore (Rs82, six hours) and one bus to Madurai (Rs89, six hours) at 2.30pm.

Getting Around

The government tourist office rents out bicycles for Rs15 per hour. **Gokulam Bike Hire** (☎ 9447237165; per day Rs250; ☾ 7.30am-7pm) has several motorbikes for hire, as does SN Restaurant (per day Rs250).

Autorickshaws ply the hills around Munnar with bone-shuddering efficiency; they charge from Rs150 to nearby places and up to Rs650 for a full day's sightseeing.

AROUND MUNNAR

Eravikulam National Park (Indian/foreigner Rs15/200; ☾ 7am-6pm Sep-May), 16km from Munnar, is home to the endangered, but almost tame, *Nilgiri tahr* (a type of mountain goat). From Munnar, an autorickshaw/taxi costs Rs150/300 return; a government bus takes you the final 4km from the checkpoint (Rs20).

Chinnar Wildlife Sanctuary (☾ 7am-6pm), about 10km past Marayoor and 60km northeast of Munnar, hosts deer, leopards, elephants and the endangered grizzled giant squirrel. Trekking (Rs100 for three hours) and tree house (single/double Rs1000/1250) or hut stays (single Rs1500 to Rs2500, double Rs1800 to Rs3000) within the sanctuary are available, as well as ecotour programs like river-trekking, cultural visits, and waterfall treks (around Rs100). For details contact the Forest Information Centre in Munnar. Buses from Munnar heading to Coimbatore can drop you off at Chinnar (Rs31, 1½ hours).

Top Station, on Kerala's border with Tamil Nadu, has spectacular views over the Western Ghats. From Munnar, four daily buses (Rs26, from 7.30am) make the steep 32km climb in around an hour. Taxis (Rs800) and rickshaws (Rs400) also make the return trip from Munnar.

Thattekkad Bird Sanctuary (☎ 0485-2588302; Indian/foreigner Rs10/100; ☾ 6am-6pm) is a serene 25-sq-km park, home to over 270 species, including Malabar grey hornbills, jungle nightjar, grey drongo, darters and rarer species like the Sri Lankan frogmouth. You can hire private guides (Rs100 to Rs150) in the sanctuary, and there's a canteen with basic food and drinks just inside the gate. To stay in the **Treetop Machan** (d incl meals Rs2500) in the sanctuary contact the assistant wildlife warden (☎ 0485-2588302) at Kothamangalam. Otherwise, **Hornbill Inspection Bungalow** (☎ 0484-2310324; www.thehornbillcamp.com; s/d Rs1200/2400) has basic rooms outside the sanctuary. A better option is staying in the **homestay** (per person incl meals Rs700) of eager Ms Sudah, who greets most foreign visitors at the sanctuary gate. For accommodation with a little more style, visit the lovely **Birds Lagoon Resort** (☎ 0485-2572444; www.birdslagoon.com; Palamatton, Thattekkad; r incl breakfast Rs2500-3500; ⊠ ⊡). Set deep in the villages near Thattekkad, this low-key resort lies on a seasonal lake among spacious and manicured grounds. The basic rooms here are roomy and very comfy, with lots of wood trim and lamp lighting. The whole place feels refreshingly remote and is particularly popular with visiting ornithologists. It's 16km from Kothamangalam.

Thattekkad is on the Ernakulam–Munnar road. Take a direct bus from either Ernakulam (Rs29, two hours) or Munnar (Rs51, three hours) to Kothamangalam, from where a Thattekkad bus travels the final 12km (Rs6, 25 minutes).

PARAMBIKULAM WILDLIFE SANCTUARY

Possibly the most protected environment in South India – it's nestled behind three dams in a valley surrounded by Keralan and Tamil Nadu sanctuaries – **Parambikulam Wildlife Sanctuary** (www.parambikulam.org; Indian/foreigner Rs10/100, camera Rs25; ☯ 7am-6pm) constitutes 285 sq km of Kipling-storybook scenery and wildlife-spotting goodness. It's home to elephants, bison, gaur, sloths, sambar, crocodiles, tigers, panthers and some of the largest teak trees in Asia. The sanctuary is best avoided during monsoon (June to August) and it sometimes closes in March and April.

Contact the **ecocare centre** (☎ 04253-245025) in Palakkad to arrange tours of the park, hikes and stays on the reservoir's freshwater island (Rs600 to Rs4000). There are 150 beds in **treetop huts** (from Rs2500) throughout the park; book through the ecocare centre.

You have to enter the park from Pollachi (40km from Coimbatore and 49km from Palakkad; see p1108) in Tamil Nadu. There are at least two buses in either direction between Pollachi and Parambikulam via Anamalai daily (Rs15, 1½ hours). The nearest train station is Coimbatore, Tamil Nadu, from where you can board buses to Pollachi.

CENTRAL KERALA

KOCHI (COCHIN)
☎ 0484 / pop 1.36 million

Serene Kochi has been drawing traders and explorers to its shores for over 600 years, and today stands as a living homage to a vibrant past unlike any other. Nowhere in India could you find such a melange: giant fishing nets from China, a 400-year-old synagogue, ancient mosques and Portuguese houses, all mixed in with the crumbling residuum of the British Raj. The result is an unlikely blend of medieval Portugal, Holland and an English village grafted onto the tropical Malabar Coast. It's a delightful place to spend some time and nap in some of India's finest heritage accommodation.

Mainland Ernakulam is the hectic transport and cosmopolitan hub of Kochi, while the historical towns of Fort Cochin and Mattancherry remain wonderfully serene – thick with the smell of the past where goats still outnumber rickshaws on the history-laden streets.

Orientation
Kochi is made up of a gaggle of islands and peninsulas that includes mainland Ernakulam; the islands of Willingdon, Bolgatty and Gundu; Fort Cochin and Mattancherry on the southern peninsula; and Vypeen and Vallarpadam Islands. All are linked by bridges or ferries. The train station, bus stand and KTDC Tourist Reception Centre are in Ernakulam, while Fort Cochin and Mattancherry have all the historical sites and most of the better-value accommodation.

Information
BOOKSHOPS
Current Books (Map p1018; ☎ 3231590; Market Rd; ☯ 9.30am-7.30pm Mon-Sat) A branch of DC Books.
DC Books (Map p1018; ☎ 2391295; Banerji Rd, Ernakulam; ☯ 9.30am-7.30pm Mon-Sat) A typically great English-language selection.
Idiom Bookshop Fort Cochin (Map p1016; ☎ 2217075; Bastion St; ☯ 9am-9pm Mon-Sat, 10am-6pm Sun); Mattancherry (Map p1016; ☎ 2225604; opposite boat jetty; ☯ 10am-6pm) Huge range of quality new and used books.

INTERNET ACCESS
Cafe de Net (Map p1016; Bastion St, Fort Cochin; per hr Rs30; ☯ 9am-10.30pm) This old-timer may have DOS-era computers, but the breezy upstairs location is hard to beat.
Net Park (Map p1018; Convent Rd, Ernakulam; per hr Rs15; ☯ 9am-9pm)

KERALA

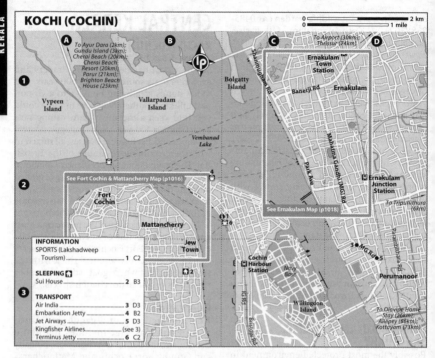

KOCHI (COCHIN)

INFORMATION
SPORTS (Lakshadweep
Tourism).................................... 1 C2

SLEEPING ⌂
Sui House................................. 2 B3

TRANSPORT
Air India................................... 3 D3
Embarkation Jetty.................... 4 B2
Jet Airways............................... 5 D3
Kingfisher Airlines................(see 3)
Terminus Jetty.......................... 6 C2

Net Point (Map p1018; Carrier Station Rd, Ernakulam; per hr Rs20; ⏱ 9.30am-9.30pm)

Sify iWay (Map p1016; per hr Rs30; ⏱ 9.30am-10pm) Fast computers in a spacious upstairs cafe setting above the Shop-n-Save.

MEDICAL SERVICES
Lakeshore Hospital (Off map p1018; ☎ 2701032; NH Bypass, Marudu) Has the best medical facilities in the city. It's 8km southeast of central Ernakulam.

MONEY
There are scores of ATMs along Mahatma Gandhi (MG) Rd in Ernakulam, and a few in Fort Cochin.

Thomas Cook (Map p1018; ☎ 2369729; Palal Towers, MG Rd; ⏱ 9.30am-5.30pm Mon-Sat)

UAE Exchange (⏱ 9.30am-6pm Mon-Sat, to 1.30pm Sun); Ernakulam (Map p1018; ☎ 2383317; Perumpillil Bldg, MG Rd); Fort Cochin (Map p1016; ☎ 2216231; Amravathi Rd) A reliable place for foreign exchange and changing travellers cheques.

POST
College post office (Map p1018; ☎ 2369302; Convent Rd, Ernakulam; ⏱ 9am-4pm Mon-Fri, to 9pm Sat)

Ernakulam post office branches Hospital Rd (Map p1018; ☎ 2355467; ⏱ 9am-8pm Mon-Sat, 10am-5pm Sun); MG Rd (Map p1018); Broadway (Map p1018)

Main post office (Map p1016; Post Office Rd, Fort Cochin; ⏱ 9am-5pm Mon-Fri, to 3pm Sat)

TOURIST INFORMATION
There's a tourist information counter at the airport. Many places distribute a brochure that includes a neat map and walking tour entitled 'Historical Places in Fort Cochin'.

Government of India Tourist Office (Map p1016; ☎ 2668352; indtourismkochi@sify.com; Willingdon Island; ⏱ 9am-5.30pm Mon-Fri, to 1pm Sat) Range of brochures and maps of India.

KTDC Tourist Reception Centre Ernakulam (Map p1018; ☎ 2353234; Shanmugham Rd, Ernakulam; ⏱ 8am-7pm) Fort Cochin (Map p1016; ☎ 2216567; Calvathy Rd; ⏱ 10am-5pm Mon-Sat) Also organises tours.

Tourist Desk Information Counter Ernakulam (Map p1018; ☎ 2371761; touristdesk@satyam.net.in; ⏱ 8.30am-6pm); Fort Cochin (Map p1016; ☎ 2216129) A private tour agency knowledgable about Kochi and beyond.

Tourist Police Ernakulam (Map p1018; ☎ 2353234; ⏱ 8am-6pm); Fort Cochin (Map p1016; ☎ 2215055; ⏱ 24hr)

Sights

FORT COCHIN

At the very the tip of Fort Cochin sit the unofficial emblems of Kerala's backwaters: cantilevered **Chinese fishing nets** (Map p1016). A legacy of traders from the 1400 AD court of Kubla Khan, these enormous, spiderlike contraptions require at least four people to operate their counterweights at high tide. Unfortunately, modern fishing techniques are making these labour-intensive methods less and less profitable.

The **Indo-Portuguese Museum** (Map p1016; ☎ 2215400; Indian/foreigner Rs10/25; ☉ 9am-1pm & 2-6pm Tue-Sun), in the garden of the Bishop's House, preserves the heritage of one of India's earliest Catholic communities, including vestments, silver processional crosses and altarpieces from the Cochin diocese. The basement contains remnants of the Portuguese Fort Immanuel.

Believed to be India's oldest European-built church, **St Francis Church** (Map p1016; Bastion St) was originally constructed in 1503 by Portuguese Franciscan friars. The edifice that stands here today was built in the mid-16th century to replace the original wooden structure. Adventurer Vasco da Gama, who died in Cochin in 1524, was buried on this spot for 14 years before his remains were taken to Lisbon – you can still visit his tombstone in the church.

The **Dutch Cemetery** (Map p1016; Beach Rd), consecrated in 1724, contains the worn and dilapidated graves of Dutch traders and soldiers; it's gates are normally locked but you can ask the caretaker at St Francis Church if you want to have a look around.

The imposing Catholic **Santa Cruz Basilica** (Map p1016; cnr Bastion St & KB Jacob Rd) was originally built on this site in 1506, though the current building dates to 1902. Inside you'll find artefacts from the different eras in Kochi and a striking pastel-coloured interior.

MATTANCHERRY PALACE

Built by the Portuguese in 1555, **Mattancherry Palace** (Dutch Palace; Map p1016; ☎ 2226085; Bazaar Rd; admission Rs2; ☉ 10am-5pm Sat-Thu) was a rather generous gift presented to the Raja of Kochi, Veera Kerala Varma (1537–61), as a gesture of goodwill. More probably, it was a used as a sweetener to securing trading privileges. The Dutch renovated the palace in 1663, hence its alternative name, the Dutch Palace.

The star attractions here are the astonishingly preserved Hindu **murals**, depicting scenes from the Ramayana, Mahabharata and Puranic legends in intricate detail. The central hall on the 1st floor is now a portrait gallery of maharajas from 1864. There's an impressive collection of palanquins (hand-carried carriages), bejewelled outfits and splendidly carved ceilings in every room. The ladies' bedchamber downstairs features a cheerful Krishna using his six hands and two feet to engage in foreplay with eight very happy milkmaids. Photography is prohibited.

PARDESI SYNAGOGUE & JEW TOWN

This **synagogue** (Map p1016; admission Rs2; ☉ 10am-noon & 3-5pm Sun-Thu, closed Jewish hols), originally built in 1568, was partially destroyed by the Portuguese in 1662, and rebuilt two years later when the Dutch took Kochi. It features an ornate gold pulpit and intricate, hand-painted, willow-pattern floor tiles from Canton, China. It's magnificently illuminated by chandeliers (from Belgium) and coloured-glass lamps. The graceful clock tower was built in 1760. There is an upstairs balcony for women who worshipped separately according to Orthodox rites. Note that shorts or sleeveless tops are not allowed inside.

The synagogue is smack bang in the middle of **Jew Town** (Map p1016), a bustling port area and centre of the Kochi spice trade. Scores of small firms huddle together in old, dilapidated buildings and the air is filled with the biting aromas of ginger, cardamom, cumin, turmeric and cloves. These days the lanes around the Dutch Palace and synagogue are packed with more antique and tourist-curio shops than pungent spices. Look out for the Jewish names on some of the buildings.

ART GALLERIES

Kochi is a leader in encouraging local contemporary artists.

Draavidia Art & Performance Gallery (Map p1016; ☎ 3096812; Bazaar Rd; ☉ 9am-5pm) Shows off art by Keralan artists in an airy upstairs gallery. It also holds classical music concerts (Rs100) from November to March at 6pm.

Kashi Art Gallery (Map p1016; ☎ 215769; Bazaar Rd, Mattancherry; ☉ 10am-12.30pm & 2-6pm) The pioneer of Fort Cochin's art revival, Kashi displays changing exhibitions of local artists.

Heritage Art (Map p1016; Tower Rd; ☉ 10am-6pm) A tiny little gallery showing a small selection of works by local artists.

KERALA

FORT COCHIN & MATTANCHERRY

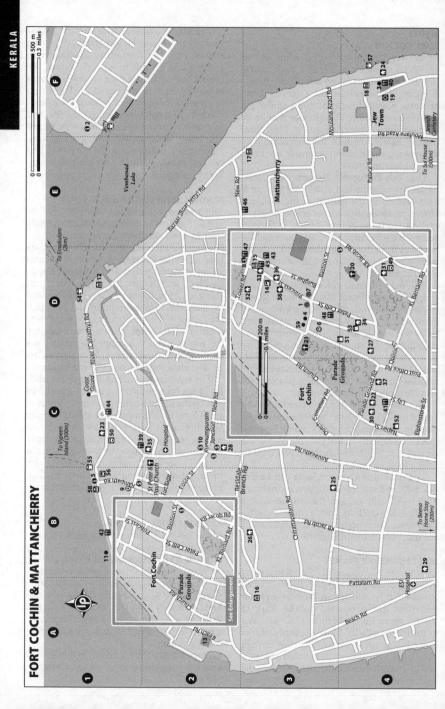

Activities

SWIMMING

Nonguests can swim at the small pool of **Grande Residencia Hotel** (Map p1016; Princess St, Fort Cochin) for Rs500 per person. For a dip in the ocean, you can make a day trip out to the attractive **Cherai beach** on Vypeen Island (see p1026).

AYURVEDA

Ayur Dara (2502362; www.ayurdara.com; Murik-kumpadam, Vypeen Island; treatment €20 per day; 9am-5pm) Run by third-generation ayurvedic practitioner Dr Subhash, this delightful waterside treatment centre specialises in long-term treatments. It's 4km from the Vypeen Island ferry (autorickshaw Rs40). By appointment only.

Ayush (Map p1016; 6456566; KB Jacob Rd, Fort Cochin; massage from Rs700; 8.30am-7pm) Part of an India-wide chain of ayurvedic centres, this place also does long-term treatments.

Kerala Ayurveda (Kerala Ayurveda Pharmacy Ltd; Map p1018; 2378198; www.kaplayurveda.com; AM Thomas Rd, Ernakulam; massage from Rs500; 7am-7pm) This government-approved centre comes recommended for all types of ayurvedic treatments.

Courses

Mrs Leelu Roy runs a popular cooking class called **Cook & Eat** (Map p1016; 2215377; simonroy@hotmail.com; Quiros St; class Rs500; 11am & 6pm) in her great big family kitchen. Several of the homestays in towns are also happy to organise impromptu cooking demonstrations and classes for their guests.

The Kerala Kathakali Centre (p1023) has lessons in classical **Kathakali** dance, music and make-up (from Rs350 per hour). Contact Suji (09895860646) for more details.

For a crash course in the martial art of **kalarippayat**, head out to Ens Kalari (p1023), a famed training centre. Short courses from one week to one month cost Rs2500 to Rs8500 (including accommodation).

Tours

The private Tourist Desk Information Counter (p1014) runs popular full-day, **houseboat backwater tours** (Rs550) through local canals and lagoons. A canoe trip through smaller canals and villages is included, as is lunch and hotel pick-ups. See the boxed text, p1003, for more information.

The KTDC (p1014) also has half-day backwater tours (Rs350) at 8.30am and 2pm, and tourist **motor-boat tours** around Fort Cochin (Rs100) at the same times. It has full-day houseboat backwater trips at 8.30am (Rs650), where you stop to see local weaving factories, spice gardens and, most importantly, toddy tapping!

Most hotels and tourist offices can arrange a day trip out to the **Elephant training camp** (7am-6pm) at Kudanadu, 50km from

KERALA

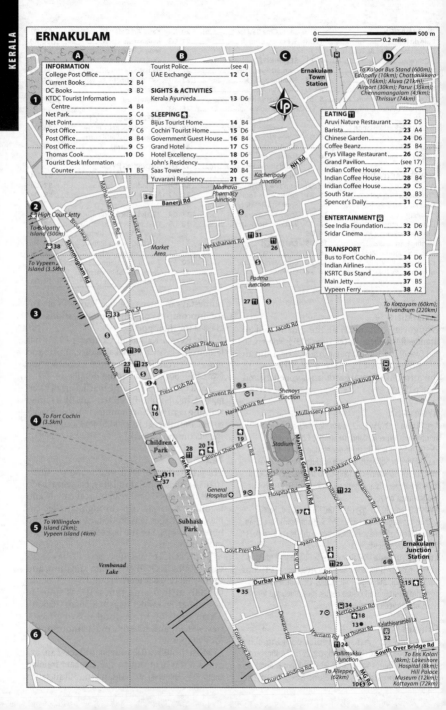

ERNAKULAM

0 — 500 m
0 — 0.2 miles

INFORMATION		
College Post Office	1	C4
Current Books	2	B4
DC Books	3	B2
KTDC Tourist Information Centre	4	B4
Net Park	5	C4
Net Point	6	D5
Post Office	7	C6
Post Office	8	B4
Post Office	9	C5
Thomas Cook	10	D6
Tourist Desk Information Counter	11	B5
Tourist Police	(see 4)	
UAE Exchange	12	C4

SIGHTS & ACTIVITIES

Kerala Ayurveda	13	D6

SLEEPING

Bijus Tourist Home	14	B4
Cochin Tourist Home	15	D6
Government Guest House	16	B4
Grand Hotel	17	C5
Hotel Excellency	18	D6
John's Residency	19	C4
Saas Tower	20	B4
Yuvarani Residency	21	C5

EATING

Aruvi Nature Restaurant	22	D5
Barista	23	A4
Chinese Garden	24	D6
Coffee Beanz	25	B4
Frys Village Restaurant	26	C2
Grand Pavilion	(see 17)	
Indian Coffee House	27	C3
Indian Coffee House	28	B4
Indian Coffee House	29	C5
South Star	30	B3
Spencer's Daily	31	C2

ENTERTAINMENT

See India Foundation	32	D6
Sridar Cinema	33	A3

TRANSPORT

Bus to Fort Cochin	34	D6
Indian Airlines	35	C6
KSRTC Bus Stand	36	D4
Main Jetty	37	B5
Vypeen Ferry	38	A2

Ernakulam Town Station

To Kaloor Bus Stand (600m); Edapally (10km); Chottanikkara (16km); Aluva (21km); Airport (30km); Parur (35km); Chennamangalam (43km); Thrissur (74km)

NH Rd

Kacheripady Junction

Madhava Pharmacy Junction

Banerji Rd

High Court Jetty

To Bolgatty Island (500m)

To Vypeen Island (3.5km)

Mathai Manjoran Rd

Broadway

Shanmugham Rd

Market Rd

Jew St

Market Area

Veekshanam Rd

Padma Junction

Marine Walk

Gopala Prabhu Rd

AL Jacob Rd

Rajaji Rd

To Kottayam (60km); Trivandrum (220km)

Ammankovil Rd

Press Club Rd

Convent Rd

Shenoys Junction

Narakathara Rd

Mullassery Canal Rd

To Fort Cochin (3.5km)

Children's Park

Cannon Shed Rd

Park Ave

TG Rd

Stadium

Mahatma Gandhi (MG) Rd

Mahakavi G Rd

Kalikamuri Rd

General Hospital

Hospital Rd

PT Usha Rd

Chittoor Rd

To Willingdon Island (2km); Vypeen Island (4km)

Subhash Park

Karikkat Rd

Convent Rd

Ernakulam Junction Station

Govt Press Rd

Layam Rd

Club Rd

Josi Junction

Vembanad Lake

Durbar Hall Rd

Dewans Rd

Nettipadam Rd

Foreshore Rd

Warriam Rd

AM Thomas Rd

Kalathiparambil La

Pallimukku Junction

Church Landing Rd

To Alleppey (62km)

MG Rd

South Over Bridge Rd

To Ens Kalari (8km); Lakeshore Hospital (8km); Hill Palace Museum (12km); Kottayam (72km)

Kathrikadavu Rd

Kalathiparambil Rd

Kochi. Here you can go for a ride (Rs200) and even help out with washing the gentle beasts if you arrive at 8am. Entry is free, though the elephant trainers will expect a small tip. A return trip out here in a taxi should cost around Rs900 to Rs1000.

Festivals & Events
In January/February, the eight-day **Ernakulathappan Utsavam festival** culminates in a procession of 15 decorated elephants, ecstatic music and fireworks.

Sleeping
Fort Cochin is an ideal place to escape the noise and chaos of the mainland – it's tranquil and romantic, with some excellent accommodation choices. Its homestay scene has ballooned recently, with hundreds of family houses offering near-identical, large and clean, budget rooms.

Ernakulam is much cheaper and more convenient for onward travel, but the ambiance and accommodation choices there are less than inspiring. Regardless of where you stay, book ahead during December and January.

FORT COCHIN
Budget
Royal Grace Tourist Home (Map p1016; ☎ 2216584; Amaravathi Rd; r Rs350-500) This old-timer is one of the rare budget stalwarts still left in Fort Cochin. There are loads of rooms on offer in a large multistorey building, each with little more than a bed, four walls and a teeny-tiny bathroom.

Princess Inn (Map p1016; ☎ 2217073; princessinnfortkochi@gmail.com; Princess St; s Rs350, d Rs400-600) One of the few places that sticks valiantly to its budget guns, the exceptionally friendly Princess Inn is a shining example of what a fresh lick of paint can do: sprucing up what would otherwise be dull, tiny rooms with cheery bright colours. The comfy communal spaces are a treat, and the three large, front-facing rooms are particularly excellent value.

Mother Tree (Map p1016; ☎ 3220996; www.hotelmothertree.com; KL Bernard Master Rd; r Rs600, with AC Rs800;) There are just a few miniscule rooms in this compact homestay, but the hip and colourful paint job, immaculate cleanliness and neat rooftop chill-out space make this place worth seeking out.

Green Woods Bethlehem (Map p1016; ☎ 3247791; greenwoodsbethlehem1@vsnl.net; opposite ESI Hospital;

r Rs800-900) Owner Sheeba looks ready to sign your adoption papers the minute you walk through her front door. What might just be the cutest guest house in Kochi lies in a quiet residential area cocooned in its own thick jungle of plants and soaring palms. The rooms in this multistorey building are humble but cosy, all lovingly decorated with homely bits and bobs. The included breakfast is served in the fantastic, leafy rooftop cafe, where cooking classes/demonstrations are often held.

Sonnetta Residency (Map p1016; ☎ 2215744; www.sonnettaresidency.com; Princess St; r Rs800, with AC Rs1200;) Right in the thick of the Fort Cochin action, the plain rooms at this Portuguese-era building are pretty small, but come with nice touches like curtains and indoor plants to make you feel at home.

Two other homestays worth checking out:
Costa Gama Home Stay (Map p1016; ☎ 2216122; www.stayincochin.com; Thamaraparambu Rd; r Rs550-600) Cosy little place that gets rave reviews from travellers.
Beena Home Stay (Kadathanad; ☎ 2215458; www.homestaykochi.com; KB Jacob Rd; s Rs600, d Rs800-1000, d with AC Rs1300-1500;) Offers simple rooms and a ridiculously friendly welcome.

Midrange
Delight Home Stay (Map p1016; ☎ 2217658; www.delightfulhomestay.com; Post Office Rd; r Rs1000-1500, with AC Rs2500;) And delightful it is. The uniquely styled rooms here have been marvellously remodelled and are eminently alluring. There's frilly white woodwork all around, a charming little garden, and an imposing sitting room covered in wall-to-wall polished teak.

Spencer Home (Map p1016; ☎ 2215049; spencerhomestyfc@rediffmail.com; Parade Ground Rd; d Rs1200) This handsomely restored heritage home has top-value, snug rooms set around a charming little garden courtyard. It has great period highlights, like high wood-beam ceilings and amazingly intricate antique locks, and breakfast is served garden-side, in front of your room.

Walton's Homestay (Map p1016; ☎ 2215309; www.waltonshomestay.com; Princess St; r Rs1200-2000;) The fastidious Mr Walton offers big and light rooms in his guest house, all decked out in white with blue trim. There's a lush garden out the back, a large secondhand bookshop downstairs, and a communal breakfast is included in the price. The bird-filled garden has one lovely AC garden cottage available for rent (d Rs2000).

Raintree Lodge (Map p1016; ☎ 3251489; www.fort cochin.com; Peter Celli St; r Rs2000; 🏠) The intimate and comfortable rooms at the Raintree flirt with boutique-hotel status. Each room has a great blend of modern and period decor fused with well-designed flair. Try to get an upstairs room with a (tiny) balcony.

Bernard Bungalow (Map p1016; ☎ 2216162; www .bernardbungalow.com; Parade Ground Rd; r Rs2500-3500; 🏠) This gracious place is in a generously sized 350-year-old house that boasts a large collection of interesting rooms. The house has polished floorboards, wooden window shutters, balconies and verandas, and is filled with lovely period furniture that gives it that 1940s summer cottage look.

Sui House (Off map p1014; ☎ 2227078; suihouse@ gmail.com; Maulana Azad Rd; r Rs3500; 🏠) This luxury homestay is the home of the owner of gorgeous Caza Maria (right). There are just two mammoth AC en-suite rooms in this large family villa, painted either turquoise or yellow. Both rooms are breezy and bright, each filled with a range of elegant antique pieces. The sumptuous communal drawing room is filled with more fetching antiques, and a hearty breakfast is served in the outdoor courtyard.

Also worth checking out:

Daffodil Home Stay (Map p1016; ☎ 2218686; www .daffodilhomestay.com; Njaliparambu Junction; r Rs800, with AC Rs1500-2000; 🏠) Big and brightly painted modern rooms, with an upstairs carved-wood Keralan balcony.

Fort Heaven Residency (Map p1016; ☎ 2215588; www.fortheavenresidency.com; Amravathi Rd; r Rs950, with AC Rs1350; 🏠) Massive rooms in a very spacious and comfy house with a huge lawn.

Top End

our pick Old Harbour Hotel (Map p1016; ☎ 2218006; www.oldharbourhotel.com; Tower Rd; r incl tax Rs7500-14600; 🏠 💻 🏊) Set around an idyllic garden, with lily ponds and a small pool, the dignified Old Harbour is housed in a 300-year-old Dutch/Portuguese heritage building and is one of the best luxury deals around. The elegant mix of period and modern styles and bright colour accents are luxurious without being over the top, lending the place a much more intimate feel than some of the more grandiose competition. Many rooms here face directly onto the garden, and some sport plant-filled, open-air bathrooms.

Malabar House (Map p1016; ☎ 2216666; www.mala barhouse.com; Parade Ground Rd; r €220, ste incl breakfast €300-360; 🏠 💻 🏊) What may just be one of the fanciest boutique hotels in Kerala, Malabar flaunts its uberhip blend of modern colours and period fittings like it's not even trying. It has a restaurant, wine bar and tapas bar on the premises. While the suites are huge and lavishly appointed, the standard rooms are a little short on space.

Brunton Boatyard (Map p1016; ☎ 2215461; brunton boatyard@cghearth.com; River Rd; r Rs17,500-25,000; 🏠 💻 🏊) This imposing hotel faithfully reproduces 16th- and 17th-century Dutch and Portuguese architecture in it's grand complex. All of the rooms look out over the harbour, and have bathtub and balconies with a refreshing sea breeze that's beats AC any day.

MATTANCHERRY & JEW TOWN

Caza Maria (Map p1016; ☎ 3258837; cazamaria@rediff mail.com; Jew Town Rd; r incl breakfast Rs3000-4500; 🏠) Right in the heart of Jew Town, this unique place has just two enormous and sumptuously decorated heritage rooms overlooking the bazaar. Fit for a maharaja, the idiosyncratic style here has to be seen to be believed – with each high-ceilinged room painted in bright colours, filled to the brim with first-rate antiques and with tall windows looking onto the bustling market street below.

ERNAKULAM
Budget

Cochin Tourist Home (Map p1018; ☎ 2377577; Caravara Rd; s/d from Rs175/275, r with AC Rs750; 🏠) This ultra-budget cheapie opposite Erankulam Junction train station is fine for an emergency kip if you arrive late or have to leave early. Rooms are scruffy but reasonably hygienic.

Saas Tower (Map p1018; ☎ 2365319; www.saastower .com; Cannon Shed Rd; s/d Rs350/550, with AC from Rs650/1000; 🏠) They say they have 'facilities to match your fantasies' – but you'd need pretty dull fantasies to justify that tag line. The predictably standard and straightforward rooms, filled with almost-pink wooden furniture, are made more attractive by the handy location near the boat jetty and above a decent restaurant.

John's Residency (Map p1018; ☎ 2355395; TG Rd; r Rs400-600, with AC Rs1200; 🏠) It's a shame that the funky, almost boutiquey, yellow foyer design isn't replicated throughout this small hotel. Still, the rooms are fastidiously clean and come with red curtains that give it a moody, almost arty, feel during the day.

Bijus Tourist Home (Map p1018; ☎ 2361661; www .bijustouristhome.com; Market Rd; s/d from Rs440/690, d with AC Rs1300; ✷) This friendly, popular choice is handy for the main jetty and has slightly dated, though excellently maintained rooms that still manage to look smart. The place is very efficiently run.

Midrange

Hotel Excellency (Map p1018; ☎ 2378251; www.hotel excellency.com; Nettipadam Rd; s/d from Rs650/750, with AC Rs950/1050; ✷ ▢) This businesslike hotel has white-tiled and sterile hallways more reminiscent of a hospital, but the lamp-lit rooms are more welcoming and come with spotless bathrooms.

Government Guest House (Map p1018; ☎ 2360502; Shanmughan Rd; s/d Rs850/1200; ✷) We secretly love Kerala's government guest houses – they always manage to be the best deal in town. Right in the city's heart and near the sea, this massive eight-storey monolith of a building has huge, perfectly neat rooms. The place probably won't win any style awards soon, but considering some of the upper-floor rooms have balconies with sweeping sea vistas, this is still unbeatable value.

Yuvarani Residency (Map p1018; ☎ 2377040; www .yuvaraniresidency.com; MG Rd; s/d from Rs950/1200, with AC Rs1500/1850; ✷) Even though all that glitters is not gold here, these almost-swanky rooms are perfectly comfortable and finished with all the stylish dark-wood fixtures your heart desires. It's set back from MG Rd enough to shield the noise.

Grand Hotel (Map p1018; ☎ 2382061; www.grandho telkerala.com; MG Rd; s/d from Rs1800/2100; ✷) This funky 1960s hotel oozes the sort of retro styling that modern hotels would kill to re-create. The large rooms are very neat, with parquet floors and large modern bathrooms, and the foyer has cool lounges and groovy art deco chairs. One of the more interesting places to stay in Ernakulam.

AROUND KOCHI

ourpick Olavipe Homestay (Map p1016; ☎ 0478-2522255; www.olavipe.com; Olavipe; s/d incl meals Rs7000/1000) This gorgeous 1890s traditional Syrian-Christian home is on a 16-hectare farm surrounded by backwaters, 28km south of Kochi. A restored mansion of rosewood and glistening teak, it has several large and breezy rooms – all skilfully finished with original period decor (only the ceiling fans are new). There are lots of shady awnings and sitting areas, a fascinating archive with six generations of family history, and the gracious owners will make you feel like a welcome friend rather than a guest. A taxi to/from Fort Cochin is Rs600 to Rs700.

Eating & Drinking

Covert beer consumption is *de rigueur* at most of the Fort Cochin restaurants, and more expensive in the licensed ones (Rs80 to Rs165).

FORT COCHIN

Teapot (Map p1016; Peter Celli St; snacks Rs30-50, meals Rs125-175) This stylish haunt is the perfect venue for 'high tea', with quality teas, sandwiches and full meals served in chic-minimalist, airy rooms. Witty tea-themed accents include loads of antique teapots, tea chests for tables and a gnarled, tea-tree based glass table. The death by chocolate here (Rs50) is truly cocoa homicide. Trust us.

Solar Cafe (Map p1016; Bazaar Rd; meals Rs30-75; ☽ 10am-6pm) This arty and funky cafe at Draavidia Gallery (p1015) serves up organic breakfasts and lunches in a brightly coloured and friendly setting. There's a fun open kitchen and the upstairs veranda seating overlooks the hubbub of the street below.

Oy's Restaurant (Map p1016; Burgher St; meals Rs60-175) This new addition to the dining scene is one of the hippest looking restaurants in Kochi. The setting is groovy lounge-like: with low-slung couches backed by bamboo; low glass-topped tables; and a bass-heavy chill-out soundtrack. The Southeast Asian–focused dishes are original and reasonably good – try the grilled prawns with crunchy vegetables (Rs145).

Casa Linda (Map p1016; Dispensary Rd; mains Rs65-250) This modern dining room above the hotel of the same name might not be much to look at, but it's all about the food here. Chef Dipu once trained with a Frenchman and whips up delicious local Keralan dishes alongside French imports like Poisson de la Provencale (fish fried in oil and herbs, Provence style). The Keralan dry-fried coconut prawns (Rs140), made to a loving mother's recipe, are scrumptious.

ourpick Dal Roti (Map p1016; Lily St; meals Rs70-170; ☽ lunch & dinner) You'll hear the buzz about this place before you even arrive in town – it's the best food in Fort Cochin. Friendly and knowledgable owner Ramesh will hold your hand through his expansive North Indian menu, which even sports its own glossary,

KERALA

TRADITIONAL KERALAN ARTS

Kathakali

The art form of Kathakali crystallised at around the same time as Shakespeare was scribbling his plays, though elements of it stem from 2nd-century temple rituals. The Kathakali performance is the dramatised presentation of a play, usually based on the Hindu epics the Ramayana, the Mahabharata and the Puranas. All the great themes are covered – righteousness and evil, frailty and courage, poverty and prosperity, war and peace.

Drummers and singers accompany the actors, who tell the story through their precise movements, particularly mudras (hand gestures) and facial expressions. Traditionally, performances took place in temple grounds and went from 8pm until dawn; shorter performances in other locales are now also popular.

Preparation for the performance is lengthy and disciplined. Paint, fantastic costumes, ornamental headpieces and meditation transform the actors both physically and mentally into the gods, heroes and demons they are about to play.

You can see cut-down performances in tourist hot spots all over the state, and there are Kathakali schools in Trivandrum (see p985) and near Thrissur (see p1029) that encourage visitors.

Kalarippayat

Kalarippayat is an ancient tradition of martial training and discipline, still taught throughout Kerala. Some believe it is the forerunner of all martial arts, with roots tracing back to the 12th-century skirmishes among Kerala's feudal principalities.

Masters of *kalarippayat,* called Gurukkal, teach their craft inside a special arena called a *kalari*. The *kalari* is part gymnasium, part school and part temple. Its construction follows traditional principles: its rectangular design is always aligned east–west and Hindu deities are represented in each corner.

Kalarippayat movements – the foundation of choreography that uses the actors' bodies and gestures as tools of expression – can be traced in Kerala's performing arts, such as Kathakali and *kootiattam,,* and in ritual arts such as *theyyam*.

Theyyam

Kerala's most popular ritualistic art form, *theyyam,* is believed to pre-date Hinduism, originating from folk dances performed during harvest celebrations. An intensely local ritual, it's often performed in *kavus* (sacred groves) throughout northern Kerala.

Theyyam refers both to the shape of the deity/hero portrayed, and to the actual ritual. There are around 450 different *theyyams*, each with a distinct costume; face paint, bracelets, breastplates, skirts, garlands and especially headdresses are exuberant, intricately crafted and sometimes huge (up to 6m or 7m tall).

During performances, each protagonist loses his physical identity and speaks, moves and blesses the devotees as if he were that deity. There is frenzied dancing and wild drumming, and a surreal, otherworldly atmosphere is created, the kind of atmosphere in which a deity indeed might, if it so desired, manifest itself in human form.

The *theyyam* season is October to May, during which time there will be an annual ritual at each of the hundreds of *kavus*. *Theyyam*s are often held to bring good fortune to important events, such as marriages and housewarmings. See p1034 for details on how to find one.

and help you dive in to his delicious range of vegetarian, eggetarian and nonvegetarian options. The setting is chic minimalist, with whitewashed walls and bench seating, helping you focus on the yummy dishes here.

Kashi Art Cafe (Map p1016; Burgher St; breakfast/lunch Rs85/90; 8.30am-7.30pm) An institution in Fort Cochin, this place has a hip-but-casual vibe, along with hip-but-casual service. The coffee is

as strong as it should be and the daily Western breakfast and lunch specials are excellent. A small gallery shows off local artists.

Malabar Junction (Map p1016; ☎ 2216666; Parade Ground Rd; mains Rs280-1000) Set in an open-sided pavilion, the classy restaurant at Malabar House is movie-star cool. There's a seafood-based, European-style menu and Grover's Estate wine (quaffable, Indian) is served. The signature dish is the impressive seafood platter with grilled vegetables (Rs980).

Also recommended:

New Ananda Bhavan (Map p1016; River Rd; dishes Rs14-40) Herbivores: make a beeline for this basic but spotless veggie hole-in-the-wall restaurant.

Salt 'n' Pepper (Map p1016; Tower Rd; dishes Rs40-120; ⏲ 24hr) Superbly average food, but the street-side tables bustle nightly with punters having a 'special teapot' tipple (Rs100).

Behind the Chinese fishing nets are a couple of **fishmongers** (Map p1016; seafood per kg Rs50-300), from whom you can buy fish (or prawns, scampi, lobster), then take your selection to a shack where they will cook it and serve it to you (fish about Rs40 per kg).

MATTANCHERRY & JEW TOWN

Ramathula Hotel (Map p1016; Kayees Junction, Mattancherry; biryani Rs35-40; ⏲ lunch & dinner) This place is legendary among locals for its chicken and mutton biryanis – get here early or you'll miss out. It's better known by the chef's name, Kayees.

Caza Maria (Map p1016; Bazaar Rd; mains around Rs100-200) With cooks trained by a travelling Frenchman, this is an enchanting, bright blue space with funky music and a changing daily menu of North Indian, South Indian and French dishes.

ERNAKULAM

Frys Village Restaurant (Map p1018; Veekshanam Rd; dishes Rs35-100; ⏲ lunch & dinner; ❄) This cavernous family restaurant is one of the best places in town for authentic Keralan food, especially for seafood like *pollichathu* (fish in banana leaves) or crab roast (Rs50 to Rs100 depending on size).

Aruvi Nature Restaurant (Map p1018; Chittoor Rd; meals around Rs50) An interesting twist on the traditional Keralan set meal – the whole menu here is created according to ayurveda principles and contains no dairy, spicy peppers or salt. And it's still damned tasty – definitely worth a try!

South Star (Map p1018; Shanmughan Rd; meals Rs50-100; ❄) This upmarket version of the Bimbis chain of restaurants is in a dark, moodily lit space that's plushed out in nice chairs and dark-wood tables. The bulky menu has North and South Indian victuals, as well as a massive choice of Chinese dishes.

Grand Pavilion (Map p1018; MG Rd; meals Rs80-350; ❄) This is the restaurant at the Grand Hotel

and is as retro-stylish as the hotel itself. It serves a tome of a menu that covers dishes from the West, North India, South India and most of the rest of the Asian continent. The *meen pollichathu* (fish cooked in banana leaves, Rs150) here gets the thumbs up.

Other options:

Spencer's Daily (Map p1018; Veekshanam Rd; ⏲ 7.30am-10.30pm) Well-stocked supermarket.

Indian Coffee House (Map p1018; Cannon Shed Rd) Also has branches on Jos Junction and MG Rd near Padma Junction.

Coffee Beanz (Map p1018; Shanmugham Rd; breakfasts Rs30-75; ⏲ lunch & dinner; ❄) For a hip coffee hit.

Barista (Map p1018; Bay Pride Mall; Marine Walk; snacks Rs50-70; ⏲ lunch & dinner; ❄) Branch of the Indian coffee chain with great location on the sea.

Entertainment

CINEMAS

Sridar Cinema (Map p1018; Shanmugham Rd, Ernakulam; tickets Rs40) Screens films in Malayalam, Hindi, Tamil and English.

KATHAKALI

There are several places in Kochi where you can view Kathakali (see the boxed text, opposite). The performances are certainly made for tourists, but they're also a good introduction to this intriguing art form. The standard program starts with the intricate make-up application, followed by a commentary on the dance and then the performance.

See India Foundation (Map p1018; ☎ 2376471; Kalathiparambil Lane, Ernakulam; admission Rs150; ⏲ make-up 6pm, show 7-8pm) One of the oldest Kathakali theatres in Kerala, it has small-scale shows with an emphasis on the religious and philosophical roots of Kathakali.

Kerala Kathakali Centre (Map p1016; ☎ 2217552; www.kathakalicentre.com; KB Jacob Rd, Fort Cochin; admission Rs150; ⏲ make-up 5pm, show 6.30-8pm) In a massive new theatre, this place specialises in grand, showy performances and provides useful translations of the night's story.

KALARIPPAYAT

Examples of this fast-paced traditional martial art can now be easily seen in Fort Cochin. The Kerala Kathakali Centre (above) holds one-hour performances at its old theatre (Map p1016) opposite Brunton Boatyard nightly at 7pm (Rs150).

If you want to see real professionals have a go at it, it's best to travel out to **Ens Kalari**

(Off map p1018; ☎ 2700810; www.enskalari.org.in; Nettoor, Ernakulam), a renowned *kalarippayat* learning centre 8km southeast of Ernakulam. They hold one-hour demonstrations Monday to Saturday at 7pm (one day's notice required, admission by donation).

Shopping

Broadway in Ernakulam (p1018) is good for local shopping, spice shops, clothing and a bazaar feel. Around Convent and Market Rds there's a huddle of tailors, and on and around Market Rd, between Jew St and Press Club Rd, is the textiles centre. On Jew Town Rd in Mattancherry (Map p1016) there's a plethora of Kashmiri-run shops selling everything from genuine antiques, to cheap knock-offs. Many shops in Fort Cochin operate lucrative commission rackets, with autorickshaw drivers getting huge kickbacks (which are added to your price) just for dropping tourists at their door.

Fabindia (Map p1016; ☎ 2217077; www.fabindia.com; Napier St, Fort Cochin; ⏰ 10am-8pm) This popular chain of stores has oodles of fine Indian textiles, fabrics, clothes and home linens as well as accessories, personal care products and homewares.

Cinnamon (Map p1016; ☎ 2217124; Post Office Rd, Fort Cochin; ⏰ 10am-7pm Mon-Sat) Cinnamon sells gorgeous Indian-designed clothing, jewellery and homewares in an ultrachic white retail space.

Niraamaya (Map p1016; ☎ 3263465; Quiros St, Fort Cochin; ⏰ 10am-5pm) Popular throughout Kerala, Niraamaya sells 'ayurvedic' clothing and fabrics – all made of organic cotton, coloured with natural herb dyes, or infused with ayurvedic oils. The clothing is very simple, but makes for an original gift.

Getting There & Away
AIR

The following airlines have offices in Kochi:
Air India (Map p1014; ☎ 2351295; MG Rd; ⏰ 9.30am-1pm & 1.45-5.30pm Mon-Sat)
Indian Airlines (Map p1018; ☎ 2370238; Durbar Hall Rd; ⏰ 9.45am-1pm & 1.45-5pm)
Jet Airways (Map p1014; ☎ 2358582; MG Rd; ⏰ 9am-5pm Mon-Sat, to 1.30pm Sun)
Kingfisher Airlines (Map p1014; ☎ 2351144; 2nd fl, Sreekandath Rd; ⏰ 9.30am-6pm Mon-Sat)

Low-cost airlines **Paramount Airways** (☎ 2610404-5), **IndiGo** (☎ 4029316) and **Spice Jet** (☎ 18001803333) have offices at the airport. See the table below, for sample fares and flights.

DOMESTIC FLIGHTS FROM ERNAKULAM

Destination	Airline	Fare (US$)	Duration (hr)	Frequency
Agatti	IT	145	1½	5 weekly
Bengaluru	9W	84	1¼	1 daily
	IT	84	1¼	3 daily
Chennai	IC	88	1	3 weekly
	9W	85	1½	1 daily
	IT	85	1½	3 daily
	I7	81	1	3 daily
Delhi	IC	200	3	1 daily
	9W	136	3	2 daily
	IT	121	4	1 daily
	6R	89	4	1 daily
Goa	IT	75	4	1 daily
Kozhikode	IC	85	1	1 daily
	IT	85	1	1 daily
Mumbai	IC	120	2	1 daily
	9W	111	2	2 daily
	IT	85	2	2 daily
	SG	77	2	1 daily
Trivandrum	IC	85	¾	2 daily
	IT	85	¾	1 daily

Note: Fares are oneway. Airline codes: IC – Indian Airlines; 9W – Jet Airways; IT – Kingfisher; I7 – Paramount Airways; 6E – IndiGo; SG – SpiceJet.

MAJOR BUSES FROM ERNAKULAM

The following bus services operate from the KSRTC bus stand (Map p1018).

Destination	Fare (Rs)	Duration (hr)	Frequency
Alleppey	39	1½	every 20 minutes
Bengaluru	249 (AC 448)	14	eight daily
Calicut	129	5	hourly
Chennai	425 (AC 650)	16	one daily
Coimbatore	118	4½	nine daily
Kannur	146	8	seven daily
Kanyakumari	197	8	two daily
Kollam	91	3½	every 20 minutes
Kothamangalam	29	2	every 30 minutes
Kottayam	46	2	every 20 minutes
Kumily (for Periyar)	115	5	eight daily
Madurai	174	9	two daily
Munnar	80	5½	every 45 minutes
Mangalore	270	12	one daily
Thrissur	51	2	every 15 minutes
Trivandrum	135	5	every 20 minutes

BUS

The **KSRTC bus stand** (Map p1018; ☎ 2372033; ☺ reservations 6am-10pm) is in Ernakulam next to the railway halfway between the two train stations. Many buses passing through Ernakulam originate in other cities – you may have to join the scrum when the bus pulls in. You can make reservations up to five days in advance for buses originating here. There's a separate window for reservations to Tamil Nadu. See above for more information on buses from Ernakulam.

Several private bus companies have super-deluxe, AC, video buses to Bengaluru, Chennai, Mangalore and Coimbatore; prices are around 75% higher than government buses. There are stands selling tickets all over Ernakulam. **Kaloor bus stand** is the main private bus station; its 1km north of the city.

TRAIN

Ernakulam has two train stations, Ernakulam Town and Ernakulam Junction, with reservations for both made at the Ernakulam Junction **reservations office** (☎ 132; ☺ 8am-8pm Mon-Sat, 8am-2pm Sun).

There are trains to Trivandrum (2nd class/ AC chair Rs56/238, 4½ hours), via either Alleppey (Rs25/135, 1½ hours) and Kollam (Rs46/188, 3½ hours), or via Kottayam (Rs6/ 142, 1½ hours). Trains also run to Thrissur (Rs29/131, 1½ hours), Calicut (Rs55/180, 4½ hours) and Kannur (Rs70/276, 6½ hours). For long-distance trains, see p1026.

Getting Around
TO/FROM THE AIRPORT

Kochi International Airport (Off map p1018; ☎ 2610113; www.cochin-airport.com) is at Nedumbassery, 30km northeast of Ernakulam. Taxis to/from Ernakulam cost around Rs500, and to/from Fort Cochin around Rs650. Ernakulam's mad traffic means that the trip can take over 1½ hours in the daytime, though usually less than one hour at night.

BOAT

Ferries are the fastest form of transport between Fort Cochin and the mainland. The jetty on the eastern side of Willingdon Island is called **Embarkation** (Map p1014); the west one, opposite Mattancherry, is **Terminus** (Map p1014); and the main stop at Fort Cochin is **Customs** (Map p1016), with another stop at the **Mattancherry Jetty** near the synagogue (Map p1016). One-way fares are all around Rs3.

Ernakulam

There are services to both Fort Cochin jetties (Customs and Mattancherry) every 25 to 50 minutes (5.55am to 9.30pm) from Ernakulam's **main jetty** (Map p1018).

Ferries also run every 20 minutes or so to Willingdon and Vypeen Islands (6am to 10pm).

Fort Cochin

Ferries run from Customs Jetty to Ernakulam between 6.20am and 9.50pm. Ferries also hop between Customs Jetty and Willingdon

MAJOR TRAINS FROM ERNAKULAM

The following are major long-distance trains departing from Ernakulam Town.

Destination	Train No & Name	Fare* (Rs)	Duration (hr)	Departures
Bengaluru	6525 *Bangalore Exp*	270/724/986	13	6.05pm
Chennai	2624 *Chennai Mail*	303/791/1066	12	7.15pm
Delhi	2625 *Kerala Exp***	599/1621/2220	46	3.40pm
Goa	6312 *Bikaner Exp*	320/862/1179	15	8.00pm (Sat only)
Kanyakumari	6526 *Kanyakumari Exp*	167/431/580	8	10.10am
Mangalore	6329 *Malabar Exp*	200/525/711	10½	11.45pm
Mumbai	6382 *Mumbai Exp*	473/1320/1815	40	1.00pm

*Sleeper/3AC/2AC
**Departs from Ernakulam Junction

Island 18 times a day from 6.40am to 9.30pm (Monday to Saturday).

Car and passenger ferries cross to Vypeen Island from Fort Cochin virtually nonstop from 6am until 10pm.

LOCAL TRANSPORT

There are no real bus services between Fort Cochin and Mattancherry Palace, but it's an enjoyable 30-minute walk through the busy warehouse area along Bazaar Rd. Autorickshaws should cost around Rs20, but you'll need to haggle. Most autorickshaw trips around Ernakulam shouldn't cost more than Rs25.

To get to Fort Cochin after ferries stop running, catch a bus in Ernakulam on MG Rd (Rs8, 45 minutes), south of Durbar Hall Rd. From Fort Cochin, buses head out to Ernakulam from opposite the Vypeen Island ferry jetty. Taxis charge round-trip fares between the islands, even if you only go one way – Ernakulam Town train station to Fort Cochin should cost around Rs170.

Scooters/Enfields can be hired for Rs250/450 per day from **Vasco Tourist Information Centre** (Map p1016; ☎ 2216215; vascoinformations@yahoo.co.uk; Bastion St, Fort Cochin).

AROUND KOCHI
Tripunithura

Hill Palace Museum (Off map p1018; ☎ 0484-2781113; admission Rs20; ☉ 9am-12.30pm & 2-4.30pm Tue-Sun) at Tripunithura, 12km southeast of Ernakulam en route to Kottayam, was formerly the residence of the Kochi royal family and is an impressive 49-building palace complex. It now houses the collections of the royal families, as well as 19th-century oil paintings, old coins, sculptures and paintings, and temple models. From Ernakulam catch the bus to Tripunithura from MG Rd or Shanmugham Rd, behind the Tourist Reception Centre (Rs5, 45 minutes); an autorickshaw should cost around Rs250 return with one-hour waiting time.

Cherai Beach

On Vypeen Island, 25km from Fort Cochin, **Cherai beach** might just be Kochi's best-kept secret. It's a lovely stretch of as-yet undeveloped white sand, with miles of lazy backwaters just a few hundred metres from the seafront. Best of all, it's close enough to visit on a day trip from Kochi.

If you plan on staying for more than a day, there are a few low-key resorts here.

Run by the same folk who own Salt 'n' Pepper restaurant in Fort Cochin, **Brighton Beach House** (☎ 0484-221855, 9947440449; www.brightonbeachhouse.org; r Rs850, with AC Rs1200; ☉ Nov-Mar) has a few basic rooms in a small building right near the shore. The beach is rocky here, but the place is wonderfully secluded, filled with hammocks to loll in, and has a neat, elevated stilt-restaurant that serves perfect sunset views with dinner.

An excellent collection of distinctive cottages lying around a meandering lagoon, **Cherai Beach Resort** (☎ 0484-2416949; www.cheraibeachresorts.com; Vypeen Island; r Rs2000-3000, with AC Rs4200-4500; ☒ ▢) has the beach on one side and backwaters on the other. Bungalows are individually designed using natural materials, with either curving walls or split-levels or lookouts onto the backwaters. There's even a tree growing inside one room. The restaurant serves daily buffets (breakfast/lunch/dinner Rs150/300/350). Check out a few different rooms to find one to your liking.

To get here from Fort Cochin, catch a car-ferry to Vypeen Island (per person/scooter Rs1.50/3) and either hire an autorickshaw from the jetty (around Rs270) or catch one of the frequent buses (Rs14, one hour).

Parur & Chennamangalam

Nowhere is the tightly woven religious cloth that is India more apparent than in Parur, 35km north of Kochi. Here, one of the oldest **synagogues** (admission Rs2; ☾ 9am-5pm Tue-Sun) in Kerala, at Chennamangalam, 8km from Parur, has been fastidiously renovated. Inside you can see notable door and ceiling wood reliefs in dazzling colours, while just outside lies the oldest tombstone in India – inscribed with the Hebrew date corresponding to 1269. The Jesuits first arrived in Chennamangalam in 1577 and there's a **Jesuit church** and the ruins of a Jesuit college nearby. Nearby are a **Hindu temple** on a hill overlooking the Periyar River, a 16th-century **mosque**, and Muslim and Jewish **burial grounds**.

In Parur town, you'll find the **agraharam** (place of Brahmins) – a small street of closely packed and brightly coloured houses origi-nally settled by Tamil Brahmins.

Parur is compact, though Chennamangalam is best visited with a guide. **Indoworld** (Map p1016; ☎ 2218947; www.indoworldtours.com; Princess St; ☾ 8am-8pm Mon-Sat, to 2.30pm Sun) can organise tours (around Rs600 plus guide).

Buses for Parur leave from the KSRTC bus stand in Kochi (Rs16, one hour, every 10 minutes). From Parur catch a bus (Rs3) or autorickshaw (Rs50) to Chennamangalam.

THRISSUR (TRICHUR)
☎ 0487 / pop 330,100

While the rest of Kerala has its fair share of celebrations, Thrissur remains the cul-tural cherry on the festival cake. With a list of energetic and highly spirited festivals as long as a temple-elephant's trunk, the region supports several institutions that nurse the dying classical Keralan performing arts back to health. This busy, bustling place is home to a community of Nestorian Christians, whose denomination dates back to the 3rd century AD. The popular performing-arts school Kerala Kalamandalam (p1029) and Sri Krishna Temple (33km northeast of Thrissur; p1029) are nearby. Plan to get here during the rambunctious festival season (November to mid-May).

Orientation & Information
There are several ATMs around town.
DTPC office (District Tourism Promotion Council; ☎ 2320800; Palace Rd; ☾ 10am-5pm Mon-Sat)
Lava Rock Internet Cafe (Kuruppam Rd; per hr Rs25; ☾ 8.30am-9.30pm)
Paragon Web Inc (2nd fl, High Rd; per hr Rs20; ☾ 8.30am-9.30pm)
UAE Money Exchange (☎ 2445668; TB Rd; ☾ 9am-5.30pm Mon-Sat, 9.30am-1pm Sun)

Sights & Activities
One of the oldest in the state, **Vadakkunathan Kshetram Temple** crowns the hill at the epi-centre of Thrissur. Finished in classic Keralan architecture, only Hindus are allowed inside, though the mound surrounding the temple has sweeping metropolis views and is a popu-lar spot to loiter. Thrissur is also famed for its numerous churches, including **Our Lady of Lourdes Cathedral**, a massive cathedral with an underground shrine; **Puttanpalli (New) Church** with its towering, pure-white spires; and the **Chaldean (Nestorian) Church**, which is unique in its complete lack of pictorial representations of Jesus.

The **Archaeology Museum** (admission Rs6; ☾ 9am-1pm, 2pm-4.30pm Tue-Sun) is housed in the 200-year-old Sakthan Thampuran Palace. Wandering through its arrow-guided maze you get to see some neat artefacts, includ-ing 12th-century Keralan bronze sculp-tures, earthenware pots big enough to cook children in, and an extraordinary 1500kg wooden treasury box covered in locks and iron spikes.

Festivals & Events
In a state where festivals are a way of life, Thrissur still manages to stand out for tem-ple revelry. Highlights here include **Thrissur Pooram** (April/May) – the most colour-ful and biggest of Kerala's temple festivals with wonderful processions of elephants; **Uthralikavu Pooram** (March/April), whose climactic day sees 20 elephants circling the shrine; and **Thypooya Maholsavam** (January/February), with a spectacular *kavadiyattam* (a form of ritualistic dance) procession in which dancers carry tall, ornate structures called *kavadis*.

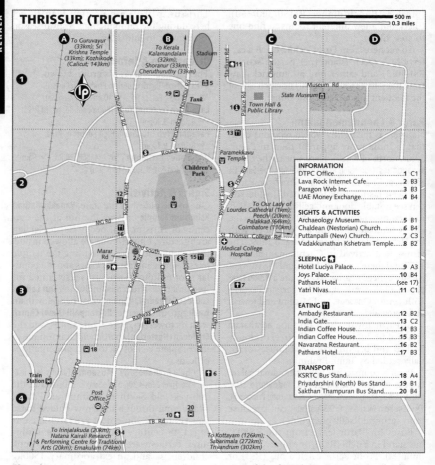

THRISSUR (TRICHUR)

INFORMATION	
DTPC Office.....................................1	C1
Lava Rock Internet Cafe.................2	B3
Paragon Web Inc...........................3	B3
UAE Money Exchange....................4	B4

SIGHTS & ACTIVITIES	
Archaeology Museum.....................5	B1
Chaldean (Nestorian) Church..........6	B4
Puttanpalli (New) Church...............7	C3
Vadakkunathan Kshetram Temple.....8	B2

SLEEPING	
Hotel Luciya Palace........................9	A3
Joys Palace.................................10	B4
Pathans Hotel.....................(see 17)	
Yatri Nivas.................................11	C1

EATING	
Ambady Restaurant......................12	B2
India Gate..................................13	C2
Indian Coffee House.....................14	B3
Indian Coffee House.....................15	B3
Navaratna Restaurant..................16	B2
Pathans Hotel.............................17	B3

TRANSPORT	
KSRTC Bus Stand.........................18	A4
Priyadarshini (North) Bus Stand....19	B1
Sakthan Thampuran Bus Stand......20	B4

Sleeping

Pathans Hotel (☎ 2425620; www.pathansresidentialhotel .com; Round South; s/d from Rs275/395, with AC Rs585/788; ✷) With no-frills rooms at no-frills prices, this is probably the best budget value in town. The basic and clean rooms are on the 5th and 6th floors here and have TV and occasional hot water.

Yatri Nivas (☎ 2332333; Stadium Rd; r Rs460, with AC Rs690; ✷) This government-run hotel is opposite the town stadium on a refreshingly quiet street. Set around scruffy gardens, it has large, plain rooms and service as slow as molasses.

Hotel Luciya Palace (☎ 2424731; luciapalace@ hotmail.com; s/d Rs666/777, with AC Rs888/999; ✷) In a cream, colonial-themed building, this is

one of the few places in town that has some character. Sitting in a quiet cul-de-sac, this grandiose-looking hotel has comfortable and spacious rooms, though some of the rooms without air-conditioning are nicer than the air-con ones.

Joys Palace (☎ 2429999; www.joyshotels.com; TB Rd; s/d from Rs1500/1800; ✷) This showy tower that looks like an ornate 10-storey meringue caters to Thrissur's jet set. Thankfully, the rooms are not too over the top, are quite comfy and have big windows to enjoy the upper floor's sweeping views. There's a 2nd-floor restaurant with an outdoor balcony (buffet breakfast/lunch/dinner Rs205/240/260) and an cool glass-fronted elevator that feels like a fun-park ride.

Eating

Pathans Hotel (1st fl, Round South; dishes from Rs25) A little cafeteria-like, this atmospheric place is popular with families for lunch (thali Rs40) and has a sweets counter downstairs.

Ambady Restaurant (Round West; dishes Rs25-60) A little way off the street, this breezy semi-outdoor place is a huge hit with families tucking into several different varieties of set meals.

India Gate (Town Hall Rd; dishes Rs25-60) In the same building as the HDFC Bank, this is a bright, pure-veg place serving an unbeatable range of dosas (Rs45 to Rs60), including jam, cheese and cashew versions, and *uttapams* (thick savoury rice pancake – a Tamil Nadu version of a pizza; Rs25 to Rs40).

Navaratna Restaurant (Round West; dishes Rs45-90; ⓨ lunch & dinner) Cool dark and intimate, this is the classiest joint to eat in town. Expect lots of veg and nonveg dishes from North India served in arctic AC surrounds. Great lunchtime meals for Rs70.

The Indian Coffee House has branches at Round South and Railway Station Rd.

Getting There & Away

BUS

KSRTC buses leave around every 30 minutes from the KSRTC bus stand bound for Trivandrum (Rs183, 7½ hours), Ernakulam (Kochi, Rs51, two hours), Calicut (Rs80, 3½ hours), Palakkad (Rs41, 1½ hours) and Kottayam (Rs81, four hours). Hourly buses go to Coimbatore (Rs68, three hours). From here there are buses to Ponnani (Rs31, 1½ hours) and Prumpavoor (Rs37, two hours), where you can connect with buses bound for Munnar.

Regular services also chug along to Guruvayur (Rs22, one hour), Irinjalakuda (Rs15, one hour) and Cheruthuruthy (Rs18, 1½ hours). Two private bus stands (Sakthan Thampuran and Priyadarshini) have more frequent buses to these destinations, though the chaos involved in navigating each station hardly makes using them worthwhile.

TRAIN

Services run regularly to Ernakulam (2nd class/AC chair Rs29/131, 1½ hours) and Calicut (Rs39/157, three hours). There are also regular trains running to Palakkad (sleeper/3AC/2AC Rs101/188/258, 1½ hours) via Shoranur.

AROUND THRISSUR

The Hindu-only **Sri Krishna Temple** at Guruvayur, 33km northwest of Thrissur, is perhaps the most famous in Kerala. Said to have been created by Guru, preceptor of the gods, and Vayu, god of wind, the temple is believed to date from the 16th century and is renowned for its healing powers. An annual and spectacular **Elephant Race** is held here in February or March.

Kerala Kalamandalam (☎ 04884-262418; www .kalamandalam.org), 32km northeast of Thrissur at Cheruthuruthy, is a champion of Kerala's traditional-art renaissance. Using an ancient Gurukula system of learning, students undergo intensive study in Kathakali, *mohiniyattam* (classical dance), *kootiattam*, percussion, voice and violin. Structured **visits** (per person incl lunch US$25; ⓨ 9.30am-1pm) are available, including a tour around the theatre and classes. Individually tailored introductory courses are offered one subject at a time (between six and 12 months; around Rs1500 per month, plus Rs1500 for accommodation).

Natana Kairali Research & Performing Centre for Traditional Arts (☎ 0480-2825559; natana kairali@gmail.com), 20km south of Thrissur near Irinjalakuda, offers training in traditional arts, including rare forms of puppetry and dance. Short appreciation courses lasting up to a month are sometimes available to keen foreigners (about Rs250 per class). In December each year, the centre holds five days of *mohiniyattam* (dance of the temptress) performances, a form of classical Keralan women's dance.

Regular bus services connect each of these destinations with Thrissur (see left).

NORTHERN KERALA

KOZHIKODE (CALICUT)

☎ 0495 / pop 880,168

Always a prosperous trading town, Calicut was once the capital of the formidable Zamorin dynasty. Vasco da Gama first landed near here in 1498, on his way to snatch a share of the subcontinent for king and country (Portugal that is). These days, trade depends mostly on exporting Indian labour to the Middle East. There's not a lot for tourists to see, though it's a nice break in the journey and the jumping-off point for Wayanad Wildlife Sanctuary.

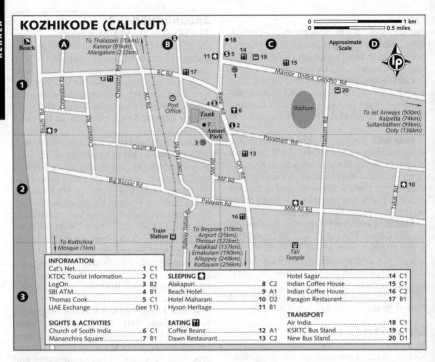

KOZHIKODE (CALICUT)

INFORMATION		
Cat's Net	1	C1
KTDC Tourist Information	2	C1
LogOn	3	B2
SBI ATM	4	B1
Thomas Cook	5	C1
UAE Exchange	(see 11)	

SIGHTS & ACTIVITIES		
Church of South India	6	C1
Mananchira Square	7	B1

SLEEPING		
Alakapuri	8	C2
Beach Hotel	9	A1
Hotel Maharani	10	D2
Hyson Heritage	11	B1

EATING		
Coffee Beanz	12	A1
Dawn Restaurant	13	C2

Hotel Sagar	14	C1
Indian Coffee House	15	C1
Indian Coffee House	16	C2
Paragon Restaurant	17	B1

TRANSPORT		
Air India	18	C1
KSRTC Bus Stand	19	C1
New Bus Stand	20	D1

Information

There are HDFC and State Bank of India ATMs in town.

Cat's Net (Mavoor Rd; per hr Rs25; ⏱ 9am-9pm) Fast computers.

KTDC Tourist Information (☎ 2373862; GH Rd) Cursory tourist information.

UAE Exchange (☎ 2762772; Bank Rd; ⏱ 9.30am-6pm Mon-Sat, to 1.30pm Sun)

LogOn (Ansari Park; per hr Rs25; ⏱ 9am-9pm)

Thomas Cook (☎ 2762681; Bank Rd; ⏱ 9.30am-5.30pm Mon-Sat)

Sights

Mananchira Square was the former courtyard of the Zamorins and preserves the original spring-fed tank. The 650-year-old **Kuttichira Mosque** is located in an attractive wooden four-storey building that is supported by impressive wooden pillars and painted brilliant aqua, blue and white. Burnt down by the Portuguese in 1510, it was rescued and rebuilt to tell the tale. The central **Church of South India** was established by Swiss missionaries in 1842 and has unique Euro-Keralan architecture.

Sleeping

Alakapuri (☎ 2723451-54; www.alakapurihotels.com; MM Ali Rd; s/d from Rs200/550, with AC Rs500/650; ⚡) Built motel-style around a green lawn (complete with fountain!) this place is off the road and quieter than most. Rooms come in different sizes and prices and, while a little scuffed, are tidy and reasonable value.

Hotel Maharani (☎ 2723101; www.hotelmaharani.com; Taluk Rd; d from Rs550, with AC from Rs1200; ⚡) This massive, hospital-like block lies secluded at the eastern end of town, surrounded by palms and greenery. Rooms are big, though spartan and a bit worn. Some hush time is almost guaranteed.

Hyson Heritage (☎ 4081000; www.hysonheritage.com; Bank Rd; s/d from Rs750/850, with AC from Rs1000/1300; ⚡) At this business-focused place you get a fair bit of swank for your rupee. The standard rooms are tidy, spacious and comfortable, while the massive deluxe AC rooms come with bathtubs and average art.

Beach Hotel (☎ 2762055; www.beachheritage.com; Beach Rd; r Rs1750; ⚡) Built in 1890 to house the Malabar British Club, this place is now a delightful 10-room hotel. Some rooms have bathtubs and secluded verandas; others have original polished wooden flooring and private balconies. All are tastefully furnished and drip with character. Dinner is often served in the trim little garden. This is easily the best place to stay in Calicut.

Eating

Hotel Sagar (Mavoor Rd; dishes Rs10-80; 6am-2am) With a dark wood interior and latticework on the front, this eatery is a tad more stylish than the competition. Veg and nonveg thali meals are served, with yummy biryanis (including fish, Rs60) and other dishes offered at lunchtime.

Coffee Beanz (RC Rd; snacks Rs25-80, meals Rs40-180; 12pm-10pm) The local franchise of our favourite coffee-chain, this jazzy, modern AC joint offers the usual gamut of coffee options (Rs20 to Rs70), as well as great-value lunchtime-special meals (from Rs45 to Rs60). Snacks and full meals also available.

Paragon Restaurant (Kannur Rd; dishes Rs40-195) Bypass the slightly dingy old section of this always-packed restaurant and head straight to the bright-yellow, modern and swish dining area with separate AC room. The menu is embarrassingly vast, with lots of fish, chicken and veg options. The food is scrumptious.

Dawn Restaurant (GH Rd; dishes Rs75-180, lunch buffet Rs200) The restaurant at the Hotel Malabar does multicuisine well, serving inventive Indian dishes and Keralan specials to a soundtrack of dull muzak.

For tasty, cheap snacks and great coffee, hit the Indian Coffee House on Mavoor Rd or GH Rd.

Getting There & Away

AIR

Air India (2771974; Eroth Centre, Bank Rd) flies daily to Mumbai (US$110), Chennai (US$85) and Kochin (US$85). **Jet Airways** (2740518; 29 Mavoor Rd) has one daily flight to Mumbai (US$95), while **Kingfisher** (18002333131; airport) flies to Chennai (US$75), Mangalore (US$85) and Kochi (US$85).

BUS

The **KSRTC bus stand** (Mavoor Rd) has buses to Bengaluru (Bangalore, via Mysore, Rs210, AC Rs351, eight hours, 10 daily), Mangalore (Rs163, seven hours, three daily) and to Ooty (Rs86, 5½ hours, four daily). There are frequent buses to Thrissur (Rs80, 3½ hours), Trivandrum (via Alleppey and Ernakulam; Rs268, 10 hours, eight daily) and Kottayam (Rs162, seven hours, 13 daily). For Wayanad district, buses leave every 15 minutes heading to Sultanbatheri (Rs62, three hours) via Kalpetta (Rs48, two hours).

The New Bus Stand, further east along Mavoor Rd, has long-distance private buses.

TRAIN

The train station is 1km south of Mananchira Sq. There are trains to Mangalore (sleeper/3AC/2AC Rs108/305/423, five hours), Kannur (Rs32/130, two hours), Ernakulam (2nd class/AC chair Rs55/180, 4½ hours) via Thrissur (Rs39/157, three hours), and all the way to Trivandrum (sleeper/3AC/2AC Rs190/505/691, 11 hours).

Heading southeast, there are trains to Coimbatore (sleeper/3AC/2AC Rs101/271/388, 4½ hours), via Palakkad (Rs101/216/300, 3½ hours). These trains then head north to the centres of Bengaluru, Chennai and Delhi.

Getting Around

Calicut has a glut of autorickshaws and, curiously, most are happy to use the meter. It costs about Rs10 from the station to the KSRTC bus stand or most hotels.

WAYANAD WILDLIFE SANCTUARY

 04936 / pop 780,200

Ask any Keralan what the prettiest part of their state is and most will whisper: Wayanad. Encompassing part of a remote forest reserve that spills into Tamil Nadu, Wayanad's landscape is a green medley of rice paddies, verdant untouched forests and the odd spice plantation. With only rudimentary tourist infrastructure, the region gets surprisingly few visitors, a shame since it's one of the few places you're almost guaranteed to spot wild elephants.

Orientation & Information

The sanctuary, covering an area of 345 sq km, consists of two separate pockets – **Muthanga** in the east and bordering Tamil Nadu, and **Tholpetty** in the north bordering Karnataka. Three major towns in Wayanad district make good bases for exploring the sanctuary – **Kalpetta** in the south, **Sultanbatheri** (also known as Sultan Battery) in the east and **Mananthavadi** in the northwest.

KERALA

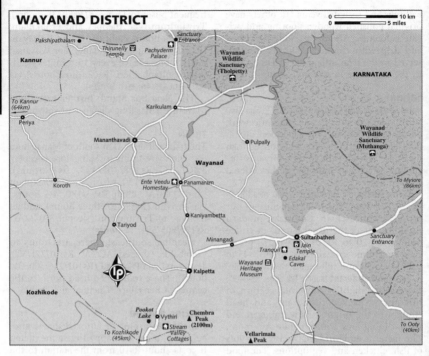

WAYANAD DISTRICT

The somewhat disorganised **DTPC office** (☎ 04936-202134; www.dtpcwayanad.com; Kalpetta; ☽ 10am-5pm Mon-Sat) at Kalpetta can help organise tours, permits and trekking. There are UAE Exchange offices in Kalpetta and Sultanbatheri, and Federal Bank and Canara Bank ATMs can be found in each of the three main towns, as can a smattering of internet cafes.

Sights & Activities

VISITING THE SANCTUARY

Entry to both parts of the **sanctuary** (Indian/foreigner Rs10/100, camera/video Rs25/150; ☽ 7am-5pm) is only permitted as part of a guided trek or **jeep safari**, both of which can be arranged at the sanctuary entrances.

At **Tholpetty** (☎ 04935-250853; jeep tour incl guide Rs500), the 1½-hour jeep tours (7am to 9am and 3pm to 5pm) are a great way to spot wildlife. Rangers organise **guided treks** (up to 5 people Rs1600; ☽ 8am-2pm) from here.

At **Muthanga** (☎ 271010; jeep tour incl guide Rs350), two-hour jeep tours are available in the mornings and afternoons, and, at the time of research, all day guided walks (Rs500 to Rs800) were being planned for the near future.

The DTPC, as well as most hotels, arrange guided jeep tours (up to five people Rs1500 to Rs1800) of the Muthanga sanctuary and surrounding Wayanad sights.

AYURVEDA

For ayurvedic treatments, visit the **Kannur Ayurvedic Centre** (☎ 0436-203001; www.ayurvedawaya nad.com; Kalpetta; r Rs500), a small, government-certified and family-run clinic in Kalpetta. Ayurvedic massage start at Rs500, longer treatments like full 21-day panchakarma cleansing cost around Rs9100, plus Rs120 for food and Rs500 for accommodation per day. There are also daily yoga classes.

OTHER SIGHTS & ACTIVITIES

There are some top opportunities for independent **trekking** around the district, including a climb to the top of Chembra Peak, at 2100m the area's tallest summit; Vellarimala, with great views and lots of wildlife-spotting opportunities; and Pakshipathalam, a formation of large boulders deep in the forest. Permits are necessary and can be arranged at forest offices in South or North

Wayanad. The DTPC office in Kalpetta organises trekking guides (Rs600 per day), camping equipment (around Rs250 per person) and transport – pretty much anything you might need to get you hiking. It also runs four-hour bamboo **rafting trips** (Rs1000) from June to September.

Thought to be one of the oldest on the subcontinent, **Thirunelly Temple** (dawn-dusk) is 10km from Tholpetty. While non-Hindus cannot enter, the ancient and intricate pillars and stone carvings, set against a soaring backdrop of mist-covered peaks, is an astounding sight no matter what your creed.

The 13th-century **Jain temple** (8am-noon & 2pm-6pm), near Sultanbatheri, has splendid stone carvings and is an important monument to the region's strong historical Jain presence. Close by, near Ambalavayal, are the **Edakal Caves** (admission Rs10; 9am-5pm), with petroglyphs thought to date back over 3000 years and jaw-dropping views of Wayanad district. In the same area, **Wayanad Heritage Museum** (Ambalavayal; admission Rs10; 9am-5pm) exhibits headgear, weapons, pottery, carved stone and other artefacts dating back to the 15th century that shed light on Wayanad's significant Adivasi population.

The picture-perfect **Pookot Lake** (admission Rs10; 9am-6pm) is 3km before Vythiri. Geared up for visitors, it has well-maintained gardens, a cafeteria, playground and paddle/row boats for hire (Rs30/50 per 20 minutes). It gets packed on the weekends, though feels quite peaceful during the week.

Sleeping & Eating

There are forest serambys (wooden huts; double without bathroom Rs1000) near the entrances of both Tholpetty and Muthanga, though you'll have to bring your own food. Contact either sanctuary office for bookings, or the **wildlife warden** (04936-220454; 10am-5pm Mon-Sat) at Sultanbatheri.

PPS Tourist Home (04936-203431; www.ppstouristhome.com; Kalpetta; s/d Rs250/340, deluxe r Rs500-600;) This agreeable and friendly place in the middle of Kalpetta has budget rooms in a motel-like compound that are clean, fair sized and comfy. Management can arrange trips around Wayanad (Rs1700 per carload) and hikes up Chembra Peak (Rs600 plus permit fees, six hours).

Hotel Regency (04936-220512; www.issacsregency.com; Sultanbatheri; s/d from Rs495/750, with AC from Rs1100/1200;) The pick of Sultanbatheri's

---

PANCHAKARMA – DETOX THE HARD WAY

Ayurveda, Kerala's ancient approach to health and wellbeing, proposes two fundamental methods of healing: *shaman chikitsa* and panchakarma *chikitsa*. While *shaman chikitsa* uses external herbal-medicinal preparations to heal the body of minor ills, the more intense system of panchakarma *chikitsa* (bodily purification) is used to treat more serious ailments.

In what is essentially an intense detox regime, panchakarma uses a combination of five types of different therapies (*panchakarma* means 'five actions') to rid the body of built-up endotoxins. These include: *vaman* – therapeutic vomiting; *virechan* – purgation; *vasti* – enemas; *nasya* – elimination of toxins through the nose; and *raktamoksha* – detoxification of the blood. Before panchakarma begins, the body is first prepared over several days with a special diet, oil massages (*snehana*) and herbal steam-baths (*swedana*). Only then can real treatment begin. Depending on the patient's ailments, vomiting may be induced using herbal concoctions, diarrhoea provoked using natural laxatives, the nasal passages may be flushed with oils, herbs may be inserted into the rectum as enemas, and the blood may be flushed through bloodletting (cutting) and the use of leeches. Treatment lasts for a minimum of 15 days, with 21 days the norm.

Although it may sound pretty grim, panchakarma purification might only use a few of these treatments at a time, with therapies like bloodletting and leeches only used in rare cases. Still, this is no spa holiday. Many tourist-geared ayurvedic clinics offer basic oil massage and the like, but for genuine panchakarma you will need to visit an ayurvedic doctor who can prescribe a cleansing treatment individually tailored to your needs. Conveniently located clinics that offer three-week purification regimes include Dr Franklin's Panchakarma Institute in Kovalam (p992), Eden Garden in Varkala (p994), Janakanthi Panchakarma Centre in Kollam (p997), Ayurveda: Sree Krishna in Alleppey (p999), Kannur Ayurvedic Centre in Wayanad (opposite). Expect to pay from around Rs800 to Rs2000 per day for treatment, with accommodation charges extra.

bunch of hotels, this quiet and no-nonsense place has routine, large and relatively tidy rooms in a U-shaped building. The deluxe rooms differ from the standard ones in price only.

Pachyderm Palace (☎ reservations 0484-2371761; touristdesk@satyam.net.in; Tholpetty; r per person incl meals Rs1250-1500) This rambling house lies just outside the gate of Tholpetty Wildlife Sanctuary – very handy for early morning treks, tours and wildlife viewing. The varied rooms are very simple and tidy, with one great stilt-bungalow on offer that's surrounded by forest. The Keralan food served here is excellent, and free morning/night animal-spotting safaris are included in the price.

Ente Veedu Homestay (☎ 04935-220008; www.ente veedu.co.in; Panamaram; r incl breakfast Rs2000-2500; 🖳) In a stunning location overlooking sprawling banana plantations and rice paddies, this isolated homestay halfway between Kalpetta and Manthavady is definitely worth seeking out. Surrounded by bucolic villages, it has several large rooms that come thoughtfully and colourfully furnished. Two rooms are bamboo lined and offer private balconies. There are hammocks and wicker lounges here to enjoy the sensational views. Call to arrange a pick-up.

our pick **Stream Valley Cottages** (☎ 04936-255860; www.streamvalleycottages.com; Vythiri; d Rs3000) These wonderful modern cottages lie on the banks of a small stream, several hundred metres off the main road (2.5km before Vythiri). Each cottage has loads of space, separate sitting areas, large private verandas, stylish dark-wood interiors and comes with a hushed soundtrack of singing birds and bubbling brooks. Traditional Keralan meals are available (Rs300 per day).

Tranquil (☎ 04936-220244; www.tranquilresort.com; Kuppamudi Estate, Kolagapara; s/d Rs10,100/12,750, deluxe Rs14,350/18,000; 🏊) This charming and luxurious homestay is in the middle of 160 hectares of pepper, coffee, vanilla and cardamom plantations. The elegant house has sweeping verandas filled with plants and handsome furniture. The owners are excellent hosts and arrange tours of the area (included). Prices include meals and tax.

Getting There & Around
Buses brave the winding roads between Calicut and Sultanbatheri (Rs62), via Kalpetta (Rs48), every 30 minutes. Private buses also run between Kannur and Mananthavadi every 45 minutes (Rs53, 2½ hours). From Sultanbatheri, one 8am bus heads out for Ooty (Rs84, four hours), with a second one passing through town at around 1pm. Buses for Mysore (Rs75, three hours) leave every 30 minutes or so.

Plenty of private buses connect Mananthavadi, Kalpetta and Sultanbatheri every 10 to 20 minutes during daylight hours (Rs14 to Rs26, 45 minutes to 1¼ hours). From Mananthavadi, regular buses also head to Tholpetty (Rs12.50, 45 minutes). You can hire jeeps to get from one town to the next for around Rs400 to Rs600 each way.

There are plenty of autorickshaws for short trips within the towns, and the DTPC can help arrange car hire (from around Rs1500 per day).

KANNUR (CANNANORE)
☎ 0497 / pop 498,200

Under the Kolathiri rajas, Kannur was a major port bristling with international trade – explorer Marco Polo christened it a 'great emporium of spice trade'. Since then, the usual colonial suspects, including the Portuguese, Dutch and British, have had a go at exerting their influence on the region. Today it is an unexciting, though agreeable, town known mostly for its weaving industry and cashew trade, with an excellent beach at Costa Malabari and incredible *theyyam* possession performances (see p1022).

Information
The **DTPC Office** (☎ 2706336; 🕙 10am-5pm Mon-Sat), opposite the KSRTC bus stand, supplies basic maps of Kannur. There are Federal Bank and State Bank of India ATMs adjacent to the bus stand. A **UAE Exchange** (☎ 2709022; City Centre, Fort Rd; 🕙 9.30am-6pm Mon-Sat, to 1.30pm Sun) office changes travellers cheques and cash; it's located in City Centre mall, five minutes from the train station.

Sights
Kannur is the best place to see the spirit-possession ritual called **theyyam** (see boxed text, p1022); on most nights of the year there should be a *theyyam* ritual on somewhere in the vicinity. The easiest way to find out about *theyyam* is to contact Kurien at Costa Malabari (see opposite). Alternatively, you can visit the **Kerala Folklore Academy** (☎ 2778090),

near Chirakkal Pond Valapattanam, 20km north of Kannur, where you can see vibrantly coloured costumes up close and sometimes catch a performance.

The Portuguese built **St Angelo Fort** (admission free; 9am-6pm) in 1505 from brilliantly red laterite stone on a promontory a few kilometres south of town. It has a serene garden and excellent views of nearby palm-fringed beaches.

Established in 1955, the **Loknath Weavers' Co-operative** (2726330; 8.30am-5.30pm Mon-Sat) is one of the oldest in Kannur and occupies a large building busily clicking with the sound of looms. You can stop by for a quick tour and visit the small shop here that displays the fruits of their labours. It's 4km south of Kannur.

This region is also known for the manufacture of *beedis,* those tiny Indian cigarettes deftly rolled inside green leaves. One of the largest, and purportedly best, manufacturers is the **Kerala Dinesh Beedi Co-Operative** (2835280; 8am-5pm Tue-Sat), with a factory at Thottada, 7km south of Kannur. Either of these cooperatives is a Rs80 to Rs100 (return) autorickshaw ride from Kannur town.

Kairail (0460-2243460), located 20km north of Kannur, offers rice-barge trips on the unspoilt northern Kerala backwaters. Day cruises (10am to 4pm) for up to 10 people cost Rs3500, or you can rent a barge by the hour (Rs1500 per hour).

Sleeping & Eating

Government Guest House (2706426; d Rs220, with AC Rs575;) As usual, a government guest house comes through with the goods. This place has several buildings near the water, but rooms in the 'new block,' which are enormous, simply and tastefully furnished and sport balconies that looking right onto the sea, are phenomenal value.

Hotel Meridian Palace (2761676; Bellard Rd; s Rs225-500, d Rs275-550, d with AC Rs700-1000) Located in the market area opposite the main train station. There's a bewildering array of budget rooms on offer here. If you manage to decide on one, chances are it will be clean, basic and convenient for an early train departure.

Mascot Beach Resort (2708445; www.mascotresort .com; s/d Rs700/900, with AC from Rs1000/1200;) A few hundred metres south of the Government Guest House, this place also has grand views of the ocean from its neat and comfy AC

rooms, though the budget options are a bit dowdy and filled with '80s bling.

Kannur Beach House (0497-2708360, 9847184535; www.kannurbeachhouse.com; Thottada Beach; r per person incl meals Rs1100) Near Costa Malabari and in an idyllic spot right behind the beach, the large rooms in this traditional Keralan building are presentably furnished and boast handsome large wooden shutters – though unfortunately no mosquito screens or nets. Each room comes with either a balcony or porch to enjoy the sensational ocean sunset views through swaying palms. It's 8km from Kannur.

our pick Costa Malabari (reservations 0484-2371761; touristdesk@satyam.net.in; Thottada Beach; r per person incl meals Rs1250) In a small village and five minutes' walk from an idyllic beach, Costa Malabari pioneered tourism in this area with its spacious rooms in an old hand-loom factory. There's a huge communal space, comfy lounging areas outside, and extra rooms now offered in two other nearby houses – one perched dramatically on a sea cliff. The home-cooked Keralan food is plentiful and, frankly, might just be some of the best in the country. Kurien, your gracious host, is an expert on the astonishing *theyyam* ritual (see boxed text, p1022) and can help arrange a visit. It's 8km from Kannur town; a rickshaw/taxi from the train station is around Rs100/200.

Getting There & Away

There are frequent daily buses to Mysore (Rs186, eight hours) and a few to Mangalore (Rs107, four hours). Most departures for Calicut (Rs51, 2½ hours) and Ernakulam (Rs186, eight hours) leave in the afternoon and evening. There's one daily bus to Ooty (via Wayanad, Rs113, nine hours) at 10pm. Frequent private buses to Mananthavadi (for Wayanad, Rs53, 2½ hours) leave from the private bus stand between the KSRTC stand and the train station.

There are several daily trains to Mangalore (sleeper/3AC/2AC Rs101/220/306, three hours), Calicut (2nd class/AC chair Rs32/130, two hours) and Ernakulam (Rs70/276, 6½ hours).

BEKAL & AROUND
 0467

Bekal and nearby Palakunnu and Udma, in Kerala's far north, host a handful of pretty

KERALA

white-sand beaches begging for DIY exploration. As yet there are few decent places to stay and getting around can be a real pain, though off-the-beaten-track adventurers may revel in discovering the place before it's turned into the next Kovalam. Because it's a predominantly Muslim area, it's important to keep local sensibilities in mind, especially at the beach.

The laterite-brick **Bekal Fort** (Indian/foreigner Rs5/100; 8am-5pm), built between 1645 and 1660, sits on Bekal's rocky headland and houses a small Hindu temple and plenty of goats. Next door, **Bekal beach** (admission Rs5) encompasses a grassy park and a long, beautiful stretch of sand that turns into a circus on weekends and holidays when local families descend here for rambunctious leisure time. Isolated **Kappil Beach**, 6km north of Bekal, has fine sand and calm water, but beware of shifting sandbars.

Located 22km south of Bekal, **Bekal Boat Stay** (0467-2282633; www.bekalboatstay.com; Kottappuram, Nileshwar) is one of the first enterprises in the region to offer overnight houseboat trips around the Valiyaparamba backwaters (Rs7000/9500 per 24 hours for two/four people). It has just four boats – all considerably more rustic than those on offer in Alleppey.

Sleeping & Eating

Sleeping options are pretty dire in the area, with lots of cheap, poor quality hotels scattered between Kanhangad (12km south) and Kasaragod (10km north).

Hotel Bekal International (0467-2204271; www.hotelbekal.com; Kanhangad; s/d from Rs200/350, d with AC from Rs700;) A relatively comfortable, if unexciting, midrange option 10km south of Bekal Fort. This huge complex has a green fetish, in everything from walls to '70s chairs, and a big choice of spacious, immaculate (green) rooms.

Gitanjali Heritage (9447469747; www.gitanjaliheritage.com; s/d with meals Rs2500/3500) Five kilometres from Bekal, this lovely homestay lies surrounded by rice paddies, deep among Kasaragod's inland villages. It's an intimate heritage home with comfortable, higgledy-piggledy rooms filled with ancestral furniture and polished wood. Call ahead for pick-ups.

Bekal Beach Camp (0946267792; www.bekalbeachcamp.com; Pallikara; r incl meals & taxes Rs3500) This is the hands-down winner for Bekal's 'most

atmospheric place to stay' award. It's camping in style here, with luxury canvas cabins scattered around the secluded end of Bekal beach among a small grove of palms. Each cabin has lots of space and is fitted out with comfy beds, lamps and fun en-suite toilets. Constant sea breezes and perfect sunset vistas come standard, as do hammocks on its private beach.

Getting There & Around

A couple of local trains stop at Fort Bekal station, right on Bekal beach. Kanhangad, 12km south, is a major train stop, while Kasaragod, 10km to the north, is the largest town in the area. Both Kanhangad and Kasaragod have frequent buses running to and from Bekal (around Rs10, 20 minutes). An autorickshaw from Bekal Junction to Kappil beach is around Rs30.

LAKSHADWEEP

pop 60,700

Comprising a string of 36 palm-covered coral islands 300km off the coast of Kerala, Lakshadweep is as stunning as it is isolated. Only 10 of these islands are inhabited, mostly with Sunni Muslim fishermen, and foreigners are only allowed to stay on a few of these. With fishing and coir production the main sources of income, local life on the islands remains highly traditional, and a caste system divides the islanders between Koya (land owners), Malmi (sailors) and Melachery (farmers).

The real attraction of the islands lies under the water: the 4200 sq km of pristine archipelago lagoons, unspoiled coral reefs and warm waters are a magnet for flipper-toting travellers and divers alike. Lakshadweep can only be visited on a pre-organised package trip – all listed accommodation prices are for the peak October to May season and include permits and meals. Diving, snorkelling, kayaking, boat trips, sailing and jaunts to nearby islands can be arranged by most resorts.

Information

SPORTS (Society for the Promotion of Recreational Tourism & Sports; Map p1014; 0484-2668387; www.lakshadweeptourism.com; IG Rd, Willingdon Island; 10am-5pm Mon-Sat) is the main organisation for tourist information.

PERMITS

Foreigners are limited to staying in pricey resorts; a special permit (one month's notice) is required and organised by tour operators, hotels or SPORTS in Kochi. Most of the Islands have only recently been opened up to foreigners, who are now allowed to stay on Bangaram, Agatti, Kadmat, Minicoy and Kavaratti islands.

Getting There & Away

Kingfisher Airlines (www.flykingfisher.com) flies five times a week between Kochi and Agatti Island (US$145 each way) – check the airline's website for the latest information. A 1½-hour transfer by boat from Agatti to Bangaram costs US$50 return. A fast 25-seater boat plies the waters between Agatti and Kadmat for Rs750 each way.

There are scheduled boat departures from Kochi to Kadmat and Mincoy islands between October and May (return including food in AC seat/four-berth/two-berth cabin, Rs3500/6000/8000, 18 to 20 hours each way). Get in touch with SPORTS in Kochi for details.

BANGARAM ISLAND

The 50-hectare island is fringed with pure sand, and the sight of the moon slipping beneath the lagoon horizon is very nearly worth the expense.

Bangaram Island Resort (☎ 0484-2668221; www.cghearth.com; r full board Oct-Apr €300, 4-person deluxe cottages €550) is run by the CGH Earth group and administered from its hotel in Kochi. Shop around before you leave home – some tourist agents can secure better deals than others.

AGATTI ISLAND

The village located on this 2.7-sq-km island has several mosques, which you can visit if dressed modestly. There's no alcohol on the island.

Agatti Island Beach Resort (☎ 0484-2362232; www.agattiislandresorts.com; s/d full board €100/140, with AC €140/190; ❄) sits on two beaches at the southern tip of the island and offers a range of packages. The resort has simple, low-rise beach cottages, designed to be comfortably cool without AC, and a restaurant for 20 people.

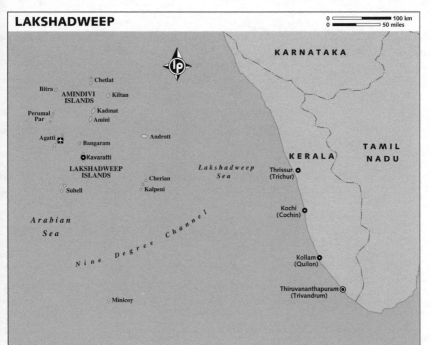

KERALA

DIVING

Lakshadweep is a diver's dream, with excellent visibility and an embarrassment of marine life living on undisturbed coral reefs. The best time to dive is between mid-October and mid-May when the seas are calm and visibility is 20m to 40m. During the rough monsoon many dive outfits close up shop.

Lacadives (☎ 022-66627381-82; www.lacadives.com; E-20 Everest Bldg, Taredo Rd, Mumbai) runs dive centres on Bangaram and Kadmat Islands. Costs can vary: a CMAS one-star course costs US$500, while experienced divers pay from US$50 per dive (including equipment hire), with discounts available for multiple dives. Information is available through the hotels or directly through Lacadives in Mumbai. The diving school on Agatti Island is run by **Goa Diving** (☎ 0832-2555117; www.goadiving.com).

From Kadmat Island, dives range from 9m to 40m in depth. Some of the better sites include North Cave, the Wall, Jack Point, Shark Alley, the Potato Patch, Cross Currents and Sting Ray City. Around Bangaram good spots include the 32m-deep wreck of the *Princess Royale*, Manta Point, Life, Grand Canyon and the impressive sunken reef at Perumal Par.

For a guide to environmentally friendly diving, see the boxed text, p110.

KADMAT ISLAND

Kadmat Beach Resort (☎ 0484-2668387; laksports _2004@vsnl.net; s/d Rs2500/4000, with AC Rs3000/5000; ✖) is administered by SPORTS (p1036) and can be reached by overnight boat from Kochi (p1037).

MINICOY ISLAND

You can now stay on the remote island of Minicoy in newly built cottages at **Swaying Palm** (☎ 0484-2668387; laksports_2004@vsnl.net; s/d Rs2500/4000, with AC Rs3000/5000; ✖). See p1037 for boat transport from Kochi.

Tamil Nadu

Many foreign travellers come to India seeking something 'old', a sense of living connection to traditions older than the culture they've left.

For many Indians, that same sense of age is achieved in Tamil Nadu, homeland of one of humanity's living classical civilisations, a people whose culture has grown, but in many ways not fundamentally altered, since the Greeks sacrificed goats to Zeus.

Here you can listen to one of the oldest dialogues in the human conversation: that of South India and her Dravidian inhabitants, whose cultural heart beats here at the tip of the subcontinental triangle. Haggle with a local merchant and they're using the same slang Roman sailors heard on the streets of Mamallapuram almost 2000 years ago.

But this state is as dynamic as it is drenched in history. In Tamil Nadu's famous temples, fire-worshipping devotees smear tikka on their brows before heading to IT offices to develop new software applications. Deep green rice paddies, sandstone rock carvings, ubiquitous white sarongs and next-generation Windows; here, India has one foot in the 21st century and the other in the poetry of one of the oldest literary languages on Earth.

When you visit, try to reach the ends of India, where three oceans mingle and avatars of God worship God on the beach. See the tiger-prowled hills of the Nilgiris, the Mother Temple of the triple-breasted, fish-eyed goddess and the Mountain of Fire, where the Destroyer and Dancer of the Universe manifests himself as a pillar of flame. It's all packed into a state that manages to remain fiercely distinct from India, while exemplifying her oldest and most adventurous edges.

HIGHLIGHTS

- Explore the past in one of India's most ancient states in the palaces and temples of **Thanjavur** (Tanjore; p1084)

- Breathe in the cool air, the colonialism, the quirkiness of **Ooty** (Udhagamandalam; p1112)

- Enjoy steak. Or yoga. Or steak *and* yoga in the former French colony of **Puducherry** (Pondicherry; p1071)

- Join the pilgrims and devotees filing into Madurai's **Sri Meenakshi Temple** (p1095), a riot of Dravidian sculpture.

- Pick through the ruins of **Mamallapuram** (Mahabalipuram; p1059) by sunset, then gorge on fresh seafood

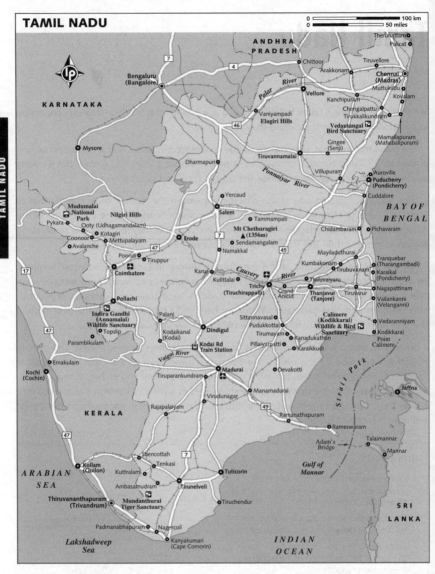

History

It's ironic that the bearers of the torch of South Indian identity may have their origins in Punjab and Pakistan. The early Indus civilisations display elements of Dravidian thought, language, culture and art, including a meditating god seated in the lotus position. This may be the world's first depiction of the yogi archetype, who has come to symbolise, for many, Asian spirituality.

The nomadic Aryans drove the Dravidians south around 1500 BC. Here, a classical language and classical civilisations developed, cushioned by geography against North Indian invasion. By 300 BC the region was controlled by three major dynasties – Cholas in the

FAST FACTS

Population 62.1 million
Area 130,058 sq km
Capital Chennai (Madras)
Main language Tamil
When to go November to March

east, Pandyas in the central area and Cheras in the west. This was the classical period of Tamil literature and myth – the Sangam Age – when kingdoms were ruled by feuding poet-kings and romantic epics; a visitor at the time described the Tamils as favouring rose petals over gold.

The Tamils developed their own aesthetic style, constructing huge cities that rivalled population centres in China and Europe, and magnificent steeped temples that wouldn't look out of place in Mayan Central America. Although each kingdom left notable achievements, the Cholas deserve some special mention. This remarkable nation maintained one of the great maritime empires of history, extending its influence to Cambodia, Vietnam and Indonesia and spreading Tamil ideas of reincarnation, karma and yogic practice to Southeast Asia. The end result of this cross-pollination was architectural wonders like Angkor Wat, the intellectual gestation of Balinese Hinduism and much of the philosophy associated with classical Buddhism.

Before the Mughals could fully extend their reach to India's tip, in 1640 the British negotiated the use of Madraspatnam (now Chennai) as a trading post. Subsequent interest by the French, Dutch and Danes led to continual conflict and, finally, almost total domination by the British, when the region became known as the Madras Presidency. Small pocketed areas, including Puducherry (Pondicherry) and Karaikal, remained under French control.

Many Tamils played a significant part in India's struggle for Independence, which was finally won in 1947. In 1956 the Madras Presidency was disbanded and Tamil Nadu was established as an autonomous state.

DEFINING DRAVIDIANS

The Tamils consider themselves the standard bearers of Dravidian – pre-Aryan Indian – civilisation. Their culture, language and history are distinctive from North India (although more related than some Tamil nationalists claim), and their ability to trace Tamil identity to classical antiquity is a source of considerable pride.

During the Indus Valley period (2600–1900 BC), the nomadic Aryans drove the city-dwelling Dravidians south while incorporating elements of the latter's beliefs into their holy texts, the Vedas. Take vegetarianism; before contact, the Aryans were known to have a penchant for meat (especially beef). The marriage of Aryan rituals and Dravidian concepts like renunciation, karma and reincarnation laid the groundwork for the development of early Hinduism.

But the Aryan insistence on segregating their dark-skinned Dravidian subjects may have been the foundation of caste as well. Early edicts make it clear: the paler the complexion, the higher the caste. South–North and class tensions were encouraged by the British, who used these strains to facilitate divide-and-conquer policies.

Ever since Indian independence in 1947, Tamil politicians have railed against caste (which they see as favouring light-skinned Brahmins) and Hindi (as unrelated to Tamil as Russian). The post-independence 'Self Respect' movement, influenced by Marxism, mixed South Indian communal values with class warfare rhetoric and spawned Dravidian political parties that remain major regional powers today. Anti-Hindi riots have defaced thousands of Hindi street signs here, and for a period in the late 1950s activists called for Dravida Nadu (Home of the Dravidians), an independent South Indian nation.

Although calls for separatism are past, Tamil nationalism is still in vogue. Many Tamil politicians loudly defend the Tamil Tigers, the same organisation that assassinated Rajiv Gandhi in 1991 (imagine a viable, sitting opposition party in your country openly supporting a group that killed your president or prime minister to get an idea of how separate some Tamil parties still consider themselves from India), and there is an unfortunate prejudice amongst the generally tolerant Tamils towards anything Sinhalese. Throughout the state, male politicians don a white shirt and white *mundu* (sarong), the official uniform of Tamil pride.

TOP FIVE TEMPLES

Tamil Nadu is nirvana for anyone wanting to explore South Indian temple culture and architecture. Many of the temples are important places of pilgrimage for Hindus, where daily *puja* (offering or prayer) rituals and colourful festivals will leave a deep impression on even the most temple-weary traveller. Other temples stand out for their stunning architecture, soaring *gopurams* (gateway towers) and intricately carved, pillared *mandapams* (pavilions in front of the temple). Almost all have free admission. There are so many that it pays to be selective, but the choice is subjective. Here's our top five:

- Sri Meenakshi Temple (p1095), Madurai
- Arunachaleswar Temple (p1069), Tiruvannamalai
- Brihadishwara Temple (p1084), Thanjavur (Tanjore)
- Sri Ranganathaswamy Temple (p1089), Trichy (Tiruchirappalli)
- Nataraja Temple (p1079), Chidambaram

Information

The state tourism body is **Tamil Nadu Tourism** (www.tamilnadutourism.org), which runs tourist offices of varying uselessness in most cities and large towns, plus a reliably average chain of hotels. You can also check www.tamilnadu-tourism.com for package-tour options.

ACCOMMODATION

Accommodation costing more than Rs200 in Tamil Nadu (but not Puducherry) is subject to a government 'luxury' tax – 5% on rooms between Rs200 and Rs500, 10% on rooms between Rs501 and Rs1000, and 12.5% on rooms over Rs1000. There's often an additional 'service tax' at upmarket hotels. Prices throughout this chapter do not include tax, unless stated otherwise. The best lodging in the state is in Mamallapuram, which boasts some excellent quirky backpacker lodges; Puducherry, with its old colonial villages (and some newer, more stylish digs); and the Victorian guest houses of Ooty and Kodaikanal.

PERMITS

As well as for the areas listed following, permits are required for trekking in some areas of the Nilgiri Hills around Mudumalai National Park (see p1118). Reputable guides should have the required permits for tourist trekking; researchers and academics need to apply separately.

Conservator of Forests (Map pp1044-5; ☎ 24321139; 8th fl, Panangal Bldg, 1 Jeenis Salai, Saidapet, Chennai) The Conservator of Forests issues permits for all areas other than the Vedantangal Bird Sanctuary, but will only do so for researchers.

Wildlife Warden's Office (WWO; Map pp1044-5; ☎ 24321471; 4th fl, DMS Office, 259 Anna Salai, Teynampet, Chennai) Issues permits in advance for accommodation at Vedantangal Bird Sanctuary.

Dangers & Annoyances

The big draw in Tamil Nadu is the 5000-some temples, but this is a very religious state, and non-Hindus are generally not allowed inside inner sanctums. This can be frustrating, as large areas of the best temples are essentially inaccessible to many travellers. Even non-resident Indians can be subject to scrutiny, and non-Indian Hindus may have to provide proof of conversion. Temple touts are fairly common and can be a nuisance, but don't dismiss every one as a scammer. There are many excellent guides here and they deserve both your time and rupees; use your best judgement, ask other travellers which guides they'd recommend and be on the lookout for badge-wearing official guides, who tend to be excellent resources.

Don't expect the Hindi slang you picked up in Rishikesh to go over well here. The Tamils are fiercely proud of their language and some consider Hindi to be North Indian cultural imperialism (see boxed text, p1041). North Indian tourists are often as confused as you are down here; more Tamils speak English than Hindi.

CHENNAI (MADRAS)

☎ 044 / pop 6.6 million

No matter how determined you are, you'd be pretty hard pressed to find much to gush about when it comes to Chennai. The streets

---

FESTIVALS IN TAMIL NADU

Many of Tamil Nadu's most colourful festivals revolve around temples – there's something going on somewhere in the state all year round.

International Yoga Festival (4-7 Jan; Puducherry, p1071) Puducherry's ashrams and yoga culture are put on show with workshops, classes and music and dance events. Held throughout the city, the event attracts yoga masters from all over India.

Pongal (mid-Jan; statewide) As the rice boils over the new clay pots, this festival symbolises the prosperity and abundance a fruitful harvest brings. For many, the celebrations begin with temple rituals, followed by family gatherings. Later it's the animals, especially cows, which are honoured for their contribution to the harvest.

International Music festival (Jan; Thiruvaiyaru, p1087) Held near Thanjavur, this music festival is held in honour of the saint and composer Thyagaraja.

Teppam (Float) Festival (Jan/Feb; Madurai, p1097) A popular event held on the full moon of the Tamil month of Thai, when statues of deities are floated on the huge Mariamman Teppakkulam Tank.

Natyanjali Dance Festival (Feb/Mar; Chidambaram, p1079) This five-day festival attracts performers from all over the country to the Nataraja Temple to celebrate Nataraja (Shiva) – Lord of the Dance.

Chithrai Festival (Apr/May; Madurai, p1094) The main event on Madurai's busy festival calendar is this 14-day event that celebrates the marriage of Meenakshi to Sundareswarar (Shiva). The deities are wheeled around the Sri Meenakshi Temple in massive chariots that form part of long, colourful processions.

Summer festivals (May-Jun; Ooty, p1112 & Kodaikanal, p1103) Tamil Nadu's hill stations both hold similar festivals which feature boat races on the lake, horse racing (in Ooty), flower shows and music.

Bastille Day (14 Jul; Puducherry, p1072) Street parades and a bit of French pomp and ceremony are all part of the fun at this celebration.

Karthikai Deepam Festival (Nov/Dec; statewide) Held during full moon, Tamil Nadu's 'festival of lights' is celebrated throughout the state with earthenware lamps and firecrackers, but the best place to see it is Tiruvannamalai (see boxed text, p1070), where the legend began.

Festival of Carnatic Music & Dance (mid-Dec–mid-Jan; Chennai, p1054) One of the largest of its type in the world, this festival is a celebration of Tamil music and dance.

Mamallapuram Dance Festival (Dec-Jan; Mamallapuram, p1059) A four-week dance festival showcasing dances from all over India, with many performances on an open-air stage against the imposing backdrop of Arjuna's Penance. Dances include the Bharata Natyam (Tamil Nadu), Kuchipudi (Andhra Pradesh) tribal dance, Kathakali (Kerala drama); there are also puppet shows and classical music performances. Performances are held only from Friday to Sunday.

---

are clogged with traffic, the weather oppressively hot, the air heavy with smog, and sights of any interest are uncooperatively thin on the ground. Even the movie stars, as one Chennaiker put it, are 'not that hot'.

While it may not boast the money of Mumbai (Bombay) or the buzz of Bengaluru (Bangalore), Chennai does feel friendlier than most cities its size. Chennai is so modest you wouldn't even know it's an economic powerhouse, much less a queen of showbiz: India's fourth-largest city is its most humble.

The major transport hub of the region, this 70-sq-km city is a conglomerate of urban villages connected by a maze of roads ruled by hard-line rickshaw drivers. Its central location and excellent plane, train and bus connections actually make it an interesting alternative entry point into India. If you do happen to be caught here between connections, it's certainly worth your while poking around the markets of George Town or taking a sunset stroll along pretty Marina Beach.

HISTORY

Chennai and surrounds have been attracting seafaring traders for centuries. As long as 2000 years ago, its residents traded and haggled with Chinese, Greek, Phoenician, Roman and Babylonian merchants. The Portuguese and the Dutch muscled in on this lucrative trade in the 16th century. The British, initially content to purchase spices and other goods from the Dutch, soon had enough of that and in 1639 established a settlement in the fishing village of Madraspatnam. The British East India Company erected Fort St George in 1653.

By the 18th century, the British East India Company had to contend with the French. Robert Clive (Clive of India), a key player in the British campaign, recruited an army of 2000 sepoys (Indian soldiers in British

TAMIL NADU

CHENNAI (MADRAS)

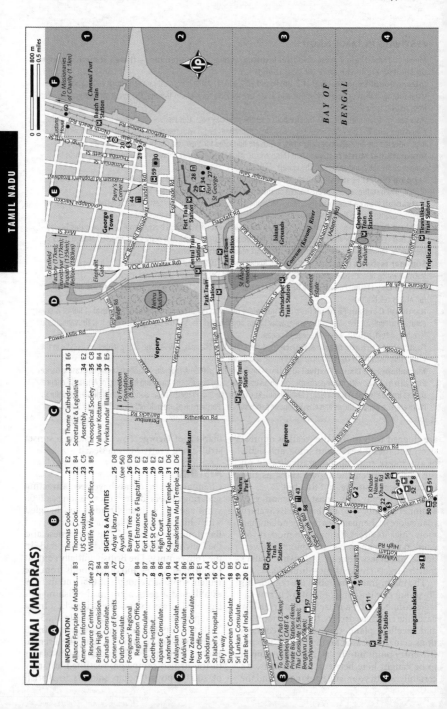

INFORMATION

Alliance Française de Madras..1	B3
American Information	
Resource Center.............(see 23)	
British High Comission............2	B4
Canadian Consulate....................3	B4
Conservator of Forests...............4	A7
Dutch Consulate..........................5	C7
Foreigners' Regional	
Registration Office...................6	B4
German Consulate.......................7	B7
Goethe-Institut...........................8	B4
Japanese Consulate.....................9	B6
Landmark....................................10	B4
Malaysian Consulate..................11	A4
Maldives Consulate....................12	B6
New Zealand Consulate.............13	B5
Post Office.................................14	E1
Sahodaran..................................15	A4
St Isabel's Hospital...................16	C6
Sify i-way.................................17	C5
Singaporean Consulate.............18	B5
Sri Lankan Consulate................19	C5
State Bank of India...................20	E1

Thomas Cook............................21	E2
Thomas Cook............................22	B4
US Consulate.............................23	C5
Wildlife Warden's Office...........24	B5

SIGHTS & ACTIVITIES

Adyar Library..............................25	D8
Ayush....................................(see 56)	
Banyan Tree................................26	D8
Fort Entrance & Flagstaff...........27	E2
Fort Museum..............................28	E2
Fort St George............................29	E2
High Court...................................30	E2
Kapaleeshwarar Temple.............31	D6
Ramakrishna Mutt Temple..........32	D6

San Thome Cathedral.................33	E6
Secretariat & Legislative	
Assembly...................................34	E2
Theosophical Society.................35	C8
Valluvar Kottam.........................36	B4
Vivekanandar Illam....................37	E5

800 m
0.5 miles

BAY OF BENGAL

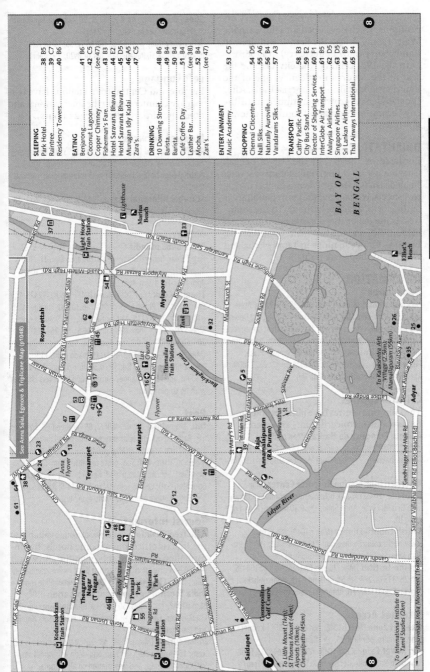

SLEEPING
Park Hotel	38 B5
Raintree	39 C7
Residency Towers	40 B6

EATING
Benjarong	41 B6
Coconut Lagoon	42 C5
Copper Chimney	(see 47)
Fisherman's Fare	43 B3
Hotel Saravana Bhavan	44 E2
Hotel Saravana Bhavan	45 D5
Murugan Idly Kadai	46 A5
Zara's	47 C5

DRINKING
10 Downing Street	48 B6
Barista	49 B4
Barista	50 B4
Café Coffee Day	51 B4
Leather Bar	(see 38)
Mocha	52 B4
Zara's	(see 47)

ENTERTAINMENT
Music Academy	53 C5

SHOPPING
Chennai Citicentre	54 D5
Nalli Silks	55 A6
Naturally Auroville	56 B4
Varadarams Silks	57 A3

TRANSPORT
Cathy Pacific Airways	58 B3
City Bus Stand	59 E2
Director of Shipping Services	60 F1
InterGlobe Air Transport	61 B5
Malaysia Airlines	62 D5
Singapore Airlines	63 D5
Sri Lankan Airlines	64 B5
Thai Airways International	65 B4

service) and launched a series of military expeditions which developed into the Carnatic Wars. Facing defeat, the French withdrew to Pondicherry (now Puducherry) in 1756.

In the 19th century, the city became the seat of the Madras Presidency, one of the four divisions of British Imperial India. After Independence, growth continued until the city became the significant southern gateway it is today.

ORIENTATION
Bordered on the east by the Bay of Bengal, Chennai is a sprawling combination of several small districts. George Town, a jumble of narrow streets, bazaars and the court buildings, is in the north, near the harbour. To the southwest is the major thoroughfare of Anna Salai (Mount Rd) and the two main train stations: Egmore, for destinations in Tamil Nadu, and Central, for interstate trains.

INFORMATION
Bookshops
Higginbothams (Map p1048; ☎ 28513519; 116 Anna Salai; ☿ 9am-8pm Mon-Sat, 10.30am-7.30pm Sun) Decent English-language book selection. Has a branch at the airport.
Landmark (☿ 9am-9pm Mon-Sat, 10.30am-9pm Sun) Anna Salai (Map p1048; ☎ 28495995; Spencer Plaza, Phase II); Nungambakkam (Map pp1044-5; ☎ 28221000; Apex Plaza, Nungambakkam High Rd)

Cultural Centres
The following centres have libraries and sometimes sponsor concerts, films and events.
Alliance Française de Madras (Map pp1044-5; ☎ 28279803; www.af-madras.org; 24/40 College Rd, Nungambakkam; ☿ 9am-7pm Mon-Fri, 9.30am-1.30pm Sat)
American Information Resource Center (Map pp1044-5; ☎ 28112000; http://americanlibrary.in.library .net; Gemini Circle, Anna Salai; ☿ 9.30am-5pm Mon-Fri) Bring ID.
British Council Library (Map p1048; ☎ 42050600; www.britishcouncilonline.org; 737 Anna Salai; ☿ 11am-7pm Mon-Sat) Monthly membership is Rs200.
Goethe-Institut (Max Mueller Bhavan; Map pp1044-5; ☎ 28331314/2; 4 5th St, Rutland Gate, Nungambakkam; ☿ 9am-4pm Mon-Fri, library 11am-6pm Tue-Sat)

Internet Access
Internet Zone (Map p1048; ☎ 42145885; 1 Kennet Lane, Egmore; per hr Rs25; ☿ 8am-10pm)
Log In Net Cafe (Map p1048; ☎ 52141648; 35 Triplicane High Rd, Triplicane; per hr Rs15; ☿ 9am-11pm)

SGee (Map p1048; ☎ 42310391; 20 Vallabha Agraharam St, Triplicane; per hr Rs20; ☿ 24hr)
Sify i-way (Map pp1044-5; ☎ 6551755; 59 Dr Radhakrishnan Salai, Royapettah; per hr Rs20; ☿ 24hr)

Left Luggage
Egmore and Central train stations have left-luggage counters, as do the international and domestic airports (Rs10 per 24 hours).

Medical Services
Apollo Hospital (Map p1048; ☎ 28293333, emergency 28290792; www.apollohospitals.com; 21 Greams Lane) Cutting-edge hospital popular with international 'medical tourists'.
St Isabel's Hospital (Map pp1044-5; ☎ 24662611; 18 Oliver Rd, Mylapore)

Money
State Bank of India George Town (Map pp1044-5; 22 Rajaji Salai, George Town; ☿ 10am-4pm Mon-Fri, 10am-1pm Sat); Anna Salai (Map p1048; Anna Salai; ☿ 10am-4pm Mon-Fri, 10am-1pm Sat)
Thomas Cook Anna Salai (Map p1048; ☎ 28492423/4; Spencer Plaza, Phase I; ☿ 9.30am-6.30pm); Egmore (Map p1048; ☎ 28553276; 45 Montieth Rd; ☿ 9.30am-6pm Mon-Sat); George Town (Map pp1044-5; ☎ 25342374; 20 Rajaji Salai; ☿ 9.30am-6pm Mon-Sat); Nungambakkam (Map pp1044-5; ☎ 28274941; Eldorado Bldg, 112 Nungambakkam High Rd; ☿ 9.30am-6.30pm Mon-Fri, 9.30am-noon Sat) Changes currency and travellers cheques with no commission.

Post
DHL (Map p1048; ☎ 4214886/7; 85 Pantheon Rd, Egmore; ☿ 8am-7pm) For secure international parcel delivery.
Post office Anna Salai (Map p1048; ☿ 8am-8.30pm Mon-Sat, 10am-4pm Sun, poste restante 10am-6pm Mon-Sat); Egmore (Map p1048; Kennet Lane; ☿ 10am-6pm Mon-Sat); George Town (Map pp1044-5; Rajaji Salai; ☿ 8am-8.30pm Mon-Sat, 10am-4pm Sun)

Tourist Information
The free **CityInfo** (www.explocity.com), available at the tourist office and at some hotels, has information on restaurants, nightlife and what's on. Also check out **Chennai Best** (www.chennaibest .com) and **Chennai Online** (www.chennaionline.com).
India Tourism Development Corporation (ITDC; Map p1048; ☎ 28281250; www.attindiatourism.com; 29 Cherian Cres, Egmore; ☿ 10am-5.30pm Mon-Sat) Hotel and tour bookings only.
Indiatourism (Map p1048; ☎ 28460285; indtour@vsnl .com; 154 Anna Salai; ☿ 9am-6pm Mon-Fri, 9am-1pm Sat) Good for maps and information on all of India.

Tamil Nadu Tourism Complex (TTDC; Map p1048; ☎ 25367850; www.tamilnadutourism.org; 2 Wallajah Rd, Triplicane; ☒ 10am-5.30pm Mon-Fri) Brochure-filled state tourist offices from all over India. The tour-booking desk at the Tamil Nadu office (☎ 25383333) is open 24 hours.

Travel Agencies
Madura Travel Service (Map p1048; ☎ 28192002; www.maduratravel.com; Kennet Lane, Egmore; ☒ 24hr) **SP Travels & Tours** (Map p1048; ☎ 28604001; sptravels1@eth.net; 90 Anna Salai, Triplicane; ☒ 9.30am-6.30pm Mon-Sat)

Visa Extensions
Foreigners' Regional Registration Office (Map pp1044-5; ☎ 28251721; Shastri Bhavan, Haddows Rd, Nungambakkam; ☒ 9.30am-noon Mon-Fri) With some complicated wrangling and copious doses of patience, some travellers have managed to procure visa extensions here. Theoretically, they take 10 days to process.

DANGERS & ANNOYANCES
While it may seem that Chennai autorickshaw drivers take pride in being the city's biggest annoyance, this is probably just a coincidence: convincing a driver to use the meter is a Vatican-certified miracle; fares border on the astronomical; and post-arrival disputes over pre-agreed fares are not uncommon. Avoid paying up front.

Tempting offers of Rs50 'tours' of the city sound too good to be true. They are. Expect to spend the day being dragged from one shop or emporium to another.

If you have a serious problem with a driver, mentioning a call to the **traffic police** (☎ 103) can defuse the conflict. See p1058 for details on other modes of transport.

SIGHTS
Egmore & Central Chennai
GOVERNMENT MUSEUM
Housed across several British-built buildings known as the Pantheon Complex, this excellent **museum** (Map p1048; ☎ 28193238; www .chennaimuseum.org; 486 Pantheon Rd, Egmore; Indian/foreigner Rs15/250, camera/video Rs200/500; ☒ 9.30am-5pm Sat-Thu) is Chennai's best.

The main building has a respectable **archaeological section** representing all the major South Indian periods, including Chola, Vijayanagar, Hoysala and Chalukya. Don't miss the intricate marble reliefs on display from Amaravathi temple in Andhra Pradesh (p976). Further along is a **natural history and zoology** section with a motley collection of skeletons and stuffed birds and animals.

In Gallery 3, the **bronze gallery** has a superb and beautifully presented collection of Chola art. Among the impressive pieces is the bronze of Ardhanariswara, the androgynous incarnation of Shiva and Parvati.

The same ticket gets you into the **National Art Gallery**, the **children's museum** and a small **modern art gallery**, all located in the same complex.

VALLUVAR KOTTAM
This **memorial** (Map pp1044-5; Valluvar Kottam High Rd, Kodambakkam; ☒ 9am-7.30pm) honours the Tamil

---

THE ICE HOUSE
Before it was a shrine to Swami Vivekananda (see p1048), this beautiful, pink wedding-cake building on Chennai's promenade served as the town's sole refrigerator.

From Boston, USA, Frederic Tudor – known as the 'Ice King' – was the first to bring the cooling magic of ice to the subcontinent in 1833. Chipped off in huge blocks from New England's wintry slopes and cleverly wrapped in insulating woodchips, nearly two-thirds of the precious cargo survived its maiden sea voyage to Calcutta aboard the clipper *Tuscany*. These precious and ephemeral goods (the first real whitegoods) were highly prized by British expatriates of the East India Company. Soon, insulated depots were being built in Calcutta, Bombay and Madras to store the ice upon its arrival; Madras' dainty Victorian-style 'Ice House' was built for this purpose around 1842. The Ice King's business was successful for decades, until the discovery of ice-making through steaming led to its eventual collapse in 1880, when the Ice House was sold to Biligiri Iyengar of Madras.

In 1897, Swami Vivekananda had returned from the USA, passing through Madras and spending nine days as a guest at the Ice House. After his departure, a short-lived shrine was established in the basement of the building with the help of its owner. The government then acquired the building in 1917 and used it variously as different hostels and a school until 1997, when the Tamil government dedicated the building as a permanent exhibit of Swami Vivekananda's life.

TAMIL NADU

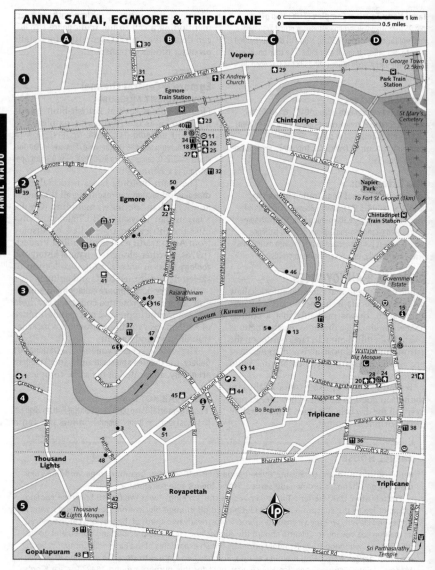

ANNA SALAI, EGMORE & TRIPLICANE

poet Thiruvalluvar and his classic work, the *Thirukural*. A weaver by trade, Thiruvalluvar lived around the 1st century BC in what is present-day Chennai and wrote this famed poem, providing a moral code for millions of followers. The three-level memorial replicates ancient Tamil architecture and boasts an immense 35m chariot, as well as an enor-mous auditorium and inscriptions of the *Thirukural*'s 1330 couplets.

VIVEKANANDAR ILLAM

The **Vivekananda House** (Map pp1044-5; ☎ 28446188; Kamarajar Salai, Triplicane; adult/child Rs2/1; ☑ 10am-1pm & 3-7pm Thu-Tue) is interesting not only for the dis-plays on the famous 'wandering monk', but

INFORMATION			SLEEPING			Spencer's Daily	(see 45)
Apollo Hospital	1	A4	Broad Lands Lodge	20	D4	Vasanta Bhavan	40 B1
Australian Consulate	2	C4	Cristal Guest House	21	D4	Vasantha Bhavan	(see 23)
British Council Library	3	B4	Hotel Ashoka	22	B2		
DHL	4	B2	Hotel Chandra Park	23	B1	DRINKING	
Higginbothams	5	C3	Hotel Comfort	24	D4	Café Coffee Day	41 A3
India Tourism Development			Hotel Pandian	25	B2		
Corporation (ITDC)	6	B4	Hotel Regent	26	B2	ENTERTAINMENT	
Indiatourism	7	B4	Masa	27	B2	Sathyam Cinema	42 A5
Internet Zone	8	B2	Paradise Guest House	28	D4		
Landmark	(see 45)		Royal Regency	29	C1	SHOPPING	
Log In Net Cafe	9	D3	Salvation Army Red Shield Guest			Amethyst	43 A5
Madura Travel Service	(see 8)		House	30	B1	Fabindia	44 C4
Post Office (Anna Salai)	10	C3	YWCA International Guest			Fabindia	(see 45)
Post Office (Egmore)	11	B2	House	31	B1	Spencer Plaza	45 B4
SGee	12	D4					
SP Travels & Tours	13	C3	EATING			TRANSPORT	
State Bank of India	14	C4	Amethyst	(see 43)		Air Canada	46 C3
Tamil Nadu Tourism Complex			Annapurna	32	B2	Air France	(see 50)
(TTDC)	15	D3	Hotel Comfort	(see 24)		Air India	47 B3
Thomas Cook	16	B3	Hotel Saravana Bhavan	33	C3	American Airlines	48 A5
Thomas Cook	(see 45)		Hotel Saravana Bhavan	34	B2	Indian Airlines	(see 47)
			Hotel Saravana Bhavan	35	A5	Jet Airways	49 B3
SIGHTS & ACTIVITIES			Jam Bazaar	36	D4	Kingfisher Airlines	(see 47)
Government Museum	17	A2	Ponnusamy Hotel	37	B3	KLM	50 B2
Mahabodhi Society of Sri Lanka	18	B2	Ratna Cafe	38	D4	Lufthansa	51 B4
National Art Gallery	19	A3	Sparky's Diner	39	A2	Private Bus Stand	(see 34)

also for the semicircular structure in which it's housed (see boxed text, p1047). Swami Vivekananda stayed here briefly in 1897 and preached his ascetic philosophy to adoring crowds. The museum houses a collection of photographs and memorabilia from the swami's life, a gallery of religious historical paintings and the 'meditation room' where Vivekananda stayed. Free one-hour meditation classes are held on Wednesday nights at 7pm.

South Chennai

Chennai's most active and impressive temple, the ancient Shiva **Kapaleeshwarar Temple** (Map pp1044–5; Kutchery Rd, Mylapore; ⊗ 4am-noon & 4-8pm) is constructed in the Dravidian style and displays the architectural elements – rainbow-coloured *gopuram* (gateway tower), *mandapams* (pavilions in front of a temple) and a huge tank – found in the famous temple cities of Tamil Nadu.

The tranquil, leafy grounds of the **Ramakrishna Mutt Temple** (Map pp1044–5; RK Mutt Rd; ⊗ 4.30-11.45am & 3-9pm, puja 8am) are a world away from the chaos and crazy rickshaw drivers outside. Orange-clad monks glide around and there's a reverential feel here. The temple itself is a handsome shrine constructed in themes paying homage to India's major religions. It's open to followers of any faith for meditation.

Originally built by the Portuguese in 1504, then rebuilt in neo-Gothic style in 1893, **San**

Thome Cathedral (Map pp1044–5; ☎ 24985455; Kamarajar Salai) is a soaring Roman Catholic church between Kapaleeshwarar Temple and Marina Beach. In the basement is a chapel housing the tomb of St Thomas the Apostle (Doubting Thomas), who it is said brought Christianity to the subcontinent in the 1st century.

During an early morning or evening stroll along the 13km sandy stretch of **Marina Beach** (Map pp1044–5) you'll pass cricket matches, kids flying kites, fortune-tellers, fish markets and families enjoying the sea breeze. This beach was especially hard hit during the 2004 tsunami, with around 200 recorded casualties, most of them children. Don't swim here – strong rips make it dangerous.

Between the Adyar River and the coast, the 100 hectares of the **Theosophical Society** (Map pp1044–5; Lattice Bridge Rd; ⊗ 8-10am & 2-5pm Mon-Fri, 8-10am Sat) provide one of the few peaceful retreats from the city. The sprawling grounds contain a church, mosque, Buddhist shrine and Hindu temple. There's a huge variety of native and introduced trees, including a famed 400-year-old **banyan tree** whose branches offer reprieving shade for over 40,000 sq ft. The **Adyar Library** (⊗ 9am-5pm) here has an immense collection of books on religion and philosophy, from thousand-year-old Buddhist scrolls to intricate, handmade 19th-century bibles. If you're interested in the Theosophical Society's philosophy, call into the public relations office and chat with the director.

TRADITIONAL TRADERS

George Town, the area that grew around the fort, retains much of its original flavour. This is the wholesale centre of Chennai (Madras). Many backstreets, bordered by NSC Bose Rd, Krishna Koil St, Mint St and Rajaji Salai, are entirely given over to selling one particular type of merchandise as they have for hundreds of years – paper goods in Anderson St, fireworks in Badrian St and so on. Even if you're not in the market for anything, wander the mazelike streets to see another aspect of Indian life flowing seamlessly from the past into the present.

George Town
FORT ST GEORGE

Finished around 1653 by the British East India Company, the **fort** (Map pp1044-5; 10am-5pm) has undergone many facelifts over the years. Inside the vast perimeter walls is now a precinct housing the **Secretariat & Legislative Assembly**. The 46m-high **flagstaff** at the main entrance is a mast salvaged from a 17th-century shipwreck.

The **Fort Museum** (25670389; Indian/foreigner Rs5/100, video Rs25; 10am-5pm Sat-Thu) has military memorabilia from the British and French East India Companies, as well as the Raj and Muslim administrations.

HIGH COURT

Built in 1892, this red Indo-Saracenic structure at Parry's Corner is said to be the largest judicial building in the world after the Courts of London. You can wander around the court buildings (Map pp1044–5) and sit in on sessions.

Other Sights
LITTLE MOUNT & ST THOMAS MOUNT

It is believed that from around AD 58, St Thomas lived in hiding at **Little Mount** (Chinnamalai; off Map pp1044-5; Saidapet). The cave still bears what some believe to be Thomas' handprint, left when he escaped through an opening that miraculously appeared. Three kilometres on, **St Thomas Mount** (Parangi Malai) is thought to be the site of Thomas' martyrdom in AD 72. Both mounts are about 1km from the Saidapet and St Thomas Mount train stations, respectively.

ACTIVITIES

Go for a 45-minute *abhyangam* (oil treatment; Rs650) or an extended ayurvedic treatment at **Ayush** (Map pp1044-5; 65195195; www.leverayush.com; 6 Khader Nawaz Khan Rd, Nungambakkam; 7am-7pm). It also offers one-hour yoga classes (Rs150) or 21-day courses (Rs1200).

COURSES
Language

International Institute of Tamil Studies (off Map pp1044-5; 22540992; www.ulakaththamizh.org; Central Polytechnic Campus, Adyar) Runs intensive one-month courses in Tamil.

Meditation

Mahabodhi Society of Sri Lanka (Map p1048; 28192458; 12 Kennet Lane, Egmore) Dharma talks, meditation and special *pujas* (offerings or prayers) on full-moon and other days.

TAMIL LITERATURE

The Tamil language is the oldest and purest of India's four Dravidian languages, and Tamil literature boasts an illustrious history spanning over two millennia.

The earliest era of Tamil writing was the Sangam period (from the first century BC to the 5th century AD); remains of the writing of this era have been gathered into two collections known as the Eight Anthologies and the Ten Idyls. Secular writing of this time was rich with images of everyday life – seasons, plants, animals and places.

The medieval period that followed saw Jain, Buddhist and Muslim influences take control of the Tamil region, with didactic Tamil texts of the time leading a religious renaissance. Tamil literature from this period was famed for its wealth of ancient morals and values, and is still considered some of the most important world literature of the era.

The changing socio-political scene of Tamil Nadu continued to inspire Tamil writing, with the most recent, modern period of Tamil literature owing its roots to influences from colonial British writers of the 19th century.

A MODERN CLASSIC – THE ENFIELD BULLET

The classic lines, the guttural purr – to motoring enthusiasts India's Enfield motorcycle is as unmistakable as the silhouette of the Taj Mahal. The iconic Enfield Bullet has been manufactured in India since 1955, boasting the longest production run of any bike anywhere in the world.

The Enfield story begins in country England, where the factory of George Townsend Jr first took a stab at making newfangled bicycles in the 1880s. The following decade the company also started supplying rifle parts to a factory in Enfield, assuming the name Royal Enfield and stamping the slogan 'made like a gun' on their bicycles. Their first twin-engine motorbike was introduced in 1909.

During WWI demand for Enfield's two-wheeled transport boomed. The famous 'Bullet' moniker was first applied to Enfield's 1931 four-valve, single cylinder bike, a machine that was in high demand during WWII.

The 350cc Bullet was first manufactured in India by Madras Motors in 1955 to supply the Indian Army. During the 1970s increasing competition from Japan's light and compact scooters forced Enfield's UK factories to close up shop. By this time, Enfield India was still soldiering on, a practically independent company that made their own modifications to the original Bullet design to better suit the subcontinent. By 1989, Enfield India was exporting their sought-after vintage-styled bikes – made to the same specifications for over 30 years – back to the UK and Europe.

The original Bullet remains in production today at the **Enfield Factory** (☎ 42230245; www.royalenfield.com; Tiruvottiyur), 17km outside of Chennai. Half-hour tours (Rs600) run on Saturdays at 10.30am. Enfield's legendary motorbikes, designed in 1955 but manufactured just last week, truly give meaning to the term 'modern-day classic'.

Vivekanandar Illam (Map pp1044-5; ☎ 28446188; Kamarajar Salai, Triplicane) Free one-hour classes on Wednesday nights at 7pm.

TOURS

TTDC (p1046) conducts half-day city tours (non-AC/AC Rs125/180) and day trips to Mamallapuram (non-AC/AC Rs350/500), Puducherry (non-AC Rs400) and Tirupathi (AC Rs665). Book at ITDC (p1046) or TTDC.

SLEEPING

Hotels in Chennai are pricier than in the rest of Tamil Nadu and don't as a rule offer much bang-for-your-buck.

Egmore, on and around chaotic Kennet Lane, is best for budget accommodation, as is the Triplicane High Rd area, which is a little further out and mildly less chaotic. Egmore is also where you'll find the majority of midrange sleeping options, while the top-end hotels lie further out in leafy, southwest Chennai.

Many hotels in Chennai fill up by noon.

Budget
EGMORE
Salvation Army Red Shield Guest House (Map p1048; ☎ 25321821; 15 Ritherdon Rd; dm/r Rs100/300; ⊠) Though bordering on the dingy, this surprisingly popular cheapie lies in a quiet spot north of Egmore station. The bathrooms make only the most basic concessions to hygiene, though the staff here are helpful. Checkout is 9am.

Hotel Regent (Map p1048; ☎ 28191801; 11 Kennet Lane; s/d Rs200/350) The pick of the litter when it comes to budget digs in them 'ere parts. The frequently cleaned rooms are located around a courtyard and blissfully set back from much of Kennet Lane's mayhem.

Masa (Map p1048; ☎ 28193954; 15 Kennet Lane; s/d from Rs270/460) The grotty and windowless abodes here will usually reward a last-ditch effort of finding a room if all other places are full (as they often are).

YWCA International Guest House (Map p1048; ☎ 25324234; ywcaigh@indiainfo.com; Poonamallee High Rd; s/d/tr from Rs600/750/1000; ⊠) Set around sprawling, green and shady grounds right near the train station, the YWCA still manages to offer up healthy doses of hush. Rooms are housed in an oversized building, where the dregs of colonial-era charm still hang around the hallway lounge. The old rooms adhere to the most demanding levels of cleanliness.

TRIPLICANE
Cristal Guest House (Map p1048; ☎ 28513011; 34 CNK Rd; s/d Rs150/200) In a modern building adhering

to the white-tile-on-every-surface school of interior design, the clean abodes here win our 'cheapest rooms in Chennai' award.

Paradise Guest House (Map p1048; ☎ 28594252; paradisegh@hotmail.com; 17 Vallabha Agraharam St; s/d/tr from Rs250/300/400; ✖) Travellers agree that the Paradise boasts some of the best-value digs on this street. Expect sparkling white tiles, a breezy rooftop, friendly staff and hot water by the steaming bucket.

Broad Lands Lodge (Map p1048; ☎ 28545573; broadlandshotel@yahoo.com; 18 Vallabha Agraharam St; s/d from Rs300/400, without bathroom from Rs270/300) At this old-school favourite of the dreadlocked brigade, the warrens of rooms puncture a creaky colonial-era building like holes in Swiss cheese. Strangely, visitors don't seem to mind the barebone, idiosyncratic rooms, the plain concrete floors or the dank shared bathrooms – perhaps the leafy, subdued courtyards and happy communal vibe trumps these shortcomings.

Midrange
EGMORE
Hotel Pandian (Map p1048; ☎ 28191010; 15 Kennet Lane; s/d from Rs700/1100; ✖) This decent pad bridges the budget and midrange categories with slightly dated, wood-panelled rooms that are kept in reasonably good nick.

Hotel Chandra Park (Map p1048; ☎ 28191177; www .hotelchandrapark.com; 9 Gandhi Irwin Rd; s/d with AC incl breakfast from Rs850/950; ✖) With other hotels practically doubling their prices every year, the Chandra Park prices remain mysteriously low. Standard rooms are small but have clean towels and tight, white sheets. Throw in a hearty buffet breakfast and classy front lobby, and this place offers superb value by Chennai standards.

Hotel Ashoka (Map p1048; ☎ 28553377; www.ballal grouphotels.com; 47 Pantheon Rd; s/d Rs905/1250, with AC Rs1250/1500; ✖) If a 1950s Miami architect was asked to design a space-age hotel on Mars, the Ashoka might be what he'd come up with. The novelty of the funky design will soon wear off, however, and you'll be left with old-school rooms covered in a thousand layers of paint and filled with musty air. The cottages (single/double Rs2400/2800) have more of an Austin Powers ambience: lush red carpeting, fridges and cocoonlike tubs.

Royal Regency (Map p1048; ☎ 25611777; www.royal regency.co.in; 26-27 Poonamallee High Rd; r from Rs2300; ✖) The splashes of colour adorning the outside of this hotel, smack-bang between Central and Egmore train stations, cannot be missed. It's

all very businesslike inside, sparsely furnished and offering the minimum needed for a solid night's sleep.

TRIPLICANE
Hotel Comfort (Map p1048; ☎ 28587661; www.hotel comfortonline.com; 22 Vallabha Agraharam St; s/d from Rs1100/1200; ✖) Fresh from a major round of renovations, the immaculate rooms here now offer goodies like flat-screen TVs and bright-orange bathrooms. Perfectly comfy.

Top End
The following hotels have central AC and multicuisine restaurant and bar, and they accept credit cards. Unless stated otherwise, checkout is noon.

Residency Towers (Map pp1044-5; ☎ 28156363; www .theresidency.com; Sir Theagaraya Nagar Rd, T Nagar; s/d from Rs5000/5500; ✖ 🖳 ▣ ✖) At this price, it's like Residency Towers doesn't know what a good thing it has going: five-star elegance with a lot more personality. Every floor is decorated differently, but rooms all have sliding doors in front of windows to block out light and noise, dark-wood furniture and thoughtful touches.

our pick Raintree (Map pp1044-5; ☎ 24304050; www.raintreehotels.com; 120 St Mary's Rd, Mylapore; s/d from Rs7500/8500; ✖ 🖳 ▣) A rarity in Chennai, this ecofriendly lodge oozes personality from every pore. Floors are made of bamboo, wastewater is treated and used for gardening, and electricity conservation holds pride of place. But then the sleek, minimalist rooms are some of the most stylish and comfortable around, and the rooftop infinity pool (which doubles as insulation) has a gorgeous wooden terrace with views of the sea.

Park Hotel (Map pp1044-5; ☎ 42676000; www .theparkhotels.com; 601 Anna Salai; s/d from Rs11,000/13,000; ✖ 🖳) We love this uberchic boutique hotel, which flaunts stylish elements like frosted-glass partitions, towering indoor bamboo gardens and oversized doors. The rooms are petite but have all the mod cons, including funky bathrooms separated from the boudoir by an opaque glass wall. It's all pretty swish, and as a bonus you have the trendy Leather Bar (p1054) on the premises.

EATING
Chennai is packed with classic 'meals' joints, which serve thalis (traditional South Indian 'all-you-can-eat' meals) for lunch and dinner, and tiffin (snacks) such as *idlis* (rice dump-

lings) and dosas (paper-thin lentil-flour pancakes) the rest of the day. It's tempting – and feasible – to eat every meal at one of Chennai's dozen Saravana Bhavan restaurants (below), where you can count on quality vegetarian food.

The Mylapore area has many good independent restaurants, so head there if you're looking for something more refined.

Restaurants
EGMORE
Vasanta Bhavan (Map p1048; 33 Gandhi Irwin Rd; mains Rs40-60; ☻ 5am-11pm) Excellent 'meals' (Rs40). The older Vasantha Bhavan down the street at No 10 is not as good but has more charm and also sweets.

Annapurna (Map p1048; ☎ 28523037; 23 Pantheon Rd; mains Rs40-60; ☻ lunch & dinner Mon-Sat, lunch Sun) A bustling hole-in-the-wall that serves up a lip-smacking taste of Bengal in Chennai's Egmore district. Try the *bhetki paturi* (fish baked in banana leaves). Yum.

Ponnusamy Hotel (Map p1048; Wellington Estate, 24 Ethiraj Rd; mains Rs40-85; ☻ lunch & dinner) This well-known non-veg place serves curry, biryani (steamed rice with meat or vegetables) and Chettinad specialities. Look out for interesting options like pigeon fry and rabbit masala.

Hotel Saravana Bhavan Egmore (Map p1048; 21 Kennet Lane; ☻ 6am-10.30pm); George Town (Map pp1044–5; 209 NSC Bose Rd); Mylapore (Map pp1044–5; 101 Dr Radhakrishnan Salai; ☻ 7am-11pm); Thousand Lights (Map p1048; 293 Peter's Rd; ☻ lunch & dinner); Triplicane (Map p1048; Shanthi Theatre Complex, 48 Anna Salai; ☻ 7am-11pm) Dependably delish, 'meals' at the Saravana Bhavans run around Rs50, though the Mylapore locale has some 'special meals' for Rs95 and up. The Thousand Lights branch is more upscale, with an Rs180 buffet and silver cutlery.

Fisherman's Fare (Map pp1044–5; ☎ 28362071; Major Ramanathan Salai (Spur Tank Rd); meals Rs110-300; ☻ 11am-10pm) This small, spotless, AC dining room gets packed to the rafters come lunchtime, with punters digging into well-prepared fish fare ranging from shrimp to fish curries to tandoori fish. There's a great lunchtime special for Rs155.

Sparky's Diner (Map p1048; ☎ 42144206; Ramanathan Salai (Spur Tank Rd); meals Rs140-250; ☻ lunch & dinner) Sparky's is a wall-to-wall homage to kitsch. This expat-run 'American' diner is plastered with US state licence plates and movie posters, has Sinatra crooning on the radio, and decks its waiters out in baseball shirts. Look out for

OK American specials like deep-fried chicken or Cajun gumbo.

TRIPLICANE
Ratna Cafe (Map p1048; ☎ 28487181; 255 Triplicane High Rd; dishes Rs25-60) Though often crowded and cramped, Ratna is renowned in Triplicane and beyond for its scrumptious *idlis* and the hearty doses of *sambar* (soupy lentil dish with cubed vegetables) that go with it.

Hotel Comfort (Map p1048; 22 Vallabha Agraharam; mains Rs30-100; ☻ dinner) The menu is typical Indian and Chinese, but the rooftop garden is green, cosy and relaxed. Beer is served.

GOPALAPURAM
Amethyst (Map p1048; ☎ 28353581; 14 Padmavathi Rd; meals Rs105-260; ☻ 10am-10pm) Set in a stunning lemon-coloured, colonial-era building, this place is comfortably posh. The lush garden setting and patio dining takes the cake for restaurant ambience. Expect comfy couches, tasteful antique furniture and afternoon tea with lovely cucumber-and-mint-chutney sandwiches.

MYLAPORE & AROUND
Murugan Idly Kadai (Map pp1044–5; ☎ 42025076; 77 GN Chetty Rd; T Nagar; dishes Rs30-60) Those in the know generally agree this particular branch of the small chain serves some of the best *idli* and South Indian meals in town. We heartily concur.

Coconut Lagoon (Map pp1044–5; ☎ 42020428; cnr Cathedral & TTK Rds, Alwarpet; mains Rs55-200; ☻ noon-3pm & 7-11.45pm) Excellent Keralan and Goan fare with a focus on seafood delicacies, such as *kari meen polli chathu* (fish masala steamed in banana leaf).

Zara's (Map pp1044–5; ☎ 28111462; 74 Cathedral Rd, Teynampet; tapas Rs70-250; ☻ 1-3pm & 6.30-11pm) Though this tiny place is a little tough to find, seekers will be rewarded by this ultracool tapas bar. Expect genuine Spanish flavour: everything from squid and olives to tortilla and sangria. Three-course lunch specials with wine or beer are a decent deal at Rs225/245 for veg/non-veg. The bar here doubles as a popular hang-out in it's own right (see p1054).

Copper Chimney (Map pp1044–5; ☎ 28115770; 74 Cathedral Rd, Teynampet; mains Rs140-250; ☻ noon-3pm & 6-11.30pm) Vegetarians might want to give this meat-centric place a wide berth, but others will drool over the yummy North Indian tandoori dishes served among plush furnishings.

Benjarong (Map pp1044-5; ☎ 24322640; 537 TTK Rd, Alwarpet; mains Rs140-500; ⏰ lunch & dinner) From the finely crafted furniture and calming ambience to the attentive service and superbly presented food, this Thai restaurant is an experience. Most mains are around Rs200.

Self-Catering

Jam Bazaar (Map p1048; cnr Ellis Rd & Bharathi Salai, Triplicane) Animated market bursting with fruit, vegetables and spices.

Spencer's Daily (Map p1048; ☎ 42140784; Spencer Plaza, Anna Salai; ⏰ 9.30am-9pm)

DRINKING
Cafes

Chennai is very much in the throes of India's cappuccino addiction.

Mocha (Map pp1044-5; D Khader Nawaz Khan Rd, Nungambakkam; coffee Rs20-180; ⏰ 11am-11pm) The young and beautiful come here for coffee, hookahs (water pipes; Rs195 to Rs245) and snacks (Rs50 to Rs150). Lovely outdoor garden.

Popular coffee chains are dotted around Chennai, including **Barista** (Map pp1044-5; Rosy Towers, Nungambakkam High Rd & D Khader Nawaz Khan Rd, Nungambakkam; coffee Rs20-50; ⏰ 7.30am-11.30pm) and **Café Coffee Day** (coffee Rs20-50; ⏰ 10am-11pm) Egmore (Map p1048; Alsa Mall, Montieth Rd); Nungambakkam (Map pp1044-5; 123/124 Nungambakkam High Rd).

Bars & Nightclubs

Chennai's nightlife scene throbs that little bit more every year, though it's no Bengaluru or Mumbai yet. It doesn't help that bars and clubs are supposed to close at midnight and are restricted to hotels.

Zara's (Map pp1044-5; ☎ 28111462; 74 Cathedral Rd, Teynampet; cocktails Rs230-350; ⏰ 1-3pm & 6.30-11pm) Where the cool people come on weekends for tapas (see p1053), sangria, house-infused vodka (jalapeño, almond, cinnamon) and inventive mocktails. Dress nice.

Geoffrey's Pub (off Map pp1044-5; ☎ 24757788; Radha Park Inn Hotel, 171 Jawaharlal Nehru Salai, Arumbakkam; ⏰ 6-11pm Wed-Mon) This modern version of the English pub is one of the few places in Chennai that hosts live music nightly. Not always great music, but music nonetheless. The atmosphere is casual, with Kollywood types occasionally gracing the place with their presence.

Leather Bar (Map pp1044-5; ☎ 42144000; Park Hotel, 601 Anna Salai; ⏰ 6-11pm) Thankfully 'leather' refers to floor and wall coverings rather than kinky jock-straps and dungeons. This modish pad has talented mixologists dishing up fancy drinks and DJs spinning happy dance tunes.

10 Downing Street (Map pp1044-5; ☎ 43546565; North Boag Rd, T Nagar; ⏰ 6-11pm) Also worth checking out, this English-themed pub is often packed with a mixed bag of punters.

ENTERTAINMENT
Classical Music & Dance

If you happen to be in Chennai around mid-December to mid-January, you're in for a treat: the Festival of Carnatic Music & Dance (see the boxed text, p1043) is a massive showcase of classical Tamil music and dance. Turn

---

KOLLYWOOD BLING

Tamil film fans – and they're known for their fanaticism – will tell you that their movies have always been technically superior to Hindi films. Far from living in Bollywood's shadow, Kollywood – named for Kodambakkam, the neighbourhood preferred by many studios and film people – has its own tradition of filmmaking founded on high-quality production, slightly more realistic plot lines and much more realistic heroes (ie they like them chubby and moustachioed).

Kollywood style, though, is changing. Bollywood's famous 'masala' format – that crowd-pleasing mix of drama, comedy, romance and action – is rubbing off on Tamil films, and vice versa. Bollywood's been remaking Tamil blockbusters, while the big-name celebs in Mumbai (Bombay) are working in Kollywood.

Kollywood comes second to Bollywood for revenue, and some say it even rivals it for distribution – with obsessed Tamil fans queuing up not only in Tamil Nadu's 1800 cinemas, but also in Sri Lanka, Malaysia, South Africa, Europe and the USA. Meanwhile, some Hindi film studios, hearing the ch-ching of Kollywood's success, have begun to get in on the action and produce Tamil films themselves – films which, to be sure, will be remade someday in Bollywood. And the circle begins again.

up to hear lectures, see demonstrations and view numerous concerts held around the Tamil capital.

Music Academy (Map pp1044–5; ☎ 28115162; cnr TKK Rd & Cathedral Rd) This is Chennai's most popular public venue for Carnatic classical music and Bharata Natyam dance. Many performances are free.

Kalakshetra Arts Village (off Map pp1044–5; ☎ 24521169; kshetra@vsnl.com; Dr Muthulakshmi Rd, Tiruvanmiyu; ☽ 10am-6pm) Founded in 1936, Kalakshetra is committed to reviving classical dance and music. Check out one of their regular performances, or a class (9am to 11am and 2pm to 4.30pm Monday to Friday). Four-month courses in music and dance cost Rs750 per month.

Cinema

Chennai has more than 100 cinemas, a reflection of the vibrant film industry here (see boxed text, opposite). Most screen Tamil films, but **Sathyam Cinema** (Map p1048; ☎ 28512425; 8 Thiruvika Rd, Royapettah; tickets Rs65-120) often shows English-language films alongside local fare.

SHOPPING

Theagaraya Nagar (aka T Nagar; Map pp1044–5) has great shopping, especially at Pondy Bazaar and around Panagal Park. Nungambakkam's shady D Khader Nawaz Khan Rd (Map pp1044–5) is an exceedingly pleasant lane of shops, cafes and galleries.

Most of the finest Kanchipuram silks turn up in Chennai (and Bengaluru), so consider doing your silk shopping here.

Amethyst (Map p1048; ☎ 28351627; 14 Padmavathi Rd, Gopalapuram; ☽ 11am-8pm) See what's the latest at this collection of shops in Sundar Mahal, a lovely heritage building. Clothes, Indo-Western jewellery, lacquer-ware and other home decor by India's hottest designers.

Fabindia Spencer Plaza (Map p1048; ☎ 42158015; Anna Salai; ☽ 11am-8pm); Woods Rd (Map p1048; ☎ 42027015; ☽ 10am-8pm) The Woods Rd shop has home and food sections, along with fabulous clothes.

Naturally Auroville (Map pp1044–5; ☎ 28330517; D Khader Nawaz Khan Rd, Nungambakkam; ☽ 10.30am-8pm Mon-Sat, 11.30am-7pm Sun) *Objets* (pottery, bedspreads, scented candles) and fine foods (organic coffees, breads and cheeses) from Auroville.

The best commercial shopping malls include **Spencer Plaza** (Map p1048; Anna Salai) and

Chennai Citicentre (Map pp1044–5; Dr Radhakrishnan Salai, Mylapore).

For silks, check out:

Nalli Silks (Map pp1044–5; ☎ 24344115; 9 Nageswaran Rd, T Nagar; ☽ 9.30am-9.30pm) The granddaddy of silk shops.

Varadarams Silks (Map pp1044–5; ☎ 28363867; 88 Harrington Rd, Chetpet; ☽ 10am-7.30pm Mon-Sat) Low-priced Kanchipuram silk.

GETTING THERE & AWAY
Air
AIRPORTS
Anna International Airport (☎ 22560551) in Tirusulam, 16km southwest of the centre, is efficient and not too busy, making Chennai a good entry or exit point. **Kamaraj domestic terminal** (☎ 22560551) is next door.

DOMESTIC AIRLINES
Domestic airlines with offices in Chennai include:

Indian Airlines (Map p1048; ☎ 28578153/4; airport 22561906; 19 Rukmani Lakshmi Pathy Rd (Marshalls Rd), Egmore)

IndiGo (☎ 22560286; airport)

Jet Airways (Map p1048; ☎ domestic 39893333, international 1800 225522; 41/43 Montieth Rd, Egmore; ☽ 9am-8pm Mon-Sat, 9am-7pm Sun) Also flies internationally.

Kingfisher Airlines (Map p1048; ☎ 28584366; 19 Rukmani Lakshmi Pathy Rd (Marshalls Rd), Egmore) Also has international flights.

Paramount Airways (☎ 22561667-70; airport)

SpiceJet (☎ 1800 1803333; airport)

INTERNATIONAL AIRLINES
Air Canada (Map p1048; ☎ 28582817; 8 Audithanar Rd, Egmore)

Air France (Map p1048; ☎ 1800 1800033; 42 Pantheon Rd, Egmore)

Air India (Map p1048; ☎ 1800 1801407; 19 Rukmani Lakshmi Pathy Rd (Marshalls Rd), Egmore)

American Airlines (Map p1048; ☎ 18001807300; Prince Centre, 248 Pathari Rd, Thousand Lights)

Cathay Pacific Airways (Map pp1044–5; ☎ 42988400; 47 Major Ramanathan Salai (Spur Tank Rd), Chetpet)

Gulf Air (☎ 28554417; airport)

InterGlobe Air Transport (Map pp1044–5; ☎ 28226149; Maalavika Centre, MGR Salai (Kodambakkam High Rd), Nungambakkam) For Air New Zealand, South African, United, Delta and Virgin Atlantic ticketing changes.

KLM (Map p1048; ☎ 1800 1800044; 42 Pantheon Rd, Egmore)

DOMESTIC FLIGHTS FROM CHENNAI (MADRAS)

Destination	Airline	Fare (US$)	Duration (hr)	Frequency
Bengaluru	IC	86	¾	2 daily
	9W	76	1	4 daily
	I7	71	¾	2 daily
	6E	63	1	daily
Delhi	IC	128	2½	4 daily
	9W	123	2½	4 daily
	6E	95	2½	3 daily
Goa	IC	130	1¼	3 weekly
	I7	101	1¼	daily
	6E	77	2½	daily
Hyderabad	IC	79	1	2 daily
	9W	74	1	3 daily
	I7	71	1	3 daily
	6E	56	1	daily
Kochi	IC	98	1	3 weekly
	9W	85	1	daily
	I7	81	1	3 daily
Kolkata	IC	138	2	daily
	9W	123	2	daily
	6E	82	2	2 daily
Mumbai	IC	145	2	4 daily
	9W	115	2	6 daily
	SG	84	2	2 daily
Port Blair	IC	136	2	daily
	9W	98	2	2 daily
Trivandrum	IC	95	1½	daily
	I7	91	1¼	2 daily
	9W	75	1½	daily

Note: Fares are one-way only.
Airline codes: 6E – IndiGo, 9W – Jet Airways, I7 – Paramount, IC – Indian Airlines, SG – SpiceJet.

Lufthansa (Map p1048; ☎ 30213500, airport 22569393; 167 Anna Salai) No walk-ins.
Malaysia Airlines (Map pp1044–5; ☎ 42191919; 90 Dr Radhakrishnan Salai, Mylapore)
Singapore Airlines (Map pp1044–5; ☎ 28473976; Westminster, 108 Dr Radhakrishnan Salai, Mylapore)
Sri Lankan Airlines (Translanka Air Travels; Map pp1044–5; ☎ 43921100; 4 Kodambakkam High Rd, Nungambakkam)
Thai Airways International (Map pp1044–5; ☎ 42173311; 31 Haddows Rd, Nungambakkam)

Boat

Passenger ships sail from the George Town harbour to Port Blair in the Andaman Islands (see p1125) every 10 days or so. The **Director of Shipping Services** (Map pp1044–5; ☎ 25226873; fax 25220841; Shipping Corporation Bldg, Rajaji Salai, George Town; ☉ 10am-4pm Mon-Sat) sells tickets (Rs1932 to Rs6221) for the 60-hour trip. You will need two photographs and three photocopies each of your passport identity page and visa.

Bus

Most Tamil Nadu (SETC) and other government buses operate from the insanely chaotic **Chennai Mofussil Bus Terminus** (CMBT; off Map pp1044–5; ☎ 23455858, 24794705; Jawaharlal Nehru Salai, Koyambedu), better known as Koyambedu CMBT, 7km west of town.

Buses 15 or 15B from Parry's Corner or Central train station, and 27B from Anna Salai or Egmore train station, all head there (Rs4, 45 minutes). An autorickshaw charges around Rs150 for the same ride.

SETC, Karnataka (KSRTC) and Andhra Pradesh (APRSTC) bus services cover the destinations listed in the boxed text (opposite), usually in the morning and late afternoon.

BUS SERVICES FROM CHENNAI (MADRAS)

Destination	Fare (Rs)	Duration (hr)	Frequency
Bengaluru	170-260	9	every 30min
Chidambaram	80-90	7	18 daily
Coimbatore	210-290	11½	every 30min
Ernakulam (Kochi)	425-650	16	daily
Hyderabad	350-400	12	5 daily
Kodaikanal	200-220	14	daily
Madurai	155-190	10	every 20min
Mamallapuram	40	2	every 15-30min
Mysore	200-235	11	10 daily
Ooty	250-310	14	2 daily
Puducherry	50-85	4	every 20min
Thanjavur	120-135	9	hourly
Tirupathi	60-70	4	every 30min
Trichy	120-185	8	every 15-30min
Trivandrum	325-425	17	6 daily

Several companies operate Volvo AC buses to the same destinations from the less overwhelming private-bus station next door; try **KPN** (☎ 24797998) or **Rathi Meena** (☎ 24791494). There's another, smaller private bus stand (Map p1048) opposite Egmore train station. These superdeluxe buses usually leave at night and cost two to three times more than ordinary buses.

Train

Interstate trains and those heading west generally depart from Central train station (Map pp1044–5), while trains heading south depart from Egmore (Map p1048). The **Train Reservation Complex** (☎ general 139, reservations 1361; ⊙ 8am-8pm Mon-Sat, 8am-2pm Sun) is in a separate 10-storey building just west of Central station;

MAJOR TRAINS FROM CHENNAI (MADRAS)

Destination	Train No & name	Fare (Rs)	Duration (hr)	Departure
Bengaluru	2007 *Shatabdi Exp**	530/1015	5	6am CC
	2609 *Bangalore Exp*	121/412	6½	1.20pm CC
Delhi	2615 *Grand Trunk Exp*	547/1504/2017	35	7.15pm CC
	2621 *Tamil Nadu Exp*	547/1504/2017	33	10pm CC
Coimbatore	6627 *West Coast Exp*	225/594/806	8½	11.30am CC
Goa	7311 *Vasco Exp***	359/973/1329	22	1.40pm CC
Hyderabad	2759 *Charminar Exp*	326/857/1159	14	6.10pm CC
	2603 *Hyderabad Exp*	311/812/1095	13	4.45pm CC
Kochi	6041 *Alleppey Exp*	283/761/1036	11¾	9.15pm CC
Kolkata	2842 *Coromandel Exp*	479/1284/1751	27	8.45am CC
	2840 *Howrah Mail*	479/1284/1751	28½	11.35pm CC
Madurai	6127 *MS Guruvayur Exp*	225/594/806	8½	7.50am CE
	2635 *Vaigai Exp*	145/499	8	12.25pm CE
Mumbai	1042 *Mumbai Exp*	399/1085/1486	26	11.45am CC
	2164 *Chennai Exp*	419/1114/1517	23	6.50am CE
Mysore	2007 *Shatabdi Exp**	675/1284	7	6am CC
	6222 *Mysore Exp*	224/594/806	10½	11.30pm CC
Tirupathi	6053 *Tirupathi Exp*	71/229	3	1.50pm CC
Trichy	2605 *Pallavan Exp*	115/392	5½	3.30pm CE
Trivandrum	2695 *Trivandrum Exp*	356/938/1272	15¾	4pm CC

Departure codes: CC – Chennai Central, CE – Chennai Egmore
*Daily except Tuesday; ** Fridays only
Shatabdi fares are chair/executive; Express and Mail fares are 2nd/chair car for day trains, sleeper/3AC/2AC for overnight trains

TAMIL NADU

the Foreign Assistance Tourist Cell is on the 1st floor. Egmore's **booking office** (☎ 28194579) keeps the same hours.

GETTING AROUND
To/From the Airport
The cheapest way to reach the airport is by MRTS train to Tirusulam station, 300m across the road from the terminals (Rs6). An auto-rickshaw will cost you at least Rs200/300 for a day/night trip.

Both terminals have prepaid taxi kiosks, where tickets are Rs270/450 for non-AC/AC to Egmore or Anna Salai/Triplicane.

Autorickshaw
Rickshaw drivers in Chennai have the scruples of a scorpion, with astronomical fares routinely quoted for both locals and tourists alike. Since you have no chance of getting a driver to use the meter, expect to pay at least Rs25 for a short trip down the road. From Egmore to George Town, Triplicane or Anna Salai will cost around Rs50, to Nungambakkam Rs60. Prices are at least 25% higher after 10pm. There's a prepaid booth outside Central station.

See p1047 for more details on Chennai's autorickshaws.

Bus
Chennai's bus system is worth getting to know. The main city bus stand (Map pp1044–5) is at Parry's Corner, and fares are between Rs4 and Rs10. Some useful routes are listed below.

Car & Taxi
For an extended hire, organise a driver through a travel agent or large hotel. You

CHENNAI BUS ROUTES

Bus No	Route
1	Parry's-Central-Triplicane
5D	Koyambedu CMBT-Guindy-Adyar-Mylapore
9, 10	Parry's-Central-Egmore-T Nagar
11/11A	Parry's-Anna Salai-T Nagar
15B	Parry's-Central-Koyambedu CMBT
18	Parry's-Saidapet
19S	Parry's-Central-Adyar
27B	Egmore-Chetpet-Koyambedu CMBT
31	Parry's-Central-Vivekananda House
32	Central-Triplicane-Vivekanand House
51M	T Nagar-St Thomas Mount

might pay a little more, but the driver should be reliable and you'll have a point of contact should something go wrong. Non-AC rates are around Rs500 per half-day (five hours) within the city, and Rs5 per kilometre (with a daily 250km minimum) beyond city limits.

For slightly more expensive and reliable AC cabs, you can call **Manjoo Cabs** (☎ 23813083; manjoocabs@yahoo.com), a drivers' cooperative.

Train
Efficient MRTS trains run every 15 minutes from Beach station to Fort, Park (at Central Station), Egmore, Chetpet, Nungambakkam, Kodambakkam, Mambalam, Saidapet, Guindy, St Thomas Mount, Tirusulam (for the airport), and on down to Tambaram. The second line branches off at Park and hits Light House and Tirumailar (at Kapaleeshwarar Temple). Tickets cost between Rs5 and Rs10.

NORTHERN TAMIL NADU

CHENNAI TO MAMALLAPURAM
Chennai's sprawl peters after an hour or two heading south, at which point Tamil Nadu becomes open road, red dirt, khaki sand and blue skies. Currently this stretch of sand – known as the Coromandel Coast – is the only area of Tamil Nadu's 1076km coastline that's being developed for traditional beachside tourism. Small resorts, artist colonies and roadside plazas dot the way to Mamallapuram, and real-estate development signs sprout like mushrooms.

There's a tropical bohemian groove floating around Injambalkkam village, site of the **Cholamandal Artists' Village** (☎ 044-4926092; admission free; ⏰ 9.30am-6.30pm). This 4-hectare artists' cooperative (18km south of Chennai) is a serene muse away from the world and a quiet chance to both see and purchase contemporary Indian art direct from the source. There are two simple studio-cum-guest-houses available for visiting artists only (Rs500 per day; book well in advance).

As Cholamandal is to contemporary Indian expression, **DakshinaChitra** (☎ 044-27472603; www.dakshinachitra.net; Indian adult/student Rs75/30, foreign adult/student Rs200/75; ⏰ 10am-6pm Wed-Mon) is to traditional arts and crafts. Located about 12km south of Cholamandal, this is a jumble of open-air museum, preserved village and artisan workshops – another well-worth-it stop (especially for the kids) for learning about the Dravidian crafts of Tamil Nadu, Kerala, Karnataka and Andhra Pradesh. Of special note are 17 refurbished heritage houses and recreated village-scapes. DakshinaChitra means 'A Picture of the South', which is essentially what you're provided via local pottery, silk-weaving, puppet-building and basket-making workshops, traditional theatre performances and art studios. A delightfully cool 12-room **guest house** (☎ 98414 22149; r Rs550, with AC Rs800; 🞱) is in the grounds, though you might want to check your visit is not coinciding with a school overnight excursion.

You can ditch the inimitable cultural heritage of one of India's oldest states for a day at one of India's largest amusement parks, **MGM Dizzee World** (☎ 044-24981005; www.mgmdizzeeworld.com; adult/child Rs350/300; 🕙 10am-7.30pm), just north of the Crocodile Bank.

One of the best institutions of its kind in India, **Crocodile Bank** (☎ 044-27472447; www.madras crocodilebank.org; adult/child Rs30/15, camera/video Rs10/75; 🕙 8am-5.30pm Tue-Sun), 40km south of Chennai, is a fascinating peek into a world of reptiles culled from your best dinosaur dreams, and an incredible conservation trust to boot. The Bank does crucial work towards protecting the critically endangered gharial, an enormous but harmless (to humans) species of crocodilian with a long, thin nose that feeds on fish. There are thousands of other reptiles here, including the Indian mugger and saltwater crocs of the Andaman and Nicobar Islands. If you've got an open evening on the weekend, come for the **night safari** (adult/child Rs60/20; 🕙 7-8.30pm Sat & Sun), when you can shine a flashlight over the water and catch the staring eyes of thousands of the Bank's local residents.

We weren't able to visit on our last trip, but if you love your dolphins (or water slides), **Dolphin City** (☎ 04114-46370; 🕙 10am-7pm), 6km south of Crocodile Bank, is a huge water-park complex that features daily dolphin and sea-lion shows, plus a nice range of water slides, pools and kiddie rides.

About 5km north of Mamallapuram in the village of Salavankuppam, beside the East Coast Rd, the **Tiger Cave** is a rock-cut shrine, possibly dating from the 7th century. It's dedicated to Durga and has a small *mandapam* featuring a crown of carved *yali* (mythical lion creature) heads.

To reach these places, take any bus heading south from Chennai to Mamallapuram and ask to be let off at the appropriate destination.

An AC taxi for a full-day tour costs about Rs1500; an autorickshaw will run Rs650 to Rs800. You can swim along the coast, but beware of strong currents and tides as there are no lifeguards around.

MAMALLAPURAM (MAHABALIPURAM)
☎ 044 / pop 12,345

Mamallapuram is a tossed salad: ancient archaeological wonders, a fine, if windy strip of sand, good biryani in local *dhabas* (snack bars) and cheap internet in the traveller ghetto, one of the few in Tamil Nadu. But don't think of it as only the latter; this World Heritage Site was once a major seaport and second capital of the Pallava kings, and a saunter through the town's great carvings and temples at sunset, when the sandstone turns bonfire orange and blood red and modern carvers *tink-tink* with their chisels on the street, enflames the imagination.

And then…you wander down Othavadai Cross St. There are the mellow trills of Jack Johnson. Bob Marley flags hang from the balconies. Stores sell things from Tibet, 'Indian' clothes that few Indians would probably ever wear, toilet paper, hand sanitiser and used books, and you know you have landed, once again, in the Kingdom of Backpackistan.

'Mal', as many travellers call it, is less than two hours by bus from Chennai. Its beach, cheap accommodation, handicraft shops and Tamil Nadu's most highly regarded dance festival (see boxed text, p1043) make it easy to see why many travellers make a beeline here straight from Chennai.

Orientation
Mamallapuram village is tiny and laid-back, with most of the action on East Raja, Othavadai and Othavadai Cross Sts; the last runs parallel to the beach. The surrounding sites of interest can be explored on foot or by bicycle.

Information
BOOKSHOPS
JK Bookshop (☎ 9840442853; 144 Othavadai St; 🕙 8.30am-9pm) A small bookshop where you can buy or swap books in several languages, including English, French and German. Proceeds support village schools established by the owner.

EMERGENCY
All Women Police station (GK Mandapam St)
Police station (Kovalam Rd)

INTERNET ACCESS

Internet access is everywhere.

AM Communication (cnr Othavadai and East Raja St; per hr Rs40; ☾ 9am-9pm)

Lakshmi Lodge Internet (5 Othavadai Cross St; per hr Rs40; ☾ 9am-10pm)

MEDICAL SERVICES

Suradeep Hospital (☎ 27442390; 15 Thirukkulam St; ☾ 24hr) Recommended by travellers.

MONEY

LKP Forex (East Raja St; ☾ 9.30am-6.30pm Mon-Sat)

State Bank of India ATM (East Raja St; ☾ 24hr)

POST

Post office (☾ 8am-4pm Mon-Fri) Located just down and to the east of the tourist office.

TOURIST INFORMATION

Tourist office (☎ 27442232; Kovalam Rd; ☾ 10am-5.45pm Mon-Fri)

Sights

You can easily spend a full day exploring the temples, *mandapams* and rock carvings around Mamallapuram. Apart from the Shore Temple and Five Rathas, admission is free. Official guides from the Archaeological Survey of India can be found at archaeological sites and hired for Rs50 (give more if the tour is good); they're well worth the money.

SHORE TEMPLE

Standing like a magnificent fist of rock-cut elegance overlooking the sea, the **Shore Temple** (combined ticket with Five Rathas Indian/foreigner Rs10/250, video Rs25; ☾ 6.30am-6pm) symbolises the heights of Pallava architecture and the maritime ambitions of the Pallava kings. Its small size belies its excellent proportion and the supreme quality of the carvings, many of which have been eroded into vaguely Impressionist embellishments. Originally constructed in the 7th century, it was later rebuilt by Narasimhavarman II and houses two central shrines to Shiva. The layout is meant to resemble the perfect cosmic body, with the head and heart located over the spire that dominates the structure. Facing east and west, the original linga (phallic images of Shiva) captured the sunrise and sunset. The temple is believed to be the last in a series of buildings that extended along a since submerged coastline; this theory gained credence during the 2004 tsunami, when re-ceding waters revealed the outlines of what may have been sister temples. The building is now protected from further erosion by a huge rock wall, and like many of Mamallapuram's sights, it's spectacularly floodlit at night.

FIVE RATHAS

Carved from single pieces of rock, the **Five Rathas** (Five Rathas Rd; combined ticket with Shore Temple Indian/foreigner Rs10/250, video Rs25; ☾ 6.30am-6pm) are low-laying monoliths that huddle in more ancient subtlety than grandeur. Each temple is dedicated to a Hindu god and named for one of the Pandavas, the five hero-brothers of the epic Mahabharata, plus their common wife, Draupadi.

The shrines are meant to resemble chariots (*ratha* is Sanskrit for chariot), and were hidden in the sand until excavated by the British 200 years ago. Outside each *ratha* is a carving of an animal mount of the gods. Taken together, the layout theme of God, Pandava and animal mount is remarkable for its architectural consistency, considering everything here was cut from single chunks of rock.

The first *ratha*, **Draupadi Ratha**, on the left after you enter the gate, is dedicated to Draupadi and the goddess Durga, who represents the sacred femininity and fertility of the Indian soil. The goddess looks out at her worshippers from a carved lotus throne, while outside, a huge sculpted lion stands guard.

Behind the goddess shrine, a huge Nandi (bull, vehicle of Shiva) heralds the chariot of the most important Pandava. **Arjuna Ratha** is appropriately dedicated to Shiva, the most important deity of the Pallavas. Other gods, including the Vedic Indra, are depicted on the outer walls.

Look around the lintels of the middle temple, **Bhima Ratha**, and you'll notice faded faces that some archaeologists believe possess Caucasian features, evidence of Mamallapuram's extensive trade ties with ancient Rome. Inside is a shrine to Vishnu.

Guides may tell you the carving of Pallava king Narasimhavarman on **Dharmaraja Ratha**, the tallest of the chariots, resembles an Egyptian pharaoh, suggesting even earlier trade ties across the Indian Ocean. The theory is tantalising, but not terribly well substantiated. The final *ratha*, **Nakula-Sahadeva Ratha**, is dedicated to Indra and has a fine sculptured elephant standing nearby. As you enter the gate, approaching from the north, you see its back first, hence its name **gajaprishthakara**

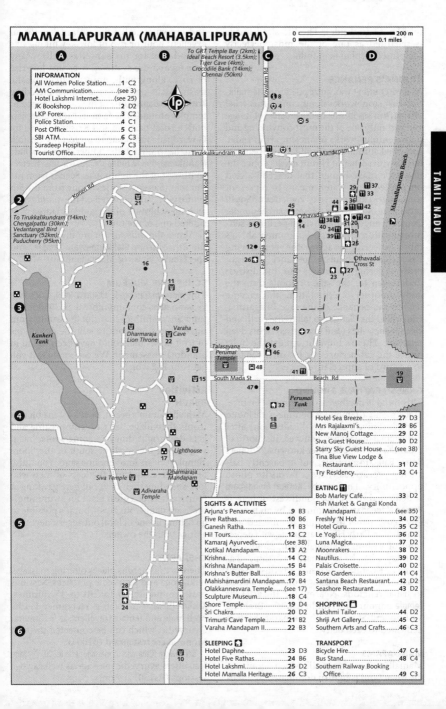

MAMALLAPURAM (MAHABALIPURAM)

0 — 200 m
0 — 0.1 miles

INFORMATION
All Women Police Station.......1 C2
AM Communication............(see 3)
Hotel Lakshmi Internet......(see 25)
JK Bookshop.........................2 D2
LKP Forex............................3 C2
Police Station.......................4 C1
Post Office...........................5 C1
SBI ATM..............................6 C3
Suradeep Hospital................7 C3
Tourist Office.......................8 C1

To GRT Temple Bay (2km);
Ideal Beach Resort (3.5km);
Tiger Cave (4km);
Crocodile Bank (14km);
Chennai (50km)

To Tirukkalikundram (14km);
Chengalpattu (30km);
Vedantangal Bird
Sanctuary (52km);
Puducherry (95km)

Kanheri Tank

Dharmaraja Lion Throne

Varaha Cave

Talasayana Perumal Temple

Kanheri Tank

Siva Temple

Adivaraha Temple

Dharmaraja Mandapam

Lighthouse

Perumai Tank

TAMIL NADU

Mamallapuram Beach

Othavadai St

Othavadai Cross St

South Mada St

Beach Rd

SIGHTS & ACTIVITIES
Arjuna's Penance....................9 B3
Five Rathas.........................10 B6
Ganesh Ratha.......................11 B3
Hi! Tours.............................12 C2
Kamaraj Ayurvedic..........(see 38)
Kotikal Mandapam..............13 A2
Krishna...............................14 C2
Krishna Mandapam.............15 B4
Krishna's Butter Ball...........16 B3
Mahishamardini Mandapam..17 B4
Olakkannesvara Temple....(see 17)
Sculpture Museum..............18 C4
Shore Temple......................19 D4
Sri Chakra..........................20 D2
Trimurti Cave Temple..........21 B2
Varaha Mandapam II...........22 B3

SLEEPING
Hotel Daphne......................23 D3
Hotel Five Rathas................24 B6
Hotel Lakshmi.....................25 D2
Hotel Mamalla Heritage.......26 C3

Hotel Sea Breeze.................27 D3
Mrs Rajalaxmi's...................28 B6
New Manoj Cottage.............29 D2
Siva Guest House................30 D2
Starry Sky Guest House....(see 38)
Tina Blue View Lodge &
   Restaurant.......................31 D2
Try Residency......................32 C4

EATING
Bob Marley Café.................33 D2
Fish Market & Gangai Konda
   Mandapam...................(see 35)
Freshly 'N Hot 34 D2
Hotel Guru.........................35 C2
Le Yogi..............................36 D2
Luna Magica.......................37 D2
Moonrakers........................38 D2
Nautilus.............................39 D2
Palais Croisette...................40 D2
Rose Garden.......................41 C4
Santana Beach Restaurant....42 D2
Seashore Restaurant...........43 D2

SHOPPING
Lakshmi Tailor....................44 D2
Shriji Art Gallery.................45 C2
Southern Arts and Crafts......46 C3

TRANSPORT
Bicycle Hire........................47 C4
Bus Stand...........................48 C4
Southern Railway Booking
   Office..............................49 C3

(elephant's backside). The life-sized image is regarded as one of the most perfectly sculptured elephants in India.

ARJUNA'S PENANCE

As if we couldn't wax more poetic on Mamallapuram's stonework, along comes this **relief carving** (West Raja St), one of the greatest of its age and certainly one of the most convincing and unpretentious works of ancient art in India. Inscribed into a huge boulder, the penance bursts with scenes of Hindu myth (notice the *nagas,* or snake-beings, that descend a cleft once filled with water, meant to represent the Ganges) and everyday vignettes of South Indian life. A herd of elephants marches under armies of angels, while Arjuna performs self-mortification so he can be granted Shiva's most powerful weapon, the god-slaying Pasupata. In Hinduism, 'penance' does not mean suffering that erases sins, but distress undertaken for the sake of boons from the gods. Another interpretation: the carving depicts the penance of the sage Bhagaritha, who asked the Ganges to fall to the earth and cleanse the ashes (and ergo, sins) of his dead relatives. There's humour amidst the holy: notice the cat performing his own penance to a crowd of appreciative mice.

GANESH RATHA & AROUND

This *ratha* is northwest of Arjuna's Penance. Once a Shiva temple, it became a shrine to Ganesh (Shiva's elephant-headed son) after the original lingam was removed. Just north of the *ratha* is a huge boulder known as **Krishna's Butter Ball**. Immovable, but apparently balancing precariously, it's a favourite photo opportunity. The nearby **Kotikal Mandapam** is dedicated to Durga. Southwest of here is **Varaha Mandapam II**, dominated by an incredibly active panel of Vishnu manifested as a boar avatar. Early Hindu art is rife with depictions of Vishnu in animal form, as opposed to today, when he is primarily worshipped as Rama or Krishna, which suggests this nascent phase of Hindu theology was more closely tied to tribal religions. Nearby, the **Trimurti Cave Temple** honours the Hindu trinity – Brahma, Vishnu and Shiva – with a separate section dedicated to each deity.

MANDAPAMS

Mamallapuram's main hill, which dominates the town (and is in turn dominated by a red-and-brownstone lighthouse), makes for an excellent hour or two of low-key hiking (it's a good spot for the sunset as well). Many *mandapams* are scattered over this low rise of rock, along with, unfortunately, plastic trash. Focus on the *mandapams,* including **Krishna Mandapam**, one of the earliest rock-cut temples around. The famous carving depicts both a rural pastiche and Krishna lifting up Govardhana mountain to protect his kinsfolk from the wrath of Indra. Other shrines include **Mahishamardini Mandapam**, just a few metres southwest of the lighthouse. Scenes from the Puranas (Sanskrit stories dating from the 5th century AD) are depicted on the *mandapam,* with the sculpture of the goddess Durga considered one of the finest.

Above the *mandapam* are the remains of the 8th-century **Olakkannesvara Temple**, and spectacular views of Mamallapuram.

SCULPTURE MUSEUM

This **museum** (East Raja St; adult/child Rs2/1, camera Rs10; ◷ 9am-5.30pm) contains more than 3000 sculptures and paintings that run the gamut from interesting stonework to still-life depictions of fruit bowls that could have been found in grandma's basement. We can safely say: you get your Rs2 worth.

Activities
BEACH

Mamallapuram's beach, or at least the bit that fronts the village, isn't exactly pristine and gets downright dingy in some spots, but if you walk a bit north or south of the Shore Temple it clears into very fine sand. You'll also be further away from the leers of men who love spending their days out here gawking at tourists. It's not a great place for swimming – there are dangerous rips – but it's possible to go fishing in one of local outriggers; negotiate a price with the owner.

THERAPIES

There are numerous places offering massage, reiki, yoga and ayurvedic practices. Sessions cost around Rs350 for 30 to 45 minutes. **Krishna** (Siesta; Othavadai St) is recommended by both male and female travellers, as is Kamaraj Ayurvedic, which can be contacted through Moonrakers restaurant (p1064).

Sri Chakra (Othavadai St; massage per hr Rs300; ◷ 8am-9pm) offers ayurvedic massage as well as yoga sessions (Rs150) at 7am.

There are many other operators in town with similar rates and timings. As always, and especially for such an intimate service, ask fellow travellers, question the massage therapist carefully and if you have any misgivings, don't proceed.

Tours

Hi! Tours (☎ 27443360; www.hi-tours.com; 123 East Raja St) runs bicycle tours to sights like the Tiger Cave. Tours run from 8am to 2pm and include guide and lunch. Hi! Tours also organises day trips to Kanchipuram (p1065) and Vedantangal Bird Sanctuary (p1065).

Sleeping

BUDGET

Hotel Five Rathas (r from Rs100) Tucked into the alleys across from the Five Rathas, this place has clean concrete rooms that have been livened up with murals that look like Hindu temple art pressed through an acid trip. It's an idiosyncratic place run by a sweet old man, but be aware the psychedelic character doesn't just apply to the decor.

Mrs Rajalaxmi's (☎ 27442460; from r Rs150) Like many of the family-run hotels near the Five Rathas, this is a friendly and homey spot. The rooms are basic, but fresh coats of paint and a transitory clientele of eccentrics give this spot a bit of character.

Tina Blue View Lodge & Restaurant (☎ 27442319; 34 Othavadai St; r Rs150-300) Tina is one of Mamallapuram's originals and kind of looks it, but remains deservedly popular for its whitewashed walls, pale-blue accents and tropically pleasant garden, if not its facilities, which are getting a bit rusty.

Lakshmi Lodge (☎ 27442463; 5 Othavadai Cross St; d Rs200-500, with AC Rs850; ⌧ ▣ ▣) The Lakshmi is a backpacker standard with a huge number of rooms on offer and a plethora of travel services (internet, taxi booking etc) available on the ground floor. There's a tanklike swimming pool (empty in the off-season) and friendly (if slightly overbearing owners) thrown in free of charge.

Starry Sky Guest House (☎ 27443726; 2B Othavadai Cross St; d from Rs250; ⌧) The title isn't a misnomer – you can get nice views of the night sky from the rooftop verandah of this hotel, which otherwise offers clean and cheap rooms that are good value for money.

Siva Guest House (☎ 27443534; sivaguesthouse@hotmail.com; 2 Othavadai Cross St; d Rs250, with AC Rs800; ⌧) Deservedly popular with travellers, Siva gets consistently good reports. Rooms are spotless and each has a small verandah.

our pick Hotel Daphne (☎ 27442811; hoteldaphne1@yahoo.com; 17 Othavadai Cross St; d Rs350, with AC Rs750; ⌧) This cubist complex conceals spotless rooms that resemble Ikea showpieces that somehow stumbled into India. It's a decided step above the rest of the backpacker-blah accommodation, and the upper-floor rooms are great spots for eating wind, lazing about and generally vegetating.

MIDRANGE & TOP END

New Manoj Cottage (☎ 9840387095; newmanojcottage@yahoo.com; 136 Fisherman Colony; r Rs500-700) The unsigned Manoj (it's across from New Papillon Le Bistro restaurant) is a family-run homestay with three spacious and well-kept rooms that are the easy equivalent of most midrange accommodation in town.

Hotel Sea Breeze (☎ 27443035; www.nivalink.com/seabreeze; Othavadai Cross St; r from Rs900; ⌧ ▣) The Sea Breeze is a nice hotel of the reliably middle-class beachfront-escape school of design, but the real draw is the pool, which nonguests can use for Rs150.

Try Residency (☎ 27442728; tryresidency@gmail.com; East Raja St; r Rs800, with AC Rs1300; ⌧) Rooms are exceptionally large and some overlook Mamallapuram's algae-laden tank (mmmm). There's not a lot of character, but if you need some Western-style amenities, it's not a bad option.

Hotel Mamalla Heritage (☎ 27442060; www.hotelmamallaheritage.com; 104 East Raja St; s/d with AC from Rs1100/1900; ⌧ ▣) In town, this corporate-y place has large, comfortable rooms, all with fridge, and charmingly friendly service. The pool's a decent size, and there's a quality veg and rooftop restaurant.

Ideal Beach Resort (☎ 27442240; www.idealresort.com; s/d Rs4000/5000, cottages from Rs5000; ⌧ ▣ ▣) With a landscaped garden setting and comfortable rooms or cottages, this low-key beachfront resort is popular with package tours and Chennai expats. The design is small and secluded enough to have an intimate atmosphere and there's a lovely open-air poolside restaurant. It's about 3.5km north of town.

GRT Temple Bay (☎ 27443636; www.grttemplebay.com; r from Rs8000; ⌧ ▣ ▣) This is the best of the luxury resorts that lays to the north of town. It's got everything you need to feel like waterfront royalty, including 24-hour service, a spa, sauna, health club and prices that are probably a little much all things considered.

Eating & Drinking

Restaurateurs near Othavadai Cross St provide open-air ambience, decent Western mains and bland Indian curries. If you want real Indian food, there are good cheap stalls near the bus stand and fish market. Most places – licensed or not – serve beer, but be sensitive to the 11pm local curfew; if you persuade a restaurant to allow you to linger over drinks, it's the owner, not you, who faces a hefty fine. That said, on an almost rotating basis one restaurant in town will either bribe the cops or dare to break curfew, and this place ends up being where the party is come 11pm. All places listed are open for breakfast, lunch and dinner.

Palais Croisette (8 Othavadai St; mains Rs40-120) On the roof of Hotel Ramakrishna, the Palais manages very nice pasta (put it this way: it came recommended by an Italian traveller) and similarly good fresh seafood.

Rose Garden (Beach Rd; mains around Rs50) This is one of the better biryani shops in a town that's surprisingly full of joints serving this tasty Muslim treat. The other spot locals recommend for similar fare (and prices) is the unaffiliated Hotel Guru, located behind the fish market. Expect a barren atmosphere and great food at both spots.

Freshly 'N Hot (Othavadai Cross St; mains from Rs50) Yes, the name makes no sense, and we're not sure it's some cute misspelling either, considering the guys who run this open-air cafe have so many other Western standards down. Especially the ice coffee: hands down the best in town.

Nautilus (Othavadai Cross St; mains from Rs50) The Nautilus seems perpetually buzzing with every traveller you've ever met talking about how much they loved/hated/got-ripped-off-in Goa/Varanasi/Hampi/Cochi while eating eggs on toast and drinking smoothies.

Moonrakers (34 Othavadai St; mains Rs60-150) Like it or not, you'll likely end up here at some stage; it's the sort of place that magnetises travellers. Probably because it's a three-storey resto-bar complex that dominates the backpacker-ghetto streetscape. Food is OK, ambience is better and beer is enjoyable from the top-floor verandah.

Le Yogi (☎ 27442571; Othavadai St; mains Rs70-150) This is probably the best Western food in town. The steaks, pastas and pizzas are genuine and tasty (if small), service is stellar, and

the airy dining area, with wooden accents, flickering candlelight and billowing fabrics, is romantic as all get out.

Beachside Bob Marley Café, Seashore Restaurant, Santana Beach Restaurant and Luna Magica are all recommended for fresh seafood; you'll get a good plate of fish for around Rs150.

Shopping

Mamallapuram wakes to the sound of sculptors' chisels on granite, and you'll inevitably be approached by someone trying to sell you everything from a Rs90 stone pendant to a Rs400,000 Ganesh that needs to be lifted with a mobile crane. There are lots of good art galleries, tailors and antique shops here. For clothes, we recommend **Lakshmi Tailor** (Othavadai St), across from Moonrakers. Nice prints and original art can be found at **Shriji Art Gallery** (11/1 Othavadai St) and expensive but beautiful curios culled from local homes at **Southern Arts and Crafts** (☎ 27443675; 72 East Raja St).

Getting There & Away

There are at least 30 buses a day running to/from Chennai (Rs25, two hours, 30 daily). To Chennai airport take bus 108B (Rs25, two hours, four daily). There are also at least nine daily buses to Puducherry (Rs35, two hours) and Kanchipuram (Rs20, two hours, 11 daily) via Tirukkalikundram.

Taxis are available from the bus station. Long-distance trips require plenty of bargaining. It's about Rs900 to Chennai or the airport.

You can make train reservations at the **Southern Railway Booking Office** (East Raja St).

Getting Around

The easiest way to get around is on foot, though on a hot day it's quite a hike to see all the monuments. Bicycles or mopeds (we recommend the former; Mamallapuram is pretty small) can be rented through most guest houses and at numerous stalls along East Raja St.

AROUND MAMALLAPURAM

About 14km west of Mamallapuram in Tirukkalikundram is the hilltop **Vedagirishvara Temple** (admission Rs2; ⏰ 8.30am-1pm & 5-7pm) dedicated to Shiva. It's often called the Eagle Temple; according to legend two eagles come here each day at noon from Varanasi, a good

2000km away (they often don't turn up on time). It might also be called the Eagle Temple because that's what you should be if you want to visit the shrine.

You climb (and climb and climb) the 550 smooth steps to the hilltop bare-footed. Once there, the temple contains two beautiful shrines, as well as incredible views over the rich green rice paddies in every direction. It's lovely – if busy – in the late afternoon, but the middle of the day (while making for a hot climb) is very peaceful when the temple itself is closed. You can get here by bus or bicycle from Mamallapuram.

VEDANTANGAL BIRD SANCTUARY

Located about 52km southwest of Mamallapuram, this wildlife **sanctuary** (admission Rs5; 6am-6pm) is an important breeding ground for waterbirds – cormorants, egrets, herons, ibises, spoonbills, storks, grebes and pelicans – that migrate here from October to March. At the height of breeding season (December and January) there can be up to 30,000 birds nesting in the mangroves. The best viewing times are early morning and late afternoon; head for the watchtower and look down on the noisy nests across the water.

Basic rooms are available at the **Forest Department Resthouse** (d Rs300), 500m before the sanctuary. You're supposed to book in advance with the **Wildlife Warden's Office** (WWO; Map pp1044-5; ☎ 24321471; 4th fl, DMS Office, 259 Anna Salai, Teynampet) in Chennai – good luck – but in practice the caretaker will probably find a room if one's available. You may or may not be offered food if you arrive unexpectedly; if you have transport, it's 10km or so to the nearest evening food stall.

To get here by public transport, first get to Chengalpattu, an hour's bus ride from Mamallapuram. From here you can take a bus to Vedantangal via Padalam, where you may have to change buses at the road junction. Most Vedantangal buses go directly to the sanctuary entrance, others to the village bus station, from where the sanctuary is a 1km walk south. Visitors also often make a day trip by AC taxi from Mamallapuram; this should cost around Rs1000.

KANCHIPURAM

☎ 044 / pop 188,763

The old capital of the Pallava dynasty is a typical Tamil Nadu temple town: modern India

at her frenetic best dappled with houses of worship that form a veritable dialogue with history in stone. Kanchi (as it's often called) is also a centre of silk production and famed for its high-quality saris. It's usually (and best) visited as a day trip from Mamallapuram or Chennai, as there's not a lot to see outside of the justifiably famous temples.

Orientation & Information

The city is on the main Chennai–Bengaluru road, 76km southwest of Chennai. There's no tourist office, but for information online check out www.hellokanchipuram.com. On Kamaraja St there's a small cluster of cheap internet cafes. Changing travellers cheques can be a hassle, so it's best to use local ATMs.

Googly (144 Kamaraja St; per hr Rs25; 9am-9pm) Internet access.
ICICI Bank ATM (Gandhi Rd)
Netcafé (148 Kamaraja St; per hr Rs25; 9am-9pm) Internet access.
State Bank of India ATM (Hospital Rd)

Sights

All temples are open from 6am to 12.30pm and 4pm to 8.30pm. Most have free admission.

KAILASANATHA TEMPLE

The oldest temple in Kanchi is the most impressive, not for its size but weight of historical presence. Dedicated to Shiva, the Kailasanatha Temple was built by the Pallava king Rajasimha in the 7th century. The low-slung sandstone compound is chock-a-block with fascinating carvings, including many half-animal deities that were in vogue during the period of early Dravidian architecture.

The remaining fragments of 8th-century murals are visible reminders of how magnificent the original temple must have looked. There are 58 small shrines honouring Shiva and Parvati and their sons, Ganesh and Murugan.

It's worth your while to hire an official guide from the Archaeological Survey of India (Rs50). Non-Hindus are allowed into the inner sanctum here, where there is a prismatic lingam – the largest in town and third-largest in Asia.

SRI EKAMBARANATHAR TEMPLE

This Shiva temple is one of the largest in the city, covering 12 hectares and dominated by a 59m-high *gopuram*. The carvings feel alive

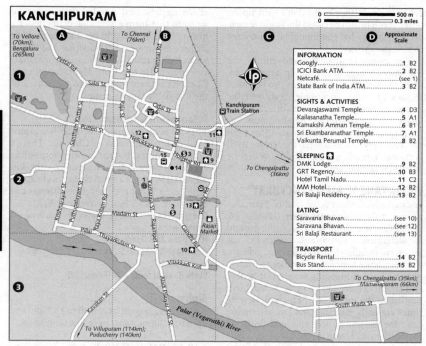

and beautiful, but still weighted with five centuries of history; they were chiselled by artisans in 1509 during the Vijayanagar empire. The temple's name is said to derive from Eka Amra Nathar – Lord of the Mango Tree – and there is an old mango tree, with four branches representing the four Vedas (sacred Hindu texts) on site. Of the five elemental temples of Shiva, this is the shrine of Earth.

According to legend, the goddess Kamakshi worshipped Shiva here in the form of a linga made of sand, which still lies at the heart of the temple, inscribed with carvings of 108 smaller lingam. Unfortunately non-Hindus cannot see the mirror chamber, an electricity-free room that worshippers enter with candles. The central image of Shiva is reflected in the candlelight across the mirrored walls, creating countless images of the god that allude to his infinite presence.

KAMAKSHI AMMAN TEMPLE

This imposing temple is dedicated to the goddess Parvati in her guise as Kamakshi (She Whose Eyes Awaken Desire). To the right of the temple's entrance is the marriage hall, with

wonderful ornate pillars, and directly ahead is the main shrine topped with a golden *vimana* (legendary flying chariot). Again, non-Hindus cannot enter the sanctum, where Kamakshi/Parvati is depicted, uncharacteristically, in the lotus position. Each February/March carriages housing statues of the temple deities are hauled through the streets; this procession should not be missed if you're in the vicinity.

DEVARAJASWAMI TEMPLE

Dedicated to Vishnu, this enormous **monument** (admission Rs2, camera/video Rs5/100) was built by the Vijayanagars and is among the most impressive of Kanchipuram's temples. It has a beautifully sculptured '1000-pillared' hall (only 96 of the original 1000 remain) as well as a marriage hall commemorating the wedding of Vishnu and Lakshmi. One of the temple's most notable features is a huge chain carved from a single piece of stone which can be seen at each corner of the *mandapam*. The temple is supposedly the place to go to receive cures from lizard-related illnesses thanks to twin silver and gold-plated reptiles that crawl over the temple ceiling, where they devour platinum cockroaches (kidding).

KANCHIPURAM & KUNG FU?

One of Asia's most famous historical personalities is Bodhidharma, a Buddhist monk credited with bringing Chan Buddhism – better known by its Japanese title, 'Zen' – to China. Like King Arthur, Bodhidharma's historical origins are lost to legend, and he may actually be an amalgamation of several real-life individuals, but many sources say he was born in the 5th century in Kanchipuram. Supposedly, Bodhidharma travelled to China, where he taught and popularised Chan Buddhism, which later spread to Korea and Japan. Legends also say Bodhidharma instructed disciples at the Shaolin Monastery (of 'every kung fu movie ever' fame) in Varma Kalai (The Art of Vital Points), a South Indian martial art that is practised in Tamil Nadu today. In China, the self-defence style evolved into Kung Fu. We should note this version of events is disputed by many Chinese, although it carries a lot of weight in this corner of South India, where Tamil action heroes fight using moves inspired by Varma Kalai, along with good old Indian cinematic moustache-fu.

Every 40 years the waters of the temple tank are drained, revealing a huge wooden statue of Vishnu which is worshipped for 48 days. You may like to hang around for the next viewing – in 2019. Otherwise, float festivals (when deities are literally floated across the reservoir) are held on the tank three times a year.

VAIKUNTA PERUMAL TEMPLE

Roughly 1200 years old and dedicated to Vishnu, this temple was built shortly after the Kailasanatha. The cloisters inside the outer wall consist of lion pillars and are representative of the first phase in the architectural evolution of the grand 1000-pillared halls. The main shrine, which is uniquely spread over three levels, contains images of Vishnu standing, sitting, reclining and riding his preferred mount, the garuda (half-eagle, half-man). There's another monitor lizard icon here.

Sleeping & Eating

Kanchi's cheap pilgrims' lodges are shabby, but there are a few decent midrange options.

DMK Lodge (☎ 9380913144; Nellukkara St; r from Rs150) Basically a lodge for members of the DMK political party, this is a friendly spot but the rooms are pretty tatty (like every other budget place in town).

Sri Balaji Residency (☎ 47203868; sribalajiresidency@ gmail.com; 124 Railway Rd; s/d from Rs300/500; ✷) This is your best bet in town: big clean rooms at a cut-throat price with polished floors, colour TVs and an excellent restaurant downstairs.

Hotel Tamil Nadu (☎ 27222553; d Rs490, with AC Rs800; ✷) A study in government-run mediocrity, this hotel opposite the railway station has wide, airy rooms set off with scrubbed tile floors, and the character of a blank piece of paper.

MM Hotel (☎ 27227250; www.mmhotels.com; 65 Nellukkara St; d Rs650, with AC Rs990; ✷) A good-value, busy and clean hotel, frequented by Indian businesspeople. A Saravana Bhavan veg restaurant is next door, with a welcome AC dining room.

GRT Regency (☎ 27225250; www.grthotels.com; 487 Gandhi Rd; s/d Rs1750/2250; ✷ ▣) While it's not the best setting on the noisy main road, the rooms here are the probably the cleanest and most comfortable you'll find in Kanchi. There is yet another Saravana Bhavan – we like to think of it as the vegetarian McDonald's (well, a lot better) of Tamil Nadu – located here.

Getting There & Away

The busy bus stand is in the centre of town. See the boxed text (below) for services.

Regular suburban trains leave from Beach, Fort or Egmore stations in Chennai direct to Kanchipuram.

Getting Around

Bicycles can be hired (per hour/day Rs3/40) from stalls around the bus station. An autorickshaw for a half-day tour of the five main temples (around Rs200) will inevitably involve a stop at a silk shop.

BUSES FROM KANCHIPURAM

Destination	Fare (Rs)	Duration (hr)	Frequency
Bengaluru	120-150	6	2 daily
Chennai	20-24.50	2	every 10min
Mamallapuram	25	2	9 daily
Puducherry	35	3	12 daily
Tiruvannamalai	40	3	22 daily
Trichy	105	7	5 daily
Vellore	20	1½	every 15min

VELLORE

☎ 0416 / pop 386,746

For a dusty bazaar town, Vellore feels both cosmopolitan and majestic, thanks to its massive Vijayanagar fort and the Christian Medical College (CMC) Hospital, one of the finest hospitals in India. The hospital attracts international medical students as well as patients from all over India, and the town is worth a day for soaking up both its historical ambience and small-town-but-international vibe.

Information

There are several internet cafes along Ida Scudder Rd in front of the hospital.

State Bank of India (102 Ida Scudder Rd) Money can be exchanged here and there's an ATM.

Surfzone (Ida Scudder Rd) Internet cafe next to the State Bank of India.

Tourist office (☯ 10am-5.45pm Mon-Fri)

Sights

The solid walls and dry moat of the splendid **Vellore Fort** dominate the west side of town. It was built in the 16th century and passed briefly into the hands of the Marathas in 1676 and the Mughals in 1708. The British occupied the fort in 1760 following the fall of Srirangapatnam and the death of Tipu Sultan. These days it houses various government offices, parade grounds, a university, a church, an ancient mosque and a police recruiting school.

At the west side of the fort complex, the small **national government museum** (admission free;

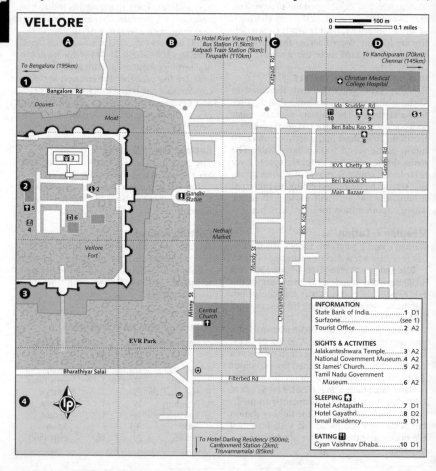

VELLORE

To Hotel River View (1km);
Bus Station (1.5km);
Katpadi Train Station (5km);
Tirupathi (110km)

To Bengaluru (195km)

To Kanchipuram (70km);
Chennai (145km)

Bangalore Rd

Douves

Moat

Ida Scudder Rd

Christian Medical College Hospital

Beri Babu Rao St

KVS Chetty St

Beri Bakkali St

Main Bazaar

Gandhi Statue

Nethaji Market

Vellore Fort

Central Church

EVR Park

Bharathiyar Salai

Filterbed Rd

To Hotel Darling Residency (500m);
Cantonment Station (2km);
Tiruvannamalai (85km)

INFORMATION	
State Bank of India	1 D1
Surfzone	(see 1)
Tourist Office	2 A2

SIGHTS & ACTIVITIES	
Jalakanteshwara Temple	3 A2
National Government Museum	4 A2
St James' Church	5 A2
Tamil Nadu Government Museum	6 A2

SLEEPING	
Hotel Ashtapathi	7 D1
Hotel Gayathri	8 D2
Ismail Residency	9 D1

EATING	
Gyan Vaishnav Dhaba	10 D1

BUSES FROM VELLORE			
Destination	Fare (Rs)	Duration (hr)	Frequency
Chennai	46-60	3	every 10min
Bengaluru	80-95	5	every 30min
Kanchipuram	20	2	every 15min
Tiruvannamalai	40	2	every 5min
Trichy (direct)	110	7	4 daily

🕒 9am-5pm Sat-Thu) contains sculptures dating back to Pallava and Chola times. Next door, pretty **St James' Church** (1846) is only open for Sunday services.

On the east side, the **Tamil Nadu government museum** (Indian/foreigner Rs5/100; 🕒 9am-5pm Sat-Thu) displays hero stones in the forecourt dating from the 8th century and depicting the stories of war heroes in battle. The dusty exhibits have seen much better days, but the small collection of tribal clothes and artefacts is interesting.

Near the fort entrance, **Jalakanteshwara Temple** (🕒 6am-1pm & 3-8pm), a gem of late Vijayanagar architecture, was built about 1566. Check out the small, detailed sculptures on the walls of the marriage hall. During the invasions by the Adil Shahis of Bijapur, the Marathas and the Carnatic nawabs (Muslim ruling princes), the temple was occupied by a garrison and temple rituals ceased. Now it's once again a place of worship.

Sleeping & Eating

Vellore's cheapest hotels are concentrated along the roads south of and parallel to the hospital, mostly catering to people in town for treatment; there are many to choose from on Beri Babu Rao St. Decent midrange hotels are scattered further afield.

Hotel Gayathri (☎ 2227714; 22 Beri Babu Rao St; s/d Rs150/230) This dingy place has impersonal service and squat toilets, but at least the shared balconies let in some light.

Hotel Ashtapathi (☎ 2224602; Ida Scudder Rd; r Rs400, with AC Rs520; ❄) It's small, clean and good value here, but ask for a room off the noisy roadside. There's a decent veg restaurant attached.

Ismail Residency (☎ 2223216; Ida Scudder Rd; s/d Rs420/575; ❄) A five-room lodge with tatty but spotless rooms, this is next door to the clean Hotel Arthy restaurant.

Hotel River View (☎ 2225251; Katpadi Rd; d Rs900, with AC Rs1300; ❄) North of the town centre and close to the bus station, this hotel benefits from a

relatively quiet location and pleasant gardens, but the 'river view' is hardly that. Rooms are spacious, the Shikar garden restaurant serves a barbecue every evening and there's a bar.

Darling Residency (☎ 2213001; 11/8 Officers Line; s/d Rs1300/1400; ❄) Recognised as the best hotel in town. The rooms are clean and comfortable, and there's even a small fitness room with exercise bike. The rooftop Aranya Roof Garden Restaurant (open lunch and dinner) is cool and breezy, serving salads (Rs25), a variety of pasta, tandoori and Chinese food for around Rs60, and good ice cream. It's recommended by visiting medicos and locals alike.

Cheap veg restaurants line Ida Scudder Rd. Try **Gyan Vaishnav Dhaba** (Ida Scudder Rd; thalis Rs25) for good Punjabi food.

Getting There & Away

BUS

The bus stand is about 500m from the Hotel River View, 1.5km to the north of town. For services, see the boxed text (left).

TRAIN

Vellore's main train station is 5km north at Katpadi. Bus 192 (Rs2) shuttles between the station and town. There are at least six daily express trains to/from Chennai Central (2nd class/sleeper Rs45/67), which continue to Bengaluru (Rs65/120).

TIRUVANNAMALAI

☎ 04175 / pop 130,567

There are temple towns, there are mountain towns, and there are temple-mountain towns where God appears as a phallus of fire. Welcome to Tiruvannamalai. About 85km south of Vellore and flanked by boulder-strewn Mt Arunachala, this is one of the five 'elemental' cities of Shiva; here the god is worshipped in his fire incarnation as Arunachaleswar (see boxed text, p1070). At each full moon Mt Arunachala swells with thousands of pilgrims who circumnavigate the base of the mountain, but at any time you'll see Shaivite priests, sadhus (spiritual men) and devotees gathered around the temple. Tiruvannamalai is also home to the Sri Ramana (also known as Sri Ramanasramam) Ashram.

Sights & Activities

ARUNACHALESWAR TEMPLE

The Arunachaleswar is awash in golden flames and the roasting scent of burning ghee, as

TAMIL NADU

befits the fire incarnation of the Destroyer of the Universe. Covering some 10 hectares, this vast **temple** (☺ 6am-1pm & 5.30-10pm) is one of the largest in India. Four large unpainted *gopurams*, one for each cardinal point, front the approaches, with the eastern tower rising 13 storeys and an astonishing 66m.

You enter Arunachaleswar through concentric rings of profanity evolving into sacredness, from the outer wall of beggars and merchants, past dark corridors recessed with bejewelled gods, and, finally, into the heart of the temple, where a roaring oven that looks like a walnut shell spewing fire is tended by temple Brahmins in front of a lingam. *Puja* is performed daily at 8am, 10am, 6pm, 8pm and 9.30pm.

MT ARUNACHALA
Known as Sonachalam (Red Mountain) in Sanskrit, this 800m-high extinct volcano dominates Tiruvannamalai and local conceptions of the element of fire, which supposedly finds its sacred abode in Arunachala's heart. On full-moon and festival days, thousands of pilgrims circumnavigate the 14km base of the mountain. If you're not quite that devoted, an autorickshaw will take you around for about Rs150. An alternative is to pick up a circle map from the ashram office, hire a bicycle (per hour Rs3) from the road near the entrance, and ride your way around.

You can make a sort of phallus pilgrimage here by visiting eight famous linga dotted around the mountain's cardinal and subcardinal spokes. Also, watch out for the field of a thousand lingam, 'planted' by domestic and overseas donors from Malaysia to America.

For a superb view of the Arunachaleswar Temple, climb part or all the way up the hill

(about four hours return). There's a signed path that leads up through village homes near the northwest corner of the temple, passing two caves, **Virupaksha** and **Skandasramam**. Sri Ramana Maharshi lived and meditated in these caves for more than 20 years from 1899 to 1922, after which he and his growing band of spiritual followers established the ashram.

SRI RAMANA ASHRAM
This tranquil **ashram** (☎ 237292; www.ramana-maharshi.org; ☺ office 8-11am & 2-5pm), 2km southwest of Tiruvannamalai, draws devotees of Sri Ramana Maharshi, a guru who died in 1950 after nearly 50 years in contemplation. It's a very relaxed place, set in green surrounds, where visitors are able to meditate or worship the shrine where the guru achieved samadhi (conscious exit from the body). Day visits are permitted but *devotees only* may stay at the ashram by applying in writing, preferably at least three months in advance.

Sleeping & Eating
Tiruvannamalai is best visited as a day trip from Puducherry. There are budget lodges around the temple, but quality is lacking. During festival time (November/December) prices can rise by a staggering 1000%.

Arunachala Ramana Home (☎ 236120; www.arhometvm.com; 70 Ramana Nagar, Chengam Rd; s/d from Rs200/300) Basic, clean and friendly, it's close to the fabulous Manna Café which answers your any need for non-Indian food, including salads (Rs25), pastas and cakes. Plenty of chai stalls and veg cafes are nearby.

Hotel Ganesh (☎ 2226701; 111A Big St; d Rs245, with AC Rs645; ✷) On the busy bazaar road running along the north side of the temple, Ganesh is

---

THE LINGAM OF FIRE

Legend has it that Shiva appeared as a column of fire on Mt Arunachala, creating the original symbol of the lingam. Each November/December full moon, the **Karthikai Deepam Festival** celebrates this legend throughout India but becomes particularly significant at Tiruvannamalai. Here, a huge fire, lit from a 30m wick immersed in 2000L of ghee, blazes from the top of Mt Arunachala for days. In homes, lamps honour Shiva and his fiery lingam. The fire symbolises Shiva's light, which eradicates darkness and evil.

At festival time up to half a million people come to Tiruvannamalai. In honour of Shiva, they scale the mountain or circumnavigate its base. On the upward path, steps quickly give way to jagged and unstable rocks. There's no shade, the sun is relentless and the journey must be undertaken in bare feet – a mark of respect to the deity. None of this deters the thousands of pilgrims who quietly and joyfully make their way to the top and the abode of their deity.

a little haven of peace and value. Some rooms are poky, but they're clean enough and the inner courtyard balcony is pleasant. There's a decent veg restaurant downstairs.

Hotel Arunai Anantha (☎ 237275; www.aruna-ianantha.com; s/d from Rs1500/2000; 🅿 🏊) The big draws at this fairly deluxe hotel, about 1km beyond the ashram, are the landscaped gardens and swimming pool. For deluxe rooms add Rs300; they're worth it for the extra size and comfort.

Getting There & Away

There are buses every half-hour to Chennai (Rs62, 3½ hours) and Vellore (Rs40, two hours). There are at least three daily buses to Puducherry (Rs31, three hours). A taxi to Puducherry (via Gingee) costs around Rs800.

Only local passenger trains use Tiruvannamalai train station – two trains a day pass through between Vellore and Villupuram (where you can change for Puducherry).

GINGEE (SENJI)
☎ 04145

Somewhere 37km east of Tiruvannamalai, nature sprinkled a smattering of marbles – rounded boulders and lumpy rocks – in shades of grey, brown and red over the flat green paddies of Tamil Nadu. Then man turned two of these stony protrusions into the **Rajagiri & Krishnagiri** (King & Queen Fort; Indian/foreigner Rs5/100; ☉ 9am-5pm). Constructed mainly in the 16th century by the Vijayanagars (though some structures date from the 13th century), these edifices, which poke out of the Tamil plain like castles misplaced by the *Lord of the Rings,* have been occupied by the Marathas, the Mughals, the French and finally, the British.

It's a good hike to the top of either fort, but along the way you'll pass through several monuments, from *gopurams* to granaries. And hassle is almost non-existent (besides a few wandering sadhus); when you're here, it's you, a few friendly Indian tourists and lots of monkeys. A walk around will take half a day, especially if you cross the road and make the steep ascent to Krishnagiri. Buildings within Rajagiri (on the south side of the road) include a Shiva temple, a mosque and – most prominent – the restored audience hall. Almost all have been marred by graffiti.

It's easy to day trip to Gingee from Puducherry (67km) or Tiruvannamalai (37km). Buses leave every 30 minutes from Tiruvannamalai (Rs11.50, one hour). Ask to be let off at 'the fort', 2km before Gingee town. An autorickshaw from Gingee to the fort costs about Rs70 one way.

PUDUCHERRY (PONDICHERRY)
☎ 0413 / pop 220,749

Let's get something clear: if you came to Puducherry (which used to be called Pondicherry and is almost always referred to as 'Pondy') expecting a Provençal village in South India, you're in for some sore disappointment, *mon ami*. Most of Pondy is Tamil Nadu: honk-scream-screech-honk-chaos Tamil Nadu. Running through Tamil Nadu is a thin trickle of colonial Pondy: some cobblestones, mustard-yellow townhouses, and here and there a shady boulevard that could put you in mind of gendarmes marching past sari-clad belles – HONK!

On top of everything are hotels, restaurants and 'lifestyle' shops that sell a vision of *vieux Asie* created by savvy entrepreneurs and embellished by Gallic creative types who arrived here on the French hippie trail. Their presence has in turn attracted Indian artists and designers, and thus, Pondy's vibe: less faded colonial *ville*, more contemporary bohemian, vaguely New Age – but also faintly Old World – node on the international travel trail.

Enjoy the shopping, the French food (hellooooo steak!), the beer (goodbye Tamil Nadu alcohol taxes – Pondy is a Union Territory) and, if you like, yoga and meditation at the Sri Aurobindo Ashram. Have a stroll past the police, who still wear red Gallic *kepi,* and imagine another time when – HONK!

Orientation

Puducherry is split from east to west by a partially covered sewer…we mean, canal. The more 'French' part of town is on the east side (towards the sea), the more typically Indian portion to the west. Nehru St and Lal Bahadur Sastri, better known as Rue Bussy, are the main east–west streets; Mahatma Gandhi (MG) Rd and Mission St are the north–south thoroughfares. Pondy's grid design makes it relatively easy to follow, although many streets have one name at one end and another at the other, while others use the French 'Rue' instead of 'Street'.

TAMIL NADU

PUDUCHERRY (PONDICHERRY)

0 —————— 200 m
0 —————— 0.1 miles

Thiyaga Raja Salai

To Quiet Beach (4km);
Reppo Beach (4km);
International
Centre for Yoga Education &
Research (5km); Serenity
Beach (6km); Auroville (10km);
Mamallapuram (95km)

To Auroville (11km);
Kanchipuram (105km);
Chennai (160km)

To Bus Stand (500m);
Villupuram (39km);
Chidambaram (70km)

Botanical
Gardens
17

To Villupuram
(38km)

To Villa Pondicherry (1km);
Chunnambar (8km);
Chidambaram (70km)

Puducherry
Train Station

To New
Lighthouse (700m)

BAY OF
BENGAL

Bharathi
Park

Government
Square

Police
HQ

Old
Lighthouse

Heritage Walk

Information

Puducherry keeps European hours and takes
a long lunch break; you can expect most
businesses to be closed from about 1pm to
3.30pm. Besides the usual Indian and Tamil
Nadu festivals, Puducherry celebrates its
Gallic roots with a nice fete come Bastille
Day (p1043).

BOOKSHOPS

French Bookshop (☎ 2338062; Suffren St; ☺ 9am-
12.30pm & 3.30-7.30pm) This small shop next to Alliance
Française carries many French titles.
Librairie Kailash (☎ 331872; 169 Lal Bahadur Shastri
St; ☺ 9.30am-1.30pm & 3.30-9pm Mon-Sat) Another
excellent collection of titles, particularly coffee-table
books, in French.

INFORMATION	
Alliance Française	**1** C5
Canara Bank	**2** C3
Citibank ATM	**3** C4
Coffee.Com	**4** B4
Focus Books	**5** C3
French Bookshop	**6** C5
French Consulate	**7** D2
ICICI Bank	**8** C1
Libraire Kailash	**9** B4
LKP Forex	(see 51)
Main Post Office	**10** C3
New Medical Centre	**11** B4
Puducherry Tourist Office	**12** D4
State Bank of India	**13** C4
UTI Bank ATM	**14** B1
Vibe	(see 56)
Wi Corner	**15** C4

SIGHTS & ACTIVITIES	
Ayurvedic Holistic Healing Centre	**16** C1
Botanical Gardens	**17** A5
Church of Our Lady of the Immaculate Conception	**18** C3
Gandhi Statue	**19** D3
Hôtel de Ville (Town Hall)	**20** D4
Jayalakshmi Fine Arts Academy	**21** C3

Notre Dame de Agnes	**22** D4
Puducherry Museum	**23** D3
Sacred Heart Church	**24** B5
Sri Aurobindo Ashram	**25** D2
Sri Aurobindo Information Centre	**26** C3
Sri Manakula Vinayagar Temple	**27** C2

SLEEPING	
Ajantha Beach Guest House	**28** D5
Calve	**29** C2
French Villa	**30** D5
Ganga Guest House	**31** A4
Hotel Continental	**32** C5
Hotel De L'Orient	**33** C5
Hotel de Pondichery	**34** D5
New Guest House	**35** C5
Park Guest House	**36** D5
Promenade	**37** D3
Richmond	**38** C5
Santhi Inn	**39** C5
Sri Aurobindo Information Centre	(see 26)
Surya Swastika Guest House	**40** C2
Villa Helena	**41** C5

EATING	
Au Feu de Bois	**42** C4

kasha ki aasha	**43** C4
La Coromandale	**44** D4
La Terrasse	**45** C5
Le Café	**46** D3
Le Club	(see 34)
Madame Shante's	**47** C4
Rendezvous	**48** C4
Satsanga	**49** C5
Surguru	**50** C3

DRINKING	
Promenade	(see 37)
Space Coffee & Arts	**51** C4

SHOPPING	
Auroboutique	(see 25)
Fabindia	**52** C5
Geethanjali	**53** C4
kasha ki aasha	(see 43)
La Boutique d'Auroville	**54** C2
Pondy Cre'Art	(see 52)
Sri Aurobindo Handmade Paper Factory	**55** C1
Vibe	**56** C4

TRANSPORT	
Bicycle Hire	**57** C5

TAMIL NADU

Vibe (☎ 4500250; 6 Rue Surcouf; ✆ 10am-7.30pm Mon-Sat) Has a decent selection of books by Indian authors.

CULTURAL CENTRES
Alliance Française (☎ 2338146; afpondy@satyam.net. in; 58 Suffren St; ✆ 9am-noon & 3-6pm Mon-Sat) The French cultural centre has a library, computer centre and art gallery, and conducts French-language classes. Films are shown on Sunday at 6pm. The monthly newsletter, *Le Petit Journal*, details forthcoming events. Maison Colombani, its associated exhibition and performance space, is on Dumas St.

INTERNET ACCESS
You won't lack for internet cafes.
Coffee.Com (236 Mission St; per 30min Rs20; ✆ 10am-1am) A popular, hip cafe, but service has suffered as it has grown in popularity.
Wi Corner (1 Caziavar St, cnr Lal Bahadur Shastri Street; per hr Rs30; ✆ 10am-10pm) Our favourite, run by the overwhelmingly friendly Mohamed. Has rocket-fast connections and wi-fi.

MEDICAL SERVICES
Lal Bahadur Shastri St between Bharathi St and MG Rd is packed with clinics, pharmacies and two 24-hour hospitals:
New Medical Centre (☎ 2228890; 470 MG Rd; ✆ 24hr)

MONEY
ATMs are plentiful.
Canara Bank ATM (45 Gingy St)

Citibank ATM (cnr Lal Bahadur Shastri St & Labourdonnais Sts)
ICICI Bank ATM (47 Mission St)
LKP Forex (☎ 2224008; 2A Labourdonnais St; ✆ 9.30am-7.30pm Mon-Fri, 9.30am-6.30pm Sat)
State Bank of India (15 Suffren St)
UTI/Axis Bank ATM (164 Bussy St)

POST
Main post office (Rangapillai St; ✆ 9am-7pm Mon-Sat, 10am-5pm Sun)

TOURIST INFORMATION
Puducherry tourist office (☎ 2339497; 40 Goubert Ave; ✆ 9am-5pm) Has enthusiastic staff and a decent free map.

Sights & Activities
FRENCH QUARTER
Pocketed away in the eastern alleys are a series of cobbled roads, white and mustard buildings in various states of romantic *déshabillé*, and a slight sense of Gallic glory gone by, otherwise known as the French Quarter. The best way to explore these streets is via Puducherry's **heritage walk**. Start at the north end of Goubert Ave, the seafront promenade, and wander south past the **French consulate** and the **Gandhi Statue**. Turn right at the **Hôtel de Ville** (town hall) on Rue Mahe Labourdonnais, past the shady **Bharathi Park**. From there it's a matter

of pottering south through **Dumas**, **Romain Rolland** and **Suffren Sts**. **Focus Books** (☎ 2345513; 204 Mission St; 9.30am-1.30pm & 3.30-9pm Mon-Sat) sells heritage walking trail brochures (Rs9). You may also want to take a look down Vysial St, between MG Rd and Mission St; locals say this tree-lined block is one of the last faithfully maintained slices of old Pondy.

SRI AUROBINDO ASHRAM
Founded in 1926 by Sri Aurobindo and a Frenchwoman known as 'the Mother' (whose visage, which you'll either find benevolent or vaguely creepy, is *everywhere* here), this **ashram** (cnr Marine St & Manakula Vinayagar Koil St) seeks to synthesise yoga and modern science. After Aurobindo's death, spiritual authority (and minor religious celebrity) passed to the Mother, who died in 1973 aged 97. A constant flow of visitors files through the **main ashram building** (8am-noon & 2-6pm Mon-Sat), which has the flower-festooned samadhi of Aurobindo and the Mother in the central courtyard.

PUDUCHERRY MUSEUM
Goodness knows how this cute little **museum** (15 St Louis St; adult/child Rs2/1; 9.40am-1pm & 2-5.20pm Tue-Sun) keeps its artefacts from rotting, considering there's a whole floor of French-era furniture sitting in the South Indian humidity. As you amble through the colonial-era building, keep an eye peeled for Pallava and Chola sculptures, a small Versailles' worth of French Union–era bric-a-brac, and coins and shards of pottery excavated from Arikamedu, a once-major seaport a few kilometres south of Puducherry that traded with the Roman Empire during the 1st century BC.

CHURCHES & TEMPLES
Puducherry has one of the best collections of over-the-top cathedrals in India. *Merci*, French missionaries. The **Church of Our Lady of the Immaculate Conception** (Mission St), completed in 1791, is a robin's-egg-blue-and-cloud-white typically Jesuit edifice, while the brown-and-white grandiosity of the **Sacred Heart Church** (Subbayah Salai) is set off by stained glass and a Gothic sense of proportion. The mellow pink-and-cream **Notre Dame de Anges** (Dumas St), built in 1858, looks sublime in the late-afternoon light. The smooth limestone interior was made using eggshells in the plaster.

But this is still India, and the Hindu faith still reigns supreme. Don't miss the chance to watch tourists, pilgrims and the curious get a head pat from the temple elephant who stands outside **Sri Manakula Vinayagar Temple** (Manakula Vinayagar Koil St; 5.45am-12.30pm & 4-9.30pm), dedicated to Ganesh and tucked down a backstreet just south of the Sri Aurobindo Ashram; the temple also contains over 40 skilfully painted friezes.

BOTANICAL GARDENS
Established by the French in 1826, the **botanical gardens** (admission free; 10am-5pm) form a green, if somewhat litter-strewn, oasis on the southwest side of town.

BEACHES
Pondy is a seaside town, but that doesn't make it a beach destination; the city's sand is a thin strip of dirty brown blah that slurps into a seawall of jagged rocks. With that said, Goubert Ave (Beach Rd) is a killer stroll, especially at dawn and dusk when everyone in town takes a constitutional or romantic stroll. There are a few decent beaches to the north and south of town. Quiet, Reppo and Serenity Beaches are all north of the centre, within 8km of Puducherry. Chunnambar, 8km south, has Paradise Beach, water sports and backwater boat cruises. Both areas are becoming inundated with high-end resorts. The tourist office (p1073) has details.

Courses
ARTS
Jayalakshmi Fine Arts Academy (☎ 2342036; goodsin@ vsnl.net.in; 221 Mission St; 9.30am-1.30pm & 3.30-8.30pm Mon-Sat, 7am-12.30pm Sun) is an established place with classes in *bharatanatyam* (dance), singing, *veena* (Indian stringed instrument), tabla (drums) and a range of other musical instruments. Private tuition fees start at Rs200 per hour for a minimum of five hours, and there's a one-off registration fee (Rs350).

YOGA & AYURVEDA
Puducherry's International Yoga Festival (p1043) is held annually in early January. **International Centre for Yoga Education & Research** (ICYER; ☎ 2241561; www.icyer.com; 16A Mettu St, Chinnamudaliarchavady, Kottukuppam) Also known as the Ananda Ashram, this renowned centre conducts annual six-month yoga teacher-training courses and 10-day summer courses.

Ayurvedic Holistic Healing Centre (☎ 6537651; 6 Sengeniammal Koil St) Performs detox services, back procedures, varna point massage, skin treatment and offers ayurvedic massages and yoga courses.

Sri Aurobindo Ashram (☎ 23396483; bureaucentral@sriaurobindoashram.org; 3 Rangapillai St) Study and/or practise yoga (see also opposite).

Tours

The local tourist office (p1073) runs half-day sightseeing tours (Rs100, 2pm to 6pm) to the water-sports complex at Chunnambar, Auroville and Sri Aurobindo Ashram. Full-day tours (Rs200, 9am to 6pm) cover the same area plus the botanical gardens, paper factory (p1077), Sacred Heart Church and a couple of Hindu temples; both tours need a minimum of six people to operate.

Sleeping

If you've been saving for a special occasion, splurge here, because Puducherry's lodgings are as good as South India gets. Local heritage houses manage to combine colonial romanticism with modern spoilage and, dare we say, French playfulness, like vintage movie posters and colour schemes that run from monochrome to neon-bright; these same rooms would likely run hundreds of dollars in the West.

BUDGET

Sri Aurobindo Ashram runs a lot of local budget accommodation. They're clean and you'll be around like-minded souls (ie the budget – and karma – conscious). But they come with rules: 10.30pm curfew and no smoking or alcohol. For information and reservations, contact the **Sri Aurobindo information centre** (☎ 2339646/8; bureaucentral@sriaurobindoashram .org; cnr Rangapillai St & Ambour Salai; ⏰ 6am-8pm).

New Guest House (☎ 2221553; 64 Romain Rolland St; d Rs100) Sparse, huge and packed with the ashram faithful; this is a great spot for those who love the monastery cubicle school of lodging.

Surya Swastika Guest House (☎ 2343092; 11 Iswaran Koil St; d Rs140-150, without bathroom Rs100) It's (decidedly) not the Ritz, but if you need clean, cheap rooms and no curfew, this is your best bet.

Hotel Continental (☎ 2225828; 48 Labourdonnais St; s/d Rs350/500; ❄) The Continental may not have much charm, but it does have clean, polished rooms and AC for a bargain price.

Park Guest House (☎ 2334412; 1 Goubert Ave; d Rs400, with AC Rs600; ❄) This is the most sought-after

ashram address in town thanks to its wonderful seafront position. All front rooms face the sea and have their own porch or balcony, and there's a large lawn area for morning yoga or meditation.

MIDRANGE & TOP END

Ganga Guest House (☎ 2222675; www.gangaguest.com; 479 Bharathi St; r Rs400-750) This old colonnaded house, swathed in red, yellow and chocolate browns, feels like the antique set of a period piece Bollywood blockbuster – posters for which decorate every room. Aim for a terrace room; they get a bit of breeze and some have balconies.

Santhi Inn (☎ 2220946; www.santhiinn.com; 57 Nehru St; r Rs600-850; ❄) The multistorey Santhi certainly isn't a heritage house, but it's a clean, corporate-y kinda spot with comfy beds and a conveniently central location.

Ajantha Beach Guest House (☎ 2338898; 1 Rue Bazar St Laurent; d with sea view Rs600-1200; ❄) The location is the main selling point – right on the beachfront promenade. The four sea-view rooms are plain but comfortable and have balconies; others are drab and windowless.

Villa Pondicherry (☎ 2356253; www.pondy.org; 23 Dr Ambedkar Salai; d from Rs650, without bathroom from Rs550; ❄) This ageing but charming colonial residence is about 1km south of the train station, next to St Francis Xavier Church. The five rooms and central lounge certainly have character and fun decor, but some may find it a little too homely. Look for the red door and small brass plaque under the verandah.

Hotel de Pondichery (☎ 2227409; 38 Dumas St; r from Rs1350-2450; ❄) Yet another heritage home, this recently renovated place has lovely colonial-style rooms and outdoor terraces. It's more Old World than luxurious, but rooms are private and quiet.

French Villa (☎ 4201545; www.thefrenchvilla.in; 51 Suffren St; r Rs1500) We're not quite sure what a 'traveller's house of colours and flavours', as the brochure states, is supposed to be, but we do think this villa – more of a cottage – is immaculately cute. The smallish scale and seashore-bright rooms are a pleasant break from Pondy's more baroque heritage-style hotels.

our pick Villa Helena (☎ 2226789; villahelena@satyam.net.in; 13 Lal Bahadur Shastri St; r Rs2200-2800; ❄) What sits Helena apart from her heritage siblings is the dash of vintage fun she overlays on respectable colonial facades. With 1930s-era

Chinese movie posters, luxurious beds and high-ceilinged rooms, you feel caught between a black-and-white colonial noir flick and a modern designer's dream.

Hotel De L'Orient (☎ 2343067; www.neemranahotels .com; 17 Romain Rolland St; r Rs3000–6000; 🅰) This is as grand as it gets in Puducherry: a restored colonial mansion with rooms that appeal to your inner pith-helmeted aristocrat. Should you need a sense of columned regal importance, the hush of breezy verandahs and the scurrying service of men in clean white uniforms, this is the place to book.

Richmond (☎ 2346363; www.theresidency.com; 12 Labourdonnais St; r incl breakfast Rs3500–4000; 🅰 🖳) The Richmond, located in an attractive yellow colonial-era edifice, manages the whole heritage with a twist of modern aesthetic very well; rooms are dark-wood accented but sleek enough to stand out to the contemporary conscious.

Calve (☎ 2224261; www.calve.in; 36 Vysial St; r incl breakfast Rs3555–5355; 🅰) This excellent heritage option, located on a quiet, tree-shaded boulevard, combines a soaring sense of high-ceilinged space with egg-white walls, flat-screen TVs, huge niche-embedded mattresses groaning under soft cushions and a warm backdrop of Burmese teak floors and banisters.

Promenade (☎ 2227750; www.sarovarhotels.com; 23 Goubert Ave; r incl breakfast Rs5200–6900; 🅰) The Promenade is a supremely modern beachfront boutique dripping with contemporary design flash. It's owned and operated by the swish Hidesign group, and is trying to magnetise itself as a centre for Puducherry's small social scene.

Eating

Puducherry is a Tamil Nadu culinary highlight; you get the best of South Indian cooking plus several restaurants specialising in well-prepped French and Italian cuisine. If you've been missing cheese and think cows are only sacred when seared medium rare, you're in luck. There's a string of cheap street stalls open past 11pm on Anna Salai and Lal Bahadur Shastri St

La Coromandale (30 Goubert Ave; mains Rs40) Tasty South Indian thalis, rice, noodles and cold drinks and a relaxed atmosphere for meeting and chatting are the attractions of this open-fronted restaurant, situated on the promenade. Beware of eccentric opening hours.

Le Café (Goubert Ave; mains Rs40-150) Situated near the Gandhi statue, this is a good spot for sandwiches, coffee (hot or ice) and clean views over the Bay of Bengal.

kasha ki aasha (☎ 2222963; www.kasha-ki-aasha. com; 23 Rue Surcouf; mains Rs60–120; ⏰ 8am-7pm Mon-Sat) You'll get a great pancake breakfast, good lunches (try the European-style thali) and delicious cakes served on the pretty rooftop of this colonial-house-cum-craftshop-cum-cafe.

Surguru (☎ 4308082; 99 Mission St; mains Rs40-100; ⏰ lunch & dinner) Simple South Indian served in a posh setting. Surguru is the fix for thali addicts who like their veg accompanied by the strongest AC this side of Chennai.

La Terrasse (☎ 2220809; 5 Subbayah Salai; pizzas Rs80-175; ⏰ Thu-Tue) This simple semi-open-air place near the southern end of the promenade has a wide menu but is best known for good pizzas and safe salads, as opposed to their Indian food (which is frankly wanting). No alcohol is served.

Madame Shante's (40 Romain Rolland St; mains Rs90-170; ⏰ lunch & dinner) This rooftop option, which does its stock-in-trade in French, with a focus on seafood (try the garlic squid), isn't quiete as polished-looking as the competition, but the food is still excellent and the ambience decidedly open-air and alluring.

Au Feu de Bois (☎ 2341821; 28 Lal Bahadur Shastri St; pizzas Rs140-230; ⏰ lunch & dinner Tue-Sun) Wood-fired pizza and only wood-fired pizza is the name of the game here, and it's a damn decent game.

Le Club (☎ 2339745; 38 Dumas St; mains Rs140-325; ⏰ lunch & dinner) This club wraps three restaurants into one, with heavy French fare, a simple garden terrace and – unique to Pondy as of our writing – Vietnamese and Southeast Asian fare in the attached Indochine.

Satsanga (☎ 2225867; 30-32 Labourdonnais St; mains Rs150-250; ⏰ lunch & dinner) This very popular backyard spot serves excellent continental cuisine and, like most places in this genre, a full Indian menu as well. The large variety of sausages and lovely homemade bread and butter goes down a particular treat, as do any of the steaks.

Rendezvous (☎ 2339132; 30 Suffren St; mains Rs150-500; ⏰ lunch & dinner Wed-Mon) The steaks here are superb, but then again, so is just about anything at this suitably romantic restaurant, where diners can lounge in AC comfort or pick at their coq au vin under the stars on the lush garden terrace.

TAMIL NADU

Drinking & Entertainment

Although this is one of the better spots in Tamil Nadu to sink a beer, closing time is a decidedly un-Gallic 11pm. If you're here on Friday or Saturday, get ready for some late-night fun, when Pondy stays open until (drum roll)…11.30pm! Break out the champagne! With low taxes on alcohol, Puducherry has a reputation for cheap booze. The reality is you'll really only find cheap beer (Rs30) in 'liquor shops' or the darkened bars attached to them. While you can sometimes get a large Kingfisher for Rs60, the better restaurants charge up to Rs100.

Space Coffee & Arts (☎ 2356253; 2 Labourdonnais St; ☸ 6-11pm) A funky little semi-open-air cafe for juice, coffee, beer, a bite and some damn fine cocktails (hello, Blue Lemonade). Staff are friendly, locals and tourists congregate here, and all in all it's the most social traveller spot in Pondy.

The Promenade (opposite) hotel bar also occasionally gets buzzing in the evenings.

Shopping

With all the yoga yuppies congregating here, Pondy is starting to specialise in the sort of boutique-chic-meets-Indian-bazaar school of fashion, accessories and souvenirs.

Sri Aurobindo Handmade Paper Factory (☎ 2334 763; 50 SV Patel Salai; ☸ 8.30am-noon & 1.30-5pm Mon-Sat) Fine handmade paper is sold here, and you can ask at the counter about tours of the factory. There's a wider choice of goods at Auroboutique near the ashram; all sales support ashram work.

Fabindia (☎ 2226010; www.fabindia.com; 59 Suffren St; ☸ 9.30am-7.30pm) Opposite Alliance Française, this shop has a good variety of quality woven goods and furnishings, traditionally made but with a contemporary feel. In operation since 1960, one of its selling points is its 'fair, equitable and helpful relationship' with village producers.

Geethanjali (☎ 4200392; 20 Lal Bahadur Shastri St; ☸ 10am-7pm Mon-Sat) The sort of place where Indiana Jones gets the sweats, this antique and curio shop sells statues, sculptures, paintings and furniture culled from Puducherry's colonial, and even pre-colonial history.

La Boutique d'Auroville (38 Nehru St; ☸ 9.30am-1pm & 3.30-8pm Mon-Sat) It's fun browsing through the crafts here, including jewellery, batiks, kalamkari (similar to batik) drawings, carpets and woodcarvings.

kasha ki aasha (☎ 2222963; www.kasha-ki-aasha .com; 23 Rue Surcouf; ☸ 8am-7pm Mon-Sat) Fabulous fabrics and gorgeous garments and crafts that are sourced directly from their makers are sold by an all-women staff in this lovely old colonial house. There's a breezy rooftop eatery (p1076) on site.

Pondy Cre'Art(☎ 4200258; 53 Suffren St; ☸ 10am-7.30pm Mon-Sat) Local and European designers get their creativity going on here with leather handbags, handmade paper journals and the sort of clothes that look like they got caught between an Indian flea market and a Soho outlet.

Vibe (☎ 4500250; 6 Rue Surcouf; ☸ 10am-7.30pm Mon-Sat) There's a lot of made-for-travellers Indian fashion hanging from the racks here; think breezy but flattering salwar kameez–inspired blouses for women and mandarin-collared cotton shirts for men. It also does a good stock-in-trade of the sleek designer homeware that screams conspicuous consumption, and sells some good books on the side, but the staff can be overbearing, following you around every room in the shop.

Getting There & Away

BUS
The bus stand is 500m west of town. See the boxed text (p1078) for details of services.

TAXI
Air-conditioned taxis from Puducherry to Chennai cost around Rs2700 and to Chennai airport Rs2500.

TRAIN
There are two direct services a day to Chennai (Rs58, five hours), and one to Tirupathy. There's a computerised booking service for southern trains at the station.

Getting Around

One of the best ways to get around Pondy is by walking. Large three-wheelers shuttle between the bus stand and Gingy St for Rs5, but they're hopelessly overcrowded. Cycle- and autorickshaws are plentiful – an autorickshaw across town costs about Rs40.

Since the streets are broad and flat, the most popular transport is pedal power. Bicycle-hire shops line many of the streets, especially MG Rd and Mission St. You'll also find hire shops in Subbayah Salai and Goubert Ave. The usual rental is Rs5/20 per hour/day, but some places ask Rs70 per day.

BUSES FROM PUDUCHERRY (PONDICHERRY)				
Destination	Fare (Rs)	Duration (hr)	Frequency	Type
Bengaluru	150	8	6 daily	Deluxe
Chennai	55	3½	83 daily	Express
Chidambaram	25	1½	50 daily	State
Coimbatore	170	9	8 daily	Deluxe
Kanchipuram	40	3	5 daily	State
Kumbakonam	35	4	6 daily	State
Mamallapuram	35	2	5 daily	State
Tiruvannamalai	40	3½	9 daily	State
Trichy	75	5	4 daily	Deluxe & State

Mopeds or motorbikes are useful for getting out to the beaches or to Auroville and can be rented from a number of shops and street stalls. The going rate is Rs150 a day for a gearless scooter and Rs175 for a motorbike.

AUROVILLE
☎ 0413 / pop 1800
Auroville is one of those ideas anyone with a whiff of New Age will love: an international community built on handfuls of soil donated by 124 countries, where dedicated souls, ignoring creed, colour and nationality, work to build a universal township and realise interconnectedness, love and good old human oneness.

On paper. In execution, Auroville is both its high ideals and some not-as-glamorous reality. Imagine over 80 rural settlements encompassing scrubby Tamil countryside, where harmony is strived for if not always realised between 1800 residents representing almost 40 nationalities. Two-thirds of Aurovillians are foreign, and outside opinions of them range from positive vibes to critics who say the town is an enclave for expats seeking a self-indulgent rustic escape.

Ultimately, Auroville encompasses all of the above, and anyone interested in the experiment may want to visit on a day trip from Puducherry. Be prepared for lots of posters celebrating 'The Mother', the French traveller-turned-guru, and founder of the Sri Aurobindo Ashram (p1074). Be warned: Auroville is not that tourist-friendly. Each settlement has its own area of expertise and most Aurovillians are busy simply getting on with their work. Still, you may get a sense of the appeal of the place after a visit to the visitor centre and the **Matrimandir**, Auroville's spiritual

heart. One of those unfortunate buildings that tries to look futuristic and ends up coming off dated, this giant golden golf ball/faux Epcot Center contains an inner chamber lined with white marble that houses a solid crystal (the largest in the world), 70cm in diameter, which you won't actually see, since the Matrimandir is not open to casual visitors. But there is a pleasant plot of **gardens** (🕑 10am-1pm & 2-4.30pm daily except Sun afternoon), from which you can spy the structure while listening to piped-in Enya-esque music; you need to pick up a pass (free) from the information service (below).

Information
There's a photographic exhibition and video room at the **Auroville Information Service** (www .auroville.org; admission free; 🕑 9am-1pm & 1.30-5.30pm), which also issues garden passes for external views of the Matrimandir (from 9.45am to 12.30pm and 1.45pm to 4pm only). In the same complex, the **visitor centre** (☎ 2622239; www .auroville.org; 🕑 9am-6pm) contains a bookshop, a nice cafe and Boutique d'Auroville, which sells Aurovillian handicrafts.

Sleeping & Eating
You can only stay in Auroville if you're serious about contributing to it. A stay of no shorter than a week is preferred and while work isn't obligatory, it's much appreciated. Accommodation isn't offered in exchange for work; rooms range from Rs150 to Rs1000, and guests are also required to contribute around Rs60 per day for the 'maintenance and development' of Auroville.

There are more than 40 guest houses in Auroville, each tied to communities with specific work missions (women's education, farming etc). The best way to match your interests with the community you'll stay in is to check out the website and, preferably, get suggestions from and make arrangements with the **Auroville Guest Service** (☎ 2622704; avguests@ auroville.org.in) before arriving.

Although there are stores and small roadside eateries in Auroville, and communities have communal dining areas, many Aurovillians gather at the Solar Kitchen – powered by solar energy – which dishes out more than 400 meals daily from its buffet. The cafe at the visitor centre is open to day visitors.

Getting There & Away
The best way to enter Auroville is from the coast road, at the village of Periyar Mudali-archavadi. Ask around as it's not well signposted. A return autorickshaw ride from Puducherry is about Rs250, but a better option is to hire a moped or bicycle. It's about 12km from Puducherry to the visitor centre.

CENTRAL TAMIL NADU

CHIDAMBARAM
☎ 04144 / pop 67,795
There's basically one reason to visit Chidambaram: The Lord of the Dance. No, put away your Michael Flatley posters – we mean the great temple complex of Nataraja, Shiva as the Dancer of the Universe. The greatest Nataraja temple in India also happens to be a Dravidian architectural highlight and one of the holiest Shiva sites in South India. Chidambaram can be visited as a day trip from Puducherry, or as a stopover between Puducherry and Kumbakonam or Trichy.

Of the many festivals, the two largest are the **10-day chariot festivals**, which are celebrated in April/May and December/January. In February/March the five-day **Natyanjali Dance Festival** (p1043) attracts performers from all over the country to celebrate Nataraja (Shiva) – Lord of the Dance.

Orientation & Information
The small town is developed around the Nataraja Temple with streets named after the cardinal points. Accommodation is close to the temple and the bus stand a five-minute walk to the southeast. The train station is about 1km further south.
Cybase (Pillaiyar Koil St; per hr Rs30; ☼ 9am-9pm) Fast internet access.

ICICI Bank ATM (Hotel Saradharam; South Car St)
Post office (North Car St; ☼ 10am-3pm Mon-Sat)
Tourist office (☎ 238739; Railway Feeder Rd; ☼ 9am-5pm Mon-Fri) Frequently deserted.
UAE Exchange (Pillaiyar Koil St; ☼ Mon-Sat) Best place in town to exchange money.

Sights
NATARAJA TEMPLE
The legend goes: one day, in a nearby forest, Shiva and Kali got into a dance-off that was judged by the assembled gods. Shiva finished his routine with a high kick to the head that Kali could not duplicate and won the title Nataraja, or Lord of the Dance. It is in this form he is worshipped at the great **Shiva temple** (☼ courtyard & shrines 6am-12.30pm & 4.30-10.30pm), which draws a regular stream of pilgrims and visitors. The region was a Chola capital from 907 to 1310 and the temple was erected during the later time of the administration, although local guides claim some of the complex was built by the Pallavas in the 6th century. The high-walled 22-hectare complex has four towering *gopurams* decked out in schizophrenic Dravidian stonework.

The main entrance, through the east *gopuram*, off East Car St, depicts the 108 sacred positions of classical Tamil dance. In the northeast of the complex, to the right as you enter, is the 1000-pillared **Raja Sabha** (King's Hall), open only on festival days, and to the left is the **Sivaganga** (Temple Tank), which is thick with mudfish and worshippers performing ritual ablutions. To the west of the entrance to the inner sanctum is a depiction of Shiva as Nataraja that is underlined by a distinctly European pair of cherubic angels. In the southwest corner of the second enclosure is the Dance Hall, decorated with 56 pillars, that marks the spot where Shiva outdanced Kali.

Cameras are not allowed inside the temple, and non-Hindus cannot enter the inner sanctum, although you can glimpse its golden roof and its 21,600 tiles (one for every breath a human takes a day). Note the lions that top the columns; symbols of Chola royalty and a reminder of who acted as patron for the temple. Also look out for temple Brahmins, who sport a specific lopsided-to-the-left-half shaved head. Nataraja images abound, wherein Shiva holds the drum that beats the rhythm of creation and the fire of destruction in his outstretched hands, ending one cycle of creation, beginning another and uniting all opposites – light and dark, good and evil.

TAMIL NADU

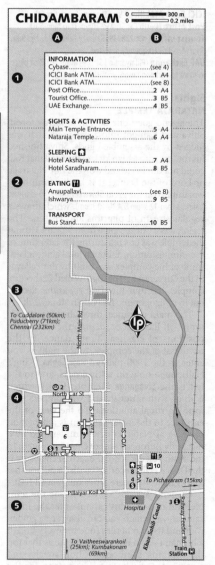

Try to catch the fire ceremony, which occurs six times a day and pulls in hundreds of worshippers who watch a ritual essentially unchanged for thousands of years. The entire complex erupts in drum beats and bells, while fires of clarified oil and butter are passed under the image of the deity, thus ensuring the cycle of creation continues.

Brahmin priests will usually guide you for a fee (anywhere from Rs30 up to Rs300, depending on the language skills and knowledge of the guide) around the temple complex. Since the Brahmins work as a cooperative to fund the temple you may wish to support this magnificent building by way of donation or hiring a guide (but don't feel bound to do so).

Sleeping & Eating

Chidambaram has many cheap pilgrims' lodges clustered around the temple; you can usually get an AC room for between Rs500 and Rs800, and non-AC for as low as Rs150, but some of these spots come off as pretty dire.

Hotel Akshaya (☎ 220192; 17/18 East Car St; r Rs300-800) Close to the temple, this hotel has a wide range of rooms that run the gamut from boxy singles to quite good value AC 'suites'.

Hotel Saradharam (☎ 221336; www.hotelsaradharam.co.in; 19 VGP St; d Rs650, with AC Rs1200; 🏠) The busy and friendly Saradharam is the top hotel in town and conveniently located across from the bus stand. It's a bit worn in corners, but it's clean and comfortable and a welcome respite from the frenzy of the town centre.

Predictably, the best places to eat are in hotels. **Anuupallavi** (mains Rs25-70; 🕑 lunch & dinner) is an excellent AC multicuisine restaurant in the Saradharam. Just across the bus stand is vegetarian **Ishwarya** (thalis Rs25; 🕑 breakfast, lunch & dinner), which does very fine thalis. There are lots of cheap veg eats in the area immediately surrounding the temple complex.

Getting There & Away

The bus stand is very central – within walking distance to the temple and accommodation. There are hourly buses to Chennai (Rs90, seven hours), and buses to Puducherry (Rs40, two hours) and Kumbakonam (Rs35, 2½ hours) run regularly. There are also five direct buses daily to Madurai (Rs150, eight hours).

Chidambaram now stands on the Chennai–Trichy gauge line; trains and services are open to Kumbakonam, Thanjavur and once a day to Rameswaram. The station is a 20-minute walk southeast of the temple (Rs40 by autorickshaw).

AROUND CHIDAMBARAM

About 15km east of town, **Pichavaram** is a peaceful backwater of mangroves and tidal flats. You can spend a pleasant hour or two being rowed around the waterways and enjoying the bird life and calm surrounds. Boat hire (per hour Rs125; maximum five people) is available every day, and is busy with local visitors at the weekend. A basic three-room **guest house** (per room Rs300) is available beside the boat-hire place, and you can order food there.

KUMBAKONAM
☎ 0435 / pop 160,767
At first glance Kumbakonam is another Indian junction town, but then you notice the temples that sprout out of this busy city like mushrooms, a reminder that this was once a seat of medieval South Indian power. It's an easy day trip from Thanjavur, and makes a good base for exploring the coastal towns of the Cauvery Delta.

There's no tourist office in Kumbakonam, and road names and signs here are more erratic than usual. The best place to exchange travellers cheques is at the **UAE Exchange** (☎ 2423212; 134 Kamarajar Rd) near the train station. You'll find an ICICI Bank ATM almost opposite **Ashok Net Café** (☎ 2433054; 24 Ayikulam Rd; per hr Rs20; ⏱ 9am-10.30pm).

Sights
Dozens of colourfully painted *gopurams* point skyward from Kumbakonam's 18 temples, most of which are dedicated to Shiva or Vishnu, but probably only the most dedicated temple-goer would tackle visiting more than a few. All temples are open from 6am to noon and 4pm to 10pm, and admission is free.

The largest Vishnu temple in Kumbakonam, with a 50m-high east gate, is **Sarangapani Temple**, just off Ayikulam Rd. The temple shrine, in the form of a chariot, was the work of the Cholas during the 12th century.

Kumbeshwara Temple, about 200m west and entered via a nine-storey *gopuram,* is the largest Shiva temple. It contains a lingam said to have been made by Shiva himself when he mixed the nectar of immortality with sand.

The 12th-century **Nageshwara Temple**, from the Chola dynasty, is also dedicated to Shiva in the guise of Nagaraja, the serpent king. On three days of the year (in April or May) the sun's rays fall on the lingam. The main shrine here is in the form of a chariot.

The huge **Mahamakham Tank**, 600m southeast of the Nageshwara Temple, is the most

TAMIL NADU

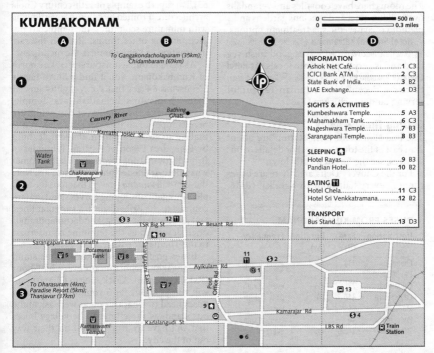

KUMBAKONAM

0 — 500 m
0 — 0.3 miles

INFORMATION
Ashok Net Café.....................1 C3
ICICI Bank ATM.....................2 C3
State Bank of India................3 B2
UAE Exchange......................4 D3

SIGHTS & ACTIVITIES
Kumbeshwara Temple............5 A3
Mahamakham Tank................6 C3
Nageshwara Temple..............7 B3
Sarangapani Temple..............8 B3

SLEEPING
Hotel Rayas.........................9 B3
Pandian Hotel......................10 B2

EATING
Hotel Chela.........................11 C3
Hotel Sri Venkkatramana.........12 B2

TRANSPORT
Bus Stand...........................13 D3

sacred in Kumbakonam. It's believed that every 12 years the waters of the Ganges flow into the tank, and at this time a festival is held; the next is due in 2016.

Sleeping & Eating

Pandian Hotel (☎ 2430397; 52 Sarangapani East St; s/d Rs140/250) You might want to sniff around the rooms (some of which are mildewed) at this budget standby, but in general you're getting good value here.

Hotel Siva International (☎ 2424013; Periya St; d from Rs300, with AC from Rs800; 🎇) Given the sheer size of this complex you're likely to find something that suits your taste amidst the labyrinthine warren of clean budget and midrange rooms. They're a bit boxy, but comfortable for their lack of character.

Hotel Rayas (☎ 2422545, 2423170; 18 Post Office Rd; d from Rs700, with AC from Rs900; 🎇) Friendly service and reliably spacious (and clean) rooms make this your best lodging option in town.

Paradise Resort (☎ 2416469; www.paradiseresort india.com; Tanjore Rd, Darasuram; r from Rs2000; 🎇) An atmospheric resort constructed around heritage buildings and thatch and teak cottages. The rooms here have cool tiles and verandahs overlooking quiet and spacious gardens and a plethora of ayurvedic spa treatment options.

Hotel Sri Venkkatramana (TSR Big St; thalis Rs25; 🕐 breakfast, lunch & dinner) serves good fresh veg food and is very popular with locals. At **Hotel Chela** (9 Ayikulam Rd; mains Rs30-80; 🕐 lunch & dinner) there's a decent North Indian restaurant serving tandoori chicken (Rs80).

Getting There & Away

The bus stand and train station are about 2km east of the town centre. For details of bus services, see the boxed text (below).

For the Cauvery Delta area there are buses running every half-hour to Karaikal (Rs16,

BUSES FROM KUMBAKONAM

Destination	Fare (Rs)	Duration (hr)	Frequency
Chennai (No 303)	113	7	every 30min
Chidambaram	22	2½	every 20min
Coimbatore	110	10	daily (7pm)
Madurai	65	5	8 daily
Puducherry	40	4½	every 20min
Thanjavur	14.50	1½	every 10min

two hours), via Tranquebar and then on to Nagapattinam.

The overnight *Rock Fort Express* is the only major train to/from Chennai (sleeper/3AC Rs130/365), going via Thanjavur and Trichy. Passenger trains run to Chidambaram (Rs31, two hours) and Thanjavur.

AROUND KUMBAKONAM

Within a very easy day-trip distance from Kumbakonam are the two superb Chola temples of Dharasuram and Gangakondacholapuram. They are comparatively unvisited and beautifully constructed, and can be enjoyed in relative peace. Along with Brihadishwara Temple (p1084) in Thanjavur, these structures are a Unesco World Heritage Site: the Great Living Chola Temples. They can be visited on a day trip from Kumbakonam, or from Thanjavur (for Dharasuram) and Chidambaram (for Gangakondacholapuram).

Dharasuram & Gangakondacholapuram

Only 4km west of Kumbakonam in the village of Dharasuram, the **Airatesvara Temple** (🕐 6am-noon & 4-8pm), constructed by Rajaraja II (1146-63), is a superb example of 12th-century Chola architecture. Fronted by columns overflowing with miniature sculptures, the temple art depicts, among other things, Shiva in the rare incarnation as Kankalamurti, the mendicant.

At Gangakondacholapuram, 35km north of Kumbakonam, you'll find a Shiva **temple** (🕐 6am-noon & 4-8pm) that's only slightly smaller than Thanjavur's Brihadishwara Temple; many believe the quality of the sculpture here is superior to its sister structure. While that's a subjective opinion, the temple, built by Rajendrea I (son of Rajaraja I, builder of Brihadishwara) does represent a latter, somewhat more developed phase of Chola art. Note the 49m-tall *vimana* (tower) that tops the temple; its elegant up-sloping curves stand in stark contrast to the Brihadishwara's angular lines, and as a result the Gangakondacholapuram is often described as the feminine counterpart to the Thanjavur edifice.

Buses go from Kumbakonam bus stand to Gangakondacholapuram every half-hour (Rs15, 1½ hours). A rickshaw to Dharasuram will run at about Rs75 roundtrip. Frequent buses head to Dharasuram as well; ask at the bus stand, as these tend to be village buses that will have to drop you off on their way out of the city.

CAUVERY DELTA

The Cauvery River is the beating heart of South Indian agriculture and, back in its day, connected the entire region via riverine routes. Today the Cauvery's delta, which spills into Tamil Nadu's east coast, is one of the prettiest and poorest parts of the state. This green and pleasant region can be visited on a lovely day drive (expect to pay Rs2000 to Rs3000 for a return taxi from Kumbakonam), although Nagapattinam, the capital of the district of the same name, can be given a pass unless you love traffic and drying fish.

Tourism infrastructure is generally of a low standard. Nagapattinam district was the worst affected part of Tamil Nadu when the 2004 tsunami struck, with up to 7000 lives lost and thousands more left homeless. Life seems to have returned to normal, although international aide projects were still very much in evidence at the time of writing.

Tranquebar (Tharangambadi)

☎ 04364

About 80km south of Chidambaram, Tranquebar was a Danish post established in 1620 by the Danish East India Company. The solid, pink-hued seafront **Danesborg Fort** (Indian/foreigner Rs5/50; ☼ 10am-1pm & 2-5.45pm Sat-Thu), occupied by the British in 1801, houses a small but fascinating **museum** on the region's Danish history. The quiet roadway leading to the fort is entered by an impressive 1792 gateway, and an exuberant Sunday service is held in the nearby 1718 church. Danish NGOs are busy restoring some of the colonial row houses in the fort's vicinity.

Stay directly opposite the fort in the exquisitely plush **Bungalow on the Beach** (☎ 288065; www.neemranahotels.com; r from Rs3000; 🍴 🖥); rooms and views are fabulous, as is the villa-like heritage setting. Just next door – and still with sea views – is the pleasant **Hotel Tamil Nadu** (☎ 288065; dm/r Rs150/600), run by the owners of Bungalow on the Beach. To get here, take a bus from Chidambaram (Rs30, 2½ hours).

Vailankanni (Velanganni)

☎ 04365 / pop 10,151

In the 15th century, a young buttermilk boy glimpsed the Virgin Mary as Our Lady of Good Health here, and her **basilica** remains one of the great cross-cultural religious icons in South India.

Housed in a neo-Gothic cathedral (elevated to the status of basilica when the Pope popped by in 1962), the Catholic Our Lady is the recipient of some distinctly Hindu worship. While one hall displays the crucifixion and the Last Supper, the main event is the altar of Our Lady, where Mary is dressed in a golden sari, adorned with garlands of flowers and anointed with the milk of smashed coconuts.

Behind the basilica is a small **museum** (admission free) that houses offerings to Mary; small gold leg icons from those who've healed a bad leg, silver heart lockets from newlyweds, even silver-and-gold stethoscopes from medical students who have passed their exams. It's an almost medieval display of reverence.

An annual nine-day festival culminates on 8 September, the celebration of Mary's birth. There's a hectically devout but amiable atmosphere, with many interested Hindu visitors.

In town there are many lodges, especially in the square by the bus station and around the basilica. **SPT Lodge** (☎ 264288; r Rs250, with AC Rs500; 🍴) – with a car on the roof…huh? – is a clean option, as is **Dayana Lodge** (☎ 263116; r Rs350, with AC Rs650; 🍴). Or ask at the Church Rooms Booking Office, also on the square.

Daily bus services travel between Chennai and Vailankanni, Coimbatore, Bengaluru, Kanyakumari and Thiruvananthapuram (Trivandrum).

Calimere (Kodikkarai) Wildlife & Bird Sanctuary

This 333-sq-km **sanctuary** (☎ 04365-253092; per person/vehicle Rs5/15; ☼ 6am-6pm), 90km southeast of Thanjavur, is noted for vast flocks of migratory curlews, terns, plovers, sandpipers, shanks and more that nest in the tidal mud flats from October to March. Unfortunately, in 2008 it also became a smuggling point for Tamil Tigers, and we weren't able to visit due to security concerns.

In the past the forest department ran two lodges here, charging Rs100 for two people. Other options included **Thambusamy Rest House** (r Rs100), 1km or so off the main road and beside the new lighthouse; you can walk to a watchtower and there's a shady, neglected garden. You'll need to bring food.

The easiest way to get to Calimere is by bus (Rs6, hourly) or taxi from Vedaranniyam, which is 12km away and linked by frequent buses to Nagapattinam or Thanjavur.

THANJAVUR (TANJORE)

☎ 04362 / pop 215,314

Here are the ochre foundation blocks of one of the most remarkable nations of Dravidian history, one of the few kingdoms to expand Hinduism beyond the Black Waters that surround India, a bedrock for aesthetic styles that spread from Madurai to the Mekong. A dizzying historical legacy was once administered from Thanjavur, ancient capital of the great Chola Empire, which today…is a chaotic, messy, modern Indian town. Oh, how the good times have gone. But their presence is still remarkably evident; past the honking buses and happy public urination are the World Heritage–listed Brihadishwara Temple and the sprawling Maratha palace complex.

Information

BBC Net (18/12 MKM Rd; per hr Rs25; ☯ 9.30am-9.30pm) Fast internet access in the basement of the Nallaiyah Shopping Complex.

ICICI Bank ATM (South Main Rd; New Bus Station)

Indian Bank ATM (Vallum Rd)

Main post office (☯ 9am-7pm Mon-Sat, 10am-4pm Sun) Near the train station.

Sify i-way (East Main Rd; per hr Rs20; ☯ 9am-11pm) Broadband goodness.

State Bank of India ATM (Hospital Rd)

Tourist office (☎ 230984; Gandhiji Rd; ☯ 10am-5.45pm Mon-Fri) On the corner of the Hotel Tamil Nadu complex.

VKC Forex (Golden Plaza, Gandhiji Rd; ☯ 9.30am-9pm) Changes cash and travellers cheques.

Sights

BRIHADISHWARA TEMPLE & FORT

Come here twice: in the morning, when the tawny sandstone begins to assert its dominance over the white dawn sunshine, and in the evening, when the rocks capture a hot palette of reds, oranges, yellows and pinks. Alright; there's no single light that best illuminates the **Brihadishwara Temple** (☯ 6am-1pm & 3-8pm), the crowning glory of Chola temple architecture. The temple was commissioned in 1010 by Rajaraja (whose name literally means 'king of kings'), a well-regarded monarch so organised he had the names and addresses of all his dancers, musicians, barbers and poets inscribed into the temple wall – better than many modern Indian institutions can manage.

Note the covered statue of Nandi (Shiva's sacred bull) – 6m long by 3m high – that faces the inner sanctum. Created from a single piece of rock, it weighs 25 tonnes and is one of India's largest Nandi statues. There's also a well-executed interpretive centre set along the side alcoves, which includes sculptures and paintings culled from the temple walls (including a particularly energetic Shiva slaying an army of demons while Buddha hovers above. Not for enlightenment either; the demons were Shiva-worshippers, and the Buddha took them on as devotees so the Destroyer could justify killing them).

Unlike most South Indian temples where the *gopurams* are the highest towers, here the 13-storey, 66m *vimana* (centre tower) dominates.

THANJAVUR ROYAL PALACE & MUSEUMS

The pink walls hold court for crows; the queen's courtyard is overrun with weeds; the inner corridors stink of bat guano. And yet…amid the decay are expertly carved bodies of gods and goddesses, sky-bright tile work, massive columns of preserved, chocolate-coloured teak and the incredible murals of one of the great dynasties of South Indian royalty. The labyrinthine complex was constructed partly by the Nayaks of Madurai and partly by the Marathas.

Walk by a local school to enter the main hall of the **palace** (Indian adult/child Rs5/2, foreign adult/child Rs50/25, incl entry to the Durbar Hall & bell tower; ☯ 9am-6pm), and follow the signs to the elegantly faded **Durbar Hall** (Royal Court). An incredible profusion of murals erupts here, unrestored and elegantly faded, bursting with geometric designs, scenes of Hindu legend and a flock of vaguely-European-yet-almost-Indian cherubs. With a torch you can peek into a 6km secret passage that runs under the palace and reeks of bat poo.

In the former Sadar Mahal Palace is the **Raja Serfoji Memorial Hall** (admission Rs2) with a small collection of thrones, weapons and photographs; there's a similar collection in the **Royal Palace Museum** (admission Rs1, camera/video Rs30/250). Many of the artefacts date from the early 19th century when the enlightened and far-sighted scholar-king Serfoji II ruled. His sixth descendant still lives here; pick up *Raja Serfoji II* (Rs25), his very readable monograph about his extraordinary ancestor, from any of the ticket desks.

An extensive **gallery** (admission Rs15, camera/video Rs30/250) of Chola bronzes sits between the Royal Palace Museum and the bell tower. Admission to a small tower is included with this fee, wherein you can see an incongruous

---

THE SOUTH INDIAN–SOUTHEAST ASIAN CONNECTION

If you're a fan of Southeast Asian temples, art and architecture, going to South India is like retracing Western art back to Greece. Which would make Tamil Nadu the cultural cradle of South India, and Thanjavur the heartland of the Cholas, something like Athens. Under Rajaraja (985–1014) and his son, Rajendra (1012–44), the Chola Empire expanded into Sri Lanka and Southeast Asia, annexing much of Sumatra and the Indo-Malay kingdom of Srivijaya. Beyond the military influence, South Indian Hindus expanded their cultural umbrella, sometimes literally: the Southeast Asian use of umbrellas as royal regalia traces directly back to South India. So do the statues of *apsaras* (heavenly nymphs), the richly embellished jewellery of court fashions from Angkor in Cambodia to Ayutthaya in Thailand (the latter name derived from the Ramayana kingdom of Ayodyah), the centrality of temples to daily life, the sense of form and space used in stone and bronze sculptures, and a common usage of Sanskrit in classical literature. Bali remains a Hindu island thanks to the cross-cultural connections of this period, and every Thai king for the past 200 years has been named Rama in honour of the prince of the Indian epic.

There's a legend of the founding of Angkor Wat, with its Chola-esque step pyramids and bas reliefs of enormous Khmer faces, which elegantly sums up this link: a Cambodian *naga* (serpent-dragon) princess would not marry any suitor until she was approached by an Indian warrior, who cast his spear into her fertile paddies (no, really). The story doesn't just link two nations, it weds their religions as well, indigenous Southeast Asian nature cults (which venerated *nagas* and other animal-deities) blending with the classical Hinduism of South India.

---

whale skeleton and a lovely lotus-style ceiling, plus a few peeling murals. Nearby, the **bell tower** is worth a climb for views right across Thanjavur and the palace itself. The spiral stone staircase is dark, narrow and slippery; watch your head and your step.

Perhaps Serfoji II's greatest contribution to posterity is the **Saraswati Mahal Library** (admission free; ⏰ 10am-1pm & 1.30-5.30pm Tue-Thu) between the gallery and the palace museum. It's a monument to both universal knowledge and an eclectic mind that collected prints of Chinese torture methods, Audubon-style sketches of Indian flora and fauna, sketches of the old London skyline and a collection of some 60,000 palm-leaf and paper manuscripts in Indian and European languages. Like few of his contemporaries, Serfoji II understood the need to preserve the Indian written canon, and today the library has converted 243 Tamil and 183 Sanskrit palm-leaf records into printed material.

Just down the road, the uninspiring **Tamil Museum** (East Main Rd; admission free; ⏰ 10am-1pm & 1.30-5.30pm Tue-Thu) houses a blasé collection of coins, carvings and cannonballs.

Sleeping
BUDGET

There's a bunch of nondescript cheap lodges opposite the central bus stand with rooms for Rs150 to Rs300 a double.

Ashoka Lodge (☎ 230022; 93 Abraham Pandithar Rd; dm/s/d Rs130/140/300, r with AC Rs525; 🛠) The Ashoka's been in business for 42 years, and is frankly looking its age. That said, the rooms are, if a little tattered, surprisingly spacious for the cost and kept clean.

Hotel Yagappa (☎ 230421; 1 Trichy Rd; d Rs195-420, with AC Rs770; 🛠) Yagappa is close to the train station and an ATM; this is a good thing. It's also getting a bit faded; this is a bad thing. But the interior is still well maintained, and rooms are clean enough for the budget-and-rail-proximate conscious.

Manees Residency (☎ 271574; www.maneesresidency.com; 2905 Srinivasam Pillai Rd; s/d Rs275/425, with AC Rs426/625; 🛠) The best high-budget/low-midrange option around, Manees provides energetic service, sparkling cleanliness and rooms that are almost shockingly sparkly for the price.

Hotel Valli (☎ 231580; arasu_tnj@rediffmail.com; 2948 MKM Rd; s/d from Rs260/500, r with AC Rs600; 🛠) Near the train station, Valli is another great bet for budget travellers. Staff are personable and the rooms themselves are spic-and-span. It's in a reasonably peaceful location beyond a bunch of greasy backyard workshops.

MIDRANGE & TOP END

Hotel Ramnath (☎ 272567; 1335 South Rampart; s/d from Rs400/450, with AC Rs650/700; 🛠) Just across from the bus stand, the Ramnath is a nice 'upmarket

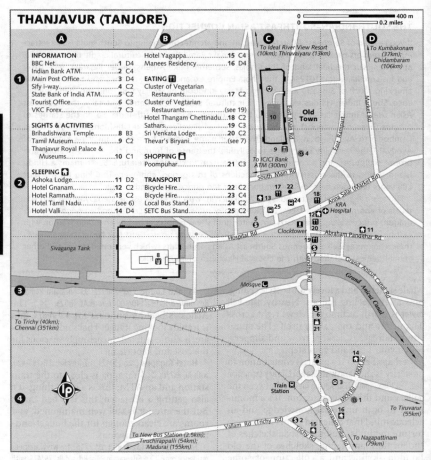

THANJAVUR (TANJORE)

INFORMATION
BBC Net.................................1 D4
Indian Bank ATM...................2 C4
Main Post Office....................3 D4
Sify i-way.............................4 C2
State Bank of India ATM.........5 C3
Tourist Office........................6 C3
VKC Forex............................7 C3

SIGHTS & ACTIVITIES
Brihadishwara Temple...........8 B3
Tamil Museum......................9 C2
Thanjavur Royal Palace &
  Museums.........................10 C1

SLEEPING
Ashoka Lodge.....................11 D2
Hotel Gnanam.....................12 C2
Hotel Ramnath....................13 C2
Hotel Tamil Nadu...............(see 6)
Hotel Valli.........................14 D4

Hotel Yagappa....................15 C4
Manees Residency...............16 D4

EATING
Cluster of Vegetarian
  Restaurants....................17 C2
Cluster of Vegtarian
  Restaurants.................(see 19)
Hotel Thangam Chettinadu....18 C2
Sathars...............................19 C3
Sri Venkata Lodge...............20 C2
Thevar's Biryani...............(see 7)

SHOPPING
Poompuhar..........................21 C3

TRANSPORT
Bicycle Hire.........................22 C2
Bicycle Hire.........................23 C4
Local Bus Stand...................24 C2
SETC Bus Stand...................25 C2

To Ideal River View Resort (10km); Thiruvaiyaru (13km)

To Kumbakonam (37km); Chidambaram (106km)

Old Town

To ICICI Bank ATM (300km)

South Main Rd

KRA Hospital

Abraham Pandithar Rd

Hospital Rd

Clocktower

Grand Anicut Canal Rd

Grand Anicut Canal

Sivaganga Tank

Mosque

Kutchery Rd

To Trichy (40km); Chennai (351km)

Gandhiji Rd

Train Station

Srinivasan Pillai Rd

Vallam Rd (Trichy Rd)

Trichy Rd

To Tiruvarur (55km)

To Nagapattinam (79km)

To New Bus Station (2.5km); Tiruchirappalli (54km); Madurai (155km)

budget' option for those who want a little bit of spoiling – fresh rooms and credit-card acceptance – with their savings.

Hotel Tamil Nadu (☎ 231325; Gandhiji Rd; d from Rs450, with AC from Rs800; ✷) The Tamil Nadu has cleaned up its act (and hiked its prices) as of late, making this former government guesthouse a cool spot for those hovering between price categories. The architecture is sultan-chic (makes sense, given this is a former royal guest house), an atmosphere accentuated by a quiet, leafy courtyard, big rooms and wide balconies.

Hotel Gnanam (☎ 278501; www.hotelgnanam.com; Anna Salai; s/d Rs1050/1250; ✷ 🖳) It's a bit of a corporate hotel, but the Gnanam is perfect for anyone needing wireless internet and

other modern amenities while plopped in Thanjavur's geographic centre.

Ideal River View Resort (☎ 250633; www.idealresort .com; s/d from Rs3000/3500; ✷ 🖳 ⛱) About 10km northwest of the city, this tranquil resort is by far the nicest place to stay near Thanjavur. Set in beautiful gardens beside the Vennar River are immaculate, brightly furnished cottages with roomy balconies.

Eating

There's a cluster of simple veg restaurants, open for breakfast, lunch and dinner, near the local bus stand and along Gandhiji Rd.

Sri Venkata Lodge (Gandhiji Rd; thalis Rs25) A few minutes from the bus station, this veg-only place does a nice thali.

Thevar's Biryani (☎ 270979; Gandhiji Rd; mains Rs30-60) Thevar's specialises in exactly what the name suggests, and it specialises in the Mughal rice dish (done up with southern influences here, like sour tamarind sauce) well.

Hotel Thangam Chetttinadu (☎ 272755; Old Bus Station, Anna Salai Rd; mains Rs30-80) A conveniently located, often locally stuffed spot that should satisfy any mixed group of vegetarians and carnivores.

Sathars (☎ 331041; 167 Gandhiji Rd; mains Rs40-95) Good service and quality food make this place popular. Downstairs is a veg restaurant with lunchtime thalis, upstairs is an AC section with great-value non-veg food.

Shopping

Thanjavur is a good place to shop for handicrafts and arts, especially around the palace. Numerous shops along East Main Rd and Gandhiji Rd sell everything from quality crafts and ready-made clothes to inexpensive kitsch. For fixed prices and hassle-free shopping, try **Poompuhar** (Gandhiji Rd; ✇ 10am-8pm Mon-Sat).

To see bronze-casters at work, call craftsman **Mr Kathirvel** (☎ 098432-35202), whose extended family have, for several generations, used the lost-wax method to make bronze artefacts in a backyard kiln; it's a window into the small cottage industries on which Indian craft still thrives. He lives out towards Vallam Rd; call for directions.

Getting There & Away

BUS

The two city bus stands are for local and SETC buses. SETC has a computerised **reservation office** (☎ 230950; ✇ 7.30am-9.30pm). The New Bus Station, 2.5km south of the centre, services local areas and destinations south. Bus 74 shuttles between the three bus stations (Rs3.50). For details of services, see the boxed text (right).

TRAIN

The station is conveniently central at the south end of Gandhiji Rd. Thanjavur is off the main Chennai–Madurai line, so there's only one express train direct to Chennai – the overnight *Rock Fort Express* (sleeper/3AC Rs181/485, 9½ hours) departing at 8.30pm. For more frequent trains north or south, including to Madurai, take a passenger train to Trichy (Rs20, 1½ hours, eight daily) and change there. There's one daily express (6.50am) and

BUSES FROM THANJAVUR (TANJORE)

Destination	Fare (Rs)	Duration (hr)	Frequency
Chennai	105-135	8	20 daily
Chidambaram*	50	4	every 30min
Kumbakonam*	15	1	every 30min
Madurai*	50	4	every 15min
Ooty	125	10	8.30pm
Trichy*	20	1½	every 5min

* New Bus Station

a couple of passenger trains to Kumbakonam (Rs10, one hour).

The *Thanjavur–Mysore Express* leaves daily at 7.15pm for Bengaluru (sleeper/3AC Rs205/493, 11 hours) and Mysore (sleeper/3AC Rs220/598, 14½ hours).

Getting Around

The main attractions of Thanjavur are close enough to walk between, but this can make for a tiring day depending on your fitness. Bicycles can be hired from stalls opposite the train station and local bus stand (per hour Rs3). An autorickshaw into town from the New Bus Station costs around Rs200.

AROUND THANJAVUR

Located about 13km north of Thanjavur, **Thiruvaiyaru** hosts the January **international music festival** (p1043) in honour of the saint and composer Thyagaraja, whose birthplace is at Tiruvarur, 55km east of Thanjavur. The **Thyagararajaswami Temple** here boasts the largest temple chariot in Tamil Nadu, which is hauled through the streets during the 10-day **car festival** in April/May. Regular bus services run from Thanjavur to Thiruvaiyaru for Rs4.

TRICHY (TIRUCHIRAPPALLI)
☎ 0431 / pop 866,354

Welcome to (more or less) the geographic centre of Tamil Nadu. Fortunately, this hub isn't just a travel junction, although it does make a good base for exploring large swatches of central Tamil Nadu. But Tiruchirappalli, universally known as Trichy, also mixes up a throbbing bazaar with several major must-see temples, including the dramatic Rock Fort and mind-boggling Sri Ranganathaswamy complex. It's very popular with Indian tourists, especially during auspicious marriage

TAMIL NADU

seasons when gorgeously clothed families abound in every hotel.

Trichy's long history dates back to before the Christian era when it was a Chola citadel. Since then it's passed into the hands of the Pallavas, Pandyas, Vijayanagars and Deccan sultans. The modern town and the Rock Fort Temple were built by the Nayaks of Madurai.

Orientation

Trichy's places of interest are scattered over a large area from north to south, but for travellers the city is conveniently split into three distinct areas. The Trichy Junction, or Cantonment, area in the south has most of the hotels and restaurants, the bus and train stations, the tourist office and the main post office. This is where you'll likely arrive and stay. The Rock Fort Temple and main bazaar area is 2.5km north of here; the other important temples are in an area called Srirangam, a further 3km to 5km north again, across the Cauvery River. Fortunately, the whole lot is connected by a good bus service.

Information

INTERNET ACCESS

Mas Media Internet (Map p1090; Williams Rd; per hr Rs10; ☽ 24hr)

Sify i-way (per hr Rs30; ☽ 9am -9pm) Chinnar Bazaar (Map p1088); Williams Rd (Map p1090); Royal Rd (Map p1090)

MEDICAL SERVICES

Seahorse Hospital (Map p1090; ☎ 2462660; Royal Rd) A large hospital in the Cantonment.

MONEY

Canara Bank (Map p1088; Chinnar Bazaar)

Delight Forex (Map p1090; Williams Rd; ☽ 9.30am-5.30pm Mon-Sat)

ICICI Bank ATM Junction Rd (Map p1090); West Boulevard Rd (Map p1088)

UTI Bank ATM Chinnar Bazaar (Map p1088); Junction Rd (Map p1090)

TOURIST INFORMATION

Tourist office (Map p1090; ☎ 2460136; 1 Williams Rd; ☽ 10am-5.45pm Mon-Fri) One of the more helpful tourism info offices in the state.

TRAVEL AGENCIES

Indian Panorama (☎ 2433372; www.indianpanorama .in) Trichy-based and covering all of India, this professional and reliable agency/tour operator is run by a New Zealand couple.

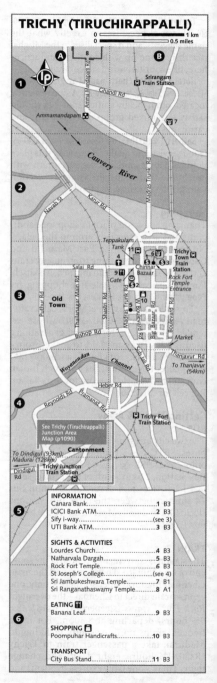

TRICHY (TIRUCHIRAPPALLI)

INFORMATION	
Canara Bank	1 B3
ICICI Bank ATM	2 B3
Sify i-way	(see 3)
UTI Bank ATM	3 B3

SIGHTS & ACTIVITIES	
Lourdes Church	4 B3
Natharvala Dargah	5 B3
Rock Fort Temple	6 B3
St Joseph's College	(see 4)
Sri Jambukeshwara Temple	7 B1
Sri Ranganathaswamy Temple	8 A1

EATING	
Banana Leaf	9 B3

SHOPPING	
Poompuhar Handicrafts	10 B3

TRANSPORT	
City Bus Stand	11 B3

Sights
ROCK FORT TEMPLE

The **Rock Fort Temple** (Map p1088; admission Rs2, camera/video Rs10/50; ☯ 6am-8pm), perched 83m high on a massive outcrop, lords over Trichy with stony arrogance. The ancient rock was first hewn by religious-minded Pallavas, who cut small cave temples into the southern face, but it was the war-savvy Nayaks who later made strategic use of the naturally fortified position. There are two main temples: **Sri Thayumanaswamy Temple**, halfway to the top (there may be some bats snoozing in the ceiling), and **Vinayaka Temple**, at the summit, dedicated to Ganesh. There are 437 stone-cut steps to climb, and the hike is worth the effort – the view is wonderful, with eagles wheeling beneath and Trichy sprawling all around into the greater Cauvery. Non-Hindus are not allowed into either temple, but occasionally – for a small fee – temple priests waive this regulation, although the inside of the Vinayaka temple isn't that impressive.

SRI RANGANATHASWAMY TEMPLE

Alright temple-philes, here's the one you've been waiting for: quite possibly the biggest temple in India. Actually, even if you're feeling templed-out, we have a feeling this **temple complex** (Map p1088; camera/video Rs50/150; ☯ 6am-1pm & 3-9pm) is going to knock your socks off. Located about 3km north of the Rock Fort, it feels more like a self-enclosed city than a house of worship, and in truth, that's the idea: entering this temple's inner sanctum requires passing through seven *gopuram* (the largest is 73m high). Inside the fourth wall is a kiosk where you can buy a ticket (Rs10) and climb the wall for a semi-panoramic view of the complex that delineates levels of existence and consciousness. You'll proceed past rings of beggars, merchants and Brahmins, then plazas of *devas* (angels) and minor deities before reaching the inner chamber, dedicated to Vishnu. Here, the god is worshipped as Sheshashayana, Vishnu who sleeps on a bed made of the king of *nagas*.

Take note of the numerous carvings and statues of *vanaras* (literally 'forest people'), monkey warriors and princesses from the Ramayana, as well as avatars (incarnations) of Vishnu in one of his animal forms, such as the half-lion Nararishma. These may have been tribal pre-Hindu deities that were folded into the religion, and remain popular objects of worship.

A **Temple Chariot Festival** where statues of the deities are paraded aboard a fine chariot is held here each January, but the most important festival is the 21-day **Vaikunta Ekadasi** (Paradise Festival) in mid-December, when the celebrated Vaishnavaite text, Tiruvaimozhi, is recited before an image of Vishnu.

Bus 1 from Trichy Junction or Rock Fort stops right outside this temple.

SRI JAMBUKESHWARA TEMPLE

If you're visiting the five elemental temples of Shiva, you need to visit **Sri Jambukeshwara Temple** (Map p1088; camera/video Rs20/150; ☯ 6am-1pm & 3-9pm), dedicated to Shiva, Parvati and the medium of water. The liquid theme of the place is realised in the central shrine, which houses a partially submerged Shiva lingam. The outer chambers are full of carvings, including several of an elephant being freed from a spider web by Shiva, which provoked the pachyderm to perform *puja* for the Destroyer.

If you're taking bus 1, ask for 'Tiruvanakoil'; the temple is about 100m east of the main road.

OTHER SIGHTS

Lourdes Church (Map p1088) is heavily decked out in Gallo-Catholic design, from neo-Gothic spires to the anguished scenes of crucifixion and martyrdom painted inside. The hush of the nave makes an interesting contrast to the frenetic activity that characterises Trichy's Hindu temples, but note the cross-religious pollination: icons of the Virgin Mary are garlanded in Hindu flower necklaces. The **Feast of Our Lady of Lourdes** is held on 11 February.

The entrance to Lourdes is on Madras Trunk Rd, and when you're finished you can escape into the green and cool campus of Jesuit **St Joseph's College** (where classes run from Intro to Javascript to Comparative Theology). You might notice signs that display a syncretic icon: a Hindu temple overlaid by a Christian cross underlined by the Muslim crescent and star. An eccentric and dusty **museum** (admission free; ☯ 10am-noon & 2-4pm Mon-Sat) contains the natural history collections of the Jesuit priests' summer excursions to the Western Ghats in the 1870s. Bang on the door and the caretaker will let you in – or not, depending on if he's there.

Natharvala Dargah (Map p1088) is another example of India's masalafication of religion. It's Islam's turn, in the form of the tomb of popular Muslim saint Natther. From a distance

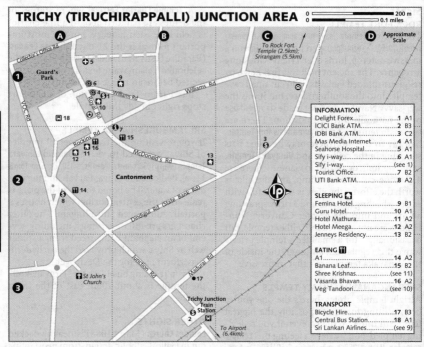

TRICHY (TIRUCHIRAPPALLI) JUNCTION AREA

INFORMATION
Delight Forex	**1** A1
ICICI Bank ATM	**2** B3
IDBI Bank ATM	**3** C2
Mas Media Internet	**4** A1
Seahorse Hospital	**5** A1
Sify i-way	**6** A1
Sify i-way	(see 1)
Tourist Office	**7** B2
UTI Bank ATM	**8** A2

SLEEPING
Femina Hotel	**9** B1
Guru Hotel	**10** A1
Hotel Mathura	**11** A2
Hotel Meega	**12** A2
Jenneys Residency	**13** B2

EATING
A1	**14** A2
Banana Leaf	**15** B2
Shree Krishnas	(see 11)
Vasanta Bhavan	**16** A2
Veg Tandoori	(see 10)

TRANSPORT
Bicycle Hire	**17** B3
Central Bus Station	**18** A1
Sri Lankan Airlines	(see 9)

the mausoleum is a minaret-ensconced compound with distinctly Arab sea-green embellishments, but the *puja*-like worship of Natther has strong Hindu overtones.

Sleeping
Most of Trichy's hotels are in the Junction/Cantonment area around the bus station and a short walk north of the train station.

BUDGET
Hotel Meega (Map p1090; ☎ 2414092; hotelmeega@rediff mail.com; 3 Rockins Rd; d Rs325, with AC Rs500; ✷) This is a good-value hotel – the rooms are smallish but clean, bright and more midrange than budget standard. There's a popular veg restaurant downstairs.

Hotel Mathura (Map p1090; ☎ 2414737; www.hotel mathura.com; 1 Rockins Rd; s/d Rs325/415, with AC Rs595/685; ✷) The Mathura is quite good value, as long as you can score a room that isn't on the bus stand side of the building (or if you can sleep through the honk of a dozen Indian air horns). Rooms are all clean and spacious.

Guru Hotel (Map p1090; ☎ 2415881; guruhotel@yahoo .com; 13A Royal Rd; s/d Rs500/600, with AC Rs700/900, ste

Rs1300; ✷) Like the Mathura, the Guru is a lovely midrange option; if anything, it comes off as cleaner and posher (especially the marble lobby) than its competitor.

MIDRANGE & TOP END
Femina Hotel (Map p1090 ☎ 2414501; try_femina@ sancharnet.in; 104C Femina Rd; d from Rs550, with AC from Rs1300; ✷ ⚑) Femina is one of those Indian business hotels that manages to be affordable even if you're on a budget – and the staff doesn't look at travellers as if they've just crawled out of a swamp. Nonguests can use the pool and small gym (per hour Rs75).

Jenneys Residency (Map p1090; ☎ 2414414; jenneys@ satyam.net.in; 3/14 McDonald's Rd; r from US$50; ✷ ⚑) Jenneys is enormous, semi-luxurious and in a relatively quiet location. The best rooms are on the top floors but all are well appointed; be aware that a 25% luxury tax will be added. Hotel facilities include a health club and a truly bizarre Wild West theme bar.

Eating
Veg Tandoori (Map p1090; Royal Rd; mains Rs15-40; ☾ breakfast, lunch & dinner) It may look tatty, but

this spot adjacent to the bus stand does a reliable line in all kinds of veg cuisine, and the best dosas we tried in Trichy. Plus, it's open late (well, past 11pm).

Shree Krishnas (Map p1090; 1 Rockins Rd; mains Rs20-40; ☙ breakfast, lunch & dinner) On the lower floor of Hotel Mathura, with a nice view of the buses playing plough-the-pedestrian across the road, this is a reliable spot for veg goodness and milky-sweet deserts.

Vasanta Bhavan (Map p1090; Rockins Rd; mains Rs20-40; ☙ breakfast, lunch & dinner) Just next door to Shree Krishnas, you can pop in here for North Indian veg – that of the paneer and naan genre – if you're tired of dosas and *idlis*.

A1 (Map p1090; Junction Rd; mains Rs25-80; ☙ lunch & dinner) The waiters clearly graduated from the Keystone Cops School of Food Service, but otherwise this pleasant AC restaurant does very tasty veg and non-veg.

Banana Leaf (Map p1088; ☎ 271101; Madras Trunk Rd; mains Rs30-90; ☙ lunch & dinner) The Leaf is the best thing going in Trichy, with an enormous menu that plucks off regional favourites from Kashmir to Kanyakumari. With that said, the speciality is the fiery, vaguely vinegary cuisine of Andhra Pradesh; if you can handle your heat, fall in love with the chicken Hyderabadi. Another branch is next to the Hotel Tamil Nadu in Trichy Junction.

Shopping

The main bazaar, which runs by the entrance to the Rock Fort, is as chaotic and crowded as you like; it constantly feels like all of Trichy is strolling the strip. The usual Indian array of plastic toys and ripped-off Bollywood VCDs is on sale. Try **Poompuhar Handicrafts** (Map p1088; West Boulevard Rd; ☙ 9am-8pm) for fixed-price crafts.

Getting There & Away

Trichy is virtually in the geographical centre of Tamil Nadu and it's well connected by air, bus and train.

AIR

As well as domestic flights, Trichy's airport has flights to Sri Lanka. **Sri Lankan Airlines** (Map p1088; ☎ 2412582; ☙ 9am-5.30pm Mon-Sat, 9am-1pm Sun), with an office at Femina Hotel, flies daily to Colombo (US$175).

BUS

Most buses head to the central bus station (Map p1090) on Rockins Rd. If you're travel-

ling to Kodaikanal, a good option is to take one of the frequent buses to Dindigul (Rs25, two hours) and change there. For details of services, see the boxed text (below).

TRAIN

Trichy is on the main Chennai–Madurai line so there are lots of rail options in either direction. Of the nine daily expresses to Chennai, the quickest are the *Vaigai Express* (2nd/chair class Rs85/312, 5½ hours) departing Trichy at 9.10am, and the *Pallavan Express,* which leaves at 6.30am. The best overnight train is the *Rock Fort Express* (sleeper/3AC Rs145/392, 7½ hours) at 9.40pm.

For Madurai the best train is the *Guruvaya Express* (2nd class/sleeper Rs47/75, three hours), which leaves at 1pm. The *Mysore Express* goes daily to Bengaluru (sleeper/3AC Rs160/450, 11½ hours) and Mysore (sleeper/3AC Rs212/562, 15 hours).

Getting Around

TO/FROM THE AIRPORT

The 7km ride into town is Rs1400 by taxi and Rs80 by autorickshaw. Otherwise, take bus 7, 59, 58 or 63 to/from the airport (30 minutes).

BICYCLE

Trichy lends itself to cycling as it's flat; it's a reasonably easy ride from Trichy Junction to the Rock Fort Temple, but a long haul to Srirangam and back. There are a couple of places on Madurai Rd near the train station where you can hire bicycles (per hr Rs5).

BUS

Trichy's local bus service is easy to use. Bus 1 (any letter) from the central bus station on

BUSES FROM TRICHY (TIRUCHIRAPPALLI)

Destination	Fare (Rs)	Duration (hr)	Frequency
Bengaluru	150	8	3 daily
Chennai	110-142	7	every 5min
Chidambaram	51	3½	hourly
Coimbatore	73	7	every 30min
Kodaikanal	62	6	3 daily
Madurai	35	3	every 10min
Ooty	100	8	daily
Puducherry	70	5	3 daily
Thanjavur	15	1½	every 5min

Rockins Rd goes every few minutes via the Rock Fort Temple, Sri Jambukeshwara Temple and the main entrance to Sri Ranganathaswamy Temple (Rs4). To see them all, get off in that order (ask the conductor or driver where the stops are), as it runs in a one-way circuit.

SOUTHERN TAMIL NADU

TRICHY TO RAMESWARAM

In between Trichy and Rameswaram is Tamil Nadu's best example of cave art, the homeland of the region's greatest traders and bankers, and a few other stop-offs that make for a good road trip (or day tour from Trichy, Madurai or Rameswaram). The following sites are, unless otherwise noted, listed in order of encounter from Trichy south to Rameswaram.

Some 34km south of Trichy is the non-descript town of **Pudukkottai**, which has historical importance in inverse proportion to its current obscurity. From 1680 to 1947 this was one of the great princely states of South India, and the relics of bygone days are on display in the wonderful **Pudukkottai Museum** (Indian/foreigner Rs3/100; 9.30am-5pm), located in a renovated palace building in Pudukkottai town. Its eclectic collection includes musical instruments, megalithic burial artefacts and some remarkable paintings and miniatures.

About 16km north of Pudukkottai is **Sittannavasal** (admission Rs100), where you'll find a small Jain cave temple that conceals magnificent vegetable-oil frescoes. The shrine is small, but the cave is widely ignored by day trippers, which means you'll likely get to appreciate these masterpieces of Jain art on your own. Note the Edenic garden paradise painted on the main ceiling, which conceals fish, mythical sea monsters and beautiful water maidens. Or try making your 'Om' echo across an acoustic masterpiece of a meditation chamber, where statues of Jain saints sit in cross-legged repose.

Simple and imposing, the renovated **Tirumayam Fort** (Indian/foreigner Rs5/100; 9am-5pm), located about 17km south of Puddukotai, is worth a climb for the 360-degree views from the battlements onto the surrounding countryside. Or you can take a shady rest with local goats under a banyan tree.

In the backstreets of small **Kanadukathan**, 10km south of Tirumayam, are the wedding-cake houses of the Chettiars, an interrelated clan of bankers, merchants and traders. The mansions of the community are decked out in the cosmopolitan goods bought home by Chettiars during their extensive trading forays: Belgian chandeliers, Italian granite, Burmese teak and artwork from around the world. To get a feel for the royal life, book a night in the **Chettinadu Mansion** (04565-273080; www.chettinadumansion.com; r from Rs3300;) or **Visalam** (04843-011711; www.cghearth.com/visalam; r from €170;), both restored and frankly fantastic heritage houses. They're pricey, but hey: you get to spend the night in a living Indian palace.

It's an easy day tour from Trichy (taxi with/without AC Rs1500/1000) or Madurai (a little more). Otherwise catch one of the many daily buses from Trichy to Karaikkudi (Rs52, three hours) and get on and off at the sights along the way. Coming from Madurai, get a bus to Karaikkudi and take a local bus or hire a taxi. Kanadukathan is about a 500m walk off the main road.

Regular buses run between Karaikkudi, via Ramanathapuram, to Rameswaram.

RAMESWARAM

04573 / pop 37,968

In the past, one did not go past here. Rameswaram was the southernmost point of sacred India; to leave her boundaries was to abandon caste and fall below the status of the lowliest skinner of sacred cows. Then Rama, incarnation of Vishnu and hero of the Ramayana, led an army of monkeys and bears to the ocean and crossed into the kingdom of (Sri) Lanka, where he defeated the demon Ravana and rescued his wife, Sita. Afterwards, prince and princess came to this spot to offer thanks to Shiva.

If all this seems like so much folklore, it's gospel for millions of Hindus, who flock to the Ramanathaswamy Temple to worship where God, essentially, worshipped God.

Apart from these pilgrims, Rameswaram is a sleepy fishing village. It's also an island, connected to the mainland by the Indira Gandhi bridge, and used to serve as a ferry link to Sri Lanka – until the Tamil Tigers went on the prowl. Tamil Sri Lankan refugees still come here by the boatload.

Orientation & Information

Most hotels and restaurants are clustered around the Ramanathaswamy Temple. The bus stand, 2km to the west, is connected by shuttle bus to the town centre.

You can't change money here but the **State Bank of India** (East Car St) has an ATM accepting international cards.

Sights

RAMANATHASWAMY TEMPLE

When Rama decided to worship Shiva, he figured he'd need a lingam to do the thing properly. Being a God, he sent a flying monkey to find the biggest lingam around – in this case, a Himalayan mountain. But the monkey took too long, so Rama's wife Sita made a simple lingam of sand, which Shiva approved of, and which is enshrined today in the centre of this **temple** (camera Rs25; ☷ 4am-1pm & 3-8.30pm). Besides housing the world's holiest sand-mound, the structure is notable for its horizon-stretching thousand-pillar halls and 22 *theerthams* (tanks), which pilgrims are expected to bathe in and drink from. The number of *theerthams* corresponds with the number of arrows in Rama's quiver, which he used to generate water on the island. Only Hindus may enter the inner sanctum.

Even when the temple is closed, it is possible to take a peaceful amble through the extensive corridors. In the evening, before the temple is closed, you may see temple Brahmins take some of the residing deities on a parade through the halls of Ramanathaswamy.

DHANUSHKODI & ADAM'S BRIDGE

Kanyakumari may technically be India's land's end, but **Dhanushkodi** plays the part better. About 18km southwest of town, this is a long, low sweep of sand, dust devils, fishing hamlets, donkeys and green waves. It's tempting to swim here, but be careful of strong rips. You can ride a passenger truck for a few rupees, or walk 2½ hours (one way!) to the edge: **Adam's Bridge**, the chain of reefs, sandbanks and islets that almost connects India with Sri Lanka, 33km away, was supposedly built by Rama and his monkey army. Buses (Rs5, hourly) from the local bus stand on East Car St stop about 4km before the beach so you have to walk the rest of the way, and an autorickshaw costs Rs250 return.

About 10km before Dhanushkodi, the **Kothandaraswamy Temple** is the only structure to

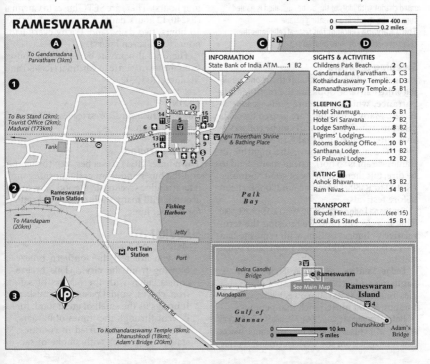

RAMESWARAM

0	400 m
0	0.2 miles

INFORMATION
State Bank of India ATM.....1 B2

SIGHTS & ACTIVITIES
Childrens Park Beach..........2 C1
Gandamadana Parvatham...3 C3
Kothandaraswamy Temple..4 D3
Ramanathaswamy Temple...5 B1

SLEEPING
Hotel Shanmuga................6 B1
Hotel Sri Saravana.............7 B2
Lodge Santhya...................8 B2
Pilgrims' Lodgings.............9 B2
Rooms Booking Office........10 B1
Santhana Lodge...............11 B2
Sri Palavani Lodge............12 B2

EATING
Ashok Bhavan..................13 B2
Ram Nivas......................14 B1

TRANSPORT
Bicycle Hire....................(see 15)
Local Bus Stand...............15 B1

To Gandamadana Parvatham (3km)

To Bus Stand (2km); Tourist Office (2km); Madurai (173km)

West St
Middle St
South Car St

Tank

Rameswaram Train Station

To Mandapam (20km)

Sannathi St
North Car St
West Car St
East Car St

Agni Theertham Shrine & Bathing Place

Palk Bay

Fishing Harbour

Jetty

Port Train Station

Port

Indira Gandhi Bridge

Mandapam

Gulf of Mannar

Rameswaram

Rameswaram Island

See Main Map

Dhanushkodi

Adam's Bridge

0	10 km
0	5 miles

To Kothandaraswamy Temple (8km); Dhanushkodi (18km); Adam's Bridge (20km)

survive a 1964 cyclone that destroyed the village. Legend has it Rama, overcome with guilt at having killed Ravana, performed a *puja* on this spot and thereafter the temple was built. It is also believed Vibhishana, brother of Sita's kidnapper Ravana, joined Rama here, prompting one of the great ethical debates in Indian literature: is it right to betray your family to be true to yourself?

GANDAMADANA PARVATHAM

This **temple**, located 3km northwest of Rameswaram, is a shrine reputedly containing Rama's footprints. The two-storey *mandapam* is on a small hill – the highest point on the island – and has good views out over the coastal landscape. Pilgrims visit at dawn and dusk.

Activities

Childrens Park Beach is a neglected splash of sand with fishing boats and some swings which might distract a wee one for a little.

Festivals & Events

Car Festival (Feb/Mar) During the festival, a huge decorated chariot with idols of the deities installed is hauled through the streets in a pulsating parade.

Thiru Kalyana (Jul/Aug) This festival celebrates the celestial marriage of Shiva and Parvati.

Sleeping & Eating

Budget travellers should call the **rooms booking office** (East Car St) opposite the main temple entrance, which can score beds as low as Rs120. Many hotels here are geared towards pilgrims, which means staff can be conservative, often refusing to take in single travellers (because, you know, the nightlife in Rameswaram is so hot). Cheap rooms tend to be dire, but there's a string of good midrange (Rs400 to Rs800) hotels around; book ahead before festivals.

Santhana Lodge (☎ 221229; West Car St; r Rs200-300) This is a decent (and we're using the term relatively) budget option, with requisite bad sheets but acceptably clean rooms and squat toilets.

Lodge Santhya (☎ 221329) Next door to Santhana Lodger, this grotty spot offers singles for as low as Rs150. You get what you pay for, but, if you must, pinch that penny.

Hotel Shanmuga (☎ 222984; 7 Middle St; d Rs380, with AC Rs750; 🌀) This is another nice midrange place, just removed from the western (main) temple

entrance. Rooms are large and connected to the outside world via HBO and CNN.

Hotel Sri Saravana (☎ 223367; South Car St; r from Rs450, with AC from Rs750; 🌀) This is a friendly, clean hotel with great service and spacious rooms, and they're not averse to single travellers. Rooms have TVs, and the ones towards the top have sea views (and increased rates).

Sri Palavani Lodge (☎ 223367; South Car St; r from Rs500, with AC from Rs800; 🌀) Next door to Shanmuga, this place offers almost identical rooms, layout and friendly service.

A number of inexpensive vegetarian restaurants such as **Ashok Bhavan** (West Car St) serve thalis for around Rs35. As you might guess there's a focus on South Indian food here, but **Ram Nivas** (West Car St; mains Rs15-40) does a nice line in North Indian veg like paneer and dhal fry. You can find fish in a few restaurants, but if you track down anything else befitting carnivores, let us know.

Getting There & Away

BUS

Buses run to Madurai every 10 minutes (Rs49, four hours). There are SETC buses to Chennai (Rs240, 12 hours, daily), Kanyakumari (Rs120, 10 hours, two daily) and Trichy every half-hour (Rs82, seven hours).

There are also private buses and minibuses from the town centre to Chennai (Rs400) and Madurai (Rs125).

TRAIN

The *Rameswaram Express* leaves for Chennai daily at 7.55pm.

Getting Around

Town buses (Rs1) travel between the temple and the bus stand from early morning until late at night. Cycling is a good way to get around, with many stalls renting old rattlers for Rs5 per hour.

MADURAI

☎ 0452 / pop 1.2 million

Do you not feel the southern breeze blowing from the city... This breeze comes laden with the odours of saffron, chives, sandal paste, and musk... It brings us the smell of good food, for it went through the fumes of bazaars, where pancakes are fried in countless stalls... It is thick with smoke of sacrifices… The wealthy city is not far off, and you need have no fear. Even if you go there alone, you will meet no danger on your way.

The Silapadikaram

Chennai may be the heart of Tamil Nadu, but Madurai claims her soul. No European-built port town this; Madurai is Tamil-borne and Tamil-rooted, one of the oldest cities in India, a metropolis that traded with ancient Rome and outlasted her destruction. Now Madurai competes with the Italian capital for 'worst traffic ever', and while the smells described in *The Silapadikaram*, the Tamil equivalent of the *Odyssey*, are still present, they're offset by the reek of petrol and piss.

Tourists, Indian and foreign, usually come here to see the temple of Sri Meenakshi Amman, a labyrinthine structure that ranks among the greatest temples of India. Otherwise, Madurai, perhaps appropriately given her age, captures many of India's most glaring dichotomies: a city centre dominated by a medieval temple, an economy increasingly driven by IT, all overlaid with the energy and excitement of a typically Indian city slotted into a much more manageable package than Chennai's sprawl.

If you happen to be here during spring, try to catch the Chitrhrai Festival, when temple images are paraded throughout the city (p1043).

History
Tamil and Greek documents record the existence of Madurai from the 4th century BC. It was popular for trade, especially in spices, and was also the home of the *sangam,* the academy of Tamil poets. Over the centuries Madurai has come under the jurisdiction of the Cholas, the Pandyas, Muslim invaders, the Hindu Vijayanagar kings, and the Nayaks, who ruled until 1781. During the reign of Tirumalai Nayak (1623–55), the bulk of the Sri Meenakshi Temple was built, and Madurai became the cultural centre of the Tamil people, playing an important role in the development of the Tamil language.

Madurai then passed into the hands of the British East India Company. In 1840 the company razed the fort, which had previously surrounded the city, and filled in the moat. Four broad streets – the Veli streets – were constructed on top of this fill and to this day define the limits of the old city.

Orientation
The main post office, tourist office and many hotels are conveniently wedged between the train station and the temple.

Information
BOOKSHOPS
Malligai Book Centre (11 West Veli St; ⏲ 9am-2pm & 4.30-9pm Mon-Sat) Opposite the train station; the left-hand side has a decent selection of English-language titles.
Turning Point Books (75 Venkatesh Towers, Town Hall Rd; ⏲ 10am-9pm Mon-Sat) A 4th-floor bookshop opposite New College with a good selection, especially the shelves on Indian religion.

INTERNET ACCESS
You can't walk without tripping over an internet cafe, including several 24-hour Sify I-Ways, but our favourite is **Chat Club** (75 Venkatesh Towers, Town Hall Rd; per hr Rs20; ⏲ 9am-11.30pm), just below Turning Point Books, where you'll find staff to be exceedingly accommodating.

MONEY
ATMs are plentiful.
Canara Bank ATM (West Perumal Maistry St)
HDFC Bank ATM (West Veli St)
ICICI Bank ATM (North Chitrai St)
State Bank of India (West Veli St) Has foreign-exchange desks and an ATM.
VKC Forex (Zulaiha Towers, Town Hall Rd; ⏲ 9am-7pm) An efficient place to change travellers cheques and cash.

POST
Main post office (West Veli St; ⏲ 9am-5pm Mon-Sat, parcel office 9.30am-7pm)

TOURIST INFORMATION
Madurai tourist office (☎ 2334757; 180 West Veli St; ⏲ 10am-5pm Mon-Fri, 11am-1pm Sat) Helpful staff when they're there, with brochures and maps. Tourist counters of sorts are also at the train station and airport.

Sights
SRI MEENAKSHI TEMPLE
The **Sri Meenakshi Temple** (camera Rs30; ⏲ 6am-12.30pm & 4-9pm), abode of the triple-breasted, fish-eyed Goddess Meenakshi Amman ('fish-eyed' is an adjective for perfect eyes in classical Tamil poetry), is considered by many to be the height of South Indian temple architecture, as vital to the aesthetic heritage of this region as the Taj Mahal is to North India. It's not so much a temple as a 6-hectare complex enclosed by 12 *gopurams,* the highest of which

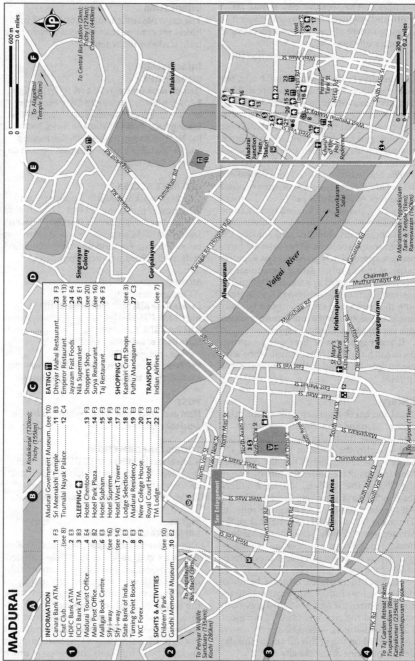

MADURAI

INFORMATION
Canara Bank ATM	1 F3
Chat Club	(see 8)
HDFC Bank ATM	2 E3
ICICI Bank ATM	3 B3
Madurai Tourist Office	4 E4
Main Post Office	5 B2
Malligai Book Centre	6 E3
Sify i-way	(see 16)
Sify i-way	(see 14)
State Bank of India	7 E3
Turning Point Books	8 E3
VKC Forex	9 F3

SIGHTS & ACTIVITIES
Children's Park	(see 10)
Gandhi Memorial Museum	10 E2
Madurai Government Museum	(see 10)
Sri Meenakshi Temple	11 B3
Tirumalai Nayak Palace	12 C4

SLEEPING 🛏
Hotel Chentoor	13 F3
Hotel Park Plaza	14 F3
Hotel Subham	15 F3
Hotel Supreme	16 F3
Hotel West Tower	17 F3
Lodge Selection	18 F3
Madurai Residency	19 F3
New College House	20 F3
Royal Court Hotel	21 E3
TM Lodge	22 F3

EATING 🍴
Dhivyar Mahal Restaurant	23 F3
Emperor Restaurant	(see 13)
Jayaram Fast Foods	24 E4
Nila Supermarket	25 E1
Shoppers Shop	(see 20)
Surya Restaurant	(see 16)
Taj Restaurant	26 F3

SHOPPING 🛍
Kashmiri Craft Shops	(see 3)
Puthu Mandapam	27 C3

TRANSPORT
Indian Airlines	(see 7)

towers 52m over Madurai, and all of which are carved with a staggering array of gods, goddesses, demons and heroes.

According to legend, the beautiful Meenakshi was born with three breasts and this prophecy: her superfluous breast would melt away when she met her husband. The event came to pass when she met Shiva and took her place as his consort. The temple of the cosmic couple was designed in 1560 by Vishwanatha Nayak and built during the reign of Tirumalai Nayak, but its history goes back 2000 years to the time when Madurai was a Pandyan capital.

Much of the temple is off-limits to non-Hindus, but lay people can enter the **Puthu Mandapam** in the east, which forms a long and impressive entrance hall that leads to the eastern *gopuram*. From here you can see the outer rings of the concentric corridors that enclose the sanctums of Meenakshi and Shiva, worshipped here as Sundareswarar, the beautiful lord. Be on the lookout for statues of deities encrusted in small balls of butter, thrown at the gods as offerings from their devout worshippers.

Also within the temple complex, housed in the 1000-Pillared Hall, is the **Temple Art Museum** (admission Rs7; 7am-7pm). It contains painted friezes and stone and brass images and good exhibits on Hindu deities.

Allow plenty of time to see this temple and be warned: shorts and socks are not allowed. Early mornings or late evenings are the best times to avoid crowds, and there's often classical dance somewhere in the complex at the weekends. 'Temple guides' charge negotiable fees, rarely below Rs200, so prepare to negotiate and be aware that they are often fronts for emporiums and tailor shops.

TIRUMALAI NAYAK PALACE

What the Meenakshi Temple is to Nayak religious architecture, the Tirumalai **palace** (Indian/foreigner Rs10/50, camera/video Rs30/100; 9am-1pm & 2-5pm) is to the secular. Unfortunately it's in a state of rot today, but the shell that remains is still impressive. The main event is the entrance gate, main hall and Natakasala (Dance Hall), with their faded yellow plasterwork, lion and *makara* (crocodile-elephant creature) sculptures and a series of fabulous murals that hints at the opulence the Nayak rulers once enjoyed. The rectangular courtyard, 75m by 52m, is known as Swargavilasa (Celestial Pavilion), and while time has taken its toll, you still get the sense the plaza fully deserved the name. The Indo-Saracenic palace was built in 1636 by the ruler whose name it bears.

There's a nightly **sound-and-light show** (admission Rs50; English 6.45pm, Tamil 8pm) which can be fun; the mosquitoes and people carrying on conversations throughout come at no extra cost. The palace is a 20-minute walk from the temple.

MUSEUMS

Housed in the *tamukkam* (old exhibition pavilion) of the Rani Mangammal is the excellent **Gandhi Memorial Museum** (admission free, camera Rs50; 10am-1pm & 2-5.30pm), set in spacious and relaxing grounds. The maze of rooms contains an impressively moving and detailed account of India's struggle for independence from 1757 to 1947, and the English-language signs pull no punches about British rule. Included in the exhibition is the blood-stained dhoti (long loincloth) that Gandhi was wearing at the time he was assassinated in Delhi in 1948 (p135); it's here because he first took up wearing the dhoti as a sign of native pride in Madurai in 1921. The **Gandhian Literary Society Bookstore** (Mon-Sat) is behind the museum.

The **Madurai Government Museum** (Indian/foreigner Rs10/100; 9.30am-5.30pm Sat-Thu) is next door in the same grounds. Inside is a neglected collection of archaeological finds, sculpture, bronzes, costumes and paintings. A shady **children's park** (admission Rs2; 10am-8pm) with pay-as-you-go rides and slides is alongside the museums' entrance driveway.

MARIAMMAN TEPPAKKULAM TANK

This vast tank, 5km east of the old city, covers an area almost equal to that of Sri Meenakshi Temple and is the site of the incredible **Teppam (Float) Festival** (p1043), held in January/February, when the Meenakshi temple deities are taken on a naval tour of their kingdom. The evening culminates in Shiva's seduction of his wife, whereupon the icons are brought back to the temple to make love and in so doing, regenerate the universe (Meenakshi's diamond nose stud is even removed so it doesn't irritate her lover). As exciting as that all sounds, the tank is empty for most of the year and primarily serves as a cricket ground for local kids. It was built by Tirumalai Nayak in 1646 and is connected to the Vaigai River by underground channels.

Tours

The tourist office organises half-day sightseeing tours that include the Tirumalai Nayak Palace and Gandhi Memorial Museum, and finish at the Sri Meenakshi Temple. Tours start at 7am and 3pm and cost Rs125 per person (minimum six people).

Sleeping

Most of Madurai's accommodation is concentrated in the area between the train station and Sri Meenakshi Temple.

BUDGET

Town Hall Rd, running eastwards from the train station, has a knot of cheap and not-so-cheerful hotels. All budget choices have squat toilets.

Lodge Selection (☎ 2342625; 70 Town Hall Rd; s/d Rs190/250) This is one of the better choices amidst the budget hotels clustered around Town Hall Rd. The upper rooms have alright views and while the rooms aren't ritzy, they're as good as you'll get for this price.

Hotel Subham (☎ 2342022; 61 West Perumal Maistry St; s/d Rs200/320, r Rs200) Some rooms here are clean, slightly airy and a good deal, but the darker, dingier ones are definitely worth a pass.

TM Lodge (☎ 2341651; www.maduraitmlodge.com; 50 West Perumal Maistry St; s/d Rs200/320, d with AC & TV Rs550; ✖) TM is efficiently run with clean linen and reasonably well-kept rooms. The upper rooms are definitely lighter and airier, some with private sit-outs.

New College House (☎ 2342971; collegehouse_mdu@ yahoo.co.in; 2 Town Hall Rd; r from Rs240, with AC from Rs660; ✖) FYI: it's spelled 'Neww College House' in case you get confused. There's some 250 rooms scattered over this concrete complex. Some are quite nice, some not-so-much, and street noise often permeates, so try and get something away from the bustle.

MIDRANGE & TOP END

Madurai's best-value accommodation is the string of midrange hotels along West Perumal Maistry St, near the train station. Rooms without AC are a bargain and worth making that step up from the budget joints, especially if you're not travelling alone. Most have rooftop restaurants with temple and sunset views.

Hotel West Tower (☎ 2346098; 42/60 West Tower St; r Rs350-525, with AC Rs700-800; ✖) On the line between budget and midrange, and in spitting distance of the temple, the West Tower has clean rooms, friendly service and a location that can't be beat.

Madurai Residency (☎ 2343140; www.madurairesidency.com; 15 West Marret St; s/d Rs425/490, r with AC from Rs850; ✖ 🖳) The service is stellar and the rooms are lovely and fresh at this winner, which has the highest rooftop restaurant in town. There's 24-hour internet in the lobby, and breakfast is included in the room rates.

Hotel Supreme (☎ 2343151; www.supremehotels.com; 110 West Perumal Maistry St; s/d from Rs550/680, r with AC from Rs1200; ✖) This is another large, well-presented hotel that is very popular – although sometimes overcrowded – with domestic tourists. You can't miss the chance to walk into Apollo, a bar built to look like a spaceship, and wonder if someone laced your lassi last night. There's good food at the on-site Surya Restaurant.

Hotel Chentoor (☎ 3042222; www.hotelchentoor.com; 106 West Perumal Maistry St; s/d Rs650/700, with AC from Rs950/1050; ✖) Chentoor has spic-and-span rooms, some of which have great temple and city views; a busy, cheap rooftop restaurant (opposite); and what surely must be the dimmest lit bar in India on the ground floor.

Hotel Park Plaza (☎ 3011111; www.hotelparkplaza.net; 114 West Perumal Maistry St; s/d Rs1075/1350; ✖) The Plaza's lobby is slightly more upmarket than its neighbours, and rooms are standard midrange: comfortable and simply furnished. The front rooms have temple views from the 3rd floor up. There's a good rooftop restaurant and the (inappropriately named) Sky High Bar – on the 1st floor.

Royal Court Madurai (☎ 4356666; www.royalcourtindia.com; 4 West Veli St; s/d Rs2800/3100; ✖ 🖳 ☎) The Royal Court manages to blend a bit of white-sheeted, hardwood-floored colonial elegance with a whole mess of modern amenities, such as wi-fi in all rooms, that makes it an excellent, centrally located top-end choice for someone who needs a bit of spoiling.

Eating

Along West Perumal Maistry St the rooftop restaurants of a string of hotels offer breezy night-time dining and temple views; most also have AC restaurants open for breakfast and lunch.

Jayaram Fast Foods (5-8 Nethaji Rd; mains Rs25-75; ☽ lunch & dinner) There's a busy (and yummy) bakery downstairs, and a crisp and clean restaurant up top that does a nice line in Indian fare, plus burgers and pizzas. While the latter aren't winning any awards, this is as good a piece of pie as you'll find in Madurai.

Taj Restaurant (☎ 2343650; 55 Town Hall Rd; mains Rs30-64; ☼ lunch & dinner) This non-veg extravaganza is packed with happily masticating families in the evening, no doubt enjoying specials like the Mughal biryani (only available Sundays) and the intriguing, occasionally offered pigeon masala.

Emperor Restaurant (☎ 2350490; 106 West Perumal Maistry St; mains Rs30-80; ☼ breakfast, lunch & dinner) It's all veg all the time at Hotel Chentoor's rooftop restaurant, but that karmic goodness is a bit undone by the fact this spot basically becomes a very popular bar come nightfall.

Dhivyar Mahal Restaurant (☎ 2342700; 21 Town Hall Rd; mains Rs30-92; ☼ lunch & dinner) One of the better multicuisine restaurants not attached to a hotel, Dhivyar Mahal is clean and bright. The usual curries go down a treat, and where else are you going to find roast leg of lamb in Madurai?

Surya Restaurant (110 West Perumal Maistry St; mains Rs45-110; ☼ dinner) The rooftop restaurant of Hotel Supreme offers a superb view over the city and a nice pure veg menu, but the winner here has got to be the cold coffee, which might as well have been brewed by God when you sip it on a dusty, hot (ie holy) day.

Taj Garden Retreat (☎ 2371601; www.tajhotels.com; 40 TPK Rd; mains from Rs150; ☼ breakfast, lunch & dinner) This indoor-outdoor restaurant is perched in the gardens above the city, with stunning sunset views. If you're hankering for spag and salad in relaxed surrounds, this is the place to come.

Street stalls selling sweets, dosas, idli and the like are ubiquitous, especially near the train station. **Shoppers Shop** (Town Hall Rd; ☼ 8am-11pm) and **Nila Supermarket** (Algarkoil Rd; ☼ 7am-11pm) are well-stocked grocery stores including a good selection of Western foods.

Shopping

Madurai teems with cloth stalls and tailors' shops, which you may notice upon being approached for the umpteenth time by a tailor tout. A great place for getting cottons and printed fabrics is Puthu Mandapam, the pillared former entrance hall at the eastern side of Sri Meenakshi Temple. Here you'll find rows of tailors, all busily treadling away and capable of whipping up a good replica of whatever you're wearing in an hour or two. Quality, designs and prices vary greatly depending on the material and complexity of the design, but you can

have a shirt made up for Rs150. Every driver, temple guide and tailor's brother will lead you to the Kashmiri craft shops in North Chitrai St, offering to show you the temple view from the rooftop – the views are good, and so is the inevitable sales pitch.

Getting There & Away

AIR

Indian Airlines (☎ 2341234, airport 2690771; West Veli St; ☼ 10am-5pm Mon-Sat) flies daily to Mumbai and Chennai. Jet Airways also flies daily to Chennai, as does newcomer **Paramount Airways** (☎ 1800 180 1234; www.paramountairways.com). Air Deccan flies daily to Bengaluru. None of these last three airlines has an office in town, but airport counters open at flight times.

BUS

Most long-distance buses arrive and depart from the **central bus station** (☎ 2580680; Melur Rd; ☼ 24hr), 6km northeast of the old city. It appears chaotic but is actually a well-organised 24-hour operation. Local buses shuttle into the city every few minutes for Rs2. There's a fixed-rate autorickshaw stand just outside the station (you'll inevitably be waved there); the fee to the train station (where most of the hotels are located) is Rs79, plus a Rs2 service charge.

Private bus companies offer super-deluxe coaches with video services to Chennai and Bengaluru (Rs220 to Rs300), but the state bus companies have similar services and while travel agencies sell tickets – often at an inflated price – you may end up on a state bus anyway. The boxed text (p1100) lists prices for government buses; some express services run to Bengaluru, Chennai, Mysore and Puducherry.

The Arapalayam bus stand, northwest of the train station on the river bank, has hourly buses to Kumili (Rs45, 4½ hours) for the Periyar Wildlife Sanctuary. There are regular services to Coimbatore (Rs75, six hours). Buses leave for Kodaikanal at 2.30pm and 8.30pm (Rs40, four to five hours), and to Palani every half-hour (Rs35, five hours).

TRAIN

Madurai Junction train station is on the main Chennai–Kanyakumari line. There are at least nine daily trains to Chennai, and three daily services to Kanyakumari.

Some other services include Madurai to Coimbatore (2nd class/sleeper Rs62/98,

BUSES FROM MADURAI

Destination	Fare (Rs)	Duration (hr)	Frequency
Bengaluru	182	12	4 daily
Chennai	144-186	10	every 30min
Chidambaram	85	8	3 daily
Kochi	144	8	2 daily
Kanyakumari	90	6	hourly
Mysore	260	16	daily (via Ooty)
Puducherry	105	8	2 daily
Rameswaram	59	4	every 30min
Trichy	40	3	every 10min
Trivandrum	215	9	2 daily

6½ hours) and Bengaluru (sleeper/3AC Rs179/502, 6 hours), as well as Trivandrum and Mumbai.

Getting Around

The airport is 12km south of town and taxis cost Rs200 to the town centre. Autorickshaws ask around Rs100. Alternatively, bus 10A from the central bus station goes to the airport, but don't rely on it being on schedule.

Central Madurai is small enough to get around on foot.

KANYAKUMARI (CAPE COMORIN)

☎ 04652 / pop 19,739

The end of India has more appeal than being the end of the road. There's a whiff of accomplishment (along with dried fish) upon making it to the tip of the country, the terminus of a narrowing funnel of rounded granite mountains – some of India's oldest – green fields plaided with silver-glinting rice paddies and slow-looping wind farms. Like all edges, there's a sense of the surreal here. You can see three seas mingle, the sunset over the moonrise and the Temple of the Virgin Sea Goddess within minutes of each other. But beyond that, Kanyakumari is a genuinely friendly village that is nice respite from the dust of the Indian road.

Orientation & Information

The main temple is right on the point of Kanyakumari and leading north from it is a small bazaar lined with restaurants, stalls and souvenir shops.

Janaki Forex (🕑 9.30am-6pm Mon-Sat) Off South Car St. Change cash and travellers cheques here.

Post office (Main Rd; 🕑 8am-6pm Mon-Fri) About 300m north of the tourist office.

Tamil Mercantile Bank ATM (Main Rd)

Tony's Internet (Sannathi St; per hr Rs50; 🕑 10am-8pm) Friendly and relatively fast.

Tourist office (☎ 246276; Main Rd; 🕑 8am-6pm Mon-Fri) Get a useful, free *In and Around Kanyakumari* brochure here – if anyone's in the office.

Sights & Activities

KUMARI AMMAN TEMPLE

We can't claim to have written the first review of this place; let's go back to the 1st-century *Periplus of the Erythraean Sea*, by an unknown Greek merchant:

> …there is another place called Comari, at which are the Cape of Comari and a harbour; hither come those men who wish to consecrate themselves for the rest of their lives, and bathe and dwell in celibacy; and women also do the same; for it is told that a goddess once dwelt here and bathed.

The legends say the *kanya* (virgin) goddess Kumari, a manifestation of the Great Goddess Devi, single-handedly conquered demons and secured freedom for the world. At this **temple** (🕑 4.30am-12.30pm & 4-8pm) pilgrims give her thanks in an intimately spaced, beautifully decorated temple, where the nearby crash of waves from three oceans can be heard through the twilight glow of oil fires clutched in vulva-shaped votive candles (a reference to the sacred femininity of the goddess). Men must remove their shirts to enter and cameras are forbidden.

GANDHI MEMORIAL

Poignantly and appropriately placed at the end of the nation Gandhi fathered is this **memorial** (admission by donation; 🕑 7am-7pm), which purposely resembles an Orissan temple embellished by Hindu, Christian and Muslim architects. The central plinth was used to store some of the Mahatma's ashes, and each year, on Gandhi's birthday (2 October), the sun's rays fall on the stone. Guides may ask for an excessive donation, but Rs10 is enough; try and keep an air of silence (even if locals don't).

KAMARAJ MEMORIAL

Just next to the Gandhi memorial is this **shrine** (🕑 until dark) to K Kamaraj, known as 'the Gandhi of the South'. One of the most powerful politicians of post-independence India, Kamaraj held the chief ministership of both Madras State and latter-day Tamil Nadu, and was instrumental in bringing Lal Bahadur Shastri and Indira Gandhi into the prime minister's seat. You can also thank the Tamil leader for school lunch, since he instituted the first free ones in Tamil Nadu in 1956. Unfortunately, the shrine is nothing but a collection of dusty blown-up photographs with barely any space given to context or explanation.

VIVEKANANDA EXHIBITION & VIVEKANANDAPURAM

This **exhibition** (Main Rd; admission Rs2; 8am-noon & 4-8pm) details the life and extensive journey across India made by the philosopher Swami Vivekananda (the 'Wandering Monk'; 1863–1902), who developed a synthesis between the tenets of Hinduism and concepts of social justice. The storyboards are a bit over-detailed; if you're overwhelmed, concentrate on enjoying the photos and Swamiji's letters, which detail his growth during his *prabrajya* (period of wandering). A more pictorial and interesting exhibition can be found at **Vivekanandapuram** (247012; admission free; 9am-1pm & 5-9pm), an ashram 3km north of town that provides a snapshot of Indian philosophy, religion, leaders and thinkers.

VIVEKANANDA MEMORIAL

Four hundred metres offshore is the rock where Swami Vivekananda meditated and chose to take his moral message beyond India's shores. A **memorial** (admission Rs10; 8am-5pm) was built in Vivekananda's memory in 1970, and reflects architectural styles drawn from all over India. It can be a loud place when packed with tourists, but the islet is big enough to provide moments of seclusion. If you really need quiet, there's a meditation chamber focused on a glowing Om symbol.

The huge **statue** on the smaller island, which looks like an Indian Colossus of Rhodes, is not of Vivekananda but Tamil poet Thiruvalluvar. India's 'Statue of Liberty' was the work of more than 5000 sculptors. It was erected in 2000 and honours the poet's 133-chapter work *Thirukural* – hence its height of exactly 133ft (40.5m).

Ferries shuttle between the port and the islands between 8am and 4pm; the cost is Rs20 round-trip.

GOVERNMENT MUSEUM

This **museum** (Main Rd; Indian/foreigner Rs5/100; 9.30am-5.30pm Sat-Thu) is overpriced and underwhelming. There's a blah display of archaeological finds and temple artefacts and some freak-show paraphernalia, like the foetus of a four-legged goat and (gasp!) a three-chambered coconut.

SEAFRONT

There's a crowded beach here and **ghats** that lead down to a lingam half submerged in a wave-driven tidal pool. Past the ice-cream and *chaat* (snack) sellers above the beach is a somewhat blasé **memorial** to victims of the 2004 tsunami.

BAYWATCH

Tired of temples? This impressive **amusement park** (246563; www.baywatch.co.in; adult/child Rs240/180; 10am-7pm) is a great way to spend the day, especially if you've got kids in tow. The entry ticket gives unlimited access to a wave pool with water slides (women should swim in at least knee-length shorts and shirt for propriety). The adjacent **wax museum** (adult/child Rs50/40), filled with Indian politicians and celebrities, promises to 'Make You Feel at London'! The park is just 1.5km west of the town centre – a rickshaw ride shouldn't be more than Rs80.

Sleeping

Some hotels, especially midrange places around the bazaar, have seasonal rates, so some prices double during April and May, and late October to January.

BUDGET

TTDC Youth Hostel (246257; dm Rs50) This hostel is part of Hotel Tamil Nadu. The dormitories and common bathrooms are foul, but you can't beat the price and the location is great.

Jothi Lodge (246316; Sannathi St; r from Rs150) Offers rooms for as low as Rs150, but they're pretty dingy.

Hotel Narmadha (246365; Kovalam Rd; r Rs200-250) This big concrete block conceals some very friendly staff and cheapo rooms that are kept reasonably clean and comfy; it's popular with pilgrims and is set to the west of the main bazaar, next to Hotel Tri-Sea.

Saravana Lodge (246007; Sannathi St; r Rs250-450) If you opt for a room without TV you can cut a pretty good deal at this place just outside the temple entrance. All rooms have private bathrooms with squat toilets.

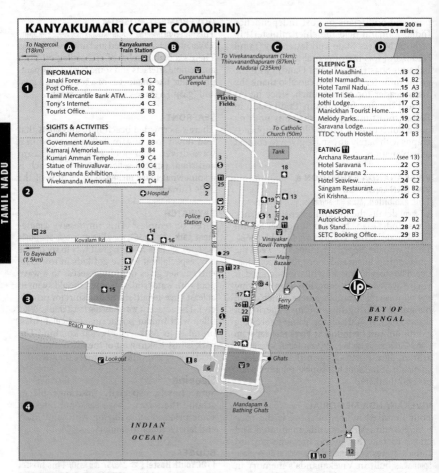

KANYAKUMARI (CAPE COMORIN)

INFORMATION
Janaki Forex.............................1	C2
Post Office..............................2	B2
Tamil Mercantile Bank ATM....3	B2
Tony's Internet.......................4	C3
Tourist Office.........................5	B3

SIGHTS & ACTIVITIES
Gandhi Memorial....................6	B4
Government Museum..............7	B3
Kamaraj Memorial...................8	B4
Kumari Amman Temple...........9	C4
Statue of Thiruvalluvar..........10	C4
Vivekananda Exhibition..........11	B3
Vivekananda Memorial...........12	D4

SLEEPING
Hotel Maadhini.....................13	C2
Hotel Narmadha....................14	B2
Hotel Tamil Nadu..................15	A3
Hotel Tri Sea........................16	B2
Jothi Lodge..........................17	C2
Manickhan Tourist Home.......18	C2
Melody Parks........................19	C2
Saravana Lodge....................20	C3
TTDC Youth Hostel...............21	B3

EATING
Archana Restaurant............(see 13)	
Hotel Saravana 1..................22	C3
Hotel Saravana 2..................23	C3
Hotel Seaview......................24	C2
Sangam Restaurant...............25	B2
Sri Krishna..........................26	C3

TRANSPORT
Autorickshaw Stand..............27	B2
Bus Stand............................28	A2
SETC Booking Office.............29	B3

MIDRANGE & TOP END

Hotel Tamil Nadu (☎ 246257; Beach Rd; r Rs450, with AC Rs750; ❄) Despite the usual quirks of a government-run hotel, this is a great location if you want to get away from the (slight) bustle of town; balcony rooms have ocean, though not temple, views.

Manickhan Tourist Home (☎ 246387; East Car St; d Rs450, with AC Rs1100; ❄) This very friendly hotel is professionally run and a real pleasure to doss in; the large rooms are all outfitted with clean bathrooms, satellite TV and, if you're willing to shell out a bit, superb sea views.

Hotel Maadhini (☎ 246787; East Car St; d Rs450, with AC Rs1100; ❄) Next door to Manickhan, this place offers almost the exact same experience (and rates).

Hotel Tri Sea (☎ 246787; Kovalam Rd; r from Rs500, with AC from Rs1200; ❄) As you walk west of the town you cannot miss the high-rise Tri Sea, which offers huge, airy rooms, most with balconies that are facing the ocean. The doors of some of the bathrooms seem to have been painted by a bored, drugged-up graphic artist, but hey, it's all in the name of quirky character.

Melody Parks (☎ 247667; Sannathi St; r from Rs1000, with AC from Rs1500; ❄) The enthusiastic staff here make you feel well at home in one of Kanyakumari's few true top-end places. In this case, you're getting an extra dose of spoiling, if much the same views and fairly plusher rooms than what's available at the nearby midrange spots.

Eating

There are plenty of fruit stalls and basic veg restaurants in the bazaar area, open for breakfast, lunch and dinner.

Sri Krishna (Sannathi St; mains Rs25-85) If you need fresh juice, good ice cream or Indian takes on pizza and burgers, try this clean and busy corner cafe.

Archana Restaurant (East Car St; mains Rs25-95) At the Hotel Maadhini, this restaurant, which serves predictable if well-executed Indian fare, is best visited in the evening when the pleasant garden area provides open-air ambience.

Hotel Seaview (East Car St; mains Rs30-150) This upmarket hotel has an excellent AC multi-cuisine restaurant specialising in fresh local seafood and posh takes on North and South Indian faves.

Sangam Restaurant (Main Rd; mains Rs40-170) It's as if the Sangam started in Kashmir, trekked across the entirety of India, and stopped here to open a restaurant that features top culinary picks culled from every province encountered along the way. The food is good, the joint is bustling, and the menu must be one of the biggest in Tamil Nadu.

Hotel Saravana has two clean, busy veg restaurants with thalis (Rs25) and good chai.

Getting There & Away

BUS

The surprisingly sedate bus stand is a 10-minute walk west of the centre along Kovalam Rd and there's a handy **SETC booking office** (⏰ 7am-9pm) on Main Rd. For details of services, see the boxed text (below).

TRAIN

The train station is about 1km north of the bazaar and temple. The daily *Chennai Egmore*

Express departs for Chennai at 5.15pm (sleeper/2AC/3AC Rs189/321/1026, 13 hours) and the 6.35am *Tiruchirappalli–Howrah Express* to Chennai departs on Saturday. The same trains also stop at Madurai and Trichy.

There are two daily express trains to Trivandrum (2nd class/3AC Rs33/183, two hours, 87km).

For the real long-haulers or train buffs, the weekly *Himsagar Express* runs all the way to Jammu Tawi (in Jammu and Kashmir; see p285), a distance of 3734km, in 66 hours – the longest single train ride in India.

THE WESTERN GHATS

Deep blue skies, pine sap breezes, dollops of purple and gold splashed from a wildflower palette and the crackle of a wood fire on perpetual late autumn nights.

The British built their summer homes here, seeking what we might call 'colonial air-con'. Because let's face it: Tamil Nadu can be hot as hell, and even the plushest rooms can't cool you off as you wander the dust clouds on the plains. Solution? The lush mountains of the Western Ghats, some of the most welcome hill heat relief in India. Rising like an impassable bulwark of evergreen and deciduous tangle from the north of Mumbai to the tip of Tamil Nadu, the Ghats (with an average elevation of 915m) contain 27% of all India's flowering plants, 60% of its medicinal plants and an incredible array of endemic wildlife. It's not just the air and (relative) lack of pollution that's refreshing, either – there's a general acceptance of quirkiness and eccentricity in the hills that is hard to find in the lowlands. Think hippie cafes, handlebar-moustachioed trekking guides and tiger-stripe earmuffs for sale in the bazaar. On the downside is the state of local tribal groups whose identity is in danger of both over-exploitation and assimilation.

KODAIKANAL (KODAI)

☎ 04542 / pop 32,969 / elev 2100m

Kodai is small, intimate, misty and mountainous; there are few more refreshing Tamil Nadu moments than boarding a bus in the heat-soaked plains and disembarking in the sharp pinch of a Kodaikanal night. It's not all cold though; during the day the weather is positively pleasant, more reminiscent of deep spring than early winter.

BUSES FROM KANYAKUMARI (CAPE COMORIN)			
Destination	Fare (Rs)	Duration (hr)	Frequency
Bengaluru	333	15	daily
Chennai	280	16	6 daily
Kodaikanal	132	10	daily
Kovalam	40	3½	daily
Madurai	76	6	8 daily
Rameswaram	108	9	2 daily
Trivandrum	31	3	2 daily

Located in the Palani knolls some 120km northwest of Madurai, Kodai clings to a mountainside draped in *sholas* (forests) of pine, gum trees and *kurinji* shrub, unique to the Western Ghats. The light, purple-blue-coloured blossoms flower every 12 years; next due date 2018. If you don't feel like waiting, the many treks by nearby dark rock faces and white waterfalls are still rewarding.

The renowned Kodaikanal International School provides a bit of cosmopolitan influence and scenes like a French teenager getting a light for his *bidi* off a Punjabi classmate, before they discuss in English Heath Ledger's performance as the Joker.

Compared to Ooty, Kodaikanal is relaxed, but it's still popular with Indian tourists (especially honeymooners). If it's summer, make sure you catch the horse races and boating during the Summer Festival (see boxed text p1043).

Orientation & Information

For a hill station, Kodai is remarkably compact and the central town area can easily be explored on foot. There are several internet cafes, and a State Bank of India ATM near the Carlton Hotel.

Alpha Net (PT Rd; per hr Rs40; ☽ 9am-10pm) By far the friendliest and fastest internet in town.

Apollo Communications (Anna Salai; per hr Rs40; ☽ 9am-8pm) Internet access.

Indian Bank (Anna Salai; ☽ 10am-2pm & 2.30-3.30pm Mon-Fri, 10am-12.30pm Sat) With foreign-exchange desk.

Kurinji Tours & Travel (☎ 240008; kurinjitravels@sancharnet.in; Club Rd; ☽ 9am-6pm) Reliable help with onward travel arrangements.

Tourist office (☎ 241675; Anna Salai; ☽ 10am-5.45pm)

HILL TRIBES OF THE NILGIRI

For centuries, the Nilgiris have been home to hill tribes. While retaining integrity in customs, dress and language, the tribes were economically, socially and culturally interdependent. The British concept of exclusive property rights disenfranchised many tribespeople, as did exploitative commercial practices that undermined their barter-based economy. Today, many eke out a living in poverty gathering honey or herbs for the ayurveda industry.

The Toda tribe's social, economic and spiritual system centred on the buffalo, whose milk and ghee was integral to their diet and used as currency – in exchange for grain, tools and medical services. Most importantly, the dairy produce provided offerings to the gods as well as fuel for the funeral pyre. It was only at the ritual for human death that the strictly vegetarian Toda killed a buffalo, not for food but to provide company for the deceased.

The Badagas are believed to have migrated to the Nilgiris from the north around 1600 AD, in the wake of Muslim invasions in the north, and are thus not officially a tribal people. With knowledge of the world outside the hills, they became effective representatives for the hill tribes. Their agricultural produce, particularly grain, added a further dimension to the hill diet.

The Kotas lived in the Kotagiri area and were considered by other tribes to be lower in status. They still undertake ceremonies in which the gods are beseeched for rains and bountiful harvests.

The Kurumbas inhabited the thick forests of the south. They gathered bamboo, honey and materials for housing, some of which were supplied to other tribes. They also engaged in a little agriculture, and at sowing and harvest times they employed the Badaga to perform rituals entreating the gods for abundant yields.

The Irulus, also from the southern slopes, produced tools and gathered honey and other forest products that they converted into brooms and incense. They are devotees of Vishnu and often perform rituals for other tribes.

British colonialism and lowland migration have undermined tribal cultural systems to the point of collapse. Displaced tribes have been 'granted' land by the Indian government, but the cultivation of land is anathema to the Toda, who see themselves as caretakers of the soil – for them, to dig into the land is to desecrate it.

Today many tribal people have assimilated to the point of invisibility. Some have fallen into destructive patterns associated with displacement and alienation. Others remain straddled across two cultures, but the tribes are in a precarious state. Although the Indian government claims 5000 hill people remain, tribal censuses put the number at 1700.

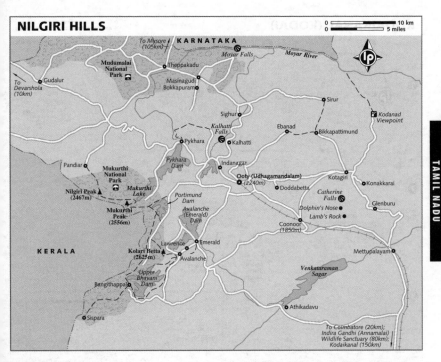

NILGIRI HILLS

Sights & Activities

WALKING & TREKKING

Assuming it's not cloaked in opaque mist, the valley views along paved **Coaker's Walk** (admission Rs2, camera Rs5; ⏰ 7am-7pm) are superb. There's no plastic allowed on the pathway, a rule flagrantly flaunted by locals, and a small **observatory** (admission Rs3) with telescope at the southern end. You can start near Greenlands Youth Hostel or Villa Retreat – where **stained glass** in the nearby Church of South India (CSI) is stunning in the morning light – and the stroll takes all of five minutes. The 5km **lake circuit** is pleasant in the early morning when you can count the kingfishers before the tourist traffic starts.

The views from **Pillar Rocks**, a 7km hike (one-way, beginning near Bryant Park), are excellent (again, assuming fine weather), and there are some wonderful hiking trails through pockets of forest, including **Bombay Shola** and **Pambar Shola**, that meander around Lower Shola Rd and St Mary's Rd. You will need a guide; talk to the staff at Greenlands Youth Hostel (p1107). Guides (per hour Rs70 to Rs100) of varying quality can also be ar-ranged through the tourist office while others will approach you in the street; the booklet *Trekking Routes in Kodaikanal* details walks ranging from 8km to 27km.

PARKS & WATERFALLS

Near the start of Coaker's Walk is **Bryant Park** (admission Rs5; ⏰ 9.30am-5pm), landscaped and stocked by the British officer after whom it's named. **Chettiar Park** (admission free; ⏰ 8.30am-5pm), about 1.5km uphill from town on the way to the Kurinji Andavar Temple, is small, pretty and landscaped. Both get crowded with school groups and canoodling couples. Nearby waterfalls include **Silver Cascade**, on the road outside Kodai and often full of in-terstate tourists bathing on the rocks, and compact **Bear Shola Falls**, in a pocket of for-est about a 20-minute walk from the town centre.

BOATING & HORSE RIDING

If you're sappy in love like a bad Bollywood song, the thing to do in Kodai is rent a pedal boat (Rs20 to Rs40), rowboat (Rs100) or Kashmiri *shikara* (covered gondola;

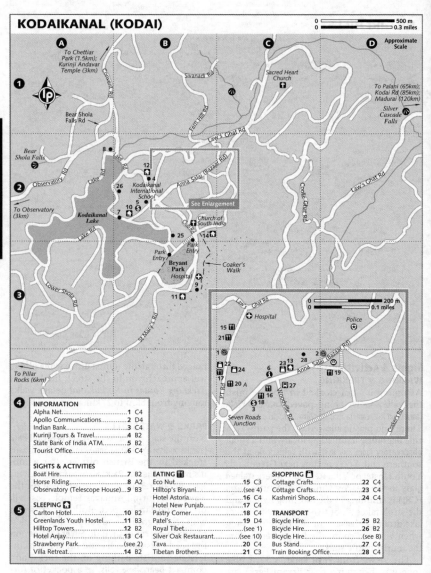

KODAIKANAL (KODAI)

TAMIL NADU

Rs140 including boatman) from either the Kodaikanal Boat & Rowing Club or Tamil Nadu Tourist Development Corporation; screechy crooning to your significant other is strictly optional.

There's a few horse hire stands on the lake. The rate is Rs180 per hour unaccompanied or Rs300 with a guide, but you can take a short ride for Rs80. Some of the horses here are in bad shape.

Sleeping

Hotel prices can jump by as much as 300% during the high season (from 1 April to 30 June). Prices listed here are low-season rates.

Most hotels in Kodai have a 9am or 10am checkout time in high season, but for the rest of the year it's usually 24 hours.

BUDGET

Greenlands Youth Hostel (☎ 240899; www.greenlandskodaikanal.com; dm Rs100, d Rs200-800) With cheap rooms and sweeping views of the valley below, this excellent lodge remains the number-one choice for budget travellers. There's a crowded dormitory and a range of rooms from basic doubles to more spacious digs with balcony, fireplace and TV. Staff are cheery, the location is peaceful and treks can be arranged.

Hotel Anjay (☎ 241809; www.hotelanjay.com; Anna Salai; d Rs400-650) The Anjay is a well-kept box of comfy, clean rooms with basic beds and amenities. Management is friendly and the hotel is centrally located.

MIDRANGE & TOP END

Strawberry Park (☎ 242340; Anna Salai; r from Rs500) Who wouldn't be attracted to a hotel with a name that sounds like a Beatles single? Rooms are huge and the bedding is thick and warm, perfect for cold Kodai evenings.

Hilltop Towers (☎ 240413; www.hilltopgroup.in; Club Rd; d/ste from Rs890/1500) Although it comes off as big, boxy and corporate, rustic accents like polished teak floors and wooden embellishments, plus very friendly staff and excellent upper-floor views, make the Hilltop a midrange standout.

Villa Retreat (☎ 240940; www.villaretreat.com; Club Rd; r Rs1089-2250, cottages Rs2813) The terrace garden of this lovely old stone-built family hotel at the northern end of Coaker's Walk offers awesome valley views. The best rooms, somewhat overpriced, are the cottages with panoramic views. Most rooms have fireplaces and TV, and there's a cosy restaurant. Prices include taxes.

Carlton Hotel (☎ 240056; www.krahejahospitality .com; Lake Rd; d/cottages Rs7000/10,000) The cream of Kodai's hotels is a magnificent five-star colonial mansion that overlooks the lake and the international school. Rooms are bright, spacious and some have private balconies with lake views. The lobby and grounds very much succeed at recreating hill station ambience, with stone walls, dark-wood flooring and roaring fireplaces that make you want to demand a scotch now, dammit, from the eager staff.

Eating
RESTAURANTS

PT Rd is the best place for cheap restaurants and it's here that most travellers and students from the international school congregate. The once-vaunted Manna Bake, a bakery popular with granola-types and backpackers, was closed at the time of research.

Tava (PT Rd; mains Rs30; ☯ lunch & dinner Thu-Tue) A clean, fast and cheap veg option, this place has a wide menu; try the cauliflower-stuffed *gobi paratha* (spicy cauliflower bread) and *sev puri* (crisp, puffy fried bread with potato and chutney).

Hotel Astoria (☎ 240524; Anna Salai; mains Rs30-50, thalis Rs35-60; ☯ breakfast, lunch & dinner) This veg restaurant is always packed with locals and tourists, especially come lunchtime when it serves excellent all-you-can-eat thalis.

Hotel New Punjab (PT Rd; mains Rs30-100; ☯ lunch & dinner) For North Indian and tandoori dishes (and any non-veg curries in general), this is the best place in Kodai.

Patel's (Anna Salai; mains Rs40; ☯ lunch & dinner) Locals and Gujaratis craving a taste of their state's delicious vegetarian cuisine crowd into this barren yet bustling cafe come dinner time.

Royal Tibet (PT Rd; mains Rs40-80; ☯ lunch & dinner) If you're missing Tibetan food, come here for the chewy but tasty *momos* (dumplings). A nearby competitor, Tibetan Brothers, offers almost the exact same menu, and while their *momos* aren't up to scratch, they do a superior *thukpa* (noodle soup).

Hilltop's Biryani (Club Rd; mains Rs55-80; ☯ lunch & dinner) There's a huge range of biryani available here, from hot Hyderabadi-style to an intriguing seafood version of the spicy rice dish.

Silver Oak Restaurant (☎ 240056; Lake Rd; buffet lunch & dinner Rs450; ☯ breakfast, lunch & dinner) The restaurant at the Carlton Hotel puts on lavish buffet meals, serving everything from steak to lasagne to paneer *makhani* (paneer cooked in creamy tomato gravy), though you might feel a bit out of place in hiking gear.

SELF-CATERING

Eco Nut (☎ 243296; PT Rd; ☯ 10am-5pm Mon-Sat) This interesting shop sells a wide range of locally produced organic health food – whole-wheat bread, muffins, cheese, salad greens – and essential oils, herbs and herb remedies.

Pastry Corner (Anna Salai; ☯ 9am-9pm) Pick up great picnic sandwiches and yummy brownies (Rs5;

after 3pm) here, or squeeze onto the benches with a cuppa to watch the world go by.

Excellent homemade chocolates and dried fruit are sold all over town.

Shopping

The many handicraft stores stock good craftwork, and several also reflect the local low-key but long-term commitment to social justice.

Cottage Crafts (☎ 240160; Anna Salai; ☼ 10am-8pm) Run by the voluntary organisation Coordinating Council for Social Concerns in Kodai (Corsock), here you'll find goods crafted by disadvantaged groups, with about 80% of the purchase price returns to the craftspeople. There's also a second branch on PT Rd.

On PT Rd you'll find small Kashmiri shops and South Indian handicrafts stalls.

Getting There & Away

The nearest train station is Kodai Rd, at the foot of the mountain, where taxis (around Rs1000) and buses (Rs15) wait. There's a **train booking office** (Anna Salai; ☼ 9am-5pm Mon-Sat, 1.30-5pm Sun) in town.

Don't expect a bus to be depart from Kodaikanal immediately. Tickets for private buses can be booked at travel agents near the bus stand. For details of main bus departures from Kodaikanal, see the boxed text, (below).

Getting Around

The central part of Kodaikanal is compact and very easy to get around on foot. There are no autorickshaws (believe it or not) but plenty of taxis willing to take you to various sightseeing points. Charges are fixed and relatively high;

BUSES FROM KODAIKANAL (KODAI)

Destination	Fare (Rs)	Duration (hr)	Frequency
Bengaluru	283	11	daily
Bengaluru *	450	11	daily
Chennai	450	11	2 daily
Coimbatore	50	5	daily
Kochi*	400	8	daily
Madurai	34	3½	hourly
Madurai*	150	3	2 daily
Ooty	250-400	8	daily
Palani	20	2	8 daily
Trichy	57	5	3 daily

*private buses

sightseeing tours cost from Rs650 to Rs1500 for a day trip.

If you fancy a ride around the lake or you're fit enough to tackle the hills, mountain bikes can be hired from several **bicycle stalls** (per hr/day Rs10/75; ☼ 8am-6pm) around the lake.

AROUND KODAIKANAL

One of the better high-end escapes in the hills, about three hours' drive below Kodaikanal off the Palani–Dindigul road, is the fabulous **Cardamom House** (☎ 0451-2556765, 09360-691793; www.cardamomhouse.com; r from Rs3000). Created with love and care by a retired Brit, this comfortable guest house – at the end of a scenic road beside bird-rich Lake Kamarajar – runs on solar power, uses water wisely, farms organically, trains and employs only locals (who produce terrific meals), and supports several village development initiatives. You'll need to book well in advance, hire a driver to take you there, and prepare for some serious relaxation.

INDIRA GANDHI (ANNAMALAI) WILDLIFE SANCTUARY

The largest of the three wildlife sanctuaries in the Western Ghats along the Tamil Nadu–Kerala border, this misty mountain park covers almost 1000 sq km of mostly teak forest and evergreen jungle. It's home to elephants, gaurs (Indian bison), tigers, panthers, spotted deer, wild boars, bears, porcupines and civet cats, and the Nilgiri tahr – commonly known as the ibex. The endangered lion-tailed macaque may also be spotted. The park has a renowned medicinal plant garden and interpretive centre (check out the astrological medicine chart and beauty hints if you're feeling travel-weary), and is home to the tribal group of Kada people, many of whom work here. The park's elephant training centre can be visited on the guided vehicle tour.

The **park reception centre** (per person Rs50, camera/video Rs10/50; ☼ day visitors 6.30am-6pm) at Topslip, where trekking guides can be arranged and where there are several lodges, is about 35km southwest of Pollachi. Wildlife is often seen on the drive in, and you can wander around the reception-centre surroundings. Access to the inner forest has traditionally been limited to tours (Rs625 for a 25-seater bus, irrespective of numbers; one hour) or guided treks (Rs70, maximum four people, four hours), but as of research private vehicles were being permitted into the park; this may be your best bet for covering the large area free of minders. Other tours and treks run on demand.

Sleeping & Eating

Forest accommodation is available at and near Topslip. It *must* be booked in advance in Pollachi at the **Wildlife Warden's Office** (WWO; ☎ 04259-2225356; Meenkarai Rd; ⊙ 9am-5pm Mon-Fri), but hours and service can be erratic. Rooms in several simple lodges at Topslip are Rs300; the somewhat more comfortable New Tree Tops lodge is Rs1000; and dorm beds are available for Rs30 at Ambulli Illam, 2km from the reception centre. There's a basic canteen at Topslip.

It's a fairly good bet you'll need to overnight in Pollachi; try **Sakthi Hotels** (☎ 04259-223050; sakthifibreproducts@vsnl.net; Coimbatore Rd; d Rs200, with AC Rs495; ⌘). You can also try to stay in Valparai, a hill town about 64km south of Pollachi that is trying to sell itself as the Nilgiris' next big tourism thing. There's the usual setting of cool valleys, tea plantations and several guest houses. These range from the serviceable **Green Hills** (☎ 04253-222262; State Bank Rd; r from Rs300; ⌘) to the posh, Victorian comfort of the **Stanmore Bungalow** (☎ 422-4351500; www.teabungalows.com; r from Rs300; ⌘), a converted British villa with suited-up butlers, tea-plantation views from the verandah and all the other paraphernalia that reminds you there will always be some corner of this land that is forever cashing in on colonial nostalgia.

Getting There & Away

The sanctuary is between Palani and Coimbatore. Regular buses travelling from both places stop at the nearest large town, Pollachi, which is also on the Coimbatore–Dindigul train line.

From Pollachi, buses leave the bus stand for Topslip at 6.15am, 11.15am and 3.15pm, returning at 9.30am, 1pm and 6.30pm. A taxi from Pollachi to the sanctuary costs around Rs800 one way. Buses from Pollachi to Valparai run throughout the day.

COIMBATORE

☎ 0422 / pop 1.46 million

Coimbatore may be one of the largest cities in Tamil Nadu, but most travellers use it as either a step towards getting into Ooty, or out of the hills and into Kerala. Which isn't a bad idea; this is a large business and junction city that's friendly enough, but short on sights. Sometimes known as the Manchester of India for its textile industry, it has plenty of accommodation and eating options if you need to spend the night.

Information

Blazenet (Nehru St; per hr Rs20; ⊙ 9am-12.30pm) Internet access.

HSBC ATM (Racecourse Rd) Next to Annalakshmi Restaurant.

ICICI ATM (Avanashi Rd) Opposite Nilgiri's Nest.

Main post office (Railway Feeder Rd; ⊙ 10am-8pm Mon-Sat, 10am-2pm Sun) A few hundred metres northwest of the train station, reached via a pedestrian underpass from the platforms.

Tourist office (⊙ 10am-5.45pm) Small office inside the train station.

Sleeping

Hotel Shri Shakti (☎ 2224225; Sastri Rd; s/d Rs195/280) There's not much character here, but there are a lot of rooms; if you need a cheap, basic place to crash that's adjacent to the bus stands, look no further.

Hotel AP (☎ 4392777; hotelap@yahoo.com; s/d from Rs195/420, d with AC Rs750; ⌘) Again: cheap, basic rooms, in this case located across from the train station. The AP's tucked into some back alleys, but you'll recognise it by its oddly cubist, Gaudi-esque exterior.

Hotel Blue Star (☎ 2230635; 369A Nehru St; s/d from Rs400/600, with AC from Rs600/850; ⌘) A sprawling hotel, this has simple, clean rooms; the top floor is much nicer than downstairs. Management is friendly and it's convenient for the bus stands.

Legend's Inn (☎ 4350000; legends_inn@yahoo.com; Geetha Hall Rd; s/d Rs700/800, with AC Rs950/1100; ⌘) The Legend is, well, a legend, with comfortable furnishings, bamboo blinds and sparkling bathrooms.

Nilgiri's Nest (☎ 4505500; nilgiriscbe@gmail.com; 739A Avanashi Rd; s/d from Rs1500/2600; ⌘) This lovely large complex feels like a vaguely kitschy hotel plunked out of the West; rooms are designed in a cool '60s mod kind of way, and decorated with tasteful Audubon-esque prints of local birdlife.

Residency (☎ 2201234; www.theresidency.com; 1076 Avanashi Rd; s/d from Rs4700/5000; ⌘ ▢ ▣) Coimbatore's finest hotel has all the five-star trimmings, along with friendly staff and immaculate rooms. There's a well-equipped health club and pool, two excellent restaurants, a coffee shop and a bookshop in the lobby.

TAMIL NADU

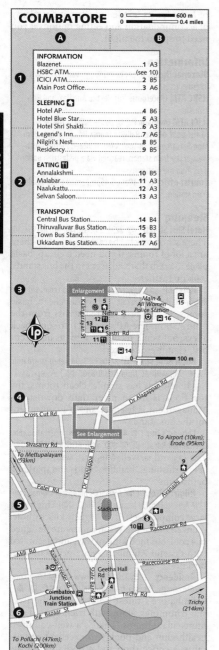

Eating

There's a fast-food hall and supermarket underneath Nilgiri's Nest (p1109).

Selvan Saloon (Sastri Rd; mains Rs20) This isn't a restaurant; it's a stall. But it's a stall that serves the best street food we had in South India: an incredibly rich and spicy mushroom curry that would shame some of the pricier dishes around. Look for the long lines, and get ready for bliss.

Malabar (7 Sastri Rd; mains Rs50-120; ☺ lunch & dinner) In the KK Residency Hotel, this restaurant specialises in Keralan and North Indian food. The Malabar chicken roast (Rs100) is a spicy treat and there are seafood choices like tandoori pomfret.

Naalukattu (Nehru St; mains Rs50-130; ☺ lunch & dinner) For the price, this is a rather gorgeous restaurant that resembles a dark-wood-accented Keralan verandah. The Malayalam-inspired food is all good, but it's the fish curry that goes down an absolute treat.

Annalakshmi (☎ 2212142; 106 Racecourse Rd; set meals Rs150; ☺ lunch & dinner Tue-Sun) The top veg restaurant in town, this is run by devotees of Swami Shatanand Saraswati; the price of your meal helps support the Shivanjali educational trust for underprivileged children.

Getting There & Away
AIR
The airport is 10km east of town. There are flights from here to Mumbai (US$100 to US$160), Delhi (US$110 to US$309), Kozhikode (Calicut; US$65 to US$100), Chennai (US$130) and Bengaluru (US$60 to US$90). Airlines include:

Air India (☎ 2399833)
Jet Airways (☎ 2243465)
Kingfisher Airlines (☎ 2214075)
Paramount Airways (☎ 3256822)
SpiceJet Airlines (☎ 1800 180 3333)

BUS
There are three bus stands in the city centre.

From Central Bus Station services depart to nearby northern destinations such as Ooty (Rs50, 3½ hours, every 30 minutes) and Mettupalayam (Rs13, one hour, every 10 minutes). From Thiruvalluvar bus station you can catch state and interstate buses to Bengaluru (Rs180 to Rs225, nine hours, 10 daily), Mysore (Rs70 to Rs95, five hours, every hour) and Chennai (Rs275, 11½ hours, seven daily). The town bus stand is for local city buses.

MAJOR TRAINS FROM COIMBATORE

Destination	Train name	Fare (Rs)	Duration (hr)	Departure
Bengaluru	Kanyakumari-Bangalore Exp	148-416	9	10.35pm daily
Chennai	Kovai Exp	116-404	7½	1.40pm daily
	Cheran Exp	116-404	8½	10pm daily
Kochi	Sabari Exp	93-261	5	8.50am daily
Madurai	Coimbatore-Madurai Exp	60-102	6	10.45pm daily
Ooty	Nilgiri Exp (via Mettupalayam)	22-35	7	5.15am daily
Pollachi	Pollachi-Podanur	24	1½	5 daily

Ukkadam bus station, south of the city, is for buses to nearby southern destinations including Palani (Rs30, three hours, every 20 minutes), Pollachi (Rs15, one hour, every five minutes) and Madurai (Rs70, five hours, every 30 minutes).

TRAIN

Coimbatore Junction is on the main line between Chennai and Ernakulam (Kerala). For Ooty, catch the daily *Nilgiri Express* at 5.15am; it connects with the miniature railway departure from Mettupalayam to Ooty at 7.10am. The whole trip to Ooty takes about seven hours. For train services, see the boxed text, above.

Getting Around

For the airport take bus 20 from the town bus stand or bus 90 from the train station (Rs4). Many buses ply between the train station and the town bus stand (Rs1.50). Autorickshaw drivers charge around Rs40 between the bus and train stations.

AROUND COIMBATORE

Isha Yoga Center

This **ashram** (☎ 0422-2515345; www.ishafoundation. org; ☼ 6am-8pm), in Poondi, 30km west of Coimbatore, is also a yoga retreat and place of pilgrimage. The centrepiece is a multi-religious temple housing the Dhyanalingam, said to be unique in that it embodies all seven chakras of spiritual energy. Visitors are welcome to the temple to meditate, or to take part in one- to two-week Isha yoga courses, for which you should register in advance.

Mettupalayam

This commercial town is the starting point for the miniature train to Ooty. There's little of interest for travellers, but if you want to avoid the 7.20am connection, there is plenty of ac-

commodation. Try **Nanda Lodge** (☎ 04254-222555; Ooty Main Rd; r from Rs231), which is basic but clean and right opposite the bus station, through which there's a short cut to the train station. **Hotel EMS Mayura** (☎ 04254-227936; 212 Coimbatore Rd; r Rs680, with AC Rs1150; 🖳), a decent enough mid-range hotel, is 2km from the train station.

COONOOR

☎ 0423 / pop 101,000 / elev 1850m

Coonoor is one of the three **Nilgiri hill stations** – Ooty, Kotagiri and Coonoor (see the Nilgiri Hills map, p1105) – that lie above the southern plains. Like Kotagiri, Coonoor is a place for quiet and isolation, which can be found in any of Upper Coonoor's accommodation, 1km to 2km above the town centre. From here you can look down over the sea of red tile rooftops to the slopes behind and soak up the peace, cool climate and beautiful scenery. Just note you get none of the above in central Coonoor, which is a bustling, honking mess.

Sights & Activities

In Upper Coonoor, the 12-hectare **Sim's Park** (adult/child Rs5/2, camera/video Rs25/250; ☼ 8.30am-6pm) is a peaceful oasis of manicured lawns and more than 1000 plant species, including magnolia, tree ferns and camellia. Buses heading to Kotagiri can drop you here.

There are several popular viewpoints around Coonoor. **Dolphin's Nose**, about 10km from town, exposes a vast panorama encompassing **Catherine Falls** across the valley. On the way back, drop into **Guernsey Tea Factory** (☎ 2230205; admission Rs10; ☼ 8am-6pm) and take a short guided tour of the fragrant processing plant. Afterwards, stop at **Lamb's Rock**, named after the British captain who created a short path to this favourite picnic spot in a pretty patch of forest, for some more amazing views past the hills into the hazy plains. The easiest way to see these sights – all on the same road –

is on a rickshaw tour for around Rs400. If you're feeling energetic, walk the 6km or so back into town from Lamb's Rock (it's mostly, but not entirely, downhill).

Sleeping & Eating

You'll need a rickshaw (or good legs) to reach all these places.

Hotel Vivek Coonoor (☎ 2230658; www.hotelvivek .com; Figure of Eight Rd; dm Rs100, r from Rs400-700) Many of the wide range of rooms here have balconies (screened to avoid the 'monkey menace') from which you can hear the tea-pickers plucking leaves below you. There's also a monster dormitory.

YWCA Wyoming Guesthouse (☎ 2234426; s/d Rs275/550) This ramshackle guesthouse, a hill-station gem of a structure nestled into an up-slope of Upper Coonoor, is a budget favourite. Although ageing and draughty, the 150-year-old colonial house oozes character with wooden terraces and serene views over Coonoor.

Tryst (☎ 2207057; www.trystindia.com; d incl breakfast & dinner Rs4000) If you're looking for a gregarious accommodation experience that's quirky and classy, check out the website of this extraordinary guest house and book ahead. It's beautifully located in a former tea plantation manager's bungalow.

Your best bet for eating is your hotel restaurant, though there are forgettable restaurants in the town centre.

Getting There & Away

Coonoor is on the miniature train line between Mettupalayam (28km) and Ooty (18km) – see p1118. Buses to Ooty (Rs6.50, one hour) and Kotagiri (Rs8, one hour) leave roughly every 15 minutes.

KOTAGIRI

☎ 04266 / pop 29,184

The oldest of the three Nilgiri hill stations, Kotagiri is about 28km from Ooty. It's a quiet, unassuming place with a forgettable town centre, but we're assuming you're not here for the nightlife. Rather, the appeal is the escape from Ooty overdevelopment: red dirt tracks in the pines, blue skies and the high green walls of the Nilgiris.

From Kotagiri you can visit **Catherine Falls**, 8km away near the Mettupalayam road (the last 3km is by foot only, and the falls only flow after rain), **Elk Falls** (6km) and **Kodanad Viewpoint** (22km), where there's a view over

the Coimbatore Plains and Mysore Plateau. A half-day taxi tour to all three will cost around Rs600. The scenery on the road to Mettupalayam is gorgeous, so you may want to detour this way if you're heading down from Ooty.

A couple of very basic lodges are in the small town centre and a splendid 1915 colonial building, **Stone House Retreat** (☎ 273300; www.naharhotels.com; r Rs2000), offers fabulous views and atmosphere but charges like a wounded bull for all extras.

Also located here are the offices of the **Keystone Foundation** (☎ 272277; www.keystone -foundation.org; Groves Hill Rd), an NGO that works to improve environmental conditions in the Nilgiris while working with, and creating better living standards for, indigenous communities. For more on their work, see the boxed text (opposite).

Buses stop at the edge of town, about 1km from the centre. Buses to Ooty depart hourly (Rs15, two hours), crossing one of Tamil Nadu's highest passes. Buses to Mettupalayam leave every 30 minutes and to Coonoor every 15 minutes.

OOTY (UDHAGAMANDALAM)

☎ 0423 / pop 93,921 / elev 2240m

Ah, Ooty. It may be a bit bustling for some tastes, but most travellers quickly fall in love with this pine-clad retreat, where trekkers congregate in front of roaring fires before setting out into the surrounding green dream. Even the typical chaos of India becomes somehow subdued in the shadow of the hills. Therein lays Ooty's charm, especially when you throw in her quirks: a jumble of Hindu temples and ecotourism, overlaid by a veneer of manicured British aesthetic and, for the hell of it, a garden dedicated to thread.

This is South India's most famous (and certainly best-named) hill station, established by the British in the early 19th century as the summer headquarters of the then-Madras government and memorably nicknamed 'Snooty Ooty'. Development ploughed through a few decades ago, but somehow old Ooty survived. The quiet, wildflower-shaded boulevards left behind by the English (think Dorset-Upon-Ghat) and the surprisingly cosmopolitan town centre (thanks, crowds of travellers and local international school students) have ended up complementing, rather than clashing with, each other.

NATURE, NATIVES & THE NILGIRIS

What are the challenges facing tribal communities in the Nilgiris today? In proportion to the rest of the population they are a minority population. They are flaunted as museum pieces. They had a tremendous synergy. But that has been lost now. The government says 5000 Adivasis are left – the Adivasis say 1700. There is an awareness among them that they are in danger of disappearing in a generation. We need to work on education and healthcare.

Is it true parts of the ayurveda industry get many herbs from the Nilgiris while employing tribal peoples at exploitative wages? That industry needs good manufacturing practices. If, from the demand side, people said they want certain requirements like fair compensation for herb gatherers, that will happen on the supply side. I very much believe the consumer has a voice here.

Can you speak about environmental campaigns here, and the challenges they've faced? There was a very good effort here to rid the Nilgiris of plastic. [The antiplastic movement] had gotten the public on their side. But you need a solution – you just can't say 'ban plastic' without providing paper or cloth bags. And you need enforcement. Just a few raids on plastic in the markets caused such a stir. With Indian tourists there's no enforcement, so they feed monkeys, toss trash and talk loudly in quiet areas.

How does tourism impact the Nilgiris? Both sides. Tourism is positive in that it keeps the economy going, especially when tea is in the dumps. The negative is what you see – pollution etc. When tourists come up, they need to be sensitised to our unique conditions then and there.

Mathew John is director of the Keystone Foundation (opposite).

The journey up to Ooty on the miniature train is romantic and the scenery stunning – try to get a seat on the left-hand side where you get the best views across the mountains. With that said, even the bus ride is pretty impressive (if not nearly as relaxing). From April to June (the *very* busy season) Ooty is a welcome relief from the hot plains, and in the colder months (October to March) you'll need warm clothing – which you can buy cheap here – as overnight temperatures occasionally drop to 0°C.

The Summer Festival, when the hills explode in colour and parties, is a great time to visit (see boxed text p1043).

Orientation & Information

The train station and bus station are next to the racecourse, which is surrounded by cheap hotels. Further downhill is the lake, while the valley slopes up on either side, studded with colonial houses and guest lodges with good views. From the bus station it's a 10-minute walk to the bazaar area and a 20-minute walk to Ooty's commercial centre, Charing Cross.

BOOKSHOPS

Higginbothams Commercial Rd (☎ 2443736; ❤ 9.30am-1pm & 3.30-7.30pm Mon-Sat); Commissioner's Rd (☎ 2442546; ❤ 9am-1pm & 2-5.30pm Mon-Sat) OK selection of contemporary English-language Indian and other fiction.

INTERNET ACCESS

Global Net (Commercial Rd; per hr Rs25; ❤ 9.30am-9pm)
Internet cafes Church Hill Rd (per hr Rs30; ❤ 10am-9pm); Commercial Rd (per hr Rs20; ❤ 10am-10pm)

LIBRARY

Nilgiri Library (Bank Rd; temporary membership Rs350; ❤ 9.30am-1pm & 2.30-6pm, reading room 9.30am-6pm, Sat-Thu) Quaint little haven in a crumbling 1867 building with a collection of more than 40,000 books, including rare titles on the Nilgiris and hill tribes.

MONEY

Canara Bank ATM (Commercial Rd)
State Bank of India (Bank Rd; ❤ 10am-4pm Mon-Fri, 10am-2pm Sat) Changes travellers cheques and has an ATM.
State Bank of India ATM (Commercial Rd)
UK Forex (Commercial Rd) Changes travellers cheques and cash.
UTI Bank ATM (Ettines Rd)

NATIONAL PARK INFORMATION

Wildlife Warden's Office (WWO; ☎ 2444098; ❤ 10am-5.45pm Mon-Fri) Manages Mudumalai National Park, including advance booking for park accommodation.

POST

Charing Cross post office (Ettines Rd; ❤ 9.30am-5.30pm Mon-Fri)
Main post office (Havelock Rd; ❤ 9am-5pm Mon-Sat) Diagonally opposite St Stephen's Church.

TAMIL NADU

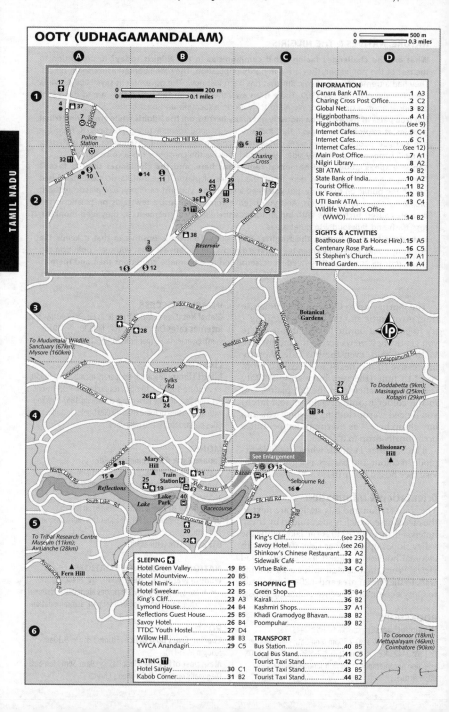

OOTY (UDHAGAMANDALAM)

INFORMATION

Canara Bank ATM.....................**1** A3	
Charing Cross Post Office........**2** C2	
Global Net.............................**3** B2	
Higginbothams......................**4** A1	
Higginbothams.....................(see **9**)	
Internet Cafes........................**5** C4	
Internet Cafes........................**6** C1	
Internet Cafes......................(see **12**)	
Main Post Office.....................**7** A1	
Nilgiri Library.........................**8** A2	
SBI ATM................................**9** B2	
State Bank of India................**10** A2	
Tourist Office.........................**11** B2	
UK Forex...............................**12** B3	
UTI Bank ATM........................**13** C4	
Wildlife Warden's Office	
(WWO)...............................**14** B2	

SIGHTS & ACTIVITIES

Boathouse (Boat & Horse Hire)..**15** A5
Centenary Rose Park................**16** C5
St Stephen's Church.................**17** A1
Thread Garden........................**18** A4

King's Cliff...........................(see **23**)
Savoy Hotel.........................(see **26**)
Shinkow's Chinese Restaurant...**32** A2
Sidewalk Café.........................**33** B2
Virtue Bake............................**34** C4

SHOPPING

Green Shop............................**35** B4
Kairali..................................**36** B2
Kashmiri Shops......................**37** A1
Khadi Gramodyog Bhavan........**38** B2
Poompuhar...........................**39** B2

TRANSPORT

Bus Station............................**40** B5
Local Bus Stand......................**41** C5
Tourist Taxi Stand...................**42** B2
Tourist Taxi Stand...................**43** B5
Tourist Taxi Stand...................**44** B2

SLEEPING

Hotel Green Valley..................**19** B5	
Hotel Mountview....................**20** B5	
Hotel Nimi's..........................**21** B5	
Hotel Sweekar.......................**22** B5	
King's Cliff...........................**23** A3	
Lymond House.......................**24** B4	
Reflections Guest House..........**25** B5	
Savoy Hotel..........................**26** B4	
TTDC Youth Hostel..................**27** D4	
Willow Hill............................**28** B3	
YWCA Anandagiri....................**29** C5	

EATING

Hotel Sanjay..........................**30** C1
Kabob Corner.........................**31** B2

TOURIST INFORMATION
Tourist office (✆ 2443977; ⊙ 10am-5.45pm Mon-Fri)
Maps, brochures and tour information.

Sights
ST STEPHEN'S CHURCH
Perched above the town centre, the immaculate **St Stephen's Church** (Church Hill Rd; ⊙ 10am-1pm & 3-5pm Mon-Sat, services 8am & 11am Sun), built in 1829, is the oldest church in the Nilgiris. Throughout its history, St Stephens has racially shifted from hosting an exclusively British congregation to an Anglo-Indian orphanage to falling under the auspices of the Church of South India. Look out for lovely stained glass, huge wooden beams hauled by elephant from the palace of Tipu Sultan some 120km away, and the sometimes kitschy, sometimes touching, slabs and plaques donated by colonial-era churchgoers. In the quiet, overgrown cemetery you'll find headstones commemorating many an Ooty Brit, including the wife and daughter of John Sullivan, the town's founder.

BOTANICAL GARDENS
Established in 1848, these lovely **gardens** (adult/child Rs10/3, camera/video Rs10/100; ⊙ 8am-6.30pm) are a living gallery of the natural fauna of the Nilgiris. Look out for a fossilised tree trunk believed to be around 20 million years old, and on busy days, roughly 20 million Indian tourists.

CENTENARY ROSE PARK
With its terraced lawns and colourful flowerbeds – best between May and July – this terraced **rose garden** (Selbourne Rd; adult/child Rs10/5, camera/video Rs30/50; ⊙ 9am-6.30pm) is a pleasant place for a stroll. There are good views over Ooty from the hilltop location.

THREAD GARDEN
Your appreciation of the **Thread Garden** (☎ 2445145; North Lake Rd; admission Rs10, camera/video Rs15/30; ⊙ 8.30am-7.30pm) rests on your love of irony and kitsch. If that threshold is low, you'll be disappointed. If it's decent, you may, if you're in a good mood, enjoy the 'miracle' (official description and just *slight* hyperbole) that is 150 species of 'plants' from around the world meticulously re-created using 'hand-wound' thread. The technique was perfected by Keralan artist Anthony Joseph and the work took 50 craftspeople

12 years to complete, which is either very impressive or kinda sad.

DODDABETTA LOOKOUT
This is it: the highest point (2633m) of the Nilgiris and one of the best **viewpoints** (admission Rs2; ⊙ 7am-6pm) around, assuming, as usual, the day is clear. It's about 10km out of town; go early for better chances of a mist-free view. Any Kotagiri buses will drop you here.

TRIBAL RESEARCH CENTRE MUSEUM
It's hard to say why you should love the this **museum** (admission free; ⊙ 10am-5pm Mon-Fri) more: for its decently executed exhibits on Nilgiri and Andaman tribal groups, or the decomposing corpses of badly stuffed local wildlife, including a rotting mongoose that just arrived from hell's deepest pit and a 'python' apparently made from several socks, a blanket and those googly eyes you buy at the local crafts store. OK: seriously, the artefacts are fantastic – you may never get the chance to hold a Stone Age bow in your life again – and descriptions of the tribes are good, if written by anthropologists with no filter from academia to normal English. The guides are either researchers who can give you an enthusiastic account of their expeditions, or some hapless local staffer who shouts 'Spear! Spear!' while gesturing at a spear. The museum is just beyond the village of M Palada, 11km from Ooty on the way to Emerald. Catch any of the frequent buses heading to M Palada and walk from there, or hire a rickshaw from Ooty for around Rs300 return.

Activities
TREKKING
Trekking is pretty much de rigeur in Ooty and the reason most travellers come here. On day trips you'll have a wander through evergreen forest, tea plantations, over lookouts, into local villages and generally, catch a bus back to town. Most guest houses will set you up with guides, or you can hire your own – plenty will offer their services to you. Expect to pay depending on the size of your group, Rs300 to Rs900 for a full-day trek. For other nearby hiking options, consider the resorts near Mudumalai National Park (see p1119).

HORSE RIDING
Alone or with a guide, you can hire horses outside the boathouse on the north side of the

lake; the rides mostly consist of a short amble along bitumen, although you can explore the woods and hills for more money. Prices run from Rs70 for a short ride to Rs150 to Rs200 for an hour, which takes you partway around the lake. Try not to pick a horse that looks too tired, as many do.

BOATING

Rowboats can be rented from the **boathouse** (⊗ 9am-5.30pm) by the artificial lake (created in 1824). Prices start from Rs60 for a two-seater pedal boat (30 minutes) and go up to Rs250 for a 15-seater motorboat (20 minutes).

HORSE RACING

Ooty's racecourse dominates the lower part of the hill station between Charing Cross and the lake. The horse-racing season runs from mid-April to June and on race days the town is a hive of activity; it's an event you can't miss if you're in town. Outside the season, the 2.4km racecourse just becomes a cricket field-cum-trash dump-cum-public toilet.

Tours

The tourist office (p1115) can put you in touch with agencies that run day trips to Mudumalai National Park via the Pykhara Dam (Rs200; minimum 15 people) starting at 9.30am and returning at 7pm, with just a quick spin through the park. Trips to Coonoor and surrounds are also possible.

A better alternative is to hire a taxi for the day and go as you please. Rates run for about Rs650 for a four-hour trip around Ooty, or Rs1200 to Rs1500 for a full day depending on where you're heading.

Sleeping

Ooty has some fantastic rustic lodges in the budget–midrange scale, gorgeous colonial residences at the high end, and even some decent backpacker dosses around the noisy bus stands. Be warned: it's a sellers' market in the high season (1 April to 15 June), when many hotel prices double and checkout time is often 9am. Prices listed here are for the low season when most places are good value.

BUDGET

YWCA Anandagiri (☎ 2442218; www.ywcaagooty.com; Ettines Rd; dm from Rs90, r & bungalow incl tax from Rs264-906) This former brewery and sprawling complex of hill cottages, dotted with brilliant clouds of flower gardens and possessing an almost Tuscan vibe, is one of the most attractive YWCAs we've ever seen. Throw in elegant lounges and fireplaces and you've got some seriously lovely budget accommodation going on.

TTDC Youth Hostel (☎ 2443665; Botanical Garden Rd; dm/d Rs100/350) This state-run hostel is reliably mediocre, clean and busy; you may want to call ahead to book a dorm bed if you're in the area.

Hotel Nimi's (☎ 2444552; s/d Rs200/300) Nimi's, opposite the train station, is a very basic lodge with rooms that are as cheap as attached-bathroom accommodation comes in Ooty. It's clean, but otherwise, don't expect a lot.

Hotel Green Valley (☎ 2444219; North Lake Rd; s/d Rs250/350) With nice views of the lake and clean, cosy rooms, Green Valley offers most of what next-door Reflections possesses (minus the on-call cooking and busy common area) at roughly half the rate.

Hotel Sweekar (☎ 2442348; Race View Rd; d Rs300-350) Probably the best value for money in town, the Sweekar hosts guests in big, rustically touched up rooms that carry a whiff of age and colonial class. The hotel occupies a traditional old Ooty cottage that sits at the end of a lavender-lined path, and is run by an incredibly friendly Bahai manager.

Reflections Guest House (☎ 2443834; North Lake Rd; d from Rs400-800) Reflections has a great common area that becomes an excellent spot for meeting other hill-bound travellers and trekkers. Unfortunately, service has suffered in inverse proportion to popularity, and the ladies who run the place can be curt in a 'Pay now', kinda way. But if you're looking to meet folks and enjoy the occasional home-cooked meal on demand, you're in the right spot.

MIDRANGE & TOP END

Hotel Mountview (☎ 2443307; Racecourse Rd; r Rs660) Perched on a quiet driveway directly above the bus station, these eight simple, enormous rooms, decked out in colonial hill-station chic, occupy an elegant old bungalow.

Willow Hill (☎ 2444037; www.willowhill.in; 58/1 Havelock Rd; d Rs900-1750) Sitting high above town, Willow Hill's large windows provide great views of Ooty. The rooms, all with wooden floors, have a distinct alpine-chalet-chic, with the most expensive rooms offering a private garden.

King's Cliff (☎ 2452888; www.kingscliff-ooty.com; Havelock Rd; d Rs1475-3575) High above Ooty on

Strawberry Hill is this gorgeous residence, the sort of colonial house with wood panelling, antique furnishings and cosy lounge where you'd expect to find Kipling sipping a sherry. In point of fact the lobby is decorated with photos of Churchill, Hitchcock, Al Capone and…Jesus. Anyways, this place drips charm and Old World polish, so book ahead and live large, Raj-style.

Lymond House (☎ 2223377; thewildstay@yahoo. com; 77 Sylks Rd; r Rs3000) If Mucha and F Scott Fitzgerald partnered up to open a hotel in Ooty, it'd probably come out looking something like this delightful restored English villa. Rooms are all ensconced in Old World/Jazz Age opulence, the dining room and gardens are gorgeous, and the period atmosphere is thick enough to swim in, while alleviated by breaths of fresh air in the form of quirky embellishments like the owner's classic car.

Savoy Hotel (☎ 2444142; www.tajhotels.com; 77 Sylks Rd; s/d from Rs5800/6800) The Savoy is one of Ooty's oldest hotels, with parts dating back to 1829. Big cottages are arranged around a beautiful garden of flowerbeds, lawns and clipped hedges. The quaint rooms have large bathrooms, polished floors, log fires and bay windows. Modern facilities include a 24-hour bar, excellent multicuisine dining room and an ayurvedic centre.

Eating

Virtue Bake (☎ 2452788; Charing Cross) If you want to see Indian kids and international students talk like American valley girls while sipping posh coffee and snacking on excellent cakes and brownies, Virtue Bake is *totally* your scene.

Hotel Sanjay (☎ 2443160; Charing Cross; mains Rs35-85; ☽ breakfast, lunch & dinner) This basic but bustling spot does excellent thalis; the Keralan style fish meal is especially tasty.

Shinkow's Chinese Restaurant (☎ 2442811; 38/83 Commissioner's Rd; mains Rs50-150; ☽ lunch & dinner) Shinkow's is an Ooty institution and the simple menu of chicken, pork, beef, fish, noodles and rice dishes is usually pretty good, if kind of uninspired.

our pick Kabob Corner (☎ Commercial Rd; mains Rs50-200; ☽ lunch & dinner) Aaargh – let your inner carnivore scream in vicious exultation after enduring the non-stop veg of South India. Here you can tear apart perfectly grilled and spiced chunks of lamb, chicken and if you like, paneer (wussy). Sop up the juices with

pillowy triangles of naan and revel in your messy return to the meat-eating fold.

Sidewalk Café (Commercial Rd; mains Rs80-250; ☽ lunch & dinner) A cross between an American diner and an Italian cafe is something you'd expect to find in Mumbai rather than the mountains, but it's a welcome change of scene. The fluorescent interior is oddly out of place in Ooty and the food is a bit overpriced, but if you're craving something Western this is as good as it gets.

Both the **Savoy Hotel** (☎ 2444142; www.tajhotels. com; 77 Sylks Rd; mains from around Rs140; ☽ lunch & dinner) and **King's Cliff** (☎ 2452888; www.kingscliff-ooty. com; Havelock Rd; mains Rs80-200; ☽ lunch & dinner) have atmospheric restaurants with log fires and quality multicuisine food. The latter has no alcohol permit, but you can BYO.

Shopping

Ooty can be a fun place to shop, but don't expect anything out of the ordinary. The main places to shop are along Commercial Rd, where you'll find Kashmiri shops as well as government outlets for Kairali and Khadi Gramodyog Bhavan. Poompuhar is on Comercial Rd. The Keystone Foundation (see boxed text, p1113) runs the **Green Shop** (☎ 2441340; Club Rd), which sells honey and organic produce harvested by local and indigenous farmers.

Getting There & Away

Without doubt the most romantic way to arrive in Ooty is aboard the miniature train, and you'll need to book ahead in the high season. Buses also run regularly up and down the mountain, both from other parts of Tamil Nadu and from Mysore in Karnataka.

BUS

The state bus companies all have **reservation offices** (☽ 9am-5.30pm) at the busy bus station. There are two routes to Karnataka – the main bus route via Gudalur and the shorter, more arduous route via Masinagudi. The latter is tackled only by minibuses and winds through 36 hairpin bends! Frequent buses leave for Mettupalayam and Coimbatore, and there's daily service to Chennai, Bengaluru and Mysore.

Connect with trains to Chennai or Kochi (Cochin, Kerala) at Coimbatore.

To get to Mudumalai National Park (Rs27, 2½ hours, 12 daily), take one of the Mysore buses that will drop you at park headquarters at Theppakadu, or one of the small buses that go via the narrow and twisting Sighur Ghat road. Some of these rolling wrecks travel only as far as Masinagudi (Rs14, 1½ hours), from where there are buses every two hours to Theppakadu.

Local buses leave every 30 minutes for Kotagiri (Rs10, two hours) and every 10 minutes to Coonoor (Rs6.50, one hour).

TRAIN

The miniature train – one of the Mountain Railways of India given World Heritage status by Unesco in 2005 – is the best way to get here. There are fine views of forest, waterfalls and tea plantations along the way, especially from the front 1st-class carriage; the steam engine pushes, rather than pulls, the train up the hill, so the front carriage leads the way. Departures and arrivals at Mettupalayam connect with those of the *Nilgiri Express,* which runs between Mettupalayam and Chennai. The miniature train departs Mettupalayam for Ooty at 7.20am daily (1st/2nd class Rs117/12, five hours, 46km). If you want a seat in either direction, be at least 45 minutes early or make a reservation (Rs25) at least 24 hours in advance.

From Ooty the train leaves at 3pm and takes about 3½ hours. There are also two daily passenger trains between Ooty and Coonoor (1½ hours).

Getting Around

Plenty of autorickshaws hang around the bus station – a ride from the train or bus stations to Charing Cross costs about Rs30, and a list of autorickshaw fixed prices is on a sign at the steps on Commercial Rd leading to the tourist information office.

Taxis cluster at several stands in town. There are fixed fares to most destinations including Coonoor (Rs400), Kotagiri (Rs600), Gudalur (Rs800), Mudumalai National Park (Rs800) and Coimbatore (Rs800).

There's a jeep hire near the main bazaar, although its best to rent these out in groups; expect to pay about 1.5 times more than local taxi fares.

MUDUMALAI NATIONAL PARK

☎ 0423

In the foothills of the Nilgiris, this 321-sq-km **park** (admission Rs35; ☉ 6.30-9am & 3-6pm) is like a classical Indian landscape painting given life sans trash: thin, spindly trees and light-slotted leaves concealing spotted chital deer and slow herds of gaur (Indian bison). Somewhere in the hills are tigers, although you're very lucky if you spot one.

Part of the Nilgiri Biosphere Reserve (3000 sq km), the park is the best place for spotting wildlife in Tamil Nadu, although there's still a good chance you won't see more than some deer and kingfishers. Vegetation ranges from grasslands to semi-evergreen forests to foothill scrub; besides the above species, panthers, wild boars, jackals and sloth bears prowl the reserve. Otters and crocodiles both inhabit the Moyar River, and the park's wild elephant population numbers about 600.

A good time to visit is between December and June although the park may be closed during the dry season (February to March). Heavy rain is common in October and November.

The admission price includes a Rs20 minibus tour.

Orientation & Information

The main service area in Mudumalai is Theppakadu, on the main road between Ooty and Mysore. Here you'll find the park's **reception centre** (☎ 526235; ☉ 6.30-9am & 3-6pm) and some park-run accommodation.

The closest village is Masinagudi, 7km from Theppakadu.

Tours

It's not possible to hike in the park and tours are limited to sanctuary minibuses; private vehicles are not allowed in the park except on the main Ooty–Mysore road that runs through it. Most people see the park via 45-minute **minibus tours** (per person Rs35 incl Rs15 park entry fee) that run between 7am and 9am and 3pm and 6pm. The tour makes a 15km loop through part of the park; passengers are told not to wear bright clothes and remain quiet, but in the land of loud saris and louder cell phones, this very rarely happens.

A much better bet is to hire a guide for a foot **trek** outside the park boundaries. Talk to the guys who hang around the park entry station, or ask at your resort – all have their own knowledgeable, English-speaking guides who charge around Rs150 for a couple of hours and Rs300 to Rs400 for a four hour walking or combined jeep-and-walking tour. Don't forget you'll need a permit to trek in some parts of the park; reputable guides should already possess the right paperwork.

Elephant rides are occasionally offered for Rs400 per group of four.

Sleeping & Eating

All budgets are catered for – there are budget and midrange lodges inside the park at Theppakadu; budget rooms and midrange cottages in Masinagudi; and midrange jungle resorts in Bokkapuram (4km south of Masinagudi). For meals at the resorts, expect to pay from Rs400 per person per day.

IN THE PARK

For most accommodation in the park, book in advance, in person, with the WWO (p1113) in Ooty. In low season, you *may* be able to get accommodation if it's available by asking directly at the park reception centre. The following three park-run places are walking distance from park reception and on the banks of the river.

Minivet Dormitory (r per person Rs35) A clean place, with two four-bed rooms, each with private bathroom with cold water only.

Theppakadu Log House (d/q Rs330/560) and **Sylvan Lodge** (d/q Rs330/560) are the pick of the places in the park. Overlooking the river, they're comfortable, well maintained and good value. There's a kitchen at Sylvan Lodge that prepares meals for booked guests.

The government-run **Tamil Nadu Hotel** (☎ 252 6580; dm/d/q Rs75/295/495) is in the same cluster of buildings; it provides basic accommodation and basic meals. Near Masinagudi, try **Bamboo Banks Farm** (☎ 2526211; www.bamboobanks.in; cottages s/d Rs825/1125), which lays a couple of kilometres out of town towards Bokkapuram. There are four big, comfortable private cottages in the lush gardens of the family-run property. The landscape is beautiful but tamed; you'll need transport to travel the few kilometres to wilderness areas.

BOKKAPURAM

This area south of Masinagudi is home to a gaggle of fine forest resorts, mostly family-run businesses with a warm, homely atmosphere, high standards and breathtaking views.

Forest Hills Guest House (☎ 2526216; www.foresthills-resort.com; s/d from Rs1400/1700, huts Rs1250) Forest Hills is a family-run, family-sized guesthouse (10 rooms on 5 hectares) with a few cute bamboo huts, some clean spacious rooms and a fabulous watchtower for wildlife-watching and birdwatching. There's a slight colonial air here with a gazebo-style bar, games rooms and a barbecue pit.

Safari Land Farm and Guest House (☎ 2526937; r from Rs1800) You can get Swiss Family Robinson in this jungle complex of well-decked-out tree houses. The views into the surrounding jungle hills are stunning, but the pace, for all the dramatic scenery, is supremely relaxed.

Jungle Retreat (☎ 2526469; www.jungleretreat.com; dm Rs473, bamboo huts/standard r Rs1969/2532, tree house Rs4500) This is one of the most stylish resorts in the area, with lovingly built stone cottages decked out in classic furniture and sturdy bamboo huts, all spread out to give a feeling of seclusion. It's possible to camp, and there's a dormitory for groups. The bar, restaurant and common area is a great place to meet fellow travellers and the owners are knowledgeable and friendly, with a large area of private forest at their disposal. All prices include taxes.

Getting There & Away

Buses from Ooty to Mysore and Bengaluru stop at Theppakadu (Rs24, 2½ hours, 11 daily). Bus services run every two hours between Theppakadu and Masinagudi.

The longer route that these buses take to or from Ooty is via Gudalur (67km). The direct route to Masinagudi, however, is an interesting 'short cut' (Rs10, 1½ hours, 36km) which involves taking one of the small government buses that make the trip up (or down) the torturous Sighur Ghat road. The bends are so tight and the gradient so steep that large buses simply can't use it. Private minibuses heading to Mysore also use this route but if you want to get off at Masinagudi, you'll have to pay the full fare (Rs125).

TAMIL NADU

Andaman & Nicobar Islands

Andaman & Nicobar Islands

On old maps, the Andamans and Nicobars were the kind of islands whose inhabitants were depicted with dog heads or faces in their chests, surrounded by sea serpents coiled around a tempest-lashed sea known to Indians as Kalapani: The Black Waters. These were the islands that someone labelled, with a shaky hand, 'Here be Monsters'.

Likely, those maps were drawn by an early traveller who realised they had found a Very Good Thing and didn't want to share it with the rest of us.

Because the Andaman and Nicobar Islands are, unambiguously and without hyperbole, tropical bliss. If it weren't for the tragic fact their indigenous populations have largely been wiped out and displaced, they'd be practically perfect. That depressing addendum aside, what's the attraction here?

Blue, blue, blue and blue: oceans and skies, streaked with silver sheets of flying fish. Primeval jungle cut by muddy rivers that run past villages as old as India itself, where some inhabitants still literally live in the Stone Age. Snow-white beaches melting under flame-and-purple sunsets, all populated by a friendly masala of South and Southeast Asian settlers and their laid-back descendants.

Unfortunately the Nicobars are off limits to tourists, but that still leaves hundreds of islands to explore. When you do choose to wander, it will likely be by ferry. When the salt cuts the waves and dolphins shimmer in front of the next oncoming Eden, you'll know you've found a wholly unexpected island allure to India.

HIGHLIGHTS

- Regress to infantile laziness and happiness on **Neil Island** (p1134)
- Snorkel and socialise on **Havelock Island** (p1133)
- Interact with a small town yet multicultural cast of Indians in **Port Blair** (p1127)
- Take a road trip through the jungle heart of the Andamans around **Mayabunder** and **Diglipur** (p1135)
- Find Butler Bay; call God; say thanks for paradise on **Little Andaman** (p1137)

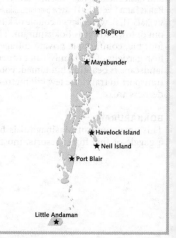

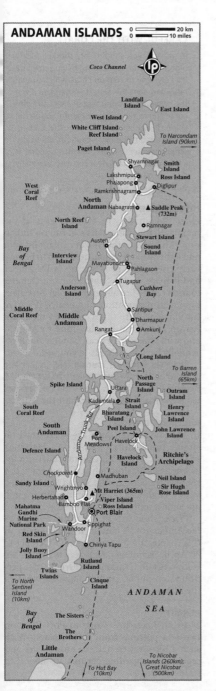

ANDAMAN ISLANDS

0   20 km
0   10 miles

Coco Channel

Landfall Island
East Island
West Island
White Cliff Island
Reef Island
To Narcondam Island (90km)
Paget Island
Shyamnagar
Smith Island
Lakshmipur
Ross Island
Phaiapong
Diglipur
Ramkrishnagram
West Coral Reef
North Andaman
Nabagram
Saddle Peak (732m)
North Reef Island
Ramnagar
Bay of Bengal
Austen
Stewart Island
Interview Island
Sound Island
Mayabunder
Pahlagaon
Anderson Island
Tugapur
Cuthbert Bay
Middle Coral Reef
Middle Andaman
Santipur
Rangat
Dharmapur
Amkunj
Long Island
To Barren Island (65km)
Spike Island
North Passage Island
Uttara
Outram Island
South Coral Reef
Kadamtala
Strait Island
Bharatang Island
Henry Lawrence Island
South Andaman
Peel Island
John Lawrence Island
Port Meadows
Havelock
Defence Island
Havelock Island
Ritchie's Archipelago
Checkpoint
Madhuban
Neil Island
Sandy Island
Wrightmyo
Mt Harriet (365m)
Sir Hugh Rose Island
Herbertabad
Viper Island
Mahatma Gandhi Marine National Park
Bamboo Flat
Ross Island
Port Blair
Red Skin Island
Wandoor
Sippighat
Jolly Buoy Island
Chiriya Tapu
Rutland Island
Twins Islands
To North Sentinel Island (10km)
Cinque Island
ANDAMAN SEA
Bay of Bengal
The Sisters
The Brothers
Little Andaman
To Nicobar Islands (260km); Great Nicobar (500km)
To Hut Bay (10km)

ANDAMAN & NICOBAR ISLANDS

History

The date of initial human settlement in the Andamans and Nicobars is lost to history. Anthropologists say stone-tool crafters have lived here for 2000 years, and scholars of human migration believe local indigenous tribes have roots in Negrito and Malay ethnic groups in Southeast Asia. Otherwise, these specks in the sea have been a constant source of legend to outside visitors.

Even the name 'Andaman' is thought to derive from 'Hanuman'; the Hindu monkey god supposedly used the islands as a stepping stone between India and Sri Lanka (although that really doesn't make geographic sense). The 10th-century Persian adventurer Buzurg Ibn Shahriyar described an island chain inhabited by cannibals, a story Marco Polo repeated with the slight embellishment that the natives had dog heads. With that said, stories of cannibalism may have been inflated by Malay pirates, who liked to use the archipelago as a secret raiding base. Tablets in Thanjavur (Tanjore) in Tamil Nadu named the archipelago Timaittivu: The Impure Islands.

None of the above was exactly tourism brochure stuff, but visitors kept coming: the Marathas in the late 17th century and 200 years later, the British, who used the Andamans as a penal colony for political dissidents. When WWII rolled around, some islanders greeted the invading Japanese as liberators, but despite installing Indian politicians as (puppet) administrators, the Japanese military proved to be far harsher occupiers than the British.

Following Independence in 1947, the Andaman and Nicobar Islands were incorporated into the Indian Union. Migration from the mainland has inflated their population from a few thousand to more than 350,000; many of these arrivals were Bengali refugees fleeing the chaos of partition. During this influx, tribal land rights and environmental protection were often disregarded, and while some conditions are improving, the indigenous tribes remain largely in decline.

Many of the aftershocks of the 2004 Indian Ocean earthquake were concentrated off the coast of the islands, which were doubly devastated by the resulting tsunami and vibrations from the actual quakes. The Nicobars were especially hard hit; some estimate a fifth of the population was killed. Numerous citizens were relocated to Port Blair after the tsunami, and many have yet to return to their homes. But by and large normalcy has returned, along with tourists, although places like Little Andaman remain practically deserted by visitors (so visit).

Climate

Sea breezes keep temperatures within the 23°C to 31°C range and the humidity at around 80% all year. The southwest (wet) monsoons come to the islands between roughly mid-May and early October, and the northeast (dry) monsoons between November and December. Be warned: bad weather can seriously muck up your travel itinerary since ferry services are cancelled if the sea is too rough.

Geography & Environment

The islands form the peaks of the Arakan Yoma, a mountain range that begins in Western Myanmar (Burma) and extends into the ocean running all the way to Sumatra in Indonesia.

The isolation of the Andaman and Nicobar Islands has led to the evolution of many endemic plant and animal species. Of 62 identified mammals, 32 are unique to the islands, including the Andaman wild pig, crab-eating macaque, masked palm civet and species of tree shrews and bats. Almost 50% of the islands' 250 bird species are endemic, including ground-dwelling megapodes, *hawabills* (swiftlets) and the emerald Nicobar pigeon. The isolated beaches provide excellent breeding grounds for turtles, and inland rivers are prowled by saltwater crocodiles. While dolphins are frequently sighted, the once abundant dugongs have all but vanished.

Mangroves are an important aspect of the landscape, offering a natural protective barrier between land and sea. Further inland the forests contain important tree species, including the renowned padauk – a hardwood with light and dark colours occurring in the same tree.

FAST FACTS

Population 356,265
Area 8248 sq km
Telephone code ☎ 03192
Main languages Hindi, Bengali, Tamil
When to go December to early April

> **CAREFUL WITH THE CORAL!**
>
> In general, you should only snorkel during high tide in the Andamans. During low tide it's very easy to step on coral, which irreparably damages the delicate organisms. Even the sweep of a strong flipper kick can harm coral. You're also risking a painful sea urchin spine if you set your feet on the seabed. Divers need to be extra cautious about descents near reefs; colliding with the coral at a hard pace with full gear is environmentally disastrous.

Information

Even though they're 1000km east of the mainland, the Andamans still run on Indian time. This means that it can be dark by 5pm and light by 4am; people here tend to be very early risers. The peak season is December and January, and in September and October tourists can fill literally every bed in Port Blair; book accommodation in advance if you're travelling at these times. The wet monsoon season runs from roughly June to August, and while the weather can be foul, you'll essentially have the islands to yourself.

Andaman & Nicobar Tourism (A&N Tourism; Map p1128; ☎ 232747; www.tourism.andaman.nic.in; Kamaraj Rd, Port Blair; ☷ 8.30am-1pm & 2-5pm Mon-Fri, 8.30am-noon Sat) is the main tourism body for the islands.

ACCOMMODATION

In the low season there are great deals on simple beach huts on Neil and Havelock Islands; some huts with shared toilet run for as low as Rs50, although you'll generally pay somewhere between Rs150 and Rs250 (still a steal!). High-end resorts, on the other hand, are almost uniformly overpriced.

Prices shoot up in the peak season (15 December to 15 January). Prices given in this chapter are for midseason (1 October to 30 April, excluding peak). May to September is low season. Camping is currently not permitted on public land or national parks in the islands.

PERMITS

Most civil servants come to Port Blair on two-year postings from the mainland. With such a turnover of staff, be aware rules and regulations regarding permits are subject to sudden changes.

ISLAND INDIGENES

The Andaman and Nicobar Islands' indigenous peoples constitute just 12% of the population and, in most cases, their numbers are decreasing.

Onge

Two-thirds of Little Andaman's Onge Island was taken over by the Forest Department and 'settled' in 1977. The 100 or so remaining members of the Onge tribe live in a 25-sq-km reserve covering Dugong Creek and South Bay. Anthropologists say the Onge population has declined due to demoralisation through loss of territory.

Sentinelese

The Sentinelese, unlike the other tribes in these islands, have consistently repelled outside contact. For years, contact parties arrived on the beaches of North Sentinel Island, the last redoubt of the Sentinelese, with gifts of coconuts, bananas, pigs and red plastic buckets, only to be showered with arrows, although some encounters have been a little less hostile. About 150 Sentinelese remain.

Andamanese

Now numbering only about 40, it seems impossible the Andamanese can escape extinction. There were around 7000 Andamanese in the mid-19th century, but friendliness to colonisers was their undoing, and by 1971 all but 19 of the population had been swept away by measles, syphilis and influenza epidemics. They've been resettled on tiny Strait Island.

Jarawa

The 350 remaining Jarawa occupy the 639-sq-km reserve on South and Middle Andaman Islands. In 1953 the chief commissioner requested an armed sea plane bomb Jarawa settlements and their territory has been consistently disrupted by the Andaman Trunk Rd, forest clearance and settler and tourist encroachment. Hardly surprisingly, most Jarawa remain hostile to contact.

Shompen

Only about 250 Shompen remain in the forests on Great Nicobar. Seminomadic hunter-gatherers who live along the riverbanks, they have resisted integration and avoid areas occupied by Indian immigrants.

Nicobarese

The 30,000 Nicobarese are the only indigenous people whose numbers are not decreasing. The majority have converted to Christianity and been partly assimilated into contemporary Indian society. Living in village units led by a head man, they farm pigs and cultivate coconuts, yams and bananas. The Nicobarese, who probably descended from people of Malaysia and Myanmar, inhabit a number of islands in the Nicobar group, centred on Car Nicobar, the region worst affected by the 2004 tsunami.

An Indian anthropologist tells us expeditions to the Sentinelese (a traditional pastime of visiting dignitaries who want to be seen roughing it in the Andamans) have ceased, which may be a good thing, as contact with the 'civilised' world continues to devastate other tribes. In 2008, eight Onge died after drinking washed-ashore chemicals they mistook for alcohol, evidence of the danger of alcoholism in the native community. In the same year, violent encounters flared between the Jarawa and poachers and intruders who illegally entered their reserve, resulting in the deaths of both settlers and Jarawas.

ANDAMAN & NICOBAR ISLANDS

All foreigners need a permit to visit the Andaman Islands; it's issued free on arrival. The 30-day permit (which can be extended to 45 days), allows foreigners to stay in Port Blair. Overnight stays are also permitted on South and Middle Andaman (excluding tribal areas), North Andaman (Diglipur), Long Island, North Passage, Little Andaman (excluding tribal areas), and Havelock and Neil Islands.

The permit also allows day trips to Jolly Buoy, South Cinque, Red Skin, Ross, Narcondam, Interview and Rutland Islands, as well as The Brothers and The Sisters.

To obtain the permit, air travellers simply present their passport and fill out a form on arrival at Port Blair airport. Permits are usually issued for as long as you ask, up to the 30-day maximum.

Boat passengers will probably be met by an immigration official on arrival, but if not should seek out the immigration office at Haddo Jetty immediately. Keep your permit on you at all times – you won't be able to travel without it. Police frequently ask to see it, especially when you're disembarking on other islands, and hotels will need permit details. Check current regulations regarding boat travel with:

Andaman & Nicobar Tourism (A&N Tourism; Map p1128; ☎ 238473; www.tourism.andaman.nic.in; Kamaraj Rd, Port Blair; ☼ 8.30am-1pm & 2-5pm Mon-Fri, 8.30am-noon Sat)

Foreigners' Registration Office Chennai (☎ 044-23454970, 044-28278210); Kolkata (☎ 033-22470549, 033-22473300)

Shipping Corporation of India (SCI; www.shipindia.com) Chennai (☎ 044-5231401; Jawahar Bldg, 6 Rajaji Salai); Kolkata (☎ 033-2482354; 1st fl, 13 Strand Rd); Port Blair (Map p1128; ☎ 233347/233590; Aberdeen Bazaar)

National Parks & Sanctuaries

Additional permits are required to visit some national parks and sanctuaries. To save a lot of running around, take advantage of the 'single window' system for permits and information at the A&N Tourism office (p1127) in Port Blair, where there's now also a **Forestry Department Desk** (☼ 8.30-11am & 2.30-4.30pm Mon-Sat). Here you can find out whether a permit is needed, how to go about getting it, how much it costs and whether it is in fact possible to get one (it's not always).

If you plan to do something complicated, you'll be sent to the **Chief Wildlife Warden** (CWW; Map p1128; ☎ 233321; Haddo Rd; ☼ 8.30am-noon & 1-4pm Mon-Fri) where your application should consist of a letter stating your case, the name of the boat and the dates involved; all things being equal, the permit should be issued within the hour.

For most day permits it's not the hassle but the cost. For areas such as Mahatma Gandhi Marine National Park, and Ross and Smith Islands near Diglipur, the permits cost Rs50/500 for Indians/foreigners. For Saddle Peak National Park, also near Diglipur, the cost is Rs25/250.

Students with valid ID often only pay minimal entry fees, but must produce a letter from the Chief Wildlife Warden in Port Blair authorising the discount.

The Nicobar Islands are normally off limits to all except Indian nationals engaged in research, government business or trade.

Activities
DIVING

The Andamans are one of the world's great diving locations, as much for their relative isolation as their crystal-clear waters, superb coral and kaleidoscopic marine life.

The main dive season – depending on the monsoon – runs from roughly November to April, but trips still occur during the summer wet season, from roughly June to August (you will just be closer to the shore). And diving conditions are generally fine in September and October; there's just rain to contend with.

Centres offer fully equipped boat dives, discover scuba diving courses (around US$100), open water (US$350) and advanced courses (US$300), as well as Divemaster training. Prices vary depending on the location, number of participants and duration of the course, but diving in the Andamans runs around Rs2000/3000 for a single/double boat dive. In national parks there's an additional cost of Rs1000 per person per day payable directly to the park.

Havelock Island is far and away the main diving centre in the islands, although some outfits were expanding onto Neil at the time of research.

Barefoot Scuba (Map p1133; ☎ 282181; www.barefootindia.com) Based at Café del Mar at No 3 Village, this dive operation is connected with Barefoot at Havelock resort.

Blue Lagoon Divers (Map p1133; ☎ 091-9933201327; www.divingandaman.com) Based out of Eco Villa at No 2 Village.

Dive India (Map p1133; ☎ 091-9932082204; www.diveindia.com) Based at Island Vinnie's Tropical Beach Cabanas, midway between No 3 and 5 Villages.

SNORKELLING

Much easier and cheaper to arrange than diving, snorkelling can be highly rewarding. Havelock Island is one of the best, and cer-

---

ISLAND LIFE

Most people don't visit the Andamans for their culture, unless they're interested in researching the islands' tribal populations. But there is a just-as-fascinating 'new' home-grown culture here born of the settlement of pioneers from across India and nearby Myanmar (Burma). You'd be hard pressed to find such a cosmopolitan mix of South and Southeast Asians in what amounts to a series of small towns and villages, rather than large, multicultural cities; it comes as quite a relaxing surprise to see Bengalis, Keralans, Telugus and Karens (from Myanmar) chatting and sharing tea amidst swaying palms.

And locals appear to appreciate their idyllic surrounds. Today, most residents of the Andamans are native born, although many have travelled to the mainland for hospital visits or schooling. Mostly, they seem to loathe it. It's not uncommon to hear comments such as 'I can't stand the mainland'. One local said to us, 'I was born here, raised here, and I'll die here. Whenever I step on the mainland, I just want to be back in the islands.'

Andamaners and Nicobarans are generally laid-back, friendly and fair-minded, as the following episode illustrates.

I was taking an autorickshaw in Rangat and hadn't agreed to a price beforehand. Not feeling like arguing, I handed the driver Rs20 at the end of the ride – more, I thought, than I owed.

As I walked away, the driver yelled, 'Sir! Sir!' I sighed, not wanting to argue, and turned around – to see the auto driver holding out Rs5 change.

Adam Karlin

---

tainly easiest, places for snorkelling as many accommodation places organise boat trips out to otherwise inaccessible coral reefs and islands, and you can snorkel offshore on Neil Island.

The closest place to Port Blair for snorkelling is North Bay. Other relatively easily accessible snorkelling sites include Red Skin and Jolly Buoy, near Wandoor.

SURFING

Intrepid surfing travellers have been whispering about Little Andaman (p1137) since it first opened up to foreigners several years ago. Although the island is still quite remote, surfers continue to drift here for the reliable waves off the east coast. **SEAL** (http://seal-asia.com) offers a couple of live-aboard surfing charters a year, with pick-up and drop-off in Port Blair, between mid-March and mid-May.

FISHING

The Andamans also have game fishing opportunities. The occasional charter boat out of Phuket (Thailand) makes **live-aboard trips** (www.andamanisland-fishing.com), usually around March.

Getting There & Away

AIR

There are daily flights to Port Blair from Delhi, Kolkata (Calcutta) and Chennai (Madras), although flights from Delhi and Kolkata are often routed through Chennai. Fares run between US$250 and US$400 round-trip depending on how early you book; some airlines offer one-way flights for as low as US$50, but these need to be booked months in advance. At the time of research, **Kingfisher Airlines** (☎ 18002093030; www.flykingfisher.com) had the cheapest last-minute flights to the islands. Other options include **Air India** (Chennai ☎ 044-285554747; Kolkata ☎ 033-22822356; Port Blair ☎ 230949; www.airindia.com) and **JetLite** (Chennai ☎ 044-22560909; Kolkata ☎ 033-25110901; Port Blair ☎ 244364; www.jetlite.com).

There's been talk for some years about direct flights from Phuket (Thailand) to Port Blair, but for now, it's still talk. Check the **A&N Tourism** (www.tourism.andaman.nic.in) website for updates.

BOAT

Ah, the infamous boat to Port Blair. Depending on who you ask, it's either 'the only *real* way to get to the Andamans, man' or a hassle and a half. The truth lies somewhere in between; the ferry from the mainland is probably nicer than you expect, but it ain't Carnival Cruise lines. There are usually four to six sailings a month between Port Blair and the Indian mainland – fortnightly to/from Kolkata (56 hours) and weekly (in high season) to/from Chennai (60 hours) on vessels operated by

Shipping Corporation of India (SCI; www.shipindia.com; Chennai ☎ 044-5231401; Kolkata ☎ 033-2482354; Port Blair Map p1128; ☎ 233347/233590; Aberdeen Bazaar). The schedule is erratic, so call SCI in advance. Updated schedules and fares can be found at www.and.nic.in/spsch/sailing.htm.

Take sailing times with a large grain of salt – travellers have reported sitting on the boat at Kolkata harbour for up to 12 hours, or waiting to dock near Port Blair for several hours. With hold-ups and variable weather and sea conditions, the trip can take three to four days. The service from Chennai goes via Car Nicobar once a month, taking an extra two days, but only residents may disembark. There is usually a service once a month from Visakhapatnam in Andhra Pradesh (see p974 for more details).

If you're buying your return ticket in Port Blair, go to the 1st floor of the A&N Tourism office where they can reserve you a berth under the tourist-quota system; you then take the approval letter to the Directorate of Shipping Services' ticket office at Phoenix Bay Jetty. This process can take some days, so it's simpler to arrange return tickets on the mainland when purchasing your outward ticket.

Classes vary slightly between boats, but the cheapest is bunk (Rs1700 to Rs1960), followed by 2nd class B (Rs3890), 2nd class A (Rs5030), 1st class (Rs6320) and deluxe cabins (Rs7640). The MV *Akbar* also has AC dorm berths (Rs3290). Pricewise, higher-end tickets cost as much, if not more, than a plane ticket. If you go bunk, prepare for waking up to a chorus of men 'hwwaaaaching' and spitting, little privacy and toilets that tend to get…unpleasant after three days at sea. That said, it's a good way to meet locals.

Food (tiffin for breakfast, thalis for lunch and dinner) costs around Rs150 per day and pretty much consists of glop on rice. Bring something (fruit in particular) to supplement your diet. Some bedding is supplied, but if you're travelling bunk class, bring a sleeping sheet. Many travellers take a hammock to string up on deck.

There is no official ferry between Port Blair and Thailand, but if there are yachts around you could try to crew. Some travellers wonder if it's possible to get from the Andamans to Myanmar (Burma) by sea. Legally, you can't, although we hear it's been done by those with their own boats. Be aware you are risking imprisonment or worse from the Indian and Burmese navies if you give this a go.

Getting Around

All roads – and ferries – lead to Port Blair, and you'll inevitably spend a night or two here booking onward travel. The main island group – South, Middle and North Andaman – is connected by road, with ferry crossings and bridges. Cheap state and more expensive private buses run south from Port Blair to Wandoor, and north to Bharatang, Rangat, Mayabunder and finally to Diglipur, 325km north of the capital. The Jarawa reserve closes to most traffic at around 3pm; thus, buses that pass through the reserve leave from around 4am up till 11am. Private jeeps and minivans connect many villages; these are hop-on, hop-off affairs, but you can hire a whole vehicle for an inflated price.

A boat is the only way to reach most islands, and while ferry travel is romantic, ferry ticket offices will become the hell of your life. Expect the worst: hot waits, slow service, queue-jumping and a rugby scrum to the ticket window. To hold your spot and advance in line you need to be a little aggressive (but don't be a jerk). Or be a woman; the queues for ladies are a godsend if you can join them, but they really only apply in Port Blair. You can buy tickets the day you travel by arriving at the appropriate jetty an hour beforehand, but this is risky during high season and not a guarantee on Havelock any time of year. In towns like Rangat, ferry ticket offices usually open between Never-O'clock and Go-to-Hell.

There are regular boat services to Havelock and Neil Islands, as well as Rangat, Mayabunder, Diglipur and Little Andaman. If all else fails, fishermen may be willing to give you a ride for around Rs2000 between, say, Port Blair and Havelock. A schedule of sailing times can be found at www.and.nicin/spsch/iisailing.htm.

A subsidised interisland helicopter service runs from Port Blair to Little Andaman (Rs1488, 35 minutes, Tuesday, Friday and Saturday), Havelock Island (Rs850, 20 minutes, Tuesday; 40 minutes, Saturday, via Neil Island) and Diglipur via Mayabunder (Rs2125 or Rs1915 from Mayabunder, one hour, Tuesday). Bookings must be made through the **Civil Aviation office** (☎ 230480) in Port Blair.

Mainland train bookings can be made at the **Railway Bookings office** (☒ 8am-12.30pm & 1-2pm), located in the Secretariat's office south

---

FESTIVALS IN THE ANDAMAN ISLANDS

The 10-day **Island Tourism Festival** is held in Port Blair, usually in January. Dance groups come from surrounding islands and the mainland, and various cultural perform-ances are held at the Exhibition Complex. One of the festival's more bizarre aspects is the Andaman dog show, but there's also a flower show, a baby show and a fancy-dress competition! For information, check the **A&N Tourism** (www.tourism.andaman.nic.in) website.

Subhash Mela is held every January on Havelock to celebrate the birthday of free-dom fighter Subhas Chandra Bose; expect a fun week of dance, readings and other cultural bric-a-brac.

---

of Aberdeen Bazaar; your hotel owners should also be able to help with any onward rail enquires.

PORT BLAIR
pop 100,186

Port Blair deserves more credit than it receives from the mobs of travellers who rush through it on the way to Havelock Island. Green, laid-back and surprisingly cosmopolitan, it's an incredibly attractive town that sprawls over jungly hills culled from Jurassic Park and sev-eral deep-blue bays that fuzz into a soft-focus seascape horizon. You'd be hard pressed to find such a vibrant mix of Indian Ocean inhab-itants – Bengalis, Tamils, Nicobarese, Burmese and Telugus – anywhere, let alone in what's basically a very friendly small town. Whatever your opinions on the place, you're inevitably here for a day or two as 'PB' is the only place to reliably access the internet, withdraw money and book onward travel in the islands.

Orientation

Most of the hotels, the bus stand and inter-island ferries from Phoenix Bay Jetty are around the Aberdeen Bazaar area. The airport is about 4km south of town.

Information
EMERGENCY
Aberdeen Police Station (☎ 232400, 232100; MG Rd)
GB Pant Hospital (☎ 232102; GB Pant Rd)
Secretariat office (A&N office; ☎ 232579; Rajbhawan Secretariat Complex, Kamraj Road)

INTERNET ACCESS
There are quite a few internet places in Aberdeen Bazaar; try **Net World** (per hr Rs40; ☼ 9am-8.30pm), by the Clock Tower.

MONEY
Port Blair is the only place in the Andamans where you can change cash or travellers cheques, and find an ATM. There's a Western Union office by the post office.
Axis Bank ATM (MA Rd)
Canara Bank (Clock Tower)
ICICI Bank ATM (cnr Foreshore & MA Rds)
Island Travels (☎ 233358; islandtravels@yahoo.com; Aberdeen Bazaar; ☼ 9am-1pm & 2-6pm Mon-Sat) One of several travel agencies with foreign-exchange facilities.
State Bank of India (MA Rd; ☼ 9am-noon & 1-3pm Mon-Fri, 10am-noon Sat) Travellers cheques and foreign currency can be changed here.
UTI Bank ATM (cnr MG Rd & Haddo Rd; Aberdeen Bazaar)

POST
Main post office (MG Rd; ☼ 9am-5pm Mon-Sat)

TOURIST INFORMATION
Andaman & Nicobar Tourism (A&N Tourism; ☎ 232747; www.tourism.andaman.nic.in; Kamraj Rd; ☼ 8.30am-1pm & 2-5pm Mon-Fri, 8.30am-noon Sat) This is the main island tourist office, and the place to book government accommodation (between 8am and 11.30am and 2pm and 3pm) and get wildlife permits. Staff are helpful, if laid-back.
India Tourism (☎ 233006; 2nd fl, 189 Junglighat Main Rd; ☼ 8.30am-12.30pm & 1-5pm Mon-Fri)

Sights & Activities
CELLULAR JAIL NATIONAL MEMORIAL
A former British prison that is now a shrine to the political dissidents it once jailed, **Cellular Jail National Memorial** (GB Pant Rd; admission Rs5, cam-era/video Rs10/50; ☼ 9am-12.30pm & 1.30-5pm Tue-Sun) is worth visiting to understand the important space the Andamans occupy in India's na-tional memory. Built over a period of 18 years in 1890, the original seven wings contained 698 cells radiating from a central tower. Like many political prisons, Cellular Jail became something of a university for freedom fight-ers, who exchanged books, ideas and debates despite walls and wardens.

A **sound-and-light show** (adult/child Rs20/10) con-sisting of voice-over conversations between the 'spirit' of the jail and its former inhabitants borders on being powerful, if it weren't for frequent interruptions by cheesy synthesiser

ANDAMAN & NICOBAR ISLANDS

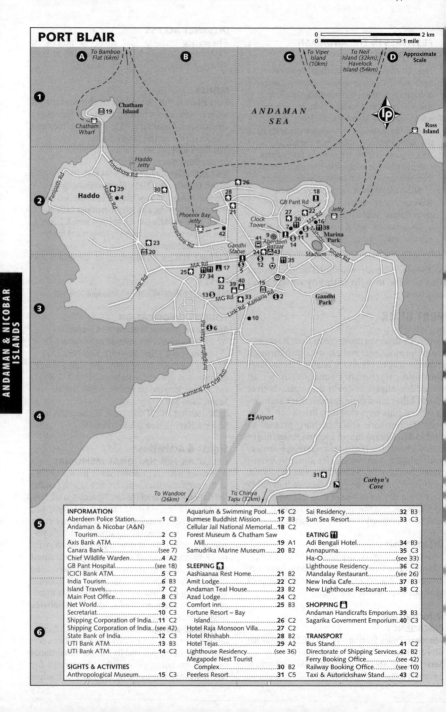

PORT BLAIR

INFORMATION
Aberdeen Police Station	**1** C3
Andaman & Nicobar (A&N) Tourism	**2** C3
Axis Bank ATM	**3** C2
Canara Bank	(see 7)
Chief Wildlife Warden	**4** A2
GB Pant Hospital	(see 18)
ICICI Bank ATM	**5** C3
India Tourism	**6** B3
Island Travels	**7** C2
Main Post Office	**8** C3
Net World	**9** C2
Secretariat	**10** C3
Shipping Corporation of India	**11** C2
Shipping Corporation of India	(see 42)
State Bank of India	**12** C3
UTI Bank ATM	**13** B3
UTI Bank ATM	**14** C2

SIGHTS & ACTIVITIES
Anthropological Museum	**15** C3
Aquarium & Swimming Pool	**16** C2
Burmese Buddhist Mission	**17** B3
Cellular Jail National Memorial	**18** C2
Forest Museum & Chatham Saw Mill	**19** A1
Samudrika Marine Museum	**20** B2

SLEEPING
Aashiaanaa Rest Home	**21** B2
Amit Lodge	**22** C2
Andaman Teal House	**23** B2
Azad Lodge	**24** C2
Comfort Inn	**25** B3
Fortune Resort – Bay Island	**26** C2
Hotel Raja Monsoon Villa	**27** C2
Hotel Rhishabh	**28** B2
Hotel Tejas	**29** A2
Lighthouse Residency	(see 36)
Megapode Nest Tourist Complex	**30** B2
Peerless Resort	**31** C5

Sai Residency	**32** B3
Sun Sea Resort	**33** C3

EATING
Adi Bengali Hotel	**34** B3
Annapurna	**35** C3
Ha-O	(see 33)
Lighthouse Residency	**36** C2
Mandalay Restaurant	(see 26)
New India Cafe	**37** B3
New Lighthouse Restaurant	**38** C2

SHOPPING
Andaman Handicrafts Emporium	**39** B3
Sagarika Government Emporium	**40** C3

TRANSPORT
Bus Stand	**41** C2
Directorate of Shipping Services	**42** B2
Ferry Booking Office	(see 42)
Railway Booking Office	(see 10)
Taxi & Autorickshaw Stand	**43** C2

riffs and patriotic song recitals sung by a Bollywood backup ensemble. It's still worth seeing; shows are in Hindi nightly at 6pm and English at 7.15pm, but check ahead. No refunds for bad weather.

ANTHROPOLOGICAL MUSEUM

The best **museum** (☎ 232291; MG Rd; Indian/foreigner Rs10/50; 🕑 9am-1pm & 1.30-4.30pm Fri-Wed) in Port Blair provides a thorough and sympathetic portrait of the islands' indigenous tribal communities. The glass display cases may be old school, but they don't feel anywhere near as ancient as the simple geometric patterns etched into a Jarawa chest guard, a skull left in a Sentinelese lean-to or the totemic spirits represented by Nicobarese shamanic sculptures. Pick up a pamphlet (Rs20) on indigenous culture, written by local anthropologists, in the gift shop.

SAMUDRIKA MARINE MUSEUM

Run by the Indian Navy, this is probably the best science **museum** (☎ 232012, ext 2214; Haddo Rd; adult/child Rs10/5, camera/video Rs20/40; 🕑 9am-5.30pm Tue-Sun) in Port Blair (which isn't saying much). The exhibits could be flashier, but they're at least largely accurate and informative, especially as concerns the islands' ecosystem, tribal communities, plants, animals and marine life.

FOREST MUSEUM & CHATHAM SAW MILL

Located on Chatham Island (reached by a road bridge), the **saw mill** (admission Rs2; 🕑 8am-2.30pm Mon-Sat) was set up by the British in 1836 and was one of the largest wood processors in Asia. Inside is the forest museum, which displays locally grown woods, including padauk, and has displays on the history of timber milling on the island. It may not be to everyone's taste – especially conservationists – but it gives a different perspective on the islands' history and economy.

AQUARIUM & SWIMMING POOL

You found Nemo! Or his formaldehyde-preserved corpse, which screams in silent accusation at you from the rows of glass jars that constitute this ghoulish **aquarium** (Mahabir Singh Rd; adult/child Rs5/3; 🕑 9am-1pm & 2-4.45pm Thu-Tue, closed 2nd Sat of month). There's also tanks of living tropical fish lining the walls that are about as impressive as a decent pet shop. Opposite the aquarium, the Olympic-sized public **swimming pool** (admission Rs25; 🕑 Mon-Sat) is clean enough,

and open to men only 6.30am to 8am and 5pm to 6pm, to women only 4pm to 5pm, and to families 6pm to 7pm.

CORBYN'S COVE

No one comes to Port Blair for the beach, but if you need a sand fix, Corbyn's Cove, 7km south of town, is your best bet. It's a small curve of coast backed by palms that's popular with locals and Indian tourists, and it's a good spot for swimming and sunset. An autorickshaw ride from town costs about Rs200.

BURMESE BUDDHIST MISSION

This tiny bell-shaped stupa (shrine) is not particularly impressive, but it's an incongruous example of Burmese Buddhist architecture in India and a reminder that you're way closer to Southeast Asia than the subcontinent.

Tours

A&N Tourism runs Port Blair city tours (Rs52), as well tours to Ross Island (Rs75), Mt Harriet (Rs157), Wandoor via spice and rubber plantations (Rs105), Corbyn's Cove (Rs52), Chiriya Tapu (Rs105) snorkelling trips to Jolly Buoy and Redskin Islands (Rs450), and a tour of Ross and Viper Islands and North Bay (Rs360). Trip times vary throughout the week; check with the A&N Tourism office (p1127) for full details.

Sleeping

Prices are higher than the mainland, and you need to book ahead in high season.

BUDGET

Azad Lodge (☎ 242646; MA Rd, Aberdeen Bazaar; r Rs200) Probably the best budget option in town, Azad's rooms are clean, cheap and come with attached bathrooms including sit-down flush toilets – what more do you need?

Comfort Inn (☎ 919932086969; 36 MA Rd; r Rs300) No, it's not the American motel corporation, but a small hotel located above Temptations restaurant. Quality is about the same as the US chain: so-so but perfectly passable rooms.

our pick Aashiaanaa Rest Home (☎ 09447217008; Marine Hill; r Rs300-700; 🖳) Run by the incredibly friendly Shadab and his lovely family, the Aashiaanaa has a lot of 'As' in the name and love in its heart. Rooms are spotless and spacious, and the more expensive ones have nice views over town. It's conveniently just up the hill from the main jetty.

ANDAMAN & NICOBAR ISLANDS

Sai Residency (☎ 212737; r Rs400, with AC Rs600; 🖫) This small, family run affair has some spic-and-span rooms in a central location; you will find it situated behind a cluster of mechanics' stalls behind the Burmese Buddhist Mission.

Hotel Raja Monsoon Villa (☎ 241133; s/d Rs400/550, with AC Rs550/900; 🖫) Centrally located, this tatty, clean and friendly hotel is in a side street of small shops and tea stalls opposite the town's main mosque.

Andaman Teal House (☎ 232642; Haddo Rd; d Rs400, with AC Rs800; 🖫) The local government guest house sprawls over a garden onto a hill that offers some nice sea views, but a lot of the rooms, particularly non-AC ones, are worn down. Bookings must be made through A&N Tourism (p1127).

MIDRANGE

Amit Lodge (☎ 230657; Medical Rd; r Rs600-750; 🖫) Service could use a swift kick and a lesson in smiling, but otherwise this is a fine hotel with breezy balconies that overlooks a bluff near Cellular Jail.

Hotel Tejas (☎ 230360; hotel_tejas@yahoo.co.in; Haddo Rd; d Rs650, with AC Rs950; 🖫) Sparkling rooms of the linoleum-floor-and-comfy-enough-bed sort perch over a hill, a tangled clump of jungle and a sweeping view of Haddo Jetty.

Hotel Rhisabh (☎ 238223; hotelrishabh@yahoo.co.in; Marine Hill; d Rs950, with AC Rs1400; 🖫) On top of Marine Hill, the Rhishabh primarily caters to well-heeled Indian families on holiday. The rooms and facilities are bright white and comfortable, if kind of boring, and some have good views over town.

Lighthouse Residency (☎ 238918; ashraf.lhresidency@gmail.com; MA Rd, Aberdeen Bazaar; r from Rs1000-1200; 🖫) On top of the restaurant of the same name, the Lighthouse is a bit overpriced for what it offers, which are perfectly pleasant rooms with TVs and, at the more expensive end, good views of the waterfront.

Sun Sea Resort (☎ 238330; www.sunsearesort-andamans.com; MG Rd; s/d from Rs1500/2000; 🖫) Despite there being no sea anywhere nearby, this hotel is still a winner, as plush as (if not plusher than) most of the high-end resorts for about half the price.

TOP END

Major credit cards are accepted at the following and prices include breakfast.

Megapode Nest Tourist Complex (☎ 232076, 232207; aniidco@vsnl.com; off Haddo Rd; s/d from Rs2000/2500, cottages Rs3500; 🖫) Despite having a name that sounds like a villain's lair in a Nintendo game, this is the best top-end deal in town, primarily because the prices allow it to straddle the midrange border. A complex of rooms and cottages slopes down to the sparkling sea, with the best ones styled like traditional Nicobari huts.

Peerless Resort (☎ 22172153; www.peerlesshotels.com; s/d Rs3000/3900, cottage d Rs5000; 🖫) The location is the main plus for Peerless Resort – just back from Corbyn's Cove Beach. Rooms have undergone a fairly major renovation, but they're still overpriced for what you get; they're clean and that's about it.

Fortune Resort – Bay Island (☎ 234101; www.fortunehotels.in; Marine Hill; s/d from Rs4500/5000; 🖫 🖫) Port Blair's top hotel boasts a great location, perched above the ocean with fine sea views from its terraced garden and balcony restaurant. The rooms, while comfortable with polished floors, balconies, and island bric-a-brac, are small; make sure to ask for a sea-facing room.

Eating

Port Blair has a good range of North and South Indian restaurants, reflecting its diverse population of settlers from across India.

New India Cafe (MA Rd; mains from Rs30) There's not terribly much 'new' about this rather worn locals' favourite. You will find well-done vegetarian and nonvegetarian from across India, and breakfast omelettes are surpassingly scrumptious.

Adi Bengali Hotel (MA Rd; mains from Rs30) This energetic canteen does a brisk stock-in-trade in spicy fish curries and other West Bengal staples. Everything's prepared pretty well, if the usual clientele of silent, satisfied Bengali labourers is any proof.

Annapurna (MG Rd; mains from Rs40) Annapurna is an extremely popular veg option that looks like a high-school cafeteria and serves consistently good karma-friendly fare, ranging from crisp southern dosas (paper-thin lentil-flour pancakes) to rich North Indian–style curries.

Lighthouse Residency (MA Rd, Aberdeen Bazaar; mains Rs45-140; ✆ lunch & dinner) The Lighthouse is lit like a fluorescent nightmare, but the air-conditioning is cranked, the beer's cold and Thai and Chinese dishes make a welcome addition to the Indian favourites. Try the fish tikka – well-grilled goodness, if dinky portions.

Ha-O (MG Rd; mains Rs60-140) The onsite restaurant for Sun Sea Resort (p1130) is one of the better up-market eateries in town, well-regarded for its tandoori grill and excellent North Indian of the heavy Punjabi curry sort.

New Lighthouse Restaurant (Marina Park; mains Rs80-250, seafood Rs150-400) The New Lighthouse is the sort of open-air seafood place autorickshaw drivers recommend because they assume this is what Port Blair tourists are looking for. Unfortunately, it's breezy and open air because it's kind of falling apart, but hey, if you want fresh, whole grilled fish, lobster or crab, they got you covered here.

Mandalay Restaurant (Marine Hill; ☺ breakfast, lunch & dinner) If you need to splurge, you can do a lot worse than the Mandalay's excellent buffet (breakfast Rs200, lunch and dinner Rs350), heavy with Indian and Western faves served on either an attractive deck or in a not-quite-as-appealing Burmese-themed interior.

Shopping

Aberdeen Bazaar is lined with stalls selling cheap clothing and household goods. 'Island' crafts (the same tiki tat you can find anywhere) are available from a handful of emporiums and speciality shops. Most of the shells on sale are collected legally – a good emporium can show proof of this – but, as always, be aware of your home country's restrictions on importing them.

Andaman Handicrafts Emporium (☎ 240141; MG Rd, Middle Point; ☺ 10am-7pm)

Sagarika Government Emporium (MG Rd, Middle Point; ☺ 10am-7pm)

Getting There & Away

See p1125 for details on transport to and from the Andaman Islands.

BOAT

Most interisland ferries depart from Phoenix Bay Jetty. Advance tickets for boats can be purchased from the ticket counters at the ferry booking office between 9am and 4pm the day before travel. On some boats tickets can be purchased on the boat, but in high season you risk missing out.

From Chatham Wharf there are hourly passenger ferries to Bamboo Flat (Rs3, 15 minutes).

BUS

There are four daily buses to Wandoor (Rs10, 1½ hours). Daily buses run at 4.30am to Diglipur (Rs150, 12 hours) and at 5am and 10.30am to Mayabunder (Rs110, nine hours) via Rangat. The above represents a mix of private and government services; private buses are inevitably more expensive and generally more comfortable. Their 'offices' (a guy with a ticket book) are located across from the main bus stand; they'll likely find you if you look confused enough.

If you want to take the scenic 48km road trip to Bamboo Flat and Mt Harriet, there's a bus at 8.15am and 4pm (Rs18, 1½ hours); returning by ferry will take only 15 minutes.

Getting Around

The central area is easy enough to walk around, but to get out to Corbyn's Cove, Haddo or Chatham Island you'll need some form of transport. A taxi or autorickshaw from the airport to Aberdeen Bazaar costs around Rs60. From Aberdeen Bazaar to Phoenix Bay Jetty is about Rs20 and to Haddo Jetty it's around Rs35.

Bicycles are good for getting around the town and the immediate Port Blair area. They can be hired from stalls in Aberdeen Bazaar for around Rs40 per day.

AROUND PORT BLAIR & SOUTH ANDAMAN

Ross Island

Visiting Ross Island feels like discovering a jungle-clad Lost City, à la Angkor Wat, where the ruins happen to be Victorian English rather than ancient Khmer. The former administrative headquarters for the British in the Andamans, **Ross Island** (admission Rs20) is an essential half-day trip from Port Blair. In its day, little Ross was fondly called the 'Paris of the East' (along with Pondicherry, Saigon etc...). But the cute title, vibrant social scene and tropical gardens were all wiped out by the double whammy of a 1941 earthquake and the invasion of the Japanese (who left behind some machine-gun nests that are great fun to poke around in).

Today the old English architecture is still standing, even as it is swallowed by a green wave of fast-growing jungle. Landscaped paths cross the island and most of the buildings are labelled. There's a small museum with historical displays and photos of Ross Island in its heyday, and a small park where resident deer nibble on bushes.

Ferries to Ross Island (Rs16, 20 minutes) depart from the jetty behind the aquarium in Port Blair at 8.30am, 10.30am, 12.30pm and 2pm Thursday to Tuesday; check when you buy your ticket, as times can be affected by tides.

Viper Island & North Bay

The afternoon boat trip to **Viper Island** (admission Rs5) is worthwhile to see the sobering remains of the ochre-coloured brick jail and the gallows built by the British in 1867. The formidable name comes from a wrecked 19th-century British trading ship nearby. Harbour cruises leave from the jetty behind the aquarium daily at 3pm (Rs60 to Rs75, 45 minutes each way); there are more frequent boats on Wednesday. **North Bay** is the most easily accessible snorkelling bay to Port Blair. A **combined boat tour** (per person Rs300; ⏰ 9.30am-5pm) to Ross and Viper Islands and North Bay leaves daily from the aquarium jetty, allowing 2½ hours to snorkel and explore the bay.

Mt Harriet

Mt Harriet (365m) is across the inlet, north of Port Blair, and there's a road up to the top with good views and bird-watching. To reach Mt Harriet, take the Bamboo Flat passenger ferry (Rs3, 15 minutes) from Chatham Jetty. From Bamboo Flat the road runs 7km along the coast up the summit. Taxis will do the trip for around Rs250 if you don't want to walk.

Wandoor

Wandoor, a tiny speck of a village 29km southwest of Port Blair, is the jumping-off point for **Mahatma Gandhi Marine National Park** (Indian/foreigner Rs50/500), which covers 280 sq km and comprises 15 islands of mangrove creeks, tropical rainforest and reefs supporting 50 types of coral. The marine park's snorkelling sites at **Jolly Buoy** and **Red Skin** islands are popular day trips from Wandoor Jetty (Rs300). That said, if Havelock or Neil Islands are on your Andamans itinerary, it's probably easier and cheaper to wait until you reach them for your underwater experience; unless you're willing to pay through the nose, boats simply don't linger long enough for you to get a good snorkelling experience.

Buses run from Port Blair to Wandoor (Rs8, 1½ hours). About 2km beyond the Wandoor Jetty are quiet, sandy beaches with some excellent snorkelling.

Chiriya Tapu

Chiriya Tapu, 30km south of Port Blair, is a tiny village of beaches, mangroves, and about 2km south, some of the best snorkelling outside Havelock and Neil Islands. There are seven buses a day to the village from Port Blair (Rs8, 1½ hours) and it's possible to arrange boats from here to Cinque Island. Port Blair's zoo was in the process of moving its animals to a new **biological park** here at the time of research; it should be open by the time you read this.

Cinque Island

The uninhabited islands of North and South Cinque, connected by a sandbar, are part of the wildlife sanctuary south of Wandoor. The islands are surrounded by coral reefs, and are among the most beautiful in the Andamans.

Only day visits are allowed, but unless you're on one of the day trips occasionally organised by travel agencies, you need to get permission in advance from the Chief Wildlife Warden (p1124). The islands are two hours by boat from Chiriya Tapu or 3½ hours from Wandoor, and are covered by the Mahatma Gandhi Marine National Park permit (Indian/foreigner Rs50/500).

HAVELOCK ISLAND

With snow-white beaches, teal shallows, dark jungle hills, a coast crammed with beach huts and backpackers from around the world (including roughly a division of Israeli Defence Force leavers), Havelock's one of those budget-travel tropical gems that, in a few years, will have the same cachet as Ko Pha Ngang. If not the nightlife; there are quietly buzzing social scenes concentrated around the common area of the beach hut resorts, but nothing approaching full-moon party madness. Besides for doing nothing, Havelock is a popular spot for snorkelling and diving. Most travellers make a beeline here from Port Blair.

Inhabited by Bengali settlers since the 1950s, Havelock is about 54km northeast of Port Blair and covers 100 sq km. Only the northern third of the island is settled, and each village is referred to by a number. Boats dock at the jetty at No 1 Village; the main bazaar is 2km south at No 3 Village; and most of the accommodation is strung along the east

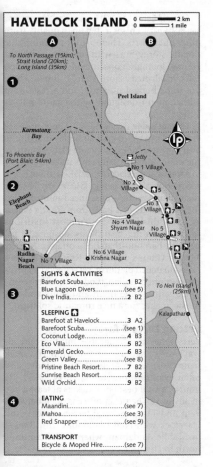

HAVELOCK ISLAND

To North Passage (15km);
Strait Island (20km);
Long Island (35km)

Peel Island

Karmatang Bay

To Phoenix Bay
(Port Blair; 54km)

Jetty
No 1 Village
No 2 Village
Elephant Beach
No 3 Village
No 4 Village
Shyam Nagar   No 5 Village
No 6 Village
Radha Nagar Beach   No 7 Village   Krishna Nagar

To Neil Island
(25km)

Kalapathar

SIGHTS & ACTIVITIES
Barefoot Scuba.........................1 B2
Blue Lagoon Divers...............(see 5)
Dive India.................................2 B2

SLEEPING
Barefoot at Havelock..............3 A2
Barefoot Scuba.....................(see 1)
Coconut Lodge........................4 B3
Eco Villa....................................5 B2
Emerald Gecko........................6 B3
Green Valley..........................(see 8)
Pristine Beach Resort.............7 B2
Sunrise Beach Resort..............8 B2
Wild Orchid..............................9 B2

EATING
Maandini...............................(see 7)
Mahoa....................................(see 3)
Red Snapper ....(see 9)

TRANSPORT
Bicycle & Moped Hire...........(see 7)

coast between villages No 2 and No 5. Internet access was spotty at time of research; some small shops offers unreliable link-ups, but don't expect to stay connected here.

Sights & Activities

The prettiest and most popular sweep of sand here is **Radha Nagar Beach**, also known as **beach No 7**. It's a beautiful curve of sugar fronted by perfectly spiralled waves, all backed by native forest that might have grown out of a postcard. And the sunsets? Pretty damn nice. The drive out to the beach, located on the northwestern side of the island about 12km from the jetty, runs through the green dream that is inland Havelock (autorickshaws will take you for about Rs150). Ten minutes' walk along the

beach to the northwest is the gorgeous **'lagoon'**, another gem of sheltered sand and crystalline water, and in peak season you can take an **elephant ride** (adult/child Rs20/10) through the jungle.

Elephant Beach, where there's good snorkelling, is further north and reached by a 40-minute walk through a muddy elephant logging trail; it's well-marked (off the cross-island road), but hard going after rain. The beach itself virtually disappeared after the tsunami and at high tide it's impossible to reach – ask locally. Lots of snorkelling charters come out this way, and there are lifeguards who will reprimand anyone who litters – God bless them.

A highlight of Havelock is **snorkelling** or **fishing**, and the best way to do either is on a boat trip organised by your hotel. Trips cost from Rs1000 to Rs2000, depending on the number of people going, distance involved etc – if you go with a good-sized group you may pay as low as Rs250 per head. Snorkelling gear is widely available on Havelock from resorts and small restaurants, and is generally very low quality. Havelock is also the premier spot for **scuba diving** on the Andamans; see p1124 for more information.

Some resorts can organise guided **jungle treks** for keen walkers or bird-watchers, but be warned the forest floor turns to glug after rain. The inside rainforest is a spectacular, emerald cavern, and the **bird-watching** – especially on the forest fringes – is rewarding; look out for the blue-black racket-tailed drongo trailing his fabulous tail feathers and, by way of contrast, the brilliant golden oriole.

About 5km beyond No 5 Village, you'll find Kalapathar, where an **elephant training camp** is sometimes open to visitors. Beyond Kalapathar the road passes another pristine beach and then peters out into forest.

The local **bazaar** in No 2 Village is a good spot for an evening stroll; it's like being back in mainland India, except you can crank the chaos down from an anarchic '10' to a tropically languid '5'.

Sleeping & Eating

Most hotels in Havelock are of the cluster of beach hut genre. They all claim to be 'eco' huts ('eco' apparently meaning 'cheap building material'), but they are great value for money, especially in low season.

There are occasional crackdowns on booze here, but you can almost always buy grog at the 'wine shop' in No 1 Village. Unless otherwise noted, all listed accommodation have passable menus of backpacker-oriented Western and Indian food. If you desire something more authentically Indian, head to the cheap food stalls in town (No 1 Village) or the main bazaar (No 2 Village).

The following listings run north to south.

Eco Villa (☎ 091-9933201327; huts Rs200-1500) The thatch and hut complex for Blue Lagoon Divers (p1124) has a spacious feel to it and gets pretty damn romantic at night, when the moon rises over deep-blue ocean evenings. Larger, midrange huts are very good, two-storey value for money.

Barefoot Scuba (☎ 282181; www.barefootindia.com; cabanas with bathroom Rs4100-10,600; ⊠) Barefoot's main diving centre (p1124) has some of the best upmarket accommodation on the island: well-endowed Nicobari cottages, AC Andaman villas and semi-contemporary split-level apartments that face directly over the sea.

Pristine Beach Resort (☎ 282344; alexpristine@hotmail.com; huts Rs100-150, cottages with bathroom Rs250-400) One of the better beach-hut options; Pristine's beach really is just that, and the hammock to hut to tree ratio is scientifically sound. The nearby restaurant Maandini (mains Rs30 to Rs60) was a popular hang-out of the pasta-and-curry genre during research.

Green Valley (☎ 99-33298075; huts from Rs50) Green Valley is the only beach-hut complex that's not actually on the water. Instead, it's set back in a copse of palm and coconut trees that provide nice shade over the cheapest lodging in town. The huts are exactly the same as the ones you'll find in the standard beach resorts, although bathrooms are shared.

Sunrise Beach Resort (huts Rs150-400) Sunrise offers the same thatched goodness as every other resort on Havelock – what sets it apart is a long, awning-topped communal hall where everyone eats and does arts and crafts. It kinda feels like kindergarten for budget travellers.

Wild Orchid (☎ 282472; www.wildorchidandaman. com; d cottages from Rs2000, with AC from Rs2500; ⊠) Set back from a secluded beach, this is a mellow, friendly place with tastefully furnished cottages designed in traditional Andamanese style. The restaurant, Red Snapper (mains Rs100 to Rs350), is one of few genuinely good places to eat on the island and scores on ambience. Fresh seafood is usually available (often caught by the owner or guests!).

Emerald Gecko (☎ 282170; www.emerald-gecko.com; huts Rs500-2000) This is a step up in quality from other hut resorts. There are four comfortable double-storey huts with open-roofed bathrooms, lovingly constructed from bamboo rafts that drifted ashore from Myanmar. There are some budget huts too, and a restaurant with a menu designed by the same folk as Wild Orchid.

Coconut Lodge (huts Rs150-300) These huts are arranged in a weird circular outlay that directs everyone to a raised, concrete platform where the entire lodge usually ends up carousing.

Barefoot at Havelock (☎ 282151, in Port Blair 237656; www.barefootindia.com; cottages Rs3600-5300; ⊠) For the location alone – ensconced in bird-filled forest grounds just back from Radha Nagar Beach – this is Havelock's most luxurious resort, boasting beautifully designed timber and bamboo-thatched cottages. Nearby Mahoa (mains Rs200 to Rs500), set on a raised thatched platform, serves good if small-proportioned Italian food that, when combined with a blue night and some ambient music, makes for a nice romantic splurge.

Getting There & Away

Ferry times are changeable, but there are always direct sailings to and from Havelock from Port Blair at least once daily, and often twice or more (tourist ferry Rs150, 2½ hours). You'd best book tickets at least a day in advance. The ticket office is open between 9am and 11am. Several ferries a week link Havelock with Neil Island and with Rangat in Middle Andaman, where buses continue north to Diglipur.

Getting Around

A local bus connects the jetty and villages on a roughly hourly circuit, but having your own transport is useful here. You can rent mopeds or motorbikes (per day from Rs250) and bicycles (per day Rs40 to Rs50) from the shop outside Pristine Beach Resort, from the stall with the sign in Village No 3, or ask at your hotel.

An autorickshaw from the jetty to No 3 Village is Rs30, to No 5 is Rs50 and to No 7 is Rs150 to Rs200.

NEIL ISLAND

Gbknjbhnm. Sorry, that's what happens when you fall asleep on your keyboard, or in the sand, a hammock or wherever. Because that's life on Neil Island: you arrive, say 'Nice!', and then you either dive or become more indolent than a Roman emperor after lunch. You're about 40km from Port Blair, a short ferry ride from Havelock and several universes away from life at home. Oh OK, it's not all torpor; you can swim, snorkel, bike, go on jungle treks, bdbjdkbnbmzzzzzzzzzz.

Whoops.

Sights & Activities

Neil Island's beaches are numbered 1 to 5, and the road distance between them is 8km. **No 1** is the prettiest and most accessible, a 40-minute walk west of the jetty and village. Most of the accommodation places are close to here and the island's best **snorkelling** is around the coral reef at the far (western) end of this beach. There's a good sunset viewpoint out this way that becomes a communal spot in the sand for tourists and locals come early evening. At low tide it's difficult getting over the coral into the water; conversely, at high tide the beach is underwater (it's kind of ironic how hard it can be to swim here given you're in the middle of the ocean).

No 2 Beach, on the north side of the island, has a natural bridge formation in the water; a cycle ride and short walk will take you to it. A track up the small hill behind Gyan Garden Restaurant leads to a **viewpoint** across the island and out to sea. At time of research, beaches No 3 and 4 were undeveloped. **No 5 Beach**, reached via the village road to the eastern side of the island, is an enclosed stretch with a bit of swell. It's a pleasant bike ride out here (about 5km from the village); just cycle to the end of the road, and walk 50m or so straight ahead to the beach.

You might be able to hire snorkelling gear around town (per day Rs100), but don't bank on it. Hire of a fishing boat to go to offshore snorkelling or fishing spots will cost between Rs1000 and Rs2000 depending on how far out you want to travel, how long you choose to snorkel etc; several people can usually fit on board. Bicycles are available for hire at several shops in the village (per day Rs40).

Sleeping & Eating

In the village there's a market, a few shops, a couple of basic restaurants and the A&N Tourism guesthouse. West of the jetty along No 1 Beach are three small 'resorts'; all have great locations and serve mediocre food.

The first place you come to, about 500m from the village market, **Cocon Huts** (☎ 282528; huts Rs50, cottages Rs350-400) has a good waterfront ambience. It was closed for renovation during our visit and has a reputation as a local drinking hole, but still comes recommended by travellers.

Tango Beach Resort (☎ 270364; huts Rs50-250, cottages Rs500) and **Pearl Park Resort** (☎ 282510; huts Rs100-250, cottages & rooms Rs400-1000) are technically two different resorts, but their proximity and same-same-ness makes them feel like identical sides of a double-headed coin. They both offer nice thatch huts, less interesting if more comfortable concrete rooms, flower-bedecked gardens, friendly communal areas and good service. OK, there is one difference: Tango has pet kittens; Pearl Park keeps puppies.

For a charmless, government-run hotel, **Hawa Bill Nest** (☎ 282630; dm Rs150, d Rs800; 🍴) offers pretty cosy digs. Five minutes' walk from the village beach, it's convenient if not as atmospheric as the other options; book at A&N Tourism (p1127) in Port Blair.

Providing somewhat erratic service out of season, but popular when/if they're up and running, Gyan Garden Restaurant and Green Heaven Restaurant are two informal and relaxed outdoor eateries and hang-outs between the village and No 1 Beach.

Getting There & Around

A ferry makes a round trip each morning from Phoenix Bay Jetty in Port Blair (Rs36, two hours). Twice a week the Rangat ferry calls at Neil after Havelock, which is useful if you want to visit both islands.

An autorickshaw will take you to No 1 Beach from the jetty for Rs50.

MIDDLE & NORTH ANDAMAN

The Andamans aren't just sun and sand. They're also jungle that feels as primeval as the Jurassic and as thick as the Amazon, a green tangle of ancient forest that could have been birthed in Mother Nature's subconscious. This shaggy, wild side of the islands can be seen on a long, loping bus ride up the Andaman Trunk Rd (ATR). Going to Diglipur by road thrusts you onto bumpy roads framed by antediluvian trees and roll-on, roll-off ferries that cross red-tannin rivers prowled by saltwater crocodiles.

But there's a negative side to riding the ATR: the road cuts through the homeland of the Jarawa and has brought the tribe into incessant contact with the outside world. Modern India and tribal life do not seem able to coexist – every time Jarawa and settlers interact, misunderstandings have led to friction, confusion and at worst, violent attacks and death. Indian anthropologists and indigenous rights groups like Survival International have called for the ATR to be closed; its status is under review as of this writing (see p1123).

The first major town north of Port Blair is Rangat. There's not much here, but you could hire a private dinghy to take you to **Long Island**, which has a couple of good beaches that will very likely be deserted – namely Lalaji and Marg Bay. Expect to pay Rs500 to Rs800 for boat hire. **Hawksbill Nest** (☎ 279022; four-bed dm Rs600, d Rs450, with AC Rs850; ✸) is about 15 minutes north of Rangat, and any northbound bus will drop you there; bookings must be made at A&N Tourism (p1127) in Port Blair. Hawksbill turtles nest on the beaches of nearby Cuthbert Bay between November and February.

If you need to stay in town there are several awful lodges that charge from Rs150 to Rs300 a night. You can get to Rangat several times a week from Port Blair or Havelock Island by ferry (Rs80/25, nine hours) or daily by bus (Rs90, eight hours). Ferries are more likely to cancel due to bad weather here. The ticket office, with fickle hours (ostensibly 10am to 3pm), is on the north edge of town.

Mayabunder & Around

In 'upper' Middle Andaman, there are several villages inhabited by Karen, members of a Burmese hill tribe that were relocated here during the British colonial period. In Mayabunder, stop at **Sea'n'Sand** (☎ 273454; r Rs200-500), a simple lodge, restaurant and bar overlooking the water 1km south of the town centre. Run by an extended Karen family, it's low-key and will appeal to travellers looking for an experience away from the crowds. You can go on a range of **boat-based day tours** (per tour from Rs500-2500) that, depending on the season, may include visits to **Forty One Caves** where *hawabills* make their highly prized edible nests; snorkelling off **Avis Island**; or a coast-and-forest-wilderness experience on **Interview Island**.

Mayabunder, 71km north of Rangat, is linked by daily buses from Port Blair (Rs120, 10 hours) and by once- or twice-weekly ferries.

Diglipur & Around

Don't expect too much out of Diglipur, three hours by road above Mayabunder and the northernmost major town in the Andamans. It's basically a muddy bazaar and you'll likely head straight for Kalipur, where you'll find lodging and vistas of the ocean and outlying islands. Ferries arrive at Aerial Bay Jetty from where it's 11km southwest to Diglipur, the bus stand and Administration Block, where boat tickets can be booked. Kalipur is on the coast 8km southeast of the jetty.

SIGHTS & ACTIVITIES

Like lovely tropical counterweights, the twin islands of **Smith** and **Ross** are connected by a narrow sandbar. Since this is designated as a marine sanctuary, you must get a permit (Indian/foreigner Rs50/500) from the **Forest Office** (✸ 6am-2pm Mon-Sat) opposite Aerial Bay Jetty to visit. You can charter a boat to take you for the day from the village for around Rs700.

At 732m, **Saddle Peak** is the highest point in the Andamans. You can trek through subtropical forest to the top and back from Kalipur in about six hours; the views from the peaks onto the archipelago are incredible. Again, a permit is required from the Forest Office (Indian/foreigner Rs25/250) and a local guide will make sure you don't get lost – ask at Pristine Beach Resort. **Snorkelling** is possible behind the small island off the beach near Pristine Beach Resort, and just around the coast at Radha Nagar.

Leatherback and green turtles nest along the Diglipur coastline between December and March.

SLEEPING & EATING

There are two places to stay opposite each other at Kalipur, 8km southeast of the Aerial Bay Jetty. Buses run along this route (Rs8); an autorickshaw costs about Rs100.

Pristine Beach Resort (☎ 201837; huts Rs200-700) Huddled among the palms between paddy fields and the beach, Pristine is a pretty spot with several simple bamboo huts on stilts, a restaurant and friendly owners. It gets very busy in peak season.

Turtle Resort (☎ 272553; r Rs400, with AC800; ✸) Set on a small hill with rural views from the balconies, this A&N Tourism hotel is comfy if a little musty. It's best to book ahead through A&N Tourism (p1127) in Port Blair, though you'll likely be able to get a room on-site if one's available.

GETTING THERE & AWAY

Diglipur, located about 80km north of Mayabunder, is served by daily buses to/from Port Blair (Rs150, 12 hours), as well as buses to Mayabunder (Rs30 to Rs50, 2½ hours) and Rangat (Rs70, 4½ hours). There are also daily ferries from Port Blair to Diglipur, returning overnight from Diglipur (seat/berth Rs81/150, 10 hours).

LITTLE ANDAMAN

Named Gaubolambe by the indigenous Onge, Little Andaman is as far south as you can go in the islands. There's an end of the world (in tropical paradise) feeling here: barely any tourists visit, the locals are so friendly they feel like family and the island itself is a gorgeous fist of mangroves, jungle and teal plucked from a twinkle in nature's eye.

Located about 120km south of Port Blair, the main settlement here is Hut Bay, a pleasant small town that primarily produces smiling Bengalis and Tamils. North of here you'll find isolated beaches as fresh as bread out of the oven. **Netaji Nagar Beach**, 11km north of Hut Bay, and **Butler Bay**, a further 3km north, are gorgeous and great for surfing. Inland, the **White Surf** and **Whisper Wave waterfalls** offer a forest experience; they're pleasant falls and

you may be tempted to swim in the rock pools, but beware local crocodiles. The **Andaman and Nicobar Islands Forest Plantation Development Corporation** (ANIFPDC; ☎ 232752) runs much of the tourism on Little Andaman and may or may not be manning Rs20 ticket booths at the above locations. They also, ostensibly, operate elephants treks into the jungle, boating and bird-watching fun near Butler Bay creek, and a Red Oil Palm plantation 11km north of Hut Bay.

There are plenty of cheap thali and tiffin places in Hut Bay (we recommend the unnamed Bengali eatery across from the police station). Sleepingwise there's only a few places to stay on the island. Vvet House, Cozy Cave and Green Grace lodges are all operated by ANIFPDC and offer comfy if uninspired rooms running from Rs150 to Rs300; you can get an AC room in Green Grace for Rs300/600 (single/double) and there's a Rs100 dorm in Cozy Cave. The independent **Sealand Tourist Home** (☎ 284525) next to Vvet House, offers much the same prices and accommodation as above.

Ferries land at Hut Bay Jetty on the east coast; from there the beaches lay to the north. Buses (Rs10) leave when they want for Butler Bay, or you can hire a local jeep (Rs100). Boats sail to Little Andaman from Port Blair daily – the trip there is eight hours, while the return is a six-hour speedboat trip.

ANDAMAN & NICOBAR ISLANDS

Directory

CONTENTS

ACCOMMODATION

India has a broad spectrum of accommodation, from grungy backpacker hotels with concrete floors and cold 'bucket' showers to opulent palaces with every conceivable comfort. Most big towns and tourist centres have something for all budgets, but rates vary widely around the country making it best to see this book's individual chapters (Sleeping sections) for accommodation costs in the areas you intend visiting. Also see p1141. Keep in mind that popular tourist centres usually witness a significant price hike during the tourist season and can fill up fast at these times, making advance reservations wise.

> **BOOK ACCOMMODATION ONLINE**
>
> For more accommodation reviews and recommendations by Lonely Planet authors, check out www.lonelyplanet.com/hotels. You'll find the insider low-down on the top places to stay. Best of all, you can usually book online.

Room quality can vary considerably *within* hotels so try to inspect a few rooms first. Avoid carpeted rooms at cheaper hotels unless you like the smell of mouldy socks. For the lowdown on hotel bathrooms, read p1140. Sound pollution can be irksome (especially in urban hubs); pack good-quality earplugs and request a room that doesn't face a busy road. It's a good idea to keep your door locked, as some staff can have the annoying habit of knocking and automatically walking in without first seeking your permission.

Credit cards are accepted at most top-end hotels and many midrange places; budget hotels invariably require cash. Most hotels ask for a deposit at check in – ask for a receipt and be wary of any request to sign a blank impression of your credit card. If the hotel insists, consider going to the nearest ATM and paying cash. Verify the check-out time when you check-in – some hotels have a fixed check-out time (usually 10am or noon), while others give you 24-hour check-out. Reservations by phone without a deposit are usually fine, but call to confirm the booking the day before you arrive.

Be aware that in tourist hot spots (eg Rajasthan, Varanasi), hotels may 'borrow' the name of a thriving competitor to confuse travellers, paying commissions to taxi and rickshaw drivers who bring them unsuspecting customers. Make sure that you know the *exact* name of your preferred hotel, and confirm that you have indeed been taken to the right hotel before you pay the driver (p1140).

Accommodation Options

As well as conventional hotels, there are atmospheric guest houses in traditional village homes and colonial-era properties with faded

---

PRACTICALITIES

- Electricity is 230V to 240V, 50 Hz AC, and sockets are the three-round-pin variety (two-pin sockets are also found). Blackouts are common, particularly during summer and the monsoon.

- Officially India is metric. Terms you're likely to hear are: lakhs (one lakh = 100,000) and crores (one crore = 10 million).

- Major English-language dailies include the *Hindustan Times, Times of India, Indian Express, Hindu, Statesman, Telegraph, Daily News & Analysis (DNA)* and *Economic Times*. Regional English-language and local-vernacular publications are found nationwide.

- Incisive current-affairs reports are printed in *Frontline, India Today,* the *Week, Tehelka* and *Outlook*.

- The national (government) TV broadcaster is Doordarshan. More people watch satellite and cable TV; English-language channels include BBC, CNN, Cartoon Network, Star Movies, HBO, Discovery and MTV. TV program (and radio) details appear in most major daily newspapers.

- Government-controlled All India Radio (AIR) nationally transmits local and international news. There are also private FM channels broadcasting music, current affairs, talkback and more.

Raj charm. Standout options in this book are indicated by **our pick**.

BUDGET & MIDRANGE HOTELS

Apart from some character-filled exceptions – such as traditional wood or stone guest houses in remote mountain areas – most budget and midrange hotels are modern-style concrete blocks. Shared bathrooms (often with squat toilets) are usually only found at the cheapest lodgings. Most rooms have ceiling fans and better rooms have electric mosquito-killers and/or window nets, though cheaper rooms may lack windows altogether. Bringing your own sheet (or a sleeping-bag liner) is a sound policy – some cheap hotels have sheets with more holes and stains than a string vest at an oyster-eating contest! Apart from that, many budget hotels don't provide a top sheet so you could find yourself sleeping under (dodgy) bed-covers that haven't been washed for years. Away from tourist areas, cheaper hotels may

---

CARBON-MONOXIDE POISONING

Some mountain areas rely on charcoal burners for warmth, but these should be avoided due to the risk of fatal carbon-monoxide poisoning. The thick, mattresslike blankets used in many mountain areas are amazingly warm once you get beneath the covers. If you're still cold, improvise a hot-water bottle by filling your drinking-water bottle with boiled water and covering it with a sock.

---

not take foreigners because they don't have the necessary foreigner-registration forms.

Midrange hotels usually offer extras such as cable/satellite TV and air-conditioning, although some just have (noisy) 'air-coolers' that cool air by blowing it over cold water. They're better than nothing, but no challenge to real air-conditioning, especially during the monsoon.

Note that some hotels lock their doors at night. Members of staff may sleep in the lobby but waking them up can be a challenge. Let the hotel know in advance if you'll be arriving or coming back to your room late in the evening.

CAMPING

There are few official camping sites in India, but campers can usually find hotels with gardens where they can camp for a nominal fee and use the bathroom facilities. Wild camping is often the only accommodation option on trekking routes. In mountain areas, you'll also find summer-only tented camps, with accommodation in semipermanent 'Swiss tents' with attached bathrooms.

DORMITORY ACCOMMODATION

A number of hotels have cheap dormitories, though these may be mixed and, in less touristy places, full of drunken drivers – not ideal conditions for single women. More traveller-friendly dorms are found at the handful of hostels run by the YMCA, YWCA and Salvation Army as well as at HI-associated hostels. Tourist bungalows run by state governments and railway

> **GET TO KNOW YOUR BATHROOM**
>
> Most of India's midrange hotels and all top-end ones have sit-down toilets with toilet paper and soap supplied. In ultra-cheap hotels, and in places off the tourist trail, squat toilets are the norm and toilet paper is rarely provided. Squat toilets are variously described as 'Indian-style', 'Indian' or 'floor' toilets, while the sit-down variety may be called 'Western' or 'commode' toilets. In a few places, you'll find the curious 'hybrid toilet', a sit-down version with footpads on the edge of the bowl.
>
> Terminology for hotel bathrooms varies across India. 'Attached bath', 'private bath' or 'with bath' means that the room has its own en-suite bathroom. 'Common bath', 'no bathroom' or 'shared bath' means communal bathroom facilities.
>
> Not all rooms have hot water. 'Running', '24-hour' or 'constant' water means that hot water is available round-the-clock (not always the case in reality). 'Bucket' hot water is only available in buckets (sometimes for a small charge).
>
> Many places use wall-mounted electric geysers (water heaters) that need to be switched on up to an hour before use. Note that the geyser's main switch can sometimes be located outside the bathroom.
>
> Hotels that advertise 'room with shower' may be misleading – sometimes the shower is just a pipe sticking out of the wall. Meanwhile, some hotels surreptitiously disconnect showers to cut costs, while showers at other places render a mere trickle of water.
>
> In this book, hotel rooms have their own private bathroom unless otherwise indicated.

retiring rooms may also offer inexpensive dorm beds.

GOVERNMENT ACCOMMODATION & TOURIST BUNGALOWS

The Indian government maintains a network of guest houses for travelling officials and public workers, known variously as rest houses, dak bungalows, circuit houses, PWD (Public Works Department) bungalows and forest rest houses. These places may accept travellers if no government employees need the rooms, but permission is sometimes required from local officials and you'll probably have to find the *chowkidar* (caretaker) to open the doors.

'Tourist bungalows' are run by state governments – rooms are usually midpriced (some with cheap dorms) and have varying standards of cleanliness and service. Some state governments also run chains of more expensive hotels, including some lovely heritage properties. Details are normally available through the state tourism office.

HOMESTAYS/B&BS FOR PAYING GUESTS

Known as homestays, or B&Bs, these family-run guest houses will appeal to those seeking a small-scale, uncommercial setting with home-cooked meals. Standards range from mud-and-stone huts with hole-in-the-floor toilets to comfortable middle-class homes. Contact the local tourist office for a full list of participating families.

Some travellers love the experience, while others have reported feeling stifled by the often close tabs kept on them by over-protective (usually for caring reasons) families, and/or obliged to return home at a reasonable hour of night because they aren't given a key.

RAILWAY RETIRING ROOMS

Most large train stations have basic rooms for travellers in possession of an ongoing train ticket or Indrail Pass. Some are grim, others are surprisingly pleasant, but all are noisy from the sound of passengers and trains. Nevertheless, they're useful for early-morning train departures and there's usually a choice of dormitories or private rooms (24-hour checkout).

TEMPLES & PILGRIMS' REST HOUSES

Accommodation is available at some ashrams (spiritual retreats), gurdwaras (Sikh temples) and *dharamsalas* (pilgrims' guest houses) for a donation, but these places have been established for genuine pilgrims so please exercise judgment about the appropriateness of staying (some regional chapters have further details). Always abide by any protocols.

TOP-END & HERITAGE HOTELS

India has plenty of top-end properties, from modern five-star chain hotels to unique heritage abodes (eg palaces). Most top-end hotels have rupee rates for Indian guests and US dollar rates for foreigners (including Non-

Resident Indians, or NRIs). Officially, you're supposed to pay the dollar rates in foreign currency or by credit card, but many places will accept rupees adding up to the dollar rate (verify this when checking-in).

The Government of India tourism website, **Incredible India** (www.incredibleindia.org), has a useful list of palaces, forts and other erstwhile royal retreats that accept paying guests – click on the 'Royal Retreats' heading.

Costs

Given that the cost of budget, midrange and top-end hotels varies so much across India it would be misleading of us to provide a 'national' price range for each category. The best way to gauge accommodation costs for the regions you intend visiting is to go directly to the Sleeping sections of this book's regional chapters. Keep in mind that most establishments raise tariffs annually, so the prices may have risen by the time you read this. Regional chapters' will also proffer specific details about locally relevant factors such as seasonal cost variations.

Accommodation listings in this book are arranged in price order, from cheapest to most expensive. Tariffs don't include taxes unless otherwise stated. All room costs include en-suite bathrooms unless otherwise mentioned.

As blackouts are common (especially during summer and the monsoon), double-check that the hotel has a back-up generator if you're paying for electric 'extras' such as air-conditioners and TVs.

SEASONAL VARIATIONS

Hotels in popular tourist hang-outs crank up their prices in the high season, which usually coincides with the best weather for the area's sights and activities – normally summertime in the mountains (around June to October), and the cooler months in the plains (around October to mid-February). In areas popular with foreign tourists, there's an additional peak period over Christmas and New Year. At other times, these hotels offer significant discounts. It's always worth trying your luck and asking for a discount if the hotel seems quiet.

Many temple towns have additional peak seasons around major festivals and pilgrimages – for festival details see the Events Calendar chapter and the 'Festivals in…' boxed texts in regional chapters. For any major festival, make advance accommodation arrangements.

TAXES & SERVICE CHARGES

State governments slap a variety of taxes on hotel accommodation (except at the cheaper hotels), and these are added to the cost of your room. Taxes vary from state to state and are detailed in the regional chapters. Many upmarket hotels also levy an additional 'service charge' (usually around 10%). Rates quoted in this book's regional chapters exclude taxes unless otherwise indicated.

BUSINESS HOURS

Official business hours are from 9.30am to 5.30pm Monday to Friday, but many offices open later and close earlier. Apart from Sundays, government offices in many states remain closed on alternate (usually second and fourth) Saturdays. Most offices have an official lunch hour from around 1pm. Shops generally open around 10am and operate until 6pm or later; some close on Sunday (or another day of the week; see regional chapters). Note that curfews apply in some areas, notably Kashmir and the Northeast States. Airline offices generally stick to standard business hours Monday to Saturday.

Most banks are open from 10am to 2pm on weekdays (until 4pm in some areas), and from 10am to noon (or 1pm) on Saturday. Exact branch hours vary from town to town so check locally. Foreign-exchange offices may open longer and operate daily.

Main post offices are open from around 10am to 5pm on weekdays (though some postal services may not be offered in the afternoon), and until noon on Saturday. Some larger post offices have a full day on Saturday and a half-day on Sunday.

Restaurant timings vary regionally – most open from around 8am to 10pm daily. Exceptions are noted in the regional chapters.

CHILDREN

India is wonderfully accepting of children, however extra caution is needed in hot and crowded conditions. Pay particular attention to hygiene and be *very* vigilant around traffic. It's also advisable to keep children away from monkeys and stray dogs, which can carry all sorts of diseases. See Lonely Planet's *Travel with Children,* and the Travelling With

DIRECTORY

Children section of Lonely Planet's **Thorn Tree Travel Forum** (www.lonelyplanet.com/thorntree) for more detailed advice.

Practicalities

ACCOMMODATION
Many hotels have 'family rooms' and almost all will provide an extra bed for a small additional charge, though cots are less common. Upmarket hotels may offer baby-sitting facilities and/or kids activity programs and should also have cable TV with English-language children's channels (many cheaper hotels have cartoons only in Hindi).

DISCOUNTS
On Indian trains, children aged under four travel for free and those aged five to 11 pay half-price. Most airlines charge 10% of the adult fare for infants (under two years old) and 50% for under-11s.

Many tourist attractions have a reduced entry fee for children under 12 (see regional chapters).

FOOD & DRINK
Children are welcome at most restaurants, but usually it's just upmarket places and fast-food chains that have highchairs and children's menus. Across India, nappy-changing facilities are usually restricted to the (often cramped) restaurant toilet.

Unfamiliar food may initially present a hurdle for some kids, but Western fast food is widely available and snacks such as *pakoras* (deep-fried battered vegetables) and *dosas* (savoury crepes) should appeal. As long as it's peeled or washed in purified water, fruit is also good. Bottled water, cartons of fruit juice and soft drinks are easily found. Some children will enjoy sweet milky *chai* (tea).

HEALTH
Avoiding tummy upsets can be a daily challenge – see p1196 for more advice. Note that rabid animals can also pose a risk. If your child takes special medication it's wise to bring along an adequate stock. Check with a doctor before departure about recommended jabs and drug courses for children.

TRANSPORT
Long-distance road travel should include sufficient food and toilet stops as travel sickness can be a problem, particularly on rough roads. On public transport, children may be expected to give their seat to adults, meaning long journeys with a child on your lap. Note that child seats in rented cars are rare (inquire when booking).

Trains are usually the most comfortable mode of transport, especially for long trips. Internal air travel can save time and tempers.

TRAVEL WITH INFANTS
Standard baby products such as disposable nappies (diapers), wet wipes and milk powder can be bought in most large cities and tourist centres, but aren't reliably found elsewhere (so stock up). If you've got a finicky baby, consider bringing powdered milk or baby food from home. Also bring along high-factor sunscreen, a snug-fitting wide-brimmed hat and a washable changing mat for covering dirty surfaces. Breastfeeding in public is generally not condoned by Indian society.

Sights & Activities
It's a good idea to initially allow a few days for your child to simply acclimatise to India's explosion of sights, sounds, smells and tastes, before launching into any big trips around the country.

In terms of attractions, there are numerous options that will keep kids happy, from beaches and wildlife parks to planetariums and sound-and-light shows – see regional chapters for details.

India's bounty of festivals may also capture your child's imagination, although some may be overwhelmed by the crowds. For festival details see the Events Calendar chapter , and the 'Festivals in…' boxed texts at the start of regional chapters.

CLIMATE
India is so vast that climatic conditions in the far north have little relation to those of the extreme south. Generally speaking, the country has a three-season year – the hot, the wet and the cool. See p20.

COURSES
You can pursue all sorts of courses in India, from yoga and meditation to cooking and Hindi. To find out about new courses, inquire at tourist offices, ask fellow travellers, and browse local newspapers and noticeboards. Also see the Activities chapter and, for cooking courses, p91.

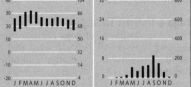

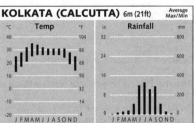

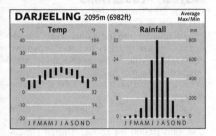

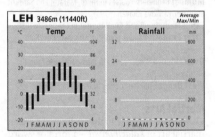

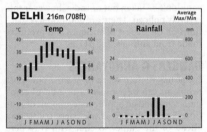

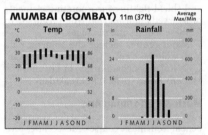

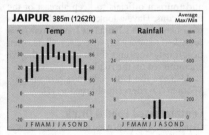

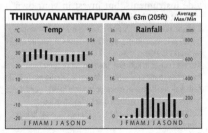

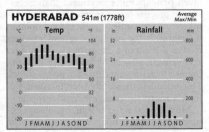

Arts & Crafts

Some recommended arts and crafts courses include the following.

Madhya Pradesh & Chhattisgarh Saathi has courses in Bastar tribal arts (p724).

Mumbai The Khatwara Institute (p793) offers assorted courses (for women only) that include *mehndi* and block-printing.

Rajasthan Jhunjhunu (p192) and Udaipur (p218) have painting courses.

Languages

The places that are listed below offer language courses, some requiring a minimum time commitment.

Delhi Basic Hindi classes at Delhi's Central Hindi Directorate (p139).

Himachal Pradesh Long and short courses in Tibetan at McLeod Ganj (p375).

Kerala Short courses in Malayalam, Hindi and Sanskrit at Vijnana Kala Vedi Cultural Centre (p1006).

Mumbai Beginners' courses in Hindi, Marathi and Sanskrit at Bharatiya Vidya Bhavan (p793).

Tamil Nadu Hindi and Tamil courses in Chennai (p1050).

Uttar Pradesh Various places in Varanasi offer Hindi courses (p446).

Uttarakhand Hindi courses in Mussoorie (p467) and Rishikesh (p478).

West Bengal Tibetan courses in Darjeeling (p554).

Martial Arts

Courses are available in the traditional Keralan martial art of *kalarippayat* – a form of sword and shield fighting incorporating elements of ayurveda and *marma* (the precursor to Chinese acupressure massage).

Major centres include the Vijnana Kala Vedi Cultural Centre (p1006) in Kottayam, CVN Kalari Sangham (p985) in Trivandrum, and Ens Kalari (p1023) in Ernakulam.

Music & Performing Arts

Allow at least several weeks to derive any real benefit from music courses. Most centres provide instruments, but invest in your own if you intend playing back home.

Karnataka Classical Indian dance classes at Nrityagram (p913) in Hessaraghatta, and tabla classes at Shruthi Musical Works (p918) in Mysore.

Kerala Courses in Kathakali (Keralan dance opera) and *kootiattam* (traditional Sanskrit drama) in Trivandrum (p985), Kathakali and Kathakali make-up in Kochi (p1017), and dance centres near Thrissur (p1029) and Kottayam (p1006).

Kolkata Aurobindo Bhawan (p518) has classical Indian dance classes.

Rajasthan Tabla, flute, singing and *kathak* (Indian classical dance) courses in Pushkar (p197), Jaipur (p174) and Udaipur (p218).

Tamil Nadu Courses in *bharatanatyam* (classical dance), singing and various musical instruments in Puducherry (p1074); Kalakshetra Arts Village (p1054) in Chennai offers courses in classical Tamil dance and music.

Uttar Pradesh Varanasi has several places where you can learn musical instruments or classical dance (p446).

Uttarakhand Classical dance and musical instrument classes in Rishikesh (p478).

Tea Appreciation

Details about interesting tea training courses can be found on p543.

Yoga & Holistic Therapies

India has thousands of yoga centres offering long courses and daily classes as well as courses in ayurveda, meditation and other therapies. See p113 for details.

CUSTOMS REGULATIONS

Visitors are allowed to bring 1L each of wine and spirits and 200 cigarettes or 50 cigars or 250g of tobacco into India duty-free. Officials sometimes ask tourists to enter expensive items such as video cameras and laptop computers on a 'Tourist Baggage Re-export' form to ensure they're taken out of India at the time of departure.

Technically you're supposed to declare any amount of cash/travellers cheques over US$5000/10,000 on arrival. Indian rupees shouldn't be taken out of India, however this is rarely policed. There are additional restrictions on the export of antiques and products made from animals; see p1158.

DANGERS & ANNOYANCES

India has its fair share of scams, but most problems can be avoided with a bit of common sense and an appropriate amount of caution. Scams change as tricksters try to stay ahead of the game, so chat with travellers and tourism officials to keep abreast of the latest cons. Have a look at the India branch of Lonely Planet's **Thorn Tree Travel Forum** (www .lonelyplanet.com/thorntree), where travellers often post timely warnings about problems they've encountered on the road.

Also see the Dos & Don'ts box on p62. Women travellers should read p1170.

Contaminated Food & Drink

In past years, some private medical clinics have given patients more treatment than necessary to procure larger payments from travel-insurance companies – get a second opinion if possible. In the late 1990s, several travellers died as a result of a dangerous scam in Agra and Varanasi after being fed food spiked with bacteria by restaurants linked to dodgy clinics. This scam has thankfully been quashed, but there's always the chance it could reappear.

Most bottled water is legit, but always ensure the lid seal is intact and check that the bottom of the bottle hasn't been tampered with. Crush plastic bottles after use to prevent them being misused later, or better still, bring along water-purification tablets or a filtration system to avoid adding to India's plastic-waste mountain.

Drugs
Possession and use of drugs is illegal in India. A few towns allow the legal (controlled) sale of bhang (marijuana) for religious reasons, but elsewhere, courts treat possession of cannabis as severely as possession of heroin.

In the Kullu region of Himachal Pradesh, dozens of travellers have disappeared or been murdered in the hills, with suspicion falling on local drug gangs; read Warning – Fatal Vacations, p350. Don't assume strangers are harmless because they share your interest in drugs.

Also see p1151.

Festivals
The sheer mass of humanity at many of India's festivals provides an incredible spectacle, but every year pilgrims are crushed or trampled to death on temple processions and train platforms. Be extra careful around large crowds at these times, and travel on conventional trains rather than special pilgrim services.

Care is also needed during the Holi festival (p27). Foreigners get doused with water and coloured dye like everyone else, and a few people have been scarred by dodgy chemicals. Consider buying a cheap set of throwaway clothes specifically for this festival. There's also a tradition of guzzling alcohol and bhang during Holi, and female travellers have been hassled by spaced-out blokes; it's wise for women to avoid venturing onto the streets alone.

Overpricing & Photography
There are circumstances where it's best to agree on prices beforehand so as to avoid being over-charged, whether it's eating in places without menus or flagging down an autorickshaw. Apart from the money issue, prior price-setting could also deflect potentially ugly misunderstandings later.

On the photographic front, something to be aware of – apart from propriety issues (see the Photography Etiquette section in the Dos & Don'ts box on p62) – is that some travellers have reported getting approval when photographing a person, only to have that same individual demand money afterwards. Use your instincts and when uncertain, avoid taking pictures of people.

Rebel Violence
India has a number of (sometimes armed) dissident groups championing various causes. These groups have employed the same tried and tested techniques of rebel groups everywhere – assassinations and bomb attacks on government infrastructure, public transport, religious centres, tourist sites and markets. For further information read p57.

Most of the time, India is no more dangerous than anywhere else, but certain areas are particularly prone to insurgent violence – specifically Kashmir, the Northeast States, some remote tribal regions and, less frequently, parts of Bihar and West Bengal. Curfews and strikes can close the roads (as well as banks, shops etc) for days on end in sensitive regions like Kashmir.

International terrorism is as much of a risk in Europe or America, so this is no reason not to go to India, but it makes sense to check the local security situation carefully before travelling (especially in high-risk areas). See regional chapters for more information.

Scams
There are various scams, predominantly in tourist hubs, designed to separate travellers from their money.

Be highly suspicious of strangers' claims that you can purchase goods cheaply in India and sell them easily at a profit elsewhere. Precious stones and carpets are favourites for this long-running con. Operators who practise such schemes are deceptively friendly, pouring out sob stories about not being able to obtain an export licence etc. And therein lies the opportunity for you to 'get rich quick' – by carrying or mailing the goods home and selling them to the trader's (non-existent) overseas representatives at a profit. Some may show you (forged) testimonials from other travellers. Without exception, the goods are worth a fraction of what you paid and the 'representatives' never materialise. Also read the boxed text, p179.

It also pays to be cautious when sending goods home. Shops have been known to swap high-value items for junk when posting goods to home addresses. If you have any doubts, send the package yourself from the post office. Be careful when paying for souvenirs with a credit card. Government shops are usually legitimate; private souvenir shops have been known to surreptitiously run off extra copies of the credit-card imprint slip, used for phoney transactions later. Insist that the trader carries out any credit-card transaction on the counter in front of you. Alternatively, take out cash from an ATM to avoid this risk altogether.

While it's only a minority of traders who are involved in dishonest schemes, many souvenir vendors are knee-deep in the commission racket (opposite).

Swimming

Dozens of locals and foreigners drown every year on Goa's beaches alone, even confident swimmers who venture into (deceptively) calm seas (see p861). Be aware that the sea can have very dangerous rips, undertows and currents; always inquire locally to find out safe places to swim and preferably have someone keep a watch while you take a paddle. Apart from the ocean, there are also deceptively strong currents in many rivers, including the Ganges.

Never venture into the water after consuming alcohol.

Transport Scams

Many private travel agencies make extra cash by scamming travellers for tours and travel tickets. Make sure you're clear what is included in the price of any tour (get this in writing) to avoid charges for hidden 'extras' later on.

Be cautious of anyone offering tours to Kashmir in Delhi and other traveller centres. Some travel agents exploit travellers' safety concerns to make extra money from tours that you can do just as easily (and safely) on public transport. Always check the security situation before you travel and make your own tour arrangements after you arrive to cut out these dodgy middlemen.

Tours to Srinagar's houseboats from Delhi should definitely be avoided – read p292.

When buying a bus, train or plane ticket anywhere other than the registered office of the transport company, make certain you're getting the ticket class you paid for. It's not uncommon for travellers to book a deluxe bus or AC train berth and arrive to find a bog-standard ordinary bus or a less comfortable sleeper seat.

Theft & Druggings

Theft is a risk in India, as it is anywhere else. On buses and trains, keep luggage securely locked (minipadlocks and chains are available at many train stations) and lock your bags to the metal baggage racks or the wire loops found under seats; padlocking your bags to the roof racks on buses is also a sensible policy.

Thieves tend to target popular tourist train routes, such as Delhi to Agra. Be extra alert just before the train departs; thieves often take advantage of the confusion and crowds. Airports are another place to exercise caution; after a long flight you're unlikely to be at your most alert.

Occasionally, tourists (especially those travelling solo) are drugged and robbed during train or bus journeys; a friendly stranger strikes up a conversation, offers you a spiked drink (to send you to sleep), then makes off with everything you have. It's often best to politely decline drinks or food offered by strangers (use your instincts) – stomach upsets are a convenient excuse.

Unfortunately some travellers make their money go further by helping themselves to other peoples – take extra care in dormitories. For lost credit cards, immediately call the international lost/stolen number; for lost/stolen travellers cheques, contact the American Express or Thomas Cook office in Delhi (p121).

A good travel-insurance policy is essential (see p1149); keep the emergency contact details handy and familiarise yourself with the claims procedure. Keep photocopies of your passport identity page and visa page, separately from your passport, as well as a copy of your airline ticket. You could also email scans to yourself.

The safest place for your money and your passport is next to your skin, either in a concealed money belt or a secure place under your shirt. If you carry your money in a wallet, keep it in your front trouser pocket, never the back pocket (the 'pickpocket's friend').

It's wise to peel off at least US$100 and store it away separately from your main stash; however, keep your main stash and other valuables on your person. Also, separate big currency notes from small bills so you don't publicly display large wads of cash when paying for services or checking into hotels.

In hotels, *never* leave your money or valuable documents in your room (no, not even under mattresses) when you go out. Better hotels, however, will have a safe for valuables. For peace of mind, you may also want to use your own padlock at hotels where doors are locked with a padlock (common at cheaper hotels). If you cannot lock your hotel room securely from the inside at night, stay somewhere else.

Touts & Commission Agents

With so many businesses dependent on tourism, competition is cut-throat. Many hotels and shops drum up extra business by paying commission to local fixers who bring tourists through the doors. These places tend to be unpopular for a reason – prices will invariably be raised (by as much as 50%) to pay the fixer's commission. To get around this, ask taxis or rickshaws to drop you at a landmark rather than at your intended destination, so you can walk in alone and pay the normal price.

Train and bus stations are often swarming with touts – if anyone asks if this is your first trip to India, say you've been here several times, as this is usually a ruse to gauge your vulnerability. You'll often hear stories about the hotels that refuse to pay commissions being 'full', 'under renovation' or 'closed'. Check things out yourself. Be very sceptical of phrases like 'my brother's shop' and 'special deal at my friend's place'.

On the flip side, touts can be beneficial if you arrive in a town without a hotel reservation when some big festival is on, or during the peak season – they'll know which places have beds.

Touts can be particular bothersome in Delhi. A good way to avoid tout hassles is to arrange hotel pick-ups where possible, especially when arriving in a big city for the first time.

Trekking

Trekking off the beaten track always carries risks and India is often poorly set up for independent trekkers. We strongly recommend hiring local guides and porters or joining an organised trek before heading off into potentially dangerous terrain; see p112 for more information.

DISCOUNTS
Seniors

Some airlines offer discounts (of up to 50%) on domestic air travel for Indian citizens aged 65 or over (inquire when booking). However, promotional fares and internet tickets on airlines are often cheaper than discounted full fares. Anyone over 60 is entitled to a 30% discount on the cost of train travel (foreigners should bring passports as proof of age).

Student & Youth Travel

Student cards are of limited use nowadays as most concessions are based on age. Hostels run by the Indian Youth Hostels Association are part of the HI network; an HI card sometimes entitles you to discount rates. YMCA/YWCA members also receive discounts on accommodation.

Foreigners under 30 years of age receive a 25% discount on some domestic air tickets (inquire when booking). This applies to full-price tickets, so standard fares for budget airlines may be cheaper still.

EMBASSIES & HIGH COMMISSIONS IN INDIA

Most foreign diplomatic missions are based in Delhi, but several nations operate consulates in other Indian cities (see websites, where provided, in the following Delhi addresses). Many missions have certain timings for visa applications, usually mornings, but phone for details.

These are just some of the many foreign missions found in India.

Australia Chennai (Map p1048; ☎ 044-28601160; 512 Raheja Towers, 177 Anna Salai, Anna Salai); Delhi (Map pp126-7; ☎ 011-41399900; www.ausgovindia.com; 1/50G Shantipath, Chanakyapuri); Mumbai (Map pp780-1; ☎ 022-6669 2000; 36 Maker Chambers VI, 3rd fl, 220 Nariman Point)

Bangladesh Delhi (Map pp122-3; ☎ 011-24121394; www.bhcdelhi.org; EP39 Dr Radakrishnan Marg, Chanakyapuri); Kolkata (Map pp504-5; ☎ 033-22475208; 9 Circus Ave)

Bhutan (Map pp126-7; ☎ 011-26889230; Chandragupta Marg, Chanakyapuri, Delhi)

Canada Chennai (Map pp1044-5; ☎ 044-28330888; 18 Khader Nawaz Khan Rd); Delhi (Map pp126-7; ☎ 011-41782000; www.dfait-maeci.gc.ca/new-delhi; 7/8 Shantipath, Chanakyapuri); Mumbai (Map p786; ☎ 022-67494444; 6th fl, Fort House, 221 Dr DN Rd)

France Delhi (Map pp126-7; ☎ 011-24196100; www .france-in-india.org; 2/50E Shantipath, Chanakyapuri); Mumbai (Map pp780-1; ☎ 022-66694000; 7th fl, Hoechst House, Nariman Point)

DIRECTORY

Germany Chennai (Map pp1044-5; ☎ 044-24301600; 9 Boat Club Rd, RA Puram); Delhi (Map pp126-7; ☎ 011-26871837; www.new-delhi.diplo.de; 6/50G Shantipath, Chanakyapuri); Kolkata (Map pp504-5; ☎ 033-24791141; 1 Hastings Park Rd, Alipore); Mumbai (Map pp780-1; ☎ 022-22832422; 10th fl, Hoechst House, Nariman Point)

Israel Delhi (Map pp126-7; ☎ 011-30414500; http://delhi.mfa.gov.il; 3 Aurangzeb Rd); Mumbai (Map pp780-1; ☎ 022-22822822/22819993; Earnest House, 16th fl, NCPA Marg, Nariman Point)

Italy Delhi (Map pp126-7; ☎ 011-26114355; www.ambnewdelhi.esteri.it; 50E Chandragupta Marg, Chanakyapuri); Mumbai (Map pp780-1; ☎ 022-23804071; Kanchanjunga, 1st fl, 72G Deshmukh Marg, Kemp's Corner)

Japan Chennai (Map pp1044-5; ☎ 044-24323860; 12/1, Cenetoph Rd 1st St, Teynampet); Delhi (Map pp126-7; ☎ 011-26876564; www.in.emb-japan.go.jp; 50G Shantipath, Chanakyapuri); Mumbai (Map pp780-1; ☎ 022-23517101; 1 ML Dahanukar Marg, Cumballa Hill)

Malaysia Chennai (Map pp1044-5; ☎ 044-28226888; 44 Tank Bund Rd, Nungambakkam); Delhi (Map pp126-7; ☎ 011-26111291; www.kln.gov.my/perwakilan/newdelhi; 50M Satya Marg, Chanakyapuri); Mumbai (Map p796; ☎ 022-26455751/2; Notan Plaza, 4th fl, Turner Rd, Bandra West)

Maldives Chennai (Map pp1044-5; ☎ 044-24331696; Balaji Dental & Craniofacial Hospital, 30, KB Dasan Rd, Teynampet); Delhi (Map pp122-3; ☎ 011-41435701; www.maldiveshighcom.in/; B2 Anand Niketan); Kolkata (Map p512; ☎ 033-22485400; Ground fl, Hastings Chambers, KS Roy Rd) Hidden around the side of the building down an alley off KS Roy Rd; Mumbai (Map p786; ☎ 022-22078041; 212A Maker Bhawan No 3, New Marine Lines, Churchgate); Trivandrum (off Map p984; ☎ 0471-2558189; 13/1245 TC, Kumarapuram)

Myanmar Delhi (Map pp126-7; ☎ 011-24678822; 3/50F Nyaya Marg); Kolkata (Map pp504-5; ☎ 033-24851658; 57K Ballygunge Circular Rd)

Nepal Delhi (Map pp126-7; ☎ 011-23327361; Barakhamba Rd); Kolkata (Map pp504-5; ☎ 033-24561224; 1 National Library Ave, Alipore)

Netherlands Chennai (Map pp1044-5; ☎ 044-43535381; 76 Venkatakrisha Rd, Mandaveli); Delhi (Map pp126-7; ☎ 011-24197600; http://india.nlembassy.org/; 6/50F Shantipath, Chanakyapuri); Mumbai (Map p786; ☎ 022-22194200; Forbes Bldg, Home St, Fort)

New Zealand Chennai (Map pp1044-5; ☎ 044-28112472; Rane Engine Valves Ltd, 132 Cathedral Rd); Delhi (Map pp126-7; ☎ 011-26883170; www.nzembassy.com; 50N Nyaya Marg, Chanakyapuri); Mumbai (Map pp780-1; ☎ 022-23520022; Aashiana, 1st fl, 5 Altamount Rd, Breach Candy)

Pakistan (Map pp126-7; ☎ 011-24676004; 2/50G Shantipath, Chanakyapuri, Delhi)

Singapore Chennai (Map pp1044-5; ☎ 044-28158207; 17-A North Boag Rd, T. Nagar); Delhi (Map pp126-7; ☎ 011-46000915; www.mfa.gov.sg/newdelhi; E6 Chandragupta Marg); Mumbai (Map pp780-1; ☎ 022-22043205; Maker Chambers IV, 10th fl, 222 Jamnalal Bajaj Rd, Nariman Point)

South Africa Delhi (Map pp122-3; ☎ 011-26149411; www.dha.gov.za; B18 Vasant Marg, Vasant Vihar); Mumbai (Map pp780-1; ☎ 022-23513725; Gandhi Mansion, 20 Altamount Rd, Cumballa Hill)

Sri Lanka Chennai (Map pp1044-5; ☎ 044-24987896; 196 TTK Rd, Alwarpet); Delhi (Map pp126-7; ☎ 011-23010201; www.newdelhi.mission.gov.lk; 27 Kautilya Marg, Chanakyapuri); Mumbai (Map p786; ☎ 022-22045861; Mulla House, 34 Homi Modi St, Fort)

Switzerland Delhi (Map pp126-7; ☎ 011-26878372; www.eda.admin.ch; Nyaya Marg, Chanakyapuri); Mumbai (Map pp780-1; ☎ 022-22884563-65; 102 Maker Chambers IV, 10th fl, 222 Jamnalal Bajaj Marg, Nariman Point)

Thailand Chennai (off Map pp1044-5; ☎ 044-42300730; 21/22 Arunachalam Rd, Kotturpuram); Delhi (Map pp126-7; ☎ 011-26118104; www.thaiemb.org.in; 56N Nyaya Marg, Chanakyapuri); Kolkata (Map pp504-5; ☎ 033-24407836; 18B Mandeville Gardens, Gariahat); Mumbai (Map pp780-1; ☎ 022-22823535; Dalamal House, 1st fl, Jamnalal Bajai Marg, Nariman Point)

UK Chennai (Map pp1044-5; ☎ 044-42192151; 20 Anderson Rd); Delhi (Map pp126-7; ☎ 011-26872161; www.ukinindia.com; Shantipath, Chanakyapuri); Kolkata (Map p510; ☎ 033-22885172; 1 Ho Chi Minh Sarani); Mumbai (Map pp780-1; ☎ 022-66502222; Naman Chambers, C/32 G Block Bandra Kurla Complex, Bandra East)

USA Chennai (Map pp1044-5; ☎ 044-28574242; Gemini Circle, 220 Anna Salai); Delhi (Map pp126-7; ☎ 011-24198000; http://newdelhi.usembassy.gov/; Shantipath, Chanakyapuri); Kolkata (Map p510; ☎ 033-39842400; 5/1 Ho Chi Minh Sarani); Mumbai (Map pp780-1; ☎ 022-23633611; Lincoln House, 78 Bhulabhai Desai Rd, Breach Candy)

FOOD

Nowhere in the world makes such an inspired use of spices as India. To get a taste of what's on offer read the Food & Drink chapter and the Eating sections of the regional chapters. For opening hours see p1141 and the book's Eating sections.

GAY & LESBIAN TRAVELLERS

Technically, homosexual relations for men are illegal in India and the penalties for transgression can theoretically be up to life imprisonment. There's no law against lesbian sexual relations.

Foreigners are unlikely to be targeted by India's homosexuality laws, but members of the Indian community have been campaigning against this legislation for years. The campaign to repeal 'Section 377' has recently attracted some high-profile supporters – for more information read p64.

There are low-key gay scenes in a number of cities including Mumbai, Delhi, Kolkata, Bengaluru and Chandigarh (Gay Pride marches have been held at some of these centres).

However India is, broadly speaking, a conservative society and public displays of affection are generally frowned upon for heterosexual couples as well as gay and lesbian couples. In fact, men holding hands can be more commonly seen than with heterosexual couples, though this is generally a sign of friendship rather than sexual orientation.

Publications & Websites

To tap into Delhi's gay scene, join the Gay Delhi email list: send a blank email to gaydelhi-subscribe@yahoogroups.com. There are regular socials and this is also a point of contact for the Delhi Frontrunners & Walkers, a weekly running and walking group.

For further information (including local events) have a look at **Indian Dost** (www.indiandost.com/gay.php), **Gay Bombay** (www.gaybombay.org), **Humrahi** (www.geocities.com/WestHollywood/Heights/7258) and **Humsafar** (www.humsafar.org).

Support Groups

There are support groups in a number of Indian cities that include the following.

Several organisations exist in Bengaluru: **Good As You** (www.sawnet.org/orgns/good_as_you.html; Bengaluru) is a support group for gay, lesbian, bisexual and transgender people. Meanwhile, the NGO **Swabhava** (Map p902; ☎ 080-22230959; http://swabhava_trust.tripod.com; 4th fl MS Plaza, No 1, Old No 566, 13th A Cross, 4th Main, Sampangiramnagar, Bengaluru) works directly with issues affecting lesbians, gays, bisexuals and transgender people in ways that include publications, advocacy, counselling and training programs. It also operates the **Sahaya Helpline** (☎ 080-22230959). Volunteer opportunities exist. **Sangama** (Map p902; ☎ 080-23438840/23438843; www.sangama.org; 9 Ababil Patil Cheluvappa St, JC Nagar, Bengaluru) deals with crisis intervention and provides a community outreach service for gay and bisexual men and women, transgenders and *hijras* (transvestites and eunuchs).

In Kolkata, the **Counsel Club** (☎ 033-23598130; counselclub93@hotmail.com; c/o Ranjan, Post Bag No 794, Kolkata) provides support for gays, lesbians, transgenders and bisexuals and arranges monthly meetings. The associated **Palm Avenue Integration Society** (integration99@rediffmail.com; c/o Pawan, Post Bag No 10237, Kolkata) offers health advice. There's also a library service; opening times and directions are by request. **Sappho** (☎ 033-24419995; www.sapphokolkata.org; Kolkata) operates as a support group for lesbian, bisexual and transgender women.

In Chennai, **Sahodaran** (Map pp1044-5; ☎ 044-8252869; www.sahodaran.faithweb.com; 127 Sterling Rd, 1st fl, Nungambakkam, Chennai) is a support group for gay men. It holds social-group meetings and activities.

In Mumbai, the **Humsafar Trust** (Map p796; ☎ 022-26673800; www.humsafar.org; Old BMC Bldg, Vakola Post Office, Nehru Rd, Vakola, Santa Cruz East, Mumbai) runs gay and transgender support groups and advocacy programs. Their drop-in centre in Santa Cruz East hosts workshops and has a library; it's also the place to pick up a copy of the pioneering gay-and-lesbian magazine *Bombay Dost* and is one of the venues for 'Sunday High', a monthly screening of queer-interest films.

HOLIDAYS

In India there are officially three national public holidays: Republic Day (26 January), Independence Day (15 August) and Gandhi Jayanti (2 October). Every state celebrates its own official holidays, which cover bank holidays for government workers as well as major religious festivals – usually Diwali, Dussehra and Holi (Hindu), Nanak Jayanti (Sikh), Eid al-Fitr (Muslim), Mahavir Jayanti (Jain), Buddha Jayanti (Buddhist) and Easter and Christmas (Christian). For more on religious festivals, see the Events Calendar chapter.

Most businesses (offices, shops etc) and tourist sites close on public holidays, but transport is usually unaffected. It's wise to make transport and hotel reservations well in advance if you intend visiting during major festivals.

INSURANCE

Every traveller should take out travel insurance – if you can't afford it, you can't afford the consequences if something does go wrong. Make sure that your policy covers theft of property and medical treatment, as well as air evacuation. Be aware that some policies place restrictions on potentially dangerous activities such as scuba-diving, skiing, motorcycling, trekking, paragliding and climbing. When hiring a motorcycle in India, make sure the rental policy includes at least third-party insurance; see p1184.

There are hundreds of different policies so read the small print carefully and make sure your activities are covered. In some areas, trekking agents may only accept customers who have cover for emergency helicopter evacuation. Some policies pay doctors and hospitals directly; others expect you to pay upfront and claim the money back later (keep all documentation for your claim). It's crucial to get a police report in India if you've had anything stolen; insurance companies may refuse to reimburse you without one. Also see p1191.

For insurance recommendations, click www.lonelyplanet.com/travel_services.

INTERNET ACCESS

Internet cafes are widespread in India and connections are usually reasonably fast, except in more remote areas. Bandwidth load tend to be lowest in the early morning and early afternoon. Internet charges vary regionally (see regional chapters), usually falling anywhere between Rs20 and Rs65 per hour and often with a 15 to 30-minute minimum.

It's a good idea to write and save your messages in a text application before pasting them into your browser – power cuts can be common and all too often your hard-crafted email can vanish into the ether. Be wary of sending sensitive financial information from internet cafes; some places are able to use keystroke-capturing technology to access passwords and emails. Using online banking on any nonsecure system is generally unwise.

If you're travelling with a laptop many internet cafes can supply you with internet access over a LAN Ethernet cable, or you can join an international roaming service with an Indian dial-up number, or take out an account with a local Internet Service Provider (ISP); inquire locally. Make sure your modem is compatible with the telephone and dial-up system in India (an external global modem may be necessary).

Another useful investment in India is a fuse-protected universal AC adaptor to protect your circuit board from power surges.

Plug adaptors are widely available throughout India, but bring spare plug fuses from home. Wi-fi access is available in an ever-increasing number of hotels (mostly top-end properties and a growing number of midrange ones) and some coffee shops in larger cities, but again, avoid sending credit-card details or other personal data over a wireless connection. For more information on travelling with a portable computer try www.teleadapt.com.

In this book, hotels offering internet access to guests are marked by 🖳 . See p24 for useful India-specific web resources.

LAUNDRY

Almost all hotels (of every budget) offer a same- or next-day laundry service. Most employ the services of dhobi-wallahs – washermen and women who will diligently bash your wet clothes against rocks and scrubbing boards, returning them spotlessly clean and ironed, but possibly missing a button or two. If you don't think your clothes will stand up to the treatment, wash them yourself or give them to a drycleaner. Washing powder can be bought cheaply virtually everywhere. Note that some hotels ban washing clothes in their rooms.

Most laundries and hotels charge per item (you'll usually be required to submit a list with your dirty clothes). It can take longer to dry clothes during the (humid) monsoon.

LEGAL MATTERS

If you're in a sticky legal situation, immediately contact your embassy (p1147). However, be aware that all your embassy may be able to do is monitor your treatment in custody and arrange a lawyer. In the Indian justice system, the burden of proof can often be on the accused and stints in prison before trial are not unheard of.

You should always carry your passport; police are entitled to ask you for identification at any time.

Antisocial Behaviour

Recent laws have made smoking any form of tobacco in public illegal throughout India. The punishment (which is variably enforced) for breaking this rule is a fine of at least Rs200. People are free to smoke inside their homes and in most open spaces such as streets (heed any signs stating otherwise). A number of Indian cities have also banned spitting and littering.

WARNING: BHANG LASSI

Although it's rarely printed in menus, some restaurants in popular tourist centres will clandestinely whip up bhang lassi, a yoghurt and iced-water beverage laced with cannabis (occasionally other narcotics). Commonly dubbed 'special lassi', this often potent concoction can cause varying degrees of ecstasy, drawn-out delirium, hallucination, nausea and paranoia. Note that some travellers have been ill for several days, robbed, or hurt in accidents, after drinking this fickle brew. A few towns have legal (controlled) bhang outlets such as the Bhang Shop in Jaisalmer (p245).

Drugs

Possession of any illegal drug is regarded as a criminal offence. If convicted, the *minimum* sentence is 10 years, with very little chance of remission or parole.

Cases can take months (even several years) to appear before a court, while the accused may have to wait in prison, and there's usually a hefty monetary fine on top of any custodial sentence. The police have been getting particularly tough on foreigners who use drugs, so you should take this risk very seriously. Note that travellers have been targeted in sting operations in Manali and other backpacker enclaves.

Marijuana grows wild in various parts of India, but consuming it is still an offence, except in towns where bhang is legally sold for religious rituals.

MAPS

Maps available inside India are of variable quality. Some of the better map series include TTK Discover India, **Nest & Wings** (www.nestwings .com), **Eicher** (http://maps.eicherworld.com/) and **Nelles** (www.nelles-verlag.de). The **Survey of India** (www.sur veyofindia.gov.in) also publishes decent city, state and country maps, but some titles are rather frustratingly restricted for security reasons. All of these maps are available at good bookshops, or you can buy them online from Delhi's **India Map Store** (www.indiamapstore.com).

Throughout India, most state-government tourist offices stock basic local maps. These are often dated and lacking in essential detail, but are fine for general orientation purposes.

MONEY

The Indian rupee (Rs) is divided into 100 paise (p), but paise coins are becoming increasingly rare. Coins come in denominations of 5p, 10p, 20p, 25p and 50p, and Rs1, Rs2 and Rs5; notes come in Rs5, Rs10, Rs20, Rs50, Rs100, Rs500 and Rs1000 (this last one is handy for large bills but can pose problems in regards to getting change for small services). The Indian rupee is linked to a basket of currencies and its value is generally stable; see the inside front cover of this book for exchange rates.

ATMs linked to international networks are common in most urban centres throughout India. However, carry cash or travellers cheques as backup in case the power goes down, the ATM is out of order, your card is rejected, or you lose or break your plastic.

You need to present your passport whenever you officially change currency or travellers cheques (don't forget to keep money-exchange receipts in case you need to change excess rupees into foreign currency before departing India). Commission for foreign exchange still exists but is usually nominal. For information about costs, see p21.

Read p1146 for tips on keeping money safe during your trip.

ATMs

Modern 24-hour ATMs are found in most urban centres across the country, though the ATM may not always be in the same place as the bank branch. The most commonly accepted cards are Visa, MasterCard, Cirrus, Maestro and Plus. Some banks in India that accept foreign cards include Citibank, HDFC, ICICI, HSBC and the State Bank of India. Away from major towns, always carry cash or travellers cheques as back-up.

Banks usually impose higher charges on international transactions, but this may be cancelled out by the favourable exchange rates between banks. Reduce charges by making larger transactions less often. Before your trip, check whether your card can reliably access banking networks in India and ask for details of charges. Some travellers have reported their home banks blocking use of cards, making it advisable to notify your bank that you'll be using it in India (provide dates); also take along your bank's phone number (as even some pre-warned banks have automated programs that detect and block nonroutine banking).

DIRECTORY

Note that some ATMs can snatch back money if you don't remove it within around 30 seconds. Conversely, other machines can take more than 30 seconds to actually release cash, so don't panic if the money doesn't appear instantaneously.

The ATMs listed in this book's regional chapters accept foreign cards (but not necessarily all types of cards). Always keep the emergency lost-and-stolen numbers for your credit cards in a safe place, separate from your cards, and report any loss or theft immediately.

Black Market

Black-market moneychangers do exist in India but legal moneychangers are so common that there's no reason to use them, except to possibly change small amounts of cash at land border crossings. As a rule, if someone approaches you on the street and offers to change money, you're probably being set up for a scam.

Cash

Major currencies such as US dollars, British pounds and euros are easy to change throughout India, although some bank branches insist on travellers cheques only. Quite a few banks also accept other currencies such as Australian and Canadian dollars, and Swiss francs. Private moneychangers deal with a wider range of currencies, but Pakistani, Nepali and Bangladeshi currency can be harder to change away from the border. When travelling off the beaten track, always carry an adequate stock of rupees.

Whenever changing money, check every note. Banks staple bills together into bricks, which puts a lot of wear and tear on the currency. Don't accept any filthy, ripped or disintegrating notes, as these may be difficult to use.

It can be tough getting change in India (particularly at small shops, taxis etc) making it wise to maintain a stock of smaller currency. Try to stockpile Rs10, Rs20 and Rs50 notes.

Officially, you cannot take rupees out of India, but this is laxly enforced. However, you can change any leftover rupees back into foreign currency, most easily at the airport (some banks have a Rs1000 minimum). You may be required to present encashment certificates or credit-card/ATM receipts, and you may also have to show your passport and airline ticket.

Credit Cards

Credit cards are accepted at a growing number of shops, upmarket restaurants, and midrange and top-end hotels, and you can also usually use them to pay for flights and train tickets. However, be wary of scams; see p1145. Cash advances on major credit cards are also possible at some banks without ATMs. MasterCard and Visa are the most widely accepted cards; for details about whether you can access home accounts in India, inquire at your bank before leaving.

Encashment Certificates

By law, all foreign currency must be changed at official moneychangers or banks. For every (official) foreign-exchange transaction, you'll receive an encashment certificate (receipt), which will allow you to re-exchange rupees into foreign currency when departing India. You'll need to have encashment certificates totalling the amount of rupees you intend changing back to foreign currency. Printed receipts from ATMs are also accepted as evidence of an international transaction at most banks.

Traditionally, money-exchange receipts have also been required when paying for tourist-quota train tickets in rupees, but this requirement has been relaxed.

International Transfers

If you run out of money, someone back home can wire you cash via moneychangers affiliated with **Moneygram** (www.moneygram.com) or **Western Union** (www.westernunion.com). A fee is added to the transaction. To collect cash, bring your passport and the name and reference number of the person who sent the funds.

Moneychangers

Private moneychangers are usually open for longer hours than banks, and they're found almost everywhere (many also double as internet cafes and travel agents). Compare rates with those at the bank and, as elsewhere, check you are given the correct amount. Upmarket hotels may also change money, but their rates are usually not as competitive as the banks or private moneychangers.

Tipping, Baksheesh & Bargaining

In tourist restaurants or hotels, a service fee is usually already added to your bill and tipping is optional. Elsewhere, a tip is appreciated. Hotel bellboys and train/airport porters appreciate anything around Rs50 to carry heavy bags, and hotel staff should be given similar gratuities for services above and beyond the call of duty. It's not mandatory to tip taxi or rickshaw drivers, but it's good to tip drivers who are honest about the fare. If you hire a car with driver for more than a couple of days, a tip is recommended for good service – details on p1181.

Baksheesh can loosely be defined as a 'tip', and it covers everything from alms for beggars to bribes.

Many Indians implore tourists not to hand out sweets, pens or money to children, as it encourages them to beg. To make a lasting difference, donate to a reputable school or charitable organisation (see p1165).

When it comes to shopping, apart from fixed-price shops (such as government emporiums and fair-trade cooperatives), bargaining is the norm; read the Art of Haggling boxed text, p1161.

Travellers Cheques

All major brands are accepted in India, but some banks may only accept cheques from American Express (Amex) and Thomas Cook. Pounds sterling and US dollars are the safest currencies, especially in smaller towns. Charges for changing travellers cheques vary from place to place and bank to bank.

Always keep an emergency cash stash in case you lose your travellers cheques, and keep a record of the cheques' serial numbers separate from your cheques, along with the proof-of-purchase slips, encashment vouchers and photocopied passport details. If you lose your cheques, contact the American Express or Thomas Cook office in Delhi (see p121).

To replace lost travellers cheques, you need the proof-of-purchase slip and the numbers of the missing cheques (some places require a photocopy of the police report and a passport photo). If you don't have the numbers of your missing cheques, Amex (or whichever company has issued them) will contact the place where you bought them.

PHOTOGRAPHY

For useful tips and techniques on travel photography, read Lonely Planet's travel photography guides, including *Travel Photography, Landscape Photography, Wildlife Travel Photography, Urban Travel Photography* and *People Photography*.

Digital

Memory cards for digital cameras are available from photographic shops in most large cities and towns. However, the quality of memory cards is variable – some don't carry the advertised amount of data. Expect to pay upwards of Rs500 for a 1GB card. To be safe, regularly back up your memory card to CD; internet cafes may offer this service for Rs60 to Rs110 per disk. Some photographic shops make prints from digital photographs for roughly the standard print-and-processing charge.

Print & Slide

Colour-print film-processing facilities are readily available in most urban centres. Film is relatively cheap and the quality is usually good, but you'll only find colour-slide film in the major cities and tourist traps. On average, developing costs around Rs5 per 4x6 print, plus Rs20 for processing. Passport photos are available from many photo shops for around Rs100 to Rs125 (four visa-size shots).

Always check the use-by date on local film and slide stock. Make sure you get a sealed packet and that you're not handed a roll that's been sitting in a glass cabinet in the sunshine for the last few months. Be wary of buying film from street hawkers – unscrupulous characters have been known to load old/damaged film into new-looking canisters. It's best to only buy film from reputable stores – and preferably film that's been refrigerated.

Restrictions

India is touchy about anyone taking photographs of military installations – this can include train stations, bridges, airports, military sites and sensitive border regions. Photography from the air is officially prohibited, although airlines rarely enforce this.

Many places of worship – such as monasteries, temples and mosques – also prohibit photography. Respect these proscriptions and always ask when in doubt, as taking photographs of forbidden images can cause serious offence. See p62 for etiquette about photographing people.

POST

India has the biggest postal network on earth, with over 155,500 post offices. Mail and posterestante services are generally good, although the speed of delivery will depend on the efficiency of any given office. Airmail is faster and more reliable than sea mail, although it's best to use courier services (such as DHL) to send and receive items of value; expect to pay around Rs3000 per kilogram to Europe, Australia or the USA. Private couriers are often cheaper, but goods may be repacked into large packages to cut costs and things sometimes go missing.

Receiving Mail

To receive mail in India, ask senders to address letters to you with your surname in capital letters and underlined, followed by poste restante, GPO (main post office), and the city or town in question. Many 'lost' letters are simply misfiled under given/first names, so check under both your names and ask senders to provide a return address in case you don't collect your mail. Letters sent via poste restante are generally held for around one to two months before being returned. To claim mail, you'll need to show your passport. It's best to have any parcels sent to you by registered post.

Sending Mail

Posting letters/aerogrammes to anywhere overseas costs Rs20/15, while Rs12 is the usual cost for international postcards. For postcards, stick on the stamps *before* actually writing on them, as post offices can give you as many as four stamps per card. Sending a letter overseas by registered post adds Rs15 to the stamp cost.

In terms of posting parcels, some post offices can be relatively straightforward while others involve multiple counters and lots of queuing. Some services are only offered at certain times of the day (often mornings, but check locally).

Prices vary depending on weight (including packing material) and you have a choice of airmail (delivery in one to three weeks), sea mail (two to four months), or Surface Air-Lifted (SAL) – a curious hybrid where parcels travel by both air and sea (around one month). Parcels must be packed up in white linen and the seams sealed with wax. Local tailors offer this service, or there may be a parcel-packing service at the post office itself. Carry a permanent marker to write on the parcel any information requested by the desk. The post office can provide the necessary customs declaration forms and these must be stitched or pasted to the parcel. If the contents

are a gift under the value of Rs1000, you won't have to pay duty at the delivery end.

Parcel post has a maximum of 20kg to 30kg depending on the destination, and charges vary depending on whether you go by air or sea (prices on application).

A small package costs Rs40 (up to 100g) to any country and Rs30 per additional 100g (up to a maximum of 2000g; different charges apply for higher weights than this). You also have the option of the EMS (express mail service; delivery within three days) for around 30% more than the normal airmail price.

Books or printed matter can go by (inexpensive) international book post for Rs350 (maximum 5kg), but the package must be wrapped with a hole that reveals the contents for inspection by customs – tailors are experienced in creating this in such a way that nothing falls out. The website for **India Post** (www.indiapost.gov.in) has an online calculator for assorted domestic and international postal tariffs.

Be cautious with places that offer to mail things to your home address after you have bought them. Government emporiums are usually fine, but for most other places it pays to do the posting yourself.

SHOPPING

India is an Aladdin's cave of retail goodies, with rambunctious bazaars and swanky boutiques beckoning shoppers with twinkling gemstones, startling sculptures, sumptuous silks, village artworks, colourful shawls, handsome carpets and oodles of glorious handicrafts.

Every region has its own special arts and crafts, usually showcased in state emporiums and cottage industries' (fair-trade) cooperatives. These shops normally charge fair fixed prices; almost everywhere else, you'll have to don your haggling hat (read the Art of Haggling boxed text, p1161). Opening hours for shops vary (consult the Shopping sections of regional chapters).

Be cautious when buying items that include delivery to your country of residence, and be wary of being led to shops by smooth-talking touts (see p1147). Exporting antiques is prohibited (read p1158).

Bronze Figures, Pottery, Stone Carving & Terracotta

In southern India and parts of the Himalaya, small images of deities are created by the age-

---

RESPONSIBLE SHOPPING

Overall, a comparatively small proportion of the money brought to India by tourism reaches people in rural areas. Travellers can make a greater contribution by shopping at community cooperatives, set up to protect and promote traditional cottage industries, and to provide education, training and a sustainable livelihood at the grassroots level. Many of these projects focus on refugees, low-caste women, tribal people and others living on society's fringes.

The quality of products sold at cooperatives is high and the prices are usually fixed, which means you won't have to haggle. A share of the sales money is channelled directly into social projects such as schools, healthcare, training and other advocacy programs for socially disadvantaged groups. Shopping at the national network of Khadi & Village Industries emporiums will also contribute to rural communities.

Wherever you travel, keep your eyes peeled for fair-trade cooperatives and also see this book's regional chapters for recommendations, where they exist.

---

old lost-wax process. A wax figure is made, a mould is formed around it, and the wax is melted and poured out and replaced with molten metal; the mould is then broken open to reveal the figure inside. Figures of Shiva as dancing Nataraja are the most popular items, but you can also find images of Buddha and numerous deities from the Hindu pantheon.

The West Bengalese also employ the lost-wax process to make Dokra tribal bell sculptures, while in the Bastar region of Chhattisgarh, the Ghadwa Tribe has an interesting twist on the lost-wax process by using a fine wax thread to cover the metal mould, leaving a lattice-like design on the final product.

In Buddhist areas, you can find very striking bronze statues of Buddha and the Tantric gods, finished off with finely polished and painted faces.

In Mamallapuram (p1064) in Tamil Nadu, craftsmen using local granite and soapstone have revived the ancient artistry of the Pallava sculptors; souvenirs range from tiny stone elephants to enormous deity statues weighing half a tonne. Tamil Nadu is also known for the bronzeware from Thanjavur (p1087) and Trichy (Tiruchirappalli; p1087).

A number of places produce attractive terracotta work, ranging from vases and decorative flowerpots to terracotta images of deities, and children's toys.

Jaipur (p179) in Rajasthan specialises in blue-glazed pottery with floral and geometric motifs. At temples across India you can buy small clay or plaster effigies of Hindu deities.

Carpets

Carpet-making is a living craft in India, with workshops across the country producing fine wool and silkwork in traditional and contemporary designs. The finest carpets are produced in Kashmir and the Buddhist heartlands of Ladakh, Himachal Pradesh, Sikkim and West Bengal. Carpet-making is also a major revenue earner for Tibetan refugees; most refugee settlements have cooperative carpet workshops. You can also find reproductions of tribal Turkmen and Afghan designs in states such as Uttar Pradesh. Antique carpets usually aren't antique – unless you buy from an internationally reputable dealer; stick to 'new' carpets.

The price of a carpet will be determined by the number and the size of the hand-tied knots, the range of dyes and colours, the intricacy of the design and the material. Silk carpets cost more and look more luxurious, but wool carpets usually last longer. Expect to pay upwards of US$200 for a good quality 90cm by 1.5m (or 90cm by 1.8m, depending on the region) wool carpet, and around US$2000 for a similar sized carpet in silk. Tibetan carpets are cheaper, reflecting the relative simplicity of the designs; many refugee cooperatives sell 90cm by 1.5m carpets for around US$100 or less.

A number of people buy carpets under the mistaken belief that they can be sold for a profit back home. Unless you really know your carpets and the carpet market in your home country, it's best to buy a carpet simply because you love it. Many places can ship carpets home for a fee – although it may be safest to send things independently to avoid scams (depending on the shop; use your instinct) – or you can carry them in the plane's hold (allow 5kg to 10kg of your baggage allowance for a 90cm by 1.5m carpet).

DIRECTORY

CARPETS & CHILD LABOUR

Children have been employed as carpet weavers in the subcontinent for centuries, and many child-care charities from within and beyond India are campaigning against the use of child labour by the carpet industry. Although it's impossible to get accurate figures, various published reports suggest there are upwards of 100,000 child carpet weavers in India.

Unfortunately, the issue is more complicated than it first appears. In many areas, education is often not an option, for both economic and cultural reasons, and the alternative to child labour may not be school but hunger for the whole family. We encourage travellers to buy from carpet-weaving cooperatives that employ adult weavers *and* provide education for their children, breaking the cycle of child labour.

India's **Carpet Export Promotion Council** (www.india-carpets.com) is campaigning to eliminate child labour from the carpet industry by penalising factories that use children, and by founding schools to provide an alternative to carpet-making. Ultimately, the only thing that can stop child labour is compulsory education for children. However, the economic and social obstacles are significant, often making new initiatives difficult to implement.

Unfortunately for the buyer, there's no easy way of knowing whether a carpet has been made by children. Shops are unlikely to admit to using child labour and most of the international labelling schemes for carpets have been discredited. The carpets produced by Tibetan refugee cooperatives are almost always made by adults, while Uttar Pradesh is the undisputed capital of child labour in India. Government emporiums and charitable cooperatives are usually the best places to buy.

In both Kashmir and Rajasthan, you can also find coarsely woven woollen *numdas* (or *namdas*), which are much cheaper than knotted carpets. Various regions manufacture flat-weave *dhurries* (kilimlike cotton rugs), including Kashmir, Himachal Pradesh, Rajasthan and Uttar Pradesh. Kashmiris also produce striking *gabbas*, made from chain-stitched wool or silk.

Jewellery

Virtually every town in India has at least one bangle shop. These sell an extraordinary variety ranging from colourful plastic and glass to shiny brass and silver.

Heavy folk-art silver jewellery can be bought in various parts of the country, particularly in Rajasthan – Jaipur (p179), Udaipur (p223) and Pushkar (p200) are good places to find silver jewellery pitched at foreign tastes. Jaipur is also renowned for its precious and semiprecious gems – and gem scams (see p1145 and p179). Throughout India you can find finely crafted gold and silver rings, anklets, earrings, toe rings, necklaces and bangles, and pieces can often be crafted to order.

Chunky Tibetan jewellery made from silver (or white metal) and semiprecious stones is sold all over India. Many pieces feature Buddhist motifs and text in Tibetan script, including the famous mantra *Om Mani Padme Hum*. Some of the pieces sold in Tibetan

centres such as McLeod Ganj and Leh are genuine antiques but be aware that there's a huge industry in India, Nepal and China making artificially aged souvenirs. If you feel like being creative, loose beads of agate, turquoise, carnelian and silver are widely available. Buddhist meditation beaded strings made of gems or wood also make good souvenirs.

Pearls are produced by most seaside states. They're a speciality of Hyderabad (p967) and pearls are crafted into jewellery in many other areas. You'll find them at most state emporiums. Prices vary depending on the colour and shape – you pay more for pure white pearls or rare colours like black. Perfectly round pearls are generally more expensive than misshapen or elongated pearls however the quirky shapes of Indian pearls can actually be more alluring than the perfect round balls. A single strand of seeded pearls can cost as little as Rs300, but better-quality pearls start at around Rs700.

Cuttack in Orissa (p666) is famed for its lacelike silver filigree work known as *tarakasi*. A silver framework is made and then filled in with delicate curls and ribbons of thin silver.

Leatherwork

As cows are sacred in India, leatherwork is made from buffalos, camels, goats or some other substitute. Kanpur in Uttar Pradesh is the country's major leatherwork centre.

Most large cities offer a smart range of modern leather footwear at very reasonable prices, some stitched with zillions of sparkly sequins – marvellous partywear!

Chappals, those wonderful (often curly-toed) leather sandals, are sold throughout India but are particularly good in the Maharashtran cities of Kolhapur, Pune and Matheran. The states of Punjab and Rajasthan (especially Jaipur) are famed for jootis (traditional, often pointy-toed slip-in shoes).

In Bikaner (Rajasthan), artisans decorate camel hide with gold to produce beautiful mirror frames, boxes and bottles, while in Indore in Madhya Pradesh, craftspeople stretch leather over wire and cloth frameworks to make cute toy animals. In most big cities you'll find well-made, competitively priced leather handbags, wallets, belts and other accessories.

Metalwork & Marble

You'll find copper and brassware throughout India. Candleholders, trays, bowls, tankards and ashtrays are particularly popular buys. In Rajasthan and Uttar Pradesh, the brass is inlaid with exquisite designs in red, green and blue enamel. *Bidri* – a form of damascening where silver is inlaid in gunmetal (an alloy of zinc, copper, lead and tin) – is used to make boxes and ornaments in Bidar (Karnataka); see the boxed text on *bidri*, p952.

Many Tibetan religious objects are created by inlaying silver in copper; prayer wheels, ceremonial horns and traditional document cases are all inexpensive buys. Resist the urge to buy *kangling* (Tibetan horns) and *kapala* (ceremonial bowls) made from inlaid human leg bones and skulls – they are illegal!

In all Indian towns, you can find *kadhai* (Indian woks, also known as *balti*) and other items of cookware for incredibly low prices. Beaten-brass pots are particularly attractive, while steel storage vessels, copper-bottomed cooking pans and steel thali trays are also popular souvenirs.

The people of Bastar in Chhattisgarh discovered a method of smelting iron some 35,000 years ago. Similar techniques are used today to create abstract depictions of spindly, pointillist animal and human figures, which are often also made into functional items such as lamp stands and coat racks.

A sizable cottage industry has sprung up in Agra reproducing the ancient Mughal art

form of *pietra dura* (inlaying marble with semiprecious stones). The inspiration for most pieces comes from the Taj Mahal.

Musical Instruments

Quality Indian musical instruments are mostly available in the larger cities, especially Kolkata, Varanasi and Delhi. Prices vary according to the quality – and sound – of the instrument.

Decent tabla sets with a wooden tabla (tuned treble drum) and metal *doogri* (bass tone drum) cost upwards of Rs3000. Cheaper sets are generally heavier and often sound inferior.

Sitars range anywhere from Rs4000 to Rs20,000 (possibly even more). The sound of each sitar will vary with the wood used and the shape of the gourd, so try a few. Note that some cheaper sitars can warp in colder or hotter climates. On any sitar, make sure the strings ring clearly and check the gourd carefully for damage. Spare string sets, sitar plectrums and a screw-in 'amplifier' gourd are sensible additions.

Other popular instruments include the *shehnai* (Indian flute), the *sarod* (like an Indian lute), the harmonium and the *esraj* (similar to an upright violin). Conventional violins are great value – prices start at Rs3000, while Kolkata is especially known for its quality acoustic guitars (from just Rs2500), which are exported worldwide.

Paintings

Reproductions of Indian miniature paintings are widely available but the quality varies, with the cheaper ones having less detail and mostly using inferior materials. Udaipur (p223) and Bikaner in Rajasthan have a particularly good range of shops specialising in modern reproductions on paper and silk, or you can browse Delhi's numerous state emporiums.

In places such as Kerala and Tamil Nadu, you'll come across miniature paintings on leaf skeletons portraying domestic life, rural scenes and deities. In Andhra Pradesh you can buy exquisite cloth paintings called *kalamkari,* which depict deities and historic events; see www.kalamkariart.org for more on this interesting art form.

The artists' community of Raghurajpur (p657) near Puri (Orissa) preserves the age-old art of *pattachitra* painting. Cotton or *tassar* (silk cloth) is covered with a mixture of

PROHIBITED EXPORTS

To protect India's cultural heritage, the export of certain antiques is prohibited. Many 'old' objects are fine, but the difficulties begin if something is verifiably more than 100 years old. Reputable antique dealers know the laws and can make arrangements for an export-clearance certificate for any old items that you're permitted to export. If in doubt, contact Delhi's **Archaeological Survey of India** (Map pp126-7; ☎ 011-23010822; www.asi.nic.in; Janpath; ☒ 9.30am-1pm & 2-6pm Mon-Fri) next to the National Museum. The rules may seem stringent but the loss of artworks and traditional buildings in places such as Ladakh, Himachal Pradesh, Gujarat and Rajasthan, due to the international trade in antiques and carved windows and doorframes, has been alarming. Look for quality reproductions instead.

The Indian Wildlife Protection Act bans any form of wildlife trade. Don't buy any products that endanger threatened species and habitats – doing so can result in heavy fines and even imprisonment. This includes ivory, *shahtoosh* shawls (made from the down of rare Tibetan antelopes), and anything made from the fur, skin, horns or shell of any endangered species. Products made from certain rare plants are also banned.

Note that your home country may have additional laws forbidding the import of restricted items and wildlife parts. The penalties can be severe so know the law before you buy.

gum and chalk; it's then polished, and images of deities and scenes from Hindu legends are painted on with exceedingly fine brushes. Orissa also produces *chitra pothi*, where images are etched onto dried palm-leaf sections with a fine stylus.

Bihar's unique folk art is Mithila (or Madhubani) painting, an ancient art form preserved by the women of Madhubani (see p573). These captivating paintings are most easily found in Patna but are also sold in big city emporiums. Over in Khajuraho, the Adivart Tribal & Folk Art Museum (p685) sells original Bhili paintings.

In all Tibetan Buddhist areas, including Sikkim, parts of Himachal Pradesh and Ladakh, you can find exquisite *thangkas* (rectangular Tibetan paintings on cloth) of Tantric Buddhist deities and ceremonial mandalas. Some perfectly reproduce the glory of the murals in India's medieval gompas (Buddhist monasteries); others are much simpler. Prices vary, but bank on at least Rs3000 for a decent quality *thangka* of A3 size, a lot more for large intricate *thangkas*. The selling of antique *thangkas* is illegal, and you would be unlikely to find the real thing anyway.

Throughout the country (especially in big cities like Delhi, Mumbai and Kolkata) look out for shops and galleries selling brilliant contemporary paintings by local artists.

Papier-Mâché

Artisans in Srinagar (p286) have been producing lacquered papier-mâché for centuries, and papier-mâché-ware is now sold right across India. The basic shape is made in a mould from layers of paper (often recycled newsprint), then painted with fine brushes and lacquered for protection. Prices depend upon the complexity and quality of the design, and the amount of gold leaf used. Many pieces feature patterns of animals and flowers, or hunting scenes from Mughal miniature paintings. You can find papier-mâché bowls, boxes, letter holders, coasters, trays, lamps and Christmas decorations (stars, crescent moons, balls and bells). Weight for weight, these are probably the most cost-effective souvenirs in India but you need to transport them carefully.

Rajasthan is *the* place to buy colourful papier-mâché puppets, which are typically sold as a pair – depicting a husband and wife.

Shawls, Silk & Saris

Indian shawls are famously warm and light-weight – they're often better than the best down jackets. It's worth buying one to use as an emergency blanket on cold night journeys. Shawls are made from all sorts of wool, from lamb's wool to fibres woven from yak, goat and angora-rabbit hair. Many are embroidered with intricate designs. However it's illegal to buy *shahtoosh* shawls, as rare Tibetan antelopes are killed to provide the wool.

The undisputed capital of the Indian shawl is the Kullu Valley in Himachal Pradesh, with dozens of women's cooperatives producing very fine woollen pieces – for further details see p356.

Ladakh and Kashmir are major centres for *pashmina* (wool shawl) production – you'll pay at least Rs6000 for the authentic article – however be aware that many so-called *pashmina* shawls are actually made from a mixture of yarns. Also see the boxed text on p328. Shawls from the Northeast States are famously warm, with bold geometric designs. In Sikkim and West Bengal, you may also find fantastically embroidered Bhutanese shawls. Gujarat's Kutch region produces some particularly distinctive woollen shawls, patterned with subtle embroidery and mirrorwork. Handmade shawls and tweeds can also be found in Ranikhet and Almora in Uttarakhand.

Saris are a very popular souvenir, especially given that they can be easily adapted to other purposes (from cushion covers to skirts). Real silk saris are the most expensive, and the silk usually needs to be washed before it becomes soft. The 'silk capital' of India is Kanchipuram (p1065) in Tamil Nadu, but you can also find fine silk saris (and cheaper scarves) in centres that include Varanasi, Mysore and Kolkata. Assam is renowned for its *muga, endi* and *pat* silks (produced by different species of silkworms), which are widely available in Guwahati. You'll pay upwards of Rs3000 for a quality embroidered silk sari.

Patan (p738), in Gujarat, is the centre for the ancient and laborious craft of *patola*-making – every thread in these fine silk saris is individually hand-dyed before weaving, and patterned borders are woven with real gold. Slightly less involved versions are produced in Rajkot (p768) – only the warp threads are dyed. Gold thread is also used in the famous *kota doria* saris of Kota in Rajasthan.

Aurangabad (p821), in Maharashtra, is the traditional centre for the production of *himroo* shawls, sheets and saris, which are made from a blend of cotton, silk and silver thread. Silk and gold-thread saris produced at Paithan (near Aurangabad) are some of India's finest – prices range from around Rs6000 to a mind-blowing Rs300,000. Other states that are famous for sari production include Madhya Pradesh for *maheshwari* (cotton saris from Maheshwar), *chanderi* saris (silk saris from Chanderi) and Bishnupur (West Bengal) for *baluchari* saris, which employ a traditional form of weaving with untwisted silk thread.

Textiles

Textile production is India's major industry and around 40% takes place at the village level, where it's known as *khadi* (homespun cloth) – hence the government-backed *khadi* emporiums around the country. These inexpensive superstores sell all sorts of items made from homespun cloth, including the popular Nehru jackets and kurta pyjamas (long shirt and loose-fitting trousers) with sales benefiting rural communities.

You'll find a truly amazing variety of weaving and embroidery techniques around India. In tourist centres such as Goa, Rajasthan and Himachal Pradesh, textiles are stitched into popular items such as shoulder bags, wall hangings, cushion covers, bedspreads, clothes and much more. For information about the beautiful embroidery and other textile work of Kutch, read the boxed text on p774.

Appliqué is an ancient art in India, with most states producing their own version, often featuring abstract or anthropomorphic patterns. The traditional lampshades and *pandals* (tents) used in weddings and festivals are usually produced using the same technique.

In Adivasi (tribal) areas of Gujarat and Rajasthan, small pieces of mirrored glass are embroidered onto fabric, creating eye-catching bags, cushion covers and wall hangings. Jamnagar, in Gujarat, is famous for its vibrant *bandhani* (tie-dye work) used for saris, scarves, and anything else that stays still for long enough. Ahmedabad (p727) is a good place to buy Gujarati textiles, and Vadodara (p739) is renowned for block-printed fabrics used for bedspreads and dress material.

Block-printed and woven textiles are sold by fabric shops all over India, often in vivid colour combinations. Each region has its own speciality. The India-wide chain-store **Fabindia** (www.fabindia.com) is one retail outlet striving to preserve traditional patterns and fabrics, transforming them into highly accessible items for home decoration, and Indian and Western-style fashions.

Orissa has a reputation for bright appliqué and *ikat* (a Southeast-Asian technique where thread is tie-dyed before weaving). The town of Pipli (p652), between Bhubaneswar and Puri, produces some particularly striking appliqué work. The techniques used to create *kalamkari* cloth paintings in Andhra Pradesh (a centre for this ancient art is Sri Kalahasti –

DIRECTORY

see p978) and Gujarat are also used to make lovely wall hangings and lamp shades.

Lucknow (p428), in Uttar Pradesh, is noted for hand-woven embroidered *chikan* cloth, which features incredibly intricate floral motifs. Punjab is famous for the attractively folksy *phulkari* embroidery (flowerwork with stitches in diagonal, vertical and horizontal directions), while women in West Bengal use chain stitches to make complex figurative designs called *kantha*. A similar technique is used to make *gabba*, women's kurtas and men's wedding jackets in Kashmir.

Batik can be found throughout India. It's often used for saris and *salwar kameez* (traditional dresslike tunic and trouser combination for women). City boutiques flaunt particularly trendy *salwar kameez* in a staggering array of fabrics and styles. Big Indian cities such as Mumbai, Bengaluru and Delhi are top spots to pick up haute couture by talented Indian designers, as well as moderately priced Western fashions.

Woodcarving

Woodcarving is an ancient art form throughout India. In Kashmir, walnut wood is used to make finely carved wooden screens, tables, jewellery boxes and trays, inspired by the decorative trim of houseboats. Willow cricket bats are another Kashmiri speciality.

Sandalwood carvings of Hindu deities is one of Karnataka's specialities, but you'll pay a king's ransom for the real thing – a 10cm-high Ganesh costs around Rs3000 in sandalwood, compared to Rs300 in kadamb wood. However, the sandalwood will release fragrance for years. Wood inlay is one of Bihar's oldest crafts – you'll find wooden wall hangings, tabletops, trays and boxes inlaid with metals and bone. The religious icons produced from wood inlay in Goa also have a certain chintzy appeal.

At places like Udaipur in Rajasthan, you can buy brightly painted figures of Hindu deities carved from mango wood. In many parts of Rajasthan you can also find fabric printing blocks carved from teak wood.

The carved wooden massage wheels and rollers available at many Hindu pilgrimage sites make good gifts for friends and family back home.

Buddhist woodcarvings are a speciality of Sikkim, Ladakh, Arunachal Pradesh and all Tibetan refugee areas. You'll find wall plaques

of the eight lucky signs, dragons and *chaam* masks, used for ritual dances. Most of the masks are artless reproductions, but you can sometimes find genuine *chaam* masks made from lightweight whitewood or papier-mâché from Rs3000 upwards.

Other Buys

It's little surprise that Indian spices are snapped up by tourists. Virtually all towns have shops and bazaars selling locally made spices at great prices. Karnataka, Kerala, Uttar Pradesh, Rajasthan and Tamil Nadu produce most of the spices that go into garam masala (the 'hot mix' used to flavour Indian curries), while the Northeast States and Sikkim are known for black cardamom and cinnamon bark.

Attar (essential oil mostly made from flowers) shops can be found right around the country. Mysore (p914) is especially famous for its sandalwood oil, while Mumbai is a major centre for the trade of traditional fragrances, including valuable *oud,* made from a rare mould that grows on the bark of the agarwood tree. Ooty and Kodaikanal (both in Tamil Nadu) produce aromatic and medicinal oils from herbs, flowers and eucalyptus.

Indian incense is exported worldwide, with Bengaluru (p901) and Mysore (p914) being major producers, and incense from Auroville (p1078) also well regarded.

Meanwhile, a speciality of Goa is feni (liquor distilled from coconut milk or cashews) – a head-spinning spirit that often comes in decorative bottles.

Quality Indian tea is sold in Darjeeling and Kalimpong (both in West Bengal), Assam and Sikkim, as well as parts of South India. There are also commendable tea retailers in Delhi (see p153) and other urban hubs.

In Bhopal (p689), in Madhya Pradesh, colourful *jari* shoulder bags, embroidered with beads, are a speciality. Also on the portables front, the Northeast States are noted for their beautiful hand-woven baskets and wickerwork – each tribe has its own unique basket shape.

Jodhpur (p230), among other places, is famed for its antiques (but check out p1158 before buying).

In towns with Buddhist communities, such as McLeod Ganj, Leh, Manali, Gangtok, Kalimpong and Darjeeling, keep an eye out for 'Buddha shops' selling devotional objects

---

THE ART OF HAGGLING

Government emporiums, fair-trade cooperatives, department stores and modern shopping centres almost always charge fixed prices. Anywhere else you need to bargain. Shopkeepers in tourist hubs are accustomed to travellers who have lots of money and little time to spend it, so you can often expect to be charged double or triple the 'real' price. Souvenir shops are generally the most notorious.

The first 'rule' to haggling is never to show too much interest in the item you've got your heart set upon. Secondly, resist purchasing the first thing that takes your fancy. Wander around and price items, but don't make it too obvious – if you return to the first shop the vendor will know it's because they are the cheapest (resulting in less haggling leeway).

Decide how much you would be happy paying and then express a casual interest in buying. If you have absolutely no idea of what something should really cost, start by slashing the price by half. The vendor will, most likely, look utterly aghast, but you can now work up and down respectively in small increments until you reach a mutually agreeable price. You'll find that many shopkeepers lower their so-called 'final price' if you head out of the store saying you'll 'think about it'.

Haggling is a way of life in India and is usually taken in good spirit. It should never turn ugly. Always keep in mind exactly how much a rupee is worth in your home currency to put things in perspective. If a vendor seems to be charging an unreasonably high price, simply look elsewhere.

---

such as prayer flags, singing bowls, hand-bells and prayer wheels.

Fine-quality handmade paper – often fashioned into cards, boxes and notebooks – is worth seeking out, with good places to start including Puducherry (p1071), Delhi (p153) and Mumbai (p804).

Hats are also popular – the Assamese make decorated reed-pith sun hats, and Tibetan refugees produce woollen hats, gloves and scarves, which are sold nationwide. There's also the traditional caps worn by men and women of Himalayan tribes; they're available at many towns in Himachal Pradesh.

India has a phenomenal range of books at very competitive prices, including gorgeous leather-bound titles. Music CDs by local musicians are also red-hot value.

So much to buy, so little luggage space… Happy shopping!

SOLO TRAVELLERS

Tourist hubs such as Goa, Rajasthan, Kerala, Manali, McLeod Ganj, Leh, Agra and Varanasi are good places to meet fellow travellers, swap stories, get up-to-the-minute travel tips and find others to travel with. You may also be able to find travel companions on Lonely Planet's **Thorn Tree Travel Forum** (www.lonelyplanet .com/thorntree). Throughout India, travellers often move in roughly the same direction, so it's not unusual to see the same faces over and over again on your trip.

Although most solo travellers experience no major problems in India, some less honourable souls (locals and travellers alike) view lone tourists as an easy target for theft. Don't be paranoid, but like anywhere else in the world, it's wise to stay on your toes in unfamiliar surroundings.

Perhaps the most significant issue facing solo travellers is cost. Single-room rates at guest houses and hotels are sometimes not much lower than double rates; some midrange and top-end places don't even offer a single tariff. However, it's always worth trying to negotiate a lower rate for single occupancy.

In terms of transport, you'll save money if you find others to share taxis and autorickshaws. This is also advisable if you intend hiring a car with driver for longer trips. Solo bus travellers may be able to get the 'co-pilot' (near the driver) seat on buses, which not only has a good view out front, but is also handy if you've got a big bag.

It's worth noting that there have been muggings on single men wandering around isolated areas, even during the day. Information specific to women can be found on p1170.

TELEPHONE

There are few payphones in India, but private PCO/STD/ISD call booths do the same job, offering inexpensive local, interstate and international calls at lower prices than calls made from hotel rooms (especially top-end ones). These booths are found extensively around the country, many open 24 hours. A digital meter displays how much the call is costing and usually provides a printed receipt when the call is finished. Faxes can be sent from quite a few call centres.

Recent years have seen phone costs slide, thanks to competition. There are variations (depending on the operator and destination); in Delhi, for instance, a Vodafone PCO booth charges around Rs1 per minute for an STD call, while international calls hover between Rs5 and Rs10 per minute.

Some booths also offer a 'call-back' service – you ring home, provide the phone number of the booth and wait for people at home to call you back, for a fee of around Rs10 on top of the cost of the preliminary call.

Useful online resources include the **Yellow Pages** (www.indiayellowpages.com) and **Justdial** (www.justdial.com).

Note that getting a line can be difficult in remote country and mountain areas – an engaged signal may just mean that the exchange is overloaded, so keep trying.

Mobile Phones

India is mobile-phone crazy and there's roaming coverage for international GSM phones in most cities and large towns. Mobile-phone numbers in India usually have 10 digits, typically starting with 9. To avoid expensive roaming costs (often highest for incoming calls), get hooked up to the local mobile-phone network. Note that mobiles bought in some countries may be locked to a particular network; you'll have to get the phone unlocked, or buy a local phone (available from Rs2000) to use an Indian SIM card.

Getting connected is inexpensive and, overall, relatively straightforward (larger cities are easiest). Foreigners need to supply one passport photo (take two, just in case) and a photocopy of their passport identity and visa pages (some places will do the photocopying for you).

In most Indian towns you simply buy a prepaid mobile-phone kit (SIM card and phone number, plus an allocation of calls) from around Rs150 from a phone shop or local PCO/STD/ISD booth, internet cafe or grocery store. Thereafter, you must purchase new credits on that network, sold as scratch cards in shops and call centres. Credit must usually be used within a set time limit and

costs vary with the amount of credit on the card. The amount you pay for a credit top-up is not the amount you get on your phone – state taxes and service charges come off first. For some networks, recharge cards are being replaced by direct credit, where you pay the vendor and the credit is deposited straight to your phone – ask which system is in use before you buy.

Calls made within the state or city in which you bought the SIM card are cheap – Rs1 per minute – and you can call internationally for less than Rs10 per minute. SMS messaging is even cheaper. Usually, the more credit you have on your phone, the cheaper the call rate. However, some travellers have reported unreliable signals and problems with international texting (with messages or replies being delayed or failing to get through).

The most popular (and reliable) companies include Airtel, Vodaphone and BSNL. Note that most SIM cards are state specific; they can be used in other states, but you pay for calls at roaming rates and you'll be charged for incoming calls as well as outgoing calls. If, for example, you buy a SIM card in Delhi, calls ex-Delhi will be around Rs1.50 per minute, while the charge to receive a call from anywhere in India (ex-Delhi) is Rs1 per minute.

As the mobile-phone industry continues to evolve, mobile rates, suppliers and coverage are all likely to develop over the life of this book.

Phone Codes

Regular phone numbers have an area code followed by up to eight digits. The government is slowly trying to bring all numbers in India onto the same system, so area codes may change and new digits may be added to numbers with limited warning.

To make a call *to* India from overseas, dial the international access code of the country you're in, then 91 (international country code for India), then the area code (drop the initial zero when calling from abroad), then the local number.

To make an international call *from* India, dial 00 (international access code from India), then the country code of the country you're calling, then the area code and the local number.

Also available is the Home Country Direct service, which gives you access to the international operator in your home country. For the price of a local call, you can then make reverse-charge (collect) or phonecard calls. The number is typically constructed ☎ 000 + the country code of your home country + 17. Some countries and their numbers:

Country	Number
Australia	☎ 0006117
Germany	☎ 0004917
Italy	☎ 0003917
Japan	☎ 0008117
Netherlands	☎ 0003117
New Zealand	☎ 0006417
UK	☎ 0004417
USA	☎ 000117

TIME

India is 5½ hours ahead of GMT/UTC, 4½ hours behind Australian Eastern Standard Time (EST) and 10½ hours ahead of American EST. The local standard time is known as IST (Indian Standard Time), although some affectionately dub it 'Indian Stretchable Time'. The floating half-hour was added to maximise daylight hours over such a vast country.

TOILETS

Public toilets are most easily found in major cities and tourist sites, with some of the most hygienic being those built by Sulabh International – also see p138. The cleanest toilets (usually with sit-down and squat choices) are most reliably found at modern restaurants, shopping complexes and cinemas. It's always a good idea to carry your own toilet paper, just in case.

When it comes to effluent etiquette, especially beyond urban centres, locals may use the 'hand-and-water' technique, which involves cleaning one's bottom with a small jug of water and the left hand.

Also see p1140.

TOURIST INFORMATION
Local Tourist Offices

In addition to the Government of India tourist offices (also known as 'India Tourism') each state maintains its own network of tourist offices. These vary in their efficiency and usefulness – some are run by enthusiastic souls who go out of their way to help, others are basically a vehicle for the sale of State Tourism Development Corporation tours. Most of the tourist offices have free brochures and often a free (or inexpensive) local map (for further map information see p1151).

The first stop for information should be the tourism website of the Government of India, **Incredible India** (www.incredibleindia.org); for details of its regional offices around India, click on the 'Help Desk' tab at the top of the homepage.

See regional chapters for contact details of relevant tourist offices.

Tourist Offices Abroad

The Government of India operates the following tourist offices abroad.

Australia (☎ 02-9221 9555; info@indiatourism.com. au; Level 5, 135 King St, Glasshouse Shopping Complex, Sydney, NSW, 2000)

Canada (☎ 416-962 3787; info@indiatourismcanada.ca; 60 Bloor St, West Ste 1003, Toronto, M4 W3 B8)

China (☎ 86-1065686294; beijing@indiatourism.org.cn; 29th fl, East Tower, LG Twin Towers, B-12 Jianguomenwai Dajie, Chaoyang District)

Dubai (☎ 971-4-2274848; goirto@eim.ae; NASA Bldg, AL Maktoum Rd, Deira, UAE)

France (☎ 01 4523 3045; indtourparis@aol.com; 11-13 Bis Blvd Haussmann, F-75009 Paris)

Germany (☎ 069-2429490; office@india-tourism.com; Basler Strasse 48, D-60329 Frankfurt Am-Main 1)

Italy (☎ 02-8053506; info@indiatourismmilan.com; Via-Albricci 9, Milan 20122)

Japan (☎ 03-3571 5062; indtourt@smile.ocn.ne.jp; Art Masters Ginza Bldg, 6th-9th fl, 6-5-12 Ginza, Chuo-Ku, Tokyo 104-0061)

Netherlands (☎ 020-6208991; info@indiatourismamsterdam.com; Rokin 9/15, 1012 KK Amsterdam)

Singapore (☎ 65-6235 3800; indtour.sing@pacific.net .sg; 20 Kramat Lane, 01-01 United House, 228773)

South Africa (☎ 011-3250880; goito@global.co.za; Craighall 2024, Hyde Lane, Lancaster Gate, Johannesburg 2000)

UK (☎ 0207-4373677; london5@indiatouristoffice.org; 7 Cork St, London W1S 3LH)

USA Los Angeles (☎ 213-380 8855; indiatourismla@aol .com; Suite 204, 3550 Wilshire Boulevard, CA, 900102485); New York (☎ 212-586 4901; ny@itonyc.com; Suite 1808, 1270 Ave of Americas, NY, 10020)

TRAVEL PERMITS

Access to certain parts of India – particularly disputed border areas – is controlled by an often-complicated permit system. A permit known as an Inner-Line Permit (ILP) is required to visit certain parts of Himachal Pradesh, Ladakh, Uttarakhand and Sikkim that lie close to the disputed border with China/Tibet. Obtaining the ILP is basically a formality, but travel agents must apply on

DIRECTORY

your behalf for certain areas, including many trekking routes passing close to the border. ILPs are issued by regional magistrates and district commissioners, either directly to travellers (for free) or through travel agents (for a fee). See p331 (Himachal Pradesh), p300 (Ladakh), p499 (Uttarakhand) and p587 (Sikkim) for additional information.

Entering parts of the Northeast States is much more complex – for comprehensive details read p610.

We recommend that you double-check with tourism officials to see if permit requirements have undergone any recent changes before you head out to these areas.

TRAVELLERS WITH DISABILITIES

India's crowded public transport, crush of humanity and variable infrastructure can test even the hardiest able-bodied traveller. If you have a physical disability or you are vision impaired, these can pose even more of a challenge.

India has a very limited number of hotels that are wheelchair-friendly (almost exclusively top end), making it highly advisable to make pre-trip inquiries and book ground-floor rooms at hotels that lack adequate facilities. Some restaurants and offices have ramps, but most tend to have at least one step. Staircases are often steep and lifts frequently stop at mezzanines between floors. Footpaths and pavements, where they exist, can be riddled with holes, littered with debris and packed with pedestrians, hindering movement. If you use crutches, bring along spare rubber caps for the tips as they're likely to wear down quickly.

Given these challenges, if your mobility is considerably restricted you may like to ease the stress by travelling with an able-bodied companion. Additionally, hiring a car with driver will make moving around a whole lot easier (see p1181); if you use a wheelchair, make sure the car-hire company can provide an appropriate vehicle to carry it.

To obtain further advice pertaining to your specific requirements, consult your doctor before heading to India. A number of organisations may also be able to proffer further information or at least point you in the right direction – good places to start include **Mobility International USA** (MIUSA; www.miusa.org), **Access-Able Travel Source** (www.access-able.com), **Global Access News** (www.globalaccessnews.com), **Royal Association for Disability & Rehabilitation** (RADAR; www.radar.org.uk) and **Accessible Journeys** (www.disabilitytravel.com).

VISAS

You must get a visa *before* arriving in India and these are available at Indian missions worldwide. Most people travel on the standard six-month tourist visa. Student visas and business visas have strict conditions (consult the Indian embassy for details). An onward travel ticket is a requirement for most visas, but this isn't always enforced (check in advance). Note that your passport needs to be valid for at least six months beyond your intended stay in India.

Six-month multiple-entry tourist visas (valid from the date of issue) are granted to nationals of most countries regardless of whether one stays that long or not. You can enter and leave as often as you like, but you can only spend a total of 180 days in the country, starting from the date of issue. There are additional restrictions on travellers from Bangladesh and Pakistan, as well as certain Eastern European, African and Central Asian countries. Check any special conditions for your nationality with the Indian embassy in your country.

Visas are priced in the local currency and may have an added service fee (contact your country's Indian embassy for current prices).

Extended visas are possible for people of Indian origin (excluding those in Pakistan and Bangladesh) who hold a non-Indian passport and live abroad.

For visas lasting more than six months, you're supposed to register at the Foreigners' Regional Registration Office (FRRO; see below) within 14 days of arriving in India; inquire about these special conditions when you apply for your visa.

Visa Extensions

Fourteen-day visa extensions are theoretically possible at the discretion of the **Ministry of Home Affairs** (Map pp126-7; ☎ 011-23385748; Jaisalmer House, 26 Man Singh Rd, Delhi; ⏰ inquiries 9-11am Mon-Fri) but don't get your hopes up. The only circumstances where this might conceivably happen are in *extreme* medical emergencies or if you were robbed of your passport just before you planned to leave the country (at the end of your visa). If you run low on time, consider doing the 'visa run' over to Bangladesh or Nepal and applying for another tourist visa there.

If you do find yourself needing to request an extension (again, there has to be a very good reason), you should contact the **Foreigners' Regional Registration Office** (FRRO; Map pp122-3; ☎ 011-26195530; frrodelhi@hotmail.com; Level 2,

East Block 8, Sector 1, Rama Krishna (RK) Puram, Delhi; (☼ 9.30am-5.30pm Mon-Fri), just around the corner from the Hyatt Regency hotel. This is also the place to come for a replacement visa if you need your lost/stolen passport replaced (required before you can leave the country). Note that regional FRROs are even less likely to grant an extension.

Assuming you meet the stringent criteria, the FRRO is permitted to issue an extension of 14 days (free for nationals of most countries; inquire on application). You must bring your confirmed air ticket, one passport photo (take two, just in case) and a photocopy of your passport identity and visa pages. Note that this system is designed to get you out of the country promptly with the correct official stamps, not to give you two extra weeks of travel.

VOLUNTEERING

Many charities and international aid agencies work in India and there are numerous opportunities for volunteers. However, you're much more likely to be of help if you commit for at least a month. Better international volunteer agencies will work to make sustainable changes, letting the process be guided and informed by local people. It may be possible to find a placement after you arrive in India, but charities and NGOs normally prefer volunteers who have applied in advance and been approved for the kind of work involved.

Agencies Overseas

There are scores of international volunteering agencies, and it can be bewildering trying to assess which ones have ethical policies. Agencies that offer short projects in lots of different countries whenever you want to go are almost always tailoring projects to the volunteer rather than finding the right volunteer for the work that needs to be done. Look for projects that will derive benefits from your existing skills.

The organisation **Ethical Volunteering** (www .ethicalvolunteering.org) has some excellent guidelines for choosing an ethical sending agency.

There are some tried and tested international projects, such as Britain's **Voluntary Service Overseas** (VSO; www.vso.org.uk), that volunteer in various professional roles, though the time commitment can be up to several years. The international organisation **Indicorps** (www.indicorps.org) matches volunteers to projects across India in all sorts of fields, particularly social development. There are special fel-

lowships for people of Indian descent living outside India.

Jamyang Foundation (www.jamyang.org) may be able to arrange volunteer placements for teachers in Zanskar and Himachal Pradesh.

Mondo Challenge (www.mondochallenge.org/india) has opportunities, from teaching to community projects, for volunteers in West Bengal and Ladakh.

Many Indian NGOs also offer volunteer work; for listings click on www.indianngos .com.

To find sending agencies in your area, read Lonely Planet's *Volunteer,* the *Gap Year Book* and the *Career Break Book,* or use the internet – some good starting sites include **World Volunteer Web** (www.worldvolunteerweb.org), **Working Abroad** (www.workingabroad.com) and **Worldwide Volunteering** (www.worldwidevolunteering.org.uk).

Aid Programs in India

Following are listings of programs in India that may have opportunities for volunteers. It's best to contact them in advance, rather than turning up on the doorstep expecting to automatically be offered a position. Donations of money or clothing may also be welcomed. Note that unless otherwise indicated, volunteers are expected to cover their own costs (accommodation, food, transport etc).

Some of the organisations below may have other branches in India; see websites for details.

ANDHRA PRADESH

Blue Cross of Hyderabad (off Map p958; ☎ 040-23544355; www.bluecrosshyd.in; Rd No 35, Jubilee Hills, Hyderabad) runs a 2-acre shelter with 600 animals at the western edge of Hyderabad. It works to rescue and adopt sick animals, and vaccinate and sterilise stray dogs. Volunteers can help in the shelter, grooming, feeding and caring for shelter animals, or in the office.

The **Confederation of Voluntary Associations** (COVA; Map p958; ☎ 040-24572984; www.covanetwork.org; 20-4-10, Charminar, Hyderabad) is an umbrella organisation for around 800 NGOs in Andhra Pradesh working with women, children, civil liberties and sustainable agriculture. Volunteers are matched with programs that need their skills (long-term volunteers preferred).

With an animal hospital and sanctuary, **Karuna Society for Animals & Nature** (☎ 08555-287214; www.karunasociety.org; 2/138/C Karuna Nilayam, Prasanthi Nilayam Post, Anantapur) rescues and treats sick, abandoned and mistreated animals. Volunteers can help with caretaking operations; a one-month, full-time minimum commitment is needed, as are vaccinations.

BIHAR

There are opportunities for volunteer teachers, carers, health professionals and other roles in schools and community projects around Bihar, both long and short term. See p578 for details.

CHHATTISGARH

Saathi (☎ 07786-242852; saathibastar@yahoo.co.in; Kondagaon, Chhattisgarh; training & daily board Rs400, weekly materials Rs500; ☷ 8am-6pm Mon-Sat) encourages tribal people in production of terracotta, woodcarving and metalwork. Volunteers with design and craft knowledge are welcome.

DELHI

The magazine *First City* lists various local NGOs that welcome volunteers and financial aid.

There are two branches of Mother Teresa's Kolkata-based order **Missionaries of Charity** Nirmal Hriday (Map pp122-3; ☎ 011-65731435; 1 Magazine Rd); Shishu Bhavan (Map pp122-3; ☎ 011-23950181; 12 Commissioners Lane), which welcome volunteers (weekdays only). Shishu Bhavan looks after infants (female volunteers only), while Nirmal Hriday cares for the sick, destitute and dying.

The **Concern India Foundation** (Map pp122-3; ☎ 011-26224482; delhi@concernindia.org; Room A52, 1st fl, Amar Colony, Lajpat Nagar 4) may be able to link volunteers with current projects around the country; contact them well in advance for information.

Near the Hotel Namaskar in Paharganj, **Salaam Baalak Trust** (Map p142; ☎ 011-23681803; www.salaambaalaktrust.com; Chandiwalan, Main Bazaar, Paharganj) provides shelter, food, education and other support to Delhi's homeless street children. You can help by sponsoring a child for Rs28,500 per year, funding individual projects, or donating clothes, toys, blankets, books and computers. Volunteer English teachers, doctors, and computer experts are welcome. Another way you can help is by taking a tour with a street child – see p139.

SOS Children's Village (Map pp126-7; ☎ 011-24359734; www.soscvindia.org; A7 Nizammudin West) assists orphaned, abandoned and destitute children. There are periodic openings for volunteers to teach English for a minimum of two years (apply in advance through the local SOS office in your own country); you should have a teaching qualification.

GOA

Goa's leading environmental group, the **Goa Foundation** (☎ 0832-2256479; www.goafoundation.org; G-8 Feira Alta, Mapusa) runs occasional volunteer programs, including litter clean-ups (contact them for current details).

The British-based organisation **Children Walking Tall** (☎ 09822-124802; www.childrenwalkingtall.com; 'The Mango House,' near Vrundavan Hospital, Karaswada, Mapusa) has opportunities for volunteer childcare workers, teachers and medics at its projects for homeless children and orphans near Mapusa. The minimum placement is three months and every volunteer needs a criminal-background check.

For more options see the boxed text, p875.

GUJARAT

Mother Teresa's Kolkata-based **Missionaries of Charity** (☎ 079-27559050; 831/1 Bhimjipura, Nara Wadaj, Ahmedabad) has a branch in Ahmedabad that takes care of abandoned infants (female volunteers only).

Also in Ahmedabad is the **Animal Help Foundation** (Map p728; ☎ 079-2867698; www.ahf.org.in/; 5 Retreat, Shahibaug, Ahmedabad), which helps destitute animals, including street dogs and the thousands of birds wounded during the Makar Sakranti kite festival. Opportunities exist for vets and animal carers.

HARYANA & PUNJAB

Volunteers can assist the work of the **Nek Chand Foundation** (☎ 01923-856644; www.nekchand.com; 1 Watford Rd, Radlett, Herts, WD7 8LA, UK), which helps maintain and preserve the mosaics of the Nek Chand Fantasy Rock Garden in Chandigarh (p257).

HIMACHAL PRADESH

McLeod Ganj is the volunteering capital of Himachal Pradesh, with numerous opportunities to work with Tibetan refugees, both long- and short-term. See p376 for more details.

About 6km south of Manali in the village of Rangri, the **Himalayan Buddhist Cultural School** (☎ 01902-251845; palkithakur@yahoo.com) has placements for experienced teachers who are willing to volunteer for six months or more. Contact them in advance.

Volunteer placements for experienced teachers can be arranged at Buddhist nunnery schools in Spiti and Kinnaur through the US-based **Jamyang Foundation** (www.jamyang.org).

Kullu Project (☎ 94181-02083; kulluproject.web.officelive.com) arranges volunteers to work with schools and orphanages in the Kullu Valley.

JAMMU & KASHMIR

Volunteering in Jammu and the Kashmir Valley is complicated by the security situation, but there are various opportunities in Zanskar and Ladakh. Many Buddhist monastery schools need experienced teachers of English for long-term volunteer placements, and there are also tours that clean the rubbish from remote areas. Also have a look at p307.

The British-based charity **International Society for Ecology & Culture** (www.isec.org.uk) works to promote sustainable development in rural parts of Ladakh. There are one-month placements on rural farms that aim to give Ladakhis control over their future and foster cross-cultural understanding; contact them directly to find out exactly how you can help.

The local NGO **Ladakh Ecological Development Group** (Map p304; ☎ 01982-253221; www.ledeg.org; Ecology Centre, Leh) is involved in environmental education and sustainable development.

Tibet Heritage Fund (www.tibetheritagefund.org) is working on the preservation of old Leh in Ladakh. Those qualified and experienced in art restoration or architecture might be able to help (check their website).

Many international agencies that send volunteers also offer placements, such as the **Jamyang Foundation** (www.jamyang.org); see p1165 for more information.

KARNATAKA

Bengaluru's **Ashoka Trust for Research in Ecology & the Environment** (ATREE; ☎ 080-23533942; www.atree.org; 659 5th A Main Rd, Hebbal, Bengaluru) is committed to sustainable development issues related to conservation and biodiversity. It takes volunteers who have experience or a keen interest in conservation and environmental issues.

Equations (☎ 080-25457607; www.equitabletourism.org; 415, 2nd C Cross, 4th Main Rd, OMBR Layout, Banaswadi Post, Bengaluru) works to promote 'holistic tourism' and protect local communities from exploitation through lobbying, local training programs and research publications.

It may be possible to volunteer at the Bengaluru gay-and-lesbian support group Swabhava – see p1149.

KERALA

The UK-registered charity **Kerala Link** (www.kerala-link.org) places volunteers at one of their partner institutions located in rural Kerala, including a special-needs children's school. Contact them online for current volunteer opportunities lasting from six weeks to six months.

KOLKATA

Mother Teresa's **Missionaries of Charity** (www.motherteresa.org) has volunteering opportunities at several care homes around Kolkata, including Nirmal Hriday (home for the dying), Prem Dan (for the sick and mentally ill) and Shishu Bhavan (for orphaned children). For further details see p509 and the boxed text on p514.

The **Situational Management & Inter-Learning Establishment** (SMILE; ☎ 033-25376621; www.smilengo.org; Udayrajpur, Madhyamgram, No 9 Rail Gate) is an NGO that works with destitute young people in Kolkata. It runs a residential children's home and provides direct assistance to homeless children at Sealdah train station. Volunteers are accepted for two-week placements in work camps and longer stays that last up to a year (you pay a fee to participate, which covers your meals and accommodation).

Started in 1979, **Calcutta Rescue** (Map p510; ☎ /fax 033-22175675; www.calcuttarescue.org; 4th fl, 85 Collins St) provides medical care and health education for the poor and disadvantaged of Kolkata and other parts of West Bengal. The organisation has six- to nine-month openings for experienced medical staff, teachers and administrators; contact them directly for current vacancies.

Run by vets who are volunteers, the **Calcutta Society for the Prevention of Cruelty to Animals** (CSPCA; Map p512; ☎ 033-22367738; http://calcuttaspca.org/; 276 BB Ganguly St) cares for stray and domestic animals in Kolkata and is a campaigner for animal rights. Qualified vets can volunteer at the veterinary surgery on BB Ganguly Rd, but a minimum of one month is preferred.

Samaritans (☎ 033-22295920; http://thecalcuttasamaritans.org; 48 Ripon Rd) welcomes caring listeners and donations.

MADHYA PRADESH

Sambhavna Trust (Map p690; ☎ 0755-2730914; sam bavna@sancharnet.in; Bafna Colony, Berasia Rd, Bhopal) was established to help victims of the 1984 Bhopal Disaster – see the boxed text on p691.

Global Village (☎ 07686-272819; ajay.awasthi@ gmail.com), based outside Khajuraho, principally targets environmental problems but also supports local education as well as working towards curbing more disturbing problems such as child prostitution. More information can be found on p686.

Rehwa Society (☎ 07283-273203; www.rehwasociety .org; Maheshwar) is a craft cooperative where profits are used for the weavers' welfare. For further details, including volunteering, see p708.

MAHARASHTRA

Based near Phaltan, the **Nimbkar Agricultural Research Institute** (☎ 02166-222396; www.nariphaltan .org; Phaltan-Lonand Rd, Tambmal, Phaltan) has a focus on sustainable development, animal husbandry and renewable energy. Volunteer internships lasting two to six months are available for agriculture, engineering and science graduates to assist with the research.

Located 30km from Pune is **Sadhana Village** (off Map p847; ☎ 020-25380792; www.sadhana-village .org; Priyankit, 1 Lokmanya Colony, Pune), a residential-care centre for intellectually disabled adults. Volunteers (prepared to commit to at least two months) assist in workshops, cultural activities and community-development programs for women and children. Meals and accommodation are provided but the organisation receives no government funding so donations are appreciated.

Volunteering options are available at **Anandwan** (http://mss.niya.org; Maharogi Sewa Samiti, Waroa, Chandrapur) ashram, founded by social activist Baba Amte, and its satellite ashrams in the region. However, do write in advance. Also see the boxed text on p830.

MUMBAI

In Mumbai, **Child Rights & You** (CRY; off Map pp780-1; ☎ 022-23063647/51; www.cry.org; 189A Anand Estate, Sane Guruji Marg, Mahalaxmi) fundraises for more than 300 projects India-wide, including ones that help deprived children. Volunteers can assist with campaigns (online and on the ground), research, surveys and media. A six-week commitment is required.

The **Vatsalya Foundation** (off Map pp780-1; ☎ 022-24962115; www.thevatsalyafoundation.org; Anand Niketan, King George V Memorial, Dr E Moses Rd, Mahalaxmi) works with Mumbai's street children, focusing on rehabilitation into mainstream society. There are long- and short-term opportunities in teaching and sports activities.

Volunteers can support English and art classes, design workshops or do research or data analysis at **Apne Aap Women Worldwide** (Map pp780-1; ☎ 022-32015597; www.apneaap.org; Chandramani Budh Vihar Municipal School, 4th fl, 13th Lane, Kamathipura), an anti-trafficking organisation that works in legal protection and provides learning and livelihood training to women's and teenage girls' groups. There are also volunteer possibilities with their offices in Kolkata, Bihar and Delhi.

Concern India Foundation (Map p786; ☎ 022-22852270; www.concernindia.org; 3rd fl, Ador House, 6 K Dubash Marg) supports development-oriented organisations working with vulnerable members of the community. The focus is on establishing sustainable projects run by local people. The foundation can arrange volunteer placements matched to your skills and interests in Mumbai and around India (six months minimum). Many of the field jobs require Hindi.

Saathi (Map pp780-1; ☎ 022-23009117; www.saathi .org; Agripada Municipal School, Farooque Umarbhouy Lane, Agripada) works with adolescent youths living on the street. Volunteers should be willing to commit to at least three months and work full-time (six days per week) for the organisation. There's a range of volunteering possibilities, but those interested in working directly with adolescents should speak some Hindi. The organisation also gives information sessions and tours of the neighbourhoods where it works with a Rs1000 donation.

The **Welfare of Stray Dogs** (Map p786; ☎ 022-23733433, 9819100808; www.wsdindia.org; H1 Chambers, B Bharocha Rd, Kala Ghoda) works to improve the lives of street dogs by eradicating rabies, sterilising, educating the public about strays and finding adoptive homes. Volunteers can walk dogs, mind kennels, treat street dogs (training and rabies shot required), manage stores, educate kids in school programs or fundraise.

ORISSA

The **Wildlife Society of Orissa** (☎ 0674-2311513; www .wildlifeorissa.org; A320, Sahid Nagar, Bhubaneswar) may accept volunteers to help with its work to save endangered species in Orissa, especially the olive ridley turtle (also see p661).

RAJASTHAN

The Jaipur branch of Mother Teresa's Kolkata-based **Missionaries of Charity** (Map pp170-1; ☎ 0141-2365804; Vardhman Path, C-Scheme, Jaipur) provides a refuge for the destitute, many of whom are mentally ill or disabled.

Assisting people with cerebral palsy and other neural conditions, **Disha – Centre for Special Education, Vocational Training & Rehabilitation** (☎ 0141-2393319; www.dishafoundation.org; Disha Path, Nirman Nagar-C, Jaipur) operates a centre providing special education, home management, staff training, counselling and advocacy. Volunteers are needed in the fields of physiotherapy, speech therapy, special education, sports, arts and crafts and vocational counselling.

The laudable animal hospital **Help in Suffering** (☎ 0141-3245673; www.his-india.org.au; Maharani Farm, Durgapura, Jaipur) welcomes qualified voluntary vets (three-/six-/12-month commitments). Apply first in writing.

Also in Jaipur is the **SOS Children's Village** (☎ 0141-2280262; www.sos-childrensvillages.org; Jhotwara Rd, Jaipur), located opposite Petal Factory, which cares for and educates children and young adults. Volunteers teach English and help the children with their homework for a minimum of one year. The parent organisation SOS Kinderdorf International runs several dozen programs across India, employing unmarried women, abandoned wives and widows as carers for orphaned, destitute and abandoned children.

The NGO **Marwar Medical & Relief Society** (☎ 0291-2545210; www.mandore.com; c/o Mandore Guest House, Dadawari Lane, Mandore) works to address drug-addiction problems and provide medical services and education in the Jodhpur district. Guests at its guest house in Mandore and other volunteers are accepted on short-term development and education projects in local villages.

Jaipur's **Ladli** (off Map pp170-1; ☎ 9829011124; www.ladli.org; 74 Govindpuri, Rakdi, Sodala, Jaipur) provides vocational training for abused, orphaned and destitute children. Volunteers work in child care and teach English; placements last two months to a year.

Seva Mandir (off Map p214; ☎ 0294-2451041; www.sevamandir.org; Old Fatehpura, Udaipur) is involved in health promotion, literacy programs and developing natural resources. Development interns can observe and participate in development work for a minimum period of two weeks; apply via the website.

Also in Udaipur, the animal hospital **Animal Aid Society** (off Map p214; ☎ 0294-2513359; www.animaidsociety.org; c/o Pratap Singh Rathore, 27C Neemach Mata Scheme, Dewali, Udaipur) accepts trained veterinary staff and other animal-loving volunteers to help rescue and treat injured stray animals and street dogs at its veterinary clinic in Chota Hawala village.

The **Urmul Trust** (off Map p250; ☎ 0151-2523093; Urmul Bhawan, Ganganagar Rd, Bikaner) provides primary health care and education to hundreds of villages in Rajasthan, as well as promoting rights for women. Volunteer placements (minimum one month) are available in social welfare, teaching, health care and other projects. The Urmul Trust is located inside Urmul Dairy (next to the bus terminal).

SIKKIM

Placements for volunteer teachers at schools in Sikkim can be arranged through the British-based charity **Himalayan Education Lifeline Programme** (HELP; ☎ 01227 263055; www.help-education.org; Mansard House, 30 Kingsdown Park, Whitstable, Kent CT5 2DF, UK). See the website for comprehensive details.

Teaching placements in Sikkim can also be arranged through the **Muyal Liang Trust** (☎ 020-7229 4774; 53 Blenheim Crescent, London W11 2EG UK).

TAMIL NADU

In Chennai, there are volunteer opportunities at the **Missionaries of Charity** (off Map pp1044-5; ☎ 044-25956928; 79 Main Rd, Royapuram, Chennai), which is part of Mother Teresa's Kolkata-based care operation.

The **Freedom Foundation** (off Map pp1044-5; ☎ 044-25567228; www.thefreedomfoundation.org; 15 United Colony, Red Hills Rd, Kolathur, Chennai) provides services to people living with HIV/AIDs, including treatment at its clinic and work-skills training. It also campaigns for HIV education and prevention. There are opportunities for counsellors, trainers, teachers and carers.

The international eye-care charity **Unite for Sight** (www.uniteforsight.org/intl_volunteer) has month-long openings for volunteer assistants, teachers, nurses and optical-health professionals to help at its partner eye-care clinics in Chennai and around India; see the website for details.

The NGO **Rural Institute for Development Education** (RIDE; off Map p1066; ☎ 04112-268393; 46 Periyar Nagar, Little Kanchipuram) works with numerous villages in Kanchipuram to remove children from forced labour and into transition

DIRECTORY

schools. Volunteers can contribute in teaching, administrative and support roles.

In Chennai, the **Rejuvenate India Movement** (RIM; off Map pp1044-5; ☎ 044-22235133; www.india-movement.org; A1 Monisha Sriram Flats, 9 Kulothungan Cross St, Chittlapakkam, Chennai) can arrange short- and long-term placements for skilled volunteers on development projects run by partner NGOs in over a dozen villages in Tamil Nadu. There are also opportunities in Karnataka. Spoken Hindi is an asset.

In Kotagiri is the **Keystone Foundation** (www.keystone-foundation.org), an NGO that strives to improve environmental conditions in the Nilgiris while working with, and creating better living standards for, indigenous communities.

UTTAR PRADESH

In Varanasi, the **Learn for Life Society** (www.learn-for-life.org), which can be contacted through the **Brown Bread Bakery** (Map p444; ☎ 0542-2403566; brownbreadbakery@yahoo.co.in), has volunteer opportunities at its small school for disadvantaged children; consult the website for details and also see p445.

The **Sankat Mochan Foundation** (☎ 0542-2313884; vmbganga@satyam.net.in; Tulsi Ghat), a charity dedicated to cleaning up the Varanasi stretch of the Ganges River (see the boxed text on p446), welcomes volunteers to help with research and administration.

UTTARAKHAND

Volunteers can help the **Uttaranchal Forest Development Corporation** (www.uafdc.in), based in Dehra Dun, with animal rescue and Gujjar tribal village development projects in Rajaji National Park. The best contact for these projects is the **Mahesh Yogi Organisation** (☎ 01334-220910, mobile 9837100215; mohansindia@gmail.com) at Mohan's Adventure Tours in Haridwar (p471).

The grassroots **Rural Organisation for Social Elevation** (ROSE; ☎ 05963-241081; www.rosekanda.org; Sonargaon Village, PO Kanda, Bageshwar) is based in Kanda village, near Bageshwar. Volunteers live with a local family for one to six months, helping out with cooking, teaching, field work and building projects.

In Ghangaria village in the Valley of Flowers, the Eco Development Committee runs conservation projects between June and October. Contact the Nature Interpretation Centre (p485).

WEST BENGAL

In Darjeeling, **Hayden Hall** (Map p550; ☎ 0354-2253228; min@haydenhall.com; 42 Laden La Rd, Darjeeling) has volunteer opportunities (minimum six months) for people with health-care and preschool-teaching backgrounds.

Human Wave (☎ 033-26852823; http://humanwave-volunteer.org; 52 Tentultala Lane, Mankundu, Hooghly) runs community development and health schemes in West Bengal, including volunteer projects in the Sunderbans and youth projects in Kolkata.

The organic **Makaibari Tea Estate** (slg_rajah@sancharnet.in; www.makaibari.com; Pankhabari Rd, Kurseong) has an established program that places volunteers in health, education and agriculture jobs that benefit plantation workers. It's popular with gap-year students.

WOMEN TRAVELLERS

Broadly speaking, India is a conservative society, and the skimpy clothing and culturally inappropriate behaviour of a minority of foreign women appears to have had somewhat of a ripple effect on the perception of foreign women in general. One unfortunate consequence of this is that many female travellers have reported some form of sexual harassment while in India – predominantly lewd comments and invasion of privacy, sometimes groping. Most cases are reported in urban centres of North India and prominent tourist towns elsewhere.

While there's no need to be paranoid, you should be aware that your behaviour and dress code are under scrutiny, particularly away from cosmopolitan cities like Mumbai and the tourist-accustomed beaches of Goa. Getting constantly stared at is something you'll have to live with. Don't allow it to get the better of you. It's best to refrain from returning male stares, as this may be considered a come-on; dark glasses can help, while MP3-players and books are useful accessories for averting unwanted conversations.

Other harassment women have encountered include provocative gestures, jeering, getting 'accidentally' bumped into on the street and being followed. Exuberant special events such as the Holi festival can be notorious for this. Women travelling with a male partner are less likely to be hassled. However, mixed couples of Indian and non-Indian descent may get disapproving stares, even if neither individual actually lives in India.

Ultimately, there are no sure-fire ways of shielding yourself from sexual harassment, even if you do everything 'right' – use your own judgement and instincts, and err on the side of caution if you're unsure.

On the personal hygiene front, sanitary pads are widely available but tampons are usually restricted to pharmacies in big cities and some tourist towns (even then, the choice may be limited). Carry additional stocks for travel off the beaten track.

Clothing

Warding off sexual harassment is often a matter of adjusting your behaviour to match the prevailing social norms. Avoiding culturally inappropriate clothing can help enormously. Steer clear of sleeveless tops, shorts, miniskirts (ankle-length skirts are recommended) and any other skimpy, see-through or tight-fitting attire. Baggy clothing that masks the contours of your body is the way to go. Draping a *dupatta* (long scarf) over T-shirts is another good way of staving off unwanted stares.

In some areas, such as Goa and Mumbai, there's generally a more liberal attitude towards dress. But away from these areas, take your cues from local women. Most Indian women wear saris, *salwar kameez,* or long shorts and a T-shirt whenever swimming in public view. When returning from the beach, use a sarong to avoid stares and glares on the way back to your hotel.

Wearing Indian-style clothes makes a positive impression and can considerably deflect harassment. The *salwar kameez* is regarded as respectable attire and wearing it will show your respect for local dress etiquette. This elegant, flowing outfit is also surprisingly cool in the hot weather, and the *dupatta* (long scarf) worn with it is very handy if you visit a shrine that requires your head to be covered. If you don't wish to wear a *salwar kameez,* a smart alternative is a kurta (long shirt) worn over jeans or trousers.

Going into public wearing a *choli* (sari blouse) or a sari petticoat (which some foreign women mistake for a skirt) is rather like strutting around half dressed – avoid it. You can read personal experiences proffered by fellow women travellers at www.journeywoman.com.

Staying Safe

Women have reported being molested by masseurs and other therapists, especially in tourist centres such as Varanasi and McLeod Ganj. No matter where you are, try to check the reputation of any teacher or therapist before going to a solo session. If you feel uneasy at any time, leave. For gynaecological health issues, most women prefer to seek out a female doctor.

To keep conversations with unknown men short, get to the point as quickly and politely as possible – getting involved in an inane conversation with someone you barely know can be misinterpreted as a sign of sexual interest. Questions and comments such as 'Do you have a boyfriend?' or 'You're looking very beautiful' are indicators that the conversation may be taking a steamy tangent. Some women prepare in advance by wearing a pseudo wedding ring, or by announcing early on in the conversation that they're married or engaged (regardless of the reality).

If you still get the uncomfortable feeling that a guy is encroaching on your space, he probably is. A firm request to keep away usually does the trick, especially if your tone is loud and curt enough to draw the attention of passers-by. Alternatively, the silent treatment (not responding to questions at all) can be remarkably effective.

When interacting with men on a day-to-day basis, follow local women's cues and instead of shaking hands say *namaste* – the traditional, respectful Hindu greeting.

Female filmgoers will probably feel more comfortable (and lessen the chances of potential harassment) by going to the cinema with a companion. At hotels, get into the habit of keeping your door locked, as staff (particularly at budget places) can knock and automatically walk in without waiting for your permission.

Lastly, it's wise to arrive in towns before dark. Don't walk alone at night and avoid wandering alone in isolated areas even during daylight.

Taxis & Public Transport

Officials recommend that solo women prearrange an airport pick-up from their hotel if their flight is scheduled to arrive after dark. If that's not possible, in Delhi (and some other cities) you can avail of a prepaid radio cab service such as **Easycabs** (see p161) – it's more expensive than the regular prepaid taxis, but promotes itself as a safe service, with drivers that have been vetted as part of their recruitment. If you do catch a regular prepaid taxi,

DIRECTORY

make a point of (in front of the driver) writing down the car registration and driver's name, and giving it to one of the airport police.

Avoid taking taxis alone late at night (when many roads are deserted) and never agree to have more than one man (the driver) in the car – ignore claims that this is 'just my brother' or 'for more protection'. Women are advised against wearing expensive-looking jewellery as it can make them a target for muggers.

On trains and buses, being a woman has some advantages. Women are able to queue-jump without consequence, and on trains there are special ladies-only carriages. Solo women have reported less hassle by opting for the more expensive classes on trains, especially for overnight trips. If you're travelling overnight in a three-tier carriage, try to get the uppermost berth, which will give you more privacy (and distance from potential gropers).

On public transport, don't hesitate to return any errant limbs, put some item of luggage in between you, be vocal (so as to attract public attention, thus shaming the fellow), or simply find a new spot.

Transport

CONTENTS

GETTING THERE & AWAY

The following sections contain information on transport to, from and around India. Flights, tours and other tickets may also be booked online at www.lonelyplanet.com/bookings.

ENTERING THE COUNTRY

Entering India by air or land is relatively straightforward, with standard immigration and customs procedures (p1144). It's wise to pre-arrange an airport pick-up if arriving at night.

Passport

To enter India you need a valid passport, visa (see p1164) and an onward/return ticket. Your passport should be valid for at least six months beyond your intended stay in India. If your passport is lost or stolen, immediately contact your country's representative (see p1147). Keep photocopies of your airline ticket and the identity and visa pages of your passport in case of emergency. Check with the Indian embassy in your home country for any special conditions that may exist for your nationality.

THINGS CHANGE...

The information in this chapter is particularly vulnerable to change. Check directly with the airline or a travel agent to make sure you understand how a fare (and the ticket you may buy) works and be aware of the security requirements for international travel. Shop carefully. The details given in this chapter should simply be regarded as pointers and not as a substitute for your own careful, up-to-date research.

TRANSPORT

AIR
Airports & Airlines

India has four main gateways for international flights (see the following list); however, there are a number of other cities servicing international carriers – for details see regional chapters and www.indianairports.com. India is a big country, so arrange to fly into the airport that's nearest to the area you'll be visiting.

Chennai (Madras; MAA; Anna International Airport; ☎ 044-22560551; www.chennaiairport.com)
Delhi (DEL; Indira Gandhi International Airport; ☎ 011-25661000; www.newdelhiairport.in)
Kolkata (Calcutta; CCU; Netaji Subhash Chandra Bose International Airport; ☎ 033-25118787; www.calcuttaairport.com)
Mumbai (Bombay; BOM; Chhatrapati Shivaji International Airport; ☎ 022-26813000; www.csia.in)

AIRLINES FLYING TO/FROM INDIA

India's national carrier is **Air India** (www.airindia.com), of which the former state-owned domestic carrier, Indian Airlines, is now a part, following a merger deal. Well-regarded private airline **Jet Airways** (www.jetairways.com) also operates a number of international flights, as do several other Indian carriers (see p1178). Consult the websites for current route and fare information.

Other airlines flying to and from India (websites have up-to-date contact details):
Aeroflot (www.aeroflot.org)
Air Canada (www.aircanada.com)
Air France (www.airfrance.com)
Alitalia (www.alitalia.com)
American Airlines (www.aa.com)

CLIMATE CHANGE & TRAVEL

Climate change is a serious threat to the ecosystems that humans rely upon, and air travel is the fastest-growing contributor to the problem. Lonely Planet regards travel, overall, as a global benefit, but believes we all have a responsibility to limit our personal impact on global warming.

FLYING & CLIMATE CHANGE

Pretty much every form of motorised travel generates CO2 (the main cause of human-induced climate change) but planes are far and away the worst offenders, not just because of the sheer distances they allow us to travel, but because they release greenhouse gases high into the atmosphere. The statistics are frightening: two people taking a return flight between Europe and the US will contribute as much to climate change as an average household's gas and electricity consumption over a whole year.

CARBON OFFSET SCHEMES

Climatecare.org and other websites use 'carbon calculators' that allow travellers to offset the level of greenhouse gases they are responsible for with financial contributions to sustainable travel schemes that reduce global warming – including projects in India, Honduras, Kazakhstan and Uganda.

Lonely Planet, together with Rough Guides and other concerned partners in the travel industry, supports the carbon offset scheme run by climatecare.org. Lonely Planet offsets all of its staff and author travel.

For more information check out our website: www.lonelyplanet.com

Austrian Airlines (www.aua.com)
Biman Bangladesh Airlines (www.biman-airlines.com)
British Airways (www.british-airways.com)
Cathay Pacific Airways (www.cathaypacific.com)
Drukair (www.drukair.com.bt)
El Al Israel Airlines (www.elal.co.il)
Emirates (www.emirates.com)
Finnair (www.finnair.com)
Gulf Air (www.gulfairco.com)
Japan Airlines (www.jal.com)
Kenya Airways (www.kenya-airways.com)
KLM – Royal Dutch Airlines (www.klm.com)
Kuwait Airways (www.kuwait-airways.com)
Lufthansa (www.lufthansa.com)
Malaysia Airlines (www.malaysiaairlines.com)
Nepal Airlines (www.royalnepal-airlines.com)
Pakistan International Airlines (www.piac.com.pk)
Qantas Airways (www.qantas.com.au)
Qatar Airways (www.qatarairways.com)
Singapore Airlines (www.singaporeair.com)
South African Airways (www.flysaa.com)
Sri Lankan Airlines (www.srilankan.aero)
Swiss International Airlines (www.swiss.com)
Thai Airways International (www.thaiair.com)

Departing India

Most airlines no longer require reconfirmation of international tickets, although it's still a good idea to call to check that flight times haven't changed. The majority of airlines ask you to check in three hours before international departures – remember to factor in the Indian traffic when planning your trip to the airport.

Most Indian airports have free luggage trolleys, but porters will eagerly offer to lug your load for a negotiable fee. For flights originating in India, hold bags must be passed through the X-ray machine in the departures hall and baggage tags are required for the security check for all cabin bags, including cameras.

Tickets

An onward or return air ticket is usually a condition of the Indian tourist visa, so few visitors buy international tickets inside India. Only designated travel agencies can book international flights, but fares may be the same if you book directly with the airlines. Departure tax and other charges are included in airline tickets.

Given the fluctuating prices of international travel to India, it's best to contact a travel agent or surf the web to get up-to-the-minute fares and flight schedules. Note that internet fares often offer the best deals – here are some good places to start:

Ebookers (www.ebookers.com)
Expedia (www.expedia.com)
Flight Centre (www.flightcentre.com)
Flights.com (www.tiss.com)
STA Travel (www.statravel.com)

Travelocity (www.travelocity.com)
Yatra (www.yatra.com)

Africa
There are direct flights to India from South Africa and East Africa. **Rennies Travel** (www.rennies travel.com) and **STA Travel** (www.statravel.co.za) have offices throughout southern Africa. Check their websites for branch locations.

Asia
STA Travel is prolific in Asia, with branches in Bangkok (www.statravel.co.th), Singapore (www.statravel.com.sg), Hong Kong (www .statravel.com.hk) and Japan (www.statravel .co.jp). Another resource in Japan is **No 1 Travel** (www.no1-travel.com); in Hong Kong try **Four Seas Travel** (www.fourseastravel.com). At least one airline offers flights to India from Bangladesh, the Maldives, Myanmar, Nepal, Pakistan and Sri Lanka; consult local travel agencies or the internet for current details.

Australia
Most flights from Australia involve a stopover, with the stopover destination depending on the carrier. Popular agents include **STA Travel** (www.statravel.com.au) and **Flight Centre** (www.flight centre.com.au). Also see www.travel.com.au.

Canada
From eastern and central Canada, most flights go via Europe; from Vancouver and the west coast, flights go via Asia. **Travel Cuts** (www.travel cuts.com) is Canada's national student travel agency. For online bookings try www.expedia .ca and www.travelocity.ca.

Continental Europe
There are connections to Indian cities from most European capitals, either directly or with a stop. For discount fares, try the agencies in the following lists or visit the big online ticket agencies. **STA Travel** (Austria www.statravel.at; Denmark www .statravel.dk; Norway www.statravel.no; Sweden www.statravel. se; Switzerland www.statravel.ch) and Last Minute have regional websites for nations across Europe.

FRANCE
Recommended agencies:
Anyway (www.anyway.fr)
Lastminute (www.lastminute.fr)
Nouvelles Frontières (www.nouvelles-frontieres.fr)
OTU Voyages (www.otu.fr)
Voyageurs du Monde (www.vdm.com)

GERMANY
Recommended agencies:
Expedia (www.expedia.de)
Just Travel (www.justtravel.de)
Lastminute (www.lastminute.de)
STA Travel (www.statravel.de)

ITALY
One recommended agency is **CTS Viaggi** (www .cts.it).

NETHERLANDS
One recommended agency is **Airfair** (www.air fair.nl).

SPAIN
One recommended agency is **Barcelo Viajes** (www.barceloviajes.com).

Middle East
Recommended agencies:
Al Rais Travel (www.alrais.com) In Dubai.
Egypt Panorama Tours (www.eptours.com) In Cairo.
Israel Student Travel Association (www.issta.co.il) In Jerusalem.
Orion-Tour (www.oriontour.com) In Istanbul.

New Zealand
Flights between India and New Zealand go via Southeast Asia. Both **Flight Centre** (www .flightcentre.co.nz) and **STA Travel** (www.statravel.co.nz) have branches throughout the country.

South America
Recommended agencies:
ASATEJ (www.asatej.com) In Argentina.
Ividiomas (www.ividiomas.com) In Venezuela.
Student Travel Bureau (www.stb.com.br) In Brazil.

UK & Ireland
Discount air travel is big business in London. Advertisements for many travel agencies appear in the travel pages of the weekend broadsheet newspapers, in *Time Out* and *Evening Standard*, and in the free online magazine *TNT* (www.tntmagazine.com).
Recommended travel agencies:
Ebookers (www.ebookers.com)
Flight Centre (www.flightcentre.co.uk)
Last Minute (www.last-min.com)
North South Travel (www.northsouthtravel.co.uk)
Quest Travel (www.questtravel.com)
STA Travel (www.statravel.co.uk)
Trailfinders (www.trailfinders.co.uk)
Travel Bag (www.travelbag.co.uk)

TRANSPORT

USA

Discount travel agencies in the USA are known as consolidators (although you won't see a sign on the door saying 'Consolidator'). San Francisco is the ticket-consolidator capital of the USA, although some good deals can certainly be found in Los Angeles, New York and other big cities.

Recommended for online bookings:

American Express Travel (www.itn.net)
CheapTickets (www.cheaptickets.com)
Expedia (www.expedia.com)
Lowestfare.com (www.lowestfare.com)
Orbitz (www.orbitz.com)
STA Travel (www.sta.com)
Travelocity (www.travelocity.com)

LAND
Border Crossings

Although most visitors fly into India, the overland route from Nepal is popular, and smaller numbers of travellers enter India from Pakistan and Bangladesh. For more on these routes, consult Lonely Planet's *Istanbul to Kathmandu,* or see the 'Europe to India overland' section on www.seat61.com/India.htm.

If you enter India by bus or train you'll be required to disembark at the border for standard immigration and customs checks. You *must* have a valid Indian visa in advance as no visas are available at the border. The standard Indian tourist visa allows multiple entries within a six-month period – see p1164.

Drivers of cars and motorbikes will need the vehicle's registration papers, liability insurance and an international drivers' permit in addition to their domestic licence.

You'll also need a *Carnet de passage en douane,* which acts as a temporary waiver of import duty. To find out the latest requirements for the paperwork and other important driving information, contact your local automobile association.

See p1181 and p1184 for more on car and motorcycle travel.

BANGLADESH

Foreigners can use four of the land crossings between Bangladesh and India, all in West Bengal or the Northeast States. Exiting Bangladesh overland is complicated by red tape – if you enter by air, you require a road permit (or 'change of route' permit) to leave by land. There have been reports of people managing to leave without a change of route

permit, and others being turned back for not having one. To apply for visa extensions and change-of-route permits you will need to visit the **Immigration and Passport Office** (☎ 889750; Agargaon Rd; ☺ Sat-Thu) in Dhaka. Some travellers have also reported problems exiting Bangladesh overland with the visa issued on arrival at Dhaka airport.

Heading from India to Bangladesh, tourist visas should be obtained in advance from a Bangladeshi mission (see p1147). See also boxed texts, p641 and p636.

Heading from Bangladesh to India, you have to prepay the exit tax (Tk300); this must be paid in advance at a Sonali Bank branch (either in Dhaka, another big city, or at the closest branch to the border).

Kolkata to Dhaka

There are many daily bus services from Kolkata to Dhaka, crossing the India–Bangladesh border at Benapol – see p529 for more information. There's also a train link between Kolkata and Dhaka – see p530. The border post for the train is Darsana – your Bangladeshi visa needs to have this marked on it for you to be able to purchase a ticket.

Siliguri to Chengrabandha/Burimari

This minor northern border crossing is accessible from Siliguri in West Bengal, with regular direct buses to Chengrabandha. From here you can catch buses on to Rangpur, Bogra and Dhaka. See boxed text, p545, for more details.

Shillong to Sylhet

This little-used crossing offers a handy back route from northeast India to Bangladesh. Share 4WDs run every morning from Bara Bazaar in Shillong to the border post at Dawki. From Dawki you can walk or catch a taxi to the bus station in Tamabil, which has regular buses to Sylhet – see boxed text, p641, for more information.

Agartala to Dhaka

This border is close to Dhaka, along Akhaura Rd, near Agartala in India. The distance between Dhaka and Agartala is 155km. For more information see boxed text, p636.

BHUTAN

Phuentsholing is the main entry and exit point between India and Bhutan; you need a Bhutanese visa to enter the country and are required to book a tour with a registered tour operator in Bhutan, which can be done directly through an affiliated travel agency abroad. As entry requirements need advance planning and are subject to change, we recommend you consult a travel agent or Bhutanese embassy for up-to-the-minute details. Also see www.tourism.gov.bt and Lonely Planet's *Bhutan*.

Siliguri/Kolkata to Phuentsholing
Buses from Kolkata and Siliguri to Phuentsholing are run by Bhutan Transport Services. From Kolkata, there's a direct bus at 7am (see p529). See boxed text, p545, for details on travel from Siliguri.

NEPAL
Even though the security situation in Nepal has improved greatly over recent years, officials advise that travellers check the current security status before crossing into Nepal by land – local newspapers and international news websites are good places to start.

Political and weather conditions permitting, there are five land border crossings between India and Nepal:
- Sunauli in Uttar Pradesh to Bhairawa in central Nepal
- Raxaul in Bihar to Birganj in central Nepal
- Panitanki in West Bengal to Kakarbhitta in eastern Nepal
- Jamunaha in Uttar Pradesh to Nepalganj in western Nepal
- Banbassa in Uttaranchal to Mahendranagar in western Nepal

Visas are available at all the border crossings but payment is due in US dollars and you need two recent passport photos. Alternatively, obtain a visa in advance from a Nepalese mission (see p1147).

Sunauli to Bhairawa
This is the easiest crossing for Delhi or Varanasi, with connections on to Kathmandu, Pokhara and Lumbini. From Varanasi regular buses leave for Sunauli (non-AC/AC Rs172/215, 10 hours), or you can travel by train to Gorakhpur (p454) and take a local bus to Sunauli (Rs56, three hours) from there. See boxed text, p456, for information about crossing the border.

Raxaul to Birganj
This crossing is convenient for Kolkata, Patna and the eastern plains, and there are onward connections to Kathmandu. Daily buses run to Raxaul from Patna and Kolkata, but it's more comfortable to jump on the daily *Mithila Express* train from Kolkata. For more details about crossing the border, see boxed text, p574.

Panitanki to Kakarbhitta
This is the handiest crossing for Darjeeling, Sikkim and the Northeast States. Buses and share 4WDs run to the border from Siliguri and several other towns in West Bengal, and you can explore the eastern Terai as you travel on to Kathmandu. See boxed text, p545, for details about crossing the border.

Jamunaha to Nepalganj
Plenty of domestic tourists cross into Nepal at Jamunaha in Uttar Pradesh, but most foreign travellers stick to more convenient crossings. However, Nepalganj is a useful gateway for Nepal's Royal Bardia National Park and there are frequent onward flights to Kathmandu. Buses run regularly from Lucknow to Rupaidha Bazar (seven hours), a short rickshaw ride from the Jamunaha border post. Alternatively, you can take a train to Nanpara, and change to a bus or taxi for the 17km trip to the border.

Banbassa to Mahendranagar
This back route into Nepal from Banbassa (Uttarakhand) provides access to the little-visited western Terai. However, the route is often blocked by flooding and landslides during (and soon after) the monsoon. Daily buses to Banbassa leave Delhi's **Anand Vihar bus stand** (off Map pp122-3; ☎ bookings 011-22141611) several times daily (Rs184, 10 hours). See boxed text, p499, for information about crossing the border.

PAKISTAN
Given the rocky relationship between India and Pakistan, crossing by land depends on the current state of relations between the two countries – check locally. Assuming the crossings are open, there are routes into Pakistan from Delhi, Amritsar (Punjab) and Rajasthan by bus or train. The bus route from Srinagar to Pakistan-administered Kashmir is currently only open to Indian citizens.

You must have a visa to enter Pakistan, and it's easiest to obtain this from the Pakistan mission in your home country. At the time of writing, the **Pakistan embassy** (☎ 011-24676004; 2/50G Shantipath, Chanakyapuri; ✆ applications 8-11am Mon-Fri) in Delhi was issuing 90-day tourist visas for most nationalities in around five days, *but* this office may stop issuing visas at times of political tension. If you do apply within India, you'll need a letter of recommendation from your home embassy as well as the usual application forms and two passport photos.

Attari to Wagah (Amritsar to Lahore)
The main transit point between India and Pakistan is the border post between Attari, near Amritsar, and Wagah, near Lahore. For details about crossing the border, see 'India–Pakistan Border at Attari/Wagah' (p275) and the boxed text, p275. Try to coordinate your crossing with the spectacular closing of the border ceremony – see boxed text, p276.

Delhi to Lahore
There are direct bus and train services between Delhi and Lahore. However, these services can get crowded, and clearing the border formalities can take anywhere between two and five hours – compared to one or two hours if you travel independently. Security has been tightened but is still a lingering concern following the bomb attack on a Delhi–Lahore train in 2007 that claimed almost 70 lives.

The Lahore Bus Service leaves from Delhi's **Dr Ambedkar Bus Station office** (☎ 011-23318180, 23712228; Delhi Gate; ✆ 9am-7pm Mon-Sat) at 6am daily, arriving in Lahore around 12 hours later. The fare is Rs1500 one way (advance bookings are essential). The baggage limit is 20kg per person (Rs60 per extra kilogram, with a maximum of 15kg) plus one piece of hand luggage.

The *Samjhauta Express* train leaves the Old Delhi train station (purchase tickets here) on Wednesday and Sunday at 10.50pm and arrives at the Indian border crossing of Attari at 7am. Passengers then disembark for customs checks and visa procedures, before reboarding for the 30-minute trip to Lahore. Tickets cost Rs270 in sleeper class.

Rajasthan to Pakistan
After years of wrangling, the weekly *Thar Express* (aka *JU MBF Link Express*) train from Jodhpur (Rajasthan) to the border crossing

at Munabao/Khokrapar and onto Karachi (Pakistan) resumed in early 2006. Schedules can be erratic, so check locally in Jodhpur for departure times. For more details see p238.

SEA
There are several sea routes between India and surrounding islands but none leave Indian sovereign territory – see p1180. There has long been talk of a passenger ferry service between southern India and Colombo in Sri Lanka but this has yet to materialise. Inquire locally to see if there has been any progress.

GETTING AROUND

AIR
India has a competitive domestic airline industry. Airline seats can be booked directly by telephone, through travel agencies or cheaply over the internet. Domestic airlines set rupee fares for Indian citizens, while foreigners may be charged US dollar fares (usually payable in rupees).

Reconfirmation is normally only required if your ticket was bought outside India, but, to be safe, it doesn't hurt to call a few days ahead. Airlines may issue a replacement for lost tickets, but refunds are rare. For details of airfare discounts see p1147.

The recommended check-in time for domestic flights is one hour before departure, and hold luggage must be X-rayed and stamped before you check in. Every item of cabin baggage needs a baggage label, which must be stamped as part of the security check (don't forget to collect tags at the check-in counter). Flights to sensitive destinations (eg Kashmir and Ladakh) have extra security restrictions: cabin baggage may be completely prohibited and batteries usually need to be removed from all electronic items and placed in the hold. You may also need to identify your bags on the tarmac before they are loaded on the plane. Officially, photography at airports and from the air is prohibited.

The usual baggage allowance is 20kg (10kg for smaller aircraft) in economy class, and 30kg in business.

Airlines in India
Recent years have witnessed a surge in domestic flights (and resulting price wars) around the country due to industry deregulation.

STOP PRESS: DOMESTIC AIRLINE CHANGES!

Recent years have seen various domestic airline mergers and name changes in India – these were still unfolding at the time of going to press, so be aware that there may be changes over the life of this book. We've used airline office names that were applicable on the ground at the time of research.

Keep in mind that although Air India and Indian Airlines have merged, some offices across the country may still be using the old name of Indian Airlines. Kingfisher Airlines and Air Deccan have also merged, with their offices now going by the names of Kingfisher Airlines and, its budget carrier, Kingfisher Red. Meanwhile, JetLite (which used to be known as Air Sahara) is a subsidiary of Jet Airways.

Be aware that some dodgy travel agencies may try to confuse travellers with name changes.

Two well-established players are Air India (of which Indian Airlines is now a part) and Jet Airways. Then there are India's new budget airlines, offering discounted fares on a variety of domestic sectors.

Competition among carriers means that fares frequently change and airlines are constantly adopting all sorts of promotional offers. It's advisable to consult travel agencies and the web for up-to-the-minute details about the best fares and routes. Taxes can add a considerable amount to airfares. At the time of writing, the airlines in the following list were operating across various destinations in India – see regional chapters for specifics about routes, fares and booking offices.

Air India (www.airindia.com) India's national carrier (which now includes Indian Airlines) operates many domestic and international flights.

GoAir (www.goair.in) Low-cost carrier.

IndiGo (www.goindigo.in) Another budget airline.

Jagson Airlines (www.jagsonairline.com) Among other destinations, it uses tiny Dornier planes to access small runways in Himachal Pradesh.

Jet Airways (www.jetairways.com) Rated by many as India's best airline, with growing domestic and international services.

JetLite (www.jetlite.com) Jet Airways' budget carrier.

Kingfisher Airlines (www.flykingfisher.com) Yep, it's an airline owned by a beer company, offering domestic flights and a few international ones.

Kingfisher Red (www.flykingfisher.com/kingfisher-red .aspx) Kingfisher Airlines' low-cost option.

Spicejet (www.spicejet.com) Budget carrier.

A useful site for booking domestic flights online is www.makemytrip.com.

Helicopter Services

Several companies, including **Pawan Hans Helicopters** (www.pawanhans.nic.in), offer helicopter shuttle services in limited regions – relevant regional chapters contain details.

BICYCLE

There are no restrictions on bringing a bicycle into the country. However, bicycles sent by sea can take a few weeks to clear customs in India, so it's better to fly bikes in. Having said that, it may actually be cheaper – and less of a hassle – to hire or buy a bicycle in India itself. Mountain bikes with off-road tyres give the best protection against India's many potholed and puncture-prone roads. Roadside cycle mechanics abound but you should still bring spare tyres and brake cables, lubricating oil and a chain repair kit, and plenty of puncture repair patches. Bikes can often be carried for free, or for a small luggage fee, on the roof of public buses – handy for uphill stretches. Contact your airline for information about transporting your bike and customs formalities in your home country.

Read up on bicycle touring before you travel – Rob Van Der Plas' *Bicycle Touring Manual* and Stephen Lord's *Adventure Cycle-Touring Handbook* are good places to start. Consult local cycling magazines and cycling clubs for useful information and advice. The **Cycling Federation of India** (Map pp126-7; ☎ 011-23753528; www.cyclingfederationofindia.org; 12 Pandit Pant Marg; ⏱ 10am-5pm Mon-Fri) can provide local information.

Road rules are virtually nonexistent throughout most of India, and cities and national highways can be hazardous places to cycle, so, where possible, stick to back roads. Be conservative about the distances you expect to cover – an experienced cyclist can manage around 60km to 100km a day on the plains, 40km to 60km on sealed mountain roads and 40km or less on dirt roads.

Hire

Tourist centres and other places where travellers congregate are the easiest spots to find bicycles for hire – simply inquire locally. Prices vary, with most places charging anywhere between Rs30 and Rs80 per day for a roadworthy, Indian-made bicycle (mountain bikes, where available, are usually upwards of Rs350 per day). Hire places may require a cash security deposit (avoid leaving your airline ticket or passport).

Purchase

A top place to buy anything bicycle-related is Delhi's Jhandewalan Cycle Market (Map pp122–3), which has imported and domestic new and secondhand bikes and spare parts. Mountain bikes with reputable brands that include Hero (www.herocycles.com) and Atlas (www.atlascyclesonepat.com) generally start at around Rs3000. Reselling is usually fairly easy – ask at local cycle or hire shops or put up an advert on travel noticeboards. If you purchased a new bike and it's still in reasonably good condition, you should be able to get back around 50% of what you originally paid.

BOAT

Scheduled ferries connect mainland India to Port Blair in the Andaman Islands (see p1125). The trip takes around 60 hours from Chennai (see p1056) or around 56 hours from Kolkata (see p528). There are also sporadic ferries from Visakhapatnam (Andhra Pradesh) to the Andaman Islands (p974).

Between October and May, there are boat services from Kochi (Kerala) to the Lakshadweep Islands (see p1037).

There are also numerous shorter ferry services across rivers, from chain pontoons to coracles, and various boat cruises – see the regional chapters and the Activities chapter p108 for more information.

BUS

Buses are generally the cheapest way to get around India, although most travellers prefer trains for long-distance journeys. Services are fast and frequent, and buses are the only way to get around many mountainous areas. However, roads in curvaceous terrain can be especially perilous; buses are often driven with wilful abandon, and accidents are always a risk. Avoid night buses unless there's no alternative, as driving conditions are more hazardous and drivers may also be suffering from lack of sleep. All buses make snack and toilet stops (some more frequently than others), providing a break from the rattle and shake but possibly adding hours to journey times.

Buses run by the state government bus companies are usually the most reliable option (if there's a breakdown, another bus will be sent to pick up passengers), and seats can usually be booked up to a month in advance. Private buses tend to be either more expensive (but with greater comfort), or cheaper, but drivers can be notorious speed-demons and conductors tend to cram on as many passengers as possible to maximise profits. On top of that, there isn't usually a backup plan for private buses – if your bus breaks down, you may be waiting for an awfully long time. Earplugs are a boon on all long-distance buses to muffle the often deafening music. On any bus, try to sit between the axles to minimise the bumpy effect of potholes.

Luggage is either stored in compartments underneath the bus (sometimes for a small fee) or it can be carried on the roof (arrive at least an hour ahead of the departure time, as some buses cover the roof-stored bags with a large sheet of canvas, making it inconvenient/impossible for last-minute additions). If your bags go on the roof, make sure they're securely locked, and tied to the metal baggage rack – some unlucky travellers have seen their belongings go bouncing off the roof on bumpy roads! Theft is a minor risk so keep an eye on your bags at snack and toilet stops and *never* leave your day-pack or valuables unattended inside the bus.

Share 4WDs complement the bus service in many mountain areas – see p1186.

Classes

Both state and private companies offer 'ordinary' buses – ageing rattletraps, often with wonky windows that blast in dust – or more expensive 'deluxe' buses, which range from less decrepit versions of ordinary buses to flashy Volvo tour buses with AC and reclining two-by-two seating. Travel agencies in many tourist towns offer relatively expensive private two-by-two buses, which tend to leave and terminate at conveniently central stops. Be warned that agencies have been known to book people onto ordinary buses at superdeluxe prices. If possible book directly with the bus company – many state tourist offices

ROAD DISTANCES (km)

	Agra	Bengaluru (Bangalore)	Chennai (Madras)	Delhi	Jaipur	Jaisalmer	Jodhpur	Kolkata (Calcutta)	Mumbai (Bombay)	Panaji (Panjim)	Thiruvananthapuram (Trivandrum)	Varanasi
Agra	---											
Bengaluru (Bangalore)	1833	---										
Chennai (Madras)	1957	337	---									
Delhi	206	2039	2163	---								
Jaipur	230	1875	2072	253	---							
Jaisalmer	839	2080	2394	858	614	---						
Jodhpur	562	1961	2275	585	332	277	---					
Kolkata (Calcutta)	1285	1824	1621	1491	1515	2129	2423	---				
Mumbai (Bombay)	1196	995	1332	1405	1152	1085	966	1916	---			
Panaji (Panjim)	1736	576	913	1945	1692	1625	1506	2120	540	---		
Thiruvananthapuram (Trivandrum)	2468	2876	716	837	2678	2611	2492	2337	1526	986	---	
Varanasi	607	1747	2002	813	837	1446	1169	678	1579	1803	2718	---

TRANSPORT

run their own reliable deluxe bus services. Timetables and destinations may be displayed on signs or billboards at travel agencies and tourist offices.

Costs

The cheapest buses are 'ordinary' government buses, but prices vary from state to state (consult regional chapters). Add around 50% to the ordinary fare for deluxe services, double the fare for AC, and triple or quadruple the fare for a two-by-two service.

Reservations

Most deluxe buses can be booked in advance – usually up to a month in advance for government buses – at the bus station or local travel agencies. Reservations are rarely possible on 'ordinary' buses and travellers often get left behind in the mad rush for a seat. To maximise your chances of securing a seat, either send a travelling companion ahead to grab some space, or pass a book or article of clothing through an open window and place it on an empty seat. This 'reservation' method rarely fails. If you board a bus midway through its journey, you'll often have to stand until a seat becomes free.

At many bus stations there's a separate women's queue, although this isn't always obvious because signs are often in Hindi and men frequently join the melee. Women have an unspoken right to elbow their way to the front of any bus queue in India, so don't be shy, ladies!

CAR

Few people bother with self-drive car rental – not only because of the challenging driving conditions, but also because hiring a car with driver is wonderfully affordable in India, particularly if several people share the cost. Seatbelts are either nonexistent or of variable quality.

Hiring a Car & Driver

Hiring a car with driver is an excellent way to see several places in one day, and the cost slides if you find other travellers to split the fare. Most towns have taxi stands or car-hire companies where you can arrange short or long tours (see regional chapters).

TRANSPORT

Be aware that not all hire cars are licensed to travel beyond their home state. Even those vehicles that are licensed to enter different states have to pay extra (often hefty) state taxes, which will add to the rental charge – confirm the amount when booking so that you don't get a nasty surprise later!

Ask for a driver who speaks some English and knows the region you intend visiting. Try to see the car and meet the driver before paying any money. For multiday trips, the charge should cover the driver's meals and accommodation. Drivers should make their own sleeping and eating arrangements.

Finally, it's *essential* to set the ground rules from day one. Many travellers have complained of having their holiday marred by their driver. To avoid anguish later, politely but firmly let the driver know from the outset that you're the boss.

COSTS

The cost of charter trips depends on the distance and the terrain (driving on mountain roads uses more petrol, hence the higher cost). One-way trips usually cost the same as return ones (to cover the petrol and driver charges for getting back to base). Petrol should be included in the quoted price.

Hire charges vary from state to state. Some taxi unions set a time limit or a maximum kilometre distance for day trips – if you go over, you'll have to pay extra. To avoid potential misunderstandings, ensure you get *in writing* what you've been promised (quotes should include petrol, sightseeing stops, all your chosen destinations, and meals and accommodation for the driver). If a driver asks you for money to pay for petrol en route because he is short of cash, get receipts so you can be reimbursed later.

For sightseeing day trips around a single city, expect to pay anywhere upwards of Rs700/800 for a non-AC/AC car with an eight-hour, 80km limit per day (extra charges apply beyond this).

A tip is customary at the end of your journey; Rs125 per day is fair (more if you're really pleased with the driver's service).

Self-Drive Hire

Self-drive car hire is possible in India's larger cities but, given the hair-raising driving conditions, most travellers opt for a car with driver. International rental companies with representatives in India include **Budget** (www .budget.com) and **Hertz** (www.hertz.com); you'll need an international drivers' permit and your own domestic licence.

HITCHING

For a negotiable fee, truck drivers supplement the bus service in some remote areas. However, as drivers rarely speak English, you may have difficulty explaining where you wish to go, and working out how much is a fair price to pay. Beware that truck drivers have a reputation for driving under the influence of alcohol. As anywhere, women are strongly advised against hitching alone or even as a pair. Always use your instincts.

LOCAL TRANSPORT

Buses, cycle-rickshaws, autorickshaws, taxis, boats and urban trains provide transport around India's cities. On any form of transport without a fixed fare, agree on the price *before* you start your journey and make sure that it covers your luggage and every passenger. If you don't, you're likely to encounter a heated altercation when you get to your destination. Even where local transport is metered, drivers may refuse to use the meter, demanding an elevated 'fixed' fare. If this happens, insist on the meter – if that fails, find another vehicle.

Costs for public transport vary from town to town (consult regional chapters). Fares usually increase at night (by up to 100%) and some drivers charge a few rupees extra for luggage. Carry plenty of small bills for taxi and rickshaw fares as drivers rarely have change.

Some taxi/autorickshaw drivers are involved in the commission racket – for more information see p1147.

Autorickshaw, Tempo & Vikram

The Indian autorickshaw is basically a three-wheeled motorised contraption with a tin or canvas roof and sides, providing room for two passengers (although you'll often see many more bodies squeezed in) and limited luggage. You may also hear autorickshaws being referred to as autos, scooters, riks or tuk-tuks. Autorickshaws are mostly cheaper than taxis and are usually metered, although getting the driver to turn on the meter can be a challenge.

Travelling by auto is great fun, but the clunky two-stroke engines can be smelly and noisy, and the open windows allow in blasts of

---

THE BRAVE BRO

In Ladakh, Arunachal Pradesh and Sikkim, the Border Roads Organisation (BRO) 'build(s) roads in the sky', including some of the world's highest motorable passes. Risking life and limb to keep the roads open, the BRO has a wicked sense of humour when it comes to driver warnings:

■ Overtaker beware of Undertaker.

■ Better to be Mister Late than a late Mister.

■ Go easy on my curves.

■ Stop gossiping, let him drive.

■ Love thy neighbour, but not while driving.

---

air – which can be a boon or a curse, depending on the ambient temperature and the level of pollution outside.

Tempos and *vikrams* (large tempos) are basically outsized autorickshaws with room for more passengers, running on fixed routes for a fixed fare. In country areas, you may also see the fearsome-looking 'three-wheeler' – a crude, tractorlike tempo with a front wheel on an articulated arm.

Boat

Various kinds of local boats offer transport across and down rivers in India, from big car ferries to wooden canoes and wicker coracles – see regional chapters for details. Most of the larger boats carry bicycles and motorcycles for a fee.

Bus

Urban buses, particularly in the big cities, are fume-belching, human-stuffed mechanical monsters that travel at breakneck speed (except during morning and evening rush hours, when they can be endlessly stuck in traffic). It's usually far more convenient and comfortable to opt for an autorickshaw or taxi.

Cycle-Rickshaw

A cycle-rickshaw is a pedal cycle with two rear wheels, supporting a bench seat for passengers. Most have a canopy that can be raised in wet weather, or lowered to provide extra space for luggage. Most of the big cities have phased out (or reduced) the number of cycle-rickshaws, but they are still a major means of

local transport in many smaller towns. Fares must be agreed upon in advance – it's a good idea to speak to locals to get an idea of what is a fair price for the distance you intend travelling. Tips are always appreciated, given the slog involved.

Kolkata is the last bastion of the human-powered rickshaw, a hand-cart on two wheels pulled directly by the rickshaw-wallah.

Taxi

Most towns have taxis, and these are usually metered. However, getting drivers to use the meter can be a major hassle. Drivers often claim that the meter is broken and proceed to request a hugely elevated 'fixed' fare instead. Threatening to get another taxi will often miraculously fix the meter. In tourist areas especially, some taxis flatly refuse to use the meter – if this happens, just find another cab. To avoid fare-setting shenanigans, use prepaid taxis where possible (regional chapters contain details).

Getting a metered ride is only half the battle. Meters are almost always outdated, so fares are calculated using a combination of the meter reading and a complicated 'fare adjustment card'. Predictably, this system is open to abuse. If you spend a few days in any town, you'll soon get a feel for the difference between a reasonable fare and a blatant rip-off. Be aware that many taxi drivers supplement their earnings with commissions – see p1147.

Other Local Transport

In some towns, *tongas* (horse-drawn two-wheelers) and *victorias* (horse-drawn carriages) still operate. Kolkata has a tram network, and both Delhi and Kolkata have

---

PREPAID TAXIS

Most Indian airports and many train stations have a prepaid-taxi booth, normally just outside the terminal building. Here, you can book a taxi for a fixed price (which will include baggage) and thus avoid commission scams. However, officials advise holding on to the payment coupon until you reach your chosen destination, in case the driver has any other ideas! Smaller airports and stations may have prepaid autorickshaw booths instead.

---

efficient underground train systems. Mumbai, Delhi and Chennai, among other centres, have suburban trains that leave from ordinary train stations. See regional chapters for comprehensive details.

MOTORCYCLE

Despite the traffic challenges, India is an amazing country for long-distance motorcycle touring. Motorcycles generally handle the pitted roads better than four-wheeled vehicles, and you'll have the added bonus of being able to stop when and where you want. However, motorcycle touring can be quite an undertaking – there are some popular motorcycle tours (see opposite) for those who don't want the rigmarole of going it alone.

The classic way to motorcycle round India is on an Enfield Bullet, still built to the original 1940s specifications. As well as making a satisfying chugging sound, these bikes are fully manual, making them easy to repair (parts can be found almost everywhere in India). On the other hand, Enfields are often less reliable than many of the newer, Japanese-designed bikes.

The most preferred starting point for motorcycle tours is Delhi, and popular destinations include Rajasthan, South India and Ladakh. Weather is an important factor to consider – for the best times to visit different areas see the Fast Facts boxes at the start of regional chapters. To cross from neighbouring countries, check the latest regulations and paperwork requirements from the relevant diplomatic mission.

Driving Licence

To hire a motorcycle in India, technically you're required to have a valid international drivers' permit in addition to your domestic licence. In tourist areas, some places may rent out a motorcycle without asking for a driving permit/licence, but you won't be covered by insurance in the event of an accident, and may also face a fine.

Fuel & Spare Parts

Petrol and engine oil are widely available in the plains, but petrol stations are widely spaced in the mountains. If you intend to travel to remote regions, ensure you carry enough extra fuel (seek local advice about fuel availability before setting off). At the time of writing, petrol cost around Rs56 per litre.

If you're going to remote regions it's also important to carry basic spares (valves, fuel lines, piston rings etc). Spare parts for Indian and Japanese machines are widely available in cities and larger towns. Delhi's Karol Bagh is a good place to find parts for all Indian and imported bikes.

For all machines (particularly older ones), make sure you regularly check and tighten all nuts and bolts, as Indian roads and engine vibration tend to work things loose quite quickly. Check the engine and gearbox oil level regularly (at least every 500km) and clean the oil filter every few thousand kilometres. Given the road conditions, the chances are you'll make at least a couple of visits to a puncture-wallah – start your trip with new tyres and carry spanners to remove your own wheels.

Hire

Plenty of places rent out motorcycles for local trips and longer tours. Japanese- and Indian-made bikes in the 100cc to 150cc range are cheaper than the big 350cc to 500cc Enfields. As a deposit, you'll need to leave a large cash lump sum (ensure you get a receipt that also stipulates the refundable amount), your passport or your air ticket; it's strongly advisable to avoid leaving your air ticket and passport, the latter of which you'll need to check in at hotels and which the police can demand to see at any time.

One consistently reliable company for long-term rentals is Lalli Motorbike Exports (opposite). For three weeks' hire, a 500cc Enfield costs Rs17,000; a European style is Rs22,000; and a 350cc costs Rs15,000. The price includes excellent advice and an invaluable crash course in Enfield mechanics and repairs.

See the regional chapters for other recommended rental companies and their charges.

Insurance

Only hire a bike with third-party insurance – if you hit someone without insurance, the consequences can be very costly. Reputable companies will include third-party cover in their policies. Those that don't probably aren't trustworthy.

You must also arrange insurance if you buy a motorcycle (usually you can organise this through the person selling the bike). The minimum level of cover is third-party insurance – available for Rs400 to Rs500 per year. This will cover repair and medical costs for any other vehicles, people or property you might hit, but no cover for your own machine.

Comprehensive insurance (recommended) costs upwards of Rs500 per year.

Organised Motorcycle Tours

Dozens of companies offer organised motorcycle tours around India with a support vehicle, mechanic and guide. Below are some reputable outfits (see websites for contact details, itineraries and prices):

Blazing Trails (www.blazingtrailstours.com)
Classic Bike Adventure (www.classic-bike-india.com)
Ferris Wheels (www.ferriswheels.com.au)
H-C Travel (www.hctravel.com)
Himalayan Roadrunners (www.ridehigh.com)
Indian Motorcycle Adventures (http://homepages.ihug.co.nz/~gumby)
Lalli Singh Tours (www.lallisingh.com)
Moto Discovery (www.motodiscovery.com)
Royal Expeditions (www.royalexpeditions.com)
Saffron Road Motorcycle Tours (www.saffronroad.com)
Shepherds Realms (www.asiasafari.com)
Wheel of India (www.wheelofindia.com)

Purchase

If you're planning a longer tour, consider purchasing a motorcycle. Secondhand bikes are widely available and the paperwork is a lot easier than buying a new machine. Finding a secondhand motorcycle is a matter of asking around. Check travellers' noticeboards and approach local motorcycle mechanics and other bikers.

In Delhi, the area around Hari Singh Nalwa St in Karol Bagh has dozens of motorcycle and parts shops, but plenty of dodgy dealers. We consistently receive good reports about **Lalli Motorbike Exports** (☎ 011-28750869; www.lallisingh .com; 1740-A/55 (basement), Hari Singh Nalwa St, Abdul Aziz Rd, Karol Bagh). Run by the knowledgeable Lalli Singh, this place sells and rents out Enfields and parts, and buyers get a crash course in running and maintaining these lovable but temperamental machines.

A decent firm in Mumbai is **Allibhai Premji Tyrewalla** (☎ 022-23099313; www.premjis.com; 205 Dr D Bhadkamkar (Lamington) Rd), which sells new and secondhand motorcycles with a buy-back option.

In Jaipur (Rajasthan) a recommended place for hiring, fixing or purchasing a motorcycle is Rajasthan Auto Centre (see p182).

COSTS

A well looked after secondhand 350cc Enfield will cost anywhere from Rs18,000 to Rs40,000, while a more modern version, with European-style configuration, costs Rs40,000 to Rs50,000; the 500cc model is Rs45,000 to Rs75,000. A useful website for Enfield models is www.royalenfield.com.

It's advisable to get any secondhand bike serviced before you set off. When re-selling your bike, expect to get between half and two-thirds of the price you paid if the bike is still in reasonable condition. Shipping an Indian bike overseas is complicated and expensive – ask the shop you bought the bike from to explain the process.

As well as the cost of the bike, you'll have to pay for insurance – see opposite. Helmets are available for Rs500 to Rs2000, and extras like panniers, luggage racks, protection bars, rearview mirrors, lockable fuel caps, petrol filters and extra tools are easy to come by. One useful extra is a customised fuel tank, which will increase the range you can cover between fuel stops. An Enfield 500cc gives about 25km/L: the 350cc model gives slightly more.

OWNERSHIP PAPERS

There's plenty of paperwork associated with owning a motorcycle. The registration papers are signed by the local registration authority when the bike is first sold and you'll need these papers when you buy a secondhand bike. Foreign nationals cannot change the name on the registration. Instead, you must fill out the forms for a change of ownership and transfer of insurance. If you buy a new bike, the company selling it must register the machine for you, adding to the cost.

For any bike, the registration must be renewed every 15 years (for around Rs5000) and you must make absolutely sure that it states the 'fitness' of the vehicle, and that there are no outstanding debts or criminal proceedings associated with the bike. The whole process is complicated and it makes sense to seek advice from the company selling the bike. Allow around two weeks to tackle the paperwork and get on the road.

Road Conditions

Given the varied road conditions, India can be challenging for novice riders. Hazards range from cows and chickens crossing the carriageway to broken-down trucks, pedestrians on the road, and perpetual potholes and unmarked speed humps. Rural roads sometimes have grain crops strewn across them to be threshed

TRANSPORT

by passing vehicles – a serious sliding hazard for bikers.

Try not to cover too much territory in one day and avoid travelling after dark – many vehicles drive without lights, and dynamo-powered motorcycle headlamps are useless at low revs while negotiating around potholes. On busy national highways expect to average 50km/h without stops; on winding back roads and dirt tracks this can drop to 10km/h.

For long hauls, transporting your bike by train can be a convenient option. Buy a standard train ticket for the journey, then take your bike to the station parcel office with your passport, registration papers, driver's licence and insurance documents. Packing-wallahs will wrap your bike in protective sacking for around Rs150 to Rs250 and you must fill out various forms and pay the shipping fee – around Rs2000 to Rs3500 (charges are less on an ordinary train) – plus an insurance fee of 1% of the declared value of the bike. Bring the same paperwork to collect your bike from the goods office at the other end. If the bike is left waiting at the destination for more than 24 hours, you'll pay a storage fee of around Rs50 to Rs100 per day.

SHARE 4WDS

In mountain areas, share 4WDs supplement the bus service, charging similar fixed fares. Although nominally designed for five to six passengers, most share 4WDs squeeze in many more people. The seats beside and immediately behind the driver are more expensive than the cramped bench seats at the rear. Four-wheel-drives only leave when full, and it is not uncommon for everyone to bail out of a half-full 4WD and pile into a fuller vehicle that is ready to depart. Drivers will leave immediately if you pay for all the empty seats in the vehicle.

Four-wheel-drives run from 4WD stands and 'passenger stations' at the junctions of major roads; ask locals to point you in the right direction. See this book's regional chapters for routes and fares. In some states, 4WDs are known as 'sumos' after the Tata Sumo, a popular 4WD.

Be warned that some people can suffer from travel sickness, particularly on winding mountain roads. Be prepared to give up your window seat to queasy fellow passengers.

TOURS

Tours are available all over India, run by tourist offices, local transport companies and travel agencies. Organised tours can be an inexpensive way to see several places on one trip, although you rarely get much time at each place. If you arrange a tailor-made tour, you'll have more freedom about where you go and how long you stay.

Drivers may double as guides, or you can hire a qualified local guide for a fee. In tourist towns, be wary of touts claiming to be professional guides. Ask the local tourist office about recommended (approved) guides and ask to see evidence from guides who claim to be accredited. Assess the experience of trekking guides by asking about routes, distances and the type of terrain involved – vague answers should set off alarm bells.

On any overnight tour or trek, ensure that all the necessary equipment is provided (eg first-aid kits, camping gear) and inspect everything before you set off. Always confirm (in writing) exactly what the quoted price includes (food, accommodation, transport, trekking equipment, guide fees etc).

See the Tours sections in the regional chapters for details about local tours. For more information about treks and tours, read the Activities chapter (p105).

International Tour Agencies

Many international companies offer tours to India, from straightforward sightseeing trips to adventure tours and activity-based holidays. To find current tours that match your interests, quiz travel agents and surf the web. Some good places to start your tour hunt:

Dragoman (www.dragoman.com) One of several reputable overland tour companies offering trips on customised vehicles.

Exodus (www.exodustravels.co.uk) A wide array of specialist trips, including tours with a holistic, wildlife and adventure focus.

India Wildlife Tours (www.india-wildlife-tours.com) All sorts of wildlife tours, plus 4WD/horse/camel safaris and bird-watching.

Indian Encounter (www.indianencounters.com) Special-interest tours that include wildlife spotting, trekking, river-rafting and Ayurvedic treatments.

Intrepid Travel (www.intrepidtravel.com) Appealing possibilities, from wildlife tours to sacred rambles.

Peregrine Adventures (www.peregrine.net.au) Popular cultural and trekking tours.

Sacred India Tours (www.sacredindia.com) Includes tours with a holistic focus such as yoga and Ayurveda, as well as architectural and cultural tours.

World Expeditions (www.worldexpeditions.com.au) An array of options that includes trekking and cycling tours.

TRAIN

Travelling by train is a terrific way to traverse India. Trains offer a smoother ride than buses, and are especially recommended for long journeys that include overnight travel. India's rail network is one of the world's most extensive, prices are reasonable, and the experience of travelling on an Indian train is a reason to travel all by itself.

An estimated 18 to 20 million people travel by train in India *every day* and Indian Railways is the largest utility employer on earth, with roughly 1.5 million workers. There are around 6900 train stations scattered across the country.

At first, the process of booking a seat can seem bewildering, but behind the scenes things are astonishingly well organised – see Reservations (p1189) for tips on buying a ticket. Some cities also have suburban train networks, although these can be very crowded during peak hours.

Train services to certain destinations are often increased during major festivals, but, tragically, almost every year people are crushed to death in stampedes on overcrowded platforms. Also be mindful of potential passenger drugging and theft – see p1146. Be aware that train trips can be delayed at any time of the journey, so, to avoid stress, factor some leeway into your travel plans.

We've listed useful trains throughout this book but there are hundreds more services. The best way of sourcing updated railway information is to use relevant internet sites such as **Indian Railways** (www.indianrail.gov.in) and the useful www.seat61.com/India.htm. There's also *Trains at a Glance* (Rs35), available at many train station bookstands and better bookshops/newsstands, but it's published annually so it's not as up to date as websites. Nevertheless, it offers comprehensive timetables covering all the main lines.

Big stations often have English-speaking staff who can help with choosing the best train. At smaller stations, midlevel officials such as the deputy station master usually speak English. It's also worth approaching tourist office staff if you need advice about booking tickets, deciding train classes etc. The nationwide railways inquiries number is ☎ 139.

Classes

Trains and seats come in a variety of classes. Express and mail trains usually have general (2nd class) compartments with unreserved seating – often a real free-for-all – and a series of more comfortable compartments that you can reserve. On day trains, there may be a chair-car with padded reclining seats and (usually) AC, or an executive chair car, with better seats and more space.

For overnight trips, you have several choices. 'Sleeper' berths are arranged in groups of six, with two roomier berths across the aisle, in air-cooled carriages. Air-conditioned carriages have either three-tier AC (3AC) berths, in the same configuration as sleepers, or two-tier AC (2AC) berths in groups of four on either side of the aisle. Some trains also have flashier 1st-class AC (1AC) berths, with a choice of two- or four-berth compartments with locking doors.

Bedding is provided in all AC sleeping compartments and there is usually a meal service, plus regular visits from the coffee- and chai-wallah. In sleeper class, bring your own bedding (a warm Indian shawl is perfect for the job). In all sleeping compartments, the lower berths convert to seats for daytime use. If you'd rather sleep, book an upper berth. Note that there is usually a locked door between the reserved and unreserved carriages – if you get trapped on the wrong side, you'll have to wait until the next station to change.

There are also special train services connecting major cities. Shatabdi express trains are same-day services with seating only, in AC chair and executive chair cars. Both classes are comfortable, but the tinted-glass windows can cut down the views a fair bit. The clearest views

---

TOP FIVE SCENIC TRAIN JOURNEYS

A handful of delightful toy trains still ply the metre-gauge lines from the plains to the hills, offering sterling views and a hint of colonial-era charm. Here are our top five scenic rail journeys.

- Darjeeling Himalayan Railway ('Toy Train'; (p552)
- Mettupalayam-Ooty Miniature Train (p1118)
- Shimla Toy Train (p341)
- Matheran Toy Train (p835)
- Visakhapatnam through Eastern Ghats (p974)

TRANSPORT

RAILWAY RAZZLE DAZZLE

India offers an enticing choice of tailored train journeys for tourists seeking to ride the rails with flair. Fares usually include accommodation on board, tours, admission fees and all or most meals, and there are normally child concessions – inquire when booking.

The most popular of the stylish bunch is the *Palace on Wheels* (www.palaceonwheelsindia .com), which operates week-long tours of Rajasthan, departing from Delhi. The itinerary includes Jaipur, Jaisalmer, Jodhpur, Ranthambore National Park, Chittorgarh, Udaipur, Keoladeo Ghana National Park and Agra. Fit-for-a-maharaja carriages are sumptuously decked out and there are dining cars, a bar, a lounge and a library. From October to March, the total fare (seven nights) per person is US$3920/2905/2380 for single/double/triple occupancy. In September and April it costs US$2905/2205/1820. Book in advance online.

Visiting Bikaner and Shekhawati, in Rajasthan, is the *Heritage on Wheels* (www.heritageonwheels .net), a three-night trip that departs from Jaipur. Rates per person per night are US$300/200/150 for single/double/triple occupancy. Book online.

In Maharashtra, the *Deccan Odyssey* offers seven nights of luxury covering the main tourist spots of Maharashtra and Goa. The train leaves from Mumbai (Bombay), heading south through the resorts and port towns of the Konkan Coast to Goa, then looping inland to Pune, Aurangabad (for Ellora), Jalgaon (for Ajanta) and Nasik. From October to March, fares per person per night start at US$540/390/320 for single/double/triple occupancy (US$415/320/260 in September and April). You can do the trip for a minimum of three days; the seven-day package costs an extra US$100 if you'd like guided tours of Mumbai and Goa. Make reservations through Mumbai's **Maharashtra Tourism Development Corporation** (MTDC; ☎ 022-22845678; www.maharashtratourism .gov.in; Madame Cama Rd, Nariman Point, Mumbai).

The Golden Chariot (www.thegoldenchariot.co.in) takes visitors through Karnataka (with a brief stop in Goa) in style. Three different tour packages are available: Bengaluru (Bangalore)–Bengaluru (Monday to Monday); Bengaluru–Goa (Monday to Sunday); and Goa–Goa (Sunday to Sunday). All of the latter packages visit Karnataka's major sights, including Bengaluru, Mysore, Belur, Halebid, Kabini, Hampi and Badami, with a pit stop in Goa. It runs throughout the year. Rates per person per night start at single/double/triple Rs15,800/11,800/9600 (April to August) and Rs19,400/14,000/11,400 (September to March). Bookings can be made online or at the offices of Bengaluru's **Karnataka State Tourism Development Corporation** (KSTDC; Kasturba Rd ☎ 080-22275883; Badami House, Kasturba Rd; St Mark's Rd ☎ 080-41329211; Karnataka Tourism House, 8 Papanna Lane, St Mark's Rd).

With a sacred rather than luxurious focus, the *Mahaparinirvan Express* (aka *Buddhist Circuit Special*), which runs from October to March, tours Buddhist sites (including Lumbini in Nepal; visa required). The eight-day tour leaves from Delhi, visiting Gaya, Bodhgaya, Rajgir, Nalanda, Varanasi (visits to Sarnath and the Ganges), Gorakhpur, Kushinagar, Lumbini, Gonda (for Sravasti) and Agra, before returning to Delhi. It costs US$150/125/95 in 1st/2nd/3rd class per person per night on a twin-share basis (single occupancy hotel rooms can be arranged at an extra charge). For further information, and bookings, head to www.irctc.co.in.

---

are from the barred but unglazed windows of non-AC sleeper and general carriages.

Rajdhani express trains are long-distance overnight services between Delhi and state capitals, with a choice of 1AC, 2AC, 3AC and 2nd class. Reserved tickets on both Shatabdi and Rajdhani trains are slightly more expensive but fares include meals. Prices of all tickets reflect the level of comfort – see the Costs section (right). In all classes, a padlock and a length of chain are useful for securing your luggage to the baggage racks.

For a very helpful description of the various train classes (including pictures) see http://www.seat61.com/India.htm#classes.

Costs

Fares are calculated by distance and class of travel – as shown in the boxed text, opposite. Rajdhani and Shatabdi trains are slightly more expensive, but the price includes meals. Most air-conditioned carriages have a catering service (meals are brought to your seat). In unreserved classes it's a good idea to carry portable snacks. Seniors can avail of discounted train tickets – see p1147.

To find out which trains travel between any two destinations, go to www.trainenquiry .com and click on 'Find Your Train' – type in the name of the two destinations (you may then be prompted to choose from a list of stations) and you'll get a list of every train (with the name, number and arrival/departure times). Then, armed with these details, you can find the fare for your chosen train by going to www.indianrail.gov.in and clicking on 'Fare Enquiry'.

Major stations offer 'retiring rooms', which can be handy if you have a valid ongoing ticket or Indrail Pass – see p1140. Another useful facility is the left-luggage office (cloakroom), where locked bags (only) can be stored for a small daily fee if you have a valid train ticket. For peace of mind, chain your bag to the baggage rack and check the opening times to make sure you can get your bag back when you need it.

Reservations

No reservations are required for general (2nd class) compartments. You can reserve seats in all chair-car, sleeper, and 1AC, 2AC and 3AC carriages up to 60 days in advance at any station with a computerised booking system. Advance bookings are strongly recommended for all overnight journeys.

The reservation procedure is reasonably straightforward – obtain a reservation slip from the information window and fill in the name of the departure station, the destination station, the class you want to travel in and the name and number of the train (this is where *Trains at a Glance* comes into its own, or, see the Costs section, opposite, for how to get the required details on the internet). You then join the long queue to the ticket window, where your ticket

will be printed. Women should avail of the separate women's queue – if there isn't one, go to the front of the regular queue.

In larger cities, there are dedicated ticket windows for foreigners and credit-card payments. Elsewhere, you'll have to join a general queue and pay cash in rupees. A special tourist quota is set aside for foreign tourists travelling between popular stations. These seats can only be booked at dedicated reservation offices in major cities (details are given in this book's regional chapters), and you need to show your passport and visa as ID. The government has fairly recently changed the rules, allowing foreigners to pay for tourist quota seats in rupees, British pounds, US dollars or euros, in cash or Thomas Cook and American Express travellers cheques (change is given in rupees). However, quite a few offices still ask to see foreign exchange certificates before accepting payment in rupees.

Trains are frequently overbooked, but many passengers cancel. You can buy a ticket on the 'wait list' and try your luck. A refund is available if you fail to get a seat – ask the ticket office about your chances. Refunds are available on any ticket, even after departure, with a penalty – the rules are complicated so check when you book.

If you don't want to go through the hassle of buying a ticket yourself, many travel agencies and hotels will purchase your train ticket for a commission, although beware of ticket scams (eg being sold a cheaper class than requested, at a higher class fare).

Internet bookings are also possible on the website www.irctc.co.in, and you can choose an e-ticket, or have the ticket sent to you inside India by courier. The website www.seat61 .com/India.htm has some excellent advice on online bookings – scroll down to the 'How to buy tickets – from outside India' heading.

EXPRESS TRAIN FARES IN RUPEES

Distance (km)	1AC	2AC	3AC	Chair car (CC)	Sleeper (SL)	Second (II)
100	542	322	158	122	56	35
200	794	430	256	199	91	57
300	1081	556	348	271	124	78
400	1347	693	433	337	154	97
500	1613	830	519	404	185	116
1000	2628	1352	845	657	301	188
1500	3328	1712	1070	832	381	238
2000	4028	2072	1295	1007	461	288

TRANSPORT

Reserved tickets show your seat/berth number (or wait-list number) and the carriage number. When the train pulls in, keep an eye out for your carriage number written on the side of the train (station staff can point you in the right direction if you get confused). A list of names and berths is also posted on the side of each reserved carriage – a beacon of light for panicking travellers!

It's wise to book well ahead if you plan on travelling during Indian holidays or festivals, when seats can fill up incredibly fast.

Train Passes

The Indrail Pass permits unlimited rail travel for the period of its validity, but it offers limited savings and you must still make reservations. Passes are available for one to 90 days of travel and you can book through certain overseas travel agencies, or station ticket offices in major Indian cities – click on the Information/International Tourist link on www.indianrail.gov.in for further details, including prices. There's no refund for either lost or partially used tickets.

Health Dr Trish Batchelor

CONTENTS

There is huge geographical variation in India, from tropical beaches to the Himalaya mountains. So environmental issues like heat, cold and altitude can cause health problems. Hygiene is poor in most regions so food and water-borne illnesses are common. Many insect-borne diseases are present, particularly in tropical areas. Medical care is basic in many areas (especially beyond the larger cities) so it's essential to be well prepared before travelling to India.

Travellers tend to worry about contracting infectious diseases when in the tropics, but these rarely cause serious illness or death in travellers. Pre-existing medical conditions and accidental injury (especially traffic accidents) account for most life-threatening problems. Becoming ill in some way, however, is very common. Fortunately, most travellers' illnesses can be prevented with some common-sense behaviour or treated with a well-stocked traveller's medical kit – however, never hesitate to consult a doctor while on the road, as self-diagnosis can be hazardous.

The following advice is a general guide only and certainly does not replace the advice of a doctor trained in travel medicine.

BEFORE YOU GO

Pack medications in their original, clearly labelled containers. A signed and dated letter from your physician describing your medical conditions and medications, including generic names, is very useful. If carrying syringes or needles, be sure to have a physician's letter documenting their medical necessity. If you have a heart condition, bring a copy of your ECG taken just prior to travelling.

If you take any regular medication, bring double your ordinary needs in case of loss or theft. You'll be able to buy quite a few medications over the counter in India without a doctor's prescription, but it can be difficult to find some of the newer drugs, particularly the latest antidepressant drugs, blood-pressure medications and contraceptive pills.

INSURANCE

Even if you are fit and healthy, don't travel without health insurance – accidents do happen. Declare any existing medical conditions you have – the insurance company will check if your problem is pre-existing and will not cover you if it is undeclared. You may require extra cover for adventure activities such as rock climbing and scuba diving. If your health insurance doesn't cover you for medical expenses abroad, consider getting extra insurance. If you're uninsured, emergency evacuation is expensive, bills of over US$100,000 are not uncommon.

It's a good idea to find out in advance if your insurance plan will make payments directly to providers or if it will reimburse you later for overseas health expenditures (in India, doctors usually expect payment in cash). Some policies offer lower and higher medical-expense options; the higher ones are chiefly for countries that have extremely high medical costs, such as the United States. You may prefer a policy that pays doctors or hospitals directly rather than you having to pay on the spot and claim from your insurance company later. However be aware that most medical facilities in India require immediate payment. If you do have to claim later, make sure you keep all relevant documentation. Some policies ask that you telephone back (reverse charges) to a centre in your home country where an immediate assessment of your problem will be made.

HEALTH

HEALTH

MEDICAL CHECKLIST

Recommended items for a personal medical kit:

- Antifungal cream, eg Clotrimazole
- Antibacterial cream, eg Mupirocin
- Antibiotic for skin infections, eg Amoxicillin/Clavulanate or Cephalexin
- Antihistamine – there are many options, eg Cetrizine for daytime and Promethazine for night
- Antiseptic, eg Betadine
- Antispasmodic for stomach cramps, eg Buscopam
- Contraceptive
- Decongestant, eg Pseudoephedrine
- DEET-based insect repellent
- Diarrhoea medication – consider an oral rehydration solution (eg Gastrolyte), diarrhoea 'stopper' (eg Loperamide) and antinausea medication (eg Prochlorperazine). Antibiotics for diarrhoea include Norfloxacin or Ciprofloxacin; for bacterial diarrhoea Azithromycin; for giardia or amoebic dysentery Tinidazole.
- First-aid items such as scissors, elastoplasts, bandages, gauze, thermometer (but not mercury), sterile needles and syringes, safety pins and tweezers
- Ibuprofen or another anti-inflammatory
- Indigestion tablets, eg Quick Eze or Mylanta
- Iodine tablets (unless you are pregnant or have a thyroid problem) to purify water
- Laxative, eg Coloxyl
- Migraine medication if you suffer from migraines
- Paracetamol
- Pyrethrin to impregnate clothing and mosquito nets
- Steroid cream for allergic or itchy rashes, eg 1% to 2% hydrocortisone
- High-factor sunscreen and wide-brimmed hat
- Throat lozenges
- Thrush (vaginal yeast infection) treatment, eg Clotrimazole pessaries or Diflucan tablet
- Ural or equivalent if prone to urine infections

VACCINATIONS

Specialised travel-medicine clinics are your best source of up-to-date information; they stock all available vaccines and can give specific recommendations for your trip. The doctors will take into account factors such as past vaccination history, the length of your trip, activities you may be undertaking and underlying medical conditions, such as pregnancy.

Most vaccines don't give immunity until *at least* two weeks after they're given, so visit a doctor four to eight weeks before departure. Ask your doctor for an International Certificate of Vaccination (otherwise known as the 'yellow booklet'), which will list all the vaccinations you've received.

Recommended Vaccinations

The World Health Organization (WHO) recommends the following vaccinations for travellers going to India (as well as being up to date with measles, mumps and rubella vaccinations):

Adult diphtheria and tetanus Single booster recommended if none in the previous 10 years. Side effects include sore arm and fever.

Hepatitis A Provides almost 100% protection for up to a year; a booster after 12 months provides at least another 20 years' protection. Mild side effects such as headache and sore arm occur in 5% to 10% of people.

Hepatitis B Now considered routine for most travellers. Given as three shots over six months. A rapid schedule is also available, as is a combined vaccination with Hepatitis

A. Side effects are mild and uncommon, usually headache and sore arm. In 95% of people lifetime protection results.

Polio Only one booster is required as an adult for life-time protection. Inactivated polio vaccine is safe during pregnancy.

Typhoid Recommended for all travellers to India, even those only visiting urban areas. The vaccine offers around 70% protection, lasts for two to three years and comes as a single shot. Tablets are also available, but the injection is usually recommended as it has fewer side effects. Sore arm and fever may occur.

Varicella If you haven't had chickenpox, discuss this vaccination with your doctor.

These immunisations are recommended for long-term travellers (more than one month) or those at special risk (seek further advice from your doctor):

Japanese B Encephalitis Three injections in all. Booster recommended after two years. Sore arm and headache are the most common side effects. In rare cases, an allergic reaction comprising hives and swelling can occur up to 10 days after any of the three doses.

Meningitis Single injection. There are two types of vaccination: the quadravalent vaccine gives two to three years' protection; meningitis group C vaccine gives around 10 years' protection. Recommended for long-term backpackers aged under 25.

Rabies Three injections in all. A booster after one year will then provide 10 years' protection. Side effects are rare – occasionally headache and sore arm.

Tuberculosis (TB) A complex issue. Adult long-term travellers are usually recommended to have a TB skin test before and after travel, rather than vaccination. Only one vaccine given in a lifetime.

Required Vaccinations

The only vaccine required by international regulations is yellow fever. Proof of vaccination will only be required if you have visited a country in the yellow-fever zone within the six days prior to entering India. If you are travelling to India from Africa or South America, you should check to see if you require proof of vaccination.

INTERNET RESOURCES

There is a wealth of travel-health advice on the internet – www.lonelyplanet.com is a good place to start. Some other suggestions:

Centers for Disease Control and Prevention (CDC; www.cdc.gov) Good general information.

MD Travel Health (www.mdtravelhealth.com) Provides complete travel-health recommendations for every country, updated daily.

World Health Organization (WHO; www.who.int/ith) Its helpful book *International Travel & Health* is revised annually and is available online.

FURTHER READING

Lonely Planet's *Healthy Travel – Asia & India* is a handy pocket size and packed with useful information, including pre-trip planning, emergency first aid, immunisation and disease information, and what to do if you get sick on the road. Other recommended references include *Travellers' Health* by Dr Richard Dawood and *Travelling Well* by Dr Deborah Mills – check out the website of **Travelling Well** (www.travellingwell.com.au).

IN TRANSIT

DEEP VEIN THROMBOSIS (DVT)

Deep vein thrombosis (DVT) occurs when blood clots form in the legs during plane flights, chiefly because of prolonged immobility. The longer the flight, the greater the risk. Though most blood clots are reabsorbed uneventfully, some may break off and travel through the blood vessels to the lungs, where they may cause life-threatening complications.

The chief symptom of DVT is swelling or pain of the foot, ankle or calf, usually but not always on just one side. When a blood clot travels to the lungs, it may cause chest pain and difficulty in breathing. Travellers with any of these symptoms should immediately seek medical attention.

To prevent the development of DVT on long flights, walk about the cabin, perform isometric compressions of the leg muscles (ie contract the leg muscles while sitting), drink plenty of fluids, and avoid alcohol and tobacco.

JET LAG & MOTION SICKNESS

Jet lag is common when crossing more than five time zones; it results in insomnia, fatigue, malaise and/or nausea. To avoid jet lag try drinking plenty of fluids (nonalcoholic) and eating light meals. Upon arrival, seek exposure to natural sunlight and readjust your schedule (for meals, sleep etc) as soon as possible.

Antihistamines such as dimenhydrinate (Dramamine), promethazine (Phenergan) and meclizine (Antivert, Bonine) are usually the first choice for treating motion sickness. Their main side effect is drowsiness. One herbal

HEALTH

alternative is ginger, which works wonders for some people.

IN INDIA

AVAILABILITY OF HEALTH CARE

Medical care is hugely variable in India, especially beyond the big cities. Some cities now have clinics catering specifically to travellers and expatriates. These clinics are usually more expensive than local medical facilities, but are worth utilising, as they should offer a higher standard of care. Additionally, they understand the local system, and are aware of the most reputable local hospitals and specialists. They may also liaise with insurance companies should you require evacuation. Recommended clinics are listed under Information sections in the regional chapters of this book. It is usually difficult to find reliable medical care in rural areas.

Self-treatment may be appropriate if your problem is minor (eg traveller's diarrhoea), you are carrying the relevant medication and you cannot attend a recommended clinic. However, if you suspect you may potentially have a serious disease, especially malaria, do not waste time; travel to the nearest quality facility to receive attention. It is always better to be assessed by a doctor than to rely on self-treatment.

Before buying medication over the counter, always check the use-by date and ensure the packet is sealed. Don't accept items that have been poorly stored (eg lying in a glass cabinet exposed to the sunshine).

INFECTIOUS DISEASES
Avian Flu

'Bird flu' or Influenza A (H5N1) is a subtype of the type A influenza virus. This virus typically infects birds and not humans; however,

in 1997 the first documented case of bird-to-human transmission was recorded in Hong Kong. Currently, very close contact with dead or sick birds is the principal source of infection and bird-to-human transmission does not easily occur.

Symptoms include high fever and typical influenza-like symptoms with rapid deterioration, leading to respiratory failure and death in many cases. The early administration of antiviral drugs, such as Tamiflu, is recommended to improve the chances of survival. At this time it is not routinely recommended for travellers to carry Tamiflu with them – rather, immediate medical care should be sought if bird flu is suspected.

There is currently no vaccine available to prevent bird flu. For up-to-date information check these two websites:

- www.who.int/en/
- www.avianinfluenza.com.au

Coughs, Colds & Chest Infections

Around 25% of travellers to India will develop a respiratory infection. This usually starts as a virus and is exacerbated by environmental conditions, such as pollution in the cities, or cold and altitude in the mountains. Commonly a secondary bacterial infection will intervene – marked by fever, chest pain and coughing up discoloured or blood-tinged sputum. If you have the symptoms of an infection seek medical advice or consider commencing a general antibiotic.

Dengue Fever

This mosquito-borne disease is becomingly increasingly problematic in the tropical world, especially in the cities. As there is no vaccine available it can only be prevented by avoiding mosquito bites. The mosquito that carries dengue bites day and night, so use insect avoidance measures at all times. Symptoms include high fever, severe headache and body ache (dengue was previously known as 'breakbone fever'). Some people develop a rash and experience diarrhoea. There is no specific treatment, just rest and paracetamol – do not take aspirin as it increases the likelihood of haemorrhaging. Make sure you see a doctor to be diagnosed and monitored.

Hepatitis A

A problem throughout the region, this food-and water-borne virus infects the liver, causing jaundice (yellow skin and eyes), nausea and lethargy. There is no specific treatment for hepatitis A, you just need to allow time for the liver to heal. All travellers to India should be vaccinated against hepatitis A.

Hepatitis B

The only sexually transmitted disease that can be prevented by vaccination, hepatitis B is spread by body fluids. The long-term consequences can include liver cancer and cirrhosis.

Hepatitis E

Transmitted through contaminated food and water, hepatitis E has similar symptoms to hepatitis A, but is far less common. It is a severe problem in pregnant women and can result in the death of both mother and baby. There is currently no vaccine, and prevention is by following safe eating and drinking guidelines.

HIV

HIV is spread via contaminated body fluids. Avoid unsafe sex, unsterile needles (including in medical facilities) and procedures such as tattoos. The growth rate of HIV in India is one of the highest in the world – also see p63.

Influenza

Present year-round in the tropics, influenza (flu) symptoms include fever, muscle aches, a runny nose, cough and sore throat. It can be severe in people over the age of 65 or in those with medical conditions such as heart disease or diabetes – vaccination is recommended for these individuals. There is no specific treatment, just rest and paracetamol.

Japanese B Encephalitis

This viral disease is transmitted by mosquitoes and is rare in travellers. Like most mosquito-borne diseases it is becoming a more common problem in affected countries. Most cases occur in rural areas and vaccination is recommended for travellers spending more than one month outside of cities. There is no treatment, and a third of infected people will die while another third will suffer permanent brain damage. Ask your doctor for further details.

Malaria

For such a serious and potentially deadly disease, there is an enormous amount of misinformation concerning malaria. You must get expert advice as to whether your trip actually puts you at risk. For most rural areas, especially, the risk of contracting malaria far outweighs the risk of any tablet side effects. Before you travel, seek medical advice on the right medication and dosage for you.

Malaria is caused by a parasite transmitted by the bite of an infected mosquito. The most important symptom of malaria is fever, but general symptoms, such as headache, diarrhoea, cough or chills, may also occur. Diagnosis can only be properly made by taking a blood sample.

Two strategies should be combined to prevent malaria – mosquito avoidance and antimalarial medications. Most people who catch malaria are taking inadequate or no antimalarial medication.

Travellers are advised to prevent mosquito bites by taking these steps:

- Use a DEET-containing insect repellent on exposed skin. Wash this off at night, as long as you are sleeping under a mosquito net. Natural repellents such as citronella can be effective, but must be applied more frequently than products containing DEET.
- Sleep under a mosquito net impregnated with pyrethrin.
- Choose accommodation with proper screens and fans (if not air-conditioned).
- Impregnate clothing with pyrethrin in high-risk areas.
- Wear long sleeves and trousers in light colours.
- Use mosquito coils.
- Spray your room with insect repellent before going out for your evening meal.

There are a variety of medications available. The effectiveness of the chloroquine and Paludrine combination is now limited in many parts of South Asia. Common side effects include nausea (40% of people) and mouth ulcers.

The daily tablet doxycycline is a broad-spectrum antibiotic that has the added benefit of helping to prevent a variety of tropical diseases, including leptospirosis, tick-borne disease and typhus. The potential side effects include photosensitivity (a tendency to sunburn), thrush (in women), indigestion, heartburn, nausea and interference with the contraceptive pill. More serious side effects include ulceration of the oesophagus – you can help prevent this by taking your tablet

HEALTH

with a meal and a large glass of water, and never lying down within half an hour of taking it. It must be taken for four weeks after leaving the risk area.

Lariam (mefloquine) has received much bad press, some of it justified, some not. This weekly tablet suits many people. Serious side effects are rare but include depression, anxiety, psychosis and having fits. Anyone with a history of depression, anxiety, other psychological disorders or epilepsy should not take Lariam. It is considered safe in the second and third trimesters of pregnancy. Tablets must be taken for four weeks after leaving the risk area.

The newer drug Malarone is a combination of atovaquone and proguanil. Side effects are uncommon and mild, most commonly nausea and headache. It is the best tablet for scuba divers and for those on short trips to high-risk areas. It must be taken for one week after leaving the risk area.

Rabies

This uniformly fatal disease is spread by the bite or possibly even the lick of an infected animal – most commonly a dog or monkey. You should seek medical advice immediately after any animal bite and commence post-exposure treatment. Having pre-travel vaccination means the postbite treatment is greatly simplified. If an animal bites you, gently wash the wound with soap and water, and apply iodine-based antiseptic. If you are not pre-vaccinated you will need to receive rabies immunoglobulin as soon as possible, and this is very difficult to obtain in much of India.

STDs

Sexually transmitted diseases most common in India include herpes, warts, syphilis, gonorrhoea and chlamydia. People carrying these diseases often have no signs of infection. Condoms will prevent gonorrhoea and chlamydia but not warts or herpes. If after a sexual encounter you develop any rash, lumps, discharge or pain when passing urine, seek immediate medical attention. If you have been sexually active during your travels, have an STD check on your return home.

Tuberculosis

While TB is rare in travellers, those who have significant contact with the local population (such as medical and aid workers and long-term travellers) should take precautions. Vaccination is usually only given to children under the age of five, but adults at risk are recommended to have pre- and post-travel TB testing. The main symptoms are fever, cough, weight loss, night sweats and fatigue.

Typhoid

This serious bacterial infection is also spread via food and water. It gives a high and slowly progressive fever and headache, and may be accompanied by a dry cough and stomach pain. It is diagnosed by blood tests and treated with antibiotics. Vaccination is recommended for all travellers who are spending more than a week in India. Be aware that vaccination is not 100% effective, so you must still be careful with what you eat and drink.

TRAVELLER'S DIARRHOEA

This is by far the most common problem affecting travellers in India – between 30% and 70% of people will suffer from it within two weeks of starting their trip. In over 80% of cases, travellers' diarrhoea is caused by a bacteria (there are numerous potential culprits), and thus responds promptly to treatment with antibiotics. Treatment with antibiotics will depend on your situation – how sick you are, how quickly you need to get better, where you are etc.

Travellers' diarrhoea is defined as the passage of more than three watery bowel actions within 24 hours, plus at least one other symptom, such as fever, cramps, nausea, vomiting or feeling generally unwell.

Treatment consists of staying well hydrated; rehydration solutions like Gastrolyte are the best for this. Antibiotics such as norfloxacin, ciprofloxacin or azithromycin should kill the bacteria quickly.

Loperamide is just a 'stopper' and doesn't get to the cause of the problem. It can be helpful, though (eg if you have to go on a long bus ride). Don't take loperamide if you have a fever or blood in your stools. Seek medical attention quickly if you do not respond to an appropriate antibiotic.

Amoebic Dysentery

Amoebic dysentery is very rare in travellers but is often misdiagnosed by poor-quality labs. Symptoms are similar to bacterial diarrhoea: fever, bloody diarrhoea and generally feeling unwell. You should always seek reliable medical care if you have blood in your

DRINKING WATER

- Never drink tap water.

- Bottled water is generally safe – check the seal is intact at purchase.

- Avoid ice unless you know it has been safely made.

- Be careful of fresh juices served at street stalls in particular – they may have been watered down or may be served in unhygienic jugs/glasses.

- Boiling water is usually the most efficient method of purifying it.

- The best chemical purifier is iodine. It should not be used by pregnant women or those with thyroid problems.

- Water filters should also filter out viruses. Ensure your filter has a chemical barrier such as iodine and a small pore size (less than four microns).

diarrhoea. Treatment involves two drugs: Tinidazole or Metronidazole to kill the parasite in your gut and then a second drug to kill the cysts. If left untreated complications such as liver or gut abscesses can occur.

Giardiasis

Giardia is a parasite that is relatively common in travellers. Symptoms include nausea, bloating, excess gas, fatigue and intermittent diarrhoea. The parasite will eventually go away if left untreated but this can take months; the best advice is to seek medical treatment. The treatment of choice is Tinidazole, with Metronidazole being a second-line option.

ENVIRONMENTAL HAZARDS
Air Pollution

Air pollution, particularly vehicle pollution, is an increasing problem in most of India's urban hubs. If you have severe respiratory problems, speak with your doctor before travelling to India. This pollution also causes minor respiratory problems, such as sinusitis, dry throat and irritated eyes. If troubled by the pollution, leave the city for a few days and get some fresh air.

Diving & Surfing

Divers and surfers should seek specialised advice before they travel to ensure their medical kit contains treatment for coral cuts and tropical ear infections, as well as the standard problems. Divers should ensure their insurance covers them for decompression illness – get specialised dive insurance through an organisation such as **Divers Alert Network** (DAN; www .danasiapacific.org). Have a dive medical before you leave your home country – there are certain medical conditions that are incompatible with diving.

Food

Eating in restaurants is generally the biggest risk factor for contracting travellers' diarrhoea. Ways to avoid it include eating only freshly cooked food, and avoiding shellfish and food that has been sitting in buffets. Peel all fruit, cook vegetables and soak salads in iodine water for at least 20 minutes. Eat in busy restaurants with a high turnover of customers. Also read the box, p90.

Heat

Many parts of India, especially down south, are hot and humid throughout the year. For most people it takes at least two weeks to adapt to the hot climate. Swelling of the feet and ankles is common, as are muscle cramps caused by excessive sweating. Prevent these by avoiding dehydration and excessive activity in the heat. Take it easy when you first arrive. Don't eat salt tablets (they aggravate the gut); drinking rehydration solution or eating salty food helps. Treat cramps by stopping activity, resting, rehydrating with double-strength rehydration solution and gently stretching.

Dehydration is the main contributor to heat exhaustion. Symptoms include feeling weak; headache; irritability; nausea or vomiting; sweaty skin; a fast, weak pulse; and a normal or slightly elevated body temperature. Treatment involves getting out of the heat and/or sun, fanning the sufferer and applying cool, wet cloths to the skin, laying the sufferer flat with their legs raised and rehydrating with water containing one-quarter teaspoon of salt per litre. Recovery is usually rapid and it is common to feel weak for some days afterwards.

Heat stroke is a serious medical emergency. Symptoms come on suddenly and include weakness, nausea, a hot dry body with a body temperature of over 41°C, dizziness, confusion, loss of coordination, fits, and eventually collapse and loss of consciousness. Seek medical help and commence cooling by getting the person

HEALTH

out of the heat, removing their clothes, fanning them and applying cool wet cloths or ice to their body, especially to the groin and armpits.

Prickly heat is a common skin rash in the tropics, caused by sweat being trapped under the skin. The result is an itchy rash of tiny lumps. Treat it by moving out of the heat and into an air-conditioned area for a few hours and by having cool showers. Creams and ointments clog the skin so they should be avoided. Locally bought prickly-heat powder can be helpful.

Tropical fatigue is common in long-term expatriates based in the tropics. It's rarely due to disease and is caused by the climate, inadequate mental rest, excessive alcohol intake and the demands of daily work in a different culture.

Altitude Sickness

If you are going to altitudes above 3000m, you should get information on preventing, recognising and treating Acute Mountain Sickness (AMS). The biggest risk factor for developing altitude sickness is going too high too quickly – you should follow a conservative acclimatisation schedule such as can be found in all good trekking guides – and you should *never* go to a higher altitude when you have any symptoms that could be altitude related. There is no way to predict who will get altitude sickness and it is often the younger, fitter members of a group who succumb.

Symptoms usually develop during the first 24 hours at altitude but may be delayed up to three weeks. Mild symptoms include headache, lethargy, dizziness, difficulty sleeping and loss of appetite. AMS may become more severe without warning and can be fatal. Severe symptoms include breathlessness, a dry, irritative cough (which may progress to the production of pink, frothy sputum), severe headache, lack of coordination and balance, confusion, irrational behaviour, vomiting, drowsiness and unconsciousness.

Treat mild symptoms by resting at the same altitude until recovery, which usually takes a day or two. Paracetamol or aspirin can be taken for headaches. If symptoms persist or become worse, however, immediate descent is necessary; even 500m can help. Drug treatments should never be used to avoid descent or to enable further ascent.

The drugs acetazolamide and dexamethasone are recommended by some doctors for the prevention of AMS; however, their use is controversial. They can reduce the symptoms, but they may also mask warning signs; severe and fatal AMS has occurred in people taking these drugs.

To prevent acute mountain sickness:

- Ascend slowly – have frequent rest days, spending two to three nights at each rise of 1000m.
- It is always wise to sleep at a lower altitude than the greatest height reached during the day, if possible. Also, once above 3000m, care should be taken not to increase the sleeping altitude by more than 300m per day.
- Drink extra fluids. The mountain air is dry and cold, and moisture is lost as you breathe.
- Eat light, high-carbohydrate meals.
- Avoid alcohol and sedatives.

Insect Bites & Stings

Bedbugs don't carry disease but their bites can be very itchy. They live in the cracks of furniture and walls and then migrate to the bed at night to feed on you. You can treat the itch with an antihistamine. Lice inhabit various parts of your body but most commonly your head and pubic area. Transmission is via close contact with an infected person. They can be difficult to treat and you may need numerous applications of an antilice shampoo such as pyrethrin. Pubic lice are usually contracted from sexual contact.

Ticks are contracted after walking in rural areas. Ticks are commonly found behind the ears, on the belly and in armpits. If you have had a tick bite and experience symptoms such as a rash at the site of the bite or elsewhere, fever or muscle aches, you should see a doctor. Doxycycline prevents tick-borne diseases.

Leeches are found in humid rainforest areas. They do not transmit any disease but their bites are often intensely itchy for weeks afterwards and can easily become infected. Apply an iodine-based antiseptic to any leech bite to help prevent infection.

Bee and wasp stings mainly cause problems for people who are allergic to them. Anyone with a serious bee or wasp allergy should carry an injection of adrenalin (eg an Epipen) for emergency treatment. For others pain is the main problem – apply ice to the sting and take painkillers.

Skin Problems

Fungal rashes are common in humid climates. There are two common fungal rashes that affect travellers. The first occurs in moist areas, such as the groin, armpits and between the toes. It starts as a red patch that slowly spreads and is usually itchy. Treatment involves keeping the skin dry, avoiding chafing and using an antifungal cream such as clotrimazole or Lamisil. *Tinea versicolor* is also common – this fungus causes small, light-coloured patches, most commonly on the back, chest and shoulders. Consult a doctor.

Cuts and scratches become easily infected in humid climates. You should take meticulous care of any cuts and scratches to prevent complications such as abscesses. Immediately wash all wounds in clean water and apply antiseptic. If you develop signs of infection (increasing pain and redness), see a doctor. Divers and surfers should be particularly careful with coral cuts, as they easily become infected.

Sunburn

Even on a cloudy day sunburn can occur rapidly. Always use a strong sunscreen (at least factor 30), making sure to reapply after a swim, and always wear a wide-brimmed hat and sunglasses outdoors. Avoid lying in the sun during the hottest part of the day (10am to 2pm). You can get burnt very easily when you are at high altitudes, so be vigilant once above 3000m. If you become sunburnt, stay out of the sun until you have recovered, apply cool compresses and, if necessary, take painkillers for the discomfort. One per cent hydrocortisone cream applied twice daily is also helpful.

WOMEN'S HEALTH

In most places in India, supplies of sanitary products (pads, rarely tampons) are readily available. Birth-control options may be limited, so bring adequate supplies of your own form of contraception. Heat, humidity and antibiotics can all contribute to thrush. Treatment is with antifungal creams and pessaries such as clotrimazole. A practical alternative is a single tablet of Fluconazole (Diflucan). Urinary-tract infections can be precipitated by dehydration or long bus journeys without toilet stops; bring suitable antibiotics. For gynaecological health issues, seek out a female doctor.

Pregnant women should receive specialised advice before travelling. The ideal time to travel is in the second trimester (between 16 and 28 weeks), when the risk of pregnancy-related problems is at its lowest and pregnant women generally feel at their best. Always carry a list of reputable medical facilities available at your destination and ensure you continue your standard antenatal care at these facilities. Avoid rural travel in areas with poor transport and substandard medical facilities. Most of all, ensure that your travel-insurance policy covers all pregnancy-related possibilities, including premature labour.

Malaria is a high-risk disease for pregnant women, and WHO recommends that pregnant women do *not* travel to areas with Chloroquine-resistant malaria. None of the more effective antimalarial drugs are completely safe in pregnancy.

Travellers' diarrhoea can quickly lead to dehydration and result in inadequate blood flow to the placenta. Many of the drugs used to treat various diarrhoea bugs are not recommended in pregnancy. Azithromycin is generally considered safe.

HEALTH

Language

CONTENTS

There is no one 'Indian' language as such. This is part of the reason why English is still widely spoken more than 50 years after the British left India and why it's still the official language of the judiciary.

Eighteen languages are recognised by the constitution, and these fall into two major groups: Indic (also called Indo-Aryan) and Dravidian. Additionally, over 1600 minor languages and dialects were listed in the latest census. With so many languages, the scope for misunderstanding can be easily appreciated!

The Indic languages are a branch of the Indo-European group of languages (to which English belongs). The Indic languages were spoken by the Central Asian peoples who invaded what is now India. The Dravidian languages such as Tamil are native to South India, although they have been influenced by Sanskrit and Hindi over the years.

Most of India's languages have their own script, but written English can also be quite common; in some states, such as Gujarat, you'll hardly see a word of it, whereas in Himachal Pradesh virtually everything is in English. An Rs5 or larger banknote shows the scripts of 14 of India's languages. As well as Hindi and English there's a list of 12 other languages: from the top, they are Assamese, Bengali, Gujarati, Kannada, Kashmiri, Malayalam, Marathi, Oriya, Punjabi, Sanskrit, Tamil, Telugu and Urdu. (See the boxed text, opposite, for more information.)

Major efforts have been made to promote Hindi as the national language of India and to gradually phase out English. A stumbling block to this plan is that Hindi is the predominant language in the north, but it bears little relation to the Dravidian languages of the south. Subsequently, very few people in the south speak Hindi. It is from here, particularly in the state of Tamil Nadu, that the most vocal opposition to the countrywide adoption of Hindi comes, along with the strongest support for the retention of English.

For many educated Indians, English is virtually their first language, and for the large number of Indians who speak more than one language, English is often their second tongue. Thus it's very easy to get around India with English, but it's always good to know at least a little of the local language.

HINDI

Hindi is written from left to right in Devanagari script. While the script may be unfamiliar, English speakers will recognise many of Hindi's grammatical features.

For a far more comprehensive guide to Hindi, get a copy of Lonely Planet's *Hindi, Urdu & Bengali* phrasebook.

PRONUNCIATION

Most Hindi sounds are similar to their English counterparts, but there are a few tricky ones. There's a difference between 'aspirated' and 'unaspirated' consonants – the aspirated

INDIA'S OFFICIAL LANGUAGES

Assamese State language of Assam, and spoken by nearly 60% of that state's population. Dates back to the 13th century.

Bengali Spoken by nearly 200 million people (mostly in what is now Bangladesh), and the state language of West Bengal. Developed as a language in the 13th century.

Gujarati State language of Gujarat, it is an Indic language.

Hindi The most important Indian language, although it is only spoken as a mother tongue by about 20% of the population, mainly in the area known as the Hindi-belt, the cow-belt or Bimaru, which includes Bihar, Madhya Pradesh, Rajasthan and Uttar Pradesh. This Indic language is the official language of the Indian government, the states already mentioned, plus Haryana and Himachal Pradesh.

Kannada State language of Karnataka, spoken by about 65% of that state's population.

Kashmiri Kashmiri speakers account for about 55% of the population of Jammu and Kashmir. It is an Indic language written in the Perso-Arabic script.

Konkani A Dravidian language spoken by people in the Goa region.

Malayalam A Dravidian language, and the state language of Kerala.

Manipuri An Indic language of the northeast region.

Marathi An Indic language dating back to around the 13th century, Marathi is the state language of Maharashtra.

Nepali The predominant language of Sikkim, where around 75% of the people are ethnic Nepalis.

Oriya An Indic language, it is the state language of Orissa where it is spoken by around 90% of the population.

Punjabi Another Indic language, this is the state language of Punjab. Although based on Devanagari (the same script as Hindi), it is written in a 16th-century script known as Gurumukhi, which was created by the Sikh guru, Guru Angad.

Sanskrit One of the oldest languages in the world, and the language of classical India. All the Vedas and classical literature such as the Mahabharata and the Ramayana were written in this Indic language.

Sindhi A significant number of Sindhi speakers are found in what is now Pakistan, although the greater number are in India. In Pakistan, the language is written in a Perso-Arabic script, while in India it uses the Devanagari script.

Tamil An ancient Dravidian language at least 2000 years old, and the state language of Tamil Nadu. It is spoken by 65 million people.

Telugu The Dravidian language spoken by the largest number of people, it is the state language of Andhra Pradesh.

Urdu This is the state language of Jammu and Kashmir. Along with Hindi, it evolved in early Delhi. While Hindi was largely adopted by the Hindu population, the Muslims embraced Urdu, and so the latter is written in the Perso-Arabic script and includes many Persian words.

---

ones are pronounced with a strong puff of air, like saying 'h' after the sound. There are also 'retroflex' consonants, produced by curling the tongue up and back to make contact with the ridge of tissue behind the top teeth. The transliteration system we've used for Hindi in this language guide is designed to be as simple as possible, and for this reason it doesn't distinguish between all the sounds of spoken Hindi.

It's important to pay attention to the pronunciation of vowels and especially to their length, eg **a** compared to **aa**. The combination **ng** after a vowel indicates that it is nasalised (ie pronounced through the nose).

Vowels

a	as the 'u' in 'sun'
aa	as in 'father'
ai	as in 'hair' before a consonant; as in 'aisle' at the end of a word
au	as in 'haul' before a consonant; as the 'ou' in 'ouch' at the end of a word
e	as in 'they'
ee	as the 'ee' in 'feet'
i	as in 'sit'
o	as in 'shot'
oo	as the 'oo' in 'fool'
u	as in 'put'

Consonants

ch	as in 'cheese'
g	always as in 'gun', never as in 'age'
r	slightly trilled
y	as in 'yak'
g	as in 'go'

ACCOMMODATION

Where is the (best/cheapest) hotel?
sab se (achaa/sastaa) hotal kahaang hai?

Please write the address.
zaraa us kaa pataa lik deejiye

Do you have any rooms available?
kyaa koee kamraa kaalee hai?

I'd like to share a dorm.
maing dorm me teharnaa chaahtaa/ee hoong (m/f)

EMERGENCIES

Help!	*mada keejiye!*
Stop!	*ruko!*
Thief!	*chor!*
Call a doctor!	*daaktar ko bulaao!*
Call an ambulance!	*embulains le aanaa!*
Call the police!	*pulis ko bulaao!*
I'm lost.	*maing raastaa bhool gayaa/ gayee hoong* (f/m)

Where is the ...?	*... kahaang hai?*
police station	*taanaa*
toilet	*gusalkaanaa*

I wish to contact my embassy/consulate.
maing apne embassy ke sebaat
katnaa logõ chaahtaa/chaahtee hoong (f/m)

How much for ...?	*... kaa kiraayaa kitnaa hai?*
one night	*ek din*
one week	*ek hafte*

I'd like a ...	*mujhe ... chaahiye*
double room	*dabal kamraa*
room with a bathroom	*gusalkaanevaalaa kamraa*
single room	*singal kamraa*

May I see it?
kyaa maing kamraa dek saktaa/ee hoong? (m/f)
Is there any other room?
koee aur kamraa hai?
Where's the bathroom?
gusalkaanaa kahaang hai?

bed	*palang*
blanket	*kambaal*
key	*chaabee*
shower	*shaavar*
toilet paper	*taailet pepar*
water (cold/hot)	*paanee (tandaa/garam)*
with a window	*kirkeevaalaa*

CONVERSATION & ESSENTIALS

Hello.	*namaste/namskaar*
Goodbye.	*namaste/namskaar*
Yes.	*jee haang*
No.	*jee naheeng*

'Please' is usually conveyed through the polite form of the imperative, or through other expressions. This book uses polite expressions and the polite forms of words.

Thank you.	*shukriyaa/danyavaad*
You're welcome.	*koee baat naheeng*
Excuse me/Sorry.	*kshamaa keejiye*
How are you?	*aap kaise/kaisee haing?* (m/f)
Fine, and you?	*maing teek hoong aap sunaaiye*
What's your name?	*aap kaa shubh naam kyaa hai?*

DIRECTIONS

Where's a/the ...	*... kahaang hai?*
bank	*baink*
consulate	*kaungnsal*
embassy	*dootaavaas*
Hindu temple	*mandir*
mosque	*masjid*
post office	*daakkaanaa*
public phone	*saarvajanik fon*
public toilet	*shauchaalay*
Sikh temple	*gurudvaaraa*
town square	*chauk*

Is it far from/near here?
kyaa voh yahaang se door/nazdeek hai?

SIGNS

प्रवेश/अन्दर	Entrance
निकार/बाहर	Exit
खुला	Open
बन्द	Closed
अन्दर आना [निषिि/मना] है	No Entry
धूम्रपान करना [निषिि/मना] है	No Smoking
निषिि	Prohibited
गर्म	Hot
ठंडा	Cold
शोचालय	Toilets

HEALTH

Where is a/the ...?	*... kahaang hai?*
clinic	*davaakaanaa*
doctor	*daaktar*
hospital	*aspataal*

I'm sick.	*maing beemaar hoong*
antiseptic	*ainteeseptik*
antibiotics	*ainteebayotik*
aspirin	*(esprin) sirdard kee davaa*
condoms	*nirodak*
contraceptives	*garbnirodak*
diarrhoea	*dast*
medicine	*davaa*
nausea	*gin*
syringe	*sooee*
tampons	*taimpon*

LANGUAGE DIFFICULTIES

Do you speak English?
   kyaa aap ko angrezee aatee hai?
Does anyone here speak English?
   kyaa kisee ko angrezee aatee hai?
I understand.
   maing samjhaa/ee
I don't understand.
   maing naheeng samjhaa/ee
Please write it down.
   zaraa lik deejiye

NUMBERS

Whereas we count in tens, hundreds, thousands, millions and billions, the Indian numbering system uses tens, hundreds, thousands, hundred thousands and ten millions. A hundred thousand is a *laakh*, and 10 million is a *krore*. These two words are almost always used in place of their English equivalents.

Once in the thousands, written numbers have commas every two places, not three.

1	*ek*
2	*do*
3	*teen*
4	*chaar*
5	*paangch*
6	*chai*
7	*saat*
8	*aat*
9	*nau*
10	*das*
11	*gyaarah*
12	*bara*
13	*terah*
14	*chaudah*
15	*pandrah*
16	*solah*
17	*satrah*
18	*attaarah*
19	*unnees*
20	*bees*
21	*ikkees*
22	*baaees*
30	*tees*
40	*chaalees*
50	*pachaas*
60	*saat*
70	*sattar*
80	*assee*
90	*nabbe/navve*
100	*sau*

1000	*hazaar*
100,000	*ek laak* (written 1,00,000)
10,000,000	*ek krore* (written 1,00,00,000)

SHOPPING & SERVICES

Where's the nearest ...?
sab se karib ... kah hai?

bookshop	*kitaab kee dukaan*
chemist/pharmacy	*davaaee kee dukaan*
general store	*dukaan*
market	*baazaar*
washerman	*dobee*

Where can I buy ...?
maing . . . kah kareed sakta hoong?
I'd like to buy ...
mujhe ... karidnaa hai

clothes	*kapre*
colour film	*rangin film*
envelope	*lifaafaa*
handicrafts	*haat kee banee cheeze*
magazines	*patrikaae*
map	*nakshaa*
newspaper (in English)	*(angrezee kaa) akbaar*
paper	*kaagaz*
razor	*ustaraa*
soap	*saabun*
stamp	*tikat*
toothpaste	*manjan*
washing powder	*kaprre done kaa saabun*

a little	*toraa*
big	*baraa*
enough	*kaafee*
more	*aur*
small	*chotaa*
too much/many	*bahut/adik*

How much is this?
   is kaa daam kyaa hai?
I think it's too expensive.
   yeh bahut mahegaa/i hai (m/f)
Can you lower the price?
   is kaa daam kam keejiye?
Do you accept credit cards?
   kyaa aap vizaa kaard vagairah lete ha?

TIME & DATES

What time is it?
   kitne baje haing?/taaim kyaa hai?
It's (10) o'clock.
   (das) baje haing
It's half past two.
   daaee baje haing

When?	kab?
now	ab
today	aaj
tomorrow/yesterday	kal (while kal is used for both, the meaning is made clear by context)

day	din
evening	shaam
month	maheenaa
morning	saveraa/subhaa
night	raat
week	haftaa
year	saal/baras

Monday	somvaar
Tuesday	mangalvaar
Wednesday	budvaar
Thursday	guruvaar/brihaspativaar
Friday	shukravaar
Saturday	shanivaar
Sunday	itvaar/ravivaar

TRANSPORT

How do we get to ...? ... kaise jaate haing?

When is the ... bus? ... bas kab jaaegee?
first	pehlaa/pehlee
next	aglaa/aglee
last	aakiree

What time does the ... leave?
... kitne baje jaayegaa/jaayegee? (m/f)
What time does the ... arrive?
... kitne baje pahungchegaa/pahungchegee? (m/f)
boat	naav (f)
bus	bas (f)
plane	havaaee jahaaz (m)
train	relgaaree (f)

I'd like a ... ticket.
mujhe ek ... tikat chaahiye
one way	ek-tarafaa
return	do-tarafaa

1st class	pratam shreni
2nd class	dviteey shreni

TAMIL

Tamil is the official language in the South Indian state of Tamil Nadu and the Union Territory of Puducherry (Pondicherry). It is one of the major Dravidian languages of South India.

SCRIPT & TRANSLITERATION

Tamil has its own alphabetic script which has not been included in this language guide. The transliteration system used here is intended as a simplified method for representing the sounds of Tamil using the Roman alphabet.

PRONUNCIATION

Like Hindi, the Tamil sound system includes a number of retroflex consonants, which are pronounced by curling the tongue up and back so that the tip makes contact with the ridge of tissue on the roof of the mouth. For the sake of simplicity, in this language guide we haven't distinguished the retroflex consonants from their nonretroflex counterparts. You'll find that your meaning will still be clear from the context of what you're saying.

Vowels

a	as the 'u' in 'run'
aa	as in 'rather'
ai	as in 'aisle'
au	as the 'ow' in 'how'
e	as in 'met'
ee	as in 'meet'
i	as in 'bit'
o	as in 'hot'
oo	as in 'rule'
u	as in 'chute'

Consonants

g	as in 'go'
k	as in 'kit'
ñ	as the 'ni' in 'onion'
s	as in 'sit'
zh	as the 's' in 'pleasure'

ACCOMMODATION

Do you have any rooms available?
araikal kitaikkumaa?
for one/two people
oruvar/iruvarukku
for one/two nights
oru/irantu iravukal
How much is it per night/per person?
oru iravukku/oru nabarukku evallavu?
Is breakfast included?
kaalai sirruntiyutan serttaa?

EMERGENCIES

Help!	utavi!
Leave me alone!	ennai taniyaaka irukkavitu!
Go away!	tolaintu po!
Call a doctor!	taaktarai kooppitavum!
Call the police!	poleesai kooppitavum!
I'm lost.	naan vazhi taviritten

camping ground	tangumitam
guesthouse	viruntinar vituti
hotel	hotal/vituti
youth hostel	ilaiñar vituti

CONVERSATION & ESSENTIALS

Hello.	vanakkam
Goodbye.	poyittu varukiren
Yes/No.	aam/illai
Please.	tayavu seytu
Thank you.	nanri
You're welcome.	nallatu varuka
Excuse me/Sorry.	mannikkavum
Do you speak English?	neenkal aankilam pesuveerkalaa?
How much is it?	atu evvalavu?
What's your name?	unkal peyar enna?
My name is ...	en peyar ...

DIRECTIONS

Where is (a/the) ...?	... enke irukkiratu?
Go straight ahead.	neraaka sellavum
Turn left.	valatu pakkam tirumbavum
Turn right.	itatu pakkam tirumbavum
far	tooram
near	arukil

NUMBERS

0	boojyam
1	ondru
2	iranyu
3	moonru
4	naanku
5	aintu
6	aaru
7	ezhu
8	ettu
9	onpatu
10	pattu
100	nooru
1000	aayiram
2000	irantaayiram
100,000	latsam (written 1,00,000)
1,000,000	pattu latsam (written 10,00,000)
10,000,000	koti (written 1,00,00,000)

SIGNS

வழி உள்ளே	Entrance
வழி வெளியே	Exit
திறந்த	Open
மூடிய	Closed
தகவல்	Information
அனுமதி இல்லை	Prohibited
காவல் நிலையம்	Police Station
மலசலகூடம்	Toilets
ஆண்	Men
பெண	Women

SHOPPING & SERVICES

What time does it open/close?
tirakkum/mootum neram enna?

bank	vangi
chemist/ pharmacy	aruntukkataikkaarar/ maruntakam
... embassy	... tootarakam
my hotel	en unavu vituti
market	maarkket
newsagency	niyoos ejensi
post office	tabaal nilayam
public phone	potu tolaipesi
stationers	elutuporul vanikar
tourist information office	surrulaa seyti totarpu aluvalakam

big	periya
small	siriya

TIME & DATES

What time is it ?	mani ettanai?
afternoon	matiyam
day	pakal
month	maatam
morning	kaalai
night	iravu
today	inru
tomorrow	naalai
week	vaaram
yesterday	nerru

Monday	tinkal
Tuesday	sevvaay
Wednesday	putan
Thursday	viyaazhan
Friday	velli
Saturday	sani
Sunday	ñaayiru

LANGUAGE

TRANSPORT

When does the	*eppozhutu atutta ...*
next ... leave/arrive?	*varum/sellum?*
boat	*pataku*
bus (city)	*peruntu (nakaram/ulloor)*
bus (intercity)	*peruntu (veliyoor)*
train	*rayil*

I'd like a one-way/return ticket.
enakku oru vazhi/iru vazhi tikket venum

1st class	*mutalaam vakuppu*
2nd class	*irantaam vakuppu*
bus/trolley stop	*peruntu nilayam*
left luggage	*tavara vitta saamaan*
timetable	*kaala attavanais*
train station	*rayil nilayam*

I'd like to hire a ...	*enakku ... vaatakaikku venum*
bicycle	*saikkil*
car	*kaara*

Also available from Lonely Planet:
India phrasebook

LANGUAGE

Glossary

This glossary is a sample of the words and terms you may come across during your Indian wanderings. For definitions of food and drink, see p92.

abbi – waterfall

Abhimani – eldest son of *Brahma*

Abhimanyu – son of *Arjuna*

acharya – revered teacher; spiritual guide

Adivasi – tribal person

agarbathi – incense

Agasti – legendary Hindu sage revered in the south as he is credited with introducing Hinduism and developing the Tamil language

Agni – major deity in the *Vedas;* mediator between men and the gods; also fire

ahimsa – discipline of nonviolence

AIR – All India Radio; the national broadcaster

air-cooler – big, noisy, water-filled fan

amrita – immortality

Ananda – *Buddha's* cousin and personal attendant

Ananta – snake on which *Vishnu* reclined

Andhaka – 1000-headed demon, killed by *Shiva*

angrezi – foreigner

anikut – dam

anna – 16th of a rupee; no longer legal tender

Annapurna – form of *Durga;* worshipped for her power to provide food

apsara – heavenly nymph

Aranyani – Hindu goddess of forests

Ardhanari – *Shiva's* half-male, half-female form

Arishta – *daitya* who, having taken the form of a bull, attacked *Krishna* and was killed by him

Arjuna – *Mahabharata* hero and military commander who married *Subhadra*, took up arms and overcame many demons; he had the *Bhagavad Gita* related to him by *Krishna*, led Krishna's funeral ceremony and finally retired to the Himalaya

Aryan – Sanskrit for 'noble'; those who migrated from Persia and settled in northern India

ashram – spiritual community or retreat

ashrama – Hindu system; there are three stages in life recognised by this system – *brahmachari, grihastha* and *sanyasin* – but this kind of merit is only available to the upper three castes

ASI – Archaeological Survey of India; an organisation involved in monument preservation

atman – soul

attar – essential oil usually made from flowers and used as a base for perfumes

autorickshaw – noisy, three-wheeled, motorised contraption for transporting passengers, livestock etc for short distances; found throughout the country, they are cheaper than taxis

Avalokitesvara – in *Mahayana* Buddhism, the *bodhisattva* of compassion

avatar – incarnation, usually of a deity

ayurveda – ancient and complex science of Indian herbal medicine and healing

azad – Urdu for 'free', as in Azad Jammu and Kashmir

azan – Muslim call to prayer

baba – religious master or father; term of respect

babu – clerk

bagh – garden

bahadur – brave or chivalrous; an honorific title

baksheesh – tip, donation (alms) or bribe

Balarama – brother of *Krishna*

bandar – monkey

bandh – general strike

bandhani – tie-dye

banian – T-shirt or undervest

baniya – moneylender or trader

banyan – Indian fig tree; spiritual to many Indians

baoli – see *baori*

baori – well, particularly a step-well with landings and galleries; in Gujarat it is more commonly referred to as a *baoli*

barasingha – deer

basti – slum

bearer – like a butler

begum – Muslim princess; woman of high rank

Bhagavad Gita – Hindu Song of the Divine One; *Krishna's* lessons to *Arjuna*, the main thrust of which was to emphasise the philosophy of *bhakti;* it is part of the *Mahabharata*

Bhairava – the Terrible; refers to the eighth incarnation of *Shiva* in his demonic form

bhajan – devotional song

bhakti – surrendering to the gods; faith

bhang – dried leaves and flowering shoots of the marijuana plant

bhangra – rhythmic Punjabi music/dance

Bharat – Hindi for India

Bharata – half-brother of *Rama;* ruled while Rama was in exile

bhavan – house, building; also spelt bhawan

bheesti – see *bhisti*

Bhima – *Mahabharata* hero; the brother of *Hanuman* and renowned for his great strength

bhisti – water carrier

bhoga-mandapa – Orissan hall of offering

bhojanalya – snack bar in Rajasthan, known elsewhere as dhaba

bidi – small, hand-rolled cigarette

bindi – forehead mark (often dot-shaped) worn by women

BJP – Bharatiya Janata Party

Bodhi Tree – tree under which *Buddha* sat when he attained enlightenment

bodhisattva – literally 'one whose essence is perfected wisdom'; in *Early Buddhism*, bodhisattva refers only to *Buddha* during the period between his conceiving the intention to strive for Buddhahood and the moment he attained it; in *Mahayana* Buddhism, to one who renounces *nirvana* in order to help others attain it

Bollywood – India's answer to Hollywood; the film industry of Mumbai (Bombay)

Brahma – Hindu god; worshipped as the creator in the *Trimurti*

brahmachari – chaste student stage of the *ashrama* system

Brahmanism – early form of Hinduism that evolved from Vedism (see *Vedas*); named after *Brahmin* priests and *Brahma*

Brahmin – member of the priest/scholar *caste*, the highest Hindu *caste*

Buddha – Awakened One; the originator of Buddhism; also regarded by Hindus as the ninth incarnation of *Vishnu*

Buddhism – see *Early Buddhism*

bugyal – high-altitude meadow

bund – embankment or dyke

burka – one-piece garment used by conservative Muslim women to cover themselves from head to toe

cantonment – administrative and military area of a Raj-era town

caravanserai – traditional accommodation for camel caravans

Carnatic music – classical music of South India

caste – a Hindu's hereditary station (social standing) in life; there are four castes: *Brahmin, Kshatriya, Vaishya* and *Shudra*

cenotaph – monument honouring a dead person whose body is somewhere else

chaam – ritual masked dance performed by some Buddhist monks in *gompas* to celebrate the victory of good over evil and of Buddhism over pre-existing religions

chaitya – Sanskrit form of 'cetiya', meaning shrine or object of worship; has come to mean temple, and more specifically, a hall divided into a central nave and two side aisles by a line of columns, with a votive *stupa* at the end

chakra – focus of one's spiritual power; disc-like weapon of *Vishnu*

Chamunda – form of *Durga;* armed with a scimitar, noose and mace, and clothed in elephant hide, her mission was to kill the demons Chanda and Munda

chandra – moon, or the moon as a god

Chandragupta – Indian ruler in the 3rd century BC

chappals – sandals or leather thonglike footwear; flip-flops

char dham – four pilgrimage destinations of Badrinath, Kedarnath, Yamunotri and Gangotri

charas – resin of the marijuana plant; also referred to as 'hashish'

charbagh – formal Persian garden, divided into quarters (literally 'four gardens')

charpoy – simple bed made of ropes knotted together on a wooden frame

chedi – see *chaitya*

chela – pupil or follower, as George Harrison was to Ravi Shankar

chhatri – *cenotaph* (literally 'umbrella')

chikan – embroidered cloth (speciality of Lucknow)

chillum – pipe of a hookah; commonly used to describe the pipes used for smoking *ganja*

chinkara – gazelle

chital – spotted deer

chogyal – king

choli – sari blouse

chomos – Tibetan Buddhist nuns

chorten – Tibetan for *stupa*

choultry – pilgrim's rest house; also called *'dharamsala'*

chowk – town square, intersection or marketplace

chowkidar – night watchman, caretaker

chuba – dress worn by Tibetan women

Cong (I) – Congress Party of India; also known as Congress (I)

coolie – labourer or porter (may be considered derogatory)

CPI – Communist Party of India

CPI (M) – Communist Party of India (Marxist)

crore – 10 million

dacoit – bandit (particularly armed bandit), outlaw

dada – paternal grandfather or elder brother

dagoba – see *stupa*

daitya – demon or giant who fought against the gods

dak – staging post, government-run accommodation

Dalit – preferred term for India's *Untouchable* caste; see also *Harijan*

Damodara – another name for *Krishna*

dargah – shrine or place of burial of a Muslim saint

darshan – offering or audience with someone; auspicious viewing of a deity

darwaza – gateway or door

Dasaratha – father of *Rama* in the *Ramayana*

Dattatreya – *Brahmin* saint who embodied the *Trimurti*

Delhiite – resident of Delhi

desi – local, Indian

deul – temple sanctuary

devadasi – temple dancer

Devi – *Shiva's* wife; goddess

dhaba – basic restaurant or snack bar

dham – holiest pilgrimage places of India

dharamsala – pilgrim's rest house

dharma – for Hindus, the moral code of behaviour or social duty; for Buddhists, following the law of nature, or path, as taught by *Buddha*

dharna – nonviolent protest

dhobi – person who washes clothes; commonly referred to as *dhobi*-wallah

dhobi ghat – place where clothes are washed

dhol – traditional double-sided drum

dholi – man-carried portable 'chairs'; people are carried in them to hilltop temples etc

dhoti – long loincloth worn by men; like a *lungi*, but the ankle-length cloth is then pulled up between the legs

dhurrie – rug

Digambara – 'Sky-Clad'; Jain group that demonstrates disdain for worldly goods by going naked

dikpala – temple guardian

Din-i-Ilahi – Akbar's philosophy asserting the common truth in all religions

diwan – principal officer in a princely state; royal court or council

Diwan-i-Am – hall of public audience

Diwan-i-Khas – hall of private audience

dowry – money and/or goods given by a bride's parents to their son-in-law's family; it's illegal but still widely exists in many arranged marriages

Draupadi – wife of the five Pandava princes in the *Mahabharata*

Dravidian – general term for the cultures and languages of the deep south of India, including Tamil, Malayalam, Telugu and Kannada

dukhang – Tibetan prayer hall

dun – valley

dupatta – long scarf for women often worn with the *salwar kameez*

durbar – royal court; also a government

Durga – the Inaccessible; a form of *Shiva*'s wife, *Devi*, a beautiful, fierce woman riding a tiger/lion; a major goddess of the *Shakti* sect

dwarpal – doorkeeper; sculpture beside the doorways to Hindu or Buddhist shrines

Early Buddhism – any of the schools of Buddhism established directly after *Buddha*'s death and before the advent of *Mahayana*; a modern form is the *Theravada* (Teaching of the Elders) practised in Sri Lanka and Southeast Asia; Early Buddhism differed from the *Mahayana* in that it did not teach the *bodhisattva* ideal

elatalam – small hand-held cymbals

election symbols – identifying symbols for the various political parties, used to canvas illiterate voters

Emergency – period in the 1970s during which Indira Gandhi suspended many political rights

Eve-teasing – sexual harassment

fakir – Muslim who has taken a vow of poverty; may also apply to other ascetics

filmi – slang term describing anything to do with Indian movies

gabba – appliquéd Kashmiri rug

gaddi – throne of a Hindu prince

gali – lane or alleyway

Ganesh – Hindu god of good fortune; elephant-headed son of *Shiva* and *Parvati*, he is also known as Ganpati and his vehicle is a ratlike creature

Ganga – Hindu goddess representing the sacred Ganges River; said to flow from *Vishnu*'s toe

ganj – market

ganja – dried flowering tips of the marijuana plant

gaon – village

garh – fort

gari – vehicle; 'motor gari' is a car and 'rail gari' is a train

Garuda – man-bird vehicle of *Vishnu*

gaur – Indian bison

Gayatri – sacred verse of *Rig-Veda* repeated mentally by *Brahmins* twice a day

geyser – hot-water unit found in many bathrooms

ghat – steps or landing on a river, a range of hills or a road up hills

ghazal – Urdu song derived from poetry; poignant love themes

giri – hill

Gita Govinda – erotic poem by Jayadeva relating *Krishna*'s early life as *Govinda*

godmen – commercially minded gurus

godown – warehouse

gompa – Tibetan Buddhist monastery

Gonds – aboriginal Indian race, now mainly found in the jungles of central India

goonda – ruffian or tough

Gopala – see *Govinda*

gopi – milkmaid; *Krishna* was fond of them

gopuram – soaring pyramidal gateway tower of *Dravidian* temples

gora – white person, European

Govinda – *Krishna* as a cowherd; also just cowherd

grihastha – householder stage of the *ashrama* system; followers discharge their duty to ancestors by having sons and making sacrifices to the gods

gufa – cave

gumbad – dome on an Islamic tomb or mosque

gurdwara – Sikh temple

Gurmukhi – script of the *Guru Granth Sahib*; Punjabi script

guru – holy teacher; in Sanskrit literally *'goe'* (darkness) and *'roe'* (to dispel)

Guru Granth Sahib – Sikh holy book

haat – village market

haj – Muslim pilgrimage to Mecca

haji – Muslim who has made the *haj*

hammam – Turkish bath; public bathhouse

Hanuman – Hindu monkey god, prominent in the *Ramayana,* and a follower of *Rama*

Hara – one of *Shiva*'s names

Hari – another name for *Vishnu*

Harijan – name (no longer considered acceptable) given by Mahatma Gandhi to India's *Untouchable caste,* meaning 'children of god'

hartal – strike

hashish – see *charas*

hathi – elephant

haveli – traditional, often ornately decorated, residences, particularly those found in Rajasthan and Gujarat

hijab – headscarf used by Muslim women

hijra – eunuch, transvestite

Hinayana – see *Early Buddhism*

Hiranyakasipu – *daitya* king killed by *Narasimha*

hookah – water pipe used for smoking *ganja* or strong tobacco

howdah – seat for carrying people on an elephant's back

iftar – breaking of the *Ramadan* fast at sunset

ikat – fabric made with thread which is tie-dyed before weaving

imam – Muslim religious leader

imambara – tomb dedicated to a Shiite Muslim holy man

IMFL – Indian-made foreign liquor

Indo-Saracenic – style of colonial architecture that integrated Western designs with Islamic, Hindu and Jain influences

Indra – significant and prestigious Vedic god; god of rain, thunder, lightning and war

Ishwara – another name given to *Shiva;* lord

Jagadhatri – Mother of the World; another name for *Devi*

jagamohan – assembly hall

Jagannath – Lord of the Universe; a form of *Krishna*

jali – carved lattice (often marble) screen; also refers to the holes or spaces produced through carving timber or stone

Janaka – father of *Sita*

Jataka – tale from *Buddha*'s various lives

jauhar – ritual mass suicide by immolation, traditionally performed by Rajput women at times of military defeat to avoid being dishonoured by their captors

jawan – policeman or soldier

jheel – swampy area

jhuggi – shanty settlement; also called *basti*

jhula – bridge

ji – honorific that can be added to the end of almost anything as a form of respect; thus 'Babaji', 'Gandhiji'

jihad – holy war (Islam)

JKLF – Jammu and Kashmir Liberation Front

jooti – traditional, often pointy-toed, slip-in shoes; commonly found in North India

juggernaut – huge, extravagantly decorated temple 'car' dragged through the streets during certain Hindu festivals

jumkahs – earrings

jyoti linga – most important shrines to *Shiva,* of which there are 12

kabaddi – traditional game (similar to tag)

Kailasa – sacred Himalayan mountain; home of *Shiva*

Kali – ominous-looking evil-destroying form of *Devi;* commonly depicted with dark skin, dripping with blood, and wearing a necklace of skulls

Kalki – White Horse; future (10th) incarnation of *Vishnu* which will appear at the end of Kali-Yug, when the world ceases to be; has been compared to *Maitreya* in Buddhist cosmology

Kama – Hindu god of love

kameez – woman's shirtlike tunic; see also *salwar kameez*

Kanishka – important king of the Kushana empire who reigned in the early Christian era

Kanyakumari – Virgin Maiden; another name for *Durga*

kapali – sacred bowl made from a human skull

karma – Hindu, Buddhist and Sikh principle of retributive justice for past deeds

Kartikiya – Hindu god of war, *Shiva*'s son

kata – Tibetan prayer shawl, traditionally given to a *lama* when pilgrims come into his presence

kathputli – puppeteer; also known as *putli*-wallah

Kedarnath – name of *Shiva* and one of the 12 *jyoti linga*

khadi – homespun cloth; Mahatma Gandhi encouraged people to spin this rather than buy English cloth

Khalistan – former Sikh secessionists' proposed name for an independent Punjab

Khalsa – Sikh brotherhood

Khan – Muslim honorific title

kho-kho – traditional game (similar to tag); less common variation on *kabbadi*

khol – black eyeliner

khur – Asiatic wild ass

kiang – wild ass found in Ladakh

kirtan – Sikh devotional singing

koil – Hindu temple

kolam – see *rangoli*

kompu – C-shaped metal trumpet

kos minar – milestone

kot – fort

kothi – residence or mansion

kotwali – police station

Krishna – *Vishnu*'s eighth incarnation, often coloured blue; he revealed the *Bhagavad Gita* to *Arjuna*

Kshatriya – Hindu *caste* of soldiers or administrators; second in the *caste* hierarchy

kund – lake or tank; Toda village

kurta – long shirt with either short collar or no collar

Kusa – one of *Rama*'s twin sons

lakh – 100,000

Lakshmana – half-brother and aide of *Rama* in the *Ramayana*

Lakshmi – *Vishnu*'s consort, Hindu goddess of wealth; she sprang forth from the ocean holding a lotus

lama – Tibetan Buddhist priest or monk

lathi – heavy stick used by police, especially for crowd control

Laxmi – see *Lakshmi*

lehanga – very full skirt with a waist cord

lhamo – Tibetan opera

lingam – phallic symbol; auspicious symbol of *Shiva*; plural 'linga'

lok – people

Lok Sabha – lower house in the Indian parliament (House of the People)

loka – realm

Losar – Tibetan new year

lungi – worn by men, this loose, coloured garment (similar to a sarong) is pleated by the wearer at the waist to fit

machaan – observation tower

madrasa – Islamic seminary

maha – prefix meaning 'great'

Mahabharata – Great Hindu Vedic epic poem of the *Bharata* dynasty; containing approximately 10,000 verses describing the battle between the Pandavas and the Kauravas

Mahabodhi Society – founded in 1891 to encourage Buddhist studies

Mahadeva – Great God; *Shiva*

Mahadevi – Great Goddess; *Devi*

Mahakala – Great Time; *Shiva* and one of 12 *jyoti linga*

mahal – house or palace

maharaja – literally 'great king'; princely ruler

maharana – see *maharaja*

maharao – see *maharaja*

maharawal – see *maharaja*

maharani – wife of a princely ruler or a ruler in her own right

mahatma – literally 'great soul'

Mahavir – last *tirthankar*

Mahayana – the 'greater-vehicle' of Buddhism; a later adaptation of the teaching that lays emphasis on the *bodhisattva* ideal, teaching the renunciation of *nirvana* in order to help other beings along the way to enlightenment

Mahayogi – Great Ascetic; *Shiva*

Maheshwara – Great Lord; *Shiva*

Mahisa – Hindu demon

mahout – elephant rider or master

Mahratta – see *Maratha*

maidan – open (often grassed) area; parade ground

Maitreya – future *Buddha*

Makara – mythical sea creature and *Varuna*'s vehicle; crocodile

mala – garland or necklace

mali – gardener

mandal – shrine

mandala – circle; symbol used in Hindu and Buddhist art to symbolise the universe

mandapa – pillared pavilion, temple forechamber

mandi – market

mandir – temple

mani stone – stone carved with the Tibetan-Buddhist mantra *'Om mani padme hum'* ('Hail the jewel in the lotus')

mani walls – Tibetan stone walls with sacred inscriptions

mantra – sacred word or syllable used by Buddhists and Hindus to aid concentration; metrical psalms of praise found in the *Vedas*

Mara – Buddhist personification of that which obstructs the cultivation of virtue, often depicted with hundreds of arms; also the god of death

Maratha – central Indian people who controlled much of India at various times and fought the Mughals and Rajputs

marg – road

Maruts – Hindu storm gods

masjid – mosque

mata – mother

math – monastery

maund – unit of weight now superseded (about 20kg)

maya – illusion

mehndi – henna; ornate henna designs on women's hands (and often feet), traditionally for certain festivals or ceremonies (eg marriage)

mela – fair or festival

memsahib – Madam; respectful way of addressing women

Meru – mythical mountain found in the centre of the earth; on it is *Swarga*

mihrab – mosque 'prayer niche' that faces Mecca

mithuna – pairs of men and women; often seen in temple sculpture

Moghul – see *Mughal*

Mohini – *Vishnu* in his female incarnation

moksha – liberation from *samsara*

monsoon – rainy season

morcha – mob march or protest

mudra – ritual hand movements used in Hindu religious dancing; gesture of *Buddha* figure

muezzin – one who calls Muslims to prayer, traditionally from the minaret of a mosque

Mughal – Muslim dynasty of subcontinental emperors from Babur to Aurangzeb

mujtahid – divine

mullah – Muslim scholar or religious leader

Mumbaikar – resident of Mumbai (Bombay)

mund – village

muntjac – deer

murti – statue, often of a deity

nadi – river

Naga – mythical serpentlike beings capable of changing into human form

namaskar – see *namaste*

namaste – traditional Hindu greeting (hello or goodbye), often accompanied by a respectful small bow with the hands together at the chest or head level; also *namaskar*

namaz – Muslim prayers

Nanda – cowherd who raised *Krishna*

Nandi – bull, vehicle of *Shiva*

Narasimha – man-lion incarnation of *Vishnu*

Narayan – incarnation of *Vishnu* the creator

Narsingh – see *Narasimha*

natamandir – dancing hall

Nataraja – *Shiva* as the cosmic dancer

nautch – dance

nautch girls – dancing girls

nawab – Muslim ruling prince or powerful landowner

Naxalites – ultra-leftist political movement begun in West Bengal as a peasant rebellion; characterised by violence

Nilakantha – form of *Shiva;* his blue throat is a result of swallowing poison that would have destroyed the world

nilgai – antelope

nirvana – ultimate aim of Buddhists and the final release from the cycle of existence

niwas – house, building

nizam – hereditary title of the rulers of Hyderabad

noth – the Lord (Jain)

NRI – Non-Resident Indian; of economic significance to modern India

nullah – ditch or small stream

Om – sacred invocation representing the essence of the divine principle; for Buddhists, if repeated often enough with complete concentration, it leads to a state of emptiness

Osho – the late Bhagwan Shree Rajneesh, a popular, controversial guru

paan – mixture of betel nut and leaves for chewing

padma – lotus; another name for the Hindu goddess *Lakshmi*

padyatra – 'foot journey' made by politicians to raise support at village level

pagal – insane, crazy; often said in jest

pagoda – see *stupa*

paise – the Indian rupee is divided into 100 paise

palanquin – boxlike enclosure carried on poles on four men's shoulders; the occupant sits inside on a seat

Pali – the language, related to Sanskrit, in which the Buddhist scriptures were recorded; scholars still refer to the original Pali texts

palia – memorial stone

palli – village

Panchatantra – series of traditional Hindu stories about the natural world, human behaviour and survival

panchayat – village council

pandal – marquee

pandit – expert or wise person; sometimes used to mean a bookworm

Parasurama – *Rama* with the axe; sixth incarnation of *Vishnu*

Parsi – adherent of the Zoroastrian faith

Partition – formal division of British India in 1947 into two separate countries, India and Pakistan

Parvati – another form of *Devi*

pashmina – fine woollen shawl

patachitra – Orissan cloth painting

PCO – Public Call Office, from where you can make local, interstate and international phone calls

peepul – fig tree, especially a bo tree

peon – lowest-grade clerical worker

pietra dura – marble inlay work characteristic of the Taj Mahal

pinjrapol – animal hospital run by Jains

pir – Muslim holy man; title of a Sufi saint

POK – Pakistan Occupied Kashmir

pradesh – state

pranayama – study of breath control; meditative practice

prasad – temple-blessed food offering

puja – literally 'respect'; offering or prayers

pujari – temple priest

pukka – proper; a Raj-era term

pukka sahib – proper gentleman

punka – cloth fan, swung by pulling a cord

Puranas – set of 18 encyclopaedic Sanskrit stories, written in verse, relating to the three gods, dating from the 5th century AD

purdah – custom among some conservative Muslims (also adopted by some Hindus, especially the Rajputs) of keeping women in seclusion; veiled

Purnima – full moon; considered to be an auspicious time

putli-wallah – puppeteer; also known as *kathputli*

qawwali – Islamic devotional singing

qila – fort

Quran – the holy book of Islam, also spelt Koran

Radha – favourite mistress of *Krishna* when he lived as a cowherd

raga – any of several conventional patterns of melody and rhythm that form the basis for freely interpreted compositions

railhead – station or town at the end of a railway line; termination point

raj – rule or sovereignty; British Raj (sometimes just Raj) refers to British rule

raja – king; sometimes *rana*

rajkumar – prince

Rajput – Hindu warrior *caste,* former rulers of northwestern India

Rajya Sabha – upper house in the Indian parliament (Council of States)

rakhi – amulet

Rama – seventh incarnation of *Vishnu*

Ramadan – Islamic holy month of sunrise-to-sunset fasting (no eating, drinking or smoking); also referred to as Ramazan

Ramayana – story of *Rama* and *Sita* and their conflict with *Ravana;* one of India's best-known epics

rana – king; sometimes *raja*

rangoli – elaborate chalk, rice-paste or coloured powder design; also known as *kolam*

rani – female ruler or wife of a king

ranns – deserts

rasta roko – roadblock set up for protest purposes

rath – temple chariot or car used in religious festivals

rathas – rock-cut *Dravidian* temples

Ravana – demon king of Lanka who abducted *Sita;* the titanic battle between him and *Rama* is told in the *Ramayana*

rawal – nobleman

rickshaw – small, two- or three-wheeled passenger vehicle

Rig-Veda – original and longest of the four main *Vedas*

rishi – any poet, philosopher, saint or sage; originally a sage to whom the hymns of the *Vedas* were revealed

Road – railway town that serves as a communication point to a larger town off the line, eg Mt Abu and Abu Road

rudraksh mala – strings of beads used in *puja*

Rukmani – wife of *Krishna;* died on his funeral pyre

sadar – main

sadhu – ascetic, holy person, one who is trying to achieve enlightenment; often addressed as *'swamiji'* or *'babaji'*

safa – turban

sagar – lake, reservoir

sahib – respectful title applied to a gentleman

salai – road

salwar – trousers usually worn with a *kameez*

salwar kameez – traditional dresslike tunic and trouser combination for women

samadhi – in Hinduism, ecstatic state, sometimes defined as 'ecstasy, trance, communion with God'; in Buddhism, concentration; also a place where a holy man has been cremated/buried, usually venerated as a shrine

sambalpuri – Orissan fabric

sambar – deer

samsara – Buddhists, Hindus and Sikhs believe earthly life is cyclical; you are born again and again, the quality of these rebirths being dependent upon your *karma* in previous lives

sangam – meeting of two rivers

sangeet – music

sangha – community of Buddhist monks and nuns

Sankara – *Shiva* as the creator

sanyasin – like a *sadhu;* a wandering ascetic who has renounced all worldly things as part of the *ashrama* system

Saraswati – wife of *Brahma,* goddess of learning; sits on a white swan, holding a *veena*

Sat Sri Akal – Sikh greeting

Sati – wife of *Shiva;* became a *sati* ('honourable woman') by immolating herself; although banned more than a century ago, the act of *sati* is still (very) occasionally performed

satra – Hindu Vaishnavaite monastery and centre for art

satsang – discourse by a swami or guru

satyagraha – nonviolent protest involving a hunger strike, popularised by Mahatma Gandhi; from Sanskrit, literally meaning 'insistence on truth'

Scheduled Castes – official term used for the *Untouchable* or *Dalit caste*

sepoy – formerly an Indian solider in British service

serai – accommodation for travellers

seva – voluntary work, especially in a temple

shahadah – Muslim declaration of faith ('There is no God but Allah; Mohammed is his prophet')

Shaivism – worship of *Shiva*

Shaivite – follower of *Shiva*

shakti – creative energies perceived as female deities; devotees follow Shaktism

sharia – Islamic law

sheesha – see *hookah*

shikara – gondola-like boat used on lakes in Srinagar (Kashmir)

shikhar – hunting expedition

shirting – material from which shirts are made

Shiva – Destroyer; also the Creator, in which form he is worshipped as a *lingam*

shola – virgin forest

shree – see *shri*

shri – honorific male prefix; Indian equivalent of 'Respected Sir'

shruti – heard

Shudra – *caste* of labourers

sikhara – Hindu temple-spire or temple

Singh – literally 'lion'; a surname adopted by Sikhs

sirdar – leader or commander

Sita – Hindu goddess of agriculture; more commonly associated with the *Ramayana*

sitar – Indian stringed instrument

Siva – see *Shiva*

Skanda – another name for *Kartikiya*

sonam – *karma* accumulated in successive reincarnations

sree – see *shri*

sri – see *shri*

stupa – Buddhist religious monument composed of a solid hemisphere topped by a spire, containing relics of *Buddha;* also known as a 'dagoba' or 'pagoda'

Subhadra – *Krishna's* incestuous sister

Subrahmanya – another name for *Kartikiya*

Sufi – Muslim mystic

Sufism – Islamic mysticism

suiting – material from which suits are made

Surya – the sun; a major deity in the *Vedas*
sutra – string; list of rules expressed in verse
swami – title of respect meaning 'lord of the self'; given to initiated Hindu monks
swaraj – independence
Swarga – heaven of *Indra*
sweeper – lowest *caste* servant, performs the most menial tasks

tabla – twin drums
tal – lake
taluk – district
tandava – *Shiva's* cosmic victory dance
tank – reservoir; pool or large receptacle of holy water found at some temples
tantric Buddhism – Tibetan Buddhism with strong sexual and occult overtones
tatty – woven grass screen soaked in water and hung outside windows to cool the air
tempo – noisy three-wheeler public transport vehicle; bigger than an autorickshaw
thakur – nobleman
thangka – Tibetan cloth painting
theertham – temple *tank*
Theravada – orthodox form of Buddhism practised in Sri Lanka and Southeast Asia that is characterised by its adherence to the Pali canon; literally 'dwelling'
thiru – holy
tikka – mark Hindus put on their foreheads
tilak – auspicious forehead mark of devout Hindu men
tirthankars – the 24 great Jain teachers
tonga – two-wheeled horse or pony carriage
topi – cap
torana – architrave over a temple entrance
toy train – narrow-gauge train; mini-train
trekkers – jeeps; hikers
Trimurti – triple form; the Hindu triad of *Brahma, Shiva* and *Vishnu*
Tripitaka – classic Buddhist scriptures, divided into three categories, hence the name 'Three Baskets'
tripolia – triple gateway

Uma – *Shiva's* consort; light
Untouchable – lowest *caste* or 'casteless', for whom the most menial tasks are reserved; the name derives from the belief that higher castes risk defilement if they touch one; formerly known as *Harijan,* now *Dalit*
Upanishads – esoteric doctrine; ancient texts forming part of the *Vedas;* delving into weighty matters such as the nature of the universe and soul

urs – death anniversary of a revered Muslim; festival in memory of a Muslim saint

vaastu – creation of a cosmically favourable environment
Vaishya – member of the Hindu *caste* of merchants
Valmiki – author of the *Ramayana*
Vamana – fifth incarnation of *Vishnu,* as the dwarf
varku – sacred flute made from a thigh bone
varna – concept of *caste*
Varuna – supreme Vedic god
Vedas – Hindu sacred books; collection of hymns composed in preclassical Sanskrit during the second millennium BC and divided into four books: *Rig-Veda,* Yajur-Veda, Sama-Veda and Atharva-Veda
veena – stringed instrument
vihara – Buddhist monastery, generally with central court or hall off which open residential cells, usually with a *Buddha* shrine at one end; resting place
vikram – *tempo* or a larger version of the standard *tempo*
vimana – principal part of Hindu temple
vipassana – insight meditation technique of *Theravada* Buddhism in which mind and body are closely examined as changing phenomena
Vishnu – part of the *Trimurti; Vishnu* is the Preserver and Restorer who so far has nine *avatars:* the fish Matsya; the tortoise Kurma; the wild boar Naraha; *Narasimha; Vamana; Parasurama; Rama; Krishna;* and *Buddha*

wadi – hamlet
wallah – man; added onto almost anything, eg *dhobi*-wallah, chai-wallah, taxi-wallah
wavs – step-wells, northern India
wazir – title of chief minister used in some former Muslim princely states

yagna – self-mortification
yakshi – maiden
yali – mythical lion creature
yantra – geometric plan said to create energy
yatra – pilgrimage
yatri – pilgrim
yogini – female goddess attendants
yoni – female fertility symbol

zakat – tax in the form of a charitable donation, one of the five 'Pillars of Islam'
zamindar – landowner
zari – gold or silver thread used in weaving
zenana – area of an upperclass home where women are secluded; women's quarters

The Authors

SARINA SINGH
Coordinating Author, Haryana & Punjab

After finishing a business degree in Melbourne, Sarina bought a one-way ticket to India where she completed a Sheraton corporate traineeship before working as a freelance journalist and foreign correspondent. After four years in the subcontinent she returned to Australia, pursued postgraduate journalism qualifications and wrote/directed an award-nominated documentary film. She has worked on 30 Lonely Planet books, is the author of *Polo in India,* and has also written articles for many international publications including *National Geographic Traveler.* For this book, Sarina commissioned Christopher Kremmer and William Dalrymple and also wrote Destination India, Getting Started, Events Calendar, History, The Culture, Food & Drink, Activities, Directory, Transport, Glossary, and the Delicious India and Festive India sections.

LINDSAY BROWN
Rajasthan, Gujarat

After completing a PhD on evolutionary genetics and a stint as a science editor and a sojourn on the subcontinent, Lindsay started working for Lonely Planet. Lindsay is a former Publishing Manager of the Outdoor Activity guides at Lonely Planet, and he returns to the subcontinent to trek, write and photograph whenever possible. He has also contributed to Lonely Planet's *South India, Nepal, Bhutan, Rajasthan, Delhi & Agra* and *Pakistan & the Karakoram Highway* guides, among others.

MARK ELLIOTT
Kolkata (Calcutta), Jammu & Kashmir

Mark has been making forays to the subcontinent since a 1984 trip that lined his stomach for all eventualities. For this edition he returned to the underrated metropolis of Kolkata, was utterly inspired by the deep yet light-hearted spirituality of Ladakh and managed to dodge riots, hartals and curfews around Kashmir. After weeks of delay due to blockades and political unrest, he finally managed to travel the Srinagar to Jammu road soon after it reopened. When not researching travel guides Mark lives a blissfully quiet suburban life with his beloved Belgian bride, Danielle, who found him at a Turkmen camel market. The camel would have been cheaper!

PAUL HARDING
Himachal Pradesh, Uttarakhand

Paul has been drawn back to India and all its chaos many times since first landing in Delhi more than a decade ago. As a travel writer and photographer, he's travelled from Kanyakumari to the Himalaya, slept in palaces and fleapits and consumed plenty of Kingfisher beer. On this trip Paul explored the wonderful Himalayan states of Himachal Pradesh and Uttarakhand, riding knee-trembling mountain roads, managing to get a round of golf in near Shimla, and wishing he had more time for trekking. Paul has written for numerous magazines and Lonely Planet guides, including *South India, Goa* and *Istanbul to Kathmandu.* He lives near the beach in Melbourne, Australia.

ABIGAIL HOLE
Delhi

Abigail Hole visited India around 15 years ago, rattling around the north –
to Delhi, Manali, Kashmir and Punjab – before melting in Rajasthan during
the hot season. She's returned at least every couple of years. This is the
third time she's contributed to Lonely Planet's *India*, and she wrote the
first edition of the *Rajasthan, Delhi & Agra* guide. Having researched the
capital for this book, she now can't wait to get an excuse to return, explore
some more, shop some more, wander through more Mughal gardens and
try more *Dilli-ki-chaat*. She has also written on India for various magazines
and newspapers.

PATRICK HORTON
Bihar & Jharkhand, Sikkim, Northeast States

Patrick, writer and photographer, was born with restless feet. He travelled
extensively in his native Britain before hitting the around-the-world trail
and ending up in Melbourne. His journeys lead him to the more arcane
areas of the world including North Korea, Eritrea, Kosovo, East Timor, Serbia,
Tonga, Cuba and riding a motorcycle over the Himalaya. But he is forever
returning to India, a place that he considers another home. This research
trip to uncover the jewels of Northeast India, Sikkim, Bihar and Jharkhand
completes a long-held ambition to visit every state in India.

KATE JAMES
West Bengal, Orissa

Melbourne-born Kate grew up in Ooty, where her parents taught at an
international school. Her family holidayed across the subcontinent for eight
years, carrying the very first edition of Lonely Planet *India* and memorably
spending Christmas 1980 in a tribal village on the border of Andhra Pradesh
and Orissa. Country and suburban journalism in Australia led Kate to an in-
house editing job at Lonely Planet and then into a freelance writing and
editing career. She is the author of *Women of the Gobi*. This is her first book
as an author for Lonely Planet.

AMY KARAFIN
Mumbai (Bombay), Andhra Pradesh

Indian in several former lives, Amy Karafin headed straight to India after
university for an extended trip that would turn out to be karmically ordained.
She spent the next few years alternating between New York and faraway
lands until, fed up with the irony of being a travel editor in a Manhattan
cubicle, she relinquished her MetroCard and her black skirts to make a living
on the road. She's been freelancing seminomadically ever since, spending
big chunks of time in Senegal, Guinea and India. She lives mostly in Brooklyn
now, but also sometimes in Mumbai and Dakar.

ADAM KARLIN · Tamil Nadu, Andaman & Nicobar Islands

Adam was a 23-year old backpacker in South India when the Tamil bandit Veerappan was killed near his hostel. A few days later, he filed his first international news story on the 'Jungle Cat's' death. A month later, Adam was being interrogated by Tamil Tigers while reporting on the Sri Lankan civil war. The Tamils and their homeland have had a place in his heart ever since, and he jumped at the opportunity to go back to South India for Lonely Planet. While he'll always love Tamil Nadu, he was pleasantly surprised to discover Eden umpteen times during his first visit to the Andamans, too.

ANIRBAN DAS MAHAPATRA · Maharashtra, Karnataka

Six years into his career as an Indian journalist, Anirban Mahapatra has almost perfected the art of selling outlandish story ideas to his editors to routinely beat the confines of his office cubicle and scoot off to far-flung corners of the country. Now based in Delhi, he's trundled through Maharashtra and Karnataka several times in the past, once even in a mad-hat attempt to retrace the steps of 15th-century Russian explorer Afanasy Nikitin. His primary reason for going south, however, is to significantly endanger the local marine life (oh the crabs!) while he's there, and wash it all down with some fresh draught in beer-town Bengaluru. He's also a writer and photographer, and this is his first Lonely Planet assignment on the road.

DANIEL McCROHAN · Uttar Pradesh, Madhya Pradesh & Chhattisgarh

Straight out of school and with the travelling experience of...well, a school-boy, Daniel's first trip to India blew him away. Complete pandemonium was the best way he could describe it at the time. Fifteen years later and with numerous India trips under his money belt, he still revels in trying to make sense of the chaos. Daniel has now travelled extensively throughout almost half the states in India. Exploring tribal Chhattisgarh was a first for him this time, and a major highlight, but he will forever remember this particular research trip as the one that finally gave him his first tiger-sighting – after 14 unsuccessful attempts.

AMELIA THOMAS · Goa

Amelia Thomas is a writer and journalist working throughout India and the Middle East. She has worked on numerous Lonely Planet titles, and her book *The Zoo on the Road to Nablus,* telling the true story of the last Palestinian zoo, was published in 2008. Her four small children, aged between 10 months and five years, enjoy accompanying her on assignments – particularly the Goan kind, which sees them conducting their own research into sandcastles, rock pools and Indian ice cream. Her forthcoming book, 'Hypnosis!' tells the incredible, colourful tale of Abbé de Faria, Goan priest and hypnotist extraordinaire.

RAFAEL WLODARSKI Kerala, Tamil Nadu (Chennai)

After completing degrees in marketing and psychology in Melbourne, Rafael vowed never to use them and set off on a short around-the-world trip. Nine years and five passports later, he is yet to come home. Rafael spent his entire 20s travelling overland through the Middle East, the Indian subcontinent, and North and South America. He managed to get lost in India for six months along the way, and relished coming back to Kerala to update this edition. He currently lives somewhere between San Francisco, London and Zanzibar.

CONTRIBUTING AUTHORS

William Dalrymple was born in Scotland and wrote the highly acclaimed bestseller *In Xanadu* when he was 22. *City of Djinns* won the Thomas Cook Travel Book Award and the *Sunday Times* Young British Writer of the Year Award. *White Mughals* won the Wolfson Prize for History 2003 and his most recent book, *The Last Mughal,* won the Crossword Indian Book of the Year Prize and the Duff Cooper Memorial Prize. His next work, *Nine Lives,* will be published by Bloomsbury in October. William wrote the 'Last Mughal' boxed text in the History chapter.

Christopher Kremmer is the author of four books imbued with the history, culture and conflicts of modern Asia. They include the bestselling *Inhaling the Mahatma,* a journey to the heart of the Indian identity, and *Bamboo Palace,* a ground-breaking quest to uncover the fate of the missing royal family of Laos. His superb portrait of Afghanistan, *The Carpet Wars,* follows the lives of Afghan carpet weavers and sellers amid the torment of war and religious extremism. He is currently writing a novel set in Australia. Christopher wrote the 'India' boxed text in The Culture chapter.

David Lukas lives on the edge of Yosemite National Park where he studies and writes about the natural world. He has contributed environment chapters to about 28 Lonely Planet guides and is the author of the recent *A Year of Watching Wildlife.* When not writing about plants and animals, he leads nature tours and programs. David wrote the Environment chapter..

Behind the Scenes

THIS BOOK

When the first edition of India emerged in 1981 it was the biggest, most complicated and most expensive project we'd tackled at Lonely Planet. Thirteen editions on, it's still a sprawling beast of a book. This is Sarina Singh's fifth stint as coordinating author. As well as researching Haryana & Punjab, she led a crack team of authors: Lindsay Brown (Rajasthan, Gujarat), Mark Elliott (Kolkata, Jammu & Kashmir), Paul Harding (Uttar Pradesh, Uttarakhand), Abigail Hole (Delhi), Patrick Horton (Sikkim, Bihar & Jharkand, Northeastern States), Kate James (West Bengal, Orissa), Amy Karafin (Andhra Pradesh, Mumbai), Adam Karlin (Tamil Nadu, Andaman & Nicobar Islands), Anirban Das Mahapatra (Maharashtra, Karnataka), Daniel McCrohan (Uttar Pradesh, Madhya Pradesh & Chhattisgarh), Amelia Thomas (Goa) and Rafael Wlodarski (Kerala, Chennai). David Lukas wrote the Environment chapter and the Health chapter was adapted from text written by Dr Trish Batchelor. William Dalrymple wrote the 'Last Mughal' boxed text in the History chapter and Christopher Kremmer wrote the 'India' boxed text in the Culture chapter.

This guidebook was commissioned in Lonely Planet's Melbourne office, and produced by the following:

Commissioning Editors Sam Trafford, Will Gourlay, Suzannah Shwer, Shawn Low
Coordinating Editor Alison Ridgway
Coordinating Cartographer Hunor Csutoros
Coordinating Layout Designer Carlos Solarte
Managing Editor Brigitte Ellemor
Managing Cartographers Adrian Persoglia, David Connolly
Managing Layout Designers Laura Jane, Indra Kilfoyle
Assisting Editors Janice Bird, Adrienne Costanzo, Kate Evans, Carly Hall, Helen Koehne, Alan Murphy, Joanne Newell, Katie O'Connell, Kristin Odijk, Martine Power, Saralinda Turner, Fionn Twomey, Helen Yeates
Assisting Cartographers Alissa Baker, Ildiko Bogdanovits, Xavier Di Toro, Joshua Geoghegan, Joanne Luke, Amanda Sierp
Assisting Layout Designers Nicholas Colicchia, Jacqui Saunders, Cara Smith
Cover Image research provided by lonelyplanetimages.com
Project Managers Chris Girdler, Eoin Dunlevy

Thanks to Lucy Birchley, Melanie Dankel, Sally Darmody, Mark Germanchis, Robyn Loughnane, Caroline Megaloeconomou, Wayne Murphy, John Taufa, Juan Winata

THANKS
SARINA SINGH

In India, thanks to those kind souls who made life on the road less bumpy, especially Hitender,

THE LONELY PLANET STORY

Fresh from an epic journey across Europe, Asia and Australia in 1972, Tony and Maureen Wheeler sat at their kitchen table stapling together notes. The first Lonely Planet guidebook, *Across Asia on the Cheap*, was born.

Travellers snapped up the guides. Inspired by their success, the Wheelers began publishing books to Southeast Asia, India and beyond. Demand was prodigious, and the Wheelers expanded the business rapidly to keep up. Over the years, Lonely Planet extended its coverage to every country and into the virtual world via lonelyplanet.com and the Thorn Tree message board.

As Lonely Planet became a globally loved brand, Tony and Maureen received several offers for the company. But it wasn't until 2007 that they found a partner whom they trusted to remain true to the company's principles of travelling widely, treading lightly and giving sustainably. In October of that year, BBC Worldwide acquired a 75% share in the company, pledging to uphold Lonely Planet's commitment to independent travel, trustworthy advice and editorial independence.

Today, Lonely Planet has offices in Melbourne, London and Oakland, with over 500 staff members and 300 authors. Tony and Maureen are still actively involved with Lonely Planet. They're travelling more often than ever, and they're devoting their spare time to charitable projects. And the company is still driven by the philosophy of *Across Asia on the Cheap*: 'All you've got to do is decide to go and the hardest part is over. So go!'

Kalpana Kumari and Janmejaye Singh for adopting me as family; and Mamta, Anup and Abhinav Bamhi for being first-rate stress banishers. Kudos to all at LP who worked their magic on the manuscripts, with heartfelt thanks, especially, to the tenacious authors for months of slog – I'm deeply grateful. On a personal note, warm thanks to Chris Kremmer and William Dalrymple for being so delightful to work with; to frost-free Nick, for grace and understanding; and to my parents, for being so extraordinarily cool.

LINDSAY BROWN

Thanks to the many people in Rajasthan and Gujarat who shared their interest and expertise. In particular I would like to thank Dicky Singh and Satinder Singh in Jaipur, Joshi in Jodhpur, Loise and Chanesar in Jaisalmer, Gouri in Bikaner, and Mr Sorathia in Junagadh. For his good humour and prowess on the road, a huge thanks to Saleem. Thanks to fellow author Sarina Singh, and thanks to Jenny, Pat and Sinead at home.

MARK ELLIOTT

Eternal thanks as ever to my beloved wife (Danielle Systermans) and to my unbeatable parents: constant sources of love, help and inspiration. Thanks too to all at LP, notably Sam Trafford for sending me to Kashmir at such an intriguing moment and Sarina for being such a pleasure to work with. In India, thank you to Jai Chand and family, Rouf John, Jos and Scot, Tom and Hanna, Mona and Suzanne, Maud and Niamh, Brian and Megan, Birgit Bernhard, Evangeline Dimichele and so many others.

ABIGAIL HOLE

So many thanks to Sarina for her wisdom and insider advice, to my other co-authors, especially Daniel, Amelia, Mark and Patrick, to CEs Sam Trafford, Shawn Low, and Will Gourlay, and to everyone in production. Huge thanks to Jyoti, Niranjan and Sumeet Desai. Gratitude also to Pawas Prasoon at Delhi Tourism, to Rajinder, to Murad and Tannie Baig, to Srishti Bajaj, and to Mark Morris. Et merci beaucoup, Alex Lieury and Mathieu Chanard. Not forgetting Luca, Mum and Ant for making this all possible. My part in this book is dedicated to Omi, my inspiring, beautiful grandmother, who died while I was away.

AMY KARAFIN

My sincere thanks go to the people of Andhra Pradesh and Bombay for putting up with my questions and for having created such fascinating places. I'm also deeply grateful to Akash Bhartiya,

assistant researcher, Hindi tutor and loyal kulfi partner; Mom and Dad; Manik and Surekha Bhartiya; Sarina Singh, Sam Trafford and Will Gourlay; Malini and Hari Hariharan; Jayasree Anand and Sandhya Kanneganti; Raghu Raman; Sunjoy Monga; the original members of the Barry Karafin International Executive Club; Hervé, Charlie and Hernan; and SN Goenka and everyone at Dhamma Pattan, Dhamma Nagajjuna, Dhamma Vijaya and Dhamma Khetta. Bhavatu sabba mangalam.

ADAM KARLIN

Thanks: Abi in Trichy, Santosh in Coonoor, Mani in Kumbakonam, Kumar in Mamallapuram, Selvam in Tirumayam, Shadab, BK Das and DK Das in Port Blair, the Indian Army men in Diglipur and Rakesh and Anthony in Chennai. Huge ups to Prabil and Amit in Little Andaman. Also: cheers to Stephanie et Francois, Em, Ellie and Becky, Simone, Moran, Charlie, Danny and Sophie, Lara and Andy and every other companion met on the road.

PAUL HARDING

Thank you, as always, to Rajinder Kumar in Delhi for hospitality and, in particular, the shopping tips. In Haridwar, Sanjeev Mehta was again a mine of information and a gracious host. In McLeod thanks to the guys at Contact and Lla. In Manali, thanks to Mr Thakur and in Naggar to Ravi Sharma. In Kausani thanks to Vipin Upreti and his staff. Thanks also to the travellers I met who shared their stories and experiences, particularly Kenric who popped up everywhere! Thanks with love to Hannah at home. Last but not least, thanks to Sarina Singh for her brilliant support, to Sam Trafford for being a great CE and to the editors and cartos at LP for their hard work.

PATRICK HORTON

No author can hope to produce anything worthwhile without the assistance of people on the ground. My really big thanks go to Hermanta Dass of Network Travels. As driver, guide and friend he got me around this special region, laughed at my jokes and was always ready to join me in a late night Kingfisher after the day's work was done, (usually after 9pm). As a person who knows everyone in tourism in the Northeast, he was able to browbeat and persuade those responsible for granting those pesky permits to let me in so that I could visit every state, the first author in many years to be able to do so. In Sikkim I could have got nowhere without Tensing Namgyal of Namgyal Tours and Travels who likewise eased permits and provided transport and guides.

BEHIND THE SCENES

KATE JAMES

Chris and Luffy kept the home fires smoking: thanks, boys. At LP, thanks to the rolling CE team, Sarina Singh, editor Alison Ridgway and carto Mandy Sierp. In Orissa, thanks to Bijaya and Tutu at Discover Tours, and Pulak and Claire at Grass Routes. In West Bengal, thanks go to Andrew Pulger, Debal Deb and especially to Martyn Brown at Kali Travel Home. Thanks to fellow travellers who shared jeeps, beers and useful information: especially to Jo, Sarah and Naomi for instant friendship at just the right time; and to Gary for showing me the Diwali fireworks over Puri.

ANIRBAN DAS MAHAPATRA

Many thanks to editors Sam Trafford, Shawn Low, Will Gourlay and Suzannah Shwer; carto Adrian Persoglia and the entire team at Lonely Planet; and my fellow authors, who put their heads and hearts into this book. Sarina, thanks a ton for your help and guidance – I owe you many beers! On the ground, thanks to the wonderful people of the Deccan, the energetic Mrs Ramu at the Bengaluru KSTDC office, fellow scribes Bishakha Sarkar, Abhijit Mitra, Swagata Sen and Nirmala Ravindran, Shama Pawar for her help in Hampi and Anegundi, and Sivakumar, Gajanan and Ashok for their enthusiastic driving. Finally, to Shohini for her help, patience

SEND US YOUR FEEDBACK

We love to hear from travellers – your comments keep us on our toes and help make our books better. Our well-travelled team reads every word on what you loved or loathed about this book. Although we cannot reply individually to postal submissions, we always guarantee that your feedback goes straight to the appropriate authors, in time for the next edition. Each person who sends us information is thanked in the next edition – and the most useful submissions are rewarded with a free book.

To send us your updates – and find out about Lonely Planet events, newsletters and travel news – visit our award-winning website: lonelyplanet.com/contact.

Note: we may edit, reproduce and incorporate your comments in Lonely Planet products such as guidebooks, websites and digital products, so let us know if you don't want your comments reproduced or your name acknowledged. For a copy of our privacy policy visit lonelyplanet.com/privacy.

and encouragement, and to our house dogs for generally making life a breeze!

DANIEL MCCROHAN

Thanks to all the travellers I met for top advice and amusing banter, especially Lo Tallon, Jourdain Gadoury, Dan Snuggs and James Ashton. In Agra, a big thanks to Ramesh at Tourist Rest House for all your help statewide. In Lucknow, a warm appreciation for Naheed for city tips and for having such a great homestay, while thanks go to Sheevendra at Bandavgarh and Dhanya at Pench for indispensible tiger park knowledge. As always, my biggest thank you goes to my family in the UK and to Taotao in China for all your love and patience.

AMELIA THOMAS

Many thanks, first, to Pinky and her fabulous family, without whom everyday life would have been impossible. Thanks, too, to Shilpa, for the soft landing, and to Tanya, Shubangi and the second Pinky, who do such wonderful work with our tinies. Thanks to Sarina, Sam, Will, Alison, the other authors, and the team at LP for being great to work with, as always; to Nich and Cheryl for the morning bhaji paus and evening G&Ts; and to Cassidy, Tyger, Cairo, Gal and Zeyah for forsaking the Middle East to set up camp, instead, on the shores of the Arabian Sea.

RAFAEL WLODARSKI

Thanks goes out to the all the helpful folk who smoothed my speedy path through India, particularly the staff at tourist and KTDC offices far and wide. A big bucket of thanks goes out to the people that went beyond the call of duty to help make this book possible: Dayar, taxi driver MK Sekhran in Kottayam, Prabhath (Joseph) in Kollam, Rottu in Trivandrum, Saji in Kovalam, Siddharth from Locadives, and a huge thanks to PJ Varghese, Kurien & Mr Vanu. Thanks also to Sarina Singh for her steady captainship and to Sam Trafford for sending me to India. Very special thanks are reserved, as always, for Suzanna, and for my mum.

OUR READERS

Many thanks to the travellers who used the last edition and wrote to us with helpful hints, useful advice and interesting anecdotes:

A Ruchika Abbi, Hywel Abbott, Alexandra Abed, Pauline Abetti, Erika Abrams, Ria-Maria Adams, Roger Adams, Joakim Adamsson, R K Agrawal, Emilio Agusti, Ji Ahn, Cinthya Albert, Tyler Ambrose, Lorenzo Ambrosini, Dana Amit, Gabriele Ammermann, Brooks Anderson, Emma Andreasson, Eric Andresen, Karen Andresen, James Andrew, Cristiano Annamaria, Islam Ansari, Tim Antonov, Hentry Argaio, Matthias Armbruster, Graeme And D'Lorna

Armstrong, Esther Arumugam, Jeanette Asquith, Melissa Atkinson, David Austin, Akash Avani, Roberto Avigliano **B** Karsten Bachem, Shagun Bagga, Wanda Baginska, Kuba Baginski, Jessica Bagnall, Magdalena Balcerek, Clare Ballard, Arvind Bangay, Girdhari Bapna, Karen Barfoot, Afifa Barkallah, Tim Barnet, Monica Basak, Frederic Nadeau, Sandi Bassett, Liz Bate, Chris Baumann, Whalie Bayer, Felix Bayne, Krista Beard, Corthay Beatrice, Matthew Beaufort, Petra Beckmann, Vicki Beddage, Don Beddage, Susanne Bell, Arjen Beltman, Nelly Bencomo, Denise Benitez, Stephen Benrad, Adam Bentel, Edo And Simone Berger-Bleumink, Maiken Berle, Geoff Berman, Graham Beswick, Maureen Beyrend, Pushpa Bhamu, Sanjay Bhargav, Hemu Bhati, Vinod Bhatt, Sara Bianchi, Emilia Bianco, Dave Bick, Mir Bilal, Chandan Bisht, Liz Bissett, Mike Bissett, Lisa Blachut, Ollie Blake, Monique Blandin, Carl Bloch, Azul Blue, Maria Emanuela Boccafoschi, Sohel Bohra, Eric Borgman, Suryakumar Boriah, Dana Borne, Gesine Bornschein, Irene Bos, Sinead Boylan, Raanan Bracha, Steve Braithwaite, Seana Brandon, Lucy Brasset, Bethia Brehmer, Martin Breidenbach, Martin Brewerton, Olivier Briand, Helen Briggs, Sophie Broadbent, Michael Brodrick, Julia Brukner, S Buckley, Piotr Bukal, Jutta Bürger, Trevor Burley, Vishal Burman, Sheona Burrow, Bernhard Buser **C** Leopoldina Caccia Dominioni, Eric Caldeira, Mauricio Campos, Sara Cantini, Katie Carlile, Jackie Carman, Peter Carpenter, James Caudwell, Jeff Caulfield, Stefania Cavaliere, Drew Cavendish-Grey, Veronica Cedillos, Aynur Celik, Sudipto Chakraborti, Eric Chan, Louise Chang, Chin-Fan Chang, Francoise Charpin, Jack Chia, Sam Chillingworth, Gill Devesey Chris Glassar, Virginia And Barry Christian, Chantel Chu, Richard Chubb, Rebecca Chung, Katie Church, David Cintra, Tom Clark, Wayne Clarkson, Emily Clayson, Pamela Clayton , Phillippa Clements, Tereza Cleverley, Eugnia Clima, Angela Clyburn, Dawn Cochrane, Dave Cochrane, Margret Coghill, Michele Cogo, Peter Colbert, Salemla Colegrave, Pierre Collins, Robin Conz, Martha Conzalez, Brian Cook, David Cookson, Nathan Corcoran, Goncalo Costa, Shannan Courtenay, Sylvain Couture, Amrit Coyle, Colleen Crawford, The Crichards, Elena Cris, Jane Cross, Liz Cunniffe, Yvonne Cunningham, Kyle Cunningham, David Curits, Hayley Curran, Steve Curry, Letizia Cutino **D** Anne D'Heygers, Loes D'Hooghe, Akelei D'Hulster, Beverley D'Silva, Martin Dannemora, Peter Dantoft, Natasha Dar, Pratik Das, Kunal Datta, Allison Davies, Alan Davis, Simon Davis, Tim Dawson, Patricia De Bordes, Marc De Galan, Hanne De Glas, Jeroen De Graaf, Daan De Leeuw, Marina De Silva, Liton Deb, Josh Decker, Christophe Defilippi, Eduardo Delgado, Brian Dell, Angélique Denis, Ella Dennison, Sharon Depauw, Robert Derash, Simon Derrick, Tom Deterre, Ine Deviaene, Peter Devitt, Cyndy Devlin, Felix Dieterich, Jane Dixon, Anne Dobson, Mike Dodson, Stephan Doerrenberg, Mariella Donalisio, Federico Donatini, Pieter Bas Donkersteeg, Jane Downing, Christine Drane, Jonathan Drennan, Jamie Duffy, Ron And Gillian Dugmore, Peter Dundas, Mary Dunne, Ahmed Durvesh, Shawn Duthie **E** Melanie Easton, Susan Edwards, Andre Effing, Wanessa El Amri, Brian Ellis, Andrew Ellis, Roger Elmitt, Tamir Epstein, Anna Eriksson, Sean Erwin, Adam Estroff, Angela Exworth, Frank Eyhorn **F** Lisa Fabian, Angelo Fanelli, Allison Febey, Sol Feldman, Ewa Ferens, Maria Fergusson, Alfonso Fernandez Bonilla, Shelly Sol Fhima, Max Field, Daniel Fiott, Miriam Fisher, Jane Fisher, Dave Fisher, Rachel Fitzsimons, Nicola Fleck, Mary Flynn, Andrew Flynn, Candice Foong, Alex Forbes, Polly Forbes, Jayne Forbes, Patrick Ford, Veronique Fortin, Christopher Fowler, Augustin Fragniere, Laura Frank, Gary Fraser, Kelly Frazer, Sarah French, Valerie French, Joachim Frenz, Anneli Friis, Almut Fues **G** Jose Gabriel, Mansi Gandhi Shah, Sourav Garg, Ben Garrison, Gary Gary, Sophia Gee, Yigal Gelb, Mr Gergely, Mrs Gergely, Elsbeth Geukers, David Gibson, Klari Gidofalvy, Graham Gilbert, Max Ginpil, Sky Girl, Oded Givony, Karen Gleave, Barry John Glover, Olivier Godfroid, Laura Godsall, Mira Goetsch, Bethan Goldsmith, Omar Goller, Emily Goodacre, David Goodman, Harinder Goolry, Kim Goris, Daisy Goschalk, Melanie Goudreau, Rebecca Gough, Jordan Goulding, Stuart Graham, Amparo Granada, Jeremy Grange, Janis Gravelis, Oliver Gray, Abby Grayzel, Pat Grediagin, Rick Green, Karolien Greenacre, Eva Gregory, Tobias Gresser, Rachel Grierson, Tessa Griffith, Glen Griffiths, Yvette and Patrick Groothedde, Petra Grosskinsky Jeckelmann, Martin Grubinger, Martin Grznar, Sreejata Guha, Christine Guiao, Markus Gully, Arun Gupta, Rohit Gupta, Michael Gurman, Kristian Gustavussen, Sašo Gyergyek **H** Nadav Haber, Yuval Hadash, Keith Hainge, Catherine Halbleib, Jolin Haley, Valerie Hall, Amy Hall, Julie Hamilton, Martin Hanner, Martin Rune Hansen, Aaron Harnett, Morgan Harrington, Penny Harris, Joanne Harrison, Denise Hart, Rainer Haseneder, Nick Hassell, Margaret Hathaway, Lianne Haug, Jan Hayes, Kevin Heasman, Olaf Heischel, Katherine Heitz, Magnus Hellbom, Knut-Erik Helle, Christoph Heller, Gerard Helmink, Sam Henderson, Oliver Henrich, Jaan Henrik, Fred Henry, Daria Hepps, Markku Hietala, Harri Hietanen, Anna Hildebrandt, Sarah Hine, Katy Hinton, Alexandra Hinz, Nora Hippmann, Anthony Hitchin, Michael Hoather, Moshe Hoffman, Richard Hogan, Robert Holder, Brent Holland, Isak Holmgren, Wade Holowaty, Atsuko Honda, H P Hope-Stone, Sara Hopkins, Kevin Hopkins, Ashley Howard, Joan Howe, Virginia Huang, Katrin Hubens, Nick Huggard ,Kay Hughes, Jakobien Huisman, Alain Grootaers, James Humphrey, Russell Huntington, Michael Hvidtfeldt **I** Ulf Ingesson, John Isaacs, Israel, Ramdas Iyer **J** Pasqual Jabaloyas, Jacqui, Muriel Jacquinet, Markus Jahn, Shilpa Jain, Rochelle Jakeman, Dusan Jakl, Hamish Jenkinson, Amy Jenner, Amadeo Jensana, Peter Jensen, Cecilia Jensen, Peter Jensen, Miguel Jimenez Calderon, Guy Jobling, Guyy Jobling, Stein Johannes Kolnes, Rouf John, Kent Johnson, Ezra Johnson, Keegan Johnson, Julia Jones, Barcanan Joni, Laura Jorgensen, Nikki Lee Ormerod, Annie Joseph, Linda Joyce **K** Nanhie K, Vinny Kahlon, Anneli Käll, Chitra Kankiah, Randhir Kapoor, Karam, Margriet Katoen, Erez Katsav, Sarah Katz, Ben Kaufman, Rupinder Kaur, Zehavit Kehat, Andrew Kelly, Istvan Kerekes, Mahendra Singh Khamesra, Basim Khan, Siddharth Khandelwal, Puneet Khanna, Jacqueline Kim, Anthony King, Justine Kirby, Emmi Kivela, Marijke Klaver, Louise Kleinbergs, Brigitte Klemens, Mariam Klik, Joanna Kosiska, Gregory Kluyskens, Christine Knight, Sara Knight, Chris Joshua & Dylan, Alan Koepcke, Nina Kolisnyk, Kartik Koolwal, Murielle Kopitzke, Itai Kran, Joseph Kreamer, Anna-Louise Noe Kristensen, Stephan Kruisman, Simon Küffer, Michael Kuhn, Maayan Kum, Pratima Kumar, Sanjay Kumar, Pappu Kumar **L** Olivier Lacourse, Marlene Lagimodiere, Elaine Lam, Christian Lanciai, Andree Lanfranconi, Anna-Maria Lappalainen, Fred Lars-

Erik, Anna-Kristina Larsson, Rachel Lauer, Roy Lavens, Louiza Lawrence, Francis Lawrence, Joseph Lawson, Ramakrishnan Laxman, Ronan Le Gouellec, Youen Le Ru, Mandy Leader, Anne Lebel, Anoesjka Lechner, Steve Ledahawsky, Jaemoon Lee, Jean-Marc Legras, Lynne Legros, Bas Lemmens, Jan-Pleun Lens, Alexis Leon, Jurij Leskovec, Frederic Levesque, Jean-Paul Lew, Malcolm Lewena, Ofer Li-D'Or, Allison Lichter, Catarina Lilliehöök, Kemmy Lim, Audrey Lin, Chris Lin, Stephanie Lindinger, Adam Lineberry, Brenda Link Williams, Alona Lisitsa, Asha Lobo, Hedda Loimer, Sarah Lois Lois, Paolo Lolli, Jose Lomas, Luz Lomeli, Amy Looker, Amadeo Lopez, Renato Losio, Joe Lucas, Cornelius Luedtke, Sonia Luna **M** Adrian Ma, Mona Maamari, Wolfram Machatsch, Catherine Macmanus, Jerald Macmurray, Franco Magnani, John Mahood, Penny Mahood, Bettina Mair, Brigitte Malou, Fiona Manning, Vasilis Marambos, William Marcose, Peter Marsden, Sally Marshall, Roland Martensson, Claire Martin, Gillian Martin, Jessica Martin, Maria And Barbara Marx, Joshua Mastadi, Gerald Masure, Erika Matthei, Andres Matute, Daniel Maughan, Deb Maurer, Salvador Correia, Heath Mcallister, Bronwyn Mcbride, Andrew Mccarthy, Claudia Mcglynn, Twid Mcgrath, Iain Mcintyre, Joel Meadows, Steve Meldrum, Ruth Meller, Eliane Menghetti, Eitan Merhavy, Ben Merven, Barbara Metzger, H Meyer, Monika Meyer-Baron, Michael Miclon, Charlene Mills, Patrick Mills, Dani Milner, Mimi Mimi, Matt Mitton, Barbara Moccetti-Bänziger, Barbara Müller-Junker, Dennis Mogerman, Pulak Mohanty, Shivanand Mohanty, Sara Monteiro, Bruce Moon, Sandeep Moonka, Anthony Moore, Alex And Helen Moore, Zuzana Moravcova, Jane Morgan, Patrice Morris, Christopher Morse, Ashley Morton, Megan Mossip, David Mould, Melissa Mouldin, Dave Moyer, Miroslava Mrazova, Christina Mueller, Wanjiru Mukoma, Aaldrik Mulder, Julian Muller, Aramia Munro, Ross Munro Burnell, Daniel Musikant, Arttu Muukkonen **N** Latha Nachiyamai, Robert Nagle, Ranjana Nair, Aileen Nandi, Surekha Narain, Rocky Narang, Serhat Narsap, Eric Neemann, Tal Neuberger, Michaela Newell, Alon Newman, Lisa Ngan-Hing, Dang Hoang Nguyen, Thoms Nicl, Erik Niinemaa, Judith Nijeboer, Mildred Noordam, Josiane Noreau, Mette Nørholm, Louisa North, Miia Nykänen-Khaling, Kristoffer Nyrop **O** Daniel O'Kelly, Aoife O'Sullivan, Abigael Ogada-Osir, Barbara Okugbeni, Ernes Olaxa, Savary De Beauregard Olivier, Sarah Olsen, Mirjam Olsthoorn, Stefan Op De Woerd, Ruby Ormeno, Henriette Orth, Ashok Otwal **P** Himanshu J Padhya, T P Padmarajaiah, Thea Pagani, Susan Parker, Erna Parker, Tricia Parry, Kate Partridge, Frederic Pasqualini, Menaka Patki, Karin Peen, Tom Pengelly, Bob Percival, Vanesa Perez, Stephanie Perrot, Anna Pers, Annemarie Pestalozzi, Hugh Peto, Robert Pfohman, Caroline Phillips, Perminder Phull, Margaret Pichlbauer, Kim Pickering, Elena Pike, Catherine Pinard, Doeko Pinxt, Deby Pippin, Prue Plovanic, Daniel Pole, Chris Pollard, Mandy Poppen, Sue Popper, Sue Popper, Walesa Porcellato, Charlotte Pothuizen, Byran Potter, Xavier Poultney, Kate Pounder, Meris Powell, Rebekah Powell, Suraj Pradhan, Niven Prasad, Wolfgang Preikschat, Jesse Prest, Mr Prohaska, Mrs Prohaska, Steve Pyer **Q** Juliet Quintero **R** Roopesh R, Ngawang Rabgyal, Mahesh Raja, Kumar Rajeev, Sue Rand, Olga Rando, Subash Rao, Sharon Raphael, Jürg Rauschenbach, Richard Rawson, Prad Ray, Shuvjit Ray, Laura Rees, Simon Reid, Willa Reiffel, Barrie Reiffel, Brenda Remmers, Simone Resch, Elizabeth Rhodes, Scott Rice, Antoine Richard, Kathryn Richards, Edana Richardson, Alastair Richardson, Stuart Riddle, Jonathan Riley, Laura Rives, Sian Roberts, Gwil Roberts, Tim Roberts, Lisbeth Rofhök, Corroenne Romain, Patrick Roman, Zanchi Romana, Jean-Paul Roques, Ortwin Rosner, Sebastian Roth, Isabelle-Jasmin Roth, Marko Rowlan, Christopher Rowland, Christopher Rowland, Mukut Roychoudhury, Philip Rubbens, Jens Rubner, Ernie Rumpel, Pia Russo, Bas Rutjens **S** Priya Saha, Richard Samuel, Pedro Sánchez Cuadrado, Saswati Sarkar, Pranjal Sarma, Vakaris Šaulys, Peter Schack, Ben Schill, Dorothee Schilling, Ansel Schmidt, Hans Dieter Schmitt, Simon Scholl, Marieke Scholz, Melissa Schreiber, Fer Schroeders, Esther Schuller, Carla Emilia Schulmeyer, Evan Schwartz, Chris Scorer, Jeff Sedoff, Sanjeev Sehgal, Andrew Seltzer, Min Seong Kim, Sunil Seth, Zubin Sethna, Steve Sexauer, Pritesh Shah, Mayank Shah, Dinesh Shah, Ute Shaktawat, Ohad Shamian, John Shanley, Ann Shannon, Erika Shantz, Mahdi Shariati Moghaddam, S Sharma, Nitesh Sharma, Mary Sharp, Sandy Sharratt, John Sheridan, Rae Sheridan, Yulia Shitko, Ido Shlomo, Chris Shorrock, Upendra Shrimali, Noga Shteiman, Doug Shult, Kelsie Shute, Celine Sicre, Debra Siegel, David Silvester, Uwe Simmer, Elke Kummer, Andrew Simon, Sindhu Sindhu, Sarabjeet Singh, Jatinder Singh, Bhupinder Singh, Carina Skareby, Alex Slaets, Mike Slone, Natalie Smart, Neill Smith, Wendy Smith, Aidan Smith, Kelli Smith, Preston Smith, Jon Smith, Bob Smith, Patrick Smith, Remco Snoeij, Edmund So, Eva Sokolowski, Laura Sola, Madhulika Somasekhar, Young Sook Song, Peter Spalding, Tony Sparkes, Dianne Spencer, Colette Spillane, Ariane St-Louis, Blazej Stachowiak, Hamsa Stainton, Dick Stammes, Claudia Stampfli, Bauer Stephen, Caleb Stewart, Melanie Stokking, Diane Strong, Tom Stuart, Karen Stubbs, Ana Sofia Suarez, Gaz Summer, Nicholas Summers, Edwin Sumun, Marjon Sutherland, Zsolt Suto, William Swallow, Raju Swami, Mark Swan, Martina Swart, Gyoergy Szell, Monika Szyszlowska **T** Cheerharan T, Joseph Tami, Sabine Tamm, Christine Tandon, Dharmesh Tanna , Anne Tansey, Samantha Taylor, Chad Taylor, David Taylor, Dan Taylor, Jt Taylor , Genevieve Tearle, Rishi Tejwani, Akis Temperidis, James Theobold, Mia Theuns, Mathew Thomas, Steve Thompson, Richard Thorne, Adrienne Tibbits, Bernard Tiffany, Alex Tindle, Anjali Tirkey, Egle Tiskevciute, Regis Titeca, Jonathan Tomlinson, Giulia Tonini, Nick Toon, Jan Trabandt, Alejandro Trénor, Els Troch, Virginia Trujillo, Periklis Tsoukalas, Rossana Turchetto, Helen Turner, Jane Twist **U** Alexia Uhia, Derek Uram, Reuben Urban, Ute, Julia Uvarov **V** Juha Valimaki, Simon Valque, Michael Van Bregt, Caroline Van De Velde, Paul Van Den Haak, Nynke And Dominique Van Der Schaaf / De Oliveira, Colin Van Huijstee, Emma Van Leest, Huub Van Loon, Rob Van Vroonhoven, Christopher Vandewalle, Audrey Vanel, Lal Vattiyankotu, Mike Vayda , Puja Vedi, Venkat, Evert Verheijen, Mahitosh Verma, Eric Vermeeren, Ron & Cécile Versleijen Brouwer, Alex Villard, Vincent Vleugel, Krista Vogels, Elisabeth Volquardts, Linda Voorwinde **W** Felix Wagner, Terry Wainwright, Elke Wakefield, David Waknine, Margot Walbert, Dani Waldispuehl, Ben Walker, Angela Wall, Anna Walton, Lisa Warden, Jay Waronker, Dorothy Jayne Watkins, Brenda Weinberg, Bill Weir, Jonathan Weitsman, Maureen Welch, Dave Wells, Marion White,

Ramby White, Rachel Whitney, Alex Whittam, Juliet Widdup, Marielle Wiggers, Ellen Wigmore, David Wijgerse, Gareth Wilce, Amber Williams, Nicola Williams, Sky Williamson, Helen Willoughby, Chris Wills, Lou Wilson, Klaus Winterling, Alex Withey, Laura & Jim Wittke, Gili Wolff, Joanna Wood, Beverly Wood, Carolyn Woodley, Brad Wootton **Y** Jim Yen, Ilanit Yoel, Bae Yongyeon, Sara Young, Craig Young, Sara Young, David Young, Josef Yu **Z** Rimma Zakirow, Rimma Zakirow, Corinne Zakravsky, Romana Zanchi, Francesco Zaratin, Annemarie Zeeman, Gernot Zimmermann

ACKNOWLEDGMENTS
Many thanks to the following for the use of their content:

Globe on title page ©Mountain High Maps 1993 Digital Wisdom, Inc.

Excerpt from *Shilappadikaram* (The Ankle Bracelet) by Prince Iiango Adigal, translated by Alain Daniélou, copyright ©1965 by Alain Daniélou. Reprinted by permission of New Directions Publishing Corp.

Index

INDEX

INDEX

INDEX

GreenDex

The following organisations have been selected by our authors because they demonstrate a commitment to sustainability. We've selected restaurants that have an organic focus or refill water bottles with safe, drinkable water and use local produce, funnelling profits back into the community. We've listed businesses and not-for-profits for diverse reasons: some use solar power and have composting toilets; others support refugees by providing them with employment or reinvest profits into local groups. Ecolodges and trekking organisations that take care of the natural environment and minimise our impact on it are also mentioned here.

For more green tips, see Responsible Trekking (p114). If you think we've omitted someone here, email us at www.lonelyplanet.com/contact. For more information about sustainable tourism and Lonely Planet, see www.lonelyplanet.com/responsibletravel.

MAP LEGEND

ROUTES

Tollway	Mall/Steps
Freeway	Tunnel
Primary	Pedestrian Overpass
Secondary	Walking Tour
Tertiary	Walking Tour Detour
Lane	Walking Trail
Under Construction	Walking Path
Unsealed Road	Track
One-Way Street	

TRANSPORT

Ferry	Rail
Metro	Rail (Underground)
Bus Route	Tram

HYDROGRAPHY

River, Creek	Canal
Intermittent River	Water
Swamp	Lake (Dry)
Mangrove	Lake (Salt)
Reef	Mudflats

BOUNDARIES

International	Regional, Suburb
State, Provincial	Ancient Wall
Disputed	Cliff

AREA FEATURES

Airport	Land
Area of Interest	Mall
Beach, Desert	Market
Building	Park
Campus	Reservation
Cemetery, Christian	Rocks
Cemetery, Other	Sports
Forest	Urban

POPULATION

CAPITAL (NATIONAL)	CAPITAL (STATE)
Large City	Medium City
Small City	Town, Village

SYMBOLS

Sights/Activities
- Beach
- Buddhist
- Castle, Fortress
- Christian
- Hindu
- Islamic
- Jain
- Jewish
- Monument
- Museum, Gallery
- Point of Interest
- Pool
- Ruin
- Sikh
- Skiing
- Trail Head
- Zoo, Bird Sanctuary

Eating
- Eating

Drinking
- Drinking
- Café

Entertainment
- Entertainment

Shopping
- Shopping

Sleeping
- Sleeping
- Camping

Transport
- Airport, Airfield
- Border Crossing
- Bus Station
- General Transport
- Parking Area
- Petrol Station
- Taxi Rank

Information
- Bank, ATM
- Embassy/Consulate
- Hospital, Medical
- Information
- Internet Facilities
- Police Station
- Post Office, GPO
- Telephone
- Toilets

Geographic
- Lighthouse
- Lookout
- Mountain, Volcano
- National Park
- Pass, Canyon
- River Flow
- Waterfall

LONELY PLANET OFFICES

Australia
Head Office
Locked Bag 1, Footscray, Victoria 3011
☎ 03 8379 8000, fax 03 8379 8111
talk2us@lonelyplanet.com.au

USA
150 Linden St, Oakland, CA 94607
☎ 510 250 6400, toll free 800 275 8555
fax 510 893 8572
info@lonelyplanet.com

UK
2nd fl, 186 City Rd,
London EC1V 2NT
☎ 020 7106 2100, fax 020 7106 2101
go@lonelyplanet.co.uk

Published by Lonely Planet Publications Pty Ltd
ABN 36 005 607 983

© Lonely Planet Publications Pty Ltd 2009

© photographers as indicated 2009

Cover photograph: Vivid pink turbans dot the landscape at the Kithalai Fair, Narlai, Jodhpur, Rajasthan, Keren Su/Lonely Planet Images. Many of the images in this guide are available for licensing from Lonely Planet Images: www.lonelyplanetimages.com.

Mixed Sources
Product group from well-managed forests and other controlled sources
www.fsc.org Cert no. SGS-COC-005002
© 1996 Forest Stewardship Council